ANTHOLOGY OF

THIRD EDITION

ILLUSTRATED BY FRITZ EICHENBERG

Children's Literature

EDNA JOHNSON · EVELYN R. SICKELS

FRANCES CLARKE SAYERS

HOUGHTON MIFFLIN COMPANY

Boston · The Riverside Press Cambridge

The Riverside Press

CAMBRIDGE MASSACHUSETTS

PRINTED IN THE U.S.A.

COPYRIGHTS AND ACKNOWLEDGMENTS

DOROTHY ALDIS — "Windy Wash Day," from *Child Life Magazine.*

APPLETON-CENTURY-CROFTS, INC. — "The Flower-fed Buffaloes," from *Going to the Stars* by Vachel Lindsay; copyright, 1926, D. Appleton & Co.; reprinted by permission of the publishers Appleton-Century-Crofts, Inc. Illustration by A. B. Frost from *Uncle Remus* (Trade-Mark Reg. U.S. Pat. Office): *His Songs and His Sayings* by Joel Chandler Harris, published by Appleton-Century-Crofts, Inc.

EDWARD ARNOLD (PUBLISHERS) LTD., London — "Pandora" and "Prometheus the Firebringer," from *Orpheus with His Lute* by W. M. L. Hutchinson.

BANKS UPSHAW AND COMPANY — "Caballito, Caballito," from *Mother Goose on the Rio Grande* by Frances Alexander and others, copyright 1944.

BRANDT & BRANDT — "Nancy Hanks," from *A Book of Americans,* Rinehart & Company, copyright © 1933 by Rosemary and Stephen Vincent Benet. "The Ballad of William Sycamore," from *The Collected Works of Stephen Vincent Benet,* Rinehart & Company, copyright © 1922 by Stephen Vincent Benet, copyright renewed 1950 by Rosemary Carr Benet. "In Just-spring," by E. E. Cummings, from *Poems 1923–1954,* Harcourt, Brace and Company, copyright © 1923, 1951 by E. E. Cummings.

THE CLARENDON PRESS, Oxford — Selections from the *Oxford Nursery Rhyme Book,* assembled by Iona and Peter Opie; selections from the *Oxford Dictionary of Nursery Rhymes,* edited by Iona and Peter Opie.

PADRAIC COLUM — "Phaethon," "Bellerophon," and "The Seven Sleepers," from *The Forge in the Forest* by Padraic Colum (Macmillan, 1925); "Orpheus,"

Williams; also for granting permission to use *Pelle's New Suit* by Elsa Beskow; "The Canoe in the Rapids," from *The Talking Cat and Other Stories of French Canada*, copyright 1952 by Natalie Savage Carlson; selection from *The Wheel on the School*, copyright 1954 by Meindert De Jong; selection from *The Adventures of Tom Sawyer* by Mark Twain; "Incident," from *Color* by Countee Cullen; "Trucks," from *I Go A-Traveling* by James S. Tippett.

LUCIEN HARRIS — "The Wonderful Tar-Baby" and "Brer Rabbit's Astonishing Prank," by Joel Chandler Harris.

HARVARD UNIVERSITY PRESS — "Determination of the Seasons" and "Origin of the Pleiades," from *Tales of the North American Indians* by Stith Thompson.

THE HOGARTH PRESS LTD., London — selections from *Sandy Andy and Other Scottish Nursery Rhymes* by Norah and William Montgomerie.

HOLIDAY HOUSE — "The General's Horse," from *Padre Porko* by Robert Davis, and an illustration by Fritz Eichenberg from the same book.

HENRY HOLT AND COMPANY, INC. — "The Goat Well," from *Fire on the Mountain* by Harold Courlander, Wolf Leslau, and Robert W. Kane, copyright 1950 by Henry Holt and Company, Inc.; "Thor Gains His Hammer" and "Thor's Unlucky Journey," from *Thunder of the Gods* by Dorothy Hosford, copyright 1952 by Dorothy Hosford; selections from *A Rocket in My Pocket* by Carl Withers, copyright 1948 by Henry Holt and Company, Inc.; "The Last Word of a Bluebird," from *Mountain Interval* by Robert Frost, copyright 1916, 1921 by Henry Holt and Company, Inc., copyright 1944 by Robert Frost; "Stopping by Woods on a Snowy Evening" and "The Pasture," from *Complete Poems of Robert Frost*, copyright 1923 by Henry Holt and Company, Inc., copyright 1951 by Robert Frost; "Fog" and "Lost," from *Chicago Poems* by Carl Sandburg, copyright 1916 by Henry Holt and Company, Inc., copyright 1944 by Carl Sandburg; by permission of the publishers.

HOUGHTON MIFFLIN COMPANY — "An Athos Legend," from *Tales of Christophilos* by Joice M. NanKivell, copyright 1954 by Joice Mary Loch and Panos Ghikas; "How the Seven Brothers Saved Their Sister," from *Tales of the Cheyennes* by Grace Jackson Penney, copyright 1953 by Grace Jackson Penney; *The Little House* by Virginia Lee Burton, copyright 1942 by Virginia Lee Demetrios; "Old Fire Dragaman," from *The Jack Tales* by Richard Chase, copyright 1943 by Richard Chase; from *Young Lafayette* by Jeanette Eaton, copyright 1932 by Jeanette Eaton; from *Johnny Tremain* by Esther Forbes, copyright 1943 by Esther Forbes Hoskins; "The Cat and the Parrot," from *How to Tell Stories to Children* by Sara Cone Bryant, copyright 1905; "The Camel's Complaint," from *The*

Admiral's Caravan by Charles E. Carryl; "Song of Greatness," from *Children Sing in the Far West* by Mary Austin; from *In the Days of Giants* by Abbie Farwell Brown; from *Squirrels and Other Fur-Bearing Animals* by John Burroughs; from *More About Me* by John Drinkwater; from *The Wonder Garden* by Frances Jenkins Olcott; from *Old Greek Folk Stories Told Anew* by Josephine Preston Peabody; *A Prayer for Little Things* by Eleanor Farjeon; "Wizard Frost," by Frank Dempster Sherman. "Riddles in the Dark," from *The Hobbit* by J. R. R. Tolkien, copyright 1938, reprinted by permission of Houghton Mifflin Company and George Allen & Unwin Ltd., London.

ALFRED A. KNOPF, INC. — "The Weasel," by Sally Carrighar, originally published in *The Saturday Evening Post* under the title of "Forest Buccaneer" and here reprinted from *One Day on Beetle Rock* by Sally Carrighar, by permission of Alfred A. Knopf, Inc.; copyright 1943 by The Curtis Publishing Company. Selection from *Hans Christian Andersen: A Great Life in Brief* by Rumer Godden, reprinted by permission of Alfred A. Knopf, Inc.; copyright 1954 by Rumer Godden. "Luna, la Luna," reprinted from *The Hungry Moon: Mexican Nursery Tales* by Patricia Fent Ross, by permission of Alfred A. Knopf, Inc.; copyright 1946 by Alfred A. Knopf, Inc. "Cinderella and the Glass Slipper," "The Sleeping Beauty," and "The Hare and the Hedgehog," from *Told Again* by Walter de la Mare, by permission of Alfred A. Knopf, Inc., and Richard de la Mare; copyright 1927 by Walter de la Mare. "Youth" from *The Dream Keeper* by Langston Hughes, by permission of Alfred A. Knopf, Inc.; copyright 1932 by Alfred A. Knopf, Inc. "The Frog" and "The Yak," from *Cautionary Verses* by Hilaire Belloc, by permission of Alfred A. Knopf, Inc., and A. D. Peters, London. "Measure Me, Sky!" from *Slow Wall: Poems Together with Nor Without Music* by Leonora Speyer, reprinted by permission of Alfred A. Knopf, Inc.; copyright 1926, 1946 by Leonora Speyer. "Escape" and "Velvet Shoes," from *Collected Poems of Elinor Wylie*, reprinted by permission of Alfred A. Knopf, Inc.; copyright 1921, 1932 by Alfred A. Knopf, Inc. *Peter and the Wolf* by Serge Prokofieff, reprinted by permission of Alfred A. Knopf, Inc. "How the Coyote Danced with the Blackbirds," reprinted from *Zuñi Folk Tales* by Frank Hamilton Cushing, by permission of Alfred A. Knopf, Inc.; copyright 1901 by Emily T. M. Cushing, copyright 1931 by Alfred A. Knopf, Inc.

J. B. LIPPINCOTT COMPANY — "The Flea," from *Picture Tales from Spain* by Ruth Sawyer, copyright 1936 by J. B. Lippincott Company, published by J. B. Lippincott Company; selections from *Picture Rhymes from Foreign Lands* by Rose Fyleman, copyright 1935 by Rose Fyleman, published by J. B. Lippincott Company; "Hercules: The Eleventh Task," from *Heroic Tales from Greek Mythology* by Katharine Pyle, copyright 1928, 1955 by Walter Pyle, published by

For

Anne Carroll Moore

WRITER, CRITIC, AND PIONEER IN LIBRARY WORK WITH CHILDREN

FOREWORD

This new edition of the *Anthology of Children's Literature*, like its predecessors, seeks to relate children and their books to the values and verities of literature. The chief intent of the editors has been threefold: first, to arouse interest in the books from which the contents of this anthology derive; second, to place these materials in fresh relation to the present; and third, to give the adult reader, not final judgments, but the desire and the tools to develop his own critical ability, appreciation, and taste in the field of children's literature.

In structure the third edition has not been radically changed from the second, though within the framework there is much that is new. The general introduction and the fourteen section introductions are all new, as are most of the headnotes. The five sections dealing with traditional literature — nursery rhymes, fables, folk tales, myths and legends, and hero stories — have been strengthened by additions, substitutions, and rearrangements. Under "Folk Tales," for example, 26 countries or regions are represented by 80 tales, as against 18 countries with 66 tales in the previous edition. The former separate section "Folklore That Has Inspired Good Music" has this time been omitted, for its main purpose was to give information that has since become generally available through published lists of recordings.

In presenting tales from folklore, legend, myth, and epic, the editors have taken pains to choose the versions best suited for telling aloud — Wanda Gág's robust renderings of Grimm, for example, and Walter de la Mare's sensitive retellings of folk stories. Other distinguished storytellers represented in this book include Marie Shedlock, Seumas MacManus, Padraic Colum, Ella Young, Eleanor Farjeon, Ruth Sawyer, and Mary Gould Davis. Storytelling values are further emphasized in the headnotes, and a new article on storytelling, with practical suggestions, appears as Appendix A.

Nonsense verse, nature writing, biography, and travel and history have been treated as distinct genres in separate sections, rather than subdivisions of larger categories as before. These, and the sections on fantasy, fiction, and poetry, have also been strengthened and brought up to date. A sampling of names new to this edition in these areas includes Rachel Carson, Hendrik Van

Loon, J. R. R. Tolkien, Rumer Godden, and Meindert De Jong; Robert McCloskey, Elizabeth Yates, Elizabeth Chesley Baity, Mary Norton, and Sally Carrighar; Ogden Nash, E. E. Cummings, T. S. Eliot, Dylan Thomas, and Dame Edith Sitwell. In the poetry section, the omission of many older poems which are now found in most poetry collections has made possible a fuller representation of modern poets, an enriched offering for older or exceptional children, and the inclusion of some mint-new favorites for younger children.

Because the picture book has become a kind of literature in its own right, a new section is devoted to it. Although the picture-book story depends on its illustration and book design for its fullest communication, the purpose here is to increase general awareness and appreciation of this unique blending of the literary and graphic arts, as well as to present fifteen distinguished texts that are strong enough to stand on their own merit apart from their particular formats.

Finally, a new section of "Sacred Writings" replaces the "Old Testament Stories" of the former edition. It includes selections from the New Testament as well as the Old, some extracts from the scriptures of the world's religions, a group of prayers, and three saints' legends of universal appeal.

All bibliographies have been compiled anew, as have the graded reading lists. The appendixes have been revised and brought up to date, and Appendix D, on "Illustrators of Children's Books," has been wholly rewritten to present and illustrate criteria of design, line, and style in the work of artists.

In preparing this edition a new editor, Frances Clarke Sayers, has joined the two former editors. Like the one, she has approached the anthology as a teacher of Children's Literature in the English Department of a university, for she is now at the University of California at Los Angeles. Like the other editor, she is a former children's librarian, having served eleven years as Superintendent of Work with Children in the New York Public Library.

The editors wish to express their thanks to Fritz Eichenberg for undertaking the illustration of this edition. His specially designed cartouches, endleaves, and spot drawings capture the verities of pleasure in children's literature and help to give this anthology a sense of that unity of purpose, through diversity of subject matter, that has been an underlying aim.

EVELYN R. SICKELS

CONTENTS

INTRODUCTION: THE KEYS OF CANTERBURY · xxix

Around the World in Nursery Rhymes

INTRODUCTION 3

Mother Goose Nursery Rhymes

1. Pat-a-cake, pat-a-cake 6
2. This little pig went to market 6
3. To market, to market 6
4. Hickory, dickory, dock 6
5. Bye, baby bunting 6
6. Hush-a-bye, baby, on the tree top 6
7. Rock-a-bye, baby, thy cradle is green 6
8. Hey, diddle, diddle 6
9. Ding, dong, bell 6
10. Pussy cat, pussy cat 7
11. Little Boy Blue 7
12. Little Miss Muffet 7
13. Ride a cock-horse to Banbury Cross 7
14. Baa, baa, black sheep 7
15. Little Jack Horner 7
16. Little Tommy Tucker 7
17. Tom, Tom, the piper's son 7
18. Mary, Mary, quite contrary 7
19. Georgie Porgie, pudding and pie 7
20. Hickety, pickety, my black hen 7
21. Humpty Dumpty sat on a wall 8
22. A diller, a dollar, a ten o'clock scholar 8
23. Hark, hark, the dogs do bark 8
24. Goosey, goosey gander 8
25. Great A, little a 8
26. Rub-a-dub dub, three men in a tub 8
27. Jack be nimble 8
28. Bow, wow, wow 8
29. Barber, barber, shave a pig 8
30. Bless you, bless you, burnie-bee 8
31. Rain, rain, go away 8
32. The north wind doth blow 8
33. As Tommy Snooks and Bessy Brooks 8
34. Diddle, diddle, dumpling, my son John 9
35. Lucy Locket lost her pocket 9
36. Peter, Peter, pumpkin eater 9
37. Curly locks, Curly locks 9
38. Jack Sprat could eat no fat 9
39. Cock a doodle doo! 9
40. I had a little pony 9
41. If I had a donkey that wouldn't go 9
42. Jack and Jill went up the hill 9
43. Little Bo-peep has lost her sheep 9
44. Cushy cow, bonny, let down thy milk 10
45. A farmer went trotting upon his grey mare 10
46. Boys and girls come out to play 10
47. What are little boys made of? 10
48. Charley Wag, Charley Wag 10
49. A cat came fiddling out of a barn 10
50. I had a little hen 10
51. I'll tell you a story 10
52. How many miles to Babylon? 11
53. There was a little man, and he had a little gun 11
54. As I was going to Banbury 11
55. Six little mice sat down to spin 11
56. Three young rats with black felt hats 11
57. Hot-cross buns! 11
58. Cross patch 11
59. I saw a ship a-sailing 11
60. Wee Willie Winkie runs through the town 12
61. Bobby Shaftoe's gone to sea 12
62. I had a little nut tree 12
63. Gray goose and gander 12
64. Johnny shall have a new bonnet 12
65. Lavender's blue 12
66. I love sixpence 12
67. If I'd as much money as I could spend 12
68. There was an old woman, and what do you think? 13
69. There was an old woman who lived in a shoe 13
70. There was an old woman tossed up in a basket 13
71. There was an old woman had three sons 13

NOTE: *See also the alternate Contents by Ages and Grades on page 1219.*

72. There was an old woman, as I've
    heard tell   13
73. There was a crooked man   13
74. Doctor Foster went to Gloucester   13
75. Solomon Grundy   13
76. The lion and the unicorn   14
77. When good King Arthur ruled this
    land   14
78. Old King Cole   14
79. A carrion crow sat on an oak   14
80. Four and twenty tailors   14
81. Snail, snail   14
82. Mr. East gave a feast   14
83. See a pin and pick it up   14
84. Where are you going, my pretty maid? 15
85. One misty, moisty morning   15
86. What's in the cupboard?   15
87. I had a little husband   15
88. My little old man and I fell out   15
89. As I was going to sell my eggs   15
90. Simple Simon met a pieman   15
91. The Queen of Hearts   15
92. This is the house that Jack built   16
93. Dame, get up and bake your pies   16
94. I saw three ships come sailing by   17
95. Thirty days hath September   17
96. The boughs do shake and the bells do
    ring   17

Mother Goose Ballads

97. Old Mother Goose when she wanted to
    wander   17
98. Old Mother Hubbard   18
99. Jenny Wren fell sick   18
100. Who killed Cock Robin?   19
101. A Frog he would a-wooing go   19
102. There were three jovial Welshmen   20
103. Can you make a cambric shirt   21

John Newbery's Mother Goose

104. Three wise men of Gotham   22
105. There was an old man, and he had a
     calf   22
106. There was an old woman lived under
     the hill   22
107. See saw, Margery Daw   22
108. Here's A, B, and C   22
109. There was a man of Thessaly   23

Singing Games, Jingles, Counting-out Rhymes

110. One, two, buckle my shoe   23
111. Sing a song of sixpence   23
112. Pease porridge hot   24
113. London Bridge is broken down   24
114. Gay go up and gay go down   24
115. Lady Queen Anne she sits in the sun 25
116. Oh, the brave old Duke of York   25
117. Pop Goes the Weasel   25
118. The Twelve Days of Christmas   25
119. I am a gold lock   26
120. I went up one pair of stairs   26
121. See-saw sacradown   27
122. Intery, mintery, cutery, corn   27
123. Eins, zwei, Polizei   27
124. Un, deux, trois, j'irai dans le bois 27
125. Une fill' a battu   27

Riddles, Paradoxes, Tongue Trippers

126. Long legs, crooked thighs   28
127. Thirty white horses   28
128. In marble halls as white as milk   28
129. As round as an apple   28
130. Black within and red without   28
131. Elizabeth, Elspeth, Betsy, and Bess 28
132. I have a little sister, they call her Peep,
     Peep   28
133. Two legs sat on three legs   28
134. Little Nancy Etticoat   28
135. Hick-a-more, Hack-a-more   28
136. As I was going to St. Ives   29
137. If all the seas were one sea   29
138. If all the world was apple pie   29
139. I saw a fishpond all on fire   29
140. A man in the wilderness asked me   29
141. Betty Botter bought some butter   29
142. How much wood would a woodchuck
     chuck   29
143. Peter Piper pick'd a peck of pepper 29

Nursery Rhymes of Many Lands

144. Little Girl (Arabian)   30
145. The Five Toes (Chinese)   30
146. Lady Bug (Chinese)   30
147. Thistle-Seed (Chinese)   30
148. Blind Man's Buff (Chinese)   30

149. Old Chang the Crab (*Chinese*)   31
150. Fishing (*Danish*)   31
151. Jonathan (*Dutch*)   31
152. Gretchen (*Dutch*)   31
153. The Goblin (*French*)   31
154. Mee, Ray, Doh (*German*)   31
155. An angel came as I lay in bed (*Hebrew*)   31
156. Twelfth Night (*Italian*)   32
157. New Year's Day (*Japanese*)   32
158. Luna, la Luna (*Mexican*)   32
159. Caballito (*Mexican*)   32
160. Tradja of Norway (*Norwegian*)   32
161. Husky Hi (*Norwegian*)   32
162. Mushrooms (*Russian*)   32
163. Dance to your daddy (*Scottish*)   32
164. A wee bird sat upon a tree (*Scottish*)   33
165. Lady, Lady Landers (*Scottish*)   33
166. The cock and the hen (*Scottish*)   33
167. Sandy Candy (*Scottish*)   33
168. John Smith's a very guid man (*Scottish*)   33
169. Haily Paily (*Scottish*)   33
170. Well I Never! (*Spanish*)   33
171. To the Shop (*Welsh*)   33

American Chants and Jingles

172. Yankee Doodle went to town   34
173. I asked my mother for fifty cents   34
174. A bear went over the mountain   34
175. I'm going to Lady Washington's   34
176. Monday's child is fair of face   34
177. Five little squirrels sat up in a tree   34
178. I've got a rocket in my pocket   34

BIBLIOGRAPHY   35

Nonsense

INTRODUCTION   41

Old Greek Nonsense Rhymes

Little Hermogenes is so small   45
Look at Marcus and take warning   45
I boiled hot water in an urn   45
If a Pig Wore a Wig, *Christina Rosselli*   45
Mr. Punchinello   45
Three Children Sliding on the Ice   45

Laura E. Richards

Eletelephony   46
The High Barbaree   46
The Monkeys and the Crocodile   46
Mrs. Snipkin and Mrs. Wobblechin   46
The Owl and the Eel and the Warming-Pan   47
The Great Panjandrum Himself, *Samuel Foote*   47
The Camel's Complaint, *Charles E. Carryl*   47

Lewis Carroll

The Walrus and the Carpenter   48
'Tis the Voice of the Lobster   49
The Crocodile   49
The White Rabbit's Verses   49
Jabberwocky   50
The Gardener's Song   50
The Beaver's Lesson   51

Edward Lear

Nonsense Alphabet   53
The Jumblies   55
The Owl and the Pussy-Cat   56
Mr. and Mrs. Discobbolos   56
The Duck and the Kangaroo   57
The Quangle Wangle's Hat   57
The Table and the Chair   58
The Broom, the Shovel, the Poker and the Tongs   59
The Courtship of the Yonghy-Bonghy-Bò   59
Limericks   60
The Frog, *Hilaire Belloc*   61
The Yak, *Hilaire Belloc*   61
The Eel, *Ogden Nash*   62
The Guppy, *Ogden Nash*   62

BIBLIOGRAPHY   62

Picture Books

INTRODUCTION   67

A Apple Pie, *Kate Greenaway*   72
Johnny Crow's Garden, *L. Leslie Brooke*   72
The Story of the Three Bears,
    L. Leslie Brooke   73
The Story of the Three Little Pigs,
    L. Leslie Brooke   75
The Story of Little Black Sambo,
    Helen Bannerman   77
Noël for Jeanne-Marie, *Françoise*   78
The Tale of Peter Rabbit, *Beatrix Potter*   79

Millions of Cats, *Wanda Gág*   81
Pelle's New Suit, *Elsa Beskow*   83
Little Toot, *Hardie Gramatky*   83
The Little House, *Virginia Lee Burton*   86
Ola, *Ingri and Edgar Parin d'Aulaire*   88
Dick Whittington and His Cat,
    Marcia Brown   90
The 500 Hats of Bartholomew Cubbins,
    Dr. Seuss   93
Mei Li, *Thomas Handforth*   99

BIBLIOGRAPHY   103

Fables

INTRODUCTION   111

Aesop's Fables

The Wind and the Sun   114
A Wolf in Sheep's Clothing   114
A Lion and a Mouse   114
The Shepherd's Boy and the Wolf   114
The Town Mouse and the Country Mouse   115
The Crow and the Pitcher   115
The Dog and His Shadow   115
The Fox and the Crow   115
The Dog in the Manger   115
The Jackdaw and the Borrowed Plumes   116
The Hare and the Tortoise   116
The Goose with the Golden Eggs   116
The Grasshopper and the Ants   116
The Lark and Its Young   116
Belling the Cat   117
The Fox and the Grapes   117
The Miller, His Son, and the Ass   117

The Panchatantra and Bidpai Fables

The Brâhman's Goat   117
The Poor Man and the Flask of Oil   118
The Crow and the Partridge   118
The Tiger, the Brâhman, and the Jackal   119

Jataka Tales

The Spirit that Lived in a Tree   120
The Banyan Deer   121
The Hare that Ran Away   122

Persian Fable

The Seeds and the Wheat   123

Translated from Apion

Androcles and the Lion   123

La Fontaine's Fables

The Dove and the Ant, *Marianne Moore*   124
The Fox and the Goat, *Marianne Moore*   124
The Camel and the Flotsam,
    Marianne Moore   125
The Dairymaid and Her Milk-Pot,
    Marianne Moore   125

Modern Fables

The Blind Men and the Elephant,
    John G. Saxe   126
The Moth and the Star, *James Thurber*   126

BIBLIOGRAPHY   127

Folk Tales

INTRODUCTION 131

Germany

Jakob and Wilhelm Grimm

The Elves 136
The Wolf and the Seven Little Kids 137
The Golden Goose 138
The Bremen Town Musicians 140
The Brother and Sister 142
Hansel and Gretel, *Wanda Gág* 145
The Fisherman and His Wife,
   Wanda Gág 149
Rapunzel, *Wanda Gág* 154
Snow White and the Seven Dwarfs,
   Wanda Gág 156
Rumpelstiltskin 162

Gone Is Gone, *Wanda Gág* 164
The Sorcerer's Apprentice, *Richard Rostron* 167

France

Little Red Riding-Hood, *Charles Perrault* 170
Drakestall, *Andrew Lang* 171
Cinderella and the Glass Slipper,
   Walter de la Mare 174
The Sleeping Beauty, *Walter de la Mare* 180
Beauty and the Beast, *Andrew Lang* 185
Toads and Diamonds, *Charles Perrault* 193

England

The Hare and the Hedgehog,
   Walter de la Mare 195

Joseph Jacobs

The Old Woman and Her Pig 197
Henny-Penny 198
Teeny-Tiny 199
Jack and the Beanstalk 200
Molly Whuppie 203
The Three Sillies 205
Master of All Masters 206
The Well of the World's End 207
The History of Tom Thumb 209
Tamlane 211
The King o' the Cats 212

Ireland

King O'Toole and His Goose,
   Joseph Jacobs 214
Billy Beg and the Bull, *Seumas MacManus* 216
The Bee, the Harp, the Mouse, and the
   Bum-Clock, *Seumas MacManus* 220
Jack and the King Who Was a Gentleman,
   Seumas MacManus 224
Kate Mary Ellen, *Padraic Colum* 227
The Children of Lir, *Ella Young* 230

Scotland

The Faery Flag of Dunvegan,
   Barbara Ker Wilson 235

Spain

The Flea, *Ruth Sawyer* 239
The Tinker and the Ghost,
   Ralph Boggs and Mary Gould Davis 242
The General's Horse, *Robert Davis* 244

Italy

The Priceless Cats, *M. A. Jagendorf* 247

Russia

Seven Simeons, *Boris Artzybasheff* 250
The Little Humpbacked Horse,
   Post Wheeler 258
Mr. Samson Cat, *Valéry Carrick* 265
Peter and the Wolf, *Serge Prokofieff* 267

Czechoslovakia

Budulinek, *Parker Fillmore* 269
The Twelve Months, *Parker Fillmore* 271

Poland

The Jolly Tailor Who Became King,
   Lucia Borski and Kate Miller 276

XX CONTENTS

Finland

The Bear Says "North," *Parker Fillmore*   280
Mighty Mikko, *Parker Fillmore*   281
Hidden Laiva, *James Cloyd Bowman and Margery Bianco*   285

Scandinavia

Peter Christen Asbjörnsen

The Three Billy-Goats-Gruff   290
The Pancake   291
The Ram and the Pig Who Went into the Woods   292
Gudbrand on the Hillside   294
Boots and His Brothers   296
The Princess on the Glass Hill   298
East o' the Sun and West o' the Moon   303
The Lad Who Went to the North Wind   308
The Cat on the Dovrefell   310

The Talking Pot, *Mary C. Hatch*   311

China

Ah Tcha the Sleeper, *Arthur Bowie Chrisman*   313
The Magic Monkey, *Plato and Christina Chan*   316

Japan

The Tongue-cut Sparrow, *Lafcadio Hearn*   318

India

Numskull and the Rabbit, *Arthur W. Ryder*   319
The Cat and the Parrot, *Sara Cone Bryant*   322

Arabia

Aladdin and the Wonderful Lamp, *Andrew Lang*   324

Turkey

Three Fridays, *Alice Geer Kelsey*   331

Canada

The Canoe in the Rapids, *Natalie Savage Carlson*   333

American Regional Tales

Alaskan Eskimo Tale
Mr. Crow Takes a Wife, *Charles E. Gillham*   336

Southern Negro Tales
The Wonderful Tar-Baby, *Joel Chandler Harris*   339
Brer Rabbit's Astonishing Prank, *Joel Chandler Harris*   341

Southern Mountain Tale
Old Fire Dragaman, *Richard Chase*   343

Tall Tales
Paul Bunyan, *Esther Shephard*   346
Slue-foot Sue Dodges the Moon, *James Cloyd Bowman*   349

Mexico

Why the Burro Lives with the Man, *Catherine Bryan and Mabra Madden*   355
The Princess and José, *Anita Brenner*   357

South America

The Tale of the Lazy People, *Charles J. Finger*   358

The West Indies

From Tiger to Anansi, *Philip M. Sherlock*   365

Ethiopia

The Goat Well, *Harold Courlander and Wolf Leslau*   367

BIBLIOGRAPHY   370

Myths and Legends

INTRODUCTION 385

Myths of Ancient Greece

Note on Greek Mythology 388
Demeter, *Edith Hamilton* 389
Prometheus the Firebringer,
  W. M. L. Hutchinson 391
Pandora, *W. M. L. Hutchinson* 394
The Curse of Echo, *Elsie Buckley* 396
Cupid and Psyche, *Edith Hamilton* 399
Orpheus, *Padraic Colum* 404
Baucis and Philemon, *Edith Hamilton* 406
Daphne, *Frances Jenkins Olcott* 407
Phaethon, *Padraic Colum* 408
Bellerophon, *Padraic Colum* 410
Icarus and Daedalus,
  Josephine Preston Peabody 412
Atalanta's Race, *Padraic Colum* 413
The Judgment of Midas,
  Josephine Preston Peabody 416

Norse Myths

Note on Norse Mythology 417
Odin Goes to Mimir's Well,
  Padraic Colum 418
How Frey Won Gerda the Giant Maiden,
  Padraic Colum 419
The Magic Apples, *Abbie Farwell Brown* 422
Balder and the Mistletoe,
  Abbie Farwell Brown 427
Thor Gains His Hammer, *Dorothy Hosford* 432
Thor's Unlucky Journey, *Dorothy Hosford* 434
The Quest of the Hammer,
  Abbie Farwell Brown 438

North American Indian Myths

Determination of the Seasons,
  Stith Thompson 444
How Glooskap Found the Summer,
  Charles Godfrey Leland 444
The Story of the First Woodpecker,
  Florence Holbrook 446
The Locust and the Coyote,
  Aileen B. Nusbaum 447
How the Coyote Danced with the
  Blackbirds, *Frank Hamilton Cushing* 448
Why the Ant Is Almost Cut in Two,
  Alice Marriott 450
Origin of the Pleiades, *Stith Thompson* 452
How the Seven Brothers Saved Their
  Sister, *Grace Jackson Penney* 452

South American Myth

The Legend of the Palm Tree,
  Margarida Estrela Bandeira Duarte 456

Hawaiian Myth

How Kana Brought Back the Sun and Moon
  and Stars, *Padraic Colum* 457

Greek Legends

Why the Monks of Athos Use a Samantron,
  Joice M. NanKivell 459
The Seven Sleepers, *Padraic Colum* 460

BIBLIOGRAPHY 463

Heroes of Epic and Romance

INTRODUCTION 469

Greece

Odysseus and the Cyclops, *Padraic Colum* 474
Perseus, *Edith Hamilton* 476
Hercules: The Eleventh Task,
  Katharine Pyle 480
How Jason Lost His Sandal in Anauros,
  Charles Kingsley 483

England

Beowulf's Fight with Grendel,
  Hamilton Wright Mabie 487
How St. George Fought the Dragon,
  Marion Lansing 492
King Arthur and His Sword,
  Sidney Lanier 493
Robin Hood and Little John,
  Howard Pyle 499

Ireland

The Wonder Smith and His Son,
    Ella Young   503
Cuchulain's Wooing, Eleanor Hull   507

Scandinavia

Sigurd's Youth, Padraic Colum   512

Germany

Fafnir, the Dragon, James Baldwin   517

France

The Song of Roland, Merriam Sherwood   522

Spain

The Cid, Merriam Sherwood   528

Finland

The Kalevala: The Two Suitors,
    Babette Deutsch   533

India

Rama: The March to Lanka,
    Dhan Gopal Mukerji   538

Persia

Zal, Helen Zimmern   541

BIBLIOGRAPHY   544

Fantasy

INTRODUCTION   551

Hans Christian Andersen

    The Real Princess   554
    Five Peas in a Pod   554
    The Candles   556
    Thumbelisa   558
    The Wild Swans   563
    The Steadfast Tin Soldier   571
    The Tinder Box   573
    The Nightingale   577
    The Emperor's New Clothes   582
    The Ugly Duckling   584
    The Swineherd   589
    The Fir Tree   591

Adventures of Pinocchio: Pinocchio's First
    Pranks, Carlo Collodi   596
Peter Pan in Kensington Gardens:
    Lock-Out Time, James M. Barrie   598
Alice's Adventures in Wonderland:
    Down the Rabbit-Hole and
    The Rabbit Sends in a Little Bill,
    Lewis Carroll   603

Just So Stories: How the Camel Got His
    Hump, Rudyard Kipling   609
The Story of Doctor Dolittle: The Rarest
    Animal of All, Hugh Lofting   610
Rabbit Hill: Little Georgie Sings a Song,
    Robert Lawson   612
The Wind in the Willows: The Wild Wood,
    Kenneth Grahame   616
The Little Prince (selection),
    Antoine de Saint-Exupéry   622
Many Moons, James Thurber   624
Mary Poppins Opens the Door:
    The Marble Boy, Pamela Travers   629
The Borrowers (selection), Mary Norton   638
The Hobbit: Riddles in the Dark,
    J. R. R. Tolkien   645
Half Magic: What Happened to Katharine,
    Edward Eager   652
Gulliver's Travels: FROM A Voyage to
    Lilliput, Jonathan Swift   663
The King of the Golden River,
    John Ruskin   669

BIBLIOGRAPHY   682

Sacred Writings and Legends of the Saints

INTRODUCTION 691

Bible Selections

Joseph and His Brethren (abridged),
Genesis 26–46 695
The Story of Ruth (abridged), Ruth 1–2 703
The Visit of the Magi, Matthew 2:1–12 705
The Prodigal Son, Luke 15:11–32 705
Charity, I Corinthians 13 706

Songs from the Bible
The Two Paths, Proverbs 4:10–19 706
The Tree and the Chaff, Psalm 1 707
The Lord Is My Shepherd, Psalm 23 707
The Earth Is the Lord's, Psalm 24 707
God Is Our Refuge and Strength,
Psalm 46 708
Abiding in the Shadow of the Almighty,
Psalm 91 708
I Will Lift Up Mine Eyes, Psalm 121 709
Praise Ye the Lord, Psalm 150 709

Prayers

May the strength of God pilot me,
St. Patrick 709

Lord, make me an instrument of Thy peace,
St. Francis of Assisi 710
God be in my head, and in my
understanding 710
What God gives, and what we take,
Robert Herrick 710
Lord, purge our eyes to see,
Christina Rossetti 710
Give us grace and strength,
Robert Louis Stevenson 710

"Golden Words"

"Golden Words" from Sacred Writings 711

Legends of the Saints

St. Jerome and the Lion and the Donkey,
Helen Waddell 713
The Truce of the Wolf; a Legend of St.
Francis of Assisi, Mary Gould Davis 715
St. Nicholas, Eleanor Farjeon 719

BIBLIOGRAPHY 722

Earth, Sky, and Sea

INTRODUCTION 729

Wagtail: Wagtail's World Grows Wider,
Alice Crew Gall and Fleming H. Crew 731
Children of the Sea: The Dolphin's Tale,
Wilfrid S. Bronson 733
The Cricket, Jean Henri Fabre 736
Walden: The Battle of the Ants and The
Loon, Henry David Thoreau 738
Vulpes the Red Fox (selection), John and
Jean George 740
One Day on Beetle Rock: The Weasel,
Sally Carrighar 743
Squirrels and Other Fur-Bearers: The Mink,
John Burroughs 745

A Hind in Richmond Park:
Bird Migration on the Pampas,
W. H. Hudson 746
Far Away and Long Ago: Flamingoes,
W. H. Hudson 749
Beneath the Tropic Seas: Sponges,
William Beebe 749
Men, Microscopes, and Living Things:
Between the Heights and the Depths,
Katherine B. Shippen 751
The Sea Around Us: The Moving Tides,
Rachel L. Carson 753

BIBLIOGRAPHY 756

Biography

INTRODUCTION 767

Columbus Sails: The Ambassador,
   C. Walter Hodges 769
Amos Fortune, Free Man: Auctioned for
   Freedom, *Elizabeth Yates* 771
Leader by Destiny: George Washington,
   the Boy, *Jeanette Eaton* 776
Young Lafayette: The Great Adventure
   Begins, *Jeanette Eaton* 782
Daniel Boone: Boonesborough,
   James Daugherty 787
Audubon: Many Trails and a Snug Cabin,
   Constance Rourke 791

Abraham Lincoln: His Good Stepmother,
   Genevieve Foster 793
Abe Lincoln Grows Up: "Peculiarsome"
   Abe, *Carl Sandburg* 795
Hans Christian Andersen, *Rumer Godden* 798
Invincible Louisa: "Little Women,"
   Cornelia Meigs 802
Clara Barton of the Red Cross,
   Jeannette Covert Nolan 810
Madame Curie: Four Years in a Shed,
   Eve Curie 814
Albert Schweitzer, *Joseph Gollomb* 818

BIBLIOGRAPHY 820

Travel and History

INTRODUCTION 827

The Story of Mankind: The Setting of the
   Stage, *Hendrik Van Loon* 831
Americans Before Columbus: The Vikings
   Find and Lose America,
   Elizabeth Chesley Baity 833
Vast Horizons: The Polos,
   Mary Seymour Lucas 835
Hakluyt's Voyages: The Deliverance,
   Richard Hakluyt 840
Of Courage Undaunted: Lewis and Clark,
   James Daugherty 841

George Washington's World:
   The Declaration of Independence,
   Genevieve Foster 845
Captain Scott's Last Expedition: The Last
   March, *from the Diary of Captain
   Robert Scott* 847
North to the Orient: Point Barrow,
   Anne Morrow Lindbergh 849
Wind, Sand, and Stars: The Elements,
   Antoine de Saint-Exupéry 853
The Great Heritage: We Have Tomorrow,
   Katherine B. Shippen 858

BIBLIOGRAPHY 859

Fiction

INTRODUCTION 865

Poppy Seed Cakes (selection), *Margery Clark* 867
The Little Wooden Doll (selection),
   Margery Williams Bianco 868
Little Girl with Seven Names,
   Mabel Leigh Hunt 869
Little House in the Big Woods: Summer-
   time, *Laura Ingalls Wilder* 881
Heidi: In the Pasture, *Johanna Spyri* 885

The Fair American: The New Cabin Boy,
   Elizabeth Coatsworth 892
Rufus M. (selection), *Eleanor Estes* 895
Hans Brinker: Hans and Gretel Find a
   Friend, *Mary Mapes Dodge* 900
Hitty: I Go Up in the World,
   Rachel L. Field 903
Blue Willow: The Shack, *Doris Gates* 908
The Wheel on the School (selection),
   Meindert De Jong 914

Caddie Woodlawn: Breeches and Clogs,
  Carol Ryrie Brink   922
Downright Dencey: The Former Time,
  Caroline Dale Snedeker   926
The Good Master: The Round-up,
  Kate Seredy   931
Lassie Come-Home: A Long Journey's
  Beginning, Eric Knight   935
Homer Price: The Doughnuts,
  Robert McCloskey   938
Call It Courage: Drums, Armstrong Sperry   942
Adam of the Road: A Blush of Boys,
  Elizabeth Janet Gray   945
Men of Iron (selection), Howard Pyle   949
The Trumpeter of Krakow: The Man Who
  Wouldn't Sell His Pumpkin,
  Eric P. Kelly   951

Master Simon's Garden: The Edge of the
  World, Cornelia L. Meigs   955
Rolling Wheels: Over the Divide,
  Katharine Grey   961
The Adventures of Tom Sawyer: Tom
  Meets Becky, Mark Twain   963
Treasure Island (selection),
  Robert Louis Stevenson   969
Robinson Crusoe (selection), Daniel Defoe   976
Johnny Tremain: Salt-Water Tea,
  Esther Forbes   981
The Silver Pencil (selection),
  Alice Dalgliesh   986
All-American: A Lesson in Citizenship,
  John R. Tunis   989

BIBLIOGRAPHY   993

Poetry

INTRODUCTION   1001

Fairies, Fay, and Far Away

The Fairies, William Allingham   1004
The Fairies, Rose Fyleman   1004
A Fairy Went A-Marketing, Rose Fyleman   1005
The Little Elf, John Kendrick Bangs   1005
The Elves' Dance   1005
Here We Come A-Piping   1006
Some One, Walter de la Mare   1006
Overheard on a Saltmarsh, Harold Monro   1006
Escape, Elinor Wylie   1006
"Over Hill, Over Dale,"
  William Shakespeare   1007
"Where the Bee Sucks,"
  William Shakespeare   1007
Queen Mab, William Shakespeare   1007
"You Spotted Snakes,"
  William Shakespeare   1007
The Song of Wandering Aengus,
  William Butler Yeats   1008
A Song of Sherwood, Alfred Noyes   1008
The King of China's Daughter,
  Edith Sitwell   1009

Wind, Woods, and Weather

Laughing Song, William Blake   1010
Waiting, Harry Behn   1010

Spring, William Blake   1010
The Echoing Green, William Blake   1011
In Just-spring, E. E. Cummings   1011
March, William Wordsworth   1011
Little Wind, Kate Greenaway   1012
Who Has Seen the Wind?
  Christina Rossetti   1012
The Wind, Robert Louis Stevenson   1012
Windy Wash Day, Dorothy Aldis   1012
The Kite, Harry Behn   1012
Song (April), William Watson   1013
April, Sara Teasdale   1013
Home Thoughts from Abroad,
  Robert Browning   1013
April and May, Ralph Waldo Emerson   1013
The Pasture, Robert Frost   1013
Dandelion, Hilda Conkling   1014
To the Dandelion, James Russell Lowell   1014
Daffodils, William Wordsworth   1014
To Daffodils, Robert Herrick   1014
Pussy Willows, Rowena Bastin Bennett   1015
Sweet Peas, John Keats   1015
Rain, Robert Louis Stevenson   1015
The Rain, Rowena Bastin Bennett   1015
Rubber Boots, Rowena Bastin Bennett   1015
The Umbrella Brigade, Laura E. Richards   1015
Cape Ann, T. S. Eliot   1016
In Arden Forest, William Shakespeare   1016
A Morning Song, William Shakespeare   1016
Loveliest of Trees, Alfred Edward Housman   1017

Trees, *Harry Behn* 1017
The Bridge, *Christina Rossetti* 1017
The Painted Desert,
    Elizabeth Coatsworth 1017
Yucca, *Ann Nolan Clark* 1018
Fog, *Carl Sandburg* 1018
Lost, *Carl Sandburg* 1018
The Branch, *Elizabeth Madox Roberts* 1018
Song of the Brook, *Alfred, Lord Tennyson* 1019
Minnows, *John Keats* 1019
The Lake Isle of Innisfree,
    William Butler Yeats 1020
I Meant to Do My Work Today,
    Richard Le Gallienne 1020
The Cloud, *Percy Bysshe Shelley* 1020
Glimpse in Autumn, *Jean Starr Untermeyer* 1021
The Morns are Meeker than They Were,
    Emily Dickinson 1021
Autumn Fires, *Robert Louis Stevenson* 1021
A Vagabond Song, *Bliss Carman* 1022
Color in the Wheat, *Hamlin Garland* 1022
The Last Word of a Bluebird, *Robert Frost* 1022
Something Told the Wild Geese,
    Rachel Field 1022
To the Fringed Gentian,
    William Cullen Bryant 1023
Hallowe'en, *Harry Behn* 1023
What Am I? *Dorothy Aldis* 1023
God's World, *Edna St. Vincent Millay* 1023
To Autumn, *John Keats* 1024
Wizard Frost, *Frank Dempster Sherman* 1024
The Frost Pane, *David McCord* 1024
The Snowflake, *Walter de la Mare* 1025
For Snow, *Eleanor Farjeon* 1025
Velvet Shoes, *Elinor Wylie* 1025
Stopping by Woods on a Snowy Evening,
    Robert Frost 1025
Lines from "Snowbound," *John Greenleaf
    Whittier* 1026
"When Icicles Hang by the Wall,"
    William Shakespeare 1026
An Almanac, *William Sharp* 1026
The Wakeupworld, *Countee Cullen* 1027

Surge of the Sea

At the Sea-side, *Robert Louis Stevenson* 1027
The Shell, *David McCord* 1027
A Sea Song, *Allan Cunningham* 1027
Sea-Fever, *John Masefield* 1028
A Wanderer's Song, *John Masefield* 1028
From "Swimmers," *Louis Untermeyer* 1028

Little Creatures

Little Things, *James Stephens* 1029
A Prayer for Little Things,
    Eleanor Farjeon 1029
The Mouse, *Elizabeth Coatsworth* 1029
The City Mouse, *Christina Rossetti* 1030
Little Snail, *Hilda Conkling* 1030
The Little Turtle, *Vachel Lindsay* 1030
Our Mr. Toad, *David McCord* 1030
The Caterpillar, *Christina Rossetti* 1031
Firefly, *Elizabeth Madox Roberts* 1031
Fireflies, *Winifred Welles* 1031
On the Grasshopper and Cricket,
    John Keats 1031
The Wasp, *William Sharp* 1031
The Blackbird, *Humbert Wolfe* 1032
The Sandpiper, *Celia Thaxter* 1032
Bantam Rooster, *Harry Behn* 1032
Red Rooster, *Hilda Conkling* 1032
Mrs. Peck-Pigeon, *Eleanor Farjeon* 1033
Duck's Ditty, *Kenneth Grahame* 1033
Market Square, *A. A. Milne* 1033
The Squirrel 1034
Clover for Breakfast, *Frances Frost* 1034
Milk for the Cat, *Harold Monro* 1034
The Mysterious Cat, *Vachel Lindsay* 1035
I Like Little Pussy, *Jane Taylor* 1035
Mary's Lamb, *Sarah Josepha Hale* 1036
The Lamb, *William Blake* 1036

Good Day and Good Night

Softly, Drowsily, *Walter de la Mare* 1036
The Sounds in the Morning,
    Eleanor Farjeon 1037
Song for a Little House, *Christopher Morley* 1037
The Swing, *Robert Louis Stevenson* 1037
My Shadow, *Robert Louis Stevenson* 1037
The Land of Counterpane,
    Robert Louis Stevenson 1038
Pirate Story, *Robert Louis Stevenson* 1038
The Little Land, *Robert Louis Stevenson* 1038
Bed in Summer, *Robert Louis Stevenson* 1039
Pretending, *Harry Behn* 1039
Hiding, *Dorothy Aldis* 1040
Circus, *Eleanor Farjeon* 1040
Whistles, *Dorothy Aldis* 1041
The Little Whistler, *Frances Frost* 1041
Troubles, *Dorothy Aldis* 1041
Radiator Lions, *Dorothy Aldis* 1041
Mumps, *Elizabeth Madox Roberts* 1041
Washing, *John Drinkwater* 1042

Twos, *John Drinkwater* 1042
Miss T., *Walter de la Mare* 1042
Tired Tim, *Walter de la Mare* 1042
The Barber's, *Walter de la Mare* 1042
Boys' Names, *Eleanor Farjeon* 1043
Girls' Names, *Eleanor Farjeon* 1043
General Store, *Rachel Field* 1043
Taxis, *Rachel Field* 1043
Motor Cars, *Rowena Bastin Bennett* 1043
Trucks, *James S. Tippett* 1044
Song of the Train, *David McCord* 1044
Skyscrapers, *Rachel Field* 1044
Animal Crackers, *Christopher Morley* 1044
Evening, *Harry Behn* 1045
Nod, *Walter de la Mare* 1045
What the Rattlesnake Said, *Vachel Lindsay* 1045
The Moon's the North Wind's Cooky,
   Vachel Lindsay 1045
Full Moon, *Walter de la Mare* 1045
Silver, *Walter de la Mare* 1046
The White Window, *James Stephens* 1046
Stars, *Sara Teasdale* 1046
Night, *Sara Teasdale* 1046
The Night Will Never Stay,
   Eleanor Farjeon 1046
Nurse's Song, *William Blake* 1046
Cradle Song, *William Blake* 1047
Sleep, Baby, Sleep 1047
An Indian Lullaby 1047
Lullaby of an Infant Chief, *Sir Walter Scott* 1047
Wynken, Blynken, and Nod, *Eugene Field* 1048
Sweet and Low, *Alfred, Lord Tennyson* 1048
Seal Lullaby, *Rudyard Kipling* 1049
Good Night, *Thomas Hood* 1049

Christmas, Christmas!

While Shepherds Watched Their Flocks by
   Night, *Nahum Tate* 1049
O Little Town of Bethlehem,
   Phillips Brooks 1050
Cradle Hymn, *Martin Luther* 1050
Christmas Morning,
   Elizabeth Madox Roberts 1050
A Christmas Folk-Song,
   Lizette Woodworth Reese 1051
God Rest Ye Merry, Gentlemen,
   Dinah Maria Mulock Craik 1051
"Some Say . . . ," *William Shakespeare* 1051
I Wonder as I Wander 1051
A Visit from St. Nicholas,
   Clement C. Moore 1052

The Grace of Understanding

Measure Me, Sky! *Leonora Speyer* 1053
Beauty, *E-Yeh-Shure (Louise Abeita)* 1053
Barter, *Sara Teasdale* 1053
Wings, *Victor Hugo* 1054
My Heart Leaps Up, *William Wordsworth* 1054
I Never Saw a Moor, *Emily Dickinson* 1054
Do You Fear the Wind? *Hamlin Garland* 1054
A Song of Greatness, *Mary Austin* 1054
A Chant Out of Doors,
   Marguerite Wilkinson 1054
Fern Hill, *Dylan Thomas* 1055
Miracles, *Walt Whitman* 1056
Give Me the Splendid Silent Sun,
   Walt Whitman 1056
I Hear America Singing, *Walt Whitman* 1056
The Commonplace, *Walt Whitman* 1057
Atlantic Charter, *Francis Brett Young* 1057
Lincoln, *John Gould Fletcher* 1057
Abraham Lincoln Walks at Midnight,
   Vachel Lindsay 1057
Nancy Hanks, *Rosemary Carr and Stephen
   Vincent Benét* 1058
"When to the Sessions of Sweet Silent
   Thought," *William Shakespeare* 1058
Incident, *Countee Cullen* 1058
Ring Around the World, *Annette Wynne* 1059

Ballads and Tales

Get Up and Bar the Door 1059
Sir Patrick Spens 1060
Robin Hood and Little John 1060
The Keys of Canterbury 1063
Hiawatha's Childhood,
   Henry Wadsworth Longfellow 1063
Paul Revere's Ride,
   Henry Wadsworth Longfellow 1065
Barbara Frietchie, *John Greenleaf Whittier* 1067
The Flower-fed Buffaloes, *Vachel Lindsay* 1068
The Ballad of William Sycamore,
   Stephen Vincent Benét 1068
Lochinvar, *Sir Walter Scott* 1069
The Charge of the Light Brigade,
   Alfred, Lord Tennyson 1070
The Sands of Dee, *Charles Kingsley* 1070
Annabel Lee, *Edgar Allan Poe* 1071
The Pied Piper of Hamelin,
   Robert Browning 1071
The Admiral's Ghost, *Alfred Noyes* 1075
The Creation, *James Weldon Johnson* 1076
BIBLIOGRAPHY 1078

Appendixes

Appendix A

Storytelling   1083
BIBLIOGRAPHY   1088

Appendix B

The Story of Children's Literature   1090
BIBLIOGRAPHY   1107

Appendix C

Early Writings   1109
  Little Goody Two-Shoes   1110
  A Day of Misfortunes, *Maria Edgeworth*   1123
  A Hymn in Prose, *Letitia Aikin Barbauld* 1126
  The Butterfly's Ball, *William Roscoe* 1127
  Murdoch's Rath, *Juliana Horatia Ewing* 1128
BIBLIOGRAPHY   1131

Appendix D

Illustrators of Children's Books   1132
BIBLIOGRAPHY   1148

Appendix E

The Newbery and Caldecott Awards   1149

Appendix F

Graded Reading Lists   1152

Appendix G

Biographical Sketches   1174

Appendix H

Pronouncing Glossary   1216

CONTENTS BY AGES AND GRADES · 1219

INDEX · 1225

INTRODUCTION: THE KEYS OF CANTERBURY

"Oh lady, I will give you
The keys of Canterbury,
If you will be my bride,
My sweet and only dear,
And walk along with me anywhere."

ENGLISH FOLK SONG

THIS OLD SINGING GAME evokes a melody in the mind and an image of incomparable treasure. Part of the spell, to be sure, lies in the music which accompanies it, but the words in themselves are potent and full of mystery. The word *Canterbury!* How smooth its balance on the tongue. At sight and sound of it, echoes of Chaucer's pilgrimage shake through the mind and the Cathedral itself looms up on the plain. Who was the gentleman who had possession of the keys, to give away at will? And what treasure would the lady command by their ownership? No one knows! One can fit the meaning to one's own purpose. For those who encounter the song here, the keys of Canterbury shall represent the keys to Literature; for Literature is an edifice as many-towered and as spirit-lifting as any cathedral man has sent skyward. ("We see the shape from start to finish," writes Virginia Woolf.[1] "It (the book) is a barn; a pig-sty, or a cathedral.")

Literature is the term we use to define excellence in writing; "writings in which expression and form, in connection with ideas of permanent and universal interest, are characteristic or essential features, as poetry, romance, history, biography, essays, etc." This is the definition given in the *American College Dictionary,* and a good one it is, too, as good as the botanical definition of a flower. But the trick is to recognize the flower on sight, to enjoy it, and to be impelled by that enjoyment to impart to others one's own pleasure or exaltation. The obligation to impart is increased when the response of children is involved, since theirs is the future and the opportunity to advance the boundaries of taste and accomplishment, for a whole generation.

The startling fact is that children's literature, at least a third of it, derives from the same sources as does the literature of the adult world: the primitive beginnings — epic, saga, the folk tale, mythology, poetry, romance. True, the form in which the *Iliad* and the *Odyssey, Beowulf,* and *King Arthur* are given to children is a less complex form, but the emotion, the driving force of the

---

[1] In the chapter "How Should One Read a Book": Virginia Woolf, *The Second Common Reader* (Harcourt, Brace, New York, 1932), p. 291.

xxix

story, the pitch of absolute sincerity which characterize these literatures are common ground for child and adult alike.

The difference between literature for children and literature for adults lies in choice of subject matter rather than in the depth of feeling or the quality of writing. Children are not prepared for and not interested in psychological intricacies, or the love between men and women, or social controversies, or politics, or the anguish of self-doubt, or the explorations of man's relation to the unknown. And yet, by intuition and premonition, they recognize some of these unknowns as foreshadowing the life that lies ahead. For that reason, the literature which is symbolic is significant. They grasp the symbol, and feel secure because they have a key, to be used as needed.

The interests of children are extensive: knowledge, play, imaginative adventure, exploration of worlds known and unknown; or to break it down further, science, history, biography, anthropology, archaeology, poetry, religion — and above all, an interest in stories, for there is no substitute for fiction as a means of discovering the infinite varieties of experience which befall human beings. All of these are subjects to be lifted above the ordinary by the gift of literature. No one has described that quality, that edge of perception, which is recognized as literature, as eloquently as has Paul Hazard, distinguished scholar, Professor of Comparative Literature at the Sorbonne, and one of the few to consider books for children from the broad base of literature as a whole:

> I like books that remain faithful to the very essence of art [he writes]. Namely; those that offer to children an intuitive and direct way of knowledge, a simple beauty capable of being perceived immediately, arousing in their souls a vibration which will endure all their lives. . . .
>
> And books that awaken in them not maudlin sentimentality but sensibility; that enable them to share in great human emotions; that give them respect for universal life — that of animals, of plants; that teach them not to despise everything that is mysterious in creation and in man. . . .
>
> I like books of knowledge . . . when they have tact and moderation; when, instead of pouring out so much material on a child's soul that it is crushed, they plant in it a seed that will develop from the inside. . . . I like them especially when they distill from all the different kinds of knowledge the most difficult and the most necessary — that of the human heart.[2]

But how is one to recognize these attributes, if by some mischance one's own childhood was devoid of reading? The definitions and statements and allegories describing literature are all very well, but there is only one way to learn to recognize it for oneself. And that is to read! To the reading must be added the act of judging, and of deciding what is worthy of the children for whom one is responsible. If you are without experience in the literature of childhood, trust yourself to the inspired readers, men and women whose own love of literature spills over into their books and articles, and infects us like a happy contagion: Walter de la Mare, Anne Carroll Moore, Alice Jordan, C. S. Lewis, A. A. Milne, Clifton Fadiman, Horace Scudder, Anne T. Eaton — and Paul Hazard. These are among the best. Read what they have read, and

2 Paul Hazard, *Books, Children and Men* (The Horn Book, Inc., Boston, 1944), pp. 42–43.

girls rather than for adults. *Current Books, Senior Booklist* is published by the same board.

Children's Catalog, compiled by Marion L. Mc-Connell and Dorothy H. West. H. W. Wilson Company, 950–972 University Ave., New York, N.Y. Ninth ed.

A classified catalog of 3,204 children's books with descriptive notes, recommended for public and school libraries with an author, title, and subject index. Kept up-to-date with annual supplements.

Distinguished Books of the Year, an annual list compiled by the Children's Library Association of the American Library Association, 50 E. Huron Street, Chicago 11, Illinois.

Available in leaflet form from the Association and also published in library and educational periodicals.

Growing Up with Books, an annual list published by the R. R. Bowker Company, 62 West 45th St., New York 36.

Available at quantity rates.

The Horn Book Magazine, a bi-monthly, published by The Horn Book, Inc., 585 Boylston Street, Boston 16, Mass.

A distinguished magazine devoted entirely to the field of children's literature.

McCall's List of 100 Best Books for Children, selected for *McCall's* by Virginia Haviland, Ruth Gagliardo, and Elizabeth Nesbitt. McCall Corporation, P.O. Box 1390, Grand Central Station, New York 17.

McCall's Magazine asked three distinguished women in the field of children's literature to choose one hundred books which they considered the best for children to grow on.

Recommended Children's Books of the Current Year, compiled under the direction of Louise Davis, children's book review editor of the *Library Journal,* 62 West 45th St., New York 36. 1957.

Books are professionally evaluated by librarians.

Science Books for Boys and Girls, 1952–55, prepared by Nora Beust and Paul Blackwood. The Office of Education, Washington 25, D.C.

Seven Stories High — The Child's Own Library, compiled by Anne Carroll Moore. F. E. Compton & Co., 1000 N. Dearborn St., Chicago, Illinois.

Reprinted from Compton's Pictured Encyclopedia. One of the most widely used of all basic lists, it was originally compiled and frequently revised by Anne Carroll Moore. It grew out of her wide experience as Superintendent of Work with Children in the New York Public Library.

Starred Books from the Library Journal, edited by Peggy Melcher and published by the *Library Journal,* 62 West 45th St., New York 16. 1955.

Seven hundred complete reviews of the best books for children of the last 17 years as evaluated by children's librarians.

Your Reading, prepared and published by the National Council of Teachers of English, 704 South 6th St., Champaign, Illinois.

Published in two sections, *Junior High School List* and *Senior High School List.*

measure your mind against theirs, and where you find yourself wanting in appreciation of *Wind in the Willows* or *And Now Miguel*, hold yourself accountable, and try again, or reach beyond in another direction. Read in the company of children, for their reactions and insights will help you to fresh vision and perception. Read as deeply as you can, and after a while you will recognize for yourself the *signatures of literature*.

Among them are, *the emotion of the author:* In every piece of literature — poem, story, biography, or a life cycle of the weasel — the extent of the personal involvement of the author in his subject determines the reach of his power to touch and inform the emotion of the reader. Here is an excerpt from the autobiography of the naturalist W. H. Hudson. Once it is read, it is unforgettable, because it expresses so passionate a love for his own boyhood, spent in South America.

> To climb trees and put my hand down in the deep hot nest of the Bien-te-veo and feel the hot eggs. . . . To lie on a grassy bank with the blue water between me and beds of tall bulrushes, listening to the mysterious sounds of the wind and of hidden rails and coots and courlans conversing together in strange human-like tones. . . . To lie on my back on the rust-brown grass in January and gaze up at the wide hot whitey-blue sky, peopled with millions and myriads of glistening balls of thistle-down, ever, ever floating by; to gaze and gaze until they are to me living things and I, in an ecstasy, am with them, floating in that immense shining void![3]

Originality of concept: This, of course, is among the first signs of greatness. *Alice in Wonderland* comes first to mind, in this connection, because it and its sequel, *Alice Through the Looking Glass*, are unlike any other books ever written. Fantasy is apt to yield treasure here, because it invites originality by the nature of its being.

The revelation of life is a third sign of literature: the means by which the specific incident or observation is related to the universal experience of man. Slight, delicate, tender, or on a large and heroic scale, how endlessly fascinating are the testaments to the human spirit which literature records.

Mastery of style, and the suitability of style to concept: These are discernible in literature, for the written structure breathes for the work and surges through it like a tide of life blood. As children read, they come to feed upon the pleasures of good writing, and so nourish their own abilities, of comprehension and expression.

These, then, are among the keys of Canterbury. And the master key unlocks the Treasure of Enjoyment! "Mere literary knowledge is of slight importance," writes Alfred Whitehead. "The only thing that matters is, how it is known. The facts related are nothing. Literature only exists to express and develop that imaginative world which is our life, the kingdom which is within us. The literary side of a technical education should consist in an effort to make the pupils enjoy literature. It does not matter what they know, but the enjoyment is vital."[4]

---

[3] W. H. Hudson, *Far Away and Long Ago* (E. P. Dutton, New York, 1918), p. 294.
[4] Alfred Whitehead, *The Aims of Education* (Macmillan, New York, 1921), pp. 88–89.

BIBLIOGRAPHY

Books and Reading

Bennett, James O'Donnell. *Much Loved Books; Best Sellers of the Ages*. Boni & Liveright, 1927.

Cecil, Lord David. *The Fine Art of Reading*. Bobbs-Merrill, 1957.

Center, Stella S. *The Art of Book Reading*. Charles Scribner's Sons, 1952.

Drew, Elizabeth. *The Enjoyment of Literature*. W. W. Norton, 1935.

Eastman, Max. *The Literary Mind: Its Place in an Age of Science*. Charles Scribner's Sons, 1931.

Erskine, John. *The Delight of Great Books*. Bobbs-Merrill, 1928.

Fadiman, Clifton, ed. *Reading I've Liked*. Simon & Schuster, 1941.

Finger, Charles. *After the Great Companions; a Free Fantasia on a Lifetime of Reading*. E. P. Dutton, 1934.

Forster, E. M. *Aspects of the Novel*. Harcourt, Brace, 1949.

Guérard, Albert. *Preface to World Literature*. Henry Holt, 1940.

Highet, Gilbert. *A Clerk of Oxenford, Essays on Literature and Art*. Oxford University Press, 1954.

Highet, Gilbert. *People, Places and Books*. Oxford University Press, 1953.

Jackson, Holbrook. *The Reading of Books*. Charles Scribner's Sons, 1947.

Loveman, Amy. *"I'm Looking for a Book . . ."* Dodd, Mead, 1936.

Powys, John Cowper. *Enjoyment of Literature*. Simon & Schuster, 1938.

Quiller-Couch, Sir Arthur. *On the Art of Reading*. G. P. Putnam's Sons, 1920.

Read, Sir Herbert Edward. *The Nature of Literature*. Horizon, 1956.

Santayana, George. *Essays in Literary Criticism;* ed. by Irving Singer. Charles Scribner's Sons, 1956.

Stefferud, Alfred, ed. *Wonderful World of Books*. Houghton Mifflin, 1952.

Trilling, Lionel. *The Liberal Imagination; Essays on Literature and Society*. Doubleday, 1953. (Anchor Books)

Van Doren, Mark. *A Liberal Education*. Henry Holt, 1943.

Woolf, Virginia. *The Common Reader*. Harcourt, Brace, 1925.

Books on Reading for Children

Arbuthnot, May Hill. *Children and Books*. Scott, Foresman, rev. ed. 1957.

A comprehensive study of children and their books by a well-known Associate Professor of Education at Western Reserve University.

Becker, May Lamberton. *First Adventures in Reading*. J. B. Lippincott, rev. ed. 1947.

Friendly, helpful counsel concerning books from babyhood to teen-age. The author's genuine enthusiasm is contagious and delightful. In *Adventures in Reading*, Mrs. Becker tells about books for young adults.

Chase, Mary Ellen. *Recipe for a Magic Childhood;* illus. by George and Doris Hauman. Macmillan, 1952.

The author, formerly a professor of English Literature at Smith College, recalls her happy childhood in which books played a vital and absorbing part. First appeared as an article in the *Ladies' Home Journal*, May 1951.

Crouch, Marcus, comp. *Chosen for Children, An Account of the Books Which Have Been Awarded the Library Association Carnegie Medal, 1936–1957*. The Library Association, London, 1957.

Dalgliesh, Alice. *First Experiences with Literature*. Charles Scribner's Sons, 1937.

Discriminating discussion of literature for children in kindergarten and primary grades.

Duff, Annis. *"Bequest of Winds"; a Family's Pleasures with Books.* Viking Press, rev. ed. 1954.

A refreshing account of reading experiences shared by two children and their parents.

Duff, Annis. *"Longer Flight": A Family Grows Up with Books.* Viking Press, 1955.

The author continues her adventures in reading with her children now grown older.

Eaton, Anne Thaxter. *Reading with Children.* Viking Press, 1940.

A stimulating book which has grown out of the author's experience with children and books for more than twenty years as librarian of the Lincoln School, Teachers College, Columbia University.

Eaton, Anne Thaxter. *Treasure for the Taking.* Viking Press, rev. ed. 1957.

First published in 1946 as a companion to the author's *Reading for Children*, this excellent compilation has been fully revised. Brief, penetrating comments on the titles listed in 63 categories provide a sure guide to books that will delight children of all ages.

Fenner, Phyllis. *The Proof of the Pudding: What Children Read.* John Day, 1957.

An informal, lively discussion "about some of the best liked books of all time, telling a little about them, why a child likes them, and approximately how old a child is when he reads them." The book is an outgrowth of the author's thirty-two years as a librarian.

Hazard, Paul. *Books, Children and Men;* trans. from the French by Marguerite Mitchell. The Horn Book, Inc., 1947.

An eminent French scholar discusses with charm and clear insight the national traits in relation to books for children. A distinguished addition to the books on the history and criticism of children's literature.

Meigs, Cornelia, and others. *A Critical History of Children's Literature;* decorations by Vera Bock. Macmillan, 1953.

A survey of children's books in English from earliest times to the present, prepared in four parts under the editorship of Cornelia Meigs. Contents: Part 1, Roots in the Past up to 1840, by Cornelia Meigs; Part 2, Widening Horizons 1840–1890, by Anne Eaton; Part 3, A Rightful Heritage 1890–1920, by Elizabeth Nesbitt; Part 4, The Golden Age 1920–1950, by Ruth Hill Viguers.

Miller, Bertha Mahony, and Elinor Whitney Field, eds. *Newbery Medal Books: 1922–1955 with their Authors' Acceptance Papers and Related Material chiefly from the Horn Book Magazine.* Horn Book Papers, Vol. I. The Horn Book, Inc., 1955.

A richly rewarding book which constitutes a history of the Newbery awards through the year 1955. The winning books are presented in chronological arrangement. This is the first volume of a series which will reprint papers originally published in the *Horn Book.*

Miller, Bertha Mahony, and Elinor Whitney Field, eds. *Caldecott Medal Books: 1938–1957 with the Artists' Acceptance Papers and Related Material chiefly from the Horn Book Magazine.* Horn Book Papers, Vol. II. The Horn Book, Inc., 1957.

Everyone interested in the graphic arts and illustration will find this companion volume to *Newbery Medal Books: 1922–1955* extremely valuable. It contains the acceptance speeches of the artists, their biographies, a format note and a brief résumé of each book, an article on Randolph Caldecott, the artist for whom the medal was named, and a critical analysis "What Is a Picture Book?" by Esther Averill.

Moore, Anne Carroll. *My Roads to Childhood; Views and Reviews of Children's Books.* Doubleday, 1939.

Discriminating criticism and helpful booklists. Material first appeared under the titles *Roads to Childhood* (1920); *New Roads to Childhood* (1923); and *Crossroads to Childhood* (1926).

Moore, Anne Carroll. *The Three Owls.* 3 volumes. Vol. 1, Macmillan, 1925; Vols. 2 and 3, Coward-McCann, 1928 and 1931.

In 1924, under the editorship of Stuart Sherman and continuing until 1930 under that of Irita Van Doren, Miss Moore conducted a distinctive page of contemporary criticism of children's books known as "The Three Owls." These three volumes are made up of papers selected from that page, with many essays by Miss Moore.

Munson, Amelia H. *An Ample Field: Books and Young People.* American Library Association, 1950.

A love of reading and the author's own delight in sharing books is implicit in this inspirational guide to book selection for young adults.

Smith, Irene. *A History of the Newbery and Caldecott Medals.* Viking Press, 1957.

The author reviews the events that led to the founding of the awards; describes the procedures by which the winners are selected; appraises the books that have received the awards; lists the runners-up; and discusses the influence of these awards in upholding high standards in writing and illustration.

Smith, Lillian H. *The Unreluctant Years: a Critical Approach to Children's Literature.* American Library Association, 1953.

Out of a long and distinguished career as head of the Boys and Girls House of the Toronto Public Library, the author shares with the reader some of the joy that has been hers in a close familiarity with the books children love. In her foreword she states that "the aim of this book is to consider children's books as literature, and to discuss some of the standards by which they can be so judged."

Thompson, Jean. *Books for Boys and Girls.* Ryerson Press, rev. ed. 1954.

A thoughtful and discerning selection of books, well annotated, covering 19 categories.

Walker, Elinor. *Book Bait.* American Library Association, 1957.

Detailed notes on adult books popular with young people. Planned to help busy teachers and librarians guide teen-agers into the riches of mature reading, each title is summarized at length, with special attention to the qualities that make it attractive to young people. Helpful for individual guidance to future reading.

White, Dorothy Neal. *Books Before Five.* Oxford University Press, 1954.

Perceptive observations of a mother who kept a day-to-day record of the stories she read to her little girl between the ages of two and five years. Also of interest is the author's *About Books for Children,* a volume of fresh and original essays published by Oxford University Press in 1946.

Aids to Choosing Books

Adventuring with Books, compiled and published by the National Council of Teachers of English, 704 South 6th St., Champaign, Illinois. Rev. ed. 1956.

One thousand books recommended for kindergarten through grade six, arranged under large subject headings.

A Basic Book Collection for Elementary Grades. American Library Association, 1956. Sixth ed.

A selective, annotated list compiled by library and educational experts.

A Basic Book Collection for Junior High Schools. American Library Association, 1956. Second ed.

Similar in plan and format to the *Basic Book Collection for Elementary Grades.*

Bible Stories and Books about Religion for Children, compiled and published by the Child Study Association of America, Inc., 132 E. 74th St., New York 21. 1957.

A non-sectarian selection.

Bibliography of Books for Children, compiled and published by the Association for Childhood Education International, 1200 15th St., N.W., Washington 5, D.C. Revised 1956.

Approximately one thousand books recommended for children from ages four to twelve, arranged by subject.

The Booklist: A Guide to Current Books, published semimonthly, September through July, and monthly in August, by the American Library Association, 50 E. Huron St., Chicago 11, Illinois.

Books for the Teen-age, compiled and published by the New York Public Library, Fifth Avenue at 42nd St., New York 18.

A selective list published each year in the January issue of Branch Library Book News.

Books for Brotherhood, an annual annotated list prepared and published by the National Conference of Christians and Jews, 43 West 75th St., New York.

Books of the Year for Children, an annual list compiled and published by the Child Study Association of America, 132 E. 74th St., New York 21.

Children's Books for $1.25 or Less, compiled and published by the Association for Childhood Education International, 1200 15th St., N.W. Washington 5, D.C.

Children's Books Published in [year], compiled and published by the New York Public Library, New York 18.

Each year the Children's Department compiles a list of the best books published during the current year. The list represents the "cream of the crop" and the books are well annotated.

Children's Books Too Good to Miss, compiled by May Hill Arbuthnot and others. Western Reserve University Press, 2035 Adelbert Road, Cleveland 6, Ohio. 1953.

Two hundred titles which the compiler considers "an irreducible minimum of books which every child should be exposed to and helped to enjoy."

Current Books, Junior Booklist of the Secondary Education Board, Milton 86, Mass. 1957.

Annotations are written especially for the boys and

Around the World in Nursery Rhymes

KATE GREENAWAY'S ALPHABET (*circ. 1885*) *is the source of the decorative initials at the beginning of the section introductions. The initials have been redrawn especially for this anthology by Marion Phinney.*

"Imagination not unbridled, but which has not yet known the bridle. Caprice not unchained, but unaware of any chain." [1]

LITERATURE OF THE NURSERY IS well-nigh universal. Every country has its share of nursery rhymes and lullabies. Fortunate the child who early catches a glimpse of a world larger than his own through some acquaintance with a song from over the water or the other side of the earth. The child who inherits the English tongue has as his birthright a tradition of nursery rhymes which is singularly ample, robust, and enduring. Rooted in poetry, it is innately attuned to a child's concept of the world. Sense and nonsense exist together in sweet reasonableness, and one giddy scene follows another in an atmosphere charged with wonder. This mirrors the world as young children see it. "To a child in its first years," says Eleanor Farjeon, "the prosaic and the wondrous are on equal terms. It is as easy for a child to believe in an unnamable terror as a pain in the finger; or in an untellable rapture as the cake on its plate." [2]

Music is the first appeal of Mother Goose; the felicity of sound, the elemental pulse of its rhythm, certain as a heart beat and as basic to a child's impulse to make patterns of movement with his body. *Dance to your daddy, / My little babby, / Dance to your daddy, / My little lamb. //*

Variety of rhyme and meter continually surprise the ear, the pace changing as quickly as the scene and cast of characters. *Bow, wow, wow, / Whose dog art thou? / Little Tom Tinker's dog, / Bow, wow, wow. // Gay go up and gay go down, / To ring the bells of London town. // Charlie Wag, Charlie Wag, / Ate the pudding and left the bag. //*

What drama is packed in this brief, abrupt verse: Miss Muffet and the spider; Peter Pumpkin-eater stowing his wife away in a pumpkin shell. What perception of men and women: *My little old man and I fell out, / How shall we bring this matter about? / Bring it about as well as you can, / And get you gone, you little old man! //* What mirth and merrymaking: *Hey, diddle, diddle, / The cat and the fiddle . . . // Boys and girls come out to play, / The moon doth shine as bright as day. // A cat came fiddling out of a*

---

[1] Paul Hazard, *Books, Children and Men* (The Horn Book, Inc., Boston, 1944), p. 82.
[2] Eleanor Farjeon, *Magic Casements* (Allen and Unwin, London, 1941), p. 31.

barn. // What kindness and cruelty: *If I had a donkey that wouldn't go / Would I beat him? Oh no, no. / I'd put him in the barn and give him some corn, / The best little donkey that ever was born.* // *As I was going to sell my eggs, / I met a man with bandy legs; / Bandy legs and crooked toes, / I tripped up his heels and he fell on his nose.* //

What a parade of the workaday world: the farmer, the dairy maid, the baker, and the butcher. What portrayal of the professions: soldiers, sailors, doctors, lawyers, and preaching men; and whole processions of craftsmen; tinkers, tailors, barbers, and smiths. What an array of companionable animals: dogs and cats, sheep, cows, donkeys, hens, geese — and innumerable mice, with and without tails.

What a world in miniature that touches upon even the greatest themes: romantic love, and the inevitability of fate and character: *Bobby Shaftoe's gone to sea, / Silver buckles at his knee; / He'll come back and marry me, / Bonny Bobby Shaftoe.* // *There was an old woman had three sons, / Jerry and James and John. / Jerry was hung and James was drowned, / John was lost and never was found, / So there was an end of her three sons, / Jerry and James and John.* // All classes of society tumble across the pages of Mother Goose: kings and queens, lords and ladies, the wise and the foolish, thieves, rogues, and honest men; pedlars, and gypsies, and pipers playing "Over the hills and far away."

Not only rhyme and melody and revelation enhance Mother Goose, but the very essence of poetry is here: the recurring miracle of phrase that evokes such images of pure delight as to reverberate through the mind, echo upon echo. *As fair as a lily, as white as a swan.* // *The boughs do shake and the bells do ring.* // *I had a little nut tree, / Nothing would it bear / But a silver nutmeg / And a golden pear.* //

"This is the key of the kingdom." So runs one of the old rhymes. This might well be said of Mother Goose as a whole, for here is the dawn of humor, nonsense, and imagination; the quick awareness of the multiple wonders of the world; and a first appreciation of the bite and beauty of words. To all these kingdoms, Mother Goose is the key.

In England, this traditional literature is known as Nursery Rhymes, probably because that institution of the English home, the Nanny, was second only to children themselves in the transmitting of the rhymes. In America, the old comforting term of Mother Goose has somehow held. That name first appeared, not in England, but in France, where the phrase, "Tales of My Mother Goose," formed a part of the frontispiece to Charles Perrault's famous collection of fairy tales, published in Paris in the year 1697. The French expression, "contes de ma mère l'oye," was in common use, having the same meaning as the comparable English phrase, "an old wives' tale." [3] No doubt the old peasant woman who tended the geese was the accepted symbol of the storyteller.

[3] *Perrault's Tales of Mother Goose. The Dedication Manuscript of 1695, Reproduced in Collotype Facsimile with Introduction and Critical Text,* by Jacques Barchilon (Pierpont Morgan Library, New York, 1956), Vol. II, chap. 2, p. 37.

The earliest record of the translation of the Perrault tales into English stands at 1729.[4] It was John Newbery, the energetic bookseller of St. Paul's churchyard, who first had the wit to match the term Mother Goose to a collection of the traditional rhymes, and to issue them under the title, *Mother Goose's Melody or Sonnets for the Cradle,* in 1760. These "soporific sonnets," to quote from its anonymous preface, consisted of some fifty of the rhymes, followed by a selection of the incidental lyrics from Shakespeare, all under the running head of *Mother Goose's Melody.* This little volume brought together, between its Dutch flowery-gilt-paper covers, the incomparable heritage of the English tongue: Shakespeare and Mother Goose. No doubt William Shakespeare himself had fed upon the fruit of the great tree we know as Mother Goose. *O Mistress mine, where are you roaming? / O, stay and hear! your true love's coming, / That can sing both high and low. //* How easily Mother Goose could lay claim to this melody and the sharpness of its image!

We think of the rhymes of Mother Goose as the special province of childhood. Their lineage goes back to beginnings in which the adult mind reveled, found release and recreation. Old ballads, chapbooks and song books, stage plays, folk songs; the jibes of political satire, bits of singing games, riddles, relics of ritual, ceremony, and incantation — these are the seedbeds of the hardy perennials that have blossomed and endured in the nursery.

The most thorough and scholarly account of the old rhymes is to be found in one of the notable books of this century, *The Oxford Dictionary of Nursery Rhymes,* edited by Iona and Peter Opie. This book, six years in the making, cites the earliest recording in print of each rhyme, and in many cases gives variants. The alphabetical arrangement of the verses, the wealth of contemporary pictorial examples, the thorough notes and comments, the "Index of notable figures associated with the invention, diffusion or illustration of the nursery rhymes," the evidence of the vast enjoyment of the compilers at their task, make it an exhilarating piece of scholarship and give fresh testimony to the vigor and the humanity of Mother Goose. Small wonder, then, that for children the nursery rhyme is "the beginning of wisdom."

[4] *The Oxford Dictionary of Nursery Rhymes,* edited by Iona and Peter Opie (Oxford University Press, New York, 1951), pp. 39–40.

MOTHER GOOSE NURSERY RHYMES [1]

✑ English and American ✑

1

Pat-a-cake, pat-a-cake, baker's man,
Bake me a cake as fast as you can;
Pat it and prick it, and mark it with T,
Put it in the oven for Tommy and me.

2

This little pig went to market,
This little pig stayed at home,
This little pig had roast beef,
This little pig had none,
And this little pig cried, Wee-wee-
    wee-wee-wee,
I can't find my way home.

3

To market, to market,
    To buy a fat pig,
Home again, home again,
    Jiggety-jig.
To market, to market,
    To buy a fat hog,
Home again, home again,
    Jiggety-jog.

4

Hickory, dickory, dock,
The mouse ran up the clock.
    The clock struck one,
    The mouse ran down,
Hickory, dickory, dock.

[1] Unless otherwise stated, the nursery rhymes are
from *The Oxford Nursery Rhyme Book,* assembled by
Iona and Peter Opie (Oxford University Press).

5

Bye, baby bunting,
Daddy's gone a-hunting,
Gone to get a rabbit skin
To wrap the baby bunting in.

6

Hush-a-bye, baby, on the tree top,
When the wind blows the cradle will rock;
When the bough breaks the cradle will fall,
Down will come baby, cradle, and all.

7

Rock-a-bye, baby, thy cradle is green;
Father's a nobleman, mother's a queen;
And Betty's a lady, and wears a gold ring;
And Johnny's a drummer, and drums for the
    king.

8

Hey, diddle, diddle,
The cat and the fiddle,
The cow jumped over the moon;
The little dog laughed
To see such sport,
And the dish ran away with the spoon.

9

Ding, dong, bell,
Pussy's in the well.
Who put her in?
Little Johnny Green.
Who pulled her out?
Little Tommy Stout.

What a naughty boy was that
To try to drown poor pussy cat,
Who never did him any harm,
And killed the mice in his father's barn.

10

Pussy cat, pussy cat,
Where have you been?
I've been to London
To look at the Queen.
Pussy cat, pussy cat,
What did you there?
I frightened a little mouse
Under her chair.

11

Little Boy Blue,
Come blow your horn,
The sheep's in the meadow,
The cow's in the corn.

Where is the boy
Who looks after the sheep?
He's under a haycock
Fast asleep.

Will you wake him?
No, not I,
For if I do,
He's sure to cry.

12

Little Miss Muffet
Sat on a tuffet,
Eating her curds and whey;
There came a big spider,
Who sat down beside her
And frightened Miss Muffet away.

13

Ride a cock-horse to Banbury Cross,
To see a fine lady upon a white horse;
Rings on her fingers and bells on her toes,
And she shall have music wherever she goes.

14

Baa, baa, black sheep,
Have you any wool?
Yes, sir, yes, sir,

Three bags full;
One for the master,
And one for the dame,
And one for the little boy
Who lives down the lane.

15

Little Jack Horner
Sat in the corner,
Eating a Christmas pie;
He put in his thumb,
And pulled out a plum,
And said, What a good boy am I!

16

Little Tommy Tucker
Sings for his supper:
What shall we give him?
White bread and butter.
How shall he cut it
Without e'er a knife?
How will he be married
Without e'er a wife?

17

Tom, Tom, the piper's son,
Stole a pig and away he run;
The pig was eat,
And Tom was beat,
And Tom went howling down the street.

18

Mary, Mary, quite contrary,
How does your garden grow?
With silver bells and cockle shells,
And pretty maids all in a row.

19

Georgie Porgie, pudding and pie,
Kissed the girls and made them cry;
When the boys came out to play,
Georgie Porgie ran away.

20

Hickety, pickety, my black hen,
She lays eggs for gentlemen;
Gentlemen come every day
To see what my black hen doth lay.

21

Humpty Dumpty sat on a wall,
Humpty Dumpty had a great fall;
All the King's horses and all the King's men
Couldn't put Humpty together again.

22

A diller, a dollar,
A ten o'clock scholar,
What makes you come so soon?
You used to come at ten o'clock,
But now you come at noon.

23

Hark, hark,
The dogs do bark,
The beggars are coming to town;
Some in rags,
And some in jags,
And one in a velvet gown.

24

Goosey, goosey gander,
Whither shall I wander?
Upstairs and downstairs
And in my lady's chamber.
There I met an old man
Who would not say his prayers,
I took him by the left leg
And threw him down the stairs.

25

Great A, little a,
Bouncing B,
The cat's in the cupboard
And can't see me.

26

Rub-a-dub dub,
Three men in a tub,
And who do you think they be?
The butcher, the baker,
The candlestick-maker;
Turn 'em out, knaves all three![2]

[2] From W. A. Wheeler, *Mother Goose's Melodies*
(Houghton Mifflin).

27

Jack be nimble,
Jack be quick,
Jack jump over
The candlestick.

28

Bow, wow, wow,
Whose dog art thou?
Little Tom Tinker's dog,
Bow, wow, wow.

29

Barber, barber, shave a pig,
How many hairs will make a wig?
Four and twenty, that's enough.
Give the barber a pinch of snuff.

30

Bless you, bless you, burnie-bee,
Tell me when my wedding be;
If it be tomorrow day,
Take your wings and fly away.
Fly to the east, fly to the west,
Fly to him I love the best.

31

Rain, rain, go away,
Come again another day,
Little Johnny wants to play.

32

The north wind doth blow,
And we shall have snow,
And what will poor Robin do then?
Poor thing.
He'll sit in a barn,
And keep himself warm,
And hide his head under his wing,
Poor thing.

33

As Tommy Snooks and Bessy Brooks
Were walking out one Sunday,
Says Tommy Snooks to Bessy Brooks,
Tomorrow will be Monday.

34

Diddle, diddle, dumpling, my son John,
Went to bed with his trousers on;
One shoe off, and one shoe on,
Diddle, diddle, dumpling, my son John.

35

Lucy Locket lost her pocket,
Kitty Fisher found it;
Not a penny was there in it,
Only ribbon round it.

36

Peter, Peter, pumpkin eater,
Had a wife and couldn't keep her;
He put her in a pumpkin shell
And there he kept her very well.

Peter, Peter, pumpkin eater,
Had another, and didn't love her;
Peter learned to read and spell,
And then he loved her very well.

37

Curly locks, Curly locks,
Wilt thou be mine?
Thou shalt not wash dishes
Nor yet feed the swine;
But sit on a cushion
And sew a fine seam,
And feed upon strawberries,
Sugar and cream.

38

Jack Sprat could eat no fat,
His wife could eat no lean,
And so between them both, you see,
They licked the platter clean.

39

Cock a doodle doo!
My dame has lost her shoe,
My master's lost his fiddling stick,
And knows not what to do.

Cock a doodle doo!
What is my dame to do?
Till master finds his fiddling stick
She'll dance without her shoe.

Cock a doodle doo!
My dame has found her shoe,
And master's found his fiddling stick,
Sing doodle doodle doo.

Cock a doodle doo!
My dame will dance with you,
While master fiddles his fiddling stick
For dame and doodle doo.

40

I had a little pony,
His name was Dapple Gray;
I lent him to a lady
To ride a mile away.
She whipped him, she slashed him,
She rode him through the mire;
I would not lend my pony now,
For all the lady's hire.

41

If I had a donkey that wouldn't go,
Would I beat him? Oh no, no.
I'd put him in the barn and give him some
corn,
The best little donkey that ever was born.[3]

42

Jack and Jill went up the hill,
To fetch a pail of water;
Jack fell down, and broke his crown,
And Jill came tumbling after.

43

Little Bo-peep has lost her sheep,
And doesn't know where to find them;
Leave them alone, and they'll come home,
Bringing their tails behind them.

Little Bo-peep fell fast asleep,
And dreamt she heard them bleating;
But when she awoke, she found it a joke,
For they were still a-fleeting.

Then up she took her little crook,
Determined for to find them;

[3] From *The Oxford Dictionary of Nursery Rhymes*,
ed. Iona and Peter Opie (Oxford University Press).

She found them indeed, but it made her
    heart bleed,
    For they'd left their tails behind them.

It happened one day, as Bo-peep did stray
    Into a meadow hard by,
There she espied their tails side by side,
    All hung on a tree to dry.

She heaved a sigh, and wiped her eye,
    And over the hillocks went rambling,
And tried what she could, as a shepherdess
    should,
    To tack again each to its lambkin.

44

Cushy cow, bonny, let down thy milk,
And I will give thee a gown of silk;
A gown of silk and a silver tee,
If thou wilt let down thy milk for me.

45

A farmer went trotting upon his grey mare,
    Bumpety, bumpety, bump!
With his daughter behind him so rosy and
    fair,
    Lumpety, lumpety, lump!

A raven cried, Croak! and they all tumbled
    down,
    Bumpety, bumpety, bump!
The mare broke her knees and the farmer
    his crown,
    Lumpety, lumpety, lump!

The mischievous raven flew laughing away,
    Bumpety, bumpety, bump!
And vowed he would serve them the same
    the next day,
    Lumpety, lumpety, lump!

46

Boys and girls come out to play,
The moon doth shine as bright as day.
Leave your supper and leave your sleep,
And join your playfellows in the street.
Come with a whoop and come with a call,
Come with a good will or not at all.
Up the ladder and down the wall,
A half-penny loaf will serve us all;

You find milk, and I'll find flour,
And we'll have a pudding in half an hour.

47

What are little boys made of, made of?
What are little boys made of?
    Frogs and snails
    And puppy-dogs' tails,
That's what little boys are made of.

What are little girls made of, made of?
What are little girls made of?
    Sugar and spice
    And all things nice,
That's what little girls are made of.

48

Charley Wag, Charley Wag,
Ate the pudding and left the bag.[4]

49

A cat came fiddling out of a barn,
With a pair of bagpipes under her arm;
She could sing nothing but fiddle-de-dee,
The mouse has married the bumble-bee;
Pipe, cat — dance, mouse —
We'll have a wedding at our good house.[5]

50

I had a little hen, the prettiest ever seen;
She washed me the dishes, and kept the house
    clean;
She went to the mill to fetch me some flour.
She brought it home in less than an hour;
She baked me my bread, she brewed me my
    ale,
She sat by the fire and told many a fine tale.[5]

51

I'll tell you a story
About Jack a Nory,
And now my story's begun;
I'll tell you another
Of Jack and his brother,
And now my story is done.

[4] From *The Oxford Dictionary of Nursery Rhymes*,
ed. Iona and Peter Opie (Oxford University Press).
[5] From W. A. Wheeler, *Mother Goose's Melodies*
(Houghton Mifflin).

52

How many miles to Babylon?
Three-score and ten.
Can I get there by candle-light?
Yes, and back again.
If your heels are nimble and light,
You may get there by candle-light.

53

There was a little man, and he had a little
    gun,
  And his bullets were made of lead, lead,
    lead;
He went to the brook, and shot a little duck,
  Right through the middle of the head,
    head, head.

He carried it home to his old wife Joan,
  And bade her a fire for to make, make,
    make,
To roast the little duck he had shot in the
    brook,
  And he'd go and fetch her the drake, drake,
    drake.

54

As I was going to Banbury,
Upon a summer's day,
My dame had butter, eggs, and fruit,
And I had corn and hay;
Joe drove the ox, and Tom the swine,
Dick took the foal and mare;
I sold them all — then home to dine,
From famous Banbury fair.

55

Six little mice sat down to spin;
Pussy passed by and she peeped in.
What are you doing, my little men?
Weaving coats for gentlemen.
Shall I come in and cut off your threads?
No, no, Mistress Pussy, you'd bite off our
    heads.
Oh, no, I'll not; I'll help you to spin.
That may be so, but you don't come in.

56

Three young rats with black felt hats,
Three young ducks with white straw flats,

Three young dogs with curling tails,
Three young cats with demi-veils,
Went out to walk with two young pigs
In satin vests and sorrel wigs;
But suddenly it chanced to rain
And so they all went home again.

57

Hot-cross buns!
Hot-cross buns!
One a penny, two a penny,
Hot cross buns!

Hot-cross buns!
Hot-cross buns!
If you have no daughters,
Give them to your sons.[6]

58

Cross patch,
Draw the latch,
Sit by the fire and spin;
Take a cup
And drink it up,
Then call your neighbors in.

59

I saw a ship a-sailing,
  A-sailing on the sea;
And O! it was all laden
  With pretty things for thee!

There were comfits in the cabin,
  And apples in the hold;
The sails were made of silk,
  And the masts were made of gold!

The four and twenty sailors,
  That stood between the decks,
Were four and twenty white mice,
  With chains about their necks.

The captain was a duck,
  With a packet on his back;
And when the ship began to move,
  The captain said, "Quack! quack!"[6]

[6] From W. A. Wheeler, *Mother Goose's Melodies*
(Houghton Mifflin).

60

Wee Willie Winkie runs through the town,
Upstairs and downstairs in his nightgown,
Rapping at the window, crying through the
    lock,
Are the children in their beds, for now it's
    eight o'clock?

61

Bobby Shaftoe's gone to sea,
Silver buckles at his knee;
He'll come back and marry me,
    Bonny Bobby Shaftoe.

Bobby Shaftoe's bright and fair,
Combing down his yellow hair,
He's my ain for evermair,
    Bonny Bobby Shaftoe.

62

I had a little nut tree,
    Nothing would it bear
But a silver nutmeg
    And a golden pear;
The king of Spain's daughter
    Came to visit me,
And all for the sake
    Of my little nut tree.
I skipped over water,
    I danced over sea,
And all the birds in the air
    Couldn't catch me.

63

Gray goose and gander,
    Waft your wings together,
And carry the good king's daughter
    Over the one-strand river.

64

Johnny shall have a new bonnet,
    And Johnny shall go to the fair,
And Johnny shall have a blue ribbon
    To tie up his bonny brown hair.

And why may not I love Johnny?
And why may not Johnny love me?
And why may not I love Johnny
    As well as another body?

And here's a leg for a stocking,
    And here's a leg for a shoe,
And he has a kiss for his daddy,
    And two for his mammy, I trow.

And why may not I love Johnny?
And why may not Johnny love me?
And why may not I love Johnny
    As well as another body?

65

Lavender's blue, diddle, diddle,
    Lavender's green;
When I am king, diddle, diddle,
    You shall be queen.

Call up your men, diddle, diddle,
    Set them to work,
Some to the plough, diddle, diddle,
    Some to the cart.

Some to make hay, diddle, diddle,
    Some to thresh corn,
Whilst you and I, diddle, diddle,
    Keep ourselves warm.

66

I love sixpence, jolly little sixpence,
    I love sixpence better than my life;
I spent a penny of it, I lent a penny of it,
    And I took fourpence home to my wife.

Oh, my little fourpence, jolly little four-
    pence,
    I love fourpence better than my life;
I spent a penny of it, I lent a penny of it,
    And I took twopence home to my wife.

Oh, my little twopence, jolly little twopence,
    I love twopence better than my life;
I spent a penny of it, I lent a penny of it,
    And I took nothing home to my wife.

Oh, my little nothing, jolly little nothing,
    What will nothing buy for my wife?
I have nothing, I spend nothing,
    I love nothing better than my wife.

67

If I'd as much money as I could spend,
I never would cry old chairs to mend;

Old chairs to mend, old chairs to mend;
I never would cry old chairs to mend.

68

There was an old woman,
   And what do you think?
She lived upon nothing
   But victuals and drink:
Victuals and drink
   Were the chief of her diet,
And yet this old woman
   Could never keep quiet.

69

There was an old woman who lived in a
   shoe;
She had so many children she didn't know
   what to do;
She gave them some broth without any
   bread;
She whipped them all soundly and put them
   to bed.

70

There was an old woman tossed up in a
   basket,
   Seventeen times as high as the moon;
Where she was going I couldn't but ask it,
   For in her hand she carried a broom.
Old woman, old woman, old woman,
   quoth I,
Where are you going to up so high?
To brush the cobwebs off the sky!
May I go with you? Aye, by-and-by.

71

There was an old woman had three sons,
   Jerry and James and John.
Jerry was hung and James was drowned,
John was lost and never was found,
So there was an end of her three sons,
   Jerry and James and John.[7]

72

There was an old woman, as I've heard tell,
She went to market her eggs for to sell;
She went to market all on a market day,
And she fell asleep on the king's highway.

There came a peddler whose name was Stout,
He cut her petticoats all round about;
He cut her petticoats up to the knees,
Which made the old woman shiver and
   freeze.

When this little old woman first did wake,
She began to shiver and she began to shake;
She began to wonder and she began to cry,
"O! deary, deary me, this is none of I!"

"But if it be I as I hope it be,
I've a little dog at home, and he'll know me;
If it be I, he'll wag his tail
And if it be not I, he'll loudly bark and
   wail!"

Home went the little woman all in the dark,
Up got the little dog, and he began to bark;
He began to bark; so she began to cry,
"O! deary, deary me, this is none of I!"[8]

73

There was a crooked man, and he went a
   crooked mile;
He found a crooked sixpence against a
   crooked stile;
He bought a crooked cat, which caught a
   crooked mouse,
And all lived together in a little crooked
   house.[8]

74

Doctor Foster went to Gloucester
In a shower of rain;
He stepped in a puddle, up to his middle,
And never went there again.[8]

75

Solomon Grundy
Born on a Monday,
Christened on Tuesday,
Married on Wednesday,
Took ill on Thursday,
Worse on Friday,
Died on Saturday,
Buried on Sunday;
This is the end
Of Solomon Grundy.

[7] From *The Oxford Dictionary of Nursery Rhymes*, ed. Iona and Peter Opie (Oxford University Press).

[8] From W. A. Wheeler, *Mother Goose's Melodies* (Houghton Mifflin).

76

The lion and the unicorn
　　Were fighting for the crown;
The lion beat the unicorn
　　All round about the town.

Some gave them white bread,
　　And some gave them brown;
Some gave them plum cake
　　And drummed them out of town.

77

When good King Arthur ruled this land,
　　He was a goodly king;
He stole three pecks of barley-meal,
　　To make a bag-pudding.

A bag-pudding the king did make,
　　And stuffed it well with plums:
And in it put great lumps of fat,
　　As big as my two thumbs.

The king and queen did eat thereof,
　　And noblemen beside;
And what they could not eat that night
　　The queen next morning fried.[9]

78

Old King Cole
Was a merry old soul,
And a merry old soul was he;
He called for his pipe,
And he called for his bowl,
And he called for his fiddlers three.

Every fiddler, he had a fiddle,
And a very fine fiddle had he;
Twee tweedle-dee, tweedle-dee, went the
　　fiddlers,
Oh, there's none so rare,
As can compare
With King Cole and his fiddlers three![9]

79

A carrion crow sat on an oak,
Watching a tailor shape his cloak.
　　Sing heigh ho, the carrion crow,
　　Fol de riddle, lol de riddle, hi ding do.

[9] From W. A. Wheeler, *Mother Goose's Melodies* (Houghton Mifflin).

The carrion crow began to rave,
And called the tailor a crooked knave.
　　Sing heigh ho, the carrion crow,
　　Fol de riddle, lol de riddle, hi ding do.

Wife, bring me my old bent bow,
That I may shoot yon carrion crow.
　　Sing heigh ho, the carrion crow,
　　Fol de riddle, lol de riddle, hi ding do.

The tailor he shot and missed his mark,
And shot his own sow through the heart.
　　Sing heigh ho, the carrion crow,
　　Fol de riddle, lol de riddle, hi ding do.

Wife, bring brandy in a spoon,
For our old sow is in a swoon.
　　Sing heigh ho, the carrion crow,
　　Fol de riddle, lol de riddle, hi ding do.

80

Four and twenty tailors
　　Went to kill a snail,
The best man among them
　　Durst not touch her tail;
She put out her horns
　　Like a little Kyloe cow,
Run, tailors, run,
　　Or she'll kill you all e'en now.

81

Snail, snail,
Come out of your hole,
Or else I'll beat you
As black as coal.

Snail, snail,
Put out your horns,
I'll give you bread
And barley corns.

82

Mr. East gave a feast;
Mr. North laid the cloth;
Mr. West did his best;
Mr. South burnt his mouth
With eating a cold potato.

83

See a pin and pick it up,
All the day you'll have good luck;

See a pin and let it lay,
Bad luck you'll have all day.

84

Where are you going, my pretty maid?
I'm going a-milking, sir, she said.
May I go with you, my pretty maid?
You're kindly welcome, sir, she said.
What is your father, my pretty maid?
My father's a farmer, sir, she said.
What is your fortune, my pretty maid?
My face is my fortune, sir, she said.
Then I can't marry you, my pretty maid!
Nobody asked you, sir, she said.[10]

85

One misty, moisty morning,
    When cloudy was the weather,
I met a little old man
    Clothed all in leather.

He began to compliment,
    And I began to grin,
How do you do, and how do you do,
    And how do you do again?[11]

86

What's in the cupboard?
Says Mr. Hubbard.
A knuckle of veal,
Says Mr. Beal.
Is that all?
Says Mr. Ball.
And enough too,
Says Mr. Glue;
And away they all flew.

87

I had a little husband,
    No bigger than my thumb;
I put him in a pint-pot
    And there I bade him drum.
I bought a little horse
    That galloped up and down;
I bridled him, and saddled him
    And sent him out of town.

I gave him some garters
    To garter up his hose,
And a little silk handkerchief
    To wipe his pretty nose.

88

My little old man and I fell out,
How shall we bring this matter about?
Bring it about as well as you can,
And get you gone, you little old man![12]

89

As I was going to sell my eggs,
I met a man with bandy legs;
Bandy legs and crooked toes,
I tripped up his heels and he fell on his
    nose.[12]

90

Simple Simon met a pieman,
    Going to the fair;
Says Simple Simon to the pieman,
    Let me taste your ware.

Says the pieman to Simple Simon,
    Show me first your penny;
Says Simple Simon to the pieman,
    Indeed I have not any.

Simple Simon went a-fishing,
    For to catch a whale;
All the water he had got
    Was in his mother's pail.

Simple Simon went to look
    If plums grew on a thistle;
He pricked his fingers very much,
    Which made poor Simon whistle.

He went for water in a sieve
    But soon it all fell through;
And now poor Simple Simon
    Bids you all adieu.

91

The Queen of Hearts,
She made some tarts,
    All on a summer's day;

---

[10] From Andrew Lang, *The Nursery Rhyme Book*
(Frederick Warne).

[11] From W. A. Wheeler, *Mother Goose's Melodies*
(Houghton Mifflin).

[12] From *The Oxford Dictionary of Nursery Rhymes*,
ed. Iona and Peter Opie (Oxford University Press).

The Knave of Hearts
He stole those tarts
  And took them clean away.

The King of Hearts
Called for the tarts,
  And beat the knave full sore;
The Knave of Hearts
Brought back the tarts,
  And vowed he'd steal no more.

92

This is the house that Jack built.

This is the malt
That lay in the house that Jack built.

This is the rat,
That ate the malt
That lay in the house that Jack built.

This is the cat,
That killed the rat,
That ate the malt
That lay in the house that Jack built.

This is the dog,
That worried the cat,
That killed the rat,
That ate the malt
That lay in the house that Jack built.

This is the cow with the crumpled horn,
That tossed the dog,
That worried the cat,
That killed the rat,
That ate the malt
That lay in the house that Jack built.

This is the maiden all forlorn,
That milked the cow with the crumpled horn,
That tossed the dog,
That worried the cat,
That killed the rat,
That ate the malt
That lay in the house that Jack built.

This is the man all tattered and torn,
That kissed the maiden all forlorn,
That milked the cow with the crumpled horn,
That tossed the dog,

That worried the cat,
That killed the rat,
That ate the malt
That lay in the house that Jack built.

This is the priest all shaven and shorn,
That married the man all tattered and torn,
That kissed the maiden all forlorn,
That milked the cow with the crumpled horn,
That tossed the dog,
That worried the cat,
That killed the rat,
That ate the malt
That lay in the house that Jack built.

This is the cock that crowed in the morn,
That waked the priest all shaven and shorn,
That married the man all tattered and torn,
That kissed the maiden all forlorn,
That milked the cow with the crumpled horn,
That tossed the dog,
That worried the cat,
That killed the rat,
That ate the malt
That lay in the house that Jack built.

This is the farmer sowing his corn,
That kept the cock that crowed in the morn,
That waked the priest all shaven and shorn,
That married the man all tattered and torn,
That kissed the maiden all forlorn,
That milked the cow with the crumpled horn,
That tossed the dog,
That worried the cat,
That killed the rat,
That ate the malt
That lay in the house that Jack built.

93

Dame, get up and bake your pies,
  Bake your pies, bake your pies;
Dame, get up and bake your pies,
  On Christmas day in the morning.

Dame, what makes your maidens lie,
  Maidens lie, maidens lie;
Dame, what makes your maidens lie,
  On Christmas day in the morning?

Dame, what makes your ducks to die,
  Ducks to die, ducks to die;

Dame, what makes your ducks to die,
  On Christmas day in the morning?

Their wings are cut and they cannot fly,
  Cannot fly, cannot fly;
Their wings are cut and they cannot fly,
  On Christmas day in the morning.

94

I saw three ships come sailing by,
  Come sailing by, come sailing by,
I saw three ships come sailing by,
  On New-Year's day in the morning.

And what do you think was in them then,
  Was in them then, was in them then?
And what do you think was in them then,
  On New-Year's day in the morning?

Three pretty girls were in them then,
  Were in them then, were in them then,
Three pretty girls were in them then,
  On New-Year's day in the morning.

One could whistle, and one could sing,
  And one could play on the violin;
Such joy there was at my wedding,
  On New-Year's day in the morning.

95

Thirty days hath September,
April, June, and November;
All the rest have thirty-one,
Excepting February alone,
And that has twenty-eight days clear
And twenty-nine in each leap year.

96

The boughs do shake and the bells do ring,
So merrily comes our harvest in,
Our harvest in, our harvest in,
So merrily comes our harvest in.

We've ploughed, we've sowed,
We've reaped, we've mowed,
We've got our harvest in.

MOTHER GOOSE BALLADS

97

Old Mother Goose,
  When she wanted to wander,
Would ride through the air
  On a very fine gander.

Mother Goose had a house,
  'Twas built in a wood,
Where an owl at the door
  For sentinel stood.

She had a son Jack,
  A plain-looking lad,
He was not very good,
  Nor yet very bad.

She sent him to market,
  A live goose he bought;
See, mother, says he,
  I have not been for nought.

Jack's goose and her gander
  Grew very fond;
They'd both eat together,
  Or swim in the pond.

Jack found one fine morning,
  As I have been told,
His goose had laid him
  An egg of pure gold.

Jack ran to his mother
　　The news for to tell,
She called him a good boy,
　　And said it was well.

Jack sold his good egg
　　To a merchant untrue,
Who cheated him out of
　　A half of his due.

Then Jack went a-courting
　　A lady so gay,
As fair as the lily,
　　And sweet as the May.

The merchant and squire
　　Soon came at his back,
And began to belabour
　　The sides of poor Jack.

Then old Mother Goose
　　That instant came in,
And turned her son Jack
　　Into famed Harlequin.

She then with her wand
　　Touched the lady so fine,
And turned her at once
　　Into sweet Columbine.

98

Old Mother Hubbard
Went to the cupboard
To get her poor dog a bone;
But when she came there
The cupboard was bare,
And so the poor dog had none.

She went to the baker's
To buy him some bread;
But when she came back
The poor dog was dead.

She went to the joiner's
To buy him a coffin;
But when she came back
The poor dog was laughing.

She took a clean dish
To get him some tripe;
But when she came back
He was smoking a pipe.

She went to the tavern
For white wine and red;
But when she came back
The dog stood on his head.

She went to the hatter's
To buy him a hat;
But when she came back
He was feeding the cat.

She went to the barber's
To buy him a wig;
But when she came back
He was dancing a jig.

She went to the fruiterer's
To buy him some fruit;
But when she came back
He was playing the flute.

She went to the tailor's
To buy him a coat;
But when she came back
He was riding a goat.

She went to the cobbler's
To buy him some shoes;
But when she came back
He was reading the news.

She went to the seamstress
To buy him some linen;
But when she came back
The dog was spinning.

She went to the hosier's
To buy him some hose;
But when she came back
He was dressed in his clothes.

The dame made a courtesy,
The dog made a bow;
The dame said, "Your servant,"
The dog said, "Bow, wow!"

99

Jenny Wren fell sick
　　Upon a merry time,
In came Robin Redbreast
　　And brought her sops and wine.

Eat well of the sop, Jenny,
    Drink well of the wine.
Thank you, Robin, kindly,
    You shall be mine.

Jenny Wren got well,
    And stood upon her feet;
And told Robin plainly,
    She loved him not a bit.

Robin he got angry,
    And hopped upon a twig,
Saying, Out upon you, fie upon you!
    Bold faced jig!

100

Who killed Cock Robin?
    "I," said the Sparrow,
    "With my bow and arrow,
I killed Cock Robin."

Who saw him die?
    "I," said the Fly,
    "With my little eye,
And I saw him die."

Who caught his blood?
    "I," said the Fish,
    "With my little dish,
And I caught his blood."

Who made his shroud?
    "I," said the Beadle,
    "With my little needle,
And I made his shroud."

Who shall dig his grave?
    "I," said the Owl,
    "With my spade and showl,
And I'll dig his grave."

Who'll be the parson?
    "I," said the Rook,
    "With my little book,
And I'll be the parson."

Who'll be the clerk?
    "I," said the Lark,
    "If it's not in the dark,
And I'll be the clerk."

Who'll carry him to the grave?
    "I," said the Kite.
    "If 'tis not in the night,
And I'll carry him to his grave."

Who'll carry the link?
    "I," said the Linnet,
    "I'll fetch it in a minute,
And I'll carry the link."

Who'll be the chief mourner?
    "I," said the Dove,
    "I mourn for my love,
And I'll be chief mourner."

Who'll bear the pall?
    "We," said the Wren,
    Both the cock and the hen,
"And we'll bear the pall."

Who'll sing a psalm?
    "I," said the Thrush,
    As she sat in a bush,
"And I'll sing a psalm."

And who'll toll the bell?
    "I," said the Bull,
    "Because I can pull";
And so, Cock Robin, farewell.

All the birds in the air
    Fell to sighing and sobbing,
    When they heard the bell toll
For poor Cock Robin.

101

A Frog he would a wooing go,
    Heigho, says Rowley,
Whether his mother would let him or no.
    With a rowley powley, gammon and
        spinach,
    Heigho, says Anthony Rowley!

So off he set with his opera hat,
    Heigho, says Rowley,
And on the road he met with a rat.
    With a rowley powley, gammon and
        spinach,
    Heigho, says Anthony Rowley!

"Pray, Mr. Rat, will you go with me,"
Heigho, says Rowley,
"Kind Mrs. Mousey for to see?"
With a rowley powley, gammon and
spinach,
Heigho, says Anthony Rowley!

When they came to the door of Mousey's hall,
Heigho, says Rowley,
They gave a loud knock and they gave a loud
call.
With a rowley powley, gammon and
spinach,
Heigho, says Anthony Rowley!

"Pray, Mrs. Mouse, are you within?"
Heigho, says Rowley,
"Oh, yes, kind sirs, I'm sitting to spin."
With a rowley powley, gammon and spin-
ach,
Heigho, says Anthony Rowley!

"Pray, Mrs. Mouse, will you give us some
beer?"
Heigho, says Rowley,
"For Froggy and I are fond of good cheer."
With a rowley powley, gammon and
spinach,
Heigho, says Anthony Rowley!

"Pray, Mr. Frog, will you give us a song?"
Heigho, says Rowley,
"But let it be something that's not very long."
With a rowley powley, gammon and
spinach,
Heigho, says Anthony Rowley!

"Indeed, Mrs. Mouse," replied the frog,
Heigho, says Rowley,
"A cold has made me as hoarse as a dog."
With a rowley powley, gammon and
spinach,
Heigho, says Anthony Rowley!

"Since you have caught cold, Mr. Frog,"
Mousey said,
Heigho, says Rowley,
"I'll sing you a song that I have just made."
With a rowley powley, gammon and
spinach,
Heigho, says Anthony Rowley!

But while they were all a merry-making,
Heigho, says Rowley,
A cat and her kittens came tumbling in.
With a rowley powley, gammon and
spinach,
Heigho, says Anthony Rowley!

The cat she seized the rat by the crown;
Heigho, says Rowley,
The kittens they pulled the little mouse
down.
With a rowley powley, gammon and
spinach,
Heigho, says Anthony Rowley!

This put Mr. Frog in a terrible fright,
Heigho, says Rowley,
He took up his hat, and he wished them
good night.
With a rowley powley, gammon and
spinach,
Heigho, says Anthony Rowley!

But as Froggy was crossing over a brook,
Heigho, says Rowley,
A lily-white duck came and gobbled him up.
With a rowley powley, gammon and
spinach,
Heigho, says Anthony Rowley!

So there was an end of one, two, and three,
Heigho, says Rowley,
The Rat, the Mouse, and the little Frog-gee!
With a rowley powley, gammon and
spinach,
Heigho, says Anthony Rowley!

102

There were three jovial Welshmen,
As I have heard them say,
And they would go a-hunting
Upon St. David's day.

All the day they hunted,
And nothing could they find,
But a ship a-sailing,
A-sailing with the wind.

One said it was a ship,
The other he said nay;
The third said it was a house,
With the chimney blown away.

And all the night they hunted,
  And nothing could they find
But the moon a-gliding,
  A-gliding with the wind.

One said it was the moon,
  The other he said nay;
The third said it was a cheese,
  And half o't cut away.

And all the day they hunted,
  And nothing could they find
But a hedgehog in a bramble-bush,
  And that they left behind.

The first said it was a hedgehog;
  The second he said nay;
The third it was a pin-cushion,
  And the pins stuck in wrong way.

And all the night they hunted,
  And nothing could they find
But a hare in a turnip field,
  And that they left behind.

The first said it was a hare;
  The second he said nay;
The third said it was a calf,
  And the cow had run away.

And all the day they hunted,
  And nothing could they find
But an owl in a holly-tree,
  And that they left behind.

One said it was an owl;
  The other he said nay;
The third said 'twas an old man
  And his beard growing gray.

103

Can you make a cambric shirt,
  Parsley, sage, rosemary, and thyme,
Without any seam or needlework?
  And you shall be a true lover of mine.

Can you wash it in yonder well,
  Parsley, sage, rosemary, and thyme,
Where never sprung water, nor rain ever fell?
  And you shall be a true lover of mine.

Can you dry it on yonder thorn,
  Parsley, sage, rosemary, and thyme,
Which never bore blossom since Adam was
    born?
  And you shall be a true lover of mine.

Now you've asked me questions three,
  Parsley, sage, rosemary, and thyme,
I hope you'll answer as many for me,
  And you shall be a true lover of mine.

Can you find me an acre of land,
  Parsley, sage, rosemary, and thyme,
Between the salt water and the sea sand?
  And you shall be a true lover of mine.

Can you plough it with a ram's horn,
  Parsley, sage, rosemary, and thyme,
And sow it all over with one pepper-corn?
  And you shall be a true lover of mine.

Can you reap it with a sickle of leather,
  Parsley, sage, rosemary, and thyme,
And bind it up with a peacock's feather?
  And you shall be a true lover of mine.

When you have done and finished your work,
  Parsley, sage, rosemary, and thyme,
Then come to me for your cambric shirt,
  And you shall be a true lover of mine.

JOHN NEWBERY'S MOTHER GOOSE

Matthew Prior, in his life of Oliver Gold-smith, says there is a probability that Goldsmith had a hand in preparing the Mother Goose's Melody as it was first issued by Newbery. It is true that Goldsmith began as a hack writer for John Newbery about the time this little 3 × 4½" volume was supposed to have been published; but as Newbery himself says nothing in his foreward about Goldsmith and definitely states on the title page that he took the rhymes from the "lips of the Old British nurses," Gold-smith's connection seems not more than a pos-sibility. As a guess, might it not be possible that the "maxims" after each rhyme came from the fertile brain of Goldsmith? Are they, or are they not, in harmony with his character? This whole question could be an interesting subject for study.

Another interesting fact to be noted is that Newbery considered Shakespeare's lyrics suit-able reading for children of the Mother Goose age; for the last part of Mother Goose's Melody contained the best known of the lyrics, some of which small children might well claim as their own.

104

Three wise men of Gotham,
    They went to sea in a bowl,
And if the bowl had been stronger,
My song had been longer.

It is long enough. Never lament the loss of what is not worth having. — Boyle.

105

There was an old man,
    And he had a calf,
    And that's half.

He took him from the stall
And put him on the wall,
    And that's all.

Maxim. Those who are given to tell all they know, generally tell more than they know.

106

There was an old woman
Lived under the hill,
And if she's not gone
She lives there still.

This is a self-evident proposition which is the very essence of truth. *She lived under the hill, and if she's not gone, she lives there still.* Nobody will presume to contradict this. — Creusa.

107

See saw, Margery Daw,
Jacky shall have a new master;
Jacky must have but a penny a day,
Because he can work no faster.

It is a mean and scandalous practice in authors to put notes to things that deserve no notice. — Grotius.

108
A Learned Song

Here's A, B, and C,
D, E, F, and G,
H, I, K, L, M, N, O, P, Q,
R, S, T, U,
W, X, Y, and Z.

And here's the child's dad,
Who is sagacious and discerning,
And knows this is the fount of learning.

This is the most learned ditty in the world,
for indeed, there is no song can be made with
out the aid of this, it being the *gamut* and
ground-work of them all. — Mope's *Geography of the Mind.*

109
ALEXANDER'S SONG

There was a man of Thessaly,
And he was wondrous wise,

He jumped into a quick-set hedge,
And scratched out both his eyes;
And when he saw his eyes were out,
With all his might and main,
He jumped into another hedge,
And scratched them in again.

How happy it was for the man to scratch
his eyes in again, when they were scratched
out! But he was a blockhead or would have
kept himself out of the hedge, and not been
scratch'd at all. — Wiseman's *New Way to
Wisdom.*

SINGING GAMES, JINGLES, COUNTING-OUT RHYMES

110

1, 2,
Buckle my shoe;

3, 4,
Knock at the door;

5, 6,
Pick up sticks;

7, 8,
Lay them straight;

9, 10,
A big fat hen;

11, 12,
Dig and delve;

13, 14,
Maids a-courting;

15, 16,
Maids in the kitchen;

17, 18,
Maids in waiting;

19, 20,
My plate's empty.

111

Sing a song of sixpence,
A pocket full of rye;
Four and twenty blackbirds,
Baked in a pie.

When the pie was opened,
The birds began to sing;
Was not that a dainty dish,
To set before the king?

The king was in his counting-house,
Counting out his money;

The queen was in the parlour,
  Eating bread and honey.

The maid was in the garden,
  Hanging out the clothes,
When down came a blackbird
  And pecked off her nose.

112

Pease porridge hot,
Pease porridge cold,
Pease porridge in the pot,
  Nine days old.
Some like it hot,
Some like it cold,
Some like it in the pot
  Nine days old.

113

London Bridge is broken down,
  Dance o'er my Lady Lee;
London Bridge is broken down,
  With a gay lady.

How shall we build it up again?
  Dance o'er my Lady Lee;
How shall we build it up again?
  With a gay lady.

Build it up with silver and gold,
  Dance o'er my Lady Lee;
Build it up with silver and gold,
  With a gay lady.

Silver and gold will be stole away,
  Dance o'er my Lady Lee;
Silver and gold will be stole away,
  With a gay lady.

Build it up with iron and steel,
  Dance o'er my Lady Lee;
Build it up with iron and steel,
  With a gay lady.

Iron and steel will bend and bow,
  Dance o'er my Lady Lee;
Iron and steel will bend and bow,
  With a gay lady.

Build it up with wood and clay,
  Dance o'er my Lady Lee;

Build it up with wood and clay,
  With a gay lady.

Wood and clay will wash away,
  Dance o'er my Lady Lee;
Wood and clay will wash away,
  With a gay lady.

Build it up with stone so strong,
  Dance o'er my Lady Lee;
Huzza! 'twill last for ages long,
  With a gay lady.

114

Gay go up and gay go down,
To ring the bells of London town.

Bull's eyes and targets,
Say the bells of St. Marg'ret's.

Brickbats and tiles,
Say the bells of St. Giles'.

Oranges and lemons,
Say the bells of St. Clement's.

Pancakes and fritters,
Say the bells of St. Peter's.

Two sticks and an apple,
Say the bells at Whitechapel.

Old Father Baldpate,
Say the slow bells at Aldgate.

Maids in white aprons,
Say the bells at St. Catherine's.

Pokers and tongs,
Say the bells at St. John's.

Kettles and pans,
Say the bells at St. Anne's.

You owe me five farthings,
Say the bells of St. Martin's.

When will you pay me?
Say the bells at Old Bailey.

When I grow rich,
Say the bells at Shoreditch.

Pray, when will that be?
Say the bells at Stepney.

I'm sure I don't know,
Say the bells at Bow.

Here comes a candle to light you to bed,
Here comes a chopper to chop off your
  head.

115

Lady Queen Anne she sits in the sun,
As fair as a lily, as white as a swan;
Come taste my lily, come smell my rose,
Which of my maidens do you choose?
The ball is ours and none of yours,
Go to the wood and gather flowers.
Cats and kittens now stay within,
While we young maidens walk out and in.

116

Oh, the brave old Duke of York,
  He had ten thousand men;
He marched them up to the top of the
  hill,
  And he marched them down again.
And when they were up, they were up,
  And when they were down, they were
  down,
And when they were only half way up,
  They were neither up nor down.

117

POP GOES THE WEASEL

Up and down the City Road,
  In and out the Eagle,
That's the way the money goes,
  Pop goes the weasel!

Half a pound of tuppenny rice,
  Half a pound of treacle,
Mix it up and make it nice,
  Pop goes the weasel!

Every night when I go out
  The monkey's on the table;
Take a stick and knock it off,
  Pop goes the weasel!

118

THE TWELVE DAYS OF CHRISTMAS

*"Among our traditional games, some con-
sist of a dialogue in which the answer is set in
cumulative form. These include the game
known as* The Twelve Days of Christmas *which
was played on Twelfth-Day night by the assembled company before eating mince-pies and
twelfth cake. In the game of* Twelve Days *each
player in succession repeated the gifts of the
day, and raised his fingers and hand according
to the number which he named. Each answer
included one that had gone before, and forfeits
were paid for each mistake that was made."* —
From Lina Eckenstein, *Comparative Studies in
Nursery Rhymes* (Duckworth, London, 1906).

The first day of Christmas,
My true love sent to me
A partridge in a pear tree.

The second day of Christmas,
My true love sent to me
Two turtle doves, and
A partridge in a pear tree.

The third day of Christmas,
My true love sent to me
Three French hens,
Two turtle doves, and
A partridge in a pear tree.

The fourth day of Christmas,
My true love sent to me
Four colly birds,
Three French hens,
Two turtle doves, and
A partridge in a pear tree.

The fifth day of Christmas,
My true love sent to me
Five gold rings,
Four colly birds,
Three French hens,
Two turtle doves, and
A partridge in a pear tree.

The sixth day of Christmas,
My true love sent to me
Six geese a-laying,
Five gold rings,

Four colly birds,
Three French hens,
Two turtle doves, and
A partridge in a pear tree.

The seventh day of Christmas,
My true love sent to me
Seven swans a-swimming,
Six geese a-laying,
Five gold rings,
Four colly birds,
Three French hens,
Two turtle doves, and
A partridge in a pear tree.

The eighth day of Christmas,
My true love sent to me
Eight maids a-milking,
Seven swans a-swimming,
Six geese a-laying,
Five gold rings,
Four colly birds,
Three French hens,
Two turtle doves, and
A partridge in a pear tree.

The ninth day of Christmas,
My true love sent to me
Nine drummers drumming,
Eight maids a-milking,
Seven swans a-swimming,
Six geese a-laying,
Five gold rings,
Four colly birds,
Three French hens,
Two turtle doves, and
A partridge in a pear tree.

The tenth day of Christmas,
My true love sent to me
Ten pipers piping,
Nine drummers drumming,
Eight maids a-milking,
Seven swans a-swimming,
Six geese a-laying,
Five gold rings,
Four colly birds,
Three French hens,
Two turtle doves, and
A partridge in a pear tree.

The eleventh day of Christmas,
My true love sent to me
Eleven ladies dancing,
Ten pipers piping,
Nine drummers drumming,
Eight maids a-milking,
Seven swans a-swimming,
Six geese a-laying,
Five gold rings,
Four colly birds,
Three French hens,
Two turtle doves, and
A partridge in a pear tree.

The twelfth day of Christmas,
My true love sent to me
Twelve lords a-leaping,
Eleven ladies dancing,
Ten pipers piping,
Nine drummers drumming,
Eight maids a-milking,
Seven swans a-swimming,
Six geese a-laying,
Five gold rings,
Four colly birds,
Three French hens,
Two turtle doves, and
A partridge in a pear tree.

The two rhymes which follow are a game. Number one (1) speaks first; number two (2), who is ignorant of the joke, takes the lines marked 2.

119

1. I am a gold lock.
   2. I am a gold key.
1. I am a silver lock.
   2. I am a silver key.
1. I am a brass lock.
   2. I am a brass key.
1. I am a lead lock.
   2. I am a lead key.
1. I am a monk lock.
   2. I am a monk key (monkey).[1]

120

1. I went up one pair of stairs.
   2. Just like me.

[1] From Andrew Lang, *The Nursery Rhyme Book* (Frederick Warne).

1. I went up two pairs of stairs.
2. Just like me.
1. I went into a room.
2. Just like me.
1. I looked out of a window.
2. Just like me.
1. And there I saw a monkey.
2. Just like me.[2]

121

See-saw sacradown,
   Which is the way to London town?
One foot up and the other foot down,
   And that is the way to London town.

122

Intery, mintery, cutery, corn,
Apple seed and briar thorn;
Wire, briar, limber lock,
Five geese in a flock,
Sit and sing by a spring,
O-U-T, and in again.

123
GERMAN

Eins, zwei, Polizei,
Drei, vier, Offizier,
Fünf, sechs, alte Hex,
Sieben, acht, gute Nacht,
Neun, zehn, auf wiedersehen.

One, two, policeman blue,
Three, four, captain of the corps,
Five, six, a witch on two sticks,
Seven, eight, the hour is late,
Nine, ten, we meet again.[3]

[2] Ibid.

124
FRENCH

Un, deux, trois, j'irai dans le bois,
Quatre, cinq, six, chercher les cerises,
Sept, huit, neuf, dans mon panier neuf,
Dix, onze, douze, elles seront toutes rouges.

One, two, three, to the wood goes she,
Four, five, six, cherries she picks,
Seven, eight, nine, in her basket fine,
Ten, eleven, twelve, (she said),
All the cherries are red, red, red![3]

125
FRENCH

Une fill' a battu
Le roi d'Angleterre.

Tout est regagné
Par une bergère.

Nous pouvons danser,
Nous n'aurons plus de guerre.

A maiden's wondrous fame, I sing
She broke the pride of England's King.

All that we lost in our distress
Has been won back by a shepherdess.

Now, dance, dance, dance away,
There'll be no war for many a day![3]

[3] From Henry Bett, *Nursery Rhymes and Tales* (Holt).

RIDDLES, PARADOXES, TONGUE TRIPPERS

126

Long legs, crooked thighs,
Little head and no eyes.
(*A pair of tongs*)

127

Thirty white horses
Upon a red hill,
Now they stamp,
Now they champ,
Now they stand still.
(*Teeth*)

128

In marble halls as white as milk,
Lined with a skin as soft as silk,
Within a fountain crystal clear,
A golden apple doth appear.
No doors there are to this stronghold,
Yet thieves break in and steal the gold.
(*Egg*)

129

As round as an apple, as deep as a cup,
And all the king's horses can't pull it up.
(*Well*)

130

Black within and red without;
Four corners round about.
(*Chimney*)

131

Elizabeth, Elspeth, Betsy, and Bess
They all went together to seek a bird's nest.
They found a bird's nest with five eggs in;
They each took one, and left four in.
(*One girl*)

132

I have a little sister, they call her Peep,
   Peep;
She makes the waters deep, deep, deep;
She climbs the mountains high, high, high;
Poor little creature, she has but one eye.
(*A star*)

133

Two legs sat on three legs,
With one leg in his lap;
In comes four legs,
And runs away with one leg,
Up jumps two legs,
Catches up three legs,
Throws it after four legs
And makes him bring back one leg.
(*Two legs — a man*)
(*Three legs — a stool*)
(*One leg — leg of meat*)
(*Four legs — a dog*)

134

Little Nancy Etticoat,
With a white petticoat,
And a red nose;
She has no feet or hands,
The longer she stands
The shorter she grows.
(*A candle*)

135

Hick-a-more, Hack-a-more,
Hung on a kitchen door;
   Nothing so long,
   And nothing so strong,
As Hick-a-more, Hack-a-more,
Hung on the kitchen door.
(*A sunbeam*)

136

As I was going to St. Ives,
I met a man with seven wives,
Each wife had seven sacks,
Each sack had seven cats,
Each cat had seven kits:
Kits, cats, sacks, and wives,
How many were there going to St. Ives?
(One) [1]

137

If all the seas were one sea,
What a *great* sea that would be!
And if all the trees were one tree,
What a *great* tree that would be!
And if all the axes were one axe,
What a *great* axe that would be!
And if all the men were one man,
What a *great* man he would be!
And if the *great* man took the *great* axe,
And cut down the *great* tree,
And let it fall into the *great* sea,
What a splish splash *that* would be!

138

If all the world was apple pie,
    And all the sea was ink,
And all the trees were bread and cheese,
    What should we have for drink?

139

I saw a fishpond all on fire
I saw a house bow to a squire
I saw a parson twelve feet high
I saw a cottage near the sky
I saw a balloon made of lead
I saw a coffin drop down dead
I saw two sparrows run a race
I saw two horses making lace
I saw a girl just like a cat
I saw a kitten wear a hat
I saw a man who saw these too
And said though strange they all were true.

140

A man in the wilderness asked me,
How many strawberries grow in the sea.
I answered him, as I thought good,
As many red herrings as swim in the wood.

141

Betty Botter bought some butter,
But, she said, the butter's bitter;
If I put it in my batter
It will make my batter bitter,
But a bit of better butter
Will make my batter better.
So she bought a bit of butter
Better than her bitter butter,
And she put it in her batter
And the batter was not bitter.
So 'twas better Betty Botter bought a bit
    of better butter.

142

How much wood would a woodchuck chuck
If a woodchuck could chuck wood?
A woodchuck would chuck as much as he
    would chuck
If a woodchuck could chuck wood. [2]

143

The entire alphabet is treated in this same way in Peter Piper's Practical Principles of Plain and Perfect Pronunciation *published by J. Harris and Son in 1819. Caroline Hewins included the* Peter Piper Alphabet *in its original form in her book* A Mid-Century Child and Her Books, *recollections of her own childhood reading. The alphabet may also be found in Caroline M. Hewins Her Book, by Jennie D. Lindquist, published by The Horn Book, Inc., in 1954. To have heard Miss Hewins recite this tongue-tripping alphabet is an unforgettable experience. She called it her one parlor trick.*

Peter Piper pick'd a Peck of Pepper;
Did Peter Piper pick a Peck of Pepper?
If Peter Piper pick'd a Peck of Pepper,
Where's the Peck of Pepper Peter Piper
    pick'd?

---

[1] The solution is "one" or "none" according to how the question is read. If the question is "How many wives, sacks, cats, and kittens went to St. Ives?" the answer is "None."

[2] From Maud and Miska Petersham, *The Rooster Crows; A Book of American Rhymes and Jingles* (Macmillan).

NURSERY RHYMES OF MANY LANDS

144
LITTLE GIRL
(Arabian)

I will build you a house
If you do not cry,
A house, little girl,
As tall as the sky.

I will build you a house
Of golden dates,
The freshest of all
For the steps and gates.

I will furnish the house
For you and for me
With walnuts and hazels
Fresh from the tree.

I will build you a house,
And when it is done
I will roof it with grapes
To keep out the sun.[1]

145
THE FIVE TOES
(Chinese)

This little cow eats grass,
This little cow eats hay,
This little cow drinks water,
This little cow runs away,
This little cow does nothing,
But just lie down all day;
   We'll whip her.[2]

[1] From Rose Fyleman, *Picture Rhymes from Foreign Lands* (Lippincott).
[2] From I. T. Headland, *Chinese Mother Goose Rhymes* (Revell).

146
LADY BUG
(Chinese)

Lady-bug, lady-bug,
Fly away, do,
Fly to the mountain,
And feed upon dew,
Feed upon dew,
And sleep on a rug,
And then run away
Like a good little bug.[2]

147
THISTLE-SEED
(Chinese)

Thistle-seed, thistle-seed,
  Fly away, fly,
The hair on your body
  Will take you up high;
Let the wind whirl you
Around and around,
You'll not hurt yourself
When you fall to the ground.[2]

148
BLIND MAN'S BUFF
(Chinese)

A peacock feather
On a plum-tree limb,
You catch me,
And I'll catch him.

All come and see!
All come and see!
A black hen laid a white egg for me.[2]

149
OLD CHANG THE CRAB
(Chinese)

Old man Chang, I've oft heard it said,
You wear a basket upon your head;
You've two pairs of scissors to cut your
    meat,
And two pairs of chopsticks with which you
    eat.[3]

150
FISHING
(Danish)

Row to the fishing-ground, row away,
How many fish have you caught to-day?
One for my father and one for my
    mother
One for my sister and one for my brother;
One for you and another for me
And one for the fisher who went to sea.[4]

151
'JONATHAN
(Dutch)

Jonathan Gee
Went out with his cow;
He climbed up a tree
And sat on a bough.
He sat on a bough
And it broke in half,
And John's old cow
Did nothing but laugh.[4]

152
GRETCHEN
(Dutch)

Little Dutch Gretchen sat in the kitchen,
Eating some nice sauerkraut,
When the little dog Schneider
Came and sat down beside her,
And little Dutch Gretchen went out.[5]

[3] Ibid.
[4] From Rose Fyleman, Picture Rhymes from Foreign Lands (Lippincott).
[5] From Alice Daglish and Ernest Rhys, The Land of Nursery Rhyme (Dutton).

153
THE GOBLIN
(French)

A goblin lives in our house, in our house, in
    our house,
A goblin lives in our house all the year
    round.
He bumps
And he jumps
And he thumps
And he stumps.
He knocks
And he rocks
And he rattles at the locks.
A goblin lives in our house, in our house,
    in our house,
A goblin lives in our house all the year
    round.[6]

154
MEE, RAY, DOH
(German)

Me, Ray, Doh,
Pussy's in the snow;
Back she comes, oh, what a sight,
Wearing little boots of white;
Jimminy, oh, Jimminy, oh Jimminy, oh Jo!

Me, Ray, Doh,
Where shall pussy go?
By the fire she shall remain,
Lick her stockings clean again;
Jimminy, oh Jimminy, oh Jimminy, oh Jo! [6]

155
(Hebrew)

An angel came as I lay in bed;
I will give you wings — the angel said;
I will give you wings that you may fly
To the country of Heaven above the sky.

My beautiful angel flew away,
He came not again by night or by day;
Angels are busy with many things,
And he has forgotten to send the wings.[6]

[6] From Rose Fyleman, Picture Rhymes from Foreign Lands (Lippincott).

156
TWELFTH NIGHT
(*Italian*)

Saw, saw;
White are the sheep,
Blue are the doves' eggs,
Jesus send us sleep.
Here comes Twelfth Night,
Everyone's in bed,
Three gold crowns he
Wears on his head.
Here comes the servant
With a white filly,
And here comes the Lady,
White as a lily.[6]

157
NEW YEAR'S DAY
(*Japanese*)

How many nights, oh, how many nights,
Till New Year's Day, when we fly our kites,
When we spin our tops, when we run and
    play?
Oh, how many nights till New Year's Day?

How many nights must still go by
Till we send our shuttlecocks up to the sky,
Till our balls go bouncing, bouncing away?
Hurry up, hurry up, New Year's Day.[6]

158
(*Mexican*)

Luna, la Luna
Comiendo su tuna
Echando las cáscaras
En la laguna.

Oh, Moon, little Moon,
My tuna you take;
But you throw the peelings
Into the lake.[7]

159
CABALLITO
(*Mexican*)

Caballito, Caballito,
No me tambu, no me tumba;

A galope y a galope.
Recio, recio, recio.
¡Que viva Antonio!

Little pony, little pony
Do not throw me, do not throw me:
Galloping, galloping,
Watch us go!
Long live Antonio.[8]

160
TRADJA OF NORWAY
(*Norwegian*)

Little Tradja of Norway,
She sat in the doorway,
Eating her reindeer-broth;
There came a big badger
And little Miss Tradja
Soon carried her meal farther North.[9]

161
HUSKY HI
(*Norwegian*)

Husky hi, husky hi,
Here comes Kerry galloping by.
She carries her husband tied in a sack,
She carries him home on her horse's back.
Husky hi, husky hi,
Here comes Kerry galloping by![10]

162
MUSHROOMS
(*Russian*)

Lucky is the mushrooms' mother,
Her daughters grow so fast —
Born on Saturday, grown by Sunday,
Waiting to be courted Monday.[10]

163
(*Scottish*)

Dance to your daddy,
My little babby,
Dance to your daddy, my little lamb;
You shall have a fishy

---

6 *Ibid.*
7 From Patricia Fent Ross, *The Hungry Moon; Mexican Nursery Tales* (Knopf). "Tuna" (line 6) is a fruit that grows on a cactus plant.

8 From Frances Alexander and others, *Mother Goose on the Rio Grande* (Banks Upshaw, Dallas).
9 From Alice Daglish and Ernest Rhys, *The Land of Nursery Rhyme* (Dutton).
10 From Rose Fyleman, *Picture Rhymes from Foreign Lands* (Lippincott).

In a little dishy,
You shall have a fishy when the boat comes
  in.[11]

164
(Scottish)

A wee bird sat upon a tree,
When the year was dune and auld,
And aye it cheepit sae peetiously,
"My, but it's cauld, cauld." [12]

165
(Scottish)

Lady, Lady Landers,
Lady, Lady Landers,
Tak up yer coat
Aboot yer heid,
And flee awa
Tae Flanders.
Flee ower firth,
And flee ower fell,
Flee ower pool,
And rinnin well,
Flee ower muir,
And flee ower mead,
Flee ower livin,
Flee ower deid,
Flee ower corn,
And flee ower lea,
Flee ower river,
Flee ower sea,
Flee ye east,
Or flee ye west,
Flee till him
That loes me best. [12]

166
(Scottish)

The cock and the hen,
The deer in the den,
Shall drink in the clearest fountain.
The venison rare
Shall be my love's fare,
And I'll follow him over the mountain.[12]

167
(Scottish)

Sandy Candy
Blaws his hown

Ten mile
Amo the corn.[12]

168
(Scottish)

John Smith's a very guid man,
Teaches scholars now and than,
And when he's dune he taks a dance,
Up tae London, doon tae France.[12]

169
(Scottish)

Haily Paily
Sits on the sands,
Combs her hair
Wi her lily-white hands.[12]

170
WELL I NEVER!
(Spanish)

Two little mice went tripping down the
  street,
Pum catta-pum chin chin,
One wore a bonnet and a green silk skirt,
One wore trousers and a nice clean shirt;
Pum catta-pum chin chin.

One little hen went tripping down the street,
Pum catta-pum chin chin,
One little hen very smart and spry,
With a wig-wagging tail and a wicked little
  eye,
Pum catta-pum chin chin.[18]

171
TO THE SHOP
(Welsh)

I have a little pony
Rising four years old,
His shoes are made of silver
His bit is made of gold.

Into town I'll send him
To fetch a great big sack
Of tea and sugar-candy
For Mary and for Jack.[13]

11 From *The Oxford Dictionary of Nursery Rhymes*, ed. Iona and Peter Opie (Oxford University Press).

12 From Norah and William Montgomerie, *Sandy Candy and Other Scottish Nursery Rhymes* (Hogarth Press, London).

13 From Rose Fyleman, *Picture Rhymes from Foreign Lands* (Lippincott).

AMERICAN CHANTS AND JINGLES

172

Yankee Doodle went to town
Riding on a pony,
Stuck a feather in his hat
And called it Macaroni.[1]

173

I asked my mother for fifty cents
To see the elephant jump the fence.
He jumped so high
He reached the sky
And never came back till the Fourth of
July.[1]

174

A bear went over the mountain,
A bear went over the mountain,
A bear went over the mountain
To see what he could see!

The other side of the mountain,
The other side of the mountain,
The other side of the mountain
Was all that he could see.[1]

175

I'm going to Lady Washington's
To get a cup of tea
And five loaves of gingerbread,
So don't you follow me.[1]

176

Monday's child is fair of face,
Tuesday's child is full of grace,
Wednesday's child is full of woe,
Thursday's child has far to go,
Friday's child is loving and giving,
Saturday's child works hard for a living,
But the child that is born on the Sabbath day
Is blythe and bonny and good and gay.[1]

177

Five little squirrels sat up in a tree,
The first one said, "What do I see?"
The second one said, "A man with a gun."
The third one said, "Then we'd better run."
The fourth one said. "Let's hide in the
shade."
The fifth one said, "I'm not afraid."
Then BANG went the gun, and how they did
run.[2]

178

I've got a rocket
In my pocket;
I cannot stop to play.
Away it goes!
I've burnt my toes.
It's Independence Day.[2]

[1] From Maud and Miska Petersham, *The Rooster Crows; a Book of American Rhymes and Jingles* (Macmillan).
[2] From Carl Withers, *A Rocket in My Pocket; the Rhymes and Chants of Young Americans* (Holt).

BIBLIOGRAPHY

Opie, Iona and Peter, eds. *The Oxford Dictionary of Nursery Rhymes;* illus. with historical plates. Oxford University Press, 1951.

A scholarly work done with consummate skill and filled with fascinating notes. The editors are leading authorities on eighteenth-century children's literature and chapbooks. They have brought together more than 500 traditional rhymes, giving their individual histories, literary associations, variations, and parallels in other languages. In the introduction they describe the different types of rhymes, the earliest collections, theories dealing with their origin, and the possible identity of Mother Goose. A book for adults with imagination who care for poetry and folklore.

Opie, Iona and Peter, eds. *The Oxford Nursery Rhyme Book.* Oxford University Press, 1955.

A unique collection of 800 nursery rhymes. More than 400 illustrations are reproductions of woodcuts from the earliest children's books and chapbooks of the eighteenth and nineteenth centuries. Engravings by both Thomas and John Bewick are included. Supplementing the early reproductions are 150 illustrations by Joan Hassall.

Bett, Henry. *Nursery Rhymes and Tales; Their History and Origin.* Henry Holt, 1924.

A brief introduction to the history of nursery rhymes and folk tales. First published in England.

Eckenstein, Lina. *Comparative Studies in Nursery Rhymes.* Duckworth (London), 1906.

Traces the folk origins of Mother Goose rhymes.

Sackville-West, Virginia. *Nursery Rhymes; an Essay;* illus. by Philippe Julian. Michael Joseph (London), 1950.

The author shows that folklore, mythology, and history all combine in the making of nursery rhymes, but she contends that it is "the inherent music of the nursery jingle" that preserves it in loving remembrance.

Mother Goose Nursery Rhymes

Book of Nursery and Mother Goose Rhymes; ed. and illus. by Marguerite de Angeli. Doubleday, 1954.

An excellent collection containing 376 rhymes, including some of the longer and many of the less familiar ones.

The Boyd Smith Mother Goose; texts carefully collated and verified by Laurence Elmendorf; illus. by E. Boyd Smith. G. P. Putnam's Sons, 1919.

Invaluable for reference because it contains the text of *Mother Goose's Melody* (c.1760) as issued by John Newbery from his bookshop at the Sign of the Bible and Sun in St. Paul's churchyard, London; and that of *The Original Mother Goose's Melody* (c.1785), the first American collection of nursery rhymes, printed by Isaiah Thomas of Worcester, Mass.

Ditties for the Nursery; ed. by Iona Opie and illus. by Monica Walker. Oxford University Press, 1954.

"Rhymes which delighted children in the reign of George III . . . published about 1805 under the title *Original Ditties for the Nursery, So Wonderfully Contrived that they may be either Sung or Said by Nurse or Baby.*" Children of today will delight in many of these unfamiliar rhymes of yesterday. The illustrations have vitality and charm.

The Gay Mother Goose; with drawings by Françoise. Charles Scribner's Sons, 1938.

Over seventy familiar rhymes selected by Alice Dalgliesh and Françoise. The charm of the illustrations lies in their likeness to those the children draw for themselves.

Lavender's Blue; a Book of Nursery Rhymes; comp. by Kathleen Lines; pictures by Harold Jones. Franklin Watts, 1954.

A beautifully illustrated book with eighty-one pages in full color reproduced from lithographs on stone. The sheets were printed in England. This edition is distinguished not only for its illustrations but for its inclusion of many little-known nursery rhymes.

Little Mother Goose; illus. by Jessie Willcox Smith. Dodd, Mead, reissued in 1954.

Because of its small size, excellent selection, and childlike pictures, this edition, first published in 1918, remains a great favorite.

Mother Goose; or, The Old Nursery Rhymes; illus. by Kate Greenaway. Frederick Warne, n.d.

A slender book containing a limited number of rhymes with charming, characteristic illustrations.

Mother Goose; Seventy-Seven Verses; with pictures by Tasha Tudor. Oxford University Press, 1944.

A small book with pictures in soft pastels which appeal especially to little girls.

Mother Goose's Melodies; or, Songs for the Nursery; ed. by W. A. Wheeler. Houghton Mifflin.

An interesting edition illustrated with old-fashioned woodcuts. It contains a history of the apocryphal Dame Vergoose of Boston. First published in 1869. Excellent for reference.

Nursery Rhyme Book; ed. by Andrew Lang; illus. by L. Leslie Brooke. Frederick Warne, new edition, 1947.

This book has been a mainstay for over half a century. The origin and history of some of the rhymes is given in the preface. Delightful interpretative illustrations.

The Real Mother Goose; with pictures by Blanche Fisher Wright. Rand McNally, 1916.

One of the best editions for the youngest children, containing the more familiar rhymes with brightly colored pictures.

Ring o' Roses; a Nursery Rhyme Picture Book; with numerous drawings in color and in black and white by L. Leslie Brooke. Frederick Warne.

An ideal first book for very young children with L. Leslie Brooke's inimitable illustrations.

Singing Games

Bertail, Inez, ed. *Complete Nursery Song Book;* illus. by Walt Kelly. Lothrop, Lee & Shepard, 1954.

Favorite nursery songs with simple piano arrangements and directions for singing games and finger plays.

Chase, Richard, comp. *Hullabaloo, and Other Singing Folk Games;* illus. by Joshua Tolford; with six piano settings by Hilton Rufty. Houghton Mifflin, 1949.

Verses, tunes, and directions for eighteen traditional American-English singing games, folk games, and figure dances.

Henius, Frank, ed. *Songs and Games of the Americas;* illus. by Oscar Fabrés. Charles Scribner's Sons, 1943.

Thirty-eight songs and games from Mexico and most of the countries of Central and South America, translated from Spanish, Portuguese, and French. Music included.

Jacobs, Gertrude, comp. *The Chinese-American Song and Game Book;* illus. by Chao Shih Chen; music by Virginia and Richard Mather. A. S. Barnes, 1944.

Eighteen Chinese singing games with words given in both Chinese and English. The delicate drawings are the work of a young Chinese girl.

Writers' Program. *Spanish-American Song and Game Book.* A. S. Barnes, 1942.

Games which have been sung and played in New Mexico for generations. Directions are given in both Spanish and English. Music is included.

Nursery Rhymes Set to Music, Play Rhymes, and Chants

Crane, Walter. *Baby's Bouquet; a Fresh Bunch of Old Rhymes and Tunes;* arranged and decorated by Walter Crane. Frederick Warne, 1900.

Thirty-seven nursery rhymes set to music. A companion volume to *The Baby's Opera,* which contains thirty-six of the more familiar Mother Goose rhymes.

Fish, Helen Dean, comp. *Four & Twenty Blackbirds; Nursery Rhymes of Yesterday recalled for Children of Today;* illus. by Robert Lawson. J. B. Lippincott (A Stokes Book), 1937.

An excellent collection of little-known nursery rhymes and ballads. Simple music is given for many of the rhymes. Robert Lawson's illustrations make it a delightful picture book. A brief historical note for each rhyme is given in the Contents.

Kapp, Paul. *A Cat Came Fiddling, and Other Rhymes of Childhood;* illus. by Irene Haas; introduction by Burl Ives. Harcourt, Brace, 1956.

Fifty-seven delightful nonsense verses and nursery rhymes set to music.

Moffat, Alfred. *Our Old Nursery Rhymes;* the original tunes harmonized by Alfred Moffat; illus. by H. Willebeek LeMair. David McKay, 1911.

Thirty Mother Goose rhymes with music. Full-page illustrations in delicate color. *Little Songs of Long Ago* is a companion volume.

Petersham, Maud and Miska, comps. *The Rooster Crows; a Book of American Rhymes and Jingles;* illustrated by the compilers. Macmillan, 1945.

American rhymes and jingles, finger games, rope-skipping rhymes, counting-out rhymes, and other game rhymes, delightfully illustrated. Awarded the Caldecott medal, 1946.

Taylor, Margaret, comp. *Did You Feed My Cow?;* illus. by Paul Galdone. Thomas Y. Crowell, 1956.

Contemporary play rhymes collected over a period of years as the author heard them from boys and girls to whom the rhymes had been handed down and who made them their own.

Wheeler, Opal. *Sing Mother Goose;* illus. by Marjorie Torrey. E. P. Dutton, 1945.

Fifty-two of the best-loved Mother Goose rhymes set to music.

Withers, Carl, comp. *A Rocket in my Pocket; the Rhymes and Chants of Young Americans;* illus. by Susanne Suba. Henry Holt, 1948.

Over four hundred rhymes, chants, game songs, tongue twisters current today. The compiler collected the material while he was doing field work with children in New York City and many regions of the United States.

Wood, Ray, comp. *Fun in American Folk Rhymes;* with drawings by Ed Hargis; introduction by Carl Carmer. J. B. Lippincott, 1952.

American folk rhymes, ballads, counting-out, skipping, and jump-rope rhymes. A companion volume to the author's *American Mother Goose.*

Folk Songs

Boni, Margaret Bradford, ed. *Fireside Book of Folk Songs;* arranged for the piano by Norman Lloyd; illus. by Alice and Martin Provensen. Simon & Schuster, 1947.

Planned for family or group singing. Includes nursery rhymes and ballads besides favorite songs of yesterday. Colorful illustrations add to the distinction of the book.

Carmer, Carl, comp. *America Sings; Stories and Songs of Our Country's Growing;* musical arrangements by Edwin John Stringham; illus. by Elizabeth Carmer. Alfred A. Knopf, 1942.

A distinguished anthology of folk songs and tales reflecting America's work and growth.

Gordon, Dorothy. *Sing It Yourself; Folk Songs of All Nations;* illus. by Alida Conover. E. P. Dutton, 1932.

Folk songs from the British Isles, France, Germany, Norway, and Russia, besides those from America.

Seeger, Ruth. *American Folk Songs for Children in Home, School and Nursery School;* illus. by Barbara Cooncy. Doubleday, 1948.

Folk songs from all parts of America. Introductory chapters discuss the value of folk music for children. A book for children, parents, and teachers.

Seeger, Ruth. *Animal Folk Songs for Children; Traditional American Songs;* illus. by Barbara Cooney. Doubleday, 1950.

Songs of the woods, fields, farm, and ranch are collected in this companion volume to *American Folk Songs for Children.*

Seeger, Ruth. *American Folk Songs for Christmas;* illus. by Barbara Cooney. Doubleday, 1953.

Folk songs based on Christmas themes.

Wheeler, Opal. *Sing for Christmas; a Round of Christmas Carols and Stories of Carols;* illus. by Gustaf Tenggren. E. P. Dutton, 1943.

An excellent choice of Christmas music. Colorful illustrations.

Nursery Rhymes of Other Lands

Elkin, R. H., trans. *Old Dutch Nursery Rhymes;* illus. by H. Willebeek LeMair; original tunes harmonized by J. Rönten. David McKay, 1917.

A companion volume to *Our Old Nursery Rhymes* and *Little Songs of Long Ago.*

Fyleman, Rose, trans. *Picture Rhymes from Foreign Lands;* illus. by Valéry Carrick. J. B. Lippincott, 1935. (A Stokes Book)

Rhythm, humor, and nonsense run through these folk rhymes for children from France, Germany, Spain, Norway, Russia, China, Japan, and other countries.

Headland, I. T., trans. *Chinese Mother Goose Rhymes;* illus. with photographs. Revell, 1900.

Over one hundred nursery rhymes translated from the Chinese and illustrated with photographs taken by the translator in China.

Nonsense

*" . . . this laughing heartsease, this indefinable
'cross' between humour, phantasy and a sweet
unreasonableness . . . "* [1]

HAT NONSENSE!" WHETHER THIS
be a term of praise or opprobrium depends upon the inflection of the voice.
It may mean indignation and complete dismissal of the topic as unworthy of
notice. It could mean the quick recognition of an art, the gentle art of nonsense: "that divine lunacy that God has given to men as a holiday of the intellect." [2] Gentle it may be, but it is never weak or merely silly. True nonsense is like the paw of a kitten, all seeming fur and feathers on the surface,
but beneath its softest gesture against airy nothingness lie claw, sinew, and
bone. The rules of nonsense are as exacting as those which govern the writing
of a play or a sonnet. Nonsense is the art of rearranging immutable laws
in such a way as to set logic, order, authority, or accepted standards of behavior slightly awry. It offers fantastic perspective on the familiar landscape,
and heightens the common day with a pretense of irresponsibility.

The art of nonsense seems to belong especially to the English-speaking
people, and most of all to the English themselves. They have a "solemn love
of nonsense," a unique appreciation of it as well as a master hand at creating
it. The great age of nonsense flowered in the nineteenth century. Whether
the Victorian sense of well-being, bred by the prosperity of the age, was responsible for this peak of accomplishment, or whether the repressions of the
time found an outlet in the high jinks of nonsense is a matter of conjecture.
The fact remains that the Victorian era produced giants of the art and set an
enduring standard of excellence. The Oxford don, Charles Lutwidge Dodgson,
setting free his intellectual disciplines of mathematics and logic by assuming
the name Lewis Carroll, created two whole worlds of nonsense, *Alice's Adventures in Wonderland* and *Through the Looking-Glass,* a feat of imaginative
prowess which is not likely to be equaled. The great novelists of the time
romped through nonsense also: William Makepeace Thackeray, for example,
in his nonsense pantomime, *The Rose and the Ring;* and Charles Dickens in

[1] Walter de la Mare, "Lewis Carroll," in *The Eighteen-Eighties, Essays by Fellows of the
Royal Society of Literature,* ed. by Walter de la Mare (The University Press, Cambridge,
England, 1930), p. 218.
[2] G. K. Chesterton, "Gilbert and Sullivan," *ibid.,* p. 142.

41

his *Magic Fishbone*, giving typical nonsense perspective to the characteristic size of Victorian families —

> They had nineteen children and were always having more. Seventeen of these children took care of the baby and Alicia, the eldest, took care of them all. Their ages varied from seven years to seven months.

Edward Lear, by profession a landscape painter, by choice the beloved companion of children, ushered in the great time with his *Book of Nonsense* (1846), which preceded by nineteen years the publication of *Alice's Adventures in Wonderland*. His inner eye had caught sight of the old Mother Goose rhyme,

> There was an old man of Tobago
> Who lived on rice, gruel, and sago,
> Till, much to his bliss,
> His physician said this,
> To a leg, sir, of mutton you may go.

He took to this form like a duck to water, making it his own and producing hundreds of limericks, each with its drama of triumph or frustration, as abrupt, sharp, and hilarious as Mother Goose herself. *Nonsense Songs, Stories, Botany and Alphabets* followed in 1871; *More Nonsense, Pictures, Rhymes,* in 1872; *Laughable Lyrics,* in 1877; and a final *Nonsense Songs and Stories,* in 1895. In the hands of Lear, nonsense often sweeps over into the realm of poetry; *The Courtship of the Yonghy-Bonghy-Bò* and *The Jumblies* have the felicity of music and the power to evoke a longing for the unattainable that is at once childlike and mystical:

> Far and few, far and few,
>   Are the lands where the Jumblies live;
> Their heads are green, and their hands are blue,
>   And they went to sea in a sieve.

To the gifts of his inventive play, his sense of melody, his prodigious manipulation of words and sounds is added the power of his incisive line with which he illustrates his own inspired absurdities. There is no end of delight in the writing and drawing of this "Lord High Bosh and Nonsense Producer," as he once titled himself. Gilbert and Sullivan extended the boundaries of nonsense to include the adult audience in their comic operas, a crowning musical diadem upon the great age of nonsense.

America is not without its disciples of the art, Laura E. Richards' free-flowing fancy creating nonsense as gay, bubbling, and irrepressible as Lear himself. *The Peterkin Papers* of Lucretia Hale comprises a nonsense world inhabited by familiar zanies and loveable people not quite accustomed to reasoned sensibility; and in our own time, the verse of Ogden Nash and the fables of James Thurber thrive in a latitude a little north-north-east of actuality. The American habit of exaggeration and the "tall tale" show that there is something native to nonsense in our heritage.

Any attempt to study the methods of nonsense can arrive at only a portion of the truth, since this genius, like any other, defies definition, and the spirit escapes analysis. There is satisfaction, however, in an attempt to discover the stuff of which nonsense is made, and pleasure in the pursuit. Much of it seems to consist of *an inspired selection and arrangement of incongruities.* "The owl and the eel and the warming-pan/They went to call on the soap-fat man,"/ sings Laura Richards.[3] This cast of characters is an example of the inevitable rightness of inspiration. Substitute any other fowl and fish and household appliance, and the whole drama falls flat; no other combination can equal the exquisite exactitude of this nonsense trio. In Mother Goose a cow jumps over the moon. Now a cow is by temperament and physiology the most unlikely barnyard animal to succeed at the broad jump. It is the juxtaposition of deed with disposition that produces the nonsense. The elopement of the Owl and the Pussycat in Lear's great romance of the nursery affords the same pleasure in incongruity.

Much nonsense grows out of the meaning of words and the confusion that results when meaning is changed by accent or context. There are some people for whom the word entrance, meaning the opposite of exit, is always read en-tránce, with the accent on the second syllable. And that, of course, is a door of a different color. The changes wrought by the substitution of one letter or syllable for another are also sources of innocent merriment. Lewis Carroll is a master at this type of manipulation:

> "I only took the regular course."
> "What was that?" inquired Alice.
> "Reeling and Writhing, of course, to begin with," the Mock Turtle replied; "and then the different branches of Arithmetic—Ambition, Distraction, Uglification, and Derision." [4]

The sound of words and the taste of them on the tongue is a major source of nonsense. The true lover of nonsense must abandon rigid insistence on the proper use of the word, and accept as true in spirit the meaning the nonsense author bestows upon it. "Have you seen a crocodile in these promiscuous parts?" asks the Elephant's Child in Kipling's story of *How the Elephant Got His Trunk.* If the use of "promiscuous" in this context troubles you, you are no true lover of sublime distortion. And again, in *How the Rhinoceros Got His Skin,* the cake that the Parsee man baked is the most delectable cake in all of literature, because it smelled "most sentimental."

The invention of words is characteristic of your true nonsense writer. This is no mean achievement, for the word must appear to both the ear and the eye to come of a long and legitimate lineage of Latin or Greek. It must seem authentic, no mere babbling of sound without genuine structure. A small dictionary could be compiled of Lear's wonderful words: *borascible* (to describe the "Old Person of Bangor/ Whose face was distorted with anger"), *oblivorous,*

[3] In *Tirra Lirra.*
[4] *Alice's Adventures in Wonderland,* chap. 9.

dolomphirus; whole geographies of countries which do not exist, but should; and creatures unknown before he invented them, the Pobble, the Jumblies, and the Yonghy-Bonghy-Bò.

Language, sound, and combinations of sounds are a source of playful exploration for children. They invent languages, collect words they delight in, make up words and give names to objects, like the Master of All Masters in the fairy tale. They laugh at the tricks their own speech plays upon them. "Look, Dad," a small child calls across the summer lawn, "I'm turning somersaults. In winter will I turn wintersaults?"

In this world of nonsense, young children find themselves happily at home. It is a world they understand because it mirrors the shifting boundaries between the real and the impossible which exist in their own minds. "Reality for the child is both more arbitrary and better regulated than for us," says Jean Piaget, the Swiss philosopher and psychologist. "It is more arbitrary, because *nothing is impossible,* and nothing obeys casual laws. But whatever may happen, it can be accounted for, for behind the most fantastic events which he believes in, the child will always discover motives which are sufficient to justify them; just as the world of the primitive races is peopled with a wealth of arbitrary intentions, but is devoid of chance." [5]

For children, nonsense is a confirmation of experience, a language peculiarly their own, and the laughter it provokes is the most genuine mirth of childhood.

[5] Jean Piaget, *Language and Thought of the Child,* trans. Marjorie Gabain (Meridian Books, New York), p. 216.

NONSENSE

Old Greek Nonsense Rhymes[1]

Little Hermogenes is so small
He can't reach anything down at all;
Though it's on the ground, he must let it
    lie —
For he's so short that it's still too high.

Lucilius (c. A.D. 50)

Look at Marcus and take warning:
  Once he tried to win a race,
Ran all night, and in the morning
  Hadn't passed the starting place!

Lucilius

I boiled hot water in an urn
  Till it was cold as ice;
I blew the fire to make it burn,
  Which froze it in a trice.

After *Nicarchus (c. A.D. 200)*

If a Pig Wore a Wig[2]

CHRISTINA ROSSETTI

If a pig wore a wig,
What could we say?
Treat him as a gentleman,
  And say, "Good day."
If his tail chanced to fail,
What could we do?
Send him to the tailoress
  To get one new.

[1] From *The Book of Nonsense*, ed. Roger Lancelyn
Green (Dutton).
[2] From Christina Rossetti, *Sing-Song* (Macmillan).

Mr. Punchinello[3]

Mother, I want to be married
To Mister Punchinello,
To Mister Punch, to Mister Chin,
  to Mister Nell, to Mister Lo,
Pun — Chin — Nell — Lo —
To Mister Punchinello!

Three Children Sliding on the Ice[4]

*Iona and Peter Opie give the earliest date
of this "choice piece of drollery" as 1651, which
disproves the authorship of either John Gay
or Oliver Goldsmith to whom it has been
ascribed.*

Three children sliding on the ice
  Upon a summer's day;
As it fell out, they all fell in,
  The rest they ran away.

Now had these children been at home,
  Or sliding on dry ground,
Ten thousand pounds to one penny
  They had not all been drowned.

You parents all that children have,
  And you that have got none,
If you would have them safe abroad,
  Pray keep them safe at home.

[3] From *Tom Tiddler's Ground; a Book of Poetry
for Children*, chosen by Walter de la Mare (Collins).
[4] From *The Oxford Dictionary of Nursery Rhymes*
ed. Iona and Peter Opie (Oxford University Press).

Eletelephony[5]

LAURA E. RICHARDS

Once there was an elephant,
Who tried to use the telephant —
No! No! I mean an elephone
Who tried to use the telephone —
(Dear me! I am not certain quite
That even now I've got it right.)

Howe'er it was, he got his trunk
Entangled in the telephunk;
The more he tried to get it free,
The louder buzzed the telephee —
(I fear I'd better drop the song
Of elephop and telephong!)

The High Barbaree[5]

LAURA E. RICHARDS

*"Sailing down along the coast
Of the High Barbaree."*
— *Old Song*

As I was sailing down the coast
Of High Barbaree,
I chanced to see a Muffin Bird
A-sitting in a tree.

Oh, mournfully he sang,
And sorrowful he sat,
Because he was a-frightened of
The Crum-pet Cat!

The Crumpet Cat is little known;
He sits him under trees,
And watches for the Muffin Bird
His palate for to please.

And then he opens wide his mouth,
The cruel Crumpet Cat,
And the Muffin Bird falls into it,
Just — like — that!

I left the ship, I gained the shore,
And to the tree I hied,
Just as the Cat was opening
His jaws wide, wide!

[5] From Laura E. Richards, *Tirra Lirra: Rhymes Old
and New* (Little, Brown).

I waved my arms and shouted loud,
"Shoo! shoo! SHOO!"
And off the Cat went flumpering,
And off the birdie flew.

MORAL

When you sail the Barbaree,
Mind what you're about!
Always carry with you
A good loud shout!

When you see a Crumpet Cat,
Let your shout be heard;
For you may save the life of
A pretty Muffin Bird!

The Monkeys and the Crocodile[5]

LAURA E. RICHARDS

Five little monkeys
Swinging from a tree;
Teasing Uncle Crocodile,
Merry as can be.
Swinging high, swinging low,
Swinging left and right:
"Dear Uncle Crocodile,
Come and take a bite!"

Five little monkeys
Swinging in the air;
Heads up, tails up,
Little do they care.
Swinging up, swinging down,
Swinging far and near:
"Poor Uncle Crocodile,
Aren't you hungry, dear?"

Four little monkeys
Sitting in the tree;
Heads down, tails down,
Dreary as can be.
Weeping loud, weeping low,
Crying to each other:
"Wicked Uncle Crocodile,
To gobble up our brother!"

Mrs. Snipkin and Mrs. Wobblechin[5]

LAURA E. RICHARDS

Skinny Mrs. Snipkin,
With her little pipkin,

Sat by the fireside a-warming of her toes.
Fat Mrs. Wobblechin,
With her little doublechin,
Sat by the window a-cooling of her nose.

Says this one to that one,
"Oh! you silly fat one,
Will you shut the window down? You're
    freezing me to death!"
Says that one to t'other one,
"Good gracious, how you bother one!
There isn't air enough for me to draw my
    precious breath!"

Skinny Mrs. Snipkin,
Took her little pipkin,
Threw it straight across the room as hard as
    she could throw:
Hit Mrs. Wobblechin
On her little doublechin,
And out of the window a-tumble she did go.

The Owl and the Eel and the Warming-Pan [6]

LAURA E. RICHARDS

The owl and the eel and the warming-pan,
They went to call on the soap-fat man.
The soap-fat man he was not within:
He'd gone for a ride on his rolling-pin.
So they all came back by the way of the town,
And turned the meeting-house upside down.

The Great Panjandrum Himself [7]

SAMUEL FOOTE

So she went into the garden to cut a cabbage
    leaf to make an apple-pie;
And at the same time a great she-bear,
    coming down the street, pops its head
    into the shop.
What! no soap? So he died, and she very
    imprudently married the Barber;
And there were present the Picninnies, and
    the Joblillies, and the Garyulies,

6 *Ibid.*
7 From *A Book of Nonsense Verse, Prose, and Pictures,* collected by Ernest Rhys (Dutton).

And the great Panjandrum himself, with the
    little round button at top;
And they all fell to playing the game of catch-
    as-catch-can,
Till the gunpowder ran out at the heels of
    their boots.

The Camel's Complaint [8]

CHARLES E. CARRYL

Canary-birds feed on sugar and seed,
    Parrots have crackers to crunch;
And, as for the poodles, they tell me the
    noodles
Have chickens and cream for their lunch.
    But there's never a question
    About my digestion —
ANYTHING *does* for me!

Cats, you're aware, can repose in a chair,
    Chickens can roost upon rails;
Puppies are able to sleep in a stable,
    And oysters can slumber in pails.
    But no one supposes
    A poor Camel dozes —
ANY PLACE *does* for me!

Lambs are inclosed where it's never exposed,
    Coops are constructed for hens;
Kittens are treated to houses well heated,
    And pigs are protected by pens.
    But a Camel comes handy
    Wherever it's sandy —
ANYWHERE *does* for me!

People would laugh if you rode a giraffe,
    Or mounted the back of an ox;
It's nobody's habit to ride on a rabbit,
    Or try to bestraddle a fox.
    But as for a Camel, he's
    Ridden by families —
ANY LOAD *does* for me!

A snake is as round as a hole in the ground,
    And weasels are wary and sleek;
And no alligator could ever be straighter
    Than lizards that live in a creek.

8 From Charles E. Carryl, *The Admiral's Caravan* (Houghton Mifflin).

But a Camel's all lumpy
And bumpy and humpy —
ANY SHAPE *does* for me!

The Walrus and the Carpenter [9]

LEWIS CARROLL

The sun was shining on the sea,
  Shining with all his might;
He did his very best to make
  The billows smooth and bright —
And this was odd, because it was
  The middle of the night.

The moon was shining sulkily,
  Because she thought the sun
Had got no business to be there
  After the day was done —
"It's very rude of him," she said,
  "To come and spoil the fun!"

The sea was wet as wet could be,
  The sands were dry as dry.
You could not see a cloud, because
  No cloud was in the sky;
No birds were flying overhead —
  There were no birds to fly.

The Walrus and the Carpenter
  Were walking close at hand;
They wept like anything to see
  Such quantities of sand —
"If this were only cleared away,"
  They said, "it would be grand!"

"If seven maids with seven mops
  Swept it for half a year,
Do you suppose," the Walrus said,
  "That they could get it clear?"
"I doubt it," said the Carpenter,
  And shed a bitter tear.

"O Oysters, come and walk with us!"
  The Walrus did beseech.
"A pleasant walk, a pleasant talk,
  Along the briny beach;
We cannot do with more than four,
  To give a hand to each."

9 From Lewis Carroll, *Through the Looking-Glass.*

The eldest Oyster looked at him,
  But never a word he said;
The eldest Oyster winked his eye,
  And shook his heavy head —
Meaning to say he did not choose
  To leave the oyster-bed.

But four young Oysters hurried up,
  All eager for the treat;
Their coats were brushed, their faces
    washed,
  Their shoes were clean and neat —
And this was odd, because, you know,
  They hadn't any feet.

Four other Oysters followed them,
  And yet another four;
And thick and fast they came at last,
  And more, and more, and more —
All hopping through the frothy waves,
  And scrambling to the shore.

The Walrus and the Carpenter
  Walked on a mile or so,
And then they rested on a rock
  Conveniently low —
And all the little Oysters stood
  And waited in a row.

"The time has come," the Walrus said,
  "To talk of many things:
Of shoes — and ships — and sealing-wax —
  Of cabbages — and kings —
And why the sea is boiling hot —
  And whether pigs have wings."

"But wait a bit," the Oysters cried,
  "Before we have our chat;
For some of us are out of breath,
  And all of us are fat!"
"No hurry!" said the Carpenter.
  They thanked him much for that.

"A loaf of bread," the Walrus said,
  "Is what we chiefly need;
Pepper and vinegar besides
  Are very good indeed —
Now, if you're ready, Oysters dear,
  We can begin to feed."

"But not on us!" the Oysters cried,
  Turning a little blue.

"After such kindness, that would be
  A dismal thing to do!"
"The night is fine," the Walrus said.
  "Do you admire the view?

"It was so kind of you to come!
  And you are very nice!"
The Carpenter said nothing but,
  "Cut us another slice.
I wish you were not quite so deaf —
  I've had to ask you twice!"

"It seems a shame," the Walrus said,
  "To play them such a trick.
After we've brought them out so far,
  And made them trot so quick!"
The Carpenter said nothing but,
  "The butter's spread too thick!"

"I weep for you," the Walrus said;
  "I deeply sympathize."
With sobs and tears he sorted out
  Those of the largest size,
Holding his pocket-hankerchief
  Before his streaming eyes.

"O Oysters," said the Carpenter,
  "You've had a pleasant run!
Shall we be trotting home again?"
  But answer came there none —
And this was scarcely odd, because
  They'd eaten every one.

'Tis the Voice of the Lobster [10]

Lewis Carroll

'Tis the voice of the Lobster; I heard him
    declare,
"You have baked me too brown, I must sugar
    my hair."
As a duck with its eyelids, so he with his nose
Trims his belt and his buttons, and turns out
    his toes.
When the sands are all dry, he is gay as a lark,
And will talk in contemptuous tones of the
    Shark:
But when the tide rises and sharks are
    around,
His voice has a timid and tremulous sound.

10 From Lewis Carroll, *Alice's Adventures in Won
derland.*

I passed by his garden, and marked with one
    eye
How the Owl and the Panther were sharing
    a pie:
The Panther took pie-crust and gravy and
    meat,
While the Owl had the dish as its share of
    the treat.
When the pie was all finished, the Owl, as
    a boon,
Was kindly permitted to pocket the spoon;
While the Panther received knife and fork
    with a growl,
And concluded the banquet —

The Crocodile [10]

Lewis Carroll

How doth the little crocodile
  Improve his shining tail,
And pour the waters of the Nile
  On every golden scale!

How cheerfully he seems to grin!
  How neatly spreads his claws,
And welcomes little fishes in
  With gently smiling jaws!

The White Rabbit's Verses [10]

Lewis Carroll

They told me you had been to her,
  And mentioned me to him;
She gave me a good character,
  But said I could not swim.

He sent them word I had not gone.
  (We know it to be true.)
If she should push the matter on,
  What would become of you?

I gave her one, they gave him two,
  You gave us three or more;
They all returned from him to you,
  Though they were mine before.

If I or she should chance to be
  Involved in this affair,
He trusts to you to set them free,
  Exactly as we were.

My notion was that you had been
  (Before she had this fit)
An obstacle that came between
  Him and ourselves and it.

Don't let him know she liked them best,
  For this must ever be
A secret, kept from all the rest,
  Between yourself and me.

Jabberwocky [1]

Lewis Carroll

'Twas brillig, and the slithy toves
  Did gyre and gimble in the wabe:
All mimsy were the borogoves,
  And the mome raths outgrabe.

"Beware the Jabberwock, my son!
  The jaws that bite, the claws that catch!
Beware the Jubjub bird, and shun
  The frumious Bandersnatch!"

He took his vorpal sword in hand:
  Long time the manxome foe he sought —
So rested he by the Tumtum tree,
  And stood awhile in thought.

And, as in uffish thought he stood,
  The Jabberwock, with eyes of flame,
Came whiffling through the tulgey wood,
  And burbled as it came!

One, two! One, two! And through and
    through
  The vorpal blade went snicker-snack!
He left it dead, and with its head
  He went galumphing back.

"And hast thou slain the Jabberwock?
  Come to my arms, my beamish boy!
O frabjous day! Callooh! Callay!"
  He chortled in his joy.

'Twas brillig, and the slithy toves
  Did gyre and gimble in the wabe:
All mimsy were the borogoves,
  And the mome raths outgrabe.

[1] From Lewis Carroll, *Through the Looking-Glass.*

The Gardener's Song [2]

Lewis Carroll

He thought he saw an Albatross
  That fluttered round the lamp;
He looked again, and found it was
  A Penny-Postage-Stamp.
"You'd best be getting home," he said;
  "The nights are very damp!"

He thought he saw an Argument
  That proved he was the Pope;
He looked again, and found it was
  A Bar-of-Mottled-Soap.
"A fact so dread," he faintly said,
  "Extinguishes all hope!"

He thought he saw a Banker's-Clerk
  Descending from the bus;
He looked again, and found it was
  A Hippopotamus.
"If this should stay to dine," he said,
  "There won't be much for us!"

He thought he saw a Buffalo
  Upon the chimney-piece;
He looked again, and found it was
  His Sister's-Husband's-Niece.
"Unless you leave this house," he said,
  "I'll send for the police!"

He thought he saw a Coach-and-Four
  That stood beside his bed;
He looked again, and found it was
  A Bear without a head.
"Poor thing!" he said — "poor, silly thing!
  It's waiting to be fed!"

He thought he saw a Garden-Door
  That opened with a key;
He looked again, and found it was
  A Double-Rule-of-Three.
"And all its mystery," he said,
  "Is clear as day to me!"

He thought he saw a Kangaroo
  That worked a coffee-mill;
He looked again, and found it was
  A Vegetable-Pill.

[2] From Lewis Carroll, *The Story of Sylvie and Bruno.*

"Were I to swallow this," he said,
   "I should be very ill!"

He thought he saw a Rattlesnake
   That questioned him in Greek;
He looked again, and found it was
   The Middle-of-Next-Week.
"The one thing I regret," he said,
   "Is that it cannot speak!"

The Beaver's Lesson[3]

LEWIS CARROLL

They sought it with thimbles, they sought it
      with care;
   They pursued it with forks and hope;
They threatened its life with a railway-share;
   They charmed it with smiles and soap.

Then the Butcher contrived an ingenious
      plan
   For making a separate sally;
And had fixed on a spot unfrequented by
      man,
   A dismal and desolate valley.

But the very same plan to the Beaver
      occurred:
   It had chosen the very same place:
Yet neither betrayed, by a sign or a word,
   The disgust that appeared in his face.

Each thought he was thinking of nothing but
      "Snark"
   And the glorious work of the day;
And each tried to pretend that he did not
      remark
   That the other was going that way.

But the valley grew narrow and narrower
      still,
   And the evening got darker and colder,
Till (merely from nervousness, not from
      good-will)
   They marched along shoulder to shoulder.

Then a scream, shrill and high, rent the
      shuddering sky,
   And they knew that some danger was near:

[3] From Lewis Carroll, *The Hunting of the Snark.*

The Beaver turned pale to the tip of its tail,
   And even the Butcher felt queer.

He thought of his childhood, left far, far
      behind —
   That blissful and innocent state —
The sound so exactly recalled to his mind
   A pencil that squeaks on a slate!

" 'Tis the voice of the Jubjub!" he suddenly
      cried.
   (This man, that they used to call "Dunce.")
"As the Bellman would tell you," he added,
      with pride,
   "I have uttered that sentiment once.

" 'Tis the note of the Jubjub! Keep count,
      I entreat,
   You will find I have told it you twice.
'Tis the song of the Jubjub! The proof is
      complete,
   If only I've stated it thrice."

The Beaver had counted with scrupulous
      care,
   Attending to every word:
But it fairly lost heart, and outgrabe in
      despair,
   When the third repetition occurred.

It felt that, in spite of all possible pains,
   It had somehow contrived to lose count,
And the only thing now was to rack its poor
      brains
   By reckoning up the amount.

"Two added to one — if that could but be
      done,"
   It said, "with one's fingers and thumbs!"
Recollecting with tears how, in earlier years,
   It had taken no pains with its sums.

"The thing can be done," said the Butcher,
      "I think.
   The thing must be done, I am sure.
The thing shall be done! Bring me paper
      and ink,
   The best there is time to procure."

The Beaver brought paper, portfolio, pens,
   And ink in unfailing supplies:

While strange, creepy creatures came out of
their dens,
And watched them with wondering eyes.

So engrossed was the Butcher, he heeded
them not,
As he wrote with a pen in each hand,
And explained all the while in a popular
style
Which the Beaver could well understand.

"Taking Three as the subject to reason
about —
A convenient number to state —
We add Seven, and Ten, and then multiply
out
By One Thousand diminished by Eight.

"The result we proceed to divide, as you
see,
By Nine Hundred and Ninety and Two:
Then subtract Seventeen, and the answer
must be
Exactly and perfectly true.

"The method employed I would gladly ex-
plain,
While I have it so clear in my head,
If I had but the time and you had but the
brain —
But much yet remains to be said.

"In one moment I've seen what has hitherto
been
Enveloped in absolute mystery,
And without extra charge I will give you at
large
A Lesson in Natural History."

In his genial way he proceeded to say
(Forgetting all laws of propriety,
And that giving instruction, without intro-
duction,
Would have caused quite a thrill in
Society),

"As to temper, the Jubjub's a desperate
bird,
Since it lives in perpetual passion:
Its taste in costume is entirely absurd —
It is ages ahead of the fashion:

"But it knows any friend it has met once
before:
It never will look at a bribe:
And in charity-meetings it stands at the door,
And collects — though it does not sub-
scribe.

"Its flavor when cooked is more exquisite
far
Than mutton, or oysters, or eggs:
(Some think it keeps best in an ivory jar,
And some, in mahogany kegs:)

"You boil it in sawdust: you salt it in glue:
You condense it with locusts and tape:
Still keeping one principal object in view —
To preserve its symmetrical shape."

The Butcher would gladly have talked till
next day,
But he felt that the Lesson must end,
And he wept with delight in attempting to
say
He considered the Beaver his friend:

While the Beaver confessed, with affectionate
looks
More eloquent even than tears,
It had learned in ten minutes far more than
all books
Would have taught it in seventy years.

They returned hand-in-hand, and the Bell-
man, unmanned
(For a moment) with noble emotion,
Said, "This amply repays all the wearisome
days
We have spent on the billowy ocean!"

Such friends as the Beaver and Butcher
became
Have seldom, if ever, been known;
In winter or summer, 'twas always the same —
You could never meet either alone.

And when quarrels arose — as one frequently
finds
Quarrels will, spite of every endeavor —
The song of the Jubjub recurred to their
minds,
And cemented their friendship forever!

Nonsense Alphabet [4]

EDWARD LEAR

a

A was once an apple pie,
  Pidy,
  Widy,
  Tidy,
  Pidy,
  Nice insidy,
  Apple pie!

b

B was once a little bear,
  Beary,
  Wary,
  Hairy,
  Beary,
  Taky cary,
  Little bear.

c

C was once a little cake
  Caky,
  Baky,
  Maky,
  Caky,
  Taky caky,
  Little cake!

d

D was once a little doll,
  Dolly,
  Molly,
  Polly,
  Nolly,
  Nursy dolly,
  Little doll!

e

E was once a little eel,
  Eely,
  Weely,
  Peely,
  Eely,
  Twirly, tweely,
  Little eel!

[1] Edward Lear, *The Complete Nonsense Book* (Dodd, Mead, 1942) is the source of this and the following selections from Lear.

f

F was once a little fish,
  Fishy,
  Wishy,
  Squishy,
  Fishy,
  In a dishy,
  Little fish!

g

G was once a little goose,
  Goosy,
  Moosy,
  Boosy,
  Goosy,
  Waddly-woosy,
  Little goose!

h

H was once a little hen,
  Henny,
  Chenny,
  Tenny,
  Henny,
  Eggsy-any,
  Little hen?

i

I was once a bottle of ink,
  Inky,
  Dinky,
  Thinky,
  Inky,
  Blacky minky,
  Bottle of ink!

j

J was once a jar of jam,
  Jammy,
  Mammy,
  Clammy,
  Jammy,
  Sweety, swammy,
  Jar of jam!

k

K was once a little kite,
  Kity,
  Whity,

Flighty,
Kity,
Out of sighty,
Little kite!

l

L   was once a little lark,
Larky,
Marky,
Harky,
Larky,
In the parky,
Little lark!

m

M   was once a little mouse,
Mousy,
Bousy,
Sousy,
Mousy,
In the housy,
Little mouse!

n

N   was once a little needle,
Needly,
Tweedly,
Threedly,
Needly,
Whisky wheedly,
Little needle!

o

O   was once a little owl,
Owly,
Prowly,
Howly,
Owly,
Browny fowly,
Little owl!

p

P   was once a little pump
Pumpy,
Slumpy,
Flumpy,
Pumpy,
Dumpy, thumpy,
Little pump!

q

Q   was once a little quail,
Quaily,
Faily,
Daily,
Quaily,
Stumpy-taily,
Little quail!

r

R   was once a little rose,
Rosy,
Posy,
Nosy,
Rosy,
Blows-y, grows-y,
Little rose!

s

S   was once a little shrimp,
Shrimpy,
Nimpy,
Flimpy,
Shrimpy,
Jumpy, jimpy,
Little shrimp!

t

T   was once a little thrush,
Thrushy,
Hushy,
Bushy,
Thrushy,
Flitty, flushy,
Little thrush!

u

U   was once a little urn,
Urny,
Burny,
Turny,
Urny,
Bubbly, burny,
Little urn!

v

V   was once a little vine,
Viny,
Winy,

Twiny,
Viny,
Twisty-twiny,
Little vine!

w

W was once a little whale,
Whaly,
Scaly,
Shaly,
Whaly,
Tumbly-taily,
Little whale!

x

X was once a great king Xerxes,
Xerxy,
Perxy,
Turxy,
Xerxy,
Linxy, lurxy,
Great king Xerxes!

y

Y was once a little yew,
Yewdy,
Fewdy,
Crudy,
Yewdy,
Growdy, grewdy,
Little yew!

z

Z was once a piece of zink,
Tinky,
Winky,
Blinky,
Tinky,
Tinky, minky,
Piece of zink!

The Jumblies

EDWARD LEAR

They went to sea in a sieve, they did;
   In a sieve they went to sea:
In spite of all their friends could say,
On a winter's morn, on a stormy day,
   In a sieve they went to sea.

And when the sieve turned round and round,
And every one cried, "You'll all be drowned!"
They called aloud, "Our sieve ain't big;
But we don't care a button, we don't care
      a fig:
   In a sieve we'll go to sea!"
      Far and few, far and few,
   Are the lands where the Jumblies live:
      Their heads are green, and their hands
      are blue;
      And they went to sea in a sieve.

They sailed away in a sieve, they did,
   In a sieve they sailed so fast,
With only a beautiful pea-green veil
Tied with a ribbon, by way of a sail,
   To a small tobacco-pipe mast.
And every one said who saw them go,
"Oh! won't they be soon upset, you know?
For the sky is dark, and the voyage is
      long;
And, happen what may, it's extremely wrong
   In a sieve to sail so fast."
      Far and few, far and few,
   Are the lands where the Jumblies live:
      Their heads are green, and their hands
      are blue;
      And they went to sea in a sieve.

The water it soon came in, it did;
   The water it soon came in:
So, to keep them dry, they wrapped their feet
In a pinky paper all folded neat;
   And they fastened it down with a pin.
And they passed the night in a crockery-jar;
And each of them said, "How wise we are!
Though the sky be dark, and the voyage be
      long,
Yet we never can think we were rash or
      wrong,
   While round in our sieve we spin."
      Far and few, far and few,
   Are the lands where the Jumblies live:
      Their heads are green, and their hands
      are blue;
      And they went to sea in a sieve.

And all night long they sailed away;
   And when the sun went down,
They whistled and warbled a moony song
To the echoing sound of a coppery gong,
   In the shade of the mountains brown.

"O Timballoo! How happy we are
When we live in a sieve and a crockery-jar!
And all night long, in the moonlight pale,
We sail away with a pea-green sail
  In the shade of the mountains brown."
    Far and few, far and few,
      Are the lands where the Jumblies live:
    Their heads are green, and their hands
      are blue;
    And they went to sea in a sieve.

They sailed to the Western Sea, they did. —
  To a land all covered with trees:
And they bought an owl, and a useful cart,
And a pound of rice, and a cranberry-tart,
  And a hive of silvery bees;
And they bought a pig, and some green jack-
    daws,
And a lovely monkey with lollipop paws,
  And forty bottles of ring-bo-ree,
    And no end of Stilton cheese.
    Far and few, far and few,
      Are the lands where the Jumblies live:
    Their heads are green, and their hands
      are blue;
    And they went to sea in a sieve.

And in twenty years they all came back, —
  In twenty years or more;
And every one said, "How tall they've grown!
For they've been to the Lakes, and the Tor-
    rible Zone,
  And the hills of the Chankly Bore."
And they drank their health, and gave them
    a feast
Of dumplings made of beautiful yeast;
And every one said, "If we only live,
We, too, will go to sea in a sieve,
  To the hills of the Chankly Bore."
    Far and few, far and few,
      Are the lands where the Jumblies live:
    Their heads are green, and their hands
      are blue;
    And they went to sea in a sieve.

The Owl and the Pussy-Cat

EDWARD LEAR

The Owl and the Pussy-Cat went to sea
  In a beautiful pea-green boat:

They took some honey, and plenty of money
  Wrapped up in a five-pound note.
The Owl looked up to the stars above,
  And sang to a small guitar,
"O lovely Pussy, O Pussy, my love,
What a beautiful Pussy you are,
      You are,
      You are!
What a beautiful Pussy you are!"

Pussy said to the Owl, "You elegant fowl,
  How charmingly sweet you sing!
Oh! let us be married; too long we have tar-
    ried:
  But what shall we do for a ring?"
They sailed away, for a year and a day,
  To the land where the bong-tree grows;
And there in a wood a Piggy-wig stood,
  With a ring at the end of his nose,
      His nose,
      His nose,
With a ring at the end of his nose.

"Dear Pig, are you willing to sell for one
    shilling
  Your ring?" Said the Piggy, "I will."
So they took it away, and were married next
    day
  By the Turkey who lives on the hill.
They dined on mince and slices of quince,
  Which they ate with a runcible spoon;
And hand in hand, on the edge of the sand,
  They danced by the light of the moon,
      The moon,
      The moon,
  They danced by the light of the moon.

Mr. and Mrs. Discobbolos

EDWARD LEAR

Mr. and Mrs. Discobbolos
  Climbed to the top of a wall.
And they sate to watch the sunset sky,
And to hear the Nupiter Piffkin cry,
  And the Biscuit Buffalo call.
They took up a roll and some Camomile tea,
And both were as happy as happy could be,
  Till Mrs. Discobbolos said, —
    "Oh! W! X! Y! Z! *

* The rhyme scheme calls for the English pronunciation, zed.

It has just come into my head,
Suppose we should happen to fall!!!!!
                Darling Mr. Discobbolos!"

"Suppose we should fall down flumpetty,
   Just like pieces of stone,
On to the thorns, or into the moat,
What would become of your new green coat?
   And might you not break a bone?
It never occurred to me before,
That perhaps we shall never go down any
      more!"
      And Mrs. Discobbolos said,
      "Oh, W! X! Y! Z!
      What put it into your head
      To climb up this wall, my own
                Darling Mr. Discobbolos?"

Mr. Discobbolos answered,
   "At first it gave me pain,
And I felt my ears turn perfectly pink
When your exclamation made me think
   We might never get down again!
But now I believe it is wiser far
To remain for ever just where we are."
      And Mr. Discobbolos said,
      "Oh! W! X! Y! Z!
      It has just come into my head
      We shall never go down again,
                Dearest Mrs. Discobbolos!"

So Mr. and Mrs. Discobbolos
   Stood up and began to sing, —
"Far away from hurry and strife
Here we will pass the rest of life,
   Ding a dong, ding dong, ding!
We want no knives nor forks nor chairs,
No tables nor carpets nor household cares;
      From worry of life we've fled;
      Oh! W! X! Y! Z!
      There is no more trouble ahead,
      Sorrow or any such thing,
                For Mr. and Mrs. Discobbolos!"

The Duck and the Kangaroo

EDWARD LEAR

Said the Duck to the Kangaroo,
   "Good gracious! how you hop
Over the fields, and the water too,
   As if you never would stop!

My life is a bore in this nasty pond;
And I long to go out in the world beyond:
   I wish I could hop like you,"
   Said the Duck to the Kangaroo.

"Please give me a ride on your back,"
   Said the Duck to the Kangaroo:
"I would sit quite still, and say nothing but
      'Quack'
   The whole of the long day through;
And we'd go the Dee, and the Jelly Bo Lee,
Over the land, and over the sea:
   Please take me a ride! oh, do!"
   Said the Duck to the Kangaroo.

Said the Kangaroo to the Duck,
   "This requires some little reflection.
Perhaps, on the whole, it might bring me
      luck:
   And there seems but one objection;
Which is, if you'll let me speak so bold,
Your feet are unpleasantly wet and cold,
   And would probably give me the roo-
Matiz," said the Kangaroo.

Said the Duck, "As I sate on the rocks,
   I have thought over that completely;
And I bought four pairs of worsted socks,
   Which fit my web-feet neatly;
And, to keep out the cold, I've bought a
      cloak;
And every day a cigar I'll smoke;
   All to follow my own dear true
   Love of a Kangaroo."

Said the Kangaroo, "I'm ready,
   All in the moonlight pale;
But to balance me well, dear Duck, sit steady,
   And quite at the end of my tail."
So away they went with a hop and a bound;
And they hopped the whole world three
      times round.
   And who so happy, oh! who,
   As the Duck and the Kangaroo?

The Quangle Wangle's Hat

EDWARD LEAR

On the top of the Crumpetty Tree
   The Quangle Wangle sat,

But his face you could not see,
  On account of his Beaver Hat.
For his Hat was a hundred and two feet
    wide,
With ribbons and bibbons on every side,
And bells, and buttons, and loops, and lace,
So that nobody ever could see the face
    Of the Quangle Wangle Quee.

The Quangle Wangle said
  To himself on the Crumpetty Tree,
"Jam and jelly, and bread
  Are the best of food for me!
But the longer I live on this Crumpetty Tree
The plainer than ever it seems to me
That very few people come this way
And that life on the whole is far from gay!"
    Said the Quangle Wangle Quee.

But there came to the Crumpetty Tree
  Mr. and Mrs. Canary;
And they said, "Did ever you see
  Any spot so charmingly airy?
May we build a nest on your lovely Hat?
Mr. Quangle Wangle, grant us that!
O please let us come and build a nest
Of whatever material suits you best,
      Mr. Quangle Wangle Quee!"

And besides, to the Crumpetty Tree
  Came the Stork, the Duck, and the Owl;
The Snail and the Bumble-Bee,
  The Frog and the Fimble Fowl
(The Fimble Fowl, with a Corkscrew leg);
And all of them said, "We humbly beg
We may build our homes on your lovely
    Hat, —
Mr. Quangle Wangle, grant us that!
    Mr. Quangle Wangle Quee!"

And the Golden Grouse came there,
  And the Pobble who has no toes,
And the small Olympian bear,
  And the Dong with a luminous nose.
And the Blue Baboon who played the flute,
And the Orient Calf from the Land of Tute,
And the Attery Squash, and Bisky Bat, —
All came and built on the lovely Hat
      Of the Quangle Wangle Quee.

And the Quangle Wangle said
  To himself on the Crumpetty Tree,

"When all these creatures move
  What a wonderful noise there'll be!"
And at night by the light of the Mulberry
    moon
They danced to the Flute of the Blue Baboon,
On the broad green leaves of the Crumpetty
    Tree,
And all were as happy as happy could be,
      With the Quangle Wangle Quee.

The Table and the Chair

EDWARD LEAR

Said the Table to the Chair,
"You can hardly be aware
How I suffer from the heat
And from chilblains on my feet.
If we took a little walk,
We might have a little talk;
Pray let us take the air,"
Said the Table to the Chair.

Said the Chair unto the Table,
"Now, you *know* we are not able:
How foolishly you talk,
When you know we *cannot* walk!"
Said the Table with a sigh,
"It can do no harm to try.
I've as many legs as you:
Why can't we walk on two?"

So they both went slowly down,
And walked about the town
With a cheerful bumpy sound
As they toddled round and round;
And everybody cried,
As they hastened to their side,
"See! the Table and the Chair
Have come out to take the air!"

But in going down an alley,
To a castle in a valley,
They completely lost their way,
And wandered all the day;
Till, to see them safely back,
They paid a Ducky-quack,
And a Beetle, and a Mouse,
Who took them to their house.

Then they whispered to each other,
"O delightful little brother,

What a lovely walk we've taken!
Let us dine on beans and bacon."
So the Ducky and the leetle
Browny-Mouse and the Beetle
Dined, and danced upon their heads
Till they toddled to their beds.

The Broom, the Shovel, the Poker and the Tongs

EDWARD LEAR

The Broom and the Shovel, the Poker and
    Tongs,
They all took a drive in the Park;
And they each sang a song, ding-a-dong,
    ding-a-dong!
Before they went back in the dark.
Mr. Poker he sate quite upright in the coach;
Mr. Tongs made a clatter and clash;
Miss Shovel was dressed all in black (with a
    brooch);
Mrs. Broom was in blue (with a sash).
    Ding-a-dong, ding-a-dong!
    And they all sang a song.

"O Shovely so lovely!" the Poker he sang,
   "You have perfectly conquered my heart.
Ding-a-dong, ding-a-dong! If you're pleased
    with my song,
I will feed you with cold apple-tart.
When you scrape up the coals with a delicate
    sound,
   You enrapture my life with delight,
Your nose is so shiny, your head is so round,
   And your shape is so slender and bright!
    Ding-a-dong, ding-a-dong!
    Ain't you pleased with my song?"

"Alas! Mrs. Broom," sighed the Tongs in his
    song,
   "Oh! is it because I'm so thin,
And my legs are so long, — ding-a-dong,
    ding-a-dong! —
That you don't care about me a pin?
Ah! fairest of creatures, when sweeping the
    room,
   Ah! why don't you heed my complaint?
Must you needs be so cruel, you beautiful
    Broom,
   Because you are covered with paint?

    Ding-a-dong, ding-a-dong!
    You are certainly wrong."

Mrs. Broom and Miss Shovel together they
    sang,
   "What nonsense you're singing to-day!"
Said the Shovel, "I'll certainly hit you a
    bang!"
Said the Broom, "And I'll sweep you
    away!"
So the coachman drove homeward as fast as
    he could,
   Perceiving their anger with pain;
But they put on the kettle, and little by little
   They all became happy again.
    Ding-a-dong, ding-a-dong!
    There's an end of my song.

The Courtship of the Yonghy-Bonghy-Bò

EDWARD LEAR

On the coast of Coromandel
   Where the early pumpkins blow,
    In the middle of the woods
    Lived the Yonghy-Bonghy-Bò.
Two old chairs, and half a candle —
One old jug without a handle —
    These were all his worldly goods:
    In the middle of the woods,
    These were all the worldly goods,
    Of the Yonghy-Bonghy-Bò,
    Of the Yonghy-Bonghy-Bò.

Once, among the Bong-trees walking
   Where the early pumpkins blow,
    To a little heap of stones
    Came the Yonghy-Bonghy-Bò.
There he heard a Lady talking,
To some milk-white Hens of Dorking —
   " 'Tis the Lady Jingly Jones!
    On that little heap of stones
    Sits the Lady Jingly Jones!"
    Said the Yonghy-Bonghy-Bò,
    Said the Yonghy-Bonghy-Bò.

"Lady Jingly! Lady Jingly!
   Sitting where the pumpkins blow,
    Will you come and be my wife?"
    Said the Yonghy-Bonghy-Bò.

"I am tired of living singly —
On this coast so wild and shingly —
    I'm a-weary of my life;
    If you'll come and be my wife,
    Quite serene would be my life!"
Said the Yonghy-Bonghy-Bò,
Said the Yonghy-Bonghy-Bò.

"On this Coast of Coromandel
  Shrimps and watercresses grow,
    Prawns are plentiful and cheap,"
  Said the Yonghy-Bonghy-Bò.
"You shall have my chairs and candle,
And my jug without a handle!
    Gaze upon the rolling deep
    (Fish is plentiful and cheap);
    As the sea, my love is deep!"
  Said the Yonghy-Bonghy-Bò,
  Said the Yonghy-Bonghy-Bò.

Lady Jingly answered sadly,
  And her tears began to flow, —
    "Your proposal comes too late,
    Mr. Yonghy-Bonghy-Bò!
I would be your wife most gladly!"
(Here she twirled her fingers madly,)
    "But in England I've a mate!
    Yes! you've asked me far too late,
    For in England I've a mate,
    Mr. Yonghy-Bonghy-Bò!
    Mr. Yonghy-Bonghy-Bò!

"Mr. Jones (his name is Handel, —
  Handel Jones, Esquire, & Co.)
    Dorking fowls delights to send,
    Mr. Yonghy-Bonghy-Bò!
Keep, oh, keep your chairs and candle,
And your jug without a handle, —
    I can merely be your friend!
    Should my Jones more Dorkings send,
    I will give you three, my friend!
    Mr. Yonghy-Bonghy-Bò!
    Mr. Yonghy-Bonghy-Bò!

"Though you've such a tiny body,
  And your head so large doth grow, —
    Though your hat may blow away,
    Mr. Yonghy-Bonghy-Bò!
Though you're such a Hoddy Doddy,
Yet I wish that I could modi-
    fy the words I needs must say!
    Will you please to go away?

    That is all I have to say,
    Mr. Yonghy-Bonghy-Bò!
    Mr. Yonghy-Bonghy-Bò!"

Down the slippery slopes of Myrtle,
  Where the early pumpkins blow,
    To the calm and silent sea
    Fled the Yonghy-Bonghy-Bò.
There, beyond the Bay of Gurtle,
Lay a large and lively Turtle.
    "You're the Cove," he said, "for
        me;
    On your back beyond the sea,
    Turtle, you shall carry me!"
  Said the Yonghy-Bonghy-Bò,
  Said the Yonghy-Bonghy-Bò.

Through the silent-roaring ocean
  Did the Turtle swiftly go;
    Holding fast upon his shell
    Rode the Yonghy-Bonghy-Bò.
With a sad primeval motion
Towards the sunset isles of Boshen
    Still the Turtle bore him well.
    Holding fast upon his shell,
    "Lady Jingley Jones, farewell!"
  Sang the Yonghy-Bonghy-Bò.
  Sang the Yonghy-Bonghy-Bò.

From the Coast of Coromandel
  Did that Lady never go;
    On that heap of stones she mourns
    For the Yonghy-Bonghy-Bò.
On the Coast of Coromandel,
In his jug without a handle
    Still she weeps, and daily moans;
    On that little heap of stones
    To her Dorking Hens she moans,
  For the Yonghy-Bonghy-Bò,
  For the Yonghy-Bonghy-Bò.

Limericks

EDWARD LEAR

There was an Old Man in a tree,
Who was horribly bored by a Bee;
When they said, "Does it buzz?" he replied,
    "Yes, it does!
It's a regular brute of a Bee."

There was an old man in a tree,
Whose whiskers were lovely to see;
But the birds of the air pluck'd them
    perfectly bare,
To make themselves nests in that tree.

There was a Yong Lady whose nose
Was so long that it reached to her toes;
So she hired an Old Lady, whose conduct was
    steady,
To carry that wonderful nose.

There is a young lady, whose nose,
Continually prospers and grows;
When it grew out of sight, she exclaimed in
    a fright,
"Oh! Farewell to the end of my nose!"

There was an Old Man on whose nose
Most birds of the air could repose;
But they all flew away at the closing of day,
Which relieved that Old Man and his nose.

There was a Young Lady of Norway,
Who casually sat in a doorway;
When the door squeezed her flat, she ex-
    claimed, "What of that?"
This courageous Young Lady of Norway.

There was an Old Man who said, "Hush!
I perceive a young bird in this bush!"
When they said, "Is it small?" he replied,
    "Not at all;
It is four times as big as the bush!"

There was an Old Man of the East,
Who gave all his children a feast;
But they all ate so much, and their conduct
    was such,
That it killed that Old Man of the East.

There was an old person of Ware,
Who rode on the back of a bear:
When they ask'd, "Does it trot?" he said,
    "Certainly not!
He's a Moppsikon Floppsikon bear!"

There was an old man on the Border,
Who lived in the utmost disorder;
He danced with the cat, and made tea in his
    hat,
Which vexed all the folks on the Border.

There was an old man, who when little
Fell casually into a kettle;
But, growing too stout, he could never get
    out,
So he passed all his life in that kettle.

The Frog [5]

HILAIRE BELLOC

Be kind and tender to the frog,
    And do not call him names,
As 'Slimy skin,' or 'Polly-wog,'
    Or likewise 'Ugly James,'
Or 'Gap-a-grin,' or 'Toad-gone-wrong,'
    Or 'Bill Bandy-knees':
The frog is justly sensitive
    To epithets like these.
No animal will more repay
    A treatment kind and fair;
At least so lonely people say
    Who keep a frog (and, by the way,
They are extremely rare.)

The Yak [5]

HILAIRE BELLOC

As a friend to the children commend me the
    Yak.
    You will find it exactly the thing:
It will carry and fetch, you can ride on its
    back,
    Or lead it about with a string.

The Tartar who dwells on the plains of
    Tibet
    (A desolate region of snow)
Has for centuries made it a nursery pet,
    And surely the Tartar should know!

Then tell your papa where the Yak can be
    got,
    And if he is awfully rich
He will buy you the creature — or else he
    will not.
    (I cannot be positive which.)

[5] From Hilaire Belloc, *Cautionary Verses* (Knopf).

The Eel [6]

OGDEN NASH

I don't mind eels
Except as meals
And the way they feels.

[6] From Ogden Nash, *Family Reunion* (Little, Brown).

The Guppy [7]

OGDEN NASH

Whales have calves,
Cats have kittens,
Bears have cubs,
Bats have bittens,
Swans have cygnets,
Seals have puppies,
But guppies just have little guppies.

[7] From Ogden Nash, *Versus* (Little, Brown).

BIBLIOGRAPHY

Carroll, Lewis, *pseud. Alice's Adventures in Wonderland* and *Through the Looking-Glass;* with ninety-two illustrations by John Tenniel. Macmillan, n.d. (New Children's Classics)

Both stories contain some of the best nonsense ever written.

Carroll, Lewis, *pseud. The Hunting of the Snark; an Agony in Eight Fits;* with nine illustrations by Henry Holiday. Macmillan, 1927.

A nonsense narrative poem first published in 1876, reissued with the original illustrations.

Charles, Robert Henry. *Roundabout Turn;* illus. by L. Leslie Brooke. Frederick Warne, 1930.

This delightful bit of wise nonsense was written by the Chief Inspector of the Elementary Schools in England. Leslie Brooke read it in *Punch* where it was first published, and it so delighted him that he asked if he might illustrate it. The result is this charming picture book about the toad who lived on Albury Heath and set out to see if the world was really round.

Green, Roger Lancelyn, ed. *The Book of Nonsense;* illus. by Charles Folkard, Tenniel, Lear, Shepard, and others. E. P. Dutton, 1956. (Children's Illustrated Classics)

Classic nonsense selections going back to the ancient Greeks and continuing down through the ages.

Lear, Edward. *The Complete Nonsense Book;* containing all of the original pictures and verses together with new material; ed. by Lady Strachey of Sutton Court. Dodd, Mead, 1942.

The accentuated rhythm, the grotesque drawings, and the exaggeration appeal to a child's sense of humor.

Lear, Edward. *The Jumblies, and Other Nonsense Verses and The Pelican Chorus;* illus. by L. Leslie Brooke. Frederick Warne, 1954.

One of the most pleasing picture books.

Lear, Edward. *Nonsense Songs;* with drawings by L. Leslie Brooke. Frederick Warne, 1954.

Nineteen nonsense verses taken from the author's *Book of Nonsense.* This volume includes the poems from *The Jumblies and Other Nonsense Verses* and *Pelican Chorus and Other Nonsense Verses* published separately.

Rhys, Ernest, comp. *Book of Nonsense Verse, Prose and Pictures.* E. P. Dutton, 1928.

Contains Lear's *Limericks, Jolly Beggar,* and other rhymes; nonsense rhymes from *Alice in Wonderland; Struwwelpeter;* and nonsense rhymes from *Mother Goose's Melody.*

Richards, Laura E. *Tirra Lirra; Rhymes Old and New;* introduction by May Hill Arbuthnot; illus. by Marguerite Davis. Little, Brown, new edition, 1955.

Nonsense verses published in the *St. Nicholas* a generation ago, with some of the author's more recent rhymes.

References for the Adult

Cammaerts, Emile. *The Poetry of Nonsense.* E. P. Dutton, 1926.

Essays by a Belgian poet on the spirit of nonsense and its expression in poetry and art.

Chesterton, Gilbert K. "A Defense of Nonsense," in *Stories, Essays and Poems.* E. P. Dutton. (Everyman's Library)

A brief but profound discussion. "This simple sense of wonder at the shapes of things, and at their exuberant independence of our intellectual standards and our trivial definitions, is the basis of spirituality as it is the basis of nonsense."

De la Mare, Walter. "Lewis Carroll," in *The Eighteen-Eighties, Essays by Fellows of the Royal Society of Literature;* ed. by Walter de la Mare. Cambridge University Press, 1930. Also separate, published by Faber (London).

The limericks of Edward Lear as well as the imagination of Lewis Carroll are explored in this perceptive essay on nonsense.

Empson, William. "Alice in Wonderland," in *Some Versions of the Pastoral,* New Directions; also Chatto & Windus (London), 1935.

A critical approach to the mind of Carroll as well as an appreciation of his genius. The work of a distinguished contemporary critic.

Sewell, Elizabeth. *The Field of Nonsense.* Chatto & Windus (London), 1952.

Nonsense is described as a game of the spirit as well as of the intellect, based upon the work of Edward Lear and Lewis Carroll. An original piece of scholarship.

Suggestions for Further Reading
Edward Lear

Davidson, Angus. *Edward Lear, Landscape Painter and Nonsense Poet 1812–1888.* E. P. Dutton, 1939.

"How pleasant to know Mr. Lear!" through this biography of the English artist and limerick writer.

Lear, Edward. *Letters of Edward Lear to Chichester Fortescue, Lord Carlingford, and Frances, Countess Waldegrave;* ed. by Lady Strachey. Unwin (London), 1908.

Letters written between 1847 and 1864 which contain many interesting anecdotes. The introduction includes Lear's own account of his work.

Laura E. Richards

Coatsworth, Elizabeth. "Laura E. Richards," *The Junior Bookshelf,* March, 1924.

Eaton, Anne Thaxter. "Laura E. Richards," *The Horn Book Magazine,* Vol. 17, July–Aug. 1941, pp. 247–255.

Mahony, Bertha E. "Salute to Laura E. Richards," *The Horn Book Magazine,* Vol. 17, July–Aug. 1941, p. 245.

Richards, Laura E. *Stepping Westward.* Appleton-Century-Crofts, 1931.

Mrs. Richards' autobiography reads like a story, revealing a singularly rich and happy life.

Viguers, Ruth Hill. "Laura E. Richards, Joyous Companion," *The Horn Book Magazine;* Pt. I, April 1956; Pt. II, June 1956; Pt. III, October 1956; Pt. IV, December 1956.

Picture
Books

"The great and golden rule of art, as well as of life, is this: That the more distinct, sharp, and wiry the bounding line, the more perfect the work of art, and the less keen and sharp, the greater is the evidence of weak imagination, plagiarism, and bungling. . . . Leave out this line and you leave out life itself." [1]

ASK A GROUP OF ADULTS, TAKEN AT random — teachers, students, parents, or librarians — what they consider most important in a picture book for children, and the majority answer will probably be "Color!" It is a natural first response in a people who are assaulted by color on every hand, at almost every waking moment of their day. Color is the major ally in the advertising, packaging, and marketing of all the products on the shelves of supermarkets. It assails us in the cars that crowd the highways; it beckons from every billboard and poster. "In living color," says the voice of television. Even the mail boxes have surrendered their traditional khaki to the bright triad of the red, white, and blue.

Certainly the mystery of color is one to which the child responds with perhaps a clearer understanding of its emotive power than the adult, whose sensitivity to color may well have been dulled by excess of it. For this over-exposure has resulted in a tendency on the part of the adult to accept as appropriate to childhood anything that has color, with little regard for the other components which are basic to excellence in the art of the picture book: namely, the text itself, the relation of the pictures to the text, the artist's mastery of lineal rhythm, spatial balance, and harmony of color, and his endowment of a unique, personal style.

In the realm of children's literature, the picture book may be defined as a book which depends largely upon its pictorial quality as the medium for its tale telling, its revelation of fact or fancy. Because a child can absorb pictures and understand their meaning before he has mastered the skill of reading, the picture book becomes his earliest experience in following events in ordered sequence; his first venture beyond himself into an imaginary world in which he feels concern and sympathy for some protagonist, be it duck, rabbit, train, truck, or tractor. The picture book constitutes a beginning awareness of drama,

[1] William Blake. Quoted in Herbert Read, *The Meaning of Art* (Penguin Books, 1949), p. 122.

67

characterization, and moods of joy or sorrow. In brief, the picture book is not only an introduction to literature, but it becomes a kind of literature in its own right. It is a medium which must be perceived, on the one hand, in terms of pictorial art, and on the other, in terms of the art of writing.

The relationship between picture and text is a subtle one; it is, in the distinguished books, a felicitous marriage between two different modes of expression. In certain marriages between human beings there seems to emerge a quality or characteristic aura that partakes of both partners yet does not exist entirely in either, a quality that results from the combination of their personalities and from the bonds between them. So it is with picture books. The words that tell the story are extended and enhanced by the pictures; but the pictures, too, carry their burden of narration, and many a child, picture book in hand, can glean the gist of the story though he cannot read a word. In certain classic picture books, one is hardly conscious of the transition of the eye from picture to text, so close is their relationship, so subtle the interplay between the written word and the artist's image. Wanda Gág's *Millions of Cats,* L. Leslie Brooke's stories of *Johnny Crow,* Kurt Wiese's pictures for *The Story About Ping* by Marjorie Flack, Marie Ets's *Play With Me,* with its perfection of story, picture, and perception of childhood: these are typical of complete and fulfilled artistry in picture-book making.

With foreign picture books, of course, the text is nonexistent for the majority of readers. But books by foreign artists, no matter what the accompanying language, should be given equal consideration by those who choose books for children, for a child's first introduction to other climes, customs, costumes, and landscapes may well come from familiarity with foreign picture books. The imagination stretches and grows by association with the concepts, style, and vision of artists bred in an atmosphere different from our own. The world may be encompassed through the eye, and groundwork laid for the concept of the universality of man, as well as of art.

When Edmund Evans of Racquet Court, Fleet Street, London, perfected a process of color printing from wood blocks, in 1856, he invited three artists of the day to join him in producing a series of picture books for children, known as "toy books." Those three artists were Kate Greenaway, Randolph Caldecott, and Walter Crane. They have come to be looked upon as the founders of the picture-book tradition in English and American children's books. A study of their individual approaches to their assignments may well serve to reveal some facets of the art of picture-book making.

Of the three, Randolph Caldecott was the greatest, and the medal given annually to the most distinguished picture book of the year bears his name. To the task of picture-book making he brought two great attributes. The first was the gift of line. He had a well-nigh superb control of line. He could make it move, leap, soar. Look at the delineating ability of Caldecott! A sharp, clear, nervous line which echoes and reaffirms every turn of his mind: a line that can be exact and delicate, or robust and vigorous. From Caldecott the informed eye learns to recognize the fact that this lineal quality is basic to every other attribute of the picture book. "In discussing the linear aspect of a work of art," writes the art critic MacKinley Helm, "it is necessary to distinguish between 'line' and 'lines.' Line is essentially the outline of forms. It is not necessarily something which is drawn; frequently it is merely indicated. Some painters draw their designs (with 'lines') and fill them with color. In such a case the work is principally linear. Others, like Rouault, draw unmistakable boundary lines between forms or objects, or, like Renoir, simply differentiate their forms by means of color and light."[2] Here the writer is speaking of formal painting, but his definition of the lineal element applies to the art of the picture book as well as to the more formal art. Caldecott's drawing is lineal by virtue of his mastery of lines. Beatrix Potter's line is no less definite because it is indicated by means of color and light, as strong in exactitude as that of Caldecott himself.

The second great gift of Caldecott was his ability to extend the meaning of the text; to enhance and enliven it; to play and sport with it in an exuberance born of his own wit and imagination. Observe especially the series of quick, spontaneous sketches that intersperse the pages of colored illustration. What sport he has with the old rhymes and songs: the battle between the dogs in "Where are you going, my pretty maid?" which matches the exchange of words between the milkmaid and the young man who was above her station. Follow the story of the elopement of the dish with the spoon in "Hey Diddle Diddle, the Cat and the Fiddle." There is nothing in the old rhyme which says anything about how the parents of the spoon felt at the turn of events, or who the parents were, or what were the subsequent results of it all. But Randolph Caldecott has made it a tale of "star-crossed lovers" as eloquent as words.

Walter Crane perhaps parallels the method of Rouault, as MacKinley Helm defines it in the quotation above. He draws unmistakable boundaries, setting them off with contrasting masses of brilliant color. He was concerned with design, as well as with color; the design of the whole page in the book, as well as the picture on the page. His pictures have the flat, static quality of Japanese prints, combined with the ordered clutter of a rich, theatrical background. One learns to perceive the meaning of his design by looking at the varieties of ways in which he crowds the space, leading the eye to follow prolific details to its ordered climax. Page follows page, in more than Oriental splendor. There is a glory of color here, rich mounting of picture and print, as in a tapestry — but the flowing quality of line that runs through Caldecott's books like a great tide is missing.

The third member of this triumvirate was Kate Greenaway. Hers was the happy combination of author-artist that accounts for the success of many present-day picture books. In *Under the Window* and *Marigold Garden*, she wrote the verse that graces the pages she designed and illustrated. Her greatest attribute was her distinctive style: it has charm and delicacy, a poetic element, and yet it is vigorous. She drew with exquisite exactitude flowers, garlands, wreaths, and gardens. Hers was a pictorial world of light and sunshine, and joyous children in pursuit of childlike pleasures: games, toys, teas,

[2] MacKinley Helm, *Modern Mexican Painters* (Harper, New York, 1941), p. 113.

parties, and unequaled processions and ceremonials that wend their way across the pages of her books. She had little power to manipulate line, and the dancing feet and skipping shoes never quite get off the ground. One suspects that she dressed her children in long frocks in order to avoid delineating bending knees and nimble ankles. But the intensity of her feeling for the freedom and gaiety of childhood is apparent in everything she essayed. The utter naturalness of the children triumphs, as does the aura of grace and felicity. Kate Greenaway is matchless in charm and delicacy, without the weakness of sentimentality.

Styles have changed since the days of Racquet Court. New methods of reproducing picture and color have increased the artist's range, making compensatory demands upon his knowledge of the technical skills involved in the field of graphic arts. The present-day makers of picture books function amid the changing trends in art, new social concepts, the pressures of educational theory, and the vast influences of advertising and commercial art. In addition, mass production tends to reduce taste to a conforming mediocrity. We become conditioned to expect every book to look like every other. Yet the endless possibilities for variety in the arrangement of patterns in space, in the rhythm of line, in the mood and tone of color, in the symmetry between parts and the whole, and above all, the imprint of each artist's individuality upon the book, the style by which he declares his uniqueness — these remain timeless integrities, and happily there are many artists who uphold them.

Children of today may respond to a great variety of lineal invention, ranging from the classic strength and simplicity of Jean Charlot's line to the intricate fabrications of Dr. Seuss's galloping absurdities; from the delicate precision of Maurice Sendak to the running improvisation of Louis Slobodkin. Form is defined in the enclosing boundaries of Roger Duvoisin's versatility, or stated boldly by the juxtaposition of strong masses of color in the books of Paul Rand, where design takes precedence over all other components. Color ranges from the subtleties of Ludwig Bemelmans' *Madeline* to the bold clamor of Nicolas Mordvinoff, whose invention shocks the eye of the timid traditionalist but delights the children.

Fashions in the writing of picture books have also changed. The traditional approach has been to acclaim stories which, though written for the youngest children, held to the structure and canons of good writing: plot, characterization, conflict and resolution, with variations of mood, atmosphere, sense of place — all the elements that endow the reading of fiction with infinite fascination. Beatrix Potter remains the supreme genius of the nursery because she has mastered the discipline of the dramatist as well as of the artist. Her little stories are models of structure as well as of feeling. She never hesitates to create suspense, present moral issues, or show the inevitability of character. The endearing Peter Rabbit acts in accordance with his own greedy nature, and suffers tragic consequences. And this is said to the youngest children, in the space of moments, in terms they recognize as comparable to their own experience of life.

In today's picture books there seems to be a trend away from structural strength. A whole school of "mood books" has developed, in which a static, descriptive text, usually about the weather or the seasons of the year, is made the basis for a series of pictures — some of great distinction — which attempts to transcend the inaction of the text through the use of brilliant color and intricate design. Children, however, respond with greater enthusiasm to the book that has a story to tell, or that has some climax of feeling, if not of action.

No anthology can fully explore or explain the stature of this segment of children's literature — the picture book. Some of the great artists of our time have contributed to it, men and women whose pictures hang upon the walls of museums and galleries: Candido Portinari; Doris Lee; James Daugherty; Taro Yashima; Wanda Gág; Conrad Buff; Jean Charlot; Georges Schreiber. Others have made themselves masters of the unique art of the picture book: Nicolas Mordvinoff; Leonard Weisgard; Fritz Eichenberg; Marcia Brown; Leo Politi; Marie Ets. The names crowd the page, and no mere mention of names is adequate recognition of the originality, the imagination, the inventive genius which has gone into the making of picture books. So rich is this body of work, so fresh and vigorous the interpretations of the artists, that those concerned with children are obligated to explore it. The books are available. No need to be content with the arch, the coy, the sentimental, and the insincere; nor to accept the vulgarity of cheap books. The only way to know how to judge picture books is to look long at the best of them, with newly opened eyes.

This anthology makes no attempt to reproduce pictures with the texts from the books. So often the book as a whole is a work of art: story, picture, type, paper, binding — the very shape and heft of it to the hand, that to show a part only results in vitiating the whole. The stories given here are strong enough to stand on their own as stories, and deserve to live beyond and outside of a particular, perishable edition, but they should be seen in their original formats to be fully known and appreciated.

When one explores picture books in the company of children, it becomes clear how great is the impact of picture and story on their minds. The best books confirm the innate good taste of children and set upon their imaginations a seal of excellence, giving them standards of values in life as well as in art. The picture book sets the compass, as it were, for the whole journey.

PICTURE BOOKS

A Apple Pie

❧ *This alphabet nursery rhyme was well known as early as the latter part of the seventeenth century. Two centuries later, Kate Greenaway made it into an enchanting picture book* [1] *with quaintly dressed little girls and boys skipping through the the pages as they merrily devour an apple pie.*

A was an apple-pie;
B bit it,
C cut it,
D dealt it,
E eat it,
F fought for it,
G got it,
H had it,
 I inspected it,
J jumped for it,
K kept it,
L longed for it,
M mourned for it,
N nodded at it,
O opened it,
P peeped in it,
Q quartered it,
R ran for it,
 S stole it,
T took it,
U upset it,
V viewed it,
W wanted it,
X, Y, Z and ampersand
All wished for a piece in hand.

[1] *A Apple Pie,* illustrated by Kate Greenaway
(Frederick Warne, 1886).

Johnny Crow's Garden [2]

L. LESLIE BROOKE

❧ *Several generations of children in both England and America have loved this delightful nonsense picture book which had its beginnings in the artist's own childhood. As a small boy, Leslie Brooke loved the stories about Johnny Crow which his father, a novelist, told him. When he grew up and had two sons of his own, he in turn told them about Johnny Crow. At the suggestion of his wife, he made a picture book of the genial bird. A few years later came* Johnny Crow's Party, *and thirty years later he wrote and illustrated* Johnny Crow's New Garden *for his small grandson Peter Brooke.*

Johnny Crow
Would dig and sow
Till he made a little Garden.

And the Lion
Had a green and yellow Tie on
In Johnny Crow's Garden.

And the Rat
Wore a Feather in his Hat
But the Bear
Had nothing to wear
In Johnny Crow's Garden.

So the Ape
Took his Measure with a Tape
In Johnny Crow's Garden.

[2] Complete text from *Johnny Crow's Garden,* written and illustrated by L. Leslie Brooke (Frederick Warne, 1903).

Then the Crane
Was caught in the Rain
In Johnny Crow's Garden.

And the Beaver
Was afraid he had a Fever
But the Goat
Said:
"It's nothing but his Throat!"
In Johnny Crow's Garden.

And the Pig
Danced a Jig
In Johnny Crow's Garden.

Then the Stork
Gave a Philosophic Talk
Till the Hippopotami
Said: "Ask no further 'What am I?'"
While the Elephant
Said something quite irrelevant
In Johnny Crow's Garden.

And the Goose —
Well,
The Goose *was* a Goose
In Johnny Crow's Garden.

And the Mouse
Built himself a little House
Where the Cat
Sat down beside the Mat
In Johnny Crow's Garden.

And the Whale
Told a very long Tale
In Johnny Crow's Garden.

And the Owl
Was a funny old Fowl
And the Fox
Put them all in the Stocks
In Johnny Crow's Garden.

But Johnny Crow
He let them go
And they all sat down
   to their dinner in a row
In Johnny Crow's Garden!

The Story of the Three Bears [a]

~§ *Until recently, this story was generally attributed to Robert Southey, for it was printed in the fourth volume of his miscellany* The Doctor *(1837). But a manuscript in the Osborne Collection of the Toronto Public Library, entitled* The Story of the Three Bears *metrically related, with illustrations locating it at Cecil Lodge in September 1831 by Eleanor Mure,[4] seems to prove that the nursery tale was not original with Southey. However, Southey had never claimed that the story was an original work. The dedication in the Mure manuscript reads: "The celebrated nursery tale put into verse and embellished with drawings for a birthday present to Horace Broke Sept: 26: 1831." This would imply that the story was in existence prior to 1831. In both the Mure manuscript and the Southey story the heroine is a little old woman. Goldilocks had not yet made her appearance.*

L. Leslie Brooke has drawn the most delightful pictures for the version given below. His creative imagination adds captivating details which not only interpret but extend the spirit of the story. His charming attention to detail and his gentle humor have never been more clearly shown. He included this story in his Golden Goose Book,[5] *which is an ideal first book of nursery tales.*

Once upon a time there were three Bears, who lived together in a house of their own, in a wood. One of them was a Little Wee Bear, and one was a Middle-sized Bear, and the other was a Great Big Bear. They had each a bowl for their porridge: a little bowl for the Little Wee Bear; and a middle-sized bowl for the Middle-sized Bear; and a great bowl for the Great Big Bear. And they had each a chair to sit in: a little chair for the Little Wee Bear; and a middle-sized chair for the Middle-sized Bear; and a great chair for the Great Big Bear. And they had each

[a] Text from *English Fairy Tales;* retold by Flora Annie Steel (Macmillan, 1918).

[4] *Children's Literature: Books and Manuscripts;* an exhibition November 19, 1954 through February 28, 1955 (The Pierpont Morgan Library, New York, 1954), Item 124.

[5] *The Golden Goose Book;* illustrated by L. Leslie Brooke (Frederick Warne, 1906).

a bed to sleep in: a little bed for the Little Wee Bear; and a middle-sized bed for the Middle-sized Bear; and a great bed for the Great Big Bear.

One day, after they had made the porridge for their breakfast and poured it into their porridge-bowls, they walked out into the wood while the porridge was cooling that they might not burn their mouths by beginning too soon, for they were polite, well-brought-up Bears. And while they were away, a little girl called Goldilocks, who lived at the other side of the wood and had been sent on an errand by her mother, passed by the house and looked in at the window. And then she peeped in at the keyhole, for she was not at all a well-brought-up little girl. Then seeing nobody in the house she lifted the latch. The door was not fastened, because the Bears were good Bears who did nobody any harm and never suspected that anybody would harm them. So Goldilocks opened the door and went in; and well pleased was she when she saw the porridge on the table. If she had been a well-brought-up little girl she would have waited till the Bears came home, and then, perhaps, they would have asked her to breakfast; for they were good Bears — a little rough or so, as the manner of Bears is, but for all that very good-natured and hospitable. But she was an impudent, rude little girl, and so she set about helping herself.

First she tasted the porridge of the Great Big Bear, and that was too hot for her. Next she tasted the porridge of the Middle-sized Bear, but that was too cold for her. And then she went to the porridge of the Little Wee Bear, and tasted it, and that was neither too hot nor too cold, but just right, and she liked it so well, that she ate it all up, every bit!

Then Goldilocks, who was tired, for she had been catching butterflies instead of running on her errand, sat down in the chair of the Great Big Bear, but that was too hard for her. And then she sat down in the chair of the Middle-sized Bear, and that was too soft for her. But when she sat down in the chair of the Little Wee Bear, that was neither too hard, nor too soft, but just right. So she seated herself in it, and there she sat till the bottom of the chair came out, and down she

came, plump upon the ground; and that made her very cross, for she was a bad-tempered little girl.

Now, being determined to rest, Goldilocks went upstairs into the bedchamber in which the Three Bears slept. And first she lay down upon the bed of the Great Big Bear, but that was too high at the head for her. And next she lay down upon the bed of the Middle-sized Bear, and that was too high at the foot for her. And then she lay down upon the bed of the Little Wee Bear, and that was neither too high at the head, nor at the foot, but just right. So she covered herself up comfortably, and lay there till she fell fast asleep.

By this time the Three Bears thought their porridge would be cool enough for them to eat it properly; so they came home for breakfast. Now careless Goldilocks had left the spoon of the Great Big Bear standing in his porridge.

"SOMEBODY HAS BEEN AT MY PORRIDGE!"

said the Great Big Bear in his great, rough, gruff voice.

Then the Middle-sized Bear looked at his porridge and saw the spoon was standing in it too.

"SOMEBODY HAS BEEN AT MY PORRIDGE!"

said the Middle-sized Bear in his middle-sized voice.

Then the Little Wee Bear looked at his, and there was the spoon in the porridge-bowl, but the porridge was all gone!

"Somebody has been at my porridge and has eaten it all up!"

said the Little Wee Bear in his little wee voice.

Upon this the Three Bears, seeing that someone had entered their house, and eaten up the Little Wee Bear's breakfast, began to look about them. Now the careless Goldilocks had not put the hard cushion straight when she rose from the chair of the Great Big Bear.

"SOMEBODY HAS BEEN SITTING IN MY CHAIR!"

said the Great Big Bear in his great, rough, gruff voice.

And the careless Goldilocks had squatted down the soft cushion of the Middle-sized Bear.

"SOMEBODY HAS BEEN SITTING IN MY CHAIR!"

said the Middle-sized Bear in his middle-sized voice.

"Somebody has been sitting in my chair,
and has sat the bottom through!"

said the Little Wee Bear in his little wee voice.

Then the Three Bears thought they had better make further search in case it was a burglar; so they went upstairs into their bedchamber. Now Goldilocks had pulled the pillow of the Great Big Bear out of its place.

"SOMEBODY HAS BEEN LYING IN MY BED!"

said the Great Big Bear in his great, rough, gruff voice.

And Goldilocks had pulled the bolster of the Middle-sized Bear out of its place.

"SOMEBODY HAS BEEN LYING IN MY BED!"

said the Middle-sized Bear in his middle-sized voice.

But when the Little Wee Bear came to look at his bed, there was the bolster in its place!

And the pillow was in its place upon the bolster.

And upon the pillow ——?

There was Goldilocks' yellow head — which was not in its place, for she had no business there.

"Somebody has been lying in my bed, —
and here she is still!"

said the Little Wee Bear in his little wee voice.

Now Goldilocks had heard in her sleep the great, rough, gruff voice of the Great Big Bear; but she was so fast asleep that it was no more to her than the roaring of wind, or the rumbling of thunder. And she had heard the middle-sized voice of the Middle-

sized Bear, but it was only as if she had heard someone speaking in a dream. But when she heard the little wee voice of the Little Wee Bear, it was so sharp and so shrill, that it awakened her at once. Up she started, and when she saw the Three Bears on one side of the bed, she tumbled herself out at the other and ran to the window. Now the window was open, because the Bears, like good, tidy Bears, as they were, always opened their bedchamber window when they got up in the morning. So naughty, frightened little Goldilocks jumped; and whether she broke her neck in the fall or ran into the wood and was lost there or found her way out of the wood and got whipped for being a bad girl and playing truant no one can say. But the Three Bears never saw anything more of her.

The Story of the Three Little Pigs[6]

L. Leslie Brooke has taken this favorite nursery tale and given it fresh life with his inimitable drawings. He has a genius for entering into the spirit of the story he is illustrating, and his evident enjoyment is expressed in his pictures. His drawings are full of action and merriment and they have a storytelling quality all their own. This story is included in The Golden Goose Book[7] and it is also published as a separate picture book.

Once upon a time when pigs spoke rhyme
And monkeys chewed tobacco,
And hens took snuff to make them tough,
And ducks went quack, quack, quack, O!

There was an old sow with three little pigs, and as she had not enough to keep them, she sent them out to seek their fortune. The first that went off met a man with a bundle of straw, and said to him,

"Please, man, give me that straw to build me a house."

Which the man did, and the little pig built

[6] Text from Joseph Jacobs, *English Fairy Tales* (Putnam, 1892).

[7] *The Golden Goose Book*, illus. L. Leslie Brooke (Frederick Warne, 1906).

a house with it. Presently came along a wolf, and knocked at the door, and said,

"Little pig, little pig, let me come in."

To which the pig answered.

"No, no, by the hair of my chiny chin chin."

The wolf then answered to that,

"Then I'll huff, and I'll puff, and I'll blow your house in."

So he huffed, and he puffed, and he blew his house in, and ate up the little pig.

The second little pig met a man with a bundle of furze and said,

"Please, man, give me that furze to build a house."

Which the man did, and the pig built his house. Then along came the wolf, and said,

"Little pig, little pig, let me come in."

"No, no, by the hair of my chiny chin chin."

"Then I'll puff, and I'll huff, and I'll blow your house in."

So he huffed, and he puffed, and he puffed and he huffed, and at last he blew the house down, and he ate up the little pig.

The third little pig met a man with a load of bricks, and said,

"Please, man, give me those bricks to build a house with."

So the man gave him the bricks, and he built his house with them. So the wolf came, as he did to the other little pigs, and said,

"Little pig, little pig, let me come in."

"No, no, by the hair on my chiny chin chin."

"Then I'll huff, and I'll puff, and I'll blow your house in."

Well, he huffed, and he puffed, and he huffed and he puffed, and he puffed and huffed; but he could *not* get the house down. When he found that he could not, with all his huffing and puffing, blow the house down, he said,

"Little pig, I know where there is a nice field of turnips."

"Where?" said the little pig.

"Oh, in Mr. Smith's home-field, and if you will be ready tomorrow morning I will call for you, and we will go together, and get some for dinner."

"Very well," said the little pig, "I will be ready What time do you mean to go?"

"Oh, at six o'clock."

Well, the little pig got up at five and got the turnips before the wolf came (which he did about six), who said,

"Little pig, are you ready?"

The little pig said, "Ready! I have been and come back again and got a nice potful for dinner."

The wolf felt very angry at this, but thought that he would be up to the little pig somehow or other, so he said,

"Little pig, I know where there is a nice apple-tree."

"Where?" said the pig.

"Down at Merry-Garden," replied the wolf, "and if you will not deceive me, I will come for you at five o'clock tomorrow and get some apples."

Well, the little pig bustled up the next morning at four o'clock, and went off for the apples, hoping to get back before the wolf came; but he had farther to go and had to climb the tree, so that just as he was coming down from it, he saw the wolf coming, which, as you may suppose, frightened him very much. When the wolf came up he said:

"Little pig, what! are you here before me? Are they nice apples?"

"Yes, very," said the little pig. "I will throw you down one."

And he threw it so far, that, while the wolf was gone to pick it up, the little pig jumped down and ran home. The next day the wolf came again and said to the little pig,

"Little pig, there is a fair at Shanklin this afternoon; will you go?"

"Oh, yes," said the pig, "I will go; what time shall you be ready?"

"At three," said the wolf. So the little pig went off before the time as usual and got to the fair and bought a butter-churn, which he was going home with, when he saw the wolf coming. Then he could not tell what to do. So he got into the churn to hide, and by so doing turned it round, and it rolled down the hill with the pig in it, which frightened the wolf so much, that he ran home without going to the fair. He went to the little pig's house and told him how frightened he had been by a great round thing which came down the hill past him. Then the little pig said,

"Hah, I frightened you then. I had been to the fair and bought a butter-churn; and when I saw you, I got into it, and rolled down the hill."

Then the wolf was very angry indeed and declared he *would* eat up the little pig, and that he would get down the chimney after him. When the little pig saw what he was about, he hung on the pot full of water and made up a blazing fire and, just as the wolf was coming down, took off the cover and in fell the wolf; so the little pig put on the cover again in an instant, boiled him up, and ate him for supper and lived happy ever afterwards.

The Story of Little Black Sambo [8]

Helen Bannerman

❧ *Mrs. Bannerman was born in Edinburgh but spent thirty years of her married life in India. In 1889, when she was returning to India after leaving her two little girls at home in Scotland for their education, she wrote this story to send home to amuse them. She wrote it partly to comfort herself too, for it was hard to be separated from her children and she had a long journey ahead of her.*

Critics have called the story "a miracle of simplicity and drama." Perhaps part of the charm lies in the happy choice of incidents and in the ingenious way little Sambo of India overcomes apparently impossible difficulties.

Once upon a time there was a little black boy, and his name was Little Black Sambo.

And his Mother was called Black Mumbo.

And his Father was called Black Jumbo.

And Black Mumbo made him a beautiful little Red Coat, and a pair of beautiful little Blue Trousers.

And Black Jumbo went to the Bazaar, and bought him a beautiful Green Umbrella, and a lovely little Pair of Purple Shoes with Crimson Soles and Crimson Linings.

And then wasn't Little Black Sambo grand?

So he put on all his Fine Clothes, and went out for a walk in the Jungle. And by and by he met a Tiger. And the Tiger said to him, "Little Black Sambo, I'm going to eat you up!" And Little Black Sambo said, "Oh! Please Mr. Tiger, don't eat me up, and I'll give you my beautiful little Red Coat." So the Tiger said, "Very well, I won't eat you this time, but you must give me your beautiful little Red Coat." So the Tiger got poor Little Black Sambo's beautiful little Red Coat, and went away saying, "Now I'm the grandest Tiger in the Jungle."

And Little Black Sambo went on, and by and by he met another Tiger, and it said to him, "Little Black Sambo, I'm going to eat you up!" And Little Black Sambo said, "Oh! Please Mr. Tiger, don't eat me up, and I'll give you my beautiful little Blue Trousers." So the Tiger said, "Very well, I won't eat you this time, but you must give me your beautiful little Blue Trousers." So the Tiger got poor Little Black Sambo's beautiful little Blue Trousers, and went away saying, "Now I'm the grandest Tiger in the Jungle."

And Little Black Sambo went on and by and by he met another Tiger, and it said to him, "Little Black Sambo, I'm going to eat you up!" And Little Black Sambo said, "Oh! Please Mr. Tiger, don't eat me up, and I'll give you my beautiful little Purple Shoes with Crimson Soles and Crimson Linings."

But the Tiger said, "What use would your shoes be to me? I've got four feet, and you've got only two; you haven't got enough shoes for me."

But Little Black Sambo said, "You could wear them on your ears."

"So I could," said the Tiger: "that's a very good idea. Give them to me, and I won't eat you this time."

So the Tiger got poor Little Black Sambo's beautiful little Purple Shoes with Crimson Soles and Crimson Linings, and went away saying, "Now I'm the grandest Tiger in the Jungle."

And by and by Little Black Sambo met another Tiger, and it said to him, "Little Black Sambo, I'm going to eat you up!" and

[8] Complete text from Helen Bannerman, *The Story of Little Black Sambo* (Lippincott, 1923).

Little Black Sambo said, "Oh! Please Mr. Tiger, don't eat me up, and I'll give you my beautiful Green Umbrella." But the Tiger said, "How can I carry an umbrella, when I need all my paws for walking with?"

"You could tie a knot on your tail and carry it that way," said Little Black Sambo. "So I could," said the Tiger. "Give it to me, and I won't eat you this time." So he got poor Little Black Sambo's beautiful Green Umbrella, and went away saying, "Now I'm the grandest Tiger in the Jungle."

And poor Little Black Sambo went away crying, because the cruel Tigers had taken all his fine clothes.

Presently he heard a horrible noise that sounded like "Gr-r-r-r-rrrrrrr," and it got louder and louder. "Oh! dear!" said Little Black Sambo, "there are all the Tigers coming back to eat me up! What shall I do?" So he ran quickly to a palm-tree, and peeped round it to see what the matter was.

And there he saw all the Tigers fighting, and disputing which of them was the grandest. And at last they all got so angry that they jumped up and took off all the fine clothes, and began to tear each other with their claws, and bite each other with their great big white teeth.

And they came, rolling and tumbling right to the foot of the very tree where Little Black Sambo was hiding, but he jumped quickly in behind the umbrella. And the Tigers all caught hold of each other's tails, as they wrangled and scrambled, and so they found themselves in a ring round the tree.

Then, when the Tigers were very wee and very far away, Little Black Sambo jumped up, and called out, "Oh! Tigers! why have you taken off all your nice clothes? Don't you want them any more?" But the Tigers only answered, "Gr-r-rrrrr!"

Then Little Black Sambo said, "If you want them, say so, or I'll take them away." But the Tigers would not let go of each other's tails, and so they could only say "Gr-r-r-r-rrrrrrr!"

So Little Black Sambo put on all his fine clothes again and walked off.

And the Tigers were very, very angry, but still they would not let go of each other's tails. And they were so angry that they ran round the tree, trying to eat each other up, and they ran faster and faster, till they were whirling round so fast that you couldn't see their legs at all.

And they still ran faster and faster and faster, till they all just melted away, and there was nothing left but a great big pool of melted butter (or "ghi," as it is called in India) round the foot of the tree.

Now Black Jumbo was just coming home from his work, with a great big brass pot in his arms, and when he saw what was left of all the Tigers he said, "Oh! what lovely melted butter! I'll take that home to Black Mumbo for her to cook with."

So he put it all into the great big brass pot, and took it home to Black Mumbo to cook with.

When Black Mumbo saw the melted butter, wasn't she pleased! "Now," said she, "we'll all have pancakes for supper!"

So she got flour and eggs and milk and sugar and butter, and she made a huge big plate of most lovely pancakes. And she fried them in the melted butter which the Tigers had made, and they were just as yellow and brown as little Tigers.

And then they all sat down to supper. And Black Mumbo ate Twenty-seven pancakes, and Black Jumbo ate Fifty-five, but Little Black Sambo ate a Hundred and Sixty-nine, because he was so hungry.

Noël for Jeanne-Marie [9]

FRANÇOISE

With the first picture book Jeanne-Marie Counts Her Sheep, *the little French girl won a very special place in the hearts of small children. In the story given here, Jeanne-Marie tells her white sheep, Patapon, that Christmas is near and she wonders what Father Christmas will put in her wooden shoes. Drama and suspense enter the story when Patapon realizes that perhaps Father Christmas will not be able to leave a gift for a little sheep who has no shoes to put by the fireplace. Children are delighted with the way Jeanne-Marie handles the situation.*

[9] Complete text from *Noël for Jeanne-Marie,* by Françoise (Scribner, 1953).

Françoise, the author-artist, has a rare gift of seeing the world through the eyes of a very young child, and she knows just what little children like. There is a charming freshness and variety of design in her pictures, which are drawn with skill and distinction. Both the rhythmic text and the storytelling power of the illustrations delight small children.

It is winter time. The snow is falling. Jeanne-Marie says to her white sheep Patapon: "Noël will soon be here. I am so happy, so happy, Patapon."

Patapon answers: "Noël? I do not know about Noël. Tell me about Noël, Jeanne-Marie. Tell me about Noël."

"Listen, Patapon," says Jeanne-Marie. "Noël is the birthday of the little Jesus. And there is something more about Noël. If you are very good, Father Noël brings you presents. He comes in the night. No one sees him, no one at all. I put my wooden shoes near the chimney and Father Noël fills them with presents. You will see, Patapon, you will see. . . ."

Patapon jumps in the gold brown hay. Patapon answers: "I have four little black shoes. But I can't take them off and I can't put them near the chimney. Father Noël will not leave any present for me, Jeanne-Marie."

"Patapon," says Jeanne-Marie, "what do you think Father Noël will bring to me? Maybe a bright red kerchief with little white stars, Patapon."

Patapon answers: "Yes, you will get a new bright red kerchief. But I have no shoe to put near the chimney, and Father Noël won't leave any present for me, Jeanne-Marie."

"Patapon," says Jeanne-Marie, "maybe Father Noël will bring me a new doll carriage. And you, Patapon, you will be the doll! We'll have lots and lots of fun, riding in the country!"

Patapon answers: "Yes — but I have no shoe and Father Noël will not leave any present for me."

"Patapon," says Jeanne-Marie. "Maybe I'll get a manger, with the 'santons' — the little Jesus, the ox and the ass, the Kings, and all the little people who come to see the baby and to bring him gifts."

Patapon answers: "Yes, you will get a manger, with all the little people: the shepherds and the sheep, and the Kings with their gifts. But I have no shoe to put near the chimney, and Father Noël will not leave any present for me, Jeanne-Marie!"

"Patapon," says Jeanne-Marie, "if you are very good maybe you will get something, anyway."

So Jeanne-Marie goes to the old man who makes wooden shoes. She buys a tiny pair for Patapon.

Now it is the night before Christmas. Jeanne-Marie puts her best wooden shoes near the chimney. She puts Patapon's little new ones near by. Then Jeanne-Marie goes to sleep. And listen! Do you know what happened?

Father Noël came in the night. No one saw him. No one at all. Not even lambs. Not even Patapon, for Patapon was fast asleep in the gold brown hay. But . . .

On Christmas morning all the little santons were smiling in Jeanne-Marie's shoes. And . . . and . . . in the tiny wooden shoes there was a present for Patapon, too — a yellow satin ribbon with a bow, and a tinkling bell!

Patapon was so pleased with her present that she jumped here and there in the gold brown hay, Ding! Ding! Ding! sang the little bell. Noël! Noël! Noël!

The Tale of Peter Rabbit [1]

BEATRIX POTTER

This story is one of the best-loved of all the nursery classics. Beatrix Potter wrote it first in the form of a letter to amuse a little invalid boy, Noël Moore, the five-year-old son of her former German governess, and she illustrated the letter with pen-and-ink sketches. Noël loved the story and cherished the letter. (He grew up to be a clergyman.) Years later when Beatrix Potter thought of publishing the little story, she borrowed the letter. She copied the drawings, added a few more, made the story

[1] Complete text from Beatrix Potter, *The Tale of Peter Rabbit* (Frederick Warne, 1903).

a little longer, and submitted it to a publisher. It was politely rejected. After it had been turned down by six publishers, Beatrix Potter drew out her savings from the Post Office savings bank and had a modest edition of 450 copies privately printed at a cost of £11. But it was not until Frederick Warne and Company decided to publish it with colored illustrations that the little story came into its own. It sold for a shilling and carried a royalty of threepence a copy. The fame of Peter Rabbit spread rapidly. At the time of Beatrix Potter's death in 1943 the book had been translated into five languages and had sold several million copies. Beatrix Potter wrote over twenty of these little animal stories, but Peter Rabbit, Benjamin Bunny, and The Tailor of Gloucester are the best.

Once upon a time there were four little Rabbits, and their names were —

Flopsy,
Mopsy,
Cotton-tail,
and Peter.

They lived with their Mother in a sand-bank, underneath the root of a very big fir-tree.

"Now, my dears," said old Mrs. Rabbit one morning, "you may go into the fields or down the lane, but don't go into Mr. McGregor's garden: your Father had an accident there; he was put in a pie by Mrs. McGregor. Now run along, and don't get into mischief; I am going out."

Then old Mrs. Rabbit took a basket and her umbrella, and went through the wood to the baker's. She bought a loaf of brown bread and five currant buns.

Flopsy, Mopsy, and Cotton-tail, who were good little bunnies, went down the lane to gather blackberries; but Peter who was very naughty, ran straight away to Mr. McGregor's garden, and squeezed under the gate!

First he ate some lettuces and some French beans; and then he ate some radishes; and then, feeling rather sick, he went to look for some parsley.

But round the end of a cucumber frame, whom should he meet but Mr. McGregor!

Mr. McGregor was on his hands and knees planting out young cabbages, but he jumped up and ran after Peter, waving a rake and calling out, "Stop thief!"

Peter was most dreadfully frightened; he rushed all over the garden, for he had forgotten the way back to the gate.

He lost one of his shoes among the cabbages, and the other shoe amongst the potatoes.

After losing them, he ran on four legs and went faster, so that I think he might have got away altogether if he had not unfortunately run into a gooseberry net, and got caught by the large buttons on his jacket. It was a blue jacket with brass buttons, quite new.

Peter gave himself up for lost, and shed big tears; but his sobs were overheard by some friendly sparrows, who flew to him in great excitement, and implored him to exert himself.

Mr. McGregor came up with a sieve, which he intended to pop upon the top of Peter; but Peter wriggled out just in time, leaving his jacket behind him. And rushed into the toolshed, and jumped into a can. It would have been a beautiful thing to hide in, if it had not had so much water in it.

Mr. McGregor was quite sure that Peter was somewhere in the toolshed, perhaps hidden underneath a flower-pot. He began to turn them over carefully, looking under each.

Presently Peter sneezed — "Kertyschoo!" Mr. McGregor was after him in no time, and tried to put his foot upon Peter, who jumped out of the window, upsetting three plants. The window was too small for Mr. McGregor and he was tired of running after Peter. He went back to his work.

Peter sat down to rest; he was out of breath and trembling with fright, and he had not the least idea which way to go. Also he was very damp with sitting in that can.

After a time he began to wander about, going lippity — lippity — not very fast, and looking all around.

He found a door in a wall; but it was locked, and there was no room for a fat little rabbit to squeeze underneath.

An old mouse was running in and out over the stone door-step, carrying peas and beans to her family in the wood. Peter asked her the way to the gate, but she had such a large pea in her mouth that she could not answer.

She only shook her head at him. Peter began to cry.

Then he tried to find his way straight across the garden, but he became more and more puzzled. Presently, he came to a pond where Mr. McGregor filled his water-cans. A white cat was staring at some goldfish; she sat very, very still, but now and then the tip of her tail twitched as if it were alive. Peter thought it best to go away without speaking to her; he had heard about cats from his cousin, little Benjamin Bunny.

He went back towards the toolshed, but suddenly, quite close to him, he heard the noise of a hoe — scr-r-ritch, scratch, scratch, scritch. Peter scuttered underneath the bushes. But presently, as nothing happened, he came out, and climbed upon a wheelbarrow, and peeped over. The first thing he saw was Mr. McGregor hoeing onions. His back was turned toward Peter, and beyond him was the gate!

Peter got down very quietly off the wheelbarrow, and started running as fast as he could go, along a straight walk behind some black-currant bushes.

Mr. McGregor caught sight of him at the corner, but Peter did not care. He slipped underneath the gate, and was safe at last in the wood outside the garden.

Mr. McGregor hung up the little jacket and the shoes for a scare-crow to frighten the blackbirds.

Peter never stopped running or looked behind him till he got home to the big fir-tree.

He was so tired that he flopped down upon the nice soft sand on the floor of the rabbit hole, and shut his eyes. His mother was busy cooking; she wondered what he had done with his clothes. It was the second little jacket and pair of shoes that Peter had lost in a fortnight!

I am sorry to say that Peter was not very well during the evening.

His mother put him to bed, and made some camomile tea; and she gave a dose of it to Peter!

"One table-spoonful to be taken at bed-time."

But Flopsy, Mopsy, and Cotton-tail had bread and milk and blackberries for supper.

Millions of Cats [2]

Wanda Gág

Here is a picture book which is original in conception, yet it has the enduring quality of a folk tale. A little old man goes in search of one little kitten to keep his lonely wife company and comes back with "hundreds of cats, thousands of cats, millions and billions and trillions of cats." Children love the lilting refrain. The drawings have strength and vitality, and the rhythmic design of pictures and text is beautifully balanced.

Once upon a time there was a very old man and a very old woman. They lived in a nice clean house which had flowers all around it, except where the door was. But they couldn't be happy because they were so very lonely.

"If we only had a cat!" sighed the very old woman.

"A cat?" asked the very old man.

"Yes, a sweet little fluffy cat," said the very old woman.

"I will get you a cat, my dear," said the very old man.

And he set out over the hills to look for one. He climbed over the sunny hills. He trudged through the cool valleys. He walked a long, long time and at last he came to a hill which was quite covered with cats.

Cats here, cats there,
Cats and kittens everywhere,
Hundreds of cats,
Thousands of cats,
Millions and billions and trillions of cats.

"Oh," cried the old man joyfully, "now I can choose the prettiest cat and take it home with me!" So he chose one. It was white.

But just as he was about to leave, he saw another one all black and white and it seemed just as pretty as the first. So he took this one also.

But then he saw a fuzzy gray kitten way over here which was every bit as pretty as the others, so he took it too.

[2] Complete text from Wanda Gág, *Millions of Cats* (Coward-McCann, 1928).

And now he saw one way down in a corner which he thought too lovely to leave, so he took this too.

And just then, over here, the very old man found a kitten which was black and very beautiful.

"It would be a shame to leave that one," said the very old man. So he took it.

And now, over there, he saw a cat which had brown and yellow stripes like a baby tiger.

"I simply must take it!" cried the very old man; and he did.

So it happened that every time the very old man looked up, he saw another cat which was so pretty he could not bear to leave it, and before he knew it, he had chosen them all.

And so he went back over the sunny hills and down through the cool valleys, to show all his pretty kittens to the very old woman.

It was very funny to see those hundreds and thousands and millions and billions and trillions of cats following him.

They came to a pond.

"Mew, mew! We are thirsty!" cried the

Hundreds of cats,
Thousands of cats,
Millions and billions and trillions of cats.

"Well, here is a great deal of water," said the very old man.

Each cat took a sip of water, and the pond was gone!

"Mew, mew! Now we are hungry!" said the

Hundreds of cats,
Thousands of cats,
Millions and billions and trillions of cats.

"There is much grass on the hills," said the very old man.

Each cat ate a mouthful of grass and not a blade was left!

Pretty soon the very old woman saw them coming.

"My dear!" she cried, "What are you doing? I asked for one little cat, and what do I see? —

Cats here, cats there,
Cats and kittens everywhere,

Hundreds of cats,
Thousands of cats,
Millions and billions and trillions of cats.

"But we can never feed them all," said the very old woman. "They will eat us out of house and home."

"I never thought of that," said the very old man. "What shall we do?"

The very old woman thought for a while and then she said, "I know! We will let the cats decide which one we should keep."

"Oh yes," said the very old man; and he called to the cats, "Which one of you is the prettiest?"

"I am!"

"I am!"

"No, I am!"

"No, I am the prettiest!"

"I am!"

"No, I am! I am! I am!" cried hundreds and thousands and millions and billions and trillions of voices, for each cat thought itself the prettiest.

And they began to quarrel.

They bit and scratched and clawed each other and made such a great noise that the very old man and the very old woman ran into the house as fast as they could. They did not like such quarreling. But after a while the noise stopped, and the very old man and the very old woman peeped out of the window to see what had happened. They could not see a single cat!

"I think they must have eaten each other all up," said the very old woman. "It's too bad!"

"But look!" said the very old man, and he pointed to a bunch of high grass. In it sat one little frightened kitten. They went out and picked it up. It was thin and scraggly.

"Poor little kitty," said the very old woman.

"Dear little kitty," said the very old man. "How does it happen that you were not eaten up with all those hundreds and thousands and millions and billions and trillions of cats?"

"Oh, I'm just a very homely little cat," said the kitten, "So when you asked who was the prettiest, I didn't say anything. So nobody bothered about me."

They took the kitten into the house, where the very old woman gave it a warm bath and brushed its fur until it was soft and shiny.

Every day they gave it plenty of milk — and soon it grew nice and plump.

"And it is a very pretty cat, after all!" said the very old woman.

"It is the most beautiful cat in the whole world," said the very old man. "I ought to know, for I've seen —

Hundreds of cats,
Thousands of cats,
Millions and billions and trillions of cats —

and not one was as pretty as this one."

Pelle's New Suit[3]

Elsa Beskow

A satisfying realistic picture-storybook that tells how Pelle's fine blue suit of clothes was made from the wool of his lamb. The story is told not only in text, but also in full-page pictures in color by the author-artist.

There was once a little Swedish boy whose name was Pelle. Now, Pelle had a lamb which was all his own and which he took care of all by himself.

The lamb grew and Pelle grew. And the lamb's wool grew longer and longer, but Pelle's coat only grew shorter!

One day Pelle took a pair of shears and cut off all the lamb's wool. Then he took the wool to his grandmother and said: "Granny dear, please card this wool for me!"

"That I will, my dear," said his grandmother, "if you will pull the weeds in my carrot patch for me."

So Pelle pulled the weeds in Granny's carrot patch and Granny carded Pelle's wool.

Then Pelle went to his other grandmother and said. "Grandmother dear, please spin this wool into yarn for me!"

"That will I gladly do, my dear," said his grandmother, "if while I am spinning it you will tend my cows for me."

And so Pelle tended Grandmother's cows and Grandmother spun Pelle's yarn.

[3] Complete text from Elsa Beskow, *Pelle's New Suit* (Harper, 1929).

Then Pelle went to a neighbor who was a painter and asked him for some paint with which to color his yarn.

"What a silly little boy you are!" laughed the painter. "My paint is not what you want to color your wool. But if you will row over to the store to get a bottle of turpentine for me, you may buy yourself some dye out of the change from the shilling."

So Pelle rowed over to the store and bought a bottle of turpentine for the painter, and bought for himself a large sack of blue dye out of the change from the shilling.

Then he dyed his wool himself until it was all, all blue.

And then Pelle went to his mother and said: "Mother dear, please weave this yarn into cloth for me."

"That will I gladly do," said his mother, "if you will take care of your little sister for me."

So Pelle took good care of his little sister, and Mother wove the wool into cloth.

Then Pelle went to the tailor: "Dear Mr. Tailor, please make a suit for me out of this cloth."

"Is that what you want, you little rascal?" said the tailor. "Indeed I will, if you will rake my hay and bring in my wood and feed my pigs for me."

So Pelle raked the tailor's hay and fed his pigs.

And then he carried in all the wood. And the tailor had Pelle's suit ready that very Saturday evening.

And on Sunday morning Pelle put on his new suit and went to his lamb and said: "Thank you very much for my new suit, little lamb."

"Ba-a-ah," said the lamb, and it sounded almost as if the lamb were laughing.

Little Toot[4]

Hardie Gramatky

Mr. Gramatky has created a captivating new character in the fun-loving little tugboat

[4] Complete text from Hardie Gramatky, *Little Toot* (Putnam, 1939).

*in New York harbor. Irresponsible Little Toot
is far too pleased with himself to do any real
work until one day he takes part in a rescue and
earns the right to be called a hero. Mr. Gramatky,
who tells and illustrates his story with evident
enjoyment, got his idea from watching the tugboats on the East River from his studio window. The reader gets the genuine feel of the
waterfront in both pictures and text. The nauti-
cal blues and greens and stormy black match
perfectly the bravado of Little Toot.*

At the foot of an old, old wharf lives the
cutest, silliest little tugboat you ever saw.
A *very* handsome tugboat with a brand-new
candy-stick smokestack.

His name is Little Toot. And this name
he came by through no fault of his own.
Blow hard as he would, the only sound that
came out of his whistle was a gay, small
-toot-toot-toot.

But what he couldn't create in sound,
Little Toot made up for in smoke. From his
chubby smokestack he would send up a
volley of smoke balls which bubbled over
his wake like balloons. Hence, when he got
all "steamed up," Little Toot used to feel
very important . . .

Then the flag at his masthead would dance
like the tail of a puppy dog when he's
happy . . .

And he flaunted his signals like a man-
o'-war.

Now, the river where Little Toot lives is
full of ships. They come from ports all over
the world, bringing crews who speak strange
tongues, and bringing even stranger cargoes
— hides from Buenos Aires, copra from the
South Seas, whale oil from the Antarctic, and
fragrant teas from distant Asia. So there is
always work for tugboats to do, either pushing ships into the docks to be unloaded, or
else pulling them into the stream and down
the channel to the ocean to begin a new
voyage.

So a tugboat's life is a busy, exciting one,
and Little Toot was properly right in the
middle of it. His father, Big Toot, is the
biggest and fastest tugboat on the river.
Why, Big Toot can make *more* smoke and
kick up *more* water than any two of the
other boats put together.

As for Grandfather Toot, he is an old sea

dog who breathes smoke . . . and tells of
his mighty deeds on the river.

You'd think that Little Toot, belonging
to such an important family, would have his
mind on work. But no. Little Toot hated
work. He saw no sense in pulling ships fifty
times bigger than himself all the way down
to the ocean. And he was scared of the wild
seas that lay in wait outside the channel,
beyond where the harbor empties into the
ocean.

Little Toot had no desire to be tossed
around. He preferred the calm water of the
river itself, where he could always find plenty
of fun. Like gliding, for example . . .

Or playing thread-the-needle around the
piers.

Or, what was even fancier, cutting
figure 8's . . .

Little Toot liked nothing better than to
make a really fine figure 8. First you throw
your weight on one side, then on the other.
And the result never failed to delight him,
although his antics annoyed the hard-
working tugboats awfully.

But he kept on making figure 8's that
grew bigger and bigger until one day, carried
away by the joy of it all, he made one so
big it took up the whole river. Indeed, there
was hardly room for it between the two
shores . . .

And no room at all for a big tug named
J. G. McGillicuddy, which was bound downstream to pick up a string of coal barges
from Hoboken. J. G. McGillicuddy had
little love for other tugboats, anyway, and a
frivolous one like Little Toot made him mad.

This by itself was bad enough; but, unfortunately for Little Toot, the other tugboats
had seen what had happened. So they began
to make fun of him, calling him a sissy who
only knew how to play . . .

Poor Little Toot. He was ashamed and
angry, but there was nothing he could do
about it except blow those silly smoke
balls . . .

But the more he blew, the more the other
boats laughed at him.

Little Toot couldn't stand it. He fled to
his favorite hiding place alongside the wharf,
where his taunting friends could not reach
him; and there he just sat and sulked.

After he had moped a while Little Toot saw, headed down the river, a great ocean liner.

And pulling it were four tugboats, with his own father Big Toot right up in front.

The sight of that brave, bustling work made Little Toot think. He thought harder than ever in his life, and then — all of a sudden — a great idea burst over him. He *wouldn't* be a silly, frivolous little tugboat any more. He would work like the best of them. After all, wasn't he the son of Big Toot, the mightiest tug on the river? Well, he would make Big Toot proud of him. He'd show them all! Full of ambition, he started eagerly downstream.

He sidled hopefully up to one big ship after another, tooting for them to heave a towline. But they supposed he was still only a nuisance, and would have nothing to do with him. Oscar, the Scandinavian, rudely blew steam in his face . . .

. . . And the others were too busy with their own affairs to notice a bothersome little tug. They knew him too well!

But the rudest of all was a great transatlantic liner which blasted him right out of the water.

That was too much for Little Toot. He wasn't wanted anywhere or by anyone. With his spirits drooping he let the tide carry him where it willed. He was so *lonesome* . . .

Floating aimlessly downstream he grew sadder and sadder until he was utterly miserable. He was sunk so deep in his own despair he didn't even notice that the sky had grown dark and that the wind was whipping up into a real storm.

Suddenly he heard a sound that was like no sound he had ever heard before —

It was the *Ocean*. The Great Ocean that Little Toot had never seen. And the noise came from the waves as they dashed and pounded against the rocks.

But that wasn't all. Against the black sky climbed a . . .

. . . brilliant, flaming rocket.

When Little Toot looked hard, he saw, jammed between two huge rocks, an ocean liner which his father had towed many times up and down the river.

It was truly a terrible thing to see . . .

Little Toot went wild with excitement! He began puffing those silly balls of smoke out of his smokestack . . .

And as he did, a wonderful thought struck him. Why, those smoke balls could probably be seen 'way up the river, where his father and grandfather were. So he puffed a signal, thus . . .

S. O. S.

'Way up the river they saw it . . .

Of course they had no idea who was making the signals, but they knew it meant "come quickly." So they all dropped what they were doing to race to the rescue.

Out from many wharves steamed a great fleet —

   big boats,
    little boats,
     fat ones,
    and skinny ones . . .

. . . With Big Toot himself right in the lead, like an admiral at the head of his fleet . . .

Just in time, too, because Little Toot, still puffing out his S.O.S., was hard put to it to stay afloat.

One wave spun him around till he was dizzy; and another tossed him up so high he was glad when a spiral-shaped wave came along for him to glide down on . . .

Before he could spit the salt water out of his smokestack, still another wave came along and tossed him up again . . .

It looked as though he'd never get down.

All this was pretty awful for a tugboat that was used to the smooth water of the river. What made it terrifying was the fact that out of the corner of his eye, when he was thus hung on a wave, Little Toot saw that the fleet wasn't able to make headway against such fierce seas.

Even Grandfather Toot was bellowing he had never seen such a storm.

Little Toot was scared green . . .

Something had to be done. But all that Little Toot had ever learned to do was blow out those silly smoke balls.

Where he was, the channel was like a narrow bottle neck with the whole ocean trying to pour in at once.

That was why the fleet couldn't make any

headway. The force of the seas simply swept them back . . .

Indeed, they were on the verge of giving up entirely when suddenly above the storm they heard a gay, familiar toot . . .

It was Little Toot. Not wasting his strength butting the waves as they had done. But bouncing from crest to crest, like a rubber ball. The pounding hurt like everything, but Little Toot kept right on going.

And when Big Toot looked out to sea through his binoculars, he saw the crew on the great vessel throw a line to Little Toot.

It was a wonderful thing to see. When the line was made fast, Little Toot waited for a long moment . . .

And then, when a huge wave swept under the liner, lifting it clear of the rocks, he pulled with all of his might. *The liner came free!*

The people on board began to cheer . . .

And the whole tugboat fleet insisted upon Little Toot's escorting the great boat back into the harbor.

Little Toot was a hero! And Grandfather Toot blasted the news all over the river.

Well, after that Little Toot became quite a different fellow. He even changed his tune . . .

And it is said that he can haul as big a load as his father can . . .

. . . that is, when Big Toot hasn't a very big load to haul . . .

The Little House [5]

VIRGINIA LEE BURTON

⋙ *The talented author-artist has endowed the little house with an endearing personality. Located in the country, it quietly watches the changing of the seasons and, with the passing years, the gradual encroachment of the city. The pictures, bright and detailed, give a highly dramatic effect to the story. The skillful use of color suggests day and night and the different aspects of the seasons in both country and city. Children like to point out the little house in each picture, and it becomes increasingly difficult to*

[5] Complete text from Virginia Lee Burton, *The Little House* (Houghton Mifflin, 1942).

find as it is hemmed in by more and more tall buildings and elevated tracks. In the end, the reader has the joy of seeing the forlorn, shabby little house moved back into the green and sunny country where it can hear the birds sing, watch the sun rise and set, and see the stars at night. In 1943 Virginia Lee Burton won the Caldecott medal for this book, which was chosen as the most distinguished picture book of the year.

Once upon a time there was a Little House way out in the country. She was a pretty Little House and she was strong and well built. The man who built her so well said, "This Little House shall never be sold for gold or silver and she will live to see our great-great-grandchildren's great-great-grandchildren living in her."

The Little House was very happy as she sat on the hill and watched the countryside around her. She watched the sun rise in the morning and she watched the sun set in the evening. Day followed day, each one a little different from the one before . . . but the Little House stayed just the same.

In the nights she watched the moon grow from a thin new moon to a full moon, then back again to a thin old moon; and when there was no moon she watched the stars. Way off in the distance she could see the lights of the city. The Little House was curious about the city and wondered what it would be like to live there.

Time passed quickly for the Little House as she watched the countryside slowly change with the seasons. In the Spring, when the days grew longer and the sun warmer, she waited for the first robin to return from the South. She watched the grass turn green. She watched the buds on the trees swell and the apple trees burst into blossom. She watched the children playing in the brook.

In the long Summer days she sat in the sun and watched the trees cover themselves with leaves and the white daisies cover the hill. She watched the gardens grow, and she watched the apples turn red and ripen. She watched the children swimming in the pool.

In the Fall, when the days grew shorter and the nights colder, she watched the first frost turn the leaves to bright yellow and orange and red. She watched the harvest gathered and the apples picked. She watched the children going back to school.

In the Winter, when the nights were long and the days short, and the countryside covered with snow, she watched the children coasting and skating. Year followed year. . . . The apple trees grew old and new ones were planted. The children grew up and went away to the city . . . and now at night the lights of the city seemed brighter and closer.

One day the Little House was surprised to see a horseless carriage coming down the winding country road. . . . Pretty soon there were more of them on the road and fewer carriages pulled by horses. Pretty soon along came some surveyors and surveyed a line in front of the Little House. Pretty soon along came a steam shovel and dug a road through the hill covered with daisies. . . . Then some trucks came and dumped big stones on the road, then some trucks with little stones, then some trucks with tar and sand, and finally a steam roller came and rolled it all smooth, and the road was done.

Now the Little House watched the trucks and automobiles going back and forth to the city. Gasoline stations . . . roadside stands . . . and small houses followed the new road. Everyone and everything moved much faster now than before.

More roads were made, and the countryside was divided into lots. More houses and bigger houses . . . apartment houses and tenement houses . . . schools . . . stores . . . and garages spread over the land and crowded around the Little House. No one wanted to live in her and take care of her any more. She couldn't be sold for gold or silver, so she just stayed there and watched.

Now it was not so quiet and peaceful at night. Now the lights of the city were bright and very close, and the street lights shone all night. "This must be living in the city," thought the Little House, and didn't know whether she liked it or not. She missed the field of daisies and the apple trees dancing in the moonlight.

Pretty soon there were trolley cars going back and forth in front of the Little House. They went back and forth all day and part of the night. Everyone seemed to be very busy and everyone seemed to be in a hurry.

Pretty soon there was an elevated train going back and forth above the Little House. The air was filled with dust and smoke, and the noise was so loud that it shook the Little House. Now she couldn't tell when Spring came, or Summer or Fall, or Winter. It all seemed about the same.

Pretty soon there was a subway going back and forth underneath the Little House. She couldn't see it, but she could feel and hear it. People were moving faster and faster. No one noticed the Little House any more. They hurried by without a glance.

Pretty soon they tore down the apartment houses and tenement houses around the Little House and started digging big cellars . . . one on each side. The steam shovels dug down three stories on one side and four stories on the other side. Pretty soon they started building up. . . . They built up twenty-five stories on one side and thirty-five stories on the other.

Now the Little House only saw the sun at noon, and didn't see the moon or stars at night at all because the lights of the city were too bright. She didn't like living in the city. At night she used to dream of the country and the field of daisies and the apple trees dancing in the moonlight.

The Little House was very sad and lonely. Her paint was cracked and dirty. . . . Her windows were broken and her shutters hung crookedly. She looked shabby . . . though she was just as good a house as ever underneath.

Then one fine morning in Spring along came the great-great-granddaughter of the man who built the Little House so well. She saw the shabby Little House, but she didn't hurry by. There was something about the Little House that made her stop and look again. She said to her husband, "That Little House looks just like the Little House my grandmother lived in when she was a little girl, only *that* Little House was way out in the country on a hill covered with daisies and apple trees growing around."

They found out it was the very same house, so they went to the Movers to see if the Little House could be moved. The Movers looked the Little House all over and said, "Sure, this house is as good as ever. She's built so well we could move her anywhere." So they jacked up the Little House and put her on wheels. Traffic was held up for hours as they slowly moved her out of the city.

At first the Little House was frightened, but after she got used to it she rather liked it. They rolled along the big road, and they rolled along the little roads, until they were way out in the country. When the Little House saw the green grass and heard the birds singing, she didn't feel sad any more. They went along and along, but they couldn't seem to find just the right place. They tried the Little House here, and they tried her there. Finally they saw a little hill in the middle of a field . . . and apple trees growing around. "There," said the great-great-granddaughter, "that's just the place."

"Yes, it is," said the Little House to herself.

A cellar was dug on top of the hill and slowly they moved the house from the road to the hill. The windows and shutters were fixed and once again they painted her a lovely shade of pink. As the Little House settled down on her new foundation, she smiled happily. Once again she could watch the sun and moon and stars. Once again she could watch Spring and Summer and Fall and Winter come and go.

Once again she was lived in and taken care of. Never again would she be curious about the city . . . Never again would she want to live there . . . The stars twinkled above her . . . A new moon was coming up . . . It was Spring . . . and all was quiet and peaceful in the country.

Ola [6]

INGRI AND EDGAR PARIN D'AULAIRE

This distinguished picture book of Norway tells of a small boy's adventure on his skis in the snow, of his trip to Lapland with a peddler, to a fishing village on the Arctic, then home again. The large drawings in full color were made directly on lithograph stones and are instinct with the atmosphere of the country. Small chil-

[6] Complete text from Ingri and Edgar Parin d'Aulaire, *Ola* (Doubleday, 1932).

dren claim Ola as a real friend as they go with him on one of their first adventures in a strange country.

Far up in the north the sun is afraid to show his pale face in winter. But the moon and the stars love the sparkling frost. They gleam fairylike through the long night and the arctic lights leap across the sky in cold, silent flames. They glitter on the snow and the ice of a long, mountainous country down below. In their magic light the country looks like a huge silver spoon, thousands of miles long. This is Norway. And it is the strangest country in the world. It is so crowded with mountains, forests, huge trolls, redcapped gnomes, and alluring Hulder-maidens that only a few human people have room to live there.

In this country there is a forest, in winter a very strange forest. For under the heavy burden of snow the trees turn into a crowd of solemn creatures. In the middle of the forest there was a small house. And in this house there lived a small boy. Ola was his name. His eyes were light blue, his tousled hair was yellow, and his face was rosy from much fresh air. With sleepy eyes Ola peered out through the tangle of frost roses on his window. The flaring arctic lights had awakened him and he decided to put on his clothes and go out for a while to look around. Strange adventures might wait for him, behind the quaint paintings on the old door. So he opened the door and went out.

At the gate a moose was standing, and some hares played quietly around Ola while he fastened his skis to his feet. But when he wanted to join their play they scampered, frightened, to all sides. A small hare was so stupid, it ran just in front of Ola's skis. "Run on, my seven-league boots," said Ola to his skis. "Let us see if we can catch that hare."

For a long time he followed the hare and could not overtake it. But when he came to a very steep slope, his skis started to race down so fast that they caught up with the hare. Quick-witted Ola squatted down and grabbed it. Down the slope they flew, faster and faster, and right over a high bank.

Some girls happened to be standing under

the bank. When a white hare and a red cap fell at their feet, right from the sky, they were sure it was a gnome who wanted to play hide-and-seek with them.

They looked all over for the gnome. But instead of a gnome they saw Ola high up in a pine tree, hanging by his skis. "I caught hold of these branches," he boasted. "Help me down, you silly girls." So they did. And they told him they were Siri and Turi, Randi and Guri, Mari and Kari and Gro, and he might come along to see a wedding in the next valley.

Ola joined the girls and they rushed down to a big farm where the buildings played merry-go-round around a birch tree.

From the big storehouse scullery maids were carrying all kinds of delicious food. There was butter and brown goat-cheese shaped like animals and castles. There were stacks of flat-bread, large as millstones and thin as leaves, and trout and meat and porridge and cakes. There was also a big bowl of ale, and on its surface swam small drinking vessels like ducks on a pond.

The children heard music from the main house, so they ran to a window and peeped in.

At the fireplace sat an old fiddler, playing and singing, and at a long table the wedding party was seated. The bride looked just like a princess with a huge silver crown on her head, and the groom had silver buttons wherever there was a place on his suit. The bridal feast was to last for several days, and this was just a light meal to give the wedding party strength for the long ride to church.

When lunch was over the whole party came out and climbed into sleighs. They started off and the children hung on behind. The girls were soon thrown off, only Ola managed skillfully to keep on. Up hill and down hill they flew.

But suddenly, as they approached the church, a howling black dragon rushed out from a cave. It plowed through the drifts that blocked its way, throwing the snow this way and that and covering the whole wedding party. "The dragon swallowed me," thought Ola, and he did not dare to move. The parson and the sexton helped the others out of the snow and they stepped into the

church as if nothing had happened. Only a red cap was left over as it did not belong to any of the party.

After a while Per peddler passed and stopped to pick up the red cap. He was surprised to find a yellow tuft beneath. As he pulled, Ola came up. Ola was afraid Per peddler would laugh at him if he told him about the dragon. So he said: "I just dug myself a house like the Lapps."

"So?" said Per peddler. "But the Lapps don't live like that. They live in tents and have reindeers. I am on my way there now."

"Please, peddler, take me along," Ola begged.

"All right," said Per peddler. "You may help me carry."

They traveled over mountains and valleys and rivers and lakes, always to the north. The days grew shorter and shorter till at last the sun did not show himself at all. At noon there was just a dim light. The roads ended, but Ola and Per peddler went on and on.

At last they met a Lapp who was herding a flock of reindeer. The deer were all digging for moss under the snow. Nearby were the Lapp tents. While Per peddler was busy trading, Ola stared at the reindeer and Lapp children just as curiously as they stared at him.

Then Ola and Per peddler went on south again over wild mountains where a furious storm was raging. Suddenly Per peddler's huge knapsack blew open and all his nice goods were scattered about. Not far away there was a fishing village on the shore of the Arctic Ocean. "Don't worry," said Per to Ola. "While I go to get new goods, you can go fishing."

The first thing Per peddler did when he came to the fishing village was to buy Ola a fisherman's outfit and, dressed in that, Ola at once got work. All day long he spent out on the fishing grounds, pulling in cod. Ola liked it. Sometimes his boat was deep in a wave valley and the fishermen in the boats nearby looked as if they were sitting in water up to their necks. Sometimes his boat was high on a water mountain and Ola could see hundreds of other fisherboats gathered from all parts of Norway.

The fishermen told Ola that strange people

live in small houses at the bottom of the sea, and they have lots of goats grazing on their grass roofs. But these goats are very greedy for the tidbits of the fishing hooks, and to their owners' horror the goats get drawn right up and change into codfish. The fishermen showed Ola bits of goats' beards on the chins of the codfish.

They took Ola to a place where the water was boiling and whirling around a black cliff. "That is the Maelstrom," they said. "Here at the bottom a man and his wife sit quarreling over their huge kettle of food. He stirs this way and she stirs that way, and the water becomes so terribly rough that no ship can sail across."

In the evening when they came back to the harbour, they all worked together, preparing the codfish. They cleaned the fish and hung them on racks to dry, and the livers they steamed into delicious codliver oil. They gave Ola a very large fish for himself and a can of codliver oil.

All of a sudden spring was there. The codfish went off to the great ocean, and the fishermen sold their catch and sailed for their far-away homes.

Ola decided that he would go home, too. He had heard that he could go most of the way by ship. So as he saw a boat lying deserted at the shore, he crawled into it and rowed off.

He had not rowed far, however, when the wind blew the clouds right down over him. In the fog Ola could not see his hand before his face. But he rowed on. Suddenly his hair stood upright on his head, for he heard a terrible howl as from many wild animals.

But the fog lifted, and there he saw a boat loaded with cats. "These terrible cats," said the man who rowed the boat, "they are furious because I took them away from the birds' islets so the birds may hatch in peace."

On one of the islets Ola saw a little girl crying. "I want my kitten back," she sobbed. "Never mind," said Ola. "You'll get your kitten back in the fall. Show me the birds now." "All right," said the little girl. "You can help me gather eiderdown. I'll give you an empty sack."

Among the grass and heather the eiderducks were sitting on their nests. The nests were softly lined with down, and the birds did not mind when the children took some of it away.

After they had filled the sacks with down they climbed a steep cliff. Here millions of cormorants, gulls, sea-parrots, and auks had their nests.

At the top of the cliff a crowd of children came running toward them. "Look at our beautiful midnight sun!" they cried. "It won't set for many weeks, and all that time we may be up all night." Ola looked and saw hundreds of cliffs shaped like strange animals. The red sun rolled along their backs. Suddenly he saw a ship sailing southward between the cliffs, and on deck he recognized Per peddler. Per peddler had chartered the ship and loaded it with dried cod. Now he was on his way to Bergen to sell it.

"Wait, wait," cried Ola, "take me along home!" Per peddler stopped the ship, and the children let Ola down on a rope. The little girl said he might keep the sack with down which he carried.

And with his down, his fish, and his codliver oil Ola boarded the ship and sailed homeward.

Dick Whittington and His Cat [7]

MARCIA BROWN

This versatile author-artist is a storyteller with both words and pictures. Here she retells the famous folk tale in vigorous prose well suited to the story hour. She has a rare talent for suiting the type of illustration to her subject matter. For Dick Whittington, her choice of the bold line of the linoleum block matches perfectly the robust story and its period. The pictures, in dull gold and black, combine lively action with a fine sense of design.

Long ago in England there lived a little boy named Dick Whittington. Dick's father and mother died when he was very young, and as he was too small to work, he had a hard time of it. The people in the village

[7] Complete text from *Dick Whittington*, told and cut in linoleum by Marcia Brown (Scribner, 1950).

were poor and could spare him little more than the parings of potatoes and now and then a crust of bread. He ran about the country as ragged as a colt, until one day he met a wagoner on his way to London. "Come along with me," said the wagoner. So off they set together.

Now Dick had heard of the great city of London. It was said that the people who lived there were all fine gentlemen and ladies, that there was singing and music all day long, and that the streets were paved with gold. As for the gold, "I'd be willing to get a bushel of that," said Dick to himself.

But when Dick got to London, how sad he was to find the streets covered with dirt instead of gold! And there he was in a strange place, without food, without friends, and without money. Dick was soon so cold and hungry that he wished he were back sitting by a warm fire in a country kitchen. He sat down in a corner and cried himself to sleep.

A kind gentleman saw him there and said, "Why don't you go to work, my lad?"

"That I would," said Dick, "if I could get anything to do."

"Come along with me," said the gentleman, and he led Dick to a hayfield. There he worked hard and lived merrily until the hay was made.

Now Dick was again forlorn. He wandered back to town, fainting for want of food, and laid himself down at the door of Mr. Fitzwarren, a rich merchant.

Here the cook saw him, and being an ill-natured hussy, she called out, "On your way there, lazy rogue, or would you like a scalding to make you jump?"

Just then Mr. Fitzwarren came home to dinner. When he saw the dirty, ragged boy lying in his doorway, he said to him, "What ails you, boy? You look old enough to work."

"Sir, I am a poor country lad," said Dick. "I have neither father nor mother nor any friend in the world. I would be glad to work, but I've had no food for three days." Dick then tried to get up, but he was so weak he fell down again.

"Take this lad into the house," Mr. Fitzwarren ordered his servants. "Give him meat and drink. When he is stronger he can help the cook with her dirty work."

Now Dick would have lived happily with this worthy family if he had not been bumped about by the cook.

"Look sharp there, clean the spit, empty the dripping pan, sweep the floor! Step lively or —!" And down came the ladle on the boy's shoulders. For the cook was always roasting and basting, and when the spit was still, she basted his head with a broom or anything else she could lay her hands on. When Mr. Fitzwarren's daughter, Alice, saw what was going on, she warned the cook, "Treat that boy more kindly or leave this house!"

Besides the crossness of the cook, Dick had another hardship. His bed was placed in a garret where there were so many rats and mice running over his bed he could never get to sleep.

But one day a gentleman gave Dick a penny for brushing his shoes. The next day Dick saw a girl in the street with a cat under her arm. He ran up to her. "How much do you want for that cat?" he asked.

"Oh, this cat is a good mouser," said the girl. "She will bring a great deal of money."

"But I have only a penny in the world," said Dick, "and I need a cat badly." So the girl let him have it.

Dick hid his cat in the garret because he was afraid the cook would beat her too. He always saved part of his dinner for her, and Miss Puss wasted no time in killing or frightening away all the rats and mice. Now Dick could sleep as sound as a top.

Not long after this, Mr. Fitzwarren had a ship ready to sail. He called all his servants into the parlor and asked them what they chose to send to trade. All the servants brought something but poor Dick. Since he had neither money nor goods, he couldn't think of sending anything.

"I'll put some money down for him," offered Miss Alice, and she called Dick into the parlor.

But the merchant said, "That will not do. It must be something of his own."

"I have nothing but a cat," said Dick.

"Fetch your cat, boy," said the merchant, "and let her go!"

So Dick brought Puss and handed her over to the captain of the ship with tears in his eyes. "Now the rats and mice will keep me awake all night again," he said. All the company laughed, but Miss Alice pitied Dick and gave him some half-pence to buy another cat.

While Puss was beating the billows at sea, Dick was beaten at home by the cross cook. She used him so cruelly and made such fun of him for sending his cat to sea that the poor boy decided to run away. He packed the few things he had and set out early in the morning on All-Hallows Day. He walked as far as Halloway and sat down on a stone to rest. While he was sitting there wondering which way to go, the Bells of Bow began to ring. Dong! Dong!

They seemed to say to him:

"Turn again, Whittington,
Lord Mayor of London."

"Lord Mayor of London!" said Dick to himself. "What wouldn't I give to be Lord Mayor of London and ride in such a fine coach! I'll go back and I'll take the cuffings of the cook, if I'm to be Lord Mayor of London." So home he went. Luckily, he got into the house and about his business before the old cook came downstairs.

Meanwhile the ship with the cat on board was long beating about at sea. The winds finally drove it on the coast of Barbary. Here lived the Moors, a people unknown to the English. They came in great numbers on board to see the sailors and the goods which the captain wanted to trade.

The captain sent some of his choicest goods to the king of the country. The king was so well pleased that he invited the captain and his officer to come to his palace, about a mile from the sea.

Here they were placed on rich carpets, flowered with gold and silver. The king and queen sat at the upper end of the room, and dinner was brought in. No sooner had the servants set down the dishes than an amazing number of rats and mice rushed in. They helped themselves from every dish, scattering pieces of meat and gravy all about.

The captain in surprise turned to the nobles and asked, "Are not these vermin offensive?"

"Oh yes," said they, "very offensive! The King would give half of his treasure to be rid of them. They not only ruin his dinner, but also attack him in his chamber, even in his bed! He has to be watched while he is sleeping for fear of them!"

The captain jumped for joy. He remembered Whittington and his cat and told the king he had a creature on board the ship that would soon destroy the mice. The king's heart heaved so high at this good news that his turban dropped off his head. "Bring this creature to me!" he cried. "Vermin are dreadful in a court! If she will do what you say, I will load your ship with ivory, gold dust and jewels in exchange for her."

Away flew the captain to the ship, while another dinner was got ready. With Puss under his arm, he returned to the palace just in time to see the rats about to devour the second dinner. At first sight of the rats and mice the cat sprang from the captain's arms. Soon she had laid most of them dead at her feet, while the rest fled to their holes.

The king rejoiced to see his old enemies destroyed. The queen asked to see Miss Puss. When the captain presented the cat, the queen was a little afraid to touch a creature that had made such havoc among the rats and mice. Finally she stroked her and said, "Puttey, puttey, puttey," for she had not learned English. The captain put the cat on the queen's lap, where she purred and played with her majesty's hand and then sang herself to sleep.

When the king learned that Miss Puss and her kittens would keep the whole country free from rats and mice, he bargained for the whole ship's cargo. He gave ten times as much for Miss Puss as for all the rest.

When the ship was loaded, the captain and his officer took leave of their majesties. A breeze springing up, they hurried on board and set sail for England.

The sun was scarcely up one morning when Mr. Fitzwarren stole from his bed to count over the cash. He had just sat down at his desk in the counting house when somebody came tap, tap-tap at the door.

"Who's there?"

"A friend. I bring you news of the good ship Unicorn!"

The merchant bustled up in such a hurry that he forgot his gout. He opened the door.

There stood the captain and his officer with a cabinet of jewels and a bill of lading. The merchant lifted up his eyes and thanked Heaven for such a prosperous voyage. They told him about the cat and showed him the caskets of diamonds and rubies they had brought for Dick.

At that the merchant cried out:

"Go call him and tell him of his fame,
And call him Mr. Whittington by name."

Dick was scouring pots in the kitchen and did not want to come into the clean parlor. "The floor is polished, and my shoes are dirty and full of nails." But the merchant made him come in and sit down.

He took Dick by the hand and said, "Mr. Whittington, I sent for you to congratulate you upon your good fortune. The captain has sold your cat to the king of Barbary. She has brought you more riches than I am worth in the world. May you long enjoy them!"

When they showed him the caskets of jewels, Dick laid the whole at his master's feet, but Mr. Fitzwarren refused it. He offered them to his mistress and his good friend Miss Alice, but they too refused the smallest part. Dick then rewarded the captain and ship's crew for the care they had taken of Puss, and distributed presents to all the servants, even to his old enemy, the cook.

Mr. Fitzwarren advised Mr. Whittington to send for tradesmen to dress him like a gentleman, and offered him his house until he could provide himself with a better. Now when Dick's face was washed, his hair curled, his hat cocked, and he was dressed in a rich suit of clothes, he turned out a genteel young fellow.

In a little time he dropped his sheepish behavior and soon became a sprightly companion. Miss Alice, who formerly looked on him with pity, now saw him in quite another light.

When Mr. Fitzwarren noticed how fond they were of each other, he proposed a match between them. Both parties cheerfully consented.

The Lord Mayor in his coach, Court of Aldermen, Sheriffs, company of stationers, and a number of eminent merchants attended the wedding ceremony. And afterwards all were treated to an elegant entertainment.

Whittington and his bride were called the happiest couple in England. He was chosen Sheriff and was three different times elected Lord Mayor of London. In the last year of his mayoralty Whittington entertained King Henry the Fifth and his Queen.

"Never had Prince such a subject," said Henry, and Whittington replied, "Never had subject such a King!"

The Five Hundred Hats of Bartholomew Cubbins [8]

DOCTOR SEUSS

An original and spontaneous fanciful tale about a small boy and his miraculous crop of hats, written by the gifted author-artist of And to Think That I Saw It on Mulberry Street.

In the beginning, Bartholomew Cubbins didn't have five hundred hats. He had only one hat. It was an old one that had belonged to his father and his father's father before him. It was probably the oldest and the plainest hat in the whole Kingdom of Didd, where Bartholomew Cubbins lived. But Bartholomew liked it — especially because of the feather that always pointed straight up in the air.

The Kingdom of Didd was ruled by King Derwin. His palace stood high on the top of the mountain. From his balcony he looked down over the houses of all his subjects — first, over the spires of the noblemen's castles, across the broad roofs of the rich men's mansions, then over the little houses of the townsfolk, to the huts of the farmers far off in the fields.

[8] Complete text from Doctor Seuss, *The 500 Hats of Bartholomew Cubbins* (Vanguard Press, 1938).

It was a mighty view and it made King Derwin feel mighty important.

Far off in the fields, on the edge of a cranberry bog, stood the hut of the Cubbins family. From the small door Bartholomew looked across the huts of the farmers to the houses of the townsfolk, then to the rich men's mansions and the noblemen's castles, up to the great towering palace of the king. It was exactly the same view that King Derwin saw from his balcony, but Bartholomew saw it backward.

It was a mighty view, but it made Bartholomew Cubbins feel mighty small.

Just after sunrise one Saturday morning, Bartholomew started for town. He felt very happy. A pleasant breeze whistled through the feather in his hat. In his right hand he carried a basket of cranberries to sell at the market. He was anxious to sell them quickly and bring the money back home to his parents.

He walked faster and faster till he got to the gates of the town.

The sound of silver trumpets rang through the air. Hoofbeats clattered on the cobbled streets.

"Clear the way! Clear the way! Make way for the king!"

All the people rushed for the sidewalks. They drove their carts right up over the curbstones. Bartholomew clutched his basket tighter.

Around the corner dashed fifty trumpeters on yellow-robed horses. Behind them on crimson-robed horses came the King's Own Guards.

"Hats off to the king!" shouted the captain of the King's Own Guards.

On came the king's carriage — white and gold and purple. It rumbled like thunder through the narrow street.

It swept past Bartholomew. Then suddenly its mighty brakes shrieked. It lurched — and then it stopped. The whole procession stood still.

Bartholomew could hardly believe what he saw. Through the side window of the carriage, the king himself was staring back — straight back at him. Bartholomew began to tremble.

"Back up!" the king commanded the royal coachman.

The royal coachman shouted to the royal horses. The King's Own Guards shouted to their crimson-robed horses. The trumpeters shouted to their yellow-robed horses. Very slowly the whole procession backed down the street, until the king's carriage stopped right in front of Bartholomew.

The king leaned from his carriage window and fixed his eyes directly on Bartholomew Cubbins. "Well . . .? Well . . .?" he demanded.

Bartholomew shook with fright. "I ought to say something," he thought to himself. But he could think of nothing to say.

"Well?" demanded the king again. "Do you or do you *not* take off your hat before your king?"

"Yes, indeed, Sire," answered Bartholomew, feeling greatly relieved. "I *do* take off my hat before my king."

"Then take it off this very instant," commanded the king, more loudly than before.

"But, Sire, my hat *is* off," answered Bartholomew.

"Such impudence!" shouted the king, shaking an angry finger. "How dare you stand there and tell me your hat is off!"

"I don't like to say you are wrong, Sire," said Bartholomew very politely, "but you see my hat *is* off." And he showed the king the hat in his hand.

"If that's your hat in your hand," demanded the king, "what's that on your head?"

"On my head?" gasped Bartholomew. There did seem to be something on his head. He reached up his hand and touched a hat!

The face of Bartholomew Cubbins turned very red. "It's a hat, Sire," he stammered, "but it *can't* be mine. Someone behind me must have put it on my head."

"I don't care *how* it got there," said the king. "You take it off." And the king sat back in his carriage.

Bartholomew quickly snatched off the hat. He stared at it in astonishment. It was exactly the same as his own hat — the same size, the same color. And it had exactly the same feather.

"By the crown of my fathers!" roared the king, again leaning out of the carriage window. "Did I or did I *not* command you to take off your hat?"

"You did, Sire . . . I took it off . . . I took it off twice."

"Nonsense! There is still a hat upon your head."

"Another hat?" Again Bartholomew reached up his hand and touched a hat.

"Come, come, what is the meaning of all this?" demanded the king, his face purple with rage.

"I don't know, Sire," answered Bartholomew. "It never happened to me before."

The king was now shaking with such fury that the carriage rocked on its wheels and the royal coachman could hardly sit in his seat. "Arrest this impudent trickster!" shouted the king to the captain of the King's Own Guards. "We'll teach him to take off his hat."

The royal coachman cracked his long whip. The king's carriage swung forward up the street toward the palace.

But the captain of the King's Own Guards leaned down from his big brass saddle and grabbed Bartholomew Cubbins by his shirt. Away flew Bartholomew's basket! The cranberries bounced over the cobblestones and rolled down into the gutter.

With a jangling of spurs and a clatter of horseshoes, the captain and Bartholomew sped up the winding street toward the palace. Out of the narrow streets, on up the hill! Bartholomew clung to the captain's broad back. On and on they galloped, past the bright gardens of the wealthy merchants. Higher and higher up the mountain, on past the walls of the noblemen's castles . . .

Flupp! . . . the sharp wind whisked off Bartholomew's hat. *Flupp. Flupp!* . . . two more flew off. *Flupp Flupp* flew another . . . and another. ". . . 4 . . . 5 . . . 6 . . . 7 . . ." Bartholomew kept counting as the hats came faster and faster. Lords and ladies stared from the windows of their turrets, wondering what the strange stream of hats could mean.

Over the palace drawbridge they sped — through the great gates, and into the courtyard. The captain pulled in his reins.

"His Majesty waits in the throne room," said a guard, saluting the captain.

"The throne room!" The captain dropped Bartholomew to the ground. "I'd certainly hate to be in your shoes," he said, shaking his head sadly.

For a moment Bartholomew was terribly frightened. "Still," he thought to himself, "the king can do nothing dreadful to punish me, because I really haven't done anything wrong. It would be cowardly to feel afraid."

Bartholomew threw back his shoulders and marched straight ahead into the palace. "Follow the black carpet," said the guard at the door. All through the long hallway Bartholomew could hear the muttering of voices behind heavy doors. "He won't take off his hat?" "No, he won't take off his hat."

Bartholomew walked on till he stood in the very middle of the throne room. The king, in a long scarlet robe, was sitting on his throne. Beside him stood Sir Alaric, keeper of the king's records. He wore in his belt, instead of a sword, a long silver ruler. Lords and noblemen of the court stood solemn and silent.

The king looked down at Bartholomew severely. "Young man, I'll give you one more chance. Will you take off your hat for your king?"

"Your Majesty," said Bartholomew as politely as he possibly could, "I will — but I'm afraid it won't do any good." And he took off his hat — and it didn't do any good. Another hat sat on Bartholomew's head. He took off hat after hat after hat after hat until he was standing in the middle of a great pile of hats.

The lords and noblemen were so astonished they couldn't even speak. Such a thing had never happened in the throne room before.

"Heavens!" said Sir Alaric, keeper of the records, blinking behind his triangular spectacles. "He's taken off forty-five!"

"And there were three more down in the town," said the king.

"And you must add on eighty-seven more that blew off my head as we galloped up the hill," said Bartholomew, trying to be helpful.

"One hundred and thirty-five hats! Most

unusual," said Sir Alaric, writing it down on a long scroll.

"Come, come," said the king impatiently. "Sir Alaric, what do you make of all this nonsense?"

"Very *serious* nonsense, Your Majesty," answered Sir Alaric. "I advise you to call in an expert on hats."

"Excellent," agreed the king. "Ho, Guard! Fetch in Sir Snipps, maker of hats for all the fine lords."

Into the throne room marched the smallest man, wearing the tallest hat that Bartholomew had ever seen. It was Sir Snipps. Instead of a sword, he wore at his side a large pair of scissors.

"Take a look at this boy's hat," commanded the king. Sir Snipps looked at Bartholomew Cubbins's hat and sniffed in disgust. Then he turned to the king and bowed stiffly. "Your Majesty, I, Sir Snipps, am the maker of hats for all the fine lords. I make hats of cloth of gold, fine silks and gems and ostrich plumes. You ask *me* what *I* think of *this* hat? Pooh! It is the most ordinary hat I ever set eyes on."

"In that case," said the king, "it should be very simple for you to take it off."

"Simple, indeed," mumbled Sir Snipps haughtily, and, standing on his tiptoes, he pushed his pudgy thumb at Bartholomew's hat and knocked it to the floor. Immediately another appeared on Bartholomew's head.

"Screebees!" screamed Sir Snipps, leaping in the air higher than he was tall. Then he turned and ran shrieking out of the throne room.

"Dear me!" said the king, looking very puzzled. "If Snipps can't do it, this *must* be more than an ordinary hat."

"One hundred and thirty-six," wrote Sir Alaric, wrinkling his brow. "Your Majesty, I advise that you call in your Wise Men."

"A fine idea!" said the king. "Ho, Guard! bring me Nadd. Nadd knows about everything in all my kingdom."

In came an old, old man. He looked at the hat on Bartholomew's head, and he looked at the pile of hats on the floor.

"Nadd, my Wise Man, can you take off his hat?" asked the king. Nadd shook his head solemnly — solemnly no.

"Then fetch me the father of Nadd," commanded the king. "He knows about everything in all my kingdom and in all the world beyond."

In came an even older man. But when he looked at Bartholomew's hats, the father of Nadd merely locked his fingers across his beard and said nothing.

"Then bring me the father of the father of Nadd!" ordered the king. "He knows about everything in all my kingdom, in all the world beyond, and in all other worlds that may happen to be."

Then came the oldest man of them all. But he just looked at Bartholomew and nibbled nervously at the end of his beard.

"Does this mean there is *no one* in my whole kingdom who can take off this boy's hat?" bellowed the king in a terrifying voice.

A small voice came up through the balcony window. "What's the matter, Uncle Derwin?" To Bartholomew, it sounded like the voice of a boy.

The king stepped out on the balcony and leaned over the marble railing. "There's a boy in here . . . just about your age," the king said. "He won't take off his hat."

Bartholomew tiptoed up behind the king and looked down. There stood a boy with a big lace collar — a very proud little boy with his nose in the air. It was the Grand Duke Wilfred, nephew of the king.

"You send him down here," said the Grand Duke Wilfred. "*I'll* fix him."

The king thought for a minute. He pushed back his crown and scratched his head. "Well . . . maybe you can. There's no harm in trying."

"Take him to the Grand Duke Wilfred!" commanded the king. And two of the King's Own Guards led Bartholomew out of the throne room.

"Pooh!" said the Grand Duke Wilfred, looking at Bartholomew's hat and laughing meanly. "*That* hat won't come off? You stand over there." He pointed to a corner where the wall curved out. "I need a little target practice with my bow and arrow."

When Bartholomew saw that the Grand Duke Wilfred had only a child's bow, he didn't feel frightened. He spoke up proudly, "*I* can shoot with my father's big bow."

"My bow's plenty big enough for shooting hats — especially hats like yours," answered Wilfred. And he let fly an arrow. zzZ!... it grazed Bartholomew's forehead and nipped off his hat. Away it blew, and over the parapet. But another hat appeared on his head. zzZ!...zzZ!...zzZ!...the arrows flew...till the grand duke's whole bagful of arrows was gone. And still a hat sat upon Bartholomew's head.

"It's not fair," cried the grand duke. "It's not fair!" He threw down his bow and stamped upon it.

"One hundred and fifty-four hats!" gulped Sir Alaric.

"These hats are driving me mad!" The king's voice rang out through all the palace. "Why waste time with a *child's* bow and arrow. Fetch me the mightiest bow and arrow in all my realm — fetch the yeoman of the bowmen!"

"Yeoman of the bowmen," echoed all the lords and noblemen of the court.

A gigantic man strode out across the terrace. His bow was as big as the branch of a tree. The arrow was twice as long as Bartholomew, and thicker than his wrist.

"Yeoman of the bowmen," said the king, "shoot off this boy's hat...and make it *stay* off!"

Bartholomew was trembling so hard that he could scarcely stand straight. The yeoman bent back his mighty bow.

G-r-r-zibb!...Like a mad giant hornet the arrow tore through the air toward Bartholomew Cubbins.

G-r-r-zapp!...The sharp arrowhead bit through his hat and carried it off — on and on for a full half mile.

G-r-r-zopp!...It plunked to a stop in the heart of an oak tree. Yet there on Bartholomew's head sat another hat.

The face of the yeoman of the bowmen went white as the palace walls. "It's black magic!" he shrieked.

"Black magic, that's *just what it is*," sighed the king with relief. "I should have thought of that before. That makes things simple. Back to the throne room! Call my magicians!"

In the whole throne room there wasn't a sound as loud as a breath. But from the spiral stairs that led down from the southwest tower came the shuffling of slow, padded feet. The magicians were coming! Low and slow, they were chanting words that were strange...

"Dig a hole five furlongs deep,
Down to where the night snakes creep,
Mix and mold the mystic mud,
Malber, Balber, Tidder, Tudd."

In came seven black-gowned magicians, and beside each one stalked a lean black cat. They circled around Bartholomew Cubbins muttering deep and mysterious sounds.

"Stop this useless muttering," ordered the king. "I want a chant that will charm away this boy's hat."

The magicians huddled over Bartholomew and chanted.

"Winkibus
Tinkibus
Fotichee
Klay,
Hat on this demon's head,
Fly far away!
Howl, men, howl away
Howl away, howl away,
Yowl, cats, yowl away,
Yowl away, yowl away!
Hat on this demon's head,
Seep away, creep away, leap away, gleap away,
Never come back!"

"A mighty good chant," said the king, looking very pleased. "Are you sure it will work?"

All the magicians nodded together.

"But," said the king, looking puzzled, "there still *seems* to be a hat upon his head. How long will it take for the charm to work?"

"Be calm, oh, Sire, and have no fears,"

chanted the magicians.

"Our charm will work in ten short years."

"*Ten years!*" gasped the king. "Away, fools!" he shouted. "Out of my sight! I can't wait *ten years* to get rid of his hat. Oh, dear, what *can* I do...what CAN I do?"

"If I were king," whispered the Grand Duke Wilfred, "I'd chop off his head."

"A dreadful thought," said the king, biting his lip. "But I'm afraid I'll have to."

"Young man," he said to Bartholomew Cubbins, and he pointed to a small door at the end of the room, "march down those steps to the dungeon and tell the executioner to chop off your head."

Bartholomew's heart sank into his boots, but he did as the king commanded. "I *must* take off my hat," he said to himself as he started down the long black stairway. "This is my last chance." One hat after another he tore from his head ". . . 156 . . . 157 . . . 158 . . ." It grew colder and damper. ". . . 217 . . . 218 . . . 219 . . ." Down . . . down . . . down. ". . . 231 . . . 232 . . . 233 . . ." It seemed to Bartholomew he must be in the very heart of the mountain.

"Who's there?" said a voice from the blackness.

Bartholomew turned a corner and stepped into the dungeon.

The executioner was whistling and swinging his axe idly, because at the moment he had nothing to do. In spite of his business, he really seemed to be a very pleasant man.

"The king says you must chop off my head," said Bartholomew.

"Oh, I'd hate to," said the executioner, looking at him with a friendly smile. "You seem like such a nice boy."

"Well . . . the king says you have to," said Bartholomew, "so please get it over with."

"All right," sighed the executioner, "but first you've got to take off your hat."

"Why?" asked Bartholomew.

"I don't know," said the executioner, "but it's one of the rules. I can't execute anyone with his hat on."

"All right," said Bartholomew, "you take it off for me."

The executioner leaned across the chopping block and flipped off Bartholomew's hat.

"What's this?" he gasped, blinking through the holes in his mask, as another hat sat on Bartholomew's head. He flipped this one off . . . then another and another.

"Fiddlesticks!" grunted the executioner, throwing his axe on the floor. "I can't execute you at all." And he shook hands with Bartholomew and sent him back upstairs to the king.

The king had been taking a nap on the throne. "What are you doing back here?" he said to Bartholomew, angry at being awakened.

"I'm sorry, Your Majesty," explained Bartholomew. "My head can't come off with my hat on . . . It's against the rules."

"So it can't," said the king, leaning back wearily. "Now how many hats does that make altogether?"

"The executioner knocked off thirteen . . . and I left 178 more on the dungeon steps," answered Bartholomew.

"Three hundred and forty-six hats," mumbled Sir Alaric from behind his scroll.

"Uncle Derwin," yawned the Grand Duke Wilfred, "I suppose I'll have to do away with him. Send him up to the highest turret and I, in person, will push him off."

"Wilfred! I'm surprised at you," said the king. "But I guess it's a good idea."

So the king and the grand duke led Bartholomew Cubbins toward the highest turret.

Up and up and up the turret stairs he climbed behind them.

"This is my *last* — my *very last* chance," thought Bartholomew. He snatched off his hat. "Three hundred and forty-seven!" He snatched off another. He pulled and he tore and he flung them behind him. ". . . 398 . . . 399 . . ." His arms ached from pulling off hats. But still the hats came. Bartholomew climbed on.

". . . 448 . . . 449 . . . 450 . . ." counted Sir Alaric, puffing up the stairs behind him.

Suddenly Sir Alaric stopped. He looked. He took off his triangular spectacles and wiped them on his sleeve. And then he looked again. *The hats began to change!* Hat 451 had, not one, but *two* feathers! Hat 452 had three . . . and 453 also had three *and a little red jewel!* Each new hat was fancier than the hat just before.

"Your Majesty! Your Majesty!" cried out Sir Alaric.

But the king and the grand duke were 'way up where they couldn't hear. They had already reached the top of the highest turret. Bartholomew was following just behind.

"Step right out here and get out on that wall," snapped the Grand Duke Wilfred. "I can't wait to push you off."

But when Bartholomew stepped up on the wall, they gasped in amazement. He was wearing the most beautiful hat that had ever been seen in the Kingdom of Didd. It had a ruby larger than any the king himself had ever owned. It had ostrich plumes, and cockatoo plumes, and mockingbird plumes, and paradise plumes. Beside *such* a hat even the king's crown seemed like nothing.

The Grand Duke Wilfred took a quick step forward. Bartholomew thought his end had come at last.

"Wait!" shouted the king. He could not take his eyes off the magnificent hat.

"I *won't* wait," the grand duke talked back to the king. "I'm going to push him off now. That new big hat makes me madder than ever." And he flung out his arms to push Bartholomew off.

But the king was quicker than Wilfred. He grabbed him by the back of his fine lace collar. "This is to teach you," His Majesty said sternly, "that grand dukes *never* talk back to their king." And he turned the Grand Duke Wilfred over his knee and spanked him soundly, right on the seat of his royal silk pants.

"And now," smiled the king, lifting Bartholomew down from the wall, "it would be nice if you'd sell me that wonderful hat!"

". . . 498 . . . 499 . . ." broke in the tired voice of Sir Alaric, who had just arrived at the top of the steps, "and *that* . . ." he pointed to the hat on Bartholomew's head, "makes exactly 500!"

"*Five Hundred!*" exclaimed the king. "Will you sell it for five hundred pieces of gold?"

"Anything you say, Sire," answered Bartholomew. "You see . . . I've never sold one before."

The king's hands trembled with joy as he reached for the hat.

Slowly, slowly, Bartholomew felt the weight of the great hat lifting from his head. He held his breath. . . . Then suddenly he felt the cold evening breezes blow through his hair. His face broke into a happy smile. The head of Bartholomew Cubbins was bare!

"Look, Your Majesty! *Look!*" he shouted to the king.

"No! *You* look at *me*," answered the king.

And he put the great hat on right over his crown.

Arm in arm, the king and Bartholomew went down to the counting-room to count out the gold. Then the king sent Bartholomew home to his parents . . . no basket on his arm, no hat on his head, but with five hundred pieces of gold in a bag.

And the king commanded that the hat he had bought, and all the other hats, too, be kept forever in a great crystal case by the side of his throne.

But neither Bartholomew Cubbins, nor King Derwin himself, nor anyone else in the Kingdom of Didd could ever explain how the strange thing had happened. They only could say it just "happened to happen" and was not very likely to happen again.

Mei Li[9]

THOMAS HANDFORTH

During the six years Thomas Handforth lived in Peking, he delighted in making sketches of traditional Chinese life and customs. Sword dancers, stilt walkers, jugglers, fortune tellers, peddlers, and priests came to pose for him. One day the idea occurred to him that he would like to put these picturesque friends of his into a picture book for children. While he was trying to decide on the principal character, he met Mei Li and was so charmed with her that he knew he had found the perfect heroine for his story. Mei Li promptly brought her little friends to be drawn, and her small white dog and her duck. Gradually the book took shape, and for the extraordinarily beautiful lithographs the artist was awarded the Caldecott medal for the most distinguished picture book of the year.

In North China, near the Great Wall, is a city shut in by a Wall. Not far from the city in the snow-covered country is a house with a wall round it, too. Inside the house on the morning before New Year's Day, everyone was very busy. Mei Li, a little girl with a candle-top pigtail, was scrubbing and sweeping and dusting. Her mother, Mrs.

9 Complete text from Thomas Handforth, *Mei Li* (Doubleday, 1938).

Wang, was baking and frying and chopping. Her brother, San Yu, was fixing and tasting and mixing. A fine feast was being prepared for the Kitchen God, who would come at midnight to every family in China to tell them what they must do during the coming year.

Only Uncle Wang sat without working. He was talking and laughing and singing of the sights to be seen in the city. Often, with his camels, he went there to sell vegetables; so he knew.

San Yu stopped to listen happily, because his mother had just told him that he could go that day to the New Year Fair in the city.

Mrs. Wang stopped to listen cheerily because she thought of the red candles and paper money that San Yu would bring back to please the Kitchen God.

Mei Li stopped to listen sadly because little girls always had to stay home.

"Eiya! Eiya!" she whimpered to herself, wagging her candle-top. "If I always stay at home, what can I be good for? I am going to take my lucky treasures and have adventures like San Yu."

Into the pocket of her winter big coat Mei Li packed her three lucky pennies and her three lucky marbles — one lapis blue, one coral red, and one jade green.

Then she followed San Yu little by little through the courtyard, being careful to wish a happy New Year to the ducks and pigs.

"New rejoicing, Mrs. Ugly Pig!" she said, bowing politely. "New rejoicing, Stupid Mr. Duck!" she said, again bowing politely.

When no one was looking she slipped quickly through the gate.

Outside the gate Mei Li caught up with San Yu.

"Please, San Yu, take me on the ice sled with you as far as the city gate," she whispered.

"What can a girl do at the Fair?" scoffed San Yu.

"I will give you my lapis-blue marble if you will," said Mei Li.

And San Yu whispered back, "Can-Do."

Then Igo, the small white dog, begged to go, too. San Yu's thrush did not want to be left at home either. So San Yu, Mei Li, Igo and the thrush all set out together on an ice sled. A man pulled it, slipping and sliding down the frozen canal.

They zipped and they whizzed along the snow-white canal. Soon they came to the bridge just outside the city. There Mei Li gave one of her lucky pennies to a hungry beggar girl.

"Thank you, thank you!" said the girl, whose name was Lidza.

"What fun for a girl to go to the Fair! A lucky penny will bring you luck. But remember! You must be back before the Big Gate closes, or you will not be able to leave the city and go home tonight. And then you could not greet the Kitchen God."

Across the bridge a donkey was waiting for them. San Yu, Mei Li, the thrush and Igo climbed on his back, and jerkity-jerk he trotted off through the gate in the thick wall.

Now they were inside the city, trotting along a wide street.

They saw people riding in rickshas, and people on camels, ladies in glass carriages, men on shaggy Mongol ponies, and other boys and girls on donkeys. And all of them were dressed in their finest clothes, and all of them were going merrily to enjoy the New Year holiday. It was just as exciting as Uncle Wang had said.

It was lunchtime when they arrived at the Great Square. There some of the city children were eating bean-curd sweets and buying sugared fruits on long sticks.

Mei Li wanted candy too, but even more she wanted a firecracker. She spent her second penny on firecrackers. She was too frightened to shoot them off herself, so she gave them to San Yu and ran away with her fingers in her ears.

"Bang! Bang!" popped the crackers.

"Pooh! Pooh!" sneered San Yu. "Girls are always afraid. What *can* a girl do at the New Year Fair?"

"Lots of things," said Mei Li. "Look at those girls in the circus over there. They can walk on stilts. They can balance on a tightrope. They can throw pots and pans in the air with their feet. And so can I!"

She ran to a circus girl who looked strong. "Oh, please, will you hold me upside down in the palm of your hand?" Mei Li begged. "I want to try it."

The circus girl lifted her high in the air. Mei Li balanced all right, but her legs wobbled a little.

"Ho!" jeered San Yu. "Anyone can learn that kind of trick. But only boys can be real actors!" San Yu had dressed himself up as a wise old man with a silly long beard. He was performing with one of the boys in the traveling show who was dressed like an emperor with a crown like a pot of flowers. They were singing songs together in high squeaky voices.

Girls couldn't be actors, Mei Li knew. She looked around for something else to do. There in one corner of the Fairgrounds, was a black bear with a ring in his nose. She would show San Yu how brave she was. She would make the bear do tricks!

Mei Li's candle-top trembled as she held out a bit of beancake to the bear. The bear bounced up and down and flapped his padded paws, begging for the cake.

"That's a tottering, *tame* old bear," shouted San Yu. "Watch me while I hunt a wild, wicked lion!"

"Mercy!" squealed Mei Li. "That long-eared thing is not a lion, but two boys with a mask and a straw tail. Be careful not to shoot them!"

Mei Li ran now to join some girls who were riding circus ponies. Her pony pranced around the ring, and her candle-top bobbed up and down as she danced on his back. She was beginning to feel like a real circus performer, but suddenly she missed San Yu.

She hurried down the street and found him at the Bridge of Wealth. Under the Bridge of Wealth hung a little bell, and under the bell lay a skinny, wrinkled priest who mumbled, "Ring the bell with a penny, and you will have money for all the year."

"Oh," wailed Mei Li, "my last lucky penny, and the bell is so tiny! I'm sure I could never hit it. Here, San Yu, you throw it for me." And she gave her last penny to San Yu.

"Ting-ling!" tinkled the bell.

"Ho, I am rich!" sang San Yu. "Igo and I are going to buy a kite. Look after my thrush while I'm gone."

"Oh," spluttered Mei Li, and her candle-top whisked with rage, "my last lucky penny! What can I do now?" She started sadly up a near-by hill. And there at the top, under a gnarled old pine tree, sat a smooth young priest telling fortunes with bamboo sticks.

"Tell me a fine fortune and I'll give you my coral-red marble," pleaded Mei Li. "My brother is going to be rich, and I want to be as lucky as he."

"You will rule over a kingdom," replied the priest, waving his magic wand over the sticks and taking the coral-red marble.

Mei Li ran happily down the hill. Surely, if the fortune sticks said she was going to rule a kingdom she would. But how could she rule a kingdom unless she was a princess? And who ever heard of a princess without a crown?

At the foot of the hill she met some girls who were all dressed up to go to the Fair. Mei Li told them about the fortune and they helped her to make a crown with a jade-green marble fixed in front.

Mei Li's candle-top wagged proudly above it as she strutted down the street. This was much more fun than performing in a circus. She came to a large toy shop.

Surely a princess with a crown could visit a toy shop, even though she had no lucky pennies to spend, thought Mei Li. Inside there were rows upon rows of tiny figures, priests, peddlers, dancing girls, wise men, musicians, monkeys and deer.

"Perhaps," thought Mei Li, as she played, "they are all here to honor me!" But the little figures were made of painted wood, and very soon Mei Li left them.

The next room was bright with New Year lanterns made to look like fishes. All the bulgy fishy eyes stared at her.

"They are looking at my lovely crown," thought Mei Li, and her candle-top swished with vanity.

In the next hall, large grasshopper, crab, turtle and moth lanterns stared at her. But the Princess Mei Li did not feel happy with such big, unpleasant bugs. She had never seen any like those in the walled garden at home. She hurried outdoors.

Outdoors a strong wind was blowing. Suddenly a gray hawk swooped through the cold sky. Mei Li pressed San Yu's thrush close to her, so that the hawk could not hurt it.

She ran as quickly as she could toward the market place. The hawk swooped close, and closer, and closer still!

"Poor little thrush!" thought Mei Li, her candle-top stiff with fright. "What can I do to save you?"

Just then a large goose escaped from its basket. Quickly Mei Li crawled under the basket and lay still as dead.

Thump! Thump! Thump! beat her heart. "Haw! Haw! Haw!" echoed some throaty snorts.

"Those 'haws' are not hawk 'haws'," Mei Li said to her thrush. She peeked through a hole in the basket and saw three clumsy camels laughing at her.

"Ha! Ha! Ha!" came from the other side, and three deep voices said, "There's the rascal we're looking for!"

"Bandits!" thought Mei Li. Again she lay still as dead, and her heart beat Thump! Thump! Thump!

Then she felt a tug, tug, tugging at her candle-top and a tug, tug, tugging at her trousers, and a yap, yap, yapping in her ear and a yap, yap, yapping at her feet. It was Igo.

"Tee-hee-hee!" hooted San Yu, who had been hiding behind a baby camel. "That wasn't a hawk chasing you, it was only my kite."

"You are brave for a girl, to protect San Yu's thrush, but don't you know your own uncle in his fur hat?" said Uncle Wang. "I have been hunting for you all day, and if we don't hurry back on the camels, before the city gate closes, we'll not get home tonight to greet the Kitchen God."

"Up we go," said Uncle Wang, and he climbed on the first camel, holding Mei Li safely in front of him. San Yu and his thrush sat on the second camel, and Igo rode proudly by himself on the third.

And then the camels, with the riders between their humps and the baby camel tagging behind, gallumphed through the evening light. Faster and faster they raced through the darkening streets: through the falling sparks of bursting New Year rockets. They were too late! The city gate was swinging closed!

But no! Lidza, the beggar girl, was holding the heavy door open with her feet. She knew that Mei Li must be home by midnight to greet the Kitchen God. And even five policemen and five soldiers could not force her away until Mei Li was through the gate.

Faster and faster the camels sped on and up and on and down through the hills that looked like dragons in the dark night.

Mei Li's pennies were gone. Her marbles were gone. Her crown was lost. She was so hungry that her stomach ached, and so tired that her candle-top lay flat on her head. Prancing ponies, bouncing bears and long-eared lions seemed to be following her. She had forgotten she was a princess.

And surely no kingdom could be as nice as home. How glad she was at the sight of her house among the trees behind the wall!

"Oh, the best part of going to the Fair is getting home," cried Mei Li, as Uncle Wang lifted her down from the camel's back. "And we are still in time for the New Year feast."

"Do not be sad because you have brought home no presents," said Mrs. Wang to San Yu. "You have brought us the princess who rules our hearts." And while she waited to greet the Kitchen God, Mei Li wondered: "Even Mamma knows that I am a princess just as the fortune sticks said, but where can my kingdom be?"

At midnight, when the Kitchen God appeared behind the flame and smoke of burning incense, behind the honey cakes and dumplings which Mrs. Wang had cooked for him, he said solemnly, blinking at Mei Li, "This house is your kingdom and palace. Within its walls all living things are your loyal, loving subjects."

Mei Li sighed happily, "It will do for a while, anyway."

This is the thrifty princess,
Whose house is always clean,
No dirt within her kingdom
Is ever to be seen.

Her food is fit
For a king to eat,
Her hair and clothes
Are always neat.

BIBLIOGRAPHY

Ardizzone, Edward, author illustrator. *Little Tim and the Brave Sea Captain.* Oxford University Press, new edition, 1955. (K–Grade 2)

A picture book of distinction which a young English artist made for his small son. The water colors, filled with drama and realism, show an understanding of seas and ships. *Tim All Alone* was awarded the first Kate Greenaway medal in 1957. This English award corresponds to the Caldecott medal in America.

Aulaire, Ingri and Edgar Parin d', author-illustrators. *Children of the Northlights.* Viking Press, 1935. (Grades 2–4)

After reading *Ola,* children will enjoy this story of Lise and Lasse in Lapland. The picture book is the happy result of the D'Aulaires' long journey by boat and sled into the north of Norway.

Bannerman, Helen, author-illustrator. *The Story of Little Black Sambo.* J. B. Lippincott, 1923. (K–Grade 3)

Further adventures of this favorite nursery hero are found in *Sambo and the Twins.*

Bemelmans, Ludwig, author-illustrator. *Madeline.* Simon & Schuster, 1939. (Grades 1–3)

Bemelmans has a genius for creating a sense of place. Here he creates the spell of Paris as he tells the story of Madeline, a child who does not take kindly to the regimentation of a French boarding school. *Madeline's Rescue* was awarded the Caldecott medal in 1954.

Beskow, Elsa, author-illustrator. *Pelle's New Suit;* trans. by Marion Letcher Woodburn. Harper & Brothers, n.d. (K–Grade 3)

A picture book from Sweden with twelve full-page illustrations in color.

Brooke, L. Leslie, author-illustrator. *Johnny Crow's Party.* Frederick Warne, 1907. (K–Grade 3)

This equally delightful picture book follows *Johnny Crow's Garden.*

Brown, Marcia, author-illustrator. *Little Carousel.* Charles Scribner's Sons, 1946. (K–Grade 2)

A captivating picture book that tells what happened when Mr. Corelli brought his little carousel to a city street.

Brown, Margaret Wise. *The Little Island,* by Golden MacDonald, *pseud.;* illus. by Leonard Weisgard. Doubleday, 1946. (Grades 1–3)

On a little island in the ocean there lived lobsters, seals, spiders, and kingfishers. Once a kitten came ashore and learned the secret of being an island from a wise and talkative fish. Brilliant pictures show the changing seasons on the island. Awarded the Caldecott medal in 1947.

Brown, Margaret Wise. *Wheel on the Chimney;* illus. by Tibor Gergely. J. B. Lippincott, 1954. (K–Grade 3)

A thoroughly satisfying picture book of the stork migration between Hungary and Africa. The artist's striking double-page spreads of storks in flight convey a sense of the beauty and mystery of bird flight.

Brunhoff, Jean de, author-illustrator. *The Story of Babar, the Little Elephant;* trans. from the French by Merle S. Haas. Random House, 1933. (Grades 1–3)

A gay, sophisticated, yet childlike picture book of Babar, the little elephant who ran away from the jungle, found consolation in the exhilaration of city life, and then returned to the jungle to be crowned king of the elephants.

Burton, Virginia Lee, author-illustrator. *Mike Mulligan and His Steam Shovel.* Houghton Mifflin, 1939. (Grades 1–3)

A picture book which happily combines realistic and imaginative elements touched with humor. Mike remains faithful to his outmoded steam shovel, Mary Ann, and together they dig a strange home for themselves in the town of Popperville. The artist received the Caldecott medal in 1943 for her picture book *The Little House.*

Caldecott, Randolph, illustrator. *Picture Books.* 4 vols. Frederick Warne, 1878–85. (K–Grade 3)

This talented artist, for whom the annual American picture book award is named, has taken sixteen favorite nursery rhymes and made them into picture books. His drawings, distinguished for simplicity of line, are full of action and spirited humor.

Chönz, Selina. *A Bell for Ursli;* illus. by Alois Carigiet. Oxford University Press, 1950. (K–Grade 3)

Rhyming text and radiant water colors tell the story of a little boy who lives high in the mountains of Switzerland. The beauty and charm of the Swiss edition have been retained in the American printing.

Clark, Ann Nolan. *In My Mother's House;* illus. by Velino Herrera. Viking Press, 1941. (Grades 2–4)

The simple day-to-day life of a Pueblo Indian child in the Southwest is told in quiet, cadenced prose. The drawings, by a distinguished Indian mural painter, add distinction to the book.

Daugherty, James, author-illustrator. *Andy and the Lion.* Viking Press, 1938. (Grades 1–3)

A vigorous, modern version of the famous Greek fable of Androcles and the Lion, illustrated with masterly drawings.

Ets, Marie Hall, author-illustrator. *Play With Me.* Viking Press, 1955. (K–Grade 2)

There is a rare quality to this sensitive story of a little girl who tries to play with the wild creatures of the meadow. They all run away from her. Then, when she sits perfectly still, one by one, they come to her. *In the Forest* tells of a little boy's meeting with the animals of the forest.

Flack, Marjorie, author-illustrator. *Angus and the Ducks.* Doubleday, 1930. (K–Grade 2)

An amusing story of a little Scotch terrier whose curiosity led him to slip under the hedge. Children will want to follow his adventures in *Angus and the Cat* and *Angus Lost.*

Flack, Marjorie. *The Story of Ping;* illus. by Kurt Wiese. Viking Press, 1933. (Grades 1–3)

A small classic which tells of a Peking duckling's night of adventure on the Yangtze River. The pictures heighten the delight of the story.

Françoise, *pseud.,* author-illustrator. *Jeanne-Marie Counts Her Sheep.* Charles Scribner's Sons, 1951. (K–Grade 1)

A little French girl counts the number of lambs her sheep may have, and plans what she will buy with the money from their wool. Followed by *Springtime for Jeanne-Marie; Noël for Jeanne-Marie;* and *Jeanne-Marie in Gay Paris.*

Gág, Wanda, author-illustrator. *A B C Bunny;* hand-lettered by Howard Gág. Coward-McCann, 1933. (K–Grade 2)

Soft-toned lithographs full of rhythm combine with sparkling verse to tell by way of the alphabet an absorbing story of a rabbit.

Gág, Wanda, author-illustrator. *Snippy and Snappy.* Coward-McCann, 1931. (K–Grade 3)

After *Millions of Cats* children will enjoy this story of two little field mice who venture forth

in search of cheese and are rescued just as they are about to investigate a mouse trap.

Geisel, Theodor Seuss, author-illustrator. *And to Think That I Saw It on Mulberry Street.* Vanguard Press, 1937. (K–Grade 3)

A small boy's imagination peoples a prosaic street with strange and marvelous creations. Children will want to read the other delightful nonsense tales by this author.

Graham, Al. *Timothy Turtle;* illus. by Tony Palazzo. Viking Press, 1946. (Grades 1–3)

Timothy Turtle was not satisfied with his life and longed for fame, but after an exciting journey over Took-a-Look hill he was glad to return to his ferrying business.

Gramatky, Hardie, author-illustrator. *Little Toot.* G. P. Putnam's Sons, 1939. (K–Grade 2)

Small boys and their fathers will enjoy this story of the saucy little tugboat.

Hader, Berta and Elmer, author-illustrators. *The Big Snow.* Macmillan, 1948. (K–Grade 3)

Delicate pictures in color and in black and white show the animals of the woods preparing for winter. Then comes the snow and through the long winter the animals and birds are fed by two kindly folk who live on the hillside. Awarded the Caldecott medal in 1949.

Handforth, Thomas, author-illustrator. *Mei Li.* Doubleday, 1938. (Grades 1–3)

Mr. Handforth made the distinguished drawings while living in China. Both illustrations and text picture with fidelity the traditional Chinese life. Awarded the Caldecott medal in 1939.

Langstaff, John. *Frog Went A-Courtin';* retold by John Langstaff; pictures by Feodor Rojankovsky. Harcourt, Brace, 1955. (Grades 1–3)

Many versions of the well-known ballad have contributed to the making of this new American version illustrated by rollicking drawings in color. Awarded the Caldecott medal in 1956. The two gifted collaborators have created a delightful new version of another old rhyme in their more recent picture book *Over in the Meadow;* the exquisite drawings capture the magic and wonder of nature.

Leaf, Munro. *The Story of Ferdinand;* illus. by Robert Lawson. Viking Press, 1936. (Grades 1–4)

Any self-respecting bull in Spain goes in for bullfighting, but not Ferdinand. He preferred to smell flowers. This is the story of what happened when Ferdinand found himself in the arena.

Lipkind, William. *Finders Keepers;* illus. by Nicolas Mordvinoff. Harcourt, Brace, 1951. (K–Grade 3)

The dilemma of two dogs with one bone, told in crisp text and pictures distinguished by droll imagination. Awarded the Caldecott medal in 1952. *The Two Reds* is a story of a red-haired boy and a red-furred cat.

McCloskey, Robert, author-illustrator. *Make Way for Ducklings.* Viking Press, 1941. (K–Grade 3)

A truly American picture book. Mr. and Mrs. Mallard and their eight ducklings make their home on an island in the Charles River. Aided by an Irish policeman, Mrs. Mallard and her ducklings march sedately through Boston traffic to reach the pond in the Public Garden where peanuts and popcorn are plentiful. Awarded the Caldecott medal in 1942. *Blueberries for Sal* and *One Morning in Maine* are equally delightful. *Time of Wonder* received the Caldecott medal in 1958.

McGinley, Phyllis. *All Around the Town;* illus. by Helen Stone. J. B. Lippincott, 1948. (K–Grade 3)

Poems of the sights and sounds of the city present the letters of the alphabet with an ingenious use of the phonetics of each letter. Fine interpretative drawings.

Morrow, Elizabeth. *The Painted Pig; a Mexican Picture Book;* illus. by René d'Harnoncourt. Alfred A. Knopf, 1930. (Grades 2–4)

A Mexican picture book with distinguished illustrations tells how Pita and Pedro search for a painted pig bank.

Minarik, Else Holmelund. *Little Bear;* illus. by Maurice Sendak. Harper & Brothers, 1957. (Grades 1–3)

Easy text and engaging pictures tell of four events in the life of Little Bear.

Politi, Leo, author-illustrator. *The Song of the Swallows.* Charles Scribner's Sons, 1949. (K–Grade 3)

A tender, poetic story of Little Juan and how he helped ring the bells at the Capistrano Mission to welcome the swallows as they came flying in from the sea on St. Joseph's day. Pictures are in soft colors. Awarded the Caldecott medal in 1950.

Potter, Beatrix, author-illustrator. *The Tailor of Gloucester.* Frederick Warne, 1903. (Grades 1–4)

After reading the Peter Rabbit books, children will enjoy this beautiful little Christmas story of a poor tailor and his cat who lived "in the time of swords and periwigs." John Masefield calls this little book "a gem of English prose."

Rey, H. A., author-illustrator. *Curious George.* Houghton Mifflin, 1941. (K–Grade 2)

The zestful activity of a small monkey and the difficulty he has in getting used to the city before he goes to live in a zoo are told in simple text and bright pictures. Followed by *Curious George Gets a Job; Curious George Rides a Bike,* and *Curious George Wins a Medal.*

Sayers, Frances Clarke. *Bluebonnets for Lucinda;* illus. by Helen Sewell. Viking Press, 1934. (Grades 1–3)

The story of how Lucinda saw bluebonnets growing in Texas in the spring of the year, and how she tamed the geese with her music box. A happy combination of author and artist.

Tresselt, Alvin. *White Snow, Bright Snow;* illus. by Roger Duvoisin. Lothrop, Lee & Shepard, 1947. (K–Grade 3)

Poetic text and full-page illustrations in soft blue accented with touches of red and yellow convey the beauty of the first snowfall, the activities of winter, and the approach of spring. Awarded the Caldecott medal in 1948.

Ward, Lynd, author-illustrator. *The Biggest Bear.* Houghton Mifflin, 1952. (K–Grade 2)

A thoroughly American picture book which had its roots in the author's own childhood. Johnny Orchard longed for a bearskin to hang on his barn, but the bear he found was much too little to shoot. Johnny kept him as a pet, but the bear became more and more of a problem as he grew up. How Johnny found a home for his bear makes a heartwarming story told almost entirely by the pictures. Awarded the Caldecott medal in 1953.

Yashima, Taro, *pseud.,* author-illustrator. *Crow Boy.* Viking Press, 1955. (K–Grade 3)

The author-artist has created a sensitive picture book from the poignant memory of his own childhood in Japan. A shy, lonely mountain boy leaves his home at dawn and returns at sunset to go to a village school. He is ignored by his classmates until an understanding teacher shows them that Crow Boy has much to give them. The pictures are in glowing colors. *The Umbrella* has the same tender, poignant quality in both pictures and text.

References for the Adult

See also bibliography following "Illustrators of Children's Books" in the Appendix.

Brown, Marcia. "Distinction in Picture Books," *The Horn Book Magazine,* Vol. 25, Sept.–Oct. 1949, pp. 382–395.

Dalgliesh, Alice. "Small Children and Books," *The Horn Book Magazine,* Vol. 9, Feb. 1933, pp. 158–163.

Duff, Annis. *"Bequest of Wings"; a Family's Pleasures with Books.* Viking Press, rev. ed. 1954.

"The Man of It," pp. 39–58.

Eaton, Anne Thaxter. *Reading with Children.* Viking Press, 1940.

"Through Magic Doorways," pp. 41–65.

Meigs, Cornelia, and others. *A Critical History of Children's Literature.* Macmillan, 1953.

"The March of Picture Books," by Elizabeth Nesbitt, pp. 399–416; "The Artist as Storyteller," by Ruth Hill Viguers, pp. 582–590.

Miller, Bertha Mahony, and Elinor Whitney Field, eds. *Caldecott Medal Books: 1938–1957.* The Horn Book, Inc., 1957.

A companion volume to *Newbery Medal Books: 1922–1955.* Contains the acceptance speeches of the artists, their biographies, a brief résumé of each book, an introductory paper on Randolph Caldecott, the artist for whom the medal is named, and a critical analysis "What Is a Picture Book?" by Esther Averill.

Mitchell, Marguerite. "Artists and Picture Books," *The Horn Book Magazine,* Vol. 13, May–June 1937, pp. 139–143.

Sayers, Frances Clarke. "Through These Sweet Fields," *The Horn Book Magazine,* Vol. 18, Nov. 1942, pp. 436–444.

Smith, Lillian H. *The Unreluctant Years; a Critical Approach to Children's Literature.* American Library Association, 1953.

"Picture Books," pp. 115–129.

The D'Aulaires

Aulaire, Ingri and Edgar Parin d'. "Working Together on Books for Children," *The Horn Book Magazine,* Vol. 16, Aug. 1940, pp. 247–255.

Mahony, Bertha E. "Ingri and Edgar d'Aulaire," *The Horn Book Magazine,* Vol. 16, Aug. 1940, pp. 257–264.

Massee, May. "Ingri and Edgar Parin d'Aulaire: A Sketch," *The Horn Book Magazine,* Vol. 11, Sept.–Oct. 1935, pp. 265–270.

L. Leslie Brooke

The L. Leslie Brooke Number. *The Horn Book Magazine,* Vol. 17, May–June 1941.

Moore, Anne Carroll. "Leslie Brooke: Pied Piper of English Picture Books," in *My Roads to Childhood.* Doubleday, 1939, pp. 267–271.

Virginia Lee Burton

Burton, Virginia Lee. "Making Picture Books," *The Horn Book Magazine,* Vol. 19, July 1943, pp. 228–232.

Hogarth, Grace Allen. "Virginia Lee Burton, Creative Artist," *The Horn Book Magazine,* Vol. 19, July 1943, pp. 221–227.

Françoise

Dalgliesh, Alice. "Françoise Speaks to Children," *The Horn Book Magazine,* Vol. 29, Dec. 1953, pp. 442–446.

Wanda Gág

Wanda Gág Memorial Number. *The Horn Book Magazine,* Vol. 23, May 1947.

Dobbs, Rose. "All Creation, Wanda Gág and Her Family," *The Horn Book Magazine,* Vol. 11, Nov.–Dec. 1935, pp. 367–373.

Thomas Handforth

Thomas Handforth Memorial Number. *The Horn Book Magazine,* Oct. 19, 1950.

Coatsworth, Elizabeth. A review of Thomas Handforth's *Mei Li,* in *The Horn Book Magazine,* Vol. 15, May–June 1939, pp. 149–151.

The Petershams

Green, Irene Smith. "Maud and Miska Petersham," *The Horn Book Magazine,* Vol. 22, July 1946, pp. 248–253.

Leo Politi

Livsey, Rosemary. "Leo Politi, Friend of All," *The Horn Book Magazine,* Vol. 25, March–April 1949, pp. 97–108.

Beatrix Potter

The Art of Beatrix Potter; with an Appreciation by Anne Carroll Moore. Frederick Warne, 1955.

"The Art of Beatrix Potter is a revelation of the hidden sources of her powers as a creator of children's books of great originality and timeless value. . . . To those who have known Beatrix Potter's books from childhood and have shared them with children, turning these pages becomes a veritable treasure hunt for the familiar and a fresh discovery of the artist herself." – From the Appreciation. See also Dorothy P. Lathrop's review in *The Horn Book Magazine,* Vol. 31, Sept.–Oct. 1935, pp. 331–356.

De la Mare, Walter. "Peter Rabbit, Beatrix Potter and Friends," *The New York Times Book Review*, Sept. 7, 1952.

Lane, Margaret. *The Tale of Beatrix Potter; a Biography*. Frederick Warne, 1946.
A skillful treatment of the influences in the life of Beatrix Potter which helped develop her genius.

Mahony, Bertha E. "Beatrix Potter and Her Nursery Classics," *The Horn Book Magazine*, Vol. 17, May–June 1941, pp. 230–238.

Nesbitt, Elizabeth. "Classics in Miniature — Beatrix Potter," in Cornelia Meigs and others, *A Critical History of Children's Literature*. Macmillan, 1953. Pp. 344–355.

"Peter Rabbit's Birthday." *Life Magazine*, Dec. 6, 1952, p. 113.

Potter, Beatrix. "Over the Hills and Far Away," *The Horn Book Magazine*, Vol. 5, Feb. 1921, pp. 3–10.

"Beatrix Potter in Letters," *The Horn Book Magazine*, Vol. 20, May–June 1946, pp. 214–224.

Reed, Elizabeth Connell. "The Little Potters," *The Horn Book Magazine*, Vol. 31, Dec. 1935, pp. 433–442.

Stevens, Elizabeth H. "A Visit to Mrs. Tiggy-Winkle," *The Horn Book Magazine*, April 1958, pp. 131–136.

Fables

"Fables in sooth are not what they appear;
Our moralists are mice, and such small deer.
We yawn at sermons, but we gladly turn
To moral tales, and so amused, we learn."[1]

W

HEN THE ANIMAL TALE IS TOLD
with an acknowledged moral purpose, it becomes a *fable.*"[2] Thus does Stith
Thompson, the great scholar of folklore, define the genre which is familiar to
us all. So universal is the knowledge of such stories as *The Dog in the Manger,
The Lion and the Mouse,* and *The Boy Who Cried Wolf,* that we seem to
have been born knowing them. They are almost part of our intuitive knowledge, and few can chart the day and hour in which they were first encountered.

Children, and other readers of folklore, are quite accustomed to a world in
which beasts and men speak a common language, change worlds and shapes
upon occasion, render help to one another, or wage wars of wit and cunning.
The anthropomorphic treatment of animals is a source of entertainment even
in the sophistication of our own day. Witness the popularity of Pogo in the
comic strips, and of the animated cartoon on the moving picture screen.

No doubt the fable is derived from the habit of the primitive mind which
considered animals as the equal of man, or possessed of magical powers beyond
him. "What is characteristic of primitive mentality is not its logic but its
general sentiment of life . . . ," writes Ernst Cassirer. "Primitive man by no
means lacks the ability to grasp the empirical differences of things. But in
his conception of nature and life all these differences are obliterated by a
stronger feeling; the deep conviction of a fundamental and indelible *solidarity
of life* that bridges over the mutiplicity and variety of its single forms."[3]

When the familiar animals of folklore were made to bear upon their backs
the burden of a moral, the *fable* was born, marking the development of a
degree of sophistication in man. The fables as we know them owe their wide
dissemination, not to the oral tradition of folklore, but to two great written
or literary sources, one in India and the other in Greece. "Of the five or six
hundred fables belonging to the two literary traditions of India and Greece,"
says Stith Thompson, "fewer than fifty seem to have been recorded from oral

[1] Jean de la Fontaine.
[2] Stith Thompson, *The Folktale* (Dryden Press, New York, 1946), p. 10.
[3] Ernst Cassirer, *An Essay on Man* (Doubleday Anchor Books), p. 109.

storytellers." [4] The Greek cycle of fables is ascribed to the authorship of one Aesop, about whose origins, fate, and writing there are as many legends as those surrounding Homer. He was a Greek slave at Samos, living some time in the sixth century B.C., says one account, a swarthy man (Aesop means black) and deformed, with a sharp wit that enabled him to say through the medium of the fable what he dared not say directly, in criticism of his time.

The English scholar Joseph Jacobs has proved that the fables of Aesop came mainly from a collection made in 300 B.C. by Demetrius Phalerus, founder of the Alexandrian Library; therefore, he says, "The answer to the question 'who wrote Aesop?' is simple: 'Demetrius of Phaleron.' " [5] Whatever their origin, they early became the heritage of the English tongue, since Aesop's fables were translated from the French and published by England's first printer, William Caxton, in 1484. Sir Roger L'Estrange, in 1692, made the best and largest collection of fables in English, especially designed for the reading of children, including some not attributed to Aesop. The Croxall edition of 1722 was also addressed to children. This edition, together with that of Thomas James in 1848, formed the basis for the most distinguished collection of Aesop's fables published in America, the one edited and illustrated by Boris Artzybasheff. [6]

A second cycle of fables has its origins in India, the great Hindu collection known as the *Panchatantra*, or the *Five Books*. This was in existence as early as 200 B.C. These fables are characterized by an intricate interweaving of story within story, a scheme which is common to the Orient, as the *Arabian Nights* exemplifies. The animals of these fables, unlike those of the simpler tales of Aesop, do not act in accordance with their basic animal character. They are, rather, human beings wearing animal masks, giving voice to wit and wisdom in epigrammatic verse quoted from sacred writings. "It is as if the animals in some English beast fable were to justify their actions by quotations from Shakespeare and the Bible." [7] The fables of Aesop, taken as a whole, afford shrewd observations on the behavior of man, but those of the *Panchatantra* come closer to forming a philosophy of life.

> Not rank, but character, is birth;
> It is not eyes, but wits that see;
> True wisdom 'tis to cease from wrong;
> Contentment is prosperity. [8]

These same fables, in their Arabic version, are known as *The Fables of Bidpai*. A second ancient source of fable, originating in the East, are the *Jataka* tales. They are stories clustered about the central theme of the myriad births of the Buddha who, in accordance with the Buddhistic belief in the transmigration

4 Stith Thompson, *The Folktale*, p. 218.

5 Joseph Jacobs, *Aesop's Fables* (first edition, 1864; latest, 1926), Introduction. Quoted in Percy Muir, *English Children's Books* (Batsford, London, 1954), p. 24.

6 Published by the Viking Press, 1933.

7 Arthur W. Ryder, trans., *Gold's Gloom, Tales from the Panchatantra* (University of Chicago Press, 1925), p. 2.

8 *Ibid.*, p. 17.

of the soul, suffered himself to be born in many shapes of the animal world and the world of nature. The earliest version of the well-loved *Henny Penny* and the *Tar Baby* story can be traced to this source.

Marie Shedlock, the noted English storyteller, whose influence as artist and teacher reached far beyond the boundaries of her own country, made a distinguished collection of the Jataka tales (*Eastern Stories and Legends*), directly relating them to children in her versions to be told or read aloud. In addition to the typical moral purpose of the fable, these stories have about them an aura of compassion. They seem remarkably contemporary in the light of Albert Schweitzer's statement of belief: "a reverence for life."

Of all the tellers of fables, only one has been called *Le Fablier*, the Fabler, and that one is Jean de la Fontaine (1621–1695). Using the fables of Aesop as a basis, drawing upon other fables of the medieval world, and inventing some of his own, he made the telling of them an art, and himself the master storyteller. He gave verse form to the tales, relating them to his own time and country, painting them, as it were, in a French landscape, and satirizing, with gentle humor, his contemporaries. He endowed the tales, as he himself stated, with "a certain piquancy . . . originality and humor. When I say humor I do not mean jocosity, but an alluring, irresistible something that can be imparted to any subject however serious." [9] The fables of La Fontaine are one of the pillars of French literature, and the children of France know them by heart, as they know their prayers.

Some educators question the suitability of fables for children, forgetting perhaps that while children shun moralizing they are drawn to morality. The drama of the fable, the animal characters, and the quick flash of its single illustration of a truth — these hold the attention of children. Fables are like small, bright pebbles picked up from the shore, stored in the pocket as reminders of past experience, and held in the mind when needed.

The selection of fables for this anthology has been made as broad as possible, including examples of folk fables from different nations as well as many derived from literary sources. Many of the best-known fables have been omitted, because the primary emphasis has been put upon those which have the greatest appeal for children.

[9] From La Fontaine's Preface, given in *The Fables of La Fontaine,* trans. Marianne Moore (Viking Press, New York, 1954), p. 7.

FABLES

❧ Aesop's Fables ❧

The Wind and the Sun

Once upon a time when everything could talk, the Wind and the Sun fell into an argument as to which was the stronger. Finally they decided to put the matter to a test; they would see which one could make a certain man, who was walking along the road, throw off his cape. The Wind tried first. He blew and he blew and he blew. The harder and colder he blew, the tighter the traveler wrapped his cape about him. The Wind finally gave up and told the Sun to try. The Sun began to smile and as it grew warmer and warmer, the traveler was comfortable once more. But the Sun shone brighter and brighter until the man grew so hot, the sweat poured out on his face, he became weary, and seating himself on a stone, he quickly threw his cape to the ground. You see, gentleness had accomplished what force could not.

really does not pay to pretend to be what you are not.

A Lion and a Mouse

A Mouse one day happened to run across the paws of a sleeping Lion and wakened him. The Lion, angry at being disturbed, grabbed the Mouse, and was about to swallow him, when the Mouse cried out, "Please, kind Sir, I didn't mean it; if you will let me go, I shall always be grateful; and, perhaps, I can help you some day." The idea that such a little thing as a Mouse could help him so amused the Lion that he let the Mouse go. A week later the Mouse heard a Lion roaring loudly. He went closer to see what the trouble was and found his Lion caught in a hunter's net. Remembering his promise, the Mouse began to gnaw the ropes of the net and kept it up until the Lion could get free. The Lion then acknowledged that little friends might prove great friends.

A Wolf in Sheep's Clothing

A certain Wolf, being very hungry, disguised himself in a Sheep's skin and joined a flock of sheep. Thus, for many days he could kill and eat sheep whenever he was hungry, for even the shepherd did not find him out. One night after the shepherd had put all his sheep in the fold, he decided to kill one of his own flock for food; and without realizing what he was doing, he took out the wolf and killed him on the spot. It

The Shepherd's Boy and the Wolf

A mischievous Shepherd's Boy used to amuse himself by calling, "Wolf, Wolf!" just to see the villagers run with their clubs and pitchforks to help him. After he had called this more than once for a joke and had laughed at them each time, they grew angry. One day a Wolf really did get among the sheep, and the Shepherd Boy called "Wolf, Wolf!" in vain. The villagers went on with their work, the Wolf killed what he wanted of the sheep, and the Shepherd Boy learned that liars are not believed, even when they do tell the truth.

The Town Mouse and the Country Mouse

A Country Mouse was very happy that his city cousin, the Town Mouse, had accepted his invitation to dinner. He gave his city cousin all the best food he had, such as dried beans, peas, and crusts of bread. The Town Mouse tried not to show how he disliked the food and picked a little here and tasted a little there to be polite. After dinner, however, he said, "How can you stand such food all the time? Still I suppose here in the country you don't know about any better. Why don't you go home with me? When you have once tasted the delicious things I eat, you will never want to come back here." The Country Mouse not only kindly forgave the Town Mouse for not liking his dinner, but even consented to go that very evening to the city with his cousin. They arrived late at night; and the City Mouse, as host, took his Country Cousin at once to a room where there had been a big dinner. "You are tired," he said. "Rest here, and I'll bring you some real food." And he brought the Country Mouse such things as nuts, dates, cake, and fruit. The Country Mouse thought it was all so good, he would like to stay there. But before he had a chance to say so, he heard a terrible roar, and looking up, he saw a huge creature dash into the room. Frightened half out of his wits, the Country Mouse ran from the table, and round and round the room, trying to find a hiding place. At last he found a place of safety. While he stood there trembling he made up his mind to go home as soon as he could get safely away; for, to himself, he said, "I'd rather have common food in safety than dates and nuts in the midst of danger."

The Crow and the Pitcher

A thirsty Crow, after looking in vain for water to drink, at last saw some in the bottom of a pitcher. Seeing this water made him more thirsty than ever, and he began to plan how he could get it. He finally hit upon a scheme. By dropping pebbles into the pitcher and doing so until he brought the water near enough to the top so that he could reach it, he had all he wanted. Then he said to himself, "Well, I know now, that little by little does the trick."

The Dog and His Shadow

A Dog, carrying a piece of meat in his mouth, was crossing a stream on a narrow foot-bridge. He happened to look into the water and there he saw his Shadow, but he thought it another dog with a piece of meat larger than his. He made a grab for the other dog's meat; but in doing so, of course, he dropped his own; therefore was without any, and thus learned that greediness may cause one to lose everything.

The Fox and the Crow

A Fox once saw a Crow making off with a piece of cheese in its beak and made up his mind he was going to get it. "Good-morning, friend Crow," he called. "I see your feathers are as black and shining and beautiful as ever. You are really a beautiful bird. It is too bad your voice is poor! If that were lovely too, you would, without question, be the Queen of Birds." The Crow, rather indignant that the Fox doubted the beauty of her voice, began to caw at once. Of course the cheese dropped; and as the Fox put his paw on it he yelled, "I have what I wanted — and let me give you a bit of advice — Don't trust flatterers."

The Dog in the Manger

A cross, selfish Dog went to rest one hot afternoon in a manger. When the tired Ox came in from the field and wanted to eat his hay, the Dog barked at him so that he dared not try it. "To keep others from having what they need," said the Ox to himself, "when you can't use it yourself, is the meanest selfishness I know."

The Jackdaw and the Borrowed Plumes

A Jackdaw once found some Peacock feathers. Wishing to make himself beautiful, he stuck them in among his own and tried to pass himself off as a Peacock. But the Peacocks recognized him at once and drove him from their midst, pulling out the false feathers as they did so. The poor Jackdaw went back to his own kind. The other Jackdaws, however, were so disgusted with his behavior, that they also refused to let him stay with them. "For," they said, "fine feathers do not make fine birds and it is silly to be proud of borrowed plumes."

The Hare and the Tortoise

A Hare was once boasting about how fast he could run when a Tortoise, overhearing him, said, "I'll run you a race." "Done," said the Hare and laughed to himself; "but let's get the Fox for a judge." The Fox consented and the two started. The Hare quickly outran the Tortoise, and knowing he was far ahead, lay down to take a nap. "I can soon pass the Tortoise whenever I awaken." But unfortunately, the Hare overslept himself; therefore when he awoke, though he ran his best, he found the Tortoise was already at the goal. He had learned that "Slow and steady wins the race."

The Goose with the Golden Eggs

Once upon a time a Man had a Goose that laid a Golden Egg every day. Although he was gradually becoming rich, he grew impatient. He wanted to get all his treasure at once; therefore he killed the Goose. Cutting her open, he found her — just like any other goose, and he learned to his sorrow that it takes time to win success.

The Grasshopper and the Ants

On a beautiful sunny winter day some Ants had their winter store of food out to dry. A Grasshopper came by and gazed hungrily at the food. As the Ants paid no attention to him, he finally said, "Won't you please give me something to eat? I'm starving." "Did you not store away food last summer for use now?" asked the Ants. "No," replied the Grasshopper, "I was too busy enjoying myself in dancing and singing." "Well, then," said the Ants, "live this winter on your dancing and singing, as we live on what we did. No one has a right to play all the time, or he will have to suffer for it."

The Lark and Its Young

A Mother Lark had a nest of young birds in a field of ripe grain. One day when she came home, she found the little birds much excited. They reported that they had heard the owner of the field say it was time to call the Neighbors to help them gather the grain, and they begged the Mother Lark to take them away. "Do not worry," she said, "if he is depending upon his neighbors, the work won't begin today. But listen carefully to what the Farmer says each time he comes and report to me." The next day, again while their mother was getting their food, the Farmer came and exclaimed, "This field needs cutting badly; I'll call my Relatives over to help me. We'll get them here tomorrow." The excited young birds reported this news to their Mother upon her return. "Never mind," she said, "I happen to know these Relatives are busy with their own grain; they won't come. But continue to keep your ears open and tell me what you hear." The third day, when the Farmer came, he saw the grain was getting overripe, and turning to his Son, said, "We can't wait longer; we'll hire some men tonight, and tomorrow we'll begin cutting." When the Mother Lark heard these words, she said to her Children, "Now we'll have to move; when people decide to do things themselves instead of leaving such work to others, you may know they mean business."

Belling the Cat

One time the Mice were greatly bothered by a Cat; therefore, they decided to hold a meeting to talk over what could be done about the matter. During the meeting, a Young Mouse arose and suggested that a bell be put upon the Cat so that they could hear him coming. The suggestion was received with great applause, when an Old Mouse arose to speak. "That's all right," he said, "but who of us would dare to hang a bell around the Cat's neck?" Seeing their looks of fear, he added, "You know it is often much easier to suggest a plan than to carry it out."

The Fox and the Grapes

A hungry Fox happened to be passing along a Vineyard where many fine bunches of grapes were hanging high on the arbor. The Fox leaped to get some, time and time again. Failing to do so and weary with jumping, he finally gave up, and as he trotted away he said to himself, "I didn't want them anyway; I know they must still be sour."

The Miller, His Son, and the Ass

A Miller with his Son were one time driving an ass to market to sell it. Some young people passing by made fun of them for walking when the ass might be carrying one of them. Upon hearing them, the father had the boy get on the ass and was walking along happily until an old man met them. "You lazy rascal," he called to the boy, "to ride and let your poor old father walk!" The son, red with shame, quickly climbed off the ass and insisted that his father ride. Not long after, they met another who cried out,

"How selfish that father is — to ride and let his young son walk!"

At that the Miller took his Son up on the ass with himself, thinking he had at last done the right thing. But alas, he hadn't, for the next person they met was more critical than the others. "You should be ashamed of yourself," he said, "to be both riding that poor little beast; you are much better able to carry it."

Discouraged but willing to do right, the Miller and his Son got off the ass, bound its legs together on a long pole, and thus carried it on to the market. When they entered town, however, they made such a funny sight that crowds gathered about them laughing and shouting. This noise frightened the ass so much that he kicked himself free and, tumbling into the river, was drowned. The Miller, now disgusted, called to his Son to come along, and they rushed back home. "Well," said the father, "we have lost the ass, but we have learned one thing — that when one tries to please everybody, he pleases none, not even himself."

The Panchatantra and Bidpai Fables
The Brâhman's Goat[1]

The strong, deft, clever rascals note,
Who robbed the Brâhman of his goat.

In a certain town lived a Brâhman named Friendly who had undertaken the labor of maintaining the sacred fire. One day in the month of February, when a gentle breeze was blowing, when the sky was veiled in clouds and a drizzling rain was falling, he went to another village to beg a victim for the sacrifice, and said to a certain man: "O sacrificer, I wish to make an offering on the approaching day of the new moon. Pray give me a victim." And the man gave him a plump goat, as prescribed in Scripture. This he put through its paces, found it sound, placed it on his shoulder, and started in haste for his own city.

Now on the road he was met by three rogues whose throats were pinched with hunger. These, spying the plump creature on his shoulder, whispered together: "Come now! If we could eat that creature, we

[1] From *Gold's Gloom, Tales from the Panchatantra,* trans. from the Sanskrit by Arthur Ryder (University of Chicago Press).

should have the laugh on this sleety weather. Let us fool him, get the goat, and ward off the cold."

So the first of them changed his dress, issued from a by-path to meet the Brâhman, and thus addressed the man of pious life: "O pious Brâhman, why are you doing a thing so unconventional and so ridiculous? You are carrying an unclean animal, a dog, on your shoulder. Are you ignorant of the verse:

> The dog and the rooster,
> The hangman, the ass,
> The camel, defile you:
> Don't touch them, but pass."

At that the Brâhman was mastered by anger, and he said: "Are you blind, man, that you impute doghood to a goat?" "Brâhman," said the rogue, "do not be angry. Go whither you will."

But when he had traveled a little farther, the second rogue met him and said: "Alas, hold sir, alas! Even if this dead calf was a pet, still you should not put it on your shoulder. For the proverb says:

> Touch not unwisely man or beast
> That lifeless lie:
> Else, gifts of milk and lunar fast
> Must purify."

Then the Brâhman spoke in anger: "Are you blind, man? You call a goat a calf." And the rogue said: "Holy sir, do not be angry. I spoke in ignorance. Do as you will."

But when he had walked only a little farther through the forest, the third rogue, changing his dress, met him and said: "Sir, this is most improper. You are carrying a donkey on your shoulder. Yet the proverb tells you:

> If you should touch an ass — be it
> In ignorance or not —
> You needs must wash your clothes and bathe,
> To cleanse the sinful spot.

Pray drop this thing, before another sees you."

So the Brâhman concluded that it was a goblin in quadruped form, threw it on the ground, and made for home, terrified. Mean-

while, the three rogues met, caught the goat, and carried out their plan.

And that is why I say:

> The strong, deft, clever rascals note, . . .

and the rest of it.

The Poor Man and the Flask of Oil

There once was a Poor Man living in a house next to a wealthy Merchant who sold oil and honey. As the Merchant was a kind neighbor, he one day sent a flask of oil to the Poor Man. The Poor Man was delighted, and put it carefully away on the top shelf. One evening, as he was gazing at it, he said aloud, "I wonder how much oil there is in that bottle. There is a large quantity. If I should sell it, I could buy five sheep. Every year I should have lambs, and before long I should own a flock. Then I should sell some of the sheep, and be rich enough to marry a wife. Perhaps we might have a son. And what a fine boy he would be! So tall, strong, and obedient! But if he should disobey me," and he raised the staff which he held in his hand, "I should punish him thus." And he swung the staff over his head and brought it heavily to the ground, knocking, as he did so, the flask off the shelf, so that the oil ran over him from head to foot.

The Crow and the Partridge

A Crow flying across a road saw a Partridge strutting along the ground. "What a beautiful gait that Partridge has!" said the Crow. "I must try to see if I can walk like him." She alighted behind the Partridge and tried for a long time to learn to strut. At last the Partridge turned around and asked the Crow what she was about. "Do not be angry with me," replied the Crow. "I have never before seen a bird who walks as beautifully as you can, and I am trying to learn to walk like you." "Foolish bird," responded the Partridge. "You are a Crow and should walk like a Crow. You would look silly if you were to strut like a Partridge." But the

Crow went on trying to learn to strut, until she had finally forgotten her own gait, and she never learned that of the Partridge. Be yourself if you want to be your best.

The Tiger, the Brâhman, and the Jackal[2]

Once upon a time a tiger was caught in a trap. He tried in vain to get out through the bars, and rolled and bit with rage and grief when he failed.

By chance a poor Brâhman came by. "Let me out of this cage, O pious one!" cried the tiger.

"Nay, my friend," replied the Brâhman mildly, "you would probably eat me if I did."

"Not at all!" swore the tiger with many oaths; "on the contrary, I should be forever grateful, and serve you as a slave!"

Now when the tiger sobbed and sighed and wept and swore, the pious Brâhman's heart softened, and at last he consented to open the door of the cage. "What a fool you are! What is to prevent my eating you now, for after being cooped up so long I am just terribly hungry!"

In vain the Brâhman pleaded for his life; the most he could gain was a promise to abide by the decision of the first three things he chose to question as to the justice of the tiger's action.

So the Brâhman first asked a pipal tree what it thought of the matter, but the pipal tree replied coldly, "What have you to complain about? Don't I give shade and shelter to every one who passes by, and don't they in return tear down my branches to feed their cattle? Don't whimper — be a man!"

Then the Brâhman, sad at heart, went farther afield till he saw a buffalo turning a well-wheel; but he fared no better for it, for it answered, "You are a fool to expect gratitude! Look at me! While I gave milk, they fed me on cotton-seed and oil-cake; but now I am dry they yoke me here, and give me refuse as fodder!"

[2] From Flora Annie Steel, *Tales of the Punjab* (Macmillan).

The Brâhman, still more sad, asked the road to give him its opinion.

"My dear sir," said the road, "how foolish you are to expect anything else! Here am I, useful to everybody, yet all, rich and poor, great and small, trample on me as they go past, giving me nothing but the ashes of their pipes and the husks of their grain!"

On this the Brâhman turned back sorrowfully, and on the way he met a jackal, who called out, "Why, what's the matter, Mr. Brâhman? You look as miserable as a fish out of water!"

Then the Brâhman told him all that had occurred. "How very confusing!" said the jackal, when the recital was ended; "would you mind telling me over again? for everything seems so mixed up!"

The Brâhman told it all over again, but the jackal shook his head in a distracted sort of way, and still could not understand.

"It's very odd," said he sadly, "but it all seems to go in at one ear and out at the other! I will go to the place where it all happened, and then perhaps I shall be able to give a judgment."

So they returned to the cage, by which the tiger was waiting for the Brâhman, and sharpening his teeth and claws.

"You've been away a long time!" growled the savage beast, "but now let us begin our dinner."

"Our dinner!" thought the wretched Brâhman, as his knees knocked together with fright; "what a remarkably delicate way of putting it!"

"Give me five minutes, my lord!" he pleaded, "in order that I may explain matters to the jackal here, who is somewhat slow in his wits."

The tiger consented, and the Brâhman began the whole story over again, not missing a single detail, and spinning as long a yarn as possible.

"Oh, my poor brain! oh, my poor brain!" cried the jackal, wringing his paws. "Let me see! how did it all begin? You were in the cage, and the tiger came walking by ———"

"Pooh!" interrupted the tiger, "what a fool you are! *I* was in the cage."

"Of course!" cried the jackal, pretending to tremble with fright; "yes! I was in the cage — no, I wasn't — dear! dear! where are my wits? Let me see — the tiger was in the Brâhman, and the cage came walking by — no, that's not it either! Well, don't mind me, but begin your dinner, for I shall never understand!"

"Yes, you shall!" returned the tiger, in a rage at the jackal's stupidity; "I'll make you understand! Look here — I am the tiger ——"

"Yes, my lord!"

"And that is the Brâhman ——"

"Yes, my lord!"

"And that is the cage ——"

"Yes, my lord!"

"And I was in the cage — do you understand?"

"Yes — no — Please my lord ——"

"Well?" cried the tiger, impatiently.

"Please, my lord! — how did you get in?"

"How! — why, in the usual way, of course!"

"Oh dear me! — my head is beginning to whirl again! Please don't be angry, my lord, but what is the usual way?"

At this the tiger lost patience, and, jumping into the cage, cried, "This way! Now do you understand how it was?"

"Perfectly!" grinned the jackal, as he dexterously shut the door; "and if you will permit me to say so, I think matters will remain as they were!"

❧ Jataka Tales ❧

The Spirit that Lived in a Tree [3]

And it came to pass that the Buddha was re-born as a Tree-Spirit. Now there reigned (at Benares) at that time a King who said to himself: "All over India, the kings live in palaces supported by many a column. *I* will build me a palace resting on one column only — then shall I in truth be the chiefest of all kings."

Now in the King's Park was a lordly Sal tree, straight and well-grown, worshiped by

[3] From Marie L. Shedlock, *Eastern Stories and Legends* (Dutton).

village and town; and to this tree even the Royal Family also paid tribute, worship, and honor. And then suddenly there came an order from the King that the tree should be cut down.

And the people were sore dismayed; but the woodmen, who dared not disobey the orders of the King, came to the Park with hands full of perfumed garlands and, encircling the tree with a string, fastened to it a nosegay of flowers; and kindling a lamp, they did worship, exclaiming: "O Tree, on the seventh day must we cut thee down, for so hath the King commanded. Now let the Deities who dwell within thee go elsewhither; and since we are only obeying the King's command, let no blame fall upon us, and no harm come to our children because of this."

And the Spirit who lived in the tree, hearing these words, reflected within himself and said: "These builders are determined to cut down this tree and to destroy my place of dwelling. Now my life lasts only as long as this tree. And lo! all the young Sal trees that stand around, where dwell the Deities, my kinsfolk — and they are many — will be destroyed! My own destruction does not touch me so near as the destruction of my children; therefore must I protect their lives." Accordingly, at the hour of midnight, adorned in divine splendor, he entered into the magnificent chamber of the King and, filling the whole chamber with a bright radiance, stood weeping beside the King's pillow. At the sight of him, the King, overcome with terror, said: "Who art thou, standing high in the air, and why do thy tears flow?"

And the Tree-God made answer: "Within thy realm I am known as the Lucky-Tree. For sixty thousand years have I stood, and all have worshiped me; and though they have built many a house, and many a town, no violence has been done to me. Spare thou me, also, O King."

Then the King made answer and said: "Never have I seen so mighty a trunk, so thick and strong a tree; but I will build me a palace, and thou shalt be the only column on which it shall rest, and thou shalt dwell there for ever."

And the Tree said: "Since thou art resolved to tear my body from me, I pray thee cut me down gently, one branch after another — the root last of all."

And the King said: "O Woodland Tree! what is this thou askest of me? It were a painful death to die. One stroke at the root would fell thee to the ground. Why wouldst thou die piecemeal?"

And the Tree made answer: "O King! My children, the young Sal trees, all grown at my feet; they are prosperous and well sheltered. If I should fall with one mighty crash, behold these young children of the forest would perish also!"

And the King was greatly moved by this spirit of sacrifice, and said: "O great and glorious Tree! I set thee free from thy fear; and because thou wouldst willingly die to save thy kindred, thou shalt not be cut down. Return to thy home in the Ancient Forest."

The Banyan Deer [4]

Long ago the Bodisat came to life as a deer. When he was born he was of a golden color; his eyes were like round jewels; his horns were white as silver; his mouth was red as a cluster of kamala flowers; his hoofs were as bright and hard as lacquer-work; his tail as fine as the tail of a Thibetan ox; and his body as large in size as a foal's.

He lived in the forest with an attendant herd of five hundred deer, under the name of the King of the Banyan Deer; and not far from him there dwelt another deer, golden as he, under the name of the Monkey Deer, with a like attendant herd.

The King of that country was devoted to hunting, never ate without meat, and used to summon all the townspeople to go hunting every day to the destruction of their ordinary work. The people thought, "This King puts an end to all our work. Suppose we make a park, provide food and drink for the deer. Then we will drive them into the park, close the entrance and deliver them to the King."

This they did, surrounding the very place where the Banyan Deer and the Monkey Deer were living. When the King heard this, he

[4] From Marie L. Shedlock, *Eastern Stories and Legends* (Dutton).

went to the park, and seeing there the two golden-colored deer, he granted them their lives. But henceforth he would go himself to shoot the deer and bring it home. Sometimes his cook would go and shoot one. The deer, as soon as they saw the boy, would quake with fear of Death, and run away; but when they had been hit once or twice, they became weary or wounded and were killed. And the herd told their King, who sent for the Monkey Deer and said: "Friend, almost all the Deer are being destroyed. Now, though they certainly must die, yet henceforth let them not be wounded with arrows. Let the deer take it by turns to go to the place of execution. One day let the lot fall on my herd, and the next day on yours."

He agreed, and thenceforth the deer whose turn it was used to go and lie down after placing his neck on the block of execution. And the cook used to come and carry off the one he found lying there.

But one day the lot fell upon a roe in the Monkey Deer who was with young. She went to the Monkey Deer and said: "Lord! I am with young. When I have brought forth my son, we will both take our turn. Order the bows to pass me by."

"I cannot make your lot," said he, "fall upon the others. You know well enough it has fallen upon you. Go away!" Receiving no help from him, she went to the Bodisat and told him the matter. He listened to her quietly and said: "Be it so! Do you go back. I will relieve you of your turn." And he went himself and laid his head on the block of execution.

The cook, seeing him, exclaimed: "The King of the Deer whose life was promised to him is lying in the place of execution. What does it mean?" And he went hastily, and told the King.

The King no sooner heard it than he mounted his chariot and proceeded with a great retinue to the place, and beholding the Bodisat, said: "My friend, the King of the Deer! Did I not grant you your life? Why are you lying here?"

"O great King! A roe with young came and told me that the lot had fallen upon her. Now I could not ask another to take her place, so I, giving my life for her, have lain down. Harbor no further suspicion, O great King!"

"My Lord, the golden-colored King of the Deer! I never yet saw, even among men, one so full of forbearance, kindness and compassion. I am pleased with thee in this matter! Rise up. I grant your lives, both to you and to her!"

"But though we be safe, what shall the rest do, O King of men?"

"Then I grant their lives to the rest, my Lord."

"Thus, then, great King, the deer in the park will have gained security, but what will the others do?"

"They also shall not be molested."

"Great King! even though the deer dwell secure, what shall the rest of the four-footed creatures do?"

"They shall also be free from fear."

"Great King, even though the quadrupeds are in safety, what shall the flock of birds do?"

"Well, I grant the same boon to them."

"Great King! the birds then will obtain peace; but what of the fish who dwell in the water?"

"They shall have peace as well."

Then the Great Being having interceded with the king for all creatures said:

"Walk in righteousness, O great King! Doing justice to fathers and mothers, to townsmen and landsmen, you shall enter, when your body is dissolved, the happy world of Heaven."

The roe gave birth to a son as beautiful as buds of flowers; and he went to playing about with the Monkey Deer's herd. But when its mother saw that, she said, "My son, henceforth go not in his company. You may keep to the Banyan Deer's herd."

Now after that, the deer, secure of their lives, began to eat men's crops. And the men dared not strike them or drive them away, recollecting how it had been granted to them that they should dwell secure. So they met together in front of the King's palace, and told the matter to the King.

"When I was well pleased, I granted to the leader of the Banyan herd a boon," said he. "I may give up my kingdom but not my oaths! Begone with you! Not a man in my kingdom shall be allowed to hurt the deer."

When the Banyan King heard that, he assembled his herd, and said:

"Henceforth you are not allowed to eat other people's crops." And so forbidding them, he sent a message to the men: "Henceforth let the husbandmen put up no fence to guard their crops: but let them tie leaves round the edge of the field as a sign."

From that time, they say, the sign of the tying of the leaves was seen in the fields, and from that time not a single deer trespassed beyond it: for such was the instruction they received from (their King) the Bodisat.

And the Bodisat continued thus his life long to instruct the deer, and passed away with his herd, according to his deeds.

The Hare that Ran Away [5]

And it came to pass that the Buddha (to be) was born again as a Lion. Just as he had helped his fellow-men, he now began to help his fellow-animals, and there was a great deal to be done. For instance, there was a little nervous Hare who was always afraid that something dreadful was going to happen to her. She was always saying: "Suppose the Earth were to fall in, what would happen to me?" And she said this so often that at last she thought it really was about to happen. One day, when she had been saying over and over again, "suppose the Earth were to fall in, what would happen to me?" she heard a slight noise; it really was only a heavy fruit which had fallen upon a rustling leaf, but the little Hare was so nervous she was ready to believe anything, and she said in a frightened tone: "The Earth is falling in." She ran away as fast as she could go; presently she met an old brother Hare, who said: "Where are you running to, Mistress Hare?"

And the little Hare said: "I have no time to stop and tell you anything. The Earth is falling in, and I am running away."

"The Earth is falling in, is it?" said the old brother Hare, in a tone of much astonishment; and he repeated this to his brother

[5] From Marie L. Shedlock, *Eastern Stories and Legends* (Dutton).

hare, and he to his brother hare, and he to his brother hare, until at last there were a hundred thousand brother hares, all shouting. "The Earth is falling in." Now presently the bigger animals began to take the cry up. First the deer, and then the sheep, and then the wild boar, and then the buffalo, and then the camel, and then the tiger, and then the elephant.

Now the wise Lion heard all this noise and wondered at it. "There are no signs," he said, "of the Earth falling in. They must have heard something." And then he stopped them all short and said: "What is this you are saying?"

And the Elephant said: "I remarked that the Earth was falling in."

"How do you know this?" asked the Lion.

"Why, now I come to think of it, it was the Tiger that remarked it to me."

Then the Tiger said: "I had it from the Camel," and the Camel said: "I had it from the Buffalo." And the buffalo from the wild boar, and the wild boar from the sheep, and the sheep from the deer, and the deer from the hares, and the hares said: "Oh! we heard it from that little Hare."

And the Lion said: "Little Hare, what made you say that the Earth was falling in?"

And the little Hare said: "I saw it."

"You saw it?" said the Lion. "Where?"

"Yonder by the tree."

"Well," said the Lion, "come with me and I will show you how ———"

"No, no," said the Hare, "I would not go near that tree for anything, I'm so nervous."

"But," said the Lion, "I am going to take you on my back." And he took her on his back, and begged the animals to stay where they were until they returned. Then he showed the little Hare how the fruit had fallen upon the leaf, making the noise that had frightened her, and she said: "Yes, I see — the Earth is not falling in." And the Lion said: "Shall we go back and tell the other animals?"

And they went back. The little Hare stood before the animals and said: "The Earth is not falling in." And all the animals began to repeat this to one another, and they dispersed gradually, and you heard the words more and more softly:

"The Earth is not falling in," etc., etc., etc., until the sound died away altogether.

⊰ A Persian Fable ⊱
The Seeds and the Wheat [6]

There was once a man who entered a field of Wheat and stole some of the ripe grain. The owner of the field demanded why he had stolen the Wheat. The thief replied, "My Lord, I have not stolen any Wheat belonging to you. You planted only the Seeds, and what I took was the ripe Wheat. Why do you call me a thief?" The two men went before a Judge and asked him, "Which of us is right and which is wrong?" The Judge answered, "The one who sowed the Seed is right, and he who did not sow the Seed is wrong. The Seed is the origin of the Wheat. How should he who did not sow have any right to the Wheat that grew from it?"

⊰ Translated from Apion ⊱
Androcles and the Lion

⊰ *Arthur Gilchrist Brodeur, in the University of California Publications on Modern Philology (vol. XI, p. 197 ff.), shows very conclusively that this story is not a folk tale of Oriental origin, but a sophisticated story by Apion. Aulus Gellius, who lived in the second century, in his* Noctes Atticae *[vol. V, chap. XIV], tells this story as taken from Apion's book, the* Aegyptiaca, *now lost, wherein Apion says he saw the Androcles story "from the moment of the lion's entry into the Circus until the ultimate conclusion." As a corroboration, Brodeur points out that Seneca, in his* De Beneficiis, *who was also in Rome part of the time Apion was, tells of seeing such an incident; but Seneca goes on to say that the man had once been the lion's trainer. As Apion was born in Oasis in the Libyan Desert, Brodeur shows how natural it would be for Apion to motivate the lion's gratitude as he did.*

Androcles, a runaway slave, had fled to a forest for safety. He had not been there long when he saw a Lion who was groaning with

6 From Stanislas Julien, *Les Avadanes.*

pain. He started to flee, but when he realized that the Lion did not follow but only kept on groaning, Androcles turned and went to it. The Lion, instead of rushing at him, put out a torn and bloody paw. Androcles, seeing the poor beast was in pain and wanting to help it, went up, took its paw, and examined it. Discovering a large thorn, the man pulled it out and thus relieved the pain. The grateful Lion in return took Androcles to its cave and every day brought him food. Sometime later both were captured and taken to Rome. The slave was condemned to be killed by being thrown to the Lion, which had not had food for several days. Androcles was led into the arena in the presence of the Emperor and his court, and at the same time the Lion was loosed. It came headlong toward its prey, but when it came near Androcles, instead of pouncing upon him, it jumped up and fawned upon him like a friendly dog. The Emperor was much surprised and called to him Androcles who told his story. The Emperor freed both the slave and the Lion, for he thought such kindness and such gratitude were deserving of reward.

✎ *La Fontaine's Fables* ✐

The Dove and the Ant [7]

Near a pure rivulet a dove came down and
   drank;
Then a thirsty ant fell forward, almost sank,
And one might have seen the midget struggling helplessly,
Too frustrated each time, to reach what it
   desired.
The dove's quick action proved that mercy
   was not dead
When she bore and loosed a straw from overhead
To act as an earthwork whenever her friend
   tired.
    It was a successful ruse.
But a churl by chance had crept up without
   shoes,
And carried a crossbow to bag birds for his
   pot.

[7] From Marianne Moore, trans., *The Fables of La Fontaine* (Viking Press).

Venus' bird then tempted its use;
His eye grew bright at thought of the dainty
   dove he'd caught
And he was about to bring it down — hard-
   hearted sot —
   When the ant pinched his heel; where-
    upon
   The lout turned his head before he shot;
The pigeon had heard and then was gone,
So no supper for churl as a result of his toil.
"No penny, no pigeon possible."

The Fox and the Goat [8]

Captain Fox was padding along sociably
With Master Goat whose horns none would
   care to oppose,
Though he could not see farther than the
   end of his nose;
Whereas the fox was practiced in chicanery.
Thirst led them to a well and they simulta-
   neously
   Leaped in to look for water there.
After each had drunk what seemed a suffi-
   ciency,
The fox said to the goat, "Well, friend, and
   from here where?
We can't be always drinking, Master Goat,
   can we?
Put your feet up; your horns will rise to that
   degree,
Push against the wall until your rump is
   snugged in;
   I'll climb you like a ladder then,
   Up the back, up the horns again,
   In that way, as you have seen,
   Before long I'll be where we first stood
   And can draw you up if you think good."
— "Genius," said the goat. "By my beard,
   what finesse!
   Nothing like a fox's wit;
   A ruse on which I could not have hit;
   A superlative mind, I confess."
The fox leaped out of the well; the goat had
   to stay down —
   Harangued as by a sage in a gown
   About patience and experience;
Yes; told: "If Heaven had only given you as
   good sense
As the beard on your chin's an exceptional
   one,

[8] *Ibid.*

You'd not be an adventurer
Into wells, as you have been. Therefore
    good-by, I must depart.
Strain up high; each leap can be a new start.
    As for me, I'm due far from here;
I can't stand about as if at an inn."

Better think of the outcome before you begin.

The Camel and the Flotsam [9]

A man, encountering a camel,
Fled, shocked by a sight so novel.
Another ventured near. A third then braved
    what they had feared;

    The curiosity was snared.
We grow accustomed to what at first made
    us afraid,
Though before so alarming we had shivered
    with dread.
    Having seen it, we are prepared
    When we encounter it afterward.
Since I've broached this topic, a word might
    be added
    About some watchmen who were de-
    luded
By a form at sea. They were so intimidated
    Each of them said he could swear
    That what he saw was a man of war;
Then concluded a fireship was being moored;
    Then a wherry; then something tied
    with a cord,
    And then some flotsam that swung and
    swirled.

    Ah yes, how much I've seen in the world,
    For which these anecdotes account —
Far off, immense; but close at hand to what
    does it amount!

The Dairymaid and Her Milk-Pot [9]

Perrette's milk-pot fitted her head-mat just
    right —
    Neatly quilted to grip the pot tight.

[9] From Marianne Moore, trans., *The Fables of La Fontaine* (Viking Press).

Then she set off to market and surely walked
    well,
In her short muslin dress that encouraged
    long strides,
Since to make better time she wore shoes with
    low heel
    And had tucked up her skirt at the sides.
    Like summer attire her head had grown
    light,
    Thinking of what she'd have bought by
    night.
In exchange for the milk, since supposing it
    gone,
She'd buy ten times ten eggs and three hens
    could be set.
Taking care all hatched out, she'd not lose
    more than one
    And said, "Then there'll be pullets to
    sell.
I'll raise them at home; it is quite within
    reason,
    Since shrewd Master Fox will be doing
    well
If I can't shortly buy a young pig and grow
    bacon.
The one I had bought would be almost half
    grown;
He'd need next to no feed — almost nothing
    at all;
When he's sold I'll have funds — good hard
    cash to count on.
Then with room at the barn for some stock
    in the stall,
I could buy cow and calf if the pig had sold
    high;
If I'd not had a loss, I'd add sheep by and
    by."
Perrette skipped for joy as she dreamt of
    what she'd bought.
The crock crashed. Farewell, cow, calf, fat
    pig, eggs not hatched out.
The mistress of wealth grieved to forfeit for-
    ever
    The profits that were mounting.
    How ask her husband to forgive her
    Lest he beat her as was fitting?
    And thus ended the farce we have
    watched:
*Don't count your chickens before they
    are hatched.*

❧ Modern Fables ❧

The Blind Men and the Elephant [10]

JOHN G. SAXE

It was six men of Indostan
 To learning much inclined,
Who went to see the Elephant
 (Though all of them were blind),
That each by observation
 Might satisfy his mind.

The First approached the Elephant,
 And happening to fall
Against his broad and sturdy side,
 At once began to bawl:
"God bless me! but the Elephant
 Is very like a wall!"

The Second, feeling of the tusk,
 Cried, "Ho! what have we here
So very round and smooth and sharp?
 To me 'tis mighty clear
This wonder of an Elephant
 Is very like a spear!"

The Third approached the animal,
 And happening to take
The squirming trunk within his hands,
 Thus boldly up and spake:
"I see," quoth he, "the Elephant
 Is very like a snake!"

The Fourth reached out his eager hand,
 And felt about the knee.
"What most this wondrous beast is like
 Is mighty plain," quoth he;
" 'Tis clear enough the Elephant
 Is very like a tree!"

The Fifth, who chanced to touch the ear
 Said, "E'en the blindest man
Can tell what this resembles most;
 Deny the fact who can,
This marvel of an Elephant
 Is very like a fan!"

The Sixth no sooner had begun
 About the beast to grope,

Than, seizing on the swinging tail
 That fell within his scope,
"I see," quoth he, "the Elephant
 Is very like a rope!"

And so these men of Indostan
 Disputed loud and long,
Each in his own opinion
 Exceeding stiff and strong.
Though each was partly in the right,
 And all were in the wrong!

The Moth and the Star [11]

JAMES THURBER

❧ *James Thurber's* Many Moons, *well loved fantasy, is actually an elaboration of a fable, but here he catches the true spirit of fable, with its moral precept, its economy of expression and its single example by way of illustration. The humor lies in his skillful use of an archaic form in a contemporary idiom.*

A young and impressionable moth once set his heart on a certain star. He told his mother about this and she counseled him to set his heart on a bridge lamp instead. "Stars aren't the thing to hang around," she said; "Lamps are the thing to hang around." "You get somewhere that way," said the moth's father. "You don't get anywhere chasing stars." But the moth would not heed the words of either parent. Every evening at dusk when the star came out he would start flying toward it and every morning at dawn he would crawl back home worn out with his vain endeavor. One day his father said to him, "You haven't burned a wing in months, boy, and it looks to me as if you were never going to. All your brothers have been badly burned flying around street lamps and all your sisters have been terribly singed flying around house lamps. Come on, now, get out of here and get yourself scorched! A big strapping moth like you without a mark on him!"

The moth left his father's house, but he would not fly around street lamps and he would not fly around house lamps. He went

10 From John Godfrey Saxe, *Poems* (Boston, 1852).

11 Reprinted by permission, © The New Yorker Magazine, Inc.

right on trying to reach the star, which was four and one-third light years, or twenty five trillion miles, away. The moth thought it was just caught in the top branches of an elm. He never did reach the star, but he went right on trying, night after night, and when he was a very, very old moth he began to think that he really had reached the star

and he went around saying so. This gave him a deep and lasting pleasure, and he lived to a great old age. His parents and his brothers and his sisters had all been burned to death when they were quite young.

MORAL: Who flies afar from the sphere of our sorrow is here today and here to morrow.

BIBLIOGRAPHY

Aesop

Aesop's Fables; ed. and illus. with wood engravings by Boris Artzybasheff. Text based on the Croxall edition of 1722 and the James edition of 1848. Viking Press, 1933. (Grades 5–8)
A beautiful edition, distinguished in format.

Aesop's Fables; from the translations of Thomas James and George Tyler Townsend; introduction by Angelo Patri; illus. by Glen Rounds. J. B. Lippincott, 1949. (Lippincott Classics) (Grades 5–8)
More than one hundred of the fables with illustrations admirably suited to the text.

Aesop's Fables; with drawings by Fritz Kredel. Grosset & Dunlap, 1947. (Illustrated Junior Library) (Grades 5–8)
Preface gives the origin and history of the fables and a short sketch of the life of Aesop.

The Fables of Aesop; ed. by Joseph Jacobs; illus. by Kurt Wiese. Macmillan, 1950. (New Children's Classics) (Grades 4–6)
First published in 1894. Based upon the two-volume edition of *The Fables of Aesop* first printed by William Caxton, edited by Joseph Jacobs, and published by David Nutt, London, 1889. Dr. Jacobs stated that he "felt at liberty to retell the fables in such a way as to interest children." His collection has long been considered a basic source of Aesop's fables for boys and girls.

Fables of India

The Panchatantra. *The Panchatantra;* trans. from the Sanskrit by Arthur W. Ryder. University of Chicago Press, 1925. (Adult)
In his introduction Dr. Ryder states that this translation was made "to extend accurate and joyful acquaintance with one of the world's masterpieces." Panchatantra in Sanskrit means "five books." Each of the five books is a story by itself with shorter stories interwoven much in the same manner as the framework of the *Arabian Nights.* An invaluable source for students of folklore.

Bidpai. *The Tortoise and the Geese, and Other Fables of Bidpai;* retold by Maude Barrows Dutton; illus. by E. Boyd Smith. Houghton Mifflin, 1908. (Grades 3–4)
According to tradition, Bidpai was a sage of India who lived about 300 B.C. All his accumulated wisdom he put into his fables. In the Middle Ages "Bidpai" referred to the narrator of animal fables, or to the collection itself, known in Arabic as *Fables of Bidpai.*

Jatakas. *Jataka Tales;* retold by Ellen C. Babbitt; illus. by Ellsworth Young. Appleton-Century, 1912. (Grades 4–5)
Fables chiefly about animals, taken from one of the sacred books of the Buddhists. Followed by *More Jataka Tales* and *Twenty Jataka Tales.* These are the best of the retelling of the Buddha stories.

Gaer, Joseph. *The Fables of India;* illus. by Randy Monk. Little, Brown, 1955. (Grades 5–9)
Animal fables different from and yet intriguingly similar to those of the Western world. A retelling of the animal fables from the *Panchatantra,* the *Hitopadesa,* and the *Jatakas.*

Shedlock, Marie. *Eastern Stories and Legends;* foreword by Professor T. W. Rhys Davids; intro. by Anne Carroll Moore. E. P. Dutton, 1920. (Grades 3–5)
Stories of the Buddha rebirths based upon the translations from Pali made by Professor Rhys Davids.

Fables of France

La Fontaine, Jean de. *Fables of La Fontaine;* trans. by Marianne Moore. Viking Press, 1954. (Adult)

This new translation of the fables by an American poet is an important literary achievement. Miss Moore has followed the original text with fidelity and has added the flavor of her own keen wit and sense of form.

La Fontaine, Jean de. *Fables;* trans. by Margaret Wise Brown; illus. by André Hellé. Harper & Brothers, 1940. (Grades 3–4)

Fables from Hellé's La Fontaine picture book.

Samivel. *Rufus the Fox;* adapted from the French by Margery Bianco. Harper & Brothers, 1937. (Grades 3–5)

Mrs. Bianco has retold in rhyme the story from the French beast-epic of Reynard the Fox.

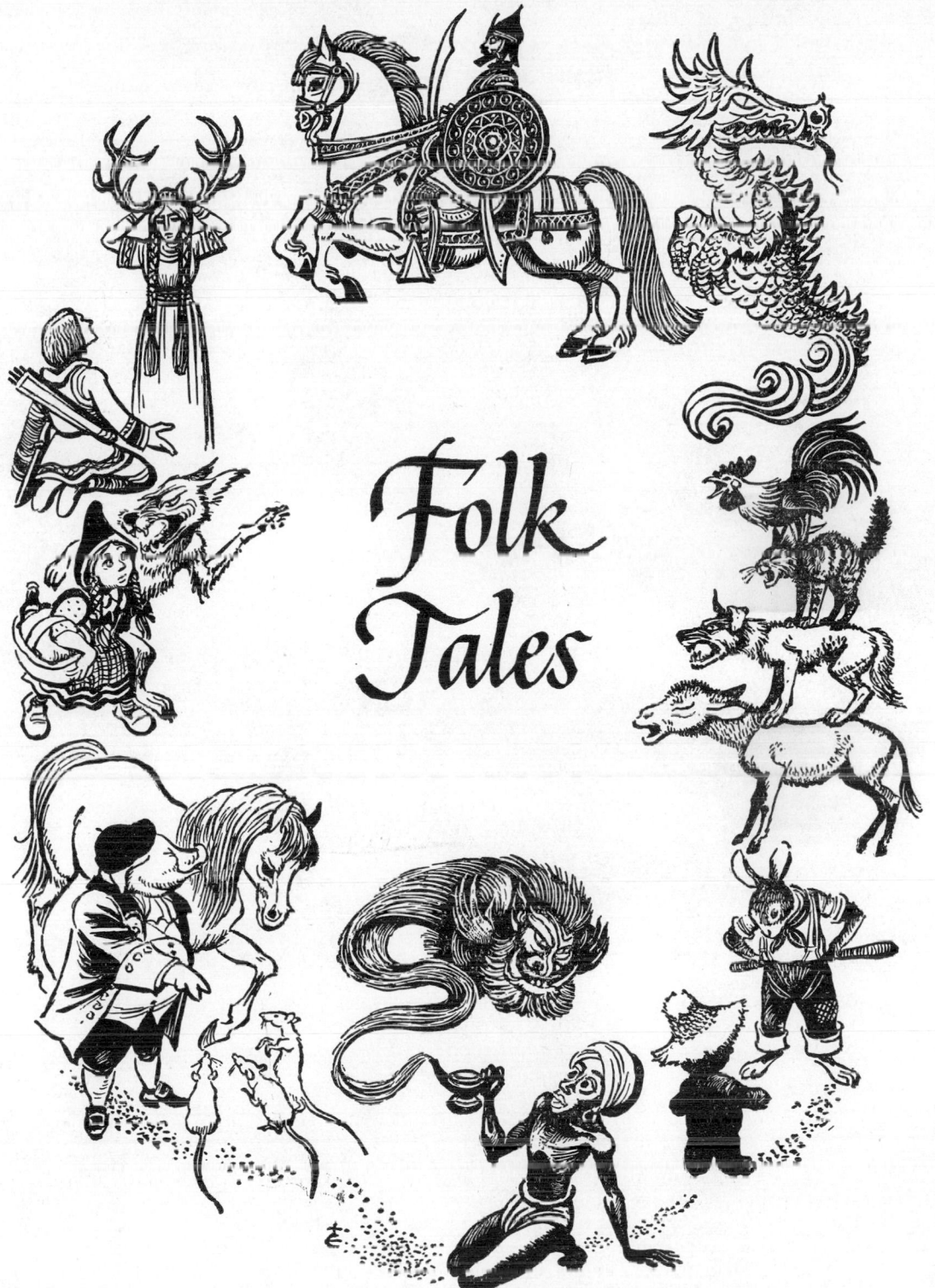

Folk
Tales

"We have another past besides the past that history tells us about, a past which is in us, in individuals, more livingly than the recorded past. It is a past in which men slowly arrived at self consciousness while building up the community, the arts and the laws." [1]

S OLD AS LANGUAGE, FOLK TALES have encircled the world. They are the most gifted travelers, adapting themselves to culture after culture, yet keeping a hard core of individuality, holding to the initial point of the story, the essence of its conceptive idea. Wherever people gathered, in market places, about the hearths of homes, at tasks of weaving or sowing or planting — the stories told were not only the entertainment, but the philosophy and the living tradition of masses of unlettered people.

They were preserved, altered, adapted by the devices of storytellers, and they have outlived succeeding generations of man through the simple mediums of the human voice and memory. The vast reservoir of folk tales lies within the great oral tradition that makes up the body of folklore, one of the major divisions, the other categories being *Myth and Legend, Fable, Ballads and Romances, Epics and Sagas*. The reader of folk tales soon discovers certain types of stories which occur over and over. The *Märchen*, for one, a term borrowed from the studies of the Grimm brothers, and described by the great American folklore scholar, Stith Thompson, as being stories which move "in an unreal world without definite locality or definite characters and [are] filled with the marvelous. In this never-never land humble heroes kill adversaries, succeed to kingdoms, and marry princesses." [2] Stories about animals are another clear group, told not with a didactic or practical purpose, as is the fable, but simply relating the adventures of animals as protagonists, as in the tale of "The Bremen Town Musicians." The cumulative story is a recognizable type, winding up in successive incidents, like the story of "The Old Woman and Her Pig," in fascinating patterns of repetition and incantation. The drolls form a recurring pattern, stories of numskulls and simpletons, full of exaggerated nonsense. Then there are the stories of the real and practical world, husbands who are to mind the house, and wives who know how to handle a foolish husband, greeting him with love, as in the Norwegian story of "What the Goodman Does Is Sure to Be Right," or beating him thoroughly,

---

[1] From Introduction to *Grimm's Fairy Tales* (Pantheon Books, New York, 1944).
[2] Stith Thompson, *The Folktale* (Dryden Press, New York, 1946), p. 8.

as happens in the English version of the same story, "Mr. Vinegar." The *pourquoi* stories are typical of folk tales, the "why" stories, being legends of explanation, such as "Why the bear is stumpy-tailed," or "Why the chipmunk's back is striped."

When manuscript copying and printing made possible the collection of these stories, they appeared as basic material for some of the great storytellers of the Middle Ages, such as Chaucer and Boccaccio. The crude chapbooks, too, in their first printings, used these stories as their subject matter. But the folk tale as a vast history of man's past was not recognized for its true worth by educated men until the middle of the nineteenth century. Then came the great awakening.

In 1785, at Hanau in Hesse-Cassel, Jakob Grimm was born. A year later, Wilhelm Grimm followed him into the world, and the two brothers, growing up with four other children in the family, were drawn together in a relationship that was to last through their lifetime. Since their father was a lawyer, they decided to follow his profession when they came of age, and they studied law at the University at Marburg. Their professor of law was interested in the legends of the Middle Ages and in the songs of the minnesingers. His interest must have influenced the two young students, for they turned from the law to a study of the German language, its history and structure. Jakob's German Grammar is one of the great works in language study. In the process of their linguistic studies, they came upon the stories which country people had by heart, and they decided to make them the subject of study. *Die Brüder Grimm,* as they signed themselves, were the first collectors of folklore to recognize in the raw material of the tales a source for the scientific study of the race which had produced them. They were the first to glimpse the ethnographical worth of the folk tale. They understood also the importance of preserving the language in which the stories were told. They were concerned "to let the speech of the people break directly into print" and were scrupulous in their elimination of extraneous elements in the stories, or of an oversophistication. Their chief informant was Frau Katherina Viehmann (1755–1815) who knew the stories as the people told them, and through her tellings the Grimms preserved the characteristic simplicity, strength, crudity and patterns of the tales.

In the preface to the first edition of the second volume, published in 1815, Wilhelm Grimm described the methods of the great, natural storyteller, Frau Viehmann: "She recounts her stories thoughtfully, accurately, with uncommon vividness and evident delight . . . Anyone believing that the traditional matherials are easily falsified and carelessly preserved, and hence cannot survive over a long period, should hear how close she always keeps to her story and how zealous she is for its accuracy. . . . Among people who follow the old life ways without change, attachment to inherited patterns is stronger than we, impatient for variety, can realize."

The first volume of the *Kinder- und Hausmärchen* was published in 1812, a second volume in 1815, and a third in 1822. Successive revised editions followed through the years. The two brothers opened up the gates to a new world of scholarship which was as old as time. In their wake, scholar after scholar sought out the hidden pockets of folklore in his own region, and made fresh discovery: Elias Lönnrot (1802–1884) in Finland; Peter Asbjörnsen (1812–1885) and his friend and collaborator Jörgen Moe (1813–1882) in Norway, with George Dasent (1817–1896) translating their work into the English. In England, Andrew Lang (1844–1912) and Joseph Jacobs (1854–1916) were among the leaders of the movement.

Fast upon the steps of the nineteenth-century discovery of the folk tale came the succeeding waves of scholarly research, each with its version of the origin of the tales. For early in the process of collecting, it became apparent that the same story appeared in places far removed from one another. How was the wide dissemination of the folk tale to be explained, and where did it originate? One theory, that of the linguistic scholars, held that the tales came from a common language (Indo-European theory). Another held that they came from a common locality, probably India. A third said that the tales were really only broken-down myths, the detritus of a great, encompassing mythology based on the interpretation of nature; the proponents of this theory offered rather far-fetched proof by saying, for example, that when the wolf ate Red Riding-Hood, it was only symbolic of the night swallowing up the day. Then came the anthropologist, who said that the reason the same tales were found all over the world was because primitive man, wherever he may be geographically or in whatever stage of historical development, thinks like every other primitive man, and that similar ideas generated similar tales. None of these theories could hold all of the truth, and scholars and scientists would quickly dispute each theory as it evolved.

Modern students of folklore follow the scheme of study which was originated in Finland, under the leadership of Julius and Kaarle Krohn, father and son, who evolved a scientific method of studying the folk tale by means of a thorough study of its history and geography; a historical-geographical method which brings together all the variants of a story and traces its history and travel. In this plan, "each of the hundreds of tale types must be submitted to exhaustive study — and in the end the results of these studies synthesized into adequate generalizations."[3] The stories are studied, not only by type, but by motif, which is "the smallest element in a tale having power to persist in tradition,"[4] such as the recurring motif of the wicked stepmother, or the youngest son. The Finnish movement resulted in a world organization of folklore scholars and enthusiasts. One of its greatest achievements centers in America, in the *Motif-Index of Folk-Literature* edited by Stith Thompson, who occupied the only Chair of Folklore in the United States at the University of Indiana. Even the most casual reader of folklore, upon looking into this Index, will catch a glimpse of the magnitude of the work and will gain a new respect for the mystery and miraculous power of the whole realm of folklore.

One curious episode in the history of the folk tale precedes the influence of the Brothers Grimm, occurring in the century before them. The place was France, at the time of Louis XIV, a time of elegance and intellectual brilliance.

[3] Stith Thompson, *The Folktale*, p. 396.
[4] *Ibid.*, p. 415.

The yeast of folklore was discovered by the grandees of the court, who toyed with the writing of fairy tales, as a later court was to play-act the role of bucolic shepherdess and shepherd. Charles Perrault was a member of that court, a lawyer, prominent in the affairs of the French Academy, and fond of children, since it was he who procured for the children of Paris the right to play in the gardens of the Tuileries, which others would have held sacred to the Crown. In 1697, Perrault gave into the hand of the printer a book of fairy tales, which he said his son had written, taking down the tales from an old nurse. It is generally supposed that the son did not write them, and that the senior Perrault protected his dignity by this invention. The book contained eight immortal stories: "The Sleeping Beauty," "Red Riding-Hood," "Blue Beard," "Puss in Boots," "Diamonds and Toads," "Cinderella," "Riquet with the Tuft," and "Hop o' my Thumb." Perrault seems intuitively to have honored the simplicity, lucidity, and directness of the folk tale, making these qualities his own. Other writers of the period — Madame d'Aulnoy and Madame de Beaumont — made the fairy tale a mirror of the court, decorating it with sophistication and overburdening it with observations of a moral nature. Perrault relished the tales himself, and let them speak for themselves without any interference other than his gift as storyteller. It was a germinal book for the whole of Europe and a salvation for children who had little to read but lessons and tracts of moral precepts.

All of this is of very little concern to children. They ask for fairy tales, knowing exactly what to expect in return. The word *fairy* comes originally from the Latin *fatum*, fate, through the Old French and Middle French *féerie*, meaning the land of the fée or fates, into the Middle English *faerie*. Spenser with his Faerie Queene and Shakespeare with his Titania are no doubt responsible for the concept of fairies as dainty, small, beautiful creatures, from which, alas, the modern concept of them as all tinsel and star dust portrays them in a degenerative state. They are, in the folk tale, unpredictable forces, like Nature herself, sometimes benign, often cruel and malicious. In the minds of children, they promise the marvelous, the miraculous, and the just.

With passionate devotion, children read fairy tales, never tiring of the elemental themes and the images of magic. Sometimes the insatiable hunger endures through years of childhood, until at last the child emerges into a new maturity, free of the golden spell, laden with pollen, like an inebriate bee. From his reading of the folk tale, the child gains a yea-saying faith in the ultimate goodness of life, a recognition of the threat of evil in the world and even in himself, with magic weapons to conquer it. He gains the habit of wonder; a robust sense of humor; the ability to find enchantment in the most common day, and the power to thrust his imagination beyond himself and the limits of ignorance.

Everything is clear in the fairy tale. One knows exactly where to place one's sympathy. The issues are soon stated, with no unnecessary subtleties of emotion, no bewildering wavering between cause and effect. Everyone acts according to his nature, and the stories move in strong, direct action to the always expected end, where the good come to glory and joy, and evil is punished as befits it, with primitive symbols of suffering. The structure and style of the tales accustom the reader to the art of writing at its best, for there is economy of language, nothing that does not move to the ultimate finish, and yet there is imagery, there are flashes of poetic insight and the clear echoes of spoken words and individual ways of saying things. "She was so lovely, there was no end to her loveliness." "Billy, my boy, you and I must undergo great scenery." "My blessing be on you till the sea loses its saltiness and the trees forget to bud in the springtime." "Clippety, lippety, lippety, clippety, here come Brer Rabbit just as sassy as a jay-bird."

The brutality and cruelty in the tales is disturbing to many people who cannot bear to give children knowledge of cruelty and violence, though it is difficult to know how they are to avoid such knowledge, being children of the twentieth century, in which there have been two world wars, such degradation of human dignity as man had never before known, and the mushroom-shaped cloud shadowing the universe. It is well to remember that what is read for oneself, without experience of horror, is never as vivid as that which has been given the unconscious emotion of the spoken voice. If the story-teller cannot describe the fate of the first two little pigs without crunching the bones, the tale is not for her. To read of horror may even fulfill some need, to know symbolically what the threat may be. To hear it brings it closer to reality; but to see it, in pictures, is to define it too clearly and to shut off the protection of only half knowing. That is why, for many children who saw Walt Disney's *Snow White* at too early an age, it was only the story of a terrible witch.

Certain authorities feel that folk tales should not be given to younger children, before they have come to a knowledge of their own reality in the world. This brings up the question of what is reality for the young child, and of our ability to define it. The most eloquent discussion of this matter is to be found in Lewis Mumford's book *Green Memories,* an account of the childhood of his own son who was killed in the war. The Mumfords had held to the theory that "the immediate visible environment, visible and meaningful, that is, to grownups, is the real one in which the child should live." Accordingly, the factual and pragmatic was stressed in the education of the young Geddes, but this did not banish some inner world of terror, the existence of which the boy confessed, when he was grown. Lewis Mumford continues:

> Surely, the minds of children are full of memories and forebodings that anticipate and reinforce [the] more tangible threats of inhumanity: the wildest folk tale, the most brutal fairy story, do fuller justice to their reality than a factual account of a walk to school; and we fooled ourselves when we thought that any antiseptic efforts of ours to keep the germs of fantasy from incubating could banish the child's sense of the mysterious, the inscrutable, the terrible, the overwhelming. In repressing this life of fantasy and subordinating it to our own practical interests, we perhaps made it take more devious forms, or at least gave the demonic a free hand without conjuring up any angelic powers to fight on the other side. We did not get rid of the dragon: we only banished St. George.[5]

[5] Lewis Mumford, *Green Memories* (Harcourt, Brace, New York, 1947), p. 65.

GERMANY

The Elves [1]

(The Elves and the Shoemaker)

A common folk theme is one in which good fairies secretly help good mortals, not only without asking reward but in some cases objecting to payment.

There was once a shoemaker, who, through no fault of his own, became so poor that at last he had nothing left but just enough leather to make one pair of shoes. He cut out the shoes at night, so as to set to work upon them next morning; and as he had a good conscience, he laid himself quietly down in his bed, committed himself to heaven, and fell asleep. In the morning, after he had said his prayers, and was going to get to work, he found the pair of shoes made and finished, and standing on his table. He was very much astonished, and could not tell what to think, and he took the shoes in his hand to examine them more nearly; and they were so well made that every stitch was in its right place, just as if they had come from the hand of a master-workman.

Soon after a purchaser entered, and as the shoes fitted him very well, he gave more than the usual price for them, so that the shoemaker had enough money to buy leather for two more pairs of shoes. He cut them out at night, and intended to set to work the next morning with fresh spirit; but that was not to be, for when he got up they were already finished, and a customer even was not lack-

[1] From Jakob and Wilhelm Grimm, *Household Stories,* trans. Lucy Crane (Macmillan, 1926).

ing, who gave him so much money that he was able to buy leather enough for four new pairs. Early next morning he found the four pairs also finished, and so it always happened; whatever he cut out in the evening was worked up by the morning, so that he was soon in the way of making a good living, and in the end became very well to do.

One night, not long before Christmas, when the shoemaker had finished cutting out, and before he went to bed, he said to his wife,

"How would it be if we were to sit up tonight and see who it is that does us this service?"

His wife agreed, and set a light to burn. Then they both hid in a corner of the room, behind some coats that were hanging up, and then they began to watch. As soon as it was midnight they saw come in two neatly formed naked little men, who seated themselves before the shoemaker's table, and took up the work that was already prepared, and began to stitch, to pierce, and to hammer so cleverly and quickly with their little fingers that the shoemaker's eyes could scarcely follow them, so full of wonder was he. And they never left off until everything was finished and was standing ready on the table, and then they jumped up and ran off.

The next morning the shoemaker's wife said to her husband, "Those little men have made us rich, and we ought to show ourselves grateful. With all their running about, and having nothing to cover them, they must be very cold. I'll tell you what; I will make little shirts, coats, waistcoats, and breeches for them, and knit each of them a pair of stockings, and you shall make each of them a pair of shoes."

The husband consented willingly, and at night, when everything was finished, they laid the gifts together on the table, instead of the cut-out work, and placed themselves so that they could observe how the little men would behave. When midnight came, they rushed in, ready to set to work, but when they found, instead of the pieces of prepared leather, the neat little garments put ready for them, they stood a moment in surprise, and then they testified the greatest delight. With the greatest swiftness they took up the pretty garments and slipped them on, singing,

> "What spruce and dandy boys are we
> No longer cobblers we will be."

Then they hopped and danced about, jumping over the chairs and tables, and at last they danced out at the door.

From that time they were never seen again; but it always went well with the shoemaker as long as he lived, and whatever he took in hand prospered.

The Wolf and the Seven Little Kids [2]

&_ The wolf is most often the villain animal in beast tales. He frequently victimizes sheep, who are held in some contempt among the old storytellers. In a general sense, the form of this story is cumulative._

There was once on a time an old goat who had seven little kids and loved them with all the love of a mother for her children. One day she wanted to go into the forest and fetch some food. So she called all seven to her and said, "Dear children, I have to go into the forest; be on your guard against the wolf; if he comes in, he will devour you all — skin, hair, and all. The wretch often disguises himself, but you will know him at once by his rough voice and his black feet." The

2 From Jakob and Wilhelm Grimm, _Household Tales,_ trans. Margaret Hunt (G. Bell and Son, London, 1884).

kids said, "Dear mother, we will take good care of ourselves; you may go away without any anxiety." Then the old one bleated and went on her way with an easy mind.

It was not long before some one knocked at the house-door and cried, "Open the door, dear children: your mother is here and has brought something back with her for each of you." But the little kids knew that was the wolf by the rough voice. "We will not open the door," cried they. "Thou art not our mother. She has a soft, pleasant voice, but thy voice is rough; thou art the wolf!" Then the wolf went away to a shopkeeper and bought himself a great lump of chalk, ate this and made his voice soft with it. Then he came back, knocked at the door of the house, and cried, "Open the door, dear children, your mother is here and has brought something back with her for each of you." But the wolf had laid his black paws against the window, and the children saw them and cried, "We will not open the door; our mother has not black feet like thee: thou art the wolf!" Then the wolf ran to a baker and said, "I have hurt my feet, rub some dough over them for me." And when the baker had rubbed his feet over, he ran to the miller and said, "Strew some white meal over my feet for me." The miller thought to himself, "The wolf wants to deceive some one," and refused; but the wolf said, "If thou wilt not do it, I will devour thee." Then the miller was afraid and made his paws white for him. Truly men are like that.

So now the wretch went for the third time to the house-door, knocked at it, and said, "Open the door for me, children, your dear little mother has come home and has brought every one of you something back from the forest with her." The little kids cried "First show us thy paws that we may know if thou art our dear little mother." Then he put his paws in through the window, and when the kids saw that they were white, they believed that all he said was true and opened the door. But who should come in but the wolf! They were terrified and wanted to hide themselves. One sprang under the table, the second into the bed, the third into the stove, the fourth into the kitchen, the fifth into the cupboard, the sixth under the washing-bowl, and the seventh into the clock-case. But the wolf found them all and used no great ceremony; one after the other he swallowed them down his throat. The youngest in the clock-case was the only one he did not find. When the wolf had satisfied his appetite, he took himself off, laid himself down under a tree in the green meadow outside, and began to sleep. Soon afterwards the old goat came home again from the forest. Ah! what a sight she saw there! The house-door stood wide open. The table, chairs, and benches were thrown down, the washing-bowl lay broken to pieces, and the quilts and pillows were pulled off the bed. She sought her children, but they were nowhere to be found. She called them one after another by name, but no one answered. At last, when she came to the youngest, a soft voice cried, "Dear mother, I am in the clock-case." She took the kid out, and it told her that the wolf had come and had eaten all the others. Then you may imagine how she wept over her poor children.

At length in her grief she went out, and the youngest kid ran with her. When they came to the meadow, there lay the wolf by the tree and snored so loud that the branches shook. She looked at him on every side and saw that something was moving and struggling in his gorged body. "Ah, heavens," said she, "is it possible that my poor children whom he has swallowed down for his supper can be still alive?" Then the kid had to run home and fetch scissors, and a needle and thread, and the goat cut open the monster's stomach, and hardly had she made one cut, than one little kid thrust its head out, and when she had cut farther, all six sprang out one after another, and were all still alive, and had suffered no injury whatever, for in his greediness the monster had swallowed them down whole. What rejoicing there was! Then they embraced their dear mother, and jumped like a tailor at his wedding. The mother, however, said, "Now go and look for some big stones, and we will fill the wicked beast's stomach with them while he is still asleep." Then the seven kids dragged the stones thither with all speed and put as many of them into his stomach as they could

get in; and the mother sewed him up again in the greatest haste, so that he was not aware of anything and never once stirred.

When the wolf at length had had his sleep out, he got on his legs; and as the stones in his stomach made him very thirsty, he wanted to go to a well to drink. But when he began to walk and to move about, the stones in his stomach knocked against each other and rattled. Then cried he,

"What rumbles and tumbles
    Against my poor bones?
I thought 'twas six kids,
    But it's naught but big stones."

And when he got to the well and stooped over the water and was just about to drink, the heavy stones made him fall in and there was no help, but he had to drown miserably. When the seven kids saw that, they came running to the spot and cried aloud, "The wolf is dead! The wolf is dead!" and danced for joy round about the well with their mother.

The Golden Goose [3]

❧ *This tale has the very common motif of three brothers starting out to seek their fortunes; with the youngest and supposedly stupid brother eventually successful in his quest. Sometimes his success is the result of chance; sometimes of a kindness he shows, as in this story; and sometimes he wins because he is really the clever one of the three, as in* Boots and His Brothers.

There was a man who had three sons. The youngest was called Dummling — which is much the same as Dunderhead, for all thought he was more than half a fool — and he was at all times mocked and ill-treated by the whole household.

It happened that the eldest son took it into his head one day to go into the wood to cut fuel; and his mother gave him a nice pasty and a bottle of wine to take with him, that he might refresh himself at his work.

[3] From Jakob and Wilhelm Grimm, *Household Tales*, ed. and partly trans. anew by Marian Edwardes (Dent, London, 1922).

As he went into the wood, a little old man bid him good day and said, "Give me a little piece of meat from your plate, and a little wine out of your bottle, for I am very hungry and thirsty." But this clever young man said, "Give you my meat and wine? No, I thank you, I should not have enough left for myself"; and away he went. He soon began to cut down a tree; but he had not worked long before he missed his stroke and cut himself and was forced to go home to have the wound dressed. Now it was the little old man that sent him this mischief.

Next went out the second son to work; and his mother gave him too a pasty and a bottle of wine. The same little old man met him also and asked him for something to eat and drink. But he too thought himself very clever, and said, "The more you eat the less there will be for me; so go your way!" The little man took care that he too should have his reward, and the second stroke that he aimed against a tree hit him on the leg, so that he too was forced to go home.

Then Dummling said, "Father, I should like to go and cut wood too." But his father said, "Your brothers have both lamed themselves; you had better stay at home, for you know nothing about the business of wood-cutting." But Dummling was very pressing; and at last his father said, "Go your way! You will be wiser when you have smarted for your folly." His mother gave him only some dry bread and a bottle of sour beer. But when he went into the wood, he met the little old man, who said, "Give me some meat and drink, for I am very hungry and thirsty." Dummling said, "I have only dry bread and sour beer; if that will suit you, we will sit down and eat it, such as it is, together." So they sat down; and when the lad pulled out his bread, behold it was turned into a rich pasty; and his sour beer, when they tasted it, was delightful wine. They ate and drank heartily; and when they had done, the little man said, "As you have a kind heart, and have been willing to share everything with me, I will send a blessing upon you. There stands an old tree; cut it down, and you will find something at the root." Then he took his leave and went his way.

Dummling set to work and cut down the tree; and when it fell, he found, in a hollow under the roots, a goose with feathers of pure gold. He took it up and went on to a little inn by the roadside where he thought to sleep for the night on his way home. Now the landlord had three daughters; and when they saw the goose, they were very eager to see what this wonderful bird could be and wished very much to pluck one of the feathers out of its tail. At last the eldest said, "I must and will have a feather." So she waited till Dummling was gone to bed and then seized the goose by the wing; but to her great wonder there she stuck, for neither hand nor finger could she get away again. Then in came the second sister and thought to have a feather too; but the moment she touched her sister, there she too hung fast. At last came the third, and she also wanted a feather; but the other two cried out, "Keep away! for Heaven's sake, keep away!" However, she did not understand what they meant. "If they are there," thought she, "I may as well be there too." So she went up to them; but the moment she touched her sisters she stuck fast and hung to the goose as they did. And so they kept company with the goose all night in the cold.

The next morning Dummling got up and carried off the goose under his arm. He took no notice at all of the three girls, but went out with them sticking fast behind. So wherever he traveled, they too were forced to follow, whether they would or no, as fast as their legs could carry them.

In the middle of a field the parson met them; and when he saw the train, he said, "Are you not ashamed of yourselves, you bold girls, to run after a young man in that way over the fields? Is that good behavior?" Then he took the youngest by the hand to lead her away; but as soon as he touched her he too hung fast and followed in the train, though sorely against his will; for he was not only in rather too good plight for running fast, but just then he had a little touch of the gout in the great toe of his right foot. By and by up came the clerk; and when he saw his master, the parson, running after the three girls, he wondered greatly and said, "Holla! holla! your reverence! whither so fast? There is a christening today." Then he ran up and took him by the gown; when, lo and behold, he stuck fast too. As the five were thus trudging along, one behind another, they met two laborers with their mattocks coming from work; and the parson cried out lustily to them to help him. But scarcely had they laid hands upon him when they too fell into the rank; and so they made seven, all running together after Dummling and his goose.

Now Dummling thought he would see a little of the world before he went home; so he and his train journeyed on, till at last they came to a city where there was a king who had an only daughter. The princess was of so thoughtful and moody a turn of mind that no one could make her laugh; and the king had made known to all the world that whoever could make her laugh should have her for his wife. When the young man heard this, he went to her with his goose and all its train; and as soon as she saw the seven all hanging together and running along, treading on each other's heels, she could not help bursting into a long and loud laugh. Then Dummling claimed her for his wife and married her; and he was heir to the kingdom, and lived long and happily with his wife.

But what became of the goose and the goose's tail I never could hear.

The Bremen Town Musicians[4]

(The Traveling Musicians)

❧ Though this tale can be placed in the cumulative class, it has also well-developed action. It is one of the most popular beast tales, not only because the characters are familiar friends of children, but because they have been or are about to be abused but are finally successful. Such action calls upon the child's sympathy and sense of justice.

There was once an ass whose master had made him carry sacks to the mill for many a

[4] From Jakob and Wilhelm Grimm, *Household Stories*, trans. Lucy Crane (Macmillan, 1926).

long year, but whose strength began at last to fail, so that each day as it came found him less capable of work. Then his master began to think of turning him out, but the ass, guessing that something was in the wind that boded him no good, ran away, taking the road to Bremen; for there he thought he might get an engagement as town musician. When he had gone a little way he found a hound lying by the side of the road panting, as if he had run a long way.

"Now, Holdfast, what are you so out of breath about?" said the ass.

"Oh dear!" said the dog, "now I am old, I get weaker every day, and can do no good in the hunt; so, as my master was going to have me killed, I have made my escape; but now, how am I to gain a living?"

"I will tell you what," said the ass, "I am going to Bremen to become town musician. You may as well go with me, and take up music too. I can play the lute, and you can beat the drum."

And the dog consented, and they walked on together. It was not long before they came to a cat sitting in the road, looking as dismal as three wet days.

"Now then, what is the matter with you, old shaver?" said the ass.

"I should like to know who would be cheerful when his neck is in danger," answered the cat. "Now that I am old my teeth are getting blunt, and I would rather sit by the oven and purr than run about after mice, and my mistress wanted to drown me; so I took myself off; but good advice is scarce, and I do not know what is to become of me."

"Go with us to Bremen," said the ass, "and become town musician. You understand serenading."

The cat thought well of the idea, and went with them accordingly. After that the three travelers passed by a yard, and a cock was perched on the gate crowing with all his might.

"Your cries are enough to pierce bone and marrow," said the ass; "what is the matter?"

"I have foretold good weather for Lady-Day, so that all the shirts may be washed and dried; and now on Sunday morning company is coming, and the mistress has told the cook that I must be made into soup, and this evening my neck is to be wrung, so that I am crowing with all my might while I can."

"You had much better go with us, Chanticleer," said the ass. "We are going to Bremen. At any rate, that will be better than dying. You have a powerful voice, and when we are all performing together it will have a very good effect."

So the cock consented, and they went on all four together.

But Bremen was too far off to be reached in one day, and towards evening they came to a wood, where they determined to pass the night. The ass and the dog lay down under a large tree; the cat got up among the branches, and the cock flew up to the top, as that was the safest place for him. Before he went to sleep he looked all round him to the four points of the compass, and perceived in the distance a little light shining, and he called out to his companions that there must be a house not far off, as he could see a light, so the ass said,

"We had better get up and go there, for these are uncomfortable quarters." The dog began to fancy a few bones, not quite bare, would do him good. And they all set off in the direction of the light, and it grew larger and brighter, until at last it led them to a robber's house, all lighted up. The ass, being the biggest, went up to the window, and looked in.

"Well, what do you see?" asked the dog.

"What do I see?" answered the ass; "here is a table set out with splendid eatables and drinkables, and robbers sitting at it and making themselves very comfortable."

"That would just suit us," said the cock.

"Yes, indeed, I wish we were there," said the ass. Then they consulted together how it should be managed so as to get the robbers out of the house, and at last they hit on a plan. The ass was to place his forefeet on the window-sill, the dog was to get on the ass's back, the cat on the top of the dog, and lastly the cock was to fly up and perch on the cat's head. When that was done, at a given signal they all began to perform their music. The ass brayed, the dog barked, the cat mewed, and the cock crowed; then they burst

through into the room, breaking all the panes of glass. The robbers fled at the dreadful sound; they thought it was some goblin and fled to the wood in the utmost terror. Then the four companions sat down to table, made free with the remains of the meal, and feasted as if they had been hungry for a month. And when they had finished they put out the lights, and each sought out a sleeping-place to suit his nature and habits. The ass laid himself down outside on the dunghill, the dog behind the door, the cat on the hearth by the warm ashes, and the cock settled himself in the cockloft, and as they were all tired with their long journey they soon fell fast asleep.

When midnight drew near, and the robbers from afar saw that no light was burning and that everything appeared quiet, their captain said to them that he thought that they had run away without reason, telling one of them to go and reconnoiter. So one of them went and found everything quite quiet; he went into the kitchen to strike a light, and taking the glowing fiery eyes of the cat for burning coals, he held a match to them in order to kindle it. But the cat, not seeing the joke, flew into his face, spitting and scratching. Then he cried out in terror, and ran to get out at the back door, but the dog, who was lying there, ran at him and bit his leg; and as he was rushing through the yard by the dunghill the ass struck out and gave him a great kick with his hindfoot; and the cock, who had been wakened with the noise, and felt quite brisk, cried out, "Cock-a-doodle-doo!"

Then the robber got back as well as he could to his captain, and said, "Oh dear! in that house there is a grewsome witch, and I felt her breath and her long nails in my face; and by the door there stands a man who stabbed me in the leg with a knife; and in the yard there lies a black specter, who beat me with his wooden club; and above, upon the roof, there sits the justice, who cried, 'Bring that rogue here!' And so I ran away from the place as fast as I could."

From that time forward the robbers never ventured to that house, and the four Bremen town musicians found themselves so well off where they were that there they stayed. And the person who last related this tale is still living, as you see.

The Brother and Sister[5]

The usual story of Hansel and Gretel is made up of two parts. In the first, we learn how the children happened to be wandering and living alone in a wood and their experiences at the home of the wicked fairy. Part Two tells of their escape from the witch's house and the succeeding adventures in trying to keep free of the witch as she pursues them. The opera, Hansel and Gretel, *takes up the first half of the story.* The Brother and Sister *deals with their adventures in the second part and gives the happy ending.*

The brother took his sister's hand and said to her,

"Since our mother died we have had no good days; our stepmother beats us every day, and if we go near her she kicks us away; we have nothing to eat but hard crusts of bread left over; the dog under the table fares better; he gets a good piece every now and then. If our mother only knew, how she would pity us! Come, let us go together out into the wide world!"

So they went, and journeyed the whole day through fields and meadows and stony places, and if it rained the sister said, "The skies and we are weeping together."

In the evening they came to a great wood, and they were so weary with hunger and their long journey, that they climbed up into a high tree and fell asleep.

The next morning, when they awoke, the sun was high in heaven, and shone brightly through the leaves. Then said the brother, "Sister, I am thirsty; if I only knew where to find a brook, that I might go and drink! I almost think that I hear one rushing." So the brother got down and led his sister by the hand, and they went to seek the brook. But their wicked stepmother was a witch, and had known quite well that the two children had run away, and had sneaked after them, as only witches can, and had laid a spell on

[5] From Jakob and Wilhelm Grimm, *Household Stories*, trans. Lucy Crane (Macmillan, 1926).

all the brooks in the forest. So when they found a little stream flowing smoothly over its pebbles, the brother was going to drink of it; but the sister heard how it said in its rushing,

"He a tiger will be who drinks of me,
Who drinks of me a tiger will be!"

Then the sister cried, "Pray, dear brother, do not drink, or you will become a wild beast, and will tear me in pieces."

So the brother refrained from drinking, though his thirst was great, and he said he would wait till he came to the next brook. When they came to a second brook the sister heard it say,

"He a wolf will be who drinks of me,
Who drinks of me a wolf will be!"

Then the sister cried, "Pray, dear brother, do not drink, or you will be turned into a wolf, and will eat me up!"

So the brother refrained from drinking, and said, "I will wait until we come to the next brook, and then I must drink, whatever you say; my thirst is so great."

And when they came to the third brook the sister heard how in its rushing it said,

"Who drinks of me a fawn will be,
He a fawn will be who drinks of me!"

Then the sister said, "O my brother, I pray drink not, or you will be turned into a fawn, and run away far from me."

But he had already kneeled by the side of the brook and stooped and drunk of the water, and as the first drops passed his lips he became a fawn.

And the sister wept over her poor lost brother, and the fawn wept also, and stayed sadly beside her. At last the maiden said, "Be comforted, dear fawn, indeed I will never leave you."

Then she untied her golden girdle and bound it round the fawn's neck, and went and gathered rushes to make a soft cord, which she fastened to him; and then she led him on, and they went deeper into the forest. And when they had gone a long long way, they came at last to a little house, and the maiden looked inside, and as it was empty she thought, "We might as well live here."

And she fetched leaves and moss to make a soft bed for the fawn, and every morning she went out and gathered roots and berries and nuts for herself, and fresh grass for the fawn, who ate out of her hand with joy, frolicking round her. At night, when the sister was tired, and had said her prayers, she laid her head on the fawn's back, which served her for a pillow, and softly fell asleep. And if only the brother could have got back his own shape again, it would have been a charming life. So they lived a long while in the wilderness alone.

Now it happened that the King of that country held a great hunt in the forest. The blowing of the horns, the barking of the dogs, and the lusty shouts of the huntsmen sounded through the wood, and the fawn heard them and was eager to be among them.

"Oh," said he to his sister, "do let me go to the hunt; I cannot stay behind any longer," and begged so long that at last she consented.

"But mind," said she to him, "come back to me at night. I must lock my door against the wild hunters, so, in order that I may know you, you must knock and say, 'Little sister, let me in,' and unless I hear that I shall not unlock the door."

Then the fawn sprang out, and felt glad and merry in the open air. The King and his huntsmen saw the beautiful animal, and began at once to pursue him, but they could not come within reach of him, for when they thought they were certain of him he sprang away over the bushes and disappeared. As soon as it was dark he went back to the little house, knocked at the door, and said, "Little sister, let me in."

Then the door was opened to him, and he went in, and rested the whole night long on his soft bed. The next morning the hunt began anew, and when the fawn heard the hunting-horns and the tally-ho of the huntsmen he could rest no longer, and said, "Little sister, let me out, I must go."

The sister opened the door and said, "Now, mind you must come back at night and say the same words."

When the King and his hunters saw the fawn with the golden collar again, they chased him closely, but he was too nimble and swift for them. This lasted the whole day, and at last the hunters surrounded him, and one of them wounded his foot a little, so that he was obliged to limp and go slowly. Then a hunter slipped after him to the little house, and heard how he called out, "Little sister, let me in," and saw the door open and shut again after him directly. The hunter noticed all this carefully, went to the King, and told him all he had seen and heard. Then said the King, "Tomorrow we will hunt again."

But the sister was very terrified when she saw that her fawn was wounded. She washed his foot, laid cooling leaves round it, and said, "Lie down on your bed, dear fawn, and rest, that you may be soon well." The wound was very slight, so that the fawn felt nothing of it the next morning. And when he heard the noise of the hunting outside, he said, "I cannot stay in, I must go after them; I shall not be taken easily again!"

The sister began to weep, and said, "I know you will be killed, and I left alone here in the forest, and forsaken of everybody. I cannot let you go!"

"Then I shall die here with longing," answered the fawn; "when I hear the sound of the horn I feel as if I should leap out of my skin."

Then the sister, seeing there was no help for it, unlocked the door with a heavy heart, and the fawn bounded away into the forest, well and merry. When the King saw him, he said to his hunters, "Now, follow him up all day long till the night comes, and see that you do him no hurt."

So as soon as the sun had gone down, the King said to the huntsmen: "Now, come and show me the little house in the wood."

And when he got to the door he knocked at it, and cried, "Little sister, let me in!"

Then the door opened, and the King went in, and there stood a maiden more beautiful than any he had seen before. The maiden shrieked out when she saw, instead of the fawn, a man standing there with a gold crown on his head. But the King looked kindly on her, took her by the hand, and said, "Will you go with me to my castle, and be my dear wife?"

"Oh yes," answered the maiden, "but the

fawn must come too. I could not leave him." And the King said, "He shall remain with you as long as you live, and shall lack nothing." Then the fawn came bounding in, and the sister tied the cord of rushes to him, and led him by her own hand out of the little house.

The King put the beautiful maiden on his horse, and carried her to his castle, where the wedding was held with great pomp; so she became lady Queen, and they lived together happily for a long while; the fawn was well tended and cherished, and he gamboled about the castle garden.

Now the wicked stepmother, whose fault it was that the children were driven out into the world, never dreamed but that the sister had been eaten up by wild beasts in the forest, and that the brother, in the likeness of a fawn, had been slain by the hunters. But when she heard that they were so happy, and that things had gone so well with them, jealousy and envy arose in her heart, and left her no peace, and her chief thought was how to bring misfortune upon them.

Her own daughter, who was as ugly as sin, and had only one eye, complained to her, and said, "I never had the chance of being a Queen."

"Never mind," said the old woman, to satisfy her; "when the time comes, I shall be at hand."

After a while the Queen brought a beautiful baby-boy into the world, and that day the King was out hunting. The old witch took the shape of the bedchamber woman, and went into the room where the Queen lay, and said to her, "Come, the bath is ready; it will give you refreshment and new strength. Quick, or it will be cold."

Her daughter was within call, so they carried the sick Queen into the bathroom, and left her there. And in the bathroom they had made a great fire, so as to suffocate the beautiful young Queen.

When that was managed, the old woman took her daughter, put a cap on her, and laid her in the bed in the Queen's place, gave her also the Queen's form and countenance, only she could not restore the lost eye. So, in order that the King might not remark it, she had to lie on the side where there was no eye. In the evening, when the King came home and heard that a little son was born to him, he rejoiced with all his heart, and was going at once to his dear wife's bedside to see how she did. Then the old woman cried hastily,

"For your life, do not draw back the curtains, to let in the light upon her; she must be kept quiet." So the King went away, and never knew that a false Queen was lying in the bed.

Now, when it was midnight, and everyone was asleep, the nurse, who was sitting by the cradle in the nursery and watching there alone, saw the door open, and the true Queen come in. She took the child out of the cradle, laid it in her bosom, and fed it. Then she shook out its little pillow, put the child back again, and covered it with the coverlet. She did not forget the fawn either; she went to him where he lay in the corner, and stroked his back tenderly. Then she went in perfect silence out at the door, and the nurse next morning asked the watchmen if any one had entered the castle during the night, but they had seen no one. And the Queen came many nights, and never said a word; the nurse saw her always, but she did not dare speak of it to any one.

After some time had gone by in this manner, the Queen seemed to find voice, and said one night,

"My child my fawn twice more I come to see,
Twice more I come, and then the end must be."

The nurse said nothing, but as soon as the Queen had disappeared she went to the King and told him all. The King said, "Ah, heaven! what do I hear! I will myself watch by the child tomorrow night."

So at evening he went into the nursery, and at midnight the Queen appeared, and said,

"My child my fawn once more I come to see,
Once more I come, and then the end must be."

And she tended the child, as she was accustomed to do before she vanished. The King dared not speak to her, but he watched again the following night, and heard her say,

"My child my fawn this once I come to see,
This once I come, and now the end must be."

Then the King could contain himself no longer, but rushed towards her, saying, "You are no other than my dear wife!"

Then she answered, "Yes, I am your dear wife," and in that moment, by the grace of heaven, her life returned to her, and she was once more well and strong. Then she told the King the snare that the wicked witch and her daughter had laid for her. The King had them both brought to judgment, and sentence was passed upon them. The daughter was sent away into the wood, where she was devoured by the wild beasts, and the witch was burned, and ended miserably.

And as soon as her body was in ashes the spell was removed from the fawn, and he took human shape again; and then the sister and brother lived happily together until the end.

Hansel and Gretel [6]

In 1931, Wanda Gág, the distinguished artist-author of Millions of Cats and The A B C Bunny, was given a complete edition of Grimm's Fairy Tales, in their original German, by her friend and fellow-artist Carl Zigrosser, Curator of Prints in the Philadelphia Museum of Art. It was a gift which was to have beneficent reverberations. Wanda Gág knew these stories by heart, for she was brought up on them. Born in Minnesota of pioneer Bohemian stock, she grew up in the German-speaking community of New Ulm, where these stories were native to the air she breathed. She was peculiarly fitted, therefore, for the task she set herself — to make her own translation of certain of the tales, and to illustrate them. The result, over a period of years, was the appearance of an endearing series of books, some consisting of only one story, such as Snow White and the Seven Dwarfs, others being collections of stories, Tales from Grimm, Three Gay Tales from Grimm, and finally More Tales from Grimm, which unhappily was not fully completed, as far as the illustrations were concerned, at the time of her death.

Wanda Gág's translations have a subtle warmth about them, a simplicity of style and presentation which gives them an appeal for children who are at the beginning of their exploration of folklore. She is absolutely true to the folk spirit, and gives added sharpness to dialogue and characterization. Five of the stories as freely translated by her are included in this anthology. But the complete work of art is to be seen in the books themselves, appealing in size and format, and illustrated by her characteristically encircling line, which heightens the comfortable atmosphere of peasant interiors, gives intimacy to landscape, and emphasizes the humorous and robust quality of the tales.

Hansel and Gretel is one of the best loved of fairy tales, with its comestible house, its malevolent witch, the friendship of birds, and the courage of the children themselves. In the original German version, when the death of the witch is described, the text reads, "Oh, then she began to howl quite horribly, but Gretel ran away, and the godless witch was miserably burnt to death." Wanda Gág omits all mention of God, removes the event from any relationship to human suffering, and makes it what it is — a symbol of justice, in a nonsense rigmarole: "The old one cried, and frizzled and fried, but no one heard. That was the end of her, and who cares?"

In a little hut near the edge of a deep, deep forest lived a poor woodchopper with his wife and his two children, Hansel and Gretel.

Times were hard. Work was scarce and the price of wood was high. Many people were starving, and our poor woodchopper and his little brood fared as badly as all the rest.

One evening after they had gone to bed, the man said to his wife, "I don't know what will become of us. All the potatoes are gone, every head of cabbage is eaten, and there is only enough rye meal left for a few loaves of bread."

"You are right," said his wife, who was not the children's real mother, "and there is nothing for us to do but take Hansel and Gretel into the woods and let them shift for themselves."

She was a hard-hearted woman and did not much care what became of the children. But the father loved them dearly and said, "Wife, what are you saying? I would never have the heart to do such a thing!"

"Oh well then," snapped the stepmother,

[6] From Tales from Grimm, trans. Wanda Gág (Coward-McCann, 1936).

"if you won't listen to reason, we'll all have to starve." And she nagged and scolded until the poor man, not knowing what else to say, consented to do it. "May heaven keep them from harm," he sighed.

Hunger had kept the children awake that night, and, lying in their trundle-beds on the other side of the room, they had heard every word their parents had said. Gretel began to cry softly but her brother Hansel whispered, "Don't worry, little sister; I'll take care of you."

He waited until the father and mother were sleeping soundly. Then he put on his little jacket, unbarred the back door and slipped out. The moon was shining brightly, and the white pebbles which lay in front of the house glistened like silver coins. Hansel bent down and gathered as many of the shiny pebbles as his pockets would hold. Then he tiptoed back to bed and told Gretel he had thought of a very good plan for the morrow.

At break of day the mother came to wake the children. "Get up, you lazy things," she said, "we're off to the forest to gather wood. Here is a piece of bread for each of you. Don't eat it until noon; it's all you'll get today."

Gretel carried both pieces of bread in her apron because, of course, Hansel's pockets were so full of pebbles. They were soon on their way to the forest: the mother first with a jug of water, the father next with an ax over his shoulder, Gretel with the bread and Hansel bringing up the rear, his pockets bulging with pebbles. But Hansel walked very slowly. Often he would stand still and look back at the house.

"Come, come, Hansel!" said the father. "Why do you lag behind?"

"I'm looking at my little white kitten, papa. She's sitting on the roof and wants to say good-by."

"Fool!" said the mother. "That's not your kitten. That's only the morning sun shining on the chimney."

But Hansel lingered on and dropped the pebbles behind him, one at a time, all along the way.

It was a long walk, and Hansel and Gretel became very tired. At last the mother called a halt and said, "Sit down, children, and rest yourselves while we go off to gather some wood. If you feel sleepy you can take a little nap."

Hansel and Gretel sat down and munched their bread. They thought their father and mother were nearby, because they seemed to hear the sound of an ax. But what they heard was not an ax at all, only a dry branch which was bumping against a dead tree in the wind.

By and by the two little children became so drowsy they lay down on the moss and dropped off to sleep. When they awoke it was night and they were all alone.

"Oh Hansel, it's so dark! Now we'll never find our way home," said Gretel, and began to cry.

But Hansel said, "Don't cry, little sister. Just wait until the moon is out; I'll find the way home."

Dawn was stealing over the mountains when they reached their home, and with happy faces they burst in at the door. When their mother saw them standing before her, she was taken aback. But then she said, "Why, you naughty children! Where have you been so long? I began to think you didn't want to come back home."

She wasn't much pleased but the father welcomed them joyfully. He had lain awake all night worrying over them.

Luckily, things now took a turn for the better, and for several weeks the woodchopper was able to earn enough money to keep his family from starving. But it did not last, and one evening the children, still awake in their trundle-beds, heard the mother say to the father: "I suppose you know there's only one loaf of bread left in the house, and after that's eaten, there's an end to the song. We must try once more to get rid of the children, and this time we'll take them still deeper into the woods, so our sly Hansel can't find his way back."

As before, the father tried to talk her out of it, but the hard-hearted stepmother wouldn't listen to him. He who says A must also say B, and because the father had given in the first time, he had to give in this time as well.

Hansel saw that he would have to get up and gather pebbles again, and as soon as his parents were asleep, he crept out of bed. But alas! the door was locked now and he had to go back to bed and think of a different plan.

The next day everything happened as it had the first time. Hansel and Gretel were each given a crust of bread and then they all went forth into the forest. Hansel brought up the rear as before, and kept straggling behind the rest.

"Come, come, Hansel!" said the father. "Why do you lag behind?"

"I see my pet dove, papa. It is sitting on the roof and wants to say good-by to me."

"Fool!" said the mother. "That's not your dove. That's only the morning sun shining on the chimney."

But Hansel kept on loitering because he was again busy making a trail to guide them back home. And what do you think he did this time? He had broken his bread-crust into tiny pieces and now he was carefully scattering the crumbs, one by one, behind him on the path.

They had to walk even farther than before, and again the parents went to gather wood, leaving Hansel and Gretel behind. At noon Gretel shared her bread with Hansel, and then they both fell asleep.

When they awoke, it was dark and they were all alone. This time Gretel did not cry because she knew Hansel had scattered crumbs to show them the way back. When the moon rose, Hansel took her hand and said, "Come, little sister, now it's time to go home."

But alas! when they looked for the crumbs they found none. Little twittering birds which fly about in the woods and glades, had eaten them all, all up.

The two unhappy children walked all that night and the next day too, but the more they looked for the way, the more they lost it. They found nothing to eat but a few sour berries; and at last, weak and hungry, they sank down on a cushion of moss and fell asleep.

It was now the third morning since they had left their home. They started to walk again, but they only got deeper and deeper into the wood.

They felt small and strange in the large,

silent forest. The trees were so tall and the shade was so dense. Flowers could not grow in that dim, gloomy place — not even ferns. Only pale waxy mushrooms glowed faintly among the shadows, and weird lichens clung to the tree-trunks. Suddenly, into the vast green silence fell a ripple of sound so sweet, so gay, so silvery, that the children looked up in breathless wonder. A little white bird sat there in a tree; and when its beautiful song was ended, it spread its wings and fluttered away with anxious little chirps as though it wished to say, "Follow me! Follow me!"

Hansel and Gretel followed gladly enough, and all at once they found themselves in a fair flowery clearing at the edge of which stood a tiny cottage.

The children stood hand in hand and gazed at it in wonder. "It's the loveliest house I ever saw," gasped Gretel, "and it looks good enough to eat."

They hurried on, and as they reached the little house, Hansel touched it and cried, "Gretel! It *is* good enough to eat."

And, if you can believe it, that's just what it was. Its walls were made of gingerbread, its roof was made of cake. It was trimmed with cookies and candy, and its window-panes were of pure transparent sugar. Nothing could have suited the children better and they began eating right away, they were so hungry! Hansel plucked a cookie from the roof and took a big bite out of it. Gretel munched big slabs of sugar-pane which she had broken from the window.

Suddenly a honey voice came floating from the house. It said:

Nibble, nibble, nottage,
Who's nibbling at my cottage?

To which the children said mischievously:

It's only a breeze,
Blowing down from the trees.

At this, the door burst open, and out slithered a bent old woman, waggling her head and leaning on a knotted stick. Hansel stopped munching his cookie and Gretel stopped crunching her sugar-pane. They were frightened — and no wonder! The Old One was far from beautiful. Her sharp nose bent down to meet her bristly chin. Her face, all folds and wrinkles, looked like an old shriveled pear; and she had only three teeth, two above and one below, all very long and yellow.

When the Old One saw that the children were turning to run away, she said in sugary tones, "Ei, ei! my little darlings, what has brought you here? Come right in and stay with me. I'll take good care of you."

She led them inside, and there in the middle of the room was a table neatly spread with toothsome dainties: milk, pancakes and honey, nuts, apples and pears.

While the children were eating their fill, the Old One made up two little beds which stood at one end of the room. She fluffed up the feather bed and puffed up the pillows, she turned back the lily-white linen, and then she said: "There, my little rabbits — a downy nest for each of you. Tumble in and slumber sweetly."

As soon as Hansel and Gretel were sound asleep, the Old One walked over and looked at them.

"Mm! Mm! Mm!" she said. "They're mine for certain!"

Now why should she do that? Well, I must tell you the real truth about the Old One. She wasn't as good and friendly as she pretended to be. She was a bad, bad witch who had built that sweet and sugary house on purpose to attract little children. Witches have ruby-red eyes and can hardly see at all, but oh! how they can smell with those long sharp noses of theirs! What they can smell is human beings; and that morning, as Hansel and Gretel were wandering around in the forest, the Old One knew it well enough. Sniff! sniff! sniff! went her nose — she had been sniffing and waiting for them all day.

The next morning while the two little innocents were still sleeping peacefully, the Old One looked greedily at their round arms and rosy cheeks. "Mm! Mm! Mm!" she mumbled. "Juicy morsels!"

She yanked Hansel out of bed, dragged him into the back yard, and locked him up in the goose-coop. Hansel screamed and cried but it did him no good.

Then the Old One went into the house,

gave Gretel a rough shake and cried, "Up with you, lazy bones. Make haste and cook some food for your brother. He's out in the goose-coop and if we feed him well, ei! ei! what a tasty boy he'll make!"

When Gretel heard this she burst into tears, but the Old One gave her a cuff on the ears and said, "Stop howling, you fool. Pick up your legs and do as I tell you."

Each day Gretel had to cook big pots full of fattening food for Hansel, and each morning the Old One hobbled out to the goose-coop and cried, "Hansel, let me see your finger so I can tell how fat you're getting."

But Hansel never showed her his finger. He always poked out a dry old bone, and the Old One, because of her red eyes, never knew the difference. She thought it really was his finger, and wondered why it was that he did not get fat.

When four weeks had passed and Hansel seemed to stay thin, the Old One became impatient and said to Gretel, "Hey there, girl! Heat up a big kettle of water. I'm tired of waiting and, be he fat or lean, I'm going to have Hansel for my supper tonight."

Gretel cried and pleaded with her. But the Old One said, "All that howling won't do you a bit or a whit of good. You might as well spare your breath."

She built a roaring fire in the stove and said to Gretel, "First we'll do some baking. I've mixed and kneaded the dough, and the loaves are all ready for the oven." Then she opened the oven door and added in a sweet voice, "Do you think it's hot enough for the bread, Gretel dear? Just stick your head in the oven and see, there's a good girl!"

Gretel was about to obey, when a bird (the same white bird which had led them out of the forest) began to sing a song. It seemed to Gretel he was singing:

> Beware, beware,
> Don't look in there.

So Gretel didn't look into the oven. Instead she said to the Old One, "Well, I really don't know how to go about it. Couldn't you first show me how?"

"Stupid!" cried the Old One. "It's easy enough. Just stick your head way in and give a good look around. See? Like this!"

As the Old One poked her horrid old head into the oven, Gretel gave her a push and a shove, closed the oven door, bolted it swiftly and ran away. The Old One called and cried, and frizzled and fried, but no one heard. That was the end of her, and who cares?

Gretel was already in the back yard. "Hansel!" she cried. "We are free!" She opened the door of the goose-coop and out popped Hansel. The children threw their arms about each other and hopped and skipped around wildly.

But now there came a soft whirr in the air. The children stopped dancing and looked up. The good white bird and many others — all the twittering birds from the fields and glades — were flying through the air and settling on the cake-roof of the gingerbread house.

On the roof was a nest full of pearls and sparkling gems. Each little forest-bird took out a pearl or a gem and carried it down to the children. Hansel held out his hands, and Gretel held up her apron to catch all these treasures, while the little white bird sat on the roof and sang:

> Thank you for the crumbs of bread,
> Here are gems for you instead.

Now Hansel and Gretel understood that these were the very same birds who had eaten up their crumbs in the forest, and that this was how they wished to show their thanks.

As the birds fluttered away, Hansel said, "And now, little sister, we must make haste and get out of this witchy wood. As for me, I got very homesick sitting in that goose-coop week after week."

"And I," said Gretel. "Yes, I've been homesick too. But, Hansel, here we are so far from home, and how can we ever find our way back?"

Ho, what luck! There was the little white bird fluttering ahead of them once more. It led them away and soon they were in a green meadow. In front of them lay a big, big pond. How to get over it! As Hansel and Gretel stood on the shore wondering what to do, a large swan came floating by, and the children said:

> Float, swan, float!
> Be our little boat.

The swan dipped its graceful head, raised it and dipped it again — that meant yes. When the swan had taken the children, one by one, to the other shore, they thanked it prettily and patted its long curved neck. Near the water's edge ran a neat little path. Hansel and Gretel followed it, and now the trees and the fields began to look familiar. Soon they saw their father's house gleaming through the trees and they ran home as fast as they could. The father, who had been grieving and looking for his lost children all this time, was sitting in front of the hearth gazing sadly into the fire. As the door burst open and his two little ones ran in with shouts and laughter, his eyes filled with tears of joy. He hugged them and kissed them, and all he could say was: "My treasures, my little treasures!"

"Oh, as to treasures, papa," said Hansel, putting his hands into his pockets, "we'll show you some! See, now we will never have to starve again." At this, Gretel poured a shower of jewels from her apron, while Hansel added handful after handful from his pockets.

And the hard-hearted stepmother, where was she? Well, I'll tell you. When Hansel and Gretel seemed to be gone for good, the woman saw that her husband could think of nothing but his lost children. This made her so angry that she packed up her things in a large red handkerchief and ran away. She never came back, and Hansel and Gretel and their good father lived happily ever after.

The Fisherman and His Wife[7]

It would be interesting to know how the vinegar jug as a habitation came into folklore. There is Mr. Vinegar in the English story of that name; and here, in this version of The Fisherman and His Wife, *the couple are discovered in a like dwelling.*

This is a universal story, if ever there was one. Who has not known an insatiable woman,

7 From *Tales from Grimm*, trans. Wanda Gág (Coward McCann, 1936).

or a man who feels himself quite able to undertake the tasks of God himself? When anyone says "She's like the fisherman's wife," the whole tale is told.

There was once a fisherman and his wife. They lived together in a vinegar jug close by the sea, and the fisherman went there every day and fished: and he fished and he fished.

So he sat there one day at his fishing and always looked into the clear water: and he sat and he sat.

Then down went the hook, deep down, and when he pulled it up, there he had a big golden fish. And the fish said to him, "Listen, fisher, I beg of you, let me live. I am not a real fish; I am an enchanted Prince. How would it help you if you killed me? I wouldn't taste good to you anyway — put me back into the water and let me swim."

"Nu," said the man, "you needn't make so many words about it. A fish that can talk — I would surely have let him swim anyway."

With that he put him back into the clear water, and the fish went down and left a long streak of blood after him. And the fisher got up and went home to his wife in the vinegar jug.

"Husband," said the wife, "haven't you caught anything today?"

"Nay," said the man. "I caught a golden fish who said he was an enchanted Prince, so I let him swim again."

"But didn't you wish yourself something?" asked the wife.

"Nay," said the man. "What could I have wished?"

"Ach!" said the wife. "Here we live in a vinegar jug that smells so sour and is so dark: you could have wished us a little hut. Go there now and tell him — tell him we want a little hut. He will do that, surely."

"Ach!" said the man. "Why should I go there?"

"Ei!" said the wife. "After all, you caught him and let him swim again, didn't you? He will do that surely; go right there."

The man still didn't want to go, but he did not want to go against his wife's wishes, either, so he went off to the sea. As he came there, the sea was all green and yellow and not at all so clear any more. So he went and stood and said:

> Manye, Manye, Timpie Tee,
> Fishye, Fishye in the sea,
> Ilsebill my wilful wife
> Does not want my way of life.

Now the fish came swimming along and said, "Nu, what does she want then?"

"Ach!" said the man. "After all, I caught you and let you go. Now my wife says I should really have wished myself something. She doesn't want to live in the vinegar jug any more; she would dearly like to have a hut."

"Go there," said the fish. "She has that now."

So the man went home and his wife wasn't sitting in the vinegar jug any more, but there stood a little hut and she was sitting in front of it on a bench. She took his hand and said to him, "Just come in. See, now isn't that much better?"

So they went in, and in the hut was a little hall and a parlor; also a sleeping room in which stood their bed. And a kitchen and dining room, with the best of utensils laid out in the nicest way: pewter and brassware and all that belonged there. In back of the hut was a little yard with chickens and ducks, and a garden with vegetables and fruit.

"See," said the wife, "isn't that neat?"

"Yes," said the man, "and so let it be. Now we will live right contentedly."

"Nu, we'll think about that," said the wife. With that they ate something and went to bed.

So that went on for about eight or fourteen days, when the wife said: "Listen, man, the hut is much too small, and the yard and garden are so tiny. The fish might really have given us a bigger house. I want to live in a stone mansion. Go to the fish, he must give us a mansion."

"Ach, wife," said the man. "The hut is good enough — why should we want to live in a mansion?"

"Go there," said the wife. "The fish can easily do that much."

"Nay, wife," said the man, "the fish has already given us the hut. I don't want to go there again; it might displease the fish."

"Go!" said the wife. "He can do that right well and will do it gladly; you just go there."

The man's heart became heavy and he didn't want to go. He said to himself, "That is not right," but he went there anyway.

When he came to the sea, the water was all purple and gray and thick, and not green and yellow any more, but it was still quiet. So he went and stood and said:

Manye, Manye, Timpie Tee,
Fishye, Fishye in the sea,
Ilsebill my wilful wife
Does not want my way of life.

"Nu, what does she want then?" asked the fish.

"Ach!" said the man. "She wants to live in a big stone mansion."

"Go there then," said the fish, "she is standing in front of the door."

So the man left and thought he would go home, but when he reached it, there was a big stone mansion, and his wife was standing on the steps, just ready to go in. She took him by the hand and said, "Just come inside."

That he did, and in the mansion was a big hall with marble floors, and there were so many many servants, and they tore open the big doors. The walls were all bright, and covered with fine tapestries, and the rooms were full of golden chairs and tables. Crystal chandeliers hung from the ceilings, all the parlors and chambers were covered with carpets, and food and the best of wines stood on the tables so that they were ready to break.

In back of the mansion was a big courtyard with horse and cow stables, and carriages of the very best. Also there was a marvelous big garden with the most beautiful flowers and fine fruit trees. And a park — at least a half a mile long — in it were stags and deer and rabbits and all that one could ever wish for oneself.

"See?" said the wife, "isn't that beautiful?"

"Oh yes," said the man, "and so let it be. Now we will live in the beautiful mansion and be well satisfied."

"Nu, we'll think that over and sleep on it," said the wife.

With that they went to bed.

The next morning the wife woke up first. It was just daybreak, and she saw from her bed the wonderful land lying before her. The man was still sleeping, so she nudged him in his side with her elbow and said, "Man, get up and just look out of the window. See? Couldn't one become King over all that land? Go to the fish — we want to be King."

"Ach, wife!" said the man. "Why should we want to be King? I don't want to be King."

"Nu," said the wife, "if *you* don't want to be King, *I* want to be King. Go to the fish and tell him I want to be King."

"Ach, wife!" said the man, "that I don't want to tell the fish."

"Why not?" said the wife. "Go right straight there. I must be King!"

So the man went there and was right dismayed. "That is not right and is not right," he thought. He did not want to go but he went anyway. And as he came to the shore, there it was all blackish grey and the water foamed up from the bottom and it smelled all rotten. So he went and stood and said:

Manye, Manye, Timpie Tee,
Fishye, Fishye in the sea,
Ilsebill my wilful wife
Does not want my way of life.

"Nu, what does she want then?" asked the fish.

"Ach!" said the man. "She wants to be King."

"Go there then — she is all that," said the fish.

So the man went, and when he came to the mansion it had become a big castle. It had a high tower with wonderful trimmings on it, and a sentry stood before the door, and there were so many many soldiers with drums and trumpets! And as he came into the castle, he found that everything was made of marble and gold, with velvet covers and big golden tassels. Then the doors of the hall opened. There was all the court, and his wife sat on a high throne of gold and diamonds. She had a crown of pure gold on her head, and a scepter of gold and jewels in her hand. On both sides of her stood six maidens in a row, each always one head smaller than the other.

So he went and stood there and said, "Oh wife, are you now King?"

"Yes," said the wife. "Now I am King."

So he stood there and looked at her, and when he had looked at her like that for a while, he said, "Ach, wife, how nice it is that you are King! Now we have nothing more to wish for."

"Nay, man," said the wife and looked all restless. "There isn't enough to do. To me the time seems so long — I can't stand that any more. Go there to the fish. King I am, now I must also become Emperor."

"Ach wife!" said the man. "Why should you want to be Emperor?"

"Man," said she, "go to the fish. I want to be Emperor!"

"Ach wife!" said the man. "I don't want to tell that to the fish. He can't make an Emperor — that he cannot and cannot do."

"What!" said the wife. "I am King and you are my man. Will you go there right away? If he can make a King, he can make an Emperor. I want and want to be Emperor. Go there right now!"

So he had to go, but he became all scared. And as he went along like that, he thought to himself, "That doesn't and doesn't go right. Emperor is too much to ask for — the fish will get tired in the end."

With that he came to the sea. It was all black and thick, and began to ferment so that it made bubbles, and such a wild wind blew over it that the man was horrified. So he went and stood and said:

> Manye, Manye, Timpie Tee,
> Fishye, Fishye in the sea,
> Ilsebill my wilful wife
> Does not want my way of life.

"Nu, what does she want then?" asked the fish.

"Ach fish!" said the man, "she wants to be Emperor."

"Go there then," said the fish. "She is all that."

So the man went, and when he came there, the whole castle was made of polished marble with alabaster statues and golden decorations. In front of the door soldiers were marching, and they blew their trumpets and beat their drums and kettle drums. In the castle, barons and earls and dukes were walking around as servants: they opened the doors for him which were of pure gold. And when he came inside, there sat his wife on a throne which was made all of one piece of gold and was about two miles high. She wore a big golden crown which was three ells high and was set with brilliants and carbuncles. In one hand she held the scepter and in the other hand she had the imperial globe. On both sides of the throne stood the gentlemen-at-arms in two rows, one always smaller than the next: from the biggest giant who was two miles high, to the smallest dwarf who was only as big as my little finger. And in front of her stood so many many Princes and Kings!

So the man went and stood and said, "Wife, are you now Emperor?"

"Yes," said she, "I am Emperor."

So he stood there and looked at her right well, and after he had looked at her like that for a while, he said, "Ach wife, how nice it is now that you are Emperor."

"Man!" she said. "Why are you standing there like that? I am Emperor but now I want to become Pope. Go to the fish."

"Ach wife!" said the man. "What do you ask of me? You can't become Pope. There is only one Pope in Christendom; surely the fish can't make that."

"Man," said she, "I want to be Pope. Go right there. Even today I must become Pope."

"Nay, wife," said the man, "that I don't want to tell him; that won't go right, that is too much — the fish can't make you a Pope."

"Man, what chatter!" said the wife. "If he can make an Emperor, he can make a Pope as well. Get along. I am Emperor and you are my man — will you go there now?"

At that he was frightened and went there; but he felt all faint, and shook and quaked, and his knees and calves became flabby. And now such a big wind blew over the land, and the clouds flew so that it grew as dark as though it were evening. The leaves blew from the trees, the water splashed against the shore, and worked and churned as though it were boiling. And far away he saw the ships; they were in trouble, and tossed and leaped on the billows. The sky was still a little blue in the middle, but at the sides it was coming up right red as in a heavy storm.

So he went there in despair, and stood in terror and said:

> Manye, Manye, Timpie Tee,
> Fishye, Fishye in the sea,
> Ilsebill my wilful wife
> Does not want my way of life.

"Nu, what does she want then?" asked the fish.

"Ach," said the man, "she wants to be Pope."

"Go there then," said the fish. "She is that now."

So he went, and when he came home it was like a big church with palaces all around it. There he pushed his way through the crowd: inside everything was lit up with thousands and thousands of candles. His wife was dressed in pure gold and sat on an even higher throne than before and now she wore three big golden crowns, and all around her there was so much pomp and grandeur! On both sides of her, there stood two rows of candles: from the tallest, as thick as a tower, down to the smallest kitchen candle. And all the Emperors and Kings were down before her on their knees.

"Wife," said the man, and looked at her right well, "are you now Pope?"

"Yes," said she, "I am Pope."

So he went and stood and looked at her, and it was just as though he looked at the sun. After he had looked at her for a while, he said, "Ach wife, how nice it is now that you are Pope."

But she sat there stiff as a tree and did not stir or move herself. Then he said, "Well, wife, now that you are Pope you will have to be satisfied. You can't become anything more."

"That I will think over," said the wife.

With that they went to bed, but the wife was not satisfied, and her greediness did not let her sleep. She was always wondering what else she could become.

The man slept right well and soundly — he had done much running that day — but the wife could not sleep and tossed herself from one side to the other all through the night and wondered what else she could become, but could think of nothing higher.

With that the sun began to rise, and as she saw the rosy dawn she leaned over one end of the bed and looked out of the window. And when she saw the sun coming up: "Ha!" she thought, "couldn't I, too, make the sun and moon go up?"

"Man," she said, and poked him in the ribs with her elbow, "wake up, and go there to the fish. I want to be like God."

The man was still half asleep but he was so alarmed by this, that he fell out of bed. He thought he had not heard a-right and rubbed his eyes and said, "Ach wife, what are you saying?"

"Man," said she, "if I can't make the sun and moon rise and have to sit here and see that the sun and moon are going up, I can't stand that, and I won't have a peaceful moment until I can make them go up myself."

Then she looked at him in such a horrible way that a shudder ran over him.

"Go right there," she said, "I want to be like God."

"Ach wife!" said the man, and fell before her on his knees. "That the fish can't do. Emperor and Pope he can make. I beg of you, be satisfied and stay Pope."

At that she became furious and her hair flew wildly about her head. She lifted up her tunic and gave him a kick with her foot and screamed, "I can't stand it and I can't stand it any longer! Will you go?"

So he pulled on his trousers and ran away as though he were mad. But outside there was a storm and it raged so that he could hardly stay on his feet. The houses and the trees blew over and the mountains quaked. The big rocks broke off and rolled into the sea, and the sky was pitch black, and it thundered and lightened, and the sea went up into big black waves as high as church towers and mountains, and they all had a white crown of foam on their tops. So he screamed out and could hardly hear his own voice:

> Manye, Manye, Timpie Tee!
> Fishye, Fishye in the sea!
> Ilsebill my wilful wife
> Does not want my way of life.

"Nu, what does she want then?" asked the fish.

"Ach!" said the man. "She wants to make the sun and moon rise. She wants to be like God."

"Go home then," said the fish, "she's back in her vinegar jug again."

And there they are both sitting to this day.

Rapunzel [8]

After all, a fairy story is not just a fluffy puff of nothing which can be airily blown aside by a 'school of thought,' nor is it merely a tenuous bit of make believe. . . . Its roots are real and solid, reaching far back into man's past, into ancient mythology and religion, and into the lives and customs of many peoples and countries." So wrote Wanda Gág in The Horn Book *for March, 1937, in an article in which she discusses the controversy over fairy tales and speaks out in their defense.*

There is a moving spiritual quality in the story of Rapunzel, in which so much is endured for the sake of love, and the tears of the beloved have the power to heal blindness.

In a little German village lived a man and his wife. They had long wished for a child, and now at last they had reason to hope that their wish would be granted.

In their back yard was a shed which looked out upon their neighbor's garden: Often the woman would stand and look at this garden, for it was well kept and flourishing, and had lovely flowers and luscious vegetables laid out in the most tempting manner. The garden was surrounded by a high stone wall but, wall or no wall, there was not much danger of any one entering it. This was because it belonged to Mother Gothel, who was a powerful witch and was feared in all the land.

One summer's day, as the witch's garden was at its very best, the woman was again gazing from the window of her little shed. She feasted her eyes on the gay array of flowers, and she looked longingly at the many kinds of vegetables which were growing there. Her mouth watered as her eyes traveled from the long, crisp beans to the fat, green peas; from the cucumbers to the crinkly lettuce; from the carrots to the waving turnip tops. But when her glance fell upon a fine big bed of rampion (which in that country is called *rapunzel*) a strange feeling came over her. She had always been fond of rampion salad, and these plants in the witch's garden looked so fresh, so green, so tempting, that she felt she must have some, no matter what the cost.

But then she thought to herself, "It's no use. No one can ever get any of the witch's vegetables. I might as well forget about it."

Still, try as she would, she could not, could not forget. Every day she looked at the fresh green rampion, and every day her longing for it increased. She grew thinner and thinner, and began to look pale and miserable.

Her husband soon noticed this, and said, "Dear wife, what is the matter with you?"

"Oh," said she, "I have a strange desire for some of that rampion in Mother Gothel's garden, and unless I get some, I fear I shall die."

At this the husband became alarmed and as he loved her dearly, he said to himself, "Before you let your wife die, you'll get her some of those plants, no matter what the risk or cost."

Therefore, that evening at twilight, he climbed over the high wall and into the witch's garden. Quickly he dug up a handful of rampion plants and brought them to his ailing wife. She was overjoyed, and immediately made a big juicy salad which she ate with great relish, one might almost say with greed.

In fact she enjoyed it so much that, far from being satisfied, her desire for the forbidden vegetable had now increased threefold. And although she looked rosier and stronger after she had eaten the rampion salad, in a few days she became pale and frail once more.

There was nothing for the man to do but go over to the witch's garden again; and so he went, at twilight as before. He had reached the rampion patch and was about to reach out for the plants, when he stopped

[8] From *Tales from Grimm,* trans. Wanda Gág (Coward-McCann, 1936).

short, horrified. Before him stood the witch, old Mother Gothel herself!

"Oh, Mother Gothel," said the man, "please be merciful with me. I am not really a thief and have only done this to save a life. My wife saw your rampion from that window yonder, and now her longing for it is so strange and strong that I fear she will die if she cannot get some of it to eat."

At this the witch softened a little and said, "If it is as you say, I will let you take as many of the plants as are needed to make her healthy again. But only on one condition: when your first child is born, you must give it to me. I won't hurt it and will care for it like a mother."

The man had been so frightened that he hardly knew what he was doing, and so in his terror, he made this dreadful promise.

Soon after this, the wife became the mother of a beautiful baby girl, and in a short time Mother Gothel came and claimed the child according to the man's promise. Neither the woman's tears nor the man's entreaties could make the witch change her mind. She lifted the baby out of its cradle and took it away with her. She called the girl Rapunzel after those very plants in her garden which had been the cause of so much trouble.

Rapunzel was a winsome child, with long luxuriant tresses, fine as spun gold. When she was twelve years old, the witch took her off to the woods and shut her up in a high tower. It had neither door nor staircase but at its very top was one tiny window. Whenever Mother Gothel came to visit the girl, she stood under this window and called:

Rapunzel, Rapunzel,
Let down your hair.

As soon as Rapunzel heard this, she took her long braids, wound them once or twice around a hook outside the window, and let them fall twenty ells downward toward the ground. This made a ladder for the witch to climb, and in that way she reached the window at the top of the tower.

Thus it went for several years, and Rapunzel was lonely indeed, hidden away in the high tower.

One day a young Prince was riding through the forest when he heard faint music in the distance. That was Rapunzel, who was trying to lighten her solitude with the sound of her own sweet voice.

The Prince followed the sound, but all he found was a tall, forbidding tower. He was eager to get a glimpse of the mysterious singer but he looked in vain for door or stairway. He saw the little window at the top but could think of no way to get there. At last he rode away, but Rapunzel's sweet singing had touched his heart so deeply that he came back evening after evening and listened to it.

Once, as he was standing there as usual, well hidden by a tree — he saw a hideous hag come hobbling along. It was old Mother Gothel. She stopped at the foot of the tower and called:

Rapunzel, Rapunzel,
Let down your hair.

Now a pair of golden-yellow braids tumbled down from the window. The old hag clung to them and climbed up, up, up, and into the tower window.

"Well!" thought the Prince. "If that is the ladder to the song-bird's nest then I, too, must try my luck some day."

The next day at dusk, he went back to the tower, stood beneath it and called:

Rapunzel, Rapunzel,
Let down your hair.

The marvelous tresses were lowered at once. The Prince climbed the silky golden ladder, and stepped through the tiny window up above.

Rapunzel had never seen a man, and at first she was alarmed at seeing this handsome youth enter her window. But the Prince looked at her with friendly eyes and said softly, "Don't be afraid. When I heard your sweet voice, my heart was touched so deeply that I could not rest until I had seen you."

At that Rapunzel lost her fear and they talked happily together for a while. Then the Prince said, "Will you take me for your husband, and come away with me?"

At first Rapunzel hesitated. But the youth

was so pleasant to behold and seemed so good and gentle besides, that she thought to herself: "I am sure he will be much kinder to me than Mother Gothel."

So she laid her little hand in his and said, "Yes, I will gladly go with you, but I don't know how I can get away from here. If you come every day, and bring each time a skein of silk, I will weave it into a long, strong ladder. When it is finished I will climb down on it, and then you can take me away on your horse. But come only in the evening," she added, "for the old witch always comes in the daytime."

Every day the Prince came and brought some silk. The ladder was getting longer and stronger, and was almost finished. The old witch guessed nothing, but one day Rapunzel forgot herself and said, "How is it, Mother Gothel, that it takes you so long to climb up here, while the Prince can do it in just a minute—oh!"

"What?" cried the witch.

"Oh nothing, nothing," said the poor girl in great confusion.

"You wicked, wicked child!" cried the witch angrily. "What do I hear you say? I thought I had kept you safely hidden from all the world, and now you have deceived me!"

In her fury, she grabbed Rapunzel's golden hair, twirled it once or twice around her left hand, snatched a pair of scissors with her right, and ritsch, rotsch, the beautiful braids lay on the floor. And she was so heartless after this, that she dragged Rapunzel to a waste and desolate place, where the poor girl had to get along as best she could, living in sorrow and want.

On the evening of the very day in which Rapunzel had been banished, the old witch fastened Rapunzel's severed braids to the window hook, and then sat in the tower and waited. When the Prince appeared with some silk, as was his wont, he called:

> Rapunzel, Rapunzel,
> Let down your hair.

Swiftly Mother Gothel lowered the braids. The Prince climbed up as usual, but to his dismay he found, not his dear little Rapunzel, but the cruel witch who glared at him with angry, venomous looks.

"Aha!" she cried mockingly. "You have come to get your dear little wife. Well, the pretty bird is no longer in her nest, and she'll sing no more. The cat has taken her away, and in the end that same cat will scratch out your eyes. Rapunzel is lost to you; you will never see her again!"

The Prince was beside himself with grief, and in his despair he leaped out of the tower window. He escaped with his life, but the thorny thicket into which he fell, blinded him.

Now he wandered, sad and sightless, from place to place, ate only roots and berries, and could do nothing but weep and grieve for the loss of his dear wife.

So he wandered for a whole year in deepest misery until at last he chanced upon the desolate place whither Rapunzel had been banished. There she lived in wretchedness and woe with her baby twins—a boy and a girl—who had been born to her in the meantime.

As he drew near, he heard a sweet and sorrowful song. The voice was familiar to him and he hurried toward it.

When Rapunzel saw him, she flew into his arms and wept with joy. Two of her tears fell on the Prince's eyes—in a moment they were healed and he could see as well as before.

Now they were happy indeed! The Prince took his songbird and the little twins too, and together they rode away to his kingdom. There they all lived happily for many a long year.

Snow White and the Seven Dwarfs[9]

"Most like the fairies, especially in the wealth of traditions concerning them, are the dwarfs. In the countries of northern Europe they are considered as spirits of the underground." Stith Thompson so describes them

[9] Wanda Gág, Snow White and the Seven Dwarfs (Coward-McCann, 1938).

in his The Folktale: *"They are certainly more ungainly, as generally conceived, than the fairies, and are nearest in appearance to the little house-spirits which the English know as brownies and the Danes as 'nisser'"* (p. 248). *Dr. Thompson says further that "Walt Disney was particularly successful in catching the traditional conception of the dwarfs in his production of 'Snow White.'" It is interesting to note that there is some disagreement with him on this score. There are those who feel that the names and the characterization bestowed upon the Disney dwarfs were something less than true to the mystery and dignity that is traditionally their due. Dopey, Sneezy, Sleepy, and Doc — these seem unlikely names for members of the same race as Rumpelstiltskin and Tom Tit Tot. In his autobiography, Surprised by Joy, C. S. Lewis, professor of Medieval and Renaissance English Literature at Cambridge University, speaks of his delight in dwarfs, "the old, bright-hooded, snowy-bearded dwarfs we had in those days . . . before Walt Disney vulgarized the earthmen"* (p. 54).

At any rate, the story of the child among dwarfs is one of the most appealing in all folklore, with its mingled motifs of cruel stepmother and magic sleep, to be broken by Prince Charming.

Once upon a time, in the middle of winter, the snowflakes were falling like feathers from the sky. At a castle window framed in ebony sat a young Queen working at her embroidery, and as she was stitching away and gazing at the snowflakes now and then, she pricked her finger and three little drops of blood fell down upon the snow. And because the red color looked so beautiful there on the snow she thought to herself, "Oh, if I only had a little child as white as snow, as rosy red as blood, and with hair as ebon black as the window frame!"

Soon after this a baby girl was born to her — a little Princess with hair of ebon black, cheeks and lips of rosy red, and a skin so fine and fair that she was called Snow White. But when the child was born the Queen died.

After a year had passed, the King married a second time. His new wife, who was now Queen, was very beautiful but haughty and proud and vain — indeed, her only wish in

life was to be the fairest in the land. She had a mirror, a magic one, and when she looked in it she would say:

"Mirror, Mirror, on the wall,
Who's the fairest one of all?"

and the mirror would reply:

"Oh Queen, thou art the fairest in the land."

With this the Queen was well content for she knew that her mirror always spoke the truth.

The years flowed on, and all this time Snow White was growing up — and growing more beautiful each year besides. When she was seven years old she was fair as the day, and there came a time when the Queen stood in front of her mirror and said:

"Mirror, Mirror, on the wall,
Who's the fairest one of all?"

and this time the mirror answered:

"Queen, thou art of beauty rare
But Snow White with ebon hair
Is a thousand times more fair."

At this the Queen became alarmed and turned green and yellow with envy. And whenever she saw Snow White after that, her heart turned upside down within her — that was how much she hated the innocent child for her beauty. These envious feelings grew like weeds in the heart of the Queen until she had no peace by day or by night. At last she could bear it no longer. She sent for a royal huntsman and told him to take the child into the woods and do away with her. "And bring me a token," she added, "so that I may be sure you've obeyed me."

So the huntsman called Snow White and led her into the woods but before he could harm her, she burst into tears and said, "Oh please, dear hunter, have mercy! If you will let me go, I'll gladly wander away, far away into the wildwood and I'll never come back again."

The huntsman was glad enough to help the sweet innocent girl, so he said, "Well, run away then, poor child, and may the beasts of the wood have mercy on you." As a token he brought back the heart of a wild boar, and the wicked Queen thought it was Snow White's. She had it cooked and ate it, I am sorry to say, with salt and great relish.

Little Snow White wandered off into the depths of the wildwood. Above her were leaves and leaves and leaves, about her the trunks of hundreds of trees, and she didn't know what to do. She began to run, over jagged stones and through thorny thickets. She passed many wild animals on the way, but they did not hurt her. She ran all day, through woods and woods and over seven high high hills. At last, just at sunset, she came upon a tiny hut in a wooded glen. The door was open and there was no one at home, so she thought she would stay and rest herself a little.

She went in and looked around. Everything was very small inside, but as neat and charming as could be, and very very clean. At one end of the room stood a table decked in white, and on it were seven little plates, seven little knives and forks and spoons, and seven little goblets. In front of the table, each in its place, were seven little chairs; and at the far side of the room were seven beds, one beside the other, all made up with coverlets as pure and white as plum blossoms.

Snow White was hungry and thirsty, so she took from each little plate a bit of vegetable and a bite of bread, and from each little goblet a sip of sweet wine. She had become very tired, too, from all her running, and felt like taking a nap. She tried one bed after another but found it hard to choose the one which really suited her.

The first little bed was too hard.
The second little bed was too soft.
The third little bed was too short.
The fourth little bed was too narrow.
The fifth little bed was too flat.
The sixth little bed was too fluffy.
But the seventh little bed was just right so she lay down in it and was soon fast asleep.

After the sun had set behind the seventh hilltop and darkness had crept into the room, the masters of the little hut came home — they were seven little dwarfs who dug all day and hacked away at the hills, in search of gems and gold. They lit their seven little lights and saw right away that someone had been there, for things were not quite the same as they had left them in the morning.

Said the first little dwarf, "Who's been sitting in my chair?"

Said the second little dwarf, "Who's been eating from my plate?"

Said the third, "Who's been nibbling at my bread?"

Said the fourth, "Who's been tasting my vegetables?"

Said the fifth, "Who's been eating with my fork?"

And the sixth, "Who's been cutting with my knife?"

And the seventh, "Who's been drinking from my little goblet?"

Now the first little dwarf turned around, and saw a hollow in his bed and said, "Someone's been sleeping in my bed."

And the second little dwarf looked at his bed and said, "Someone's been sleeping in mine too. It's rumpled."

And the third said, "In mine too, it's all humped up and crumpled."

And the fourth said, "In mine too. It's full of wrinkles."

And the fifth said, "And mine. It's full of crinkles."

And the sixth said, "Mine too. It's all tumbled up and jumbled."

But the seventh cried, "Well, someone's been sleeping in my bed, *and here she is!*"

The others came crowding around, murmuring and whispering in wonderment at the sight, "Ei! Ei!" they said, "how beautiful is this child!" They brought their tiny lights and held them high, and looked and looked and looked. So pleased were they with their new little guest that they did not even wake her, but let her sleep in the bed all night. The seventh dwarf now had no bed, to be sure, but he slept with his comrades, one hour with each in turn until the night was over.

In the morning when Snow White awoke and saw seven little men tiptoeing about the room, she was frightened, but not for long. She soon saw that they were friendly little folk, so she sat up in bed and smiled at them. Now that she was awake and well rested, she looked more lovely than ever, with her rosy cheeks and big black eyes. The seven little dwarfs circled round her in new admiration and awe, and said, "What is your name, dear child?"

"They call me Snow White," said she.

"And how did you find your way to our little home?" asked the dwarfs. So she told them her story.

All seven stood around and listened, nodding their heads and stroking their long long beards, and then they said, "Do you think you could be our little housekeeper — cook and knit and sew for us, make up our beds and wash our little clothes? If you will keep everything tidy and homelike, you can stay with us, and you shall want for nothing in the world."

"Oh yes, with all my heart!" cried Snow White. So there she stayed, and washed and sewed and knitted, and kept house for the kindly little men. Every day the seven dwarfs went off to one of the seven hills to dig for gems and gold. Each evening after sunset they returned, and then their supper had to be all ready and laid out on the table. But every morning before they left they would warn Snow White about the Queen.

"We don't trust her," they said. "One of these days she'll find out that you are here. So be careful, child, and don't let anyone into the house."

The dwarfs were right. One day the Queen, just to make sure, stood in front of her mirror and said:

"Mirror, Mirror, on the wall,
Who's the fairest one of all?"

and the mirror replied:

"Thou are very fair, Oh Queen,
But the fairest ever seen
Dwells within the wooded glen
With the seven little men."

The Queen turned green with fury when she heard this, for now she knew that the huntsman had deceived her, and that Snow White was still alive.

Day and night she sat and pondered, and wondered what to do, for as long as she was not the fairest in the land, her jealous heart gave her no rest. At last she thought out a plan: she dyed her face and dressed herself to look like a peddler woman. She did it so well that no one would have known her, and then, with a basketful of strings and laces, she made her way over the seven hills to the home of the seven dwarfs. When she reached it she knocked at the little door and cried, "Fine wares for sale! Fine wares for sale!"

Snow White peeped out of the window and said, "Good day, my dear woman, what have you there in your basket?"

"Good wares! Fine wares!" said the woman. "Strings, cords and laces, of all kinds and colors," and she held up a loop of gaily colored bodice laces.

Snow White was entranced with the gaudy trifle and she thought to herself, "The dwarfs were only afraid of the wicked Queen, but surely there can be no harm in letting this honest woman into the house." So she opened the door and bought the showy laces.

"Child," said the woman as she entered the little room, "what a sight you are with that loose bodice! Come, let me fix you up with your new laces, so you'll look neat and trim for once."

Snow White, who suspected nothing, stood up to have the new gay laces put into her bodice, but the woman worked quickly and laced her up so tightly that Snow White lost her breath and sank to the floor.

"Now!" cried the Queen as she cast a last look at the motionless child, "now you have *been* the fairest in the land!"

Luckily this happened just as the sun was sinking behind the seventh hill, so it was not long before the dwarfs came trudging home from work. When they saw their dear little Snow White lying there, not moving, not talking, they were deeply alarmed. They lifted her up, and when they saw how tightly she was laced, they hurriedly cut the cords in two. And in that moment Snow White caught her breath again, opened her eyes, and all was well once more.

When the dwarfs heard what had happened they said, "That was no peddler woman, Snow White; that was the wicked Queen. So please beware, dear child, and let no one into the house while we're gone."

By this time the Queen had reached her home, so she rushed to her mirror and said:

> "Mirror, Mirror, on the wall,
> Who's the fairest one of all?"

and to her dismay it answered as before:

> "Thou art very fair, Oh Queen,
> But the fairest ever seen
> Dwells within the wooded glen
> With the seven little men."

At this the Queen's fury knew no bounds and she said, "But now, my pretty one — now I'll think up something which *will* be the end of you!" And soon she was very busy.

You will not be surprised, I am sure, when I tell you that this wicked creature was skilled in the arts of witchcraft; and with the help of these arts she now worked out her second scheme. She fashioned a comb — a beautiful golden comb, but a poisonous one. Then, disguising herself as a different old woman, she crossed the seven hills to the home of the seven dwarfs. When she reached it she knocked at the door and cried as before, "Good wares for sale! Fine wares! For sale! For sale!"

Snow White peeped out of the window but this time she said, "You may as well go on your way, good woman. I am not allowed to let anyone in."

"Very well!" said the old woman. "You needn't let me in, but surely there can be no harm in *looking* at my wares," and she held up the glittering poisonous comb.

Snow White was so charmed by it that she forgot all about the dwarfs' warning and opened the door. The old woman stepped inside and said in honeyed tones, "Why don't you try it on right now, my little rabbit? Look, I'll show you how it should be worn!"

Poor Snow White, innocent and trusting, stood there with sparkling eyes as the woman thrust the comb into her ebon hair. But as soon as the comb touched her head, the poison began to work, and Snow White sank to the floor unconscious.

"You paragon of beauty!" muttered the Queen. "That will do for you, I think."

She hurried away just as the sun was sinking behind the seventh hill, and a few minutes later the dwarfs came trudging home from work. When they saw Snow White lying there on the floor, they knew at once that the Queen had been there again. Quickly they searched, and soon enough they found the glittering poisonous comb which was still fastened in the girl's black hair. But at the very moment that they pulled it out, the poison lost its power and Snow White opened her eyes and sat up, as well as ever before.

When she told the seven dwarfs what had happened, they looked very solemn and said, "You can see, Snow White, it was not an old woman who came, but the wicked Queen in disguise. So please, dear child, beware! Buy nothing from anyone and let no one, no one at all, into the house while we're gone!"

And Snow White promised.

By this time the Queen had reached her home and there she stood in front of her mirror and said:

> "Mirror, Mirror, on the wall,
> Who's the fairest one of all?"

and the mirror answered as before:

> "Thou are very fair, Oh Queen,
> But the fairest ever seen
> Dwells within the wooded glen
> With the seven little men."

When she heard this, the Queen trembled with rage and disappointment. "I must, I *will* be the fairest in the land!" she cried, and away she went to a lonely secret chamber where no one ever came. There, by means of her wicked witchery, she fashioned an apple. A very beautiful apple it was, so waxy white and rosy red that it made one's mouth water to look at it. But it was far from being as good as it looked, for it was so artfully made that half of it — the rosiest half — was full of poison.

When the Queen had finished this apple she put it into a basket with some ordinary apples, and disguised herself as a peasant-wife. She crossed the seven hills to the home of the seven dwarfs and knocked at the door as before.

Snow White peeped out of the window and said, "I am not allowed to let anyone in, nor to buy anything either — the seven dwarfs have forbidden it."

"Suits me," said the peasant-wife, "I can easily sell my fine apples elsewhere. Here, I'll give you one for nothing."

"No," said Snow White, "I'm not allowed to take anything from strangers."

"Are you afraid? Of poison, perhaps?" said the woman. "See, I'll cut the apple in two and I myself will eat half of it to show you how harmless it is. Here, you can have the nice rosy half, I'll take the white part."

By this time Snow White's mouth was fairly watering for the luscious-looking fruit, and when the woman took a big bite out of the white half and smacked her lips, the poor girl could bear it no longer. She stretched her little hand out through the window, took the rosy half of the apple and bit into it. Immediately she sank to the floor and knew no more.

With a glance of glee and a laugh over-loud, the Queen cried, "Now, you! White as snow, red as blood and black as ebony — *now* let the dwarfs revive you!"

She could scarcely wait to get home to her mirror and say:

"Mirror, Mirror, on the wall,
Who's the fairest one of all?"

and to her joy it said:

"Oh Queen, thou art the fairest in the land!"

Now there was peace at last in the heart of the Queen — that is, as much peace as can ever be found in a heart full of envy and hate.

After the wicked Queen had gone away, the sun sank down behind the seventh hill and the dwarfs came trudging home from work. When they reached their little home, no light gleamed from its windows, no smoke streamed from its chimney. Inside all was dark and silent — no lamps were lit and no supper was on the table. Snow White lay on the floor and no breath came from her lips.

At this sight the seven little dwarfs were filled with woe, for well they knew that this was once more the work of the wicked Queen.

"We must save her!" they cried, and hur-

ried here and there. They lit their seven lights, then took Snow White and laid her on the bed. They searched for something poisonous but found nothing. They loosened her bodice, combed her hair and washed her face with water and wine, but nothing helped: the poor child did not move, did not speak, did not open her eyes.

"Alas!" cried the dwarfs. "We have done all we could, and now Snow White is lost to us forever!"

Gravely they shook their heads, sadly they stroked their beards, and then they all began to cry. They cried for three whole days and when at last they dried their tears, there lay Snow White, still motionless to be sure, but so fresh and rosy that she seemed to be blooming with health.

"She is as beautiful as ever," said the dwarfs to each other, "and although we cannot wake her, we must watch her well and keep her safe from harm."

So they made a beautiful crystal casket for Snow White to lie in. It was transparent all over so that she could be seen from every side. On its lid they wrote in golden letters:

Snow White — A Princess

and when it was all finished they laid Snow White inside and carried it to one of the seven hilltops. There they placed it among the trees and flowers, and birds of the wood came and mourned for her, first an owl, then a raven, and last of all a little dove.

Now only six little dwarfs went to dig in the hills every day, for each in his turn stayed behind to watch over Snow White so that she was never alone.

Weeks and months and years passed by, and all this time Snow White lay in her crystal casket and did not move or open her eyes. She seemed to be in a deep deep sleep, her face as fair as a happy dream, her cheeks as rosy as ever. The flowers grew gaily about her, the clouds flew blithely above. Birds perched on the crystal casket and trilled and sang, the woodland beasts grew tame and came to gaze in wonder.

Some one else came too and gazed in wonder — not a bird or a rabbit or a deer, but a young Prince who had lost his way while wandering among the seven hills. When he saw the motionless maiden, so beautiful and rosy red, he looked and looked and looked. Then he went to the dwarfs and said, "Please let me take this crystal casket home with me and I will give you all the gold you may ask for."

But the dwarfs shook their heads and said, "We would not give it up for all the riches in the world."

At this the Prince looked troubled and his eyes filled with tears.

"If you won't take gold," he said, "then please give her to me out of the goodness of your golden hearts. I know not why, but my heart is drawn toward this beautiful Princess. If you will let me take her home with me, I will guard and honor her as my greatest treasure."

When they heard this, the kind little dwarfs took pity on the Prince and made him a present of Snow White in her beautiful casket.

The Prince thanked them joyfully and called for his servants. Gently they placed the crystal casket on their shoulders, slowly they walked away. But in spite of all their care, one of the servants made a false step and stumbled over a gnarly root. This joggled the casket, and the jolt shook the piece of poisoned apple right out of Snow White's throat. And lo! she woke up at last and was as well as ever. Then all by herself she opened the lid, sat up, and looked about her in astonishment.

The Prince rushed up and lifted her out of the casket. He told her all that had happened and begged her to be his bride. Snow White consented with sparkling eyes, so they rode away to the Prince's home where they prepared for a gay and gala wedding.

But while this was going on in the Prince's castle, something else was happening in that other castle where lived the wicked Queen. She had been invited to a mysterious wedding, so she dressed herself in her festive best and stood in front of her mirror and said:

"Mirror, Mirror, on the wall,
  Who's the fairest one of all?"

and the mirror answered:

"Thou art very fair, Oh Queen,
  But the fairest ever seen
  Is Snow White, alive and well,
  Standing 'neath a wedding bell."

When she heard this, the Queen realized that it was Snow White's wedding to which she had been invited. She turned purple with rage, but still she couldn't stay away. It would have been better for her if she had, for when she arrived she was given a pair of red hot shoes with which she had to dance out her wicked life. But as to all the rest — the Prince and his Princess Snow White, and the seven little dwarfs — they all lived happily ever after.

Rumpelstiltskin [1]

❧ *Riddles are a frequent motif in folk tales. Versions of this tale can be found among most of the early peoples. Besides the riddle motif, we find here the device of testing the truth of a previous statement. In the French version, the falsehood is different, and told for a reason less satisfactory than this one. There are also other but minor changes.*

There was once a miller who was poor, but he had one beautiful daughter. It happened one day that he came to speak with the king. and, to give himself consequence, he told him that he had a daughter who could spin gold out of straw. The king said to the miller, "That is an art that pleases me well; if thy daughter is as clever as you say, bring her to my castle tomorrow, that I may put her to the proof."

When the girl was brought to him, he led her into a room that was quite full of straw, and gave her a wheel and spindle, and said, "Now set to work, and if by the early morning thou hast not spun this straw to gold thou shalt die." And he shut the door himself, and left her there alone.

And so the poor miller's daughter was left there sitting, and could not think what to do for her life; she had no notion how to set to

[1] From Jakob and Wilhelm Grimm, *Household Stories*, trans. Lucy Crane (Macmillan, 1926).

work to spin gold from straw, and her distress grew so great that she began to weep. Then all at once the door opened, and in came a little man, who said, "Good evening, miller's daughter; why are you crying?"

"Oh!" answered the girl, "I have got to spin gold out of straw, and I don't understand the business."

Then the little man said, "What will you give me if I spin it for you?"

"My necklace," said the girl.

The little man took the necklace, seated himself before the wheel, and whirr, whirr, whirr! three times round and the bobbin was full; then he took up another, and whirr, whirr, whirr; three times round, and that was full; and so he went on till the morning, when all the straw had been spun, and all the bobbins were full of gold. At sunrise came the king, and when he saw the gold he was astonished and very much rejoiced, for he was very avaricious. He had the miller's daughter taken into another room filled with straw, much bigger than the last, and told her that as she valued her life she must spin it all in one night.

The girl did not know what to do, so she began to cry, and then the door opened, and the little man appeared and said, "What will you give me if I spin all this straw into gold?"

"The ring from my finger," answered the girl.

So the little man took the ring, and began again to send the wheel whirring round, and by the next morning all the straw was spun into glistening gold. The king was rejoiced beyond measure at the sight, but as he could never have enough of gold, he had the miller's daughter taken into a still larger room full of straw, and said, "This, too, must be spun in one night, and if you accomplish it you shall be my wife." For he thought, "Although she is but a miller's daughter, I am not likely to find any one richer in the whole world."

As soon as the girl was left alone, the little man appeared for the third time and said, "What will you give me if I spin the straw for you this time?"

"I have nothing left to give," answered the girl.

"Then you must promise me the first child

you have after you are queen," said the little man.

"But who knows whether that will happen?" thought the girl; but as she did not know what else to do in her necessity, she promised the little man what he desired, upon which he began to spin, until all the straw was gold. And when in the morning the king came and found all done according to his wish, he caused the wedding to be held at once, and the miller's pretty daughter became a queen.

In a year's time she brought a fine child into the world, and thought no more of the little man; but one day he came suddenly into her room, and said, "Now give me what you promised me."

The queen was terrified greatly, and offered the little man all the riches of the kingdom if he would only leave the child; but the little man said, "No, I would rather have something living than all the treasures of the world."

Then the queen began to lament and to weep, so that the little man had pity upon her.

"I will give you three days," said he, "and if at the end of that time you cannot tell my name, you must give up the child to me."

Then the queen spent the whole night in thinking over all the names that she had ever heard, and sent a messenger through the land to ask far and wide for all the names that could be found. And when the little man came next day, (beginning with Caspar, Melchior, Balthazar) she repeated all she knew, and went through the whole list, but after each the little man said, "That is not my name."

The second day the queen sent to inquire of all the neighbors what the servants were called, and told the little man all the most unusual and singular names, saying, "Perhaps you are called Roast-ribs, or Sheepshanks, or Spindleshanks?" But he answered nothing but "That is not my name."

The third day the messenger came back again, and said, "I have not been able to find one single new name; but as I passed through the woods I came to a high hill, and near it was a little house, and before the house burned a fire, and round the fire danced a comical little man, and he hopped on one leg and cried,

"Today do I bake, tomorrow I brew,
    The day after that the queen's child comes in;
And oh! I am glad that nobody knew
    That the name I am called is Rumpelstiltskin!"

You cannot think how pleased the queen was to hear that name, and soon afterwards, when the little man walked in and said, "Now, Mrs. Queen, what is my name?" she said at first, "Are you called Jack?"

"No," answered he.

"Are you called Harry?" she asked again.

"No," answered he. And then she said,

"Then perhaps your name is Rumpelstiltskin!"

"The devil told you that! the devil told you that!" cried the little man, and in his anger he stamped with his right foot so hard that it went into the ground above his knee; then he seized his left foot with both his hands in such a fury that he split in two, and there was an end of him.

Gone Is Gone [2]

The war between the sexes, and the debate of who works the harder in this world, man or woman — these have been subjects for stories since the earliest time. Here is a tribute to the capabilities of woman. The complaining male is put in his place. There are numskull motifs in this story: the cow taken to the roof to graze; the cider left running in the cellar.

This story does not appear in Grimm. Wanda Gág places it in Bohemia. A Scandinavian version is called The Husband Who Was to Mind the House, *and is to be found in Gudrun Thorne-Thomsen's book,* East o' the Sun and West o' the Moon *(Row, Peterson). Stith Thompson reports the tale as having a ballad form in English-speaking countries.*

This is an old, old story which my grandmother told me when I was a little girl. When she was a little girl her grandfather had told it to her, and when he was a little peasant boy in Bohemia, his mother had told

[2] Wanda Gág, *Gone Is Gone* (Coward-McCann, 1935).

it to him. And where she heard it, I don't know, but you can see it is an old old story, and here it is, the way my grandmother used to tell it.

It is called . . .

GONE IS GONE
and it is the story of a man who wanted to do housework

This man, his name was Fritzl -- his wife, her name was Liesi. They had a little baby, Kinndli by name, and Spitz who was a dog.

They had one cow, two goats, three pigs, and of geese they had a dozen. That's what they had.

They lived on a patch of land, and that's where they worked.

Fritzl had to plow the ground, sow the seeds and hoe the weeds. He had to cut the hay and rake it too, and stack it up in bunches in the sun. The man worked hard, you see, from day to day.

Liesi had the house to clean, the soup to cook, the butter to churn, the barn yard and the baby to care for. She, too, worked hard each day as you can plainly see.

They both worked hard, but Fritzl always thought that he worked harder. Evenings when he came home from the field, he sat down, mopped his face with his big red handkerchief, and said: "Hu! How hot it was in the sun today, and how hard I did work. Little do you know, Liesi, what a man's work is like, little do you know! *Your* work now, 'tis nothing at all."

"'Tis none too easy," said Liesi.

"None too easy!" cried Fritzl. "All you do is to putter and potter around the house a bit — surely there's nothing hard about such things."

"Nay, if you think so," said Liesi, "we'll take it turn and turn about tomorrow. I will do your work, you can do mine. I will go out in the fields and cut the hay, you can stay here at home and putter and potter around. You wish to try it — yes?"

Fritzl thought he would like that well enough — to lie on the grass and keep an eye on his Kinndli-girl, to sit in the cool shade and churn, to fry a bit of sausage and cook a little soup. Ho! that would be easy! Yes, yes, he'd try it.

Well, Licsi lost no time the next morning. There she was at peep of day, striding out across the fields with a jug of water in her hand and the scythe over her shoulder.

And Fritzl, where was he? He was in the kitchen, frying a string of juicy sausages for his breakfast. There he sat, holding the pan over the fire, and as the sausage was sizzling and frizzling in the pan, Fritzl was lost in pleasant thoughts.

"A mug of cider now," that's what he was thinking. "A mug of apple cider with my sausage — that would be just the thing."

No sooner thought than done.

Fritzl set the pan on the edge of the fire place, and went down into the cellar where there was a big barrel full of cider. He pulled the bung from the barrel and watched the cider spurt into his mug, sparkling and foaming so that it was a joy to see.

But Hulla! What was that noise up in the kitchen — such a scuffle and clatter! Could it be that Spitz-dog after the sausages? Yes, that's what it was, and when Fritzl reached the top of the stairs, there he was, that dog, dashing out of the kitchen door with the string of juicy sausages flying after him.

Fritzl made for him, crying, "Hulla! Hulla! Hey, hi, ho, hulla!" But the dog wouldn't stop. Fritzl ran, Spitz ran too. Fritzl ran fast, Spitz ran faster, and the end of it was that the dog got away and our Fritzl had to give up the chase.

"Na, na! What's gone is gone," said Fritzl, shrugging his shoulders. And so he turned back, puffing and panting, and mopping his face with his big red handkerchief.

But the cider, now! Had he put the bung back in the barrel? No, that he hadn't, for here he was still holding the bung in his fist.

With big fast steps Fritzl hurried home, but it was too late, for look! the cider had filled the mug and had run all over the cellar besides.

Fritzl looked at the cellar full of cider. Then he scratched his head and said, "Na, na! What's gone is gone."

Well, now it was high time to churn the butter. Fritzl filled the churn with good rich cream, took it under a tree and began to churn with all his might. His little Kinndli was out there too, playing Moo-cow among

the daisies. The sky was blue, the sun right gay and golden, and the flowers, they were like angels' eyes blinking in the grass.

"This is pleasant now," thought Fritzl, as he churned away. "At last I can rest my weary legs. But wait! What about the cow? I've forgotten all about her and she hasn't had a drop of water all morning, poor thing."

With big fast steps Fritzl ran to the barn, carrying a bucket of cool fresh water for the cow. And high time it was, I can tell you, for the poor creature's tongue was hanging out of her mouth with the long thirst that was in her. She was hungry too, as a man could well see by the looks of her, so Fritzl took her from the barn and started off with her to the green grassy meadow.

But wait! There was that Kinndli to think of — she would surely get into trouble if he went out to the meadow. No, better not take the cow to the meadow at all. Better keep her nearby on the roof. The roof? Yes, the roof! Fritzl's house was not covered with shingles or tin or tile — it was covered with moss and sod, and a fine crop of grass and flowers grew there.

To take the cow up on the roof was not so hard as you might think, either. Fritzl's house was built into the side of a hill. Up the little hill, over a little shed, and from there to the green grassy roof. That was all there was to do and it was soon done.

The cow liked it right well up there on the roof and was soon munching away with a will, so Fritzl hurried back to his churning.

But Hulla! Hui! What did he see there under the tree? Kinndli was climbing up on the churn — the churn was tipping! spilling! falling! and now, there on the grass lay Kinndli, all covered with half-churned cream and butter.

"So that's the end of our butter," said Fritzl, and blinked and blinked his blue eyes. Then he shrugged his shoulders and said, "Na, na! What's gone is gone."

He picked up his dripping Kinndli and set her in the sun to dry. But the sun, now! It had climbed high up into the heavens. Noontime it was, no dinner made, and Liesi would soon be home for a bite to eat.

With big fast steps Fritzl hurried off to the garden. He gathered potatoes and onions, carrots and cabbages, beets and beans, turnips, parsley and celery.

"A little of everything, that will make a good soup," said Fritzl as he went back to the house, his arms so full of vegetables that he could not even close the garden gate behind him.

He sat on a bench in the kitchen and began cutting and paring away. How the man did work, and how the peelings and parings did fly!

But now there was a great noise above him. Fritzl jumped to his feet.

"That cow," he said, "she's sliding around right much up there on the roof. She might slip off and break her neck."

Up on the roof went Fritzl once more, this time with loops of heavy rope. Now listen carefully, and I will tell you what he did with it. He took one end of the rope and tied it around the cow's middle. The other end of the rope he dropped down the chimney and this he pulled through the fireplace in the kitchen below.

And then? And then he took the end of the rope which was hanging out of the fireplace and tied it around his own middle with a good tight knot. That's what he did.

"Oh yo! Oh ho!" he chuckled. "That will keep the cow from falling off the roof." And he began to whistle as he went on with his work.

He heaped some sticks on the fireplace and set a big kettle of water over it.

"Na, na!" he said. "Things are going as they should at last, and we'll soon have a good big soup! Now I'll put the vegetables in the kettle — "

And that he did.

"And now I'll put in the bacon — "

And that he did too.

"And now I'll light the fire — "

But that he never did, for just then, with a bump and a thump, the cow slipped over the edge of the roof after all; and Fritzl — well, he was whisked up into the chimney and there he dangled, poor man, and couldn't get up and couldn't get down.

Before long, there came Liesi home from the fields with the water jug in her hand and the scythe over her shoulder.

But Hulla! Hui! What was that hanging over the edge of the roof? The cow? Yes, the cow, and half-choked she was, too, with her eyes bulging and her tongue hanging out.

Liesi lost no time. She took her scythe — and ritsch! rotsch! — the rope was cut, and there was the cow wobbling on her four legs, but alive and well, heaven be praised!

Now Liesi saw the garden with its gate wide open. There were the pigs and goats and all the geese too. They were full to bursting, but the garden, alas! was empty.

Liesi walked on, and now what did she see? The churn upturned, and Kinndli there in the sun, stiff and sticky with dried cream and butter.

Liesi hurried on. There was Spitz-dog on the grass. He was full of sausages and looked none too well.

Liesi looked at the cellar. There was the cider all over the floor and halfway up the stairs besides.

Liesi looked in the kitchen. The floor! It was piled high with peelings and parings, and littered with dishes and pans.

At last Liesi saw the fireplace. Hu! Hulla! Hui! What was that in the soup-kettle? Two arms were waving, two legs were kicking, and a gurgle, bubbly and weak-like, was coming up out of the water.

"Na, na! What can this mean?" cried Liesi. She did not know (but we do — yes?) that when she saved the cow outside, something happened to Fritzl inside. Yes, yes, as soon as the cow's rope was cut, Fritzl, poor man, he dropped down the chimney and crash! splash! fell right into the kettle of soup in the fireplace.

Liesi lost no time. She pulled at the two arms and tugged at the two legs — and there, dripping and spluttering, with a cabbage-leaf in his hair, celery in his pocket, and a sprig of parsley over one ear, was her Fritzl.

"Na, na, my man!" said Liesi. "Is that the way you keep house — yes?"

"Oh Liesi, Liesi!" sputtered Fritzl. "You're right — that work of yours, 'tis none too easy."

" 'Tis a little hard at first," said Liesi, "but tomorrow, maybe, you'll do better."

"Nay, nay!" cried Fritzl. "What's gone is gone, and so is my housework from this day on. Please, please, my Liesi — let me go back to my work in the fields, and never more will I say that my work is harder than yours."

"Well then," said Liesi, "if that's how it is, we surely can live in peace and happiness for ever and ever."

And that they did.

The Sorcerer's Apprentice [3]

❧ *This is a modern version of a tale which is more than eighteen hundred years old. The story tells of a sorcerer's apprentice who, during his master's absence, invokes the magic words that start the broom fetching water; but alas, he cannot remember the mystical charm that will stop the broom. Soon the house is flooded, but the fortuitous arrival of the master-magician saves the day. Goethe wrote a ballad based upon this story, and in 1897 the French composer, Paul Dukas, wrote an orchestral scherzo which was inspired directly by Goethe's poem, but remotely by this old tale.*

Many years ago, in far-off Switzerland, there lived a sorcerer. That is, this story took place many years ago. For all we know, the sorcerer may be living yet. His name then was Willibald, which is a little odd, but no stranger than he was. He was tall and thin, and his nose was long and pointed to match. He wore long, loose, trailing gowns. What was left of his hair was white. A small black cap sat on the back of his head.

He was not a very ordinary sorcerer. For instance, his fellow sorcerers specialized in disappearing in puffs of smoke. Then they would bob up, at a moment's notice, in places far away from where they had been a second before. But Willibald felt such tricks were beneath his dignity. To him they were a trifle show-offy. *He* traveled from place to place on a donkey. Of course, this took a good deal more time. But no one knew better than he did that he was no ordinary sorcerer, and that his customers would wait.

However, he did have a weakness for service. It was his habit to command pieces of furniture — chairs, tables, footstools, even

[3] Richard Rostron, *The Sorcerer's Apprentice* (Morrow, 1941).

brooms — to do his bidding. Of course, once in a while a passer-by would be frightened out of his wits to see a table capering along the street with a bucket of water on its top. But this didn't happen often. The sorcerer lived way on the edge of town on a street that wasn't at all fashionable. And he was usually very careful not to let anyone see him work his spells. Not even Fritzl, his apprentice, knew how it was done.

Fritzl was a boy who was learning the sorcery business. He wasn't very bright or industrious. He made mistakes, spilled things, and was a general nuisance. In fact, only Willibald's patience saved him from being sent home in disgrace.

Of course, Fritzl was very pleased to have most of the unpleasant chores done for him. He didn't have to dust, or sweep, or scrub, or fetch water for the tank in the sorcerer's cellar workshop. Willibald used a good deal of water in his spells. And all this happened in the days before there were such things as faucets and sinks and city water supplies.

But in spite of all this, Fritzl wasn't satisfied. There were times when the sorcerer would go away and leave him to do all the work himself. Fritzl disliked those days terribly. So he decided to learn the spell his master used on the furniture. One day he crept to the top of the cellar stairs and peeped over. Willibald was busy stirring something in a kettle over the fire.

He stopped stirring to reach for a piece of firewood, and then exclaimed, "Out of wood again! That boy! Fritzl! Fritzl!"

Fritzl trembled, but didn't answer. He was afraid his master would guess that he had been spying.

"Fritzl! Where *is* that boy? Never here when you want him." The sorcerer grumbled a bit. Then he stopped stirring, and went over and stood a broom against the wall. He stepped back three paces, and forward two paces, and clapped his hands three times. Then he said, "Lif! Luf! Laf! Broom, fetch firewood!"

The broom immediately appeared to have arms — somewhat thin ones, and rather splintery, but still, arms. It came toward the stairs, hopping and thumping along on its straws. Willibald went back to his stirring, and Fritzl waited till the broom had thumped past his hiding place. Then he quietly crept away. Now he knew the spell, and he felt quite pleased with himself. He wouldn't have to work nearly so hard when old Willibald went off and left him to do everything alone.

There came a day when the sorcerer had to go off on business to the other side of town in a great hurry. In fact, he was almost tempted to travel in a puff of smoke instead of on his donkey. But he remembered in time who he was and soon he and his donkey were clip-clopping down the street. But before he went, he said to Fritzl:

"This place is a mess. While I'm gone you set about clearing it out. And be sure to scrub the cellar floor clean. I dropped a spell I was mixing last night, and it's left quite a large stain. I'm expecting a visitor from the Sorcerers' Society of Silesia in a few days and I don't want him to think I'm in the habit of spilling things. And then don't forget to refill the water tub in the workshop." You see, Willibald was very vain of the reputation he had of being no ordinary sorcerer.

When his master had gone, Fritzl went to work with a broom. He swept clouds of dust — both star and earth — in all directions. Then he started on the furniture, wiping and polishing till everything shone. After that he went downstairs to the workshop and scrubbed the floor there. The stain was very large and very dark, and he scrubbed a long time. By the time he had finished, the water tub was empty. It was a warm day and he had worked very hard. The idea of making many trips to the river with the water bucket didn't appeal to him at all.

Then he had an idea: Why not let the broom fetch the water? Of course, if old Willibald found out, he would very likely, be terribly angry. But surely the tub would be full by the time the sorcerer returned and no one would ever know. So Fritzl thought, and he wasted no time in thinking any further.

He seized the broom, stood it up against the wall, stepped back three paces, forward two paces, as he had seen Willibald do, then clapped his hands three times and said the magic words: "Lif! Luf! Laf! Broom, fetch water from the river!" He was delighted when the broom's arms appeared and it picked up the water bucket and started — thump-athump-athump! — up the stairs.

Soon it was back, and before Fritzl knew what was happening, it had tilted the bucket and flung the water across the room with a splash. Then it was off again — thump-athump-athump! — before Fritzl could stop it.

The water ran about and got in Fritzl's shoes, which wasn't very comfortable. He thought: "Well, perhaps I didn't think fast enough. When it comes back I'll make it put the water in the tub instead of spilling it out on the floor."

Almost before he knew it, the broom had returned. As soon as it appeared at the top of the stairs with another bucket of water, Fritzl called out: "Don't throw it. Pour it in the tub!" But the broom paid no heed, flung the water as before, and went off — thump-athump-athump! — for more.

Poor Fritzl was frantic. "Something is wrong here," he thought. "Perhaps I'd better do the job myself and not try to get it done by magic." And when the broom returned again, he clapped his hands three times and cried: "Lif! Luf! Laf! Broom, stop fetching water!" But once more the broom paid no heed and flung the water across the room. And again it went off — thump-athump-athump! — for more.

Again and again the broom went back and forth, each time fetching and sloshing out a bucket of water and returning to the river for another. Fritzl became desperate. The water rose higher and higher until it reached his knees. Everything — even the big water tub — started floating around the room. And Fritzl's panic grew and grew. At last he seized an ax and next time the broom came with a bucket of water, he swung wildly and split it down the middle. But instead of stopping, the two pieces went merrily on. Each piece grew another arm, and another bucket appeared from nowhere. Off they went — thump-athump-athump! — to the river.

Higher and higher the flood mounted. The two brooms came and went faster and faster. Fritzl wept and pleaded. **He repeated** snatches of spells he had heard his master use. He tried to get out of the cellar, but the water had floated the wooden steps out of place. The brooms went on and on and the water rose and rose.

Just as it rose to his chin, Fritzl heard the clip-clop of his master's donkey coming along the street. Then he heard the donkey stop and Willibald coming in the front door. "Help! Help!" he cried.

Willibald quickly appeared at the top of the stairs. "What goes on here?" he howled. Just then the brooms came in with more water and sloshed it down the stairs. Willibald was in the way and his gown was drenched. And there is nothing quite so angry as a wet sorcerer.

"Help, Master, quick!" poor Fritzl wailed. "I tried to make the broom fetch water, and then it wouldn't stop. Do something, before I drown!"

"Dumbhead!" roared Willibald. "I ought to let you drown. It's just what you deserve!" As he said this, he jumped hastily aside, for the brooms could be heard thump-athump-athumping into the house. When they appeared, the sorcerer clapped his hands *four* times. Then he gabbled a long string of words. But Fritzl didn't hear them, for just then the water tub bumped against his head. He lost his footing and went under the water with a gurgle.

Next thing he knew, he was lying on the floor coughing and gasping. He looked around him. The water was gone. In fact, there wasn't anything in the cellar that was even wet. The steps were back in their places in the stairs. One broom stood quietly and peacefully in the woodbox, with a bucket beside it. The other broom and bucket had disappeared.

Fritzl looked fearfully up at his master. The sorcerer stood at the top of the stairs, sputtering and fuming with rage. "Get out of my sight, you blockhead! I've reached the end of my patience! Go on, get out! Go back where you came from!" And he clapped his hands quite a bit and stamped his foot — the left one — and a puff of smoke appeared on the floor beside Fritzl.

The puff of smoke grew and grew. As it grew it moved over and covered the apprentice. He shut his eyes in fright. He felt himself being lifted and heard a whistling in his ears like the wind. Then he was dropped with a hard bump. When he opened his eyes, he saw he was in his mother's front yard.

Fritzl lived to be a very old man, but he never saw the sorcerer again. And he didn't want to. In the fine summer evenings he would sit and tell stories to his grandchildren. They liked best the story of old Willibald and the broom. They remembered it and told it to their grandchildren. And *they* told it to *their* grandchildren. And so it has come down to us.

FRANCE

Little Red Riding-Hood [1]

⅜ This tale, too, has many versions, and the question of whether to use this with its realistic ending or one of those with a softened ending is still a debatable one. Three reasons led to the choice of the version given here: first, most children are too ignorant of the meaning of death to be hurt by this ending; second, children have logical minds, and this is the logical climax; third, some children may enjoy this form of the story, as adults enjoy seeing a tragedy on the stage.

There was once upon a time a little village girl, the prettiest ever seen or known, of whom her mother was dotingly fond. Her grandmother was even fonder of her still, and had a little red hood made for the child, which suited her so well that wherever she went she was known by the name of Little Red Riding-Hood.

One day, her mother having baked some cakes, said to her, "Go and see how your grandmother is getting on, for I have been told she is ill; take her a cake and this little jar of butter." Whereupon Little Red Riding-Hood started off without delay towards the village in which her grandmother lived. On her way she had to pass through a wood, and there she met that sly old fellow, Mr. Wolf, who felt that he should very much like to eat her up on the spot, but was afraid to do so, as there were woodcutters at hand in the forest.

He asked her which way she was going, and the poor child, not knowing how dangerous it is to stop and listen to a wolf, answered: "I am going to see my grandmother and am taking a cake and a little jar of butter, which my mother has sent her."

"Does she live far from here?" asked the Wolf.

"Oh, yes!" replied Little Red Riding-Hood, "on the further side of the mill that you see down there; hers is the first house in the village."

"Well, I was thinking of going to visit her myself," rejoined the Wolf, "so I will take this path, and you take the other, and we will see which of us gets there first."

The Wolf then began running off as fast as he could along the shorter way, which he had chosen, while the little girl went by the longer way, and amused herself with stopping to gather nuts, or run after butterflies, and with making little nosegays of all the flowers she could find.

It did not take the Wolf long to reach the grandmother's house. He knocked, tap, tap.

"Who is there?"

"It is your granddaughter, Little Red Riding-Hood," answered the Wolf, imitating the child's voice. "I have brought a cake and a little jar of butter, which my mother has sent you."

The good grandmother, who was ill in bed, called out, "Pull the bobbin, and the latch will go up." The Wolf pulled the bobbin, and the door opened. He leaped on to the poor old woman and ate her up in less than no time, for he had been three days without food. He then shut the door again and laid himself down in the grandmother's bed to wait for Little Red Riding-Hood. Presently she came and knocked at the door, tap, tap.

[1] From Charles Perrault, *Fairy Tales* (Dutton, 1916).

"Who is there?" Little Red Riding-Hood was frightened at first, on hearing the Wolf's gruff voice, but thinking that her grandmother had a cold, she answered:

"It is your granddaughter, Little Red Riding-Hood. I have brought a cake and a little jar of butter, which my mother has sent you."

The Wolf called out, his time in rather a softer voice, "Pull the bobbin, and the latch will go up." Little Red Riding-Hood pulled the bobbin, and the door opened.

When the Wolf saw her come in, he hid himself under the bedclothes and said to her, "Put the cake and the little jar of butter in the cupboard and come into bed with me."

Little Red Riding-Hood undressed and went to the bedside and was very much astonished to see how different her grandmother looked to what she did when she was up and dressed.

"Grandmother," she exclaimed, "what long arms you have!"

"All the better to hug you with, my little girl."

"Grandmother, what long legs you have!"

"All the better to run with, child."

"Grandmother, what long ears you have!"

"All the better to hear with, child."

"Grandmother, what large eyes you have!"

"All the better to see with, child."

"Grandmother, what large teeth you have!"

"All the better to eat you with!"

And saying these words, the wicked Wolf sprang out upon Little Red Riding-Hood and ate her up.

Drakestail[2]

One of the most charming of the beast tales. Here are magic, a hero mistreated but self-confident, and the hero's final success, all told in a simple, direct manner. The climax is so nonchalantly met by Drakestail that the child-listener accepts it quite satisfied, and the adult reader is equally delighted, although for another reason.

[2] From Andrew Lang, *The Red Fairy Book* (Longmans, Green, 1947).

Drakestail was very little, that is why he was called Drakestail; but tiny as he was he had brains, and he knew what he was about, for having begun with nothing he ended by amassing a hundred crowns. Now the King of the country, who was very extravagant and never kept any money, having heard that Drakestail had some, went one day in his own person to borrow his hoard; and, my word, in those days Drakestail was not a little proud of having lent money to the King. But after the first and second year, seeing that they never even dreamed of paying the interest, he became uneasy, so much so that at last he resolved to go and see His Majesty himself and get repaid. So one fine morning Drakestail, very spruce and fresh, takes the road, singing: "Quack, quack, quack, when shall I get my money back?"

He had not gone far when he met friend Fox, on his rounds that way.

"Good-morning, neighbor," says the friend, "where are you off to so early?"

"I am going to the King for what he owes me."

"Oh! take me with thee!"

Drakestail said to himself: "One can't have too many friends." . . . "I will," says he, "but going on all-fours you will soon be tired. Make yourself quite small, get into my throat — go into my gizzard and I will carry you."

"Happy thought!" says friend Fox.

He takes bag and baggage and presto! is gone like a letter into the post.

And Drakestail is off again, all spruce and fresh, still singing: "Quack, quack, quack, when shall I have my money back?"

He had not gone far when he met his lady-friend Ladder, leaning on her wall.

"Good-morning, my duckling," says the lady friend, "whither away so bold?"

"I am going to the King for what he owes me."

"Oh! take me with thee!"

Drakestail said to himself: "One can't have too many friends." . . . "I will," says he, "but with your wooden legs you will soon be tired. Make yourself quite small, get into my throat — go into my gizzard and I will carry you."

"Happy thought!" says my friend Ladder, and nimble, bag and baggage, goes to keep company with friend Fox.

And "Quack, quack, quack." Drakestail is off again, singing and spruce as before. A little farther he meets his sweetheart, my friend River, wandering quietly in the sunshine.

"Thou, my cherub," says she, "whither so lonesome, with arching tail, on this muddy road?"

"I am going to the King, you know, for what he owes me."

"Oh! take me with thee!"

Drakestail said to himself: "One can't have too many friends." . . . "I will," says he, "but you who sleep while you walk will soon be tired. Make yourself quite small, get into my throat — go into my gizzard and I will carry you."

"Ah, happy thought!" says my friend River.

She takes bag and baggage and glou, glou, glou, she takes her place between friend Fox and my friend Ladder.

And "Quack, quack, quack." Drakestail is off again singing.

A little farther on he meets comrade Wasp's-nest, manoeuvring his wasps.

"Well, good-morning, friend Drakestail," said comrade Wasp's-nest, "where are we bound for so spruce and fresh?"

"I am going to the King for what he owes me."

"Oh! take me with thee!"

Drakestail said to himself, "One can't have too many friends." . . . "I will," says he, "but with your battalion to drag along, you will soon be tired. Make yourself quite small, go into my throat — get into my gizzard and I will carry you."

"By Jove! that's a good idea!" says comrade Wasp's-nest.

And left file! he takes the same road to join the others with all his party. There was not much more room, but by closing up a bit they managed. . . . And Drakestail is off again singing.

He arrived thus at the capital and threaded his way straight up the High Street, still running and singing "Quack, quack, quack, when shall I get my money back?" to the great astonishment of the good folks, till he came to the King's palace.

He strikes with the knocker: "Toc! toc!"

"Who is there?" asks the porter, putting his head out of the wicket.

"'Tis I, Drakestail. I wish to speak to the King."

"Speak to the King! . . . That's easily said. The King is dining, and will not be disturbed."

"Tell him that it is I, and I have come he well knows why."

The porter shuts his wicket and goes up to say it to the King, who, with all his ministers, was just sitting down to dinner.

"Good, good!" said the King laughing. "I know what it is! Make him come in and put him with the turkeys and chickens."

The porter descends.

"Have the goodness to enter."

"Good!" says Drakestail to himself, "I shall now see how they eat at court."

"This way, this way," says the porter. "One step further. . . . There, there you are."

"How? what? in the poultry yard?"

Fancy how vexed Drakestail was!

"Ah! so that's it," says he. "Wait! I will compel you to receive me. Quack, quack, quack, when shall I get my money back?" But turkeys and chickens are creatures who don't like people that are not as themselves. When they saw the newcomer and how he was made and when they heard him crying too, they began to look black at him.

"What is it? What does he want?"

Finally they rushed at him all together to overwhelm him with pecks.

"I am lost!" said Drakestail to himself, when by good luck he remembers his comrade friend Fox, and he cries:

"Reynard, Reynard, come out of your earth,
    Or Drakestail's life is of little worth."

Then friend Fox, who was only waiting for these words, hastens out, throws himself on the wicked fowls, and quick! quack! he tears them to pieces; so much so that at the end of five minutes there was not one left alive. And Drakestail, quite content, began to sing again, "Quack, quack, quack, when shall I get my money back?"

When the King who was still at table heard this refrain, and the poultry woman came to tell him what had been going on in the yard, he was terribly annoyed.

He ordered them to throw this tail of a drake into the well, to make an end of him.

And it was done as he commanded. Drakestail was in despair of getting himself out of such a deep hole, when he remembered his lady friend, the Ladder.

"Ladder, Ladder, come out of thy hold,
Or Drakestail's days will soon be told."

My friend Ladder, who was only waiting for these words, hastens out, leans her two arms on the edge of the well, then Drakestail climbs nimbly on her back, and hop! he is in the yard, where he begins to sing louder than ever.

When the King, who was still at table and laughing at the good trick he had played his creditor, heard him again reclaiming his money, he became livid with rage.

He commanded that the furnace should be heated, and this tail of a drake thrown into it, because he must be a sorcerer.

The furnace was soon hot, but this time Drakestail was not so afraid; he counted on his sweetheart, my friend River.

"River, River, outward flow,
Or to death Drakestail must go."

My friend River hastens out, and errouf! throws herself into the furnace, which she floods with all the people who had lighted it; after which she flowed growling into the hall of the palace to the height of more than four feet.

And Drakestail, quite content, begins to swim, singing deafeningly, "Quack, quack, quack, when shall I get my money back?"

The King was still at table and thought himself quite sure of his game; but when he heard Drakestail singing again and when they told him all that had passed, he became furious and got up from table brandishing his fists.

"Bring him here, and I'll cut his throat! bring him here quick!" cried he.

And quickly two footmen ran to fetch Drakestail.

"At last," said the poor chap, going up the great stairs, "they have decided to receive me."

Imagine his terror when, on entering, he sees the King as red as a turkey cock, and all his ministers attending him, standing sword in hand. He thought this time it was all up with him. Happily, he remembered that there was still one remaining friend, and he cried with dying accents:

"Wasp's-nest, Wasp's-nest, make a sally,
Or Drakestail nevermore may rally."

Hereupon the scene changes.

"Bs, bs, bayonet them!" The brave Wasp's-nest rushes out with all his wasps. They threw themselves on the infuriated King and his ministers, and stung them so fiercely in the face that they lost their heads, and not knowing where to hide themselves they all jumped pell-mell from the window and broke their necks on the pavement.

Behold Drakestail much astonished, all alone in the big saloon and master of the field. He could not get over it.

Nevertheless, he remembered shortly what he had come for to the palace, and improving the occasion, he set to work to hunt for his dear money. But in vain he rummaged in all the drawers; he found nothing; all had been spent.

And ferreting thus from room to room he came at last to the one with the throne in it and feeling fatigued, he sat himself down on it to think over his adventure. In the meanwhile the people had found their King and his ministers with their feet in the air on the pavement, and they had gone into the palace to know how it had occurred. On entering the throne-room, when the crowd saw that there was already someone on the royal seat, they broke out in cries of surprise and joy:

"The King is dead, long live the King!
Heaven has sent us down this thing."

Drakestail, who was no longer surprised at anything, received the acclamations of the people as if he had never done anything else all his life.

A few of them certainly murmured that a Drakestail would make a fine King; those who knew him replied that a knowing Drakestail was a more worthy King than a spendthrift like him who was lying on the pavement. In short, they ran and took the crown off the head of the deceased, and placed it on that of Drakestail, whom it fitted like wax.

Thus he became King.

"And now," said he after the ceremony, "ladies and gentlemen, let's go to supper. I am so hungry!"

Cinderella and the Glass Slipper [3]

◈§ *No version of this immortal tale equals the flavor of this retelling, with its measured details of costume and festival, its clear portrait of an endearing young girl, its evocation of snow and the winter night, its moments of magic and romance. The great poet's touch is everywhere apparent — in the wisdom of the fairy godmother, as well as in her magic: "What's being old, my dear? Merely little by little and less by less"; the command of words that seem colloquial and spoken, the language of the folk tale: "She never stayed mumpish or sulky," ". . . the two elder sisters squinnied down out of their window." Yet the structure of the tale remains intact, the wicked sisters are justly punished, and the incident of the snipping off of their big toe and heel is let stand, with no fear of nightmare to follow.*

There were once upon a time three sisters who lived in an old, high, stone house in a street not very far from the great square of the city where was the palace of the King. The two eldest of these sisters were old and ugly, which is bad enough. They were also sour and jealous, which is worse. And simply because the youngest (who was only their half-sister) was gentle and lovely, they hated her.

While they themselves sat in comfort in their fine rooms upstairs, she was made to live in a dark, stone-flagged kitchen with nothing but rats, mice, and cockroaches for company. There, in a kind of cupboard, she slept. By day she did the housework — cooking and scrubbing and sweeping and scouring. She made the beds, she washed their linen, she darned their stockings, she mended their clothes. She was never in bed till midnight; and summer or winter, she had to

[3] From Walter de la Mare, *Told Again* (Knopf, 1927).

be up every morning at five, to fetch water, to chop up the firewood and light the fires. In the blind, frozen mornings of winter she could scarcely creep about for the cold.

Yet, in spite of all this, though she hadn't enough to eat, though her sisters never wearied of nagging and scolding at her, or of beating her, either, when they felt in the humour, she soon forgot their tongues and bruises. She must have been happy by nature, just as by nature a may-tree is covered with leaves and blossom, or water jets out of a well-spring. To catch sight of a sunbeam lighting up the kitchen wall now and then, or the moonlight stealing across the floor, or merely to wake and hear the birds shrilling at daybreak, was enough to set her heart on fire.

She would jump out of bed, say her prayers, slip into her rags, wash her bright face under the pump, comb her dark hair; then, singing too, not like the birds, but softly under her breath, would begin her work. Sometimes she would set herself races against the old kitchen clock; or say to herself, "When I've done this and this and this and *this*, I'll look out of the window." However late it was before the day was finished, she made it a rule always to sit for a little while in front of the great kitchen fire, her stool drawn close up to the hearth among the cinders. There she would begin to dream even before she fell asleep; and in mockery her sisters called her Cinderella.

They never left her at peace. If they could not find work for her to do, they made it; and for food gave her their crusts and bits left over. They hated her, and hated her all the more because, in spite of their scowls and grumblings, she never stayed mumpish or sulky, while her cheeks ever grew fairer and her eyes brighter. She couldn't help it. Since she felt young and happy, she couldn't but seem so.

Now all this may have been in part because Cinderella had a fairy godmother. This fairy godmother had come to her christening, and well the sisters remembered it. This little bunched-up old woman had a hump on her back, was dressed in outlandish clothes and a high steeple hat, and the two impudent trollops (who even then tried to make themselves look younger than they were) had called her "Old Stump-Stump," had put out their tongues at her, and laughed at every word she said.

But except for one slow piercing look at them out of her green eyes (after which they laughed no more), the old woman had paid them no heed. She had stooped over Cinderella's wooden cradle and gazed a long time at her sleeping face, then, laying her skinny fore-finger on the mite's chin, she had slowly nodded — once, twice, thrice. If every nod meant a fairy gift, then what wonder Cinderella had cheeks like a wild rose, eyes clear as dewdrops, and a tongue like a blackbird's?

Now Cinderella, of course, could not remember her christening; and her godmother had never been seen or heard of since. She seemed to have quite forgotten her godchild; and when one day Cinderella spoke of her to her sisters, they were beside themselves with rage.

"Godmother, forsooth!" they cackled. "Crazy old humpback! Much she cares for you, Miss Slut! Keep to your cinders; and no more drowsing and dreaming by the fire!"

So time went on, until at last Cinderella was so used to their pinchings and beatings and scoldings that she hardly noticed them. She kept out of their company as much as she could, almost forgot how to cry, was happy when she was alone, and was never idle.

Now a little before Christmas in the year when Cinderella was eighteen, the King sent out his trumpeters to proclaim that on Twelfth Night there was to be a great Ball at the Palace, with such dancing and feasting and revelry as had never been known in that country before. Bonfires were to be lit on the hills, torches in the streets. There were to be stalls of hot pies, eels, sweetmeats, cakes and comfits in the market-place. There were to be booths showing strange animals and birds and suchlike; and the fountains in the city were to run that night with wine. For the next day after it would be the twenty-first birthday of the King's only son. When the people heard the proclamation of the King's trumpeters, there were wild rejoicings, and they at once began to make ready for the feast.

In due time there came to the old stone house where the three sisters lived the King's Lord Chamberlain. At sound of the wheels of his coach the two elder sisters squinnied down out of their window and then at once scuttled downstairs to lock Cinderella up in the kitchen, in case he should see not only her rags, but her lovely young face. He had come, as they guessed, to bring them the King's command that they should attend the great Ball. "I see, madam, three are invited," he said, looking at his scroll.

"Ay," said they, as if in grief, "but only two of us are left." So he bowed and withdrew.

After that the two old sisters scarcely stopped talking about the Ball. They could think of nothing else. They spent the whole day and every day in turning out their chests and wardrobes in search of whatever bit of old finery they could lay hands on. For hours together they sat in front of their great looking-glass, smirking this way and languishing that, trying on any old gown or cloak they could find — slippers and sashes, wigs and laces and buckles and necklaces, and never of the same mind for two minutes together. And when they weren't storming at Cinderella, they were quarreling and wrangling between themselves.

As for Cinderella, from morning to night she sat stitching and stitching till she could scarcely see out of her young eyes or hold her needle. The harder she worked and the more she tried to please them, the worse they fumed and flustered. They were like wasps in a trap.

At last came the night of the Ball. The streets were ablaze with torches and bonfires. In every window burned wax tapers. Shawls and silks of all the colours of the rainbow dangled from sill and balcony. Wine red and golden gushed from the fountains. Everywhere there was feasting and merriment, laughter and music. At one end of the city was a booth of travelling bears, which were soon so crammed with buns and honeycomb that they could only sit and pant; and at the other was a troupe of Barbary apes that played on every kind of instrument of music.

Besides which, there was a singing Mermaid; a Giant, with a dwarf on his hat-brim; and a wild man from the Indies that gulped down flaming pitch as if it were milk and water.

The country people, all in their best and gayest clothes (and they came from far and near as if to a Fair), had brought their children even to the youngest, and stood gazing and gaping at the dressed-up lords and ladies in their coaches and carriages on their way to the Palace. There were coaches with six horses, and coaches with four; and a fat, furred, scarlet-silked postillion to each pair. The whole city under the tent of the starry night flared bright as a peepshow.

But Cinderella hadn't a moment even to peer down from an upper window at these wonders. She hardly knew whether she was on her head or her heels. And when at last her two old sisters — looking in their wigs and powder more like bunched-up fantastic monkeys than human beings — had at last rolled off in their hired carriage to the Palace, she was so tired she could scarcely creep upstairs.

After tidying up the litter in their bedrooms, and making a pot of soup to be kept simmering for them till they came home, she drew her stool up to the kitchen fire, with not even the heart to look out of the window. She had never before felt so lonely or wretched, and as she sat there in the red glow of the smouldering coals, before even she knew it was there, a tear rolled down her cheek and splashed with a sizzle into the hot ashes. She ached all over. Nevertheless she poked up the fire again, swept up the ashes, began to sing a little to herself, forgot to go on, and as she did so set to wondering what *she* would be doing now if she herself had gone to the Palace. "But since you can't be in two places at once, my dear," she suddenly laughed out loud, "why here you must stay."

By now it had grown quieter in the streets, and against the black of the window in the wintry night snow was falling. Sitting on her stool among the cinders, Cinderella listened to the far-away strains of music. But these too died away as she listened; utter silence came with the snow; and in a minute or two she would have fallen fast asleep.

Indeed, all was so hushed at last in the vacant kitchen that the ashes, like pygmy bells in a belfry, tinkled as they fell; a cricket began shrilly churring from a crevice in the hob, and she could hear the tiny *tic-a-tac-tac* of the mice as they came tippeting and frisking round her stool. Then, suddenly, softly, and without warning, there sounded out of the deep hush a gentle knock-knocking at the door.

Cinderella's drowsy eyes opened wide. The mice scuttled to their wainscot. Then all was still again. What stranger was this, come in the dark and the snow? Maybe, thought Cinderella, it was only the wind in the ivy. But no, yet again there sounded that gentle knocking — there could be no mistake of that. So Cinderella rose from her stool, lit the tallow candle in an old copper candlestick, and, lifting the latch, peered out into the night.

The stars of huge Orion were wildly shaking in the dark hollow of the sky; the cold air lapped her cheek; and the garden was mantled deep and white as wool with snow. And behold on the doorstep stood a little old humpbacked woman, with a steeple hat on her head, and over her round shoulders a buckled green cloak that came down to her very heels.

"Good-evening, my dear," said the old woman. "I see you don't know who *I* am?" Her green eyes gleamed in the candlelight as she peered into the gloom of the kitchen. "And why, pray, are you sitting here alone, when all the world is gone to the Ball?"

Cinderella looked at her — at her green far-set eyes and long hooked nose, and she smiled back at the old woman and begged her to come in. Then she told her about the Ball.

"Ahai!" said the old woman, "and I'll be bound to say, my dear, you'd like to go too. Ay, so I thought. Come, then, there's no time to waste. Night's speeding on. Put on your gown and we'll be off to the Palace at once."

Now her sisters had strictly forbidden Cinderella to stir from the house in their absence. Bread and water for three days they had threatened her with if she so much as opened the door. But she knew in her heart they had not told her the truth about the Ball. She knew she had been invited to go too; and now she was not so frightened of them as she used to be. None the less, she could only smile in reply to the old woman, and all she could say was: "It's very kind of you, ma'am. I should dearly like to go to the Ball, and I'm sorry; but I've nothing to go in."

Now the old woman was carrying in her hand (for she stooped nearly double) a crutch or staff, and she said, "Ahai! my dear! Rags and skin, eh? So it's nothing but a gown you need. *That's* soon mended."

With that, she lifted a little her crutch into the air, and as if at a sign and as if an owl had swooped in out of the night, there floated in through the open door out of the darkness and snow a small square Arabian leather trunk, red and gold, with silver hinges and a silver lock.

The old woman touched the lock with her crutch and the lid flew open. And beneath the lid there lay a gown of spangled orient muslin edged with swansdown and seed pearls and white as hoar-frost. There was a fan of strange white feathers, too, and a wreath of green leaves and snow-flowers, such flowers as bloom only on the tops of the mountains under the stars.

"So there's the gown!" said the old woman with a cackle. "Now hasten, my dear. Polish up those bright young cheeks of yours, and we'll soon get a-going."

Cinderella ran off at once into the scullery, put her face under the pump, and scrubbed away until her cheeks were like wild roses, and her hands like cuckoo-flowers. She came back combing her hair with all that was left of her old comb, and then and there, in front of the kitchen fire, shook herself free of her rags and slipped into the muslin gown. Whereupon she looked exactly like a rose-bush dazzling with hoar-frost under the moon.

The old woman herself laced up the silver laces, and herself with a silver pin pinned the wreath of green leaves and snow-flowers in Cinderella's dark hair, then kissed her on both cheeks. As they stood there together, yet again the far-away music of fiddle and trumpet came stealing in through the night air

from the Palace. And suddenly Cinderella frowned, and a shadow stole over her face.

"But look, ma'am," said she, "just look at my old shoes!" For there they stood, both of them together by the hearth, two old battered clouts that had long been friends in need and in deed, but had by now seen far too much of the world. The old woman laughed and stooped over them.

"Why," she said, "what's being old, my dear? Merely little by little, and less by less." As she said these words, she jerked up the tip of her crutch again, and, behold, the two old patched-up shoes seemed to have floated off into another world and come back again. For in their stead was a pair of slippers the like of which Cinderella had never seen or even dreamed of. They were of spun glass and lined with swansdown, and Cinderella slipped her ten toes into them as easily as a minnow slips under a stone.

"Oh, Godmother! Look!" she cried. "And now I am ready!"

"Ahai!" said the old woman, pleased to her very heart-strings with her happy young god-daughter. "And how, pray, are we going to get through the snow?"

"I think, do you know, dear Godmother," said Cinderella, frowning a little, "I should love to *walk*." Her Godmother pointed with her crutch and, looking at Cinderella with her sharp green eyes, said:

> "Never grumbling, nought awry;
> Always willing, asks no why;
> Patient waiting, free as air —
> What's that pumpkin over there?"

Then Cinderella looked at the old summer pumpkin in the corner by the dresser that had been put by for pie in the winter, and didn't know what to say.

"Bring it a little closer, my dear," said her Godmother. So Cinderella lifted the great pumpkin in her bare arms and laid it down by the hearth. Once more the old woman waved her crutch, and behold, the pumpkin swelled and swelled before Cinderella's very eyes; it swelled in its faded mottled green till it was as huge as a puncheon of wine, and then split softly open. And before Cinderella could so much as sigh with surprise and delight, there, on its snow-slides, stood a small, round-topped, green and white coach.

"Ahai!" breathed the old woman again, and out of their holes came scampering a round dozen of house mice, which, with yet another wave of her crutch, were at once transformed into twelve small deer, like gazelles, with silver antlers, and harness of silver, bridles and reins. Six of them stood out in the snow under the stars, four of them in the kitchen, and two in the entry. Then out from a larger hole under the shelf where the pots and pans were kept, and behind which was the stone larder with its bacon and cheeses, brisked four smart black rats; and these also were changed and transmogrified as if at a whisper, and now sat up on the coach, two in front and two behind — a sharp-nosed coachman and three dapper footmen. And the coachman sat with the long reins in his hand, waiting for Cinderella to get in.

Then the old woman said:

"And now, my dear, I must leave you. There's but one thing you must remember. Be sure to hasten away from the Palace before the clock has finished tolling twelve. Midnight, my dear. The coach will be waiting, and you must haste away home."

Cinderella looked at her Godmother, and for the second time that evening a tear rolled glittering down her cheek. Oddly enough, though this was a tear of happiness, it was *exactly* like the tear that had rolled down her cheek in her wretchedness as she sat alone.

"Oh, dear, dear Godmother, how can I thank you?" she said.

"Well, my dear," said the old woman, "if you don't know how, why you can't. And if you can't, why, you needn't." And she kissed her once more.

Then Cinderella stepped into the coach. The old woman lifted her crutch. The coachman cracked his whip. The deer, with their silver clashing antlers and silver harness, scooped in the snow their slender hoofs, and out of the kitchen off slid the coach into a silence soft as wool. On, on, under the dark starry sky into streets still flaming and blazing with torches and bonfires, it swept, bearing inside of it not only the last of the King's guests, but by far the loveliest. As for the people still abroad, at sight of it and of Cinderella they opened their mouths in the utmost astonishment, then broke into a loud huzza. But Cinderella heard not a whisper — she was gone in a flash.

When she appeared in the great ball-room, thronged with splendour, its flowers vying in light with its thousands of wax candles in sconce and chandelier, even the fiddlers stopped bowing an instant to gaze at such a wonder. Even so much as one peep at Cinderella was a joy and a marvel.

The Prince himself came down from the dais where sat his father and mother, and himself led Cinderella to the throne. They danced together once, they danced together twice, and yet again. And Cinderella, being so happy and lovely, and without scorn, pride or vanity in her face, everyone there delighted to watch her, except only her two miserable half-sisters, who sat in a corner under a bunch of mistletoe and glared at her in envy and rage.

Not that they even dreamed who she was. No, even though they were her half-sisters, and had lived in the same house with her since she was a child. But then, who could have supposed this was the slattern and drudge they had left at home among her cinders?

But how swiftly slips time away when the heart is happy! The music, the radiant tapers, the talking and feasting — the hours melted like hoar-frost in the sun. And even while Cinderella was once more dancing with the Prince, his dark eyes looking as if he himself were half a-dream, Cinderella heard again the great bell of the Palace clock begin to toll: *One-two-three* . . .

"Oh!" she sighed, and her heart seemed to stand still, "I hear a clock!"

And the Prince said: "Never heed the clock. It is telling us only how little time we have, and how well we should use it." *Five — six — seven* . . .

But "Oh!" Cinderella said, "what time is it telling?"

And the Prince said, "Midnight."

With that, all the colour ebbed out of her young cheeks. She drew herself away from the Prince, and ran off as fast as her feet could carry her. Straight out of the ball-room she scampered, down the long corridor, down yet another, and down the marble staircase. But as she turned at the foot of the staircase, she stumbled a little, and her left slipper slipped off. Cinderella could not wait. Eleven strokes had sounded, and as she leapt breathlessly into the coach there boomed out the twelfth. She was not a moment too soon.

Presently after, yet as if in no time, she found herself at home again in the cold black kitchen. Nothing was changed, though the fire was out, the candle but a stub. There in its corner by the potboard lay the pumpkin. And here as of old sat she herself, shivering a little in her rags on her three-legged stool among the cinders, and only the draughty door ajar and a few tiny plumes of swansdown on the flagstone for proof that she had ever stirred from the house.

But for these, all that had passed might have been a dream. But Cinderella was far too happy for that to be true, and her face was smiling as she looked into the cold ashes of the fire. She looked and she pondered; and while she was pondering, it was as if a voice had asked her a question, "Why is your foot so cold?"

She looked down, and to her dismay saw on one foot a glass slipper, and on the other nothing but an old black stocking. The old woman's magic had come and gone, but it had forgotten a slipper. And even while Cinderella was thinking what she should do, there came a loud pealing of the bell above her head, and she knew that her sisters had come back from the Ball.

So, one foot shod and one foot stockinged, she hastened upstairs with the soup, and helped her sisters to get to bed. Never before had they been in such a rage. Nothing she could do was right. They pinched her when she came near, and flung their slippers at her when she went away; and she soon knew what was amiss. They could talk of nothing else but the strange princess (as they thought her) who had come late to the Ball and with her witcheries had enchanted not only the young Prince but even the King and Queen and the whole Court, down to the very dwarfs, imps, and pages. Their tired old eyes squinted with envy, and they seemed so worn-out and wretched that Cinderella longed to comfort them if only but just to say: "But why trouble about her? *She* will never come back again."

She was thankful at any rate they were too busy with their tongues to notice her feet; and at last she slipped downstairs, *clip-clop, clip-clop,* and was soon safe in bed and asleep.

The very next day the royal trumpeters were trumpeting in the streets once more. Even the Prince had not been able to run as fast as Cinderella, and had come out into the snowy night only just in time to see her coach of magic vanish into the dark. But he had picked up her slipper as he came back.

Proclamation was sounded that anyone who should bring tidings of this lovely young stranger or of her slipper, should be richly rewarded. But Cinderella in her kitchen heard not even an echo of the trumpeters. So they trumpeted in vain.

Then the King sent out his Lord Chamberlain with six pages to attend him. They were bidden search through the city, house by house. And one of the pages carried before the Lord Chamberlain the glass slipper on a crimson cushion with tassels of pearls. At each house in turn, every lady in it was bidden try on the slipper, for the King was determined to find its owner, unless indeed she was of the undiscoverable Courts of Faërie. For most of the ladies the slipper was too high in the instep; for many it was too narrow in the tread; and for all it was far too short.

At last, the Lord Chamberlain came to the house of the three sisters. The two old sisters had already heard what passed when the page brought in the slipper. So the elder of them with a pair of tailor's shears had snipped off a big toe, and bound up her foot with a bandage. But even this was of no avail. For when she tried, in spite of the pain, to push her foot into it, the slipper was far too narrow. The second sister also, with a great cook's knife, had secretly carved off a piece of her heel, and had bound that foot up with a bandage. But even this was of no avail. For push and pull as she might, the shoe was at least an inch too short.

The Lord Chamberlain looked angrily at the sisters.

"Is there any other lady dwelling in this house?" he said.

The two sisters narrowed their eyes one at the other, and lied and said, "No." Yet even at that very moment there welled in a faint singing as if out of the very bowels of the earth.

The Lord Chamberlain said, "What voice is that I hear?"

The two sisters almost squinted as they glanced again each at the other, and the one said it was a tame popinjay: and the other that it was the creaking of the pump.

"Then," said the Lord Chamberlain, "the pump has learned English!" He at once sent two of his pages to seek out the singer whose voice he had heard, and to bring her into his presence. So Cinderella had to appear before him in her rags, just as she was. But when she saw the glass slipper on the crimson cushion, she almost laughed out loud.

The Lord Chamberlain, marvelling at her beauty, said: "Why do you smile, my child?"

She said, "Because, my lord, I have a slipper exactly like that one myself. It's in a drawer in the kitchen dresser." And when one of the pages had brought the other slipper, behold, Cinderella's two feet with both their heels and all their ten toes slipped into them as easily as a titmouse into its nest.

When Cinderella was brought to the King and the Queen, they received her as if she were a long-lost daughter. Far and near, once more, at her wedding, the bonfires blazed all night among the hills, the fountains in the market-place ran with wine, there were stalls of venison pies, black puddings and eels, sweetmeats, cakes and comfits, and such a concourse of strangers and noblemen in the city as it had never contained before.

Of Cinderella's guests of honour the first was a humpity-backed old woman muffled up in a green mantle, who ate nothing, and drank nothing, and said nothing; but smiled and smiled and smiled.

As for the elder sisters, they sat at home listening to the wedding bells clashing their changes in the steeples. The one being without a heel to her left foot, and the other without a big toe, they walked lame ever afterwards. And their neighbors, laughing at their folly, called them the Two Old Stumpstumps.

The Sleeping Beauty [4]

Sleeping Beauty *was one of the eight immortal tales of Charles Perrault, first published in France in 1697, with its first translation into English given the probable date of 1765; the translator, R. Samber.*

The Brothers Grimm found the tale prevalent in the regions they studied and it appears in their collection under the title Little Briar Rose. *This loving retelling by Walter de la Mare heightens the imagery and the romance.*

There lived long ago a King and a Queen, who, even though they loved one another, could not be wholly happy, for they had no children. But at last, one night in April — and a thin wisp of moon was shining in the light of the evening sky — a daughter was born to them. She was a tiny baby, so small that she could have been cradled in a leaf of one of the water-lilies in the moat of the castle. But there were no bounds to the joy of the King and Queen.

In due time they sent out horsemen all over the country, to invite the Fairy Women to her christening. Alas, that one of them should have been forgotten! There were wild hills and deep forests in that country, and it was some days before everything was ready. But then there was great rejoicing in the castle, and all day long came the clattering of horses' hoofs across the drawbridge over the moat; and not only horses, but much stranger beasts of burden, for some of the Fairy Women had journeyed from very far away. And each of them brought a gift — fine, rare, and precious — for the infant Princess.

When the merriment was nearly over, and most of the guests were gone, and the torches were burning low in the great hall, a bent-up old Fairy Woman — the oldest and most potent of them all — came riding in towards the

[4] From Walter de la Mare, *Told Again* (Knopf, 1927).

castle on a white ass, with jangling bells upon
its harness and bridle.

Without pausing or drawing rein, she rode
on, over the drawbridge, and into the hall,
nor stayed her ass until it stood beside the
great chair where sat the chief nurse of the
Princess, the infant asleep on a velvet cushion
on her lap. The ass lifted its head and
snuffed at the golden tassel of the cushion, as
if it might be hay. Long and steadfastly this
old Fairy Woman gazed down on the harmless child, lying asleep there, and her rage
knew no bounds. At last she raised her eyes,
and glaring round on the King and Queen
from under the peak of her black mantle,
she uttered these words:

"Plan as you may, the day will come,
When in spinning with spindle, she'll prick her
    thumb.
Then in dreamless sleep she shall slumber on
Till years a hundred have come and gone."

Then, mantling herself up again, she
clutched at her bridle-rein, wheeled her
jangling ass about in the hall, rode off, and
was gone.

Now, if the King and Queen had remembered to invite this revengeful Fairy
Woman to the Christening Feast, all might
have been well. But to grieve at their folly
was in vain. The one thing left to them
was to keep unceasing watch over the child,
and to do all in their power to prevent what
the old Fairy Woman had foretold from
coming true. The King sent messengers
throughout his kingdom far and near, proclaiming that every spindle in his realm
should be destroyed or brought at once to
the castle. There they were burnt. Anyone
after that who was found to be hiding a
spindle away at once lost his head.

Many years went by, until the King and
Queen seldom recalled what the evil-wishing
Fairy Woman had said. The Princess, as she
grew up, first into a child, then into a maid,
became ever more beautiful; and she was of
a gentle nature, loving and lovable. Indeed,
because they feared to sadden her heart with
the thought that anyone had ever boded ill
of her, she was never told of what had happened after her christening, or of the Fairy
Woman on the white ass.

Now, nothing more delighted the young
Princess than to wander over the great
castle and to look out of its many windows,
and to peep out through the slits in its thick
walls. But there was one turret into which
for a long time she never succeeded in finding her way. She would look up at it from
the green turf beneath and long to see into it.
Everywhere else she had been, but not there.

However, one evening in April she came
by chance to a secret door that she had never
till then noticed. There was a key in its iron
lock. Glancing over her shoulder, she turned
the key, opened the door, and ran as fast
as she could up the winding stone steps beyond it.

Every now and then appeared a window-
slit, and at one she saw the bright, young,
new moon in the sky, like a sickle of silver;
and at another the first stars beginning to
prickle into the East. But at the top of the
staircase she came to another door.

Here she stopped to peep through the
latch-hole, and in the gloom beyond she saw
an old, grey, stooping woman hunched up
in a hood of lamb's wool. She was squatting
on a stool, and now she leant a little this
way and now she leant a little that way, for
with her skinny fingers she was spinning flax
with a spindle.

The Princess watched her intently, and at
last, though she was unaware of it, breathed
a deep sigh at the latch-hole, for the sight
of the twirling spindle had so charmed her
mind that her body had almost forgotten to
breathe.

At sound of this sigh the old woman at
once stayed in her spinning, and, without
moving, apart from tremulous head and
hand, called softly:

"If thou wouldst see an old woman spin,
    Lift up the latch and enter in!"

The Princess, knowing of no harm, lifted
the latch and went in.

It was cold and dark in the thick-walled
room, and when she drew near, the old
woman began again to croon over her work;
and these were the words she said:

"Finger and thumb you twirl and you twine,
    Twisting it smooth and sleek and fine."

She span with such skill and ease, her right hand drawing the strands from the cleft stick or distaff, while her left twisted and stayed, twisted and stayed, that the Princess longed to try too.

Then the old woman, laying her bony fingers that were cold as a bird's claws on the Princess's hand, showed her how to hold the spindle, and at last bade her take it away and practise with it, and to come again on the morrow. But never once did she raise her old head from beneath her hood or look into the Princess's face.

For some reason which she could not tell, the Princess hid the spindle in a fold of her gown as she hastened back to her room. But she had been gone longer than she knew, and already the King and Queen were anxiously looking for her and were now come for the second time to her room seeking her. When they saw her, safely returned, first they sighed with relief, and then they began to scold her for having been away so long without reason.

And the Princess said: "But surely, mother, what is there to be frightened of? Am I not old enough yet to take care of myself?"

She laughed uneasily as (with the spindle hidden in the folds of her gown) she sat on her bedside, her fair hair dangling down on to its dark-blue quilted coverlet.

The King said: "Old enough, my dear, why yes. But wise enough? Who can say?"

The Queen said, "What are you hiding in your hand, my dear, in the folds of your gown?"

The Princess laughed again and said it was a secret.

"Maybe," said the Princess, "it is a flower, or maybe it is a pin for my hair, or maybe it is neither of these; but this very night I will show it you." And again she laughed.

So for the moment they were contented, she was so gay and happy. But when the King and Queen had gone away and were closeted together in their own private room, their fears began to stir in them again, and they decided that the very next day they would tell the Princess of the Fairy Woman and warn her against her wiles.

But, alas! even when the King and Queen were still talking together, the Princess had taken out the spindle again, and was twisting it in her hand. It was a pretty, slender thing, made cunningly out of the wood of the coral-berried prickwood or spindle-tree, but at one end sharp as a needle. And as she twisted and stayed, twisted and stayed, wondering as she did so why her young fingers were so clumsy, there sounded suddenly in the hush of the evening the wild-yelling screech of an owl at her window. She started, the spindle twisted in her hand, and the sharp point pricked deep into her thumb.

Before even the blood had welled up to the size of a bead upon her thumb, the wicked magic of the Fairy Woman began to enter into her body. Slowly, drowsily, the Princess's eyelids began to descend over her dark blue eyes; her two hands slid softly down on either side of her; her head drooped lower and lower towards her pillow. She put out her two hands, as if groping her way; sighed; sank lower; and soon she had fallen fast, fast asleep.

Not only the Princess, either. Over the King and Queen, as they sat talking together, a dense, stealthy drowsiness began to descend, though they knew not what had caused it, and they too, in a little while, were mutely slumbering in their chairs. The Lord Treasurer, alone with his money bags, the Astronomer over his charts, the ladies in their chamber, the chief butler in his pantry, and the cooks with their pots and ladles, and the scullions at their basting and boiling, and the maids at their sewing and sweeping — over each and every one of them this irresistible drowsiness descended, and they too were soon asleep.

The grooms in the stables, the gardeners in the garden, the huntsmen and the bee-keepers and the herdsmen and the cowmen and the goat-girl and the goose-girl; the horses feeding at their mangers, the hounds in their kennels, the pigs in their sties, the hawks in their cages, the bees in their skeps, the hens on their roosting sticks, the birds in the trees and bushes — even the wakeful robin hopping upon the newly-turned clods by the hedgeside, drooped and drowsed; and a deep slumber overwhelmed them one and all.

The fish in the fish-ponds, the flies crawling on the walls, the wasps hovering over the sweetmeats, the moths flitting in search of some old clout in which to lay their eggs, stayed one and all where the magic had found them. All, all were entranced — fell fast, fast asleep.

Throughout the whole castle there was no sound or movement whatsoever, but only the gentle sighings and murmurings of a deep, unfathomable sleep.

Darkness gathered over its battlements and the forests around it; the stars kindled in the sky; and then, at last, the April night gone by, came dawn and daybreak and the returning sun in the East. It glided slowly across the heavens and once more declined into the west; but still all slept on. Days, weeks, months, years went by. Time flowed on, without murmur or ripple, and, wonder of wonders, its passing brought no change.

The Princess, who had been young and lovely, remained young and lovely. The King and Queen aged not at all. They had fallen asleep talking, and the King's bearded mouth was still ajar. The Lord High Chancellor in his gown of velvet, his head at rest upon his money bags, looked not a moment older, though old indeed he looked. A fat scullion standing at a table staring at his fat cheeks and piggy eyes in the bottom of a copper pot continued to stand and stare, and the reflection of those piggy eyes and his tow-coloured mop at the bottom of it changed not at all. The flaxen-haired goose-girl with her switch and her ball of cowslips sat in the meadow as still and young and changeless as her geese. And so it was throughout the castle — the living slumbered on, time flowed away.

But with each returning spring the trees in the garden grew taller and greener, the roses and brambles flung ever wider their hooked and prickled stems and branches. Bindweed and bryony and woodbine and traveller's joy mantled walls and terraces. Wild fruit and bushes of mistletoe flaunted in the orchards. Moss, greener than samphire and seaweed, crept over the stones. The roots of the water-lilies in the moat swelled to the girth of Asian serpents; its water shallowed; and around the castle there sprang up, and every year grew denser, an immense thorny hedge of white-thorn and

briar, which completely encircled it at last with a living wall of green.

At length, nine-and-ninety winters with their ice and snow and darkness had come and gone, and the dense thorn-plaited hedge around the castle began to show the first tiny knobs that would presently break into frail green leaf; the first of spring was come again once more. Wild sang the missel-thrush in the wind and rain. The white-thorn blossomed; the almond-tree; the wilding peach. Then returned the cuckoo, its *cuck-oo* echoing against the castle's walls; and soon the nightingale, sweet in the far thickets.

At last, a little before evening of the last day of April, a Prince from a neighboring country, having lost his way among mountains that were strange to him in spite of his many wanderings, saw from the hillside the distant turrets of a castle.

Now, when this Prince was a child his nurse had often told him of the sleeping Princess and of the old Fairy Woman's spell, and as he stared down upon the turrets from the hillside the thought came to him that this might be the very castle itself of this old story. So, with his hounds beside him, he came riding down the hill, until he approached and came nearer to the thicket-like hedge that now encircled it even beyond its moat, as if in warning that none should spy or trespass further.

But, unlike other wayfarers who had come and gone, this Prince was not easily turned aside. Having tied his hunting-horn to a jutting branch, he made a circuit and rode round the hedge until he came again to the place from which he had started and where his horn was left dangling. But nowhere had he found any break or opening or make-way in the hedge. "Then," thought he, "I must hack my way through." So a little before dark he began to hack his way through with his hunting-knife.

He slashed and slashed at the coarse, prickly branches, pressing on inch by inch until his hands were bleeding and his hunting-gloves in tatters. Darkness came down, and at midnight he hadn't won so much as half-way through the hedge. So he rested himself, made a fire out of the dry twigs and branches, and, exhausted and wearied out, lay down intending to work on by moonlight. Instead, he unwittingly fell fast asleep. But while he slept, a little wind sprang up, and carried a few of the glowing embers of the Prince's fire into the tindery touchwood in the undergrowth of the hedge. There the old, dead leaves began to smoulder, then broke into flame, and by dawn the fire had burnt through the hedge and then stayed. So that when beneath the bright morning sky, wet with dew but refreshed with sleep, the Prince awoke, his way was clear.

He crept through the ashen hole into the garden beyond, full of great trees, many of them burdened with blossom. But there was neither note of bird nor chirp of insect. He made his way over the rotting drawbridge, and went into the castle. And there, as they had fallen asleep a hundred years ago, he saw the King's soldiers and retainers. Outside the guard-house sat two of them, mute as mummies, one with a dice-box between his fingers, for they had been playing with the dice when sleep had come over them a hundred years ago.

At last the Prince came to the bedchamber of the Princess; its door stood ajar, and he looked in. For a while he could see nothing but a green dusk in the room, for its stone windows were overgrown with ivy. He groped slowly nearer to the bed, and looked down upon the sleeper. Her faded silks were worn thin as paper and crumbled like tinder at a touch, yet Time had brought no change at all in her beauty. She lay there in her loveliness, the magic spindle still clasped in her fingers. And the Prince, looking down upon her, had never seen anything in the world so enchanting or so still.

Then, remembering the tale that had been told him, he stooped, crossed himself, and gently kissed the sleeper, then put his hunting-horn to his lips, and sounded a low, but prolonged clear blast upon it, which went echoing on between the stone walls of the castle. It was like the sound of a bugle at daybreak in a camp of soldiers. The Princess sighed; the spindle dropped from her fingers, her lids gently opened, and out of her dark eyes she gazed up into the young man's face. It was as if from being as it were

a bud upon its stalk she had become suddenly a flower; and they smiled each at the other.

At this same moment the King, too, stirred, lifted his head, and looked about him uneasily, as if in search of something. But seeing the dark beloved eyes of the Queen moving beneath their lids, he put out his hand and said, "Ah, my dear!" as if he were satisfied. The Lord High Chancellor, lifting his grey beard from his money table, began to count again his money. The ladies began again to laugh and to chatter over their embroideries. The fat chief butler rose up from stooping over his wine-bottles in the buttery. The cooks began to stir their pots; the scullions began to twist their spits; the grooms began to groom their horses; the gardeners to dig and prune. The huntsmen rode out to their hunting; the cowman drove in his cows; the goat-girl her goats; and the goose-girl in the meadow cried "Ga! ga!" to her geese. There was a neighing of horses and a baying of hounds and a woofing of pigs and a mooing of cows. There was a marvellous shrill crowing of cocks and a singing of birds and a droning of bees and a flitting of butterflies and a buzzing of wasps and a stirring of ants and a cawing of rooks and a murmuration of starlings. The round-eyed robin hopped from clod to clod, and the tiny wren, with cocked-up tail, sang shrill as a bugle amid the walls of the orchards.

For all living things within circuit of the castle at sound of the summons of the Prince's horn had slipped out of their long sleep as easily as a seed of gorse in the hot summer slips out of its pod, or a fish slips from out under a stone. Hearts beat pit-a-pat, tongues wagged, feet clattered, pots clashed, doors slammed, noses sneezed: and soon the whole castle was as busy as a newly-wound clock.

The seventh day afterwards was appointed for the marriage of the Prince and the Princess. But when word was sent far and near, bidding all the Fairy Women to the wedding — and these think no more of time than fish of water — one of them again was absent. And since — early or late — she never came, it seems that come she couldn't. At which the King and Queen heartily rejoiced. The dancing and feasting, with music of harp and pipe and drum and tabor, continued till daybreak; for, after so long a sleep, the night seemed short indeed.

Beauty and the Beast [5]

The vogue of the French court of Louis XIV which set the grandees playing at the writing of fairy tales was responsible for the creation of Perrault's Histoires ou Contes du Temps Passé; avec des Moralités, *which we know as Perrault's Fairy Tales. It produced less clearsighted followers, such as Countess d'Aulnoy (Marie Catherine La Mothe), whose stories "contained some scraps of folklore" but were vitiated by a profuse and ornamental style. The White Cat has endured, and as edited by Rachel Field and illustrated by Elizabeth MacKinstry (Macmillan, 1928) it has been given pictorial realization of great distinction. Among the writers of this school was Gabrielle Susanne Barbot de Gallos de Villeneuve, and to her we owe the immortal story of* Beauty and the Beast. *It is sometimes attributed to yet another writer of the time, Madame de Beaumont, because her version of the story so often appears in books addressed primarily to children, but there is no doubt who the author is, for it first appeared in the famous encyclopedia of this literature,* Le Cabinet des Fées (1785–89) *which ran into forty-one volumes.* Beauty and the Beast *is one of the most enduring variations on the great theme of the redemption of ugliness through the power of love.*

The version given here is that of Andrew Lang, who made his own adaptation from the account of Madame Villeneuve. It appears in what is certainly one of the best-loved books of all the books of childhood — Andrew Lang's Blue Fairy Book, *which was first published in 1889, at a time when the fairy tale and the traditional tales of folklore were not highly regarded as reading for children. (Mrs. Molesworth and Juliana Horatia Ewing then held the center of the stage, as writers of realism and Victorian manners.) The* Blue Fairy Book, *followed by* The Red Fairy Book (1890), *set the style for an upsurge of interest in the fairy tale. It will be remembered that Andrew Lang*

5 From Andrew Lang, *The Blue Fairy Book* (Longmans, Green, 1948).

was a scholar as well as a storyteller; he supported the anthropological theory of the origin of the folk tale.

Once upon a time, in a far-off country, there lived a merchant who was enormously rich. As he had six sons and six daughters, however, who were accustomed to having everything they fancied, he did not find he had a penny too much. But misfortunes befell them. One day their house caught fire and speedily burned to the ground, with all the splendid furniture, books, pictures, gold, silver and precious goods it contained. The father suddenly lost every ship he had upon the sea, either by dint of pirates, shipwreck or fire. Then he heard that his clerks in distant countries, whom he had trusted entirely, had proved unfaithful. And at last from great wealth he fell into the direst poverty.

All that he had left was a little house in a desolate place at least a hundred leagues from the town. The daughters at first hoped their friends, who had been so numerous while they were rich, would insist on their staying in their houses, but they soon found they were left alone. Their former friends even attributed their misfortunes to their own extravagance and showed no intention of offering them any help.

So nothing was left for them but to take their departure to the cottage, which stood in the midst of a dark forest. As they were too poor to have any servants, the girls had to work hard, and the sons, for their part, cultivated the fields to earn their living. Roughly clothed, and living in the simplest way, the girls regretted unceasingly the luxuries and amusements of their former life. Only the youngest daughter tried to be brave and cheerful.

She had been as sad as anyone when misfortune first overtook her father, but soon recovering her natural gaiety, she set to work to make the best of things, to amuse her father and brothers as well as she could, and to persuade her sisters to join her in dancing and singing. But they would do nothing of the sort, and because she was not as doleful as themselves, they declared this miserable life was all she was fit for. But she was really far prettier and cleverer than they were. Indeed, she was so lovely she was always called Beauty.

After two years, their father received news that one of his ships, which he had believed lost, had come safely into port with a rich cargo. All the sons and daughters at once thought that their poverty was at an end and wanted to set out directly for the town; but their father, who was more prudent, begged them to wait a little, and though it was harvest time, and he could ill be spared, determined to go himself to make inquiries.

Only the youngest daughter had any doubt but that they would soon again be as rich as they were before. They all loaded their father with commissions for jewels and dresses which it would have taken a fortune to buy; only Beauty did not ask for anything. Her father, noticing her silence, said:

"And what shall I bring for you, Beauty?"

"The only thing I wish for is to see you come home safely," she answered.

But this reply vexed her sisters, who fancied she was blaming them for having asked for such costly things. Her father, however, was pleased, but as he thought she certainly ought to like pretty presents, he told her to choose something.

"Well, dear Father," she said, "as you insist upon it, I beg that you will bring me a rose. I have not seen one since we came here, and I love them so much."

The merchant set out, only to find that his former companions, believing him to be dead, had divided his cargo between them. After six months of trouble and expense he found himself as poor as when he started on his journey. To make matters worse, he was obliged to return in the most terrible weather. By the time he was within a few leagues of his home he was almost exhausted with cold and fatigue. Though he knew it would take some hours to get through the forest, he resolved to go on. But night overtook him, and the deep snow and bitter frost made it impossible for his horse to carry him any farther.

The only shelter he could get was the hollow trunk of a great tree, and there he crouched all the night, which seemed to him the longest he had ever known. The howling of the wolves kept him awake, and when at last day broke the falling snow had covered up every path, and he did not know which way to turn.

At length he made out some sort of path, but it was so rough and slippery that he fell down more than once. Presently it led him into an avenue of trees which ended in a splendid castle. It seemed to the merchant very strange that no snow had fallen in the avenue of orange trees, covered with flowers and fruit. When he reached the first court of the castle he saw before him a flight of agate steps. He went up them and passed through several splendidly furnished rooms.

The pleasant warmth of the air revived him, and he felt very hungry; but there seemed to be nobody in all this vast and splendid palace. Deep silence reigned everywhere, and at last, tired of roaming through empty rooms and galleries, he stopped in a room smaller than the rest, where a clear fire was burning and a couch was drawn up cosily before it. Thinking this must be prepared for someone who was expected, he sat down to wait till he should come and very soon fell into a sweet sleep.

When his extreme hunger wakened him after several hours, he was still alone; but a little table, with a good dinner on it, had been drawn up close to him. He lost no time in beginning his meal, hoping he might soon thank his considerate host, whoever it might be. But no one appeared, and even after another long sleep, from which he awoke completely refreshed, there was no sign of anybody, though a fresh meal of dainty cakes and fruit was prepared upon the little table at his elbow.

Being naturally timid, the silence began to terrify him, and he resolved to search once more through all the rooms; but it was of no use, there was no sign of life in the palace! Then he went down into the garden, and though it was winter everywhere else, here the sun shone, the birds sang, the flowers bloomed, and the air was soft and sweet. The merchant, in ecstasies with all he saw and heard, said to himself:

"All this must be meant for me. I will go this minute and bring my children to share all these delights."

In spite of being so cold and weary when he reached the castle, he had taken his horse to the stable and fed it. Now he thought he would saddle it for his homeward journey, and he turned down the path which led to the stable. This path had a hedge of roses on each side of it, and the merchant thought he had never seen such exquisite flowers. They reminded him of his promise to Beauty, and he stopped and had just gathered one to take to her when he was startled by a strange noise behind him. Turning round, he saw a frightful Beast, which seemed to be very angry and said in a terrible voice:

"Who told you you might gather my roses? Was it not enough that I sheltered you in my palace and was kind to you? This is the way you show your gratitude, by stealing my flowers! But your insolence shall not go unpunished."

The merchant, terrified by these furious words, dropped the fatal rose and, throwing himself on his knees, cried, "Pardon me, noble sir. I am truly grateful for your hospitality, which was so magnificent I could not imagine you would be offended by my taking such a little thing as a rose."

But the Beast's anger was not lessened by his speech.

"You are very ready with excuses and flattery," he cried. "But that will not save you from the death you deserve."

Alas, thought the merchant, if my daughter Beauty could only know into what danger her rose has brought me! And in despair he began to tell the Beast all his misfortunes and the reason of his journey, not forgetting to mention Beauty's request.

"A king's ransom would hardly have procured all that my other daughters asked for," he said. "But I thought I might at least take Beauty her rose. I beg you to forgive me, for you see I meant no harm."

The Beast said, in a less furious tone, "I will forgive you on one condition — that you will give me one of your daughters."

"Ah," cried the merchant, "if I were cruel enough to buy my own life at the expense of one of my children's, what excuse could I invent to bring her here?"

"None," answered the Beast. "If she comes at all she must come willingly. On no other condition will I have her. See if any of them is courageous enough, and loves you enough, to come and save your life. You seem to be an honest man so I will trust you to go home. I give you a month to see if any of your daughters will come back with you and stay here, to let you go free. If none of them is willing, you must come alone, after bidding them good-bye forever, for then you will belong to me. And do not imagine that you can hide from me, for if you fail to keep your word I will come and fetch you!" added the Beast grimly.

The merchant accepted this proposal. He promised to return at the time appointed, and then, anxious to escape from the presence of the Beast, he asked permission to set off at once. But the Beast answered that he could not go until the next day.

"Then you will find a horse ready for you," he said. "Now go and eat your supper and await my orders."

The poor merchant, more dead than alive, went back to his room, where the most delicious supper was already served on the little table drawn up before a blazing fire. But he was too terrified to eat and only tasted a few of the dishes, for fear the Beast should be angry if he did not obey his orders. When he had finished, the Beast warned him to remember their agreement and to prepare his daughter exactly for what she had to expect.

"Do not get up tomorrow," he added, "until you see the sun and hear a golden bell ring. Then you will find your breakfast waiting for you, and the horse you are to ride will be ready in the courtyard. He will also bring you back again when you come with your daughter a month hence. Farewell. Take a rose to Beauty, and remember your promise!"

The merchant lay down until the sun rose. Then, after breakfast, he went to gather Beauty's rose and mounted his horse, which carried him off so swiftly that in an instant he had lost sight of the palace. He was still wrapped in gloomy thoughts when it stopped before the door of his cottage.

His sons and daughters, who had been uneasy at his long absence, rushed to meet him, eager to know the result of his journey which, seeing him mounted upon a splendid horse and wrapped in a rich mantle, they supposed to be favorable. But he hid the truth from them at first, only saying sadly to Beauty as he gave her the rose:

"Here is what you asked me to bring you. Little you know what it has cost."

Presently he told them his adventures from beginning to end, and then they were all very unhappy. The girls lamented loudly over their lost hopes, and the sons declared their father should not return to the terrible castle. But he reminded them he had promised to go back. Then the girls were very angry with Beauty and said it was all her fault. If she had asked for something sensible this would never have happened.

Poor Beauty, much distressed, said to them, "I have indeed caused this misfortune, but who could have guessed that to ask for a rose in the middle of summer would cause so much misery? But as I did the mischief it is only just that I should suffer for it. I will therefore go back with my father to keep his promise."

At first nobody would hear of it. Her father and brothers, who loved her dearly, declared nothing should make them let her go. But Beauty was firm. As the time drew near she divided her little possessions between her sisters, and said good-bye to everything she loved. When the fatal day came she encouraged and cheered her father as they mounted together the horse which had brought him back. It seemed to fly rather than gallop, but so smoothly that Beauty was not frightened. Indeed, she would have enjoyed the journey if she had not feared what might happen at the end of it. Her father still tried to persuade her to go back, but in vain.

While they were talking the night fell. Then, to their great surprise, wonderful colored lights began to shine in all directions, and splendid fireworks blazed out before them; all the forest was illuminated. They even felt pleasantly warm, though it had been bitterly cold before. They reached the avenue of orange trees and saw that the palace was brilliantly lighted from roof to ground, and music sounded softly from the courtyard.

"The Beast must be very hungry," said Beauty, trying to laugh, "if he makes all this rejoicing over the arrival of his prey." But, in spite of her anxiety, she admired all the wonderful things she saw.

When they had dismounted, her father led her to the little room. Here they found a splendid fire burning, and the table daintily spread with a delicious supper.

Beauty, who was less frightened now that she had passed through so many rooms and seen nothing of the Beast, was quite willing to begin, for her long ride had made her very hungry. But they had hardly finished their meal when the noise of the Beast's footsteps was heard approaching, and Beauty clung to her father in terror, which became all the greater when she saw how frightened he was. But when the Beast really appeared, though she trembled at the sight of him, she made a great effort to hide her horror, and saluted him respectfully.

This evidently pleased the Beast. After looking at her he said, in a tone that might have struck terror into the boldest heart, though he did not seem to be angry:

"Good evening, old man. Good evening, Beauty."

The merchant was too terrified to reply, but Beauty answered sweetly, "Good evening, Beast."

"Have you come willingly?" asked the Beast. "Will you be content to stay here when your father goes away?"

Beauty answered bravely that she was quite prepared to stay.

"I am pleased with you," said the Beast. "As you have come of your own accord, you may remain. As for you, old man," he added, turning to the merchant, "at sunrise tomorrow take your departure. When the bell rings, get up quickly and eat your breakfast, and you will find the same horse waiting to take you home."

Then turning to Beauty, he said, "Take your father into the next room, and help him choose gifts for your brothers and sisters. You will find two traveling trunks there; fill them as full as you can. It is only just that you should send them something very precious as a remembrance."

Then he went away, after saying, "Good-bye, Beauty; good-bye, old man." Beauty was beginning to think with great dismay of her father's departure, but they went into the next room, which had shelves and cupboards all round it. They were greatly surprised at the riches it contained. There were splendid dresses fit for a queen, with all the ornaments to be worn with them, and when Beauty opened the cupboards she was dazzled by the gorgeous jewels lying in heaps upon every shelf. After choosing a vast quantity, which she divided between her sisters — for she had made a heap of the wonderful dresses for each of them — she opened the last chest, which was full of gold.

"I think, Father," she said, "that, as the gold will be more useful to you, we had better take out the other things again, and fill the trunks with it."

So they did this, but the more they put in, the more room there seemed to be, and at last they put back all the jewels and dresses they had taken out, and Beauty even added as many more of the jewels as she could carry at once. Even then the trunks were not too full, but they were so heavy an elephant could not have carried them!

"The Beast was mocking us!" cried the merchant. "He pretended to give us all these things, knowing that I could not carry them away."

"Let us wait and see," answered Beauty. "I cannot believe he meant to deceive us. All we can do is to fasten them up and have them ready."

So they did this and returned to the little room where they found breakfast ready. The merchant ate his with a good appetite, as the Beast's generosity made him believe he might perhaps venture to come back soon and see Beauty. But she felt sure her father was leaving her forever, so she was very sad when the bell rang sharply.

They went down into the courtyard, where two horses were waiting, one loaded with the two trunks, the other for him to ride. They were pawing the ground in their impatience to start, and the merchant bade Beauty a hasty farewell. As soon as he was mounted he went off at such a pace she lost sight of him in an instant. Then Beauty began to cry and wandered sadly back to her own room. But she soon found she was very

sleepy, and as she had nothing better to do she lay down and instantly fell asleep. And then she dreamed she was walking by a brook bordered with trees, and lamenting her sad fate, when a young prince, handsomer than anyone she had ever seen, and with a voice that went straight to heart, came and said to her:

"Ah, Beauty, you are not so unfortunate as you suppose. Here you will be rewarded for all you have suffered elsewhere. Your every wish shall be gratified. Only try to find me out, no matter how I may be disguised, for I love you dearly, and in making me happy you will find your own happiness. Be as true-hearted as you are beautiful, and we shall have nothing left to wish for."

"What can I do, Prince, to make you happy?" said Beauty.

"Only be grateful," he answered, "and do not trust too much to your eyes. Above all, do not desert me until you have saved me from my cruel misery."

After this she thought she found herself in a room with a stately and beautiful lady, who said to her, "Dear Beauty, try not to regret all you have left behind you; you are destined for a better fate. Only do not let yourself be deceived by appearances."

Beauty found her dreams so interesting that she was in no hurry to awake, but presently the clock roused her by calling her name softly twelve times. Then she rose and found her dressing-table set out with everything she could possibly want, and when her toilet was finished, she found dinner waiting in the room next to hers. But dinner does not take very long when one is alone, and very soon she sat down cosily in the corner of a sofa, and began to think about the charming prince she had seen in her dream.

"He said I could make him happy," said Beauty to herself. "It seems, then, that this horrible Beast keeps him a prisoner. How can I set him free? I wonder why they both told me not to trust to appearances? But, after all, it was only a dream, so why should I trouble myself about it? I had better find something to do to amuse myself."

So she began to explore some of the many rooms of the palace. The first she entered was lined with mirrors. Beauty saw herself reflected on every side and thought she had never seen such a charming room. Then a bracelet which was hanging from a chandelier caught her eye, and on taking it down she was greatly surprised to find that it held a portrait of her unknown admirer, just as she had seen him in her dream. With great delight she slipped the bracelet on her arm and went on into a gallery of pictures, where she soon found a portrait of the same handsome prince, as large as life, and so well painted that as she studied it he seemed to smile kindly at her.

Tearing herself away from the portrait at last, she passed into a room which contained every musical instrument under the sun, and here she amused herself for a long while in trying them and singing. The next room was a library, and she saw everything she had ever wanted to read as well as everything she had read. By this time it was growing dusk, and wax candles in diamond and ruby candlesticks lit themselves in every room.

Beauty found her supper served just at the time she preferred to have it, but she did not see anyone or hear a sound, and though her father had warned her she would be alone, she began to find it rather dull.

Presently she heard the Beast coming and wondered tremblingly if he meant to eat her now. However, he did not seem at all ferocious, and only said gruffly:

"Good evening, Beauty."

She answered cheerfully and managed to conceal her terror. The Beast asked how she had been amusing herself, and she told him all the rooms she had seen. Then he asked if she thought she could be happy in his palace; and Beauty answered that everything was so beautiful she would be very hard to please if she could not be happy. After about an hour's talk Beauty began to think the Beast was not nearly so terrible as she had supposed at first. Then he rose to leave her, and said in his gruff voice:

"Do you love me, Beauty? Will you marry me?"

"Oh, what shall I say?" cried Beauty, for she was afraid to make the Beast angry by refusing.

"Say yes or no without fear," he replied.

"Oh, no, Beast," said Beauty hastily.

"Since you will not, good night, Beauty," he said.

And she answered, "Good night, Beast," very glad to find her refusal had not provoked him. After he was gone she was very soon in bed and dreaming of her unknown prince.

She thought he came and said, "Ah, Beauty! Why are you so unkind to me? I fear I am fated to be unhappy for many a long day still."

Then her dreams changed, but the charming prince figured in them all. When morning came her first thought was to look at the portrait and see if it was really like him, and she found it certainly was.

She decided to amuse herself in the garden, for the sun shone, and all the fountains were playing. She was astonished to find that every place was familiar to her, and presently she came to the very brook and the myrtle trees where she had first met the prince in her dream. That made her think more than ever he must be kept a prisoner by the Beast.

When she was tired she went back to the palace and found a new room full of materials for every kind of work — ribbons to make into bows and silks to work into flowers. There was an aviary full of rare birds, which were so tame they flew to Beauty as soon as they saw her and perched upon her shoulders and her head.

"Pretty little creatures," she said, "how I wish your cage was nearer my room that I might often hear you sing!" So saying she opened a door and found to her delight that it led into her own room, though she had thought it was on the other side of the palace.

There were more birds in a room farther on, parrots and cockatoos that could talk, and they greeted Beauty by name. Indeed, she found them so entertaining that she took one or two back to her room, and they talked to her while she was at supper. The Beast paid her his usual visit and asked the same questions as before, and then with a gruff good night he took his departure, and Beauty went to bed to dream of her mysterious prince.

The days passed swiftly in different amusements, and after a while Beauty found another strange thing in the palace, which often pleased her when she was tired of being alone. There was one room which she had not noticed particularly; it was empty, except that under each of the windows stood a very comfortable chair. The first time she had looked out of the window it seemed a black curtain prevented her from seeing anything outside. But the second time she went into the room, happening to be tired, she sat down in one of the chairs, when instantly the curtain was rolled aside, and a most amusing pantomime was acted before her. There were dances and colored lights, music and pretty dresses, and it was all so gay that Beauty was in ecstasies. After that she tried the other seven windows in turn, and there was some new and surprising entertainment to be seen from each of them so Beauty never could feel lonely any more. Every evening after supper the Beast came to see her, and always before saying good night asked her in his terrible voice:

"Beauty, will you marry me?"

And it seemed to Beauty, now she understood him better, that when she said, "No, Beast," he went away quite sad. Her happy dreams of the handsome young prince soon made her forget the poor Beast, and the only thing that disturbed her was being told to distrust appearances, to let her heart guide her, and not her eyes. Consider as she would, she could not understand.

So everything went on for a long time, until at last, happy as she was, Beauty began to long for the sight of her father and her brothers and sisters. One night, seeing her look very sad, the Beast asked her what was the matter. Beauty had quite ceased to be afraid of him. Now she knew he was really gentle in spite of his ferocious looks and his dreadful voice. So she answered that she wished to see her home once more. Upon hearing this the Beast seemed sadly distressed, and cried miserably:

"Ah, Beauty, have you the heart to desert an unhappy Beast like this? What more do you want to make you happy? Is it because you hate me that you want to escape?"

"No, dear Beast," answered Beauty softly,

"I do not hate you, and I should be very sorry never to see you any more, but I long to see my father again. Only let me go for two months, and I promise to come back to you and stay for the rest of my life."

The Beast, who had been sighing dolefully while she spoke, now replied, "I cannot refuse you anything you ask, even though it should cost me my life. Take the four boxes you will find in the room next to your own and fill them with everything you wish to take with you. But remember your promise and come back when the two months are over, for if you do not come in good time you will find your faithful Beast dead. You will not need any chariot to bring you back. Only say good-bye to all your brothers and sisters the night before you come away and, when you have gone to bed, turn this ring round upon your finger, and say firmly, 'I wish to go back to my palace and see my Beast again.' Good night, Beauty. Fear nothing, sleep peacefully, and before long you shall see your father once more."

As soon as Beauty was alone she hastened to fill the boxes with all the rare and precious things she saw about her, and only when she was tired of heaping things into them did they seem to be full. Then she went to bed, but could hardly sleep for joy. When at last she began to dream of her beloved prince she was grieved to see him stretched upon a grassy bank, sad and weary, and hardly like himself.

"What is the matter?" she cried.

But he looked at her reproachfully, and said, "How can you ask me, cruel one? Are you not leaving me to my death perhaps?"

"Ah, don't be so sorrowful!" cried Beauty. "I am only going to assure my father that I am safe and happy. I have promised the Beast faithfully I will come back, and he would die of grief if I did not keep my word!"

"What would that matter to you?" asked the prince. "Surely you would not care?"

"Indeed I should be ungrateful if I did not care for such a kind beast," cried Beauty indignantly. "I would die to save him from pain. I assure you it is not his fault he is so ugly."

Just then a strange sound woke her —

someone was speaking not very far away; and opening her eyes she found herself in a room she had never seen before, which was certainly not as splendid as those she had seen in the Beast's palace. Where could she be? She rose and dressed hastily and then saw that the boxes she had packed the night before were all in the room. Suddenly she heard her father's voice and rushed out to greet him joyfully. Her brothers and sisters were astonished at her appearance, for they had never expected to see her again. Beauty asked her father what he thought her strange dreams meant and why the prince constantly begged her not to trust to appearances. After much consideration he answered:

"You tell me yourself that the Beast, frightful as he is, loves you dearly and deserves your love and gratitude for his gentleness and kindness. I think the prince must mean you to understand you ought to reward him by doing as he wishes, in spite of his ugliness."

Beauty could not help seeing that this seemed probable; still, when she thought of her dear prince who was so handsome, she did not feel at all inclined to marry the Beast. At any rate, for two months she need not decide but could enjoy herself with her sisters. Though they were rich now, and lived in a town again and had plenty of acquaintances, Beauty found that nothing amused her very much. She often thought of the palace, where she was so happy, especially as at home she never once dreamed of her dear prince, and she felt quite sad without him.

Then her sisters seemed quite used to being without her, and even found her rather in the way, so she would not have been sorry when the two months were over but for her father and brothers. She had not the courage to say good-bye to them. Every day when she rose she meant to say it at night, and when night came she put it off again, until at last she had a dismal dream which helped her to make up her mind.

She thought she was wandering in a lonely path in the palace gardens, when she heard groans. Running quickly to see what could be the matter, she found the Beast stretched out upon his side, apparently dying. He re-proached her faintly with being the cause of his distress, and at the same moment a stately lady appeared, and said very gravely:

"Ah, Beauty, see what happens when people do not keep their promises! If you had delayed one day more, you would have found him dead."

Beauty was so terrified by this dream that the very next evening she said good-bye to her father and her brothers and sisters, and as soon as she was in bed she turned her ring round upon her finger, and said firmly:

"I wish to go back to my palace and see my Beast again."

Then she fell asleep instantly, and only woke up to hear the clock saying, "Beauty, Beauty," twelve times in its musical voice, which told her she was really in the palace once more. Everything was just as before, and her birds were so glad to see her, but Beauty thought she had never known such a long day. She was so anxious to see the Beast again that she felt as if suppertime would never come.

But when it came no Beast appeared. After listening and waiting for a long time, she ran down into the garden to search for him. Up and down the paths and avenues ran poor Beauty, calling him. No one answered, and not a trace of him could she find. At last, she saw that she was standing opposite the shady path she had seen in her dream. She rushed down it and, sure enough, there was the cave, and in it lay the Beast — asleep, so Beauty thought. Quite glad to have found him, she ran up and stroked his head, but to her horror he did not move or open his eyes.

"Oh, he is dead, and it is all my fault!" cried Beauty, crying bitterly.

But then, looking at him again, she fancied he still breathed. Hastily fetching some water from the nearest fountain, she sprinkled it over his face, and to her great delight he began to revive.

"Oh, Beast, how you frightened me!" she cried. "I never knew how much I loved you until just now, when I feared I was too late to save your life."

"Can you really love such an ugly creature as I am?" asked the Beast faintly. "Ah, Beauty, you came only just in time. I was dying because I thought you had forgotten your promise. But go back now and rest, I shall see you again by-and-by."

Beauty, who had half expected he would be angry with her, was reassured by his gentle voice and went back to the palace, where supper was awaiting her. And afterward the Beast came in as usual and talked about the time she had spent with her father, asking if she had enjoyed herself and if they had all been glad to see her.

Beauty quite enjoyed telling him all that had happened to her. When at last the time came for him to go, he asked, as he had so often asked before:

"Beauty, will you marry me?"

She answered softly, "Yes, dear Beast."

As she spoke a blaze of light sprang up before the windows of the palace; fireworks crackled and guns banged, and across the avenue of orange trees, in letters all made of fireflies, was written: *Long live the prince and his bride.*

Turning to ask the Beast what it could all mean, Beauty found he had disappeared, and in his place stood her long-loved prince! At the same moment the wheels of a chariot were heard upon the terrace, and two ladies entered the room. One of them Beauty recognized as the stately lady she had seen in her dreams; the other was so queenly that Beauty hardly knew which to greet first. But the one she already knew said to her companion:

"Well, Queen, this is Beauty, who has had the courage to rescue your son from the terrible enchantment. They love each other, and only your consent to their marriage is wanting to make them perfectly happy."

"I consent with all my heart," cried the queen. "How can I ever thank you enough, charming girl, for having restored my dear son to his natural form?" And then she tenderly embraced Beauty and the prince, who had meanwhile been greeting the fairy and receiving her congratulations.

"Now," said the fairy to Beauty, "I suppose you would like me to send for all your brothers and sisters to dance at your wedding?"

And so she did, and the marriage was celebrated the very next day with the utmost

splendor, and Beauty and the prince lived happily ever after.

Toads and Diamonds[6]

In this, one of the most popular fairy tales, we find several motifs: the abused child, a fairy, and kindness begetting kindness — all topped by poetic justice.

There was once a widow who had two daughters. The elder was so like her mother in temper and face that to have seen the one was to have seen the other. They were both so disagreeable and proud, that it was impossible to live with them. The younger, who was the exact portrait of her father in her kindly and polite ways, was as beautiful a girl as one could see. As we are naturally fond of those who resemble us, the mother doted on her elder daughter, while for the younger she had a most violent aversion and made her take her meals in the kitchen and work hard all day. Among other things that she was obliged to do, this poor child was forced to go twice a day to fetch water from a place a mile or more from the house and carry back a large jug filled to the brim. As she was standing one day by this spring, a poor woman came up to her and asked the girl to give her some water to drink.

"Certainly, my good woman," she replied, and the beautiful girl at once stooped and rinsed out the jug; and then, filling it with water from the clearest part of the spring, she held it up to the woman, continuing to support the jug, that she might drink with great comfort.

Having drunk, the woman said to her, "You are so beautiful, so good and kind, that I cannot refrain from conferring a gift upon you," for she was really a fairy, who had taken the form of a poor village woman, in order to see how far the girl's kind-heartedness would go. "This gift I make you," continued the fairy, "that with every word you speak, either a flower or a precious stone will fall from your mouth."

The girl had no sooner reached home than

[6] From Charles Perrault, *Fairy Tales* (Dutton, 1916).

her mother began scolding her for being back so late. "I am sorry, mother," said she, "to have been out so long," and as she spoke, there fell from her mouth six roses, two pearls, and two large diamonds.

The mother gazed at her in astonishment.

"What do I see!" she exclaimed. "Pearls and diamonds seem to be dropping from her mouth! How is this, my daughter?" — It was the first time she had called her daughter. The poor child related in all simplicity what had happened, letting fall quantities of diamonds in the course of her narrative. "I must certainly send my other daughter there," said the mother. "Look, Fanchon, see what falls from your sister's mouth when she speaks! Would you not be glad to receive a similar gift? All you have to do is go and fetch water from the spring and if an old woman asks you for some to drink, to give it to her nicely and politely."

"I should like to see myself going to the spring," answered the rude, cross girl.

"I insist on your going," rejoined the mother, "and that at once."

The elder girl went off, still grumbling; with her she took the handsomest silver bottle she could find in the house.

She had no sooner arrived at the spring, than she saw a lady magnificently dressed walking towards her from the wood, who approached and asked for some water to drink. It was the same fairy who had appeared to the sister, but she had now put on the airs and apparel of a princess, as she wished to see how far this girl's rudeness would go.

"Do you think I came here just to draw water for you?" answered the arrogant and unmannerly girl; "I have, of course, brought this silver bottle on purpose for you to drink from, and all I have to say is — drink from it if you like!"

"You are scarcely polite," said the fairy, without losing her temper; "however, as you are so disobliging, I confer this gift upon you, that with every word you speak a snake or a toad shall fall from your mouth."

Directly her mother caught sight of her, she called out, "Well, my daughter!"

"Well, my mother!" replied the ill-tempered girl, throwing out as she spoke two vipers and a toad.

"Alack!" cried the mother, "what do I see? This is her sister's doing, but I will pay her out for it," and, so saying, she ran towards the younger with intent to beat her. The unhappy girl fled from the house, and went and hid herself in a neighboring forest. The King's son, who was returning from hunting, met her, and seeing how beautiful she was, asked her what she was doing there all alone, and why she was crying.

"Alas! sir, my mother has driven me from home."

The King's son, seeing five or six pearls and as many diamonds falling from her mouth as she spoke, asked her to explain how this was, and she told him all her tale. The King's son fell in love with her; and thinking that such a gift as she possessed was worth more than any ordinary dower brought by another, he carried her off to his father's palace, and there married her.

As for her sister, she made herself so hated that her own mother drove her from the house. The miserable girl, having gone about in vain trying to find someone who would take her in, crept away into a corner of a wood and there died.

ENGLAND

The Hare and the Hedgehog [1]

⋸ç This version of a well-known Grimm's fairy tale follows the original closely, and yet it clearly shows the touch of a poet and master storyteller, who by subtle means makes the story essentially English. In the German version, the time is autumn, and the buckwheat is in bloom. For Walter de la Mare, the time is spring, and cowslips and broom mark the scene as English. With what finesse he sharpens the wit and irony of the tale, slipping in words that taste richly on the tongue! In the German version, the Hedgehog speaks like a peasant: "Hold your tongue, woman. Don't begin to discuss things which are matters for men. Be off, dress yourself and come with me." In the conversation as De la Mare reports it, the Hedgehog is rather a country squire, and the picture of a comfortable nursery and a well-run establishment is summoned to the mind's eye. "Leave all this fussing and titivating," says the Hedgehog. "The children can dry themselves. Come with me."

What sport he makes of the moral! "When a man marries, he should take a wife who looks just as he himself looks," reads the German text. De la Mare renders the moral with particularity: "And lucky it was for the hedgehog he had the good sense to marry a wife like himself, and not a weasel, or a wombat, or a whale."

Early one Sunday morning, when the cowslips or paigles were showing their first honey-sweet buds in the meadows and the broom was in bloom, a hedgehog came to his little door to look out at the weather. He

¹ From Walter de la Mare, *Told Again* (Knopf, 1927).

stood with arms a-kimbo, whistling a tune to himself — a tune no better and no worse than the tunes hedgehogs usually whistle to themselves on fine Sunday mornings. And as he whistled, the notion came into his head that, before turning in and while his wife was washing the children, he might take a little walk into the fields and see how his young nettles were getting on. For there was a tasty beetle lived among the nettles; and no nettles — no beetles.

Off he went, taking his own little private path into the field. And as he came stepping along around a bush of blackthorn, its blossoming now over and its leaves showing green, he met a hare; and the hare had come out to look at his spring cabbages.

The hedgehog smiled and bade him a polite "Good morning." But the hare, who felt himself a particularly fine sleek gentleman in this Sunday sunshine, merely sneered at his greeting.

"And how is it," he said, "*you* happen to be out so early?"

"I am taking a walk, sir," said the hedgehog.

"A walk!" sniffed the hare. "I should have thought you might use those bandy little legs of yours to far better purpose."

This angered the hedgehog, for as his legs were crooked by nature, he couldn't bear to have bad made worse by any talk about them.

"You seem to suppose, sir," he said, bristling all over, "that you can do more with your legs than I can with mine."

"Well, perhaps," said the hare, airily.

"See here, then," said the hedgehog, his beady eyes fixed on the hare, "I say you *can't.* Start fair, and I'd beat you nowt to ninepence. Ay, every time."

"A race, my dear Master Hedgehog!" said the hare, laying back his whiskers. "You must be beside yourself. It's *childish.* But still, what will you wager?"

"I'll lay a Golden Guinea to a Bottle of Brandy," said the hedgehog.

"Done!" said the hare. "Shake hands on it, and we'll start at once."

"Ay, but not quite so fast," said the hedgehog. "I have had no breakfast yet. But if you will be here in half an hour's time, so will I."

The hare agreed, and at once took a little frisky practice along the dewy green border of the field, while the hedgehog went shuffling home.

"He thinks a mighty deal of himself," thought the hedgehog on his way. "But we shall see what we *shall* see." When he reached home he bustled in and looking solemnly at his wife said:

"My dear, I have need of you. In all haste. Leave everything and follow me at once into the fields."

"Why, what's going on?" says she.

"Why," said her husband, "I have bet the hare a Guinea to a Bottle of Brandy that I'll beat him in a race, and you must come and see it."

"Heavens! husband," Mrs. Hedgehog cried, "are you daft? Are you gone crazy? You! Run a race with a hare!"

"Hold your tongue, woman," said the hedgehog. "There are things simple brains cannot understand. Leave all this fussing and titivating. The children can dry themselves; and you come along at once with me." So they went together.

"Now," said the hedgehog, when they reached the ploughed field beyond the field which was sprouting with young green wheat, "listen to me, my dear. This is where the race is going to be. The hare is over there at the other end of the field. I am going to arrange that he shall start in that deep furrow, and I shall start in this. But as soon as I have scrambled along a few inches and he can't see me, I shall turn back. And what *you,* my dear, must do is this: When he comes out of his furrow *there,* you must be

sitting puffing like a porpoise *here.* And when you see him, you will say, 'Ahah! so you've come at last?' Do you follow me, my dear?" At first Mrs. Hedgehog was a little nervous, but she smiled at her husband's cunning, and gladly agreed to do what he said.

The hedgehog then went back to where he had promised to meet the hare, and he said, "Here I am, you see; and very much the better, sir, for a good breakfast."

"How shall we run," simpered the hare scornfully, "down or over; sideways, longways; three legs or altogether? It's all one to me."

"Well, to be honest with you," said the hedgehog, "let me say this. I have now and then watched you taking a gambol and disporting yourself with your friends in the evening, and a pretty runner you are. But you never keep straight. You all go round and round, and round and round, scampering now this way, now that and chasing one another's scuts as if you were crazy. And as often as not you run uphill! But you can't run *races* like that. You must keep straight; you must begin in one place, go steadily on, and end in another."

"I could have told you that," said the hare angrily.

"Very well then," said the hedgehog. "You shall keep to that furrow, and I'll keep to this."

And the hare, being a good deal quicker on his feet than he was in his wits, agreed.

"One! Two! Three! — and AWAY!" he shouted, and off he went like a little whirlwind up the field. But the hedgehog, after scuttling along a few paces, turned back and stayed quietly where he was.

When the hare came out of his furrow at the upper end of the field, the hedgehog's wife sat panting there as if she would never be able to recover her breath, and at sight of him she sighed out, "Ahah! sir, so you've come at last?"

The hare was utterly shocked. His ears trembled. His eyes bulged in his head. "You've run it! You've run it!" he cried in astonishment. For she being so exactly like her husband, he never for a moment doubted that her husband she actually was.

"Ay," said she, "but I was afraid you had gone lame."

"Lame!" said the hare, "lame! But there, what's one furrow? 'Every time' was what you said. We'll try again."

Away once more he went, and he had never run faster. Yet when he came out of his furrow at the bottom of the field, there was the hedgehog! And the hedgehog laughed, and said: "Ahah! So here you are again! At last!" At this the hare could hardly speak for rage.

"Not enough! not enough!" he said. "Three for luck! Again, again!"

"As often as you please, my dear friend," said the hedgehog. "It's the long run that really counts."

Again, and again, and yet again the hare raced up and down the long furrow of the field, and every time he reached the top, and every time he reached the bottom, there was the hedgehog, as he thought, with his mocking, "Ahah! So here you are again! At last!"

But at length the hare could run no more. He lay panting and speechless; he was dead beat. Stretched out there, limp on the grass, his fur bedraggled, his eyes dim, his legs quaking, it looked as if he might fetch his last breath at any moment.

So Mrs. Hedgehog went off to the hare's house to fetch the Bottle of Brandy; and, if it had not been the best brandy, the hare might never have run again.

News of the contest spread far and wide. From that day to this, never has there been a race to compare with it. And lucky it was for the hedgehog he had the good sense to marry a wife like himself, and not a weasel, or a wombat, or a whale!

The Old Woman and Her Pig [2]

A cumulative tale that has a quick unwinding after a slow build-up.

An old woman was sweeping her house, and she found a little crooked sixpence. "What," said she, "shall I do with this little

[2] From Joseph Jacobs, *English Fairy Tales* (Putnam, 1892).

sixpence? I will go to market, and buy a little pig."

As she was coming home, she came to a stile: but the piggy wouldn't go over the stile.

She went a little further, and she met a dog. So she said to him: "Dog! dog! bite pig; piggy won't go over the stile; and I shan't get home tonight." But the dog wouldn't.

She went a little further, and she met a stick. So she said: "Stick! stick! beat dog! dog won't bite pig; piggy won't get over the stile; and I shan't get home tonight." But the stick wouldn't.

She went a little further, and she met a fire. So she said: "Fire! fire! burn stick; stick won't beat dog; dog won't bite pig; piggy won't get over the stile; and I shan't get home tonight." But the fire wouldn't.

She went a little further, and she met some water. So she said: "Water! water! quench fire; fire won't burn stick; stick won't beat dog; dog won't bite pig; piggy won't get over the stile; and I shan't get home tonight." But the water wouldn't.

She went a little further, and she met an ox. So she said: "Ox! ox! drink water; water won't quench fire; fire won't burn stick; stick won't beat dog; dog won't bite pig; piggy won't get over the stile; and I shan't get home tonight." But the ox wouldn't.

She went a little further, and she met a butcher. So she said: "Butcher! butcher! kill ox; ox won't drink water; water won't quench fire; fire won't burn stick; stick won't beat dog; dog won't bite pig; piggy won't get over the stile; and I shan't get home tonight." But the butcher wouldn't.

She went a little further, and she met a rope. So she said: "Rope! rope! hang butcher; butcher won't kill ox; ox won't drink water; water won't quench fire; fire won't burn stick; stick won't beat dog; dog won't bite pig; piggy won't get over the stile; and I shan't get home tonight." But the rope wouldn't.

She went a little further, and she met a rat. So she said: "Rat! rat! gnaw rope; rope won't hang butcher; butcher won't kill ox; ox won't drink water; water won't quench fire; fire won't burn stick; stick won't beat dog; dog won't bite pig; piggy won't get over the stile; and I shan't get home tonight." But the rat wouldn't.

She went a little further, and she met a cat. So she said: "Cat! cat! kill rat; rat won't gnaw rope; rope won't hang butcher; butcher won't kill ox; ox won't drink water; water won't quench fire; fire won't burn stick; stick won't beat dog; dog won't bite pig; piggy won't get over the stile; and I shan't get home tonight." But the cat said to her, "If you will go to yonder cow, and fetch me a saucer of milk, I will kill the rat." So away went the old woman to the cow.

But the cow said to her: "If you will go to yonder hay-stack and fetch me a handful of hay, I'll give you the milk." So away went the old woman to the hay-stack; and she brought the hay to the cow.

As soon as the cow had eaten the hay, she gave the old woman the milk; and away she went with it in a saucer to the cat.

As soon as the cat had lapped up the milk, the cat began to kill the rat; the rat began to gnaw the rope; the rope began to hang the butcher; the butcher began to kill the ox; the ox began to drink the water; the water began to quench the fire; the fire began to burn the stick; the stick began to beat the dog; the dog began to bite the pig; the little pig in a fright jumped over the stile; and so the old woman got home that night.

Henny-Penny [3]

(*Chicken-Little*)

Henny-Penny, *a more consistently cumulative beast tale, is also repetitive. Practically the same story is told under the title* Chicken-Licken *and in* The Hare that Ran Away.

One day Henny-Penny was picking up corn in the cornyard when — whack! — something hit her upon the head. "Goodness gracious me!" said Henny-Penny; "the sky's a-going to fall; I must go and tell the king."

So she went along, and she went along, and she went along till she met Cocky-Locky. "Where are you going, Henny-Penny?" says

³ From Joseph Jacobs, *English Fairy Tales* (Putnam, 1892).

Cocky-Locky. "Oh! I'm going to tell the king the sky's a-falling," says Henny-Penny. "May I come with you?" says Cocky-Locky. "Certainly," says Henny-Penny. So Henny-Penny and Cocky-Locky went to tell the king the sky was falling.

They went along, and they went along, and they went along till they met Ducky-Daddles. "Where are you going to, Henny-Penny and Cocky-Locky?" says Ducky-Daddles. "Oh! we're going to tell the king the sky's a-falling," said Henny-Penny and Cocky-Locky. "May I come with you?" says Ducky-Daddles. "Certainly," said Henny-Penny and Cocky-Locky. So Henny-Penny, Cocky-Locky, and Ducky-Daddles went to tell the king the sky was a-falling.

So they went along, and they went along, and they went along, till they met Goosey-Poosey. "Where are you going to, Henny-Penny, Cocky-Locky, and Ducky-Daddles?" said Goosey-Poosey. "Oh! we're going to tell the king the sky's a-falling," said Henny-Penny and Cocky-Locky and Ducky-Daddles. "May I come with you?" said Goosey-Poosey. "Certainly," said Henny-Penny, Cocky-Locky, and Ducky-Daddles. So Henny-Penny, Cocky-Locky, Ducky-Daddles, and Goosey-Poosey went to tell the king the sky was a-falling.

So they went along, and they went along, and they went along, till they met Turkey-Lurkey. "Where are you going, Henny-Penny, Cocky-Locky, Ducky-Daddles, and Goosey-Poosey?" says Turkey-Lurkey. "Oh! we're going to tell the king the sky's a-falling," said Henny-Penny, Cocky-Locky, Ducky-Daddles, and Goosey-Poosey. "May I come with you, Henny-Penny, Cocky-Locky, Ducky-Daddles, and Goosey-Poosey?" said Turkey-Lurkey. "Oh, certainly, Turkey-Lurkey," said Henny-Penny, Cocky-Locky, Ducky-Daddles, and Goosey-Poosey. So Henny-Penny, Cocky-Locky, Ducky-Daddles, Goosey-Poosey, and Turkey-Lurkey all went to tell the king the sky was a-falling.

So they went along, and they went along, and they went along, till they met Foxy-Woxy; and Foxy-Woxy said to Henny-Penny, Cocky-Locky, Ducky-Daddles, Goosey-Poosey, and Turkey-Lurkey: "Where are you going, Henny-Penny, Cocky-Locky,

Ducky-Daddles, Goosey-Poosey, and Turkey-Lurkey?" And Henny-Penny, Cocky-Locky, Ducky-Daddles, Goosey-Poosey, and Turkey-Lurkey said to Foxy-Woxy: "We're going to tell the king the sky's a-falling." "Oh! but this is not the way to the king, Henny-Penny, Cocky-Locky, Ducky-Daddles, Goosey-Poosey, and Turkey-Lurkey," says Foxy-Woxy; "I know the proper way; shall I show it to you?" "Oh, certainly, Foxy-Woxy," said Henny-Penny, Cocky-Locky, Ducky-Daddles, Goosey-Poosey, and Turkey-Lurkey. So Henny-Penny, Cocky-Locky, Ducky-Daddles, Goosey-Poosey, Turkey-Lurkey, and Foxy-Woxy all went to tell the king the sky was a-falling.

So they went along, and they went along, and they went along, till they came to a narrow and dark hole. Now this was the door of Foxy-Woxy's cave. But Foxy-Woxy said to Henny-Penny, Cocky-Locky, Ducky-Daddles, Goosey-Poosey, and Turkey-Lurkey: "This is the short way to the king's palace; you'll soon get there if you follow me. I will go first and you come after, Henny-Penny, Cocky-Locky, Ducky-Daddles, Goosey-Poosey, and Turkey-Lurkey." "Why of course, certainly, without doubt, why not?" said Henny-Penny, Cocky-Locky, Ducky-Daddles, Goosey-Poosey, and Turkey-Lurkey.

So Foxy-Woxy went into his cave, and he didn't go very far, but turned around to wait for Henny-Penny, Cocky-Locky, Ducky-Daddles, Goosey-Poosey, and Turkey-Lurkey. So at last at first Turkey-Lurkey went through the dark hole into the cave. He hadn't got far when "Hrumph," Foxy-Woxy snapped off Turkey-Lurkey's head and threw his body over his left shoulder. Then Goosey-Poosey went in, and "Hrumph," off went her head and Goosey-Poosey was thrown beside Turkey-Lurkey. Then Ducky-Daddles waddled down, and "Hrumph," snapped Foxy-Woxy, and Ducky-Daddles' head was off and Ducky-Daddles was thrown alongside Turkey-Lurkey and Goosey-Poosey. Then Cocky-Locky strutted down into the cave, and he hadn't gone far when "Snap, Hrumph!" went Foxy-Woxy and Cocky-Locky was thrown alongside of Turkey-Lurkey, Goosey-Poosey, and Ducky-Daddles.

But Foxy-Woxy had made two bites at Cocky-Locky; and when the first snap only

hurt Cocky-Locky but didn't kill him, he called out to Henny-Penny. But she turned tail and off she ran home; so she never told the king the sky was a-falling.

Teeny-Tiny [4]

&ξ *This story, too, is in the repetitive form of a cumulative tale. Its charm for children lies, first, in the constant repetition of "teeny-tiny," and then, if well read, in the explosive ending, "Take it!"*

Once upon a time there was a teeny-tiny woman who lived in a teeny-tiny house in a teeny-tiny village. Now, one day this teeny-tiny woman put on her teeny-tiny bonnet and went out of her teeny-tiny house to take a teeny-tiny walk. And when this teeny-tiny woman had gone a teeny-tiny way, she came to a teeny-tiny gate; so the teeny-tiny woman opened the teeny-tiny gate and went into a teeny-tiny churchyard. And when this teeny-tiny woman had got into the teeny-tiny churchyard, she saw a teeny-tiny bone on a teeny-tiny grave, and the teeny-tiny woman said to her teeny-tiny self, "This teeny-tiny bone will make me some teeny-tiny soup for my teeny-tiny supper." So the teeny-tiny woman put the teeny-tiny bone into her teeny-tiny pocket and went home to her teeny-tiny house.

Now when the teeny-tiny woman got home to her teeny-tiny house, she was a teeny-tiny bit tired; so she went up her teeny-tiny stairs to her teeny-tiny bed and put the teeny-tiny bone into a teeny-tiny cupboard. And when this teeny-tiny woman had been to sleep a teeny-tiny time, she was awakened by a teeny-tiny voice from the teeny-tiny cupboard, which said,

"Give me my bone!"

And this teeny-tiny woman was a teeny-tiny frightened; so she hid her teeny-tiny head under the teeny-tiny clothes and went to sleep again. And when she had been to sleep again a teeny-tiny time, the teeny-tiny

4 From Joseph Jacobs, *English Fairy Tales* (Putnam, 1892).

voice again cried out from the teeny-tiny cupboard a teeny-tiny louder,

"Give me my bone!"

This made the teeny-tiny woman a teeny-tiny more frightened; so she hid her teeny-tiny head a teeny-tiny farther under the teeny-tiny clothes. And when the teeny-tiny woman had been to sleep again a teeny-tiny time, the teeny-tiny voice from the teeny-tiny cupboard said again a teeny-tiny louder,

"Give me my bone!"

And this teeny-tiny woman was a teeny-tiny bit more frightened, but she put her teeny-tiny head out of the teeny-tiny clothes and said in her loudest teeny-tiny voice, "TAKE IT!"

Jack and the Beanstalk [5]

&⟨ *This story is often classified as a droll, that is, a story of the blunders, often comic in character, of a stupid person. Compare this with* Gudbrand on the Hillside *and* The Bee, the Harp, the Mouse, and the Bum-Clock.

There was once upon a time a poor widow who had an only son named Jack and a cow named Milky-White. And all they had to live on was the milk the cow gave every morning, which they carried to the market and sold. But one morning Milky-White gave no milk, and they didn't know what to do.

"What shall we do, what shall we do?" said the widow, wringing her hands.

"Cheer up, mother, I'll go and get work somewhere," said Jack.

"We've tried that before, and nobody would take you," said his mother; "we must sell Milky-White and with the money start shop or something."

"All right, mother," says Jack; "it's market-day today, and I'll soon sell Milky-White, and then we'll see what we can do."

So he took the cow's halter in his hand, and off he started. He hadn't gone far when

[5] From Joseph Jacobs, *English Fairy Tales* (Putnam, 1892).

he met a funny-looking old man, who said to him: "Good morning, Jack."

"Good morning to you," said Jack, and wondered how he knew his name.

"Well, Jack, and where are you off to?" said the man.

"I'm going to market to sell our cow here."

"Oh, you look the proper sort of chap to sell cows," said the man; "I wonder if you know how many beans make five."

"Two in each hand and one in your mouth," says Jack, as sharp as a needle.

"Right you are," says the man, "and here they are, the very beans themselves," he went on, pulling out of his pocket a number of strange-looking beans. "As you are so sharp," says he, "I don't mind doing a swop with you — your cow for these beans."

"Go along," says Jack; "wouldn't you like it?"

"Ah! you don't know what these beans are," said the man; "if you plant them overnight, by morning they grow right up to the sky."

"Really?" said Jack; "you don't say so."

"Yes, that is so, and if it doesn't turn out to be true you can have your cow back."

"Right," says Jack, and hands him over Milky-White's halter and pockets the beans.

Back goes Jack home, and as he hadn't gone very far, it wasn't dusk by the time he got to his door.

"Back already, Jack?" said his mother; "I see you haven't got Milky-White, so you've sold her. How much did you get for her?"

"You'll never guess, mother," says Jack.

"No, you don't say so. Good boy! Five pounds, ten, fifteen, no, it can't be twenty."

"I told you you couldn't guess. What do you say to these beans; they're magical, plant them over-night and —"

"What!" says Jack's mother, "have you been such a fool, such a dolt, such an idiot, as to give away my Milky-White, the best milker in the parish, and prime beef to boot, for a set of paltry beans? Take that! Take that! Take that! And as for your precious beans here they go out of the window. And now off with you to bed. Not a sup shall you drink, and not a bit shall you swallow this very night."

So Jack went upstairs to his little room in

the attic, and sad and sorry he was, to be sure, as much for his mother's sake, as for the loss of his supper.

At last he dropped off to sleep.

When he woke up, the room looked so funny. The sun was shining into part of it, and yet all the rest was quite dark and shady. So Jack jumped up and dressed himself and went to the window. And what do you think he saw? Why, the beans his mother had thrown out of the window into the garden had sprung up into a big beanstalk, which went up and up and up till it reached the sky. So the man spoke truth after all.

The beanstalk grew up quite close past Jack's window; so all he had to do was to open it and give a jump on to the beanstalk which ran up just like a big ladder. So Jack climbed, and he climbed, and he climbed, and he climbed, and he climbed, and he climbed, and he climbed till at last he reached the sky. And when he got there he found a long broad road going as straight as a dart. So he walked along, and he walked along, and he walked along till he came to a great big tall house, and on the doorstep there was a great big tall woman.

"Good morning, mum," says Jack, quite polite-like. "Could you be so kind as to give me some breakfast?" For he hadn't had anything to eat, you know, the night before, and was as hungry as a hunter.

"It's breakfast you want, is it?" says the great big tall woman, "It's breakfast you'll be if you don't move off from here. My man is an ogre and there's nothing he likes better than boys broiled on toast. You'd better be moving on or he'll soon be coming."

"Oh! please mum, do give me something to eat, mum. I've had nothing to eat since yesterday morning, really and truly, mum," says Jack. "I may as well be broiled as die of hunger."

Well, the ogre's wife was not half so bad after all. So she took Jack into the kitchen and gave him a chunk of bread and cheese and a jug of milk. But Jack hadn't half finished these when thump! thump! thump! the whole house began to tremble with the noise of someone coming.

"Goodness gracious me! It's my old man," said the ogre's wife, "what on earth shall I

do? Come along quick and jump in here." And she bundled Jack into the oven just as the ogre came in.

He was a big one, to be sure. At his belt he had three calves strung up by the heels, and he unhooked them and threw them down on the table and said: "Here, wife, broil me a couple of these for breakfast. Ah! what's this I smell?

> Fee-fi-fo-fum,
> I smell the blood of an Englishman,
> Be he alive, or be he dead
> I'll have his bones to grind my bread."

"Nonsense, dear," said his wife, "you're dreaming. Or perhaps you smell the scraps of that little boy you liked so much for yesterday's dinner. Here, you go and have a wash and tidy up, and by the time you come back your breakfast'll be ready for you."

So off the ogre went, and Jack was just going to jump out of the oven and run away when the woman told him not. "Wait till he's asleep," says she; "he always has a doze after breakfast."

Well, the ogre had his breakfast, and after that he goes to a big chest and takes out of it a couple of bags of gold, and down he sits and counts till at last his head began to nod, and he began to snore till the whole house shook again.

Then Jack crept out on tiptoe from his oven, and as he was passing the ogre he took one of the bags of gold under his arm, and off he pelters till he came to the beanstalk, and then he threw down the bag of gold, which of course fell into his mother's garden, and then he climbed down, and climbed down till at last he got home and told his mother and showed her the gold and said, "Well, mother, wasn't I right about the beans? They are really magical, you see."

So they lived on the bag of gold for some time, but at last they came to the end of it, and Jack made up his mind to try his luck once more up at the top of the beanstalk. So one fine morning he rose up early, and got on to the beanstalk, and he climbed, and he climbed, and he climbed, and he climbed, and he climbed, and he climbed till at last he came out on to the road again and up to the great big tall house he had been to before.

There, sure enough, was the great big tall woman a-standing on the doorstep.

"Good morning, mum," says Jack, as bold as brass, "could you be so good as to give me something to eat?"

"Go away, my boy," said the big tall woman, "or else my man will eat you up for breakfast. But aren't you the youngster who came here once before? Do you know, that very day, my man missed one of his bags of gold."

"That's strange, mum," said Jack, "I dare say I could tell you something about that; but I'm so hungry I can't speak till I've had something to eat."

Well, the big tall woman was so curious that she took him in and gave him something to eat. But he had scarcely begun munching it as slowly as he could when thump! thump! thump! they heard the giant's footstep, and his wife hid Jack away in the oven.

All happened as it did before. In came the ogre as he did before, said: "Fee-fi-fo-fum," and had his breakfast off three broiled oxen. Then he said: "Wife, bring me the hen that lays the golden eggs." So she brought it, and the ogre said: "Lay," and it laid an egg all of gold. And then the ogre began to nod his head and to snore till the house shook.

Then Jack crept out of the oven on tiptoe and caught hold of the golden hen and was off before you could say "Jack Robinson." But this time the hen gave a cackle which woke the ogre, and just as Jack got out of the house he heard him calling: "Wife, wife, what have you done with my golden hen?"

And the wife said: "Why, my dear?"

But that was all Jack heard, for he rushed off to the beanstalk and climbed down like a house on fire. And when he got home he showed his mother the wonderful hen, and said "Lay" to it; and it laid a golden egg every time he said, "Lay."

Well, Jack was not content, and it wasn't very long before he determined to have another try at his luck up there at the top of the beanstalk. So one fine morning, he rose up early and got on to the beanstalk, and he climbed, and he climbed, and he climbed, and he climbed till he got to the top. But this time he knew better than to go straight to the ogre's house. And when he got near

it, he waited behind a bush till he saw the ogre's wife come out with a pail to get some water, and then he crept into the house and got into the copper. He hadn't been there long when he heard thump! thump! thump! as before, and in came the ogre and his wife.

"Fee-fi-fo-fum, I smell the blood of an Englishman," cried out the ogre. "I smell him, wife, I smell him."

"Do you, my dearie?" says the ogre's wife. "Then, if it's that little rogue that stole your gold and the hen that laid the golden eggs he's sure to have got into the oven." And they both rushed to the oven. But Jack wasn't there, luckily, and the ogre's wife said: "There you are again with your fee-fi-fo-fum. Why of course it's the boy you caught last night that I've just broiled for your breakfast. How forgetful I am, and how careless you are not to know the difference between live and dead after all these years."

So the ogre sat down to the breakfast and ate it, but every now and then he would mutter: "Well, I could have sworn ——" and he'd get up and search the larder and the cupboards and everything, only, luckily, he didn't think of the copper.

After breakfast was over, the ogre called out, "Wife, wife, bring me my golden harp." So she brought it and put it on the table before him. Then he said: "Sing!" and the golden harp sang most beautifully. And it went on singing till the ogre fell asleep and commenced to snore like thunder.

Then Jack lifted up the copper-lid very quietly and got down like a mouse and crept on hands and knees till he came to the table, when up he crawled, caught hold of the golden harp and dashed with it towards the door. But the harp called out quite loud: "Master! Master!" and the ogre woke up just in time to see Jack running off with his harp.

Jack ran as fast as he could, and the ogre came rushing after and would soon have caught him only Jack had a start and dodged him a bit and knew where he was going. When he got to the beanstalk the ogre was not more than twenty yards away when suddenly he saw Jack disappear like, and when he came to the end of the road he saw Jack underneath climbing down for dear life.

Well, the ogre didn't like trusting himself to such a ladder, and he stood and waited; so Jack got another start. But just then the harp cried out: "Master! Master!" and the ogre swung himself down on to the beanstalk, which shook with his weight. Down climbs Jack, and after him climbed the ogre. By this time Jack had climbed down, and climbed down, and climbed down till he was very nearly home. So he called out: "Mother! Mother! bring me an axe; bring me an axe." And his mother came rushing out with the axe in her hand, but when she came to the beanstalk she stood stock still with fright, for there she saw the ogre with his legs just through the clouds.

But Jack jumped down and got hold of the axe and gave a chop at the beanstalk which cut it half in two. The ogre felt the beanstalk shake and quiver, so he stopped to see what was the matter. Then Jack gave another chop with the axe, and the beanstalk was cut in two and began to topple over. Then the ogre fell down and broke his crown, and the beanstalk came toppling after.

Then Jack showed his mother his golden harp, and what with showing that and selling the golden eggs Jack and his mother became very rich, and he married a great princess, and they lived happy ever after.

Molly Whuppie [6]

A rare tale this, distinguished by the fact that the youngest child who outwits the giant and wins a kingdom is a girl! There is a rich mixture of motifs here: the deception of the giant's wife by the bag trick, the stealing of objects from the giant — these echo and re-echo through tale after tale. The incident of changing night dresses, or necklaces, goes back to an ancient Greek source.

The storyteller will discover that this version comes ready for the telling. It appeals to well-nigh every age and is pleasurable to know, with its image of the bridge of one hair and its refrains: "Woe worth ye, Molly Whuppie" and "Twice yet, carle, I'll come to Spain."

[6] From Joseph Jacobs, *English Fairy Tales* (Putnam, 1892).

Once upon a time there was a man and a wife had too many children, and they could not get meat for them, so they took the three youngest and left them in a wood. They travelled and travelled and could see never a house. It began to be dark, and they were hungry. At last they saw a light and made for it; it turned out to be a house. They knocked at the door, and a woman came to it, who said: "What do you want?" They said: "Please let us in and give us something to eat." The woman said: "I can't do that, as my man is a giant, and he would kill you if he comes home." They begged hard. "Let us stop for a little while," said they, "and we will go away before he comes." So she took them in, and set them down before the fire, and gave them milk and bread; but just as they had begun to eat, a great knock came to the door, and a dreadful voice said:

"Fee, fie, fo, fum,
I smell the blood of some earthly one.

Who have you there, wife?" "Eh," said the wife, "it's three poor lassies cold and hungry, and they will go away. Ye won't touch 'em, man." He said nothing, but ate up a big supper, and ordered them to stay all night. Now he had three lassies of his own, and they were to sleep in the same bed with the three strangers. The youngest of the three strange lassies was called Molly Whuppie, and she was very clever. She noticed that before they went to bed the giant put straw ropes round her neck and her sisters', and round his own lassies' necks, he put gold chains. So Molly took care and did not fall asleep, but waited till she was sure every one was sleeping sound. Then she slipped out of the bed, and took the straw ropes off her own and her sisters' necks, and took the gold chains off the giant's lassies. She put the straw ropes on the giant's lassies and the gold chains on herself and her sisters, and lay down. And in the middle of the night up rose the giant, armed with a great club, and felt for the necks with the straw. It was dark. He took his own lassies out of bed on to the floor, and battered them until they were dead, and then lay down again, thinking he had managed finely. Molly thought it time she and her sisters were off and away, so she wakened them and told them to be quiet, and they slipped out of the house. They all got out safe, and they ran and ran, and never stopped until morning, when they saw a grand house before them. It turned out to be a king's house: so Molly went in, and told her story to the king. He said: "Well, Molly, you are a clever girl, and you have managed well; but, if you would manage better, and go back, and steal the giant's sword that hangs on the back of his bed, I would give your eldest sister my eldest son to marry." Molly said she would try. So she went back, and managed to slip into the giant's house, and crept in below the bed. The giant came home, and ate up a great supper, and went to bed. Molly waited until he was snoring, and she crept out, and reached over the giant and got down the sword; but just as she got it out over the bed it gave a rattle, and up jumped the giant, and Molly ran out at the door and the sword with her; and she ran, and he ran, till they came to the "Bridge of one hair"; and she got over, but he couldn't, and he says, "Woe worth ye, Molly Whuppie! never ye come again." And she says: "Twice yet, carle, I'll come to Spain." So Molly took the sword to the king, and her sister was married to his son.

Well, the king he says: "Ye've managed well, Molly; but if ye would manage better, and steal the purse that lies below the giant's pillow, I would marry your second sister to my second son." And Molly said she would try. So she set out for the giant's house, and slipped in, and hid again below the bed, and waited till the giant had eaten his supper, and was snoring sound asleep. She slipped out and slipped her hand below the pillow, and got out the purse; but just as she was going out the giant wakened, and ran after her; and she ran, and he ran, till they came to the "Bridge of one hair," and she got over, but he couldn't and he said, "Woe worth ye, Molly Whuppie! never you come again." "Once yet, carle," quoth she, "I'll come to Spain." So Molly took the purse to the king, and her second sister was married to the king's second son.

After that the king says to Molly: "Molly, you are a clever girl, but if you would do better yet, and steal the giant's ring that he wears on his finger, I will give you my youngest son for yourself." Molly said she would try. So back she goes to the giant's house, and hides herself below the bed. The giant wasn't long ere he came home, and, after he had eaten a great big supper, he went to his bed, and shortly was snoring loud. Molly crept out and reached over the bed, and got hold of the giant's hand, and she pulled and she pulled until she got off the ring; but just as she got it off the giant got up, and gripped her by the hand and he says, "Now I have caught you, Molly Whuppie, and, if I had done as much ill to you as ye have done to me, what would ye do to me?"

Molly says: "I would put you into a sack, and I'd put the cat inside wi' you, and the dog aside you, and a needle and thread and a shears and I'd hang you up upon the wall, and I'd go to the wood, and choose the thickest stick I could get, and I would come home, and take you down, and bang you till you were dead."

"Well, Molly," says the giant, "I'll just do that to you."

So he gets a sack, and puts Molly into it, and the cat and the dog beside her, and a needle and thread and shears, and hangs her up upon the wall, and goes to the wood to choose a stick.

Molly she sings out: "Oh, if ye saw what I see."

"Oh," says the giant's wife, "what do ye see, Molly?"

But Molly never said a word but, "Oh, if ye saw what I see!"

The giant's wife begged that Molly would take her up into the sack till she would see what Molly saw. So Molly took the shears and cut a hole in the sack, and took out the needle and thread with her, and jumped down and helped the giant's wife up into the sack, and sewed up the hole.

The giant's wife saw nothing, and began to ask to get down again; but Molly never minded, but hid herself at the back of the door. Home came the giant, and a great big tree in his hand, and he took down the sack, and began to batter it. His wife cried, "It's me, man"; but the dog barked and the cat mewed, and he did not know his wife's voice. But Molly came out from the back of the door, and the giant saw her and he after her; and he ran, and she ran, till they came to the "Bridge of one hair," and she got over but he couldn't; and he said, "Woe worth you, Molly Whuppie! never you come again." "Never more, carle," quoth she, "will I come again to Spain."

So Molly took the ring to the king, and she was married to his youngest son, and she never saw the giant again.

The Three Sillies [7]

⊷ The Three Sillies is the most enduring of the drolls, the numskull stories. Stith Thompson says that it is told "in all parts of Europe and well out into Siberia. Versions apparently based upon English originals have been found in Virginia, and close parallels exist in Africa." For the storyteller, this story catches the interest of babes and sires, the wise and foolish of all ages. It is basic to any repertory.

Once upon a time there was a farmer and his wife who had one daughter, and she was courted by a gentleman. Every evening he used to come and see her, and stop to supper at the farmhouse, and the daughter used to be sent down into the cellar to draw the beer for supper. So one evening she had gone down to draw the beer, and she happened to look up at the ceiling while she was drawing, and she saw a mallet stuck in one of the beams. It must have been there a long, long time, but somehow or other she had never noticed it before, and she began a-thinking. And she thought it was very dangerous to have that mallet there, for she said to herself: "Suppose him and me was to be married, and we was to have a son, and he was to grow up to be a man, and come down into the cellar to draw the beer, like as I'm doing now, and the mallet was to fall on his head and kill him, what a dreadful thing it would be!" And she put down the candle and the jug, and sat herself down and began a-crying.

Well, they began to wonder upstairs how

7 From Joseph Jacobs, *English Fairy Tales* (Putnam, 1892).

it was that she was so long drawing the beer, and her mother went down to see after her, and she found her sitting on the settle crying, and the beer running over the floor. "Why, whatever is the matter?" said her mother. "Oh, mother!" says she, "look at that horrid mallet! Suppose we was to be married, and was to have a son, and he was to grow up, and was to come down to the cellar to draw the beer, and the mallet was to fall on his head and kill him, what a dreadful thing it would be!" "Dear, dear! what a dreadful thing it would be!" said the mother, and she sat her down aside of the daughter and started a-crying too. Then after a bit the father began to wonder that they didn't come back, and he went down into the cellar to look after them himself, and there they two sat a-crying, and the beer running all over the floor. "Whatever is the matter?" says he. "Why," says the mother, "look at that horrid mallet. Just suppose, if our daughter and her sweetheart was to be married, and was to have a son, and he was to grow up, and was to come down into the cellar to draw the beer, and the mallet was to fall on his head and kill him, what a dreadful thing it would be!" "Dear, dear, dear! so it would!" said the father, and he sat himself down aside of the other two, and started a-crying.

Now the gentleman got tired of stopping up in the kitchen by himself, and at last he went down into the cellar too, to see what they were after; and there they three sat a-crying side by side, and the beer running all over the floor. And he ran straight and turned the tap. Then he said: "Whatever are you three doing, sitting there crying, and letting the beer run all over the floor?" "Oh!" says the father, "look at that horrid mallet! Suppose you and our daughter was to be married, and was to have a son, and he was to grow up, and was to come down into the cellar to draw the beer, and the mallet was to fall on his head and kill him!" And then they all started a-crying worse than before. But the gentleman burst out a-laughing, and reached up and pulled out the mallet, and then he said: "I've travelled many miles, and I never met three such big sillies as you three before; and now I shall start out on my travels again, and when I can find three bigger sillies than you three, then I'll come back and marry your daughter." So he wished them good-bye, and started off on his travels, and left them all crying because the girl had lost her sweetheart.

Well, he set out, and he travelled a long way, and at last he came to a woman's cottage that had some grass growing on the roof. And the woman was trying to get her cow to go up a ladder to the grass, and the poor thing durst not go. So the gentleman asked the woman what she was doing. "Why, lookye," she said, "look at all that beautiful grass. I'm going to get the cow on to the roof to eat it. She'll be quite safe, for I shall tie a string round her neck, and pass it down the chimney, and tie it to my wrist as I go about the house, so she can't fall off without my knowing it." "Oh, you poor silly!" said the gentleman, "you should cut the grass and throw it down to the cow!" But the woman thought it was easier to get the cow up the ladder than to get the grass down, so she pushed her and coaxed her and got her up, and tied a string round her neck, and passed it down the chimney, and fastened it to her own wrist. And the gentleman went on his way, but he hadn't gone far when the cow tumbled off the roof, and hung by the string tied round her neck, and it strangled her. And the weight of the cow tied to her wrist pulled the woman up the chimney, and she stuck fast half-way and was smothered in the soot.

Well, that was one big silly.

And the gentleman went on and on, and he went to an inn to stop the night, and they were so full at the inn that they had to put him in a double-bedded room, and another traveller was to sleep in the other bed. The other man was a very pleasant fellow, and they got very friendly together; but in the morning, when they were both getting up, the gentleman was surprised to see the other hang his trousers on the knobs of the chest of drawers and run across the room and try to jump into them, and he tried over and over again, and couldn't manage it; and the gentleman wondered whatever he was doing it for. At last he stopped and wiped his face with his handkerchief. "Oh dear," he says, "I do think trousers are the most awkwardest kind of clothes that ever were. I can't think who could have invented such things. It takes me the best part of an hour to get into mine every morning, and I get so hot! How do you manage yours?" So the gentleman burst out a-laughing, and showed him how to put them on; and he was very much obliged to him, and said he never should have thought of doing it that way.

So that was another big silly.

Then the gentleman went on his travels again; and he came to a village, and outside the village there was a pond, and round the pond was a crowd of people. And they had got rakes, and brooms, and pitchforks, reaching into the pond; and the gentleman asked what was the matter. "Why," they say, "matter enough! Moon's tumbled into the pond, and we can't rake her out anyhow!" So the gentleman burst out a-laughing, and told them to look up into the sky, and that it was only the shadow in the water. But they wouldn't listen to him, and abused him shamefully, and he got away as quick as he could.

So there was a whole lot of sillies bigger than the three sillies at home. So the gentleman turned back home again and married the farmer's daughter, and if they didn't live happy for ever after, that's nothing to do with you or me.

Master of All Masters [8]

❧ *Another droll, but constructed in an entirely different way. The contrast between the brevity of the tale and the girl's long-winded warning of the fire causes the shock of surprise which is the basis of comedy.*

A girl once went to the fair to hire herself for servant. At last a funny-looking old gentleman engaged her, and took her home to his house. When she got there, he told her that he had something to teach her, for that in his house he had his own names for things.

8 From Joseph Jacobs, *English Fairy Tales* (Putnam, 1892).

He said to her: "What will you call me?"

"Master or mister, or whatever you please, sir," says she.

He said: "You must call me 'master of all masters.' And what would you call this?" pointing to his bed.

"Bed or couch, or whatever you please, sir."

"No, that's my 'barnacle.' And what do you call these?" said he pointing to his pantaloons.

"Breeches or trousers, or whatever you please, sir."

"You must call them 'squibs and crackers.' And what would you call her?" pointing to the cat.

"Cat or kit, or whatever you please, sir."

"You must call her 'white-faced simminy.' And this now," showing the fire, "what would you call this?"

"Fire or flame, or whatever you please, sir."

"You must call it 'hot cockalorum,' and what this?" he went on, pointing to the water.

"Water or wet, or whatever you please, sir."

"No, 'pondalorum' is its name. And what do you call all this?" asked he as he pointed to the house.

"House or cottage, or whatever you please, sir."

"You must call it 'high topper mountain.'"

That very night the servant woke her master up in a fright and said: "Master of all masters, get out of your barnacle and put on your squibs and crackers. For white-faced simminy has got a spark of hot cockalorum on its tail, and unless you get some pondalorum, high topper mountain will be all on hot cockalorum". . . . .
. . . . That's all.

The Well of the World's End [9]

⊷§ The recurring motif of the disenchantment of a person doomed to appear in animal form until his head is severed from his body is the central theme of this English version which in

[9] From Joseph Jacobs, *English Fairy Tales* (Putnam, 1892).

the Grimm collection is known as The Frog Prince. Jacobs has given it a form well suited to the storyteller. Often, in a folk tale, one comes upon a phrase that is sheer poetry. "The well of the world's end" is such a phrase, with its power to evoke a sense of mystery and doom. And the refrain, "my hinny, my heart" is another bit which is utterly poetic.

Once upon a time, and a very good time it was, though it wasn't in my time, nor in your time, nor any one else's time, there was a girl whose mother had died, and her father married again. And her stepmother hated her because she was more beautiful than herself, and she was very cruel to her. She used to make her do all the servant's work, and never let her have any peace. At last, one day, the stepmother thought to get rid of her altogether; so she handed her a sieve and said to her: "Go, fill it at the Well of the World's End and bring it home to me full, or woe betide you." For she thought she would never be able to find the Well of the World's End, and, if she did, how could she bring home a sieve full of water?

Well, the girl started off, and asked every one she met to tell her where was the Well of the World's End. But nobody knew, and she didn't know what to do, when a queer little old woman, all bent double told her where it was, and how she could get to it. So she did what the old woman told her, and at last arrived at the Well of the World's End. But when she dipped the sieve in the cold, cold water, it all ran out again. She tried and she tried again, but every time it was the same; and at last she sat down and cried as if her heart would break.

Suddenly she heard a croaking voice, and she looked up and saw a great frog with goggle eyes looking at her and speaking to her.

"What's the matter, dearie?" it said.

"Oh, dear, oh dear," she said, "my stepmother has sent me all this long way to fill this sieve with water from the Well of the World's End, and I can't fill it no how at all."

"Well," said the frog, "if you promise me to do whatever I bid you for a whole night long, I'll tell you how to fill it."

So the girl agreed, and the frog said:

"Stop it with moss and daub it with clay,
And then it will carry the water away";

and then it gave a hop, skip, and jump, and went flop into the Well of the World's End.

So the girl looked about for some moss, and lined the bottom of the sieve with it, and over that she put some clay, and then she dipped it once again into the Well of the World's End; and this time, the water didn't run out, and she turned to go away.

Just then the frog popped up its head out of the Well of the World's End, and said: "Remember your promise."

"All right," said the girl; for thought she, "what harm can a frog do me?"

So she went back to her stepmother, and brought the sieve full of water from the Well of the World's End. The stepmother was angry as angry, but she said nothing at all.

That very evening they heard something tap tapping at the door low down, and a voice cried out:

"Open the door, my hinny, my heart,
Open the door, my own darling;
Mind you the words that you and I spoke,
Down in the meadow, at the World's End Well."

"Whatever can that be?" cried out the stepmother, and the girl had to tell her all about it, and what she had promised the frog.

"Girls must keep their promise," said the stepmother. "Go and open the door this instant." For she was glad the girl would have to obey a nasty frog.

So the girl went and opened the door, and there was the frog from the Well of the World's End. And it hopped, and it hopped, and it jumped, till it reached the girl, and then it said:

"Lift me to your knee, my hinny, my heart:
Lift me to your knee, my own darling;
Remember the words you and I spoke,
Down in the meadow by the World's End Well."

But the girl didn't like to, till her stepmother said: "Lift it up this instant, you hussy! Girls must keep their promises!"

So at last she lifted the frog up on to her lap, and it lay there for a time, till at last it said:

"Give me some supper, my hinny, my heart,
Give me some supper, my darling;
Remember the words you and I spake,
In the meadow, by the Well of the World's End."

Well, she didn't mind doing that, so she got it a bowl of milk and bread, and fed it well. And when the frog had finished, it said:

"Go with me to bed, my hinny, my heart,
Go with me to bed, my own darling;
Mind you the words you spake to me,
Down by the cold well, so weary."

But that the girl wouldn't do, till her stepmother said: "Do what you promised, girl; girls must keep their promises. Do what you're bid, or out you go, you and your froggie."

So the girl took the frog with her to bed, and kept it as far away from her as she could. Well, just as the day was beginning to break what should the frog say but:

"Chop off my head, my hinny, my heart,
Chop off my head, my own darling;
Remember the promise you made to me,
Down by the cold well so weary."

At first the girl wouldn't, for she thought of what the frog had done for her at the Well of the World's End. But when the frog said the words over again, she went and took an axe and chopped off its head, and lo! and behold, there stood before her a handsome young prince, who told her that he had been enchanted by a wicked magician, and he could never be unspelled till some girl would do his bidding for a whole night, and chop off his head at the end of it.

The stepmother was surprised indeed when she found the young prince instead of the nasty frog, and she wasn't best pleased, you may be sure, when the prince told her that he was going to marry her stepdaughter because she had unspelled him. But married they were, and went away to live in the castle of the king, his father, and all the stepmother had to console her was, that it was all through her that her stepdaughter was married to a prince.

The History of Tom Thumb [1]

Tiny characters as well as adventure always interest children, and here both are united to make this one of the most popular tales. It is interesting to read Andersen's Thumbelisa as a literary variant.

In the days of the great Prince Arthur, there lived a mighty magician, called Merlin, the most learned and skillful enchanter the world has ever seen.

This famous magician, who could take any form he pleased, was traveling about as a poor beggar; and being very tired, he stopped at the cottage of a ploughman to rest himself and asked for some food.

The countryman bade him welcome; and his wife, who was a very good-hearted woman, soon brought him some milk in a wooden bowl and some coarse brown bread on a platter.

Merlin was much pleased with the kindness of the ploughman and his wife; but he could not help noticing that though everything was neat and comfortable in the cottage, they both seemed to be very unhappy. He therefore asked them why they were so melancholy, and learned that they were miserable because they had no children.

The poor woman said, with tears in her eyes: "I should be the happiest creature in the world if I had a son; although he was no bigger than my husband's thumb, I would be satisfied."

Merlin was so much amused with the idea of a boy no bigger than a man's thumb, that he determined to grant the poor woman's wish. Accordingly, in a short time after, the ploughman's wife had a son, who, wonderful to relate! was not a bit bigger than his father's thumb.

The queen of the fairies, wishing to see the little fellow, came in at the window while the mother was sitting up in the bed admiring him. The queen kissed the child, and, giving it the name of Tom Thumb, sent for some of the fairies, who dressed her little godson according to her orders:

[1] From Joseph Jacobs, *English Fairy Tales* (Putnam, 1892).

An oak-leaf hat he had for his crown;
His shirt of web by spiders spun;
And jacket wove of thistle's down;
His trowsers were of feathers done.
His stockings, of apple-rind, they tie
With eyelash from his mother's eye:
His shoes were made of mouse's skin,
Tann'd with the downy hair within.

Tom never grew any larger than his father's thumb, which was only of ordinary size; but as he got older he became very cunning and full of tricks. When he was old enough to play with the boys and had lost all his own cherry-stones, he used to creep into the bags of his playfellows, fill his pockets and, getting out without their noticing him, would again join in the game.

One day, however, as he was coming out of a bag of cherry-stones, where he had been stealing as usual, the boy to whom it belonged chanced to see him. "Ah, ah! my little Tommy," said the boy, "so I have caught you stealing my cherry-stones at last, and you shall be rewarded for your thievish tricks." On saying this, he drew the string tight round his neck, and gave the bag such a hearty shake, that poor little Tom's legs, thighs, and body were sadly bruised. He roared out with pain and begged to be let out, promising never to steal again.

A short time afterwards his mother was making a batter-pudding; and Tom, being very anxious to see how it was made, climbed up to the edge of the bowl; but his foot slipped, and he plumped over head and ears into the batter, without his mother noticing him, who stirred him into the pudding-bag, and put him in the pot to boil.

The batter filled Tom's mouth and prevented him from crying; but, on feeling the hot water, he kicked and struggled so much in the pot, that his mother thought that the pudding was bewitched; and, pulling it out of the pot, she threw it outside the door. A poor tinker, who was passing by, lifted up the pudding; and, putting it into his budget, he then walked off. As Tom had now got his mouth cleared of the batter, he then began to cry aloud, which so frightened the tinker that he flung down the pudding and ran away. The pudding being broke to pieces by the fall, Tom crept out covered all over with the batter and walked home. His mother, who was very sorry to see her darling in such a woeful state, put him into a teacup and soon washed off the batter, after which she kissed him and laid him in bed.

Soon after the adventure of the pudding, Tom's mother went to milk her cow in the meadow, and she took him along with her. As the wind was very high, for fear of being blown away, she tied him to a thistle with a piece of fine thread. The cow soon observed Tom's oak-leaf hat and, liking the appearance of it, took poor Tom and the thistle at one mouthful. While the cow was chewing the thistle, Tom was afraid of her great teeth, which threatened to crush him in pieces, and he roared out as loud as he could: "Mother, mother!"

"Where are you, Tommy, my dear Tommy?" said his mother.

"Here, mother," replied he, "in the red cow's mouth."

His mother began to cry and wring her hands; but the cow, surprised at the odd noise in her throat, opened her mouth and let Tom drop out. Fortunately his mother caught him in her apron as he was falling to the ground, or he would have been dreadfully hurt. She then put Tom in her bosom and ran home with him.

Tom's father made him a whip of barley straw to drive the cattle with, and having one day gone into the fields, Tom slipped a foot and rolled into the furrow. A raven, which was flying over, picked him up and flew with with him over the sea and there dropped him.

A large fish swallowed Tom the moment he fell into the sea, which was soon after caught, and bought for the table of King Arthur. When they opened the fish in order to cook it, every one was astonished at finding such a little boy, and Tom was quite delighted at being free again. They carried him to the king, who made Tom his dwarf, and he soon grew a great favorite at court; for by his tricks and gambols he not only amused the king and queen but also all the Knights of the Round Table.

It is said that when the king rode out on horseback, he often took Tom along with him; and if a shower came on, Tom used to creep into his majesty's waist coat pocket, where he slept till the rain was over.

King Arthur one day asked Tom about his parents, wishing to know if they were as small as he was, and whether they were well off. Tom told the king that his father and mother were as tall as anybody about the court, but in rather poor circumstances. On hearing this, the king carried Tom to his treasury, the place where he kept all his money, and told him to take as much money as he could carry home to his parents, which made the poor little fellow caper with joy. Tom went immediately to procure a purse, which was made of a water-bubble, and then returned to the treasury, where he received a silver three-penny-piece to put into it.

Our little hero had some difficulty in lifting the burden upon his back; but he at last succeeded in getting it placed to his mind, and set forward on his journey. However, without meeting with any accident and after resting himself more than a hundred times by the way, in two days and two nights he reached his father's house in safety.

Tom had traveled forty-eight hours with a huge silver-piece on his back and was almost tired to death, when his mother ran out to meet him and carried him into the house. But he soon returned to court.

As Tom's clothes had suffered much in the batter-pudding and the inside of the fish, his majesty ordered him a new suit of clothes, and to be mounted as a knight on a mouse.

It was certainly very diverting to see Tom in this dress and mounted on the mouse, as he rode out a-hunting with the king and nobility, who were all ready to expire with laughter at Tom and his fine prancing charger.

The king was so charmed with his address that he ordered a little chair to be made, in order that Tom might sit upon his table, and also a palace of gold, a span high, with a door an inch wide, to live in. He also gave him a coach, drawn by six small mice.

The queen was so enraged at the honors conferred on Sir Thomas that she resolved to ruin him and told the king that the little knight had been saucy to her.

The king sent for Tom in great haste; but being fully aware of the danger of royal anger, he crept into an empty snail-shell, where he lay for a long time until he was almost starved with hunger, but at last he ventured to peep out, and seeing a fine large butterfly on the ground near the place of his concealment, he got close to it and, jumping astride on it, was carried up into the air. The butterfly flew with him from tree to tree and from field to field, and at last returned to the court, where the king and nobility all strove to catch him; but at last poor Tom fell from his seat into a watering pot, in which he was almost drowned.

When the queen saw him, she was in a rage, and said he should be beheaded; and he was put into a mouse trap until the time of his execution.

However, a cat, observing something alive in the trap, patted it about till the wires broke and set Thomas at liberty.

The king received Tom again into favor, which he did not live to enjoy, for a large spider one day attacked him; and although he drew his sword and fought well, yet the spider's poisonous breath at last overcame him.

> He fell dead on the ground where he stood,
> And the spider suck'd every drop of his blood.

King Arthur and his whole court were so sorry at the loss of their little favorite that they went into mourning and raised a fine white marble monument over his grave with the following epitaph:

> Here lies Tom Thumb, King Arthur's knight,
> Who died by a spider's cruel bite.
> He was well known in Arthur's court,
> Where he afforded gallant sport;
> He rode a tilt and tournament,
> And on a mouse a-hunting went.
> Alive he filled the court with mirth;
> His death to sorrow soon gave birth.
> Wipe, wipe your eyes, and shake your head
> And cry — Alas! Tom Thumb is dead!

Tamlane [2]

Here is an example of a motif very common in all folk tales, the hero stolen by a fairy queen. Not all such tales end so happily.

[2] From Joseph Jacobs, *More English Fairy Tales* (Putnam, 1894).

Young Tamlane was son of Earl Murray, and Burd Janet was daughter of Dunbar, Earl of March. And when they were young they loved one another and plighted their troth. But when the time came near for their marrying, Tamlane disappeared, and none knew what had become of him.

Many, many days after he had disappeared, Burd Janet was wandering in Carterhaugh Wood, though she had been warned not to go there. And as she wandered she plucked the flowers from the bushes. She came at last to a bush of broom and began plucking it. She had not taken more than three flowerets when by her side up started young Tamlane.

"Where come ye from, Tamlane, Tamlane?" Burd Janet said; "and why have you been away so long?"

"From Elfland I come," said young Tamlane. "The Queen of Elfland has made me her knight."

"But how did you get there, Tamlane?" said Burd Janet.

"I was hunting one day, and as I rode widershins round yon hill, a deep drowsiness fell upon me, and when I awoke, behold! I was in Elfland. Fair is that land and gay, and fain would I stop but for thee and one other thing. Every seven years the Elves pay their tithe to the Nether world, and for all the Queen makes much of me, I fear it is myself that will be the tithe."

"Oh, can you not be saved? Tell me if aught I can do will save you, Tamlane?"

"One only thing is there for my safety. Tomorrow night is Hallowe'en, and the fairy court will then ride through England and Scotland, and if you would borrow me from Elfland you must take your stand by Miles Cross between twelve and one o' the night, and with holy water in your hand you must cast a compass all around you."

"But how shall I know you, Tamlane?" quoth Burd Janet, "amid so many knights I've ne'er seen before?"

"The first court of Elves that come by let pass. The next court you shall pay reverence to, but do naught nor say aught. But the third court that comes by is the chief court of them, and at the head rides the Queen of all Elfland. And I shall ride by her side upon a milk-white steed with a star in my crown; they give me this honor as being a christened knight. Watch my hands, Janet, the right one will be gloved but the left one will be bare, and by that token you will know me."

"But how to save you, Tamlane?" quoth Burd Janet.

"You must spring upon me suddenly, and I will fall to the ground. Then seize me quick, and whatever change befall me, for they will exercise all their magic on me, cling hold to me till they turn me into a red-hot iron. Then cast me into this pool and I will be turned back into a mother-naked man. Cast then your green mantle over me, and I shall be yours, and be of the world again."

So Burd Janet promised to do all for Tamlane, and next night at midnight she took her stand by Miles Cross and cast a compass round her with holy water.

Soon there came riding by the Elfin court; first over the mound went a troop on black steeds, and then another troop on brown. But in the third court, all on milk-white steeds, she saw the Queen of Elfland, and by her side a knight with a star in his crown, with right hand gloved and the left bare. Then she knew this was her own Tamlane, and springing forward she seized the bridle of the milk-white steed and pulled its rider down. And as soon as he had touched the ground she let go the bridle and seized him in her arms.

"He's won, he's won amongst us all," shrieked out the eldritch crew, and all came around her and tried their spells on young Tamlane.

First they turned him in Janet's arms like frozen ice, then into a huge flame of roaring fire. Then, again, the fire vanished and an adder was skipping through her arms, but still she held on; and then they turned him into a snake that reared up as if to bite her, and yet she held on. Then suddenly a dove was struggling in her arms, and almost flew away. Then they turned him into a swan, but all was in vain, till at last he was turned into a red-hot glaive, and this she cast into a well of water and then he turned back into a mother-naked man. She quickly cast her green mantle over him, and young Tamlane was Burd Janet's for ever.

Then sang the Queen of Elfland as the court turned away and began to resume its march:

"She that has borrowed young Tamlane
    Has gotten a stately groom,
She's taken away my bonniest knight,
    Left nothing in his room.

"But had I known, Tamlane, Tamlane,
    A lady would borrow thee,
I'd hae ta'en out thy two grey eyne,
    Put in two eyne of tree.

"Had I but known, Tamlane, Tamlane,
    Before we came from home,
I'd hae ta'en out thy heart o' flesh,
    Put in a heart of stone.

"Had I but had the wit yestreen
    That I have got today,
I'd paid the Fiend seven times his teind
    Ere you'd been won away."

And then the Elfin court rode away, and Burd Janet and young Tamlane went their way homewards and were soon after married after young Tamlane had again been sained by the holy water and made Christian once more.

The King o' the Cats[3]

⚜ *Here is a tale for the storyteller on Hallowe'en. This story occurs in many regions. Stith Thompson defines the motif to which it belongs as "Spirit leaves when report is made of death of one of his kind." But the greatest effect is to be had when it is a cat that is summoned, for the story seems to belong to the cat's nature.*

One winter's evening the sexton's wife was sitting by the fireside with her big black cat, Old Tom, on the other side, both half asleep and waiting for the master to come home. They waited and they waited, but still he didn't come, till at last he came

[3] From Joseph Jacobs, *More English Fairy Tales* (Putnam, 1894).

rushing in, calling out, "who's Tommy Tildrum?" in such a wild way that both his wife and his cat stared at him to know what was the matter.

"Why, what's the matter?" said his wife, "and why do you want to know who Tommy Tildrum is?"

"Oh, I've had such an adventure. I was digging away at old Mr. Fordyce's grave when I suppose I must have dropped asleep, and only woke up by hearing a cat's *Miaou*."

"*Miaou!*" said Old Tom in answer.

"Yes, just like that! So I looked over the edge of the grave, and what do you think I saw?"

"Now, how can I tell?" said the sexton's wife.

"Why, nine black cats all like our friend Tom here, all with a white spot on their chestesses. And what do you think they were carrying? Why, a small coffin covered with a black velvet pall, and on the pall was a small coronet all of gold, and at every third step they took they cried all together, *Miaou —*"

"*Miaou!*" said Old Tom again.

"Yes, just like that!" said the Sexton; "and as they came nearer and nearer to me I could see them more distinctly, because their eyes shone out with a sort of green light. Well, they all came towards me, eight of them carrying the coffin, and the biggest cat of all walking in front for all the world like — but look at our Tom, how he's looking at me. You'd think he knew all I was saying."

"Go on, go on," said his wife; "never mind Old Tom."

"Well, as I was a-saying, they came towards me slowly and solemnly, and at every third step crying all together, *Miaou —*"

"*Miaou!*" said Old Tom again.

"Yes, just like that, till they came and stood right opposite Mr. Fordyce's grave, where I was, when they all stood still and looked straight at me. I did feel queer, that I did! But look at Old Tom; he's looking at me just like they did."

"Go on, go on," said his wife; "never mind Old Tom."

"Where was I? Oh, they all stood still looking at me, when the one that wasn't carrying the coffin came forward and, staring at me, said to me — yes, I tell 'ee, *said* to me, with a squeaky voice, 'Tell Tom Tildrum that Tim Toldrum's dead,' and that's why I asked you if you knew who Tom Tildrum was, for how can I tell Tom Tildrum Tim Toldrum's dead if I don't know who Tom Tildrum is?"

"Look at Old Tom, look at Old Tom!" screamed his wife.

And well he might look, for Tom was swelling and Tom was staring, and at last Tom shrieked out, "What — old Tim dead! then I'm the King o' the Cats!" and rushed up the chimney and was never more seen.

IRELAND

King O'Toole and His Goose [1]

Irish fairy tales are in two main classes: the humorous, such as this, with a certain earthiness; and the beautiful, with great delicacy and charm, such as The Land of the Heart's Desire *by William Butler Yeats.*

Och, I thought all the world, far and near, had heerd of King O'Toole — well, well but the darkness of mankind is untollable! Well, sir, you must know, as you didn't hear it afore, that there was a king, called King O'Toole, who was a fine old king in the old ancient times, long ago; and it was he that owned the churches in the early days. The king, you see, was the right sort; he was the real boy and loved sport as he loved his life, and hunting in particular; and from the rising o' the sun, up he got and away he went over the mountains after the deer; and fine times they were.

Well, it was all mighty good, as long as the king had his health; but, you see, in the course of time the king grew old, by raison he was stiff in his limbs, and when he got stricken in years, his heart failed him, and he was lost entirely for want o' diversion, because he couldn't go a-hunting no longer; and, by dad, the poor king was obliged at last to get a goose to divert him. Oh, you may laugh if you like, but it's truth I'm telling; and the way the goose diverted him was this-a-way: You see, the goose used to swim across the lake and go diving for trout and catch fish on a Friday for the king, and

[1] From Joseph Jacobs, *Celtic Fairy Tales* (Putnam, 1893).

flew every other day round about the lake, diverting the poor king. All went on mighty well until, by dad, the goose got stricken in years like her master and couldn't divert him no longer; and then it was that the poor king was lost entirely. The king was walkin' one mornin' by the edge of the lake, lamentin' his cruel fate, and thinking of drowning himself, that could get no diversion in life, when all of a sudden, turning round the corner, whom should he meet but a mighty decent young man coming up to him.

"God save you," says the king to the young man.

"God save you kindly, King O'Toole," says the young man.

"True for you," says the king. "I am King O'Toole," says he, "prince and plennypennytinchery of these parts," says he; "but how came ye to know that?" says he.

"Oh, never mind," says Saint Kavin.

You see it was Saint Kavin, sure enough — the saint himself in disguise and nobody else. "Oh, never mind," says he, "I know more than that. May I make bold to ask how is your goose, King O'Toole?" says he.

"Blur-an-agers, how came ye to know about my goose?" says the king.

"Oh, no matter; I was given to understand it," says Saint Kavin.

After some more talk the king says, "What are you?"

"I'm an honest man," says Saint Kavin.

"Well, honest man," says the king, "and how is it you make your money so aisy?"

"By makin' old things as good as new," says Saint Kavin.

"Is it a tinker you are?" says the king.

"No," says the saint; "I'm no tinker by

trade, King O'Toole; I've a better trade than a tinker," says he — "What would you say," says he, "if I made your old goose as good as new?"

My dear, at the word of making his goose as good as new, you'd think the poor old king's eyes were ready to jump out of his head. With that the king whistled, and down came the poor goose, just like a hound, waddling up to the poor cripple, her master, and as like him as two peas. The minute the saint clapt his eyes on the goose, "I'll do the job for you," says he, "King O'Toole."

"By Jaminee!" says King O'Toole, "if you do, I'll say you're the cleverest fellow in the seven parishes."

"Oh, by dad," says Saint Kavin, "you must say more nor that — my horn's not so soft all out," says he, "as to repair your old goose for nothing; what'll you gi' me if I do the job for you? — that's the chat," says Saint Kavin.

"I'll give you whatever you ask," says the king; "isn't that fair?"

"Divil a fairer," says the saint, "that's the way to do business. Now," says he, "this is the bargain I'll make with you, King O'Toole: will you gi' me all the ground the goose flies over, the first offer, after I make her as good as new?"

"I will," says the king.

"You won't go back on your word?" says Saint Kavin.

"Honor bright!" says King O'Toole, holding out his fist.

"Honor bright!" says Saint Kavin, back again, "it's a bargain. Come here!" says he to the poor old goose — "come here, you unfortunate ould cripple, and it's I that'll make you the sporting bird." With that, my dear, he took up the goose by the two wings — "Criss o' my cross an you," says he markin' her to grace with the blessed sign at the same minute — and throwing her up in the air, "whew," says he, jist givin' her a blast to help her; and with that, my jewel, she took to her heels, flyin' like one o' the eagles themselves, and cutting as many capers as a swallow before a shower of rain.

Well, my dear, it was a beautiful sight to see the king standing with his mouth open, looking at his poor old goose flying as light

as a lark, and better than ever she was; and when she lit at his feet, patted her on the head, and "Ma vourneen," says he, "but you are the darlint o' the world."

"And what do you say to me," says Saint Kavin, "for making her the like?"

"By Jabers," says the king, "I say nothing beats the art o' man, barring the bees."

"And do you say no more nor what?" says Saint Kavin.

"And that I'm beholden to you," says the king.

"But will you gi'e me all the ground the goose flew over?" says Saint Kavin.

"I will," says King O'Toole, "and you're welcome to it," says he, "though it's the last acre I have to give."

"But you'll keep your word true," says the saint.

"As true as the sun," says the king.

"It's well for you, King O'Toole, that you said that word," says he; "for if you didn't say that word, the divil the bit o' your goose would ever fly agin."

When the king was as good as his word, Saint Kavin was pleased with him; and then it was that he made himself known to the king. "And," says he, "King O'Toole, you're a decent man, for I only came here to try you. You don't know me," says he, "because I'm disguised."

"Musha! then," says the king, "who are you?"

"I'm Saint Kavin," said the saint, blessing himself.

"Oh, queen of heaven!" says the king, making the sign of the cross between his eyes and falling down on his knees before the saint; "is it the great Saint Kavin," says he, "that I've been discoursing all this time without knowing it," says he, "all as one as if he was a lump of a gossoon? — and so you're a saint?" says the king.

"I am," says Saint Kavin.

"By Jabers, I thought I was only talking to a dacent boy," says the king.

"Well, you know the difference now," says the saint. "I'm Saint Kavin," says he, "the greatest of all the saints."

And so the king had his goose as good as new to divert him as long as he lived; and the saint supported him after he came into his property, as I told you, until the day of his death — and that was soon after; for the poor goose thought he was catching a trout one Friday; but, my jewel, it was a mistake he made — and instead of a trout, it was a thieving horse-eel; and instead of the goose killing a trout for the king's supper — by dad, the eel killed the king's goose — and small blame to him; but he didn't ate her, because he darn't ate what Saint Kavin had laid his blessed hands on.

Billy Beg and the Bull [2]

This tale defies precise classification; it has the cruel stepmother at the beginning; it has an unknown boy successful. True, he is a king's son, but he does not trade on that fact. Its magic comes from an animal, as in The Little Humpbacked Horse; *and lastly, it has the Cinderella episode of a shoe left behind. The plot, therefore, is unusually complex for a folk tale.*

Once on a time when pigs was swine, there was a King and a Queen, and they had one son, Billy, and the Queen gave Billy a bull that he was very fond of, and it was just as fond of him. After some time the Queen died, and she put it as her last request on the King that he would never part Billy and the bull; and the King promised that, come what might, come what may, he would not. After the Queen died the King married again, and the new Queen didn't take to Billy Beg, and no more did she like the bull, seeing himself and Billy so thick. But she couldn't get the King on no account to part Billy and the bull; so she consulted with a hen-wife what they could do as regards separating Billy and the bull. "What will you give me," says the hen-wife, "and I'll very soon part them?" "Whatever you ask," says the Queen. "Well and good then," says the hen-wife, "you are to take to your bed, making pretend that you are bad with a complaint, and I'll do the rest of it." And, well and good, to her bed she took, and none of the doctors could do anything for her, or make out what was her

[2] From Seumas MacManus, *In Chimney Corners* (Doubleday, 1899).

complaint. So the Queen asked for the hen-wife to be sent for. And sent for she was, and when she came in and examined the Queen, she said there was one thing, and only one, could cure her. The King asked what was that, and the hen-wife said it was three mouthfuls of the blood of Billy Beg's bull. But the King wouldn't on no account hear of this, and the next day the Queen was worse, and the third day she was worse still, and told the King she was dying, and he'd have her death on his head. So, sooner nor this, the King had to consent to Billy Beg's bull being killed. When Billy heard this he got very down in the heart entirely, and he went doitherin' about, and the bull saw him and asked him what was wrong with him that he was so mournful; so Billy told the bull what was wrong with him, and the bull told him to never mind but keep up his heart, the Queen would never taste a drop of his blood. The next day then the bull was to be killed, and the Queen got up and went out to have the delight of seeing his death. When the bull was led up to be killed, says he to Billy, "Jump up on my back till we see what kind of a horseman you are." Up Billy jumped on his back, and with that the bull leapt nine mile high, nine mile deep and nine mile broad, and came down with Billy sticking between his horns. Hundreds were looking on dazed at the sight, and through them the bull rushed, and over the top of the Queen killing her dead, and away he galloped where you wouldn't know day by night, or night by day, over high hills, low hills, sheep-walks, and bullock-traces, the Cove of Cork, and old Tom Fox with his bugle horn. When at last they stopped, "Now then," says the bull to Billy, "you and I must undergo great scenery, Billy. Put your hand," says the bull, "in my left ear, and you'll get a napkin, that, when you spread it out, will be covered with eating and drinking of all sorts, fit for the King himself." Billy did this, and then he spread the napkin, and ate and drank to his heart's content, and he rolled up the napkin and put it back in the bull's ear again. "Then," says the bull, "now put your hand into my right ear and you'll find a bit of a stick; if you wind it over your head three times, it will be turned into a sword and give you the strength of a thousand men besides your own, and when you have no more need of it as a sword, it will change back into a stick again." Billy did all this. Then says the bull, "At twelve o'clock the morrow I'll have to meet and fight a great bull." Billy then got up again on the bull's back, and the bull started off and away where you wouldn't know day by night, or night by day, over high hills, low hills, sheep-walks and bullock-traces, the Cove of Cork, and old Tom Fox with his bugle horn. There he met the other bull, and both of them fought, and the like of their fight was never seen before or since. They knocked the soft ground into hard, and the hard into soft, the soft into spring wells, the spring wells into rocks, and the rocks into high hills. They fought long, and Billy Beg's bull killed the other and drank his blood. Then Billy took the napkin out of his ear again and spread it out and ate a hearty good dinner. Then says the bull to Billy, says he, "At twelve o'clock tomorrow, I'm to meet the bull's brother that I killed the day, and we'll have a hard fight." Billy got on the bull's back again, and the bull started off and away where you wouldn't know day by night, or night by day, over high hills, low hills, sheep-walks, and bullock-traces, the Cove of Cork, and old Tom Fox with his bugle horn. There he met the bull's brother that he killed the day before, and they set to, and they fought, and the like of the fight was never seen before or since. They knocked the soft ground into hard, the hard into soft, the soft into spring wells, the spring wells into rocks, and the rocks into high hills. They fought long, and at last Billy's bull killed the other and drank his blood. And then Billy took out the napkin out of the bull's ear again and spread it out and ate another hearty dinner. Then says the bull to Billy, says he — "The morrow at twelve o'clock I'm to fight the brother to the two bulls I killed — he's a mighty great bull entirely, the strongest of them all; he's called the Black Bull of the Forest, and he'll be too able for me. When I'm dead," says the bull, "you, Billy, will take with you the napkin, and you'll never be hungry; and the stick, and you'll be able to overcome everything that

comes in your way; and take out your knife and cut a strip of the hide off my back and another strip off my belly and make a belt of them, and as long as you wear them you cannot be killed." Billy was very sorry to hear this, but he got up on the bull's back again, and they started off and away where you wouldn't know day by night or night by day, over high hills, low hills, sheep-walks and bullock-traces, the Cove of Cork and old Tom Fox with his bugle horn. And sure enough at twelve o'clock the next day they met the great Black Bull of the Forest, and both of the bulls to it, and commenced to fight, and the like of the fight was never seen before or since; they knocked the soft ground into hard ground, and the hard ground into soft, and the soft into spring wells, and the spring wells into rocks, and the rocks into high hills. And they fought long. But at length the Black Bull of the Forest killed Billy Beg's bull and drank his blood. Billy Beg was so vexed at this that for two days he sat over the bull neither eating or drinking, but crying salt tears all the time. Then he got up, and he spread out the napkin, and ate a hearty dinner, for he was very hungry with his long fast; and after that he cut a strip of the hide off the bull's back, and another off the belly, and made a belt for himself, and taking it and the bit of stick, and the napkin, he set out to push his fortune; and he traveled for three days and three nights till at last he came to a great gentleman's place. Billy asked the gentleman if he could give him employment, and the gentleman said he wanted just such a boy as him for herding cattle. Billy asked what cattle would he have to herd and what wages would he get. The gentleman said he had three goats, three cows, three horses and three asses that he fed in an orchard; but that no boy who went with them ever came back alive, for there were three giants, brothers, that came to milk the cows and the goats every day, and killed the boy that was herding; so if Billy liked to try, they wouldn't fix the wages till they'd see if he would come back alive. "Agreed, then," said Billy. So the next morning he got up and drove out the three goats, the three cows, the three horses, and the three asses to the orchard and commenced to feed them. About the middle of the day Billy heard three terrible roars that shook the apples off the bushes, shook the horns on the cows, and made the hair stand up on Billy's head; and in comes a frightful big giant with three heads, and begun to threaten Billy. "You're too big," says the giant, "for one bite and two small for two. What will I do with you?" "I'll fight you," says Billy, says he, stepping out to him and swinging the bit of stick three times over his head, when it changed into a sword and gave him the strength of a thousand men besides his own. The giant laughed at the size of him, and says he, "Well, how will I kill you? Will it be by a swing by the back, a cut of the sword, or a square round of boxing?" "With a swing by the back," says Billy, "if you can." So they both laid holds, and Billy lifted the giant clean off the ground, and fetching him down again sunk him in the earth up to his armpits. "Oh, have mercy," says the giant. But Billy, taking his sword, killed the giant, and cut out his tongues. It was·evening by this time, so Billy drove home the three goats, three cows, three horses, and three asses, and all the vessels in the house wasn't able to hold all the milk the cows give that night.

"Well," says the gentleman, "This beats me, for I never saw anyone coming back alive out of there before, nor the cows with a drop of milk. Did you see anything in the orchard?" says he. "Nothing worse nor myself," says Billy. "What about my wages, now," says Billy. "Well," says the gentleman, "you'll hardly come alive out of the orchard the morrow. So we'll wait till after that." Next morning his master told Billy that something must have happened to one of the giants, for he used to hear the cries of three every night, but last night he only heard two crying. "I don't know," says Billy, "anything about them." That morning after he got his breakfast Billy drove the three goats, three cows, three horses, and three asses into the orchard again, and began to feed them. About twelve o'clock he heard three terrible roars that shook the apples off the bushes, the horns on the cows, and made the hair stand up on Billy's head, and in comes a frightful big giant, with six heads, and he told Billy he had killed his brother yesterday,

but he would make him pay for it the day. "Ye're too big," says he, "for one bite and too small for two, and what will I do with you?" "I'll fight you," says Billy, swinging his stick three times over his head, and turning it into a sword, and giving him the strength of a thousand men besides his own. The giant laughed at him, and says he, "How will I kill you — with a swing by the back, a cut of the sword, or a square round of boxing?" "With a swing by the back," says Billy, "if you can." So the both of them laid holds, and Billy lifted the giant clean off the ground and fetching him down again, sunk him in it up to the arm-pits. "Oh, spare my life!" says the giant. But Billy, taking up his sword, killed him and cut out his tongues. It was evening by this time, and Billy drove home his three goats, three cows, three horses, and three asses; and what milk the cows gave that night overflowed all the vessels in the house, and, running out, turned a rusty mill that hadn't been turned before for thirty years. If the master was surprised seeing Billy coming back the night before, he was ten times more surprised now.

"Did you see anything in the orchard the day?" says the gentleman. "Nothing worse nor myself," says Billy. "What about my wages now," says Billy. "Well, never mind about your wages," says the gentleman, "till the morrow, for I think you'll hardly come back alive again," says he. Well and good, Billy went to his bed, and the gentleman rose in the morning; says he to Billy, "I don't know what's wrong with two of the giants; I only heard one crying last night." "I don't know," says Billy, "they must be sick or something." Well, when Billy got his breakfast that day again, he set out to the orchard, driving before him the three goats, three cows, three horses, and three asses; and sure enough about the middle of the day he hears three terrible roars again, and in comes another giant, this one with twelve heads on him; and if the other two were frightful, surely this one was ten times more so. "You villain, you," says he to Billy, "you killed my two brothers, and I'll have my revenge on you now. Prepare till I kill you," says he; "you're too big for one bite and too small for two; what will I do with you?" "I'll fight you," says Billy, shaping out and winding the bit of stick three times over his head. The giant laughed heartily at the size of him, and says he, "What way do you prefer being killed? Is it with a swing by the back, a cut of the sword, or a square round of boxing?" "A swing of the back," says Billy. So both of them again laid holds, and my brave Billy lifts the giant clean off the ground, and fetching him down again, sunk him down to his arm-pits in it. "Oh, have mercy; spare my life," says the giant. But Billy took his sword, and, killing him, cut out his tongues. That evening he drove home his three goats, three cows, three horses, and three asses, and the milk of the cows had to be turned into a valley where it made a lough three miles long, three miles broad, and three miles deep, and that lough has been filled with salmon and white trout ever since. The gentleman wondered now more than ever to see Billy back the third day alive. "Did you see nothing in the orchard the day, Billy?" says he. "No, nothing worse nor myself," says Billy. "Well, that beats me," says the gentleman. "What about my wages now?" says Billy. "Well, you're a good mindful boy, that I couldn't easy do without," says the gentleman, "and I'll give you any wages you ask for the future." The next morning says the gentleman to Billy, "I heard none of the giants crying last night, however it comes. I don't know what has happened to them." "I don't know," says Billy, "they must be sick or something." "Now, Billy," says the gentleman, "you must look after the cattle the day again, while I go to see the fight." "What fight?" says Billy. "Why," says the gentleman, "it's the king's daughter is going to be devoured by a fiery dragon, if the greatest fighter in the land, that they have been feeding specially for the last three months, isn't able to kill the dragon first. And if he's able to kill the dragon, the king is to give him the daughter in marriage." "That will be fine," says Billy. Billy drove out his three goats, three cows, three horses, and three asses to the orchard that day again; and the like of all that passed that day to see the fight with the man and the fiery dragon, Billy never witnessed before. They went in coaches and carriages, on horses and jackasses, riding and walking, crawling and creeping. "My tight little fellow," says a man that was passing to Billy, "why don't you come to see the great fight?" "What would take the likes of me there?" says Billy. But when Billy found them all gone, he saddled and bridled the best black horse his master had and put on the best suit of clothes he could get in his master's house and rode off to the fight after the rest. When Billy went there, he saw the king's daughter with the whole court about her on a platform before the castle, and he thought he never saw anything half as beautiful; and the great warrior that was to fight the dragon was walking up and down on the lawn before her, with three men carrying his sword, and everyone in the whole country gathered there looking at him. But when the fiery dragon came up with twelve heads on him, and every mouth of him spitting fire, and let twelve roars out of him, the warrior ran away and hid himself up to the neck in a well of water; and all they could do they couldn't get him to come and face the dragon. Then the king's daughter asked if there was no one there to save her from the dragon and get her in marriage. But not one stirred. When Billy saw this, he tied the belt of the bull's hide round him, swung his stick over his head and went in, and after a terrible fight entirely, killed the dragon. Everyone then gathered about to find who the stranger was. Billy jumped on his horse and darted away sooner than let them know; but just as he was getting away the king's daughter pulled the shoe off his foot. When the dragon was killed the warrior that had hid in the well of water came out; and cutting the heads off the dragon, he brought them to the king, and said that it was he who killed the dragon, in disguise; and he claimed the king's daughter. But she tried the shoe on him and found it didn't fit him; so she said it wasn't him and that she would marry no one only the man the shoe fitted. When Billy got home he changed his clothes again, and had the horse in the stable, and the cattle all in before his master came. When the master came, he began telling Billy about the wonderful day they had entirely, and about the warrior hiding in the well of water, and about the grand stranger that came down out of the sky in a cloud on a black horse, and killed the fiery dragon, and then vanished in a cloud again, "and now," says he, "Billy, wasn't that wonderful?" "It was, indeed," says Billy, "very wonderful entirely." After that it was given out over the country that all the people were to come to the king's castle on a certain day, till the king's daughter would try the shoe on them, and whoever it fitted she was to marry them. When the day arrived Billy was in the orchard with the three goats, three cows, three horses, and three asses, as usual; and the like of all the crowds that passed that day going to the king's castle to get the shoe tried on, he never saw before. They went in coaches and carriages, on horses and jackasses, riding and walking, and crawling and creeping. They all asked Billy was not he going to the king's castle, but Billy said, "Arrah, what would be bringin' the likes of me there?" At last when all the others had gone, there passed an old man with a very scarecrow suit of rags on him, and Billy stopped him and asked him what boot would he take and swap clothes with him. "Just take care of yourself, now," says the old man, "and don't be playing off your jokes on my clothes, or maybe I'd make you feel the weight of this stick." But Billy soon let him see it was in earnest he was, and both of them swapped suits, Billy giving the old man boot. Then off to the castle Billy started, with the suit of rags on his back and an old stick in his hand; and when he come there, he found all in great commotion trying on the shoe, and some of them cutting down their foot, trying to get it to fit. But it was all of no use, the shoe could be got to fit none of them at all, and the king's daughter was going to give up in despair when the wee ragged looking boy, which was Billy, elbowed his way through them, and says he, "Let me try it on; maybe it would fit me." But the people when they saw him, all began to laugh at the sight of him, and "Go along out of that, you example you," says they, shoving and pushing him back. But the king's daughter saw him, and called on them by all manner of means to let him come up and try on the shoe. So Billy went up, and all the people looked on,

breaking their hearts laughing at the conceit of it. But what would you have of it, but to the dumfounding of them all, the shoe fitted Billy as nice as if it was made on his foot for a last. So the king's daughter claimed Billy as her husband. He then confessed that it was he that killed the fiery dragon; and when the king had him dressed up in a silk and satin suit, with plenty of gold and silver ornaments, everyone gave in that his like they never saw afore. He was then married to the king's daughter, and the wedding lasted nine days, nine hours, nine minutes, nine half minutes and nine quarter minutes, and they lived happy and well from that day to this.

The Bee, the Harp, the Mouse, and the Bum-Clock [3]

This droll is a more detailed version of the Jack and the Beanstalk *theme. The Irish flair for embellishment of style and incident is apparent. The motif of the mirthless princess is included, a frequent theme of the folk tale.*

Once there was a widow, and she had one son, called Jack. Jack and his mother owned just three cows. They lived well and happy for a long time; but at last hard times came down on them, and the crops failed, and poverty looked in at the door, and things got so sore against the poor widow that for want of money and for want of necessities she had to make up her mind to sell one of the cows.

"Jack," she said one night, "go over in the morning to the fair to sell the branny cow."

Well and good: in the morning my brave Jack was up early, and took a stick in his fist and turned out the cow, and off to the fair he went with her; and when Jack came into the fair, he saw a great crowd gathered in a ring in the street. He went into the crowd to see what they were looking at, and there in the middle of them he saw a man with a wee, wee harp, a mouse, and bum-clock [cockroach], and a bee to play the harp. And when the

[3] From Seumas MacManus, *Donegal Fairy Stories* (Lippincott, 1926).

man put them down on the ground and whistled, the bee began to play and the mouse and the bum-clock to dance, and there wasn't a man or woman, or a thing in the fair, that didn't begin to dance also; and the pots and pans, and the wheels and reels jumped and jigged, all over the town, and Jack himself and the branny cow were as bad as the next.

There was never a town in such a state before or since; and after a while the man picked up the bee, the harp, and the mouse, and the bum-clock and put them into his pocket; and the men and women, Jack and the cow, the pots and pans, wheels and reels, that had hopped and jigged, now stopped, and every one began to laugh as if to break its heart. Then the man turned to Jack. "Jack," says he, "how would you like to be master of all these animals?"

"Why," says Jack, "I should like it fine."

"Well, then," says the man, "how will you and me make a bargain about them?"

"I have no money," says Jack.

"But you have a fine cow," says the man. "I will give you the bee and the harp for it."

"O, but," Jack says, says he, "my poor mother at home is very sad and sorrowful entirely, and I have this cow to sell and lift her heart again."

"And better than this she cannot get," says the man. "For when she sees the bee play the harp, she will laugh if she never laughed in her life before."

"Well," says Jack, says he, "that will be grand."

He made the bargain. The man took the cow; and Jack started home with the bee and the harp in his pocket, and when he came home, his mother welcomed him back.

"And Jack," says she, "I see you have sold the cow."

"I have done that," says Jack.

"Did you do well?" says the mother.

"I did well and very well," says Jack.

"How much did you get for her?" says the mother.

"O," says he, "it was not for money at all I sold her, but for something far better."

"O, Jack! Jack!" says she, "what have you done?"

"Just wait until you see, mother," says he, "and you will soon say I have done well."

Out of his pocket he takes the bee and the harp and sets them in the middle of the floor, and whistles to them, and as soon as he did this the bee began to play the harp, and the mother she looked at them and let a big, great laugh out of her, and she and Jack began to dance, the pots and pans, the wheels and reels began to jig and dance over the floor, and the house itself hopped about also.

When Jack picked up the bee and the harp again, the dancing all stopped, and the mother laughed for a long time. But when she came to herself, she got very angry entirely with Jack, and she told him he was a silly, foolish fellow, that there was neither food nor money in the house, and now he had lost one of her good cows also. "We must do something to live," says she. "Over to the fair you must go tomorrow morning, and take the black cow with you and sell her."

And off in the morning at an early hour brave Jack started and never halted until he was in the fair. When he came into the fair, he saw a big crowd gathered in a ring in the street. Said Jack to himself, "I wonder what are they looking at."

Into the crowd he pushed, and saw the wee man this day again with a mouse and a bum-clock, and he put them down in the street and whistled. The mouse and the bum-clock stood up on their hind legs and got hold of each other and began to dance there and jig; and as they did there was not a man or woman in the street who didn't begin to jig also, and Jack and the black cow, and the wheels and the reels, and the pots and pans, all of them were jigging and dancing all over the town, and the houses themselves were jumping and hopping about, and such a place Jack or any one else never saw before.

When the man lifted the mouse and the bum-clock into his pocket, they all stopped dancing and settled down, and everybody laughed right hearty. The man turned to Jack. "Jack," said he, "I am glad to see you; how would you like to have these animals?"

"I should like well to have them," says Jack, says he, "only I cannot."

"Why cannot you?" says the man.

"O," says Jack, says he, "I have no money, and my poor mother is very down-hearted. She sent me to the fair to sell this cow and bring some money to lift her heart."

"O," says the man, says he, "if you want to lift your mother's heart, I will sell you the mouse; and when you set the bee to play the harp and the mouse to dance to it, your mother will laugh if she never laughed in her life before."

"But I have no money," says Jack, says he, "to buy your mouse."

"I don't mind," says the man, says he, "I will take your cow for it."

Poor Jack was so taken with the mouse and had his mind so set on it, that he thought it was a grand bargain entirely, and he gave the man his cow and took the mouse and started off for home; and when he got home his mother welcomed him.

"Jack," says she, "I see you have sold the cow."

"I did that," says Jack.

"Did you sell her well?" says she.

"Very well indeed," says Jack, says he.

"How much did you get for her?"

"I didn't get money," says he, "but I got value."

"O, Jack! Jack!" says she, "what do you mean?"

"I will soon show you that, mother," says he, taking the mouse out of his pocket and the harp and the bee, setting all on the floor; and when he began to whistle the bee began to play, and the mouse got up on its hind legs and began to dance and jig, and the mother gave such a hearty laugh as she never laughed in her life before. To dancing and jigging herself and Jack fell, and the pots and pans and the wheels and reels began to dance and jig over the floor, and the house jigged also. And when they were tired of this, Jack lifted the harp and the mouse and the bee and put them in his pocket, and his mother she laughed for a long time.

But when she got over that, she got very down-hearted and very angry entirely with Jack. "And O, Jack," she says, "you are a stupid, good-for-nothing fellow. We have neither money nor meat in the house, and here you have lost two of my good cows, and I have only one left now. Tomorrow morning," she says, "you must be up early and take this cow to the fair and sell her. See to get something to lift my heart up."

"I will do that," says Jack, says he. So he went to his bed, and early in the morning he was up and turned out the spotty cow and went to the fair.

When Jack got to the fair, he saw a crowd gathered in a ring in the street. "I wonder what they are looking at, anyhow," says he. He pushed through the crowd, and there he saw the same wee man he had seen before, with a bum-clock; and when he put the bum-clock on the ground, he whistled, and the bum-clock began to dance, and the men, women, and children in the street, and Jack and the spotty cow began to dance and jig also, and everything on the street and about it, the wheels and reels, the pots and pans, began to jig, and the houses themselves began to dance likewise. And when the man lifted the bum-clock and put it in his pocket, everybody stopped jigging and dancing and every one laughed loud. The wee man turned and saw Jack.

"Jack, my brave boy," says he, "you will never be right fixed until you have this bum-clock, for it is a very fancy thing to have.

"O, but," says Jack, says he, "I have no money."

"No matter for that," says the man: "you have a cow, and that is as good as money to me."

"Well," says Jack, "I have a poor mother who is very downhearted at home, and she sent me to the fair to sell this cow and raise some money and lift her heart."

"O, but Jack," says the wee man, "this bum-clock is the very thing to lift her heart, for when you put down your harp and bee and mouse on the floor and put the bum-clock along with them, she will laugh if she never laughed in her life before."

"Well, that is surely true," says Jack, says he, "and I think I will make a swap with you."

So Jack gave the cow to the man and took the bum-clock himself and started for home. His mother was glad to see Jack back and says she, "Jack, I see that you have sold the cow."

"I did that, mother," says Jack.

"Did you sell her well, Jack?" says the mother.

"Very well indeed, mother," says Jack.

"How much did you get for her?" says the mother.

"I didn't take any money for her, mother, but value," says Jack and he takes out of his pocket the bum-clock and the mouse, and set them on the floor and began to whistle, and the bee began to play the harp and the mouse and the bum-clock stood up on their hind legs and began to dance, and Jack's mother laughed very hearty, and everything in the house, the wheels and the reels, and the pots and pans went jigging and hopping over the floor, and the house itself went jigging and hopping about likewise.

When Jack lifted up the animals and put them in his pocket, everything stopped, and the mother laughed for a good while. But after a while, when she came to herself and saw what Jack had done and how they were now without either money, or food, or a cow, she got very, very angry at Jack and scolded him hard, and then sat down and began to cry.

Poor Jack, when he looked at himself, confessed that he was a stupid fool entirely. "And what," says he, "shall I now do for my poor mother?" He went out along the road, thinking and thinking, and he met a wee woman who said, "Good-morrow to you, Jack," says she, "how is it you are not trying for the King's daughter of Ireland?"

"What do you mean?" says Jack.

Says she: "Didn't you hear what the whole world has heard, that the King of Ireland has a daughter who hasn't laughed for seven years; and he has promised to give her in marriage and to give the kingdom along with her, to any man who will take three laughs out of her."

"If that is so," says Jack, says he, "it is not here I should be."

Back to the house he went and gathers together the bee, the harp, the mouse, and the bum-clock, and putting them into his pocket; he bade his mother good-by and told her it wouldn't be long till she got good news from him and off he hurries.

When he reached the castle, there was a ring of spikes all round the castle and men's heads on nearly every spike there.

"What heads are these?" Jack asked one of the King's soldiers.

"Any man that comes here trying to win the King's daughter and fails to make her laugh three times, loses his head and has it stuck on a spike. These are the heads of the men that failed," says he.

"A mighty big crowd," says Jack, says he. Then Jack sent word to tell the King's daughter and the King that there was a new man who had come to win her.

In a very little time the King and the King's daughter and the King's court all came out and sat themselves down on gold and silver chairs in front of the castle and ordered Jack to be brought in until he should have his trial. Jack, before he went, took out of his pocket the bee, the harp, the mouse, and the bum-clock, and he gave the harp to the bee, and he tied a string to one and the other, and took the end of the string himself, and marched into the castle yard before all the court, with his animals coming on a string behind him.

When the Queen and the King and the court and the princes saw poor ragged Jack with his bee, and mouse, and bum-clock hopping behind him on a string, they set up one roar of laughter that was long and loud enough; and when the King's daughter herself lifted her head and looked to see what they were laughing at and saw Jack and his paraphernalia, she opened her mouth and she let out of her such a laugh as was never heard before.

Then Jack dropped a low courtesy, and said, "Thank you, my lady; I have one of the three parts of you won."

Then he drew up his animals in a circle, and began to whistle, and the minute he did, the bee began to play the harp, and the mouse and the bum-clock stood up on their hind legs, got hold of each other, and began to dance, and the King and the King's court and Jack himself began to dance and jig, and everything about the King's castle, pots and pans, wheels and reels and the castle itself began to dance also. And the King's daughter, when she saw this, opened her mouth again, and let out of her a laugh twice louder than she let before; and Jack, in the middle of his jigging, drops another courtesy, and says, "Thank you, my lady; that is two of the three parts of you won."

Jack and his menagerie went on playing and dancing, but Jack could not get the third laugh out of the King's daughter, and the poor fellow saw his big head in danger of going on the spike. Then the brave mouse came to Jack's help and wheeled round upon its heel, and as it did so its tail swiped into the bum-clock's mouth, and the bum-clock began to cough and cough and cough. And when the King's daughter saw this she opened her mouth again, and she let out the loudest and hardest and merriest laugh that was ever heard before or since; and, "Thank you, my lady," says Jack, dropping another courtesy; "I have all of you won."

Then when Jack stopped his menagerie, the King took himself and the menagerie within the castle. He was washed and combed and dressed in a suit of silk and satin with all kinds of gold and silver ornaments, and then was led before the King's daughter. And true enough she confessed that a handsomer and finer fellow than Jack she had never seen, and she was very willing to be his wife.

Jack sent for his poor old mother and brought her to the wedding, which lasted nine days and nine nights, every night better than the other. All the lords and ladies and gentry of Ireland were at the wedding. I was at it, too, and got brogues, broth and slipper of bread and came jigging home on my head.

Jack and the King Who Was a Gentleman [4]

🥀 *Lucky the storyteller who has a touch of Irish in him and can recreate the music of the language as the Irish say it, with its cadence, its accompanying trill of the r's and its rich arrangement of words; for the Irish have "a great delight in the flow of language."*

[4] From Seumas MacManus, *In Chimney Corners* (Doubleday, 1899).

In the English version of Jack and the Beanstalk, *the old refrain goes:*

> *"Fee, fi, fo, fum*
> *I smell the blood of an Englishman."*

But in the Irish version of the same tale, the refrain is as follows:

> *"Fee, fi, fo, fum*
> *I feel the smell of a melodious lying Irishman*
> *Under my sod of a country."*

Here is a "whopping" story, with its element of exaggeration, its tall tales, and the winning of a princess besides.

Well, childre: wanst upon a time, when pigs was swine, there was a poor widdy woman lived all alone with her wan son Jack in a wee hut of a house, that on a dark night ye might aisily walk over it by mistake, not knowin' at all, at all, it was there, barrin' ye'd happen to strike yer toe again' it. An' Jack an' his mother lived for lee an' long, as happy as hard times would allow them, in this wee hut of a house, Jack sthrivin' to 'arn a little support for them both by workin' out, an' doin' wee turns back an' forrid to the neighbors. But there was one winter, an' times come to look black enough for them — nothin' to do, an' less to ate, an' clothe themselves as best they might; an' the winther wore on, gettin' harder an' harder, till at length when Jack got up out of his bed on a mornin', an' axed his mother to make ready the drop of stirabout for their little brakwus as usual, "Musha, Jack, *a mhic,*" says his mother, says she, "the malechist — thanks be to the Lord! — is as empty as Paddy Ruadh's donkey that used to ate his brakwus at supper-time. It stood out long an' well, but it's empty at last, Jack, an' no sign of how we're goin' to get it filled again — only we trust in the good Lord that niver yet disarted the widow and the orphan — He'll not see us wantin', Jack."

"The Lord helps them that help themselves, mother," says Jack back again to her.

"Thrue for ye, Jack," says she, "but I don't see how we're goin' to help ourselves."

"He's a mortial dead mule out an' out that hasn't a kick in him," says Jack. "An', mother, with the help of Providence — not comparin' the Christian to the brute baste — I have a kick in me yet; if you thought ye could only manage to sthrive along the best way you could for a week, or maybe two weeks, till I get back again off a little journey I'd like to undhertake."

"An' may I make bould to ax, Jack," says his mother to him, "where would ye be afther makin' the little journey to?"

"You may that, then, Mother," says Jack. "It's this: You know the King of Munsther is a great jintleman entirely. It's put on him, he's so jintlemanly, that he was niver yet known to make use of a wrong or disrespectable word. An' he prides himself on it so much that he has sent word over all the known airth that he'll give his beautiful daughter — the loveliest picthur in all Munsther, an' maybe in all Irelan', if we'd say it — an' her weight in goold, to any man that in three trials will make him use the unrespectful word, an' say, 'Ye're a liar!' But every man that tries him, an' fails, loses his head. All sorts and descriptions of people, from prences an' peers down to bagmen an' beggars, have come from all parts of the known world to thry for the great prize, an' all of them up to this has failed, an' by consequence lost their heads. But, mother dear," says Jack, "where's the use in a head to a man if he can't get mail for it to ate? So I'm goin' to thry me fortune, only axin' your blissin' an' God's blissin' to help me on the way."

"Why, Jack, a thaisge," says his mother, "it's a dangersome task; but as you remark, where's the good of the head to ye when ye can't get mail to put in it? So, I give ye my blissin', an' night, noon, an' mornin' I'll be prayin' for ye to prosper."

An' Jack set out, with his heart as light as his stomach, an' his pocket as light as them both together; but a man 'ill not travel far in ould Irelan' (thanks be to God!) on the bare-footed stomach — as we'll call it — or it'll be his own fault if he does; an' Jack didn't want for plenty of first-class aitin' an' dhrinkin' lashin's an' laivin's, and pressin' him to more. An' in this way he thravelled away afore him for five long days till he come to the King of Munsther's castle. And when he was comed there he rattled on the gate, an' out come the king.

"Well, me man," says the king, "what might be your business here?"

"I'm come here, your Kingship," says Jack, mighty polite, an' pullin' his forelock, be raison his poor ould mother had always insthructed him in the heighth of good breedin' "I'm come here, your R'yal Highness," says Jack, "to thry for yer daughter."

"Hum!" says the king. "Me good young man," says he, "don't ye think it a poor thing to lose yer head?"

"If I lose it," says Jack, "sure one consolation 'ill be that I'll lose it in a glorious cause."

An' who do ye think would be listenin' to this same deludherin' speech of Jack's, from over the wall, but the king's beautiful daughter herself. She took an eyeful out of Jack, an' right well plaised she was with his appearance, for —

"Father," says she at once, "hasn't the boy as good a right to get a chance as another? What's his head to you? Let the boy in," says she.

An' sure enough, without another word, the King took Jack within the gates, an' handin' him over to the sarvints, tould him to be well looked afther an' cared for till mornin'.

Next mornin' the King took Jack with him an' fetched him out into the yard. "Now then, Jack," says he, "we're goin' to begin. We'll drop into the stables here, and I'll give you your first chance."

So he took Jack into the stables an' showed him some wondherful big horses, the likes of which poor Jack never saw afore, an' everyone of which was the heighth of the side wall of the castle an' could step over the castle walls, which were twenty-five feet high, without strainin' themselves.

"Them's purty big horses, Jack," says the King. "I don't suppose ever ye saw as big or as wondherful as them in yer life."

"Oh, they're purty big indeed," says Jack, takin' it as cool as if there was nothin' whatsomever astonishin' to him about them. "They're purty big indeed," says Jack, *for this counthry*. But at home with us in Donegal we'd only count them little nags, shootable for the young ladies to dhrive in pony-carriages."

"What!" says the King, "do ye mane to tell me ye have seen bigger in Donegal?"

"Bigger!" says Jack. "Phew! Blood alive, yer Kingship, I seen horses in my father's stable that could step over your horses with-out thrippin'. My father owned one big horse — the greatest, I believe, in the world again."

"What was he like?" says the King.

"Well, yer Highness," says Jack, "it's quite beyond me to tell ye what he was like. But I know when we wanted to mount it could only be done by means of a step-laddher, with nine hundred and ninety steps to it, every step a mile high, an' you had to jump seven mile off the topmost step to get on his back. He ate nine ton of turnips, nine ton of oats, an' nine ton of hay, in the day an' it took ninety-nine men in the daytime, an' ninety-nine more in the night-time, carrying his feeds to him; an' when he wanted a drink, the ninety-nine men had to lead him to a lough that was nine mile long, nine mile broad, an' nine mile deep, an' he used to drink it dry every time," says Jack, an' then he looked at the King, expectin' he'd surely have to make a liar of him for that.

But the King only smiled at Jack, an' says he, "Jack, that was a wonderful horse en-tirely, an' no mistake."

Then he took Jack with him out into the garden for his second trial, an' showed him a beeskep, the size of the biggest rick of hay ever Jack had seen; an' every bee in the skep was the size of a thrush, an' the queeny bee as big as a jackdaw.

"Jack," says the King, says he, "isn't them wondherful bees? I'll warrant ye, ye never saw anything like them?"

"Oh, they're middlin' — middlin' fairish," says Jack — "for this countbry. But they're nothin' at all to the bees we have in Donegal. If one of our bees was flying across the fields," says Jack, "and one of your bees happened to come in its way, an' fall into our bee's eye, our bee would fly to the skep, an' ax another bee to take the mote out of his eye."

"Do you tell me so, Jack?" says the King. "You must have great monsthers of bees."

"Monsthers," says Jack. "Ah, yer High-ness, monsthers is no name for some of them. I remimber," says Jack, says he, "a mighty great breed of bees me father owned. They were that big that when my father's new castle was a-buildin' (in the steddin' of the old one which he consaived to be too small for a man of his mains), and when the work-men closed in the roof, it was found there was a bee inside, an' the hall door not bein' wide enough, they had to toss the side wall to let it out. Then the queeny bee — ah! she was a wondherful baste entirely!" says Jack. "Whenever she went out to take the air she used to overturn all the ditches and hedges in the country; the wind of her wings tossed houses and castles; she used to swallow whole flower gardens; an' one day she flew against a ridge of mountains nineteen thou-sand feet high and knocked a piece out from top to bottom, an' it's called Barnesmore Gap to this day. This queeny bee was a great trouble an' annoyance to my father, seein' all the harm she done the naybours round about; and once she took it in her head to fly over to England, an' she created such mischief an' disolation there that the King of Englan' wrote over to my father if he didn't come immaidiately an' take home his queeny bee that was wrackin' an' ruinin' all afore her he'd come over himself at the head of all his army and wipe my father off the face of the airth. So my father ordhered me to mount our wondherful big horse that I tould ye about, an' that could go nineteen mile at every step, an' go over to Englan' an' bring home our queeny bee. An' I mounted the horse an' started, an' when I come as far as the sea I had to cross to get over to Englan', I put the horse's two fore feet into my hat, an' in that way he thrashed the sea dry all the way across an' landed me safely. When I come to the King of Englan' he had to supply me with nine hundred and ninety-nine thousand men an' ninety-nine thousand mile of chains an' ropes to catch the queeny bee an' bind her. It took us nine years to catch her, nine more to tie her, an' nine years and nine millions of men to drag her home, an' the King of Englan' was a beggar afther from that day till the day of his death. Now what do ye think of that bee?" says

Jack, thinkin' he had the King this time sure enough,

But the King was a cuter one than Jack took him for, an' he only smiled again, an' says he, —

"Well, Jack, that was a wondherful great queeny bee entirely."

Next, for poor Jack's third an' last chance, the King took him to show him a wondherful field of beans he had, with every beanstalk fifteen feet high an' every bean the size of a goose's egg.

"Well, Jack," says the King, says he, "I'll engage ye never saw more wondherful beanstalks than them?"

"Is it them?" says Jack. "Arrah, man, yer Kingship," says he, "they may be very good — for this counthry; but sure we'd throw them out of the ground for useless afthershoots in Donegal. I mind one bean-stalk in partickler, that my father had for a show an' a cur'osity, that he used to show as a great wondher entirely to sthrangers. It stood on ninety-nine acres of ground, it was nine hundred mile high, an' every leaf covered nine acres. It fed nine thousand horses, nine thousand mules, an' nine thousand jackasses for nineteen years. He used to send nine thousand harvestmen up the stalk in spring to cut and gather off the soft branches at the top. They used to cut these off when they'd reach up as far as them (which was always in the harvest time), an' throw them down, an' nine hundred and ninety-nine horses an' carts were kept busy for nine months carting the stuff away. Then the harvestmen always reached down to the foot of the stalk at Christmas again."

"Faix, Jack," says the King, "it was a wondherful bean-stalk, that, entirely."

"You might say that," says Jack, trying to make the most of it, for he was now on his last leg. "You might say that," says he. "Why, I mind one year I went up the stalk with the harvestmen, an' when I was nine thousand mile up, doesn't I miss my foot, and down I come. I fell feet foremost, and sunk up to my chin in a whinstone rock that was at the foot. There I was in a quandhary — but I was not long ruminatin' till I hauled out my knife, an' cut off my head, an' sent it home to look for help. I watched after it,

as it went away, an' lo an' behould ye, afore it had gone half a mile I saw a fox set on it, and begin to worry it. 'By this an' by that,' says I to meself, 'but this is too bad!' — an' I jumped out an' away as hard as I could run, to the assistance of my head. An' when I come up, I lifted my foot, an' give the fox three kicks, an' knocked three kings out of him — every one of them a nicer an' a better jintleman than you."

"Ye're a liar, an' a rascally liar," says the King.

"More power to ye!" says Jack, givin' three buck leaps clean into the air, "an' it's proud I am to get you to confess it; for I have won yer daughter."

Right enough the King had to give up to Jack the daughter — an' be the same token, from the first time she clapped her two eyes on Jack she wasn't the girl to gainsay him — an' her weight in goold. An' they were both of them marrid, an' had such a weddin' as surpassed all the weddin's ever was heerd tell of afore or since in that country or in this. An' Jack lost no time in sendin' for his poor ould mother, an' neither herself nor Jack ever after knew what it was to be in want. An' may you an' I never know that same naither.

Kate Mary Ellen [5]

Here we have a typical Irish folk tale of the less robust, less humorous kind. And yet the fact that the fairies, who are supposed to be wiser than human beings, found themselves sixty years late in keeping an appointment has a sly touch of humor. One finds here obedience and the just reward for obedience bestowed by the fairies in spite of their own disappointment.

There was a little girl hereabout and her name was Kate Mary Ellen. She was as good a child as ever put a shawl across her head. Her people had only one cow and Kate Mary Ellen used to be minding it along the grassy sides of the road. One Saint Patrick's day she thought she would pluck herself a bunch of the shamrock that grew inside that fort. The

[5] From Padraic Colum, *A Boy in Eirinn* (Dutton, 1929).

people used to say that the shamrock that grew there had a splash of blood on it and Kate Mary Ellen would fain have a bunch that would be so remarkable. So when the cow got into a good piece of grass, Kate Mary Ellen left her and went up to the fort. She had trouble in getting in, for there were sloe bushes and blackthorn bushes round it like a fence. But she got through at last, and there was clear ground with old twisted thorn trees growing round.

Kate Mary Ellen plucked a piece of shamrock and looked to see if there was anything remarkable on it at all. When she looked round again she saw a little fellow looking at her from behind a hawthorn bush. By the size of him and by the shape of his boots she knew he was a fairy man. And behind every hawthorn bush Kate Mary Ellen saw a couple more. She was that flustered that she stood without moving a limb.

Then one who had sharp eyes and a very high look said to her, "Are you an obedient child?"

"I am, sir," said Kate Mary Ellen.

"Then," said he, "take these shamrocks in your hand and go and stand on the bridge. A coach will be passing and you must contrive to stop it. Inside of it will be a big man, and all you will have to do is to hand him your bunch of shamrocks and say to him, 'Daniel O'Connell, the fairy people of Ireland will not go against you.' Will you be able to do that?"

"I will, sir," says Kate Mary Ellen.

"Say the words after him," said another of the fairies, a middling sharp-looking little fellow.

"Daniel O'Connell, the fairies of Ireland won't go against you," says Kate Mary Ellen.

"That's it," says the high-looking fairy man, "and now let you make your way to the bridge, and I'll send one of my men to look after your cow till you come back."

Away went Kate Mary Ellen. She got down the slope that goes down from the fort, and then she came racing back. The fairies were all standing consulting together.

"I suppose," says Kate Mary Ellen, "that's the bridge on the Old Road that I'm to go to?"

"It's the road that the coaches travel that you're to go to," says the second fairy, very severe.

"There's no bridge upon that road," says Kate Mary Ellen.

"Go and stand on the bridge and do the Commander's bidding," says the second fairy back to her.

"Yes, sir," says Kate Mary Ellen, and with that she made off.

"She never stopped running until she was on the Old Road. The grass was growing nigh to the middle of it, for nothing ever traveled it except a goose or an ass. Kate Mary Ellen stationed herself on the bridge, and waited and waited. All she heard going past was an odd trout that leaped in the stream below. She began to get anxious on account of her cow; there was no sign of a coach high up or low down, and at last she started off running to Martin Murphy's house.

"Will there be any coach on the Old Road today?" says she, as soon as she came in the door.

Martin Murphy was sitting at the fire, and he turned round on that.

"A coach," says he. "A coach on the Old Road," says he again. "What would there be a coach on the Old Road for? Sure it's thirty years since a car itself went traveling that road."

"And will Daniel O'Connell not be coming the way?" says Kate Mary Ellen.

"Daniel O'Connell," says Martin Murphy. "What do they be teaching you at all in school? Don't you know that it's sixty years since Daniel O'Connell was walking the ground of Ireland?"

Well, at that Kate Mary Ellen made off. Her heart was twisted with concern for the cow. She made for the fort, and got through the blackthorns and sloe bushes. The fairies were standing there with trailing cloaks on them and little swords in their belts. They were consulting together, and they all looked very anxious.

"Well," says the second fairy, "and what did he say?"

"He's not coming that way at all, and it's long since a coach went over the road."

"Could it be that we're late?" says the commander.

"Not at all," says the second of them. "But in case he went early we'll take horse."

"Yes," says the commander, "we'll take horse this minute, and we'll wait for him at Tara. The little girl will have to come with us, for it is appointed to her to hand the shamrock to the Liberator. Show her how to mount the bramble," says he, "and let us be off on the minute."

They gave Kate Mary Ellen a bramble, and put a dock-leaf on it for a side-saddle; the commander stamped his foot, and they were clear of the fort and were galloping through the air in a moment.

"We mustn't come up to the Hill," says the second of the fairies, "for the crowds of the world are sure to be on Tara today. We'll get off at the back of the hill and ride over quietly."

The wind that was before them they overtook, and the red wind of March that was behind did not overtake them. They rode on and on, and they were soon at Tara.

They came down on a little field.

"And now," says the second fairy, "we'll let on that we're huntsmen and gallop up to them. The crowds of the world are sure to be on the Hill, but we'll keep to the outside of them."

With that they galloped through fields and over ditches, and they came up to the Hill of Tara. And all that was before them was a wide grassy place with cattle grazing over it. There was no sign of a person on the Hill at all.

"We're late for the meeting," says one of them.

"We're a day late for the meeting," says another of them.

"We're a year late for the meeting," says a third of them.

"Ay, and twenty years late for the meeting," says a fourth one of them.

"You're sixty years late for the meeting," says Kate Mary Ellen, speaking up to them.

All the fairies shook their heads at the one that was second.

"You're to blame for this," says the commander, looking very severe at him.

The second of the fairies went down on his knees immediately. "My lord," says he, lifting his hands, "don't blame me. It was only this morning I received notice of the meeting from Clourie Com."

The commander looked at them all very severely. "It's no wonder," says he, "that above ground and below ground affairs are in the state they're in. Mount horses and make no stop nor stay until we strike hoofs on our own courtyard."

They mounted, and if they came at a run they went back at a race. When they struck hoof on the fort the ground opened and they went down. They took a turning to the right and came to a little forge. In they went, Kate Mary Ellen with them. The like of what she saw there never came to her eyes since or before. It wasn't a face that was looking towards them, but the top of a head that was as bald and as smooth as a goose's egg. The beard that grew down was all round the fellow like an apron. He was a little old fellow sitting on a stool, and his legs were twisted like the stems of the hawthorn tree. His hands were under his head, and Kate Mary Ellen never saw them. Only the top of his bald head was to be seen.

"When you took that man into your service did you know what age he was?" says the commander to the second fairy.

"I thought I did, my lord," says he.

"Well, whatever age he told you he was, he's a thousand years older than that same," says the commander. "It's no wonder our time has all gone wrong, and that we're sixty years slow in our reckoning. Start Clourie Com carving his tombstone, and by the time he has that done he'll be ripe for his burial. And as for you, young girl," says he, "I found you serviceable and agreeable. You'll get your cow in the hollow and you can go home or stay on the road, as it pleases yourself. Bring the bunch of shamrock with you. Dip it in the well of the fort, and it will remain everlasting. And on the Saint Patrick's Day that the cherry tree in your grandmother's yard is blown down, stand at the cross roads and give the bunch to a young man you'll see riding by. He'll be on his way to Tara, too, and you'll tell him that the fairies of Ireland will not go against him. We missed Dan O'Connell, but we'll not miss him. And," says he, "lest it should be said," says he, "that those who help the fairies get nothing for their service, the next time you're at the well in the pasture field lift up the flagstone," says he, "and you'll find a little pan of gold."

The Children of Lir[6]

~§ *This tragic tale of jealousy, suffering, and remorse comes out of the poetic mythology of Ireland. The characters are not human beings, but belong to the "Tuatha De Danaan," the gods of Celtic belief. Unlike the gods of most mythologies, the Celtic deities were not worshiped or placated by sacrifice and ritual. Nor did they dwell in some region removed from earth. The Norse gods lived in Valhalla, a region in the sky, and there they shared immortality with heroes who had died gloriously in battle. To the Greeks, Mt. Olympus was the region beyond earth where the gods lived and from which they directed the affairs of man. But to the Celtic mind, the earth of Ireland itself and the waters that washed its shores, these were the ultimate paradise, the Land of the Ever-Young. The Celtic fairy belongs to the people of Danaan, and to this day, the mounds and hills of Ireland are believed to hold special magic, being the dwelling place of the gods themselves. William Butler Yeats in his play,* The Land of Heart's Desire, *describes the paradise as*

"*. . . a land where even the old are fair, And even the wise are merry of tongue.*"

Ella Young, whose version is given here, was a member of the group of brilliant men and women who, working with Yeats and Lady Gregory, Dr. Douglas Hyde, Padraic Colum, and many others, reinterpreted Celtic legend, epic, and myth. The result was a renaissance of literature — novels, stories, and drama — which, in the first quarter of this century, won the admiration of the world, and gave fresh impetus to the study of traditional literature.

Long ago when the Tuatha De Danaan lived in Ireland there was a Great King called Lir. He had four children — Fionnuala, Aodh, Fiacra, and Conn. Fionnuala was the

[6] From *Celtic Wonder Tales,* retold by Ella Young (Dutton).

eldest and she was as beautiful as sunshine in blossomed branches; Aodh was like a young eagle in the blue of the sky; and his two brothers, Fiacra and Conn, were as beautiful as running water.

In those days sorrow was not known in Ireland: the mountains were crowned with light, and the lakes and rivers had strange star-like flowers that shook a rain of jewelled dust on the white horses of the De Danaans when they came down to drink. The horses were swifter than any horses that are living now and they could go over the waves of the sea and under deep lake-water without hurt to themselves. Lir's four children had each one a white horse and two hounds that were whiter than snow.

Every one in Lir's kingdom loved Fionnuala, and Aodh, and Fiacra, and Conn, except their step-mother, Aoifa. She hated them, and her hatred pursued them as a wolf pursues a wounded fawn. She sought to harm them by spells and witchcraft. She took them in her chariot to the Lake of Darvra in Westmeath. She made them bathe in the lake and when they were coming out of the water she struck them with a rod of enchantment and turned them into four white swans.

"Swim as wild swans on this lake," she said, "for three hundred years, and when that time is ended swim three hundred years on the narrow sea of the Moyle, and when that time is ended swim three hundred years on the Western Sea that has no bounds but the sky."

Then Fionnuala, that was a swan, said:

"O Wicked Woman, a doom will come upon you heavier than the doom you have put on us and you will be more sorrowful than we are to-day. And if you would win any pity in the hour of your calamity tell us now how we may know when the doom will end for us."

"The doom will end when a king from the North weds a queen from the South; when a druid with a shaven crown comes over the sea; when you hear the sound of a little bell that rings for prayers."

The swans spread their wings and flew away over the lake. They made a very sorrowful singing as they went, lamenting for themselves.

When the Great King, their father, knew the sorrow that had come to him, he hastened down to the shore of the lake and called his children. They came flying to him, four white swans, and he said:

"Come to me, Fionnuala; come Aodh; come Conn; come Fiacra." He put his hands on them and caressed them and said: "I cannot give you back your shapes till the doom that is laid on you is ended, but come back now to the house that is mine and yours, White Children of my Heart."

Then Fionnuala answered him:

"The shadow of the woman who ensnared us lies on the threshold of your door: we cannot cross it."

And Lir said:

"The woman who ensnared you is far from any home this night. She is herself ensnared, and fierce winds drive her into all the restless places of the earth. She has lost her beauty and become terrible; she is a Demon of the Air, and must wander desolate to the end of time — but for you there is the firelight of home. Come back with me."

Then Conn said:

"May good fortune be on the threshold of your door from this time and for ever, but we cannot cross it, for we have the hearts of wild swans and we must fly in the dusk and feel the water moving under our bodies; we must hear the lonesome cries of the night. We have the voices only of the children you knew; we have the songs you taught us — that is all. Gold crowns are red in the fire-light, but redder and fairer is dawn."

Lir stretched out his hands and blessed his children. He said:

"May all beautiful things grow henceforth more beautiful to you, and may the song you have be melody in the heart of whoever hears it. May your wings winnow joy for you out of the air, and your feet be glad in the water-ways. My blessing be on you till the sea loses its saltness and the trees forget to bud in springtime. And farewell, Fionnuala, my white blossom; and farewell Aodh, that was the red flame of my heart; and farewell, Conn, that brought me gladness; and farewell, Fiacra, my treasure. Lonesome it is for you, flying far off in places strange to you; lonesome it is for me without you.

Bitter it is to say farewell, and farewell, and nothing else but farewell."

Lir covered his face with his mantle and sorrow was heavy on him, but the swans rose into the air and flew away calling to each other. They called with the voices of children, but in their heart was the gladness of swans when they feel the air beneath them and stretch their necks to the freedom of the sky.

Three hundred years they flew over Lake Darvra and swam on its waters. Often their father came to the lake and called them to him and caressed them; often their kinsfolk came to talk with them; often harpers and musicians came to listen to the wonder of their singing. When three hundred years were ended the swans rose suddenly and flew far and far away. Their father sought them, and their kinsfolk sought them, but the swans never touched earth or rested once till they came to the narrow Sea of the Moyle that flows between Ireland and Scotland. A cold stormy sea it was, and lonely. The swans had no one to listen to their singing, and little heart for singing amid the green curling bitter waves. The storm-wind beat roughly on them, and often they were separated and calling to one another without hope of an answer. Then Fionnuala, for she was the wisest, said:

"Let us choose a place of meeting, so that when we are separated and lost and wandering each one will know where to wait for the others."

The swans, her brothers, said it was a good thought; they agreed to meet together in one place, and the place they chose was Carraig-na-Ron, the Rock of the Seals. And it was well they made that choice, for a great storm came on them one night and scattered them far out over the sea. Their voices were drowned in the tempest and they were driven hither and thither in the darkness.

In the pale morning Fionnuala came to the Rock of the Seals. Her feathers were broken with the wind and draggled with the saltness of the sea and she was lamenting and calling on Aodh and Fiacra and Conn.

"O Conn, that I sheltered under my feathers, come to me! O Fiacra, come to me! O Aodh, Aodh, Aodh, come to me!"

And when she did not see them, and no voice answered, she made a sore lamentation and said:

"O bitter night that was blacker than the doom of Aoifa at the first to us! O three that I loved! O three that I loved! The waves are over your heads and I am desolate!"

She saw the red sun rising, and when the redness touched the waters, Conn came flying to her. His feathers were broken with the wind and draggled with the saltness of the sea. Fionnuala gathered him under her wings and comforted him, and she said:

"The day would not seem bitter to me now if only Aodh and Fiacra were come."

In a little while Fiacra came to her over the rough sea. She sheltered and comforted him with her wings, and she cried over the waters:

"O Aodh, Aodh, Aodh, come to me!"

The sun was high in the heavens when Aodh came, and he came with his feathers bright and shining and no trace of the bitter storm on him.

"O where have you been, Aodh?" said Fionnuala and Fiacra and Conn to him.

"I have been flying where I got sight of our kinsfolk. I have seen the white steeds that are swifter than the winds of March, and the riders that were comrades to us when we had our own shapes. I have seen both Aodh and Fergus, the two sons of Bove Dearg."

"O tell us, Aodh, where we may get sight of them!" said the swans.

"They are at the river mouth of the Bann," said Aodh. "Let us go there, and we may see them though we cannot leave the Moyle."

So much gladness came on all the swans that they forgot their weariness and the grievous buffeting of the storm and they rose and flew to the river mouth of the Bann. They saw their kinsfolk, the beautiful company of the Faery Host, shining with every colour under heaven and joyous as the wind in Springtime.

"O tell us, dear kinsfolk," said the swans, "how it is with our father?"

"The Great King has wrapped his robes of beauty about him, and feasts with those from whom age cannot take youth and light-heartedness," said Fergus.

"Ah," said Fionnuala, "he feasts and it is well with him! The joy-flame on his hearth cannot quench itself in ashes. He cannot hear us calling through the night — the wild swans, the wanderers, the lost children."

The Faery Host was troubled, seeing the piteous plight of the swans, but Aodh, that was a swan said to Fergus, his kinsman and comrade:

"Do not cloud your face for us, Fergus; the horse you ride is white, but I ride a whiter — the cold curling white wave of the sea."

Then Fiacra said:

"O Fergus, does my own white horse forget me, now that I am here in the cold Moyle?"

And Conn said:

"O Fergus, tell my two hounds that I will come back to them some day."

The memory of all beautiful things came on the swans, and they were sorrowful, and Fionnuala said:

"O beautiful comrades, I never thought that beauty could bring sorrow: now the sight of it breaks my heart," and she said to her brothers: "Let us go before our hearts are melted utterly."

The swans went over the Moyle then, and they were lamenting, and Fionnuala said:

"There is joy and feasting in the house of Lir to-night, but his four children are without a roof to cover them."

"It is a poor garment our feathers make when the wind blows through them: often we had the purple of kings' children on us.

"We are cold to-night, and it is a cold bed the sea makes: often we had beds of down with embroidered coverings.

"Often we drank mead from gold cups in the house of our father; now we have the bitterness of the sea and the harshness of sand in our mouths.

"It is weariness — O a great weariness — to be flying over the Moyle: without rest, without companions, without comfort.

"I am thinking of Angus to-night: he has the laughter of joy about him for ever.

"I am thinking to-night of Mananaun, and of white blossoms on silver branches.

"O swans, my brothers, I am thinking of

beauty, and we are flying away from it for ever."

The swans did not see the company of the Faery Host again. They swam on the cold stormy sea of the Moyle, and they were there till three hundred years were ended.

"It is time for us to go," said Fionnuala, "we must seek the Western Sea."

The swans shook the water of the Moyle from their feathers and stretched out their wings to fly.

When they were come to the Western Sea there was sorrow on them, for the sea was wilder and colder and more terrible than the Moyle. The swans were on that sea and flying over it for three hundred years, and all that time they had no comfort, and never once did they hear the foot-fall of hound or horse or see their faery kinsfolk.

When the time was ended, the swans rose out of the water and cried joyfully to each other: "Let us go home now, the time is ended!"

They flew swiftly, and yet they were all day flying before they came to the place where Lir had his dwelling; when they looked down they saw no light in the house, they heard no music, no sound of voices. The many-coloured house was desolate and all the beauty was gone from it; the white hounds and the bright-maned horses were gone, and all the beautiful glad-hearted folk of the Sidhe.

"Every place is dark to us!" said Conn. "Look at the hills!"

The swans looked at the hills they had known, and every hill and mountain they could see was dark and sorrowful: not one had a star-heart of light, not one had a flame-crown, not one had music pulsing through it like a great breath.

"O Aodh, and Conn, and Fiacra," said Fionnuala, "beauty is gone from the earth: we have no home now!"

The swans hid themselves in the long dank grass, till morning. They did not speak to each other; they did not make a lamentation; they were silent with heaviness of grief. When they felt the light of morning they rose in the air and flew in wide circles seeking their kinsfolk. They saw the dwellings of strangers, and a strange people tending flocks

and sowing corn on plains where the Tuatha De Danaan had hunted white stags with horns of silver.

"The grief of all griefs has come upon us!" said Fionnuala. "It is no matter now whether we have the green earth under us or bitter sea-waves: it is little to us now that we are in swans' bodies."

Her brothers had no words to answer her; they were dumb with grief till Aodh said:

"Let us fly far from the desolate house and the dead hills. Let us go where we can hear the thunder of the Western Sea."

The swans spread their wings and flew westward till they came to a little reedy lake, and they alit there and sheltered themselves, for they had no heart to go farther.

They took no notice of the days and often they did not know whether it was the moon or the sun that was in the sky, but they sang to each other, and that was all the comfort they had.

One day, while Fionnuala was singing, a man of the stranger-race drew near to listen. He had the aspect of one who had endured much hardship. His garments were poor and ragged. His hair was bleached by sun and rain. As he listened to the song a light came into his eyes and his whole face grew beautiful. When the song ended he bowed himself before the swans and said:

"White Swans of the Wilderness, ye have flown over many lands. Tell me, have ye seen aught of Tir-nan-Oge, where no one loses youth; or Tir-na-Moe, where all that is beautiful lives for ever; or Moy-Mell, that is so honey-sweet with blossom?"

"Have we seen Tir-nan-Oge? It is our own country! We are the children of Lir the King of it."

"Where is that country? How may one reach it? Tell me!"

"Ochone! It is not anywhere on the ridge of the world. Our father's house is desolate!"

"Ye are lying, to make sport for yourselves! Tir-nan-Oge cannot perish — rather would the whole world fall to ruin!"

"O would we had anything but the bitterness of truth on our tongues!" said Aodh. "Would we could see even one leaf from those trees with shining branches where the many-coloured birds used to sing! Ochone!

Ochone! for all the beauty that has perished with Tir-nan-Oge!"

The stranger cried out a loud sorrowful cry and threw himself on the ground. His fingers tore at the roots of the grass. His body writhed and trembled with grief.

The children of Lir wondered at him, and Aodh said:

"Put away this fierceness of grief and take consolation to yourself. We, with so much heavier sorrow, have not lamented after this fashion."

The stranger raised himself: his eyes blazed like the eyes of a hunted animal when it turns on the hunters.

"How could your sorrow be equal to mine? Ye have dwelt in Tir-nan-Oge; ye have ridden horses whiter than the snow of one night and swifter than the storm-wind; ye have gathered flowers in the Plain of Honey. But I have never seen it — never once! Look at me! I was born a king! I have become an outcast, the laughing stock of slaves! I am Aibric the wanderer! — I have given all — all, for the hope of finding that country. It is gone now — it is not anywhere on the round of the world!"

"Stay with us," said Fiacra, "and we will sing for you, and tell you stories of Tir-nan-Oge."

"I cannot stay with you! I cannot listen to your songs! I must go on seeking; seeking; seeking while I live. When I am dead my dreams will not torment me. I shall have my fill of quietness then."

"Can you not believe us when we tell you that Tir-nan-Oge is gone like the white mists of morning? It is nowhere."

"It is in my heart, and in my mind, and in my soul! It burns like fire! It drives me like a tireless wind! I am going. Farewell!"

"Stay!" cried Aodh, "we will go with you. There is nothing anywhere for us now but brown earth and drifting clouds and wan waters. Why should we not go from place to place as the wind goes, and see each day new fields of reeds, new forest trees, new mountains? O, we shall never see the star-heart in any mountain again!"

"The mountains are dead," said Conn.

"The mountains are not dead," said Aibric. "They are dark and silent, but they are not dead. I know. I have cried to them in the night and laid my forehead against theirs and felt the beating of their mighty hearts. They are wiser than the wisest druid, more tender than the tenderest mother. It is they who keep the world alive."

"O," said Fionnuala, "if the mountains are indeed alive let us go to them; let us tell them our sorrowful story. They will pity us and we shall not be utterly desolate."

Aibric and the swans journeyed together, and at dusk they came to a tall beautiful mountain — the mountain that is called Nephin, in the West. It looked dark and sombre against the fading sky, and the sight of it, discrowned and silent, struck chill to the hearts of the wild swans: they turned away their heads to hide the tears in their eyes. But Aibric stretched his hands to the mountains and cried out:

"O beautiful glorious Comrade, pity us! Tir-nan-Oge is no more, and Moy-Mell is lost for ever! Welcome the children of Lir, for we have nothing left but you and the earth of Ireland!"

Then a wonder happened.

The star-heart of Nephin shone out — magnificent — tremulous — coloured like a pale amethyst.

The swans cried out to each other:

"The mountain is alive! Beauty has come again to the earth! Aibric, you have given us back the Land of Youth!"

A delicate faery music trembled and died away and was born again in the still evening air, and more and more the radiance deepened in the heart of Nephin. The swans began to sing most sweetly and joyously, and at the sound of that singing the star-heart showed in mountain after mountain till every mountain in Ireland pulsed and shone.

"Crown yourselves, mountains!" said Aodh, "that we may know the De Danaans are still alive and Lir's house is builded now where old age cannot wither it!"

The mountains sent up great jewelled rays of light so that each one was crowned with a rainbow; and when the Children of Lir saw that splendour they had no more thought of the years they had spent over dark troublous waters, and they said to each other:

"Would we could hear the sound of the

little bell that rings for prayers, and feel our swan-bodies fall from us!"

"I know the sound of a bell that rings for prayers," said Aibric, "and I will bring you where you can hear it. I will bring you to Saint Kemoc and you will hear the sound of his bell."

"Let us go," said the swans, and Aibric brought them to the Saint. The Saint held up his hands and blessed God when he saw them, and he besought them to remain a while and to tell him the story of their wanderings. He brought them into his little church and they were there with him in peace and happiness relating to him the wonders of the Land of Youth. It came to pass then that word reached the wife of King Largnen concerning the swans: she asked the king to get them for her, and because she demanded them with vehemence, the king journeyed to the Church of Saint Kemoc to get the swans.

When he was come, Saint Kemoc refused to give him the swans and Largnen forced

his way into the church to take them. Now, he was a king of the North, and his wife was a queen of the South, and it was ordained that such a king should put an end to the power of Aoifa's spell. He came to the altar, and the swans were close to it. He put his hands on the swans to take them by force. When he touched them the swan-feathers dwindled and shrivelled and became as fine dust, and the bodies of Lir's children became as a handful of dust, but their spirits attained to freedom and joined their kinsfolk in the Land-of-the-Ever-Living.

It was Aibric who remembered the story of the children of Lir, because he loved them. He told the story to the people of Ireland, and they were so fond of the story and had such pity for Lir's children that they made a law that no one was to hurt a wild swan, and when they saw a swan flying they would say:

"My blessing with you, white swan, for the sake of Lir's children!"

SCOTLAND

The Faery Flag of Dunvegan[1]

For centuries Dunvegan Castle has been the ancestral home of the chiefs of the MacLeod clan. In folklore, the castle is famous for its Faery Flag, now a tattered remnant of faded silk with "elf-spots" in red stitching. It can be seen today preserved under glass in the drawing-room of the castle, with the following inscription, "Given by the fairies to Ian, 4th Chief, about 1380. It brought victory to the Clan at the battle of Glendale in 1490,

[1] From Scottish Folk-Tales and Legends, retold by Barbara Ker Wilson (Oxford University Press, 1954).

and at the battle of the Wall, Trumpan (Waternish) in 1580."

For over a thousand years, Dunvegan Castle, which stands in the west of Skye, has been the home of the MacLeods of MacLeod. Across the waters of Loch Dunvegan, many chieftains have gone forth in times now passed to lead the clansmen against their hereditary enemies, the MacDonalds of Eigg, who were long known as the lawless Lords of the Isles. And perhaps the most treasured possession of the Clan MacLeod is the Faery Flag, which has been passed on from generation to generation until the story of its origin has become a famous legend.

In far distant ages there was once a chief of the Clan MacLeod who was called Malcolm. On a day when the waters of Loch Dunvegan reflected a summer sky, and the heather splashed its glorious purple over the hills, he took a fair lady of the faery folk to be his bride; and for a little while he and his faery wife dwelt peacefully together in the grey Castle of Dunvegan. But the faery folk could never find perfect happiness in the land of men; and when she had borne a fine son to her lord, Malcolm's fair lady felt a great longing to rejoin her own people; a longing far stronger than the love she had for her mortal husband. And because he could not bear to see his beloved wife unhappy, Malcolm said that he would himself escort her upon the path that led back to her own country. So it happened that this faery woman took fond leave of her tiny child as he lay in his cradle, and went with her husband across the Loch to take the road that would lead her home once more.

And although it was just such a bright summer's day as that on which he had first brought her to the castle as his bride, yet it seemed to Malcolm that the waters of the Loch were dark and dowly, so heavy was the grief that lay upon him. When they came to the far shore, he carried his lady from the boat in his arms, and gently set her upon the ground. Then he accompanied her a little upon her way; but when they reached the span of grey stones that was known as the Faery Bridge, she bade him come no farther, and went on her path alone. Never a backward look she gave; and Malcolm saw his fair wife no more.

Now that very night a great feast was held in the hall of the castle, to celebrate the birth of Malcolm's son, who would one day succeed his noble father as Chief of the Clan MacLeod. And heavy-hearted as he was, Malcolm had perforce to join in the rejoicing and revelry, for this feast was held by ancient tradition. Besides, he himself felt a great pride in his child, destined to be the future MacLeod of MacLeod.

Many clansmen filled the great hall, which blazed with the light of a hundred torches; and the castle servants ran to and fro bearing platters heaped high with succulent venison and flasks full of the good golden ale. And throughout the night the brave pibroch sounded as the men of the Clan MacCrimmon, hereditary pipers to the Clan MacLeod, played stirring music for Malcolm's guests.

In a turret far removed from the noisy gathering in the great hall, the babe who was the cause of all this rejoicing lay quietly asleep in his cradle. His nurse sat beside him as he slept, imagining to herself the cheerful company and the good cheer that would be filling the hall. She was but a girl, young and comely; and as the moon rose high and shone into the solitary turret, a great desire came upon her to take just one peep at the gay revelry. She glanced at the sleeping child; and it seemed that he lay quiet and tranquil enough. So she rose softly to her feet and tiptoed across the rush-strewn floor. Then she fled swiftly along the twisting, moonlit passage-ways and down the winding steps until the skirl of the pipes beat full upon her ears and she came into the great hall. For a while she sat at the far end of the hall, intent on the gaiety and merriment all around her; and when she had feasted her eyes enough, she got up again and prepared to go back to the turret. But as she rose to go, a sudden fear set her heart lurching. For Malcolm himself rose up from his place at the high table and looked in her direction.

"Oh, black the moment that ever I thought to leave the bairn alone," she thought, "for the anger of MacLeod will surely be raised against me."

But although Malcolm had indeed fixed his gaze on her, it did not occur to him that she had done wrong in joining the feasting; for he supposed that she would have left the child in the care of some other servant while she was away from his side. So he called out to her in a voice that had no anger in it, and commanded her to fetch his son before all the company, that he might show the clansmen their future chief.

Trembling with relief, the nurse slipped away to do his bidding, hoping earnestly in her heart that no harm had come to the child in her absence.

Now after the babe had been left alone in the turret, he had slept on for a while in peace. But soon an owl flew past outside with a weird screech, and this disturbed the child, so that he woke in fright. When no one came to comfort him and rock him to sleep again, he started crying; and the sound echoed forlornly through the deserted room.

But though no human ears heard his crying, in a manner unknown to men it reached the hearing of his faery mother as she dwelt in the midst of her own Fair Folk. And dear as her earth-born child was to her heart, by eldritch means she hastened to be beside him and comfort him when no one else was near. She might not take him in her arms; but instead she spread over him a shining faery covering of grass-green silk, embroidered with elf spots and wrought with unearthly skill. As soon as the child felt this faery covering, which brought the comfort of a mother's embrace, he stopped his crying and smiled a little as he settled down to sleep again. And seeing her babe so peaceful and serene, his mother went from his side.

When the child's anxious nurse came back to the turret, she was thankful beyond speech to see how peaceful her young charge lay. But when she saw the covering that lay over him, she was aware that faery folk had been beside him; for she knew the faeries' own green hue, and she recognized the elf spots embroidered on the silk. Yet the bairn himself had taken no harm; and as she sent up a prayer of thankfulness that it was not some changeling child she had discovered lying there, she vowed never again to leave him alone.

Then she took the child in her arms, still wrapped in his faery covering, and bore him to the great hall, according to MacLeod's command. As she neared the feasting and revelry, a sound of enchanted music swept along the passage-ways behind her. It filled the air and hovered over the child in her arms, drowning the sound of the MacCrimmons' pipes, whose pibroch died away as everyone in the great hall fell silent in amazement. And as MacLeod and all his clansmen sat listening, they heard the sweet voices of a faery host chanting the legend that was to be remembered as long as there was a man living to bear the name MacLeod.

They sang that the child's green covering was a faery flag, the gift of the Little People to the Clan MacLeod, to remain in their possession so long as that great name was known in Scotland. And they foretold that the waving of the flag would save the Clan in the midst of three great dangers; but that on no account was it ever to be waved for a trivial reason.

Then, as Malcolm and the clansmen listened, motionless, and the nurse still clasped the babe in her arms, the faery voices changed. On a lower and more sombre note they prophesied the curse that would fall upon the Clan MacLeod if ever they disregarded the true value of their faery gift, and waved the flag at a time other than that of dire necessity.

For then it would come to pass that three dreadful events would follow the waving of the flag, in whatever age or century it might take place. The heir to MacLeod of MacLeod would shortly die; the group of rocks at Dunvegan which were called the Three Maidens would fall into the hands of a Campbell; and at a time when a red fox brought forth her young in a turret of the castle, the glory of the MacLeods would depart, they would lose a great part of their lands, and there would not be sufficient men left in the Chief's own family to row a boat over Loch Dunvegan.

The Little People had bequeathed their gift and pronounced the curse that attended it; and their voices died away as a mist dissolves on the hill-side, until there was not a wisp nor a whisper left.

Then Malcolm rose from his place, and took the faery flag from about his son. Carefully he smoothed its green folds and gave instructions that it should be placed in an iron casket of fine workmanship, that would henceforth be borne at the head of the clansmen whenever they went to do battle. And he decreed that none but MacLeod of MacLeod himself should ever take out the flag, to unfurl it and wave it aloft.

In time, Malcolm departed from this earth, and his son after him. And generations passed by, with the faery flag still safely in the keeping of the clan, until there came a day when the MacDonalds came in great force against the MacLeods. For the old enmity of the two clans still raged fiercely, although there was many a marriage between a MacLeod and a MacDonald. Indeed, it is said of them that they were constantly putting rings on each other's fingers, and dirks into each other's hearts. On this occasion the MacDonalds were determined to humble the pride of the MacLeods for ever, and after landing at Waternish, they advanced to Trumpan and sacked the church there.

Meanwhile, the Chief of MacLeod had rowed across Loch Dunvegan to lead his clansmen against the MacDonalds; and at Trumpan a battle took place that raged long and hotly. At length, however, it was clear that the MacLeods, hard-pressed, were being forced to give ground to the MacDonalds; and it was obvious that to overcome the invaders they must rely on a strength other than that of the claymore and the dirk.

It was then that the Chief of MacLeod called for the iron casket that held the faery flag. He undid the clasps and lifted out the frail square of green silk, thinking to himself that surely it was for no trivial reason he now called on the faery power. In the midst of the battle the flag was held aloft in the sight of all the clansmen, who watched in awe as it unfurled and waved above them.

Immediately, there was a change in the fortune of the fight, for it seemed to the MacDonalds that the MacLeod forces had suddenly become reinforced, and were swelled in strength. Thinking themselves outnumbered, they faltered and fell back, and the MacLeods pressed home their advantage and carried the day in triumph. This was the first occasion on which the power of the faery flag was invoked and proven.

The cause of the second unfurling of the flag was of a different nature. Once again the fortunes of the clan were threatened; but not by an enemy who wielded a claymore or hurled a dirk. A plague fell upon their cattle, until there was scarcely a beast left that was untouched by the murrain. The clansmen were overcome with great hardship, for upon their cattle depended the greater part of their livelihood and welfare. When the Chief of MacLeod saw the distress that

had fallen on his people, and realized how few beasts were left in the pastures, he knew that if the prosperity of the clan were to be restored, he must call on a power beyond human strength. So he brought forth the faery flag from its iron casket, and he said, as his ancestor had said before him:

"Now surely it is for no trivial reason that I call on the faery power."

Then the flag was raised aloft, and it unfurled and waved over the stricken land. From that moment, not another beast was touched by the plague, and many on whom the murrain had already descended, recovered. And this was the second occasion on which the power of the faery flag was invoked and proven.

Time passed, and the faery flag was handed from Chief to Chief as the generations went by. In the year 1799 a man called Buchanan was employed as factor to MacLeod of MacLeod. Now like everyone else, he had learnt the legend of the faery flag, and knew also of the curse — as yet unfulfilled — that attended it. But he was a sceptical man, and scorned to put his belief in any superstitious fancy. He declared that the flag was no more than a square of rotting silk, and the legend merely a tale that old wives whispered to each other.

One day, at a time when the MacLeod himself was away from Dunvegan, Buchanan decided to test the curse for himself, and explode once for all the superstitions that hung about the flag. There was an English blacksmith in the village; and it was he whom Buchanan employed to force open the iron casket containing the flag; for the key to the casket was always in the possession of the Chief. When the lid was up, he took out the frail green square and waved it in the air. And surely no man could have thought of a more trivial reason for invoking the faery power.

To those who had never doubted the strength of the faery curse, the events that followed appeared inevitable. In a short while, the heir to MacLeod was blown up in H.M.S. *Charlotte,* and the Maidens were sold to Angus Campbell of Esnay. And it came to pass, exactly as the faery voices had foretold so long ago, that a tame fox belonging to a Lieutenant Maclean, who was staying in Dunvegan Castle, brought forth her young in the west turret; and at this time the MacLeod fortunes began to decline, and a great part of their estates was sold. Although the prosperity of the clan was gradually retrieved, much of its glory vanished for ever; and there was a time not long distant when there were only three MacLeods

left in the Chief's own family: not sufficient to row a four-oared boat over Loch Dunvegan.

Today the faery flag remains in a glass case in Dunvegan Castle; and all who know its strange history stop to wonder at this threadbare piece of ancient silk, brown with age, on which the embroidered elf spots may still be discerned.

SPAIN

The Flea [1]

&§ *The helpful animals of folklore! They are myriad in every culture. In this Spanish tale, the ant, the beetle, and the mouse make possible the shepherd's winning of the princess. However, this story takes an unprecedented turn, for if the princess will have none of the shepherd, by the same token he will have none of her, preferring to take his treasure and return to the mountains, to marry one of his own kind.*

The artful hand of a fine storyteller is perceptible in this version. Ruth Sawyer is a distinguished collector of tales as well as a teller of them, and her mastery of the written word as well as of the spoken is responsible for the sure dramatic development of the plot, and the flavor of locale and custom.

Once there was and was not a King of Spain. He loved to laugh; he loved a good joke as well as any common fellow. Best of all he loved a riddle.

One day he was being dressed by his chamberlain. As the royal doublet was be-

[1] From Ruth Sawyer, *Picture Tales from Spain* (Lippincott, 1936).

ing slipped over the royal head, a flea jumped from the safe hiding-place of the stiff lace ruff. He landed directly upon the King.

Quicker than half a wink the King clapped his hand over the flea and began to laugh. "*Por Dios*, a flea! Who ever heard of a King of Spain having a flea? It is monstrous — it is delicious! We must not treat her lightly, this flea. You perceive, My Lord Chamberlain, that having jumped on the royal person, she has now become a royal flea. Consider what we shall do with her."

But the chamberlain was a man of little wit. He could clothe the King's body but he could not add one ribbon or one button to the King's imagination. "I have it!" said the King at last, exploding again into laughter. "We will pasture out this flea — in a great cage — large enough for a goat — an ox — an elephant. She shall be fed enormously. When she is of a proper size I will have her killed and her skin made into a tambourine. The Infanta, my daughter, shall dance to it. We will make a fine riddle out of it. Whichever suitor that comes courting her who can answer the riddle shall marry with her. *There* is a royal joke worthy of a

King! Eh, my Lord Chamberlain? And we will call the flea Felipa."

In his secret heart the chamberlain thought the King quite mad; but all he answered was: "Very good, Your Majesty," and went out to see that proper pasturage was provided for Felipa.

At the end of a fortnight the flea was as large as a rat. At the end of a month she was as large as a cat who might have eaten that rat. At the end of a second month she was the size of a dog who might have chased that cat. At the end of three months she was the size of a calf.

The King orderd Felipa killed. The skin was stretched, dried, beaten until it was as soft, as fine, as silk. Then it was made into a tambourine, with brass clappers and ribbons — the finest tambourine in all of Spain.

The Infanta, whose name was Isabel, but who was called Belita for convenience, learned to dance with Felipa very prettily; and the King himself composed a rhyme to go with the riddle. Whenever a suitor came courting, the Infanta would dance and when she had finished, the King would recite:

> "Belita — Felipa — they dance well together —
> Belita — Felipa; now answer me whether
> You know this Felipa — this *animalita*.
> If you answer right, then you marry Belita."

Princes and dukes came from Spain and Portugal, France and Italy. They were not dull-witted like the chamberlain and they saw through the joke. The King was riddling about the tambourine. It was made from parchment and they knew perfectly well where parchment came from. So a prince would answer: "A goat, Your Majesty." And a duke would answer: "A sheep, Your Majesty" — each sure he was right. And the Infanta would run away laughing and the King would roar with delight and shout: "Wrong again!"

But after a while the King got tired of this sheep and goat business. He wanted the riddle guessed; he wanted the Infanta married. So he sent forth a command that the next suitor who failed to guess the riddle should be hung — and short work made of it, too.

That put a stop to the princes and dukes. But far up in the Castilian highlands a shepherd heard about it. He was young, but not very clever. He thought — it would be a fine thing for a shepherd to marry an Infanta, so he said to his younger brother: "Manuelito — you shall mind the sheep and goats; I will go to the King's palace."

But his mother said: "Son, you are a *tonto*. How should you guess a riddle when you cannot read or write, and those who can have failed? Stay at home and save yourself a hanging."

Having once made up his mind, nothing would stop him — not even fear. So his mother baked him a *tortilla* to carry with him, gave him her blessing and let him go.

He hadn't gone far when he was stopped by a little black ant. "Señor Pastor," she cried, "give me a ride to the King's court in your pocket."

"La Hormiguita, you cannot ride in my pocket. There is a *tortilla* there which I shall have for my breakfast. Your feet are dirty from walking, and you will tramp all over it."

"See, I will dust off my feet on the grass here and promise not to step once on the *tortilla*."

So the shepherd put the ant into his shepherd pouch and tramped on. Soon he encountered a black beetle who said: "Señor Pastor — give me a ride to the King's court in your pocket."

"El Escarabajo, you cannot ride in my pouch. There is a *tortilla* there which I shall presently have for my breakfast — and who wants a black beetle tramping all over his breakfast!"

"I will fasten my claws into the side of your pouch and not go near the *tortilla*."

So the shepherd took up the beetle and carried him along. He hadn't gone far when he came up with a little gray mouse who cried: "Señor Pastor, give me a ride to the King's court in your pouch."

But the shepherd shook his head. "Ratonperez, you are too clumsy and I don't like the flavor of your breath. It will spoil my *tortilla* that I intend to have for my breakfast."

"Why not eat the *tortilla* now and then

the breakfast will be over and done with," and Ratonperez said it so gently, so coaxingly, that the shepherd thought it was a splendid idea. He sat down and ate it. He gave a little crumb to La Hormiguita, a crumb to El Escarabajo and a big crumb to Ratonperez. Then he went on his road to the King's court carrying the three creatures with him in his pouch.

When he reached the King's palace he was frightened, frightened. He sat himself down under a cork tree to wait for his courage to grow.

"What are you waiting for?" called the ant, the beetle and Ratonperez all together.

"I go to answer a riddle. If I fail I shall be hanged. That isn't so pleasant. So I wait where I can enjoy being alive for a little moment longer."

"What is the riddle?"

"I have heard that it has to do with something called Felipa that dances, whoever she may be."

"Go on and we will help you. Hurry, hurry, it is hot in your pouch."

So the shepherd climbed the palace steps, asked for the King and said that he had come to answer the riddle.

The guard passed him on to the footman, saying, *"Pobrecito!"*

The footman passed him on to the lackey, saying, *"Pobrecito!"*

The lackey passed him on to the court chamberlain, saying, *"Pobrecito!"* And it was his business to present him to the King.

The King shook his head when he saw the shepherd-staff in his hand and the shepherd-pouch hanging from his belt, and he said: "A shepherd's life is better than no life at all. Better go back to your flocks."

But the shepherd was as rich in stubbornness as he was poor in learning. He insisted he must answer the riddle. So the Infanta came and danced with the tambourine and the King laughed and said his rhyme:

> "Belita — Felipa — they dance well together —
> Belita — Felipa; now answer me whether
> You know this Felipa — this *animalita*.
> If you answer right, then you marry Belita."

The shepherd strode over and took the tambourine from the hand of the Infanta.

He felt the skin carefully, carefully. To himself he said: "I know sheep and I know goats; and it isn't either."

"Can't you guess?" whispered the black beetle from his pouch.

"No," said the shepherd.

"Let me out," said the little ant; "perhaps I can tell you what it is." So the shepherd unfastened the pouch and La Hormiguita crawled out, unseen by the court. She crawled all over the tambourine and came back whispering, "You can't fool me. I'd know a flea anywhere, any size."

"Don't take all day," shouted the King. "Who is Felipa?"

"She's a flea," said the shepherd.

Then the court was in a flutter.

"I don't want to marry a shepherd," said the Infanta.

"You shan't," said the King.

"I'm the one to say 'shan't'," said the shepherd.

"I will grant you any other favor," said the Infanta.

"I will grant you another," said the King.

"It was a long journey here, walking," said the shepherd. "I would like a cart to ride home in."

"And two oxen to draw it," whispered the black beetle.

"And two oxen to draw it," repeated the shepherd.

"You shall have them," said the King.

"And what shall I give you?" asked the Infanta.

"Tell her you want your pouch filled with gold," whispered Ratonperez.

"That's little enough," said the Infanta.

But while the royal groom was fetching the cart and oxen; and the lord of the exchequer was fetching a bag of gold; Ratonperez was gnawing a hole in the pouch. When they came to pour in the gold, it fell through as fast as water, so that all around the feet of the shepherd it rose like a shining yellow stream.

"That's a lot of gold," said the King at last.

"It's enough," said the shepherd. He took his cart, filled it with the gold, drove back to the highlands of Castile. He married a shepherd's daughter, who never had to do anything but sit in a rocking-chair and fan herself all day. And that's a contented life, you might say — for anyone who likes it.

The Tinker and the Ghost [2]

A well-known folklore scholar and a distinguished storyteller combine talents in this superb ghost story. Ralph Boggs discovered the story in Spain. There are several widespread motifs here, the re-assembling of the ghost, member by member — legs, trunk, arms, and head — and the return from the dead to pay a debt. The folklore of Spain and Latin America shows the influence of the Church upon folklore sources. This tale is no exception. The second author, Mary Gould Davis, was formerly Supervisor of Storytelling in the New York Public Library. The storyteller's ear for dialogue, the eye for detail, are apparent here. Note the shades of difference in the repeated descriptions of the eggs cooking — six incidents of frying eggs and bacon, each told with an element of individuality. This device aids the storyteller in learning the story, and prevents the necessary repetition of fact from seeming monotonous.

On the wide plain not far from the city of Toledo there once stood a great gray Castle. For many years before this story begins no one had dwelt there, because the Castle was haunted. There was no living soul within its walls, and yet on almost every night in the year a thin, sad voice moaned and wept and wailed through the huge, empty rooms. And on All Hallows' Eve a ghostly light appeared in the chimney, a light that flared and died and flared again against the dark sky.

Learned doctors and brave adventurers had tried to exorcise the ghost. And the next morning they had been found in the great hall of the Castle, sitting lifeless before the empty fireplace.

Now one day in late October there came to the little village that nestled around the

[2] From Ralph Steele Boggs and Mary Gould Davis, *Three Golden Oranges and Other Spanish Folk Tales* (Longmans, Green, 1936).

Castle walls a brave and jolly tinker whose name was Esteban. And while he sat in the market place mending the pots and pans the good wives told him about the haunted Castle. It was All Hallows' Eve, they said, and if he would wait until nightfall he could see the strange, ghostly light flare up from the chimney. He might, if he dared go near enough, hear the thin, sad voice echo through the silent rooms.

"If I dare!" Esteban repeated scornfully. "You must know, good wives, that I — Esteban — fear nothing, neither ghost nor human. I will gladly sleep in the Castle tonight, and keep this dismal spirit company."

The good wives looked at him in amazement. Did Esteban know that if he succeeded in banishing the ghost the owner of the Castle would give him a thousand gold reales?

Esteban chuckled. If that was how matters stood, he would go to the Castle at nightfall and do his best to get rid of the thing that haunted it. But he was a man who liked plenty to eat and drink and a fire to keep him company. They must bring to him a load of faggots, a side of bacon, a flask of wine, a dozen fresh eggs and a frying pan. This the good wives gladly did. And as the dusk fell, Esteban loaded these things on the donkey's back and set out for the Castle. And you may be very sure that not one of the village people went very far along the way with him!

It was a dark night with a chill wind blowing and a hint of rain in the air. Esteban unsaddled his donkey and set him to graze on the short grass of the deserted courtyard. Then he carried his food and his faggots into the great hall. It was dark as pitch there. Bats beat their soft wings in his face, and the air felt cold and musty. He lost no time in piling some of his faggots in one corner of the huge stone fireplace and in lighting them. As the red and golden flames leaped up the chimney Esteban rubbed his hands. Then he settled himself comfortably on the hearth.

"*That* is the thing to keep off both cold and fear," he said.

Carefully slicing some bacon he laid it in the pan and set it over the flames. How good it smelled! And how cheerful the sound of its crisp sizzling!

He had just lifted his flask to take a deep drink of the good wine when down the chimney there came a voice — a thin, sad voice — and *"Oh me!"* it wailed, *"Oh me! Oh me!"*

Esteban swallowed the wine and set the flask carefully down beside him.

"Not a very cheerful greeting, my friend," he said, as he moved the bacon on the pan so that it should be equally brown in all its parts. "But bearable to a man who is used to the braying of his donkey."

And *"Oh me!"* sobbed the voice. *"Oh me! Oh me!"*

Esteban lifted the bacon carefully from the hot fat and laid it on a bit of brown paper to drain. Then he broke an egg into the frying pan. As he gently shook the pan so that the edges of his egg should be crisp and brown and the yolk soft, the voice came again. Only this time it was shrill and frightened.

"Look out below," it called. *"I'm falling."*

"All right," answered Esteban, "only don't fall into the frying pan."

With that there was a thump, and there on the hearth lay a man's leg! It was a good leg enough and it was clothed in the half of a pair of brown corduroy trousers.

Esteban ate his egg, a piece of bacon and drank again from the flask of wine. The wind howled around the Castle and the rain beat against the windows.

Then, *"Look out below,"* called the voice sharply. *"I'm falling!"*

There was a thump, and on the hearth there lay a second leg, just like the first!

Esteban moved it away from the fire and piled on more faggots. Then he warmed the fat in the frying pan and broke into it a second egg.

And, *"Look out below!"* roared the voice. And now it was no longer thin, but strong and lusty. *"Look out below! I'm falling!"*

"Fall away," Esteban answered cheerfully. "Only don't spill my egg."

There was a thump, heavier than the first two, and on the hearth there lay a trunk. It was clothed in a blue shirt and a brown corduroy coat.

Esteban was eating his third egg and the last of the cooked bacon when the voice called again, and down fell first one arm and then the other.

"Now," thought Esteban, as he put the frying pan on the fire and began to cook more bacon. "Now there is only the head. I confess that I am rather curious to see the head."

And: "LOOK OUT BELOW!" thundered the voice. "I'M FALLING — FALLING!"

And down the chimney there came tumbling a head!

It was a good head enough, with thick black hair, a long black beard and dark eyes that looked a little strained and anxious. Esteban's bacon was only half cooked. Nevertheless, he removed the pan from the fire and laid it on the hearth. And it is a good thing that he did, because before his eyes the parts of the body joined together, and a living man — or his ghost — stood before him! And *that* was a sight that might have startled Esteban into burning his fingers with the bacon fat.

"Good evening," said Esteban. "Will you have an egg and a bit of bacon?"

"No, I want no food," the ghost answered. "But I will tell you this, right here and now. You are the only man, out of all those who have come to the Castle, to stay here until I could get my body together again. The others died of sheer fright before I was half finished."

"That is because they did not have sense enough to bring food and fire with them," Esteban replied coolly. And he turned back to his frying pan.

"Wait a minute!" pleaded the ghost. "If you will help me a bit more, you will save my soul and get me into the Kingdom of Heaven. Out in the courtyard, under a cypress tree, there are buried three bags — one of copper coins, one of silver coins, and one of gold coins. I stole them from some thieves and brought them here to the Castle to hide. But no sooner did I have them buried than the thieves overtook me, murdered me and cut my body into pieces. But they did not find the coins. Now you come with me and dig them up. Give the copper coins to the Church, the silver coins to the poor, and keep the gold coins for yourself. Then I will have expiated my sins and can go to the Kingdom of Heaven."

This suited Esteban. So he went out into the courtyard with the ghost. And you should have heard how the donkey brayed when he saw them!

When they reached the cypress tree in a corner of the courtyard: "Dig," said the ghost.

"Dig yourself," answered Esteban.

So the ghost dug, and after a time the three bags of money appeared.

"Now will you promise to do just what I asked you to do?" asked the ghost.

"Yes, I promise," Esteban answered.

"Then," said the Ghost, "strip my garments from me."

This Esteban did, and instantly the ghost disappeared, leaving his clothes lying there on the short grass of the courtyard. It went straight up to Heaven and knocked on the Gate. St. Peter opened it, and when the spirit explained that he had expiated his sins, gave him a cordial welcome.

Esteban carried the coins into the great hall of the castle, fried and ate another egg and then went peacefully to sleep before the fire.

The next morning when the village people came to carry away Esteban's body, they found him making an omelette out of the last of the fresh eggs.

"Are you alive?" they gasped.

"I am," Esteban answered. "And the food and the faggots lasted through very nicely. Now I will go to the owner of the Castle and collect my thousand gold *reales*. The ghost has gone for good and all. You will find his clothes lying out in the courtyard.

And before their astonished eyes he loaded the bags of coins on the donkey's back and departed.

First he collected the thousand gold *reales* from the grateful lord of the Castle. Then he returned to Toledo, gave the copper coins to the *cura* of his church, and faithfully distributed the silver ones among the poor. And on the thousand *reales* and the golden coins he lived in idleness and a great contentment for many years.

The General's Horse [3]

The character of the beneficent pig, Padre Porko, in Spanish folklore presents an interesting series of conjectures. Where did he come from? For the pig is somehow not indigenous to Spain, as he would seem to be to England or Ireland, where he is the most important domestic animal. He came apparently from a time earlier than the Moors, even earlier than the Romans and the Visigoths. L. R. Muirhead, in his guide book Southern Spain and Portugal *(Macmillan, 1929), describes early stone carvings which depict the pig. He suggests that these carvings stem from the original Iberic stock, which was Celtic, in a time which predates Moors and Romans.*

Padre Porko is thoroughly Spanish now, whatever his origin. Señor Don Padre Porko! The special friend of orphans and animals, a benevolent spirit, to whom people entrust their hope of good fortune. "We'll leave it to Padre Porko," they say. Robert Davis, a gifted American newspaper correspondent, had these tales direct from the mouth of a native storyteller, during an assignment in Spain. The book from which this story is taken is one of the most endearing in format, with its definitive illustrations by Fritz Eichenberg.

It was a misty-moisty evening. The drops of rain fell from the tips of the leaves, with a "plop," into the puddles underneath. The wind blew the branches of the umbrella pine against the windows of the Padre's house. It was the sort of weather when no person or animal was willingly out-of-doors. The honest creatures of the air, the forest and the earth had long been asleep.

The Widow Hedge-Hog had washed the supper dishes, swept the hearth with her tail, warmed the Padre's flannel pajamas, and gone home to her family under the apple tree.

Before his fire the Padre dozed. He had eaten three plates of heavenly stewed carrots for his supper, and every now and then he rubbed his stomach gently, to help them digest. The tapping of the branches on the window and the falling of the rain made a soothing music. Upon the shelf above the

[3] From Robert Davis, *Padre Porko, The Gentlemanly Pig* (Holiday House, 1939).

chimney stood a polished red apple. The Padre was trying to decide whether he should eat the apple or smoke his pipe before crawling into bed for a good night's sleep.

"Rat-a-tat-tat-tat," suddenly sounded the knocker on his door.

"My Goodness Gracious," he exclaimed, pushing his feet into his red slippers. "Who can be out on a night like this? It must be someone in real trouble."

"Who is there?" he called, putting his sensitive nose to the keyhole. He could learn more through his nose than many people can learn through their ears and eyes.

"It is Antonio, the stable-boy from the General's."

"Come in, come in," invited the Padre, seating himself again, and taking out his pipe.

The door opened and a dripping figure stepped inside. Very politely he waited on the door-mat, his cap in his hand.

"Your Honor will please to excuse me for coming so late," he said. "But it was only tonight that the General said he would send me away in disgrace. My Grandmother told me that Your Honor is the Godfather of all Spanish boys who do not have real fathers, so you will please to excuse my coming."

The Padre was reaching up for the red apple. "She told you the truth, Antonio. You sit here and eat this apple, while I put tobacco in my pipe." With a skillful movement of his left hind foot the Padre kicked dry branches upon the fire.

"And don't be in any hurry, Antonio. Take all the time you need. Tell me the very worst. Whatever the trouble, we can put it right."

"It is about the white horse," Antonio began, "the fat, white one, that the General rides in parades, at the head of his soldiers. He can't walk. It is his left front hoof." The boy gulped it out in a single breath.

"They say that it is my fault, that I made him fall when I rode him for exercise. But it's not true. I always go slowly, and turn corners at a walk."

"Let's go and see," said the Padre, going to the closet for his rubber coat. "And here's a cape for you to put around your shoulders."

Once at the General's, the Padre and Antonio hung their wet things in the harness-room and unhooked the door of the box stall where the white horse lived. He was a superb animal, but he stood with one front foot off the floor.

"Excuse me, Your Excellency, but can you tell me the cause of Your Excellency's lameness?"

The great beast pricked up his ears. "The cause of it!" he snorted. "Why a three day old colt would know that much, and yet these stupid doctors and professors have been pestering me for two weeks. A wire nail has gone into the tender center of my foot. It has no head. You cannot see it. The idiots, and they pretend to know so much."

"I thought as much," murmured the Padre, sympathetically. "And will Your Excellency co-operate with us, if we try to get the nail out?"

"Won't I, though!" The horse snorted again. "Why, I haven't been able to touch this foot to the ground for sixteen days."

"This is a case for the Rat Family, and for no one else," said the Padre to himself. He trotted over to a hole in the stable floor. His voice, as he leaned over the opening, was a soft whine through his nose. "Is the lady of the house at home?"

A gray muzzle appeared. "I am only a poor widow, Don Porko; my husband was caught in a trap last harvest time. But if my children and a poor soul like me can be of any help to you, you are more than welcome to our best."

"Indeed you can, Mrs. Furrynose," said the Padre with enthusiasm. "We animals are going to do what none of the veterinary professors knew how to do. Listen carefully. Of all the rats in this town which one has the strongest teeth?" Other heads had joined Mother Furrynose at the opening, and now they all answered in a single unanimous squeak, "Uncle Israel, down at the flour-mill."

"Good," said the Padre. "And now, Mrs. Furrynose, I want you to listen once more. Will you send your oldest boy for Uncle Israel right away? Tell him that Padre Porko needs all the husky boy and girl rats in this town at the General's stable in half-an-hour."

Before the Padre had finished his request, a sleek rat was out of the hole and running toward the door. "You can count on us, Chief," he called.

Hardly ten minutes had passed when a peculiar noise was heard outside the stable. It was like the wind blowing the dry leaves in October. It was a rustling, a bustling, a scratching, a scraping, a marching of countless feet. Uncle Israel entered at the head of his tribe. He was an old-fashioned Quaker rat, gray and gaunt, and the size of a half-grown kitten. When he smiled he showed his remarkable teeth, sharp as razors and the color of ivory. He motioned to his brown-coated army and they lined up in rows around the wall, watching him and the Padre with shoe-button eyes.

"I'm not so strong as I used to be," apologized Uncle Israel, "except for my teeth. I don't want to boast, but none of these young rats can hold on to things as hard as I can. As soon as I got your message I brought my relatives. We will do anything you say, Padre." The rows of heads nodded in agreement.

"Thank you for coming, Uncle Israel," said the Padre. "In a minute I'll explain what our work is going to be. First we must tell the General's horse our plan."

He stood by the shoulder of the white horse and spoke in his most persuasive way. "Your Excellency, we are ready for the operation that will cure your foot. But we must be sure of your co-operation. It may hurt, I'm afraid, especially at first."

"It can't hurt more than my hoof aches right now. Go ahead," said the horse.

"We must uncover the end of the nail so that Uncle Israel can grip it in his beautiful teeth. Please bend back your foot."

The General's horse rested his foot on the straw, with the under side showing, and Uncle Israel, placing one paw on either edge of the tender V, began to gnaw, his teeth cutting in like a machine. Presently he sat up, squeaking excitedly. "I have it. It's right there. It's like a piece of wire. But I can get a good hold on it. What next, Padre?"

"Antonio," ordered the Padre, "bring the halters that hang in the harness room, and tie the ropes one to the other. And you, Uncle Israel, slip your head through this loop in the leather. We will run the long rope out across the stable floor so that everyone can find a hold. Take your time, Uncle Israel, everything depends upon your teeth. When you are ready for us to pull, wiggle your tail."

Things worked like clock-work. Uncle Israel held on. Three hundred young rats strained and pulled on the rope. The General's horse winced with the pain. The Padre walked up and down like a captain in a battle. But the nail in the foot of the white horse did not budge.

Padre Porko had an idea. "Widow Furry-nose, what would give you the most pleasure in the world?"

The lady replied quickly. "To bury that deceitful black cat up at the miller's." Everybody sat up and clapped his paws.

"Well, young people," said the Padre, "think that you are pulling the hearse to the graveyard, and that the miller's black cat is in it. Wouldn't you manage to get that hearse to the graveyard? Pull like that."

The floor of the barn seemed alive. It was a rippling, gray-brown carpet of straining small bodies. The teeth of Uncle Israel were locked in a death grip. Padre Porko walked back and forth, singing, "Horrible cat, get her buried, haul the hearse."

And, inch by inch, a long, thin, villainous nail came out of the horse's foot.

Then what a racket! Everyone was squirming, and squeaking, and jumping and rolling over, and tickling and nipping tails, and telling how strong he was. The white horse and Antonio admired Uncle Israel's teeth. And all of his nephews and nieces and grandchildren were so proud of him that they kissed him on both whiskers. Padre Porko kept repeating, "I'm proud of you. Great work! I always say that we animals can do anything, if we will work together."

But it was the General's horse who brought the evening to its perfect close. He whinnied into the Padre's ear, "Please translate to Antonio that if he will unlock the oat box I'm sure our friends would enjoy a light lunch. The General himself would be the first to propose it. He will be very thankful when he visits the stable tomorrow and finds me trotting on four legs."

Mrs. Furrynose and Uncle Israel had the young people sit in circles of ten, while Antonio passed the refreshments, pouring a little pile of oats in the center of each circle. Over three hundred guests were served but their table manners were excellent. No one snatched or grabbed, or gobbled his food. Everyone said, "If you please," and "Thank you," and "Excuse me for talking when my mouth is full."

When the crunching was at its height, Uncle Israel made a speech. "Padre Porko, Your Excellency, and friends, relatives and neighbors, this is a proud and happy night for me. In all my life my teeth never did such good work before. They helped this noble white horse, and they enabled us rats to aid the Padre in one of his kind acts. But, also, tonight, my teeth brought me to the attention of a lovely lady, Madame Furrynose, and I am delighted to say that she will not be a widow much longer. One and all, you are invited to the wedding, which will be held next Sunday afternoon in the flour-mill, while the miller is at church. And the Padre Porko has promised to send word to all dogs

and cats of the town that none of our guests are to be caught while going, coming or at the party." A hurricane of cheers and clapping followed the speech.

The pink nose of the white horse pushed through the window of his stall, and the merrymakers looked up. "May I, too, offer a wedding present to these worthy friends? Every night I will leave a handful of grain in the corner of my manger. They will find it there for their midnight lunch. A wedded pair with such polite manners can be trusted not to disturb the repose of a hard-working old horse."

The morning sun crept along the stable wall until it shone directly upon the sleeping Antonio. He sat up and rubbed his eyes. How did it happen that he was not in his bed, but in the box stall of the General's horse? And the horse was stamping with the foot that had been lame. Queerer still, the grain box was open and half the oats were gone. And what was the meaning of the four halter ropes tied together?

These are questions which Antonio never could answer. But when he told this story to his children, he was no longer a stable boy. He was the head trainer of all the General's racing horses.

ITALY

The Priceless Cats[1]

§ This is an Italian variation of the story Dick Whittington and His Cat, which the author heard many years ago in Perugia. The

[1] From M. A. Jagendorf, The Priceless Cats and Other Italian Folk Stories (Vanguard Press, 1956).

surprising new ending adds a piquant touch to the old tale.

Among the ancient Romans there was a proverb that those who are greedy never have enough, and since the Romans were Italians, the proverb still holds true. In the golden city of Venice they tell a tale that proves this time-old saying.

There lived in that city by the sea two merchants who were neighbors. Both were rich. Both had grand palaces on the green, shimmering canal, with proud gondolas tied to cinnabar-and-yellow-striped poles. And both had lovely young children who were friendly and played with one another. As for the merchants, one was as different from the other as a black pebble from a shining ruby.

One was hard and sharp and greedy, wanting whatever he saw, whether he needed it or not, while the other was generous and good, working to help not only himself but others as well. The two merchants knew each other and spoke to each other, but when it came to business, Mr. Greedy-Wolf was wary and watchful, not trusting anyone — not even himself.

So time went by, with these two buying and selling, working and growing.

Came a day when Giovanni, the good merchant, set out on a far journey to trade for spices, which were much sought after in Europe then.

He loaded his vessels with toys and corals and silks and beautiful glassware to exchange for pepper and cinnamon and vanilla and curries and other scented spices that grew on the islands far away.

He sailed for days and weeks and then came to the rich East, where he traded from island to island, with benefit to himself and satisfaction to the islanders.

One sparkling morning he came to a harbor that was as still as a graveyard, with masts hanging like tombstones. The streets and the markets were quiet as the night.

The merchant and some of his men walked about — disturbed by their own footsteps. Where were the hustling and bustling townspeople dressed in colorful clothes? Where were the smells of spices and the cries of vendors that usually filled the air of a busy city?

Finally the traders from Venice met two men who took them before the King. The ruler sat on his throne with a sorrowful face and head bowed low. Courtiers stood around, no different from the King.

"Can we trade with your people, Your Majesty?" the Venetian merchant said. "We have rich goods from our land that we would gladly exchange for spices."

"Master merchant," said the ruler, "our spices are ravaged, our grain is destroyed, our food is ruined. It is a wonder we are alive, because of the terrible plague that has come over our land. Everything is slowly being destroyed — even our clothes."

"And what is this terrible plague that has brought your land such unhappiness, Your Majesty?"

"Gnawing rats and scuttling mice! They are in our homes and clothes and in our fields and roads. We have set traps for them and we have strewn poison in the pantries, but that has done more harm to our animals than to the pests. There seems to be no remedy for this curse."

"Have you no cats?" the merchant asked.

"Cats? What are cats?"

"Why, cats are furry little animals like small dogs, and they are the mortal enemies of mice and rats, destroying them wherever they find them!"

"Where can I find these cats?" the King cried. "I'll pay anything for them!"

"Your Majesty," Don Giovanni said, "you do not have to pay for cats. We have many of them on our ship, and I will gladly give you a present of some; I am certain your pests will soon be gone."

The King thanked the merchant, almost with tears in his eyes, and within an hour the merchant brought two fine cats — one, a black Tom as fierce as he was big, and the other a lovely tiger-striped lady cat who was famous for having many kittens and catching even more mice.

The King and the islanders looked with awe and wonder at the two animals, for they had never seen cats before, and when they saw them set to work at once on the mice and rats, they were so overjoyed that they wanted to sing and dance.

The King was grateful from the bottom of his heart and wanted to prove this to the merchant, so he showered him and his crew with bales of spices and gleaming jewels, with sweet-smelling sandalwood and carved ivory, beautiful as a song.

When the merchant and his crew sailed home, they were so happy and contented that even the wind and the waves knew it and led their vessel swiftly back to Venice.

And the joy of Don Giovanni's family was great when he reached home, and great was the excitement of his fellow merchants of Venice when they saw his royal cargo.

Don Giovanni met Don Cesare, his neighbor, before the golden church of San Marco, that treasury of beauty in the world. They spoke of this and that, about the journey and the trading, and then Don Giovanni told Don Cesare how he had traded the richest merchandise of all for just a pair of common cats. Don Cesare's tongue nearly hung out with greed and envy when they parted.

Thereafter, day and night, Don Cesare could think only of how Don Giovanni had gained a treasure by giving away two worthless cats that any Venetian would pay to get rid of. He had no peace, and he was more restless than a horse with a thorn in its side. Green jealousy and greed ate into him like fire in dry grass, until he could stand it no longer. He had to go to that island and bring back as big, if not a bigger, treasure than had Don Giovanni.

He fitted out a splendid ship filled with the best of goods, golden vessels, brocades, carved corals. With such gifts the generous King should give him twice — no, three times — as many riches as he had given Don Giovanni.

Soon Don Cesare reached the island. He told the King he was a friend of Don Giovanni. The King received him with open arms, only too happy to welcome a friend of the man who, by his generous gift, had rid the island of the terrible pests.

Don Cesare told the King he, too, had brought him gifts — gifts much more valuable than those of Don Giovanni. Then he presented his gifts of golden cups and carved corals, rich brocades and gilded embroideries — the richest Venice could show — to prove his friendship.

Truly the emperor was overwhelmed by this show of unselfish generosity. He was a simple and an honest man, and appreciative as well, and he thought hard how he could repay the friendship shown by Don Cesare.

Try as he would, he could think of nothing rich enough and fine enough.

In the end he called together his counsellors to decide what to give to Don Cesare in return for the lavish presents, which, the King thought, Don Cesare had given out of the kindness of his heart.

Each elder had his say. In the end, one rich in wisdom arose and said, "Oh, King, this man from Venice has given to you and to us things that will be a joy to look at for years to come. Truly, we in our little island have no gifts to equal his. We could give him spices and perfumes and woods, but these are simple things growing freely in our land. They come and go every year. But there is one thing we possess now that is of great value in this world.

"Not so long ago we were cursed with a pest that nearly destroyed us. The rats and mice overran our land, starved our children, and covered our homes with filth. Then we received a priceless gift that made us once again a free and happy people. Since that time, those precious cat animals have increased in number, and we can well afford to give some of them away, precious as they are to us. I would therefore say to give to Don Cesare, that most unselfish Venetian, two of those invaluable cats. I am sure they will bring to him as great a blessing as they have brought to us."

King and counsellors thought this a splendid and wise suggestion. A cage of solid gold was made, and the King himself chose as the proper gift the two prettiest and most playful kittens that could be found.

Then the King set a day for the great royal audience to present the merchant with his reward. All the counsellors came, and as many people as the room could hold, and then the merchant appeared before the King. He came with light steps and greedy thoughts, thinking of the riches he would reap now — riches that would surely be greater than those Don Giovanni had received.

There were blowing of trumpets and beating of drums and many falderal speeches of friendship on the part of the merchant.

In the end the royal master said, "Don Cesare, you came to our land and gave me kindly gifts freely from the goodness of your heart. That is a fine thing for a man to do. And, as the saying goes, from seeds of goodness grow rich purple plums of goodness. I and my counsellors thought for a long time how to reward you properly for such unselfish generosity, and finally we decided on the most valuable gift we have.

"When my people and my land were in their greatest distress, a countryman of yours saved us by giving us a gift. It was a gift more precious than gold or diamonds or spices. We have been unable to think of anything more wonderful than the same gift for you. We know it will bring you the same joy and peace it has brought to us. Soldiers, bring the golden cage with the royal gift for Don Cesare!"

Then two soldiers came in with the golden cage in which the two little kittens were playing in a way that was a joy to behold.

The soldiers stopped with the cage before the merchant. The King smiled happily, as did the courtiers and the people.

The merchant looked at the kittens, but he could not say a word, and when he saw everyone beaming and smiling at him, he had to smile, too — a smile that stretched from ear to ear. . . . Soon after he sailed homeward.

Shall I tell you how he felt? Well, I will. The first few days he was full of fury and hatred, and not a man could speak to him. Then, little by little, he began to see how fate had played a joke on him that he could not change with all his riches and all his power. And, slowly, like the trickle of a single crystal drop of water, he began to think that perhaps jealousy and greed were the wrong seeds for the flowers he wanted in life.

He never said a word to anyone in Venice about what had happened, but it was noticed that he acted more kindly toward people, and that he no longer raced so wildly after gold and riches as he had done before.

RUSSIA

Seven Simeons[1]

❧ *The artist Artzybasheff has given us one of the finest of Russian folk tales. The spirit of old Russia is clearly shown — the peasants' blind obedience to their ruler, and their pride in the land. The author's decorative illustrations for this book make it one of the most distinguished examples of American book design.*

Beyond the high mountains and the dark forests, beyond the great rivers and the blue seas, in a certain kingdom upon a certain

[1] Boris Artzybasheff, *Seven Simeons* (Viking Press, 1937).

flat place, stood a city. In this city lived a king and the king's name was Douda.

King Douda was wise, King Douda was rich, and he was strong, for he had a strong army; so strong it was that nobody knew just how strong, not even his own generals.

Of big cities he had forty times forty, with ten palaces in each, each with a silver door, crystal windows, and a roof of gold, and of the best gold, too!

To advise him in matters of state he had nine old men, all with long white beards and large wise heads, all with more brains than enough; they always told him the truth!

Would you not think that a king like

Douda should have been happy? Not at all! There he was: rich, wise, powerful, and, moreover, he was very good-looking! So good-looking was King Douda that his beauty could not be imagined, nor described with a pen, nor told about in a tale. Yet he was very unhappy. He was sad because he could not find a worthy maiden for a bride, a princess who would be as good-looking as himself.

Once as he sat on a golden chair in his garden upon the shores of the sea, thinking about his misfortune, he saw a ship sail up to the dock before his palace. The sailors dropped anchor, furled their sails, and then laid a plank to come ashore.

King Douda thought to himself: "The sailors sail upon many seas and see marvels quite unknown. I shall ask them if in their travels they have not heard of some princess who is as good-looking as myself."

The sailors were brought to the King and they bowed before him in the best manner. A cup of wine was served to them; when they had drunk the wine and wiped their beards, King Douda said to them:

"It is well known that you sail upon the seas and see many marvels. Now tell us in all truth and honesty, isn't there some king or mighty prince who has a daughter as good looking as myself? For King Douda to be a worthy bride, for this great kingdom to be a worthy queen?"

The sailors thought and then thought some more; then the eldest one said, "Aye, I have heard that far beyond the distant sea, upon an island, there is a mighty kingdom. And the king has a daughter, Princess Helena, who is as good-looking as yourself. But this fair maiden is not a bride for you!"

Here the King became angry. "How dare you speak so to me, King Douda? Where is this island, what is the name of it, and who knows the way there?"

"It is called Boozan Island, and it is not near," replied the mariner. "Ten years of travel by the watery way, and the way to it we do not know. But even should we know it, judge for yourself. Ten years sailing there, ten years sailing back, adds twenty. By that time the fair lady will age, and girlish beauty is not like the taxpayer's duty: it's here today but gone tomorrow."

King Douda became pensive. "Well," he said, "it's to my sorrow. But as a reward for you, sailors, I give you a grant. You may take your ship to any part of my kingdom and pay neither tax nor duty!"

The sailors bowed low and departed, but the King sat there on his golden chair, in the garden upon the shores of the sea, thinking. And his thoughts were like entangled black threads. He could never find the end to them.

Douda was sad, but then he thought, "if I go hunting and have some fun, I may lose my sorrow in the fields; in the dark forest I might drop it. Then by tomorrow I might think how I could marry this beautiful princess."

The King's huntsmen blew their horns loud, the King's horsemen came galloping out, and King Douda rode forth to hunt, to forget his sorrow and to have some fun.

They were riding over the plains and through the dark forests, up the hills, and down the valleys looking for white geese and swans, for black bears and red foxes, when suddenly they came upon a beautiful field of wheat, shining like gold in the sun. When his hunting party had galloped through the field, King Douda reined in his horse and looked back in admiration.

"That is very fine wheat," he said. "One can see that the man who tilled this soil must be a good worker. Should all the fields throughout my kingdom be plowed and seeded like this one, there would be so much bread that my people could never eat it up, even in a lifetime!"

And King Douda ordered that the man who plowed the field should be found. The King's horsemen galloped off to do as they were told and shortly came upon seven youths sitting under a tree. Goodly lads they were, dressed in white linen shirts, themselves very handsome and so much alike that you could not tell them apart. They sat in the shade eating their dinner, a loaf of rye bread and plenty of good, clear, spring water.

"Hey, whose field is this here, with the golden wheat shining in the sun?"

"Ours!" said the seven in one voice. "By us plowed and by us seeded."

"And who may you fellows be, and whose people?"

"We are subjects of our good King Douda. To each other we are brothers; by name we are called Simeon."

The King's horsemen rode back and took the seven brothers with them, so that the King could see them for himself. The King liked the brothers and spoke to them very kindly, asking them who they were, and why and how.

"We are simple folk," said the first Simeon, "and your peasants, Douda. To each other we are brothers by the same father of the same mother, and the name we answer to is Simeon. Our old father taught us to pray to God; to serve our King faithfully; to pay our taxes regularly; and to till the soil without surcease. 'If you, my sons, aren't lazy,' he said, 'if you plow the soil in the proper way and seed it in the right season, it will reward you. It will give bread for you to eat and, when the time comes and you are old and tired, it will make a soft place for your rest.' Our father also told us to learn different trades. 'A craft,' said father, 'is not a heavy burden, but it is good to know one against a rainy day. The best aid is some useful trade,' he said."

King Douda was pleased with this simple speech.

"Good fellows!" he said. "Very good fellows! And what may be the trades you have learned from your father?"

Answered the first Simeon,

"Mine is a simple one. If I should be given the right tools and plenty of bricks, I can build a tower higher than the clouds, almost to the very sky."

"Good!" said the King. "Let's hear from the others."

Answered the second Simeon,

"My skill isn't much. Should my brother build this tower, I could climb to the top of it and from there I could see all the kingdoms of the world. I could tell what's going on in every one of them."

"This is very good," said the King. "And the next?"

Answered the third Simeon,

"My trade is an easy one. When you, Douda, need ships for your royal navy they are built by real masters, men of great learning and experience. But should you order me, I shall take an axe and go to it: slap, dash, a tap and a clout, and your ship is turned out! But then, my ship would be a crude, home-made thing. While the real ship takes a year to sail, mine is back in an hour; while the real ship takes ten years to sail, mine is there in a week. Such an artless, crude thing this ship would be."

"Very nice," said the King. "And what about you?"

Answered the fourth Simeon,

"My trade is easy! Should my brother build this ship, I could sail it to the ends of the earth. And if some enemy starts after it or a great storm breaks out over the sea, I shall make the ship go down, I shall hide it deep down below, in the watery depths. But when the danger is over I can bring it up again upon the blue waters of the sea."

"Not bad," said the King. "However, I have heard of it being done in our Navy, the first part of it at any rate. Next!"

Answered the fifth Simeon,

"My trade is that of a simple blacksmith. If you should give me a scrap of iron, I can fashion a gun for you. This gun will shoot by itself and never miss."

"Splendid!" said the King. "But, please, go on."

Answered the sixth Simeon,

"Of my skill I am ashamed to tell. If my brother shoots anything I can always recover it. Be it in the sky or in the forest, be it in the deep sea or behind a cloud, I shall go down, I shall climb up and always bring back what the gun shoots."

"Dear me! This is the best of all," said King Douda, because he was very much pleased with the Simeons' modesty. "Our thanks to you all for your good, simple words. It is true, what your father has told you, 'A craft is not a heavy burden, but it is good to know one against a rainy day.' Come with me to my City. I wish to see for myself what you can do."

The seven Simeons bowed low before Douda, and said in one voice, "You are our high and mighty Douda and if such be your pleasure we are your humble servants."

But the King remembered the seventh

brother. "And you, Simeon, what is the trade you have learned from your father?"

Answered the seventh Simeon,

"I have learned nothing from him! Not that I haven't tried, but it flew into one ear and out of the other. I do have some skill in one thing, but I would rather not mention it."

"Speak!" exclaimed King Douda. "What is this secret thing?"

"No, Douda! First I must have your promise, your royal pledge that after I've told you, you will forgive me and let me keep my head in the same place it is now."

"Be it so!" said the King. "I give you my royal word."

The seventh Simeon looked around, stepped from foot to foot, coughed, and then spoke,

"My talent, King Douda, should remain hidden, because instead of its being rewarded, men's heads are chopped off for such ability. My skill is this: there isn't a treasure, be it concealed, locked up or buried, be it behind a door, a lock, or a bar, that I cannot have, should I take a fancy to it."

"What's that?" exclaimed King Douda. "I will not put up with it, it's too grave a matter!"

The King was very displeased and angry. "No, there is no excuse for a thief, no mercy for such a vicious villain. I shall have you put to death; I shall lock you up in the darkest dungeon and keep you there behind iron bars till you forget this skill!"

"But, King Douda, you have heard the old saying, 'He who is not caught, is not a thief.' If I had my fancy I could have even your kingdom's treasury. With all its gold I could have a palace built as good as your own! But such is my simplicity, that my only guilt is that I am telling you the truth."

"This is a most provoking situation," the King said. "I have given you my royal pledge, but to let you go free is to ask for trouble. You must be, for safety, locked up. Hey, jailors, take this man, clamp irons upon him and toss him into the darkest dungeon. From this day forward he is not to see the light of day, nor the bright sun nor the silver moon.

"As for you other Simeons, you are in my favor. Come with me and do what you were taught by your father, so that I can see it for myself."

The six Simeons went to the King's City as they were told, but the seventh was locked in a dark, damp place.

When they came to the city, the first Simeon was promptly given plenty of bricks and the proper tools to set to work. The tower grew up so fast and so high that the King, as he was looking at it, had to hold his crown with one hand and shade his eyes with the other. It almost reached to the sun.

The second Simeon, when the tower was ready, climbed to the top of it. He looked East, North, West and South, and he listened. Then he came down and told what was going on in the world, which king was fighting a war, which king was planning a war, and which one had had enough and was suing for peace. Then, besides, he told of such secret things that the King smiled and his Court laughed themselves blue in the face.

The third Simeon lost no time. He rolled up his sleeves, took an axe and went to work. Slap, dash, a tap and a clout, and the ship was turned out! When King Douda rode to the shore to see it, the ship's flags waved, silken sails were blown full by the wind, and the brass cannons fired the salute. But what was best, the ship had silver strings for its rigging and the sailors played good music on it. The fourth Simeon sailed the ship upon the blue waters. When it was out in the open sea, he took it by its carved prow and made it go down like a stone! It seemed as if there never had been a ship upon the water, but an hour later he brought it up again, and a nice big fish, besides, for the King's supper.

While King Douda was amusing himself with the ship, the fifth Simeon had his smithy ready, the iron hot, and before long he had fashioned the gun, the gun which shoots by itself and never misses!

There was an eagle flying high in the sky. It flew up to the sun and was looking at it. The King spoke to the fifth brother,

"See," he said, "if you can shoot that foolish bird. It flies, looking at the sun, as if there were nothing better to do!"

The fifth Simeon only smiled. He loaded

his gun with a silver bullet, aimed — bang!
And the eagle came tumbling down head first
and legs last. But before it fell to the ground
the sixth Simeon caught it on a silver platter
and brought it to the King.

"I like that!" said the King. "That was
very well done and we are much pleased with
you and your brothers. We shall reward you.
To show our appreciation you may go to
the royal kitchen to rest and have a good
dinner."

The six Simeons bowed low and went to
the kitchen as they were told. But just as
they began to eat their soup, the King's Jester
came rushing in waving his cap with little
bells on it.

"Here, here, you blockheads!" the Jester
cried. "You country bumpkins! A fine time
you pick out to eat your dinner. Come,
King Douda is asking for you!"

The brothers ran to the King's chambers.
What great disaster could have happened?
They saw standing by the door all the King's
men, his Sergeants, Lieutenants, Major-Generals, Senators, and the Best People. The
King himself sat on his golden chair looking
pensive.

"Listen," he said to the Simeons. "I am
very pleased with you, my good fellows. But
my Generals and my Senators had a thought.
If you, second Simeon, can see the world from
the top of your tower, you must go up and
look. For I am told that somewhere beyond
the Great Sea is an island. On this island is
a king and the king has a daughter. I am
told that this princess is as good-looking as
myself."

The second Simeon ran to the tower without delay. From the tower he looked this
way and that way, then came down and reported.

"King Douda, your command I have carried out. I looked beyond the Great Sea and
I saw Boozan Island. From what I see the
king there is very proud and unfriendly. He
sits in his palace and talks like this: 'I have
a daughter, beautiful Helena, and nowhere
in the world is there a king or a prince
worthy of her hand. Should one come here
to woo her, I would declare war on him! I
would chop off his head and burn his kingdom to ashes!'"

"But how big is his army?" asked Douda.
"And how far is his kingdom from my
kingdom?"

"To make a rough guess, to sail there
would take ten years less two days, but should
a storm break out it might take a bit longer.
I did see the king's army, too. It was training in the field, but there were not many: a
hundred thousand lancers, a hundred thousand gunners, and of his horsemen about the
same number. The king also has another
army in reserve. It never goes any place but
is fed and groomed for some emergency."

King Douda thought very long, then exclaimed,

"I do want to marry beautiful Helena!"
After he had exclaimed this the Generals
and Senators kept silent and only tried to
hide behind each other's backs.

"If I may speak, Sir," said the third Simeon, and he coughed a little. "I would say,
Sir, but I am only a simple man and have no
education, I would say, that although my
ship is a crude, home-made thing, it could
bring the Princess. While the real ship takes
ten years to sail, mine would be there in a
week."

"Now we are getting somewhere!" said
Douda. "Hey, my brave Generals and wise
Senators, think quickly! Should I, your King
Douda, win beautiful Helena by war or shall
we first try diplomacy? I now give you my
promise that he who brings her to me shall
be in my favor. He shall be made the Lord
High Keeper of the Kingdom's Treasury
and can help himself to it!"

All were silent as before, and there was a
shuffling of feet as the Generals and Senators
tried to hide behind each other's backs. King
Douda frowned and was about to speak an
angry word to them when, as if someone had
asked for it, the King's Jester jumped forward. The Jester shook his cap with the little
golden bells on it and exclaimed,

"Here, here, you wise men! Your heads
are big, your beards are long but all your
brains aren't worth a song. Have you, King
Douda, forgotten the old saying, that sometimes even the prickly thorn, for an ass
might serve as corn? The seventh Simeon
may be of good service to you! He is the one
to go to Boozan Island. He can steal the

Princess to be your bride. Then, should her father declare war upon us, it will take him ten years of sailing to get here. But a lot can happen in ten years. I heard once that somewhere some wizard promised some king that within ten years he would teach a horse to sing like a nightingale."

"By my crown, you are right!" cried Douda. "Thanks to you, Fool! As reward I shall order another bell to be sewed on your cap and a cookie given to each of your children."

The Jester was pleased because he took great pride in the little bells and, to show his appreciation, he stood on his head.

Now, by the King's command, the heavy iron doors were opened, and the seventh Simeon was led out and brought before the King.

"Certainly I can steal the Princess," said Simeon. "It shouldn't be much trouble. She is not a precious pearl kept under seven locks. Order, Douda, the ship to be loaded with fine cloths and ivory, with Persian rugs and precious stones. Then I and my brothers will sail to Boozan Island and bring back the beautiful Princess to be your bride."

There was great hustle and bustle in the kingdom. By the King's order the ship was loaded and in less time than it takes to braid the hair on a bald man's head, the brothers said good-bye and were off.

Their ship sailed upon the waters of the Great Sea. Its carved prow cut the waves like a sharp plow. Then before they had time to say "What a jolly good ride," in the distant blue, Boozan Island appeared to the brothers' view.

They saw Boozan Island, all black with bristling guns. The great armies were marching all over it to the beating of drums. The King's spare army was there too, being fed and groomed. From their high tower the King's sentries spied the ship and cried out with loud voice, "Hold, drop the anchor! Answer us! Who are you and why do you come here?"

The seventh Simeon replied, "We are peaceful merchants and bear no arms. We have fine cloths and ivory, Persian rugs and precious stones. And what we sell is not dear. For a mouse's tail you can buy a whale! Besides, we have nice presents for your King."

When the King heard of it, he ordered the Simeons brought to his royal palace. The brothers loaded up a little boat with what they had, and came ashore as they were told.

In the great hall of the royal palace the Boozan King was sitting on a throne with Princess Helena by his side. So lovely she was that her beauty could not be imagined or described, or told about in a tale. She had golden hair, rosy cheeks, and eyes so sweet, so gentle, that if you saw her, all you could say would be, "Oh, how beautiful is the Princess!"

But the seventh Simeon said, "We are peaceful merchants from beyond the sea. We came here to sell, to buy, and to trade. And we brought a few little presents for Your Majesty, should you honor us by their acceptance."

Saying this he bowed low and his brothers unrolled their precious cloths of most luscious quality, and rare velvets, quite priceless. They spread out the marvels of carved ivory and round pearls. Rich cloaks, sewed with gold, all gold, solid gold. They sparkled like fire! Bracelets, earrings, necklaces, diamonds, rubies, and sapphires.

When she saw the treasures the Princess clapped her hands, exclaiming with delight, "Aren't they lovely! Many thanks to you, dear strangers, for your beautiful gifts."

"Oh, but no!" answered the seventh Simeon. "Those are just trifles for you to give to your servants. The cloths are for the chambermaids to use as rags and the round pearls for the kitchen boys to play marbles with. We do have real treasures too, but being afraid of not pleasing Your Majesty, we left them on our ship. If only, wise beautiful Princess, you would honor us by coming to our ship to see and to choose for yourself, you could have all and the ship itself as well. What good to us are all the jewels in the world after we've seen your lovely eyes?"

The Princess was pleased with his simple words and she asked her father, "Father dear, may I go? I shall see and choose for myself and bring back something for you, too."

The Boozan King thought awhile and then

he said, "Well, dear daughter, if you must, you must. But you shall go there on my royal ship which has a hundred guns on it, with one hundred of the Best Warriors and a thousand other soldiers, just in case something should happen."

The royal ship left the shore. Upon it were many of the Best Warriors and other soldiery and one hundred guns. When they reached the Simeons' ship, the Princess went aboard it, climbing up its crystal stairs. The seventh Simeon led her from cabin to cabin, from one hold to another, showing her everything and telling her stories. And the stories he told her were so good that beautiful Helena forgot the time.

But the fourth Simeon had not forgotten. He took the ship by its carved prow, he made it go down and he hid it deep down below in the watery depths. The Best Warriors when they saw this, bellowed like bulls, and the thousand other soldiers hung their heads and only stood blinking and looking into the water. Then, because there was nothing they could do, they turned the royal ship back to shore and went to tell the King of this unexpected, unheard-of misfortune.

The Boozan King, when he heard of it cried bitterly, saying, "Oh, my dear beautiful daughter! God has punished me for my stubborn pride. I thought there was no king or prince worthy of your hand, and I guarded you like a precious jewel. But now you lie dead in the watery depths among seaweed and coral." Then he turned to the Best Warriors. "And you, you blockheads, why didn't you look? Off to jail with you while I think of a punishment so severe that even your childen and grandchildren will remember it!"

While the Boozan King raved and lamented, the brothers' ship was streaking under the water like a silver fish. Then, with the island left far behind them, the fourth Simeon brought it up again to sail upon the calm blue waters of the sea.

But the Princess began to think of the time. "I must go home. If I don't go very soon my father might become angry." As she said this she came up on deck and lo, there was no Boozan Island! Only the blue sea around and the blue sky above. Now it

would seem the rest would be easy — the brothers had their prize and were sailing home. But no — there is more to this story.

The Princess knew some magic. She raised up her hands, looked to the sky, and turned into a beautiful bird of many colors. She spread her wings and flew away. Here the fifth Simeon lost no time. He loaded his gun with a silver bullet, aimed — bang! And the bird fell down, shot in the wing. But before it reached the water the sixth Simeon caught it in his hands. Then the bird turned into a little silver fish and slipped out into the deep water. Simeon caught the fish too, but in his very hands it turned into a little gray mouse and went running around the deck. But Simeon pounced on it quicker than a cat, and in his hands the little mouse became the beautiful Princess once more, and this time for good. Because this was all the magic the beautiful Princess knew.

It was early, early in the morning when King Douda sat at the crystal window of his palace, thinking. "Could the brothers bring the Princess? Would the brothers come back at all?" And he gazed upon the blue waters of the sea lost in thought. He could not sleep, he could not eat, or go hunting, or join a feast. The beautiful Princess was on his mind.

King Douda looked upon the waters. "What is it there? Is it a white gull flying or a ship sailing?" Yes! It was the brothers' ship flying home. The flags waving, silken sails blown full by the wind, and good music played by the sailors upon its rigging.

The signal gun boomed from the shore. Now the ship drew nearer and dropped anchor. Its sails were furled, a plank was laid ashore and the Princess came off the ship. She was as beautiful as the bright sun in the morning, as lovely as the heavenly stars of the night!

King Douda rejoiced when he saw her. "Run," he said, "all my Sergeants, Lieutenants, Major-Generals and the Best People, fire the cannons, blow the trumpets, and sound the bells! Run, greet the Princess, your future queen."

They all ran to do as they were told and spread the precious carpets and opened wide the gates. Even the King himself ran out to welcome Helena to his kingdom. He took her by the hands and led her to his palace, saying, "Please, my beautiful Helena, make yourself at home. We have heard about your beauty but truly it is greater than we had hoped. But, if you say the word, I shall send you back to your dear father. I cannot be so cruel as to keep you here by force!"

Here the Princess looked upon King Douda and, as she looked at him, it seemed to her as if the sun itself danced in the sky, as if the sea played music and the mountains broke out in a song!

What more can one say? The Princess saw how good-looking Douda was and she fell in love with him.

It was not long thereafter that the seven Simeons were sent back to the Boozan King bearing a letter from his daughter, Helena. She wrote, "Our King and my dear Father: I have found the man worthy of my hand and I shall marry him so soon as we have your blessing. The High and Mighty King Douda, my future husband and your son-in-law, sends to you his envoys with greetings and best wishes. And we both hope that you will come to our wedding."

They sailed swiftly beyond the sea and in less time than it takes to tell about it the seven brothers reached Boozan Island. The King's great armies were assembled upon a big square. In the middle of the square rose a scaffold and on the scaffold stood the King's headsman holding a shiny axe. The King had ordered put to death all of the Best Warriors and the thousand other soldiers who had guarded his daughter. "Chop off their heads!" he said. "All of them, from the first to the last!"

"Stop! Do not chop!" cried the seventh Simeon from the ship's poop. "We have brought you a letter from your daughter."

So delighted was the Boozan King when he read the letter that he said, "Let the fools go. I forgive them. It must have been God's own will that my dear daughter should marry King Douda."

The brothers were given a great feast and sent back with the King's blessing for the wedding. He himself could not go because of important matters of state which required his direct attention, such as training his army and seeing that his spare army was well groomed.

Faster than before, the brothers sailed back towards their own home. In no time, in the distant blue, King Douda's kingdom appeared in their view.

"Our thanks to you, my good fellows," said King Douda cheerfully, when the Simeons stood before him and the Princess. "It was well done and we are both very happy. Now you can ask for anything you desire. Should you like to be my generals, I shall make you my Field Marshals. But should you rather be my Senators I shall make you my Prime Ministers. Then you can have all the gold and silver you need."

The first brother bowed low before the King and replied, "We seven brothers are only simple folk and your peasants, Douda. It is not for us to strut at the Royal Court. We shouldn't know when to stand up or when to sit down, or what to wear and when! But give us leave to go back to our field. By us it was plowed and by us seeded and now its golden wheat shines in the sun. One thing we beg of you. Let our seventh brother go with us. Forgive him his talent. He is not the first to have it nor will he be the last!"

"Be it so," said the King. "But we are very sorry you cannot stay for our wedding. It's going to be such a fine party!"

The wedding day soon arrived and there was great merriment and joy in the land. Good King Douda married the Princess Helena and they both were so good-looking that all the people cheered and cried, "Hurrah!"

The church bells pealed, the flags waved and the cannons fired the salutes until they burst.

It was a fine party! I should know because I was there myself and danced to the gay music till I couldn't dance any more!

And now, my gentle friends, we are at the tale's end. For what was good in it, praise it; but for the rest forgive the poor story-teller. A wrong word is not like the bird in a cage. If ever a word flies out, no man can jump and catch it. In this I have no doubt!

The Little Humpbacked Horse [2]

One of the first things the reader notices in this story is the old-Russian atmosphere, not only the names, and such words as "versts," but the acts of the brothers. Ivan climbs on top of the Russian stove to take a nap; the two older brothers kiss each other when they make a bargain; and a head man who comes out with soldiers to disperse the crowd wears fur footgear.

Across the wide sea-ocean, on the further side of high mountains, beyond thick forests, in a village that faced the sky, there once lived an old peasant who had three sons. The eldest, Danilo, was the most knowing lad in the place; the second, Gavrilo, was neither clever nor dull; and the youngest, who was named Ivan, was called a dullard, because while his brothers, after they had sowed their wheat and threshed it, drove to town and went merrymaking, he cared to do nothing but lie in the corner on the stove and sleep. So the whole neighborhood called him "Little Fool Ivan."

Now one morning when the peasant went to his stack, he found to his dismay that someone in the night had stolen some of the hay; so that evening he sent his eldest son to watch for the thief.

Danilo, accordingly, took his ax and his hayfork and went to the field. On this night there was a biting frost and heavy snow, and he said to himself, "Why should I freeze myself stiff to save a little worthless fodder?" So, finding a warm corner, he lay down, wrapped himself in his thick fur coat and went to sleep.

In the morning he saw that some of the hay had been stolen. He rolled himself well in the snow, went home, and knocked at the door till his father let him in.

"Didst thou see the thief?" asked the peasant.

"I heard him prowling not far off," answered Danilo; "but I shouted, and he dared not come nearer. However, I have had a terrible night, thou mayst be sure! It was bitter cold, and I am frozen to the marrow!"

2 From Post Wheeler, *Russian Wonder Tales* [Beechhurst Press, New York, 1946].

His father praised him, calling him a good son, and the next night sent his second son to watch.

So Gavrilo took his hatchet and his long knife and went to the field. Now on this night it was raining, and he said to himself, "They say my brother is cleverer than I, but I am at least knowing enough to take care of myself; and why should I stand all night wet to the skin for the sake of a little dried grass?" So, having found a sheltered spot, he lay down, covered himself with his warm cloak and went to sleep.

In the morning he saw that more of the hay had been stolen. He went to a brook, poured water over his clothing so that it was drenched, went home, and knocked at the door till it was opened.

"Didst thou see the thief?" asked his father.

"I did," Gavrilo answered, "and laid hold of his coat and gave him such a beating that he will remember it. But the rascal tore away and ran so fast that I could not catch him. But I have had a night for my pains, I can tell you! The rain poured every minute, and I am soaked to the bones!"

His father praised him likewise, calling him a brave fellow till he was as proud as a cock with five hens, and the next evening said to Little Fool Ivan: "Now, my son, it is thy turn to watch, but thou art such a simpleton thou canst not even keep the sparrows from the peas. It will be small use for thee to go."

However, Little Fool Ivan climbed down from the stove, put a crust of bread under his coat and went whistling off to the field. He did not lie down as his brothers had done, but went about the whole field, looking on every side; and when the moon rose he sat down under a bush, counted the stars in the sky and ate his crust with a good appetite.

Suddenly, just at midnight, he heard the neigh of a horse; and looking out from the bush he saw a wonderful mare, as white as snow, with a golden mane curled in little rings.

"So," said Little Fool Ivan to himself, "thou art, then, the thief of our hay! Only come a little nearer, and I will be on thy back as tight as a locust!" The mare came nearer and nearer and at last, choosing the right moment, Ivan leaped out, seized her tail and jumped on to her back, wrong side before.

The white mare's eyes darted forth lightning. She curled her neck like a snake, reared on her hind legs and shot off like an arrow. She raced over fields, she flew like a bird over ditches, she galloped like the wind along mountains and dashed through thick forests. But run as she would, and rear and snort as she might, she could not throw off Little Fool Ivan. He clung to her tail and stuck to her back like a burr.

At last, just as day was beginning to dawn, the mare stopped and, panting, spoke to him with a human voice. "Well, Ivan," said she, "since thou canst sit me, it seems thou must possess me. Take me home, and give me a place to rest for three days. Only, each morning just at sunrise, let me out to roll in the dew. And when the three days are up, I will bear thee three such colts as were never heard of before. Two of them will be Tzar's horses, of brown and gray, and these thou mayst sell if thou choosest. But the third will be a little humpbacked stallion only three feet high with ears a foot long and him thou shalt neither sell for gold nor give as a gift to anyone whatsoever. So long as thou art in the white world he shall be thy faithful servant. In winter he will show thee how to be warm, and when thou dost hunger he will show thee where to find bread. In return for these three colts, thou shalt release me and give me my freedom."

Little Fool Ivan agreed. He rode the white mare home, hid her in an empty shepherd's corral, whose entrance he covered with a horse-cloth and went home and knocked at the door till his brothers let him in.

When they saw him, they began to question him. "Well, no doubt thou didst see the thief! Perhaps thou didst even catch him! Tell us."

"To be sure I did," he replied. "I jumped on the thief's back and laid hold of the villain's tail, and we ran a thousand versts or more. My neck was nearly broken in the end, and ye may believe I am tired!" So saying he climbed on to the stove without taking off even his bark sandals, and went to sleep, while his brothers and his father roared with laughter at the story, not a word of which, of course, they believed.

Little Fool Ivan kept the white mare hidden from all other eyes. For three mornings he rose at daybreak and let her out to roll on the dewy meadow and on the fourth morning, he went to the corral and found beside her, as she had promised, three colts. Two were most beautiful to see; they were of brown and gray, their eyes were like blue sapphires, their manes and tails were golden and curled in little rings, and their hoofs were of diamond, studded with pearls. But the third was a tiny horse like a toy, with two humps on his back and ears a foot long.

Ivan was overjoyed. He thanked the white mare; and she, released, curled her neck like a snake, reared on her hind legs and shot off like an arrow. Then he began to admire the three colts, especially the little humpbacked one which frisked like a dog about Ivan's knees, clapping his long ears together from playfulness and dancing up and down on his little hoofs. He kept them hidden, as he had the white mare, in the shepherd's corral, letting them out each morning at sunrise to roll in the dew and spending many hours petting them, talking to them, currying their coats till they shone like silver and braiding their golden manes.

Time went on (but whether it was three weeks or three years that flew away matters little, since one need not run after them) till it befell, one day, that his eldest brother, Danilo, who had been to town for a holiday, returned late at night and, missing his way in the darkness, stumbled into the shepherd's corral. Hearing a sound, he made a light and to his astonishment saw the three young horses.

"So-ho!" he thought. "Now I understand why Little Fool Ivan spends so much time in this old corral!" He ran to the house and woke his brother Gavrilo. "Come quickly," he said, "and see what three horses our young idiot of a brother has found for himself!" And Gavrilo followed him as fast as he could, straight across a nettle field barefoot, since he did not wait to put on his boots.

When they came to the corral the two fine horses were neighing and snorting. Their eyes were burning like beautiful blue candles and their curling gold manes and tails and their hoofs of diamond and pearls filled the two brothers with envy. Each looked at them so long that he was nearly made blind of one eye. Then Danilo said:

"They say it takes a fool to find a treasure. But where in the white world could Little Fool Ivan have got these marvelous steeds? As for thee and me, brother, we might search our heads off and we would find not even two roubles!"

"That is true," answered Gavrilo. "We should have the horses, and not Little Fool Ivan. Now I have an idea. Next week is the Fair at the capital. Many foreigners will come in ships to buy linen and it is said that even Tzar Saltan will be there. Let us come here by night and take the horses thither and sell them. They will fetch a great price and we will divide it equally between us two. Thou knowest what a good time we could have with the money; and while we are slapping our full purses and enjoying ourselves, our dolt of an Ivan will not be able to guess where his horses have gone visiting. What sayest thou? Let us shake hands upon it."

So the two brothers agreed, kissed each other, crossed themselves, and went home planning how to spend the money they should get for the horses.

When the next week came round, accordingly, they said a prayer before the holy images, asked their father's blessing, and departed to the Fair. When they had gone some distance, however, they returned to the village secretly after nightfall, took the two fine horses out of the corral, and again set out for the capital.

Next morning, when Ivan came to the corral, he found to his grief that the beautiful pair had vanished. There was left only the little humpbacked horse that was turning round and round before him, capering, clapping his long ears together and dancing up and down for joy. Ivan began to weep salt tears. "O my horses, brown and gray!" he cried; "my good steeds with golden manes! Did I not caress you enough? What wretch — may he tumble through a bridge — hath stolen you away?"

At this the humpbacked horse neighed and spoke in a human voice: "Don't worry, little master," he said. "It was thy brothers who took them away, and I can take thee to them. Sit on my back and hold fast by my ears, and have a care not to fall off!" So Little Fool Ivan sat on his back, holding up his feet lest they drag on the ground, and laid hold of his ears; and the pony shook himself till his little mane quivered, reared on his hind legs, snorted three times and shot away like an arrow, so fast that the dust curled under his feet. And almost before Ivan had time to take breath, he was versts away on the highroad to the capital.

When his brothers saw Little Fool Ivan coming after them like the wind, on his toy horse, they knew not what to do. "For shame, ye rascals!" shouted he as he overtook them. "Ye may be more clever than I, but I have never stolen your steeds!"

"Our dear little brother!" said Danilo. "There is little use denying. We took thy two horses, but we did so with no thought of wrong to thee. As thou knowest, this has been a poor season with our crops and a bad harvest, and for despair I and Gavrilo have been like to hang ourselves. When we came by chance upon these two steeds, we considered that thou hadst little knowledge of bargaining and trading, and doubtless knew not their worth, whereas we could get for them at least a thousand roubles at the Fair. With this money we could help our little father, as thou wouldst wish; and we purposed to buy besides for thee a red cap and new boots with red heels. So if we have erred, do thou forgive us."

"Well," answered Little Fool Ivan, "thy words sound fair enough. If this was your thought, go and sell my two horses, but I will go with you." So, though they wished him well strangled, the two brothers had no choice but to take him with them, and thus they came to the capital.

Now when they reached the market-place where the traders were assembled, so wonderful were the two steeds that the people swarmed about them, buzzing like bees in a hive, till for the press no one could pass either in or out, and there was great commotion. Perceiving this, the head man sent a crier, who blew on a gold trumpet and shouted in a loud voice: "O merchants and buyers! crowd not, but disperse one and all!" But they would not move from the horses. Then the head man rode out himself in slippers and fur cap with a body of soldiers, who cleared the way with their whips, so that he came to the middle of the market and saw the horses with his own eyes.

"God's world is wonderful!" he cried, rubbing his head. "What marvels doth it hold!" And bidding the crier proclaim that no buyer should buy them, he rode to the Palace, came to the presence of the Tzar, and told him of them.

The Tzar could not sit still for curiosity. He ordered his state carriage and rode at once to the market; and when he saw the horses, tugging at their halters and gnawing their bits, with their eyes shining like sapphires, their curling golden manes, and hoofs of diamond and pearls, he could not take his eyes from them. He examined them on both sides, called to them with caressing words, patted their backs, and stroked their manes, and asked who owned them.

"O Tzar's Majesty," said Little Fool Ivan, "I am their master."

"What wilt thou take for them?" asked the Tzar.

"Thrice five caps full of silver," answered Ivan, "and five roubles beside."

"Good," said the Tzar, and ordered the money given him. Then ten grooms, with gray hair and golden uniforms, led the pair to the royal stables. On the way, however, the horses knocked the grooms down, bit to pieces the bridles, and ran neighing to Ivan.

Then the Tzar called him to his presence, and said: "It seems that my wonderful steeds will obey only thee. There is no help but that I make thee my Chief Equerry and Master of my Stables." And he ordered the crier at once to proclaim the appointment. So Little Fool Ivan called his brothers Danilo and Gavrilo, gave to them the fifteen caps full of silver, and the five roubles beside, kissed them, bade them not neglect their father but to care for him in his old age, and led the two horses to the royal stables, while a great throng of people followed, watching the little humpbacked horse who went dancing after them up the street.

The telling of a tale is quick but time itself passes slowly. Five weeks went by, while Ivan wore red robes, ate sweet food, and slept his fill. Each morning at sunrise, he took the horses to roll in the dew on the open field and fed them with honey and white wheat until their coats shone like satin. But the more the Tzar praised him the more envious many in the Court were of him. As the saying is, one need not be rich only so he have curly hair and is clever; and because Little Fool Ivan had succeeded so easily, people hated him, and the one who hated him most was the officer who had been the Tzar's Master of Horse before his coming. Each day this man pondered how he might bring about Ivan's ruin, and at night he would creep to the stables and lie hid in the wheat bins, hoping to catch his rival in some fault.

When this failed, he went to all those Court officials who were envious of the new favorite and bade them hang their heads and go about with sorrowful faces, promising, when the Tzar asked the cause, to tell him what would ruin Little Fool Ivan. They did so, and the Tzar, noticing their sad looks, asked:

"O Boyars, why are ye cast down and crestfallen?"

Then he who had given this counsel stood forth, and said: "O Tzar's Majesty! not for ourselves do we grieve, but we fear thy new Master of the Stables is a wizard and an evil-doer and familiar with Black Magic. For he doth boast openly that he could fetch thee, if he chose, in addition to thy two wonderful steeds, the fabled Pig with the Golden Bristles and the Silver Tusks, with her twenty sucklings, who live in the hidden valley of the Land of the South."

Hearing this, the Tzar was wroth. "Bring before me this wild boaster," he said, "and he shall make good his words without delay!" Thereupon they ran to the stables, where Little Fool Ivan lay asleep, and kicked him wide awake and brought him to the Tzar, who looked at him angrily and said: "Hear my command. If in three days thou hast not brought hither from the hidden valley of the Land of the South the Pig with the Golden Bristles and Silver Tusks, together with her twenty sucklings, I will deliver thee to an evil death!"

Little Fool Ivan went to the stable weeping bitterly. Hearing him coming the little humpbacked horse began to dance and to flap its ears together for joy, but as soon as he saw his master's tears he almost began to sob himself. "Why art thou not merry, little master?" he asked. "Why does thy head hang lower than thy shoulders?"

Ivan embraced and kissed the little horse, and told him the task the Tzar had laid upon him. "Do not weep," said the pony; "I can help thee. Nor is this service so hard a one. Go thou to the Tzar and ask him a bucket of golden corn, a bucket of silver wheat, and a silken lasso."

So Ivan went before the Tzar and asked, as he had been bidden, for the wheat, the corn, and the silken lasso, and brought them to the stables. "Now," said the little hump-backed horse, "lie down and sleep, for the morning holds more wisdom than the evening."

Little Fool Ivan lay down to sleep, and next morning the pony waked him at dawn. "Mount me now," he said, "with thy grain and thy silken rope, and we will be off, for the way is far."

Ivan put the silver wheat and the golden corn into stout bags, slung them across the pony's neck, and with his silken lasso wound about his waist, mounted; and the little humpbacked horse darted away like an eagle. He scoured wide plains, leaped across swift rivers, and sped along mountain ridges; and after running without pause for a day and a night, he stopped in a deep valley on the edge of a dreary wood and said: "Little master, this is the Land of the South, and in this valley lives the Pig with the Golden Bristles. She comes each day to root in this forest. Take thou the golden corn and the silver wheat and pour them on the ground in two piles, at some distance apart and conceal thyself. When the Pig comes she will run to the corn, but the sucklings will begin to eat the wheat; and while the mother is not by, thou mayst secure them. Bring them to me and tie them to my saddle with the silken lasso, and I will bear thee back. As for the Pig, she will follow her sucklings."

Little Fool Ivan did all as the little horse bade him. He entered the forest, put the corn and wheat in two piles, hid himself in a thicket near the latter, and rested till evening, when there came a sound of grunting; and the Pig with the Golden Bristles and Silver Tusks led her young into the forest. She saw the corn and at once began to eat it, while the twenty sucklings ran to the wheat. He caught them, one by one, tied them with the silken lasso, and, hastening to the little horse, made them fast to his saddle-bow. Scarce had he mounted when the Pig perceived them and, seeing her sucklings borne away, came running after them, erecting her golden bristles and gnashing her silver tusks.

The little humpbacked horse sped away like a flash back along the road they had come with the Pig pursuing them; and, after running without stop for a night and a day, they arrived after dark at the Tzar's capital. Little Fool Ivan rode to the Palace court-yard, set down there the twenty suckling-pigs, still tied by the silken lasso, went to the stables and fell asleep.

In the morning the Tzar was greatly astonished to see that Little Fool Ivan had performed the task and was delighted to possess the new treasure. He sent for his Master of Horse and praised him and gave him a rich present, so that the envious ones thereat were made still more envious.

So, after some days, these came to the Tzar and said: "Thy Master of Horse, O Tzar's Majesty, doth boast now that the bringing of the wonderful Pig with her twenty sucklings was but a small service, and that he could, if he but chose, bring to thee the Mare with Seven Manes and her seven fierce stallions that graze on a green meadow between the crystal hills of the Caucasus."

Then, in more anger than before, the Tzar bade them bring Little Fool Ivan to his presence and said sternly: "Heed my royal word. If in seven days thou hast not brought hither from between the crystal hills of the Caucasus the Seven-Maned Mare with her seven stallions, I will send thee where the crows shall pick thy bones!"

Little Fool Ivan went weeping to the little humpbacked horse and told him of the Tzar's new command. "Grieve not, little master," said the other; "let not thy bright head droop. I can aid thee. Nor is this service too hard a one. Go thou to the Tzar and demand that he prepare at once a stone stable with one door opening into it and another opening out. Ask also for a horse's skin and an iron hammer of twelve poods * weight."

Ivan obeyed. He demanded the stable, the horse's skin and the iron hammer, and when all was ready the little horse said: "Lie down and sleep now, little master. The morning is wiser than the evening." Little Fool Ivan lay down and slept, and next morning at daybreak the pony waked him. Ivan tied the horse's skin to the saddle-bow, slung the hammer about his neck and mounted; and the little humpbacked horse darted away like a swallow, till the dust curled about his legs like a whirlwind. When he had run three days and four nights without rest, he stopped between two crystal hills and said:

"Yonder lies the green meadow whereon each evening grazes the Mare with Seven Manes and her seven fierce stallions. Take now thy horse's skin and sew me within it, and presently the mare will come and will set upon me with her teeth. While she rends the skin from me, do thou run and strike her between her two ears with thy twelve pood hammer, so that she will be stunned. Mount me then in haste, and thou mayst lead her after thee; and as for the seven stallions, they will follow."

So Little Fool Ivan sewed the little horse in the horse's skin; and when the mare with the seven stallions came, the stallions stood afar off, but the mare set upon him and rent the skin from him. Then Ivan ran and struck her with the iron hammer and stunned her, and instantly, holding by her seven manes, leaped to the back of the little humpbacked horse.

Scarce had he mounted, when the seven fierce stallions saw him and came galloping after them, screaming with rage. But the little humpbacked horse was off like a dart back along the road they had come, and when they had traveled without stopping three nights and four days, they arrived at the Tzar's capital. Little Fool Ivan rode to the

stone stable that had been built, went in at one door, and leaving therein the Mare with the Seven Manes, rode out of the other and barred it behind him; and the seven stallions, following the mare, were caught. Then Ivan went to his own place and went to sleep.

When they reported to the Tzar that this time also Little Fool Ivan had performed his task, the Tzar was more rejoiced than before and bestowed high rank and all manner of honors upon him, till, for hatred and malice, the envious ones were beside themselves.

They conferred together and coming before the Tzar, they said: "O Tzar's Majesty! to bring thee the mare and the stallions, thy Master of Horse boasteth now, was but a small service, saying that if he willed he could fetch thee from across three times nine lands, where the little red sun rises, the beautiful Girl-Tzar, whom thou hast so long desired for thy bride, who lives on the sea-ocean in a golden boat, which she rows with silver oars."

Then was the Tzar mightily angered. "Summon this boaster again before me," he commanded; and when Little Fool Ivan was come in, he bade him bring him the lovely Girl-Tzar within twelve days or pay the forfeit with his head. So, for the third time, Ivan went weeping to the little humpbacked horse and told him the Tzar's will.

"Dry thy tears, little master," said the other, "for I can assist thee. This is not, after all, the hardest service. Go thou to the Tzar and ask for two handkerchiefs cunningly embroidered in gold, a silken tent woven with gold thread and with golden tent-poles, gold and silver dishes, and all manner of wines and sweetmeats."

Ivan lost no time in obeying and when they were ready brought them to the stables. "Lie down and sleep now," said the little horse. "Tomorrow is wiser than today." Accordingly Little Fool Ivan lay down and slept till the little horse woke him at daybreak. He put all that had been prepared into a bag and mounted, and the little humpbacked horse sped away like the wind.

For six days they rode, a hundred thousand versts, till they reached a forest at the very end of the world, where the little red sun

* One pood — about forty pounds.

rises out of the blue sea-ocean. Here they stopped and Ivan alighted.

"Pitch now thy tent on the white sand," said the little horse. "In it spread thy embroidered handkerchiefs and on them put the wine and the gold and silver plates piled with sweetmeats. As for thee, do thou hide behind the tent and watch. From her golden boat the Girl-Tzar will see the tent and will approach it. Let her enter it and eat and drink her fill. Then go in, seize and hold her, and call for me." So saying, he ran to hide himself in the forest.

Ivan pitched the tent, prepared the food and wine, and lying down behind the tent, made a tiny hole in the silk through which to see, and waited. And before long the golden boat came sailing along over the blue sea-ocean. The beautiful Girl-Tzar alighted to look at the splendid tent and seeing the wine and sweetmeats, entered and began to eat and drink. So graceful and lovely was she that no tale could describe her and Little Fool Ivan could not gaze enough. He forgot what the little horse had told him and he was still peering through the hole in the silk when the beautiful maiden sprang up, left the tent, leaped into her golden boat, and the silver oars carried her far away on the sea-ocean.

When the little humpbacked horse came running up, Ivan too late repented of his folly. "I am guilty before thee!" he said. "And now I shall never see her again!" and he began to shed tears.

"Never mind," said the little horse. "She will come again tomorrow, but if thou failest next time we must needs go back without her, and thy head will be lost."

Next day Little Fool Ivan spread the wines and sweetmeats and lay down to watch as before; and again the lovely Girl-Tzar came rowing in her golden boat and entered the tent and began to regale herself. And while she ate and drank, Ivan ran in and seized and held her and called to the little horse. The girl cried out and fought to be free, but when she saw how handsome Little Fool Ivan was, she quite forgot to struggle. He mounted and put her before him on the saddle, and the humpbacked horse dashed away like lightning along the road they had come.

They rode six days and on the seventh they came again to the capital, and Little Fool Ivan — with a sad heart, since he had fallen in love with her himself — brought the lovely girl to the Palace.

The Tzar was overjoyed. He came out to meet them, took the maiden by her white hand, seated her beside him beneath a silken curtain on a cushion of purple velvet, and spoke to her tender words. "O Girl-Tzar, to whom none can be compared!" he said. "My Tzaritza that is to be! For how long have I not slept, either by night or in the white day, for thinking of thine eyes!"

But the beautiful Girl-Tzar turned from him and would not answer, and again and again he tried his wooing, till at length she said: "O Tzar, thou art wrinkled and gray, and hast left sixty years behind thee, while I am but sixteen. Should I wed thee, the Tzars of all Tzardoms would laugh, saying that a grandfather had taken to wife his grandchild."

Hearing this, the Tzar was angry. "It is true," he said, "that flowers do not bloom in winter and that I am no longer young. But I am nevertheless a great Tzar."

Then she replied: "I will wed no one who hath gray hairs and who lacks teeth in his head. If thou wilt but grow young again, then will I wed thee right willingly."

"How can a man grow young again?" he asked.

"There is a way, O Tzar," she said, "and it is thus: Order three great caldrons to be placed in thy courtyard. Fill the first with cold water, the second with boiling water, and the third with boiling mare's milk. He who bathes one minute in the boiling milk, two in the boiling water, and three in the cold water, becomes instantly young and so handsome that it cannot be told. Do this and I will become thy Tzaritza, but not otherwise."

The Tzar at once bade them prepare in the courtyard the three caldrons, one of cold water, one of boiling water, and one of boiling mare's milk, minded to make the test. The envious courtiers, however, came to him and said: "O Tzar's Majesty! this is a strange thing, and we have never heard that a man can plunge into boiling liquid and not be scalded. We pray thee, therefore, bid thy Master of Horse bathe before thee; then mayest thou be assured that all is well." And this counsel seemed to the Tzar good and he straightway summoned Little Fool Ivan and bade him prepare to make the trial.

When Ivan heard the Tzar's command he said to himself, "So I am to be killed like a sucking-pig or a chicken!" and he went sorrowfully to the stables and told the little humpbacked horse. "Thou hast found for me the Pig with the Golden Bristles," he said, "the Seven-Maned Mare, and the beautiful Girl-Tzar; but now these are all as nothing, and my life is as worthless as a boot sole!" And he began to weep bitterly.

"Weep not, little master," said the little horse. "This is indeed a real service that I shall serve thee. Now listen well to what I say. When thou goest to the courtyard, before thou strippest off thy clothes to bathe, ask of the Tzar to permit them to bring to thee thy little humpbacked horse, that thou mayest bid him farewell for the last time. He will agree; and when I am brought there, I shall gallop three times around the three kettles, dip my nose in each, and sprinkle thee. Lose not a moment then, but jump instantly in the caldron of boiling milk, then into the boiling water, and last into the cold water."

Scarcely had he instructed him when the Boyars came to bring Ivan to the courtyard. All the Court Ministers were there to see and the place was crowded with people, while the Tzar looked on from a balcony. The two caldrons were boiling hot, and servants fed the great fires beneath them with heaps of fuel. Little Fool Ivan bowed low before the Tzar and prepared for the bath.

But having taken off his coat, he bowed again and said: "O Tzar's Majesty! I have but one favor to ask. Bid them bring hither my little humpbacked horse that I may embrace him once more for the last time!" The Tzar was in good humor thinking he was so soon to regain his youth and he consented, and presently the little horse came running into the courtyard, dancing up and down and clapping his long ears together. But as soon as he came to the three caldrons he galloped three times round them, dipped his

nose into each and sprinkled his master; and without waiting a moment Little Fool Ivan threw off his clothes and jumped into the caldrons, one after the other. And while he had been good-looking before, he came from the last caldron so handsome that his beauty could neither be described with a pen nor written in a tale.

Now when the Tzar saw this, he could wait no longer. He hastened down from the balcony and without waiting to undress, crossed himself and jumped into the boiling milk. But the charm did not work in his case, and he was instantly scalded to death.

Seeing the Tzar was dead, the Girl-Tzar came to the balcony and spoke to the people, saying: "Thy Tzar chose me to be his Tzaritza. If thou wilt, I will rule this Tzardom, but it shall be only as the wife of him who brought me from mine own!"

The people, well pleased, shouted: "Health to Tzar Ivan!" And so Little Fool Ivan led the lovely Girl-Tzar to the church and they were married that same day.

Then Tzar Ivan ordered the trumpeters to blow their hammered trumpets and the butlers to open the bins, and he made in the Palace a feast like a hill, and the Boyars and Princes sat at oak tables and drank from golden goblets and made merry till they could not stand on their feet.

But Little Fool Ivan, with his Tzaritza, ruled the Tzardom wisely and well and grew never too wise to take counsel of his little humpbacked horse.

Mr. Samson Cat[3]

The definitive collection of Russian folk tales, comparable to the work of Jakob and Wilhelm Grimm in Germany, and to the accomplishment of Peter Asbjörnsen and Jörgen Moe in Scandinavia, is that made by A. N. Afanas'ev (1826–71). The English edition, Russian Fairy Tales, *was published by Pantheon Books (1945). Afanas'ev was an ethnologist who saw in the folk tales a clue to some of the basic characteristics of the Russian people. His collection was made over a period of eleven*

[3] From Valéry Carrick, *Picture Tales from the Russian* (Lippincott).

years. One of the stories in that collection is called The Ram, the Cat, and the Twelve Wolves. Mr. Samson Cat, *which is given here, is a version of the same story. Valéry Carrick has domesticated the story by changing the wild animals into the more familiar barnyard types but the plot is the same, and the theme remains untouched, namely, the power of fear to distort the facts.*

In his introduction to the Russian tales, Roman Jakobsen points out the interesting fact that only one-third of the Russian fairy tales are common to Western European sources, and one-third are totally unknown to Western Europe. The reader of folk tales will soon recognize the fact that only in Russian folklore is the witch, Baba Yaga, equipped with a house on chicken legs, which gives her an added degree of mobility, and no other lore has the Firebird and the Sea King.

Once upon a time a cat came running out of a certain village, and a fox came running out of a certain forest, and they met.

"How do you do?" said the fox. "How do you do?" said the cat. "What's your name?" said the fox. "Mr. Samson Cat, and what's yours?" "They call me Widow Fox." "Let's live together," said the cat. "Very well," said the fox. And so they settled down in Widow Fox's cottage.

One day Mr. Cat went out for a walk to gather berries in the forest, when a hare came running along. He never noticed the cat and jumped right on to the top of him.

Mr. Cat said: "F-r-r-r!" and the hare took fright and set off running so fast, that you could see his heels twinkle, and he was gone! Then the hare met a wolf, and said to him: "As I was running past Widow Fox's cottage, an unheard-of beast jumped right on to the top of me, he was so big and so dreadful! He was just going to swallow me up alive, only my legs saved me!" "I must go and have a look," said the wolf. "Don't, he will eat you up!" said the hare. Nevertheless the wolf went off to Widow Fox's cottage. And just then Widow Fox and Mr. Samson Cat had dragged a dead sheep into their courtyard, and were hard at it behind the fence, gobbling him up.

When Widow Fox had had enough, she came out at the gate, and there Mr. Wolf came up to her. He could hear how Mr. Cat was going on behind the fence, and said to Widow Fox: "Who is that there in your courtyard, Widow Fox?" "That's the mighty Mr. Samson Cat. He killed a sheep in a fight and now he's eating it. You'd better go away quickly, or else the same thing will happen to you." Meantime Mr. Cat was working hard at the sheep and crying: "Mee-ow, mee-ow!" And Mr. Wolf thought he was saying: "Not en*ough*, not en*ough*," and he thought: "Good gracious, he hasn't had enough after eating a whole sheep!" and he grew frightened and ran away. And as he was running he saw a pig rubbing his side against a tree. And he said to him: "Have you heard the news? We shan't be able to make a living in *this* forest any more; Widow Fox has got a dreadful animal living with her, the mighty Mr. Samson Cat. He eats four sheep a day, and then says he hasn't had enough." And Mr. Pig flapped his ears and winked his eye and said: "I should like to have a look at this beast!" "What are you thinking of!" said Mr. Wolf, "you'd better not go near the place!"

And while they were standing and talking, a bear came up, and Mr. Pig said to him: "Uncle Bruin, have you heard the news? Widow Fox has a beast living with her called the mighty Mr. Samson Cat. He eats ten oxen a day, and then says he hasn't had enough!" "What a terrible thing," said Bruin, "I *should* like to see that beast!"

So they discussed this way and that, and sent Mr. Pig to Widow Fox to ask if they might just with one eye have a peep at Mr. Samson Cat. And Mr. Pig came to Widow Fox and said: "How do you do? how do you do, Widow Fox? We have heard tell of your Mr. Samson and we should so like to have a look at him. Do please tell us how this could be arranged without the danger of his eating us up!" And Widow Fox thought for a bit and then said: "This is how you must arrange it: bake a *lot* of pies and get a *lot* of honey, and invite us to come and see you. *Perhaps* he won't do you any harm then." And Mr. Pig was delighted and ran back to his friends and told Mr. Wolf and Mr. Bruin: "Widow Fox says: 'Bake a *lot* of pies and get a *lot* of honey, and we will come and see you, and *perhaps* the mighty Mr. Samson Cat won't eat you all up.' " And so Bruin began to get the honey, Mr. Wolf began to bake the pies, and Mr. Pig began to tidy up, and get ready to receive the expected guests.

And they baked a *lot* of pies, and got a *lot* of honey, and Bruin said: "I shall get up into a tree; from there I shall see better when the guests begin to arrive." And so he climbed up.

And Mr. Wolf said: "For a whole day I've been working at those pies. I shall go and rest for a bit under this log." And he crawled under the log and lay down there.

And Mr. Pig said: "I have got hot all over, making everything tidy. I shall go and get into the shade for a bit." And he went and hid in the brushwood.

Meanwhile Widow Fox and the mighty Mr. Samson Cat came along, and their hosts were not there! Bruin was up an oak, Mr. Wolf under a log, and Mr. Pig in the brushwood. So there was nothing to be done but start eating without their hosts, and Widow Fox went for the honey while Mr. Cat got to work on the stuffed pies.

Suddenly Mr. Cat heard something rustling in the grass, and this was Mr. Pig's tail rustling from fright. Mr. Cat thought: "I expect that's a mouse," and dashed off and caught Mr. Pig by the tail.

Mr. Pig squealed and ran off as hard as he could, and ran his snout straight into the stump of a tree.

Mr. Cat was really just as much frightened himself, and jumped on to the tree. At this Bruin's paws grew weak from fright, and he fell plump down from the tree right on to the top of the log under which Mr. Wolf was lying.

And Mr. Wolf thought: "My end has come," and he jumped out from under the log and started off running as hard as he could go. And it was not till evening that Mr. Wolf, Mr. Pig and Bruin met again and told each other their experiences.

Mr. Pig said: "Well I never! The way he caught hold of my tail and dashed my head against the stump!" And Bruin said: "The stump was nothing! He tore out the whole oak tree by the roots and began to shake it. How could I possibly hold on? I was lucky not to fall into his jaws." And Mr. Wolf said: "And the way he put me one on with that oak tree! Well, that *is* a beast, if you like!" And they all began to shake their heads and said: "Well, that *is* a beast, if you like! There's no mistake about Mr. Samson Cat!"

Peter and the Wolf [4]

This old Russian folk tale was chosen by the Russian composer, Serge Prokofieff, as the subject for a musical fairy tale which he wrote to help children identify orchestral instruments. Each character in the story is represented by a corresponding instrument in the orchestra; Peter by the string quartet; the bird by the flute; the duck by the oboe; the cat by the clarinet in a low register; the grandfather by the bassoon; the wolf by three horns; the shots of the hunters by the kettle and bass drums.

Early one morning Peter opened the gate and went out into the big green meadow. On the branch of a birch tree sat a little bird — Peter's friend. When he saw Peter he chirped at him gaily, "All's quiet here."

Soon a duck came waddling around. She was very happy to see that Peter had not closed the gate, and so decided to have a nice swim in the deep pond in the meadow. As soon as the little bird saw the duck, he flew down and settled himself in the grass beside her. Shrugging his shoulders he said, "What kind of a bird are *you* if you can't fly?" To which the duck replied, "What kind of a bird are *you* if you can't swim?" and dived into the pond. They argued and argued, the duck swimming in the pond, the little bird hopping back and forth along the bank. Suddenly, something caught Peter's eye.

It was a cat crawling through the grass. The cat said to herself, "The bird is busy arguing. If I could only have him for my dinner!" Stealthily she crept toward him on her velvet paws.

"Oh, look out!" cried Peter.

Quickly the bird flew up into the tree while the duck quacked angrily at the cat —

[4] Serge Prokofieff, *Peter and the Wolf* (Knopf).

from the middle of the pond. The cat crawled round and round the tree and thought, "Is it worth climbing up so high? By the time I get there the bird will have flown away."

All at once Grandpapa came out. He was angry because Peter had gone to the meadow. "The meadow is a dangerous place," he cried. "What if a wolf should come out of the forest? — What would you do then?" Peter paid no attention to Grandpapa's words.

Boys like Peter are not afraid of wolves. Grandpapa took Peter by the hand, led him home — and locked the gate.

No sooner had Peter gone than a big grey wolf *did* come out of the forest. In a twinkling the cat sprang up into the tree. The duck quacked and in her great excitement jumped out of the pond.

No matter how hard the duck tried to run, she couldn't escape the wolf. He was getting nearer and nearer. He was catching up with her — there — he got her — and swallowed her with a single gulp!

And now this is how things stood: the cat was sitting on one branch up in the tree, the bird was sitting on another — not too close to the cat, while the wolf walked round and round the tree, looking at them both with greedy eyes. In the meantime, Peter, without the slightest fear, stood behind the closed gate, watching all that was going on. Presently, he ran into the house, found a strong rope, hurried back and climbed up the high stone wall. One of the branches of the tree, around which the wolf was pacing stretched out over this high wall. Grabbing hold of this branch, Peter climbed over into

the tree. He said to the bird, "Fly down and circle around the wolf's head, but take care that he doesn't catch you!" The bird almost touched the wolf's head with his wings, while the wolf snapped furiously at him from this side — and that. How that bird did worry the wolf! And oh! how the wolf tried to catch him! But the bird was far too clever for him.

Meanwhile, Peter had made a lasso, and letting it down very carefully — he caught the wolf by the tail and pulled with all his might. Feeling himself caught, the wolf began to jump wildly, trying to get loose. But Peter had tied the other end of the rope to the tree, and the wolf's jumping only made the rope tighter around his tail! Just then, who should come out of the woods but the hunters who were following the wolf's trail, and shooting as they came. From his perch in the tree Peter cried out to them: "You don't need to shoot. The bird and I have already caught him! Please help us take him to the zoo."

The hunters were only too willing. And now you can just imagine the triumphant procession! Peter at the head — after him the hunters, leading the wolf — and winding up the procession, Grandpapa and the cat. Grandpapa shook his head reprovingly. "This is all very well, but what if Peter had *not* caught the wolf — what then!" Above them flew the little bird, merrily chirping, "Aren't we smart, Peter and I? See what *we* have caught!" And if you had listened very carefully, you could have heard the duck quacking away inside the wolf, because in his haste the wolf had swallowed her whole — and the duck was still alive.

Budulinek [1]

⊷§ *An adventure story, a model of construction, choice of incident, and motivation, as far as younger children are concerned. It speaks to them with authority, and seems to mirror the world as they feel it. Parker Fillmore, in his introduction to the collection in which it occurs, states that it is one of five nursery tales which make up a section of Czech, Moravian, or Slovak tradition. He had it first by word of mouth, and then substantiated his discovery in the written records of old tales.*

There was once a little boy named Budulinek. He lived with his old Granny in a cottage near a forest.

Granny went out to work every day. In the morning when she went away she always said:

"There, Budulinek, there's your dinner on the table and mind, you mustn't open the door no matter who knocks!"

One morning Granny said:

"Now, Budulinek, today I'm leaving you some soup for your dinner. Eat it when dinner time comes. And remember what I always say: don't open the door no matter who knocks."

She went away and pretty soon Lishka, the sly old mother fox, came and knocked on the door.

"Budulinek!" she called. "You know me! Open the door! Please!"

Budulinek called back:

"No, I mustn't open the door."

But Lishka, the sly old mother fox, kept on knocking.

[1] From Parker Fillmore, *The Shoemaker's Apron* (Harcourt, Brace, 1920).

"Listen, Budulinek," she said: "if you open the door, do you know what I'll do? I'll give you a ride on my tail!"

Now Budulinek thought to himself:

"Oh, that would be fun to ride on the tail of Lishka, the fox!"

So Budulinek forgot all about what Granny said to him every day and opened the door.

Lishka, the sly old thing, came into the room and what do you think she did? Do you think she gave Budulinek a ride on her tail? Well, she didn't. She just went over to the table and gobbled up the bowl of soup that Granny had put there for Budulinek's dinner and then she ran away.

When dinner time came Budulinek hadn't anything to eat.

In the evening when Granny came home, she said:

"Budulinek, did you open the door and let any one in?"

Budulinek was crying because he was so hungry, and he said:

"Yes, I let in Lishka, the old mother fox, and she ate up all my dinner, too!"

Granny said:

"Now, Budulinek, you see what happens when you open the door and let some one in. Another time remember what Granny says and don't open the door."

The next morning Granny cooked some porridge for Budulinek's dinner and said:

"Now, Budulinek, here's some porridge for your dinner. Remember: while I'm gone you must not open the door no matter who knocks."

Granny was no sooner out of sight than Lishka came again and knocked on the door.

"Oh, Budulinek!" she called. "Open the door and let me in!"

But Budulinek said:

"No, I won't open the door!"

"Oh, now, Budulinek, please open the door!" Lishka begged. "You know me! Do you know what I'll do if you open the door? I'll give you a ride on my tail! Truly I will!"

Budulinek thought to himself:

"This time maybe she will give me a ride on her tail."

So he opened the door.

Lishka came into the room, gobbled up Budulinek's porridge, and ran away without giving him any ride at all.

When dinner time came Budulinek hadn't anything to eat.

In the evening when Granny came home she said:

"Budulinek, did you open the door and let any one in?"

Budulinek was crying again because he was so hungry, and he said

"Yes, I let in Lishka, the old mother fox, and she ate up all my porridge, too!"

"Budulinek, you're a bad boy!" Granny said. "If you open the door again, I'll have to spank you! Do you hear?"

The next morning before she went to work, Granny cooked some peas for Budulinek's dinner.

As soon as Granny was gone he began eating the peas, they were so good.

Presently Lishka, the fox, came and knocked on the door.

"Budulinek!" she called. "Open the door! I want to come in!"

But Budulinek wouldn't open the door. He took his bowl of peas and went to the window and ate them there where Lishka could see him.

"Oh, Budulinek!" Lishka begged. "You know me! Please open the door! This time I promise you I'll give you a ride on my tail! Truly I will!"

She just begged and begged until at last Budulinek opened the door. Then Lishka jumped into the room and do you know what she did? She put her nose right into the bowl of peas and gobbled them all up!

Then she said to Budulinek:

"Now get on my tail and I'll give you a ride!"

So Budulinek climbed on Lishka's tail

and Lishka went running around the room faster and faster until Budulinek was dizzy and just had to hold on with all his might.

Then, before Budulinek knew what was happening, Lishka slipped out of the house and ran swiftly off into the forest, home to her hole, with Budulinek still on her tail! She hid Budulinek down in her hole with her own three children and she wouldn't let him out. He had to stay there with the three little foxes and they all teased him and bit him. And then wasn't he sorry he had disobeyed his Granny! And, oh, how he cried!

When Granny came home she found the door open and no little Budulinek anywhere. She looked high and low, but no, there was no little Budulinek. She asked every one she met had they seen her little Budulinek, but nobody had. So poor Granny just cried and cried, she was so lonely and sad.

One day an organ-grinder with a wooden leg began playing in front of Granny's cottage. The music made her think of Budulinek.

"Organ-grinder," Granny said, "here's a penny for you. But, please, don't play any more. Your music makes me cry."

"Why does it make you cry?" the organ-grinder asked.

"Because it reminds me of Budulinek," Granny said, and she told the organ-grinder all about Budulinek and how somebody had stolen him away.

The organ-grinder said:

"Poor Granny! I tell you what I'll do: as I go around and play my organ I'll keep my eyes open for Budulinek. If I find him I'll bring him back to you."

"Will you?" Granny cried. "If you bring me back my little Budulinek I'll give you a measure of rye and a measure of millet and a measure of poppy seed and a measure of everything in the house!"

So the organ-grinder went off and everywhere he played his organ he looked for Budulinek. But he couldn't find him.

At last one day while he was walking through the forest he thought he heard a little boy crying. He looked around everywhere until he found a fox's hole.

"Oho!" he said to himself. "I believe that wicked old Lishka must have stolen Budulinek! She's probably keeping him here with her own three children! I'll soon find out."

So he put down his organ and began to play. And as he played he sang softly:

> "One old fox
> And two, three, four,
> And Budulinek
> He makes one more!"

Old Lishka heard the music playing and she said to her oldest child:

"Here, son, give the old man a penny and tell him to go away because my head aches."

So the oldest little fox climbed out of the hole and gave the organ-grinder a penny and said:

"My mother says, please will you go away because her head aches."

As the organ-grinder reached over to take the penny, he caught the oldest little fox and stuffed him into a sack. Then he went on playing and singing:

> "One old fox
> And two and three
> And Budulinek
> Makes four for me!"

Presently Lishka sent out her second child with a penny and the organ-grinder caught the second little fox in the same way and stuffed it also into the sack. Then he went on grinding his organ and softly singing:

> "One old fox
> And another for me,
> And Budulinek
> He makes the three."

"I wonder why that old man still plays his organ," Lishka said and sent out her third child with a penny.

So the organ-grinder caught the third little fox and stuffed it also into the sack. Then he kept on playing and singing softly:

> "One old fox —
> I'll soon get you! —
> And Budulinek
> He makes just two."

At last Lishka herself came out. So he caught her, too, and stuffed her in with her children. Then he sang:

> "Four naughty foxes
> Caught alive!
> And Budulinek
> He makes the five!"

The organ-grinder went to the hole and called down:

"Budulinek! Budulinek! Come out!"

As there were no foxes left to hold him back, Budulinek was able to crawl out.

When he saw the organ-grinder he cried and said:

"Oh, please, Mr. Organ-Grinder, I want to go home to my Granny!"

"I'll take you home to your Granny," the organ-grinder said, "but first I must punish these naughty foxes."

The organ-grinder cut a strong switch and gave the four foxes in the sack a terrible beating until they begged him to stop and promised that they would never again do anything to Budulinek.

Then the organ-grinder let them go and he took Budulinek home to Granny.

Granny was delighted to see her little Budulinek and she gave the organ-grinder a measure of rye and a measure of millet and a measure of poppy seed and a measure of everything else in the house.

And Budulinek never again opened the door!

The Twelve Months [2]

◄§ *This Czech tale is one of the best in Nemcova's collection. It really is another version of the French story* Toads and Diamonds. *However, as it is made more complicated by cumulative repetition, it builds up better to a climax. And yet, to a child reader, the marriage of the heroine to a mere farmer may not be so interesting as her marriage to a prince; and the contrast with* Toads and Diamonds *is unforgettable.*

There was once a woman who had two girls. One was her own daughter, the other

[2] From Parker Fillmore, *The Shoemaker's Apron* (Harcourt, Brace, 1920).

a stepchild. Holena, her own daughter, she loved dearly, but she couldn't bear even the sight of Marushka, the stepchild. This was because Marushka was so much prettier than Holena. Marushka, the dear child, didn't know how pretty she was, and so she never understood why, whenever she stood beside Holena, the stepmother frowned so crossly.

Mother and daughter made Marushka do all the housework alone. She had to cook and wash and sew and spin and take care of the garden and look after the cow. Holena, on the contrary, spent all her time decking herself out and sitting around like a grand lady.

Marushka never complained. She did all she was told to do and bore patiently their everlasting fault-finding. In spite of all the hard work she did, she grew prettier from day to day, and in spite of her lazy life, Holena grew uglier.

"This will never do," the stepmother thought to herself. "Soon the boys will come courting, and once they see how pretty Marushka is, they'll pay no attention at all to my Holena. We had just better do all we can to get rid of that Marushka as soon as possible."

So they both nagged Marushka all day long. They made her work harder, they beat her, they didn't give her enough to eat, they did everything they could think of to make her ugly and nasty. But all to no avail. Marushka was so good and sweet that, in spite of all their harsh treatment, she kept on growing prettier.

One day in the middle of January Holena took the notion that nothing would do but she must have a bunch of fragrant violets to put in her bodice.

"Marushka!" she ordered sharply. "I want some violets. Go out to the forest and get me some."

"Good heavens, my dear sister!" cried poor Marushka. "What can you be thinking of? Whoever heard of violets growing under the snow in January?"

"What, you lazy little slattern!" Holena shouted. "You dare to argue with me! You go this minute and if you come back without violets, I'll kill you!"

The stepmother sided with Holena and, taking Marushka roughly by the shoulder, she pushed her out of the house and slammed the door.

The poor child climbed slowly up the mountain-side, weeping bitterly. All around the snow lay deep with no track of man or beast in any direction. Marushka wandered on and on, weak with hunger and shaking with cold.

"Dear God in heaven," she prayed, "take me to yourself away from all this suffering."

Suddenly ahead of her she saw a glowing light. She struggled toward it and found at last that it came from a great fire that was burning on the top of the mountain. Around the fire there were twelve stones, one of them much bigger and higher than the rest. Twelve men were seated on the stones. Three of them were very old and white; three were not so old; three were middle-aged; and three were beautiful youths. They did not talk. They sat silent gazing at the fire. They were the Twelve Months.

For a moment Marushka was frightened and hesitated. Then she stepped forward and said, politely:

"Kind sirs, may I warm myself at your fire? I am shaking with cold."

Great January nodded his head and Marushka reached her stiff fingers toward the flames.

"This is no place for you, my child," Great January said. "Why are you here?"

"I'm hunting for violets," Marushka answered.

"Violets? This is no time to look for violets with snow on the ground!"

"I know that, sir, but my sister, Holena, says I must bring her violets from the forest or she'll kill me, and my mother says so, too. Please, sir, won't you tell me where I can find some?"

Great January slowly stood up and walked over to the youngest Month. He handed him a long staff and said:

"Here, March, you take the high seat."

So March took the high seat and began waving the staff over the fire. The fire blazed up and instantly the snow all about began to melt. The trees burst into bud; the grass revived; the little pink buds of the daisies appeared; and, lo, it was spring!

While Marushka looked, violets began to peep out from among the leaves, and soon it was as if a great blue quilt had been spread on the ground.

"Now, Marushka," March cried, "there are your violets! Pick them quickly!"

Marushka was overjoyed. She stooped down and gathered a great bunch. Then she thanked the Months politely, bade them good day, and hurried away.

Just imagine Holena and the stepmother's surprise when they saw Marushka coming home through the snow with her hands full of violets. They opened the door and instantly the fragrance of the flowers filled the cottage.

"Where did you get them?" Holena demanded rudely.

"High up in the mountain," Marushka said. "The ground up there is covered with them."

Holena snatched the violets and fastened them in her waist. She kept smelling them herself all afternoon and she let her mother smell them, but she never once said to Marushka:

"Dear sister, won't you take a smell?"

The next day, as she was sitting idle in the chimney corner, she took the notion that she must have some strawberries to eat. So she called Marushka and said:

"Here you, Marushka, go out to the forest and get me some strawberries."

"Good heavens, my dear sister," Marushka said, "where can I find strawberries this time of year? Whoever heard of strawberries growing under the snow?"

"What, you lazy little slattern!" Holena shouted. "You dare to argue with me! You go this minute, and if you come back without strawberries, I'll kill you!"

Again the stepmother sided with Holena and, taking Marushka roughly by the shoulder, she pushed her out of the house and slammed the door.

Again the poor child climbed slowly up the mountain-side, weeping bitterly. All around the snow lay deep with no track of man or beast in any direction. Marushka wandered on and on, weak with hunger and shaking with cold. At last she saw ahead of her the glow of the same fire that she had seen the day before. With happy heart she hastened to it. The Twelve Months were seated as before with Great January on the high seat.

Marushka bowed politely and said:

"Kind sirs, may I warm myself at your fire? I am shaking with cold."

Great January nodded and Marushka reached her stiff fingers toward the flames.

"But Marushka," Great January said, "why are you here again? What are you hunting now?"

"I'm hunting for strawberries," Marushka answered.

"Strawberries? But, Marushka, my child, it is winter and strawberries do not grow in the snow."

Marushka shook her head sadly.

"I know that, sir, but my sister, Holena, says I must bring her strawberries from the forest or she will kill me, and my mother says so, too. Please, sir, won't you tell me where I can find some?"

Great January slowly stood up and walked over to the Month who sat opposite him. He handed him the long staff and said:

"Here, June, you take the high seat."

So June took the high seat and began waving the staff over the fire. The flames blazed high, and with the heat the snow all about melted instantly. The earth grew green; the trees decked themselves in leaves; the birds began to sing; flowers bloomed and, lo, it was summer! Presently little starry white blossoms covered the ground under the beech trees. Soon these turned to fruit, first green, then pink, then red, and, with a gasp of delight, Marushka saw that they were ripe strawberries.

"Now, Marushka," June cried, "there are your strawberries! Pick them quickly!"

Marushka picked an apronful of berries. Then she thanked the Months politely, bade them good-bye, and hurried home.

Just imagine again Holena and the stepmother's surprise as they saw Marushka coming through the snow with an apronful of strawberries!

They opened the door and instantly the fragrance of the berries filled the house.

"Where did you get them?" Holena demanded rudely.

"High up in the mountain," Marushka answered, "under the beech trees."

Holena took the strawberries and gobbled and gobbled and gobbled. Then the stepmother ate all she wanted. But it never occurred to either of them to say:

"Here, Marushka, you take one."

The next day, when Holena was sitting idle, as usual, in the chimney corner, the notion took her that she must have some red apples. So she called Marushka and said:

"Here you, Marushka, go out to the forest and get me some red apples."

"But, my dear sister," Marushka gasped, "where can I find red apples in winter?"

"What, you lazy little slattern, you dare to argue with me! You go this minute, and if you come back without red apples, I'll kill you!"

For the third time the stepmother sided with Holena and, taking Marushka roughly by the shoulder, pushed her out of the house and slammed the door.

So again the poor child went out to the forest. All around the snow lay deep with no track of man or beast in any direction. This time Marushka hurried straight to the mountain-top. She found the Months still seated about their fire with Great January still on the high stone.

Marushka bowed politely and said:

"Kind sirs, may I warm myself at your fire? I am shaking with cold."

Great January nodded, and Marushka reached her stiff fingers toward the flames.

"Why are you here again, Marushka?" Great January asked. "What are you looking for now?"

"Red apples," Marushka answered. "My sister, Holena, says I must bring her some red apples from the forest or she will kill me, and my mother says so, too. Please sir, won't you tell me where I can find some?"

Great January slowly stood up and walked over to one of the older Months. He handed him the long staff and said:

"Here, September, you take the high seat."

So September took the high seat and began waving the staff over the fire. The fire burned and glowed. Instantly the snow disappeared. The fields about looked brown and yellow and dry. From the trees the leaves dropped one by one and a cool breeze scattered them over the stubble. There were not many flowers, old wild asters on the hillside, and meadow saffron in the valleys, and under the beeches ferns and ivy. Presently Marushka spied an apple tree weighted down with ripe fruit.

"There, Marushka," September called, "there are your apples. Gather them quickly."

Marushka reached up and picked one apple. Then she picked another.

"That's enough, Marushka!" September shouted. "Don't pick any more!"

Marushka obeyed at once. Then she thanked the Months politely, bade them good-bye, and hurried home.

Holena and her stepmother were more surprised than ever to see Marushka coming through the snow with red apples in her hands. They let her in and grabbed the apples from her.

"Where did you get them?" Holena demanded.

"High up on the mountain," Marushka answered. "There are plenty of them growing there."

"Plenty of them! And you only brought us two!" Holena cried angrily. "Or did you pick more and eat them yourself on the way home?"

"No, no, my dear sister," Marushka said. "I haven't eaten any, truly I haven't. They shouted to me not to pick any more."

"I wish the lightning had struck you dead!" Holena sneered. "I've a good mind to beat you!"

After a time the greedy Holena left off her scolding to eat one of the apples. It had so delicious a flavor that she declared she had never in all her life tasted anything so good. Her mother said the same. When they had finished both apples, they began to wish for more.

"Mother," Holena said, "go get me my fur cloak. I'm going up the mountain myself. No use sending that lazy little slattern again, for she would only eat up all the apples on the way home. I'll find that tree and when I pick the apples, I'd like to see anybody stop me!"

The mother begged Holena not to go out

in such weather, but Holena was headstrong and would go. She threw her fur cloak over her shoulders and put a shawl on her head and off she went up the mountain-side.

All around the snow lay deep with no track of man or beast in any direction. Holena wandered on and on determined to find those wonderful apples. At last she saw a light in the distance and when she reached it she found it was the great fire about which the Twelve Months were seated.

At first she was frightened, but, soon growing bold, she elbowed her way through the circle of men and without so much as saying, "By your leave," she put out her hands to the fire. She hadn't even the courtesy to say: "Good-day."

Great January frowned.

"Who are you?" he asked in a deep voice. "And what do you want?"

Holena looked at him rudely.

"You old fool, what business is it of yours who I am or what I want!"

She tossed her head airily and walked off into the forest.

The frown deepened on Great January's brow. Slowly he stood up and waved the staff over his head. The fire died down. Then the sky grew dark; an icy wind blew over the mountain; and the snow began to fall so thickly that it looked as if someone in the sky were emptying a huge feather bed.

Holena could not see a step before her. She struggled on and on. Now she ran into a tree, now she fell into a snowdrift. In spite of her warm cloak her limbs began to weaken and grow numb. The snow kept on falling, the icy wind kept on blowing.

Did Holena at last begin to feel sorry that she had been so wicked and cruel to Marushka? No, she did not. Instead, the colder she grew, the more bitterly she reviled Marushka in her heart, the more bitterly she reviled even the good God Himself.

Meanwhile, at home her mother waited for her and waited. She stood at the window as long as she could, then she opened the door and tried to peer through the storm. She waited and waited, but no Holena came.

"Oh dear, oh dear, what can be keeping her?" she thought to herself. "Does she like those apples so much that she can't leave them, or what is it? I think I'll have to go out myself and find her."

So the stepmother put her fur cloak about her shoulders, threw a shawl over her head, and started out.

She called: "Holena! Holena!" but no one answered.

She struggled on and on up the mountain-side. All around the snow lay deep with no track of man or beast in any direction.

"Holena! Holena!"

Still no answer.

The snow fell fast. The icy wind moaned on.

At home Marushka prepared the dinner and looked after the cow. Still neither Holena nor the stepmother returned.

"What can they be doing all this time?" Marushka thought.

She ate her dinner alone and then sat down to work at the distaff.

The spindle filled and daylight faded, and still no sign of Holena and her mother.

"Dear God in heaven, what can be keeping them!" Marushka cried anxiously. She peered out the window to see if they were coming.

The storm had spent itself. The wind had died down. The fields gleamed white in the snow, and up in the sky the frosty stars were twinkling brightly. But not a living creature was in sight. Marushka knelt down and prayed for her sister and mother.

The next morning she prepared breakfast for them.

"They'll be very cold and hungry," she said to herself.

She waited for them, but they didn't come. She cooked dinner for them, but still they didn't come. In fact they never came, for they both froze to death on the mountain.

So our good little Marushka inherited the cottage and the garden and the cow. After a time she married a farmer. He made her a good husband and they lived together very happily.

POLAND

The Jolly Tailor Who Became King [1]

⪥ *In making her collection*, The Jolly Tailor and Other Fairy Tales, *Mrs. Borski chose stories most representative of Polish folklore. Stories she had told over and over again to Polish children in their own tongue, she translated for English-speaking children. The favorite,* The Jolly Tailor, *is reprinted below. A lively story, full of humor, it tells of impossible happenings that seem perfectly logical and satisfactory.*

Once upon a time, in the town of Taidaraida, there lived a merry little Tailor, Mr. Joseph Nitechka. He was a very thin man and had a small beard of one hundred and thirty-six hairs.

All tailors are thin, reminding one of a needle and thread, but Mr. Nitechka was the thinnest of all, for he could pass through the eye of his own needle. He was so thin that he could eat nothing but noodles, for they were the only thing which could pass down his throat. But for all this, he was a very happy man, and a handsome one, too, particularly on holidays when he braided his beard.

Now Mr. Nitechka would have lived very happily in Taidaraida had it not been for a Gypsy. She happened to be in the town when she cut her foot. In her trouble she went to the Tailor, who darned the skin so carefully and so neatly that not a scar could be seen.

[1] From Lucia Merecka Borski and Kate B. Miller, *The Jolly Tailor and Other Fairy Tales* (Longmans, Green, 1925).

The Gypsy was so grateful that she read Nitechka's future from his hand:

"If you leave this town on a Sunday and walk always Westward, you will reach a place where you will be chosen King!"

Nitechka laughed at this. But that very night he dreamt that he indeed became a King, and that from great prosperity he grew so fat that he looked like an immense barrel. Upon waking he thought:

"Maybe it is true? Who knows? Get up, Mr. Nitechka, and go West."

He took a bundle with a hundred needles and a thousand miles of thread, a thimble, an iron, and a pair of very big scissors, and started out to find the West. He asked first one and then another in the town of Taidaraida where the West was. But no one knew. Finally he asked an old man, a hundred and six years old, who upon thinking awhile said:

"West must be there where the sun sets."

This seemed so wise to Nitechka that he went that way. But he had not gone far when a gust of wind blew across the field — not a very strong gust — but, because Mr. Nitechka was so exceedingly thin, just strong enough to carry him off.

The Tailor flew through the air, laughing heartily at such a ride. Soon, however, the wind became tired and let him down to earth. He was much bewildered and did not come to his senses until someone shouted:

"What is this?"

Mr. Nitechka looked around and saw that he was in a wheat field and that the wind had thrown him right into the arms of a Scarecrow. The Scarecrow was very elegant in a blue jacket and a broken stovepipe hat, and his trousers were only a bit torn. He had two sticks for feet and also sticks for hands.

Nitechka took off his little cap, bowed very low, saying in his thin voice:

"My regards to the honorable Sir. I beg your pardon if I stepped on your foot. I am Mr. Nitechka, the Tailor."

"I am very much pleased to meet such a charming man," answered the Scarecrow. "I am Count Scarecrow and my coat of arms is Four Sticks. I watch the sparrows here so that they will not steal wheat, but I give little heed to them. I am uncommonly courageous and would like to fight only with lions and tigers, but this year they very seldom come to eat the wheat. Where are you going, Mr. Nitechka?"

Nitechka bowed again and hopped three times as he was very polite and he knew that well-bred men thus greeted each other.

"Where do I go, Mr. Count? I am going Westward to a place where I will become King."

"Is it possible?"

"Of course! I was born to be a King. And perhaps you, Mr. Count, would like to go with me; it will be merrier."

"All right," answered the Scarecrow. "I am already weary of being here. But please, Mr. Nitechka, mend my clothes a bit, because I might like to marry someone on the way; and so I should be neat and handsome."

"With great pleasure!" said Nitechka. He went to work, and in an hour the Scarecrow had a beautiful suit and a hat almost like new. The sparrows in the field laughed at him a little, but he paid no attention to them as he walked with great dignity with Mr. Nitechka.

On the way the two became great friends. They generally slept in a wheat field, the Tailor tying himself to the Scarecrow with a piece of thread so that the wind could not carry him off again. And when dogs fell upon them, the Scarecrow, who was very brave because of his profession, tore out his foot and threw it after them. Then he tied it again to his body.

Once in the evening they spied a light through the trees.

"Let us go there; maybe they will let us pass the night," said Nitechka.

"By all means, let us do them the honor," answered Count Scarecrow.

As they drew nearer they saw that it was a strange house because it could walk. It stood on four feet and was turning around.

"The owner of the house must be a gay man," whispered the Tailor. "He dances all the time."

They waited until the door came round to them and then went into the house. It was indeed a very strange house. Although it was summer, immense logs of wood burned in the stove, and on the fire sat a nobleman warming himself. From time to time he took a glowing coal in his hands and swallowed it with great pleasure. Upon noticing the travelers, he went over to them, bowed and said:

"Is it not Mr. Nitechka and Count Scarecrow?"

They were speechless with astonishment to think that he should know them, but said nothing. Mr. Nitechka hopped up three times and Count Scarecrow took off his hat. The nobleman continued:

"Stay with me for supper and tomorrow you may go your way. I will call my wife, my daughter, and my other relatives."

He clapped his hands and suddenly a large company appeared. The host's daughter was very beautiful, but when she laughed, it was as if a horse had neighed in a meadow. She took an instant liking to Nitechka and told him she would very much like to have him for her husband. They sat down to supper, Nitechka and Count Scarecrow on a bench, and all the others on iron pots filled with glowing coals.

"Do not wonder, dear Sirs," the host said, "that we sit thus, for our family always feels very cold."

They served soup in a big caldron and Nitechka was just putting his spoon to his lips, when Count Scarecrow pulled his coat and whispered:

"Mr. Nitechka, don't eat, for this is hot pitch!"

So pretending that they liked the soup, they spilt it under the table. Then a strange looking servant brought a new dish of rats in a black sauce, and later he served fried locust, lob-worms with parmesan cheese like noodles, and, for dessert, old, bad eggs.

Nitechka and Count Scarecrow threw everything under the table, becoming more and more frightened.

All at once the host said:

"Do you know, Mr. Nitechka, that the King has just died in Pacanów [Patsanoff]?"

"Where is Pacanów, is it far?" asked the Tailor.

"A crow can fly to that town in two days. And do you know they are seeking a King there, and he who marries my daughter will become King?"

The girl neighed like an old horse at this and threw her arms around Nitechka's neck.

"Let's run away!" murmured Count Scarecrow.

"But I can't find the door. There is no help," replied Nitechka.

Soon, however, the whole family became very gay, and presently the host said:

"We will drink to your health and sing merrily. Mr. Nitechka, do you know a song?"

"Yes, indeed," said Nitechka, "and a very nice one."

Saying this, he whispered to Count Scarecrow:

"Watch, brother, and when the door is behind us, shout!"

Then he got up, took off his cap and in his thin little voice began to sing the only song he knew.

> "Sing praises to the Holy Virgin,
> Sing praises to Her Wondrous Name!"

At the mention of the Virgin, the whole family rose to their feet, and ran around the room, sprawling and shouting and cursing. Nitechka said nothing, but simply continued his song. He could feel the house running somewhere with them, and so he sang and sang like the thinnest pipe in the organ. When he had finished the song, he began to sing it over again. At that moment everything disappeared, and only a terrible wind blew.

Terrified, Nitechka and Count Scarecrow found themselves alone in a huge meadow. Then they gave thanks for their delivery and Nitechka said:

"They were awful devils, but we overpowered them."

"I frightened them so much," boasted Count Scarecrow.

They continued their way toward Pacanów, where dwelt the famous smiths who shoe the goats, a beautiful old town, where the King had died. When after seven days of adventures they reached Pacanów, they were greatly astonished. All around the town it was sunshiny and pleasant; but over Pacanów the rain poured from the sky as from a bucket.

"I won't go in there," said the Scarecrow, "because my hat will get wet."

"And even I do not wish to become King of such a wet kingdom," said the Tailor.

Just then the townspeople spied them and rushed toward them, led by the Burgomaster riding on a shod goat.

"Dear Sirs," they said, "maybe you can help us."

"And what has happened to you?" asked Nitechka.

"Deluge and destruction threaten us. Our King died a week ago, and since that time a terrible rain has come down upon our gorgeous town. We can't even make fires in our houses, because so much water runs through the chimneys. We will perish, honorable Sirs!"

"It is too bad," said Nitechka very wisely.

"Oh, very bad! And we are most sorry for the late King's daughter, as the poor thing can't stop crying and this causes even more water."

"That makes it still worse," replied Nitechka, still more wisely.

"Help us, help us!" continued the Burgomaster. "Do you know the immeasurable reward the Princess promised to the one who stops the rain? She promised to marry him and then he will become King."

"Truly?" cried Nitechka. "Count Scarecrow, let's go to the town. We ought to try to help them."

They were led through the terrible rain to the Princess, who upon seeing Nitechka, cried out:

"Oh, what a handsome youth!"

He hopped three times and said:

"Is it true, Princess, that you will marry the one who stops the rain?"

"I vowed I would."

"And if I do it?"

"I will keep my promise."

"And I shall become a King?"

"You will, O beautiful youth."

"Very well," answered the Tailor. "I am going to stop the rain."

So saying he nodded to Count Scarecrow and they left the Princess.

The whole population, full of hope, gathered around them. Nitechka and the Scarecrow stood under an umbrella and whispered to each other.

"Listen, Scarecrow, what shall we do to make the rain stop falling?"

"We have to bring back pleasant weather."

"But how?"

"Ha! Let's think!"

But for three days they thought and the rain fell and fell and fell. Suddenly Nitechka gave a cry of joy like a goat's bleating.

"I know where the rain comes from!"

"Where from?"

"From the sky!"

"Eh!" grumbled the Scarecrow. "I know that too. Surely it doesn't fall from the bottom to the top, but the other way around."

"Yes," said Nitechka, "but why does it fall over the town only, and not elsewhere?"

"Because elsewhere is nice weather."

"You're stupid, Mr. Count," said the Tailor. "But tell me, how long has it rained?"

"They say since the King died."

"So you see! Now I know everything! The King was so great and mighty that when he died and went to Heaven he made a huge hole in the sky."

"Oh, oh, true!"

"Through the hole the rain poured and it will pour until the end of the world if the hole isn't sewed up!"

Count Scarecrow looked at him in amazement.

"In all my life I have never seen such a wise Tailor," said he.

They rejoiced greatly, went to the Burgomaster, and ordered him to tell the townspeople that Mr. Joseph Nitechka, a citizen of the town of Taidaraida, promised to stop the rain.

"Long live Mr. Nitechka! Long may he live!" shouted the whole town.

Then Nitechka ordered them to bring all the ladders in the town, tie them together, and lean them against the sky. He took a hundred needles and, threading one, went up the ladders. Count Scarecrow stayed at the bottom and unwound the spool on which there was a hundred miles of thread.

When Nitechka got to the very top he saw that there was a huge hole in the sky, a hole as big as the town. A torn piece of the sky hung down, and through this hole the water poured.

So he went to work and sewed and sewed for two days. His fingers grew stiff and he became very tired but he did not stop. When he had finished sewing he pressed out the sky with the iron and then, exhausted, went down the ladders.

Once more the sun shone over Pacanów. Count Scarecrow almost went mad with joy, as did all the other inhabitants of the town. The Princess wiped her eyes that were almost cried out, and throwing herself on Nitechka's neck, kissed him affectionately.

Nitechka was very happy. He looked around, and there were the Burgomaster and Councilmen bringing him a golden scepter and a gorgeous crown and shouting:

"Long live King Nitechka! Long live he! Long live he! And let him be the Princess' husband and let him reign happily!"

So the merry little Tailor reigned happily for a long time, and the rain never fell in his kingdom. In his good fortune Nitechka did not forget his old friend, Count Scarecrow, but he appointed him the Great Warden of the Kingdom to drive away the sparrows from the royal head.

FINLAND

The Bear Says "North" [1]

In his introduction to the collection from which this story is taken, Parker Fillmore states his belief that this story, with fifteen others which he defines as a "Nursery epic," is related to the Beast Epic of Reynard the Fox. It is not a debased form of that great satire on Church and State which has been current in Europe since the twelfth century, but rather the very roots from which the cycle springs. In other words, the simpler stories reflecting in animal form traits of Finnish peasant character antedate the more sophisticated Reynard cycle.

This brief tale has a measure of sophistication and wit, showing Fox in his traditional role of trickster and wise man.

One day while Osmo, the Bear, was prowling about the woods he caught a Grouse.

"Pretty good!" he thought to himself. "Wouldn't the other animals be surprised if they knew old Osmo had caught a Grouse!"

He was so proud of his feat that he wanted all the world to know of it. So, holding the Grouse carefully in his teeth without injuring it, he began parading up and down the forest ways.

"They'll all certainly envy me this nice plump Grouse," he thought. "And they won't be so ready to call me awkward and lumbering after this, either!"

Presently Mikko, the Fox, sauntered by. He saw at once that Osmo was showing off and he determined that the Bear would not

[1] From Parker Fillmore, *Mighty Mikko* (Harcourt, Brace, 1922).

get the satisfaction of any admiration from him. So he pretended not to see the Grouse at all. Instead he pointed his nose upwards and sniffed.

"Um! Um!" grunted Osmo, trying to attract attention to himself.

"Ah," Mikko remarked, casually, "is that you, Osmo? What way is the wind blowing to-day? Can you tell me?"

Osmo, of course, could not answer without opening his mouth, so he grunted again hoping that Mikko would have to notice why he couldn't answer. But the Fox didn't glance at him at all. With his nose still pointed upwards he kept sniffing the air.

"It seems to me it's from the South," he said. "Isn't it from the South, Osmo?"

"Um! Um! Um!" the Bear grunted.

"You say it is from the South, Osmo? Are you sure?"

"Um! Um!" Osmo repeated, growing every moment more impatient.

"Oh, not from the South, you say. Then from what direction is it blowing?"

By this time the Bear was so exasperated by Mikko's interest in the wind when he should have been admiring the Grouse that he forgot himself, opened his mouth, and roared out:

"North!"

Of course the instant he opened his mouth, the Grouse flew away.

"Now see what you've done!" he stormed angrily. "You've made me lose my fine plump Grouse!"

"I?" Mikko asked. "What had I to do with it?"

"You kept asking me about the wind until I opened my mouth — that's what you did!"

The Fox shrugged his shoulders.

"Why did you open your mouth?"

"Well, you can't say 'North!' without opening your mouth, can you?" the Bear demanded.

The Fox laughed heartily.

"See here, Osmo, don't blame me. Blame yourself. If I had had that Grouse in my mouth and you had asked me about the wind, I should never have said, 'North!'"

"What would you have said?" the Bear asked.

Mikko, the rascal, laughed harder than ever. Then he clenched his teeth and said:

"East!"

Mighty Mikko [2]

Helpful animals, the stupid ogre, the winning of wealth and a princess by the humble, kind, and dispossessed — these three favorite motifs in a combination deriving from Finnish folklore make Mighty Mikko *a story of endless satisfaction. The reader will recognize the lineaments of Perrault's* Puss in Boots *and the English tale of* Dick Whittington.

There was once an old woodsman and his wife who had an only son named Mikko. As the mother lay dying the young man wept bitterly.

"When you are gone, my dear mother," he said, "there will be no one left to think of me."

The poor woman comforted him as best she could and said to him:

"You will still have your father."

Shortly after the woman's death, the old man, too, was taken ill.

"Now, indeed, I shall be left desolate and alone," Mikko thought, as he sat beside his father's bedside and saw him grow weaker and weaker.

"My boy," the old man said just before he died, "I have nothing to leave you but the three snares with which these many years I have caught wild animals. Those snares now belong to you. When I am dead, go

2 From Parker Fillmore, *Mighty Mikko* (Harcourt, Brace, 1922).

into the woods and if you find a wild creature caught in any of them, free it gently and bring it home alive."

After his father's death, Mikko remembered the snares and went out to the woods to see them. The first was empty and also the second, but in the third he found a little red Fox. He carefully lifted the spring that had shut down on one of the Fox's feet and then carried the little creature home in his arms. He shared his supper with it and when he lay down to sleep the Fox curled up at his feet. They lived together some time until they became close friends.

"Mikko," said the Fox one day, "why are you so sad?"

"Because I'm lonely."

"Pooh!" said the Fox. "That's no way for a young man to talk! You ought to get married! Then you wouldn't feel lonely!"

"Married!" Mikko repeated. "How can I get married? I can't marry a poor girl because I'm too poor myself and a rich girl wouldn't marry me."

"Nonsense!" said the Fox. "You're a fine well set up young man and you're kind and gentle. What more could a princess ask?"

Mikko laughed to think of a princess wanting him for a husband.

"I mean what I say!" the Fox insisted. "Take our own Princess now. What would you think of marrying her?"

Mikko laughed louder than before.

"I have heard," he said, "that she is the most beautiful princess in the world! Any man would be happy to marry her!"

"Very well," the Fox said, "if you feel that way about her then I'll arrange the wedding for you."

With that the little Fox actually did trot off to the royal castle and gain audience with the King.

"My master sends you greetings," the Fox said, "and he begs you to loan him your bushel measure."

"My bushel measure!" the King repeated in surprise. "Who is your master and why does he want my bushel measure?"

"Ssh!" the Fox whispered as though he didn't want the courtiers to hear what he was saying. Then slipping up quite close to the King he murmured in his ear:

"Surely you have heard of Mikko, haven't you? — Mighty Mikko as he's called."

The King had never heard of any Mikko who was known as Mighty Mikko but, thinking that perhaps he should have heard of him, he shook his head and murmured:

"H'm! Mikko! Mighty Mikko! Oh, to be sure! Yes, yes, of course!"

"My master is about to start off on a journey and he needs a bushel measure for a very particular reason."

"I understand! I understand!" the King said, although he didn't understand at all, and he gave orders that the bushel measure which they used in the storeroom of the castle be brought in and given to the Fox.

The Fox carried off the measure and hid it in the woods. Then he scurried about to all sorts of little out of the way nooks and crannies where people had hidden their savings and he dug up a gold piece here and a silver piece there until he had a handful. Then he went back to the woods and stuck the various coins in the cracks of the measure. The next day he returned to the King.

"My master, Mighty Mikko," he said, "sends you thanks, O King, for the use of your bushel measure."

The King held out his hand and when the Fox gave him the measure he peeped inside to see if by chance it contained any trace of what had recently been measured. His eye of course at once caught the glint of the gold and silver coins lodged in the cracks.

"Ah!" he said, thinking Mikko must be a very mighty lord indeed to be so careless of his wealth; "I should like to meet your master. Won't you and he come and visit me?"

This was what the Fox wanted the King to say but he pretended to hesitate.

"I thank your Majesty for the kind invitation," he said, "but I fear my master can't accept it just now. He wants to get married soon and we are about to start off on a long journey to inspect a number of foreign princesses."

This made the King all the more anxious to have Mikko visit him at once for he thought that if Mikko should see his daughter before he saw those foreign princesses he might fall in love with her and marry her. So he said to the Fox:

"My dear fellow, you must prevail on your master to make me a visit before he starts out on his travels! You will, won't you?"

The Fox looked this way and that as if he were too embarrassed to speak.

"Your Majesty," he said at last, "I pray you pardon my frankness. The truth is you are not rich enough to entertain my master and your castle isn't big enough to house the immense retinue that always attends him."

The King, who by this time was frantic to see Mikko, lost his head completely.

"My dear Fox," he said, "I'll give you anything in the world if you prevail upon your master to visit me at once! Couldn't you suggest to him to travel with a modest retinue this time?"

The Fox shook his head.

"No. His rule is either to travel with a great retinue or to go on foot disguised as a poor woodsman attended only by me."

"Couldn't you prevail on him to come to me disguised as a poor woodsman?" the King begged. "Once he was here, I could place gorgeous clothes at his disposal."

But still the Fox shook his head.

"I fear Your Majesty's wardrobe doesn't contain the kind of clothes my master is accustomed to."

"I assure you I've got some very good clothes," the King said. "Come along this minute and we'll go through them and I'm sure you'll find some that your master would wear."

So they went to a room which was like a big wardrobe with hundreds and hundreds of hooks upon which were hung hundreds of coats and breeches and embroidered shirts. The King ordered his attendants to bring the costumes down one by one and place them before the Fox.

They began with the plainer clothes.

"Good enough for most people," the Fox said, "but not for my master."

Then they took down garments of a fine grade.

"I'm afraid you're going to all this trouble for nothing," the Fox said. "Frankly now don't you realize that my master couldn't possibly put on any of these things!"

The King, who had hoped to keep for his own use his most gorgeous clothes of all, now ordered these to be shown.

The Fox looked at them sideways, sniffed them critically, and at last said:

"Well, perhaps my master would consent to wear these for a few days. They are not what he is accustomed to wear but I will say this for him: he is not proud."

The King was overjoyed.

"Very well, my dear Fox, I'll have the guest chambers put in readiness for your master's visit and I'll have all these, my finest clothes, laid out for him. You won't disappoint me, will you?"

"I'll do my best," the Fox promised.

With that he bade the King a civil good day and ran home to Mikko.

The next day as the Princess was peeping out of an upper window of the castle, she saw a young woodsman approaching accompanied by a Fox. He was a fine stalwart youth and the Princess, who knew from the presence of the Fox that he must be Mikko, gave a long sigh and confided to her serving maid:

"I think I could fall in love with that young man if he really were only a woodsman!"

Later when she saw him arrayed in her father's finest clothes — which looked so well on Mikko that no one even recognized them as the King's — she lost her heart completely and when Mikko was presented to her she blushed and trembled just as any ordinary girl might before a handsome young man. All the Court was equally delighted with Mikko. The ladies went into ecstasies over his modest manners, his fine figure, and the gorgeousness of his clothes, and the old graybeard Councilors, nodding their heads in approval, said to each other:

"Nothing of the coxcomb about this young fellow! In spite of his great wealth see how politely he listens to us when we talk!"

The next day the Fox went privately to the King, and said:

"My master is a man of few words and quick judgment. He bids me tell you that your daughter, the Princess, pleases him mightily and that, with your approval, he will make his addresses to her at once."

The King was greatly agitated and began:

"My dear Fox — "

But the Fox interrupted him to say:

"Think the matter over carefully and give me your decision tomorrow."

So the King consulted with the Princess and with his Councilors and in a short time the marriage was arranged and the wedding ceremony actually performed!

"Didn't I tell you?" the Fox said, when he and Mikko were alone after the wedding.

"Yes," Mikko acknowledged, "you did promise that I should marry the Princess. But, tell me, now that I am married what am I to do? I can't live on here forever with my wife."

"Put your mind at rest," the Fox said. "I've thought of everything. Just do as I tell you and you'll have nothing to regret. To-night say to the King: 'It is now only fitting that you should visit me and see for yourself the sort of castle over which your daughter is hereafter to be mistress!' "

When Mikko said this to the King, the King was overjoyed for now that the marriage had actually taken place he was wondering whether he hadn't perhaps been a little hasty. Mikko's words reassured him and he eagerly accepted the invitation.

On the morrow the Fox said to Mikko:

"Now I'll run on ahead and get things ready for you."

"But where are you going?" Mikko said, frightened at the thought of being deserted by his little friend.

The Fox drew Mikko aside and whispered softly:

"A few days' march from here there is a very gorgeous castle belonging to a wicked old dragon who is known as the Worm. I think the Worm's castle would just about suit you."

"I'm sure it would," Mikko agreed. "But how are we to get it away from the Worm?"

"Trust me," the Fox said. "All you need do is this: lead the King and his courtiers along the main highway until by noon to-morrow you reach a crossroads. Turn there to the left and go straight on until you see the tower of the Worm's castle. If you meet any men by the wayside, shepherds or the like, ask them whose men they are and show no surprise at their answer. So now, dear master, farewell until we meet again at your beautiful castle."

The little Fox trotted off at a smart pace and Mikko and the Princess and the King attended by the whole Court followed in more leisurely fashion.

The little Fox, when he had left the main highway at the crossroads, soon met ten woodsmen with axes over their shoulders. They were all dressed in blue smocks of the same cut.

"Good day," the Fox said politely. "Whose men are you?"

"Our master is known as the Worm," the woodsmen told him.

"My poor, poor lads!" the Fox said, shaking his head sadly.

"What's the matter?" the woodsmen asked.

For a few moments the Fox pretended to be too overcome with emotion to speak. Then he said:

"My poor lads, don't you know that the King is coming with a great force to destroy the Worm and all his people?"

The woodsmen were simple fellows and this news threw them into great consternation.

"Is there no way for us to escape?" they asked.

The Fox put his paw to his head and thought.

"Well," he said at last, "there is one way you might escape and that is by telling every one who asks you that you are the Mighty Mikko's men. But if you value your lives never again say that your master is the Worm."

"We are Mighty Mikko's men!" the woodsmen at once began repeating over and over. "We are Mighty Mikko's men!"

A little farther on the road the Fox met twenty grooms, dressed in the same blue smocks, who were tending a hundred beautiful horses. The Fox talked to the twenty grooms as he had talked to the woodsmen and before he left them they, too, were shouting:

"We are Mighty Mikko's men!"

Next the Fox came to a huge flock of a thousand sheep tended by thirty shepherds all dressed in the Worm's blue smocks. He stopped and talked to them until he had them roaring out:

"We are Mighty Mikko's men!"

Then the Fox trotted on until he reached the castle of the Worm. He found the Worm himself inside lolling lazily about. He was a huge dragon and had been a great warrior in his day. In fact his castle and his lands and his servants and his possessions had all been won in battle. But now for many years no one cared to fight him and he had grown fat and lazy.

"Good day," the Fox said, pretending to be very breathless and frightened. "You're the Worm, aren't you?"

"Yes," the dragon said, boastfully, "I am the great Worm!"

The Fox pretended to grow more agitated. "My poor fellow, I am sorry for you! But of course none of us can expect to live forever. Well, I must hurry along. I thought I would just stop and say good-by."

Made uneasy by the Fox's words, the Worm cried out:

"Wait just a minute! What's the matter?"

The Fox was already at the door but at the Worm's entreaty he paused and said over his shoulder:

"Why, my poor fellow, you surely know, don't you? that the King with a great force is coming to destroy you and all your people!"

"What!" the Worm gasped, turning a sickly green with fright. He knew he was fat and helpless and could never again fight as in the years gone by.

"Don't go just yet!" he begged the Fox. "When is the King coming?"

"He's on the highway now! That's why I must be going! Good-by!"

"My dear Fox, stay just a moment and I'll reward you richly! Help me to hide so that the King won't find me! What about the shed where the linen is stored? I could crawl under the linen and then if you locked the door from the outside the King could never find me."

"Very well," the Fox agreed, "but we must hurry!"

So they ran outside to the shed where the

linen was kept and the Worm hid himself under the linen. The Fox locked the door, then set fire to the shed, and soon there was nothing left of that wicked old dragon, the Worm, but a handful of ashes.

The Fox now called together the dragon's household and talked them over to Mikko as he had the woodsmen and the grooms and the shepherds.

Meanwhile the King and his party were slowly covering the ground over which the Fox had sped so quickly. When they came to the ten woodsmen in blue smocks, the King said:

"I wonder whose woodsmen those are."

One of his attendants asked the woodsmen and the ten of them shouted out at the top of their voices:

"We are Mighty Mikko's men!"

Mikko said nothing and the King and all the Court were impressed anew with his modesty.

A little farther on they met the twenty grooms with their hundred prancing horses. When the grooms were questioned, they answered with a shout:

"We are Mighty Mikko's men!"

"The Fox certainly spoke the truth," the King thought to himself, "when he told me of Mikko's riches!"

A little later the thirty shepherds when they were questioned made answer in a chorus that was deafening to hear:

"We are Mighty Mikko's men!"

The sight of the thousand sheep that belonged to his son-in-law made the King feel poor and humble in comparison and the courtiers whispered among themselves:

"For all his simple manner, Mighty Mikko must be a richer, more powerful lord than the King himself! In fact it is only a very great lord indeed who could be so simple!"

At last they reached the castle which from the blue smocked soldiers that guarded the gateway they knew to be Mikko's. The Fox came out to welcome the King's party and behind him in two rows all the household servants. These, at a signal from the Fox, cried out in one voice:

"We are Mighty Mikko's men!"

Then Mikko in the same simple manner that he would have used in his father's mean

little hut in the woods bade the King and his followers welcome and they all entered the castle where they found a great feast already prepared and waiting.

The King stayed on for several days and the more he saw of Mikko the better pleased he was that he had him for a son-in-law.

When he was leaving he said to Mikko:

"Your castle is so much grander than mine that I hesitate ever asking you back for a visit."

But Mikko reassured the King by saying earnestly:

"My dear father-in-law, when first I entered your castle I thought it was the most beautiful castle in the world!"

The King was flattered and the courtiers whispered among themselves:

"How affable of him to say that when he knows very well how much grander his own castle is!"

When the King and his followers were safely gone, the little red Fox came to Mikko and said:

"Now, my master, you have no reason to feel sad and lonely. You are lord of the most beautiful castle in the world and you have for wife a sweet and lovely Princess. You have no longer any need of me, so I am going to bid you farewell."

Mikko thanked the little Fox for all he had done and the little Fox trotted off to the woods.

So you see that Mikko's poor old father, although he had no wealth to leave his son, was really the cause of all Mikko's good fortune, for it was he who told Mikko in the first place to carry home alive anything he might find caught in the snares.

Hidden Laiva, or the Golden Ship[3]

Finnish and Scandinavian scholars have done more to collect their native folk tales than have any others since the days of the Grimm brothers in Germany. In Finland alone, over

3 From James Cloyd Bowman and Margery Bianco, *Tales from a Finnish Tupa* (Albert Whitman, 1936).

30,000 of these tales have been brought together. In addition, the great national epic, the Kalevala, has been published. This epic is comparable to the Sagas of Iceland and the Nibelungen Ring in representing the national spirit.

In olden days there lived a woodsman whose name was Toivo. Every day, with his bow and arrows slung across his shoulder, he used to wander through the wild forests of Finland. One day in his wanderings he came to a high jagged mountain where no man had ever set foot before. For this was the mountain where the Gnomes lived, and there in a dark hidden cavern lay Hiitola, the Gnomes' home.

When the Gnomes saw Toivo, they all crowded round him and began shouting: "You come at just the right moment! If you will settle our quarrel and help us to divide our gold fairly between us, we will give you money and a golden ship."

It happened that the parents of these Gnomes had died just a few days before, and the Gnomes had fallen heir to all their wealth. They were very busy trying to divide it up. The whole mountain side was strewn with golden spoons and golden dishes and golden carriages. There was a lot of money, too, great shining gold pieces lying all about. The Gnomes were very greedy; each wanted to have more than his own share and so they couldn't come to any agreement about it all.

Toivo stared about him at all this wealth strewn around. More beautiful than the dishes or carriages was a ship of gold that stood on a high rock shining in the sun. The ship caught Toivo's eye at once.

"How do you make this ship go?" he asked the Gnomes.

The largest of the Gnomes stepped forward. He had a turned-up nose, a shaggy pointed red beard and short bandy legs. He hopped into the golden ship and said:

"Why, you just lift this upper what-you-may-call-it with your hand, and push the lower one with your foot, and the ship will race with the wind like a wild tern."

As soon as Toivo had learned the trick, he made a bargain with the Gnomes.

"If you will give me the golden ship and fill it with golden spoons and dishes, and fill my pockets with money, I'll show you how to settle your quarrel."

"Agreed!" shouted the Gnomes, and they began scrambling about in a great hurry to do as he asked.

Toivo set an arrow to his bow and said: "I am going to shoot an arrow, and the first one to find it will be your King. He will settle your affairs."

"That's wonderful! Now we'll be happy again," shouted the Gnomes.

Toivo stretched his bow and sent the arrow whistling through the air. All the Gnomes went rushing after it. Then Toivo jumped into the golden ship, he pulled with his hand and he pushed with his foot, there was a loud whir-rr, and the ship leaped down the steep mountain and far out across the sea.

Soon after Toivo brought it to a perfect landing before the King's castle.

It happened that the King's daughter was on the castle steps at that very moment. She was sitting with her chin in her hands, dreaming of the day that some brave prince would come riding up to marry her, when all at once she saw the golden ship.

"This must surely be a prince from some wonderful country," she said to herself, "to come riding over land and sea in a ship like that!"

And she came dancing down the castle steps.

"Take me in your golden ship, dear Prince, she said, "and I will be your bride!"

But Toivo could only stammer, "Sweet Princess, you're making a big mistake, I'm merely Toivo, a common woodsman. I'm not good enough to touch the shoes on your feet. There are plenty of Kings' sons who would be glad and proud to be your husband!"

But the Princess was so excited about the golden ship and the golden spoons and the golden dishes that she didn't care whether Toivo was only a woodsman or what he was.

"It doesn't matter a bit," she said. "Take me in your ship, that's all, and I'll be your bride."

"You're making fun of me," Toivo answered her. "No one but a King's son would be good enough for the likes of you."

The Princess ran into the castle and back again, her arms heaped with costly clothes.

"Dress up in these," she laughed, "and you'll be a Prince too!" And back she ran to fetch food and drink.

Toivo was so humble he dared not even lay a finger on those fine clothes. He felt that he was not even good enough to be the Princess's servant. And he gazed at her in fear and trembling as she paced back and forth before the golden ship, begging him to marry her.

But at the end of seven days he saw that she was really unhappy because he refused her, so he said:

"Gentle Princess, if you really want to make a bargain with a humble woodsman, step into the ship."

As soon as she was seated, he fell on his knees and asked:

"Where would you like to sail, gentle Princess, in this golden ship?"

"To the very middle of the sea. I've heard tell there is an island there ten miles long where the berry bushes are loaded to the ground with red and purple fruit, and where the birds sing day and night."

Toivo pushed with his hand and pulled with his foot, and off flew the golden ship, right down to the center of an island, and stopped there. Toivo jumped out and ran to look for the purple and red berries.

The first berries that he found were yellow. Toivo tasted them, and before he knew what was happening he fell to the ground in a deep sleep. The Princess waited impatiently for him to come back. At first she thought he was lost. But after three days she decided that he had deserted her, and she grew very angry.

"Die here, you low-bred knave!" she cried. "I shall turn the golden ship round and sail right home again."

So she pulled with her hand and pushed with her foot, and flew back to the castle, while poor Toivo still lay sprawled out on the ground fast asleep.

At the end of another day, Toivo woke up. He searched everywhere, but he could not find the golden ship nor the Princess. His beautiful golden spoons and dishes were gone, too. All he had left was a pocketful of money.

As he hunted high and low, he grew faint with hunger. Before him was a bush laden with purple berries. Toivo filled his left pocket with the fruit, thrust a berry into his mouth and began crunching it between his teeth. All at once he felt horns growing out from his head, monstrous pronged horns like the antlers of a wild moose. They were heavy and they hurt terribly.

"It would be better if I'd stayed hungry," he thought. "These horns are driving me crazy! If a ship should come, the sailors will take me for a wild beast and shoot me."

As he looked for some safe place in which to hide, he saw a bush with red berries on it. He filled his right pocket this time, and crunched one of the red berries between his teeth. No sooner had he done so than the heavy horns fell by magic from his head and he became the most handsome man in the world.

Next day a ship appeared over the edge of the sea. Toivo ran up and down the beach shouting to the sailors. "Take me with you, good friends, take me away before I die on this island. Bring me to the King's castle and I will pay you well."

The sailors gladly took Toivo and set him down before the King's castle. There he walked through the garden and came to a clear sparkling pool. He sat down on the edge of the pool and dipped his tired feet in the water.

It so happened that the King's Butler was coming to draw water. He said to Toivo:

"My good man, tired you may be, but if the King hears that you've been dipping your dusty feet into his drinking water, he'll have you head cut off!"

"My good sir," said Toivo, "the water will soon be clear again, but I'm sorry for my mistake. Let me show you a secret."

And he took a shining red berry from his right pocket and gave it to the Butler. The Butler crunched the berry between his teeth, and at once became the handsomest man in the kingdom, next of course to Toivo himself. He was so delighted that he hid Toivo in a corner of the pantry where the King would not find him.

At dinner time the Princess saw how wonderfully changed the Butler was in his looks, and it made her very curious.

"What has made you so handsome all of a sudden?" she asked him.

"I met a man in the garden who gave me a shining red berry," he whispered. "I ate it, and the charm worked. I became as you now see me."

"Find that man," the Princess said. "Tell him if he'll only make me beautiful too, I'll marry him."

"I'm afraid he's gone," the Butler said. "He wanted to hide, because he was afraid someone would cut his head off if they found him here."

"Tell him not to be frightened," the Princess said. "I will protect him. Bring him into the secret chamber and I'll give him food and drink."

The Butler went to fetch Toivo, and when they returned they found the Princess waiting with food and drink all set out. When the Princess saw Toivo, he was so handsome that she did not know him at all. While he was eating she said:

"If you can make me as beautiful as you are handsome, I'll be your bride."

Toivo became hot with anger, for he thought the Princess had grown tired of him on the island and had run away, stealing his golden ship and leaving him there to die. He did not know of the long time she had waited there.

"No, gentle Princess," he said. "I'm only a poor servant. There is many a king's son who would gladly marry you."

"Only believe me," she said. "I will dress you in a uniform of a General in the King's Army. I will fill your pockets with gold. I will give you a magic golden ship! Only please, please make me as beautiful as you are handsome, and let us be married."

"Very well," said Toivo at last. "Have it your way. Eat this berry."

He took a purple berry from his left pocket, and as the Princess crunched the berry between her teeth a pair of monstrous pronged horns grew out from her head, as heavy and huge as the horns of a wild elk!

As for Toivo, he got very frightened at what he had done, and ran off to hide.

The Princess set up a great hullabaloo, and everyone came running. When the King saw the horns he tried to cut them away, but they were hard as iron and firmly fixed to her head. So then he ordered his two strongest soldiers to follow behind the Princess everywhere she went and carry the weight of the horns while she walked.

No wonder the whole court was upset! The King and Queen and all the ladies and gentlemen in waiting could talk of nothing but the poor Princess and her terrible plight. In despair the King at last sent soldiers into every part of his kingdom with this message:

"Whoever will cure the King's daughter by removing her monstrous horns shall receive the hand of the King's daughter in marriage and be raised to the highest command in the King's Army."

From every part of the kingdom came doctors and healers and magicians. They tried all their medicines and potions, all their spells and wonders. But it was wasted work, for the horns still remained.

At last, after many days, Toivo came forward from the crowd and knelt before the King, saying:

"O King, please let me try my cure."

"I doubt if you can do anything, my lad," the King said. "You can see for yourself how all these wise men have failed, one after another. They have eaten and drunk to their own luck, but my poor daughter remains the same."

"But, King, I am the only one who knows the right charm," Toivo begged. "If you'll let me try, I'm sure I can take away the horns."

"Try, then, and if the horns do fall from my daughter's head, I'll make you the highest general in my army."

"Send all these doctors and healers away," said Toivo, "and command your soldiers to make merry, for I will surely make your daughter the most beautiful woman in the kingdom."

So the King commanded all the doctors and healers and magicians to go home, and the soldiers to make merry, while Toivo was left alone to work his cure.

Toivo said to the maidservant:

"Go, girl, and put dry sticks in the *sauna* (bath house) hearth. Make a hot fire to heat the stones in the Princess's bath house."

And to the page boy he said:

"Run quick to the deep wild forest, boy, and fetch me three long straight willow twigs. With these I will make the horns disappear."

The *sauna* was made ready with warm water and heated stones. The long straight willow twigs were brought and laid in the bath house, too. Then Toivo called for the Princess. He sent the maidservant outside and shut the door. He set the Princess on a bench. He tore the clothing from her shoulders and began to beat her soundly with the willow twigs.

"I'll teach you to run away with my golden ship and leave me to die in the middle of the sea!" he shouted between the strokes. "I'll teach you, you cruel woman, to steal my golden spoons and my golden dishes! I am Toivo, the man you promised to marry if I would take you to a far-off island! I'll teach you!"

The Princess's shoulders were soon red and welted from the blows of the willow twigs. She cried:

"Stop beating me, stop beating me, poor man, and I'll explain everything. Only stop, and I promise never to harm you again!"

"Very well then, explain," said Toivo gruffly.

"It was like this," the Princess began. "For three long days and nights I waited for you. I can't tell you how lonely it seemed, there on that island in the middle of the sea. Every moment I expected some horrible monster to come and swallow me alive. I felt sure you had deserted me, and you can't blame me for being so frightened that I flew back home in your golden ship. How can you doubt that I loved you from the very beginning, and still do!"

When Toivo heard this he threw away the willow twigs and fell on his knees before her. "Forgive me, forgive me for being angry with you, gentle Princess! I will never lift my hand against you again."

As he spoke, Toivo drew a shining red berry from his right pocket. The Princess crunched it between her teeth; at once the ugly horns fell from her head and her face became as fair as a new-blown rose.

Toivo called the maidservant. She dressed the Princess in fine linen; upon her head she set the tall bridal crown, covered with jewels, and upon her feet soft shoes woven of the finest white birch bark in all the King's land.

When the people saw the Princess in her white robe, her thick golden braids falling to her knees, her blue eyes shining and her skin like the fairest rose-petal, they knew she had become the most beautiful woman in the kingdom.

The King was so happy he declared a holiday throughout the whole land. Everywhere people ate, drank and danced all night long. Toivo became the King's highest general. He married his Princess and they all lived happily ever after.

SCANDINAVIA

The Three Billy-Goats-Gruff [1]

~§ *This cumulative beast tale is an almost perfectly constructed short story. It wastes no words; the action moves with rapidity; and the satisfactory ending to the action is tied off with a couplet which children love to repeat.*

Once on a time there were three Billy-Goats who were to go up to the hillside to make themselves fat, and the family name of the three goats was "Gruff."

On the way up was a bridge, over a burn they had to cross; and under the bridge lived a great ugly Troll, with eyes as big as saucers and a nose as long as a poker.

First of all came the youngest Billy-Goat-Gruff to cross the bridge.

"Trip, trap; trip, trap!" went the bridge.

"WHO'S THAT tripping over my bridge?" roared the Troll.

"Oh! it is only I, the tiniest Billy-Goat-Gruff; and I'm going up to the hillside to make myself fat," said the Billy-Goat, with such a small voice.

"Now, I'm coming to gobble you up," said the Troll.

"Oh, no! pray don't take me. I'm too little, that I am," said the Billy-Goat. "Wait a bit till the second Billy-Goat-Gruff comes; he's much bigger."

"Well! be off with you," said the Troll.

A little while after came the second Billy-Goat-Gruff to cross the bridge.

"Trip, Trap! Trip, Trap! Trip, Trap!" went the bridge.

[1] From Peter Christen Asbjörnsen, *Popular Tales from the Norse,* trans. G. W. Dasent (Putnam, 1908).

"WHO'S THAT tripping over my bridge?" roared the Troll.

"Oh! it's the second Billy-Goat-Gruff, and I'm going up to the hillside to make myself fat," said the Billy-Goat, who hadn't such a small voice.

"Now, I'm coming to gobble you up," said the Troll.

"Oh, no! don't take me. Wait a little till the big Billy-Goat-Gruff comes; he's much bigger."

"Very well; be off with you," said the Troll.

But just then up came the big Billy-Goat-Gruff.

"Trip, Trap! Trip, Trap! Trip, Trap!" went the bridge, for the Billy-Goat was so heavy that the bridge creaked and groaned under him.

"WHO'S THAT tramping over my bridge?" roared the Troll.

"It's I! THE BIG BILLY-GOAT-GRUFF," said the Billy-Goat, who had a big hoarse voice of his own.

"Now, I'm coming to gobble you up," roared the Troll.

> "Well, come along! I've got two spears,
>   And I'll poke your eyeballs out at your ears,
>   I've got besides two curling-stones,
>   And I'll crush you to bits, body and bones."

That was what the big Billy-Goat said; so he flew at the Troll and poked his eyes out with his horns, and crushed him to bits, body and bones, and tossed him out into the burn, and after that he went up to the hillside. There the Billy-Goats got so fat they were scarcely able to walk home again;

and if the fat hasn't fallen off them, why they're still fat; and so ——

> Snip, snap, snout,
> This tale's told out.

The Pancake[2]

❧ *This repetitive, cumulative tale is found in many countries and is so full of amusing action and speech that it is no surpise to find it modernized in* The Gingerbread Boy.

Once on a time there was a goody who had seven hungry bairns, and she was frying a Pancake for them. It was a sweet-milk Pancake, and there it lay in the pan bubbling and frizzling so thick and good, it was a sight for sore eyes to look at. And the bairns stood round about, and the goodman sat by and looked on.

"Oh, give me a bit of Pancake, mother dear: I am so hungry," said one bairn.

"Oh, darling mother," said the second.

"Oh, darling, good mother," said the third.

"Oh, darling, good, nice mother," said the fourth.

"Oh, darling, pretty, good, nice mother," said the fifth.

"Oh, darling, pretty, good, nice, clever mother," said the sixth.

"Oh, darling, pretty, good, nice, clever, sweet mother," said the seventh.

So they begged for the Pancake all round, the one more prettily than the other; for they were so hungry and so good.

"Yes, yes, bairns, only bide a bit till it turns itself" – she ought to have said, "till I get it turned" — "and then you shall have some – a lovely sweet-milk Pancake; only look how fat and happy it lies there."

When the Pancake heard that it got afraid, and in a trice it turned itself all of itself, and tried to jump out of the pan; but it fell back into it again t'other side up, and so when it had been fried a little on the other side, too, till it got firmer in its flesh, it sprang out on the floor, and rolled off like a wheel through the door and down the hill.

[2] From Peter Christen Asbjörnsen, *Tales from the Fjeld*, trans. G. W. Dasent (Putnam, 1908).

"Holloa! Stop, Pancake!" and away went the goody after it, with the frying-pan in one hand and the ladle in the other, as fast as she could, and her bairns behind her, while the goodman limped after them last of all.

"Hi! won't you stop? Seize it! Stop, Pancake," they all screamed out, one after another, and tried to catch it on the run and hold it, but the Pancake rolled on and on, and in the twinkling of an eye it was so far ahead that they couldn't see it, for the Pancake was faster on its feet than any of them.

So when it had rolled a while it met a man.

"Good day, Pancake," said the man.

"God bless you, Manny-Panny," said the Pancake.

"Dear Pancake," said the man, "don't roll so fast; stop a little and let me eat you."

"When I have given the slip to Goody-Poody, and the goodman, and seven squalling children, I may well slip through your fingers, Manny-Panny," said the Pancake, and rolled on and on till it met a hen.

"Good day, Pancake," said the hen.

"The same to you, Henny-Penny," said the Pancake.

"Pancake, dear, don't roll so fast; bide a bit and let me eat you up," said the hen.

"When I have given the slip to Goody-Poody, and the goodman, and seven squalling children, and Manny-Panny, I may well slip through your claws, Henny-Penny," said the Pancake, and so it rolled on like a wheel down the road.

Just then it met a cock.

"Good day," said the cock.

"The same to you, Cocky-Locky," said the Pancake.

"Pancake, dear, don't roll so fast, but bide a bit and let me eat you up."

"When I have given the slip to Goody-Poody, and the goodman, and seven squalling children, and to Manny-Panny, and Henny-Penny, I may well slip through your claws, Cocky-Locky," said the Pancake, and off it set rolling away as fast as it could; and when it had rolled a long way it met a duck.

"Good day, Pancake," said the duck.

"The same to you, Ducky-Lucky."

"Pancake, dear, don't roll away so fast; bide a bit and let me eat you up."

"When I have given the slip to Goody-Poody, and the goodman, and seven squalling children, and Manny-Panny, and Henny-Penny, and Cocky-Locky, I may well slip through your fingers, Ducky-Lucky," said the Pancake, and with that it took to rolling and rolling faster than ever; and when it had rolled a long, long way it met a goose.

"Good day, Pancake," said the goose.

"The same to you, Goosey-Poosey."

"Pancake, dear, don't roll so fast; bide a bit and let me eat you up."

"When I have given the slip to Goody-Poody, and the goodman, and seven squalling children, and Manny-Panny, and Henny-Penny, and Cocky-Locky, and Ducky-Lucky, I can well slip through your feet, Goosey-Poosey," said the Pancake, and off it rolled.

So when it had rolled a long, long way farther, it met a gander.

"Good day, Pancake," said the gander.

"The same to you, Gander-Pander," said the Pancake.

"Pancake, dear, don't roll so fast; bide a bit and let me eat you up."

"When I have given the slip to Goody-Poody, and the goodman, and seven squalling children, and Manny-Panny, and Henny-Penny, and Cocky-Locky, and Ducky-Lucky, and Goosey-Poosey, I may well slip through your feet, Gander-Pander," said the Pancake, and it rolled off as fast as ever.

So when it had rolled a long, long time it met a pig.

"Good day, Pancake," said the pig.

"The same to you, Piggy-Wiggy," said the Pancake, which, without a word more, began to roll and roll like mad.

"Nay, nay," said the pig, "you needn't be in such a hurry; we two can go side by side and see each other over the wood; they say it is not safe in there."

The Pancake thought there might be something in that, and so they kept company. But when they had gone awhile, they came to a brook. As for Piggy, he was so fat he swam safely across; it was nothing to him; but the poor Pancake couldn't get over.

"Seat yourself on my snout," said the pig, "and I'll carry you over."

So the Pancake did that.

"Ouf, ouf," said the pig, and swallowed the Pancake at one gulp; and the poor Pancake could go no farther, why—this story can go no farther either.

The Ram and the Pig Who Went into the Woods [3]

 This Scandinavian story is really only another version of The Bremen Town Musicians. *The motive for leaving home is the same in both, but the differences between the two tales offer an interesting study.*

There was once upon a time a ram, who was being fattened up for killing. He had therefore plenty to eat, and he soon became round and fat with all the good things he got. One day the dairymaid came, and gave him some more food.

"You must eat, ram," she said; "you'll not be long here now, for tomorrow we are going to kill you."

"There's an old saying, that no one should sneer at old women's advice, and that advice and physic can be had for everything except death," thought the ram to himself; "but perhaps I might manage to escape it this time."

And so he went on eating till he was full, and when he was quite satisfied he ran his horns against the door, burst it open, and set off to the neighboring farm. There he made straight for the pigsty, to look for a pig with whom he had struck up an acquaintance on the common, since when they had always been good friends and got on well together.

"Good day, and thanks for your kindness last time we met," said the ram to the pig.

"Good day, and thanks to you," said the pig.

"Do you know why they make you so comfortable, and why they feed you and look after you so well?" said the ram.

"No," said the pig.

"There are many mouths to feed on this farm, you must know," said the ram; "they are going to kill you and eat you."

[3] From Peter Christen Asbjörnsen, *Fairy Tales from the Far North* (Century, 1895).

"Are they?" said the pig. "Well, much good it may do them!"

"If you are of the same mind as I, we will go into the woods and build a house and live by ourselves; there is nothing like having a home of your own, you know," said the ram.

Yes, the pig was quite willing. "It's nice to be in fine company," said he, and off they started.

When they had got a bit on the way they met a goose.

"Good day, my good people, and thanks for your kindness last time we met," said the goose. "Where are you off to?"

"Good day, and thanks to you," said the ram. "We had it altogether too comfortable at our place, so we are off to the woods to live by ourselves. In your own house you are your own master, you know," said he.

"Well, I'm very comfortable where I am," said the goose; "but why shouldn't I join you? Good company makes the day shorter," said she.

"But neither hut nor house can be built by gabbling and quacking," said the pig. "What do you think you can do?"

"Good counsel and skill may do as much as a giant's will," said the goose. "I can pluck moss and stuff it into the crevices, so that the house will be warm and comfortable."

Well, she might come with them, thought the pig, for he liked the place to be warm and cozy.

When they had gone a bit on the way — the goose was not getting along very fast — they met a hare, who came scampering out of the wood.

"Good day, my good people, and thanks for your kindness the last time we met," said the hare. "How far are you going today?" said he.

"Good day, and thanks to you," said the ram; "we had it altogether too comfortable at our place, so we are off to the woods to build a house and live by ourselves. When you have tried both East and West, you'll find that a home of your own is after all the best," said he.

"Well, I have, of course, a home in every bush," said the hare; "but I have often said to myself in the winter that if I lived till the summer I would build a house, so I have a good mind to go with you and build one after all," said he.

"Well, if the worst comes to the worst, we might take you with us to frighten the dogs away," said the pig, "for you couldn't help us to build the house, I should say."

"There is always something for willing hands to do in this world," said the hare. "I have teeth to gnaw pegs with, and I have paws to knock them into the walls, so I'll do very well for a carpenter; for 'good tools make good work,' as the man said, when he skinned his mare with an auger," said the hare.

Well, he might come with them and help to build the house; there could be no harm in that.

When they had got a bit farther on the way they met a cock.

"Good day, my good people, and thanks for your kindness last time we met," said the cock; "where are you all going today?" he said.

"Good day, and thanks to you," said the ram; "we had it altogether too comfortable at our place, so we are off to the woods to build a house and live by ourselves. 'For unless at home you bake, you'll lose both fuel and cake,' " said he.

"Well, I am comfortable enough, where I am," said the cock, "but it's better to have your own roost than to sit on a stranger's perch and crow; and that cock is best off who has a home of his own," said he. "If I could join such fine company as yours, I too would like to go to the woods and build a house."

"Well, flapping and crowing is all very well for noise, but it won't cut joists," said the pig. "You can't help us to build a house," he said.

"It is not well to live in a house where there is neither dog nor cock," said the cock; "I am early to rise and early to crow."

"Yes, 'early to rise makes one wealthy and wise,' so let him come with us!" said the pig. He was always the heaviest sleeper. "Sleep is a big thief, and steals half one's life," he said.

So they all set off to the woods and built the house. The pig felled the trees and the ram dragged them home; the hare was the carpenter, and gnawed pegs and hammered them into walls and roof; the goose plucked moss and stuffed it into the crevices between the logs; the cock crew and took care that they did not oversleep themselves in the mornings, and when the house was ready and the roof covered with birch-bark and thatched with turf, they could at least live by themselves, and they were all both happy and contented.

"It's pleasant to travel both East and West, but home is, after all, the best," said the ram.

But a bit farther into the wood two wolves had their lair, and when they saw that a new house had been built hard by they wanted to know what sort of folks they had got for neighbors. For they thought, "a good neighbor is better than a brother in a foreign land, and it is better to live among good neighbors than to be known far and wide."

So one of them made it his business to call there and ask for a light for his pipe. The moment he came inside the door the ram rushed at him, and gave him such a butt with his horns that the wolf fell on his head into the hearth; the pig snapped and bit, the goose nipped and pecked, the cock flew up on a rafter and began to crow and cackle, and the hare became so frightened that he scampered and jumped about, both high and low, and knocked and scrambled about from one corner of the room to the other.

At last the wolf managed to get out of the house.

"Well, to know one's neighbors is to add to one's wisdom," said the wolf who was waiting outside; "I suppose you had a grand reception, since you stayed so long. But what about the light? I don't see either pipe or smoke," said he.

"Yes, that was a nice light I got, and a nice lot of people they were," said he who had been inside. "Such treatment I never met with before, but 'as you make your bed so you must lie,' and 'an unexpected guest must put up with what he gets,'" said the wolf. "No sooner had I got inside the door than the shoemaker threw his last at me, and I fell on my head in the middle of the forge; there sat two smiths, blowing bellows

and pinching and snipping bits of flesh off me with red-hot tongs and pincers; the hunter rushed about the room looking for his gun, but as luck would have it, he couldn't find it. And up on the rafters sat some one beating his arms about and shouting: 'Let's hook him! let's hook him! Sling him up! sling him up!' and if he had only got hold of me I should never have got out alive."

Gudbrand on the Hillside [4]

◄§ *The action at the beginning of this story is very like that of* Jack and the Beanstalk *and of* The Bee, the Harp, the Mouse, and the Bum-Clock. *But after the foolish exchanges are made, this tale takes a sudden, unexpected turn and leads to a very different, though equally satisfactory, conclusion.*

There was once upon a time a man whose name was Gudbrand. He had a farm which lay far away up on the side of a hill, and therefore they called him Gudbrand on the Hillside.

He and his wife lived so happily together and agreed so well, that whatever the man did the wife thought it so well done that no one could do it better. No matter what he did, she thought it was always the right thing.

They lived on their own farm, and had a hundred dollars at the bottom of their chest and two cows in their cowshed. One day the woman said to Gudbrand:

"I think we ought to go to town with one of the cows and sell it, so that we may have some ready money by us. We are pretty well off, and ought to have a few shillings in our pocket like other people. The hundred dollars in the chest we mustn't touch, but I can't see what we want with more than one cow. It will be much better for us to sell one as I shall then have only one to look after instead of the two I have now to mind and feed."

Yes, Gudbrand thought, that was well and sensibly spoken. He took the cow at once and went to town to sell it; but when he got there no one would buy the cow.

[4] From Peter Christen Asbjörnsen, *Fairy Tales from the Far North* (Century, 1895).

"Ah, well!" thought Gudbrand, "I may as well take the cow home again. I know I have both stall and food for it, and the way home is no longer than it was here." So he strolled homeward again with the cow.

When he had got a bit on the way he met a man who had a horse to sell, and Gudbrand thought it was better to have a horse than a cow, and so he changed the cow for a horse.

When he had gone a bit farther he met a man who was driving a fat pig before him, and then he thought it would be better to have a fat pig than a horse, and so he changed with the man.

He now went a bit farther, and then he met a man with a goat, and, as he thought it was surely better to have a goat than a pig, he changed with the man who had the goat.

Then he went a long way, till he met a man who had a sheep; he changed with him, for he thought it was always better to have a sheep than a goat.

When he had gone a bit farther, he met a man with a goose; and so he changed the sheep for the goose. And when he had gone a long, long way he met a man with a cock; he changed the goose with him, for he thought, "It is surely better to have a cock than a goose."

He walked on till late in the day, when he began to feel hungry. So he sold the cock for sixpence and bought some food for himself.

"For it is always better to keep body and soul together than to have a cock," thought Gudbrand.

He then set off again homeward till he came to his neighbor's farm and there he went in.

"How did you get on in town?" asked the people.

"Oh, only so-so," said the man; "I can't boast of my luck, nor can I grumble at it either." And then he told them how it had gone with him from first to last.

"Well, you'll have a fine reception when you get home to your wife," said the neighbor. "Heaven help you! I should not like to be in your place."

"I think I might have fared much worse," said Gudbrand; "but whether I have fared well or ill, I have such a kind wife that she never says anything, no matter what I do."

"Aye, so you say; but you won't get me to believe it," said the neighbor.

"Shall we have a wager on it?" said Gudbrand. "I have a hundred dollars in my chest at home; will you lay the same?"

So they made the wager and Gudbrand remained there till the evening, when it began to get dark, and then they went together to the farm.

The neighbor was to remain outside the door and listen, while Gudbrand went in to his wife.

"Good evening!" said Gudbrand when he came in.

"Good evening!" said the wife. "Heaven be praised you are back again."

"Yes, here I am!" said the man. And then the wife asked him how he had got on in town.

"Oh, so-so," answered Gudbrand; "not much to brag of. When I came to town no one would buy the cow, so I changed it for a horse."

"Oh, I'm so glad of that," said the woman; "we are pretty well off and we ought to drive to church like other people, and when we can afford to keep a horse I don't see why we should not have one. Run out, children, and put the horse in the stable."

"Well, I haven't got the horse after all," said Gudbrand; "for when I had got a bit on the way I changed it for a pig."

"Dear me!" cried the woman, "that's the very thing I should have done myself. I'm so glad of that, for now we can have some bacon in the house and something to offer people when they come to see us. What do we want with a horse? People would only say we had become so grand that we could no longer walk to church. Run out, children, and let the pig in."

"But I haven't got the pig either," said Gudbrand, "for when I got on a bit farther on the road I changed it for a milch goat."

"Dear! dear! how well you manage everything!" cried the wife. "When I really come to think of it, what do I want with the pig? People would only say, 'over yonder they eat up everything they have.' No, now I have a goat I can have both milk and cheese and keep the goat into the bargain. Let in the goat, children."

"But I haven't got the goat either," said Gudbrand; "when I got a bit on the way I changed the goat and got a fine sheep for it."

"Well!" shouted the woman, "you do everything just as I should wish it — just as if I had been there myself. What do we want with a goat? I should have to climb up hill and down dale to get it home at night. No, when I have a sheep I can have wool and clothes in the house, and food as well. Run out, children, and let in the sheep."

"But I haven't got the sheep any longer," said Gudbrand, "for when I had got a bit on the way I changed it for a goose."

"Well, thank you for that!" said the woman; "and many thanks too! What do I want with a sheep? I have neither wheel nor spindle, and I do not care either to toil and drudge making clothes; we can buy clothes now as before. Now I can have goose-fat, which I have so long been wishing for, and some feathers to stuff that little pillow of mine. Run, children, and let in the goose."

"Well, I haven't got the goose either," said Gudbrand. "When I got a bit farther on the way I changed it for a cock."

"Well, I don't know how you can think of it all!" cried the woman. "It's just as if I had done it all myself. — A cock! Why, it's just the same as if you'd bought an eight-day clock, for every morning the cock will crow at four, so we can be up in good time. What do we want with a goose? I can't make goose-fat and I can easily fill my pillow with some soft grass. Run, children, and let in the cock."

"But I haven't got a cock either," said Gudbrand, "for when I had got a bit farther I became so terribly hungry I had to sell the cock for sixpence and get some food to keep body and soul together."

"Heaven be praised you did that!" cried the woman. "Whatever you do, you always do the very thing I could have wished. Besides, what did we want with the cock? We are our own masters and can lie as long as we like in the mornings. Heaven be praised! As long as I have got you back again, who manage everything so well, I shall neither want cock, nor goose, nor pig, nor cow."

Gudbrand then opened the door. "Have I won the hundred dollars now?" he asked. And the neighbor was obliged to confess that he had.

Boots and His Brothers [5]

Here is another "Jack" tale, also with the motif of the youngest son's success. The story is also symbolic of Man's curiosity which has made him master of natural resources.

Once on a time there was a man who had three sons, Peter, Paul, and John. John was Boots, of course, for he was the youngest. I can't say the man had anything more than these three sons, for he hadn't one penny to rub against another, and so he told his sons over and over again that they must go into the world and try to earn their bread, for there was nothing to be looked for but starving to death.

Not far away from the man's cottage stood the king's palace, and, you must know, just against the king's windows was a great oak, which was so stout and big that it took all the light away from the king's palace. The king had said that he would give many, many dollars to the man who could fell the oak, but no one was man enough for that, for as soon as ever one chip of the oak's trunk flew off, two grew in its stead. A well, too, the king wanted dug, that would hold water for the whole year; all his neighbors had wells, but he had none, and he thought that was a shame. So the king said that he would give to any man who could dig a well which would hold water for the whole year round, both money and goods; but no one could do it, for the king's palace lay high, high up on a hill, and a man could dig but a few inches before he came upon the living rock.

But as the king had set his heart on having these two things done, he had it given out far and wide, in all the churches of his kingdom, that he who could fell the big oak in the king's courtyard, and dig him a well that would hold water the whole year round, should have the Princess and half the

[5] From Peter Christen Asbjörnsen, *Popular Tales from the Norse*, trans. G. W. Dasent (Putnam, 1908).

kingdom. Well, you may easily know there was many a man who came to try his luck; but for all their hacking and hewing, and all their digging and delving, it was no good. The oak got stouter and bigger at every stroke, and the rock didn't get softer either. So one day those three brothers thought they'd set off and try, too, and their father hadn't a word against it; for even if they didn't get the Princess and half the kingdom, it might happen that they would get a place somewhere with a good master; and that was all he wanted. So when the brothers said they thought of going to the palace, their father said "yes" at once. So Peter, Paul, and Jack went off from their home.

Well, they hadn't gone far before they came to a firwood, and up along one side of a steep hillside, and as they went, they heard something hewing and hacking away up on the hill among the trees.

"I wonder now what it is that is hewing away up yonder," said Jack.

"You're always so clever with your wonderings," said Peter and Paul both at once. "What wonder is it, pray, that a woodcutter should stand and hack up on a hillside?"

"Still, I'd like to see what it is, after all," said Jack, and up he went.

"Oh, if you're such a child, 'twill do you good to go and take a lesson," bawled out his brothers after him.

But Jack didn't care for what they said: he climbed the steep hillside towards where the noise came, and when he reached the place, what do you think he saw? Why, an axe that stood there hacking and hewing all of itself, at the trunk of a fir.

"Good day," said Jack. "So you stand here all alone and hew, do you?"

"Yes; here I've stood and hewed and hacked a long, long time, waiting for you," said the Axe.

"Well, here I am at last," said Jack, as he took the axe, pulled it off its haft, and stuffed both head and haft into his wallet.

So when he got down again to his brothers, they began to jeer and laugh at him.

"And now, what funny thing was it you saw up yonder upon the hillside?" they said.

"Oh, it was only an axe we heard," said Jack.

So when they had gone a bit farther, they came under a steep spur of rock, and up there they heard something digging and shoveling.

"I wonder now," said Jack, "what it is digging and shoveling up yonder at the top of the rock."

"Ah, you're always so clever with your wonderings," said Peter and Paul again, "as if you'd never heard a woodpecker hacking and pecking at a hollow tree."

"Well, well," said Jack, "I think it would be a piece of fun just to see what it really is."

And so he set off to climb the rock, while the others laughed and made fun of him. But he didn't care a bit for that; up he climbed, and when he got near the top, what do you think he saw? Why a spade that stood there digging and delving.

"Good day," said Jack. "So you stand here all alone, and dig and delve!"

"Yes, that's what I do," said the Spade, "and that's what I've done this many a long day, waiting for you."

"Well, here I am," said Jack again, as he took the spade and knocked it off its handle, and put it into his wallet and then went down again to his brothers.

"Well, what was it, so rare and strange," said Peter and Paul, "that you saw up there at the top of the rock?"

"Oh, nothing more than a spade," said Jack; "that was what we heard."

So they went on again a good bit, till they came to a brook. They were thirsty, all three, after their long walk, and so they lay down beside the brook to have a drink.

"I wonder now," said Jack, "where all this water comes from."

"I wonder if you are right in your head," said Peter and Paul in one breath. "If you're not mad already, you'll go mad very soon with your wonderings. Where the brook comes from, indeed! Have you never heard how water rises from a spring in the earth?"

"Yes; but still I've a great fancy to see where this brook comes from," said Jack.

So up alongside the brook he went, in spite of all that his brothers bawled after him. Nothing could stop him. On he went. So, as he went up, the brook got smaller and smaller, and at last, a little way farther on, what do you think he saw? Why, a great walnut, and out of that the water trickled.

"Good day!" said Jack again. "So you lie here, and trickle and run down all alone?"

"Yes, I do," said the Walnut; "and here have I trickled and run this many a long day, waiting for you."

"Well, here I am," said Jack, as he took a lump of moss, and plugged up the hole, that the water mightn't run out. Then he put the walnut into the wallet and ran down to his brothers.

"Well, now," said Peter and Paul, "have you found out where the water comes from? A rare sight it must have been!"

"Oh, after all it was only a hole it ran out of," said Jack; and so the others laughed and made game of him again; but Jack didn't mind that a bit.

"After all, I had the fun of seeing it," said he.

So when they had gone a bit farther, they came to the king's palace; but as all the men in the kingdom had heard how they might win the Princess and half the realm, if they could only fell the big oak and dig the king's well, so many had come to try their luck that the oak was now twice as stout and big as it had been at first, for two chips grew for every one they had hewed out with their axes, as I daresay you all bear in mind. So the king had now laid it down as a punishment, that if any one tried and couldn't fell the oak, he should be put on a barren island, and both his ears were to be chopped off. But the two brothers didn't let themselves be scared by that; they were quite sure they could fell the oak, and Peter, as he was the eldest, was to try his hand first; but it went with him as with all the rest who had hewn at the oak; for every chip that he cut out, two grew in its place. So the king's men seized him, cut off his ears, and put him out on the island.

Now Paul, he was to try his luck, but he fared just the same; when he had hewn two or three strokes, they began to see the oak grow, and so the king's men seized him, too, and clipped his ears, and put him out on the island; and his ears they clipped closer, because they said he should have taken a lesson from his brother.

So now Jack was to try.

"If you *will* look like a marked sheep,

we're quite ready to clip your ears at once, and then you'll save yourself some bother," said the king, for he was very angry with him for his brothers' sake.

"Well, I'd like just to try first," said Jack, and so he got leave. Then he took his axe out of his wallet and fitted it to its haft.

"Hew away!" said he to his axe; and away it hewed, making the chips fly again, so that it wasn't long before down came the oak.

When that was done Jack pulled out his spade; and fitted it to its handle.

"Dig away!" said he to the spade; and so the spade began to dig and delve till the earth and rock flew out in splinters, and so he had the well soon dug out, you may believe.

And when he had got it as big and deep as he chose, Jack took out his walnut and laid it in one corner of the well, and pulled the plug of moss out.

"Trickle and run," said Jack; and so the nut trickled and ran, till the water gushed out of the hole in a stream, and in a short time the well was brimful.

Thus Jack had felled the oak which shaded the king's palace, and dug a well in the palace yard, and so it was that he got the Princess and half the kingdom, as the king had said; but it was lucky for Peter and Paul that they had lost their ears, else they had heard each hour and day how every one said, "Well, after all, Jack wasn't so much out of his mind when he took to wondering."

The Princess on the Glass Hill [6]

◁§ The beginning of this story is almost identical with that of the Russian tale, The Little Humpbacked Horse. The development of the action, however, is more like that in Atalanta's Race.

Once on a time there was a man who had a meadow, which lay high up on the hillside, and in the meadow was a barn, which he had built to keep his hay in. Now, I must tell you there hadn't been much in the barn for the last year or two, for every Saint

[6] From Peter Christen Asbjörnsen, *Popular Tales from the Norse*, trans. G. W. Dasent (Putnam, 1908).

John's night, when the grass stood greenest and deepest, the meadow was eaten down to the very ground the next morning, just as if a whole drove of sheep had been there feeding on it over night. This happened once, and it happened twice; so that at last the man grew weary of losing his crop of hay, and said to his sons — for he had three of them, and the youngest was named Boots, of course — that now one of them must just go and sleep in the barn in the outlying field when Saint John's night came, for it was too good a joke that his grass should be eaten, root and blade, this year, as it had been the last two years. So whichever of them went he must keep a sharp lookout; that was what their father said.

Well, the eldest son was ready to go and watch the meadow; trust him for looking after the grass! It shouldn't be his fault if man or beast, or the fiend himself, got a blade of grass. So, when evening came, he set off to the barn and lay down to sleep; but a little later on in the night there came such a clatter, and such an earthquake, that walls and roof shook, and groaned, and creaked; then up jumped the lad and took to his heels as fast as ever he could; nor dared he once look round till he reached home; and as for the hay, why, it was eaten up this year just as it had been twice before.

The next Saint John's night, the man said again it would never do to lose all the grass in the outlying field year after year in this way, so one of the sons must trudge off to watch it, and watch it well, too. Well, the next oldest son was ready to try his luck. So off he went and lay down to sleep in the barn as his brother had done before him; but as night came on, there came a rumbling and quaking of the earth, worse even than on the last Saint John's night. When the lad heard it, he got frightened, and took to his heels as though he were running a race.

Next year the turn came to Boots; but when he made ready to go, the other two began to laugh, and make game of him, saying:

"You're just the man to watch the hay, that you are; you who have done nothing all your life but sit in the ashes and toast yourself by the fire."

Boots did not care a pin for their chattering, and stumped away, as evening drew on, up the hillside to the outlying field. There he went inside the barn and lay down; but in about an hour's time the barn began to groan and creak, so that it was dreadful to hear.

"Well," said Boots to himself; "if it isn't any worse than this I can stand it well enough."

A little while after there came another creak and an earthquake, so that the litter in the barn flew about the lad's ears.

"Oh," said Boots to himself; "if it isn't any worse than this, I daresay I can stand it out."

But just then came a third rumbling, and a third earthquake, so that the lad thought walls and roof were coming down on his head; but it passed off, and all was still as death about him.

"It'll come again, I'll be bound," thought Boots; but no, it did not come again; still it was and still it stayed; but after he had lain a little while he heard a noise as if a horse were standing just outside the barn-door, and cropping the grass. He stole to the door and peeped through a chink; and there stood a horse feeding away. So big and fat and grand a horse, Boots had never set eyes on; by his side on the grass lay a saddle and bridle, and a full set of armor for a knight, all of brass, so bright that the light gleamed from it.

"Ho, ho!" thought the lad; "it's you, is it, that eats up our hay? I'll soon put a spoke in your wheel; just see if I don't."

So he lost no time, but took the steel out of his tinder-box and threw it over the horse; then it had no power to stir from the spot and became so tame that the lad could do what he liked with it. He got on its back and rode off with it to a place which no one knew of, and there he put up the horse. When he got home his brothers laughed and asked how he fared.

"You didn't lie long in the barn, even if you had the heart to go as far as the field."

"Well," said Boots, "all I can say is, I lay in the barn till the sun rose, and neither saw nor heard anything; I can't think what there was in the barn to make you both so afraid."

"A pretty story!" said his brothers; "but we'll soon see how you watched the meadow." So they set off, but when they reached it, there stood the grass as deep and thick as it had been the night before.

Well, the next Saint John's night it was the same story over again; neither of the elder brothers dared to go out to the outlying field to watch the crop; but Boots, he had the heart to go, and everything happened just as it had happened the year before. First a clatter and an earthquake, then a greater clatter and another earthquake, and so on a third time; only this year the earthquakes were far worse than the year before. Then all at once, everything was as still as death, and the lad heard how something was cropping the grass outside the barn-door, so he stole to the door and peeped through a chink; and what do you think he saw? Why, another horse standing right up against the wall, and chewing and champing with might and main. It was far finer and fatter than that one which came the year before; and it had a saddle on its back and a bridle on its neck and a full suit of mail for a knight lay by its side, all of silver, and as grand as you would wish to see.

"Ho, ho!" said Boots to himself; "it's you that gobbles up our hay, is it? I'll soon put a spoke in your wheel"; and with that he took the steel out of his tinder-box and threw it over the horse's crest, which stood still as a lamb. Well, the lad rode this horse, too, to the hiding place where he kept the other one; and after that he went home.

"I suppose you'll tell us," said one of the brothers, "there's a fine crop this year, too, in the hayfield."

"Well, so there is," said Boots; and off ran the others to see, and there stood the grass thick and deep, as it was the year before; but they didn't give Boots softer words for all that.

Now, when the third Saint John's eve came, the two elder still hadn't the heart to

lie out in the barn and watch the grass, for they had got so scared the night they lay there before, that they couldn't get over the fright; but Boots, he dared to go; and, to make a long story short, the very same thing happened this time as had happened twice before. Three earthquakes came, one after the other, each worse than the one which went before; and when the last came, the lad danced about with the shock from one barn wall to the other; and after that, all at once, it was as still as death. Now when he had lain a little while he heard something tugging away at the grass outside the barn; so he stole again to the door-chink and peeped out, and there stood a horse close outside — far, far bigger and fatter than the two he had taken before.

"Ho, ho!" said the lad to himself; "it's you, is it, that comes here eating up our hay? I'll soon put a spoke in your wheel, I'll soon stop that." So he caught up his steel and threw it over the horse's neck, and in a trice it stood as if it were nailed to the ground, and Boots could do as he pleased with it. Then he rode off with it to the hiding place where he kept the other two, and then went home. When he got there his two brothers made game of him as they had done before, saying they could see he had watched the grass well, for he looked for all the world as if he were walking in his sleep, and many other spiteful things they said; but Boots gave no heed to them, only asking them to go and see for themselves; and when they went, there stood the grass as fine and deep this time as it had been twice before.

Now, you must know that the king of the country where Boots lived had a daughter, whom he would give only to the man who could ride up over the hill of glass, for there was a high, high hill, all of glass, as smooth and slippery as ice, close by the king's palace. Upon the tip-top of the hill, the king's daughter was to sit, with three golden apples in her lap, and the man who could ride up and carry off the three golden apples was to have half of the kingdom and the princess for his wife. This the king had stuck up on all the church doors in his realm, and had given it out in many other kingdoms besides.

Now, this princess was so lovely that all who set eyes on her fell over head and ears in love with her whether they would or not. So I needn't tell you how all the princes and knights who heard of her were eager to win her, as a wife, and half of the kingdom besides; and how they came riding from all parts of the world on high prancing horses, and clad in the grandest clothes, for there wasn't one of them who hadn't made up his mind that he, and he alone, was to win the princess.

When the day of trial came, which the king had fixed, there was such a crowd of princes and knights under the glass hill, that it made one's head to whirl to look at them; and everyone in the country who could even crawl along was off to the hill, for they were all eager to see the man who was to win the princess.

The two elder brothers set off with the rest; but as for Boots, they said outright he shouldn't go with them, for if they were seen with such a dirty changeling, all begrimed with smut from cleaning their shoes and sifting cinders in the dusthole, they said folk would make game of them.

"Very well," said Boots; "it's all one to me. I can go alone, and stand or fall by myself."

Now when the two brothers came to the hill of glass, the knights and princes were all hard at it, riding their horses till they were all in a foam; but it was no good, by my troth; for as soon as ever the horses set foot on the hill, down they slipped, and there wasn't one who could get a yard or two up; and no wonder, for the hill was as smooth as a sheet of glass and as steep as a house-wall. But all were eager to have the princess and half the kingdom. So they rode and slipped, and slipped and rode, and still it was the same story over again. At last their horses were so weary that they could scarce lift a leg, and in such a sweat that the lather dripped from them, and so the knights had to give up trying any more. The king was just thinking that he would proclaim a new trial for the next day, to see if they would have better luck, when all at once a knight came riding up on so brave a steed that no one had ever seen the like of it in his born

days, and the knight had mail of brass, and the horse, a brass bit in its mouth, so bright that the sunbeams shone from it. Then all the others called out to him that he might just as well spare himself the trouble of riding up the hill, for it would lead to no good; but he gave no heed to them, and put his horse at the hill, and up it went like nothing for a good way, about a third of the height; and when he had got so far, he turned his horse and rode down again. So lovely a knight the princess thought she had never seen; and while he was riding she sat and thought to herself — "Would to heaven he might only come up, and down the other side."

And when she saw him turning back, she threw down one of the golden apples after him, and it rolled down into his shoe. But when he got to the bottom of the hill he rode off so fast that no one could tell what had become of him. That evening all the knights and princes were to go before the king, that he who had ridden so far up the hill might show the apple the princess had thrown; but there was no one who had anything to show. One after the other they all came, but not a man of them could show the apple.

At evening, the brothers of Boots came home too, and had a long story to tell about the riding up the hill.

"First of all," they said, "there was not one of the whole lot who could get so much as a stride up; but at last came one who had a suit of brass mail, and a brass bridle and saddle, all so bright that the sun shone from them a mile off. He was a chap to ride, just! He rode a third of the way up the hill of glass and he could easily have ridden the whole way up, if he chose; but he turned round and rode down thinking, maybe, that was enough for once."

"Oh! I should so like to have seen him, that I should," said Boots, who sat by the fireside, and stuck his feet into the cinders as was his wont.

"Oh!" said his brothers, "you would, would you? You look fit to keep company with such high lords, nasty beast that you are, sitting there amongst the ashes."

Next day the brothers were all for setting

off again; and Boots begged them this time, too, to let him go with them and see the riding; but no, they wouldn't have him at any price, he was too ugly and nasty, they said.

"Well, well," said Boots; "if I go at all, I must go by myself. I'm not afraid."

So when the brothers got to the hill of glass, all the princes and knights began to ride again, and you may fancy they had taken care to shoe their horses sharp; but it was no good — they rode and slipped, and slipped and rode, just as they had done the day before, and there was not one who could get as far as a yard up the hill. And when they had worn out their horses, so that they could not stir a leg, they were all forced to give it up as a bad job. The king thought he might as well proclaim that the riding should take place the next day for the last time, just to give them one chance more; but all at once it came across his mind that he might as well wait a little longer to see if the knight in the brass mail would come this day too. Well, they saw nothing of him; but all at once came one riding on a steed far, far braver and finer than that on which the knight of brass had ridden, and he had silver mail, and a silver saddle and bridle, all so bright that the sunbeams gleamed and glanced from far away. Then the others shouted out to him again, saying he might as well hold hard and not try to ride up the hill, for all his trouble would be thrown away; but the knight paid no attention to them, and rode straight at the hill and right up it, till he had gone two thirds of the way, and then he wheeled his horse round and rode down again. To tell the truth, the princess liked him still better than the knight in brass, and she sat and wished he might only be able to come right to the top, and down the other side; but when she saw him turning back, she threw the second apple after him, and it rolled into his shoe. But as soon as ever he had come down the hill of glass, he rode off so fast that no one knew what became of him.

At evening when all were to go before the king and the princess, that he who had the golden apple might show it, in they went, one after the other; but there was no one who had any golden apple to show. The two

brothers, as they had done on the former day, went home and told how things had gone, and how all had ridden at the hill and none got up.

"But, last of all," they said, "came one in a silver suit, and his horse had a silver bridle and a silver saddle. He was just a chap to ride; and he got two-thirds up the hill, and then turned back. He was a fine fellow and no mistake; and the princess threw the second gold apple to him."

"Oh!" said Boots, "I should so like to have seen him too, that I should."

"A pretty story," they said. "Perhaps you think his coat of mail was as bright as the ashes you are always poking about and sifting, you nasty, dirty beast."

The third day everything happened as it had happened the two days before. Boots begged to go and see the sight, but the two wouldn't hear of his going with them. When they got to the hill there was no one who could get so much as a yard up it; and now all waited for the knight in silver mail, but they neither saw nor heard of him. At last came one riding on a steed, so brave that no one had ever seen his match; and the knight had a suit of golden mail, and a golden saddle, and bridle, so wondrous bright that the sunbeams gleamed from them a mile off. The other knights and princes could not find time to call out to him not to try his luck, for they were amazed to see how grand he was. He rode at the hill, and tore up it like nothing, so that the princess hadn't even time to wish that he might get up the whole way. As soon as ever he reached the top, he took the third golden apple from the princess's lap, and then turned his horse and rode down again. As soon as he got down, he rode off at full speed, and out of sight in no time.

Now, when the brothers got home at evening, you may fancy what long stories they told, how the riding had gone off that day; and amongst other things, they had a deal to say about the knight in golden mail.

"He was just a chap to ride!" they said; "so grand a knight isn't to be found in the whole world."

"Oh!" said Boots, "I should so like to have seen him, that I should."

"Ah!" said his brothers, "his mail shone a deal brighter than the glowing coals which you are always poking and digging at; nasty, dirty beast that you are."

Next day all the knights and princes were to pass before the king and the princess — it was too late to do so the night before, I suppose — that he who had the golden apple might bring it forth, but one came after another, first the princes and then the knights, and still no one could show the gold apple.

"Well," said the king, "someone must have it, for it was something that we all saw with our own eyes, how a man came and rode up and bore it off."

He commanded that everyone who was in the kingdom should come up to the palace and see if he could show the apple. Well, they all came, one after another, but no one had the golden apple, and after a long time the two brothers of Boots came. They were the last of all, so the king asked them if there was no one else in the kingdom who hadn't come.

"Oh, yes," said they. "We have a brother, but he never carried off the golden apple. He hasn't stirred out of the dusthole on any of the three days."

"Never mind that," said the king; "he may as well come up to the palace like the rest."

So Boots had to go up to the palace.

"How, now," said the king; "have you got the golden apple? Speak out!"

"Yes, I have," said Boots; "here is the first, and here is the second, and here is the third one, too"; and with that he pulled all three golden apples out of his pocket, and at the same time threw off his sooty rags, and stood before them in his gleaming golden mail.

"Yes!" said the king; "you shall have my daughter and half my kingdom, for you well deserve both her and it."

So they got ready for the wedding, and Boots got the princess for his wife, and there was great merry-making at the bridal-feast, you may fancy, for they could all be merry though they couldn't ride up the hill of glass; and all I can say is, that if they haven't left off their merry-making yet, why, they're still at it.

East o' the Sun and West o' the Moon[7]

⋙ *It is interesting to note certain likenesses in this story to other tales. First of all, the prince is disguised and comes to a house seeking shelter from the cold. In the second place, the heroine, disobeying orders, talks too much; tries to discover who her husband is; and as a result, has to go through long trials and many tests before she wins him back. A very similar situation, in part, is found in Cupid and Psyche.*

Once on a time there was a poor husbandman who had so many children that he hadn't much of either food or clothing to give them. Pretty children they all were; but the prettiest was the youngest daughter, who was so lovely there was no end to her loveliness.

So one day, 'twas on a Thursday evening late in the fall of the year, the weather was wild and rough outside. It was cruelly dark, and rain fell and wind blew, till the walls of the cottage shook again and again. There they all sat round the fire busy with this thing and that. Just then, all at once something gave three taps on the window-pane. The father went out to see what was the matter; and when he got out of doors, what should he see but a great big White Bear.

"Good evening to you," said the White Bear.

"The same to you," said the man.

"Will you give me your youngest daughter? If you will, I'll make you as rich as you are now poor," said the Bear.

Well, the man would not be at all sorry to be so rich; but still he thought he must have a bit of a talk with his daughter first; so in he went and told them how there was a great White Bear waiting outside, who had given his word to make them rich if he could only have the youngest daughter.

The lassie said "No!" outright. Nothing could get her to say anything else; so the man went out and settled it with the White Bear, that he should come again the next Thursday evening and get an answer. Mean-

[7] From Peter Christen Asbjörnsen, *Popular Tales from the Norse*, trans. G. W. Dasent (Putnam, 1908)

time the man talked to his daughter and kept telling her of all the riches they would get; and how well off she would be herself. At last she thought better of it, and washed and mended her rags, made herself as smart as she could, and was ready to start. I can't say her packing gave her much trouble.

Next Thursday evening came the White Bear to fetch her; and she got upon his back with her bundle, and off they went. When they had gone a bit of the way, the White Bear said,

"Are you afraid?"

"No," she said.

"Well! mind and hold tight by my shaggy coat, and there's nothing to fear," said the Bear.

So she rode a long, long way, till they came to a great steep hill. There on the face of it, the White Bear gave a knock; and a door opened, and they came into a castle, where there were many rooms lit up; rooms gleaming with silver and gold; and there was a table ready laid, and it was all as grand as it could be. The White Bear gave her a silver bell; and when she wanted anything, she had only to ring it, and she would get what she wanted at once.

Well, after she had eaten and drunk, and evening wore on, she got sleepy after her journey and thought that she would like to go to bed; so she rang the bell; and she had scarce taken hold of it before she came into a chamber where there were two beds made, as fair and white as any one could wish to sleep in, with silken pillows and curtains and gold fringe. All that was in the room was gold or silver; but when she had gone to bed, and put out the light, a man came in and lay down on the other bed. That was the White Bear, who threw off his beast shape at night; but she never saw him, for he always came after she put the light out, and before the day dawned he was up and gone again. So things went on happily for a while; but at last she began to grow silent and sorrowful; for she went about all day alone and she longed to go home and see her father and mother, and brothers and sisters, and that was why she was so sad and sorrowful, because she couldn't get to them.

"Well, well!" said the Bear, "perhaps there's a cure for all this; but you must promise me one thing, not to talk alone with your mother, but only when the rest are by to hear; for she will take you by the hand and try to lead you into a room alone to talk; but you must mind and not do that, else you'll bring bad luck to both of us."

So one Sunday, the White Bear came and said now they could set off to see her father and mother. Well, off they started, she sitting on his back; and they went far and long. At last they came to a grand house, and there her brothers and sisters were running about out of doors at play, and everything was so pretty, 'twas a joy to see.

"This is where your father and mother live now," said the White Bear; "but don't forget what I told you, else you'll make us both unlucky."

No, bless you, she'd not forget, and when she had reached the house, the White Bear turned right about and left her.

Then she went in to see her father and mother, and there was such joy, there was no end of it. None of them thought that they could thank her enough for all she had done for them. Now, they had everything they wished, as good as good could be, and they all wanted to know how she got on where she lived.

Well, she said, it was very good to live where she did; she had all she wished. What she said beside I don't know; but I don't think any of them had the right end of the stick, or that they got much out of her. But so in the afternoon, after they had finished their dinner, all happened as the White Bear had said. Her mother wanted to talk with her alone in her bed-room; but she minded what the White Bear had said, and wouldn't go upstairs.

"Oh, what we have to talk about will keep," she said, and put her mother off. But somehow or other, her mother got around her at last, and she had to tell the whole story. So she said, how every night, when she had gone to a bed, a man came and lay down on the other bed in her room as soon as she had put out the light, and how she never saw him, because he was always up and away before the morning dawned; and how she went woeful and sorrowful, for she thought she should so like to see him, and how all day long she walked about there alone, and how dull, and dreary, and lone-some it was.

"My!" said her mother; "it may well be a Troll sleeping in your room! But now I'll teach you a lesson how to set eyes on him. I'll give you a bit of candle, which you can carry in your bosom. Just light that while he is asleep; but take care not to drop the tallow on him."

Yes, she took the candle, and hid it in her bosom, and as night drew on the White Bear came to fetch her away.

But when they had gone a bit of the way, the Bear asked her if all hadn't happened as he had said.

Well, she couldn't say it hadn't.

"Now mind," said he, "if you have listened to your mother's advice, you have brought bad luck on us both, and then all that has passed between us will be as nothing."

"No," she said, "I haven't listened to my mother's advice."

When she reached home, and had gone to bed, it was the old story over again. There came a man and lay down on the other bed; but at dead of night, when she heard him sleeping, she got up and struck a light, lit the candle, and let the light shine on him, and she saw that he was the loveliest Prince she had ever set eyes on and she fell so deep in love with him on the spot, that she thought that she couldn't live if she didn't give him a kiss then and there. And so she did; but as she kissed him, she dropped three hot drops of tallow on his shirt and he woke up.

"What have you done?" he cried; "now you have made us both unlucky, for had you held out only for this one year, I had been freed. For I have a stepmother who has be-witched me, so that I am a White Bear by day, and a Man by night. But now all ties are snapt between us; now I must set off from you to her. She lives in a castle which stands EAST O' THE SUN AND WEST O' THE MOON, and there, too, is a Princess with a nose three ells long, and she's the wife I must have now."

She wept and took it ill, but there was no help for it; go he must.

Then she asked him if she mightn't go with him.

No, she mightn't.

"Tell me the way, then," she said, "and I'll search you out; that surely I may get leave to do."

"Yes, you may do that," he said; "but there is no way to that place. It lies EAST O' THE SUN AND WEST O' THE MOON, and thither you'll never find your way."

The next morning when she awoke, both Prince and castle were gone, and there she lay on a little green patch in the midst of the gloomy thick wood, and by her side lay the same bundle of rags she had brought with her from her old home.

When she had rubbed the sleep out of her eyes, and wept till she was tired, she set out on her way, and walked many, many days, till she came to a lofty crag. Under it sat an old hag, and played with a gold apple which she tossed about. Her the lassie asked if she knew the way to the Prince, who lived with his stepmother in the castle that lay EAST O' THE SUN AND WEST O' THE MOON, and who was to marry the Princess with a nose three ells long.

"How did you come to know about him?" asked the old hag; "but maybe you are the lassie who ought to have had him?"

Yes, she was.

"So, so; it's you, is it?" said the old hag. "Well, all I know about him is, that he lives in the old castle that lies EAST O' THE SUN AND WEST O' THE MOON, and thither you'll come late or never; but still you may have the loan of my horse and on him you may ride to the next neighbor. Maybe she'll be able to tell you; and when you get there, just give the horse a switch under the left ear, and beg him to be off home; and, stay, this golden apple may you take with you."

So she got upon the horse and rode a long, long time, 'till she came to another crag, under which sat another old hag, with a gold carding-comb. Her the lassie asked if she knew the way to the castle that lay EAST O' THE SUN AND WEST O' THE MOON, and she an-swered, like the first old hag, that she knew nothing about it except it was east o' the sun and west o' the moon.

"And thither you'll come, late or never;

but you shall have the loan of my horse to my next neighbor; maybe she'll tell you all about it; and when you get there, just switch the horse under the left ear and beg him to be off home."

And this old hag gave her the golden carding-comb; it might be she'd find some use for it, she said. So the lassie got up on the horse, and rode a far, far way, and a weary time; and so at last she came to another great crag, under which sat another hag, spinning with a golden spinning-wheel. Her, too, the lassie asked if she knew the way to the Prince, and where the castle was that lay EAST O' THE SUN AND WEST O' THE MOON. So it was the same thing over again.

"Maybe it's you who ought to have had the Prince?" said the old hag.

Yes, it was.

But she, too, didn't know the way a bit better than the others. East o' the sun and west o' the moon it was, she knew — that was all.

"And thither you'll come, late or never; but I'll lend you my horse, and then I think you'd best ride to the East Wind and ask him; maybe he knows those parts, and can blow you thither. But when you get to him, you need only to give the horse a switch under the left ear, and he'll trot home himself."

And so, too, she gave the girl the gold spinning-wheel. "Maybe you'll find use for it," said the old hag.

Then on she rode many, many days, a weary time, before she got to the East Wind's house; but at last she did reach it, and then she asked the East Wind if he could tell her the way to the Prince who dwelt east o' the sun and west o' the moon. Yes, the East Wind often heard tell of the Prince and the castle, but he couldn't tell the way for he had never blown so far.

"But if you will, I'll go to my brother, the West Wind; maybe he knows, for he is much stronger. So, if you'll just get on my back, I'll carry you thither."

Yes, she got on his back, and they went briskly along.

When they got there they went into the West Wind's house; and the East Wind said the lassie he had brought was the one who ought to have had the Prince who lived in the castle EAST O' THE SUN AND WEST O' THE MOON; and so she had set out to seek him, and how he had come with her, and would be glad to know if the West Wind knew how to get to the castle.

"Nay," said the West Wind, "so far I've never blown; but if you will, I'll go with you to our brother the South Wind, for he's much stronger than either of us, and he has flapped his wings far and wide. Maybe he'll tell you. You can get on my back, and I'll carry you to him."

Yes, she got on his back, and so they traveled to the South Wind and were not so very long on the way.

When they got there, the West Wind asked him if he could tell the lassie the way to the castle that lay EAST O' THE SUN AND WEST O' THE MOON, for it was she who ought to have had the Prince who lived there.

"You don't say so! That's she, is it?" said the South Wind.

"Well, I have blustered about in most places in my time, but so far have I never blown; but if you will, I'll take you to my brother the North Wind; he is the strongest of the whole lot of us and if he doesn't know where it is, you'll never find any one in the world to tell you. You can get on my back and I'll carry you thither."

Yes! she got on his back and away he went from his house at a fine rate. And this time, too, she wasn't long on the way.

When they got to the North Wind's house, he was so wild and cross, cold puffs came from him a long way off.

"BLAST YOU BOTH, WHAT DO YOU WANT?" he roared out to them ever so far off, so that it struck them with an icy shiver.

"Well," said the South Wind, "you needn't be so foul-mouthed, for here I am, your brother, the South Wind, and here is the lassie who ought to have had the Prince who dwells in the castle that lies EAST O' THE SUN AND WEST O' THE MOON; and now she wants to ask you if you ever were there, and can tell her the way, for she would be so glad to find him again."

"YES, I KNOW WELL ENOUGH WHERE IT IS," said the North Wind;

"once in my life I blew an aspen-leaf thither, but I was so tired I couldn't blow a puff for ever so many days after. But if you really wish to go thither, and aren't afraid to come along with me, I'll take you on my back and see if I can blow you thither."

Yes! with all her heart; she must and would get thither if it were possible in any way; and as for fear, however madly he went, she wouldn't be at all afraid.

"Very well, then," said the North Wind. "but you must sleep here tonight, for we must have the whole day before us if we're to get thither at all."

Early the next morning the North Wind woke her, and puffed himself up, and blew himself out, and made himself so stout and big 'twas gruesome to look at him; and so off they went high through the air as if they would never stop till they got to the world's end.

Down below there was such a storm; it threw down long tracts of wood and many houses, and when it swept over the great sea ships foundered by the hundreds.

They tore on and on — no one can believe how far they went — and all the while they still went over the sea, and the North Wind got more and more weary, and so out of breath he could scarcely bring out a puff; and his wings drooped and drooped, till at last he sank so low that the crests of the waves dashed over his heels.

"Are you afraid?" said the North Wind.

No, she wasn't.

But they weren't very far from land; and the North Wind had still enough strength left in him that he managed to throw her up on the shore under the windows of the castle which lay EAST o' THE SUN AND WEST o' THE MOON; but then he was so weak and worn out he had to stay there and rest many days before he could get home again.

Next morning the lassie sat under the castle window and began to play with the gold apple; and the first person she saw was the Long-nose who was to have the Prince.

"What do you want for your gold apple, you lassie?" said the Long-nose, and threw up the window.

"It's not for sale for gold or money," said the lassie.

"If it's not for sale for gold or money, what is it that you will sell it for? You may name your own price," said the Princess.

"Well! if I may get to the Prince who lives here and be with him tonight, you shall have it," said the lassie.

Yes! she might; that could be arranged. So the Princess got the gold apple; but when the lassie came up to the Prince's bed-room at night he was fast asleep; she called him and shook him, and between whiles she wept sore; but for all she could do she couldn't wake him up. Next morning as soon as day broke, came the Princess with the long nose, and drove her out again.

So in the daytime she sat down under the castle windows and began to card with her golden carding-comb, and the same thing happened again. The Princess asked what she wanted for it; and she said it wasn't for sale for gold or money, but if she might get leave to go to the Prince and be with him for the night, the Princess should have it. But when she went up, she found him asleep again, and she called, and she shook him, and wept, and prayed, and she couldn't get life into him; and as soon as the first gray peep of day came, then came the Princess with the long nose, and chased her out again.

So in the daytime, the lassie sat down outside under the castle window, and began to spin with her golden spinning-wheel, and that, too, the Princess with the long nose wanted to have. So she raised the window and asked what the lassie wanted for it. The lassie said, as she had said before, it wasn't for sale for gold or money; but if she might go up to the Prince who was there, and be there alone that night, the Princess might have it.

Yes! she might do that and welcome. But now you must know there were some Christian folk who had been carried off thither, and as they sat in their room, which was next the Prince, they had heard how a girl had been in there, and wept and prayed, and called to him two nights running, and they told that to the Prince.

That evening when the Princess came with her sleeping potion, the Prince made as if he drank, but threw the drink over his shoulder for he could guess what kind of a drink it was. So when the lassie came in she found the Prince wide awake; and then she told him the whole story of how she came thither.

"Ah," said the Prince, "you've come just in the nick of time for tomorrow is to be our wedding-day; and now I won't have the Long-nose, for you are the only lassie in the world who can set me free. I'll say I want to see what my wife is fit for and beg her to wash the shirt which has the three spots of tallow on it; she'll say yes, for she doesn't know 'tis you who put them there; but that's work for Christian folk, and not for a pack of Trolls; and so I'll say that I won't have any other for my bride than she who can wash them out, and ask you to do it."

The next day, when the wedding was to be, the Prince said,

"First of all, I want to see what my bride is fit for."

"Yes," said the stepmother with all her heart.

"Well," said the Prince, "I've got a fine shirt which I'd like for my wedding shirt; but somehow it has got three spots of tallow on it which I must have washed out; and I have sworn never to take any other bride than the lassie who is able to do that. If she can't she's not worth having."

Well, that was no great thing, they said; so they agreed, and she with the long nose began to wash away as hard as ever she could, but the more she rubbed and scrubbed, the bigger the spots grew.

"Ah," said the old hag, her mother, "you can't wash; let me try."

But she hadn't long taken the shirt in hand before it got far worse than ever, and with all her rubbing, and wringing, and scrubbing, the spots grew bigger and blacker, and the darker and uglier the shirt.

Then all the other Trolls began to wash; but the longer it lasted, the blacker and uglier the shirt grew, till at last it was as black all over as if it had been up the chimney.

"Ah," said the Prince, "you're none of you worth a straw; you can't wash. Why there, outside, sits a beggar lassie. I'll be bound she knows how to wash better than the whole lot of you. *Come in, lassie!*" he shouted.

Well, in she came.

"Can you wash this shirt clean, lassie?" he said.

"I don't know," she said, "but I think I can."

And almost before she had taken it and dipped it in the water, it was as white as the driven snow, and whiter still.

"Yes, you are the lassie for me," said the Prince.

At that the old hag flew into such a rage, she burst on the spot, and the Princess with the long nose did the same, and the whole pack of Trolls after her — at least I've never heard a word about them since.

As for the Prince and the Princess, they set free all the poor Christian folk who had been carried off and shut up there; and they took with them all the silver and gold, and flitted away as far as they could from the castle that lay EAST O' THE SUN AND WEST O' THE MOON.

The Lad Who Went to the North Wind [8]

✒ *The exchange of a non-magical object for a magical one is a motif often found in folk tales. Here the hero is a normal boy, determined to have his rights. The action moves swiftly to a satisfactory ending.*

Once on a time there was an old widow who had one son, and as she was poorly and weak, her son had to go into the storehouse to fetch meal for cooking; but when he got outside the storehouse, and was just going down the steps, there came the North Wind, puffing and blowing, caught up the meal, and so away with it through the air. Then the lad went back into the storehouse for more; but when he came out again on the steps, if the North Wind didn't come again and carry off the meal with a puff; and more than that, he did so a third time. At this the lad got very angry; and as he thought it hard that the North Wind should behave so, he thought he'd just look him up and ask him to give up his meal.

8 From Peter Christen Asbjörnsen, *Popular Tales from the Norse*, trans. G. W. Dasent (Putnam, 1908).

So off he went, but the way was long, and he walked and walked; but at last he came to the North Wind's house.

"Good day," said the lad, and "thank you for coming to see us yesterday."

"GOOD DAY," answered the North Wind, for his voice was loud and gruff, "AND THANKS FOR COMING TO SEE ME. WHAT DO YOU WANT?"

"Oh," answered the lad, " I only wished to ask you to be so good as to let me have back the meal you took from me on the storehouse steps, for we haven't much to live on; and if you're to go snapping up the morsel we have there'll be nothing for it but to starve."

"I haven't got your meal," said the North Wind; "but if you are in such need, I'll give you a cloth which will get you everything you want, if you only say, 'Cloth, spread yourself, and serve up all kinds of good dishes.' "

With this the lad was well content. But, as the way was so long he couldn't get home in one day, he turned into an inn on the way; and when they were going to sit down to supper, he laid the cloth on a table which stood in the corner and said —

"Cloth, spread yourself, and serve up all kinds of good dishes." He had scarce said it, before the cloth did as it was bid; and all who stood by thought it a fine thing, but most of all the landlord. So, when all was fast asleep, at the dead of night, he took the lad's cloth, and put another in its stead, just like the one he had got from the North Wind, but which couldn't so much as serve up a bit of dry bread.

When the lad woke, he took his cloth and went off with it, and that day he got home to his mother.

"Now," said he, "I've been to the North Wind's house, and a good fellow he is, for he gave me this cloth, and when I only say to it, 'Cloth, spread yourself, and serve up all kinds of good dishes,' I get any sort of food I please."

"All very true, I dare say," said his mother; "but seeing is believing; and I shan't believe it till I see it."

So the lad made haste, drew out a table, laid the cloth on it and said —

"Cloth, spread yourself, and serve up all kinds of good dishes."

But never a bit of dry bread did the cloth serve up.

"Well," said the lad, "there's no help for it but to go to the North Wind again"; and away he went.

So he came to where the North Wind lived late in the afternoon.

"Good evening!" said the lad.

"Good evening!" said the North Wind.

"I want my rights for that meal of ours which you took," said the lad; "for as for the cloth I got, it isn't worth a penny."

"I've got no meal," said the North Wind; "but yonder you have a ram which coins nothing but golden ducats as soon as you say to it —

" 'Ram, ram! make money!' "

So the lad thought this a fine thing; but as it was too far to get home that day, he turned in for the night at the same inn where he had slept before.

Before he called for anything, he tried the truth of what the North Wind had said of the ram; and found it all right; but when the landlord saw that, he thought it was a famous ram, and when the lad had fallen asleep, he took another which couldn't coin gold ducats, and changed the two.

Next morning off went the lad; and when he got home to his mother, he said,

"After all, the North Wind is a jolly fellow; for now he has given me a ram which can coin gold ducats if I only say, 'Ram, ram! make money!' "

"All very true, I dare say," said his mother; "but I shan't believe any such stuff until I see the ducats made."

"Ram, ram! make money!" said the lad; but if the ram made anything it wasn't money.

So the lad went back to the North Wind, and blew him up, and said the ram was worth nothing, and he must have his rights for the meal.

"Well," said the North Wind; "I've nothing else to give you but that old stick in the corner yonder; but it's a stick of that kind that if you say,

" 'Stick, stick! lay on!' it lays on till you say,

" 'Stick, stick! now stop!' "

So, as the way was long, the lad turned in

this night again, to the landlord; but as he could pretty well guess how things stood as to the cloth and the ram, he lay down at once on the bench and began to snore, as if he were asleep.

Now the landlord, who easily saw that the stick must be worth something hunted up one which was like it. When he heard the lad snore, he was going to change the two; but just as he was about to take it the lad bawled out,

"Stick! stick! lay on!"

So the stick began to beat the landlord, till he jumped over the chairs and tables and benches and yelled and roared,

"Oh, my! oh, my! bid the stick be still, else it will beat me to death, and you shall have back both your cloth and your ram."

When the lad thought the landlord had got enough, he said,

"Stick, stick! now stop!"

Then he took the cloth and put it into his pocket, and went home with his stick in his hand, leading the ram by a cord round its horns; and so he got his rights for the meal he had lost.

The Cat on the Dovrefell [9]

❧ The noted novelist, G. B. Stern, has called this one of the greatest cat stories in all literature. So it is, though no cat appears in it. For the storyteller who seeks a Christmas story which is non-religious, this offers a solution. Here is one more typical folk-tale comment on man's ability to best the forces of Might and Darkness by his own wit and sense of humor.

Once on a time there was a man up in Finnmark who had caught a great white bear, which he was going to take to the King of Denmark. Now, it so fell out, that he came to the Dovrefell just about Christmas Eve, and there he turned into a cottage where a man lived, whose name was Halvor, and asked the man if he could get house-room there for his bear and himself.

[9] From Peter Christen Asbjörnsen, Popular Tales from the Norse, trans. G. W. Dasent (Putnam, 1908).

"Heaven never help me, if what I say isn't true!" said the man; "but we can't give anyone house-room just now, for every Christmas Eve such a pack of Trolls come down upon us, that we are forced to flit, and haven't so much as a house over our own heads, to say nothing of lending one to anyone else."

"Oh?" said the man, "if that's all, you can very well lend me your house; my bear can lie under the stove yonder, and I can sleep in the side-room."

Well, he begged so hard, that at last he got leave to stay there; so the people of the house flitted out, and before they went, everything was got ready for the Trolls; the tables were laid, and there was rice porridge, and fish boiled in lye, and sausages, and all else that was good, just as for any other grand feast.

So, when everything was ready, down came the Trolls. Some were great, and some were small; some had long tails, and some had no tails at all; some, too, had long, long noses; and they ate and drank, and tasted everything. Just then one of the little Trolls caught sight of the white bear, who lay under the stove; so he took a piece of sausage and stuck it on a fork, and went and poked it up against the bear's nose, screaming out:

"Pussy, will you have some sausage?"

Then the white bear rose up and growled, and hunted the whole pack of them out of doors, both great and small.

Next year Halvor was out in the wood, on the afternoon of Christmas Eve, cutting wood before the holidays, for he thought the Trolls would come again; and just as he was hard at work, he heard a voice in the wood calling out:

"Halvor! Halvor!"

"Well," said Halvor, "here I am."

"Have you got your big cat with you still?"

"Yes, that I have," said Halvor; "she's lying at home under the stove, and what's more, she has now got seven kittens, far bigger and fiercer than she is herself."

"Oh, then, we'll never come to see you again," bawled out the Troll away in the wood, and he kept his word; for since that time the Trolls have never eaten their Christmas brose with Halvor on the Dovrefell.

The Talking Pot [10]

This story of the magic pot — the thieving pot, in some retellings — is one of three which are known only in Scandinavia and the Baltic countries. Parallel versions remain as yet undiscovered. The story as given here is taken from a larger collection translated and compiled by Jens Christian Bay (Danish Fairy and Folk Tales, Harper, 1899, a book long out of print). Dr. Bay's translation was made from the text of Svend Grundtvig, the great collector in Denmark during the middle years of the nineteenth century.

Once upon a time there was a man so poor that he had nothing in the world but a wife, a house, and one lone cow. And after a time, he got even poorer than that, and so he had to take the cow to market and sell her.

On the way he met a fine-faced stranger. "Well, my good man," said the stranger, "whither away with that fat cow?"

"To market, and thank you," said the man, though the cow was far from fat.

"Then perhaps you will sell her to me," said the stranger.

Yes, the farmer would sell and gladly, provided the price were twenty dollars or more.

The stranger shook his head. "Money I cannot give you," he said. "But I have a wonderful pot that I will trade you," and he showed the farmer a three-legged iron pot with a handle that was tucked under his arm.

Now, truth to tell, there was nothing at all wonderful-looking about the pot, and it might have hung in any chimney in the country. Besides, the poor man had nothing to put in it, neither food nor drink, so he declined to make the trade. "Money I need, and money I must have," he said, "so you may keep your wonderful pot."

But hardly had he said these words than the pot began to speak. "Take me, take me," cried the pot, "and you'll never have cause to rue it." And so the man changed his mind and made the trade, for if the pot could talk, then surely it could do other things, too.

Home he now returned, and when he reached there, he hid the pot in the stable

[10] From Mary C. Hatch, *13 Danish Tales* (Harcourt, Brace, 1947).

where the cow had always been kept, for he wanted to surprise his wife. Then he went inside. "Well, good wife," he said, "fetch me a bit to eat and a sup to drink, for I've walked a long mile and back today."

But his wife would do none of it till she heard about her husband's success at the market. "Did you make a fine bargain?" she asked.

"Fine as fine," said her husband.

"That is well," nodded the wife, "for we've a hundred places to use the money."

But it wasn't a money bargain. No indeed, exclaimed her husband.

Not a money bargain! Well, pray then, what had the good man gotten for the cow, cried the wife, and she would not rest till her husband had taken her to the barn and showed her the three-legged pot tied up to the stall.

And then the good wife *was* angry! Trading a fine, fat cow — though truth to tell it was neither fine nor fat — for a common black pot that might hang in anyone's chimney.

"You are stupid as a goose," cried the wife. "Now what will we do for food and drink? If you were not so tough, I do believe I would stew you!" And she started to shake her husband. But before she could do the poor man much damage, the pot began to speak again.

"Clean me, and shine me, and put me on the fire," said the pot, and at that the woman sang a different tune. "Well!" she said. "If you can talk, perhaps you can do other things, too." And she took the pot and scrubbed it and polished it, and then hung it over the fire.

"I will skip, I will skip," said the pot.

"How far will you skip?" asked the woman.

"Up the hill, and down the dale, and into the rich man's house," cried the little pot, and with that, it jumped down from the hook, and skipping across the room, went out the door, and up the road to the rich man's house. Here the rich man's wife was making fine cakes and puddings, and the pot jumped up on the table and settled there still as a statue.

"Well!" exclaimed the rich man's wife. "You are just what I need for my finest pudding." Then she stirred in sugar and spices, and raisins and nuts, a whole host of good things, and the pot took them all without a murmur. In a few minutes, the pudding was made, and the woman picked up the pot and put it on the fire. But down the pot jumped and skipped to the door.

"Dear me," exclaimed the woman. "What are you doing, and where are you going?"

"I'm bound for home to the poor man's house," cried the little pot, and away it went skipping up the road till it was back at the poor man's little cottage.

When the couple saw that the pot had brought them a fine pudding, the finest they had ever seen, they were very pleased, and the farmer said, "Now, my good wife, did I not make a good bargain when I traded our poor old cow for this wonderful pot?"

"Indeed you did," said his wife, and she fell to eating the pot's fine pudding.

The next morning, the pot again cried, "I will skip, I will skip!" And the wife said, "How far will you skip?"

"Up hill and down dale, and into the rich man's barn," the little pot replied, and out the house and up the road it went skipping, straight to the rich man's barn.

The rich man's servants were threshing grain, and the pot skipped to the center of the floor and stood there still as a statue.

"Well!" said one of the threshers. "Here is just the pot to hold a bushel of grain," and he poured in a sackful. But this took up no room at all, and so he poured in another and another till there was not a grain of anything left in the whole barn.

"A most peculiar pot!" exclaimed the men. "Though it looks as if it had hung in any number of chimneys." And then they tried to lift it, but it slid away from them and went skipping across the floor.

"Dear me," cried the men. "What are you doing, and where are you going?"

"I'm bound for home to the poor man's house," said the pot, and out the door it skipped, and though the men ran after it, they were left huffing and puffing far behind.

When the little pot reached home again, it poured out the wheat in the poor man's barn, and there was enough to make bread and cakes for years to come.

But that was not the end of its good deeds, for on the third morning it said again, "I will skip, I will skip!" And the old wife asked, "Where will you skip?" And it answered, "Up hill and down dale to the rich man's house," and out the house it ran at once.

Now the rich man was in his counting house counting out his money, and when the little pot arrived, up it jumped on the table, right in the midst of all the gold pieces.

"What a fine pot," cried the rich man. "Just the thing for my money." And into the pot he tossed handful after handful of money till not one piece was left loose on the table. Then he picked up his treasure to hide it in his money cupboard, but the pot slipped from his fingers and hopped to the door.

"Stop, stop," cried the rich man. "You have all my money."

"But not yours for long," said the pot. "I carry it home to the poor man's house," and out the room it skipped and back to the poor man's cottage. There it poured out the golden treasure, and the old couple cried aloud with delight.

"Now you have enough," said the pot, and indeed they did, enough and more, too, and so the wife washed the pot carefully and put it aside.

But in the morning, the pot was off again, straight for the rich man's house, and when the rich man saw it, he cried, "There is the wicked pot that stole my wife's pudding, and my wheat, and all my gold. But it shall bring everything back, every last farthing and more." Then he grabbed the pot, but bless my soul, if he didn't stick fast! And though he tugged and he pulled, he couldn't get free.

"I will skip, I will skip," said the pot.

"Well, skip to the North Pole," cried the man, still furiously trying to free himself, and at that, away went the pot and the man with it. Up the hill they waltzed and down the hill, and never once did they stop, not even to say hello or good-bye at the old couple's cottage, for the pot was in a great hurry. The North Pole, you know, is far, far away, even for a fast-skipping pot.

CHINA

Ah Tcha the Sleeper

⋙ *This subtle story is an excellent example of the treatment of a folk tale in the hands of an artist who has given it the stamp of his individuality without destroying the integrity of the folklore spirit. It is a "pourquoi" story because it tells the origin of tea. The recurring motif of witches and cats as symbols of darkness and evil is present here, and it is rich in details of the culture from which it comes.*

The story first appeared in Shen of the Sea, *the Newbery award winner of 1926, a book which consists of sixteen stories. The author heard them first from a Chinese shopkeeper whom he had consulted about typical Chinese foods, information he needed for a story he was in the process of writing. That encounter led to friendship and a revelation of the Chinese spirit, which Arthur Chrisman brilliantly made his own.*

Years ago, in southern China, lived a boy, Ah Tcha by name. Ah Tcha was an orphan, but not according to rule. A most peculiar orphan was he. It is usual for orphans to be very, very poor. That is the world-wide custom. Ah Tcha, on the contrary, was quite wealthy. He owned seven farms, with seven times seven horses to draw the plow. He owned seven mills, with plenty of breezes to spin them. Furthermore, he owned seven thousand pieces of gold, and a fine white cat.

The farms of Ah Tcha were fertile, were wide. His horses were brisk in the furrow. His mills never lacked for grain, nor wanted

1 From Arthur Bowie Chrisman, *Shen of the Sea* (Dutton, 1925).

for wind. And his gold was good sharp gold, with not so much as a trace of copper. Surely, few orphans have been better provided for than the youth named Ah Tcha. And what a busy person was this Ah Tcha. His bed was always cold when the sun arose. Early in the morning he went from field to field, from mill to mill, urging on the people who worked for him. The setting sun always found him on his feet, hastening from here to there, persuading his laborers to more gainful efforts. And the moon of midnight often discovered him pushing up and down the little teakwood balls of a counting board, or else threading cash, placing coins upon a string. Eight farms, nine farms he owned, and more stout horses. Ten mills, eleven, another white cat. It was Ah Tcha's ambition to become the richest person in the world.

They who worked for the wealthy orphan were inclined now and then to grumble. Their pay was not beggarly, but how they did toil to earn that pay which was not beggarly. It was go, and go, and go. Said the ancient woman Nu Wu, who worked with a rake in the field: "Our master drives us as if he were a fox and we were hares in the open. Round the field and round and round, hurry, always hurry." Said Hu Shu, her husband, who bound the grain into sheaves: "Not hares, but horses. We are driven like the horses of Lung Kuan, who ..." It's a long story.

But Ah Tcha, approaching the murmurers, said, "Pray be so good as to hurry, most excellent Nu Wu, for the clouds gather blackly, with thunder." And to the scowling husband he said, "Speed your work, I beg you,

313

honorable Hu Shu, for the grain must be under shelter before the smoke of Evening Rice ascends."

When Ah Tcha had eaten his Evening Rice, he took lantern and entered the largest of his mills. A scampering rat drew his attention to the floor. There he beheld no less than a score of rats, some gazing at him as if undecided whether to flee or continue the feast, others gnawing — and who are you, nibbling and caring not? And only a few short whisker-lengths away sat an enormous cat, sleeping the sleep of a mossy stone. The cat was black in color, black as a crow's wing dipped in pitch, upon a night of inky darkness. That describes her coat. Her face was somewhat more black. Ah Tcha had never before seen her. She was not his cat. But his or not, he thought it a trifle unreasonable of her to sleep, while the rats held high carnival. The rats romped between her paws. Still she slept. It angered Ah Tcha. The lantern rays fell on her eyes. Still she slept. Ah Tcha grew more and more provoked. He decided then and there to teach the cat that his mill was no place for sleepy heads.

Accordingly, he seized an empty grain sack and hurled it with such exact aim that the cat was sent heels over head. "There, old Crouch-by-the-hole," said Ah Tcha in a tone of wrath. "Remember your paining ear, and be more vigilant." But the cat had no sooner regained her feet than she . . . changed into . . . Nu Wu, the old woman who worked in the fields . . . a witch. What business she had in the mill is a puzzle. However, it is undoubtedly true that mills hold grain, and grain is worth money. And that may be an explanation. Her sleepiness is no puzzle at all. No wonder she was sleepy, after working so hard in the field, the day's length through.

The anger of Nu Wu was fierce and instant. She wagged a crooked finger at Ah Tcha, screeching: "Oh, you cruel money-grubber. Because you fear the rats will eat a pennyworth of grain you must beat me with bludgeons. You make me work like a slave all day — and wish me to work all night. You beat me and disturb my slumber. Very well, since you will not let me sleep,

I shall cause you to slumber eleven hours out of every dozen. . . . Close your eyes." She swept her wrinkled hand across Ah Tcha's face. Again taking the form of a cat, she bounded downstairs.

She had scarce reached the third step descending when Ah Tcha felt a compelling desire for sleep. It was as if he had taken gum of the white poppy flower, as if he had tasted honey of the gray moon blossom. Eyes half closed, he stumbled into a grain bin. His knees doubled beneath him. Down he went, curled like a dormouse. Like a dormouse he slumbered.

From that hour began a change in Ah Tcha's fortune. The spell gripped him fast. Nine-tenths of his time was spent in sleep. Unable to watch over his laborers, they worked when they pleased, which was seldom. They idled when so inclined — and that was often, and long. Furthermore, they stole in a manner most shameful. Ah Tcha's mills became empty of grain. His fields lost their fertility. His horses disappeared — strayed, so it was said. Worse yet, the unfortunate fellow was summoned to a magistrate's *yamen,* there to defend himself in a lawsuit. A neighbor declared that Ah Tcha's huge black cat had devoured many chickens. There were witnesses who swore to the deed. They were sure, one and all, that Ah Tcha's black cat was the cat at fault. Ah Tcha was sleeping too soundly to deny that the cat was his. . . . So the magistrate could do nothing less than make the cat's owner pay damages, with all costs of the lawsuit.

Thereafter, trials at court were a daily occurrence. A second neighbor said that Ah Tcha's black cat had stolen a flock of sheep. Another complained that the cat had thieved from him a herd of fattened bullocks. Worse and worse grew the charges. And no matter how absurd, Ah Tcha, sleeping in the prisoner's cage, always lost and had to pay damages. His money soon passed into other hands. His mills were taken from him. His farms went to pay for the lawsuits. Of all his wide lands, there remained only one little acre — and it was grown up in worthless bushes. Of all his goodly buildings, there was left one little hut, where the boy spent most of his time, in witch-imposed slumber.

Now, near by in the mountain of Huge Rocks Piled, lived a greatly ferocious *loong*, or, as foreigners would say, a dragon. This immense beast, from tip of forked tongue to the end of his shadow, was far longer than a barn. With the exception of length, he was much the same as any other *loong*. His head was shaped like that of a camel. His horns were deer horns. He had bulging rabbit eyes, a snake neck. Upon his many ponderous feet were tiger claws, and the feet were shaped very like sofa cushions. He had walrus whiskers, and a breath of red-and-blue flame. His voice was like the sound of a hundred brass kettles pounded. Black fish scales covered his body, black feathers grew upon his limbs. Because of his color he was sometimes called *Oo Loong*. From that it would seem that *Oo* means neither white nor pink.

The black *loong* was not regarded with any great esteem. His habit of eating a man — two men if they were little — every day made him rather unpopular. Fortunately, he prowled only at night. Those folk who went to bed decently at nine o'clock had nothing to fear. Those who rambled well along toward midnight, often disappeared with a sudden and complete thoroughness.

As every one knows, cats are much given to night skulking. The witch cat, Nu Wu was no exception. Midnight often found her miles afield. On such a midnight, when she was roving in the form of a hag, what should approach but the black dragon. Instantly the *loong* scented prey, and instantly he made for the old witch.

There followed such a chase as never was before on land or sea. Up hill and down dale, by stream and wood and fallow, the cat woman flew and the dragon coursed after. The witch soon failed of breath. She panted. She wheezed. She stumbled on a bramble and a claw slashed through her garments too close for comfort. The harried witch changed shape to a cat, and bounded off afresh, half a li at every leap. The *loong* increased his pace and soon was close behind, gaining. For a most peculiar fact about the *loong* is that the more he runs the easier his breath comes, and the swifter grows his speed. Hence, it is not surprising that his fiery breath was presently singeing the witch cat's back.

In a twinkling the cat altered form once more, and as an old hag scuttled across a turnip field. She was merely an ordinarily powerful witch. She possessed only the two forms — cat and hag. Nor did she have a gift of magic to baffle or cripple the hungry black *loong*. Nevertheless, the witch was not despairing. At the edge of the turnip field lay Ah Tcha's miserable patch of thick bushes. So thick were the bushes as to be almost a wall against the hag's passage. As a hag, she could have no hope of entering such a thicket. But as a cat, she could race through without hindrance. And the dragon would be sadly bothered in following. Scheming thus, the witch dashed under the bushes — a cat once more.

Ah Tcha was roused from slumber by the most outrageous noise that had ever assailed his ears. There was such a snapping of bushes, such an awful bellowed screeching that even the dead of a century must have heard. The usually sound-sleeping Ah Tcha was awakened at the outset. He soon realized how matters stood — or ran. Luckily, he had learned of the only reliable method for frightening off the dragon. He opened his door and hurled a red, a green, and a yellow firecracker in the monster's path.

In through his barely opened door the witch cat dragged her exhausted self. "I don't see why you couldn't open the door sooner," she scolded, changing into a hag. "I circled the hut three times before you had the gumption to let me in."

"I am very sorry, good mother. I was asleep." From Ah Tcha.

"Well, don't be so sleepy again," scowled the witch, "or I'll make you suffer. Get me food and drink."

"Again, honored lady, I am sorry. So poor am I that I have only water for drink. My food is the leaves and roots of bushes."

"No matter. Get what you have — and quickly."

Ah Tch reached outside the door and stripped a handful of leaves from a bush. He plunged the leaves into a kettle of hot water and signified that the meal was prepared. Then he lay down to doze, for he had been awake fully half a dozen minutes and the desire to sleep was returning stronger every moment.

The witch soon supped and departed, without leaving so much as half a "Thank you." When Ah Tcha awoke again, his visitor was gone. The poor boy flung another handful of leaves into his kettle and drank quickly. He had good reason for haste. Several times he had fallen asleep with the cup at his lips — a most unpleasant situation, and scalding. Having taken several sips, Ah Tcha stretched him out for a resumption of his slumber. Five minutes passed . . . ten minutes . . . fifteen. . . . Still his eyes failed to close. He took a few more sips from the cup and felt more awake than ever.

"I do believe," said Ah Tcha, "that she has thanked me by bewitching my bushes. She has charmed the leaves to drive away my sleepiness."

And so she had. Whenever Ah Tcha felt tired and sleepy — and at first that was often — he had only to drink of the bewitched leaves. At once his drowsiness departed. His neighbors soon learned of the bushes that banished sleep. They came to drink of the magic brew. There grew such a demand that Ah Tcha decided to set a price on the leaves. Still the demand continued. More bushes were planted. Money came.

Throughout the province people called for "the drink of Ah Tcha." In time they shortened it by asking for "Ah Tcha's drink," then for "Tcha's drink," and finally for "Tcha."

And that is its name at present, "Tcha," or "Tay," or "Tea," as some call it. And one kind of Tea is still called "Oo Loong" — "Black Dragon."

The Magic Monkey [2]

⋙ We find in this ancient Chinese tale the belief in the importance of knowledge. The hero has such a curiosity to see and understand everything about him that he attends a school for magic. When he and Teacher disagree as

[2] From Plato and Christina Chan, *The Magic Monkey*, adapted from an old Chinese legend (McGraw-Hill, Whittlesey House, 1944).

to the purpose of such education, Magic Monkey, after several interesting adventures, returns home. Here he uses his magic power to rid the homeland of the Demon of Havoc. This part of the story is told below.

He was not sorry in the least to be home again. He had had enough of school, anyway, and had learned all he wanted to know. He could fly, couldn't he? And he had the Magic Wand, didn't he, and knew all the secrets of transformations. What other monkey knew more?

All his friends were glad to see him home again. They crowded around him and told him they certainly missed him. They needed him home badly, too. For something very serious had happened. Their country was being invaded. The wicked Demon of Havoc was starting a war and causing a lot of trouble.

"Can't you do something about it?" they asked Magic Monkey.

Now the Demon of Havoc was a terrible monster. He had never had a good thought in all his life. He had never done a good deed. He had never even been polite to anybody. In fact, he enjoyed being as wicked as wicked could be, and the worse he was the better he liked it. He did wrong continually just for the sake of doing wrong. And he liked to torment and annoy others and make war upon them with the least bit of an excuse.

So when he saw how happy the monkeys were in their magic land, he decided he would destroy that happiness as quickly as he could. He summoned his army and marched right to the very edge of the magic land.

"Destroy the monkeys!" he cried. "Capture Magic Monkey, their King. Put an end to them all!"

Magic Monkey faced him, alone and unarmed. He was not the least bit afraid.

"Ha! Ha! Ha!" cried the Demon of Havoc, spitting fire, and flourishing his sword. "Where is your army, silly monkey?"

And Magic Monkey yelled back, "Here is my army, you big fool!"

Magic Monkey had really learned a great many things at school. He had been a very smart pupil even if he had once politely told

Teacher he knew nothing. He knew how to make all sorts of transformations. So he suddenly yanked a handful of hair from his head, bit the hairs into tiny bits, and threw them into the air. And quickly each hair changed into a small monkey.

There were hundreds and hundreds of them, and away they dashed to attack the Demon of Havoc. They swarmed around him like bees, biting him on the arms and legs, dashing into his eyes, and making him half blind with rage. Some tickled him on the nose and made him sneeze. The Demon of Havoc had a terrible time. He wanted to fight and he had to sneeze, too. The monkeys biting him made him itch. He could not drop his sword and scratch himself. So he jumped around like mad, swung his sword in the air, and howled with rage.

"Let me at you!" he cried to Magic Monkey, and dashed forward.

Probably he would have cut off Magic Monkey's head right then and there, if Magic Monkey hadn't been smart, and . . .

Suddenly Magic Monkey transformed himself into an enormous oak tree, with a trunk bigger around than ten big barrels, and huge branches that reached almost to the sky. It was the largest tree that had ever been, and the Demon had to stop and stare in complete amazement.

Also, at this point, the monkey army suddenly stopped its attack upon the Demon of Havoc and jumped into the branches of the tree. There they were, hundreds and hundreds and hundreds of them, jabbering and jabbering, making faces at the Demon, and throwing acorns at him.

At first the Demon did not quite know what had happened. First he had seen Magic Monkey. Then he had vanished. Then, where Magic Monkey had stood was a tree. It made the Demon of Havoc madder than ever. He guessed the real truth and was furious.

"You can't fool me that way!" he cried. "You think because you can make transformations you will outwit me. Not so. I'll show you!"

With his sword he began chopping at the tree. However . . .

Magic Monkey was too smart for the Demon of Havoc even at this frightening moment. So he suddenly transformed himself into a blade of grass. The Demon looked everywhere, but could not find him. He turned around and around and around, and almost stepped on Magic Monkey a couple of times.

Afraid that this might really happen, and if it did it would be good-bye for him, for he would be crushed to earth, Magic Monkey quickly made yet another transformation. He was standing behind the Demon of Havoc, so he changed himself into a great big billy-goat!

And then, running swiftly, he butted right into the Demon of Havoc and knocked him flat upon the ground.

Then quickly, before the Demon could pick himself up, Magic Monkey took the needle, the Magic Wand, from behind his ear.

"Grow larger — and larger — and larger!" he cried.

And suddenly the Magic Wand, instead of being a needle, became a huge pillar — bigger than the tree even. To the Magic Monkey it was light as a needle, so he lifted it high above his head, and then . . .

He brought the pillar down upon the Demon of Havoc and crushed him flat into the earth. Down and down and down he pushed the pillar — and down and down and down — lower and lower and lower sank the Demon — and was no more!

Then Magic Monkey turned the pillar back into a needle again, put it behind his ear, dusted off his hands, and grinned with great joy.

"That finishes you — Demon of Havoc — for good and all!" he said. "I guess Teacher will be proud of me now. I have certainly put my magic to a very good use."

All the monkeys applauded and cheered and hailed him as a great hero.

"He is the smartest monkey that has ever lived!" they said.

"We are happy to have him as our King!"

"He is indeed, now and forever more, Magic Monkey!"

And they lifted him upon their shoulders, marched around singing and shouting — and everyone was happy forever after.

JAPAN

The Tongue-cut Sparrow [1]

Retribution for the cruel and greedy, reward for the gentle and kind of heart — this is the pattern of justice of which each culture dreams, if the folklore mirrors, as it does, the ideals of its creators. This charming story from the Japanese states it with perfect balance of cause and effect. Lafcadio Hearn, Greek-Irish American, who adopted Japan as the home of his spirit, tells the story with becoming style.

'Tis said that once upon a time a cross old woman laid some starch in a basin intending to put it in the clothes in her wash-tub; but a sparrow that a woman, her neighbor, kept as a pet ate it up. Seeing this, the cross old woman seized the sparrow and saying, "You hateful thing!" cut its tongue and let it go.

When the neighbor woman heard that her pet sparrow had got its tongue cut for its offense, she was greatly grieved, and set out with her husband over mountains and plains to find where it had gone, crying: "Where does the tongue-cut sparrow stay? Where does the tongue-cut sparrow stay?"

At last they found its home. When the sparrow saw that its old master and mistress had come to see it, it rejoiced and brought them into its house and thanked them for their kindness in old times and spread a table for them, and loaded it with *sake* and fish till there was no more room, and made its wife and children and grandchildren all serve the table. At last, throwing away its drinking-cup, it danced a jig called the

[1] From Lafcadio Hearn, *Japanese Fairy Tales* (Liveright, 1924).

sparrow's dance. Thus they spent the day. When it began to grow dark, and they began to talk of going home, the sparrow brought out two wicker baskets and said: "Will you take the heavy one, or shall I give you the light one?" The old people replied: "We are old, so give us the light one: it will be easier to carry it." The sparrow then gave them the light basket and they returned with it to their home. "Let us open and see what is in it," they said. And when they had opened it and looked they found gold and silver and jewels and rolls of silk. They never expected anything like this. The more they took out the more they found inside. The supply was inexhaustible. So that house at once became rich and prosperous. When the cross old woman who had cut the sparrow's tongue out saw this, she was filled with envy, and went and asked her neighbor where the sparrow lived, and all about the way. "I will go too," she said, and at once set out on her search.

Again the sparrow brought out two wicker baskets and asked as before: "Will you take the heavy one, or shall I give you the light one?"

Thinking the treasure would be great in proportion to the weight of the basket, the old woman replied: "Let me have the heavy one." Receiving this, she started home with it on her back; the sparrow laughing at her as she went. It was as heavy as a stone and hard to carry; but at last she got back with it to her house.

Then when she took off the lid and looked in, a whole troop of frightful devils came bouncing out from the inside and at once tore the old woman to pieces.

INDIA

Numskull and the Rabbit [1]

It should be a matter of pride to American scholarship that the most highly acclaimed translation, in India itself, of the Sanskrit text of the Panchatantra into English is that made by Arthur W. Ryder, the American Sanskrit scholar. The preface to the Indian publication of the English text — the title page bears the imprint of the Jaico Publishing House, Bombay (1949) — has this to say of the Ryder translation: "It is the best of all existing Panchatantra translations in any foreign language."

Current among the Indian populace for at least five thousand years, probably longer, the animal stories which make up the Panchatantra have been told among all peoples of the world through more than twenty centuries. The original collection, in Sanskrit, numbered about eighty-four tales. In their travels through the ages, the stories underwent many changes, not only in regard to their form, color, and setting, but even as to their total numerical strength.

A maimed and garbled version was printed by Caxton, in English, and an even earlier printing in German was one of the first printed books in Europe. In 1859 Theodor Benfey, the noted German Sanskrit scholar, provided a literal and faithful translation in the German language of the Kashmir recension — a recension which is recognized by Oriental scholars as the most authoritative in existence. Benfey's Sanskrit studies were largely responsible for one of the major theories of the origins of folk tales, namely, that the tales had a common origin in India. That theory has been rather thoroughly exploded, but Benfey's studies resulted in incomparably increased knowledge of

the whole field of folklore, and his translation of the Panchatantra remains a pivotal accomplishment. He proved that "the Hindus, even before their acquaintance with the animal fables of Aesop which they received from the Greeks, had invented their own compositions of a similar kind, and a great many of them at that" (Stith Thompson, The Folktale, p. 376). "The difference between their (the Hindu) conceptions and those of the Aesop fables," says Mr. Benfey in his introduction to his Panchatantra, "consisted in general in the fact that whereas the Aesopic writer had his animals act in accordance with their own special nature, the Indic fable treated the animals without regard to their special nature, as if they were merely men masked in animal form." The Indian fable is didactic in intent, the wise conduct of life its theme, whereas the Aesopic fable is often a comment on traits of human nature or a cautionary tale. The Indian fable reflects the Hindu belief in the transmigration of souls. It bears also the characteristic trick of style in which one story is told within the frame of another, like a series of boxes within boxes. The readers of The Arabian Nights will find the pattern familiar.

> Intelligence is power. But where
> Could power and folly make a pair?
> The rabbit played upon his pride
> To fool him; and the lion died.

In a part of a forest was a lion drunk with pride, and his name was Numskull. He slaughtered the animals without ceasing. If he saw an animal, he could not spare him.

So all the natives of the forest — deer, boars, buffaloes, wild oxen, rabbits, and others — came together, and with woebegone countenances, bowed heads, and knees clinging to the ground, they undertook to beseech

1 From *The Panchatantra*, trans. from the Sanskrit by Arthur W. Ryder (University of Chicago Press, 1925).

obsequiously the king of beasts. "Have done, O King, with this merciless, meaningless slaughter of all creatures. It is hostile to happiness in the other world. For the Scripture says:

"A thousand future lives
    Will pass in wretchedness
For sins a fool commits
    His present life to bless.

"What wisdom in a deed
    That brings dishonor fell,
That causes loss of trust,
    That paves the way to hell?

And yet again:

"The ungrateful body, frail
    And rank with filth within,
Is such that only fools
    For its sake sink in sin.

"Consider these facts, and cease, we pray, to slaughter our generations. For if the master will remain at home, we will of our own motion send him each day for his daily food one animal of the forest. In this way neither the royal sustenance nor our families will be cut short. In this way let the king's duty be performed. For the proverb says:

"The king who tastes his kingdom like
    Elixir, bit by bit,
Who does not overtax its life,
    Will fully relish it.

"The king who madly butchers men,
    Their lives as little reckoned
As lives of goats, has one square meal,
    But never has a second.

"A king desiring profit, guards
    His world from evil chance;
With gifts and honors waters it
    As florists water plants.

"Guard subjects like a cow, nor ask
    For milk each passing hour:
A vine must first be sprinkled, then
    It ripens fruit and flower.

"The monarch-lamp from subjects draws
    Tax-oil to keep it bright:
Has any ever noticed kings
    That shone by inner light?

"A seedling is a tender thing,
    And yet, if not neglected,
It comes in time to bearing fruit:
    So subjects well protected.

"Their subjects form the only source
    From which accrue to kings
Their gold, grain, gems, and varied drinks,
    And many other things.

"The kings who serve the common weal
    Luxuriantly sprout;
The common loss is kingly loss,
    Without a shadow of a doubt."

After listening to this address, Numskull said: "Well, gentlemen, you are quite convincing. But if an animal does not come to me every day as I sit here, I promise you I will eat you all." To this they assented with much relief, and fearlessly roamed the wood. Each day at noon one of them appeared as his dinner, each species taking its turn and providing an individual grown old, or religious, or grief-smitten, or fearful of the loss of son or wife.

One day a rabbit's turn came, it being rabbit day. And when all the thronging animals had given him directions, he reflected: "How is it possible to kill this lion — curse him! Yet after all,

"In what can wisdom not prevail?
    In what can resolution fail?
What cannot flattery subdue?
    What cannot enterprise put through?

I can kill even a lion."

So he went very slowly, planning to arrive tardily, and meditating with troubled spirit on a means of killing him. Late in the day he came into the presence of the lion, whose throat was pinched by hunger in consequence of the delay, and who angrily thought as he licked his chops: "Aha! I must kill all the animals the first thing in the morning."

While he was thinking, the rabbit slowly drew near, bowed low, and stood before him. But when the lion saw that he was tardy and too small at that for a meal, his soul flamed with wrath, and he taunted the rabbit, saying: "You reprobate! First, you are too small for a meal. Second, you are tardy. Because of this wickedness I am going to kill you, and tomorrow morning I shall extirpate every species of animal."

Then the rabbit bowed low and said with deference: "Master, the wickedness is not mine, nor the other animals'. Pray hear the cause of it." And the lion answered: "Well, tell it quick, before you are between my fangs."

"Master," said the rabbit, "all the animals recognized today that the rabbits' turn had come, and because I was quite small, they dispatched me with five other rabbits. But in mid-journey there issued from a great hole in the ground a lion who said: 'Where are *you* bound? Pray to your favorite god.' Then I said: 'We are traveling as the dinner of lion Numskull, our master, according to agreement.' 'Is that so?' said he. 'This forest belongs to me. So all the animals, without exception, must deal with me — according to agreement. This Numskull is a sneak thief. Call him out and bring him here at once. Then whichever of us proves stronger shall be king and shall eat all these animals.' At his command, master, I have come to you. This is the cause of my tardiness. For the rest, my master is the sole judge."

After listening to this, Numskull said: "Well, well, my good fellow, show me that sneak thief of a lion, and be quick about it. I cannot find peace of mind until I have vented on him my anger against the animals. He should have remembered the saying:

"Land and friends and gold at most
    Have been won when battles cease;
If but one of these should fail,
    Do not think of breaking peace.

"Where no great reward is won,
    Where defeat is nearly sure,
Never stir a quarrel, but
    Find it wiser to endure."

"Quite so, master," said the rabbit. "Warriors fight for their country when they are insulted. But this fellow skulks in a fortress. You know he came out of a fortress when he held us up. And an enemy in a fortress is hard to handle. As the saying goes:

"A single royal fortress adds
    More military force

Than do a thousand elephants,
    A hundred thousand horse.

"A single archer from a wall
    A hundred foes forfends;
And so the military art
    A fortress recommends.

"God Indra used the wit and skill
    Of gods in days of old,
When Devil Gold-mat plagued the world,
    To build a fortress-hold.

"And he decreed that any king
    Who built a fortress sound
Should conquer foemen. This is why
    Such fortresses abound."

When he heard this, Numskull said: "My good fellow, show me that thief. Even if he is hiding in a fortress, I will kill him. For the proverb says:

"The strongest man who fails to crush
    At birth, disease or foe,
Will later be destroyed by that
    Which he permits to grow.

And again:

"The man who reckons well his power,
    Nor pride nor vigor lacks,
May single-handed smite his foes
    Like Rama-with-the-ax."

"Very true," said the rabbit. "But after all it was a mighty lion that I saw. So the master should not set out without realizing the enemy's capacity. As the saying runs:

"A warrior failing to compare
    Two hosts, in mad desire
For battle, plunges like a moth
    Headforemost into fire.

And again:

"The weak who challenge mighty foes
    A battle to abide,
Like elephants with broken tusks,
    Return with drooping pride."

But Numskull said: "What business is it of yours? Show him to me, even in his fortress." "Very well," said the rabbit. "Follow me, master." And he led the way to a well, where he said to the lion: "Master, who can endure your majesty? The moment he saw you, that thief crawled clear into his hole. Come, I will show him to you." "Be quick about it, my good fellow," said Numskull.

So the rabbit showed him the well. And the lion, being a dreadful fool, saw his own reflection in the water, and gave voice to a great roar. Then from the well issued a roar twice as loud, because of the echo. This the lion heard, decided that his rival was very powerful, hurled himself down, and met his death. Thereupon the rabbit cheerfully carried the glad news to all the animals, received their compliments, and lived there contentedly in the forest.

And that is why I say:

Intelligence is power . . .

and the rest of it.

The Cat and the Parrot [2]

⚬ *This nonsense story has its origins in the folklore of India. The version given by W. H. D. Rouse in* The Talking Thrush (*Dutton, o.p.*) *gives the cat good cause for his initial treatment of the parrot. But here is the version which best suits the storyteller, and young children find it well-nigh irresistible in this form. It has the cumulative and repetitive scheme which invariably weaves a spell; it is true to the egocentric character of cats with their inner conviction of superiority; its towering improbability makes it a tale worthy of Paul Bunyan; and the justice of its happy conclusion, even for the villain, is vastly satisfying. The Czech variant is called* Kuratko the Terrible *and may be found in* The Shoemaker's Apron, *by Parker Fillmore.*

Once there was a cat, and a parrot. And they had agreed to ask each other to dinner, turn and turn about: first the cat should ask the parrot, then the parrot should invite the cat, and so on. It was the cat's turn first.

Now the cat was very mean. He provided nothing at all for dinner except a pint of milk, a little slice of fish, and a biscuit. The parrot was too polite to complain, but he did not have a very good time.

When it was his turn to invite the cat,

[2] From Sara Cone Bryant, *How to Tell Stories to Children* (Houghton Mifflin, 1905).

he cooked a fine dinner. He had a roast of meat, a pot of tea, a basket of fruit, and, best of all, he baked a whole clothes-basketful of little cakes! — little, brown, crispy, spicy cakes! Oh, I should say as many as five hundred. And he put four hundred and ninety-eight of the cakes before the cat, keeping only two for himself.

Well, the cat ate the roast, and drank the tea, and sucked the fruit, and then he began on the pile of cakes. He ate all the four hundred and ninety-eight cakes, and then he looked round and said: —

"I'm hungry; haven't you anything to eat?"

"Why," said the parrot, "here are my two cakes, if you want them?"

The cat ate up the two cakes, and then he licked his chops and said, "I am beginning to get an appetite; have you anything to eat?"

"Well, really," said the parrot, who was now rather angry, "I don't see anything more, unless you wish to eat me!" He thought the cat would be ashamed when he heard that — but the cat just looked at him and licked his chops again, — and slip! slop! gobble! down his throat went the parrot!

Then the cat started down the street. An old woman was standing by, and she had seen the whole thing, and she was shocked that the cat should eat his friend. "Why, cat!" she said, "how dreadful of you to eat your friend the parrot!"

"Parrot, indeed!" said the cat. "What's a parrot to me? — I've a great mind to eat you, too." And — before you could say "Jack Robinson" — slip! slop! gobble! down went the old woman!

Then the cat started down the road again, walking like this, because he felt so fine. Pretty soon he met a man driving a donkey. The man was beating the donkey, to hurry him up, and when he saw the cat he said, "Get out of my way, cat; I'm in a hurry and my donkey might tread on you."

"Donkey, indeed!" said the cat, "much I care for a donkey! I have eaten five hundred cakes, I've eaten my friend the parrot, I've eaten an old woman, — what's to hinder my eating a miserable man and a donkey?"

And slip! slop! gobble! down went the old man and the donkey.

Then the cat walked on down the road,

jauntily, like this. After a little, he met a procession, coming that way. The king was at the head, walking proudly with his newly married bride, and behind him were his soldiers, marching, and behind them were ever and ever so many elephants, walking two by two. The king felt very kind to everybody, because he had just been married, and he said to the cat, "Get out of my way, pussy, get out of my way, — my elephants might hurt you."

"Hurt me!" said the cat, shaking his fat sides. "Ho, ho! I've eaten five hundred cakes, I've eaten my friend the parrot, I've eaten an old woman, I've eaten a man and a donkey; what's to hinder my eating a beggarly king?"

And slip! slop! gobble! down went the king; down went the queen; down went the soldiers, — and down went all the elephants!

Then the cat went on, more slowly; he had really had enough to eat, now. But a little farther on he met two land-crabs, scuttling along in the dust. "Get out of our way, pussy," they squeaked.

"Ho, ho ho!" cried the cat in a terrible voice. "I've eaten five hundred cakes, I've eaten my friend the parrot, I've eaten an old woman, a man with a donkey, a king, a queen, his men-at-arms, and all his elephants; and now I'll eat you too."

And slip! slop! gobble! down went the two land-crabs.

When the land-crabs got down inside, they began to look around. It was very dark, but they could see the poor king sitting in a corner with his bride on his arm; she had fainted. Near them were the men-at-arms, treading on one another's toes, and the elephants, still trying to form in twos, — but they couldn't, because there was not room. In the opposite corner sat the old woman, and near her stood the man and his donkey. But in the other corner was a great pile of cakes, and by them perched the parrot, his feathers all drooping.

"Let's get to work!" said the land-crabs. And, snip, snap, they began to make a little hole in the side, with their sharp claws. Snip, snap, snip, snap, — till it was big enough to get through. Then out they scuttled.

Then out walked the king, carrying his bride; out marched the men-at-arms; out tramped the elephants, two by two; out came the old man, beating his donkey; out walked the old woman, scolding the cat; and last of all, out hopped the parrot, holding a cake in each claw. (You remember, two cakes was all he wanted?)

But the poor cat had to spend the whole day sewing up the hole in his coat!

ARABIA

Aladdin and the Wonderful Lamp[1]

❧ *This tale of adventure is from an old collection, one which, if not the greatest collection of short stories, is without doubt the best known* — The Arabian Nights' Entertainments, *or* The Thousand and One Nights. *The book as a whole is built in the "frame-story" manner, like the* Panchatantra. *One anecdote leads to another until the tales are sometimes four and five deep. Thus the beautiful but clever narrator, Scheherazade, interested the Sultan, her new husband, who had previously had his wives killed the next day after marriage; and when she had managed to stay alive a thousand and one nights he naturally yielded and let her live on. A few of these tales, as* Aladdin, *are suitable for children and have always been favorites.*

There once lived a poor tailor, who had a son called Aladdin, a careless, idle boy who would do nothing but play all day long in the streets with little idle boys like himself. This so grieved the father that he died; yet, in spite of his mother's tears and prayers, Aladdin did not mend his ways. One day, when he was playing in the streets as usual, a stranger asked him his age, and if he was not the son of Mustapha the tailor. "I am, sir," replied Aladdin; "but he died a long while ago." On this the stranger, who was a famous African magician, fell on his neck and kissed him, saying: "I am your uncle,

[1] From *Arabian Nights,* collected and edited by Andrew Lang (Longmans, Green, 1898).

and knew you from your likeness to my brother. Go to your mother and tell her I am coming." Aladdin ran home and told his mother of his newly found uncle. "Indeed, child," she said, "your father had a brother, but I always thought he was dead." However, she prepared supper, and bade Aladdin seek his uncle, who came laden with wine and fruit. He presently fell down and kissed the place where Mustapha used to sit, bidding Aladdin's mother not to be surprised at not having seen him before, as he had been forty years out of the country. He then turned to Aladdin, and asked him his trade, at which the boy hung his head, while his mother burst into tears. On learning that Aladdin was idle and would learn no trade, he offered to take a shop for him and stock it with merchandise. Next day he bought Aladdin a fine suit of clothes and took him all over the city, showing him the sights, and brought him home at nightfall to his mother, who was overjoyed to see her son so fine.

Next day the magician led Aladdin into some beautiful gardens a long way outside the city gates. They sat down by a fountain and the magician pulled a cake from his girdle, which he divided between them. They then journeyed onwards till they almost reached the mountains. Aladdin was so tired that he begged to go back, but the magician beguiled him with pleasant stories, and led him on in spite of himself. At last they came to two mountains divided by a narrow valley, "We will go no farther," said the false uncle. "I will show you something wonderful; only do you gather up sticks while I kindle a fire." When it was lit the

324

magician threw on it a powder he had about him, at the same time saying some magical words. The earth trembled a little and opened in front of them, disclosing a square flat stone with a brass ring in the middle to raise it by. Aladdin tried to run away, but the magician caught him and gave him a blow that knocked him down. "What have I done, uncle?" he said piteously; whereupon the magician said more kindly: "Fear nothing, but obey me. Beneath this stone lies a treasure which is to be yours, and no one else may touch it; so you must do exactly as I tell you." At the word treasure Aladdin forgot his fears, and grasped the ring as he was told, saying the names of his father and grandfather. The stone came up quite easily, and some steps appeared. "Go down," said the magician; "at the foot of those steps you will find an open door leading into three large halls. Tuck up your gown and go through them without touching anything, or you will die instantly. These halls lead into a garden of fine fruit trees. Walk on till you come to a niche in a terrace where stands a lighted lamp. Pour out the oil it contains, and bring it me." He drew a ring from his finger and gave it to Aladdin, bidding him prosper.

Aladdin found everything as the magician had said, gathered some fruit off the trees, and having got the lamp, arrived at the mouth of the cave. The magician cried out in a great hurry: "Make haste and give me the lamp." This Aladdin refused to do until he was out of the cave. The magician flew into a terrible passion, and throwing some more powder on to the fire, he said something, and the stone rolled back into its place.

The magician left Persia forever, which plainly showed that he was no uncle of Aladdin's, but a cunning magician, who had read in his magic books of a wonderful lamp, which would make him the most powerful man in the world. Though he alone knew where to find it, he could only receive it from the hand of another. He had picked out the foolish Aladdin for this purpose, intending to get the lamp and kill him afterwards.

For two days Aladdin remained in the dark crying and lamenting. At last he clasped his hands in prayer, and in so doing, rubbed the ring, which the magician had forgotten to take from him. Immediately an enormous and frightful genie rose out of the earth, saying: "What wouldst thou with me? I am the Slave of the Ring, and will obey thee in all things." Aladdin fearlessly replied: "Deliver me from this place!" whereupon the earth opened, and he found himself outside. As soon as his eyes could bear the light he went home, but fainted on the threshold. When he came to himself, he told his mother what had passed, and showed her the lamp and the fruits he had gathered in the garden, which were in reality precious stones. He then asked for some food. "Alas! child," she said, "I have nothing in the house, but I have spun a little cotton and will go and sell it." Aladdin bade her keep her cotton, for he would sell the lamp instead. As it was very dirty she began to rub it, that it might fetch a higher price. Instantly a hideous genie appeared and asked what she would have. She fainted away, but Aladdin, snatching the lamp, said boldly: "Fetch me something to eat!" The genie returned with a silver bowl, twelve silver plates containing rich meats, two silver cups, and two bottles of wine. Aladdin's mother, when she came to herself, said: "Whence comes this splendid feast?" "Ask not, but eat," replied Aladdin. So they sat at breakfast till it was dinner-time and Aladdin told his mother about the lamp. She begged him to sell it, and have nothing to do with devils. "No," said Aladdin, "since chance hath made us aware of its virtues, we will use it, and the ring likewise, which I shall always wear on my finger." When they had eaten all the genie had brought, Aladdin sold one of the silver plates, and so on until none were left. He then had recourse to the genie, who gave him another set of plates, and thus they lived for many years.

One day Aladdin heard an order from the Sultan proclaimed that everyone was to stay at home and close his shutters while the Princess, his daughter, went to and from the bath. Aladdin was seized by a desire to see her face, which was very difficult, as she always went veiled.

He hid himself behind the door of the

bath and peeped through a chink. The Princess lifted her veil as she went in, and looked so beautiful that Aladdin fell in love with her at first sight. He went home so changed that his mother was frightened. He told her he loved the Princess so deeply that he could not live without her, and meant to ask her in marriage of her father.

His mother, on hearing this, burst out laughing; but Aladdin at last prevailed upon her to go before the Sultan and carry his request. She fetched a napkin and laid in it the magic fruits from the enchanted garden, which sparkled and shone like the most beautiful jewels. She took these with her to please the Sultan, and set out, trusting in the lamp.

The Grand Vizier and the lords of council had just gone in as she entered the hall and placed herself in front of the Sultan. He took no notice of her. She went every day for a week, and stood in the same place. When the council broke up on the sixth day the Sultan said to his Vizier: "I see a certain woman in the audience-chamber every day carrying something in a napkin. Call her next time, that I may find out what she wants." Next day, at a sign from the Vizier, she went up to the foot of the throne and remained kneeling till the Sultan said to her: "Rise, good woman, and tell me what you want." She hesitated, so the Sultan sent away all but the Vizier, and bade her speak freely, promising to forgive her beforehand for anything she might say. She then told him of her son's violent love for the Princess. "I prayed him to forget her," she said, "but in vain; he threatened to do some desperate deed if I refused to go and ask your Majesty for the hand of the Princess. Now I pray you to forgive not me alone, but my son Aladdin." The Sultan asked her kindly what she had in the napkin, whereupon she unfolded the jewels and presented them. He was thunderstruck, and turning to the Vizier said: "What sayest thou? Ought I not to bestow the Princess on one who values her at such a price?" The Vizier, who wanted her for his own son, begged the Sultan to withhold her for three months, in the course of which he hoped his son would contrive to make him a richer present. The Sultan granted this, and told Aladdin's mother that, though he consented to the marriage, she must not appear before him again for three months.

Aladdin waited patiently for nearly three months; but after two had elapsed, his mother, going into the city to buy oil, found everyone rejoicing, and asked what was going on. "Do you not know," was the answer, "that the son of the Grand Vizier is to marry the Sultan's daughter tonight?" Breathless, she ran and told Aladdin, who was overwhelmed at first, but presently bethought him of the lamp. He rubbed it, and the genie appeared, saying: "What is thy will?" Aladdin replied: "The Sultan, as thou knowest, has broken his promise to me, and the Vizier's son is to have the Princess. My command is that tonight you bring hither the bride and bridegroom." "Master, I obey," said the genie. Aladdin then went to his chamber, where, sure enough, at midnight the genie transported the bed containing the Vizier's son and the Princess. "Take this new-married man," he said, "and put him outside in the cold, and return at daybreak." Whereupon the genie took the Vizier's son out of bed, leaving Aladdin with the Princess. "Fear nothing," Aladdin said to her; "you are my wife, promised to me by your unjust father, and no harm shall come to you." The Princess was too frightened to speak, and passed the most miserable night of her life, while Aladdin lay down beside her and slept soundly. At the appointed hour the genie fetched in the shivering bridegroom, laid him in his place, and transported the bed back to the palace.

Presently the Sultan came to wish his daughter good-morning. The unhappy Vizier's son jumped up and hid himself, while the Princess would not say a word, and was very sorrowful. The Sultan sent her mother to her, who said: "How comes it, child, that you will not speak to your father? What has happened?" The Princess sighed deeply, and at last told her mother how, during the night, the bed had been carried into some strange house, and what had passed there. Her mother did not believe her in the least, but bade her rise and consider it an idle dream.

The following night exactly the same thing happened, and next morning, on the Princess's refusing to speak, the Sultan threatened to cut off her head. She then confessed all, bidding him ask the Vizier's son if it were not so. The Sultan told the Vizier to ask his son, who owned the truth, adding that, dearly as he loved the Princess, he had rather die than go through another such fearful night, and wished to be separated from her. His wish was granted, and there was an end of feasting and rejoicing.

When the three months were over, Aladdin sent his mother to remind the Sultan of his promise. She stood in the same place as before, and the Sultan, who had forgotten Aladdin, at once remembered him, and sent for her. On seeing her poverty the Sultan felt less inclined than ever to keep his word, and asked his Vizier's advice, who counseled him to set so high a value on the Princess that no man living could come up to it. The Sultan then turned to Aladdin's mother, saying: "Good woman, a Sultan must remember his promises, and I will remember mine, but your son must first send me forty basins of gold brimful of jewels, carried by forty black slaves, led by as many white ones, splendidly dressed. Tell him that I await his answer." The mother of Aladdin bowed low and went home, thinking all was lost. She gave Aladdin the message, adding: "He may wait long enough for your answer!" "Not so long, mother, as you think," her son replied. "I would do a great deal more than that for the Princess." He summoned the genie, and in a few moments the eighty slaves arrived, and filled up the small house and garden. Aladdin made them set out to the palace, two and two, followed by his mother. They were so richly dressed, with such splendid jewels in their girdles, that everyone crowded to see them and the basins of gold they carried on their heads.

They entered the palace and, after kneeling before the Sultan, stood in a half-circle round the throne with their arms crossed, while Aladdin's mother presented them to the Sultan. He hesitated no longer, but said: "Good woman, return and tell your son that I wait for him with open arms." She lost no time in telling Aladdin, bidding him make haste. But Aladdin first called the genie.

"I want a scented bath," he said, "a richly embroidered habit, a horse surpassing the Sultan's, and twenty slaves to attend me. Besides this, six slaves, beautifully dressed, to wait on my mother; and lastly, ten thousand pieces of gold in ten purses." No sooner said than done.

Aladdin mounted his horse and passed through the streets, the slaves strewing gold as they went. Those who had played with him in his childhood knew him not, he had grown so handsome. When the Sultan saw him he came down from his throne, embraced him, and led him into a hall where a feast was spread, intending to marry him to the Princess that very day. But Aladdin refused, saying, "I must build a palace fit for her," and took his leave.

Once home, he said to the genie: "Build me a palace of the finest marble, set with jasper, agate, and other precious stones. In the middle you shall build me a large hall with a dome, its four walls of massy gold and silver, each side having six windows, whose lattices, all except one which is to be left unfinished, must be set with diamonds and rubies. There must be stables and horses and grooms and slaves; go and see about it!"

The palace was finished by next day, and the genie carried him there and showed him all his orders faithfully carried out, even to the laying of a velvet carpet from Aladdin's palace to the Sultan's. Aladdin's mother then dressed herself carefully, and walked to the palace with her slaves, while he followed her on horseback. The Sultan sent musicians with trumpets and cymbals to meet them, so that the air resounded with music and cheers. She was taken to the Princess, who saluted her and treated her with great honor. At night the Princess said good-bye to her father, and set out on the carpet for Aladdin's palace, with his mother at her side, and followed by the hundred slaves. She was charmed at the sight of Aladdin, who ran to receive her. "Princess," he said, "blame your beauty for my boldness if I have displeased you." She told him that, having seen him, she willingly obeyed her father in this matter. After the wedding had taken place Aladdin led her into the hall, where a feast was spread, and she supped with him, after which they danced till midnight.

Next day Aladdin invited the Sultan to see the palace. On entering the hall with the four-and-twenty windows, with their rubies, diamonds, and emeralds, he cried: "It is a world's wonder! There is only one thing that surprises me. Was it by accident that one window was left unfinished?" "No, sir, by design," returned Aladdin. "I wished your Majesty to have the glory of finishing this palace." The Sultan was pleased, and sent in the best jewelers in the city. He showed them the unfinished window, and bade them fit it up like the others. "Sir," replied their spokesman, "we cannot find jewels enough." The Sultan had his own fetched, which they soon used, but to no purpose, for in a month's time the work was not half done. Aladdin, knowing that their task was vain, bade them undo their work and carry the jewels back, and the genie finished the window at his command. The Sultan was surprised to receive his jewels again, and visited Aladdin, who showed him the window finished. The Sultan embraced him, the envious Vizier meanwhile hinting that it was the work of enchantment.

Aladdin had won the hearts of the people by his gentle bearing. He was made captain of the Sultan's armies, and won several battles for him; but remained modest and courteous as before and lived thus in peace and content for several years.

But far away in Africa the magician remembered Aladdin and by his magic arts discovered that Aladdin, instead of perishing miserably in the cave, had escaped and had married a Princess with whom he was living in great honor and wealth. He knew that the poor tailor's son could only have accomplished this by means of the lamp and traveled night and day till he reached the capital of China, bent on Aladdin's ruin. As he passed through the town he heard people talking everywhere about a marvelous palace.

"Forgive my ignorance," he said. "What is this palace you speak of?"

"Have you not heard of Prince Aladdin's palace," was the reply, "the greatest wonder of the world? I will direct you if you have a mind to see it."

The magician thanked him who spoke, and having seen the palace knew that it had been raised by the genie of the lamp and became half-mad with rage. He determined to get hold of the lamp and again plunge Aladdin into the deepest poverty.

Unluckily, Aladdin had gone a-hunting for eight days, which gave the magician plenty of time. He bought a dozen copper lamps, put them into a basket, and went to the palace, crying, "New lamps for old!" followed by a jeering crowd.

The Princess, sitting in the hall of twenty-four windows, sent a slave to find out what the noise was about, who came back laughing, so that the Princess scolded her.

"Madam," replied the slave, "who can help laughing to see an old fool offering to exchange fine new lamps for old ones?"

Another slave, hearing this, said: "There is an old one on the cornice there which he can have." Now, this was the magic lamp, which Aladdin had left there, as he could not take it out hunting with him.

The Princess, not knowing its value, laughingly bade the slave take it and make the exchange. She went and said to the magician: "Give me a new lamp for this." He snatched it and bade the slave take her choice, amid the jeers of the crowd. Little he cared, but left off crying his lamps, and went out of the city gates to a lonely place, where he remained till nightfall, when he pulled out the lamp and rubbed it. The genie appeared and at the magician's command carried him, together with the palace and the Princess in it, to a lonely place in Africa.

Next morning the Sultan looked out of the window toward Aladdin's palace and rubbed his eyes, for it was gone. He sent for the Vizier and asked what had become of the palace. The Vizier looked out too, and was lost in astonishment. He again put it down to enchantment, and this time the Sultan believed him, and sent thirty men on horseback to fetch Aladdin in chains. They met him riding home, bound him, and forced him to go with them on foot. The people, however, who loved him, followed, armed, to see that he came to no harm. He was carried before the Sultan, who ordered the executioner to cut off his head. The executioner made Aladdin kneel down, bandaged his eyes, and raised his scimitar to strike. At that instant the Vizier, who saw that the crowd had forced their way into the courtyard and were scaling the walls to rescue Aladdin, called to the executioner to stay his hand. The people, indeed, looked so threatening that the Sultan gave way and ordered Aladdin to be unbound, and pardoned him in the sight of the crowd. Aladdin now begged to know what he had done. "False wretch!" said the Sultan, "come hither," and showed him from the window the place where his palace had stood. Aladdin was so amazed that he could not say a word. "Where is my palace and my daughter?" demanded the Sultan. "For the first I am not so deeply concerned, but my daughter I must have, and you must find her or lose your head." Aladdin begged for forty days in which to find her, promising if he failed, to return and suffer death at the Sultan's pleasure. His prayer was granted, and he went forth sadly from the Sultan's presence. For three days he wandered about like a madman, asking everyone what had become of his palace, but they only laughed and pitied him. He came to the banks of a river, and knelt down to say his prayers before throwing himself in. In so doing he rubbed the magic ring he still wore. The genie he had seen in the cave appeared, and asked his will. "Save my life, genie," said Aladdin, "and bring my palace back." "That is not in my power," said the genie; "I am only the Slave of the Ring; you must ask him of the lamp." "Even so," said Aladdin, "but thou canst take me to the palace, and set me down under my dear wife's window." He at once found himself in Africa, under the window of the Princess, and fell asleep out of sheer weariness.

He was awakened by the singing of the birds, and his heart was lighter. He saw plainly that all his misfortunes were owing to the loss of the lamp, and vainly wondered who had robbed him of it.

That morning the Princess rose earlier than she had done since she had been carried into Africa by the magician, whose company she was forced to endure once a day. She, however, treated him so harshly that he dared not live there altogether. As she was dressing, one of her women looked out and saw Aladdin.

The Princess ran and opened the window, and at the noise she made Aladdin looked up. She called to him to come to her, and great was the joy of these lovers at seeing each other again.

After he had kissed her Aladdin said: "I beg of you, Princess, in God's name, before we speak of anything else, for your own sake and mine, tell me what has become of an old lamp I left on the cornice in the hall of twenty-four windows when I went hunting."

"Alas!" she said, "I am the innocent cause of our sorrows," and told him of the exchange of the lamp.

"Now I know," cried Aladdin, "that we have to thank the African magician for this! Where is the lamp?"

"He carries it about with him," said the Princess. "I know, for he pulled it out of his breast to show me. He wishes me to break my faith with you and marry him, saying that you were beheaded by my father's command. He is forever speaking ill of you, but I only reply to him by my tears. If I persist in doing so, I doubt not but he will use violence."

Aladdin comforted her and left her for awhile. He changed clothes with the first person he met in the town and having bought a certain powder, returned to the Princess, who let him in by a little side door. "Put on your most beautiful dress," he said to her, "and receive the magician with smiles, leading him to believe that you have forgotten me. Invite him up to sup with you and say you wish to taste the wine of his country. He will go for some and while he is gone, I will tell you what to do." She listened carefully to Aladdin and when he left her, arrayed herself gayly for the first time since she left China. She put on a girdle and headdress of diamonds, and, seeing in a glass that she was more beautiful than ever, received the magician, saying, to his great amazement: "I have made up my mind that Aladdin is dead, and that all my tears will not bring him back to me, so I am resolved to mourn no more, and have therefore invited you to sup with me; but I am tired of the wines of China, and would fain taste those of Africa." The magician flew to his cellar, and the Princess put the powder Aladdin had given her in her cup. When he returned she asked him to drink her health in the wine of Africa, handing him her cup in exchange for his, as a sign she was reconciled to him. Before drinking the magician made her a speech in praise of her beauty, but the Princess cut him short, saying: "Let us drink first, and you shall say what you will afterwards." She set her cup to her lips and kept it there, while the magician drained his to the dregs and fell back lifeless. The Princess then opened the door to Aladdin, and flung her arms round his neck; but Aladdin put her away, bidding her leave him, as he had more to do. He then went to the dead magician, took the lamp out of his vest, and bade the genie carry the palace and all in it back to China. This was done, and the Princess in her chamber only felt two little shocks, and little thought she was at home again.

The Sultan, who was sitting in his closet, mourning for his lost daughter, happened to look up, and rubbed his eyes, for there stood the palace as before! He hastened thither, and Aladdin received him in the hall of the four-and-twenty windows, with the Princess at his side. Aladdin told him what had happened, and showed him the dead body of the magician, that he might believe. A ten days' feast was proclaimed, and it seemed as if Aladdin might now live the rest of his life in peace; but it was not to be.

The African magician had a younger brother, who was, if possible, more wicked and more cunning than himself. He traveled to China to avenge his brother's death, and went to visit a pious woman called Fatima, thinking she might be of use to him. He entered her cell and clapped a dagger to her breast, telling her to rise and do his bidding on pain of death. He changed clothes with her, colored his face like hers, put on her veil, and murdered her, that she might tell no tales. Then he went towards the palace of Aladdin, and all the people, thinking he was the holy woman, gathered round him.

kissing his hands and begging his blessing. When he got to the palace there was such a noise going on round him that the Princess bade her slave look out of the window and ask what was the matter. The slave said it was the holy woman, curing people by her touch of their ailments, whereupon the Princess, who had long desired to see Fatima, sent for her. On coming to the Princess, the magician offered up a prayer for her health and prosperity. When he had done, the Princess made him sit by her, and begged him to stay with her always. The false Fatima, who wished for nothing better, consented, but kept his veil down for fear of discovery. The Princess showed him the hall, and asked him what he thought of it. "It is truly beautiful," said the false Fatima. "In my mind it wants but one thing." "And what is that?" said the Princess. "If only a roc's egg," replied he, "were hung up from the middle of this dome, it would be the wonder of the world."

After this the Princess could think of nothing but the roc's egg, and when Aladdin returned from hunting he found her in a very ill humor. He begged to know what was amiss, and she told him that all her pleasure in the hall was spoilt for the want of a roc's egg hanging from the dome. "If that is all," replied Aladdin, "you shall soon be happy." He left her and rubbed the lamp, and when the genie appeared commanded him to bring a roc's egg. The genie gave such a loud and terrible shriek that the hall shook. "Wretch!" he cried, "is it not enough that I have done everything for you, but you must command me to bring my master and hang him up in the midst of this dome? You and your wife and your palace deserve to be burnt to ashes, but that this request does not come from you, but from the brother of the African magician, whom you destroyed. He is now in your palace disguised as the holy woman — whom he murdered. He it was who put that wish into your wife's head. Take care of yourself, for he means to kill you." So saying, the genie disappeared.

Aladdin went back to the Princess, saying his head ached, and requesting that the holy

Fatima should be fetched to lay her hands on it. But when the magician came near, Aladdin, seizing his dagger, pierced him to the heart. "What have you done?" cried the Princess. "You have killed the holy woman!" "Not so," replied Aladdin, "but a wicked magician," and told her of how she had been deceived.

After this Aladdin and his wife lived in peace. He succeeded the Sultan when he died, and reigned for many years, leaving behind him a long line of kings.

TURKEY

Three Fridays [1]

Here is a jest, a witty story, one of the many that revolve about the Hodja. The word Hodja is the Turkish title for a Moslem priest who is both teacher and judge. He is traditionally kind, human, and so beloved that fun may be poked at him with utter safety. He himself has an impish sense of humor. The imagery of the Orient is reflected in these stories. One of the gifts of the folk tale is its indirect revelation of manners, customs, and sense of place.

There was just one day of each week that worried Nasr-ed-Din Hodja. On six days he was as free as a butterfly. He could talk with his friends in the market place or ride his donkey to a nearby village. He could work in the vineyards or go hunting in the hills. He could lounge in the coffee house or sit in the sun in his own courtyard. There was nothing to hurry him to be at a certain place at a certain time to do a certain thing.

But Friday was different. It was much different. That was the day when all good Mohammedans went to their mosques. Because Nasr-ed-Din Hodja, years before, had attended the school for priests, he was expected each Friday to mount the pulpit

[1] From Alice Geer Kelsey, *Once the Hodja* (Longmans, Green, 1943).

of the mosque at a certain time and preach a sermon. That was all very well when he had something to say, but there were many Fridays when his mind was as empty as that of his own little gray donkey. It was one thing to swap stories with the men in the coffee house and quite another to stand alone in the high pulpit and talk to a mosque full of people. The men, each squatting on his own prayer rug on the floor, looked up at him with such solemn faces. Then there was the fluttering in the balcony behind the lattices, which told him that the women were waiting too. Of course, the chanting, which came before the sermon, was not hard because all the men joined in that, bowing till they touched their foreheads to the floor in the Nemaz. But the sermon — that was hard.

One Friday he walked more slowly than ever through the cobblestoned streets of Ak Shehir. He saw the veiled women slipping silently past him on their way to the latticed balcony of the mosque. He saw the men in their best clothes hurrying to the mosque to hear his sermon. But what sermon? He stopped at the mosque door to leave his shoes. He pattered with the other men across the soft thick rugs. But they could squat on the rugs, while he had to climb into the high pulpit.

Perhaps the beauty of the mosque would

give him an idea. He looked up at the blues and reds and whites of the intricate tracery on the ceiling, but not a thought came. He looked at the rich yellows and reds of the mosaics on the walls, but there was no help there. He looked at the men's faces staring up at him. He heard the tittering in the latticed balcony where the veiled women sat. He must say something.

"Oh, people of Ak Shehir!" He leaned on the pulpit and eyed them squarely. "Do you know what I am about to say to you?"

"No!" boomed from the rugs where the men squatted.

"No!" floated down in soft whispers from the latticed balcony, whispers not meant for any ears beyond the balcony.

"You do not know?" said Nasr-ed-Din Hodja, shaking his head and looking from one face to another. "You are sure you do not know? Then what use would it be to talk to people who know nothing at all about this important subject. My words would be wasted on such ignorant people."

With that, the Hodja turned and climbed slowly down the pulpit steps. His eyes lowered, he walked with injured dignity through the crowds of men. He slipped on his shoes at the mosque door, and was out in the sunshine — free until next Friday.

That day came all too soon. The Hodja mingled with the crowds going to the mosque. His coarse, home-knit stockings pattered across the deep colorful rugs. He climbed the steps to the high pulpit. He looked down at the sea of solemn faces. He heard the rustling behind the lattices of the balcony. He had hoped that this week he could think of a sermon, but the carvings of the doorway did not help him, nor the embroidered hangings of the pulpit, nor the pigeons fluttering and cooing at the window. Still, he must say something.

"Oh, people of Ak Shehir!" intoned the Hodja, gesturing with both hands. "Do you know what I am about to say to you?"

"Yes," boomed the men who remembered what had happened when they said "No" last week.

"Yes," echoed in soft whispers from the balcony.

"You know what I am going to say?" said the Hodja, shrugging first one shoulder and then the other. "You are sure you know what I am going to say? Then I need not say it. It would be a useless waste of my golden words if I told you something that you already knew."

The Hodja turned and again climbed down the pulpit steps. He picked his way with unhurried dignity among the men. He scuffed into his shoes and escaped into the sunshine. Another free week was ahead of him.

But the best of weeks end. The third Friday found him once more climbing the pulpit steps, with not a word worth saying in that solemn mosque. The ancient Arabic writing on the bright ceiling had no help for him. The flickering candles in the large round chandelier winked at him but said nothing. Even the big Koran in front of him might have had blank pages instead of its fine Arabic words and its illuminated borders. Men's faces looked up at him expectantly. Bright eyes peered through the lattices of the women's balcony. The time had come again when he must speak.

"Oh, people of Ak Shehir!" declaimed the Hodja as he groped helplessly for an idea. "Do you know what I am about to say to you?"

"No," came from those who were thinking of the last Friday.

"Yes," came from those who were thinking of the Friday before that.

"Some of you know and some of you do not know!" The Hodja rubbed his hands together and beamed down at the men. "How very fine! Now let those who know tell those who do not know!"

The Hodja was humming to himself as he came down from the pulpit, two steps at a time. He nodded and smiled as he threaded his way through the men. Some thought he bowed and smiled toward the latticed balcony, but others said the good Hodja would not have made so bold. He picked his own worn shoes from the rows and rows by the mosque door. The sunshine was warm and friendly. The birds were singing and there was the fragrance of hawthorn blossoms in the air.

The Hodja had not a worry in the world — not till another Friday should come around.

CANADA

The Canoe in the Rapids [1]

&8 *Mrs. Carlson retells with skill and keen wit the French-Canadian folk tales that her great-great uncle, Michel Meloche, told her mother as a child, and which, in turn, her mother told to her. The story given here is a particular favorite and produces many a chuckle.*

Once in another time, François Ecrette was an adventurer in the woods. Every winter he went north with Sylvain Gagnon. They trapped foxes, beavers, minks and any furred creature that would step into their traps.

When spring came and the ice in the river melted, the two men would load their furs into a canoe and paddle down the swift current to sell their winter's catch to the trader.

It was one such spring that François and Sylvain headed south with the finest catch that they had ever made. If only they could beat the other trappers to the trading post, they could make a fine bargain.

"A-ah, we will be rich men," said Sylvain, who already could hear the *tintin* of coins in his deep pockets.

"Yes," answered François, "if we get through the Devil's Jaws safely."

Nowhere on any of the rivers of Canada was there such a fearsome place. In the Devil's Jaws, there were waterfalls that roared and whirlpools that spun a boat about like a dry leaf. It was as if the river fell into a panic itself when squeezed into the Devil's Jaws and tried to run away in every direction.

1 From Natalie Savage Carlson, *The Talking Cat, and Other Stories of French Canada* (Harper, 1952).

"That's true," said Sylvain, "but you are lucky to have me for a partner. Nowhere in all Canada is there such a skillful boatman as Sylvain Gagnon."

Sylvain drew the cold air in through his nose puffed out his chest with it.

So François Ecrette felt safe and happy, even though the worst ordeal of the long trip was ahead of them.

They loaded the canoe with their bundles of furs and their provisions. For days they paddled down the river, singing gay songs to pass away the long hours.

One late afternoon they beached their boat on the bank and made for a clearing on the hill. They built a campfire, and François started to roast a young rabbit he had shot. He hung it over the coals by spearing it on a green willow branch.

"We must eat well," said Sylvain, "for we are close to the Devil's Jaws. We will need all our strength for that pull and push."

"But it will soon be dark," François reminded him. "Shouldn't we camp here all night so we can go through the rapids in daylight?"

"Pou, pou," laughed Sylvain, "what a scared rabbit you are! I can paddle at night as well as by day. I could shoot the Devil's Jaws with my eyes closed and a beaver riding on my paddle."

François rubbed his stubbly chin.

"My faith," he exclaimed, "I am the luckiest man in the world to have you for a partner, Sylvain Gagnon. I don't believe you have fear of anything."

As if to test the truth of this, an angry growl came from behind the bushes. Both men jumped to their feet, François seizing

333

his rifle as he did so. The bushes broke open and a big brown bear came through them. He walked slowly on all fours, shuffling from this paw to that paw, and from that paw to this paw. Straight toward the two trappers he came.

François lifted his rifle to his shoulder and took careful aim. He pulled the trigger. Plink! Nothing happened. There was no bullet in the rifle because it had been used on the rabbit.

The bear gave another angry growl. He rose on his hind legs and walked toward François like a man, shuffling from this paw to that paw.

François dropped the gun and ran for his life. Already Sylvain Gagnon was far ahead of him, his fur coat making him look like a bear that ran too fast to shuffle from this paw to that paw. François made for a big tree, but he didn't have time to climb it as the bear was almost on him. So around the tree he ran. And behind him followed the bear. Round and round and round the tree ran François and the bear. Any little bird looking down from the treetop wouldn't have known whether the bear was chasing François Ecrette or François was chasing the bear. The trapper ran so fast that he was more behind the bear than in front of him. And as the bear ran around the tree, he clawed the air angrily. But his sharp claws only tore the bark from the tree. And if François had anything at all to be thankful for, it was that the ragged shreds flying through the air were bark from the tree and not skin from his back.

Around and around and around went the man and the beast. The bear got dizzy first. He ran slower and slower. Finally he broke away from the tree and went staggering away, first to this side and then to that side. And as he reeled and stumbled, he knocked his head into one tree trunk after another. Bump — bump — bump.

François lost no time in finding another tree to climb, for the tree they had been running around had been stripped of its bark as far up as a bear could reach. As he climbed, he could hear the bump, bump, bump of the bear's head as he stumbled into tree trunks.

Panting and dizzy himself, François settled into a crotch of the tree. Now where was that false friend, Sylvain Gagnon, who had left him to face the bear alone? He called and called but there was no answer. Perhaps the bear had eaten Sylvain. A-tout-tou, what bad luck that would be when there was still the Devil's Jaws ahead! How could he ever get through those treacherous waters without the skillful boatman Sylvain Gagnon?

And how could he get safely from the tree to the boat? Perhaps the bear was waiting for him among the bushes. The sleepy sun soon went to bed and it grew dark. It became colder than ever. François Ecrette's arms and legs were numb.

At last he jerkily lowered himself from the tree. He looked about in every direction, but it was too dark to see anything. He sniffed and sniffed like a bear, for if a bear can smell a man, maybe a man can smell a bear. But all François could smell was the sharp, icy air of early spring. Slowly he made his way down the hill toward the place they had left the canoe.

Then great joy filled the heart of François Ecrette. Although the trees blackened the river, a faint moonlight glimmered through them. Its pale light fell upon a figure hunched in the bow of the canoe with the fur coat pulled up over its ears.

"Sylvain," cried François, "you are safe after all. Why didn't you come back to me?"

But Sylvain must have felt a deep shame, for he only put his head down between his arms and made a sad, apologetic sound.

"Believe me, my friend," said François, "I'm certainly glad you escaped, for we have a terrible ride ahead of us this night. Do you think we better try the rapids after all?"

But his companion resolutely straightened up and squared his shoulders in the fur coat. François pushed the boat into the stream, leaped aboard and grabbed a paddle. Silently they floated into the current; then the slender canoe headed for the dangers ahead.

"My faith, it is good to have you in this boat with me," cried François. "This current is like a bolt of lightning."

The boat raced faster and faster. Instead of paddling for speed, François had to spend his strength flattening the paddle like a brake. The trees made a dark tunnel of the river course so that François could barely see his companion's stout back.

On, on they went. The frail canoe sped in a zigzag flight like a swallow. François Ecrette's sharp ear caught the distant roar of the rapids.

"Brace yourself, Sylvain," he cried, "for the boat is now in your hands. I will help you as much as I can."

So he plied his paddle from this side to that side and from that side to this side. The river had become like an angry, writhing eel. He heard the waterfall ahead and began paddling like mad so the canoe would shoot straight and true. The least slant of the boat and the churning current would turn it over and over, and swallow them both.

François felt the icy wind and the cold spray on his face as they plunged over the waterfall and bobbed in the whirlpool below. He fought the churning, frothing waters that he could hear more than see. His muscles tightened like iron and the air blew up his lungs.

"My faith, but it's a good thing to have such a boatman as Sylvain Gagnon guiding this canoe," rejoiced François. "In such a current as this, no other man could bring a boat through safely. I will forget the way he deserted me when that big brown bear attacked us."

All danger was not over yet, for the stern of the canoe was sucked into the outer rim of a whirlpool. The lurch of the boat wrenched François Ecrette's back like a blow from a giant hammer. The canoe spun around completely. For fully ten minutes, there was such a battle with the churning waters as François had never known before. Around and around, up and down rocked the canoe, with François fiercely wielding his paddle. If it hadn't been for the soothing figure in front of him, he would have given up in fright.

Finally the canoe straightened out and leaped straight ahead. The roar of the rapids grew fainter. François let his paddle drag and relaxed.

"My faith," he gasped. "I thought that was the last of us for sure. You have saved us both, Sylvain Gagnon. No boatman in all

Canada but you could have gotten us out of that Devil's trap."

But his modest companion only shrugged his shoulders and humped lower into the bow.

Then because François was worn out from his paddling, he decided to take a little nap. With no other partner but Sylvain would he have dared doze off. But Sylvain had proved his mettle in getting them through the rapids, and the waters ahead were slow and peaceful. So François rested his paddle, closed his eyes and fell into a deep sleep.

When he awoke, it was morning. The sun had chased the shadows out from under the trees, and the river sparkled in the friendliest kind of way.

François rubbed the sleep out of his eyes.

"Ah, Sylvain," he yawned, "what a night we had in the rapids. If it hadn't been for you — a-tou-tou-tou-tou!"

For François Ecrette's partner in the canoe was not Sylvain Gagnon, the great boatman, but the big brown bear of the clearing!

François jumped up and gave a blood-curdling shriek. The bear slowly turned around and looked at him. He shook his great furry head as if to shake his brains back into their right place after they had been knocked apart by the tree trunks. He gave a low threatening growl.

François didn't wait any longer. He dived into the river and furiously swam through the icy water. After what seemed a sinner's lifetime, he reached the frosty shore. When he looked back at the river, he had a last glance of the canoe, full of furs, disappearing among the trees with the big brown bear standing in the bow.

Now this was a fine how-does-it-make of trouble. Here was François all alone in the wilderness without Sylvain, furs, provisions or even a dry match.

Luckily the trading post couldn't be too far away now. François gathered dry wood and started a fire in the Indian way, by rubbing two sticks together. Then he stood as close to the fire as he could, to dry out his clothes. He scorched and steamed like the uneaten rabbit back on the sharp stick in the clearing.

At last he was dry enough to brave the

cold walk down the river bank. He set out slowly. The branches scratched his hands and face. His boots sloshed and squashed through the slush of early spring.

It was late afternoon by the time he reached the trader's village. Everyone seemed surprised to see him alive.

"Your canoe was found caught in a log jam below here, with bear tracks on the shore," said the trader. "We thought a bear had carried you off."

"But the furs," cried François. "What happened to them? Were they lost?"

"They are all safe," said the trader. "Your friend Sylvain Gagnon arrived only a little while ago. He helped me check through them."

Then a familiar face appeared in the crowd.

"François, my good friend," cried Sylvain. "I got a ride back with a party of Indians. But how did you ever get the canoe through the rapids all by yourself?"

"Sylvain, my false friend," retorted the trapper, "I was not alone. The big brown bear who chased me in the clearing was with me."

Then François Ecrette shivered and shook in a way that had nothing to do with the cold spring afternoon or his damp clothing.

So all turned out well for François Ecrette in the end. But he never went on any more trapping trips with Sylvain Gagnon. You see, my friends, one who turns into a big brown bear when you need him most is not a true friend.

AMERICAN REGIONAL TALES

⊷§ *Alaskan* §⊷

Mr. Crow Takes a Wife[1]

⊷§ *In this story from Eskimo folklore, one feels close to the process of creation involved in the making of a folk tale. In the bleak landscape of the Arctic there is little upon which the imagination may feed. But the flights of birds are there, to be watched and studied, and the sharing of life with animals. So the Eskimos have made stories about birds, giving them, as is usual in the process, the speech and the basic*

[1] From Charles E. Gillham, *Beyond the Clapping Mountains, Eskimo Stories from Alaska* (Macmillan, 1947).

urges of man, and equipping them with sleds and kayaks resembling their own. But with the anthropomorphic element there is also astonishing accuracy concerning the habits of bird and beast.

The collector of these tales, a biologist in the employ of the U.S. Government, spent eight summers studying water fowl and animal life in the region; nor did he neglect the study of man. "In each Eskimo village is a Kashmin," he reports, *"or 'Man House.' Men and boys gather there and listen to the stories of the Medicine Men."*

Elsewhere in this collection, the term The Clapping Mountains *is explained. "There are two high mountains that are very close together. All the birds who fly South must pass between them. Every little while they clap*

*together, just as you clap your hands, and any-
one caught between them is crushed to death."*

Once upon a time there lived an old crow.
He really was not a bad fellow, but he was
rather proud and puffed up about himself
and he thought he was very wise. Mr. Crow
was as black as coal and in those days he had
a long tail about which he was rather vain.
He was unhappy, though, for he did not
have a wife. Several of the birds he asked
to marry him had refused.

"We know you are quite wise, Mr. Crow,
but you are such a greedy bird. We like
grass and tender roots to eat. You hunt old
dead things along the beach and you seldom
eat the nice food we do. No, Mr. Crow," the
birds replied, "we do not want to marry you."

So Mr. Crow was sad as fall came on and
he saw the birds leaving to go south. He
could see long strings of geese and other birds
as they headed south, driving their bird sleds
through the sky. He looked up, and coming
right over him were Mr. White-fronted Goose
and his family. The old gander was in front,
pulling, in the harness and, behind, his wife
held the handle bars of the sled. The children were riding.

"Hello there, Mr. White-front," the old
crow called. "Have you any daughters who
would like to marry? I am looking for a
wife and I would like to go south for the
winter."

Mr. Goose looked down at Mr. Crow, but
he kept on pulling away at his sky sled. "No,
Mr. Crow," he replied, "my daughters are
rather young to marry. Besides, you do not
eat the things we do and you would always
be away, hunting along the seashore. That
is a lovely boat you are building, but our
girls do not need a boat; they can all swim."

So the white-fronted geese went on their
way.

Mr. Crow continued to work on his boat.
He had an adz, a queer tool that all the
Eskimo people use. They can take a round
log and chop along it and make it up into
boards. So the old crow worked on as another
flock of geese came by. They were emperor
geese, and Mr. Crow looked up at them. The
old gander was pulling the sled and he
leaned into the harness, for he was very

strong. In the sled his one child, a girl
goose, was riding. His wife was riding on the
runners and holding the handle bars. They
were really a beautiful family, with their
pretty pearl-gray backs and their white heads
flashing in the sun.

"Hello, Mr. Emperor Goose," the old crow
called to the family. "That is a beautiful
daughter you have. Do you think she would
care to marry me? I would like to go with
you to the birdland for the winter."

Mr. Emperor Goose looked down at Mr.
Crow, and the girl goose blushed. "I do not
know, Mr. Crow. Maybe it will be all right
if our daughter is willing. That is a fine
kayak you are building; but she really needs
none, for she can swim very well." The old
gander stopped near the igloo to talk it over.
He took off the harness he wore while pulling
the sky sled, and sat down on the grass.
"What do you think about it, Mamma?" he
asked Mrs. Emperor Goose.

"I suppose it is all right," she said, looking
at Mr. Crow and his long tail. "He really is
making a lovely kayak and he would not be
such a bad-looking son-in-law. I am afraid,
though, he would have trouble keeping up
with us as we go to the birdland for the
winter. We go very fast, for our sky sled is
not heavily loaded. What if he should fall
off as we cross the big wide ocean?"

"Oh, I am quite strong," Mr. Crow
bragged, and he arched his long tail as he
saw that Mrs. Goose had noticed it. "I can
pull the sky sled, myself, and I will not get
tired when we cross the big wide ocean. Just
wait until I put on my parka and my water
boots and close the igloo door. I am all
ready to leave."

Mr. Crow was so excited that he worked
quickly. "What a lovely goose girl the young
Emperor woman is," he thought. How he
would show off before them when he took
his turn pulling the sky sled! Soon Mr. Crow
was all ready.

"You had better ride behind on the runners and hold the handle bars," Mr. Emperor
Goose told the old crow. "It is really quite
hard work and I do not think you are strong
enough to do it."

"Nonsense," said Mr. Crow, putting on
the harness. "I will pull the sled through the

sky, and you ride on the runner, Mr. Goose, and hold to the handle bars."

Mr. Crow set off as fast as he could go. He wanted to show the young goose girl how strong he was, and he pulled as hard as he could.

"Mercy," said Mrs. Emperor Goose, "we certainly are going fast! We should be to the big wide ocean tonight if we go this swiftly. Mr. Crow is really quite strong."

So the old crow pulled all the harder. The goose girl and her mother rode on the sky sled, and Mr. Emperor Goose held the handle bars and rode on the runner. They passed several families of other birds who were not pulling their sky sleds so fast. All of them were surprised to see Mr. Crow doing all the work.

After quite a distance the old crow grew tired. He had never been so fagged out in all his life. He was sorry, now, that he had not let Mr. Emperor Goose pull, in the harness, and his wings hurt so that he could hardly go another foot.

"Here, Mr. Crow," the Emperor Goose said, "let me pull the sky sled."

"Oh, I can pull it, Mr. Goose," and the old crow spurted up a bit. "I really am very strong. I think I can pull the sled clear to the land where the birds live." He pulled all the harder, but he was getting very weak.

At last the old gander went up and took the harness from Mr. Crow. "You ride behind and hold the handle bars," he told him. "I will pull the sky sled for a while."

Poor Mr. Crow was so tired he was almost dead. His lovely tail, which had streamed out behind, now drooped down. He hung on to the handle bars, and Mr. Emperor Goose went like the wind. Soon they came to the big wide ocean and started right across. When they were halfway, Mr. Crow was still gasping for breath. Suddenly they hit a rough cloud of air and the sky sled gave a terrible bounce. The poor old crow fell right off behind. He was so tired that he could not even say a word, and on went Mr. Goose with the sled. Mrs. Emperor Goose and the daughter were looking ahead, enjoying the ride. They did not know that Mr. Crow had fallen right over the big wide ocean.

The old crow flapped as hard as he could

to keep from falling into the big wide ocean. His beautiful tail was drooping and he was very weary. "Goodness," he said, "the goose people do not know that I have fallen off the sled and they are going on without me. I do not think I can ever fly the rest of the way across the big wide ocean."

Mr. Crow flapped his tired wings as strongly as he could, but he kept getting lower and lower in the sky. Soon he was only a few feet above the waves and he knew that soon he would fall right in if he did not flap his wings harder.

"Oh, I am going to drown," he thought, "and I was just going to marry the beautiful goose girl. Why did I ever act so foolish and try to pull the sky sled so fast?"

As he got closer down to the water, Mr. Crow looked ahead. He could still see Mr. Emperor Goose pulling his sled, and right beneath him he could see the shore of the big wide ocean. If he could only fly a little farther! Mr. Crow flapped and flapped, but he just could not make it. At last a big wave touched his wing; then another touched his tail and — kerplop! — the old crow fell right into the water. The shore was only a few feet away.

How Mr. Crow did wish that he had learned to swim like the geese! He went clear under and down to the bottom. Giving a kick with his feet, up he came again. The salty water from the big wide ocean got into Mr. Crow's nose and went down his throat. He choked terribly. Down he went and up he came again. He had salty water in his eyes and he was gasping. Surely, now, he would drown. Just then a big wave larger than the others washed Mr. Crow right out onto the sand. Hastily he dragged his long wet tail up away from the edge of the water.

For a long time Mr. Crow lay on the sand and gasped for breath; the water in his mouth tasted very bad and he had a stomach-ache. At last he sat up, took off his parka, and wrung the water out of it. Then he shook the water from his long tail and felt better. He rested again, then jumped into the air and followed along in the tracks that the sled had made in the sky. He must catch up with Mr. Goose and his lovely daughter.

After some time Mr. Crow saw the emperor geese. They had stopped their sled down near a lot of other birds. He saw the white-fronted geese, the snow geese, and the black brants. Even the little sandpipers were there with a tiny sled, and Mr. King Eider Duck had a very fancy one made of walrus ivory.

"We were worried about you, Mr. Crow," Mr. Emperor Goose said. "What happened to you? I could not turn my sky sled around, for we were over the big wide ocean. I knew that one so strong as you could get here all right by himself."

The old crow did not tell Mr. Emperor Goose what had happened, for he was rather ashamed of the way he had acted. Instead he asked, "What are all of these birds waiting here for? Why don't we go ahead to the south?"

"It is the Canadian geese and the curlews," Mrs. Emperor Goose answered him. "They are always late, and each year we have had to wait for them here. You see, we all try to meet here and fly through the Clapping Mountains together."

Poor Mr. Crow, he was so tired! And when Mrs. Emperor Goose spoke of the Clapping Mountains, he felt worse. "Heavens," he thought, "I forgot all about the Clapping Mountains. They are likely to catch me this time, because I am so tired I cannot fly very fast."

At last Mr. Emperor Goose grew impatient. "I think I will go ahead," he told his wife. "I am tired of having to wait every year for the Canadian geese and the curlews." So Mr. Goose put on his pulling harness and Mrs. Goose and the goose girl got into the sled. "We must fly very hard," Mr. Emperor Goose said. "You, Mr. Crow, hold the handle bars, but do not ride on the runner. You had better flap your wing and help me to make more speed."

Away they went like the very wind.

Mr. Crow did the very best he could, but he could only flap feebly along. "Hurry faster, Mr. Crow," the Emperor Goose called back. "We will be sure to be caught in the Clapping Mountains."

The big gander pulled very hard and Mr. Crow, hanging on to the handle bars, could not even fly hard enough to keep up. His

long tail streamed out behind, and he was badly frightened. Just as Mr. Emperor Goose got through the mountains, they began to tremble; in a second they clapped together as hard as they could. Mr. Crow gave a terrible squawk, for his long tail was caught between the straight walls. They cut his long feathers off short, so that he did not have any more tail than a chicken.

How foolish Mr. Crow felt with his beautiful tail gone! The goose girl even laughed, and that made him feel more silly than ever.

"If you ask me," said Mr. Emperor Goose, "I think it helps your looks decidedly not to have that silly tail waving out behind. What good is it anyway? It is only in the way and you could never swim with it on."

So the old crow felt a little better and he found that it was easier to fly, too. Mrs. Emperor Goose even started asking him about Hooper Bay, and the goose girl smiled at him.

When they reached the Aleutian Islands, Mr. Emperor Goose said that this was the place they would spend the winter. As soon as Mr. Crow had an igloo built, a great feast was held and Mr. Crow and the goose girl were married. Mr. Crow, by this time, had almost forgotten all about his nice long tail that he had lost up in the Clapping Mountains, and the other birds didn't seem to notice it at all. Ever since that time, the crows have had short tails.

It is good for one always to try to pull his share of the load, but he should not be so silly as to think he can do it all.

❧ Southern Negro Tales ❧

The Wonderful Tar-Baby[2]

JOEL CHANDLER HARRIS

❧ *The old Negro, Uncle Remus, tells these beloved animal stories to a little boy who lives on a Southern plantation. The folk tales, which were probably brought over from Africa by*

2 From Joel Chandler Harris, *Uncle Remus, His Songs and His Sayings* (Appleton Century, 1935).

the slaves, are rich in humor. Four generations of children in America have laughed with glee at Brer Rabbit's triumph over his old enemy, Brer Fox, and at the astonishing pranks of the other "creeturs." Of all the stories, The Wonderful Tar-Baby is perhaps the favorite. While the dialect in the Uncle Remus stories may be difficult for some children to read, no child should miss this rich heritage of Negro folklore. The stories are invaluable for storytelling and for reading aloud.

"One day atter Brer Rabbit fool 'im wid dat calamus root, Brer Fox went ter wuk en got 'im some tar, en mix it wid some turkentime, en fix up a contrapshun wat he call a Tar-Baby, en he tuck dish yer Tar-Baby en he sot 'er in de big road, en den he lay off in de bushes fer to see wat de news wuz gwineter be. En he didn't hatter wait long, nudder, kaze bimeby here come Brer Rabbit pacin' down de road — lippity-clippity, clippity-lippity — dez ez sassy ez a jay-bird. Brer Fox, he lay low. Brer Rabbit come prancin' long twel he spy de Tar-Baby, en den he fotch up on his behime legs like he wuz 'stonished. De Tar-Baby, she sot dar, she did, en Brer Fox, he lay low.

" 'Mawnin'!' sez Brer Rabbit, sezee — 'nice wedder dis mawnin',' sezee.

"Tar-Baby ain't sayin' nothin', en Brer Fox, he lay low.

" 'How duz yo' sym'tums seem ter segashuate?' sez Brer Rabbit, sezee.

"Brer Fox, he wink his eye slow, en lay low, en de Tar-Baby, she ain't sayin' nothin'.

" 'How you come on, den? Is you deaf?' sez Brer Rabbit, sezee. 'Kaze if you is, I kin holler louder,' sezee.

"Tar-Baby stay still, en Brer Fox, he lay low.

" 'Youer stuck up, dat's w'at you is,' says Brer Rabbit, sezee, 'en I'm gwineter kyore you, dat's w'at I'm a gwineter do,' sezee.

"Brer Fox, he sorter chuckle in his stummuck, he did, but Tar-Baby ain't sayin' nothin'.

" 'I'm gwineter larn you howter talk ter 'specttubble fokes ef hit's de las' ack,' sez Brer Rabbit, sezee. 'Ef you don't take off dat hat en tell me howdy, I'm gwineter bus' you wide open,' sezee.

"Tar-Baby stay still, en Brer Fox, he lay low.

"Brer Rabbit keep on axin' 'im, en de Tar-Baby she keep on sayin' nothin', twel present'y Brer Rabbit draw back wid his fis', he did, en blip he tuck 'er side er de head. Right dar's whar he broke his merlasses jug. His fis' stuck, en he can't pull loose. De tar hilt 'im. But Tar-Baby, she stay still, en Brer Fox, he lay low.

" 'Ef you don't lemme loose, I'll knock you agin,' sez Brer Rabbit, sezee, en wid dat he fotch 'er a wipe wid de udder han', en dat stuck. Tar-Baby, she ain't sayin' nothin', en Brer Fox, he lay low.

" 'Tu'n me loose, fo' I kick de natal stuffin' outten you,' sez Brer Rabbit, sezee, but de Tar-Baby, she ain't sayin' nothin'. She des hilt on, en den Brer Rabbit lose de use er his feet in de same way. Brer Fox, he lay low. Den Brer Rabbit squall out dat ef de Tar-Baby don't tu'n 'im loose he butt 'er cranksided. En den he butted, en his head got stuck. Den Brer Fox, he sa'ntered fort', lookin' des ez innercent ez one er yo' mammy's mockin'-birds.

" 'Howdy, Brer Rabbit,' sez Brer Fox, sezee. 'You look sorter stuck up dis mawnin',' sezee, en den he rolled on de groun', en laughed en laughed twel he couldn't laugh no mo'. 'I speck you'll take dinner wid me dis time, Brer Rabbit. I done laid in some calamus root, en I ain't gwineter take no skuse,' sez Brer Fox, sezee.

.   .   .   .

" 'You been runnin' roun' here sassin' atter me a mighty long time, but I speck you done come ter de een 'er de row. You bin cuttin' up yo' capers en bouncin' 'roun' in dis neighberhood ontwel you come ter b'leeve yo'se'f de boss er de whole gang. En den youer allers some'rs whar you got no bizness,' sez Brer Fox, sezee. 'Who ax you fer ter come en strike up a 'quaintance wid dish yer Tar-Baby? En who stuck you up dar whar you iz? Nobody in de roun' worril. You des tuck en jam yo'se'f on dat Tar-Baby widout waitin' fer enny invite,' sez Brer Fox, sezee, 'en dar you is' en dar you'll stay twel I fixes up a bresh-pile and fires her up, kaze I'm gwineter bobby-cue you dis day, sho,' sez Brer Fox, sezee.

"Den Brer Rabbit talk mighty 'umble.

" 'I don't keer w'at you do wid me, Brer Fox,' sezee, 'so you don't fling me in dat brier-patch. Roas' me, Brer Fox,' sezee, 'but don't fling me in dat brier-patch,' sezee.

" 'Hit's so much trouble fer ter kindle a fier,' sez Brer Fox, sezee, 'dat I speck I'll hatter hang you,' sezee.

" 'Hang me des ez high as you please, Brer Fox,' sez Brer Rabbit, sezee, 'but do fer de Lord's sake don't fling me in dat brier-patch,' sezee.

" 'I ain't got no string,' sez Brer Fox, sezee, 'en now I speck I'll hatter drown you,' sezee.

" 'Drown me des ez deep ez you please, Brer Fox,' sez Brer Rabbit, sezee, 'but do don't fling me in dat brier-patch,' sezee.

" 'Dey ain't no water nigh,' sez Brer Fox, sezee, 'en now I speck I'll hatter skin you,' sezee.

" 'Skin me, Brer Fox,' sez Brer Rabbit, sezee, 'snatch out my eyeballs, t'ar out my years by de roots, en cut off my legs,' sezee, 'but do please, Brer Fox, don't fling me in dat brier-patch,' sezee.

"Co'se Brer Fox wanter hurt Brer Rabbit bad ez he kin, so he cotch 'im by de behime legs en slung 'im right in de middle er de brier-patch. Dar wuz a considerbul flutter whar Brer Rabbit struck de bushes, en Brer Fox sorter hang 'roun' fer ter see w'at wuz gwineter happen. Bimeby he hear somebody call 'im, en way up de hill he see Brer Rabbit settin' cross-legged on a chinkapin log koamin' de pitch outen his har wid a chip. Den Brer Fox know dat he bin swop off mighty bad. Brer Rabbit wuz bleedzed fer ter fling back some er his sass, en he holler out:

" 'Bred en bawn in a brier-patch, Brer Fox — bred en bawn in a brier-patch!' en wid dat he skip out des ez lively ez a cricket in de embers."

Brer Rabbit's Astonishing Prank [3]

JOEL CHANDLER HARRIS

Joel Chandler Harris wrote a friend in regard to his Uncle Remus stories: "I seem to see before me the smiling faces of thousands of children — some young and fresh, and some wearing the friendly marks of age, but all children at heart — and not an unfriendly face among them. And out of the confusion, and while I am trying hard to speak the right word, I seem to hear a voice lifted above the rest, saying, 'You have made some of us happy.' And so I feel my heart fluttering and my lips trembling, and I have to bow silently and turn away, and hurry back into the obscurity that fits me best."

"I 'speck dat 'uz de reas'n w'at make old Brer Rabbit git 'long so well, kaze he aint copy atter none er de yuther creeturs," Uncle Remus continued, after a while. "W'en he make his disappearance 'fo' um, hit 'uz allers in some bran new place. Dey aint known wharbouts fer ter watch out fer 'im. He wuz de funniest creetur er de whole gang. Some folks moughter call him lucky, en yit, w'en he git in bad luck, hit look lak he mos' allers come out on top. Hit look mighty kuse now, but 't wa'n't kuse in dem days, kaze hit 'uz done gun up dat, strike 'im w'en you might en whar you would, Brer Rabbit wuz de soopless creetur gwine.

"One time, he sorter tuck a notion, ole Brer Rabbit did, dat he'd pay Brer B'ar a call, en no sooner do de notion strike 'im dan he pick hisse'f up en put out fer Brer B'ar house."

"Why, I thought they were mad with each other," the little boy exclaimed.

"Brer Rabbit make he call w'en Brer B'ar en his fambly wuz off fum home," Uncle Remus explained, with a chuckle which was in the nature of a hearty tribute to the crafty judgment of Brother Rabbit.

"He sot down by de road, en he see um go by — old Brer B'ar en ole Miss B'ar, en der two twin-chilluns, w'ich one un um wuz name Kubs en de t'er one wuz name Klibs."

The little boy laughed, but the severe seriousness of Uncle Remus would have served for a study, as he continued:

"Ole Brer B'ar en Miss B'ar, dey went 'long ahead, en Kubs en Klibs, dey come shufflin'

---

[3] From Joel Chandler Harris, *Nights with Uncle Remus* (Houghton Mifflin, 1883).

en scramblin' 'long behime. W'en Brer Rabbit see dis, he say ter hisse'f dat he 'speck he better go see how Brer B'ar gittin' on; en off he put. En 't wa'n't long n'er 'fo' he 'uz ransackin' de premmuses same like he 'uz sho' 'nuff patter-roller. W'iles he wuz gwine 'roun' peepin' in yer en pokin' in dar, he got ter foolin' 'mong de shelfs, en a bucket er honey w'at Brer B'ar got hid in de cubbud fall down en spill on top er Brer Rabbit, en little mo'n he'd er bin drown. Fum head ter heels dat creetur wuz kiver'd wid honey; he wa'n't des only bedobble wid it, he wuz des kiver'd. He hatter set dar en let de natal sweetness drip outen he eyeballs 'fo' he kin see he han' befo' 'im, en den, atter he look 'round little, he say to hisse'f, sezee:

" 'Heyo, yer! W'at I gwine do now? If I go out in de sunshine, de bumly-bees en de flies dey'll swom up'n take me, en if I stay yer, Brer B'ar'll come back en ketch me, en I dunner w'at in de name er gracious I gwine do.'

"Ennyhow, bimeby a notion strike Brer Rabbit, en he tip 'long twel he git in de woods, en w'en he git out dar, w'at do he do but roll in de leafs en trash en try fer ter rub de honey off'n 'im dat a-way. He roll, he did, en de leafs dey stick; Brer Rabbit roll, en de leafs dey stick, en he keep on rollin' en de leafs keep on stickin', twel atter w'ile Brer Rabbit wuz de mos' owdashus-lookin' creetur w'at you ever sot eyes on. En ef Miss Meadows en de gals could er seed 'im den en dar, dey wouldn't er bin no mo' Brer Rabbit call at der house; 'deed, en dat dey would n't.

"Brer Rabbit, he jump 'roun', he did, en try ter shake de leafs off'n 'im, but de leafs, dey aint gwine ter be shuck off. Brer Rabbit, he shake en he shiver, but de leafs dey stick; en de capers dat creetur cut up out dar in de woods by he own-alone se'f wuz scan'lous — dey wuz dat; dey wuz scan'lous.

"Brer Rabbit see dis wa'n't gwine ter do, en he 'low ter hisse'f dat he better be gittin' on todes home, en off he put. I 'speck you done year talk er deze yer booggers w'at gits atter bad chilluns," continued Uncle Remus, in a tone so seriously confidential as to be altogether depressing; "well, den, des 'zactly dat a-way Brer Rabbit look, en ef you'd er seed 'im you'd er made sho' he de gran'-daddy er all de booggers. Brer Rabbit pace 'long, he did, en ev'y motion he make, de leafs dey'd go *swishy-swushy, splushy-splishy,* en, fum de fuss he make en de way he look, you'd er tuck 'im ter be de mos' suvvigus varment w'at disappear fum de face er de yeth sence ole man Noah let down de drawbars er de ark en tu'n de creeturs loose; en I boun' ef you'd er stuck up long wid 'im, you'd er been mighty good en glad ef you'd er got off wid dat.

"De fus' man w'at Brer Rabbit come up wid wiz ole Sis Cow, en no sooner is she lay eyes on 'im dan she h'ist up 'er tail in de elements, en put out like a pack er dogs wuz atter 'er. Dis make Brer Rabbit laff, kaze he know dat w'en a ole settle' 'oman like Sis Cow run 'stracted in de broad open day-time, dat dey mus' be sump'n' mighty kuse 'bout dem leafs en dat honey, en he keep on a-rackin' down de road. De nex' man w'at he meet wuz a black gal tollin' a whole passel er plantation shotes, en w'en de gal see Brer Rabbit come prancin' 'long, she fling down 'er basket er corn en des fa'rly fly, en de shotes, dey tuck thoo de woods, en sech n'er racket ez dey kick up wid der runnin', en der snortin', en der squealin' aint never bin year in dat settlement needer befo' ner since. Hit keep on dis a-way long ez Brer Rabbit meet anybody — dey des broke en run like de Ole Boy wuz atter um.

"C'ose, dis make Brer Rabbit feel monst'us biggity, en he 'low ter hisse'f dat he 'speck he better drap 'roun' en skummish in de neighborhoods er Brer Fox house. En w'iles he wuz stannin' dar runnin' dis 'roun' in he min', yer come old Brer B'ar en all er he fambly. Brer Rabbit, he git crossways de road, he did, en he sorter sidle todes um. Ole Brer B'ar, he stop en look, but Brer Rabbit, he keep on sidlin' todes um. Ole Miss B'ar, she stan' it long ez she kin, en den she fling down 'er parrysol en tuck a tree. Brer B'ar look lak he gwine ter stan' his groun', but Brer Rabbit he jump straight up in de a'r en gin hisse'f a shake, en, bless yo' soul, honey! ole Brer B'ar make a break, en dey tells me he to' down a whole panel er fence gittin' 'way fum dar. En ez ter Kubs en Klibs, dey tuck der hats in der han's, en dey went skaddlin' thoo de bushes des same ez a drover er hosses."

"And then what?" the little boy asked.

"Brer Rabbit p'raded on down de road," continued Uncle Remus, "en bimeby yer come Brer Fox en Brer Wolf, fixin' up a plan fer ter nab Brer Rabbit, en dey wuz so intents on der confab dat dey got right on Brer Rabbit 'fo' dey seed 'im; but, gentermens! w'en dey is ketch a glimpse un 'im, dey gun 'im all de room he want. Brer Wolf, he try ter show off, he did, kase he wanter play big 'fo' Brer Fox, en he stop en ax Brer Rabbit who is he. Brer Rabbit, he jump up en down in de middle er de road, en holler out:

" 'I'm de Wull-er-de-Wust. I'm de Wull-er-de-Wust, en youer de man I'm atter!'

"Den Brer Rabbit jump up en down en make lak he gwine atter Brer Fox en Brer Wolf, en de way dem creeturs lit out fum dar wuz a caution.

"Long time atter dat," continued Uncle Remus, folding his hands placidly in his lap, with the air of one who has performed a pleasant duty, — "long time atter dat, Brer Rabbit come up wid Brer Fox en Brer Wolf, en he git behime a stump, Brer Rabbit did, en holler out:

" 'I'm de Wull-er-de-Wust, en youer de mens I'm atter!'

"Brer Fox en Brer Wolf, dey broke, but 'fo' dey got outer sight en outer year'n', Brer Rabbit show hisse'f, he did, en laugh fit ter kill hisse'f. Atterwuds, Miss Meadows she year 'bout it, en de nex' time Brer Fox call, de gals dey up en giggle, en ax 'im ef he aint feard de Wull-er-de-Wust mought drap in."

❧ Southern Mountain Tales ❧

Old Fire Dragaman [4]

❧ *The Jack Tales of Richard Chase are American versions or variants of European folk tales. They are contemporary examples of the process of survival and adaptation so characteristic of folklore. Richard Chase found a pocket of survival at Beech Creek, North Caro-*

4 From *The Jack Tales,* ed. Richard Chase (Houghton Mifflin Company, 1943).

lina. There, in the keeping of mountain folk, who have been telling these stories since the first English settlers came to that region, he found the tales, listened, and set them down in the speech of the people. The roots and origins are clearly visible. Here is Jack of the beanstalk and Jack the giant killer. Jack is the hero of all these stories. He is the American prototype of Boots, the youngest son who is hero of the Scandinavian folk tale. In the notes to these tales, scholars have traced the stories to their sources in Grimm and other collections, including the English epic Beowulf. It is fascinating to explore the naturalization of the story. See what happens to the old refrain of Fee, fi, fo, fum when it becomes American and Southern:

> "Fee! Faw! Fumm!
> I smell the blood of a English-mum.
> Bein' he dead or bein' he alive,
> I'll grind his bones
> To eat with my pones."

The story given here is the one which is said to derive from Beowulf. Certainly, like the epic, it concerns an underground monster who must be destroyed. In this form, it is an astonishingly vital tale for the storyteller.

One time Jack and his two brothers, Will and Tom, were all of 'em a-layin' around home; weren't none of 'em doin' no good, so their daddy decided he'd set 'em to work. He had him a tract of land out in a wilderness of a place back up on the mountain. Told the boys they could go up there and work it. Said he'd give it to 'em. Hit was a right far ways from where anybody lived at, so they fixed 'em up a wagonload of rations and stuff for housekeepin' and pulled out.

There wasn't no house up there, so they cut poles and notched 'em up a shack. They had to go to work in a hurry to get out any crop and they set right in to clearin' 'em a newground. They decided one boy 'uld have to stay to the house till twelve and do the cookin'.

First day Tom and Jack left Will there. Will went to fixin' around and got dinner ready, went out and blowed the horn to call Tom and Jack, looked down the holler and there came a big old giant steppin' right up the mountain. Had him a pipe about four foot long, and he had a long old blue beard that dragged on the ground.

When Will saw the old giant was headed right for the house, he ran and got behind the door, pulled it back on him and scrouged back against the wall a-shakin' like a leaf. The old giant came on to the house, reached in and throwed the cloth back off the dishes, eat ever'thing on the table in one bite and sopped the plates. Snatched him a chunk of fire and lit his pipe; the smoke came a-bilin' out. Then he wiped his mouth and went on back down the holler with that old pipe a-sendin' up smoke like a steam engine.

Tom and Jack came on in directly, says, "Why in the world ain't ye got us no dinner, Will?"

"Law me!" says Will. "If you'd 'a seen what I just seen you'd 'a not thought about no dinner. An old Fire Dragaman came up here, eat ever' bite on the table, and sopped the plates."

Tom and Jack laughed right smart at Will.

Will says, "You all needn't to laugh. Hit'll be your turn tomorrow, Tom."

So they fixed up what vittles they could and they all went back to work in the new-ground.

Next day Tom got dinner, went out and blowed the horn. There came Old Fire Dragaman —

"Law me!" says Tom. "Where'll I get?"

He ran and scrambled under the bed. Old Fire Dragaman came on up, eat ever'thing there was on the table, sopped the plates, and licked out all the pots. Lit his old pipe and pulled out down the holler, the black smoke a-rollin' like comin' out a chimley. Hit was a sight to look at.

Will and Jack came in, says, "Where's our dinner, Tom?"

"Dinner, the nation! Old Fire Dragaman came back up here. Law me! Hit was the beatin'-est thing I ever seen!"

Will says, "Where was you at, Tom?"

"Well, I'll tell ye," says Tom; "I was down under the bed."

Jack laughed, and Will and Tom says, "You just wait about laughin', Jack. Hit'll be your time tomorrow."

Next day Will and Tom went to the new-ground. They got to laughin' about where Jack 'uld hide at when Old Fire Dragaman came.

Jack fixed up ever'thing for dinner, went out about twelve and blowed the horn. Looked down the wilder-ness, there was Old Fire Dragaman a-comin' up the hill with his hands folded behind him and a-lookin' around this way and that.

Jack went on back in the house, started puttin' stuff on the table. Never payed no attention to the old giant, just went right on a-fixin' dinner. Old Fire Dragaman came on up.

Jack was scoopin' up a mess of beans out the pot, says, "Why, hello, daddy."

"Howdy, son."

"Come on in, daddy. Get you a chair. Dinner's about ready; just stay and eat with us."

"No, I thank ye. I couldn't stay."

"Hit's on the table. Come on sit down."

"No. I just stopped to light my pipe."

"Come on, daddy. Let's eat."

"No, much obliged. I got no time."

Old Fire Dragaman reached in to get him a coal of fire, got the biggest chunk in the fireplace, stuck it down in his old pipe, and started on back. Jack took out and follered him with all that smoke a-bilin' out; watched where he went to, and saw him go down a big straight hole in the ground.

Will and Tom came on to the house, saw Jack was gone.

Will says, "I reckon that's the last of Jack. I'll bet ye a dollar Old Fire Dragaman's done took him off and eat him. Dinner's still on the table."

So they set down and went to eatin'. Jack came on in directly.

Will says, "Where'n the world ye been, Jack? We 'lowed Old Fire Dragaman had done eat ye up."

"I been watchin' where Old Fire Dragaman went to."

"How come dinner yet on the table?"

"I tried my best to get him to eat," says Jack. "He just lit his old pipe and went on back. I follered him, saw him go down in a big hole out yonder."

"You right sure ye ain't lyin', Jack?"

"Why, no," says Jack. "You boys come with me and you can see the place where he went in at. Let's us get a rope and basket so we can go in that hole and see what's down there."

So they got a big basket made out of splits, and gathered up a long rope they'd done made out of hickory bark, and Jack took 'em on down to Old Fire Dragaman's den.

"Will, you're the oldest," says Jack; "we'll let you go down first. If you see any danger, you shake the rope and we'll pull ye back up."

Will got in the basket, says, "You recollect now; whenever I shake that rope, you pull me out of here in a hurry."

So they let him down. Directly the rope shook, they jerked the basket back out, says, "What'd ye see, Will?"

"Saw a big house. Hit's like another world down there."

Then they slapped Tom in the basket and let him down; the rope shook, they hauled him up.

"What'd you see, Tom?"

"Saw a house and the barn."

Then they got Jack in the basket, and let him down. Jack got down on top of the house, let the basket slip down over the eaves and right on down in the yard. Jack got out, went and knocked on the door.

The prettiest girl Jack ever had seen came out. He started right in to courtin' her, says, "I'm goin' to get you out of here."

She says, "I got another sister in the next room yonder, prettier'n me. You get her out too."

So Jack went on in the next room. That second girl was a heap prettier'n the first, and Jack went to talkin' to her and was a-courtin' right on. Said he'd get her out of that place.

She says, "I got another sister in the next room, prettier'n me. Don't you want to get her out too?"

"Well, I didn't know they got any prettier'n you," says Jack, "but I'll go see."

So he went on in. Time Jack saw that 'un he knowed she was the prettiest girl ever lived, so he started in right off talkin' courtin' talk to her; plumb forgot about them other two.

That girl said to Jack, says, "Old Fire Dragaman'll be back here any minute now. Time he finds you here he'll start in spittin' balls of fire."

So she went and opened up an old chest, took out a big swoard and a little vial of ointment, says, "If one of them balls of fire hits ye, Jack, you rub on a little of this medicine right quick, and this here swoard is the only thing that will hurt Old Fire Dragaman. You watch out now, and kill him if ye can."

Well, the old giant came in the door directly, saw Jack, and com-menced spittin' balls of fire all around in there, some of 'em big as pumpkins. Jack he went a-dodgin' around tryin' to get at the old giant with that swoard. Once in a while one of them fireballs 'uld glance him, but Jack rubbed on that ointment right quick and it didn't even make a blister. Fin'ly Jack got in close and clipped him with that swoard, took his head clean off.

Then Jack made that girl promise she'd marry him. So she took a red ribbon and got Jack to plat it in her hair. Then she gave Jack a wishin' ring. He put it on his finger and they went on out and got the other two girls.

They were awful pleased. They told Jack they were such little bits of children when the old giant catched 'em they barely could recollect when they first came down there.

Well, Jack put the first one in the basket and shook the rope. Will and Tom hauled her up, and when they saw her they commenced fightin' right off to see which one would marry her.

She told 'em, says, "I got another sister down there."

"Is she any prettier'n you?" says Will.

She says to him, "I ain't sayin'."

Will and Tom chunked the basket back down in a hurry. Jack put the next girl in, shook the rope. Time Will and Tom saw her, they both asked her to marry, and went to knockin' and beatin' one another over gettin' *her*.

She stopped 'em, says, "We got one more sister down there."

"Is she prettier'n you?" says Will.

She says to him, "You can see for yourself."

So they slammed the basket back down, jerked that last girl out.

"Law me!" says Will. "This here's the one I'm a-goin' to marry."

"Oh, no, you ain't!" Tom says. "You'll marry me, won't ye now?"

"No," says the girl, "I've done promised to marry Jack."

"Blame Jack," says Will. "He can just stay in there." And he picked up the basket and rope, throwed 'em down the hole.

"There ain't nothin' much to eat down there," says the girl; "he'll starve to death."

"That's just what we want him to do," says Will, and they took them girls on back up to the house.

Well, Jack eat ever'thing he could find down there, but in about three days he saw the rations were runnin' awful low. He scrapped up ever' bit there was left and then he was plumb out of vittles; didn't know what he'd do.

In about a week Jack had com-menced to get awful poor. Happened he looked at his hand, turned that ring to see how much he'd fallen off, says, "I wish I was back home settin' in my mother's chimley corner smokin' my old chunky pipe."

And next thing, there he was.

Jack's mother asked him how come he wasn't up at the newground. Jack told her that was just exactly where he was started.

When Jack got up there, Will and Tom were still a-fightin' over that youngest girl. Jack came on in the house and saw she still had that red ribbon in her hair, and she came over to him, says, "Oh, Jack!"

So Jack got the youngest and Tom got the next 'un, and that throwed Will to take the oldest.

And last time I was down there they'd done built 'em three pole cabins and they were all doin' pretty well.

ᵛᔕ Tall Tales ᔕᵛ
Paul Bunyan⁵

ᔕ *The Paul Bunyan stories center on a legendary hero of the lumber camps of the*

⁵ From Esther Shephard, *Paul Bunyan* (Harcourt, Brace, 1924).

American Northwest. This giant lumberjack is noted for his prodigious feats and the size of his logging operations. The narrator usually claimed acquaintance with Paul and the stories were told in competition. Figures and dimensions often varied with the audience, as the storyteller "lays on all the traffic will bear." As to the origin of the stories, Esther Shephard says, "Some evidence points to a French-Canadian origin among the loggers of Quebec or northern Ontario, who may even have brought them from the old country; the name, then, may be a derivative of the French-Canadian word bongyenne. *But other evidences point just as strongly to an American beginning, possibly in Michigan or Wisconsin." Whatever their origin may be, these tall tales are a unique contribution of the American frontier to the world's folklore.*

Well, the way I was sayin', Paul had been figgurin' on where he was goin' to go next, and so then that mornin' he made up his mind.

"I'll go West," he says. "Reckon there'll be loggin' enough for me to do out there for a year or two anyway."

He'd heard about the Big Trees they had out there, and he'd seen the tops of some of 'em when he'd been out cruisin' one Sunday, and then Ole had told him about 'em too — he'd seen some of 'em from the top of the cornstalk the time he was up. And some fellows that had come into camp from the West told him about some outfit that was loggin' out there on the Coast on a big scale, and Paul, naturally, wanted to come out and show that fellow how to log.

And so he made up his mind to go right away.

Paul was goin' to show Joe how to log, and he wasn't goin' to let him get ahead of him, and so, as soon as he got his land staked out, he went back East and got the Blue Ox and other camp equipment. Paul went back to the Ottawa country where he'd left some of his stuff when he'd been loggin' there a long time ago, and then of course the equipment he had to take out of North Dakota, and then a lot of new stuff from Chicago, donkey engines, and cable, and railroad cars, and what-not, and a lot of other new-fangled things he was goin' to use.

"I'll beat 'em at their own game," he says.

And Babe was good for freightin' too. Just as good as for any other kind of woods work.

.   .   .   .

When Paul and Babe come to a piece of thick woods, Paul generally went ahead of the Ox to make a road for him, where the timber was thick, and it was kind of swampy — like in the Lake of the Woods country. He'd have his axe in his hand — the big one with the sixteen-foot cuttin' surface and the wove grass handle — and he'd swing it back and forth in front of him as he went along and make a road for the Ox. The trees would just fall crosswise across the road as soon as he got past, big end for little end and little end for big end, and make as fine a corduroy as you'd ever want to see, and then the Ox would come along behind.

I used to like to see 'em — Paul comin' through the woods that way slashin' with his axe, with the clean timber road layin' there behind him, and the streak of light showin' through the dark pine trees, and the big Blue Ox comin' along there behind with the load, chewin' his cud as easy and peaceful as if he'd been goin' into his barn in Paul's camp on the Red River.

That's the way Paul done most of his freightin', but sometimes he went farther south across the plains.

.   .   .   .

I remember one time I was with him on one of those trips when he was bringin' some stuff out, and he had a calf that he'd bought from some farmer in Iowa that he was bringin' with him to butcher for his camp on the Skagit, when he'd be just about the right size then, and so he took him along on this tote-trip he was makin' across the plains. And after the first day we stopped overnight at a cabin near Billings, Montana.

The young fellow who was homesteadin' there said he'd put the calf in the barn for the night, so's he'd be protected from the weather some, and Paul of course was glad at that, because he knowed that would keep the meat more tender, and he told him, sure, that would be fine, if he had room enough.

"Well, then, I'll do that," says the homesteader.

And so then we put the calf in the barn, and we put up for the night.

Well, the next mornin' when we got up and went outside, somethin' about the place looked kind of funny and we didn't hardly know at first what it was, but finally one of 'em says:

"I know what's the matter. The barn's gone."

And sure enough when we looked, where it'd been there was only a pile of straw now, bein' blowed about by the wind.

So then of course we all begun lookin' around to find out what'd become of it, but we couldn't see it nowheres. It hadn't been burned, we knowed that, because if it had of there would of been some ashes, and there wasn't nothin', only just straw and a few boards of the old floor, just as if it'd been lifted right up and carried away by the wind. And then we happened to think the calf was in the barn too.

Well, we didn't hardly know what it was could of come about, and so then Holloway — that's the young fellow homesteadin' — happened to think he had a pair of field glasses somewheres about the place. For he'd used to a been a forest ranger before, and so that's how he happened to have the glasses there. Well, he brought 'em out, and we looked around, and finally one of us spied the barn way off in the distance away off towards the south.

"And gee! it's movin'!" he said.

"No, sure not. There ain't wind enough to be movin' it now. There might of been in the night, but there sure ain't now — no wind at all to speak of."

"But it's movin' just the same. And there's a kind of funny thing on top of it."

Well, we got our saddle ponies and rode on out there and we found the barn, and I'll be blamed if there inside of it wasn't that calf of Paul's.

Or I shouldn't of said inside it, for he was mostly outside.

You know he'd growed so fast in the night he'd grown clean out of it and here was the four sides of the barn hangin' around his legs. He sure was the limit for growin' fast.

.   .   .   .

Some of the finest loggin' Paul done after he come West was in the Inland Empire. Course it wasn't an Inland Empire then, but just a big inland sea, and it was around the shores of this lake and on an island in the northwest corner of it that Paul Bunyan logged. It was pretty near my favorite loggin' with Paul, that year was.

.   .   .   .

I know when we first come down there Paul went out to cut a tree down one day. He cut away for a couple of hours, and then he went round to see how much he had left to chop before he'd get through, and here if he didn't find two Irishmen choppin' away on the other side of the tree and they'd been choppin' there for over three years, they said, ever since the spring of the Long Rain just about three years before that. It seems some boss had sent 'em in there to cut that tree down and that's all the farther they'd got, and I suppose the boss had forgot all about 'em a long time ago.

They was all overgrown with beards and they was lean and hungry, of course, and kind of wild too and queer from havin' been away from civilization so long and not havin' seen nobody for such a long time.

Paul felt mighty sorry for 'em and so he said he'd see what he could do, and he went back to his own side again and got his other axe and chopped away a little faster, because the men was starvin' to death, and between 'em in an hour or so they got it down.

And then I'll be blamed after all that trouble if the old tree wasn't hollow.

.   .   .   .

Loggin' on the island and around the inland sea was sure mighty handy. For one thing, there wasn't no waste. You could cut up the main part of the tree into them special lengths Paul was gettin' out that year, and then you could cut up all the limbs into just ordinary size logs and that way there wasn't no waste at all. And all them small logs filled up the spaces between the big ones and made a nice solid-lookin' job of it.

The way Paul done, he just cut the trees around the edge of the island first — the first row of 'em all around — and fell them right out into the lake where they'd be all ready for the drive, and filled in on top with them smaller logs, and then the next row of trees on top of the first ones, and the next row on top of that, and so on, one circle layin' right inside and at the same time kind of on top of the next circle, till the whole island was one solid pile of logs, way till you got to the center, to the mountain. Mount Pasco was right up in the middle of the island and that's where we had the camp, of course. Not a very high mountain but kind of big and flat, with a crater in the top of it, and a hollow where you could cook the soup always by natural heat.

And then the trees from the sides of the lake he cut out in the water too, but we finished up the island first. From the south shore of the lake when you got away from it far enough the island used to look like a great big hotcake layin' out there, all nice and brown, and kind of high in the middle like it had plenty of good egg and soda in it, and then kind of a little uneven around the edge like a good hotcake always ought to be.

It was sure as pretty a raft of logs as you'd ever want to see, and the biggest one I ever knowed of Paul havin'. The sunshine was mighty bright there in the Inland Empire and used to lay over them brown logs out there so you could almost see the air movin' in heat waves above them, even though everything else was still, and out over the blue sea too, till you couldn't hardly look at it, it was so bright. Loggin' there was different from most of the loggin' we'd done, and we liked it.

And then when we got the raft all ready and everythin' layin' just the way we wanted it, Paul went down to the southwest corner of the lake and plowed out an outlet for it. He was goin' to take most of them logs to China, so he figgured from that corner would be the best way to get out to the ocean. And then, when he got the river finished and about half filled up with water and slicked out over the top so it would be slippery, he turned the lake right into it.

Runnin' out so fast there, of course, the inland sea right away begun to slant from the northeast to the southwest, and the whole hotcake of logs just slid right off the island and floated right down to the outlet and then pretty soon the logs from the sides begun to slide in after it trailin' along behind, till goin' down the river it looked like a great big sea turtle with its hair streamin' out behind it. And it wasn't long till it was gone and clean out of sight. And so that loggin' was over.

. . . .

There's many conflictin' stories about how Paul dug the Columbia River, but of course there's only one right one and that's the one I was just tellin' about the Inland Empire. I was right there and I saw how it was done. When Paul got his raft of logs finished and was ready to take 'em out, he just went out there and plowed out the river. And there wasn't nothin' to it at all. He plowed it out first and then filled it up with water and evened it out so it would be nice and smooth for his logs to slide over. On a windy day in the Gorge when an east wind is blowin' you can see the hole yet in the water where Paul never put in the last bucketful when he was evenin' it out.

. . . .

Well, there's stories, and stories. I don't suppose I've heard 'em all. His old friends all remember him, and any of 'em will tell you about Paul. And some of 'em wishes a good many times that he was back here loggin' again; even the young fellows who never knowed him, but have only just heard about him, would of liked pretty well to've been in on the good old times, I guess.

Slue-foot Sue Dodges the Moon [6]

🔏 *The American folk tale is a Johnny-Come-Lately as compared to the long heritage of the oral tradition. But it holds to many of the true patterns of folklore — indigenous humor, clear characterization, swift action and denouement. The absurdity of a country as big as America, and the enormity of the task facing the settlers and the workmen, provided a natural breeding ground for the story of exaggeration, the Tall*

[6] From James Cloyd Bowman, *Pecos Bill, the Greatest Cowboy of All Time* (Albert Whitman, 1937).

Tale. The industrial frontiers of lumbering and cattle raising gave us the roots of two typical folk tale cycles. Paul Bunyan represents the folk image of the lumber worker, and Pecos Bill of the cowboy. Slue-foot Sue's story seems almost prophetic in this time of the launching of satellite moons. Slue-foot Sue almost made it in her own person.

"Has Slue-foot Sue learned to ride a broncho yet as good as a catfish?" asked Gun Smith with a sharp look at Pecos Bill's face.

Pecos took a few seconds to pull himself together before he attempted to answer.

"Sue's a wonderful broncho buster," he said wistfully. "She takes to a cayuse as naturally as a porcupine quill takes to a broncho's heels. You see, on one of my trips I roped a calico pony and gentled it. Later I took it along up to Pinnacle Mountain and taught her to ride it."

"And has her mother said she could wear cowpuncher pants?" Gun Smith laughed.

"Well, yes and no," Pecos explained. "You see, Gun Smith, the mother and Sue are something like you and Moon. They've got strong minds of their own. Sue was determined to wear chaps like a cowman, and her mother was equally determined that she should wear a skirt. Finally they compromised, which is better than you and Moon have done. And so Sue wears both — one over the top of the other, you understand."

"All dressed up, eh, Pecos?" laughed Gun Smith.

"Yes, but this is only half of it. The mother says Sue's now got to wear one of those big spring-steel bustles the English think're so smart. Which would be all right in its way if the bustle didn't make it ten times harder for Sue to keep in the saddle when her broncho is galloping. Every time the horse strikes the ground the spring in the bustle just naturally throws her up into the air. And she looks like one of those six-weeks-old blackbirds that ain't yet quite got all the tail feathers."

"You told her that, Pecos?" inquired Gun Smith.

"Tell her!" Pecos Bill exclaimed. "Of course I did. Why, we both laughed about it till we almost cried. Finally she said, 'If you had a wife, Pecos, would you force her to wear both skirt and chaps? And would you force her to wear spring-steel bustles when she goes riding?' And I replied, 'If I ever have a wife, she can wear any old thing she wants.'"

"Then what did she say?" Gun Smith asked, hiding his rising excitement.

"Why, if you must know, what she said was, 'How I do wish I were your wife.' 'You mean that?' I asked, drawing in a deep breath, I can tell you. 'But isn't there anything you would refuse me?' she queried growing very serious. 'Absolutely nothing in the world,' I told her and I meant it at the moment. But then I thought I'd better make myself a little clearer, so I explained, 'That is, I'd let you do everything except ride Widow Maker. Once he threw the best rider I knew onto the top of Pike's Peak, and, of course, I don't want anything like that to happen to the one woman I love.'

"'Of course not,' Sue replied much disappointed. And she sure was pouting when she told me. 'Then you don't think I can ride as well as you. Just wait till I can get this old skirt and this spring-steel bustle off, and I'll show you I can ride, even Widow Maker!'

"I asked her, 'Do you really wish you were my wife?' And she replied, 'I don't know anybody whose wife I'd wish to be half so much.' 'Well then, Sue,' I said, 'Keep right on wishing, and it won't be long.'"

"But you don't mean to tell me that you really mean to marry this girl!" Gun Smith demanded coolly.

"Of course I mean to marry Sue. That's just the reason I'm inviting you and Chuck and Moon and the others along to the wedding, so that you can be my bridesmen or groomsmaids or whatever it is you call them. We've sent back East for a minister, and he's due to arrive at Pinnacle Mountain this morning."

There was, of course, great excitement at the I. X. L. Ranch when it was noised about that Pecos Bill was to wed the vivacious Sue. One minute the cowmen laughed in an uproar; the next minute they were like a nest of hornets. For come to think of it, it was funny — and no joke — at the same time.

Pecos Bill married? They couldn't believe it.

When the day arrived, Pecos Bill started with his men in the direction of Pinnacle Mountain. He rode a little ahead, very solemn and quiet, as though lost in dreams. After two or three hours he found he couldn't possibly poke along with the others. He wanted to be with his Sue. "I think I'll ride on ahead," he called suddenly. And before anybody could answer, he had given free rein to Widow Maker, and all that the others could see then was a yellowish cloud of dust.

As Gun Smith and the others followed as fast as their bronchos could carry them, they put their feelings into words.

"What'll we do with a woman at I. X. L. Ranch?"

"There ain't no room for a skirt 'round our outfit!"

"No mistake about that, Pecos Bill is sure loco this time."

"With a woman around, Pecos Bill won't be worth as much as a lop-eared maverick."

"Well, judgin' from past experience, we should give him credit for havin' at least a grain of horse sense."

When Gun Smith and Moon and the others arrived at Pinnacle Mountain they asked the mother if she had seen anything of Pecos Bill.

"Colonel Bill, if you please!" she answered proudly with raised eyebrows. "The Colonel and my daughter are out horseback riding, thank you. Won't you come right along in and make yourselves comfortable until they return? I'm sorry, but my lord and his Eminence, the Right Reverend Doctor Hull, are walking. They're taking a little constitutional before the ceremony begins, don't you know. You'll have to excuse me for the minute — I'm so sorry — but, you see, I am obliged to superintend the dinner."

"So she's already made a Colonel of our Pecos!" Gun Smith snorted under his breath.

"She couldn't think of havin' her daughter marry anybody less than a Colonel, *don't you know!*" Chuck added in disgust.

"I wonder she hasn't made him a Sir Knight of the Garter, or at very least a General!" Mushmouth continued.

"She's made a strong gesture in that direction. The other royal titles'll follow soon enough," Chuck replied, with an amused smile. "Lucky she didn't get hold of any of the rest of us or hard tellin' what kind of monkeys we'd become!"

After a short while the men could hear voices outside. Slue-foot Sue was saying in a nervous, petulant way: "But after we're married you've just got to let me ride Widow Maker! You simply must, I say! You must! You must!"

"But, Sue dear," Colonel Pecos Bill replied with quiet firmness, "you wouldn't thank me if I let you break your neck on the spot, would you?"

"Oh! It's the same old story I've been hearing all my life, wherever I turn! It's can't! Can't! Can't, all the while! But I want you to know that I *will* ride Widow Maker! I say I will! I will!! I will!!! I'll show you that I can ride your old broncho as well as you or any other cowman! I'm no longer a baby, remember that!"

"But, Sue dear," Colonel Bill answered with quiet patience, "don't worry any more about it. There, now, that's the way I like you to smile. We'll see about it after the wedding."

"Right you are," laughed the girlish voice. "We shall see! We shall see!" she ended, believing she had won her victory.

When Pecos and Sue entered, the men got to their feet stiffly with hats in hand. "Well, when did you arrive?" Pecos began. "Sue, here are my friends . . . This is Gun Smith, this, my brother Chuck, and this, Moon Hennessey."

Sue gave each of the men a warm greeting. "It is just perfectly lovely of you to come so far to witness this important event. The Colonel and I surely do appreciate it. By the way, who is going to be the best man?"

"I rather believe," exclaimed Gun Smith, "that I'd prefer, if it makes no difference to you, to act in the capacity of a groomsmaid or a bridesman, as you might say."

"How wonderful of you!" Sue laughed heartily. "You have put it quaintly, indeed."

All the others joined in the joyous spirit of the occasion, and soon everybody was entirely at ease and happy.

When Slue-foot Sue and Colonel Bill ap-

peared later for the wedding ceremony, the bride was dressed in a dazzling white satin gown. The wide skirt draped itself in flowing, lacy lines over the wide-spreading hoops; the train extended half across the room; and the steel-spring bustle looked very smart indeed! But dearest of all was the sweet face of the bride herself.

The Right Reverend Doctor Hull was quite charmed with the bride. "My lord," he whispered, "I've not seen Sue's equal in years — not in many years!"

Colonel Bill himself had given no little attention to his clothes. He had, in fact, ridden at least two thousand miles to collect the very best of everything that was to be had. His high-heeled boots, with fancy hand stitching, were polished till they shone like a pair of mirrors. His spurs were of solid gold. He was carrying an imported hat he had ridden seven hundred miles to purchase. Its band was of the best Mexican bead work. He had a pair of breeches he had purchased in California. They were sort of lavender with inch-square checks. His shirt was of white silk and his vest of red satin that was intended by its creator to set every woman's eyes aflame. His coat was covered with delicate Mexican bead work, too.

It was little wonder he was so proud of himself that he carried his head cocked decidedly over his left shoulder. He was so entirely happy that the corners of his mouth almost touched the tops of his ears. In fact, there wasn't a thing to criticize in Pecos Bill's clothes. He was gotten together exactly right for the occasion.

Just before the couple stood in place for the ceremony the Right Reverend gentleman whispered to my lord: "It seems the least bit weird, even though it is deucedly picturesque, to see the bridegroom dressed so entirely out of accord with His Majesty's London costumer's latest togs."

"Oh, I don't mind, since the Colonel is every inch a man, don't you know," my lord smiled in reply. "I rather approve of his costume."

All the boys were feeling very gay and hardly able to wait for things to start. Mushmouth had brought along his lip-piano to play the wedding march. Bullfrog Doyle was fidgeting about, all set to accompany him by dancing a different tune with each foot. Everyone was bursting with fun. That is, all except Sue's mother, who turned so cold that her stare froze on her face like an Egyptian mummy.

And Slue-foot Sue had an even greater shock in store for her mother. For just before the ceremony was about to begin, she gave a whoop and rushed from the room. A moment later she returned, arrayed in sombrero, woolen shirt, chaps, high-heeled boots, jingling spurs and flaming red breeches. "Ee-Yow!" she called. "A cowboy bride for the greatest cowboy in the world," and swung her hat about her head.

Everyone was completely fascinated by the daring of the beautiful woman. It was evident, judging by the brief moment that she took to make the change, that she must have worn the cowboy clothes under her wedding gown.

In her excitement one thing was wrong, however. She had forgotten that she was still wearing her steel-spring bustle. She had it on now, and although everyone knew at once that a bustle wasn't the thing to wear with chaps and spurs, nobody dared make a suggestion that would spoil the girlish bride's feeling of freedom and happiness.

When her mother saw Sue she fairly choked with annoyance. She tried to speak, but the words stuck in her throat. And Sue, seeing her mother speechless, leapt out of the room with another explosive "Ee-Yow!" This action proved quite too much for the mother's highly excited nerves and she threw up her hands and fainted in a heap on the floor. Colonel Bill flew to help the good woman like the chivalrous gentleman that he was.

This was just the chance Sue was looking for. Quick as a flash she ran pell-mell to where Widow Maker was tied and released him. The faithful horse saw her coming and let out a terrific whinny of distress. Colonel Bill instantly understood what Widow Maker meant and almost dropped the mother on the floor in his haste to rescue his bride.

But alas! Pecos was a fraction of a second too late. He and the others reached the door just in time to see Slue-foot Sue flying upward through the air out of a cloud of dust.

The poor girl, in fact, had been bucked so high that she had to duck her head to let the moon go by. Pecos stood wringing his hands and looking wildly in the direction of his vanishing bride. After an hour and a half of intense anguish on his part, Sue fell back to earth with the speed of a meteor. She struck exactly in the middle of the spring-steel bustle and rebounded like a rocket, and again the sky completely swallowed her up.

Colonel Bill had often found himself in the middle of many a bad fix; but this was the first time in his life he had ever had to admit that he was absolutely helpless and beaten from the start.

When the mother finally revived and discovered she was entirely deserted, she trotted out on the steps to see what could be happening that was of so much more interest than herself. When she saw Sue again fall like a thunderstone and rebound like a cannon ball, she tried to speak, but instead she again fainted dead away. His Eminence happened to discover her a little while later and beckoned to the astonished Gun Smith and Moon Hennessey to carry her into the house.

Chuck and Mushmouth and the others were so excited by the sudden disaster they couldn't think of a thing to do except to stand open-mouthed and watch for the next return trip of Sue. Back she came, only to go up again. After three or four hours of this suspense, Gun Smith had a bright idea. He found his way over to where the Colonel was pacing back and forth with clenched fists, watching in the general direction whence the bride had last flown, and said:

"Pecos, why in the name of creation don't you lasso her next time she comes flyin' down?"

"I had already thought of that," replied Pecos from the depth of an ocean of despair, "but I'm afraid the rope would cut her in two. Just think of the terrific speed she's traveling!"

"But can't you catch her in your arms or somethin'?" Gun Smith continued hopefully.

"I might, if it wasn't for that confounded

steel-spring bustle; but with that on, I'm sure it would kill us both!"

After ten or a dozen of these lightning-like bounces, Sue began to realize her novel situation. Once, as she came whizzing past, she succeeded in timing her shrieks just right, so that her Colonel heard:

"S-t-o-p m-e!"

When Pecos was entirely unable to do this Sue tried to shout other of her wishes; but her words sounded only like a siren as she flew whizzing away into the sky.

After a prolonged conference with His Eminence, my lord walked over to where the Colonel was waiting and said emphatically: "I say, Colonel, why don't you stop her?"

"Why don't you stop her yourself?" retorted Pecos.

"But, don't you know, I didn't start her!"

"And neither did I!" replied Pecos. "The fact is, I did everything possible to prevent the calamity. But you know Sue!"

"But, how shall I say, it's surely your fault. You tempted her with your bucking broncho!"

"I didn't tempt her, I'm telling you. The very name of the horse should have been a warning," Pecos replied, out of patience. "I told her it was risky to ride Widow Maker!"

"Evidently you know very little about women," my lord declared. "When you said your horse was dangerous, it was the best way to make her want to ride him. That's women for you."

Despite their argument, Slue-foot Sue kept right on bouncing up and down. During the second day Pecos began to collect his wits and throw strings of dried beef around Sue's neck to keep her from starving to death. By timing his arm perfectly with her rebound, he was able to thus lasso food around her neck nearly every time he tried.

Since there didn't seem to be any end in sight to Sue's bouncing, Gun Smith and Chuck and Moon Hennessey thought they might just as well set out for the I. X. L. Ranch. There was nothing they could do and the entire household was so completely disrupted that they were famished for something to eat. Besides, there might be a stampede on back home or something worse.

Pecos gave them his permission to go, and as soon as they were out of reach of Pinnacle Mountain they began to laugh themselves sick. Gun Smith started, remarking with straight face:

"Slue-foot Sue is sure one prize *bouncin'* bride!"

Mushmouth burst out with a verse of *The Little Black Bull Came Bawling Down the Mountain,*

Rusty Peters shouted:

"I'm a riding son of thunder of the sky,
I'm a broncho twisting wonder on the fly.
Hey, you earthlings, shut your winders,
We're a-ripping clouds to flinders —
If the blue-eyed darling kicks at you, you die."

As he finished, Chuck took it up:

"I want to be a cowboy and with the cowboys stand,
   Big spurs upon my bootheels and a lasso in my
      hand;
   My hat broad-brimmed and belted upon my head
      I'll place,
   And wear my chaparajos with elegance and grace."

"But I won't ever try to ride that sky-scrapin' Widow Maker, not after what's happened to the fair Sue," roared Gun Smith. "I love my life too well!"

So the cowboys went joyously back to their work. But back on Pinnacle Mountain Pecos was neither joyous nor happy. After three days of ceaseless watching, he was able to estimate the time it would take Sue to come to rest. During the first, there had been an hour and a half between succeeding rebounds; during the second day an hour and a quarter; and during the third day only an hour. At this rate he could plainly understand that she still had two or three more days to go before stopping.

Night and day Pecos Bill stood and watched helplessly. Each night he built a gypsy fire so that Sue might know he had not deserted her.

At last, at the end of the sixth day, Pecos succeeded in lassoing Sue and in carrying her in to her prostrate mother.

"The wretch! The wretch! The wretch!" snapped the mother.

"Colonel Bill's to blame," insisted my lord.

Slue-foot Sue was too exhausted even to cry. She lay with a wan, helpless, pathetic little smile playing silently around her mouth. After a week or two she began listlessly to talk, but in a strange, quiet, mouse-like whisper. The vivacious, romantic Sue that had been was no more.

"Wouldn't it be best, Pecos, if our marriage were never to take place after all?" she said appealingly one afternoon a week later, as Pecos sat faithfully beside her bed. "You see, I won't want ever to ride a broncho again, nor even look at a catfish. I'm entirely cured. I want to go back with Mother to a world where things are at least partly civilized."

The mother, who was listening, called my lord and His Eminence. Together they decided to release Colonel Bill from all future obligations as regards Sue.

It was another new experience for Pecos Bill when he was obliged to take a lasting farewell of Sue. There were ever so many things he wanted to say, but, like the wise man that he was, he kept them all discreetly under the middle of his tongue.

He kissed Sue's hand in silence, took up his Stetson and walked with mixed feelings out where Widow Maker was patiently waiting. He leapt astride and rode, and rode, and rode, without hesitating, across the endless country. He crossed Canada, skirted the valleys of the Platte, of the Missouri, of the Arkansas, and of the Rio Grande. In silence he rode here and there among the mountains, along the rivers, and across the rolling mesa. And everywhere he went he told his troubles to the Coyotes and the other animals, and they all told him theirs. There wasn't a thing any of them could do about anything.

"But if I can't do anything about Sue, there's plenty else I can turn my hand to," mused Pecos as he rode sadly along.

The first day he amused himself by putting horns on all the toads he met. The second day he put the thorns on the mesquite trees and cactuses. The third day he cried so hard his tears started the Butte Falls in Montana. The fourth day he used up all the prickly pear leaves in Idaho wiping his eyes, they smarted so. The fifth day he turned all the corn flowers and blue bottles into bachelor's buttons.

When Pecos Bill finally rode into the I. X. L. Ranch he was wistful and sad. Something fine had gone from his life, never to return.

"Oh, no, it isn't as you think," Pecos replied when Gun Smith asked him why he looked so down and out. "Fate never intended me to be a husband. I'm awfully glad Slue-foot Sue and the others found it out so soon. I just wasn't cut out for a husband, you might say. No, boys, that's not what's got me downhearted.

"What's really troubling me, Gun Smith, is the coming of the Nesters and the Hoemen," Pecos continued. "Everywhere, by the side of the Platte and down the Missouri and across the Arkansas and along the Rio Grande, civilization is on the march. Covered wagons and shacks are multiplying by leaps and bounds, barbed wire is being stretched, and homesteads are becoming permanent! The days of the free grass range are gone forever!"

"You don't mean it!" Gun Smith exclaimed, not sure he could believe his ears.

"The railroads and the barbed wire are turning the trick. I've just come from visiting all the range land and I know what I'm talking about. It won't be long now until we'll have got our herds together and rushed our cattle to the nearest packing house. Of course, there are a few things we'll have to do before we start the drive."

Pecos Bill concluded by singing a song he had improvised along the way:

"Oh, it's squeak! squeak! squeak!
    Hear them stretching of the wire.
The Nester brand is on the land;
    I reckon I'll retire.
'Twas good to live when all the sod
    Without no fence or fuss,
Belonged in partnership to God,
    The Government and us.
While progress toots her brassy horn
    And makes her Hoe-men buzz,
I thank the Lord I wasn't born
    No later than I wuz."

MEXICO

Why the Burro Lives with the Man [1]

❧ *A "pourquoi" beast tale from Mexico gives a logical reason for the donkey's attachment to man. Even though that attachment is not one of affection, the burro is honest in his dealings with the one whose protection from wild animals he seeks.*

Benito, the burro, lived on the mesa to hide from the mountain lion. When he first came there to live, he trembled every time he looked toward the mountains that had once been his home.

"How fortunate I am," he said, "to have found this friendly mesa! Indeed, I am fortunate to be alive. The lion ate my friends and relatives one by one. Again and again he tried to have me for his dinner." Benito closed his eyes to shut out the thought.

Now the only food Benito found on the mesa was sagebrush and cactus. Said he one day, "This is poor fare for an honest burro. How I long for some green grass and a drink of cool water! Starving is almost as bad as being chased by the lion. But what can I do? I cannot go back to the mountains, though I am sick and tired of this kind of food. Surely there must be some place where I can live in safety and still have enough to eat."

As the days passed, Benito became more and more indignant whenever he thought of the mountain lion.

Said he, "My patience with that fellow is at an end! He can't do this to me! Why should I be afraid of him? The next time

[1] From Catherine Bryan and Mabra Madden, *The Cactus Fence* (Macmillan, 1943).

we meet I will teach him a lesson." And he pranced across the mesa playing he was chasing his enemy. He ended the chase by kicking a bush, saying, "That for you, you miserable cat! Now you will know better than to cross the path of Benito, the burro."

At that very moment his sharp ears caught a sound from behind. In terror he turned, and there, sitting on a rock, smiling from ear to ear, was none other than Don Coyote!

"Good day to you, Señor Benito," said Don Coyote. "It is indeed a pleasure to see you again. How do you like your new home?"

"Must you always sneak up from behind?" said Benito. "You frightened me out of my wits. I thought it was the mountain lion. See how upset I am! Have you no respect for the feelings of others?"

"My dear, dear friend!" said Don Coyote. "I am beginning to wonder if you are glad to see me. After all, we have known each other for a long time. Yes? No?"

"I know you only too well!" answered Benito. "How did you happen to find me?"

"I figured it out," replied Don Coyote. "This morning I met the mountain lion. He said, 'Do you know where Benito is?' 'No,' I said, 'I do not.' Then I thought to myself, 'Now where could Benito be? He could be in only one of two places — either here or there. He is not here; therefore he is there. Now where is there? Why, over there on the mesa, of course.' So, just to make sure, I thought I would pay you a visit and, sure enough, here I am and there you are!"

"Did you tell the mountain lion all of that?" asked Benito angrily.

"No-o. Not exactly," answered Don Coyote, "although he did say he would make it worth my while if I found out."

"You are a villain!" cried Benito. "You would sell me to the lion. You deserve to be kicked!"

"How you misjudge me!" said Don Coyote. "I would not tell the lion your whereabouts, especially for the few bones he had to offer. While talking with him I said to myself, 'I like Benito. He is a good burro. Here is a chance to do him a favor. I will go over to the mesa and have a talk with him and, if he will listen to reason, perhaps we can arrive at a bargain.'" And Don Coyote looked at Benito out of the corner of his eye.

"He is a sly rogue," thought Benito. "I will listen to him although I know there is a skunk in the bush." To Don Coyote he said, "What do you propose to do for me?"

"My friend," said Don Coyote, "the lion wants you for his dinner. Should he learn you are on the mesa, you will again have to run for your life. It is not a pleasant thought, is it?"

"I do not like to think of it," said Benito.

"How would you like to live where you would be safe from the lion and at the same time have enough to eat and drink?"

"You interest me!" replied Benito. "Pray continue."

"At the foot of those hills," said Don Coyote, pointing to a patch of green, "there lives a man. He is the only creature the lion fears. The animals that live behind his fence are safe. They do his work and he gives them food and a place in the barnyard."

"To work for the man means changing one's way of living," said Benito.

"It is better to change one's way of living than to perish," said Don Coyote.

"A fence keeps one from going where one chooses," said Benito.

"A fence keeps one from being eaten by the mountain lion," said Don Coyote.

"Why have you taken such an interest in my safety?" asked Benito. "What do you expect to gain from it?"

"My friend," said Don Coyote, "when I think of that cruel mountain lion that eats harmless creatures, I shudder. I do not want him to eat you. I want to know you are safe and out of harm's way."

"Is that all that keeps you from being happy?" asked Benito.

"Now that you have mentioned it," said Don Coyote, "there is one more thing I would like to do. I will tell you all, and you will know that I have a tender heart. I know the man has some chickens. He keeps them in a barnyard like the other animals. They beg the man to set them free. I have heard their pleadings. It is pitiful!" And Don Coyote wiped a tear from his eye.

"I have tried to rescue them many times," he continued, "but each time the man refuses to listen. I offered him land, gold, diamonds — in fact, everything one could desire. He simply would not listen to reason. It has distressed me greatly.

"Then today I had a happy thought. I said to myself, 'Without me Benito would never have thought of going to the man for protection from the lion. In return he will surely be willing to help me help those poor, dear chickens. The peg that fastens the door of the henhouse is too high for me to reach. Tonight, after the man goes to bed, Benito will pull out the peg. I will then take the chickens, one by one, to my cave in the hills where they will once again be happy.'"

Benito looked Don Coyote straight in the eye. Said he, "I am an honest burro. If I live with the man I will give him an honest day's work for my food. I will have nothing to do with your scheme to steal his chickens."

"So that is how you repay me for trying to save your life!" cried Don Coyote. "It will serve you right if you are eaten by the lion."

"Take that!" cried Benito, giving Don Coyote a kick that sent him rolling.

Don Coyote scrambled to his feet. "You stupid burro!" he cried. "You will regret that kick! Now I will take the bones from the lion."

"Then take that, and that, and that!" cried Benito as he kicked the coyote again and again.

"You will pay dearly for those kicks, Señor Burro," cried Don Coyote. "I will help the lion eat you."

"Take that for the lion!" cried Benito, and he gave such a mighty kick that it rolled the angry coyote over the edge of the mesa. Benito watched him pick himself out of a bed of cactus.

"Hee-haw," laughed Benito as Don Coyote loped away toward the mountains.

"Well," said Benito at last, "that is that. What else is there left for me to do but go to the house of the man? It is better to live than to die." And, so saying, he departed.

From that day to this he has lived with the man. He has not always been happy, but you cannot drive him away. And when he remembers how he kicked Don Coyote he laughs and sings, "Hee-haw, hee-haw, hee-haw!"

The Princess and José [2]

Here is an ancient riddle decked out as a piece of Mexican folklore. Riddles are a common occurrence in the folk tale, and have held the storyteller's attention as prime sources of wit and the matching of wits. However, they occur most frequently in Eastern tales. The Princess and José belongs to a definite type as defined by Stith Thompson, the "out-riddling the judge," the larger, related group being stories in which the princess is won by the hero's ability to answer a riddle rather than to propose one. The especial charm of this story lies in the incident which describes the princess bringing her husband his lunch, in full panoply of royal horse and carriage, as he works in the field with his peon brothers. The story has its origin in Spanish lore, but it wears a Mexican serape.

José was a good boy and very polite. He liked to learn about other places. So one day he decided to go and see the world.

He was walking along the road when he was arrested. Some soldiers arrested him.

"Why do you arrest me?" said José. "I haven't done anything wrong."

"You look like a thief," they said. "Besides, we need prisoners to build the roads."

"I am not a thief," José said, "and I don't see why I should work on the roads if I don't want to, especially if I am not paid for it."

"Prisoners aren't paid." That was what the soldiers told him.

José stood in the middle of the road and the soldiers were all around him, and he

[2] From Anita Brenner, *The Boy Who Could Do Anything* (William R. Scott, 1942).

made a speech. They took their guns off their shoulders and listened. He said, "It is not fair to make people work and not pay for it. I will not do it."

"If you won't work, then you go to jail," said the soldiers. And there he was. In jail. "And if you don't work, you don't eat," they said, so there he was in jail, and hungry.

Now the king of this place had a daughter. She was the princess. She was very beautiful and also very kind. When she heard about José she took a basket and packed it full of things to eat, enough for breakfast and dinner and supper. She put in eggs and bread and cake and milk and a whole roast chicken, and pork and beans and chili, of course, and a pineapple and some chocolate candy. She covered it up with a fine white napkin and she got into her golden coach and went to the jail.

There were many prisoners in the jail. They were all going to be shot, one by one. This was because the king had nothing to do. He loved games and riddles but they were all old ones and he was tired of them, so he was peevish. Every time he was peevish he always had somebody shot. That is the way kings are.

Every morning the princess came to the jail with a basket on her arm. It had José's food in it. The soldiers let her in. They winked and smiled and said, "The princess must be in love with José."

"But it is very sad, they cannot marry because José has to be shot," one soldier said.

"Yes, he will be the very first one because he wouldn't work on the roads," said another soldier.

"The next time the king feels like shooting some one, it will be José's turn. Too bad."

But the princess said to José, "I am looking for a way to save you."

One morning the king woke up feeling very cross. He had nothing to do and so he was cross. He decided that José would be shot that day. The princess saw how cross he was so she ran to José and whispered something, and then she ran out again to where the soldiers were all lined up ready to shoot him.

Everybody was watching. Suddenly the princess spread out a sheet that was nine feet long. Four soldiers had to hold it up. It had something written on it in big red letters. It said, "Father, if he tells you a riddle that you can't guess, will you spare his life?"

"Yes," said the king, "certainly I will. Of course. Naturally." He called to José, "If you tell me a riddle that I can't guess, I will spare your life."

There was José in the middle of all the soldiers. He looked at the king, then he looked at the princess, then he looked wise. "What is it that goes first on four legs, then on two legs, and then on three legs?" he asked.

The king thought. He thought and thought. He scratched his head until his crown fell off and then he thought some more, but he couldn't guess. "All right," said the king, "your life is saved. But what is the answer?"

"Why, it's very simple. It is yourself. When you were a baby you crawled on all fours. Now you are a man and you walk on two legs. When you grow old, you will have a cane. That will be three. See? First four, then two, then three."

The king was surprised. It was so simple. "José must be pretty clever to think of something like that," he said. "It is all right if he wants to marry the princess." So they

married. They had a big party and they all ate and sang and danced and José opened the jail and let all the other prisoners out.

So they lived in the palace happily but José wanted to go and see things and, besides, he wanted to visit his family. He dressed himself in his old clothes, the poor man's clothes he was wearing when the soldiers arrested him, and he went home.

In the morning, his father and brothers went out to work in the fields. José went with them. At noon his mother brought a basket with his father's dinner in it, and his brothers' wives brought baskets for them.

"Won't you have some dinner?" said José's father and brothers, for José had no basket.

"Oh, no thank you. I'll have my dinner later," said José carelessly.

At that moment they saw a golden coach coming along the road. Then came two other coaches full of soldiers, and some more soldiers on horses. It was the princess in her golden coach, sitting inside with her basket and the soldiers were the escort, because when kings and princesses go any place it is like a parade.

José's family was frightened when they saw the soldiers. They wondered if anybody was going to be arrested, but José said carelessly, "Oh, that's nothing. It's just my wife bringing my dinner."

SOUTH AMERICA

The Tale of the Lazy People[1]

❧ Charles Finger, the author of Tales from Silver Lands, collected these stories from all parts of South America. This one comes from

[1] From Charles J. Finger, Tales From Silver Lands (Doubleday, 1924).

Colombia. From it we learn not only why there are so many monkeys but also why they throw nuts and branches at people passing through the forest. Tales from Silver Lands won the Newbery award in 1925.

Long, long ago there were no monkeys, and the trees were so full of fruit, and the vines of grapes, that people became lazy, and at last did little but eat and sleep, being too idle to carry away the rinds and skins of the fruit that they lived on, and certainly too lazy to clean their thatched houses.

It was very pleasant at first, but soon not so pleasant, for winged things that bit and stung came in thousands to feed on the things thrown aside, and they too grew lazy, finding so much to eat ready at hand, and when people tried to brush them away there was a loud and angry buzz and much irritated stinging, so that soon every one was wonder-struck, not knowing exactly what to do. For a time it seemed easier to move the little village to a new spot and to build new houses, for the dwellings were light affairs and in a day or less a good house could be built. But then they lived by a lake from which the water for drinking was taken, and as it was but a little body of water, it was not long before the people had built right round the still pool and so were back again at the starting place. As for the stinging flies, they were soon worse than the mosquitoes, while a great wasp with pink head and legs and bands of black and gold on its body, though very pretty to see, was worst of all. So it was no easy matter to know what to do, and there was much talk and much argument, and all that the people agreed on was that something had to be done, and that, very soon.

One day there came to the village a queer and rather faded kind of man, ragged and tattered and torn as though he had scrambled for miles through the thorn-bush forest. He had rough yellow hair, and queer wrinkles at the corners of his eyes which made him look as if he were smiling. It was late in the afternoon when he came and the people were taking their rest after the noon meal, so no one took much notice of him although he went here and there, looking at things, and so walked round the lake. But the curiosity of everyone was excited when he was seen to make a basket, which he did quickly, and then commence to gather up the fruit skins and rinds in one place. Now and then some one or other raised himself in his hammock, with a mind to talk to him, but it seemed almost too much trouble, and when

some great blue-winged butterfly fluttered past or some golden-throated humming-bird flashed in the sunlight, their eyes wandered away from the old man and they forgot him again. So the sunlight died and the forest was a velvet blackness and everyone slept, though the old man still worked on, and the next morning when the people awoke he was still working diligently, though he had but a small place cleared after all.

The very thought that any one would work all night made the head man shiver with a kind of excitement, yet he was very curious to know why the stranger went to so much trouble, seeing that he neither lived there nor was of the lake men. At the same time it made his spirit droop to think that, if the place was to be cleared up, he and everyone else had a mountain of work in sight. So Tera, the head man, called to Cuco, who was his servant, telling him to bring the stranger to him, and Cuco, who was very respectful, said that he would attend to it. Then Cuco did his part by calling Yana and delivering the message to him. And Yana in turn told his servant, Mata, who told his servant, Pera, who told his servant, Racas, who told a boy, so that at last the message reached the old man. Then back went the old man, handed by the boy to Racas, by Racas to Pera, by Pera to Mata, by Mata to Yana, and by Yana to Cuco, so that at last he stood before Tera, the head man, and the others, being curious to know what was afoot, gathered about.

"What is your name, from where do you come, and what do you want?" asked Tera, putting his three questions at once, to save trouble. Then the head man looked at those about him with a little frown, as much as to say, "Note how wisely I act," and each man who had heard, seeing that the head man looked his way, nodded at his neighbor, as though calling attention to the wisdom of the head man, so all went very well. But the little old man stood there very simply, making no fuss at all and quite unimpressed with the greatness of the great man.

"I want to work," he answered. "I want to be told what you want done and to see that it is done."

To be sure, the language that he spoke was

one new to those who listened, but somehow they seemed to understand. But the thing that he said they found truly astonishing and could hardly believe their ears. But the head man, though as astonished as any one there, quickly regained his composure and asked this question:

"What is your trade?"

"I have no trade," said the old man. "But I get things done."

"What kind of things?"

"All kinds of things."

"Do you mean big things, like house-building and all that?" asked the head man.

"Yes. And little things too, which are really big things when you come to consider," said the old man, but that seemed an odd if not a silly thing to say, the head man thought.

"Little things left undone soon become big things," explained the old man, and waved his hand in the direction of a heap of fruit skins and husks near by.

"Yes. Yes. But you must not preach to us, you know," said Tera a little testily. "Tell me the names of the trades you have."

So the little old man began to tell, naming big things and very little things, things important and things not important at all, and having finished, asked very politely whether any one there had anything to be done. As for pay he said that he wanted none at all and would take none, and he said that because some of those gathered about him began offering him things.

For instance, Pera said: "If you work for me, I will let you have one fish out of every ten that you catch, for I am a fisherman." And Racas pushed him aside, saying: "But I will do better, for I am supposed to be fruit gatherer and will give you two things for every ten you gather." And so it went, each bidding higher than his neighbor, until it came to the turn of the man whose duty it was to gather the rinds and fruit skins. He said, "I will let you have, not one out of ten, nor two out of ten, nor five out of ten that you gather, but ten out of ten, if you will work for me." At that the old man said quite positively that he would take no pay at all.

No more was said then and the little old man turned away without as much as bowing to the head man, seeing which the head man waved his hand and said: "You may go, and so that you will lose no time, you need not bow to me." And all the rest gathered there said very hastily: "Nor need you bow to me, either."

The old man took small notice of any one, but went away singing, for he had a gay, light-hearted disposition, and having reached the place he had cleared, he took flat pieces of wood and began cutting out figures like little men, and each figure had a kind of handle that looked like a long tail. Nor did he cease whittling until he had made at least twenty wooden figures for each man in the village. Being finished he stood up to stretch his legs and straighten his back, and when the people asked him what the little figures were for, he shrugged his shoulders but spoke never a word. Then he lifted the figures that he had made, one by one, and set them upright in the sand until there was a long row of them, and took his place in front of them, like a general before his army. It was beautiful to look at, for one figure was as like another as one pin is like another, and for a moment even the old man stood admiring the line. After a moment he waved his hand in a peculiar way, spoke some magic word, and waved his hand again, at which each of the figures came to life and nodded its head, seeing which all the people laughed and clapped their hands. The ragged man bade them make no noise, but watch.

"Since you do not like to work," he said, "I have made twenty figures for each of you, and they will work for you without pay, doing what you require them to do; only observe this, you must not give any figure more than one particular job. And now let each man or woman clap his hands three times, then call out the name of the thing to be done."

When he had said this, the figures started running, twenty gathering in a circle about each man there, bowing from the hips and straightening themselves again, so that their tails of wood went up and down like pump-handles.

"Now see," said the ragged man, "you have things to work for you, and as I call out, the figures will stand forth, each ready to do his task." And he began calling, thus:

"Armadillo hunters, stand forth!" and a hundred and more active figures ran together like soldiers.

So he named others in order as:

Bread-makers.

Cassava gatherers.

Despolvadores, who would gather up dust.

Esquiladors, who would shear the goats.

Farsante men, whose work was to amuse tired men.

Guardas, to keep order about the place.

Horneros, or bakers.

Industriosos, who were to do odd jobs everywhere.

Jumentos, whose work it was to carry burdens.

Labradores, to do heavy work and clear away garbage.

Moledores, to grind the corn.

Narradores, who told stories, related gossip and so.

Olleros, or pot makers.

Pocilga figures, to attend to the pigs.

Queseros, to make cheese from goat's milk.

Rumbosos, or proud-looking things to walk in parades.

Servidores, or food carriers.

Trotadores, to run errands.

Vaqueros, to attend to the cows.

So everyone was well pleased and each one had his twenty figures to do all that needed to be done, and all that day there was a great scraping and cleaning and carrying and currying and hurrying and scurrying. Silently the little figures worked, never stopping, never tiring, never getting in one another's way, and all that the living people had to do was to rest and watch the men of wood, and keep their brains free for higher things. For it must be remembered that before the old man came there with his wonderful gift, the people had complained there was so much to be done that they had no time to write poems or to make songs or to create music, and that with the daily tasks abolished their brains would be more active.

Not two days had passed before the children of the place complained that they did not have a chance and that they had so much to do, what with hunting for things lost, looking after their small brothers and sisters, keeping things in order, trying to remember things they were told, cleaning things, and a dozen other tasks, that they really had no time to play, much less to study. So they went in a body to the old man and asked him to give each child twenty figures to do odd things. There was a great deal of fire and expression in his eyes when he made answer that if the children really needed help he would lose no time in providing it. But the young people were quite positive that they were overworked, and the long and short of it was that the old man whittled out many, many more figures, and in another twenty-four hours each and every boy and girl had his own

Abaniquero, or fan maker, so that none had to pluck a palm leaf.

Baliquero figure, to carry letters and messages.

Cabrero, to look after the goats.

Desalumbrado, to hunt for things in the dark.

Enseñador, or private teacher, who was never to scold.

Florista, to save them the trouble of gathering flowers.

Guasón figure, to amuse them.

Hojaldarista, whose work it was to make cakes.

Juego figure, to arrange games.

Keeper of things.

Lector, to read and tell stories.

Mimo, to act as clown.

Niñera, to look after younger children.

Obediencia figure, to make others obey.

Postor, to buy things for them.

Quitar figures, to take things away when children tired.

Recordación figures, or rememberers.

Solfeadors, to sing to them.

Tortada men, to make pies.

Volantes, as servants.

So things seemed to be going very well, and before a month had passed in all that place there was not a thing out of order, soiled, broken, bent, lost, misplaced, undone, unclean, or disorderly. Neither man nor woman nor child had to worry; dinners were always prepared, fruits gathered, beds made, houses in perfect order, and all was spick and span. All that the grown-up people had to do was to look on, and no one was proud of the order in his house because every other house in the place was as orderly. As for the children, they had nothing at all to do but to eat, drink, rest, and sleep. Then, presently, more figures were called for as this one or that wanted a larger house, a finer garden, or grander clothes.

But as the wooden figures became more numerous and as no figure could do more than one task, the ragged man had to make figures for the figures and servants for the servants, for as things went on, there had to be more fruit gatherers, more water carriers, more scavengers, more cooks, because the figures had to eat and drink. Thus it came to pass that before long, instead of there being twenty figures for each man, there were sixty or seventy, with new ones coming from the old man's knife every day. Soon the lively manikins were everywhere, inside houses as well as outside, thick as flies in summer and certainly a great deal more persistent, for there could be no closing of doors against the manikins. Indeed, had anything like that been attempted there would have been a great cry for special door-openers. So, many houses were quite cluttered with wooden men, those who were on duty rushing about until it made the head swim to look at them, and those who were resting or sleeping, for soon they learned to rest and to sleep, lying about the floors, piled up in corners, or hanging to rafters by their tails. All that increase in help had made for the production of a thousand or more guardas, whose task it was to keep order, and they were everywhere, alert and watchful and officious, and the real people had to step about very gingerly sometimes, to avoid treading on them and annoying them.

At last there came a day when the people began to grow a little tired of doing nothing, and they told one another that a little help was a very good thing, but help in excess, too much of a good thing altogether. So there was a meeting and much talk and the manikin narrators, whose duty it was to carry gossip and the news, were very busy, rushing from here to there with their scraps of information.

"It is very clear that something must be done," said Tera, the head man.

"But everything *is* being done," answered the little old man. "If *everything* is done, something *must* be done."

"I did not mean that," said Tera, who seemed a little testy. "I meant to say that these wooden men must be kept in their places."

"But they *are* in their places," replied the old man. "Their place is everywhere because they do everything, so they are in their places."

"You see, the days are so very long, so very dull," said the man who wished to have time that he might become a poet. "At the shut of day we are not weary."

"We do not want to be petted," said another.

"The trouble is," sighed a fat man, "you can't be happy when everything is done for you."

"And we don't want to be nobodies," shouted another.

Another said very mournfully: "It seems to me that when these wooden things do things with our things, then the things that they do and make and care for are not our things."

"Too many 'things' in that speech," said the fat man.

"Well, there are too many things," answered the other. "Look at me. I used to be gardener and now I'm nothing. When my garden is dug and planted and tended and watered and the very flowers plucked by these wooden things, and when other wooden things pick up the leaves and pull the weeds and do everything, then my garden does not seem to be mine." He added after awhile: "I hope you know what I mean, because it is not very clear to me, yet it is so. I remember — "

At that the little old man put up his hand and said: "But that is against the contract. You must not try to remember, really you must not, because there are manikins to do all the remembering, if you please."

"Well, but I think — " began the man, when he was again interrupted.

"Please do not think," said the little old man. "We have things to do the thinking, if you please." He thought for a moment, his bent forefinger on his lips, then he said: "I'll see what can be done. It is clear that you are not satisfied, although you have everything that you asked for and certainly all the time that you want."

"Let us do something," murmured Tera.

"I'm afraid there is nothing that you can do," said the little old man, "because, as you see, everything is done, and when everything is done it is quite clear that something cannot be left to be done. The only thing that is clear is that there is nothing to be done."

At that the meeting broke up and each went to his own hammock to think things over, and soon the general cry was: "We must have elbow room." And hearing that, the little old man went to work and whittled more figures of wood, a whole army of them, ten for each living man, woman, and child, and in voices that creaked like wooden machinery they marched hither and thither, crying: "Elbow room. Elbow room!"

Soon there was confusion. It was manikin against manikin for a time, the Elbow-roomers thrusting and pushing the other working manikins, some going about their work with frantic haste, others interfering with them, clutching at them and at the things they carried, a tangled knot of them sometimes staggering, to go down with a crash. Soon in every house was a jangling tumult, manikins and men running about in houses and dashing out into the open spaces outside; the noise of slamming doors and breaking pots; the clamor of animals. Above all could be heard everywhere cries of "We want elbow room! We want elbow room!" Soon men were running away from the houses with those strange swift manikins hanging to them, sometimes beating them, while other manikins threw things out of the doors and through windows, food and household things. And excited children fled too, while their manikins ran at their sides, some chattering, some acting the clown as was their duty, some telling stories as they ran, while other strange little figures of wood ran bearing heavy burdens. It was all a dreadful mix-up with no one knowing what to do, no one knowing where to go, and everywhere the manikins who were guardas, or order keepers, ran about, tripping people and manikins alike in the effort to stop the rush. But when the day was near its end there were no people in the houses and the hammocks swung idly, for all the men and women and children, even the white-haired grandfathers and grandmothers, had fled to the further side of the lake, where they could have elbow room, leaving the houses and all that was in them to the manikins.

The next day, the people plucked their fruit for themselves and it seemed as though fruit was never sweeter. The water that they carried from the lake tasted better and cooler than water had for many a long day, and when night came they were happily tired and slept well, without any manikin to swing their hammocks and sing to them. And in the morning they woke early to discover the pink and gold of the sunrise most wonderful to see, and there was music in the sound of the wind among the grasses. So as the day passed they were both amazed and astonished at the wonderful and beautiful things that they had almost forgotten, the sight of butterflies fluttering from flower to flower, the shadows chasing across the hills, the richness of the green earth and the blueness of the sky, the gold of sunlight on the leaves, the rippling water and the bending trees; indeed the memory of the manikin days was like a fearful nightmare. Very light-hearted then they grew and the world was full of the music of their laughter and song, and briskly they worked, enjoying it all, building new houses and making things to put in them.

Meanwhile in the village things had gone queerly. For one thing the Elbow-room-ers kept up their crowding and pushing, so that the manikins trying to work at their old tasks (and there were many who went on just as before) were sadly hindered. There were other figures of wood with nothing to do, since the people they served were gone, and these fell to quarreling among themselves and grew mischievous. For instance, the pot makers and the pot cleaners fell out, and the pot cleaners started to break the pots so that the pot makers would have more work to do. That meant that the clay gatherers and the clay diggers had to work harder;

then because they worked harder, though to be sure all their work meant nothing and was little more than idle bustle, they grew hungrier and wanted more to eat. Because of all that the fruit gatherers had more to do and the water carriers had to work harder and the cassava bread makers had to bake as they had never baked before. That brought the fire builders into it, and of course the wood gatherers also, for they too had to work harder and to eat more, so still more work came on the food bringers. And all the time the Elbow-room-ers rushed about, always in groups of ten, driving and commanding, rushing on workers and sweeping them aside. So everywhere were little figures hurrying one after the other, going to and fro, busy about nothing, quarreling about nothing, fighting about nothing.

The trouble came when the Elbow-room-ers interfered with the dogs and the cats, the goats and the hens, pushing and hustling them. For the animals, disliking all disorder and clatter, fell upon the manikins, workers and idlers alike. Seeing that, the household utensils took a hand and the very pots and kettles ran or rolled or fell, spilling hot water over the wooden things with pump-handle tails. The very embers from the fires leaped into the fray. All the while from the metates in which the corn had been ground came a low growling, and the growling formed itself into words:

> Day by day you tortured us —
> Grind, grind, grind.

> Holi! Holi!
> Huqui! Huqui!
> Grind, grind, grind.

> Bring to us the torturers —
> Grind, grind, grind.

> Let them feel our power now —
> Grind! *Grind!* GRIND!

So the metates turned and turned, going round and round without hands, and presently an Elbow-room-er that was struggling with a corn-grinder stumbled, and both fell between the grinding stones and in a moment were crushed to powder. In a flash house utensils and animals learned the new trick, and in every house manikins were pushed into the grinding stones. Then sparks began to fly and roofs to catch on fire and manikins bolted here and there in confusion, sometimes jamming in doorways, there were so many and all in such disorder. Then came dazzling, flickering lightning and a great rain, so that for very safety the manikins fled to the forest and climbed the trees. And there they have lived ever since, for they grew hair and became monkeys. But the remembrance of all that passed stayed with them, and in their hearts to this very day is no love for man, and for that very reason when a Christian passes through a forest he must look well to himself, lest the manikins in revenge try to hurt him by casting nuts and branches at his head.

THE WEST INDIES

From Tiger to Anansi [1]

The origin of this story lies in Africa. It was brought to the West Indies by slaves, no doubt, who remembered this tale and others from their tribal fires. It became adapted to the new locale, reflecting the modes, manners, customs, climate, and landscape of the new place. Some of the Anansi stories parallel the Uncle Remus stories of the South in our own country. They come from the same source.

Anansi is a fascinating character, sometimes a man, sometimes a spider. In the West Indies, he is called "ceiling Thomas," because when he is a spider, the walls are his walking ground.

Once upon a time and a long long time ago the Tiger was king of the forest.

At evening when all the animals sat together in a circle and talked and laughed together, Snake would ask,

"Who is the strongest of us all?"

"Tiger is strongest," cried the dog. "When Tiger whispers the trees listen. When Tiger is angry and cries out, the trees tremble."

"And who is the weakest of all?" asked Snake.

"Anansi," shouted dog, and they all laughed together. "Anansi the spider is weakest of all. When he whispers no one listens. When he shouts everyone laughs."

Now one day the weakest and strongest came face to face, Anansi and Tiger. They met in a clearing of the forest. The frogs hiding under the cool leaves saw them. The bright green parrots in the branches heard them.

When they met, Anansi bowed so low that his forehead touched the ground. Tiger did not greet him. Tiger just looked at Anansi.

"Good morning, Tiger," cried Anansi. "I have a favor to ask."

"And what is it, Anansi?" said Tiger.

"Tiger, we all know that you are strongest of us all. This is why we give your name to many things. We have Tiger lilies, and Tiger stories and Tiger moths and Tiger this and Tiger that. Everyone knows that I am weakest of all. This is why nothing bears my name. Tiger, let something be called after the weakest one so that men may know my name too."

"Well," said Tiger, without so much as a glance toward Anansi, "what would you like to bear your name?"

"The stories," cried Anansi. "The stories that we tell in the forest at evening time when the sun goes down, the stories about Br'er Snake and Br'er Tacumah, Br'er Cow and Br'er Bird and all of us."

Now Tiger liked these stories and he meant to keep them as Tiger stories. He thought to himself, How stupid, how weak this Anansi is. I will play a trick on him so that all the animals will laugh at him. Tiger moved his tail slowly from side to side and said, "Very good, Anansi, very good. I will let the stories be named after you, if you do what I ask."

"Tiger, I will do what you ask."

"Yes, I am sure you will, I am sure you will," said Tiger, moving his tail slowly from side to side. "It is a little thing that I ask. Bring me Mr. Snake alive. Do you know Snake who lives down by the river, Mr. Anansi? Bring him to me alive and you can have the stories."

[1] From Philip M. Sherlock, *Anansi, the Spider Man: Jamaican Folk Tales.* Copyright 1954 by Philip Sherlock. Reprinted by permission of the publishers, Thomas Y. Crowell Company, New York.

Tiger stopped speaking. He did not move his tail. He looked at Anansi and waited for him to speak. All the animals in the forest waited. Mr. Frog beneath the cool leaves, Mr. Parrot up in the tree, all watched Anansi. They were all ready to laugh at him.

"Tiger, I will do what you ask," said Anansi. At these words a great wave of laughter burst from the forest. The frogs and parrots laughed. Tiger laughed loudest of all, for how could feeble Anansi catch Snake alive?

Anansi went away. He heard the forest laughing at him from every side.

That was on Monday morning. Anansi sat before his house and thought of plan after plan. At last he hit upon one that could not fail. He would build a Calaban.

On Tuesday morning Anansi built a Calaban. He took a strong vine and made a noose. He hid the vine in the grass. Inside the noose he set some of the berries that Snake loved best. Then he waited. Soon Snake came up the path. He saw the berries and went toward them. He lay across the vine and ate the berries. Anansi pulled at the vine to tighten the noose, but Snake's body was too heavy. Anansi saw that the Calaban had failed.

Wednesday came. Anansi made a deep hole in the ground. He made the sides slippery with grease. In the bottom he put some of the bananas that Snake loved. Then he hid in the bush beside the road and waited.

Snake came crawling down the path toward the river. He was hungry and thirsty. He saw the bananas at the bottom of the hole. He saw that the sides of the hole were slippery. First he wrapped his tail tightly around the trunk of a tree, then he reached down into the hole and ate the bananas. When he was finished he pulled himself up by his tail and crawled away. Anansi had lost his bananas and he had lost Snake, too.

Thursday morning came. Anansi made a Fly Up. Inside the trap he put an egg. Snake came down the path. He was happy this morning, so happy that he lifted his head and a third of his long body from the ground. He just lowered his head, took up the egg in his mouth, and never even touched the trap. The Fly Up could not catch Snake.

What was Anansi to do? Friday morning came. He sat and thought all day. It was no use.

Now it was Saturday morning. This was the last day. Anansi went for a walk down by the river. He passed by the hole where Snake lived. There was Snake, his body hidden in the hole, his head resting on the ground at the entrance to the hole. It was early morning. Snake was watching the sun rise above the mountains.

"Good morning, Anansi," said Snake.

"Good morning, Snake," said Anansi.

"Anansi, I am very angry with you. You have been trying to catch me all week. You set a Fly Up to catch me. The day before you made a Slippery Hole for me. The day before that you made a Calaban. I have a good mind to kill you, Anansi."

"Ah, you are too clever, Snake," said Anansi. "You are much too clever. Yes, what you say is so. I tried to catch you, but I failed. Now I can never prove that you are the longest animal in the world, longer even than the bamboo tree."

"Of course I am the longest of all animals," cried Snake. "I am much longer than the bamboo tree."

"What, longer than that bamboo tree across there?" asked Anansi.

"Of course I am," said Snake. "Look and see." Snake came out of the hole and stretched himself out at full length.

"Yes, you are very, very long," said Anansi, "but the bamboo tree is very long, too. Now that I look at you and at the bamboo tree I must say that the bamboo tree seems longer. But it's hard to say because it is farther away."

"Well, bring it nearer," cried Snake. "Cut it down and put it beside me. You will soon see that I am much longer."

Anansi ran to the bamboo tree and cut it down. He placed it on the ground and cut off all its branches. Bush, bush, bush, bush! There it was, long and straight as a flagstaff.

"Now put it beside me," said Snake.

Anansi put the long bamboo tree down on the ground beside Snake. Then he said:

"Snake, when I go up to see where your

head is, you will crawl up. When I go down to see where your tail is, you will crawl down. In that way you will always seem to be longer than the bamboo tree, which really is longer than you are."

"Tie my tail, then!" said Snake. "Tie my tail! I know that I am longer than the bamboo, whatever you say."

Anansi tied Snake's tail to the end of the bamboo. Then he ran up to the other end.

"Stretch, Snake, stretch, and we will see who is longer."

A crowd of animals were gathering round. Here was something better than a race. "Stretch, Snake, stretch," they called.

Snake stretched as hard as he could. Anansi tied him around his middle so that he should not slip back. Now one more try. Snake knew that if he stretched hard enough he would prove to be longer than the bamboo.

Anansi ran up to him. "Rest yourself for a little, Snake, and then stretch again. If you can stretch another six inches you will be longer than the bamboo. Try your hardest. Stretch so that you even have to shut your eyes. Ready?"

"Yes," said Snake. Then Snake made a mighty effort. He stretched so hard that he had to squeeze his eyes shut. "Hooray!" cried the animals. "You are winning, Snake. Just two inches more."

And at that moment Anansi tied Snake's head to the bamboo. There he was. At last he had caught Snake, all by himself.

The animals fell silent. Yes, there Snake was, all tied up, ready to be taken to Tiger. And feeble Anansi had done this. They could laugh at him no more.

And never again did Tiger dare to call these stories by his name. They were Anansi stories forever after, from that day to this.

ETHIOPIA

The Goat Well[1]

❧ One of the traits of Harold Courlander as storyteller is the scientific spirit which informs his versions. He is an anthropologist turned storyteller. The texts run true to folklore form, without extraneous material; all the original strength of structure and of directness stands out clearly. We are indebted to him for making available the folk tales of little-known regions.

"The folklore of Ethiopia," says Mr. Courlander, "represents a cross current of influences of the Middle East, Africa, and the West. Present-day semantic cultures — Christian and

Moslem — overlie the older traditions. The country has endured invasions of Greeks, Portuguese, and other Europeans, and these have left a residue of influence on local customs of the Ethiopians." The result is a rich and unique heritage, a source of inspiration for the storyteller.

A man named Woharia was once traveling across the plateau when he came to an abandoned house. He was tired and hungry, so he rested in the house and ate some of his bread, called injera. When he was about to leave he heard the baa-ing of a goat. He looked in all directions, but he saw nothing except the dry brown landscape. He heard the goat again, and finally he went to the

[1] From Harold Courlander and Wolf Leslau, *The Fire on the Mountain and Other Ethiopian Stories* (Holt, 1950).

old well and looked down into it. There, standing on the dry bottom, was the animal, which had somehow fallen in while searching for water to drink.

"What luck!" Woharia said. He climbed down and tied a rope around the goat, and then he came up and began to pull her out of the well.

Just at this moment a Cunama trader, with three camels loaded with sacks of grain, approached him. He greeted Woharia and asked if he might have water there for his thirsty camels.

"Naturally, if there were water here you would be welcome to it," Woharia said. "But unfortunately this is only a goat well."

"What is a goat well?" the Cunama asked.

"What do you think? It's a well that produces goats," Woharia said, and he pulled on his rope again until he got the goat to the top.

"This is really extraordinary!" the Cunama said. "I've never before heard of a goat well!"

"Why, I suppose you're right," Woharia said. "They aren't very common."

"How does it work?" the Cunama trader asked.

"Oh, it's simple enough," Woharia said. "Every night you throw a pair of goat's horns into the well, and in the morning you find a goat. Then all you have to do is draw her out."

"Unbelievable!" the Cunama said. "Man, how I'd like to own such a well!"

"So would everyone else," Woharia said, untying the goat and letting her run loose. "But few people can afford to buy such an unusual thing."

"Well, I'll tell you," the Cunama said, thinking very hard. "I'm not a rich man, but I'll pay you six bags of durra grain for it."

Woharia laughed.

"That wouldn't pay for many goats," he said.

"I'll give you twelve bags of durra, all that my camels are carrying!" the Cunama said anxiously.

Woharia smiled and shook his head.

"Seven goats a week," he said as though he were talking to himself. "Thirty goats

a month. Three hundred sixty-five goats a year . . ."

But the Cunama had set his heart on owning the well.

"Look at my young sleek camels! I have just bought them in Keren! Where will you ever find better camels than these? I'll give you my twelve bags of grain and my three camels also. I'd give you more, but I own nothing else in the whole world, I swear it to you!"

Woharia thought silently for a moment.

"Since you want it so much, I'll sell it to you," he said finally.

The Cunama leaped down from his camel and embraced Woharia.

"For this goodness may you live long!" he said. "May Allah bring you many good things to give you joy!"

"Ah," Woharia said, looking at the camels, "he has already done so."

He took the three camels loaded with grain, his goat, and his few other possessions, and prepared to leave.

"Before you go, tell me your name?" the Cunama asked.

"People call me Where-I-Shall-Dance," Woharia replied. And then he went away to the south, leaving the Cunama with the well.

The Cunama was very impatient to begin getting goats from the well. When evening came, he dropped two goat's horns into it and lay down in the house to sleep. The next morning, when it was barely light, he rushed out again to draw up his first goat, but when he peered into the well, he saw nothing except the old horns he had thrown in.

He became very anxious.

"There must be some mistake!" he said to himself.

That evening he threw down two more horns, and again in the morning he rushed out to get his first goat, but once more he saw only the old goat's horns there. This time he was very worried. He scoured the country to find old goat's horns, and he threw armful after armful into the well. And all night long he sat by the well shouting into it:

"Goats, are you there? Goats, are you there?"

But nothing at all happened. When morning came at last the Cunama was angry and unhappy. He realized that he had been duped by his own anxiousness to get the well. There was nothing left to do but to go out and find the man who had taken his camels and his precious grain.

The trader traveled southward, as Woharia had done. At last, when night had fallen, he came to a village. When he arrived in the village square, where many people were gathered, he went up to them and asked:

"Do you know Where-I-Shall-Dance?"

"Why, it doesn't matter, dance anywhere you like," the people answered. "Dance right here if you wish!" And they began to sing and make music for him.

"No, no, you don't understand," he said. "What I want to know is, do you know Where-I-Shall-Dance?"

"Yes, dance here!" they said again.

The Cunama was very angry because he thought the people were making fun of him, so he went out of the village and continued his journey southward, stopping only to sleep at the edge of the road.

The next day, he came to another village, and he went to the market place and said in a loud voice:

"Does anybody know Where-I-Shall-Dance?"

The people gathered around him instantly and shouted:

"Dance here! Dance here!"

They clapped their hands and a drummer came and beat his drum, and everyone waited for the Cunama to dance.

He turned and fled from the village, believing that the people were ridiculing him. Again, he came to a village, and again he asked:

"Do you know Where-I-Shall-Dance?"

And once more the people began clapping their hands and answered:

"Yes, dance here!"

The same thing happened in every village

the man entered. He began to feel very hopeless, and sometimes thought he might even be losing his mind. He began to be afraid to ask his question. Finally, one day, he came to the village of the chief of the district. When he asked his question here and the people gave him the usual answer, the news was carried to the chief, who immediately sent for him.

"Now, what sort of nonsense is this?" the chief asked. "You ask the people where you should dance and then you refuse to dance."

The unhappy man told how he had bought the dry well in exchange for his three young camels and his grain. The chief listened sympathetically. He remembered that a man named Woharia had recently settled in a nearby village, and that he had come with three camels and twelve bags of grain.

"Sit down and rest," the chief said. "I will handle this matter now."

He sent a messenger to Woharia, and when the messenger found him he said, as he had been instructed:

"There is a man waiting to see you at the house of the chief. His name is What-I-Shall-Do. The chief wishes you to come at once."

Woharia went immediately to the house of the chief, and the servants let him in.

"What can I do for you?" the chief asked.

"Why, do you know What-I-Shall-Do?" Woharia asked.

"Yes, I know what you shall do," the chief said. "You shall give back the Cunama trader his three camels and his twelve bags of grain."

Woharia was crestfallen and ashamed. He gave the Cunama back the camels and the grain. The Cunama took them and went out. As he passed through the market place the people shouted:

"Dance here! Dance here!"

And the trader was so happy that this time he danced in the market place.

BIBLIOGRAPHY

General Collections

Arbuthnot, May Hill, comp. *Time for Fairy Tales, Old and New;* illus. by John Averill and others. Scott, Foresman, 1952.

A representative collection of folk tales, myths, epics, fables, and modern fanciful tales for children.

Association for Childhood Education. Literature Committee. *Told Under the Green Umbrella; Old Stories for New Children;* illus. by Grace Gilkison. Macmillan, 1930.

A discriminating choice of twenty-six favorite stories mostly from folklore.

Baker, Augusta, ed. *The Talking Tree; Fairy Tales from 15 Lands;* illus. by Johannes Troyer. J. B. Lippincott, 1955.

A storyteller's selection of fairy tales from folk tale collections now out of print.

De la Mare, Walter, ed. *Animal Stories.* Charles Scribner's Sons, 1940.

The editor has selected, and in some cases, entirely rewritten these stories taken mostly from folklore. In the preface he traces the development of the animal folk tale.

Dobbs, Rose, ed. *Once Upon a Time; Twenty Cheerful Tales to Read and Tell;* illus. by Flavia Gág. Random House, 1950. (K–Grade 2)

Familiar folk fables and stories of nature, animals, and people and a few tales just for fun.

Hutchinson, Veronica, comp. *Chimney Corner Stories; Tales for Little Children;* collected and retold; illus. by Lois Lenski. G. P. Putnam's Sons, 1925. (Grades 3–5)

The aim has been to include in one volume stories of unquestioned merit that have found favor with little children. A second collection, *Chimney Corner Fairy Tales,* contains thirteen well-known fairy tales from many countries.

Lang, Andrew, ed. *The Blue Fairy Book;* illus. by Ben Kutcher; foreword by Mary Gould Davis. Longmans, Green, new edition, 1948. (Grades 4–6)

The stories included in the color fairy books have been gathered from many countries and sources. *The Blue Fairy Book,* first published in 1889, is made up almost entirely of old favorites, tales from Perrault and Madame d'Aulnoy as well as stories from Germany and Norway.

Scudder, Horace E., ed. *Book of Fables and Folk Stories.* Houghton Mifflin, 1919. (Grades 4–5)

This book, still popular since it was first published in 1882, contains the more familiar fables and folk tales.

United Nations Women's Guild. *Ride with the Sun;* ed. by Mr. Courlander for the United Nations Women's Guild; illus. by Roger Duvoisin. McGraw-Hill (Whittlesey House), 1955. (Grades 4–7)

An anthology of folk tales and stories from the sixty countries of the United Nations.

Wiggin, Kate Douglas, and Nora Archibald Smith, eds. *The Fairy Ring;* illus. by Elizabeth MacKinstry. Doubleday, 1906. (Crimson Classics) (Grades 4–6)

This volume and the companion books *Magic Casements, Tales of Laughter,* and *Tales of Wonder* contain stories from the folklore of many nations. Useful for reading aloud and for storytelling.

Africa

Courlander, Harold, and George Herzog. *The Cow-Tail Switch and Other West African Stories;* illus. by Mayde Lee Chastain. Henry Holt, 1947. (Grades 4–7)

These stories, still told in the jungle villages and seacoast towns, were gathered by the authors on expeditions to Africa.

Courlander, Harold, and Wolf Leslau. *Fire on the Mountain, and Other Ethiopian Stories;* illus. by Robert W. Kane. Henry Holt, 1950. (Grades 5–7)

A companion volume to *The Cow-Tail Switch.* Many of the stories are very short, similar to Aesop's fables.

Courlander, Harold, and Albert Kofi Prempeh. *The Hat-Shaking Dance and Other Tales from the Gold Coast;* illus. by Enrico Arno. Harcourt, Brace, 1956. (Grades 3–6)

Wise and humorous folk tales from the Ashanti people of the African Gold Coast.

Kalibala, Ernest, and Mary Gould Davis. *Wakaima and the Clay Man, and Other African Folk Tales;* illus. by Avery Johnson. Longmans, Green, 1946. (Grades 3–5)

Wakaima the rabbit, Wango the leopard, and Wankima the monkey are some of the characters in these folk tales of East Africa. The title story is reminiscent of *The Tar Baby,* from the Uncle Remus stories.

Marais, Joseph. *Koos, the Hottentot; Tales of the Veld;* illus. by Henry Stahlhut. Alfred A. Knopf, 1945. (Grades 4–7)

Folk tales from the South African veld recorded by the author as he heard them from his old Hottentot nurse, Koos. They give the reader a sense of the strangeness and beauty of Africa.

Arabia

Arabian Nights. *Arabian Nights, Tales of Wonder and Magnificence;* selected and adapted by Padraic Colum; illus. by Lynd Ward. Macmillan, 1953. (New Children's Classics) (Grades 5–7)

The best retelling of the Arabian Nights for children. Text is based on Edward Lane's translation of *The Thousand and One Nights* (1838–40). Mr. Colum says, "The stories are representative and an effort has been made to bring children near to the original literature and to the wonderful Saracenic civilization." The Introduction includes an admirable discussion of the history of the Arabian Nights and its place in world literature.

Arabian Nights. *Arabian Nights;* collected and edited by Andrew Lang; illus. by Vera Bock; with a foreword by Mary Gould Davis. Longmans, Green, 1946. (Grades 5–7)

First published in 1898. Based on the French translation by Antoine Galland. The decorative type of illustration is in keeping with the Oriental setting. One of the best editions for its selection, illustrations, and foreword.

Arabian Nights. *Arabian Nights; Their Best Known Tales;* ed. by Kate Douglas Wiggin and Nora A. Smith; illus. by Maxfield Parrish. Charles Scribner's Sons, 1937. (Scribner Illustrated Classics) (Grades 5–7)

The editors have retold these tales taken mainly from Scott's edition and from the Lane translation.

Brown, Marcia. *The Flying Carpet;* told from *The Arabian Nights;* illus. by the author. Charles Scribner's Sons, 1956. (Grades 2–4)

A gorgeous picture book full of Oriental atmosphere.

Canada

Carlson, Natalie Savage. *Alphonse, That Bearded One;* illus. by Nicolas Mordvinoff. Harcourt, Brace, 1954. (Grades 3–5)

Out of French Canada comes this robust and rollicking tall tale of a bear cub trained by his master, the shrewd Jeannot Vallar, to be a soldier. When Vallar is conscripted, he sends Alphonse in his place.

Carlson, Natalie Savage. *Sashes Red and Blue;* illus. by Rita Fava. Harper, 1956. (Grades 4–6)

More French-Canadian folk tales filled with fun and wisdom.

Carlson, Natalie Savage. *The Talking Cat and Other Stories of French Canada;* pictures by Roger Duvoisin. Harper, 1952. (Grades 4–6)

Thoroughly delightful stories which the author heard from her mother who heard them from a French-Canadian great uncle. A fresh contribution to folklore.

Hooke, Hilda Mary. *Thunder in the Mountains; Legends of Canada;* illus. by Clare Bice. Oxford University Press, 1947. (Grades 4–6)

Indian legends from Nova Scotia and Labrador to the plains of Saskatchewan and the Lands of the Sunset. Retold with sincerity and vigor.

Macmillan, Cyrus. *Glooskap's Country; and Other Indian Tales;* illus. by John Hall. Oxford University Press, 1956. (Grades 5–7)

These tales begin with stories of Glooskap, the supernatural hero of the Micmac Indians of Eastern Canada, and move west over the prairies to the Pacific Coast.

China

Bishop, Claire. *Five Chinese Brothers;* illus. by Kurt Wiese. Coward-McCann, 1938. (Grades 1–3)

A dramatic retelling of an old Chinese folk tale made into a picture book by Kurt Wiese's interpretative drawings. Excellent for storytelling.

Carpenter, Frances. *Tales of a Chinese Grandmother;* illus. by Malthé Hasselriis. Doubleday, 1937. (Grades 5–7)

Chinese folk tales and legends retold with the full flavor of the Orient.

Chan, Christina. *Magic Monkey;* adapted from an old Chinese legend by Plato and Christina Chan. McGraw-Hill. (Whittlesey House), 1944. (Grades 3–5)

See book note on page 316. Read also *The Good Luck Horse,* another Chinese legend retold and illustrated by a twelve-year-old Chinese boy, Plato Chan.

Chrisman, Arthur Bowie. *Shen of the Sea;* illus. by Else Hasselriis. E. P. Dutton, 1925. (Grades 5–8)

Stories which have a folklore quality tell the origin of tea, chopsticks, dragons, etc. Awarded the Newbery medal in 1926.

Lim, Sian-tek. *Folk Tales from China;* illus. by William Arthur Smith. John Day, 1944. (Grades 6–8)

Age-old tales from the folk literature and history of China. Read also *More Folk Tales from China.*

Ritchie, Alice. *The Treasure of Li-Po;* illus. by T. Ritchie. Harcourt, Brace, 1949. (Grades 4–7)

Original fairy tales which, while not traditional, have an authentic Chinese flavor.

Czechoslovakia

Fillmore, Parker. *Czechoslovak Fairy Tales;* illus. by Jan Matulka. Harcourt, Brace, 1919. (Grades 4–6)

Fifteen folk tales retold with a fine appreciation of fancy, fun and fairies.

Fillmore, Parker. *The Shoemaker's Apron;* illus. by Jan Matulka. Harcourt, Brace, 1920. (Grades 4–6)

Twenty Czechoslovakian folk tales drawn from original sources and retold by an accomplished storyteller with a keen appreciation of their humor.

England

Brooke, L. Leslie. *Golden Goose Book.* Frederick Warne, 1906. (K–Grade 3)

An ideal first book of fairy tales. Contains the nursery classics, *The Three Bears, Three Little Pigs, Tom Thumb,* and *The Golden Goose.* Captivating illustrations.

Brown, Marcia. *Dick Whittington and His Cat;* told and cut in linoleum by Marcia Brown. Charles Scribner's Sons, 1950. (Grades 1–3)

This fascinating retelling of the famous tale is simpler than most of the versions. Children will enjoy the many illustrations. There is a picture for each short paragraph of text.

De la Mare, Walter. *Told Again; Old Tales Told Again;* illus. by A. H. Watson. Alfred A. Knopf, 1927. (Grades 3–5)

Favorite fairy tales retold by an English poet whose poetic imagination gives them fresh charm.

Jacobs, Joseph, ed. *English Fairy Tales;* illus. by J. D. Batten. G. P. Putnam's Sons; 3rd ed. rev., 1892. (Grades 4–6)

Joseph Jacobs was a born storyteller as well as a student of folklore. This is one of the best collections of fairy tales of any country. In retelling the stories, Jacobs has preserved their humor and dramatic power. *More English Fairy Tales* is another indispensable collection.

Reeves, James. *English Fables and Fairy Stories;* illus. by Joan Kiddell-Monroe. Oxford University Press, 1954. (Oxford Myths and Legends) (Grades 4–7)

Contains many of the familiar folk tales. Mr. Reeves embellishes the stories a little more than Joseph Jacobs.

Steel, Flora Annie. *English Fairy Tales Retold;* illus. by Arthur Rackham. Macmillan, 1918. (Grades 4–6)

A fine collection of forty of the most familiar and best-loved folk tales.

Finland

Bowman, James Cloyd, and Margery Bianco. *Tales from a Finnish Tupa:* from a translation by Aili Kolehmainen; illus. by Laura Bannon. Albert Whitman, 1937. (Grades 4–6)

An outstanding collection of folk tales for children which is also invaluable to students of folklore and to storytellers.

Fillmore, Parker. *Mighty Mikko; a Book of Finnish Fairy Tales and Folk Tales;* illus. by Jay Van Everen. Harcourt, Brace, 1922. (Grades 4–6)

The author's version of Finnish stories, many of which have variants in the folk tales of other countries.

France

Aulnoy, Marie, Comtesse d'. *The White Cat, and Other Old French Fairy Tales;* arranged by Rachel Field; illus. by Elizabeth MacKinstry. Macmillan, 1928. (Grades 4–6)

A beautiful book with illustrations in the manner of the eighteenth century.

Brown, Marcia. *Stone Soup;* illus. by the author. Charles Scribner's Sons, 1947. (Grades 1–3)

A delightful picture book which gives new life to the old tale of the wily soldiers who got their meal by hoodwinking a whole village of peasants.

Perrault, Charles. *All the French Fairy Tales;* retold, with a foreword by Louis Untermeyer;

illus. by Gustave Doré. Didier, 1946. (Grades 4–6)

A combined edition of *French Fairy Tales* and *More French Fairy Tales*. The superb Gustave Doré pictures in gravure have been used to illustrate the stories.

Perrault, Charles, and Mme. d'Aulnoy. *Fairy Tales;* illus. by Charles Robinson. E. P. Dutton, 1916. (Grades 4–6)

Contains eight of the Perrault tales and *The Benevolent Frog* and *Princess Rosette* by Mme. d'Aulnoy.

Perrault, Charles. *Cinderella, or The Little Glass Slipper;* trans. and illus. by Marcia Brown. Charles Scribner's Sons, 1954. (Grades 1–3)

Marcia Brown has given a fresh imaginative interpretation to this story which knows no barrier of time or country. Her pictures are touched with humor, gaiety, and magic. Awarded the Caldecott medal in 1955.

Perrault, Charles. *Puss in Boots;* freely trans. and illus. by Marcia Brown. Charles Scribner's Sons, 1952. (Grades 1–3)

A gay, spirited picture book in the French tradition.

Picard, Barbara L. *French Legends, Tales, and Fairy Stories;* illus. by Joan Kiddell-Monroe. Oxford University Press, 1955. (Oxford Myths and Legends) (Grades 5–8)

Folk tales from the French provinces and selections from the hero tales and courtly stories of the Middle Ages, retold with skill.

Germany

Grimm, Jakob and Wilhelm. *Grimm's Fairy Tales;* complete edition with 212 illustrations by Josef Scharl. Pantheon Books, 1944.

The only complete edition of the tales gathered by the Grimm brothers, with strikingly original illustrations by a distinguished Bavarian artist. Padraic Colum's Introduction and Joseph Campbell's Folklorists Commentary will be of special interest to the student of folklore, but the book in its attractive format will be enjoyed by the whole family.

Grimm, Jakob and Wilhelm. *The House in the Wood, and Other Fairy Stories;* with drawings by L. Leslie Brooke. Frederick Warne, 1944. (Grades 3–5)

An excellent selection for younger children.

Grimm, Jakob and Wilhelm. *Household Stories from the Collection of the Brothers Grimm;* trans. from the German by Lucy Crane; illus.

by Johannes Troyer. Macmillan, 1954. (New Children's Classics) (Grades 4–6)

One of the best translations. The original edition was illustrated by Walter Crane in 1882.

Grimm, Jakob and Wilhelm. *More Tales from Grimm;* freely trans. and illus. by Wanda Gág. Coward-McCann, 1947. (Grades 4–6)

A companion volume to *Tales from Grimm*. It contains some of the stories not so well known. Both text and illustrations are distinguished. The foreword by Carl Zigrosser tells about the artist's background and her method of illustration.

Grimm, Jakob and Wilhelm. *Snow White and the Seven Dwarfs;* freely trans. and illus. by Wanda Gág. Coward-McCann, 1938. (Grades 2–4)

The well-loved tale is told with a childlike simplicity combined with strength and beauty.

Grimm, Jakob and Wilhelm. *Tales from Grimm;* freely trans. and illus. by Wanda Gág. Coward-McCann, 1936. (Grades 4–6)

A thoroughly satisfying and delightful edition from the standpoint of both text and pictures. Wanda Gág is a translator and artist of rare genius. Her translations retain the quality of the spoken story. She explains her theory of free translation in the introduction.

Grimm, Jakob and Wilhelm. *Three Gay Tales from Grimm;* freely trans. and illus. by Wanda Gág. Coward McCann, 1943. (Grades 3–5)

Wanda Gág tells in her delightful text and inimitable pictures the stories of the *Clever Wife, Three Feathers,* and *Goose Hans.*

Hawaii

Colum, Padraic. *Legends of Hawaii;* illus. by Don Forrer. Yale University Press, 1937. (Grades 8–9)

Selections from the author's two volumes, *At the Gateway of the Day* and *Bright Islands.*

India

Beling, Mabel Ashe. *The Wicked Goldsmith;* illus. by Owen Smith. Harper, 1941. (Grades 6–9)

Stories of ancient India, including one from the *Ramayana* and one from the *Mahabharata.*

Jacobs, Joseph, ed. *Indian Fairy Tales;* gathered from the Hindoos; illus. by J. D. Batten. G. P. Putnam's Sons, 1892. (Grades 4–6)

Stories from the Jatakas or birth stories of Buddha; the fables of Bidpai; and other Sanskrit tales. The

Notes and References are of value to the story-teller.

Steel, Flora Annie. *Tales of the Punjab;* told by the people; with illustrations by J. Lockwood Kipling and notes by R. C. Temple. Macmillan, 1894. (Grades 6–8)

Good for storytelling and reading aloud.

Indonesia

Courlander, Harold. *Kantchil's Lime Pit and Other Stories from Indonesia;* illus. by Robert W. Kane. Harcourt, Brace, 1950. (Grades 5–9)

Stories about wise and foolish men, and tales of animals. Best loved are the stories about Kantchil, the tiny mouse deer only a foot high.

Ireland

Bennett, Richard. *Little Dermot and the Thirsty Stones, and Other Irish Folk Tales;* illus. by the author. Coward-McCann, 1953. (Grades 4–6)

A retelling of some of the Irish tales from County Cork and County Kerry.

Colum, Padraic. *The Big Tree of Bunlahy; Stories of My Own Countryside;* illus. by Jack Yates. Macmillan, 1933. (Grades 5–8)

The people of Bunlahy gather around their big tree and listen to stories told by Old Cuckoo, the Clock-Mender, the Shoemaker's Daughter, the Scholar, and others.

Jacobs, Joseph, ed. *Celtic Fairy Tales;* illus. by John D. Batten. G. P. Putnam's Sons, 1893. (Grades 4–6)

Stories of the rich folk-fancy of the Welsh, Scottish, and Irish Celts. Longer stories and more detailed than those in Jacobs' *English Fairy Tales.*

MacManus, Seumas, comp. *Donegal Wonder Book.* J. B. Lippincott, 1926. (Grades 5–7)

Heroic tales told with robust humor and a fine compelling rhythm.

MacManus, Seumas, comp. *Well o' the World's End;* illus. by Richard Bennett. Devin-Adair, 1955. (Grades 4–6)

Folk tales which Seumas MacManus heard at the nightly telling of stories by the cottage turf fires in the Donegal Highlands.

O'Faolain, Eileen. *Irish Sagas and Folk Tales;* illus. by Joan Kiddell-Monroe. Oxford University Press, 1954. (Oxford Myths and Legends) (Grades 4–7)

A good introduction to the wonders of Irish folklore. Mrs. O'Faolain retells the sagas with a simplicity that retains the dignity of the original tales.

Young, Ella. *Celtic Wonder Tales Retold.* E. P. Dutton, n.d. (Grades 5–8)

Stories of the Gubbaun Saor, told by the Irish poet and student of folklore.

Young, Ella. *The Unicorn with Silver Shoes;* illus. by Robert Lawson. Longmans, Green, 1932. (Grades 4–6)

In rhythmic prose the Irish poet tells the tale of Ballor, the King's son, and his adventures in the Land of the Ever Young. Wit and laughter and the wonder of childhood are in these stories which were told long ago in Dublin for the children of "Æ."

Italy

Botsford, Florence H. *Picture Tales from the Italian;* illus. by Grace Gilkison. J. B. Lippincott, 1929. (Grades 3–5)

Simple stories, one from each of the provinces of Italy.

Capuana, Luigi. *Italian Fairy Tales;* trans. by Dorothy Emmrich; illus. by Margaret Freeman. E. P. Dutton, 1929. (Grades 5–7)

Folk tales which are classics in Italy. In translating them into English Miss Emmrich has succeeded in keeping the humor and liveliness.

Jagendorf, Moritz A. *The Priceless Cats and Other Italian Folk Stories;* illus. by Gioia Fiamenghi. Vanguard Press, 1956. (Grades 3–6)

Mr. Jagendorf heard these stories while in Italy. He has told them with a directness and a simplicity that makes them excellent for storytelling.

Japan

Hearn, Lafcadio, and others. *Japanese Fairy Tales;* illus. by "Kay"; with an introduction by Phyllis Fenner. Liveright, 1953. (Grades 4–6)

These charming tales, variants of folk tales from other countries, preserve the spirit of the originals yet have the added delicate beauty that is distinctly Japanese.

Uchida, Yoshiko. *The Dancing Kettle, and Other Japanese Folk Tales;* illus. by Richard C. Jones. Harcourt, Brace, 1949. (Grades 3–5)

These stories were told to the author when she was a child. Excellent for storytelling.

Uchida, Yoshiko. *The Magic Listening Cap;* illus. by the author. Harcourt, Brace, 1955. (Grades 4–7)

Wise and humorous folk tales retold with rhythmic simplicity.

Korea

Jewett, Eleanore. *Which Was Witch? Tales of Ghosts and Magic from Korea;* illus. by Taro Yashima. Viking Press, 1953. (Grades 4–7)

Good for storytelling and reading aloud.

So-Un, Kim. *The Story Bag. A Collection of Korean Folk Tales;* trans. by Setsu Higashi; illus. by Kim Eui-hwan. Charles E. Tuttle, 1955.

A charming book which will interest the storyteller.

Mexico

Brenner, Anita. *The Boy Who Could Do Anything; and Other Mexican Folk Tales;* retold by Anita Brenner; illus. by Jean Charlot. William R. Scott, 1942. (Grades 4–6)

Many of these stories stem from ancient Indian mythology before the Spanish conquest, yet they often include modern touches showing how each generation adds to the telling of a story.

Purnell, Idella, and John Weatherwax, eds. *The Talking Bird; an Aztec Story Book; Tales Told to Little Paco by His Grandfather;* illus. by Frances Purnell Dehlsen. Macmillan, 1930. (Grades 4–6)

Miss Purnell lived in Mexico for several years and Mr. Weatherwax is a student of Mexican folklore.

Ross, Patricia. *In Mexico They Say;* illus. by Henry C. Pitz. Alfred A. Knopf, 1942. (Grades 4–7)

Fourteen folk tales combining the elements of fantasy and superstition with realism.

Persia (Iran)

Kelsey, Alice Geer. *Once the Mullah; Persian Folk Tales;* illus. by Kurt Werth. Longmans, Green, 1954. (Grades 4–6)

Mullah Nasr-ed-din is the Persian double of the beloved Hodja of the Turks. Young readers delight in the ingenuity the Mullah displays in getting himself out of tight spots.

Persian Fairy Tales; decorated by Valenti Angelo. Peter Pauper Press, 1939.

Folk tales of Persia told for older boys and girls.

Poland

Bernhard, Josephine, trans. *The Master Wizard and Other Polish Tales;* revised and adapted by E. Frances La Valley; illus. by Marya Werten. Alfred A. Knopf, 1934. (Grades 4–6)

Tales of magic and strange adventure which were told about the fireside by Mrs. Bernhard's grandmother.

Borski, Lucia, and Kate Miller, trans. *The Jolly Tailor and Other Fairy Tales;* illus. by Kazimir Klepacki. Longmans, Green, 1925. (Grades 4–6)

One of the best sources of Polish folk tales. In her foreword Mary Gould Davis tells of Mrs. Borski's experience in telling these tales to American children before they were published in book form.

Borski, Lucia, trans. *Polish Folk Tales;* illus. by Erica Gorecka-Egan. Sheed & Ward, 1947. (Grades 4–6)

Tales which the translator heard in Poland as a child. Years later she told them to children in Story Hours in the New York Public Library.

Russia

Artzybasheff, Boris. *Seven Simeons; a Russian Tale;* retold and illus. by Boris Artzybasheff. Viking Press, 1937. (Grades 3–5)

A delightfully subtle and humorous tale of seven brothers who used their magic to help their king. The decorative and imaginative drawings in four colors are superb.

Carrick, Valéry. *Picture Tales from the Russian;* trans. by Nevill Forbes. J. B. Lippincott, 1913. (A Stokes Book) (Grades 2–4)

Simple, amusing folk tales for little children.

Deutsch, Babette, and Avrahm Yarmolinsky. *Tales of Faraway Folk;* illus. by Irena Lorentowicz. Harper, 1952. (Grades 3–5)

A poet, a scholar, and an artist have combined their efforts to produce this excellent collection of ten tales from Central Asia and the Caucasus.

Downing, Charles. *Russian Tales and Legends;* illus. by Joan Kiddell-Monroe. Oxford University Press, 1957. (Oxford Myths and Legends) (Grades 4–7)

The author has drawn his material from many regions of traditional Russia, from the Ukraine to eastern Siberia.

Ershov, Petr Pavlovich. *Little Magic Horse; a Russian Tale;* trans. by Tatiana Balkoff

Drowne; illus. by Vera Bock. Macmillan, 1942. (Grades 5-8)

The story of the little humpbacked horse, written over a hundred years ago by Ershov, is a great favorite with Russian children. This is the first English translation in rhymed verse. The distinguished illustrations express perfectly the drollery and magic of the text.

Papashvily, George and Helen. *Yes and No Stories; a Book of Georgian Folk Tales;* illus. by Simon Lissim. Harper, 1946. (Grades 6-9)

There is a freshness to these tales that makes them good reading.

Ransome, Arthur. *Old Peter's Russian Tales;* illus. by Dmitri Mitrokhin. Thomas Nelson & Sons, 1917. (Grades 4-6)

The author heard these tales from the peasants while he was a correspondent for the *Manchester Guardian* and the *London Daily Mail.* The stories are well told with many humorous touches.

Reyher, Rebecca. *My Mother is the Most Beautiful Woman in the World;* pictures by Ruth Gannett. Howell, Soskin, 1945. (Grades 3-5)

This charming Russian folk tale is based on the proverb, "We do not love people because they are beautiful, but they seem beautiful to us because we love them." The colorful illustrations catch the spirit of the story.

Wheeler, Post. *Russian Wonder Tales;* containing twelve of the famous Bilibin illustrations in color. Beechhurst Press, rev. ed. 1946. (Grades 6-8)

Tales of the Caucasus retold by a scholar. First published in 1912. This edition adds four new stories.

Zeitlin, Ida. *Skazki: Tales and Legends of Old Russia;* illus. by Theodore Nadejen. George H. Doran, 1926. (Grades 6-8)

Thirteen stories retold from versions of Afanasiev, Pushkin, the Russian poet, and Zhukovsky. *Skazki* represents the old Russian culture.

Scandinavia

Asbjörnsen, Peter Christen. *East of the Sun and West of the Moon;* illus. by Hedvig Collin. Macmillan, 1953. (New Children's Classics) (Grades 5-7)

Stories are chosen from the Dasent translation of Asbjörnsen and Moe first published in 1859. The illustrations by the Danish artist are well suited to the spirit of the text.

Asbjörnsen, Peter Christen, and Jörgen Moe. *East of the Sun and West of the Moon;* twenty-one Norwegian folk tales; ed. and illus. by

Ingri and Edgar Parin d'Aulaire. Viking Press, 1938. (Grades 5-7)

Striking full-page lithographs distinguish this volume. In the introduction the artist-editors tell of the fine feeling the Norse people have for their heritage of folklore.

Hatch, Mary. *13 Danish Tales;* illus. by Edgun. Harcourt, Brace, 1947. (Grades 4-7)

These stories, retold with unusual charm, are based on J. Christian Bay's translation entitled *Danish Fairy and Folk Tales,* first published in 1809.

Hatch, Mary. *More Danish Tales;* illus. by Edgun. Harcourt, Brace, 1949. (Grades 3-5)

Gay, humorous tales skillfully retold from Sven Grundtvig's *Folkaeventyr.* Excellent for storytelling.

Jones, Gwyn. *Scandinavian Legends and Folk-Tales;* illus. by Joan Kiddell-Monroe. Oxford University Press, 1956. (Oxford Myths and Legends) (Grades 5-7)

Stories from Denmark, Iceland, Norway, and Sweden are grouped under the headings, "Princes and Trolls," "Tales from the Ingle-Nook," "From the Land of Ice and Fire," and "Kings and Heroes."

Thorne-Thomsen, Gudrun, ed. *East o' the Sun and West o' the Moon with other Norwegian folk tales.* Row, Peterson, rev. ed. 1946. (Grades 3-5)

Twenty-five folk tales retold by a noted storyteller with a fine appreciation of the spirit of the original sources.

Undset, Sigrid, ed. *True and Untrue and Other Norse Tales;* illus. by Frederick T. Chapman. Alfred A. Knopf, 1945. (Grades 4-7)

Based on the original stories of Asbjörnsen and Moe. The author's foreword, "The Adventure Story of the Folk Tale," is of great value to the storyteller.

Scotland

Grierson, Elizabeth. *Scottish Fairy Book;* illus. by Morris Meredith Williams. J. B. Lippincott, 1910. (Grades 4-6)

Stories selected from Scottish folk tales and ballads retold with fine poetic feeling.

Wilson, Barbara Ker. *Scottish Folk-Tales and Legends;* illus. by Joan Kiddell-Monroe. Oxford University Press, 1954. (Oxford Myths and Legends) (Grades 5-7)

A fresh, vivid retelling of traditional tales of great beauty, homely tales of comic adventure, and proud clan legends.

South America

Bandeira Duarte, Margarida Estrela. *The Legend of the Palm Tree;* illus. by Paulo Werneck. Grosset & Dunlap, 1940. (Grades 3–4)

How the palm tree became the "good tree of Providence."

Finger, Charles. *Tales from Silver Lands;* woodcuts by Paul Honoré. Doubleday, 1924. (Grades 5–7)

Folk tales of the Indians of Brazil, which Mr. Finger gathered first-hand from the Indians he met in his wanderings. The book was awarded the Newbery medal in 1925.

Henius, Frank, comp. *Stories from the Americas;* collected and trans. by Frank Henius; illus. by Leo Politi. Charles Scribner's Sons, 1944. (Grades 4–6)

Some of these stories came from Europe and were modified and changed by the countries to which they came. Selected by Latin-Americans as stories that are favorites with the children of their countries.

Lovelace, Maud and Delos. *The Golden Wedge; Indian Legends of South America;* illus. by Charlotte Anna Chase. Thomas Y. Crowell, 1942. (Grades 5–7)

Early creation myths and legends of South America.

Spain

Boggs, Ralph Steele, and Mary Gould Davis. *Three Golden Oranges; and Other Spanish Folk Tales;* illus. by Emma Brock. Longmans, Green, 1936. (Grades 5–6)

The stories, collected and rewritten in Spain, preserve the full flavor of authentic folklore.

Davis, Robert. *Padre Porko; the Gentlemanly Pig;* illus. by Fritz Eichenberg. Holiday House, 1948. (Grades 4–6)

First published in 1939. The 1948 edition contains two additional stories as humorous and delightful as the earlier ones.

Sawyer, Ruth. *Picture Tales from Spain;* illus. by Carlos Sanchez. J. B. Lippincott, 1936. (Grades 4–6)

These eleven native folk tales were told in Spanish to the author by a sailor, a goatherd, and a muleteer. In retelling them in English Ruth Sawyer has kept the native humor and freshness.

Switzerland

Carpenter, Frances. *Tales of a Swiss Grandmother;* illus. by Ernest Bieler. Doubleday, 1940. (Grades 5–7)

Well-told tales from Swiss history, folklore, and legend.

Duvoisin, Roger. *Three Sneezes and Other Swiss Tales;* illus. by the author. Alfred A. Knopf, 1941. (Grades 4–6)

The author, who heard these folk tales during his childhood in Switzerland, has retold them with vigor and humor.

Turkey

Kelsey, Alice Geer. *Once the Hodja;* illus. by Frank Dobias. Longmans, Green, 1943. (Grades 4–6)

Nasr-ed-din Hodja is a simple country fellow with a talent for doing wise things foolishly and foolish things wisely.

United States

Cothran, Jean, ed. *With a Wig, with a Wag, and Other American Folk Tales;* illus. by Clifford N. Geary. David McKay, 1954. (Grades 3–5)

Told with admirable brevity, these tales for younger children range from New England to California, Louisiana to the Northwest. Good material for storytelling.

Field, Rachel, ed. *American Folk and Fairy Tales;* illus. by Margaret Freeman. Charles Scribner's Sons, 1929. (Grades 6–8)

Twenty-one stories chosen because they were genuinely American and grouped under the headings: Indian Legends, Negro Stories, Louisiana Folk Tales, Paul Bunyan, Tone Beaver, and Southern Mountain Stories.

Sawyer, Ruth. *Journey Cake, Ho!;* illus. by Robert McCloskey. Viking Press, 1953. (K–Grade 3)

A noted storyteller and a gifted artist have combined their talents to produce this rollicking American version of *The Pancake.*

Alaskan Eskimo

Gillham, Charles Edward. *Beyond the Clapping Mountains; Eskimo Stories from Alaska;* illus. by Chanimun. Macmillan, 1943. (Grades 3–5)

The author, who spent eight summers in Alaska as a biologist for the United States government, heard these stories from an Eskimo. The line drawings are by an Eskimo girl.

North American Indian

Bell, Corydon. *John Rattling-Gourd of Big Cove;* illus. by the author. Macmillan, 1955. (Grades 4–5)

Tales of wonder, myth, and legend which are the rich heritage of the Cherokee Indians.

De Angulo, Jamie. *Indian Tales;* illus. by the author; foreword by Carl Carmer. A. A. Wyn, 1953. (Grades 4–6)

A poet's feeling for language and an anthropologist's understanding of peoples distinguish this collection of legends.

Grinnell, George Bird. *Blackfeet Indian Stories.* Charles Scribner's Sons, 1931. (Grades 4–6)

Stories handed down for generations among the Blackfeet Indians. Read also the author's *Blackfeet Lodge Tales.*

Hogner, Dorothy C. *Navajo Winter Nights; Folk Tales and Myths of the Navajo Indians;* illus. by Nils Hogner. Thomas Nelson & Sons, 1935. (Grades 4–6)

Author and illustrator gathered material while on a trip to the Navajo reservations in Arizona and New Mexico.

Marriott, Alice Lee. *Winter-telling Stories;* illus. by Roland Whitehorse. Thomas Y. Crowell, 1947. (Grades 4–7)

A fresh and unusual group of stories which the Kiowas, a tribe of the Plains Indians, tell of their hero Saynday, who was also a great trickster. The pictures are drawn by a Kiowa Indian.

Martin, Frances. *Nine Tales of Coyote;* illus. by Dorothy McEntee. Harper, 1950. (Grades 4–6)

Stories about Coyote, the medicine man of the Numipu Indians, who could change himself into an animal.

Martin, Frances. *Nine Tales of Raven;* illus. by Dorothy McEntee. Harper, 1951. (Grades 4–6)

Tales of the Alaskan Eskimos, the Canadian Indians, and the Indians of Washington and Oregon.

Peck, Leigh. *Don Coyote;* illus. by Virginia Lee Burton. Houghton Mifflin, 1942. (Grades 4–6)

Folk tales and fables about the coyote, many from Mexican and Indian sources. The coyote is the southwestern counterpart of Brer Rabbit.

Penney, Grace Jackson. *Tales of the Cheyennes;* illus. by Walter Richard West. Houghton Mifflin, 1953. (Grades 4–7)

Traditional tales of the Cheyenne Indians.

Running, Corinne. *When Coyote Walked the Earth;* illus. by Richard Bennett. Henry Holt, 1949. (Grades 4–6)

Authentic tales of the American Indians of the Pacific Northwest, built around the all-powerful coyote who ruled the animal world before the

first Indians came. Skillfully retold so that the rhythm of the speaking voice is sustained in the prose.

North American Negro

Duncan, Eula Griffin. *Big Road Walker;* based on stories told by Alice Cannon; illus. by Fritz Eichenberg. J. B. Lippincott, 1940. (Grades 5–8)

Negro tall tales of the giant, Big Road Walker, which were told to the author by a Negro cook in North Carolina.

Harris, Joel Chandler. *Complete Tales of Uncle Remus;* comp. by Richard Chase; illus. by A. B. Frost and Frederick Church. Houghton Mifflin, 1954. (Grades 5–8)

All the beloved folk tales of Brer Rabbit and his friends collected for the first time in one volume.

Harris, Joel Chandler. *Uncle Remus; His Songs and His Sayings;* illus. by A. B. Frost. Appleton, 1921. (Grades 5–8)

These plantation stories were first published in the Atlanta, Georgia, *Constitution* in 1880.

Southern Mountain Folk

Chase, Richard, ed. *Grandfather Tales; American-English Folk Tales;* illus. by Berkeley Williams, Jr. Houghton Mifflin, 1948. (Grades 4–7)

A distinct contribution to American folklore. Mr. Chase has gathered old songs and tales from the mountain people of North Carolina, Virginia, Kentucky, and Alabama. In his preface he states that he took a free hand in the telling and that he put each tale together from different versions and from his own experience in telling them.

Chase, Richard, ed. *The Jack Tales;* illus. by Berkeley Williams, Jr. Houghton Mifflin, 1943. (Grades 4–7)

These variants of the European folk tales of simple Jack, who always comes out ahead, have taken on the native wit of the Appalachian Mountains where generations of mountain folk have made them their own.

Tall Tales

Blair, Walter. *Tall Tale America; a Legendary History of our Humorous Heroes;* illus. by Glen Rounds. Coward-McCann, 1944. (Grades 5–8)

The fabulous achievements of the legendary heroes of folklore are retold in an extravagantly humorous vein.

Bontemps, Arna. *Fast Sooner Hound;* illus. by Virginia Lee Burton. Houghton Mifflin, 1942. (Grades 1–4)

This tall tale of the long-legged, lop-eared hound that could out-run any train comes from the folklore of the Old West. The drawings are full of action and humor.

Bowman, James Cloyd. *Pecos Bill, the Greatest Cowboy of All Time;* pictures by Laura Bannon. Albert Whitman, 1937. (Grades 6–9)

Robust tall tales from the cowboy saga of Pecos Bill retold with imagination and vigor.

Carmer, Carl. *The Hurricane's Children; Tales from Your Neck o' the Woods;* illus. by Elizabeth Black Carmer. Farrar, 1937. (Grades 7–9)

Humorous American folk tales including Paul Bunyan, Febold Feboldsen, and others.

Felton, Harold W. *Fire-Fightin' Mose;* illus. by Aldren A. Watson; foreword by B. A. Botkin. Alfred A. Knopf, 1955. (Grades 6–8)

Subtitled: "Being an account of the life and times of the world's greatest fire fighter, member of the New York City Volunteer Fire Department, and of the Company of Lady Washington, Engine No. 40, a machine of greatest excellence, known as the White Ghost."

Felton, Harold W. *John Henry and His Hammer;* illus. by Aldren A. Watson. Alfred A. Knopf, 1950. (Grades 5–8)

This version is a little more literary than Shapiro's *John Henry and the Double-Jointed Steam Drill,* and not so robust.

Felton, Harold W., ed. *Legends of Paul Bunyan;* illus. by Richard Bennett. Alfred A. Knopf, 1947. (Grades 7–9)

Stories, songs and poems arranged in chronological order beginning with Paul Bunyan's unusual birth.

Felton, Harold W. *Pecos Bill, Texas Cowpuncher;* illus. by Aldren A. Watson. Alfred A. Knopf, 1949. (Grades 7–9)

The preposterous adventures of Pecos Bill, "the greatest cowboy of them all," are told with dry humor by the author in the colloquial speech of the Southwest.

Malcolmson, Anne, and Dell J. McCormick. *Mister Stormalong;* illus. by Joshua Tolford. Houghton Mifflin, 1952. (Grades 5–9)

Fabulous adventures of Stormalong, the legendary Paul Bunyan of the sea, who stood several fathoms tall and skippered a ship as long as all Cape Cod.

Malcolmson, Anne B. *Yankee Doodle's Cousins;* illus. by Robert McCloskey. Houghton Mifflin, 1941. (Grades 5–9)

Stories of both real and legendary characters who have become heroes of American folklore. The robust and humorous illustrations are admirably suited to the text.

Rounds, Glen. *Ol' Paul, the Mighty Logger;* illus. by the author. Holiday House, 1949. (Grades 4–8)

"Being a true account of the seemingly incredible exploits and inventions of the great Paul Bunyan" (subtitle).

Shapiro, Irwin. *Yankee Thunder; the Legendary Life of Davy Crockett;* illus. by James Daugherty. Julian Messner, 1944. (Grades 6–9)

The legendary stories about Davy Crockett have been blended into a tall tale which follows Davy from Tennessee to the White House and to the South Seas.

Shephard, Esther. *Paul Bunyan;* illus. by Rockwell Kent. Harcourt, Brace, 1941. (Grades 7–9)

One of the best versions of the Paul Bunyan tales. The author collected these stories from the loggers in Washington, Oregon, and British Columbia. She has told the stories just as she heard the men in the lumber camps tell them. First published in 1924.

Wales

Jones, Gwyn. *Welsh Legends and Folk Tales,* retold by Gwyn Jones; illus. by Joan Kiddell-Monroe. Oxford University Press, 1955. (Oxford Myths and Legends) (Grades 5–9)

A distinguished Welsh folklorist has brought together an interesting collection of ancient Celtic tales and legends.

West Indies

Belpré, Pura. *Perez and Martina;* illus. by Carlos Sanchez. Frederick Warne, 1932. (Grades 2–4)

A droll nonsense tale of Puerto Rico beloved by all Spanish-speaking children.

Belpré, Pura. *The Tiger and the Rabbit and Other Tales;* illus. by Kay Petersen Parker. Houghton Mifflin, 1946. (Grades 3–6)

Puerto Rican folk tales, rich in atmosphere. Written from the memory of the author's childhood.

Courlander, Harold. *Uncle Bouqui of Haiti;* decorated by Lucy Herndon Crockett. William Morrow, 1942. (Grades 4–6)

Uncle Bouqui, kind and gentle, with unbounded faith in his own cleverness, and Ti Malice, sly and crafty, are two unique characters from the folklore of Haiti.

Johnson, Gyneth. *How the Donkeys Came to Haiti and Other Tales;* illus. by Angelo di Benedetto. Devin-Adair, 1949. (Grades 4–6)

The author lived in rural Haiti and heard these tales told at native "sings." The folk tales probably came from Africa years ago and have acquired Spanish and French embellishments.

Sherlock, Philip M. *Anansi, the Spider Man;* illus. by Marcia Brown. Thomas Y. Crowell, 1954. (Grades 4–6)

A delightful collection of folk tales of the West Indies about Anansi, who was a man when things went well, but in times of danger became a spider. Retold with humor, warmth, and vitality.

Yugoslavia

Fillmore, Parker. *The Laughing Prince; a Book of Jugoslav Fairy Tales and Folk Tales;* illus. by Jay Van Everen. Harcourt, Brace, 1921. (Grades 4–6)

Fourteen southern Slav stories including Bulgarian tales and those of other Balkan peoples. Relatively unknown stories told with humor.

References for the Adult

Thompson, Stith. *The Folktale.* Dryden Press, 1946.

Long years of research, teaching, and writing form the background for this scholarly work in which the author, one of the foremost authorities on the subject, discusses the universality of the folk tale; traces the spread of folk tales; and analyzes types of tales and their place in the primitive culture of the American Indian.

Arnold, Matthew. *On the Study of Celtic Literature and Other Essays.* E. P. Dutton, 1932.

Especially "Folklore," pp. 13–136.

Clough, Ben C. *The American Imagination at Work: Tall Tales and Folk Tales.* Alfred A. Knopf, 1947.

Davidson, Levette J. *A Guide to American Folklore.* University of Denver Press, 1951.

Keightley, Thomas. *The Fairy Mythology.* Bell (London), 1892.

Krappe, Alexander Haggerty. *The Science of Folk-lore.* Methuen (London), 1930.

Kready, Laura F. *A Study of Fairy Tales.* Houghton Mifflin, 1916.

Lang, Andrew. *Custom and Myth.* Longmans, Green, 1930.

Leach, Maria, ed. *Funk & Wagnalls Standard Dictionary of General Folklore, Mythology and Legend.* 2 vols. Funk & Wagnalls, 1949–1950.

The richness, vitality, and range of world folklore, mythology, and legend are revealed in this major reference work compiled not only for the folklorist but also for the general reader.

Ramsey, Eloise, comp. *Folklore for Children and Young People.* The American Folklore Society, Philadelphia, 1952.

A critical and descriptive bibliography compiled for use in the elementary and intermediate school.

Rugoff, Milton, ed. *A Harvest of World Folk Tales.* Viking Press, 1949.

Yeats, William Butler. *Folk and Fairy Tales of the Irish Peasantry.* Walter Scott Pub. Co. (London), 1888.

Chapters and Commentary

Afanasiev, Alexander N. *Russian Fairy Tales;* trans. by Norbert Guterman; illus. by A. Alexeieff. Pantheon Books, 1945.

Contains a valuable Folkloristic Commentary by Roman Jakobson, pp. 631–651.

Arbuthnot, May Hill. *Children and Books.* Scott, Foresman, rev. ed. 1957.

"Old Magic," Chapter 11, pp. 231–253; "Using Folk Tales with Children," Chapter 12, pp. 255–270.

Botkin, Benjamin A., ed. *A Treasury of American Folklore.* Crown Pub. Co., 1944.

Foreword by Carl Sandburg. Introduction of interest to the student of folklore.

Carmer, Carl. *America Sings.* Alfred A. Knopf, 1942.

Introduction, pp. 7–11.

Carmer, Carl, and Mary Gould Davis. *Folklore.* Two articles reprinted from Compton's Pictured Encyclopedia. F. E. Compton & Co., 1950.

De la Mare, Walter. *Animal Stories.* Charles Scribner's Sons, 1940.

Introduction, pp. xiii–lvi. Mr. De la Mare traces the development of the animal folktale and comments on the stories.

Duff, Annis. *"Bequest of Wings"; A Family's Pleasures with Books.* Viking Press, 1944.

"A Brief for Fairy Tales," Chapter XIV, pp. 170–181.

Eaton, Anne Thaxter. *Reading with Children.* Viking Press, 1940.

"Over the Edge of the World," Chapter IV, pp. 65–88.

Grimm, Jakob and Wilhelm. *Grimm's Fairy Tales;* complete edition with 212 illustrations by Josef Scharl. Pantheon Books, 1944.

Introduction by Padraic Colum. Folkloristic Commentary by Joseph Campbell: "The Work of the Brothers Grimm," pp. 833–839; "The Types of Stories," pp. 840–845; "The History of the Tales," pp. 846–856; "The Question of Meaning," pp. 857–864.

Hazard, Paul. *Books, Children and Men.* The Horn Book, Inc., 1944.

"Perrault's Fairy Tales," pp. 5–10; "France," pp. 121–128; "The Brothers Grimm," pp. 152–157; "Fairy Tales and Their Meaning," pp. 157–161.

Jacobs, Joseph, ed. *English Fairy Tales; More English Fairy Tales;* etc. G. P. Putnam's Sons.

In each of Joseph Jacobs' collections of fairy tales he gives valuable information for the student of folklore in the preface and in a section called "Notes and References."

Meigs, Cornelia, and others. *A Critical History of Children's Literature.* Macmillan, 1953.

"A Rightful Heritage: The Return of the Fairy Tale," pp. 199–321; "Looking to the Past — Folk and Fairy Tales," pp. 448–460.

Moore, Annie E. *Literature Old and New for Children.* Houghton Mifflin, 1934.

"Folk Tales," Chapter 4, pp. 78–120.

Smith, Lillian H. *The Unreluctant Years.* American Library Association, 1953.

"The Art of the Fairy Tale," Chapter 4, pp. 44–64.

Undset, Sigrid, ed. *True and Untrue and Other Norse Tales.* Alfred A. Knopf, 1945.

"The Adventure of the Folk Tale," pp. 1–27.

Wanda Gág

Gág, Wanda. *Growing Pains; an Autobiography.* Coward-McCann, 1940.

Scott, Alma. *Wanda Gág, the Story of an Artist.* University of Minnesota Press, 1949.

The Grimm Brothers

Gooch, G. P. "Jakob Grimm," in *History and Historians in the Nineteenth Century.* Longmans, Green, 1913.

Ker, W. P. "Jacob Grimm," in *Collected Essays.* Macmillan, 1925. Vol. 2, pp. 222–233.

Joseph Jacobs

Hays, May Bradshaw. "Memories of My Father, Joseph Jacobs," *The Horn Book Magazine,* Vol. 28, Dec. 1952, pp. 385–392.

Andrew Lang

Andrew Lang; Being the Andrew Lang Lecture Delivered Before the University of St. Andrews, December 1927. Oxford University Press, 1928.

Green, Roger Lancelyn. *Andrew Lang: A Critical Biography.* Edmund Ward (Leicester, Eng.), 1946.

Repplier, Agnes. "Andrew Lang," *Catholic World,* Vol. 96, Dec. 1912, pp. 289–297.

Ella Young

Colum, Padraic. *Ella Young, an Appreciation.* Longmans, Green, 1931.

Young, Ella. *Flowering Dusk: Things Remembered Accurately and Inaccurately; an Autobiography.* Longmans, Green, 1945.

Myths and Legends

"To be surprised, to wonder, is to begin to understand. This is the sport, the luxury, special to the intellectual man. The gesture characteristic of his tribe consists in looking at the world with eyes wide open in wonder. . . . This faculty of wonder is . . . the one which leads the intellectual man through life in the perpetual ecstasy of the visionary. . . . Hence it was that the ancients gave Minerva (the Goddess of Wisdom) her owl, the bird with ever-dazzled eyes." [1]

F ALL THE CREATURES ON THIS earth, only man has asked questions; only man endlessly pursues the Dark Bird of Unknowing, gathering up each feather his shafts loosen from the great wings. Feather by feather, he seeks to conquer his prey, and in so doing, to unravel the riddles governing his own world, and the worlds beyond, if such there be.

Primitive man, living without science, surrounded by mystery and terror, had three approaches to knowledge: his observation of the natural world, his practical experience of life, and his imagination. With this equipment he gave such order as he could to his life, creating explanations for the mysteries which surrounded him, and by this means coming to terms with them. He invested everything with life: trees, stones, the very tools he had himself fashioned. He invented gods, casting them in the image of man and beast such as he himself knew, giving them shapes that were gigantic, or grotesque, or horrible, in order that their powers would be above his own. Having formed them, he worshipped them, begged for their favor, propitiated them with sacrifice and ritual, and made them guardians of such moral law and ethics as evolved from his society. "Now it is a canon of religious study," writes Gilbert Murray, "that all gods reflect the social state, past or present, of their worshippers." [2]

Myths, then, are in part science, because like science they attempt to relate

[1] José Ortega y Gasset, *The Revolt of the Masses* (W. W. Norton and Company, New York, 1932), p. 12.

[2] Gilbert Murray, *Five Stages of Greek Religion* (Columbia University Press, New York, 1925), p. 67.

cause and effect; in part religion, since many of them seek to explain the unknown, man's relationship to it, and to give patterns to ritual and worship; in part social and moral law, since ethics and morality evolve from belief.

Stories from mythology — the myths of nature, the accounts of the old gods — have a clarity about them, a flashing, brilliant symbolism that draws the imagination of children. Practiced in the art of bestowing life upon objects about them — toys, chairs, beds, broomsticks, or umbrellas — children recognize the logic of myth, matching their own childlike imagination with that of the childhood of the world.

How spacious are the stories in concept, how ingenious and how greatly "charged with marvels." C. S. Lewis analyzes their exceptional quality when he says,

> . . . the myth does not essentially exist in words at all. We all agree that the story of Balder is a great myth, a thing of inexhaustible value. But of whose version — whose words — are we thinking when we say this?
>
> For my own part, the answer is that I am not thinking of any one's words. No poet, as far as I know or can remember, has told this story supremely well. I am not thinking of any particular version of it. If the story is anywhere embodied in words, that is almost an accident. What really delights and nourishes me is a particular pattern of events, which would equally delight and nourish if it had reached me by some medium which involved no words at all — say by a mime, or a film, and I think this is true of all such stories.[3]

In addition to the originality of concept, and the clarity of myth, the child recognizes an atmosphere native to his inborn sense of wonder. This sense of wonder, inherent in most children, is perhaps the greatest gift the child brings into the world. In all our processes of education, this attribute should be nourished, sustained, and guaranteed survival. Unfortunately, it is too soon lost. In the modern world, replete with marvels, the emphasis is put upon the practical aspects of life — science, the organizations of society, the ways in which goods are manufactured and distributed; and the feeling of wonder, the basic response to the miraculous, is dulled and stunted. "We have been given tools for an intenser form of existence," says Ortega y Gasset, "but no feeling for their historic duties; they [the masses] have been hurriedly inoculated with the pride and power of modern instruments, but not with their spirit."[4]

Myth, folk tales, the epic and saga — the heritage of the whole great oral tradition, with its conviction of belief, its fresh, first-seeing of the world — these give children a lasting background of wonder and condition them to see the world with "ever-dazzled" eyes.

The Greek myths and the Norse are the prime sources of mythology for the Western world. The earliest written record of the Greek mythology — probably the highest development in the evolution of myth — is in the *Iliad*,

---

[3] From *George Macdonald, An Anthology*, edited by C. S. Lewis (The Macmillan Company, New York, 1947), p. 15.

[4] Ortega y Gasset, *The Revolt of the Masses*, p. 55.

attributed to Homer, and dated around the year 1000 B.C. Hundreds of years before the written record, the tales and beliefs had been created, changed, evolved, until we know them as the Golden Age of Greece. The *Iliad* and Homer's succeeding *Odyssey* contain some of the greatest stories the world will ever know.

Other sources of Greek mythology exist in the Homeric hymns, fragmentary odes to the gods, and in the writing of Hesiod, seven hundred years before the birth of Christ. The great dramatists of Greece, Aeschylus (525–456 B.C.), Sophocles (496–406 B.C.), and Euripides (480–406 B.C.), wrote their towering tragedies against the background of this mythology, thrusting deep into the motives of gods and men in their relationships with one another.

When Rome conquered Greece, the Romans took over the religion of the Greeks, adapting it to their own practical minds, less poetic and less spiritual than the Greek manner of thinking. They gave the gods new names and were slightly condescending to them. We owe to the Roman writer, Ovid, our knowledge of many of the stories. His *Metamorphoses* gives account of the Greek gods, with wit and impudence. The Romans believed in them with less ardor than the Greeks. For the Romans, they were celestial pets to be presented on promenade.

The Norse mythology, dark, heroic, and austere like the region which produced it, reaches its highest written or literary expression in one famous manuscript book, known as the *Elder* or *Poetic Edda*. It was created in Iceland, the long work of Icelandic bards who emerged as spokesmen for a culture made up of Norsemen, exiled from Scandinavia to Iceland. The author is unknown, and its date not certain, some scholars placing it as late as the latter part of the thirteenth century. The *Younger* or *Prose Edda* is the work of one man, Snorri Sturluson, a great artist-historian of the medieval age. From these two sources come the *Völsunga Saga*. The *Nibelungenlied* of the Germanic people bears a relationship to them.

Each culture "declares itself" in its mythology, and the comparative reading of myths affords an understanding of individual characteristics, but gives above all a growing sense of the elements that are universal to the mind of man. Nor does mythology belong only to the past, and the long-dead cultures which it survives. The stuff of myth works in our minds today. "Religion, philosophies, arts, the social forms of primitive and historic man, prime discoveries in science and technology, the very dreams that blister sleep, boil up from the basic ring of myth."[5]

[5] Joseph Campbell, *The Hero with a Thousand Faces* (Pantheon Books, New York, 1949), p. 3.

MYTHS OF ANCIENT GREECE

Note on Greek Mythology

One of the remarkable elements in Greek mythology is the relationship between gods and men. Indeed, the Greek spirit created its gods in the image of men and women, perfect in proportion, noble in appearance, crowned with beauty. The Greek gods were only men and women raised to a sublime scale, powerful to be sure, but bearing celestial faults that were comfortably human. Jealousy and envy, the thirst for revenge, greed of possession and the deceptive heart — these seem strange attributes in those who are worshipped. And yet these very human characteristics made it possible for the gods to move with such ease between two worlds, their own and that of man, taking sides in quarrels, sponsoring one hero against another, jealous of the measure of devotion accorded them by mortals, and often falling in love with mortal maid or youth and so creating whole dynasties of half-gods.

Yet the moral law existed, a deep recognition of a sublimity above both gods and men. Underlying the Greek's joy in nature, his celebration of the wonder of Man, his worship of beauty and proportion, his delight in life itself, lay the deeper awareness of order and the obligation to sustain an ideal nobility. "The myths are firmly built into two dramatic cycles," writes H. D. F. Kitto in his study of the Greek mind, "which are among the supreme achievements of the human mind: *dramas about the birth and growth of reason, order and mercy among gods and man alike.*"[1]

The gods were said to dwell upon Olympus, a

[1] H. D. F. Kitto, *The Greeks* (Penguin Books), p. 202.

mountain or a region somewhere in the heavens. The Olympians were Zeus (whom the Romans called Jupiter), chief of all the gods and high authority among them; Hera (Juno) his wife, always the jealous and watchful spouse, and with good reason; Ares (Mars), god of War and son of Zeus and Hera; Athena (Minerva), goddess of Wisdom, sprung full grown from the head of Zeus; Apollo, god of Light; Aphrodite (Venus), goddess of Love; Hermes (Mercury), the messenger of the gods; Artemis (Diana), goddess of the Moon; Hestia (Vesta), sister of Zeus, a virgin goddess sacred to the hearth; Poseidon (Neptune), brother of Zeus, ruler of the sea and the world under the sea; Hades (Pluto), a second brother of Zeus and ruler of the region of the Dead, under the earth; Hephaestus (Vulcan), the blacksmith of the gods, the maker and shaper of things, said to be the son of Zeus.

Lesser gods dwelling on Olympus were Eros (Cupid), god of Love; Hebe, goddess of youth and cupbearer to the gods; Iris, the goddess of the Rainbow; and the Muses and Graces, "two bands of lovely sisters."

Countless other gods were worshipped by the Greeks. Among the gods of the Earth, there was Demeter (Ceres), mother of every growing thing, and Dionysus (Bacchus), the god of the vine. Before the gods, there had been the Titans, whom the gods overthrew. And before the Titans, dark and terrible creatures born of Mother Earth and Father Heaven, so malformed that Father Heaven imprisoned them in secret places of the earth. Of all his children, Father Heaven let live in freedom Cronus, the Titan, and the Cyclopes, the giants with one eye.

Cronus overcame his father, and ruled for untold ages, with his sister-queen Rhea (Ops).

Zeus, their son, waged war against his father with the help of his five brothers and sisters, and Cronus was destroyed. In that great battle, two Titans took part, Prometheus siding with Zeus, and Atlas siding with Cronus. After the victory of Zeus, Atlas was doomed as punishment to bear upon his shoulders forever the great pillar that holds apart earth and sky.

The range of Greek mythology is enormous, representing as it does the evolution of a religion based upon earlier, manifold beliefs. The stories vary from as simple a parable as the story of Midas, who loved gold above all else, to the complex and ennobling concept of Prometheus. Whatever one reads of them — the flower myths, the explanations of natural phenomena, or the tales of gods and men — the vitality of their spirit touches and informs almost every facet of contemporary life.

Demeter [2]

(Ceres and Persephone)

"This story is told only in a very early poem, one of the earliest of the Homeric Hymns, dating from the eighth or the beginning of the seventh century. The original has the marks of early Greek poetry, great simplicity and directness and delight in the beautiful world. Demeter was the goddess of marriage and fertility. The story of the loss of her daughter Persephone, and the mother's search for her, are the ancient Greek's explanation of summer and winter." — Edith Hamilton.

Demeter had an only daughter, Persephone (in Latin, Proserpine), the maiden of the spring. She lost her and in her terrible grief she withheld her gifts from the earth, which turned into a frozen desert. The green and flowering land was icebound and lifeless because Persephone had disappeared.

The lord of the dark Underworld, the king of the multitudinous dead, carried her off when, enticed by the wondrous bloom of the narcissus, she strayed too far from her companions. In his chariot drawn by coal-black steeds he rose up through a chasm in the

2 From Edith Hamilton, *Mythology* (Little, Brown, 1942).

earth, and grasping the maiden by the wrist set her beside him. He bore her away, weeping, down to the Underworld. The high hills echoed her cry and the depths of the sea, and her mother heard it. She sped like a bird over sea and land seeking her daughter. But no one would tell her the truth, "no man nor god, nor any sure messenger from the birds." Nine days Demeter wandered, and all that time she would not taste of ambrosia or put sweet nectar to her lips. At last she came to the Sun and he told her all the story: Persephone was down in the world beneath the earth, among the shadowy dead.

Then a still greater grief entered Demeter's heart. She left Olympus; she dwelt on earth, but so disguised that none knew her, and, indeed, the gods are not easily discerned by mortal men. In her desolate wanderings she came to Eleusis and sat by the wayside near a wall. She seemed an aged woman, such as in great houses care for the children or guard the storerooms. Four lovely maidens, sisters, coming to draw water from the well, saw her and asked her pityingly what she did there. She answered that she had fled from pirates who had meant to sell her as a slave, and that she knew no one in this strange land to go to for help. They told her that any house in the town would welcome her, but that they would like best to bring her to their own if she would wait there while they went to ask their mother. The goddess bent her head in assent, and the girls, filling their shining pitchers with water, hurried home. Their mother, Metaneira, bade them return at once and invite the stranger to come, and speeding back they found the glorious goddess still sitting there, deeply veiled and covered to her slender feet by her dark robe. She followed them, and as she crossed the threshold to the hall where the mother sat holding her young son, a divine radiance filled the doorway and awe fell upon Metaneira.

She bade Demeter be seated and herself offered her honey-sweet wine, but the goddess would not taste it. She asked instead for barley-water flavored with mint, the cooling draft of the reaper at harvest time and also the sacred cup given the worshipers at

Eleusis. Thus refreshed, she took the child and held him to her fragrant bosom and his mother's heart was glad. So Demeter nursed Demophoön, the son that Metaneira had borne to wise Celeus. And the child grew like a young god, for daily Demeter anointed him with ambrosia and at night she would place him in the red heart of the fire. Her purpose was to give him immortal youth.

Something, however, made the mother uneasy, so that one night she kept watch and screamed in terror when she saw the child laid in the fire. The goddess was angered; she seized the boy and cast him on the ground. She had meant to set him free from old age and from death, but that was not to be. Still, he had lain upon her knees and slept in her arms and therefore he should have honor throughout his life.

Then she showed herself the goddess manifest. Beauty breathed about her and a lovely fragrance; light shone from her so that the great house was filled with brightness. She was Demeter, she told the awestruck women. They must build her a great temple near the town and so win back the favor of her heart.

Thus she left them, and Metaneira fell speechless to the earth and all there trembled with fear. In the morning they told Celeus what had happened and he called the people together and revealed to them the command of the goddess. They worked willingly to build her a temple, and when it was finished Demeter came to it and sat there — apart from the gods in Olympus, alone, wasting away with longing for her daughter.

That year was most dreadful and cruel for mankind over all the earth. Nothing grew; no seed sprang up; in vain the oxen drew the plowshare through the furrows. It seemed the whole race of man would die of famine. At last Zeus saw that he must take the matter in hand. He sent the gods to Demeter, one after another, to try to turn her from her anger, but she listened to none of them. Never would she let the earth bear fruit until she had seen her daughter. Then Zeus realized that his brother must give way. He told Hermes to go down to the Underworld and to bid the lord of it let his bride go back to Demeter.

Hermes found the two sitting side by side, Persephone shrinking away, reluctant because she longed for her mother. At Hermes' words she sprang up joyfully, eager to go. Her husband knew that he must obey the word of Zeus and send her up to earth away from him, but he prayed her as she left him to have kind thoughts of him and not be so sorrowful that she was the wife of one who was great among the immortals. And he made her eat a pomegranate seed, knowing in his heart that if she did so she must return to him.

He got ready his golden car and Hermes took the reins and drove the black horses straight to the temple where Demeter was. She ran out to meet her daughter as swiftly as a Maenad runs down the mountain-side. Persephone sprang into her arms and was held fast there. All day they talked of what had happened to them both, and Demeter grieved when she heard of the pomegranate seed, fearing that she could not keep her daughter with her.

Then Zeus sent another messenger to her, a great personage, none other than his revered mother Rhea, the oldest of the gods. Swiftly she hastened down from the heights of Olympus to the barren, leafless earth, and standing at the door of the temple she spoke to Demeter.

Come, my daughter, for Zeus, far-seeing, loud-
thundering, bids you.
Come once again to the halls of the gods where you
shall have honor,
Where you will have your desire, your daughter, to
comfort your sorrow
As each year is accomplished and bitter winter is
ended.
For a third part only the kingdom of darkness shall
hold her.
For the rest you will keep her, you and the happy
immortals.
Peace now. Give men life which comes alone from
your giving.

Demeter did not refuse, poor comfort though it was that she must lose Persephone for four months every year and see her young loveliness go down to the world of the dead. But she was kind; the "Good Goddess," men always called her. She was sorry for the desolation she had brought about. She made the fields once more rich with abundant fruit and the whole world bright with flowers and green leaves. Also she went to the princes of Eleusis who had built her temple and she chose one, Triptolemus, to be her ambassador to men, instructing them how to sow the corn. She taught him and Celeus and the others her sacred rites, "mysteries which no one may utter, for deep awe checks the tongue. Blessed is he who has seen them; his lot will be good in the world to come."

> Queen of fragrant Eleusis,
> Giver of earth's good gifts,
> Give me your grace, O Demeter.
> You, too, Persephone, fairest,
> Maiden all lovely, I offer
> Song for your favor.

Prometheus the Firebringer[3]

⊰ *Here is one of the greatest of Greek myths: the story of the Immortal who so loved mankind that he defied Zeus, and endured endless torture in order that Man might have the gift of fire. This is much more than an origin myth. Prometheus is the symbol of the questioning mind, the one individual who dares to challenge the very laws of the universe and the godhead. Aeschylus made him the hero of an epic trilogy of dramas, of which only the second one,* Prometheus Bound, *has come down to us. Subsequent poets and philosophers have envisioned him as the prototype of the rebel, the savior of mankind, the fighter against tyranny and injustice.*

In the beginning of the reign of Zeus, his bosom friend and counsellor was Prometheus, by whose wisdom he had balked the Titans of their revenge. But ere long the young King of the Sky became jealous of that very wisdom to which he owed so much, and fell to doubting the loyalty of his chief helper.

He began to say to himself that as Prometheus had forsaken Cronos in his hour of need, so he would forsake Zeus, should he foresee the coming of some yet mightier god. Had he not, moreover, interceded for Cronos,

[3] From W. M. L. Hutchinson, *Orpheus with His Lute* (Longmans, Green, 1926).

and given him a sure refuge in those Happy Isles that lay beyond the range of lightning-flash or thunderstone — and was he not, perhaps, already conspiring with the exiled Titan brethren to restore their ancient king?

Now, what mainly bred suspicion in the mind of Zeus was this: Prometheus, though he came duly to council and to feast in the heavenly halls, seemed ever impatient to be gone upon some business of his own in the world below. It fell on a day that Zeus sat banqueting, throned in splendor such as mortal eye hath not seen, and surrounded by the glorious company of the Olympians, his brothers and sisters, and Prometheus rose up from his place and made to depart, after his wont. And Zeus asked him:

"What is it you will find on earth, Prometheus, fairer than this house of mine, that you are in such haste to leave?"

"Nothing fairer, nor so fair," answered Prometheus, with a smile, "but something sweeter to me. For bethink you, King of us all, that you were born where now you reign, but I am no native of the Sky; to me, a son of Earth, the green glens of Arcadia are dearer than all your starry pomp."

So he went his way, but Zeus sat frowning in his place, for the answer misliked him. Presently he called to him the blithe-faced Hermes, his herald and messenger, and bade him follow Prometheus and watch what he did in those glens that he loved better than the golden houses of heaven.

"It is for no good end," he said wrathfully, "that the Titan hides his doings from my view under the dense covert of his oakwoods."

Straightway Hermes put on his shining, winged sandals that bear him over sea and land more swiftly than bird can fly, and sped upon his errand. When he came again, Zeus asked him what he had seen.

"King of gods," said Hermes, smiling, "have no fear that Prometheus will plot anything against us Olympians. He recks not of us; all his delight is in the race of puny mortals whom he made out of the clay to pleasure old Cronos; and as for his business in Arcadia, it is neither more nor less than devising their welfare.

"He has taught them, it seems, to fashion rude tools and weapons of horn and bone and flint, to build themselves huts, to till and sow the ground, and many other arts that the men of the Gold and Silver Ages knew nothing of. I heard some among them speak of him — they call him the Great Brother whose wisdom helps to lighten their hard lot, and there was word also of a wondrous gift he has promised to bestow on them ere long."

"What gift is that?" asked Zeus uneasily.

"They do not know," answered Hermes; "but Prometheus has told them that it will be to them *a good servant and a bad master.*"

Now Zeus was troubled at these tidings, for he did not believe that the great Titan would thus befriend mere mortals, creatures of a day, without some deep design. In time, perhaps, he would teach them so much that they would become wiser than gods — nay, this unknown gift he had promised them might be some potent charm that would make them strong enough to defy the Lord of the thunder!

Zeus pondered long what this gift might be, but he could make no guess at it. So, when the Immortals were again gathered to the banquet, he put forth a riddle to them all, saying "What is it that is *a good servant and a bad master?*"

Some said one thing, some another; but Prometheus knew that Hermes had spied upon him in Arcadia, and whispered in his ear, "Minion of Zeus, if you would win favor with your master, say *It is fire.*" And Hermes said it, laughing, after his wont; for he himself never bore ill-will to any one, and dreamed not that a quarrel was toward between his lord and the Titan.

Zeus no sooner heard the answer of Hermes than he perceived that fire was indeed the gift Prometheus was minded to bestow upon men, which, as yet, was unknown to mortals, and burned only beneath the earth and on the sacred Hearth of the gods on high. He resolved to defeat the purpose of Prometheus, whatever it might be, and, rising up, he said:

"You have heard, Olympians, my riddle and its answer. Now hear and obey my command. Let none dare to profane the thrice-holy element of fire by bestowing it on mortals, but be it for ever consecrate to the use of the gods alone. Swift vengeance will I take on him who shall transgress this my law."

The rest of the Immortals hastily promised obedience, but Prometheus began to plead earnestly with Zeus for the race of mortals, bidding him remember the want and hardship they must endure now that Earth no longer gave her increase freely as in the Age of Gold. Without fire, he said, mankind could not warm their shivering frames in the winter season, nor forge weapons of metal to defend themselves from beasts of prey, nor bring to perfection any of those helpful crafts that he had begun to teach them.

"Forbid them fire," he cried, "and you forbid them all hope of rising above the life of animals; their doom is sure, they must be savages to the end."

But Zeus would not hearken to his pleading, for he could not see that the heart of Prometheus was filled with compassion and loving-kindness for helpless man, being indeed blinded by his jealous mistrust.

"What are this folk of clay to me?" he said disdainfully. "They were not made for my pleasure, that I should show them favor — nay, they belong to Cronos, who bade you provide him new worshippers when he had destroyed the race of Silver. For his sake they are hateful to me, and I have a mind to cut them off as he did those others, and people Earth with a race that has known no other gods but me."

Prometheus made him no answer, but gave him a look at once proud and mournful, and in a little while he departed without word of farewell. And after that he came no more to the board of Zeus. But when some days had passed, Zeus looked forth upon the earth and saw pillars of blue smoke rising among the trees in all the valleys of Arcadia.

For Prometheus had taken fire from the Hearth of the gods by stealth, and brought it to men in a hollow wand of fennel that served him instead of a staff. He had shown them how to make open hearths of sun-baked clay in their poor dwellings, and how to kindle dry wood thereon with the new gift, and they cried aloud for joy and wonder as they saw the scarlet flowers of flame blossom from the dead boughs.

Then was Zeus wroth indeed; in the first moment of his fury he stretched forth his hand to his thunderbolts with intent to hurl them upon the land of Arcadia and utterly consume every living thing therein. But he bethought him suddenly of a better way to wreak vengeance upon the rebel Prometheus, and he stayed his hand. Thunderbolts could not slay the Titan, since he was immortal, and to destroy the land and men he loved would be but small satisfaction, for he could soon make himself another folk in some country fairer than Arcadia.

"These men shall not die," said the angry god, "but I will devise such evils for them that they shall desire death rather than life, and Prometheus shall see their misery and be powerless to succor them. That shall be his keenest pang among the torments I will heap upon him."

Now there are two giant Twins whose lot it is to serve him that sits upon the throne of heaven, be he who he may, and the gods call them Kratos and Bia, that is to say, Might and Force. These Zeus called before him, and having laid certain commands on them, he sent them to the Forge of the Cyclopes in Mount Etna, which he had given to the lame smith-god, Hephaestus, the cunning craftsman of the Olympians, to be his workshop.

Meanwhile Prometheus, not ignorant of his doom, betook himself to the house of his brother, Epimetheus, and said to him:

"Brother, I am bound on a far journey, and must bid farewell to you and to Arcadia, our pleasant home, for the Fates will have it so. Grieve not, nor be amazed at the things you will shortly hear concerning me, since all that must befall me I have foreseen with unshaken mind, but take good heed to yourself and beware above all else of receiving any gift from Zeus."

With that he took leave of his brother, and returned to his own house, to await those whom he knew would come speedily, and that night he went unresisting with Kratos, Bia, and Hephaestus to his place of punishment.

There is a ravine of ice-clad rocks upon the peak of huge Mount Caucasus, so walled about with gaunt black precipices, so ghastly in its frozen desolation, that it might seem a very temple of Death, where nothing living had ever come since the making of the world. Not the tiniest, lowliest plant that grows peeps from the crannies of its jagged cliffs; no voice of beast or bird ever echoes there, save the scream of a famished eagle far aloft.

Yet it is a solitude without peace, for night and day fierce gusts sweep through the gorge, now wailing like spirits in torment, now with uproar so hideous that to hear it would drive a man from his wits. The bright snow that lies deep on the mountain head is whirled away by those pitiless blasts before it can mantle the unsightly masses of rock that bestrew the floor of the ravine or the lightning-scarred crags whence they have fallen.

Hither now came the captive Titan, led by the ministers of Zeus. They had bound him with fetters of brass and with chains of iron, which Hephaestus had wrought, being so commanded, but sorely against his will. For he and all the Olympians loved Prometheus because of his great and gracious ways, and had they dared, would have interceded for him with their King. But Kratos and Bia, who were by nature without pity, exulted over their mighty prisoner, and when they were now come to the place Zeus had appointed and saw that Hephaestus stood gazing sorrowfully upon him, they were enraged.

"Hephaestus!" cried Kratos fiercely, "why loiter you now? Have you a mind to take sides with this Firestealer, or have you so soon forgot the charge Zeus gave you by my mouth?"

"I would he had given it to some other," muttered the lame god.

"Have a care, Haltfoot, that he overhear you not," answered Kratos tauntingly. "It is well seen you are loth to do his bidding, and if you make not better speed your pity may shortly be needed for your own plight."

"Savage that you are," retorted Hephaestus, "what needs your rude urging? I know, and will perform the sentence of Zeus, but none that has not, like you, a heart of stone, could joy in such a task. Come, let us about it, and hold your peace the while."

Forthwith Kratos and Bia caused Prometheus to stand upright against a huge pillar of rock, and they held up his arms above his head, while Hephaestus bound him to the pillar by the neck and wrists and ankles, riveting his fetters to the rock with nails of adamant. Slowly he plied his hammer, slowly he limped to and fro, and as he worked he heavily sighed. Meantime Kratos feasted his eyes on the sight, and exclaimed impatiently against his slackness.

"Bind him faster, Hephaestus!" he cried. "Drive home this spike through the iron collar, that he may not turn his head to right or left! Look you, how loose sits this manacle! Another rivet, I pray you, lest the cunning rebel shake himself free. So — have you done at last? Ah, ha! Prometheus! could not all your foresight save you from this pass? Now learn, too late, what it is to be the Friend of Man and the Foe of Zeus!"

Never a word answered Prometheus, but Hephaestus angrily bade Kratos and Bia begone, for they had done their office. As they sullenly withdrew, he turned to the motionless figure against the pillar and spoke parting words.

"Son of Earth," he said, "not more unwelcome are those bonds to you who wear them than was the forging of them to me. Alas! that my skill is put to such a proof — that I must bind one of race divine in these shackles which no power can break! Ah! rash Prometheus, why did you flout the majesty of Zeus for the sake of worthless mortals? Know you not that a newcomer makes ever a stern master, jealous of his honor?

"Loth am I to leave you thus, but I can avail you nothing; nor see I whence you are to look for any deliverer. Here, then, you must bide, shut out from sight and speech of gods or men by these eternal walls; here, unsheltered in the scorching blaze of noon you will pray for the coming of starry-kirtled Night, albeit to you she brings no solace, but only exchange of torment — the arrows of frost for the arrows of the sun. Ay, where nought else ever changes, dear to your sleepless eyes shall be the comings of morn and eve."

Having thus spoken, Hephaestus also went his way with halting steps, and all was silence for a space in that prison-house. Then a great cry broke from the Titan in his anguish:

"O Earth, Mother of all, O radiant Sky and free Winds of heaven, behold what wrongs are mine! Yea, I call on the Sun's pure splendor, and the multitudinous smile of Ocean waves, and you, O Founts of the rivers, to witness what outrage an Immortal suffers at an Immortal's hand. Behold these shameful bonds, this living tomb where I must wrestle alone with never-ending pain — to this the new Lord of the world has doomed Prometheus for no other crime than giving man fire from heaven."

He paused awhile, communing with his own heart, then said, "Yet why do I lament? All this I foresaw from the beginning, and knew at how great a price I must win for mankind the thrice-blessed gift of fire, whereby alone they shall attain to mastery in every art that ministers to life. Nor will I upbraid the tyrant who has thus repaid my ancient kindness. Not he, but resistless Fate, has decreed my doom, and he also in the hour ordained, must learn to submit, as I do."

Pandora[4]

In this myth we have really the second chapter on the beginnings of things — of the first woman, Pandora; of our troubles; of hope. Hesiod (Theogony, 570–612) is the source for the statement that Pandora was the first woman; and in his Works and Days (54–105) he tells that Hope alone was left in the box. The similarity to the story of Eve's temptation and fall cannot be overlooked. In another version, Epimetheus is no less culpable than Pandora; for he might have stopped her had he not been likewise curious.

Now while Prometheus comforted his heart with the thought of what mankind would be able to accomplish by means of fire, Zeus sat pondering how he might frus-

[4] From W. M. L. Hutchinson, *Orpheus with His Lute* (Longmans, Green, 1926).

trate that good gift with some countervailing evil. For it is a law to all the Immortals, that none may take away what another has bestowed, nor could even he now deprive mortals of their new possession. He purposed, therefore, to send them some gift so baneful that they should be never free from misery their lives long, and thus to fill up the measure of his vengeance upon Prometheus.

After long thought, he called Hephaestus to him and said, "Hephaestus, I have devised a new thing, that has not its like in earth or heaven; now put forth all your skill, for you must forthwith make it, according to the fashion I will tell you."

"Of what shall I make it?" asked Hephaestus.

"Of whatever you can find most fair," said Zeus. "Mingle together all things loveliest, sweetest, and best, but look, that you also mingle therewith the opposites of each."

So Hephaestus took gold and dross, wax and flint, pure snow and mud of the highways, honey and gall; he took the bloom of the rose and the toad's venom, the voice of laughing water and the peacock's squall; he took the sea's beauty and its treachery; the dog's fidelity, the wind's inconstancy; the cruelty of the tiger and the mother-bird's heart of love. All these, and other contraries past number, he blended cunningly into one substance, and this he molded into the shape that Zeus described to him.

When it was finished, Hephaestus looked upon his handiwork and said, "We have made no new thing, but the image of a goddess."

"Nay," said Zeus, "we have made the First Woman," and with that he breathed upon the image, and it lived, and looked upon them wonderingly, as one suddenly awakened.

Then he called all the Olympians to behold the First Woman, and they marveled at the beauty of her, for in truth she was fair as any goddess.

They cried that they would each offer her some gift on this her birthday, and so they did; the goddesses arrayed her in glorious apparel, Hephaestus decked her with jewels of cunning workmanship, and every god gave her some precious thing. Last of all, Zeus himself placed in her hands a casket of lustrous amber, richly overwrought with flowers and fruit of the pomegranate, and having two golden snakes for handles.

"Behold, Immortals," he said, "this new fair creature of my shaping thought, endowed with every earthly loveliness, laden with heaven's choicest treasures! Shall she not be named Pandora, All-Gifted? Seems she not even as a bride adorned for her husband? But she is no mate for an Olympian, for she is mortal; come, let us send her to wed with Epimetheus, in token that we bear him no ill-will for his rebel brother's sake."

The Olympians were well pleased, for they knew not the guileful intent of Zeus, and straightway he bade Hermes lead Pandora to the house of Epimetheus, and say to him, "The King of Gods, in sign of his goodwill towards you, sends you this peerless bride, who brings with her in this casket such a dowry as he only can bestow."

So Hermes brought the First Woman to Arcadia. Now when Epimetheus saw her beauty, and heard why she was come, he could scarce contain himself for joy at his good fortune, and he received the bride with her casket into his house, and wedded her that day, without once remembering the warning Prometheus gave him, not to take any gift from Zeus. But on the morrow it came back to his mind, and he repented of what he had done; for this was his nature, that he was never wise until too late. From this he had his name of Epimetheus, which means After-Thought, even as his brother was called Prometheus, that is Fore-Thought, because he was wise concerning things yet to come.

Epimetheus now reflected that the dowry Zeus had given his bride was doubtless meant to work him some deadly harm, and he asked Pandora if she knew what lay in her amber box.

"No, my husband," said she, "but I will fetch the box from our chamber and we will open it and see. I long to know what the great King of the Immortals has bestowed on us."

"Bide here, Pandora," said the Titan, "and listen well to what I shall say. My mind misgives me that yonder casket holds some evil secret, and he who sent it is not a friend but a subtle enemy. I was warned erewhile to take no gift at his hand, but in my folly I paid little heed. Now since what is done cannot be undone, and the gift is under my roof, here let it stay; but I charge you on your love and obedience, never open the casket. For whatever it holds can do us no mischief while we keep it fast shut, and it is itself so royal-rich and beautiful a thing that I have no heart to cast it away."

Pandora was glad that she might keep the wondrous box, and every day she viewed it with delight as it shone like translucent gold in the sunlight. But after a while she wearied of that pleasure, and began to wonder more and more what might be hidden within it. Many a time, alone in her chamber, she sat gazing at the casket until longing to learn its secret so nearly overcame her that she arose and went hastily forth, vowing to look on it no more.

At last, in an accursed hour, she could resist her desire no longer; she laid her hand upon the lid, and raised it gently — very gently, half-fearful of what she might see. Quick as thought out flew a swarm of tiny winged sprites, soaring and drifting upwards like breeze-blown tufts of thistledown, and they vanished like a wreath of smoke through the open doorway.

With a startled cry Pandora closed the box — but, alas! too late; one glance had shown her it was empty, and she sat down and wept tears of disappointment. Now had she known what she had done, she must have grieved a thousand times more bitterly, for the sprites she had let loose were all the cares and woes and fell diseases that afflict mankind, and from that hour to this they fly abroad upon earth, pursuing hapless mortals from the cradle to the grave. Such was the dower that the First Woman brought with her into the world.

Epimetheus found his wife weeping, and she told him what had befallen, and he forgave her, and said, "Half the fault is mine, because I left the casket in your keeping. It seems that it is as much a woman's nature to be over-curious as it is mine to be wise too late."

And he forbore to reproach her, although he now knew well enough by his power of after-thought, what those sprites were. He asked Pandora if she was sure they had all escaped, and she said "Yes." But by and by she thought she would look again, and when she opened the casket, she saw there was still one left, clinging beneath the gold rim that held up the lid, with its rainbow wings drooping as if broken. And something told Pandora that the name of it was Hope.

What did Pandora do when she found Hope was left in the casket? She pitied the fairy thing, because it seemed half dead, and she laid it in her bosom, to warm it back to life. But when she had cherished it awhile, Hope crept into her heart, and made its abode there; and being comforted, it inhabits ever since the hearts of mortals.

The Curse of Echo [5]

⋲§ *Two nature myths are included in this story: the origin of the echo and the origin of the flower, narcissus. To the Greeks, each flower bore a second blessing beside the initial one of its existence. As Edith Hamilton points out in her* Mythology, *Greece is not a fertile land, but rugged and rocky, and the up-cropping of spring's wild flowers in such earth seems a double miracle.*

In an early Homeric Hymn of the seventh or eighth century, the story is told of the creation of the first narcissus. Zeus set it blooming in the vale of Enna, where its blossoms served to entice Persephone away from her companions gathering flowers there, so that she was alone when the chasm opened before her, and Pluto, the king of the regions of the Dead, rose from the pit in his black chariot and carried her away.

Ovid is the source for the story of Echo and Narcissus (Metamorphoses, iii, 356–401). Echo, the lovely nymph, beguiled Juno with her stories in order that Jupiter might have time to escape from his latest affair of the heart. When Juno discovered the ruse, she wreaked bitter vengeance upon Echo, by robbing her of her voice, except for the purpose of repeating a

5 From Elsie Buckley, *Children of the Dawn* (Stokes, 1908).

fragment of what is said to her. In the version given here, it is the mischief of the nymphs which Echo seeks to hide from Hera. This retelling includes a fine piece of wisdom for the storyteller, "for the best tale-tellers are those who can lie, but who mingle in with their lies some grains of truth which they have picked from their own experience."

In the flowery groves of Helicon Echo was once a fair nymph who, hand in hand with her sisters, sported along the green lawns and by the side of the mountain-streams. Among them all her feet were the lightest and her laugh the merriest, and in the telling of tales not one of them could touch her. So if ever any among them were plotting mischief in their hearts, they would say to her,

"Echo, thou weaver of words, go thou and sit beside Hera in her bower, and beguile her with a tale that she come not forth and find us. See thou make it a long one, Echo, and we will give thee a garland to twine in thy hair."

And Echo would laugh a gay laugh, which rang through the grove.

"What will you do when she tires of my tales?" she asked.

"When that time comes we shall see," said they.

So with another laugh she would trip away and cast herself on the grass at Hera's feet. When Hera looked upon Echo her stern brow would relax, and she would smile upon her and stroke her hair.

"What hast thou come for now, thou sprite?" she would ask.

"I had a great longing to talk with thee, great Hera," she would answer, "and I have a tale — a wondrous new tale — to tell thee."

"Thy tales are as many as the risings of the sun, Echo, and each one of them as long as an old man's beard."

"The day is yet young, mother," she would say, "and the tales I have told thee before are as mud which is trampled underfoot by the side of the one I shall tell thee now."

"Go to, then," said Hera, "and if it pleases me I will listen to the end."

So Echo would sit upon the grass at Hera's feet, and with her eyes fixed upon her face she would tell her tale. She had the gift of words, and, moreover, she had seen and heard many strange things which she alone could tell of. These she would weave into romances, adding to them as best pleased her, or taking from them at will; for the best of tale-tellers are those who can lie, but who mingle in with their lies some grains of truth which they have picked from their own experience. And Hera would forget her watchfulness and her jealousies, and listen entranced, while the magic of Echo's words made each scene live before her eyes. Meanwhile the nymphs would sport to their hearts' content and never fear her anger.

But at last came the black day of reckoning when Hera found out the prank which Echo had played upon her so long, and the fire of her wrath flashed forth like lightning.

"The gift whereby thou hast deceived me shall be thine no more," she cried. "Henceforward thou shalt be dumb till someone else has spoken, and then, even if thou wilt, thou shalt not hold thy tongue, but must needs repeat once more the last words that have been spoken."

"Alas! alas!" cried the nymphs in chorus.

"Alas! alas!" cried Echo after them, and could say no more, though she longed to speak and beg Hera to forgive her. So did it come to pass that she lost her voice, and could only say that which others put in her mouth, whether she wished it or no.

Now, it chanced one day that the young Narcissus strayed away from his companions in the hunt, and when he tried to find them he only wandered further, and lost his way upon the lonely heights of Helicon. He was now in the bloom of his youth, nearing manhood, and fair as a flower in spring, and all who saw him straightway loved him and longed for him. But, though his face was smooth and soft as maiden's, his heart was hard as steel; and while many loved him and sighed for him, they could kindle no answering flame in his breast, but he would spurn them, and treat them with scorn, and go on his way, nothing caring. When he was born, the blind seer Teiresias had prophesied concerning him,

"So long as he sees not himself he shall live and be happy."

And his words came true, for Narcissus cared for neither man nor woman, but only for his own pleasure; and because he was so fair that all who saw him loved him for his beauty, he found it easy to get from them what he would. But he himself knew nought of love, and therefore but little of grief; for love at the best brings joy and sorrow hand in hand, and if unreturned, it brings nought but pain.

Now, when the nymphs saw Narcissus wandering alone through the woods, they, too, loved him for his beauty, and they followed him wherever he went. But because he was a mortal they were shy of him, and would not show themselves, but hid behind the trees and rocks so that he should not see them; and amongst the others Echo followed him, too. At last, when he found he had really wandered astray, he began to shout for one of his companions.

"Ho, there! where art thou?" he cried.

"Where art thou?" answered Echo.

When he heard the voice, he stopped and listened, but he could hear nothing more. Then he called again.

"I am here in the wood — Narcissus."

"In the wood — Narcissus," said she.

"Come hither," he cried.

"Come hither," she answered.

Wondering at the strange voice which answered him, he looked all about, but could see no one.

"Art thou close at hand?" he asked.

"Close at hand," answered Echo.

Wondering the more at seeing no one, he went forward in the direction of the voice. Echo, when she found he was coming towards her, fled further, so that when next he called, her voice sounded far away. But wherever she was, he still followed after her, and she saw that he would not let her escape; for wherever she hid, if he called, she had to answer, and so show him her hiding-place. By now they had come to an open space in the trees, where the green lawn sloped down to a clear pool in the hollow. Here by the margin of the water she stood, with her back to the tall, nodding bulrushes, and as Narcissus came out from the trees she wrung her hands, and the salt tears dropped from her eyes; for she loved him, and longed to speak to him, and yet she could not say a word. When he saw her he stopped.

"Art thou she who calls me?" he asked.

"Who calls me?" she answered.

"I have told thee, Narcissus," he said.

"Narcissus," she cried, and held out her arms to him.

"Who art thou?" he asked.

"Who art thou?" said she.

"Have I not told thee," he said impatiently, "Narcissus?"

"Narcissus," she said again, and still held out her hands beseechingly.

"Tell me," he cried, "who art thou and why dost thou call me?"

"Why dost thou call me?" said she.

At this he grew angry.

"Maiden, whoever thou art, thou hast led me a pretty dance through the woods, and now thou dost nought but mock me."

"Thou dost nought but mock me," said she.

At this he grew yet more angry, and began to abuse her, but every word of abuse that he spoke she hurled back at him again. At last, tired out with his wanderings and with anger, he threw himself on the grass by the pool, and would not look at her nor speak to her again. For a time she stood beside him weeping, and longing to speak to him and explain, but never a word could she utter. So at last in her misery she left him, and went and hid herself behind a rock close by. After a while, when his anger had cooled down somewhat, Narcissus remembered he was very thirsty, and noticing for the first time the clear pool beside him, he bent over the edge of the bank to drink. As he held out his hand to take the water, he saw looking up towards him a face which was the fairest face he had ever looked on, and his heart, which never yet had known what love was, at last was set on fire by the face in the pool. With a sigh he held out both his arms towards it, and the figure also held out two arms to him, and Echo from the rock answered back his sigh. When he saw the figure stretching out towards him and heard the sigh, he thought that his love was returned, and he bent down closer to the water and whispered, "I love thee."

"I love thee," answered Echo from the rock.

At these words he bent down further, and tried to clasp the figure in his arms, but as he did so, it vanished away. The surface of the pool was covered with ripples, and he found he was clasping empty water to his breast. So he drew back and waited awhile, thinking he had been over-hasty. In time, the ripples died away and the face appeared again as clear as before, looking up at him longingly from the water. Once again he bent towards it, and tried to clasp it, and once again it fled from his embrace. Time after time he tried, and always the same thing happened, and at last he gave up in despair, and sat looking down into the water, with the teardrops falling from his eyes; and the figure in the pool wept, too, and looked up at him with a look of longing and despair. The longer he looked, the more fiercely did the flame of love burn in his breast, till at length he could bear it no more, but determined to reach the desire of his heart or die. So for the last time he leaned forward, and when he found that once again he was clasping the empty water, he threw himself from the bank into the pool, thinking that in the depths, at any rate, he would find his love. But he found nought but death among the weeds and stones of the pool, and knew not that it was his own face he loved reflected in the water below him. Thus were the words of the prophet fulfilled, "So long as he sees not himself he shall live and be happy."

Echo, peeping out from the rock, saw all that had happened, and when Narcissus cast himself into the pool, she rushed forward, all too late, to stop him. When she found she could not save him, she cast herself on the grass by the pool and wept and wept, till her flesh and her bones wasted away with weeping, and nought but her voice remained and the curse that was on her. So to this day she lives, a formless voice haunting rocks and caves and vaulted halls. Herself no man has seen since the day Narcissus saw her wringing her hands for love of him beside the nodding bulrushes, and no man ever shall see again. But her voice we all have heard repeating our words when we thought that no one was by; and though now she will say whatever we bid her, if once the curse

were removed, the cry of her soul would be, "Narcissus, Narcissus, my love, come back — come back to me!"

By the side of the clear brown pool, on the grass that Echo had watered with her tears, there sprang up a sweet-scented flower, with a pure white face and a crown of gold. And to this day in many a land men call that flower "Narcissus," after the lad who, for love of his own fair face, was drowned in the waters of Helicon.

Cupid and Psyche [6]

This story is found only in the work of Apuleius, a Latin writer of the second century. Psyche is the Greek word for the soul, and the word from which our own word psychology derives. Cupid of course was the god of Love. Love and the Soul! These are themes that have engaged the mind of man through the centuries, and no doubt will continue to do so till the end of time.

The Norwegian folk tale, with one of the most beautiful names in all folklore, East o' the Sun and West o' the Moon, is essentially the same story, removed from any association with the gods, but stating the same themes of the necessity for trust in love, the anguish easily borne if it be for the sake of love, and its glorious triumph in the end.

There was once a king who had three daughters, all lovely maidens, but the youngest, Psyche, excelled her sisters so greatly that beside them she seemed a very goddess consorting with mere mortals. The fame of her surpassing beauty spread over the earth, and everywhere men journeyed to gaze upon her with wonder and adoration and to do her homage as though she were in truth one of the immortals. They would even say that Venus herself could not equal this mortal. As they thronged in ever-growing numbers to worship her loveliness no one any more gave a thought to Venus herself. Her temples were neglected; her altars foul with cold ashes; her favorite towns deserted and falling in ruins. All the honors once hers were

6 From Edith Hamilton, *Mythology* (Little, Brown, 1942).

now given to a mere girl destined some day to die.

It may well be believed that the goddess would not put up with this treatment. As always when she was in trouble she turned for help to her son, that beautiful winged youth whom some call Cupid and others Love, against whose arrows there is no defense, neither in heaven nor on the earth. She told him her wrongs and as always he was ready to do her bidding. "Use your power," she said, "and make the hussy fall madly in love with the vilest and most despicable creature there is in the whole world." And so no doubt he would have done, if Venus had not first shown him Psyche, never thinking in her jealous rage what such beauty might do even to the God of Love himself. As he looked upon her it was as if he had shot one of his arrows into his own heart. He said nothing to his mother, indeed he had no power to utter a word, and Venus left him with the happy confidence that he would swiftly bring about Psyche's ruin.

What happened, however, was not what she had counted on. Psyche did not fall in love with a horrible wretch, she did not fall in love at all. Still more strange, no one fell in love with her. Men were content to look and wonder and worship — and then pass on to marry someone else. Both her sisters, inexpressibly inferior to her, were splendidly married, each to a king. Psyche, the all-beautiful, sat sad and solitary, only admired, never loved. It seemed that no man wanted her.

This was, of course, most disturbing to her parents. Her father finally traveled to an oracle of Apollo to ask his advice on how to get her a good husband. The god answered him, but his words were terrible. Cupid had told him the whole story and had begged for his help. Accordingly Apollo said that Psyche, dressed in deepest mourning, must be set on the summit of a rocky hill and left alone, and that there her destined husband, a fearful winged serpent, stronger than the gods themselves, would come to her and make her his wife.

The misery of all when Psyche's father brought back this lamentable news can be imagined. They dressed the maiden as though for her death and carried her to the hill with greater sorrow than if it had been to her tomb. But Psyche herself kept her courage. "You should have wept for me before," she told them, "because of the beauty that has drawn down upon me the jealousy of Heaven. Now go, knowing that I am glad the end has come." They went in despairing grief, leaving the lovely helpless creature to meet her doom alone, and they shut themselves in their palace to mourn all their days for her.

On the high hilltop in the darkness Psyche sat, waiting for she knew not what terror. There, as she wept and trembled, a soft breath of air came through the stillness to her, the gentle breathing of Zephyr, sweetest and mildest of winds. She felt it lift her up. She was floating away from the rocky hill and down until she lay upon a grassy meadow soft as a bed and fragrant with flowers. It was so peaceful there, all her trouble left her and she slept. She woke beside a bright river; and on its bank was a mansion stately and beautiful as though built for a god, with pillars of gold and walls of silver and floors inlaid with precious stones. No sound was to be heard; the place seemed deserted and Psyche drew near, awestruck at the sight of such splendor. As she hesitated on the threshold, voices sounded in her ear. She could see no one, but the words they spoke came clearly to her. The house was for her, they told her. She must enter without fear and bathe and refresh herself. Then a banquet table would be spread for her. "We are your servants," the voices said, "ready to do whatever you desire."

The bath was the most delightful, the food the most delicious, she had ever enjoyed. While she dined, sweet music breathed around her: a great choir seemed to sing to a harp, but she could only hear, not see, them. Throughout the day, except for the strange companionship of the voices, she was alone, but in some inexplicable way she felt sure that with the coming of the night her husband would be with her. And so it happened. When she felt him beside her and heard his voice softly murmuring in her ear, all her fears left her. She knew without seeing him that here was no monster or shape of terror, but the lover and husband she had longed and waited for.

This half-and-half companionship could not fully content her; still she was happy and time passed swiftly. One night, however, her dear though unseen husband spoke gravely to her and warned her that danger in the shape of her two sisters was approaching. "They are coming to the hill where you disappeared, to weep for you," he said; "but you must not let them see you or you will bring great sorrow upon me and ruin to yourself." She promised him she would not, but all the next day she passed in weeping, thinking of her sisters and herself unable to comfort them. She was still in tears when her husband came and even his caresses could not check them. At last he yielded sorrowfully to her great desire. "Do what you will," he said, "but you are seeking your own destruction." Then he warned her solemnly not to be persuaded by anyone to try to see him, on pain of being separated from him forever. Psyche cried out that she would never do so. She would die a hundred times over rather than live without him. "But give me this joy," she said: "to see my sisters." Sadly he promised her that it should be so.

The next morning the two came, brought down from the mountain by Zephyr. Happy and excited, Psyche was waiting for them. It was long before the three could speak to each other; their joy was too great to be expressed except by tears and embraces. But when at last they entered the palace and the elder sisters saw its surpassing treasures; when they sat at the rich banquet and heard the marvelous music, bitter envy took possession of them and a devouring curiosity as to who was the lord of all this magnificence and their sister's husband. But Psyche kept faith; she told them only that he was a young man, away now on a hunting expedition. Then filling their hands with gold and jewels, she had Zephyr bear them back to the hill. They went willingly enough, but their hearts were on fire with jealousy. All their own wealth and good fortune seemed to them as nothing compared with Psyche's, and their envious anger so worked in them

that they came finally to plotting how to ruin her.

That very night Psyche's husband warned her once more. She would not listen when he begged her not to let them come again. She never could see him, she reminded him. Was she also to be forbidden to see all others, even her sisters so dear to her? He yielded as before, and very soon the two wicked women arrived, with their plot carefully worked out.

Already, because of Psyche's stumbling and contradictory answers when they asked her what her husband looked like, they had become convinced that she had never set eyes on him and did not really know what he was. They did not tell her this, but they reproached her for hiding her terrible state from them, her own sisters. They had learned, they said, and knew for a fact, that her husband was not a man, but the fearful serpent Apollo's oracle had declared he would be. He was kind now, no doubt, but he would certainly turn upon her some night and devour her.

Psyche, aghast, felt terror flooding her heart instead of love. She had wondered so often why he would never let her see him. There must be some dreadful reason. What did she really know about him? If he was not horrible to look at, then he was cruel to forbid her ever to behold him. In extreme misery, faltering and stammering, she gave her sisters to understand that she could not deny what they said, because she had been with him only in the dark. "There must be something very wrong," she sobbed, "for him so to shun the light of day." And she begged them to advise her.

They had their advice all prepared beforehand. That night she must hide a sharp knife and a lamp near her bed. When her husband was fast asleep she must leave the bed, light the lamp, and get the knife. She must steel herself to plunge it swiftly into the body of the frightful being the light would certainly show her. "We will be near," they said, "and carry you away with us when he is dead."

Then they left her torn by doubt and distracted what to do. She loved him; he was her dear husband. No; he was a horrible serpent and she loathed him. She would kill him — She would not. She must have certainty — She did not want certainty. So all day long her thoughts fought with each other. When evening came, however, she had given the struggle up. One thing she was determined to do: she would see him.

When at last he lay sleeping quietly, she summoned all her courage and lit the lamp. She tiptoed to the bed and holding the light high above her she gazed at what lay there. Oh, the relief and the rapture that filled her heart. No monster was revealed, but the sweetest and fairest of all creatures, at whose sight the very lamp seemed to shine brighter. In her first shame at her folly and lack of faith, Psyche fell on her knees and would have plunged the knife into her own breast if it had not fallen from her trembling hands. But those same unsteady hands that saved her betrayed her, too, for as she hung over him, ravished at the sight of him and unable to deny herself the bliss of filling her eyes with his beauty, some hot oil fell from the lamp upon his shoulder. He started awake: he saw the light and knew her faithlessness, and without a word he fled from her.

She rushed out after him into the night. She could not see him, but she heard his voice speaking to her. He told her who he was, and sadly bade her farewell. "Love cannot live where there is no trust," he said, and flew away. "The God of Love!" she thought. "He was my husband, and I, wretch that I am, could not keep faith with him. Is he gone from me forever? . . . At any rate," she told herself with rising courage, "I can spend the rest of my life searching for him. If he has no more love left for me, at least I can show him how much I love him." And she started on her journey. She had no idea where to go; she knew only that she would never give up looking for him.

He meanwhile had gone to his mother's chamber to have his wound cared for, but when Venus heard his story and learned that it was Psyche whom he had chosen, she left him angrily alone in his pain, and went forth to find the girl of whom he had made

her still more jealous. Venus was determined to show Psyche what it meant to draw down the displeasure of a goddess.

Poor Psyche in her despairing wanderings was trying to win the gods over to her side. She offered ardent prayers to them perpetually, but not one of them would do anything to make Venus their enemy. At last she perceived that there was no hope for her, either in heaven or on earth, and she took a desperate resolve. She would go straight to Venus; she would offer herself humbly to her as her servant, and try to soften her anger. "And who knows," she thought, "if he himself is not there in his mother's house." So she set forth to find the goddess who was looking everywhere for her.

When she came into Venus' presence the goddess laughed aloud and asked her scornfully if she was seeking a husband since the one she had had would have nothing to do with her because he had almost died of the burning wound she had given him. "But really," she said, "you are so plain and ill-favored a girl that you will never be able to get you a lover except by the most diligent and painful service. I will therefore show my good will to you by training you in such ways." With that she took a great quantity of the smallest of the seeds, wheat and poppy and millet and so on, and mixed them all together in a heap. "By nightfall these must all be sorted," she said. "See to it for your own sake." And with that she departed.

Psyche, left alone, sat still and stared at the heap. Her mind was all in a maze because of the cruelty of the command; and, indeed, it was of no use to start a task so manifestly impossible. But at this direful moment she who had awakened no compassion in mortals or immortals was pitied by the tiniest creatures of the field, the little ants, the swift-runners. They cried to each other, "Come, have mercy on this poor maid and help her diligently." At once they came, waves of them, one after another, and they labored separating and dividing, until what had been a confused mass lay all ordered, every seed with its kind. This was what Venus found when she came back, and very angry she was to see it. "Your work is by no means over," she said. Then she gave Psyche a crust of bread and bade her sleep on the ground while she herself went off to her soft, fragrant couch. Surely if she could keep the girl at hard labor and half starve her, too, that hateful beauty of hers would soon be lost. Until then she must see that her son was securely guarded in his chamber where he was still suffering from his wound. Venus was pleased at the way matters were shaping.

The next morning she devised another task for Psyche, this time a dangerous one. "Down there near the riverbank," she said, "where the bushes grow thick, are sheep with fleeces of gold. Go fetch me some of their shining wool." When the worn girl reached the gently flowing stream, a great longing seized her to throw herself into it and end all her pain and despair. But as she was bending over the water she heard a little voice from near her feet, and looking down saw that it came from a green reed. She must not drown herself, it said. Things were not as bad as that. The sheep were indeed very fierce, but if Psyche would wait until they came out of the bushes toward evening to rest beside the river, she could go into the thicket and find plenty of the golden wool hanging on the sharp briars.

So spoke the kind and gentle reed, and Psyche, following the directions, was able to carry back to her cruel mistress a quantity of the shining fleece. Venus received it with an evil smile. "Someone helped you," she said sharply. "Never did you do this by yourself. However, I will give you an opportunity to prove that you really have the stout heart and the singular prudence you make such a show of. Do you see that black water which falls from the hill yonder? It is the source of the terrible river which is called hateful, the river Styx. You are to fill this flask from it." That was the worst task yet, as Psyche saw when she approached the waterfall. Only a winged creature could reach it, so steep and slimy were the rocks on all sides, and so fearful the onrush of the descending waters. But by this time it must be evident to all the readers of this story (as, perhaps, deep in her heart it had become evident to Psyche herself) that although

each of her trials seemed impossibly hard, an excellent way out would always be provided for her. This time her savior was an eagle, who poised on his great wings beside her, seized the flask from her with his beak and brought it back to her full of the black water.

But Venus kept on. One cannot but accuse her of some stupidity. The only effect of all that had happened was to make her try again. She gave Psyche a box which she was to carry to the underworld and ask Proserpine to fill with some of her beauty. She was to tell her that Venus really needed it, she was so worn-out from nursing her sick son. Obediently as always Psyche went forth to look for the road to Hades. She found her guide in a tower she passed. It gave her careful directions how to get to Proserpine's palace, first through a great hole in the earth, then down to the river of death, where she must give the ferryman, Charon, a penny to take her across. From there the road led straight to the palace. Cerberus, the three-headed dog, guarded the doors, but if she gave him a cake he would be friendly and let her pass.

All happened, of course, as the tower had foretold. Proserpine was willing to do Venus a service, and Psyche, greatly encouraged, bore back the box, returning far more quickly than she had gone down.

Her next trial she brought upon herself through her curiosity and, still more, her vanity. She felt that she must see what that beauty-charm in the box was; and, perhaps, use a little of it herself. She knew quite as well as Venus did that her looks were not improved by what she had gone through, and always in her mind was the thought that she might suddenly meet Cupid. If only she could make herself more lovely for him! She was unable to resist the temptation; she opened the box. To her sharp disappointment she saw nothing there; it seemed empty. Immediately, however, a deadly languor took possession of her and she fell into a heavy sleep.

At this juncture the God of Love himself stepped forward. Cupid was healed of his wound by now and longing for Psyche. It is a difficult matter to keep Love imprisoned.

Venus had locked the door, but there were the windows. All Cupid had to do was to fly out and start looking for his wife. She was lying almost beside the palace, and he found her at once. In a moment he had wiped the sleep from her eyes and put it back into the box. Then waking her with just a prick from one of his arrows, and scolding her a little for her curiosity, he bade her take Proserpine's box to his mother and he assured her that all thereafter would be well.

While the joyful Psyche hastened on her errand, the god flew up to Olympus. He wanted to make certain that Venus would give them no more trouble, so he went straight to Jupiter himself. The Father of Gods and Men consented at once to all that Cupid asked – "Even though," he said, "you have done me great harm in the past – seriously injured my good name and my dignity by making me change myself into a bull and a swan and so on . . . However, I cannot refuse you."

Then he called a full assembly of the gods, and announced to all, including Venus, that Cupid and Psyche were formally married, and that he proposed to bestow immortality upon the bride. Mercury brought Psyche into the palace of the gods, and Jupiter himself gave her the ambrosia to taste which made her immortal. This, of course, completely changed the situation. Venus could not object to a goddess for her daughter-in-law; the alliance had become eminently suitable. No doubt she reflected also that Psyche, living up in heaven with a husband and children to care for, could not be much on the earth to turn men's heads and interfere with her own worship.

So all came to a most happy end. Love and the Soul (for that is what Psyche means) had sought and, after sore trials, found each other; and that union could never be broken.

Orpheus[7]

How great the imagination which could encompass in one definitive story the magnitude and mystery of music! It is done in this love story of Orpheus and Eurydice (or Eurydike), in which Death itself breaks immutable laws, so moving is the power of music.

Virgil told the story first. The poet Apollonius, a third century Greek, in his work Argonautica *places Orpheus among the Argonauts who, led by Jason, went in search of the Golden Fleece. The lyre of Orpheus sped the tasks of the rowers on that long journey, calmed the anger of the men, and saved the Argonauts from the wiles of the Sirens, for the music of Orpheus drowned out the voices of the Sirens which, had they been harkened to, would have drawn the men to shipwreck and disaster.*

Many were the minstrels who, in the early days of the world, went amongst men, telling them stories of the Gods, of their wars and their births, and of the beginning of things. Of all these minstrels none was so famous as Orpheus; none could tell truer things about the Gods; he himself was half divine, and there were some who said that he was in truth Apollo's son.

But a great grief came to Orpheus, a grief that stopped his singing and his playing upon the lyre. His young wife, Eurydike, was taken from him. One day, walking in the garden, she was bitten on the heel by a serpent; straightway she went down to the World of the Dead.

Then everything in this world was dark and bitter for the minstrel of the Gods; sleep would not come to him, and for him food had no taste. Then Orpheus said, "I will do that which no mortal has ever done before; I will do that which even the Immortals might shrink from doing; I will go down into the World of the Dead, and I will bring back to the living and to the light my bride, Eurydike."

Then Orpheus went on his way to the cavern which goes down, down to the World of the Dead – the Cavern Tainaron. The trees showed him the way. As he went on, Orpheus played upon his lyre and sang; the trees heard his song and were moved by his grief, and with their arms and their heads they showed him the way to the deep, deep cavern named Tainaron.

Down, down, down by a winding path

[7] From Padraic Colum, *Orpheus; Myths of the World* (Macmillan, 1930).

Orpheus went. He came at last to the great gate that opens upon the World of the Dead. And the silent guards who keep watch there for the Rulers of the Dead were astonished when they saw a living being coming towards them, and they would not let Orpheus approach the gate.

The minstrel took the lyre in his hands and played upon it. As he played, the silent watchers gathered around him, leaving the gate unguarded. As he played the Rulers of the Dead came forth, Hades and Persephone, and listened to the words of the living man.

"The cause of my coming through the dark and fearful ways," sang Orpheus, "is to strive to gain a fairer fate for Eurydike, my bride. All that is above must come down to you at last, O Rulers of the most lasting World. But before her time has Eurydike been brought here. I have desired strength to endure her loss, but I cannot endure it. And I have come before you, Hades and Persephone, brought here by love."

When Orpheus said the name of love, Persephone, the queen of the dead, bowed her young head, and bearded Hades, the king, bowed his head also. Persephone remembered how Demeter, her mother, had sought her all through the world, and she remembered the touch of her mother's tears upon her face. And Hades remembered how his love for Persephone had led him to carry her away from the valley where she had been gathering flowers. He and Persephone stood aside, and Orpheus went through the gate and came amongst the dead.

Still upon his lyre he played. Tantalos — who for his crime had been condemned to stand up to his neck in water and yet never be able to assuage his thirst — Tantalos heard, and for a while did not strive to put his lips toward the water that ever flowed away from him; Sisyphos — who had been condemned to roll up a hill a stone that ever rolled back — Sisyphos heard the music that Orpheus played, and for a while he sat still upon his stone. Ixion, bound to a wheel, stopped its turning for a while; the vultures abandoned their torment of Tityos; the daughters of Danaos ceased to fill their jars; even those dread ones, the Erinyes,

who bring to the dead the memories of all their crimes and all their faults, had their cheeks wet with tears.

In the throng of the newly-come dead Orpheus saw Eurydike. She looked upon her husband, but she had not the power to come near him. But slowly she came when Hades, the king, called her. Then with joy Orpheus took her hands.

It would be granted them — no mortal ever gained such privilege before — to leave, both together, the World of the Dead, and to abide for another space in the World of the Living. One condition there would be — that on their way up neither Orpheus nor Eurydike should look back.

They went through the gate and came out amongst the watchers that are around the portals. These showed them the path that went up to the World of the Living. That way they went, Orpheus and Eurydike, he going before her.

Up and through the darkened ways they went, Orpheus knowing that Eurydike was behind him, but never looking back upon her. As he went his heart was filled with things to tell her — how the trees were blossoming in the garden she had left; how the water was sparkling in the fountain; how the doors of the house stood open; how they, sitting together, would watch the sunlight on the laurel bushes. All these things were in his heart to tell her who came behind him, silent and unseen.

And now they were nearing the place where the cavern opened on the world of the living. Orpheus looked up toward the light from the sky. Out of the opening of the cavern he went; he saw a white-winged bird fly by. He turned around and cried, "O Eurydike, look upon the world I have won you back to!"

He turned to say this to her. He saw her with her long dark hair and pale face. He held out his arms to clasp her. But in that instant she slipped back into the gloom of the cavern. And all he heard spoken was a single word, "Farewell!" Long, long had it taken Eurydike to climb so far, but in the moment of his turning around she had fallen back to her place amongst the dead. For Orpheus had looked back.

Back through the cavern Orpheus went again. Again he came before the watchers of the gate. But now he was not looked at nor listened to; hopeless, he had to return to the World of the Living.

The birds were his friends now, and the trees and the stones. The birds flew around him and mourned with him; the trees and stones often followed him, moved by the music of his lyre. But a savage band slew Orpheus and threw his severed head and his lyre into the River Hebrus. It is said by the poets that while they floated in mid-stream the lyre gave out some mournful notes, and the head of Orpheus answered the notes with song.

And now that he was no longer to be counted with the living, Orpheus went down to the World of the Dead, going down straightway. The silent watchers let him pass; he went amongst the dead, and he saw his Eurydike in the throng. Again they were together, Orpheus and Eurydike, and them the Erinyes could not torment with memories of crimes and faults.

Baucis and Philemon [8]

⋐§ "Ovid is the only source for this story. It shows especially well his love of details and the skillful way he uses them to make a fairy tale seem realistic. The Latin names of the gods are used." — Edith Hamilton.

In the Phrygian hill-country there were once two trees which all the peasants near and far pointed out as a great marvel, and no wonder, for one was an oak and the other a linden, yet they grew from a single trunk. The story of how this came about is a proof of the immeasurable power of the gods, and also of the way they reward the humble and the pious.

Sometimes when Jupiter was tired of eating ambrosia and drinking nectar up in Olympus and even a little weary of listening to Apollo's lyre and watching the Graces dance, he would come down to the earth, dis-

8 From Edith Hamilton, *Mythology* (Little, Brown, 1942).

guise himself as a mortal and go looking for adventures. His favorite companion on these tours was Mercury, the most entertaining of all the gods, the shrewdest and the most resourceful. On this particular trip Jupiter had determined to find out how hospitable the people of Phrygia were. Hospitality was, of course, very important to him, since all guests, all who seek shelter in a strange land, were under his especial protection.

The two gods, accordingly, took on the appearance of poor wayfarers and wandered through the land, knocking at each lowly hut or great house they came to and asking for food and a place to rest in. Not one would admit them; every time they were dismissed insolently and the door barred against them. They made trial of hundreds; all treated them in the same way. At last they came upon a little hovel of the humblest sort, poorer than any they had yet found, with a roof made only of reeds. But here, when they knocked, the door was opened wide and a cheerful voice bade them enter. They had to stoop to pass through the low entrance, but once inside they found themselves in a snug and very clean room, where a kindly-faced old man and woman welcomed them in the friendliest fashion and bustled about to make them comfortable.

The old man set a bench near the fire and told them to stretch out on it and rest their tired limbs, and the old woman threw a soft covering over it. Her name was Baucis, she told the strangers, and her husband was called Philemon. They had lived in that cottage all their married life and always been happy. "We are poor folk," she said, "but poverty isn't so bad when you're willing to own up to it, and a contented spirit is a great help, too." All the while she was talking, she was busy doing things for them. The coals under the ashes on the dark hearth she fanned to life until a cheerful fire was burning. Over this she hung a little kettle full of water and just as it began to boil her husband came in with a fine cabbage he had got from the garden. Into the kettle it went, with a piece of the pork which was hanging from one of the beams. While this cooked Baucis set the table with her trembling old hands. One table-leg was too short, but she propped it up with a bit of broken dish. On the board she placed olives and radishes and several eggs which she had roasted in the ashes. By this time the cabbage and bacon were done, and the old man pushed two rickety couches up to the table and bade his guests recline and eat.

Presently he brought them cups of beechwood and an earthenware mixing bowl which held some wine very like vinegar, plentifully diluted with water. Philemon, however, was clearly proud and happy at being able to add such cheer to the supper and he kept on the watch to refill each cup as soon as it was emptied. The two old folks were so pleased and excited by the success of their hospitality that only very slowly a strange thing dawned upon them. The mixing bowl kept full. No matter how many cups were poured out from it, the level of the wine stayed the same, up to the brim. As they saw this wonder each looked in terror at the other, and dropping their eyes they prayed silently. Then in quavering voices and trembling all over they begged their guests to pardon the poor refreshments they had offered. "We have a goose," the old man said, "which we ought to have given your lordships. But if you will only wait, it shall be done at once." To catch the goose, however, proved beyond their powers. They tried in vain until they were worn out, while Jupiter and Mercury watched them greatly entertained.

But when both Philemon and Baucis had had to give up the chase panting and exhausted, the gods felt that the time had come for them to take action. They were really very kind. "You have been hosts to gods," they said, "and you shall have your reward. This wicked country which despises the poor stranger will be bitterly punished, but not you." They then escorted the two out of the hut and told them to look around them. To their amazement all they saw was water. The whole countryside had disappeared. A great lake surrounded them. Their neighbors had not been good to the old couple; nevertheless standing there they wept for them. But of a sudden their tears were dried by an overwhelming wonder. Before their eyes the tiny, lowly hut which had been their home for so long was turned into a stately pillared

temple of whitest marble with a golden roof. "Good people," Jupiter said, "ask whatever you want and you shall have your wish." The old people exchanged a hurried whisper, then Philemon spoke. "Let us be your priests, guarding this temple for you — and oh, since we have lived so long together, let neither of us ever have to live alone. Grant that we may die together."

The gods assented, well pleased with the two. A long time they served in that grand building, and the story does not say whether they ever missed their little cozy room with its cheerful hearth. But one day standing before the marble and golden magnificence they fell to talking about that former life, which had been so hard and yet so happy. By now both were in extreme old age. Suddenly as they exchanged memories each saw the other putting forth leaves. Then bark was growing around them. They had time only to cry, "Farewell, dear companion." As the words passed their lips they became trees, but still they were together. The linden and the oak grew from one trunk.

From far and wide people came to admire the wonder, and always wreaths of flowers hung on the branches in honor of the pious and faithful pair.

Daphne [9]

&§ The story of why Daphne was changed into a laurel was originally told by Ovid (Metamorphoses, 452–567). It shows how even Apollo, god of the sun, music, and poetry, could not escape the power of Cupid, but it was unfortunate that his first love should be Daphne who had forsworn love and had made her father promise never to make her marry. Consequently, when Apollo fell in love with her, it was in vain; and when she called upon her father for help, he was duty bound to aid her. The story also accounts for the use by the Greeks of the laurel wreath as a reward of merit, especially for poetry.

In ancient times, when Apollo left his Shining Palace in the Sun, to roam the earth,

9 From Frances Jenkins Olcott, The Wonder Garden (Houghton Mifflin, 1919).

he met Cupid, who with bended bow and drawn string was seeking human beings to wound with the arrows of love.

"Silly boy," said Apollo, "what do you with the warlike bow? Such burden best befits my shoulders, for did I not slay the fierce serpent, the Python, whose baleful breath destroyed all that came nigh him? Warlike arms are for the mighty, not for boys like you! Do you carry a torch with which to kindle love in human hearts, but no longer lay claim to my weapon, the bow!"

But Cupid replied in anger: "Let your bow shoot what it will, Apollo, but my bow shall shoot *you!*"

Then Cupid rose up, and beating the air with his wings, drew two magic arrows from his quiver. One was of shining gold, and with its barbed point could he inflict wounds of love. The other arrow was of dull silver, and its wound had the power to engender hate.

The silver arrow Cupid let fly into the breast of Daphne, the daughter of the River-King Peneus; and forthwith she fled away from the homes of men and hunted beasts in the forest.

With the golden arrow Cupid grievously wounded Apollo, who, fleeing to the woods, saw there the nymph Daphne pursuing the deer, and straightway he fell in love with her beauty. Her golden locks hung down upon her neck, her eyes were like stars, her form was slender and graceful and clothed in clinging white. Swifter than the light wind she flew, and Apollo followed after.

"O Nymph! daughter of Peneus," he cried, "stay, I entreat you! Why do you fly as a lamb from the wolf, as a deer from the lion, or as a dove with trembling wings flees from the eagle! I am no common man! I am no shepherd! You know not, rash maid, from whom you are flying! Jupiter is my sire. Mine own arrow is unerring; but, alas! Cupid's aim is truer, for he has made his wound in my heart! Alas! wretched me! though I am that great one who discovered the art of healing, yet this love may not be healed by my herbs or my skill!"

But Daphne stopped not at these words; she flew from him with timid step. The winds fluttered her garments, the light breezes spread her flowing locks behind her. Swiftly Apollo drew near, even as the keen greyhound draws near to the frightened hare he is pursuing.

With trembling limbs Daphne turned to the river, the home of her father, Peneus. Close behind her was Apollo. She felt his breath on her hair and his hand on her shoulder. Her strength was spent, she grew pale, and in faint accents she implored the river:

"Oh, save me, my Father, save me from Apollo-of-the-Golden-Beams!"

Scarcely had she thus spoken before a heaviness seized her limbs. Her breast was covered with bark, her hair grew into green leaves and her arms into branches. Her feet, a moment before so swift, became rooted to the ground. And Daphne was no longer a nymph, but a green laurel tree.

When Apollo beheld this change, he cried out and embraced the tree, and kissed its leaves.

"Beautiful Daphne," he said, "since you cannot be my bride, yet shall you be my tree. Henceforth my hair, my lyre, and my quiver shall be adorned with laurel. Your wreaths shall be given to conquering chiefs, to winners of fame and joy; and as my head has never been shorn of its locks, so shall you wear your green bay leaves, winter and summer — forever!"

Apollo ceased speaking, and the laurel bent its new-made boughs in assent, and its stem seemed to shake and its leaves to murmur gently.

Phaethon[1]

The story of Phaethon is most fully told in Ovid's Metamorphoses (*i, 750ff.; ii, 366*). *The scorched earth is supposed to account for deserts. Phaethon has also been identified with the sun, his "fall" representing a blazing sunset.*

It is a story typical of youth eager to assume work beyond its capabilities, eager to win recognition among its peers, eager to claim unique heritage and position.

[1] From Padraic Colum, *The Forge in the Forest* (Macmillan, 1925).

His fiery steeds and his gleaming chariot the Sun-God, Helios, gave over to the young man Phaethon. The shining doors were rolled open and the steeds stood there, pawing the ground and sniffing the wind that blew towards them; yoked to the steeds was the gleaming chariot.

These were the horses and this was the chariot that, journeying through the heavens, brought light and warmth to men. None but Helios himself had ever driven them before. Now Helios stood there and the light was gone from his face. "O Phaethon, O my son," he cried, "thou art being given what thou hast claimed. But before thou dost take the reins, stay and consider! Thou art half mortal, and only the immortals may drive these fiery steeds and this gleaming chariot through the course of the heavens."

But the young man, Phaethon, sprang into the chariot and took in his hands the reins that were across the necks of the fiery steeds.

"Long did I live on earth," he said, "without name and without honour; now I would have the world know that I am indeed the son of bright Helios. Thou didst swear to let me have a token that I, Phaethon, am indeed thy son, and this is the token that I claim — to be let drive thy steeds and thy chariot through the course of the heavens for a single day."

"Renounce thy desire before it is too late, and stay in my shining halls, known to mortals and immortals as my son, the son of Helios who brings light and warmth to the world."

But already the young man had shaken the reins; the fiery steeds sprang forward, and the shining doors of their stable rolled back. Something more his father said to him, but Phaethon did not hear his words. The bright wheels spun round and the chariot of Helios took its course through the sky.

The brightness of their tossing manes made Phaethon exultant; the swiftness of the steeds as they swept along the brightening path through the heavens filled him with delight, and his heart was lifted with pride as he held the reins that guided the course of the horses.

"I — I," he cried in his pride, "I, the name-less son of Klymene, my mother, have the horses of Helios under my hands; I drive my father's gleaming chariot through the heavens; I, Phaethon, will be remembered, and all men must speak of me, because for a single day I am bringing them light and warmth."

He thought of the time he had bade farewell to Klymene, his mother; he thought of how he had come into the bright halls of Helios; he thought of how he had heard his father speak of him, praising his beauty, and of how pride had grown in him then and a resolve to have his father grant him a token that would make the world know that he, Phaethon, was indeed the son of Helios. His father had sworn that he would grant him any token that he might ask.

"And what other token might I ask than this? — to have their reins in my hands and these fiery steeds sweeping forward upon the brightening path. O brightness of fire! What was it that my father said about none but an immortal being able to drive the steeds of Helios? I drive them. I am half mortal, but now that I have driven the fiery steeds and the gleaming chariot I feel that I am become immortal! Immortal, immortal, im-mortal!" he cried, as he went through the brightening heavens, "immortal Phaethon!"

But the immortal horses knew that hands that were not immortal held their reins. They knew that the weakness of one who dies was in the hold that was upon them. They swerved aside from their path in the heavens. They plunged and plunged, going farther off their course. And upon earth men looked up and said, "A portent in the heavens! The steeds of Helios are rushing here and there!"

To Phaethon the horses were but tossing their manes; the bright wheels were but spinning as they should spin. He stood upright in the chariot, holding the reins, and he spoke:

"Are these the hands of one who is half immortal? These hands that hold and guide the horses of Helios! But must men speak always of the horses of Helios? Would that there was a way of making men below wonder at their course today! Wonder, and then know that not Helios but another, one younger and more daring than he, has hands upon the reins today!"

Plunging and plunging, the horses went farther and farther off their course. They went too far from their course in the blue heavens. Earth withered as they came too near. Fire sprang up, fire, and again, fire! The trees on the plains crackled, and dropped branches, and burned. On the mountains the forests took fire. Now there were mountains burning with fire that went up to the sky.

He knew now that the steeds had gone from their course. He tried to guide them back. The fiery steeds turned savage eyes and bared teeth upon him. They tossed their heads; the wheels spun faster and faster, and the chariot rocked as they rushed and plunged along.

Fires went up in the cities of men; in the rivers and lakes the waters dried up; men lay dying upon the earth. The young man Phaethon, knowing his hands too weak to guide them, shouted to the fiery steeds.

Zeus, the ever-watchful, saw Phaethon's course through the heavens, saw the plunging steeds and the fires going up on the earth, and he knew that all life might be destroyed by the horses and chariot coming nearer and nearer to the earth. He gathered the clouds together, making a veil between the chariot and the world of men. And then he flung his lightning on young Phaethon. The lightning of Zeus tore him from the chariot, and the horses, now that they no longer felt his hands upon the reins, staggered back to their course. Feebly now they went on. Feebly they finished their journey, but they won back to the shining stables that had been built for them by Hephaestos beside the gleaming halls of Helios.

Down, down into the seething sea young Phaethon fell. But he was not lost in the sea. The daughters of Hesperus found him and lifted his body out of the depths of the sea. They made a tomb for him on the seashore, and they wrote above his tomb, "Young Phaethon fell from his father's chariot, but even so he lost nothing of his glory, for his heart was set upon the doing of great things."

Bellerophon[2]

&§ *It might be helpful to relate a few points connected with the background of this myth. The Iliad (v, 179) is responsible for the description of the Chimaera, and Pausanias (ii, 31; lv, 31) tells the story which accounts for Pegasus as the symbol for poetry. The story states that when Mount Helicon was so entranced by the songs of the Muses and began to rise toward heaven, Pegasus stopped its ascent by stamping on the ground. At that the Hippocrene (horse fountain) burst forth and became known as the Spring of the Muses. It is an easy step from this point to make the flying horse, Pegasus, the symbol for the flights of poetry. This is the heritage from which the neon light "At the sign of the flying horse" stems.*

Often he watched the eagle in the air; as his gaze followed it on its way he would shout out his own name, "Bellerophon, Bellerophon!" As his name came back to him from the high rocks it seemed to him to be a prophecy of the time when he, too, would mount up and go the way of the eagle. He owned a bright sword and he knew that his spirit was braver and stronger than the spirits of those who were around him. And yet he had to serve a grudging King, and fresh labours and harassments came to him every day.

Once as he came back from his labour, the eyes of King Proetus's Queen rested upon the bright youth. "How beautiful he is, this Bellerophon," the Queen said. She spoke to him and would have him speak to her. But Bellerophon turned from Proetus's Queen — Proetus whom he had to serve. Then the Queen went to King Proetus, and, falsely accusing Bellerophon, had him sent away. But she had him sent away from slavery into dangers. He was commanded to go to the King of Lykia, and he went bearing tablets that told that King to thrust him into danger and still more danger.

"Thou must slay the Chimaera for me," said the King of Lykia; "thou must slay the Chimaera that appears in the sky and affrights all of us." Even then the Chimaera

[2] From Padraic Colum, *The Forge in the Forest* (Macmillan, 1925).

appeared in the sky. It had the head of a lion, the body of a goat, and the tail of a dragon. It filled the bright sky with horror and darkness. Then Bellerophon vowed that he would slay the monster; he would slay it, not because the King commanded him to slay it, but because the monster filled the beautiful depths that he loved with blackness. "I will slay the Chimaera for thee, O King," Bellerophon said, and he laid his hand on his bright sword as he spoke, "I will slay the Chimaera, and I will bring its lion's head into thy hall."

But how would he come to the Chimaera that went through the bright spaces of the sky? It came upon the tops of high mountains, and there Bellerophon would come upon it and slay it. But even as he sharpened his bright sword to go to the mountains and seek the Chimaera there, a whisper came to Bellerophon and told him that he should mount up to slay the Chimaera. And the whisper told him of a horse that grazed on far pastures, the horse Pegasus that had wings. And if he could come upon Pegasus and bridle him and mount him he could slay with his bright sword the Chimaera in the sky.

Then Bellerophon went forth bearing his sword and carrying the bridle that would hold Pegasus, the winged horse. He went forth, and in his own wild pastures he came upon Pegasus. The youth saw the winged horse feeding upon lotuses and springing across the water-courses. White was Pegasus, with white wings and dainty hoofs, and a heavy mane that tossed as he bounded along. It was easy to see that no bridle had ever gone upon Pegasus.

All day Bellerophon, the strong youth, followed after Pegasus. The horse bounded away, hardly noticing his pursuer. On the second day Bellerophon came suddenly upon Pegasus. He was drinking at a certain spring. Bellerophon seized the winged horse by the mane, and strove to hold him. But Pegasus trampled and kicked and at last broke away from Bellerophon. Afterwards he saw the winged horse only in the air, or drinking with his head raised from the spring every moment.

Often when he was worn out with watching and the chase, it would seem to Bellerophon that he never would be able to capture the horse Pegasus; he never would be able to slay the Chimaera, and he would have to go back and bear whatever doom the King of Lykia would lay upon him. And then he would see the sky being filled with the blackness and horror of the Chimaera, and he would resolve once more that he would be the one who would slay the monster.

One night a dream came to him. The goddess Pallas Athene appeared in his dream, and she said to him that any mortal who had such resolve as he had and who strove as he strove to carry out his resolve would have help from the immortals. She whispered to him of a philtre that would tame the horse Pegasus. Then he awoke, and he found in the hollow of his shield a cup that had a liquid in it—a liquid that was red like burning iron.

Bellerophon waited, hidden, at the spring that Pegasus came to. He seized the horse by the mane, and he poured into his mouth and between his teeth the liquid that he had found. Then Pegasus became tame under his hand. He put the bridle upon him. With the bright sword in his hand he mounted up to slay the Chimaera that even then filled the sky with blackness and horror.

And now he was in the air at last. As he went above the earth he shouted out his name, "Bellerophon, Bellerophon!" He knew now how magnificent that name was — the name for the rider of the skies, the conqueror of the Chimaera. He rose above where the eagle flew. He looked down and saw the fields and houses and towns of men. He would always soar above them, Bellerophon thought.

He saw the Chimaera near him, the monster that had the head of a lion, the body of a goat, and the tail of a dragon. Pegasus screamed, and would have kept back from the monster. But Bellerophon rode to meet the darkening thing. It breathed out fire that scorched him. But Bellerophon fought with it, using his bright sword. At last he struck into its body and brought the Chimaera from the sky down to the ground.

He rode Pegasus beside where it lay. He

sprang off and cut the lion-head off the monster that lay there. Then Pegasus, screaming because the monster's blood had come upon him, reddening his white sides, fled away. Bellerophon, as he saw the winged horse go, knew that he could never recapture him, and knew that he could never again soar above the fields and the houses and the towns of men.

Into the hall of the King of Lykia he went, bringing the lion-head of the Chimaera. And then, because he saw an eagle soaring in the blue of the air, he wept. Before him, as he knew, there were long and weary wanderings over the face of the earth. He wept, knowing what was gone from him and what was before him. And then he rejoiced, for he knew that the pure spaces over him would never again be filled with the blackness and horror of the Chimaera.

Icarus and Daedalus [3]

~§ *Daedalus is the Greek word for cunning worker. In the Greek mythology he was an artisan, sculptor, and architect, and figures largely in the early legends of Crete, where this story begins. One authority says the name Daedalus is merely symbolical of the early Greek art; for after he landed in Sicily, he never flew again, but devoted himself to architecture and built many temples. He was also given credit for inventing many tools and carpentry in general.*

Among all those mortals who grew so wise that they learned the secrets of the gods, none was more cunning than Daedalus.

He once built, for King Minos of Crete, a wonderful Labyrinth of winding ways so cunningly tangled up and twisted around that, once inside, you could never find your way out again without a magic clue. But the king's favor veered with the wind, and one day he had his master architect imprisoned in a tower. Daedalus managed to escape from his cell; but it seemed impossible to leave the island, since every ship

3 From Josephine Preston Peabody, *Old Greek Folk Stories Told Anew* (Houghton Mifflin, 1897).

that came or went was well guarded by order of the king.

At length, watching the sea-gulls in the air — the only creatures that were sure of liberty — he thought of a plan for himself and his young son Icarus, who was captive with him.

Little by little, he gathered a store of feathers great and small. He fastened these together with thread, molded them in with wax, and so fashioned two great wings like those of a bird. When they were done, Daedalus fitted them to his own shoulders, and after one or two efforts, he found that by waving his arms he could winnow the air and cleave it, as a swimmer does the sea. He held himself aloft, wavered this way and that with the wind, and at last, like a great fledgling, he learned to fly.

Without delay, he fell to work on a pair of wings for the boy Icarus, and taught him carefully how to use them, bidding him beware of rash adventures among the stars. "Remember," said the father, "never to fly very low or very high, for the fogs about the earth would weigh you down, but the blaze of the sun will surely melt your feathers apart if you go too near."

For Icarus, these cautions went in at one ear and out by the other. Who could remember to be careful when he was to fly for the first time? Are birds careful? Not they! And not an idea remained in the boy's head but the one joy of escape.

The day came, and the fair wind that was to set them free. The father bird put on his wings, and, while the light urged them to be gone, he waited to see that all was well with Icarus, for the two could not fly hand in hand. Up they rose, the boy after his father. The hateful ground of Crete sank beneath them; and the country folk, who caught a glimpse of them when they were high above the tree-tops, took it for a vision of the gods — Apollo, perhaps, with Cupid after him.

At first there was a terror in the joy. The wide vacancy of the air dazed them — a glance downward made their brains reel. But when a great wind filled their wings, and Icarus felt himself sustained, like a halcyon-bird in the hollow of a wave, like a child uplifted by his mother, he forgot everything in the world but joy. He forgot Crete and the other islands that he had passed over: he saw but vaguely that winged thing in the distance before him that was his father Daedalus. He longed for one draft of flight to quench the thirst of his captivity: he stretched out his arms to the sky and made toward the highest heavens.

Alas for him! Warmer and warmer grew the air. Those arms, that had seemed to uphold him, relaxed. His wings wavered, drooped. He fluttered his young hands vainly — he was falling — and in that terror he remembered. The heat of the sun had melted the wax from his wings; the feathers were falling, one by one, like snowflakes; and there was none to help.

He fell like a leaf tossed down by the wind, down, down, with one cry that over took Daedalus far away. When he returned, and sought high and low for the poor boy, he saw nothing but the bird-like feathers afloat on the water, and he knew that Icarus was drowned.

The nearest island he named Icaria, in memory of the child; but he, in heavy grief, went to the temple of Apollo in Sicily, and there hung up his wings as an offering. Never again did he attempt to fly.

Atalanta's Race [4]

> *Atalanta had been forewarned not to marry, as marriage would be her ruin; there-fore, she had made a vow which she thought would stop any suitor. But as one sees from this story, it did not; and her marriage was the cause of her ruin. She and Hippomenes were so happy that they forgot to pay honor to Venus, who caused them to be changed into a pair of lions. It is interesting to note that the device of throw-ing the apples is the same one used in the Scan-dinavian fairy tale,* The Princess on the Glass Hill.

There are two Atalantas, ... the Hunt-ress, and another who is noted for her speed

[4] From Padraic Colum, *The Golden Fleece, and the Heroes Who Lived Before Achilles* (Macmillan, 1921).

of foot and her delight in the race — the daughter of Schoeneus, King of Boeotia, Atalanta of the Swift Foot.

So proud was she of her swiftness that she made a vow to the gods that none would be her husband except the youth who won past her in the race. Youth after youth came and raced against her, but Atalanta, who grew fleeter and fleeter of foot, left each one of them far behind her. The youths who came to the race were so many, and the clamor they made after defeat was so great, that her father made a law that, as he thought, would lessen their number. The law that he made was that the youth who came to race against Atalanta and who lost the race should lose his life into the bargain. After that the youths who had care for their lives stayed away from Boeotia.

Once there came a youth from a far part of Greece into the country that Atalanta's father ruled over. Hippomenes was his name. He did not know of the race, but having come into the city and seeing the crowd of people, he went with them to the course. He looked upon the youths who were girded for the race, and he heard the folk say amongst themselves, "Poor youths, as mighty and as high-spirited as they look, by sunset the life will be out of each of them, for Atalanta will run past them as she ran past the others." Then Hippomenes spoke to the folk in wonder, and they told him of Atalanta's race and of what would befall the youths who were defeated in it. "Unlucky youths," cried Hippomenes, "how foolish they are to try to win a bride at the price of their lives!"

Then, with pity in his heart, he watched the youths prepare for the race. Atalanta had not yet taken her place, and he was fearful of looking upon her. "She is a witch," he said to himself; "she must be a witch to draw so many youths to their deaths, and she, no doubt, will show in her face and figure the witch's spirit."

But even as he said this, Hippomenes saw Atalanta. She stood with the youths before they crouched for the first dart in the race. He saw that she was a girl of a light and a lovely form. Then they crouched for the race; then the trumpets rang out, and the youths and the maiden darted like swallows over the sand of the course.

On came Atalanta, far, far ahead of the youths who had started with her. Over her bare shoulders her hair streamed, blown backward by the wind that met her flight. Her fair neck shone, and her little feet were like flying doves. It seemed to Hippomenes as he watched her that there was fire in her lovely body. On and on she went as swift as the arrow that the Scythian shoots from his bow. And as he watched the race, he was not sorry that the youths were being left behind. Rather would he have been enraged if one came near overtaking her, for now his heart was set upon winning her for his bride, and he cursed himself for not having entered the race.

She passed the last goal mark and she was given the victor's wreath of flowers. Hippomenes stood and watched her and he did not see the youths who had started with her — they had thrown themselves on the ground in their despair.

Then wild, as though he were one of the doomed youths, Hippomenes made his way through the throng and came before the black-bearded King of Boeotia. The king's brows were knit, for even then he was pronouncing doom upon the youths who had been left behind in the race. He looked upon Hippomenes, another youth who would make the trial, and the frown became heavier upon his face.

But Hippomenes saw only Atalanta. She came beside her father; the wreath was upon her head of gold, and her eyes were wide and tender. She turned her face to him, and then she knew by the wildness that was in his look that he had come to enter the race with her. Then the flush that was on her face died away, and she shook her head as if she were imploring him to go from that place.

The dark-bearded king bent his brows upon him and said, "Speak, O youth, speak and tell us what brings you here."

Then cried Hippomenes as if his whole life were bursting out with his words: "Why does this maiden, your daughter, seek an easy renown by conquering weakly youths in the race? She has not striven yet. Here stand I, one of the blood of Poseidon, the god of the sea. Should I be defeated by her in the race, then, indeed, might Atalanta have something to boast of."

Atalanta stepped forward and said: "Do not speak of it, youth. Indeed, I think that it is some god, envious of your beauty and your strength, who sent you here to strive with me and to meet your doom. Ah, think of the youths who have striven with me even now! Think of the hard doom that is about to fall upon them! You venture your life in the race, but indeed I am not worthy of the price. Go hence, O stranger youth; go hence and live happily, for indeed I think that there is some maiden who loves you well."

"Nay, maiden," said Hippomenes, "I will enter the race and I will venture my life on the chance of winning you for my bride. What good will my life and my spirit be to me if they cannot win this race for me?"

She drew away from him then and looked upon him no more, but bent down to fasten the sandals upon her feet. And the black-bearded king looked upon Hippomenes and said, "Face, then, this race tomorrow. You will be the only one who will enter it. But bethink thee of the doom that awaits thee at the end of it." The king said no more, and Hippomenes went from him and from Atalanta, and he came again to the place where the race had been run.

He looked across the sandy course with its goal marks, and in his mind he saw again Atalanta's swift race. He would not meet doom at the hands of the king's soldiers, he knew, for his spirit would leave him with the greatness of the effort he would make to reach the goal before her. And he thought it would be well to die in that effort and on that sandy place that was so far from his own land.

Even as he looked across the sandy course now deserted by the throng, he saw one move across it, coming toward him with feet that did not seem to touch the ground. She was a woman of wonderful presence. As Hippomenes looked upon her, he knew that she was Aphrodite, the goddess of beauty and of love.

"Hippomenes," said the immortal goddess,

"the gods are mindful of you who are sprung from one of the gods, and I am mindful of you because of your own worth. I have come to help you in your race with Atalanta, for I would not have you slain, nor would I have that maiden go unwed. Give your greatest strength and your greatest swiftness to the race, and behold! here are wonders that will prevent the fleet-footed Atalanta from putting all her spirit into the race."

And then the immortal goddess held out to Hippomenes a branch that had upon it three apples of shining gold.

"In Cyprus," said the goddess, "where I have come from, there is a tree on which these golden apples grow. Only I may pluck them. I have brought them to you, Hippomenes. Keep them in your girdle, and in the race you will find out what to do with them, I think."

So Aphrodite said, and then she vanished, leaving a fragrance in the air and the three shining apples in the hands of Hippomenes. Long he looked upon their brightness. They were beside him that night, and when he arose in the dawn he put them in his girdle. Then, before the throng, he went to the place of the race.

When he showed himself beside Atalanta, all around the course were silent, for they all admired Hippomenes for his beauty and for the spirit that was in his face; they were silent out of compassion, for they knew the doom that befell the youths who raced with Atalanta.

And now Schoeneus, the black-bearded king, stood up, and he spoke to the throng, saying: "Hear me all, both young and old: this youth, Hippomenes, seeks to win the race from my daughter, winning her for his bride. Now, if he be victorious and escape death, I will give him my dear child, Atalanta, and many fleet horses besides as gifts from me, and in honor he shall go back to his native land. But if he fail in the race, then he will have to share the doom that has been meted out to the other youths who raced with Atalanta hoping to win her for a bride."

Then Hippomenes and Atalanta crouched for the start. The trumpets were sounded and they darted off.

Side by side with Atalanta Hippomenes went. Her flying hair touched his breast, and it seemed to him that they were skimming the sandy course as if they were swallows. But then Atalanta began to draw away from him. He saw her ahead of him, and then he began to hear the words of cheer that came from the throng — "Bend to the race, Hippomenes! Go on, go on! Use your strength to the utmost!" He bent himself to the race, but farther and farther from him Atalanta drew.

Then it seemed to him that she checked her swiftness a little to look back at him. He gained on her a little. And then his hand touched the apples that were in his girdle. As it touched them, it came into his mind what to do with the apples.

He was not far from her now, but already her swiftness was drawing her farther and farther away. He took one of the apples into his hand and tossed it into the air so that it fell on the track before her.

Atalanta saw the shining apple. She checked her speed and stooped in the race to pick it up. And as she stooped, Hippomenes darted past her, and went flying toward the goal that now was within his sight.

But soon she was beside him again. He looked, and he saw that the goal marks were far, far ahead of him. Atalanta with the flying hair passed him, and drew away and away from him. He had not speed to gain upon her now, he thought, so he put his strength into his hand and he flung the second of the shining apples. The apple rolled before her and rolled off the course. Atalanta turned off the course, stooped and picked up the apple.

Then did Hippomenes draw all his spirit into his breast as he raced on. He was now nearer to the goal than she was. But he knew that she was behind him, going lightly where he went heavily. And then she went past him. She paused in her speed for a moment and she looked back on him.

As he raced on, his chest seemed weighted down and his throat was crackling dry. The goal marks were far away still, but Atalanta was nearing them. He took the last of the golden apples into his hand. Perhaps she was now so far that the strength of his throw would not be great enough to bring the apple before her.

But with all the strength he could put into his hand he flung the apple. It struck the course before her feet and then went bounding wide. Atalanta swerved in her race and followed where the apple went. Hippomenes marveled that he had been able to fling it so far. He saw Atalanta stoop to pick up the apple, and he bounded on. And then, although his strength was failing, he saw the goal marks near him. He set his feet between them and then fell down on the ground.

The attendants raised him up and put the victor's wreath upon his head. The concourse of people shouted with joy to see him victor. But he looked around for Atalanta and he saw her standing there with the golden apples in her hands. "He has won," he heard her say, "and I have not to hate myself for bringing a doom upon him. Gladly, gladly do I give up the race, and glad am I that it is this youth who has won the victory from me."

She took his hand and brought him before the king. Then Schoeneus, in the sight of all the rejoicing people, gave Atalanta to Hippomenes for his bride, and he bestowed upon him also a great gift of horses. With his dear and hard won bride, Hippomenes went to his own country, and the apples that she brought with her, the golden apples of Aphrodite, were reverenced by the people.

The Judgment of Midas [5]

◆§ Midas was the name of several Phrygian kings. Ovid (Metamorphoses, xi, 85–145) tells how our legendary Midas came into contact with Dionysus (god of the vine), who, as a reward for helping him, granted Midas' request to have everything he touched turn into gold. When Midas realized he would starve to death, he successfully begged to be freed from this power. Still Midas did not learn his lesson. He became a follower of Pan, the woodland god of hunters, fishermen, and shepherds, who

[5] From Josephine Preston Peabody, Old Greek Folk Stories Told Anew (Houghton Mifflin, 1897).

played the reed pipes so beautifully that all living things mourned or rejoiced according to his tune. This power so went to Pan's head that he challenged Apollo to a contest of ability. Apollo saw fit to punish not Pan but his faithful follower Midas, who remained loyal to Pan.

Pan came at length to be such a wonderful piper with his syrinx (for so he named his flute) that he challenged Apollo to make better music if he could. Now the sun-god was also the greatest of divine musicians, and he resolved to punish the vanity of the country-god, and so consented to the test. For judge they chose the mountain Tmolus, since no one is so old and wise as the hills. And, since Tmolus could not leave his home, to him went Pan and Apollo, each with his followers, oreads and dryads, fauns, satyrs, and centaurs.

Among the worshipers of Pan was a certain Midas, who had a strange story. Once a king of great wealth, he had chanced to befriend Dionysus, god of the vine, and when he was asked to choose some good gift in return, he prayed that everything he touched might be turned into gold. Dionysus smiled a little when he heard this foolish prayer, but he granted it. Within two days King Midas learned the secret of that smile, and begged the god to take away the gift that was a curse. He had touched everything that belonged to him, and little joy did he have of his possessions! His palace was as yellow a home as a dandelion to a bee, but not half so sweet. Row upon row of stiff golden trees stood in his garden; they no longer knew a breeze when they heard it. When he sat down to eat, his feast turned to treasure uneatable. He learned that a king may starve, and he came to see that gold cannot replace the live, warm gifts of the Earth. Kindly Dionysus took back the charm, but from that day King Midas so hated gold that he chose to live far from luxury, among the woods and fields. Even here he was not to go free from misadventure.

Tmolus gave the word, and Pan uprose with his syrinx, and blew upon the reeds a melody so wild and yet so coaxing that the squirrels came, as if at a call, and the birds hopped down in rows. The trees swayed with a longing to dance, and the fauns looked at one another and laughed for joy. To their furry little ears, it was the sweetest music that could be.

But Tmolus bowed before Apollo, and the sun-god rose with his golden lyre in his hands. As he moved, light shook out of his radiant hair as raindrops are showered from the leaves. His trailing robes were purple, like the clouds that temper the glory of a sunset, so that one may look upon it. He touched the strings of his lyre, and all things were silent with joy. He made music, and the woods dreamed. The fauns and satyrs were quite still; and the wild creatures crouched, blinking, under a charm of light that they could not understand. To hear such a music cease was like bidding farewell to father and mother.

With one accord they fell at the feet of Apollo, and Tmolus proclaimed the victory his. Only one voice disputed that award.

Midas refused to acknowledge Apollo lord of music — perhaps because the looks of the god dazzled his eyes unpleasantly, and put

him in mind of his foolish wish years before. For him there was no music in a golden lyre!

But Apollo would not leave such dull ears unpunished. At a word from him they grew long, pointed, furry, and able to turn this way and that (like a poplar leaf) — a plain warning to musicians. Midas had the ears of an ass, for everyone to see!

For a long time the poor man hid this oddity with such skill that we might never have heard of it. But one of his servants learned the secret, and suffered so much from keeping it to himself that he had to unburden his mind at last. Out into the meadows he went, hollowed a little place in the turf, whispered the strange news into it quite softly, and heaped the earth over again. Alas! a bed of reeds sprang up there before long, and whispered in turn to the grass-blades. Year after year they grew again, ever gossiping among themselves; and to this day, with every wind that sets them nodding together, they murmur, laughing, *"Midas has the ears of an ass: Oh, hush, hush!"*

NORSE   MYTHS

Note on Norse Mythology

The source of our knowledge of the Norse myths is the *Eddas* — the *Elder* or *Poetic Edda,* and the *Younger* or *Prose Edda* (see the introduction to this section, page 387). From these we learn of the gods and their enemies, the frost giants; of the dwelling-place of each group; of Yggdrasill, the huge ash tree that supports the universe, and of the three Norns (Fates) that care for it; and of Ragnarok. In the Norse mythology, as well as in the Greek, the giants

were older than the gods, who had wrested the power from their predecessors, though not in the same manner. In the Norse mythology, twelve ranking gods and twenty-four goddesses dwelt in Asgard; whereas only five Greek gods and five goddesses lived on Olympus. Loki, the god of mischief, has no counterpart among the Greek gods. It is true he was really a giant, but he had forced himself among the gods so that he was considered almost one of them. It was he who brought about Ragnarok (the twilight of the gods) and their final overthrow as well as his own death. For the Norse gods were not immortal; they had to partake of Iduna's apples to keep young and strong; the Greek gods could not be destroyed. They were immortal and invincible. But in Norse mythology there was always the threat of impending doom. The gods knew that in the end they would be destroyed, but they were determined to die resisting. To them a heroic death was not defeat but victory.

Odin Goes to Mimir's Well [1]

Odin, the All-father, was supreme among gods and men. He was the god of wisdom, knowledge, and poetry. He was also the god of war and of the dead. In Valhalla, he presided over the banquets of the heroes who were slain in battle. Seated on his throne in his golden palace, Gladsheim, he looked out over all the world. Perched on his shoulders were his two black ravens, Hugin (Thought) and Munin (Memory), who flew daily over the earth and brought back news to him. When they told him only of shadows and dark forebodings, Odin felt that he must seek more wisdom. Then it was that he told his queenly wife Frigga that he must leave Asgard for a while and go to Mimir's well, there to change what knowledge he had into wisdom so that he might deal as wisely as possible with the dark events when they happened.

And so Odin, no longer riding on Sleipner, his eight-legged steed; no longer wearing his golden armour and his eagle-helmet, and without even his spear in his hand, travelled through Midgard, the World of Men, and made his way towards Jötunheim, the Realm of the Giants.

No longer was he called Odin All-Father, but Vegtam the Wanderer. He wore a cloak of dark blue and he carried a traveller's staff in his hands. And now, as he went towards Mimir's Well, which was near to Jötunheim, he came upon a Giant riding on a great Stag.

Odin seemed a man to men and a giant to giants. He went beside the Giant on the great Stag and the two talked together. "Who art thou, O brother?" Odin asked the Giant.

[1] From Padraic Colum, *The Children of Odin* (Macmillan, 1920).

"I am Vafthrudner, the wisest of the Giants," said the one who was riding on the Stag. Odin knew him then. Vafthrudner was indeed the wisest of the Giants, and many went to strive to gain wisdom from him. But those who went to him had to answer the riddles Vafthrudner asked, and if they failed to answer the Giant took their heads off.

"I am Vegtam the Wanderer," Odin said, "and I know who thou art, O Vafthrudner. I would strive to learn something from thee."

The Giant laughed, showing his teeth. "Ho, ho," he said, "I am ready for a game with thee. Dost thou know the stakes? My head to thee if I cannot answer any question thou wilt ask. And if thou canst not answer any question that I may ask, then thy head goes to me. Ho, ho, ho. And now let us begin."

"I am ready," Odin said.

"Then tell me," said Vafthrudner, "tell me the name of the river that divides Asgard from Jötunheim?"

"Ifling is the name of that river," said Odin. "Ifling that is dead cold, yet never frozen."

"Thou hast answered rightly, O Wanderer," said the Giant. "But thou hast still to answer other questions. What are the names of the horses that Day and Night drive across the sky?"

"Skinfaxe and Hrimfaxe," Odin answered. Vafthrudner was startled to hear one say the names that were known only to the Gods and to the wisest of the Giants. There was only one question now that he might ask before it came to the stranger's turn to ask him questions.

"Tell me," said Vafthrudner, "what is the name of the plain on which the last battle will be fought?"

"The Plain of Vigard," said Odin, "the plain that is a hundred miles long and a hundred miles across."

It was now Odin's turn to ask Vafthrudner questions. "What will be the last words that Odin will whisper into the ear of Baldur, his dear son?" he asked.

Very startled was the Giant Vafthrudner at that question. He sprang to the ground and looked at the stranger keenly.

"Only Odin knows what his last words to

Baldur will be," he said, "and only Odin would have asked that question. Thou art Odin, O Wanderer, and thy question I cannot answer."

"Then," said Odin, "if thou wouldst keep thy head, answer me this: what price will Mimir ask for a draught from the Well of Wisdom that he guards?"

"He will ask thy right eye as a price, O Odin," said Vafthrudner.

"Will he ask no less a price than that?" said Odin.

"He will ask no less a price. Many have come to him for a draught from the Well of Wisdom, but no one yet has given the price Mimir asks. I have answered thy question, O Odin. Now give up thy claim to my head and let me go on my way."

"I give up my claim to thy head," said Odin. Then Vafthrudner, the wisest of the Giants, went on his way, riding on his great Stag.

It was a terrible price that Mimir would ask for a draught from the Well of Wisdom, and very troubled was Odin All-Father when it was revealed to him. His right eye! For all time to be without the sight of his right eye! Almost he would have turned back to Asgard, giving up his quest for wisdom.

He went on, turning neither to Asgard nor to Mimir's Well. And when he went towards the South he saw Muspelheim, where stood Surtur with the Flaming Sword, a terrible figure, who would one day join the Giants in their war against the Gods. And when he turned North he heard the roaring of the cauldron Hvergelmer as it poured itself out of Niflheim, the place of darkness and dread. And Odin knew that the world must not be left between Surtur, who would destroy it with fire, and Niflheim, that would gather it back to Darkness and Nothingness. He, the eldest of the Gods, would have to win the wisdom that would help to save the world.

And so, with his face stern in front of his loss and pain, Odin All-Father turned and went towards Mimir's Well. It was under the great root of Yggdrasill — the root that grew out of Jötunheim. And there sat Mimir, the Guardian of the Well of Wisdom, with his deep eyes bent upon the deep water. And Mimir, who had drunk every day from the Well of Wisdom, knew who it was that stood before him.

"Hail, Odin, Eldest of the Gods," he said.

Then Odin made reverence to Mimir, the wisest of the world's beings. "I would drink from your well, Mimir," he said.

"There is a price to be paid. All who have come here to drink have shrunk from paying that price. Will you, Eldest of the Gods, pay it?"

"I will not shrink from the price that has to be paid, Mimir," said Odin All-Father.

"Then drink," said Mimir. He filled up a great horn with water from the well and gave it to Odin.

Odin took the horn in both his hands and drank and drank. And as he drank all the future became clear to him. He saw all the sorrows and troubles that would fall upon Men and Gods. But he saw, too, why the sorrows and troubles had to fall, and he saw how they might be borne so that Gods and Men, by being noble in the days of sorrow and trouble, would leave in the world a force that one day, a day that was far off indeed, would destroy the evil that brought terror and sorrow and despair into the world.

Then when he had drunk out of the great horn that Mimir had given him, he put his hand to his face and he plucked out his right eye. Terrible was the pain that Odin All-Father endured. But he made no groan nor moan. He bowed his head and put his cloak before his face, as Mimir took the eye and let it sink deep, deep into the water of the Well of Wisdom. And there the Eye of Odin stayed, shining up through the water, a sign to all who came to that place of the price that the Father of the Gods had paid for his wisdom.

How Frey Won Gerda the Giant Maiden[2]

How Frey Won Gerda the Giant Maiden *is the most allegorical of the myths given here. Frey, god of spring, rain, and sunshine, woos*

[2] From Padraic Colum, *The Children of Odin* (Macmillan, 1920).

Gerda, thus in spring starting the growth of seeds which have been lying fallow all winter. But only with the help of Skirner, the warm south wind, can Frey bring about the warm days with their growing vegetation.

Frey, chief of the Vanir, longed to have sight of his sister who had been from Asgard for so long. (You must know that this happened during the time when Freya was wandering through the world, seeking her husband, the lost Odur.) Now there was in Asgard a place from which one could overlook the world and have a glimpse of all who wandered there. That place was Hlidskjalf, Odin's lofty Watch-Tower.

High up into the blue of the air that Tower went. Frey came to it and he knew that Odin All-Father was not upon Hlidskjalf. Only the two wolves, Geri and Freki, that crouched beside Odin's seat at the banquet, were there, and they stood in the way of Frey's entrance to the Tower. But Frey spoke to Geri and Freki in the language of the Gods, and Odin's wolves had to let him pass.

But, as he went up the steps within the Tower, Frey, chief of the Vanir, knew that he was doing a fateful thing. For none of the High Gods, not even Thor, the Defender of Asgard, nor Baldur, the Best-beloved of the Gods, had ever climbed to the top of that Tower and seated themselves upon the All-Father's seat. "But if I could see my sister once I should be contented," said Frey to himself, "and no harm can come to me if I look out on the world."

He came to the top of Hlidskjalf. He seated himself on Odin's lofty seat. He looked out on the world. He saw Midgard, the World of Men, with its houses and towns, its farms and people. Beyond Midgard he saw Jötunheim, the Realm of the Giants, terrible with its dark mountains and its masses of snow and ice. He saw Freya as she went upon her wanderings, and he marked that her face was turned towards Asgard and that her steps were leading towards the City of the Gods. "I have contented myself by looking from Hlidskjalf," said Frey to himself, "and no harm has come to me."

But even as he spoke his gaze was drawn to a dwelling that stood in the middle of the ice and snow of Jötunheim. Long he gazed upon that dwelling without knowing why he looked that way. Then the door of the house was opened and a Giant maiden stood within the doorway. Frey gazed and gazed on her. So great was the beauty of her face that it was like starlight in that dark land. She looked from the doorway of the house, and then turned and went within, shutting the door.

Frey sat on Odin's high seat for long. Then he went down the steps of the Tower and passed by the two wolves, Geri and Freki, that looked threateningly upon him. He went through Asgard, but he found no one to please him in the City of the Gods. That night sleep did not come to him, for his thoughts were fixed upon the loveliness of the Giant maid he had looked upon. And when morning came he was filled with loneliness because he thought himself so far from her. He went to Hlidskjalf again, thinking to climb the Tower and have sight of her once more. But now the two wolves, Geri and Freki, bared their teeth at him and would not let him pass, although he spoke to them again in the language of the Gods.

He went and spoke to wise Niörd, his father. "She whom you have seen, my son," said Niörd, "is Gerda, the daughter of the Giant Gymer. You must give over thinking of her. Your love for her would be an ill thing for you."

"Why should it be an ill thing for me?" Frey asked.

"Because you would have to give that which you prize most for the sake of coming to her."

"That which I prize most," said Frey, "is my magic sword."

"You will have to give your magic sword," said his father, the wise Niörd.

"I will give it," said Frey, loosening his magic sword from his belt.

"Bethink thee, my son," said Niörd. "If thou givest thy sword, what weapon wilt thou have on the day of Ragnarök, when the Giants will make war upon the Gods?"

Frey did not speak, but he thought the day

of Ragnarök was far off. "I cannot live without Gerda," he said, as he turned away.

There was one in Asgard who was called Skirnir. He was a venturesome being who never cared what he said or did. To no one else but Skirnir could Frey bring himself to tell of the trouble that had fallen on him — the trouble that was the punishment for his placing himself on the seat of the All-Father.

Skirnir laughed when he heard Frey's tale. "Thou, A Van, in love with a maid of Jötunheim! This is fun indeed! Will ye make a marriage of it?"

"Would that I might even speak to her or send a message of love to her," said Frey. "But I may not leave my watch over the Elves."

"And if I should take a message to Gerda," said Skirnir the Venturesome, "what would my reward be?"

"My boat Skidbladnir or my boar Golden Bristle," said Frey.

"No, no," said Skirnir. "I want something to go by my side. I want something to use in my hand. Give me the magic sword you own."

Frey thought upon what his father said, that he would be left weaponless on the day of Ragnarök, when the Giants would make war upon the Gods and when Asgard would be endangered. He thought upon this, and drew back from Skirnir, and for a while he remained in thought. And all the time thick-set Skirnir was laughing at him out of his wide mouth and his blue eyes. Then Frey said to himself, "The day of Ragnarök is far off, and I cannot live without Gerda."

He drew the magic sword from his belt and he placed it in Skirnir's hand. "I give you my sword, Skirnir," he said. "Take my message to Gerda, Gymer's daughter. Show her this gold and these precious jewels, and say I love her, and that I claim her love."

"I shall bring the maid to you," said Skirnir the Venturesome.

"But how wilt thou get to Jötunheim?" said Frey, suddenly remembering how dark the Giants' land was and how terrible were the approaches to it.

"Oh, with a good horse and a good sword one can get anywhere," said Skirnir. "My horse is a mighty horse, and you have given me your sword of magic. To-morrow I shall make the journey."

Skirnir rode across Bifröst, the Rainbow Bridge, laughing out of his wide mouth and his blue eyes at Heimdall, the Warder of the Bridge to Asgard. His mighty horse trod the earth of Midgard, and swam the river that divides Midgard, the World of Men, from Jötunheim, the Realm of the Giants. He rode on heedlessly and recklessly, as he did all things. Then out of the iron forests came the monstrous wolves of Jötunheim, to tear and devour him and his mighty horse. It was well for Skirnir that he had in his belt Frey's magic sword. Its edge slew and its gleam frighted the monstrous beasts. On and on Skirnir rode on his mighty horse. Then he came to a wall of fire. No other horse but his mighty horse could go through it. Skirnir rode through the fire and came to the dale in which was Gymer's dwelling.

And now he was before the house that Frey had seen Gerda enter on the day when he had climbed Hlidskjalf, Odin's Watch-Tower. The mighty hounds that guarded Gymer's dwelling came and bayed around him. But the gleam of the magic sword kept them away. Skirnir backed his horse to the door, and made his horse's hooves strike against it.

Gymer was in the feast hall drinking with his Giant friends, and he did not hear the baying of the hounds nor the clatter that Skirnir made before the door. But Gerda sat spinning with her maidens in the hall. "Who comes to Gymer's door?" she said.

"A warrior upon a mighty horse," said one of the maidens.

"Even though he be an enemy and one who slew my brother, yet shall we open the door to him and give him a cup of Gymer's mead," said Gerda.

One of the maidens opened the door and Skirnir entered Gymer's dwelling. He knew Gerda amongst her maidens. He went to her and showed her the rich gold and the precious jewels that he had brought from Frey. "These are for you, fairest Gerda," he said, "if you will give your love to Frey, the Chief of the Vanir."

"Show your gold and jewels to other maidens," said Gerda. "Gold and jewels will never bring me to give my love."

Then Skirnir the Venturesome, the heedless of his words, drew the magic sword from his belt and held it above her. "Give your love to Frey, who has given me this sword," he said, "or meet your death by the edge of it."

Gerda, Gymer's daughter, only laughed at the reckless Skirnir. "Make the daughters of men fearful by the sharpness of Frey's sword," she said, "but do not try to frighten a Giant's daughter with it."

Then Skirnir the Reckless, the heedless of his words, made the magic sword flash before her eyes, while he cried out in a terrible voice, saying a spell over her:

> Gerd, I will curse thee;
> Yes, with this magic
> Blade I shall touch thee;
> Such is its power
> That, like a thistle,
> Withered 'twill leave thee,
> Like a thistle the wind
> Strips from the roof.

Hearing these terrible words and the strange hissings of the magic sword, Gerda threw herself on the ground, crying out for pity. But Skirnir stood above her, and the magic sword flashed and hissed over her. Skirnir sang:

> More ugly I'll leave thee
> Than maid ever was;
> Thou wilt be mocked at
> By men and by Giants;
> A Dwarf only will wed thee;
> Now on this instant
> With this blade I shall touch thee,
> And leave thee bespelled.

She lifted herself on her knees and cried out to Skirnir to spare her from the spell of the magic sword.

"Only if thou wilt give thy love to Frey," said Skirnir.

"I will give my love to him," said Gerda. "Now put up thy magic sword and drink a cup of mead and depart from Gymer's dwelling."

"I will not drink a cup of your mead nor shall I depart from Gymer's dwelling until you yourself say that you will meet and speak with Frey."

"I will meet and speak with him," said Gerda.

"When will you meet and speak with him?" asked Skirnir.

"In the wood of Barri nine nights from this. Let him come and meet me there."

Then Skirnir put up his magic sword and drank the cup of mead that Gerda gave him. He rode from Gymer's house, laughing aloud at having won Gerda for Frey, and so making the magic sword his own for ever.

Skirnir the Venturesome, the heedless of his words, riding across Bifröst on his mighty horse, found Frey standing waiting for him beside Heimdall, the Warder of the Bridge to Asgard.

"What news dost thou bring me?" cried Frey. "Speak, Skirnir, before thou dost dismount from thine horse."

"In nine nights from this thou mayst meet Gerda in Barri Wood," said Skirnir. He looked at him, laughing out of his wide mouth and his blue eyes. But Frey turned away, saying to himself:

> Long is one day;
> Long, long two.
> Can I live through
> Nine long days?

Long indeed were these days for Frey. But the ninth day came and in the evening Frey went to Barri Wood. And there he met Gerda, the Giant maid. She was as fair as when he had seen her before the door of Gymer's house. And when she saw Frey, so tall and noble looking, the Giant's daughter was glad that Skirnir the Venturesome had made her promise to come to Barri Wood. They gave each other rings of gold. It was settled that the Giant maid should come as a bride to Asgard.

The Magic Apples [3]

ᴈ§ *Hoenir is said to have helped Odin create the first human beings; therefore, it was natural*

[3] From Abbie Farwell Brown, *In the Days of Giants* (Houghton Mifflin, 1902).

for Hoenir to be Odin's companion on any adventure. As for Loki, he was always ready for adventure or mischief. It is interesting to compare this story with that episode of the Nibelungenlied in which the giants get from Wotan (Odin) Freia, whose presence is necessary to the well-being of the gods; in this story they must not only get Idun, but the apples that keep the gods young and strong. In both stories Odin is helpless in retrieving the loss; Loki is successful in each case.

It is not very amusing to be a king. Father Odin often grew tired of sitting all day long upon his golden throne in Valhalla above the heavens. He wearied of welcoming the new heroes whom the Valkyries brought him from wars upon the earth, and of watching the old heroes fight their daily deathless battles. He wearied of his wise ravens, and the constant gossip which they brought him from the four corners of the world; and he longed to escape from every one who knew him to some place where he could pass for a mere stranger, instead of the great king of the Aesir, the mightiest being in the whole universe, of whom every one was afraid.

Sometimes he longed so much that he could not bear it. Then — he would run away. He disguised himself as a tall old man, with white hair and a long gray beard. Around his shoulders he threw a huge blue cloak, that covered him from top to toe, and over his face he pulled a big slouch hat, to hide his eyes. For his eyes Odin could not change — no magician has ever learned how to do that. One was empty; he had given the eye to the giant Mimir in exchange for wisdom.

Usually Odin loved to go upon these wanderings alone; for an adventure is a double adventure when one meets it single-handed. It was a fine game for Odin to see how near he could come to danger without feeling the grip of its teeth. But sometimes, when he wanted company, he would whisper to his two brothers, Hoenir and red Loki. They three would creep out of the palace by the back way; and, with a finger on the lip to Heimdal, the watchman, would silently steal over the rainbow bridge which led from Asgard into the places of men and dwarfs and giants.

Wonderful adventures they had, these three, with Loki to help make things happen. Loki was a sly, mischievous fellow, full of his pranks and his capers, not always kindly ones. But he was clever, as well as malicious; and when he had pushed folk into trouble, he could often help them out again, as safe as ever. He could be the jolliest of companions when he chose, and Odin liked his merriment and his witty talk.

One day Loki did something which was no mere jest nor easily forgiven, for it brought all Asgard into danger. And after that Father Odin and his children thought twice before inviting Loki to join them in any journey or undertaking. This which I am about to tell was the first really wicked deed of which Loki was found guilty, though I am sure his red beard had dabbled in secret wrongs before.

One night the three high gods, Odin, Hoenir, and Loki, stole away from Asgard in search of adventure. Over mountains and deserts, great rivers and stony places, they wandered until they grew very hungry. But there was not food to be found — not even a berry or a nut.

Oh, how footsore and tired they were! And oh, how faint! The worst of it ever is that — as you must often have noticed — the heavier one's feet grow, the lighter and more hollow becomes one's stomach; which seems a strange thing, when you think of it. If only one's feet became as light as the rest of one feels, folk could fairly fly with hunger. Alas! this is not so.

The three Aesir drooped and drooped, and seemed on the point of starving, when they came to the edge of a valley. Here, looking down, they saw a herd of oxen feeding on the grass.

"Hola!" shouted Loki. "Behold our supper!" Going down into the valley, they caught and killed one of the oxen, and, building a great bonfire, hung up the meat to roast. Then the three sat around the fire and smacked their lips, waiting for the meat to cook. They waited for a long time.

"Surely, it is done now," said Loki, at last; and he took the meat from the fire. Strange to say, however, it was raw as ere the fire was lighted. What could it mean? Never before had meat required so long a time to roast. They made the fire brighter and re-hung the beef for a thorough basting, cooking it even longer than they had done at first. When again they came to carve the meat, they found it still uneatable. Then, indeed, they looked at one another in surprise.

"What can this mean?" cried Loki, with round eyes.

"There is some trick!" whispered Hoenir, looking around as if he expected to see a fairy or a witch meddling with the food.

"We must find out what this mystery betokens," said Odin thoughtfully. Just then there was a strange sound in the oak-tree under which they had built their fire.

"What is that?" Loki shouted, springing to his feet. They looked up into the tree, and far above in the branches, near the top, they spied an enormous eagle, who was staring down at them, and making a queer sound, as if he were laughing.

"Ho-ho!" croaked the eagle. "I know why your meat will not cook. It is all my doing, masters."

The three Aesir stared in surprise. Then Odin said sternly: "Who are you, Master Eagle? And what do you mean by those rude words?"

"Give me my share of the ox, and you shall see," rasped the eagle, in his harsh voice. "Give me my share, and you will find that your meat will cook as fast as you please."

Now the three on the ground were nearly famished. So, although it seemed very strange to be arguing with an eagle, they cried, as if in one voice: "Come down, then, and take your share." They thought that, being a mere bird, he would want but a small piece.

The eagle flapped down from the top of the tree. Dear me! What a mighty bird he was! Eight feet across the wings was the smallest measure, and his claws were as long and strong as ice-hooks. He fanned the air like a whirlwind as he flew down to perch beside the bonfire. Then in his beak and claws he seized a leg and both shoulders of the ox, and started to fly away.

"Hold, thief!" roared Loki angrily, when he saw how much the eagle was taking. "That is not your share; you are no lion, but you are taking the lion's share of our feast. Begone, Scarecrow, and leave the meat as you found it!" Thereat, seizing a pole, he struck at the eagle with all his might.

Then a strange thing happened. As the great bird flapped upward with his prey, giving a scream of malicious laughter, the pole which Loki still held stuck fast to the eagle's back, and Loki was unable to let go of the other end.

"Help, help!" he shouted to Odin and to Hoenir, as he felt himself lifted off his feet. But they could not help him. "Help, help!" he screamed, as the eagle flew with him, now high, now low, through brush and bog and briar, over treetops and the peaks of mountains. On and on they went, until Loki thought his arm would be pulled out, like a weed torn up by the roots. The eagle would not listen to his cries nor pause in his flight, until Loki was almost dead with pain and fatigue.

"Hark you, Loki," screamed the eagle, going a little more slowly; "no one can help you except me. You are bewitched, and you cannot pull away from this pole, nor loose the pole from me, until I choose. But if you will promise what I ask, you shall go free."

Then Loki groaned: "O eagle, only let me go, and tell me who you really are, and I will promise whatever you wish."

The eagle answered: "I am the giant Thiasse, the enemy of the Aesir. But you ought to love me, Loki, for you yourself married a giantess."

Loki moaned: "Oh, yes! I dearly love all my wife's family, great Thiasse. Tell me what you want of me?"

"I want this," quoth Thiasse gruffly. "I am growing old, and I want the apples which Idun keeps in her golden casket, to make me young again. You must get them for me."

Now these apples were the fruit of a magic tree, and were more beautiful to look at and more delicious to taste than any fruit that ever grew. The best thing about them was that whoever tasted one, be he ever so old, grew young and strong again. The apples belonged to a beautiful lady named Idun, who kept them in a golden casket. Every morning the Aesir came to her to be refreshed and made over by a bite of her precious fruit. That is why in Asgard no one ever waxed old or ugly. Even Father Odin, Hoenir, and Loki, the three travelers who had seen the very beginning of everything, when the world was made, were still sturdy and young. And so long as Idun kept her apples safe, the faces of the family who sat about the table of Valhalla would be rosy and fair like the faces of children.

"O friend giant!" cried Loki. "You know not what you ask! The apples are the most precious treasure of Asgard, and Idun keeps watch over them as if they were dearer to her than life itself. I never could steal them from her, Thiasse; for at her call all Asgard would rush to the rescue, and trouble would buzz about my ears like a hive of bees let loose."

"Then you must steal Idun herself, apples and all. For the apples I must have, and you have promised, Loki, to do my bidding."

Loki sniffed and thought, thought and sniffed again. Already his mischievous heart was planning how he might steal Idun away. He could hardly help laughing to think how angry the Aesir would be when they found their beauty-medicine gone forever. But he hoped that, when he had done this trick for Thiasse, now and then the giant would let him have a nibble of the magic apples; so that Loki himself would remain young long after the other Aesir were grown old and feeble. This thought suited Loki's malicious nature well.

"I think I can manage it for you, Thiasse," he said craftily. "In a week I promise to bring Idun and her apples to you. But you must not forget the great risk which I am running, nor that I am your relative by marriage. I may have a favor to ask in return, Thiasse."

Then the eagle gently dropped Loki from his claws. Falling on a soft bed of moss Loki jumped up and ran back to his traveling companions, who were glad and surprised to see him again. They had feared that the eagle was carrying him away to feed his young eaglets in some far-off nest. Ah, you may be sure that Loki did not tell them who the eagle really was, nor confess the wicked promise which he had made about Idun and her apples.

After that the three went back to Asgard, for they had had adventure enough for one day.

The days flew by, and the time came when Loki must fulfill his promise to Thiasse. So one morning he strolled out into the meadow where Idun loved to roam among the flowers. There he found her, sitting by a tiny spring, holding her precious casket of apples on her lap. She was combing her long golden hair, which fell from under a wreath of spring flowers, and she was very beautiful. Her green robe was embroidered with buds and blossoms of silk in many colors, and she wore a golden girdle about her waist. She smiled as Loki came, and tossed him a posy, saying: "Good-morrow, red Loki. Have you come for a bite of my apples? I see a wrinkle over each of your eyes which I can smooth away."

"Nay, fair lady," answered Loki politely, "I have just nibbled of another apple, which I found this morning. Verily, I think it is sweeter and more magical than yours."

Idun was hurt and surprised.

"That cannot be, Loki," she cried. "There are no apples anywhere like mine. Where found you this fine fruit?" and she wrinkled up her little nose scornfully.

"Oho! I will not tell any one the place," chuckled Loki, "except that it is not far, in a little wood. There is a gnarled old apple-tree, and on its branches grow the most beautiful red-cheeked apples you ever saw. But you could never find it."

"I should like to see these apples, Loki, if only to prove how far less good they are than mine. Will you bring me some?"

"That I will not," said Loki teasingly. "Oh, no! I have my own magic apples now, and folk will be coming to me for help instead of to you."

Idun began to coax him, as he had guessed that she would; "Please, please, Loki, show me the place!"

"Well, then, because I love you, Idun, better than all the rest, I will show you the place, if you will come with me. But it must be a secret — no one must ever know."

All girls like secrets.

"Yes — yes!" cried Idun eagerly. "Let us steal away now, while no one is looking."

This was just what Loki hoped for.

"Bring your own apples," he said, "that we may compare them with mine. But I know mine are better."

"I know mine are the best in all the world," returned Idun, pouting. "I will bring them, to show you the difference."

Off they started together, she with the golden casket under her arm; and Loki chuckled wickedly as they went. He led her for some distance farther than she had ever strayed before, and at last she grew frightened.

"Where are you taking me, Loki?" she cried. "You said it was not far. I see no little wood, no old apple tree."

"It is just beyond, just a little step beyond," he answered. So on they went. But that little step took them beyond the boundary of Asgard — just a little step beyond, into the space where the giants lurked and waited for mischief.

Then there was a rustling of wings, and whirr-rr-rr! Down came Thiasse in his eagle dress. Before Idun suspected what was happening, he fastened his claws into her girdle and flapped away with her, magic apples and all, to his palace in Jotunheim, the Land of Giants.

Loki stole back to Asgard, thinking that he was quite safe, and that no one would discover his villainy. At first Idun was not missed. But after a little the gods began to feel signs of age, and went for their usual bite of her apples. Then they found that she had disappeared, and a great terror fell upon them. Where had she gone? Suppose she should not come back!

The hours and days went by, and still she did not return. Their fright became almost a panic. Their hair began to turn gray, and their limbs grew stiff and gouty so that they hobbled down Asgard streets. Even Freia, the loveliest, was afraid to look in her mirror, and Balder, the beautiful, grew pale and haggard. The happy land of Asgard was like a garden over which a burning wind had blown — all the flower-faces were faded and withered, and springtime was turned into yellow fall.

If Idun and her apples were not quickly found, the gods seemed likely to shrivel and blow away like autumn leaves. They held a council to inquire into the matter, endeavoring to learn who had seen Idun last, and whither she had gone. It turned out that one morning Heimdal had seen her strolling out of Asgard with Loki, and no one had seen her since. Then the gods understood; Loki was the last person who had been with her — this must be one of Loki's tricks. They were filled with anger. They seized and bound Loki and brought him before the council. They threatened him with torture and with death unless he should tell the truth. And Loki was so frightened that finally he confessed what he had done.

Then indeed there was horror in Asgard. Idun stolen away by a wicked giant! Idun and her apples lost, and Asgard growing older every minute! What was to be done? Big Thor seized Loki and threw him up in the air again and again, so that his heels touched first the moon and then the sea; you can still see the marks upon the moon's white face. "If you do not bring Idun back from the land of your wicked wife, you shall have worse than this!" he roared. "Go and bring her now."

"How can I do that?" asked Loki, trembling.

"That is for you to find," growled Thor. "Bring her you must. Go!"

Loki thought for a moment. Then he said: "I will bring her back if Freia will loan me her falcon dress. The giant dresses as an eagle. I, too, must guise me as a bird, or we cannot outwit him."

Then Freia hemmed and hawed. She did not wish to loan her feather dress, for it was very precious. But all the Aesir begged; and finally she consented.

It was a beautiful great dress of brown feathers and gray, and in it Freia loved to skim like a falcon among the clouds and stars. Loki put it on, and when he had done so he looked exactly like a great brown hawk. Only his bright black eyes remained the same, glancing here and there, so that they lost sight of nothing.

With a whirr of his wings Loki flew off to the north, across mountains and valleys and great river Ifing, which lay between Asgard and Giant Land. And at last he came to the palace of Thiasse the giant.

It happened, fortunately, that Thiasse had gone fishing in the sea, and Idun was left alone, weeping and broken-hearted. Presently she heard a little tap on her window, and, looking up, she saw a great brown bird perching on the ledge. He was so big that Idun was frightened and gave a scream. But the bird nodded pleasantly and croaked: "Don't be afraid, Idun. I am a friend. I am Loki, come to set you free."

"Loki! Loki is no friend of mine. He brought me here," she sobbed. "I don't believe you came to save me."

"That is indeed why I am here," he replied, "and a dangerous business it is, if Thiasse should come back before we start for home."

"How will you get me out?" asked Idun doubtfully. "The door is locked, and the window is barred."

"I will change you into a nut," said he, "and carry you in my claws."

"What of the casket of apples?" queried Idun. "Can you carry that also?"

Then Loki laughed long and loudly.

"What welcome to Asgard do you think I should receive without the apples?" he cried. "Yes, we must take them, indeed."

Idun came to the window, and Loki, who was a skillful magician, turned her into a nut and took her in one claw, while in the other he seized the casket of apples. Then off he whirred out of the palace grounds and away toward Asgard's safety.

In a little while Thiasse returned home, and when he found Idun and her apples gone, there was a hubbub, you may be sure! However, he lost little time by smashing mountains and breaking trees in his giant rage; that fit was soon over. He put on his eagle plumage and started in pursuit of the falcon.

Now an eagle is bigger and stronger than any other bird, and usually in a long race he can beat even the swift hawk who has an hour's start. Presently Loki heard behind him the shrill scream of a giant eagle, and his heart turned sick. But he had crossed the great river, and already was in sight of Asgard. The aged Aesir were gathered on the rainbow bridge watching eagerly for Loki's return; and when they spied the falcon with the nut and the casket in his talons, they knew who it was. A great cheer went up, but it was hushed in a moment, for they saw the eagle close after the falcon; and they guessed that this must be the giant Thiasse, the stealer of Idun.

Then there was a great shouting of commands, and a rushing to and fro. All the gods, even Father Odin and his two wise ravens, were busy gathering chips into great heaps on the walls of Asgard. As soon as Loki, with his precious burden, had fluttered weakly over the wall, dropping to the ground beyond, the gods lighted the heaps of chips which they had piled, and soon there was a wall of fire, over which the eagle must fly. He was going too fast to stop. The flames roared and crackled, but Thiasse flew straight into them, with a scream of fear and rage. His feathers caught fire and burned, so that he could no longer fly, but fell headlong to the ground inside the walls. Then Thor, the Thunder-Lord, and Týr, the mighty war-king, fell upon him and slew him, so that he could never trouble the Aesir any more.

There was great rejoicing in Asgard that night, for Loki changed Idun again to a fair lady; whereupon she gave each of the eager gods a bit of her life-giving fruit, so that they grew young and happy once more, as if all these horrors had never happened.

Not one of them, however, forgot the evil part which Loki had played in these doings. They hid the memory, like a buried seed, deep in their hearts. Thenceforward the word of Loki and the honor of his name were poor coin in Asgard; which is no wonder.

Balder and the Mistletoe [4]

Balder, the youngest son of Odin and Frigg, was god of light and peace and of the beautiful and the wise. The mistletoe has always figured in myths; it is supposed to have been the golden bough which Aeneas plucked

[4] From Abbie Farwell Brown, *In the Days of Giants* (Houghton Mifflin, 1902).

to use as a key to Hades. This myth has two interpretations. Like the Greek myth of Demeter, it may explain the seasons, or it may be a further forewarning of the fall of the gods at the hands of the giants in the last great battle. This victory of the ice giants may represent the coming of the ice age.

Now at this time Balder the beautiful had a strange dream. He dreamed that a cloud came before the sun, and all Asgard was dark. He waited for the cloud to drift away, and for the sun to smile again. But no; the sun was gone forever, he thought; and Balder awoke feeling very sad. The next night Balder had another dream. This time he dreamed that it was still dark as before; the flowers were withered and the gods were growing old; even Idun's magic apples could not make them young again. And all were weeping and wringing their hands as though some dreadful thing had happened. Balder awoke feeling strangely frightened, yet he said no word to Nanna his wife, for he did not want to trouble her.

When it came night again Balder slept and dreamed a third dream, a still more terrible one than the other two had been. He thought that in the dark, lonely world there was nothing but a sad voice, which cried, "The sun is gone! The spring is gone! Joy is gone! For Balder the beautiful is dead, dead, dead!"

This time Balder awoke with a cry, and Nanna asked him what was the matter. So he had to tell her of his dream, and he was sadly frightened; for in those days dreams were often sent to folk as messages, and what the gods dreamed usually came true. Nanna ran sobbing to Queen Frigg, who was Balder's mother, and told her all the dreadful dream, asking what could be done to prevent it from coming true.

Now Balder was Queen Frigg's dearest son. Thor was older and stronger, and more famous for his great deeds; but Frigg loved far better gold-haired Balder. And indeed he was the best-loved of all the Aesir; for he was gentle, fair and wise, and wherever he went folk grew happy and light-hearted at the very sight of him, just as we do when we first catch a glimpse of spring peeping

over the hilltop into Winterland. So when Frigg heard of Balder's woeful dream, she was frightened almost out of her wits.

"He must not die! He shall not die!" she cried. "He is so dear to all the world, how could there be anything which would hurt him?"

And then a wonderful thought came to Frigg. "I will travel over the world and make all things promise not to injure my boy," she said. "Nothing shall pass my notice. I will get the word of everything."

So first she went to the gods themselves, gathered on Ida Plain for their morning exercise; and telling them of Balder's dream, she begged them to give the promise. Oh, what a shout arose when they heard her words!

"Hurt Balder! — our Balder! Not for the world, we promise! The dream is wrong — there is nothing so cruel as to wish harm to Balder the beautiful!" they cried. But deep in their hearts they felt a secret fear which would linger until they should hear that all things had given their promise. What if harm were indeed to come to Balder! The thought was too dreadful.

Then Frigg went to see all the beasts who live in field or forest or rocky den. Willingly they gave their promise never to harm hair of gentle Balder. "For he is ever kind to us," they said, "and we love him as if he were one of ourselves. Not with claws or teeth or hoofs or horns will any beast hurt Balder."

Next Frigg spoke to the birds and fishes, reptiles and insects. And all — even the venomous serpents — cried that Balder was their friend, and that they would never do aught to hurt his dear body. "Not with beak or talon, bite or sting or poison fang, will one of us hurt Balder," they promised.

After doing this, the anxious mother traveled over the whole world, step by step; and from all the things that are she got the same ready promise never to harm Balder the beautiful. All the trees and plants promised; all the stones and metals; earth, air, fire, and water; sun, snow, wind, and rain, and all diseases that men know — each gave to Frigg the word of promise which she wanted. So at last, footsore and weary, she came back to Asgard with the joyful news that Balder must be safe, for that there was nothing in the world but had promised to be his harmless friend.

Then there was rejoicing in Asgard, as if the gods had won one of their great victories over the giants. The noble Aesir and the heroes who had died in battle upon the earth, and who had come to Valhalla to live happily ever after, gathered on Ida Plain to celebrate the love of all nature for Balder.

There they invented a famous game, which was to prove how safe he was from the bite of death. They stationed Balder in the midst of them, his face glowing like the sun with the bright light which ever shone from him. And as he stood there unarmed and smiling, by turns they tried all sorts of weapons against him; they made as if to beat him with sticks, they stoned him with stones, they shot at him with arrows and hurled mighty spears straight at his heart.

It was a merry game, and a shout of laughter went up as each stone fell harmless at Balder's feet, each stick broke before it touched his shoulders, each arrow overshot his head, and each spear turned aside. For neither stone nor wood nor flinty arrow-point nor barb of iron would break the promise which each had given. Balder was safe with them, just as if he were bewitched. He remained unhurt among the missiles which whizzed about his head, and which piled up in a great heap around the charmed spot whereon he stood.

Now among the crowd that watched these games with such enthusiasm, there was one face that did not smile, one voice that did not rasp itself hoarse with cheering. Loki saw how everyone and everything loved Balder, and he was jealous. He was the only creature in all the world that hated Balder and wished for his death. Yet Balder had never done harm to him. But the wicked plan that Loki had been cherishing was almost ripe, and in this poison fruit was the seed of the greatest sorrow that Asgard had ever known.

While the others were enjoying their game of love, Loki stole away unperceived from Ida Plain, and with a wig of gray hair, a long

gown, and a staff, disguised himself as an old woman. Then he hobbled down Asgard streets till he came to the palace of Queen Frigg, the mother of Balder.

"Good-day, my lady," quoth the old woman, in a cracked voice. "What is that noisy crowd doing yonder in the green meadow? I am so deafened by their shouts that I can hardly hear myself think."

"Who are you, good mother, that you have not heard?" said Queen Frigg in surprise. "They are shooting at my son Balder. They are proving the word which all things have given me — the promise not to injure my dear son. And that promise will be kept."

The old crone pretended to be full of wonder. "So, now!" she cried. "Do you mean to say that every single thing in the whole world has promised not to hurt your son? I can scarce believe it; though, to be sure, he is as fine a fellow as I ever saw." Of course this flattery pleased Frigg.

"You say true, mother," she answered proudly, "he is a noble son. Yes, everything has promised — that is, everything except one tiny little plant that is not worth mentioning."

The old woman's eyes twinkled wickedly. "And what is that foolish little plant, my dear?" she asked coaxingly.

"It is the mistletoe that grows in the meadow west of Valhalla. It was too young to promise, and too harmless to bother with," answered Frigg carelessly.

After this her questioner hobbled painfully away. But as soon as she was out of sight from the Queen's palace, she picked up the skirts of her gown and ran as fast as she could to the meadow west of Valhalla. And there sure enough, as Frigg had said, was a tiny sprig of mistletoe growing on a gnarled oak-tree. The false Loki took out a knife which she carried in some hidden pocket and cut off the mistletoe very carefully. Then she trimmed and shaped it so that it was like a little green arrow, pointed at one end, but very slender.

"Ho, ho!" chuckled the old woman. "So you are the only thing in all the world that is too young to make a promise, my little mistletoe. Well, young as you are, you must go on an errand for me today. And maybe you shall bear a message of my love to Balder the beautiful."

Then she hobbled back to Ida Plain, where the merry game was still going on around Balder. Loki quietly passed unnoticed through the crowd, and came close to the elbow of a big dark fellow who was standing lonely outside the circle of weapon-throwers. He seemed sad and forgotten, and he hung his head in a pitiful way. It was Höd, the blind brother of Balder.

The old woman touched his arm. "Why do you not join the game with the others?" she asked, in her cracked voice. "Are you the only one to do your brother no honor? Surely, you are big and strong enough to toss a spear with the best of them yonder."

Höd touched his sightless eyes madly. "I am blind," he said. "Strength I have, greater than belongs to most of the Aesir. But I cannot see to aim a weapon. Besides, I have no spear to test upon him. Yet how gladly would I do honor to dear Balder!" and he sighed deeply.

"It were a pity if I could not find you at least a little stick to throw," said Loki, sympathetically. "I am only a poor old woman, and of course I have no weapon. But ah — here is a green twig which you can use as an arrow, and I will guide your arm, poor fellow."

Höd's dark face lighted up, for he was eager to take his turn in the game. So he thanked her, and grasped eagerly the little arrow which she put into his hand. Loki held him by the arm, and together they stepped into the circle which surrounded Balder. And when it was Höd's turn to throw his weapon, the old woman stood at his elbow and guided his big arm as it hurled the twig of mistletoe towards where Balder stood.

Oh, the sad thing that befell! Straight through the air flew the little arrow, straight as magic and Loki's arm could direct it. Straight to Balder's heart it sped, piercing through jerkin and shirt and all, to give its bitter message of "Loki's love," as he had said. And that was the end of sunshine and spring and joy in Asgard, for the dream had come true, and Balder the beautiful was dead.

When the Aesir saw what had happened, there was a great shout of fear and horror, and they rushed upon Höd, who had thrown the fatal arrow.

"What is it? What have I done?" asked the poor blind brother, trembling at the tumult which had followed his shot.

"You have slain Balder!" cried the Aesir. "Wretched Höd, how could you do it?"

"It was the old woman — the evil old woman, who stood at my elbow and gave me a little twig to throw," gasped Höd. "She must be a witch."

Then the Aesir scattered over Ida Plain to look for the old woman who had done the evil deed; but she had mysteriously disappeared.

"It must be Loki," said wise Heimdal. "It is Loki's last and vilest trick."

"Oh, my Balder, my beautiful Balder!" wailed Queen Frigg, throwing herself on the body of her son. "If I had only made the mistletoe give me the promise, you would have been saved. It was I who told Loki of the mistletoe — so it is I who have killed you. Oh, my son, my son!"

But Father Odin was speechless with grief. His sorrow was greater than that of all the others, for he best understood the dreadful misfortune which had befallen Asgard. Already a cloud had come before the sun, so that it would never be bright day again. Already the flowers had begun to fade and the birds had ceased to sing. And already the Aesir had begun to grow old and joyless — all because the little mistletoe had been too young to give a promise to Queen Frigg.

"Balder the beautiful is dead!" the cry went echoing through all the world, and everything that was sorrowed at the sound of the Aesir's weeping.

Balder's brothers lifted up his beautiful body upon their great war shields and bore him on their shoulders down to the seashore. For, as was the custom in those days, they were going to send him to Hela, the Queen of Death, with all the things he best had loved in Asgard. And these were — after Nanna his wife — his beautiful horse, and his ship Hringhorni. So that they would place Balder's body upon the ship with his horse beside him, and set fire to this wonderful funeral pile. For by fire was the quickest passage to Hela's kingdom.

But when they reached the shore, they found that all the strength of all the Aesir was unable to move Hringhorni, Balder's ship, into the water. For it was the largest ship in the world and it was stranded far up the beach.

"Even the giants bore no ill-will to Balder," said Father Odin. "I heard the thunder of their grief but now shaking the hills. Let us for this once bury our hatred of that race and send to Jotunheim for help to move the ship."

So they sent a messenger to the giantess Hyrrockin, the hugest of all the Frost People. She was weeping for Balder when the message came.

"I will go, for Balder's sake," she said. Soon she came riding fast upon a giant wolf, with a serpent for the bridle; and mighty she was, with the strength of forty Aesir. She dismounted from her wolf-steed, and tossed the wriggling reins to one of the men-heroes who had followed Balder and the Aesir from Valhalla. But he could not hold the beast, and it took four heroes to keep him quiet, which they could only do by throwing him upon the ground and sitting upon him in a row. And this mortified them greatly.

Then Hyrrockin the giantess strode up to the great ship and seized it by the prow. Easily she gave a little pull and presto! it leaped forward on its rollers with such force that sparks flew from the flint stones underneath and the whole earth trembled. The boat shot into the waves and out toward open sea so swiftly that the Aesir were likely to have lost it entirely, had not Hyrrockin waded out up to her waist and caught it by the stern just in time.

Thor was angry at her clumsiness, and raised his hammer to punish her. But the other Aesir held his arm.

"She cannot help being so strong," they whispered. "She meant to do well. She did not realize how hard she was pulling. This is no time for anger, brother Thor." So Thor spared her life, as indeed he ought, for her kindness.

Then Balder's body was borne out to the ship and laid upon a pile of beautiful silks, and furs, and cloth-of-gold, and woven sunbeams which the dwarfs had wrought. So that his funeral pyre was more grand than anything which had ever been seen. But when Nanna, Balder's gentle wife, saw them ready to kindle the flames under this gorgeous bed, she could bear her grief no longer. Her loving heart broke, and they laid her beside him, that they might comfort each other on their journey to Hela. Thor touched the pile gently with his hammer that makes the lightning, and the flames burst forth, lighting up the faces of Balder and Nanna with a glory. Then they cast upon the fire Balder's war-horse, to serve his master in the dark country to which he was about to go. The horse was decked with a harness all of gold, with jewels studding the bridle and headstall. Last of all Odin laid upon the pyre his gift to Balder, Draupnir, the precious ring of gold which the dwarf had made, from which every ninth night there dropped eight other rings as large and brightly golden.

"Take this with you, dear son, to Hela's palace," said Odin. "And do not forget the friends you leave behind in the now lonely halls of Asgard."

Then Hyrrockin pushed the great boat out to sea, with its bonfire of precious things. And on the beach stood all the Aesir watching it out of sight, all the Aesir and many besides. For there came to Balder's funeral great crowds of little dwarfs and multitudes of huge frost giants, all mourning for Balder the beautiful. For this one time they were all friends together, forgetting their quarrels of so many centuries. All of them loved Balder, and were united to do him honor.

The great ship moved slowly out to sea, sending up a red fire to color all the heavens. At last it slid below the horizon softly, as you have often seen the sun set upon the water, leaving a brightness behind to lighten the dark world for a little while.

This indeed was the sunset for Asgard. The darkness of sorrow came in earnest after the passing of Balder the beautiful.

Thor Gains His Hammer[5]

The Norse mythology is largely doom-ridden and heroic, a grim concept, in which the gods know that they face ultimate destruction. Yet within this framework, there are some stories which have the character of a folk tale, showing the gods concerned with affairs of battle and survival, and helped by magic, as men were. This is such a tale, this story of the forging of the mighty hammer which was to protect the gods against all evil, and which made Thor the most powerful, after Odin.

Loki made much trouble for the gods with his evil pranks and his malice. But there was one time his mischief worked for good in the end. Thor might never have owned his wonderful hammer had it not been for Loki. It came about in this way:

Thor had a beautiful wife whose name was Sif. Her hair was long and yellow and shone like gold in the sunlight. Thor was proud of her.

One day, while Sif lay sleeping under the trees where Iduna's apples grew, Loki cut off all her hair. He did it for a prank. When Sif woke and discovered the loss of her beautiful hair, she went weeping to Thor.

"This is the work of that rascal Loki," cried Thor angrily. "I'll break every bone in his body."

He rushed off to look for Loki. It was not long before he found him and seized him.

Loki was filled with terror when he saw Thor's anger. He begged for mercy, but Thor would not let him go.

"Wait, O mighty Thor," begged Loki. "Don't punish me and I will get new hair for Sif. I will find hair of real gold that will shine in the sunlight and will grow like other hair."

"How will you do that?" said Thor.

"I will go to the Dark Elves, to the Sons of Ivaldi, and ask them to make the hair for me," said Loki. "They can make every kind of wondrous thing."

Thor gave his consent.

"But remember," he cried, shaking Loki so that his teeth chattered in his head. "If

[5] From Dorothy Hosford, *Thunder of the Gods* (Holt, 1952).

you don't bring back hair that will grow like other hair, I will break every bone in your body. And it must be as long and beautiful as Sif's own hair. Now go."

Loki was only too glad to set out. The dwarfs lived deep within the mountains and he had a long journey to make.

When Loki came to the dwelling place of the Dark Elves they said that they could perform his task. They made the hair, and they made two other gifts as well. They made the spear Gungnir, which became Odin's possession, and they made the magic ship, Skidbladnir.

On his way home with the gifts Loki met another dwarf named Brock. Loki was feeling pleased with himself and proud of his success. At once he made a wager with Brock.

"See what I have," cried Loki. "I'll wager my head that your brother Sindri can't make three gifts as precious as these."

Sindri was famed among the dwarfs and Brock knew how great was his brother's skill.

"I'll take that wager," said Brock. "Come with me. We will go to the smithy and we will see what Sindri can make."

Brock explained the wager to his brother and Sindri started the fire in the forge. The flames lit up the far corners of the dwarfs' cave. When it was hot enough Sindri laid within the fire a pig's hide. He handed the bellows to Brock and told him to work them without ceasing until he should return. Then he left the cave.

As soon as Sindri had gone Loki changed himself into a huge fly. He lit upon Brock's hand and stung him. But Brock kept the bellows working and did not let go.

When Sindri returned he took the work out of the fire. It was a boar, a wild pig with mane and bristles of gold.

Then Sindri placed gold in the fire and bade Brock work the bellows as before. This time the fly settled on Brock's neck and stung twice as hard. But Brock did not let go of the bellows. When Sindri returned he took out of the fire the golden ring which is called Draupnir.

For the third gift Sindri placed iron in the fire. "Keep the bellows going, Brock, or all will be spoiled," said Sindri, as he left the smithy.

This was Loki's last chance and the fly settled between Brock's eyes and stung his eyelids so hard that the blood ran down. The pain and the blood blinded him. Brock had to pause to sweep the fly away. He let go of the bellows with one hand and only for an instant. But the fire died down.

At that moment Sindri returned and said that what was in the hearth had come near to being spoiled. He took the work out of the fire and it was a hammer.

Sindri gave the three gifts to Brock. "Take these to the gods," he said, "and see whose gifts will win the wager."

Loki and Brock set off for Asgard, the home of the gods, each bearing his gifts. The gods were called together and met in the great council hall named Gladsheim. They took their places on the high seats. It was agreed that Odin and Thor and Frey should decide whose gifts were best.

Loki presented his gifts first. He gave Thor the golden hair for Sif, to Odin he gave the spear Gungnir, and to Frey the ship Skidbladnir, telling the virtues of each. As soon as it was placed upon Sif's head the hair would grow like other hair. The spear Gungnir would never fall short of its mark; and the ship Skidbladnir would always find favoring winds, no matter in what direction it was set. Yet it could be folded like a napkin and placed in Frey's pocket, if he so wished.

Then Brock offered his gifts. He gave to Odin the golden ring which is called Draupnir.

"Every ninth night eight other rings like itself will drop from it," said Brock.

He gave the boar, which was called Gold-Mane, to Frey.

"No horse can run through the air or over the sea with such swiftness," said Brock. "And you can always find your way by the light which shines from its mane and bristles of gold, no matter how black and dark the night may be."

Brock gave the hammer to Thor.

"The name of the hammer is Mjollnir," he told Thor. "With it you can strike as hard a blow as you please at whatever comes in your way. You can hurl it as far as you like, and it will always find its mark and return to your hand. Yet, if you wish, you can make the hammer small and put it in your pocket."

The hammer had only one fault, though Brock did not mention that. The handle was a little short. That was because Loki had caused Brock to drop the bellows.

Odin and Thor and Frey held a council. They decided that Brock's gifts were best, for Thor's hammer was the most valuable gift of all. This was just the weapon the gods needed in their wars against the Frost-Giants. The giants had better beware. Now Thor could hurl his mighty hammer at them and catch it again in his hand.

Odin rose to his feet and announced to all that Brock had won the wager.

Brock immediately demanded Loki's head.

"What good is my head to you?" cried Loki. "I will give you a great sum of gold for a ransom. You will be the richest of all the dwarfs."

Dwarfs love gold, but Brock would have none of it, and said that Loki must keep to the terms of his bargain.

"Then catch me if you can!" cried Loki.

In an instant he was far off, for he had on the shoes which would carry him through air and over water in the twinkling of an eye.

Brock begged Thor to catch Loki. Thor was still angry with Loki and willing enough to do so. Thor asked Frey to lend him the boar Gold-Mane. He leapt on the boar's back and away he went through the air. Before long he had brought Loki back to Asgard.

Brock was ready to cut off his head, but Loki cried: "My head, yes! But not an inch of my neck. I did not wager my neck."

How could Brock cut off Loki's head without touching his neck? Brock had to let it go at that.

"If I had my brother's awl I would sew your mischief-speaking lips together," he cried out in anger.

No sooner had he spoken than the awl was there and of itself pierced Loki's lips. Then Brock sewed them together with a thong. Not that it troubled Loki much, for when Brock was gone he ripped out the thongs.

Loki, as usual, got off with little punishment. But the gods were much richer for their new gifts.

Thor's Unlucky Journey [6]

◄§ *The symbolism of this story is richly inventive, for this story of Thor's feats of strength against the Frost Giants has in it the Norse belief in the scheme of the world, with its reference to the Midgard Serpent who encircled the world. Several origin stories are included, such as the drinking of the sea by Thor, which accounts for the Ebb Tide; and Fire and Thought are given personification. It is a good story to tell, with its similes of strength, its exaggerations, and its progressively difficult trials. It is typically Norse in feeling, since the god Thor was not completely victorious over his adversaries.*

Thor, the god of thunder, was indeed one of the mightiest of the gods. His battles against the Frost-Giants were many. They knew to their sorrow how great he was. Yet it cannot be said that Thor was victor in all his encounters with the giants. There was one adventure in which he was not so lucky.

One day Thor started off in his chariot, driving his goats. Loki went with him. Toward the end of the day they came to the house of a farmer and decided to stay there for the night. Thor's goats could always provide a meal for him. Thor slaughtered his goats and skinned them and had them cooked for supper. He invited the farmer and his wife and their son and daughter to share the meal. The name of the son was Thjalfi and the daughter was named Roskva. Thor told the farmer and his family to throw all the bones down on the skins of the goats, when they had finished their meal. The hides were spread out on the ground a little way from the fire. They did as they were told, except Thjalfi, who was somewhat greedy. He broke one of the bones to get at the sweet-tasting marrow.

[6] From Dorothy Hosford, *Thunder of the Gods* (Holt, 1952).

In the morning Thor rose. He went over to the goatskins spread on the ground. When he raised his hammer high over the bones the goats sprang to life again. They were just as before except that one of them limped on a hind leg. When Thor saw this he knew someone had disobeyed him and had broken a thigh bone. His brows grew dark with anger and he gripped the handle of his hammer so fiercely that his knuckles grew white. The countryman and his family were terrified when they saw Thor's wrath.

"Have mercy, O Thor," they cried, "we will pay you for the harm we have done. We will give you our house and our cattle and our land. We will give all we own. Have mercy on us, O Mighty One."

When Thor saw how frightened they were he forgot his anger. As payment he agreed to take the son and daughter of the countryman into his service. Thjalfi and Roskva have ever since been with Thor.

They started off again on their journey, leaving the goats behind. They walked until they came to the sea. They waded right through the sea and up to the shore on the other side. In a little while they reached a dark forest and all day they traveled through it. Thjalfi, who was swift-footed beyond all other men, carried Thor's wallet in which were the provisions for the journey. This was not country in which much could be found along the way.

As it grew dark they looked about for a place to spend the night. They found a house with a wide door that stood open the whole length of the house. The house was dark and quiet and they decided to take shelter here for the night. They went in and settled themselves to sleep.

About midnight they heard a great noise. The earth trembled as from an earthquake. They looked about for some place to hide themselves and discovered a smaller doorway leading into a side room. Loki and Thjalfi and Roskva hid themselves in the farthest corner of this room, but Thor sat in the doorway, with his hammer in his hand, ready to meet the danger.

When the light of morning came they all went outside. Roskva began to prepare breakfast. Thor said that he would walk about and have a look at things. A little way off he came upon a huge giant stretched out asleep on the ground. He was snoring mightily and the earth shook beneath him. Then Thor knew what the rumbling and the roaring in the night had been. Thor buckled on his belt of strength, but just at that moment the giant woke and sat up. It is said that Thor, for once in his life, had no desire to strike a blow.

Instead he asked the giant what his name was. "I am called Skrymir," said the giant, "but I have no need to ask your name. I know well that you are Asa-Thor. But what have you done with my glove?"

As he spoke he stooped and picked up a great glove lying at some distance on the ground. This was what Thor and the others had mistaken in the dark for a house. The smaller doorway into the side room was the opening into the thumb.

"Shall we travel together?" said the giant. Thor agreed. First they had breakfast, each party eating from its own provisions.

Then Skrymir suggested that they put all the food into one sack. Thor agreed. So Skrymir put Thor's wallet into his sack. He tied the mouth of the sack and flung it over his shoulder.

They started on their journey. Skrymir strode ahead of them with such long strides that it was not easy to keep up with him. They traveled all day. When night came Skrymir found them a place to rest under a wide-spreading oak tree. He flung the sack from his shoulder to the ground.

"Now I am going to sleep," said Skrymir. "You can take your supper from the sack if you like." He lay down a little way off and at once was fast asleep.

The others were hungry. Thor began to untie the sack so they might have food. Though he pulled and turned and twisted the rope, the knot would not loosen at all. The more Thor struggled, the angrier he grew. Suddenly he seized his hammer with both hands. He went over to where Skrymir lay and dealt him a blow on the head.

Skrymir woke up and said: "What was that? Did a leaf fall on me? Have you had your supper, Thor?"

Thor said they had and were getting ready to sleep. Then they went under another oak and prepared to rest, but they did not feel very safe.

About midnight Thor heard Skrymir snoring so that the woods shook with the sound. He went to where the giant lay and flourishing his hammer above his head, he brought it down with such force that the giant's skull was dented.

Skrymir woke up. "Now what is that?" he said. "Has an acorn fallen on me? How is it with you, Thor?"

Thor said that it was only midnight and there was still time for sleeping.

"I just happened to waken," said Thor. Then he went back to his place speedily.

Skrymir stretched out again. Thor lay quiet, but he was not asleep. He thought that if he could give Skrymir just one more blow, the giant would not see day again. Just before dawn Thor heard Skrymir snoring. Running to where he lay, Thor struck him such a mighty blow on the temple that the hammer sank into the skull up to its handle.

But Skrymir sat up and stroked his cheek. "Did a twig fall on my face? Are you awake, Thor? It is almost day, and time we were on our way."

They prepared to start their journey. Then Skrymir said: "You have no long way to go now to reach the home of the giants. But let me give you a word of advice: don't brag too much of your prowess there, for Utgard-Loki and his men have little patience with the boasting of such small fellows as you. Perhaps it would be wiser if you did not go at all. Yet if you are determined to keep on your journey, take the way to the east. My road lies north, to those mountains you see beyond you."

Skrymir flung the sack of food over his shoulder and was gone without another word. It has never been said that the others were sorry to see him go.

Thor and his companions traveled all morning. About noon they caught sight of a great castle standing in the middle of a plain. The top of it was so high that they had to bend their heads back before they could see it. The gate to the castle was locked. Thor went up to it and tried to open it, but could not move it. So they crept in between the bars. They saw before them a huge hall and went toward it. The door was open and they went inside.

There they saw many men sitting about on benches and none of them could be called small men. Utgard-Loki, king of the giants, was among them. They went before him and saluted him. He took his time to look them over, laughing at them scornfully through his teeth.

"There is no need to ask news of a long journey," said Utgard-Loki. "Is this stripling Asa-Thor? Or am I wrong? Tell us in what you are skilled, you and your fellows. For no one is allowed to remain among us who cannot do some thing better than other men."

Loki, who was standing behind the others, spoke up. "There is one thing I am ready to wager at once, and that is that I can eat faster than anyone here."

"We shall soon find out," answered Utgard-Loki.

Then he shouted for a man named Logi to come to the center of the hall to try his skill with Loki. A great trencher of food was brought and placed upon the floor. Loki and Logi sat down at each end of it and began to eat with all their might. They met in the middle of the trencher. Loki had eaten all the meat from the bones, but Logi had consumed the meat and the bones and the trencher as well. So Loki was beaten at this game.

"What is that young man able to do?" asked Utgard-Loki, pointing to Thjalfi.

"I am willing to try a race with someone," answered Thjalfi.

"You will need to be swift of foot," said Utgard-Loki.

They all went outside. The level plain was a good place for running a race. Utgard-Loki called a small fellow named Hugi. He told him to run against Thjalfi.

They started. Hugi was far enough ahead that he met Thjalfi as he turned back at the end of the course.

"You will have to stretch your legs more than that, Thjalfi, if you are to win," said Utgard-Loki. "Yet it is true that never have men come here who could run so well."

When they ran the second trial Hugi was so far ahead that when he turned back at the end of the course, Thjalfi had still the length of a bow shot to run.

"Well run," said Utgard-Loki, "but I cannot think that Thjalfi will win if you should run a third time."

Thjalfi ran the third time with all his might, and he was the swiftest of men. Yet Hugi had come to the end of the course and turned back before Thjalfi had reached the middle of it.

All agreed that Hugi had won the race.

Then they went inside the hall and Utgard-Loki asked Thor in what way he would try his skill. "We have heard great things of your prowess, Thor," said he.

"I will drink with anyone who cares to drink," said Thor.

"Very good," said Utgard-Loki. He called his serving boy to bring the great horn from which the henchmen sometimes drank.

"It is considered a good drink if you can empty this horn at one draught," said Utgard-Loki. "Some among us must drink twice, but there is not any man here who cannot drain it in three draughts."

Thor took the horn. He thought it not too large, though it seemed somewhat long. Thor was thirsty. He put the horn to his lips and took a long, deep draught. He thought to himself that he would not have to take more than one drink. But when he had to stop for breath and put the horn down he saw, to his surprise, that there was but little less in it than there had been before.

"Well," said Utgard-Loki, "that was a pretty good drink. But if anyone had told me that Asa-Thor could not drink more than this I would not have believed it. No doubt you will drain it this time."

Thor answered nothing. He put his mouth to the horn again and drank as long as he could hold his breath. When he paused it seemed to him that it had gone down even less than before. Yet at least one could now tilt the horn a little without spilling it.

"Well," said Utgard-Loki, "can you finish that in one more draught? It seems to me that you have perhaps left overmuch for the last drink. It cannot be said that you are as great here among us as you are among the gods, unless you are more skilled in other games than in this."

Thor grew angry. He put the horn to his mouth and drank with all his might. He struggled with it and drank as long as he could, but when he had to put the horn down again it was still almost full. Yet it could be said that a little space had been made in it. But Thor would drink no more.

"It can be plainly seen that you are not so great as we thought you were," said Utgard-Loki. "Will you try your skill at other games, since you won no praise in this one?"

"I will risk it," said Thor. "Yet I know that at home among the gods my drink would not have seemed so little."

"We have a game among us that does not amount to much," said Utgard-Loki. "Our young boys like to play it. It is to lift my cat from the floor. Indeed I would not have dared to mention it had I not seen that Asa-Thor is by no means as great as we thought he was."

There leaped forth upon the hall floor a large gray cat. Thor put one hand down under the middle of its body and stretched upward. But the more he stretched the more the cat arched its back. Though he stretched as high as he could the cat only lifted one foot off the floor. And Thor had to give up that game.

"The game went just as I thought it would," said Utgard-Loki. "The cat is very great, and Thor is low and little beside the huge men who are here with us."

"Call me little if you will," cried Thor, "but let anyone here come and wrestle with me. For now I am angry."

"I see no man here who would not hold it a disgrace to wrestle with you," said Utgard-Loki looking about the benches. "Let my old nurse, Elli, be called. Thor can wrestle with her if he wishes. She has thrown men who have seemed to me no less strong than Thor."

There appeared an old woman, bent with age. Thor grappled with her, but the more he struggled the firmer she stood. He could in no way throw her. She began to try some tricks of her own and Thor tottered. Then Thor went down upon one knee.

Utgard-Loki came up and bade them cease wrestling. "There is no need now," said he, "for Thor to challenge any of my men."

It was now toward evening. Utgard-Loki showed Thor and his companions to a seat at one of the benches. They remained throughout the night and were treated with great hospitality.

When morning came Thor and the others rose and made ready to leave. Utgard-Loki himself came into the hall. He ordered a table set for them with every kind of food and drink. When they had eaten, he went to see them on their way. As they were about to part, Utgard-Loki said:

"What think you, Thor, of this journey? Have you met any man mightier than yourself?"

"What I have done here will gain me small praise," answered Thor. "What troubles me most is that you will think me a man of little might."

"Now that you are out of the castle, I will tell you something," said Utgard-Loki. "If I live and prevail, Thor, you will never come into it again. This I know, by my troth, you should never have come into it at all had I known what strength you had! You nearly had us all in great peril."

Utgard-Loki went on speaking; "I have tricked you, Thor. It was I whom you met in the wood. I tied the sack of food with troll-iron, so that you could not undo it. When you went to smite me with the hammer I brought a mountain between us, though you could not see it. Otherwise the first blow would have slain me. Do you see that mountain with the three valleys, one deeper than the others? Those are the marks of your blows.

"It was the same with the games you played against my henchmen," continued Utgard-Loki. "There you were tricked, too. Loki was hungry and ate ravenously, but he who was called Logi was Fire and he devoured the trencher as well as the meat. Thjalfi ran the race with Hugi, who is Thought — and how could Thjalfi outrun Thought?"

"And how did you trick me, Utgard-Loki?" said Thor.

"When you drank from the horn, Thor,

it seemed to you to go down slowly. But that was a wonder I could hardly believe even when I saw. For the other end of the horn was in the sea itself, though you knew it not. When you look at the sea you will notice how the water has drawn back. From hence we shall call that the Ebb Tide.

"And my gray cat was not as it appeared to be. It was the Midgard Serpent itself which is twined about the whole earth. It was the same with the wrestling match. It was a marvel that you withstood so long and bent only one knee. You struggled with Old Age and all men must give in to Old Age at last.

"And now," said Utgard-Loki, "it is best that we part. It will be better for us both if you come not here again. I will defend my castle with every trick I know, so that you shall get no power over me."

When Thor knew he had been tricked, he seized his hammer and would have hurled it at Utgard-Loki. But the giant had disappeared. Thor turned toward the castle, thinking to crush it with a blow from the hammer. It was gone also. There was nothing before them but the green and level plain.

So Thor turned back, with the others, and made his way to Thrudvang, his own realm. Already his thoughts were busy as to how he might be revenged.

"One day," said Thor to himself, "I will seek out the Midgard Serpent. We shall see if I be 'little and low.'"

The Quest of the Hammer [7]

⋐ *Thor, the strongest of the gods, was the oldest son of Odin. Besides his wonderful hammer, which returned to his hand after he had thrown it, he had a belt of strength which doubled his power when he wore it, and an iron glove which he wore when he threw his hammer. Though Thor usually walked, he had a goat-drawn cart or chariot; and its rolling wheels gave out the sound of thunder; the thunderbolt came when his hammer flew back to his hand. As the possessor of these powerful weapons and as the strongest god, Thor was*

[7] From Abbie Farwell Brown, *In the Days of Giants* (Houghton Mifflin, 1902).

the greatest defender of the gods against their enemies, the giants. Thor was also the patron of the peasants and laboring classes, and Thor's day has become our Thursday.

One morning Thor the Thunderer awoke with a yawn, and stretching out his knotted arm, felt for his precious hammer, which he kept always under his pillow of clouds. But he started up with a roar of rage, so that all the palace trembled. The hammer was gone!

Now this was a very serious matter, for Thor was the protector of Asgard, and Miölnir, the magic hammer which the dwarf had made, was his mighty weapon, of which the enemies of the Aesir stood so much in dread that they dared not venture near. But if they should learn that Miölnir was gone, who could tell what danger might not threaten the palaces of heaven?

Thor darted his flashing eye into every corner of Cloud Land in search of the hammer. He called his fair wife, Sif of the golden hair, to aid in the search, and his two lovely daughters, Thrude and Lora. They hunted and they hunted; they turned Thrudheim upside down, and set the clouds to rolling wonderfully, as they peeped and pried behind and around and under each billowy mass.

Thor's yellow beard quivered with rage, and his hair bristled on end like the golden rays of a star, while all his household trembled.

"It is Loki again!" he cried. "I am sure Loki is at the bottom of this mischief!" For since the time when Thor had captured Loki for the dwarf Brock and had given him over to have his bragging lips sewed up, Loki had looked at him with evil eyes; and Thor knew that the red rascal hated him most of all the gods.

But this time Thor was mistaken. It was not Loki who had stolen the hammer — he was too great a coward for that. And though he meant, before the end, to be revenged upon Thor, he was waiting until a safe chance should come, when Thor himself might stumble into danger, and Loki need only to help the evil by a malicious word or two; and this chance came later, as you shall hear in another tale.

Meanwhile Loki was on his best behavior, trying to appear very kind and obliging; so when Thor came rumbling and roaring up to him, demanding, "What have you done with my hammer, you thief?" Loki looked surprised, but did not lose his temper nor answer rudely.

"Have you indeed missed your hammer, brother Thor?" he said, mumbling, for his mouth was still sore where Brock had sewed the stitches. "That is a pity; for if the giants hear of this, they will be coming to try their might against Asgard."

"Hush!" muttered Thor, grasping him by the shoulder with his iron fingers. "That is what I fear. But look you, Loki: I suspect your hand in the mischief. Come, confess."

Then Loki protested that he had nothing to do with so wicked a deed. "But," he added wheedlingly, "I think I can guess the thief; and because I love you, Thor, I will help you to find him."

"Humph!" growled Thor. "Much love you bear to me! However, you are a wise rascal, the nimblest wit of all the Aesir, and it is better to have you on my side than on the other, when giants are in the game. Tell me, then: who has robbed the Thunder-Lord of his bolt of power?"

Loki drew near and whispered in Thor's ear. "Look, how the storms rage and the winds howl in the world below! Someone is wielding your thunder-hammer all unskillfully. Can you not guess the thief? Who but Thrym, the mighty giant who has ever been your enemy and your imitator, and whose fingers have long itched to grasp the short handle of mighty Miölnir, that the world may name him Thunder-Lord instead of you. But look! What a tempest! The world will be shattered into fragments unless we soon get the hammer back."

Then Thor roared with rage. "I will seek this impudent Thrym!" he cried. "I will crush him into bits, and teach him to meddle with the weapon of the Aesir!"

"Softly, softly," said Loki, smiling maliciously. "He is a shrewd giant, and a mighty. Even you, great Thor, cannot go to him and pluck the hammer from his hand as one would slip the rattle from a baby's pink fist. Nay, you must use craft, Thor; and it is I

who will teach you, if you will be patient."

Thor was a brave, blunt fellow, and he hated the ways of Loki, his lies and his deceit. He liked best the way of warriors — the thundering charge, the flash of weapons, and the heavy blow; but without the hammer he could not fight the giants hand to hand. Loki's advice seemed wise, and he decided to leave the matter to the Red One.

Loki was now all eagerness, for he loved difficulties which would set his wit in play and bring other folk into danger. "Look, now," he said. "We must go to Freia and borrow her falcon dress. But you must ask; for she loves me so little that she would scarce listen to me."

So first they made their way to Folkvang, the house of maidens, where Freia dwelt, the loveliest of all in Asgard. She was fairer than fair, and sweeter than sweet, and the tears from her flower-eyes made the dew which blessed the earth-flowers night and morning. Of her Thor borrowed the magic dress of feathers in which Freia was wont to clothe herself and flit like a great beautiful bird all about the world. She was willing enough to lend it to Thor when he told her that by its aid he hoped to win back the hammer which he had lost; for she well knew the danger threatening herself and all the Aesir until Miölnir should be found.

"Now will I fetch the hammer for you," said Loki. So he put on the falcon plumage, and, spreading his brown wings, flapped away up, up, over the world, down, down, across the great ocean which lies beyond all things that men know. And he came to the dark country where there was no sunshine nor spring, but it was always dreary winter; where mountains were piled up like blocks of ice, and where great caverns yawned hungrily in blackness. And this was Jotunheim, the land of the Frost Giants.

And lo! when Loki came thereto he found Thrym the Giant King sitting outside his palace cave, playing with his dogs and horses. The dogs were as big as elephants, and the horses were as big as houses, but Thrym himself was as huge as a mountain; and Loki trembled, but he tried to seem brave.

"Good-day, Loki," said Thrym, with the

terrible voice of which he was so proud, for he fancied it was as loud as Thor's. "How fares it, feathered one, with your little brothers, the Aesir, in Asgard halls? And how dare you venture alone in this guise to Giant Land?"

"It is an ill day in Asgard," sighed Loki, keeping his eye warily upon the giant, "and a stormy one in the world of men. I heard the winds howling and the storms rushing on the earth as I passed by. Some mighty one has stolen the hammer of our Thor. Is it you, Thrym, greatest of all giants — greater than Thor himself?"

This the crafty one said to flatter Thrym, for Loki well knew the weakness of those who love to be thought greater than they are.

Then Thrym bridled and swelled with pride, and tried to put on the majesty and awe of noble Thor; but he only succeeded in becoming an ugly, puffy monster.

"Well, yes," he admitted. "I have the hammer that belonged to your little Thor; and now how much of a lord is he?"

"Alack!" sighed Loki again, "weak enough he is without his magic weapon. But you, O Thrym — surely your mightiness needs no such aid. Give me the hammer, that Asgard may no longer be shaken by Thor's grief for his precious toy."

But Thrym was not so easily to be flattered into parting with his stolen treasure. He grinned a dreadful grin, several yards in width, which his teeth barred like jagged boulders across the entrance to a mountain cavern.

"Miölnir the hammer is mine," he said, "and I am Thunder-Lord, mightiest of the mighty. I have hidden it where Thor can never find it, twelve leagues below the sea-caves, where Queen Ran lives with her daughters, the white-capped Waves. But listen, Loki. Go tell the Aesir that I will give back Thor's hammer. I will give it back upon one condition — that they send Freia the beautiful to be my wife."

"Freia the beautiful!" Loki had to stifle a laugh. Fancy the Aesir giving their fairest flower to such an ugly fellow as this! But he only said politely, "Ah, yes; you demand our Freia in exchange for the little hammer? It is a costly price, great Thrym. But I will be your friend in Asgard. If I have my way, you shall soon see the fairest bride in all the world knocking at your door. Farewell!"

So Loki whizzed back to Asgard on his falcon wings; and as he went he chuckled to think of the evils which were likely to happen because of his words with Thrym. First he gave the message to Thor — not sparing of Thrym's insolence, to make Thor angry; and then he went to Freia with the word for her — not sparing of Thrym's ugliness, to make her shudder. The spiteful fellow!

Now you can imagine the horror that was in Asgard as the Aesir listened to Loki's words. "My hammer!" roared Thor. "The villain confesses that he has stolen my hammer, and boasts that he is Thunder-Lord! Gr-r-r!"

"The ugly giant!" wailed Freia. "Must I be the bride of that hideous old monster, and live in his gloomy mountain prison all my life?"

"Yes; put on your bridal veil, sweet Freia," said Loki maliciously, "and come with me to Jotunheim. Hang your famous starry necklace about your neck, and don your bravest robe; for in eight days there will be a wedding, and Thor's hammer is to pay."

Then Freia fell to weeping. "I cannot go! I will not go!" she cried. "I will not leave the home of gladness and Father Odin's table to dwell in the land of horrors! Thor's hammer is mighty, but mightier the love of the kind Aesir for their little Freia! Good Odin, dear brother Frey, speak for me! You will not make me go?"

The Aesir looked at her and thought how lonely and bare would Asgard be without her loveliness; for she was fairer than fair, and sweeter than sweet.

"She shall not go!" shouted Frey, putting his arms about his sister's neck.

"No, she shall not go!" cried all the Aesir with one voice.

"But my hammer," insisted Thor. "I must have Miölnir back again."

"And my word to Thrym," said Loki, "that must be made good."

"You are too generous with your words," said Father Odin sternly, for he knew his brother well. "Your word is not a gem of great price, for you have made it cheap."

Then spoke Heimdal, the sleepless watchman who sits on guard at the entrance to the rainbow bridge which leads to Asgard; and Heimdal was the wisest of the Aesir, for he could see into the future, and knew how things would come to pass. Through his golden teeth he spoke, for his teeth were all of gold.

"I have a plan," he said. "Let us dress Thor himself like a bride in Freia's robes, and send him to Jotunheim to talk with Thrym and to win back his hammer."

But at this word Thor grew very angry. "What! dress me like a girl!" he roared. "I should never hear the last of it! The Aesir will mock me, and call me 'maiden'! The giants, and even the puny dwarfs, will have a lasting jest upon me! I will not go! I will fight! I will die, if need be! But dressed as a woman I will not go!"

But Loki answered him with sharp words, for this was a scheme after his own heart. "What, Thor!" he said. "Would you lose your hammer and keep Asgard in danger for so small a whim? Look, now: if you go not, Thrym with his giants will come in a mighty army and drive us from Asgard; then he will indeed make Freia his bride, and moreover he will have you for his slave under the power of his hammer. How like you this picture, brother of the thunder? Nay, Heimdal's plan is a good one, and I myself will help to carry it out."

Still Thor hesitated; but Freia came and laid her white hand on his arm, and looked up into his scowling face pleadingly.

"To save me, Thor," she begged. And Thor said he would go.

Then there was great sport among the Aesir, while they dressed Thor like a beautiful maiden. Brünhilde and her sisters, the nine Valkyrie, daughters of Odin, had the task in hand. How they laughed as they brushed and curled his yellow hair, and set upon it the wondrous headdress of silk and pearls! They let out seams, and they let down hems, and set on extra pieces, to make it larger, and so they hid his great limbs and knotted arms under Freia's fairest robe of scarlet; but beneath it all he would wear his shirt of mail and his belt of power that gave him double strength. Freia herself twisted about his neck her famous necklace of starry jewels, and Queen Frigg, his mother, hung at his girdle a jingling bunch of keys, such as was the custom for the bride to wear at Norse weddings. Last of all, that Thrym might not see Thor's fierce eyes and the yellow beard, that ill became a maiden, they threw over him a long veil of silver white which covered him to the feet. And there he stood, as stately and tall a bride as even a giant might wish to see; but on his hands he wore his iron gloves, and they ached for but one thing — to grasp the handle of the stolen hammer.

"Ah, what a lovely maid it is!" chuckled Loki; "and how glad will Thrym be to see this Freia come! Bride Thor, I will go with you as your handmaiden, for I would fain see the fun."

"Come, then," said Thor sulkily, for he was ill-pleased, and wore his maiden robes with no good grace. "It is fitting that you go; for I like not these lies and maskings, and I may spoil the mummery without you at my elbow."

There was loud laughter above the clouds when Thor, all veiled and dainty-seeming, drove away from Asgard to his wedding, with maid Loki by his side. Thor cracked his whip and chirruped fiercely to his twin goats with golden hoofs, for he wanted to escape the sounds of mirth that echoed from the rainbow bridge, where all the Aesir stood watching. Loki, sitting with his hands meekly folded like a girl, chuckled as he glanced up at Thor's angry face; but he said nothing, for he knew it was not good to joke too far with Thor, even when Miölnir was hidden twelve leagues below the sea in Ran's kingdom.

So off they dashed to Jotunheim, where Thrym was waiting and longing for his beautiful bride. Thor's goats thundered along above the sea and land and people far below, who looked up wondering as the noise rolled overhead. "Hear how the thunder rumbles!" they said. "Thor is on a long journey tonight." And a long journey it was, as the tired goats found before they reached the end.

Thrym heard the sound of their approach, for his ear was eager. "Hola!" he cried. "Someone is coming from Asgard — only one of Odin's children could make a din so fearful. Hasten, men, and see if they are bringing Freia to be my wife."

Then the lookout giants stepped down from the top of his mountain, and said that a chariot was bringing two maidens to the door.

"Run, giants, run!" shouted Thrym, in a fever at this news. "My bride is coming! Put silken cushions on the benches for a great banquet, and make the house beautiful for the fairest maid in all space! Bring in all my golden-horned cows and my coal-black oxen, that she may see how rich I am, and heap all my gold and jewels about to dazzle her sweet eyes! She shall find me richest of the rich; and when I have her — fairest of the fair — there will be no treasure that I lack — not one!"

The chariot stopped at the gate, and out stepped the tall bride, hidden from head to foot, and her handmaiden muffled to the chin. "How afraid of catching cold they must be!" whispered the giant ladies, who were peering over one another's shoulders to catch a glimpse of the bride, just as the crowd outside the awning does at a wedding nowadays.

Thrym had sent six splendid servants to escort the maidens: these were the Metal Kings, who served him as lord of them all. There was the Gold King, all in cloth of gold, with fringes of yellow bullion, most glittering to see; and there was the Silver King, almost as gorgeous in a suit of spangled white; and side by side bowed the dark Kings of Iron and Lead, the one mighty in black, the other sullen in blue; and after them were the Copper King, gleaming ruddy and brave, and the Tin King, strutting in his trimmings of gaudy tinsel which looked nearly as well as silver but were more economical. And this fine troop of lackey kings most politely led Thor and Loki into the palace, and gave them the best, for they never suspected who these seeming maidens really were.

And when evening came there was a wonderful banquet to celebrate the wedding.

On a golden throne sat Thrym, uglier than ever in his finery of purple and gold. Beside him was the bride, of whose face no one had yet caught even a glimpse; and at Thrym's other hand stood Loki, the waiting-maid, for he wanted to be near to mend the mistakes which Thor might make.

Now the dishes at the feast were served in a huge way, as befitted the table of giants: great beeves roasted whole, on platters as wide across as a ship's deck; plum-puddings as fat at feather-beds, with plums as big as footballs; and a wedding cake like a snow-capped haymow. The giants ate enormously. But to Thor, because they thought him a dainty maiden, they served small bits of everything on a tiny gold dish. Now Thor's long journey had made him very hungry, and through his veil he whispered to Loki, "I shall starve, Loki! I cannot fare on these nibbles. I must eat a goodly meal as I do at home." And forthwith he helped himself to such morsels as might satisfy his hunger for a little time. You should have seen the giants stare at the meal which the dainty bride devoured!

For first under the silver veil disappeared by pieces a whole roast ox. Then Thor made eight mouthfuls of eight pink salmon, a dish of which he was very fond. And next he looked about and reached for a platter of cakes and sweetmeats that was set aside at one end of the table for the lady guests, and the bride ate them all. You can fancy how the damsels drew down their mouths and looked at one another when they saw their dessert disappear; and they whispered about the table, "Alack! if our future mistress is to sup like this day by day, there will be poor cheer for the rest of us!" And to crown it all, Thor was thirsty, as well he might be; and one after another he raised to his lips and emptied three great barrels of mead, the foamy drink of the giants. Then indeed Thrym was amazed, for Thor's giant appetite had beaten that of the giants themselves.

"Never before saw I a bride so hungry," he cried, "and never before one half so thirsty!"

But Loki, the waiting-maid whispered to him softly, "The truth is, great Thrym, that my dear mistress was almost starved. For eight days Freia has eaten nothing at all, so eager was she for Jotunheim."

Then Thrym was delighted, you may be sure. He forgave his hungry bride, and loved her with all his heart. He leaned forward to give her a kiss, raising a corner of her veil; but his hand dropped suddenly, and he started up in terror, for he had caught the angry flash of Thor's eye, which was glaring at him through the bridal veil. Thor was longing for his hammer.

"Why has Freia so sharp a look?" Thrym cried. "It pierces like lightning and burns like fire."

But again the sly waiting-maid whispered timidly, "Oh, Thrym, be not amazed! The truth is, my poor mistress's eyes are red with wakefulness and bright with longing. For eight nights Freia has not known a wink of sleep, so eager was she for Jotunheim."

Then again Thrym was doubly delighted, and he longed to call her his very own dear wife. "Bring in the wedding gift!" he cried. "Bring in Thor's hammer, Miölnir, and give it to Freia, as I promised; for when I have kept my word she will be mine — all mine!"

Then Thor's big heart laughed under his woman's dress, and his fierce eyes swept eagerly down the hall to meet the servant who was bringing in the hammer on a velvet cushion. Thor's fingers could hardly wait to clutch the stubby handle which they knew so well; but he sat quite still on the throne beside ugly old Thrym, with his hands meekly folded and his head bowed like a bashful bride.

The giant servant drew nearer, nearer, puffing and blowing, strong though he was, beneath the mighty weight. He was about to lay it at Thor's feet (for he thought it so heavy that no maiden could lift it or hold it in her lap), when suddenly Thor's heart swelled, and he gave a most unmaidenly shout of rage and triumph. With one swoop he grasped the hammer in his iron fingers; with the other arm he tore off

the veil that hid his terrible face, and trampled it under foot; then he turned to the frightened king, who cowered beside him on the throne.

"Thief!" he cried. "Freia sends you this as a wedding gift!" And he whirled the hammer about his head, then hurled it once, twice, thrice, as it rebounded to his hand; and in the first stroke, as of lightning, Thrym rolled dead from his throne; in the second stroke perished the whole giant household — these ugly enemies of the Aesir; and in the third stroke the palace itself tumbled together and fell to the ground like a toppling playhouse of blocks.

But Loki and Thor stood safely among the ruins, dressed in their tattered maiden robes, a quaint and curious sight; and Loki, full of mischief now as ever, burst out laughing.

"Oh, Thor! if you could see" — he began; but Thor held up his hammer and shook it gently as he said:

"Look now, Loki: it was an excellent joke, and so far you have done well — after your crafty fashion, which likes me not. But now I have my hammer again and the joke is done. From you, nor from another, I brook no laughter at my expense. Henceforth, we will have no mention of this masquerade, nor of these rags which now I throw away. Do you hear, red laughter?"

And Loki heard, with a look of hate, and stifled his laughter as best he could; for it is not good to laugh at him who holds the hammer.

Not once after that was there mention in Asgard of the time when Thor dressed him as a girl and won his bridal gift from Thrym the giant.

But Miölnir was safe once more in Asgard, and you and I know how it came there; so some one must have told. I wonder if red Loki whispered the tale to some outsider, after all? Perhaps it may be so, for now he knew how best to make Thor angry; and from that day when Thor forbade his laughing, Loki hated him with the mean little hatred of a mean little soul.

NORTH AMERICAN INDIAN MYTHS

Determination of the Seasons [1]

(Tahltan)

❧ *This tale and* How Glooskap Found the Summer *are interesting when considered together, since they show very different causes for the seasons. This one is clearly a beast tale in which the weaker animal wins, and belongs to that class of myths which explain how the present world came to be what it is. Glooskap may be typed not only as an explanation of the world-as-it-is, but also as a tale about this world and "the other world." The fact that the symbol for Glooskap is the snowshoe rabbit suggests a comparison with the* Jatakas, *and Buddha's transformations into one wild animal or another, when he would return to earth. Glooskap is not represented as an animal, but neither is he definitely represented in the human form.*

Once Porcupine and Beaver quarreled about the seasons. Porcupine wanted five winter months. He held up one hand and showed his five fingers. He said, "Let the winter months be the same in number as the fingers on my hand." Beaver said, "No," and held up his tail, which had many cracks or scratches on it. He said, "Let the winter months be the same in number as the scratches on my tail." Now they quarreled and argued. Porcupine got angry and bit off his thumb. Then, holding up his hand with the four fingers, he said emphatically, "There must be only four winter months." Beaver became a little afraid, and gave in. *For this*

reason porcupines have four claws on each foot now.

Since Porcupine won, the winter remained four months in length, until later Raven changed it a little. Raven considered what Porcupine and Beaver had said about the winters, and decided that Porcupine had done right. He said, "Porcupine was right. If the winters were made too long, people could not live. *Henceforth the winters will be about this length,* but they will be variable. I will tell you of the *gaxewisa* month, when people will meet together and talk. At that time of the year people will ask questions (or propound riddles) and others will answer. If the riddle is answered correctly, then the person who propounded it must answer, 'Fool-Hen.'" Raven chose this word because the fool-hen has a shorter beak than any other game-bird. "If people guess riddles correctly at this time of year, then the winter will be short, and the spring come early."

How Glooskap Found the Summer [2]

(Algonquin)

In the long-ago time before the first white men came to live in the New World, and when people lived always in the early red morning before sunrise, a mighty race of Indians lived in the northeastern part of the

---

[1] From Stith Thompson, *Tales of the North American Indians* (Harvard University Press, 1929).

[2] From Charles Godfrey Leland, *The Algonquin Legends of New England* (Houghton Mifflin, 1884).

New World. Nearest the sunrise were they, and they called themselves Wawaniki — Children of Light. Glooskap was their lord and master. He was ever kind to his people, and did many great works for them.

Once, in Glooskap's day, it grew very cold; snow and ice were everywhere, fires would not give enough warmth; the corn would not grow, and his people were perishing with cold and famine. Then Glooskap went very far north where all was ice. He came to a wigwam in which he found a giant, a great giant — for he was Winter. It was his icy breath that had frozen all the land. Glooskap entered the wigwam and sat down. Then Winter gave him a pipe, and as he smoked, the giant told tales of the olden times when he, Winter, reigned everywhere; when all the land was silent, white, and beautiful. The charm fell upon Glooskap; it was the frost charm. As the giant talked on and on, Glooskap fell asleep; and for six months he slept like a bear; then the charm fled, as he was too strong for it, and he awoke.

Soon after he awoke, his talebearer, Tatler the Loon, a wild bird who lived on the shores of the lakes, brought him strange news. He told of a country far off to the south where it was always warm: there lived a queen, who could easily overcome the giant, Winter. So Glooskap, to save his people from cold and famine and death, decided to go and find the queen.

Far off to the seashore he went, and sang the magic song which the whales obey. Up came his old friend, Blob the Whale. She was Glooskap's carrier and bore him on her back when he wished to go far out to sea. Now the whale always had a strange law for travelers. She said to Glooskap, "You must shut your eyes tight while I carry you; to open them is dangerous; if you do that, I am sure to go aground on a reef or sand-bar, and cannot get off, and you may be drowned."

Glooskap got on her back, and for many days the whale swam, and each day the water grew warmer and the air more balmy and sweet, for it came from spicy shores. The odors were no longer those of salt, but of fruits and flowers.

Soon they found themselves in shallow waters. Down in the sand the clams were singing a song of warning. "O big Whale," they sang, "keep out to sea, for the water here is shallow."

The whale said to Glooskap, who understood the language of all creatures, "What do they say?"

But Glooskap, wishing to land at once, said, "They tell you to hurry, for a storm is coming."

Then the whale hurried until she was close to the land, and Glooskap opened his left eye and peeped. At once the whale stuck hard and fast on the beach, so that Glooskap, leaping from her head, walked ashore on dry land.

The whale, thinking she could never get off, was very angry. But Glooskap put one end of his strong bow against the whale's jaw, and taking the other end in his hands, he placed his feet against the high bank, and with a mighty push, he sent her out into the deep water. Then, to keep peace with the whale, he threw her a pipe and a bag of Indian tobacco, and the whale, pleased with the gift, lighted the pipe and sailed far out to sea.

Far inland strode Glooskap and at every step it grew warmer, and the flowers began to come up and talk with him. He came to where there were many fairies dancing in the forest. In the center of the group was one fairer than all the others; her long brown hair was crowned with flowers and her arms filled with blossoms. She was the queen Summer.

Glooskap knew that here at last was the queen who by her charms could melt old Winter's heart, and force him to leave. He caught her up, and kept her by a crafty trick. The Master cut a moose-hide into a long cord; as he ran away with Summer, he let the end trail behind him. The Fairies of Light pulled at the cord, but as Glooskap ran, the cord ran out, and though they pulled, he left them far behind.

So at last he came to the lodge of old Winter, but now he had Summer in his bosom; and Winter welcomed him, for he hoped to freeze Glooskap to sleep again.

But this time the Master did the talking. This time his charm was the stronger, and ere long the sweat ran down Winter's face;

he knew that his power was gone; and the charm of Frost was broken. His icy tent melted. Then Summer used her strange power and everything awoke. The grass grew, the fairies came out, and the snow ran down the rivers, carrying away the dead leaves. Old Winter wept, seeing his power gone.

But Summer, the queen, said, "I have proved that I am more powerful than you. I give you now all the country to the far North for your own, and there I shall never disturb you. Six months of every year you may come back to Glooskap's country and reign as of old, but you will be less severe. During the other six months, I myself will come from the South and rule the land."

Old Winter could do nothing but accept her offer. In the late autumn he comes back to Glooskap's country and reigns six months; but his rule is softer than in olden times. And when he comes, Summer runs home to the warm Southland. But at the end of six months, she always comes back to drive old Winter away to his own land, to awaken the northern land, and to give it the joys that only she, the queen, can give. And so, in Glooskap's old country, Winter and Summer, the hoary old giant and the beautiful fairy queen, divide the rule of the land between them.

The Story of the First Woodpecker [3]

A story of tribal life, accompanied by magic and transformation, this myth — like the Pancake story — is found in a similar form among many other primitive peoples, but in no other version is the old woman turned into a woodpecker. Such punishment shows how very close the Indians were to nature.

In the days of long ago the Great Spirit came down from the sky and talked with men. Once as he went up and down the earth, he came to the wigwam of a woman.

[3] From Florence Holbrook, *A Book of Nature Myths* (Houghton Mifflin, 1902).

He went into the wigwam and sat down by the fire, but he looked like an old man, and the woman did not know who he was.

"I have fasted for many days," said the Great Spirit to the woman. "Will you give me some food?" The woman made a very little cake and put it on the fire. "You can have this cake," she said, "if you will wait for it to bake." "I will wait," he said.

When the cake was baked, the woman stood and looked at it. She thought, "It is very large. I thought it was small. I will not give him so large a cake as that." So she put it away and made a small one. "If you will wait, I will give you this when it is baked," she said, and the Great Spirit said, "I will wait."

When that cake was baked, it was larger than the first one. "It is so large that I will keep it for a feast," she thought. So she said to her guest, "I will not give you this cake, but if you will wait, I will make you another one." "I will wait," said the Great Spirit again.

Then the woman made another cake. It was still smaller than the others had been at first, but when she went to the fire for it, she found it the largest of all. She did not know that the Great Spirit's magic had made each cake larger, and she thought, "This is a marvel, but I will not give away the largest cake of all." So she said to her guest, "I have no food for you. Go to the forest and look there for your food. You can find it in the bark of the trees, if you will."

The Great Spirit was angry when he heard the words of the woman. He rose up from where he sat and threw back his cloak. "A woman must be good and gentle," he said, "and you are cruel. You shall no longer be a woman and live in a wigwam. You shall go out into the forests and hunt for your food in the bark of trees."

The Great Spirit stamped his foot on the earth, and the woman grew smaller and smaller. Wings started from her body and feathers grew upon her. With a loud cry she rose from the earth and flew away to the forest.

And to this day all woodpeckers live in the forest and hunt for their food in the bark of trees.

The Locust and the Coyote [4]

(Zuñi)

This beast tale has a moral if one wants to find it; perhaps its moral is the same as that of How the Coyote Danced with the Blackbirds, *and similar to that of the fable* The Crow and the Partridge, *but the lesson here is less emphasized than in the fable. In many folk tales the coyote is represented as a stupid beast.*

In the days of the ancients, there lived south of Hálona an old Coyote; and over near the headland of rocks, in a crooked, old piñon tree, lived a Locust.

One day the Coyote went out hunting, leaving his large family of children and his old wife at home.

It was a fine day and the old Locust crawled out of his home, and along one of the bare branches of the piñon tree, where, hooking his feet firmly into the bark, he began to sing and play his flute.

It was just at this time that the Coyote happened to come along. He heard the little Locust singing at the top of his voice:

"Locust, Locust, playing a flute,
    Away up above on the pine tree bough,
    Closely clinging,
    Playing a flute,
    Playing a flute!"

"Delight of my senses!" called out the Coyote, squatting down on his haunches, and looking up, with his ears pricked and his mouth grinning. "Delight of my senses! How finely you play your flute!"

"Do you think so?" said the Locust, continuing his song.

"Goodness yes!" cried the Coyote, as he came nearer. "What a fine song it is! Please teach it to me. I would like to sing it to my old wife, and to my children. I have a great many children."

"All right," said the Locust. "Now listen well." And he sang his song again.

"Delightful!" cried the Coyote. "Now, shall I try?"

[4] From Aileen B. Nusbaum, *Zuñi Indian Tales* (Putnam, 1926).

"Yes, try," said the old Locust.

Then in a very hoarse voice the Coyote half growled and half sang what the Locust had sung. "That is really very good, don't you think so?" he asked the Locust.

"Well — fairly," said the little creature.

"Now then, let us sing it together." And while the Locust piped shrilly, the Coyote sang gruffly.

"There now!" he exclaimed. "I am a fine fellow!" And without waiting to say another word, he whisked away toward his home. As he was running along he kept repeating the song to himself, and he thought little of where he was going. Therefore he did not notice an old Gopher peering at him ahead on the trail. Now this old Gopher laid a trap for him in his hole.

The Coyote came trotting along, singing merrily, when suddenly he tumbled heels over head into the Gopher's hole. He sneezed, began to cough and to rub the sand out of his eyes, and then jumping up, he said many wicked things to the old Gopher, who laughed at him far down in one of his cellars.

The Coyote scrambled out of the hole, and tried to recall his song, but found that he had forgotten it.

"You lubber-cheeked old Gopher!" he cried out. "You have made me forget my lovely song. Well — I will run back and get the old Locust to sing it over again. If he can sit there singing to himself, why can't he sing it to me?" So he ran back as fast as he could. When he arrived at the piñon tree, sure enough, there was the old Locust still sitting and singing.

"O, how lucky that you are here, my friend!" said the Coyote. "A fat-sided old Gopher dug a hole right in my path; and I went along singing your delightful song, and was so busy with it that I fell headlong into the trap he had set for me. I was so startled that, on my word, I forgot all about the song, and I have come back to ask you to sing it for me again."

"Very well," said the Locust. "Be more careful this time." So he sang the song over.

"Splendid! Surely I'll not forget it this time," cried the Coyote. He whisked about, and away he ran toward his home south of Hálona. "Let's see how it goes. O, yes!" And he commenced to sing.

Now this frightened a flock of Pigeons, and they came fluttering out of the bushes at his very feet, with such whizzing and whistling that the Coyote nearly tumbled over backwards, he was so scared. And between his fright and his anger at the birds, he was so much shaken up that he again forgot his song.

Now the Locust thought that something of the kind would happen, and he did not like the Coyote very well anyway, so he decided to play him a trick, and teach him a lesson in the minding of his own affairs.

First, catching tight hold of the bark, he swelled himself up and strained until his back split open; then he walked right out of his old skin, and crawling down the tree, found a little quartz stone, which, being light colored and clear, would make his skin look like himself. He took the stone up the tree and carefully placed it in the empty skin. Then he glued the back together with a little pitch, and left the false Locust sticking to the bark. After he had finished, he flew away to a neighboring tree.

And during this time the Coyote had met the Pigeons and had again forgotten his song. "I'll just go and get him to sing it over again. The silly old fellow must be still there piping away." And he ran back as fast as his legs would carry him.

"Ah wah!" he panted. "I'm all tired out with this running back and forth. But no matter; I see you are still there, my friend. I had dreadfully bad luck. I nearly stepped on some ugly, gray-backed Pigeons, and they flew up into the air with such a racket that it startled me so — I — forgot the song. Now, my friend, will you not be good enough to sing it once more for me?"

But the Locust said nothing.

"Why, what's the matter? Don't you hear me?" yelled the Coyote, running nearer, and looking closely at the Locust. "I say, I have lost my song, and I want you to sing it for me again. Will you, or will you not?" Then he waited — but the Locust on the piñon tree said never a word.

"Look here, are you going to sing for me or not?" growled the Coyote, getting angry. There was no reply of course.

The Coyote stretched out his nose, and wrinkled up his lips, and snarled, "Look here, do you see my teeth? Well, I'll ask you just four times more to sing for me, and if you don't sing then, I'll snap you in two, I tell you. Will-you-sing-for-me? Once. Will-you-sing-for-me? Twice. Two more times, look out! Will-you-sing-for-me? Are you crazy? Do you see my teeth? Only once more. Will-you-sing-for-me?"

And the Locust in the tree said nothing at all.

"Ah! Wha!" yelled the Coyote, and he made a quick jump in the air, and snapped the Locust skin off the branch. He bit so hard that the stone broke his teeth, and he rolled in the sand and howled and wriggled with pain. Then he got up and shook his head, and ran away with his tail between his legs.

And the old Locust sat in the other piñon tree and sang his song, and played his flute just for the joy of it, and because the sun was shining.

How the Coyote Danced with the Blackbirds [5]

(Zuñi)

This "pourquoi" story is reminiscent of the fable The Jackdaw and the Borrowed Plumes. *Note that the fable is terse and to the point, as a fable should be, whereas this story is deftly developed to the climax and the moral left to the reader's inference.*

One late autumn day in the times of the ancients, a large council of Blackbirds were gathered, fluttering and chattering, on the smooth, rocky slopes of Gorge Mountain, northwest of Zuñi. Like ourselves, these birds, as you are well aware, congregate together in autumn time, when the harvests are ripe, to indulge in their festivities before going into winter quarters; only we do not

5 From Frank Hamilton Cushing, *Zuñi Folk Tales* (Knopf).

move away, while they, on strong wings and swift, retreat for a time to the Land of Ever-lasting Summer.

Well, on this particular morning they were making a great noise and having a grand dance, and this was the way of it: They would gather in one vast flock, somewhat orderly in its disposition, on the sloping face of Gorge Mountain — the older birds in front, the younger ones behind — and down the slope, chirping and fluttering, they would hop, hop, hop, singing:

"Ketchu, Ketchu, oñtila, oñtila,
Ketchu, Ketchu, oñtila, oñtila!
Ashokta a yá-à-laa Ke-e-tchu,
Oñtila,
Oñtila!"—.
"Blackbirds, blackbirds, dance away, O, dance away, O!
Blackbirds, blackbirds, dance away, O, dance away, O!
Down the Mountain of the Gorges, Blackbirds,
Dance away, O!
Dance away, O!"

and, spreading their wings, with many a flutter, flurry, and scurry, keh, keh — keh, keh — keh, keh — keh, keh — they would fly away into the air, swirling off in a dense, black flock, circling far upward and onward; then, wheeling about and darting down, they would dip themselves in the broad spring which flows out at the foot of the mountain, and return to their dancing place on the rocky slope.

A Coyote was out hunting (as if he could catch anything, the beast!) and saw them, and was enraptured.

"You beautiful creatures!" he exclaimed. "You graceful dancers! Delight of my senses! How do you do that, anyway? Couldn't I join in your dance — the first part of it, at least?"

"Why, certainly; yes," said the Blackbirds. "We are quite willing," the masters of the ceremony said.

"Well," said the Coyote, "I can get on the slope of the rocks and I can sing the song with you; but I suppose that when you leap off into the air I shall have to sit there pat-ting the rock with my paw and my tail and singing while you have the fun of it."

"It may be," said an old Blackbird, "that

we can fit you out so that you can fly with us."

"Is it possible!" cried the Coyote. "Then by all means do so. By the Blessed Immor-tals! Now, if I am only able to circle off into the air like you fellows, I'll be the big-gest Coyote in the world!"

"I think it will be easy," resumed the old Blackbird. "My children," said he, "you are many, and many are your wing feathers. Contribute each one of you a feather to our friend." Thereupon the Blackbirds, each one of them, plucked a feather from his wing. Unfortunately they all plucked feath-ers from the wings on the same side.

"Are you sure, my friend," continued the old Blackbird, "that you are willing to go through the operation of having these feathers planted in your skin? If so, I think we can fit you out."

"Willing? — why, of course I am willing." And the Coyote held up one of his arms, and, sitting down, steadied himself with his tail. Then the Blackbirds thrust in the feathers all along the rear of his forelegs and down the sides of his back, where wings ought to be. It hurt, and the Coyote twitched his mustache considerably; but he said nothing. When it was done, he asked: "Am I ready now?"

"Yes," said the Blackbirds, "we think you'll do."

So they formed themselves again on the upper part of the slope, sang their songs, and hopped along down with many a flutter, flurry, and scurry — Keh, keh, keh, keh, keh, keh — and away they flew off into the air.

The Coyote, somewhat startled, got out of time but followed bravely, making heavy flops; but, as I have said before, the wings he was supplied with were composed of feathers all plucked from one side, and therefore he flew slanting and spirally and brought up with a whack, which nearly knocked the breath out of him, against the side of the mountain. He picked himself up, and shook himself, and cried out: "Hold! Hold! Hold on, hold on there!" to the fast-disappearing Blackbirds. "You've left me behind!"

When the birds returned, they explained: "Your wings are not quite thick enough, friend; and, besides, even a young Blackbird, when he is first learning to fly, does just this sort of thing that you have been doing — makes bad work of it."

"Sit down again," said the old Blackbird. And he called out to the rest: "Get feathers from your other sides also, and be careful to select a few strong feathers from the tips of the wings, for by means of these we cleave the air, guide our movements, and sustain our flight."

So the Blackbirds all did as they were bidden, and after the new feathers were planted, each one plucked out a tail-feather, and the most skillful of the Blackbirds inserted these feathers into the tip of the Coyote's tail. It made him wince and "yip" occasionally; but he stood it bravely and reared his head proudly, thinking all the while: "What a splendid Coyote I shall be! Did ever anyone hear of a Coyote flying?"

The procession formed again. Down the slope they went, hoppity-hop, hoppity-hop, singing their song, and away they flew into the air, the Coyote in their midst. Far off and high they circled and circled, the Coyote cutting more eager pranks than any of the rest. Finally they returned, dipped themselves again into the spring, and settled on the slopes of the rocks.

"There, now," cried out the Coyote, with a flutter of his feathery tail, "I can fly as well as the rest of you."

"Indeed, you do well!" exclaimed the Blackbirds. "Shall we try it again?"

"Oh, yes! Oh, yes! I'm a little winded," cried the Coyote, "but this is the best fun I ever had."

The Blackbirds, however, were not satisfied with their companion. They found him less sedate than a dancer ought to be, and, moreover, his irregular cuttings-up in the air were not to their taste. So the old ones whispered to one another: "This fellow is a fool, and we must pluck him when he gets into the air. We'll fly so far this time that he will get a little tired and cry to us for assistance."

The procession formed, and hoppity-hop, hoppity-hop, down the mountain slope they went, and with many a flutter and flurry flew off into the air. The Coyote, unable to restrain himself, even took the lead. On and on and on they flew, the Blackbirds and the Coyote, and up and up and up, and they circled round and round, until the Coyote found himself missing a wing stroke occasionally and falling out of line; and he cried out, "Help! Help, friends, help!"

"All right!" cried the Blackbirds, "Catch hold of his wings; hold him up!" cried the old ones. And the Blackbirds flew at him; and every time they caught hold of him (the old fool all the time thinking they were helping) they plucked out a feather, until at last the feathers had become so thin that he began to fall, and he fell and fell and fell — flop, flop, flop, he went through the air — the few feathers left in his forelegs and sides and the tip of his tail just saving him from being utterly crushed as he fell with a thud to the ground. He lost his senses completely, and lay there as if dead for a long time. When he awoke, he shook his head sadly, and, with a crestfallen countenance and tail dragging between his legs, betook himself to his home over the mountains.

The agony of that fall had been so great and the heat of his exertions so excessive that the feathers left in his forelegs and tail-tip were all shriveled up into little ugly black fringes of hair. His descendants were many.

Therefore, you will often meet coyotes to this day who have little black fringes along the rear of their forelegs, and the tips of their tails are often black. Thus it was in the days of the ancients.

Thus shortens my story.

Why the Ant Is Almost Cut in Two [6]
(Kiowa)

❧ *Ritual, belief, and a "pourquoi" story are combined in this tale from the mythology of the Kiowa Indians, taken down by a noted anthropologist, Alice Marriott, and recorded in her book* Winter-Telling Stories. *According to ritual, these stories must be told only in the winter season. Saynday, the trickster-god, con-*

[6] From Alice Marriott, *Winter-Telling Stories.* Copyright 1947 by Alice Marriott. Reprinted by permission of the publishers, Thomas Y. Crowell Company, New York.

siders here the mystery of death and the tragedy of the young who die. Making himself small, it was with the lowly ant that he chose to discuss these matters.

Sayday was coming along, and as he came he saw little Red Ant with a big sack over her shoulder. Little Red Ant was different in those early days. Her head and her body were all in one piece, with no neck between them. When she carried her big round sack it looked like one ball carrying another and rolling along the ground.

"Hello, there," said Sayday. "You look as if you were hot."

"I am hot," said little Red Ant. "It's a hot day."

"Sit down and rest," said Sayday, "and let's talk things over."

"All right," said little Red Ant.

They sat down and rested in the shade of a prickly pear, and Sayday made himself small enough to talk comfortably to little Red Ant.

"I've been thinking a lot," said Sayday.

"What have you been thinking about?" asked little Red Ant.

"I've been thinking about death," said Sayday. "My world and my people have been going on quite a while now, and things are beginning to get old and die sometimes."

"What's wrong with that?" said little Red Ant. "It makes room for new people."

"The people who die don't like it," said Sayday.

"There isn't any way to make them stop dying," said little Red Ant.

"No, but there might be a way to bring them back," said Sayday. "I've been thinking and thinking and thinking and thinking about it, and I think I know a way to bring them back when they've been dead four days."

"Well, it sounds rather silly to me," said little Red Ant.

"I don't see anything silly about it," said Sayday.

"I think it is," said little Red Ant. "The way things are now, the people who die off are old. They've had a good time and lived life out. When they go, it doesn't hurt them. Then there is a place for a new person to come along and enjoy life. I think the new ones ought to have a turn."

"That's the way it is now," said Sayday, "but maybe it won't always be that way. Maybe some of the young people will get killed off by accident. Then we ought to have some way to bring them back so they can enjoy their full lives."

"I don't think you need to," said little Red Ant. "If they're so stupid they go and get killed, it's just their own faults."

"All right," said Sayday. "I wanted to know what you thought. Now that I know, I will let there be death. When things and people die, they won't come back to this world any more. Now I have to go and see some more of my world. Goodbye."

And he and little Red Ant went their separate ways.

Four days later Sayday was coming back, and he came to that same prickly pear. There was mourning and crying all around. He looked down on the ground and saw little Red Ant. She was sitting in the shade of the prickly pear and crying as if her heart would break. Sayday made himself little again, and sat down beside her.

"What's the matter?" said Sayday.

"Oh, it's my son," said little Red Ant.

"What happened to your son?" said Sayday.

"A buffalo stepped on him," answered little Red Ant, "and now he's all gone dead."

"That's too bad," said Sayday.

"It's terrible," said little Red Ant.

And before Sayday could do anything, she pulled his knife out of his belt and cut herself almost in two, just above her shoulders. Sayday thought there had been enough dying already for one morning, so he took the knife away before she could cut herself clear in two.

"There," he said, "you see how it is. That's the way people feel when some one they love dies. They want to die too. If you'd let me have my way, your son would have come back at the end of four days. But you thought there would be too many people in the world if that happened. So now you know why I wanted to do that. For all the rest of the world, people will keep on dying. And for all the rest of the world, you will go around cut almost in two, to remind you of what you did to everybody."

And that's the way it was, and that's the way it is, to this good day.

Origin of the Pleiades [7]

(Onondaga)

The Indian story of the origin of the seven stars that form the cluster, the Pleiades, differs from any of the various explanations found in Greek mythology. Moreover, in all Greek versions the Pleiades were originally girls, not boys as here.

A long time ago a party of Indians went through the woods toward a good hunting-ground, which they had long known. They traveled several days through a very wild country, going on leisurely and camping by the way. At last they reached Kan-ya-ti-yo, "the beautiful lake," where the gray rocks were crowned with great forest trees. Fish swarmed in the waters, and at every jutting point the deer came down from the hills around to bathe or drink of the lake. On the hills and in the valleys were huge beech and chestnut trees, where squirrels chattered, and bears came to take their morning and evening meals.

The chief of the band was Hah-yah-no, "Tracks in the water," and he halted his party on the lake shore that he might return thanks to the Great Spirit for their safe arrival at this good hunting-ground. "Here will we build our lodges for the winter, and may the Great Spirit, who has prospered us on our way, send us plenty of game, and health and peace." The Indian is always thankful.

The pleasant autumn days passed on. The lodges had been built, and hunting had prospered, when the children took a fancy to dance for their own amusement. They were getting lonesome, having little to do, and so they met daily in a quiet spot by the lake to have what they called their jolly dance. They had done this a long time, when one day a very old man came to them. They had seen no one like him before. He was dressed in white feathers, and his white hair shone like silver. If his appearance was strange, his words were unpleasant as well. He told them they must stop their dancing, or evil would happen to them. Little did the children heed, for they were intent on their sport, and again and again the old man appeared, repeating his warning.

The mere dances did not afford all the enjoyment the children wished, and a little boy, who liked a good dinner, suggested a feast the next time they met. The food must come from their parents, and all these were asked when they returned home. "You will waste and spoil good victuals," said one. "You can eat at home as you should," said another, and so they got nothing at all. Sorry as they were for this, they met and danced as before. A little to eat after each dance would have made them happy indeed. Empty stomachs cause no joy.

One day, as they danced, they found themselves rising little by little into the air, their heads being light through hunger. How this happened they did not know, but one said, "Do not look back, for something strange is taking place." A woman, too, saw them rise, and called them back, but with no effect, for they still rose slowly above the earth. She ran to the camp, and all rushed out with food of every kind, but the children would not return, though their parents called piteously after them. But one would even look back, and he became a falling star. The others reached the sky, and are now what we call the Pleiades, and the Onondagas Oot-kwa-tah. Every falling or shooting star recalls the story, but the seven stars shine on continuously, a pretty band of dancing children.

How the Seven Brothers Saved Their Sister [8]

(Cheyenne)

In this American Indian myth of the Pleiades, the seven stars were once brothers. In

[7] From Stith Thompson, *Tales of the North American Indians* (Harvard University Press, 1929).

[8] From Grace Jackson Penney, *Tales of the Cheyennes* (Houghton Mifflin, 1953).

*Greek mythology, they were seven sisters pur-
sued by Orion, the hunter, upon whom Zeus
took pity, helping them to escape by changing
them into stars. This poetic tale from the Cheyennes seems to reveal the role of woman in that
culture. The theme of pursuit is here, and the
transformation into stars, but the hunter is the
terrible double-teethed Bull of the Buffaloes.*

Long and long ago, there lived among the
Cheyennes an old woman and her young
granddaughter. They had no other relatives,
and lived together in a little lodge, where
the grandmother taught the young girl, Red
Leaf, to make fine beaded robes and moccasins. Nowhere in all the tribe was there a
better robe-maker than Red Leaf.

Now it so happened that not very far from
there lived seven brothers. They had no
father, no mother, and no sisters. The seven
of them lived together, with the youngest,
Moksois, staying at home to take care of the
camp while the six older brothers went out
to hunt.

"Grandmother," said Red Leaf, one day,
"I would like to have Moksois and his
brothers to be my brothers. They are great
hunters, and could bring home food for us
all. They have no sister, so I could keep
their lodge, and cook their food, and make
their moccasins."

Her grandmother thought that was a fine
idea, so she helped Red Leaf select seven of
her nicest robes, and seven pairs of her best
moccasins. These she carried over to the
lodge of the seven brothers.

The six brothers were hunting, and Moksois was down at the creek getting water
when she came to the lodge, but she went
in, anyway, and put one of the robes and a
pair of moccasins on each of the seven beds.
When he got back with the water, she was
stirring the pot of soup on the fire. They
talked, and then he saw the robes and the
moccasins.

"Where did these fine moccasins and robes
come from?" he asked.

"I brought them. I thought it would be a
good thing for us all if I became your sister,"
Red Leaf answered, still stirring the soup.

"It suits me," Moksois said. "But I'll have
to ask my brothers about it."

When the brothers came home from the
hunt and found the fine new robes and moccasins, and learned that Red Leaf wanted to
be their sister, they thought it was a good
arrangement.

So that was the way it was, from then on.
They all lived together, very comfortably.
The brothers hunted, and Red Leaf took
care of the meat they brought home, and
made their robes and moccasins, and Moksois helped by bringing in water, and keeping plenty of wood for the fire.

But there came a day when everything
was changed. Moksois took his bow and
arrows and went out to hunt chipmunks.
He wandered farther from the lodge than he
thought. While he was gone, a giant buffalo
bull came to the lodge and took Red Leaf
and ran away with her.

He was the Double-Teethed Bull, strange
mysterious bull, strongest of all the buffalo.
He was different from the other buffalo, for
he had teeth in his upper and in his lower
jaw, and he ruled over them.

When Moksois returned to the lodge, he
found it partly torn down, and the tracks of
the great bull coming in and going out. He
was very much afraid. Tears ran down his
face while he searched for his sister. When
he saw his brothers coming home from the
hunt, he ran to them, crying, "A great bull
has stolen our sister."

The brothers knew the tracks were those
of the great Double-Teethed Bull. They
began to mourn and cry. "What can we do
to save our sister? The Double-Teethed Bull
is so powerful we can do nothing against
him. He cannot be killed."

At last, one said, "We can't just sit here.
Let's get busy and build four strong corrals,
one inside the other. Then we'll go and
try to get our sister away from him. That
way, if we can get her, we will have some
strong place to bring her."

This they did, piling big logs together and
bracing them like a fort. When all four were
finished, little Moksois went out and gathered anthills and brought them back in his
robe. He scattered the ants and sand in a
line all around the inside of the smallest
corral.

Then the seven brothers followed the

tracks of their sister and the great bull for a long time. At last they came to the top of a high hill, from which they could look far across the plain. There they saw a great herd of buffalo, covering the plain as far as the eye could see. In the center of the herd was a large open space, and in the open space sat their sister, with the great bull lying on the ground close by. No other buffalo were near them.

The brothers had brought their medicine sacks with them. One was made from the skin of a blackbird, one from that of a crow, one from a coyote skin, and one from the skin of a tiny yellow bird. Little Moksois' medicine sack was made of tanned buffalo hide, made in the shape of a half-moon, and he carried the skin of a gopher inside it.

The eldest brother took the blackbird skin in his hand, and it changed into a live blackbird. He told the bird to fly down and try to get close enough to their sister to tell her they were there.

He flew close to Red Leaf, where she sat on the ground, half-covered by her robe. He tried to talk to her, but the great bull saw him there and rumbled, "Blackbird, what are you trying to do? Are you a spy? Go away, or I will look at you and you will fall to the ground, dead." The blackbird was afraid of his power, so he flew back to the brothers.

The second brother sent the coyote that came alive from the coyote-skin medicine sack. The coyote was very clever. He slipped around far to the south, and came up on the other side of the herd. Then he went limping through the buffalo, acting as though he were sick and crippled.

But the Double-Teethed Bull was not fooled. He shook his heavy horns at him and said, "Coyote, I think you are a spy. Go away, before I look at you and you die. . . ."

So Coyote was afraid to stay. He went back to the brothers. This time they tried the crow. He flew in close, lighting on the ground, and pecking as though gathering food, then flying a little closer and lighting again. But the bull suspected him. "Go away, crow. Don't come any closer. You're trying to do something bad. I think I'll just look at you. Then you will fall down dead. . . ." Crow didn't wait. He flew away, back to the brothers, waiting on the hill.

The last to go was the tiny yellow bird. He was so tiny that he crept along through the grass, among the buffalo, without any of them seeing him, even the great bull. He slipped under Red Leaf's robe and said to her, "Red Leaf, your brothers are yonder on the hill. They will try to save you. They sent me to tell you what to do. Just cover yourself all over with your robe, and pretend to go to sleep. Then wait."

The great bull snorted, and rumbled in his throat, but he didn't see the little yellow bird as he crept back through the herd. When he got back to the hill, the brothers took council among themselves. Moksois said, "Now it is my turn to do something. Everyone be quiet. I will try to put the Double-Teethed Bull to sleep so we can do something."

So he lay down on the ground with his half-moon medicine sack by his head and shut his eyes. Everyone kept very still, waiting. After a time, he opened his eyes and arose. "Blackbird, fly down and see if the bull is asleep," he said.

When the blackbird came back, he said he'd seen the great bull, sleeping soundly, with his nose against the ground.

"That is good," said Moksois. "I am to blame for the Double-Teethed Bull stealing our sister. Now I will get her back. All of you wait here, but be ready to run away when I get back."

He opened his half-moon medicine sack and took the gopher skin out and laid it on the ground. Instantly, it became a live gopher, and started to dig with its long sharp claws. Moksois stayed right beside the gopher and followed it into the hole it was digging.

The gopher made a tunnel straight to where Red Leaf lay, covered by her robe. Moksois came up under the robe and took her by the hand and led her back along the gopher hole to where the brothers waited.

They took their sister, and as fast as they could, they ran toward home, to the shelter of the strong corrals they had built. But Moksois stayed behind, to keep watch on the herd. He wanted to see what happened when the great bull found Red Leaf gone. He felt very brave. "I will stay here and watch," he said. "I am not afraid. Let the Double-

Teethed Bull look at me. He can't kill me with one of his looks."

The great bull heaved himself to his feet and shook himself all over. Then he walked over to Red Leaf's robe, still spread out on the ground over the gopher hole, and sniffed at it. When he saw she was gone, he bellowed and pawed the ground, throwing clouds of dust into the air. He tossed and hooked the robe with his sharp horns until he tore it to shreds.

All the buffalo were excited and milling around, pawing and bellowing. Then the bull saw the gopher hole. He sniffed at it, then began to run back over the ground the same direction Moksois and Red Leaf had gone through the tunnel. All the other buffalo followed him, charging at great speed; heads down, stirring up such a cloud of dust that it was like the smoke from a prairie fire.

Moksois watched them from the hill, but before they got too near, he put an arrow in his bow and shot it as far as he could, toward home. The instant the arrow touched the ground, Moksois was beside it. That was part of his power. He kept shooting his arrows until he reached the lodge.

"Get ready, the buffalo are coming," he cried. And they all got inside the log corrals and kept watch. In a little while, the great herd of buffalo came in sight, galloping over the plain, with the huge bull out in front. When they saw the corrals, they stopped and waited while an old cow walked slowly nearer.

"Come back with me, Red Leaf. The Double-Teethed Bull wants you," she called to them. "If you don't return, he will come and get you himself."

Moksois said, "Tell him to come, if he dares." But before she had gone very far, he shot the old cow, and she fell to the ground. Three other messengers came, asking Red Leaf to come back to the Double-Teethed Bull, and making threats. Each time Moksois gave them the same answer. Each time he shot them before they got back to the great bull. Only the last one got near enough to give him Moksois' message.

Then the great bull was terribly angry. He pranced and pawed. He hooked the ground and bellowed defiance. Head down, he charged the corral at a fast gallop, the herd thundering behind.

"Come out," he roared to the girl. "Come out. Don't you know who I am?"

Red Leaf was trembling and crying. She begged her brothers to let her go. "He will kill you all. Let me go. . . . It may save you . . ."

But Moksois said, "Don't be afraid. Don't cry. I will kill the bull."

When the Double-Teethed Bull heard Moksois say that, he was furious. He charged the corral and hooked his horns in the logs, tossing them aside like sticks. The churning, bellowing herd charged the other corrals, one after another, scattering the logs like straws in the wind. But when they came to the place where Moksois had made the line inside with the anthills, every grain of sand had become a big rock, making a strong rock corral, that stopped the buffalo charge.

Again and again the buffalo charged the wall, hurling the great stones in every direction, like pebbles. The eldest brother said, "Even these rocks can't stand against him. He will be inside, next time. . . ."

Their sister cried, "Let me go . . . let me go outside, or he will kill you all."

But Moksois said again, "Don't be afraid. Stay here. I still have power . . ." Then he shot his arrow straight up into the air, just as high as he could shoot it. And as high as it went, there stood a tall tree, reaching into the sky.

"Now, hurry, climb up there," he cried, helping his sister into the tree. Quickly, all the brothers climbed up into the branches. But just as Moksois climbed to the lowest limb, the Double-Teethed Bull broke through the rocks with a terrible bellow that shook the hills.

He charged and charged the tree, tearing off great slivers with his sharp horns. But just as fast as he tossed a piece of wood aside, it joined back to the tree the same as it had been before.

Moksois only waited to shoot his last arrow at the powerful bull, before he followed his brothers and his sister up and up the tree, until they went into the sky. There they became the seven stars. The girl is the head star, and the little one, off to one side by itself, is little Moksois, still keeping guard.

SOUTH AMERICAN MYTH

The Legend of the Palm Tree[1]

❧ *The publication of this story in English has an interesting history. Some years ago, as part of the Good Neighbor policy toward Latin America, some American publishers sent a library of North American books to South America. When the library was on exhibit in Rio de Janeiro, the people were so delighted that they determined to return the compliment. They decided to make available to the boys and girls of North America one of their favorite stories for children. They chose* The Legend of the Palm Tree; *had it translated from the Portuguese; commissioned a noted Brazilian artist to make the illustrations; had the book printed and bound in Brazil; and sent ten thousand copies to a publisher in North America. This edition has long since been exhausted, but you may read below the ancient legend of how the palm tree became, for the natives of Brazil, the "good Tree of Providence."*

The tribe was living in happiness. The sun warmed the huts, ripening the fruits. Sometimes the clouds covered the sun and the rain fell, refreshing the plantations, swelling the rivers. But after the rain the sun became hot. So hot that it dried up the rivers and killed the plants and animals.

The Indians prayed and danced, begging their God Tupan to send them rain once more, to quench the thirst of the plants and animals. But their prayers were in vain. The sun continued burning . . . Indians and animals died; the vultures came and devoured them where they fell.

Of all the tribe there remained in the end

[1] Margarida Estrela Bandeira Duarte, *The Legend of the Palm Tree* (Grosset & Dunlap, 1940).

only two Indians and their child. Abandoning their home, they set forth in search of a happier land. They traveled during the whole night. For food they had only roots to chew.

The burning sun was again high in the sky when the boy came upon a lonely palm tree waving its green branches in the desert. Under the scant shade of this palm tree they paused to rest. Overcome by fatigue, the parents fell asleep. Only the little boy remained awake. He was afraid. . . .

While he was praying to the God Tupan to help them, he suddenly heard a voice calling him.

Looking up he saw an Indian woman in the top of the palm tree. She said to him: "My name is Carnauba. I am here to help you. Many years ago my tribe, too, suffered from the long dry season. I helped my people all I could. When I died the Moon changed me into this tree that I may save the stricken. Do as I advise you and you shall yet be happy.

"Cut open my trunk and quench your thirst with my sap. Eat my fruits and you will be hungry no more. Take one of my roots and cook it. Drink this medicine and it will heal you. Put my leaves to dry and beat them. From them you will get my wax, a gray and perfumed powder, with which you will light your way in the moonless nights. From the straw that remains, weave your hat and your mat.

"Now you must do something for me: plant my little nuts in order that there may grow a plantation of palm trees. Then you may build your hut with the timber from my trunk."

The boy did everything just as the Indian

woman had told him. Some years later a large plantation of palm trees stood swaying where the desert once had been.

The young Indian, now grown to man-hood, said good-by to his parents, as he set forth to carry to the Indians, near and far, the coconuts of the good Tree of Providence, as the happy natives of Brazil call it today.

HAWAIIAN MYTH

How Kana Brought Back the Sun and Moon and Stars[1]

&ᓑ *Whether or not this story refers to a period comparable to what we know as the ice age is not clear. It does not seem to represent the chaos in Genesis before the Lord created the sun, moon, and stars, since it definitely refers to their previous existence and to their having been stolen.*

Once the Sun and the Moon and the Stars were taken away; they were taken away by Ka-hoa-alii, and the people of the world would still be in cold and darkness if Kana and his brother Niheu had not gone to find them and bring them back.

You have been told about Kana, the youth who could stretch himself upward until his body was as thin as the thread of a spider's web, and you have been told about Niheu, his brother, who carried a war-club so great that, by resting one end of it in his canoe and putting the other end against a cliff, he could walk from his canoe to the land, and you have been told about Uli, Kana's and Niheu's wise grandmother.

This story begins with Niheu. Once when he was crossing the Island of Hawaii he heard about Ka-hoa-alii's man and how he kept the people fishing and cooking for him; the people were pitying themselves and com-plaining when Niheu came amongst them.

[1] From Padraic Colum, *The Bright Islands* (Yale University Press, 1925).

Then Niheu saw Ka-hoa-alii's man, and he flung his club at him; the stroke of the great club knocked Ka-hoa-alii's man over. And after he had flung his club Niheu went on to his grandmother's house. He told her what he had done. She was made afraid, and she told him that trouble would come be-cause of his mischief. "Go," she said, "and find your brother Kana, and bring him here to us, for we shall need his help."

But before he went, Uli made him help her fix a long rope that she had. She took the rope and she tied it to the post of her house, and she brought the end of it down to the seashore, and she tied it to a great stone there. The people wondered, and Niheu wondered at what Uli did. Then Niheu went off to find his brother Kana.

Meanwhile, Ka-hoa-alii had heard what Uli's grandson had done to his man. "I will punish Niheu for this, and I will punish all the people of Hawaii," he said. "Now I will take away the Sun and the Moon and the Stars from their sky. I will leave the people in cold and darkness; only where I am will there be warmth and light."

Niheu found his brother, and he started with him for their grandmother's house. While they were on their way the darkness came, for the Sun was taken out of the sky suddenly. But as they went on, they struck against the rope that Uli had stretched from the post of her house to the stone on the seashore. Holding the rope, they came to the house. Kana did not go within, for no house was high enough to hold him. The two of them saw their grandmother seated by a blazing fire with lights all around her.

"So you have come," said their grandmother to them. "You are the only two in all the world that can bring the Sun and the Moon and the Stars back into our sky. Ka-hoa-alii has taken them away, and you must go to where Ka-hoa-alii is. Before I tell you what to do, do you, Kana, stretch yourself upward, and see if there is any light in the sky."

Kana stretched himself upward until his head was near the sky. He looked around, and he saw a little light in it. He brought himself down again, and he told his grandmother what he had seen.

Then said Uli: "You, Kana, and you, Niheu, will have to go to the country that Ka-hoa-alii rules over. Go straight toward the place that the Sun used to rise in. The fine rain will fall on you and the cold will get into your bones, but go on and on until you come to where an old woman sits at the bottom of a cliff. She is my sister; Luahine-kai-kapu she is named, and she is blind. Tell her that you are Uli's grandchildren, and she will direct you to the country that Ka-hoa-alii rules over."

So Kana and Niheu started off from their grandmother's house. They went in a straight line toward the place that the Sun used to rise in. As they went on, the fine rain fell on them and the cold went into their bones. Kana took up Niheu and carried him on. But still the fine rain fell on them and still the cold crept into their bones. Then, when they came to the place that is called Kaha-kae-kaea, Niheu lay down to die.

Kana left him wrapped in leaves under a loulu palm and went on. He came to where an old woman sat at the bottom of a cliff; she was blind, and he knew that she was Luahine-kai-kapu, his grandmother's sister.

"Whose child are you?" said Luahine-kai-kapu to Kana.

"Your sister's Uli's grandchild," said Kana.

"What have you come for?" said she.

"I have come to get the Sun and the Moon and the Stars that Ka-hoa-alii has taken from our sky; I am the only one who can bring them back. Show me the way to Ka-hoa-alii's country."

"I have no eyes," said Luahine-kai-kapu; "I cannot see to show you the way."

"Lie down under this coconut tree," said Kana. Luahine-kai-kapu lay down. Kana picked off the young shoots of the coconut and called out to her, "Luahine-kai-kapu, turn your face toward the sky." She turned her face up as directed; Kana then threw the two young shoots at her eyes.

Then he struck her in the eyes, and she jumped up and cried out with a loud voice, "Oh, I am killed!" Kana then said to her, "Be quiet and rub your eyes." The old woman began rubbing her eyes. After she had done this, she cried out that she was able to see as before.

"Before I send you into the country of Ka-hoa-alii, I shall have to do something to make your hands different," said Luahine-kai-kapu. She took ku-kui-nut and charcoal and she pounded them together and she made a paste. She rubbed the paste she had made on the great hands of Kana. "Now," said she, "you have hands like the hands of Ka-hoa-alii." Then she told him what to do when he came to the place where Ka-hoa-alii lived.

She set a fire before him to guide him, and she set a wind at his back to help him on. And helped on by the wind and guided by the fire, Kana came at last to the borders of Ka-hoa-alii's country. Then the fire died down, and he had no guide to go before him. But still the wind helped him on.

He came to the place where Ka-hoa-alii was. He hid and watched him. Ka-hoa-alii would lift up a great stone that covered a hole in the sky, and take food up in his hands and feast with his attendants. And when they had feasted, they would go into the house and play games. Thus Ka-hoa-alii and his attendants passed the day; they feasted and they played games, and they played games and they feasted.

Kana did what Luahine-kai-kapu told him to do. He watched all they did. When they had gone into the house, he went to the great stone. He lifted it up. He propped it up with his feet. Then he put his two hands down into the hole.

Those below put things into his hands. They were things to eat. Kana flung them away, and put his hands down again. Those below put water into his hands. He emptied the water out. Kana put his hands down again. Those below put birds into his hands; he took them up and let them fly around; they were the birds that cry when darkness is going. Now as they flew around they cried, "Kia-wea! Kia-wea!"

He put his hands down again. Now his hands were filled with Stars. He took them up and flung them into the sky. There they stayed — the Stars that we still see. He lowered his hands again. The Moon was put into his hands. He put the Moon into the blue sky with the Stars, and it stayed there, giving light.

Kana put his hands down again. This time a single bird was put into his hands. He took it up and put it beside him. It was the crowing cock. He put his hands down once more; the warm Sun was put into his hands. He held the bright Sun up. He put it into the sky. The cock beside him crowed.

The cock crew, and Ka-hoa-alii, hearing it crow, came out of his house. He saw Kana standing there, and he saw the Sun shining in the sky. He went toward Kana to kill him, but he saw how tall and how strong Kana was, and he was afraid to touch him. And Kana, seeing that Ka-hoa-alii was afraid of him, demanded from him the Water of Life, the Water of Kane, so that he might restore his brother with it. Ka-hoa-alii gave him the Water of Kane.

Kana then went to Kaha-kae-kaea. His brother Niheu was there, wrapped in leaves under the loulu palm. He gave him the Water of Life, and life came back again to Niheu. Afterward Ka-hoa-alii came to where they were. He gave them a canoe made out of white chicken feathers, and in that canoe Kana and Niheu returned to Hawaii. They went to their grandmother's house, and they saw the Sun in the heavens, and the Moon following the Sun, and Stars with the Moon. And never again were these bright lights taken out of our sky.

GREEK LEGENDS

Why the Monks of Athos Use a Samantron [1]

→§ *In regions where life remains unsophisticated, it is sometimes possible to see legend in the making, and to observe the naïve, creative folk spirit — poetic, uninstructed and creative — in operation. The book from which this legend is taken succeeds in giving such a picture of present-day regions in Greece. This story bears the marks of a true legend, "an*

[1] From Joice M. NanKivell, *Tales of Christophilos* (Houghton Mifflin, 1954).

unauthentic story handed down by tradition, and popularly regarded as historical."

They got to the monastery of Zographou just as a monk came out of the important-looking front door to beat the *samantron*, which was a board swinging from the branches of a big tree.

He beat on it with a hammer.

"Rum-a-tum-tum — Bang! Crash!" And from far and near came the sound of other samantrons, beating all the world to dinner.

"Rum-a-tum-tum — rum-a-tum-tum — Come and be saved —"

A nice old monk came out of the forest and sat on a stone beside Christophilos.

"Aren't you going in to dinner?" asked Christophilos.

He laughed and shook his head, then he took a handful of walnuts from his pocket and gave them to Christophilos.

He wore a high, frayed black hat with a cardboard brim fixed on it to shade his eyes from the sun. His beard was long, and his feet were bare. His scanty gray hair hung down below his hat.

"This servant of God eats no bread, but only what God sends him."

He settled his bare feet in the dust, with the toes spread out.

"Why should I spend my days thinking of the sound of the samantron until my stomach aches for food. I have better things to think of. There are too many nuts if I am hungry. A man has only to look to find food, for food is all around us. But most men listen, they only know one hour from another by the samantron. Rum-a-tum-tum — rum-a-tum-tum, come and be saved, come and be saved. As it was in the very old days, so it is now." He beat on his knees with his sharp bony fingers: "Rum-a-tum-tum, rum-a-tum-tum — come and be saved — "

"I don't understand," said Christophilos.

"My poor boy, why should you? Few schoolmasters teach anything worth knowing, and how can they? They know nothing at all. I will tell you something." He wagged his thin finger in Christophilos's face. "There is something that all the monks, and a few other people know. Why do we use samantrons and not bells?"

Christophilos shook his head.

. . . .

"Ah, you see even your world close beside Athos doesn't know that, and it is from times older than the oldest living man! When Noah built the Ark, my boy, he found he had one board left over. He worried and worried about that board. While he worried the Lord God held up all the clouds with his hands and not a single drop of rain fell, but the Lord God cried to Noah, and told him to think quickly as he did not want to hold up those clouds forever! Then Noah began to think quickly, and an idea came to him,

poof, pat, just as a beetle flies through a window! He ran and hung the board from the branches of a tree, and he lifted his hammer. Bang! Bang! Rum-a-tum-tum, rum-a-tum-tum — come and be saved —

"All the animals heard it, and they came up out of the forests and valleys, and down from the high places; two and two, and two and two, as the monks walk today. The jackals, and the hares, and the spiders, and all the insects and the birds; and when the last tortoise was safely in, Noah stopped beating on the samantron and went into the Ark and shut the door. Then the Lord God slipped the clouds out of his hands, and it rained and rained and rained; and everyone who knows anything at all will tell you that story is true."

The Seven Sleepers [2]

No wonder that Sleep has held the imagination of man, from the earliest time to the revelations of Sigmund Freud. It is a common happening, but none the less mysterious for that. This story concerns a legend of the early Christian era. But before that time was Sleeping Beauty *from the dawn of folklore and the Nigerian folk tale which tells of the blessing of sleep,* The Town Where No One Slept. *The story of the long sleep which awaits the moment of awakening is a recurring tale. The armies of Frederick Barbarossa, sleeping until he shall return to call them to arms; and our own* Rip Van Winkle; *these too belong to this mythology of sleep.*

The roots of the Cedars of Lebanon grew down into that cavern, and in their tangles a thousand bats huddled together. Every seven years the dog that was Malchus's dog wakened up: raising his head he would see his master and his master's six friends lying, one beside the other, fast asleep.

The dog that was Malchus's dog would smell around, but nothing would come to him except the smell that he had known in burrows — the smell of dry earth. There would be no stir in the air around him;

[2] From Padraic Colum, *The Forge in the Forest* (Macmillan, 1925).

there would be no movement upon the ground; there would be no daylight. The thousand bats, high above him, made no sound and gave no stir. With his head raised, the dog that was Malchus's dog would look at his master, expecting that his voice would come to him. No voice would come, and the dog would turn round, and lie down, and sleep again.

Every seven years for fifty times seven years the dog would wake up; still his master and his master's six friends lay there, their flesh upon them, and the bloom of youth upon their flesh. Then, one day, light streamed into the cavern, for the stones that had been set at its mouth were removed. The dog waked up; seeing the daylight, the dog barked. Malchus, his master, waked up. And then the other six sleepers awakened.

They awakened and they said to one another, "We have slept; even through the hours of our great danger we slept." They saw daylight streaming in and each said, "It is not as we thought it was." Each thought that he had had a dream of the cavern being closed upon them by their persecutors with immovable stones.

For these youths had been persecuted by Decius, Emperor of the Romans, King of the Four Quarters of the Earth, having dominion over seventy-two Kings. The Emperor had been moved to persecute the Christians of the city of Ephesus. He had a proclamation made, saying that all who would not go into the pagan temples and make sacrifice to the pagan idols should be cut to pieces by his soldiers; he himself rode on his horse into the city to see that his command was carried out.

Nearly all who were in the city forsook the Christian faith. But there were seven youths who would not forsake it, nor go into the pagan temples and make sacrifice to the pagan idols. These seven were friends who were devoted to one another, and their names were Malchus, Marcian, Dionysius, John, Serapion, Maximian, and Constantine.

They stole from the city and they went towards the mountain Celion, and the dog that was Malchus's dog followed them. They hid within a cavern. Then one went back to the city to buy food. The shopkeeper who sold him meal made a little rent in the bag so that the meal trickled out, leaving a track where he went. And the Emperor, mounted on his horse, followed this track and came to the cavern where the seven had hidden themselves. He signed to his followers, and they drew heavy stones, and they closed up the entrance of the cavern. "In a while," the Emperor said, "none will be left alive in Ephesus or around it who have the Christian faith." And the Emperor rejoiced as he said this. The seven in the cavern sat together; they saw the daylight being shut out, and they knew from the scornful shouts of those outside that they had been shut in so that they never could leave the cavern. They sat there talking to one another, and weeping and consoling one another. Then they slept. The dog that was Malchus's dog crept close to them, and he, too, slept, but every seven years he awakened.

And after a hundred years, and another hundred, and a third hundred years had passed, a man came to the side of that mountain, and seeking weighty stones for the building of a roadway, he took away the stones that were at the mouth of the cavern. It was then that the daylight streamed in on where they lay. It was then that the dog that was Malchus's dog barked. It was then that they wakened up — Malchus, Marcian, Dionysius, John, Serapion, Maximian, and Constantine. It was then that each said, "It is not as I thought; the mouth of the cavern is not closed upon us."

They were hungry. Malchus told his friends that he would steal into the city, and buy bread and bring it back to them. They let him go, and he went out of the cavern, and down the side of the mountain, and along the road that went to the city of Ephesus. When he came before the gate of the city he nearly fell backward in astonishment. For behold! over the gate of the city was the cross of the Christian faith. He thought that this could be nothing but a trick to bring back to the city the Christians who had fled from it. And in greater fear than ever he went through the gate and into the city.

He had lived in a wide street in that city,

but now he went down by-ways and lane-ways so that he might not be met by those who knew him. He came to a baker's shop that was away from the main part of the town, and he went within. He saluted the baker, and the baker returned his salutation in the name of Christ. Malchus was fearful, thinking that the words were said to trap him, but he pretended not to have heard what the baker said. He took the loaves from him, and handed him a silver coin in payment.

When the baker received the coin he looked at Malchus sharply. He then went to the back of the shop and spoke to some who were there. Malchus was about to steal out of the shop when the baker came and laid hands on him, saying, "Nay, you must not go until you have told us where the treasure is that you found." "I found no treasure," Malchus said to him. "Where, then, did you get the ancient coin that you have given me in payment for the loaves? Assuredly you have found a treasure." And when the baker said this to him Malchus gave himself up for lost, for he thought that this talk about treasure was but a pretence to hold him until they examined him on the charge of being a Christian.

The men in the baker's shop laid hold on Malchus, and they put a rope around his neck, and they dragged him into the market-place. They said to those who crowded around, "Here is one who has found a treasure that must be given to the Emperor, and we would have a reward for making him reveal where that treasure now is." And Malchus, in the market-place, looked all round him. He saw no one there whom he knew, and he could see that no one in the crowd knew him. He said to those who were around, "Tell me, I implore you, what city is this that I have come into?" They said, "You are playing the madman, pretending that you do not know that this is the great city of Ephesus."

It was then that Malchus saw coming through the crowd one in the robes of a Christian Bishop. "Who is the youth, and why is he being treated by the Ephesians in this way?" he asked. And Malchus heard those around him say, "He has offered a coin of the reign of an ancient Emperor in payment for loaves of bread, and he dares to say that it is of the money that his parents gave him. Assuredly he has found a treasure, but he will tell none of the Ephesians where the treasure now is."

Malchus saw that the one who came to him was indeed a Bishop, and he was more and more bewildered. The Bishop came and spoke tenderly to him. Then said Malchus, "I implore you to tell me where the Emperor Decius has gone to." The Bishop said, "Decius is not our Emperor's name. There has not been an Emperor of the name of Decius for three hundred years." And then he said, "If, as you say, you have parents and friends living in the city of Ephesus, tell us their names, so that we may bring them to you."

Then Malchus gave the names of his parents, and the names of the friends he knew in Ephesus. No one in the crowd had heard of them. The Bishop then told him that he might go to the place where he thought his parents lived. Malchus went there, the Bishop and the people following him. And when he came to the place where his parents' house had stood, behold! what he saw there was a pool of water with birds dipping their wings in it.

When he saw this he wept. Then to the Bishop and those who were with the Bishop he said, "I do not understand what I look upon. I thought that I was in great danger in coming here, thinking that it was only yesterday that the Christians of Ephesus were being put to the sword. But I see the cross surmounting the churches, and I see the Christian Bishop having authority. And yet it is to me as if I had come into a city of the dead. Let me, I pray you, go back to the cavern where I left my companions."

The Bishop signed to those who were guarding him, and they let Malchus go. He went, and they followed him, towards the mountain Celion. He entered the cavern. He saw his six friends, Marcian, Dionysius, John, Serapion, Maximian, and Constantine, and they welcomed him joyfully. He gave them the bread he had brought and they ate, and were elated. But when they asked of him what signs he saw of the persecution of Christians in Ephesus, he wept. And then he told them that all they had known in Ephesus had passed away, the good with the evil, and that there was no persecution of Christians there, and that the cross was reared in triumph over the churches and over the gate of the city, and that their parents and all whom they knew were dead and long passed away. His friends listened to him in wonder. And while he was still speaking, the Bishop came into the cavern where they were. "Bless us, Holiness," the seven youths said to him. "Nay, it is you should bless me and bless the people of Ephesus," the Bishop said, "seeing that it was on you that God bestowed the most signal favour — the favour of keeping you in life to witness the triumph of the cross in Ephesus and in the whole of the east of the world." Then the Bishop led them without, and the seven stood on the side of the mountain, and blessed the people who came that way towards them, on the morning of Easter, carrying the cross.

As they stood there, it seemed to the seven of them — to Malchus, Marcian, Dionysius, John, Serapion, Maximian, and Constantine — that every clod within was making melody, such music came to them from the cavern. Again they went within. Then they lay down as before and the dog that was Malchus's dog lay near them. And lying there their souls went from them, and they passed out of this life. Then the flesh fell away from them, and only their bones and the bones of the dog that was Malchus's dog were left in the cavern. And, behold! a rose tree grew up where they had lain, and its branches spread out and grew over the mouth of the cavern, wreathing it in roses. Ever afterwards, in that cavern and around it, there was the scent of roses.

BIBLIOGRAPHY

Mythology

Bulfinch, Thomas. *Mythology: The Age of Fable; The Age of Chivalry; Legends of Charlemagne.* Modern Library, 1934.

Thomas Bulfinch, the son of the famous Boston architect, was the first to popularize the classic myths in America. He published *The Age of Fable* in 1855, *The Age of Chivalry* in 1858, and *The Romance of the Middle Ages* in 1863. All three are found in this volume, which has become a standard reference book.

Gayley, Charles Mills, ed. *Classic Myths in English Literature and in Art.* Ginn, rev. and enl. ed. 1911.

Greek, Roman, and Norse myths and hero stories. Based on Bulfinch's *Age of Fable.* For reference use.

Hamilton, Edith. *Mythology;* illus. by Steele Savage. Little, Brown, 1942. (Grades 6–8)

Scholarship and imagination vitalize the retelling of these Greek, Roman, and Norse myths. Invaluable both as a reference book and for reading. Excellent introduction and notes.

Lum, Peter. *The Stars in Our Heavens; Myths and Fables;* illus. by Anne Marie Jauss. Pantheon Books, 1948. (Grades 7–9)

Myths, legends, and fables interpret what the Chinese, Babylonians, and Norsemen saw in the heavens.

Smith, Ruth, ed. *The Tree of Life; Selections from the Literature of the World's Religions;* illus. by Boris Artzybasheff. Viking Press, 1942.

Selected writings from the literature of the mythologies and religions of all ages.

Greece and Rome

Benson, Sally. *Stories of the Gods and Heroes;* illus. by Steele Savage. Dial Press, 1940. (Grades 5–8)

Based on Bulfinch, this is one of the best versions for children. Illustrations interpret the spirit of the text.

Buckley, Elsie. *Children of the Dawn: Old Tales of Greece;* illus. by F. C. Papé. Stokes, 1908. (Grades 5–7)

Admirable versions which convey the beauty and vitality of the old Greek tales.

Bulfinch, Thomas. *A Book of Myths: Selections from Bulfinch's "Age of Fable"*; illus. by Helen Sewell. Macmillan, 1942. (Grades 6–9)

In her illustrations Helen Sewell has interpreted the classic Greek design in a modern manner.

Colum, Padraic. *The Forge in the Forest*; illus. by Boris Artzybasheff. Macmillan, 1925. (Grades 5–7)

A spirited and poetic rendering of the old Greek myths of Phaethon, the Seven Sleepers, Bellerophon, and others.

Galt, Thomas. *The Rise of the Thunderer*; illus. by John Mackey. Thomas Y. Crowell, 1954. (Grades 5–8)

An authentic but modernized version of the Greek story of creation and the struggle of the gods to gain supremacy over heaven and earth. The book may serve as an introduction to more literary retelling of the myths.

Guerber, Hélène Adeline. *Myths of Greece and Rome*. American Book Co., 1921.

The myths are retold with special reference to literature and art. A useful reference book.

Hawthorne, Nathaniel. *A Wonder Book and Tanglewood Tales*; illus. by Gustaf Tenggren. Houghton Mifflin, n.d. (Riverside Bookshelf) (Grades 5–7)

Opinions differ as to the excellence of Hawthorne's versions of the Greek myths. Some consider them "little masterpieces of prose." Others think that Hawthorne took too great a liberty with them; that he romanticized and embroidered them until the strength and vigor of the original myths were lost. Hawthorne himself states that his retellings had a Gothic and romantic touch which was the spirit of his age.

Hutchinson, Winifred. *Orpheus with His Lute*; illus. by Dugald Stewart Walker. Longmans, Green, 1926. (Grades 6–8)

Fifteen Greek myths are woven into a lengthened and poetic telling of *Orpheus and Eurydice*.

Schwab, Gustav. *Gods and Heroes; Myths and Epics of Ancient Greece*. Pantheon Books, 1946.

Greek myths and epics from Homer translated from the German text and its Greek sources by Olga Marx and Ernest Morwitz. Illustrated with 100 sketches from Greek vase paintings. An excellent introduction by Werner Jaeger. For older boys and girls and for adults.

Iceland and Scandinavia (Norse)

Brown, Abbie Farwell. *In the Days of Giants; a Book of Norse Tales*; illus. by E. Boyd Smith. Houghton Mifflin, 1902. (Grades 3–5)

A good introduction to Norse mythology. Stories are told with humor and imagination.

Colum, Padraic. *Children of Odin*; illus. by Willy Pogány. Macmillan, 1920. (Grades 5–7)

The stories of the Norse sagas from the Twilight of the Gods to the Fall of Asgard. Told as a connected narrative in rhythmic poetic prose.

Hosford, Dorothy. *Thunder of the Gods*; illus. by Claire and George Louden. Henry Holt, 1952. (Grades 4–7)

Fifteen Norse myths retold in dignified prose which captures the boisterous good humor of the Icelandic *Eddas*.

Legends

Gibson, Katherine. *The Golden Bird and Other Stories*; illus. by E. G. Sommer. Macmillan, 1927. (Grades 5–8)

Legends of Egypt, Greece, Persia, China, and France. This collection grew out of Miss Gibson's story hour at the Cleveland Museum of Art.

France

Reynard the Fox. *Rogue Reynard*; based upon the Beast Saga; written by Andre Norton (*pseud.*); illus. by Laura Bannon. Houghton Mifflin, 1947. (Grades 4–7)

Retold in prose retaining enough of the archaic to give it the right flavor.

Hawaii

Colum, Padraic. *Legends of Hawaii*; illus. by Don Forrer. Yale University Press, 1937. (Grades 6–8)

Selections from the author's two volumes, *At the Gateway of the Day* and *The Bright Islands*.

Ireland

Buck, Alan. *The Harper's Daughter*; illus. by Richard Bennett. Oxford University Press, 1940. (Grades 7–9)

A poetic retelling of one of the world's most famous stories, the Irish legend of Deirdre.

Stephens, James. *Irish Fairy Tales*; illus. by Arthur Rackham. Macmillan, 1920. (Grades 8–9)

The legends of Fionn, leader of the Fianna, and father of Oisin, retold by a poet.

Italy

Davis, Mary Gould. *The Truce of the Wolf and Other Tales of Old Italy*; illus. by Jay Van Everen. Harcourt, Brace, 1931. (Grades 4–6)

Six of the seven stories are retold from old Italian legends. The story of "Nanni" is Miss Davis' own creation.

Japan

Coatsworth, Elizabeth. *The Cat Who Went to Heaven;* illus. by Lynd Ward. Macmillan, 1930. (Grades 5–7)

A Japanese legend retold in poetic prose. Awarded the Newbery medal in 1931.

North America

Irving, Washington. *Rip Van Winkle and The Legend of Sleepy Hollow;* illus. by Maud and Miska Petersham. Macmillan, 1951. (New Children's Classics) (Grades 6–9)

Famous old legends of the Hudson Valley.

South America

Bandeira Duarte, Margarida Estrela. *The Legend of the Palm Tree;* illus. by Paulo Werneck. Grosset & Dunlap, 1940. (Grades 3–4)

How the palm tree became the "good tree of Providence." See note on page 456.

Lovelace, Maud and Delos. *The Golden Wedge; Indian Legends of South America;* illus. by Charlotte Anna Chase. Thomas Y. Crowell, 1942. (Grades 5–7)

Early creation myths and legends of South America.

Spain

Irving, Washington. *The Alhambra; Palace of Mystery and Splendor;* selected and arranged by Mabel Williams; illus. by Louis Slobodkin. Macmillan, 1953. (New Children's Classics) (Grades 7–9)

The 1953 edition has been reset and has a new illustrator. The legends have been popular since they first appeared in 1832.

References for the Adult

Arbuthnot, May Hill. *Children and Books.* Scott, Foresman, rev. ed. 1957.

"Myths," pp. 288–306.

Bett, Henry. *English Legends;* illus. from drawings by Eric Fraser. B. T. Batsford (London), 1950.

Chase, Richard. *Quest for Myth.* Louisiana State University Press, 1949.

"The central premise of this book is that myth is literature and therefore a matter of aesthetic experience and the imagination." — Preface.

Colum, Padraic. *Orpheus, Myths of the World;* with twenty engravings by Boris Artzybasheff. Macmillan, 1930.

A scholarly addition to the study of mythology because of the fine retelling of the myths and the valuable discussion of their significance and characteristics.

Dawson, Warren. *The Bridle of Pegasus; Studies in Magic, Mythology and Folklore.* Methuen (London), 1930.

Frazer, Sir James George. *The Golden Bough: A Study in Magic and Religion.* 1 volume, abridged edition. Macmillan, 1951.

In this one volume the author has expertly compressed the wealth of invaluable material contained in the original twelve-volume edition dealing with the development of magic, customs, social practices, and religion among primitive men and women.

Lawton, William Cranston. *The Soul of the Mythology.* Yale University Press, 1923.

Livingston, Richard William. *The Legacy of Greece.* Oxford University Press, 1921.

Moore, Annie E. *Literature Old and New for Children.* Houghton Mifflin, 1934.

"Myths," Chapter 6, pp. 138–175.

Munch, Peter. *Norse Mythology: Legends of Gods and Heroes;* trans. from the Norwegian by Sigurd Bernhard Hustveld. American Scandinavian Foundation, 1926.

Rolleston, T. W. *Myths and Legends of the Celtic Race.* Farrar, 2nd rev. ed. 1934.

Smith, Lillian H. *The Unreluctant Years; A Critical Approach to Children's Literature.* American Library Association, 1951.

"Gods and Men," Chapter 5, pp. 65–79.

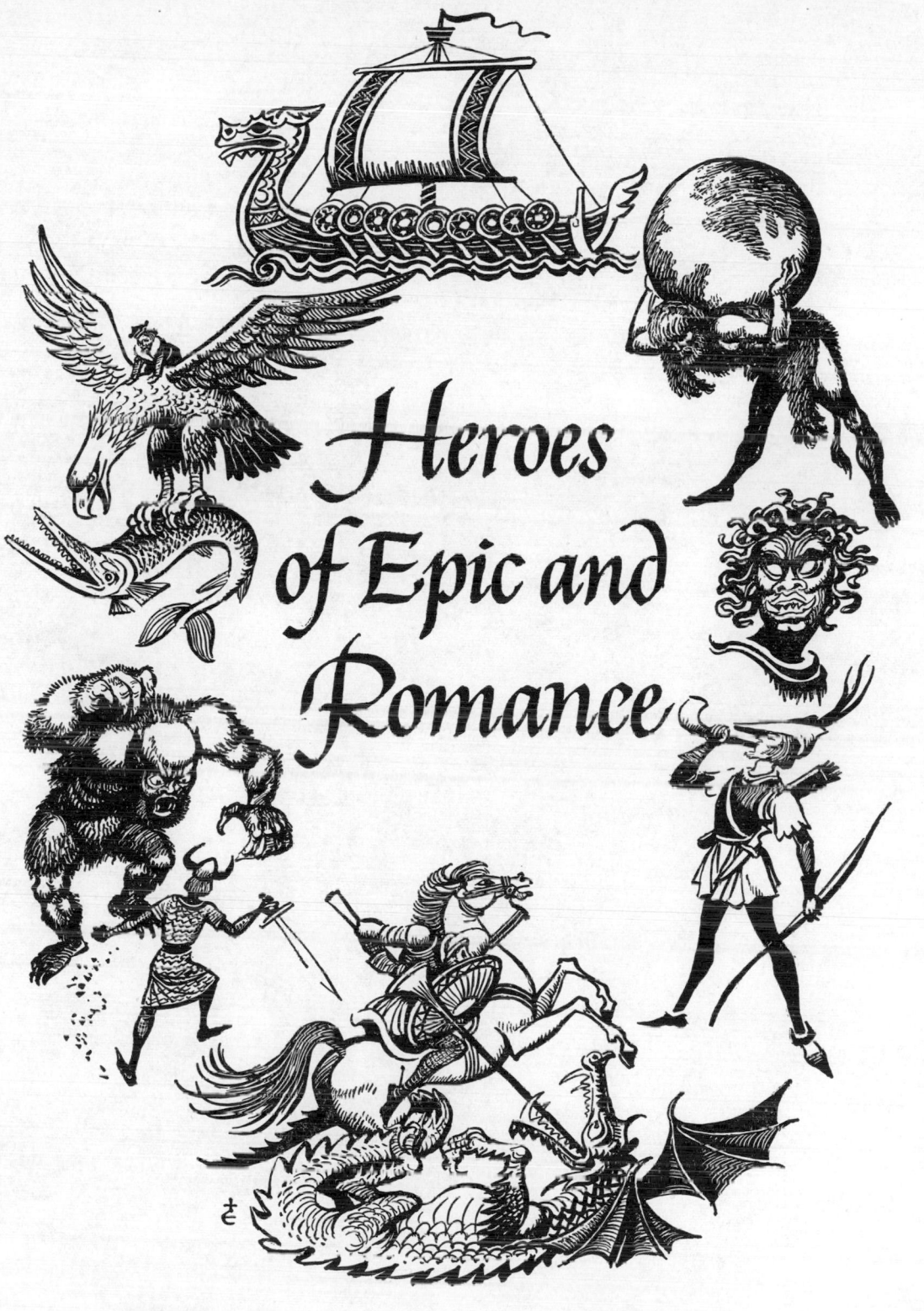

Heroes
of Epic and
Romance

WHERE READING IS CONCERNED, there is a tide in the minds of children which "taken at the flood" leads on to victory; a victory for the imagination and for a lasting upsurge of spirit. The tide comes to flood in "the middle years" of childhood, the years between nine to twelve and upwards, when children, having mastered the mechanics of reading, turn to books in a fever of interest and excitement. These are the years when children are eager to know everything at once: science, history, biography — all knowledge, as well as to discover what it means to be human, and especially what it means to be an adult.

Children in these years, reading "like a thirst," find much of what they seek in the matchless splendor of the old tales from the epic literature of the world. The grandeur of the tales; the basic, elemental emotions which they portray; the simple dignity they sustain; the unwavering nobility of the hero, even in defeat; the concept of courage and loyalty; the emphasis on physical prowess; the vigor; the clearly outlined action; the poetry and passionate feeling — these are the elements which strike hard on the minds of children with lasting effect.

The epic is a poem of extended length made up of traditional stories clustered about a central hero or group of heroes. It is large in scope, eloquent in expression, embodying the highest ideals of the culture from which it springs. Saga is the name given to the epics of the Northmen, the people of Iceland and Scandinavia, which have their origins largely in the *Eddas*. The epic is mainly pre-Christian, though here and there reference to some Christian symbol may occur as though interpolated, as in *Beowulf*. The origins reach back to the undated past. The written form stretches from a thousand years before Christ (the *Iliad*) to the time spanning the ninth and thirteenth centuries.

The Romance, such as the *Song of Roland* and the tales of chivalry which make up the Arthurian cycle, differs from the epic only in its reflection of the spread of Christianity in the Middle Ages. The one overpowering theme, characteristic of this literature, is the emerging recognition of the individual man, of man as hero, with courage enough to confront even the ultimate doom of fate.

[1] Richard Hakluyt.

The intensity of feeling in which these tales were engendered is certainly one of the prime reasons for their hold on the imaginations of children. The epics are the expression, not of one poet's conviction and emotion, but of a whole culture's interpretation of the experience of life, and of man's ideal role in a particular society. To be sure, certain individual poets may have had great influence in molding the final, written form, but the inner meaning, the symbols, the religious beliefs and codes of ethics that form the background for the telling, these have been hammered out of centuries of communal life. At some period of great flowering in the culture, the ideal hero evolves to become the image for the future, a source of pride, energy, and inspiration. Nation after nation, culture after culture, have rallied to this self-created ideal, until the epic, saga, and romance become sacred tradition by which men and women lived, waged war, made and unmade kings. They provided what Bernard Berenson describes as "orgies of communal self-importance,"[2] a basis for a primal and exulting nationalism.

As a culture experienced a period of action, triumph, and accomplishment, or produced a leader with qualities of greatness, the actuality took on the character of legend, a mixture of fact and idealized fiction. The era and the events were nurtured in the minds of generations, kept alive by tellings and retellings of bards, scops, troubadours, minnesingers, and jongleurs, to emerge at last as the *Iliad,* the *Odyssey,* the saga, the definitive epic of the culture. The history of the development of these tales is fascinating reading in itself: to find the shadowy beginning, to trace the germinal ideas through the mutations to its final form; to see how incident becomes universal, how actuality takes on the height of the ideal — all this wrought and changed by the concepts of the race and by the might and imagination of the storytellers.

In 778, in the valley of Roncesvalles in the Pyrenees, a minor skirmish occurred between the forces of Charlemagne and the Basques. It was an incident of no strategic importance. The small force was under the command of one Roland, Prefect of the Marches of Brittany, who, with his men, perished in that action. Three hundred years later, this incident has become a Holy War between the armies of Charlemagne and the Saracens; and Roland, its hero, the most noble warrior and "gentle count" of the French court. His deeds are celebrated in song, chanted about the courts of Europe by one Taillefer, "a jongleur whom a very brave heart ennobled."[3] It is to Taillefer that the authorship of the *Song of Roland,* the great epic of France, is attributed. Countless singers had sung before him, but his version gave the legend its fated form, which made it epic. French schoolboys of today still have by heart certain verses from this poem. It surely echoed in the ears of William the Conqueror at Hastings, who saw himself no doubt as Charlemagne. "No modern opera or play ever approached the popularity of the 'Chanson,'" writes Henry Adams in his great book on the medieval world. "None has ever expressed with anything like the same completeness the society that

[2] Bernard Berenson, *Aesthetics and History in the Visual Arts* (Pantheon Books, New York, 1948), p. 92.

[3] Henry Adams, *Mont-Saint-Michel and Chartres* (Houghton Mifflin Company, Boston), p. 21.

produced it. Chanted by every minstrel — known by heart, from beginning to end, by every man and woman and child, lay or clerical — translated into every tongue — more intensely felt, if possible, in Italy and Spain than in Normandy and England — perhaps most effective, as a work of art, when sung by the Templars in their great castles in the Holy Land. . . ."[4]

No modern hero, no "Superman" or creature from outer space, can ever command such intensity of emotion as the heroes of epic and romance. They are the apogee of the societies which produced them, in a climate which was primarily naïve, direct, and un-self-conscious; the climate of childhood itself.

The symbolism of the epics is the second quality which captures the minds of children. Beyond the pattern of events, magnificent in their vitality and invention, beyond the adventure, gory and violent, there is the larger framework of the allegory. "Every great literature has always been allegorical," says G. K. Chesterton. "The *Iliad* is only great because all life is a battle, the *Odyssey* because all life is a journey, the *Book of Job* because all life is a riddle."[5]

No one is quicker to sense the meaning, the clear indication of the promise of life, than children, encountering the great allegories of struggle and attainment which the epic literature affords. When the poor and unlettered Hans Christian Andersen set out as a boy of fourteen to seek his fortune in the great city of Copenhagen, he comforted his mother with assurances of his own understanding by telling her that it was quite simple. "People have at first an immense deal of adversity to go through, and then they will be famous."[6]

This is precisely a child's interpretation of the adult world, and it is the world of the epic. Andersen was unschooled, but his father had read to him the classic drama of the Danish theater, and his grandmother had steeped his mind in the folklore. He knew the portents and the symbols. Society has changed immeasurably since the days of the epics. Naïveté, simple faith, and the single ideal of individual courage in combat — these threads no longer run as clear in color nor as straightway to the ultimate design — except for children. For them, the singleness of purpose, the exuberance, the exaltation, and the glory of the epics remain an incomparable experience.

Edwin Muir, the English poet, born in the Orkney Islands, gives testimony, in his autobiography, to the instinctive rightness of the heroic age in the years of childhood. He did not know the stories in his childhood, but as a poet, writing about the Greek legends, he instinctively felt them as having happened in his youth, in the setting he knew as a child. He describes his first trials at writing poetry:

> I wrote in baffling ignorance, blundering and perpetually making mistakes. I must have been influenced by something, since we all are, but when I try to find out what it was that influenced me, I can only think of the years of childhood which I spent on my father's farm in the little island of Wyre in

---

[4] *Ibid.*, p. 31.

[5] From "A Defense of Nonsense," in *Stories, Essays, and Poems,* by G. K. Chesterton (Everyman's Library, Dent, London), p. 126.

[6] Hans Christian Andersen, *The True Story of My Life* (Longman, London, 1847), p. 30.

Orkney, and the beauty I apprehended then, before I knew there was beauty. These years had come alive, after being forgotten for so long, and when I wrote about horses they were my father's plough-horses as I saw them when I was four or five; and a poem on Achilles pursuing Hector round the walls of Troy was really a resuscitation of the afternoon when I ran away, in real terror, from another boy as I returned from school. The bare landscape of the little island became, without my knowing it, a universal landscape over which Abraham and Moses and Achilles and Ulysses and Tristram and all sorts of pilgrims passed; and Troy was associated with the Castle, a mere green mound, near my father's house.[7]

The universal landscape! It is the landscape of youth, peopled with heroes out of a time when no other landscape existed.

One would expect such tribute from a poet. But here is a man of science, Dr. Hans Zinsser, describing with characteristic gusto and individuality his first encounter with the *Iliad* and the *Odyssey*. During the First World War, he was sent to Serbia with the Red Cross Typhus Commission. In the course of time, he had a brief visit in Greece, a period of waiting between steamers. "I saw the Parthenon, Corinth, and the lovely Achian hills on which the daphne — Apollo's beloved — was in flower," he writes.

> In a bookstore I picked up secondhand texts with translations of the *Odyssey* and of *Thucydides*. And with their help I renewed some of the adventures of my youth — remembering the resounding voice of the great schoolmaster, Julius Sachs, rolling forth the mighty vowels of Homeric periods with impressive wagging of his Olympian beard. And I felt glad that I had been a dishonest little boy. For while many good boys were conscientiously learning which verbs governed the dative or the ablative . . . I — in a back seat — was following the great classicist with a well-concealed 'trot'. . . . And I pondered on the stupidity of most classical teaching, which smothers what might be the most thrilling intellectual adventure of youth under rubbish heaps of syntax and grammar. Why not read all these things with a good trot, for those who have a talent and taste for it to pick up a reading knowledge, if they will; but for all who have any slumbering seeds of imagination, to sit for a while on Olympus with the henpecked Zeus, the shrew Hera, and the emancipated Pallas Athena; to be tossed on the seas with Odysseus; to be turned into a pig by Circe! sweat inside the Trojan horse; fight with the Nazi-Spartans or the Parisian Athenians — in short, to be subjected for an impressionable time to the magnificent pageant of Greek mythology and history which leaves an indelible imprint for which no Montessori, sex education, teachers' college psychology, or self-expression pedagogy can ever substitute. All this I thought as I gazed upon the Parthenon at night. . . .[8]

The epic spirit does not belong entirely to the past. It still refreshes, revives and inspirits persons and peoples who draw upon it for an intensification of inner strength. In Iceland, the most literate country in the world, the

[7] Edwin Muir, *An Autobiography* (The Hogarth Press, London, 1954), p. 206.

[8] Hans Zinsser, *As I Remember Him, the Biography of R. S.* (Little, Brown, Boston, 1940), pp. 229–230.

"new editions of the sagas continue to be best sellers," and everyone knows by heart passages straight out of the *Elder Edda,* and the *Younger Edda* of Snorri Sturluson.[9] In India, where illiteracy runs high, the unlettered and unschooled know from memory the tales from the great Indian epic, the *Ramayana,*

> chanted from memory hundreds of years before it was committed to writing. It was written down about 300 B.C. Even then no Hindu bothers to read it. The people prefer to learn it by word of mouth. And instead of reading aloud as a man reads Shakespeare, Hindus on the contrary chant their classics from memory. . . . In the streets of India you can hear the epics quoted within the folk language as a part of the people's speech. In a word, the Hindu classics are not a thing remote from the people's utterances but contribute to them as springs flow into a living stream.[10]

When Ireland fought for recognition as a separate nation, she turned to the ancient Celtic epics as inspiration, as fuel to feed the blaze by which she sustained her individuality. The Celtic Revival brought forth a brilliant theater, as well as poetry and drama and political action. Ella Young, the Irish poet and storyteller, gave as her share to the Nationalist movement the telling of the stories of Cuchulain and Finn, epic heroes of early Ireland, to the illiterate newsboys of the Dublin streets, who came together in stores and lofts, after work, to hear her stories and, by listening, to feel themselves a part of their own great past.

The one book which Lawrence of Arabia carried in his saddle bags, during the hard years he worked among the Arabs, was Thomas Malory's *Morte Darthur,* the epic of England.

This world of epic is large in meaning to children who find it at the strategic time. Perhaps a commensurate obligation lies upon adults to make this great experience available to children, through the spoken word, as well as by means of books, so that even the non-reading child may come into his rightful heritage.

9 Evelyn Stefánsson, *Here Is the Far North* (Charles Scribner's Sons, 1957), p. 102.
10 Dhan Gopal Mukerji, *Rama, the Hero of India* (Dutton, New York, 1930), p. xl.

GREECE

Odysseus and the Cyclops[1]

⋙ *Certain stories are great in themselves, even in the barest outline. The incidents they describe are of such magnitude, so large in concept, so unequaled in invention, that they unlock the mind, and the reader and listener can never again reassemble his individual habit of thought within its former tight and tidy confines. These tales burst through boundaries and set free his imagination. Of this stature is the story of the wise Odysseus in the face of overwhelming odds. The drama is heightened by Padraic Colum's device of telling it in the first person, as Odysseus himself might have spoken it.*

Later we came to the land of the Cyclôpes, a giant people. There is a waste island outside the harbour of their land, and on it there is a well of bright water that has poplars growing round it. We came to that empty island, and we beached our ships and took down our sails.

As soon as the dawn came we went through the empty island, starting the wild goats that were there in flocks, and shooting them with our arrows. We killed so many wild goats there that we had nine for each ship. Afterwards we looked across to the land of the Cyclôpes, and we heard the sound of voices and saw the smoke of fires and heard the bleating of flocks of sheep and goats.

I called my companions together and I said, "It would be well for some of us to go

1 From Padraic Colum, *The Adventures of Odysseus and the Tale of Troy* (Macmillan, 1918).

to that other island. With my own ship and with the company that is on it I shall go there. The rest of you abide here. I will find out what manner of men live there, and whether they will treat us kindly and give us gifts that are due to strangers — gifts of provisions for our voyage."

We embarked and we came to the land. There was a cave near the sea, and round the cave there were mighty flocks of sheep and goats. I took twelve men with me and I left the rest to guard the ship. We went into the cave and found no man there. There were baskets filled with cheeses, and vessels of whey, and pails and bowls of milk. My men wanted me to take some of the cheeses and drive off some of the lambs and kids and come away. But this I would not do, for I would rather that he who owned the stores would give us of his own free will the offerings that were due to strangers.

While we were in the cave, he whose dwelling it was, returned to it. He carried on his shoulder a great pile of wood for his fire. Never in our lives did we see a creature so frightful as this Cyclops was. He was a giant in size, and, what made him terrible to behold, he had but one eye, and that single eye was in his forehead. He cast down on the ground the pile of wood that he carried, making such a din that we fled in terror into the corners and recesses of the cave. Next he drove his flocks into the cave and began to milk his ewes and goats. And when he had the flocks within, he took up a stone that not all our strength could move and set it as a door to the mouth of the cave.

The Cyclops kindled his fire, and when

it blazed up he saw us in the corners and recesses. He spoke to us. We knew not what he said, but our hearts were shaken with terror at the sound of his deep voice.

I spoke to him saying that we were Agamemnon's men on our way home from the taking of Priam's City, and I begged him to deal with us kindly, for the sake of Zeus who is ever in the company of strangers and suppliants. But he answered me saying, "We Cyclôpes pay no heed to Zeus, nor to any of thy gods. In our strength and our power we deem that we are mightier than they. I will not spare thee, neither will I give thee aught for the sake of Zeus, but only as my own spirit bids me. And first I would have thee tell me how you came to our land."

I knew it would be better not to let the Cyclops know that my ship and my companions were at the harbour of the island. Therefore I spoke to him guilefully, telling him that my ship had been broken on the rocks, and that I and the men with me were the only ones who had escaped utter doom.

I begged again that he would deal with us as just men deal with strangers and suppliants, but he, without saying a word, laid hands upon two of my men, and swinging them by the legs, dashed their brains out on the earth. He cut them to pieces and ate them before our very eyes. We wept and we prayed to Zeus as we witnessed a deed so terrible.

Next the Cyclops stretched himself amongst his sheep and went to sleep beside the fire. Then I debated whether I should take my sharp sword in my hand, and feeling where his heart was, stab him there. But second thoughts held me back from doing this. I might be able to kill him as he slept, but not even with my companions could I roll away the great stone that closed the mouth of the cave.

Dawn came, and the Cyclops awakened, kindled his fire and milked his flocks. Then he seized two others of my men and made ready for his mid-day meal. And now he rolled away the great stone and drove his flocks out of the cave.

I had pondered on a way of escape, and I had thought of something that might be done to baffle the Cyclops. I had with me a great skin of sweet wine, and I thought that if I could make him drunken with wine I and my companions might be able for him. But there were other preparations to be made first. On the floor of the cave there was a great beam of olive wood which the Cyclops had cut to make a club when the wood should be seasoned. It was yet green. I and my companions went and cut off a fathom's length of the wood, and sharpened it to a point and took it to the fire and hardened it in the glow. Then I hid the beam in a recess of the cave.

The Cyclops came back in the evening, and opening up the cave drove in his flocks. Then he closed the cave again with the stone and went and milked his ewes and his goats. Again he seized two of my companions. I went to the terrible creature with a bowl of wine in my hands. He took it and drank it and cried out, "Give me another bowl of this, and tell me thy name that I may give thee gifts for bringing me this honey-tasting drink."

Again I spoke to him guilefully and said, "Noman is my name. Noman my father and my mother call me."

"Give me more of the drink, Noman," he shouted. "And the gift that I shall give to thee is that I shall make thee the last of thy fellows to be eaten."

I gave him wine again, and when he had taken the third bowl he sank backwards with his face upturned, and sleep came upon him. Then I, with four companions, took that beam of olive wood, now made into a hard and pointed stake, and thrust it into the ashes of the fire. When the pointed end began to glow we drew it out of the flame. Then I and my companions laid hold on the great stake and, dashing at the Cyclops, thrust it into his eye. He raised a terrible cry that made the rocks ring and we dashed away into the recesses of the cave.

His cries brought other Cyclôpes to the mouth of the cave, and they, naming him as Polyphemus, called out and asked him what ailed him to cry. "Noman," he shrieked out, "Noman is slaying me by guile." They answered him saying, "If no man is slaying thee, there is nothing we can do for thee, Polyphemus. What ails thee has been sent to thee by the gods." Saying this, they went away from the mouth of the cave without attempting to move away the stone.

Polyphemus then, groaning with pain, rolled away the stone and sat before the mouth of the cave with his hands outstretched, thinking that he would catch us as we dashed out. I showed my companions how we might pass by him. I laid hands on certain rams of the flock and I lashed three of them together with supple rods. Then on the middle ram I put a man of my company. Thus every three rams carried a man. As soon as the dawn had come the rams hastened out to the pasture, and, as they passed, Polyphemus laid hands on the first and the third of each three that went by. They passed out and Polyphemus did not guess that a ram that he did not touch carried out a man.

For myself, I took a ram that was the strongest and fleeciest of the whole flock and I placed myself under him, clinging to the wool of his belly. As this ram, the best of all his flock, went by, Polyphemus, laying his hands upon him, said, "Would that you, the best of my flock, were endowed with speech, so that you might tell me where Noman, who has blinded me, has hidden himself." The ram went by him, and when he had gone a little way from the cave I loosed myself from him and went and set my companions free.

We gathered together many of Polyphemus' sheep and we drove them down to our ship. The men we had left behind would have wept when they heard what had happened to six of their companions. But I bade them take on board the sheep we had brought and pull the ship away from that land. Then when we had drawn a certain distance from the shore I could not forbear to shout my taunts into the cave of Polyphemus. "Cyclops," I cried, "you thought that you had the company of a fool and a weakling to eat. But you have been worsted by me, and your evil deeds have been punished."

So I shouted, and Polyphemus came to the mouth of the cave with great anger in his heart. He took up rocks and cast them at the ship and they fell before the prow. The men bent to the oars and pulled the ship away or it would have been broken by the rocks he cast. And when we were further away I shouted to him:

"Cyclops, if any man should ask who it was set his mark upon you, say that he was Odysseus, the son of Laertes."

Then I heard Polyphemus cry out, "I call upon Poseidon, the god of the sea, whose son I am, to avenge me upon you, Odysseus. I call upon Poseidon to grant that you, Odysseus, may never come to your home, or if the gods have ordained your return, that you come to it after much toil and suffering, in an evil plight and in a stranger's ship, to find sorrow in your home."

So Polyphemus prayed, and, to my evil fortune, Poseidon heard his prayer. But we went on in our ship rejoicing at our escape. We came to the waste island where my other ships were. All the company rejoiced to see us, although they had to mourn for their six companions slain by Polyphemus. We divided amongst the ships the sheep we had taken from Polyphemus' flock and we sacrificed to the gods. At the dawn of the next day we raised the sails on each ship and we sailed away.

Perseus[2]

◄§ "*This story is on the level of the fairy story. Hermes and Athena act like the fairy godmother in* Cinderella. *The magical wallet and cap belong to the properties fairy tales abound in everywhere. . . . Many poets allude to it. The description of Danaë in the wooden chest was the most famous passage of a famous poem by Simonides of Ceos, a great lyric poet who lived in the sixth century. The entire story is told by both Ovid and Apollodorus. The latter, probably a hundred years later than Ovid, is here the superior of the two. His account is simple and straightforward; Ovid's extremely verbose — for instance, he takes a hundred lines to kill the sea serpent. I have followed Apollodorus, but I have added the fragment from Simonides, and short quotations from other poets, notably Hesiod and Pindar.*"

— *Edith Hamilton*

[2] From Edith Hamilton, *Mythology* (Little, Brown, 1942).

King Acrisius of Argos had only one child, a daughter, Danaë. She was beautiful above all the other women of the land, but this was small comfort to the king for not having a son. He journeyed to Delphi to ask the god if there was any hope that some day he would be the father of a boy. The priestess told him no, and added what was far worse: that his daughter would have a son who would kill him.

The only sure way to escape that fate was for the king to have Danaë instantly put to death — taking no chances, but seeing to it himself. This Acrisius would not do. His fatherly affection was not strong, as events proved, but his fear of the gods was. They visited with terrible punishments those who shed the blood of kindred. Acrisius did not dare slay his daughter. Instead, he had a house built all of bronze and sunk underground, but with part of the roof open to the sky so that light and air could come through. Here he shut her up and guarded her.

So Danaë endured, the beautiful,
To change the glad daylight for brass-bound walls,
And in that chamber secret as the grave
She lived a prisoner. Yet to her came
Zeus in the golden rain.

As she sat there through the long days and hours with nothing to do, nothing to see except the clouds moving by overhead, a mysterious thing happened, a shower of gold fell from the sky and filled her chamber. How it was revealed to her that it was Zeus who had visited her in this shape we are not told, but she knew that the child she bore was his son.

For a time she kept his birth secret from her father, but it became increasingly difficult to do so in the narrow limits of that bronze house, and finally one day the little boy — his name was Perseus — was discovered by his grandfather. "Your child!" Acrisius cried in great anger. "Who is his father?" But when Danaë answered proudly, "Zeus," he would not believe her. One thing only he was sure of, that the boy's life was a terrible danger to his own. He was afraid to kill him for the same reason that had kept him from killing her, fear of Zeus and

the Furies who pursue such murderers. But if he could not kill them outright, he could put them in the way of tolerably certain death. He had a great chest made, and the two placed in it. Then it was taken out to sea and cast into the water.

In that strange boat Danaë sat with her little son. The daylight faded and she was alone on the sea.

When in the carven chest the winds and waves
Struck fear into her heart she put her arms,
Not without tears, round Perseus tenderly.
She said, "O son, what grief is mine.
But you sleep softly, little child,
Sunk deep in rest within your cheerless home,
Only a box, brass-bound. The night, this darkness
  visible,
The scudding waves so near to your soft curls,
The shrill voice of the wind, you do not heed,
Nestled in your red cloak, fair little face."

Through the night in the tossing chest she listened to the waters that seemed always about to wash over them. The dawn came, but with no comfort to her, for she could not see it. Neither could she see that around them there were islands rising high above the sea, many islands. All she knew was that presently a wave seemed to lift them and carry them swiftly on and then, retreating, leave them on something solid and motionless. They had made land; they were safe from the sea, but they were still in the chest with no way to get out.

Fate willed it — or perhaps Zeus, who up to now had done little for his love and his child — that they should be discovered by a good man, a fisherman named Dictys. He came upon the great box and broke it open and took the pitiful cargo home to his wife who was as kind as he. They had no children and they cared for Danaë and Perseus as if they were their own. The two lived there many years, Danaë content to let her son follow the fisherman's humble trade, out of harm's way. But in the end more trouble came. Polydectes, the ruler of the little island, was the brother of Dictys, but he was a cruel and ruthless man. He seems to have taken no notice of the mother and son for a long time, but at last Danaë attracted his attention. She was still radiantly beautiful even though Perseus by now was full grown, and Polydectes fell in love with her. He wanted her, but he did not want her son, and he set himself to think out a way of getting rid of him.

There were some fearsome monsters called Gorgons who lived on an island and were known far and wide because of their deadly power. Polydectes evidently talked to Perseus about them; he probably told him that he would rather have the head of one of them than anything else in the world. This seems practically certain from the plan he devised for killing Perseus. He announced that he was about to be married and he called his friends together for a celebration, including Perseus in the invitation. Each guest, as was customary, brought a gift for the bride-to-be, except Perseus alone. He had nothing he could give. He was young and proud and keenly mortified. He stood up before them all and did exactly what the king had hoped he would do, declared that he would give him a present better than any there. He would go off and kill Medusa and bring back her head as his gift. Nothing could have suited the king better. No one in his senses would have made such a proposal. Medusa was one of the Gorgons.

> And they are three, the Gorgons, each with wings
> And snaky hair, most horrible to mortals.
> Whom no man shall behold and draw again
> The breath of life.

— for the reason that whoever looked at them was turned instantly into stone. It seemed that Perseus had been led by his angry pride into making an empty boast. No man unaided could kill Medusa.

But Perseus was saved from his folly. Two great gods were watching over him. He took ship as soon as he left the king's hall, not daring to see his mother first and tell her what he intended, and he sailed to Greece to learn where the three monsters were to be found. He went to Delphi, but all the priestess would say was to bid him seek the land where men eat not Demeter's golden grain, but only acorns. So he went to Dodona, in the land of oak trees, where the talking oaks were which declared Zeus's will and where the Selli lived who made their bread from acorns. They could tell him,

however, no more than this, that he was under the protection of the gods. They did not know where the Gorgons lived.

When and how Hermes and Athena came to his help is not told in any story, but he must have known despair before they did so. At last, however, as he wandered on, he met a strange and beautiful person. We know what he looked like from many a poem, a young man with the first down upon his cheek when youth is loveliest, carrying, as no other young man ever did, a wand of gold with wings at one end, wearing a winged hat, too, and winged sandals. At sight of him hope must have entered Perseus' heart, for he would know that this could be none other than Hermes, the guide and the giver of good.

This radiant personage told him that before he attacked Medusa he must first be properly equipped, and that what he needed was in the possession of the Nymphs of the North. To find the nymphs' abode, they must go to the Gray Women who alone could tell them the way. These women dwelt in a land where all was dim and shrouded in twilight. No ray of sun looked ever on that country, nor the moon by night. In that gray place the three women lived, all gray themselves and withered as in extreme old age. They were strange creatures, indeed, most of all because they had but one eye for the three, which it was their custom to take turns with, each removing it from her forehead when she had had it for a time and handing it to another.

All this Hermes told Perseus and then he unfolded his plan. He would himself guide Perseus to them. Once there Perseus must keep hidden until he saw one of them take the eye out of her forehead to pass it on. At that moment, when none of the three could see, he must rush forward and seize the eye and refuse to give it back until they told him how to reach the Nymphs of the North.

He himself, Hermes said, would give him a sword to attack Medusa with — which could not be bent or broken by the Gorgon's scales, no matter how hard they were. This was a wonderful gift, no doubt, and yet of what use was a sword when the creature to be struck by it could turn the swordsman into stone before he was within striking distance? But another great deity was at hand to help. Pallas Athena stood beside Perseus. She took off the shield of polished bronze which covered her breast and held it out to him. "Look into this when you attack the Gorgon," she said, "You will be able to see her in it as in a mirror, and so avoid her deadly power."

Now, indeed, Perseus had good reason to hope. The journey to the twilight land was long, over the stream of Ocean and on to the very border of the black country where the Cimmarians dwell, but Hermes was his guide and he could not go astray. They found the Gray Women at last, looking in the wavering light like gray birds, for they had the shape of swans. But their heads were human and beneath their wings they had arms and hands. Perseus did just as Hermes had said, he held back until he saw one of them take the eye out of her forehead. Then before she could give it to her sister, he snatched it out of her hand. It was a moment or two before the three realized they had lost it. Each thought one of the others had it. But Perseus spoke out and told them he had taken it and that it would be theirs again only when they showed him how to find the Nymphs of the North. They gave him full directions at once; they would have done anything to get their eye back. He returned it to them and went on the way they had pointed out to him. He was bound, although he did not know it, to the blessed country of the Hyperboreans, at the back of the North Wind, of which it is said: "Neither by ship nor yet by land shall one find the wondrous road to the gathering place of the Hyperboreans." But Perseus had Hermes with him, so that the road lay open to him, and he reached that host of happy people who are always banqueting and holding joyful revelry. They showed him great kindness: they welcomed him to their feast, and the maidens dancing to the sound of flute and lyre paused to get for him the gifts he sought. These were three: winged sandals, a magic wallet which would always become the right size for whatever was to be carried in it, and, most important of all, a cap which made the wearer invisible. With these and Athena's shield and Hermes' sword, Perseus was ready for the Gorgons. Hermes knew where they lived, and leaving the happy land the two flew back across Ocean and over the sea to the Terrible Sisters' island.

By great good fortune they were all asleep when Perseus found them. In the mirror of the bright shield he could see them clearly, creatures with great wings and bodies covered with golden scales and hair a mass of twisting snakes. Athena was beside him now as well as Hermes. They told him which one was Medusa and that was important, for she alone of the three could be killed; the other two were immortal. Perseus on his winged sandals hovered above them, looking, however, only at the shield. Then he aimed a stroke down at Medusa's throat and Athena guided his hand. With a single sweep of his sword he cut through her neck and, his eyes still fixed on the shield with never a glance at her, he swooped low enough to seize the head. He dropped it into the wallet which closed around it. He had nothing to fear from it now. But the two other Gorgons had awakened and, horrified at the sight of their sister slain, tried to pursue the slayer. Perseus was safe; he had on the cap of darkness and they could not find him.

So over the sea rich-haired Danaë's son,
Perseus, on his wingèd sandals sped,
Flying swift as thought.
In a wallet all of silver,
A wonder to behold,
He bore the head of the monster,
While Hermes, the son of Maia,
The messenger of Zeus,
Kept ever at his side.

On his way back he came to Ethiopia and alighted there. By this time Hermes had left him. Perseus found, as Hercules was later to find, that a lovely maiden had been given up to be devoured by a horrible sea serpent. Her name was Andromeda and she was the daughter of a silly, vain woman,

That starred Ethiop queen who strove
To set her beauty's praise above
The sea-nymphs, and their power offended.

She had boasted that she was more beautiful than the daughters of Nereus, the sea-god. An absolutely certain way in those days to draw down on one a wretched fate was to claim superiority in anything over any deity; nevertheless, people were perpetually doing so. In this case the punishment for the arrogance the gods detested fell not on Queen Cassiopeia, Andromeda's mother, but on her daughter. The Ethiopians were being devoured in numbers by the serpent; and, learning from the oracle that they could be freed from the pest only if Andromeda were offered up to it, they forced Cepheus, her father, to consent. When Perseus arrived, the maiden was on a rocky ledge by the sea, chained there to wait for the coming of the monster. Perseus saw her and on the instant loved her. He waited beside her until the great snake came for its prey; then he cut its head off just as he had the Gorgon's. The headless body dropped back into the water; Perseus took Andromeda to her parents and asked for her hand, which they gladly gave him.

With her he sailed back to the island and his mother, but in the house where he had lived so long he found no one. The fisherman Dictys' wife was long since dead, and the two others, Danaë and the man who had been like a father to Perseus, had had to fly and hide themselves from Polydectes, who was furious at Danaë's refusal to marry him. They had taken refuge in a temple, Perseus was told. He learned also that the king was holding a banquet in the palace and all the men who favored him were gathered there. Perseus instantly saw his opportunity. He went straight to the palace and entered the hall. As he stood at the entrance, Athena's shining buckler on his breast, the silver wallet at his side, he drew the eyes of every man there. Then before any could look away, he held up the Gorgon's head; and at the sight one and all, the cruel king and his servile courtiers, were turned into stone. There they sat, a row of statues, each, as it were, frozen stiff in the attitude he had struck when he first saw Perseus.

When the islanders knew themselves freed from the tyrant, it was easy for Perseus to find Danaë and Dictys. He made Dictys king of the island, but he and his mother decided that they would go back with Andromeda to Greece and try to be reconciled to Acrisius, to see if the many years that had passed since he had put them in the chest had not softened him so that he would be glad to receive his daughter and grandson. When they reached Argos, however, they found that Acrisius had been driven away from the city, and where he was no one could say. It happened that soon after their arrival, Perseus heard that the King of Larissa, in the North, was holding a great athletic contest, and he journeyed there to take part. In the discus-throwing when his turn came and he hurled the heavy missile, it swerved and fell among the spectators. Acrisius was there on a visit to the king, and the discus struck him. The blow was fatal and he died at once.

So Apollo's oracle was again proved true. If Perseus felt any grief, at least he knew that his grandfather had done his best to kill him and his mother. With his death their troubles came to an end. Perseus and Andromeda lived happily ever after. Their son, Electryon, was the grandfather of Hercules.

Medusa's head was given to Athena, who bore it always upon the aegis, Zeus's shield, which she carried for him.

Hercules: The Eleventh Task [3]

Hercules was the greatest hero of Greece. He possessed magnificent strength. He was the son of Zeus by a mortal wife. The goddess Hera (Juno), wife of Zeus, never forgave Hercules for being Zeus' son and persecuted him throughout his life. She it was who brought on his madness and caused him to kill his wife and their three sons. When sanity returned, Hercules was grief-stricken, and as punishment exiled himself. Then in his great desire to be purified, he consulted the oracle at Delphi. The priestess told him that only a terrible penance could purge him. She bade him go to Eurystheus, King of Mycenae, and submit to whatever he demanded. She then promised him that if he performed the tasks set him, he would

[3] From Katharine Pyle, *Heroic Tales from Greek Mythology* (Lippincott, 1928).

become immortal. Eurystheus, urged on by Hera, imposed upon Hercules twelve tasks, each one of which was well-nigh impossible. They were called The Twelve Labors of Hercules and were fixed in legend as early as the fifth century B.C. They involved the following:

1. *To slay the Nemean lion, a beast no weapons could kill.*
2. *To slay the Lernean hydra, a creature with nine heads, one of which was immortal.*
3. *To bring back alive the Arcadian stag with antlers of gold.*
4. *To destroy a great boar that lived on Mount Erymantis.*
5. *To clean the Augean stables in a single day.*
6. *To drive away the Stymphalian birds.*
7. *To take captive the savage bull of Crete.*
8. *To catch the man-eating horses of Diomedes, King of Thrace.*
9. *To bring back the girdle of Hippolyta, Queen of the Amazons.*
10. *To capture the oxen of the monster Geryon.*
11. *To bring back the Golden Apples of the Hesperides.*
12. *To bring up from Hades the three-headed dog Cerberus.*

Now when Zeus and Hera had been married, to their wedding feast had come all the gods and goddesses, bringing with them gifts. Demeter brought a tree that bore most wondrous golden apples, and the immortal pair were greatly pleased with this. Zeus made a garden in the farthest west, and called it the Garden of the Hesperides, and he set the tree in the midst of it. A sleepless dragon coiled about its trunk to guard it, and four fair nymphs called the Daughters of the West were set to watch both tree and dragon.

And now Eurystheus commanded Hercules to bring him these golden apples of the Hesperides.

Hercules set forth as he was commanded, but now he wandered aimlessly; for he knew not in which direction the garden lay, nor could he find any who could tell him though he asked all whom he met. At last in his wanderings he came to the river Rhône and sat to rest beside its brink, and as he sat there he saw the naiads at play in its waters,

and he called to them, "Fair nymphs, out of your kindness, tell me if you can, where I may find the Garden of the Hesperides."

Then the nymphs ceased from play and raised themselves waist-high above the waters; and, seeing how great and tall the stranger was, they called to him, "Art thou Hercules?" for even in their river they had heard of him.

Hercules answered, "I am he."

Then the nymphs said, "Most gladly would we tell thee, if we could, where to find that garden, but few know save only the gods themselves. Nereus, the son-in-law of Oceanus, knows, and only a while ago we saw him by the sea asleep upon a rock. Hasten and thou still mayest find him there. Then catch and hold him fast until he tells thee. This he will be loath to do, and he will turn himself in thy grasp into many shapes, but do not let him go, and in the end he will be forced to tell thee."

Then Hercules thanked the kindly nymphs and followed the river on and down to the sea, and there, as they had said, he found Nereus still asleep upon the rock. His hair and beard were green and rough, and more like water weeds than hair, and two horns grew from his forehead. Then Hercules seized him with his mighty hands and woke him, and Nereus struggled to free himself and panted, "Let me go!" but Hercules would not; and suddenly the sea god turned himself into a slippery fish, but Hercules held him still. Afterward Nereus changed into a writhing serpent, then into a great three-headed dog that snapped and snarled at the hands that held him; after that he changed into a stream that almost slipped through Hercules' fingers, and then into an enormous water bird that beat him with its wings, but still he held it. Then at last Nereus turned back into his own shape again and panting cried, "Why dost thou hold me thus? What wouldst thou have of me?"

Hercules answered, "Tell me where to find the Garden of the Hesperides, and how to bring thence the golden apples, and I will let thee go."

Nereus replied, "The garden lies far to the west in Libya, but no mortal hand may pluck those apples. Only Atlas, the mighty

Titan who upholds the sky upon his shoulders, may pluck them. Seek him first. If he will aid thee it is well, but if not thou needst not hope ever to gain those apples."

Then Hercules asked where he might find Atlas, and Nereus said, "Seek him too in Libya. And now let me go."

So Hercules loosed his hold, and Nereus slipped from his hands and plunged down into the sea.

But Hercules journeyed on to Libya, and he came to where a giant stood guarding the way, and the giant called to him, "I am Antaeus, the wrestler; none may pass this way unless they first have wrestled with me."

Hercules answered, "That will I gladly do," and he cast aside his lion skin and club and sprang at Antaeus, and they wrestled together up and down, and despite the giant's size, again and still again Hercules threw him, but always Antaeus started up again from the earth stronger than before, and Hercules could not understand the reason for it. But this giant was the son of Terra, as the earth is called, and all his strength flowed into him from her. The closer his body came to her, the stronger he grew. Then at last, after having thrown him many times, Hercules guessed his secret, and he caught the giant with his mighty hands, and instead of casting him down he heaved him up and held him high so that he could not touch the ground; and Antaeus struggled, and cried out, and strove to slip from his hands and fall to earth, and could not; slowly all the strength went out of him, till at last he hung, a helpless thing, in the hands of Hercules.

Then Hercules killed him and cast his body to the ground, for he knew that now not even his mother Earth could again put life into him.

But after this Hercules lost his way and wandered from Libya on into other countries; so he came to India, where Phoebus had his palace, and to the Caucasus where Prometheus lay bound; and Prometheus saw him even from afar and called him, "Hasten thy steps, O Hercules! For ages long I have awaited thee, and now thou has come at last!"

Then Hercules drew near, and looked with wonder on Prometheus, and on the eagles that hovered over him, for though from childhood he had heard the story of Prometheus, he scarcely had believed that it was true. But now Prometheus told him with his own mouth of all his sufferings, and Hercules, filled with wrath and pity, drove away the eagles, and broke the fetters that held Prometheus, and set him free. So it was that the favored son of Zeus freed the one whom Zeus himself had bound.

And now Prometheus told Hercules that he wandered from his way, and bade him retrace his steps to Libya, and he told him where to find Atlas.

So Hercules went back the way that he had come, and after long journeying he came again to Libya and to the place of which Prometheus had told him, and there he saw Atlas towering high above him, with his head among the clouds and the sky resting on his shoulders. Then Hercules called to him, "Ho, Atlas! with thy head among the clouds, canst thou hear me?"

And Atlas answered, "I can hear. Who art thou, calling there below in such a mighty voice? What seekest thou here?"

Hercules answered, "I am Hercules, the son of Zeus." And he told the Titan how he had been made subject to Eurystheus, and of how it was the will of the gods that he should carry out the king's commands until he had performed twelve labors. "So far," he said, "I have accomplished all the tasks that he has set for me; but now he has commanded me to bring to him the golden apples of the Hesperides, and this I cannot do without thy aid."

Atlas asked, "How can I aid thee? If I ceased from holding up the skies, even for a moment, they would fall upon the earth and both would be destroyed together."

Hercules replied, "I will myself support the sky in thy place, if thou wilt fetch the apples," and to this Atlas agreed. But Hercules lacked in height, so he climbed up a mountain and stood upon its top, and he cast off his lion skin and bared his back, and Atlas shifted the weight of the sky to his shoulders; slowly and carefully he shifted it, but even so, the sky was shaken so that many of the stars fell from their places, and people were terrified, fearing the whole of the heavens was about to fall.

Then Atlas strode away toward the west, and Hercules stood there with his shoulders bowed under the weight, and always the weight seemed heavier, and he was glad when, after a time, he heard Atlas returning, and he called, "Make haste, O Atlas, and take back the sky, for even already I am wearied of it."

Atlas said, "I was wearied long ago, and now I will myself carry the apples to King Eurystheus, and thou shalt stay here in my place."

Then Hercules was afraid, thinking that he might never be released, but he hid his fear and he said, "If I am to take thy place, let me at least spread my lion's skin on the rocks, for they are hard and rough beneath my feet."

Then Atlas agreed, and he put down the apples and took back the sky, thinking that presently he would again give it over to Hercules. But Hercules said, "It is thy task to support the sky, as it is mine to carry out the orders of Eurystheus. Thou wouldst have tricked me in this thing, but instead thou hast thyself been tricked. Farewell, O Atlas!"

And he took up the apples and returned with them to Eurystheus, leaving Atlas there with the weight of the heavens resting still upon his shoulders.

How Jason Lost His Sandal in Anauros[4]

> The avid reader of traditional tales, epics, and stories finds himself fascinated by the occurrence and recurrence of motif, themes, attitudes, and incidents in sources which seem far removed from one another. One of the best-loved Christian legends is the story of St. Christopher, who bore the Christ Child upon his back across a swiftly flowing stream. Here is the same story, but it is Jason, he who set out on the impossible quest for the Golden Fleece, who crosses the flood, and it is the goddess Hera he befriends.

[4] From Charles Kingsley, The Heroes (Macmillan, 1855).

> The cycle of stories in which Jason is hero was written by a poet of the third century B.C., Apollonius of Rhodes; its title, Argonautica. Pindar, the Greek lyric poet (438 B.C.), made Jason the subject of one of his most famous odes, and Euripides (485 B.C.) based his great tragedy Medea upon the Jason story. This retelling of the story is from a book belonging to the Victorian era, but it remains one of the most vigorous and spirited sources for children.

And ten years came and went, and Jason was grown to be a mighty man. Some of his fellows were gone, and some were growing up by his side. Asclepius was gone into Peloponnese, to work his wondrous cures on men; and some say he used to raise the dead to life. And Heracles was gone to Thebes, to fulfill those famous labours which have become a proverb among men. And Peleus had married a sea-nymph, and his wedding is famous to this day. And Aeneas was gone home to Troy, and many a noble tale you will read of him, and of all the other gallant heroes, the scholars of Cheiron the just. And it happened on a day that Jason stood on the mountain, and looked north and south and east and west; and Cheiron stood by him and watched him, for he knew that the time was come.

And Jason looked and saw the plains of Thessaly, where the Lapithai breed their horses; and the lake of Boibé, and the stream which runs northward to Peneus and Tempe; and he looked north, and saw the mountain wall which guards the Magnesian shore; Olympus, the seat of the Immortals, and Ossa, and Pelion, where he stood. Then he looked east and saw the bright blue sea, which stretched away forever toward the dawn. Then he looked south, and saw a pleasant land, with white-walled towns and farms, nestling along the shore of a land-locked bay, while the smoke rose blue among the trees; and he knew it for the bay of Pagasai, and the rich lowlands of Haemonia, and Iolcos by the sea.

Then he sighed, and asked: "Is it true what the heroes tell me, that I am heir of that fair land?"

"And what good would it be to you, Jason, if you were heir of that fair land?"

"I would take it and keep it."

"A strong man has taken it and kept it long. Are you stronger than Pelias the terrible?"

"I can try my strength with his," said Jason. But Cheiron sighed, and said: —

"You have many a danger to go through before you rule in Iolcos by the sea; and many a woe; and strange troubles in strange lands, such as man never saw before."

"The happier I," said Jason, "to see what man never saw before."

And Cheiron sighed again, and said: "The eaglet must leave the nest when it is fledged. Will you go to Iolcos by the sea? Then promise me two things before you go."

Jason promised, and Cheiron answered: "Speak harshly to no soul whom you may meet, and stand by the word which you shall speak."

Jason wondered why Cheiron asked this of him; but he knew that the Centaur was a prophet, and saw things long before they came. So he promised, and leapt down the mountain, to take his fortune like a man.

He went down through the arbutus thickets, and across the downs of thyme, till he came to the vineyard walls, and the pomegranates and the olives in the glen; and among the olives roared Anauros, all foaming with a summer flood.

And on the bank of Anauros sat a woman, all wrinkled, gray, and old; her head shook palsied on her breast, and her hands shook palsied on her knees; and when she saw Jason, she spoke whining: "Who will carry me across the flood?"

Jason was bold and hasty, and was just going to leap into the flood; and yet he thought twice before he leapt, so loud roared the torrent down, all brown from the mountain rains, and silver-veined with melting snow; while underneath he could hear the boulders rumbling like the tramp of horsemen or the roll of wheels, as they ground along the narrow channel, and shook the rocks on which he stood.

But the old woman whined all the more: "I am weak and old, fair youth. For Hera's sake, carry me over the torrent."

And Jason was going to answer her scorn-

fully, when Cheiron's words came to his mind.

So he said: "For Hera's sake, the Queen of the Immortals on Olympus, I will carry you over the torrent, unless we both are drowned midway."

Then the old dame leapt upon his back, as nimbly as a goat; and Jason staggered in, wondering; and the first step was up to his knees.

The first step was up to his knees, and the second step was up to his waist; and the stones rolled about his feet, and his feet slipped about the stones; so he went on staggering and panting, while the old woman cried from off his back: —

"Fool, you have wet my mantle! Do you make game of poor old souls like me?"

Jason had half a mind to drop her, and let her get through the torrent by herself; but Cheiron's words were in his mind, and he said only: "Patience, mother; the best horse may stumble some day."

At last he staggered to the shore, and set her down upon the bank; and a strong man he needed to have been, or that wild water he never would have crossed.

He lay panting awhile upon the bank, and then leapt up to go upon his journey; but he cast one look at the old woman, for he thought, "She should thank me once at least."

And as he looked, she grew fairer than all women, and taller than all men on earth; and her garments shone like the summer sea, and her jewels like the stars of heaven; and over her forehead was a veil, woven of the golden clouds of sunset; and through the veil she looked down on him, with great soft heifer's eyes; with great eyes, mild and awful, which filled all the glen with light.

And Jason fell upon his knees, and hid his face between his hands.

And she spoke — "I am the Queen of Olympus, Hera the wife of Zeus. As thou hast done to me, so will I do to thee. Call on me in the hour of need, and try if the Immortals can forget."

And when Jason looked up, she rose from off the earth, like a pillar of tall white cloud, and floated away across the mountain peaks, toward Olympus the holy hill.

Then a great fear fell on Jason; but after a while he grew light of heart; and he blessed old Cheiron, and said — "Surely the Centaur is a prophet, and guessed what would come to pass, when he bade me speak harshly to no soul whom I might meet."

Then he went down toward Iolcos, and as he walked, he found that he had lost one of his sandals in the flood.

And as he went through the streets, the people came out to look at him, so tall and fair was he; but some of the elders whispered together; and at last one of them stopped Jason, and called to him — "Fair lad, who are you, and whence come you; and what is your errand in the town?"

"My name, good father, is Jason, and I come from Pelion up above; and my errand is to Pelias your king; tell me then where his palace is."

But the old man started, and grew pale, and said, "Do you not know the oracle, my son, that you go so boldly through the town, with but one sandal on?"

"I am a stranger here, and know of no oracle; but what of my one sandal? I lost the other in Anauros, while I was struggling with the flood."

Then the old man looked back to his companions; and one sighed and another smiled; at last he said — "I will tell you, lest you rush upon your ruin unawares. The oracle in Delphi has said, that a man wearing one sandal should take the kingdom from Pelias, and keep it for himself. Therefore beware how you go up to his palace, for he is the fiercest and most cunning of all kings."

Then Jason laughed a great laugh, like a war-horse in his pride — "Good news, good father, both for you and me. For that very end I came into the town."

Then he strode on toward the palace of Pelias, while all the people wondered at his bearing.

And he stood in the doorway and cried, "Come out, Pelias the valiant, and fight for your kingdom like a man."

Pelias came out wondering, and "Who are you, bold youth?" he cried.

"I am Jason, the son of Aeson, the heir of all this land."

Then Pelias lifted up his hands and eyes, and wept, or seemed to weep; and blessed the heavens which had brought his nephew to him, never to leave him more. "For," said he, "I have but three daughters, and no son to be my heir. You shall be my heir then, and rule the kingdom after me, and marry whichsoever of my daughters you shall choose; though a sad kingdom you will find it, and whosoever rules it a miserable man. But come in, come in, and feast."

So he drew Jason in, whether he would or not, and spoke to him so lovingly and feasted him so well, that Jason's anger passed; and after supper his three cousins came into the hall, and Jason thought that he should like well enough to have one of them for his wife.

But at last he said to Pelias, "Why do you look so sad, my uncle? And what did you mean just now, when you said that this was a doleful kingdom, and its ruler a miserable man?"

Then Pelias sighed heavily again and again and again, like a man who had to tell some dreadful story and was afraid to begin; but at last —

"For seven long years and more have I never known a quiet night; and no more will he who comes after me, till the golden fleece be brought home."

Then he told Jason the story of Phrixus, and of the golden fleece; and told him, too, which was a lie, that Phrixus's spirit tormented him, calling to him day and night. And his daughters came, and told the same tale (for their father had taught them their parts), and wept, and said, "Oh, who will bring home the golden fleece, that our uncle's spirit may have rest; and that we may have rest also, whom he never lets sleep in peace?"

Jason sat awhile, sad and silent; for he had often heard of that golden fleece; but he looked on it as a thing hopeless and impossible for any mortal man to win it.

But when Pelias saw him silent, he began to talk of other things, and courted Jason more and more, speaking to him as if he was certain to be his heir, and asking his advice about the kingdom; till Jason, who was young and simple, could not help saying to himself, "Surely he is not the dark man whom people call him. Yet why did he drive my father out?" And he asked Pelias boldly, "Men say that you are terrible, and a man of blood; but I find you a kind and hospitable man; and as you are to me, so will I be to you. Yet why did you drive my father out?"

Pelias smiled and sighed: "Men have slandered me in that, as in all things. Your father was growing old and weary, and he gave the kingdom up to me of his own will. You shall see him to-morrow, and ask him; and he will tell you the same."

Jason's heart leapt in him, when he heard that he was to see his father; and he believed all that Pelias said, forgetting that his father might not dare to tell the truth.

"One thing more there is," said Pelias, "on which I need your advice; for though you are young, I see in you a wisdom beyond your years. There is one neighbour of mine, whom I dread more than all men on earth. I am stronger than he now, and can command him: but I know that if he stay among us, he will work my ruin in the end. Can you give me a plan, Jason, by which I can rid myself of that man?"

After awhile, Jason answered, half laughing, "Were I you, I would send him to fetch that same golden fleece; for if he once set forth after it you would never be troubled with him more."

And at that a bitter smile came across Pelias's lips, and a flash of wicked joy into his eyes; and Jason saw it, and started; and over his mind came the warning of the old man, and his own one sandal, and the oracle, and he saw that he was taken in a trap.

But Pelias only answered gently, "My son, he shall be sent forthwith."

"You mean me?" cried Jason, starting up, "because I came here with one sandal?" And he lifted his fist angrily, while Pelias stood up to him like a wolf at bay; and whether of the two was the stronger and the fiercer, it would be hard to tell.

But after a moment Pelias spoke gently — "Why then so rash, my son? You, and not I, have said what is said; why blame me for what I have not done? Had you bid me love the man of whom I spoke, and make him my son-in-law and heir, I would have obeyed you; and what if I obey you now, and send the man to win himself immortal fame? I have not harmed you, or him. One thing at least I know, that he will go, and that gladly: for he has a hero's heart within him; loving glory, and scorning to break the word which he has given."

Jason saw that he was entrapped: but his second promise to Cheiron came into his mind, and he thought, "What if the Centaur were a prophet in that also, and meant that I should win the fleece!" Then he cried aloud, —

"You have well spoken, cunning uncle of mine! I love glory, and I dare keep to my word. I will go and fetch this golden fleece. Promise me but this in return, and keep your word as I keep mine. Treat my father lovingly while I am gone, for the sake of the all-seeing Zeus; and give me up the kingdom for my own, on the day that I bring back the golden fleece."

Then Pelias looked at him and almost loved him, in the midst of all his hate; and said, "I promise, and I will perform. It will be no shame to give up my kingdom to the man who wins that fleece."

Then they swore a great oath between them; and afterwards both went in, and lay down to sleep.

But Jason could not sleep, for thinking of his mighty oath, and how he was to fulfil it, all alone, and without wealth or friends. So he tossed a long time upon his bed, and thought of this plan and of that; and sometimes Phrixus seemed to call him, in a thin voice, faint and low, as if it came from far across the sea — "Let me come home to my fathers and have rest." And sometimes he seemed to see the eyes of Hera, and to hear her words again, — "Call on me in the hour of need, and see if the Immortals can forget."

And on the morrow he went to Pelias, and said, "Give me a victim, that I may sacrifice to Hera." So he went up, and offered his sacrifice; and as he stood by the altar, Hera sent a thought into his mind; and he went back to Pelias, and said —

"If you are indeed in earnest, give me two heralds, that they may go round to all the princes of the Minuai, who were pupils of the Centaur with me, that we may fit out a ship together, and take what shall befall."

At that Pelias praised his wisdom, and hastened to send the heralds out; for he said in his heart, "Let all the princes go with him, and like him, never return; for so I shall be lord of all the Minuai, and the greatest king in Hellas."

ENGLAND

Beowulf's Fight with Grendel [1]

🙚 *Anglo-Saxon poetry is not like ours. Each line is divided into two parts with a pause in the middle and two accents in each half. Instead of rhyme it makes use of alliteration; that is, beginning sounds of accented syllables are repeated. For a modern example of alliteration, see Tennyson's poem* The Song of the Brook:

> *I slip, I slide, I gloom, I glance*
> *Among my skimming swallows.*

Nor does Anglo-Saxon poetry employ stanza form. There is no humor; and the poetry is filled with kennings — *metaphorical terms with conventional meaning. Mr. Mabie has avoided kennings in the translation given below, but examples are "the ring-giver," meaning a king; and "the gannet's bath," meaning the sea. Beowulf is an Anglo-Saxon epic composed not earlier than the eighth century. Though it stands at the beginning of English literature, the scene of the poem is the region around the Baltic Sea, and the hero is Scandinavian, representing the spirit of the Vikings.*

Old King Hrothgar built for himself a great palace, covered with gold, with benches all round outside, and a terrace leading up to it. It was bigger than any hall men had ever heard of, and there Hrothgar sat on his throne to share with men the good things

[1] From Hamilton Wright Mabie, *Legends Every Child Should Know* (Doubleday, 1906).

God had given him. A band of brave knights gathered round him, all living together in peace and joy.

But there came a wicked monster, Grendel, out of the moors. He stole across the fens in the thick darkness, and touched the great iron bars of the door of the hall, which immediately sprang open. Then, with his eyes shooting out flame, he spied the knights sleeping after battle. With his steel finger-nails the hideous fiend seized thirty of them in their sleep. He gave yells of joy, and sped as quick as lightning across the moors, to reach his home with his prey.

When the knights awoke, they raised a great cry of sorrow, whilst the aged king himself sat speechless with grief. None could do battle with the monster, he was too strong, too horrible for anyone to conquer. For twelve long years Grendel warred against Hrothgar; like a dark shadow of death he prowled round-about the hall, and lay in wait for his men on the misty moors. One thing he could not touch, and that was the king's sacred throne.

Now there lived in a far-off land a youngster called Beowulf, who had the strength of thirty men. He heard of the wicked deeds of Grendel, and the sorrow of the good King Hrothgar. So he had made ready a strong ship, and with fourteen friends set sail to visit Hrothgar, as he was in need of help. The good ship flew over the swelling ocean like a bird, till in due time the voyagers saw shining white cliffs before them. Then they knew their journey was at an end; they made fast their ship, grasped their weapons, and thanked God that they had had an easy voyage.

Now the coast guard spied them from a tower. He set off to the shore, riding on horseback, and brandishing a huge lance.

"Who are you," he cried, "bearing arms and openly landing here? I am bound to know from whence you come before you make a step forward. Listen to my plain words, and hasten to answer me."

Beowulf made answer that they came as friends, to rid Hrothgar of his wicked enemy Grendel, and at that the coast guard led them on to guide them to the king's palace. Downhill they ran together, with a rushing sound of voices and armed tread, until they saw the hall shining like gold against the sky. The guard bade them go straight to it, then, wheeling round on his horse, he said, "It is time for me to go. May the Father of All keep you in safety. For myself, I must guard the coast."

The street was paved with stone, and Beowulf's men marched along, following it to the hall, their armor shining in the sun and clanging as they went. They reached the terrace, where they set down their broad shields. Then they seated themselves on the bench, while they stacked their spears together and made themselves known to the herald.

Hrothgar speedily bade them welcome. They entered the great hall with measured tread, Beowulf leading the way. His armor shone like a golden network, and his look was high and noble, as he said, "Hail, O King! To fight against Grendel single-handed have I come. Grant me this, that I may have this task alone, I and my little band of men. I know that the terrible monster despises weapons, and therefore I shall bear neither sword, nor shield, nor buckler. Hand-to-hand I will fight the foe, and death shall come to whomsoever God wills. If death overtakes me, then will the monster carry away my body to the swamps, so care not for my body, but send my armor to my king. My fate is in God's hands."

Hrothgar loved the youth for his noble words, and bade him and his men sit down to the table and merrily share the feast, if they had a mind to do so. As they feasted, a minstrel sang with a clear voice. The queen, in cloth of gold, moved down the hall and handed the jeweled cup of mead to the king and all the warriors, old and young. At the right moment, with gracious words, she brought it to Beowulf. Full of pride and high purpose, the youth drank from the splendid cup, and vowed that he would conquer the enemy or die.

When the sun sank in the west, all the guests arose. The king bade Beowulf guard the house, and watch for the foe. "Have courage," he said, "be watchful, resolve on success. Not a wish of yours shall be left unfulfilled, if you perform this mighty deed."

Then Beowulf lay down to rest in the hall, putting off from him his coat of mail, helmet, and sword.

Through the dim night Grendel came stealing. All slept in the darkness, all but one! The door sprang open at the first touch that the monster gave it. He trod quickly over the paved floor of the hall; his eyes gleamed as he saw a troop of kinsmen lying together asleep. He laughed as he reckoned on sucking the life of each one before day broke. He seized a sleeping warrior, and in a trice had crunched his bones. Then he stretched out his hand to seize Beowulf on his bed. Quickly did Beowulf grip his arm; he stood up full length and grappled with him with all his might, till his fingers cracked as though they would burst. Never had Grendel felt such a grip; he had a mind to go, but could not. He roared, and the hall resounded with his yells, as up and down he raged, with Beowulf holding him in a fast embrace. The benches were overturned, the timbers of the hall cracked, the beautiful hall was all but wrecked. Beowulf's men had seized their weapons and thought to hack Grendel on every side, but no blade could touch him. Still Beowulf held him by the arm; his shoulder cracked, and he fled, wounded to death, leaving hand, arm, and shoulder in Beowulf's grasp. Over the moors, into the darkness, he sped as best he might, and to Beowulf was the victory.

Then, in the morning, many a warrior came from far and near. Riding in troops, they tracked the monster's path, where he had fled stricken to death. In a dismal pool he had yielded up his life.

Racing their horses over the green turf, they reached again the paved street. The golden roof of the palace glittered in the sunlight. The king stood on the terrace and gave thanks to God. "I have had much woe," he said, "but this lad, through God's might, has done the deed that we, with all our wisdom, could not do. Now I will heartily love you, Beowulf, as if you were my son. You shall want for nothing in this world, and your fame shall live forever."

The palace was cleansed, the walls hung anew with cloth of gold, the whole place was made fair and straight, for only the roof had been left altogether unhurt after the fight.

A merry feast was held. The king brought fourth out of his treasures a banner, helmet, and mail coat. These he gave to Beowulf; but more wonderful than all was a famous sword handed down to him through the ages. Then eight horses with golden cheekplates were brought within the court; one of them was saddled with King Hrothgar's own saddle, decorated with silver. Hrothgar gave all to Beowulf, bidding him enjoy them well. To each of Beowulf's men he gave rich gifts. The minstrels sang; the queen, beautiful and gracious, bore the cup to the king and Beowulf. To Beowulf she, too, gave gifts; mantle and bracelets and collar of gold. "Use these gifts," she said, "and prosper well! As far as the sea rolls your name shall be known."

Great was the joy of all till evening came. Then the hall was cleared of benches and strewn with beds. Beowulf, like the king, had his own bower this night to sleep in. The nobles lay down in the hall, at their heads they set their shields and placed ready their helmets and their mail coats. Each slept, ready in an instant to do battle for his lord.

So they sank to rest, little dreaming what deep sorrow was to fall on them.

Hrothgar's men sank to rest, but death was to be the portion of one. Grendel the monster was dead, but Grendel's mother still lived. Furious at the death of her son, she crept to the great hall, and made her way in, clutched an earl, the king's dearest friend, and crushed him in his sleep. Great was the uproar, though the terror was less than when Grendel came. The knights leapt up, sword in hand; the witch hurried to escape, she wanted to get out with her life.

The aged king felt bitter grief when he heard that his dearest friend was slain. He sent for Beowulf, who, like the king, had had his own sleeping bower that night. The youth stood before Hrothgar and hoped that all was well.

"Do not ask if things go well," said the sorrowing king, "we have fresh grief this morning. My dearest friend and noblest knight is slain. Grendel you yourself destroyed through the strength given you by God, but another monster has come to avenge his death. I have heard the country folk say that there were two huge fiends to be seen stalking over the moors, one like a woman, as near as they could make out, the the other had the form of a man, but was huger far. It was he they called Grendel. These two haunt a fearful spot, a land of untrodden bogs and windy cliffs. A waterfall plunges into the blackness below, and twisted trees with gnarled roots overhang it. An unearthly fire is seen gleaming there night after night. None can tell the depth of the stream. Even a stag, hunted to death, will face his foes on the bank rather than plunge into those waters. It is a fearful spot. You are our only help, dare you enter this horrible haunt?"

Quick was Beowulf's answer: "Sorrow not, O King! Rouse yourself quickly, and let us track the monster. Each of us must look for death, and he who has the chance should do mighty deeds before it comes. I promise you Grendel's kin shall not escape me, if she hide in the depths of the earth or of the ocean."

The king sprang up gladly, and Beowulf and his friends set out. They passed stony banks and narrow gullies, the haunts of goblins.

Suddenly they saw a clump of gloomy trees, overhanging a dreary pool. A shudder ran through them, for the pool was blood-red.

All sat down by the edge of the pool, while the horn sounded a cheerful blast. In the water were monstrous sea-snakes, and on jutting points of land were dragons and strange beasts: they tumbled away, full of rage, at the sound of the horn.

One of Beowulf's men took aim at a monster with his arrow, and pierced him through, so that he swam no more.

Beowulf was making ready for the fight. He covered his body with armor lest the fiend should clutch him. On his head was a white helmet decorated with figures of boars worked in silver. No weapon could hurt it. His sword was a wonder treasure, with an edge of iron; it had never failed any one who needed it in battle.

"Be like a father to my men, if I perish," said Beowulf to Hrothgar, "and send the rich gifts you have given me to my king. He will see that I had good fortune while life lasted. Either I will win fame, or death shall take me."

He dashed away, plunging headlong into the pool. It took nearly the whole day before he reached the bottom, and while he was still on his way the water-witch met him. For a hundred years she had lived in those depths. She made a grab at him, and caught him in her talons, but his coat of mail saved him from her loathsome fingers. Still she clutched him tight, and bore him in her arms to the bottom of the lake; he had no power to use his weapons, though he had courage enough. Water-beasts swam after him and battered him with their tusks.

Then he saw that he was in a vast hall, where there was no water, but a strange, unearthly glow of firelight. At once he began to fight, but the sword would not bite — it failed its master in his need; for the first time its fame broke down. Away Beowulf threw it in anger, trusting to the strength of his hands. He cared nothing for his own life, for he thought but of honor.

He seized the witch by the shoulder and swayed her so that she sank on the pavement. Quickly she recovered, and closed in on him; he staggered and fell, worn out. She sat on him, and drew her knife to take his life, but his good mail coat turned the point. He stood up again, and then truly God helped him, for he saw among the armor on the wall an old sword of huge size, the handiwork of giants. He seized it, and smote with all his might, so that the witch gave up her life.

His heart was full of gladness, and light, calm and beautiful as that of the sun, filled the hall. He scanned the vast chamber, and saw Grendel lying there dead. He cut off his head as a trophy for King Hrothgar, whose men the fiend had killed and devoured.

Now those men who were seated on the banks of the pool watching with Hrothgar saw that the water was tinged with blood. Then the old men spoke together of the brave Beowulf, saying they feared that they would never see him again. The day was waning fast, so they and the king went homeward. Beowulf's men stayed on, sick at heart, gazing at the pool. They longed, but did not expect, to see their lord and master.

Under the depths, Beowulf was making his way to them. The magic sword melted in his hand, like snow in sunshine; only the hilt remained, so venomous was the fiend that had been slain therewith. He brought nothing more with him than the hilt and Grendel's head. Up he rose through the waters where the furious sea-beasts before had chased him. Now not one was to be seen; the depths were purified when the witch lost her life. So he came to land, bravely swimming, bearing his spoils. His men saw him, they thanked God, and ran to free him of his armor. They rejoiced to get sight of him, sound and whole.

Now they marched gladly through the highways to the town. It took four of them to carry Grendel's head. On they went, all fourteen, their captain glorious in their midst. They entered the great hall, startling the king and queen, as they sat at meat, with the fearful sight of Grendel's head.

Beowulf handed the magic hilt to Hrothgar, who saw that it was the work of giants of old. He spake to Beowulf, while all held their peace, praised him for his courage, said that he would love him as his son, and bade him be a help to mankind, remembering not to glory in his own strength, for he held it from God, and death without more ado might subdue it altogether. "Many, many treasures," he said, "must pass from me to you tomorrow, but now rest and feast."

Gladly Beowulf sat down to the banquet, and well he liked the thought of the rest.

When day dawned, he bade the king farewell with noble words, promising to help him in time of need. Hrothgar with tears and embraces let him go, giving him fresh gifts of hoarded jewels. He wept, for he loved Beowulf well, and knew he would never see him any more.

The coast guard saw the gallant warriors coming, bade them welcome, and led them to their ship. The wind whistled in the sails, and a pleasant humming sound was heard as the good ship sped on her way. So Beowulf returned home, having done mighty deeds and gained great honor.

In due time Beowulf himself became King, and well he governed the land for fifty years. Then trouble came.

A slave, fleeing from his master, stumbled by an evil chance into the den of a dragon. There he saw a dazzling hoard of gold, guarded by the dragon for three hundred winters. The treasure tempted him, and he carried off a tankard of gold to give to his master, to make peace with him.

The dragon had been sleeping; now he awoke, and sniffed the scent of an enemy along the rock. He hunted diligently over the ground; he wanted to find the man who had done the mischief in his sleep. In his rage he swung around the treasure mound, dashing into it now and again to seek the jeweled tankard. He found it hard to wait until evening came, when he meant to avenge with fire the loss of his treasure.

Presently the sun sank, and the dragon had his will. He set forth, burning all the cheerful homes of men; his rage was felt far and wide. Before dawn he shot back again to his dark home, trusting in his mound and in his craft to defend himself.

Now Beowulf heard that his own home had been burnt to the ground. It was a great grief to him, almost making him break out in a rage against Providence. His breast heaved with anger.

He meant to rid his country of the plague, and to fight the dragon single-handed. He would have thought it shame to seek him with a large band, he who, as a lad, had killed Grendel and his kin. As he armed for the fray, many thoughts filled his mind; he remembered the days of his youth, and manhood. "I fought many wars in my youth," he said, "and now that I am aged, and the keeper of my people, I will yet again seek the enemy and do famously."

He bade his men await him on the mountain-side. They were to see which of the two would come alive out of the tussle.

There the aged king beheld where a rocky archway stood, with a stream of fire gushing from it; no one could stand there and not be scorched. He gave a great shout, and the dragon answered with a hot breath of flame. Beowulf, with drawn sword, stood well up to his shield, when the burning dragon, curved like an arch, came headlong upon him. The shield saved him but little; he swung up the sword to smite the horrible monster, but its edge did not bite. Sparks flew around him on every side; he saw that the end of his days had come.

His men crept away to the woods to save their lives. One, and one only, Wiglaf by name, sped through the smoke and flame to help his lord.

"My Lord Beowulf!" he cried, "with all your might defend life; I will support you to the utmost."

The dragon came on in fury; in a trice the flames consumed Wiglaf's shield, but, nothing daunted, he stepped under the shelter of Beowulf's as his own fell in ashes about him. The king remembered his strength of old, and he smote with his sword with such force that it stuck in the monster's head, while splinters flew all around. His hand was so strong that, as men used to say, he broke any sword in using it, and was none the worse for it.

Now, for the third time, the dragon rushed upon him, and seized him by the neck with his poisonous fangs. Wiglaf, with no thought for himself, rushed forward, though he was scorched with the flames, and smote the dragon lower down than Beowulf had done before. With such effect the sword entered the dragon's body that from that moment the fire began to cease.

The king, recovering his senses, drew his knife and ended the monster's life. So these two together destroyed the enemy of the people. To Beowulf that was the greatest moment of his life, when he saw his work completed.

The wound that the dragon had given him began to burn and swell, for the poison had entered it. He knew that the tale of his days was told. As he rested on a stone by the mound, he pondered thoughtfully, looking on the cunning work of the dwarfs of old, the stone arches on their rocky pillars. Wiglaf, with tender care, unloosed his helmet and brought him water, Beowulf discoursing the while: "Now I would gladly have given my armor to my son, had God granted me one. I have ruled this people fifty years, and no king has dared attack them. I have held my own with justice, and no friend has lost his life through me. Though I am sick with deadly wounds, I have comfort in this. Now go quickly, beloved Wiglaf; show me the ancient wealth that I have won for my people, the gold and brilliant gems, that I may then contentedly give up my life."

Quickly did Wiglaf enter the mound at the bidding of his master. On every side he saw gold and jewels and choice vases, helmets and bracelets, and overhead a marvelous banner, all golden, gleaming with light, so that he could scan the surface of the floor and see the curious treasured hoards. He filled his lap full of golden cups and platters, and also took the brilliant banner.

He hastened to return with his spoils, wondering, with pain, if he should find his king still alive. He bore his treasures to him, laid them on the ground, and again sprinkled him with water. "I thank God," said the dying king, "that I have been permitted to win this treasure for my people; now they will have all that they need. But I cannot be any longer here. Bid my men make a lofty mound on the headland overlooking the sea, and there place my ashes. In time to come men shall call it Beowulf's Barrow; it shall tower aloft to guide sailors over the stormy seas."

The brave king took from his neck his golden collar, took his helmet and his coronet, and gave them to his true knight, Wiglaf. "Fate has swept all my kinsmen away," said he, "and now I must follow them."

That was his last word, as his soul departed from his bosom, to join the company of the just.

Of all kings in the world, he was, said his men, the gentlest to his knights and the most desirous of honor.

How St. George Fought the Dragon[2]

St. George is said to have been born in Cappadocia (Asia Minor) of Christian parents. The legend is that he was put to death by the Roman Emperor Diocletian because he protested against that emperor's persecutions of the Christians. His connection with the dragon goes back to the end of the sixth century, and the story was told by one Jacobus de Voragine in his Golden Legends. *He has been the national saint of England since the First Crusade, when he is supposed to have given miraculous help to Godfrey de Bouillon.*

And by my pen I will recite
Saint George's deeds, an English knight.

Away back in the second century after Christ, many hundred years before the coming of King Arthur, the ancient city of Coventry gave birth to Saint George, the first Christian hero of England, who was also the first knight-errant that ever sought adventure in foreign lands. He deemed it dishonorable, when he grew to be a man, to spend his time at home in idleness, and not achieve somewhat by valor and prowess, so he set out from England in search of worthy adventure.

After many months of travel by sea and land George came in his journeyings to Egypt, which country was then greatly annoyed by a dangerous dragon. It is a fearsome description of him that the minstrel of that day gives.

Within that country there did rest
A dreadful dragon, fierce and fell,
Whereby they were full sore oppressed.
Who by his poisonous breath each day
Did many of the city slay.
His skin more hard than brass was found,
That sword nor lance could pierce nor wound.

2 From Marion Florence Lansing, *Page, Squire, and Knight* (Ginn, 1910).

This terrible dragon had ranged up and down the country for twenty-four years, killing many and leaving devastation in his path.

George, seeking for shelter one night, was told this tale by an old hermit at whose door he knocked. Only on days when an innocent maiden was offered up to be swallowed alive, the old man told him, did the dragon cease to give forth this poisonous breath, against which no man living could stand. But now, alas! all the maidens had been offered up. In all Egypt there was none left but the king's daughter, and on the morrow she must give herself to the dragon unless some brave knight could be found who should have courage to encounter him and kill him. To such a knight the king had promised to give his daughter in marriage and the crown of Egypt after his death.

The tale of this terrible monster and the news of the royal reward so fired the English knight that he vowed that he would either save the king's daughter or lose his own life in so glorious an enterprise. He took his repose with the old hermit that night, and at sunrise buckled on his armor and journeyed to the valley where the king's daughter was to be offered up. The bold knight had scarce entered the valley where the dragon had his abode, when the fiery monster caught sight of him and sent forth from his leathern throat a sound more terrible than thunder. George turned and beheld the dreadful sight. The size of this fell dragon was fearful to behold, for his length from his shoulder to his tail was more than fifty feet, and the scales on his body shone like glittering brass. The knight rode against him with all his speed, thrusting his spear straight at the fiery dragon's jaws, but it broke to splinters against those brass-like scales.

> The dragon then 'gan him assail,
> And smote our hero with his tail;
> Then down before him went horse and man,
> Two ribs of George were bruiséd then.
> Up started George with right good will,
> And after ran the dragon still.
> The dragon was aggrievéd sore,
> And smote at George more and more.
> Long and hard was the fight
> Between the dragon and the knight.

At last George hit him under the right wing, which was the only place where there were no scales. He smote so hard with his sword that it went in up to the hilt, and the dragon fell lifeless on the ground.

Thus within the view of the maiden who was waiting to be offered up he slew the dragon.

> When as that valiant champion there
> Had slain the dragon in the field,
> To court he brought the lady fair,
> Which to all hearts much joy did yield.

When the people of the city saw him coming with the dragon's head upon his spear, they began to ring the bells, and brought him into town with great procession. Not only in Egypt but in all the world he was held in great honor, and was made welcome in every place wherever he journeyed for that brave deed. In those days he was reckoned one of the seven great champions of the world, and so dearly did all knights hold him in remembrance in later days that they called upon him for aid in battle, thinking of him as a saint in heaven; and the story goes, as you have read, that when the knights were in great danger at Jerusalem, he did appear to Godfrey and the army and signed them on to enter and conquer the Holy City. Many times the soldiers returned from battle with the tale of how, when the day was going against them and they had prayed for aid, they had seen Saint George appear in white armor, with the blood-red cross on his shoulder and the dragon on his shield, and always thereafter the soldiers pushed forward with fresh enthusiasm and won the day, shouting,

> "Saint George of merry England,
> The sign of victory."

King Arthur and His Sword [3]

⊰ Though it seems certain that there never was a King Arthur, it seems equally sure there was a chieftain of that name. Interwoven with the story of Arthur as a historical character are

[3] From Sidney Lanier, The Boy's King Arthur (Scribner, 1917).

mythical, romantic, and fairy-like elements. The legend shows the influence of the Charlemagne cycle in the appearance of the three ladies at his birth, as at that of Ogier. The influence of the northern hero-myths is shown in the episode where Arthur has to pull the sword from the stone to prove his right to be king, just as Sigmund pulls the sword from the ash tree to prove his right to be a leader. Tennyson's stories of Arthur, with which we are most familiar, are very misleading both as to the character of King Arthur and the few facts as given in the earliest poems. In English literature, the wellspring of the Arthurian stories is Malory's translation of the French Morte Darthur *(1470); this is the version followed in the retelling below.*

It befell in the days of the noble Utherpendragon, when he was King of England, that there was born to him a son who in after time was King Arthur. Howbeit the boy knew not he was the king's son. For when he was but a babe the king commanded two knights and two ladies to take the child bound in rich cloth of gold, "and deliver him to what poor man you meet at the postern gate of the castle." So the child was delivered unto Merlin, and so he bare it forth unto Sir Ector, and made an holy man to christen him, and named him Arthur; and so Sir Ector's wife nourished him. Then within two years King Uther fell sick of a great malady; and thereof he died. Then stood the realm in great danger a long while, for every lord made him strong, and many weened (thought) to have been king. And so, by Merlin's counsel, all the lords of England came together in the greatest church of London on Christmas morn before it was day, to see if God would not show by some miracle who should be king. And when the first mass was done there was seen in the church-yard, against the high altar, a great stone foursquare, like to a marble stone, and in the midst thereof was an anvil of steel, a foot of height, and therein stuck a fair sword naked by the point, and letters of gold were written about the sword that said thus: WHO SO PULLETH OUT THIS SWORD OF THIS STONE AND ANVIL, IS RIGHTWISE KING BORN OF ENGLAND.

So when all the masses were done, all the lords went for to behold the stone and the sword. And when they saw the scripture, some assayed (tried) such as would have been king. But none might stir the sword nor move it.

"He is not yet here," said the archbishop, "that shall achieve the sword, but doubt not God will make him to be known. But this is my counsel," said the archbishop, "that we let purvey (provide) ten knights, men of good fame, and they to keep this sword."

And upon New Year's day the barons let make a tournament for to keep the lords together, for the archbishop trusted that God would make him known that should win the sword. So upon New Year's day when the service was done the barons rode to the field.

And so it happened that Sir Ector rode to the jousts, and with him rode Sir Kay, his son, and young Arthur that was his nourished brother. But Sir Kay had lost his sword, for he had left it at his father's lodging, and so he prayed young Arthur to ride for his sword. "I will with a good will," said Arthur, and rode fast after the sword; and when he came home, the lady and all were gone out to see the jousting. Then was Arthur wroth, and said to himself, "I will ride to the church-yard and take the sword with me that sticketh in the stone, for my brother Sir Kay shall not be without a sword this day." And so when he came to the church-yard Arthur alighted and tied his horse to the stile, and so went to the tent, and found no knights there, for they were all at the jousting: and so he handled the sword by the handles, and lightly and fiercely he pulled it out of the stone, and took his horse and rode his way till he came to his brother Sir Kay, and delivered him the sword. And as soon as Sir Kay saw the sword, he wist (knew) well that it was the sword of the stone, and so he rode to his father, Sir Ector, and said: "Sir, lo here is the sword of the stone; wherefore I must be king of this land." When Sir Ector beheld the sword, he returned again and came to the church, and there they alighted, all three, and went into the church, and anon he made Sir Kay to swear upon a book how he came to that sword.

"Sir," said Sir Kay, "by my brother Arthur, for he brought it to me."

"How gate (got) you this sword?" said Sir Ector to Arthur.

"Sir, I will tell you. When I came home for my brother's sword, I found nobody at home for to deliver me his sword, and so I thought my brother Sir Kay should not be swordless, and so I came thither eagerly and pulled it out of the stone without any pain."

"Found ye any knights about this sword?" said Sir Ector.

"Nay," said Arthur.

"Now," said Sir Ector to Arthur, "I understand that you must be king of this land."

"Wherefore I?" said Arthur.

"Sir," said Ector, "for there should never man have drawn out this sword but he that shall be rightwise king of this land. Now let me see whether ye can put the sword there as it was and pull it out again."

"That is no mastery," said Arthur; and so he put it in the stone. Therewith Sir Ector assayed to pull out the sword, and failed.

"Now assay," said Sir Ector to Sir Kay. And anon he pulled at the sword with all his might but it would not be. "Now assay shall ye," said Sir Ector to Arthur.

"I will well," said Arthur, and pulled it out easily. And therewithal Sir Ector kneeled down to the earth, and Sir Kay.

"Alas," said Arthur, "mine own dear father and brother, why kneel ye to me?"

"Nay, nay, my lord Arthur, it is not so: I was never your father nor of your blood, but I wote (know) well ye are of an higher blood than I weened (thought) you were." And then Sir Ector told him all. Then Arthur made great moan when he understood that Sir Ector was not his father.

"Sir," said Ector unto Arthur, "will ye be my good and gracious lord when ye are king?"

"Else were I to blame," said Arthur, "for ye are the man in the world that I am most beholding (obliged) to, and my good lady and mother your wife, that as well as her own hath fostered and kept me. And if ever it be God's will that I be king, as ye say, ye shall desire of me what I may do, and I shall not fail you."

"Sir," said Sir Ector, "I will ask no more of you but that you make my son, your fostered brother Sir Kay, seneschal of all your lands."

"That shall be done, sir," said Arthur, "and more by the faith of my body; and never man shall have that office but he while that he and I live."

There withal they went unto the archbishop, and told him how the sword was achieved, and by whom. And upon the twelfth day all the barons came thither for to assay to take the sword. But there afore them all, there might none take it out but only Arthur; wherefore there were many great lords wroth, and said, "It was great shame unto them all and the realm to be governed by a boy of no high blood born." And so they fell out at that time, that it was put off till Candlemas, and then all the barons should meet there again. But always the ten knights were ordained for to watch the sword both day and night; and so they set a pavilion over the stone and the sword, and five always watched. And at Candlemas many more great lords came thither for to have won the sword, but none of them might prevail. And right as Arthur did at Christmas he did at Candlemas, and pulled out the sword easily, whereof the barons were sore aggrieved, and put it in delay till the high feast of Easter. And as Arthur sped afore, so did he at Easter; and yet there were some of the great lords had indignation that Arthur should be their king, and put it off in delay till the feast of Pentecost.

And at the feast of Pentecost all manner of men assayed to pull at the sword that would assay, and none might prevail; but Arthur pulled it out afore all the lords and commons that were there, wherefore all the commons cried at once: "We will have Arthur unto our king; we will put him no more in delay; for we all see that it is God's will that he shall be our king, and who that holdeth against it we will slay him." And therewithal they kneeled down all at once, both rich and poor, and cried Arthur mercy, because they had delayed him so long. And Arthur forgave it them, and took the sword between both his hands, and offered it upon the altar where the archbishop was, and so was he made knight of the best man that was there. And so anon was the coronation made, and there

496 ANTHOLOGY OF CHILDREN'S LITERATURE

was he sworn to the lords and commons for to be a true king, to stand with true justice from henceforth all the days of this life. Also then he made all lords that held of the crown to come in, and to do service as they ought to do. And many complaints were made unto King Arthur of great wrongs that were done since the death of King Uther, of many lands that were bereaved of lords, knights, ladies and gentlemen. Wherefore King Arthur made the lands to be given again unto them that owned them. When this was done that the king had stablished all the countries about London, then he let make Sir Kay seneschal of England; and Sir Baudwin of Britain was made constable; and Sir Ulfius was made chamberlain; and Sir Brastias was made warden to wait upon the north from Trent forwards, for it was that time for the most part enemy to the king.

Then on a day there came into the court a squire on horseback, leading a knight before him wounded to the death, and told him there was a knight in the forest that had reared up a pavilion by a well (spring) side, "and hath slain my master, a good knight, and his name was Miles; wherefore I beseech you that my master may be buried, and that some good knight may revenge my master's death." Then was in the court great noise of the knight's death, and every man said his advice. Then came Griflet, that was but a squire, and he was but young, of the age of King Arthur, so he besought the king, for all his service that he had done, to give him the order of knighthood.

"Thou art full young and tender of age," said King Arthur, "for to take so high an order upon thee."

"Sir," said Griflet, "I beseech you to make me a knight."

"Sir," said Merlin, "it were pity to leese (lose) Griflet, for he will be a passing good man when he cometh to age, abiding with you the term of his life; and if he adventure his body with yonder knight at the fountain, he shall be in great peril if ever he come again, for he is one of the best knights of the world, and the strongest man of arms."

"Well," said King Arthur. So, at the desire of Griflet, the king made him knight.

"Now," said King Arthur to Sir Griflet, "sithen (since) that I have made thee knight, thou must grant me a gift."

"What ye will, my lord," said Sir Griflet.

"Thou shalt promise me, by the faith of thy body, that when thou has jousted with the knight at the fountain, whether it fall (happen) that ye be on foot or on horseback, that in the same manner ye shall come again unto me without any question or making any more debate."

"I will promise you," said Griflet, "as ye desire." Then Sir Griflet took his horse in great haste, and dressed his shield, and took a great spear in his hand, and so he rode a great gallop till he came to the fountain, and thereby he saw a rich pavilion, and thereby under a cloth stood a fair horse well saddled and bridled, and on a tree a shield of divers colors, and a great spear. Then Sir Griflet smote upon the shield with the end of his spear, that the shield fell down to the ground.

With that came the knight out of the pavilion, and said, "Fair knight, why smote ye down my shield?"

"For I will joust with you," said Sir Griflet.

"It were better ye did not," said the knight, "for ye are but young and late made knight, and your might is nothing to mine."

"As for that," said Sir Griflet, "I will joust with you."

"That is me loth," said the knight, "but sith (since) I must needs, I will dress me thereto; but of whence be ye?" said the knight.

"Sir, I am of King Arthur's court." So they ran together that Sir Griflet's spear all to-shivered (shivered all to pieces) and therewithal he smote Sir Griflet through the shield and the left side, and brake the spear, that the truncheon stuck in his body, that horse and knight fell down.

When the knight saw him lie so on the ground he alighted, and was passing heavy, for he wend (weened) he had slain him, and then he unlaced his helm and got him wind, and so with the truncheon he set him on his horse, and betook him to God, and said he had a mighty heart, and if he might live he would prove a passing good knight. And so Sir Griflet rode to the court, whereas great moan was made for him. But through good leeches (surgeons) he was healed and his life saved.

And King Arthur was passing wroth for the hurt of Sir Griflet. And by and by he commanded a man of his chamber that his best horse and armor "be without the city or (before) tomorrow day." Right so in the morning he met with his man and his horse, and so mounted up and dressed his shield, and took his spear, and bade his chamberlain tarry there till he came again. And so King Arthur rode but a soft pace till it was day, and then was he ware of three churls which chased Merlin, and would have slain him. Then King Arthur rode unto them a good pace, and cried to them: "Flee, churls." Then were they afraid when they saw a knight, and fled away. "O Merlin," said King Arthur, "here hadst thou been slain for thy craft, had I not been."

"Nay," said Merlin, "not so, for I could save myself if I would, and thou art more near thy death than I am, for thou goest towards thy death, and God be not thy friend."

So, as they went thus talking, they came to the fountain, and the rich pavilion by it. Then King Arthur was aware where a knight sat all armed in a chair. "Sir Knight," said King Arthur, "for what cause abidest thou here? That there may no knight ride this way but if he do joust with thee?" said the king. "I rede (advise) thee leave that custom," said King Arthur.

"This custom," said the knight, "have I used and will use, maugre (in spite of) who saith nay; and who is grieved with my custom, let him amend it that will."

"I will amend it," said King Arthur.

"And I shall defend it," said the knight. Anon he took his horse, and dressed his shield, and took a spear, and they met so hard either on other's shield, that they all to-shivered (shivered all to pieces) their spears. Therewith King Arthur drew his sword. "Nay, not so," said the knight, "it is fairer that we twain run more together with sharp spears."

"I will well," said King Arthur, "an (if) I had any (more) spears."

"I have spears enough," said the knight. So there came a squire, and brought two good spears, and King Arthur took one and he the other. So they spurred their horses, and came together with all their mights, that either brake their spears to their hands. Then Arthur set hand on his sword. "Nay," said the knight, "ye shall do better; ye are a passing good jouster as ever I met withal, and for the love of the high order of knighthood let us joust once again."

"I assent me," said King Arthur. Anon there were brought two great spears, and every knight gat a spear, and therewith they ran together that Arthur's spear all to-shivered. But the other knight hit him so hard in midst of the shield that horse and man fell to the earth, and therewith Arthur was eager, and pulled out his sword, and said, "I will assay thee, Sir Knight, on foot, for I have lost the honor on horseback."

"I will be on horseback," said the knight. Then was Arthur wroth, and dressed his shield towards him with his sword drawn. When the knight saw that, he alight, for him thought no worship to have a knight at such avail, he to be on horseback, and he on foot, and so he alight and dressed his shield unto Arthur. And there began a strong battle with many great strokes, and so hewed with their swords that the cantels (pieces, of armor or of flesh) flew in the fields, and much blood they bled both, that all the place there as they fought was over-bled with blood, and thus they fought long, and rested them, and then they went to the battle again, and so hurtled together like two rams that either fell to the earth. So at the last they smote together, that both their swords met even together. But the sword of the knight smote King Arthur's sword in two pieces, wherefore he was heavy. Then said the knight unto Arthur, "Thou art in my danger whether me list to save thee or slay thee, and but thou yield thee as overcome and recreant thou shalt die."

"As for death," said King Arthur, "welcome be it when it cometh, but as to yield me to thee as recreant, I had liever die than to be so shamed." And therewithal the king leapt unto Pellinore, and took him by the middle, and threw him down, and raced off his helm. When the knight felt that, he was adread, for he was a passing big man of might, and anon he brought King Arthur under him, and raced off his helm, and would have smitten off his head.

Therewithal came Merlin, and said: "Knight, hold thy hand, for an (if) thou slay that knight, thou puttest this realm in the greatest damage that ever realm was in, for this knight is a man of more worship than thou wottest of."

"Why, who is he?" said the knight.

"It is King Arthur."

Then would he have slain him for dread of his wrath, and heaved up his sword, and therewith Merlin cast an enchantment on the knight, that he fell to the earth in a great sleep. Then Merlin took up King Arthur, and rode forth upon the knight's horse. "Alas," said King Arthur, "what hast thou done, Merlin? hast thou slain this good knight by thy crafts? There lived not so worshipful a knight as he was; I had liever than the stint (loss) of my land a year, that he were on live."

"Care ye not," said Merlin, "for he is wholer than ye, for he is but on sleep, and will awake within three hours. I told you," said Merlin, "what a knight he was; here had ye been slain had I not been. Also, there liveth not a better knight than he is, and he shall do you hereafter right good service, and his name is Pellinore, and he shall have two sons, that shall be passing good men."

Right so the king and he departed, and went unto an hermit that was a good man and a great leech. So the hermit searched all his wounds and gave him good salves; and the king was there three days, and then were his wounds well amended that he might ride and go. So Merlin and he departed, and as they rode, Arthur said, "I have no sword."

"No force," said Merlin, "hereby is a sword that shall be yours, an (if) I may." So they rode till they came to a lake, which was a fair water and a broad, and in the middest of the lake King Arthur was ware of an arm clothed in white samite, that held a fair sword in the hand. "Lo," said Merlin, "yonder is that sword that I spake of." With that they saw a damsel going upon the lake.

"What damsel is that?" said Arthur.

"That is the Lady of the Lake," said Merlin; "and this damsel will come to you anon, and then speak ye fair to her that she will give you that sword." Anon withal came the damsel unto Arthur and saluted him, and he her again.

"Damsel," said Arthur, "what sword is that, that yonder the arm holdeth above the water? I would it were mine, for I have no sword."

"Sir king," said the damsel, "that sword is mine, and if ye will give me a gift when I ask it you, ye shall have it."

"By my faith," said Arthur, "I will give you what gift ye will ask."

"Well," said the damsel, "go ye into yonder barge and row yourself to the sword, and take it and the scabbard with you, and I will ask my gift when I see my time."

So King Arthur and Merlin alighted and tied their horses to two trees, and so they went into the ship, and when they came to the sword that the hand held, King Arthur took it up by the handles, and took it with him. And the arm and the hand went under the water; and so they came unto the land and rode forth. And then King Arthur saw a rich pavilion: "What signifieth yonder pavilion?"

"It is the knight's pavilion," said Merlin, "that ye fought with last, Sir Pellinore, but he is out, he is not there; he hath ado with a knight of yours, that hight (was named) Egglame, and they have fought together, but at the last Egglame fled, and else he had been dead, and he hath chased him to Caerleon, and we shall anon meet with him in the high way."

"It is well said," quoth King Arthur, "now have I a sword, and now will I wage battle with him and be avenged on him."

"Sir, ye shall not do so," said Merlin, "for the knight is weary of fighting and chasing, so that ye shall have no worship to have ado with him; also he will not lightly be matched of one knight living; and therefore my counsel is that ye let him pass, for he shall do you good service in short time, and his sons after his days. Also ye shall see that day in short space, that ye shall be right glad to give him your sister to wife."

"When I see him," said King Arthur, "I will do as ye advise me."

Then King Arthur looked upon the sword and liked it passing well.

"Whether liketh you better," said Merlin, "the sword or the scabbard?"

"Me liketh better the sword," said King Arthur.

"Ye are more unwise," said Merlin, "for the scabbard is worth ten of the sword, for while ye have the scabbard upon you ye shall leese (lose) no blood be ye never so sore wounded, therefore keep well the scabbard alway with you."

So they rode on to Caerleon, and by the way they met with Sir Pellinore. But Merlin had done such a craft that Pellinore saw not Arthur, and so he passed by without any words.

"I marvel," said the king, "that the knight would not speak."

"Sir," said Merlin, "he saw you not, for an (if) he had seen you he had not lightly departed."

So they came unto Caerleon, whereof the knights were passing glad; and when they heard of his adventures, they marveled that he would jeopard his person so alone. But all men of worship said it was merry to be under such a chieftain that would put his person in adventure as other poor knights did.

Robin Hood and Little John [4]

&s *The popularity of Robin Hood, even in this day of science fiction and space exploration, is due no doubt to the fact that here is a hero who upholds the ideals of fair play, champions the cause of the poor and weak against the tyranny of the wealthy and the mighty, and leads a life in the greenwood which appeals to the enduring belief that the pastoral way of existence is the ideal one. Above all, Robin Hood is a man of action.*

He is a folk hero; his feats and adventures have their origins in the popular ballads of the common people. Whether he ever existed is debatable, but exist he does as an ideal of medieval England, a free man in a ruthless world, with a generous sense of humor and a passion for justice.

[4] From Howard Pyle, *The Merry Adventures of Robin Hood of Great Renown in Nottinghamshire* (Scribner, 1883).

The earliest appearance of his name in print occurs in the poem Piers Plowman, *by William Langland, in the fourteenth century. Many of the chapbooks of the early eighteenth century were devoted to accounts of him, in ballad form. From such stuff epics have been formed, but though one can see, in these scattered sources, the outlines of an epic hero, no poet emerged to give the majesty of epic form to the crude tales.*

Howard Pyle (1853–1911), the American author, artist and teacher, brought up on ballads and old tales, gave the stories of Robin Hood an epic stature for young readers. The Merry Adventures of Robin Hood, published in 1883, is a glorious re-creation of the medieval world, true in every detail to the spirit of the age, and to the idealization which the era awakens in the minds of children. The vivid, poetic text is sustained and extended by his own superb illustrations in clear line and strong design.

Up rose Robin Hood one merry morn when all the birds were singing blithely among the leaves, and up rose all his merry men, each fellow washing his head and hands in the cold brown brook that leaped laughing from stone to stone. Then said Robin: "For fourteen days have we seen no sport, so now I will go abroad to seek adventures forthwith. But tarry ye, my merry men all, here in the greenwood; only see that ye mind well my call. Three blasts upon the bugle horn I will blow in my hour of need; then come quickly, for I shall want your aid."

So saying, he strode away through the leafy forest glades until he had come to the verge of Sherwood. There he wandered for a long time, through highway and byway, through dingly dell and forest skirts. Now he met a fair buxom lass in a shady lane, and each gave the other a merry word and passed their way; now he saw a fair lady upon an ambling pad, to whom he doffed his cap, and who bowed sedately in return to the fair youth; now he saw a fat monk on a pannier-laden ass; now a gallant knight, with spear and shield and armor that flashed brightly in the sunlight; now a page clad in crimson; and now a stout burgher from good Nottingham Town, pacing along with serious footsteps; all these sights he saw, but adventure found he none. At last he took a road by the forest skirts; a bypath that dipped toward a broad, pebbly stream spanned by a narrow bridge made of a log of wood. As he drew nigh this bridge, he saw a tall stranger coming from the other side. Thereupon Robin quickened his pace, as did the stranger likewise; each thinking to cross first.

"Now stand thou back," quoth Robin, "and let the better man cross first."

"Nay," answered the stranger, "then stand back thine own self, for the better man, I wot, am I."

"That will we presently see," quoth Robin; "and meanwhile stand thou where thou art, or else, by the bright brow of Saint Ælfrida, I will show thee right good Nottingham play with a clothyard shaft betwixt thy ribs."

"Now," quoth the stranger, "I will tan thy hide till it be as many colors as a beggar's cloak, if thou darest so much as touch a string of that same bow that thou holdest in thy hands."

"Thou pratest like an ass," said Robin, "for I could send this shaft clean through thy proud heart before a curtal friar could say grace over a roast goose at Michaelmastide."

"And thou pratest like a coward," answered the stranger, "for thou standest there with a good yew bow to shoot at my heart, while I have nought in my hand but a plain blackthorn staff wherewith to meet thee."

"Now," quoth Robin, "by the faith of my heart, never have I had a coward's name in all my life before. I will lay by my trusty bow and eke my arrows, and if thou darest abide my coming, I will go and cut a cudgel to test thy manhood withal."

"Ay, marry, that will I abide thy coming, and joyously, too," quoth the stranger; whereupon he leaned sturdily upon his staff to await Robin.

Then Robin Hood stepped quickly to the coverside and cut a good staff of round oak, straight, without flaw, and six feet in length, and came back trimming away the tender stems from it, while the stranger waited for him, leaning upon his staff, and whistling as he gazed roundabout. Robin observed him furtively as he trimmed his staff, measuring him from top to toe from out the corner of his eye, and thought that he had never seen a lustier or a stouter man. Tall was Robin, but taller was the stranger by a head and a neck, for he was seven feet in height. Broad was Robin across the shoulders, but broader was the stranger by twice the breadth of a palm, while he measured at least an ell around the waist.

"Nevertheless," said Robin to himself, "I will baste thy hide right merrily, my good fellow"; then, aloud, "Lo, here is my good staff, lusty and tough. Now wait my coming, an thou darest, and meet me, an thou fearest not; then we will fight until one or the other of us tumble into the stream by dint of blows."

"Marry, that meeteth my whole heart!" cried the stranger, twirling his staff above his head, betwixt his fingers and thumb, until it whistled again.

Never did the Knights of Arthur's Round Table meet a stouter fight than did these two. In a moment Robin stepped quickly upon the bridge where the stranger stood; first he made a feint, and then delivered a blow at the stranger's head that, had it met its mark, would have tumbled him speedily into the water; but the stranger turned the blow right deftly, and in return gave one as stout, which Robin also turned as the stranger had done. So they stood, each in his place, neither moving a finger's breadth back, for one good hour, and many blows were given and received by each in that time, till here and there were sore bones and bumps, yet neither thought of crying "Enough!" or seemed likely to fall from off the bridge. Now and then they stopped to rest, and each thought that he never had seen in all his life before such a hand at quarterstaff. At last Robin gave the stranger a blow upon the ribs that made his jacket smoke like a damp straw thatch in the sun. So shrewd was the stroke that the stranger came within a hair's breadth of falling off the bridge; but he regained himself right quickly, and, by a dexterous blow, gave Robin a crack on the crown that caused the blood to flow. Then Robin grew mad with anger, and smote with all his might at the other; but the stranger warded the blow, and once again thwacked Robin, and this time so fairly that he fell heels over head into the water, as the queen pin falls in a game of bowls.

"And where art thou now, good lad?" shouted the stranger, roaring with laughter.

"Oh, in the flood and floating adown with the tide," cried Robin; nor could he forbear laughing himself at his sorry plight. Then, gaining his feet, he waded to the bank, the little fish speeding hither and thither, all frightened at his splashing.

"Give me thy hand," cried he, when he had reached the bank, "I must needs own thou art a brave and a sturdy soul, and, withal, a good stout stroke with the cudgels. By this and by that, my head hummeth like to a hive of bees on a hot June day."

Then he clapped his horn to his lips, and winded a blast that went echoing sweetly down the forest paths. "Ay, marry," quoth he again, "thou are a tall lad, and eke a brave one, for ne'er, I trow, is there a man betwixt here and Canterbury Town could do the like to me that thou hast done."

"And thou," quoth the stranger, laughing, "takest thy cudgeling like a brave heart and a stout yeoman."

But now the distant twigs and branches rustled with the coming of men, and suddenly a score or two of good stout yeomen, all clad in Lincoln green, burst from out the covert, with merry Will Stutely at their head.

"Good master," cried Will, "how is this? Truly thou art all wet from head to foot, and that to the very skin."

"Why, marry," answered jolly Robin, "yon stout fellow hath tumbled me neck and crop into the water, and hath given me a drubbing beside."

"Then shall he not go without a ducking and eke a drubbing himself!" cried Will Stutely. "Have at him, lads!"

Then Will and a score of yeomen leaped upon the stranger, but though they sprang quickly they found him ready and felt him strike right and left with his stout staff, so that, though he went down with press of numbers, some of them rubbed cracked crowns before he was overcome.

"Nay, forbear!" cried Robin, laughing until his sore sides ached again; "he is a right good man and true, and no harm shall befall him. Now hark ye, good youth, wilt thou stay with me and be one of my band? Three suits of Lincoln green shalt thou have each year, beside forty marks in fee, and share with us whatsoever good shall befall us. Thou shalt eat sweet venison and quaff the stoutest ale, and mine own good right-hand man shalt thou be, for never did I see such a cudgel-player in all my life before. Speak! wilt thou be one of my good merry men?"

"That know I not," quoth the stranger, surlily, for he was angry at being so tumbled about. "If ye handle yew bow and apple shaft no better than ye do oaken cudgel, I wot ye are not fit to be called yeomen in my country; but if there be any men here that can shoot a better shaft than I, then will I bethink me of joining with you."

"Now, by my faith," said Robin, "thou art a right saucy varlet, sirrah; yet I will stoop to thee as I never stooped to man before. Good Stutely, cut thou a fair white piece of bark four fingers in breadth, and set it fourscore yards distant on yonder oak. Now, stranger, hit that fairly with a gray goose shaft and call thyself an archer."

"Ay, marry, that will I," answered he. "Give me a good stout bow and a fair broad arrow, and if I hit it not, strip me and beat me blue with bow-strings."

Then he chose the stoutest bow amongst them all, next to Robin's own, and a straight gray goose shaft, well-feathered and smooth, and stepping to the mark — while all the band, sitting or lying upon the greensward, watched to see him shoot — he drew the arrow to his cheek and loosed the shaft right deftly, sending it so straight down the path that it clove the mark in the very center. "Aha!" cried he, "mend thou that if thou canst"; while even the yeomen clapped their hands at so fair a shot.

"That is a keen shot, indeed," quoth Robin; "mend it I cannot, but mar it I may, perhaps."

Then taking up his own good stout bow and notching an arrow with care, he shot with his very greatest skill. Straight flew the arrow, and so true that it lit fairly upon the stranger's shaft and split it into splinters. Then all the yeomen leaped to their feet and shouted for joy that their master had shot so well.

"Now, by the lusty yew bow of good Saint Withold," cried the stranger, "that is a shot indeed, and never saw I the like in all my life before! Now truly will I be thy man henceforth and for aye. Good Adam Bell was a fair shot, but never shot he so!"

"Then have I gained a right good man this day," quoth jolly Robin. "What name goest thou by, good fellow?"

"Men call me John Little whence I came," answered the stranger.

Then Will Stutely, who loved a good jest, spoke up. "Nay, fair little stranger," said he, "I like not thy name and fain would I have it otherwise. Little art thou, indeed, and small of bone and sinew; therefore shalt thou be christened Little John, and I will be thy godfather."

Then Robin Hood and all his band laughed aloud until the stranger began to grow angry.

"An thou make a jest of me," quoth he to Will Stutely, "thou wilt have sore bones and little pay, and that in short season."

"Nay, good friend," said Robin Hood, "bottle thine anger, for the name fitteth thee well. Little John shalt thou be called henceforth, and Little John shall it be. So come, my merry men, and we will go and prepare a christening feast for this fair infant."

So turning their backs upon the stream, they plunged into the forest once more, through which they traced their steps till they reached the spot where they dwelt in the depths of the woodland. There had they built huts of bark and branches of trees, and made couches of sweet rushes spread over with skins of fallow deer. Here stood a great oak tree with branches spreading broadly around, beneath which was a seat of green moss where Robin Hood was wont to sit at feast and at merry-making with his stout men about him. Here they found the rest of the band, some of whom had come in with a brace of fat does. Then they all built great fires and after a time roasted the does and broached a barrel of humming ale. Then when the feast was ready, they all sat down, but Robin Hood placed Little John at his right hand, for he was henceforth to be the second in the band.

Then, when the feast was done, Will Stutely spoke up. "It is now time, I ween, to christen our bonny babe, is it not so, merry boys?" And "Aye! Aye!" cried all, laughing till the woods echoed with their mirth.

"Then seven sponsors shall we have," quoth Will Stutely; and hunting among all the band he chose the seven stoutest men of them all.

"Now, by Saint Dunstan," cried Little John, springing to his feet, "more than one of you shall rue it an you lay finger upon me."

But without a word they all ran upon him at once, seizing him by his legs and arms and holding him tightly in spite of his struggles, and they bore him forth while all stood around to see the sport. Then one came forward who had been chosen to play the priest because he had a bald crown, and in his hand he carried a brimming pot of ale. "Now who bringeth this babe?" asked he right soberly.

"That do I," answered Will Stutely.

"And what name callest thou him?"

"Little John call I him."

"Now Little John," quoth the mock priest, "thou hast not lived heretofore, but only got thee along through the world, but henceforth thou wilt live indeed. When thou livedst not, thou wast called John Little, but now that thou dost live indeed, Little John shalt thou be called, so christen I thee." And at these last words he emptied the pot of ale upon Little John's head.

Then all shouted with laughter as they saw the good brown ale stream over Little John's beard and trickle from his nose and chin, while his eyes blinked with the smart of it. At first he was of a mind to be angry, but he found he could not because the others were so merry; so he, too, laughed with the rest. Then Robin took this sweet, pretty babe, clothed him all anew from top to toe in Lincoln green, and gave him a good stout bow, and so made him a member of the merry band.

IRELAND

The Wonder Smith and His Son[1]

⋙ *The tales of the Gubbaun Saor are stories out of an early mythology of Ireland, scattered accounts of a god, the Gubbaun Saor, who was the Wonder Smith, the world maker, the creator. His son was known as Lugh of the Long Hand, the god of the sun. Now the Gubbaun had no son of his own. He had only a daughter, Aunya. He thought a daughter a poor creature to whom to teach all the cleverness of his craft. One day, as he sat bemoaning his fate, didn't a woman come along who was sad in a like cause. She had only a son, and she was willing to give her life for a daughter. They exchanged children. It was a bargain the Gubbaun was to rue, for his son was no smith. He was a poet, a singer of songs, and he would do nothing but play on his reed pipe and sit in the sun. How the Gubbaun regained his daughter and in the end had both son and daughter together is told in part here.*

Ella Young gathered these stories from the storytellers in remote regions of Ireland. It was she who discovered them. They are among the most witty, most beautiful, and most humane clusters of traditional stories. The Celtic love of nature; the exuberant love of language and the mirth and wit; the exceptional role of woman in a primitive culture: these are shown forth in tellings characteristic of the Celtic turn of mind.

The Gubbaun Saor sat outside in the sunshine, but it's little joy he had of the good day. He was wringing his hands and making lamentation.

1 From Ella Young, *The Wonder Smith and His Son* (Longmans, Green, 1927).

"Ochone! Ochone!" he said, "my share of sorrow and the world's misfortune! Why was I given any cleverness at all, with nothing but a daughter to leave it to? Ochone!"

At that he heard a lamentation coming down the road. It was a woman raising an ullagone, clapping her hands like one distracted. She stopped when she came to the Gubbaun.

"What has happened to you, Jewel of the World," said she, "to be making lamentations?"

"Why wouldn't I make lamentations," said the Gubbaun, "when I have no one but a daughter to leave my cleverness to? 'Tis a hard thing to have all the trades in the world, and no one but a daughter to learn them!"

"'The topmost berry is always sweet," said the woman, "and the red apple that is beyond us draws our hearts. You are crying salt tears for a son, and I would give the world for a daughter."

"O, what good is a daughter!" said the Gubbaun. "What good's a girl to a man that has robbed the crows of their cleverness and taught tricks to the foxes?"

"Maybe you'd be worse off," said the woman, "if you had a son. Isn't it myself that is making a hand-clapping and shedding the salt tears of my eyes because of the son I've got — a heart-scald from sunrise to candle-light!"

"'Tis you," said the Gubbaun, "that don't know how to manage a son. He'd be a lamb of gentleness if I had him."

"O then take him," said the woman, "and give me your daughter. I'll be well content with the bargain!"

It was agreed between them, then and

there. The Gubbaun took the son and the woman got the daughter. She went away after that and left no tidings of herself: she thought it likely the Gubbaun would rue the bargain.

The Gubbaun started to teach the son. He had systems and precepts and infallible methods of teaching, but the boy would not learn. He would do nothing but sit in the sunshine and play little tunes on a flute he had made. He grew up like that.

"Clever as I am," said the Gubbaun, "the woman that got my daughter got the better of me. If I had Aunya back again, 'tis I that would be praising the world. My share of grief and misfortune! Why did I give the red apple for the unripe crab?"

He beat his hands together and lamented: but the son in a pool of sunshine played a faery reel, and two blackbirds danced to it.

How the Gubbaun Tried His Hand at Match-making

One day the Gubbaun roused himself:

"What my son needs," said he, "is a clever woman for a wife, and 'tis I that will choose one."

He gave out the news to the countryside, and many a woman came bragging of the daughter she had.

"The eye that looks on its own sees little blemish," said the Gubbaun. "I'll take no cleverness on hearsay: before I make a match for my son, I must talk to the girl he is to get."

It would take a year to tell of the girls that came, with their mothers to put a luck-word on them, and the girls that went, disheartened from the Gubbaun Saor. He outbaffled them with questions. He tripped and bewildered them with his cleverness. There was not a girl in the country-side wise enough to please him. Three girls, with a great reputation, came from a distance.

When the first girl came, the Gubbaun showed her a room heaped up with gold and treasure and the riches of the world.

"That is what the woman will get that marries my son," said he.

"There would be good spending in that pile!" said the girl. "You could be taking the full of your two hands out of it from morning till night every day in the year."

" 'Tis not you will be taking the full of your two hands out of it," said the Gubbaun. "My son will get a wiser woman."

The second girl came. The Gubbaun showed her the heap of treasure.

"I'll put seven bolts and seven bars on it," she said, "and in a hundred years it will not grow less!"

" 'Tis not you will put the bolts and bars on it," said the Gubbaun. "My son will get a wiser woman."

The third girl came. The Gubbaun showed her the heap of treasure.

"Big as it is," said she, "it will be lonesome if it is not added to!"

"I wonder," said the Gubbaun, "if you have the wit to add to it."

"Try me," said the girl.

"I will," said the Gubbaun. "Bargain with me for a sheepskin."

"If you have the wit to sell," said she, "I have the wit to buy. Show me the skin and name your price."

He showed the skin; he named his price. It was a small price. She made it smaller. The Gubbaun gave in to her.

"You have a bargain in it," said the Gubbaun; "the money-handsel to me."

"You'll get that," said she, "when I have the skin."

"That's not my way at all," said the Gubbaun, "I must have the skin and the price of it."

"May Death never trip you till you get it!"

"I will get it from a woman that will come well out of the deal — and know her advantage!"

"May your luck blossom," said the girl, " 'tis ransacking the faery hills you'll be: or bargaining with the Hag of the Ford."

"Health and Prosperity to yourself!" said the Gubbaun.

She went out from him at that, but the Gubbaun sat with his mind turned inward, considering, considering — and considering.

How the Son of the Gubbaun Met with Good Luck

"It would be well for you to be raising a hand on your own behalf, now," said the

Gubbaun Saor to his Son, "you can draw the birds from the bushes with one note of your flute: maybe you can draw luck with a woman. If you have the luck to get the daughter I gave in exchange for yourself, our good days will begin."

The Son of the Gubbaun got to his feet. "I could travel the world," he said, "with my reed-flute and the Hound that came to me out of the Wood of Gold and Silver Yew Trees." With that he gave a low call, and a milk-white Hound came running to the door.

"Is it without counsel and without advice and without a road-blessing," cried the Gubbaun, "that you are setting out to travel the world? How will you know what girl has the fire of wisdom in her mind? What sign, what token will you ask of her?"

"'Tis you that have wisdom: give me an advice," said the Son.

"Take the sheepskin," said the Gubbaun, "and set yourself to find a buyer for it. The girl that will give you the skin and the price of it is the girl that will bring good-luck across this threshold. The day and the hour that you find her, send home the Hound that I may know of her and set out the riches of this house."

"Tree of Wisdom," said the Son, "bear fruit and blossom on your branches. The road-blessing now to me."

"My blessing on the road that is smooth," said the Gubbaun, "and on the rough road through the quagmire. A blessing on night with the stars; and night when the stars are quenched. A blessing on the clear sky of day; and day that is choked with the thunder. May my blessing run before you. May my blessing guard you on the right hand and on the left. May my blessing follow you as your shadow follows. Take my road-blessing," said the Gubbaun.

"The shelter of the Hazel Boughs to you, Salmon of Wisdom," said the Son.

He set out then with the Hound to travel the solitary places and the marts of the world. He shook the dust of many a town from his feet, but the sheepskin remained on his shoulder. A cause of merriment that skin was; a target for shafts of wit; a shaming of face to the man that carried it. It found its way into proverbs and wonder tales, but it never found the bargain-clinch of a buyer.

If it hadn't been for the Hound, and the reed-flute, and the share of songs that he had, the Son of the Gubbaun Saor would have been worn to a skin of misery like a dried-up crab-apple!

One day, in the teeth of the North Wind, he climbed a hill gap and came all at once on a green plain. There was only one tree in that plain, but everywhere scarlet blossoms trembled through the grass. Beneath the tree was a well: and from the well a girl came towards him. Her heavy hair was like spun gold. She walked lightly and proudly. The Son of the Gubbaun thought it long till he could change words with her.

"May every day bring luck and blessing to you," he cried.

"The like wish to yourself," said she, "and may your load be light."

"A good wish," said he, "I have far to carry my load."

"How far?" asked the girl.

"To the world's end, I think."

"Are you under enchantment?" said she. "Did a Hag of the Storm put a spell on you; or a Faery-Woman take you in her net?"

"'Tis the net of my father's wisdom that I am caught in," said he. "I must carry this sheepskin, my grief! till a woman gives me the price of it: and the skin itself, in the clinch of a good buyer's bargain."

"You need go no farther for that," said the girl. "Name your price for the skin."

He named his price. She took the skin. She plucked the wool from it. She gave him the skin and the price together.

"Luck on your hand," said he, "is the bargain a good one?"

"It is," said she, "I have fine pure wool for the price of a skin. May the price be a luck-penny!"

"You are the Woman my father brags of," cried the Son. "My Choice, My Share of the World you are, if you will come with me."

"I will come," said the girl.

The Son of the Gubbaun Saor called to the Hound.

"Swift One," he said, "our fortunes have blossomed. Set out now, and don't let the wind that is behind you catch you up, or the wind that is in front of you out-race you, till you lie down by the Gubbaun Saor's threshold."

The Hound stretched himself in his running. He was like a salmon that silvers in mid-leap; like the wind through a forest of sedges; like the sun-track on dark waters: and he was like that in his running till he lay down by the Gubbaun Saor's threshold.

HOW THE GUBBAUN SAOR WELCOMED HOME HIS DAUGHTER

Many a time the Gubbaun looked forth to see was the Hound coming. He was tired of looking forth. He flung himself on the bench he had carved, by the hearth-stone.

"I wish I never had a son!" he said. "I wish I were a young boy, wandering idly, or lying in a wood of larches with the wind stirring the tops of them. There is joy in the slanting stoop of the sea-hawk, but a man builds weariness for himself!"

He went to the door and looked forth.

The Wood of the Ridge stood blackly against the dawn. There was a great stillness. The earth seemed to listen. Suddenly the wood was full of singing voices. A brightness moved in it low down; brightness that grew, and grew; and neared; milkwhite. The Hound! The Hound, Failinis, at last!

He broke, glittering, from the wood, and came with great leaps to the Gubbaun. The Gubbaun put his two hands about the head of the Hound.

"Treasure," he cried. "Swift-footed Jewel! Bringer of good tidings! It is time now to pile up the fires of welcome. It is time now to set my house in order. A hundred thousand welcomes!"

The Hound lay down by the door-stone.

The Gubbaun strewed green scented boughs on his threshold, plumes of the larch, branches of ash and quicken. Thorn in blossom he strewed; and marsh-mint; and frocken; and odorous red pine. He wondered if it was for Aunya — or for a stranger.

The Gubbaun piled up a fire of welcome. Beneath it he put nine sacred stones taken from the cavern of the Dragon of the Winds. He laid hazelwood on the pile for wisdom;

and oak for enduring prosperity; and blackthorn boughs to win favour of the stars. Quicken wood he had; and ancient yew; and silver-branched holly. Ash, he had, too, on the pile; and thorn; and wood of the appletree. These things of worth he had on the pile. With incantations and ceremonies he built it, and with rites such as Druids use in the hill-fires that welcome the Spring and the coming of the Gods of Dana.

The Gubbaun set out the riches of his house; the beaten metals; the wild-beast skins; the broidered work. "If it is Aunya," thought he, "and her mind matches my own, she will care more for wide skiey spaces than for any roof-tree shaped by a tool." He thought of a wide stone-scattered plain; of great wings in the night — and his eyes changed colour. The Gubbaun had every colour in his eyes: they were gray at times like the twilight; green like the winter dawn; amber like bog-water in sunlight.

The Gubbaun considered the riches of his house. He looked at the walls he had built; the secret contrivances, the strange cunning engines he had fashioned. "I was bought," he said to himself, "with a handful of tools! Yet to make — and break — and remake — that is the strong-handed choice."

Outside, joyously, rose the baying of the Hound. They were coming! The Gubbaun set fire a-leap in the piled-up wood and ran to meet them.

Flames licked out; flames that were azure; and orange; and sapphire; and blinding white. They lifted themselves like crowned serpents. They hissed. They danced. They leaped into the air. They spread themselves. They blossomed. They found voice. They sang.

"Have you looked on a fire hotter or stronger than this?" asked the Gubbaun of the girl.

She looked on the flame. She said: "The Wind from the South has more warmth and more strength than all the ceremonial fires in Erin." And as she said it, her eyes that were blue like hyacinths in Spring turned gray like lake-water in shadow.

"It is Aunya," thought the Gubbaun, "she has the wisdom of the hills: I wonder has she the wisdom of the hearth."

He took her by the hand, he showed her his finest buildings; his engines; his secret contrivances. "What is your word on these?" he asked.

"You need no word," said the girl, "and well you know it! When the full tide is full, it is full; to-day, and to-morrow no less. Tear stone from stone of these walls in the hope to surpass them — you can do no more than raise them again, fitting each block to its fellow. Trust your own wit on your work, for it's a pity of him that trusts a woman!"

"You are Aunya," cried the Gubbaun, "you are Aunya, the treasure I lost in my youth. You were a dream in my mind when every precious stone was my covering. A hundred thousand welcomes, Aunya! This house is yours, and all its riches yours! The hearth-flame yours! The roof-tree yours!"

"The reddest sun-rise," said Aunya, "is the soonest quenched. You will bid me go from this house one day, without looking backwards to it. All I ask against that day is your oath to let me carry my choice of three arm-loads of treasure out of this house."

"There is no day in all the days of the year that you will get a hard word from me, Aunya, for now my Tree of Life is the holly: no wind of misfortune can blow the leaves from it."

"Bind your oath on my asking," said Aunya.

Then said the Gubbaun:

"On the strong Sun I bind my oath,
My oath to Aunya:
If I deny three treasure-loads to her,
May the strong Sun avenge her.

On the wise Moon I bind my oath,
My oath to Aunya:
If I rue my oath
Let the wise Moon give judgment.

On the kind Earth I bind my oath,
My oath to Aunya.
On the stones of the field;
On running water;
On growing grass.
Let the tusked boar avenge it!
Let the horned stag avenge it!
Let the piast of the waters avenge it!
On the strong Sun I bind my oath."

"It is enough, my Treasure and my Jewel of Wisdom!" said Aunya.

So Aunya, daughter of the Gubbaun Saor, came home.

Cuchulain's Wooing[2]

◢§ *Two major epics of the pre-Christian Celtic world revolve about heroes of epic proportions, Cuchulain, the Hound of Ulster, and Finn, the central figure in a group of stories concerning the* fiana, *a band of warriors. The Cuchulain cycle, which numbers more than a hundred tales, is the earlier. The tales are placed, in time, as evolving from the life of 400 B.C. to the first century of the Christian era. The earliest written documentation of them is not earlier than the eleventh century.*

"Between the time of their invention for the entertainment of the chiefs and kings of Ireland to the time of their incorporation in the great books which contain the bulk of the tales, they were handed down by word of mouth, every bard and professional storyteller (of whom there was at least one in every great man's house) being obliged to know by heart a great number of these romances and prepared at any moment to recite those he might be called upon to give."
— Eleanor Hull (Introduction, p. 10, Cuchulain, the Hound of Ulster).

The earliest written source is known as The Book of the Dun Cow, *named for the color of the piece of parchment upon which it was written, which was compiled in 1100 in the monastery of Clonmacnois on the Shannon.*

The Finn cycle is three hundred years later. It has less unity than the Cuchulain cycle, is more romantic and less heroic, though the beauty of some of its separate stories is very great. Finn is perhaps closer to the people of Ireland, the stories concerning him having elements of the folktale.

It was on a day of the days of summer that Emer, daughter of Forgall the Wily, sat on a bench before her father's door, at his fort that is called Lusk to-day, but which in olden days men spoke of as the Gardens of the Sun-god Lugh, so sunny and so fair and fertile was that plain, with waving meadow-

2 From Eleanor Hull, *Cuchulain, the Hound of Ulster* (Crowell).

grass and buttercups, and the sweet may-blossom girdling the fields. Close all about the fort the gardens lay, with apple-trees shedding their pink and white upon the playing fields of brilliant green; and all the air was noisy with the buzz of bees, and with the happy piping of the thrush and soft low cooing of the doves. And Emer sat, a fair and noble maid, among her young companions, foster-sisters of her own, who came from all the farms and forts around to grow up with the daughters of the house, and learn from them high-bred and gentle ways, to fashion rich embroideries such as Irish women used to practise as an art, and weaving, and fine needlework, and all the ways of managing a house. And as they sat round Emer, a bright comely group of busy girls, they sang in undertones the crooning tender melodies of ancient Erin; or one would tell a tale of early wars, and warrior feasts or happenings of the gods, and one would tell a tale of lover's joys or of the sorrows of a blighted love, and they would sigh and laugh and dream that they too loved, were wooed, and lost their loves.

And Emer moved about among the girls, directing them; and of all maids in Erin, Emer was the best, for hers were the six gifts of womanhood, the gift of loveliness, the gift of song, the gift of sweet and pleasant speech, the gift of handiwork, the gifts of wisdom and of modesty. And in his distant home in Ulster, Cuchulain heard of her. For he was young and brave, and women loved him for his nobleness, and all men wished that he should take a wife. But for awhile he would not, for among the women whom he saw, not one of them came up to his desires. And when they urged him, wilfully he said: "Well, find for me a woman I could love, and I will marry her." Then sent the King his heralds out through every part of Ulster and the south to seek a wife whom Cuchulain would care to woo. But still he said the same, "This one, and this, has some bad temper or some want of grace, or she is vain or she is weak, not fitted as a mate to such as I. She must be brave, for she must suffer much; she must be gentle, lest I anger her; she must be fair and noble, not alone to give me pleasure as her spouse, but that all men may think of

her with pride, saying, 'As Cuchulain is the first of Ulster's braves, the hero of her many fighting-fields, so is his wife the noblest and the first of Erin's women, a worthy mate for him.'"

So when the princely messengers returned, their search was vain; among the daughters of the chiefs and noble lords not one was found whom Cuchulain cared to woo. But one who loved him told him of a night he spent in Forgall's fort, and of the loveliness and noble spirit of Forgall's second girl Emer, the maiden of the waving hair, but just grown up to womanhood. He told him of her noble mien and stately step, the soft and liquid brightness of her eyes, the colour of her hair, that like to ruddy gold fresh from the burnishing, was rolled round her head. Her graceful form he praised, her skilfulness in song and handiwork, her courage with her father, a harsh and wily man, whom all within the house hated and feared but she. He told him also that for any man to win the maiden for his wife would be a troublesome and dangerous thing, for out of all the world, her father Forgall loved and prized but her, and he had made it known that none beneath a king or ruling prince should marry her, and any man who dared to win her love, but such as these, should meet a cruel death; and this he laid upon his sons and made them swear to him upon their swords, that any who should come to woo the girl should never leave the fort alive again.

All that they said but made Cuchulain yet the more desire to see the maid and talk with her. "This girl, so brave, so wise, so fair of face and form," he pondered with himself, "would be a fitting mate for any chief. I think she is the fitting mate for me."

So on the very day when Emer sat upon her playing-fields, Cuchulain in the early morn set forth in all his festal garb in his chariot with his prancing steeds, with Laeg before him as his charioteer, and took the shortest route towards the plain of Bray, where lie the Gardens of the Sun-god Lugh. The way they went from Emain lay between the Mountains of the Wood, and thence along the High-road of the Plain, where once the sea had passed; across the marsh that bore the name the Whisper of the Secret of the Gods. Then driving on towards the River Boyne they passed the Ridge of the Great Sow, where not far off is seen the fairy haunt of Angus, God of Beauty and of Youth; and so they reached the ford of Washing of the Horses of the Gods, and the fair, flowering plains of Lugh, called Lusk to-day.

Now all the girls were busied with their work, when on the highroad leading to the fort they heard a sound like thunder from the north, that made them pause and listen in surprise.

Nearer and nearer yet it came as though at furious pace a band of warriors bore down towards the house. "Let one of you see from the ramparts of the fort," said Emer, "what is the sound we hear coming towards us." Fiall, her sister, Forgall's eldest girl, ran to the top of the rath or earthen mound that circled round the playing-fields, and looked out towards the north, shading her eyes against the brilliant sun. "What do you see there?" asked they all, and eagerly she cried: "I see a splendid chariot-chief coming at furious pace along the road. Two steeds, like day and night, of equal size and beauty, come thundering beneath that chariot on the plain. Curling their manes and long, and as they come, one would think fire darted from their curbed jaws, so strain and bound they forward; high in the air the turf beneath their feet is thrown around them, as though a flock of birds were following as they go. On the right side the horse is grey, broad in the haunches, active, swift and wild; with head erect and breast expanded, madly he moves along the plain, bounding and prancing as he goes. The other horse jet-black, head firmly knit, feet broad-hoofed, firm, and slender; in all this land never had chariot-chief such steeds as these."

"Heed not the steeds," the girls replied, "tell us, for this concerns us most, who is the chariot-chief who rides within?"

"Worthy of the chariot in which he rides is he who sits within. Youthful he seems, as standing on the very borders of a noble manhood, and yet I think his face and form are older than his years. Gravely he looks, as though his mind revolved some serious

thought, and yet a radiance as of the summer's day enfolds him round. About his shoulders a rich five-folded mantle hangs, caught by a brooch across the chest sparkling with precious gems, above his white and gold-embroidered shirt. His massive sword rests on his thigh, and yet I think he comes not here to fight. Before him stands his charioteer, the reins held firmly in his hand, urging the horses onward with a goad."

"What like is he, the charioteer?" demand the girls again.

"A ruddy man and freckled," answered Fiall; "his hair is very curly and bright-red, held by a bronze fillet across his brow, and caught at either side his head in little cups of gold, to keep the locks from falling on his face. A light cloak on his shoulders, made with open sleeves, flies back in the wind, as rapidly they course along the plain." But Emer heard not what the maiden said, for to her mind there came the memory of a wondrous youth whom Ulster loved and yet of whom all Erin stood in awe. Great warriors spoke of him in whispers and with shaking of the head. They told how when he was a little child, he fought with full-grown warriors and mastered them; of a huge hound that he had slain and many feats of courage he had done. Into her mind there came a memory, that she had heard of prophets who foretold for him a strange and perilous career; a life of danger, and an early death. Full many a time she longed to see this youth, foredoomed to peril, yet whose praise should ring from age to age through Erin; and in her mind, when all alone she pondered on these things, she still would end: "This were a worthy mate! This were a man to win a woman's love!" And half aloud she uttered the old words: "This were a man to win a woman's love!"

Now hardly had the words sprung to her lips, when the chariot stood before the door, close to the place where all the girls were gathered. And when she saw him Emer knew it was the man of whom she dreamed. He wished a blessing to them, and her lovely face she lifted in reply. "May God make smooth the path before thy feet," she gently said. "And thou, mayest thou be safe from every harm," was his reply. "Whence comest thou?" she asked; for he had alighted from his seat and stood beside her, gazing on her face. "From Conor's court we come," he answered then; "from Emain, kingliest of Ulster's forts, and this the way we took. We drove between the Mountains of the Wood, along the High-road of the Plain, where once the sea had been; across the Marsh they call the Secret of the Gods, and to the Boyne's ford named of old the Washing of the Horses of the Gods. And now at last, O maiden, we have come to the bright flowery Garden-grounds of Lugh. This is the story of myself, O maid; let me now hear of thee." Then Emer said: "Daughter am I to Forgall, whom men call the Wily Chief. Cunning his mind and strange his powers; for he is stronger than any labouring man, more learned than any Druid, more sharp and clever than any man of verse. Men say that thou art skilled in feats of war, but it will be more than all thy games to fight against Forgall himself; therefore be cautious what thou doest, for men cannot number the multitude of his warlike deeds nor the cunning and craft with which he works. He has given me as a bodyguard twenty valiant men, their captain Con, son of Forgall, and my brother; therefore I am well protected, and no man can come near me, but that Forgall knows of it. To-day he is gone from home on a warrior expedition, and those men are gone with him; else, had he been within, I trow he would have asked thee of thy business here."

"Why, O maiden, dost thou talk thus to me? Dost thou not reckon me among the strong men, who know not fear?" "If thy deeds were known to me," she said, "I then might reckon them; but hitherto I have not heard of all thy exploits." "Truly, I swear, O maiden," said Cuchulain, "that I will make my deeds to be recounted among the glories of the warrior-feats of heroes." "How do men reckon thee?" she said again. "What then is thy strength?" "This is my strength," he said. "When my might in fight is weakest, I can defend myself alone against twenty. I fear not by my own might to fight with forty. Under my protection a hundred are secure. From dread of me, strong warriors avoid my path, and come not against me in

the battlefield. Hosts and multitudes and armed men fly before my name."

"Thou seemest to boast," said Emer, "and truly for a tender boy those feats are very good; but they rank not with the deeds of chariot-chiefs. Who then were they who brought thee up in these deeds of which thou boastest?"

"Truly, O maiden, King Conor is himself my foster-father, and not as a churl or common man was I brought up by him. Among chariot-chiefs and champions, among poets and learned men, among the lords and nobles of Ulster, have I been reared, and they have taught me courage and skill and manly gifts. In birth and bravery I am a match for any chariot-chief; I direct the counsels of Ulster, and at my own fort at Dun Dalgan they come to me for entertainment. Not as one of the common herd do I stand before thee here to-day, but as the favourite of the King and darling of all the warriors of Ulster. Moreover, the god Lugh the Long-handed is my protector, for I am of the race of the great gods, and his especial foster-child. And now, O maiden, tell me of thyself; how in the sunny plains of Lugh hast thou been reared within thy father's fort?" "That I will tell thee," said the girl. "I was brought up in noble behaviour as every queen is reared; in stateliness of form, in wise, calm speech, in comeliness of manner, so that to me is imputed every noble grace among the hosts of the women of Erin."

"Good, indeed, are those virtues," said the youth; "and yet I see one excellence thou hast not noted in thy speech. Never before, until this day, among all women with whom I have at times conversed, have I found one but thee to speak the mystic ancient language of the bards, which we are talking now for secrecy one with the other. And all these things are good, but one is best of all, and that is, that I love thee, and I think thou lovest me. What hinders, then, that we should be betrothed?" But Emer would not hasten, but teasing him, she said, "Perhaps thou hast already found a wife?" "Not so," said he, "and by my right-hand's valour here I vow, none but thyself shall ever be my wife." "A pity it were, indeed, thou shouldst not have a wife," said Emer, playing with him still; "see, here is Fiall, my elder sister, a clever girl and excellent in needlework. Make her thy wife, for well is it known to thee, a younger sister in Ireland may not marry before an elder. Take her! I'll call her hither." Then Cuchulain was vexed because she seemed to play with him. "Verily and indeed," he said, "not Fiall, but thee, it is with whom I am in love; and if thou weddest me not, never will I, Cuchulain, wed at all."

Then Emer saw that Cuchulain loved her, but she was not satisfied, because he had not yet done the deeds of prime heroes, and she desired that he should prove himself by champion feats and deeds of valour before he won her as his bride.

So she bade him go away and prove himself for a year by deeds of prowess to be indeed a worthy mate and spouse for her, and then, if he would come again she would go with him as his one and only wife. But she bade him beware of her father, for she knew that he would try to kill him, in order that he might not come again. And this was true, for every way he sought to kill Cuchulain, or to have him killed by his enemies, but he did not prevail.

When Cuchulain had taken farewell of Emer and gained her promise, he returned to Emain Macha. And that night the maidens of the fort told Forgall that Cuchulain had been there and that they thought that he had come to woo Emer; but of this they were not sure, because he and Emer had talked together in the poet's mystic tongue, that was not known to them. For Emer and Cuchulain talked on this wise, that no one might repeat what they had said to Forgall.

And for a whole year Cuchulain was away, and Forgall guarded the fort so well that he could not come near Emer to speak with her; but at last, when the year was out, he would wait no longer, and he wrote a message to Emer on a piece of stick, telling her to be ready. And he came in his war-chariot, with scythes upon its wheels, and he brought a band of hardy men with him, who entered the outer rampart of the fort and carried off Emer, striking down men on every side. And Forgall followed them to the earthen out-works, but he fell over the rath, and was taken up lifeless. And Cuchulain placed Emer and her foster-sister in his chariot, carrying with them their garments and ornaments of gold and silver, and they drove northward to Cuchulain's fort at Dun Dalgan, which is Dundalk to-day.

And they were pursued to the Boyne, and there Cuchulain placed Emer in a house of safety, and he turned and drove off his enemies who followed him, pursuing them along the banks and destroying them, so that the place, which had before been called the White Field, was called the Turf of Blood from that day. Then he and Emer reached their home in safety, nor were they henceforth parted until death.

SCANDINAVIA

Sigurd's Youth[1]

Sigurd is the Scandinavian name for the German hero Siegfried. He is represented as the perfect example of his race. The Scandinavian story as found in the Eddas *differs in details from the German version of the* Nibelungenlied, *but good authorities are inclined to believe there is a historical basis for these legends, though opinions differ as to which of the exploits are fact (except, of course, the dragon story) and which are fiction.*

In Midgard, in a northern kingdom, a king reigned whose name was Alv; he was wise and good, and he had in his house a foster-son whose name was Sigurd.

Sigurd was fearless and strong; so fearless and so strong was he that he once captured a bear of the forest and drove him to the King's Hall. His mother's name was Hiordis. Once, before Sigurd was born, Alv and his father who was king before him went on an expedition across the sea and came into another country. While they were yet afar off they heard the din of a great battle. They came to the battlefield, but they found no living warriors on it, only heaps of slain. One warrior they marked: he was whitebearded and old and yet he seemed the noblest-looking man Alv or his father had ever looked on. His arms showed that he was a king amongst one of the bands of warriors.

They went through the forest searching for survivors of the battle. And, hidden in a

[1] From Padraic Colum, *The Children of Odin* (Macmillan, 1920).

dell in the forest, they came upon two women. One was tall with blue, unflinching eyes and ruddy hair, but wearing the garb of a serving-maid. The other wore the rich dress of a queen, but she was of low stature and her manner was covert and shrinking.

When Alv and his father drew near, the one who had on her the raiment of a queen said, "Help us, lords, and protect us, and we will show you where a treasure is hidden. A great battle has been fought between the men of King Lygni and the men of King Sigmund, and the men of King Lygni have won the victory and have gone from the field. But King Sigmund is slain, and we who are of his household hid his treasure and we can show it to you."

"The noble warrior, white-haired and white-bearded, who lies yonder — is he King Sigmund?"

The woman answered, "Yes, lord, and I am his queen."

"We have heard of King Sigmund," said Alv's father. "His fame and the fame of his race, the Volsungs, is over the wide world."

Alv said no word to either of the women, but his eyes stayed on the one who had on the garb of a serving-maid. She was on her knees, wrapping in a beast's skin two pieces of a broken sword.

"You will surely protect us, good lords," said she who had on the queenly dress.

"Yea, wife of King Sigmund, we will protect you and your serving-maid," said Alv's father, the old king.

Then the women took the warriors to a wild place on the seashore and they showed them where King Sigmund's treasure was hidden amongst the rocks: cups of gold and mighty armrings and jeweled collars. Prince Alv and his father put the treasure on the ship and brought the two women aboard. Then they sailed from that land.

That was before Sigurd, the foster-son of King Alv, was born.

Now the mother of Alv was wise and little of what she saw escaped her noting. She saw that of the two women that her son and her husband had brought into their kingdom, the one who wore the dress of the serving-maid had unflinching eyes and a high beauty, while the one who wore the queenly dress was shrinking and unstately. One night when all the women of the household were sitting round her, spinning wool by the light of torches in the hall, the queen-mother said to the one who wore the queenly garb:

"Thou art good at rising in the morning. How dost thou know in the dark hours when it wears to dawn?"

The one clad in the queenly garb said, "When I was young I used to rise to milk the cows, and I waken ever since at the same hour."

The queen-mother said to herself, "It is a strange country in which the royal maids rise to milk the cows."

Then she said to the one who wore the clothes of the serving-maid:

"How dost thou know in the dark hours when the dawn is coming?"

"My father," she said, "gave me the ring of gold that I wear, and always before it is time to rise I feel it grow cold on my finger."

"It is a strange country, truly," said the queen-mother to herself, "in which the serving-maids wear rings of gold."

When all the others had left she spoke to the two women who had been brought into her country. To the one who wore the clothes of a serving-maid, she said:

"Thou art the queen."

Then the one who wore the queenly clothes said, "Thou art right, lady. She is the queen, and I cannot any longer pretend to be other than I am."

Then the other woman spoke. Said she: "I am the queen as thou hast said — the queen of King Sigmund who was slain. Because a king sought for me I changed clothes with my serving-maid, my wish being to baffle those who might be sent to carry me away.

"Know that I am Hiordis, a king's daughter. Many men came to my father to ask for me in marriage, and of those that came there were two whom I heard much of: one was King Lygni and the other was King Sigmund of the race of the Volsungs. The king, my father, told me it was for me to choose between these two. Now King Sigmund was old, but he was the most famous warrior in the whole world, and I chose him rather than King Lygni.

"We were wed. But King Lygni did not lose desire of me, and in a while he came against King Sigmund's kingdom with a great army of men. We hid our treasure by the sea-shore, and I and my maid watched the battle from the borders of the forest. With the help of Gram, his wondrous sword, and his own great warrior strength, Sigmund was able to harry the great force that came against him. But suddenly he was stricken down. Then was the battle lost. Only King Lygni's men survived it, and they scattered to search for me and the treasure of the King.

"I came to where my lord lay on the field of battle, and he raised himself on his shield when I came, and he told me that death was very near him. A stranger had entered the battle at the time when it seemed that the men of King Lygni must draw away. With the spear that he held in his hand he struck at Sigmund's sword, and Gram, the wondrous sword, was broken in two pieces. Then did King Sigmund get his death-wound. 'It must be I shall die,' he said, 'for the spear against which my sword broke was Gungnir, Odin's spear. Only that spear could have shattered the sword that Odin gave my fathers. Now must I go to Valhalla, Odin's Hall of Heroes.'

"'I weep,' I said, 'because I have no son who might call himself of the great race of the Volsungs.'

"'For that you need not weep,' said Sigmund, 'a son will be born to you, my son and yours, and you shall name him Sigurd. Take now the broken pieces of my wondrous sword and give them to my son when he shall be of warrior age.'

"Then did Sigmund turn his face to the

ground and the death-struggle came on him. Odin's Valkyrie took his spirit from the battle-field. And I lifted up the broken pieces of the sword, and with my serving-maid I went and hid in a deep dell in the forest. Then your husband and your son found us and they brought us to your kingdom where we have been kindly treated, O Queen."

Such was the history that Hiordis, the wife of King Sigmund, told to the mother of Prince Alv.

Soon afterwards the child was born to her that was Sigmund's son. Sigurd she named him. And after Sigurd was born, the old king died and Prince Alv became king in his stead. He married Hiordis, she of the ruddy hair, the unflinching ways, and the high beauty, and he brought up her son Sigurd in his house as his foster-son.

Sigurd, the son of Sigmund, before he came to warrior's age, was known for his strength and his swiftness and for the fearlessness that shone round him like a glow. "Mighty was the race he sprang from, the Volsung race," men said, "but Sigurd will be as mighty as any that have gone before him." He built himself a hut in the forest that he might hunt wild beasts and live near to one who was to train him in many crafts.

This one was Regin, a maker of swords and a cunning man besides. It was said of Regin that he was an enchanter and that he had been in the world for longer than the generations of men. No one remembered, nor no one's father remembered, when Regin had come into that country. He taught Sigurd the art of working in metals and he taught him, too, the lore of other days. But ever as he taught him he looked at Sigurd strangely, not as a man looks at his fellow, but as a lynx looks at a stranger beast.

One day Regin said to young Sigurd, "King Alv has thy father's treasure, men say, and yet he treats thee as if thou wert thrall-born."

Now Sigurd knew that Regin said this that he might anger him and thereafter use him to his own ends. He said, "King Alv is a wise and a good king, and he would let me have riches if I had need of them."

"Thou dost go about as a foot-boy, and not as a king's son."

"Any day that it likes me I might have a horse to ride," Sigurd said.

"So thou dost say," said Regin, and he turned from Sigurd and went to blow the fire of his smithy.

Sigurd was made angry and he threw down the irons on which he was working and he ran to the horse-pastures by the great River. A herd of horses was there, gray and black and roan and chestnut, the best of the horses that King Alv possessed. As he came near to where the herd grazed he saw a stranger near, an ancient but robust man, wearing a strange cloak of blue and leaning on a staff to watch the horses. Sigurd, though young, had seen kings in their halls, but this man had a bearing that was more lofty than any king's he had ever looked on.

"Thou art going to choose a horse for thyself," said the stranger to Sigurd.

"Yea, father," Sigurd said.

"Drive the herd first into the river," said the stranger.

Sigurd drove the horses into the wide river. Some were swept down by the current, others struggled back and clambered up the bank of the pastures. But one swam across the river, and throwing up his head neighed as for a victory. Sigurd marked him; a gray horse he was, young and proud, with a great flowing mane. He went through the water and caught this horse, mounted him, and brought him back across the river.

"Thou hast done well," said the stranger. "Grani, whom thou hast got, is of the breed of Sleipner, the horse of Odin."

"And I am of the race of the sons of Odin," cried Sigurd, his eyes wide and shining with the very light of the sun. "I am of the race of the sons of Odin, for my father was Sigmund, and his father was Volsung, and his father was Rerir, and his father was Sigi, who was the son of Odin."

The stranger, leaning on his staff, looked on the youth steadily. Only one of his eyes was to be seen, but that eye, Sigurd thought, might see through a stone. "All thou hast named," the stranger said, "were as swords of Odin to send men to Valhalla, Odin's Hall of Heroes. And of all that thou hast named there were none but were chosen by Odin's Valkyries for battles in Asgard."

Cried Sigurd, "Too much of what is brave and noble in the world is taken by Odin for his battles in Asgard."

The stranger leaned on his staff and his head was bowed. "What wouldst thou?" he said, and it did not seem to Sigurd that he spoke to him. "What wouldst thou? The leaves wither and fall off Ygdrasil, and the day of Ragnarök comes." Then he raised his head and spoke to Sigurd. "The time is near," he said, "when thou mayst possess thyself of the pieces of thy father's sword."

Then the man in the strange cloak of blue went climbing up the hill and Sigurd watched him pass away from his sight. He had held back Grani, his proud horse, but now he turned him and let him gallop along the river in a race that was as swift as the wind.

Mounted upon Grani, his proud horse, Sigurd rode to the Hall and showed himself to Alv, the king, and to Hiordis, his mother. Before the Hall he shouted out the Volsung name, and King Alv felt as he watched him that this youth was a match for a score of men, and Hiordis, his mother, saw the blue flame of his eyes and thought to herself that his way through the world would be as the way of the eagle through the air.

Having shown himself before the Hall, Sigurd dismounted from Grani, and stroked and caressed him with his hands and told him that he might go back and take pasture with the herd. The proud horse breathed fondly over Sigurd and bounded away.

Then Sigurd strode on until he came to the hut in the forest where he worked with the cunning smith Regin. No one was in the hut when he entered. But over the anvil, in the smoke of the smithy fire, there was a work of Regin's hands. Sigurd looked upon it, and a hatred for the thing that was shown rose in him.

The work of Regin's hands was a shield, a great shield of iron. Hammered out on that shield and colored with red and brown colors was the image of a dragon, a dragon lengthening himself out of a cave. Sigurd thought it was the image of the most hateful thing in the world, and the light of the smithy fire falling on it, and the smoke of the smithy fire rising round it, made it seem verily a dragon living in his own element of fire and reek.

While he was still gazing on the loathly image, Regin, the cunning smith, came into the smithy. He stood by the wall and he watched Sigurd. His back was bent; his hair fell over his eyes that were all fiery, and he looked like a beast that runs behind the hedges.

"Aye, thou dost look on Fafnir the dragon, son of the Volsungs," he said to Sigurd. "Mayhap it is thou who wilt slay him."

"I would not strive with such a beast. He is all horrible to me," Sigurd said.

"With a good sword thou mightst slay him and win for thyself more renown than ever thy father had," Regin whispered.

"I shall win renown as my fathers won renown, in battle with men and in conquest on kingdoms," Sigurd said.

"Thou art not a true Volsung or thou wouldst gladly go where most danger and dread is," said Regin. "Thou hast heard of Fafnir the dragon, whose image I have wrought here. If thou dost ride to the crest of the hills thou mayst look across to the desolate land where Fafnir has his haunt. Know that once it was fair land where men had peace and prosperity, but Fafnir came and made his den in a cave near by, and his breathings made it the barren waste that men call Gnita Heath. Now, if thou art a true Volsung, thou wilt slay the dragon, and let that land become fair again, and bring the people back to it and so add to King Aly's domain."

"I have nought to do with the slaying of dragons," Sigurd said. "I have to make war on King Lygni, and avenge upon him the slaying of Sigmund, my father."

"What is the slaying of Lygni and the conquest of his kingdom to the slaying of Fafnir the dragon?" Regin cried. "I will tell thee what no one else knows of Fafnir the dragon. He guards a hoard of gold and jewels the like of which was never seen in the world. All this hoard you can make yours by slaying him."

"I do not covet riches," Sigurd said.

"No riches is like to the riches that Fafnir guards. His hoard is the hoard that the Dwarf Andvari had from the world's early days. Once the gods themselves paid it over as a ransom. And if thou wilt win this hoard thou wilt be as one of the gods."

"How dost thou know that of which thou speakst, Regin?" Sigurd said.

"I know, and one day I may tell thee how I know."

"And one day I may harken to thee. But speak to me no more of this dragon. I would have thee make a sword, a sword that will be mightier and better shapen than any sword in the world. Thou canst do this, Regin, for thou art accounted the best sword-smith amongst men."

Regin looked at Sigurd out of his small and cunning eyes and he thought it was best to make himself active. So he took the weightiest pieces of iron and put them into his furnace and he brought out the secret tools that he used when a master-work was claimed from his hands.

All day Sigurd worked beside him, keeping the fire at its best glow and bringing water to cool the blade as it was fashioned and re-fashioned. And as he worked he thought only about the blade and about how he would make war upon King Lygni, and avenge the man who was slain before he himself was born.

All day he thought only of war and of the beaten blade. But at night his dreams were not upon wars nor shapen blades but upon Fafnir the dragon. He saw the heath that was left barren by his breath, and he saw the cave where he had his den, and he saw him crawling down from his cave, his scales glittering like rings of mail, and his length the length of a company of men on the march.

The next day he worked with Regin to shape the great sword. When it was shapen with all the cunning Regin knew it looked indeed a mighty sword. Then Regin sharp-ened it and Sigurd polished it. And at last he held the great sword by its iron hilt.

Then Sigurd took the shield that had the image of Fafnir the dragon upon it and he put the shield over the anvil of the smithy. Raising the great sword in both his hands he struck full on the iron shield.

The stroke of the sword sheared away some of the shield, but the blade broke in Sigurd's hands. Then in anger he turned on Regin, crying out, "Thou hast made a knave's sword for me. To work with thee again! Thou must make me a Volsung's sword."

Then he went out and called to Grani, his horse, and mounted him and rode to the river bank like the sweep of the wind.

Regin took more pieces of iron and began to forge a new sword, uttering as he worked runes that were about the hoard that Fafnir the dragon guarded. And Sigurd that night dreamt of glittering treasure that he coveted not, masses of gold and heaps of glittering jewels.

He was Regin's help the next day and they both worked to make a sword that would be mightier than the first. For three days they worked upon it, and then Regin put into Sigurd's hands a sword, sharpened and pol-ished, that was mightier and more splendid looking than the one that had been forged before. And again Sigurd took the shield that had the image of the dragon upon it and he put it upon the anvil. Then he raised his arms and struck his full blow. The sword cut through the shield, but when it struck the anvil it shivered in his hands.

He left the smithy angrily and called to Grani, his proud horse. He mounted and rode on like the sweep of the wind.

Later he came to his mother's bower and stood before Hiordis.

"A greater sword must I have," said he, "than one that is made of metal dug out of the earth. The time has come, Mother, when thou must put into my hands the broken pieces of Gram, the sword of Sig-mund and the Volsungs."

Hiordis measured him with the glance of her eyes, and she saw that her son was a mighty youth and one fit to use the sword of Sigmund and the Volsungs. She bade him go with her to the King's Hall. Out of the great stone chest that was in her chamber she took the beast's skin and the broken blade that was wrapped in it. She gave the pieces into the hands of her son. "Behold the halves of Gram," she said, "of Gram, the mighty sword that in the far-off days Odin left in the Branstock, in the tree of the house of Volsung. I would see Gram new-shapen in thy hands, my son."

Then she embraced him as she had never embraced him before, and standing there with her ruddy hair about her she told him of the glory of Gram and of the deeds of his fathers in whose hands the sword had shone.

Then Sigurd went to the smithy, and he wakened Regin out of his sleep, and he made him look on the shining halves of Sigmund's sword. He commanded him to make out of these halves a sword for his hand.

Regin worked for days in his smithy and Sigurd never left his side. At last the blade was forged, and when Sigurd held it in his hand fire ran along the edge of it.

Again he laid the shield that had the image of the dragon upon it on the anvil of the smithy. Again, with his hands on its iron hilt, he raised the sword for a full stroke.

He struck, and the sword cut through the shield and sheared through the anvil, cutting away its iron horn. Then did Sigurd know that he had in his hands the Volsungs' sword. He went without and called to Grani, and like the sweep of the wind rode down to the river's bank. Shreds of wool were floating down the water. Sigurd struck at them with his sword, and the fine wool was divided against the water's edge. Hardness and fineness, Gram could cut through both.

That night Gram, the Volsungs' sword, was under his head when he slept, but still his dreams were filled with images that he had not regarded in the day time; the shrine of a hoard that he coveted not, and the gleam of the scales of a dragon that was too loathly for him to battle with.

GERMANY

Fafnir, the Dragon [1]

⮡ *Sigurd, the Scandinavian, and Siegfried, the German, are two names for the same hero whose parallel stories are to be found in the Völsunga Saga of Iceland and the Nibelungenlied of Germany.*

The root story is part of the Elder Edda, the great and earliest source of Scandinavian epic which, after hundreds of years of oral transmission, was written down by an unknown author in the twelfth or thirteenth century. The Völsunga Saga has an air of greater primitiveness than has the Nibelungenlied. Some scholars hold that the Nibelungen saga traveled north to Iceland and that the Scandinavian version preserves the earlier form of the original. Both are

[1] From James Baldwin, *The Story of Siegfried* (Scribner, 1882).

tales of immense grandeur, tragedy, pathos and heroic humanity.

The story of the slaying of Fafnir can hardly be read by the opera devotee without the "leitmotifs" of Wagner's opera cycle ringing in the ears. His four great operas tell the story of the Nibelung family and their destruction wrought by the curse of the gold which they desired greatly. The slaying of a dragon, wherever it occurs, always stirs the blood, since it is so universal a symbol of the triumph of good over evil.

Regin took up his harp, and his fingers smote the strings; and the music which came forth sounded like the wail of the winter's wind through the dead tree-tops of the forest. And the song which he sang was full of grief and wild hopeless yearning for the things which were not to be. When he had ceased, Siegfried said, —

"That was indeed a sorrowful song for one to sing who sees his hopes so nearly realized. Why are you so sad? Is it because you fear the curse which you have taken upon yourself? or is it because you know not what you will do with so vast a treasure, and its possession begins already to trouble you?"

"Oh, many are the things I will do with that treasure!" answered Regin; and his eyes flashed wildly, and his face grew red and pale. "I will turn winter into summer; I will make the desert places glad; I will bring back the golden age; I will make myself a god: for mine shall be the wisdom and the gathered wealth of the world. And yet I fear" —

"What do you fear?"

"The ring, the ring — it is accursed! The Norns, too, have spoken, and my doom is known. I cannot escape it."

"The Norns have woven the woof of every man's life," answered Siegfried. "To-morrow we fare to the Glittering Heath, and the end shall be as the Norns have spoken."

And so, early the next morning, Siegfried mounted Greyfell, and rode out towards the desert land that lay beyond the forest and the barren mountain range; and Regin, his eyes flashing with desire, and his feet never tiring, trudged by his side. For seven days they wended their way through the thick greenwood, sleeping at night on the bare ground beneath the trees, while the wolves and other wild beasts of the forest filled the air with their hideous howlings. But no evil creature dare come near them, for fear of the shining beams of light which fell from Greyfell's gleaming mane. On the eighth day they came to the open country and to the hills, where the land was covered with black boulders and broken by yawning chasms. And no living thing was seen there, not even an insect, nor a blade of grass; and the silence of the grave was over all. And the earth was dry and parched, and the sun hung above them like a painted shield in a blue-black sky, and there was neither shade nor water anywhere. But Siegfried rode onwards in the way which Regin pointed out, and faltered not, although he grew faint with

thirst and with the overpowering heat. Towards the evening of the next day they came to a dark mountain wall which stretched far out on either hand, and rose high above them, so steep that it seemed to close up the way, and to forbid them going farther.

"This is the wall!" cried Regin. "Beyond this mountain is the Glittering Heath, and the goal of all my hopes."

And the little old man ran forward, and scaled the rough side of the mountain, and reached its summit, while Siegfried and Greyfell were yet toiling among the rocks at its foot. Slowly and painfully they climbed the steep ascent, sometimes following a narrow path which wound along the edge of a precipice, sometimes leaping from rock to rock, or over some deep gorge, and sometimes picking their way among the crags and cliffs. The sun at last went down, and one by one the stars came out; and the moon was rising, round and red, when Siegfried stood by Regin's side, and gazed from the mountain-top down upon the Glittering Heath which lay beyond. And a strange, weird scene it was that met his sight. At the foot of the mountain was a river, white and cold and still; and beyond it was a smooth and barren plain, lying silent and lonely in the pale moonlight. But in the distance was seen a circle of flickering flames, ever changing, — now growing brighter, now fading away, and now shining with a dull, cold light, like the glimmer of the glowworm or the foxfire. And as Siegfried gazed upon the scene, he saw the dim outline of some hideous monster moving hither and thither, and seeming all the more terrible in the uncertain light.

"It is he!" whispered Regin, and his lips were ashy pale, and his knees trembled beneath him. "It is Fafnir, and he wears the Helmet of Terror! Shall we not go back to the smithy by the great forest, and to the life of ease and safety that may be ours there? Or will you rather dare to go forward, and meet the Terror in its abode?"

"None but cowards give up an undertaking once begun," answered Siegfried. "Go back to Rhineland yourself, if you are afraid; but you must go alone. You have brought me thus far to meet the dragon of the heath, to win the hoard of the swarthy elves, and to rid the world of a terrible evil. Before the setting of another sun, the deed which you have urged me to do will be done."

Then he dashed down the eastern slope of the mountain, leaving Greyfell and the trembling Regin behind him. Soon he stood on the banks of the white river, which lay between the mountain and the heath; but the stream was deep and sluggish, and the channel was very wide. He paused a moment, wondering how he should cross; and the air seemed heavy with deadly vapors, and the water was thick and cold. While he thus stood in thought, a boat came silently out of the mists, and drew near; and the boatman stood up and called to him, and said, —

"What man are you who dares come into this land of loneliness and fear?"

"I am Siegfried," answered the lad; "and I have come to slay Fafnir, the Terror."

"Sit in my boat," said the boatman, "and I will carry you across the river."

And Siegfried sat by the boatman's side; and without the use of an oar, and without a breath of air to drive it forward, the little vessel turned, and moved silently towards the farther shore.

"In what way will you fight the dragon?" asked the boatman.

"With my trusty sword Balmung I shall slay him," answered Siegfried.

"But he wears the Helmet of Terror, and he breathes deathly poisons, and his eyes dart forth lightning, and no man can withstand his strength," said the boatman.

"I will find some way by which to overcome him."

"Then be wise, and listen to me," said the boatman. "As you go up from the river you will find a road, worn deep and smooth, starting from the water's edge, and winding over the moor. It is the trail of Fafnir, adown which he comes at dawn of every day to slake his thirst at the river. Do you dig a pit in this roadway, — a pit narrow and deep, — and hide yourself within it. In the morning, when Fafnir passes over it, let him feel the edge of Balmung."

As the man ceased speaking, the boat touched the shore, and Siegfried leaped out. He looked back to thank his unknown friend, but neither boat nor boatman was to be seen. Only a thin white mist rose slowly from the cold surface of the stream, and floated upwards and away towards the mountain-tops. Then the lad remembered that the strange boatman had worn a blue hood bespangled with golden stars, and that a gray kirtle was thrown over his shoulders, and that his one eye glistened and sparkled with a light that was more than human. And he knew that he had again talked with Odin. Then, with a braver heart than before, he went forward, along the river bank, until he came to Fafnir's trail, — a deep, wide furrow in the earth, beginning at the river's bank, and winding far away over the heath, until it was lost to sight in the darkness. The bottom of the trail was soft and slimy, and its sides had been worn smooth by Fafnir's frequent travel through it.

In this road, at a point not far from the river, Siegfried, with his trusty sword Balmung, scooped out a deep and narrow pit, as Odin had directed. And when the gray dawn began to appear in the east he hid himself within this trench, and waited for the coming of the monster. He had not long to wait; for no sooner had the sky begun to redden in the light of the coming sun than the dragon was heard bestirring himself. Siegfried peeped warily from his hiding place, and saw him coming far down the road, hurrying with all speed, that he might quench his thirst at the sluggish river, and hasten back to his gold; and the sound which he made was like the trampling of many feet and the jingling of many chains. With bloodshot eyes, and gaping mouth, and flaming nostrils, the hideous creature came rushing onwards. His sharp, curved claws dug deep into the soft earth; and his bat-like wings, half trailing on the ground, half flapping in the air, made a sound like that which is heard when Thor rides in his goat-drawn chariot over the dark thunder clouds. It was a terrible moment for Siegfried, but still he was not afraid. He crouched low down in his hiding place, and the bare blade of the trusty Balmung glittered in the morning light. On came the hastening feet and the flapping wings: the red gleam from the monster's flaming nostrils lighted up the trench where Siegfried lay.

He heard a roaring and a rushing like the sound of a whirlwind in the forest; then a black, inky mass rolled above him, and all was dark. Now was Siegfried's opportunity. The bright edge of Balmung gleamed in the darkness one moment, and then it smote the heart of Fafnir as he passed. Some men say that Odin sat in the pit with Siegfried, and strengthened his arm and directed his sword, or else he could not thus have slain the Terror. But, be this as it may, the victory was soon won. The monster stopped short, while but half of his long body had glided over the pit; for sudden death had overtaken him. His horrid head fell lifeless upon the ground; his cold wings flapped once, and then lay, quivering and helpless, spread out on either side; and streams of thick black blood flowed from his heart, through the wound beneath, and filled the trench in which Siegfried was hidden, and ran like a mountain torrent down the road towards the river. Siegfried was covered from head to foot with the slimy liquid, and, had he not quickly leaped from his hiding place, he would have been drowned in the swift-rushing stream.

The bright sun rose in the east, and gilded the mountain tops, and fell upon the still waters of the river, and lighted up the treeless plains around. The south wind played gently against Siegfried's cheeks and in his long hair, as he stood gazing on his fallen foe. And the sound of singing birds, and rippling waters, and gay insects, — such as had not broken the silence of the Glittering Heath for ages, — came to his ears. The Terror was dead, and Nature had awakened from her sleep of dread. And as the lad leaned upon his sword, and thought of the deed he had done, behold! the shining Greyfell, with the beaming, hopeful mane, having crossed the now bright river, stood by his side. And Regin, his face grown wondrous cold, came trudging over the meadows; and his heart was full of guile. Then the mountain vultures came wheeling downward to look upon the dead dragon; and with them were two ravens, black as midnight. And when Siegfried saw these ravens he knew them to be Odin's birds, — Hugin, thought, and Munin, memory. And they alighted on the ground near by; and the lad listened to hear what they would say. Then Hugin flapped his wings, and said, —

"The deed is done. Why tarries the hero?"

And Munin said, —

"The world is wide. Fame waits for the hero."

And Hugin answered, —

"What if he win the Hoard of the Elves? That is not honor. Let him seek fame by nobler deeds."

Then Munin flew past his ear, and whispered, —

"Beware of Regin, the master! His heart is poisoned. He would be thy bane."

And the two birds flew away to carry the news to Odin in the happy halls of Gladsheim.

When Regin drew near to look upon the dragon, Siegfried kindly accosted him: but he seemed not to hear; and a snaky glitter lurked in his eyes, and his mouth was set and dry, and he seemed as one walking in a dream.

"It is mine now," he murmured: "it is all mine, now, — the Hoard of the swarthy elf-folk, the garnered wisdom of ages. The strength of the world is mine. I will keep, I will save, I will heap up; and none shall have part or parcel of the treasure which is mine alone."

Then his eyes fell upon Seigfried; and his cheeks grew dark with wrath, and he cried out, —

"Why are you here in my way? I am the lord of the Glittering Heath: I am the master of the Hoard. I am the master, and you are my thrall."

Siegfried wondered at the change which had taken place in his old master; but he only smiled at his strange words, and made no answer.

"You have slain my brother!" Regin cried; and his face grew fearfully black, and his mouth foamed with rage.

"It was my deed and yours," calmly answered Siegfried. "I have rid the world of a Terror: I have righted a grievous wrong."

"You have slain my brother," said Regin; "and a murderer's ransom you shall pay!"

"Take the Hoard for your ransom, and let us each wend his way," said the lad.

"The Hoard is mine by rights," answered Regin still more wrathfully. "I am the master, and you are my thrall. Why stand you in my way?"

Then, blinded with madness, he rushed at Siegfried as if to strike him down; but his foot slipped in a puddle of gore, and he pitched headlong against the sharp edge of Balmung. So sudden was this movement, and so unlooked for, that the sword was twitched out of Siegfried's hand, and fell with a dull splash into the blood-filled pit before him; while Regin, slain by his own rashness, sank dead upon the ground. Full of horror, Siegfried turned away, and mounted Greyfell.

"This is a place of blood," said he, "and the way to glory leads not through it. Let the Hoard still lie on the Glittering Heath: I will go my way hence; and the world shall know me for better deeds than this."

And he turned his back on the fearful scene, and rode away; and so swiftly did Greyfell carry him over the desert land and the mountain waste, that, when night came, they stood on the shore of the great North Sea, and the white waves broke at their feet. And the lad sat for a long time silent upon the warm white sand of the beach, and Greyfell waited at his side. And he watched the stars as they came out one by one, and the moon, as it rose round and pale, and moved like a queen across the sky. And the night wore away, and the stars grew pale, and the moon sank to rest in the wilderness of waters. And at day-dawn Siegfried looked towards the west, and midway between sky and sea he thought he saw dark mountain tops hanging above a land of mists that seemed to float upon the edge of the sea.

While he looked, a white ship, with sails all set, came speeding over the waters towards him. It came nearer and nearer, and the sailors rested upon their oars as it glided into the quiet harbor. A minstrel, with long white beard floating in the wind, sat at the prow; and the sweet music from his harp was wafted like incense to the shore. The vessel touched the sands: its white sails were reefed as if by magic, and the crew leaped out upon the beach.

"Hail, Siegfried the Golden!" cried the harper. "Whither do you fare this summer day?"

"I have come from a land of horror and dread," answered the lad; "and I would fain fare to a brighter."

"Then go with me to awaken the earth from its slumber, and to robe the fields in their garbs of beauty," said the harper. And he touched the strings of his harp, and strains of the softest music arose in the still morning air. And Siegfried stood entranced, for never before had he heard such music.

FRANCE

The Song of Roland[1]

‹§ The Epic and the Saga are largely pre-Christian in ideals, concepts and social structure. With the introduction of the Romance, Christianity emerges as background and motivating force. The term Romance *is applied to the long stories, basically epic in feeling, theme, and poetic form, which were recited in the Romance languages — those languages which derive from Rome, namely, Latin, French, Italian, Spanish, and Portuguese. Later, the term* Romance *came to be applied to any story in which unprecedented events take place, or the possibilities of life are heightened beyond the probabilities of actual experience.*

The Holy Wars of the Crusades, the passionate response of Europe to the image of Christ, and the adoration of the Virgin Mary which inspired the great cathedrals of medieval Europe — these were the subjects also of the medieval Romance. The legend of the Holy Grail became part of the old King Arthur cycle. A new regard for the position of woman in society, the growth of the chivalric ideal, knightly quest and devout dedication to a cause, these were the themes that bridged the old pagan world of the epic and the Christian world of the future.

In the Song of Roland, *the origins of which are discussed in the introduction to this section (page 470), Christianity had not yet become the dominating theme. It was not of God, nor of Christ, nor the Virgin, not even of his own true love that Roland thought when he came to die, but only of Charlemagne, his liege lord, and of "Sweet France." To be sure he proffered his right-hand glove to God, but this was the traditional act of homage between the feudal*

[1] From Merriam Sherwood, trans., *The Song of Roland* (Longmans, Green, 1938).

knight and his lord. The mysteries of Christ and of the Virgin had not yet overwhelmed the imagination of the feudal world when the deeds of Roland were sung.

THE BLOWING OF THE HORN

Count Roland beheld the great losses among his men. He called Oliver, his companion-at-arms:

"Fair Sir, beloved Comrade, what do you think is to be done? Behold how many vassals strew the ground! We may well weep for France, the Sweet, the Fair. What barons she has lost! Ah, my King, my Friend, why are not you here? Oliver my Brother, what can we do? How shall we send him word?"

Said Oliver:

"I know not how. I had rather die than that dishonor should be told of us."

Said Roland:

"I will sound my horn, and Charles will hear it as he crosses the pass. I swear to you, the Franks will return."

Said Oliver:

"Shameful would that be, bringing dishonor upon all your kin, dishonor which would last all their lives. When I bade you sound your horn, you refused. If you do it now, 'twill be against my counsel. To blow it now were cowardice. Why, both your arms are bloody!"

The Count answered:

"'Tis that I have struck fair blows."

Said Roland:

"Stiff is our fight. I will blow my horn, and King Charles will hear it."

Said Oliver:

"That were no knightly deed! When I bade you blow it, Comrade, you refused. If

522

the King had been with us, we should have had no hurt. Those who are with him are not to blame."

Said Oliver:

"By this beard of mine, if I see again my noble sister Aude, your Betrothed, never shall you lie in her embrace!"

Said Roland:

"Why are you angry with me"

The other answered:

"This is all your fault; for valor with sense is not madness. Measure is worth more than foolhardiness. The French are dead through your thoughtlessness. Never more shall we serve Charles. If you had taken my advice, my Lord would have returned. We should have won this battle, with King Marsile either dead or captured. Your prowess, Roland, woe the day we saw it! Charlemagne will never again have us to help him. Never will there be such a man until the day of judgment. You will die and France will be dishonored. Our loyal companionship dissolves today. Before evening falls, heavy will be our parting!"

The Archbishop heard them quarreling. He spurred his horse with his spurs of pure gold. He rode up to them and began to chastise them:

"Sir Roland, and you, Sir Oliver, in God's name I beg of you, do not quarrel! Blowing the horn would not help us now; nevertheless, it would be better to do it. Let the King come back; he will be able to avenge us. Those of Spain must not go home exulting. Our countrymen will dismount here. They will find us dead and cut to pieces. They will place us in biers on the backs of pack-horses, and will weep for us in grief and pity. They will bury us within the hallowed ground of churches, that we be not devoured by wolves or bears or dogs."

Roland replied:

"Well spoken, Sire!"

Roland placed his horn to his lips. He made a mighty effort, blowing with all his strength. High were the peaks and long the bugle's voice. They heard it echoing for thirty long leagues. Charles and all his followers heard it. Said the King:

"Our men are doing battle!"

Ganelon answered him:

"If another said that, 'twould be taken for a lie!"

Count Roland blew his horn, with great effort and in pain, so hard that the bright blood gushed from his mouth and his brain burst from his temples. The sound of his horn carried far. Charles heard it as he crossed the pass. So did Duke Naimes. The French listened. Said the King:

"Hark! That is Roland's horn! He would never have blown it if he were not doing battle."

Ganelon replied:

"There is no battle! You are old and hoary and white-haired; such words make you seem a very child. For you know the mighty pride of Roland. 'Tis a wonder that God hath suffered it so long. He even took Noples without your command. The Saracens within came forth and fought the good vassal Roland. Then he flooded the fields to wash away the blood, that no trace might appear. For a single hare he will blow his horn all day. Now he is perchance carrying out some wager before his peers. There is no people under heaven that would dare seek him in the field. Ride on! What are you stopping for? The Great Land is far away ahead of us!"

Count Roland's mouth was filled with blood. His brain had burst from his temples. He blew his horn in pain and anguish. Charles heard it, and so did his Frenchmen. Said the King:

"That bugle carries far!"

Duke Naimes replied:

"'Tis that a hero blows the blast! I am sure there is a battle. He who now asks you to do nothing has betrayed Roland. Arm yourselves and shout your battle-cry. Succor your noble followers. You can hear plainly that Roland is in despair."

The Emperor had his bugles blown. The French dismounted, and armed themselves with hauberks and helmets, and with swords adorned with gold. They had noble shields and lances stout and long, and pennons white and red and blue. All the barons of the army mounted their chargers. They spurred rapidly through the length of the pass. Not one but said to the other:

"If we should see Roland before he dies, we would deal great blows by his side!"

Of what avail such words? They had waited too long!

The light of evening shone. Against the sun the armor flashed, hauberks and helmets flaming, and shields painted with flowers, and spears and gilded pennons. The Emperor rode in wrath, and the French in sorrow and anger. Not one was there who did not weep bitterly, filled with a great fear for Roland. The King had Count Ganelon seized and given into custody, to the cooks of the household. He summoned the chief cook of them all, Besgon:

"Guard him well, as it behooves to keep such a felon! He has betrayed my followers."

Besgon received him, and set upon him a hundred scullions, among the best and the worst. They pulled out hairs from his beard and his mustache. Each one struck him four blows with his fist. They beat him with sticks and staves, put a chain around his neck and chained him like a bear, then placed him on a pack-horse, to his shame. Thus they kept him, until such time as they gave him back to Charlemagne.

High were the peaks, and shadowy and tall; the valleys, deep; and swift, the streams. The clarions sounded in the van and in the rear, all taking up and prolonging the voice of Roland's horn. The Emperor rode in wrath; and the French, sorrowful and angry. Not one was there but wept and lamented, praying God to protect Roland until they might all join him on the field of battle. What blows they would deal by his side! Of what avail their prayers? Prayers could not help them now. They had waited too long and could not arrive in time.

In great anger rode King Charles. Over his byrnie flowed his hoary beard. All the barons of France dug in their spurs. Not one was there but lamented that they were not beside Roland the Captain as he fought the Saracens of Spain. So great was his anguish, methinks he was about to give up the ghost. O Lord, what men, the sixty left in his company! Never did king or captain have better.

The Last Stand of the Rearguard

Roland looked over the mountains and the heath. Of those of France how many he saw lying dead! Like a gentle knight he wept for them:

"Noble Lords, may God have mercy on you! May he grant paradise to all your souls! May he make them to lie among the holy flowers! Never saw I better vassals than you. How long and constantly have you served me! What great countries have you conquered for Charles! But woe the day that the Emperor took you into his household! Land of France, O most sweet country, today forlorn and ravaged! Barons of France, I see you dying for me. I cannot fight for you or save you. May God, Who never lied, help you! Oliver my Brother, I must not fail you. I shall die of grief, if I am slain by nothing else. Sir Comrade, let us go smite once more!"

Count Roland returned to the fight. Wielding Durendal, he struck like a knight. He cut through the middle Faldrun of Pui and twenty-four of the Pagans most renowned. Never will any man have such desire to avenge himself. As the stag flees before the hounds, so fled the Pagans before Roland. Said the Archbishop:

"Bravo! Well done! Such valor as that befits a knight who bears good arms and sits a good steed. In battle he should be fierce and strong; otherwise, he is not worth fourpence, but should be a monk in some monastery, praying without cease for our sins!"

Roland answered:

"Smite, nor spare them!"

At these words the French began to fight once more. Heavy were the losses of the Christians. When a man knows that there will be no quarter, he puts up a brave defense in such a battle. That is why the French were as fierce as lions.

Lo! There came Marsile, riding in lordly wise on a horse that he called Gaignon. He dug in his spurs and went to smite Bevon, lord of Dijon and of Beaune. He pierced his shield and rent his hauberk, striking him dead without doing him other hurt. Then he slew Ivorie and Ivon, and, along with them, Gerard of Roussillon. Count Roland was not far away. He said to the Pagan:

"The Lord God give thee ill! Wickedly thou slayest my companions. Thou shalt feel a blow of mine before we part. This very day shalt thou learn the name of my sword!"

He rode in knightly wise to strike him. The Count cut off the King's right hand. Then he severed the head of Jurfaleu the Blond, King Marsile's son. The Pagans cried out:

"Help us, Mahound! Ye Gods of ours, avenge us on Charles! He has placed in our land scoundrels who, even at the risk of dying for it, will not flee the field!"

The one said to the other: "Well then, let us flee!"

At these words a hundred thousand took to their heels. No matter who might bid them, they would not return. Of what avail their flight? Marsile might flee, but his uncle remained, the Caliph, Lord of Carthage, Alferne, and Garmalie, and of Ethiopia — a cursed land; he held sway over the black race. They have big noses and large ears. More than fifty thousand of them were assembled there. They charged fierce and furiously, then shouted the Pagan battle-cry. Said Roland:

"This is our martyrdom! Now I know well that we have not long to live; but he is a traitor who does not first sell himself dear. Strike, my Lords, with your furbished swords! Do battle for your dead and for your lives, that sweet France may not be dishonored by us! When Charles my Lord shall come to this field and, beholding the punishment we have wrought upon the Saracens, shall find for every one of our men fifteen Pagans slain he will not fail to bless us."

The Parting of Roland and Oliver

When Roland saw the accursed people, blacker than any ink, with no spot of white except their teeth, he said:

"Now I know for certain that we shall die today. Strike, Frenchmen, for I am starting the fight anew!"

Said Oliver:

"Cursed be the last to strike!"

At these words the French fell upon the Pagans, who, when they saw how few were the French, were filled with pride and comfort. Said one to the other:

"The Emperor is in the wrong!"

The Caliph bestrode a sorrel horse. He dug in his gilded spurs, and struck Oliver from behind in the middle of his back. He rent the white hauberk, even to the body. He thrust the spear clean through his breast. Then he said:

"You have received a rude blow! Alas for you that Charlemagne left you at the pass! He has wronged us, nor is it right that he boast of it: for, in you alone, I have avenged my people!"

Oliver felt himself wounded to the death. He grasped Hauteclaire, whose steel was burnished, and smote the Caliph on his pointed gilt helmet, striking off its painted flowers and crystals. He split open his head down to the small front teeth, shook the sword, and struck him dead. Then he said:

"Pagan, curses on thee! I do not say that Charles has not lost, but thou wilt not be able to boast to wife or to any lady, in the kingdom whence thou art, that thou hast taken from me a penny's-worth, or hast done scathe to me or to any other."

Then he cried out to Roland to help him.

Oliver felt that he was wounded mortally. He would never have his fill of avenging himself. He hurled himself into the press, striking like a baron. He slashed through spear-shafts and bucklers, cut off feet and hands, cleft saddles and flanks. Whoever had seen him dismember the Saracens, flinging one dead upon the other, might indeed mind him of a doughty vassal! Nor did he forget the battle-cry of Charles. "Montjoie!" he shouted loud and clear. He called to Roland, his friend and peer:

"Sir Comrade, come to my side! With bitter sorrow we must part today!"

Roland looked into the face of Oliver. It was wan, discolored, livid, pale. The bright blood streaked his body, the clots falling to the ground.

"O Lord," said the Count, "now I know not what to do. Sir Comrade, alack for your prowess! Never will there be a man to equal thee! Ah, sweet France, how art thou pillaged today of good vassals! How art thou confounded and laid low! The Emperor will suffer great scathe."

With these words he swooned on his horse. Behold Roland swooned and Oliver wounded unto death. Oliver had lost so much blood that his vision was troubled. He could not see clearly enough to recognize mortal man, far or near. As he approached his comrade he struck him on his jeweled and gilded helmet, cleaving it as far as the nose-piece; but he did not reach the flesh. At that blow Roland looked at him, and asked him gently and softly:

"Sir Comrade, are you doing this of your own wish? This is Roland, who has always loved you well! You have struck me without challenging me first!"

Said Oliver:

"Now I know you, for I hear you speak. I cannot see you, but may the Lord God do so! I struck you. Forgive me, I pray!"

Roland answered:

"You did not hurt me. I forgive you here before God."

At these words the one bowed to the other. Thus, in great love, they parted.

Oliver felt the anguish of death approaching. Both his eyes turned in his head. He lost his sense of hearing and of sight. He dismounted and lay on the ground. He confessed his sins in a loud voice, both his hands clasped toward heaven, and prayed God to grant him Paradise and to bless Charles and sweet France, and, above all men, his comrade Roland. His heart failed, his helmet sank, his whole body fell upon the ground. Dead was the Count, no longer might he live. Roland the Brave wept for him and mourned. Never on earth will you hear of a man more sorrowful.

Roland saw that his friend was dead, saw him lying, face down, on the ground. Very gently he began to lament him:

"Sir Comrade, alas for your bold courage! We have been together for years and for days. You have never done me harm, nor I you. Since you are dead, it is my grief that I live!"

With these words the Marquis fainted on his horse Veillantif. He was held on by his stirrups of fine gold; thus, wheresoever he might go, he could not fall off.

THE DEATH OF ROLAND

Roland felt that death was near. His brain issued forth from his ears. He prayed God for his peers, that He would call them. Then, for himself, he prayed to the Angel Gabriel.

He took his horn, that no one might reproach him; and, in his other hand, his sword Durendal. More than a bowshot toward Spain, into a fallow field, he went. He climbed upon a knoll, where, under two fair trees, there were four blocks of stone, cut from marble. He fell down on his back on the green grass. There he swooned, for death was near him.

High were the mountains and very high the trees. Four blocks of stone were there, of shining marble. On the green grass Count Roland had fainted. All the time a Saracen was watching him, and feigning death as he lay among the slain. He had smeared his body and his face with blood. He got to his feet and hastened to run forward. Handsome was he, and strong, and of great prowess. In his pride he was seized with a mortal madness. He laid hold of Roland, of his body and of his weapons, and he spoke these words:

"Vanquished is Charles's nephew! I will bear away this sword of his to Araby!"

As he pulled at it, the Count came a little to his senses. Roland was conscious that his sword was being taken from him. He opened his eyes and spoke these words:

"Methinks thou art not one of ours!"

He grasped his horn, which he had no wish to lose, and struck the Pagan on the helmet, jeweled and gold-adorned. He shattered the steel and his head and his bones. Both his eyes burst from their sockets and he fell dead at Roland's feet. Said the Count:

"Pagan lout, how hadst thou the presumption to lay hold of me, whether rightly or wrongly? No man shall hear of this without deeming thee a fool. The large end of my horn has been cracked; the crystal and the gold have been knocked off."

Roland felt that his sight was going. He got to his feet, exerting all his strength. All color had left his face. Before him there was a dark stone. In grief and anger he struck ten blows upon it. The steel grated, but did not break or nick.

"Ah!" said the Count. "Help me, Saint Mary! Ah, Durendal, good Sword, alas for thee! Since I am dying, I am no longer thy keeper. How many pitched battles have I won with thee! Conquered how many wide lands, which Charles of the Hoary Beard now holds! May no man have thee who would flee from another! A good vassal has long carried you. Never will there be such a one in France the Holy!"

Roland struck on the stone of sardonyx. The steel grated but it did not crack or chip. When he saw that he could not break it, he began to lament it to himself:

"Ah, Durendal, how fair and bright and white art thou! How thou dost sparkle and flame in the sun! Charles was in the vales of Maurienne, when God sent him word from heaven by His angel that he should give thee to a count and captain. Then was I girt with thee by the noble King, the great King. With thee I conquered for him Anjou and Brittany; with thee I conquered for him Poitou and Maine. For him I conquered with thee Normandy the Free. With thee I conquered for him Provence and Aquitaine and Lombardy and all Romagna. With thee I conquered for him Bavaria and all Flanders and Burgundy and all Apulia, Constantinople, whose homage he received, and Saxony, where he does what he will. With thee I conquered for him Scotland, Wales and Ireland; and England, which he considered crownland. With thee how many lands and countries have I conquered for Charles of the Hoary Beard to rule! For this sword I have dolor and grief. Rather would I die than leave it among the Pagans. God! Father! Let not France be thus shamed!"

Roland smote a dark stone. He chipped off more of it than I can say. The sword crunched but did not break or shiver. Instead, it rebounded toward heaven. When the Count saw that he could not break it, he bewailed it very softly to himself:

"Ah, Durendal, how beautiful thou art, and holy! In thy golden hilt are relics a-plenty: a tooth of Saint Peter and some of Saint Basil's blood, and hair of my Lord Saint Denis; and there is a piece of Saint Mary's dress. It is not right for Pagans to have thee; thou shouldst be served by Christians. May coward never wield thee! Wide are the lands I shall have conquered with you, for Charles of the Hoary Beard to rule — lands which have brought the Emperor power and riches."

Roland felt that death was taking hold of him. From his head it was descending toward his heart. Beneath a pine tree he went running. He lay down on his face on the green grass. Under him he placed his sword and his horn. He turned his head toward the Pagan people. This he did because he wished that Charles and all his men should say that he, the gentle Count, died conquering. He confessed himself again and again. For his sins he offered God his glove.

Roland felt that his time was short. He lay on a sharp peak, facing Spain. With one hand he struck his breast:

"God, by Thy power forgive my sins, great and small, which I have committed from the hour that I was born until this day when I am slain!"

He held out his right glove toward God. The angels of heaven descended to him.

Count Roland lay beneath a pine tree. He had turned his face toward Spain. He began to mind him of many things: of how many lands he had conquered, of sweet France, of the men of his kin, of Charlemagne his Lord, who had fostered him. He could not help but weep and sigh. Yet himself he would not forget. He confessed his sins and prayed God for mercy:

"True Father, Who never liest, Thou Who didst raise Lazarus from the dead, and save Daniel from the lions, keep, I pray Thee, my soul from all perils arising from the sins I have committed in my life!"

He offered his right glove to God. Saint Gabriel took it from his hand. On his arm his head was resting. With clasped hands he went to his death. God sent to him His angel Cherubin and Saint Michael of the Peril of the Sea. Saint Gabriel came with them. Together they bore the soul of the Count to Paradise.

SPAIN

The Cid[1]

⁊ *The epic poem of Spain is titled* El Cantar de Mio Cid, *the poem of the Cid. Its author is unknown, the date of its final form fixed as being about 1140. A long poem, in meandering meter, it celebrates the deeds of a great warrior, one Rodrigo (or Ruy) Diaz de Bivar, who was in actual life a doughty campaigner in the wars between Spain and the Moors, though his accomplishments could hardly have equaled the dimensions of his legend. More narrowly the biography of one man rather than encompassing the spirit of a whole people,* The Cid *is not as great in scope as* The Song of Roland. *It suffers the lack of the greatest imagination in shaping its final form. "Had the matter of* The Cid *come into the hands of a poet who was not only a master of story-telling, but the possessor of literary art, as was the poet of the Iliad, our poem would have had more echo in the world." — John Clark* (A History of Epic Poetry, *Oliver and Boyd, Edinburgh, 1900).*

The selection here given comes toward the end of the tale, when the Cid gains his highest recognition from his king, and those who have wronged him are called to account.

He who in lucky hour was born did not linger. He put on his legs hose of good cloth, and over these shoes richly adorned. He donned a shirt of fine linen as bright as the sun, all its loops of gold and silver and its wristbands well-fitting — for he had ordered this. Over that he put a tunic of finest brocade, worked in gold embroideries that glistened wherever they were. Then he put on a crimson furred robe with borders of gold —

[1] From Merriam Sherwood, trans., *The Tale of the Warrior Lord* (Longmans, Green, 1930).

the Cid Campeador always wore it. On his head was a coif of fine linen, worked in gold, rightly made, so that the hair of the good Cid Campeador could not be pulled out. He wore his beard long, and he tied it with a cord. This he did because he wanted to protect all his person against insult. Over all he put a mantle of great price, in which everyone there could see something worth looking at.

With those hundred whom he had commanded to get ready, he mounted quickly and rode out of San Servando. Thus the Cid went prepared to the court. At the outside gate he dismounted properly. The Cid and all his followers went in with prudence. He was in the middle, with the hundred around him. When they saw him who in lucky hour was born coming into the court, the good King Don Alfonso rose to his feet, and so did the Count Don Enrique and the Count Don Ramón, and after that, you may know, all the rest. With great honor did they receive him who in lucky hour was born. But the Curly-Head of Grañón, García Ordóñez, and the others in the party of the Heirs of Carrión, would not rise.

The King said to the Cid: "Come and sit here by me, Campeador, on this bench that you gave me as a gift. Although it does not please some people, you are better than We."

Then he who had won Valencia spoke his thanks:

"Sit on your bench as King and Lord. I shall take my seat here with all these my men."

What the Cid said was very pleasing to the King. Then the Cid sat down on a bench of turned work. The hundred who were guarding him took their places around him. All who were in the court were gazing at the Cid, with his long beard tied with a cord. Truly he seemed a baron by his dress. The Heirs of Carrión could not look at him for shame. Then the good King Don Alfonso rose to his feet:

"Listen, followers, and may the Creator keep you! Since I became King I have held more than two courts. One was in Burgos and the other in Carrión. This third one I have come to hold today at Toledo, for love of the Cid — he who in lucky hour was born — so that he may have satisfaction of the Heirs of Carrión. They have done him great wrong, and we all know it. Let Don Enrique and Don Ramón be judges of this case, as well as you other counts who are not of the party of the Heirs of Carrión. Put your minds, all of you, for you are wise, to finding out the right, since I do not want the wrong. On the one side and the other let us be at peace today. I swear by Saint Isidore that he who disturbs my court shall leave my kingdom and lose my love. I am on the side that is in the right. Now let the Cid Campeador plead. We shall see what the Heirs of Carrión will answer."

The Cid kissed the hand of the King and rose to his feet:

"I thank you much as my King and Lord, for calling this court for love of me.

"This is my case against the Heirs of Carrión: In deserting my daughters they did me no dishonor; for it is you who married them, King, and you will know what to do about that today. But when they took my daughters from Valencia the Great I loved my sons-in-law dearly, and I gave them two swords, Colada and Tizón — which I had won as a baron should — that they might do honor to themselves and serve you with them. When they left my daughters in the Oak-Wood of Corpes they wished to have naught to do with me and lost my love. Let them give me back my swords, since they are no longer my sons-in-law."

The Judges decreed: "All this is just."

Said the Count Don García: "Let our side talk this over."

Then the Heirs of Carrión went apart, with all their relatives and followers who were there. They discussed the matter quickly and agreed on this plan:

"The Cid Campeador shows us great favor, since he does not ask redress today for the insult to his daughters. We shall easily arrange things with the King Don Alfonso. Let us give the Cid his swords, since he thus ends his plea, and when he has them, the court will adjourn. The Cid Campeador will have no further satisfaction of us."

They went back into the court with this speech:

"Your grace, O King Don Alfonso, you are our Lord! We cannot deny that he gave us two swords. Since he asks for them and wants them back, we wish to give them to him in your presence."

They drew out the swords Colada and Tizón, and placed them in the hand of the King their Lord. As they drew forth the swords all the court was lighted up. The hilts and the quillons were all of gold. The nobles of the court were struck with wonder.

The Cid took the swords. He kissed the hands of the King. He went back to the bench from which he had arisen. He held the swords in his hands and examined them both. They could not have exchanged them for others, for the Cid knew them well. He was all joyful and he smiled from his heart. He lifted his hand and took hold of his beard:

"By this beard that no one has plucked, with these shall be avenged Doña Elvira and Doña Sol!"

He called his nephew Don Pedro by name. He held out his arm and gave him the sword Tizón:

"Take it, nephew, it will now have a better lord."

To Martín Antolínez, the worthy man of Burgos, he held out his arm, and gave him the sword Colada:

"Martín Antolínez, my worthy vassal, take Colada — I won it from a good lord, from Ramón Berenguer of Barcelona the Great. I give it to you to keep well. I know that, if you have the chance, you will win great fame and honor with it."

He kissed the Cid's hand and took the sword. Then the Cid Campeador rose up:

"Thanks to the Creator, and to you, Lord

King! I am content as regards my swords, *Colada* and *Tizón*. But I have another complaint against the Heirs of Carrión. When they took my two daughters from Valencia I gave them, in gold and in silver, three thousand marks. While I was doing this they were finishing what they had on hand. Let them give me back my wealth, since they are no longer my sons-in-law."

Then you would have seen the Heirs of Carrión complain! Said the Count Don Ramón:

"Say yes or no!"

The Heirs of Carrión answered:

"We gave the Cid Campeador his swords so that he would not ask us for anything else, for that ended his suit."

The Count Don Ramón answered:

"An it please the King, this is our opinion: that you should give satisfaction to the Cid for what he complains of."

Said the good King:

"You have my permission."

The Cid Campeador rose to his feet:

"Those riches that I gave you, give them back to me, or make me an accounting."

Then the Heirs of Carrión went aside. They could not agree in counsel, for the riches were great, and the Heirs of Carrión had spent them. They went back with their decision and spoke their wishes:

"He who won Valencia presses us overmuch, since longing for our wealth thus seizes him. We will pay him from our heritages in the lands of Carrión."

Since they acknowledged the debt, the Judges said:

"If this please the Cid we do not forbid it. But in our judgment we decree it thus: that you pay it back here in the court."

At these words the King Don Alfonso spoke:

"We know this suit well: that the Cid Campeador demands satisfaction. I have two hundred of those three thousand marks. The Heirs of Carrión between them gave them to me. I wish to return them, since the brothers are ruined. Let them give them to the Cid, to him who in lucky hour was born. Since they have to pay their debt, I do not want the money."

Fernando González spoke: "We have no wealth in money."

Then the Count Don Ramón answered:

"You have spent the gold and the silver. We pronounce in judgment before the King Don Alfonso: Let them pay it in kind and let the Campeador accept it."

Then the Heirs of Carrión saw that they must pay. You would have seen many a courser led up, many a strong mule, and many a seasoned palfrey; and many a good sword and all kinds of arms brought. The Cid took all this as they priced it in the court. The Heirs of Carrión paid him who in lucky hour was born all but the two hundred marks that King Alfonso held. They had to borrow from others, for their own wealth was not enough. They got out of that affair badly mocked at, you may be sure!

The Cid took those goods. His men kept them and guarded them. After this was done, they thought of other things. The Cid spoke:

"Your grace, O Lord King, for the love of charity! I cannot forget my greatest complaint. Hear me, all ye of the court, and let my wrong grieve you! I cannot leave the Heirs of Carrión, who so evilly dishonored me, without a challenge. Speak, how have I wronged you, Heirs of Carrión: in jest or in earnest or in any way? If I have I will make amends, according to the judgment of the court. Wherefore did you tear off the sheaths of my heart? At your departure from Valencia I gave you my daughters, with very great honor and numerous goods. Since you did not want them, O traitorous hounds, why did you take them from Valencia their heritage? Wherefore did you strike them with girths and with spurs? You left them alone, in the Oak-Wood of Corpes, with the wild beasts and the birds of the forest. You are dishonored by all you did to them. If you do not make amends for this, let this court pronounce judgment."

The Count Don García rose to his feet:

"Your grace, O King, the best of all Spain! The Cid is growing used to the king's solemn court! He has let his beard grow and wears it long. Some are afraid of him and the rest he terrifies. Those of Carrión are of such high birth that they ought not to have sought his daughters . . . Who ever gave them for wives? They did right to leave them. Whatever the Cid may say we prize no whit!"

Then the Campeador took hold of his beard:

"Thanks be to God, who rules heaven and earth! My beard is long because it was grown with care. What ails you, Count, to insult my beard? Since it first began to grow it has been nurtured with joy. No son of woman born has ever seized me by it — nor has son of Moor or of Christian plucked out a strand — as I did out of yours, Count, in the Castle of Cabra! When I took Cabra, and you by the beard, there was no youngster who did not get a good handful. The part I plucked has not even yet grown as long as the rest — I have the strand here in my purse."

Fernando González rose to his feet. You shall hear what he said, in a loud voice:

"End your case, Cid. All your wealth is paid back. Let not the quarrel grow between us and you. We are by birth Counts of Carrión. We ought to marry daughters of kings or of emperors; daughters of the petty nobles were not fitting for us. We did right to leave our wives. We think more of ourselves for it, you may know, and not less."

The Cid Ruy Díaz looked at Pedro Vermúdez:

"Speak, Pedro Mudo, the Mute, Baron who art so silent! I have their wives for daughters and thou for first cousins. When they say such things to me they are giving thee earfuls. If I answer, thou mayest not fight."

Pedro Vermúdez tried to speak. His tongue was held back, for he stammered, and he could not begin. But, once started, you may know, he did not stop:

"I will tell you, Cid, you are always doing that: calling me Pedro Mudo, the Mute, in the courts. You know well that I cannot help it. But in what I have to do I will not be found wanting!

"Thou liest, Fernando, in all thou hast said. Through the Campeador you gained much honor. I will tell you what you are like. Remember when we were fighting near Valencia the Great; thou didst ask the first blows of the loyal Campeador; thou didst see a Moor and go to attack him; thou didst flee before reaching him. If I had not succored thee the Moor would have played a bad joke on thee. I left thee behind and fought with him. I routed him with the first

blows. I gave thee his horse, and kept it all a secret. Until today I have not disclosed it to anyone. Before the Cid and before everybody thou didst boast that thou hadst slain the Moor and done a deed worthy of a baron. They all believed thee, for they did not know the truth. Thou art handsome, but thou art not brave! Tongue without hands, how darest thou speak?

"Say, Fernando, admit this: Dost thou not remember the adventure of the lion in Valencia, when the Cid was sleeping and the lion broke loose? And thou, Fernando, what didst thou do in thy fear? Thou didst hide behind the bench of the Cid Campeador! Thou didst hide, Fernando; wherefore thou hast the less fame today. We surrounded the bench to protect our Lord — until the Cid awoke, he who conquered Valencia. He rose from the bench and went towards the lion, who put his head down and waited for the Cid. He let the Cid take him by the neck and put him in his cage. When the good Campeador came back he saw his vassals standing around. He asked for his sons-in-law but neither was to be seen. I defy you as a villain and traitor. I will fight this out here, before the King Don Alfonso, for the daughters of the Cid, Doña Elvira and Doña Sol. By having left them you are dishonored. They are women and you, men. In every way they are worth more than you. If it please the Creator, when the battle takes place thou wilt confess this in the guise of a traitor! Of all that I have said I shall prove the truth."

The speech of those two ended there. You shall hear now what Diego González said:

"We are by birth counts of the purest blood. Would that those marriages had never been made — to give me for father-in-law the Cid Don Rodrigo! We do not yet repent of having left his daughters. They may sigh as long as they live. What we did to them will be a reproach to them. I will fight for this with the boldest of all: that we did honor to ourselves in leaving them."

Martín Antolínez rose to his feet:

"Be silent, traitor, mouth without truth! Thou shouldst not forget the adventure of the lion. Thou didst flee through the door and hide in the courtyard. Thou didst take refuge behind the wine-press beam. Thou didst not wear again thy mantle or thy tunic! I will fight, without fail, to prove this: the daughters of the Cid are more honored, you may know, in every way, than you, by your leaving them. After the combat thou wilt say with thy mouth that thou art a traitor and hast lied in all thou hast said."

The speech of these two ceased. Asur González came into the palace, his ermine mantle and his tunic dragging. He came red-faced, for he had just breakfasted. There was little discretion in what he said:

"What ho, Barons! Who ever saw such a misfortune? Who would have said we should gain honor from the Cid of Vivar? Let him go to the Ubierna River to grind his millstones and collect his toll of corn, as is his wont! Who would have said he would marry with those of Carrión?"

Then Muño Gustioz rose to his feet:

"Be still, villain, wicked and traitorous! Thou goest to breakfast before going to pray. Thou dost belch in the faces of those to whom thou givest the kiss of peace in church. Thou speakest truth to neither friend nor lord. Thou art false to all and, more, to the Creator. I do not care to have a share in thy friendship. I shall make thee confess that thou art such as I say."

Said King Alfonso: "Let the case rest. Those who have challenged shall fight, so help me God!"

Just as they finished, lo, two knights came through the court. One was called Ojarra and the other Iñigo Jiménez. One came from the Heir of Navarre and the other from the Heir of Aragon. They kissed the hands of the King Don Alfonso. They asked his daughters of the Cid Campeador, to be Queens of Navarre and of Aragon, in honorable and lawful marriage. At this news, all the court was silent to listen. The Cid Campeador rose to his feet:

"Your grace, King Alfonso, you are my Lord! I thank the Creator for this, that they ask me for my daughters, from Navarre and from Aragon. You, not I, married them before. My daughters are in your hands. I will do nothing without your command."

The King arose. He bade the court keep silence:

"I beg of you, Cid, perfect Campeador, to be pleased to accept, and I shall give my consent. Let this marriage be authorized today in this court, for it will add to your honor and your lands and your fiefs."

The Cid arose and kissed the King's hands:

"Since it pleases you, I give my consent, Lord."

Then the King said: "God give you good guerdon! To you, Ojarra, and to you, Iñigo Jiménez, I authorize this marriage of the daughters of the Cid, Doña Elvira and Doña Sol; that he give them to you for the Heirs of Navarre and of Aragon, in honorable and lawful marriage."

Ojarra and Iñigo Jiménez rose to their feet. They kissed the hands of the King Don Alfonso, and then of the Cid Campeador. They promised and swore the feudal oath, with their hands between those of the Cid, that it should be as they had said or better. Many of that court were pleased, but not the Heirs of Carrión. Minaya Alvar Fáñez rose to his feet:

"I ask your grace as my King and Lord — and may this not displease the Cid Campeador! I have not bothered you during all this court; now I should like to speak of somewhat that concerns me."

Said the King: "I shall be pleased to hear you. Speak, Minaya, what you will."

"I beg you, all you of the court, to give heed to me, for I have a great quarrel with the Heirs of Carrión. I, as representative of King Alfonso, gave them my cousins. They took them honorably and lawfully to wife. The Cid Campeador gave them great wealth. They left his daughters to our hurt. I defy them as wicked men and traitors. Heirs of Carrión, you are Beni-Gómez, descended from Gómez Díaz, of a family which has brought forth counts of worth and valor. But we know well what they are like now. I thank the Creator for this: that the Heirs of Navarre and of Aragon have asked for my cousins, Doña Elvira and Doña Sol. Before, you held them in your arms as equals; now you must kiss their hands and call them 'Queen'. You will have to serve them, however much you may dislike it. Thanks be to the God of Heaven and to the King Don Alfonso, thus does the honor of the Cid Campeador grow!"

FINLAND

The Kalevala
The Two Suitors [1]

❧ The forming of the Kalevala, the cycle of traditional myth, lore, and stories of heroic action belonging to the Finnish people, affords interesting comment on the whole process by which epic comes into being, because it was given its final form as late as the nineteenth century.

The Kalevala consists of 22,793 verses, arranged into some fifty runes or cantos. The meter of the verse is singularly familiar because Henry Wadsworth Longfellow borrowed it for his Song of Hiawatha. The mythology and the tales are the stuff of folklore, the essence of early Finnish thought, feeling, and imagination, as well as of Finland's weather and landscape.

Reaching back three thousand years, the themes were shaped, preserved, and dispersed by the bards and singers of succeeding generations. In the early part of the nineteenth century, when European interest in traditional lore was at its height, Elias Lönnrot, a Finnish Doctor of Medicine, became aware of this native cycle. He traveled the length and breadth of Finland, gathering the songs from the lips of peasant singers. In 1882, he and a companion physician, Zacharias Topelius, first published parts of the poem. Dr. Lönnrot believed that the Kalevala was a true epic, and he attempted to give it a unity of form by his arrangement of the verses in an ordered sequence. But the Kalevala is not epic, in the true meaning of the word, since it lacks a central heroic theme, and is little concerned with the fate or stature of

[1] From Babette Deutsch, Heroes of the Kalevala: Finland's Saga (Messner, 1940).

man in the universe. It is rather an idealization of Nature, a joyous, exaggerated personification of Nature, with broad symbolism of Good against Evil, and Light against Darkness.

Its heroes (the word Kalevala means Land of Heroes) are gods striving with one another, almost playfully. Yet the stories have a freshness and exuberance that is matchless, and a point of view that is distinctive. Music, the power of song, is given in no other mythological concept the magic it possesses in the Kalevala. It is the act of creation itself.

It was early morning when old Vainamoinen set out in his red boat with the blue and red sails. But he was not the first to rise that day. His lovely sister, Annikki, had wakened before daybreak and gone down to the shore to wash her clothes. She had rinsed them and wrung them out and spread them to dry, and now she stood up and looked over the sunlit water. She was surprised to see a blue speck far out among the waves. At first she thought it was a flock of wild geese, and then she mistook it for a shoal of fish, and then she thought it must be a stump riding on the billows. But finally she saw that it was the blue sail on the vessel of old Vainamoinen. She hailed him and asked him where he was going.

"Salmon-fishing," he called back. "The salmon-trout are spawning up the river."

"Don't tell me such a silly lie," said his sister. "I have often seen my father and my grandfather before him go out to capture the salmon. There were always nets in the boat, and a heap of tackle, and beating-poles. You have nothing of the sort. Where are you going?"

"I am going after wild geese. They are flying over the sound looking for food."

"I know you are lying," said Annikki. "I have seen my father and my grandfather before him go out after wild geese. They carried tight-strung bows and had their hunting-dogs with them. You have no such thing. Tell the truth, Vainamoinen: where are you going?"

"Into battle," answered the old singer. "When a mighty fight is raging I cannot sit home quietly: I must join the other heroes and give blow for blow."

"Do you think I don't know what it means to go into battle?" cried Annikki. "When my father went to fight with other heroes he had a hundred men rowing with him, and a thousand men standing in the boat, and swords heaped under the seats. Tell me honestly, Vainamoinen, where are you going?"

"Well," said the old singer, "it is true I lied a little. But now I will tell you the truth. I am going to the dark and misty Country of the North, where people eat men and they even drown heroes. But that does not matter to me, for I am going to fetch the dazzling Maiden of the North Country to be my bride."

When Annikki heard this she gathered her skirts in her hand, and letting her wash lie, she ran as fast as she could to the smithy. There she found her brother Ilmarinen, the mighty smith. He was hammering away at an iron bench with silver trimmings, and his shoulders were covered with ashes from the furnace and his head was black with soot.

"Brother," said Annikki breathlessly, "if you make me a fine shuttle and some golden ear-rings and some girdles with links of silver, I will tell you something you ought to know."

"I will do all that," answered Ilmarinen, "if your news is important. But if it isn't, I'll feed the furnace with your trinkets."

Annikki shook her head and laughed.

"Tell me, Ilmarinen," she said, "are you still thinking of that girl up in the North Country — the one who was promised to you as a reward for forging the magic Sampo?"

Annikki knew very well that the smith had been thinking of nothing else for the past two years.

"While you are welding and hammering," she went on, "making horseshoes all day and working at your sledge all night, so that you may journey to fetch your bride, someone cleverer than you is speeding there ahead of you. I have just seen Vainamoinen in a boat with a gilded prow and a copper rudder sailing for that cold and misty land."

At this news Ilmarinen let his hammer drop to the floor of the smithy.

"Annikki," he promised, "I will make you the finest shuttle. I will forge you rings for your fingers and two or three pairs of golden ear-rings and five or six girdles with links of silver. But you must do a favor for me, too, little sister. Go to the bath-house and kindle a fire of small chips there and see that the stones are properly hot, so that I can have a steam-bath. Fetch me some soap too, for I must wash off the coal-dust of a whole autumn's labor, and the soot of a whole winter's work."

At once Annikki ran and got some branches broken by the wind and burned them, and gathered stones from the river and heated them, and cheerfully fetched water from the holy well, and warmed the bath-whisks on the hot stones, and then she mixed milk and ashes and marrow-fat to make a fine soap. And all the while that she was preparing the bath-house, Ilmarinen worked at the trinkets he had promised her.

When Annikki came to tell him that the bath was ready, he gave her the rings and the ear-rings and the girdles and a splendid head-dress as well, and marched off to the bath-house. He scrubbed himself and he rubbed himself, he cleaned himself and he steamed himself. He washed his eyes till they sparkled and his face till it shone. He washed the soot from his neck till it was white as a hen's egg, and his body till it glistened. Then Annikki brought him a linen shirt and well-fitting trousers and fine stockings that his mother had woven when she was a girl. She brought him boots of Saxon make, and a blue coat with a liver-colored lining, and a woollen overcoat tailored in the latest fashion, with splendid fur to top it. She fastened a gold-embroidered belt around his waist, and gave him brightly colored gloves, and a handsome high-crowned hat that his father had worn as a bridegroom. Ilmarinen looked splendid indeed.

As soon as he was dressed in these rich clothes he told his servant to harness the chestnut stallion and yoke him to the sledge, and fetch six golden cuckoos to sit on the frame and seven blue birds to perch on the reins and sing. If he appeared in this splendor, heralded by singing birds, surely he would delight the dazzling girl and she would consent to be his bride. Then he called for a bearskin to sit on and a walrus-hide to throw over the sledge.

When the servant had provided him with all these things, Ilmarinen begged the Creator to send a fine snowfall so that his sledge might glide swiftly over the drifts. The Creator obliged him at once: the heath was soon covered with snow, and the berry bushes were white with it.

Ilmarinen cracked his whip and drove off, praying for luck. He drove for a day and another day and a third day, and on the third day, as his gay sledge went clattering along the shore, he overtook old Vainamoinen.

The smith hailed the old singer out on the waters, and Vainamoinen waited to hear what he had to say.

"Let us make a friendly compact," said Ilmarinen. "We are both setting out to win the dazzling girl for a bride. But let us agree that neither of us will seize her by force, and that neither of us will marry her against her will."

"I agree," said old Vainamoinen. "Let the girl be given to the husband of her choice, and there will be no quarrel between us." He was sure that she would choose that famous singer, that great hero, the oldest magician, the glorious Vainamoinen. As for Ilmarinen, he was sure that she would choose the mighty smith, the forger of the heavens, the welder of the magic Sampo, the handsome Ilmarinen.

So they traveled on, each by the path he had chosen. The boat sailed so fast that the shore echoed with the noise of its speed. The horse ran so swiftly that the earth resounded with the clatter of the swaying sledge.

Before long there was loud barking in the cold and misty region of the North Country. The grizzled house-dog bayed and wagged his tail to announce that strangers were nearing.

"Go, daughter," said the Master of the North Country, "find out what the house-dog is barking about."

"I have no time, father," said the girl. "I must clean the big cow-shed and grind the corn between the heavy mill-stones, and then I must sift the flour."

The Master of the North Country turned to his wife, gap-toothed old Louhi.

"Go, old woman," he said, "and see why the house-dog is making that racket."

"I have no time," said old Louhi. "I must prepare dinner. I have an enormous loaf to bake, but first I must knead the dough."

"Women are always in a hurry, and girls are always busy toasting themselves before the stove or lying in bed," complained the old man. "Go, my son," he said, "and see what the matter is."

"I have no time," said the youth. "I must sharpen the hatchet, and there is a great pile of wood that I have to cut up into faggots."

All this while the dog was out in the furthest corn-field, wagging his tail briskly and yelping without pause.

"He isn't barking for nothing," said the old Master of the North Country. "He doesn't growl at fir-trees."

So he went to find out for himself. When he reached the corn-field he saw a red boat sailing out in the bay and a gay sledge driving along the shore. The old man hurried home to his wife.

"There are strangers coming. I wonder what it means."

"We shall soon know," said crafty old Louhi. She called the little serving-maid to lay a log on the fire.

"If the log sweats blood, the strangers mean trouble, but if it oozes water, their errand is a peaceful one."

The gentle little serving-maid hastened to place the choicest log on the fire. It did not sweat blood, neither did it ooze water, but instead honey trickled from it and fell in golden drops on the hearth.

"Aha!" said old Louhi, delighted. "Those strangers must be noble suitors." And she hurried out into the court-yard. There she could see the red boat with the gilded prow coming towards the shore, and a hero handling the copper rudder. She saw too the gay sledge, with six golden cuckoos perched on the frame and seven blue birds on the reins, all singing at once, and a hero holding the reins.

Old Louhi turned to her daughter, the dazzling Maiden of the North Country.

"Which of these heroes will you choose for a husband?" she asked. "That is old Vainamoinen in the red boat. You remember the famous singer: he is bringing a cargo of treasure. In the sledge sits Ilmarinen, the smith, but he comes empty-handed. Go fetch a tankard of mead and hand it to the hero of your choice. Hand it to old Vainamoinen," she advised her daughter. "He is the wisest of all heroes. Besides, his boat is loaded with treasure."

"I do not care for treasure," answered the dazzling girl, "nor for a wise man who is old. I will marry a young man, with bright eyes and strong hands, a man like the skilful smith, Ilmarinen, who forged the magic Sampo."

"You do not want to marry a smith, my lamb," said crafty old Louhi. "You will have to scrub his sooty aprons. When you are his wife you will have to wash his sooty head."

"I don't care," said the dazzling girl. "I don't want old Vainamoinen. An old husband is a nuisance."

Just then old Vainamoinen steered his boat into the harbor and stepped out and came to the house. He was no sooner within than he reminded the dazzling girl of her promise to marry him, if he would make her a splendid boat out of the splinters of her spindle and the fragments of her shuttle.

"But have you built such a boat?" she asked.

"Yes, truly have I!" answered old Vainamoinen. "A noble ship strong to face the storms and light as a leaf on the waves."

"Oh, what do I care for seamen!" cried the dazzling girl. "As soon as it blows up they want to set sail, and if the wind is in the east, they frown and are gloomy. I do not want to marry a man who thinks only of ships."

Before old Vainamoinen could answer her, his brother the smith entered the house. The dazzling girl greeted Ilmarinen with a smile and handed him a great beaker of mead. But Ilmarinen did not taste it.

"I will not put my lips to the drink before me," he said, "until I am granted the bride for whose sake I forged the magic Sampo, and for whom I have been longing these two years."

"That is all very well," said old Louhi slyly, "you may have my daughter for your bride, but there is one task I must ask you to perform first. There is a field full of vipers that must be ploughed. It has not been touched since the Evil One, Hiisi, ploughed it long and long ago."

Ilmarinen did not know how this was to be done, and sought counsel of the dazzling girl. She told him to forge himself a coat of mail and iron shoes and a plough ornamented with silver and gold, and he would have no trouble in subduing the field of vipers. The smith took her advice, clad himself in steel and iron, hammered out the gold and silver for a great plough, and went to the open field. It was a fearsome place, thick with writhing serpents, but Ilmarinen spoke to them persuasively, and advised them to get out of the way of his sharp ploughshare. It was not long before they all slipped off and out of sight. Then he ploughed the field and came to tell old Louhi that the task was accomplished and to ask for his bride.

"You may have her," said the gap-toothed Mistress of the North Country, "if you catch the Bear and the Wolf that live in the forest of Tuoni, Lord of the Dead. Bring them to me muzzled and bridled, and the girl is yours." Crafty old Louhi knew very well that hundreds of heroes had gone on this errand, but none had ever come back.

"It will be easy for you," said the dazzling girl, when the smith told her of this second task. "You have only to sit on a rock where the spray of the waterfall sprinkles you, and there forge a muzzle of the hardest steel and an iron bit. Neither Tuoni's Bear nor his fierce Wolf can escape you then."

So Ilmarinen stood on a rock in the midst of the stream and in the spray of the waterfall forged himself what was needed. Then, with the steel muzzle in one hand and the iron bit in the other, he went to seek the beasts of Tuoni in the depths of the forest. He prayed to the Daughter of the Clouds to blind the animals with a mist so that they could not see him coming, and there in the dread forest of Tuoni he crept up on them and muzzled them with the magic bits and brought them both back to old Louhi.

"Here is the great Bear of Tuoni, and his Wolf as well. Now give me your daughter," said Ilmarinen.

"I will give you my darling," answered old Louhi, "as soon as you bring me the Pike that swims in Tuoni's River. It is fat and scaly, and it must be caught without a net, nor dare you grasp it with your hand." The old woman knew that hundreds of heroes had gone to catch Tuoni's Pike, but not one had returned from that adventure.

A third time the smith asked the maiden to help him. He could not imagine how the Pike was to be caught without using net or tackle.

"Be of good cheer, Ilmarinen," said the dazzling girl. "Forge yourself a fiery eagle, with talons of iron and claws of steel and wings like the sides of a boat. He will dive into the River of the Dead, and bring up Tuoni's terrible Pike."

So the smith went once more to the forge and forged a bird of fire and flame, as the maiden had directed. Mounted on its wings, that were broad as the sides of a boat, he flew towards the dread river. The eagle was so huge that one great wing swept the sky and the other trailed the water. His iron talons dipped into the river and he whetted his flaming beak on the cliffs. He carried Ilmarinen swiftly to the shore of Tuoni's stream, and there the two waited for the Pike to rise out of its muddy depths.

But instead of the Pike, a wicked water-sprite rose out of the river and snatched at Ilmarinen. It would have dragged him down, but the eagle took the wicked creature by the neck and nearly twisted its head off and sent it down to the black muddy bottom.

Then the Pike of Tuoni rose slowly to the surface. He was no ordinary fish. He had a tongue as long as two axe-shafts and teeth like those of a rake. His gorge was as wide

as three great rivers and his back was the length of seven boats. He opened his awful jaws and tried to seize Ilmarinen between his terrible teeth.

But the eagle was not a small bird either. His beak was a hundred fathoms long, and his tongue the length of six spears, and each of his iron talons was like five scythes. He rushed upon the Pike and struck at it fiercely. But the Pike pulled at the eagle's broad wings and tried to drag him under the water. Up the eagle soared into the air. He hovered there a moment and then he dived. He struck one savage talon into the Pike's terrific shoulders, and gave himself a purchase by fixing the other talon firmly in the rocky cliff. But he did not thrust it deep enough and his talon slipped from the rock, and the Pike slid away and dived into the water. The shoulder of the fish was almost cloven in two and his sides were scored with the marks of the eagle's steely claws, but he had escaped the great bird's clutches.

Now the furious eagle, with fiery eyes and flaming wings, swooped a third time, seized the monstrous Pike in his talons and dragged him out of the water. Then what a battle took place between the huge bird and the terrible fish! The air glittered with iron splinters. The river heaved like a sea of steel. There was a gnashing and a thrashing, as the giant struggle continued. Finally the eagle made a mighty thrust and flapping his broad wings he bore the Pike off in triumph to the top of a tall pine tree. There he ripped open the belly of the fish and tore the head from the neck and began to feast.

"Wicked eagle!" cried Ilmarinen in anger, "Why are you so greedy? You have destroyed the Pike that I was to carry back to old Louhi!"

But the eagle, having satisfied his hunger, soared off into the heavens, breaking the horns of the moon in his flight.

Then Ilmarinen took the head of the terrible Pike and carried it back to old Louhi.

"Here is a present for you," he said. "You can make a chair out of the bones in this head that will remain forever in the lofty halls of your house."

The gap-toothed Mistress of the North Country did not thank him too graciously.

She did not care that he had brought only the head of the Pike, the bones of which would truly make a noble chair, but she was angry because he had performed every task she had set him, and now she would have to give him her beautiful daughter.

As for old Vainamoinen, he was the saddest of all.

"A man should marry when he is young,"
he said gloomily, "and choose his life's companion early. It is a grief to be old and have no wife and no children."

But Ilmarinen and the dazzling girl were full of joy, and eager for the preparations for the wedding. And how the feast was arranged, and what guests were invited, and how the bride and groom fared, you shall hear.

INDIA

Rama
The March to Lanka [1]

&§ The Ramayana, *one of the two major epics of India, is an extensive and intense love story, concerning the devotion of Rama, the god-hero, and his wife Sita, who remains faithful to him through years of separation and travail. Within this framework is a wealth of stories, history, philosophy, profuse and embroidered, like the arabesques of Oriental architecture. This, and the earlier epic, the* Mahabharata, *are sacred books, as the Bible is sacred to Christian lands. Taken together, they represent the highest aspirations of Hindu thought.*

The Ramayana *is ascribed to one poet, Valmiki, as the* Iliad *is attributed to Homer, and the date of its written form, in Sanskrit, is around 300 B.C. The* Mahabharata *is three times as long as the Bible, and eight times as long as the* Iliad *and the* Odyssey *put together. Its major framework consists of the inter-family struggle of five brothers for control of their realm. These two epics, more than any other existing epic strain, remain a living accompaniment to*

[1] From Dhan Gopal Mukerji, *Rama, the Hero of India* (Dutton, 1930).

the contemporary life of the culture which produced them.

After all the monkeys had assembled in Kishkindha under King Sugriva, Rama, Hanuman, Andaga and Lakshmana made inspiring speeches to them and exactly described their coming march to Lanka. Last of all spoke Sugriva, urging them to uphold the honour of the monkey race no matter where or how.

"On the morrow," the King concluded, "we march to Kanya Kumari (Cape Comorin) the southernmost point of India. Now go home and say farewell properly to your families. Report for duty before the first sun-wing rises again above the gloom in the east!"

And the following day just as the eagle of dawn had begun to preen his golden pinions with the clamour of a thousand storms the monkeys set out for Lanka. They leaped over many trees with the agility of hawks. They cleared the rolling hills as goats clear broken fences. They drank, bathed, and swam tawny rivers. They passed as locusts spread over autumn fields. Distances vanished under their feet like sugar into the mouth of a child. Rama and Lakshmana were carried on the backs of large monkeys who worked in relays. And ere the first day was done they had covered a twentieth part of their journey.

No sooner had the sun risen and set seven times three than the cohorts of Rama stood like clamorous forests on the edge of Cape Comorin. They roared and shouted so loudly with joy that the "surge and thunder" of the Indian Ocean was drowned as a sparrow's chirp is stilled by the wind whistling in an eagle's wing. There they stood, two men surrounded by untold apes and baboons. Before them mile upon mile unfurled the blue banners of the sea. Wherever they peered the waste of waters stretched into forbidding immensity.

After sunset as soon as the bivouacs had been lighted and all the soldiers had been comfortably settled in their separate camps Rama, Lakshmana, Sugriva, Jambuban, Angada and Hanuman held a council of war. "How to span the ocean?" they questioned one another again and again. Rama said, "We cannot leap over the ocean like thee, Hanuman. Only a few tree-dwellers have thy skill and strength. There is naught for us to do but to build a bridge."

"A bridge on a vast ocean!" exclaimed Jambuban and Sugriva. But the young, such as Angada and Lakshmana, said, "It will take a long time to make. By the time it is completed Sita and most of us will have grown old and died."

Hanuman cried, "Why do I not leap over to Sita and bring her back on my neck. That will rescue her quickly and save us a long task of bridge-making." Rama smiled at them all and said, "It is not only for Sita's rescue that we have come, but also to put an end to Ravana and his demon-race. Sita is but one woman amongst many who are exposed to attack by the Rakshasas. It is not enough that we rescue her alone. We must destroy all Lanka and free all womanhood from the menace of Ravana. In order to do our task completely we must have a vast army at Lanka's door. Sita must wait until we build a bridge on which our cohorts can cross and annihilate the Rakshasas utterly."

"Sadhoo, well spoken," shouted all his listeners. But Jambuban the bear-headed monkey who was Sugriva's Dewan (prime minister) counselled, "With all the monkeys working every day every hour it will take ten years to build that bridge to Ceylon. Ten years without fighting will undermine the heart of every soldier. Bridge-building will make pacifists of our warriors. O Rama, set not out upon thy plan to span the sea."

A sombre and profound pause followed. As if it were unbearable Sugriva broke the silence. "I have pledged you, O Rama, that we shall rescue Sita for you. But I see no reason why we should toil to free all humanity from the menace of Ravana."

Lakshmana answered, "King Sugriva, it is your head, not your heart that speaks so. Prudence is a dweller in the house of reason, a miserly tenant in a narrow home. But what Rama wishes is the truth. We should slay Ravana. Let us save not only Sita but all womanhood by slaughtering the demon vipers no matter how long it takes."

Then shouted Angada and Hanuman, "Thy words have converted us, O Lakshmana. We are devotees at the shrine of thy truth. Let the bridge be built."

"But ten years of civilian work will dry up the spring of our enthusiasm," reiterated Jambuban. "An army of civilians cannot fight demons. Ferocious soldiers are needed for that."

Another pause more depressing than the previous one followed. The monkeys turned their faces toward Rama. Their instinct told them that he had a noble idea in his mind. That tiger-silencing one spoke softly like a mother to her children:

"The bridge can be built in two years. We may have to besiege Lanka for at least ten years after that."

Sugriva grumbled, "How canst thou say that?"

"I have the means by which to do it," rejoined Dasaratha's eldest-born. "Let us rest for the night with perfect peace. On the morrow, friends, we shall commence the building of the bridge."

The force behind Rama's simple words was so great that the meeting broke up without further discussion, and each monkey softly walked away to his camp to bed. Only the two men stayed together. Then, without speaking, Rama signed Lakshmana to meditate.

The two princes folded their legs and sat still praying and meditating. The stars strode across the sky and faded. The giants of the jungle roamed and clamoured while the vast army of tree-dwellers slept. But the two men prayed for the help of Heaven, for the aid of all four-footed beasts, and for the cooperation of birds. They sought also the assistance of the Sun, the moon and the seasons. Each by each the souls of the sleeping birds and beasts answered, "Yes, we will help." The heavenly bodies, too, answered, "We come, Rama, to aid you as you ask." So while the world slept, its waking soul pledged Rama to be his slave. Such is the power that prayer and meditation can create! And because Rama was fighting to save not only his own bride but all humanity the whole universe was glad to espouse his cause.

Thus that memorable night was spent. And long before the red wheel of the Sun had churned the ocean into scudding gold, purple and amber birds were swarming with stones in their beaks, leopards and lions were flinging skulls and bones of their prey into the deep, monkeys row upon row were pulling down trees and rocks, elephants were ploughing up earth with their tusks and flinging it with their trunks, even Makara (Leviathan) and his sea-concealed family rose to assist Rama in his bridge-building.

Last of all came the chipmunks. They begged to be of service. Rama with sweet thanks said, "Dip your bodies in the sea, roll yourselves in the sand, then go and shake the sand between the stones that the apes are joining together. Go, make mortar for me." The chipmunks busied themselves at once. Lo, hardly a few minutes passed when their chief crawled up to Rama's lap and said, "Some monkey flung a rock the wrong way and hit me. O Rama, I am dying." But Rama said, "I will heal you," and he stroked the chipmunk three times with his hand. The previous night's meditation had given Rama so much power that healing passed out of him and made the little beast whole in a trice. But Rama's fingers left their marks on his body so that even now India's chipmunks wear coats of three stripes. Those are the finger marks that their ancestors received at the building of the Rama-setu or Rama-causeway to Ceylon.

The sea rose and fell but it was no longer heard; the sharp chirp of stones falling from bird-beaks, the crash and smash of rock and timber, the hissing of the surf, the hammering of boulder on boulder, the sinking of mammoth granite shafts in the deep, and the singing of those who worked and enjoyed work because they could sing, drowned all else. Thus toil became a joy, and joy a serenity of the soul.

The day ended and the night was no less like day, for the moon poured effulgence from above in answer to the prayer of Rama. So the beasts of night toiled as had done those of the day. Hammering of stone on stone rang louder than the storm smiting the "sapphire-silver" sea. So numerous were the beasts at work that they wrought with "thunder-stilling" fury. Though Rama slumbered his friends toiled at night. Since they were not his slaves they forged the stone chain on the sea without regard to his presence or his absence. Toil became their joy. They loved him, hence they toiled, not lashed by overseers, not cursed by leaders.

PERSIA

Zal[1]

> Zal is the legendary hero of the Persian epic written by Firdausi (pen name) from the Book of Kings. This book is not a book as we use the term; it is a collection of legendary folk tales which was begun as early as the sixth century. These were written down, placed in the royal library, and added to through the ninth century. Firdausi, who had been commissioned to write them into verse by the ruler, completed his work of thirty-five years in 1011; the poem is now the national epic. This legend of Zal is interesting of itself, but more so when we know that Zal was the father of the greatest of all Persian heroes, Rustam; for the story of Sohrab and Rustam is one Persian tale that is widely known, thanks to Matthew Arnold.

Seistan, which is to the south of Iran, was ruled by Saum, the Pehliva, girt with might and glory, and, but for the grief that he was childless, his days were happy. Then it came to pass that a son was born unto him, beautiful of face and limb, who had neither fault nor blemish save that his hair was like unto that of an aged man. Now the women were afraid to tell Saum, lest he be wroth when he should learn that his child was thus set apart from his fellowmen. So the infant had gazed upon the light eight days ere he knew thereof. Then a woman, brave above the rest, ventured into his presence. She bowed herself unto the dust and craved of Saum the boon of speech. And he suffered her, and she spake, saying:

[1] The Epic of Kings: Hero Tales of Ancient Persia, retold from Firdusi's Shah-Nameh by Helen Zimmern (Macmillan, 1926).

"May the Lord keep and guard thee. May thine enemies be utterly destroyed. May the days of Saum the hero be happy. For the Almighty hath accomplished his desire. He hath given to him an heir, a son is born unto the mighty warrior behind the curtains of his house, a moon-faced boy, beautiful of face and limb, in whom there is neither fault nor blemish, save that his hair is like unto that of an aged man. I beseech thee, O my master, bethink thee that this gift is from God, nor give place in thine heart to ingratitude."

When Saum had listened to her words, he arose and went into the house of the women. And he beheld the babe that was beautiful of face and limb, but whose head was like unto that of an aged man. Then Saum, fearing the jeers of his enemies, quitted the paths of wisdom. He lifted his head unto heaven and murmured against the Lord of Destiny, and cried, saying:

"O thou eternally just and good, O source of happiness, incline thine ear unto me and listen to my voice. If I have sinned, if I have strayed in the paths of Ahriman, behold my repentance and pardon me. My soul is ashamed, my heart is angered for reason of this child, for will not the nobles say this boy presageth evil? They will hold me up to shame, and what can I reply to their question? It behoveth me to remove this stain, that the land of Iran be not accursed."

Thus spake Saum in his anger, railing against fate, and he commanded his servants to take the child and cast it forth out of the land.

Now there standeth far from the haunts of

men the Mount Alberz, whose head touch-
eth the stars, and never had mortal foot been
planted upon its crest. And upon it had the
Simurgh, the bird of marvel, builded her
nest. Of ebony and of sandalwood did she
build it, and twined it with aloes, so that it
was like unto a king's house, and the evil
sway of Saturn could not reach thereto. And
at the foot of this mount was laid the child
of Saum. Then the Simurgh, when she spied
the infant lying upon the ground, bereft of
clothes and wherewithal to nourish it, sucking its fingers for very hunger, darted to
earth and raised him in her talons. And she
bare him unto her nest, that her young
might devour him. But when she had
brought him her heart was stirred within
her for compassion. Therefore she bade her
young ones to spare the babe and treat him
like to a brother. Then she chose out tender
flesh to feed her guest, and tended the infant forsaken of his sire. And thus did the
Simurgh, nor ever wearied till that moons
and years had rolled above their heads, and
the babe was grown to be a youth full of
strength and beauty. And his renown filled
the land, for neither good nor evil can be
hidden for ever. And his fame spread even
unto the ears of Saum, the son of Neriman.

Then it came to pass that Saum dreamed
a dream, wherein he beheld a man riding
towards him mounted upon an Arab steed.
And the man gave him tidings of his son,
and taunted him, saying:

"O thou who hast offended against every
duty, who disownest thy son because that his
hair is white, though thine own resembleth
the silver poplar, and to whom a bird seem-
eth fit nurse for thine offspring, wilt thou
abjure all kinship with him for ever?"

Now when Saum awoke he remembered
his dream, and fear came upon him for his
sin. And he called unto him his Mubids,
and questioned them concerning the stripling of the Mount Alberz, and whether this
could be indeed his son, for surely frosts
and heat must long since have destroyed
him. Then the Mubids answered and said:

"Not so, thou most ungrateful unto God,
thou more cruel than the lion, the tiger, and
the crocodile, for even savage beasts tend
their young, whilst thou didst reject thine

own, because thou heldest the white hair
given unto him by his Creator for a reproach
in the sight of men. O faint of heart, arise
and seek thy child, for surely one whom God
hath blessed can never perish. And turn
thou unto him and pray that he forgive
thee."

When Saum had heard these words he was
contrite, and called about him his army and
set forth unto the mountains. And when
they were come unto the mount that is
raised up to the Pleiades, Saum beheld the
Simurgh and the nest, and a stripling that
was like unto himself walking around it.
And his desire to get unto him was great,
but he strove in vain to scale the crest.
Then Saum called upon God in his humility.
And God heard him, and put it into the
heart of the Simurgh to look down and behold the warrior and the army that was
with him. And when she had seen Saum
she knew wherefore the chief was come, and
she spake and said:

"O thou who hast shared this nest, I have
reared thee and been to thee a mother, for
thy father cast thee out; the hour is come to
part us, and I must give thee again unto thy
people. For thy father is Saum the hero, the
Pehliva of the world, greatest among the
great, and he is come hither to seek his son,
and splendor awaiteth thee beside him."

When the youth had heard her words his
eyes were filled with tears and his heart with
sorrow, for he had never gazed upon men,
though he had learned their speech. And he
said:

"Art thou then weary of me, or am I no
longer fit to be thy house-fellow? See, thy
nest is unto me a throne, thy sheltering wings
a parent. To thee I owe all that I am, for
thou wast my friend in need."

And the Simurgh answered him saying, "I
do not send thee away for enmity, O my son;
nay, I would keep thee beside me for ever,
but another destiny is better for thee. When
thou shalt have seen the throne and its pomp
my nest will sink in thine esteem. Go forth,
therefore, my son, and try thy fortune in
the world. But that thou mayst remember
thy nurse who shielded thee, and reared thee
amid her little ones, that thou mayst remain
under the shadow of her wings, bear with

thee this feather from her breast. And in the day of thy need cast it into the fire, and I will come like unto a cloud and deliver thee from danger."

Thus she spake, and raised him in her talons and bore him to the spot where Saum was bowed to the dust in penitence. Now when Saum beheld his son, whose body was like unto an elephant's for strength and beauty, he bent low before the Simurgh and covered her with benison. And he cried out and said:

"O Shah of birds, O bird of God, who confoundest the wicked, mayst thou be great for ever."

But while he yet spake the Simurgh flew upwards, and the gaze of Saum was fixed upon his son. And as he looked he saw that he was worthy of the throne, and that there was neither fault nor blemish in him, save only his silvery locks. Then his heart rejoiced within him, and he blessed him, and entreated his forgiveness. And he said:

"O my son, open thine heart unto the meanest of God's servants, and I swear unto thee, in the presence of Him that made us, that never again will I harden my heart towards thee, and that I will grant unto thee all thy desires."

Then he clothed him in rich robes and named him Zal, which being interpreted meaneth the aged. And he showed him unto the army. And when they had looked on the youth they saw that he was goodly of visage and of limb, and they shouted for very joy. Then the host made them ready to return unto Seistan. And the kettle-drummers rode at their head, mounted upon mighty elephants whose feet raised a cloud of dust that rose unto the sky. And the tabors were beat, and the trumpets brayed, and the cymbals clashed, and sounds of rejoicing filled the land because that Saum had found his son, and that Zal was a hero among men.

Now the news spread even unto Minuchihr that Saum was returning from the mountains with great pomp and joy. And when he had heard it he bade Nuder go forth to meet the Pehliva and bid him bring Zal unto the court. And when Saum heard the desires of his master, he obeyed and came

within his gates. Then he beheld the Shah seated upon the throne of the Kaianides, bearing his crown upon his head, and on his right hand sat Karun the Pehliva, and he bade Saum be seated on his left. And the Shah commanded Saum that he should speak. Then Saum unbosomed himself before the Shah and spake concerning his son, neither did he hide his evil deed. And Minuchihr commanded that Zal be brought before him. So the chamberlains brought him into the presence of the king, and he was clad in robes of splendor, and the king was amazed at his aspect. And he turned and said unto Saum:

"O Pehliva of the world, the Shah enjoineth you have a care of this noble youth, and guard him for the land of Iran. And teach him forthwith the arts of war, and the pleasures and customs of the banquet, for how should one that hath been reared in a nest be familiar with our ways?"

Then the Shah bade the Mubids cast Zal's horoscope, and they read that he would be a brave and prudent knight. Now when he had heard this the Pehliva was relieved of all his fears, and the Shah rejoiced and covered Saum with gifts. Arab horses did he give unto him with golden saddles, Indian swords in scabbards of gold, brocades of Roum, skins of beasts, and carpets of Ind, and the rubies and pearls were past the numbering. And slaves poured musk and amber before him. And Minuchihr also granted to Saum a throne, and a crown and a girdle of gold, and he named him ruler of all the lands that stretch from the Sea of China to that of Sind, from Zaboulistan to the Caspian. Then he bade that the Pehliva's horse be led forth, and sent him away from his presence. And Saum called down blessings upon the Shah, and turned his face towards home. And his train followed after him, and the sound of music went before them.

Then when the tidings came to Seistan that the great hero was drawing nigh, the city decked itself in festive garbs, and every man called down the blessings of Heaven upon Zal, the son of Saum, and poured gifts at his feet. And there was joy in all the land for that Saum had taken back his son.

Now Saum forthwith called about him his

Mubids, and bade them instruct the youth in all the virtues of a king.

And daily Zal increased in wisdom and strength, and his fame filled the land. And

when Saum went forth to fight the battles of the Shah, he left the kingdom under his hands, and Zal administered it with judgment and virtue.

BIBLIOGRAPHY

Greece and Rome

Church, Alfred. *The Aeneid for Boys and Girls;* retold from Virgil in simple language. Macmillan, 1918. (Grades 5–9)

A dramatic telling which keeps the spirit of the original.

Church, Alfred. *The Iliad of Homer;* retold by Alfred J. Church; illus. by John Flaxman. Macmillan, 1951. (New Children's Classics) (Grades 5–9)

The best version of the Iliad for younger boys and girls. The Flaxman drawings add much to the flavor of the text.

Church, Alfred. *The Odyssey of Homer;* retold by Alfred J. Church; illus. by John Flaxman. Macmillan, 1951. (New Children's Classics) (Grades 5–9)

The spirit of Homer is faithfully preserved in the text, and the famous Flaxman drawings add to the distinctive format.

Colum, Padraic. *The Adventures of Odysseus and the Tale of Troy;* illus. by Willy Pogány. Macmillan, 1918. (Grades 5–9)

Padraic Colum has combined the story of the *Iliad* and the *Odyssey,* telling the continuous narrative in vigorous rhythmic prose.

Colum, Padraic. *The Golden Fleece and the Heroes Who Lived Before Achilles;* illus. by Willy Pogány. Macmillan, 1934. (Grades 6–9)

Famous Greek hero tales retold by a poet.

Kingsley, Charles. *The Heroes;* illus. by Vera Bock. Macmillan, 1954. (New Children's Classics) (Grades 5–7)

First published in 1855. Kingsley's versions of these myths retain the strength and beauty of the original Greek stories.

Iceland and Scandinavia (Norse)

French, Allen. *The Story of Grettir the Strong.* E. P. Dutton, 1908. (Grades 5–8)

A fine retelling of the Icelandic saga. Based upon the translation by William Morris and Eirika Mafnusson published in 1869 under the title *The Grettis Saga.*

Hosford, Dorothy. *Sons of the Volsungs;* illus. by Frank Dobias. Henry Holt, new ed. 1949. (Grades 7–9)

A retelling in fine rhythmic prose of the story of Sigurd and Brynhilde based on the first two books of William Morris' epic poem, *The Story of Sigurd the Volsung.*

England

Hosford, Dorothy. *By His Own Might; the Battles of Beowulf;* drawings by Lasslo Matulay. Henry Holt, 1947. (Grades 6–8)

By far the best prose version of the Anglo-Saxon epic for boys and girls. Mrs. Hosford retains the heroic quality, the vigor and force of the original, achieving the effect of simplicity and dignity.

Johnson, Richard. *Saint George and the Dragon;* ed. by Alice Dalgliesh; illus. by Lois Maloy. Charles Scribner's Sons, 1941. (Grades 4–5)

Retold in simple prose for young readers.

Lanier, Sidney, ed. *The Boys' King Arthur; being Sir Thomas Malory's History of King Arthur and His Knights of the Round Table;* illus. by N. C. Wyeth. Charles Scribner's Sons, 1917. (Scribner Illustrated Classics) (Grades 6–9)

Lanier's version follows Malory's *Morte Darthur,* which was first published by Caxton in the latter part of the fifteenth century.

Macleod, Mary. *Book of King Arthur and His Noble Knights;* introduction by Angelo Patri; illus. by Henry C. Pitz. J. B. Lippincott, new ed. 1949. (Lippincott Classics) (Grades 6–9)

These stories rewritten from Malory are faithful in spirit to the original but they are easier to read than Malory or Lanier's version of Malory and they are shorter than the Howard Pyle stories.

Malcolmson, Anne, ed. *The Story of Robin Hood;* music arr. by Grace Castagnetta; designed and illus. by Virginia Lee Burton. Houghton Mifflin, 1947. (Grades 6–9)

A distinguished and notable achievement. The editing of the eighteen ballads from the Robin Hood cycle is painstaking and scholarly. Each ballad is given in modern spelling and has been cut without hurting the original story. For each ballad Grace Castagnetta has given the original English music as far as it could be found. The illustrations are remarkable in their exquisite design.

Pyle, Howard. *Merry Adventures of Robin Hood of Great Renown in Nottinghamshire;* illus. by the author. Charles Scribner's Sons, 1946. (Brandywine Edition) (Grades 5–8)

No other version is comparable to this version by Howard Pyle.

Pyle, Howard. *The Story of King Arthur and His Knights;* illus. by the author. Charles Scribner's Sons, 1933. (Brandywine Edition) (Grades 5–8)

One of the best versions of the King Arthur stories. Followed by *The Story of the Champions of the Round Table; Sir Launcelot and His Companions;* and *The Story of the Passing of Arthur.*

Ireland

Hull, Eleanor. *The Boys' Cuchulain; Heroic Legends of Ireland;* illus. by Stephen Reid. Thomas Y. Crowell, 1910. (Grades 7–9)

The story of the great legendary hero of Ireland, told with beauty and dignity.

Young, Ella. *The Tangle-Coated Horse and Other Tales; Episodes from the Fionn Saga;* illus. by Vera Bock. Longmans, Green, 1929. (Grades 7–9)

An exquisite retelling of this "oldest and strangest of the Gaelic sagas," by an Irish poet.

Young, Ella. *The Wonder Smith and His Son; a Tale from the Golden Childhood of the World;* illus. by Boris Artzybasheff. Longmans, Green, 1927. (Grades 5–7)

Fourteen tales from the legendary cycle of Gubbaun Saor, a mythological figure of Ireland. Ella Young spent twenty years collecting these old tales. They were told to her in Gaelic and she has retold them as only a poet can.

Wales

Colum, Padraic, ed. *The Island of the Mighty; being the Hero Stories of Celtic Britain retold*

from the Mabinogion; illus. by Wilfred Jones. Macmillan, 1924. (Grades 6–9)

The Welsh retellings of the King Arthur stories. Padraic Colum calls this an epic of youth, "for no other book in all the world gives us better than this book youth, and youth seen with youth's eyes."

Demark

Davis, Julia. *Swords of the Vikings;* illus. by Suzanne Lasson. E. P. Dutton, 1928. (Grades 6–9)

Stirring tales of the ancient gods and heroes of Denmark recorded by Saxo Grammaticus, the first Danish historian.

Hyde, Mark Powell. *The Singing Sword; the Story of Sir Ogier the Dane;* illus. by Philip Cheney. Little, Brown, 1930. (Grades 6–8)

Ogier, the young son of the Duke of Denmark, is left in Charlemagne's court as hostage for the good conduct of his father. He not only wins his knighthood but helps free Denmark from the oppression of the Saxons.

Finland

Deutsch, Babette. *Heroes of the Kalevala; Finland's Saga;* illus. by Fritz Eichenberg. Julian Messner, 1940. (Grades 6–9)

A distinguished retelling of the Finnish epic by a well-known poet.

France

Baldwin, James. *The Story of Roland;* illus. by Peter Hurd. Charles Scribner's Sons, 1930. (Scribner Illustrated Classics) (Grades 6–7)

Legends of Charlemagne and Roland woven into a continuous narrative.

Bulfinch, Thomas. *Legends of Charlemagne;* illus. by N. C. Wyeth. McKay, 1924. (McKay Illustrated Classics) (Grades 7–9)

Stories of the knights of Charlemagne. The Introduction gives a history of the legends.

Sherwood, Merriam, trans. *Song of Roland;* illus. by Edith Emerson. Longmans, Green, 1938. (Grades 7–9)

Based on the Oxford manuscript, this excellent prose version of the classic tale begins with Ganelon's treachery and covers the death of Roland and Oliver and the final triumph of Charlemagne over the Saracens.

Germany

Baldwin, James. *The Story of Siegfried;* illus. by Peter Hurd. Charles Scribner's Sons, 1931. (Scribner Illustrated Classics) (Grades 5–7)

The best rendition for children of the Siegfried legends based on the *Eddas,* the *Völsunga Saga,* and the *Nibelungenlied.*

Hungary

Seredy, Kate. *The White Stag;* illus. by the author. Viking Press, 1937. (Grades 7–9)

The epic story of the migration of the Huns and Magyars from Asia to Europe and the legendary founding of Hungary. The illustrations are almost breath-taking in their dramatic power. Awarded the Newbery medal in 1938.

Poland

Gorska, Halina. *Prince Godfrey; the Knight of the Star of the Nativity;* illus. by Irena Lorentowicz. Roy Publishers, 1946. (Grades 5–8)

Subtitled: "Twelve wondrous tales recorded by Master Johannes Sarabandus, His Majesty's Astrologer." This hero tale from Poland, written with sincerity and beauty, is similar in spirit to the King Arthur stories.

Spain

Sherwood, Merriam, trans. *The Tale of the Warrior Lord, El Cantar de Mio Cid;* illus. by Henry C. Pitz. Longmans, Green, 1930. (Grades 7–9)

A dramatic prose translation of the famous twelfth-century poem which recounts the great deeds of the Spanish hero, Rodrigo Diaz de Bivar, called the Cid, meaning the Chief.

China

Crane, Louise. *The Magic Spear, and Other Stories of China's Famous Heroes.* Random House, 1938. (Grades 5–6)

Material for this book was gathered by the author during her long residence in China.

India

Gaer, Joseph. *The Adventures of Rama;* illus. by Randy Monk. Little, Brown, 1954. (Grades 7–9)

A dramatic and dignified version of the great Hindu epic *Ramayana,* the ancient story of Rama and Sita and their struggles with the evils of the world. The author, who is well known for his books on the world's religions, explains in his notes the various extant versions and the evolution of the epic from earliest times.

Mahabharata. *The Five Brothers: The Story of the Mahabharata.* Adapted from the English translation of Kisari Mohan Ganguli by Elizabeth Seeger; illus. by Cyrus Le Roy Baldridge. John Day, 1948. (Grades 6–9)

One of India's two great epics which tells of the five Pandu brothers and their fight for their kingdom.

Mukerji, Dhan Gopal. *Rama, the Hero of India.* E. P. Dutton, 1930. (Grades 7–9)

Mr. Mukerji has retold in poetic prose the story of the *Ramayana,* the great epic poem of India.

Persia

Chidsey, Alan. *Rustam, Lion of Persia;* illus. by Lois Lenski. G. P. Putnam's Sons, 1930. (Grades 6–9)

Heroic epic of the Persian hero told as a connected narrative.

Zimmern, Helen, ed. *Epic of Kings; Hero Tales of Ancient Persia;* retold from Firdusi's *Shah-Nameh.* Macmillan, 1926. (Grades 8–9)

Firdusi, the great epic poet of Persia, tells the old half-mythical history of Persia including the hero tales of Zal and Rustam.

References for the Adult

Arbuthnot, May Hill. *Children and Books.* Scott, Foresman, rev. ed. 1957.

"Epics and Hero Tales," pp. 298–306.

Armstrong, Helen. "Hero Tales for Storytelling," *The Horn Book Magazine,* Vol. 25, Jan.–Feb. 1949, pp. 9–16.

Auslander, Joseph, and Frank Ernest Hill. *The Winged Horse; the Story of the Poets and Their Poetry.* Doubleday, 1927.

"Blind Homer," Chapter 4, pp. 19–30.

Colum, Padraic. *Orpheus: Myths of the World;* illus. with 20 engravings by Boris Artzybasheff. Macmillan, 1930.

Padraic Colum's introduction, "The Significance of Mythology," is of great value to the student of mythology.

Eaton, Anne Thaxter. *Reading with Children.* Viking Press, 1940.

"The World's Great Stories," Chapter VIII, pp. 135–156.

Meigs, Cornelia, and others. *A Critical History of Children's Literature.* Macmillan, 1953.

"Howard Pyle," pp. 299–313; "A Rightful Heritage," pp. 321–327; "Looking to the Past — Hero Stories," pp. 460–464.

Moore, Anne Carroll. *The Three Owls; a Book about Children's Books.* Macmillan, 1925.

"Stories out of the Youth of the World," by Louise Seaman, pp. 107–113; "Hero Tales: The Islands of the Mighty," by Padraic Colum, reviewed by Elva S. Smith, pp. 113–117; "Robin Hood's Country," pp. 232–237.

Smith, Lillian H. *The Unreluctant Years.* American Library Association, 1953.

"Heroes of Epic and Saga," Chapter 6, pp. 81–95.

Wood, Jessica. "Unafraid of Greatness," *The Horn Book Magazine;* Pt. I, April 1956, pp. 127–136; Pt. II, June 1956, pp. 212–219.

Woolf, Virginia. *The Common Reader.* Harcourt, Brace, 1925.

"On Not Knowing Greek," pp. 39–61.

Suggestions for Further Reading

Abbott, Charles D. *Howard Pyle;* introduction by N. C. Wyeth. Harper, 1925.

Chapters "Magic Casements" and "The Middle Ages" deal particularly with his books for children.

Brown, A. C. L. *Origin of the Grail Legend.* Harvard University Press, 1943.

Gaster, Theodore H. *Oldest Stories in the World.* Viking Press, 1952.

Guerber, Hélène Adeline. *Book of the Epic.* J. B. Lippincott, 1913.

Hicks, Edward. *Sir Thomas Malory, a Biography.* Harvard University Press, 1928.

Hoffman, Alice S. *The Book of the Sagas.* E. P. Dutton, 1913.

Hull, Eleanor, ed. *The Cuchulain Saga in Irish Literature.* D. Nutt (London), 1898.

Ker, W. P. *English Literature: Mediaeval.* 6th ed. Thornton Butterworth, 1932. (Home University Library)

Koht, Halvdan. *The Old Norse Sagas.* American Scandinavian Foundation, 1945.

Malory, Sir Thomas. *The Morte d'Arthur;* introduction by A. Pollard. 2 vols. Macmillan (London), 1900. (Library of English Classics)

Malory, Sir Thomas. *The Works of Sir Thomas Malory;* ed. by Eugène Vinaver. Oxford University Press, 1947.

Morris, William. *The Story of Sigurd the Volsung and the Fall of the Niblungs.* Longmans, Green, 1924.

Oakley, Thornton. "Howard Pyle," *The Horn Book Magazine,* Vol. 7, 1931, pp. 91–97.

Phillpotts, Bertha. *Edda and Saga;* trans. from the Icelandic with an introduction by Arthur Gilchrist Brodeue. American Scandinavian Foundation, 1929.

The Poetic Edda; trans. from the Icelandic with an introduction and notes by Henry Adams Bellows. American Scandinavian Foundation, 1926.

Sturluson, Snorri. *The Prose Edda;* trans. from the Icelandic with an introduction by Arthur Gilchrist Brodeue. American Scandinavian Foundation, 1929.

Fantasy

Fantasy

"True imagination is a kind of logic; it is the capacity to deduce from the nature of an experienced reality, the nature of other unexperienced realities. Upon the depth and totality of the original experience will depend the reach and validity of the imaginative process." [1]

C HILDREN USE THE TERM *Fairy Tales* to describe stories of marvels and magic; tales set in an unreal world, in which the related events are beyond the realm of possibility; tales in which science, logic, and fact are readjusted and realigned in accordance with the concept of the story.

The folk tales — all the inherited and accumulated wisdom and grandeur of the oral tradition, bearing the *anonymous authorship* of past generations — make up the great body of fairy tales. But there are other tales of wonder and imagination, whose authorship is known, the inventions of individual minds and personalities. These we call fantasies, or literary fairy tales. Among the writers of fantasy are some of the giants of literature: Shakespeare and Spenser and Dante. There are books and tales having such signatures as Hans Christian Andersen, Lewis Carroll, Kenneth Grahame, George Macdonald, J. M. Barrie, Charles Kingsley, Rudyard Kipling, out of the Victorian age; names such as A. A. Milne, James Thurber, Antoine de Saint-Exupéry, E. B. White, William Pène du Bois, and Walter de la Mare in our own day.

The margins between the interests of children and of adults become indistinct and merge, where fantasy is concerned. Jonathan Swift's satirical *Gulliver's Travels,* conceived for adults, is one the children claim for themselves. John Bunyan's spiritual allegory, *Pilgrim's Progress,* becomes for children a fairy tale, whereas Lewis Carroll's *Alice,* written for children, is the darling and delight of philosophers, poets, and statesmen.

It is perfectly obvious why children are drawn to fantasy. The great stories of imagination only confirm their sense of wonder, their hunger for adventure, their recognition of the inconsistencies in life, their premonition of fear and threat, their love of humor and nonsense. But why has the realm of fantasy appealed to so many great and original writers? It is probably because fantasy offers them freedom in which to invent worlds of their own — spiritual

[1] Herbert Read, *The Nature of Literature* (Horizon Press, New York, 1956), p. 288.

Utopias, nonsense worlds of mirth and laughter, systems immense or minute in dimension. No other field of literature affords so great an opportunity for each to express his personal vision of life as it might be, were fancy free to command.

> Tell me where is Fancy bred,
> Or in the heart or in the head?
> How begot, how nourishéd?
> Reply, reply.[2]

The heart would seem to be a chief begetter of fantasy. Some of the greatest fantasies appear to have been woven out of the most cherished experiences, the best beloved scenes, subjects, and events of the authors' lives. It is as if the writers had the ability to transmute actuality into another dimension and by so doing to crystallize the depth of their feeling. W. H. Hudson's *A Little Boy Lost* is such a transfiguration of a boyhood he loved and remembered, spent on the pampas of South America. By the same token, Robert Lawson's *Rabbit Hill* is an expression of the emotion he felt for the landscape of Connecticut, where he lived and shared the companionship of "little creatures everywhere" — especially rabbits. J. R. R. Tolkien's *The Hobbit* must have had its inception in the scholar-author's passionate devotion to his subject — the Anglo-Saxon culture and language on which he is an authority, for *The Hobbit* is a deep-running, spirited variation on old Norse and Saxon themes of dragon-haunted regions, dwarfs, ill-gotten treasure, and the righting of old wrongs. *The Wonderful Adventure of Nils,* Selma Lagerlöf's great fantasy, is compounded of her passion for Sweden — its earth, folklore, and landscape. And what is *Alice in Wonderland* but the sport and play of a mathematician and logician who transmogrifies his hobbies, his intellectual discipline, and his kinship with children into a complex dream world with a logic all its own.

A rich improvisation upon character, setting, or event is the strength of some fantasies. Hugh Lofting's *Story of Doctor Dolittle* and P. L. Travers' *Mary Poppins* are episodic in structure, rather than complete stories moving in ordered sequence to their climax and resolution. It is the uniqueness of such characters as these, and the consistency of their highly original behavior, that makes them memorable.

Fantasy is a favorite medium for allegory, a garb for saying more than one seems to say. George Macdonald is past master at integrating some of the great mysteries of life — good and evil, the experience of death, the exploration of man's relationship to God — with the stuff of fantasy, childlike in conception, and full of magical adventures. And yet his stories never teach belief or state dogma. They remain true to the deep conviction of the folk tale and the interpretive function of myth.

An intuitive writer of fantasy was Hans Christian Andersen. He understood the essential quality of the folk spirit. His fantasies are compounded of his own originality and vision, but they are rooted in the old folk tales of Denmark. To their integrity he adds his immense compassion, his reiteration of

[2] *The Merchant of Venice*, Act III, Sc. 2.

the true values of life, his marvelous inventiveness, his wit, his drama, his gift of endowing the least object with life and appropriate character, his humor; and seeing life whole, he was not afraid to include sorrow among the themes he wrought for children.

An enormous region it is, the area of fantasy, as life-enhancing as poetry, as filled with wisdom as folklore. And the canons of this realm are these: an originality of concept; a unique inner logic; the personal involvement of the authors; an innate regard for wonder and the supernatural; and a mastery of words in the writing.

The Real Princess

Hans Christian Andersen

FANTASY

The Real Princess [1]

HANS CHRISTIAN ANDERSEN

Charming as Andersen's fairy stories are, they constantly show his attitude toward society, and The Real Princess *is a good example. The proof used to show why the princess is a "real" one reflects the feeling of the poor shoemaker's son toward the higher ranks of the social order. This modern fairy tale could have been created only by one who has learned from experience how stupid is the basis of the superiority which the so-called highest classes appropriate to themselves.*

There was once a prince, and he wanted a princess, but then she must be a *real* princess. He traveled right round the world to find one, but there was always something wrong. There were plenty of princesses, but whether they were real princesses he had great difficulty in discovering; there was always something which was not quite right about them. So at last he had to come home again, and he was very sad because he wanted a real princess so badly.

One evening there was a terrible storm; it thundered and lightened and the rain poured down in torrents; indeed it was a fearful night.

In the middle of the storm somebody knocked at the town gate, and the old king himself went to open it.

It was a princess who stood outside, but she was in a terrible state from the rain and the storm. The water streamed out of her hair and her clothes, it ran in at the top of her shoes and out at the heel, but she said that she was a real princess.

"Well, we shall soon see if that is true," thought the old queen, but she said nothing. She went into the bedroom, took all the bedclothes off and laid a pea on the bedstead: then she took twenty mattresses and piled them on the top of the pea, and then twenty feather beds on the top of the mattresses. This was where the princess was to sleep that night. In the morning they asked her how she had slept.

"Oh, terribly badly!" said the princess. "I have hardly closed my eyes the whole night! Heaven knows what was in the bed. I seemed to be lying upon some hard thing, and my whole body is black and blue this morning. It is terrible!"

They saw at once that she must be a real princess when she had felt the pea through twenty mattresses and twenty feather beds. Nobody but a real princess could have such a delicate skin.

So the prince took her to be his wife, for now he was sure that he had found a real princess, and the pea was put into the Museum, where it may still be seen if no one has stolen it.

Now this is a true story.

Five Peas in a Pod [2]

HANS CHRISTIAN ANDERSEN

Andersen's stories are like no others that have been written before or since. Five Peas

[1] From Hans Christian Andersen, *Fairy Tales*, trans. Mrs. Edgar Lucas (Dutton).

[2] From Hans Christian Andersen, *More Fairy Tales*.

in a Pod *gives evidence of his originality and inventiveness, his compassion and deep understanding. Fortunate is the child who is introduced to the stories through storytelling or reading aloud, for Andersen's stories are not for the earliest fairy tale age.*

There were five peas in one pod; they were green, and the pod was green, and so they believed all the world was green — in fact, could not be otherwise. The pod grew, and the peas grew; they were arranged as it suited their house, they sat all in a row. The sun shone without and warmed the shell, and the rain came down and watered it; it was pleasant and comfortable, bright by day and dark by night — all was as it should be — and the peas grew bigger and more and more meditative as they sat there with nothing to do but to think.

"Shall I always remain sitting here?" thought one and all of the five. "Shall I not grow hard with sitting too long? It appears to me as though there must be something beyond; I have a foreboding of something more to come."

And weeks passed away; the peas grew yellow and the shell grew yellow. "All the world is turning yellow," thought they. But all at once the pod was violently shaken, torn off the bough, and human hands thrust it into a trousers-pocket, in company with several other peascods. "Now will all be discovered to us," said the Peas, and waited for what would come next.

"I should like to know which of us will go farthest," said the least of the peas; "but it will soon be known."

"Come what come may!" exclaimed the biggest.

Crash! the pod was torn open, and all the five peas rolled out into the bright sunshine; they lay in a child's hand, a little boy held them, and he declared they were just the right peas for his gun, so one was forthwith put into the gun and shot off.

"Now I fly out into the wide world; catch me if you can;" and he was gone.

"I," announced the second, "shall fly straight into the sun; it is a big peascod and the right place for me." He, too, was gone.

"We sleep while we move," declared the third and fourth; "but we get on all the same;" and they rolled for awhile on the floor before they were picked up and put into the gun. "Ah, we shall go farthest!"

"Come what come may," repeated the fifth, as he was shot into the air; and he flew up to an old balcony under an attic window, flew into a crack in the wood, filled up with moss and mould. And the moss clustered over it; there it lay hid, lost to sight, but not forgotten by our Lord.

"Come what may," again it repeated.

Within the attic dwelt a poor woman, who went out every day to clean stoves, cut firewood, and do other hard work, for she was strong and industrious, but very, very poor. And at home in the little bare chamber she left her half-grown-up only daughter, who was so thin and weakly; for a whole year she had kept her bed, it seemed she could neither live nor die.

"She will go to her little sister," said the poor mother. "Two children had I; that was more than I could provide for, so our Lord shared them with me, and took one away for Himself. I would so gladly keep the one I have left; but He will not have them separated, and she will go and join her little sister."

But the sick girl did not go; very patient and still she lay in bed the livelong day, while her mother was out at work.

It was springtime, and early one morning when the mother was just going out, the sun shone so brightly through the little window upon the floor of the attic, and the sick girl's eyes were attracted towards the lowest pane of glass. "There is something green shooting up from the window-pane; it moves in the wind."

The mother went to the window, and forced it open. "Why, it is a little tiny pea that has sprouted up with its green leaves! How could it get here in this crevice? There, now you have a little garden to look at!"

And the invalid's bed was moved nearer to the window, so that she might watch the sprouting plant while her mother was out at work.

"Mother, I believe I am better!" said the girl, that evening. "The sun shone upon me so warmly today, and the little pea thrives so well, I begin to think I shall get well too, and get out into the sunshine."

"Would you might!" said her mother, not believing it. But she was careful to tie up the little plant, that had first given her child glad thoughts of life, to a bit of wood, that it might not be broken by the wind, and she made a network of string in front of the window, that as it grew higher it should have something to cling round. And, in fact, the little plant throve well: it grew before their eyes, day by day.

"I do believe it is going to blossom!" said the poor woman one morning; and now she really began to hope and believe that her sick girl might recover; she remembered that lately she had talked with less languor, that during the last few mornings she had raised herself in bed, and had sat gazing with sparkling eyes upon her little garden, with its single plant. And the very next week the invalid sat up for more than an hour. So happily she sat in the warm sunshine; the window was open, and outside it a little white and red pea-blossom had unfolded its dainty corolla. The poor girl bowed her head and softly kissed the delicate flower. This was a feast day for mother and daughter. "Our Lord planted it Himself, and made it thrive, on purpose to give hope and pleasure to thee, my precious child, and to me through thee." And the happy mother smiled upon the flower, as though it were a good angel from heaven.

But what became of the other peas? Why, the one that flew into the wide world, crying, "Catch me if you can!" fell into the gutter, and was there picked up by a pigeon. The third and fourth shared the same fate; they too were eaten by pigeons, and thus were useful in their generation; but the second, who aspired to fly into the sun? why, he fell into the water of the gutter — sour water it was, too — and there lay for days and weeks. "I am growing charmingly fat!" quoth the Pea. "I shall tear soon, and more than I have done I believe it is not possible for pea to do. I am the most remarkable of the five from our pod." And the stagnant water was of the same mind.

Meantime the young girl stood at the attic window with beaming eyes, and the glow of health on her cheeks, and she folded her white hands over the pea-blossom, and thanked our Lord for it.

"I hold to my pea!" quoth the water in the gutter.

The Candles [3]

Hans Christian Andersen

❧ *Andersen was deeply sensitive to the soul of things. He had the ability to see a story in everything, and the rare gift of endowing common objects with life and character. It might be a darning needle, a teapot, china ornaments, a bell, or an old street lamp. In this story it is candles.*

There was a great Wax-Light that knew well enough what it was.

"I am born in wax, and molded in a form," it said. "I give more light, and burn a longer time than any other light. My place is in the chandelier, or silver candlestick."

"That must be a charming life!" said the Tallow-Candle. "I am only of tallow — only a tallow dip; but then, I comfort myself, it is always better than to be a mere taper, that is dipped only two times: I am dipped eight times, to get a decent thickness. I'm satisfied. It would, to be sure, be finer and luckier still to have been born in wax, and not in tallow; but one doesn't fix himself. They are put in great rooms, and in glass candlesticks. I live in the kitchen — but that is a good place, too; they get up all the dishes in the house there."

"There is something that is more important than eating!" said the Wax-Candle. "Good company — to see them shine, and shine yourself. There is a ball here this evening. Now I and all my family are soon to be sent for."

Scarcely was this said, when all the wax-lights were sent for — but the Tallow-Candle, too. The mistress took it in her delicate hand, and carried it out into the kitchen; there stood a little boy with a basket that was full of potatoes, and a few

[3] From Hans Christian Andersen, *Stories and Tales,* trans. Horace E. Scudder.

apples were in it, too. The good lady had given all these to the little poor boy.

"Here is a candle for you, my little friend," said she. "Your mother sits up and works far into the night — she can use this."

The lady's little daughter stood by her; and when she heard the words "far into the night," she said, eagerly, "And I'm going to sit up till night, too! We're going to have a ball, and I'm to wear big red bows for it."

How her face shone! yes, that was happiness! no wax-light could shine like the child's eyes.

"That is a blessed thing to see," thought the Tallow-Candle. "I shall never forget it, and certainly it seems to me there can be nothing more." And so the Candle was laid in the basket under the cover, and the boy took it away.

"Where am I going to now?" thought the Candle. "I shall be with poor folks; perhaps not once get a brass candlestick; but the Wax-Light is stuck in silver, and sees the finest folks! What can there be more delightful than to be a light among fine folks? That's my lot — tallow, not wax."

And so the Candle came to the poor people — a widow with three children, in a little, low studded room, right over opposite the rich house.

"God bless the good lady for what she gave!" said the mother; "it is a splendid candle — it can burn till far into the night."

And the Candle was lighted.

"Pugh!" it said. "That was a horrid match she lighted me with. One hardly offers such a thing as that to a wax-light, over at the rich house."

There also the wax-lights were lighted, and shone out over the street. The carriages rumbled up to the rich house with the guests for the ball, dressed so finely; the music struck up.

"Now they're beginning over there," felt the Tallow-Candle, and thought of the little rich girl's bright face, that was brighter than all the wax-lights. "That sight I never shall see any more."

Then the smallest of the children in the poor house came — she was a little girl — and put her arms round her brother's and sister's necks; she had something very important to tell, and must whisper it.

"We're going to have this evening — just think of it — we're going to have this evening warm potatoes!" and her face beamed with happiness. The Candle shone right at her, and saw a pleasure, a happiness, as great as was in the rich house, where the little girl said, "We are going to have a ball this evening, and I shall wear some great red bows."

"Is it such a great thing to get warm potatoes?" thought the Candle. "Well, here is just the same joy among the little things!" and it sneezed at that — that is, it sputtered — and more than that no tallow-candle could do. The table was spread, the potatoes were eaten. O, how good they tasted! It was a real feast; and then each got an apple besides, and the smallest child sang the little verse —

"Now thanks, dear Lord, I give to Thee,
That Thou again hast filléd me. Amen."

"Was not that said prettily?" asked the little girl.

"You mustn't ask that, or say it," said the mother. "You should only thank the good God, who has filled you."

And the little children went to bed, gave a good-night kiss, and fell asleep right away; and the mother sat till far into the night, and sewed, to get a living for them and herself; and from the rich house the lights shone, and the music sounded. The stars twinkled over all the houses, over the rich and over the poor, just as clear, just as kindly.

"That was in sooth a rare evening," thought the Tallow-Candle. "Do you think the wax-lights had any better time in their silver candlesticks? that I'd like to know before I am burnt out!"

And it thought of the happy children's faces, the two alike happy — the one lighted by wax-light, the other by tallow-candle.

Yes, that is the story.

Thumbelisa [4]

HANS CHRISTIAN ANDERSEN

&§ *Here we find the feminine counterpart of Tom Thumb. Thumbelisa, or Thumbelina as she is sometimes called, also travels and has adventures. In this story we see how deftly Andersen intermingles fantasy with folklore. He has taken the theme of an old tale and touched it with the magic of his imagination.*

There was once a woman who had the greatest longing for a little tiny child, but she had no idea where to get one; so she went to an old witch and said to her, "I do so long to have a little child, will you tell me where I can get one?"

"Oh, we shall be able to manage that," said the witch. "Here is a barley corn for you; it is not at all the same kind as that which grows in the peasant's field, or with which chickens are fed; plant it in a flower pot and you will see what will appear."

"Thank you, oh, thank you!" said the woman, and she gave the witch twelve pennies, then went home and planted the barley corn, and a large, handsome flower sprang up at once; it looked exactly like a tulip, but the petals were tightly shut up, just as if they were still in bud. "That is a lovely flower," said the woman, and she kissed the pretty red and yellow petals; as she kissed it the flower burst open with a loud snap. It was a real tulip, you could see that; but right in the middle of the flower on the green stool sat a little tiny girl, most lovely and delicate; she was not more than an inch in height, so she was called Thumbelisa.

Her cradle was a smartly varnished walnut shell, with the blue petals of violets for a mattress and a rose-leaf to cover her; she slept in it at night, but during the day she played about on the table where the woman had placed a plate, surrounded by a wreath of flowers on the outer edge with their stalks in water. A large tulip petal floated on the water, and on this little Thumbelisa sat and sailed about from one side of the plate to

[4] From Hans Christian Andersen, *Fairy Tales,* trans. Mrs. Edgar Lucas.

the other; she had two white horse hairs for oars. It was a pretty sight. She could sing, too, with such delicacy and charm as was never heard before.

One night as she lay in her pretty bed, a great ugly toad hopped in at the window, for there was a broken pane. Ugh! how hideous that great wet toad was; it hopped right down on to the table where Thumbelisa lay fast asleep, under the red rose-leaf.

"Here is a lovely wife for my son," said the toad, and then she took up the walnut shell where Thumbelisa slept and hopped away with it through the window, down into the garden. A great broad stream ran through it, but just at the edge it was swampy and muddy, and it was here that the toad lived with her son. Ugh! how ugly and hideous he was, too, exactly like his mother. "Koax, koax, brekke-ke-kex," that was all he had to say when he saw the lovely little girl in the walnut shell.

"Do not talk so loud or you will wake her," said the old toad; "she might escape us yet, for she is as light as thistledown! We will put her on one of the broad water lily leaves out in the stream; it will be just like an island to her, she is so small and light. She won't be able to run away from there while we get the stateroom ready down under the mud, which you are to inhabit."

A great many water lilies grew in the stream, their broad green leaves looked as if they were floating on the surface of the water. The leaf which was furthest from the shore was also the biggest, and to this one the old toad swam out with the walnut shell in which little Thumbelisa lay.

The poor, tiny little creature woke up quite early in the morning, and when she saw where she was she began to cry most bitterly, for there was water on every side of the big green leaf, and she could not reach the land at any point.

The old toad sat in the mud decking out her abode with grasses and the buds of the yellow water lilies, so as to have it very nice for the new daughter-in-law, and then she swam out with her ugly son to the leaf where Thumbelisa stood; they wanted to fetch her pretty bed to place it in the bridal chamber before they took her there. The old toad made a deep curtsey in the water before her, and said, "Here is my son, who is to be your husband, and you are to live together most comfortably down in the mud."

"Koax, koax, brekke-ke-kex," that was all the son could say.

Then they took the pretty little bed and swam away with it, but Thumbelisa sat quite alone on the green leaf and cried because she did not want to live with the ugly toad, or have her horrid son for a husband. The little fish which swam about in the water had no doubt seen the toad and heard what she said, so they stuck their heads up, wishing, I suppose, to see the little girl. As soon as they saw her, they were delighted with her, and were quite grieved to think that she was to go down to live with the ugly toad. No, that should never happen. They flocked together down in the water round about the green stem which held the leaf she stood upon, and gnawed at it with their teeth till it floated away down the stream carrying Thumbelisa away where the toad could not follow her.

Thumbelisa sailed past place after place, and the little birds in the bushes saw her and sang, "what a lovely little maid." The leaf with her on it floated further and further away and in this manner reached foreign lands.

A pretty little white butterfly fluttered round and round her for some time and at last settled on the leaf, for it had taken quite a fancy to Thumbelisa: she was so happy now, because the toad could not reach her and she was sailing through such lovely scenes; the sun shone on the water and it looked like liquid gold. Then she took her sash, and tied one end round the butterfly, and the other she made fast to the leaf which went gliding on quicker and quicker, and she with it, for she was standing on the leaf.

At this moment a big cockchafer came flying along, he caught sight of her and in an instant he fixed his claw round her slender waist and flew off with her, up into a tree, but the green leaf floated down the stream and the butterfly with it, for he was tied to it and could not get loose.

Heavens! how frightened poor little Thumbelisa was when the cockchafer carried her up into the tree, but she was most of all grieved about the pretty white butterfly which she had fastened to the leaf; if he could not succeed in getting loose he would be starved to death.

But the cockchafer cared nothing for that. He settled with her on the largest leaf on the tree, and fed her with honey from the flowers, and he said that she was lovely although she was not a bit like a chafer. Presently all the other chafers which lived in the tree came to visit them; they looked at Thumbelisa and the young lady chafers twitched their feelers and said, "she has also got two legs, what a good effect it has." "She has no feelers," said another. "She is so slender in the waist, fie, she looks like a human being." "How ugly she is," said all the mother chafers, and yet little Thumbelisa was so pretty. That was certainly also the opinion of the cockchafer who had captured her, but when all the others said she was ugly, he at last began to believe it too, and would not have anything more to do with her, she might go wherever she liked! They flew down from the tree with her and placed her on a daisy, where she cried because she was so ugly that the chafers would have nothing to do with her; and after all, she was more beautiful than anything you could imagine, as delicate and transparent as the finest rose-leaf.

Poor little Thumbelisa lived all the summer quite alone in the wood. She plaited a bed of grass for herself and hung it up under a big dock-leaf which sheltered her from the rain; she sucked the honey from the flowers for her food, and her drink was the dew which lay on the leaves in the morning. In this way the summer and autumn passed, but then came the winter. All the birds which used to sing so sweetly to her flew away, the great dock-leaf under which she had lived shriveled up leaving nothing but a dead yellow stalk, and she shivered with the cold, for her clothes were worn out; she was such a tiny creature, poor little Thumbelisa, she certainly must be frozen to death. It began to snow and every snowflake which fell upon her was like a whole shovelful upon one of us, for we are big and she was only one inch in height. Then she wrapped herself up in a withered leaf, but that did not warm her much, she trembled with the cold.

Close to the wood in which she had been living lay a large cornfield, but the corn had long ago been carried away and nothing remained but the bare, dry stubble which stood up out of the frozen ground. The stubble was quite a forest for her to walk about in: oh, how she shook with the cold. Then she came to the door of a field-mouse's home. It was a little hole down under the stubble. The field-mouse lived so cosily and warm there, her whole room was full of corn, and she had a beautiful kitchen and larder besides. Poor Thumbelisa stood just inside the door like any other poor beggar child and begged for a little piece of barley corn, for she had had nothing to eat for two whole days.

"You poor little thing," said the field-mouse, for she was at bottom a good old field-mouse. "Come into my warm room and dine with me." Then, as she took a fancy to Thumbelisa, she said, "you may with pleasure stay with me for the winter, but you must keep my room clean and tidy and tell me stories, for I am very fond of them," and Thumbelisa did what the good old field-mouse desired and was on the whole very comfortable.

"Now we shall soon have a visitor," said the field-mouse; "my neighbor generally comes to see me every week-day. He is even better housed than I am; his rooms are very large and he wears a most beautiful black velvet coat; if only you could get him for a husband you would indeed be well settled, but he can't see. You must tell him all the most beautiful stories you know."

But Thumbelisa did not like this, and she would have nothing to say to the neighbor for he was a mole. He came and paid a visit in his black velvet coat. He was very rich and wise, said the field-mouse, and his home was twenty times as large as hers; and he had much learning but he did not like the sun or the beautiful flowers, in fact he spoke slightingly of them for he had never seen them. Thumbelisa had to sing to him and she sang both "Fly away, cockchafer" and "A monk, he wandered through the meadow," then the mole fell in love with her because of her sweet voice, but he did not say anything for he was of a discreet turn of mind.

He had just made a long tunnel through the ground from his house to theirs, and he gave the field-mouse and Thumbelisa leave to walk in it whenever they liked. He told them not to be afraid of the dead bird which was lying in the passage. It was a whole bird with feathers and beak which had probably died quite recently at the beginning of the winter and was now entombed just where he had made his tunnel.

The mole took a piece of tinder-wood in his mouth, for that shines like fire in the dark, and walked in front of them to light them in the long dark passage; when they came to the place where the dead bird lay, the mole thrust his broad nose up to the roof and pushed the earth up so as to make a big hole through which the daylight shone. In the middle of the floor lay a dead swallow, with its pretty wings closely pressed to its sides, and the legs and head drawn in under the feathers; no doubt the poor bird had died of cold. Thumbelisa was so sorry for it; she loved all the little birds, for they had twittered and sung so sweetly to her during the whole summer; but the mole kicked it with his short legs and said, "Now it will pipe no more! it must be a miserable fate to be born a little bird! Thank heaven! no child of mine can be a bird; a bird like that has nothing but its twitter and dies of hunger in the winter."

"Yes, as a sensible man, you may well say that," said the field-mouse. "What *has* a bird for all its twittering when the cold weather comes? it has to hunger and freeze, but then it must cut a dash."

Thumbelisa did not say anything, but when the others turned their backs to the bird, she stooped down and stroked aside the feathers which lay over its head, and kissed its closed eyes. "Perhaps it was this very bird which sang so sweetly to me in the summer," she thought; "what pleasure it gave me, the dear pretty bird."

The mole now closed up the hole which let in the daylight and conducted the ladies to their home. Thumbelisa could not sleep at all in the night, so she got up out of her bed and plaited a large handsome mat of hay and then she carried it down and spread it all over the dead bird, and laid some soft cotton wool which she had found in the field-mouse's room close round its sides, so that it might have a warm bed on the cold ground.

"Good-bye, you sweet little bird," said she, "good-bye, and thank you for your sweet song through the summer when all the trees were green and the sun shone warmly upon us." Then she laid her head close up to the bird's breast, but was quite startled at a sound, as if something was thumping inside it. It was the bird's heart. It was not dead but lay in a swoon, and now that it had been warmed it began to revive.

In the autumn all the swallows fly away to warm countries, but if one happens to be belated, it feels the cold so much that it falls down like a dead thing, and remains lying where it falls till the snow covers it up. Thumbelisa quite shook with fright for the bird was very, very big beside her who was only one inch high, but she gathered up her courage, packed the wool closer round the poor bird, and fetched a leaf of mint which she had herself for a coverlet and laid it over the bird's head. The next night she stole down again to it and found it alive but so feeble that it could only just open its eyes for a moment to look at Thumbelisa who stood with a bit of tinder-wood in her hand, for she had no other lantern.

"Many, many thanks, you sweet child," said the sick swallow to her; "you have warmed me beautifully. I shall soon have strength to fly out into the warm sun again."

"Oh!" said she, "it is so cold outside, it snows and freezes, stay in your warm bed, I will tend you." Then she brought water to the swallow in a leaf, and when it had drunk some, it told her how it had torn its wing on a blackthorn bush, and therefore could not fly as fast as the other swallows which were taking flight then for the distant warm lands. At last it fell down on the ground, but after that it remembered nothing, and did not in the least know how it had got into the tunnel.

It stayed there all the winter, and Thumbelisa was good to it and grew very fond of it.

She did not tell either the mole or the field-mouse anything about it, for they did not like the poor unfortunate swallow.

As soon as the spring came and the warmth of the sun penetrated the ground, the swallow said good-bye to Thumbelisa, who opened the hole which the mole had made above. The sun streamed in deliciously upon them, and the swallow asked if she would not go with him, she could sit upon his back and they would fly far away into the green wood. But Thumbelisa knew that it would grieve the old field-mouse if she left her like that.

"No, I can't," said Thumbelisa.

"Good-bye, good-bye, then, you kind, pretty girl," said the swallow, and flew out into the sunshine. Thumbelisa looked after him and her eyes filled with tears, for she was very fond of the poor swallow.

"Tweet, tweet," sang the bird, and flew into the green wood.

Thumbelisa was very sad. She was not allowed to go out into the warm sunshine at all; the corn which was sown in the field near the field-mouse's house grew quite long, it was a thick forest for the poor little girl who was only an inch high.

"You must work at your trousseau this summer," said the mouse to her, for their neighbor the tiresome mole in his black velvet coat had asked her to marry him. "You shall have both woollen and linen, you shall have wherewith to clothe and cover yourself when you become the mole's wife." Thumbelisa had to turn the distaff and the field-mouse hired four spiders to spin and weave day and night. The mole paid a visit every evening and he was always saying that when the summer came to an end, the sun would not shine nearly so warmly, now it burnt the ground as hard as a stone. Yes, when the summer was over he would celebrate his marriage; but Thumbelisa was not at all pleased, for she did not care a bit for the tiresome mole. Every morning at sunrise and every evening at sunset she used to steal out to the door, and when the wind blew aside the tops of the cornstalks so that she could see the blue sky, she thought how bright and lovely it was out there, and wished so much to see the dear swallow again; but it never came back; no doubt it was a long way off, flying about in the beautiful green woods.

When the autumn came all Thumbelisa's outfit was ready.

"In four weeks you must be married," said the field-mouse to her. But Thumbelisa cried and said that she would not have the tiresome mole for a husband.

"Fiddle-dee-dee," said the field-mouse; "don't be obstinate or I shall bite you with my white tooth. You are going to have a splendid husband; the queen herself hasn't the equal of his black velvet coat; both his kitchen and his cellar are full. You should thank heaven for such a husband!"

So they were to be married; the mole had come to fetch Thumbelisa; she was to live deep down under the ground with him, and never to go out into the warm sunshine, for he could not bear it. The poor child was very sad at the thought of bidding good-bye to the beautiful sun; while she had been with the field-mouse she had at least been allowed to look at it from the door.

"Good-bye, you bright sun," she said as she stretched out her arms towards it and went a little way outside the field-mouse's house, for now the harvest was over and only the stubble remained. "Good-bye, good-bye!" she said, and threw her tiny arms round a little red flower growing there. "Give my love to the dear swallow if you happen to see him."

"Tweet, tweet," she heard at this moment above her head. She looked up; it was the swallow just passing. As soon as it saw Thumbelisa it was delighted; she told it how unwilling she was to have the ugly mole for a husband, and that she was to live deep down underground where the sun never shone. She could not help crying about it.

"The cold winter is coming," said the swallow, "and I am going to fly away to warm countries. Will you go with me? You can sit upon my back! Tie yourself on with your sash, then we will fly away from the ugly mole and his dark cavern, far away over the mountains to those warm countries where the sun shines with greater splendor than here, where it is always summer and there are heaps of flowers. Do fly with me, you sweet little Thumbelisa, who saved my life when I lay frozen in the dark earthy passage."

"Yes, I will go with you," said Thumbelisa, seating herself on the bird's back with her feet on its outspread wing. She tied her band tightly to one of the strongest feathers, and then the swallow flew away, high up in the air above forests and lakes, high up above the biggest mountains where the snow never melts; and Thumbelisa shivered in the cold air, but then she crept under the bird's warm feathers, and only stuck out her little head to look at the beautiful sights beneath it.

Then at last they reached the warm countries. The sun shone with a warmer glow than here; the sky was twice as high, and the most beautiful green and blue grapes grew in clusters on the banks and hedgerows. Oranges and lemons hung in the woods which were fragrant with myrtles and sweet herbs, and beautiful children ran about the roads playing with the large gorgeously-colored butterflies. But the swallow flew on and on, and the country grew more and more beautiful. Under magnificent green trees on the shores of the blue sea stood a dazzling white marble palace of ancient date; vines wreathed themselves round the stately pillars. At the head of these there were countless nests, and the swallow who carried Thumbelisa lived in one of them.

"Here is my house," said the swallow; "but if you will choose one of the gorgeous flowers growing down there, I will place you in it, and you will live as happily as you can wish."

"That would be delightful," she said, and clapped her little hands.

A great white marble column had fallen to the ground and lay there broken in three pieces, but between these the most lovely white flowers grew. The swallow flew down with Thumbelisa and put her upon one of the broad leaves; what was her astonishment to find a little man in the middle of the flower, as bright and transparent as if he had been made of glass. He had a lovely golden crown upon his head and the most beautiful bright wings upon his shoulders; he was no bigger than Thumbelisa. He was the angel of the flowers. There was a similar little man or woman in every flower, but he was the king of them all.

"Heavens, how beautiful he is," whispered Thumbelisa to the swallow. The little prince was quite frightened by the swallow, for it was a perfect giant of a bird to him, he who was so small and delicate, but when he saw Thumbelisa he was delighted; she was the very prettiest girl he had ever seen. He therefore took the golden crown off his own head and placed it on hers, and asked her name, and if she would be his wife, and then she would be queen of the flowers! Yes, he was certainly a very different kind of husband from the toad's son, or the mole with his black velvet coat. So she accepted the beautiful prince, and out of every flower stepped a little lady or a gentleman so lovely that it was a pleasure to look at them. Each one brought a gift to Thumbelisa, but the best of all was a pair of pretty wings from a large white fly; they were fastened on to her back, and then she too could fly from flower to flower. All was then delight and happiness, but the swallow sat alone in his nest and sang to them as well as he could, for his heart was heavy, he was so fond of Thumbelisa himself, and would have wished never to part from her.

"You shall not be called Thumbelisa," said the angel of the flower to her; "that is such an ugly name, and you are so pretty. We will call you May."

"Good-bye, good-bye," said the swallow, and flew away again from the warm countries, far away back to Denmark; there he had a little nest above the window where the man lived who wrote this story, and he sang his "tweet, tweet" to the man, and so we have the whole story.

The Wild Swans [5]

HANS CHRISTIAN ANDERSEN

⊷§ The Wild Swans *is one of Andersen's most delightful tales. What child could resist "golden*

[5] From Hans Christian Andersen, *Fairy Tales*, trans. Mrs. Edgar Lucas.

slates with diamond pencils," the magic, Elise's trials under the restraint of silence, the dramatic suspense before she is to be burned as a witch, and the almost perfect outcome when all are completely restored except one brother? In its dramatic interest this tale is surpassed only by Snow White and the Seven Dwarfs.

Far away, where the swallows take refuge in winter, lived a king who had eleven sons and one daughter, Elise. The eleven brothers — they were all princes — used to go to school with stars on their breasts and swords at their sides. They wrote upon golden slates with diamond pencils, and could read just as well without a book as with one; so there was no mistake about their being real princes. Their sister Elise sat upon a little footstool of looking-glass, and she had a picture-book which had cost the half of a kingdom. Oh, these children were very happy; but it was not to last thus for ever.

Their father, who was king over all the land, married a wicked queen who was not at all kind to the poor children; they found that out on the first day. All was festive at the castle, but when the children wanted to play at having company, instead of having as many cakes and baked apples as ever they wanted, she would only let them have some sand in a tea-cup, and said they must make-believe.

In the following week she sent little Elise into the country to board with some peasants, and it did not take her long to make the king believe so many bad things about the boys, that he cared no more about them.

"Fly out into the world and look after yourselves," said the wicked queen; "you shall fly about like birds without voices."

But she could not make things as bad for them as she would have liked; they turned into eleven beautiful wild swans. They flew out of the palace window with a weird scream, right across the park and the woods.

It was very early in the morning when they came to the place where their sister Elise was sleeping in the peasant's house. They hovered over the roof of the house, turning and twisting their long necks, and flapping their wings; but no one either heard or saw them. They had to fly away again, and they soared up towards the clouds, far out into the wide world, and they settled in a big, dark wood, which stretched down to the shore.

Poor little Elise stood in the peasant's room, playing with a green leaf, for she had no other toys. She made a little hole in it, which she looked through at the sun, and it seemed to her as if she saw her brothers' bright eyes. Every time the warm sunbeams shone upon her cheek, it reminded her of their kisses. One day passed just like another. When the wind whistled through the rose-hedges outside the house, it whispered to the roses, "Who can be prettier than you are?" But the roses shook their heads and answered, "Elise!" And when the old woman sat in the doorway reading her Psalms, the wind turned over the leaves and said to the book, "Who can be more pious than you?" "Elise!" answered the book. Both the roses and the book of Psalms only spoke the truth.

She was to go home when she was fifteen, but when the queen saw how pretty she was, she got very angry, and her heart was filled with hatred. She would willingly have turned her into a wild swan, too, like her brothers, but she did not dare to do it at once, for the king wanted to see his daughter. The queen always went to the bath in the early morning. It was built of marble and adorned with soft cushions and beautiful carpets.

She took three toads, kissed them, and said to the first, "Sit upon Elise's head when she comes to the bath, so that she may become sluggish like yourself." "Sit upon her forehead," she said to the second, "that she may become ugly like you, and then her father won't know her! Rest upon her heart," she whispered to the third. "Let an evil spirit come over her, which may be a burden to her." Then she put the toads into the clean water, and a green tinge immediately came over it. She called Elise, undressed her, and made her go into the bath; when she ducked under the water, one of the toads got among her hair, the other got on to her forehead, and the third on to her bosom. But when she stood up three scarlet poppies floated on the water; had not the creatures been poisonous, and kissed by the sorceress, they would have been changed into crimson roses, but yet they became flowers from merely having rested a moment on her head and her heart. She was far too good and innocent for the sorcery to have any power over her. When the wicked queen saw this, she rubbed her over with walnut juice, and smeared her face with some evil-smelling salve. She also matted up her beautiful hair; it would have been impossible to recognise pretty Elise. When her father saw her, he was quite horrified and said that she could not be his daughter. Nobody would have anything to say to her, except the yard dog, and the swallows, and they were only poor dumb animals whose opinion went for nothing.

Poor Elise wept, and thought of her eleven brothers who were all lost. She crept sadly out of the palace and wandered about all day, over meadows and marshes, and into a big forest. She did not know in the least where she wanted to go, but she felt very sad, and longed for her brothers, who, no doubt, like herself had been driven out of the palace. She made up her mind to go and look for them, but she had only been in the wood for a short time when night fell. She had quite lost her way, so she lay down upon the soft moss, said her evening prayer, and rested her head on a little hillock. It was very still and the air was mild, hundreds of glow-worms shone around her on the grass and in the marsh like green fire. When she gently moved one of the branches over her head, the little shining insects fell over her like a shower of stars. She dreamt about her brothers all night long. Again they were children playing together: they wrote upon the golden slates with their diamond pencils, and she looked at the picture book which had cost half a kingdom. But they no longer wrote strokes and noughts upon their slates as they used to do; no, they wrote down all their boldest exploits, and everything that they had seen and experienced. Everything in the picture-book was alive, the birds sang, and the people walked out of the book, and spoke to Elise and her brothers. When she turned over a page, they skipped back into their places again, so that there should be no confusion among the pictures.

When she woke the sun was already high; it is true she could not see it very well through the thick branches of the lofty forest trees, but the sunbeams cast a golden shimmer around beyond the forest. There was a fresh delicious scent of grass and herbs in the air, and the birds were almost ready to perch upon her shoulders. She could hear the splashing of water, for there were many springs around, which all flowed into a pond with a lovely sandy bottom. It was surrounded with thick bushes, but there was one place which the stags had trampled down and Elise passed through the opening to the water side. It was so transparent, that had not the branches been moved by the breeze, she must have thought that they were painted on the bottom, so plainly was every leaf reflected, both those on which the sun played, and those which were in shade.

When she saw her own face she was quite frightened, it was so brown and ugly, but when she wet her little hand and rubbed her eyes and forehead, her white skin shone through again. Then she took off all her clothes and went into the fresh water. A more beautiful royal child than she, could not be found in all the world.

When she had put on her clothes again, and plaited her long hair, she went to a sparkling spring and drank some of the water out of the hollow of her hand. Then she wandered further into the wood, though where she was going she had not the least idea. She thought of her brothers, and she thought of a merciful God who would not forsake her. He let the wild crab-apples grow to feed the hungry. He showed her a tree, the branches of which were bending beneath their weight of fruit. Here she made her midday meal, and, having put props under the branches, she walked on into the thickest part of the forest. It was so quiet that she heard her own footsteps, she heard every little withered leaf which bent under her feet. Not a bird was to be seen, not a ray of sunlight pierced the leafy branches, and the tall trunks were so close together that when she looked before her it seemed as if a thick fence of heavy beams hemmed her in on every side. The solitude was such as she had never known before.

It was a very dark night, not a single glowworm sparkled in the marsh; sadly she lay down to sleep, and it seemed to her as if the branches above her parted asunder, and the Saviour looked down upon her with His loving eyes, and the little angels' heads peeped out above His head and under His arms.

When she woke in the morning she was not sure if she had dreamt this, or whether it was really true.

She walked a little further, when she met an old woman with a basket full of berries, of which she gave her some. Elise asked if she had seen eleven princes ride through the wood. "No," said the old woman, "but yesterday I saw eleven swans, with golden crowns upon their heads, swimming in the stream close by here."

She led Elise a little further to a slope, at the foot of which the stream meandered. The trees on either bank stretched out their rich leafy branches towards each other, and where, from their natural growth, they could not reach each other, they had torn their roots out of the ground, and leant over the water so as to interlace their branches.

Elise said good-bye to the old woman, and walked along by the river till it flowed out into the great open sea.

The beautiful open sea lay before the maiden, but not a sail was to be seen on it, not a single boat. How was she ever to get any further? She looked at the numberless little pebbles on the beach; they were all worn quite round by the water. Glass, iron, stone, whatever was washed up, had taken their shapes from the water, which yet was much softer than her little hand. "With all its rolling, it is untiring, and everything hard is smoothed down. I will be just as untiring! Thank you for your lesson, you clear rolling waves! Some time, so my heart tells me, you will bear me to my beloved brothers!"

Eleven white swans' feathers were lying on the seaweed; she picked them up and made a bunch of them. There were still drops of water on them. Whether these were dew or tears no one could tell. It was very lonely there by the shore, but she did not feel it, for the sea was ever changing. There were more changes on it in the course of a few hours than could be seen on an inland fresh-water lake in a year. If a big black cloud arose, it was just as if the sea wanted to say, "I can look black too," and then the wind blew up and the waves showed their white crests. But if the clouds were red and the wind dropped, the sea looked like a rose-leaf, now white, now green. But, however still it was, there was always a little gentle motion just by the shore, the water rose and fell softly like the bosom of a sleeping child.

When the sun was just about to go down, Elise saw eleven wild swans with golden crowns upon their heads flying towards the shore. They flew in a swaying line, one behind the other, like a white ribbon streamer. Elise climbed up on to the bank and hid behind a bush; the swans settled close by her and flapped their great white wings.

As soon as the sun had sunk beneath the water the swans shed their feathers and became eleven handsome princes; they were Elise's brothers. Although they had altered a good deal, she knew them at once; she felt that they must be her brothers and she sprang into their arms, calling them by name. They were delighted when they recognised their little sister who had grown so big and beautiful. They laughed and cried, and told each other how wickedly their stepmother had treated them all.

"We brothers," said the eldest, "have to fly about in the guise of swans, as long as the sun is above the horizon. When it goes down we regain our human shapes. So we always have to look out for a resting place near sunset, for should we happen to be flying up among the clouds when the sun goes down, we should be hurled to the depths below. We do not live here; there is another land, just as beautiful as this, beyond the sea; but the way to it is very long and we have to cross the mighty ocean to get to it. There is not a single island on the way where we can spend the night, only one solitary little rock juts up above the water midway. It is only just big enough for us to stand upon close together, and if there is a heavy sea the water splashes over us, yet we thank our God for it. We stay there over night in our human forms, and without it we could never revisit our beloved Fatherland, for our flight takes two of the longest days in the year. We are only permitted to visit the home of our fathers once a year, and we dare only stay for eleven days. We hover over his big forest from whence we catch a glimpse of the place where we were born, and where our father lives; beyond it we can see the high church towers where our mother is buried. We fancy that the trees and bushes here are related to us; and the wild horses gallop over the moors, as we used to see them in our childhood. The charcoal burners still sing the old songs we used to dance to when we were children. This is our Fatherland, we are drawn towards it, and here we have found you again, dear little sister! We may stay here two days longer, and then we must fly away again across the ocean, to a lovely country indeed, but it is not our own dear Fatherland! How shall we ever take you with us, we have neither ship nor boat!"

"How can I deliver you!" said their sister, and they went on talking to each other, nearly all night, they only dozed for a few hours.

Elise was awakened in the morning by the rustling of the swans' wings above her; her brothers were again transformed and were wheeling round in great circles, till she lost sight of them in the distance. One of them, the youngest, stayed behind. He laid his head against her bosom, and she caressed it with her fingers. They remained together all day; towards evening the others came back, and as soon as the sun went down they took their natural forms.

"Tomorrow we must fly away, and we dare not come back for a whole year, but we can't leave you like this! Have you courage to go with us? My arm is strong enough to carry you over the forest, so surely our united strength ought to be sufficient to bear you across the ocean."

"Oh, yes! take me with you," said Elise.

They spent the whole night in weaving a kind of net of the elastic bark of the willow bound together with tough rushes; they made it both large and strong. Elise lay down upon it, and when the sun rose and the brothers became swans again, they took up the net in their bills and flew high up among the clouds with their precious sister, who was fast asleep. The sunbeams fell straight on to her face, so one of the swans flew over her head so that its broad wings should shade her.

They were far from land when Elise woke; she thought she must still be dreaming, it seemed so strange to be carried through the air so high up above the sea. By her side lay a branch of beautiful ripe berries, and a bundle of savory roots, which her youngest brother had collected for her, and for which she gave him a grateful smile. She knew it was he who flew above her head shading her from the sun. They were so high up that the first ship they saw looked like a gull floating on the water. A great cloud came up behind them like a mountain, and Elise saw the shadow of herself on it, and those of the eleven swans looking like giants. It was a more beautiful picture than any she had ever seen before, but as the sun rose higher, the cloud fell behind, and the shadow picture disappeared.

They flew on and on all day like an arrow whizzing through the air, but they went slower than usual, for now they had their sister to carry. A storm came up, and night was drawing on; Elise saw the sun sinking, with terror in her heart, for the solitary rock was nowhere to be seen. The swans seemed to be taking stronger strokes than ever; alas! she was the cause of their not being able to get on faster; as soon as the sun went down they would become men, and they would all be hurled into the sea and drowned. She prayed to God from the bottom of her heart, but still no rock was to be seen! Black clouds gathered, and strong gusts of wind announced a storm; the clouds looked like a great threatening leaden wave, and the flashes of lightning followed each other rapidly.

The sun was now at the edge of the sea. Elise's heart quaked, when suddenly the swans shot downwards so suddenly, that she thought they were falling, then they hovered again. Half of the sun was below the horizon, and there for the first time she saw the little rock below, which did not look bigger than the head of a seal above the water. The sun sank very quickly, it was no bigger than a star, but her foot touched solid earth. The sun went out like the last sparks of a bit of burning paper; she saw her brothers stand arm in arm around her, but there was only just room enough for them. The waves beat upon the rock and washed over them like drenching rain. The heavens shone with continuous fire, and the thunder rolled, peal upon peal. But the sister and brothers held each other's hands and sang a psalm which gave them comfort and courage.

The air was pure and still at dawn. As soon as the sun rose the swans flew off with Elise, away from the islet. The sea still ran high, it looked from where they were as if the white foam on the dark green water were millions of swans floating on the waves.

When the sun rose higher, Elise saw before her half floating in the air great masses of ice, with shining glaciers on the heights. A palace was perched midway a mile in length, with one bold colonnade built above another. Beneath them swayed palm trees and gorgeous blossoms as big as mill wheels. She asked if this was the land to which she was going, but the swans shook their heads, because what she saw was a mirage; the beautiful and ever changing palace of Fata Morgana. No mortal dared enter it. Elise gazed at it, but as she gazed the palace, gardens and mountains melted away, and in their place stood twenty proud churches with their high towers and pointed windows. She seemed to hear the notes of the organ, but it was the sea she heard. When she got close to the seeming churches, they changed to a great navy sailing beneath her; but it was only a sea mist floating over the waters. Yes, she saw constant changes passing before her eyes, and now she saw the real land she was bound to. Beautiful blue mountains rose before her with their cedar woods and palaces. Long before the sun went down, she sat among the hills in front of a big cave covered with delicate green creepers. It looked like a piece of embroidery.

"Now we shall see what you will dream here tonight," said the youngest brother, as he showed her where she was to sleep.

"If only I might dream how I could deliver you," she said, and this thought filled her mind entirely. She prayed earnestly to God for His help, and even in her sleep she continued her prayer. It seemed to her that she was flying up to Fata Morgana in her castle in the air. The fairy came towards her, she was charming and brilliant, and yet she was very like the old woman who gave her the berries in the wood, and told her about the swans with the golden crowns.

"Your brothers can be delivered," she said, "but have you courage and endurance enough for it? The sea is indeed softer than your hands, and it molds the hardest stones, but it does not feel the pain your fingers will feel. It has no heart, and does not suffer the pain and anguish you must feel. Do you see this stinging nettle I hold in my hand? Many of this kind grow round the cave where you sleep; only these and the ones which grow in the churchyards may be used. Mark that! Those you may pluck although they will burn and blister your hands. Crush the nettles with your feet and you will have flax, and of this you must weave eleven coats of mail with long sleeves. Throw these over the eleven wild swans and the charm is broken! But remember that from the moment you begin this work, till it is finished, even if it takes years, you must not utter a word! The first word you say will fall like a murderer's dagger into the hearts of your brothers. Their lives hang on your tongue. Mark this well!"

She touched her hand at the same moment, it was like burning fire, and woke Elise. It was bright daylight, and close to where she slept lay a nettle like those in her dream. She fell upon her knees with thanks to God and left the cave to begin her work.

She seized the horrid nettles with her delicate hands, and they burnt like fire; great blisters rose on her hands and arms, but she suffered it willingly if only it would deliver her beloved brothers. She crushed every nettle with her bare feet, and twisted it into green flax.

When the sun went down and the brothers came back, they were alarmed at finding her mute; they thought it was some new witchcraft exercised by their wicked stepmother. But when they saw her hands, they under-stood that it was for their sakes; the youngest brother wept, and wherever his tears fell, she felt no more pain, and the blisters disappeared.

She spent the whole night at her work, for she could not rest till she had delivered her dear brothers. All the following day while her brothers were away she sat solitary, but never had the time flown so fast. One coat of mail was finished and she began the next. Then a hunting-horn sounded among the mountains; she was much frightened, the sound came nearer, and she heard dogs barking. In terror she rushed into the cave and tied the nettles she had collected and woven, into a bundle upon which she sat.

At this moment a big dog bounded forward from the thicket, and another and another, they barked loudly and ran backwards and forwards. In a few minutes all the huntsmen were standing outside the cave, and the handsomest of them was the king of the country. He stepped up to Elise: never had he seen so lovely a girl.

"How came you here, beautiful child?" he said.

Elise shook her head; she dared not speak; the salvation and the lives of her brothers depended upon her silence. She hid her hands under her apron, so that the king should not see what she suffered.

"Come with me!" he said; "you cannot stay here. If you are as good as you are beautiful, I will dress you in silks and velvets, put a golden crown upon your head, and you shall live with me and have your home in my richest palace!" Then he lifted her upon his horse. She wept and wrung her hands, but the king said, "I only think of your happiness; you will thank me one day for what I am doing!" Then he darted off across the mountains, holding her before him on his horse, and the huntsmen followed.

When the sun went down, the royal city with churches and cupolas lay before them, and the king led her into the palace, where great fountains played in the marble halls, and where walls and ceilings were adorned with paintings, but she had no eyes for them, she only wept and sorrowed; passively she allowed the women to dress her in royal robes, to twist pearls into her hair, and to draw gloves on to her blistered hands.

She was dazzlingly lovely as she stood there in all her magnificence; the courtiers bent low before her, and the king wooed her as his bride, although the archbishop shook his head, and whispered that he feared the beautiful wood maiden was a witch, who had dazzzled their eyes and infatuated the king.

The king refused to listen to him, he ordered the music to play, the richest food to be brought, and the loveliest girls to dance before her. She was led through scented gardens into gorgeous apartments, but nothing brought a smile to her lips, or into her eyes, sorrow sat there like a heritage and a possession for all time. Last of all, the king opened the door of a little chamber close by the room where she was to sleep. It was adorned with costly green carpets, and made to exactly resemble the cave where he found her. On the floor lay the bundle of flax she had spun from the nettles, and from the ceiling hung the shirt of mail which was already finished. One of the huntsmen had brought all these things away as curiosities.

"Here you may dream that you are back in your former home!" said the king. "Here is the work upon which you were engaged; in the midst of your splendor, it may amuse you to think of those times."

When Elise saw all these things so dear to her heart, a smile for the first time played upon her lips, and the blood rushed back to her cheeks. She thought of the deliverance of her brothers, and she kissed the king's hand; he pressed her to his heart, and ordered all the church bells to ring marriage peals. The lovely dumb girl from the woods was to be queen of the country.

The archbishop whispered evil words into the ear of the king, but they did not reach his heart. The wedding was to take place, and the archbishop himself had to put the crown upon her head. In his anger he pressed the golden circlet so tightly upon her head as to give her pain. But a heavier circlet pressed upon her heart, her grief for her brothers, so she thought nothing of the bodily pain. Her lips were sealed, a single word from her mouth would cost her broth-

ers their lives, but her eyes were full of love for the good and handsome king, who did everything he could to please her. Every day she grew more and more attached to him, and longed to confide in him, tell him her sufferings; but dumb she must remain, and in silence must bring her labor to completion. Therefore at night she stole away from his side into her secret chamber, which was decorated like a cave, and here she knitted one shirt after another. When she came to the seventh, all her flax was worked up; she knew that these nettles which she was to use grew in the churchyard, but she had to pluck them herself. How was she to get there? "Oh, what is the pain of my fingers compared with the anguish of my heart," she thought. "I must venture out; the good God will not desert me!" With as much terror in her heart, as if she were doing some evil deed, she stole down one night into the moonlit garden, and through the long alleys out into the silent streets to the churchyard. There she saw, sitting on a gravestone, a group of hideous ghouls, who took off their tattered garments, as if they were about to bathe, and then they dug down into the freshly made graves with their skinny fingers, and tore the flesh from the bodies and devoured it. Elise had to pass close by them, and they fixed their evil eyes upon her, but she said a prayer as she passed, picked the stinging nettles and hurried back to the palace with them.

Only one person saw her, but that was the archbishop, who watched while others slept. Surely now all his bad opinions of the queen were justified; all was not as it should be with her, she must be a witch, and therefore she had bewitched the king and all the people.

He told the king in the confessional what he had seen and what he feared. When those bad words passed his lips, the pictures of the saints shook their heads as if to say: it is not so, Elise is innocent. The archbishop however took it differently, and thought that they were bearing witness against her, and shaking their heads at her sin. Two big tears rolled down the king's cheeks, and he went home with doubt in his heart. He pretended to sleep at night, but no quiet sleep came to his eyes. He perceived how Elise got up and went to her private closet. Day by day his face grew darker, Elise saw it but could not imagine what was the cause of it. It alarmed her, and what was she not already suffering in her heart because of her brothers? Her salt tears ran down upon the royal purple velvet, they lay upon it like sparkling diamonds, and all who saw their splendor wished to be queen.

She had, however, almost reached the end of her labors, only one shirt of mail was wanting, but again she had no more flax and not a single nettle was left. Once more, for the last time, she must go to the churchyard to pluck a few handfuls. She thought with dread of the solitary walk and the horrible ghouls; but her will was as strong as her trust in God.

Elise went, but the king and the archbishop followed her, they saw her disappear within the grated gateway of the churchyard. When they followed they saw the ghouls sitting on the gravestone as Elise had seen them before; and the king turned away his head because he thought she was among them, she, whose head this very evening had rested on his breast.

"The people must judge her," he groaned, and the people judged. "Let her be consumed in the glowing flames!"

She was led away from her beautiful royal apartments to a dark damp dungeon, where the wind whistled through the grated window. Instead of velvet and silk they gave her the bundle of nettles she had gathered to lay her head upon. The hard burning shirts of mail were to be her covering, but they could have given her nothing more precious.

She set to work again with many prayers to God. Outside her prison the street boys sang derisive songs about her, and not a soul comforted her with a kind word.

Towards evening she heard the rustle of swans' wings close to her window; it was her youngest brother, at last he had found her. He sobbed aloud with joy although he knew that the coming night might be her last, but then her work was almost done and her brothers were there.

The archbishop came to spend her last hours with her as he had promised the king. She shook her head at him, and by looks and gestures begged him to leave her. She had only this night in which to finish her work, or else all would be wasted, all — her pain, tears and sleepless nights. The archbishop went away with bitter words against her, but poor Elise knew that she was innocent, and she went on with her work.

The little mice ran about the floor bringing nettles to her feet, so as to give what help they could, and a thrush sat on the grating of the window where he sang all night, as merrily as he could to keep up her courage.

It was still only dawn, and the sun would not rise for an hour when the eleven brothers stood at the gate of the palace, begging to be taken to the king. This could not be done, was the answer, for it was still night; the king was asleep and no one dared wake him. All their entreaties and threats were useless, the watch turned out and even the king himself came to see what was the matter; but just then the sun rose, and no more brothers were to be seen, only eleven wild swans hovering over the palace.

The whole populace streamed out of the town gates; they were all anxious to see the witch burnt. A miserable horse drew the cart in which Elise was seated. They had put upon her a smock of green sacking, and all her beautiful long hair hung loose from the lovely head. Her cheeks were deathly pale, and her lips moved softly, while her fingers unceasingly twisted the green yarn. Even on the way to her death she could not abandon her unfinished work. Ten shirts lay completed at her feet — she labored away at the eleventh, amid the scoffing insults of the populace.

"Look at the witch how she mutters. She has never a book of psalms in her hands; no, there she sits with her loathsome sorcery. Tear it away from her, into a thousand bits!"

The crowd pressed around her to destroy her work; but just then eleven white swans flew down and perched upon the cart flapping their wings. The crowd gave way before them in terror.

"It is a sign from Heaven! She is innocent!" they whispered, but they dared not say it aloud.

The executioner seized her by the hand, but she hastily threw the eleven shirts over the swans, who were immediately transformed to eleven handsome princes; but the youngest had a swan's wing in place of an arm, for one sleeve was wanting to his shirt of mail, she had not been able to finish it.

"Now I may speak! I am innocent."

The populace who saw what had happened bowed down before her as if she had been a saint, but she sank lifeless in her brother's arms; so great had been the strain, the terror and the suffering she had endured.

"Yes, innocent she is indeed," said the eldest brother, and he told them all that had happened.

Whilst he spoke a wonderful fragrance spread around, as of millions of roses. Every faggot in the pile had taken root and shot out branches, and a great high hedge of red roses had arisen. At the very top was one pure white blossom; it shone like a star, and the king broke it off and laid it on Elise's bosom, and she woke with joy and peace in her heart.

All the church bells began to ring of their own accord, and the singing birds flocked around them. Surely such a bridal procession went back to the palace as no king had ever seen before!

The Steadfast Tin Soldier[6]

HANS CHRISTIAN ANDERSEN

This tale is beautifully written, but it is an excellent example of how the plot of a literary fairy tale is likely to be more complicated than that of a folk tale. The action is rapid and the climax swift and sure; and nothing could be more befitting such steadfastness than for the hero and heroine not only to die together but to leave behind true representations of themselves.

There were once five and twenty tin soldiers, all brothers, for they were the offspring of the same old tin spoon. Each man shouldered his gun, kept his eyes well to the

[6] From Hans Christian Andersen, *Fairy Tales*, trans. Mrs. Edgar Lucas.

front, and wore the smartest red and blue uniform imaginable. The first thing they heard in their new world, when the lid was taken off the box, was a little boy clapping his hands and crying, "Soldiers, soldiers!" It was his birthday and they had just been given to him; so he lost no time in setting them up on the table. All the soldiers were exactly alike with one exception, and he differed from the rest in having only one leg. For he was made last, and there was not quite enough tin left to finish him. However, he stood just as well on his one leg, as the others on two, in fact he is the very one who is to become famous. On the table where they were being set up, were many other toys; but the chief thing which caught the eye was a delightful paper castle. You could see through the tiny windows, right into the rooms. Outside there were some little trees surrounding a small mirror, representing a lake, whose surface reflected the waxen swans which were swimming about on it. It was altogether charming, but the prettiest thing of all was a little maiden standing at the open door of the castle. She, too, was cut out of paper, but she wore a dress of the lightest gauze, with a dainty little blue ribbon over her shoulders, by way of a scarf, set off by a brilliant spangle, as big as her whole face. The little maid was stretching out both arms, for she was a dancer, and in the dance, one of her legs was raised so high into the air that the tin soldier could see absolutely nothing of it, and supposed that she, like himself, had but one leg.

"That would be the very wife for me!" he thought; "but she is much too grand; she lives in a palace, while I only have a box, and then there are five and twenty of us to share it. No, that would be no place for her! but I must try to make her acquaintance!" Then he lay down full length behind a snuff box, which stood on the table. From that point he could have a good look at the little lady, who continued to stand on one leg without losing her balance.

Late in the evening the other soldiers were put into their box, and the people of the house went to bed. Now was the time for the toys to play; they amused themselves with paying visits, fighting battles, and giving balls. The tin soldiers rustled about in the box, for they wanted to join the games, but they could not get the lid off. The nutcrackers turned somersaults, and the pencil scribbled nonsense on the slate. There was such a noise that the canary woke up and joined in, but his remarks were in verse. The only two who did not move were the tin soldier and the little dancer. She stood as stiff as ever on tip-toe, with her arms spread out: he was equally firm on his one leg, and he did not take his eyes off her for a moment.

Then the clock struck twelve, when pop! up flew the lid of the snuff box, but there was no snuff in it, no! There was a little black goblin, a sort of Jack-in-the-box.

"Tin soldier!" said the goblin, "have the goodness to keep your eyes to yourself."

But the tin soldier feigned not to hear.

"Ah! you just wait till tomorrow," said the goblin.

In the morning when the children got up they put the tin soldier on the window frame, and, whether it was caused by the goblin or by a puff of wind, I do not know, but all at once the window burst open, and the soldier fell head foremost from the third storey.

It was a terrific descent, and he landed at last, with his leg in the air, and rested on his cap, with his bayonet fixed between two paving stones. The maid-servant and the little boy ran down at once to look for him; but although they almost trod on him, they could not see him. Had the soldier only called out, "Here I am," they would easily have found him, but he did not think it proper to shout when he was in uniform.

Presently it began to rain, and the drops fell faster and faster, till there was a regular torrent. When it was over two street boys came along.

"Look out!" said one; "there is a tin soldier! He shall go for a sail."

So they made a boat out of a newspaper and put the soldier into the middle of it, and he sailed away down the gutter; both boys ran alongside clapping their hands. Good heavens! what waves there were in the gutter,

and what a current, but then it certainly had rained cats and dogs. The paper boat danced up and down, and now and then whirled round and round. A shudder ran through the tin soldier, but he remained undaunted, and did not move a muscle, only looked straight before him with his gun shouldered. All at once the boat drifted under a long wooden tunnel, and it became as dark as it was in his box.

"Where on earth am I going to now!" thought he. "Well, well, it is all the fault of that goblin! Oh, if only the little maiden were with me in the boat it might be twice as dark for all I should care!"

At this moment a big water rat, who lived in the tunnel, came up.

"Have you a pass?" asked the rat. "Hand up your pass!"

The tin soldier did not speak, but clung still tighter to his gun. The boat rushed on, the rat close behind. Phew, how he gnashed his teeth and shouted to the bits of stick and straw.

"Stop him, stop him, he hasn't paid his toll! he hasn't shown his pass!"

But the current grew stronger and stronger, the tin soldier could already see daylight before him at the end of the tunnel; but he also heard a roaring sound, fit to strike terror to the bravest heart. Just imagine! Where the tunnel ended the stream rushed straight into the big canal. That would be just as dangerous for him as it would be for us to shoot a great rapid.

He was so near the end now that it was impossible to stop. The boat dashed out; the poor tin soldier held himself as stiff as he could; no one should say of him that he even winced.

The boat swirled round three or four times, and filled with water to the edge; it must sink. The tin soldier stood up to his neck in water, and the boat sank deeper and deeper. The paper became limper and limper, and at last the water went over his head — then he thought of the pretty little dancer, whom he was never to see again, and this refrain rang in his ears:

"Onward! Onward! Soldier!
For death thou canst not shun."

At last the paper gave way entirely and the soldier fell through — but at the same moment he was swallowed by a big fish.

Oh! how dark it was inside the fish, it was worse than being in the tunnel even; and then it was so narrow! But the tin soldier was as dauntless as ever, and lay full length, shouldering his gun.

The fish rushed about and made the most frantic movements. At last it became quite quiet, and after a time, a flash like lightning pierced it. The soldier was once more in the broad daylight, and someone called out loudly, "a tin soldier!" The fish had been caught, taken to market, sold, and brought into the kitchen, where the cook cut it open with a large knife. She took the soldier up by the waist, with two fingers, and carried him into the parlor, where everyone wanted to see the wonderful man, who had traveled about in the stomach of a fish; but the tin soldier was not at all proud. They set him up on the table, and, wonder of wonders! he found himself in the very same room that he had been in before. He saw the very same children, and the toys were still standing on the table, as well as the beautiful castle with the pretty little dancer.

She still stood on one leg, and held the other up in the air. You see she also was unbending. The soldier was so much moved that he was ready to shed tears of tin, but that would not have been fitting. He looked at her, and she looked at him, but they said never a word. At this moment one of the little boys took up the tin soldier, and without rhyme or reason, threw him into the fire. No doubt the little goblin in the snuff box was to blame for that. The tin soldier stood there, lighted up by the flame, and in the most horrible heat; but whether it was the heat of the real fire, or the warmth of his feelings, he did not know. He had lost all his gay color; it might have been from his perilous journey, or it might have been from grief, who can tell?

He looked at the little maiden, and she looked at him; and he felt that he was melting away, but he still managed to keep himself erect, shouldering his gun bravely.

A door was suddenly opened, the draught caught the little dancer and she fluttered like a sylph, straight into the fire, to the soldier, blazed up and was gone!

By this time the soldier was reduced to a mere lump, and when the maid took away the ashes next morning she found him, in the shape of a small tin heart. All that was left of the dancer was her spangle, and that was burnt as black as a coal.

The Tinder Box[7]

HANS CHRISTIAN ANDERSEN

Andersen is retelling in The Tinder Box *the folk tale* The Blue Light. *A comparison of the two makes an interesting study, for they differ in many details. Andersen's tale is much more vivid and exciting and not always quite so ethical. Note how the reader is plunged at once into the story by the very first sentence and how at the end Andersen puts in an unexpected touch of realism —* "The boys all put their fingers in their mouths and whistled" — *so as to leave the whole story on the level of possibility.*

A soldier came marching along the high road. One, two! One, two! He had his knapsack on his back and his sword at his side, for he had been to the wars and he was on his way home now. He met an old witch on the road; she was so ugly, her lower lip hung right down on to her chin.

She said, "Good evening, soldier! What a nice sword you've got, and such a big knapsack; you are a real soldier! You shall have as much money as ever you like!"

"Thank you kindly, you old witch!" said the soldier.

"Do you see that big tree!" said the witch, pointing to a tree close by. "It is hollow inside! Climb up to the top and you will see a hole into which you can let yourself down, right down under the tree! I will tie a rope round your waist so that I can haul you up again when you call!"

"What am I to do down under the tree?" asked the soldier.

"Fetch money!" said the witch. "You must

7 From Hans Christian Andersen, *Fairy Tales*, trans. Mrs. Edgar Lucas.

know that when you get down to the bottom of the tree you will find yourself in a wide passage; it's quite light there, for there are over a hundred blazing lamps. You will see three doors which you can open, for the keys are there. If you go into the first room you will see a big box in the middle of the floor. A dog is sitting on the top of it, and he has eyes as big as saucers, but you needn't mind that. I will give you my blue-checked apron, which you can spread out on the floor; then go quickly forward, take up the dog and put him on my apron, open the box and take out as much money as ever you like. It is all copper, but if you like silver better, go into the next room. There you will find a dog with eyes as big as millstones; but never mind that, put him on my apron and take the money. If you prefer gold you can have it too, and as much as you can carry, if you go into the third room. But the dog sitting on that box has eyes each as big as the Round Tower. He *is* a dog, indeed, as you may imagine! But don't let it trouble you; you only have to put him on to my apron and then he won't hurt you, and you can take as much gold out of the box as you like!"

"That's not so bad!" said the soldier. "But what am I to give you, old witch? For you'll want something, I'll be bound."

"No," said the witch, "not a single penny do I want; I only want you to bring me an old tinder box that my grandmother forgot the last time she was down there!"

"Well! tie the rope round my waist!" said the soldier.

"Here it is," said the witch, "and here is my blue-checked apron."

Then the soldier climbed up the tree, let himself slide down the hollow trunk, and found himself, as the witch had said, in the wide passage where the many hundred lamps were burning.

Now he opened the first door. Ugh! There sat the dog with eyes as big as saucers staring at him.

"You are a nice fellow!" said the soldier, as he put him on to the witch's apron, and took out as many pennies as he could cram into his pockets. Then he shut the box, and put the dog on the top of it again, and went into the next room. Hallo! there sat the dog with eyes as big as millstones.

"You shouldn't stare at me so hard; you might get a pain in your eyes!" Then he put the dog on the apron, but when he saw all the silver in the box he threw away all the coppers and stuffed his pockets and his knapsack with silver. Then he went on into the third room. Oh! how horrible! that dog really had two eyes as big as the Round Tower, and they rolled round and round like wheels.

"Good evening!" said the soldier, saluting, for he had never seen such a dog in his life; but after looking at him for a bit he thought "that will do," and then he lifted him down on to the apron and opened the chest. Preserve us! What a lot of gold! He could buy the whole of Copenhagen with it, and all the sugar pigs from the cake-women, all the tin soldiers, whips and rocking-horses in the world! That was money indeed! Now the soldier threw away all the silver he had filled his pockets and his knapsack with, and put gold in its place. Yes, he crammed all his pockets, his knapsack, his cap and his boots so full that he could hardly walk! Now, he really had got a lot of money. He put the dog back on to the box, shut the door, and shouted up through the tree, "Haul me up, you old witch!"

"Have you got the tinder box?"

"Oh! to be sure!" said the soldier. "I had quite forgotten it." And he went back to fetch it. The witch hauled him up, and there he was standing on the high road again with his pockets, boots, knapsack and cap full of gold.

"What do you want the tinder box for?" asked the soldier.

"That's no business of yours," said the witch. "You've got the money; give me the tinder box!"

"Rubbish!" said the soldier. "Tell me directly what you want with it, or I will draw my sword and cut off your head."

"I won't!" said the witch.

Then the soldier cut off her head; there she lay! But he tied all the money up in her apron, slung it on his back like a pack, put the tinder box in his pocket, and marched off to the town.

It was a beautiful town, and he went straight to the finest hotel, ordered the grandest room and all the food he liked best, because he was a rich man now that he had so much money.

Certainly the servant who had to clean his boots thought they were very funny old things for such a rich gentleman, but he had not had time yet to buy any new ones; the next day he bought new boots and fine clothes. The soldier now became a fine gentleman, and the people told him all about the grand things in the town, and about their king, and what a lovely princess his daughter was.

"Where is she to be seen?" asked the soldier.

"You can't see her at all!" they all said; "she lives in a great copper castle surrounded with walls and towers. Nobody but the king dare go in and out, for it has been prophesied that she will marry a common soldier, and the king doesn't like that!"

"I should like to see her well enough!" thought the soldier. But there was no way of getting leave for that.

He now led a very merry life; went to theatres, drove about in the King's Park, and gave away a lot of money to poor people, which was very nice of him; for he remembered how disagreeable it used to be not to have a penny in his pocket. Now he was rich, wore fine clothes, and had a great many friends who all said what a nice fellow he was — a thorough gentleman — and he liked to be told that.

But as he went on spending money every day and his store was never renewed, he at last found himself with only two pence left. Then he was obliged to move out of his fine rooms. He had to take a tiny little attic up under the roof, clean his own boots, and mend them himself with a darning needle. None of his friends went to see him, because there were far too many stairs.

One dark evening when he had not even enough money to buy a candle with, he suddenly remembered that there was a little bit in the old tinder box he had brought out of the hollow tree, when the witch helped him down. He got out the tinder box with the candle end in it and struck fire, but as the sparks flew out from the flint the door burst open and the dog with eyes as big as saucers, which he had seen down under the tree, stood before him and said, "What does my lord command?"

"By heaven!" said the soldier, "this is a nice kind of tinder box, if I can get whatever I want like this! Get me some money," he said to the dog, and away it went.

It was back in a twinkling with a big bag full of pennies in its mouth.

Now the soldier saw what a treasure he had in the tinder box. If he struck once, the dog which sat on the box of copper came; if he struck twice, the dog on the silver box came, and if he struck three times, the one from the box of gold.

He now moved down to the grand rooms and got his fine clothes again, and then all his friends knew him once more and liked him as much as ever.

Then suddenly he began to think: After all it's a curious thing that no man can get a sight of the princess! Everyone says she is so beautiful! But what is the good of that, when she always has to be shut up in that big copper palace with all the towers. Can I not somehow manage to see her? Where is my tinder box? Then he struck the flint, and, whisk, came the dog with eyes as big as saucers.

"It certainly is the middle of the night," said the soldier, "but I am very anxious to see the princess, if only for a single moment."

The dog was out of the door in an instant, and before the soldier had time to think about it, he was back again with the princess. There she was fast asleep on the dog's back, and she was so lovely that anybody could see that she must be a real princess! The soldier could not help it, but he was obliged to kiss her, for he was a true soldier.

Then the dog ran back again with the princess, but in the morning when the king and queen were having breakfast, the princess said that she had had such a wonderful dream about a dog and a soldier. She had ridden on the dog's back, and the soldier had kissed her.

"That's a pretty tale," said the queen.

After this an old lady-in-waiting had to sit

by her bed at night to see if this was really a dream, or what it could be.

The soldier longed so intensely to see the princess again that at night the dog came to fetch her. He took her up and ran off with her as fast as he could, but the old lady-in-waiting put on her galoshes and ran just as fast behind them; when she saw that they disappeared into a large house, she thought now I know where it is, and made a big cross with chalk on the gate. Then she went home and lay down, and presently the dog came back, too, with the princess. When he saw that there was a cross on the gate, he took a bit of chalk, too, and made crosses on all the gates in the town; now this was very clever of him, for the lady-in-waiting could not possibly find the gate when there were crosses on all the gates.

Early next morning the king, the queen, the lady-in-waiting, and all the court officials went to see where the princess had been.

"There it is," said the king, when he saw the first door with the cross on it.

"No, my dear husband, it is there," said the queen, who saw another door with a cross on it.

"But there is one, and there is another!" they all cried out.

They soon saw that it was hopeless to try and find it.

Now the queen was a very clever woman; she knew more than how to drive in a chariot. She took her big gold scissors and cut up a large piece of silk into small pieces, and made a pretty little bag, which she filled with fine grains of buckwheat. She then tied it on to the back of the princess, and when that was done she cut a little hole in the bag, so that the grains could drop out all the way wherever the princess went.

At night the dog came again, took the princess on his back, and ran off with her to the soldier, who was so fond of her that he longed to be a prince, so that he might have her for his wife.

The dog never noticed how the grain dropped out all along the road from the palace to the soldier's window, where he ran up the wall with the princess.

In the morning the king and the queen easily saw where their daughter had been, and they seized the soldier and threw him into the dungeons.

There he lay! Oh, how dark and tiresome it was, and then one day they said to him, "Tomorrow you are to be hanged." It was not amusing to be told that, especially as he had left his tinder box behind him at the hotel.

In the morning he could see through the bars in the little window that the people were hurrying out of the town to see him hanged. He heard the drums and saw the soldiers marching along. All the world was going; among them was a shoemaker's boy in his leather apron and slippers. He was in such a hurry that he lost one of his slippers, and it fell close under the soldier's window where he was peeping out through the bars.

"I say, you boy! Don't be in such a hurry," said the soldier to him. "Nothing will happen till I get there! But if you will run to the house where I used to live, and fetch me my tinder box, you shall have a penny! You must put your best foot foremost!"

The boy was only too glad to have the penny, and tore off to get the tinder box, gave it to the soldier, and — yes, now we shall hear.

Outside the town a high scaffold had been raised, and the soldiers were drawn up round about it, as well as crowds of the towns-people. The king and the queen sat upon a beautiful throne exactly opposite the judge and all the councillors.

The soldier mounted the ladder, but when they were about to put the rope round his neck, he said that before undergoing his punishment a criminal was always allowed the gratification of a harmless wish, and he wanted very much to smoke a pipe, as it would be his last pipe in this world.

The king would not deny him this, so the soldier took out his tinder box and struck fire, once, twice, three times, and there were all the dogs. The one with eyes like saucers, the one with eyes like millstones, and the one whose eyes were as big as the Round Tower.

"Help me! Save me from being hanged!" cried the soldier.

And then the dogs rushed at the soldiers and the councillors; they took one by the legs, and another by the nose, and threw them up many fathoms into the air; and when they fell down, they were broken all to pieces.

"I won't!" cried the king, but the biggest dog took both him and the queen and threw them after all the others. Then the soldiers became alarmed, and the people shouted, "Oh, good soldier, you shall be our king and marry the beautiful princess!"

Then they conducted the soldier to the king's chariot, and all three dogs danced along in front of him and shouted "Hurrah!" The boys all put their fingers in their mouths and whistled, and the soldiers presented arms. The princess came out of the copper palace and became queen, which pleased her very much. The wedding took place in a week, and the dogs all had seats at the table, where they sat staring with all their eyes.

The Nightingale[8]

HANS CHRISTIAN ANDERSEN

A great underlying truth is inherent in this poignant story of the Emperor's nightingale written in beautifully balanced prose, exquisite in its imagery. Here is enduring testimony to Andersen's particular genius for blending truth and art.

In China, as you know, the Emperor is a Chinaman, and all the people around him are Chinamen too. It is many years since the story I am going to tell you happened, but that is all the more reason for telling it, lest it should be forgotten. The emperor's palace was the most beautiful thing in the world; it was made entirely of the finest porcelain, very costly, but at the same time so fragile that it could only be touched with the very greatest care. There were the most extraordinary flowers to be seen in the garden; the most beautiful ones had little silver bells tied to them, which tinkled perpetually, so that one should not pass the flowers without looking at them. Every little detail in the

8 From Hans Christian Andersen, *Fairy Tales*, trans. Mrs. Edgar Lucas.

garden had been most carefully thought out, and it was so big, that even the gardener himself did not know where it ended. If one went on walking, one came to beautiful woods with lofty trees and deep lakes. The woods extended to the sea, which was deep and blue, deep enough for large ships to sail up right under the branches of the trees. Among these trees lived a nightingale, which sang so deliciously, that even the poor fisherman who had plenty of other things to do, lay still to listen to it, when he was out at night drawing in his nets. "Heavens, how beautiful it is!" he said, but then he had to attend to his business and forgot it. The next night when he heard it again he would again exclaim, "Heavens, how beautiful it is!"

Travelers came to the emperor's capital, from every country in the world; they admired everything very much, especially the palace and the gardens, but when they heard the nightingale they all said, "This is better than anything!"

When they got home they described it, and the learned ones wrote many books about the town, the palace and the garden, but nobody forgot the nightingale, it was always put above everything else. Those among them who were poets wrote the most beautiful poems, all about the nightingale in the woods by the deep blue sea. These books went all over the world, and in course of time, some of them reached the emperor. He sat in his golden chair reading and reading, and nodding his head well pleased to hear such beautiful descriptions of the town, the palace and the garden. "But the nightingale is the best of all," he read.

"What is this?" said the emperor. "The nightingale? Why, I know nothing about it. Is there such a bird in my kingdom, and in my own garden into the bargain, and I have never heard of it? Imagine my having to discover this from a book!"

Then he called his gentleman-in-waiting, who was so grand that when anyone of a lower rank dared to speak to him, or to ask him a question, he would only answer "P," which means nothing at all.

"There is said to be a very wonderful bird called a nightingale here," said the emperor.

"They say that it is better than anything else in all my great kingdom! Why have I never been told anything about it?"

"I have never heard it mentioned," said the gentleman-in-waiting. "It has never been presented at court."

"I wish it to appear here this evening to sing to me," said the emperor. "The whole world knows what I am possessed of, and I know nothing about it!"

"I have never heard it mentioned before," said the gentleman-in-waiting. "I will seek it, and I will find it!" But where was it to be found? The gentleman-in-waiting ran upstairs and downstairs and in and out of all the rooms and corridors. No one of all those he met had ever heard anything about the nightingale; so the gentleman-in-waiting ran back to the emperor, and said that it must be a myth, invented by the writers of the books. "Your imperial majesty must not believe everything that is written; books are often mere inventions, even if they do not belong to what we call the black art!"

"But the book in which I read it is sent to me by the powerful Emperor of Japan, so it can't be untrue. I will hear this nightingale, I insist upon its being here tonight. I extend my most gracious protection to it, and if it is not forthcoming, I will have the whole court trampled upon after supper!"

"Tsing-pe!" said the gentleman-in-waiting, and away he ran again, up and down all the stairs, in and out of all the rooms and corridors; half the court ran with him, for they none of them wished to be trampled on. There was much questioning about this nightingale, which was known to all the outside world, but to no one at court. At last they found a poor little maid in the kitchen. She said, "Oh heavens, the nightingale? I know it very well. Yes, indeed it can sing. Every evening I am allowed to take broken meat to my poor sick mother: she lives down by the shore. On my way back when I am tired, I rest awhile in the wood, and then I hear the nightingale. Its song brings the tears into my eyes, I feel as if my mother were kissing me!"

"Little kitchen-maid," said the gentleman-in-waiting, "I will procure you a permanent position in the kitchen and permission to see the emperor dining, if you will take us to the nightingale. It is commanded to appear at court tonight."

Then they all went out into the wood where the nightingale usually sang. Half the court was there. As they were going along at their best pace a cow began to bellow.

"O!" said a young courtier, "there we have it. What wonderful power for such a little creature; I have certainly heard it before."

"No, those are the cows bellowing, we are a long way yet from the place." Then the frogs began to croak in the marsh.

"Beautiful?" said the Chinese chaplain, "it is just like the tinkling of church bells."

"No, those are the frogs!" said the little kitchen-maid. "But I think we shall soon hear it now!"

Then the nightingale began to sing.

"There it is!" said the little girl. "Listen, listen, there it sits!" and she pointed to a little gray bird up among the branches.

"Is it possible?" said the gentleman-in-waiting. "I should never have thought it was like that. How common it looks. Seeing so many grand people must have frightened all its colors away."

"Little nightingale!" called the kitchen-maid quite loud, "our gracious emperor wishes you to sing to him!"

"With the greatest pleasure!" said the nightingale, warbling away in the most delightful fashion.

"It is just like crystal bells," said the gentleman-in-waiting. "Look at its little throat, how active it is. It is extraordinary that we have never heard it before! I am sure it will be a great success at court!"

"Shall I sing again to the emperor?" said the nightingale, who thought he was present.

"My precious little nightingale," said the gentleman-in-waiting, "I have the honor to command your attendance at a court festival tonight, where you will charm his gracious majesty the emperor with your fascinating singing."

"It sounds best among the trees," said the nightingale, but it went with them willingly when it heard that the emperor wished it.

The palace had been brightened up for the occasion. The walls and the floors which were all of china shone by the light of many thousand golden lamps. The most beautiful flowers, all of the tinkling kind, were arranged in the corridors; there was hurrying to and fro, and a great draught, but this was just what made the bells ring, one's ears were full of the tinkling. In the middle of the large reception room where the emperor sat a golden rod had been fixed, on which the nightingale was to perch. The whole court was assembled, and the little kitchen-maid had been permitted to stand behind the door, as she now had the actual title of cook. They were all dressed in their best, everybody's eyes were turned towards the little gray bird at which the emperor was nodding. The nightingale sang delightfully, and the tears came into the emperor's eyes, nay, they rolled down his cheeks, and then the nightingale sang more beautifully than ever, its notes touched all hearts. The emperor was charmed, and said the nightingale should have his gold slipper to wear round its neck. But the nightingale declined with thanks, it had already been sufficiently rewarded.

"I have seen tears in the eyes of the emperor, that is my richest reward. The tears of an emperor have a wonderful power! God knows I am sufficiently recompensed!" and then it again burst into its sweet heavenly song.

"That is the most delightful coquetting I have ever seen!" said the ladies, and they took some water into their mouths to try and make the same gurgling when anyone spoke to them, thinking so to equal the nightingale. Even the lackeys and the chambermaids announced that they were satisfied, and that is saying a great deal, they are always the most difficult people to please. Yes, indeed, the nightingale had made a sensation. It was to stay at court now, and to have its own cage, as well as liberty to walk out twice a day, and once in the night. It always had twelve footmen with each one holding a ribbon which was tied round its leg. There was not much pleasure in an outing of that sort.

The whole town talked about the marvelous bird, and if two people met, one said to the other "Night," and the other answered "Gale," and then they sighed, perfectly understanding each other. Eleven cheese-mongers' children were called after it, but they had not got a voice among them.

One day a large parcel came for the emperor, outside was written the word "Nightingale."

"Here we have another new book about this celebrated bird," said the emperor. But it was no book; it was a little work of art in a box, an artificial nightingale, exactly like the living one, but it was studded all over with diamonds, rubies, and sapphires.

When the bird was wound up, it could sing one of the songs the real one sang, and it wagged its tail which glittered with silver and gold. A ribbon was tied round its neck on which was written, "The Emperor of Japan's nightingale is very poor, compared to the Emperor of China's."

Everybody said, "Oh, how beautiful!" And the person who brought the artificial bird immediately received the title of Imperial Nightingale-Carrier in Chief.

"Now, they must sing together; what a duet that will be."

Then they had to sing together, but they did not get on very well, for the real nightingale sang in its own way, and the artificial one could only sing waltzes.

"There is no fault in that," said the music master; "it is perfectly in time and correct in every way!"

Then the artificial bird had to sing alone. It was just as great a success as the real one, and then it was so much prettier to look at, it glittered like bracelets and breast-pins.

It sang the same tune three and thirty times over, and yet it was not tired; people would willingly have heard it from the beginning again, but the Emperor said that the real one must have a turn now — but where was it? No one had noticed that it had flown out of the open window, back to its own green woods.

"But what is the meaning of this?" said the emperor.

All the courtiers railed at it, and said it was a most ungrateful bird.

"We have got the best bird though," said they, and then the artificial bird had to sing again, and this was the thirty-fourth time that they heard the same tune, but they did not know it thoroughly even yet, because it was so difficult.

The music master praised the bird tremendously, and insisted that it was much better than the real nightingale, not only as regarded the outside with all the diamonds, but the inside too.

"Because you see, my ladies and gentlemen, and the emperor before all, in the real nightingale you never know what you will hear, but in the artificial one everything is decided beforehand! So it is, and so it must remain, it can't be otherwise. You can account for things, you can open it and show the human ingenuity in arranging the waltzes, how they go, and how one note follows upon another!"

"Those are exactly my opinions," they all said, and the music master got leave to show the bird to the public next Sunday. They were also to hear it sing, said the emperor. So they heard it, and all became as enthusiastic over it, as if they had drunk themselves merry on tea, because that is a thoroughly Chinese habit.

Then they all said "Oh," and stuck their forefingers in the air and nodded their heads; but the poor fisherman who had heard the real nightingale said, "It sounds very nice, and it is very like the real one, but there is something wanting, we don't know what." The real nightingale was banished from the kingdom.

The artificial bird had its place on a silken cushion, close to the emperor's bed: all the presents it had received of gold and precious jewels were scattered round it. Its title had risen to be "Chief Imperial Singer of the Bed-Chamber," in rank number one, on the left side; for the emperor reckoned that side the important one, where the heart was seated. And even an emperor's heart is on the left side. The music master wrote five and twenty volumes about the artificial bird; the treatise was very long, and written in all the most difficult Chinese characters. Everybody said they had read and understood it, for otherwise they would have been reckoned stupid and then their bodies would have been trampled upon.

Things went on in this way for a whole year. The emperor, the court, and all the other Chinamen knew every little gurgle in the song of the artificial bird by heart; but they liked it all the better for this, and they could all join in the song themselves. Even the street boys sang "zizizi" and "cluck, cluck, cluck," and the emperor sang it too.

But one evening when the bird was singing its best, and the emperor was lying in bed listening to it, something gave way inside the bird with a "whizz." Then a spring burst, "whirr" went all the wheels and the music stopped. The emperor jumped out of bed and sent for his private physicians, but what good could they do? Then they sent for the watchmaker, and after a good deal of talk and examination, he got the works to go again somehow; but he said it would have to be saved as much as possible, because it was so worn out, and he could not renew the works so as to be sure of the tune. This was a great blow! They only dared to let the artificial bird sing once a year, and hardly that; but then the music master made a little speech using all the most difficult words. He said it was just as good as ever, and his saying it made it so.

Five years now passed, and then a great grief came upon the nation, for they were all very fond of their emperor, and he was ill and could not live, it was said. A new emperor was already chosen, and people stood about in the street, and asked the gentleman-in-waiting how their emperor was going on.

"P," answered he, shaking his head.

The emperor lay pale and cold in his gorgeous bed, the courtiers thought he was dead, and they all went off to pay their respects to their new emperor. The lackeys ran off to talk matters over, and the chambermaids gave a great coffee party. Cloth had been laid down in all the rooms and corridors so as to deaden the sound of footsteps, so it was very, very quiet. But the emperor was not dead yet. He lay stiff and pale in the gorgeous bed with its velvet hangings and heavy golden tassels. There was an open window high above him, and the moon streamed in upon the emperor, and the artificial bird beside him.

The poor emperor could hardly breathe, he seemed to have a weight on his chest, he opened his eyes and then he saw that it was Death sitting upon his chest, wearing his golden crown. In one hand he held the emperor's golden sword, and in the other his imperial banner. Round about, from among the folds of the velvet hangings peered many curious faces, some were hideous, others gentle and pleasant. They were all the emperor's good and bad deeds, which now looked him in the face when Death was weighing him down.

"Do you remember that?" whispered one after the other. "Do you remember this?" and they told him so many things, that the perspiration poured down his face.

"I never knew that," said the emperor. "Music, music, sound the great Chinese drums!" he cried, "that I may not hear what they are saying." But they went on and on, and Death sat nodding his head, just like a Chinaman, at everything that was said.

"Music, music!" shrieked the emperor. "You precious little golden bird, sing, sing! I have loaded you with precious stones, and even hung my own golden slipper round your neck, sing, I tell you, sing!"

But the bird stood silent, there was nobody to wind it up, so of course it could not go. Death continued to fix the great empty sockets of its eyes upon him, and all was silent, so terribly silent.

Suddenly, close to the window, there was a burst of lovely song; it was the living nightingale, perched on a branch outside. It had heard of the emperor's need, and had come to bring comfort and hope to him. As it sang the faces round became fainter and fainter, and the blood coursed with fresh vigour in the emperor's veins and through his feeble limbs. Even Death himself listened to the song and said, "Go on, little nightingale, go on!"

"Yes, if you give me the gorgeous golden sword; yes, if you give me the imperial banner; yes, if you give me the emperor's crown."

And Death gave back each of these treasures for a song, and the nightingale went on singing. It sang about the quiet churchyard, when the roses bloom, where the elder flower scents the air, and where the fresh grass is ever moistened anew by the tears of the mourner. This song brought to Death a longing for his own garden, and like a cold grey mist, he passed out of the window.

"Thanks, thanks!" said the emperor; "you heavenly little bird, I know you! I banished you from my kingdom, and yet you have charmed the evil visions away from my bed by your song, and even Death away from my heart! How can I ever repay you?"

"You have rewarded me," said the nightingale. "I brought the tears to your eyes, the very first time I ever sang to you, and I shall never forget it! Those are the jewels which gladden the heart of a singer; — but sleep now, and wake up fresh and strong! I will sing to you!"

Then it sang again, and the emperor fell into a sweet refreshing sleep. The sun shone in at his window, when he woke refreshed and well; none of his attendants had yet come back to him, for they thought he was dead, but the nightingale still sat there singing.

"You must always stay with me!" said the emperor. "You shall only sing when you like, and I will break the artificial bird into a thousand pieces!"

"Don't do that!" said the nightingale, "it did all the good it could! keep it as you have always done! I can't build my nest and live in this palace, but let me come whenever I like, then I will sit on the branch in the evening, and sing to you. I will sing to cheer you and to make you thoughtful too; I will sing to you of the happy ones, and of those that suffer too. I will sing about the good and the evil, which are kept hidden from you. The little singing bird flies far and wide, to the poor fisherman, and the peasant's home, to numbers who are far from you and your court. I love your heart more than your crown, and yet there is an odor of sanctity round the crown, too! — I will come, and I will sing to you! — But you must promise me one thing!" —

"Everything!" said the emperor, who stood there in his imperial robes which he had just put on, and he held the sword heavy with gold upon his heart.

"One thing I ask you! Tell no one that you have a little bird who tells you everything, it will be better so!"

Then the nightingale flew away. The attendants came in to see after their dead emperor, and there he stood, bidding them "good-morning!"

The Emperor's New Clothes [9]

HANS CHRISTIAN ANDERSEN

This story is really a gentle satire, but as usual, Andersen does not let the satire spoil the story. One thing which adds interest is the fact that it was a little boy who not only saw the truth but spoke it; a little child led them. Though this may be the point of most interest to children, to the adult the emperor's reaction to the child's revelation is a never-ending source of glee.

Many years ago there was an emperor who was so excessively fond of new clothes that he spent all his money on them. He cared nothing about his soldiers nor for the theater, nor for driving in the woods except for the sake of showing off his new clothes. He had a costume for every hour in the day, and instead of saying as one does about any other king or emperor, "He is in his council chamber," here one always said, "The emperor is in his dressing-room."

Life was very gay in the great town where he lived; hosts of strangers came to visit it every day, and among them one day two swindlers. They gave themselves out as weavers, and said that they knew how to weave the most beautiful stuffs imaginable. Not only were the colors and patterns unusually fine, but the clothes that were made of the stuffs had the peculiar quality of becoming invisible to every person who was not fit for the office he held, or if he was impossibly dull.

"Those must be splendid clothes," thought the emperor. "By wearing them I should be able to discover which men in my kingdom are unfitted for their posts. I shall distinguish the wise men from the fools. Yes, I

[9] From Hans Christian Andersen, *Fairy Tales*, trans. Mrs. Edgar Lucas.

certainly must order some of that stuff to be woven for me."

He paid the two swindlers a lot of money in advance so that they might begin their work at once.

They did put up two looms and pretended to weave, but they had nothing whatever upon their shuttles. At the outset they asked for a quantity of the finest silk and the purest gold thread, all of which they put into their own bags while they worked away at the empty looms far into the night.

"I should like to know how those weavers are getting on with the stuff," thought the emperor; but he felt a little queer when he reflected that anyone who was stupid or unfit for his post would not be able to see it. He certainly thought that he need have no fears for himself, but still he thought he would send somebody else first to see how it was getting on. Everybody in the town knew what wonderful power the stuff possessed, and everyone was anxious to see how stupid his neighbor was.

"I will send my faithful old minister to the weavers," thought the emperor. "He will be best able to see how the stuff looks, for he is a clever man and no one fulfills his duties better than he does!"

So the good old minister went into the room where the two swindlers sat working at the empty loom.

"Heaven preserve us!" thought the old minister, opening his eyes very wide. "Why, I can't see a thing!" But he took care not to say so.

Both the swindlers begged him to be good enough to step a little nearer, and asked if he did not think it a good pattern and beautiful coloring. They pointed to the empty loom, and the poor old minister stared as hard as he could but he could not see anything, for of course there was nothing to see.

"Good Heavens!" thought he, "is it possible that I am a fool. I have never thought so and nobody must know it. Am I not fit for my post? It will never do to say that I cannot see the stuffs."

"Well, sir, you don't say anything about

the stuff," said the one who was pretending to weave.

"Oh, it is beautiful! quite charming!" said the old minister looking through his spectacles; "this pattern and these colors! I will certainly tell the emperor that the stuff pleases me very much."

"We are delighted to hear you say so," said the swindlers, and then they named all the colors and described the peculiar pattern. The old minister paid great attention to what they said, so as to be able to repeat it when he got home to the emperor.

Then the swindlers went on to demand more money, more silk, and more gold, to be able to proceed with the weaving; but they put it all into their own pockets — not a single strand was ever put into the loom, but they went on as before weaving at the empty loom.

The emperor soon sent another faithful official to see how the stuff was getting on, and if it would soon be ready. The same thing happened to him as to the minister; he looked and looked, but as there was only the empty loom, he could see nothing at all.

"Is not this a beautiful piece of stuff?" said both the swindlers, showing and explaining the beautiful pattern and colors which were not there to be seen.

"I know I am not a fool!" thought the man, "so it must be that I am unfit for my good post! It is very strange though! however one must not let it appear!" So he praised the stuff he did not see, and assured them of his delight in the beautiful colors and the originality of the design. "It is absolutely charming!" he said to the emperor. Everybody in the town was talking about this splendid stuff.

Now the emperor thought he would like to see it while it was still on the loom. So, accompanied by a number of selected courtiers, among whom were the two faithful officials who had already seen the imaginary stuff, he went to visit the crafty impostors, who were working away as hard as ever they could at the empty loom.

"It is magnificent!" said both the honest officials. "Only see, Your Majesty, what a design! What colors!" And they pointed to the empty loom, for they thought no doubt the others could see the stuff.

"What!" thought the emperor; "I see nothing at all! This is terrible! Am I a fool? Am I not fit to be emperor? Why, nothing worse could happen to me!"

"Oh, it is beautiful!" said the emperor. "It has my highest approval!" and he nodded his satisfaction as he gazed at the empty loom. Nothing would induce him to say that he could not see anything.

The whole suite gazed and gazed, but saw nothing more than all the others. However, they all exclaimed with His Majesty, "It is very beautiful!" and they advised him to wear a suit made of this wonderful cloth on the occasion of a great procession which was just about to take place. "It is magnificent! gorgeous! excellent!" went from mouth to mouth; they were all equally delighted with it. The emperor gave each of the rogues an order of knighthood to be worn in their buttonholes and the title of "Gentlemen Weavers."

The swindlers sat up the whole night, before the day on which the procession was to take place, burning sixteen candles; so that people might see how anxious they were to get the emperor's new clothes ready. They pretended to take the stuff off the loom. They cut it out in the air with a huge pair of scissors, and they stitched away with needles without any thread in them. At last they said: "Now the emperor's new clothes are ready!"

The emperor, with his grandest courtiers, went to them himself, and both the swindlers raised one arm in the air, as if they were holding something, and said: "See, these are the trousers, this is the coat, here is the mantle!" and so on. "It is as light as a spider's web. One might think one had nothing on, but that is the very beauty of it!"

"Yes!" said all the courtiers, but they could not see anything, for there was nothing to see.

"Will Your Imperial Majesty be graciously pleased to take off your clothes," said the impostors, "so that we may put on the new ones, along here before the great mirror."

The emperor took off all his clothes, and the impostors pretended to give him one article of dress after the other, of the new ones which they had pretended to make. They pretended to fasten something round his waist and to tie on something; this was the train, and the emperor turned round and round in front of the mirror.

"How well His Majesty looks in the new clothes! How becoming they are" cried all the people round. "What a design, and what colors! They are most gorgeous robes!"

"The canopy is waiting outside which is to be carried over Your Majesty in the procession," said the master of ceremonies.

"Well, I am quite ready," said the emperor. "Don't the clothes fit well?" and then he turned round again in front of the mirror, so that he should seem to be looking at his grand things.

The chamberlains who were to carry the train stooped and pretended to lift it from the ground with both hands, and they walked along with their hands in the air. They dared not let it appear that they could not see anything.

Then the emperor walked along in the procession under the gorgeous canopy, and everybody in the streets and at the windows exclaimed, "How beautiful the emperor's new clothes are! What a splendid train! And they fit to perfection!" Nobody would let it appear that he could see nothing, for then he would not be fit for his post, or else he was a fool.

None of the emperor's clothes had been so successful before.

"But he has got nothing on," said a little child.

"Oh, listen to the innocent," said its father; and one person whispered to the other what the child had said. "He has nothing on; a child says he has nothing on!"

"But he has nothing on!" at last cried all the people.

The emperor writhed, for he knew it was true, but he thought "The procession must go on now," so held himself stiffer than ever, and the chamberlains held up the invisible train.

The Ugly Duckling [1]

Hans Christian Andersen

This tale is one of Andersen's best; it really pictures, in a symbolic way, Andersen's own experiences and his life in general. Andersen always felt himself a genius; and when he tried dancing, singing, playwriting, and acting for a living, and was a failure in all, he blamed society and not his own lack of ability. According to some biographers, he never was fully reconciled to having become a swan through his fairy tales; but since they did bring him honor and the recognition his nature longed for, he accepted a storyteller's fame and made the most of it.

The country was lovely just then; it was summer. The wheat was golden and the oats still green; the hay was stacked in the rich low-lying meadows, where the stork was marching about on his long red legs, chattering Egyptian, the language his mother had taught him.

Roundabout field and meadow lay great woods in the midst of which were deep lakes. Yes, the country certainly was delicious. In the sunniest spot stood an old mansion surrounded by a deep moat, and great dock leaves grew from the walls of the house right down to the water's edge; some of them were so tall that a small child could stand upright under them. In amongst the leaves it was as secluded as in the depths of a forest; and there a duck was sitting on her nest. Her little ducklings were just about to be hatched, but she was nearly tired of sitting, for it had lasted such a long time. Moreover, she had very few visitors, as the other ducks liked swimming about in the moat better than waddling up to sit under the dock leaves and gossip with her.

At last one egg after another began to crack. "Cheep, cheep!" they said. All the chicks had come to life, and were poking their heads out.

"Quack! quack!" said the duck; and then they all quacked their hardest, and looked about them on all sides among the green leaves; their mother allowed them to look

[1] From Hans Christian Andersen, *Fairy Tales*, trans. Mrs. Edgar Lucas.

as much as they liked, for green is good for the eyes.

"How big the world is to be sure!" said all the young ones; for they certainly had ever so much more room to move about, than when they were inside in the eggshell.

"Do you imagine this is the whole world?" said the mother. "It stretches a long way on the other side of the garden, right into the parson's field; but I have never been as far as that! I suppose you are all here now?" and she got up. "No! I declare I have not got you all yet! The biggest egg is still there; how long is it going to last?" and then she settled herself on the nest again.

"Well, how are you getting on?" said an old duck who had come to pay her a visit.

"This one egg is taking such a long time," answered the sitting duck, "the shell will not crack; but now you must look at the others; they are the finest ducklings I have ever seen! they are all exactly like their father, the rascal! he never comes to see me."

"Let me look at the egg which won't crack," said the old duck. "You may be sure that it is a turkey's egg! I have been cheated like that once, and I had no end of trouble and worry with the creatures, for I may tell you that they are afraid of the water. I could not get them into it, I quacked and snapped at them, but it was no good. Let me see the egg! Yes, it is a turkey's egg! You just leave it alone and teach the other children to swim."

"I will sit on it a little longer, I have sat so long already, that I may as well go on till the Midsummer Fair comes round."

"Please yourself," said the old duck, and she went away.

At last the big egg cracked. "Cheep, cheep!" said the young one and tumbled out; how big and ugly he was! The duck looked at him.

"That is a monstrous big duckling," she said; "none of the others looked like that; can he be a turkey chick? Well, we shall soon find that out; into the water he shall go, if I have to kick him in myself."

Next day was gloriously fine, and the sun shone on all the green dock leaves. The mother duck with her whole family went down to the moat.

Splash, into the water she sprang. "Quack, quack!" she said, and one duckling plumped in after the other. The water dashed over their heads, but they came up again and floated beautifully; their legs went of themselves, and they were all there, even the big ugly gray one swam about with them.

"No, that is no turkey," she said; "see how beautifully he uses his legs and how erect he holds himself: he is my own chick! after all, he is not so bad when you come to look at him properly. Quack, quack! Now come with me and I will take you into the world, and introduce you to the duckyard; but keep close to me all the time, so that no one may tread upon you, and beware of the cat!"

Then they went into the duckyard. There was a fearful uproar going on, for two broods were fighting for the head of an eel, and in the end the cat captured it.

"That's how things go in this world," said the mother duck, and she licked her bill for she wanted the eel's head herself.

"Use your legs," said she; "mind you quack properly, and bend your necks to the old duck over there! She is the grandest of them all; she has Spanish blood in her veins and that accounts for her size, and, do you see? she has a red rag round her leg; that is a wonderfully fine thing, and the most extraordinary mark of distinction any duck can have. It shows clearly that she is not to be parted with, and that she is worthy of recognition both by beasts and men! Quack now! don't turn your toes in, a well-brought-up duckling keeps his legs wide apart just like father and mother; that's it, now bend your necks, and say quack!"

They did as they were bid, but the other ducks round about looked at them and said, quite loud: "Just look there! now we are to have that tribe! just as if there were not enough of us already, and, oh, dear! how ugly that duckling is, we won't stand him!" and a duck flew at him at once and bit him in the neck.

"Let him be," said the mother; "he is doing no harm."

"Very likely not, but he is so ungainly and queer," said the biter; "he must be whacked."

"They are handsome children mother has," said the old duck with the rag round her leg; "all good looking except this one, and he is not a good specimen; it's a pity you can't make him over again."

"That can't be done, your grace," said the mother duck; "he is not handsome, but he is a thorough good creature, and he swims as beautifully as any of the others; nay, I think I might venture even to add that I think he will improve as he goes on, or perhaps in time he may grow smaller! he was too long in the egg, and so he has not come out with a very good figure." And then she patted his neck and stroked him down. "Besides he is a drake," said she; "so it does not matter so much. I believe he will be very strong, and I don't doubt but he will make his way in the world."

"The other ducklings are very pretty," said the old duck. "Now make yourselves quite at home, and if you find the head of an eel you may bring it to me!"

After that they felt quite at home. But the poor duckling which had been the last to come out of the shell, and who was so ugly, was bitten, pushed about, and made fun of both by the ducks and the hens. "He is too big," they all said; and the turkey-cock, who was born with his spurs on, and therefore thought himself quite an emperor, puffed himself up like a vessel in full sail, made for him, and gobbled and gobbled till he became quite red in the face. The poor duckling was at his wit's end, and did not know which way to turn; he was in despair because he was so ugly, and the butt of the whole duckyard.

So the first day passed, and afterwards matters grew worse and worse. The poor duckling was chased and hustled by all of them; even his brothers and sisters ill-used him; and they were always saying, "If only the cat would get hold of you, you hideous object!"

Even his mother said, "I wish to goodness you were miles away." The ducks bit him, the hens pecked him, and the girl who fed them kicked him aside.

Then he ran off and flew right over the hedge, where the little birds flew up into the air in a fright.

"That is because I am so ugly," thought the poor duckling, shutting his eyes, but he ran on all the same. Then he came to a great marsh where the wild ducks lived; he was so tired and miserable that he stayed there a whole night.

In the morning the wild ducks flew up to inspect their new comrade.

"What sort of a creature are you?" they inquired, as the duckling turned from side to side and greeted them as well as he could. "You are frightfully ugly," said the wild ducks; "but that does not matter to us, so long as you do not marry into our family!" Poor fellow! he had no thought of marriage; all he wanted was permission to lie among the bushes, and drink a little of the marsh water.

He stayed there two whole days, then two wild geese came, or rather two wild ganders. They were not long out of the shell, and therefore rather pert.

"I say, comrade," they said, "you are so ugly that we have taken quite a fancy to you; will you join us and be a bird of passage? There is another marsh close by, and there are some charming wild geese there; all sweet young ladies, who can say quack! You are ugly enough to make your fortune among them." Just at that moment, bang! bang! was heard up above, and both the wild geese fell dead among the reeds, and the water turned blood red. Bang! bang! went the guns, and whole flocks of wild geese flew up from the rushes and the shot peppered among them again.

There was a grand shooting party, and the sportsmen lay hidden round the marsh, some even sat on the branches of the trees which overhung the water; the blue smoke rose like clouds among the dark trees and swept over the pool.

The water-dogs wandered about in the swamp, splash! splash! The rushes and reeds bent beneath their tread on all sides. It was terribly alarming to the poor duckling. He twisted his head round to get it under his wing and just at that moment a frightful, big dog appeared close beside him; his tongue hung right out of his mouth and his eyes glared wickedly. He opened his great chasm of a mouth close to the duckling, showed his sharp teeth — and — splash — went on without touching him.

"Oh, thank Heaven!" sighed the duckling, "I am so ugly that even the dog won't bite me!"

Then he lay quite still while the shot whistled among the bushes, and bang after bang rent the air. It only became quiet late in the day, but even then the poor duckling did not dare to get up; he waited several hours more before he looked about and then he hurried away from the marsh as fast as he could. He ran across fields and meadows, and there was such a wind that he had hard work to make his way.

Towards night he reached a poor little cottage; it was such a miserable hovel that it could not make up its mind which way to fall even, and so it remained standing. The wind whistled so fiercely round the duckling that he had to sit on his tail to resist it, and it blew harder and harder; then he saw that the door had fallen off one hinge and hung so crookedly that he could creep into the house through the crack and by this means he made his way into the room. An old woman lived there with her cat and her hen. The cat, which she called "Sonnie," could arch his back, purr, and give off electric sparks, that is to say if you stroked his fur the wrong way. The hen had quite tiny short legs and so she was called "Chuckie-low-legs." She laid good eggs, and the old woman was as fond of her as if she had been her own child.

In the morning the strange duckling was discovered immediately, and the cat began to purr and the hen to cluck.

"What on earth is that!" said the old woman looking round, but her sight was not good and she thought the duckling was a fat duck which had escaped. "This is a capital find," said she; "now I shall have duck's eggs if only it is not a drake! we must find out about that!"

So she took the duckling on trial for three weeks, but no eggs made their appearance. The cat was the master of the house and the hen the mistress, and they always spoke of "we and the world," for they thought that they represented the half of the world, and that quite the better half.

The duckling thought there might be two opinions on the subject, but the cat would not hear of it.

"Can you lay eggs?" she asked.

"No!"

"Will you have the goodness to hold your tongue then!"

And the cat said, "Can you arch your back, purr, or give off sparks?"

"No."

"Then you had better keep your opinions to yourself when people of sense are speaking!"

The duckling sat in the corner nursing his ill-humor; then he began to think of the fresh air and the sunshine, an uncontrollable longing seized him to float on the water, and at last he could not help telling the hen about it.

"What on earth possesses you?" she asked; "you have nothing to do, that is why you get these freaks into your head. Lay some eggs or take to purring, and you will get over it."

"But it is so delicious to float on the water," said the duckling; "so delicious to feel it rushing over your head when you dive to the bottom."

"That would be a fine amusement," said the hen. "I think you have gone mad. Ask the cat about it, he is the wisest creature I know; ask him if he is fond of floating on the water or diving under it. I say nothing about myself. Ask our mistress yourself, the old woman, there is no one in the world cleverer than she is. Do you suppose she has any desire to float on the water, or to duck underneath it?"

"You do not understand me," said the duckling.

"Well, if we don't understand you, who should? I suppose you don't consider yourself cleverer than the cat or the old woman, not to mention me. Don't make a fool of yourself, child, and thank your stars for all the good we have done you! Have you not lived in this warm room, and in such society that you might have learnt something? But you are an idiot, and there is no pleasure in associating with you. You may believe me I mean you well, I tell you home truths, and there is no surer way than that, of knowing who are one's friends. You just see about laying some eggs, or learn to purr, or to emit sparks."

"I think I will go out into the wide world," said the duckling.

"Oh, do so by all means," said the hen.

So away went the duckling, he floated on the water and ducked underneath it, but he was looked askance at by every living creature for his ugliness. Now the autumn came on, the leaves in the woods turned yellow and brown; the wind took hold of them, and they danced about. The sky looked very cold, and the clouds hung heavy with snow and hail. A raven stood on the fence and croaked Caw! Caw! from sheer cold; it made one shiver only to think of it, the poor duckling certainly was in a bad case.

One evening, the sun was just setting in wintry splendor, when a flock of beautiful large birds appeared out of the bushes; the duckling had never seen anything so beautiful. They were dazzlingly white with long waving necks; they were swans, and uttering a peculiar cry they spread out their magnificent broad wings and flew away from the cold regions to warmer lands and open seas. They mounted so high, so very high, and the ugly little duckling became strangely uneasy, he circled round and round in the water like a wheel, craning his neck up into the air after them. Then he uttered a shriek so piercing and so strange, that he was quite frightened by it himself. Oh, he could not forget those beautiful birds, those happy birds, and as soon as they were out of sight he ducked right down to the bottom, and when he came up again he was quite beside himself. He did not know what the birds were, or whither they flew, but all the same he was more drawn towards them than he had ever been by any creatures before. He did not envy them in the least, how could it occur to him even to wish to be such a marvel of beauty; he would have been thankful if only the ducks would have tolerated him among them — the poor ugly creature!

The winter was so bitterly cold that the duckling was obliged to swim about in the water to keep it from freezing, but every night the hole in which he swam got smaller and smaller. Then it froze so hard that the surface ice cracked, and the duckling had to use his legs all the time, so that the ice should not close in round him: at last he was so weary that he could move no more, and he was frozen fast into the ice.

Early in the morning a peasant came along and saw him; he went out on to the ice and hammered a hole in it with his heavy wooden shoe, and carried the duckling home to his wife. There it soon revived. The children wanted to play with it, but the duckling thought they were going to ill-use him, and rushed in his fright into the milk pan, and the milk spurted out all over the room. The woman shrieked and threw up her hands, then it flew into the butter cask, and down into the meal tub and out again. Just imagine what it looked like by this time! The woman screamed and tried to hit it with the tongs, and the children tumbled over one another in trying to catch it, and they screamed with laughter — by good luck the door stood open, and the duckling flew out among the bushes and the new fallen snow — and it lay there thoroughly exhausted.

But it would be too sad to mention all the privation and misery it had to go through during that hard winter. When the sun began to shine warmly again, the duckling was in the marsh, lying among the rushes; the larks were singing and the beautiful spring had come.

Then all at once it raised its wings and they flapped with much greater strength than before, and bore him off vigorously. Before he knew where he was, he found himself in a large garden where the apple trees were in full blossom, and the air was scented with lilacs, the long branches of which overhung the indented shores of the lake! Oh! the spring freshness was so delicious!

Just in front of him he saw three beautiful white swans advancing towards him from a thicket; with rustling feathers they swam lightly over the water. The duckling recognized the majestic birds, and he was overcome by a strange melancholy.

"I will fly to them, the royal birds, and

they will hack me to pieces, because I, who am so ugly, venture to approach them! But it won't matter; better be killed by them than be snapped at by the ducks, pecked by the hens, or spurned by the henwife, or suffer so much misery in the winter."

So he flew into the water and swam towards the stately swans; they saw him and darted towards him with ruffled feathers.

"Kill me, oh, kill me!" said the poor creature, and bowing his head towards the water he awaited his death. But what did he see reflected in the transparent water?

He saw below him his own image, but he was no longer a clumsy dark gray bird, ugly and ungainly, he was himself a swan! It does not matter in the least having been born in a duckyard, if only you come out of a swan's egg!

He felt quite glad of all the misery and tribulation he had gone through; he was the better able to appreciate his good fortune now, and all the beauty which greeted him. The big swans swam round and round him, and stroked him with their bills.

Some little children came into the garden with corn and pieces of bread, which they threw into the water; and the smallest one cried out: "There is a new one!" The other children shouted with joy, "Yes, a new one has come!" And they clapped their hands and danced about, running after their father and mother. They threw the bread into the water, and one and all said that the new one was the prettiest; he was so young and handsome. And the old swans bent their heads and did homage before him.

He felt quite shy, and hid his head under his wing; he did not know what to think; he was so very happy, but not at all proud; a good heart never becomes proud. He thought of how he had been pursued and scorned, and now he heard them all say that he was the most beautiful of all beautiful birds. The lilacs bent their boughs right down into the water before him, and the bright sun was warm and cheering, and he rustled his feathers and raised his slender neck aloft, saying with exultation in his heart: "I never dreamt of so much happiness when I was the Ugly Duckling!"

The Swineherd[2]

HANS CHRISTIAN ANDERSEN

To the child, the magic of the pot and the rattle, the prince in disguise, and the poetic justice at the end are enough to make this story interesting. But the adult reader enjoys Andersen's subtle irony. This is a good story to tell to a group of older children.

There was once a poor prince; he had only quite a tiny kingdom, but it was big enough to allow him to marry, and he was bent upon marrying.

Now, it certainly was rather bold of him to say to the emperor's daughter, "Will you have me?" He did, however, venture to say so, for his name was known far and wide; and there were hundreds of princesses who would have said "Yes," and "Thank you, kindly," but see if *she* would.

Just let us hear about it.

A rose tree grew on the grave of the prince's father, it was such a beautiful rose tree; it only bloomed every fifth year, and then only bore one blossom; but what a rose that was! By merely smelling it one forgot all one's cares and sorrows.

Then he had a nightingale which sang as if every lovely melody in the world dwelt in her little throat. This rose and this nightingale were to be given to the princess, so they were put into great silver caskets and sent to her.

The emperor had them carried before him into the great hall where the princess was playing at "visiting" with her ladies-in-waiting; they had nothing else to do. When she saw the caskets with the gifts she clapped her hands with delight!

"If only it were a little pussy cat!" said she but there was the lovely rose.

"Oh, how exquisitely it is made!" said all the ladies-in-waiting.

"It is more than beautiful," said the emperor; "it is neat."

2 From Hans Christian Andersen, *Fairy Tales*, trans. Mrs. Edgar Lucas.

But the princess touched it, and then she was ready to cry.

"Fie, papa!" she said; "it is not made, it is a real one!"

"Fie," said all the ladies-in-waiting; "it is a real one!"

"Well, let us see what there is in the other casket, before we get angry," said the emperor, and out came the nightingale. It sang so beautifully that at first no one could find anything to say against it.

"Superbe! charmant!" said the ladies-in-waiting, for they all had a smattering of French, one spoke it worse than the other.

"How that bird reminds me of our lamented empress's musical box," said an old courtier. "Ah, yes, they are the same tunes, and the same beautiful execution."

"So they are," said the emperor, and he cried like a little child.

"I should hardly think it could be a real one," said the princess.

"Yes, it is a real one," said those who had brought it.

"Oh, let that bird fly away then," said the princess, and she would not hear of allowing the prince to come. But he was not to be crushed; he stained his face brown and black, and pressing his cap over his eyes, he knocked at the door.

"Good morning, Emperor," said he; "can I be taken into service in the palace?"

"Well, there are so many wishing to do that," said the emperor; "but let me see! — yes, I need somebody to look after the pigs, for we have so many of them."

So the prince was made imperial swineherd. A horrid little room was given him near the pig-sties, and here he had to live. He sat busily at work all day, and by the evening he had made a beautiful little cooking pot; it had bells all round it and when the pot boiled they tinkled delightfully and played the old tune:

"Ach du lieber Augustin,
Alles ist weg, weg, weg!" *

But the greatest charm of all about it was, that by holding one's finger in the steam one could immediately smell all the dinners that

* Alas! dear Augustin,
All is lost, lost, lost!

were being cooked at every stove in the town. Now this was a very different matter from a rose.

The princess came walking along with all her ladies-in-waiting, and when she heard the tune she stopped and looked pleased, for she could play "Ach du lieber Augustin" herself; it was her only tune, and she could only play it with one finger.

"Why, that is my tune," she said; "this must be a cultivated swineherd. Go and ask him what the instrument costs."

So one of the ladies-in-waiting had to go into his room, but she put pattens on first.

"How much do you want for the pot?" she asked.

"I must have ten kisses from the princess," said the swineherd.

"Heaven preserve us!" said the lady.

"I won't take less," said the swineherd.

"Well, what does he say?" asked the princess.

"I really cannot tell you," said the lady-in-waiting, "it is so shocking."

"Then you must whisper it." And she whispered it.

"He is a wretch!" said the princess, and went away at once. But she had only gone a little way when she heard the bells tinkling beautifully:

"Ach du lieber Augustin."

"Go and ask him if he will take ten kisses from the ladies-in-waiting."

"No, thank you," said the swineherd; "ten kisses from the princess, or I keep my pot."

"How tiresome it is," said the princess. "Then you will have to stand round me, so that no one may see."

So the ladies-in-waiting stood round her and spread out their skirts while the swineherd took his ten kisses, and then the pot was hers.

What a delight it was to them. The pot was kept on the boil day and night. They knew what was cooking on every stove in the town, from the chamberlain's to the shoemaker's. The ladies-in-waiting danced about and clapped their hands.

"We know who has sweet soup and pancakes for dinner, and who has cutlets; how amusing it is."

"Highly interesting," said the mistress of the robes.

"Yes, but hold your tongues, for I am the emperor's daughter."

"Heaven preserve us!" they all said.

The swineherd — that is to say, the prince, only nobody knew that he was not a real swineherd — did not let the day pass in idleness, and he now constructed a rattle. When it was swung round it played all the waltzes, galops and jig tunes which have ever been heard since the creation of the world.

"But this is *superbe!*" said the princess, as she walked by. "I have never heard finer compositions. Go and ask him what the instrument costs, but let us have no more kissing."

"He wants a hundred kisses from the princess!" said the lady-in-waiting.

"I think he is mad!" said the princess, and she went away, but she had not gone far when she stopped.

"One must encourage art," she said; "I am the emperor's daughter. Tell him he can have ten kisses, the same as yesterday, and he can take the others from the ladies-in-waiting."

"But we don't like that at all," said the ladies.

"Oh, nonsense! If I can kiss him you can do the same. Remember that I pay your wages as well as give you board and lodging." So the lady-in-waiting had to go again.

"A hundred kisses from the princess, or let each keep his own."

"Stand in front of me," said she, and all the ladies stood round, while he kissed her.

"Whatever is the meaning of that crowd round the pig-sties?" said the emperor as he stepped out onto the veranda; he rubbed his eyes and put on his spectacles. "Why, it is the ladies-in-waiting, what game are they up to? I must go and see!" So he pulled up the heels of his slippers, for they were shoes which he had trodden down.

Bless us, what a hurry he was in! When he got into the yard, he walked very softly and the ladies were so busy counting the kisses, so that there should be fair play, and neither too few nor too many kisses, that they never heard the emperor. He stood on tiptoe.

"What is all this?" he said when he saw what was going on, and he hit them on the head with his slipper just as the swineherd was taking the eighty-sixth kiss.

"Out you go!" said the emperor, for he was furious, and both the princess and the prince were put out of his realm.

There she stood crying, and the swineherd scolded, and the rain poured down in torrents.

"Oh, miserable creature that I am! if only I had accepted the handsome prince. Oh, how unhappy I am!"

The swineherd went behind a tree, wiped the black and brown stain from his face, and threw away his ugly clothes. Then he stepped out dressed as a prince; he was so handsome that the princess could not help curtseying to him.

"I am come to despise thee," he said. "Thou wouldst not have an honorable prince, thou couldst not prize the rose or the nightingale, but thou wouldst kiss the swineherd for a trumpery musical box! As thou hast made thy bed, so must thou lie upon it!"

Then he went back into his own little kingdom and shut and locked the door. So she had to stand outside and sing in earnest —

> "Ach du lieber Augustin,
> Alles ist weg, weg, weg!"

The Fir Tree[3]

Hans Christian Andersen

❧ *This is said to have been Andersen's favorite of all his fairy tales, though many people cannot see why. In the first place, as it is very long it would have been better divided into three parts to coincide with the three episodes: first, the tree's life in the forest — its longing for what it thought would be something better than it had; second, its experiences as a Christmas tree, which turned out to be a disappointment; and last, its neglected end that offered only temporary comfort. The sad note at the end has nothing of the heroic in it, as in the death*

[3] From Hans Christian Andersen, *Fairy Tales and Stories,* trans. H. L. Brackstad.

of the steadfast tin soldier; one does not feel here that life was worth the struggle.

Far in the forest stood a very pretty pine tree; it had plenty of space; the sunshine could reach it and it had plenty of air. Roundabout grew many bigger companions, both pines and firs; but the little pine tree was in such a hurry to grow, it did not even trouble itself about the peasant children who ran about chattering when they came to gather wild strawberries and raspberries.

They would often come with a whole jar full of berries, or with the strawberries threaded on a straw, and sit down by the little tree and exclaim: "Oh, what a pretty little one!" The pine did not at all like this. The next year it was a long joint taller, and the following year it had grown still a joint longer, for you can always tell by the joints on a pine tree how many years it has been growing.

"Oh, if I were only such a big tree as the others!" sighed the little tree, "then I might spread my branches out far around me, and from the top look out over the whole world! The birds would then build their nests among my branches, and when the wind was blowing I could make my bow just as grandly as the others over there!"

It took no pleasure in the sunshine, in the birds, or the red clouds which sailed over it morning and evening.

If it happened to be winter, and the snow lay glittering white all around it, a hare would often come running along and jump right over the little tree — oh, it was irritating! But two winters passed, and in the third the tree had grown so big that the hare had to run around it. "Oh, to grow, to grow, to become big and old, that is the only thing worth living for in this world!" thought the tree.

In the autumn the woodcutters always came and felled some of the largest trees. This was done every year, and the young pine tree, which had now grown fairly big, trembled at the thought of it; for the big noble trees fell to the ground with a crash and a groan, the branches were cut off, the trees looked quite naked, long, and lanky — they could hardly be recognized. They were then put on carts and drawn by horses out of the forest.

Where were they going? What was going to be done with them?

In the spring, when the swallows and the storks came, the tree asked them: "Do you know where they have been taken to? Did you meet them?"

The swallows did not know anything, but the stork, looking serious, nodded his head and said: "Yes, I think so. I met many new ships on my way from Egypt. They had stately masts. I think I may say they were your trees, for there was a smell of the pine about them. I bring you greetings from them; they looked stately, quite stately."

"Oh, if I were only big enough to fly across the ocean! But what is the ocean and what is it like?"

"Well, that's too long a story to explain," said the stork, and walked away.

"Rejoice in your youth," said the sunbeams; "rejoice in your fresh growth and the young life you possess."

And the wind kissed the tree and the dew wept tears over it; but the pine tree did not understand that.

As Christmas-time was drawing near, many young trees were cut down; some of them were not even as big or as old as the pine tree which was so restless and impatient, and always wanting to get away. These young trees, which were always the most beautiful, were not denuded of their branches; they were placed on a cart and drawn by horses out of the forest.

"Where are they going to?" asked the pine tree. "They are not bigger than I; there was even one which was much smaller. Why were they allowed to keep all their branches? Where are they being taken to?"

"We know! we know!" twittered the sparrows. "We have looked in at the windows down in the town! We know where they are going to! Ah! they are going to the greatest glory and splendor one can think of. We have looked in at the windows and seen that they are placed in the middle of the warm room and decorated with most beautiful things — gilt apples, honey-cakes, toys, and many hundreds of candles."

"And then?" asked the pine tree, trembling in all its branches. "And then? What happens then?"

"Well, we haven't seen anything else. It was really wonderful!"

"I wonder if I came into existence to have such a glorious career?" cried the pine tree in exultation. "That would be even better than going across the ocean. How painful this longing is! If only it were Christmas! Now I am tall and have big branches like those which were taken away last year. Oh, how I wish that I was already in the cart, that I was in the warm parlor with all that glory and splendor around me! And then? Well, then something still better must follow, something still more glorious. But what? Oh, how I suffer! How I am longing! I do not know myself what has taken possession of me."

"Rejoice in us," said the air and the sunshine; "rejoice in your fresh youth in the open!"

But the tree did not at all rejoice. It grew and grew; green, dark green, it stood there winter and summer; people who saw it said: "There's a fine tree!" And at Christmas-time it was the first to be felled. The axe cut deeply into its marrow; the tree fell to the ground with a sigh; it felt a pain, a faintness; it was unable to think of any happiness; it was sad at parting from its home, from the spot where it had sprung up; it knew it would never again see the dear old comrades, the little bushes and the flowers round about, perhaps not even the birds. To take leave of all this was not at all pleasant. The tree came to itself only when it was being unloaded in the yard and heard a man say: "That's a beauty! That's the one we'll use!"

Two grandly dressed servants then came and carried the pine tree into a large, beautiful room. On the walls around hung portraits, and near the great stove stood Chinese vases with lions on the lids. There were rocking-chairs, silken sofas, large tables covered with picture-books and toys — many hundred dollars' worth — at least that's what the children said. And the tree was placed in a great tub filled with sand, but nobody could see it was a tub, for it was covered up with some green cloth and was standing on a large, brightly colored carpet. How the tree trembled! What was going to take place? Both the servants and the ladies of the house were busy decorating it. On the branches they hung little nets cut out of colored paper; each net they filled with sweets; gilt apples and walnuts hung from it as if they had grown there, and over a hundred red, blue, and white little candles were fastened to the branches. Dolls, which looked exactly like live beings — the tree had never seen any before — hung suspended from the green branches, and at the very top of the tree was fixed a great star of tinsel gold; it was splendid, it was quite magnificent.

"Tonight," they all said; "tonight it will look glorious!"

"Oh," thought the tree, "I wish it were evening! If only the candles could be lighted soon! And what will happen then? Will the trees from the forest come and look at me? Will the sparrows fly past the window? I wonder if I shall grow fast here and remain decorated winter and summer."

Yes, it seemed to know all about it; but it suffered from a terrible barkache from all the longing, and barkache is just as bad for a tree as a backache is to us.

The candles were now lighted. What joy, what splendor! The tree trembled in all its branches at the sight of it, so that one of the candles set fire to a branch and singed it badly.

"Goodness gracious!" cried the young ladies, and set to work in all haste to put out the fire.

The tree did not even dare to tremble. Oh, it was terrible! It was so afraid of losing any of its finery that it was quite beside itself in all this splendor, when suddenly the folding doors were opened and a crowd of children rushed into the room as if they were going to upset the tree; the older people followed in a more dignified manner. The little ones stood quite silent, but only for a moment, then they shouted again till the room rang; they danced round the tree, and one present after another was plucked from it.

"What are they doing?" thought the tree. "What's going to happen?" The candles were beginning to burn down to the branches, and were then put out one after the other. The children were now allowed to strip it; they rushed at it so that all its branches creaked, and had it not been fastened to the ceiling by the top and the golden star, it would have been overturned.

The children danced round the room with their pretty toys; nobody looked at the tree except the old nurse who was looking about between the branches, but it was only to see if a fig or an apple had been forgotten.

"A story! a story!" cried the children, and dragged a fat little man toward the tree. He sat down just under it. "For then we shall be in the greenwood," he said, "and it may please the tree to listen to the story; but I will tell you only one story. Will you have the one about Ivede-Avede, or that one about Lumpy-Dumpy, who fell down the stairs, but after all came on the throne and married the princess?"

"Ivede-Avede!" cried some, "Lumpy-Dumpy!" cried others. There was such a crying and shouting, only the pine tree remained quite silent and thought: "Am I not to join in it, not do anything at all?" It had already been in it and had done all it should do.

And the man told them about Lumpy-Dumpy, who fell down the stairs, and after all came on the throne and married the princess. "The princess!" The children clapped their hands and cried: "Go on! go on!" They wanted to hear "Ivede-Avede" also, but they got only "Lumpy-Dumpy." The pine tree stood quite silent and thoughtful: the birds in the forest had never told such stories. "Lumpy-Dumpy fell down the stairs and got the princess after all. Ah, well! that's the way of the world," thought the pine tree, believing it was true because it was such a nice old man who had told it. "Ah, well, who knows! perhaps I may fall down the stairs, too, and marry a princess." And it looked forward with pleasure to being decorated again next day with lights and toys, with gold and fruits.

"Tomorrow I shall not tremble," it thought. "I'll enjoy myself thoroughly in the midst of all my glory. Tomorrow I shall again hear the story about Lumpy-Dumpy and perhaps the one about Ivede-Avede."

And the tree remained quiet and thoughtful the whole night.

In the morning the manservant and the chambermaid came into the room.

"Now the fun is going to begin again!" thought the tree; but they dragged it out of the room, up the stairs and into the garret, and there they put it away in a dark corner where the daylight could not reach. "What is the meaning of this?" thought the tree; "I wonder what I am going to do here, and what I shall hear?" And it leaned against the wall and stood thinking and thinking. It had plenty of time to do so, for days and nights passed and nobody came near it, and when somebody at last came it was only to put some big boxes away in the corner. The tree stood quite hidden and one would think it had been quite forgotten.

"Now it's winter outside!" thought the tree. "The ground is hard and covered with snow and they cannot plant me; therefore I suppose I must stand here in the shelter till the spring. How thoughtful! How kind people are! If it were only not so dark here and so terribly lonely! Not even a little hare! It was so jolly out there in the forest, when the snow was on the ground, and the hare was running about; yes, even when he jumped over me, but I did not like it at the time. Up here it is terribly lonely!"

"Squeak, squeak!" said a tiny mouse just then, and crept out of its hole; and then came another. They sniffed at the pine tree and crept up among its branches.

"It is terribly cold!" said the little mice. "Otherwise it's very nice here! Don't you think so, you old pine tree?"

"I am not at all old!" said the pine tree; "there are many much older than I."

"Where do you come from?" asked the mice, "and what do you know?" They were so dreadfully inquisitive. "Tell us about the prettiest spot on earth. Have you been there? Have you been in the larder, where there are cheeses on the shelves and hams hanging from the ceiling, where one can dance on tallow candles, and where one goes in thin and comes out fat?"

"I don't know anything about that," said the tree; "but I know the forest, where the sun shines and where the birds sing." And then it told them everything from its youth onward, and the little mice had never heard anything like it before; they listened attentively and said:

"Dear, dear! How much you must have seen! How happy you must have been!"

"I?" said the pine tree, and thought over what it had been telling them. "Well, they were very jolly times, after all!" And then it went on to tell them about Christmas Eve, when it was decorated with cakes and candles.

"Ah!" said the little mice, "how happy you must have been, you old pine tree!"

"I am not at all old," said the tree; "it is only this winter that I came from the forest. I am in my full prime, I am only a little stunted in my growth."

"How delightfully you do tell stories!" said the little mice, and the next night they came with four other little mice, to hear the tree tell stories; and the more it went on telling the more distinctly it remembered everything, and it thought to itself: "They were very jolly times, after all! But they may come again, they may come again! Lumpy-Dumpy fell down the stairs and still got the princess; perhaps I can get a princess, too." And the pine tree thought of a pretty little birch tree which grew out in the forest and which to the pine tree was as good as a real princess.

"Who is Lumpy-Dumpy?" asked the little mice. And then the pine tree told them the whole story; it remembered every single word of it, and the little mice were so delighted with it that they were ready to jump to the top of the tree. The following night there came a great many more mice and on the Sunday even two rats; but they said the story was not funny, and the little mice were sorry to hear this, for now they also thought less of it.

"Do you know only that one story?" asked the rats.

"Only that one," answered the tree. "I heard it on the happiest evening of my life, but I did not then know how happy I was."

"It's a very poor story! Don't you know any one with bacon and tallow candles in it — any story from the larders?"

"No," said the tree.

"Ah, well, thanks all the same," answered the rats, and went off to their holes.

The little mice also disappeared at last, and the tree sighed: "It was rather pleasant to have the tiny little mice sitting round me and listening to what I told them! Now that's all over as well! but I shall take care to enjoy myself when I am brought out again!"

But when did that happen? Well, early one morning some people came and rummaged about in the garret; the boxes were moved about and the tree was dragged out of its corner and thrown somewhat roughly on the floor, but one of the men dragged it toward the staircase where there was bright sunshine.

"Now life is beginning again!" thought the tree as it felt the fresh air and the first sunbeam — and then it found itself in the yard. Everything happened so quickly that the tree forgot to take a look at itself. There was so much to see all round. The yard adjoined the garden, where everything was in full bloom; the roses hung so fresh and fragrant over the little palings; the linden-trees were in blossom, and the swallows flew about and said: "quirre-virre-vit, my husband's come home!" but it was not the pine tree they meant.

"Now I shall enjoy life!" it shouted joyously, spreading its branches far out; alas! they were all withered and yellow, and it was lying in a corner amongst weeds and nettles. The tinsel star was still fixed on the top and glittered in the sunshine.

Two of the merry children who had danced round the tree at Christmas and been so fond of it were playing in the yard. The smallest rushed at it and tore off the golden star.

"Just look what is still sticking to the ugly old Christmas tree!" he said, and began trampling upon the branches till they crackled under his feet.

And the tree looked at all the splendor and freshness of the flowers in the garden and then at itself, and wished it had remained in its dark corner in the garret. It thought of its bright young days in the forest, of the merry Christmas Eve, and of the little mice which had listened so pleased to the story about Lumpy-Dumpy.

"It's all over!" said the poor tree. "If I had only enjoyed myself when I had the chance! It's all over! All over!"

And the servant man came and chopped the tree into small pieces; it made quite a large bundle. It blazed up brightly under the largest copper kettle, and sighed so deeply that every sigh was like the report of a small gun, and the children who were at play came in and seated themselves in front of the fire, looked at it and shouted, "Pop! Pop!" But at each report, which was really a deep sigh, the tree was thinking of a summer day in the forest, or a winter night out there while the stars were shining. It thought of Christmas Eve and Lumpy-Dumpy, the only story it had heard and knew how to tell — and so the tree was burned to ashes.

The boys were playing in the yard, and the youngest was wearing the tinsel star on his breast, which the tree had worn on the happiest evening of its existence. Now all that had come to an end, and so had the tree; and the story as well came to an end, to an end — and so do all stories!

Adventures of Pinocchio

Pinocchio's First Pranks [4]

CARLO COLLODI

Pinocchio is one of the most popular of all children's stories. It was written in Italy in 1880, and has been translated into many languages. The story begins by telling of a carpenter who wanted to make a table leg out of a piece of wood, but just as he was cutting it, a small voice called out, "Stop, you are hurting me!" Then, as he planed the wood, the same voice called again, "Stop, you are tickling me!" The carpenter was afraid of this talkative piece of wood, so he gave it to his friend, Geppetto, who was planning just then to make a marionette. The following chapter tells how Geppetto fashioned the little wooden figure, but this episode is only the beginning of the pranks and capers played by the mischievous Pinocchio.

4 From Carlo Collodi, *The Adventures of Pinocchio*, trans. Sarah Scott Edwards.

Geppetto's house was a poor little room on the ground floor which drew its light from the space under a stairway. The furniture could not have been more simple: a rough old chair, a tumble-down bed, and a rickety table; that was all. In the wall at the back there was a fireplace with a lighted fire, but the flame was painted and so was the earthen pot which boiled merrily and sent forth steam which seemed real, indeed, until one knew better.

Upon entering the house Geppetto quickly got out his tools and began to carve and fashion his puppet. "What shall I name him?" said he to himself. "Ah, I shall call him Pinocchio. This name will surely bring him good luck. I once knew an entire family by that name — Father Pinocchio, Mother Pinocchio and the Pinocchio children, and all of them turned out well. Why, even the richest of them was a beggar."

As soon as Geppetto had decided upon the name for his puppet he began to work in earnest and quickly made the hair, the face, then the eyes. Imagine his amazement when he saw those eyes moving and staring up into his face.

"Wooden eyes, why do you stare at me?" asked the old man, resentfully. But there was no response.

Then Geppetto made the nose, which, scarcely done, began to grow; and it grew and grew, and grew until it seemed that it would never end. Poor Geppetto tried to stop it by cutting it off, but the more he shortened it the more that impudent nose grew.

After he had finished the nose the old man fashioned the mouth. No sooner was it made than it began to jeer and laugh at Geppetto. "Stop laughing at me!" cried the old man angrily; but it was like talking to a stone wall. "Stop laughing, I tell you!" he repeated in a threatening voice. Then the mouth stopped laughing and stuck out its tongue. Geppetto did not wish to waste any time so he pretended not to see and went on working.

After the mouth the old fellow made the chin, then the neck, the shoulders, the body, the arms, and the hands. Scarcely had Geppetto finished the hands when he felt his wig lifted from his head. Looking up, what did he see? He saw his big yellow wig waving about in the hands of the puppet.

"Pinocchio, give me back my wig!" cried Geppetto. "Give it back at once!" But Pinocchio, instead of obeying, placed the wig upon his own head, almost smothering himself beneath it.

All this rude conduct made poor old Geppetto sadder than he had ever been in his life, and turning toward Pinocchio he said to him, "You naughty boy, scarcely are you made before you begin to make fun of your poor old father. That is bad, my boy, very bad," and he wiped away a tear.

There was now nothing left to make except the legs and the feet. When Geppetto had finished them, he suddenly felt a kick on the end of his nose. "It serves me right," he said to himself. "I should have known better. Alas, now it is too late."

Picking the puppet up the old man set him on the floor in order to teach the little fellow how to walk. But Pinocchio's legs were stiff and numb, and he could not move them; so Geppetto led him by the hand and showed him how to place one foot before the other.

Little by little the puppet's feet lost their numbness, and he began to walk, then to run about the room, until suddenly he darted through the door, out into the street, and was gone. Poor Geppetto ran after the puppet but could not catch him because that rascal of a Pinocchio was running and leaping like a rabbit, and his wooden feet pattering over the cobblestones made a noise like twenty peasants clattering along in their wooden shoes.

"Catch him, catch him!" shouted Geppetto; but the people along the way, seeing this wooden puppet which ran like a race-horse, stopped, enchanted, to look at him and laughed and laughed in amazement.

Fortunately, at last a policeman appeared who, hearing all this clatter and thinking it to be a colt which had escaped from its master, planted himself squarely in the middle of the street with legs apart, determined to stop the runaway and prevent further disaster.

But Pinocchio, when he saw the policeman ahead of him barricading the whole street, decided, instead of trying to pass him, to run between his legs but in this the puppet met with failure. The policeman, without even moving aside, neatly caught Pinocchio by the nose (it was an absurdly long nose, made purposely to be grabbed by policemen), and turned him over to Geppetto, who in order to punish the puppet, decided to give him a good slap on the ears. Imagine his surprise when, in searching for the ears, he could find none. Do you know why? Because, in his haste to finish the puppet, Geppetto had forgotten to make them!

The old man took Pinocchio by the back of the neck and, as he urged him along, he said, shaking his head in a threatening manner, "We are going home and when we get there we shall settle our accounts." At this Pinocchio threw himself upon the ground and refused to go farther. Immediately a crowd gathered round and began to make remarks. Some said one thing and some another. "Poor puppet," said several. "No wonder he doesn't want to go home. Who knows how hard that old rascal, Geppetto, may beat him?" And some said, meaningly, "That old fellow appears to be a gentleman but he is a regular tyrant with children. If we leave the puppet in his hands he is quite capable of doing him much harm."

The upshot of it all was that the policeman turned Pinocchio loose and led Geppetto off to prison. The poor old man could find no words with which to defend himself but bellowed like a calf, and, as he drew near the prison he sobbed and babbled, "Ungrateful son! And to think that I took such pains to make him. But it serves me right. I should have thought first."

That which happened to Pinocchio afterwards is a story which you will not believe but you may read it in the following chapters.

Peter Pan in Kensington Gardens

Lock-Out Time [5]

JAMES M. BARRIE

Peter Pan was once a real child who left home when he was only seven days old. He was trying to reach Kensington Gardens, though it was "after Lock-Out Time." Unhappily, every fairy he appealed to ran away; so he asked the birds for help. In turn he helped them and became very wise in bird lore. He did not, however, reach the Gardens by their aid, but by a boat in which he sailed down the stream into the Gardens after Lock-Out Time. He had to make clear to the fairies there, who regarded him with some hostility, that he was not an ordinary human being and wanted to be their friend; then they let him jump ashore. The fairies finally led him to their queen, who granted him the freedom of the Gardens.

It is frightfully difficult to know much about the fairies, and almost the only thing known for certain is that there are fairies wherever there are children. Long ago children were forbidden the Gardens, and at that time there was not a fairy in the place; then the children were admitted, and the fairies came trooping in that very evening. They can't resist following the children, but you seldom see them, partly because they live in the daytime behind the railings, where you are not allowed to go, and also partly because they are so cunning. They are not a bit cunning after Lock-Out, but until Lock-Out, my word!

When you were a bird you knew the fairies pretty well, and you remember a good deal about them in your babyhood, which it is a great pity you can't write down, for gradually you forget, and I have heard of children who declared that they had never once seen a fairy. Very likely if they said this in the Kensington Gardens, they were standing looking at a Fairy all the time. The reason they were cheated was that she pre-

5 From Sir James M. Barrie, *Peter Pan in Kensington Gardens* (Scribner, 1902).

tended to be something else. This is one of their best tricks. They usually pretend to be flowers, because the court sits in the Fairies' Basin, and there are so many flowers there, and all along the Baby Walk, that a flower is the thing least likely to attract attention. They dress exactly like flowers, and change with the seasons, putting on white when lilies are in and blue for bluebells, and so on. They like crocus and hyacinth time best of all, as they are partial to a bit of color, but tulips (except white ones, which are the fairy cradles) they consider garish, and they sometimes put off dressing like tulips for days, so that the beginning of the tulip weeks is almost the best time to catch them.

When they think you are not looking, they skip along pretty lively, but if you look, and they fear there is no time to hide, they stand quite still pretending to be flowers. Then, after you have passed without knowing that they were fairies, they rush home and tell their mothers they have had such an adventure. The Fairy Basin, you remember, is all covered with ground-ivy (from which they make their castor oil), with flowers growing in it here and there. Most of them really are flowers, but some of them are fairies. You never can be sure of them, but a good plan is to walk by looking the other way, and then turn round sharply. Another good plan, which David and I sometimes follow, is to stare them down. After a long time they can't help winking, and then you know for certain that they are fairies.

There are also numbers of them along the Baby Walk, which is a famous gentle place, as spots frequented by fairies are called. Once twenty-four of them had an extraordinary adventure. They were a girls' school out for a walk with the governess, and all wearing hyacinth gowns, when she suddenly put her finger to her mouth, and then they all stood still on an empty bed and pretended to be hyacinths. Unfortunately, what the governess had heard was two gardeners coming to plant new flowers in that very bed. They were wheeling a hand-cart with flowers in it, and were quite surprised to find the bed occupied. "Pity to lift them hyacinths," said the one man. "Duke's orders," replied the other, and, having emptied the cart, they dug up the boarding-school and put the poor, terrified things in it in five rows. Of course, neither the governess nor the girls dare let on that they were fairies, so they were carted far away to a potting-shed, out of which they escaped in the night without their shoes, but there was a great row about it among the parents, and the school was ruined.

As for their houses, it is no use looking for them, because they are the exact opposite of our houses. You can see our houses by day, but you can't see them by dark. Well, you can see their houses by dark, but you can't see them by day, for they are the color of night, and I never heard of anyone yet who could see night in the daytime. This does not mean that they are black, for night has its colors just as day has, but ever so much brighter. Their blues and reds and greens are like ours with a light behind them. The palace is entirely built of many-colored glasses, and it is quite the loveliest of all royal residences, but the queen sometimes complains because the common people will peep in to see what she is doing. They are very inquisitive folk, and press quite hard against the glass, and that is why their noses are mostly snubby. The streets are miles long and very twisty, and have paths on each side made of bright worsted. The birds used to steal the worsted for their nests, but a policeman has been appointed to hold on at the other end.

One of the great differences between the fairies and us is that they never do anything useful. When the first baby laughed for the first time, his laugh broke into a million pieces, and they all went skipping about. That was the beginning of fairies. They look tremendously busy, you know, as if they had not a moment to spare, but if you were to ask them what they are doing, they could not tell you in the least. They are frightfully ignorant, and everything they do is make-believe. They have a postman, but he never calls except at Christmas with his little box, and though they have beautiful schools, nothing is taught in them; the youngest child being chief person is always elected mistress, and when she has called the roll, they all go out for a walk and never come back. It is a very noticeable thing that, in fairy families, the youngest is always chief person, and usually becomes a prince or princess, and children remember this, and think it must be so among humans also, and that is why they are often made uneasy when they come upon their mother furtively putting new frills on the bassinet.

You have probably observed that your baby-sister wants to do all sorts of things that your mother and her nurse want her not to do — to stand up at sitting-down time, and to sit down at stand-up time, for instance, or to crawl on the floor when she is wearing her best frock, and so on, and perhaps you put this down to naughtiness. But it is not; it simply means that she is doing as she has seen the fairies do; she begins by following their ways, and it takes about two years to get her into the human ways. Her fits of passion, which are awful to behold, and are usually called teething, are no such thing; they are her natural exasperation, because we don't understand her, though she is talking an intelligible language. She is talking fairy. The reason mothers and nurses know what her remarks mean, before other people know, as that "Guch" means "Give it to me at once," while "Wa" is "Why do you wear such a funny hat?" is because, mixing so much with babies, they have picked up a little of the fairy language.

Of late David has been thinking back hard about the fairy tongue, with his hands clutching his temples, and he has remembered a number of their phrases which I shall tell you some day if I don't forget. He had heard them in the days when he was a thrush, and though I suggested to him that perhaps it is really bird language he is remembering, he says not, for these phrases are about fun and adventures, and the birds talked of nothing but nest-building. He distinctly remembers that the birds used to go from spot to spot like ladies at shop windows, looking at the different nests and saying, "Not my color, my dear," and "How would that do with a soft lining?" and "But will it wear?" and "What hideous trimming!" and so on.

The fairies are exquisite dancers and that is why one of the first things the baby does is to sign to you to dance to him and then to cry when you do it. They hold their great balls in the open air, in what is called a fairy ring. For weeks afterward you can see the ring on the grass. It is not there when they begin, but they make it by waltzing round and round. Sometimes you will find mushrooms inside the ring, and these are fairy chairs that the servants have forgotten to clear away. The chairs and the rings are the only telltale marks these little people leave behind them, and they would remove even these were they not so fond of dancing that they toe it till the very moment of the opening of the gates. David and I once found a fairy ring quite warm.

But there is also a way of finding out about the ball before it takes place. You know the boards which tell at what time the Gardens are to close today. Well, these tricky fairies sometimes slyly change the board on a ball night, so that it says the Gardens are to close at six-thirty, for instance, instead of at seven. This enables them to get begun half an hour earlier.

If on such a night we could remain behind in the Gardens, as the famous Maimie Mannering did, we might see delicious sights; hundreds of lovely fairies hastening to the ball, the married ones wearing their wedding rings round their waists; the gentlemen, all in uniform, holding up the ladies' trains, and linkmen running in front carrying winter cherries, which are the fairy-lanterns; the cloakroom where they put on their silver slippers and get a ticket for their wraps; the flowers streaming up from the Baby Walk to look on, and always welcome because they can lend a pin; the supper-table, with Queen Mab at the head of it, and behind her chair the lord chamberlain, who carries a dandelion on which he blows when Her Majesty wants to know the time.

The tablecloth varies according to the seasons, and in May it is made of chestnut blossom. The way the fairy servants do is this: The men, scores of them, climb up the trees and shake the branches, and the blossom falls like snow. Then the lady servants sweep it together by whisking their skirts until it is exactly like a tablecloth, and that is how they get their tablecloth.

They have real glasses and real wine of three kinds, namely, blackthorn wine, berberris wine, and cowslip wine, and the queen pours out, but the bottles are so heavy that she just pretends to pour out. There is bread-and-butter to begin with, of the size of a three-penny bit; and cakes to end with, and they are so small that they have no crumbs. The fairies sit round on mushrooms, and at first they are well-behaved and always cough off the table, and so on, but after a bit they are not so well-behaved and stick their fingers into the butter, which is got from the roots of old trees, and the really horrid ones crawl over the tablecloth chasing sugar or other delicacies with their tongues. When the queen sees them doing this, she signs to the servants to wash up and put away, and then everybody adjourns to the dance, the queen walking in front while the lord chamberlain walks behind her, carrying two little pots, one of which contains the juice of wallflower and the other the juice of Solomon's-seals. Wallflower juice is good for reviving dancers who fall to the ground in a fit, and Solomon's-seals juice is for bruises. They bruise very easily, and when Peter plays faster and faster they foot it till they fall down in fits. For, as you know without my telling you, Peter Pan is the fairies' orchestra. He sits in the middle of the ring, and they would never dream of having a smart dance nowadays without him. "P. P." is written on the corner of the invitation-cards sent out by all really good families. They are grateful little people, too, and at the princess's coming-of-age ball (they come of age on their second birthday and have a birthday every month), they gave him the wish of his heart.

The way it was done was this. The queen ordered him to kneel, and then said that for playing so beautifully she would give him the wish of his heart. Then they all gathered round Peter to hear what was the wish of his heart, but for a long time he hesitated, not being certain what it was himself.

"If I chose to go back to mother," he asked at last, "could you give me that wish?"

Now this question vexed them, for were he to return to his mother, they should lose his music, so the queen tilted her nose contemptuously and said, "Pooh! ask for a much bigger wish than that."

"Is that quite a little wish?" he inquired.

"As little as this," the queen answered, putting her hands near each other.

"What size is a big wish?" he asked.

She measured it off on her skirt and it was a very handsome length.

Then Peter reflected and said, "Well, then, I think I shall have two little wishes instead of one big one."

Of course, the fairies had to agree, though his cleverness rather shocked them, and he said that his first wish was to go to his mother, but with the right to return to the Gardens if he found her disappointing. His second wish he would hold in reserve.

They tried to dissuade him, and even put obstacles in the way.

"I can give you the power to fly to her house," the queen said, "but I can't open the door for you."

"The window I flew out at will be open," Peter said confidently. "Mother always keeps it open in the hope that I may fly back."

"How do you know?" they asked, quite surprised, and, really, Peter could not explain how he knew.

"I just do know," he said.

So as he persisted in his wish, they had to grant it. The way they gave him power to fly was this: They all tickled him on the shoulder, and soon he felt a funny itching in that part, and then up he rose higher and higher, and flew away out of the Gardens and over the housetops.

It was so delicious that instead of flying straight to his own home he skimmed away over Saint Paul's to the Crystal Palace and back by the river and Regent's Park, and by the time he reached his mother's window he had quite made up his mind that his second wish should be to become a bird.

The window was wide open, just as he knew it would be, and in he fluttered, and there was his mother lying asleep. Peter alighted softly on the wooden rail at the foot of the bed and had a good look at her. She lay with her head on her hand, and the hollow in the pillow was like a nest lined with her brown wavy hair. He remembered, though he had long forgotten it, that she always gave her hair a holiday at night. How sweet the frills of her nightgown were! He was very glad she was such a pretty mother.

But she looked sad, and he knew why she looked sad. One of her arms moved as if it wanted to go round something, and he knew what it wanted to go round.

"O mother!" said Peter to himself, "if you just knew who is sitting on the rail at the foot of the bed!"

Very gently he patted the little mound that her feet made, and he could see by her face that she liked it. He knew he had but to say "Mother" ever so softly, and she would wake up. They always wake up at once if it is you that says their name. Then she would give such a joyous cry and squeeze him tight. How nice that would be to him, but oh! how exquisitely delicious it would be to her! That, I am afraid, is how Peter regarded it. In returning to his mother he never doubted that he was giving her the greatest treat a woman can have. Nothing can be more splendid, he thought, than to have a little boy of your own. How proud of him they are! and very right and proper, too.

But why does Peter sit so long on the rail; why does he not tell his mother that he has come back?

I quite shrink from the truth, which is that he sat there in two minds. Sometimes he looked longingly at his mother, and sometimes he looked longingly at the window. Certainly it would be pleasant to be her boy again, but on the other hand, what times those had been in the Gardens! Was he so sure that he should enjoy wearing clothes again? He popped off the bed and opened some drawers to have a look at his old garments. They were still there, but he could not remember how you put them on. The socks, for instance, were they worn on the hands or on the feet? He was about to try one of them on his hand, when he had a great adventure. Perhaps the drawer had creaked; at any rate, his mother woke up, for he heard her say "Peter," as if it was the most lovely word in the language. He remained sitting on the floor and held his breath, wondering how she knew that he had come back. If she said "Peter" again, he meant to cry "Mother" and run to her. But she spoke no more, she made little moans only, and when he next peeped at her she was once more asleep, with tears on her face.

It made Peter very miserable, and what do you think was the first thing he did? Sitting on the rail at the foot of the bed, he played a beautiful lullaby to his mother on his pipe. He had made it up himself out of the way she said "Peter," and he never stopped playing until she looked happy.

He thought this so clever of him that he could scarcely resist wakening her to hear her say, "O Peter, how exquisitely you play!" However, as she now seemed comfortable, he again cast looks at the window. You must not think that he meditated flying away and never coming back. He had quite decided to be his mother's boy, but hesitated about beginning tonight. It was the second wish which troubled him. He no longer meant to make it a wish to be a bird, but not to ask for a second wish seemed wasteful, and, of course, he could not ask for it without returning to the fairies. Also, if he put off asking for his wish too long, it might go bad. He asked himself if he had not been hard-hearted to fly away without saying good-bye to Solomon. "I should like awfully to sail in my boat just one more," he said wistfully to his sleeping mother. He quite argued with her as if she could hear him. "It would be so splendid to tell the birds of this adventure," he said coaxingly. "I promise to come back," he said solemnly, and meant it, too.

And in the end, you know, he flew away. Twice he came back from the window, wanting to kiss his mother, but he feared the delight of it might awaken her, so at last he played her a lovely kiss on his pipe, and then he flew back to the Gardens.

Many nights, and even months, passed before he asked the fairies for his second wish; and I am not sure that I quite know why he delayed so long. One reason was that he had so many good-byes to say, not only to his particular friends, but to a hundred favorite spots. Then he had his last sail, and his very last sail, and his last sail of all, and so on. Again, a number of farewell feasts were given in his honor; and another comfort-able reason was that, after all, there was no hurry, for his mother would never weary of waiting for him. This last reason displeased old Solomon, for it was an encouragement to the birds to procrastinate. Solomon had several excellent mottoes for keeping them at their work, such as "Never put off laying today because you can lay tomorrow," and "In this world there are no second chances"; and yet here was Peter gaily putting off and none the worse for it. The birds pointed this out to each other, and fell into lazy habits.

But, mind you, though Peter was so slow in going back to his mother, he was quite decided to go back. The best proof of this was his caution with the fairies. They were most anxious that he should remain in the Gardens to play to them, and to bring this to pass they tried to trick him into making such a remark as "I wish the grass was not so wet," and some of them danced out of time in the hope that he might cry, "I do wish you would keep time!" Then they would have said that this was his second wish. But he smoked their design, and though on occasions he began, "I wish ——" he always stopped in time. So when at last he said to them bravely, "I wish now to go back to mother forever and always," they had to tickle his shoulders and let him go.

He went in a hurry in the end, because he had dreamt that his mother was crying, and he knew what was the great thing she cried for, and that a hug from her splendid Peter would quickly make her to smile. Oh! he felt sure of it, and so eager was he to be nestling in her arms that this time he flew straight to the window, which was always to be open for him.

But the window was closed, and there were iron bars on it, and peering inside he saw his mother sleeping peacefully with her arm around another little boy.

Peter called, "Mother! Mother!" but she heard him not; in vain he beat his little limbs against the iron bars. He had to fly back, sobbing, to the Gardens, and he never saw his dear mother again. What a glorious boy he had meant to be to her! Ah, Peter! we who have made the great mistake, how differently we should all act at the second chance! But Solomon was right — there is no second chance, not for most of us. When we reach the window of it is Lock-Out Time. The iron bars are up for life.

Alice's Adventures in Wonderland

Down the Rabbit-Hole[6]

LEWIS CARROLL

One of the greatest literary fairy tales is that by Lewis Carroll, made up of two distinct stories — Alice's Adventures in Wonderland (1865) and Through the Looking-Glass (1872). These stories differ from most literary fairy tales in that Alice never loses her individuality nor her normal mental processes. She, always herself, knows she is in an odd but magic world; it is this juxtaposition, on the author's part, of realism and fancy that makes these books unusual. The first was written under the title of Alice's Adventures Underground for Professor Liddell's little daughter Alice, at that time one of the author's little friends. When urged to have this story published, Carroll submitted it to George Macdonald (author of The Princess and the Goblin) and his family, who heartily approved of it. Then it was rewritten and added to — "The Mad Hatter's Tea Party" was one added chapter — and published under its present name.

Alice was beginning to get very tired of sitting by her sister on the bank, and of having nothing to do; once or twice she had peeped into the book her sister was reading, but it had no pictures or conversations in it, "and what is the use of a book," thought Alice, "without pictures or conversations?"

So she was considering in her own mind (as well as she could, for the hot day made her feel very sleepy and stupid), whether the pleasure of making a daisy chain would be worth the trouble of getting up and picking the daisies, when suddenly a white rabbit with pink eyes ran close by her.

There was nothing so *very* remarkable in that; nor did Alice think it so *very* much out

6 From Lewis Carroll, *Alice's Adventures in Wonderland.*

of the way to hear the Rabbit say to itself, "Oh dear! Oh dear! I shall be too late!" (when she thought it over afterward, it occurred to her that she ought to have wondered at this, but at the time it all seemed quite natural); but when the Rabbit actually *took a watch out of its waistcoat-pocket,* and looked at it, and then hurried on, Alice started to her feet, for it flashed across her mind that she had never before seen a rabbit with either a waistcoat-pocket or a watch to take out of it, and, burning with curiosity, she ran across the field after it, and was just in time to see it pop down a large rabbit hole under the hedge.

In another moment down went Alice after it, never once considering how in the world she was to get out again.

The rabbit-hole went straight on like a tunnel for some way, and then dipped suddenly down, so suddenly that Alice had not a moment to think about stopping herself before she found herself falling down what seemed to be a very deep well.

Either the well was very deep, or she fell very slowly, for she had plenty of time as she went down to look about her, and to wonder what was going to happen next. First, she tried to look down and make out what she was coming to, but it was too dark to see anything: then she looked at the sides of the well, and noticed that they were filled with cupboards and bookshelves: here and there she saw maps and pictures hung upon pegs. She took down a jar from one of the shelves as she passed; it was labeled "ORANGE MARMALADE," but to her great disappointment it was empty; she did not like to drop the jar for fear of killing somebody underneath, so managed to put it into one of the cupboards as she fell past it.

"Well!" thought Alice to herself, "after such a fall as this, I shall think nothing of tumbling down stairs! How brave they'll all think me at home! Why I wouldn't say anything about it, even if I fell off the top of the house!" (Which was very likely true.)

Down, down, down. Would the fall *never* come to an end? "I wonder how many miles I've fallen by this time?" she said aloud. "I must be getting somewhere near the center of the earth. Let me see: that would be four thousand miles down, I think" (for, you see, Alice had learnt several things of this sort in her lessons in the schoolroom, and though this was not a *very* good opportunity for showing off her knowledge, as there was no one to listen to her, still it was good practice to say it over) "yes, that's about the right distance — but then I wonder what latitude or longitude I've got to?" (Alice had not the slightest idea what latitude was, or longitude either, but she thought they were nice grand words to say.)

Presently she began again: "I wonder if I shall fall right *through* the earth! How funny it'll seem to come out among the people that walk with their heads downwards! The Antipathies, I think" (she was rather glad there *was* no one listening, this time, as it didn't sound at all the right word) "but I shall have to ask them what the name of the country is, you know. Please, ma'am, is this New Zealand or Australia?" (And she tried to curtsey as she spoke — fancy *curtseying* as you're falling through the air! Do you think you could manage it?) "And what an ignorant little girl she'll think me for asking! No, it'll never do to ask: perhaps I shall see it written up somewhere."

Down, down, down. There was nothing else to do, so Alice soon began talking again. "Dinah'll miss me very much tonight, I should think!" (Dinah was the cat.) "I hope they'll remember her saucer of milk at tea-time. Dinah, my dear! I wish you were down here with me! There are no mice in the air, I'm afraid, but you might catch a bat, and that's very like a mouse, you know. But do cats eat bats, I wonder?" And here Alice began to get rather sleepy, and went on saying to herself, in a dreamy sort of way, "Do cats eat bats? Do cats eat bats?" and sometimes, "Do bats eat cats?" for, you see, as she couldn't answer either question, it didn't much matter which way she put it. She felt that she was dozing off, and had just begun to dream that she was walking hand in hand with Dinah, and was saying to her very earnestly, "Now, Dinah, tell me the truth: did you ever eat a bat?" when suddenly, thump! thump! down she came upon a heap of sticks and dry leaves, and the fall was over.

Alice was not a bit hurt, and she jumped up on to her feet in a moment: she looked up, but it was all dark overhead; before her was another long passage, and the White Rabbit was still in sight, hurrying down it. There was not a moment to be lost: away went Alice like the wind, and was just in time to hear it say, as it turned a corner, "Oh, my ears and whiskers, how late it's getting!" She was close behind it when she turned the corner, but the Rabbit was no longer to be seen: she found herself in a long, low hall, which was lit up by a row of lamps hanging from the roof.

There were doors all round the hall, but they were all locked, and when Alice had been all the way down one side and up the other, trying every door, she walked sadly down the middle, wondering how she was ever to get out again.

Suddenly she came upon a little three-legged table, all made of solid glass; there was nothing on it but a tiny golden key, and Alice's first idea was that this might belong to one of the doors of the hall; but, alas! either the locks were too large, or the key was too small, but at any rate it would not open any of them. However, on the second time round, she came upon a low curtain she had not noticed before, and behind it was a little door about fifteen inches high: she tried the little golden key in the lock, and to her great delight it fitted!

Alice opened the door and found it led into a small passage, not much larger than a rat-hole: she knelt down and looked along the passage into the loveliest garden you ever saw. How she longed to get out of that dark hall, and wander about among those beds of bright flowers and those cool fountains, but she could not even get her head through the doorway; "and even if my head would go through," thought poor Alice, "it would be of very little use without my shoulders. Oh, how I wish I could shut up like a telescope! I think I could, if I only knew how to begin." For, you see, so many out-of-the-way things had happened lately that Alice had begun to think that very few things indeed were really impossible.

There seemed to be no use in waiting by the little door, so she went back to the table, half hoping she might find another key on it, or at any rate a book of rules for shutting people up like telescopes: this time she found a little bottle on it ("which certainly was not here before," said Alice) and tied round the neck of the bottle was a paper label with the words "DRINK ME" beautifully printed on it in large letters.

It was all very well to say "Drink me," but the wise little Alice was not going to do *that* in a hurry: "no, I'll look first," she said, "and see whether it's marked '*poison*' or not"; for she had read several nice little stories about children who had got burnt, and eaten up by wild beasts, and other unpleasant things, all because they *would* not remember the simple rules their friends had taught them, such as, that a red-hot poker will burn you if you hold it too long; and that if you cut your finger *very* deeply with a knife, it usually bleeds; and she had never forgotten that, if you drink much from a bottle marked "poison," it is almost certain to disagree with you, sooner or later.

However, this bottle was *not* marked "poison," so Alice ventured to taste it, and finding it very nice (it had, in fact, a sort of mixed flavor of cherry-tart, custard, pineapple, roast turkey, toffy, and hot buttered toast) she very soon finished it off.

*   *   *   *   *
    *   *   *
*   *   *   *

"What a curious feeling!" said Alice, "I must be shutting up like a telescope."

And so it was indeed: she was now only ten inches high, and her face brightened up at the thought that she was now the right size for going through the little door into that lovely garden. First, however, she waited for a few minutes to see if she was going to shrink further: she felt a little nervous about this, "for it might end, you know," said Alice to herself, "in my going out altogether, like a candle. I wonder what I should be like then?" And she tried to fancy what the flame of a candle looks like after the candle is blown out, for she could not remember ever having seen such a thing.

After a while, finding that nothing more happened, she decided on going into the garden at once, but, alas for poor Alice! when she got to the door, she found she had forgotten the little golden key and when she went back to the table for it, she found she could not possibly reach it; she could see it quite plainly through the glass, and she tried her best to climb up one of the legs of the table, but it was too slippery, and when she had tired herself out with trying, the poor little thing sat down and cried.

"Come, there's no use in crying like that!" said Alice to herself, rather sharply, "I advise you to leave off this minute!" She generally gave herself very good advice (though she very seldom followed it) and sometimes she scolded herself so severely as to bring tears into her eyes, and once she remembered trying to box her own ears for having cheated herself in a game of croquet she was playing against herself, for this curious child was very fond of pretending to be two people. "But it's no use now," thought poor Alice, "to pretend to be two people! Why, there's hardly enough of me left to make *one* respectable person!"

Soon her eye fell on a little glass box that was lying under the table: she opened it, and found in it a very small cake, on which the words "EAT ME" were beautifully marked in currants. "Well, I'll eat it," said Alice, "and if it makes me grow larger, I can reach the key; and if it makes me grow smaller, I can creep under the door; so either way I'll get into the garden, and I don't care which happens!"

She ate a little bit, and said anxiously to herself, "Which way? Which way?" holding her hand on the top of her head to feel which way it was growing, and she was quite surprised to find that she remained the same size: to be sure, this is what generally happens when one eats cake, but Alice had got so much into the way of expecting nothing but out-of-the-way things to happen, that it seemed quite dull and stupid for life to go on in the common way.

So she set to work, and very soon finished off the cake.

*   *   *   *
    *   *   *

The Rabbit Sends in a Little Bill[7]

Since we left Alice, at the bottom of the rabbit-hole, she has had many experiences. As she ate too much of the cake, she became very, very tall, and under another charm so short that she had to swim in a pool made by the tears she had previously shed. Rescued from that, she meets a Duck, a Dodo, a Lory, and an Eaglet, and listens to a Mouse's tale. At her inadvertent mention of Dinah, her cat, all Alice's newly found friends quickly disappear and leave her all alone. At this point she hears the patter of footsteps, and hopes it may be the Mouse, coming back to finish his story.

It was the White Rabbit, trotting slowly back again, and looking anxiously about as it went, as if it had lost something; and she heard it muttering to itself, "The Duchess! The Duchess! Oh my dear paws! Oh my fur and whiskers! She'll get me executed, as sure as ferrets are ferrets! Where *can* I have dropped them, I wonder?" Alice guessed in a moment that it was looking for the fan and the pair of white kid gloves, and she good-naturedly began hunting about for them, but they were nowhere to be seen — everything seemed to have changed since her swim in the pool, and the great hall, with the glass table and the little door, had vanished completely.

Very soon the Rabbit noticed Alice, as she went hunting about, and called out to her, in an angry tone, "Why, Mary Ann, what *are* you doing out here? Run home this moment, and fetch me a pair of gloves and a fan! Quick, now!" And Alice was so much frightened that she ran off at once in the direction it pointed to, without trying to explain the mistake that it had made.

"He took me for his housemaid," she said to herself as she ran. "How surprised he'll be when he finds out who I am! But I'd better take him his fan and gloves — that is, if I can find them." As she said this, she came upon a neat little house, on the door of which was a bright brass plate with the name "W. RABBIT" engraved upon it. She went in without knocking, and hurried upstairs,

[7] From Lewis Carroll, *Alice's Adventures in Wonderland.*

in great fear lest she should meet the real Mary Ann, and be turned out of the house before she had found the fan and gloves.

"How queer it seems," Alice said to herself, "to be going messages for a rabbit! I suppose Dinah'll be sending me on messages next!" And she began fancying the sort of thing that would happen: " 'Miss Alice! Come here directly, and get ready for your walk!' 'Coming in a minute, nurse! But I've got to watch this mouse-hole till Dinah comes back, and see that the mouse doesn't get out.' Only I don't think," Alice went on, "that they'd let Dinah stop in the house if it began ordering people about like that!"

By this time she had found her way into a tidy little room with a table in the window, and on it (as she had hoped) a fan and two or three pairs of tiny white kid gloves: she took up the fan and a pair of the gloves, and was just going to leave the room, when her eye fell upon a little bottle that stood near the looking-glass. There was no label this time with the words "DRINK ME," but nevertheless she uncorked it and put it to her lips. "I know *something* interesting is sure to happen," she said to herself, "whenever I eat or drink anything; so I'll just see what this bottle does. I do hope it'll make me grow large again, for really I'm quite tired of being such a tiny little thing!"

It did so indeed, and much sooner than she had expected: before she had drunk half the bottle, she found her head pressing against the ceiling, and had to stoop to save her neck from being broken. She hastily put down the bottle, saying to herself, "That's quite enough — I hope I shan't grow any more — As it is, I can't get out at the door — I do wish I hadn't drunk quite so much!"

Alas! It was too late to wish that! She went on growing, and growing, and very soon had to kneel down on the floor: in another minute there was not even room for this, and she tried the effect of lying down with one elbow against the door, and the other arm curled round her head. Still she went on growing, and, as a last resource, she put one arm out of the window and one foot up the chimney, and said to herself, "Now I can do no more, whatever happens. What *will* become of me?"

Luckily for Alice, the little magic bottle had now had its full effect, and she grew no larger: still it was very uncomfortable, and, as there seemed to be no sort of chance of her ever getting out of the room again, no wonder she felt unhappy.

"It was much pleasanter at home," thought poor Alice, "when one wasn't always growing larger and smaller, and being ordered about by mice and rabbits. I almost wish I hadn't gone down that rabbit-hole — and yet — and yet — it's rather curious, you know, this sort of life! I do wonder what *can* have happened to me! When I used to read fairy tales, I fancied that kind of thing never happened, and now here I am in the middle of one! There ought to be a book written about me, that there ought! And when I grow up, I'll write one — but I'm grown up now," she added in a sorrowful tone: "at least there's no room to grow up any more *here*."

"But then," thought Alice, "shall I *never* get any older than I am now? That'll be a comfort, one way — never to be an old woman — but then — always to have lessons to learn! Oh, I shouldn't like *that!*"

"Oh, you foolish Alice!" she answered herself. "How can you learn lessons in here? Why, there's hardly room for *you*, and no room at all for any lesson-books!"

And so she went on, taking first one side and then the other, and making quite a conversation of it altogether, but after a few minutes she heard a voice outside, and stopped to listen.

"Mary Ann! Mary Ann!" said the voice. "Fetch me my gloves this moment!" Then came a little pattering of feet on the stairs. Alice knew it was the Rabbit coming to look for her, and she trembled till she shook the house, quite forgetting that she was now about a thousand times as large as the Rabbit, and had no reason to be afraid of it.

Presently the Rabbit came up to the door, and tried to open it, but, as the door opened inward, and Alice's elbow was pressed hard against it, that attempt proved a failure. Alice heard it say to itself, Then I'll go round and get in at the window."

"That you won't!" thought Alice, and, after waiting till she fancied she heard the Rabbit just under the window, she suddenly spread out her hand, and made a snatch in the air. She did not get hold of anything, but she heard a little shriek and a fall, and a crash of broken glass, from which she concluded that it was just possible it had fallen into a cucumber-frame, or something of the sort.

Next came an angry voice — the Rabbit's — "Pat! Pat! Where are you?" And then a voice she had never heard before, "Sure then I'm here! Digging for apples, yer honor!"

"Digging for apples, indeed!" said the Rabbit angrily. "Here! Come and help me out of *this!*" (Sounds of more broken glass.)

"Now tell me, Pat, what's that in the window?"

"Sure, it's an arm, yer honor!" (He pronounced it "arrum.")

"An arm, you goose! Who ever saw one that size? Why, it fills the whole window!"

"Sure, it does, yer honor: but it's an arm for all that."

"Well, it's got no business there, at any rate: go and take it away!"

There was a long silence after this, and Alice could only hear whispers now and then; such as "Sure, I don't like it, yer honor, at all, at all!" "Do as I tell you, you coward!" and at last she spread out her hand again, and made another snatch in the air. This time there were *two* little shrieks, and more sounds of broken glass. "What a number of cucumber-frames there must be!" thought Alice. "I wonder what they'll do next! As for pulling me out of the window, I only wish they *could!* I'm sure *I* don't want to stay in here any longer!"

She waited for some time without hearing anything more: at last came a rumbling of little cart-wheels, and the sound of a good many voices all talking together: she made out the words: "Where's the other ladder? — Why, I hadn't to bring but one. Bill's got the other — Bill! Fetch it here, lad! — Here, put 'em at this corner — No, tie 'em together first — they don't reach half high enough yet — Oh, they'll do well enough. Don't be particular — Here, Bill! Catch hold of this rope

— Will the roof bear? — Mind that loose slate — Oh, it's coming down! Heads below!" (a loud crash) — "Now, who did that? — It was Bill, I fancy — Who's to go down the chimney? — Nay, *I* shan't! *You* do it! — *That* I won't, then! — Bill's got to go down — Here, Bill! The master says you've got to go down the chimney!"

"Oh! So Bill's got to come down the chimney, has he?" said Alice to herself. "Why, they seem to put everything upon Bill! I wouldn't be in Bill's place for a good deal; this fireplace is narrow, to be sure; but I *think* I can kick a little!"

She drew her foot as far down the chimney as she could, and waited till she heard a little animal (she couldn't guess of what sort it was) scratching and scrambling about in the chimney close above her: then, saying to herself, "This is Bill," she gave one sharp kick, and waited to see what would happen next.

The first thing she heard was a general chorus of "There goes Bill!" then the Rabbit's voice alone — "Catch him, you by the hedge!" then silence, and then another confusion of voices — "Hold up his head — Brandy now — Don't choke him — How was it, old fellow? What happened to you? Tell us all about it!"

Last came a little feeble, squeaking voice ("That's Bill," thought Alice), "Well, I hardly know — No more, thank ye; I'm better now — but I'm a deal too flustered to tell you — all I know is, something comes at me like a Jack-in-the-box, and up I goes like a sky-rocket!"

"So you did, old fellow!" said the others.

"We must burn the house down!" said the Rabbit's voice. And Alice called out, as loud as she could, "If you do, I'll set Dinah at you!"

There was a dead silence instantly, and Alice thought to herself, "I wonder what they *will* do next! If they had any sense, they'd take the roof off." After a minute or two, they began moving about again, and Alice heard the Rabbit say, "A barrowful will do, to begin with."

"A barrowful of *what?*" thought Alice. But she had not long to doubt, for the next moment a shower of little pebbles came rattling in at the window, and some of them hit her in the face. "I'll put a stop to this," she said to herself, and shouted out, "You'd better not do that again!" which produced another dead silence.

Alice noticed, with some surprise, that the pebbles were all turning into little cakes as they lay on the floor, and a bright idea came into her head. "If I eat one of these cakes," she thought, "it's sure to make *some* change in my size; and, as it can't possibly make me larger, it must make me smaller, I suppose."

So she swallowed one of the cakes, and was delighted to find that she began shrinking directly. As soon as she was small enough to get through the door, she ran out of the house, and found quite a crowd of little animals and birds waiting outside. The poor little lizard, Bill, was in the middle, being held up by two guinea-pigs, who were giving it something out of a bottle. They all made a rush at Alice the moment she appeared; but she ran off as hard as she could, and soon found herself safe in a thick wood.

"The first thing I've got to do," said Alice to herself, as she wandered about in the wood, "is to grow to my right size again; and the second thing is to find my way into that lovely garden. I think that will be the best plan."

It sounded an excellent plan, no doubt, and very neatly and simply arranged; the only difficulty was, that she had not the smallest idea how to set about it; and, while she was peering about anxiously among the trees, a little sharp bark just over her head made her look up in a great hurry.

An enormous puppy was looking down at her with large round eyes, and feebly stretching out one paw, trying to touch her. "Poor little thing!" said Alice, in a coaxing tone, and she tried hard to whistle to it, but she was terribly frightened all the time at the thought that it might be hungry, in which case it would be very likely to eat her up in spite of all her coaxing.

Hardly knowing what she did, she picked up a little bit of stick, and held it out to the puppy: whereupon the puppy jumped into the air off all its feet at once, with a yelp of delight, and rushed at the stick, and made believe to worry it; then Alice dodged behind a great thistle, to keep herself from being run over, and, the moment she appeared on the other side, the puppy made another rush at the stick, and tumbled head over heels in its hurry to get hold of it; then Alice, thinking it was very like having a game of play with a cart-horse, and expecting every moment to be trampled under its feet, ran round the thistle again; then the puppy began a series of short charges at the stick, running a very little way forward each time and a long way back, and barking hoarsely all the while, till at last it sat down a good way off, panting, with its tongue hanging out of its mouth, and its great eyes half-shut.

This seemed to Alice a good opportunity for making her escape, so she set off at once, and ran till she was quite tired and out of breath, and till the puppy's bark sounded quite faint in the distance.

"And yet what a dear little puppy it was!" said Alice, as she leaned against a buttercup to rest herself, and fanned herself with one of the leaves. "I should have liked teaching it tricks very much, if — if I'd only been the right size to do it! Oh dear! I'd nearly forgotten that I've got to grow up again! Let me see — how *is* it to be managed? I suppose I ought to eat or drink something or other; but the great question is 'What?'"

The great question certainly was "What?" Alice looked all round her at the flowers and the blades of grass, but she could not see anything that looked like the right thing to eat or drink under the circumstances. There was a large mushroom growing near her, about the same height as herself; and when she had looked under it, and on both sides of it, and behind it, it occurred to her that she might as well look and see what was on the top of it.

She stretched herself up on tiptoe, and peeped over the edge of the mushroom, and her eyes immediately met those of a large blue caterpillar, that was sitting on the top with its arms folded, quietly smoking a long hookah, and taking not the smallest notice of her or of anything else.

Just So Stories
How the Camel Got His Hump[8]

Rudyard Kipling

Kipling's Just So Stories *should be a part of every child's reading background. They are classic nonsense, and because of the author's magnificent use of words the stories should be read or told "just so."*

Now this is the next tale, and it tells how the Camel got his big hump.

In the beginning of years, when the world was so new and all, and the Animals were just beginning to work for Man, there was a Camel, and he lived in the middle of a Howling Desert because he did not want to work; and besides, he was a Howler himself. So he ate sticks and thorns and tamarisks and milkweed and prickles, most 'scruciating idle; and when anybody spoke to him he said "Humph!" Just "Humph!" and no more.

Presently the Horse came to him on Monday morning, with a saddle on his back and a bit in his mouth, and said, "Camel, O Camel, come out and trot like the rest of us."

"Humph!" said the Camel; and the Horse went away and told the Man.

Presently the Dog came to him, with a stick in his mouth, and said, "Camel, O Camel, come and fetch and carry like the rest of us."

"Humph!" said the Camel; and the Dog went away and told the Man.

Presently the Ox came to him, with the yoke on his neck and said, "Camel, O Camel, come and plough like the rest of us."

"Humph!" said the Camel; and the Ox went away and told the Man.

At the end of the day the Man called the Horse and the Dog and the Ox together, and said, "Three, O Three, I'm very sorry for you (with the world so new-and-all); but that Humph-thing in the Desert can't work, or he would have been here by now, so I am

8 From Rudyard Kipling, *Just So Stories* (Doubleday).

going to leave him alone, and you must work double-time to make up for it."

That made the Three very angry (with the world so new-and-all), and they held a palaver, and an *indaba,* and a *punchayet,* and a pow-wow on the edge of the Desert; and the Camel came chewing milkweed *most* 'scruciating idle, and laughed at them. Then he said "Humph!" and went away again.

Presently there came along the Djinn in charge of All Deserts, rolling in a cloud of dust (Djinns always travel that way because it is Magic), and he stopped to palaver and pow-wow with the Three.

"Djinn of All Deserts," said the Horse, *"is* it right for any one to be idle, with the world so new-and-all?"

"Certainly not," said the Djinn.

"Well," said the Horse, "there's a thing in the middle of your Howling Desert (and he's a Howler himself) with a long neck and long legs, and he hasn't done a stroke of work since Monday morning. He won't trot."

"Whew!" said the Djinn, whistling, "that's my Camel, for all the gold in Arabia! What does he say about it?"

"He says 'Humph!'" said the Dog; "and he won't fetch and carry."

"Does he say anything else?"

"Only 'Humph!'; and he won't plough," said the Ox.

"Very good," said the Djinn. "I'll humph him if you will kindly wait a minute."

The Djinn rolled himself up in his dust-cloak, and took a bearing across the desert, and found the Camel most 'scruciatingly idle, looking at his own reflection in a pool of water.

"My long and bubbling friend," said the Djinn, "what's this I hear of your doing no work, with the world so new-and-all?"

"Humph!" said the Camel.

The Djinn sat down, with his chin in his hand, and began to think a Great Magic, while the Camel looked at his own reflection in the pool of water.

"You've given the Three extra work ever since Monday morning, all on account of your 'scruciating idleness," said the Djinn; and he went on thinking Magics, with his chin in his hand.

"Humph!" said the Camel.

"I shouldn't say that again if I were you," said the Djinn; "you might say it once too often. Bubbles, I want you to work."

And the Camel said "Humph!" again; but no sooner had he said it than he saw his back, that he was so proud of, puffing up and puffing up into a great big lolloping humph.

"Do you see that?" said the Djinn. "That's your very own humph that you've brought upon your very own self by not working. Today is Thursday, and you've done no work since Monday, when the work began. Now you are going to work."

"How can I," said the Camel, "with this humph on my back?"

"That's made a-purpose," said the Djinn, "all because you missed those three days. You will be able to work now for three days without eating, because you can live on your humph; and don't you ever say I never did anything for you. Come out of the Desert and go to the Three, and behave. Humph yourself!"

And the Camel humphed himself, humph and all, and went away to join the Three. And from that day to this the Camel always wears a humph (we call it "hump" now, not to hurt his feelings); but he has never yet caught up with the three days that he missed at the beginning of the world, and he has never yet learned how to behave.

The Story of Doctor Dolittle
The Rarest Animal of All

HUGH LOFTING[9]

⌐ *Lovable Doctor Dolittle gives up his practice among the "best people" of Puddleby-on-the-Marsh, to become a doctor of animals, for he loves them and understands their language. He journeys to Africa and cures the monkeys of a terrible sickness. The following chapter tells how the monkeys, in gratitude, hatch a scheme to help the impoverished doctor make some money.*

[9] From Hugh Lofting, *The Story of Doctor Dolittle* (Lippincott-Stokes, 1920).

Pushmi-pullyus are now extinct. That means, there aren't any more. But long ago, when Doctor Dolittle was alive, there were some of them still left in the deepest jungles of Africa; and even then they were very, very scarce. They had no tail, but a head at each end, and sharp horns on each head. They were very shy and terribly hard to catch. The black men get most of their animals by sneaking up behind them while they are not looking. But you could not do this with the pushmi-pullyu — because, no matter which way you came towards him, he was always facing you. And besides, only one half of him slept at a time. The other head was always awake — and watching. This was why they were never caught and never seen in Zoos. Though many of the greatest huntsmen and the cleverest menagerie-keepers spent years of their lives searching through the jungles in all weathers for pushmi-pullyus, not a single one had ever been caught. Even then, years ago, he was the only animal in the world with two heads.

Well, the monkeys set out hunting for this animal through the forest. And after they had gone a good many miles, one of them found peculiar footprints near the edge of a river; and they knew that a pushmi-pullyu must be very near that spot.

Then they went along the bank of the river a little way and they saw a place where the grass was high and thick; and they guessed that he was in there.

So they all joined hands and made a great circle round the high grass. The pushmi-pullyu heard them coming; and he tried hard to break through the ring of monkeys. But he couldn't do it. When he saw that it was no use trying to escape, he sat down and waited to see what they wanted.

They asked him if he would go with Doctor Dolittle and be put on show in the Land of the White Men.

But he shook both his heads hard and said, "Certainly not!"

They explained to him that he would not be shut up in a menagerie but would just be looked at. They told him that the Doctor was a very kind man but hadn't any money; and people would pay to see a two-headed animal and the Doctor would get rich and

could pay for the boat he had borrowed to come to Africa in.

But he answered, "No. You know how shy I am — I hate being stared at." And he almost began to cry.

Then for three days they tried to persuade him.

And at the end of the third day he said he would come with them and see what kind of a man the Doctor was first.

So the monkeys traveled back with the pushmi-pullyu. And when they came to where the Doctor's little house of grass was, they knocked on the door.

The duck, who was packing the trunk, said, "Come in!"

And Chee-Chee very proudly took the animal inside and showed him to the Doctor.

"What in the world is it?" asked John Dolittle, gazing at the strange creature.

"Lord save us!" cried the duck. "How does it make up its mind?"

"It doesn't look to me as though it had any," said Jip, the dog.

"This, Doctor," said Chee-Chee, "is the pushmi-pullyu — the rarest animal of the African jungles, the only two-headed beast in the world! Take him home with you and your fortune's made. People will pay any money to see him."

"But I don't want any money," said the Doctor.

"Yes, you do," said Dab-Dab, the duck. "Don't you remember how we had to pinch and scrape to pay the butcher's bill in Puddleby? And how are you going to get the sailor the new boat you spoke of — unless we have the money to buy it?"

"I was going to make him one," said the Doctor.

"Oh, do be sensible!" cried Dab-Dab. "Where would you get all the wood and the nails to make one with? — And besides, what are we going to live on? We shall be poorer than ever when we get back. Chee-Chee's perfectly right! Take the funny-looking thing along, do!"

"Well, perhaps there is something in what you say," murmured the Doctor. "It certainly would make a nice new kind of pet. But does the er — what-do-you-call-it really want to go abroad?"

"Yes, I'll go," said the pushmi-pullyu who saw at once, from the Doctor's face, that he was a man to be trusted. "You have been so kind to the animals here — and the monkeys tell me that I am the only one who will do. But you must promise me that if I do not like it in the Land of the White Men you will send me back."

"Why, certainly — of course, of course," said the Doctor. "Excuse me, surely you are related to the Deer Family, are you not?"

"Yes," said the pushmi-pullyu — "to the Abyssinian Gazelles and the Asiatic Chamois — on my mother's side. My father's great-grandfather was the last of the Unicorns."

"Most interesting!" murmured the Doctor; and he took a book out of the trunk which Dab-Dab was packing and began turning the pages. "Let us see if Buffon says anything ——"

"I notice," said the duck, "that you only talk with one of your mouths. Can't the other head talk as well?"

"Oh, yes," said the pushmi-pullyu. "But I keep the other mouth for eating — mostly. In that way I can talk while I am eating without being rude. Our people have always been very polite."

When the packing was finished and everything was ready to start, the monkeys gave a grand party for the Doctor, and all the animals of the jungle came. And they had pineapples and mangoes and honey and all sorts of good things to eat and drink.

After they had all finished eating, the Doctor got up and said,

"My friends: I am not clever at speaking long words after dinner, like some men; and I have just eaten many fruits and much honey. But I wish to tell you that I am very sad at leaving your beautiful country. Because I have things to do in the Land of the White Men, I must go. After I have gone, remember never to let the flies settle on your food before you eat it; and do not sleep on the ground when the rains are coming. I — er — er — I hope you will all live happily ever after."

When the Doctor stopped speaking and sat down, all the monkeys clapped their hands a long time and said to one another, "Let it be remembered always among our people that he sat and ate with us, here, under the trees. For surely he is the Greatest of Men!"

And the Grand Gorilla, who had the strength of seven horses in his hairy arms, rolled a great rock up to the head of the table and said,

"This stone for all time shall mark the spot."

And even to this day, in the heart of the jungle, that stone still is there. And monkey-mothers, passing through the forest with their families, still point down at it from the branches and whisper to their children, "Sh! There it is — look — where the Good White Man sat and ate food with us in the Year of the Great Sickness!"

Then, when the party was over, the Doctor and his pets started out to go back to the seashore. And all the monkeys went with him as far as the edge of their country, carrying his trunk and bags, to see him off.

Rabbit Hill
Little Georgie Sings a Song [1]

ROBERT LAWSON

◄§ Rabbit Hill, *which received the Newbery medal in 1945, is an engaging story of a rabbit family and all the small animals who live on a Connecticut hillside. When Little Georgie, the young rabbit, discovers that New Folks are coming to live in the big house on the hill, all the animals are in a turmoil of excitement. Will the family be "planting folks" and bring back the good old days of gardens and garbage; or will they bring traps and guns and poison? In the chapter given below, Little Georgie is sent to fetch Uncle Analdas, who is old enough to be wise in the ways of men, and who might prove helpful in an emergency. Off goes Little Georgie singing a song that he has made up himself.*

It was barely daylight when Little Georgie started his journey. In spite of her worrying, Mother had managed to put up a small but nourishing lunch. This, along with a letter

[1] From Robert Lawson, *Rabbit Hill* (Viking Press, 1944).

to Uncle Analdas, was packed in a little knapsack and slung over his shoulder. Father went along as far as the Twin Bridges. As they stepped briskly down the Hill, the whole valley was a lake of mist on which rounded treetops swam like floating islands. From old orchards rose a mounting chorus as the birds greeted the new day. Mothers chirped and chuckled and scolded as they swept and tidied the nests. On the topmost branches their menfolk warbled and shrilled and mocked one another.

The houses were all asleep, even the dogs of the Fat-Man-at-the-Crossroads were quiet, but the Little Animals were up and about. They met the Gray Fox returning from a night up Weston way. He looked footsore and sleepy and a few chicken feathers still clung to his ruff. The Red Buck trotted daintily across the Black Road to wish them good luck and good morning, but Father, for once, had no time for long social conversation. This was Business, and no rabbit in the county knew his business any better than Father — few as well.

"Now, Son," he said firmly, "your mother is in a very nervous state and you are not to add to her worries by taking unnecessary risks or by carelessness. No dawdling and no foolishness. Keep close to the road but well off it. Watch your bridges and your crossings. What do you do when you come to a bridge?"

"I hide well," answered Georgie, "and wait a good long time. I look all around for dogs. I look up the road for cars and down the road for cars. When everything's clear, I run across — fast. I hide again and look around to be sure I've not been seen. Then I go on. The same thing for crossings."

"Good," said Father. "Now recite your dogs."

Little Georgie closed his eyes and dutifully recited: "Fat-Man-at-the-Crossroads: two Mongrels — Good Hill Road: Dalmatian House on Long Hill: Collie, noisy, no wind — Norfield Church corner: Police Dog, stupid, no nose — On the High Ridge, red farmhouse: Bulldog and Setter, both fat, don't bother — Farmhouse with the big barns: Old Hound, very dangerous ——" and

so on he recited every dog on the route clear up to Danbury way. He did it without a mistake and swelled with pride at Father's approving nod.

"Excellent," said Father. "Now do you remember your checks and doublings?" Little Georgie closed his eyes again and rattled off, quite fast, "Sharp right and double left, double left and double right, dead stop and back flip, right jump, left jump, false trip and briar dive."

"Splendid," said Father. "Now attend carefully. Size up your dog; don't waste speed on a plodder, you may need it later. If he's a rusher, check, double, and freeze. Your freeze, by the way, is still rather bad. You have a tendency to flick your left ear, you must watch that. The High Ridge is very open country, so keep in the shadow of the stone walls and mark the earth piles. Porkey has lots of relatives along there and if you are pressed hard, any of them will gladly take you in. Just tell them who you are, and don't forget to thank them. After a chase, hide up and take at least ten minutes' rest. And if you have to *really* run, tighten that knapsack strap, lace back your ears, put your stomach to the ground, and RUN!

"Get along with you now and mind — no foolishness. We shall expect you and Uncle Analdas by tomorrow evening at the latest."

Little Georgie crossed the Twin Bridges in perfect form, returned Father's approving wave, and was off, on his own.

It was gray and misty as he crossed Good Hill Road, and the Dalmatian still slept. So, apparently, did the Collie up the road, for all was quiet as he plodded up Long Hill. People were beginning to stir as he approached Norfield Church corner, little plumes of blue smoke were rising from kitchen chimneys, and the air was pleasant with the smell of frying bacon.

As he expected, the Police Dog rushed him there, but he wasted little time on that affair. Loping along with tantalizing slowness until they were almost on an old fallen apple tree buried in briars, he executed a dead stop, a right jump, and a freeze. The bellowing brute overran him, and plunged headlong into the thorny tangle. His agonized howls were sweet music to Little Georgie as he hopped sedately along toward the High Ridge. He wished Father had been there to see how skillfully he had worked and to note that during the freeze his left ear hadn't flickered once.

The sun was well up when he emerged on the High Ridge. On the porch of the Red Farmhouse the fat Bulldog and the Setter slept soundly, soaking up its warmth. On any other occasion Little Georgie would have been tempted to wake them to enjoy their silly efforts at running, but mindful of Father's instructions he kept dutifully on his way.

The High Ridge was a long and open strip of country, very uninteresting to Little Georgie. The view, over miles and miles of rolling woods and meadows, was very beautiful, but he didn't care especially about views. The brilliant blue sky and the bright little cream-puff clouds were beautiful too. They made him feel good, so did the warm sun, but frankly he was becoming slightly bored. So to ease his boredom he began to make a little song.

The words had been rattling round in his head for some days now and the music was there too, but he couldn't quite get them straight and fitted together. So he hummed and he sang and he whistled. He tried the words this way and that way, he stopped and started and changed the notes around, and finally he got the first line so that it suited him. So Georgie sang that line over and over again to be sure that he wouldn't forget it when he started on the second line.

It must have been this preoccupation with his song that made Little Georgie careless and almost led to his undoing. He scarcely noticed that he had passed the house with the big barns, and he was just starting to sing his first line for the forty-seventh time when there came the roaring rush of the Old Hound right on his heels, so close that he could feel the hot breath.

Instinctively Little Georgie made several wild springs that carried him temporarily out of harm's way. He paused a fraction of a second to tighten the knapsack strap and then set off at a good steady pace. "Don't waste speed on a plodder" was Father's

rule. He tried a few checks and doubles and circlings, although he knew they were pretty useless. The great fields were too bare and the Old Hound knew all the tricks. No matter how he turned and dodged, the Hound was always there, coming along at his heavy gallop. He looked for woodchuck burrows, but there were none in sight. "Well, I guess I'll have to run it out," said Little Georgie.

He pulled the knapsack strap tighter, laced back his ears, put his stomach to the ground, and RAN. And *how* he ran!

The warm sun had loosened his muscles, the air was invigorating, Little Georgie's leaps grew longer and longer. Never had he felt so young and strong. His legs were like coiled springs of steel that released themselves of their own accord. He was hardly conscious of any effort, only of his hind feet pounding the ground, and each time they hit, those wonderful springs released and shot him through the air. He sailed over fences and stone walls as though they were mole runs. Why, this was almost like flying! Now he understood what Zip the Swallow had been driving at when he tried to describe what it was like. He glanced back at the Old Hound, far behind now, but still coming along at his plodding gallop. He was old and must be tiring while he, Little Georgie, felt stronger and more vigorous at every leap. Why didn't the old fool give up and go home?

And then, as he shot over the brow of a slight rise, he suddenly knew. *He had forgotten Deadman's Brook!* There it lay before him, broad and deep, curving out in a great silvery loop. He, the son of Father, gentleman hunter from the Bluegrass, had been driven into a trap, a trap that even Porkey should have been able to avoid! Whether he turned to right or left, the loop of the creek hemmed him in and the Old Hound could easily cut him off. There was nothing for it but to jump!

This sickening realization had not reduced his speed; now he redoubled it. The slope helped and his soaring leaps became prodigious. The wind whistled through his laced-back ears. Still he kept his head, as Father would have wished him to. He picked a spot where the bank was high and firm; he spaced his jumps so they would come out exactly right.

The take-off was perfect. He put every ounce of leg muscle into that final kick and sailed out into space. Below him he could see the cream-puff clouds mirrored in the dark water; he could see the pebbles on the bottom and the silver flash of frightened minnows, dashing away from his flying shadow. Then, with a breath-taking thump, he landed, turned seven somersaults, and came up sitting in a clump of soft lush grass.

He froze, motionless except for heaving sides, and watched the Old Hound come thundering down the slope, slide to a stop and, after eyeing the water disgustedly, take his way slowly homeward, his dripping tongue almost dragging the ground.

Little Georgie did not need to remember Father's rule for a ten-minute rest after a good run. He was blown and he knew it, but he did remember his lunch, so he unstrapped the little knapsack and combined lunch and rest. He had been really scared for a moment, but as his wind came back and his lunch went down, his spirits came up.

Father would be angry, and rightly, for he had made two very stupid mistakes: he had let himself be surprised and he had run right into a dangerous trap. But that leap! Never in the history of the county had any rabbit jumped Deadman's Brook, not even Father. He marked the exact spot and calculated the width of the stream there — at least eighteen feet! And with his rising spirits the words and the notes of his song suddenly tumbled into place.

Little Georgie lay back in the warm grass and sang his song —

> New Folks coming, Oh my!
> New Folks coming, Oh my!
> New Folks coming, Oh my!
> Oh my! Oh my!

There weren't many words and there weren't many notes, and the notes just went up a little and down a little and ended where they began. Lots of people might have thought it monotonous, but it suited Little Georgie completely. He sang it loud

and he sang it soft, he sang it as a paean of triumph, a saga of perils met and overcome. He sang it over and over again.

Red-Bellied Robin, flying northward, paused in a sapling and called down, "Hi, Little Georgie, what're you doing way up here?"

"Going to fetch Uncle Analdas. Have you been by the Hill?"

"Just left there," Robin answered. "Everybody's excited. Seems there's new Folks coming."

"Yes, I know," cried Little Georgie eagerly. "I've just made a song about it. Wouldn't you like to hear it? It goes like ——"

"No, thanks," called Robin. "Getting along ——" and flew on.

Not in the least discouraged, Little Georgie sang his song a few times more while he strapped on his knapsack and took up his journey. It was a good song to walk to, too, so he sang it as he tramped the rest of the High Ridge, as he went down the Windy Hill and circled around Georgetown. He was still singing it in the late afternoon when he got clear up Danbury way.

He had just finished "Oh my!" for the four thousandth time when a sharp voice from the bushes broke in with "Oh my — *whut?*"

Little Georgie whirled. "Oh my — *goodness!*" he cried. "Why — why, it's Uncle Analdas."

"Sure is," the voice chuckled. "Uncle Analdas as ever was. Come in, Little Georgie, come in — you're a long way from home. Ef I'd been a dog, I'd got you. Surprised yer Old Man ain't learned you more care — come in, anyhow."

Although Mother had worried about the state of Uncle Analdas's home with no feminine hands around to keep things neat, she could never, in her most pessimistic moments, have pictured anything quite so disorderly as the burrow to which Little Georgie was welcomed.

It was a man's home, there could be no doubt about that, and while Little Georgie rather admired the bachelor freedom of the place, he was forced to admit that it really was extremely dirty and the fleas numerous and active. After his day in the open air, the atmosphere indoors seemed stifling and not at all fragrant. Perhaps it was the sort of tobacco that Uncle Analdas smoked — Little Georgie hoped so. His Uncle's cooking too left something to be desired — their supper consisted of one very ancient and dried-up turnip. After this meager meal, they sat outside, at Little Georgie's suggestion, and Mother's letter was produced.

"S'pose you read it to me, Georgie," said Uncle Analdas. "Seem to've mislaid them dingblasted spectacles." Little Georgie knew that he hadn't mislaid them, in fact that he didn't own any; he'd just never learned to read, but this formality always had to be gone through with, so he dutifully read:

Dear Uncle Analdas:

I hope this finds you well but I know you are lonesome with Mildred married and gone away and all and we are hoping you will spend the summer with us, as we have new Folks coming and we hope they are planting Folks and if they are we will all eat good but they may have dogs or poison or traps and spring-guns and maybe you shouldn't risk your life although you haven't much of it left but we will be looking forward to seeing you anyway.

Your loving niece,
Mollie.

There was a postscript which said, "P.S. Please don't let Little Georgie get his feet wet," but Georgie didn't read that out loud. The idea! He, Little Georgie, who had jumped Deadman's Brook, Little Georgie the Leaper, getting his feet wet!

"Well, now," cried Uncle Analdas. "Well, now, that's a real nice letter, real nice. Don't know but what I will. Certainly is dingblasted lonesome 'round here now, with Millie gone and all. And as for food —— Of all the carrot-pinchin', stingy folks I ever see, the folks around here is the stingiest, carrot-pinchin'est. Yes sir, I think I will. 'Course new Folks coming may be good and it may be bad. Either way I don't trust 'em. Don't trust old Folks neither. But with old Folks you kin tell just how much you *can't* trust 'em and with new Folks you can't tell *nothing.* Think I'll do it though, think I will. Does yer Maw still make that peavine and lettuce soup as good as she used to?"

Little Georgie assured him that she still did and wished he had a bowl of it right then. "I've made up a song about the new Folks," he added eagerly. "Would you like to hear it?"

"Don't think I would," answered Uncle Analdas. "Sleep anywheres you've a mind to, Georgie. I've got a few knickknacks to pack up and we'd ought to get an early start. I'll wake you."

Little Georgie decided to sleep outside under the bushes. The evening was quite warm and the burrow was really pretty strong. He hummed his song, as a lullaby now, and it was a good lullaby, for before he'd finished it the third time he was sound asleep.

The Wind in the Willows
The Wild Wood [2]

KENNETH GRAHAME

When Kenneth Grahame was asked why he wrote for children, among other reasons he gave was this: "Children are not merely people; they are the only really living people that have been left to us in an over-weary world." As for writing about animals in The Wind in the Willows, *he said: "Every animal, by instinct, lives according to his nature. Thereby he lives wisely, and betters the tradition of mankind. . . . Every animal is true — is, therefore, according to his nature both beautiful and good."*

The Wind in the Willows *was written or told as bedtime stories for Kenneth Grahame's small son, affectionately known in the family as "Mouse." To understand this chapter better, the reader must know that Mole had recently made the acquaintance of Water Rat, who had introduced him to Mr. Toad and had warned him against the dangers of the Wild Wood. But when Mole also wished to know Mr. Badger, the Rat said Mr. Badger was a recluse and hard to meet. This chapter reveals what adventures Mole had in the Wild Wood, adventures which led him to Mr. Badger's door.*

The Mole had long wanted to make the acquaintance of the Badger. He seemed, by

[2] From Kenneth Grahame, *The Wind in the Willows* (Scribner, 1908).

all accounts, to be such an important personage and, though rarely visible, to make his unseen influence felt by everybody about the place. But whenever the Mole mentioned his wish to the Water Rat, he always found himself put off. "It's all right," the Rat would say. "Badger'll turn up some day or other — he's always turning up — and then I'll introduce you. The best of fellows! But you must not only take him *as* you find him, but *when* you find him."

"Couldn't you ask him here — dinner or something?" said the Mole.

"He wouldn't come," replied the Rat simply. "Badger hates Society, and invitations, and dinner, and all that sort of thing."

"Well, then, supposing we go and call on *him?*" suggested the Mole.

"O, I'm sure he wouldn't like that at *all*," said the Rat, quite alarmed. "He's so very shy, he'd be sure to be offended. I've never even ventured to call on him at his own home myself, though I know him so well. Besides, we can't. It's quite out of the question, because he lives in the very middle of the Wild Wood."

"Well, supposing he does," said the Mole. "You told me the Wild Wood was all right, you know."

"O, I know, I know, so it is," replied the Rat evasively. "But I think we won't go there just now. Not *just* yet. It's a long way, and he wouldn't be at home at this time of year, anyhow, and he'll be coming along some day, if you'll wait quietly."

The Mole had to be content with this. But the Badger never came along, and every day brought its amusements, and it was not till summer was long over, and cold and frost and miry ways kept them much indoors, and the swollen river raced past outside their windows with a speed that mocked at boating of any sort or kind, that he found his thoughts dwelling again with much persistence on the solitary gray Badger, who lived his own life by himself, in his hole in the middle of the Wild Wood.

In the wintertime the Rat slept a great deal, retiring early and rising late. During his short day he sometimes scribbled poetry or did other small domestic jobs about the house; and, of course, there were always animals dropping in for a chat, and consequently there was a good deal of story-telling and comparing notes on the past summer and all its doings.

Such a rich chapter it had been, when one came to look back on it all! With illustrations so numerous and so very highly colored! The pageant of the river bank had marched steadily along, unfolding itself in scene-pictures that succeeded each other in stately procession. Purple loosestrife arrived early shaking luxuriant tangled locks along the edge of the mirror whence its own face laughed back at it. Willow-herb, tender and wistful, like a pink sunset cloud, was not slow to follow. Confrey, the purple hand-in-hand with the white, crept forth to take its place in the line; and at last one morning the diffident and delaying dog-rose stepped delicately on the stage, and one knew, as if string-music had announced it in stately chords that strayed into a gavotte, that June at last was here. One member of the company was still awaited; the shepherd-boy for the nymphs to woo, the knight for whom the ladies waited at the window, the prince that was to kiss the sleeping summer back to life and love. But when meadow-sweet, debonair and odorous in amber jerkin, moved graciously to his place in the group, then the play was ready to begin.

And what a play it had been! Drowsy animals, snug in their holes while wind and rain were battering at their doors, recalled still, keen mornings, an hour before sunrise, when the white mist, as yet undispersed, clung closely along the surface of the water; then the shock of the early plunge, the scamper along the bank, and the radiant transformation of earth, air, and water, when suddenly the sun was with them again, and gray was gold and color was born and sprang out of the earth once more. They recalled the languorous siesta of hot midday, deep in green undergrowth, the sun striking through in tiny golden shafts and spots; the boating and bathing of the afternoon, the rambles along dusty lanes and through yellow cornfields; and the long, cool evening at last, when so many threads were gathered up, so many friendships rounded, and so many adventures planned for the morrow. There was plenty to talk about on those short winter days when the animals found themselves round the fire; still, the Mole had a good deal of spare time on his hands, and so one afternoon, when the Rat in his armchair before the blaze was alternately dozing and trying over rhymes that wouldn't fit, he formed the resolution to go out by himself and explore the Wild Wood, and perhaps strike up an acquaintance with Mr. Badger.

It was a cold, still afternoon with a hard, steely sky overhead, when he slipped out of the warm parlor into the open air. The country lay bare and entirely leafless around him, and he thought that he had never seen so far and so intimately into the insides of things as on that winter day when Nature was deep in her annual slumber and seemed to have kicked the clothes off. Copses, dells, quarries, and all hidden places, which had been mysterious mines for exploration in leafy summer, now exposed themselves and their secrets pathetically, and seemed to ask him to overlook their shabby poverty for a while, till they could riot in rich masquerade as before, and trick and entice him with the old deceptions. It was pitiful in a way, and yet cheering — even exhilarating. He was glad that he liked the country undecorated, hard, and stripped of its finery. He had got down to the bare bones of it, and they were fine and strong and simple. He did not want the warm clover and the play of seeding grasses; the screens of quickset, the billowy drapery of beech and elm seemed best away; and with great cheerfulness of spirit he pushed on toward the Wild Wood, which lay before him low and threatening, like a black reef in some still, southern sea.

There was nothing to alarm him at first entry. Twigs crackled under his feet, logs tripped him, funguses on stumps resembled caricatures, and startled him for the moment by their likeness to something familiar and far away; but that was all fun, and exciting. It led him on, and he penetrated to where the light was less, and trees crouched nearer and nearer, and holes made ugly mouths at him on either side.

Everything was very still now. The dusk advanced on him steadily, rapidly, gathering in behind and before; and the light seemed to be draining away like flood-water.

Then the faces began.

It was over his shoulder, and indistinctly, that he first thought he saw a face, a little, evil, wedge-shaped face, looking out at him from a hole. When he turned and confronted it, the thing had vanished.

He quickened his pace, telling himself cheerfully not to begin imagining things or there would be simply no end to it. He passed another hole, and another, and another; and then — yes! — no! — yes! certainly a little, narrow face, with hard eyes, had flashed up for an instant from a hole, and was gone. He hesitated — braced himself up for an effort and strode on. Then suddenly, and as if it had been so all the time, every hole, far and near, and there were hundreds of them, seemed to possess its face, coming and going rapidly, all fixing on him glances of malice and hatred: all hard-eyed and evil and sharp.

If he could only get away from the holes in the banks, he thought, there would be no more faces. He swung off the path and plunged into the untrodden places of the wood.

Then the whistling began.

Very faint and shrill it was, and far behind him, when first he heard it; but somehow it made him hurry forward. Then, still very faint and shrill, it sounded far ahead of him, and made him hesitate and want to go back. As he halted in indecision, it broke out on either side, and seemed to be caught up and passed on throughout the whole length of the wood to its farthest limit. They were up and alert and ready, evidently, whoever they were! And he — he was alone, and unarmed, and far from any help; and the night was closing in.

Then the pattering began.

He thought it was only falling leaves at first, so slight and delicate was the sound of it. Then as it grew it took a regular rhythm, and he knew it for nothing else but the pat-pat-pat of little feet still a very long way off. Was it in front or behind? It seemed to be first one, and then the other, then both. It grew and it multiplied, till from every quarter as he listened anxiously, leaning this way and that, it seemed to be closing in on him. As he stood still to hearken, a rabbit came running hard toward him through the trees. He waited, expecting it to slacken pace or to swerve from him into a different course. Instead, the animal almost brushed him as it dashed past, his face set and hard, his eyes staring. "Get out of this, you fool, get out!" the Mole heard him mutter as he swung round a stump and disappeared down a friendly burrow.

The pattering increased till it sounded like sudden hail on the dry leaf-carpet spread around him. The whole wood seemed running now, running hard, hunting, chasing, closing in round something or — somebody? In panic, he began to run too, aimlessly, he knew not whither. He ran up against things, he fell over things and into things, he darted under things and dodged round things. At last he took refuge in the deep, dark hollow of an old beech tree, which offered shelter, concealment — perhaps even safety, but who could tell? Anyhow, he was too tired to run any farther, and could only snuggle down into the dry leaves which had drifted into the hollow and hope he was safe for a time. And as he lay there panting and trembling, and listened to the whistlings and the patterings outside, he knew it at last, in all its fullness, that dread thing which other little dwellers in field and hedgerow had encountered here, and known as their darkest moment — that thing which the Rat had vainly tried to shield him from — the Terror of the Wild Wood!

Meantime the Rat, warm and comfortable, dozed by his fireside. His paper of half-finished verses slipped from his knee, his head fell back, his mouth opened, and he wandered by the verdant banks of dream-rivers. Then a coal slipped, the fire crackled and sent up a spurt of flame, and he woke with a start. Remembering what he had been engaged upon, he reached down to the floor for his verses, pored over them for a minute, and then looked round for the Mole to ask him if he knew a good rhyme for something or other.

But the Mole was not there.

He listened for a time. The house seemed very quiet.

Then he called "Moly!" several times, and, receiving no answer, got up and went out into the hall.

The Mole's cap was missing from its accustomed peg. His goloshes, which always lay by the umbrella-stand, were also gone.

The Rat left the house, and carefully examined the muddy surface of the ground outside, hoping to find the Mole's tracks. There they were, sure enough. The goloshes were new, just bought for the winter, and the pimples on their soles were fresh and sharp. He could see the imprints of them in the mud, running along straight and purposeful, leading direct to the Wild Wood.

The Rat looked very grave, and stood in deep thought for a minute or two. Then he re-entered the house, strapped a belt round his waist, shoved a brace of pistols into it, took up a stout cudgel that stood in a corner of the hall, and set off for the Wild Wood at a smart pace.

It was already getting toward dusk when he reached the first fringe of trees and plunged without hesitation into the wood, looking anxiously on either side for any sign of his friend. Here and there wicked little faces popped out of holes, but vanished immediately at sight of the valorous animal, his pistols, and the great ugly cudgel in his grasp; and the whistling and pattering, which he had heard quite plainly on his first entry, died away and ceased, and all was very still. He made his way manfully through the length of the wood, to its farthest edge; then, forsaking all paths, he set himself to traverse it, laboriously working over the whole ground, and all the time calling out cheerfully, "Moly, Moly, Moly! Where are you? It's me — it's old Rat!"

He had patiently hunted through the wood for an hour or more, when at last to his joy he heard a little answering cry. Guiding himself by the sound, he made his way through the gathering darkness to the foot of an old beech tree, with a hole in it, and from out of the hole came a feeble voice, saying, "Ratty! Is that really you?"

The Rat crept into the hollow, and there he found the Mole, exhausted and still trembling. "O Rat!" he cried, "I've been so frightened, you can't think!"

"O, I quite understand," said the Rat soothingly. "You shouldn't really have gone and done it, Mole. I did my best to keep you from it. We river-bankers, we hardly ever come here by ourselves. If we have to come, we come in couples at least; then we're generally all right. Besides, there are a hundred things one has to know, which we understand all about and you don't, as yet. I mean passwords, and signs, and sayings which have power and effect, and plants you carry in your pocket, and verses you repeat, and dodges and tricks you practice; all simple enough when you know them, but they've got to be known if you're small, or you'll find yourself in trouble. Of course, if you were Badger or Otter, it would be quite another matter."

"Surely the brave Mr. Toad wouldn't mind coming here by himself, would he?" inquired the Mole.

"Old Toad?" said the Rat, laughing heartily. "He wouldn't show his face here alone, not for a whole hatful of golden guineas, Toad wouldn't."

The Mole was greatly cheered by the sound of the Rat's careless laughter, as well as by the sight of his stick and his gleaming pistols, and he stopped shivering and began to feel bolder and more himself again.

"Now, then," said the Rat presently, "we really must pull ourselves together and make a start for home while there's still a little light left. It will never do to spend the night here, you understand. Too cold, for one thing."

"Dear Ratty," said the poor Mole, "I'm dreadfully sorry, but I'm simply dead beat and that's a solid fact. You *must* let me rest here a while longer, and get my strength back, if I'm to get home at all."

"O, all right," said the good-natured Rat, "rest away. It's pretty nearly pitch-dark now, anyhow; and there ought to be a bit of a moon later."

So the Mole got well into the dry leaves and stretched himself out, and presently dropped off into sleep, though of a broken and troubled sort; while the Rat covered himself up, too, as best he might, for warmth, and lay patiently waiting, with a pistol in his paw.

When at last the Mole woke up, much refreshed and in his usual spirits, the Rat said, "Now, then! I'll just take a look outside and see if everything's quiet, and then we really must be off."

He went to the entrance of their retreat and put his head out. Then the Mole heard him saying quietly to himself, "Hullo! hullo! here — *is* — a — go!"

"What's up, Ratty?" asked the Mole.

"*Snow* is up," replied the Rat briefly; "or rather, *down*. It's snowing hard."

The Mole came and crouched beside him, and, looking out, saw the wood that had been so dreadful to him in quite a changed aspect. Holes, hollows, pools, pitfalls, and other black menaces to the wayfarer were vanishing fast, and a gleaming carpet of faery was springing up everywhere, that looked too delicate to be trodden upon by rough feet. A fine powder filled the air and caressed the cheek with a tingle in its touch, and the black holes of the trees showed up in a light that seemed to come from below.

"Well, well, it can't be helped," said the Rat, after pondering. "We must make a start, and take our chance, I suppose. The worst of it is, I don't exactly know where we are. And now this snow makes everything look so very different."

It did indeed. The Mole would not have known that it was the same wood. However, they set out bravely, and took the line that seemed most promising, holding on to each other and pretending with invincible cheerfulness that they recognized an old friend in every fresh tree that grimly and silently greeted them, or saw openings, gaps, or paths with a familiar turn in them, in the monotony of white space and black tree-trunks that refused to vary.

An hour or two later — they had lost all count of time — they pulled up, dispirited, weary, and hopelessly at sea, and sat down on a fallen tree-trunk to recover their breath and consider what was to be done. They were aching with fatigue and bruised with tumbles; they had fallen into several holes and got wet through; the snow was getting so deep that they could hardly drag their little legs through it, and the trees were thicker and more like each other than ever. There seemed to be no end to this wood, and no beginning, and no difference in it, and, worst of all, no way out.

"We can't sit here very long," said the Rat. "We shall have to make another push for it, and do something or other. The cold is too awful for anything, and the snow will soon be too deep for us to wade through." He peered about him and considered. "Look here," he went on, "this is what occurs to me. There's a sort of dell down here in front of us, where the ground seems all hilly and humpy and hummocky. We'll make our way down into that, and try and find some sort of shelter, a cave or hole with a dry floor to it, out of the snow and the wind, and there we'll have a good rest before we try again, for we're both of us pretty dead beat. Besides, the snow may leave off, or something may turn up."

So once more they got on their feet, and struggled down into the dell, where they hunted about for a cave or some corner that was dry and a protection from the keen wind and the whirling snow. They were investigating one of the hummocky bits the Rat had spoken of, when suddenly the Mole tripped up and fell forward on his face with a squeal.

"O my leg!" he cried. "O my poor shin!" and he sat up on the snow and nursed his leg in both his front paws.

"Poor old Mole!" said the Rat kindly. "You don't seem to be having much luck today, do you? Let's have a look at the leg. Yes," he went on, going down on his knees to look, "you've cut your shin, sure enough. Wait till I get at my handkerchief, and I'll tie it up for you."

"I must have tripped over a hidden branch or a stump," said the Mole miserably. "O my! O my!"

"It's a very clean cut," said the Rat, examining it again attentively. "That was never done by a branch or a stump. Looks as if it was made by a sharp edge of something in metal. Funny!" He pondered awhile, and examined the humps and slopes that surrounded them.

"Well, never mind what done it," said the Mole, forgetting his grammar in his pain. "It hurts just the same, whatever done it."

But the Rat, after carefully tying up the leg with his handkerchief, had left him and was busy scraping in the snow. He scratched and shoveled and explored, all four legs working busily, while the Mole waited impatiently, remarking at intervals, "O, *come* on, Rat!"

Suddenly the Rat cried "Hooray!" and then "Hooray-oo-ray-oo-ray-oo-ray!" and fell to executing a feeble jig in the snow.

"What *have* you found, Ratty?" asked the Mole, still nursing his leg.

"Come and see!" said the delighted Rat, as he jigged on.

The Mole hobbled up to the spot and had a good look.

"Well," he said at last, slowly, "I *see* it right enough. Seen the same sort of thing before, lots of times. Familiar object, I call it. A door-scraper! Well, what of it? Why dance jigs around a door-scraper?"

"But don't you see what it *means,* you — you dull-witted animal?" cried the Rat impatiently.

"Of course I see what it means," replied the Mole. "It simply means that some *very* careless and forgetful person has left his door-scraper lying about in the middle of the Wild Wood, *just* where it's *sure* to trip *everybody* up. Very thoughtless of him, I call it. When I get home I shall go and complain about it to — to somebody or other, see if I don't!"

"O dear! O dear!" cried the Rat, in despair at his obtuseness. "Here, stop arguing and come and scrape!" And he set to work again and made the snow fly in all directions around him.

After some further toil his efforts were rewarded, and a very shabby door-mat lay exposed to view.

"There, what did I tell you?" exclaimed the Rat in great triumph.

"Absolutely nothing whatever," replied the Mole, with perfect truthfulness. "Well, now," he went on, "you seem to have found another piece of domestic litter, done for and thrown away, and I suppose you're perfectly happy. Better go ahead and dance your jig round that if you've got to, and get it over, and then perhaps we can go on and not waste any more time over rubbish-heaps. Can we *eat* a door-mat? Or sleep under a door-mat?

Or sit on a door-mat and sledge home over the snow on it, you exasperating rodent?"

"Do — you — mean — to — say," cried the excited Rat, "that this door-mat doesn't *tell* you anything?"

"Really, Rat," said the Mole, quite pettishly, "I think we've had enough of this folly. Who ever heard of a door-mat *telling* anyone anything? They simply don't do it. They are not that sort at all. Door-mats know their place."

"Now look here, you — you thick-headed beast," replied the Rat, really angry, "this must stop. Not another word, but scrape — scrape and scratch and dig and hunt round, especially on the sides of the hummocks, if you want to sleep dry and warm tonight, for it's our last chance!"

The Rat attacked a snow-bank beside them with ardor, probing with his cudgel everywhere and then digging with fury; and the Mole scraped busily too, more to oblige the Rat than for any other reason, for his opinion was that his friend was getting lightheaded.

Some ten minutes' hard work, and the point of the Rat's cudgel struck something that sounded hollow. He worked till he could get a paw through and feel; then called the Mole to come and help him. Hard at it went the two animals, till at last the result of their labors stood full in view of the astonished and hitherto incredulous Mole.

In the side of what had seemed to be a snowbank stood a solid-looking little door, painted a dark green. An iron bell-pull hung by the side, and below it, on a small brass plate, neatly engraved in square capital letters, they could read by the aid of moonlight,

MR. BADGER

The Mole fell backwards on the snow from sheer surprise and delight. "Rat!" he cried in penitence, "you're a wonder! A real wonder, that's what you are. I see it all now! You argued it out, step by step, in that wise head of yours, from the very moment that I fell and cut my shin, and you looked at the cut, and at once your majestic mind said to itself, 'Door-scraper!' And then you turned to and found the very door-scraper that done it! Did you stop there? No. Some people

would have been quite satisfied; but not you. Your intellect went on working. 'Let me only just find a door-mat,' says you to yourself, 'and my theory is proved!' And of course you found your door-mat. You're so clever, I believe you could find anything you liked. 'Now,' says you, 'that door exists, as plain as if I saw it. There's nothing else remains to be done but to find it!' Well, I've read about that sort of thing in books, but I've never come across it before in real life. You ought to go where you'll be properly appreciated. You're simply wasted here, among us fellows. If I only had your head, Ratty ——"

"But as you haven't," interrupted the Rat, rather unkindly, "I suppose you're going to sit on the snow all night and *talk*? Get up at once and hang on to that bell-pull you see there, and ring hard, as hard as you can, while I hammer!"

While the Rat attacked the door with his stick, the Mole sprang up at the bell-pull, clutched it and swung there, both feet well off the ground, and from quite a long way off they could faintly hear a deep-toned bell respond.

The Little Prince[3]
(A Selection)

ANTOINE DE SAINT-EXUPÉRY

❧ *In reviewing* The Little Prince, *Anne Carroll Moore referred to it as "a book so fresh and different, so original yet so infused with wisdom as to take a new place among books in general."*

The Little Prince lived alone on a tiny planet. He owned a flower of great beauty and of inordinate pride. It was this pride that ruined the serenity of the Little Prince's world and started him on his travels that brought him to the earth.

In the following chapter he is in the African desert, far from his planet and the things he loved. From a fox he learns the secret of what is really important in life.

It was then that the fox appeared.

"Good morning," said the fox.

[3] From Antoine de Saint-Exupéry, *The Little Prince* (Reynal & Hitchcock, 1943).

"Good morning," the little prince responded politely, although when he turned around he saw nothing.

"I am right here," the voice said, "under the apple tree."

"Who are you?" asked the little prince, and added, "You are very pretty to look at."

"I am a fox," the fox said.

"Come and play with me," proposed the little prince. "I am so unhappy."

"I cannot play with you," the fox said. "I am not tamed."

"Ah! Please excuse me," said the little prince.

But, after some thought, he added:

"What does that mean — 'tame'?"

"You do not live here," said the fox. "What is it that you are looking for?"

"I am looking for men," said the little prince. "What does that mean — 'tame'?"

"Men," said the fox. "They have guns, and they hunt. It is very disturbing. They also raise chickens. These are their only interests. Are you looking for chickens?"

"No," said the little prince. "I am looking for friends. What does that mean — 'tame'?"

"It is an act too often neglected," said the fox. "It means to establish ties."

"'To establish ties'?"

"Just that," said the fox. "To me, you are still nothing more than a little boy who is just like a hundred thousand other little boys. And I have no need of you. And you, on your part, have no need of me. To you, I am nothing more than a fox like a hundred thousand other foxes. But if you tame me, then we shall need each other. To me, you will be unique in all the world. To you, I shall be unique in all the world. . ."

"I am beginning to understand," said the little prince. "There is a flower . . . I think that she has tamed me. . ."

"It is possible," said the fox. "On the Earth one sees all sorts of things."

"Oh, but this is not on the Earth!" said the little prince.

The fox seemed perplexed, and very curious.

"On another planet?"

"Yes."

"Are there hunters on that planet?"

"No."

"Ah, that is interesting! Are there chickens?"

"No."

"Nothing is perfect," sighed the fox.

But he came back to his idea.

"My life is very monotonous," he said. "I hunt chickens; men hunt me. All the chickens are just alike, and all the men are just alike. And, in consequence, I am a little bored. But if you tame me, it will be as if the sun came to shine on my life. I shall know the sound of a step that will be different from all the others. Other steps send me hurrying back underneath the ground. Yours will call me, like music, out of my burrow. And then look: you see the grain-fields down yonder? I do not eat bread. Wheat is of no use to me. The wheat fields have nothing to say to me. And that is sad. But you have hair that is the color of gold. Think how wonderful that will be when you have tamed me! The grain, which is also golden, will bring me back the thought of you. And I shall love to listen to the wind in the wheat. . ."

The fox gazed at the little prince, for a long time.

"Please — tame me!" he said.

"I want to, very much," the little prince replied. "But I have not much time. I have friends to discover, and a great many things to understand."

"One only understands the things that one tames," said the fox. "Men have no more time to understand anything. They buy things all ready made at the shops. But there is no shop anywhere where one can buy friendship, and so men have no friends any more. If you want a friend, tame me. . ."

"What must I do, to tame you?" asked the little prince.

"You must be very patient," replied the fox. "First you will sit down at a little distance from me — like that — in the grass. I shall look at you out of the corner of my eye, and you will say nothing. Words are the source of misunderstandings. But you will sit a little closer to me, every day. . ."

The next day the little prince came back.

"It would have been better to come back at the same hour," said the fox. "If, for example, you come at four o'clock in the afternoon, then at three o'clock I shall begin to be happy. I shall feel happier and happier as the hour advances. At four o'clock, I shall already be worrying and jumping about. I shall show you how happy I am! But if you come at just any time, I shall never know at what hour my heart is to be ready to greet you . . . One must observe the proper rites. . ."

"What is a rite?" asked the little prince.

"Those also are actions too often neglected," said the fox. "They are what make one day different from other days, one hour from other hours. There is a rite, for example among my hunters. Every Thursday they dance with the village girls. So Thursday is a wonderful day for me! I can take a walk as far as the vineyards. But if the hunters danced at just any time, every day would be like every other day, and I should never have any vacation at all."

So the little prince tamed the fox. And when the hour of his departure drew near —

"Ah," said the fox, "I shall cry."

"It is your own fault," said the little prince. "I never wished you any sort of harm; but you wanted me to tame you. . ."

"Yes, that is so," said the fox.

"But now you are going to cry!" said the little prince.

"Yes, that is so," said the fox.

"Then it has done you no good at all!"

"It has done me good," said the fox, "because of the color of the wheat fields." And then he added:

"Go and look again at the roses. You will understand now that yours is unique in all the world. Then come back to say goodbye to me, and I will make you a present of a secret."

The little prince went away, to look again at the roses.

"You are not at all like my rose," he said. "As yet you are nothing. No one has tamed you, and you have tamed no one. You are like my fox when I first knew him. He was only a fox like a hundred thousand other foxes. But I have made him my friend, and now he is unique in all the world."

And the roses were very much embarrassed.

"You are beautiful, but you are empty," he went on. "One could not die for you. To be sure, an ordinary passerby would think that my rose looked just like you — the rose that belongs to me. But in herself alone she is more important than all the hundreds of you other roses: because it is she that I have watered; because it is she that I have put under the glass globe; because it is she that I have sheltered behind the screen; because it is for her that I have killed the caterpillars (except the two or three that we saved to become butterflies); because it is she that I have listened to, when she grumbled, or boasted, or even sometimes when she said nothing. Because she is *my* rose."

And he went back to meet the fox.

"Goodbye," he said.

"Goodbye," said the fox. "And now here is my secret, a very simple secret: It is only with the heart that one can see rightly; what is essential is invisible to the eye."

"What is essential is invisible to the eye," the little prince repeated, so that he would be sure to remember.

"It is the time you have wasted for your rose that makes your rose so important."

"It is the time I have wasted for my rose —" said the little prince, so that he would be sure to remember.

"Men have forgotten this truth," said the fox. "But you must not forget it. You become responsible, forever, for what you have tamed. You are responsible for your rose. . ."

"I am responsible for my rose," the little prince repeated, so that he would be sure to remember.

Many Moons[4]

JAMES THURBER

᜞ *This is James Thurber's first story for children. It has something of the Hans Christian Andersen spirit, in that it holds an underlying meaning for adults, though that meaning is not obtrusive enough to spoil the tale for children. As in the traditional fairy story, we have a princess in distress, a problem solved in a truly*

[4] James Thurber, *Many Moons* (Harcourt, Brace, 1943).

childlike manner of reasoning when adult solu-
tions have failed, and sufficient action and sus-
pense — all important, if not all necessary, in-
gredients of any good fairy tale.

Once upon a time, in a kingdom by the sea, there lived a little princess named Lenore. She was ten years old, going on eleven. One day Lenore fell ill of a surfeit of raspberry tarts and took to her bed.

The royal physician came to see her and took her temperature and felt her pulse and made her stick out her tongue. The royal physician was worried. He sent for the king, Lenore's father, and the king came to see her.

"I will get you anything your heart desires," the king said. "Is there anything your heart desires?"

"Yes," said the princess. "I want the moon. If I can have the moon, I will be well again."

Now the king had a great many wise men who always got for him anything he wanted, so he told his daughter that she could have the moon. Then he went to the throne room and pulled a bell cord, three long pulls and a short pull, and presently the lord high chamberlain came into the room.

The lord high chamberlain was a large, fat man who wore thick glasses which made his eyes seem twice as big as they really were. This made the lord high chamberlain seem twice as wise as he really was.

"I want you to get the moon," said the king. "The Princess Lenore wants the moon. If she can have the moon, she will get well again."

"The moon?" exclaimed the lord high chamberlain, his eyes widening. This made him look four times as wise as he really was.

"Yes, the moon," said the king. "M-o-o-n, moon. Get it tonight, tomorrow at the latest."

The lord high chamberlain wiped his forehead with a handkerchief and then blew his nose loudly. "I have got a great many things for you in my time, Your Majesty," he said. "It just happens that I have with me a list of the things I have got for you in my time." He pulled a long scroll of parchment out of his pocket. "Let me see, now." He glanced at the list, frowning. "I have got ivory, apes, and peacocks, rubies, opals, and emeralds,

black orchids, pink elephants, and blue poodles, gold bugs, scarabs, and flies in amber, humming-birds' tongues, angels' feathers, and unicorns' horns, giants, midgets, and mermaids, frankincense, ambergris, and myrrh, troubadours, minstrels, and dancing women, a pound of butter, two dozen eggs, and a sack of sugar — sorry, my wife wrote that in there."

"I don't remember any blue poodles," said the king.

"It says blue poodles right here on the list, and they are checked off with a little check mark," said the lord high chamberlain. "So there must have been blue poodles. You just forget."

"Never mind the blue poodles," said the king. "What I want now is the moon."

"I have sent as far as Samarkand and Araby and Zanzibar to get things for you, Your Majesty," said the lord high chamberlain. "But the moon is out of the question. It is thirty-five thousand miles away and it is bigger than the room the princess lies in. Furthermore, it is made of molten copper. I cannot get the moon for you. Blue poodles, yes; the moon, no."

The king flew into a rage and told the lord high chamberlain to leave the room and to send the royal wizard to the throne room.

The royal wizard was a little, thin man with a long face. He wore a high red peaked hat covered with silver stars, and a long blue robe covered with golden owls. His face grew very pale when the king told him that he wanted the moon for his little daughter, and that he expected the royal wizard to get it.

"I have worked a great deal of magic for you in my time, Your Majesty," said the royal wizard. "As a matter of fact, I just happen to have in my pocket a list of the wizardries I have performed for you." He drew a paper from a deep pocket of his robe. "It begins: 'Dear Royal Wizard: I am returning herewith the so-called philosopher's stone which you claimed' — no, that isn't it." The royal wizard brought a long scroll of parchment from another pocket of his robe. "Here it is," he said. "Now, let's see. I have squeezed blood out of turnips for you, and turnips out of blood. I have produced rabbits out of silk hats, and silk hats out of rabbits. I have conjured up flowers, tambourines, and doves out of nowhere, and nowhere out of flowers, tambourines, and doves. I have brought you divining rods, magic wands, and crystal spheres in which to behold the future. I have compounded philters, unguents, and potions, to cure heartbreak, surfeit, and ringing in the ears. I have made you my own special mixture of wolfbane, nightshade, and eagles' tears, to ward off witches, demons and things that go bump in the night. I have given you seven-league boots, the golden touch, and a cloak of invisibility —"

"It didn't work," said the king. "The cloak of invisibility didn't work."

"Yes, it did," said the royal wizard.

"No, it didn't," said the king. "I kept bumping into things, the same as ever."

"The cloak is supposed to make you invisible," said the royal wizard. "It is not supposed to keep you from bumping into things."

"All I know is, I kept bumping into things," said the king.

The royal wizard looked at his list again. "I got you," he said, "horns from Elfland, sand from the Sandman, and gold from the rainbow. Also a spool of thread, a paper of needles, and a lump of beeswax — sorry, those are things my wife wrote down for me to get her."

"What I want you to do now," said the king, "is to get me the moon. The Princess Lenore wants the moon, and when she gets it, she will be well again."

"Nobody can get the moon," said the royal wizard. "It is a hundred and fifty thousand miles away, and it is made of green cheese, and it is twice as big as this palace."

The king flew into another rage and sent the royal wizard back to his cave. Then he rang a gong and summoned the royal mathematician.

The royal mathematician was a bald-headed, near-sighted man, with a skullcap on his head and a pencil behind each ear. He wore a black suit with white numbers on it.

"I don't want to hear a long list of all the things you have figured out for me since 1907," the king said to him. "I want you to figure out right now how to get the moon for the Princess Lenore. When she gets the moon, she will be well again."

"I am glad you mentioned all the things I have figured out for you since 1907," said the royal mathematician. "It so happens that I have a list of them with me."

He pulled a long scroll of parchment out of a pocket and looked at it. "Now let me see. I have figured out for you the distance between the horns of a dilemma, night and day, and A and Z. I have computed how far is Up, how long it takes to get to Away, and what becomes of Gone. I have discovered the length of the sea serpent, the price of the priceless and the square of the hippopotamus. I know where you are when you are at Sixes and Sevens, how much Is you have to have to make an Are, and how many birds you can catch with the salt in the ocean — 187,796,132, if it would interest you to know."

"There aren't that many birds," said the king.

"I didn't say there were," said the royal mathematician. "I said if there were."

"I don't want to hear about seven hundred million imaginary birds," said the king. "I want you to get the moon for the Princess Lenore."

"The moon is three hundred thousand miles away," said the royal mathematician. "It is round and flat like a coin, only it is made of asbestos, and it is half the size of this kingdom. Furthermore, it is pasted on the sky. Nobody can get the moon."

The king flew into still another rage and sent the royal mathematician away. Then he rang for the court jester. The jester came bounding into the throne room in his motley and his cap and bells, and sat at the foot of the throne.

"What can I do for you, Your Majesty?" asked the court jester.

"Nobody can do anything for me," said the king mournfully. "The Princess Lenore wants the moon, and she cannot be well till she gets it, but nobody can get it for her. Every time I ask anybody for the moon, it gets larger and farther away. There is nothing you can do for me except play on your lute. Something sad."

"How big do they say the moon is," asked the court jester, "and how far away?"

"The lord high chamberlain says it is thirty-five thousand miles away, and bigger than the Princess Lenore's room," said the king. "The royal wizard says it is a hundred and fifty thousand miles away, and twice as big as this palace. The royal mathematician says it is three hundred thousand miles away, and half the size of this kingdom."

The court jester strummed on his lute for a little while. "They are all wise men," he said, "and so they must all be right. If they are all right, then the moon must be just as large and as far away as each person thinks it is. The thing to do is find out how big the Princess Lenore thinks it is, and how far away."

"I never thought of that," said the king.

"I will go and ask her, Your Majesty," said the court jester. And he crept softly into the little girl's room.

The Princess Lenore was awake, and she was glad to see the court jester, but her face was very pale and her voice very weak.

"Have you brought the moon to me?" she asked.

"Not yet," said the court jester, "but I will get it for you right away. How big do you think it is?"

"It is just a little smaller than my thumbnail," she said, "for when I hold my thumbnail up at the moon, it just covers it."

"And how far away is it?" asked the court jester.

"It is not as high as the big tree outside my window," said the princess, "for sometimes it gets caught in the top branches."

"It will be very easy to get the moon for you," said the court jester. "I will climb the tree tonight when it gets caught in the top branches and bring it to you."

Then he thought of something else. "What is the moon made of, princess?" he asked.

"Oh," she said, "it's made of gold, of course, silly."

The court jester left the Princess Lenore's room and went to see the royal goldsmith. He had the royal goldsmith make a tiny round golden moon just a little smaller than the thumbnail of the Princess Lenore. Then

he had him string it on a golden chain so the princess could wear it around her neck.

"What is this I have made?" asked the royal goldsmith when he had finished it.

"You have made the moon," said the court jester. "That is the moon."

"But the moon," said the royal goldsmith, "is five hundred thousand miles away and is made of bronze and is round like a marble."

"That's what you think," said the court jester as he went away with the moon.

The court jester took the moon to the Princess Lenore, and she was overjoyed. The next day she was well again and could get up and go out in the gardens to play.

But the king's worries were not yet over. He knew that the moon would shine in the sky again that night, and he did not want the Princess Lenore to see it. If she did, she would know that the moon she wore on a chain around her neck was not the real moon.

So the king sent for the lord high chamberlain and said: "We must keep the Princess Lenore from seeing the moon when it shines in the sky tonight. Think of something."

The lord high chamberlain tapped his forehead with his fingers thoughtfully and said: "I know just the thing. We can make some dark glasses for the Princess Lenore. We can make them so dark that she will not be able to see anything at all through them. Then she will not be able to see the moon when it shines in the sky."

This made the king very angry, and he shook his head from side to side. "If she wore dark glasses, she would bump into things," he said, "and then she would be ill again." So he sent the lord high chamberlain away and called the royal wizard.

"We must hide the moon," said the king, "so that the Princess Lenore will not see it when it shines in the sky tonight. How are we going to do that?"

The royal wizard stood on his hands and then he stood on his head and then he stood on his feet again. "I know what we can do," he said. "We can stretch some black velvet curtains on poles. The curtains will cover all the palace gardens like a circus tent, and the Princess Lenore will not be able to see through them, so she will not see the moon in the sky."

The king was so angry at this that he waved his arms around. "Black velvet curtains would keep out the air," he said. "The Princess Lenore would not be able to breathe, and she would be ill again." So he sent the royal wizard away and summoned the royal mathematician.

"We must do something," said the king, "so that the Princess Lenore will not see the moon when it shines in the sky tonight. If you know so much, figure out a way to do that."

The royal mathematician walked around in a circle, and then he walked around in a square, and then he stood still. "I have it!" he said. "We can set off fireworks in the gardens every night. We will make a lot of silver fountains and golden cascades, and when they go off, they will fill the sky with so many sparks that it will be as light as day and the Princess Lenore will not be able to see the moon."

The king flew into such a rage that he began jumping up and down. "Fireworks would keep the Princess Lenore awake," he said. "She would not get any sleep at all and she would be ill again." So the king sent the royal mathematician away.

When he looked up again, it was dark outside and he saw the bright rim of the moon just peeping over the horizon. He jumped up in a great fright and rang for the court jester. The court jester came bounding into the room and sat down at the foot of the throne.

"What can I do for you, Your Majesty?" he asked.

"Nobody can do anything for me," said the king, mournfully. "The moon is coming up again. It will shine into the Princess Lenore's bedroom, and she will know it is still in the sky and that she does not wear it on a golden chain around her neck. Play me something on your lute, something very sad, for when the princess sees the moon, she will be ill again."

The court jester strummed on his lute. "What do your wise men say?" he asked.

"They can think of no way to hide the moon that will not make the Princess Lenore ill," said the king.

The court jester played another song, very softly. "Your wise men know everything," he said, "and if they cannot hide the moon, then it cannot be hidden."

The king put his head in his hands again and sighed. Suddenly he jumped up from his throne and pointed to the windows. "Look!" he cried. "The moon is already shining into the Princess Lenore's bedroom. Who can explain how the moon can be shining in the sky when it is hanging on a golden chain around her neck?"

The court jester stopped playing on his lute. "Who could explain how to get the moon when your wise men said it was too large and too far away? It was the Princess Lenore. Therefore, the Princess Lenore is wiser than your wise men and knows more about the moon than they do. So I will ask *her*." And before the king could stop him, the court jester slipped quietly out of the throne room and up the wide marble staircase to the Princess Lenore's bedroom.

The princess was lying in bed but she was wide awake and she was looking out the window at the moon shining in the sky. Shining in her hand was the moon the court jester had got for her. He looked very sad, and there seemed to be tears in his eyes.

"Tell me, Princess Lenore," he said mournfully, "how can the moon be shining in the sky when it is hanging on a golden chain around your neck?"

The princess looked at him and laughed. "That is easy, silly," she said. "When I lose a tooth, a new one grows in its place, doesn't it?"

"Of course," said the court jester. "And when the unicorn loses his horn in the forest, a new one grows in the middle of his forehead."

"That is right," said the princess. "And when the royal gardener cuts the flowers in the garden, other flowers come to take their place."

"I should have thought of that," said the court jester, "for it is the same way with the daylight."

"And it is the same way with the moon," said the Princess Lenore. "I guess it is the same way with everything." Her voice became very low and faded away, and the court jester saw that she was asleep. Gently he tucked the covers in around the sleeping princess.

But before he left the room, he went over to the window and winked at the moon, for it seemed to the court jester that the moon had winked at him.

Mary Poppins Opens the Door
The Marble Boy [5]

PAMELA TRAVERS

Mary Poppins, the unpredictable nursery governess in the Banks family, is a delightful new character in children's literature. Stern, efficient, yet kind, and endowed with the gift of magic, she makes the most commonplace events, such as a trip to the park (which you may read in the chapter below) take on a fantastic turn. The Mary Poppins books are classics of fantasy and nonsense. They have been translated into many languages and are the delight of children all over the world.

"And don't forget to buy me an evening paper!" said Mrs. Banks, as she handed Jane two pennies and kissed her good-bye.

Michael looked at his mother reproachfully.

"Is that all you're going to give us?" he asked. "What'll happen if we meet the ice-cream man?"

"Well," said Mrs. Banks reluctantly, "here's another sixpence. But I do think you children get too many treats. *I* didn't have ices every day when *I* was a little girl."

Michael looked at her curiously. He could not believe she had ever been a little girl. Mrs. George Banks in short skirts and her hair tied up with ribbons? Impossible!

"I suppose," he said smugly, "you didn't deserve them!"

And he tucked the sixpence carefully into the pocket of his sailor suit.

"That's fourpence for the ice creams," said Jane. "And we'll buy a *Lot-o'-Fun* with the rest."

"Out of my way, Miss, if you please!" said a haughty voice behind her.

5 From Pamela Travers, *Mary Poppins Opens the Door* (Harcourt, Brace, 1943).

As neat and trim as a fashion-plate, Mary Poppins came down the steps with Annabel. She dumped her into the perambulator and pushed it past the children.

"Now, quick march into the park!" she snapped. "And no meandering!"

Down the path straggled Jane and Michael, with John and Barbara at their heels. The sun spread over Cherry Tree Lane like a bright enormous umbrella. Thrushes and blackbirds sang in the trees. Down at the corner Admiral Boom was busily mowing his lawn.

From the distance came sounds of martial music. The band was playing at the end of the park. Along the walks went the flowery sunshades and beneath them sauntered gossiping ladies, exchanging the latest news.

The park keeper, in his summer suit — blue with a red stripe on the sleeve — was keeping an eye on everyone as he tramped across the lawns.

"Observe the rules! Keep off the grass! All litter to be placed in the baskets!" he shouted.

Jane gazed at the sunny, dreamy scene. "It's just like Mr. Twigley's box," she said with a happy sigh.

Michael put his ear to the trunk of an oak.

"I believe I can hear it growing!" he cried. "It makes a small, soft, creeping sound —— "

"*You'll* be creeping in a minute! Right back home, unless you hurry!" Mary Poppins warned him.

"No rubbish allowed in the park!" shouted the keeper, as she swept along the Lime Walk.

"Rubbish yourself!" she retorted briskly, with a haughty toss of her head.

He took off his hat and fanned his face as he stared at her retreating back. And you knew from the way Mary Poppins smiled that she knew quite well he was staring. How could he help it, she thought to herself. Wasn't she wearing her new white jacket, with the pink collar and the pink belt and the four pink buttons down the front?

"Which way are we going today?" asked Michael.

"That remains to be seen!" she answered him priggishly.

"I was only inquiring ——" Michael argued.

"Don't, then!" she advised, with a warning sniff.

"She never lets me say anything!" he grumbled under his hat to Jane. "I'll go dumb some day and then she'll be sorry."

Mary Poppins thrust the perambulator in front of her as though she were running an obstacle race.

"This way, please!" she commanded presently, as she swung the pram to the right.

And they knew, then, where they were going. For the little path that turned out of the Lime Walk led away toward the lake.

There, beyond the tunnels of shade, lay the shining patch of water. It sparkled and danced in its net of sunlight and the children felt their hearts beat faster as they ran through the shadows toward it.

"I'll make a boat, and sail it to Africa!" shouted Michael, forgetting his crossness.

"I'll go fishing!" cried Jane, as she galloped past him.

Laughing and whooping and waving their hats, they came to the shining water. All round the lake stood the dusty green benches, and the ducks went quacking along the edge, greedily looking for crusts.

At the far end of the water stood the battered marble statue of the boy and the dolphin. Dazzling white and bright it shone, between the lake and the sky. There was a small chip off the boy's nose and a line like a black thread round his ankle. One of the fingers of his left hand was broken off at the joint. And all his toes were cracked.

There he stood, on his high pedestal, with his arm flung lightly round the neck of the dolphin. His head, with its ruffle of marble curls, was bent toward the water. He gazed down at it thoughtfully with wide marble eyes. The name NELEUS was carved in faded gilt letters at the base of the pedestal.

"How bright he is today!" breathed Jane, blinking her eyes at the shining marble.

And it was at that moment that she saw the elderly gentleman.

He was sitting at the foot of the statue, reading a book with the aid of a magnifying glass. His bald head was sheltered from the sun by a knotted silk handkerchief, and lying on the bench beside him was a black top hat.

The children stared at the curious figure with fascinated eyes.

"That's Mary Poppin's favorite seat! She *will* be cross!" exclaimed Michael.

"Indeed? And when was I ever cross?" her voice inquired behind him.

The remark quite shocked him. "Why, you're *often* cross, Mary Poppins!" he said. "At least fifty times a day!"

"Never!" she said, with an angry snap. "I have the patience of a boa constrictor! I merely speak my mind!"

She flounced away and sat down on a bench exactly opposite the statue. Then she glared across the lake at the elderly gentleman. It was a look that might have killed anybody else. But the elderly gentleman was quite unaffected. He went on poring over his book and took no notice of anyone. Mary Poppins, with an infuriated sniff, took her mending-bag from the perambulator and began to darn the socks.

The children scattered round the sparkling water.

"Here's my boat!" shrieked Michael, snatching a piece of colored paper from a litter basket.

"I'm fishing," said Jane, as she lay on her stomach and stretched her hand over the water. She imagined a fishing-rod in her fingers and a line running down, with a hook and a worm. After a little while, she knew, a fish would swim lazily up to the hook and give the worm a tweak. Then, with a jerk, she would land him neatly and take him home in her hat. "Well, I never!" Mrs. Brill would say. "It's just what we needed for supper!"

Beside her the twins were happily paddling. Michael steered his ship through a terrible storm. Mary Poppins sat primly on her bench and rocked the perambulator with one foot. Her silver needle flashed in the sunlight. The park was quiet and dreamy and still.

Bang!

The elderly gentleman closed his book and the sound shattered the silence.

"Oh, I say!" protested a shrill, sweet voice. "You might have let me finish!"

Jane and Michael looked up in surprise. They stared. They blinked. And they stared again. For there, on the grass before them, stood the little marble statue. The marble dolphin was clasped in his arms and the pedestal was quite empty.

The elderly gentleman opened his mouth. Then he shut it and opened it again.

"Er — did you say something?" he said at last, and his eyebrows went up to the top of his head.

"Yes, of course I did!" the boy replied. "I was reading over your shoulder there" — he pointed toward the empty pedestal — "and you closed the book too quickly. I wanted to finish the elephant story and see how he got his trunk."

"Oh, I *beg* your pardon," said the elderly gentleman. "I had no idea — er — of such a thing. I always stop reading at four, you see. I have to get home to my tea."

He rose and folded the handkerchief and picked up the black top hat.

"Well, now that you've finished," the boy said calmly, "you can give the book to me!"

The elderly gentleman drew back, clutching the book to his breast.

"Oh, I couldn't do that, I'm afraid," he said. "You see, I've only just bought it. I wanted to read it when I was young, but the grownups always got it first. And now that I've got a copy of my own, I really feel I must keep it."

He eyed the statue uneasily as though he feared that at any moment it might snatch the book away.

"*I* could tell you about the elephant's child ——" Jane murmured shyly to the boy.

He wheeled around with the fish in his arms.

"Oh, Jane — would you really?" he cried in surprise. His marble face gleamed with pleasure.

"And I'll tell you *Yellow Dog Dingo*," said Michael, "and *The Butterfly that Stamped*."

"No!" said the elderly gentleman suddenly. "Here I am with a suit of clothes and a hat. And he's quite naked. I'll *give* him the book! I suppose," he added, with a gloomy sigh, "I was never meant to have it."

He gave the book a last long look, and, thrusting it at the marble boy, he turned away quickly. But the dolphin wriggled and caught his eye and he turned to the boy again.

"By the way," he said, curiously, "I wonder how you caught that porpoise? What did you use — a line or a net?"

"Neither," replied the boy, with a smile. "He was given to me when I was born."

"Oh — I see." The elderly gentleman nodded, though he still looked rather puzzled. "Well, I must be getting along. Good day!" He lifted the black top hat politely and hurried off down the path.

"Thank you!" the marble boy shouted after him, as he eagerly opened the book. On the fly-leaf was written, in spidery writing, "*William Weatherall Wilkins.*"

"I'll cross out his name and put mine instead." The boy smiled gaily at Jane and Michael.

"But what is your name? And how can you read?" cried Michael, very astonished.

"My name is Neleus," the boy said, laughing. "And I read with my eyes, of course!"

"But you're only a statue!" Jane protested. "And statues don't usually walk and talk. However did you get down?"

"I jumped," replied Neleus, smiling again, as he tossed his marble curls. "I was so disappointed not to finish that story that something happened to my feet. First they twitched, and then they jumped, and the next I knew I was down on the grass!" He curled his little marble toes and stamped on the earth with his marble feet. "Oh, lucky, lucky human beings to be able to do this every day! I've watched you so often, Jane and Michael, and wished I could come and play with you. And now at last my wish has come true. Oh, tell me you're glad to see me!"

He touched their cheeks with his marble fingers and crowed with joy as he danced around them. Then, before they could utter a word of welcome, he sped like a hare to the edge of the lake and dabbled his hand in the water.

"So — this is what water feels like!" he cried. "So deep and so blue — and as light as air!" He leaned out over the sparkling lake and the dolphin gave a flick of its tail and slipped from his arms with a splash.

"Catch him! He'll sink!" cried Michael quickly.

But the dolphin did nothing of the kind. It swam round the lake and threshed the water; it dived and caught its tail in its mouth and leapt in the air and dived again. The performance was just like a turn in the circus. And as it sprang, dripping, to the arms of its master, the children could not help clapping.

"Was it good?" asked Neleus enviously. And the dolphin grinned and nodded.

"Good!" cried a well-known voice behind them. "*I* call it extremely naughty!"

Mary Poppins was standing at the edge of the lake and her eyes were as bright as her darning needle. Neleus sprang to his feet with a little cry and hung his head before her. He looked very young and small and shy as he waited for her to speak.

"Who said you might get down, may I ask?" Her face had its usual look of fury.

He shook his head guiltily.

"No one," he mumbled. "My feet jumped down by themselves, Mary Poppins."

"Then they'd better jump up again, spit-spot. You've no right to be off your pedestal."

He tilted back his marble head and the sunlight glanced off his small chipped nose.

"Oh, can't I stay down, Mary Poppins?" he pleaded. "Do let me stay for a little while and play with Jane and Michael? You don't know how lonely it is up there, with only the birds to talk to!" The earnest marble eyes entreated her. "Please, Mary Poppins!" he whispered softly, as he clasped his marble hands.

She gazed down thoughtfully for a moment, as though she were making up her mind. Then her eyes softened. A little smile skipped over her mouth and crinkled the edge of her cheek.

"Well, just for this afternoon!" she said. "This one time, Neleus! Never again!"

"Never — I promise, Mary Poppins!" He gave her an impish grin.

"Do you know Mary Poppins?" demanded Michael. "Where did you meet her?" he wanted to know. He was feeling a little jealous.

"Of course I do!" exclaimed Neleus, laughing. "She's a very old friend of my father's."

"What is your father's name? Where is he?" Jane was almost bursting with curiosity.

"Far away. In the Isles of Greece. He is called the King of the Sea." As he spoke, the marble eyes of Neleus brimmed slowly up with sadness.

"What does he do?" demanded Michael. "Does he go to the City — like Daddy?"

"Oh, no. He never goes anywhere. He stands on a cliff above the sea, holding his trident and blowing his horn. Beside him my mother sits, combing her hair. And Pelias — that's my younger brother — plays at their feet with a marble shell. And all day long the gulls fly past them, making black shadows on their marble bodies, and telling them news of the harbor. By day they watch the red-sailed ships going in and out of the bay. And at night they listen to the wine-dark waters that break on the shore below."

"How lovely!" cried Jane. "But why did you leave them?"

She was thinking that she would never have left Mr. and Mrs. Banks and Michael alone on the cliffs of Greece.

"I didn't want to," said the marble boy. "But what can a statue do against men? They were always coming to stare at us — peeking and prying and pinching our arms. They said we were made a long time ago by a very famous artist. And one day somebody said — 'I'll take *him!*' — and he pointed at me. So — I had to go."

He hid his eyes for a moment behind the dolphin's fin.

"What happened then?" demanded Jane. "How did you get to our park?"

"In a packing-case," said Neleus calmly, and laughed at their look of astonishment. "Oh, we always travel that way, you know. My family is very much in demand. People want us for parks or museums or gardens. So they buy us and send us by parcel post. It never seems to occur to them that some of us might be — lonely." He choked a little on the word. Then he flung up his head with a lordly gesture. "But don't let's think about that!" he cried. "It's been much better since you two came. Oh, Jane and Michael, I know you so well — as if you were part of my family. I know about Michael's kite and his compass; and the Doulton bowl, and Robertson Ay, and the things you have for supper. Didn't you ever notice me listening? And reading the fairy-tales over your shoulders?"

Jane and Michael shook their heads.

"I know *Alice in Wonderland* by heart," he went on. "And most of *Robinson Crusoe*. And *Everything a Lady Should Know*, which is Mary Poppins's favorite. But best of all are the colored comics, especially the one called *Lot-o'-Fun*. What happened to Tiger Tim this week? Did he get away safely from Uncle Moppsy?"

"The new one comes out today," said Jane. "We'll all read it together!"

"Oh, dear! How happy I am!" cried Neleus. "The elephant's child, and a new *Lot-o'-Fun*, and my legs like the wings of a bird. I don't know when my birthday is, but I think it must be today!" He hugged the dolphin and the book in his arms and capered across the grass.

"Hi! Ting-aling-aling! Look where you're going!" the ice cream man gave a warning cry. He was wheeling his barrow along by the lake. The printed notice in front of it said:

STOP ME AND BUY ONE
WHAT WONDERFUL WEATHER!

"Stop! Stop! Stop! Stop!" cried the children wildly, as they ran toward the barrow.

"Chocolate" said Michael.

"Lemon!" cried Jane.

And the fat little twins put out their hands and gladly took what was given them.

"And wot about you!" said the ice cream man, as Neleus came and stood shyly beside him.

"I don't know what to choose," said Neleus. "I never had one before."

"Wot! Never 'ad a nice? Wot's the matter — weak stummick? A boy your size should know all about ices! 'Ere!" The ice cream man fished inside his barrow and brought out a raspberry bar. "Take this and see 'ow you like it!"

Neleus broke the bar with his marble fingers. He popped one half in the dolphin's mouth and began to lick the other.

"Delicious," he said, "much better than seaweed."

"Seaweed? I should think so! Wot's seaweed got to do with it? But — talking of seaweed, that's a nice big cod!" The ice cream man waved his hand at the dolphin. "If you took it along to the fishmonger, 'e'd give you a fancy price."

The dolphin gave its tail a flick and its face looked very indignant.

"Oh, I don't want to sell him," said Neleus quickly. "He isn't just a fish — he's a friend!"

"A fishy kind of friend!" said the man. "Why doesn't 'e tell you to put on your clothes? You'll catch your death running round stark naked. Well, no offense meant! Ting-aling! Ting-aling!" He rode away whistling and ringing his bell.

Neleus glanced at the children out of the corner of his eye and the three burst out into peals of laughter.

"Oh, dear!" cried Neleus, gasping for breath, "I believe he thinks I'm human! Shall I run and tell him he's made a mistake? That I haven't worn clothes for two thousand years and never caught even a sniffle?"

He was just about to dart after the barrow when Michael gave a shout.

"Look out! Here's Willoughby!" he cried, and swallowed the rest of his ice in one gulp.

For Willoughby, who belonged to Miss Lark, had a habit of jumping up at the children and snatching the food from their hands. He had rough, bouncy, vulgar manners and no respect for anyone. But what else could you expect of a dog who was half an airedale and half a retriever and the worst half of both?

There he came, lolloping over the grass, sticking out his tongue. Andrew, who was as well-bred as Willoughby was common, tripped gracefully after him. And Miss Lark herself followed breathlessly.

"Just out for a spin before tea!" she trilled. "Such a beautiful day and the dogs insisted —— Good gracious, what is that I see?"

She broke off, panting, and stared at Neleus. Her face, already red, grew redder, and she looked extremely indignant.

"You naughty, wicked boy!" she cried. "What are you doing to that poor fish? Don't you know it will die if it stays out of water?"

Neleus raised a marble eyebrow. The dolphin swung its tail over its mouth to hide a marble smile.

"You see?" said Miss Lark. "It's writhing in agony! You must put it back into the water this minute!"

"Oh, I couldn't do that," said Neleus quickly. "I'm afraid he'd be lonely without me." He was trying to be polite to Miss Lark. But the dolphin was not. He flapped his tail and wriggled and grinned in a very discourteous manner.

"Don't answer me back! Fish are never lonely! You are just making silly excuses."

Miss Lark made an angry gesture toward the green bench.

"I do think, Mary Poppins," she said, "you might keep an eye on the children! This naughty boy, whoever he is, must put that fish back where he got it!"

Mary Poppins favored Miss Lark with a stare. "I'm afraid that's quite impossible, ma'am. He'd have to go too far."

"Far or near — it doesn't matter. He must put it back this instant. It's cruelty to animals and it shouldn't be allowed. Andrew and Willoughby — come with me! I shall go at once and tell the Lord Mayor!"

Away she bustled, with the dogs at her heels. Willoughby, as he trotted by, winked rudely at the dolphin.

"And tell him to put his clothes on! He'll get sunburnt, running about like that!" shrieked Miss Lark, as she hurried off.

Neleus gave a little spurt of laughter and flung himself down on the grass.

"Sunburnt!" he choked. "Oh, Mary Poppins, does nobody guess I'm made of marble?"

"Humph!" replied Mary Poppins, snorting. And Neleus tossed her a mischievous smile.

"That's what the sea lions say!" he said. "They sit on the rocks and say 'Humph!' to the sunset!"

"Indeed?" she said tartly. And Jane and

Michael waited, trembling, for what was surely coming. But nothing happened. Her face had an answering look of mischief and the blue eyes and the marble eyes smiled gently at each other.

"Neleus," she said quietly, "you have ten minutes more. You can come with us to the bookstall and back."

"And then — ?" he said, with a questioning look, as he tightened his arms round the dolphin.

She did not answer. She looked across the sparkling lake and nodded toward the pedestal.

"Oh, can't he stay longer, Mary Poppins — ?" the children began to protest. But the eager question froze on their lips, for Mary Poppins was glaring.

"I said ten minutes," she remarked. "And ten minutes is what I meant. You needn't look at me like that, either. I am not a grisly gorilla."

"Oh, don't start arguing!" cried Neleus. "We mustn't waste a second!" He sprang to his feet and seized Jane's hand. "Show me the way to the bookstall!" he said. And drew her away through the spreading sunlight and over the grassy lawns.

Behind them Mary Poppins lifted the twins into the perambulator and hurried along with Michael.

Lightly across the summer grasses ran Jane and the marble boy. His curls flew out on the wind with hers and her hot breath blew on his marble cheeks. Within her soft and living fingers the marble hand grew warmer.

"This way!" she cried, as she tugged at his arm and drew him into the Lime Walk.

At the end of it, by the far gate, stood the gaily painted bookstall. A bright sign nailed above it said:

MR. FOLLY
BOOKS PAPERS AND MAGAZINES
YOU WANT THEM
I'VE GOT THEM

A frill of colored magazines hung round the bookstall; and as the children raced up, Mr. Folly popped his head through a gap in the frill. He had a round, quiet, lazy face that looked as though nothing in the world could disturb it.

"Well, if it isn't Jane Banks and friend!" he remarked mildly. "I think I can guess what you've come for!"

"*The Evening News* and *Lot-o'-Fun*," panted Jane, as she put down the pennies.

Neleus seized the colored comic and skimmed the pages quickly.

"Does Tiger Tim get away?" cried Michael, as he dashed up, breathless, behind them.

"Yes, he does!" cried Neleus, with a shout of joy. "Listen! 'Tiger Tim Escapes Clutches of Uncle Moppsy. His New Adventure with Old Man Dogface. Watch Out For Another Tiger Tim Story Next Week!'"

"Hooray!" shouted Michael, peering round the dolphin's shoulder to get a look at the pictures.

Mr. Folly was eyeing Neleus with interest. "That's a fine young whale you got there, Sonny! Seems almost 'uman. Where did you catch him?"

"I didn't," said Neleus, glancing up. "He was given to me as a present."

"Fancy that! Well, he makes a nice pet! And where do *you* come from? Where's yer Ma?"

"She's a long way from here," replied Neleus gravely.

"Too bad!" Mr. Folly wagged his head. "Dad away, too?"

Neleus smiled and nodded.

"You don't say! Goodness, you must be lonely!" Mr. Folly glanced at the marble body. "And cold as well, I shouldn't wonder, with not a stitch on your bones!" He made a jingling noise in his pocket and thrust out his hand to Neleus.

"There! Get yourself something to wear with that. Can't go around with nothing on. Pneumonia, you know! And chilblains!"

Neleus stared at the silver thing in his hand.

"What it is?" he asked curiously.

"That's a 'arf-crown," said Mr. Folly. "Don't tell me you never saw one!"

"No, I never did," said Neleus, smiling. And the dolphin gazed at the coin with interest.

"Well, I declare! You pore little chap! Stark naked and never seen a 'arf-crown! Someone ought to be taking care of you!"

Mr. Folly glanced reproachfully at Mary Poppins. And she gave him an outraged glare.

"Someone *is* taking care of him, thank you!" she said. As she spoke she unbuttoned her new white jacket and slipped it round Neleus' shoulders.

"There!" she said gruffly. "You won't be cold now. And no thanks to *you*, Mr. Folly!"

Neleus looked from the coat to Mary Poppins and his marble eyes grew wider. "You mean — I can keep it always?" he asked.

She nodded, and looked away.

"Oh, dear sweet sea lion — thank you!" he cried, and he hugged her waist in his marble arms. "Look at me, Jane, in my new white coat! Look at me, Michael, in my beautiful buttons." He ran excitedly from one to the other to show off his new possession.

"That's right," said Mr. Folly, beaming. "Much better be sure than sorry! And the 'arf-crown will buy you a nice pair of trousers — "

"Not tonight," interrupted Mary Poppins. "We're late as it is. Now best foot forward and home we go, and I'll thank you all not to dawdle."

The sun was swiftly moving westward as she trundled the pram down the Lime Walk. The band at the end of the park was silent. The flowery sunshades had all gone home. The trees stood still and straight in the shadows. The park keeper was nowhere to be seen.

Jane and Michael walked on either side of Neleus and linked their hands through his marble arms. A silence was over the human children and over the marble child between them.

"I love you, Neleus," Jane said softly. "I wish you could stay with us always."

"I love you, too," he answered, smiling. "But I must go back. I promised."

"I suppose you couldn't leave the dolphin?" said Michael, stroking the marble fin.

Jane looked at him angrily.

"Oh, Michael — how can you be so selfish! How would you like to spend your life, all alone up there on a pedestal?"

"I'd like it — if I could have the dolphin, and call Mary Poppins a sea-lion!"

"I tell you what, Michael!" said Neleus quickly. "You can't have the dolphin — he's part of me. But the half-crown isn't. I'll give you that." He pushed the money into Michael's hand. "And Jane must have the book," he went on. "But promise, Jane, and cross your heart, that you'll let me read it over your shoulder. And every week you must come to the bench and read me the new *Lot-o'-Fun*."

He gave the book a last long look and tucked it under her arm.

"Oh, I promise, Neleus!" she said faithfully, and crossed her heart with her hand.

"I'll be waiting for you," said Neleus softly. "I'll never, never forget."

"Walk up and don't chatter!" hissed Mary Poppins, as she turned toward the lake.

The perambulator creaked and groaned as it trundled on its way. But high above the creak of the wheels they could hear a well-known voice. They tiptoed up behind Mary Poppins as she walked to the shadowy water.

"I never done it!" the voice protested. "And wouldn't — not if you paid me!"

At the edge of the lake, by the empty pedestal, stood the Lord Mayor with two Aldermen. And before them, waving his arms and shouting, and generally behaving in a peculiar manner, was the park keeper.

"It's none of my doing, Your Honor!" he pleaded. "I can look you straight in the eye!"

"Nonsense, Smith!" said the Lord Mayor sternly. "You are the person responsible for the park statues. And only you could have done it!"

"You might as well confess!" advised the first Alderman.

"It won't save you, of course," the second added, "but you'll *feel* so much better!"

"But I didn't *do* it, I'm telling you!" The park keeper clasped his hands in a frenzy.

"Stop quibbling, Smith. You're wasting my time!" The Lord Mayor shook his head impatiently. "First, I have to go looking for a naked boy who I hear is maltreating some wretched fish. A salmon, Miss Lark said — or was it a halibut? And now, as if this wasn't enough, I find the most valuable of our statues is missing from its pedestal. I am shocked and disgusted. I trusted you, Smith. And look how you repay me!"

"I *am* looking. I mean, I don't *have* to look! Oh, I don't know what I'm saying, Your Grace! But I *do* know I never touched that stachew!"

The keeper glanced round wildly for help and his eye fell on Mary Poppins. He gave a cry of horrified triumph and flung out his hand accusingly.

"Your Worship, *there's* the guilty party! She done it or I'll eat me 'at!"

The Lord Mayor glanced at Mary Poppins and back to the park keeper.

"I'm ashamed of you, Smith!" He shook his head sorrowfully. "Putting the blame on a perfectly respectable, innocent young woman taking her charges for an afternoon airing! How could you?"

He bowed courteously to Mary Poppins, who returned the bow with a ladylike smile.

"Innocent! *'Er!*" the park keeper screamed. "You don't know what you're sayin', my Lord! As soon as that girl comes into the park, the place begins to go crosswise. Merry-go-rounds jumpin' up in the sky, people coming down on kites and rockets, the Prime Minister bobbing round on balloons — and it's all *your* doing — you Caliban!" He shook his fist wildly at Mary Poppins.

"Poor fellow! Poor fellow! His mind is unhinged!" said the first Alderman sadly.

"Perhaps we'd better get some handcuffs," the second whispered nervously.

"Do what you like with me! 'Ang me, why don't yer? But it wasn't me wot done it!" Overcome with misery, the park keeper flung himself against the pedestal and sobbed bitterly.

Mary Poppins turned and beckoned to Neleus. He ran to her side on marble feet and leaned his head gently against her.

"Is it time?" he whispered, glancing up.

She nodded quickly. Then bending she took him in her arms and kissed his marble brow. For a moment Neleus clung to her as though he could never let her go. Then he broke away, smothering a sob.

"Good-bye, Jane and Michael. Don't forget me!" He pressed his chilly cheek to theirs. And before they could even say a word he had darted away among the shadows and was running toward his pedestal.

"I never 'ad no luck!" wailed the keeper. "Never since I was a boy!"

"And you won't have any now, my man, unless you put back that statue." The Lord Mayor fixed him with an angry eye.

But Jane and Michael were looking neither at the park keeper nor the Lord Mayor. They were watching a curly head appear at the far side of the pedestal.

Up scrambled Neleus, over the ledge, dragging the dolphin after him. His marble body blazed white and bright in a fading shaft of sunlight. Then with a gesture, half-gay, half-sad, he put up a little marble hand and waved them all farewell. As they waved back, he seemed to tremble, but that may have been the tears in their eyes. They watched him draw the dolphin to him, so close that its marble melted to his. Then he smoothed his curls with a marble hand and bent his head and was still. Even Mary Poppins's pink-and-white jacket seemed turned to lifeless marble.

"I can't put it back if I never took it!" the park keeper went on sobbing and shouting.

"Now, see here, Smith ——" the Lord Mayor began. Then he gave a gasp and staggered sideways with his hand clasped to his brow. "My jumping giraffes! It's come back ——" he cried. "And there's something different about it!"

He peered more closely at the statue and burst into roars of delighted laughter. He took off his hat and waved it wildly and slapped the park keeper on the back.

"Smith — you rogue! So *that* was your secret! Why didn't you tell us at first, my man? It certainly is a splendid surprise! Well, you needn't go on pretending now ——"

For the park keeper, speechless with amazement, was goggling up at Neleus.

"Gentlemen!" — the Lord Mayor turned to the Aldermen — "we have sadly misjudged this poor fellow. He has proved himself not only an excellent servant of the community — but an artist as well. Do you see what he has done to the statue? He has added a little marble coat with collar and cuffs of pink. A *great* improvement, to my mind, Smith! I *never* approved of naked statues."

"Nor I!" the first Alderman shook his head.

"Certainly not!" said the second.

"Never fear, my dear Smith. You shall have your reward. From today your wages will be raised one shilling and an extra stripe will be sewn on your sleeve. Furthermore, I shall speak of you to His Majesty when I make my next report."

And the Lord Mayor, with another ceremonious bow to Mary Poppins, swept majestically away, humbly followed by the two Aldermen.

The park keeper, looking as though he were not sure if he were on his head or his heels, stared after them. Then he turned his popping eyes to the statue and stared again at that. The marble boy and his marble fish gazed thoughtfully down at the lake. They were as still and quiet and silent as they had always been.

"Now home again, home again, jiggety-jog!" Mary Poppins raised a beckoning finger and the children followed without a word. The half-crown lay in Michael's palm, burning and bright and solid. And cold as the marble hand of Neleus was the book beneath Jane's arm.

Along the walk they marched in silence thinking their secret thoughts. And presently, on the grass behind them, there came the thud of feet. They turned to find the park keeper running heavily toward them. He had taken off his coat and was waving it, like a blue-and-red flag, at the end of his walking stick. He pulled up, panting, beside the perambulator and held out the coat to Mary Poppins.

"Take it!" he said breathlessly. "I just been looking at that boy back there. He's wearin' yours — with the four pink buttons. And you'll need one when its gets chilly."

Mary Poppins calmly took the coat and slipped it over her shoulders. Her own reflection smiled conceitedly at her from the polished brass buttons.

"Thank you," she said primly, to the park keeper.

He stood before her in his shirt-sleeves, shaking his head like a puzzled dog.

"I suppose *you* understand what it all means?" he said wistfully.

"I suppose I do," she replied smugly.

And without another word, she gave the perambulator a little push and sent it bowling past him. He was still staring after her, scratching his head, as she passed through the gate of the park.

Mr. Banks, on his way home from the office, whistled to them as they crossed the lane.

"Well, Mary Poppins!" he greeted her. "You're very smart in your blue-and-red jacket! Have you joined the Salvation Army?"

"No, sir," she replied, primly. And the look she gave him made it quite clear she had no intention of explaining.

"It's the park keeper's coat," Jane told him hurriedly.

"He gave it to her just now," added Michael.

"What — Smith? He gave her the jacket of his uniform? Whatever for?" exclaimed Mr. Banks.

But Jane and Michael were suddenly silent. They could feel Mary Poppins's gimlet eyes making holes in the backs of their heads. They dared not go on with the story.

"Well, never mind!" said Mr. Banks calmly. "I suppose she did something to deserve it!"

They nodded. But they knew he would never know what she had done, not even if he lived to be fifty. They walked up the garden path beside him, clasping the coin and the book.

And as they went they thought of the child who had given them those gifts, the marble boy who for one short hour had danced and played in the park. They thought of him standing alone on his pedestal, with his arm flung lovingly round his dolphin — forever silent, forever still, and the sweet light gone from his face. Darkness would come down upon him and the stars and the night would wrap him round. Proud and lonely he would stand there, looking down upon the waters of the little lake, dreaming of the great sea and his home so far away. . . .

The Borrowers[6]

(A Selection)

MARY NORTON

Mary Norton's delightful fantasy about the tiny people who hide away in odd nooks of old houses, and live by "borrowing" what they need, was awarded the Carnegie medal in England as the outstanding children's book of its year. In this selection Arrietty, the inches-high, thirteen-year-old "Borrower" daughter, has just ventured out onto the doorstep of the house on a perilous trip of exploration.

The step was warm but very steep. "If I got down on to the path," Arrietty thought, "I might not get up again," so for some moments she sat quietly. After a while she noticed the shoe-scraper.

"Arrietty," called Pod softly, "where have you got to?"

"I just climbed down the shoe-scraper," she called back.

He came along and looked down at her from the top of the step. "That's all right," he said after a moment's stare, "but never climb down anything that isn't fixed like. Supposing one of them came along and moved the shoe-scraper — where would you be then? How would you get up again?"

"It's heavy to move," said Arrietty.

"Maybe," said Pod, "but it's movable. See what I mean? There's rules, my lass, and you got to learn."

"This path," Arrietty said, "goes round the house. And the bank does too."

"Well," said Pod, "what of it?"

Arrietty rubbed one red kid shoe on a rounded stone. "It's my grating," she explained. "I was thinking that my grating must be just round the corner. My grating looks out on to this bank."

"Your grating!" exclaimed Pod. "Since when has it been your grating?"

"I was thinking," Arrietty went on. "Suppose I just went round the corner and called through the grating to Mother?"

"No," said Pod, "we're not going to have none of that. Not going round corners."

6 From Mary Norton, *The Borrowers* (Harcourt, Brace, 1953).

"Then," went on Arrietty, "she'd see I was all right like."

"Well," said Pod, and then he half smiled, "go quickly then and call. I'll watch for you here. Not loud, mind!"

Arrietty ran. The stones in the path were firmly bedded and her light, soft shoes hardly seemed to touch them. How glorious it was to run — you could never run under the floor: you walked, you stooped, you crawled — but you never ran. Arrietty nearly ran past the grating. Yes, there it was quite close to the ground, embedded deeply in the old wall of the house; there was moss below it in a spreading, greenish stain.

Arrietty ran up to it. "Mother!" she called, her nose against the iron grille. "Mother!" She waited quietly and, after a moment, she called again.

At the third call Homily came. Her hair was coming down and she carried, as though it were heavy, the screw lid of a pickle jar, filled with soapy water. "Oh," she said in an annoyed voice, "you didn't half give me a turn! What do you think you're up to? Where's your father?"

Arrietty jerked her head sideways. "Just there — by the front door!" She was so full of happiness that, out of Homily's sight, her toes danced on the green moss. Here she was on the other side of the grating — here she was at last, on the outside — looking in!

"Yes," said Homily, "they open that door like that — the first day of spring. Well," she went on briskly, "you run back to your father. And tell him, if the morning-room door happens to be open that I wouldn't say no to a bit of red blotting paper. Mind, out of my way now — while I throw the water!"

"That's what grows the moss," thought Arrietty as she sped back to her father, "all the water we empty through the grating. . . ."

Pod looked relieved when he saw her but frowned at the message. "How's she expect me to climb that desk without me pin? Blotting paper's a curtain-and-chair job and she should know it. Come on now! Up with you!"

"Let me stay down," pleaded Arrietty, "just a bit longer. Just till you finish. They're all out. Except Her. Mother said so."

"She'd say anything," grumbled Pod, "when she wants something quick. How does she know She won't take it into her head to get out of that bed of Hers and come downstairs with a stick? How does she know Mrs. Driver ain't stayed at home today — with a headache? How does she know that boy ain't still here?"

"What boy?" asked Arrietty.

Pod looked embarrassed. "What boy?" he repeated vaguely and then went on: "Or maybe Crampfurl — "

"Crampfurl isn't a boy," said Arrietty.

"No, he isn't," said Pod, "not in a manner of speaking. No," he went on as though thinking this out, "no, you wouldn't call Crampfurl a boy. Not, as you might say, a boy — exactly. Well," he said, beginning to move away, "stay down a bit if you like. But stay close!"

Arrietty watched him move away from the step and then she looked about her. Oh, glory! Oh, joy! Oh, freedom! The sunlight, the grasses, the soft, moving air and halfway up the bank, where it curved round the corner, a flowering cherry tree! Below it on the path lay a stain of pinkish petals and, at the tree's foot, pale as butter, a nest of primroses.

Arrietty threw a cautious glance toward the front doorstep and then, light and dancey, in her soft red shoes, she ran toward the petals. They were curved like shells and rocked as she touched them. She gathered several up and laid them one inside the other . . . up and up . . . like a card castle. And then she spilled them. Pod came again to the top of the step and looked along the path. "Don't you go far," he said after a moment. Seeing his lips move, she smiled back at him: she was too far already to hear the words.

A greenish beetle, shining in the sunlight, came toward her across the stones. She laid her fingers lightly on its shell and it stood still, waiting and watchful, and when she moved her hand the beetle went swiftly on. An ant came hurrying in a busy zigzag. She danced in front of it to tease it and put out her foot. It stared at her, nonplused, waving its antennae; then pettishly, as though put out, it swerved away. Two birds came down, quarreling shrilly, into the grass below the tree. One flew away but Arrietty could see the other among the moving grass stems above her on the slope. Cautiously she moved toward the bank and climbed a little nervously in amongst the green blades. As she parted them gently with her bare hands, drops of water plopped on her skirt and she felt the red shoes become damp. But on she went, pulling herself up now and again by rooty stems into this jungle of moss and wood-violet and creeping leaves of clover. The sharp-seeming grass blades, waist high, were tender to the touch and sprang back lightly behind her as she passed. When at last she reached the foot of the tree, the bird took fright and flew away and she sat down suddenly on a gnarled leaf of primrose. The air was filled with scent. "But nothing will play with you," she thought and saw the cracks and furrows of the primrose leaves held crystal beads of dew. If she pressed the leaf these rolled like marbles. The bank was warm, almost too warm here within the shelter of the tall grass, and the sandy earth smelled dry. Standing up, she picked a primrose. The pink stalk felt tender and living in her hands and was covered with silvery hairs, and when she held the flower, like a parasol, between her eyes and the sky, she saw the sun's pale light through the veined petals. On a piece of bark she found a wood louse and she struck it lightly with her swaying flower. It curled immediately and became a ball, bumping softly away downhill in amongst the grass roots. But she knew about wood lice. There were plenty of them at home under the floor. Homily always scolded her if she played with them because, she said, they smelled of old knives. She lay back among the stalks of the primroses and they made a coolness between her and the sun, and then, sighing, she turned her head and looked sideways up the bank among the grass stems. Startled, she caught her breath. Something had moved above her on the bank. Something had glittered. Arrietty stared.

It was an eye. Or it looked like an eye. Clear and bright like the color of the sky. An eye like her own but enormous. A glaring eye. Breathless with fear, she sat up. And the eye blinked. A great fringe of lashes came curving down and flew up again out of sight. Cautiously, Arrietty moved her legs: she would slide noiselessly in among the grass stems and slither away down the bank.

"Don't move!" said a voice, and the voice, like the eye, was enormous but, somehow, hushed — and hoarse like a surge of wind through the grating on a stormy night in March.

Arrietty froze. "So this is it," she thought, "the worst and most terrible thing of all: I have been 'seen'! Whatever happened to Eggletina will now, almost certainly, happen to me!"

There was a pause and Arrietty, her heart pounding in her ears, heard the breath again drawn swiftly into the vast lungs. "Or," said the voice, whispering still, "I shall hit you with my ash stick."

Suddenly Arrietty became calm. "Why?" she asked. How strange her own voice sounded! Crystal thin and harebell clear, it tinkled on the air.

"In case," came the surprised whisper at last, "you ran toward me, quickly, through the grass . . . in case," it went on, trembling a little, "you came and scrabbled at me with your nasty little hands."

Arrietty stared at the eye; she held herself quite still. "Why?" she asked again, and again the word tinkled — icy cold it sounded this time, and needle sharp.

"Things do," said the voice. "I've seen them. In India."

Arrietty thought of her Gazeteer of the World. "You're not in India now," she pointed out.

"Did you come out of the house?"

"Yes," said Arrietty.

"From whereabouts in the house?"

Arrietty stared at the eye. "I'm not going to tell you," she said at last bravely.

"Then I'll hit you with my ash stick!"

"All right," said Arrietty, "hit me!"

"I'll pick you up and break you in half!"

Arrietty stood up. "All right," she said and took two paces forward.

There was a sharp gasp and an earthquake in the grass: he spun away from her and sat up, a great mountain in a green jersey. He had fair, straight hair and golden eyelashes. "Stay where you are!" he cried.

Arrietty stared up at him. So this was "the boy"! Breathless, she felt, and light with fear. "I guessed you were about nine," she gasped after a moment.

He flushed. "Well, you're wrong, I'm ten." He looked down at her, breathing deeply. "How old are you?"

"Fourteen," said Arrietty. "Next June," she added, watching him.

There was silence while Arrietty waited, trembling a little. "Can you read?" the boy said at last.

"Of course," said Arrietty. "Can't you?"

"No," he stammered. "I mean — yes. I mean I've just come from India."

"What's that got to do with it?" asked Arrietty.

"Well, if you're born in India, you're bilingual. And if you're bilingual, you can't read. Not so well."

Arrietty stared up at him: what a monster, she thought, dark against the sky.

"Do you grow out of it?" she asked.

He moved a little and she felt the cold flick of his shadow.

"Oh yes," he said, "it wears off. My sisters were bilingual; now they aren't a bit. They could read any of those books upstairs in the schoolroom."

"So could I," said Arrietty quickly, "if someone could hold them, and turn the pages. I'm not a bit bilingual. I can read anything."

"Could you read out loud?"

"Of course," said Arrietty.

"Would you wait here while I run upstairs and get a book now?"

"Well," said Arrietty; she was longing to show off; then a startled look came into her eyes. "Oh — " she faltered.

"What's the matter?" The boy was standing up now. He towered above her.

"How many doors are there to this house?" She squinted up at him against the bright sunlight. He dropped on one knee.

"Doors?" he said. "Outside doors?"

"Yes."

"Well, there's the front door, the back door, the gun room door, the kitchen door,

the scullery door . . . and the french windows in the drawing room."

"Well, you see," said Arrietty, "my father's in the hall, by the front door, working. He . . . he wouldn't want to be disturbed."

"Working?" said the boy. "What at?"

"Getting material," said Arrietty, "for a scrubbing brush."

"Then I'll go in the side door"; he began to move away but turned suddenly and came back to her. He stood a moment, as though embarrassed, and then he said: "Can you fly?"

"No," said Arrietty, surprised; "can you?"

His face became even redder. "Of course not," he said angrily; "I'm not a fairy!"

"Well, nor am I," said Arrietty, "nor is anybody. I don't believe in them."

He looked at her strangely. "You don't believe in them?"

"No," said Arrietty; "do you?"

"Of course not!"

Really, she thought, he is a very angry kind of boy. "My mother believes in them," she said, trying to appease him. "She thinks she saw one once. It was when she was a girl and lived with her parents behind the sand pile in the potting shed."

He squatted down on his heels and she felt his breath on her face. "What was it like?" he asked.

"About the size of a glowworm with wings like a butterfly. And it had a tiny little face, she said, all alight and moving like sparks and tiny moving hands. Its face was changing all the time, she said, smiling and sort of shimmering. It seemed to be talking, she said, very quickly — but you couldn't hear a word. . . ."

"Oh," said the boy, interested. After a moment he asked: "Where did it go?"

"It just went," said Arrietty. "When my mother saw it, it seemed to be caught in a cobweb. It was dark at the time. About five o'clock on a winter's evening. After tea."

"Oh," he said again and picked up two petals of cherry blossom which he folded together like a sandwich and ate slowly. "Supposing," he said, staring past her at the wall of the house, "you saw a little man, about as tall as a pencil, with a blue patch in his trousers, halfway up a window curtain, carrying a doll's tea cup — would you say it was a fairy?"

"No," said Arrietty, "I'd say it was my father."

"Oh," said the boy, thinking this out, "does your father have a blue patch on his trousers?"

"Not on his best trousers. He does on his borrowing ones."

"Oh," said the boy again. He seemed to find it a safe sound, as lawyers do. "Are there many people like you?"

"No," said Arrietty. "None. We're all different."

"I mean as small as you?"

Arrietty laughed. "Oh, don't be silly!" she said. "Surely you don't think there are many people in the world your size?"

"There are more my size than yours," he retorted.

"Honestly — " began Arrietty helplessly and laughed again. "Do you really think — I mean, whatever sort of a world would it be? Those great chairs . . . I've seen them. Fancy if you had to make chairs that size for everyone? And the stuff for their clothes . . . miles and miles of it . . . tents of it . . . and the sewing! And their great houses, reaching up so you can hardly see the ceilings . . . their great beds . . . the *food* they eat . . . great, smoking mountains of it, huge bogs of stew and soup and stuff."

"Don't you eat soup?" asked the boy.

"Of course we do," laughed Arrietty. "My father had an uncle who had a little boat which he rowed round in the stock-pot picking up flotsam and jetsam. He did bottom-fishing too for bits of marrow until the cook got suspicious through finding bent pins in the soup. Once he was nearly shipwrecked on a chunk of submerged shinbone. He lost his oars and the boat sprang a leak but he flung a line over the pot handle and pulled himself alongside the rim. But all that stock — fathoms of it! And the size of the stock-pot! I mean, there wouldn't be enough stuff in the world to go round after a bit! That's why my father says it's a good thing they're dying out . . . just a few, my father says, that's all we need — to keep us. Otherwise, he says, the whole thing gets" — Arrietty

hesitated, trying to remember the word — "exaggerated, he says — "

"What do you mean," asked the boy, " 'to keep us'?"

So Arrietty told him about borrowing — how difficult it was and how dangerous. She told him about the storerooms under the floor; about Pod's early exploits, the skill he had shown and the courage; she described those far-off days, before her birth, when Pod and Homily had been rich; she described the musical snuffbox of gold filigree, and the little bird which flew out of it made of kingfisher feathers, how it flapped its wings and sang its song; she described the doll's wardrobe and the tiny green glasses; the little silver teapot out of the drawing-room case; the satin bedcovers and embroidered sheets . . . "those we have still," she told him, "they're Her handkerchiefs. . . ." "She," the boy realized gradually, was his Great-Aunt Sophy upstairs, bedridden since a hunting accident some twenty years before; he heard how Pod would borrow from Her room, picking his way — in the firelight — among the trinkets on Her dressing table, even climbing Her bed-curtains and walking on Her quilt. And of how She would watch him and sometimes talk to him because, Arrietty explained, every day at six o'clock they brought Her a decanter of Fine Old Pale Madeira, and how before midnight She would drink the lot. Nobody blamed Her, not even Homily, because, as Homily would say, She had so few pleasures, poor soul, but, Arrietty explained, after the first three glasses Great-Aunt Sophy never believed in anything she saw. "She thinks my father comes out of the decanter," said Arrietty, "and one day when I'm older he's going to take me there and She'll think I come out of the decanter too. It'll please Her, my father thinks, as She's used to him now. Once he took my mother, and She perked up like anything and kept asking after her and why didn't she come any more and saying they'd watered the Madeira because once, She says, She saw a little man *and* a little woman and now she only sees a little man. . . ."

"I wish she thought I came out of the decanter," said the boy. "She gives me dictation and teaches me to write. I only see her in the mornings when she's cross. She sends for me and looks behind my ears and asks Mrs. D. if I've learned my words."

"What does Mrs. D. look like?" asked Arrietty. (How delicious it was to say "Mrs. D." like that . . . how careless and daring!)

"She's fat and has a mustache and gives me my bath and hurts my bruise and my sore elbow and says she'll take a slipper to me one of these days. . . ." The boy pulled up a tuft of grass and stared at it angrily and Arrietty saw his lip tremble. "My mother's very nice," he said. "She lives in India. Why did you lose all your worldly riches?"

"Well," said Arrietty, "the kitchen boiler burst and hot water came pouring through the floor into our house and everything was washed away and piled up in front of the grating. My father worked night and day. First hot, then cold. Trying to salvage things. And there's a dreadful draught in March through that grating. He got ill, you see, and couldn't go borrowing. So my Uncle Hendreary had to do it and one or two others and my mother gave them things, bit by bit, for all their trouble. But the king-fisher bird was spoilt by the water; all its feathers fell off and a great twirly spring came jumping out of its side. My father used the spring to keep the door shut against draughts from the grating and my mother put the feathers in a little moleskin hat. After a while I got born and my father went bor-rowing again. But he gets tired now and doesn't like curtains, not when any of the bobbles are off. . . ."

"I helped him a bit," said the boy, "with the tea cup. He was shivering all over. I suppose he was frightened."

"My father frightened!" exclaimed Arrietty angrily. "Frightened of you!" she added.

"Perhaps he doesn't like heights," said the boy.

"He loves heights," said Arrietty. "The thing he doesn't like is curtains. I've told you. Curtains make him tired."

The boy sat thoughtfully on his haunches, chewing a blade of grass. "Borrowing," he said after a while. "Is that what you call it?"

"What else could you call it?" asked Arrietty.

"I'd call it stealing."

Arrietty laughed. She really laughed. "But we *are* Borrowers," she explained, "like you're a — a human bean or whatever it's called. We're part of the house. You might as well say that the fire grate steals the coal from the coal scuttle."

"Then what is stealing?"

Arrietty looked grave. "Don't you know?" she asked. "Stealing is — well, supposing my Uncle Hendreary borrowed an emerald watch from Her dressing-table and my father took it and hung it up on our wall. That's stealing."

"An emerald watch!" exclaimed the boy.

"Well, I just said that because we have one on the wall at home, but my father borrowed it himself. It needn't be a watch. It could be anything. A lump of sugar even. But Borrowers don't steal."

"Except from human beings," said the boy.

Arrietty burst out laughing; she laughed so much that she had to hide her face in the primrose. "Oh dear," she gasped with tears in her eyes, "you are funny!" She stared upward at his puzzled face. "Human beans are *for* Borrowers — like bread's for butter!" The boy was silent awhile. A sigh of wind rustled the cherry tree and shivered among the blossoms.

"Well, I don't believe it," he said at last, watching the falling petals. "I don't believe that's what we're for at all and I don't be-lieve we're dying out!"

"Oh, goodness!" exclaimed Arrietty im-patiently, staring up at his chin. "Just use your common sense: you're the only real human bean I ever saw (although I do just know of three more — Crampfurl, Her, and Mrs. Driver). But I know lots and lots of Borrowers: The Overmantels and the Harp-sichords and the Rain-Barrels and the Linen-Presses and the Boot-Racks and the Hon. John Studdingtons and — "

He looked down. "John Studdington? But he was our grand-uncle — "

"Well, this family lived behind a picture," went on Arrietty, hardly listening, "and there were the Stove-Pipes and the Bell-Pulls and the — "

"Yes," he interrupted, "but did you see them?"

"I saw the Harpsichords. And my mother was a Bell-Pull. The others were before I was born. . . ."

He leaned closer. "Then where are they now? Tell me that."

"My Uncle Hendreary has a house in the country," said Arrietty coldly, edging away from his great lowering face; it was misted over, she noticed, with hairs of palest gold. "And four children, Harpsichords and Clocks."

"But where are the others?"

"Oh," said Arrietty, "they're somewhere." But where? she wondered. And she shivered slightly in the boy's cold shadow which lay about her, slant-wise, on the grass.

He drew back again, his fair head blocking out a great piece of sky. "Well," he said deliberately after a moment, and his eyes were cold, "I've only seen two Borrowers but I've seen hundreds and hundreds and hundreds and hundreds — "

"Oh no — " whispered Arrietty.

"Of human beings." And he sat back.

Arrietty stood very still. She did not look at him. After a while she said: "I don't believe you."

"All right," he said, "then I'll tell you — "

"I still won't believe you," murmured Arrietty.

"Listen!" he said. And he told her about railway stations and football matches and racecourses and royal processions and Albert Hall concerts. He told her about India and China and North America and the British Commonwealth. He told her about the July sales. "Not hundreds," he said, "but thousands and millions and billions and trillions of great, big, enormous people. Now do you believe me?"

Arrietty stared up at him with frightened eyes: it gave her a crick in the neck. "I don't know," she whispered.

"As for you," he went on, leaning closer again, "I don't believe that there are any more Borrowers anywhere in the world. I believe you're the last three," he said.

Arrietty dropped her face into the primrose. "We're not. There's Aunt Lupy and Uncle Hendreary and all the cousins."

"I bet they're dead," said the boy. "And what's more," he went on, "no one will ever believe I've seen *you*. And you'll be the very last because you're the youngest. One day," he told her, smiling triumphantly, "you'll be the only Borrower left in the world!"

He sat still, waiting, but she did not look up. "Now you're crying," he remarked after a moment.

"They're not dead," said Arrietty in a muffled voice; she was feeling in her little pocket for a handkerchief. "They live in a badger's set two fields away, beyond the spinney. We don't see them because it's too far. There are weasels and things and cows and foxes . . . and crows . . ."

"Which spinney?" he asked.

"I don't KNOW!" Arrietty almost shouted. "It's along by the gas-pipe — a field called Parkin's Beck." She blew her nose. "I'm going home," she said.

"Don't go," he said, "not yet."

"Yes, I'm going," said Arrietty.

His face turned pink. "Let me just get the book," he pleaded.

"I'm not going to read to you now," said Arrietty.

"Why not?"

She looked at him with angry eyes. "Because —"

"Listen," he said, "I'll go to that field. I'll go and find Uncle Hendreary. And the cousins. And Aunt Whatever-she-is. And, if they're alive, I'll tell you. What about that? You could write them a letter and I'd put it down the hole —"

Arrietty gazed up at him. "Would you?" she breathed.

"Yes, I would. Really I would. Now can I go and get the book? I'll go in by the side door."

"All right," said Arrietty absently. Her eyes were shining. "When can I give you the letter?"

"Any time," he said, standing above her. "Where in the house do you live?"

"Well —" began Arrietty and stopped. Why once again did she feel this chill? Could it only be his shadow . . . towering above her, blotting out the sun? "I'll put it somewhere," she said hurriedly, "I'll put it under the hall mat."

"Which one? The one by the front door?"
"Yes, that one."

He was gone. And she stood there alone in the sunshine, shoulder deep in grass. What had happened seemed too big for thought; she felt unable to believe it really had happened: not only had she been "seen" but she had been talked to; not only had she been talked to but she had —

"Arrietty!" said a voice.

She stood up startled and spun round: there was Pod, moon-faced, on the path looking up at her. "Come on down!" he whispered.

She stared at him for a moment as though she did not recognize him; how round his face was, how kind, how familiar!

"Come on!" he said again, more urgently; and obediently because he sounded worried, she slithered quickly toward him off the bank, balancing her primrose. "Put that thing down," he said sharply, when she stood at last beside him on the path. "You can't lug great flowers about — you got to carry a bag. What you want to go up there for?" he grumbled as they moved off across the stones. "I might never have seen you. Hurry up now. Your mother'll have tea waiting!"

The Hobbit
Riddles in the Dark[7]
J. R. R. TOLKIEN

§ *This modern classic for children, by an eminent scholar and philologist, is deeply rooted in the folklore and myth of northwest Europe. Hobbits, J. R. R. Tolkien tells us, were little folk who lived, like dwarves and elves, in ancient times now lost and forgotten. On a quest for treasure-hoard, the hobbit Bilbo has become separated from his companions, the dwarves, and is lost in a tunnel deep under a mountain.*

When Bilbo opened his eyes, he wondered if he had; for it was just as dark as with them shut. No one was anywhere near him. Just imagine his fright! He could

[7] From J. R. R. Tolkien, *The Hobbit* (Houghton Mifflin, 1937).

hear nothing, see nothing, and he could feel nothing except the stone of the floor.

Very slowly he got up and groped about on all fours, till he touched the wall of the tunnel; but neither up nor down it could he find anything: nothing at all, no sign of goblins, no sign of dwarves. His head was swimming, and he was far from certain even of the direction they had been going in when he had his fall. He guessed as well as he could, and crawled along for a good way, till suddenly his hand met what felt like a tiny ring of cold metal lying on the floor of the tunnel. It was a turning point in his career, but he did not know it. He put the ring in his pocket almost without thinking; certainly it did not seem of any particular use at the moment. He did not go much further, but sat down on the cold floor and gave himself up to complete miserableness, for a long while. He thought of himself frying bacon and eggs in his own kitchen at home — for he could feel inside that it was high time for some meal or other; but that only made him miserabler.

He could not think what to do; nor could he think what had happened; or why he had been left behind; or why, if he had been left behind, the goblins had not caught him; or even why his head was so sore. The truth was he had been lying quiet, out of sight and out of mind, in a very dark corner for a long while.

After some time he felt for his pipe. It was not broken, and that was something. Then he felt for his pouch, and there was some tobacco in it, and that was something more. Then he felt for matches and he could not find any at all, and that shattered his hopes completely. Just as well for him, as he agreed when he came to his senses. Goodness knows what the striking of matches and the smell of tobacco would have brought on him out of dark holes in that horrible place. Still at the moment he felt very crushed. But in slapping all his pockets and feeling all round himself for matches his hand came on the hilt of his little sword — the little dagger that he got from the trolls, and that he had quite forgotten; nor do the goblins seem to have noticed it, as he wore it inside his breeches.

Now he drew it out. It shone pale and dim before his eyes. "So it is an elvish blade, too," he thought; "and goblins are not very near, and yet not far enough."

But somehow he was comforted. It was rather splendid to be wearing a blade made in Gondolin for the goblin-wars of which so many songs had sung; and also he had noticed that such weapons made a great impression on goblins that came upon them suddenly.

"Go back?" he thought. "No good at all! Go sideways? Impossible! Go forward? Only thing to do! On we go!" So up he got, and trotted along with his little sword held in front of him and one hand feeling the wall, and his heart all of a patter and a pitter.

Now certainly Bilbo was in what is called a tight place. But you must remember it was not quite so tight for him as it would have been for me or for you. Hobbits are not quite like ordinary people; and after all if their holes are nice cheery places and properly aired, quite different from the tunnels of the goblins, still they are more used to tunnelling than we are, and they do not easily lose their sense of direction underground — not when their heads have recovered from being bumped. Also they can move very quietly, and hide easily, and recover wonderfully from falls and bruises, and they have a fund of wisdom and wise sayings that men have mostly never heard or have forgotten long ago.

I should not have liked to have been in Mr. Baggins' place, all the same. The tunnel seemed to have no end. All he knew was that it was still going down pretty steadily and keeping in the same direction in spite of a twist and a turn or two. There were passages leading off to the side every now and then, as he knew by the glimmer of his sword, or could feel with his hand on the wall. Of these he took no notice, except to hurry past for fear of goblins or half-imagined dark things coming out of them. On and on he went, and down and down; and still he heard no sound of anything except the occasional whirr of a bat by his ears, which startled him at first, till it became too frequent to bother about. I do not know how long he kept on like this, hating to go on, not daring to stop, on, on, until he was tireder than tired. It seemed like all the way to tomorrow and over it to the days beyond.

Suddenly without any warning he trotted splash into water! Ugh! it was icy cold. That pulled him up sharp and short. He did not know whether it was just a pool in the path, or the edge of an underground stream that crossed the passage, or the brink of a deep dark subterranean lake. The sword was hardly shining at all. He stopped, and he could hear, when he listened hard, drops drip-drip-dripping from an unseen roof into the water below; but there seemed no other sort of sound.

"So it is a pool or a lake, and not an underground river," he thought. Still he did not dare to wade out into the darkness. He could not swim; and he thought, too, of nasty slimy things, with big bulging blind eyes, wriggling in the water. There are strange things living in the pools and lakes in the hearts of mountains: fish whose fathers swam in, goodness only knows how many years ago, and never swam out again, while their eyes grew bigger and bigger and bigger from trying to see in the blackness; also there are other things more slimy than fish. Even in the tunnels and caves the goblins have made for themselves there are other things living unbeknown to them that have sneaked in from outside to lie up in the dark. Some of these caves, too, go back in their beginnings to ages before the goblins, who only widened them and joined them up with passages, and the original owners are still there in odd corners, slinking and nosing about.

Deep down here by the dark water lived old Gollum. I don't know where he came from, nor who or what he was. He was Gollum — as dark as darkness, except for two big round pale eyes. He had a boat, and he rowed about quite quietly on the lake; for lake it was, wide and deep and deadly cold. He paddled it with large feet dangling over the side, but never a ripple did he make. Not he. He was looking out of his pale lamp-like eyes for blind fish, which he grabbed with his long fingers as quick as thinking. He liked meat too. Goblin he thought good, when he could get it; but he took care they never found him out. He just throttled them from behind, if they ever came down alone anywhere near the edge of the water, while he was prowling about. They very seldom did, for they had a feeling that something unpleasant was lurking down there, down at the very roots of the mountain. They had come on the lake, when they were tunnelling down long ago, and they found they could go no further; so there their road ended in that direction, and there was no reason to go that way — unless the Great Goblin sent them. Sometimes he took a fancy for fish from the lake, and sometimes neither goblin nor fish came back.

Actually Gollum lived on a slimy island of rock in the middle of the lake. He was watching Bilbo now from the distance with his pale eyes like telescopes. Bilbo could not see him, but he was wondering a lot about Bilbo, for he could see that he was no goblin at all.

Gollum got into his boat and shot off from the island, while Bilbo was sitting on the brink altogether flummoxed and at the end of his way and his wits. Suddenly up came Gollum and whispered and hissed:

"Bless us and splash us, my precioussss! I guess it's a choice feast; at least a tasty morsel it'd make us, gollum!" And when he said *gollum* he made a horrible swallowing noise in his throat. That is how he got his name, though he always called himself "my precious."

The hobbit jumped nearly out of his skin when the hiss came in his ears, and he suddenly saw the pale eyes sticking out at him.

"Who are you?" he said, thrusting his dagger in front of him.

"What iss he, my preciouss?" whispered Gollum (who always spoke to himself through never having anyone else to speak to). This is what he had come to find out, for he was not really very hungry at the moment, only curious; otherwise he would have grabbed first and whispered afterwards.

"I am Mr. Bilbo Baggins. I have lost the dwarves and I have lost the wizard, and I don't know where I am; and I don't want to know, if only I can get away."

"What's he got in his handses?" said Gollum, looking at the sword, which he did not quite like.

"A sword, a blade which came out of Gondolin!"

"Sssss," said Gollum, and became quite polite. "Praps ye sits here and chats with it a bitsy, my preciousss. It likes riddles, praps it does, does it?" He was anxious to appear friendly, at any rate for the moment, and until he found out more about the sword and the hobbit, whether he was quite alone really, whether he was good to eat, and whether Gollum was really hungry. Riddles were all he could think of. Asking them, and sometimes guessing them, had been the only game he had ever played with other funny creatures sitting in their holes in the long, long ago, before the goblins came, and he was cut off from his friends far under the mountains.

"Very well," said Bilbo, who was anxious to agree, until he found out more about the creature, whether he was quite alone, whether he was fierce or hungry, and whether he was a friend of the goblins.

"You ask first," he said, because he had not had time to think of a riddle.

So Gollum hissed:

> *What has roots as nobody sees,*
> *Is taller than trees,*
> *Up, up it goes,*
> *And yet never grows?*

"Easy!" said Bilbo. "Mountain, I suppose."

"Does it guess easy? It must have a competition with us, my preciouss! If precious asks, and it doesn't answer, we eats it, my preciousss. If it asks us, and we doesn't answer, we gives it a present, gollum!"

"All right!" said Bilbo, not daring to disagree, and nearly bursting his brain to think of riddles that could save him from being eaten.

> *Thirty white horses on a red hill,*
> *First they champ,*
> *Then they stamp,*
> *Then they stand still.*

That was all he could think of to ask — the idea of eating was rather on his mind. It was rather an old one, too, and Gollum knew the answer as well as you do.

"Chestnuts, chestnuts," he hissed. "Teeth! teeth! my preciousss; but we has only six!" Then he asked his second:

> Voiceless it cries,
> Wingless flutters,
> Toothless bites,
> Mouthless mutters.

"Half a moment!" cried Bilbo, who was still thinking uncomfortably about eating. Fortunately he had once heard something rather like this before, and getting his wits back he thought of the answer. "Wind, wind of course," he said, and he was so pleased that he made up one on the spot. "This'll puzzle the nasty little underground creature," he thought:

> An eye in a blue face
> Saw an eye in a green face.
> "That eye is like to this eye"
> Said the first eye,
> "But in low place,
> Not in high place."

"Ss, ss, ss," said Gollum. He had been underground a long long time, and was forgetting this sort of thing. But just as Bilbo was beginning to wonder what Gollum's present would be like, Gollum brought up memories of ages and ages and ages before, when he lived with his grandmother in a hole in a bank by a river, "Sss, sss, my preciouss," he said. "Sun on the daisies it means, it does."

But these ordinary aboveground everyday sort of riddles were tiring for him. Also they reminded him of days when he had been less lonely and sneaky and nasty, and that put him out of temper. What is more they made him hungry; so this time he tried something a bit more difficult and more unpleasant:

> It cannot be seen, cannot be felt,
> Cannot be heard, cannot be smelt.
> It lies behind stars and under hills,
> And empty holes it fills.
> It comes first and follows after,
> Ends life, kills laughter.

Unfortunately for Gollum Bilbo had heard that sort of thing before; and the answer was all round him any way. "Dark!" he said without even scratching his head or putting on his thinking cap.

> A box without hinges, key, or lid,
> Yet golden treasure inside is hid,

he asked to gain time, until he could think of a really hard one. This he thought a dreadfully easy chestnut, though he had not asked it in the usual words. But it proved a nasty poser for Gollum. He hissed to himself, and still he did not answer; he whispered and spluttered.

After some while Bilbo became impatient. "Well, what is it?" he said. "The answer's not a kettle boiling over, as you seem to think from the noise you are making."

"Give us a chance; let it give us a chance, my preciouss-ss-ss."

"Well," said Bilbo, after giving him a long chance, "what about your present?"

But suddenly Gollum remembered thieving from nests long ago, and sitting under the river bank teaching his grandmother, teaching his grandmother to suck — "Eggses!" he hissed. "Eggses it is!" Then he asked:

> Alive without breath,
> As cold as death;
> Never thirsty, ever drinking,
> All in mail never clinking.

He also in his turn thought this was a dreadfully easy one, because he was always thinking of the answer. But he could not remember anything better at the moment, he was so flustered by the egg-question. All the same it was a poser for poor Bilbo, who never had anything to do with the water if he could help it. I imagine you know the answer, of course, or can guess it as easy as winking, since you are sitting comfortably at home and have not the danger of being eaten to disturb your thinking. Bilbo sat and cleared his throat once or twice, but no answer came.

After a while Gollum began to hiss with pleasure to himself: "Is it nice, my preciousss? Is it juicy? Is it scrumptiously crunchable?" He began to peer at Bilbo out of the darkness.

"Half a moment," said the hobbit shivering. "I gave you a good long chance just now."

"It must make haste, haste!" said Gollum, beginning to climb out of his boat on to the shore to get at Bilbo. But when he put his long webby foot in the water, a fish jumped out in a fright and fell on Bilbo's toes.

"Ugh!" he said, "it is cold and clammy!" —and so he guessed. "Fish! fish!" he cried. "It is fish."

Gollum was dreadfully disappointed; but Bilbo asked another riddle as quick as ever he could, so that Gollum had to get back into his boat and think.

> *No-legs lay on one-leg, two-legs sat near on three-legs, four-legs got some.*

It was not really the right time for this riddle, but Bilbo was in a hurry. Gollum might have had some trouble guessing it, if he had asked it at another time. As it was, talking of fish, "no-legs" was not so very difficult, and after that the rest was easy. "Fish on a little table, man at table sitting on a stool, the cat has the bones" that of course is the answer, and Gollum soon gave it. Then he thought the time had come to ask something hard and horrible. This is what he said:

> *This thing all things devours:*
> *Birds, beasts, trees, flowers;*
> *Gnaws iron, bites steel;*
> *Grinds hard stones to meal;*
> *Slays king, ruins town,*
> *And beats high mountain down.*

Poor Bilbo sat in the dark thinking of all the horrible names of all the giants and ogres he had ever heard told of in tales, but not one of them had done all these things. He had a feeling that the answer was quite different and that he ought to know it, but he could not think of it. He began to get frightened, and that is bad for thinking. Gollum began to get out of his boat. He flapped into the water and paddled to the bank; Bilbo could see his eyes coming towards him. His tongue seemed to stick in his mouth; he wanted to shout out: "Give me more time! Give me time!" But all that came out with a sudden squeal was:

"Time! Time!"

Bilbo was saved by pure luck. For that of course was the answer.

Gollum was disappointed once more; and now he was getting angry, and also tired of the game. It had made him very hungry indeed. This time he did not go back to the boat. He sat down in the dark by Bilbo. That made the hobbit most dreadfully uncomfortable and scattered his wits.

"It's got to ask uss a quesstion, my preciouss, yes, yess, yesss. Jusst one more quesstion to guess, yes, yess," said Gollum.

But Bilbo simply could not think of any question with that nasty wet cold thing sitting next to him, and pawing and poking him. He scratched himself, he pinched himself; still he could not think of anything.

"Ask us! Ask us!" said Gollum.

Bilbo pinched himself and slapped himself; he gripped on his little sword; he even felt in his pocket with his other hand. There he found the ring he had picked up in the passage and forgotten about.

"What have I got in my pocket?" he said aloud. He was talking to himself, but Gollum thought it was a riddle, and he was frightfully upset.

"Not fair! not fair!" he hissed. "It isn't fair, my precious, is it, to ask us what it's got in its nassty little pocketses?"

Bilbo seeing what had happened and having nothing better to ask stuck to his question, "What have I got in my pocket?" he said louder.

"S-s-s-s," hissed Gollum. "It must give us three guesseses, my preciouss, three guesseses."

"Very well! Guess away!" said Bilbo.

"Handses!" said Gollum.

"Wrong," said Bilbo, who had luckily just taken his hand out again. "Guess again!"

"S-s-s-s," said Gollum more upset than ever. He thought of all the things he kept in his own pockets: fish-bones, goblins' teeth, wet shells, a bit of bat-wing, a sharp stone to sharpen his fangs on, and other nasty things. He tried to think what other people kept in their pockets.

"Knife!" he said at last.

"Wrong!" said Bilbo, who had lost his some time ago. "Last guess!"

Now Gollum was in a much worse state than when Bilbo had asked him the egg-question. He hissed and spluttered and rocked himself backwards and forwards, and slapped his feet on the floor, and wriggled and squirmed; but still he did not dare to waste his last guess.

"Come on!" said Bilbo. "I am waiting!" He tried to sound bold and cheerful, but he did not feel at all sure how the game was going to end, whether Gollum guessed right or not.

"Time's up!" he said.

"String, or nothing!" shrieked Gollum, which was not quite fair — working in two guesses at once.

"Both wrong," cried Bilbo very much relieved; and he jumped at once to his feet, put his back to the nearest wall, and held out his little sword. But funnily enough he need not have been alarmed. For one thing Gollum had learned long long ago was never, never, to cheat at the riddle-game, which is a sacred one and of immense antiquity. Also there was the sword. He simply sat and whispered.

"What about the present?" asked Bilbo, not that he cared very much, still he felt that he had won it, pretty fairly, and in very difficult circumstances too.

"Must we give it the thing, preciouss? Yess, we must! We must fetch it, preciouss, and give it the present we promised." So Gollum paddled back to his boat, and Bilbo thought he had heard the last of him. But he had not. The hobbit was just thinking of going back up the passage — having had quite enough of Gollum and the dark water's edge — when he heard him wailing and squeaking away in the gloom. He was on his island (of which, of course, Bilbo knew nothing), scrabbling here and there, searching and seeking in vain, and turning out his pockets.

"Where iss it? Where iss it?" Bilbo heard him squeaking. "Lost, lost, my preciouss, lost, lost! Bless us and splash us! We haven't the present we promised, and we haven't even got it for ourselves."

Bilbo turned round and waited, wondering what it could be that the creature was making such a fuss about. This proved very fortunate afterwards. For Gollum came back and made a tremendous spluttering and whispering and croaking; and in the end Bilbo gathered that Gollum had had a ring — a wonderful, beautiful ring, a ring that he had been given for a birthday present, ages and ages before in old days when such rings were less uncommon. Sometimes he had it in his pocket; usually he kept it in a little hole in the rock on his island; sometimes he wore it — when he was very, very hungry, and tired of fish, and crept along dark passages looking for stray goblins. Then he might venture even into places where the torches were lit and made his eyes blink and smart; but he would be safe. O yes! very nearly safe; for if you slipped that ring on your finger, you were invisible; only in the sunlight could you be seen, and then only by your shadow, and that was a faint and shaky sort of shadow.

I don't know how many times Gollum begged Bilbo's pardon. He kept on saying: "We are ssorry; we didn't mean to cheat, we meant to give it our only pressent, if it won the competition." He even offered to catch Bilbo some nice juicy fish to eat as a consolation.

Bilbo shuddered at the thought of it. "No thank you!" he said as politely as he could.

He was thinking hard, and the idea came to him that Gollum must have dropped that ring sometime and that he must have found it, and that he had that very ring in his pocket. But he had the wits not to tell Gollum.

"Finding's keeping!" he said to himself; and being in a very tight place, I daresay, he was right. Anyway the ring belonged to him now.

"Never mind!" he said. "The ring would have been mine now, if you had found it; so you would have lost it anyway. And I will let you off on one condition."

"Yes, what iss it? What does it wish us to do, my precious?"

"Help me to get out of these places," said Bilbo.

Now Gollum had to agree to this, if he

was not to cheat. He still very much wanted just to try what the stranger tasted like; but now he had to give up all idea of it. Still there was the little sword; and the stranger was wide awake and on the look out, not unsuspecting as Gollum liked to have the things which he attacked. So perhaps it was best after all.

That is how Bilbo got to know that the tunnel ended at the water and went no further on the other side where the mountain wall was dark and solid. He also learned that he ought to have turned down one of the side passages to the right before he came to the bottom; but he could not follow Gollum's directions for finding it again on the way up, and he made the wretched creature come and show him the way.

As they went along up the tunnel together, Gollum flip-flapping at his side, Bilbo going very softly, he thought he would try the ring. He slipped it on his finger.

"Where iss it? Where iss it gone to?" said Gollum at once, peering about with his long eyes.

"Here I am, following behind!" said Bilbo slipping off the ring again, and feeling very pleased to have it and to find that it really did what Gollum said.

Now on they went again, while Gollum counted the passages to left and right: "One left, one right, two right, three right, two left," and so on. He began to get very shaky and afraid as they left the water further and further behind; but at last he stopped by a low opening on their left (going up) — "six right, four left."

"Here'ss the passage," he whispered. "It musst squeeze in and sneak down. We durstn't go with it, my preciouss, no we durstn't, gollum!"

So Bilbo slipped under the arch, and said good-bye to the nasty miserable creature; and very glad he was. He did not feel comfortable until he felt quite sure it was gone, and he kept his head out in the main tunnel listening until the flip-flap of Gollum going back to his boat died away in the darkness. Then he went down the new passage.

It was a low narrow one roughly made. It was all right for the hobbit, except when he stubbed his toes in the dark on nasty jags in the floor; but it must have been a bit low for goblins. Perhaps it was not knowing that goblins are used to this sort of thing, and go along quite fast stooping low with their hands almost on the floor, that made Bilbo forget the danger of meeting them and hurry forward recklessly.

Soon the passage began to go up again, and after a while it climbed steeply. That slowed him down. But at last after some time the slope stopped, the passage turned a corner and dipped down again, and at the bottom of a short incline he saw filtering round another corner — a glimmer of light. Not red light as of fire or lantern, but pale ordinary out-of-doors sort of light. Then he began to run. Scuttling along as fast as his little legs would carry him he turned the corner and came suddenly right into an open place where the light, after all that time in the dark, seemed dazzlingly bright. Really it was only a leak of sunshine in through a doorway, where a great door, a stone door, was left a little open.

Bilbo blinked, and then he suddenly saw the goblins: goblins in full armour with drawn swords sitting just inside the door, and watching it with wide eyes, and the passage that led to it! They saw him sooner than he saw them, and with yells of delight they rushed upon him.

Whether it was accident or presence of mind, I don't know. Accident, I think, because the hobbit was not used yet to his new treasure. Anyway he slipped the ring on his left hand — and the goblins stopped short. They could not see a sign of him. Then they yelled twice as loud as before, but not so delightedly.

"Where is it?" they cried.

"Go back up the passage!" some shouted.

"This way!" some yelled. "That way!" others yelled.

"Look out for the door," bellowed the captain.

Whistles blew, armour clashed, swords rattled, goblins cursed and swore and ran hither and thither, falling over one another and getting very angry. There was a terrible outcry, to-do, and disturbance.

Bilbo was dreadfully frightened, but he had the sense to understand what had happened and to sneak behind a big barrel which held drink for the goblin-guards, and so get out of the way and avoid being bumped into, trampled to death, or caught by feel.

"I must get to the door, I must get to the door!" he kept on saying to himself, but it was a long time before he ventured to try. Then it was like a horrible game of blindman's-buff. The place was full of goblins running about, and the poor little hobbit dodged this way and that, was knocked over by a goblin who could not make out what he had bumped into, scrambled away on all fours, slipped between the legs of the captain just in time, got up, and ran for the door.

It was still ajar, but a goblin had pushed it nearly to. Bilbo struggled but he could not move it. He tried to squeeze through the crack. He squeezed and squeezed, and he stuck! It was awful. His buttons had got wedged on the edge of the door and the door-post. He could see outside into the open air: there were a few steps running down into a narrow valley between tall mountains; the sun came out from behind a cloud and shone bright on the outside of the door — but he could not get through.

Suddenly one of the goblins inside shouted: "There is a shadow by the door. Something is outside!"

Bilbo's heart jumped into his mouth. He gave a terrific squirm. Buttons burst off in all directions. He was through, with a torn coat and waistcoat, leaping down the steps like a goat, while bewildered goblins were still picking up his nice brass buttons on the doorstep.

Of course they soon came down after him, hooting and hallooing, and hunting among the trees. But they don't like the sun: it makes their legs wobble and their heads giddy. They could not find Bilbo with the ring on, slipping in and out of the shadow of the trees, running quick and quiet, and keeping out of the sun; so soon they went back grumbling and cursing to guard the door. Bilbo had escaped.

Half Magic
What Happened to Katharine[8]

EDWARD EAGER

With the finding of a magic charm that granted half of any wish, four children were launched on a series of remarkable adventures. In the following selection, all of them — but especially nine-year-old Katharine — discover that the intrusion of twentieth-century children into the world of King Arthur and his knights creates some unforeseen problems.

Next morning there were no secret meetings before breakfast.

Jane stayed in her room and Mark stayed in his room, and in the room they shared Katharine and Martha hardly conversed at all.

Each of the children was too busy making private plans and deciding on favorite wishes.

Breakfast was eaten in silence, but not without the exchange of some excited looks. The children's mother was aware that something was in the air, and wondered what new trial lay in store for her.

When their mother had gone to work and the dishes and other loathly tasks were done, the four children gathered in Katharine and Martha's room. Katharine had already checked to see that the charm still lay in its cubbyhole, unharmed by wish of mouse or termite.

Jane had drawn up some rules.

"The wishes are to go by turns," she said. "Nobody's to make any main wish that doesn't include all the rest of us. If there have to be any smaller wishes later on in the same adventure, the person who wished the main wish gets to make them, except in case of emergency. Like if he loses the charm and one of the other ones finds it. I get to go first."

Katharine had something to say about that.

"I don't see why," she said. "You always get dibs on first 'cause you're the oldest, and

8 From Edward Eager, *Half Magic* (Harcourt, Brace, 1954).

grown ups always pick Martha 'cause she's the baby, and Mark has a wonderful double life with all this and being a boy, too! Middle ones never get any privileges at all! Besides, who hasn't had a wish of her own yet? Think back!"

It was true. Jane had had the half-fire, and Martha had made Carrie half-talk, and Mark had taken them to half of a desert island.

Jane had to agree that Katharine deserved a chance. But she couldn't keep from giving advice.

"We don't want any old visits with Henry Wadsworth Longfellow," she said. "Make it something that's fun for everybody."

"I'm going to," said Katharine. "But I can't decide between wishing we could all fly like birds and wishing we had all the money in the world."

"Those aren't any good," said Jane. "People always wish those in stories, and it never works out at *all!* They either fly too near the sun and get burned, or end up crushed under all the money!"

"We could make it *paper* money," suggested Katharine.

A discussion followed as to how many million dollars in large bills it would take to crush a person to death. By the time the four children got back to the subject of the magic charm seventeen valuable minutes had been wasted.

But now Mark had an idea.

"We've found out the charm can take us through space," he said. "What about time?"

"You mean travel around in the past?" Jane's eyes were glowing. "See Captain Kidd and Nero?"

"I've always wanted to live back in the olden romantic days," said Katharine, getting excited, too. "In days of old when knights were bold!"

The others were joining in by now. For once the four children were all in complete agreement.

"Put in about tournaments," said Mark.

"And quests," said Jane.

"Put in a good deed, too," said Martha. "Just to be on the safe side."

"Don't forget to say two times everything,"

said all three. They clustered eagerly around Katharine as she took hold of the charm.

"I wish," said Katharine, "that we may go back twice as far as to the days of King Arthur, and see two tournaments and go on two quests and do two good deeds."

The next thing the four children knew, they were standing in the midst of a crowded highway. Four queens were just passing, riding under a silken canopy. The next moment seven merry milkmaids skipped past, going a-Maying. In the distance a gallant knight was chasing a grimly giant with puissant valor, and in the other direction a grimly giant was chasing a gallant knight for all he was worth. Some pilgrims stopped and asked the four children the way to Canterbury. The four children didn't know.

But by now they were tired of the crowded traffic conditions on the King's Highway, and crossed into a field, where the grass seemed greener and fresher than any they had ever seen in their own time. A tall figure lay on the ground nearby, under an apple tree. It was a knight in full armor, and he was sound asleep.

The four children knew he was asleep, because Martha lifted the visor of his helmet and peeked inside. A gentle snore issued forth.

The knight's sword lay on the ground beside him, and Mark reached to pick it up.

Immediately the sleeping knight awoke, and sat up.

"Who steals my purse steals trash," he said, "but who steals my sword steals honor itself, and him will I harry by wood and by water till I cleave him from his brain-pan to his thigh-bone!"

"I beg your pardon, sir," said Mark.

"We didn't mean anything," said Jane.

"We're sorry," said Katharine.

The knight rubbed his eyes with his mailed fist. Instead of the miscreant thief he had expected to see, he saw Mark and Jane and Katharine and Martha.

"Who be you?" he said. "Hath some grimly foe murdered me in my sleep? Am I in Heaven? Be ye cherubim or seraphim?"

"We be neither," said Katharine. "And this isn't Heaven. We are four children."

"Pish," said the knight. "Ye be like no

children these eyes have ever beheld. Your garb is outlandish."

"People who live in tin armour shouldn't make remarks," said Katharine.

At this moment there was an interruption. A lady came riding up on a milk-white palfrey. She seemed considerably excited.

"Hist, gallant knight!" she cried.

The knight rose to his feet, and bowed politely. The lady began batting her eyes, and looking at him in a way that made the children feel ashamed for her.

"Thank Heaven I found you," she went on. "You alone of all the world can help me, if your name be Sir Launcelot, as I am let to know it is!"

The children stared at the knight, open-mouthed with awe.

"Are you really Sir Launcelot?" Mark asked him.

"That is my name," said the knight.

The four children stared at him harder. Now that he wasn't looking so sleepy they could see that it was true. No other in all the world could wear so manly a bearing, so noble a face. They were in the presence of Sir Launcelot du Lake, the greatest knight in all the Age of Chivalry!

"How is Elaine?" Katharine wanted to know right away, "and little Galahad?"

"I know not the folk you mention," said Sir Launcelot.

"Oh, yes, you do, sooner or later," said Katharine. "You probably just haven't come to them yet."

"Be ye a prophetess?" cried Sir Launcelot, becoming interested. "Can ye read the future? Tell me more!"

But the lady on the milk-white palfrey was growing impatient.

"Away, poppets!" she said, getting between the four children and Sir Launcelot. "Gallant knight, I crave your assistance. In a dolorous tower nearby a dread ogre is distressing some gentlewomen. I am Preceptress of the Distressed Gentlewoman Society. We need your help."

"Naturally," said Sir Launcelot. He whistled, and his trusty horse appeared from behind the apple tree, where it had been cropping apples. Sir Launcelot started to mount the horse.

The four children looked at each other. They did not like what they had seen of the lady at all, and they liked the way she had spoken to them even less.

Katharine stepped forward.

"I wouldn't go if I were you," she said. "It's probably a trap."

The lady gave her an evil look.

"Even so," said Sir Launcelot, "needs must when duty calls." He adjusted his reins.

Katharine drew herself up to her full four feet four.

"As you noticed before, I be a mighty prophetess!" she cried. "And I say unto you, go not where this lady bids. She will bring you nothing but disaster!"

"I shall go where I please," said Sir Launcelot.

"So there!" said the lady.

"You'll be sorry!" said Katharine.

"Enough of parley," said Sir Launcelot. "Never yet did Launcelot turn from a worthy quest. I know who ye be now. Ye be four false wizards come to me in the guise of children to tempt me from my course. 'Tis vain. Out of the way. Flee, churls. Avaunt and quit my sight, thy bones are marrowless. Giddy-up."

Sir Launcelot chirruped to his horse, and the lady chirruped to hers, and away they went, galloping down the King's Highway. The four children had to scatter to both sides to avoid the flying hooves.

Of course it was but the work of a moment and a simple problem in fractions for Katharine to wish they all had horses and could follow.

Immediately they had, and they did.

Sir Launcelot turned, and saw the four children close at his heels, mounted now on four dashing chargers.

"Away, fiends!" he said.

"Shan't!" said Katharine.

They went on.

The four children had never ridden horseback before, but they found that it came to them quite easily, though Martha's horse was a bit big for her, and she had trouble posting.

And it was particularly interesting when, every time the lady started casting loving looks at Sir Launcelot, the children would ride up close behind and make jeering noises, and Sir Launcelot would turn in his saddle and shout, "Begone, demons!" at them. This happened every few minutes. Sir Launcelot seemed to get a little bit angrier each time.

When they had ridden a goodly pace they came to a dark wood, stretching along both sides of the highway. Just at the edge of the wood, the lady cried out that her horse had cast a shoe. Sir Launcelot reined in to go to her aid. The four children stopped at a safe distance.

Then, just as Sir Launcelot was dismounting, three knights rode out of the wood. One was dressed all in red, one in green and one in black. Before the children could cry out, the knights rushed at Sir Launcelot from behind.

It was three against one and most unfair. But even so, Sir Launcelot's strength would have been as the strength of at least nine if he hadn't been taken by surprise. As it was, he had no time even to touch his hand to his sword before the three knights had seized and disarmed him, bound him hand and foot, flung him across the saddle of his own horse, and galloped off into the wood with him, a hapless prisoner.

The lady turned on the four children.

"Ha ha!" she cried. "Now they will take him to my castle, where he will lie in a deep dungeon and be beaten every day with thorns! And so we shall serve all knights of the Round Table who happen this way! Death to King Arthur!"

"Why, you false thing, you!" said Jane.

"I told him so!" said Katharine.

"Let's go home!" said Martha.

"No, we have to rescue him!" said Mark.

"Ho ho!" said the lady. "Just you try it! Your magic is a mere nothing compared with mine, elfspawn! Know that I am the great enchantress, Morgan le Fay!"

"You *would* be!" said Katharine, who didn't like being called "elfspawn," as who would? "I remember you in the books, always making trouble. I wish you'd go jump in the lake!"

Katharine wasn't thinking of the charm when she wished this, or she might have worded it differently. But that didn't stop the charm.

"Good old charm!" said Mark, as he watched what happened.

Morgan le Fay didn't go jump in the lake; she merely fell in a pool. Luckily there was a pool handy. She slid backwards off her horse and landed in it in a sitting position. And luckier still, the pool had a muddy bottom, and Morgan le Fay stuck there long enough for Katharine to make another, calmer wish, which was that she would *stay* stuck, and unable to use any of her magic, for twice as long as would be necessary.

This done, the four children turned their horses into the wood, and set about following the wicked knights. Morgan le Fay hurled a few curses after them from among the water weeds, but these soon died away in the distance.

There was no path to follow through the wood. The branches of trees hung low and thick, and the earth beneath them was damp and dark and dank, and no birds sang.

"This," said Katharine, "is what I would call a tulgey wood."

"Don't!" cried Martha. "Suppose something came whiffling through it!"

The four children pressed on. Suddenly they came to a clearing, and there amidst a tangle of lambkill and henbane and deadly nightshade they saw the witch's castle rising just ahead of them. Poison ivy mantled its walls. There were snakes in the moat and bats in the belfry. The four children did not like the look of it at all.

"What do we do now?" said Jane.

"Wish him free, of course," said Mark.

"Just stand out here and wish? That's too easy!" said Katharine.

"I'm not going inside that castle!" said Martha.

"Nay," said Katharine, who did not seem to be so docile today as she used to be. "Ye forget that I be a mighty prophetess. Trust ye unto my clever strategy!"

"Bushwah," said Mark. "Less talk and more action."

Katharine put her hand on the charm. "I wish that two doors of this castle may stand open for us," she said.

So then the children had to look for the

one door that did. They found it at last, a little back door with a small drawbridge of its own, over the moat. The drawbridge was down and the door was ajar. The children went over the drawbridge.

"Beware!" croaked the magic talking frogs in the moat.

They went in through the doorway. A long dark passage lay beyond.

"Beware!" squeaked the magic talking mice in the walls.

The children went along the passage. It wound and twisted a good deal. The magic cobwebs hanging from the ceiling brushed at their faces and caught at their clothing, trying to hold them back, but they broke away and pushed on.

At last the passage ended at a heavy doorway. From beyond it came the sound of loud voices raised in something that was probably intended to be music. The children eased the door open a crack and peeked through, into a large hall.

The red knight and the green knight and the black knight were enjoying a hearty meal, and washing down each mouthful with a draught of nut-brown ale. They were singing at the table, which was rude of them, and the words of their song were ruder still.

> *"Speak roughly to our Launcelot*
> *And beat him with a brier!*
> *And kick him in the pants a lot—*
> *Of this we never tire!*
> *We've put him in a dungeon cell*
> *And there we'll beat him very well!*
> *Clink, canikin, clink!"*

The four children looked at each other indignantly; then they peeked through again.

Some varlets had appeared in the hall. They cleared away the dishes, left the dessert platter on the table, and departed.

The dessert was a number of round plum puddings, all aflame with blazing blue brandy. The black knight stood up to serve them.

At that moment Katharine remembered a story she had once read. She decided to have some fun with the three knights.

"I wish two of those puddings were stuck to the end of your nose!" she cried, putting her hand on the charm and staring straight at the black knight, through the crack of the doorway. And immediately one of them was.

But this pudding, unlike the one in the story, was still burning blue with brandy-fire; so that not only was it humiliating to the black knight, but hurt a good deal as well. And furthermore, his long black whiskers, of which he was inordinately proud, began to singe badly. He gave a wild howl, and his face turned nearly as black as his garments, with rage.

"Ods blood, who hath played this scurvy trick upon me?" he cried, beating at his nose and whiskers with his hands, and then yelling with pain as the flames scorched his fingers.

"Tee hee hee," tittered the green knight. "You look very funny!"

The black knight whirled on him.

"Be it *you*, then, who hath played this scurvy trick?" he cried.

"No, it be not I," said the green knight, "but you look very funny, just the same!"

"Oh, I do, do I?" shouted the black knight, in a passion. And he whipped his sword out of its scabbard, and swapped off the green knight's head.

The red knight jumped to his feet.

"I say, Albemarle, that was going a bit too far!" he cried.

"Oh, I don't know," said the black knight. "He was exceedingly provoking! Come and help me get this great pudding thing off my nose!"

"Well," said the red knight, looking at him rather dubiously, "I don't know if I can, but I'll *try!*"

And he whipped *his* sword out of *its* scabbard, and swapped off the pudding from the black knight's nose. Unfortunately (for him) he swapped off a good bit of the nose, too.

The black knight gave a wild bellow and hurled himself at the red knight, sword in hand. The red knight parried his thrust. A moment later they were joined in deadly combat, leaping about the hall, smashing furniture, and hacking off parts of each other with the greatest abandon.

Behind the door, the four children shut their eyes, held their ears, and cowered trembling in each other's arms.

The combat did not last long. Two sword

blades flashed in the air, and a second later two heads fell on the floor, followed, more slowly, by two bodies.

There was a silence. Katharine hadn't meant her wish to end in such a gory and final way. But she reminded herself to be bloody, bold and resolute, and crept through the door into the hall, followed by the three others. All four averted their eyes from what they would have seen if they had looked at the floor.

"I do think you might have managed it neater," said Jane. "How can we get through to the dungeon with all these different pieces of knight lying around underfoot?"

"The point is that I managed it at all," said Katharine, more cheerfully than she felt. "And we don't have to walk; we can wish ourselves there."

She put her hand on the charm and wished that they were twice as far as the dungeon door and that she had two keys to the dungeon in her hand.

After that, of course, it was but a matter of turning the key, and out walked Sir Launcelot, followed by several dozen other knights who had also been prisoners of the enchantress and her friends, and who looked somewhat the worse for their daily beatings.

The other captive knights fell on their knees, kissing the children's hands and hailing them as their deliverers. Sir Launcelot also thanked the children quite politely, but somehow he didn't seem so happy to be free as the children had expected he would.

A moment later, when the other captive knights had left to resume their interrupted quests, the children found out why.

"You saved me by magical means?" Sir Launcelot asked.

"That's right," said Katharine, proudly. "I did it with my little charm."

"That mislikes me much," said Sir Launcelot. "I would it were otherwise."

"Well, really!" said Katharine. "I suppose you'd rather have stayed in there being beaten?"

"Sooner that," said Sir Launcelot, "than bring shame to my honor by taking unfair magical advantage of a foe, however deadly!"

"Well, if you're all that particular," said Katharine, annoyed. "I can easily put them

back together again." And she led him into the great hall, and showed him the different pieces of the three knights.

"Please do so," said Sir Launcelot.

"Shall I lock you up in the dungeon again?" asked Katharine, sarcastically. "Doesn't it hurt your conscience that I set you free?"

"That much advantage," said Sir Launcelot, "I think I can take. Some fair jailer's daughter would probably have let me out sooner or later, anyway."

"Oh, is that so?" said Katharine. "I'm sorry I troubled, I'm sure! Is there anything else?"

"Well, yes," said Sir Launcelot. "You might just fetch me my sword and armor, which these cowardly knaves have taken from me."

Thoroughly cross with him by now, Katharine wished the sword and armor back on him; then, working out the fractions carefully, she spoke the wish that was to bring the red knight, the green knight, and the black knight back to life.

It was very interesting watching the different pieces of the different-colored knights reassembling themselves on the hall floor, and the four children were sorry when it was over.

But by then something even more interesting was going on. Because by then Sir Launcelot was fighting the three knights singlehanded, and that was a sight worth coming back many centuries to see.

Sir Launcelot did not seem to appreciate the four children's interest, however.

"Go away. Thank you very much. Good-by," he called, pinning the green knight against the wall with a table, and holding the red and black ones at bay with his sword.

"Can't we help?" Mark wanted to know.

"No. Go away," said Sir Launcelot, cracking the red knight on the pate, thwacking the black knight in the chest with his backhand swing, and leaping over the table to take a whack at the green one.

"Can't we even *watch?*" Jane wailed.

"No. It makes me nervous. I want to be alone," said Sir Launcelot, ducking under the table to send the red knight sprawling, then turning to face the black and green ones again.

Katharine sighed, and made a wish.

Next moment the four children were on their horses once more, riding along the King's Highway.

"We might at least have waited in the yard," complained Martha. "Now we'll never know how it ended!"

"He'll come out on top; trust *him!*" said Katharine. "I *do* get tired of people who are always right, all the time! Anyway, we'll be seeing him again, I imagine. At the tournament."

"Gee, yes, the tournament. I was forgetting," said Mark. "When do you suppose it'll be?"

"Not for weeks, maybe, by the time here," said Katharine. "But for us, a mere wish on the charm . . . "

And she merely wished.

"I can't get used to this being rushed around," complained Martha a second later, as she found herself somewhere else for the third time in three minutes. "Where are we now, and when is it?"

"Camelot, I should think," said Katharine, "in tournament time! Look!"

Jane and Mark and Martha looked. Camelot and the field of tournament were exactly as they would have expected them to be, from the descriptions in *The Boy's King Arthur* and the wonderful books of Mr. T. H. White. Trumpets were blowing clarion calls, the pennons fluttered on the blue air, and armor flashed in the bright light, and gallant knights and trusty squires and faithful pages and ladies fair and lowly varlets were crowding into the stands in hundreds, to watch the chivalrous sport.

The four children had front-row grandstand seats, for Katharine had made that a part of her wish. She had forgotten to say anything in her wish about getting rid of the four horses, and at first these made some trouble by wanting to sit in the grandstand, too, much to the annoyance of the people sitting behind. But Katharine wished them twice as far as away, and they disappeared.

At this, the people behind got up and left in a hurry, looking back at the four children and muttering about witchcraft and sorcery.

The children paid small heed. They were too busy looking around them and drinking in the sights.

King Arthur sat enthroned on a high platform at one end of the field. The children could see him clearly, with his kind, simple, understanding face, like the warm sun come to shine on merry England. Queen Guinevere was seated at his right, and Merlin, the magician, thin and wise and graybearded, at his left.

And now the trumpets blew an extra long fanfare, and the tournament began.

Sir Launcelot was among the first to ride out on the field. The children recognized him by his armor.

"I told you he'd come out all right," said Katharine, a bit bitterly.

But when Sir Launcelot got going in that tournament, even Katharine had to admire him.

He smote down five knights with his first spear, and four knights with his second spear, and unhorsed three more with his sword, until all the people sitting round on the benches began crying out, "Oh, Gramercy, what marvelous deeds that knight doth do in that there field!"

Jane sighed a satisfied sigh. "Kind of glorious, isn't it?" she murmured.

"It's the most wonderful age in human history," said Mark, solemnly. "If only it didn't have to end!"

"Why did it?" asked Martha, who hadn't read *The Boy's King Arthur* yet.

"Partly 'cause some of the other knights got tired of being knocked down all the time and having Launcelot always win," Mark told her.

"Yes," said Katharine, in rather a peculiar voice, "it would really be a good deed, in a way, if somebody knocked *him* down for a change, wouldn't it?"

Mark gave her a sharp look, but just then Sir Launcelot started knocking down more knights, and he had to watch the field. When he looked again, Katharine wasn't there.

Mark nudged Jane hard, as a horrible thought came into his mind.

Jane turned and saw the empty spot where Katharine had been, and Mark could tell that she was having the same thought, too.

Just then there was an interruption in the tournament. A strange knight rode out on the field of combat, and straight up to King Arthur's platform.

"I crave your Majesty's permission to challenge Sir Launcelot to single combat!" cried the strange knight in a voice loud enough for the children to hear clearly from where they sat.

The hearts of Jane and Mark sank.

Even Martha now guessed the horrid truth. "How dare she?" she whispered.

"I don't know," said Mark. "She's been getting too full of herself ever since we started this wish!"

"Wait till I get her home!" said Jane grimly.

"How call they you, strange sir?" King Arthur was saying, meanwhile, "and whence do you hail?"

"They call me Sir Kath," said the strange knight, "and I hail from Toledo, Ohio."

"I know not this Toledo," said King Arthur, "but fight if you will. Let the combat begin."

The trumpets sounded another clarion call, the strange knight faced Sir Launcelot, and there began the strangest combat, it is safe to say, ever witnessed by the knights of the Round, or any other, Table.

The intrepid Katharine thought herself very clever at this moment. She had wished she were wearing two suits of armor and riding two horses, and she had wished she were two and a half times as tall and strong as Sir Launcelot, and she had wished that she would defeat him twice. And immediately here she was, wearing one suit of armor and riding one horse, and she was one and a quarter times as tall and strong, and she couldn't wait to defeat him once.

But in her cleverness she had forgotten one thing. She had forgotten to wish that she knew the rules of jousting. And here she was, facing the greatest knight in the world, and she didn't know how to start. She knew she'd win in the end, because she'd wished it that way, but what was she to do in the beginning and middle?

Before she could work out another wish

to take care of this, Sir Launcelot rode at her, struck her with his lance, and knocked her back onto her horse's tail. Then he rode at her from the opposite direction, and knocked her forward onto her horse's neck.

The crowd roared with laughter.

The feelings of Jane, Mark and Martha may well be imagined.

As for the feelings of Katharine, they knew no bounds. She still held the magic charm clutched in one hot hand, and she wasn't bothering about correct arithmetic now.

"I wish I could fight ten times as well as you, you bully! Yah!" were the words that the valiant Sir Kath spoke, upon the field. It was a cry of pure temper.

And immediately she could fight five times as well as Sir Launcelot, and everyone knows how good *he* was.

What followed would have to be seen to be believed.

Katharine came down like several wolves on the fold. She seemed to spring from all sides at once. Her sword flashed like a living thunderbolt. Her lance whipped about, now here, now there, like a snake gone mad.

"Zounds!" cried the people, and "Lackaday" and "Wurra wurra!"

Jane, Mark and Martha watched with clasped hands.

If Sir Launcelot had not been the greatest knight in the world he would never have lived to tell the tale. Even as it was, the end was swift. In something less than a trice he was unseated from his horse, fell to the ground with a crash, and did not rise again.

Katharine galloped round and round the field, bowing graciously to the applause of the crowd.

But she soon noticed that the crowd wasn't applauding very loudly. And it was only the traitorous knights like Sir Mordred and Sir Agravaine, the ones who were jealous of Launcelot, who were applauding at all.

The rest of the crowd was strangely silent. For Launcelot, the flower of knighthood, the darling of the people's hearts, the greatest champion of the Round Table, had been defeated!

Queen Guinevere looked furious. King Arthur looked sad. The attendant knights, except for the traitorous ones, looked absolutely wretched. Merlin looked as if he didn't believe it.

Jane and Mark and Martha looked as though they believed it, but didn't want to.

And it was then that the full knowledge of what she had done swept over Katharine. She had succeeded and she had failed. She, a mere girl, had defeated the greatest knight in history. But she had pretended to herself that she was doing it for a good deed and really it had been just because she was annoyed with Launcelot for not appreciating her help enough, back in Morgan le Fay's castle.

Her cheeks flamed and she felt miserable. It was hot inside her helmet suddenly, and she dragged it off. Then she remembered too late that she'd forgotten something else, when she made her wish. She had wished to be in armor, and to be on horseback, and to be tall and strong, and to win. But she had forgotten to say anything about not being Katharine any longer.

Now, as the helmet came away, her long brown hair streamed down onto her shoulders, and her nine-year-old, little-girl face blinked at the astonished crowd.

Those sitting nearest the ringside saw. Sir Mordred tittered. Sir Agravaine sneered. The mean knights who were jealous of Sir Launcelot began to laugh, and mingled with the laughter were the cruel words, "Beaten by a girl!"

Some horrid little urchins took up the cry, and made a rude song of it:

"Launcelot's a chur-ul,
  Beaten by a gir-ul!"

Sir Launcelot came to, and sat up. He heard the laughter, and he heard the song. He looked at Katharine. Katharine looked away, but not before he had recognized her. He got to his feet. There was silence all round the field; even the mean knights stopped laughing.

Sir Launcelot came over to Katharine. "Why have you done this to me?" he said.

"I didn't mean to," said Katharine. She began to cry.

With flushed cheeks but with head held high, Sir Launcelot strode to King Arthur's platform and knelt in the dust before it. In a low voice he asked leave to go on a far quest, a year's journey away at least, that he might hide his shame till by a hundred deeds of valor he would win back his lost honor and expunge the dread words, "Beaten by a girl," forever.

King Arthur did not trust himself to speak. He nodded his consent.

Queen Guinevere did not even look at Sir Launcelot, as he walked away from the field of tournament.

Katharine went on crying.

Merlin spoke a word in King Arthur's ear. King Arthur nodded. He rose, offered an arm to Guinevere, and led her from the stand. Merlin spoke another word, this time to the attendant knights. They began clearing the people from the field.

Most of the people went quietly, but three children in the front row of the grandstand put up quite a fuss, saying that they had to find their sister Katharine, who'd done something terrible, but a sister was a sister and they'd stick up for her, anyway. The knights cleared them away with the rest.

Presently, after what seemed like at least a year, Katharine found herself alone before Merlin. She was still crying.

Merlin looked at her sternly.

"Fie on your weeping," he said. "I wot well that ye be a false enchantress, come here in this guise to defeat our champion and discredit our Table Round!"

"I'm not! I didn't!" said Katharine.

"Ye be, too!" said Merlin, "and you certainly have! After today our name is mud in Camelot!"

"Oh, oh," wept Katharine.

"Silence, sorceress," said Merlin. He waved his wand at her. "I command that you appear before me in your true form!"

Immediately Katharine wasn't tall, or strong, or in armor any more, but just Katharine.

Merlin looked surprised.

"These fiends begin early!" he said. "However, doubtless ye be but the instrument of a greater power." He waved his wand again. "I command that your allies, cohorts, aids, accomplices and companions be brought hither to stand at your side!"

Jane and Mark and Martha appeared beside Katharine, looking nearly as unhappy and uncomfortable as she.

Merlin looked really quite startled. Then he shook his head sadly.

"So young," he said, "and yet so wicked!"

"We're not!" said Martha, making a rude face.

The behavior of the others was more seemly.

"You see, sir," began Mark.

"We didn't mean to," began Jane.

"Let me," said Katharine. "I started it."

And in a rush of words and tears she told Merlin everything, beginning with the charm, and her wish to travel back in time, and going on to what she had hoped to do, and what she'd done and where she'd gone wrong.

"I wanted to do a good deed," she said, "and I *did* one, when I rescued Launcelot from that old dungeon. But then he wasn't properly grateful at all, and made me undo it, so he could rescue himself, all for the sake of his old honor! And that made me cross! And just now I pretended I was defeating him so the other knights wouldn't be so jealous of him, but really I was just trying to get back at him for being so stuck-up! And I always wanted to fight in a real tournament, anyway!"

"Well, now you have," said Merlin, "and what good did you do by it? Just made everybody thoroughly unhappy!"

"I know," said Katharine.

"That's what comes of meddling," said Merlin. "There is a pattern to history, and when you try to change that pattern, no good may follow."

Katharine hung her head.

"However," went on Merlin, and to the surprise of the four children he was smiling now, "all is not lost. I have a few magic tricks of my own, you know. Let me see, how shall I handle this? I *could* turn time back, I suppose, and make it as though this day had never happened, but it would take a lot out of me."

"Really?" said Katharine in surprise. "It would be a mere nothing to *us!*"

Merlin looked at her a bit grimly.

"Oh, it would, would it?" he said.

"Oh, yes," went on Katharine happily. "I could wish Launcelot were twice as near as here again, and then I could wish that he'd defeat me twice, and then I could wish that the people would honor him twice as much as they ever did, and then I could wish . . ."

"Hold!" cried Merlin, in alarm. "A truce to your wishes, before you get us in worse trouble! I think I had best see this wonderful charm of yours." He made a pass at Katharine with his wand. "If there be any magic among you, let it appear now or forever hold its peace."

Katharine's hot hand, which for so long had clutched the charm, opened in spite of itself, and the charm lay in plain sight, on her palm.

Merlin looked at it. His eyes widened. He swept his tall hat from his head, and bowed low before the charm, three times. Then he turned to the children.

"This is a very old and powerful magic," he said. "Older and more powerful than my own. It is, in fact, too powerful and too dangerous for four children, no matter how well they may intend, to have in their keeping. I am afraid I must ask you to surrender it."

He made another pass with his wand. The charm leaped gracefully from Katharine's hand to his own.

Mark spoke.

"But it came to us in our own time," he said, "and that's a part of history, too, just as much as this is. Maybe we were *meant* to find it. Maybe there's some good thing we're supposed to do with it. There is a pattern to history, and when you try to change that pattern, no good may follow."

Merlin looked at him.

"You are a wise child," he said.

"Just average," said Mark, modestly.

"Dear me," said Merlin. "If that be so, if all children be as sensible as you in this far future time you dwell in . . ." He broke off. "What century did you say you come from?"

"We didn't," said Mark, "but it's the twentieth."

"The twentieth century," mused Merlin. "What a happy age it must be — truly the

Golden Age that we are told is to come."

He stood thinking a moment. Then he smiled.

"Very well. Go back to your twentieth century," he said, "and take your magic with you, and do your best with it. But first, I have something to say."

He held the charm at arm's length, rather as though he feared it might bite him, and addressed it with great respect.

"I wish," he said, "that in six minutes it may be as though these children had never appeared here. Except that they — and I — will remember. And I further wish that our tournament may begin all over again and proceed as originally planned by history. Only twice as much so," he added, to be on the safe side.

"Now may I have it back, please?" Katharine asked, when he had done.

"In a minute," said Merlin. "By the way, have you been making a lot of wishes lately? It feels rather worn out to me. It won't last forever, you know."

"Oh dear, we were afraid of that," said Jane. "How many more do we get?"

"That would be telling," said Merlin. "But you'd best not waste too many. It might be later than you think."

"Oh!" cried Martha. "Maybe we'll never get home!"

"Don't worry," said Merlin, smiling at her. "There are still a few wishes left for you. And one more for me." Again he held the charm out before him.

"And I thirdly wish," he said, "for the future protection of the world from the terrible good intentions of these children, and for their protection against their own folly, that this charm may, for twice the length of time that it shall be in their hands, grant no further wishes carrying said children out of their own century and country, but that they may find whatsoever boon the magic may have in store for them in their own time and place." He put the charm into Katharine's hands. "And now you'd best be going. Because in less than a minute by my wish, it will be as though you'd never appeared here. And if you aren't home when that happens, goodness knows where you *will* be!"

"But what about the good deed I wished?" said Katharine. "None of the ones I tried worked out!"

"My child," said Merlin, and his smile was very kind now, "you have done your good deed. You have brought me word that for as far into time as the twentieth century, the memory of Arthur, and of the Round Table, which I helped him to create, will be living yet. And that in that far age people will still care for the ideal I began, enough to come back through time and space to try to be of service to it. You have brought me that word, and now I can finish my work in peace, and know that I have done well. And if that's not a good deed, I should like to know what is. Now good-by. Wish quickly. You have exactly seventeen seconds."

Katharine wished.

And because their mother and Miss Bick had been worried yesterday by their being so long away, she put in that when they got home, they should only have been gone two minutes, by real time.

This was really quite thoughtful of Katharine. Perhaps she, too, like Mark the day before, had learned something during her day of adventure.

The next thing the four children knew, they were sitting together in Katharine and Martha's room, and it was still that morning, and they had only been away from home a minute. Yet that minute was packed with memories.

"Did we dream it?" Katharine asked.

"I don't think so, or we wouldn't all remember it," said Mark.

"And we all do, don't we?" said Jane.

And they all did.

"What did that last mean, that Merlin wished on the charm?" Martha wanted to know.

"It means we have to keep our wishes close to home from now on," Mark told her.

"No more travels to foreign climes," said Jane, "and I was all set to take us on a pirate ship next!"

"No more olden times," said Mark, "and I've always wanted to see the Battle of Troy!"

"You might not have liked it, once you

got there," said Katharine, from the depths of her experience. "Traveling in olden times is *hard*."

"I don't care," said Martha. "I don't care if I never travel at all. I'm glad to be home. Aren't you?"

And they all were.

Gulliver's Travels
FROM *A Voyage to Lilliput*
JONATHAN SWIFT

•§ Dean Swift, the author of this biting satire, was a much disappointed, ambitious man when he wrote Gulliver's Travels. *In it he gave vent to all his bitterness by holding up to ridicule authors, lawyers, clergymen, and, above all, governments and their rulers. As satire has a way of losing much of its force when the conditions which evoke it are either forgotten or changed,* Gulliver's Travels *now is to most readers merely a fairy-tale adventure and popular for that reason only.*

CHAPTER 1

We set sail from Bristol, May 4, 1699, and our voyage at first was very prosperous.

It would not be proper, for some reasons, to trouble the reader with the particulars of our adventures in those seas: let it suffice to inform him that in our passage from thence to the East Indies we were driven by a violent storm to the northwest of Van Diemen's Land. By an observation we found ourselves in the latitude of 30 degrees 2 minutes south. Twelve of our crew were dead by immoderate labor and ill food; the rest were in a very weak condition.

On the fifth of November, which was the beginning of summer in those parts, the weather being very hazy, the seamen spied a rock within half a cable's length of the ship; but the wind was so strong that we were driven directly upon it, and immediately split. Six of the crew, of whom I was one, having let down the boat into the sea, made a shift to get clear of the ship and the rock. We rowed, by my computation, about three leagues, till we were able to work no longer, being already spent with labor while we were in the ship. We therefore trusted ourselves to the mercy of the waves, and in about half an hour the boat was overset by a sudden flurry from the north. What became of my companions in the boat, as well as of those who escaped on the rock, or were left in the vessel, I cannot tell, but conclude they were all lost. For my own part, I swam as fortune directed me, and was pushed forward by wind and tide. I often let my legs drop and could feel no bottom; but when I was almost gone and able to struggle no longer I found myself within my depth; and by this time the storm was much abated. The declivity was so small that I walked near a mile before I got to the shore, which I conjectured was about eight o'clock in the evening.

I then advanced forward near half a mile, but could not discover any sign of houses or inhabitants; at least, I was in so weak a condition that I did not observe them. I was extremely tired, and with that and the heat of the weather, and about half a pint of brandy that I drank as I left the ship, I found myself much inclined to sleep. I lay down on the grass, which was very short and soft, where I slept sounder than ever I remember to have done in my life, and, as I reckoned, about nine hours; for when I awaked it was just daylight.

I attempted to rise, but was not able to stir; for, as I happened to lie on my back, I found my arms and legs were strongly fastened on each side to the ground, and my hair, which was long and thick, tied down in the same manner. I likewise felt several slender ligatures across my body, from my arm-pits to my thighs. I could only look upward; the sun began to grow hot, and the light offended my eyes. I heard a confused noise about me, but, in the posture I lay, could see nothing except the sky. In a little time I felt something alive moving on my left leg, which, advancing gently forward over my breast, came almost up to my chin; when, bending my eyes downward as much as I could, I perceived it to be a human creature not six inches high, with a bow and arrow in his hands and a quiver at his back. In the meantime I felt at least forty more of the same kind (as I conjectured) following the first.

I was in the utmost astonishment, and roared so loud that they all ran back in a fright; and some of them, as I was afterward told, were hurt with the falls they got by leaping from my sides upon the ground. However, they soon returned, and one of them, who ventured so far as to get a full sight of my face, lifting up his hands and eyes by way of admiration, cried out in a shrill but distinct voice, *Hekinah degul;* the others repeated the same words several times, but I then knew not what they meant.

I lay all this while, as the reader may believe, in great uneasiness; at length, struggling to get loose, I had the fortune to break the strings and wrench out the pegs that fastened my left arm to the ground; for by lifting it up to my face I discovered the methods they had taken to bind me, and at the same time, with a violent pull which gave me excessive pain, I a little loosened the strings that tied down my hair on the left side, so that I was just able to turn my head about two inches. But the creatures ran off a second time before I could seize them; whereupon there was a great shout in a very shrill accent, and after it ceased I heard one of them cry aloud, *Tolgo phonac;* when in an instant I felt above a hundred arrows discharged on my left hand, which pricked me like so many needles; and, besides, they shot another flight into the air, as we do bombs in Europe, whereof many I suppose fell on my body (though I felt them not), and some on my face, which I immediately covered with my left hand.

When this shower of arrows was over I fell a-groaning with grief and pain; and then striving again to get loose, they discharged another volley larger than the first, and some of them attempted with spears to stick me in the side; but, by good luck, I had on me a buff jerkin which they could not pierce. I thought it the most prudent method to lie still, and my design was to continue so till night, when, my left hand being already loose, I could easily free myself; and as for the inhabitants, I had reason to believe I might be a match for the greatest army they could bring against me, if they were all of the same size with him that I saw.

But fortune disposed otherwise of me. When the people observed I was quiet, they discharged no more arrows; but by the noise I heard, I knew their numbers increased; and about four yards from me, over against my right ear, I heard a knocking for above an hour, like that of people at work; when, turning my head that way as well as the pegs and strings would permit me, I saw a stage erected, about a foot and a half from the ground, capable of holding four of the inhabitants, with two or three ladders to mount it; from whence one of them, who seemed to be a person of quality, made me a long speech, whereof I understood not one syllable.

But I should have mentioned that before the principal person began his oration he cried out three times, *Langro dehul san* (these words and the former were afterward repeated and explained to me). Whereupon immediately about fifty of the inhabitants came and cut the strings that fastened the left side of my head, which gave me the liberty of turning it to the right and observing the person and gesture of him that was to speak. He appeared to be of a middle age and taller than any of the other three who attended him, whereof one was a page that held up his train, and seemed to be somewhat longer than my middle finger; the other two stood one on each side to support him. He acted every part of an orator, and I could observe many periods of threatening, and others of promises, pity, and kindness. I answered in a few words, but in the most submissive manner, lifting up my left hand and both my eyes to the sun, as calling him for a witness; and, being almost famished with hunger, having not eaten a morsel for some hours before I left the ship, I found the demands of nature so strong upon me that I could not forbear my impatience (perhaps against the strict rules of decency) by putting my finger frequently to my mouth to signify that I wanted food.

The Hurgo (for so they call a great lord, as I afterward learned) understood me very well. He descended from the stage and commanded that several ladders should be applied to my sides, on which above a hundred of the inhabitants mounted and walked toward my mouth laden with baskets full of meat, which had been provided and sent thither by the king's orders upon the first intelligence he received of me. I observed there was the flesh of several animals, but could not distinguish them by the taste. There were shoulders, legs, and loins, shaped like those of mutton and very well dressed, but smaller than the wings of a lark. I ate them by two or three at a mouthful, and took three loaves at a time, about the bigness of musket bullets. They supplied me as they could, showing a thousand marks of wonder and astonishment at my bulk and appetite.

I then made another sign that I wanted drink. They found by my eating that a small quantity would not suffice me; and, being a most ingenious people, they flung up with great dexterity one of their largest hogsheads, then rolled it toward my hand, and beat out the top; I drank it off at a draught, which I might well do, for it did not hold half a pint, and tasted like a small wine of Burgundy, but much more delicious. They brought me a second hogshead, which I drank in the same manner, and made signs for more; but they had none to give me.

When I had performed these wonders they shouted for joy and danced upon my breast, repeating several times as they did at first, *Hekinah degul.* They made me a sign that I should throw down the two hogsheads, but first warning the people below to stand out of the way, crying aloud, *Borach mivola,* and when they saw the vessels in the air there was a universal shout of *Hekinah degul.*

I confess I was often tempted, while they were passing backward and forward on my body, to seize forty or fifty of the first that came in my reach and dash them against the ground. But the remembrance of what I had felt, which probably might not be the worst they could do, and the promise of honor I made them, for so I interpreted my submissive behavior, soon drove out these imaginations. Besides, I now considered myself as bound by the laws of hospitality to a people who had treated me with so much expense and magnificence. However, in my thoughts I could not sufficiently wonder at the intrepidity of these diminutive mortals who durst venture to mount and walk upon my body, while one of my hands was at liberty, without trembling at the very sight of so prodigious a creature as I must appear to them.

After some time, when they observed that I made no more demands for meat, there appeared before me a person of high rank from His Imperial Majesty. His Excellency, having mounted on the small of my right leg, advanced forward up to my face, with about a dozen of his retinue. And, producing his credentials under the Signet Royal, which he applied close to my eyes, spoke about ten minutes without any sign of anger, but with a kind of determinate resolution, often pointing forward, which, as I afterward found, was toward the capital city, about half a mile distant, whither, it was agreed by His Majesty in council, that I must be conveyed. I answered in few words, but to no purpose, and made a sign with my hand that was loose, putting it to the other (but over His Excellency's head, for fear of hurting him or his train), and then to my own head and body, to signify that I desired my liberty. It appeared that he understood me well enough, for he shook his head by way of disapprobation, and held his hand in a posture to show that I must be carried as a prisoner. However, he made other signs to let me understand that I should have meat and drink enough and very good treatment.

Whereupon I once more thought of attempting to break my bonds; but again, when I felt the smart of their arrows upon my face and hands, which were all in blisters and many of the darts still sticking in them, and observing likewise that the number of my enemies increased, I gave tokens to let them know that they might do with me what they pleased. Upon this the Hurgo and his train withdrew with much civility and cheerful countenances.

Soon after I heard a general shout, with frequent repetitions of the words, *Peplom selan,* and I felt great numbers of people on my left side, relaxing the cords to such a degree that I was able to turn upon my right. But before this they had daubed my face and both my hands with a sort of ointment very pleasant to the smell, which in a few minutes removed all the smart of their arrows. These circumstances, added to the refreshment I had received by their victuals and drink, which were very nourishing, disposed me to sleep. I slept about eight hours, as I was afterward assured; and it was no wonder, for the physicians, by the Emperor's order, had mingled a sleepy potion in the hogsheads of wine.

It seems that, upon the first moment I was discovered sleeping on the ground after my landing, the Emperor had early notice of it by an express, and determined in council that I should be tied in the manner I have related (which was done in the night while I slept), that plenty of meat and drink should be sent to me, and a machine prepared to carry me to the capital city.

This resolution, perhaps, may appear very bold and dangerous, and I am confident would not be imitated by any prince in Europe on the like occasion; however, in my opinion, it was extremely prudent as well as generous; for, supposing these people had endeavored to kill me with their spears and arrows while I was asleep, I should certainly have awaked with the first sense of smart, which might so far have roused my rage and strength as to have enabled me to break the strings wherewith I was tied; after which, as they were not able to make resistance, so they could expect no mercy.

These people are most excellent mathematicians, and arrived to a great perfection in mechanics by the countenance and encouragement of the Emperor, who is a renowned patron of learning. This prince hath several machines fixed on wheels for the carriage of trees and other great weights. He often builds his largest men-of-war, whereof some are nine foot long, in the woods where the timber grows, and has them carried on these engines three or four hundred yards to the sea. Five hundred carpenters and engineers were immediately set at work to prepare the greatest engine they had. It was a frame of wood raised three inches from the ground, about seven foot long and four wide, moving upon twenty-two wheels. The shout I heard was upon the arrival of this engine, which, it seems, set out in four hours after my land-

ing. It was brought parallel to me as I lay. But the principal difficulty was to raise and place me in this vehicle. Eighty poles, each of one foot high, were erected for this purpose, and very strong cords, of the bigness of pack-thread, were fastened by hooks to many bandages which the workmen had girt round my neck, my hand, my body, and my legs. Nine hundred of the strongest men were employed to draw up these cords by many pulleys fastened on the poles, and thus in less than three hours I was raised and flung into the engine, and there tied fast. All this I was told, for while the whole operation was performing I lay in a profound sleep by the force of that soporiferous medicine infused into my liquor. Fifteen hundred of the Emperor's largest horses, each about four inches and a half high, were employed to draw me toward the metropolis, which, as I said, was half a mile distant.

About four hours after we began our journey I awaked by a very ridiculous accident; for, the carriage being stopped awhile to adjust something that was out of order, two or three of the young natives had the curiosity to see how I looked when I was asleep; they climbed up into the engine, and, advancing very softly to my face, one of them, an officer in the guards, put the sharp end of his half-pike a good way up into my left nostril, which tickled my nose like a straw and made me sneeze violently; whereupon they stole off unperceived, and it was three weeks before I knew the cause of my awaking so suddenly. We made a long march the remaining part of that day, and rested at night with five hundred guards on each side of me, half with torches, and half with bows and arrows, ready to shoot me if I should offer to stir. The next morning at sunrise we continued our march, and arrived within two hundred yards of the city gates about noon. The Emperor and all his court came out to meet us, but his great officers would by no means suffer His Majesty to endanger his person by mounting on my body.

At the place where the carriage stopped there stood an ancient temple, esteemed to be the largest in the whole kingdom, which, having been polluted some years before by an unnatural murder, was, according to the zeal of those people, looked on as profane, and therefore had been applied to common use, and all the ornaments and furniture carried away. In this edifice it was determined I should lodge. The great gate fronting to the north was about four foot high and almost two foot wide, through which I could easily creep. On each side of the gate was a small window not above six inches from the ground; into that on the left side the King's smith conveyed fourscore and eleven chains, like those that hang to a lady's watch in Europe, and almost as large, which were locked to my left leg with six and thirty padlocks. Over against this temple, on t'other side of the great highway, at twenty foot distance, there was a turret at least five foot high. Here the Emperor ascended, with many principal lords of his court, to have an opportunity of viewing me, as I was told, for I could not see them. It was reckoned that above a hundred thousand inhabitants came out of the town upon the same errand; and, in spite of my guards, I believe there could not be fewer than ten thousand at several times who mounted my body by the help of ladders. But a proclamation was soon issued to forbid it upon pain of death. When the workmen found it was impossible for me to break loose, they cut all the strings that bound me, whereupon I rose up with as melancholy a disposition as ever I had in my life. But the noise and astonishment of the people at seeing me rise and walk are not to be expressed. The chains that held my left leg were about two yards long, and gave me not only the liberty of walking backward and forward in a semicircle, but, being fixed within four inches of the gate, allowed me to creep in and lie at my full length in the temple.

Chapter III

My gentleness and good behavior had gained so far on the Emperor and his court, and indeed upon the army and people in general, that I began to conceive hopes of getting my liberty in a short time. I took all possible methods to cultivate this favorable disposition. The natives came by degrees to be less apprehensive of any danger from me.

I would sometimes lie down, and let five or six of them dance on my hand. And at last the boys and girls would venture to come and play at hide and seek in my hair. I had now made a good progress in understanding and speaking their language.

The horses of the army, and those of the royal stables, having been daily led before me, were no longer shy, but would come up to my very feet without starting. The riders would leap them over my hand as I held it on the ground, and one of the Emperor's huntsmen, upon a large courser, took my foot, shoe and all; which was indeed a prodigious leap. I had the good fortune to divert the Emperor one day after a very extraordinary manner. I desired he would order several sticks of two foot high, and the thickness of an ordinary cane, to be brought me; whereupon His Majesty commanded the master of his woods to give directions accordingly; and the next morning six woodmen arrived with as many carriages, drawn by eight horses to each. I took nine of these sticks, and fixing them firmly in the ground in a quadrangular figure, two foot and a half square, I took four other sticks, and tied them parallel at each corner, about two foot from the ground; then I fastened my handkerchief to the nine sticks that stood erect, and extended it on all sides till it was as tight as the top of a drum; and the four parallel sticks rising about five inches higher than the handkerchief served as ledges on each side. When I had finished my work I desired the Emperor to let a troop of his best horse, twenty-four in number, come and exercise upon this plain. His Majesty approved of the proposal, and I took them up one by one in my hands, ready mounted and armed, with the proper officers to exercise them. As soon as they got into order, they divided into two parties, performed mock skirmishes, discharged blunt arrows, drew their swords, fled and pursued, attacked and retired, and in short discovered the best military discipline I ever beheld. The parallel sticks secured them and their horses from falling over the stage; and the Emperor was so much delighted, that he ordered this entertainment to be repeated several days, and once was pleased to be lifted up and give the word of command;

and, with great difficulty, persuaded even the Empress herself to let me hold her in her close chair within two yards of the stage, from whence she was able to take a full view of the whole performance. It was my good fortune that no ill accident happened in these entertainments, only once a fiery horse that belonged to one of the captains pawing with his hoof struck a hole in my handkerchief, and his foot slipping, he overthrew his rider and himself; but I immediately relieved them both, and covering the hole with one hand, I set down the troop with the other, in the same manner as I took them up. The horse that fell was strained in the left shoulder, but the rider got no hurt, and I repaired my handkerchief as well as I could: however, I would not trust to the strength of it any more in such dangerous enterprises.

. . . .

I had sent so many memorials and petitions for my liberty, that His Majesty at length mentioned the matter, first in the cabinet, and then in a full council; where it was opposed by none, except Skyresh Bolgolam, who was pleased, without any provocation, to be my mortal enemy. But it was carried against him by the whole board, and confirmed by the Emperor. That minister was *Galbet,* or Admiral of the Realm, very much in his master's confidence, and a person well versed in affairs, but of a morose and sour complexion. However, he was at length persuaded to comply; but prevailed that the articles and conditions upon which I should be set free, and to which I must swear, should be drawn up by himself. These articles were brought to me by Skyresh Bolgolam in person, attended by two undersecretaries, and several persons of distinction. After they were read, I was demanded to swear to the performance of them; first in the manner of my own country, and afterwards in the method prescribed by their laws; which was to hold my right foot in my left hand, to place the middle finger of my right hand on the crown of my head and my thumb on the tip of my right ear.

. . . .

I swore and subscribed to these articles with great cheerfulness and content, although some of them were not so honorable as I could have wished; which proceeded wholly from the malice of Skyresh Bolgolam the High Admiral: whereupon my chains were immediately unlocked, and I was at full liberty; the Emperor himself in person did me the honor to be by at the whole ceremony. I made my acknowledgments by prostrating myself at His Majesty's feet: but he commanded me to rise; and after many gracious expressions, which, to avoid the censure of vanity, I shall not repeat, he added, that he hoped I should prove a useful servant, and well deserve all the favors he had already conferred upon me, or might do for the future.

The reader may please to observe, that in the last article for the recovery of my liberty the Emperor stipulates to allow me a quantity of meat and drink sufficient for the support of 1728 Lilliputians. Some time after, asking a friend at court how they came to fix on that determinate number, he told me that His Majesty's mathematicians, having taken the height of my body by the help of a quadrant, and finding it to exceed theirs in the proportion of twelve to one, they concluded from the similarity of their bodies, that mine must contain at least 1728 of theirs, and consequently would require as much food as was necessary to support that number of Lilliputians. By which the reader may conceive an idea of the ingenuity of that people, as well as the prudent and exact economy of so great a prince.

CHAPTER IV

The first request I made after I had obtained my liberty was, that I might have license to see Mildendo, the metropolis; which the Emperor easily granted me, but with a special charge to do no hurt either to the inhabitants or to their houses. The people had notice by proclamation of my design to visit the town. The wall which encompassed it is two foot and a half high, and at least eleven inches broad, so that a coach and horse may be driven very safely around it; and it is flanked with strong towers at ten foot distance. I stept over the great western gate, and passed very gently, and sideling, through the two principal streets; only in my short waistcoat, for fear of damaging the roofs and eaves of the houses with the skirts of my coat. I walked with the utmost circumspection to avoid treading on any stragglers, that might remain in the streets; although the orders were very strict, that all people should keep in their houses at their own peril. The garret windows and tops of houses were so crowded with spectators that I thought in all my travels I had not seen a more populous place. The city is an exact square, each side of the wall being five hundred foot long. The two great streets, which run cross and divide it into four quarters, are five foot wide. The lanes and alleys, which I could not enter, but only view them as I passed, are from twelve to eighteen inches. The town is capable of holding five hundred thousand souls. The houses are from three to five stories. The shops and markets well provided.

The Emperor's palace is in the center of the city, where the two great streets meet. It is enclosed by a wall of two foot high, and twenty foot distant from the buildings. I had His Majesty's permission to step over this wall; and the space being so wide between that and the palace, I could easily view it on every side. The outward court is a square of forty foot, and includes two other courts: in the inmost are the royal apartments, which I was very desirous to see, but found it extremely difficult, for the great gates, from one square into another, were but eighteen inches high and seven inches wide. Now the buildings of the outer court were at least five foot high, and it was impossible for me to stride over them without infinite damage to the pile, though the walls were strongly built of hewn stone, and four inches thick. At the same time the Emperor had a great desire that I should see the magnificence of his palace; but this I was not able to do till three days after, which I spent in cutting down with my knife some of the largest trees in the royal park, about an hundred yards distant from the city. Of these trees I made two stools, each about three foot high, and strong enough to bear my weight. The people having received notice a second time, I went again through the city to the palace, with my two stools in my hands. When I came to the side of the outer court, I stood upon one stool, and took the other in my hand: this I lifted over the roof, and gently set it down on the space between the first and second court, which was eight foot wide. I then stept over the buildings very conveniently from one stool to the other, and drew up the first after me with a hooked stick. By this contrivance I got into the inmost court; and lying down upon my side, I applied my face to the windows of the middle stories, which were left open on purpose, and discovered the most splendid apartments that can be imagined. There I saw the Empress and the young Princes, in their several lodgings, with their chief attendants about them. Her Imperial Majesty was pleased to smile very graciously upon me, and gave me out of the window her hand to kiss.

The King of the Golden River

John Ruskin

This story should appeal to the same age-group as does Gulliver's Travels, *and for those children it is excellent. For the young child it is too long and sophisticated (Boots and His Brothers is much better for him), though the division into chapters helps to break the length. As a piece of literature it is excellent, with its charming descriptions full of color and sound; with its vivid personification of the South-West Wind and characterization of the three brothers; and with its climax built up by repetition of incidents, so like a folk tale, yet with variation to add interest to each incident, as each brother meets the same tests but in different order.*

CHAPTER I

How the Agricultural System of the Black Brothers was Interfered with by South-West Wind, Esquire

In a secluded and mountainous part of Stiria there was, in old time, a valley of the most surprising and luxuriant fertility. It was surrounded, on all sides, by steep and rocky mountains, rising into peaks, which were always covered with snow, and from which a number of torrents descended in constant cataracts. One of these fell westward, over the face of a crag so high, that, when the sun had set to everything else, and all below was darkness, his beams still shone full upon this waterfall, so that it looked like a shower of gold. It was, therefore, called by the people of the neighborhood, the Golden River. It was strange that none of these streams fell into the valley itself. They all descended on the other side of the mountains, and wound away through broad plains and by populous cities. But the clouds were drawn so constantly to the snowy hills, and rested so softly in the circular hollow, that in time of drought and heat, when all the country round was burnt up, there was still rain in the little valley; and its crops were so heavy, and its hay so high, and its apples so red, and its grapes so blue, and its wine so rich, and its honey so sweet, that it was a marvel to everyone who beheld it, and was commonly called the Treasure Valley.

The whole of this little valley belonged to three brothers, called Schwartz, Hans, and Gluck. Schwartz and Hans, the two elder brothers, were very ugly men, with overhanging eyebrows and small dull eyes, which were always half shut, so that you couldn't see into *them,* and always fancied they saw very far into *you.* They lived by farming the Treasure Valley, and very good farmers they were. They killed everything that did not pay for its eating. They shot the blackbirds because they pecked the fruit; and killed the hedgehogs, lest they should suck the cows; they poisoned the crickets for eating the crumbs in the kitchen; and smothered the cicadas, which used to sing all summer in the lime trees. They worked their servants without any wages, till they would not work any more, and then quarreled with them, and turned them out of doors without paying them. It would have been very odd if, with such a farm, and such a system of farming, they hadn't got very rich; and very rich they *did* get. They generally contrived to keep their corn by them till it was very dear, and then sell it for twice its value; they had heaps of gold lying about on their floors, yet it was never known that they had given so much as a penny or a crust in charity; they never went to Mass; grumbled per-

petually at paying tithes; and were, in a word, of so cruel and grinding a temper as to receive from all those with whom they had any dealings the nickname of the "Black Brothers."

The youngest brother, Gluck, was as completely opposed, in both appearance and character, to his seniors as could possibly be imagined or desired. He was not above twelve years old, fair, blue-eyed, and kind in temper to every living thing. He did not, of course, agree particularly well with his brothers, or rather, they did not agree with *him.* He was usually appointed to the honorable office of turnspit, when there was anything to roast, which was not often; for, to do the brothers justice, they were hardly less sparing upon themselves than upon other people. At other times he used to clean the shoes, floors, and sometimes the plates, occasionally getting what was left of them, by way of encouragement, and a wholesome quantity of dry blows, by way of education.

Things went on in this manner for a long time. At last came a very wet summer, and everything went wrong in the country around. The hay had hardly been got in, when the haystacks were floated bodily down to the sea by an inundation; the vines were cut to pieces with the hail; the corn was all killed by a black blight; only in the Treasure Valley, as usual, all was safe. As it had rain when there was rain nowhere else, so it had sun when there was sun nowhere else. Everybody came to buy corn at the farm, and went away pouring maledictions on the Black Brothers. They asked what they liked, and got it, except from the poor people who could only beg, and several of whom were starved at their very door, without the slightest regard or notice.

It was drawing toward winter, and very cold weather, when one day the two elder brothers had gone out, with their usual warning to little Gluck, who was left to mind the roast, that he was to let nobody in, and give nothing out. Gluck sat down quite close to the fire, for it was raining very hard, and the kitchen walls were by no means dry or comfortable looking. He turned and turned, and the roast got nice and brown. "What a pity," thought Gluck, "my brothers never ask anybody to dinner. I'm sure, when they've got such a nice piece of mutton as this, and nobody else has got so much as a piece of dry bread, it would do their hearts good to have somebody to eat it with them."

Just as he spoke, there came a double knock at the house door, yet heavy and dull, as though the knocker had been tied up — more like a puff than a knock.

"It must be the wind," said Gluck; "nobody else would venture to knock double knocks at our door."

No; it wasn't the wind; there it came again very hard, and what was particularly astounding, the knocker seemed to be in a hurry, and not to be in the least afraid of the consequences. Gluck went to the window, opened it, and put his head out to see who it was.

It was the most extraordinary-looking little gentleman he had ever seen in his life. He had a very large nose, slightly brass-colored; his cheeks were very round, and very red, and might have warranted a supposition that he had been blowing a refractory fire for the last eight-and-forty hours; his eyes twinkled merrily through long silky eyelashes, his mustaches curled twice round like a corkscrew on each side of his mouth, and his hair, of a curious mixed pepper-and-salt color, descended far over his shoulders. He was about four-feet-six in height, and wore a conical pointed cap of nearly the same altitude, decorated with a black feather some three feet long. His doublet was prolonged behind into something resembling a violent exaggeration of what is now termed a "swallow-tail," but was much obscured by the swelling folds of an enormous black, glossy-looking cloak, which must have been very much too long in calm weather, as the wind, whistling round the old house, carried it clear out from the wearer's shoulders to about four times his own length.

Gluck was so perfectly paralyzed by the singular appearance of his visitor that he remained fixed without uttering a word, until the old gentleman, having performed another, and a more energetic concerto on the knocker, turned round to look after his fly-away cloak. In so doing he caught sight of Gluck's little yellow head jammed in the window, with its mouth and eyes very wide open indeed.

"Hollo!" said the little gentleman, "that's not the way to answer the door: I'm wet; let me in!"

To do the little gentleman justice, he *was* wet. His feather hung down between his legs like a beaten puppy's tail, dripping like an umbrella; and from the ends of his mustaches the water was running into his waistcoat pockets, and out again like a mill stream.

"I beg pardon, sir," said Gluck, "I'm very sorry, but I really can't."

"Can't what?" said the old gentleman.

"I can't let you in, sir — I can't indeed; my brothers would beat me to death, sir, if I thought of such a thing. What do you want, sir?"

"Want?" said the old gentleman, petulantly. "I want fire, and shelter; and there's your great fire there blazing, crackling, and dancing on the walls, with nobody to feel it. Let me in, I say; I only want to warm myself."

Gluck had had his head, by this time, so long out of the window, that he began to feel it was really unpleasantly cold, and when he turned, and saw the beautiful fire rustling and roaring, and throwing long bright tongues up the chimney, as if it were licking its chops at the savory smell of the leg of mutton, his heart melted within him that it should be burning away for nothing. "He does look *very* wet," said little Gluck; "I'll just let him in for a quarter of an hour." Round he went to the door, and opened it; and as the little gentleman walked in, there came a gust of wind through the house that made the old chimneys totter.

"That's a good boy," said the little gentleman. "Never mind your brothers. I'll talk to them."

"Pray, sir, don't do any such thing," said Gluck. "I can't let you stay till they come; they'd be the death of me."

"Dear me," said the old gentleman, "I'm very sorry to hear that. How long may I stay?"

"Only till the mutton's done, sir," replied Gluck, "and it's very brown."

Then the old gentleman walked into the kitchen, and sat himself down on the hob, with the top of his cap accommodated up the chimney, for it was a great deal too high for the roof.

"You'll soon dry there, sir," said Gluck, and sat down again to turn the mutton. But the old gentleman did *not* dry there, but went on drip, drip, dripping among the cinders, and the fire fizzed and sputtered, and began to look very black and uncomfortable: never was such a cloak; every fold in it ran like a gutter.

"I beg pardon, sir," said Gluck at length, after watching the water spreading in long, quicksilver-like streams over the floor for a quarter of an hour; "mayn't I take your cloak?"

"No, thank you," said the old gentleman.

"Your cap, sir?"

"I am all right, thank you," said the old gentleman rather gruffly.

"But — sir — I'm very sorry," said Gluck hesitatingly; "but — really, sir — you're — putting the fire out."

"It'll take longer to do the mutton, then," replied his visitor dryly.

Gluck was very much puzzled by the behavior of his guest; it was such a strange mixture of coolness and humility. He turned away at the string meditatively for another five minutes.

"That mutton looks very nice," said the old gentleman at length. "Can't you give me a little bit?"

"Impossible, sir," said Gluck.

"I'm very hungry," continued the old gentleman; "I've had nothing to eat yesterday nor today. They surely couldn't miss a bit from the knuckle!"

He spoke in so very melancholy a tone that it quite melted Gluck's heart. "They promised me one slice today, sir," said he; "I can give you that, but not a bit more."

"That's a good boy," said the old gentleman again.

Then Gluck warmed a plate, and sharpened a knife. "I don't care if I do get beaten for it," thought he. Just as he had cut a large slice out of the mutton, there came a tremendous rap at the door. The old gentle-man jumped off the hob, as if it had suddenly become inconveniently warm. Gluck fitted the slice into the mutton again, with desperate efforts at exactitude, and ran to open the door.

"What did you keep us waiting in the rain for?" said Schwartz, as he walked in, throwing his umbrella in Gluck's face. "Ay! what for, indeed, you little vagabond?" said Hans, administering an educational box on the ear, as he followed his brother into the kitchen.

"Bless my soul!" said Schwartz when he opened the door.

"Amen," said the little gentleman, who had taken his cap off and was standing in the middle of the kitchen, bowing with the utmost possible velocity.

"Who's that?" said Schwartz, catching up a rolling-pin, and turning to Gluck with a fierce frown.

"I don't know, indeed, brother," said Gluck in great terror.

"How did he get in?" roared Schwartz.

"My dear brother," said Gluck, deprecatingly, "he was so *very* wet!"

The rolling-pin was descending on Gluck's head; but, at the instant, the old gentleman interposed his conical cap, on which it crashed with a shock that shook the water out of it all over the room. What was very odd, the rolling-pin no sooner touched the cap than it flew out of Schwartz's hand, spinning like a straw in a high wind, and fell into the corner at the farther end of the room.

"Who are you, sir?" demanded Schwartz, turning upon him.

"What's your business?" snarled Hans.

"I'm a poor old man, sir," the little gentleman began very modestly, "and I saw your fire through the window, and begged shelter for a quarter of an hour."

"Have the goodness to walk out again, then," said Schwartz. "We've quite enough water in our kitchen, without making it a drying house."

"It is a cold day to turn an old man out in, sir; look at my gray hairs." They hung down to his shoulders, as I told you before.

"Ay!" said Hans, "there are enough of them to keep you warm. Walk!"

"I'm very, very hungry, sir; couldn't you spare me a bit of bread before I go?"

"Bread, indeed!" said Schwartz; "do you suppose we've nothing to do with our bread but to give it to such red-nosed fellows as you?"

"Why don't you sell your feather?" said Hans, sneeringly. "Out with you!"

"A little bit," said the old gentleman.

"Be off!" said Schwartz.

"Pray, gentlemen ——"

"Off, and be hanged!" cried Hans, seizing him by the collar. But he had no sooner touched the old gentleman's collar than away he went after the rolling-pin, spinning round and round, till he fell into the corner on the top of it. Then Schwartz was very angry, and ran at the old gentleman to turn him out; but he also had hardly touched him when away he went after Hans and the rolling-pin, and hit his head against the wall as he tumbled into the corner. And so there they lay, all three.

Then the old gentleman spun himself round with velocity in the opposite direction; continued to spin until his long cloak was all wound neatly about him, clapped his cap on his head, very much on one side (for it could not stand upright without going through the ceiling), gave an additional twist to his corkscrew mustaches, and replied with perfect coolness: "Gentlemen, I wish you a very good morning. At twelve o'clock tonight I'll call again; after such a refusal of hospitality as I have just experienced, you will not be surprised if that visit is the last I ever pay you."

"If ever I catch you here again," muttered Schwartz, coming, half frightened, out of the corner — but, before he could finish his sentence, the old gentleman had shut the house door behind him with a great bang; and there drove past the window, at the same instant, a wreath of ragged cloud that whirled and rolled away down the valley in all manner of shapes; turning over and over in the air, and melting away at last in a gush of rain.

"A very pretty business, indeed, Mr. Gluck!" said Schwartz. "Dish the mutton, sir. If ever I catch you at such a trick again — bless me, why the mutton's been cut!"

"You promised me one slice, brother, you know," said Gluck.

"Oh! and you were cutting it hot, I suppose, and going to catch all the gravy. It'll be long before I promise you such a thing again. Leave the room, sir; and have the kindness to wait in the coal-cellar till I call you."

Gluck left the room melancholy enough. The brothers ate as much mutton as they could, locked the rest in the cupboard, and proceeded to get very drunk after dinner.

Such a night as it was! Howling wind and rushing rain, without intermission! The brothers had just sense enough left to put up all the shutters, and double bar the door, before they went to bed. They usually slept in the same room. As the clock struck twelve, they were both awakened by a tremendous crash. Their door burst open with a violence that shook the house from top to bottom.

"What's that?" cried Schwartz, starting up in his bed.

"Only I," said the little gentleman.

The two brothers sat up on their bolster and stared into the darkness. The room was full of water, and by a misty moonbeam, which found its way through a hole in the shutter, they could see in the midst of it an enormous foam globe, spinning round, and bobbing up and down like a cork, on which, as on a most luxurious cushion, reclined the little old gentleman, cap and all. There was plenty of room for it now, for the roof was off.

"Sorry to incommode you," said their visitor, ironically. "I'm afraid your beds are dampish; perhaps you had better go to your brother's room; I've left the ceiling on, there."

They required no second admonition, but rushed into Gluck's room, wet through, and in an agony of terror.

"You'll find my card on the kitchen table," the old gentleman called after them. "Remember, the *last* visit."

"Pray Heaven it may!" said Schwartz, shuddering. And the foam globe disappeared.

Dawn came at last, and the two brothers looked out of Gluck's little window in the morning. The Treasure Valley was one mass of ruin and desolation. The inundation had swept away trees, crops, and cattle, and left in their stead a waste of red sand and gray mud. The two brothers crept shivering and horror-struck into the kitchen. The water had gutted the whole first floor; corn, money, almost every movable thing had been swept away, and there was left only a small white card on the kitchen table. On it, in large, breezy long-legged letters, were engraved the words:

SOUTH-WEST WIND, ESQUIRE

Chapter II

Of the Proceedings of the Three Brothers After the Visit of South-West Wind, Esquire; and How Little Gluck Had an Interview with the King of the Golden River

South-West Wind, Esquire, was as good as his word. After the momentous visit above related, he entered the Treasure Valley no more; and, what was worse, he had so much influence with his relations, the West Winds in general, and used it so effectually, that they all adopted a similar line of conduct. So no rain fell in the valley from one year's end to another. Though everything remained green and flourishing in the plains below, the inheritance of the Three Brothers was a desert. What had once been the richest soil in the kingdom, became a shifting heap of red sand; and the brothers, unable longer to contend with the adverse skies, abandoned their valueless patrimony in despair, to seek some means of gaining a livelihood among the cities and peoples of the plains. All their money was gone, and they had nothing left but some curious, old-fashioned pieces of gold plates, the last remnants of their ill-gotten wealth.

"Suppose we turn goldsmiths?" said Schwartz to Hans, as they entered the large city. "It is a good knave's trade; we can put a great deal of copper into the gold, without anyone's finding it out."

The thought was agreed to be a very good one; they hired a furnace, and turned goldsmiths. But two slight circumstances affected their trade; the first, that people did not approve of the coppered gold; the second, that the two elder brothers, whenever they had sold anything, used to leave little Gluck to mind the furnace, and go and drink out the money in the ale-house next door. So they melted all their gold, without making money enough to buy more, and were at last reduced to one large drinking mug, which an uncle of his had given to little Gluck, and which he was very fond of, and would not have parted with for the world; though he never drank anything out of it but milk and water. The mug was a very odd mug to look at. The handle was formed of two wreaths of flowing golden hair, so finely spun that it looked more like silk than metal, and these wreaths descended into, and mixed with, a beard and whiskers of the same exquisite workmanship, which surrounded and decorated a very fierce little face, of the reddest gold imaginable, right in the front of the mug, with a pair of eyes in it which seemed to command its whole circumference. It was impossible to drink out of the mug without being subjected to an intense gaze out of the side of these eyes; and Schwartz positively averred that once, after emptying it, full of Rhenish, seventeen times, he had seen them wink! When it came to the mug's turn to be made into spoons, it half broke poor little Gluck's heart; but the brothers only laughed at him, tossed the mug into the melting-pot, and staggered out to the ale-house; leaving him, as usual, to pour the gold into bars, when it was all ready.

When they were gone, Gluck took a farewell look at his old friend in the melting-pot. The flowing hair was all gone; nothing remained but the red nose, and the sparkling eyes, which looked more malicious than ever. "And no wonder," thought Gluck, "after being treated in that way." He sauntered disconsolately to the window, and sat himself down to catch the fresh evening air, and escape the hot breath of the furnace. Now this window commanded a direct view of the range of mountains, which, as I told you before, overhung the Treasure Valley, and more especially of the peak from which fell the Golden River. It was just at the close of the day, and when Gluck sat down at the window, he saw the rocks of the mountain tops, all crimson and purple with the sunset; and there were bright tongues of fiery cloud burning and quivering about them; and the river, brighter than all, fell, in a waving column of pure gold, from precipice to precipice, with the double arch of a broad purple rainbow stretched across it, flushing and fading alternately in the wreaths of spray.

"Ah!" said Gluck aloud, after he had looked at it for a while, "if that river were really all gold, what a nice thing it would be."

"No, it wouldn't, Gluck," said a clear metallic voice, close at his ear.

"Bless me! what's that?" exclaimed Gluck, jumping up. There was nobody there. He looked round the room, and under the table, and a great many times behind him, but there was certainly nobody there, and he sat down again at the window. This time he didn't speak, but he couldn't help thinking again that it would be very convenient if the river were really all gold.

"Not at all, my boy," said the same voice, louder than before.

"Bless me!" said Gluck again; "what *is* that?" He looked again into all the corners, and cupboards, and then began turning round, and round, as fast as he could in the middle of the room, thinking there was somebody behind him, when the same voice struck again on his ear. It was singing now very merrily, "Lala-lira-la", no words, only a soft running effervescent melody, something like that of a kettle on the boil. Gluck looked out of the window. No, it was certainly in the house. Upstairs, and downstairs. No, it was certainly in that very room, coming in quicker time, and clearer notes, every moment. "Lala-lira-la." All at once it struck Gluck that it sounded louder near the furnace. He ran to the opening, and looked in; yes, he saw right, it semed to be coming, not only out of the furnace, but out of the pot. He uncovered it, and ran back in a great fright, for the pot was certainly singing! He stood in the farthest corner of the room, with his hands up, and his mouth open, for a minute or two, when the singing stopped, and the voice became clear, and pronunciative.

"Hollo!" said the voice.

Gluck made no answer.

"Hollo! Gluck, my boy," said the pot again.

Gluck summoned all his energies, walked straight up to the crucible, drew it out of the furnace, and looked in. The gold was all melted, and its surface as smooth and polished as a river; but instead of reflecting little Gluck's head, as he looked in, he saw, meeting his glance from beneath the gold, the red nose and sharp eyes of his old friend of the mug, a thousand times redder and sharper than ever he had seen them in his life.

"Come, Gluck, my boy," said the voice out of the pot again, "I'm all right; pour me out."

But Gluck was too much astonished to do anything of the kind.

"Pour me out, I say," said the voice rather gruffly.

Still Gluck couldn't move.

"*Will* you pour me out?" said the voice passionately. "I'm too hot."

By a violent effort, Gluck recovered the use of his limbs, took hold of the crucible, and sloped it so as to pour out the gold. But instead of a liquid stream, there came out, first, a pair of pretty little yellow legs, then some coat tails, then a pair of arms stuck a-kimbo, and, finally, the well-known head of his friend the mug; all which articles, uniting as they rolled out, stood up energetically on the floor, in the shape of a little golden dwarf, about a foot and a half high.

"That's right!" said the dwarf, stretching out first his legs and then his arms, and then shaking his head up and down, and as far round as it would go, for five minutes, without stopping; apparently with the view of ascertaining if he were quite correctly put together, while Gluck stood contemplating him in speechless amazement. He was dressed in a slashed doublet of spun gold, so fine in its texture that the prismatic colors gleamed over it, as if on a surface of mother of pearl; and, over this brilliant doublet, his hair and beard fell full half-way to the ground in waving curls so exquisitely delicate that Gluck could hardly tell where they ended; they seemed to melt into air. The features of the face, however, were by no means finished with the same delicacy; they were rather coarse, slightly inclining to coppery in complexion, and indicative, in expression, of a very pertinacious and intractable disposition in their small proprietor. When the dwarf had finished his self-examination, he turned his small sharp eyes full on Gluck and stared at him deliberately for a minute or two. "No, it wouldn't, Gluck, my boy," said the little man.

This was certainly rather an abrupt and unconnected mode of commencing conversation. It might indeed be supposed to refer to the course of Gluck's thoughts, which had first produced the dwarf's observations out of the pot; but whatever it referred to, Gluck had no inclination to dispute the dictum.

"Wouldn't it, sir?" said Gluck, very mildly and submissively indeed.

"No," said the dwarf, conclusively. "No, it wouldn't." And with that, the dwarf pulled his cap hard over his brows, and took two turns, of three feet long, up and down the room, lifting his legs up very high, and setting them down very hard. This pause gave time for Gluck to collect his thoughts a little, and, seeing no great reason to view his diminutive visitor with dread, and feeling his curiosity overcome his amazement, he ventured on a question of peculiar delicacy.

"Pray, sir," said Gluck rather hesitatingly, "were you my mug?"

On which the little man turned sharp round, walked straight up to Gluck, and drew himself up to his full height. "I," said the little man, "am the King of the Golden River." Whereupon he turned about again, and took two more turns, some six feet long, in order to allow time for the consternation which this announcement produced in his auditor to evaporate. After which, he again walked up to Gluck and stood still, as if expecting some comment on his communication.

Gluck determined to say something at all events. "I hope your majesty is very well," said Gluck.

"Listen!" said the little man, deigning no reply to this polite inquiry. "I am the King of what you mortals call the Golden River.

The shape you saw me in, was owing to the malice of a stronger king, from whose enchantments you have this instant freed me. What I have seen of you, and your conduct to your wicked brothers, renders me willing to serve you; therefore, attend to what I tell you. Whoever shall climb to the top of that mountain from which you see the Golden River issue, and shall cast into the stream at its source three drops of holy water, for him, and for him only, the river shall turn to gold. But no one failing in his first, can succeed in a second attempt; and if anyone shall cast unholy water into the river, it will overwhelm him, and he will become a black stone." So saying, the King of the Golden River turned away and deliberately walked into the center of the hottest flame of the furnace. His figure became red, white, transparent, dazzling — a blaze of intense light — rose, trembled, and disappeared. The King of the Golden River had evaporated.

"Oh!" cried poor Gluck, running to look up the chimney after him; "Oh, dear, dear, dear me! My mug! my mug! my mug!"

CHAPTER III

How Mr. Hans Set Off on an Expedition to the Golden River, and How He Prospered Therein

The King of the Golden River had hardly made the extraordinary exit, related in the last chapter, before Hans and Schwartz came roaring into the house, very savagely drunk. The discovery of the total loss of their last piece of plate had the effect of sobering them just enough to enable them to stand over Gluck, beating him very steadily for a quarter of an hour; at the expiration of which period they dropped into a couple of chairs, and requested to know what he had got to say for himself. Gluck told them his story, of which, of course, they did not believe a word. They beat him again, till their arms were tired, and staggered to bed. In the morning, however, the steadiness with which he adhered to his story obtained him some degree of credence; the immediate consequence of which was, that the two brothers, after wrangling a long time on the knotty question, which of them should try his fortune first, drew their swords and began fighting. The noise of the fray alarmed the neighbors, who, finding they could not pacify the combatants, sent for the constable.

Hans, on hearing this, contrived to escape, and hid himself; but Schwartz was taken before the magistrate, fined for breaking the peace, and, having drunk out his last penny the evening before, was thrown into prison till he should pay.

When Hans heard this, he was much delighted, and determined to set out immediately for the Golden River. How to get the holy water was the question. He went to the priest, but the priest could not give any holy water to so abandoned a character. So Hans went to vespers in the evening for the first time in his life, and, under pretense of crossing himself, stole a cupful, and returned home in triumph.

Next morning he got up before the sun rose, put the holy water into a strong flask, and two bottles of wine and some meat in a basket, slung them over his back, took his alpine staff in his hand, and set off for the mountains.

On his way out of the town he had to pass the prison, and as he looked in at the windows, whom should he see but Schwartz himself peeping out of the bars, and looking very disconsolate.

"Good morning, brother," said Hans: "have you any message for the King of the Golden River?"

Schwartz gnashed his teeth with rage, and shook the bars with all his strength; but Hans only laughed at him, and advising him to make himself comfortable till he came back again, shouldered his basket, shook the bottle of holy water in Schwartz's face till it frothed again, and marched off in the highest spirits in the world.

It was, indeed, a morning that might have made anyone happy, even with no Golden River to seek for. Level lines of dewy mist lay stretched along the valley, out of which rose the massy mountains — their lower cliffs in pale gray shadow, hardly distinguishable from the floating vapor, but gradually ascending till they caught the sunlight, which ran in sharp touches of ruddy color along the angular crags, and pierced, in long level rays, through their fringes of spear-like pine. Far above, shot up red splintered masses of castellated rock, jagged and shivered into myriads of fantastic forms, with here and there a streak of sunlit snow, tracked down their chasms like a line of forked lightning; and, far beyond, and far above all these, fainter than the morning cloud, but purer and changeless, slept, in the blue sky, the utmost peaks of the eternal snow.

The Golden River, which sprang from one of the lower and snowless elevations, was now nearly in shadow; all but the uppermost jets of spray, which rose like slow smoke above the undulating line of the cataract, and floated away in feeble wreaths upon the morning wind.

On this object, and on this alone, Hans's eyes and thoughts were fixed; forgetting the distance he had to traverse, he set off at an imprudent rate of walking, which greatly exhausted him before he had scaled the first range of the green and low hills. He was, moreover, surprised, on surmounting them, to find that a large glacier, of whose existence, notwithstanding his previous knowledge of the mountains, he had been absolutely ignorant, lay between him and the source of the Golden River. He entered on it with the boldness of a practiced mountaineer; yet he thought he had never traversed so strange or so dangerous a glacier in his life. The ice was excessively slippery, and out of all its chasms came wild sounds of gushing water; not monotonous or low, but changeful and loud, rising occasionally into drifting passages of wild melody; then breaking off into short melancholy tones, or sudden shrieks, resembling those of human voices in distress or pain. The ice was broken into thousands of confused shapes, but none, Hans thought, like the ordinary forms of splintered ice. There seemed a curious *expression* about all their outlines — a perpetual resemblance to living features, distorted and scornful. Myriads of deceitful shadows, and lurid lights, played and floated about and through the pale blue pinnacles, dazzling and confusing the sight of the traveler; while his ears grew dull and his head giddy with the constant gush and roar of the concealed waters. These painful circumstances increased upon him as he advanced; the ice crashed and yawned into fresh chasms at his feet, tottering spires nodded around him, and fell thundering across his path; and though he had repeatedly faced these dangers on the most terrific glaciers, and in the wildest weather, it was with a new and oppressive feeling of panic terror that he leaped the last chasm, and flung himself, exhausted and shuddering, on the firm turf of the mountain.

He had been compelled to abandon his basket of food, which became a perilous encumbrance on the glacier, and had now no means of refreshing himself but by breaking off and eating some of the pieces of ice. This, however, relieved his thirst; an hour's repose recruited his hardy frame, and with the indomitable spirit of avarice, he resumed his laborious journey.

His way now lay straight up a ridge of bare red rocks, without a blade of grass to ease the foot, or a projecting angle to afford an inch of shade from the south sun. It was past noon, and the rays beat intensely upon the steep path, while the whole atmosphere was motionless and penetrated with heat. Intense thirst was soon added to the bodily fatigue with which Hans was now afflicted; glance after glance he cast on the flask of water which hung at his belt. "Three drops are enough," at last thought he; "I may, at least, cool my lips with it."

He opened the flask, and was raising it to his lips, when his eye fell on an object lying on the rock beside him; he thought it moved. It was a small dog, apparently in the last agony of death from thirst. Its tongue was out, its jaws dry, its limbs extended lifelessly, and a swarm of black ants were crawling about its lips and throat. Its eye moved to the bottle which Hans held in his hand. He raised it, drank, spurned the animal with his foot, and passed on. And he did not know how it was, but he thought that a strange shadow had suddenly come across the blue sky.

The path became steeper and more rugged every moment; and the high hill air, instead of refreshing him, seemed to throw his blood into a fever. The noise of the hill cataracts sounded like mockery in his ears; they were all distant, and his thirst increased every moment. Another hour passed, and he again

looked down to the flask at his side; it was half empty, but there was much more than three drops in it. He stopped to open it; and again, as he did so, something moved in the path above him. It was a fair child, stretched nearly lifeless on the rock, its breast heaving with thirst, its eyes closed, and its lips parched and burning. Hans eyed it deliberately, drank, and passed on. And a dark gray cloud came over the sun, and long, snake-like shadows crept up along the mountain sides. Hans struggled on. The sun was sinking, but its descent seemed to bring no coolness; the leaden weight of the dead air pressed upon his brow and heart, but the goal was near. He saw the cataract of the Golden River springing from the hillside, scarcely five hundred feet above him. He paused for a moment to breathe, and sprang on to complete his task.

At this instant a faint cry fell on his ear. He turned, and saw a gray-haired old man extended on the rocks. His eyes were sunk, his features deadly pale, and gathered into an expression of despair. "Water!" he stretched his arms to Hans, and cried feebly, "Water! I am dying."

"I have none," replied Hans; "thou hast had thy share of life." He strode over the prostrate body, and darted on. And a flash of blue lightning rose out of the East, shaped like a sword; it shook thrice over the whole heaven, and left it dark with one heavy, impenetrable shade. The sun was setting; it plunged toward the horizon like a red-hot ball.

The roar of the Golden River rose on Hans's ear. He stood at the brink of the chasm through which it ran. Its waves were filled with the red glory of the sunset; they shook their crests like tongues of fire, and flashes of bloody light gleamed along their foam. Their sound came mightier and mightier on his senses; his brain grew giddy with the prolonged thunder. Shuddering he drew the flask from his girdle, and hurled it into the center of the torrent. As he did so, an icy chill shot through his limbs; he staggered, shrieked, and fell. The waters closed over his cry. And the moaning of the river rose wildly into the night, as it gushed over

THE BLACK STONE.

CHAPTER IV
*How Mr. Schwartz Set Off on an Expedition to
the Golden River, and How He Prospered
Therein*

Poor little Gluck waited very anxiously alone in the house for Hans's return. Finding he did not come back, he was terribly frightened and went and told Schwartz in the prison, all that had happened. Then Schwartz was very much pleased, and said that Hans must certainly have been turned into a black stone, and he should have all the gold to himself. But Gluck was very sorry, and cried all night. When he got up in the morning there was no bread in the house, nor any money, so Gluck went and hired himself to another goldsmith, and he worked so hard, and so neatly, and so long every day, that he soon got money enough together to pay his brother's fine, and he went and gave it all to Schwartz, and Schwartz got out of prison. Then Schwartz was quite pleased, and said he should have some of the gold of the river. But Gluck only begged he would go and see what had become of Hans.

Now when Schwartz had heard that Hans had stolen the holy water, he thought to himself that such a proceeding might not be considered altogether correct by the King of the Golden River, and determined to manage matters better. So he took some more of Gluck's money, and went to a bad priest, who gave him some holy water very readily for it. Then Schwartz was sure it was all quite right. So Schwartz got up early in the morning before the sun rose, and took some bread and wine, in a basket, and put his holy water in a flask, and set off for the mountains. Like his brother, he was much surprised at the sight of the glacier, and had great difficulty in crossing it, even after leaving his basket behind him. The day was cloudless, but not bright; there was a heavy purple haze hanging over the sky, and the hills looked lowering and gloomy. And as Schwartz climbed the steep rock path, the thirst came upon him, as it had upon his brother, until he lifted his flask to his lips to drink. Then he saw the fair child lying near him on the rocks, and it cried to him, and moaned for water.

"Water, indeed," said Schwartz; "I haven't half enough for myself," and passed on. And as he went he thought the sunbeams grew more dim, and he saw a low bank of black cloud rising out of the West; and, when he had climbed for another hour the thirst overcame him again, and he would have drunk. Then he saw the old man lying before him on the path, and heard him cry out for water. "Water, indeed," said Schwartz, "I haven't enough for myself," and on he went.

Then again the light seemed to fade before his eyes, and he looked up, and behold, a mist, of the color of blood, had come over the sun; and the bank of black cloud had risen very high, and its edges were tossing and tumbling like the waves of the angry sea. And they cast long shadows, which flickered over Schwartz's path.

Then Schwartz climbed for another hour, and again his thirst returned; and as he lifted his flask to his lips, he thought he saw his brother Hans lying exhausted on the path before him, and, as he gazed, the figure stretched its arms to him, and cried for water. "Ha, ha," laughed Schwartz, "are you there? Remember the prison bars, my boy. Water, indeed! do you suppose I carried it all the way up here for *you?*" And he strode over the figure; yet, as he passed, he thought he saw a strange expression of mockery about its lips. And, when he had gone a few yards farther, he looked back; but the figure was not there.

And a sudden horror came over Schwartz, he knew not why; but the thirst for gold prevailed over his fear, and he rushed on. And the bank of black cloud rose to the zenith, and out of it came bursts of spiry lightning, and waves of darkness seemed to heave and float between their flashes over the whole heavens. And the sky where the sun was getting was all level, and like a lake of blood; and a strong wind came out of that sky, tearing its crimson cloud into fragments, and scattering them far into the darkness. And when Schwartz stood by the brink of the Golden River, its waves were black, like thunder clouds, but their foam was like fire; and the roar of the waters below, and the thunder above, met, as he cast the flask into the stream. And, as he did so, the lightning glared into his eyes, and the earth gave way beneath him, and the waters closed over his cry. And the moaning of the river rose wildly into the night, as it gushed over the

TWO BLACK STONES.

CHAPTER V

How Little Gluck Set Off on an Expedition to the Golden River, and How He Prospered Therein; With Other Matters of Interest

When Gluck found that Schwartz did not come back he was very sorry, and did not know what to do. He had no money, and was obliged to go and hire himself again to the goldsmith, who worked him very hard, and gave him very little money. So, after a month or two, Gluck grew tired, and made up his mind to go and try his fortune with the Golden River. "The little King looked very kind," thought he. "I don't think he will turn me into a black stone." So he went to the priest, and the priest gave him some holy water as soon as he asked for it. Then Gluck took some bread in his basket, and the bottle of water, and set off very early for the mountains.

If the glacier had occasioned a great deal of fatigue to his brothers, it was twenty times worse for him, who was neither so strong nor so practiced on the mountains. He had several bad falls, lost his basket and bread, and was very much frightened at the strange noises under the ice. He lay a long time to rest on the grass, after he had got over, and began to climb the hill just in the hottest part of the day. When he had climbed for an hour, he got dreadfully thirsty, and was going to drink like his brothers, when he saw an old man coming down the path above him, looking very feeble, and leaning on a staff. "My son," said the old man, "I am faint with thirst. Give me some of that water." Then Gluck looked at him, and when he saw that he was pale and weary, he gave him the water; "Only pray don't drink it all," said Gluck. But the old man drank a great deal, and gave him back the bottle two-thirds empty. Then he bade him good speed, and Gluck went on again merrily. And the path became

easier to his feet, and two or three blades of grass appeared upon it, and some grasshoppers began singing on the bank beside it; and Gluck thought he had never heard such merry singing.

Then he went on for another hour, and the thirst increased on him so that he thought he should be forced to drink. But, as he raised the flask, he saw a little child lying panting by the roadside, and it cried out piteously for water. Then Gluck struggled with himself, and determined to bear the thirst a little longer; and he put the bottle to the child's lips, and it drank it all but a few drops. Then it smiled on him, and got up and ran down the hill; and Gluck looked after it, till it became as small as a little star, and then turned and began climbing again. And then there were all kinds of sweet flowers growing on the rocks, bright green moss with pale pink starry flowers, and soft belled gentians, more blue than the sky at its deepest, and pure white transparent lilies. And crimson and purple butterflies darted hither and thither, and the sky sent down such pure light that Gluck had never felt so happy in his life.

Yet, when he had climbed for another hour, his thirst became intolerable again; and, when he looked at his bottle, he saw that there were only five or six drops left in it, and he could not venture to drink. And, as he was hanging the flask to his belt again, he saw a little dog lying on the rocks, gasping for breath — just as Hans had seen it on the day of his ascent. And Gluck stopped and looked at it, and then at the Golden River, not five hundred yards above him; and he thought of the dwarf's words, "that no one could succeed, except in his first attempt"; and he tried to pass the dog, but it whined piteously, and Gluck stopped again. "Poor beastie," said Gluck, "it'll be dead when I come down again, if I don't help it." Then he looked closer and closer at it, and its eye turned on him so mournfully that he could not stand it. "Confound the King and his gold, too," said Gluck; and he opened the flask, and poured all the water into the dog's mouth.

The dog sprang up and stood on its hind legs. Its tail disappeared, its ears became long, longer, silky, golden; its nose became red, its eyes became very twinkling; in three seconds the dog was gone, and before Gluck stood his old acquaintance, the King of the Golden River.

"Thank you," said the monarch; "but don't be frightened, it's all right"; for Gluck showed manifest symptoms of consternation at this unlooked-for reply to his last observation. "Why didn't you come before," continued the dwarf, "instead of sending me those rascally brothers of yours, for me to have the trouble of turning into stones? Very hard stones they make, too."

"Oh, dear me!" said Gluck, "have you really been so cruel?"

"Cruel!" said the dwarf: "they poured unholy water into my stream; do you suppose I'm going to allow that?"

"Why," said Gluck, "I am sure, sir — your Majesty, I mean — they got the water out of the church font."

"Very probably," replied the dwarf; "but," and his countenance grew stern as he spoke, "the water which has been refused to the cry of the weary and dying is unholy, though it had been blessed by every saint in heaven; and the water which is found in the vessel of mercy is holy, though it had been defiled with corpses."

So saying, the dwarf stooped and plucked a lily that grew at his feet. On its white leaves there hung three drops of clear dew. And the dwarf shook them into the flask which Gluck held in his hand. "Cast these into the river," he said, "and descend on the other side of the mountains into the Treasure Valley, and so good speed."

As he spoke, the figure of the dwarf became indistinct. The playing colors of his robe formed themselves into a prismatic mist of dewy light: he stood for an instant veiled with them as with the belt of a broad rainbow. The colors grew faint, the mist rose into the air; the monarch had evaporated.

And Gluck climbed to the brink of the Golden River and its waves were as clear as crystal, and as brilliant as the sun. And, when he cast the three drops of dew into the stream, there opened where they fell, a small circular whirlpool, into which the waters descended with a musical noise.

Gluck stood watching it for some time, very much disappointed, because not only the river was not turned into gold but its waters seemed much diminished in quantity. Yet he obeyed his friend the dwarf, and descended the other side of the mountains, towards the Treasure Valley; and, as he went, he thought he heard the noise of water working its way under the ground. And when he came in sight of the Treasure Valley, behold, a river, like the Golden River, was springing from a new cleft of the rocks above it, and was flowing in innumerable streams among the dry heaps of red sand.

And, as Gluck gazed, fresh grass sprang beside the new streams, and creeping plants grew, and climbed among the moistening soil. Young flowers opened suddenly along the river sides, as stars leap out when twilight is deepening, and thickets of myrtle, and tendrils of vine, cast lengthening shadows over the valley as they grew. And thus the Treasure Valley became a garden again, and the inheritance, which had been lost by cruelty, was regained by love.

And Gluck went and dwelt in the valley, and the poor were never driven from his door; so that his barn became full of corn, and his house of treasure. And for him, the river had, according to the dwarf's promise, become a River of Gold.

And, to this day, the inhabitants of the valley point out the place where the three drops of holy dew were cast into the stream, and trace the course of the Golden River under the ground, until it emerges in the Treasure Valley. And at the top of the cataract of the Golden River are still to be seen two BLACK STONES, round which the waters howl mournfully every day at sunset; and these stones are still called by the people of the valley

THE BLACK BROTHERS.

BIBLIOGRAPHY

Andersen, Hans Christian. *Andersen's Fairy Tales;* trans. from the Danish by Jean Hersholt; illus. by Fritz Kredel. Heritage Press, 1942. (Grades 5–7)

Jean Hersholt, the actor, was also a student and collector of Andersen. He has translated twenty-five of the tales, giving them new vitality.

Andersen, Hans Christian. *Fairy Tales and Stories;* ed. by Signe Toksvig; illus. by George and Doris Hauman. Macmillan, 1953. (New Children's Classics) (Grades 5–7)

A well-known edition containing sixteen of the best-loved stories.

Andersen, Hans Christian. *It's Perfectly True, and Other Stories;* trans. from the Danish by Paul Leyssac; illus. by Richard Bennett. Harcourt, Brace, 1938. (Grades 5–7)

Translated by the Danish actor who is an Andersen storyteller of repute. A conversational tone is stressed in the text.

Andersen, Hans Christian. *Fairy Tales;* ed. by Svend Larsen; trans. from the original Danish text by R. P. Keigwin; illus. by Vilhelm Pedersen reproduced from the original drawings in the Andersen Museum at Odense. Charles Scribner's Sons, 1951. (World Edition)

An important new translation by the well-known English-Danish scholar. Illustrated with pencil drawings by the artist who was Andersen's own choice as an illustrator of his tales. This world edition was issued from Odense, Andersen's birthplace, under the supervision of Svend Larsen, Director of the Andersen Museum at Odense.

Andersen, Hans Christian. *The Emperor's New Clothes;* designed and illus. by Virginia Lee Burton. Houghton Mifflin, 1949. (Grades 2–4)

These are the most satisfying illustrations the well-loved tale has ever had. The artist gives play to her fine sense of pageantry in depicting the magnificence of the Emperor's domain, and her sense of humor highlights the ridiculous situation with all its implications.

Andersen, Hans Christian. *The Little Mermaid;* illus. by Dorothy P. Lathrop. Macmillan, 1939. (Grades 4–6)

Miss Lathrop's delicate, sensitive illustrations interpret anew the pathos and winsomeness of the little mermaid.

Andersen, Hans Christian. *The Steadfast Tin Soldier;* trans. by M. R. James; illus. by Marcia Brown. Charles Scribner's Sons, 1953. (Grades 1–4)

A favorite Andersen story in distinguished picture-book format. Marcia Brown's fresh imaginative drawings convey the inner beauty and meaning of the story.

Andersen, Hans Christian. *The Ugly Duckling;* trans. by R. P. Keigwin; illus. by Johannes Larsen. Macmillan, 1955. (Grades 2–4)

This edition was printed in Denmark in commemoration of the 150th anniversary of the birth of Hans Andersen, on April 2, 1805. The distinguished illustrations are by the foremost Danish painter of birds.

Atwater, Richard and Florence. *Mr. Popper's Penguins;* illus. by Robert Lawson. Little, Brown, 1938. (Grades 4–6)

A rollicking good story about a mild little house painter and his two penguins. Sheer nonsense is treated in such a matter-of-fact way that it is completely convincing.

Bailey, Carolyn Sherwin. *Miss Hickory;* illus. by Ruth Gannett. Viking Press, 1946. (Grades 4–6)

A fantasy full of the charm of the New Hampshire countryside. Miss Hickory, the heroine, is a tiny country doll made of an apple-wood twig, with a hickory nut for a head. Unusually fine lithographs heighten the imaginative quality of the text.

Barrie, Sir James Matthew. *Peter Pan;* illus. by Nora S. Unwin. Charles Scribner's Sons, new ed. 1950. (Grades 4–6)

A beautiful edition with delicate line drawings. This book is part of the Barrie "Peter Pan Bequest," as the royalties go "to help the doctors and nurses cure the children who are lying ill in the Great Ormond Street Hospital for Sick Children in London."

Benary-Isbert, Margot. *The Wicked Enchantment;* trans. by Richard and Clara Winston; illus. by Enrico Arno. Harcourt, Brace, 1955. (Grades 5–8)

Fun, suspense, and present-day fantasy are skillfully combined with ancient legend in this story set in an old cathedral town in Germany. Girls especially will enjoy the book, for much of the action centers upon eleven-year-old Anemone and her dog.

Besterman, Catherine. *The Quaint and Curious Quest of Johnny Longfoot the Shoe King's Son;* illus. by Warren Chappell. Bobbs-Merrill, 1947. (Grades 3–5)

Based on an old Polish folk tale, this story has been re-created by an author who has an uncanny knack of making the characters seem real. The illustrations interpret perfectly this delightful story.

Bianco, Margery. *The Velveteen Rabbit;* illus. by William Nicholson. Doubleday, 1926. (Grades 3–5)

How the velveteen rabbit was changed by nursery magic into a live rabbit is told in a story filled with the magic of childhood. Delightful pictures.

Boston, Lucy Maria. *The Children of Green Knowe;* illus. by Peter Boston. Harcourt, Brace, 1955. (Grades 5–7)

There is real enchantment in this unusual story of a lonely boy who comes to live with his great-grandmother in an old country house in England. Perhaps it is a story *of* children rather than *for* them, because the author penetrates deeply into the mystery of a child's imagination.

Browne, Frances. *Granny's Wonderful Chair;* illus. by Emma L. Brock. Macmillan, 1924. (Children's Classics) (Grades 4–6)

These stories told to a little girl by the "chair of her grandmother" were first written in 1857 and are still enjoyed by children today.

Carroll, Lewis (Charles Lutwidge Dodgson) *Alice's Adventures in Wonderland and Through the Looking-Glass,* with ninety-two illustrations by Sir John Tenniel. Macmillan, 1950. (New Children's Classics) (Grades 3–5)

Critics agree in acclaiming "Alice" the greatest nonsense story ever written. Other good editions are the Heritage Press edition illustrated with the original John Tenniel drawings and with a foreword by John T. Winterich; and the Rainbow Classics edition with the Tenniel illustrations and an introduction by May Lamberton Becker, published by the World Publishing Company.

Collodi, Carlo (Carlo Lorenzini). *The Adventures of Pinocchio;* trans. from the Italian by Carol Della Chiesa; illus. by Attilio Mussino. Macmillan, 1951. (New Children's Classics) (Grades 4–6)

A light-hearted fantasy that is a perennial favorite.

Craik, Dinah Maria (Mulock). *The Adventures of a Brownie;* illus. by Mary Lott Seaman. Macmillan, 1924. (Little Library) (Grades 2–4)

A household of children have a mischievous brownie for a playfellow.

Dickens, Charles. *The Magic Fishbone;* illus. by F. D. Bedford. Frederick Warne, n.d. (Grades 4–6)

A gay fantasy of the Princess Alicia and her eighteen brothers and sisters. The illustrations catch the spirit of the story.

Du Bois, William Pène. *The Great Geppy;* illus. by the author. Viking Press, 1940. (Grades 3–5)

Full of spontaneous fun is this amazing tale of Geppy, the striped circus horse, who plays detective. The drawings have wit, humor, and imagination.

Du Bois, William Pène. *Twenty-one Balloons;* illus. by the author. Viking Press, 1947. (Grades 5–9)

Fabulous adventure in the best Jules Verne tradition. The author combines his rich imagination, his scientific tastes, and brilliant artistry to tell a story with no age limit. Awarded the Newbery medal in 1948.

Eager, Edward. *Half Magic;* illus. by N. M. Bodecker. Harcourt, Brace, 1954. (Grades 4–6)

The finding of an ancient coin that grants half of any wish leads four children into many surprising adventures.

Farjeon, Eleanor. *The Glass Slipper;* illus. by Ernest H. Shepard. Viking Press, 1956. (Grades 5–8)

The fairy play, *The Glass Slipper*, by Eleanor Farjeon and her brother, was successfully produced in London. This is the story of the Cinderella play expanded to book length. Miss Farjeon's rollicking sense of humor, her gift of poetic expression, and her exquisitely balanced prose give fresh beauty to this well-loved story. The Shepard illustrations add their own charm of exaggerated drollery.

Farjeon, Eleanor. *Martin Pippin in the Daisy-Field;* illus. by Isobel and John Morton-Sale. J. B. Lippincott, 1937. (A Stokes Book) (Grades 5–6)

The very spirit of the English countryside is found in these engaging stories told to the children of the girls who listened to "Martin Pippin in the Apple Orchard."

Farjeon, Eleanor. *The Silver Curlew;* illus. by Ernest Shepard. Viking Press, 1953. (Grades 4–6)

A gay story of what befell when lazy Doll Codling ate twelve dumplings, married King Nollekens, and came under the spell of the Little Black Imp.

A skillful imaginative expansion of the English folk tale *Tom Tit Tot*.

Gannett, Ruth Stiles. *My Father's Dragon;* illus. by Ruth Chrisman Gannett. Random House, 1948. (Grades 2–4)

A refreshingly original story in which a small boy rescues an oppressed baby dragon. Here is fantasy that seems perfectly plausible. The gay, robust text is matched with enchanting illustrations.

Godden, Rumer. *Impunity Jane; the Story of a Pocket Doll;* illus. by Adrienne Adams. Viking Press, 1954. (Grades 2–4)

Jane, a four-inch doll, is the heroine of this novel in miniature. For years she belonged to little girls who kept her in sedate elegance in an Early Victorian doll-house. Then one day she became the mascot of a gang of boys and plunged into a world of glorious adventure.

Godden, Rumer. *The Mousewife;* illus. by William Pène du Bois. Viking Press, 1951. (Grades 2–4)

A hauntingly tender story of a little mousewife whose devotion to a caged dove led to her sacrifice when, moved to compassion, she freed the bird. The story is based on an anecdote in Dorothy Wordsworth's Grasmere journal.

Grahame, Kenneth. *The Reluctant Dragon;* illus. by Ernest H. Shepard. Holiday House, 1953. (Grades 4–6)

This story of a small boy who made friends with a dragon first appeared as a chapter in the author's *Dream Days*.

Grahame, Kenneth. *The Wind in the Willows;* illus. by Ernest H. Shepard. Charles Scribner's Sons, new ed. 1953. (All ages)

An ageless fantasy of the little animals that live along the bank of a river that flows through the English countryside and of those that live in the wildwood. There is kindly wisdom here, a gentle humor, and sheer magic in the writing.

Hudson, William Henry. *Little Boy Lost;* illus. by Dorothy Lathrop. Alfred A. Knopf, 1920. (Grades 6–8)

A poetic, imaginative tale of South America filled with that quality the author says he liked best as a child, "the little thrills that nature itself gave me, which half frightened and fascinated at the same time, the wonder and mystery of it all."

Kingsley, Charles. *The Water-Babies;* illus. by W. Heath Robinson. Houghton Mifflin, 1923. (Riverside Bookshelf) (Grades 5–6)

Written in 1862 for his youngest son, then four years old. The author endeavors to teach lessons of nature and ethics in the guise of a fairy tale.

Kipling, Rudyard. *Just So Stories;* illus. by J. M. Gleeson. Doubleday, 1912.

Classic nonsense stories about how the elephant got his trunk; how the camel got his hump; and other fanciful tales.

Lagerlöf, Selma. *The Wonderful Adventures of Nils;* trans. from the Swedish by Velma Swanston Howard; illus. by H. Baumhauer. Pantheon Books, new ed. 1947. (Grades 5–7)

Nils, reduced to elfin size, travels over Sweden on the back of a wild goose migrating north. Natural history is combined with a delightful fairy story.

Lawson, Robert. *Rabbit Hill;* illus. by the author. Viking Press, 1944. (Grades 3–6)

An engaging fantasy about a rabbit family and all the small animals that live on a Connecticut hillside. Awarded the Newbery medal in 1945. *The Tough Winter*, a sequel, is equally delightful.

Lewis, C. S. *The Lion, the Witch, and the Wardrobe;* illus. by Pauline Baynes. Macmillan, 1950. (Grades 4–6)

While spending a holiday at an old estate in England, four children find their way through a huge wardrobe in one of the rooms to the magical land of Narnia. This is the first of seven stories telling of Narnian adventures.

Lofting, Hugh. *The Story of Doctor Dolittle;* illus. by the author. J. B. Lippincott, 1920. (A Stokes Book)

The first of the famous Doctor Dolittle books. Hugh Walpole hailed this book as "the first children's classic since 'Alice.'"

Macdonald, George. *At the Back of the North Wind;* illus. by George and Doris Hauman. Macmillan, new ed. 1953. (New Children's Classics) (Grades 5–7)

A rare quality pervades George Macdonald's fairy stories. Although they are not allegories they are filled with spiritual meaning. *The Princess and the Goblin* and *The Princess and Curdie* will be enjoyed by children a little younger.

McGinley, Phyllis. *The Plain Princess;* illus. by Helen Stone. J. B. Lippincott, 1945. (Grades 3–5)

An imaginative story that has the charm, gaiety, and wit of a traditional fairy tale.

Nesbit, E. *The Bastable Children*. Preface by Christopher Morley. Coward-McCann, 1928. (Grades 4–6)

Contains *The Treasure Seekers; The Would-Be-Goods;* and *The New Treasure Seekers*. The author writes with charm and humor about real children who always manage to become part of a fairy tale.

Norton, Mary. *The Borrowers;* illus. by Beth and Joe Krush. Harcourt, Brace, 1953. (Grades 4–7)

The author has succeeded admirably in creating a miniature world of tiny people no taller than a pencil who live in quiet old houses and skillfully "borrow" what they need. The delightful adventures of these people are continued in *The Borrowers Afield.*

O'Faolain, Eileen. *Miss Pennyfeather and the Pooka;* illus. by Aldren Watson. Random House, 1946. (Grades 4–6)

A charming and original fantasy about fairies, leprechauns, and a pooka, a fairy horse who is lured away from his mortal home to fairyland.

Parrish, Anne. *Floating Island;* illus. by the author. Harper, 1930. (Grades 4–6)

The strange adventures of Mr. and Mrs. Doll and their three children shipwrecked on the shores of a tropical island.

Pyle, Howard. *The Wonder Clock; or, Four and Twenty Marvelous Tales.* Harper, 1915. (Grades 4–6)

These stories, "one for each hour of the day," are based on old tales and legends and told in the author's inimitable way. *Pepper and Salt* is equally well liked. Both books are good for reading aloud and for storytelling.

Ruskin, John. *The King of the Golden River;* illus. by Arthur Rackham. J. B. Lippincott, 1932. (Grades 5–6)

Written in Scotland in 1841, when the author was twenty-two years old, this classic fairy story tells how a family inheritance lost by cruelty was regained by love.

Saint-Exupéry, Antoine de. *The Little Prince;* illus. by the author; trans. from the French by Katherine Woods. Reynal & Hitchcock, 1943. (Grades 5–8)

This fairy tale, written by a poet-aviator, is primarily for adults, but it will be enjoyed by the imaginative child.

Sandburg, Carl. *Rootabaga Stories;* illus. by Maud and Miska Petersham. New ed.; 2 vols. in one. Harcourt, Brace, n.d. (Grades 5–7)

Unique nonsense stories combining fantasy and the realism of the American Middle West.

Sauer, Julia. *Fog Magic;* illus. by Lynd Ward. Viking Press, 1943. (Grades 5–7)

A richly imaginative story in which the author has skillfully fused the world of today and that of a hundred years ago. Greta is a very real little girl, and the hundred-year-old village of Blue Cove, Nova Scotia, which she finds in the heart of the fog, seems equally convincing.

Stockton, Frank R. *The Bee-Man of Orn, and Other Fanciful Tales.* Charles Scribner's Sons, 1917. (Grades 5–8)

Stockton's fanciful tales are refreshingly original and are told with delightful touches of humor. There is a matter-of-factness about them that makes them seem very real. Excellent for reading aloud.

Stockton, Frank R. *Ting-a-Ling Tales;* illus. by Richard Floethe. Charles Scribner's Sons, 1955. (Grades 4–6)

Highly original and amusing stories about giants, dwarfs, and fairies. First published in 1870 with the title *Ting-a-Ling.* Long out-of-print, this is a welcome new edition.

Swift, Jonathan. *Gulliver's Travels into Several Remote Nations of the World;* illus. by Arthur Rackham. E. P. Dutton, 1952. (Children's Illustrated Classics) (Grades 6–9)

Published as a satire for adults in 1726, the book has been enjoyed as a fairy story by several generations of children.

Tarn, W. W. *The Treasure of the Isle of Mist;* illus. by Robert Lawson. G. P. Putnam's Sons, 1934. (Grades 6–8)

A charming fantasy with an underlying significance and delicate touches of humor. The author is a distinguished scholar and an authority on the third century B.C.

Thurber, James. *Many Moons;* illus. by Louis Slobodkin. Harcourt, Brace, 1943. (Grades 4–5)

There is a rare quality of tenderness and wisdom in this delicate fantasy of the little princess who wanted the moon. The sensitive drawings catch perfectly the mood of the story. Awarded the Caldecott medal in 1944. Read also *The Great Quillow.* Children and adults will both enjoy *The White Deer* and *The Thirteen Clocks.*

Tolkien, John R. R. *The Hobbit; or There and Back Again;* illus. by the author. Houghton Mifflin, 1938. (Grades 4–7)

A richly imaginative tale of a hobbit off on an adventure to recover a treasure of gold guarded by Smaug, the dragon. Older boys and girls who like heroic romance may enjoy reading the three books comprising the fabulous allegory *Lords of the Ring.*

Travers, Pamela. *Mary Poppins;* illus. by Mary Shepard. Harcourt, Brace, 1934. (Grades 4–7)

Ever since the day Mary Poppins blew in with an east wind and slid up the banister to the nursery of the Banks children, life became touched with fun and magic.

White, E. B. *Charlotte's Web;* illus. by Garth Williams. Harper, 1952. (Grades 4–6)

Only E. B. White could have written this story of Charlotte the spider, Wilbur the pig, and a little girl who could talk to animals.

References for the Adult

Arbuthnot, May Hill. *Children and Books.* Scott, Foresman, rev. ed. 1957.

"New Magic," Chapter 14, pp. 306–348.

Eaton, Anne Thaxter. *Reading with Children.* Viking Press, 1940.

"Betwixt and Between," Chapter V, pp. 88–97; "Unicorns and Common Creatures," Chapter VI, pp. 97–106.

Green, Roger Lancelyn. *Tellers of Tales.* Edmund Ward, new ed. 1953.

"Lewis Carroll," Chapter II, pp. 26–46; "George Macdonald," Chapter III, pp. 46–59; "Edith Nesbit," Chapter XIII, pp. 189–199; "James Matthew Barrie," Chapter XIV, pp. 199–213; "Rudyard Kipling," Chapter XV, pp. 213–226; "Kenneth Grahame, Beatrix Potter, and Hugh Lofting," Chapter XVI, pp. 226–239.

Hazard, Paul. *Books, Children and Men.* The Horn Book, Inc., 1944.

"Gulliver's Travels," pp. 61–69; "Hans Christian Andersen," pp. 92–106; "The Italy of Yesterday," pp. 111–121; "England (Alice in Wonderland)," pp. 135–141; "Peter Pan," pp. 161–166.

Meigs, Cornelia, and others. *A Critical History of Children's Literature.* Macmillan, 1953.

"A Landmark in Fantasy — *The Wind in the Willows,*" pp. 355–366; "Extensions of Reality," pp. 366–377; "Modern Fancy," pp. 467–482.

Moore, Anne Carroll. *The Three Owls; a Book about Children's Books.* Macmillan, 1925.

"George Macdonald," pp. 7–17; "Hans Christian Andersen," pp. 199–205; "Aristocrats and Griffins — Fanciful Tales of Frank R. Stockton," by Mary Gould Davis, pp. 249–254.

Moore, Anne Carroll. *The Three Owls.* Vol. 3. Coward-McCann, 1931.

"The Incomparable Bastables," by Donald Douglas, pp. 96–99.

Moore, Anne Carroll, and Bertha Mahony Miller, eds. *Writing and Criticism; a Book for Margery Bianco.* The Horn Book, Inc., 1951.

"The Stories of Hans Christian Andersen," by Margery Bianco, pp. 58–63.

Moore, Annie E. *Literature Old and New for Children.* Houghton Mifflin, 1934.

"Fairy Folk and Fairy Ways," Chapter 3, pp. 44–78; "Hans Christian Andersen," Chapter 8, pp. 216–257; "Modern Fanciful Tales," Chapter 11, pp. 352–388.

Smith, Lillian H. *The Unreluctant Years.* American Library Association, 1953.

"Fantasy," Chapter 10, pp. 149–163.

Essays Presented to Charles Williams. Oxford University Press, 1947.

"On Fairy Tales," by J. R. R. Tolkien, pp. 38–90; "On Stories," by C. S. Lewis, pp. 90–105.

Hans Christian Andersen

Andersen, Hans Christian. *The Story of My Life.* Riverside Press, 1871.

The Andersen-Scudder Letters; Hans Christian Andersen Correspondence with Horace Elisha Scudder. University of California Press, 1949.

De la Mare, Walter. "Hans Christian Andersen," in *Pleasures and Speculations.* Faber & Faber (London), 1940.

Godden, Rumer. *Hans Christian Andersen.* Alfred A. Knopf, 1955.

Meynell, Esther. *The Story of Hans Andersen.* Henry Schuman, Inc., 1950.

Toksvig, Signe. *The Life of Hans Christian Andersen.* Harcourt, Brace, 1934.

James M. Barrie

Asquith, Cynthia. *Portrait of Barrie.* E. P. Dutton, 1955.

Lewis Carroll

Ayres, Harry Morgan. *Carroll's Alice.* Columbia University Press, 1936.

Collingwood, Stuart. *Life and Letters of Lewis Carroll.* Century, 1899.

De la Mare, Walter. "Lewis Carroll," in *The Eighteen-Eighties, Essays by Fellows of the Royal Society of Literature;* ed. by Walter de la Mare. Cambridge University Press, 1930.

Green, Roger Lancelyn. *The Story of Lewis Carroll.* Henry Schuman, Inc., 1950.

Lennon, Florence. *Victoria Through the Looking-Glass: The Life of Lewis Carroll.* Simon & Schuster, 1945.

Eleanor Farjeon

Sayers, Frances Clarke. "Eleanor Farjeon's Room with a View," *The Horn Book Magazine*, Vol. 32, Oct. 1956, pp. 335–345.

Kenneth Grahame

Grahame, Elspeth. *First Whispers of "The Wind in the Willows."* J. B. Lippincott, 1944.

Milne, A. A. "A Household Book (Wind in the Willows)," in *Not That It Matters.* Methuen (London), 1921.

Macy, George. "Arthur Rackham and *The Wind in the Willows*," *The Horn Book Magazine*, Vol. 16, May–June 1940, pp. 153–158.

Rudyard Kipling

Gerould, Katherine Fullerton. "The Remarkable Rightness of Rudyard Kipling," *The Atlantic Monthly*, Vol. 123, Jan. 1919, pp. 12–21.

Hart, Walter Morris. *Kipling the Story-Writer.* University of California Press, 1928.

Kipling, Rudyard. *Something of Myself: for My Friends Known and Unknown; an Autobiography.* Doubleday, 1937.

Selma Lagerlöf

Berendsohn, Walter. *Selma Lagerlöf: Her Life and Work;* adapted from the German by George E. Timpson; preface by V. Sackville-West. Ivor Nicholson and Watson (London), 1931.

C. S. Lewis

Lewis, C. S. *Surprised by Joy; the Shape of My Early Life; an Autobiography.* Harcourt, Brace, 1955.

Walsh, Chad. *C. S. Lewis; Apostle to the Skeptics.* Macmillan, 1949.

George Macdonald

Macdonald, Greville. *George Macdonald and His Wife.* Dial Press, 1924.

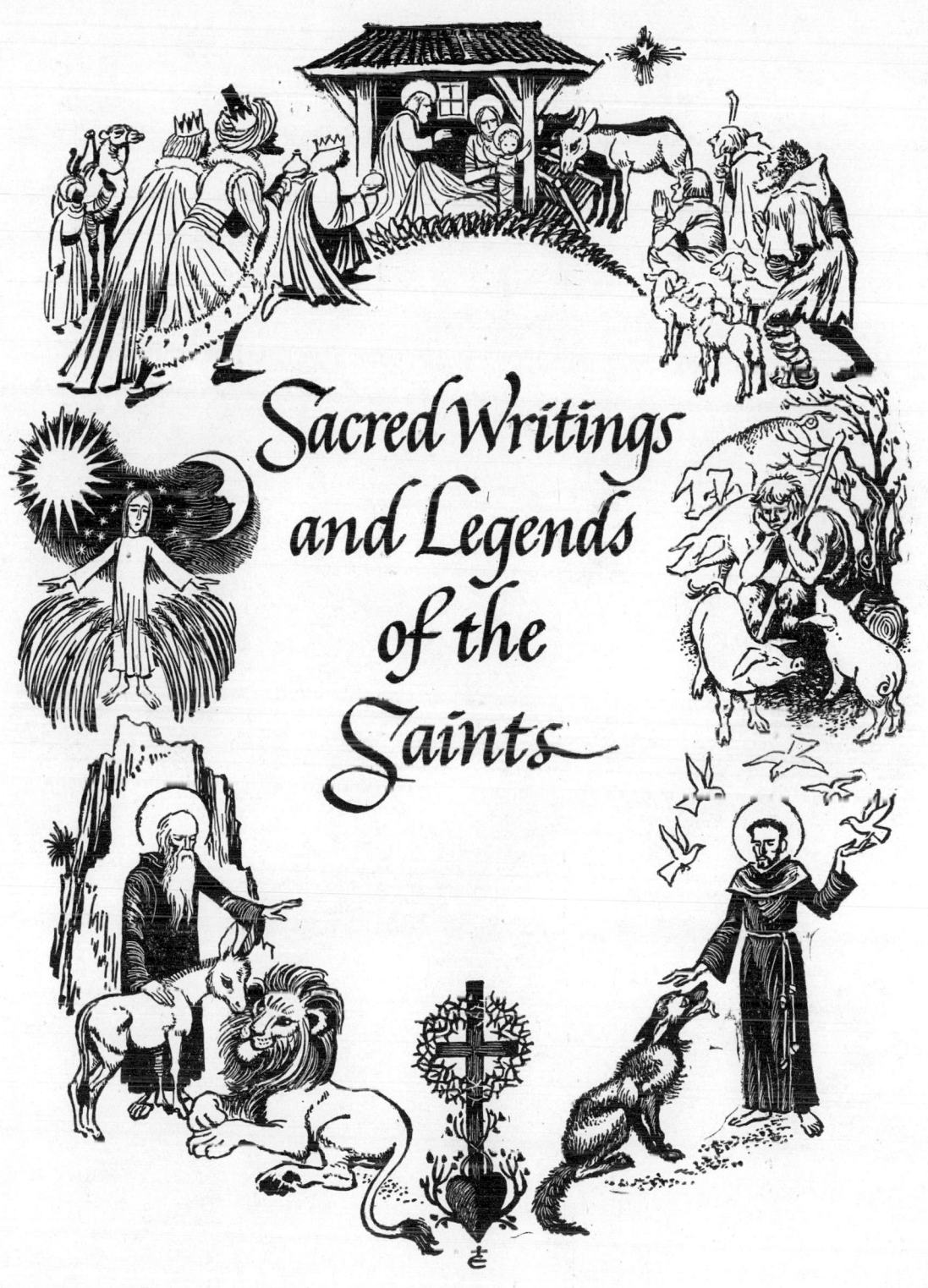

Sacred Writings and Legends of the Saints

"Apart from all questions of its religious and historical import, the Bible is an epic of the world. It unrolls a vast panorama in which the ages of the world move before us in a long train of solemn imagery, from the creation of the earth and the heavens onward." [1]

THE BIBLE IS GREAT LITERATURE, unsurpassed for its drama of human life, vitality of thought, and enduring wisdom. The King James version is a masterpiece of English literature unrivaled in its matchless simplicity, clarity, and rhythmic flow of words. How better train the ear to the beauty of English style than by listening to the King James version of the Bible read aloud? Note the felicity of phrase:

> If I take the wings of the morning,
> And dwell in the uttermost parts of the sea;
> Even there shall thy hand lead me,
> And thy right hand shall hold me.[2]

> He that dwelleth in the secret place of the Most High
> Shall abide under the shadow of the Almighty.[3]

> The eternal God is thy refuge,
> And underneath are the everlasting arms.[4]

Listen to the rhythmic quality of the prose:

> For lo, the winter is past, the rain is over and gone; the flowers appear on the earth; the time of the singing of birds is come, and the voice of the turtle is heard in our land.[5]

> And now abideth faith, hope, charity, these three; but the greatest of these is charity.[6]

Mark the beauty of diction:

> Set me as a seal upon thine heart, as a seal upon thine arm; for love is strong as death.[7]

---

[1] Sir James G. Frazer, *The Golden Bough.*   [2] Psalms 139:9, 10.   [3] Psalms 91:1.
[4] Deuteronomy 33:27.   [5] Song of Solomon 2:11, 12.   [6] I Corinthians 13:13.
[7] Song of Solomon 8:6.

Hear the ringing words from the book of Job:

> Where wast thou when I laid the foundations of the earth?
> Declare, if thou hast understanding . . .
> When the morning stars sang together,
> And all the sons of God shouted for joy?[8]

Note the majestic march of rhythm:

> Hast thou not known? Hast thou not heard that the everlasting God, the Lord, the creator of the ends of the earth, fainteth not, neither is weary? . . . He giveth power to the faint; and to them that have no might he increaseth strength. . . . They that wait upon the Lord shall renew their strength; they shall mount up with wings as eagles; they shall run, and not be weary; they shall walk and not faint.[9]

Fortunate indeed is the child who early in life hears the Bible read aloud to him. Even if he does not fully comprehend the meaning, the exquisite cadence of word and phrase and the majestic rhythms will sink deep into his consciousness and give him a basis for an appreciation of beauty of language. "And who is to say what line, what 'gracious flight of words' may fall, and take root, and grow and flower in the mind of a child?"[1]

What a rich heritage of literature the Bible contains, as many types as are found in any national literature — narrative, history, biography, philosophy, prophecy, essay, oration, and many kinds of poetry. Both the Old and New Testaments are full of incomparable stories told by storytellers who have never been surpassed in any age: the story of Joseph; that of David and Saul, including the beautiful friendship of David and Jonathan; the powerful, dramatic tale of Esther; the idyllic story of Ruth and Naomi with the unforgettable words, "Entreat me not to leave thee, or to return from following after thee, for whither thou goest, I will go and where thou lodgest, I will lodge; thy people shall be my people and thy God my God."[2] These stories have been called "epic gems in the setting of sober history."[3]

Many kinds of folklore enrich the Bible — fables, legends, ancient songs, proverbs, romances, sagas and hero tales. When our children are at the hero-worshiping age, let's make sure they have heroes worthy of their devotion. Let's give them the magnificent hero tales of Abraham, Moses, and Noah, to mention only a few of the Bible's towering personalities.

Professor Richard G. Moulton tells us that the Old Testament, in common with the literature of Greece and Rome, has been the main factor in the development of our modern prose and poetry. He reminds us that "no liberal education will be complete in which the classical and Biblical literature do

---

[8] Job 38:4, 7.

[9] Isaiah 40:28, 29, 31.

[1] Annis Duff, *"Bequest of Wings"; A Family's Pleasures with Books* (Viking Press, New York, 1944), p. 80.

[2] Ruth 1:16.

[3] Richard G. Moulton and others, *The Bible as Literature* (Thomas Y. Crowell, New York, 1896).

not stand side by side."[4]   And Laura B. Richards, referring to the Bible from a purely literary and educational point of view, says:

> No person can be considered well educated who has not some knowledge of the Old and the New Testament. Here it is not a question of vocabulary, though the infinite riches of the English language are nowhere so gloriously displayed . . . It is not a question of history, though the development of man may be profitably studied in the chronicles of a powerful and intellectual people. It is a question of knowledge against ignorance. The language, the episodes, the personages of the Bible are so interwoven with our daily speech, with the books we read, with every human utterance throughout Christendom, that our children cannot afford to be ignorant of it.[5]

Biblical phrases have indeed crept into our daily speech. We say that a man earns his living by "the sweat of his brow." He is "the salt of the earth," or a "thorn in the flesh." We may want to heap "coals of fire on his head."

We are inclined to regard the Bible as a single book, when in reality it consists of many books. The word *bible* comes from the Greek word *biblia* meaning *books*. The Bible (in the King James version) comprises sixty-six books written by more than forty authors who composed them over a period embracing a thousand years or more. This very fact that the Book of Books was written by many authors about different peoples in various epochs endows it with a quality of brotherhood. When we regard the Bible as a whole library of books, we see that it is fully as important to exercise wisdom in choosing stories and passages for our children to enjoy as it is in selecting books for them from any other library. Mrs. Duff discusses this point in her book, *"Longer Flight"*:

> In introducing books and parts of books (from the Bible) that you know are right for the age and interest of any individual child, it is reasonable to use the same kind of sensitivity to mood and occasion that functions in the successful introduction of any type of reading. . . . The nearest we have come to systematizing our presentation has been to observe the natural division of suitable material into the large categories: The stories, among which we include the accounts of the Creation, the "hero tales" (of Moses, Joseph, Noah, David, and so on), the "personal histories" (Ruth, Esther, Jonah), the Gospels and the Parables of Jesus; and poetry, in which we include, along with the true lyric, dramatic, and didactic poems, certain passages without narrative continuity and concerned with more or less abstract ideas, that have the rhythmic and emotional appeal of poetry.[6]

It is important that a child's introduction to the Bible be a joyous, happy one. Today there are many beautiful books that present Bible literature in a most attractive form. *The Christ Child* is a book of unusual beauty with illustrations in lovely color by Maud and Miska Petersham. *The First Bible,* with drawings by Helen Sewell, is an excellent introduction to the dignity and beauty of the Bible. *The Book of Books* contains the King James version

[4] *Ibid.*
[5] Laura B. Richards, *Stepping Westward* (Appleton-Century-Crofts, New York, 1931), p. 257.
[6] Annis Duff, *"Longer Flight"; A Family Grows Up with Books* (Viking Press, New York, 1955), p. 137.

of the Bible abridged and arranged with editorial comments by Wilbur Owen Sypherd "to make the selections understandable, interesting and significant as parts of a body of lasting world literature."

One God: The Ways We Worship Him, by Florence Mary Fitch, is a thoughtful, significant book that helps a child not only to understand the place of religion in his life, but to respect the religion of others. As the keynote for her book, Mrs. Fitch selects the verse from Malachi:

> Have we not all one Father?
> Hath not one God created us?[7]

She tells the story of the three great religions of America — Jewish, Catholic, and Protestant, arranged in order of antiquity. The important rituals and festivals of each faith are described and many things which are difficult to explain in text are shown in the beautiful photographs with which the book is illustrated. An eminent authority has in each case collaborated with the author and the material has been endorsed by leading educators and national organizations of these three religions.

The Tree of Life: Selections from the Literature of the World's Religions brings together testaments of beauty and faith from many lands. The editor, Ruth Smith, hopes the book will "enable children to grow up on a diet of the best from many religions as she grew up nourished by the best in the Old and New Testaments."

The truth is that no one race or no one religion has a monopoly of wisdom or the whole of the vision of God. How like a great choir is the voice of mankind praising God — though he be called by many names. With what anguished persistence does Man delineate the law and seek to live virtuously. Now, when barriers between cultures are breaking down, with the conquest of distances, it is essential that "The Grace of Understanding" keep pace with the shrinking world.

A fourteenth-century Persian poet, Háfiz, said, "The object of all religions is alike. All men seek their beloved; and all the world is love's dwelling: why talk of a mosque or a church?"[8]

In Henry David Thoreau's *Walden* there is a chapter on "Reading," which is even more applicable to the world today than when it was written. He is discussing the value and pleasure to be derived from reading the sacred books of the world, and he says: "Most men do not know that any nation but the Hebrews had a scripture. A man, any man, will go considerably out of his way to pick up a silver dollar, but here are golden words, which the wisest men of antiquity have uttered, and whose worth the wise of every succeeding age have assured us of."

For these reasons, then, this anthology adds to our native heritage of the Bible a few of the Golden Words to which Thoreau referred.

---

[7] Malachi 3:10.
[8] Moncure Daniel Conway, *The Sacred Anthology* (Trübner, London, 1874), p. 33.

BIBLE SELECTIONS

Joseph and His Brethren
(abridged)

GENESIS, CHAPTERS 26–46

And Jacob dwelt in the land of his father's sojournings, in the land of Canaan. . . . Now Israel loved Joseph more than all his children, because he was the son of his old age: and he made him a coat of many colours. And his brethren saw that their father loved him more than all his brethren; and they hated him, and could not speak peaceably unto him. And Joseph dreamed a dream, and he told it unto his brethren: and they hated him yet the more. And he said unto them, Hear, I pray you, this dream which I have dreamed: for, behold, we were binding sheaves in the field, and, lo, my sheaf arose, and also stood upright; and, behold, your sheaves came round about, and made obeisance to my sheaf. And his brethren said to him, Shalt thou indeed reign over us? or shalt thou indeed have dominion over us? And they hated him yet the more for his dreams, and for his words. And he dreamed yet another dream, and told it to his brethren, and said, Behold, I have dreamed yet a dream; and, behold, the sun and the moon and eleven stars made obeisance to me. And he told it to his father, and to his brethren; and his father rebuked him, and said unto him, What is this dream that thou hast dreamed? Shall I and thy mother and thy brethren indeed come to bow down ourselves to thee to the earth? And his brethren envied him; but his father kept the saying in mind.

And his brethren went to feed their father's flock in Shechem. And Israel said unto Joseph, Do not thy brethren feed the flock in Shechem? Come, and I will send thee unto them. And he said to him, Here I am. And he said to him, Go now, see whether it be well with thy brethren, and well with the flock; and bring me word again. So he sent him out of the vale of Hebron, and he came to Shechem. And a certain man found him, and, behold, he was wandering in the field: and the man asked him, saying, What seekest thou? And he said, I seek my brethren: tell me, I pray thee, where they are feeding the flock. And the man said, They are departed hence: for I heard them say, Let us go to Dothan. And Joseph went after his brethren, and found them in Dothan. And they saw him afar off, and before he came near unto them, they conspired against him to slay him. And they said one to another, Behold, this dreamer cometh. Come now therefore, and let us slay him, and cast him into one of the pits, and we will say, An evil beast hath devoured him: and we shall see what will become of his dreams. And Reuben heard it, and delivered him out of their hand; and said, Let us not take his life. And Reuben said unto them, Shed no blood; cast him into this pit that is in the wilderness, but lay no hand upon him: that he might deliver him out of their hand, to restore him to his father.

And it came to pass, when Joseph was come unto his brethren, that they stript Joseph of his coat, the coat of many colours that was on him; and they took him, and cast him into the pit: and the pit was empty; there was no water in it. And they sat down to eat bread: and they lifted up their eyes and looked, and, behold, a traveling company of Ishmaelites came from Gilead, with their camels bearing spicery and balm and myrrh, going to carry it down to Egypt. And Judah said unto his brethren, What profit is it if we slay our brother and conceal his blood? Come, and let us sell him to the Ishmaelites, and let not our hand be upon him; for he is our brother, our flesh. And his brethren hearkened unto him. And there passed by Midianites, merchantmen; and they drew and lifted up Joseph out of the pit, and sold Joseph to the Ishmaelites for twenty pieces of silver.

And Reuben returned unto the pit; and, behold, Joseph was not in the pit; and he rent his clothes. And he returned unto his brethren, and said, The child is not; and I, whither shall I go? And they took Joseph's coat, and killed a he-goat, and dipped the coat in the blood; and they sent the coat of many colours, and they brought it to their father; and said, This have we found: know now whether it be thy son's coat or not. And he knew it, and said, It is my son's coat; an evil beast hath devoured him; Joseph is without doubt torn in pieces. And Jacob rent his garments, and put sackcloth upon his loins, and mourned for his son many days. And all his sons and all his daughters rose up to comfort him; but he refused to be comforted; and he said, For I will go down to the grave to my son mourning. And his father wept for him.

And Joseph was brought down to Egypt; and Potiphar, an officer of Pharaoh's, the captain of the guard, an Egyptian, bought him of the hand of the Ishmaelites, which had brought him down thither. And the Lord was with Joseph, and he was a prosperous man; and he was in the house of his master, the Egyptian. And his master saw that the Lord was with him, and that the Lord made all that he did to prosper in his hand. And Joseph found grace in his sight, and he ministered unto him: and he made him overseer over his house, and all that he had he put into his hand. And it came to pass from the time that he made him overseer in his house, and over all that he had, that the Lord blessed the Egyptian's house for Joseph's sake; and the blessing of the Lord was upon all that he had, in the house and in the field. And he left all that he had in Joseph's hand; and he knew not aught that was with him, save the bread which he did eat.

And Joseph was comely, and well favoured. And it came to pass after these things, that his master's wife cast her eyes upon Joseph; and she spake to Joseph day by day, that he hearkened not unto her, to be with her. And it came to pass about this time, that he went into the house to do his work; and there was none of the men of the house there within. And she caught him by his garment, saying, Lie with me: and he left his garment in her hand, and fled, and got him out. And it came to pass, when she saw that he had left his garment in her hand and was fled forth, that she called unto the men of her house, and spake unto them, saying, See, he hath brought in an Hebrew unto us to mock us; he came unto me to lie with me, and I cried with a loud voice: and it came to pass, when he heard that I lifted up my voice and cried, that he left his garment by me, and fled, and got him out. And she laid up his garment by her, until his master came home. And she spake unto him according to these words, saying, The Hebrew servant, which thou hast brought unto us, came in unto me to mock me: and it came to pass, as I lifted up my voice and cried, that he left his garment by me, and fled out. And it came to pass, when his master heard the words of his wife which she spake unto him, saying, After this manner did thy servant to me; that his wrath was kindled. And Joseph's master took him, and put him into the prison, the place where the king's prisoners were bound: and he was there in the prison. But the Lord was with Joseph, and showed kindness unto him, and gave him favour in the sight of the keeper of the prison. And the keeper of the prison committed to Joseph's hand all the prisoners that were in the prison; and whatsoever they did there, he was the doer of it. The keeper of the prison looked not to any thing that was under his hand, because the Lord was with him; and that which he did, the Lord made it to prosper.

And it came to pass after these things,

that the butler of the king of Egypt and his baker offended their lord the king of Egypt. And Pharaoh was wroth against his two officers, against the chief of the butlers, and against the chief of the bakers. And he put them in ward in the house of the captain of the guard, into the prison, the place where Joseph was bound. And the captain of the guard charged Joseph with them, and he ministered unto them: and they continued a season in ward. And they dreamed a dream both of them, the butler and the baker of the king of Egypt, which were bound in the prison. And Joseph came in unto them in the morning, and saw them, and, behold, they were sad. And he asked Pharaoh's officers that were with him in ward in his master's house, saying, Wherefore look ye so sadly today? And they said unto him, We have dreamed a dream, and there is none that can interpret it. And Joseph said unto them, Do not interpretations belong to God? tell it me, I pray you. And the chief butler told his dream to Joseph, and said to him, In my dream, behold, a vine was before me; and in the vine were three branches: and it was as though it budded, and its blossoms shot forth; and the clusters thereof brought forth ripe grapes: and Pharaoh's cup was in my hand; and I took the grapes, and pressed them into Pharaoh's cup, and I gave the cup unto Pharaoh's hand. And Joseph said unto him, This is the interpretation of it: the three branches are three days; within yet three days shall Pharaoh lift up thine head, and restore thee unto thine office: and thou shalt give Pharaoh's cup into his hand, after the former manner when thou wast his butler. But have me in thy remembrance when it shall be well with thee, and show kindness, I pray thee, unto me, and make mention of me unto Pharaoh, and bring me out of this house: for indeed I was stolen away out of the land of the Hebrews: and here also have I done nothing that they should put me into the dungeon. When the chief baker saw that the interpretation was good, he said unto Joseph, I also was in my dream, and, behold, three baskets of white bread were on my head: and in the uppermost basket there was of all manner of bakemeats for Pharaoh; and the birds did eat them out of the basket upon

my head. And Joseph answered and said, This is the interpretation thereof: the three baskets are three days; within yet three days shall Pharaoh lift up thy head from off thee, and shall hang thee on a tree; and the birds shall eat thy flesh from off thee. And it came to pass the third day, which was Pharaoh's birthday, that he made a feast unto all his servants: and he lifted up the head of the chief butler and the head of the chief baker among his servants. And he restored the chief butler unto his butlership again; and he gave the cup unto Pharaoh's hand: but he hanged the chief baker: as Joseph had interpreted to them. Yet did not the chief butler remember Joseph, but forgat him.

And it came to pass at the end of two full years, that Pharaoh dreamed: and, behold, he stood by the river. And, behold, there came up out of the river seven kine, well favoured and fatfleshed; and they fed in the reed-grass. And, behold, seven other kine came up out of the river, ill favoured and leanfleshed; and stood by the other kine upon the brink of the river. And the ill favoured and leanfleshed kine did eat up the seven well favoured and fat kine. So Pharaoh awoke. And he slept and dreamed a second time: and, behold, seven ears of corn came up upon one stalk, rank and good. And, behold, seven ears, thin and blasted with the east wind, sprung up after them. And the thin ears swallowed up the seven rank and full ears. And Pharaoh awoke, and, behold, it was a dream. And it came to pass in the morning that his spirit was troubled; and he sent and called for all the magicians of Egypt, and all the wise men thereof: and Pharaoh told them his dream; but there was none that could interpret them unto Pharaoh. Then spake the chief butler unto Pharaoh, saying, I do remember my faults this day: Pharaoh was wroth with his servants, and put me in ward in the house of the captain of the guard, me and the chief baker: and we dreamed a dream in one night, I and he; we dreamed each man according to the interpretation of his dream. And there was with us there a young man, an Hebrew, servant to the captain of the guard; and we told him, and he interpreted to us our dreams; to each man according to his dream he did interpret. And it came to pass, as he interpreted to us, so it was; me he restored unto mine office, and him he hanged.

Then Pharaoh sent and called Joseph, and they brought him hastily out of the dungeon: and he shaved himself, and changed his raiment, and came in unto Pharaoh. And Pharaoh said unto Joseph, I have dreamed a dream, and there is none that can interpret it: and I have heard say of thee, that when thou hearest a dream thou canst interpret it. And Joseph answered Pharaoh, saying, It is not in me: God shall give Pharaoh an answer of peace. And Pharaoh spake unto Joseph, In my dream, behold, I stood upon the brink of the river: and, behold, there came up out of the river seven kine, fat-fleshed and well favoured; and they fed in the reed-grass: and, behold, seven other kine came up after them, poor and very ill favoured and leanfleshed, such as I never saw in all the land of Egypt for badness: and the lean and ill favoured kine did eat up the first seven fat kine: and when they had eaten them up, it could not be known that they had eaten them; but they were still ill favoured, as at the beginning. So I awoke. And I saw in my dream, and, behold, seven ears came up upon one stalk, full and good: and, behold, seven ears, withered, thin, and blasted with the east wind, sprung up after them: and the thin ears swallowed up the seven good ears: and I told it unto the magicians; but there was none that could declare it to me.

And Joseph said unto Pharaoh, The dream of Pharaoh is one: what God is about to do he hath declared unto Pharaoh. The seven good kine are seven years; and the seven good ears are seven years: the dream is one. And the seven lean and ill favoured kine that came up after them are seven years, and also the seven empty ears blasted with the east wind; they shall be seven years of famine. That is the thing which I spake unto Pharaoh: what God is about to do he hath showed unto Pharaoh. Behold, there come seven years of great plenty throughout all the land of Egypt; and there shall arise after them seven years of famine; and all the plenty shall be forgotten in the land of Egypt; and the famine shall consume the land; and the plenty shall not be known in the land by reason of that famine which followeth; for it shall be very grievous. And for that the dream was doubled unto Pharaoh twice, it is because the thing is established by God, and God will shortly bring it to pass. Now therefore let Pharaoh look out a man discreet and wise, and set him over the land of Egypt. Let Pharoah do this, and let him appoint overseers over the land, and take up the fifth part of the land of Egypt in the seven plenteous years. And let them gather all the food of these good years that come, and lay up corn under the hand of Pharaoh for food in the cities, and let them keep it. And the food shall be for a store to the land against the seven years of famine, which shall be in the land of Egypt; that the land perish not through the famine.

And the thing was good in the eyes of Pharaoh, and in the eyes of all his servants. And Pharaoh said unto his servants, Can we find such a one as this, a man in whom the spirit of God is? And Pharaoh said unto Joseph, Forasmuch as God hath showed thee all this, there is none so discreet and wise as thou: thou shalt be over my house, and according unto thy word shall all my people be ruled: only in the throne will I be greater than thou. And Pharaoh said unto Joseph, See, I have set thee over all the land of Egypt. And Pharaoh took off his signet ring from his hand, and put it upon Joseph's hand, and arrayed him in vestures of fine linen, and put a gold chain about his neck; and he made him to ride in the second chariot which he had; and they cried before him, Bow the knee: and he set him over all the land of Egypt. And Pharaoh said unto Joseph, I am Pharaoh, and without thee shall no man lift up his hand or his foot in all the land of Egypt. And Pharaoh called Joseph's name Zaphenathpaneah; and he gave him to wife Asenath the daughter of Poti-phera priest of On. And Joseph went out over the land of Egypt.

And Joseph was thirty years old when he stood before Pharaoh king of Egypt. And Joseph went out from the presence of Pharaoh, and went throughout all the land of Egypt. And in the seven plenteous years the earth brought forth by handfuls. And he gathered up all the food of the seven years which were in the land of Egypt, and laid up the food in the cities: the food of the field, which was round about every city, laid he up in the same. And Joseph laid up corn as the sand of the sea, very much, until he left numbering; for it was without number.

And the seven years of plenty, that was in the land of Egypt, came to an end. And the seven years of famine began to come, according as Joseph had said: and there was famine in all lands: but in all the land of Egypt there was bread. And when all the land of Egypt was famished, the people cried to Pharaoh for bread: and Pharaoh said unto all the Egyptians, Go unto Joseph; what he saith to you, do. And the famine was over all the face of the earth: and Joseph opened all the store-houses, and sold unto the Egyptians; and the famine was sore in the land of Egypt. And all countries came into Egypt to Joseph for to buy corn; because the famine was sore in all the earth.

Now Jacob saw that there was corn in Egypt, and Jacob said unto his sons, Why do ye look one upon another? And he said, Behold, I have heard that there is corn in Egypt: get you down thither, and buy for us from thence; that we may live, and not die. And Joseph's ten brethren went down to buy corn from Egypt. But Benjamin, Joseph's brother, Jacob sent not with his brethren; for he said, Lest peradventure mischief befall him. And the sons of Israel came to buy among those that came: for the famine was in the land of Canaan. And Joseph was the governor over the land; he it was that sold to all the people of the land: and Joseph's brethren came, and bowed down themselves to him with their faces to the earth.

And Joseph saw his brethren, and he knew them, but made himself strange unto them, and spake roughly with them; and he said unto them, Whence come ye? And they said, From the land of Canaan to buy food. And Joseph knew his brethren, but they knew not him. And Joseph remembered the dreams which he dreamed of them, and said unto them, Ye are spies; to see the nakedness of the land ye are come. And they said unto him, Nay, my lord, but to buy food are thy

servants come. We are all one man's sons; we are true men, thy servants are no spies. And he said unto them, Nay, but to see the nakedness of the land ye are come. And they said, We thy servants are twelve brethren, the sons of one man in the land of Canaan; and, behold, the youngest is this day with our father, and one is not. And Joseph said unto them, That is it that I spake unto you, saying, Ye are spies: hereby ye shall be proved: by the life of Pharaoh ye shall not go forth hence, except your youngest brother come hither. Send one of you, and let him fetch your brother, and ye shall be bound, that your words may be proved, whether there be truth in you: or else by the life of Pharaoh surely ye are spies. And he put them all together into ward three days.

And Joseph said unto them the third day, This do, and live; for I fear God: if ye be true men, let one of your brethren be bound in your prison house; but go ye, carry corn for the famine to your houses: and bring your youngest brother unto me; so shall your words be verified, and ye shall not die. And they did so. And they said one to another, We are verily guilty concerning our brother, in that we saw the distress of his soul, when he besought us, and we would not hear; therefore is this distress come upon us. And Reuben answered them, saying, Spake I not unto you, saying, Do not sin against the child; and ye would not hear? therefore also, behold, his blood is required. And they knew not that Joseph understood them; for there was an interpreter between them. And he turned himself about from them, and wept; and he returned to them, and spake to them, and took Simeon from among them, and bound him before their eyes. Then Joseph commanded to fill their vessels with corn, and to restore every man's money into his sack, and to give them provision for the way: and thus was it done unto them. And they laded their asses with their corn, and departed thence. And as one of them opened his sack to give his ass provender in the lodging place, he espied his money; and, behold, it was in the mouth of his sack: And he said unto his brethren, My money is restored; and, lo, it is even in my sack: and their heart failed them, and they turned trembling one to another, saying, What is this that God hath done unto us?

And they came unto Jacob their father unto the land of Canaan, and told him all that had befallen them: saying, The man, the lord of the land, spake roughly with us, and took us for spies of the country. And we said unto him, We are true men; we are no spies: we be twelve brethren, sons of our father; one is not, and the youngest is this day with our father in the land of Canaan. And the man, the lord of the land, said unto us, Hereby shall I know that ye are true men; leave one of your brethren with me, and take corn for the famine of your houses, and go your way: and bring your youngest brother unto me: then shall I know that ye are no spies, but that ye are true men: so will I deliver you your brother, and ye shall traffick in the land. And it came to pass as they emptied their sacks, that, behold, every man's bundle of money was in his sack: and when they and their father saw their bundles of money, they were afraid. And Jacob their father said unto them, Me have ye bereaved of my children: Joseph is not, and Simeon is not, and ye will take Benjamin away: all these things are against me. And Reuben spake unto his father, saying, Slay my two sons, if I bring him not to thee: deliver him into my hand, and I will bring him to thee again. And he said, My son shall not go down with you; for his brother is dead, and he only is left: if mischief befall him by the way in the which ye go, then shall ye bring down my gray hairs with sorrow to the grave.

And the famine was sore in the land. And it came to pass, when they had eaten up the corn which they had brought out of Egypt, their father said unto them, Go again, buy us a little food. And Judah spake unto him, saying, The man did solemnly protest unto us, saying, Ye shall not see my face, except your brother be with you. If thou wilt send our brother with us, we will go down and buy thee food: but if thou wilt not send him, we will not go down: for the man said unto us, Ye shall not see my face, except your brother be with you. And Israel said, Wherefore dealt ye so ill with me, as to tell the man whether ye had yet a brother? And

they said, The man asked straitly concerning ourselves, and concerning our kindred, saying, Is your father yet alive? have ye another brother? and we told him according to the tenor of these words: could we in any wise know that he would say, Bring your brother down? And Judah said unto Israel his father, Send the lad with me, and we will arise and go; that we may live, and not die, both we, and thou, and also our little ones. I will be surety for him; of my hand shalt thou require him: if I bring him not unto thee, and set him before thee, then let me bear the blame for ever: for except we had lingered, surely we had now returned a second time. And their father Israel said unto them, If it be so now, do this; take of the choice fruits of the land in your vessels, and carry down the man a present, a little balm, and a little honey, spicery and myrrh, nuts, and almonds: and take double money in your hand; and the money that was returned in the mouth of your sacks carry again in your hand; peradventure it was an oversight: take also your brother, and arise, go again unto the man: and God Almighty give you mercy before the man, that he may release unto you your other brother and Benjamin. And if I be bereaved of my children, I am bereaved.

And the men took that present, and they took double money in their hand, and Benjamin; and rose up, and went down to Egypt, and stood before Joseph. And when Joseph saw Benjamin with them, he said to the steward of his house, Bring the men into the house, and slay, and make ready; for the men shall dine with me at noon. And the man did as Joseph bade; and the man brought the men into Joseph's house. And the men were afraid because they were brought into Joseph's house; and they said, Because of the money that was returned in our sacks at the first time are we brought in; that he may seek occasion against us, and fall upon us, and take us for bondmen, and our asses. And they came near to the steward of Joseph's house, and they spake unto him at the door of the house, and said, Oh my lord, we came indeed down at the first time to buy food: and it came to pass, when we came to the lodging place, that we opened our sacks, and, behold, every man's money was in the mouth of his sack, our money in full weight: and we have brought it again in our hand. And other money have we brought down in our hand to buy food: we know not who put our money in our sacks. And he said, Peace be to you, fear not: your God, and the God of your father, hath given you treasure in your sacks: I had your money. And he brought Simeon out unto them. And the man brought the men into Joseph's house, and gave them water, and they washed their feet; and he gave their asses provender.

And they made ready the present against Joseph came at noon: for they heard that they should eat bread there. And when Joseph came home, they brought him the present which was in their hand into the house, and bowed down themselves to him to the earth. And he asked them of their welfare, and said, Is your father well, the old man of whom ye spake? Is he yet alive? And they said, Thy servant our father is well, he is yet alive. And they bowed the head, and made obeisance. And he lifted up his eyes, and saw Benjamin his brother, his mother's son, and said, Is this your youngest brother, of whom ye spake unto me? And he said, God be gracious unto thee, my son. And Joseph made haste; for his bowels did yearn upon his brother: and he sought where to weep; and he entered into his chamber, and wept there. And he washed his face, and came out; and he refrained himself, and said, Set on bread. And they set on for him by himself, and for them by themselves, and for the Egyptians, which did eat with him, by themselves: because the Egyptians might not eat bread with the Hebrews; for that is an abomination unto the Egyptians. And they sat before him, the firstborn according to his birthright, and the youngest according to his youth: and the men marvelled one with another. And he took and sent messes unto them from before him: but Benjamin's mess was five times so much as any of theirs. And they drank and were merry with him.

And he commanded the steward of his house, saying, Fill the men's sacks with food, as much as they can carry, and put every man's money in his sack's mouth. And put my cup, the silver cup, in the sack's mouth of the youngest, and his corn money. And he did according to the word that Joseph had spoken. As soon as the morning was light, the men were sent away, they and their asses. And when they were gone out of the city, and were not yet far off, Joseph said unto his steward, Up, follow after the men; and when thou dost overtake them, say unto them, Wherefore have ye rewarded evil for good? Is not this it in which my lord drinketh, and whereby he indeed divineth? ye have done evil in so doing. And he overtook them, and he spake unto them these words. And they said unto him, Wherefore speaketh my lord such words as these? God forbid that thy servants should do such a thing. Behold, the money, which we found in our sacks' mouths, we brought again unto thee out of the land of Canaan: how then should we steal out of thy lord's house silver or gold? With whomsoever of thy servants it be found, let him die, and we also will be my lord's bondmen. And he said, Now also let it be according unto your words: he with whom it is found shall be my bondman; and ye shall be blameless. Then they hasted, and took down every man his sack to the ground, and opened every man his sack. And he searched, and began at the eldest, and left at the youngest: and the cup was found in Benjamin's sack. Then they rent their clothes, and laded every man his ass, and returned to the city.

And Judah and his brethren came to Joseph's house; and he was yet there: and they fell before him on the ground. And Joseph said unto them, What deed is this that ye have done? know ye not that such a man as I can indeed divine? And Judah said, What shall we say unto my lord? what shall we speak? or how shall we clear ourselves? God hath found out the iniquity of thy servants: behold, we are my lord's bondmen, both we, and he also in whose hand the cup is found. And he said, God forbid that I should do so: the man in whose hand the cup is found, he shall be my bondman; but as for you, get you up in peace unto your father.

Then Judah came near unto him, and said, Oh my lord, let thy servant, I pray thee, speak a word in my lord's ears, and let not thine anger burn against thy servant: for thou art even as Pharaoh. My lord asked his servants, saying, Have ye a father, or a brother? And we said unto my lord, We have a father, an old man, and a child of his old age, a little one; and his brother is dead, and he alone is left of his mother, and his father loveth him. And thou saidst unto thy servants, Bring him down unto me, that I may set mine eyes upon him. And we said unto my lord, The lad cannot leave his father: for if he should leave his father, his father would die. And thou saidst unto thy servants, Except your youngest brother come down with you, ye shall see my face no more. And it came to pass when we came up unto thy servant my father, we told him the words of my lord. And our father said, Go again, buy us a little food. And we said, We cannot go down: if our youngest brother be with us, then will we go down: for we may not see the man's face, except our youngest be with us. And thy servant my father said unto us, Ye know that my wife bare me two sons: and the one went out from me, and I said, Surely he is torn in pieces; and I have not seen him since: and if ye take this one also from me, and mischief befall him, ye shall bring down my gray hairs with sorrow to the grave. Now therefore when I come to thy servant my father, and the lad be not with us; seeing that his life is bound up in the lad's life; it shall come to pass, when he seeth that the lad is not with us, that he will die: and thy servants shall bring down the gray hairs of thy servant our father with sorrow to the grave. For thy servant became surety for the lad unto my father, saying, If I bring him not unto thee, then shall I bear the blame to my father for ever. Now therefore, let thy servant, I pray thee, abide instead of the lad a bondman to my lord; and let the lad go up with his brethren. For how shall I go up to my father, and the lad be not with me? lest I see the evil that shall come on my father.

Then Joseph could not refrain himself before all them that stood by him; and he cried, Cause every man to go out from me. And there stood no man with him, while Joseph made himself known unto his brethren. And he wept aloud: and the Egyptians heard, and the house of Pharaoh heard. And Joseph said unto his brethren, I am Joseph; doth my father yet live? And his brethren could not answer him; for they were troubled at his presence. And Joseph said unto his brethren, Come near to me, I pray you. And they came near. And he said, I am Joseph your brother whom ye sold into Egypt. And now be not grieved, nor angry with yourselves, that ye sold me hither: for God did send me before you to preserve life. For these two years hath the famine been in the land: and there are yet five years in the which there shall be neither plowing nor harvest. And God sent me before you to preserve you a remnant in the earth, and to save you alive by a great deliverance. So now it was not you that sent me hither, but God; and he hath made me a father to Pharaoh, and lord of all his house, and ruler over all the land of Egypt. Haste ye, and go up to my father, and say unto him, Thus saith thy son Joseph, God hath made me lord of all Egypt: come down unto me, tarry not: and thou shalt dwell in the land of Goshen, and thou shalt be near unto me, thou, and thy flocks, and thy herds, and all that thou hast: and there will I nourish thee; for there are yet five years of famine; lest thou come children, and thy children's children, and to poverty, thou, and thy household, and all that thou hast. And, behold, your eyes see, and the eyes of my brother Benjamin, that it is my mouth that speaketh unto you. And ye shall tell my father of all my glory in Egypt, and of all that ye have seen; and ye shall haste and bring down my father hither. And he fell upon his brother Benjamin's neck, and wept; and Benjamin wept upon his neck. And he kissed all his brethren, and wept upon them: and after that his brethren talked with him.

And the fame thereof was heard in Pharaoh's house, saying, Joseph's brethren are come: and it pleased Pharaoh well, and his servants. And Pharaoh said unto Joseph, Say unto thy brethren, This do ye; lade your beasts, and go, get you unto the land of Canaan; and take your father and your households, and come unto me: and I will give you the good of the land of Egypt, and ye shall eat the fat of the land. Now thou art commanded, this do ye; take you wagons out of the land of Egypt for your little ones, and for your wives, and bring your father, and come. Also regard not your stuff; for the good of all the land of Egypt is yours. And the sons of Israel did so: and Joseph gave them wagons, according to the commandment of Pharaoh, and gave them provision for the way. To all of them he gave each man changes of raiment; but to Benjamin he gave three hundred pieces of silver, and five changes of raiment. And to his father he sent after this manner; ten asses laden with the good things of Egypt, and ten she-asses laden with corn and bread and victual for his father by the way. So he sent his brethren away, and they departed: and he said unto them, See that ye fall not out by the way.

And they went up out of Egypt, and came into the land of Canaan unto Jacob their father. And they told him, saying, Joseph is yet alive, and he is ruler over all the land of Egypt. And his heart fainted, for he believed them not. And they told him all the words of Joseph, which he had said unto them: and when he saw the wagons which Joseph had sent to carry him, the spirit of Jacob their father revived: and Israel said, It is enough; Joseph my son is yet alive: I will go and see him before I die.

And Israel took his journey with all that he had, and came to Beer-sheba, and offered sacrifices unto the God of his father Isaac. And God spake unto Israel in the visions of the night, and said, Jacob, Jacob. And he said, Here am I. And he said, I am God, the God of thy father: fear not to go down into Egypt; for I will there make of thee a great nation: I will go down with thee into Egypt; and I will also surely bring thee up again: and Joseph shall put his hand upon thine eyes. And Jacob rose up from Beer-sheba: and the sons of Israel carried Jacob their father, and their little ones, and their wives, in the wagons which Pharaoh had sent to carry him. And they took their cattle, and their goods, which they had gotten in the land of Canaan, and came into Egypt, Jacob, and all his seed with him: his sons, and his sons' sons with him, his daughters, and his sons' daughters, and all his seed brought he with him into Egypt.

The Story of Ruth

(abridged)

RUTH, CHAPTERS 1 AND 2

And it came to pass in the days when the judges judged, that there was a famine in the land. And a certain man of Beth-lehem-judah went to sojourn in the land of Moab, he, and his wife, and his two sons. And the name of the man was Elimelech, and the name of his wife Naomi, and the name of his two sons Mahlon and Chilion. And they came into the country of Moab, and continued there. And Elimelech Naomi's husband died; and she was left, and her two sons. And they took them wives of the women of Moab; and the name of the one was Orpah, and the name of the other Ruth. And they dwelled there about ten years. And Mahlon and Chilion died both of them; and the woman was left of her two children and of her husband.

Then she arose with her daughters-in-law, that she might return from the country of Moab: for she had heard in the country of Moab how that the Lord had visited his people in giving them bread. And she went forth out of the place where she was, and her two daughters-in-law with her; and they went on the way to return unto the land of Judah. And Naomi said unto her two daughters-in-law, Go, return each of you to her mother's house: the Lord deal kindly with you, as ye have dealt with the dead, and with me. The Lord grant you that ye may find rest, each of you in the house of her husband. Then she kissed them; and they lifted up their voice, and wept. And they said unto her, Nay, but we will return with thee unto thy people. And Naomi said, Turn again, my daughters; why will ye go with me? . . . nay, my daughters; for it grieveth me much for your sakes, for the hand of the Lord is gone forth against me. And they lifted up their voice, and wept again: and Orpah kissed her mother-in-law; but Ruth clave unto her. And she said, Behold, thy sister-in-law is gone back unto her people, and unto her god; return thou after thy sister-in-law. And Ruth said, Intreat me not to leave thee, and to return from following after thee: For whither thou goest, I will go; and where thou lodgest, I will lodge; thy people shall be my people, and thy God my God; where thou diest, will I die, and there will I be buried; the Lord do so to me, and more also, if aught but death part thee and me. And when she saw that she was steadfastly minded to go with her, she left speaking unto her.

So they two went until they came to Bethlehem. And it came to pass when they were come to Beth-lehem, that all the city was moved about them. And the women said, Is this Naomi? And she said unto them, Call me not Naomi, call me "Mara": for the Almighty hath dealt very "bitterly" with me. I went out full, and the Lord hath brought me home again empty: why call ye me Naomi, seeing the Lord hath testified against me, and the Almighty hath afflicted me? So Naomi returned, and Ruth the Moabitess, her daughter-in-law, with her, which returned out of the country of Moab: and they came to Beth-lehem in the beginning of barley harvest.

And Naomi had a kinsman of her husband's, a mighty man of wealth, of the family of Elimelech; and his name was Boaz. And Ruth the Moabitess said unto Naomi, Let me now go to the field, and glean among the ears of corn after him in whose sight I shall find grace. And she said unto her, Go, my daughter. And she went, and came and gleaned in the field after the reapers: and her hap was to light on the portion of the field belonging unto Boaz, who was of the family of Elimelech. And, behold, Boaz came from Beth-lehem, and said unto the reapers, The Lord be with you. And they answered him, The Lord bless thee. Then said Boaz unto his servant that was set over the reapers, Whose damsel is this? And the servant that was set over the reapers answered and said, It is the Moabitish damsel that came back with Naomi out of the country of Moab: and she said, Let me glean, I pray you, and gather after the reapers among the sheaves: so she came, and hath continued even from the morning until now, save that she tarried a little in the house. Then said Boaz unto Ruth, Hearest thou not, my daughter?

Go not to glean in another field, neither pass from hence, but abide here fast by my maidens. Let thine eyes be on the field that they do reap, and go thou after them: have I not charged the young men that they shall not touch thee? and when thou art athirst, go unto the vessels, and drink of that which the young men have drawn. Then she fell on her face, and bowed herself to the ground, and said unto him, Why have I found grace in thy sight, that thou shouldest take knowledge of me, seeing I am a stranger? And Boaz answered and said unto her, It hath fully been showed me, all that thou hast done unto thy mother-in-law since the death of thine husband: and how thou hast left thy father and thy mother, and the land of thy nativity, and art come unto a people which thou knewest not heretofore. The Lord recompense thy work, and a full reward be given thee of the Lord, the God of Israel, under whose wings thou art come to take refuge. Then she said, Let me find grace in thy sight, my lord; for that thou hast comforted me, and for that thou hast spoken kindly unto thine handmaid, though I be not as one of thine handmaidens. And at mealtime Boaz said unto her, Come hither, and eat of the bread, and dip thy morsel in the vinegar. And she sat beside the reapers: and they reached her parched corn, and she did eat, and was sufficed, and left thereof. And when she was risen up to glean, Boaz commanded his young men, saying, Let her glean even among the sheaves, and reproach her not. And also pull out some for her from the bundles, and leave it, and let her glean, and rebuke her not. So she gleaned in the field until even; and she beat out that she had gleaned, and it was about an ephah of barley.

And she took it up, and went into the city: and her mother-in-law saw what she had gleaned: and she brought forth and gave to her that she had left after she was sufficed. And her mother-in-law said unto her, Where hast thou gleaned today? and where wroughtest thou? blessed be he that did take knowledge of thee. And she showed her mother-in-law with whom she had wrought, and said, The man's name with whom I wrought today is Boaz. And Naomi said unto her daughter-in-law, Blessed be he of the Lord, who hath not left off his kindness to the living and to the dead. And Naomi said unto her, The man is nigh of kin unto us, one of our near kinsmen. And Ruth the Moabitess said, Yea, he said unto me, Thou shalt keep fast by my young men, until they have ended all my harvest. And Naomi said unto Ruth her daughter-in-law, It is good, my daughter, that thou go out with his maidens, and that they meet thee not in any other field. So she kept fast by the maidens of Boaz to glean unto the end of barley harvest and of wheat harvest; and she dwelt with her mother-in-law.

The Visit of the Magi

MATTHEW 2:1–12

Now when Jesus was born in Bethlehem of Judaea in the days of Herod the king, behold, there came wise men from the east to Jerusalem,

Saying, Where is he that is born King of the Jews? for we have seen his star in the east, and are come to worship him.

When Herod the king had heard these things, he was troubled, and all Jerusalem with him.

And when he had gathered all the chief priests and scribes of the people together, he demanded of them where Christ should be born.

And they said unto him, In Bethlehem of Judaea: for thus it is written by the prophet,

And thou Bethlehem, in the land of Juda, art not the least among the princes of Juda: for out of thee shall come a Governor, that shall rule my people Israel.

Then Herod, when he had privily called the wise men, enquired of them diligently what time the star appeared.

And he sent them to Bethlehem, and said, Go and search diligently for the young child; and when ye have found him, bring me word again, that I may come and worship him also.

When they had heard the king, they departed; and, lo, the star, which they saw in the east, went before them, till it came and stood over where the young child was.

When they saw the star, they rejoiced with exceeding great joy.

And when they were come into the house, they saw the young child with Mary his mother, and fell down, and worshipped him: and when they had opened their treasures, they presented unto him gifts; gold, and frankincense, and myrrh.

And being warned of God in a dream that they should not return to Herod, they departed into their own country another way.

The Prodigal Son

LUKE 15:11–32

And Jesus said, A certain man had two sons:

And the younger of them said to his father, Father, give me the portion of goods that falleth to me. And he divided unto them his living.

And not many days after the younger son gathered all together, and took his journey into a far country, and there wasted his substance with riotous living.

And when he had spent all, there arose a mighty famine in that land; and he began to be in want.

And he went and joined himself to a citizen of that country; and he sent him into his fields to feed swine.

And he would fain have filled his belly with the husks that the swine did eat: and no man gave unto him.

And when he came to himself, he said, How many hired servants of my father's have bread enough and to spare, and I perish with hunger!

I will arise and go to my father, and will say unto him, Father, I have sinned against heaven, and before thee,

And am no more worthy to be called thy son: make me as one of thy hired servants.

And he arose, and came to his father. But when he was yet a great way off, his father saw him, and had compassion, and ran, and fell on his neck, and kissed him.

And the son said unto him, Father, I have sinned against heaven, and in thy sight, and am no more worthy to be called thy son.

But the father said to his servants, Bring forth the best robe, and put it on him; and put a ring on his hand, and shoes on his feet:

And bring hither the fatted calf, and kill it; and let us eat, and be merry:

For this my son was dead, and is alive again; he was lost, and is found. And they began to be merry.

Now his elder son was in the field: and as he came and drew nigh to the house, he heard music and dancing.

And he called one of the servants, and asked what these things meant.

And he said unto him, Thy brother is come; and thy father hath killed the fatted calf, because he hath received him safe and sound.

And he was angry and would not go in: therefore came his father out, and intreated him.

And he answering said to his father, Lo, these years do I serve thee, neither transgressed I at any time thy commandment: and yet thou never gavest me a kid, that I might make merry with my friends:

But as soon as this thy son was come, which hath devoured thy living with harlots, thou hast killed for him the fatted calf.

And he said unto him, Son, thou art ever with me, and all that I have is thine.

It was meet that we should make merry, and be glad: for this thy brother was dead, and is alive again; and was lost, and is found.

Charity

I CORINTHIANS 13

Though I speak with the tongues of men and of angels, and have not charity, I am become as sounding brass, or a tinkling cymbal.

And though I have the gift of prophecy, and understand all mysteries, and all knowledge; and though I have all faith, so that I could remove mountains, and have not charity, I am nothing.

And though I bestow all my goods to feed the poor, and though I give my body to be burned, and have not charity, it profiteth me nothing.

Charity suffereth long, and is kind; charity envieth not; charity vaunteth not itself, is not puffed up,

Doth not behave itself unseemly, seeketh not her own, is not easily provoked, thinketh no evil;

Rejoiceth not in iniquity, but rejoiceth in the truth;

Beareth all things, believeth all things, hopeth all things, endureth all things.

Charity never faileth: but whether there be prophecies, they shall fail; whether there be tongues, they shall cease; whether there be knowledge, it shall vanish away.

For we know in part, and we prophesy in part.

But when that which is perfect is come, then that which is in part shall be done away.

When I was a child, I spake as a child, I understood as a child, I thought as a child: but when I became a man, I put away childish things.

For now we see through a glass darkly; but then face to face: now I know in part; but then shall I know even as also I am known.

And now abideth faith, hope, charity, these three; but the greatest of these is charity.

Songs from the Bible

Proverbs 4:10-19

THE TWO PATHS

Hear, O my son, and receive my sayings;
And the years of thy life shall be many.
I have taught thee in the way of wisdom;
I have led thee in right paths.
When thou goest, thy steps shall not be
    straitened;
And if thou runnest, thou shalt not stumble.
Take fast hold of instruction;
Let her not go:
Keep her;
For she is thy life.

Enter not into the path of the wicked,
And go not in the way of evil men.
  Avoid it,
    Pass not by it;
    Turn from it, and pass away.
For they sleep not, except they have done
    mischief;
And their sleep is taken away, unless they
    cause some to fall.
For they eat the bread of wickedness.
And drink the wine of violence.
But the path of the just is as the shining
    light,
  That shineth more and more unto the
    perfect day.
The way of the wicked is as darkness:
  They know not at what they stumble.

Psalm 1

THE TREE AND THE CHAFF

Blessed is the man that walketh not in the
    counsel of the ungodly,
  Nor standeth in the way of sinners,
  Nor sitteth in the seat of the scornful.
But his delight is in the law of the Lord;
  And in his law doth he meditate day and
    night.

And he shall be like a tree planted by the
    rivers of water,
  That bringeth forth its fruit in his season,
His leaf also doth not wither;
  And whatsoever he doeth shall prosper.
The ungodly are not so;
  But are like the chaff which the wind driv-
    eth away.

Therefore the ungodly shall not stand in the
    judgment,
  Nor sinners in the congregation of the
    righteous.
For the Lord knoweth the way of the right-
    eous:
  But the way of the ungodly shall perish.

Psalm 23

THE LORD IS MY SHEPHERD

The Lord is my shepherd;
I shall not want.

He maketh me to lie down in green
    pastures:
He leadeth me beside the still waters.
He restoreth my soul;
He guideth me in the paths of righteousness
    for his name's sake.
  Yea, though I walk through the valley of
    the shadow of death,
I will fear no evil;
For thou art with me;
Thy rod and thy staff, they comfort me.
Thou preparest a table before me
In the presence of mine enemies:
Thou hast anointed my head with oil;
My cup runneth over.
Surely goodness and mercy shall follow me
    all the days of my life;
And I will dwell in the house of the Lord
    forever.

Psalm 24

THE EARTH IS THE LORD'S

The earth is the Lord's, and the fulness
    thereof;
The world, and they that dwell therein.
For he hath founded it upon the seas,
And established it upon the floods.
Who shall ascend into the hill of the
    Lord?
Or who shall stand in his holy place?

He that hath clean hands, and a pure heart;
Who hath not lifted up his soul unto vanity,
Nor sworn deceitfully.
He shall receive the blessing from the
    Lord,
And righteousness from the God of his salva-
    tion.
This is the generation of them that seek
    him,
That seek thy face, O Jacob.

Lift up your heads, O ye gates;
And be ye lift up, ye everlasting doors;
And the king of glory shall come in.

Who is this king of glory?

The Lord strong and mighty,
The Lord mighty in battle.

Lift up your heads, O ye gates;
Even lift them up, ye everlasting doors;
And the king of glory shall come in.

Who is this king of glory?

The Lord of hosts,
He is the king of glory.

Psalm 46

God Is Our Refuge and Strength

God is our refuge and strength, a very
    present help in trouble.
Therefore will not we fear, though the earth
    be removed,
And though the mountains be carried into
    the midst of the sea;
Though the waters thereof roar and be
    troubled,
Though the mountains shake with the swell-
    ing thereof.

There is a river, the streams whereof shall
    make glad the city of God,
The holy place of the tabernacles of the
    Most High.
God is in the midst of her; she shall not be
    moved;
God shall help her, and that right early.
The heathen raged, the kingdoms were
    moved;
He uttered his voice, the earth melted.

    The Lord of hosts is with us;
    The God of Jacob is our refuge.

Come, behold the works of the Lord,
What desolations he hath made in the earth.
He maketh wars to cease unto the end of the
    earth;
He breaketh the bow and cutteth the spear
    in sunder;
He burneth the chariot in the fire.

Be still, and know that I am God.
I will be exalted among the heathen,
I will be exalted in the earth.

    The Lord of hosts is with us;
    The God of Jacob is our refuge.

Psalm 91

Abiding in the Shadow of the Almighty

He that dwelleth in the secret place of the
    Most High
    Shall abide under the shadow of the Al-
      mighty.
I will say of the Lord, he is my refuge and
    my fortress:
    My God; in him will I trust.

Surely he shall deliver thee from the snare
    of the fowler,
    And from the noisome pestilence.
He shall cover thee with his feathers,
    And under his wings shalt thou trust:
His truth shall be thy shield and buckler.

Thou shalt not be afraid for the terror by
    night;
    Nor the arrow that flieth by day;
Nor for the pestilence that walketh in dark-
    ness;
    Nor for the destruction that wasteth at
    noonday.

A thousand shall fall at thy side,
    And ten thousand at thy right hand;
But it shall not come nigh thee.
    Only with thine eyes shalt thou behold
And see the reward of the wicked.

Because thou hast made the Lord, which is
    my refuge,
    Even the Most High, thy habitation;
There shall no evil befall thee,
    Neither shall any plague come nigh thy
    dwelling.

For he shall give his angels charge over thee,
    To keep thee in all thy ways.
They shall bear thee up in their hands,
    Lest thou dash thy foot against a stone.
Thou shalt tread upon the lion and the
    adder;
    The young lion and the dragon
Shalt thou trample under foot.

Because he hath set his love upon me, there-
    fore will I deliver him;
    I will set him on high, because he hath
    known my name.

He shall call upon me, and I will answer
    him.
I will be with him in trouble: I will deliver
    him.
I will deliver him and honor him.
With long life will I satisfy him, and shew
    him my salvation.

Psalm 121

I WILL LIFT UP MINE EYES

I will lift up mine eyes unto the hills,
From whence cometh my help.
My help cometh from the Lord,
Which made heaven and earth.

He will not suffer thy foot to be moved;
He that keepeth thee will not slumber.
Behold, he that keepeth Israel
Shall neither slumber nor sleep.

The Lord is thy keeper;
The Lord is thy shade upon thy right
    hand.
The sun shall not smite thee by day,
Nor the moon by night.

The Lord shall preserve thee from all evil;
He shall preserve thy soul.

The Lord shall preserve thy going out and
    thy coming in
From this time forth, and even for evermore.

Psalm 150

PRAISE YE THE LORD

Praise ye the Lord.

Praise God in his sanctuary;
Praise him in the firmament of his power.

Praise him for his mighty acts;
Praise him according to his excellent great-
    ness.

Praise him with the sound of the trumpet;
Praise him with the psaltery and harp.

Praise him with the timbrel and dance;
Praise him with stringed instruments and
    organs.

Praise him upon the loud cymbals;
Praise him upon the high sounding cymbals.

Let every thing that hath breath
Praise the Lord.

Praise ye the Lord.

PRAYERS

May the strength of God pilot me, the
power of God preserve me today. May the
wisdom of God instruct me, the eye of God
watch over me, the ear of God hear me, the
word of God give me sweet talk, the hand
of God defend me, the way of God guide
me.

Christ be with me. Christ before me.

Christ after me. Christ in me.
Christ under me. Christ over me.
Christ on my right hand. Christ on my
    left hand.
Christ on this side. Christ on that side.
Christ at my back.
Christ in the head of everyone to whom
    I speak.

Christ in the mouth of every person who speaks to me.
Christ in the eye of every person who looks at me.
Christ in the ear of every person who hears me today.

St. Patrick, Ireland
Fifth Century

Lord, make me an instrument of Thy peace; where there is hatred, let me sow love; where there is injury, pardon; where there is doubt, faith; where there is despair, hope; where there is darkness, light; where there is sadness, joy.

O Divine Master, grant that I may not so much seek to be consoled as to console; to be understood as to understand; to be loved as to love. For it is in giving that we receive, it is in pardoning that we are pardoned, and it is in dying that we are born to eternal life.

St. Francis of Assisi, Italy
Thirteenth Century

God be in my head, and in my understanding;
God be in my eyes, and in my looking;
God be in my mouth, and in my speaking;
God be in my heart, and in my thinking;
God be at my end, and in my departing.

England
Fifteenth Century

What God gives, and what we take,
'Tis a gift for Christ, His sake:

Be the meal of beans and pease,
God be thanked for those and these:
Have we flesh or have we fish,
All are fragments from His dish.

Robert Herrick, England
Seventeenth Century

Lord, purge our eyes to see
Within the seed a tree,
Within the glowing egg a bird,
Within the shroud a butterfly.

Till taught by such, we see
Beyond all creatures Thee,
And hearken to Thy tender word,
And hear it, "Fear not: it is I."

Christina Rossetti, England
Nineteenth Century

Give us grace and strength to forbear and to persevere.
Give us courage and gaiety and the quiet mind.
Spare to us our friends, soften to us our enemies.
Bless us, if it may be, in all our innocent endeavors.
If it may not, give us strength to encounter that which is to come, that we may be brave in peril, constant in tribulation, temperate in wrath, and in all changes of fortune, and down to the gates of death, loyal and loving to one another.

Robert Louis Stevenson, Scotland
Nineteenth Century

"GOLDEN WORDS"

In my heart I place the feet,
The golden feet of God.
If he be mine, what can I need?
My God is everywhere:
Within, beyond man's highest word,
My God existeth still:
In sacred books, in darkest night,
In deepest, bluest sky,
In those who know the truth, and in
The faithful few on earth.[1]

Toze-Kung asked, "Is there one word which may serve as a rule for one's whole life?" Confucius answered, "Is not Reciprocity such a word? What you do not wish done to yourself, do not to others."[2]

The way of truth is like a great road. It is not difficult to know it. The evil is only that men will not seek it. Do you go home and search for it, and you will have an abundance of teachers.[3]

Without going out of the door
One can know the whole world;
Without peeping out of the window
One can see the Tao of heaven.
The further one travels
The less one knows.

Therefore the sage knows everything without travelling;
He names everything without seeing it;
He accomplishes ever.[4]

THE BRIGHTNESS

By the noon-day BRIGHTNESS,
And by the night when it darkeneth!
The Lord hath not forsaken thee, neither hath he hated thee,
And surely the future shall be better for thee than the present,
And thy Lord shall assuredly be bounteous to thee and thou be satisfied.
Did he not find thee an orphan and provide thee a home?
And he found thee erring and guided thee,
And found thee needy and enriched thee.
As to the orphan therefore wrong him not;
And as to him that asketh of thee, chide him not away;
And as for the favours of thy Lord, tell them then abroad.[5]

TO HEAVEN AND EARTH

All hail to heaven!
All hail to earth!
All hail to air!
All hail to air!
All hail to heaven!
All hail to earth!

[1] From the poet, Pattanathu (Hindu, tenth century), in Moncure Daniel Conway, *The Sacred Anthology* (Trübner, London, 1874).

[2] From the Analects of Confucius (Chinese, fifth century B.C.).

[3] From Confucianist scriptures, in Robert O. Ballou, ed., *The Bible of the World* (Viking Press, New York, 1939), p. 457.

[4] The Taoist scriptures, from *The Way* of Lao-tse (Chinese, sixth century B.C.), in Ballou, ed., *The Bible of the World.*

[5] From the Koran (the Mohammedan scriptures), in Ballou, ed., *The Bible of the World.*

My eye is sun and my breath is wind, air is
my soul and earth my body.
I verily who never have been conquered give
up my life to heaven and earth for
keeping.
Exalt my life, my strength, my deed and
action; increase my understanding and
my vigour.
Be ye my powerful keepers, watch and guard
me, ye mistresses of life and life's
creators!
Dwell ye within me, and forbear to harm
me.[6]

THE BEST HEALING

One may heal with holiness, one may heal
with the law, one may heal with the knife,
one may heal with herbs, one may heal with
the Holy Word; this one it is that will best
drive away sickness for the body of the faithful: for this one is the best-healing of all
remedies.[7]

I am Yesterday, Today and Tomorrow,
The Divine Hidden Soul who created the
gods,
And who feedeth the blessed.

[6] From the Hindu scriptures, the Atharva-Veda.
[7] From the Zoroastrian scriptures, in Ballou, ed.,
The Bible of the World.

I am Lord of the Risers from Death,
Whose Forms are the lamps in the House
of the Dead,
Whose shrine is the Earth.
When the sky is illumined with crystal,
Then gladden my road and broaden my path
And clothe me in light.
Keep me safe from the Sleeper in Darkness,
When eventide closeth the eyes of the god
And the door by the wall.
In the dawn I have opened the Sycamore;
My form is the form of all women and men,
My spirit is God.[8]

Learn, O student, the true wisdom! See
yon bush aflame with roses, like the burning
bush of Moses! Listen, and thou shall hear
if thy soul be not deaf, how from out of it,
soft and clear, speaks to thee the Lord
Almighty.[9]

He who possesses a contented mind possesses all things, even as the snake covered
with his skin needs no slippers for his feet.[10]

[8] From the Book of the Dead (Egyptian, before
700 B.C.); trans. Robert Hillyer (B. J. Brimmer Co.,
Boston, 1923).
[9] From Háfiz (Persian poet of the fourteenth century), in Conway, The Sacred Anthology.
[10] From the Hitopadesa (Sanskrit, sixth century),
in Conway, The Sacred Anthology.

LEGENDS OF THE SAINTS

St. Jerome and the Lion and the Donkey[1]

Upon a certain day as evening drew on, and the blessed Jerome sat with the brethren, as is the way of the monk, to hear the reading of the lesson and to speak good words, lo of a sudden, limping on three paws and the fourth caught up, came a mighty lion into the cloister. At sight of him a good many of the brethren fled in terror, for human frailty is but timorous. But the blessed Jerome went out to meet him as one greets an incoming guest.

And while the distance between them was shortening, the lion who had no way of speaking, it not being his nature, offered the good father as best he might his wounded paw: and the Saint, calling the brethren, gave instructions that the wounded paw should be bathed, to find why the lion went thus limping. Upon close examination, they found that the paw had been pierced by thorns. Fomentations were applied with all diligence, and the wound speedily healed.

And now, all wildness and savagery laid aside, the lion began to go to and fro among them as peaceable and domestic as any animal about the house. This the blessed Jerome observed, and spoke as follows to the brethren: "Bring your minds to bear upon this, my brethren: what, I ask you, can we find for this lion to do in the way of useful and suitable work, that will not be burdensome to him, and that he can ef-

[1] From Helen Waddell, *Beasts and Saints* (Constable, London, 1949).

ficiently accomplish? For I believe of a surety that it was not so much for the healing of his paw that God sent him hither, since He could have cured him without us, as to show us that He is anxious to provide marvellous well for our necessity."

To which the brethren gave concerted and humble response: "Thou knowest, father, that the donkey who brings us our wood from the forest pasture needs some one to look after him, and that we are always in fear that some naughty beast will devour him. Wherefore if it seem to thee good and right, let the charge of our donkey be laid upon the lion, that he may take him out to pasture, and again may bring him home."

And so it was done: the donkey was put in charge of the lion, as his shepherd: together they took the road to the pasture, and wherever the donkey grazed, there was his defender: and a sure defence he was. Nevertheless, at regular hours, that he might refresh himself and the donkey do his appointed task, the lion would come with him home.

And so for long enough it was: till one day, the donkey duly brought to his pasture, the lion felt a great weight of sluggishness come upon him, and he fell asleep. And as he lay sunk in deep slumber, it befell that certain merchants came along that road on their way to Egypt to buy oil. They saw the donkey grazing, they saw that no guardian was at hand, and seized by sudden wicked greed, they caught him and led him away.

In due course the lion roused up, knowing nothing of his loss, and set out to fetch his charge at graze. But when he was not to be seen in the accustomed pasture, constricted with anxiety and in deep distress the lion went roaring up and down, hither and thither, for the remainder of the day, seeking what he had lost. And at last, when all hope of finding the donkey was gone, he came and stood at the monastery gate.

Conscious of guilt, he no longer dared walk in as of old time with his donkey. The blessed Jerome saw him, and the brethren too, hanging about outside the gate, without the donkey, and long past his usual hour: and they concluded that he had been tempted by hunger to kill his animal. In no mind, therefore, to offer him his wonted ration, "Away with you," said they, "and finish up whatever you have left of the donkey, and fill your greedy belly." And yet even as they spoke, they were doubtful as to whether he had indeed perpetrated this crime or no.

So finally the brethren went out to the pasture whither the lion was wont to bring the animal aforesaid, and up and down they scoured, to see if they could find any trace of the slaughter. No sign of violence was to be seen: and turning home they made haste to bring their report to the blessed Jerome. He heard them, and spoke. "I entreat you, brethren," said he, "that although ye have suffered the loss of the ass, do not, nevertheless, nag at him or make him wretched. Treat him as before, and offer him his food: and let him take the donkey's place, and make a light harness for him so that he can drag home the branches that have fallen in the wood." And it was done.

So the lion did regularly his appointed task, while the time drew on for the merchants to return. Then one day, his work done, he went out, inspired as I believe, brute beast though he was, by some divine prompting, and made his way to the field. Up and down, hither and thither in circles he ran, craving some further light on the fate that had befallen his comrade. And finally, worn out but still anxious, he climbed to a rising above the highway where he might look all round him. A great way off he spied men coming with laden camels, and in front of them walked a donkey. So far off was he that he could not recognize

him. None the less he set out, stepping cautiously, to meet them.

Now it is said to be the custom in that part of the country that whenever men set out with camels on a long journey, a donkey goes in front, with the camel's halter on its neck, and the camels follow after. And now the merchants came nearer, and he recognized his donkey. With a fierce roar he charged down upon them, making a mighty din, though doing no damage to any. Crazed with terror, as they well might be, they left all they had and took to their heels, the lion meantime roaring terribly and lashing the ground with his tail: and so he drove the affrighted camels, laden as they were, back to the monastery before him.

So when this surprising sight met the brethren's gaze, the donkey pacing in the van, the lion in like fashion marching in the rear, and the laden beasts in the middle, they slipped quietly away to inform the blessed Jerome. He came out, and benevolently bade them to set open the monastery gate, enjoining them to silence. "Take their loads off these our guests," said he, "the camels, I mean, and the donkey, and bathe their feet and give them fodder, and wait to see what God is minded to show His servants."

Then, when all instructions as to the camels had been obeyed, began the lion as of old to go here and there in high feather through the cloister, flattening himself at the feet of each several brother and wagging his tail, as though to ask forgiveness for the crime that he had never committed. Whereupon the brethren, full of remorse for the cruel charge they had brought against him, would say to one another, "Behold our trusty shepherd whom so short a while ago we were upbraiding for a greedy ruffian, and God has deigned to send him to us with such a resounding miracle, to clear his character!" Meantime the blessed Jerome, aware of things to come, spoke to the brethren, saying, "Be prepared, my brethren, in all things that are requisite for refreshment: so that those who are about to be our guests may be received, as is fitting, without embarrassment."

His orders duly obeyed, and the brethren chatting with the blessed Jerome, suddenly comes a messenger with the news that there are guests without the gate, desirous to see the Father of the community. At this, the already frequently named Father commanded that the doors of the monastery be opened and the visitors brought to him. They, however, in spite of this invitation, came in blushing, and prostrated themselves at the feet of the blessed Jerome, entreating forgiveness for their fault. Gently raising them up, he admonished them to enjoy their own with thanksgiving, but not to encroach on others' goods: and in short to live cautiously, as ever in the presence of God. And this marvellous discourse ended, he bade them accept refreshment, and take again their camels and go their way.

Then with one voice they cried out, "We entreat you, Father, that you will accept, for the lamps in the church and the necessity of the brethren, half of the oil that the camels have brought: because we know and are sure that it was rather to be of service to you than for our own profit that we went down into Egypt to bargain there." To which the blessed Jerome replied, "This that you ask is indeed not right, for it would seem a great hardship that we who ought to have compassion on others and relieve their necessities by our own giving, should bear so heavy on you, taking your property away from you when we are not in need of it."

To which they answer: "Neither this food, nor any of our own property do we touch, unless you first command that what we ask shall be done. And so, as we have said, do you now accept half of the oil that the camels have brought: and we pledge ourselves and our heirs to give to you and those that come after you the measure of oil which is called a hin in each succeeding year."

So therefore, constrained and compelled by the violence of their entreaties, the blessed Jerome commanded that their prayer should be fulfilled. They partook of refreshment, and after receiving both benediction and camels, they returned exultant and jocund to their own people. But that these things were done at Bethlehem, and the fashion of their doing, is confidently related among the inhabitants of that place until this day.

The Truce of the Wolf[2]

(A Legend of St. Francis of Assisi)

In the Latin countries, particularly, the roots of pre-Christian folklore can be seen beneath the Christian legends of the saints. The bargains between beast and man were a recurring theme in folklore, but the same tales told in relation to the concept of Christian love have a special poignancy.

In Gubbio, seven hundred years ago, the winter had been a hard one. Snow had fallen more than once, and in the deep ravine that separated the two mountains behind the town the bitter, merciless winds had howled and raged day after day. Never in the history of Gubbio had the wolves been so bold and so determined. The citizens, armed with rocks and heavy staves, had risen in the night to drive them away, again and again; but night after night they returned, stealing the sheep and the young kids, raiding the hen-houses, coming boldly inside the great walls that were built to keep them out. Matteo, the baker and the strongest and bravest man in the town, said that their boldness was partly due to leadership.

"There is one great one who fears nothing," he told the anxious padre. "He catches the stones that we throw in his teeth and grinds them to powder. He comes so silently that you do not know he is there until you feel his breath on your shoulder. He is a devil, Padre. He is the Devil himself in a wolf's form."

The padre sighed. "Then we must pray to the saints to deliver us," he answered sadly.

One day, just after the New Year, the two little daughters of Gemma, the laundry woman who lived near the great gate that led out in to the ravine, went outside the gate to cut some dried heather for the donkey's bed. As dusk began to fall Gemma watched anxiously for their return. Finally she sent word to Matteo, who gathered some men about him and, passing through the gate, climbed the hill toward the caves where the wolves dwelt. Just outside the cave they

[2] From Mary Gould Davis, *The Truce of the Wolf and Other Tales of Old Italy* (Harcourt, Brace, 1931).

saw in the fading light a little red shawl and, farther on, a piece of the blue woolen dress that the older girl had been wearing. The sound of their footsteps brought from the dim shadows of the cave a snarl that made even Matteo start back. He knew that it was hopeless to attack the wolves in their own stronghold. And he knew, too, that it was too late to save the little girls. A shuddering horror swept through the town when the news became known. Mothers forbade their children to go beyond the house door, and every glimpse of Gemma's worn face brought a stab of pain and fear to the hearts of the women of Gubbio.

Late in the winter, when the courage and patience of every citizen was at its breaking-point, Gino, Matteo's eldest son, staggered into the town at dusk supported on either side by one of his companions and bleeding from a great gash in his neck and shoulder. Tired out with his long day in the fields, he had thrown himself down under an olive tree to sleep, and had waked to find the great beast at his throat. The three boys had had a terrible struggle to beat the wolf off. He had resisted them like a mad thing until a well-aimed blow from Alfredo's mattock had driven him limping away. Gino's wound festered, and when — weeks later — he came among them again his right arm hung withered and useless at his side. The evening of the attack, when the day's work was over, a meeting was held in the square of the city. Every one in Gubbio who could walk was there, men and women and children clinging fearfully to their mothers' skirts. Mounting the pedestal of the fountain where all could see him, Matteo made an impassioned speech, reciting again the long list of the crimes of the great wolf, waking in the mind and heart of every one anger and fear and grief.

"We must go to the *podestà* and ask for soldiers," he shouted. "Alone, we have failed to catch and punish this great one. We must forget our pride and ask for outside help. We *must* have peace!"

The crowd murmured in assent, the murmur rising to a sort of roar as Gemma came through the square and sat down on the pedestal at Matteo's feet. Then from the door of the church where he had been listening the padre came, and the people parted to let him through. He mounted the pedestal beside Matteo, who instantly stepped down, leaving the padre's head and shoulders outlined in the fading light and visible to them all. His slow, silvery voice, the voice that they had listened to and obeyed for so many years, seemed to clear the troubled air and to bring with it an accustomed authority and calm.

"My people," said the padre, "before we send word to the soldiers, before we ask help for Gubbio from the *podestà,* let us seek the advice of Brother Francis of Assisi. You have heard of him. You know what he has done for the troubled ones of his own town and all through Umbria. You know of his power over the beasts. It is said that they understand and even talk to him, and that he is absolutely without fear of even the wildest of them. Let us ask Brother Francis to come here to Gubbio. Let us put our trouble in his hands and abide by his decision."

Matteo shook his head doubtfully, and the padre turned to him with a little pleading gesture.

"It will mean only a little delay, Matteo," he said. "We can send a message to Assisi today. If Brother Francis can do nothing — then we must, of course, send for the soldiers." The padre's words carried great weight with the people. Matteo could see by their faces that they wanted to try his plan. He nodded.

"*Si, si,* Padre," he said almost cheerfully. "We will send for Brother Francis and see what he can do — but in my heart I fear that he can do nothing."

That very night a messenger started across the valley to Assisi, and one day a few weeks later, when spring had unfurled the gray leaves of the olive trees, when the early crocus had spread its mantle of pale lavender over the hills, a little band of brown-clad Brothers made its way up the steep hill that led to the square of Gubbio. The padre was waiting for them at the church door, and when he saw Brother Francis' face, hope leaped like a flame in his heart. Rapidly, omitting nothing, he told the story of the wolf and his sins, and Brother Francis listened, a little shadow stealing into his serene eyes.

"I understand," he said when the padre had finished. "But if this one wolf truly is the leader and controls the others, then *he* must be made to understand. You have met him with fear and violence. You must meet him without fear, and you must reason with him. You must tell him, without anger, that he is a thief and a murderer."

"But no one of us, or even no group of us, dares to go near enough this wolf to tell him anything!" the padre answered a little ruefully.

Brother Francis smiled. Then he rose and gathered his brown robe about him.

"Then I will tell him," he said quietly.

Matteo, who was standing near with a number of the men of Gubbio, protested.

"You cannot go outside the gate alone, Brother Francis," he said. "If you go, you must take us all with you. The wolf will certainly try to murder you, and only our staves and our stones can save you."

Brother Francis shook his head.

"Your staves and your stones have failed," he answered. "I will try another way now, and I go alone. My brothers may follow at a little distance — if they are not afraid. But no man of Gubbio must come outside the gate while I am on the hillside." And the men fell back before the quiet authority of his voice.

With the group of friars a little way behind him, Brother Francis went up the hill toward the caves. The sun was at its setting, and the near hill was in deep shadow while the one across the ravine was bathed in a light so concentrated, so golden, that in it the budding genestra was like points of living flame. Brother Francis stepped into the shadow and went straight up to the entrance of the first cave. There was a large stone near this entrance, and here Francis sat himself down, gathering his robe about him and turning his face toward the mouth of the cave.

"Brother Wolf," he said, "come out into the light. I would like to see and talk to you."

There was no answer from the cave. But in its shadow two eyes burned like two tiny green flames. . . . The sun sank lower. The swallows swooping overhead flew in ever narrowing circles and finally came to rest on Francis' arm and shoulder, whistling faintly.

"Be still, little brothers," said Francis softly. And the birds were still.

The friars, grown bolder in the silence, drew nearer, and Brother Leo started toward the mouth of the cave. Instantly there came a snarl, and out of the shadows sprang the great wolf. His eyes burned, his fangs showed white in his gaping red mouth, the short gray hairs stood out in a ruff around his neck. Quickly Francis lifted his hand and made the sign of the Cross. The great beast seemed to pause almost in mid-air; then he sank down beside the cave and laid his head on his crossed paws like a dog, his teeth still bared.

"If you are afraid, Brother Leo," said Francis, "move off behind the trees. There is no place for fear here." Then he turned again to the wolf.

"Brother Wolf," he said, and now the gentleness was gone from his voice and it was clear and resonant, "Brother Wolf, you have done much harm in the city of Gubbio. You have destroyed God's creatures without His leave. And not only have you slain and devoured beasts, you have also dared to kill and to destroy children who are made in the image of God. Therefore you are a murderer and worthy of the gallows, and the hand of every man in the city is against you."

He paused for a moment, and his eyes studied the huge, gaunt figure before him. He saw how every bone showed through the rough gray coat, how the short ears were scarred with many desperate battles. The green eyes were still blazing with hate and suspicion.

"But I, Brother Wolf," Francis went on more gently, "would fain make peace between you and the men of Gubbio. I would make a truce and a contract that you shall injure them no more and that they shall forgive you all your sins."

The wolf lifted his head. For a long time Francis gazed steadily at him. Slowly, slowly the fire died out of the green eyes, and there remained in them only a great hunger. Francis' face softened. Well he knew what hunger did to beasts — and to men.

"If, Brother Wolf," he went on steadily, "if it pleases you to make and to observe a peace between you and the people of Gubbio, I promise to obtain for you the cost of your maintenance from the men of the city, so that you shall never again go hungry. For well do I know that it is hunger that has driven you to these evil courses. But I beg of you now this grace. I ask your promise, Brother Wolf, that you will never do hurt again either to man or to beast. Will you promise me this?"

The lids drooped over the hungry eyes; the wolf bowed his head and made with his whole body a movement of acquiescence.

"Then, Brother Wolf," said Francis, and now his smile was like light in a dark place, "pledge me this promise, so that I may have full trust in you."

Francis held out his hand, and the great beast, rising, lifted his paw and laid it in the hand stretched out to meet it.

Francis got to his feet. His voice was as clear as a bell.

"I command you, Brother Wolf," he said, "to come now with me, fearing nothing, and we will confirm this peace before the people of Gubbio and in the Name of God."

The sun had sunk below the horizon and the valley was filled with a soft blue dusk as Francis, with the wolf at his side, his narrow gray head pressed against the brown robe, entered the city gate, the little band of friars following them. In the square the people of Gubbio — men and women and children — waited in breathless suspense for the return of the man from Assisi. As he appeared in the great portal with the shadowy form that they dreaded pressing close at his heels, a low murmur of amazement ran through the crowd. Francis passed straight on to the pedestal of the fountain, one hand resting lightly on the wolf's head. His voice, when he spoke, had in it a curious quality — the clear, joyous tone that you hear sometimes in the voice of a happy child.

"Hear me, people of Gubbio," he said. "Brother Wolf, who is here before you, has promised and pledged me his faith to make peace with you, never to injure you or harm you again in any way whatsoever. For your part you must promise him his daily sustenance in winter and in summer throughout the year. And I am bondsman for him, that he will keep and preserve through all of his life this pact of peace."

Again the murmur ran through the crowd. Matteo, his eyes shining with the wonder of it, cried eagerly, "We promise to feed him always and to keep our part of the pact! Do we not?" he added, turning to the people. And their shout in answer rang back from the mountain side. The wolf stirred uneasily, and Francis lifted the lean head in his hand and looked deep into the puzzled eyes.

"Brother Wolf," he said, "as you have pledged your word to me outside of the city to keep and preserve your promise, I desire that here again before the people of Gubbio you shall renew that pledge, and promise that you will never play me false in the surety that I have given for you."

He dropped the wolf's head and moved a pace away. A breath of doubt swept through the crowd. But Francis' face did not change. For a long moment the wolf hesitated. Then he rose and, taking one step toward Francis, he lifted the gray paw again and laid it in his hand.

At that the tension broke, and joy and wonder and relief swept through the people as a wind sweeps through a field of wheat. A woman on the outskirts of the crowd ran to her home near by and came back with a great copper pot filled with rice and gravy and vegetables which she had prepared for the evening meal. Fearlessly she went to the wolf and put it down in front of him. For an instant he sniffed it suspiciously; then his head disappeared in the pot and they could hear the eager lapping of his tongue. When he had finished every grain and licked the pot to cleanness again, he looked up into the woman's face and — *"Mille grazie, Signora,"* his eyes said. In the crowd a child laughed and clapped his hands.

And from that day the Wolf of Gubbio walked its streets as freely as one of the citizens. Every evening, winter and summer, he called at a house door, and the housewives vied with one another in preparing properly his evening meal. The children played with him, and often in the sunny noons of spring and autumn he lay stretched like a great dog in the square before the fountain. Strangers, seeing him, would wonder and perhaps be frightened. But the citizens would laugh at their fears. They would say proudly, "He will not hurt you. He is *our* wolf — the Wolf of Gubbio." When, after two peaceful years, he died of old age, they buried him in the garden of the convent. There, year after year, the oleanders shook out their white and crimson blossoms above him and the cypress trees stood like tall, dark candles beside him.

Today the citizens of Gubbio point proudly to a fresco that is painted in soft, pale colors on the walls of their great Palazzo dei Consoli. There is the little square with the fountain, exactly as it was seven hundred years ago. There are the awed and wondering people — the men and the women and the children. There is St. Francis in his brown robe, and there beside him, his head bowed under the saint's gentle hand, stands the Wolf of Gubbio.

St. Nicholas [3]

Joy had come to a certain house in Patara. A mother lay smiling on her pillows, a newborn babe lay on the head-nurse's lap, while the household women clustered round to look at him.

"There's a fine boy!" said the head-nurse proudly. "Nothing wanting to him but a name."

"What shall you call him, madam?" asked one of the women.

"His name will be Nicholas," said the mother.

"Well then, little Nicholas, come and have your first bath," said the head-nurse, and she laid the tiny baby in a basin. Cries of astonishment broke from all the women. The new-born child stood upright in the water, and clasping his hands lifted his eyes to heaven.

"Oh madam, look!"

[3] From Eleanor Farjeon, *Ten Saints* (Oxford University Press, 1936).

"Do not touch him," said the mother. "It is a miracle."

For two hours the tiny Nicholas stood with his hands clasped in his ecstasy, while the amazed women knelt about the basin, and adored him. It would hardly have surprised them if he had opened his lips and spoken, so sensible were his looks, so wise his eyes. They handled him with awe, bathing and dressing him at last as one who already knew more of holiness than they did. How else, but by divine knowledge, could he tell when Friday was come? Yet that day, when his nurse laid the baby to her breast, he turned away his head and would not suck. Not till the sun went down, and those who had fasted all day sat at their meal, would Nicholas allow a drop to pass his lips — but then he made up vigorously for lost time.

"My little wonder!" cried the nurse, dandling him as is the way of nurses. But few nurses surely had dandled a wonder like this child, who observed the fast-days before his lips could pray, and saw heaven from his bath in the hour he was born.

Nicholas grew up loving all young things. His parents, rich people of Patara in Lycia, were able to give their child more than he needed of toys and sweetmeats, money in his purse, and rich food at table. Sometimes those who have too much cannot see the needs of those who have too little, as though their own gold weighed down their eyelids and kept them shut. But when, like Nicholas, they have tender hearts, they keep their eyes open, and see the difference between rich and poor. When his parents died, he found himself a young man with a fortune which he did not wish to spend on himself.

How then would he spend it?

His friends must have wondered. He did not squander it. There were no signs of extravagance about his house or his person, and what he did with his wealth remained a secret. It is a secret that shall be kept till the end of his story.

But this may be told at once: that Nicholas had no use for his own earthly treasures, and turned his thoughts on the treasure that is in heaven. The ecstasy he had been born in never left him, and he became a servant of God.

His longing then was to see the Holy Land with his own eyes, and he took boat from Lycia to Alexandria, from which great port he would journey to Jerusalem. During the voyage, such a tempest swept sea and sky that the sailors gave up hope. The captain shouted his orders through the storm, and the men did their best to obey, but the ship tossed and strained and seemed as though she must part. All the captain's seamanship was useless. Then in the midst of the tumult a lightning-flash showed Nicholas kneeling at prayer, and his eyes were raised to heaven as though the salt waves that soaked his garments were the scented waters of his first bath.

"We are past praying for, priest!" cried the captain roughly. "Better let me lash you to a mast."

But as he spoke, the wind died down to a sigh, the black sky turned blue, the boiling sea became a sheet of silk, and the lightning vanished in the light of the sun. The sailors shouted for joy, and Nicholas said: "Nothing is ever past praying for."

"Tell us your name, priest," said the wondering captain.

"Nicholas," answered he.

"Remember it, men!" said the captain to his crew, "and if ever we are as near to death again, let us invoke the name of Nicholas."

And sailors did so then, and for centuries after, when Nicholas had joined the ranks of the saints. Many a one who prayed for aid in a storm vowed that he had seen Saint Nicholas himself standing at the ship's helm, his eyes raised to heaven, protecting the vessel and her crew from harm. And on their voyages seamen whittled little ships, and rigged them out trim and proper; and coming safely home, they hung the ships up in the sea-port churches, as a thank-offering to Saint Nicholas, their patron.

And children, who have cause to love him as much as sailors had, took Saint Nicholas for their patron too. He had a way of coming to know the needs of the young. Their pleasures were his care; so too were their pains.

It happened once in Myra, when Nicholas had become Bishop of that city, that three boys wandered into a wood on the outskirts,

and came at night to an inn. They knocked, and the Innkeeper came at once to the door. He beamed in a friendly way, and rubbed his hands. "Well, children, what may you be doing here? What do you want so late?"

"We have missed our way, Innkeeper. May we come in and sleep?"

"By all means, children, and you shall sleep without dreaming."

There is nothing to be said for this Innkeeper. He lived by robbing those who put up at his hostel. When the boys were asleep he searched their clothes, and pocketed what he found. It was not much, but the clothes themselves were worth something. And then he looked on the three boys and sighed: "They are as pink and tender as sucking-pigs! What a pity that they are not sucking-pigs! What delicious pickled pork those three would make."

No sooner thought than done. By morning the three little boys were lying in pickle in the salting-tub; and truly they slept without dreaming.

Not so the Bishop of Myra. Nicholas, lying abed in his great palace, had a dream which made him sit up in sorrow and wrath. He had seen in his vision everything that had happened, and could not rest until he had discovered if it was true. That day he wandered in the forest arrayed in his mitre and robes, and at nightfall he came to the inn, and knew it for the one he had seen in his dream. He knocked; and the Innkeeper opened, the man in the vision. He beamed on Nicholas, and rubbed his hands.

"Well, Bishop, here's an honour, to be sure! What can I do for your worship?"

"I have missed my way in the forest, Innkeeper. Can I come in and sup?"

The Innkeeper bowed him in, and gave him a seat. "What does your Worship fancy? A slice of ham? a cut of beef? or veal?"

"None of these, Innkeeper," answered Nicholas. "I have a fancy for the pork in the pickle-tub over there."

The Innkeeper glanced uneasily at his guest.

"Well, what's the matter?" asked Saint Nicholas. "Is the pork not yet salted enough?"

The Innkeeper turned white.

"Perhaps," said the Saint, "you only put it in pickle last night?"

The Innkeeper shook in his shoes so hard that he fell on the ground with his face in his hands.

"Mercy! mercy!" he wailed. "I confess! Have mercy!"

"We'll see about that," said Saint Nicholas. He crossed the room, raised his eyes to heaven, and made the sign of the Cross over the tub. The scum on the brine shivered a little, and three little sleepy-heads rose and peeped over the brim.

"Oh!" yawned the first child, "how well I have slept!"

The second stretched his arms. "Me too, without dreaming!"

"*I* dreamed," said the third child, rubbing his eyes. "I dreamed I was in Paradise."

The Innkeeper on the ground beat his breast, and wept.

Was there anything to be said for the Innkeeper? Yes, after all. Nothing is ever past praying for. Saint Nicholas knelt down with the three little boys, and put up a prayer to heaven. And even the Innkeeper was pardoned his sins, and was the better for it. He never pickled his customers again.

No wonder the Day of St. Nicholas became the children's festival. But his protection of the three little pickles is not the whole why and wherefore of that. The time has come to give away his secret, and tell in what way he liked to spend his riches when he was a young man in Patara.

There was in that city a poor nobleman who had three young daughters, so beautiful that many a youth would have sought them in marriage — but alas! they had no dowries. And without a dowry no girl, however fair, could hope for marriage in those days. So poor was the father that he had not been able to lay by a single silver piece for his eldest daughter; so poor that the time came when he knew not how to feed his children any longer. He saw no way between letting them starve, or selling them in the market, one by one, as slaves to rich men; and his heart was full of woe for the fate in store for them. As for the young maidens, they knew why their father sighed and turned pale when he looked at them. They dared

not speak of it to him, but among themselves they whispered the names of certain youths whom they loved, and must not think of.

One night the poor nobleman stood cooling his brow at his open window, thinking, as the moon sailed out of a cloud, that she was no fairer than his eldest daughter, whom to-morrow he must part with. By no other means could he save her from death, yet the means would shame both his honour and hers. While he leaned in his casement, blurring the moonlight with his tears, a heavy round object sailed into the room, and fell clinking and chinking at his feet. Stooping, the poor man picked up a plump moneybag, and he could hardly believe his eyes when he untied the string and a stream of gold pieces poured out. He counted it eagerly in little piles. He had not seen so much money for years. There was enough to dower one maiden handsomely, and he thanked heaven that now he could save his eldest daughter from shame. When morning broke he told her the glad news, and instead of going to the slave-market, the young thing ran joyously to the bazaar, to buy a silken veil, a bangle, and sweetmeats. That evening the youth she had named came to her father's house, the sweetmeats were eaten, and the lovers were betrothed.

But after dark the nobleman's heart was sore for his second daughter, who was as lovely as the starry sky he looked on through his window. For to-morrow she must go to the slave-market, since miracles surely do not happen twice. Yet this one did! He had scarcely formed the thought when a second fat round moneybag flew like a ball through the window, and it contained a dower of gold equal to that of the first. The nobleman ran out of the house too late to catch sight of the giver. Next day he told his second child to put off her sorrow, and buy herself a silken veil like her sister's. She returned from the bazaar with perfume as well, and a jar of fruits in syrup, and before the day ended she also was betrothed to the youth she wished to wed.

When evening fell the father was less unhappy than before, for what had happened twice might happen thrice; and this time he was determined to discover the unknown purse-thrower, and thank him. For he could not doubt that the good fortune of her sisters would fall to his youngest daughter, who was as sweet as the flowers that scented the night.

A little before the time was due, the nobleman stole forth and hid himself in an angle of the house; and before long a cloaked figure crept to the window, clutching in one hand a bursting money-bag. But as he aimed it at the open casement, the father came out of hiding and seized his cloak — and was amazed to see that it covered young Nicholas, the richest man in Patara. The grateful father fell on his knees, and kissed the hem of the cloak. "Nicholas, servant of God, why seek to hide yourself?"

"It is the way I prefer," said Nicholas.

"But then, your generosity will never be known!"

"Why should it be?" Nicholas seemed distressed that the mystery in which he had wrapped himself had been revealed, even to this one man. "Promise me, friend," he said, "that you will tell nobody."

"At least I must tell my children."

"The children least of all," said Nicholas. "If I choose to make young things happy by giving them presents, that is my business."

"And you won't come in and let them thank you in person?"

"I would rather they did not see me," said Nicholas. "Pray keep me dark, good sir!"

The father promised. Next day the youngest girl went to the bazaar and bought a silken veil, a necklace, and almond cakes. And she too was betrothed by evenfall.

But secrets have a way of leaking out. No doubt the three happy girls hung round their father's neck, and teased him with questions.

"Who, father, who? Who gave me my purse of gold?"

"Who, father, who? Who gave me my silken veil?"

"Dear father, who? Who gave me my handsome husband?"

"Who gave us the sweets, the fruit, the scent, and the trinkets? Who? Who? Who?" they cried, like little owls. And perhaps at last, their indulgent father whispered:

"Well! if you promise not to say a word —"

And no doubt they promised; and no doubt they told. No doubt all the girls and boys in Patara wondered whether Nicholas would come to them too one night with presents. No doubt, if their parents wished to surprise them, they hid sweetmeats in their slippers while they slept, and in the morning the children shouted to each other: "Oh look, look, look what Nicholas has brought me!" No doubt they took to leaving their shoes outside their doors, for the generous one who preferred not to be seen. No doubt, from Patara in Lycia long ago, the custom spread through Asia Minor, and crept over the border into Europe, and sailed oversea to distant continents.

And it reached the present time, when little shoes were changed for little stockings, because stockings hold quite twice as much as shoes, and one ought not to limit dear Saint Nicholas, who loves above all to be generous in secret.

BIBLIOGRAPHY

World Religions

Jones, Jessie Orton, comp. *This Is the Way; Prayers and Precepts from World Religions;* illus. by Elizabeth Orton Jones. Viking Press, 1951. (Grades 1–3)

Selections were chosen to show the underlying unity of all races and all religions and the universality of worship.

Smith, Ruth, ed. *The Tree of Life; Selections from the Literature of the World's Religions;* illus. by Boris Artzybasheff. Viking Press, 1944. (Grade 8 up)

A significant book for the thoughtful reader who will gain a knowledge of the spiritual values of the following faiths: American Indian, Norse, Hindu, Buddhist, Confucianist, Taoist, Egyptian, Babylonian, Greek, Zoroastrian, Hebrew and Christian, Mohammedan.

The Bible

The Holy Bible. Oxford Edition. Oxford University Press.

The authorized or King James Version, first published in 1611.

The Holy Bible; trans. from the Latin Vulgate; diligently compared with the Hebrew, Greek, and other editions in divers languages. Kenedy, 1914.

The authorized Catholic version.

Bible Selections

Animals of the Bible; a picture book by Dorothy P. Lathrop; with text selected by Helen Dean Fish from the King James Bible. J. B. Lippincott, 1937. (A Stokes Book) (Grades 1–4)

The artist has studied the fauna and flora of Bible lands so that each animal, bird, flower, and tree is true to natural history. Awarded the Caldecott medal in 1938.

The Book of Books; the King James Version of the English Bible, abridged and arranged with editorial comments for young readers, by W. O. Sypherd. Alfred A. Knopf, 1944. (Grades 7–9)

"Between the covers of this volume, will be found a substantial part of the writings of the Old Testament and the New Testament. . . . The introductory comments are designed to make the selections understandable, interesting, and above all, significant as parts of a body of lasting world literature." — Foreword.

A First Bible; illus. by Helen Sewell; selected and arranged by J. W. Maury. Oxford University Press, 1934. (Grades 4–6)

Stories included are those "which time has proved to be the most interesting and inspiring to youth of every age." The illustrations are full of reverence and strength.

Small Rain; Verses from the Bible; chosen by Jessie Orton Jones; illus. by Elizabeth Orton Jones. Viking Press, 1943. (Grades 1–4)

Bible verses which appeal particularly to children, illustrated from a child's point of view.

Bible Stories

Barnhart, Nancy. *The Lord Is My Shepherd; Stories from the Bible Pictured in Bible Lands;* arranged and illus. by Nancy Barnhart. Charles Scribner's Sons, 1949. (Grades 4–7)

A distinguished book in both content and format. Seventeen stories from the Old Testament and a short version of the New Testament are told reverently, keeping the beauty and dignity of the Bible text. The striking drawings are from sketches made by the artist on a visit to the Holy Land.

Gwynne, J. Harold. *The Rainbow Book of Bible Stories;* illus. by Steele Savage. World Publishing Company, 1956. (Grades 5–9)

Dr. Gwynne, a Presbyterian clergyman, has selected over one hundred of the best-loved stories from both the Old and New Testaments. Over one hundred illustrations, most of them in full color.

Hartman, Gertrude. *In Bible Days;* illus. by Kathleen Voute. Macmillan, 1948. (Grades 6–9)

Bible stories from both testaments have been selected to give a better understanding of early times and peoples of the Jewish and Christian religions.

Hurlbut, Jesse Lyman. *Hurlbut's Story of the Bible;* illus. by Ralph Pallen Coleman. John C. Winston, new ed. 1957. (Grades 5–8)

Bible stories from both testaments are arranged so that the narrative from Genesis to Revelation is in one volume.

Sherman, Henry A., and C. F. Kent, eds. *The Children's Bible.* Charles Scribner's Sons, 1922. (Grades 4–7)

Bible stories best suited to interest children have been put into simple, dignified prose.

The Old Testament

Bowie, Walter Russell. *The Bible Story for Boys and Girls: Old Testament;* illus. with color plates by different artists and with black and white decorations by Stephani and Edward Godwin. Abingdon, 1952. (Grades 5–8)

Contains the epic tales of Abraham, Joseph, Moses, David, Esther, and other less familiar characters.

Shippen, Katherine. *Moses;* frontispiece by Lili Cassel. Harper & Brothers, 1949. (Grades 6–8)

The author has brought out the dignity and beauty of the story of the Exodus and the dedication of the leader Moses.

Yates, Elizabeth, ed. *Joseph;* illus. by Nora S. Unwin. Alfred A. Knopf, 1947. (Grades 8–9)

The story of Joseph, taken from the King James Version, arranged chronologically and thoughtfully edited. Illustrated with distinctive woodcuts.

The New Testament

Bowie, Walter Russell. *The Bible Story for Boys and Girls: New Testament;* illus. with color plates by different artists and with black and white drawings by Stephani and Edward Godwin. Abingdon, 1951. (Grades 5–8)

A companion volume to *The Bible Story for Boys and Girls: Old Testament.*

Bowie, Walter Russell. *The Story of Jesus for Young People;* illus. by Robert Lawson. Charles Scribner's Sons, 1937. (Grades 3–5)

The story of Christ's life on earth told simply, in modern language.

Fitch, Florence Mary. *The Child Jesus;* illus. by Leonard Weisgard. Lothrop, Lee & Shepard, 1955. (K–Grade 3)

A story of the boy Jesus told in simple text with superb pictures in full color.

The Great Story; from the Authorized King James Version of the Bible. Harcourt, Brace, 1938. (Grades 5–8)

The life of Christ told in a continuous story selected from the King James Version of the Gospels of Matthew, Mark, Luke, and John. Illustrated with reproductions in color of fifteen famous paintings.

Jesus' Story; a Little New Testament; illus. by Maud and Miska Petersham. Macmillan, 1942. (Grades 3–5)

The life of Jesus told in the language of the King James text. The illustrations interpret the story with beauty and reverence. Available in both Protestant and Catholic editions.

Lines, Kathleen. *Once in Royal David's City; a Picture Book of the Nativity retold from the Gospels;* drawn by Harold Jones. Franklin Watts, 1956. (K–Grade 3)

The story of the first Christmas told in pictures with a line or two of text for every page. The Biblical verses are included at the back of the book.

Petersham, Maud and Miska. *The Christ Child;* as told by Matthew and Luke; illus. by Maud and Miska Petersham. Doubleday, 1931. (Grades 1–5)

A picture book of unusual beauty. The artists, who spent several months in Palestine, have rendered the story of the nativity into pictures filled with the spirit of the Holy Land.

Religion and Worship

Farjeon, Eleanor. *A Prayer for Little Things;* pictures by Elizabeth Orton Jones. Houghton Mifflin, 1945. (K–Grade 3)

A prayer for the small things that need God's care.

Field, Rachel Lyman. *Prayer for a Child;* pictures by Elizabeth Orton Jones. Macmillan, new ed. 1957. (K–Grade 3)

Although Rachel Field wrote this prayer for her small daughter, it is a prayer for all children. Awarded the Caldecott medal in 1945.

Fitch, Florence Mary. *A Book about God;* illus. by Leonard Weisgard. Lothrop, Lee & Shepard, 1953. (K–Grade 3)

In terms of the beauties and wonders of nature, author and artist explain what God is like. For children of all faiths.

Fitch, Florence Mary. *One God; the Ways We Worship Him.* Lothrop, Lee & Shepard, 1944. (All ages)

A remarkable book which will help children understand and respect religions different from their own. The author tells the story of the three great religions of America — Jewish, Catholic, and Protestant — and describes their important rituals and festivals. Illustrated with superb photographs.

Fitch, Florence Mary. *Their Search for God; Ways of Worship in the Orient.* Lothrop, Lee & Shepard, 1947. (Grades 6–9)

A companion volume to *One God,* in which the author describes with reverence and deep understanding the ways in which the peoples of the Orient worship God.

Francis of Assisi, Saint. *Song of the Sun; from the Canticle of the Sun;* illus. by Elizabeth Orton Jones. Macmillan, 1952. (K–Grade 4)

Miss Jones has written an introduction about the life of St. Francis, and the book ends with a brief story of St. Francis making the first Christmas crèche.

Johnson, Emilie Louise. *Little Book of Prayers;* illus. by Maud and Miska Petersham. Viking Press, 1941. (Grades 2–5)

Childlike prayers for each day in the week, special days, and birthdays, with a few prayers from the Bible.

Tudor, Tasha. *First Prayers;* ed. and illus. by Tasha Tudor. Oxford University Press, 1952. (K–Grade 3)

Tasha Tudor has also compiled *First Graces.* Both books are diminutive in size and illustrated with drawings in delicate colors.

Wheeler, Opal. *Sing in Praise;* music by Opal Wheeler; illus. by Marjorie Torrey. E. P. Dutton, 1946. All ages.

The best-known hymns with music and stories of the hymns. Full-page illustrations in color.

Yates, Elizabeth, comp. *Your Prayers and Mine;* decorations by Nora S. Unwin. Houghton Mifflin, 1954. (Grades 7 up)

A collection of "prayers gathered from many sources and many nations, prayers that have been used through many centuries of time."

In Bible Times

Bouquet, A. C. *Everyday Life in New Testament Times;* illus. by Marjorie Quennell and with photographs, maps and plans. Charles Scribner's Sons, 1955.

A fascinating adult book of interest to young people.

Heaton, E. W. *Everyday Life in Old Testament Times;* illus. with photographs and drawings by Marjorie Quennell. Charles Scribner's Sons, 1956.

The panorama of Israelite life from about 1250 to 586 B.C.

Terrien, Samuel. *Lands of the Bible;* illus. by William Bolin. Simon & Schuster, 1957. (Golden Historical Atlas) (Grade 7 up)

An excellent atlas and picture history designed "to show the land that shaped the people, and to depict the peoples' story against the background of their land." — Foreword.

Christmas Carols

Simon, Henry William, ed. *A Treasury of Christmas Songs and Carols;* illus. by Rafaello Busoni. Houghton Mifflin, 1955.

More than one hundred favorite carols.

Van Loon, Hendrik Willem. *Christmas Carols;* music arrangements by Grace Castagnotta; illus. by Hendrik Van Loon. Simon & Schuster, 1937.

Interesting historical notes and descriptive comments create a special atmosphere for each song.

Wasner, Franz, ed. *The Trapp-Family Book of Christmas Songs;* illus. by Agatha Trapp. Pantheon Books, 1950.

Each foreign song is given both in its original language and in English.

Wheeler, Opal. *Sing for Christmas; a Round of Christmas Carols;* illus. by Gustaf Tenggren. E. P. Dutton, 1943.

The compiler tells the stories of the carols, either how the songs came to be written or how they were sung.

Young, Percy, comp. *Carols for the Twelve Days of Christmas;* decorations by Ida Procter. Roy, 1954.

Arranged in chronological sequence for the Christmas season with quotations from the Bible.

Lives and Legends of the Saints

Beatty, Hetty Burlingame. *St. Francis and the Wolf.* Houghton Mifflin, 1953. (Grades 3–5)

The Gubbian legend of St. Francis told for younger readers.

Bishop, Claire Huchet. *Martin de Porres, Hero;* illus. by Jean Charlot. Houghton Mifflin, 1954. (Grades 6–9)

The inspiring life of the sixteenth-century Peruvian Negro who devoted his life to teaching and helping the poor. One hundred years after his death he was beatified.

Colum, Padraic. *The Legend of Saint Columba;* illus. by Elizabeth MacKinstry. Macmillan, 1935. (Grades 5–8)

The story of an Irish saint of the sixth century retold in the manner of a hero tale.

Farjeon, Eleanor. *Ten Saints;* illus. by Helen Sewell. Oxford University Press, 1936. (Grades 5–8)

The stories of St. Christopher, St. Francis, St. Nicholas, St. Patrick, and others admirably retold by a poet.

Jauss, Annie Marie. *Legends of Saints and Beasts;* illus. by the author. Aladdin, 1954. (Grades 4–6)

Four legends: St. Jerome and the Lion, St. Roch and the Dog, St. Francis and the Wolf, and St. Macarius and the Hyena. The illustrations give an idea of the manners and customs of the times.

Jewett, Sophie. *God's Troubadour; the Story of Saint Francis of Assisi;* illus. with paintings by Giotto. Thomas Y. Crowell, new ed. 1957. (Grades 5–7)

The author, while a professor of English literature at Wellesley College, made many trips to Europe and on one of these occasions, she saw the Giotto frescoes of the life of St. Francis, in Assisi, Italy, and was inspired to write this life of the beloved saint.

Waddell, Helen. *Beasts and Saints;* with woodcuts by Robert Gibbins. Constable (London), 1949. (Grades 5–7)

Although not written primarily for children, many boys and girls will enjoy these tales, taken from old chronicles, of the friendships between men and beasts.

Earth
Sky, and
Sea

Earth
Sea, and
Sea

"As never before it is the duty of parents to train their children to behold the creatures of Nature which can never lose their identities because they can only be what they already are: the flowers 'fresh and laughing as on the days of great battles,' the beasts who 'walk the earth, ignorant, while their splendor lasts, of any weakness' and, most of all, perhaps, the stars of the night sky, in all their unchanging majesty and stateliness of movement." [1]

THIS AGE OF SPACE, WITH ITS unlimited expectancy of the future, its present an actuality of fantastic discoveries and inventions, offers a strange paradox. In all this aura of the miraculous made useful, Man seems increasingly unaware of the miracle of himself and the world in which he lives. In his casual task of observing the behavior of everything in creation, including his own behavior, he loses sight of himself as a personality, an individual. He seems to have lost the power "to behold" in increasing his ability "to observe." If we are to believe our leading novelists, sociologists, playwrights, poets, and scientists, Man is in danger of dehumanizing himself, of becoming an unfeeling robot, a fitting inhabitant of Aldous Huxley's *Brave New World* or of George Orwell's depersonalized continents. The periodical literature of our day reiterates the theme. The quotation which heads this page is from an article by the poet, W. H. Auden, which appeared in *Harper's Bazaar*, July, 1956. For the *Woman's Home Companion* of the same month and year, Rachel Carson, whose masterpiece of scientific writing, *The Sea Around Us*, shook out the minds of a million readers, wrote an article entitled "Help Your Child to Wonder." In that article she said, in part:

> If I had influence with the good fairy who is supposed to preside over the christening of all children I should ask that her gift to each child be a sense of wonder so indestructible that it would last throughout life, an unfailing antidote against the boredom and disenchantments of later years, the sterile preoccupation with things that are artificial, the alienation from the sources of our strength.

[1] W. H. Auden, "An Eye for Mystery," *Harper's Bazaar*, July, 1956.

In a Commencement Address at Sarah Lawrence College, in June of 1958, Frank Lloyd Wright, the great architect, spoke to the same theme:

> The principles that build the tree will build the man. . . . That's why I think Nature should be spelled with a capital "N," not because Nature is God but because all that we can learn of God we will learn from the body of God, which we call Nature.[2]

Poet, marine biologist, and architect — each sights the danger, each sees a saving grace in an awareness of nature.

Children have, for the most part, an intuitive interest in nature, especially in relation to the creatures of the earth. They seek actually to share life with living beings, other than humans, on terms of such equality as they have known in the folktales and fables of their early reading. The reading years in which their curiosity and eagerness to know are most intent should be the foundation not only for scientific fact, and the development of any inherent scientific bent, but also for an apprehension of the Great Theme, with its magnitudinous variations.

The style in writing in the field of nature has shifted in this century from the inherited Victorian fashion of overpersonalization, with its frequently resulting sentimentality, to the straightforward explanation and observation of scientific facts, often simplified, to be sure, but accurate and true. The books for children are numerous and diverse. With the present emphasis upon science, no doubt the number will increase. There will be series of books checked for accuracy, scientifically edited, carefully documented, well illustrated, screened for vocabulary and structural simplicity. These books have their uses. But the books of lasting meaning for children are the books which capture the imagination as well as the mind. They are the work of artists as well as of scientists and naturalists. The secret of the master writers is that each is able to convey his own gift "to behold" as well as his ability as a scientific observer. Facts are stated in such a way as to imply the emotion of the author as he makes his personal discovery. The fact is made to bear, as it were, the patina of astonishment and delight with which the author himself beholds it. The great writers, some of whom are represented in this anthology, hold to the facts, but in addition they convey an exaltation of wonder, an implied worship of the marvellous. They have, in short, "an eye for mysteries."

[2] Quoted from *The New Yorker* magazine, June 14, 1958.

EARTH, SKY, AND SEA

Wagtail
'Wagtail's World Grows Wider[1]

ALICE CREW GALL AND FLEMING H. CREW

In the Foreword to Wagtail, *Albert Shields, Professor Emeritus of Education at Teachers College, Columbia University, says: "Wagtail has three distinct merits. It is scientifically accurate; it is educationally sound; it is a delightful bit of literature. No child who has once read it but will see the little world of the pool in a new and vivid light. Which is but another way of saying that a child will read it because he enjoys it, and having read it, will profit by the reading."*

From the moment he was hatched, Wagtail found the Blue Pool a wonderful place to live in. Just at first he supposed that his own particular spot in the pickerel weed was all there was to the world and was quite astonished at the number of things that went on about him.

And then one day he knew in some mysterious fashion that there was more to the world than just this, and the knowledge was so exciting that he could scarcely contain himself.

"Why, this is wonderful!" he thought, when he discovered other pickerel weeds.

"It is almost too wonderful!" he said, when he found that the Pool was filled with many lives besides his own.

But the day he slipped out of the water onto a small island of sticks that had lodged

[1] From Alice Crew Gall and Fleming H. Crew, *Wagtail* (Oxford University Press, 1932).

among the stems of the pond lilies, was the most marvelous of all!

He was almost stunned at what he saw around him.

He couldn't believe it; he simply couldn't. So he sat quite still, waiting, not knowing what might happen to him next.

The Patriarch, who was taking the afternoon sun upon the island of sticks, looked down and saw the queer little figure, something like a Tadpole and something like a Frog, yet not quite like either. "Don't be frightened," he said softly. "It's confusing just at first, but you will get used to it after a while."

"Will I?" asked Wagtail shyly. "It doesn't seem as though I ever could." "You will, though," the old Frog assured him. "Take it easy and don't rush things. I'm the Patriarch of the Pool," he added kindly, "and, if there is anything you want to know, you may ask me and I will try to tell you."

"Thank you," said Wagtail as he settled himself more comfortably; "thank you, Patriarch; I want to know about everything."

"There you go," chuckled the Patriarch; "there you go, rushing things right away! One thing at a time is a very good rule to remember, young Tadpole."

"Yes, sir," said Wagtail meekly, "where shall we begin?"

"Well," said the Patriarch thoughtfully, "let us begin with you. How much of your life do you remember up to this minute?"

"I remember the pickerel weeds," answered Wagtail promptly, "and all manner of creatures rushing about among them."

"Do you remember when you hadn't any eyes?" asked the old Frog.

"Didn't I always have eyes?" exclaimed Wagtail.

"And do you remember when you didn't have any mouth either?" went on the Patriarch, enjoying the Tadpole's surprise.

"Gracious!" said Wagtail excitedly, "you don't mean ——"

"Yes, I do," replied the old Frog; "I mean exactly that! *There was a time when you had neither eyes nor mouth.*"

Wagtail was too amazed to say anything for a minute. He sat trying to get things straightened out in his mind while the Patriarch watched him.

"Please, sir," he said at last; "please, sir, I don't seem to remember any thing so very clearly. Will you be good enough to tell about me, right from the start?"

"That's a very good spirit to show!" said the Patriarch.

He darted out his tongue after an insect that had buzzed too close to him, moved a little nearer to the Tadpole, and began his favorite pastime of story-telling.

"Suppose we start with the day you squirmed you way out of a tiny egg," he said. "You were a lively little fellow and the first things you did was to wiggle your tail as hard as you could."

"Did I?" exclaimed Wagtail; "that was pretty clever, wasn't it?"

"Not especially," returned the Patriarch dryly; "all Tadpoles do it."

"Oh," said Wagtail, a trifle embarrassed.

"But I will say," added the old Frog kindly, "that you were unusually energetic about your tail-wagging — that's where you got your name."

"Really?" said Wagtail, pleased to hear this.

"Yes," continued the Patriarch; "but you were so small that you soon grew tired and settled down on the soft, green carpet of water plants at the bottom of the Pool, to rest.

"All around you was darkness. You couldn't see because you had no eyes, and you must have wondered what the strange world was like, that you had come into."

"I don't remember it at all," said the little Tadpole. "Was I the only one who didn't have eyes?"

"Of course not," the Patriarch told him; "*no* Tadpole has eyes when he is first hatched; and none of them have mouths."

"But how did I eat if I didn't have a mouth?" inquired Wagtail.

"Well, now," said the Patriarch, swelling out his sides with importance; "*that* is something which will astonish you, I expect! You didn't eat! You lived on your little tail!"

"On my tail!" exclaimed Wagtail, very much puzzled. "What do you mean?"

"I mean," said the Patriarch, "that there was quite a bit of nourishment packed away in your tail; enough to keep you from being hungry while you waited for your mouth to grow."

"Isn't that funny!" said Wagtail, amused at this idea; "how did it ever get there?"

The Patriarch did not answer for a moment. "Well," he said presently, "I'll confess I don't know the answer to that. To tell you the truth, I've often wondered about it myself. Nobody knows the answer, I guess; it's just the way Tadpoles are made and that's all there is to it."

"It's a pretty good way, isn't it?" said Wagtail.

"It is, indeed!" answered the old Frog; and then, after a minute, he went on: "Do you know, although I have lived so long, there are still a great many things that I wonder about? I often wish I could remember more about my own Tadpole days."

Wagtail gave a little bounce upon the island of sticks.

"Were *you* a Tadpole?" he asked in amazement.

"Yes," said the old Frog; "a long time ago."

"Just like me?"

"Just like you."

This was almost too much for Wagtail to believe and he sat thinking it over for several minutes.

What an exciting thing life was, to be sure!

Suddenly a new thought occurred to him. "Will I grow to be big and strong and wonderful like you are, sometime?" he asked.

"I hope you will be a much finer Frog than I am," the Patriarch replied. "I have managed to live for a long time, though there are many dangers at the Pool; and I hope you may do the same."

"What must I do to live to be old?" asked Wagtail anxiously.

"First," said the Patriarch, looking at the little Tadpole and speaking very slowly, "you must remember this: those who stay closest to home live longest. Do not wander far from the Pool and always keep a sharp lookout."

The Tadpole caught his breath, for the old Frog sounded very solemn; but he listened carefully as the other continued:

"If you feel danger near, jump! Jump without waiting to see what it is. Jump as high and as far as you can; and into the water if possible."

"I will remember everything you have told me," promised Wagtail; "it frightens me a little, but I will remember. And now, go on and tell me what else happened to me when I was very little, won't you?"

"Well, day by day you grew. After a while your mouth appeared, your eyes came, and you grew a fine strong pair of hind legs. Your tail kept getting shorter and shorter, for you did not need it after you had a mouth to eat with, until today you have scarcely any of it left at all!"

"I haven't, have I?" exclaimed Wagtail excitedly. "And will I soon be a real frog like you?"

"Not until your front legs grow, so that you can hop," returned the Patriarch; "but you will have them before long now, I expect," he added.

"Will I?" asked Wagtail. "And what will I do then?"

But the old Frog did not answer. A widening circle of ripples showed where he had dived into the water, leaving Wagtail alone upon the island of sticks.

Children of the Sea
The Dolphin's Tale [2]
WILFRID S. BRONSON

❧ Children of the Sea *is the best of Mr. Bronson's excellent nature books for boys and*

[2] From Wilfrid S. Bronson, *Children of the Sea* (Harcourt, Brace, 1940).

girls in which he so successfully combines scientific accuracy with fancy. The selection given below is taken from the first half of the book which tells the story of a dolphin from the Florida Everglades.

We shall call the baby dolphin Tursiops because that is a name given by scientists to all the dolphins of the special breed to which this one belonged. It is a half-Latin, half-Greek name which means "looking like a fish."

Naturally his mother had no name to call him, but call him she could, as you shall see. At first it wasn't necessary, since he was always at her side. After all, he was still pretty much a part of her. She was wise, but he knew nothing. He did not even know enough to be afraid. There are dangerous animals in a Florida tidal river and in the sea, but Tursiops had no thought of these. His big idea was to stay close by his mother from whom he could obtain, as often as he pleased, a bracing drink of rich warm milk. He wanted only to be near that bigger, stronger, lovely image of himself who nibbled at him ticklingly and gave him pleasant little bouncings with her nose, lifting him to the air each time that she herself came up to blow, or gently raised his sagging tail when he was napping at the surface.

He grew very fast, partly from being so well fed and partly too, perhaps, because the almost constant swimming in a dolphin's life built up his bone and muscle rather rapidly. He began making little dashes from his mother's side, zigzagging about her as a puppy runs about an older dog upon a lawn. It was thrilling to rush out into the unknown waters in dizzy hairpin turns, always doubling quickly back. He swam swift single circles round his mother, and discovered the double circle which brought him back to her repeatedly as he criss-crossed in great foaming figure eights.

She had to keep a steady eye on him, but it was hard work, for whereas most baby mammals take long sleeps and give their mothers a chance to rest as well, Tursiops seemed to need only half as much sleep as his mother. He was forever restless, and like other playful children, he never knew when to stop. Life was almost too much fun. He often got so excited in play that he really needed squelching. For, as days passed into weeks, he tended to swim in ever-wider arcs, and suddenly one day went streaking off straightaway downstream.

Then his mother used her call, a loud whistling sound made by forcing air through a very small opening of her blowhole under water. Underwater sounds travel with great power, and her snorted scream-call leaped downstream after Tursiops, carrying its message of fear which raced through him with lightning speed from his runaway tail to his baby brain and frightened him. For the first time in his life he was afraid. Although so innocent and inexperienced, he knew that tone meant danger. It sent a chill along his spine and he wanted terribly to be back beside his mother.

Down went his flippers and flukes (good water brakes), around he came and back like a bullet, fleeing from what unseen submarine bogeyman he did not know. He leaped clear over his mother and tore around her to shake from his fins the final tingle of that first fear, and perhaps, by moving rapidly, to keep from being punished too. For, if his mother wished to, she could give an awful wallop with her tail.

After that she called him every now and then, as he played, just as a precaution. He would answer with a tenor whistle-snort, a stream of tiny bubbles rising from his blowhole like a string of pearls with a crescent pendant. These whistle-snorts served as a language, the tone and loudness changing with the different ideas that they expressed. Much of the time the two dolphins whistled merely to keep track of each other while swimming the endless windings of the slow and salty stream. At night this was more necessary, since much of the time they could not see each other. And when they slept at the surface with blowholes out in the air, the sound was more like a snoring sigh.

They would rest for five or ten minutes, tails moving gently or slowly sagging. Then a slow swim with eyes half-closed, not an interruption of slumber, but like our turning over in our beds. Next, another blinking sleep, and ever and again a snore-sigh signal.

As long as her baby's cozy snore-sigh came peacefully, the mother dolphin rested, though her tiny earholes were forever listening. Any change in the sound and she was wide awake in a wink. Should any large shape or shadow suddenly show in the surrounding water, she was instantly alert and ready to protect her precious youngster.

A great hungering shark might be about. But the shape or shadow might be only that of a gentle old sea cow, perhaps with a calf of her own.

Tursiops tried to play with a baby sea cow, much against its mother's wishes, when he met them moving along the bottom of the stream pushing on the mud with their flippers. But the baby seemed to have no wish to romp. He couldn't have kept up with Tursiops if he had tried. Instead, his mother sat up on her tail with head and "shoulders" out of water and held the baby in her "arms." And there, as with human babies, is where he nursed. She had to raise his head above the water or he'd have drowned at dinner. Tursiops soon left them to look for livelier playmates.

Looking for playmates: that was the trouble with Tursiops as he grew older. Because he was bright, he was full of curiosity about every other creature that he saw. And, like a puppy, he was everybody's friend, because dolphins are both playful and sociable. He had yet to learn that many kinds of creatures would not like his company, and indeed that some would like him all too well. For great dolphin-baby-swallowing sharks do swim into estuaries and the salty part of sluggish streams. Perhaps that is why the dolphin mother guided her inexperienced, overfriendly son upstream farther every day.

She was his most perfect playmate, after all. Only she, of all the river animals, could speed along beside him mile after mile. Where the river opened wide in lake-like places, they played at tag or swam fast races, whistling merrily. They seemed never to forget that water is a wonderfully wet and splendidly splashable stuff. Often the mother was as rambunctious as her son, for dolphins, however old, are among the gayest creatures in the world.

They would leap way out of water in their

onward rush, coming down with a spanking splash that sent water flying for thirty feet and higher in the air. Still tearing ahead, they would roll on their sides banging their heads repeatedly with lusty splashes. They lobtailed loudly, slapping the surface of the water with the flat of their tails. Or they would roll clear over and swim on their backs with jaws out, then very much like racing yachts minus masts and rigging and very low in the water.

Though appearing to have no necks, they bent that part of their bodies very readily from side to side or up and down. So with the aid of flippers and back fins, by a bend of the "neck" they could dart to either side as swiftly as a frightened fish without slowing down at all. By a deep dip of chin and tail or a lift of tail and head while going at top speed, they could turn somersaults forward or backward with the greatest of ease. Sometimes, instead of a forward somersault, they simply threw their backs and tails up and forward, causing spray to fly almost as far as when leaping clear and coming down kerplunk.

Tursiops found life a very jolly business. Without a tooth in his mouth and with no thought of any food but milk, he loved to race beside his mother into a school of big fat mullets. But while she caught them, turned them around, forced them down her throat and swallowed her fill (feeding for herself and Tursiops), he tore gaily through the school, knocking the frightened fishes about for fun. If a mullet scooted out of the school, he would chase it for the same reason a pup or kitten runs after a ball. As kittens learn by catching crickets and such small fry the better to hunt when they are cats, Tursiops learned to follow the quick dodges of the fleeing fish, a game he would some day put to work when he must get his own living directly from the sea.

When the mother dolphin had almost filled her stomach, she turned over on her back and flipped mullets into the air with her tail. Up they went following the course of a rainbow. But there was no treasure at the end, only the open mouth of the dolphin mother ready to catch them for dessert. Tursiops tried to imitate her, but his tosses mostly went wild, which hardly mattered, since he didn't intend to eat the fishes anyway.

Although there were hundreds in the panic-stricken school, he would pick one mullet out to plague especially, tossing it with his tail, racing under it and catching it. This was a cat-and-mouse performance, for he would shake it and toss it again, either with his tail or mouth, and play with the same poor fish even after it was limp and lifeless. Sometimes both dolphins played this game at once, raising their heads high out of water and tossing the mullets fifteen feet at a time. But Tursiops' fish would last longer than his mother's, because her strong, sharp teeth soon tore the wretched plaything into scraps.

Tursiops thought it sport to spring surprises. It was a jolly joke, he felt, to swim unseen below a flock of sawbill ducks moving placidly on the surface, rise suddenly amongst them with a whopping splash, and scare "the daylights" out of them as they squawked into the air. With head feathers on end and wings beating desperately, they ran over the water, rising only after a long take-off. Their frantic feet left double trails of dimples which rippled out to cross each other as Tursiops cavorted in a dolphin's glee.

Where the water was deep enough, he would leap out just below a snowy egret or a great blue heron perched on the roots of mangrove trees which lined the stream. Once a perching heron, seeing an extra large dense school of minnows moving just below it, did a most unheron-like thing. It dropped amongst them into water far too deep for its toes to touch the bottom. But instead of being bothered by this, it drifted along, lanky legs adangle, and jabbed fish after fish with great gusto. From behind, Tursiops swam swiftly and silently into the school, and with a great arch of his back heaved the heron out of the water. Up it went like a tenderfoot from the back of a bucking bronco. Only, instead of coming down again, it kept aloft on its black and blue wings, and loped away with many a blattery grunt, unable at all to see the joke.

The joke was on Tursiops when he all but stood on the end of his tail to frighten a sleepy snake-bird and got a vicious peck for his pains. He turned several somersaults whistle-screaming in agonized surprise, his distracted mother rushing about seeking something to defend him from. But besides a peck in his face he had a new idea in his head. Those long-necked things with pointed faces were better left alone, at least above the water-line. That they had a perfect right to insist on being left alone never occurred to his mischievous mind. But he had learned, at least, that most of them could take care of themselves, being very well armed.

After the snake-bird stabbed his muzzle, Tursiops was more wary of sharp-billed birds, especially waders such as herons, cranes, and ibises, which rarely got into water deep enough to allow him any advantage. Even the spoonbill was left to her supper undisturbed. But it was still impossible to resist the chance to tease those birds which swam beneath the water chasing fishes, though he was careful to avoid their bills. Jumping into the air to pester birds was one thing. When they dove deep into the stream, it was another.

Down there at least he could make masterly maneuvers and, by chasing the loons and grebes, cause them to miss the fishes they themselves were chasing. For though grebes and loons are some of the most able divers and artful dodgers under water, he was so big and swift that all thought of food forsook them when he made his playful rushes. The loons would get to the top and leave on long foot-flopping take-offs, hoo-hoo-hooing wildly. The grebes, using both feet and wings beneath the water, would stampede for the shallows and the sheltering reeds.

Even the old snake-bird, so good at "shagging" fishes under water that her other names are shag, darter, and water turkey, had to get back on her mangrove roost, shaking her dark feathers in deep disgust, when Tursiops was about. Though the lobe-toed grebes could swim five hundred feet under water in three minutes, and though the web-footed loons went even faster, such speed was not enough to protect them from being bothered by the young dolphin. He could swim rings around them and he did.

Of course Tursiops didn't spend all his time teasing. Nevertheless, the rough-and-tumble tactics of the two dolphins often worried other animals of whom they were entirely unaware. The water upstream was brackish now, getting fresher every day as they went in ever farther from the sea, deeper and deeper into the great swamp of the Everglades. Here their riotous splashing frightened hundreds of fiddler crabs into their holes in the bank. Other fiddlers which had climbed high on the buttonwoods and could not scurry to their holes were in more danger, though they didn't seem to know it. For fat raccoons would come to pick them off for supper like ripe fruit, just as they plucked oysters from mangrove roots when the tide was low.

All unaware of this, the dolphins rollicked on. The waves of their wake went rolling along the stream's edge, washing off wee insects from the overhanging plants. A mouse hunting there for seeds would be washed into the water, where a pickerel or big black bass or even a silvery snook might catch him before he could regain the shore. Only the pig-frogs, basking on the bank, enjoyed the wetting from sudden unexpected waves. This they expressed in a chorus of coarse grunts.

Souvenirs Entomologiques
The Cricket[3]

JEAN HENRI FABRE

No one knew insects more intimately than Henri Fabre. Prepared to teach mathematics, he at first picked up his science by himself. His Souvenirs Entomologiques, *which run into volumes, are filled with fascinating stories of insect life, told in the same charming manner as this one on the cricket.*

Concerning this insect, which has attracted both poet and student alike, I, the naturalist, would say that of his many interesting points, the most unique is his Home. I speak of the *Country* Cricket, for he alone, among the four varieties listed by the scientist, under-

3 Translated by Laura P. Sickels.

stands the art of creating a fixed home for himself.

The greater part of insects hide themselves in the ground, in bad weather, in a temporary refuge, obtained without labor, and abandoned without regret. The home laboriously acquired, where the insect establishes itself and which it plans never to vacate, neither in warm springtime nor in bitter winter, the cricket alone undertakes to build. He does this in view of his own tranquillity. He need not occupy himself with the chase, as does the butterfly, nor with family cares.

Upon some sunny slope in the field, he becomes proprietor of an hermitage. While all other insects wander about, sleeping under the stars, or in the shelter of cracked bark of a tree, or under a stone, or a dead leaf, the cricket, by a singular privilege, is domiciled. A serious problem this, a suitable dwelling-place, for good and all, solved by three, the cricket, the rabbit, and finally, by Man.

In my neighborhood the fox has his den where crumbling rocks in the hillside furnish the greater part of the cave. A few slight touches on the part of Reynard complete his habitation. The rabbit, more prudent and cautious, digs his hole where he sees fit, when Nature fails to offer him a passage underground which would save him labor.

The cricket surpasses them all. He disdains accidental shelter, choosing always the exact spot for his lodging, on healthy ground, exposed to light and air, and well drained. He does not profit by chance cavities in the ground, inconvenient and disappointing. He digs his chalet completely, from beginning to end — from the entrance-hall to the apartment in the extreme end. Superior to this insect, in the art of establishing a home, I see only Man. Yet he, in early days, had to dispute with wild beasts his shelter under rock or in cavern.

How shall we answer for the privilege of instinct in the lower orders of life? The cricket, one of the most humble of insects, knows to perfection how to lodge himself. He has a veritable home, an advantage unknown to many a civilized inhabitant; a peaceful retreat, the first condition of well-being, which no one around him is capable of emulating.

In the south of France, or the Midi, as we call it, a city-child who can capture a cricket thinks he owns a treasure! The tiny creature becomes a great pet. His cheery serenade breathes the joys of life in the country. Alas! his death brings mourning to the whole family. Who, at the age of sports on the greensward, has not stopped before the cabin of the Hermit! As light as you have made your step, he has heard your approach, and with a sudden recoil has descended to the bottom of his hiding-place. When you arrive the sill of the manor is deserted!

The means of coaxing the sly inhabitant to come out is a simple matter. A straw is introduced, and gently moved about in his hole. Surprised at what is going on above him, and curious as to the wherefore, he mounts from his secret apartment; he stops in the vestibule; he hesitates, trying to inform himself, while wiggling his delicate antennae; he comes to the light; he goes out, becoming an easy capture, so many happenings have confused his poor head! Should the cricket fail you on your first trial, for he sometimes becomes suspicious and resents the tickling of the straw, try emptying a glass of water into his hole! This will dislodge the simple fellow.

Adorable those days of childish races along the border of the grassy path, in search of a cricket to place in a cage, to be nourished by a leaf of lettuce! I see you again, happy days! and find you almost in your first freshness, to-day, when my blue-eyed little Paul, already master of the trick with the straw, suddenly rises from his patient position, flat on his stomach before a tiny hole. Brandishing his closed fist, he shouts, all excitement, "I've got him! I've got him!" Quick, little cricket! Slip into this paper-bag! You will be fondled and well cared for. But teach us something of the art of living!

Let us examine your lodging among the quitch-grass on this gentle slope. A little slanting gallery is dug in the ground, hardly the size of a finger. A tuft of grass half hides the entrance of the lodge; it serves as an awning and casts a discreet shadow over the sill. This is a comfort when you creep cautiously out to browse among the neighboring grasses. When all is quiet round about, you take your stand upon your terrace, in the sunshine, and give us a serenade on your delicate violin. We have learned you never use your instrument indoors.

The interior of your house is without luxury: bare walls, but not too coarse. We understand that long leisure permits the builder to smooth down rough places. At the bottom of the passage we find your sleeping-room, an alcove in a blind alley, a little more finished than the rest and more spacious. We find your dwelling, dear cricket, very simple, very clean, exempt from dampness, all conforming to the rules of hygiene. But how vast an undertaking! A gigantic tunnel, considering your delicate means for excavation.

Far from complaining of your solitary existence, you seem well satisfied with your home and with your music. You appear to appreciate the charm of a modest retreat far from the madding crowd. You seem to say:

"Let the butterflies have their freedom!
    As for me, let me live concealed."

Florian.

"Tho it rains, tho it blows, tho it thunders
    The cricket lives in peace, and chants 'cree-cree!'"

Anonymous.

Walden
The Battle of the Ants

HENRY DAVID THOREAU

⌇ *Thoreau, one of the greatest nature-lovers of America, though not a scientist, had ample time while he lived at Walden Pond to study even the smallest aspects of nature. And, unlike many scientists, he was able to express himself in clear, vivid, straightforward English. No child can read the following story without having a deeper interest in those tiny insects which are such a pest to his mother.*

One day when I went out to my wood-pile, or rather my pile of stumps, I observed two large ants, the one red, the other much larger, nearly half an inch long, and black, fiercely contending with one another. Having once got hold they never let go, but struggled and wrestled and rolled on the chips incessantly. Looking farther, I was surprised to find that the chips were covered with such combatants, that it was not a *duellum,* but a *bellum,* a war between two races of ants, the red always pitted against the black, and frequently two red ones to one black. The legions of these Myrmidons covered all the hills and vales in my wood-yard, and the ground was already strewn with the dead and dying, both red and black. It was the only battle which I have ever witnessed, the only battlefield I ever trod while the battle was raging; internecine war; the red republicans on the one hand, and the black imperialists on the other. On every side they were engaged in deadly combat, yet without any noise that I could hear, and human soldiers never fought so resolutely. I watched a couple that were fast locked in each other's embraces, in a little sunny valley amid the chips, now at noonday prepared to fight till the sun went down, or life went out. The smaller red champion had fastened himself like a vise to his adversary's front, and through all the tumblings on that field never for an instant ceased to gnaw at one of his feelers near the root, having already caused the other to go by the board; while the stronger black one dashed him from side to side, and, as I saw on looking nearer, had already divested him of several of his members. They fought with more pertinacity than bull-dogs. Neither manifested the least disposition to retreat. It was evident that their battle-cry was Conquer or die. In the meanwhile there came along a single red ant on the hill side of this valley, evidently full of excitement, who either had despatched his foe, or had not yet taken part in the battle; probably the latter, for he had lost none of his limbs; whose mother had charged him to return with his shield or upon it. Or perchance he was some Achilles, who had nourished his wrath apart, and had now come to avenge or rescue his Patroclus. He saw this unequal combat from afar — for the black were nearly twice the size of the red — he drew near with rapid pace till he stood on his guard within half an inch of the combatants;

then, watching his opportunity, he sprang upon the black warrior, and commenced his operations near the root of his right fore-leg, leaving the foe to select among his own members; and so there were three united for life, as if a new kind of attraction had been invented which put all other locks and cements to shame. I should not have wondered by this time to find that they had their respective musical bands stationed on some eminent chip, and playing their national airs the while, to excite the slow and cheer the dying combatants. I was myself excited somewhat even as if they had been men.

I took up the chip on which the three I have particularly described were struggling, carried it into my house, and placed it under a tumbler on my windowsill, in order to see the issue. Holding a microscope to the first-mentioned red ant, I saw that, though he was assiduously gnawing at the near fore-leg of his enemy, having severed his remaining feeler, his own breast was all torn away, exposing what vitals he had there to the jaws of the black warrior, whose breastplate was apparently too thick for him to pierce; and the dark carbuncles of the sufferer's eyes shone with ferocity such as war only could excite. They struggled half an hour longer under the tumbler, and when I looked again the black soldier had severed the heads of his foes from their bodies, and the still living heads were hanging on either side of him like ghastly trophies at his saddle-bow, still apparently as firmly fastened as ever, and he was endeavoring with feeble struggles, being without feelers and with only the remnant of a leg, and I know not how many other wounds, to divest himself of them; which at length, after half an hour more, he accomplished. I raised the glass, and he went off over the window sill in that crippled state. Whether he finally survived that combat, and spent the remainder of his days in some Hôtel des Invalides, I do not know; but I thought that his industry would not be worth much thereafter. I never learned which party was victorious, nor the cause of the war; but I felt for the rest of that day as if I had had my feelings excited and harrowed by witnessing the struggle, the ferocity and carnage, of a human battle before my door.

The Loon

❧ Nothing Thoreau says exaggerates the unearthly cry of the loon. This is a true nature story told in Thoreau's inimitable manner — not personifying the loon but making him a personality.

In the fall the loon (*Colymbus glacialis*) came, as usual, to molt and bathe in the pond, making the woods ring with his wild laughter before I had risen.

As I was paddling along the north shore one very calm October afternoon, for such days especially they settle on to the lakes, like the milkweed down, having looked in vain over the pond for a loon, suddenly one, sailing out from the shore toward the middle a few rods in front of me, set up his wild laugh and betrayed himself. I pursued with a paddle and he dived, but when he came up I was nearer than before. He dived again, but I miscalculated the direction he would take, and we were fifty rods apart when he came to the surface this time, for I had helped to widen the interval; and again he laughed long and loud, and with more reason than before. He manoeuvred so cunningly that I could not get within half a dozen rods of him. Each time, when he came to the surface, turning his head this way and that, he coolly surveyed the water and the land, and apparently chose his course so that he might come up where there was the widest expanse of water and at the greatest distance from the boat. It was surprising how quickly he made up his mind and put his resolve into execution. He led me at once to the widest part of the pond, and could not be driven from it. While he was thinking one thing in his brain, I was endeavoring to divine his thought in mine. It was a pretty game, played on the smooth surface of the pond, a man against a loon. Suddenly your adversary's checker disappears beneath the board, and the problem is to place yours nearest to where his will appear again. Sometimes he would come up unexpectedly on the opposite side of me, having apparently passed directly under the boat. So long-winded was he and so unweariable, that when he had swum farthest he would immediately plunge again, nevertheless; and then no wit could divine where in the deep pond, beneath the smooth surface, he might be speeding his way like a fish, for he had time and ability to visit the bottom of the pond in its deepest part. It is said that loons have been caught in the New York lakes eighty feet beneath the surface, with hooks set for trout — though Walden is deeper than that. How surprised must the fishes be to see this ungainly visitor from another sphere speeding his way amid their schools! Yet he appeared to know his course as surely under water as on the surface, and swam much faster there. Once or twice I saw a ripple where he approached the surface, just put his head out to reconnoitre, and instantly dived again. I found that it was as well for me to rest on my oars and wait his reappearing as to endeavor to calculate where he would rise; for again and again, when I was straining my eyes over the surface one way, I would suddenly be startled by his unearthly laugh behind me. But why, after displaying so much cunning, did he invariably betray himself the moment he came up by that loud laugh? Did not his white breast enough betray him? He was indeed a silly loon, I thought. I could commonly hear the splash of the water when he came up, and so also detected him. But after an hour he seemed as fresh as ever, dived as willingly and swam yet farther than at first. It was surprising to see how serenely he sailed off with unruffled breast when he came to the surface, doing all the work with his webbed feet beneath. His usual note was this demoniac laughter, yet somewhat like that of a water-fowl; but occasionally, when he had balked me most successfully and come up a long way off, he uttered a long-drawn unearthly howl, probably more like that of a wolf than any bird; as when a beast puts his muzzle to the ground and deliberately howls. This was his looning — perhaps the wildest sound that is ever heard here, making the woods ring far and wide. I concluded that he laughed in derision of my efforts, confident of his own resources. Though the sky was by this time overcast, the pond was so smooth that I could see where he broke the surface when I did not hear him. His white breast, the stillness of the air, and the smoothness of the water were all against him. At length, having come up fifty rods off, he uttered one of those prolonged howls, as if calling on the god of loons to aid him, and immediately there came a wind from the east and rippled the surface, and filled the whole air with misty rain, and I was impressed as if it were the prayer of the loon answered, and his god was angry with me; and so I left him disappearing far away on the tumultuous surface.

Vulpes, the Red Fox [4]

(A Selection)

JOHN AND JEAN GEORGE

Sound knowledge of wild-life and a deep love of the Maryland countryside are inherent in this life cycle of Vulpes, the red fox. The opening chapter of the book is given below.

Vulpes, the Red Fox, was born in a den in Maryland. It was April. The snow had gone. The woods were cold and wet. A chill rain splashed through the barren woodlands and filled the earth till it could hold no more. In the uplands the rising streams raced along their twisting beds. The river bottomlands of the Potomac swirled with muddy flood waters. Winter lingered in the cold.

In the warmth of the den spring had come. Seven foxes were born. They lay huddled against their mother's breast deep in the dark den. Their eyes were sealed. Their first want was the milk of their mother. When their hunger was satisfied the foxes dropped off to sleep. This was their life for nine days.

Vulpes knew his brothers and sisters only as whimpering cries and warm bodies that tumbled and shoved and kicked against him. He felt the cold wet nose of his mother nuzzling him, and the moist tingle of her tongue caressing him.

Then one day in the middle of April, Vulpes became aware of something new. There were dim blurred figures that accompanied the kicks and squirms. His moth-

4 From John and Jean George, *Vulpes, the Red Fox* (Dutton, 1948).

er's cold wet nose was black. Beyond the soft white fur of her breast there was a dim glow from the outside world. Vulpes could see.

He looked at all his brothers and sisters. They were gray and round. It seemed to Vulpes there were a lot of them. He looked up. His mother was looking down at him through her yellow slanting eyes. Except for the dim light at the end of the tunnel Vulpes thought this must be the whole world.

With this settled, he tumbled back to his mother's breast.

Outside the den, the red maples had burst into bloom. The brooks were lined with the yellow-green flowers of the spice bush.

The days went on and Vulpes became more and more curious about the light at the end of his world. He sat and watched it for hours at a time. It was bright and wonderful. Presently he discovered that the light changed. Sometimes it was gone for a long time. This was night. Sometimes it was gray. This was rain. Sometimes it was blacked out for a short time. At these times Vulpes caught a new smell in the musky den. He sensed another presence. This was his father bringing food to his mother.

Vulpes wondered where his father went in the light. It puzzled him. He felt he must know.

Then one day his mother darkened the tunnel and disappeared as his father had done. The little fox felt alone. The rounded den seemed large and empty. He huddled close to his brothers and sisters. They all whimpered complainingly.

When his loneliness became too great, he left his noisy kin to find his mother. He waddled down the tunnel. The light became brighter and brighter. Suddenly there was a second light. He turned his head and peered down another long tunnel. This confused the little fox. He turned to run for the safety of the darkness behind him. Before he had reached it, he felt himself being picked up by his mother. She carried him down the tunnel into the blinding light of the outside world. It was the end of April.

Vulpes found himself in what he believed was a den, a den that was huge and shining. The light was all around. One part of it was so bright he couldn't look at it. This was the sun. It was warm and pleasant. This den was so large that Vulpes could not see the end of it. This *was* the world.

The young pup scrambled unsteadily to a nearby stone. He wanted to see more of this colorful world. The spring woods abounded with color. The red keys of the maples dangled above him. A loose swirl of Virginia bluebells surrounded him, and the yellows and greens of the dog-tooth violets swept the hill below him. At the foot of the hill the old Chesapeake and Ohio Canal was fringed with the fresh greens of the willows. The willows stretched beyond the canal to the brown flood waters of the Potomac. The lacy rush of the river hung over all.

As he watched the colors of spring, Vulpes caught the movement of his shadow beneath him on the rock. As he moved, it moved with him. He looked at it. Slowly Vulpes reached out for it. Slowly the shadow reached back. As he took his paw away, the shadow did the same. Whatever he did, the shadow followed. The fuzzy outline fascinated the little fox. He ran with it. He pounced on it, and finally he lost it behind a tree. He stuck his nose out to see if it were on the other side of the tree. And there, below him, was the shadow, sticking its nose out.

He was about to spring on it when a movement at the mouth of the den caught his eye. A venturesome brother had followed him into the sunlight. Vulpes ran over and nipped him on the foot. The two foxes rolled in a mock skirmish. They found their voices in melodious "wurps" as they tumbled over and over in a cluster of pale spring beauties.

Suddenly a bolt of blue came screaming through the blossoming redbud trees overhead. Vulpes and his brother looked up to see a pair of meddlesome blue jays. They glanced toward their mother. She was calm and undisturbed. Her poise reassured them and they went back to their play.

The young foxes played on until evening. With the lengthening of the shadows came the last carol of the birds. The whistling note of the cardinal rose clear and sweet above the crystal melodies of the wood thrushes. Near the den a flurry of leaves marked the spot where a red-eyed towhee was still scratching vigorously in the wood bottoms. His sharp "Chewink" rang out through the woods. There was the plaintive wavering melody of the white-throated sparrows as they sang, "Old Sam Peabody, Peabody, Peabody, Peabody." And the "Whicherty, whicherty, whicherty," of the Maryland yellow-throats along the wet brush lands bordering the canal echoed through the bottoms.

The long hours of play had tired the little foxes and they were glad to go to bed with the birds.

As the days went by the seven pups spent more and more time playing around the den. The den was hidden in a rocky slope on the north side of the canal bank where it got the warm southern sunlight. Built long ago and now abandoned, the canal made an ideal homeland for the fox. The den was first used by an old woodchuck. Several years ago Vulpes' parents had found it and enlarged it for their own use. Back from the small rocky entrances they dug long tunnels. At the end of them they scooped out two hollows. One was where Vulpes was born, in the other his parents sometimes stored food.

Uphill from the den the hills rolled back to the distant farm lands. Sometimes Vulpes and his brothers and sisters romped in the woods behind the den. They would chase one another around the tree trunks and explore the animal trails in the spring woods.

Vulpes loved to smell the new odors he found; the chipmunks, the squirrels and the white-footed mice. Every time he caught a new scent he would bounce over to his mother and ask her who smelt like that. She would tell him who it was.

Then one afternoon Vulpes smelt an animal that was like nothing else in the woods. He looked to his mother and was alarmed to find her chasing the cubs into the den. She flashed to Vulpes' side, picked him up by the scruff of the neck and carried him off, as the voices of two boys sounded through the woods.

His father darted past him to a hiding place over the canal. Here in the tall grasses he could watch the boys without being seen. The old dog fox saw them go up the tow-path on the other side of the canal. They were carrying fishing rods on their shoulders, and would laugh and shout as they skipped stones over the water.

Presently his father came back to the den and stood before his wobbly son. This was Vulpes' first experience with man. His father warned him that this was his most dangerous enemy. With this the old fox turned around and trotted swiftly away.

Vulpes sat back on his haunches and thought of what his father had warned. Who were these animals that this great hunter feared? He decided to see for himself. He stuck his nose out of the den and sniffed the air. Then, with one eye showing around the edge of the rock, he peered down the old tow-path. Vulpes was startled to see that they walked on two feet like the birds. Surely, anything as dangerous as that, would have four legs like his father, not just two like the gentle warblers and the perky towhees. He had seen his father stalk and spring upon birds; surely, he could do the very same with men.

Vulpes was thinking very hard about these new animals when a yellow butterfly came gliding past his nose. He forgot the boys, who were now out of sight. Happily the little fox ran out into the sunlight after the butterfly. Without making a sound he leapt at the flitting insect. He chased it down the rocky bank to the water and was disappointed when the pretty little insect flitted over the canal and down the hill toward the river. Vulpes looked at the water's edge to see if he could cross and continue his chase. He put his left foot down and found it was wet and very unsafe. The ripples he made pleased him. He barked at them as they rolled away and knocked against the old dried stems of the cattails. He soon forgot the butterfly and was busy splashing his foot in the water.

The little fox yapped at a last ripple. Then he looked up at the evening sky. He was watching the colors of the fading sunset when a steady, "Urp, urp, urp, urp" in the cattails frightened him. He instinctively fell into a crouch, his head turned to one side,

his ears pointed forward. From a patch of
arrowhead in the swampy bottom of the
canal a second voice answered the first. Then
a third rose from a patch of pond lilies.
Vulpes looked from the cattails to the arrowheads to the pond lilies. He saw nothing.
Other "urps" added to the growing din. He
stared at the singing water. As he watched,
he heard another voice. It whistled meekly,
"Pe-ep, pe-ep, pe-ep, pe-ep." The noise grew
louder. It drowned out the roar of the river
in the distance.

Spotted here and there through the swampy
bottom a series of "erderps" rang out. More
and more voices joined the chorus until the
canal bed resounded with ear-splitting songs.
Never had Vulpes heard so much noise. It
hurt his ears to listen.

While he stood silently watching, a little
ripple caught his attention. Floating on the
water was a swamp cricket frog. As its
throat swelled up and it began to sing,
Vulpes saw where the "erderps" came from.
He marveled that so tiny a creature could
make so much noise. It was about as big as
the petal on the bloodroot.

On a floating twig beneath him he found
Hyla, the spring peeper. He thought Hyla
would burst, his throat swelled so as he uttered his shrill "Pe-ep."

Suddenly Vulpes realized that Pipiens, the
leopard frog, had been sitting not two feet
away from him all this time, but because
of his black-spotted green back, the little
fox thought he was an old stick in the
swamp. Pipiens blended well with the dark
waters blotched with green leaves.

All at once the frogs stopped. In the sudden silence that followed Vulpes heard the
boys returning from the river, laughing and
talking as they ran along the canal.

"Hey, look, a young fox!" one of them
shouted to the other. "Let's catch him."

"We can cross to his side on those rocks,"
the other called back.

As the boys hurried down across the rocks,
the frightened Vulpes, remembering what
his father had said, scampered to a deep
crevasse along the bank. He crawled as far
back as he could go. Trembling, he waited.

He heard the boys calling excitedly beneath him.

"Where did he go?"

"Must have gone up in those rocks somewhere," the other answered.

Vulpes was surprised that they could not
find him. He learned his most dangerous
enemy could not smell.

It wasn't long before Vulpes heard the
chorus of the frogs start up again. The boys
had given up their search and tramped
away.

He slipped cautiously from his hiding
place as his mother came gliding over the
rocks toward him. She had come to bring
her frightened pup home. He scampered
up the hill before her and tumbled into
the den.

One Day on Beetle Rock
The Weasel [5]

SALLY CARRIGHAR

*With subtle perception, the author describes
in scrupulous prose the activities of animals and
a few birds as she observes them during a typical day on Beetle Rock in the High Sierra
Mountains in California. This life of the wild
creatures is rich in drama, full of pursuit and
flight, danger and death. Miss Carrighar writes
not so much about animals as she writes from
the animal's point of view, and she is blessed
with the kind of sensitivity that enables her to
impart the "feel" of animal life. She records
her observations without sentimentality but
with deep feeling, and she combines the exactness of research with the beauty and poetry of
nature. Her book is the result of years of study
and patient watching. The chapter given below
tells of the weasel and her brood.*

Night's end had come, with its interlude
of peace, on the animal trails. The scents
that lay like vines across the forest floor were
faded now, and uninteresting. Hungry eyes
had ceased their watch of the moonlight
splashes and the plumy, shimmering tree-
tops. No heart had caught with fear when

[5] Originally published in *The Saturday Evening
Post* under the title "Forest Buccaneer" and here
reprinted from Sally Carrighar, *One Day on Beetle
Rock* (Knopf).

a twig fell or a pebble rolled. For most of the nocturnal hunters had returned to their dens, or ignored one another in a truce of weariness.

From the frail defense of an oak leaf a deer mouse stared at a passing coyote, sensing its safety by the mechanical tread of the great paws. A frog and an owl at opposite ends of the same tree closed their eyes. A black bear, trampling a new bed at the base of a cedar, broke into the burrow of a ground squirrel. With heavy eyes he saw it leap to a rock-pile; then he made a last slow turn and curled himself against the trunk.

The Weasel was not tired, and never joined a truce. She was stung by only a sharper fury when she saw the darkness seeping away beneath the trees. On the hillside where she hunted with her young she suddenly pulled herself up, sweeping the slope with her nose and eyes, trying to cup the forest in her ears for the sound of a chirp, a breath, or an earth-plug being pushed into a burrow. There was silence — proof that all the quick feet had been folded into furry flanks. She and her kits were alone in a deserted world.

The Weasel too was leading her family home, but she had stopped to try to stir up one more chase. She had chosen a slope that never furnished much excitement. The ground was a clear, smooth bed of pine and sequoia needles, with no underbrush where victims might be hiding. Even the odors beneath the Weasel's nose were of little help. For here no large obstructions, no fallen logs or gullies, had gathered the scent threads into strands. Still she whipped across the surface, vainly searching. It was not that she needed food after the night's good hunting. She was a squirrel's length stripped to a mouse's width, and was no glutton. But she was driven by insatiable hungers of the nerves.

Now she has caught the scent of a chipmunk, redolent and sweet. Perhaps it will lead her to the chipmunk's nest. She bounds along the path of odor with her tense tail high. But here is the trail of a second chipmunk crossing the first. The Weasel stops, confused. Now she follows one trail, now the other. Back and forth across the slope,

the odors weave a record of two chipmunks chasing each other. But where are the small warm bodies that left the tracings of delicious fragrance? The Weasel turns in her own tracks, comes to an angry stop. Her five young watch her. What will she do now? She'll forget the chipmunks. She stands erect, moving her nose through the air as she tries for a different scent.

Her nostrils trembled with her eagerness to find an animal odor in the smell of needles, loam, and cool dank funguses. She caught the juiciness of crushed grass mixed with faint musk. Meadow mouse! Off again, she sped along the mouse's trail towards the stream below. But the trail suddenly ended in a splash of mouse's blood and coyote scent.

The intense hope of the Weasel snapped into rage. The young ones saw her swirling over the needles like a lash. If there was another scent trail here she'd find it. She did — at this blended musk and pitchy odor left by a chickaree when he jumped from the trunk of a pine. The odor line turned to a patch of cleared earth, where he had patted down a seed, and then to the base of another pine, and up. The Weasel pursued the scent to one of the higher branches and out to the tip. From there the squirrel had leapt to another tree. That was an airy trail no enemy could follow.

The Weasel came down the tree in spirals, head first, slowly. When she reached the ground she paused, one forefoot on a root. Her eyes looked out unblinking and preoccupied. Perhaps her hungers were discouraged now — but no. Her crouched back straightened, sending her over the root in a level dash.

The Weasel young had scattered while their mother trailed the squirrel. They came flying back when a high bark told them that she had made a find at last. She was rolling over and over with the body of a chipmunk. This was not like her usual, quick death blow; again she drove her fangs through the chipmunk's fur. Then the harsh play ended. The Weasel leapt aside, allowing her kits to close in on the quiet prey.

While the brood fought over the chipmunk, their mother ran across the slope to explore the leaves beneath a dogwood thicket. By the time she returned, the shadows were thin and the chill of dawn was creeping in among the trees. Two of the young weasels munched last bites, but the others moved about slowly, only half alert, their tired legs hardly lifting their bodies above the ground. The mother bounded in among them. Her own strength still was keen but the kits needed rest, so she called them and the little pack moved down the hill.

At the base of the slope they must cross the stream. An uprooted sugar pine leaned from one side and a silvered fir snag from the other, making a bridge with a short gap in the middle. A few times when the kits were smaller one had missed his footing and had fallen into the water, but this time, tired though they were, all made the jump with safety.

The weasels' den was in a thicket, a few bounds off the top of Beetle Rock. To reach it they climbed the slope beyond the stream. When the Weasel approached the cliff from below, she often circled north and up through the brush at the end. Now she led the kits home the short way, over the Rock's broad, open terraces. They met no other animals until they came upon two gray mounds, strong with human scent. The Weasel dodged into a crack between the granite slabs. By connecting crevices she evaded the sleeping human forms and brought the kits to familiar ground beneath a shrubby oak. There, one by one, the six small creatures slipped into the earth.

Squirrels and Other Fur-Bearers
The Mink

JOHN BURROUGHS

⋘ The Mink is the factual type of nature story. Something in the way it is written reminds one of Thoreau, perhaps because it is written as a personal experience and expresses such absorbing personal interest.

In walking through the woods one day in early winter, we read upon the newly fallen snow the record of a mink's fright the night before. The mink had been traveling through the woods post-haste, not along the watercourses where one sees them by day, but over ridges and across valleys. We followed his tracks some distance to see what adventures he had met with. We tracked him through a bushy swamp, and saw where he had left it to explore a pile of rocks, then where he had taken to the swamp again, and where he had entered the more open woods. Presently the track turned sharply about, and doubled upon itself in long hurried strides. What had caused the mink to change his mind so suddenly? We explored a few paces ahead, and came upon a fox track. The mink had probably seen the fox stalking stealthily through the woods, and the sight had doubtless brought his heart into his mouth. I think he climbed a tree, and waited till the fox had passed. His track disappeared amid a clump of hemlocks, and then reappeared again a little beyond them. It described a big loop around, and then crossed the fox track only a few yards from the point where its course was interrupted. Then it followed a little watercourse, went under a rude bridge in a wood road, then mingled with squirrel tracks in a denser part of the thicket. If the mink met a muskrat or a rabbit in his travels, or came upon a grouse, or quail, or a farmer's henroost, he had the supper he was in quest of.

I followed a mink's track one morning upon the snow till I found where the prowler had overtaken and killed a muskrat by a stone wall near a little stream. The blood upon the snow and the half-devoured body of the rat told the whole story. The mink is very fond of muskrats, and trappers often use this flesh to bait their traps. I wonder if he has learned to enter the under-water hole to the muskrat's den, and then seek him in his chamber above, where the poor rat would have little chance to escape.

The mink is only a larger weasel, and has much of the boldness and bloodthirstiness of that animal. One summer day my dog Lark and I were sitting beside a small watercourse in the woods, when I saw a mink coming up the stream toward us. I sat motionless till the mink was within a few feet of us, when the dog saw him. As the dog sprang, the mink darted under a large flat stone. Lark was very fierce, and seemed to say to me, "Just lift up that stone and I will show you my way with minks." This I quickly did, and the dog sprang for the game, but he as quickly withdrew with a cry of pain as if he had touched something red-hot. The mink had got in the first blow or bite, and then effected his escape between my feet and the dog's, as if he had vanished in the air. Where he went to was a mystery. There was no hole; no depth of water; no hiding-place anywhere that I could discover or that the dog could discover, and yet the mink had disappeared. It was like some conjurer's trick.

Minks are fond of fish, and can capture them in the water. This makes them very destructive along small trout streams and ponds. I once saw a trout with an ugly gash in its side, which was doubtless the work of a mink. With a friend, I once had a camp by a trout stream in the Catskills that we named "Mink Camp," by reason of the number of minks that came every night as soon as it was dark, to devour the fishheads and entrails that we threw over on the opposite bank. We could often hear them disputing over the spoils, and in the dim light of the camp-fire could sometimes see them.

You may know the mink's track upon the snow from those of the squirrels at once. In the squirrel-track the prints of the large hind feet are ahead, with the prints of the smaller fore feet just behind them, as in the case of the rabbit. The mink, in running, usually plants his hind feet exactly upon the track of his fore feet, and closer together than the squirrel, so that his trail upon the snow is something like this:

The squirrel's track, as well as those of the rabbit and the white-footed mouse, is in form like this:

One winter day I had a good view of a mink running upon the snow and ice along the edge of a stream. He had seen or heard me, and was making a little extra speed. He bounded along with his back much arched, in a curiously stiff and mechanical sort of way, with none of the grace and ease of the squirrel. He leaped high, and cleared about two and a half feet at a bound.

A Hind in Richmond Park
Bird Migration on the Pampas [6]

W. H. HUDSON

Many favoring circumstances attended the boyhood of the naturalist-writer W. H. Hudson. He was born on the South American pampas, a land romantically untamed and beautiful. It was a paradise of bird-life when migration was on a tremendous scale. The boy Hudson saw flamingoes rise like clouds against the sky. He listened in ecstasy to the wild notes of the golden plover as he watched flock succeed flock the whole day long flying south over the great plain. Although Hudson left the pampas when a young man, the memory of it grew brighter with the passing years and his finest writing was inspired by memories of his boyhood. Of Hudson's writing, Galsworthy said, "As a simple narrator, he is well-nigh unsurpassed; as a stylist he has few equals."

The golden plover was then one of the abundant species. After its arrival in September, the plains in the neighborhood of my home were peopled with immense flocks of this bird. Sometimes in hot summers the streams and marshes would mostly dry up, and the aquatic bird population, the plover included, would shift their quarters to other districts. During one of these droughty seasons, when my age was nine, there was a marshy ground two miles from my home where a few small pools of water still remained, and to this spot the golden plover would resort every day at noon. They would appear in flocks from all quarters, flying to it like starlings in England coming in to some great roosting centre on a winter evening. I would then mount my pony and gal-

6 From W. H. Hudson, *A Hind in Richmond Park* (Dutton, 1922).

lop off joyfully to witness the spectacle. Long before coming in sight of them the noise of their voices would be audible, growing louder as I drew near. Coming to the ground, I would pull up my horse and sit gazing with astonishment and delight at the spectacle of that immense multitude of birds, covering an area of two or three acres, looking less like a vast flock than a *floor* of birds, in colour a rich deep brown, in strong contrast to the pale grey of the dried up ground all round them. A living, moving floor and a sounding one as well, and the sound too was amazing. It was like the sea, but unlike it in character since it was not deep; it was more like the wind blowing, let us say, on thousands of tight-drawn wires of varying thicknesses, vibrating them to shrill sound, a mass and tangle of ten thousand sounds. But it is indescribable and unimaginable.

Then I would put the birds up to enjoy the different sound of their rushing wings mingled with that of their cries, also the sight of them like a great cloud in the sky above me, casting a deep shadow on the earth.

The golden plover was but one of many equally if not more abundant species in its own as well as other orders, although they did not congregate in such astonishing numbers. On their arrival on the pampas they were invariably accompanied by two other species, the Eskimo curlew and the buff-breasted sandpiper. These all fed in company on the moist lands, but by-and-by the curlews passed on to more southern districts, leaving their companions behind, and the buff-breasted sandpipers were then seen to be much less numerous than the plover, about one bird to ten.

Now one autumn, when most of the emigrants to the Arctic breeding-grounds had already gone, I witnessed a great migration of this very species — this beautiful sandpiper with the habits of a plover. The birds appeared in flocks of about one to two or three hundred, flying low and very swiftly due north, flock succeeding flock at intervals of about ten or twelve minutes; and this migration continued for three days, or, at all events, three days from the first day I saw them, at a spot about two miles from my home. I was amazed at their numbers, and it was a puzzle to me then, and has been one ever since, that a species thinly distributed over the immense area of the Argentine pampas and Patagonia could keep to that one line of travel over that uniform green, sea-like country. For, outside of that line, not one bird of the kind could anywhere be seen; yet they kept so strictly to it that I sat each day for hours on my horse watching them pass, each flock first appearing as a faint buff-coloured blur or cloud just above the southern horizon, rapidly approaching then passing me, about on a level with my horse's head, to fade out of sight in a couple of minutes in the north; soon to be succeeded by another and yet other flocks in endless succession, each appearing at the same point as the one before, following the same line, as if a line invisible to all eyes except their own had been traced across the green world for their guidance. It gave one the idea that all the birds of this species, thinly distributed over tens of thousands of square miles of country, had formed the habit of assembling, previous to migration, at one starting-point, from which they set out in successive flocks of a medium size, in a disciplined order, on that marvellous journey to their Arctic breeding-grounds.

But of the smaller birds with a limited or partial migration, the military starling on his travels impressed and delighted me the most. Like a starling in shape, but larger than that bird, it has a dark plumage and scarlet breast. On the approach of winter it would appear all over the plains, not travelling in the manner of other migrants, speeding through the air, but feeding on the ground, probing the turf as starlings do, the whole flock drifting northwards at the same time. The flock, often numbering many hundreds of birds, would spread itself out, showing a long front line of scarlet breasts all turned one way, while the birds furthest in the rear would be continually flying on to drop down in advance of those at the front, so that every two or three minutes a new front line would be formed, and in this way the entire body, or army, would be slowly but continuously progressing.

How pleasant it was in those vanished years of an abundant bird life, when riding over the plain in winter, to encounter those loose, far-spread flocks with their long lines of red breasts showing so beautifully on the greensward! My memories of this bird alone would fill a chapter.

The autumnal migration, which was always a more impressive spectacle than that of the spring, began in February when the weather was still hot, and continued for three long months; for after the departure of all our own birds, the south Patagonian species that wintered with us or passed on their way to districts further north would begin to come in. During all these three long months the sight and sound of passage birds was a thing of every day, of every hour, so long as the light lasted, and after dark from time to time the cries of the night-travellers came to us from the sky — the weird laughter-like cry of rails, the shrill confused whistling of a great flock of whistling or tree duck; and, most frequent of all, the beautiful wild trisyllabic alarm cry of the upland plover.

Of this bird, the last on my list for this chapter, I must write at greater length; in the first place, for the purely sentimental reason that it was the one I loved best, and secondly, on account of the leading place it came to occupy in my mind when I thought about the problem of migration. It inhabits, or formerly inhabited, a great portion of the United States of North America, its summer or breeding home, then migrated south all the way to southern Argentina and Patagonia, and it was, I believe, most abundant on the great level pampas where I had my home. In North America it is known as the upland plover, and is also called the solitary plover and Bartram's sandpiper — for a sandpiper it is, albeit with the habits of a plover and a preference for dry lands. In the Argentine its vernacular name is Batitú, from its trisyllabic alarm note — one of the most frequently heard sounds on the pampas. It is a charming bird, white and grey with brown and yellow mottlings on its upper plumage, beautiful in its slender graceful form, with a long tail and long swallow-like pointed wings. All its motions are exceedingly graceful: it runs rapidly as a corn-crake before the rider's horse, then springs up with its wild musical cry to fly but twenty or thirty yards away and drop down again, to stand in a startled attitude flirting its long tail up and down. At times it flies up voluntarily, uttering a prolonged bubbling and inflected cry, and alights on a post or some such elevated place to open and hold its wings up vertically and continue for some time in that attitude — the artist's conventional figure of an angel.

These birds never flocked with us, even before departing; they were solitary, sprinkled evenly over the entire country, so that when out for a day on horseback I would flush one from the grass every few minutes; and when travelling or driving cattle on the pampas I have spent whole weeks on horseback from dawn to dark without being for a day out of sight or sound of the bird. When migrating its cry was heard at all hours from morning to night, from February till April: and again at night, especially when there was a moon.

Lying awake in bed, I would listen by the hour to that sound coming to me from the sky, mellowed and made beautiful by distance and the profound silence of the moonlit world, until it acquired a fascination for me above all sounds on earth, so that it lived ever after in me; and the image of it is as vivid in my mind at this moment as that of any bird call or cry, or any other striking sound heard yesterday or but an hour ago. It was the sense of mystery it conveyed which so attracted and impressed me — the mystery of that delicate, frail, beautiful being, travelling in the sky, alone, day and night, crying aloud at intervals as if moved by some powerful emotion, beating the air with its wings, its beak pointing like the needle of the compass to the north, flying, speeding on its seven-thousand-mile flight to its nesting home in another hemisphere.

Far Away and Long Ago

Flamingoes [7]

W. H. Hudson

Just before my riding days began in real earnest, when I was not yet quite confident enough to gallop off alone for miles to see the world for myself, I had my first long walk on the plain. One of my elder brothers invited me to accompany him to a water-course, one of the slow-flowing shallow marshy rivers of the pampas which was but two miles from home. The thought of the half-wild cattle we would meet terrified me, but he was anxious for my company that day and assured me that he could see no herd in that direction and he would be careful to give a wide berth to anything with horns we might come upon. Then I joyfully consented and we set out, three of us, to survey the wonders of a great stream of running water, where bulrushes grew and large wild birds, never seen by us at home, would be found. I had had a glimpse of the river before, as, when driving to visit a neighbour, we had crossed it at one of the fords and I had wished to get down and run on its moist green low banks, and now that desire would be gratified. It was for me a tremendously long walk, as we had to take many a turn to avoid the patches of cardoon and giant thistles, and by and by we came to low ground where the grass was almost waist-high and full of flowers. It was all like an English meadow in June, when every grass and every herb is in flower, beautiful and fragrant, but tiring to a boy six years old to walk through. At last we came out to a smooth grass turf, and in a little while were by the stream, which had overflowed its banks owing to recent heavy rains and was now about fifty yards wide. An astonishing number of birds were visible — chiefly wild duck, a few swans, and many waders — ibises, herons, spoonbills, and others, but the most wonderful of all were three immensely tall white-and-rose-coloured birds, wading solemnly in a row a yard or so apart from one another

some twenty yards out from the bank. I was amazed and enchanted at the sight, and my delight was intensified when the leading bird stood still and, raising his head and long neck aloft, opened and shook his wings. For the wings when open were of a glorious crimson colour, and the bird was to me the most angel-like creature on earth.

What were these wonderful birds? I asked of my brothers, but they could not tell me. They said they had never seen birds like them before, and later I found that the flamingo was not known in our neighbourhood as the water-courses were not large enough for it, but that it could be seen in flocks at a lake less than a day's journey from our home.

It was not for several years that I had an opportunity of seeing the bird again; later I have seen it scores and hundreds of times, at rest or flying, at all times of the day and in all states of the atmosphere, in all its most beautiful aspects, as when at sunset or in the early morning it stands motionless in the still water with its clear image reflected below; or when seen flying in flocks — seen from some high bank beneath one — moving low over the blue water in a long crimson line or half moon, the birds at equal distances apart, their wing-tips all but touching; but the delight in these spectacles has never equalled in degree that which I experienced on this occasion when I was six years old.

Beneath the Tropic Seas

Sponges [8]

William Beebe

⌁ *One of the least-known phenomena of the sea is the sponge. During World War II, sponges ceased to be gathered, for they are most commonly found in the Mediterranean, off the coast of the Bahamas, and off the west coast of Florida. After the war ended, the work began again. Of the five varieties found on the Florida coast, the sheep's wool is the most valu-*

[7] From W. H. Hudson, *Far Away and Long Ago* (Dutton, 1918).

[8] From William Beebe, *Beneath the Tropic Seas* (Putnam, 1928).

able. What the sponge boats bring in must be prepared for market, but that work is simple. The slimy, soft tissue soon decays out of the water and sloughs off; then the sponges are washed and beaten until the skeleton is clean, next threaded on a string, and dried. There have been some efforts to grow sponges artificially, by taking cuttings and using them for propagating, but so far these attempts have not proved profitable.

Sponges hold no mean position in the kingdom of animals, for they comprise a group equal to that which includes all backboned creatures from sharks to ourselves, and they have the honor of being the lowest living animals whose bodies consist of more than one cell.

. . . . . .

Let us enter the realm of sponges. With helmet, hose, and pump in order, I slip over the port gangway. With a last *Plop!* of air I submerge on my slim rope and slide gently down past the schooner's hull. The waves are high and the water is filled with powdered lime, and down and down I go through the heart of a liquid column of chalk — my uttermost horizon less than five feet away. A smudge at last appears beneath, and, in our present anchorage, at seven fathoms my feet touch bottom.

. . . . . .

I squat down, breathing as quietly as possible, and through the lime-filled murk I make out a scraggy sponge crag. I loosen it with my foot, and then, reaching down, tear it off and tuck it inside my belt, for I must have both hands free to climb, and untwist the hose. Before I dehelm, I hold up the sponge for safekeeping and, as soon as I reach the deck, submerge it in an aquarium.

The afternoon sun was pouring into my deck laboratory window when I placed a tiny bit of black sponge under my microscope and lost myself. There, stretching before me, lay slope after slope of brown downs, occasionally rising into a small, sharp hillock, and everywhere pitted with holes. If it had been plowed and gashed, it would have been the terrible volcanic wastes of Albemarle,

but here, instead, were mountain slopes collandered with innumerable gopher holes. Within my field of view were two oblong caves, etched deeply into the hills, and from these the perforated expanses swept downward into the awful gulfs of out-of-focusness. Having surveyed my penny-wide landscape, my eye settled to details, and suddenly I realized what I had known in the first place but had forgotten in the vividness of the mountain vision — that the whole landscape was a live, animal sponge. One of the cave mouths drew its lips together and blew forth a current of water, this being made visible by the smoke-like motes floating in it. I should not have been surprised to see the pensive, lonely eyes of the last "reluctant dragon" to appear, looking wistfully for his small boy friend. Scientifically, the sight of the cave mouth pursing its lips is an observation of considerable interest, for muscles of any kind in the integument of sponges are practically unknown.

. . . . . .

As we have seen, an active, excited sponge has, in the matter of movement, little advantage over a bit of sea moss, and yet an infant sponge, swirled out upon the current of the parent cave-mouth may found a new colony half a thousand miles away.

The eggs begin their development deep within the jelly-like tissues of the parent sponge, and one day, in company with unnumbered hosts of its fellow brood, an embryo works itself free, whirls around and around, and shoots out of the exhalant pore into the world of ocean. It looks like an infant balloon, the upper half of large, smooth cells, while those of the lower half each bear a long tail or flagellum which beats frantically upon the water. There is no unison or rhythm — each lash whips out at its own sweet will, but they do manage to beat more strongly in a backward direction, and thus the balloon forges ahead. The light attracts it, so it drifts along near the surface, its own power of propulsion being nothing in comparison with the force of winds and currents. In the course of time it acquires a distaste for the light, and therefore heads downward, and sooner or later bumps against the bottom. Here it sticks — the chance of striking a favorable spot for growth being probably one in a million. The larger cells increase rapidly and form an outer covering, the locomotor cells disappear within, and thereafter are of use in making their own private currents, whose eddies bear oxygen and particles of food to what is now a sponge.

No human being would hesitate if compelled to choose between being a seal and a seaweed. Yet there are some advantages in being rooted to one spot. The seal has to go after its meals and flee from its enemies, while a seaweed and a sponge simply sit and let the currents bring food to them.

Now and then a certain type of lucky spongelet alights on the back of a hermit crab's shell, and like a burr on a dog's coat, gets a free ride. In the case of the sponge this is for life, for it speedily dissolves the shell and forms an elastic and evergrowing coat for the fortunate crab. From now on, sponge and crab live amicably together.

. . . .

One day in April, when I had dived until I could stand it no longer, I drifted closer to the main reef of Samentin, and anchored just over a giant sponge. I had already made its acquaintance, and named an adjoining coral road "Sponge Alley." I had watched the life in and about it from a distance, had squatted beside it, observing it at close range, and finally sat upon it to rest, and to transcribe these notes with pencil upon a plate of zinc. It was larger than half a barrel and canted slightly to one side. I sent down one man who pried and cut it loose, and tied a rope around it. It was so heavy that he could barely lift it free of the bottom, to make the rope slip beneath. We drew it to the surface, but once out of water the combined efforts of four of us failed to get it over the gunwale. So down it went again, and when several hundred pounds of coral had been chopped out of its base, we had another try. This time, dealing with pure culture of sponge, we were successful. After it had been in the boat about two hours, and all the superfluous water had been drained off, its weight was little over a hundred and fifty pounds.

Men, Microscopes, and Living Things

Between the Heights and the Depths[9]

KATHERINE B. SHIPPEN

Miss Shippen has the remarkable ability to portray the past as a living factor in the life of today. In this book she traces the growth of the science of biology through the lives of the men who, from the earliest times to today, have contributed most to its development. The reader gains a clear picture of the relationship of one discovery to another, and he realizes that although man is constantly increasing his knowledge, there are still many things that he cannot yet explain. The opening chapter, which is given below, forms a background against which the lives and works of the great scientists pass in review.

High on the bleak flanks of the Himalaya Mountains, where no other animal life can survive and no green thing can grow, mountain climbers have found little jumping spiders. It is thought that they feed on pollen grains blown up to those high places by the wind. Eagles and vultures soar over those lonely peaks, though they come down to lower altitudes to rest.

Life is moving at the other extreme too, in the darkness of the ocean's floor. Strange fish live there in spite of enormous pressure and glacial cold. Some of them are furnished with phosphorescence, as if they were carrying lanterns in the ocean's dark. Here too are diatoms, the microscopic plant life of the sea, and little single-celled creatures, called radiolarians, that look like lacy snowflakes.

Between these heights and depths, as the ball of the earth moves around the sun, are all the living things we know — the trees and the grass; the spiders and the bees; the ants and the grasshoppers; the birds and bright-scaled fish; the oysters and clams; the dolphins, whales, and man himself. The earth and air and sea are filled with their activity. They are feeding and growing, re-

[9] From Katherine B. Shippen, *Men, Microscopes, and Living Things* (Viking Press, 1955).

producing their kind and dying, in endless cycles. Furry animals and those with hairy hides are moving through the forests and across the plains; birds are gathering for their great migrations; mosses and lichens, ferns and fungi, are taking nourishment from the earth and air. Clams, sponges, and corals follow their various ways.

For life is movement and activity. The only real quietness is death.

Among all the various living things, man takes his place, for he is part of them. Like all the rest he must seek nourishment, must reproduce his kind, and die.

But man is different from the other living things. He is the only one who can control the environment in which he lives. And only gradually has he become aware of the life around him. Only very recently has he understood that all living things are connected with one another like a great chain of many links, and that he himself is a part of the chain.

When he learned to use fire, to domesticate animals and cultivate the fields, he had dominion over other living things. He learned early which serpents were dangerous, which vegetables could be eaten, which animals tamed for work. He learned to live in a cave and later to build himself a house. He learned to use the furs and fleece of animals to make himself garments, because nature had given him such poor protection from the cold.

Man was different from the living things around him because he used his ingenuity to sustain his life and to control his environment.

But though man dominated the things around him he did not understand them, nor did it seem at all possible to him that there was any connection between him and them. He would have been surprised if anyone had told him that he was in any way related to a jellyfish or that the substance of a lily pad was like the stuff of which his hand was made. A jellyfish was a jellyfish, and a lily pad was a lily pad, and he was a man. There were countless plants and animals that he had never even noticed, but it did not matter.

As time passed, gifted men of various races took living things as models for designs in painting or in weaving. So in an old Egyptian papyrus you may see ducks swimming among the reeds at the edge of the Nile, or in a Persian rug a pattern of intermingled flowers. The Minoans carved animals, and painted them on the walls of their palaces more than two thousand years before Christ. Here you may see antelopes quietly feeding or startled at a sound; there fallow deer are browsing, or dogs are chasing them. The figures are carefully portrayed. The lie of the feathers on a bird's head, the teeth in a lion's mouth, the placing of the scales on the side of a fish — all these were noticed and set down. But the purpose of such work was to affirm the beauty of fish, beast, or flower, not to explain its structure. Perhaps the artist portrayed it so accurately because he could imagine nothing more perfect than its natural form.

The Greeks, with their boundless curiosity and their zest for living, were the first to be scientifically interested in living things. Hippocrates, in the seventh century before Christ, founded a school of medicine where dissections were done and a list of medicinal plants was made.

We still have a few of Hippocrates' writings; it is possible to see in them how the ancient physicians worked. One passage of his book is especially interesting, for it shows what might be called a scientific attitude toward the human body. Some people had said that certain diseases were caused by the gods, but Hippocrates wrote: "It does not matter whether you call such things divine or not. In nature all things are alike in this, that they can be traced to preceding causes. . . ."

Those early Greek scientists in Hippocrates' medical school, forever trying to seek out the causes of things, did not stop even at trying to find out the cause of life itself. All things are made of earth, air, fire, and water, they said.

But even the early Greeks did not observe nature for its own sake, but only to cure the ailments of their bodies. Aristotle was the first to watch, to try to classify, to attempt to find out how life begins, and to write down his observations. Some scientists today

believe he was the greatest natural scientist
of all time.

The questions that Aristotle asked have
not all been answered. For a long time the
books that he wrote were neglected and his
work was half forgotten. Then, one after
another, gifted, curious men took up the
work he had begun, found errors he had
made, checked facts he had established,
added new facts, until gradually science attempted to explore everything in the domain
of life from the highest mountains to the
deepest seas. Slowly man tried not merely
to dominate and use, but to understand.

The Sea Around Us
The Moving Tides [1]

RACHEL L. CARSON

⌘ The Sea Around Us *is an enthralling study
of the mystery and beauty of the ocean with
its islands, mountains, vast depths, and its fascinating sea-life. With rare skill, Rachel Carson combines scientific accuracy with poetic
imagination. Something of the rhythm and
sweeping force of the sea itself is found in her
writing. In the chapter given below, Miss Carson tells of the mysterious forces that create the
tides and the influence of the tide over the
affairs of the sea creatures.*

There is no drop of water in the ocean,
not even in the deepest parts of the abyss,
that does not know and respond to the
mysterious forces that create the tide. No
other force that affects the sea is so strong.
Compared with the tide the wind-created
waves are surface movements felt, at most,
no more than a hundred fathoms below the
surface. So, despite their impressive sweep,
are the planetary currents, which seldom in-
volve more than the upper several hundred
fathoms. The masses of water affected by
the tidal movement are enormous, as will
be clear from one example. Into one small
bay on the east coast of North America —
Passamaquoddy — 2 billion tons of water are
carried by the tidal currents twice each day;

[1] From Rachel L. Carson, *The Sea Around Us*
(Oxford University Press, 1951).

into the whole Bay of Fundy, 100 million
tons.

Here and there we find dramatic illustration of the fact that the tides affect the
whole ocean, from its surface to its floor.
The meeting of opposing tidal currents in
the Strait of Messina creates whirlpools (one
of them is Charybdis of classical fame) which
so deeply stir the waters of the strait that
fish bearing all the marks of abyssal existence,
their eyes atrophied or abnormally large,
their bodies studded with phosphorescent organs, frequently are cast up on the lighthouse beach, and the whole area yields a
rich collection of deep-sea fauna for the
Institute of Marine Biology at Messina.

The tides are a response of the mobile
waters of the ocean to the pull of the moon
and the more distant sun. In theory, there
is a gravitational attraction between every
drop of sea water and even the outermost
star of the universe. In practice, however,
the pull of the remote stars is so slight as
to be obliterated in the vaster movements
by which the ocean yields to the moon and
the sun. Anyone who has lived near tide-
water knows that the moon, far more than
the sun, controls the tides. He has noticed
that, just as the moon rises later each day
by fifty minutes, on the average, than the
day before, so, in most places, the time of
high tide is correspondingly later each day.
And as the moon waxes and wanes in its
monthly cycle, so the height of the tide
varies. Twice each month, when the moon
is a mere thread of silver in the sky, and
again when it is full, we have the highest
of the high tides, called the springs. At
these times sun, moon, and earth are directly
in line and the pull of the two heavenly
bodies is added together to bring the water
high on the beaches, and send its surf leaping upward against the sea cliffs, and draw
a brimming tide into the harbors so that
the boats float high beside their wharfs.
And twice each month, at the quarters of
the moon, when sun, moon, and earth lie
at the apexes of a triangle, and the pull of
sun and moon are opposed, we have the least
tides of the lunar month, called the neaps.

The influence of the tide over the affairs
of sea creatures as well as men may be seen

all over the world. The billions upon billions of sessile animals, like oysters, mussels, and barnacles, owe their very existence to the sweep of the tides, which brings them the food which they are unable to go in search of. By marvelous adaptations of form and structure, the inhabitants of the world between the tide lines are enabled to live in a zone where the danger of being dried up is matched against the danger of being washed away, where for every enemy that comes by sea there is another comes by land, and where the most delicate of living tissues must somehow withstand the assault of storm waves that have the power to shift tons of rock or to crack the hardest granite.

The most curious and incredibly delicate adaptations, however, are the ones by which the breeding rhythm of certain marine animals is timed to coincide with the phases of the moon and the stages of the tide. In Europe it has been well established that the spawning activities of oysters reach their peak on the spring tides, which are about two days after the full or the new moon. In the waters of northern Africa there is a sea urchin that, on the nights when the moon is full and apparently only then, releases its reproductive cells into the sea. And in tropical waters in many parts of the world there are small marine worms whose spawning behavior is so precisely adjusted to the tidal calendar that, merely from observing them, one could tell the month, the day, and often the time of day as well.

Near Samoa in the Pacific, the palolo worm lives out its life on the bottom of the shallow sea, in holes in the rocks and among the masses of corals. Twice each year, during the neap tides of the moon's last quarter in October and November, the worms forsake their burrows and rise to the surface in swarms that cover the water. For this purpose, each worm has literally broken its body in two, half to remain in its rocky tunnel, half to carry the reproductive products to the surface and there to liberate the cells. This happens at dawn on the day before the moon reaches its last quarter, and again on the following day; on the second day of the spawning the quantity of eggs liberated is so great that the sea is discolored.

The Fijians, whose waters have a similar worm, call them 'Mbalolo' and have designated the periods of their spawning 'Mbalolo lailai' (little) for October and 'Mbalolo levu' (large) for November. Similar forms near the Gilbert Islands respond to certain phases of the moon in June and July; in the Malay Archipelago a related worm swarms at the surface on the second and third nights after the full moon of March and April, when the tides are running highest. A Japanese palolo swarms after the new moon and again after the full moon in October and November.

Concerning each of these, the question recurs but remains unanswered: is it the state of the tides that in some unknown way supplies the impulse from which springs this behavior, or is it, even more mysteriously, some other influence of the moon? It is easier to imagine that it is the press and the rhythmic movement of the water that in some way brings about this response. But why is it only certain tides of the year, and why for some species is it the fullest tides of the month and for others the least movements of the waters that are related to the perpetuation of the race? At present, no one can answer.

No other creature displays so exquisite an adaptation to the tidal rhythm as the grunion —a small, shimmering fish about as long as a man's hand. Though no one can say what processes of adaptation, extending over no one knows how many millennia, the grunion has come to know not only the daily rhythm of the tides, but the monthly cycle by which certain tides sweep higher on the beaches than others. It has so adapted its spawning habits to the tidal cycle that the very existence of the race depends on the precision of this adjustment.

Shortly after the full moon of the months from March to August, the grunion appear in the surf on the beaches of California. The tide reaches flood stage, slackens, hesitates, and begins to ebb. Now on these waves of the ebbing tide the fish begin to come in. Their bodies shimmer in the light of the moon as they are borne up the beach on the crest of a wave, they lie glittering on the wet sand for a perceptible moment of time, then fling themselves into the wash of the next wave and are carried back to sea. For about an hour after the turn of the tide this continues, thousands upon thousands of grunion coming up onto the beach, leaving the water, returning to it. This is the spawning act of the species.

During the brief interval between successive waves, the male and female have come together in the wet sand, the one to shed her eggs, the other to fertilize them. When the parent fish return to the water, they have left behind a mass of eggs buried in the sand. Succeeding waves on that night do not wash out the eggs because the tide is already ebbing. The waves of the next high tide will not reach them, because for a time after the full of the moon each tide will halt its advance a little lower on the beach than the preceding one. The eggs, then, will be undisturbed for at least a fortnight. In the warm, damp, incubating sand they undergo their development. Within two weeks the magic change from fertilized egg to larval fishlet is completed, the perfectly formed little grunion still confined within the membranes of the egg, still buried in the sand, waiting for release. With the tides of the new moon it comes. Their waves wash over the places where the little masses of the grunion eggs were buried, the swirl and rush of the surf stirring the sand deeply. As the sand is washed away, and the eggs feel the touch of the cool sea water, the membranes rupture, the fishlets hatch, and the waves that released them bear them away to the sea.

But the link between tide and living creature I like best to remember is that of a very small worm, flat of body, with no distinction of appearance, but with one unforgettable quality. The name of this worm is *Convoluta roscoffensis,* and it lives on the sandy beaches of northern Brittany and the Channel Islands. Convoluta has entered into a remarkable partnership with a green alga, whose cells inhabit the body of the worm and lend to its tissues their own green color. The worm lives entirely on the starchy products manufactured by its plant guest, having become so completely dependent upon this means of nutrition that its digestive organs have degenerated. In order that the algal cells may carry on their function of photosynthesis (which is dependent upon sunlight) Convoluta rises from the damp sands of the intertidal zone as soon as the tide has ebbed, the sand becoming spotted with large green patches composed of thousands of the worms. For the several hours while the tide is out, the worms lie thus in the sun, and the plants manufacture their starches and sugars; but when the tide returns, the worms must again sink into the sand to avoid being washed away, out into deep water. So the whole lifetime of the worm is a succession of movements conditioned by the stages of the tide — upward into sunshine on the ebb, downward on the flood.

What I find most unforgettable about Convoluta is this: sometimes it happens that a marine biologist, wishing to study some related problem, will transfer a whole colony of the worms into the laboratory, there to establish them in an aquarium, where there are no tides. But twice each day Convoluta rises out of the sand on the bottom of the aquarium, into the light of the sun. And twice each day it sinks again into the sand. Without a brain, or what we would call a memory, or even any very clear perception, Convoluta continues to live out its life in this alien place, remembering, in every fiber of its small green body, the tidal rhythm of the distant sea.

BIBLIOGRAPHY

Buck, Margaret Waring. *In Woods and Fields;* illus. by the author. Abingdon, 1950. (Grades 4–8)

An informal and delightful introduction to nature study covering the northeastern part of the United States. Arrangement is first by season and then by habitat. Companion volumes are *In Yards and Gardens* and *In Ponds and Streams.*

Carrighar, Sally. *One Day at Teton Marsh;* illus. by George and Patricia Mattson. Alfred A. Knopf, 1947. (High School)

The author of *One Day on Beetle Rock* describes the effect of the first touch of winter on the animals, birds, and other wildlife that live in and around the marsh in the valley of the Teton Mountains in Wyoming.

Comstock, Anna. *Handbook of Nature-Study.* Comstock Publishing Co., 24th ed. 1939.

Based on the Cornell University nature-study leaflets, this book contains a wealth of material helpful for teachers.

Crouse, William. *Understanding Science;* illus. by Jeanne Bendick. Whittlesey House, new rev. ed. 1956. (Grades 6–9)

New material covers such areas as fusion, color TV, rockets, space platforms, earth satellites, and transistors.

Fisher, James. *The Wonderful World;* illus. in full color. Garden City, 1954. (Grades 5–8)

Brief text, richly colored illustrations, shadow-relief maps, and diagrams explain how nature and man have shaped and are shaping the world.

Huntington, Harriet E. *Let's Go Outdoors;* illus. by Preston Duncan. Doubleday, 1939. (Grades 1–4)

An invitation to small children to go outdoors and see what they can see. Companion volumes are *Let's Go to the Brook, Let's Go to the Desert,* and *Let's Go to the Seashore.*

Hyde, Margaret. *Exploring Earth and Space, the Story of the I.G.Y.* Whittlesey House, 1957. (Grades 7–9)

A challenging account of the aims and projects of more than 5,000 scientists and 55 nations cooperating in the world-wide International Geophysical Year.

Life editorial staff and Lincoln Barnett. *The World We Live In;* text adapted by Jane Werner Watson. Simon & Schuster, 1956. (Grades 5–9)

A physical history of our planet, Earth — its formation and the forms of life upon it.

Meyer, Jerome S. *The Elements; Builders of the Universe;* illus. with 68 photographs. World Publishing Co., 1957. (High School)

A stimulating introduction to the natural and man-made chemical elements that are the basis of the physical world.

Parker, Bertha Morris. *Golden Treasury of Natural History.* Simon & Schuster, 1952. (Grades 4–6)

About birds, fish, plants, trees, flowers, animals, the sun, stars, and planets. Attractively illustrated in full color. *The Golden Book of Science* (1956) is a companion volume.

Peattie, Donald Culross. *The Rainbow Book of Nature;* illus. by Rudolf Freund. World Publishing Co., 1957. (Grades 5–9)

Edwin Way Teale calls this "a wonderfully beautiful door-opening book."

Platt, Rutherford. *Walt Disney's Worlds of Nature.* Simon & Schuster, 1957. (Grades 5–8)

Interesting, informative text and three hundred color photographs from all twelve of Walt Disney's True-Life Adventure films make up a fascinating "library of wildlife."

Air and Weather

Adler, Irving. *Hurricanes and Twisters,* by Robert Irving, *pseud.* Alfred A. Knopf, 1955. (Grades 4–8)

Basic explanation of the causes, nature, and behavior of hurricanes and tornadoes.

Bell, Thelma Harrington. *Snow;* with drawings by Corydon Bell. Viking Press, 1954. (Grades 4–7)

Describes in an unusually interesting way how snowflakes are formed, their types and sizes. It also gives an account of frost, sleet, and hail.

Blough, Glenn. *Not Only for Ducks: the Story of Rain;* illus. by Jeanne Bendick. Whittlesey House, 1954. (Grades 3–5)

A simple story of the water cycle and the many forms of life dependent upon it.

Lehr, Paul, and others. *Weather*. Simon & Schuster, 1957. (Grades 7–9)

A useful handbook similar in format to other Golden Nature Guides.

Schneider, Herman. *Everyday Weather and How It Works;* pictures by Jeanne Bendick. Whittlesey House, 1951. (Grades 5–8)

An explanation of "what makes the weather" and how to read weather maps.

Tannehill, Ivan Ray. *All About the Weather;* illus. by René Martin. Random House, 1953. (Grades 4–8)

By the director of weather reporting and forecasting for the U.S. Weather Bureau.

Zim, Herbert S. *Lightning and Thunder;* illus. by James Gordon Irving. William Morrow, 1952. (Grades 4–7)

Describes the different kinds of lightning and explains causes of lightning and thunder.

Animals and Other Mammals

Andrews, Roy Chapman. *All About Whales;* illus. by Thomas W. Voter. Random House, 1954. (Grades 5–8)

Scientific facts about whales by an authority on the subject.

Bridges, William. *Zoo Babies;* illus. with photographs. William Morrow, 1953. (Grades 3–6)

True stories of some of the baby animals in New York's Bronx zoo, told by the curator of publications. Companion volumes are *Zoo Expeditions* and *Zoo Doctor*.

Bronson, Wilfrid S. *Children of the Sea;* illus. by the author. Harcourt, Brace, 1940. (Grades 6–8)

The tale of a dolphin and of its friendship with a boy who lived on the island of Nassau.

Buff, Mary and Conrad. *Dash and Dart;* illus. by Conrad Buff. Viking Press, 1942. (Grades 1–4)

The first year in the life of two fawns, told with poetic beauty. *Hurry, Scurry, and Flurry* by the same author is the story of three squirrels.

Earle, Olive. *Paws, Hoofs and Flippers;* illus. by the author. William Morrow, 1954. (Grades 5–8)

Comprehensive description of the distinguishing characteristics of mammals grouped according to types of feet.

George, John and Jean. *Masked Prowler;* illus. by Jean George. E. P. Dutton, 1956. (Grades 5–8)

After reading *Vulpes, the Red Fox*, children will enjoy this story of a raccoon.

Hegner, Robert and Jane. *Parade of the Animal Kingdom*. Macmillan, 1935. (Grades 7–9)

Natural history presented in a popular manner and illustrated with seven hundred photographs.

Henry, Marguerite. *Album of Horses;* illus. by Wesley Dennis. Rand McNally, 1951. (Grades 5–9)

A skillful text, with full-page color portraits, gives an account of twenty-two breeds of horses. *Wagging Tails; an Album of Dogs* is a companion volume.

Hogner, Dorothy. *Animal Book; American Mammals North of Mexico;* illus. by Nils Hogner. Oxford University Press, 1942. (Grades 7–9)

A well-organized handbook of mammals with stimulating text and excellent illustrations.

Liers, Emil E. *An Otter's Story;* illus. by Tony Palazzo. Viking Press, 1953. (Grades 5–8)

The dramatic story of a young otter growing up and raising a family in the North Woods. The naturalist Liers was Disney's technical adviser for his movie *Beaver Valley*.

McCracken, Harold. *Biggest Bear on Earth;* illus. by Paul Branson. J. B. Lippincott, 1943. (Grades 5–8)

A fascinating account of Little Roughneck based on the author's first-hand study of the Alaskan brown bears.

Osmond, Edward. *Animals of the World;* illus. by the author. Oxford University Press, 1956. (Grades 5–9)

Physical characteristics and habits of African and Indian elephants, Arabian and Bactrian camels, polar bears, and chimpanzees. The plant, animal, and human life native to each habitat are described.

Zim, Herbert S. *Elephants;* pictures by Joy Buba. William Morrow, 1946. (Grades 2–4)

Everything about elephants told in simple text with excellent pictures. Companion volume: *Monkeys*.

Zim, Herbert S., and Donald Hoffmeister. *Mammals; a Guide to Familiar American Species;* illus. by James Gordon Irving. Simon & Schuster, 1955. (Grades 5–9)

Gives habits and habitats for 218 species.

Archaeology

Jessup, Ronald. *The Wonderful World of Archaeology;* illus. in full color. Garden City, 1956. (Grades 5–9)

An accurate text combines with an impressive variety of paintings, diagrams, maps, and other illustrations to dramatize an exciting scientific field.

White, Anne Terry. *Lost Worlds; Adventures in Archaeology;* illus. with maps. Random House, 1941. (Grades 6–9)

The finding of four lost civilizations contains all the thrills of a great mystery.

Astronomy

Baker, Robert. *When the Stars Come Out.* Viking Press, rev. ed. 1954. (Grades 7–9)

One of the best books on astronomy. This edition has been revised to include recent astronomical discoveries. The author is a professor of astronomy at the University of Illinois. His *Introducing the Constellations* was revised in 1957.

Fenton, Carroll Lane and Mildred. *Worlds in the Sky;* illus. by the authors. John Day, 1950. (Grades 4–7)

Based on facts and principles of astronomy, yet simple enough for young children.

Freeman, Mae and Ira. *Fun with Astronomy;* illus. with photographs. Random House, 1953. (Grades 4–8)

A practical introduction to astronomy, with simple experiments by which a child can understand the principles involved in day and night and seasonal changes.

Gallant, Roy. *Exploring the Universe;* illus. by Lowell Hess. Garden City, 1956. (Grades 5–7)

Theories and discoveries of early astronomers and present-day concepts about the universe are discussed in this book which won the Thomas Alva Edison award for the best children's science book of 1956.

Reed, William Maxwell. *Stars for Sam;* ed. by Charles E. St. John; decorations by Karl Moseley. Harcourt, Brace, 1931. (Grades 5–8)

The author, a former professor of astronomy at Harvard, wrote this book for his nine-year-old nephew.

Rey, H. A. *Find the Constellations.* Houghton Mifflin, 1954. (Grades 4–8)

The aim is to make recognition of the stars easier by means of "sky-views" which show the sky throughout the year. Includes chapters on the solar system and space travel.

Schneider, Herman and Nina. *You, Among the Stars;* illus. by Symeon Shimin. William R. Scott, 1951. (Grades 3–5)

An elementary book describing the plan of the universe.

Wyler, Rose, and Gerald Ames. *The Golden Book of Astronomy;* illus. by John Polgreen. Simon & Schuster, 1955. (Grades 5–9)

A child's introduction to the wonders of the heavens and the possibilities of space travel.

Zim, Herbert S., and Robert H. Baker. *Stars; a Guide to the Constellations, Sun, Moon, Planets and Other Features of the Heavens;* illus. by James Gordon Irving. Simon & Schuster, rev. ed. 1956. (Grades 7–9)

First published in 1951, this revised edition adds new material on the universe and solar system. In *The Sun* (William Morrow, 1953) Dr. Zim explains why life on earth is dependent on light and heat from the sun.

Atomic Energy

Cooke, David C. *How Atomic Submarines are Made;* illus. with photographs. Dodd, Mead, 1957. (Grades 5–7)

Through words and pictures the author describes each step in the building of an undersea atomic-powered boat.

Haber, Heinz. *The Walt Disney Story of Our Friend the Atom;* illus. by staff artists of the Walt Disney Studio. Simon & Schuster, 1957. (Grades 5–9)

This book, striking in format, with interesting text, gives a clear, comprehensive picture of atomic energy.

Lewellen, John. *You and Atomic Energy, and Its Wonderful Uses;* illus. by Lois Fisher. Children's Press, 1949. (Grades 5–9)

Cartoon-like drawings, diagrams, and simple text explain how atomic energy is released and how it can be used for constructive purposes. The author has also written *The Mighty Atom* (Knopf, 1955).

Aviation

Ahnstrom, D. N. *The Complete Book of Jets and Rockets;* illus. with photographs and diagrams. World Publishing Co., 1957. (Grade 7 up)

The story of the discovery of jet propulsion and how it works, combined with fascinating facts about flying and heroic test pilots. *The Complete Book of Helicopters* is a companion volume.

Beeland, Lee, and Robert Wells. *Space Satellite; the Story of the Man-Made Moon;* illus. by Jack Coggins. Prentice-Hall, 1957. (Grades 5–8)

A dynamic, full-scale account of Project Vanguard.

Bendick, Jeanne. *The First Book of Airplanes;* illus. by the author. Franklin Watts, 1952. (Grades 3–6)

Starting with the rudiments of flying, the author tells of the types of planes made for various purposes. *The First Book of Space Travel* is a companion volume.

Coggins, Jack, and Fletcher Pratt. *By Space Ship to the Moon.* Random House, 1952. (Grades 5–9)

Describes a projected expedition to the moon and discusses the problems yet to be solved. *Rockets, Jets, Guided Missiles and Space Ships* gives an account of the development of rocket science.

Coombs, Charles. *Rockets, Missiles, and Moons;* illus. with photographs. William Morrow, 1957. (Grade 7 up)

A survey of developments in space travel, earth-circling satellites, and intercontinental ballistic missiles.

Dalgliesh, Alice. *Ride on the Wind;* told from *The Spirit of St. Louis,* by Charles A. Lindbergh; illus. by Georges Schreiber. Charles Scribner's Sons, 1956. (Grades 3–5)

Charles Lindbergh's boyhood and his famous flight, told from *The Spirit of St. Louis* with the cooperative interest of General Lindbergh.

Lewellen, John. *The Earth Satellite;* illus. by Ida Scheib. Alfred A. Knopf, 1957. (Grades 4–6)

A brief, clear account of the problems of launching an earth satellite, and of what scientists hoped to learn from the experiment.

Lindbergh, Charles A. *The Spirit of St. Louis.* Charles Scribner's Sons, 1953. (High School)

A distinguished account of Lindbergh's famous first flight to Paris. The book won the Pulitzer Prize for 1954.

Neurath, Marie. *New Wonders in Flying.* Lothrop, Lee & Shepard, 1957. (All ages)

Describes a collapsible plane, a gigantic tanker that can refuel four fighters at once in mid-air, and other wonders of flight.

Shippen, Katherine. *Bridle for Pegasus;* illus. by C. B. Falls. Viking Press, 1951. (Grades 7–9)

The colorful pageant of the development of flight traced through accounts of the men and women whose vision and courage turned a dream into reality.

Birds

Boulton, Rudyerd. *Traveling with the Birds;* illus. by Walter Alois Weber. Donahue, 1933. (Grades 4–6)

A picture book on bird migration with full-page pictures in color.

Earle, Olive. *Robins in the Garden;* illus. by the author. William Morrow, 1953. (Grades 1–4)

An easy-to-read factual account of a pair of robins and their family from early spring to late fall. Children a little older will enjoy *Birds and Their Nests* by the same author.

Kieran, John. *Introduction to Birds;* illus. by Don Eckelberry. Garden City, 1950. (Grades 5–9)

An entertaining introduction to the common birds of North America.

McClung, Robert M. *Ruby Throat; the Story of a Humming Bird;* illus. by the author. William Morrow, 1950. (K–Grade 3)

One year in the life of a hummingbird.

Mathews, Ferdinand S. *Book of Birds for Young People.* G. P. Putnam's Sons, 1921. (Grades 6–9)

Birds of Eastern North America, their habits and songs.

Webb, Addison. *Birds in Their Homes;* pictures by Sabra Kimball. Garden City, 1947. (Grades 3–5)

Fifty-four birds of garden, city, and country.

Zim, Herbert S., and Iran Gabrielson. *Birds;* illus. by James Gordon Irving. Simon & Schuster, 1949. (Grades 5–9)

A guide to the most familiar American birds.

Conservation

Shippen, Katherine B. *The Great Heritage;* illus. by C. B. Falls. Viking Press, 1947. (Grades 7–9)

A distinguished and scholarly appraisal of America's resources from the time the country was first settled to the present.

Smith, Frances C. *The First Book of Conservation;* illus. by René Martin. Franklin Watts, 1954. (Grades 4–7)

How wildlife, forests, plants, rivers, lakes, and the earth itself all depend on nature's interrelationships; and what man is doing to conserve and renew his natural resources.

The Earth

Pough, Frederick. *All About Volcanoes and Earthquakes;* illus. by Kurt Wiese. Random House, 1953. (Grades 5–7)

The author was former curator of physical geography and minerals at the American Museum of Natural History.

Reed, William Maxwell. *The Earth for Sam; the Story of Mountains, Rivers, Dinosaurs and Men;* drawings by Karl Moseley. Harcourt, Brace, 1930. (Grades 5–8)

Describes the changes which have taken place in the earth during various geologic periods.

Schneider, Herman and Nina. *Rocks, Rivers and the Changing Earth.* William R. Scott, 1952. (Grades 6–9)

A readable first book about geology. Line drawings give visual explanations. Simple experiments are suggested.

Sterling, Dorothy. *The Story of Caves;* illus. by Winifred Lubel. Doubleday, 1956. (Grades 5–8)

How caves are "made" and the strange creatures and formations inside them.

Zim, Herbert S. *What's Inside the Earth?;* illus. by Raymond Perlman. William Morrow, 1953. (Grades 4–6)

A book for parent and child to read together, explaining the mysteries inside the earth.

Electricity

Beeler, Nelson, and Franklyn Branley. *Experiments with Electricity;* illus. by A. W. Revell. Thomas Y. Crowell, 1949. (Grades 5–8)

The authors are experienced teachers of science.

Bendick, Jeanne. *Electronics for Young People;* illus. by the author. Whittlesey House, new rev. ed. 1955. (Grades 6–8)

This new edition has an enlarged section on atomic energy.

Epstein, Samuel and Beryl. *First Book of Electricity;* illus. by Robin King. Franklin Watts, 1953. (Grades 4–7)

A clear presentation of the ways in which electricity works, especially in the home.

Freeman, Mae and Ira. *Fun with Science;* illus. with photographs. Random House, rev. ed. 1956. (Grades 5–8)

A picture book explaining a series of experiments in physics. *Fun with Chemistry* is a companion book.

Hogben, Lancelot. *The Wonderful World of Energy;* illus. in full color. Garden City, 1957. (Grades 5–9)

The mysteries of practical physics are explained by showing how its principles are used every day.

The author also tells how man has organized nature's sources of power to work for him.

Lewellen, John. *Understanding Electronics; From Vacuum Tube to Thinking Machine;* illus. by Ida Scheib. Thomas Y. Crowell, 1957. (Grades 7–9)

Explains in a concise and thorough manner what electronics is and how it works.

Morgan, Alfred. *First Electrical Book for Boys;* illus. by the author. Charles Scribner's Sons, rev. ed. 1951. (Grades 5–8)

This edition has been brought up to date on the subjects of radio, television, radar, and electronics. *The Boys' Second Book of Radio and Electronics* was published in 1957.

Shippen, Katherine. *Bright Design;* illus. by Charles Daugherty. Viking Press, 1949. (Grades 7–9)

A graphic account of men and women from medieval times to the present who helped discover the secrets of electrical energy.

Engineering

Billings, Henry. *Bridges;* illus. by the author. Viking Press, 1956. (Grades 7–9)

Admirably clear explanations of the principles of different types of bridge construction and the engineering problems.

Ley, Willy. *Engineers' Dreams;* illus. by Isami Kashiwagi. Viking Press, 1954. (Grades 7–9)

Plans engineers have made, but which, for either political or financial reasons, have never been carried out: a tunnel under the English Channel, sea-drome islands for transocean air refueling stations, irrigation of the Jordan River valley, and harnessing power from the sun.

Ross, Frank, Jr. *The World of Engineering;* illus. with photographs. Lothrop, Lee & Shepard, 1957. (High School)

A survey of the entire field of engineering from its ancient beginnings to its myriad activities today.

Frogs and Toads

Bronson, Wilfrid S. *Polliwiggle's Progress;* illus. by the author. Macmillan, 1932. (Grades 3–5)

The life cycle of a bullfrog told in a fascinating way.

Gall, Alice Crew, and Fleming Crew. *Wagtail;* illus. by Kurt Wiese. Oxford University Press, 1932. (Grades 3–5)

The life story of a tadpole, as he changes to a frog. Children will also enjoy *Little Black Ant* by the same authors.

McClung, Robert M. *Bufo; the Story of a Toad;* illus. by the author. William Morrow, 1954. (Grades 1–3)

The story of the first three years in the life of a toad.

Zim, Herbert S. *Frogs and Toads;* illus. by Joy Buba. William Morrow, 1950. (Grades 4–6)

Explains many differences among frogs and toads.

The Human Body

Ravielli, Anthony. *Wonders of the Human Body;* illus. by the author. Viking Press, 1954. (Grades 5–8)

The body is shown as the most perfect of all machines. The book is distinguished in format.

Schneider, Herman and Nina. *How Your Body Works;* illus. by Barbara Ivins. William R. Scott, 1949. (Grades 5–8)

An excellent introduction to physiology.

Zim, Herbert S. *What's Inside of Me?;* illus. by Herschel Wartik. William Morrow, 1952. (Grades 2–5)

A simple account of the functions of the internal organs of the human body, illustrated with charts which clarify the text.

Insects

Bronson, Wilfrid S. *The Wonder World of Ants;* illus. by the author. Harcourt, Brace, 1937. (Grades 4–6)

The fascinating story of ants told by a scientist who has the happy faculty of combining scientific information with a sense of humor.

Harpster, Hilda. *Insect World;* illus. by Zhenya Gay. Viking Press, 1947. (Grades 7–9)

A comprehensive treatment of insects written with literary skill as well as scientific accuracy.

Hylander, Clarence J. *Insects on Parade;* illus. with photographs. Macmillan, 1957. (Grades 7–9)

In the parade are representatives of the common groups of insects: bugs, beetles, dragonflies, grasshoppers, moths, butterflies, flies, wasps, and ants.

Teale, Edwin Way. *The Junior Book of Insects;* illus. by the author. E. P. Dutton, 1953. (Grades 6–9)

Interesting facts about the lives and habits of the common insects, with simple instructions for collecting and studying them.

Tibbets, Albert B. *The First Book of Bees;* illus. by Hélène Carter. Franklin Watts, 1952. (Grades 4–6)

Beautiful drawings in color help dramatize the activities of the honey bees.

Williamson, Margaret. *The First Book of Bugs;* illus. by the author. Franklin Watts, 1949. (Grades 3–5)

An excellent introductory book.

Zim, Herbert S., and Clarence Cottam. *Insects;* illus. by James Gordon Irving. Simon & Schuster, 1951. (Grades 5–9)

A guide to 225 American insects.

Inventions

Darrow, Floyd, and Clarence Hylander. *The Boys' Own Book of Great Inventions.* Macmillan, 1941. (Grades 7–9)

Accounts of great inventions and how they are applied and utilized.

Hartman, Gertrude. *Machines and the Men Who Made the World of Industry;* illus. with old prints, photographs, and charts. Macmillan, 1939. (Grades 6–9)

Traces "the main steps in the great transformation that has taken place in the world during the last two centuries."

Mathematics

Hogben, Lancelot Thomas. *The Wonderful World of Mathematics;* art by André Charles Keeping and Kenneth Symonds; maps by Marjorie Saynor. Garden City, 1955. (Grades 6–9)

The dramatic story of civilization is told in brief text illumined with colorful drawings, diagrams, and signs.

Microscopes

Beeler, Nelson, and Franklyn Branley. *Experiments with a Microscope;* illus. by Anne Marie Jauss. Thomas Y. Crowell, 1957. (Grades 5–9)

How to use and operate a microscope. In treatment and format, the most attractive book now available on the subject.

Rogers, Frances. *Lens Magic;* illus. by the author. J. B. Lippincott, 1957. (Grades 7–9)

The history of the lens, how made and used in microscopes.

Shippen, Katherine B. *Men, Microscopes and Living Things;* illus. by Anthony Ravielli. Viking Press, 1955. (Grades 7–9)

Scientific progress is traced through the lives and works of the great biologists.

Yates, Raymond. *Fun with Your Microscope.* Appleton-Century-Crofts, 1943. (Grades 7–9)

A good introduction to bacteriology.

Pets

Chrystie, Frances. *Pets;* illus. by Gillett Good Griffin. Little, Brown, 1953. (Grades 6–9)

A complete handbook on the care, understanding, and appreciation of all kinds of animal pets.

Morgan, Alfred. *Pet Book for Boys and Girls;* illus. by the author and Ruth King. Charles Scribner's Sons, 1949. (Grades 4–9)

Directions for choosing suitable pets, taking care of them, and training them.

Plants and Flowers

Hoke, Alice Dickinson. *First Book of Plants;* illus. by Paul Wenck. Franklin Watts, 1953. (Grades 4–7)

A beginner's guide to botany.

Mathews, Ferdinand S. *Book of Wild Flowers for Young People;* illus. by the author. G. P. Putnam, 1923. (Grades 7–9)

Descriptions of flowers as they appear from April to October.

Stefferud, Alfred. *The Wonders of Seeds;* illus. by Shirley Briggs. Harcourt, Brace, 1956. (Grades 6–8)

The author, who is editor of the U.S. Department of Agriculture's yearbook, tells of the wonders of plant growth and the ingenious ways nature insures its continuance.

Sterling, Dorothy. *The Story of Mosses, Ferns, and Mushrooms.* Doubleday, 1955. (Grades 5–8)

Description of flowerless plants, where they live and how they reproduce.

Webber, Irma. *Travelers All; the Story of How Plants Go Places;* illus. by the author. William R. Scott, 1944. (Grades 2–4)

The author-artist, a botanist, describes simply but graphically the way in which plants and seeds are transported. Companion books are *Up Above and Down Below,* showing the parts of plants above and below the ground; *Bits That Grow Big; Where Plants Come From;* and *Anywhere*

in the World, the story of plant and animal adaptation.

Zim, Herbert S. *What's Inside of Plants?;* illus. by Herschel Warlik. William Morrow, 1952. (Grades 2–5)

Material is clearly presented in concise text and graphic drawings.

Zim, Herbert S., and Alexander Martin. *Flowers;* illus. by Rudolf Freund. Simon & Schuster, 1950. (Grades 5–9)

A guide to familiar American wild flowers.

Prehistoric Life

Andrews, Roy Chapman. *All About Dinosaurs;* illus. by Thomas W. Voter. Random House, 1953. (Grades 5–9)

Description of dinosaurs and the world in which they lived.

Baity, Elizabeth Chesley. *America Before Man;* illus. with drawings, maps, charts, and diagrams by C. B. Falls and with 31 pages of photographs. Viking Press, 1953. (Grades 7–9)

The geological history of America.

Bauman, Hans. *Caves of the Great Hunters;* trans. by Isabel and Florence McHugh. Pantheon Books, 1954. (Grades 6–9)

The true story of four French boys who in 1940 found the Lascaux Cave containing treasures of prehistoric art.

Fenton, Carroll Lane. *Prehistoric World;* with drawings by the author and color plates by James E. Allen. John Day, 1954. (Grades 4–7)

Stories of animal life in past ages.

Scheele, William E. *First Mammals;* illus. by the author. World Publishing Co., 1955. (Grades 6–9)

The author, who is Director of the Cleveland Museum of Natural History, planned this as a reference book to stimulate further reading. Companion books are *Prehistoric Animals* and *Prehistoric Man and the Primates.*

White, Anne Terry. *Prehistoric America;* illus. by Aldren Watson. Random House, 1951. (Grades 5–8)

An absorbing account of archaeological discoveries which show what primitive man was like and how he lived.

Zim, Herbert S. *Dinosaurs;* illus. by James Gordon Irving. William Morrow, 1954. (Grades 4–7)

Describes dinosaurs from the largest to the smallest and tells how they changed and why they became extinct.

Radio, Telephone, Television

Bendick, Jeanne and Robert. *Television Works Like This.* Whittlesey House, new rev. ed. 1954. (Grades 6–9)

A behind-the-scenes view of the principles, mechanics, and personnel involved in broadcasting. Contains material on color TV, educational TV, and network systems.

Floherty, John J. *The Television Story.* J. B. Lippincott, rev. ed. 1957. (Grades 7–9)

Includes new material on color television and producing television programs.

Morgan, Alfred. *Boys' First Book of Radio and Electronics;* illus. by the author. Charles Scribner's Sons, 1954. (Grades 7–9)

Gives the history of radio, explains principles of radio and electronics and shows how to apply them to homemade equipment.

Schneider, Herman and Nina. *Your Telephone and How It Works;* illus. by Jeanne Bendick. Whittlesey House, 1952. (Grades 5–9)

A step-by-step description.

Reptiles

Bronson, Wilfred S. *Turtles;* illus. by the author. Harcourt, Brace, 1945. (Grades 3–6)

Interesting and amusing information about turtles, including the care of turtles as pets.

Hoke, John. *The First Book of Snakes;* illus. by Paul Wenck. Franklin Watts, 1952. (Grades 3–5)

Fascinating information about snakes. A final section explodes some of the myths about snakes.

Holling, Holling C. *Minn of the Mississippi;* illus. by the author. Houghton Mifflin, 1951. (Grades 5–9)

In telling the story of Minn, the snapping turtle who traveled along the Mississippi's 2,500 miles, the author touches on the geography, geology, and history of the Mississippi River.

Pope, Clifford H. *Reptiles Round the World;* illus. by Helen Damrosch Tee-Van. Alfred A. Knopf, 1957. (Grades 5–8)

A simplified natural history of the snakes, lizards, turtles, and crocodiles. The author has also written *Snakes Alive and How They Live* (Viking Press, 1937).

Zim, Herbert S. *Snakes;* illus. by James Gordon Irving. William Morrow, 1949. (Grades 4–7)

Identification, anatomy, feeding, and habits of snakes found in North America. *Alligators and Crocodiles* is a companion volume. The author collaborated with Hobart M. Smith in writing *Reptiles and Amphibians,* a guide to 212 American species.

Rocks and Minerals

Cormack, Maribelle. *First Book of Stones;* illus. by M. K. Scott. Franklin Watts, 1950. (Grades 4–6)

A brief introduction to the common varieties of rocks.

Fenton, Carroll Lane and Mildred. *Rocks and Their Stories;* illus. with photographs. Doubleday, 1951. (Grades 7–9)

The authors define the distinction between "rocks" and "stones," and discuss rocks and the minerals of which they are composed.

Loomis, Frederic. *Field Book of Common Rocks and Minerals.* G. P. Putnam's Sons, 1923. (Grades 6–8)

A guide for identifying rocks and minerals of the United States and interpreting their origin and meanings.

Zim, Herbert S. *Rocks and Minerals;* illus. by Raymond Perlman. Simon & Schuster, 1957. (Grades 7–9)

Identifies more than 400 rocks, minerals, gems, and ores. Dr. Zim, in collaboration with Elizabeth Cooper, has written *Minerals: Their Identification, Uses, and How To Collect Them* (Harcourt, Brace).

Sea Life

Brindze, Ruth. *The Gulf Stream;* illus. by Hélène Carter. Vanguard Press, 1945. (Grades 4–6)

Dramatic stories of what men have learned about this great current or river which flows through the ocean.

Carson, Rachel L. *The Sea Around Us.* Oxford University Press, 1951. (Grade 8 up)

Although the book was written for adults, older boys and girls will find it absorbing reading.

Fisher, James. *The Wonderful World of the Sea;* illus. in color with maps and diagrams. Garden City, 1957. (Grades 5–8)

A sweeping panoramic picture of the sea, its nature, history, the life it shelters, and its usefulness to man.

Holling, Holling C. *Pagoo;* illus. by the author and Lucille Webster Holling. Houghton Mifflin, 1957. (Grades 4–7)

The life cycle of the hermit crab and the teeming life of the tide pool.

Johnstone, Kathleen. *Sea Treasure; a Guide to Shell Collecting;* illus. by Rudolf Freund and René Martin. Houghton Mifflin, 1957. (Grades 7–9)

Mrs. Johnstone takes the reader around the world and through the ages showing him the ways men have used sea shells.

Lane, Ferdinand. *All About the Sea;* illus. by Fritz Kredel. Random House, 1953. (Grades 4–7)

The theory of tides, what the ocean floor is like, and the creatures found in or near the sea.

Reed, William Maxwell, and Wilfrid S. Bronson. *The Sea for Sam;* ed. by F. C. Brown and Charles M. Breder, Jr.; illus. by Wilfrid S. Bronson. Harcourt, Brace, 1935. (Grades 5–8)

An excellent book for the beginning scientist.

Solar Energy

Branley, Franklyn M. *Solar Energy.* Thomas Y. Crowell, 1957. (Grades 7–9)

The science-minded reader will be fascinated with this account of solar energy and the advances already made in the field.

Halacy, D. S., Jr. *Fabulous Fireball; the Story of Solar Energy;* illus. with photographs. Macmillan, 1957. (Grade 7 up)

Once man worshiped the sun, but today he views it scientifically as a tremendous source of power.

Trees

Buff, Mary. *Big Tree;* illus. by Conrad Buff. Viking Press, 1946. (Grades 5–9)

The story of one of the giant Sequoia trees in the great redwood forests of Sequoia National Park.

Cormack, Maribelle. *First Book of Trees;* illus. by Hélène Carter. Franklin Watts, 1951. (Grades 4–7)

Fifty-seven common trees of North America are described. Full-page drawings show leaves, flowers, fruit, and the shape of the trees.

Fenton, Carroll Lane, and Dorothy Pallas. *Trees and Their World;* illus. by Carroll Lane Fenton. John Day, 1957. (Grades 4–7)

An excellent introductory book with many attractive drawings in black and white.

Selsam, Millicent. *See Through the Jungle;* illus. by Winifred Lubell. Harper & Brothers, 1957. (Grades 4–6)

A well-written and strikingly designed book about the South American rain forest. *See Through the Forest* describes plant and animal life at each level of the forest.

Webber, Irma. *Thanks to Trees.* William R. Scott, 1952. (Grades 3–5)

Explains the importance of trees, their use and conservation.

Zim, Herbert S., and Alexander C. Martin. *Trees;* illus. by Dorothea and Sy Barlowe. Simon & Schuster, 1952. (Grades 5–9)

A guide to the identification of 130 familiar American trees.

Biography

"The present generation should be provided with nice, comfortable, decent human heroes with nobility in their souls to look up to, follow, and enjoy." [1]

WORK OF BIOGRAPHY IS NO LESS a work of genuine creation than an original story. The author must be as deeply concerned and involved with the character he adopts from actuality as he is with one born of his own imagination. Nina Brown Baker, who has written a number of leading biographies for young people, once said that her husband viewed with some uneasiness each of her fresh assignments. "You fall in love with those men," he complained. There is much to be said for this approach to the writing of biography for children: to fall in love with one's subject, and to impart that love to the reader.

Like history, biography must be rooted in thorough research. The truth and the spirit of the truth must be respected, and the role of myth and legend clearly defined, so that fact and hearsay are not confused. The reality of time and place must be re-created, and yet nothing must be invented that is beyond probability and out of key with the mores of the time in which the subject lived. The general landscape, the probable weather, yes; but the long passages of contrived conversations — these should be viewed with some skepticism. The reduction of the lives of the great into page upon page of glib dialogue only serves to belittle both the mind of the child reader and the stature of the subject. Here again, source material is invaluable, and can be used with good effect for readers as young as children of the third grade and upwards, as Ingri and Edgar d'Aulaire prove in their picture-book biographies of *Pocahontas* (Doubleday, 1946) and *Benjamin Franklin* (Doubleday, 1950) and as Alice Dalgliesh demonstrates in her inspiriting biographies of Columbus (*The Columbus Story,* Scribner, 1955) and Charles Lindbergh (*Ride on the Wind,* Scribner, 1956). The English novelist, Rumer Godden, in her biography of Hans Christian Andersen, uses his stories and tales as source material, skillfully tracing the inception of the tale to an incident in his own life. This is not primarily a biography written for children; the method and the approach make it absorbing reading for anyone who knows and loves the stories of Andersen.

For children, biography serves to keep alive interest in heroes and hero

[1] Hendrik Willem Van Loon.

worship. It is fitting, therefore, that the biographer choose worthy subjects; that he show clearly wherein their heroism lay; that conflicts, discouragements, doubts, mistakes, and frustrations be made known as well as the definitive triumphs which made them heroic. The psychological study and the probe which seeks to demean or debunk a subject have no place in the biography of childhood reading. There comes a time in the reading lives of children when they seek the actuality of real people as fervently as they have sought to be one with King Arthur, Siegfried, or a mythical tribe of Space Men. For that time, only the best is worthy of their fervor.

BIOGRAPHY

Columbus Sails
The Ambassador [1]

C. WALTER HODGES

❧ *When we take up the story of Columbus given below, he has already gone through preliminary hardships — getting the chance to sail, experiencing storms at sea, scarcity of food, and, more recently, disappointment that land does not appear after evidences have been seen. His sailors are on the verge of mutiny, and Columbus has promised to turn back in three days if there is still no land in sight.*

We did not see him again all next day, which passed without event. After dark, however, toward midnight, he came out and mounted onto the poop, where he stood alone looking from point to point of all the vague, night-shadowed outlines of his ship and the distant lanterns of the others. There remained to him but fifty, forty-nine, forty-eight brief hours as commander, and after that he would never have his ships again. Don Christopher Columbus would be no more than the admiral of a dream, the discoverer of Vacancy. His life's work was at stake upon a race between Time and Distance. Over and over he must have counted these last few hours, computing their number against the miles that still might lie ahead of us — who should know how many?

He did not leave his post all night save once to fetch his cloak, which now, in the

[1] From C. Walter Hodges, *Columbus Sails* (Coward-McCann, 1950).

keen early morning, clung and flapped about him from head to foot. The wind had freshened to half a gale, and we were making a fine pace, plunging and lifting among the white horses and the gray waves. The decks were chill with spray, the air salty, rope and canvas damp with it. At the stove, Jorgé, the cook, blew and blew on his charcoal to kindle the damp wood, until the smoke started and smothered over the water. He lifted on the soup pots, which spilled hissing into the fire with every plunge of the ship. Soon the fishy smell of the soup began to blow in gusts about the deck with the smoke, amidst all the morning business of sluicing and swabbing, hauling and making trim, until the appetite was keen enough even for this too familiar diet.

Between duties we lined up and Jorgé began to ladle out the hot bowlfuls; but almost too much, even for our hunger and chilled bones, was the sour reek of the soup that morning, when smelt at close quarters.

"Worse every day," said one, sniffing in his bowl. "What stuff!"

"Jorgé the poisoner! Whew, the stink of it!"

"We'll hope it tastes better than it smells," said the Admiral's voice. He had come up unnoticed. "Give me a bowl of it, Jorgé. At least we can warm our hands on it." There was some laughter. He took the bowl and went forward up the forecastle ladder onto the prow, where he stood gazing ahead. All had been served, and the soup finished when, suddenly, he turned and hailed back:

"Stand by, all hands! Who keeps watch here? Ramón, Lopez, Ibarri, get out the nets, the grapnel! José, do you see anything ahead to starboard in the water?"

"No, Señor. Aye, now I do, though. But it keeps going awash, and I can't make out what it is. There it is again, now!"

"I can see it!" cried Roldan. "It looks like the branch of a tree!"

"A branch it is! Look, now, it's plain. Have the men ready to bring about. Bartolomeo, we must get it in at all costs."

"Ho! Helm, there! Ease her a little! Gently, gently! 'Tis too far out, I fear, Señor. We'll not get it on this tack and if we come about we may lose sight of it."

"Bring up as close as you can, then. Needs be we'll send out the boat for it. Look, Bartolomeo, I believe there are still some leaves on it. Can you see?"

"Aye, Señor; but not to be certain. Get that boat unlashed, there! José, you'll be in charge; take Sancho, Fernan, Rodrigo. Jump to it! Señor, we're nigh as close as we can make it. Shall we launch?"

"Aye, launch away!"

"Luff your helm, there! Hard over!"

The *Santa Maria* hove to with ruffling canvas, the boat was launched and pulled away. Ten minutes later she returned, slowly maneuvering the flotsam alongside to be hauled on board. It was, as the Admiral had said, a great branch in full leaf, with berries on it, only recently torn from the tree. How it had come out here was a mystery, perhaps only to be explained by the Admiral's eager face. He said nothing, but plucked off a leafy twig and handed it to the man next to him, as though to say: Let this speak for me. Then, suddenly, Gutierrez gave a cry and, thrusting his hand among the leaves of the main branch, pulled out something that had been lodged in a fork there, half-hidden under some winding seaweed. He held it out at arm's length. It was a staff of wood about three feet long, divided to a narrow fork a few inches from one end, and hollowed throughout like a pipe. What its use might have been was beyond all guessing, but none could doubt that it had been fashioned by the hand of man; for, from end to end, it was banded round with rings of crude ornamental carving whereon there were still some traces of color.

It was passed from hand to hand. Finally, the Admiral took it and lashed it to the mainmast with a piece of cord.

"It is an ambassador," he said. "Let it take the place of honor where all may see it. Even before nightfall, if it so please God, all the great lands of India will be ours. Remember the reward, then; and to it I will add my own gift — a jacket of the finest velvet to the first man who sights the shore. Let the watch be doubled. Keep your eyes sharp. Pray to the Holy Virgin and the Saints, and we shall have success!"

.   .   .   .

"What hour it is, Fernan?"

"Almost two, by the glass. Nigh time for us to turn in, thank God."

"Aye, it's raw cold out here. And I could sleep like a dog."

"Look at the Old Man, then. Still watching up there like a ghost. Does he never sleep any more?"

"After tomorrow he'll sleep, mark my words. Little we'll see of him 'til we reach port. The poor devil. I wonder . . ." The voices came softly out of the darkness near the hatch where I lay sheltered, half-dozing, wrapped in a blanket. I could not sleep.

"The clouds are rifting," said the voice again. "Looks as if we'll have a moon, after all."

"Aye, so. She's coming through. More light to see nothing by. Who's aloft this watch?"

"Rodrigo de Triana. With my warm coat on his back, too. The worse luck to him."

"Well, keep yourself warm thinking of bed. Not long now. And here comes the moon . . ."

The dim light spread like a film of snow, making everything white. It brightened. Then, from the masthead came a sudden long cry:

"Land, ho!"

I sprang to my feet. Again:

"Ahoy, below there! Land!"

From the upper deck, the Admiral's voice: "Masthead, ahoy! On what quarter!"

Men came running out on deck. Voices everywhere.

"Starboard bow! Land! Land on the starboard bow!"

The ship's company was all awake, crowding to the side, climbing into the shrouds. About two leagues ahead of us lay a dark streak like a shadow across the sea. Everyone saw it.

"The Indies!"

The covering was stripped from the gun. Powder and shot were rammed home, someone had the match blowing in his hand. "Wait, not yet!" cried Roldan, but there was no waiting. Boom! and the signal shot flashed into the night.

What if once more we are mistaken . . .? José was on the gunwale paying out the leadline. The clouds were closing again. The streak of shoreline was obscured. Could we be mistaken? Then, José's voice, suddenly:

"Bottom at twenty fathoms!"

No mistake! And as if in confirmation comes an answering cannon shot from the *Pinta*. They, too, had seen it. José called out that the water was steadily becoming shallower, and the Admiral gave the command to come about. We took in all but the squaresail and lay into the wind, awaiting daybreak. The *Pinta* brought up near-by, and the Admiral gave her a hail. As soon as her crew heard his voice, they began cheering, and the cheering and shouting went back and forth from one ship to the other. Soon the *Niña* came up with us and swung into the wind a short distance astern; and the cheering began again.

There were some hours to wait till dawn. Jorge busily lit his stove and started preparing food to put some warmth into us. "What, more soup, Jorge? Can't ye think of anything else?" laughed somebody.

"He's only got one idea in his head. Fish soup! His brains are made of it. Hey, but stand aside! Bartolomeo's got something better!"

"Give a hand, someone!" came Roldan's voice. He was staggering under the weight of a cask. "Malaga wine, shipmates! Set it down gently. Steady now!"

"A health to the Admiral!"

"The Admiral! Aye, and the Indies!" cried Mendoze. "Wealth and fortune for every man of us!"

As for Rodrigo de Triana, he was already planning how he would spend his reward money. "Out of the lot of you, it was I who sighted land!" he cried. "There was I at the masthead like a blind priest in a pulpit, couldn't see a thing, and cold as the devil! Then out comes the moon, and there it was! Land! I was near struck dumb, but when I thought of those ten thousand maravedis I found my voice all right!"

Yet I, for my part, was still uneasy, lest we were again deceiving ourselves with an illusion.

"Nay, you needn't fear on that score," said José. "This is land beyond a doubt. But what land, I wonder? Will it be India? Cathay? Zipango? What sort of people shall we find when daylight comes? By the Saints, how long it seems till then!"

But dawn came at last. Slowly the night paled from blue to gray, from gray to a mist through which, more and more clearly, appeared the land. As the day brightened, there appeared before us the long coastline, a rocky shore where thickets overhung the surf, and in one place a wide beach at the mouth of a river. Northward, a headland trailed out into the sea; to the south, from among the trees, a thread of smoke ascended into the calm air. Then, the sun came up and lit the whole scene with color. A flock of birds swerved upward and from the woods a group of little dark figures ran down onto the shore.

It was the morning of Friday, October the twelfth, in the year Fourteen Hundred and Ninety-Two.

Amos Fortune, Free Man
Auctioned for Freedom[2]

ELIZABETH YATES

⋙ *Elizabeth Yates, in her book* Amos Fortune, Free Man, *which was awarded the Newbery medal in 1951, tells a moving story of a little-known historical figure. Amos was born a prince in Africa, but when he was fifteen he was brought to America and sold as a slave.*

[2] From Elizabeth Yates, *Amos Fortune, Free Man* (Dutton, 1950).

For many years he worked as a tanner to earn the freedom which within his soul he had never lost. At the age of sixty he purchased his liberty and in later years, with his hard-earned money, he was able to buy freedom for other slaves, among them his wife Violet and her daughter Celyndia. The chapter given below comes toward the end of the book, when, in his eightieth year, Amos Fortune had become a land-owner.

With the aid of his neighbors, Amos had built his house before the winter snows came. It was a small house, like many others in the countryside, with a large central chimney and two fireplaces. At first its furnishings were of the simplest. But as the tanning went on and the iron kettle again resounded with the coins collecting in it, Amos added to their way of living things of comfort — feather beds and a writing desk, a chest of drawers and a looking glass, cheese presses and churns, a new wheel for the spinning and a larger loom. Now that he had a barn of his own and cleared fields, he bought another horse so old Cyclops might be turned out to pasture for his remaining days. A cow and a heifer took their places in the barn, and to the tools of the tanning trade were added the equipment of a farmer.

Customers came to Amos Fortune with hides and skins from considerable distances. Men who wanted work well done thought nothing of coming from as far away as Reading and Sterling in Massachusetts, as Amherst and New Ipswich in New Hampshire. The reputation of the Jaffrey tanner had grown steadily. And with a larger place, better equipment and the hire of the Burdoo boys, as well as his apprentice, Simon Peter, who was indentured to him for a period of three years, Amos was able to take on more work. People trusted him not only with skins and hides but in matters of pounds and pence.

One morning Amos opened a letter and read to Violet, " 'Sir: Please to let Mr. Joel Adams have a calf skin if mine isn't out. Let him have one of yours and I will swap or allow you for it. B. Prescott.' "

"Have you a calf skin?" Violet asked.

Amos nodded. "One of the best." And he thought with pleasure of the large barn which enabled him to keep a good stock of leather on hand against just such demands.

There was another letter from Simeon Butters asking Amos to pay Samuel Avery twelve shillings, " 'It being for value received of me,' " Amos read aloud.

Violet asked, "Can you let him have so much, Amos, not knowing when he'll pay you back?"

Amos nodded again. "We owe no one and there are coins in the kettle like a family of rabbits in a burrow." He looked at Violet and smiled the broad smile that meant more than any words. It was a debt of thanks he owed to her and would go on paying as long as he lived. She bowed her head slightly, accepting in silence what she knew in her heart was her due.

Jaffrey had a Social Library and Amos became a member of it. He read its books during the winter when tanning operations were somewhat in abeyance and discussed them with the citizens of the town. He was always well informed for he subscribed to a newspaper. His store of information, matched with his ready wit, gave him opinions that were often sought after. He was their fellow citizen, Amos Fortune, and more often than not the prefix "Mr." dignified his name. He had won his way to equality by work well done and a life well lived. But his own life was no guarantee for the lives of those who were dear to him. Celyndia, now sixteen, had many friends among the white children. But there were times when she was made to feel uneasy at school because of her color and her different ways. Violet, however, would not let her miss school. Violet knew what it was to carry through life the heavy burden of illiteracy and she did not want Celyndia to bear that along with the burden of her color. So Celyndia went bravely to school. But she was happiest when sitting beside the loom watching Violet weave or sitting at the loom and weaving herself.

The better things went with Amos, the more his heart ached for those who received the necessities of life only in the form of charity. The town had again been helping

Lois Burdoo with firewood and foodstuffs. But no matter what help she received she never seemed able to rise above her wretched lot. The children went to school in tatters, and even when given new clothes they would appear the next day with them dirty and torn. They could not seem to keep from falling down or tearing themselves on briar bushes.

After years of ineffective help, the town felt that it could not bolster Lois Burdoo any longer. She was given warning that the two oldest children would be put up to Public Vendue on the thirty-first day of December. Vendues were auctions at which townspeople could bid for the privilege of affording care to the indigent. The lowest bidder would receive the contract. It was an expedient that pioneer towns had developed to enable them to look after their poor and Jaffrey had been forced to come to it. Many of the people remembered the day in 1774 when at Town Meeting a resolution had been passed: "Voted not to raise money for the poor" and of the human suffering that had followed. For there were always poor, either through misfortune or their own inability to contend with the hard conditions surrounding them. And something had to be done. No town could free itself entirely from responsibility and auctioning off the poor was one of the means by which a township sought to meet its responsibility.

Before the beginning of each new year, notices signed by the town auctioneer were posted in public places advising of the vendue to be held. Celyndia saw one such notice and told her mother of it.

That night Violet said to Amos, "So Lois has agreed to it at last. She's putting the two oldest up to vendue."

"Not Polly!" Amos exclaimed.

"Yes, Polly and Moses."

"But Polly isn't strong enough to work as hard as she'll have to if she's vendued."

"That doesn't matter to Lois. She can't feed the children and the town can't let them starve."

Amos would not believe what Violet had told him until he went to the village late on that raw December day. Then he saw the notice posted outside the Meeting House.

There were the names of the town poor, eight in all. Some of them he knew slightly, but none so well as the two Burdoo children. Under the list of names he read,

The above will be put to the lowest bidder who shall board and nurse them in sickness and health and pay every expense for them except doctor's bills which the town will pay, and clothing which the town will provide. The contract shall continue one year from the first day of January, 1793, when those persons who shall keep them shall remove them to the place which shall next be provided for them if within the town of Jaffrey.

Amos shook his head slowly. He had not been able to keep away from slave auctions all the years he was waiting for the arrival of a young girl from Africa. Here was an auction which nothing could keep him from since the fate of a young girl he knew well was at stake.

It was a cruel cold day, that last day of the year, when Amos made his way to the Meeting House where the Vendue was being held. The wind was blowing hard and he pulled his great coat around him, tucking his chin down into the collar. There was nothing to see, for snow was on the wind and a blizzard obscured the mountain. But still it was there, Amos thought to himself. He turned toward it as he came over the crest of the hill. Stalwart and deeply grounded it was there, though winds raged around it and snow battered against it. The knowledge of its presence gave back to him some of the strength that the wind had taken from him in his walk against it up the long hill.

Entering the Meeting House he slipped quietly into a seat at the rear, hoping to be unobserved. But all who were gathered there knew someone had entered for the gust of cold wind that came through the door. Amos looked over the heads of the people at the eight luckless ones, the poor of the year who were to be despatched, sitting fearful and silent in a group near the auctioneer.

It was a strange kind of auction, this

Vendue, for there was no talk and only a little whispering among the townspeople who were present. Some of them looked shame-faced, knowing they were out to get labor in the cheapest way. Others boldly intended bidding on elderly people so they might make a few pounds off the town. All were surprised to see the tanner enter. Amos Fortune's reputation for fair dealing was such that none could think of him as taking part in a vendue.

Lois Burdoo sat in a corner huddled into her thin garments, sobbing pitifully. When Amos saw where she was, he moved over and sat beside her, stroking her hands for comfort and assurance.

The auctioneer started to address the small gathering of people, calling out his wares as if he had so much live stock at his disposal. The first to be auctioned was the fourteen year old Negro girl.

"She may be thin," he said, "but she won't cost you much to keep if she eats little. She's got a good pair of arms and those legs should carry her as far as anyone here is likely to go. What am I bid?" His eyes ranged over the crowd hopefully.

Alexander Milliken of the tavern on the slope of the mountain bid £4.

Lois Burdoo shuddered. "No, no," she murmured, "not a tavern."

Amos whispered into her ear, "It's the last bid that matters, not the first."

There were other bids, but none went lower than two pounds, ten shillings. People nodded their heads as if in agreement, for who could keep a girl in food for a year for less than that? In spite of what the auctioneer had said about the stoutness of her limbs, it was clear to see that little work would be got from a girl as thin as a child with a dazed look in her eyes and a racking cough.

"Going," the auctioneer called out, "going —"

"One pound sixteen," Amos Fortune spoke up in the voice that was clear and strong and known to so many.

The auctioneer gasped. A ripple of amazement ran through the group of people in the Meeting House.

"You must like your town to want to save it so much money," the auctioneer commented. "Going, going," he said, then in a loud voice, "gone to Mr. Amos Fortune. Polly Burdoo, one year, at £1, 16s."

Polly left the huddled cluster of the poor and ran over to her mother and Amos, turning from one to the other, still too frightened to smile at the good fortune that had come to her.

None of the others went so cheap. John Briant got the care of the Widow Combs at £5, 18s. Joseph Wilder got the Widow Cutter at £10, 16s. But the Widow Cutter was lame and so old that it would be nothing but the chimney corner for her. Twelve year old Moses Burdoo was struck off to Joseph Stewart, the first and only bidder, from that day until he was twenty-one, at £15, 15s; half to be paid at the end of one year, and if he live the other half to be paid at the end of the second year. Joseph Stewart knew the boy and had gotten work from him. He was a hard man, but the boy was like a colt and could profit by a firm hand.

"Likely his back will be sore with the beatings he'll be getting," Lois said.

"And perhaps they will do something to his soul," Amos reminded her, for he knew the boy too. "Wings can't grow without a little suffering."

Violet might have small sympathy for the shiftless Lois, but she readily took Polly to her heart, outfitting her in Celyndia's clothes and teaching her some of the duties about the house. Celyndia and Polly were near the same age and Celyndia embraced her new sister warmly. But beyond the flight of a smile across Polly's dark face and a few words, she seemed bowed forever by her lot.

When she sat dreaming by the fire Amos would sometimes call to her to break her from too long reverie and she would shake her head and blink her eyes with a start.

"Yes, Uncle Amos," she would say, eager to do his bidding.

But even if he asked her she could not say where her thoughts had been the while she had been dreaming.

Polly tried to be a help to Violet in the work of the house, but dusting cloth or broom had a way of falling from her hands. Violet would come upon her standing still and staring before her, the task she had been given to do still undone. Polly was eager to work at the loom and Celyndia spent hours showing her its simple mysteries. But as soon as Polly endeavored to do the work herself her hands would slide off the shuttle, her feet would loose their hold on the treadles and her eyes would stare before her.

"What do you think about all the time?" Celyndia asked.

But Polly could never say.

Violet, in exasperation at a simple task undone, exclaimed to Amos, "It's only your kindness that keeps her, Amos Fortune, for anyone else would have returned her to the town long ago."

He smiled in answer. What he had done had been done with good reason and he was satisfied.

Polly liked going to school with Celyndia, but after a few days she brought back a note saying there was nothing the school could do for her since she would not learn.

That evening Amos, with a piece of leather large enough for a jerkin and fine enough for a gentleman, went to see the school teacher. He offered the leather as his gift and begged leniency for Polly.

"She hasn't long with us and what she gets from you will help her where she's going," Amos said.

Because the tall old man with his keen eyes and fine carriage could not be gainsaid, the teacher agreed to keep Polly. He wondered, as he watched the tanner go on his way, who would have the girl another year, and he thought she would nowhere find the kindness that she had in the Fortune home.

Soon Polly could not raise herself from her bed, but the weaker she grew the more she smiled as if a kind of content were coming over her being. Celyndia spent hours reading to her, talking with her. Violet brought her things to eat. Amos sat beside her through the long quiet evenings. Polly asked him for stories and he told them to her, but more than all the others she asked for the story of the chariot. After he had told it they would sing together, her voice following his even though she could only whisper the words.

Violet sitting across the room at the loom and Celyndia with the spindle in her hand would join in.

One night early in November Polly asked Amos to help her sit up. He put his arms around her and held her up. She was so light that he felt if he held a flower on its stalk it could be no heavier. She held out her hands, resting her right hand in Violet's that were worn and coarse with the care she had given to others, and her left hand in Celyndia's that were supple and strong. Her eyes she kept on Amos. Peace dwelt in her face, a smile hovered over her lips, and for the first time she seemed to be seeing clearly those who were close to her. Her gaze that had always been so far away had come near at last. A small shudder passed over her body. She sat up very straight for a moment, even without the aid of Amos' arms; then she fell back into his arms.

Celyndia started to sob softly. Amos put back his head and Violet saw him shape with his lips the familiar words, "Thank you, Lord."

Violet turned to him with a question in her eyes.

Amos answered it. "I wanted her to die free. I knew she didn't have long when I bid on her, but she's had almost a year of freedom."

"She wasn't ever a slave," Violet reminded him. "She was born free."

He shook his head. "She wasn't free when she was so poor. She's gone ahead now with a smile on her face and a light in her eyes. Frightened little girl that she was, she's left that far behind and she's crossing Jordan unafraid." His face was glowing, almost as if he were sharing some of the radiance he knew had reached out to encircle Polly.

Violet looked at him. Never before had she felt so much love for this man who seemed to live to give freedom to others. "You'd set all the world free if you could, wouldn't you, Amos?"

He shook his head. "Just the part of it that I can touch. That's all any man can do." He drew the coverlet over Polly's face and reached across the bed to touch Celyndia's hands. "Don't you cry, Lyndia love, you go out and give the creatures in the barn an armful of hay. Tell them what's happened in the house and see if the barn is shut tight, for the wind is blowing cold."

Glad to have something to do, Celyndia left the room. Amos went to the fire to put on more wood, then turning around he spoke quietly to Violet.

"Once, long years ago, I thought I could set a canoe-load of my people free by breaking the bands at my wrists and killing the white man who held the weapon. I had the strength in my hands to do such a deed and I had the fire within, but I didn't do it."

"What held you back?"

Amos shook his head. "My hand was restrained and I'm glad that it was, for the years between have shown me that it does a man no good to be free until he knows how to live, how to walk in step with God."

"But Amos," Violet exclaimed, "look at the people to whom you've given freedom! Lily and Lydia, Celyndia and me, and now you've set Polly free to die happy."

"And go on living," he reminded her gently.

"How is it you're thinking of these things tonight?" she asked him. "Never before have you told me about that canoe-load of your people."

"I used to see Africa in Polly's eyes," he said, "the past and its sorrows and all that was behind, but I've not seen what was ahead for us until just now. Perhaps I saw that in her eyes, too. It's good, Violet. It will be worth the waiting for."

The next day Josiah Carey dug a grave for Polly Burdoo in the churchyard near the lot that Amos Fortune had reserved for himself. A few months later at Town Meeting it was voted to pay Amos Fortune the one pound sixteen shillings in full for keeping Polly Burdoo, even though he had not had her all the year. Amos would not use the money for their own needs. Instead, he put it away in a separate place, saying to Violet that he had a mind to do something particular with it and when he knew what it was he would tell her.

Leader by Destiny
George Washington, the Boy [3]

JEANETTE EATON

&ε§ *Many biographies have been written about George Washington, but none is better for the junior high school pupil than the one by Jeanette Eaton. In this first chapter, we see the promise of the man to be; the honest, simple-hearted, kindly person and devoted friend. His quick temper flares and as quickly dies; he knows what he wants and, in a sense, fights for it; but we see no evidence of any interest in politics, which interest he really never had.*

Through the long grass sopping wet with dew a tall boy came walking. It was half an hour before sunrise, but already light enough to show the outline of his broad-shouldered figure and fine head. After a swift glance back at the solid brick house behind him as if he were expecting someone, he climbed down the bank of the creek. He could see across it now to its border of willows and the jutting boulders against which the current rippled. Beyond the marshes lay the wide river, a tarnished mirror framed in lush foliage.

Suddenly a mockingbird from an ancient hemlock splashed the stillness with his sweet, whistling carol. And as the song ceased, a small boy scrambled between the low branches of an old willow tree. Jumping down on the bank above his elder brother, he cried reproachfully, "Why did you not awaken me before you were dressed and ready?"

Chuckling, the other said, "You were so tight asleep, Jacky, it seemed a pity." Then he added, "My traps are empty and there's nothing to see here. But there'd be time to swim before breakfast is set out."

With one joyous look of agreement the two boys leaped up the bank and started along the path past the slave quarters. Because of the deep mud bottom, dangerous as quicksand, the creek was impossible for swimming. There was nothing for it but

[3] From Jeanette Eaton, *Leader by Destiny* (Harcourt, Brace, 1938).

a walk of a mile and a half down the plantation road to the shipping wharf on the Potomac. It was a well-made road for those days, running between great blue-green fields of tobacco. The long strides of the elder boy kept Jacky trotting, but at last the pair reached the little strip of sandy beach washed by the waters of the wide river. Instantly they began slipping off their jackets.

Suddenly the tall boy pounced upon his brother and snatched him high in his arms. His deep laugh, the scream of the victim, and an enormous splash far out in deep water followed in swift succession. As a dark head came up for air and a hand waved, George swung himself to the wharf, ran down its length and dove. After a long swim under water he came up beyond the spot where Jacky was kicking and splashing in delightful contortions.

A little while later the boys sat on the edge of the wharf lacing their boots and buttoning their vests. Jacky twisted his wet hair into the pigtail which the fashion of the times required. He grunted with impatience and glanced at his companion, wishing he would talk more. Then he began a conversation himself.

"I wish you were coming home with me when I leave Wakefield, George, or that I might stay longer here. Austin and his lady allow more pleasuring than our mother does." Receiving only a nod, he added: "Betty is lonely for you, too, at the Ferry Farm. When are you coming back, George?"

Rising to his feet, the other said: "Likely when full summer is here. I promised Cousin Robin to stay with him at Chotank a bit. But first Mr. Williams would have me complete certain studies he has laid out for me." He made a wry face at the thought.

As they started down the road, the elder boy suddenly caught hold of his brother's arm and blurted out shyly, "Look, Jacky, here is something worth more than the Latin my teacher would push upon me." He jerked from his pocket a somewhat battered notebook.

"Hmm! What have you copied here? Is it poetry?"

"No. These are principles of doing the right thing at table or of meeting persons of distinction. Read the title!" He bent over his brother's shoulder, " 'Rules of Civility and Decent Behaviour in Company and Conversation.' I find them of great benefit."

But Jack was interested in something else. "How fine you have learned to write!" he exclaimed. "There is a handsome tail to your signature in this book."

Pleased, the other looked down upon the name written there. Vigorously and with a lively flourish it stood out upon the page —

Young John returned the book to its owner. "Shall you go to school in England as Lawrence and Augustine did?"

George shook his head. "I am not good at lessons — except accounting. Also, there is no money now. You know father left me but a few acres of land besides the Ferry Farm which mother has while she lives. I must fend for myself soon."

They had been walking swiftly and were nearing the spot where a grassy lane led off like an aisle between pines and cedars to a distant patch of cleared ground. Instinctively the boys glanced that way with sobered faces. Beyond view there in a peaceful semicircle lay the graves of their ancestors, and one stone, recently marked, which bore the name of Augustine Washington, their father, who had died four years before.

What the boys remembered about him was his enormous energy. Whether he was galloping around the plantation or merely talking, he was a man of force. He never tired telling his children about the Washington clan which from 1657 on had been establishing plantations through that section of Virginia, called the Northern Neck, which lies between the broad Potomac and the narrow Rappahannock rivers. Now the Washingtons were still further intermarried and scattered. Augustine had left to his seven children and his wife some five thousand acres of land in four different counties. His best properties were willed to his two oldest sons by his first wife, Lawrence and Augustine. Mary Ball Washington, the second wife, lived at the Ferry Farm on the Rappa-hannock with her daughter Betty and her three younger sons.

George, Mary Washington's eldest son, spent most of his time at Wakefield with his half-brother Augustine, called Austin for short. But the boy, who was rather a favorite in the family, stayed part of each year with his mother and went for long visits to his other half-brother, Lawrence, at his place called Mount Vernon. Now and then one of George's younger brothers would be invited by Augustine to come and stay at Wakefield also. George was always glad when it was John's turn, for he liked him better than either Charles or Samuel.

"We must hurry!" shouted Jack, suddenly breaking into a run. "We shall be late for breakfast!"

They could see the house now, and pres-ently pushed open the rustic gate and went clattering down the box-bordered flag walk. This was the rear of the house and from the small brick kitchen inside the gate — always a separate building in these Virginia places — a turbaned Negress emerged carrying a tray with covered dishes. The wide door of the mansion house stood open and from the threshold one could see through the front door opposite, at the end of the hall, the lovely green vista straight down to the edge of the creek. The hungry boys hastened into the pine-paneled dining room.

Mrs. Anne Aylette Washington, seated alone before the silver teapot, glanced up smiling to say good morning. Dazzling sun-light fell upon the bare table set with spar-kling silver, with pewter pitchers of milk and cream, a plate of cheese, a dish of preserves, and a great Spode bowl of strawberries.

Sipping her tea, their sister-in-law chatted at unheeding ears. She said her little boy was feverish from teething, reported an early morning quarrel in the slave quarters, and lamented the delay of the post from Wil-liamsburg — doubtless due, she thought, to the fact that Mr. Franklin in Philadelphia had too many irons in the fire to attend to his duties as Deputy Postmaster. At last, however, she made an announcement of in-terest. "Augustine is expecting his brother Lawrence today," she said.

George looked up with eager surprise. "Really, m'am! What brings him here?"

"I believe he is on his way to Williamsburg a little in advance of the Assembly session. I expect him for dinner." As her husband entered the room at that moment, Anne turned to him, half-petulantly, "Augustine, I've just told George that Lawrence arrives today, and look at his face! I think he would leave us tomorrow for Lawrence and Mount Vernon!"

Seating himself in an armchair at the head of the table, Augustine Washington cast a bantering glance at his half-brother. But be-fore he could speak, a Negro servant entered with a great plate of smoking corn cakes and a platter of bacon and fried fish. At once everyone's attention was fixed on making way with breakfast.

As he ate, George reflected that his sister-in-law had spoken with some justice. Al-though he had been born here at Wakefield and enjoyed the place, it was not so dear to him as Mount Vernon. Neither was the Ferry Farm across the river from the hamlet of Fredericksburg. Indeed, no estate he had ever seen could compare with his eldest brother's home one hundred and fifty miles north on the Potomac. Besides — he glanced at Augustine — certainly Austin was kind and a man of affairs, too. But Lawrence! He had been off to the Spanish wars in the West Indies. And — well — Lawrence was different.

Jack broke the long silence. Pushing back his empty plate with a sigh of satisfaction, he asked, "Shall we sail the small boat today? Or are we riding?"

Laughing, Augustine arose. "If you think to have George idle away the morning with you, John, it cannot be. He gave me his word yesterday he would help break in my colt, Phoebus. Come, let us go out to the stable and look him over."

Through the garden filed the three broth-ers. There gillyflowers and heart's-ease and early yellow roses bloomed between low hedges of privet. Before the stable door sev-eral Negroes were lounging about in low-voiced chatter. But on sight of the master they hurriedly made a pretense of activity. Augustine gave an order, and presently a big, deep-chested two-year-old of mottled gray was led out by a halter. He flung up his head nervously, rolled his eyes at the new-comers, and danced about as if defying any-one to tame him.

Shrinking back a little, Jack watched pro-ceedings with admiring interest. Calmly George drew from his pocket a barley sugar-stick, offered it to Phoebus on the palm of his hand, stroked nose and neck, and murmured soothing sounds into the restless ears. Stealth-ily the boy took a bridle from the groom. With one swift motion he slipped it on and adjusted the bit. There was a longer struggle to buckle the saddle girth. But once it was secure, George put a foot in the stirrup and vaulted to his seat.

In a quiet voice he said, "Now let go the bridle and mind his heels." For an instant he sat stroking the twisting neck.

Suddenly Phoebus sprang forward and bolted through the barnyard gate out to the grassy pasture. The battle between horse and rider had begun. Jack, clambering to the top rail of the fence, was just in time to see the first firm pull on the reins which checked the wild flight and brought the straining animal to a slower pace. Time and again the gray horse made a dash for liberty. Time and again, feeling thwarted, he plunged, reared, flung out his heels, and tried to shake off the hateful bridle.

Augustine came to stand against the fence behind his little brother. Near them gath-ered the grooms to watch and exclaim: "Law-see, dat boy kin stick!" "Seem jes' lak he grow on de saddle!" Suddenly in the distant field horse and rider disappeared behind a rise of ground.

Half an hour passed with no further view of them. At last, Augustine in dismay voiced the fear that they had dashed into the woods where it was all too easy to meet with an accident. Then beyond a distant clump of cedar trees the horse and rider reappeared. Into the stable yard they whirled. Quivering, snorting, covered with lather, Phoebus came to a dead stop.

Augustine waved his hat in air, crying, "Good boy!" The grooms clapped their hands and shouted. Jacky leaped off the fence to legs trembling with excitement and

relief. But the horseman seemed to pay no attention to the fuss. With one swing he dismounted, pulled the head of his horse around, and rubbed his nose.

"He's a good mount," he remarked in a matter-of-fact tone. "A few more trials of this kind will teach him, I'll warrant."

There might have been more praise for George, but at that instant a man in shirt-sleeves came galloping through the paddock on a small black mare. It was the overseer of the Wakefield plantation. Leaning from his saddle, he spoke to his employer in a tone of some excitement.

"Mr. Washington, a small boat has just put in from *The Heron*. The Captain sends word he has space to carry twelve hogsheads of tobacco, if we have them ready. He means to weigh anchor at high tide. Is there time to load?"

Augustine had already swung himself into the saddle. Over his pleasant face had come the shrewd look of the business executive. "Then we have but two hours!" he shouted. "Call all hands to the warehouse!" Digging his heels into the flanks of his horse, he dashed away.

Slowly George and John followed on foot through the paddock out to the grassy, uncut stretch which served as lawn from house to creek. George looked thoughtful. "A dozen hogsheads!" he mused. "What price will that fetch in the English market now, I wonder. The last load Austin shipped brought so little that he swore he meant to choose an-other London merchant."

His small brother looked at him in disgust. He couldn't bear the fearless horse-tamer to talk in that dull grown-up fashion about tobacco prices. Hastily he suggested, "We might practice wrestling under the trees here."

After a pause George answered slowly. "I had thought to paddle out to look at this merchant ship *Heron*. Would you like that?" He laughed then at Jack's joyous whoop.

By the time the boys edged the canoe be-tween the boulders of the inlet and out on the river, they could hear the faraway creak of ox-carts on their slow way down to the wharf. Through the trees they caught glimpses of figures busy about the drying shed and heard Negro voices chanting in minor cadence. Out on the water, however, it was very still. The boys dipped their paddles noiselessly, Indian fashion.

"Look!" cried George presently. "There's *The Heron* swinging at anchor. Ship ahoy!"

The boatswain leaning over the stern looked up and shouted back a greeting. Presently as the canoe drew close, he was answering with great good humor George's questions about the number of the crew and the amount of cargo aboard.

"We left a packet of goods for Colonel Thomas Lee of Stratford this morning," he said. "His sons must be great young gallants to judge by the amount of lace frills and velvet waistcoats and Russian leather boots we brought over for them from London-town."

An expression of intense interest lit up the listening face of George. Then he let go the rope of the vessel and, as it shot forward, sang out, "Good voyage to you!"

"Some day," George remarked to his brother, "I also will order satin coats and breeches from the London shops."

Unhurriedly they pushed against the current for some time. But suddenly Jack felt the canoe shoot forward and looked around to see his brother paddling for dear life. "What is it? A squall?" he asked in surprise.

George laughed. "No. Lawrence! I'd almost forgot he was coming."

There was need for haste. Hardly had the pair reached the house when they heard far down the crossroad leading to the highway the clop-clop of hoofs and the jingle of bridle rings. Anne Washington, with several house servants, was already at the gate. Standing close behind her, George watched the beautiful chestnut mare bring Lawrence closer. Behind him rode two Negro servants with rolls of luggage strapped to their saddles. At the gate Lawrence dismounted, flung his bridle to a black boy, snatched off his three-cornered hat, and in a gay voice cried, "Greetings!"

He was a young man of good height, very slender, and perfectly turned out in the fashion of the day. Flinging a smile at George, he bent low over the hand of his sister-in-law. With his powdered hair and his grace of movement, he had the air of a courtier.

George thought Augustine, who came hurrying up from the warehouse to join in the welcome, looked far more the commonplace planter. He was glad when half an hour later he went into the drawing-room that only Austin was there with the visitor. Perhaps he would get a special word with his favorite brother.

"How is it with you, boy?" asked Lawrence, with a look of affection. "How go the studies? Can you read a bit of Latin now?" Receiving a shy nod from George, he said, "Good. Now translate this — what Tiberius said about taxing the provinces, *'Boni pastoris est tondere pecus, non deglubere.'* "

George blushed, dropped his head, and pondered in glum silence. At last, catching the two young men exchanging winks, he muttered, in a sulky tone, "It signifies something about a good shepherd and his sheep."

Lawrence and Augustine laughed with the easy superiority of men who had studied the classics at English universities. "Fie!" teased the visitor. "That is a thick piece of wood you wear on your shoulders."

With a look of fury George sprang to his feet. "It is not fair to mock me thus!" he cried with blazing eyes. "I've not been at it long. Nor am I born clever — like you both! Have I had tutors and schools as you had?"

Lawrence had ceased laughing at once and leaned forward with sympathy in his sensitive face. But Augustine said sharply, "Tut, tut! Mind that temper of yours or it will get the best of you!"

Clenching his hands and breathing hard, the boy mastered his rage. "I can do some — some things well enough. I can figure and copy maps. Latin is not the whole of useful learning, is it?" Observing the kindly look bent upon him by his eldest brother, he cried out: "Lawrence, let me learn surveying. I would do something active and useful. I'm wearied of books!"

At this moment Augustine's wife entered the room to summon them to dinner and the men rose from their chairs. Lawrence placed his hand on the arm of the agitated youngster. "I understand and will see what I can do."

For this he received a look of profound gratitude, and with every trace of anger gone

George took his place at the dinner table. Presently, as the platter of ham and greens went around, he asked, "Pray tell me how are your neighbors, Mr. Fairfax and his lady and the boy Bryan?"

His brother looked pleased. "They often inquire about you. Mrs. Fairfax has been ailing. But in spite of that the house at Belvoir has been very lively. Young George, the eldest son, is back from school in England, and Lord Fairfax, Mr. William's cousin, has come to stay with him until he decides where he means to settle."

Anne Washington put down her fork with a click. "Settle? Here in America? You mean that a great lord like that will stay and not go back to London?"

Lawrence suppressed a little smile. "He is a rather sad and bitter gentleman who has lost his illusions in the world of fashion. He has come here to escape it and is looking about his vast estate to find a place suitable for building a residence." Suddenly looking at George, the speaker added, "When you come next to visit me, boy, he will doubtless take you fox-hunting. For that sport he has a passion."

George flushed with shy pleasure and put into the eyes he fixed on his brother the cry of his heart. "And when am I to come to Mount Vernon?" Reading that plea, Lawrence nodded thoughtfully.

Then the talk between the two men turned on a topic dear to them — the possibility of developing the lands beyond the Allegheny Mountains. As he spoke of the western wilderness the face of Lawrence glowed with enthusiasm. "They say that beyond the mountain range are fertile valleys ready for tilling. We should be sending settlers out to hold what was given Virginia by the Royal Charter. *We* should be pushing the fur trade with the Indians — not the Pennsylvanians. As for the French, they have even less right in that territory."

George watched Augustine nod a vigorous agreement. All the boy had ever heard about that unknown land west of the mountains fascinated him. But at this point his thoughts drifted off to the possibility of his own future. How he wished that Lawrence would take him and give him a chance! No one

could do so much for him, that he knew. Lawrence was the best of all the Washingtons.

That was probably true. After he had returned from the British expedition against Cartagena in the West Indies, Lawrence had received from his father a piece of land on the upper Potomac. There he had built a house and named the place after his commander in the war, General Vernon. With his marriage to Anne Fairfax, Lawrence had become a person of importance — an Adjutant General in the Virginia Militia and a member of the House of Burgesses. Yet for all his twenty-five hundred acres, his slaves and his many interests, Lawrence had two griefs. Since the war his health had been very uncertain and the children his wife had borne all died in infancy.

After dinner, when George had finished his lessons for the day, he went down to pitch quoits with Jack on the grass in front of the house. But he was thinking too much about Lawrence to make a good score. George had been with his brother when he took off his coat and vest in the downstairs bedroom and had been shocked at the thin frame so often shaken by coughing spells. How he wished he could help his brother! Certainly he could manage the stable. And as for farming, he knew something about it already and could master such problems. For that was the kind of learning he loved.

"I've won every game!" crowed Jacky. "You pitch too far today."

George stretched himself and yawned, then straightened up quickly at the sight of Augustine striding down from the house.

"Boy, I have news you'll like. Lawrence wants to tell you about the talk he and I had concerning your future. Go in and see him now. Tomorrow he leaves at daybreak and will have no time."

George ran up the slope and hurried into the house. For a long moment he paused in the cool hall. His mind tossed together all the fascinating bits which Lawrence had flung in air that day like confetti — the gay dinner parties at Belvoir, the meetings of the militia, fox-hunting, plans to explore the western lands, Governor Gooch's ball at Williamsburg. Here was life, adventure, glamor!

That was what he wanted — to be part of it at Mount Vernon. Would Lawrence ask him to stay there? As he tapped on the bedroom door, he felt as if he were knocking at the Wish Gate itself.

Nor did he knock in vain. Lawrence asked him to make his future home in Mount Vernon and put the invitation in a way to warm the heart of any younger brother. "I agree with what you said, George, that it would be well to have you learn surveying. I mean to have you taught fencing, also, and military tactics as a preparation for the future. You might survey my lands after a bit. For truly I am convinced that you could assist me in many ways."

So the die was cast. Late summer and fall were to be spent at the Ferry Farm and after that Lawrence would welcome his brother. This momentous conversation took place in May, 1747, when George Washington was just fifteen years and two months old. Before another spring came around he had started on his first significant adventure.

Young Lafayette
The Great Adventure Begins [4]

✍ *Lafayette, in his determination to help the American colonists in their fight for freedom, has secretly purchased a ship to take him and fellow-adventurers to America to offer their services to General Washington. While waiting for the ship to be outfitted, Lafayette visits his uncle, the Marquis de Noailles, the French Ambassador in London. The following chapter tells of that visit and the difficulties encountered before he could set off on the great adventure.*

JEANETTE EATON

It was a crowded fortnight for the visitor. He dined, supped, and even breakfasted in great houses. He rode in Hyde Park with dashing officers. One night at the opera, strolling in the lobby with his uncle between acts, he had an encounter which especially

[4] From Jeanette Eaton, *Young Lafayette* (Houghton Mifflin, 1932).

aroused his interest. On that occasion Noailles presented him to a general, resplendent in scarlet coat loaded with gold lace, white satin breeches, and formidable sword. He was Sir Henry Clinton who had been defeated by the American general, Moultrie, at Charleston in South Carolina. Gilbert wondered, as he chatted with the General, whether he were going to be sent over again and if they might some day meet on the opposite sides of a battle-line.

The man he liked best and saw most often was a young officer in the British army named Fitzpatrick. One day they even stole off by themselves, took a hackney coach for a shilling, and supped together at Devil Tavern in Fleet Street. Fitzpatrick told Gilbert all the recent news of the war. It seemed that General Washington had had a most unexpected success. On Christmas night he had crossed the Delaware River, marched all night in a snowstorm, and surprised a body of Hessians at Trenton, whom he captured almost to a man, together with their arms.

"At one time last autumn," said Fitzpatrick, "it looked as if the Americans were sure to be defeated. But their General has maneuvered in so masterly a fashion that Sir William Howe has not been able to approach Philadelphia. I believe Washington may become famous some day. He appears to be a leader of genius."

From a certain Lord Rawdon, just back from New York, Gilbert heard confirmation of this opinion. "George Washington is a Virginian," said the officer, "but his service in the French and Indian War and his work with the Continental Congress have made him known throughout the country. Everyone pins his hopes on him. Even the Tories, who are on our side, speak of him with a kind of reverence. If we could capture him, I think the war would be over."

Lafayette sent up a prayer that such would not be the case. He hugged close his hope of knowing one day this American hero. Indeed, he went about London with a boy's feeling of glee in the part he was playing. And the more candidly he declared his hope that the rebels would win, the better he seemed to be liked by the British. Even King George the Third, who had doubtless heard of the young stranger's prejudice, was very cordial in his reception of him. Gilbert was presented to the ruler at his levee and he thought there was something distinctly likable about the heavy, Germanic personage. Despite his stubborn, dull simplicity of mind, he was earnest and religious and meant his people very well. Therefore, his selfish and short-sighted policy toward the Colonies did not prevent personal loyalty even from his critics.

When the Marquis made his bow to Royalty, he was looking grand enough to justify his uncle's pride in him. He had donned his most elaborate court costume of brocaded satin, with white silk stockings, diamond buckles on his shoes, and shirt ruffles of such deep lace that, unless he shook them back, his hands were quite invisible. Still more invisible was the laughter in his heart at the picture of the monarch's astonishment had he known that before him stood a youth about to join the rebel army of America. But, at least, Louis the Sixteenth's subject was no spy. When he was invited to visit Portsmouth and observe the equipment of a new expedition to the United States, he made some excuse to refuse. It went against his sense of honor to repay hospitality by obtaining secret information.

Suddenly March, with a roaring wind and rain which made lakes of all the gutters, came hurtling into London-town and Lafayette was seized with impatience to be off. The ship he had purchased was supposed to be ready by the fifteenth, and he must rush back and see de Kalb. When he announced his intention of leaving England, however, the Marquis de Noailles was astounded.

"But why, *mon cher garçon?*" he exclaimed. "Has there not been entertainment enough? *Tiens,* you are the young lion of the town. I have compliments about you by the liter. Besides, you are bidden to another function at court and you must stay for it."

Gilbert rose from the lacquered chair his uncle had brought over to add a French touch to the Jacobean room and began to pace up and down. "Perhaps I shall return," he said, "and certainly nothing has been omitted from my enjoyment. But there is something I must do. I am not going home. Indeed, I shall not tell my family I have returned."

"Ah, so you have a secret?" The Ambassador laughed in sly approval. He could conceive only one intrigue which could pull a boy of nineteen away from such a round of gaieties. It must be a flirtation. *"Bon!* Go your way! If any inquiries are made, I shall say you are still here and slightly indisposed."

Just before he left the Embassy, Gilbert set down his entire plan for the American expedition in a pleading letter to his father-in-law. But he did not seal nor send it. He was too much afraid the Duc d'Ayen might interfere. When he arrived in Paris, he went straight to the little suburban house of the Baron de Kalb and remained there for three days. The only time he went out was to bid good-bye to Mr. Silas Deane at the apartment of one of de Kalb's friends. Then, still with his unsent letter in his pocket, he left Paris with the Baron. The farewell between the latter and his heartbroken wife and three children wrung Gilbert's tender heart and stabbed his conscience. Adrienne* would be equally grief-stricken, he was sure. Was it right for him to go? Could he risk a final interview with her or must he depart without a word? He pondered long and earnestly, but decided that to appear at home was too perilous. They might try to stop him, and his whole being was centered on getting to America.

Very gloomily he and de Kalb got into a private coach one early morning and set out for Bordeaux. Almost in silence they sat throughout the long journey, each sunk in his own thoughts. When they reached the port on the nineteenth of March, they found that few of the party had arrived and the ship not yet loaded. Gilbert had promised to buy the cargo as well as the vessel, and he was already short of cash. Nevertheless, the first thing he did to ease his melancholy was to collect a large group of officers and acquaintances and give a banquet at the finest tavern in the town.

Leaving de Kalb to supervise the preparations, he made off to the house of an uncle who was Governor of the Province of

* Gilbert's wife.

Guienne in which Bordeaux was located. While in his household he got off a letter to the Comte de Broglie and another to a titled friend in Paris. The latter he asked not only to deliver the letter he enclosed to the Duc d'Ayen, but to make peace with his family and to get from the Government at Versailles some indication that they approved his plan. After all, Lafayette was an officer in the king's regiment and naturally was loath to leave the country without some sort of official consent. He was confident that the moment they found out he was in dead earnest, both the Noailles clan and the court would send him their blessings. Yet days passed and no courier returned with news. The Marquis waited, unwilling to go without some message from Paris.

Everybody was now enrolled on the good ship *Victoire*. In addition to the thirteen officers originally listed were a great friend of de Broglie and a young American sent down by Silas Deane, named Leonard Price. Now the cargo was loaded, the sailing papers ready, and de Kalb was wild with eagerness to set forth. The French authorities were not supposed to permit a ship to leave with supplies, let alone officers, for America, and there was always danger of discovery.

Finally, in his anxiety, the Baron had the *Victoire* descend the Gironde River to a small town where they were within immediate reach of the open sea. There, at last, with his servants and luggage, Gilbert, now resolved to await news no longer, joined his companions. But the very moment he was stepping into a dory to be conveyed to the ship, a letter from his friend in Paris was handed to him. He tore it open, and at its first words his face grew pale with dismay.

They hadn't understood! They didn't approve! He was not thought a gallant knight, but a reckless and disobedient youngster. Paris was all agog, and the Duc d'Ayen in a fury was trying to get the Ministers not only to express disapproval, but to arrest the Marquis and bring him home. Gilbert was heartsick as he read. Moreover, he was alarmed. He could hardly afford openly to ignore a declared command of the king. And yet how could it be? De Broglie had been working directly with Vergennes in furthering this expedition. Surely retreat was impossible now!

In a whirl of conflicting emotion, Lafayette stepped into the boat and was rowed to the ship. The *Victoire* sailed immediately around to San Sebastien on the Spanish coast, and when they dropped anchor there, the Marquis went to de Kalb's cabin and told him the whole story.

Very wide grew the old Prussian's eyes. "I never thought you did well to leave your young wife in ignorance of your plan or to sail without saying good-bye to her," he growled reproachfully, "but I thought the Duc d'Ayen knew all about everything. I should advise you now to go back. Family quarrels are bad things. Perhaps you can sell the ship, and anyway, money is not so important to you as the approval of your relatives and the court."

Gilbert's heart sank. The idea either of letting de Kalb and the others sail without him or of giving up the whole enterprise cast him into the depths of despair. They went ashore at San Sebastien and the Marquis walked about, meditating mournfully upon his problem. The ship was taking on more cargo. Two days passed. Then one afternoon a horseman galloped into the little town and placed an envelope in the Marquis's hands.

He glanced at the contents and shouted for de Kalb. "Look at this!" he cried.

He had received nothing less than a *lettre de cachet*. That was a warrant of arrest which, in those days of imperial authority, unchecked by legal justice, could be procured from king or court enabling one individual to clap another into jail without trial. Somehow the Duc d'Ayen in his rage against his son-in-law had procured the document. It did not suggest imprisonment, but commanded him to proceed to Toulon and there await the Duc and his sister, the Comtesse de Tessé, who would escort the rebel to Italy for a pleasant exile of eight months.

"Think of my father-in-law going to such an extreme as this!" Lafayette shook the paper in front of de Kalb with a hand which trembled with indignation. "It is too much! I am not a child! Nothing shall keep me from going now."

De Kalb and he sat in a queer little Spanish inn and talked for hours. The Baron, cautious and sentimental, still urged him to return. But Gilbert repeated that he had no intention of submitting to such high-handed methods. Besides, he simply couldn't believe that the Foreign Minister was opposed to an exploit he must have helped de Broglie to organize.

"I'll return to Bordeaux, see my uncle, and send another message to Paris," said he. "You will have to await me here."

Accompanied by one servant, he got horses and set off. At the village Saint-Jean de Luz in the Basque country, which lies between France and Spain, they changed horses. The Marquis sipped a glass of wine and ate a mouthful of luncheon at the old inn there, but he felt so morose that he never even returned a dazzling smile bestowed upon him by the innkeeper's daughter who served him. Only the relentless forward gallop of his horse lulled his anxiety and misgivings.

At Bordeaux he found his uncle, the provincial Governor, far from sympathetic. Every detail of the story was known to him and the Marquis de Noailles had written from London in the greatest perturbation, certain that his nephew had brought the ambassadorial office at the Court of Saint James under grave suspicion.

Gilbert was quite upset at this and, seeing his regret, his host immediately wrote to the Hôtel de Noailles that the scapegrace was bowing to royal command and had returned from Spain. "The scapegrace" wrote also in a new attempt to win the Duc's consent to his departure. It was unthinkable that the glorious venture be tamely abandoned.

All at once there rode into Bordeaux a man with a most amazing message. He was a friend of de Broglie and one of the officers Layfayette had met at the famous farewell dinner for the members of that ill-fated first expedition. Straight from the Comte himself the herald had come to say that de Broglie had got it directly from de Vergennes that the *lettre de cachet* had been wrung from the court by the Duc d'Ayen and did not in the least represent the royal attitude toward the Marquis. There was no objection, but quite the contrary, to the sailing of

the *Victoire*. Everyone at Versailles, indeed, was singing the praises of the brave young leader and it was openly said that the Noailles were quite at fault to interfere. De Broglie's friend and messenger was himself expecting to enroll with Lafayette and was prepared to accompany him to the vessel.

So! It was all right, after all! In a single instant the face of things changed profoundly. With spirits soaring once more, Gilbert wrung the officer's hand, crying, "We'll go at once! Nothing shall stop us now!"

Naturally he did not take his uncle, the Governor, into his confidence. He sent by courier a last diplomatic missive to the Prime Minister, de Maurepas, to say that, since no answer had come from Versailles to his requests for further enlightenment, he took silence for a consent to his plan which he understood could not be official and would therefore sail immediately. Then he bade his uncle adieu, entered a post-chaise with his companion and servant, and in his uncle's presence commanded the driver to start for Marseilles. This, of course, was intended to mean that he would join the Duc d'Ayen and the Comtesse de Tessé for that journey into Italy. But almost as soon as they were well started, he changed his orders and the coach turned in mad haste for the Spanish port where the *Victoire* lay waiting.

To receive a *lettre de cachet*, however, meant that an armed force would follow to carry out its terms. Lafayette was nervous. At the first village where they stopped, he disguised himself in the costume of a courier and rode ahead of the post-chaise. Gorgeous was the scenery along the beautiful shore, but Lafayette had no eyes for it. All he thought about was getting across the border of Spain into safety, and sighed with relief when at last they entered the Basque village of Saint-Jean de Luz once more.

At the inn where he had stopped before, the weary courier went to the stable and flung himself down on a pile of straw for a brief rest. As he lay there he heard the clop-clop of wooden shoes, and looking up saw the pretty daughter of the innkeeper cross the yard and stop at the stable door. She glanced in, recognized the Marquis at once, and gave a cry of surprise to see him thus disguised.

"Szzzt!" Gilbert, who could not speak the Basque tongue, laid a finger on his lips, and by the language of gesture and expression took the girl into his confidence and begged her not to give him away. Nodding sympathetically, she disappeared.

At that very instant there came the rattle and thump of iron hooves on the flags of the courtyard. A troop of cavalry had dashed up and Gilbert saw the leader bend from his saddle to question the dark-haired lass. Had she seen any trace of the man they were seeking — a tall fellow, a young nobleman, bound on a secret mission? He spoke in French, but it was obvious to the quaking listener that the girl understood. He could not hear what she answered, but immediately after she spoke the horsemen galloped off again.

Up sprang the Marquis from his heap of straw. He mounted a fresh horse and, doffing his postilion's hat to the kind young woman, he dashed off at breakneck speed and was soon over the border-line of Spain. Early in the afternoon he reached the seaport and, as he dismounted in front of a small tavern, he was seized in the strong grasp of de Kalb.

"Donner und Blitzen! You are really here!" he roared. "Never did I expect to see you back!"

Sometime later the post-chaise and its passenger arrived. De Kalb heard the entire story and was highly delighted. Fresh provisions were bought. Everyone went aboard, and at last the Victoire set sail. It was Sunday evening, April 20, 1777.

As the vessel breasted its way into the open sea, Lafayette sent for the captain. He was a thick-set fellow with a rather surly look upon his face, and his name was Le Boursier.

"Captain," said the Marquis, "I want you to set your course straight for the nearest port on the American coast. We shall go directly across the Atlantic."

The captain wrinkled his brows, studied his thick-soled boots, and then replied: "But, Monsieur le Marquis, that is the most dangerous course. English frigates prowl that way looking for victims. Besides, my papers state that our port is the West Indies, and that's where I expect to head for."

De Kalb and several other officers were in Lafayette's cabin and they stared curiously at the two speakers. Their leader sat at the rough ship's table with his hand on his sword and his aquiline profile lifted at a proud angle. Yet he spoke in a tone of calm reasonableness.

"You see, Captain, there may be French vessels pursuing me and they are most likely to take the southern route. We will, therefore, go straight across the ocean to the American shore."

Stubbornly Le Boursier shook his head and muttered that it was impossible. Then the Marquis rose to his feet, towered over the man, and said haughtily: "Be so good as to remember that I am the owner of this vessel, bought for a certain purpose. You will obey my orders or I shall have my officers arrest you and put you in chains."

All the officers looked on approvingly. This nineteen-year-old was not a major-general for nothing. He knew how to command. Everyone felt heartened by such an exhibition of force and resolution. Its effect upon Le Boursier was immediate. He stammered out a confession that his real objection to the order was the fact that he was smuggling eight thousand dollars' worth of goods for sale in the West Indies. Lafayette's face lightened. Was that all? Pooh, he'd pay for those, also, if necessary. So the captain bowed and stumped off to give his commands, and the course was laid due west.

The moment he was gone, Gilbert flung on his cloak and went aft to watch the last of the Spanish shore. His heart was full of Adrienne. Had they told her yet that he had sailed, her husband who had gone without an embrace, a loving word, a final farewell? He wondered suddenly how he could have done it and vowed he would in the future confide everything to her. Doubtless she would have sympathized with his feeling and would have taken his part against her father. To love is to trust, and he had not loved her enough, the darling! He watched the swift twilight blot out the rugged cliffs. His last look at land for weeks to come! Suddenly the vastness of his adventure loomed over him in all its peril and uncertainty.

Not a man in the party but was affected by the same sense of loss and suspense. From one day to another there was no telling what would happen to them. Danger from storms was always supplemented by threat of attack from the English. They had only two cannon and a few antiquated muskets on board, and the ship, built like a tub, could not have fled from the most cumbersome enemy.

For days after the *Victoire* began to roll and pitch in the heavy seas, all the officers were too sick to leave their bunks. But when they finally stumbled up on deck, they were not much better off — with nothing to do except stare at the wallow and rush of gray seas. Lafayette studied English and practiced speaking it to de Kalb and young Leonard Price, the American. Moreover, he grew to know his associates, and especially liked young Major Gimat, for whom he determined to get a commission from the Continental Congress as his aide-de-camp.

As he stood beside this new friend on the high poop deck, the Marquis would say, "Major, how many days now since we left Spain?" And Gimat had counted forty before there was the slightest indication of nearing the coast of America. Almost the entire time they had had to sail dead against the wind, if wind there was. The only excitement was the possibility of being sighted by the enemy. Whenever the lookout called, "Sail ho!" everyone would rush to discover whether an English frigate was in sight. In council the group decided that since they could not fight, they had best blow themselves up rather than be captured. Most vessels were too far away to observe the *Victoire*. But one day a great ship made directly for them.

"Every man to his post!" cried the Marquis.

The officers rushed to their places. They exchanged eloquent looks and Gilbert saw Captain Le Boursier grow white with terror. As the dreadful apparition approached nearer and nearer, each man asked himself, "Is this, indeed, the end of everything?" At last they were hailed. Then — oh, the wild relief of it! — they learned it was an American ves-

sel. For a time they tried to follow in her wake, but soon fell behind.

It was not long after this thrilling moment that the wind changed, the air grew warmer, and the captain announced that they must be within a few hundred miles of the coast. At this everyone plucked up heart and fell to writing letters home. Gilbert scratched off half a dozen. But the real one, the long one, was to Adrienne.

.   .   .   .

The fifty-fourth day of that voyage was just dawning when a cry rang through the ship, "Land! Land!"

Gilbert woke out of a sound sleep. Leaping from his bunk, he scrambled into some clothes and rushed out on deck. From every cabin emerged tousled, unpowdered heads. Everyone was running pell-mell to the bow. There it was, like a mirage in the distance, the dark, uneven shadow of the shore.

"Dieu merci!" "Heaven be praised!" Thankful voices uttered the heart's cry. Leonard Price in his excitement was hugging old de Kalb. Major Gimat's eyes were full of tears. Young Lafayette, his hands tensely clasped, looked as if his eyes beheld at last the promised land where Glory waited for him.

Daniel Boone
Boonesborough [5]

JAMES DAUGHERTY

To the average boy, no early American offers more romantic thrills than Daniel Boone. The biography of this famous pioneer, written and illustrated by James Daugherty, not only brings out Boone's greatness of character, but furnishes a reliable picture of Midwestern pioneer life. No wonder the book won the Newbery award for 1940. The chapter here given tells one of the most exciting experiences of the hero's always exciting life.

A pattern of fur-clad hunters and long-eared hounds and pack-horses carrying iron

[5] From James Daugherty, *Daniel Boone* (Viking Press, 1939).

salt-kettles, trailing among the black leafless trees, made a silhouette on the blue-white snow that lay deep over the winter world of Kentucky. They were going to French Lick to boil thousands of gallons of water at the salt springs in order that desperate Boonesborough might have the salt that kept the meat from putrefying so Boonesborough could eat and live.

In the dead of winter the salt-camp at French Lick felt safe from the Indians, whose custom was to take the warpath only in the spring or summer. But one gray evening in February, as Boone was coming back to camp after a long day's hunt, he was completely surprised by an ambush of four Indian warriors. He tried to run for it, but in the deep snow it was useless. The Old Fox of Kentucky was caught again. They were the very Shawnees from whom he had escaped years ago on the Finley expedition. It was a tough, heart-breaking moment, but he had been there more than once before and had come through. Now it was a quick shift of tactics from physical action to a game of wits and bluff.

The Indians were a large war party under Chief Black Fish headed for a surprise attack on Boonesborough. Suddenly to have caught the great chief of the white men so excited them that Boone was able shrewdly to persuade them to change their plan. The silent white hunter must have turned eloquent and impressive as he stood in the midst of the savage council that was to give the tomahawk vote of life or death for the unsuspecting salt-camp. Fantastic as it sounds, nevertheless the war party agreed to leave Boonesborough till the spring, when Boone promised he would arrange a peaceable moving of the settlers farther north where they might live as adopted Shawnees. For the present the Indians would return to Chillicothe with the unscalped salt-boilers as their prisoners. All this was argued out in talk and translated back and forth by a Negro named Pompey.

Though Boone had saved the fort on the Kentucky and the salt-camp from bloody butchery by his courage and wits alone, some of the men were bitter and resentful against him as they marched half-starved and frozen

into the winter encampment of the Shawnees at Chillicothe. After a while Black Fish led a party with the white captives to Detroit to exhibit them and perhaps sell them to General Hamilton.

Detroit in 1776 was a British fort and trading post perched on the open waterway of the Great Lakes. The rich fur trade of a vast area of wild North America passed through there on the way to make fortunes in far-off King George's England. Now there was a revolution in the colonies. It would be bad for the fur business. Inside the fort the red-coated British soldiers went through their daily drill. They dreamed in their barracks of English lanes and alehouses and rosy English sweethearts.

Outside the fort the red tribes came and went at will. They traded and treated with the English soldiers and traders after their touchy, quick-changing fashion. White trappers, wild and savage as the Indians, drifted in with their fur packs to swap for ammunition and to liquor up. A trader coming in with a keg of French brandy would leave town with great bales of fine furs, and a wild drunken orgy of whooping and fighting would follow. The Indians brought in from the border raids white captives, men, women, and children, as well as scalps. For these General Hamilton, the British commander, paid fixed prices in money, Indian finery, and war paint. The black faces of African Negroes mingled in the fantastic pageant. Around these wilderness outposts surged a drama of fierce passions and violent deeds.

It was a grand show-off when Black Fish's party stalked out of the forest with the great Daniel and ten of his men as captives. The whole town thrilled to see the legendary hero of the border in the flesh. Boone was as persuasive with the British as with the Indians. He showed his commission as a captain in His British Majesty's army and told of his fictitious plan to capture Boonesborough in the spring. Hamilton was delighted with him. But when it came to selling his prisoners, Black Fish insisted that Boone was his personal property and he was not for sale, even though the general raised the price to the fabulous sum of one hundred pounds.

Boone took a long look at Detroit as he

rode back into the forest with the returning Indians. It might be the last time he would ever see white faces.

The naked Indian children stared in wonder at Daniel Boone, and the lean wolf dogs snarled and snapped, not liking his strange white smell as he sat squinting at the fire in the smoky huts of Chillicothe. He was thinking his white man's thoughts as he watched the tall idle warriors and the bronze squaws grinding corn, scraping the skins, kneading the buffalo robes to make them soft. He had done very well pretending he was an Indian, pretending he was happy and satisfied, and pleasing the great chieftain Moluntha with his clever hunting. He looked wistfully at the fat Indian ponies, thinking of a dash for freedom when the right moment came. They had washed away his white blood in the river, pulled out half his hair, and painted him with strange symbols that meant he was the adopted son of the chief Black Fish. He knew by heart the strange rhythms of the mysterious ceremonial songs and dances. He was quick to share in the red laughter or laments.

One evening he came back tired from tedious labor at the salt licks to find the braves in war paint dancing to the pounding drums and shrill war chants. Sitting in his familiar place, he watched the wild frenzies rise and sway around the flickering campfires. There were five hundred warriors preparing for a surprise attack on Boonesborough. He knew how few were the defenders and that the fort was in bad repair. The whole settlement would be utterly unprepared. His hour had come and he was ready. Before dawn he slipped out like a shadow and was gone. Now again he was the hunted fox of the wilderness with the red dogs in close pursuit.

"On the 16th I departed before sunrise in the most secret manner and arrived at Boonesborough on the 20th, after a journey of one hundred and sixty miles, during which I had but one meal." Brief autobiography. How did he know the way all the four days and nights with the Shawnee pack one jump behind?

He was not so young as he used to be, but tough and long-winded. When he came at last to the Ohio at full spring flood, he remembered he could not swim. It was the desperate tight spot he had known so often, but the angel of the wilderness showed him a leaky canoe stranded on a sand bar and he made a swift downstream crossing on the yellow waters to the Kentucky shore that he knew like the back of his hand. Familiar landmarks cheered him. He shot a buffalo and cooked his first meal in four days. He was in sight of Boonesborough. He had kept his rendezvous with Destiny.

It was a strange figure that came across the clearing into Boonesborough and said he was Daniel Boone. For weeks they had said Daniel Boone was a goner for sure this time. Even Rebecca's faith had failed, and she had returned with the family to the settlements. Boone was sorry, yet glad, too, for she was safe. His brother Israel and Jemima, his beloved daughter who had married Dick Calloway, were there to give him a warm welcome. But it was no wonder Rebecca had gone. Many a husband and father had never come back across the clearing.

The news of the coming Indian raid roused the settlers to action. The neglected log walls were repaired and everything made ready for an attack, the swift short Indian attack with which the borderers were familiar. But weeks passed and no Indians were seen. Then another escaped white man brought in news that Boone's flight had delayed the Indians. Boone then took a raiding expedition across the Ohio and burned an Indian village, getting back just a few hours ahead of the great war party of over four hundred Indians with some forty French Canadians under the direction of their officer De Quindre.

There were about fifty men and boys, besides the women and children, behind the log stockade when the Indians surrounded the clearing of Boonesborough. Instead of the usual sudden attack, an Indian came out of the woods with a white flag and by calling back and forth arranged for a parley. Every hour of delay meant a nearer hope of reinforcement coming in from Harrodsburg. Three of the defenders met Black Fish, Moluntha, and Catahecassa near the fort for a powwow. There was talk of friendship and peaceful surrender. The chief promised that the whites would be taken safely on horses to Detroit if they surrendered peaceably. There need be no bloodshed if the Americans would agree to abandon the fort.

Boone said he would explain to his people and in two days give an answer. He was glad to find that the Indians had heard from a white captive that there were several hundred defenders in the fort. The Indians believed their offer of safety was sure to be accepted.

Inside the fort the chances were talked over and argued and weighed after the democratic way of the backwoods. The odds were ten to one and worse against defense, and not a man, woman, or child would be spared if —— But the tough cantankerous spirit of the frontier urged: "Go ahead or bust." They would not have been where they were if they had not been stubborn survivors of a rough, tough, restless race who lived and died in their own independent way by the rifle, the axe, the Bible, and the plow. So they sent back the eagle's answer: "No surrender," the answer of the sassy two-year-old baby democracy, the answer of Man the Unconquerable to the hosts of darkness — "No surrender."

The iron-faced chiefs and the ornery Frenchman De Quindre took the answer grimly back to their council, while the settlers got in their cows, corn, and water from the spring without interference from the Indians. The next move was an Indian trick which was perfectly transparent to Boone, but he took the chances of playing it to win time.

The Indians proposed a grand council of nine on each side to sign a treaty of peace, after which they would depart, they said, like lambs. The council sat under the sycamore trees within rifle shot of the fort. At a wave of the hat from the delegates the riflemen in the fort were to open fire and cover the nine men's dash back when trouble started.

All day they sat in the shade and smoked, talked, and ate while a fancy treaty of peace, including a sworn allegiance to the British Crown, was agreed on, to be signed tomorrow at the same place. In the night an ambush of Indians was set around the treaty tree. The next day when the nine appeared from the fort, Black Fish met them with eighteen powerful young braves. After the signing came the two-to-one handshaking. Two Indians grabbed for each white man and a mob jumped from the laurel to finish the job. Then the nine Kentucky wildcats let loose with teeth and claws, and the fur flew. Shooting began and the nine raced for the fort. They had won the first round.

Next day there was a great hubbub in the forest, bugles blowing and orders for retreat bawled out, and the pack-horses were seen crossing the river at the ford. But the old border fox in the fort was not fooled. The gates of Boonesborough remained shut and the Indian trick failed. The real danger was an Indian rush on the gates under a heavy fire from all sides. This was what kept the riflemen waiting and watching at the portholes day and night.

But to charge across the clearing under the fire of Kentucky rifles was so contrary to the Indian way of fighting that all of De Quindre's urging for a mass attack was useless. Instead, the savages remained under cover of the woods, firing continuously. Day and night under the heavy encircling fire of the enemy, the riflemen stuck to their posts, blazing away whenever an inch of Indian hide was exposed to view. The women passed out the scant rations and scarce water, loaded guns when the firing was fast, molded bullets, comforted the children, and prayed the prayers of the pioneer faith. Each slow day under the burning sun was an eternity; each night they thanked the God of their Fathers that some protecting angel had kept the gates.

From high up in a distant tree a sniper began sending bullets inside the fort and Jemima Boone was hit. Boone drew a bead at two hundred yards on the sniper as he was reloading, and put a bullet through his head. The figure that pitched from the high tree was black Pompey. Colonel Calloway, of the old school, became irritated at Boone's cautious tactics and contrived an impressive wooden cannon. The roar and smoke of her first shot scared the Indians for about a mile out of range, but when the smoke cleared from her second blast, she had burst wide open and was permanently disabled. But she was the wonder of the wilderness as long as she lasted.

More serious was the tunnel which the enemy was driving toward the fort. It carried to the defenders the sinister fear of exploding mines that would breach the wooden walls. Day by day they could hear the digging come nearer. It wore on their strained nerves like the gnawing of a rat in the night.

Hour by hour a week dragged on. In the inky blackness of the seventh night, a bright flame suddenly shot across the clearing in a long arc and dropped on a cabin roof. It was the dreadful flaming arrow. Now they were dropping fast on the pine roofs of the cabins. Worst yet, the savages had crept across the clearing in the darkness and started fagot fires against the log palisade on all sides. The spreading glow lit up the clearing as the hungry little flames ran along the shingles. Against the glow the frantic silhouettes of the defenders trying to beat out the flames drew stinging gun fire from the enemy. Suddenly a figure leaped up on a burning roof and in a fury of flame and bullets beat out the fire. When he had finished, he calmly jumped down to safety. But the fires along the stockade were taking hold and the last remaining buckets full of precious water would be of no avail. The riflemen were standing at their posts holding their fire, waiting for the final mass attack, and women stood clutching their children. To Boone it seemed the last card had been played and lost. As the red light flickered over his set face, suddenly he felt a drop of water strike the back of his hand, and as he looked up heavy drops struck his face. In a few minutes the God-sent rain streamed down in drenching sheets. The burning stockade hissed, steamed, glowed, and went out. Something beyond human power had saved Boonesborough by the skin of its teeth.

Still the firing from the forest kept up incessantly. No one knew how near the tunnel was, but it seemed almost under their feet. The September pouring rain had soaked everyone to the bone. They would soon be passing around the last ration of food. Hope held desperately to ever slim-

mer chances. No Indian attack on a fort had ever been known to keep up so long.

Utter darkness of a night of lashing rain set in on the ninth day of the siege. In the fierce movement of the storm it seemed as though the savage demons of all the wild valley had come down for vengeance. It was a blind night when a man could not see the end of his rifle barrel. Nothing now could stop the mass rush of the savages across the clearing. The riflemen stood grimly at their posts in the pouring rain and waited. In the darkness time stopped. They shifted and growled, trying to keep their powder dry, and muttered to each other. At long last the night lifted. Out of the shapeless grayness the world was taking form. The morning came with no firing from the enemy, and the lookouts reported no signs of Indians in the forest. It looked like another false retreat. A scout or two came back with the news that the Indians were on the march this time for sure.

Then two white men crossed the clearing shouting and waving. One was Simon Kenton, who had not been able to get through the lines. It was true that the Indians had gone. The white medicine was too strong. The spirits of the forest were beaten and the white gods prevailed. A surge of wild joy was in the hearts of Boonesborough when the log gates swung open and let out the starved cattle. There was whooping and firing to welcome eighty backwoodsmen from Harrodsburg, riding in too late for a rescue but in time for the celebration.

Audubon
Many Trails and a Snug Cabin[6]

CONSTANCE ROURKE

⊰ *Audubon's birth and very early years in Haiti lie shrouded in mystery, but his boyhood in France does not. He fought a formal education by slipping out-of-doors to follow and later paint birds. The decision to send him at eighteen to America to look after Captain Audu-*

6 From Constance Rourke, *Audubon* (Harcourt, Brace, 1936).

bon's interests there was the great turning-point of his life. As a businessman Audubon was at times a success and at other times a failure, but his main interest was always in wild life, especially in birds; and America gave him the real chance to study and learn more about birds and to paint them. The passage selected, while it does not represent the general content of the chapter, does show how keen his interest was in his painting, what his problems were, and what meticulous care he gave to his work.

Audubon went on with his early plan, which was more ambitious than Wilson's, to portray American birds among their natural surroundings.

Often he made single studies. He had hardly returned from Sainte-Geneviève when he painted the brooding hunched form of a turkey buzzard, life-size, painted this so truly and substantially that the bird's whole character loomed clear against the white paper. He was steadily occupied by the complex patterning of the plumage of owls, and painted barn owls on a branch, with the Ohio and its low-lying hills dusky green in the background. He tried to solve one of the most difficult of problems, to paint a bird so that it would seem in free motion through the air, not merely set within the foreground of a scene. In a small watercolor he accomplished this, showing a bay-breasted warbler, jewel-like in grayish-green and shadowed black and tawny red, in flight — flying northward perhaps to a nesting-place in Labrador — with the pale blue hills of the Ohio beyond.

The painting of birds' eyes steadily engrossed him and he triumphed early over the problem; he was miraculously sure as to colors and shapes, and somehow by the placing of tiny sharp highlights achieved an effect of wildness which was never timidity or distraction, but the unchanging, watchful look that sets birds apart from humans.

His concern with small effects of light and color was becoming intense. He had already discovered latent tones in old wood. It happened that the use of old wood had long been a romantic convention in nature painting, introduced to create an atmosphere of melancholy decay. Audubon was to use it in many forms and textures again and again, but never according to this stale formula. He found lucent blues there, deep yellows, touches of red; he studied the bold lines of the grain in split or shattered branches and began to use these in compositions. These were not always successful, as in his early painting of the pewee flycatcher, but the decorative intention is plain, and curiously enough his use of old wood or even of lichens seldom suggested age or decay, but light and brilliance.

In these years he was clearly concerned with the conquest of design, though this grew more difficult as he used more and more exquisite natural forms. He still liked the bold outlines of birds in flight without backgrounds, with the mere placement of outlines and the patterns of spread tails and wings, and the relation of two or three birds making the decorations, as in some of his paintings of hawks. His quiet study of snowbirds in early winter on gray-black gum branches with hanging oval berries foreshadowed some of his more subtle later work. He was coming into consciousness of many forms which were always to enchant him — the pink mallow in flower, blown into changing patterns by the wind, the wild grape in fruit, and the narrow leaves of the cane.

He fronted many problems in color and pattern which he was to solve slowly, only by most patient labor and experiment. He tried to portray purple grackles stripping stalks of Indian corn, and succeeded in showing the clutching, ruthless strength of the feeding birds with a bold contrast between the yellow corn and the dark rich glow of eyes and feathers. Other paintings were taking shape — his orioles in the flowering tulip tree, his studies of the great wild turkey, the cock and the hen, and the peregrine falcons — he tried these over and again but could not please himself. He still invariably destroyed drawings or paintings when others were finished of the same subject which seemed truer. Yet with all his failures and dissatisfactions his portfolios steadily grew heavier, and overflowed with sketches of birds, leaves, flowers, fruits, insects, and — because he couldn't let them alone — squirrels and mink, otter, raccoons, opossums.

Obstacles he met in sufficient number as his plans multiplied. When he shot a rare bird, this might fall into a deep tangle where by the most determined efforts he could not reach it, or he might make a stirring discovery at so great a distance from home that when he reached his drawing table the lustrous feathers were dimmed. One cold spring he found a number of cliff swallows far down the Ohio, but the lad with whom he was hunting lost those they had shot somewhere in the woods, and it was four years before he saw cliff swallows again. He had already formed a plan to portray both the male and female of the chosen species and even the immature birds in a single painting, and he often had the experience of finding one without the others, and was obliged to wait for months or even until another season to complete his group.

But there were days of extraordinary sights, as when he saw some goshawks trailing a great crowd of swiftly flying pigeons over the Ohio. Suddenly one of them turned aside to a flock of blackbirds, and the blackbirds swiftly closed together and were like a dusky ball passing through the air. The goshawk claimed four or five of them with ease, squeezed them, dropped them into the river. As the blackbirds reached dense woods, they plunged, and the goshawk wheeled and dipped and picked up his prey from the surface of the water.

Abraham Lincoln
His Good Stepmother [7]

GENEVIEVE FOSTER

⚡ *Mrs. Foster's biography of Abraham Lincoln for younger children is a warm and understanding book. In the chapter given below, the boy Abe is nine years old. His father, Tom Lincoln, had moved the family to Pigeon Creek in Indiana, but before he had completed building a cabin, Nancy Hanks, Abe's mother, caught a fever and died. Abe and his older sister Sarah and his father were desolate without her.*

[7] From Genevieve Foster, *Abraham Lincoln* (Scribner, 1950).

A whole year passed in misery and loneliness. Then Abe's father couldn't stand it any longer. He went back to Kentucky, leaving Abe and Sarah alone with Dennis Hanks. Dennis had come to live in their cabin after Aunt Betsy died.

One dismal December day, Abe sat by the fire, scratching all the letters he could remember in the ashes, wishing he knew how to read. Every day seemed like a week, waiting for his father to come back. Abe knew why he'd gone, but that didn't make waiting any easier. Dennis had just come in with his gun, bringing a squirrel for dinner. Sarah said she'd cook it and try to make it taste good. Abe said he couldn't eat. He couldn't even swallow.

What if nobody would come? he thought. Or what if somebody came, and she didn't like them — him and Sarah? What if. . . . All of a sudden he heard horses' hooves. He ran outside. And, almost before he knew it, SHE was there. His stepmother, Sarah Bush Lincoln. He saw her first, sitting beside his father on the seat of a big wagon, piled so high with furniture that it took four horses to pull it.

On top of the pile sat two girls and a boy. They jumped down as the wagon stopped and stood staring at Abe and Sarah in their dirty, ragged clothes. Then the tall, straight woman came and stood beside them.

"These are my children," she said. "John and Sarah and Matilda Johnston." Her voice was warm and friendly. "And I suppose you are Sarah Lincoln? And you," she added slowly, "you must be Abraham."

Abe looked up. Her eyes were as friendly as her voice. She didn't even seem to see that he was too tall, or mind that he was homely. She just smiled, and so Abe smiled, too. From then to the end of his life, this second mother was to be "the best friend he had."

"Wa-al now," she said briskly, stepping into the cabin. "Fust thing for me to do is to make something for us all to eat. Meantime you young-uns go out to the horse trough. Take this soft soap and wash up good, all over."

Wash up? thought Abe, all over? in the winter? That was a mighty queer notion. But he did it, and it felt good. It felt good, too, to have a comb run through his gritty black hair. And to put on a clean shirt of the Johnston boy's. And sit down to good, hot food with eight folks around the table to eat it.

After supper, his new mother swept up the dirty cabin. But to be halfway decent, she told Abe's father, it would have to have a wood floor and a door and windows. Then he could get some lime over to Gentryville and whitewash the walls. Right away, that night, everybody must help carry in the furniture and unroll the feather beds. Abe heard something bumping in the chest as they set it down.

Next morning, when his stepmother opened it, there were two books. One was the Bible. And the other — he could hardly believe his eyes — the other was his beloved fable book.

It was *Aesop's Fables*.

"Kin you read?" his stepmother asked. Abe shook his head. "Nor kin I," she added quickly. "But you'd like to learn?" She knew the answer before he gave it. "Then I'll make sure that you git the chance, soon as there's enough settlers around here to have a school start up."

The winter Abe was thirteen, a school was started. All the children went for a few months. The others didn't half try, but Abe was different. He went over and over the words in the Speller, and practiced writing everywhere, specially on the back of the big, wooden fire shovel.

Dennis got interested, and made a pen for him out of a turkey buzzard's quill, stirred up some ink, and brought back some paper from the store at Gentryville to make into a notebook. In it Abe wrote:

Abraham Lincoln
his hand and pen.
he will be good but
god knows When

He was now fourteen. At last he could read and write! All day long, his father had

chores for him to do — hard, grubby work — but as soon as he could lay down his axe and hoe, he was turning the pages of a book, reading as if he were starved.

Tom Lincoln couldn't understand it. "It'd be different," he'd say, "if he was puny or sickly, so's he couldn't go huntin'. But for a big strappin' feller like Abe to take so to book-larnin' is jes' plain queer."

But the good stepmother understood this boy who was so different from the others. Sometimes, as she was patching or knitting, he'd have her listen while he read a funny story aloud, and they'd laugh over it together.

The first book Abe ever owned, he got from the first man he ever worked for, Mr. Josiah Crawford, a nearby farmer.

Mr. Crawford was a thin, sour man, with such a way of hanging onto money that he had more of it than any of his neighbors, and could hire them to work for him.

Tom Lincoln helped him build a new farmhouse and then sent young Abe over to work as a hired man. Abe was then only fifteen, but close to six feet tall, and strong as he was tall.

One day, Mr. Crawford and two or three other men were puzzling over how to lift a heavy log chicken coop that he wanted moved.

"Whar's Abe?" he cried in his thin, sour voice. "Off readin' again?"

"Mebbe," said one of the men, "or mebbe down by the road, talking to a stranger. You know Abe — cain't let a traveler get by without findin' out all he knows."

Just then the big boy sauntered up.

"Movin' the coop?" he drawled. "Whar to?"

The men pointed. Abe stooped down, hoisted it onto his back, carried it over and set it down, all by himself. The men were dumfounded.

Oh, Abe was strong, no doubt of that, agreed his employer, but he was lazy. He could husk corn, chop down trees, split rails faster than any two men, if he took a notion, but he'd rather read than work.

Josiah himself didn't care much about books, but he owned a few. He let Abe take one home, warning him to be careful of it. It was a biography of George Washington.

Abe could hardly wait to start it, and then he couldn't bear to stop. He read all evening, stretched out by the fire, until his father banked it with ashes and made him go to bed. Abe slept in the loft. To have the book handy as soon as it grew light, he carried it up with him, and laid it carefully between the logs. Next morning when he reached for it, his heart sank. It was soaking wet. There had been rain in the night. What could he do or say?

"Wa-al," said Josiah Crawford, shrewdly. "Seein' it's you, Abe . . . You put in three days huskin' corn, and you kin keep it."

Only three days! Abe could hardly believe it. When those three days were over the book belonged to him. The story of George Washington's life. He read it again and again. Each time it stirred him with ambition.

"I'm not always going to grub and shuck corn and split rails for a livin'," he said to Mrs. Crawford, one morning. And when she asked him what he wanted to do or be, he answered,

"The President." He half smiled as if he were joking, but his voice was serious. "Well, anyway, I'll study and get ready," he said, "and the chance may come."

Abe Lincoln Grows Up
"Peculiarsome" Abe [8]
CARL SANDBURG

❧ *The life of Lincoln is so well known to all American boys and girls that it is difficult to write a biography to attract them. Carl Sandburg has done so, however; by the straightforwardness and charm of his style, he makes the young Lincoln live. One sees this poor boy, hungering after books for what they could give him, a dreamer but a fighter, who was called lazy but was ambitious. One sympathizes with that boy and rejoices with him in his successes; yet one understands why those about him called him "peculiarsome."*

[8] From Carl Sandburg, *Abe Lincoln Grows Up* (Harcourt, Brace, 1928).

The farm boys in their evenings at Jones's store in Gentryville talked about how Abe Lincoln was always reading, digging into books, stretching out flat on his stomach in front of the fireplace, studying till midnight and past midnight, picking a piece of charcoal to write on the fire shovel, shaving off what he wrote, and then writing more — till midnight and past midnight. The next thing Abe would be reading books between the plow handles, it seemed to them. And once trying to speak a last word, Dennis Hanks said, "There's suthin' peculiarsome about Abe."

He wanted to learn, to know, to live, to reach out; he wanted to satisfy hungers and thirsts he couldn't tell about, this big boy of the backwoods. And some of what he wanted so much, so deep down, seemed to be in the books. Maybe in books he would find the answers to dark questions pushing around in the pools of his thoughts and the drifts of his mind. He told Dennis and other people, "The things I want to know are in books; my best friend is the man who'll git me a book I ain't read." And sometimes friends answered, "Well, books ain't as plenty as wildcats in these parts o' Indianny."

This was one thing meant by Dennis when he said there was "suthin' peculiarsome" about Abe. It seemed that Abe made the books tell him more than they told other people. All the other farm boys had gone to school and read *The Kentucky Preceptor*, but Abe picked out questions from it, such as "Who has the most right to complain, the Indian or the Negro?" and Abe would talk about it, up one way and down the other, while they were in the cornfield pulling fodder for the winter. When Abe got hold of a story-book and read about a boat that came near a magnetic rock, and how the magnets in the rock pulled all the nails out of the boat so it went to pieces and the people in the boat found themselves floundering in water, Abe thought it was funny and told it to other people. After Abe read poetry, especially Bobby Burns's poems, Abe began writing rhymes himself. When Abe sat with a girl, with their bare feet in the creek water, and she spoke of the moon rising, he explained to her that it was the earth moving and not the moon — the moon only seemed to rise.

John Hanks, who worked in the fields bare-footed with Abe, grubbing stumps, plowing, mowing, said: "When Abe and I came back to the house from work, he used to go to the cupboard, snatch a piece of corn bread, sit down, take a book, cock his legs up high as his head, and read. Whenever Abe had a chance in the field while at work, or at the house, he would stop and read." He liked to explain to other people what he was get-ting from books; explaining an idea to some-one else made it clearer to him. The habit was growing on him of reading out loud; words came more real if picked from the silent page of the book and pronounced on the tongue; new balances and values of words stood out if spoken aloud. When writ-ing letters for his father or the neighbors, he read the words out loud as they got writ-ten. Before writing a letter he asked ques-tions such as: "What do you want to say in the letter? How do you want to say it? Are you sure that's the best way to say it? Or do you think we can fix up a better way to say it?"

As he studied his books his lower lip stuck out; Josiah Crawford noticed it was a habit and joked Abe about the "stuck-out lip." This habit too stayed with him.

He wrote in his Sum Book or arithmetic that Compound Division was "When several numbers of Divers Denominations are given to be divided by 1 common devisor," and worked on the exercise in multiplication; "If 1 foot contains 12 inches I demand how many there are in 126 feet." Thus the schoolboy.

What he got in the schools didn't satisfy him. He went to three different schools in Indiana, besides two in Kentucky — alto-gether about four months of school. He learned his A B C, how to spell, read, write. And he had been with the other barefoot boys in butternut jeans learning "manners" under the school teacher, Andrew Crawford, who had them open a door, walk in, and say, "Howdy do?" Yet what he tasted of books in school was only a beginning, only made him hungry and thirsty, shook him with a wanting and a wanting of more and more of what was hidden between the covers of books.

He kept on saying, "The things I want to know are in books; my best friend is the man who'll git me a book I ain't read." He said that to Pitcher, the lawyer over at Rockport, nearly twenty miles away, one fall afternoon, when he walked from Pigeon Creek to Rock-port and borrowed a book from Pitcher. Then when fodder-pulling time came a few days later, he shucked corn from early day-light till sundown along with his father and Dennis Hanks and John Hanks, but after supper he read the book till midnight, and at noon he hardly knew the taste of his corn bread because he had the book in front of him. It was a hundred little things like these which made Dennis Hanks say there was "suthin' peculiarsome" about Abe.

Besides reading the family Bible and figur-ing his way all through the old arithmetic they had at home, he got hold of *Aesop's Fables, Pilgrim's Progress, Robinson Crusoe,* and Weems's *The Life of Francis Marion.* The book of fables, written or collected thou-sands of years ago by the Greek slave, known as Aesop, sank deep in his mind. As he read through the book a second and third time, he had a feeling there were fables all around him, that everything he touched and handled, everything he saw and learned had a fable wrapped in it somewhere. One fable was about a bundle of sticks and a farmer whose sons were quarreling and fighting.

There was a fable in two sentences which read, "A coachman, hearing one of the wheels of his coach make a great noise, and perceiv-ing that it was the worst one of the four, asked how it came to take such a liberty. The wheel answered that from the beginning of time, creaking had always been the privi-lege of the weak." And there were shrewd, brief incidents of foolery such as this: "A waggish, idle fellow in a country town, being desirous of playing a trick on the simplicity of his neighbors and at the same time putting a little money in his pocket at their cost, advertised that he would on a certain day show a wheel carriage that should be so con-trived as to go without horses. By silly curios-ity the rustics were taken in, and each suc-ceeding group who came out from the show were ashamed to confess to their neighbors that they had seen nothing but a wheel-barrow."

The style of the Bible, of *Aesop's Fables,* the hearts and minds back of those books, were much in his thoughts. His favorite pages in them he read over and over. Behind such proverbs as, "Muzzle not the ox that treadeth out the corn," and "He that ruleth his own spirit is greater than he that taketh a city," there was a music of simple wisdom and a mystery of common everyday life that touched deep spots in him, while out of the fables of the ancient Greek slave he came to see that cats, rats, dogs, horses, plows, ham-mers, fingers, toes, people, all had fables con-nected with their lives, characters, places. There was, perhaps, an outside for each thing as it stood alone, while inside of it was its fable.

One book came, titled, *The Life of George Washington, with Curious Anecdotes, Equal-ly Honorable to Himself and Exemplary to His Young Countrymen.* Embellished with Six Steel Engravings, by M. L. Weems, for-merly Rector of Mount Vernon Parish. It pictured men of passion and proud igno-rance in the government of England driving their country into war on the American col-onies. It quoted the far-visioned warning of Chatham to the British parliament, "For God's sake, then, my lords, let the way be instantly opened for reconciliation. I say instantly; or it will be too late forever."

The book told of war, as at Saratoga. "Hoarse as a mastiff of true British breed, Lord Balcarras was heard from rank to rank, loud-animating his troops; while on the other hand, fierce as a hungry Bengal tiger, the impetuous Arnold precipitated heroes on the stubborn foe. Shrill and terrible, from rank to rank, resounds the clash of bayonets — frequent and sad the groans of the dying. Pairs on pairs, Britons and Americans, with each his bayonet at his brother's breast, fall forward together faint-shrieking in death, and mingle their smoking blood." Washing-ton, the man, stood out, as when he wrote, "These things so harassed my heart with grief, that I solemnly declared to God, if I know myself, I would gladly offer myself a sacrifice to the butchering enemy, if I could

thereby insure the safety of these my poor distressed countrymen."

The Weems book reached some deep spots in the boy. He asked himself what it meant that men should march, fight, bleed, go cold and hungry for the sake of what they called "freedom."

"Few great men are great in everything," said the book. And there was a cool sap in the passage: "His delight was in that of the manliest sort, which, by stringing the limbs and swelling the muscles, promotes the kind-liest flow of blood and spirits. At jumping with a long pole, or heaving heavy weights, for his years he hardly had an equal."

Such book talk was a comfort against the same thing over again, day after day, so many mornings the same kind of water from the same spring, the same fried pork and corn-meal to eat, the same drizzles of rain, spring plowing, summer weeds, fall fodder-pulling, each coming every year, with the same tired feeling at the end of the day, so many days alone in the woods or the fields or else the same people to talk with, people from whom he had learned all they could teach him. Yet there ran through his head the stories and sayings of other people, the stories and say-ings of books, the learning his eyes had caught from books; they were a comfort; they were good to have because they were good by themselves; and they were still better to have because they broke the chill of the lone-some feeling.

He was thankful to the writer of *Aesop's Fables* because that writer stood by him and walked with him, an invisible companion, when he pulled fodder or chopped wood. Books lighted lamps in the dark rooms of his gloomy hours. . . . Well — he would live on; maybe the time would come when he would be free from work for a few weeks, or a few months, with books, and then he would read. . . . God, then he would read. . . . Then he would go and get at the proud secrets of his books.

His father — would he be like his father when he grew up? He hoped not. Why should his father knock him off a fence rail when he was asking a neighbor, passing by, a question? Even if it was a smart question, too pert and too quick, it was no way to handle a boy in front of a neighbor. No, he was going to be a man different from his father. The books — his father hated the books. His father talked about "too much eddication"; after readin', writin', 'rithmetic, that was enough, his father said. He, Abe Lincoln, the boy, wanted to know more than the father, Tom Lincoln, wanted to know. Already Abe knew more than his father; he was writing letters for the neighbors; they hunted out the Lincoln farm to get young Abe to find his bottle of ink with blackberry brier root and copperas in it, and his pen made from a turkey buzzard feather, and write letters. Abe had a suspicion sometimes his father was a little proud to have a boy that could write letters, and tell about things in books, and outrun and outwrestle and rough-and-tumble any boy or man in Spencer County. Yes, he would be different from his father; he was already so; it couldn't be helped.

In growing up from boyhood to young manhood, he had survived against lonesome, gnawing monotony and against floods, forest and prairie fires, snake-bites, horse-kicks, ague, chills, fever, malaria, "milk-sick."

A comic outline against the sky he was, hiking along the roads of Spencer and other counties in southern Indiana in those years when he read all the books within a fifty-mile circuit of his home. Stretching up on the long legs that ran from his moccasins to the body frame with its long, gangling arms, covered with linsey-woolsey, then the lean neck that carried the head with its surmounting coonskin cap or straw hat — it was, again, a comic outline — yet with a portent in its shadow. His laughing "Howdy," his yarns and drollery, opened the doors of men's hearts.

Starting along in his eleventh year came spells of abstraction. When he was spoken to, no answer came from him. "He might be a thousand miles away." The roaming, fathoming, searching, questioning operations of the minds and hearts of poets, inventors, beginners who take facts stark, these were at work in him. This was one sort of abstraction he knew; there was another: the blues took him; coils of multiplied melancholies wrapped their blue frustrations inside him,

all that Hamlet, Koheleth, Schopenhauer have uttered, in a mesh of foiled hopes. "There was absolutely nothing to excite ambition for education," he wrote later of that Indiana region. Against these "blues," he found the best warfare was to find people and trade with them his yarns and drolleries. John Baldwin, the blacksmith, with many stories and odd talk and eye-slants, was a help and a light.

Days came when he sank deep in the stream of human life and felt himself kin of all that swam in it, whether the waters were crystal or mud.

He learned how suddenly life can spring a surprise. One day in the woods, as he was sharpening a wedge on a log, the axe glanced, nearly took his thumb off, and left a white scar after healing.

"You never cuss a good axe," was a saying in those timbers.

Hans Christian Andersen [9]

RUMER GODDEN

◈ It was a stroke of genius to ask Rumer Godden to write the life of Hans Christian Andersen, published in celebration of the one hundred and fiftieth anniversary of the birth of the great Danish author. To the task, Rumer Godden brought her lifelong love of Andersen's stories, her painstaking research, her gift of delicate perception, and her amazing skill as a writer. In the chapter given below, she analyzes Andersen's particular genius for writing fairy tales.

It often seems that children have a telegraphic system of their own, without any wires or delivery forms; a fashion spreads among them — in Andersen's day it would have been conkers or hoops or marbles, today a space helmet, a Nancy-Anne doll or frog swimming feet — one day none of the children seems to have a certain thing, the next it is everywhere and every boy or girl has adopted it. The Andersen Tales spread quickly, first over Denmark, then into Ger-

[9] From Rumer Godden, *Hans Christian Andersen: A Great Life in Brief* (Knopf, 1954).

many, on to Sweden, England, and over the world.

But they were to be more than a fashion and soon they were found on the grownups' tables as well as in the nursery. That is what Andersen had meant: "I get hold of an idea and tell a story for the young ones," he said, "remembering all the time that father and mother are listening and we must give them something to think about too." The result was beyond anything he had expected but, when he brought out the third collection of Tales, and Heiberg, an author himself and the most sophisticated of critics, declared *The Little Mermaid* and *The Emperor's New Clothes* to be the best things H. C. Andersen had ever written, Andersen was completely bewildered.

The Little Mermaid better than *Agnete?* Though it was true that nothing he ever wrote moved him so much while writing as the fairy tale, it was written in a few days, while the poem took months of work. He was not only mystified, he was a little annoyed.

People who have not read Andersen may ask, with him, what there was in these little tales that has placed them where they are. Why these? What is it that makes them so different from Perrault or Grimm? The answer is "everything."

To begin with, they have a perfection of form that none of the others achieved; it astonished even Hertz. Each story has the essence of a poem, and a poem is not prose broken into short lines, but a distilling of thought and meaning into a distinct form, so disciplined and finely made, so knit in rhythm, that one word out of place, one word too much, jars the whole. In Andersen we are never jarred and it is this that gives the Tales their extraordinary swiftness — too often lost in translation — so that they are over almost before we have had time to take them in, and we have had the magical feeling of flying. The children, he remarked, always had their mouths a little open when he had finished; that is the feeling we have too.

But they were not written swiftly, were not the happy accidents that some people think them; anyone who has studied the original manuscripts from the first short draft of a story, through all its stages of crossings out, rewritings and alterations in Andersen's small spiky handwriting, the cuttings and pastings together, until the last draft was ready for the printer, can see how each word was weighed, and what careful pruning was done, what discipline was there. Even the discipline was skillful; Andersen never let it kill the life in his style.

That life is his hallmark. A sentence from one of Hans Andersen's Tales is utterly different from a sentence by anyone else. "The children got in the coach and drove off," Perrault or Grimm would have written, but Hans Andersen wrote: "Up they got on the coach. Good-by, Mum. Good-by, Dad. Crack went the whip, whick whack and away they dashed. Gee up! Gee up!"

"It's not writing, it's talking," the irritated Molbech had said, but, one after another, serious literary critics have found in it a source of inspiration: "From that moment," said Jacobsen, "a new prose was born in Danish literature; the language acquired grace and color, the freshness of simplicity."

That is what is lost, most of all, in English translations. The newest, by R. P. Keigwin, catch it, the Danish scholars say, as never before, but to American and English people, brought up on the sentimental verbose Andersens we have all known, these may come as a surprise. "But he makes the kitchen-maid in *The Nightingale* say 'Gosh!'" said one American critic. Precisely, because "Gosh" is nearest to the Danish of what she did say. "Where is your spunk?" the witch asks the Little Mermaid. That critic would no doubt have preferred: "Where is your courage?" but "spunk," its one syllable snapped out so quickly, is nearer to Andersen. The difference in translations can be shown by studying the story of *The Tin Soldier*. He has been called "The Dauntless Tin Soldier," "The Constant," "The Steadfast"; Mr. Keigwin uses "The Staunch." That small taut firm word "staunch" is exactly right for a little tin soldier and it has the quickness and economy of the Danish. With all their slang, the stories keep their beauty; Andersen is one of the few writers who use slang beautifully.

In the Bible we are told that God formed Man out of the dust of the earth and breathed into his nostrils . . . and Man became a living soul. Without irreverence it might be said that Hans Andersen did something like that too; he formed the stories of the dust of earth: a daisy, an old street lamp, a darning needle, a beetle, and made them live. His breath was unique; it was an alchemy of wisdom, poetry, humor, and innocence.

He was adult, a philosopher, and a lovable man; his stories are parables and have meanings that sound on and on — sometimes over our heads — after their last word is read. He was a poet and knew the whole gamut of feeling from ecstasy to black melancholy and horror. People call him sentimental; in a way he was, but in the first meaning of the word, which is not "excess of feeling" but an abounding in feeling and reflection. He was a child; children have this godlike power of giving personality to things that have none, not only toys, but sticks and stones, banister knobs and footstools, cabbages; it dies in them as they grow up, but Andersen never lost this power. "It often seems to me," he wrote, "as if every hoarding, every little flower is saying to me: 'Look at me, just for a moment, and then my story will go right into you.'" "Right into you," that is the clue. The daisy, the street lamp, the beetle — they are suddenly breathing and alive.

Once upon a time there was a bundle of matches; they were tremendously proud of their high birth. Their family tree — that's to say, the tall fir tree that each little match-stick came from — had been a huge old tree in the wood. And now the matches lay on the shelf between a tinder-box and an old iron cook-pot, and they told the other two about the time they were young. "Ah, yes," they said, "in those days, with the velvet moss at our feet, we really were on velvet. Every morning and evening we had diamond tea; that was the dew. And all day we had sunshine. . . . But then the woodcutters arrived; that was the great upheaval, and our family was all split up. Our founder and head was given a place as mainmast on board a splendid ship that could sail round the world if she liked; the other branches went to other places and, as for us, we've got the task of lighting up

for the common herd; that's how we gentlefolk come to be in the kitchen."

"Well, things have gone differently with me," said the cook-pot which stood alongside the matches. "Right from the time I first came into the world, I've been scrubbed and boiled again and again. I've got an eye for the practical and, strictly speaking, I'm No. 1 in this house. My great delight, at a time like after dinner, is to sit clean and tidy on the shelf and have a nice little chat with my friends. But except for the water-bucket, who now and then goes down into the yard, we spend all our time indoors. Our one news-bringer is the market basket, but that goes in for a lot of wild talk about the government and the people. Why, the other day there was an elderly jug so flabbergasted by what the basket said that it fell down and broke in pieces. It's a real radical, that basket, mark my words!"

"How you do chatter!" said the tinder-box; and the steel let fly at the flint, so that it gave out sparks. "Come on, let's have a cheerful evening!"

"Yes, let's discuss who belongs to the best family," said the matches.

"No, I don't like talking about myself," said the earthenware jar. "Let's have a social evening. I'll begin . . . On the shores of the Baltic, where the Danish beech trees . . ."

"It does sound interesting the way you tell it," said the broom. "One can hear at once that it's a lady telling the story; there's such a refined note running through it all."

"That's just how I feel," said the bucket, and it gave a little hop of sheer delight, and that meant "splash!" on the floor. Then the cook-pot went on with its story, and the end was every bit as good as the beginning.

The plates all rattled wth joy, and the broom took some green parsley out of the bin and crowned the cook-pot with it, knowing this would annoy the others and "If I crown her today," she thought, "then she'll crown me tomorrow."

"Now I'm going to dance," said the tongs, and dance she did — my word, what a high kick! The old chintz on the chair in the corner fairly split himself looking at it. "Now may I be crowned?" asked the tongs, and crowned she was.

"After all, they're the merest riffraff," thought the matches.

It is a whole live kitchen world. After reading it a kitchen would never seem the same place again; one is almost afraid to take a shopping basket out for fear of what it might think; it is almost as if the dustpan might speak; and notice in how few words it is told. All the stories have this economy, this startlingly quick effect. None of them, except *The Snow Queen*, which is almost a novel, is long; Andersen is verbose and boring in his novels and autobiography, but these are his poems — for that is what he always was, a poet.

Not everyone approved. There were some bad reviews. "Although the reviewer has nothing against good fairy tales for grownups," said one, "he can only find this form of literature entirely unsuitable for children . . . ought their reading, even out of school, to be merely for amusement? . . . Far from improving their minds," he said severely, "Andersen's Tales might be positively harmful. Would anyone claim that a child's sense of what is proper would be improved when it reads about a sleeping Princess riding on the back of a dog to a soldier who kisses her? . . . or that its sense of modesty be improved by reading about a woman who dined alone with a sexton in her husband's absence? Or its sense of value of human life after reading *Little and Big Claus*? As for *The Princess and the Pea* it is not only indelicate but indefensible, as the child might get the false idea that great ladies must be terribly thinskinned. . . ." The critic ended by saying: "*Little Ida's Flowers* is innocent, but it has no moral either."

We smile at such criticism, but there are others that threaten Andersen just as seriously; for instance, there is an idea now that children should be given books without shadows, books of brightness and lightness, and laughter, nothing else; perhaps the reason why these books are so lifeless is that living things have shadows.

Andersen had his dark side, a legacy from his horror of his grandfather, from the woman who tried to pin him in the lunatic cell, from the prison, and the tales with which Anne Marie and the spinning women had frightened him as a little boy and, more especially, from the customs of his time. One must remember he was writing in the first half of the nineteenth century and had spent his own childhood among ignorant, crude, and superstitious people; once he had dipped his pen in ink, both of which after *The Pen and the Inkpot* seemed despotically alive, he was carried on to the end.

Stories as vividly horrid as *The Girl Who Trod on a Loaf*, as sad as *The Shadow*, should perhaps be kept away from children altogether, but to expunge parts of them, to tell them in another way, is to destroy them, and that is desecration, not too strong a word; and almost always it is safe to trust to the children. Andersen's *The Little Mermaid* has terrible parts, the story is one of the saddest on earth, but it is also one of the very best loved.

In pictures and statues of Andersen, tiny children are shown listening to the stories. This is sentimentally false; the stories were not meant for tiny children. In Andersen's time, very little children were kept in the nursery when visitors came to the house; it was not until they were eight or nine years old that they were allowed to go down to the drawing-room or in to dessert to meet Mr. Hans Andersen and perhaps hear his Tales. Even then they did not understand the whole; they were not meant to; all Andersen wanted was that they should love them; presently, as they grew up, they would understand; to stop and explain — as conscientious mothers do — is to spoil the rhythm, the whole feeling. Let the children wonder; these are wonder tales.

How completely Andersen understood children can be seen by his letters to his child friends; he knew, to a nicety, what would please them at all ages.

When little Maria Henriques was four years old he wrote to her from the seaside:

June 7, 1870

My sweet little Marie!

I am — as you are — staying in the country. You are at Petershoi, but I am far on the other side of Copenhagen, at the forest and the sea, like you. Here it is so lovely. And I have got strawberries, big red strawberries with cream. Have you got that? They are tasting right down in the stomach.

Then I sit down on a stone down by the sea, then suddenly a big white bird comes flying, a gull; it flies right down against me so that I believe it will beat me with its wings, no, good gracious, it said: "Ma! Ma! -ri!"

"I beg your pardon?" I asked; "Ma! Ma! -ri!" it said again.

And then I understood that Ma! Ma! -ri! means "Marie!"

"Well!" I said, "is it Marie from whom you are greeting me?"

"Ja! Ja!" (in Danish, "Yes! Yes!") "Ma, ma, ri," it said.

It couldn't say it any better. It only understood gull language, and this is not much like our manner of speaking.

"Thanks for the greetings!" I said and then the gull flew away.

Then, as I was walking up in the garden came a little sparrow.

"You've been flying about so far, so far, I imagine," I said.

"Vidt, vidt" (in Danish, "Far, far"), it said.

"Have you been at Petershoi?" I asked.

"Lidt, lidt, lidt" ("A little, a little, a little"), it said.

"Did you see Marie?" I asked.

"Tidt, tidt, tidt" ("Often, often, often"), it said.

"Then you are going there again, I suppose?" I said. "Then give my greetings to Marie."

"Lidt, lidt" ("A bit, a bit"), it said.

Hasn't it been with you yet? Then it will come later, but first I will send you a letter.

It's nice to be in the country, to go bathing, to eat something or other (note: in Danish these make three rhymes), and to have a letter from your sweetheart.

H. C. ANDERSEN

Little Marie treasured that letter and kept it all her life. Children are the quickest judges and the clamor for stories, more stories, that rose from them is the answer to all criticism.

"It is easy," Andersen was to say of the Tales. "It is just as you would talk to a child. Anyone can tell them." Time has made it very plain that no one can tell them but Hans Andersen.

Invincible Louisa
"Little Women"[1]

CORNELIA MEIGS

❧ *Much of the material for* Invincible Louisa *comes from Louisa M. Alcott's autobiography;*

[1] From Cornelia Meigs, *Invincible Louisa* (Little, Brown, 1933).

but because Miss Meigs's biography deals with the facts objectively yet sympathetically, in an easy style, young readers will probably enjoy this book, whereas they might not care for the older one. We see the poverty of the Alcott family, follow Louisa's various attempts to earn money and her early failures as an author, then rejoice in her unexpected success with Little Women. Invincible Louisa *won the Newbery award in 1934.*

To one who has gone through all of her life in the ordinary sunshine and shade of bright hopes and unavoidable disappointments, it is very strange to stand, all at once, in the artificial spotlight of totally unexpected fame. From the moment her book appeared, life was entirely changed for unassuming Louisa Alcott. She simply did not know what to make of it when letters began to come pouring in, when visitors arrived in numbers scarcely less extravagant, when people pursued her everywhere to get an autograph, a word, or even nothing but a good stare at the renowned Miss Alcott, author of the new success, *Little Women.*

She had finished the book bravely, ending with Meg's engagement, since she felt that young readers would not care to go forward into the more romantic period of her heroines' lives. It was with some trepidation that she sent the whole to Mr. Niles, for he had been so obviously disappointed over the first chapters. He was equally frank now. He did not find the story as absorbing as he had hoped; it might be better, after all, to give up the idea of publishing it. But first, he would lay it before some young friends of his, girls of just the age for which it was written, to find what was their opinion.

O wise Thomas Niles, to understand that his bachelor judgment was not final in the matter and to take into consultation the only real experts, the young ladies themselves. The first to see the manuscript was his niece, Lily Almy, who lived at Longwood. She galloped through it and rendered a verdict so breathless with enthusiasm that her uncle paused and thought again. He showed it to another girl and another. Every one of them spoke of it in just the same way; they all of them loved it.

It is hard to think of *Little Women* as read for the first time; it is, to us, a tale so hallowed by the association of our mother's and our grandmother's delight in it, before our own day. A completely fresh story it was to them, a book even of a kind different from anything they had read before, a book just about themselves, so it seemed, by someone who understood them completely. It is no wonder that the first readers were enchanted with it. It is to the wisdom and appreciation of those young people that we owe the fact that *Little Women* was not hidden away forever in that spidery cupboard where Louisa's early failures were tossed in despair. We thank them from our hearts, and Mr. Niles for listening to them.

He heard their raptures with some astonishment and read the manuscript through again. On the strength of their delight in it, he decided to bring it out. We all know what followed. It was almost the first book of its kind, a direct, natural, truthful tale, with no straining after emotion and effect. It was just what girls had been starving for, although scarcely anyone knew it. Louisa did, when she refused to give up, even in the face of Thomas Niles's disappointment. He cannot be blamed for not seeing the value of the story immediately. Without his wisdom in suggesting it, in persevering with the suggestion, and in leaving the final decision to the girls themselves, there would have been no *Little Women*. There would have been only a splendid idea in the brain of a busy author who never found time to reduce it to writing or to print.

Louisa put into it everything out of her own life and those of her sisters. It was in the shabby brown house, Hillside, with its garden and fruit trees and barn, that the most happy, and the most truly childlike of her years had been spent. The house in *Little Women*, however, sounds somewhat more like the Orchard House, where the Alcotts were living when Louisa wrote the story. Hillside is more evidently Plumfield, the scene of *Little Men*. The name March rather naturally follows from the suggestion of the name May, a somewhat mild surname for that storm-tossed Abba, who lived through so many ups and downs. The Brook Farm connection with the Pratt family made John Pratt receive the name of John Brooke. He appears in one or two other stories and always the same; for his steady sincerity and goodness follow the lines of an exact portrait. Anna's contented happiness gave Louisa her knowledge, shown here and elsewhere, of what unmeasured beauty there can be in married life. Louisa put Elizabeth into the story bodily, with all her gentleness and unflinching courage. She showed May to the life, a little spoiled by the others' petting, a person of great charm and the recipient of many happy gifts, as Louisa was the dispenser of them.

The real power of the book, however, centers about Jo. She was Louisa to the life, more so, perhaps, than the author ever dreamed of making her. Louisa's honest opinion of herself was so very humble that she made not the slightest effort to dress up her counterpart in the semblance of a conventional heroine. Her picture of Jo is the farthest thing removed from flattery. She has told frankly of every drawback in her appearance and her nature, her round shoulders, her long-limbed awkwardness, her thorny moods, her headlong mistakes, her quick flashes of temper. Yet Jo is lovable beyond words and more real than any of the others. She is real because Louisa understood her even better than the rest; she stands out from the background because Louisa herself was such a magnificent character that a truthful study of her becomes, without any intention, a splendid figure also.

Louisa's kind but outwardly severe grandfather, known only during the Temple School period of their life in Boston, was put into the book as Mr. Lawrence, the grandfather of Laurie. She has declared that "Aunt March is no one," but her family say otherwise. They all see in that autocratically generous lady the reflection of no other than the great-aunt Hancock, with her connections in high places, her family tyranny and her good heart. Louisa could not remember her; but the family legend was enough, and Aunt Hancock lives on in thoroughly Aunt Hancock-ish fashion. In some of the kind relatives who were so kind to Jo and Amy, we surely see good Cousin Lizzie Wells. Not all of the minor figures can be traced to their originals; but it is safe to say that they all lived and that Louisa knew them.

With *Little Women,* Louisa achieved what she really wanted, a piece of work which she actually knew to be her best. With it she achieved also the appreciation of the world and such prosperity as gave her full power, at last, to do just what she wished. It is delightful to read of how her name came to be on every tongue; how she grew to be not merely famous, which mattered little to her, but universally loved, which mattered much. After all the years of doubting her own powers, of looking for her true field, of thinking of herself as a struggling failure, she was obliged at last to admit, even in the depths of her own soul, that she was a success.

It is a joy, also, to know of what she did with the generous prosperity which came to her so suddenly. After a whole lifetime of poverty, she felt as though the magic purse of Fortunatus was thrust, all at once, into her hands. The Alcott family now moved no more. Louisa had said, when they took up their abode in the Orchard House, that she hoped they would not stir again for twenty years. It was owing to her that they did not. She could at last make the place comfortable, the dilapidated old building which the last owner had thought fit only for firewood.

Here, in the big bedroom where the sun came flooding in, Abba Alcott, feeble now, and no longer toiling and busy, could sit all day with her knitting and sewing and the beloved books which, for so many years, there had been so little time to read. How often Louisa had said that she wanted a *sunny* room for her mother, pathetic record of the dark and cheerless lodgings into which their narrow means had frequently brought them! Her father's study was equipped with extra bookcases to hold his cherished library and the long shelves of his journals, bound by Louisa's order, so that they could be safe for generations to come. There are some tremendous ideas embodied in those journals, chiefly about education; for Bronson had theories so far in advance of his time that, even in our day, we have not caught up with all of them, although we have accepted many. It used to be thought, and not so long ago, that the

windows of a schoolroom must have white paint on all the lower panes, to keep the children from looking out, and incidentally to keep light and sunshine from coming in. It was Bronson Alcott who first opened the windows of schoolrooms to more than one kind of sunshine and who made learning brighter for all time.

It was a great and glorious day when Louisa had a furnace put into the Orchard House, so that the picturesque open fires need no longer be the sole source of heat. Not so very many years earlier, she had, one day, a dreadful battle with herself, wanting to spend a carefully saved sum of money on tickets to a concert, when, all the while, the chilly feet of her beloved family marched back and forth on cold matting in a room whose drafty floor cried aloud for a carpet. She resisted the temptation and bought the rug; but now, at last, she could do more than make a cold house a little less cold; she could make it actually warm and cheery. She thought of everything, from flannel petticoats upward, to make her beloved ones safe, comfortable, and happy in every spiritual and practical way possible.

Amongst all these matters, she thought of not one single thing to do for herself. Her own room in the house is plain and small and modestly furnished, standing today just as it did in her own time. On the table lies the shabby, black leather writing case, in which she wrote upon her knee, for she had no desk. She had begun her career of authorship on a little table in the tiny room off the Hillside garden; she had continued it in sky parlors and odd corners of casual lodgings, with so few conveniences for writers that she never missed them now. All her life, she had dreamed of what she would get for her family and had never found time for plans concerning what she might get for herself.

Meanwhile, Mr. Thomas Niles, walking with his dogs along the bank of Mystic Pond, sitting in the garden of the pleasant old Arlington house, was hatching other plans. A clever publisher was Thomas Niles, one of the most brilliant and enterprising of his time. He was watching the growing popularity of *Little Women* and presently had a new suggestion to make to Miss Alcott. The book must have a sequel.

She made almost as much demur as she had the first time. She was writing about children; no one would be interested in seeing the girls married. After long persuasion, after being shown multitudes of letters always making one and the same request, she gave in. She made one reservation, however, even as she agreed.

"I won't marry Jo to Laurie, to please anybody."

The first part of *Little Women* was published in October of the year 1868. Mr. Niles offered Louisa a certain sum for the copyright of the book, which seemed very large indeed to her unaccustomed eyes. He urged her, however, to make a different arrangement under which she would receive a royalty so long as the book was sold. It was his principle that publishing was best carried on by being as fair and as generous with the authors as it was possible to be. It is a happy record, that of his connection with Louisa Alcott. His company never had a greater success than the two achieved with *Little Women*.

He found and brought out the work of many another person who was to become famous, Jean Ingelow, Emily Dickinson, Thomas Bailey Aldrich, Susan Coolidge, Helen Hunt Jackson, Edward Everett Hale, and numberless others. Great writers of the day were his intimate friends, in spite of his odd, slow-spoken ways. It is told that Thomas Bailey Aldrich and William Dean Howells would often come into his office to see him, but would be found by others, arriving later, to be reading the morning papers, since Thomas Niles seemed to have so little to say to them. They so enjoyed the presence of this charming, silent man that they were quite content with a visit, even if it lacked conversation. He was very conservative, in spite of all his enterprise in undertaking new ventures. It is told of him that, when telephones came into use, he would never talk into one, but always had the message given and received through another person. The last of those three cousins with whom he lived says that they knew all the authors of their day, that most of them

came to the house, but that none were as delightful to have there as Louisa Alcott, who was always overflowing with good spirits and good talk, the very best company in the world.

With Thomas Niles, she formed one of those valuable friendships which were milestones in her life. He was her counselor in all literary matters, a willing and devoted guide through the rest of her career. Financial affairs were never to be difficult for her again, with such a source of income and with such good advice as to what to do with it. He began by being a friend of Bronson Alcott's — he was to end by being Louisa's literary mentor and by making her fortune.

It was no wonder, therefore, that Louisa finally heeded his urging to write a sequel to *Little Women,* to be brought out in the spring. She set herself to work in November and finished very quickly, sending him the manuscript on New Year's Day. It carried the story of the girls forward into the beginning of being grown up, into living "with their own wings," as the Dutch translator has put it. It showed Anna's wedding, with the guests dancing under the Revolutionary elm. It brought to a briefly worded end the simple tragedy of Elizabeth's short life, the Beth whom every reader has mourned, not merely because of what Louisa said of her but because of what she was.

Since neither Louisa nor May was married, it was necessary to expand into the realm of the imagination to supply the desired conclusion for the book. Amy was taken abroad, to see all those glorious things which Louisa wanted so much to have May see, when she herself first had the opportunity for travel. At Vevey, where Louisa met Ladislas, Amy was described as meeting Laurie again, and, floating on the lake, these two imaginary ones pledged their lives to each other. And as for Jo, she was dutifully provided with a husband, but what an unexpected one!

Where, everyone has wondered for all these years, where did Louisa find the model for Professor Bhaer? Is he the ideal combination of qualities which she thought might, possibly, have touched her own heart? It may be. There is a little of her father in that good Mr. Bhaer, a very little; there is a trace of Mr. Emerson in his high principles and his advice to wayward Jo. There is also something of Louisa's more distantly idealized hero, Goethe, in her Germanic make-up. No record of her own, nor any memory of her surviving family, gives evidence of there having been a real person to stand for that portrait. He is, somehow, less convincing than any of her other characters. This is not surprising, since, even in her own mind, a satisfactory lover for the counterpart of Louisa Alcott did not exist.

In the rather shadowy figure of the March girls' father, it is hard to recognize Bronson Alcott. Louisa always meant to write a book which should have her father as the central character; she spoke of it by various names, "The Cost of An Idea" or "An Old-Fashioned Boy." She had thought of it and spoken of it long before she undertook Little Women. She was so unlike Bronson that, although she was devoted to him, there were certain of his ideas which she did not truly comprehend, certain phases of his life to which she felt that she could not do justice, since she did not quite fathom the motives which lay behind them. She waited all of her life for the moment when she really would understand him fully; and she waited too long, for the book was never written. Perhaps it was because she had this plan still in view that she did not make a more striking figure out of the father of Meg, Jo, Beth, and Amy. But in one matter, we see her true affection for him coming into the very center of the stage.

In almost the last chapter of Little Women, when Jo is married, and the whole family sits about, discussing plans for the future, Jo broaches her great idea of what is to be done with Plumfield, the "beautiful old place" in the country, left her by Aunt March. She announces that she and Professor Bhaer are going to have a school there. She describes the school — it is to be for boys, for rich boys whose parents neglect them and leave them to servants, so that they have no chance for proper growing up, and for poor boys who would never have proper opportunities to learn. They are to be taught — but there is no use in going into the details of the plan.

It is, briefly, the school of which Bronson Alcott always dreamed, the perfect school which he — so nearly — knew how to put into being. The actual realization of it came as close to existing as it ever managed to, in that idea sponsored by a public-spirited man for the public schools of Germantown, in which Bronson and Abba Alcott took such happy and such brief part, during the first unclouded years of their married life. What was it that Jo said of the plan in Little Women? Her husband could "teach and train the boys in his own way," while she could keep house for them all and "feed and pet and scold them" to her heart's content. Out of the vanished years comes, in that brief passage, the vision of that glorious dream in Germantown; out of the past comes the figure of Reuben Haines with his high-collared, gray Quaker coat and his deep, farseeing eyes. He and the Alcotts had to do with the founding of two schools. One is the Germantown Academy, child of Reuben Haines's first plan, and still educating children as he hoped to educate them. That, however, is not the only school which he had a share in establishing. The other is Plumfield.

The second part of Little Women was received with as much acclaim as the first, so that Thomas Niles immediately applied to Louisa for another book to be issued the following year. He may have been a little worried, for fear, since Louisa had apparently completed the record of her own family, she might not be able to go on as successfully as she had begun. She did not need the Marches, however; but launched out into a new tale, An Old-Fashioned Girl.

The heroine of this, Polly, is not Louisa herself, but the adventures and trials through which Polly went follow very closely her own tribulations in her early effort to make a living. Louisa at the time said very little of the difficulties, the disappointments, and the slights which made those years such hard ones to a person of her sensitive, hopeful, exuberant spirits. That those hard moments made a deep impression we can now see, for so many of them come to light in her stories, along with the happiness and the unexpected adventures which fall along the way of the seeker for her daily bread. One small episode reflects very significantly Louisa's own ideas about certain matters.

In *An Old-Fashioned Girl*, someone, in Polly's hearing, refers to her single festive frock, a black silk gown, as "that inevitable dress," and calls the girl "the little black-bird." Louisa herself put on record a similar incident. "People are remarking on how familiar my best black silk has become," she says in substance. "I shall either have to get another or go home to Concord. I am going home to Concord." Her reverence for social etiquette and conventional garb was not very great. Older people who can remember say that *An Old-Fashioned Girl* is an absolutely accurate picture of Boston society in her time, with all its small customs and habits and invariable laws of procedure. As we see Polly break through some of them and express her own opinions of others, we understand fairly well what Louisa thought.

The story in its first form was very short, only seven chapters, but as before, a sequel was so loudly demanded that Louisa presently added the remainder, to make the present book. She found the characters amongst her legion of cousins and relatives in Boston and among her friends. No single person is directly recognizable, but all have the mark of reality upon them.

She had worked so hard over the second part of *Little Women* as to be quite worn out, and to show, alas, that her strength had never come back to its old vigor. A little time before the war her cousin Lizzie Wells was ill and Louisa stayed with her to nurse her. Being free for a Sunday and having missed the train to Concord, she walked home, twenty miles, and went to a party in the evening. Such boundless energy as that was never to come back to her. She was, in fact, never really well again after the hospital adventure. Although she was definitely ill through all the time that she was writing *An Old-Fashioned Girl*, she gave no hint of flagging spirits and made the story as gay as Louisa always was herself, when feeling her best.

The time had come when she had accomplished the greater part of what she had so long ago vowed that she would do. She had made her family safe and independent, she had given them comfort, and she had paid off all the old debts, which ran back to the time of the Temple School. With the ordinary affairs of life attended to, she turned to a larger and more pretentious dream which she had harbored long, as something impossibly remote. She would send May abroad, to give her the artistic education which she felt that her sister's talents richly deserved. She knew just how May longed for travel, just as she herself had longed for it. Her own desire had been laboriously and inadequately fulfilled; May's wish should be answered in full measure, heaped and running over.

She consulted a friend, Miss Alice Bartlett, as to plans. Wise and generous Miss Bartlett had a glorious idea. She, too, was going abroad and she offered to take May as her guest if Louisa would go also. Such a thing as going herself had not crossed Louisa's mind. She pondered it — not long, for she was still Louisa — and decided to go.

All the delight which she had hoped to have on that first journey and had failed to find was hers now. Louisa was not well; she had worked so hard that she never was to have any full amount of bodily ease again. But she spent small time in lamentation over that. Beyond the ordinary gift of other people, she had the capacity for enjoying herself and for knowing when she was happy. She was not hurried past German castles now, or snatched away from picturesque French villages that she longed to explore, or carried on from beautiful bright countrysides, where she liked to linger and bask in the golden warmth of Italian spring. Laughter and light-heartedness attended the progress of these three congenial spirits wherever they went. She looked all about for Ladislas, but she did not find him. Years later, he was to come to America and she was to renew her knowledge of him, but she did not see him now.

They landed at Brest and spent a sunny, delightful April in Brittany. As the summer came on, they moved forward to Geneva. Europe was, by this time, in a turmoil on account of the Franco-Prussian War, which broke out soon after they reached Switzerland. That glittering Emperor, Napoleon

III, who had tried so hard to emulate the power and magnificence of his uncle, the great Buonaparte, was making his last, super-human effort to win glory on the battlefield, and by so doing to instill new life into the dying legend of imperial glory. The Empress Eugénie was holding the reins of government at home, and, amid the ominous muttering of a discontented populace, was keeping up the outward semblance of pomp and splendor. The Emperor was ill, suffering, beside himself with nervous excitement, but still dreaming of glory, while the crash of shells and cannon roared about him, the thundering German artillery which was to bring down the French Empire forever.

"Poor old man," Louisa said of him, remembering how she had seen his Paris in its greatest glory. Switzerland was full of refugees; the Queen of Spain and her son were keeping court in a hotel in Geneva, not far from Louisa. The three Americans were interested in the romance and excitement of such great changes, but it all seemed very remote from them.

In the autumn, they moved on to Italy. Louisa wrote home of lodging in a room with a marble floor, "green doors, red carpet, blue walls, and yellow bedcovers — all so gay. It was like sleeping in a rainbow." The whole journey seemed rainbow-colored in its untroubled happiness. It did not matter to Louisa that she had pain in her bones and was often worn out. The good company and the great sights about her were enough and more to counteract all that. She wrote home from Brittany, "Ye gods, how I do sleep here," a pathetic testimonial to how she had not slept for many months past. The beautiful journey helped her, but it could not make her well. She told of how Miss Bartlett shopped briskly for antiques, May sketched with energy, and "I dawdled after them." It was a blessed relief to have time for dawdling.

While they were staying in Rome, news reached them of the death of John Pratt, Anna's husband, leaving Louisa's sister with small means and with two little boys. Louisa was broken-hearted over her sister's grief, but immediately took the steps which were characteristic of her. She took up the pen which she had meant to lay aside for a long vacation and resumed her writing, so that "John's death may not leave Anna and the dear little boys in want."

It was so that she undertook *Little Men,* and carried forward the account of the school at Plumfield, and the further chronicle, purely imaginary now, of the March family. She took no further joy in her holiday after that, since she felt that she was needed in Concord. It was decided that May should stay on for more study and that Louisa should go home.

Her father and Thomas Niles met her at the wharf, with news of the book. The manuscript of *Little Men,* arriving in the mail, almost unheralded from Rome, had been a tremendous surprise. The book was out the day Louisa got home, with such a prodigious number sold before publication that it had already achieved unprecedented honors for a story for young people. Her books had already begun to be translated into various languages. In our time, many have come to be read in practically every modern tongue.

It was always plain to Louisa, after she had been away, how feeble and old her mother seemed to become during her absence. It was true that Abba Alcott's iron strength was failing and that the change, unnoticed by those about her, was evident to any person who did not see her every day. Louisa vowed that she would never go far away from her again. She never did.

When May returned, some months later, Louisa gave into her hands, with a sigh of relief, the task of keeping house in Concord. Fame threatened to become an occupation in itself and leave Louisa no time for actual living. The visitors and the letters and the autograph albums seemed to have no end. She was asked often to speak at schools and colleges and, having a definite interest in education, she agreed whenever she could. Some people were kind and she loved to meet them; some curious, and some merely intrusive. Many who came seemed to have no idea that Miss Alcott might like a little privacy, nor did it seem to occur to them that she must have some quiet, if she were to produce any more books. To the infinitely repeated question:

"Dear Miss Alcott, are you writing anything now?" she was tempted often to answer bitterly:

"How can I?"

The years slipped by pleasantly, however, quite a number of them, without great event. *Little Men* was nearly as great a success as *Little Women*. Under demand for more books, Louisa again brought out her novel *Success*, renamed *Work,* and got it ready for publication. Two years later she wrote *Eight Cousins* and one year after that its sequel, *Rose in Bloom. Work* was widely discussed as *Moods* had been, but with no long-lived enthusiasm. The two young people's books, however, were universally beloved. Into *Eight Cousins* and its sequel she has put the general atmosphere of the enormous May connection, everyone interested in everyone else, the elders observing with watchful care just how the younger ones were growing up in "these dreadful modern times." Part of the magic of Louisa's charm for young people surely lies in the fact that she sees things through their eyes, that she depicts the ups and downs of the early adventures of life, all from the young point of view. The youthful readers all feel, entirely, that Louisa is *on their side.*

Much more of the time now she remained in Concord, so that she might be near her mother. Occasionally, as she walked along the shady streets, she would meet that old comrade, Cy, with whom she had played when she was small, who got her to jump off the beam of the barn. They never could greet each other without suddenly bursting into laughter, for the memory of those hazardous days was still common property between the brown-faced farmer, veteran of the war, and tall, stately Miss Alcott, famous authoress. Occasionally, when she felt herself able, she would go to Boston for a little, and she once spent several months in New York. In Boston, she still occasionally acted in private theatricals with all of her old spirit. There was a great fair to raise money for the preservation of the Old South Church. Louisa was the life of the whole undertaking, her special show, *Mrs. Jarley's Waxworks,* with herself as Mrs. Jarley, being a marvelous performance which was repeated every day

for a week. She was tired out by it, and at the end so hoarse that she could barely speak; but, in spite of everything, she threw tremendous zest into every scene and was an uproarious success.

When she could, she went to talk to schools, although she never could accept a quarter of the invitations which poured in upon her. She went to Philadelphia and spoke at the Germantown Academy, the surviving school which, as has been said, was born out of the plan of Reuben Haines. The boys all cheered her as she passed up School House Lane. She saw Wyck again, where she had played when she was so very little; she was taken to see her birthplace, a very old house now and soon to be demolished. At the house of her hostess, she was waited on by a delegation of young persons, grandchildren of those small pupils whom her father had taught. The group of little girls overwhelmed her with questions as to whether Beth really had scarlet fever, why Laurie did not marry Jo, who was Mr. Lawrence. She answered every query, wrote in all the autograph albums, and kissed such of those who insisted upon it. So tired was she when this interview was over that she could hardly manage to answer a second summons which came up to her room a little later. This time she was asked to come down to speak to a delegation of little boys. Unwilling to refuse any request, she came down and found only two young gentlemen, both very shy, and both sitting on the edges of their chairs. Conversation did not go forward very easily, but they were at last persuaded to tell what they had come to ask.

"Please, were the pillow fights real?"

"They were," Louisa assured them. "They were always on Saturday nights, just before the clean cases were put on for Sunday."

That was all they wished to know and they took their departure, completely satisfied.

Louisa had sent May to Europe once more during these quiet years, but was overwhelmingly glad to get her back again and to avail herself of the efficient help which May always managed to be. Abba Alcott was really an old woman now, so feeble as to need much care and to call forth great anxiety amongst those who loved her. She was happy and serene, but she was evidently not to be with them a great deal longer. In September of 1876, Louisa arranged for the third time that May should go abroad. She needed a holiday, Louisa said. It was such a happiness to May to have that artist's life which she craved; it was such a joy to Louisa to give it to her. This time, there was no question of Louisa's going also. The two daughters could not possibly be away at the same time.

May sailed on a windy, September day, some such day as that on which Louisa had first set out on her own travels. The two sisters went to the wharf together. Separations were difficult in this devoted family and were never gone through without pain and misgiving, no matter what golden promise lay in the plans which brought the parting. There was a little prayer which Louisa said to herself many times through her whole life,

"God help us all and keep us for one another."

She had said it on that day when she set out in the coach from Walpole, to try her fortune in Boston. She had said it on the day of her going away to Washington, to offer all her strength and eagerness to the service of her country. She said it now, as the ship drew out from the dock and gathered way. May, with her blue cape blowing out in the breeze, stood at the rail to wave good-bye. Louisa waved in return, gaily and bravely, her tall figure bending a little to the wind, the tendrils of her chestnut hair lifting, her face bright with the splendid hopes which sped this beloved sister on her way.

It is so, I think, that we should always remember her. At that moment, life gave her, perhaps, the supreme amount of what she had asked of it. She had won security for all those whom she loved so much, peace and happiness for her family, this final gift which she was able to make to May. That was all that Louisa had wished for; but she had something more. Warm in her heart was the knowledge that thousands of people loved her, people whom she had never seen, whose names she was never to hear.

Fame during a lifetime is something to win; but fame and affection which are to last a hundred years are seldom earned. These Louisa had, with a richness of deserving about which we love to think, as we look back at her, gay-spirited, vivid, and hopeful, waving, not to May, but to us, across the century.

Clara Barton of the Red Cross[2]

JEANNETTE COVERT NOLAN

Before Clara Barton became famous, her life was not unlike that of any well-brought-up middle-class girl of her time, except for the differences brought about by her own character. She taught school from fifteen until she was thirty, and was the first woman clerk in the Government Patent Office, a position she held when the Civil War broke out. In the government service, she had a chance to see how the wounded soldiers were neglected; and, as difficult conditions in her past life had always been a challenge which she had met and overcome, so she was determined to overcome this one. Using her own savings and collecting whatever she could from others, she organized relief nursing on the front lines, while she paid a substitute to do her work at the Patent Office. In 1864 the government appointed Clara Barton as Superintendent of Nurses; and at the close of the war, at her request, she was given the job of finding the Northern soldiers listed as missing, because, as she said, to many persons "missing" meant "desertion," and she wanted to clear the good names of the truly missing. Her success brought demands for public talks, but these came to a close in 1868 when, in the middle of a speech, her voice suddenly left her. Her doctor's advice was rest for three years, preferably abroad; and it was while abroad that she met the leaders of the European Red Cross and became convinced that America should participate in that great organization.

Clara Barton disembarked in Scotland and went from there to London, then to Paris, and then to Switzerland, to Geneva, where the climate was said to be favorable to throat afflictions. She had friends in this city: the Golays, the family of the Swiss boy for whom

2 From Jeannette Covert Nolan, *The Story of Clara Barton of the Red Cross* (Messner, 1941).

she had written letters in General Butler's base hospital in Virginia. Jules' mother and his sister were grateful to Clara Barton and never had lost sight of her. Now they wished to entertain her.

Perhaps, too, inscrutable destiny turned Clara toward Geneva — though she did not suspect it.

The Golays were charming and hospitable folk. They made their guest welcome and at ease. Their neighbors called upon her. But one morning ten dignified gentlemen who were strangers to the Golays and to Clara alike came calling. Bearded, silk-hatted, frock-coated, they were a committee from the International Convention of Geneva, with Doctor Louis Appia as leader and spokesman.

"We are here, Miss Barton," Doctor Appia announced, after an interval of ceremonious bowing, "to inquire of you, the most illustrious of American women, why the United States has refused to sign the Treaty of Geneva, which provides for the relief of sick and wounded soldiers. Your country's position is incomprehensible to us. If the treaty had originated in some monarchical government, we might credit the refusal. On the contrary, it originated in Switzerland, which is a republic older than your own. To what does America object? How can these objections be overcome? Will you not explain, madam?"

Dumbfounded, Clara stared at Doctor Appia. She had no notion whatever of either the convention or the treaty.

"Twice," continued Doctor Appia, "and formally, your government at Washington has been approached. In both instances we were rebuffed. This has amazed us." He stroked his luxuriant beard. "We had thought Americans were a humane people."

"They are," Clara asserted quickly. "The most humane people in the world."

"We had supposed their hearts would warm to a policy which would save lives, prevent cruelty ——"

"They would! No one knows so well as I how warm are American hearts."

"Then why ——"

Clara frowned. "Doctor Appia, I am quite in the dark on this topic. I have been for

years immersed in just such an enterprise as you mention, the saving of lives, the prevention of cruelty. Most of that time I was striving as an individual — and succeeding only because the innate kindliness of my countrymen sustained me in my efforts. If your convention is fair and good and effective, I am sure that America would wish to join it, and does not know she has refused. We have just been through a dreadful war, the more dreadful that it was between Americans, brother against brother. While it was in progress, Congress would consider no business except that connected with the war. Your treaty has never been submitted to the American people — of that I'm positive, or I should have heard of it."

"We have mailed much literature," Doctor Appia said.

"Printed in French?"

"And in German, yes."

"But we are an English-speaking people. Your literature could not have been widely read."

"You are a French student, Miss Barton?"

"To an extent, I am."

"Then," Doctor Appia said, nodding to the other gentlemen, "we shall leave with you this pamphlet, *Un Souvenir de Solferino*, which we respectfully ask you to study. And we shall interview you later, if we may, Miss Barton, at your convenience, to learn your opinions." He rose and bowed. All the frock coats bowed. "We devoutly hope for your sanction and your help. We all know of your great ability. No American citizen is more distinguished or beloved."

Clara took the little book into the Golays' rear garden, where the air was clear and bracing, autumn flowers colored the brick wall, and Mont Blanc loomed, snow-capped, in the distance, and there she read attentively *Un Souvenir de Solferino*.

The author, one Henri Dunant, a Swiss, had happened to be in northern Italy following the battle of Solferino, at which the Austrians were defeated by the allied armies of Italy and France. The medical corps of an army was then without any treaty protection and must trail in the wake of its own troops, whether pursuing or pursued. As an eyewitness, Monsieur Dunant saw the wounded trampled under foot, often abandoned. He encountered them, languishing, neglected, dying, in villages near the battlefront. And so appalled was he that he recruited a body of volunteers whose purpose was to mitigate the pains of all sufferers, Italians, French, and Austrians, observing no dividing lines of nationality. His pamphlet, written in 1862, was a recounting of Monsieur Dunant's experiment. In it he put the question:

"Would it not be possible to found and organize in all civilized countries permanent societies of volunteers which in time of war would render succor to the wounded *without distinction of nationality?*"

Translated into various languages, *Un Souvenir de Solferino* had challenged not only the peoples, but also the rulers of Europe. In Monsieur Dunant's native Geneva, the Société Génévoise d'Utilité Publique already existed to promote the very causes which he was urging. This organization brought together at Geneva in October, 1863, representatives of fourteen nations to draft an agreement designed to attain "the relief of the wounded in armies at the field." In August, 1864, a second convention was held, to which twenty-five sovereign states were invited, and sixteen responded by sending delegates. Here by vote an international pact was adopted, "to render neutral and immune from injury in war the sick and wounded and all who cared for them."

Since 1864, the convention had met regularly, perfecting its organization. Its emblem was a red cross on a white ground, a reversal of the white cross on red ground of the Swiss national banner and chosen as a tribute to the government of Switzerland, which had so steadfastly advanced the convention's ideals.

"There is something in this," mused Clara Barton, as she finished reading Monsieur Dunant's treatise. "A great deal. It's what I've thought of, what I talked about to David. Not the haphazard generosity of impulsive civilians — but order and system. I've dreamed of that."

She remembered the mild criticism of Doctor Appia and his gentlemen for an America which would not become officially a part of the Geneva Convention. At that meeting held in August, 1864, two Americans had been seated. They were the United States Minister to Switzerland, Mr. George C. Fogg, and the European agent of the United States Sanitary Commmission, Mr. Charles S. P. Bowles. But they had been cautioned to attend *"in an informal manner"* only, and to confine their participation merely to the giving and taking of suggestions — and there the interest of America in an international compact had ended.

"That was natural," Clara thought. "In 1864, we could not see beyond our own catastrophe. We had to get the Civil War behind us; we had our internal readjustment to make. If, as Doctor Appia says, the treaty was presented afterward to the United States Government, it must have been sidetracked in some bureau. The people have not rejected it, and wouldn't. Three years from now, when I am at home again, I shall plead for it."

What she did not know was that an attempt previously had been made to arouse the American public in behalf of the International Red Cross. At the close of the Civil War, Doctor Henry W. Bellows, president of the United States Sanitary Commission, had proposed the founding of "the American Association for the Relief of Misery of Battlefields" and had spoken with great frankness of the inadequacy of even such splendid bodies as the Sanitary Commission, which he headed. "Good intentions and humane sentiments are not alone qualified for this duty," Doctor Bellows said, and begged for the extending and universalizing of mercy toward the victims of war.

Doctor Bellows failed utterly — "ignominiously," as he later asserted. The United States Government had little time just then for philanthropies which reached outside its own borders, nor did it feel very kindly toward European monarchies for their attitude in regard to the American Civil War. Doctor Bellows acknowledged himself as thoroughly discouraged and tried no more.

Clara Barton, meditating in the Golays' garden, knew none of this. Yet, even had she been aware of the situation, her conviction that *she* must do something would probably have been the same.

Shunning the cold of mountain weather,

Clara spent the winter in Corsica. Then she returned to Switzerland, paused at Geneva, and, vexed that her throat should still be so delicate, went on to the mineral baths at Bern. Somewhat improved, she was in Bern, staying with the American consul and his wife, in July, 1870, when all Europe was electrified by Napoleon's declaration of war upon the kingdom of Prussia.

In a letter to David, Clara depicted the suspense of Switzerland as it viewed the menace of mobilizing troops. That was in the haying season. The country was very beautiful.

"It is the custom to cut all the grass fields twice and the first cutting is being done now, the field just in front of my windows is being mowed today. The cows are out on the sides of the mountains with the dairy men and women and the shepherds. There must be a lot of fruit by the promise of the trees. The peaks of the Bernese Alps, always white with snow, are in plain sight — when there is not an Indian summer haze over everything. . . . Today France and Prussia, with both Northern and Southern Germany, are armed and marching to the Rhine, and little Switzerland, bright as a diamond in her rough setting, proclaiming a neutrality which she means. Through all her valleys come her sturdy, brown-cheeked mountain farmers in their neat uniforms of blue, with knapsack and cartridge-box, forty thousand troops to line her borders and preserve her liberty at any cost."

No one could believe in war as a reality, Clara said. "Even the Prussian press said it 'could not be,' it was *zu dumm*. But the reader of history has yet to learn that nothing can be 'too foolish,' and no pretext too slight, where personal interest, royal ambition or pride are threatened. 'To the Rhine!' rings out on every side. *'Vive la guerre!'* "

Perhaps it was that same sunny afternoon, and Clara had just laid down her pen, when the procession rumbled to the portals of the American consulate. Outriders were ahead, resplendent in the flashing gold and scarlet liveries of the royal house of Baden. After them rolled a coach, rich with trappings. As the horses halted, a footman leaped down and knocked on the consul's door; with a white-gloved hand he gave a card to the consul's butler. Then the footman opened the coach door and a lady alighted.

Young and pretty, fashionably attired, she was the Grand Duchess of Baden, the daughter of King William of Prussia. She had been in the Alps, at one of her castles, but Napoleon's declaration had called her home.

"I have come these miles out of my way to see you, Miss Barton. I am a subscriber to the work of the Geneva Convention. I believe in it with all my soul. Now my country is to be involved in what will doubtless be a bitter war. Will you not aid us?"

Clara had conversed with presidents and generals and ambassadors, but never before with a grand duchess, yet she was too much the Yankee to be awed.

"I am an American," she said. "A private citizen."

"And a nurse."

"Yes, I have been that, and a sort of impromptu and amateur sanitary commissioner — — "

"Be one of us, Miss Barton!" begged the grand duchess. "We are swayed by those very emotions which dominate your heart. Our Red Cross Society is so new. It has material resources but a dearth of skilled directors, whereas your name is the synonym for efficiency. You have the habit of *getting things done*."

"I am in Bern to recuperate."

"And are you not better, Miss Barton? But do not feel that you must reply to this petition immediately. Only say that you will think about it!"

Clara was thinking about it (indeed, she'd thought of nothing else!) when, a week later, Doctor Appia with Monsieur Gustave Moynier, president of the Geneva Convention, and other officials passed through the city en route to Basel, which would be the Red Cross focal point. Again Doctor Appia spoke to Miss Barton: She understood the theory of the Red Cross now — would she not like to watch that theory translated into practice? Would she not lend herself to the emergency?

"It's strange, my being here at all," said Clara. "Almost as if foreordained. But many of the occurrences of my life have been like that. Yes, I'll follow you gentlemen to Basel."

The American consul and his wife protested. What of her throat, her voice? This was sheer idiocy and they would not permit it!

"But," Clara said, "as the Grand Duchess Louise reminded me, I am so much better. Let me go."

Basel was just at the German border. The town would surely be in the path of King William's invasion of France. Its population was in a furor of apprehension. Yet at the Red Cross headquarters calm prevailed, and the atmosphere of industry, for this was the property which the armies of both Germany and France had guaranteed protection. No cannon would be leveled upon it. Since the warehouses flew the Red Cross flag, they would be unmolested.

These warehouses Clara inspected. The stock there was much larger than any ever assembled by the United States Sanitary Commission, and every train brought into Basel barrels and crates to augment it — and also numbers of trained nurses, each with the Red Cross badge on breast or armband.

How different was this from the chaos Clara had witnessed at home! But, she sighed, if only none of it were necessary, if only peace could be kept. And, except for the greed and stupidity of men in high place, it could be. And why should one half the race be in duty bound to tie up the hurts, repair the damage, inflicted by the other half?

She had, alas, no answer.

Madame Curie
Four Years in a Shed [3]

EVE CURIE

&❧ *It was a far cry from the happy child, Marya Sklodowska, in Poland to the hard-working but equally happy physicist, Marie Curie, in Paris. Marie Curie — as we know her — was of good birth and from a devoted family. The*

[3] From Eve Curie, *Madame Curie*, trans. Vincent Sheean (Doubleday, 1937).

six children were educated and ambitious. At the age of eighteen, Marya became a governess in order that her older (and favorite) sister, Bronya, might study medicine in Paris. In turn, it was this same sister who made it possible for Marie to study physics. Marie's poverty as a student was only a preparation for what she was to endure when she and her beloved husband were working under most adverse circumstances to prove the existence of what we now call radium.

A man chosen at random from a crowd to read an account of the discovery of radium would not have doubted for one moment that radium existed: beings whose critical sense has not been sharpened and simultaneously deformed by specialized culture keep their imaginations fresh. They are ready to accept an unexpected fact, however extraordinary it may appear, and to wonder at it.

The physicist colleagues of the Curies received the news in slightly different fashion. The special properties of polonium and radium upset fundamental theories in which scientists had believed for centuries. How was one to explain the spontaneous radiation of the radioactive bodies? The discovery upset a world of acquired knowledge and contradicted the most firmly established ideas on the composition of matter. Thus the physicist kept on the reserve. He was violently interested in Pierre and Marie's work, he could perceive its infinite developments, but before being convinced he awaited the acquisition of decisive results.

The attitude of the chemist was even more downright. By definition, a chemist only believes in the existence of a new substance when he has seen the substance, touched it, weighed and examined it, confronted it with acids, bottled it, and when he has determined its "atomic weight."

Now, up to the present, nobody had "seen" radium. Nobody knew the atomic weight of radium. And the chemists, faithful to their principles, concluded: "No atomic weight, no radium. Show us some radium and we will believe you."

To show polonium and radium to the incredulous, to prove to the world the existence of their "children," and to complete their own conviction, M. and Mme. Curie were now to labor for four years.

The aim was to obtain pure radium and polonium. In the most strongly radioactive products the scientists had prepared, these substances figured only in imperceptible traces. Pierre and Marie already knew the method by which they could hope to isolate the new metals, but the separation could not be made except by treating very large quantities of crude material.

Here arose three agonizing questions:

How were they to get a sufficient quantity of ore? What premises could they use to effect their treatment? What money was there to pay the inevitable cost of the work?

Pitchblende, in which polonium and radium were hidden, was a costly ore, treated at the Saint Joachimsthal mines in Bohemia for the extraction of uranium salts used in the manufacture of glass. Tons of pitchblende would cost a great deal: a great deal too much for the Curie household.

Ingenuity was to make up for wealth. According to the expectation of the two scientists, the extraction of uranium should leave, intact in the ore, such traces of polonium and radium as the ore contains. There was no reason why these traces should not be found in the residue. And, whereas crude pitchblende was costly, its residue after treatment had very slight value. By asking an Austrian colleague for a recommendation to the directors of the mine of Saint Joachimsthal would it not be possible to obtain a considerable quantity of such residue for a reasonable price?

It was simple enough: but somebody had to think of it.

It was necessary, of course, to buy this crude material and pay for its transportation to Paris. Pierre and Marie appropriated the required sum from their very slight savings. They were not so foolish as to ask for official credits. . . . If two physicists on the scent of an immense discovery had asked the University of Paris or the French government for a grant to buy pitchblende residue, they would have been laughed at. In any case their letter would have been lost in the files of some office, and they would have had to wait

months for a reply, probably unfavorable in the end. Out of the traditions and principles of the French Revolution, which had created the metric system, founded the Normal School, and encouraged science in many circumstances, the state seemed to have retained, after more than a century, only the deplorable words pronounced by Fouquier-Tinville at the trial in which Lavoisier was condemned to the guillotine: "The Republic has no need for scientists."

But at least could there not be found, in the numerous buildings attached to the Sorbonne, some kind of suitable workroom to lend to the Curie couple? Apparently not. After vain attempts, Pierre and Marie staggered back to their point of departure, which is to say to the School of Physics where Pierre taught, to the little room where Marie had done her first experiments. The room gave on a courtyard, and on the other side of the yard there was a wooden shack, an abandoned shed, with a skylight roof in such bad condition that it admitted the rain. The Faculty of Medicine had formerly used the place as a dissecting room, but for a long time now it had not even been considered fit to house the cadavers. No floor: an uncertain layer of bitumen covered the earth. It was furnished with some worn kitchen tables, a blackboard which had landed there for no known reason, and an old cast-iron stove with a rusty pipe.

.   .   .   .

As they were taking possession of the shed, a reply arrived from Austria. Good news! By extraordinary luck, the residue of recent extractions of uranium had not been scattered. The useless material had been piled up in a no-man's-land planted with pine trees, near the mine of Saint Joachimsthal. Thanks to the intercession of Professor Suess and the Academy of Science of Vienna, the Austrian government, which was the proprietor of the state factory there, decided to present a ton of residue to the two French lunatics who thought they needed it. If, later on, they wished to be sent a greater quantity of the material, they could obtain it at the mine on the best terms. For the moment the Curies had to pay only the transportation charges on a ton of ore.

One morning a heavy wagon, like those which deliver coal, drew up in the Rue Lhomond before the School of Physics. Pierre and Marie were notified. They hurried bareheaded into the street in their laboratory gowns. Pierre, who was never agitated, kept his calm; but the more exuberant Marie could not contain her joy at the sight of the sacks that were being unloaded. It was pitchblende, *her* pitchblende, for which she had received a notice some days before from the freight station. Full of curiosity and impatience, she wanted to open one of the sacks and contemplate her treasure without further waiting. She cut the strings, undid the coarse sackcloth and plunged her two hands into the dull brown ore, still mixed with pine needles from Bohemia.

There was where radium was hidden. It was from there that Marie must extract it, even if she had to treat a mountain of this inert stuff like dust on the road.

. . . .

During the first year they busied themselves with the chemical separation of radium and polonium and they studied the radiation of the products (more and more active) thus obtained. Before long they considered it more practical to separate their efforts. Pierre Curie tried to determine the properties of radium, and to know the new metal better. Marie continued those chemical treatments which would permit her to obtain salts of pure radium.

In this division of labor Marie had chosen the "man's job." She accomplished the toil of a day laborer. Inside the shed her husband was absorbed by delicate experiments. In the courtyard, dressed in her old dust-covered and acid-stained smock, her hair blown by the wind, surrounded by smoke which stung her eyes and throat, Marie was a sort of factory all by herself.

. . . .

Radium showed no intention of allowing itself to be known by human creatures. Where were the days when Marie naïvely expected the radium content of pitchblende to be *one per cent?* The radiation of the new substance was so powerful that a tiny quantity of radium, disseminated through the ore, was the source of striking phenomena which could be easily observed and measured. The difficult, the impossible thing, was to isolate this minute quantity, to separate it from the gangue in which it was so intimately mixed.

The days of work became months and years: Pierre and Marie were not discouraged. This material which resisted them, which defended its secrets, fascinated them. United by their tenderness, united by their intellectual passions, they had, in a wooden shack, the "anti-natural" existence for which they had both been made, she as well as he.

. . . .

Whenever Pierre and Marie, alone in this poor place, left their apparatus for a moment and quietly let their tongues run on, their talk about their beloved radium passed from the transcendent to the childish.

"I wonder what *It* will be like, what *It* will look like," Marie said one day with the feverish curiosity of a child who has been promised a toy. "Pierre, what form do you imagine *It* will take?"

"I don't know," the physicist answered gently. "I should like it to have a very beautiful color. . . ."

. . . .

In the course of the years 1899 and 1900, Pierre and Marie Curie published a report on the discovery of "induced radioactivity" due to radium, another on the effects of radioactivity, and another on the electric charge carried by the rays. And at last they drew up, for the Congress of Physics of 1900, a general report on the radioactive substances, which aroused immense interest among the scientists of Europe.

. . . .

Marie continued to treat, kilogram by kilogram, the tons of pitchblende residue which were sent her on several occasions from Saint Joachimsthal. With her terrible patience, she was able to be, every day for four years, a physicist, a chemist, a specialized worker, an engineer, and a laboring man all at once. Thanks to her brain and muscle, the old tables in the shed held more and more concentrated products — products more and more rich in radium. Mme. Curie was approaching the end: she no longer stood in the courtyard, enveloped in bitter smoke, to watch the heavy basins of material in fusion. She was now at the stage of purification and of the "fractional crystallization" of strongly radioactive solutions. But the poverty of her haphazard equipment hindered her work more than ever. It was now that she needed a spotlessly clean workroom and apparatus perfectly protected against cold, heat, and dirt. In this shed, open to every wind, iron and coal dust was afloat which, to Marie's despair, mixed itself into the products purified with so much care. Her heart sometimes constricted before these little daily accidents, which took so much of her time and her strength.

Pierre was so tired of the interminable struggle that he would have been quite ready to abandon it. Of course, he did not dream of dropping the study of radium and of radioactivity. But he would willingly have renounced, for the time being, the special operation of preparing pure radium. The obstacles seemed insurmountable. Could they not resume this work later on, under better conditions? More attached to the meaning of natural phenomena than to their material reality, Pierre Curie was exasperated to see the paltry results to which Marie's exhausting effort had led. He advised an armistice.

He counted without his wife's character. Marie wanted to isolate radium and she would isolate it. She scorned fatigue and difficulties, and even the gaps in her own knowledge which complicated her task. After all, she was only a very young scientist: she still had not the certainty and great culture Pierre had acquired by twenty years' work, and sometimes she stumbled across phenomena or methods of calculation of which she knew very little, and for which she had to make hasty studies.

So much the worse! With stubborn eyes under her great brow, she clung to her apparatus and her test tubes.

In 1902, forty-five months after the day on which the Curies announced the probable existence of radium, Marie finally carried off the victory in this war of attrition: she succeeded in preparing a decigram of pure radium, and made a first determination of the atomic weight of the new substance, which was 225.

The incredulous chemists — of whom there were still a few — could only bow before the facts, before the superhuman obstinacy of a woman.

Radium officially existed.

It was nine o'clock at night. Pierre and Marie Curie were in their little house at 108 Boulevard Kellermann, where they had been living since 1900. The house suited them well. From the boulevard, where three rows of trees half-hid the fortifications, could be seen only a dull wall and a tiny door. But behind the one-story house, hidden from all eyes, there was a narrow provincial garden, rather pretty and very quiet. And from the "barrier" of Gentilly they could escape on their bicycles toward the suburbs and the woods. . . .

Old Doctor Curie, who lived with the couple, had retired to his room. Marie had bathed her child and put it to bed, and had stayed for a long time beside the cot. This was a rite. When Iréne did not feel her mother near her at night, she would call out for her incessantly, with that "Mé!" which was to be our substitute for "Mamma" always. And Marie, yielding to the implacability of the four-year-old baby, climbed the stairs, seated herself beside the child, and stayed there in the darkness until the young voice gave way to light, regular breathing. Only then would she go down again to Pierre, who was growing impatient. In spite of his kindness, he was the most possessive and jealous of husbands. He was so used to the constant presence of his wife that her least eclipse kept him from thinking freely. If Marie delayed too long near her daughter, he received her on her return with a reproach so unjust as to be comic:

"You never think of anything but that child!"

Pierre walked slowly about the room. Marie sat down and made some stitches on the hem of Iréne's new apron. One of her principles was never to buy ready-made clothes for the child: she thought them too fancy and impractical. In the days when Bronya was in Paris the two sisters cut out their children's dresses together, according to patterns of their own invention. These patterns still served for Marie.

But this evening she could not fix her attention. Nervous, she got up; then, suddenly:

"Suppose we go down there for a moment?"

There was a note of supplication in her voice — altogether superfluous, for Pierre, like herself, longed to go back to the shed they had left two hours before. Radium, fanciful as a living creature, enduring as a love, called them back to its dwelling, to the wretched laboratory.

The day's work had been hard, and it would have been more reasonable for the couple to rest. But Pierre and Marie were not always reasonable. As soon as they had put on their coats and told Doctor Curie of their flight, they were in the street. They went on foot, arm in arm, exchanging few words. After the crowded streets of this queer district, with its factory buildings, wastelands, and poor tenements, they arrived in the Rue Lhomond and crossed the little courtyard. Pierre put the key in the lock. The door squeaked, as it had squeaked thousands of times, and admitted them to their realm, to their dream.

"Don't light the lamps!" Marie said in the darkness. Then she added with a little laugh:

"Do you remember the day when you said to me, 'I should like radium to have a beautiful color'?"

The reality was more entrancing than the simple wish of long ago. Radium had something better than "a beautiful color": it was spontaneously luminous. And in the somber shed where, in the absence of cupboards, the precious particles in their tiny glass receivers were placed on tables or on shelves nailed to the wall, their phosphorescent bluish outlines gleamed, suspended in the night.

"Look! Look!" the young woman murmured.

She went forward cautiously, looked for and found a straw-bottomed chair. She sat down in the darkness and silence. Their two faces turned toward the pale glimmering, the mysterious sources of radiation, toward radium — their radium. Her body leaning forward, her head eager, Marie took up

again the attitude which had been hers an hour earlier at the bedside of her sleeping child.

Her companion's hand lightly touched her hair.

She was to remember forever this evening of glowworms, this magic.

Albert Schweitzer [4]

JOSEPH GOLLOMB

≈ *Albert Schweitzer is considered one of the greatest men of the twentieth century. Humanitarian, philosopher, theologian, organist of genius, authority on the life and works of Bach, author and lecturer, he became known the world over for his devoted work as a missionary physician in French Equatorial Africa where he established his famous hospital in Lambaréné. The chapter given below tells of an important decision that he made at the age of twenty-one.*

Albert went straight to the famous University of Strasbourg. He climbed the tower of the world-renowned Cathedral and looked down on the city, mellowed and picturesque with seventeen hundred years of history: peaked roofs with their stork nests, wooden verandas gay with flower boxes and murmurous with dovecots. Beyond them were the canals, villages, and fertile fields of the Rhine valley, and the broad, shining ribbon of the fabled river itself. Beyond that in turn was the Black Forest, home of legends and regal stags, with the huntsman's horn still sounding in the heart of the great woods.

He found a room in a house in the Old Fish Market. He did not know at the time that over a century before another youth had come to Strasbourg to study and had lived in that very room; that he, too, had climbed the Cathedral tower and, looking forward, had found life overflowing with promise.

Life more than made good its promises to young Johann Wolfgang Goethe. In the long years it gave him he became the greatest poet since Shakespeare, and made careers for himself as lawyer, scientist, painter, critic, novelist, soldier, theatrical director, political

[4] From Joseph Gollomb, *Albert Schweitzer: Genius in the Jungle* (Vanguard Press, 1949).

economist, philosopher, mathematician, administrator, and statesman.

Schweitzer would never be the universal genius that Goethe had been, but he was a greater artist in music than Goethe was at painting, and he far surpassed him in strength of character and in his compassion for suffering humanity. Nevertheless Schweitzer came to understand Goethe so well that shortly thereafter he won a prize and, later, world-wide acclaim, for his interpretation of the man, his life, and his spirit.

When he came to the university, Schweitzer was already deep in Greek and Latin, and now he added Hebrew to his studies. He found the language difficult at first, which was all he needed to make him master it. He also enrolled in the faculties of philosophy and theology, and in all took on a program that would have broken the back of an ordinary student. But then, his day had more hours in it than that of other students. When the others slept, Schweitzer delighted in staying up night after night studying, until his fellow students and the faculty decided that he could not be human.

In addition to his studies, there were the many hours of rehearsals on the organ and the recitals he gave in one country after another.

At this time he was called for the year of military service that Germany required of its educated young men. He went off with a Greek Bible in his knapsack. All that year during drills, strenuous marches, and other physically exhausting activities, his body would be doing one thing, his mind another. After twelve to sixteen hours of training, his fellow conscripts were glad to call it a day. But Schweitzer would stay up to ask searching questions of his Bible, and since his researches had not furnished satisfactory answers, he tried to work out his own.

When the year of military service was up, he returned to the university, and soon theological circles were discussing the young man who dared dispute august authorities but whose challenge had to be met.

The historic bells of the Cathedral which sounded the hours were mostly unheard by him. By day he was too absorbed in studies. Evenings he spent in talk with fellow students and professors, talk that was music to his mind, rich with harmonies, and stimulating even in its discords. After the others had gone to bed Schweitzer would go to his room to study and to write. The morning sun found him still at it, seemingly as fresh as though he had slept all night.

He made up for lost sleep, however, on week ends and on vacations at the parsonage in Günsbach, which was only a short train ride from the university. Even then for several nights there would be late hours of talk with his family.

One Whitsunday morning at home he awoke slowly out of a deep sleep, every last sinew in him so rested that he could have sung. Sunlight streaming through shaggy foliage played on the walls of his room. He could see apple blossoms and lilacs, and their scents came wafting in. Birdsong overflowed, and the breeze brought the sound of organ practice in the church, then the steeple bells rang in the festival day that it was.

He lay listening to it all and to his happiness. How generously life had dealt with him, how lavishly! A powerful body, abounding health, a teeming mind, music in every fiber, a score of skills, and a driving energy that knew no rest — nor did it seem to need any. His dearest daydreams had more than come true, and from every side there came assurance that it was all only a foretaste of what the future would be. . . .

It was too great fortune to take for granted.

His thoughts turned to the many, far too many, who had little or nothing. . . . Such sunless, poverty-stricken lives . . . bodies that had never known well-being and were little more than carriers of sickness and pain . . . minds that lived in darkness and in fear. . . . Their only dreams that did come true were nightmares. . . .

How can one have the heart to be given much and not go and share *some* of it with those others . . . much of it . . . all of it?

"To whom much is given, of him shall much be required. . . . Freely you have received, freely give. . . . Preach the word . . . heal the sick. . . ."

An honest man does not disregard such commandments. . . . He goes to those who have little and stays with them until he has made a difference in their lives. . . . How long? As long as there is misery to be relieved. . . . But there is so much of it in the world that it may swallow up a lifetime to cope with even a small part of it! . . . Well, others have done it. He had been given more than his share. Was he to hoard it all?

But other voices in him protested that talents, too, were entitled to life, growth, and fulfillment. His were only half realized. . . . He owed them something, too. . . .

He came to his decision. He would devote the next nine years to music and to science,

to teaching and to preaching, and to other "necessities of my being." Then he would put it all behind him and seek out some benighted area where he could be of direct service, "man to man," to those who had so much less than he. . . .

He was twenty-one at the time. This meant — if he kept his word — that at thirty he would turn his back on such a life as most men dream of and few achieve.

But he dressed and, putting his resolve away among his secrets, he went down smiling to breakfast with his family.

BIBLIOGRAPHY

Collections

Bailey, Carolyn Sherwin. *Children of the Handcrafts;* illus. by Grace Paull. Viking Press, 1935. (Grades 6–8)

Stories of real children who became famous in their individual crafts, including Paul Revere, the silversmith; Duncan Phyfe, the joiner; Thoreau, the pencil-maker.

Cottler, Joseph, and Haym Jaffe. *Heroes of Civilization;* illus. by F. W. Orr. Little, Brown, 1931. (Grades 5–9)

Achievements of thirty-five people who have succeeded in the fields of exploration, science, invention, biology, and medicine.

Lawson, Robert. *They Were Strong and Good;* illus. by the author. Viking Press, 1940. (Grades 4–6)

A book which emphasizes our American heritage. Robert Lawson tells the story of his four grandparents and his own father and mother, not because they were great or famous, but because they were strong and good. Awarded the Caldecott medal in 1941.

McNeer, May. *Armed with Courage;* illus. by Lynd Ward. Abingdon, 1957. (Grades 5–7)

Vivid, brief biographies of seven men and women who had great physical and spiritual courage — Father Damien, Florence Nightingale, Jane Addams, Carver, Grenfell, Schweitzer, and Gandhi.

Morgan, James. *Our Presidents; Brief Biographies of our Chief Magistrates from Washington to Truman: 1789–1949.* Macmillan, enl. ed. 1949. (Grades 7–9)

Besides the biographical sketches, a history of the Presidency is included.

Petersham, Maud and Miska. *Story of the Presidents of the United States of America;* illus. by the authors. Macmillan, 1953. (Grades 4–7) Interesting to read, useful for reference.

Richardson, Ben. *Great American Negroes;* rev. by William A. Fahey; illus. by Robert Hallock. Thomas Y. Crowell, 1956. (Grades 7–9)

Sketches of twenty-one Negroes who have added to American culture in the arts and sciences, sports and entertainment.

Shippen, Katherine. *Men of Medicine;* illus. by Anthony Ravielli. Viking Press, 1957. (High School)

A history of medical discoveries made by great scientists covering a period of five thousand years, ending with the discovery of penicillin, the "mycins," and the Salk vaccine.

Sickels, Eleanor. *In Calico and Crinoline;* illus. by Ilse Bischoff. Viking Press, 1935. (Grades 8–9)

True stories of American women who played a part in the history of their country from 1608 to 1865.

Individual Biography

Aulaire, Ingri and Edgar Parin d'. *Leif the Lucky;* illus. by the authors. Doubleday, 1941. (Grades 3–5)

The story of Leif, Erik's son, who sailed with his father to Greenland and later sailed still farther west and found the continent of America. Other picture-biographies by this talented author-artist team are *Abraham Lincoln, Benjamin Franklin, Buffalo Bill, Columbus,* and *George Washington.*

Averill, Esther. *Cartier Sails the St. Lawrence;* illus. by Feodor Rojankovsky. Harper & Brothers, new ed. 1956. (Grades 4–7)

Originally published under the title *The Voyages of Jacques Cartier,* the book is based on Cartier's own logbooks. Also by the same author and illustrator: *Daniel Boone.*

Baker, Nina Brown. *Juárez, Hero of Mexico;* illus. by Marion Greenwood. Vanguard Press, 1942. (Grades 7–9)

A well-documented account of the great patriot, the first civilian president of Mexico. The author has written many excellent biographies including *Peter the Great; Robert Bruce, King of Scots;* and *Sir Walter Raleigh.*

Becker, May Lamberton. *Presenting Jane Austen;* illus. by Edward Price. Dodd, Mead, 1952. (High School)

A perceptive biography which leads to the reading or re-reading of Jane Austen's novels. Also by the same author: *Introducing Charles Dickens.*

Commager, Henry Steele. *America's Robert E. Lee;* illus. by Lynd Ward. Houghton Mifflin, 1951. (Grades 6–8)

Written with sympathy, dignity, and respect for the great Confederate general.

Curie, Eve. *Madame Curie;* trans. by Vincent Sheean. Doubleday, 1937. (Grades 8–10)

A deeply moving story of a woman who steadfastly refused to accept defeat.

Dalgliesh, Alice. *The Columbus Story;* illus. by Leo Politi. Charles Scribner's Sons, 1955. (Grades 3–5)

The author skillfully presents the events in the life of Columbus that are most interesting to children.

Daugherty, James. *Daniel Boone;* illus. by the author. Viking Press, 1939. (Grades 5–9)

Superb lithographs and rhythmic homespun prose tell of Boone's courage and daring that contributed so much to the early expansion of America. Also by the same author: *Marcus and Narcissa Whitman.*

Davis, Robert. *Tree Toad: Adventures of the Kid Brother;* illus. by Robert McCloskey, with frontispiece by Charles Dana Gibson. J. B. Lippincott, 1942. (Grades 6–9)

This amusing account of the boyhood pranks of the author and his brother was first published as an adult book. Later it was brought out in an attractive format for boys and girls, with a foreword by Anne Carroll Moore.

Deucher, Sybil. *Edvard Grieg, Boy of the Northland;* illus. by Mary Greenwalt. E. P. Dutton, 1946. (Grades 5–8)

The story of the Norwegian composer, with simple musical arrangements of some of his best-known compositions.

Deutsch, Babette. *Walt Whitman: Builder for America;* illus. by Rafaello Busoni. Julian Messner, 1941. (High School)

An understanding presentation of the poet and his relation to the times in which he lived.

Eaton, Jeanette. *Gandhi, Fighter Without a Sword;* illus. by Ralph Ray. William Morrow, 1950. (Grades 7–9)

A luminous biography of the great spiritual and political leader. Other excellent biographies by this same author are *David Livingstone; Leader by Destiny, George Washington; Lone Journey, the Life of Roger Williams; Narcissa Whitman;* and *That Lively Man, Ben Franklin.*

Forbes, Esther. *America's Paul Revere;* illus. by Lynd Ward. Houghton Mifflin, 1946. (Grades 5–8)

Vivid prose and striking pictures combine to make an outstanding biography of a great craftsman and patriot.

Foster, Genevieve. *George Washington;* illus. by the author. Charles Scribner's Sons, 1949. (Grades 4–6)

Similar in format to the author's *Abraham Lincoln.* Although these "initial biographies" are written for younger children, the interesting text and lively illustrations appeal to older children as well.

Galt, Thomas. *Peter Zenger, Fighter for Freedom;* illus. by Ralph Ray. Thomas Y. Crowell, 1951. (Grades 7–9)

The story of New York's famous printer, and his trial in 1735 which won freedom of the press for England and America.

Godden, Rumer. *Hans Christian Andersen; a Great Life in Brief.* Alfred A. Knopf, 1955. (High School)

A sensitive biography of the beloved Danish writer whose life was poignantly reflected in his fairy tales.

Gollomb, Joseph. *Albert Schweitzer, Genius of the Jungle.* Vanguard Press, 1949. (Grades 7–9)

A splendid introduction to an extraordinary man. Based mainly on Schweitzer's own writings, it is a book to lift the spirit of both young and old interested in helping to build a better world.

Graham, Shirley, and George Lipscomb. *Dr. George Washington Carver, Scientist;* illus. by Elton C. Fax. Julian Messner, 1944. (Grades 6–9)

An inspiring biography of the great scientist and humanitarian.

Gray, Elizabeth Janet. *Penn;* illus. by George Gillett Whitney. Viking Press, 1938. (Grades 7–9)

Penn gave up wealth and position to become a Quaker. Later he was governor of the new colony of Pennsylvania. Also by this same author: *Young Walter Scott.*

Gurko, Leo. *Tom Paine, Freedom's Apostle;* illus. by Fritz Kredel. Thomas Y. Crowell, 1957. (Grades 7–9)

A significant biography of a provocative historical figure.

Hall, Anna. *Nansen;* illus. by Boris Artzybasheff. Viking Press, 1940. (Grades 7–9)

An absorbing life of the great Norwegian explorer and statesman who won the Nobel Peace Prize in 1922.

Hawthorne, Hildegarde. *Romantic Rebel; the Story of Nathaniel Hawthorne;* illus. by W. M. Berger. Appleton, 1932. (Grades 8–9)

A story-biography written by Hawthorne's grand-daughter.

Henry, Marguerite. *Benjamin West and His Cat Grimalkin;* illus. by Wesley Dennis. Bobbs-Merrill, 1947. (Grades 4–6)

The author has created a true bit of Americana with her story of the Pennsylvania Quaker boy who grew up to be called "the father of American painting."

Hodges, C. Walter. *Columbus Sails;* illus. by the author. Coward-McCann, 1940. (Grades 7–9)

An English artist brings a fresh approach to the story of the great discoverer by telling it through the eyes of men close to Columbus.

Holbrook, Stewart. *America's Ethan Allen;* illus. by Lynd Ward. Houghton Mifflin, 1949. (Grades 7–9)

A rousing biography of the leader of the Green Mountain Boys.

Hunt, Mabel Leigh. *Better Known as Johnny Appleseed;* illus. by James Daugherty; foreword by Louis Bromfield. J. B. Lippincott, 1950. (Grades 7–9)

With painstaking research and great skill the author has re-created the life of the beloved John Chapman, better known as Johnny Apple-seed. Also by the same author: *"Have You Seen Tom Thumb?"*

Jarden, Mary Louise. *The Young Brontës;* illus. by Helen Sewell. Viking Press, 1938. (Grades 7–9)

An imaginary treatment of the life of Charlotte, Emily, Branwell, and Anne, as children in the bleak parsonage on the Yorkshire moors.

Judson, Clara Ingram. *Mr. Justice Holmes;* illus. by Robert Todd. Follett, 1956. (Grades 8–10)

This inspiring life of the great American, Oliver Wendell Holmes, gives the reader a feeling of pride and deep patriotism.

Kamm, Josephine. *Gertrude Bell: Daughter of the Desert.* Vanguard Press, 1956. (Grades 7–9)

The remarkable life-story of a fascinating English-woman who became not only a mountaineer, an explorer, a historian, and archaeologist, but also a diplomat who played an important part in the formation of the kingdom of Iraq.

Kellogg, Charlotte. *Paderewski.* Viking Press, 1957. (Grades 7–9)

This deeply moving biography tells not only of Paderewski's genius as a pianist, but also of his monumental contribution to the cause of human freedom. The author was his close friend and associate in organizing relief for Poland after the First World War.

Latham, Jean. *Carry On, Mr. Bowditch;* illus. by John O'Hara Cosgrave, II. Houghton Mif-flin, 1955. (Grades 6–9)

An intensely interesting chronicle of the great navigator, Nathaniel Bowditch, which also re-creates the romantic period of the clipper ships. Awarded the Newbery medal in 1956.

Lenski, Lois. *Indian Captive: the Story of Mary Jemison;* illus. by the author. J. B. Lippin-cott, 1941. (Grades 6–9)

A fictionized but authentic story of the twelve-year-old white girl captured by the Seneca Indians in 1758.

Levinger, Elma. *Albert Einstein.* Julian Mess-ner, 1949. (Grades 7–9)

An excellent and absorbing life of one of the world's great scientists.

Long, Laura. *De Lesseps: Builder of Suez;* illus. by Clotilde Embree Funk. Longmans, Green, 1958. (Grades 5–8)

In the gigantic undertaking of building the Suez Canal, De Lesseps met each obstacle as a chal-lenge, handled the jealousy of nations with rare diplomacy, and at long last found a way to success out of failure.

McNeer, May. *America's Abraham Lincoln;* illus. by Lynd Ward. Houghton Mifflin, 1957. (Grades 5–8)

A vivid portrayal which shows the physical and spiritual growth of the boy and man.

Masani, Shakuntala. *Nehru's Story;* illus. by the author. Oxford University Press, 1949. (Grades 4–6)

This book, first written for the boys and girls of India, tells the story of the great Indian leader from the time he was a small boy.

Meadowcroft, William. *Boy's Life of Edison;* with autobiographical notes by Mr. Edison. Harper & Brothers, new ed. 1929. (Grades 6–8)

A life of the great inventor written especially for young people by a man closely associated with Edison for many years.

Meigs, Cornelia. *Invincible Louisa.* Little, Brown, 1933. (Grades 7–9)

The story of the author of *Little Women.* Illustrated with photographs of the Alcott family. Awarded the Newbery medal in 1934.

Nolan, Jeannette Covert. *Florence Nightingale;* illus. by George Avison. Julian Messner, 1946. (Grades 7–9)

A well-written, authentic life of the woman who achieved fame as a nurse in the Crimean War. Also by the same author: *The Story of Clara Barton of the Red Cross; Andrew Jackson; George Rogers Clark; John Brown;* and *Benedict Arnold.*

Norman, Charles. *John Muir.* Julian Messner, 1957. (Grades 7–9)

World-famous as a naturalist, writer, and explorer, Muir was instrumental in establishing our national parks.

Petry, Ann. *Harriet Tubman, Conductor on the Underground Railroad.* Thomas Y. Crowell, 1955. (Grades 7–9)

A sensitively written story of a heroic woman who was born a slave but escaped through the Underground Railroad and returned for others until she had helped three hundred of her people to freedom.

Politi, Leo. *The Mission Bell;* illus. by the author. Charles Scribner's Sons, 1953. (Grades 2–5)

Simple text and glowing pictures tell the inspiring story of Father Junipero Serra and how he founded the first mission settlement in California.

Purdy, Claire Lee. *He Heard America Sing; the Story of Stephen Foster;* illus. by Dorothea Cooke. Julian Messner, 1940. (Grades 6–9)

A fictionized biography of the beloved composer which also recreates a colorful section of American life.

Raverat, Gwendolen. *Period Piece.* W. W. Norton, 1953. (High School)

Delightful recollections of a Victorian childhood by the granddaughter of Charles Darwin.

Robinson, Mabel. *Runner of the Mountain Tops; the Life of Louis Agassiz;* decorations by Lynd Ward. Random House, 1939. (Grades 7–9)

The life of the Swiss immigrant who became one of America's great men and founded the Agassiz Museum at Harvard University.

Roos, Ann. *Man of Molokai; the Life of Father Damien;* illus. by Raymond Lufkin. J. B. Lippincott, 1943. (Grades 7–9)

A stirring story of Father Damien's work on the leper island of Molokai and of how his spirit of love and sacrifice ennobled all who came in contact with it.

Rourke, Constance. *Audubon;* with 12 colored plates from original Audubon prints and illustrations by James MacDonald. Harcourt, Brace, 1936. (Grades 7–9)

Distinguished by painstaking research, fine writing, and the author's enthusiasm for her subject. Also by the same author: *Davy Crockett.*

Sandburg, Carl. *Abe Lincoln Grows Up;* illus. by James Daugherty. Harcourt, Brace, 1928. (Grades 7–9)

This classic account of Lincoln's boyhood was taken from the author's *Abraham Lincoln: The Prairie Years.*

Shafter, Toby. *Edna St. Vincent Millay: America's Best-Loved Poet.* Julian Messner, 1957. (High School)

This gifted poet, at the age of thirty-one, won the Pulitzer Prize.

Shepard, Ernest H. *Drawn from Memory;* illus. by the author. J. B. Lippincott, 1957. (All Ages)

Few artists are so universally loved on both sides of the Atlantic as Ernest Shepard, the delightful illustrator of *Winnie-the-Pooh* and *Wind in the Willows.* Now, after nearly seventy years, he looks back and draws from memory with words and pictures a year of his London childhood.

Shippen, Katherine. *Leif Eriksson; First Voyager to America.* Harper & Brothers, 1951. (Grades 6–9)

A dramatic biography of the early explorer, based on the Icelandic sagas.

Steffens, Lincoln. *Boy on Horseback;* illus. by Sanford Tousey. Harcourt, Brace, 1935. (Grades 6–9)

The story of Steffens' childhood, taken from *The Autobiography of Lincoln Steffens,* reads like fiction.

Stoutenburg, Adrien, and Laura Baker. *Snowshoe Thompson;* illus. by Victor De Pauw. Charles Scribner's Sons, 1957. (Grades 7–9)

A fine, fast-moving narrative of a little-known figure in American history, John A. Thompson, who carried mail and news on skis over the rugged Sierra Nevadas in Gold Rush days.

Swenson, Eric. *The South Sea Shilling: Voyages of Captain Cook, R.N.;* illus. by Charles Michael Daugherty. Viking Press, 1952. (Grades 6–9)

A vividly sustained tale of courage and endurance.

Swift, Hildegarde. *The Edge of April; a Biography of John Burroughs;* illus. by Lynd Ward. William Morrow, 1957. (Grades 7–9)

"The most precious things of life are near at hand," wrote John Burroughs, "without money and without price. Each of you has the whole wealth of the universe at your very door."

Trease, Geoffrey. *Sir Walter Raleigh; Captain & Adventurer.* Vanguard Press, 1950. (Grades 7–9)

A brilliant biography rooted in sound research.

Waugh, Elizabeth. *Simón Bolívar: A Story of Courage;* illus. by Flora Nash DeMuth. Macmillan, 1941. (Grades 6–8)

A stirring story of the South American patriot, statesman, diplomat, and soldier.

Wheeler, Opal, and Sybil Deucher. *Franz Schubert and His Merry Friends;* illus. by Mary Greenwalt. E. P. Dutton, 1939. (Grades 4–6)

These authors have written several successful biographies of musicians for younger children, including *Sebastian Bach* and *Joseph Haydn.*

Wibberley, Leonard. *The Life of Winston Churchill.* Farrar, Straus and Cudahy, 1956. (Grades 7–9)

A lively biography of Churchill who "combines the spirit of American initiative with the traditions of the British nobility." Also by the same author: *John Barry, Father of the Navy.*

Wood, Laura. *Raymond L. Ditmars; His Exciting Career with Reptiles, Animals and Insects;* illus. with photographs. Julian Messner, 1944. (Grades 7–9)

The story of an American boy who turned a hobby into a profession and became Curator of the New York Zoological Park. Also by the same author: *Louis Pasteur* and *Walter Reed, Doctor in Uniform.*

Yates, Elizabeth. *Amos Fortune, Free Man;* illus. by Nora S. Unwin. Aladdin Books, 1950. (Grades 7–9)

A sympathetic and inspiring portrayal of a remarkable man who was born a prince in Africa, sold a slave in America, and eventually purchased his own freedom. Also by the same author: *Prudence Crandall, Woman of Courage.*

Travel
and
History

> *"All that Shakespeare says of the king,
> yonder slip of a boy that reads in the corner
> feels to be true of himself. We sympathize
> in the great moments of history, in the great
> discoveries, the great resistances, the great
> prosperities of men; because there law was
> enacted, the sea was searched, the land was
> found, or the blow was struck, for us, as we
> ourselves in that place would have done or
> applauded."* [1]

ANYONE WHO IS FORTUNATE enough to be a true lover of history is probably so endowed because, early in life, he felt himself involved in the past, as Emerson pictures his "boy in the corner." Those schooled in the texts of the first decade of this country found history a matter of dates and kings, wars and revolutions, conquests and defeats, broken up into short paragraphs and summarized in outline form at the end of the chapter. History was not for such as these unless they were fortunate enough to have a text which somehow, at some point, flowed like a story, climax following climax; or came upon a teacher who made the past live as part of their own present, and contrived to concern the children he taught in the whole fate of the human race.

Modern education interrupts the "stream of history" by making it a part of Social Studies; but in so doing, the role of the common man, the fascination of daily life through the centuries, and the connection between past and present become intimate and full of human meaning. The emphasis upon the social interpretation of history for children has resulted in a body of historical writing which is inspiriting, imaginative, and dynamic.

Man Is a Weaver, by Elizabeth Chesley Baity (Viking, 1942), *The History of Everyday Things in England,* by the Quennells (Scribner, 1918–35, 4 vols.), *Colonial Living,* by Edwin Tunis (World, 1957) — books such as these succeed in using a specific subject or topic as a clue to the greater concept of the history and progress of man. They offer opportunity, also, for a full exploration of a period, and this pattern follows the natural interests of children. Certain periods have a strong appeal for children; the life of primitive man,

[1] Ralph Waldo Emerson, "History."

the feudal period, the age of the great discoverers — these are subjects upon which many children are intent in the span of reading years between the ages of nine to twelve and thirteen. Children find exhilaration in reading history when it is based on sound, even minute scholarship, and has in addition that edge of distinctive writing which brings it into the area of literature.

The judicious use of source material strengthens the appeal of history for children. The journals, letters, and diaries of men and women and their contemporaries give immediacy to historic accounts of their accomplishments. The words of Columbus, the diaries of Jefferson, the letters that passed between father and son or husband and wife at the time of the War of the Revolution or the War Between the States — these serve to wear away the lackluster acceptance of reiterated fact piled upon fact, year after year. Suddenly, through his own words, a man is revealed, and the magnitude of his accomplishment is freshly realized. Much of the present-day child's interest in history is due to a new recognition of the appeal of source material. To read the Elizabethan prose from Hakluyt's Voyages is to know the flavor of the age, to freshen the perception, and to arouse the imagination of the reader. It was thus. And here are the very words, spoken at the time.

Certain writers show themselves steeped in and colored by the reading they have done. James Daugherty, in his books of biography and history, reveals his fervent contact with historic sources, and his books are moving and memorable as a result. In 1938, a book of unusual character appeared: *Never to Die: The Egyptians in Their Own Words,* by Josephine Mayer and Tom Prideaux (Viking Press). Here the Egyptian civilization was presented by excerpts from the sacred writings and illustrated with reproductions of Egyptian art. This book set the pace for much that was to come.

But it was the distinguished historian Hendrik Willem Van Loon who risked the heights of maturity in his interpretation of history for children. His *Story of Mankind* is a philosophical approach. He invites the judgment of children upon their past, showing them the necessity of weighing evidence in disputes, and giving them the material with which to work. His bias is toward tolerance and compassion, an opening of minds, a sharpening of perception. His humor and wit enliven the text as does the play of his rich individuality. It is significant that this book won the first Newbery award in 1922, setting a standard of achievement for all the titles which were to follow. The book put an end to the authoritarian, the bigoted, and the prejudiced points of view which so often in the past had been acceptable where children were concerned. It put an end to dullness, and gave to the generations of children caught between two World Wars a spiritual balance wheel. It is a book for children, but, like several other classics of childhood, it has leaped over boundaries of age to be acclaimed by readers of all ages who seek to know their own place in the long and enduring story of humanity.

With all the inventive, fresh ways of presenting history to children, the chronological approach still holds an appeal for young readers. Genevieve Foster, gifted writer and artist, has experimented with time in her unusual books which combine history and biography. Her *George Washington's*

World (Scribner, 1941), and *Augustus Caesar's World* (Scribner, 1947) present the contemporary world as background for the life span of the subject of her biography, and include accounts of the arts, science, and politics of the time in which her subjects lived. These richly documented, horizontal views of history are infinitely varied and interesting. This approach adds a new dimension of reality to facts which had not been formerly related to each other, and it comprises a singularly original presentation of history for children.

The outstanding tenet of writing for children in the second quarter of this century is an insistence on first-hand authenticity in science, the arts, history, biography, and travel. A renewed and vigorous research in history and biography is called for, a sound knowledge of the sciences, a lively and genuine interest on the part of the author in his subject, and the ability to inform his writing with a measure of his knowledge and his feeling. These touchstones have been substituted for a previous acceptance of much that was diluted, rewritten, and many times removed from original sources of knowledge and research.

Even the field of travel has received a new vitality from this emphasis upon direct experience, with the result that several books of marked distinction have come into being. Gone are the boring compilations of facts, wearing a weak disguise of fiction, in which an all-knowing aunt and uncle — one wonders why the parents were never able to travel — accompanied two children to a foreign land, apparently for the express purpose of giving guide-book answers to the unnatural questions the children were made to ask. Now men and women whose knowledge of the land they describe is intimate or native give accounts of the life led there, as well as the descriptive details beloved of tourists. For example, Alan Paton, the author of the distinguished novel *Cry, the Beloved Country,* has written a book for children, *The Land and People of South Africa* (Lippincott, 1955), in which he does not hesitate to present the issues of that country, with fairness, and with the same love of the land which characterized his novel. Gudrun Thorne-Thomsen's *In Norway* (Viking, 1948) is informed by the author's loving remembrance of her own childhood, while at the same time the history, modes, and manners of the country, with the lives of some of its great men, are touched upon. Evelyn Stefánsson's *Here Is the Far North* (Scribner, 1957), describing Iceland, Greenland and the Soviet Arctic, far exceeds the expectation of the usual book of travel and carries the conviction of a knowledgeable enthusiast. A new sense of responsibility informs the outstanding books which seek to acquaint children with the wider world. The immense and immediate necessity of our living together on a shrunken planet is responsible for a search for understanding and sympathy, and for the realization that the dignity of man is a term that applies to all peoples everywhere.

But though in many respects we live in an enlightened period, as far as children's literature in these areas is concerned, the need to apply critical judgment becomes increasingly acute. The truth is that the whole field of non-fiction is being somewhat exploited. Titles roll from the presses in quantities which may be far in excess of the normal and natural demands of the children themselves. The harvest is abundant, but much of the bulk is chaff. The supply may well reflect the abundance of the sources, rather than the genuine interests of the children. The very plethora of books makes it more difficult to recognize the individual, deeply felt, and well-realized expression of an author than it was when the major problem was scarcity. The judicious selection of books for children must be attained in the shadow of the great threat of our time to the inviolability of individual reaction and individual taste: namely, a mass conformity induced by mass pressures and mass markets.

TRAVEL AND HISTORY

The Story of Mankind
The Setting of the Stage[1]

HENDRIK VAN LOON

☙ *When* The Story of Mankind *was published in 1921, it presented history in a bold, original, and invigorating way. For the first time the young reader got a sweeping, universal view of history. The dead past came alive for him, and the book so fired his imagination that he wanted to find out more about this subject that suddenly seemed to be teeming with human interest. The book was awarded the Newbery Medal in 1922. It is particularly gratifying that the first award should have been given to a book which has so successfully stood the passage of time. The selection given below is the first chapter.*

We live under the shadow of a gigantic question mark.

Who are we?

Where do we come from?

Whither are we bound?

Slowly, but with persistent courage, we have been pushing this question mark further and further towards that distant line, beyond the horizon, where we hope to find our answer.

We have not gone very far.

We still know very little but we have reached the point where (with a fair degree of accuracy) we can guess at many things.

[1] From Hendrik van Loon, *The Story of Mankind* (Liveright).

In this chapter I shall tell you how (according to our best belief) the stage was set for the first appearance of man.

If we represent the time during which it has been possible for animal life to exist upon our planet by a line of this length,

———————————————

then the tiny line just below indicates the age during which man (or a creature more or less resembling man) has lived upon this earth.

Man was the last to come but the first to use his brain for the purpose of conquering the forces of nature. That is the reason why we are going to study him, rather than cats or dogs or horses or any of the other animals, who, all in their own way, have a very interesting historical development behind them.

In the beginning, the planet upon which we live was (as far as we now know) a large ball of flaming matter, a tiny cloud of smoke in the endless ocean of space. Gradually, in the course of millions of years, the surface burned itself out, and was covered with a thin layer of rocks. Upon these lifeless rocks the rain descended in endless torrents, wearing out the hard granite and carrying the dust to the valleys that lay hidden between the high cliffs of the steaming earth.

Finally the hour came when the sun broke through the clouds and saw how this little planet was covered with a few small puddles which were to develop into the mighty oceans of the eastern and western hemispheres.

Then one day the great wonder happened. What had been dead, gave birth to life.

The first living cell floated upon the waters of the sea.

For millions of years it drifted aimlessly with the currents. But during all that time it was developing certain habits that it might survive more easily upon the inhospitable earth. Some of these cells were happiest in the dark depths of the lakes and the pools. They took root in the slimy sediments which had been carried down from the tops of the hills and they became plants. Others preferred to move about and they grew strange jointed legs, like scorpions and began to crawl along the bottom of the sea amidst the plants and the pale green things that looked like jellyfishes. Still others (covered with scales) depended upon a swimming motion to go from place to place in their search for food, and gradually they populated the ocean with myriads of fishes.

Meanwhile the plants had increased in number and they had to search for new dwelling places. There was no more room for them at the bottom of the sea. Reluctantly they left the water and made a new home in the marshes and on the mudbanks that lay at the foot of the mountains. Twice a day the tides of the ocean covered them with their brine. For the rest of the time, the plants made the best of their uncomfortable situation and tried to survive in the thin air which surrounded the surface of the planet. After centuries of training, they learned how to live as comfortably in the air as they had done in the water. They increased in size and became shrubs and trees and at last they learned how to grow lovely flowers which attracted the attention of the busy big bumble-bees and the birds who carried the seeds far and wide until the whole earth had become covered with green pastures, or lay dark under the shadow of the big trees.

But some of the fishes too had begun to leave the sea, and they had learned how to breathe with lungs as well as with gills. We call such creatures amphibious, which means that they are able to live with equal ease on the land and in the water. The first frog who crosses your path can tell you all about the pleasures of the double existence of the amphibian.

Once outside of the water, these animals gradually adapted themselves more and more to life on land. Some became reptiles (creatures who crawl like lizards) and they shared the silence of the forests with the insects. That they might move faster through the soft soil, they improved upon their legs and their size increased until the world was populated with gigantic forms (which the hand-books of biology list under the names of Ichthyosaurus and Megalosaurus and Brontosaurus) who grew to be thirty to forty feet long and who could have played with elephants as a full grown cat plays with her kittens.

Some of the members of this reptilian family began to live in the tops of the trees, which were then often more than a hundred feet high. They no longer needed their legs for the purpose of walking, but it was necessary for them to move quickly from branch to branch. And so they changed a part of their skin into a sort of parachute, which stretched between the sides of their bodies and the small toes of their fore-feet, and gradually they covered this skinny parachute with feathers and made their tails into a steering gear and flew from tree to tree and developed into true birds.

Then a strange thing happened. All the gigantic reptiles died within a short time. We do not know the reason. Perhaps it was due to a sudden change in climate. Perhaps they had grown so large that they could neither swim nor walk nor crawl, and they starved to death within sight but not within reach of the big ferns and trees. Whatever the cause, the million year old world-empire of the big reptiles was over.

The world now began to be occupied by very different creatures. They were the descendants of the reptiles but they were quite unlike these because they fed their young from the "mammae" or the breasts of the mother. Wherefore modern science calls these animals "mammals." They had shed the scales of the fish. They did not adopt the feathers of the bird, but they covered their bodies with hair. The mammals however developed other habits which gave their race a great advantage over the other animals. The female of the species carried the eggs of the young inside her body until they were hatched and while all other living beings, up to that time, had left their children exposed to the dangers of cold and heat, and the attacks of wild beasts, the mammals kept their young with them for a long time and sheltered them while they were still too weak to fight their enemies. In this way the young mammals were given a much better chance to survive, because they learned many things from their mothers, as you will know if you have ever watched a cat teaching her kittens to take care of themselves and how to wash their faces and how to catch mice.

But of these mammals I need not tell you much for you know them well. They surround you on all sides. They are your daily companions in the streets and in your home, and you can see your less familiar cousins behind the bars of the zoological garden.

And now we come to the parting of the ways when man suddenly leaves the endless procession of dumbly living and dying creatures and begins to use his reason to shape the destiny of his race.

One mammal in particular seemed to surpass all others in its ability to find food and shelter. It had learned to use its forefeet for the purpose of holding its prey, and by dint of practice it had developed a hand-like claw. After innumerable attempts it had learned how to balance the whole of the body upon the hind legs. (This is a difficult act, which every child has to learn anew although the human race has been doing it for over a million years.)

This creature, half ape and half monkey but superior to both, became the most successful hunter and could make a living in every clime. For greater safety, it usually moved about in groups. It learned how to make strange grunts to warn its young of approaching danger and after many hundreds of thousands of years it began to use these throaty noises for the purpose of talking.

This creature, though you may hardly believe it, was your first "man-like" ancestor.

Americans Before Columbus
The Vikings Find and Lose America [2]

ELIZABETH CHESLEY BAITY

In Americans Before Columbus, *the author gives a fascinating panorama of American Indian migrations and cultures from the time of the Ice Age to the coming of Columbus. The chapter below tells of the first invasion of America by the white man.*

It was a cold day in the late summer of 986 A.D., and a blustering wind from the north lashed the Atlantic Ocean into great waves. The storm had been raging for days. The men in the battered little boat with the dragon carved on the prow were dead tired and half starved; they wished with all their hearts that they had never left their comfortable homes in Iceland to set sail for Greenland. Even Bjarni Herjolsson, to whom the dragon ship belonged, had to admit that the lashing winds had blown them off their course. They should long before have reached Greenland, where he was going to join his father, who had followed Eric the Red when this quick-tempered adventurer had had to leave Iceland.

At last they saw land ahead, but their hearts sank when they reached it. The shore stretched empty before them: no masts of ships, no feast-hall roofs. They were hungry for their own kind, for feasts and meetings with friends and relatives, for food and wine and songs, and for the sagas, or stories of Viking heroes which the music-making *skalds* sang to the sound of the harp. None of these things was here. When the winds died down, they turned back north again and after many days reached Greenland.

During the long winter evenings in Greenland, Bjarni often told of the unknown land that he had discovered. Among the people who asked him eager questions about it was young Leif, one of Eric's sons. As he listened, Leif's mind began to burn with the desire to explore this unknown country. Years

[2] From Elizabeth Chesley Baity, *Americans Before Columbus* (Viking Press, 1951).

later he bought a boat from Bjarni, fitted it with provisions, and persuaded thirty-five of his friends to set off on the adventure with him. He even induced old Eric the Red to lead the expedition, in order to bring it luck. Eric protested that he was too old to go, but Leif out-talked him. At last the day came when they rode down to the shore to set sail. But Eric's horse stumbled, and the old explorer fell and hurt his foot. Eric took this as a bad sign. "I am not destined to discover more countries than this in which we are now living," he told his son. "We shall no longer keep one another company."

Leif sadly said good-bye to his father and turned the dragon prow of his ship toward the land which Bjarni had sighted. They found the new land and went ashore, but it was a poor, cold place of glaciers and flat rock. Leif said, "Unlike Bjarni, we have not failed to come ashore in this country, and I shall now give it a name and call it 'Helluland' (land of flat stones)." Then the party pushed on to discover a new coast with long white beaches backed by woods. Here Leif said, "This land shall be given a name after its nature and shall be called 'Markland' (woodland)."

Then Leif turned his ship to the open sea and sailed with a northeast wind for two days. Again land was sighted.

And such land! Rich grassy meadows for the cattle, tall trees that would make wonderful ships' masts, waters that swarmed with fish. Scholars now think that this land, which Leif called "Vinland," was the coast of North America somewhere south of the Saint Lawrence River.

Leif divided his party into two groups; each day one group went exploring while the other group rested and took care of the camp. Leif ordered his men to stick together, since it would be a serious thing to be lost in this vast country. But one night the exploring party came home without Thyrker, whom Leif had loved almost as his own father since childhood. Furious and frightened, Leif started out with a searching party of twelve men. After a while they came across Thyrker, who told them in great excitement that he had discovered wild grapes. Now they could make wine! Calling

his men together the next day, Leif told them, "We will now do two things. Each day we will either gather grapes or we will fell trees for a cargo for my ship."

When the ship was loaded with wild grapes and timber, they set sail back to Greenland. His adventures earned him a new name — Leif the Lucky.

The year was 1003 A.D. Leif Ericson had brought the white man's cross and sword to the American continent — a thousand years after the time of Christ and very nearly a thousand years ago.

Other sons of Eric the Red made less lucky voyages; one was buried in America. A daughter, Freydis, half sister of Leif, led one of the five later voyages which are described in the sagas. When her companions did not please Freydis, she murdered several of them, women and children, with an ax. Other women came here; the sagas name a baby, Snorri, the first known white child born in the Americas. The histories of these expeditions were told and retold by the *skalds* who sang the sagas in the feast halls of Iceland. Three hundred years afterward, the sagas were first written down.

You may wonder how much to believe of stories that were first told three centuries before they were written down. But a careful check with historic records proves that the Icelandic sagas were very true accounts, and so we may believe that those sagas dealing with "Wineland the Good" or, as they called it, Vinland, are actual reports carried home by America's earliest known white explorers. Two Scandinavian historians, writing in 1076 and in 1140, mention the Norse discovery of Vinland, the new land beyond Thule, which may have been Iceland or the Faroe Islands. They appear to consider the discovery a fact well known to everyone.

The sagas are not the only clues to this story of the Viking explorations in the Americas. In Nova Scotia and elsewhere in the northeastern part of the United States, Viking axes, boat keels, and other objects have been found, including curiously marked stones which puzzle scholars. Olaf Strandwold has written a study called *Norse Inscriptions on American Stones*, telling about more than thirty of these stones. Some of them, he says, are road markers set up to show later explorers which way a certain party had gone. Others were put up to mark the site of religious celebrations. He reads one stone found in Braxton County, West Virginia, as an account of a colony of Norsemen who settled there; among them were people named Qn Eric, Rikar, Ole, and a woman called Guri. He dates this stone about 1037, believing that had it been later, certain Danish letter types would have been used. A second clue to the date lies in the fact that the forms of the cross and of the letter A used on this stone were given up after the first half of the eleventh century. A New England stone bearing such a cross carried a date which in our calendar would be 1031 A.D.

This Qn Eric, writes Professor Strandwold, was quite a wanderer. At one time this Viking selected the Great Mound * as the site of a Yule festival. Arriving back at his main settlement in Massachusetts, he carved on a stone: "Overland Route — Qn set the marker." A stone found in New England, says Professor Strandwold, tells that Qn Eric met his death when a boat turned over, and concludes with the words: "The ice owns Qn. O Tiv, raise him to everlasting light."

Many more Norsemen than are mentioned in the Icelandic sagas must have come to America. It may be that adventurers from Norway, unknown to the *skalds* who retold the Icelandic stories, set up other colonies far inland.

The Annals kept yearly in Iceland during the discovery period mention several visitors to the new land. In 1121 the Annals note the departure of "Eric, Bishop of Greenland," for Vinland. Nothing more is heard of Bishop Eric — unless, of course, he should be that Qn Eric who left so many marker stones in America. In 1347 the Icelandic Annals note that "A ship which had sailed to Markland came to Iceland with eighteen men on board." This note in the Icelandic Annals closes the book on the American adventure.

* The Great Mound, built long before the time of Columbus, is located near the present town of Moundsville, West Virginia.

After that, bad days came to the Viking colonists. For several hundred years the Vikings had sailed up the rivers in almost every part of Europe, leaving tall, blond rulers even in remote Russia. Now Iceland, which had been settled since 874 A.D., was no longer a prosperous settlement sending out its adventurous sons. At home in Norway there were wars and rebellions. The little colonies in Greenland, and possibly in America, whose settlers had looked forward each summer to a ship or two from the homeland, bringing news and food and wine, were neglected. Years passed; after 1347 no more ships went to Markland or Vinland. The settlements died away. Their very names were forgotten.

The saga spotlight fell upon the few individuals who returned successfully home to Iceland with their cargoes of wood and wine and their stories of Vinland the Good. But what of other colonists who may have remained in the new land? What did they think when no more ships came from home? What did they do? If Viking parties really wandered inland far enough to use the Great Mound for Yule ceremonies, their explorations were more extensive than any reported in the sagas. But America's vast spaces may have been too much for them, and their numbers too few, so that in the end they were swallowed up by the forests. The first invasion of America by the white man rippled out into silence.

Vast Horizons
The Polos [3]

MARY SEYMOUR LUCAS

❧ *The title of the book from which this selection is taken points definitely to its contents. The reader gets a picture of Europe and China at the time of the Crusades; of the rise and fall of Portugal as a great power; of the opening-up of new interests by land travels such as the Polos made; of adventures by sea such as Columbus and others dared; in short,*

[3] From Mary Seymour Lucas, *Vast Horizons* (Viking Press, 1943).

the extending of the known horizons. This chapter on the Polos is a fascinating story in itself.

By the middle of the thirteenth century, Venice had definitely jumped ahead of Genoa. Her treasury was piled high with golden ducats and her ships and merchants had control of most of the trade on the Mediterranean and Black Seas.

Among the most respected and successful of her traders were the Polo brothers, Nicolo and Maffeo. For years they traded back and forth between Venice and Constantinople and the Black Sea ports. In 1255, they decided to try their luck in the kingdom of the Tartars. Sailing to the east end of the Black Sea, they headed inland and were pleased to find friendly people and good trade. Suddenly a civil war broke out, cutting off the return route.

Boldly they decided to push on across Asia, following the great trade routes, to seek the Great Khan himself and start a rich trade. Probably they followed Rubruck's route; perhaps they even met him as he struggled westward. At length they reached Cambaluc and found Kublai on the throne. When they started home, they carried letters from him to the Pope asking him to send a hundred missionaries to convert the Mongols.

After fourteen years of marvelous adventures they reached Acre only to learn that the Pope had died and his successor had not yet been elected. There was nothing to do but wait.

Back in Venice in 1269, they found Marco, Nicolo's fifteen-year-old son, eager to hear of all they had seen, and to visit strange places. Ever since he had been old enough to wander by himself, he had spent his spare time on the wharves where the great trading ships docked, sniffing the strange, exciting smells of the East, talking to the crews, asking innumerable questions.

During the next two years, Nicolo and Maffeo made plans to return. Marco, his dreams realized, could scarcely wait for the great day, but at last it dawned, clear and warm, and they headed down the Adriatic bound for Acre. There they completed their preparations and started on their way with letters from the Pope's emissary, some sacred oil from the lamp which burned night and day in the Holy Sepulcher at Jerusalem, and, not a hundred missionaries, but two faint-hearted friars who quickly grew discouraged and turned back.

Sailing north along the coast to Ayas, they started their long journey, traveling up to Erzingan and then circling past Mount Ararat where Noah is said to have landed his ark, past a gushing fountain of oil which no one knew enough to use for fuel — the first they had ever seen — to the Tigris River, which they followed to Baghdad. Passing through the rich fields of the valley, Marco saw his first heavy-tailed sheep, with long thick tails weighing thirty pounds or more, and humped cattle, probably Brahma steers. Robbers were plentiful and travelers had to be on the alert. Once the caravan they had joined for protection was attacked and they barely escaped. At last they came to El Basra, the city from which Sinbad the Sailor began his voyages.

They took passage on a smelly little dhow which traded up and down the Persian Gulf, carrying cargoes of rotting dates. The smell of stale fish oil, which had been daubed on the boat's seams to keep out the water, nearly made them ill. The cabin was so filthy and airless that they preferred the hot decks and tried to seek some shelter from the blazing sun in the shadow of the sail.

They sighed with relief when their boat docked at Ormuz, a flourishing trade center on an island in the mouth of the Gulf. They felt the dread sirocco wind which blows every day from nine until twelve during the summer. Those who could not afford cool houses along the shore waded into the sea and stood up to their necks in water until the wind stopped blowing. To be caught in it on a sandy plain meant certain death from suffocation. Every morning they were awakened by the Mohammedan call to prayer, chanted from a high tower.

They had planned to find a ship at Ormuz and sail the rest of the way, but the Polos, used to the ships on the Mediterranean, were afraid to sail so far in a dhow, and no other ships were available. So they chose what they believed the lesser of two evils and decided to travel overland.

They headed north and presently came to the Kirman Desert. For three days they crossed sandy wastes with only an occasional well, filled with water so salty and green that it was undrinkable. The fourth day they found a river of sweet water, but their rejoicing was cut short, for it was soon swallowed by the sand and the next three days were like the first.

Joyfully leaving the desert behind them, they started across Khorasan where they heard stories of the "Old Man of the Mountain," a Mohammedan prince named Aloeddin.

He owned a beautiful valley, cut off from the rest of the world by lofty mountains. In it he built luxurious palaces and surrounded them with beautiful gardens. Conduits carried streams of wine with honey and water to all parts. Beautiful maidens lived there and spent their time singing, dancing, and playing musical instruments. A strong castle guarded the one entrance and none were allowed to enter.

Aloeddin himself lived in another valley and in his court he gathered the finest young men of the country. He talked to them of Paradise and said he had the power of admitting them.

Every once in a while he would give a chosen few a drug and while they were in coma would have them carried to his secret valley. On awakening they would believe themselves in Paradise. For a week they would be supremely happy, then once again they would be drugged and returned to court.

When they spoke with wonder of their adventure, Aloeddin told them it was but a taste of the joys they would receive after death if they served him faithfully. Consequently none were afraid to die and each was eager to give his life for his master, and Aloeddin's men were the terror of all surrounding countries.

They trailed across another desert for eight days, crossed a fertile strip where the finest melons in the world grew and came to the once great city of Balkh which had been sacked by Genghis Khan years before. For

twelve days they crossed a land inhabited only by bandits, for all others had fled for protection to stronger places. Game and fish abounded.

At last they came to Badakshan in the foothills of the Pamir Mountains. They spent several months here waiting for the snows to melt on the high passes ahead of them, and gave Marco a chance to recover more fully from an earlier attack of fever. It was here that they met a man who said he was descended from the Greek general, Alexander the Great, who had plundered that district fifteen hundred years before.

Up and up they climbed on unbelievably steep trails, twisting between jutting rocks, skirting precipitous drops of hundreds of feet, until they reached the Pamir Plateau, the "Roof of the World." They noticed that high in the mountains it took longer to boil water and that their fire did not give as much heat.

On they went into the rising sun, to old trading centers, through Kashgar, with its surrounding cotton fields, until they arrived at Khotan, where they decided to await the arrival of a caravan which they could join.

Beyond Khotan they came to the great Desert of Lop, so wide that thirty days were needed to cross it. It was said to be inhabited by evil spirits who imitated human voices and so lured those who had lagged behind their caravan far from the trail. Marco heard tales of sounds of musical instruments, of drums, and of the clashing of arms heard at night by travelers. Today these are explained by the fact that the sandhills contract and move as they cool at night, thus sounding various tones. On the other side of the desert they were met by envoys of the Khan, for news of their coming had preceded them.

Marco noticed many marvels as they passed through Cathay; perhaps the most amazing to him was a rock composed of long fibers "of the nature of the salamander, for, when woven into cloth and thrown into the fire, it remains incombustible." This, of course, was asbestos.

Leaving behind Karakorum, the old capital of the Mongols, they traveled eastward and finally arrived at Shangtu or Xanadu, where Kublai had his magnificent summer palace. With great ceremony they were ushered into the Khan's presence and bowed low before him.

Kublai nodded graciously to Nicolo and Maffeo: "Welcome, my friends," he said. "And who is this?" he added, looking at Marco who was standing in the background.

"He is my son and your servant," said Nicolo.

"He is welcome and it pleases me much," Kublai replied. From then on Marco was one of his attendants of honor and stood high in his favor.

For seventeen winters Marco felt the icy blasts sweep down from the northern steppes as he traveled far and wide as the Khan's special messenger. He learned four languages, one of them probably Chinese, so he could talk with almost anyone in the empire and satisfy his curiosity about the strange wonders he saw. Kublai delighted in the long detailed accounts of all he had seen and questioned him eagerly about this city, the crops in another place, a certain man's loyalty, and the game in a certain forest.

A year after his arrival, Kublai sent him on a diplomatic mission to Khorasan, more than halfway back across Asia. It took six months to get there and then he fell ill and had to stay for a year before he regained his strength.

When he returned to Cambaluc, he learned that a city in southern China had withstood a three years' siege. He promptly suggested that the Mongols build mangonels, early military engines for hurling three- or four-hundred-pound weights, and bombard it. Kublai was definitely interested. The machines were built and demonstrated, and won immediate approval. They were shipped south, the city surrendered after the first bombardment; the Polos stood even higher in royal favor. Marco traveled far and wide over the Eastern empire, up the Yangtze River, down into Burma, and even sailed southward to visit some of the East Indies.

At last he, his father, and uncle began to think of home. They longed to see their family and friends, to taste Italian food and wine and to breathe the salt air of the Adriatic. No doubt they thought how they could amaze their friends with tales of all

they had seen. Kublai frowned at the idea and told them to forget it. They dared not risk his anger by talking more about it, but they could not forget.

Their opportunity came when Arghun Khan, ruler of Persia under the Great Khan, sent messengers asking for a Mongol princess to be his wife. Kublai chose his daughter, the Lady Kutai, and the caravan started back. After eight weary months, they found their way blocked by war and returned to Cathay. It was then that Marco came forward and suggested that he, Nicolo, and Maffeo take the Princess to Persia by ship, and then go on to Venice for a short visit.

Fourteen great ships, each with four masts and nine sails, were equipped. With two thousand people, they left Zaitun (now Amoy) early in 1291 and sailed south, closely following the shore. Entering the Straits of Malacca they met strong head winds and were forced to wait for several months until they shifted to the northeast. These were the southwest monsoons which blow every year from May until October.

After building fortifications around the ships as guard against possible attack by unfriendly natives, Marco disappeared inland to explore. When he returned to the fleet, he found several hundred dead from the unhealthy climate. At last the wind changed. Spirits rose with the sails, and they headed across the Bay of Bengal for Ceylon, stopping at the Andaman and Nicobar Islands on the way.

They sailed up the Malabar Coast (West India) and then no one is very sure of the exact route, for Marco describes Socotra, Abyssinia, and Madagascar in detail. Probably he heard of these places when stopping along the southeastern coast of Arabia, for it is doubtful if he visited them.

At last after eighteen months at sea they reached Ormuz which they had left nearly twenty years earlier. Six hundred members of their party had died, but the Princess was still well. They landed and learned that Arghun had died, but that his nephew and successor desired Kutai for his bride.

Leaving her there, the Polos traveled north to Trebizond where they took passage in a ship bound for Venice. They arrived in 1295 and the story of their homecoming is a fine one.

One day a gondola stopped in front of the Ca' Polo in Venice and three bearded men stepped out. Their clothes, of Eastern stuff and design, were rough and tattered; their faces were bronzed by weather and lined by hardship. They spoke halting Italian with strong foreign accents. Altogether they looked more like men from the Far East than from Venice. They knocked boldly at their door and announced themselves.

Those who came to the door laughed and said: "True, Nicolo, Maffeo, and Marco Polo started for Cathay, but that was many years ago and they are long since dead. Be off before we turn the dogs on you." And the heavy door was slammed and bolted.

Again the Polos thundered against their door, and when an incautious servant drew the bolt, beat their way in. Relatives arrived from various parts of the city and finally were convinced that the three suspicious-looking strangers were indeed the long-lost members of their family.

Then there was great rejoicing. The news spread through the city and many flocked to see them. The next day a feast was arranged and all their old friends were invited.

The travelers were dressed in long robes of crimson satin. When the guests had arrived, they changed to robes of crimson damask and the first were cut up and given to the servants. Once during the dinner they disappeared, and when they returned they were dressed in crimson velvet and the damask was given to the guests. When dinner was over, they removed the velvet, divided it among the guests and appeared in the dress of wealthy Venetian merchants. Then the table was cleared, the servants sent from the room, and Marco disappeared. When he returned, he carried the ragged, travel-stained clothes which they had worn on their arrival. The guests exchanged amused glances, but they soon exclaimed in amazement as the three Polos seized knives and ripped up the seams. Cascades of rubies, emeralds, pearls, diamonds, sapphires, and other jewels tumbled out and lay in richly glowing piles in the candlelight. No longer was any one

in doubt and they were received everywhere with honor and respect.

For three years Marco was the center of attention. Men never tired of hearing the marvels of Cathay and other strange, faraway places, even though they did not believe half of what he told them. And because they thought he exaggerated, they nicknamed him "Marco Millions."

In 1298, trouble over trading rights again broke out between Venice and Genoa. The Venetian fleet, ninety strong, under Dandolo, son of the Doge, sailed south to Curzola, an island in the Adriatic off the coast of what is now Yugoslavia. There on the eighth of September, they met the Genoese who had a small but heavier fleet.

At that time the average war galley carried about two hundred rowers, forty to fifty soldiers armed with mechanical crossbows, two calkers, two attendants, one cook, the captain, and his officers, and a "gentleman-commander" who advised the captain. At Curzola, Marco, weary of staying at home, held this last position on a fine galley which he had outfitted and given to the city.

With the Lion of Saint Mark's and other gaily colored banners streaming from the mastheads, the Venetian fleet swept to the attack, oar blades flashing to the boom-boom of the kettledrums and the shrilling pipes.

In spite of having the wind against them and the morning sun in their eyes, the Venetians won an early advantage. Sharply beaked prows rammed hulls; showers of arrows hurled through space; firepots spilled their embers, and rising wisps of smoke added to the confusion. The wind freshened in gusts driving a dozen Venetian galleys ashore. The Genoese pressed forward. Twelve Venetian captains suddenly became terrified, broke through and sailed for home. The others fought bravely on. At this moment a reserve detachment of ten Genoese vessels swept from behind the island and attacked from an unsuspected quarter and clinched the victory.

With the exception of a few galleys which had foundered and those which had deserted, the entire fleet was captured by Genoa. But there was little rejoicing, for both sides had lost over three thousand men. The Genoese stripped the vessels, fired them, and set them adrift in the gathering dusk. Only a few of the finest were saved to be towed ignominiously by their sterns to Genoa in gesture of defeat.

The prisoners, seven thousand of them, had been taken from their ships in chains and paraded in triumph through the Genoese mob before being thrown into jail. Later many were ransomed by their families, but for some reason Marco was not released. However, his fame had spread to Genoa and many prominent men visited him to hear of his travels and, through their efforts, he was granted certain privileges.

One of his fellow prisoners, Rusticano, a scribe from Pisa, was greatly interested in his adventures and offered to write them down. So Marco sent home for his notebooks and for long hours dictated his story. Soon after the book was completed, a truce was signed and Marco was free. He spent the rest of his life quietly with his wife and family. When he lay dying, friends came to him and begged him, for "the peace of his soul," to deny some of the exaggerated stories he had told, but he only answered, "They are all true and I told only half of what I saw."

For hundreds of years most people who read his book laughed and said, "It's a good yarn, but such things aren't possible." Only a few of the more farseeing ones like Prince Henry of Portugal realized that for the most part it was true. And as today we say, "It's a good fish story," then people would say, "It's a Marco Polo," whenever they heard an exaggeration.

Hakluyt's Voyages
The Deliverance [4]

RICHARD HAKLUYT

Hakluyt made no voyages himself but became famous for his invaluable account of over two hundred voyages of English navigation during the reign of Queen Elizabeth. He took in-

[4] From Richard Hakluyt, *The Principal Navigations, Voyages, Traffiques and Discoveries of the English Nation, Made by Sea or Overland to the Remote and Farthest Distant Quarters of the Earth* (J. MacLehose and Sons, Glasgow, 12 vols., 1903–5).

finite pains to interview surviving seamen of various expeditions and took down their eyewitness accounts. He recorded word for word the narratives of the captains of the ships. Sir Francis Drake, Sir John Hawkins, and Sir Martin Frobisher were among his personal friends. His thrilling and fascinating record did much to create popular interest in navigation and colonization. His collection of narratives, The Principal Navigations, Voyages, Traffiques and Discoveries of the English Nation (1589–1600), *contains magnificent material which has proved to be a major source of information for all subsequent writers of sea stories including Kipling and Charles Boardman Hawes.*

The fourth of October the storm growing beyond all reason furious, the pinnace being in the wind of us, struck suddenly ahull, so that we thought she had received some grievous sea, or sprung a leak, or that her sails had failed her, because she came not with us; but we durst not hull in that unmerciful storm, but sometimes tried under our main course, sometimes with a haddock off our sail, for our ship was very leeward and most laboursome in the sea. This night we lost the pinnace and never saw her again.

The fifth our foresail was split and all to torn; then our Master took the mizzen and brought it to the foremast, to make our ship work, and with our spritsail we mended our foresail, the storm continuing without all reason in fury, with hail, snow, rain, and wind such and so mighty as that in nature it could not possibly be more: the seas such and so lofty with continual breach, that many times we were doubtful whether our ship did sink or swim.

The tenth of October, being by the accompt of our Captain and Master very near the shore, the weather dark, the storm furious, and most of our men having given over to travail, we yielded ourselves to death, without further hope of succour. Our Captain sitting in the gallery very pensive, I came and brought him some *rosa solis* to comfort him; for he was so cold that he was scarce able to move a joint. After he had drunk, and was comforted in heart, he began for the ease of his conscience to make a large repetition of his fore-passed time, and with many grievous sighs he concluded in these words:

"O most glorious God, with Whose power the mightiest things among men are matters of no moment, I most humbly beseech Thee that the intolerable burthen of my sins may through the blood of Jesus Christ be taken from me and end our days with speed, or show us some merciful sign of Thy love and our preservation."

Having thus ended, he desired me not to make known to any of the company his intolerable grief and anguish of mind, because they should not thereby be dismayed. And so suddenly, before I went from him, the sun shined clear; so that he and the Master both observed the true elevation of the Pole, whereby they knew by what course to recover the Straits. Wherewithal our Captain and Master were so revived, and gave such comfortable speeches to the company, that every man rejoiced, as though we had received a present deliverance. . . .

Of Courage Undaunted
Lewis and Clark[5]

JAMES DAUGHERTY

From the original journals of the Lewis and Clark expedition, James Daugherty has recreated one of the most splendid exploits in the history of exploration. He has captured the magnificence of disciplined bravery, the gusto, the rollicking humor of the spirit of adventure, and the beauty of the great wilderness. The expedition took two years and four months to travel the 3,555 miles from St. Louis to the Pacific, matching courage and endurance against exposure, disease, terrifying natural obstacles, and the danger of attack by Indians and wild animals. On September 23, 1806, Lewis reported in a letter to President Thomas Jefferson, "In obedience to your order, we have penetrated the Continent of North America to the Pacific Ocean." And of Meriwether Lewis, Jefferson wrote, "Of courage undaunted . . . honest, disinterested, liberal, of sound understanding and a fidelity to truth so scrupulous, that whatever he should report would be as certain as seen by ourselves; with all these quali-

[5] From James Daugherty, *Of Courage Undaunted* (Viking Press, 1951)

fications, as if selected and implanted by nature in one body for this express purpose, I could have no hesitation in entrusting the enterprise to him."

THE CORPS OF DISCOVERY

There was nothing that you would say was
   special about them.
They chawed tobacco and cussed and cater-
   wauled that
they were double-jointed, fire-eating, leather-
   necked, half-horse
half-alligator men who could lick their
   weight in wildcats.
They were picked almost at random out of
   the Ohio Valley
of Virginia, Kentucky, Tennessee, or New
   England stock,
merely a sample fistful of what American
   democracy turns out,
as you might pick a handful of leaves and
   say, These are oak.

Any state in the Union can give you ten
   thousand such
at any time, or ten times ten thousand, if
   there is a call
to stand together in time of danger,
or hold the line on land, in the sea or air,
not without bragging and grousing and a
   sour kind of humor,
sometimes terribly scared but never
broken by fear, of courage undaunted.

Sweating and rank, coarse, muscular, lanky,
level-eyed, generous minded, free speaking,
   slangy —
you don't have to go far in any city or town
   to find them;
no farther than any street corner
or factory bench, farmyard, filling station,
   public high school.
As Lincoln said, "God must have loved them
   or
he would not have made so many."

U. S. A., March 4, 1801

The bang of artillery thundered across the Potomac and echoed back from the Virginia hills.

Washington, D. C., the new capital of the United States, was saluting the inauguration of Thomas Jefferson.

At noon, Mr. Jefferson, with an escort of friends, had walked from Conrad's boarding house to the Capitol Building to be the chief actor in the ceremonies. As he entered the Senate Chamber, the waiting Congress stood while he seated himself in the chair which until a week ago he had occupied as Vice-President. Beside him on one side sat Chief Justice Marshall, on the other his defeated opponent, Aaron Burr. John Adams, the retiring president, had left the city at four o'clock that morning without waiting to greet the new President.

Mr. Jefferson rose from his seat, unfolding his tall frame to its full height. In a low voice he read to the silent Congress his inaugural address. At the end he said:

"We are all Republicans; we are all Federalists. If there be any among us who would wish to dissolve this Union or to change its Republican form, let them stand undisturbed as monuments of the safety with which error of opinion may be tolerated where reason is left free to combat it."

History was changing scenes in the great American drama, and the curtain was going up on a new act. Mr. Jefferson and the new democratic people's party, calling themselves Republicans, had ousted the aristocratic Federalists and their famous leader Alexander Hamilton. The people had been stirred to anger by the vicious Alien and Sedition Acts and had staged a second revolution, this time with ballots instead of bullets.

Wanted: A Secretary

Jefferson moved into the President's Mansion at the west end of Pennsylvania Avenue. His wife, his beloved Martha, had died many years ago. He would need a hostess to preside over the new household and manage its affairs. He invited sparkling Dolly Madison, the wife of his devoted friend and Secretary of State, James Madison, to become hostess at the President's Mansion. She brought the wit, easy grace, and ample hospitality of Virginia ways to the newly established house-hold in the draughty mansion where Abigail Adams had dried the family wash in the unfinished East Room.

The President himself did away with the stuffy ceremonies and formalities so dear to the Federalists, and got down to business. Right off he needed a personal secretary of a special sort. He did not want fancy frills but someone trustworthy and close-mouthed who was also understanding and democratic.

Himself a Virginian, he naturally thought of his beloved Charlottesville and the loyal people of Albemarle County. He remembered gallant "Mother Marks" and her coon-hunting son, Meriwether Lewis. Ten years had passed since the boy had pleaded with him to be sent on an exploring expedition across the Mississippi with the French botanist André Micheaux. Micheaux had been found to be a French secret agent and the plan had been abandoned. Jefferson learned that young Lewis was now in the United States Army.

The President wrote a letter to Commander Wilkinson, enclosing his offer to Meriwether of the post of private secretary to the President.

In the letter to Lewis, he said:

Washington, February 3, 1801

Dear Sir,

The appointment to the presidency of the U. S. has rendered it necessary for me to have a private secretary, and in selecting one I have thought it important to expect not only his capacity to aid in the private concern of the household, but also to contribute to the mass of information for the administration to acquire. ...Your knowledge of the Western country, of the army and of its interests and relations has rendered it desirable for public as well as private purposes that you should be engaged in that office....

Growing Up in Virginia

Albemarle County, lying in the shadow of the Blue Ridge Mountains, was still wild and thinly settled when William Lewis went off to the wars in 1776. He left his young wife with their children, Jane and Meriwether, at the family home on Locust Hill by Ivy Creek near Charlottesville. He served as a lieutenant, receiving no pay and providing his own equipment. That was the way Virginians felt about liberty in 1776. When he came home on leave in 1779 he contracted pneumonia and died. Later his widow married John Marks and the family moved to frontier lands in Georgia.

There were now five children in the family, Jane, Meriwether, and Reuben Lewis, and John Marks's two children, Mary and John. They were all growing up together on the edge of the Indian-infested wilderness. One night when they were camping, there was a big scare — an Indian attack. In the wild confusion Meriwether was the only one with enough presence of mind to empty a bucket of water on the campfire so that they could not be seen by an enemy lurking in the forest darkness.

Meriwether loved the woods. When he was eight years old he would go with the hounds on a coon hunt at night with torches. Neighbors said that when a treed coon saw him aim his gun, the coon would holler, "Don't shoot, Meriwether, I'll come down." Then they would slap each other on the back and roar with laughter. It was an old frontier joke that was often told about a good hunter.

Meriwether began to shoot up lean and lanky as a cornstalk. "Time you was learning about something besides coon and possum hunting," said Mother Marks in her determined way. So he went back from the border country to Charlottesville, where his uncle arranged for him to go to the school of that excellent scholar and kindly gentleman, Parson Matthew Maury.

Meriwether took his studies seriously, as he had coon hunting. In the next few years, under one teacher and another, he studied the hodgepodge of subjects that made up the education of a Virginia gentleman of that day. He studied history, Latin, geography, and mathematics, with a little botany and good manners thrown in. His spelling always remained personal and imaginative. He would spell some words three or four different ways, all of them wrong.

School vacations he loved to spend alone in the woods, drinking in the magic and mystery of their ancient peace and beauty. He liked to blaze a westward trail alone in an untrod wilderness.

When he was eighteen and through with schooling, he brought his mother back from Georgia to the old home at Locust Hill. It was a tradition of Virginia families that a young gentleman should choose as a profession the law, medicine, or the army. His father had been a soldier, so Meriwether decided on the army.

School of Experience

When President Washington called for volunteers to put down the "Whiskey Rebellion," Meriwether volunteered in the Virginia militia as a private and marched to Pittsburgh. The angry distillers of corn whiskey dispersed to set up secret stills in the vastnesses of the Alleghenies. The so-called "Whiskey Rebellion" was put down without firing a shot, and the government was safe. Meriwether was then transferred to the regular army. It was a school of action and experience in which he would learn much that he would need to know in the great adventure for which destiny had chosen him.

Soldiers were needed in the wild Northwest territories where Indians were raiding the backwoods settlements and stations, burning and scalping, in a last fierce effort to hold the forest homes of their ancestors. General St. Clair had led a poorly equipped and ill-provisioned expedition against the Indians, which had ended in defeat. After that disaster, President Washington put his old Revolutionary general, Anthony Wayne, in command of the western army to clear the Northwest of the Indians. This was "Mad Anthony" Wayne, who had taken Stony Point with the bayonet on a dark night long ago. Now his first job was to build an efficient fighting force out of the discouraged veterans and shiftless volunteers of St. Clair's army, who still remained at Pittsburgh.

First of all there must be discipline. There was daily drill in all sorts of weather, inspections and practice in the Manual of Arms. The pleasant custom of sleeping on guard duty was discouraged by a prescribed number of lashes on the bare back of the offender. There was no more talking back to superiors by independent privates; no more backslapping or poking of officers' noses by easy-going frontier militiamen. Young Lewis learned how, with axes and plenty of timber, to put up a weatherproof, bulletproof fort in the shortest possible time. He learned how an army can move warily through the wilderness without being surprised from front or rear.

When the army was ready, General Wayne put on a vigorous campaign in the forests of northern Indiana. At the battle of Fallen Timbers he decisively defeated the Indians under the great chief Tecumseh. In this campaign, Lewis renewed an old-time friendship with William Clark of Kentucky, the brother of George Rogers Clark of Vincennes and Kaskaskia fame. Lewis was assigned to the Chosen Rifle Company which Clark commanded.

They were a pair of tall, handsome soldiers, cool and proud fighters, as well as courteous gentlemen, with the gaiety of their exuberant Virginia blood. Both were experts with rifles and horses and gallant and chivalrous with the girls. They could give and take orders and carry out assignments with thoroughness and efficiency. They had the same tastes and background, with enough temperamental differences to make interesting companionship. The red-head Clark was sociable and direct, a frontiersman born and bred. Lewis was of a complex nature, sometimes moody and introspective. Lights and shadows moved behind the deep-set gray eyes that looked out under a long forelock. His long, sharp nose and sensitive mouth reminded some of his friends of the pictures of Napoleon.

Clark soon left the army and returned to Louisville. Lewis remained, to be promoted to captain, serving as paymaster for his regiment. His duties took him up and down the Mississippi and Ohio Rivers and through the Northwest wilderness to outlying army posts. He liked the order and discipline of army life, and travel through the wild country gave variety and adventure to the dullness of army routine.

Coming back to Pittsburgh headquarters in February, 1801, he found a letter awaiting him. His eyes glowed as he read:

... Your knowledge of the Western country, and of the army and of its interests and relations has rendered it desirable for public as well as private purposes that you should be engaged in that office. . . .

If these or any other views which your own reflections may suggest should present the office of my private secretary as worthy of acceptance you will make me happy in accepting it. It has been solicited by several, who will have no answer till I hear from you. Should you accept, it would be necessary that you should wind up whatever affairs you are engaged in as expeditiously as your own and the public interest will admit, and repair to this place. And that immediately on receipt of this you inform me by letter of your determination. It would be necessary that you wait on Gen. Wilkinson and obtain his approbation, and his aid in making such arrangements as may render your absence as little injurious to the service as may be. I wrote him on this subject.

Accept assurances of the esteem of Dear Sir
your friend and servant
Th: Jefferson

Lewis accepted at once. After winding up his army affairs, he rode off on the long rough road across Pennsylvania to Washington. He wondered if this could really be happening to him, or if it was only a dream, that he was to be the trusted friend of his boyhood hero and secretary to the President of the United States of America.

For ten years and more the President and his young secretary had shared the dream of an expedition of discovery and exploration beyond the Mississippi, across the unknown western wilderness to the Pacific. Now they spent hours together, planning the details that would make it a reality.

From secret sources somewhere in the mysterious Stony Mountains, two great rivers flowed east and west. The Missouri wound eastward like a great snake across the vast plains to the Mississippi. The Columbia rushed down the western slopes to the Pacific Ocean. Perhaps these rivers made an almost continuous waterway across the continent. What did all the vast wilderness between contain? No one knew.

Lewis estimated the costs of equipment and supplies, planned the route and timing and the number of men required. The President procured an authorization of the expedition from Congress "for the purpose of extending the external commerce of the United States," and an appropriation of twenty-five hundred dollars. The real purpose was to be kept a secret.

On an expedition so hazardous it was clear that there must be two leaders, so that, in case something should happen to one, the other could carry on. Lewis thought of the young men of action he had known, who were capable and courageous under fire and in difficulties. Who but red-headed Lieutenant William Clark?

With the President's approval Lewis sent off a letter to his friend in Louisville, explaining the expedition and asking Clark to share the command. He wrote:

If there is anything in this enterprise, which would induce you to participate with me in its fatigues, its dangers and its honors, believe me there is no man on earth with whom I should feel equal pleasure in sharing them as with yourself.

Would William Clark go? Would a duck take to water? Would a young Kentucky thoroughbred race? "My friend, I can assure you that no man lives with whom I would prefer to undertake and share the difficulties of such a trip than yourself. My friend, I join you with hand and heart," wrote back Billy Clark to his old comrade in arms.

The War Department refused to appoint Clark a captain, making him a second lieutenant in the Artillery. But always on the long journey it was "Captain Clark" with Lewis and the men, and the two stood equal in rank and undivided in spirit throughout the great adventure.

George Washington's World
The Declaration of Independence[6]

GENEVIEVE FOSTER

⊷§ In the introduction to George Washington's World Mrs. Foster says, "This book tells the story of George Washington's life, of the people who were living when he was, both in

[6] From Genevieve Foster, George Washington's World (Scribner, 1941).

America, and all over the world, of what they did when they were children, and how later on the pattern of their lives fitted together, and what part each played in that greatest of all adventure stories, the History of the World." The chapter given below tells of the drafting of the Declaration of Independence.

The new word, Independence, came with the year 1776, broadcast through the American colonies by a pamphlet called Common Sense. "O ye that love mankind," rang its challenging words, words that went echoing from one end of the continent to the other, "ye that dare not only to oppose tyranny but the tyrant, stand forth! Every spot in the old world is overrun with oppression. The birthday of a new world is at hand! Independence in America should date from the first musket that was fired against her." People were roused by the ringing words. In the taverns, on the plantations, on street corners and on the wharfs, in the backwoods settlements, wherever people gathered in the colonies they argued about independence.

Thomas Paine had started them talking. For the author of Common Sense was that Jack-of-all-trades but master of ideas, who had come with Benjamin Franklin's introduction to America.

"I am charmed with the sentiments of Common Sense," wrote Abigail Adams from Braintree to her husband John, in Philadelphia. "I dare say there would be no difficulty in procuring a vote from all the Assemblies of New England for Independency."

There was no difficulty in Virginia either. Virginia delegates to the Continental Congress were instructed to vote for Independence.

Except for those instructions, Thomas Jefferson was downcast as he drove from Monticello in his two-wheel gig. His young wife was very ill, and little four-year-old Martha waved a pitiful good-bye.

But it was a great satisfaction as he resumed his seat in the hall facing John Hancock, to be one of the Virginia delegates who early in June proposed the motion "That these united colonies are and of right ought to be free and independent."

"I second the motion," snapped John Adams with no hesitation.

Massachusetts and Virginia were ready for independence, but Pennsylvania and New York were not, and many other colonies were most uncertain. There were conservative law-abiding people in all the colonies, people of education and property, to whom the idea of being disloyal to their King was inconceivable.

Others were afraid of the future. "With independence established," they said, "we are in danger of being ruled by a riotous mob. If you vote for independence," they warned their friends in Congress, "you will be hanged." George III had denounced all rebels in America as traitors and the punishment for treason was hanging.

Not merely the colonies, but even members of the same family were split apart by their convictions. Thomas Jefferson and Benjamin Franklin stood for independence, but Thomas Jefferson's cousin John Randolph was a staunch Loyalist and had gone to England, leaving Tom his fine violin. Benjamin Franklin's son William, now governor of New Jersey, was also a Loyalist, and later was to act as President of the Associated Loyalists of New York City.

Endless debates and arguments filled the days of the Congress. The sound reasoning on both sides kept many delegates undecided, but gradually, John Adams said, "one after another became convinced of the truth of Independence."

A committee of five was appointed to put into writing a declaration. The three most active members were Benjamin Franklin, John Adams and Thomas Jefferson.

"You, sir," said Thomas Jefferson, turning to John Adams, "will of course draw up the declaration."

"I will not," replied the older man. "You shall do it, and I'll tell you why. You are a Virginian and a Virginian ought to head this business. I am unpopular, you are very much otherwise. Reason three . . . you can write ten times better than I can."

So Thomas Jefferson went to his lodgings and for eighteen days worked faithfully on what he had been set to write. When he had finished, crossed out and reworded a few sentences, and laid by his quill, he had written The Declaration of Independence.

Several days were taken up in discussing and changing some of the phrases, during which Benjamin Franklin with his homely humor kept the sensitive young author from becoming too disconsolate.

At last, on the fourth of July, Thomas Jefferson heard the final draft of his declaration read, voted upon and accepted.

"Thus was decided the greatest question which was ever debated in America," John Adams wrote his wife. "The second of July, 1776, will be celebrated by succeeding generations as the greatest anniversary festival — with guns, bells, bonfires and illuminations from one end of the continent to the other."

The great bronze Liberty Bell that hung in the belfry called the people of Philadelphia four days later to hear the Declaration read aloud in the square outside the State House. As a strong-voiced man stepped to the front of the small wooden platform and began to read, the last echoes of the bell caught the now well-known words:

"WHEN IN THE COURSE OF HUMAN EVENTS," he began. Silence fell as he continued: "WE HOLD THESE TRUTHS TO BE SELF-EVIDENT, THAT ALL MEN ARE CREATED EQUAL. THAT THEY ARE ENDOWED BY THEIR CREATOR WITH CERTAIN UNALIENABLE RIGHTS. THAT AMONG THESE ARE LIFE, LIBERTY AND THE PURSUIT OF HAPPINESS. . . ."

As he ended with the last word "honor," the people cheered and the Liberty Bell rang out once more.

When the copy was complete on parchment, John Hancock, as President of Congress, was the first to sign. He took his quill in hand, writing the letters larger than ever before, turning the end of the k with a more determined flourish, and with a couple of graceful scrolls he finished this, his most famous signature!

"There!" said he, "King George will have no trouble in reading that without his spectacles."

"Gentlemen, we must all hang together now," said Benjamin Franklin as he took up the quill, then added with a quirk of a smile, "or we will all hang separately."

Spoken in jest, there was sober truth behind those words. Signers of the Declaration had taken a daring step.

"I am well aware," wrote John Adams again, "of the toil and blood and treasure that it will cost us to maintain this declaration."

All knew that there was many a crisis ahead that would call for more than brave words, cheers and bell-ringing, times when only in patience, perseverance and self-sacrifice could their faith be measured.

Captain Scott's Last Expedition
The Last March[7]

From the Diary of
CAPTAIN ROBERT SCOTT

Captain Scott, the famous Antarctic explorer, was the embodiment of courage in the face of hardship and bitter disappointment. In 1910 he sailed from New Zealand in an attempt to reach the South Pole. Scott set up headquarters at Cape Evans on Ross Island and established supply stations along his route toward the Pole. In October, 1911, he started with sledges over the ice. Bad weather impeded his progress, and when he and his four companions finally arrived at the Pole on January 18, 1912, they found that Roald Amundsen had reached it only a month before. On the return trip, all five members of the party perished as a result of cruel weather and insufficient food. Later a searching party found the bodies and records in a tent which had been set up as a last camping place. The selection below, from Captain Scott's diary, tells of the last days of the expedition.

Sunday, March 11 (1912). — The sky completely overcast when we started this morning. We could see nothing, lost the tracks, and doubtless have been swaying a good deal since — 3·1 miles for the forenoon — terribly heavy dragging — expected it. Know that 6 miles is about limit of our endurance

[7] From *Captain Scott's Last Expedition* (Dodd, Mead, 1913).

now, if we get no help from wind or surfaces. We have 7 days' food and should be about 55 miles from One Ton Camp to-night, $6 \times 7 = 42$, leaving us 13 miles short of our distance, even if things get no worse. Meanwhile the season rapidly advances.

Monday, March 12. — We did 6·9 miles yesterday, under our necessary average. Things are left much the same, Oates not pulling much, and now with hands as well as feet pretty well useless. We did 4 miles this morning in 4 hours 20 minutes — we may hope for 3 this afternoon, $7 \times 6 = 42$. We shall be 47 miles from the depôt. I doubt if we can possibly do it. The surface remains awful, the cold intense, and our physical condition running down. God help us! Not a breath of favorable wind for more than a week, and apparently liable to head winds at any moment.

Wednesday, March 14. — No doubt about the going downhill, but everything going wrong for us. Yesterday we woke to a strong northerly wind with temp. —37°. Couldn't face it, so remained in camp (R. 54) till 2, then did 5¼ miles. Wanted to march later, but party feeling the cold badly as the breeze (N) never took off entirely, and as the sun sank the temp. fell. Long time getting supper in the dark (R. 55).

This morning started with southerly breeze, set sail and passed another cairn at good speed; halfway, however, the wind shifted to W. by S. or W.S.W., blew through our wind clothes and into our mits. Poor Wilson horribly cold, could not get off ski for some time. Bowers and I practically made camp, and when we got into the tent at last we were all deadly cold. Then temp. now midday down —43° and the wind strong. We *must* go on, but now the making of every camp must be more difficult and dangerous. It must be near the end, but a pretty merciful end. Poor Oates got it again in the foot. I shudder to think what it will be like to-morrow. It is only with greatest pains rest of us keep off frostbites. No idea there could be temperatures like this at this time of the year with such winds. Truly awful outside the tent. Must fight it out to the last biscuits, but can't reduce rations.

Friday, March 16, *or Saturday* 17. — Lost

track of dates, but think the last is correct. Tragedy all along the line. At lunch, the day before yesterday, poor Titus Oates said he couldn't go on; he proposed we should leave him in his sleeping bag. That we could not do, and we induced him to come on, on the afternoon march. In spite of its awful nature for him he struggled on and we made a few miles. At night he was worse and we knew the end had come.

Should this be found I want these facts recorded. Oates' last thoughts were of his Mother, but immediately before he took pride in thinking that his regiment would be pleased with the bold way in which he met his death. We can testify to his bravery. He has borne intense suffering for weeks without complaint, and to the very last was able and willing to discuss outside objects. He did not — would not — give up hope till the very end. He was a brave soul. This was the end. He slept through the night before last, hoping not to awake; but he woke in the morning — yesterday. It was blowing a blizzard. He said, "I am just going outside and may be some-time." He went out into the blizzard and we have not seen him since.

I take this opportunity of saying that we have stuck to our sick companions to the last. In case of Edgar Evans, when absolutely out of food and he lay insensible, the safety of the remainder seemed to demand his abandonment, but Providence mercifully removed him at this critical moment. He died a natural death, and we did not leave him till two hours after his death. We knew that poor Oates was walking to his death, but though we tried to dissuade him, we knew it was the act of a brave man and an English gentleman. We all hope to meet the end with a similar spirit, and assuredly the end is not far.

I can only write at lunch and then only occasionally. The cold is intense, —40° at midday. My companions are unendingly cheerful, but we are all on the verge of serious frostbites, and though we constantly talk of fetching through I don't think any of us believes it in his heart.

We are cold on the march, now, and at all times except meals. Yesterday we had to lay up for a blizzard and to-day we move dreadfully slowly. We are at No. 14 pony camp, only two pony marches from One Ton Depôt. We leave here our theodolite, a camera, and Oates' sleeping bags. Diaries, etc., and geological specimens carried at Wilson's special request, will be found with or on our sledge.

Sunday, March 18. — To-day, lunch, we are 21 miles from the depôt. Ill fortune presses, but better may come. We have had more wind and drift from ahead yesterday; had to stop marching; wind N.W., force 4. temp. —35°. No human being could face it, and we are worn out *nearly*.

My right foot has gone, nearly all the toes — two days ago I was proud possessor of best feet. These are the steps of my downfall. Like an ass I mixed a small spoonful of curry powder with my melted pemmican — it gave me violent indigestion. I lay awake and in pain all night; woke and felt done on the march; foot went and I didn't know it. A very small measure of neglect and have a foot which is not pleasant to contemplate. Bowers takes first place in condition, but there is not much to choose after all. The others are still confident of getting through — or pretend to be — I don't know! We have the last *half* fill of oil in our primus, and a very small quantity of spirit — this alone between us and thirst. The wind is fair for the moment, and that is perhaps a fact to help. The mileage would have seemed ridiculously small on our outward journey.

Monday, March 19. — Lunch. We camped with difficulty last night, and were dreadfully cold till after supper of cold pemmican and biscuit and half a pannikin of cocoa cooked over the spirit. Then, contrary to expectation, we got warm and all slept well. To-day we started in the usual dragging manner. Sledge dreadfully heavy. We are 15½ miles from the depôt and ought to get there in three days. What progress! We have two days' food but barely a day's fuel. All our feet are getting bad — Wilson's best, my right foot worst, left all right. There is no chance to nurse one's feet till we can get hot food into us. Amputation is the least I can hope for now, but will the trouble spread? That is the serious question. The weather doesn't give us a chance — the wind from N. to N.W., and —40° temp. to-day.

Wednesday, March 21. — Got within 11 miles of depôt Monday night, had to lay up all yesterday in severe blizzard. To-day forlorn hope. Wilson and Bowers going to depôt for fuel.

Thursday, March 22 and 23. — Blizzard bad as ever. — Wilson and Bowers unable to start — to-morrow last chance — no fuel and only one or two of food left — must be near the end. Have decided it shall be natural — we shall march for the depôt with or without our effects and die in our tracks.

Thursday, March 29. — Since the 21st we have had a continuous gale from W.S.W. and S.W. We had fuel to make two cups of tea apiece and bare food for two days on the 20th. Every day we have been ready to start for our depôt 11 *miles* away, but outside the door of the tent it remains a scene of whirling drift. I do not think we can hope for any better things now. We shall stick it out to the end, but we are getting weaker, of course, and the end cannot be far.

It seems a pity, but I do not think I can write more. — R. Scott.

* * * * * * *

For God's sake, look after our people.

R. Scott.

North to the Orient

Point Barrow [8]

ANNE MORROW LINDBERGH

Two outstanding features of North to the Orient *are Mrs. Lindbergh's sense of humor, which always saved any situation, and the poetic quality of her prose. Her whole approach to a new scene is that of a poet; her descriptions are often poetry itself. When the Lindberghs made this trip by air in 1931, it was indeed a real adventure. Any sort of travel toward the Arctic Circle was venturesome if not dangerous, and to make the journey by air was actually both. Before the chapter given below, Mrs. Lindbergh has told of the preliminary prep-*

[8] From Anne Morrow Lindbergh, *North to the Orient* (Harcourt, Brace, 1935).

arations, the start from the Long Island airport, the stops in Maine and at Ottawa, Canada, the flight along the southwest edge of Hudson Bay, the landings at Baker Lake and at Aklavik on the Mackenzie Delta, and finally of the take-off for Point Barrow.

"Dit-darr-darr, darr-dit-dit-darr, darr-dit-dit-dit." "WXB - - - WXB - - - WXB - - - de (from) - - - KHCAL." The blurred buzz of my own radio-sending rang in my ears. Through the cockpit cover I could see fog on the water ahead, motionless piles of light gray cotton wool with dark gray patches here and there. Out to sea the white wall of fog stood impassable and still as the ice packs from which it rose. Inland under floating islands of fog stretched the barren Arctic land. We were turning toward it as our only chance of reaching Point Barrow, the bleak northern tip of Alaska. Could we get through that night? If the weather ahead was not worse. I must get my message to the Barrow operator.

"WXB - - - WXB - - - WXB," I called to him.

"Dit-darr-dit!" A sharp clean note came through my receiver. There he was! Right on the watch, though I had called him off schedule. Then there really was a man waiting for us, I thought with relief. There really was a Point Barrow. We weren't jumping off into space. Somewhere ahead in that white wilderness a man was listening for us, guiding us in.

Now, my message: "Flying - - - thru - - - fog - - - and - - - rain - - - going - - - inland - - - wea (weather) - - - pse (please)?"

His notes came back clearly. I wrote rapidly not to miss a word, "Low - - - fog - - - bank - - - rolling - - - off - - - ice - - - now - - - clear - - - over - - - fog - - - expected - - - soon - - - pass - - - ground - - - vis (visibility) - - - one - - - mile." I poked the pad forward to my husband in the front cockpit. He glanced at it and nodded. That meant "OK. That's what I wanted to know. We'll push on."

On for hours through the unreal shifting world of soft mist. Here a cloud and there a drizzle; here a wall and there, fast melting, a hole through which gleamed the hard metallic scales of the sea. That was no mirage.

That rippling steel below us was real. If one flew into it blindly it might as well be steel. At times we seemed to be riding on its scaly back and then, with a roar, up we climbed into white blankness. No sight of land; no sight of sea or sky; only our instruments to show the position of the plane. Circling down again, my husband motioned me to reel in the antenna. We were flying too near the water. The ball-weight on the end might be snapped off. Perhaps we might even be forced to land unexpectedly on open sea and have both weight and wire torn off at the impact. His gesture was a danger signal for me and I waited, tense, for the nod and second gesture, "All right now — reel out again." At times we would come out of the fog, not into daylight but into the strange gray night. The Arctic sun just under the horizon still lit the sky with a light that did not belong to dawn or dusk. A cold gray light that seemed to grow off the ice pack.

We should be very near by now. Would we be able to get through or would we have to turn back? The fog was closing in behind us. It might be impossible to return to Aklavik. A note from the front cockpit — "Weather at Barrow?" We were flying under the fog again, too low to trail a long antenna. I reeled out a few feet of wire, which would not allow me to transmit messages but was sufficient for receiving. It all depended on the man at Barrow. If only he would go on sending in spite of our silence. We were powerless to let him know.

"Weather, weather, *weather* — send us weather," I pleaded mentally and put on my ear-phones. Silence. Wisps of fog scudded past us. No, there he was. "Darr-dit-darr, dit-dit-dit-dit," calling us. Twice, three times, four times — then silence again, waiting for us to answer. I held my breath, "Weather, weather." There he goes again. "Do - - - -u (you) - - - hear - - - me?" came the message. Silence again. He was waiting for my call. "Yes, yes," I answered silently, "but I can't send— go ahead — *weather!*"

"Darr-dit-darr; dit-dit-dit-dit." There he was again. My pencil took down the letters, slowly spelling out the message, "Fog - - - lifting - - - fast (Good man! He did it!) - - - visibility - - - two - - - miles (He did it! Good

for him!) - - - don't - - - think - - - u - - - have - - - any - - - trouble - - - find - - - lagoon." There it was — just what we wanted. I poked my husband excitedly with the pad. That operator at Barrow — he did it — we'd get through all right now. "Fog lifting, visibility two miles." Oh, what a grand man!

We could see the gray flat coast-line now and watched it closely for Barrow. That might be it — a stretch of whitish irregular blocks — houses? No, as we came nearer, they were the strange pushed-up blocks of the ice pack crushed against a little harbor. Well, *these* were houses. We had come on a small low spit of land squeezed between two seas of ice blocks. Yes, there were houses. We peered down at them eagerly, four tipsy weather-beaten shacks and a few tents, the color of the ice blocks. Can this be Barrow? I almost cried with disappointment looking at that deserted group. No sign of a person, no sign of smoke, no sign of life. It *can't* be Barrow. Childishly, my first thought ran on: "Why, that radio man said they'd have a regular Thanksgiving dinner for us. There couldn't be any dinner down there — no smoke." I felt very hungry. We circled again. "No!" I realized with relief. "No radio mast! It isn't Barrow." We followed the shore-line until we found a larger and newer group of houses between the ice pack and an open lagoon. This was Barrow, ten or twelve red roofs, numerous shacks and tents, a church steeple, and — yes, there they were — the radio masts.

We were landing on the lagoon. I pulled off two bulky pairs of flying socks and put on a pair of rubber-soled shoes for walking. Although it was not freezing weather, my feet became numb before we reached the small crowd of people on shore. A strange group huddled together in the half-light of the Arctic night. I looked at them — pointed hoods, fur parkas, sealskin boots — and thought at first, "They're *all* Eskimos." No, that must be the radio man in the khaki mackinaw. I felt a glow of gratitude and waved at him. As we climbed up the bank, the crowd of Eskimos drew back, an attitude of respect and wonder never seen in the usual crowd. As they moved a great cry arose — not a shout, but a slow deep cry of welcome. Something in it akin to the bleak land and the ice pack.

Then, after shaking of hands and a confusion of voices, I found myself running across the icy moss toward a lighted frame house. My hostess, the doctor's wife, was leading me. I stamped my numb feet on the wooden steps of her home as she pushed open the door. The warmth of a kitchen fire, the brightness of gas lamps, and a delicious smell of sweet potatoes and freshly baked muffins poured out around me and drew me in.

A long table spread for our "Thanksgiving dinner" filled the living room. White cloth, rims of plates, curves of spoons, caught the light from swinging lamps above. I looked around quickly and felt the flavor of an American home — chintz curtains drawn aside, pictures of "woodland scenes" on the walls, bright pillows on the sofa, and there, in the window, a box of climbing nasturtiums.

In the other south window I noticed a tomato plant bent under the weight of one green tomato. My hostess smiled. "That tomato won't ever ripen, you know — it hasn't enough sun — but the leaves grow and we can smell it. Even the smell of growing vegetables is good to us." I looked outside at the pale gray moss on the ground. "I didn't use the dirt around here," she went on to explain. "I tried to, at first, but it's really nothing but frozen sand. Nothing will grow in it except that moss. I carried this earth in a box all the way from Nome."

No vegetables! I tried to realize what she was explaining to me. All their provisions came in by boat once a year around the tip of Alaska from the little mining town, Nome. There was only a month or two in the summer when the icy waters were clear enough for a boat to reach Barrow, and even then the ice pack, jammed against the shore for weeks at a time, might make it impossible. This year their boat, the *Northland,* also carrying our fuel supply, was waiting a hundred miles down the coast for a change in wind to blow the ice pack offshore. "The schoolteacher and his wife are waiting for their daughter. She is on that ship."

The settlement "family" began to crowd in, piling their parkas and sealskin boots at the door of the warm room. Every member had a vital part in the life of the settlement.

The doctor and minister, our host, was leader of the community. He had built the manse in which we were staying. His son, "outside," had helped him to plan it. The doctor himself, directing the Eskimos, had measured and fitted every board and nail. He had placed special insulation in the floor, for it was impossible to have a furnace in the cellar. If you started to thaw out the ground underneath, the house might sink. And a furnace would require too much fuel in a fuel-less country. The windows, triple storm ones, were all nailed down. They were for light and not for ventilation. Windows that open and shut are always drafty. The rooms were ventilated by pipes which let in air indirectly but kept out rain and snow. Heat from the kitchen went up through ventilators in the ceiling to the bedrooms above. There were big stoves in all the rooms. The doctor installed the water tank, connected it with pipes for running water downstairs, and heated it from the stove. Aside from his work as architect and carpenter, he preached every Sunday, had a Bible class Wednesday nights, was doctor, surgeon, and dentist, and was preparing his boy for college.

His wife and another trained nurse had supervision of the hospital. The winter before there had been an epidemic of diphtheria in the settlement. The little hospital was crowded past its capacity, but they had managed all the work with only the help of a few untrained Eskimo girls.

The schoolteacher and his wife carried on their work in a frame building heated only by a stove. One of the Eskimo girls, sent from the Point Barrow School to college at Sitka, had come back to teach this year. The radio operator kept the community in touch with the outside world. Radio was their only means of communication except for the yearly boat and a few dog-team mails during the winter. He was responsible, too, for keeping the world in touch with them, sending meteorologists daily reports of the important Arctic weather. His wife was bringing up, besides a girl of nine, a six-months-old baby named Barrow (the first white child born there).

An old Scotch whaleman completed the circle as we sat at dinner. He had not been "outside" for forty years, had never seen telephones or automobiles, although radio had come to take a regular part in his life and airplanes had landed near his home several times. The Wilkins Polar Expedition had based at Barrow and a plane carrying serum had flown up the year before in the diphtheria epidemic. It was strange to realize that radio and aviation, which typify the latest advance in civilization, had vitally affected this outpost, while railroad, telephone, and telegraph had not touched it.

We sat down to a real Thanksgiving dinner. Provisions were short, but they had all pooled their supplies for a feast. Reindeer meat came out of the community cellar, a huge cave dug down in the icy ground. The radio operator carved a wild goose that had been shot near-by. Among their remaining cans of food they had found sweet potatoes, peas, and beets. There was even a salad of canned celery and fruit. Someone still had a few eggs (not fresh, of course; preserved ones), which were brought over for mayonnaise. Someone else had flour for the soda biscuits. Someone brought coffee. But the greatest treat of the evening, the most extravagant, generous touch, I did not properly appreciate. The trained nurse had grown a little parsley in the hospital window box. They had picked it to put around the platter of meat. I treated it as garniture.

On Sunday the whole Eskimo village came up the hill to the white frame church. Men in their fur jackets and big sealskin boots; women with babies on their backs under their loose fur-lined calico dresses; little children with bright slit eyes shining out of fur hoods — all padded up the hill out of their tents and shacks. Sunday service was a great occasion and they were all smiling and laughing. No one wanted to miss it. I looked for the Eskimo friends I had made in the last two or three days. "Lottie," who led us over the ice pack the day before. When she ran she heaved from one side to another like a bear. I could see her green calico dress swaying in the crowd. "Ned" and his wife, who made us a fur cap and mit-

tens. "Bert," who kept the village store and supervised the killing of the reindeer for the winter stock. We met him the day of the round-up, sledging back carcasses, cleaned and tied up in cheesecloth. Here were the Eskimo girls who helped with the Thanksgiving dinner, shy and smiling, their black hair brushed down sleekly; and the Eskimo woman who gave us a miniature whaling spear carved out of walrus tusk. They all crowded in between the wooden benches of the church. During the service there was a general shuffling and crying of babies. Whenever a baby cried too much, the mother would get up reluctantly, hitch her bundle higher up on her back, and pad out clumsily. But nothing distracted the congregation. Men, women, and children leaned forward earnestly watching the minister. Many could not understand English. Even those who had learned it in school were bewildered by psalms sung by a shepherd on a sun-parched hillside.

" 'We have gone astray like sheep,' " began the reading. Sheep, what did that mean to them? I saw stony New England pastures and those gray backs moving among blueberry bushes and junipers.

"Like the reindeer," explained the minister, "who have scattered on the tundras." The listening heads moved. They understood reindeer.

" 'Your garners will be filled.' " Big red barns, I saw, and hay wagons rumbling uphill. But the Eskimos? "Your meat cellars," the minister answered my question, "will be full of reindeer meat."

" 'Your oxen will be strong,' " read the next verse. "Your dogs for your dog teams will pull hard," continued the minister. " 'The Power of God.' " How could he explain that abstract word "Power"?

"Sometimes when the men are whaling," he started, "the boats get caught in the ice. We have to take dynamite and break up the ice to let them get out. That is power — dynamite — 'the dynamite of God.' "

"For Thine is the Kingdom, 'the dynamite,' and the Glory forever and ever. Amen," I said over to myself.

The congregation was standing up to sing. The schoolteacher's small boy, who was organist, sounded the chords. "Gloree for me — Gloree for me." A buoyant hymn generally, but sung by these people in a high singsong chant, it held a minor quality of endlessness, as though it might echo on and on over the gray tundras — "that would be gloree, gloree for me."

One morning we woke to find the weather changed. The sun was a pale moon behind the scattering mist. "Have you arranged your radio schedule?" my husband asked me. "We ought to leave." I ran down the boardwalk that covered the wet moss to the government radio shack.

The weather had not changed enough for them. Everyone was watching the manse flagpole. "Still northwest," the flag read. The ice pack still hugged the shore-line, blocking their boat, the *Northland*, off Icy Cape. "Perhaps you will fly over it!" "You can signal to them anyway!" "When you get 'outside,' perhaps you will read somewhere in the papers whether or not our boat got in. It usually has, but when it doesn't ——" They were all standing around us saying good-bye. "We have no more butter left." "Or flour." "Or tea or coffee." "I would like a package of cigarettes," admitted the radio operator with a smile. A package of cigarettes! If only we had thought to bring a few things like that. Our heavily loaded plane could not have carried much food, but a package of cigarettes, a newspaper, some fresh fruit —— I longed to have something to give them. At least we could carry out letters and messages. Someone had a daughter in China and we were going — they could hardly believe it — to China.

"Good-bye! Good-bye! We'll see you again." Perhaps the veteran whaleman would never face the blast of motor horns and the jangle of street cars, but some of the others might leave Barrow. The doctor's son was coming back to college. One of the young Eskimo men was hopefully taking a correspondence course in aviation. Poor man, he was waiting at that moment for the *Northland* to bring in his home work for the next year.

We started to put on our heavy flying clothes. Over two pairs of heavy double-weight socks I pulled on the boots they had given me. Made of sealskin, sewed and chewed into shape by the Eskimo women, they were the warmest, dryest, lightest shoes I have ever worn. My husband drew on his flying suit. His knee hit against a lump in the pocket — an orange they had given us as we left Churchill a week before! "Perhaps you'd like this," he said, half apologetically, handing it to the doctor's wife.

"An orange!" She held it in her palms for a moment as though warming her hands by its glow and then said, with the enthusiasm of a girl spending a birthday coin, "I'll tell you what we'll do! We'll give it to the baby! Wonderful — for Barrow!"

Wind, Sand, and Stars
The Elements [9]

ANTOINE DE SAINT-EXUPÉRY

ᷜ Wind, Sand, and Stars *was written for adults, and perhaps adults will appreciate more the beauty of the writing than young people, but surely no boy interested in aviation can fail to enjoy this, one of the earliest books about the different aspects of that then-new science. For Saint-Exupéry discusses the* craft *(by which he means the skill needed to fly), the men who were to do the flying, and the planes as they were in those early days, before he relates any experiences, such as are given below.*

The sky was blue. Pure blue. Too pure. A hard blue sky that shone over the scraped and barren world while the fleshless vertebrae of the mountain chain flashed in the sunlight. Not a cloud. The blue sky glittered like a new-honed knife. I felt in advance the vague distaste that accompanies the prospect of physical exertion. The purity of the sky upset me. Give me a good black storm in which the enemy is plainly visible. I can measure its extent and prepare myself for its attack. I can get my hands on my adversary. But when you are flying very high in clear

9 From Antoine de Saint-Exupéry, *Wind, Sand, and Stars*, trans. Lewis Galantière (Reynal & Hitchcock, 1939).

weather, the shock of a blue storm is as disturbing as if something collapsed that had been holding up your ship in the air. It is the only time when a pilot feels that there is a gulf beneath his ship.

Another thing bothered me. I could see on a level with the mountain peaks not a haze, not a mist, not a sandy fog, but a sort of ash-colored streamer in the sky. I did not like the look of that scarf of filings scraped off the surface of the earth and borne out to sea by the wind. I tightened my leather harness as far as it would go and I steered the ship with one hand while with the other I hung on to the longéron that ran alongside my seat. I was still flying in remarkably calm air.

Very soon came a slight tremor. As every pilot knows, there are secret little quiverings that foretell your real storm. No rolling, no pitching. No swing to speak of. The flight continues horizontal and rectilinear. But you have felt a warning drum on the wings of your plane, little intermittent rappings scarcely audible and infinitely brief, little cracklings from time to time as if there were traces of gunpowder in the air.

And then everything round me blew up.

Concerning the next couple of minutes I have nothing to say. All that I can find in my memory is a few rudimentary notions, fragments of thoughts, direct observations. I cannot compose them into a dramatic recital because there was no drama. The best I can do is to line them up in a kind of chronological order.

In the first place, I was standing still. Having banked right in order to correct a sudden drift, I saw the landscape freeze abruptly where it was and remain jiggling on the same spot. I was making no headway. My wings had ceased to nibble into the outline of the earth. I could see the earth buckle, pivot — but it stayed put. The plane was skidding as if on a toothless cogwheel.

Meanwhile, I had the absurd feeling that I had exposed myself completely to the enemy. All those peaks, those crests, those teeth that were cutting into the wind and unleashing its gusts in my direction, seemed to me so many guns pointed straight at my

defenseless person. I was slow to think, but the thought did come to me that I ought to give up altitude and make for one of the neighboring valleys where I might take shelter against a mountain-side. As a matter of fact, whether I liked it or not I was being helplessly sucked down toward the earth.

Trapped this way in the first breaking waves of a cyclone about which I learned, twenty minutes later, that at sea level it was blowing at the fantastic rate of one hundred and fifty miles an hour, I certainly had no impression of tragedy. Now, as I write, if I shut my eyes, if I forget the plane and the flight and try to express the plain truth about what was happening to me, I find that I felt weighed down, I felt like a porter carrying a slippery load, grabbing one object in a jerky movement that sent another slithering down, so that, overcome by exasperation, the porter is tempted to let the whole load drop. There is a kind of law of the shortest distance to the image, a psychological law by which the event to which one is subjected is visualized in a symbol that represents its swiftest summing up: I was a man who, carrying a pile of plates, had slipped on a waxed floor and let his scaffolding of porcelain crash.

I found myself imprisoned in a valley. My discomfort was not less, it was greater. I grant you that a down current has never killed anybody; that the expression "flattened out by a down current" belongs to journalism and not to the language of flyers. How could air possibly pierce the ground? But here I was in a valley at the wheel of a ship that was three quarters out of my control. Ahead of me a rocky prow swung to left and right, rose suddenly high in the air for a second like a wave over my head, and then plunged down below my horizon.

Horizon? There was no longer a horizon. I was in the wings of a theater cluttered up with bits of scenery. Vertical, oblique, horizontal, all of plane geometry was awhirl. A hundred transversal valleys were muddled in a jumble of perspectives. Whenever I seemed about to take my bearings, a new eruption would swing me round in a circle or send me tumbling wing over wing and I would have to try all over again to get clear of all this rubbish. Two ideas came into my mind. One was a discovery: for the first time I understood the cause of certain accidents in the mountains when no fog was present to explain them. For a single second, in a waltzing landscape like this, the flyer had been unable to distinguish between vertical mountain-sides and horizontal planes. The other idea was a fixation: the sea is flat: I shall not hook anything out at sea.

I banked — or should I use that word to indicate a vague and stubborn jockeying through the east-west valleys? Still nothing pathetic to report. I was wrestling with chaos, was wearing myself out in a battle with chaos, struggling to keep in the air a gigantic house of cards that kept collapsing despite all I could do. Scarcely the faintest twinge of fear went through me when one of the walls of my prison rose suddenly like a tidal wave over my head. My heart hardly skipped a beat when I was tripped up by one of the whirling eddies of air that the sharp ridge darted into my ship. If I felt anything unmistakably in the haze of confused feelings and notions that came over me each time one of these powder magazines blew up, it was a feeling of respect. I respected that sharp-toothed ridge. I respected that peak. I respected that dome. I respected that transversal valley opening out into my valley and about to toss me God knew how violently as soon as its torrent of wind flowed into the one on which I was being borne along.

What I was struggling against, I discovered, was not the wind but the ridge itself, the crest, the rocky peak. Despite my distance from it, it was the wall of rock I was fighting with. By some trick of invisible prolongation, by the play of a secret set of muscles, this was what was pummeling me. It was against this that I was butting my head. Before me on the right I recognized the peak of Salamanca, a perfect cone which, I knew, dominated the sea. It cheered me to think I was about to escape out to sea. But first I should have to wrestle with the gale off that peak, try to avoid its down-crushing blow. The peak of Salamanca was a giant. I was filled with respect for the peak of Salamanca.

There had been granted me one second of respite. Two seconds. Something was collecting itself into a knot, coiling itself up, growing taut. I sat amazed. I opened astonished eyes. My whole plane seemed to be shivering, spreading outward, swelling up. Horizontal and stationary it was, yet lifted before I knew it fifteen hundred feet straight into the air in a kind of apotheosis. I who for forty minutes had not been able to climb higher than two hundred feet off the ground was suddenly able to look down on the enemy. The plane quivered as if in boiling water. I could see the wide waters of the ocean. The valley opened out into this ocean, this salvation. — And at that very moment, without any warning whatever, half a mile from Salamanca, I was suddenly struck straight in the midriff by the gale off that peak and sent hurtling out to sea.

There I was, throttle wide open, facing the coast. At right angles to the coast and facing it. A lot had happened in a single minute. In the first place, I had not flown out to sea. I had been spat out to sea by a monstrous cough, vomited out of my valley as from the mouth of a howitzer. When, what seemed to me instantly, I banked in order to put myself where I wanted to be in respect of the coast-line, I saw that the coast-line was a mere blur, a characterless strip of blue; and I was five miles out to sea. The mountain range stood up like a crenelated fortress against the pure sky while the cyclone crushed me down to the surface of the waters. How hard that wind was blowing I found out as soon as I tried to climb, as soon as I became conscious of my disastrous mistake: throttle wide open, engines running at my maximum, which was one hundred and fifty miles an hour, my plane hanging sixty feet over the water, I was unable to budge. When a wind like this one attacks a tropical forest, it swirls through the branches like a flame, twists them into corkscrews, and uproots giant trees as if they were radishes. Here, bounding off the mountain range, it was leveling out the sea.

Hanging on with all the power in my engines, face to the coast, face to that wind where each gap in the teeth of the range sent forth a stream of air like a long reptile, I felt as if I were clinging to the tip of a monstrous whip that was cracking over the sea.

In this latitude the South American continent is narrow and the Andes are not far from the Atlantic. I was struggling not merely against the whirling winds that blew off the east-coast range, but more likely also against a whole sky blown down upon me off the peaks of the Andean chain. For the first time in four years of airline flying I began to worry about the strength of my wings. Also, I was fearful of bumping the sea — not because of the down currents which, at sea level, would necessarily provide me with a horizontal air mattress, but because of the helplessly acrobatic positions in which this wind was buffeting me. Each time that I was tossed, I became afraid that I might be unable to straighten out. Besides, there was a chance that I should find myself out of fuel and simply drown. I kept expecting the gasoline pumps to stop priming, and indeed the plane was so violently shaken up that in the half-filled tanks as well as in the gas line the gasoline was sloshing round, not coming through, and the engines, instead of their steady roar, were sputtering in a sort of dot-and-dash series of uncertain growls.

I hung on, meanwhile, to the controls of my heavy transport plane, my attention monopolized by the physical struggle and my mind occupied by the very simplest thoughts. I was feeling practically nothing as I stared down at the imprint made by the wind on the sea. I saw a series of great white puddles, each perhaps eight hundred yards in extent. They were running toward me at a speed of one hundred and fifty miles an hour where the down-surging wind spouts broke against the surface of the sea in a succession of horizontal explosions. The sea was white and it was green — white with the whiteness of crushed sugar and green in puddles the color of emeralds. In this tumult one wave was indistinguishable from another. Torrents of air were pouring down upon the sea. The winds were sweeping past in giant gusts as when, before the autumn harvests, they blow

a great flowing change of color over a wheatfield. Now and again the water went incongruously transparent between the white pools, and I could see a green and black sea-bottom. And then the great glass of the sea would be shattered anew into a thousand glittering fragments.

It seemed hopeless. In twenty minutes of struggle I had not moved forward a hundred yards. What was more, with flying as hard as it was out here five miles from the coast, I wondered how I could possibly buck the winds along the shore, assuming I was able to fight my way in. I was a perfect target for the enemy there on shore. Fear, however, was out of the question. I was incapable of thinking. I was emptied of everything except the vision of a very simple act. I must straighten out. Straighten out. Straighten out.

There were moments of respite, nevertheless. I dare say those moments themselves were equal to the worst storms I had hitherto met, but by comparison with the cyclone they were moments of relaxation. The urgency of fighting off the wind was not quite so great. And I could tell when these intervals were coming. It was not I who moved toward those zones of relative calm, those almost green oases clearly painted on the sea, but they that flowed toward me. I could read clearly in the water the advertisement of a habitable province. And with each interval of repose the power to feel and to think was restored to me. Then, in those moments, I began to feel I was doomed. Then was the time that little by little I began to tremble for myself. So much so that each time I saw the unfurling of a new wave of the white offensive, I was seized by a brief spasm of panic which lasted until the exact instant when, on the edge of that bubbling caldron, I bumped into the invisible wall of wind. That restored me to numbness again.

Up! I wanted to be higher up. The next time I saw one of those green zones of calm, it seemed to me deeper than before and I began to be hopeful of getting out. If I could climb high enough, I thought, I would find other currents in which I could make some headway. I took advantage of the truce to essay a swift climb. It was hard. The enemy had not weakened. Three hundred feet. Six hundred feet. If I could get up to three thousand feet, I was safe, I said to myself. But there on the horizon I saw again that white pack unleashed in my direction. I gave it up. I did not want them at my throat again; I did not want to be caught off balance. But it was too late. The first blow sent me rolling over and over and the sky became a slippery dome on which I could not find a footing.

One has a pair of hands and they obey. How are one's orders transmitted to one's hands?

I had made a discovery that horrified me: my hands were numb. My hands were dead. They sent me no message. Probably they had been numb a long time and I had not noticed it. The pity was that I had noticed it, had raised the question. That was serious. Lashed by the wind, the wings of the plane had been dragging and jerking at the cables by which they were controlled from the wheel, and the wheel in my hands had not ceased jerking a single second. I had been gripping the wheel with all my might for forty minutes, fearful lest the strain snap the cables. So desperate had been my grip that now I could not feel my hands.

What a discovery! My hands were not my own. I look at them and decided to lift a finger: it obeyed me. I looked away and issued the same order: now I could not feel whether the finger had obeyed or not. No message had reached me. I thought: "Suppose my hands were to open: how would I know it?" I swung my head round and looked again: my hands were still locked round the wheel. Nevertheless, I was afraid. How can a man tell the difference between the sight of a hand opening and the decision to open that hand, when there is no longer an exchange of sensations between the hand and the brain? How can one tell the difference between an image and an act of the will? Better stop thinking of the picture of open hands. Hands live a life of their own. Better not offer them this monstrous temptation.

And I began to chant a silly litany which went on uninterruptedly until this flight was over. A single thought. A single image. A single phrase tirelessly chanted over and over again: "I shut my hands. I shut my hands. I shut my hands." All of me was condensed into that phrase and for me the white sea, the whirling eddies, the saw-toothed range ceased to exist. There was only "I shut my hands." There was no danger, no cyclone, no land unattained. Somewhere there was a pair of rubber hands which, once they let go the wheel, could not possibly come alive in time to recover from the tumbling drop into the sea.

I had no thoughts. I had no feelings except the feeling of being emptied out. My strength was draining out of me and so was my impulse to go on fighting. The engines continued their dot-and-dash sputterings, their little crashing noises that were like the intermittent cracklings of a ripping canvas. Whenever they were silent longer than a second, I felt as if a heart had stopped beating. There! that's the end. No, they've started up again.

The thermometer on the wing, I happened to see, stood at twenty below zero, but I was bathed in sweat from head to foot. My face was running with perspiration. What a dance! Later I was to discover that my storage batteries had been jerked out of their steel flanges and hurtled up through the roof of the plane. I did not know then, either, that the ribs on my wings had come unglued and that certain of my steel cables had been sawed down to the last thread. And I continued to feel strength and will oozing out of me. Any minute now I should be overcome by the indifference born of utter weariness and by the mortal yearning to take my rest.

What can I say about this? Nothing. My shoulders ached. Very painfully. As if I had been carrying too many sacks too heavy for me. I leaned forward. Through a green transparency I saw sea-bottom so close that I could make out all the details. Then the wind's hand brushed the picture away.

In an hour and twenty minutes I had succeeded in climbing to nine hundred feet. A little to the south — that is, on my left — I could see a long trail on the surface of the sea, a sort of blue stream. I decided to let myself drift as far down as that stream. Here where I was, facing west, I was as good as motionless, unable either to advance or retreat. If I could reach that blue pathway, which must be lying in the shelter of something not the cyclone, I might be able to move in slowly to the coast. So I let myself drift to the left. I had the feeling, meanwhile, that the wind's violence had perhaps slackened.

It took me an hour to cover the five miles to shore. There in the shelter of a long cliff I was able to finish my journey south. Thereafter I succeeded in keeping enough altitude to fly inland to the field that was my destination. I was able to stay up at nine hundred feet. It was very stormy, but nothing like the cyclone I had come out of. That was over.

On the ground I saw a platoon of soldiers. They had been sent down to watch for me. I landed near-by and we were a whole hour getting the plane into the hangar. I climbed out of the cockpit and walked off. There was nothing to say. I was very sleepy. I kept moving my fingers, but they stayed numb. I could not collect my thoughts enough to decide whether or not I had been afraid. Had I been afraid? I couldn't say. I had witnessed a strange sight. What strange sight? I couldn't say. The sky was blue and the sea was white. I felt I ought to tell someone about it since I was back from so far away! But I had no grip on what I had been through. "Imagine a white sea . . . very white . . . whiter still." You cannot convey things to people by piling up adjectives, by stammering.

You cannot convey anything because there is nothing to convey. My shoulders were aching. My insides felt as if they had been crushed in by a terrible weight. You cannot make drama out of that, or out of the cone-shaped peak of Salamanca. That peak was charged like a powder magazine; but if I said so people would laugh. I would myself. I respected the peak of Salamanca. That is my story. And it is not a story.

The Great Heritage
We Have Tomorrow [10]

KATHERINE B. SHIPPEN

ᴥ *"It is not I that belong to the past, but the past that belongs to me. America is the youngest of the nations and inherits all that went before in history. And I am the youngest of America's children, and into my hands is given all her priceless heritage, to the last white star espied through the telescope, to the last great thought of the philosopher. Mine is the whole majestic past, and mine is the shining future."*
— MARY ANTIN, The Promised Land.

We now have come into the great inheritance. To our generation has been given the American earth, the richness of the forests, the wheat fields and the corn fields, the wide prairies where the cattle graze, the mines.

When the first settlers stood on the Atlantic shore they wondered what lay behind the trees that separated them from the unknown continent. Would they be strong enough, they must have wondered, to wrestle with the earth? Would they have courage to face the dangers that were in this strange place?

Now we, at the beginning of another day, take the inheritance that they have bequeathed us. As they were uncertain what might be behind the wooded hills and across the rippling rivers, so we are not quite sure what we shall find in this new world we have inherited, or what our labor may bring from it.

Shall we dig deeper into the earth, and bring up rarer treasures than they found? Will the soil bring forth richer crops because our science knows better how to plant and fertilize?

What shall we garner from the ocean? Shall we plant and harvest ocean crops, as some men think, to feed the animals and men on land? Shall we take more rich minerals from the sea water, as we are already taking magnesium? Or will the ocean tide provide a new and steady power? We do not know.

10 From Katherine B. Shippen, *The Great Heritage* (Viking Press, 1947).

Perhaps our new source of strength will lie in the release of atomic energy, of which we now know so little. It may be that we shall change one metal to another, and create new elements that do not now exist. We do not know how we may use the immense forces of light and heat which we may generate by nuclear fission.

Certainly we shall make great changes and great advances in all these ways.

But perhaps our new work, and our new achievement, will not be altogether with material things. Perhaps we shall be working with the people themselves: trying to make every man who draws his living from the American earth healthy and strong and free.

The poet Langston Hughes has written:

> We have tomorrow
> Bright before us
> Like a flame
> Yesterday, a night-gone thing
> A sun-down name
> And dawn today
> Broad arch above the road we march. *

* From Langston Hughes, *The Dream Keeper* (Knopf, 1932).

BIBLIOGRAPHY

Travel

Busoni, Rafaello. *Stanley's Africa;* illus. by the author. Viking Press, 1944. (Grades 7–9)
Stanley's dramatic meeting with Livingstone and his later expeditions as an explorer.

Duvoisin, Roger. *They Put Out to Sea; the Story of the Map;* illus. by the author. Alfred A. Knopf, 1943. (Grades 5–8)
The early traders and explorers are portrayed in this story of their contribution to history.

Follett, Helen. *Ocean Outposts;* illus. with maps by Armstrong Sperry and photographs. Charles Scribner's Sons, 1942. (Grades 7–9)
Striking photographs, fascinating maps, and lively text give essential facts about America's island possessions in the Pacific.

Gatti, Ellen and Attilio. *Here Is Africa;* photographs by Attilio Gatti and others; map by Raymond Lufkin. Charles Scribner's Sons, 1943. (Grades 7–9)
The Gattis have made ten expeditions to Africa. Superb photographs.

Hillyer, Virgil. *Child's Geography of the World;* rev. by Edward G. Huey; maps and illus. by Mary Sherwood Wright Jones. Appleton, 1951. (Grades 4–8)
The geography of the globe portrayed with originality and humor.

Iwamatsu, Tomoe. *Plenty to Watch,* by Mitsu and Taro Yashima, *pseuds.* Viking Press, 1954. (Grades 1–3)
A picture book of Japan describing the daily activities of a small village.

Kelly, Eric P. *Land of the Polish People;* illus. with photographs. J. B. Lippincott, rev. ed. 1952. (Portraits of the Nations Series) (Grades 7–9)
A brief history of Poland and its people is combined with an account of Polish music and literature.

Kennedy, Jean. *Here Is India;* photographs by Alice Schalek and others; map by Raymond Lufkin. Charles Scribner's Sons, rev. ed. 1954. (Grades 7–9)
First published in 1945, the book has been revised to give political changes in India and Pakistan.

Lucas, Mary Seymour. *Vast Horizons;* illus. and maps by C. B. Falls. Viking Press, 1943. (Grades 7–9)
The thrilling story of discovery and of the men who set out to conquer the unknown.

McNeer, May. *The Story of the Southwest;* illus. by Cornelius H. DeWitt. Harper & Brothers, 1957. (Regions of America Books) (Grades 4–7)
A panoramic guide to the Southwest, with factual text and brilliantly decorative lithographs.

Melbo, Irving Robert. *Our Country's National Parks;* 2 vols. Bobbs-Merrill, 1950. (Grades 6–9)

Authentic historical and scientific data on the twenty-eight national parks.

Paton, Alan. *Land and People of South Africa.* J. B. Lippincott, 1955. (Portraits of the Nations Series) (Grades 8–9)

A South African author gives an intimate description of the life and customs of the people.

Pyne, Mable. *Little Geography of the United States;* illus. by the author. Houghton Mifflin, 1941. (Grades 3–5)

A pictorial geography which makes an exciting introduction to the subject.

Quinn, Vernon. *Picture Map Geography of Mexico, Central America and the West Indies;* maps and drawings by Da Osimo. J. B. Lippincott, 1943. (Grades 5–8)

The maps give a graphic picture of the topography, industries, and products of the countries described. Read also the same author's *Picture Map Geography of South America* and *Picture Map Geography of the Pacific Islands.*

Stefánsson, Evelyn. *Here Is Alaska;* with a foreword by Vilhjalmur Stefánsson. Charles Scribner's Sons, 1943. (Grades 7–9)

From first-hand knowledge, Mrs. Stefánsson gives a comprehensive picture of Alaska. Illustrated with photographs.

Stefánsson, Evelyn. *Here Is the Far North;* illus. with photographs. Charles Scribner's Sons, 1957. (Grades 7–9)

The wife of the Arctic explorer has visited Greenland and Iceland and has flown the Polar Route from Los Angeles to Copenhagen.

Stockton, Frank. *Buccaneers and Pirates of Our Coasts;* illus. by George Varian and B. West Clinedinst. Macmillan, 1898. (Grades 6–9)

Stories of real pirates and their adventures in the West Indies and the Spanish Main.

Street, Alicia. *Land of the English People;* illus. with photographs. J. B. Lippincott, rev. ed. 1953. (Portraits of the Nations Series) (Grades 7–9)

Describes the English countryside and people, and outlines England's history to the coronation of Queen Elizabeth II.

Waldeck, Theodore J. *On Safari;* illus. by Kurt Wiese. Viking Press, 1940. (Grades 7–9)

The explorer-author gives a semi-autobiographical account of three journeys to Africa as a scientist and photographer.

White, Anne Terry. *Lost Worlds; Adventures in Archaeology.* Random House, 1941. (Grades 6–9)

A stimulating account of the finding of four lost civilizations.

History

Baity, Elizabeth. *Americans Before Columbus;* illus. with drawings and maps by C. B. Falls and with photographs. Viking Press, 1951. (Grades 7–9)

An absorbing study of American Indian peoples and cultures from the Asiatic migrations to the Spanish conquests. Also, *Man Is a Weaver.*

Brindze, Ruth. *Story of the Totem Pole;* illus. by Yeffe Kimball. Vanguard Press, 1951. (Grades 4–7)

The story of how the Indians, without a written language, carved their history and adventures on giant red cedars.

Buff, Mary. *Dancing Cloud; the Navajo Boy;* illus. by Conrad Buff. Viking Press, rev. ed. 1957. (Grades 3–5)

Through the exciting tale of a young Indian boy, the reader gains a vivid picture of Navajo life.

Dalgliesh, Alice. *America Begins; the Story of the Finding of the New World;* illus. by Lois Maloy. Charles Scribner's Sons, 1938. (Grades 3–5)

A picture story that will arouse the interest of young readers.

Dalgliesh, Alice. *America Builds Homes; the Story of the First Colonies;* illus. by Lois Maloy. Charles Scribner's Sons, 1938. (Grades 3–5)

How the first settlers came to America and built their homes.

Dalgliesh, Alice. *The Fourth of July Story;* illus. by Marie Nonnast. Charles Scribner's Sons, 1956. (Grades 3–6)

A book to help young children understand the meaning of one of the most colorful and dramatic American holidays. Read also *The Thanksgiving Story.*

Daugherty, James. *Of Courage Undaunted; Across the Continent with Lewis and Clark.* Viking Press, 1951. (Grades 7–9)

The story of the Lewis and Clark expedition told in stirring prose.

Duvoisin, Roger. *And There Was America;* illus. by the author. Alfred A. Knopf, 1938. (Grades 4–6)

Stories of the early explorers of America.

Earle, Alice. *Child Life in Colonial Days;* illus.

with photographs. Macmillan, 1899. (Grades 7–9)

Authentic information about American colonial children. *Home Life in Colonial Days* is a companion volume.

Foster, Genevieve. *Abraham Lincoln's World;* illus. by the author. Charles Scribner's Sons, 1944. (Grades 7–9)

Mrs. Foster discovered how difficult it is for young people to visualize events of a period in relationship to each other. Here she gives a picture of world events during Lincoln's life.

Foster, Genevieve. *Augustus Caesar's World; a Story of Ideas and Events from B.C. 44 to 14 A.D.;* illus. by the author. Charles Scribner's Sons, 1947. (High School)

A fascinating book which shows what the world was like under Roman law.

Foster, Genevieve. *Birthdays of Freedom;* illus. by the author. 2 vols. Charles Scribner's Sons, 1952 and 1957. (Grades 5–9)

Vol. I: From Early Egypt to the Fall of Rome. Vol. II: From the Fall of Rome to America's War for Freedom, July 4, 1776.

Foster, Genevieve. *George Washington's World;* illus. by the author. Charles Scribner's Sons, 1941. (Grades 7–9)

An informal, graphic, different approach to history.

Hall, Jennie. *Buried Cities;* illus. with drawings and photographs from original sources. Macmillan, 1922. (Grades 6–9)

Early life and excavations of Pompeii, Olympia, and Mycenae.

Hartman, Gertrude. *Making of a Democracy.* John Day, rev. enl. ed. 1941. (Grades 7–9)

A discussion of American democracy and its significance.

Hartman, Gertrude. *Medieval Days and Ways.* Macmillan, 1937. (Grades 6–9)

Life and society during the Middle Ages described in a simple but picturesque manner.

Hartman, Gertrude. *The World We Live In and How It Came To Be;* illus. from contemporary sources. Macmillan, 1935. (Grades 7–9)

A pictured outline of man's progress from the earliest days to the present century. *These United States and How They Came To Be* is a companion volume.

Hillyer, Virgil. *Child's History of the World.* Appleton, rev. ed. 1951. (Grades 5–8)

This edition has five new chapters bringing the story of mankind up to the end of World War II.

Hofsinde, Robert. *Indian Sign Language.* William R. Morrow, 1956. (Grades 4–8)

Shows how to form the gestures representing over 500 words in Indian sign language. *Indian Games and Crafts* is a companion volume.

Langdon, William. *Everyday Things in American Life, 1607–1776.* Charles Scribner's Sons, 1937. (Grades 7–9)

How the early colonists lived.

McNeer, May. *Mexican Story;* illus. by Lynd Ward. Ariel Books, 1953. (Grades 6–9)

A rich and telling panorama of Mexico.

Meadowcroft, Enid. *Gift of the River; a History of Ancient Egypt;* illus. and adapted from Egyptian sources by Katherine Dewey. Thomas Y. Crowell, 1937. (Grades 4–7)

A history of the Egyptians written for younger children.

Mayer, Josephine, and Tom Prideaux. *Never to Die: the Egyptians in Their Own Words.* Viking Press, 1938. (High School)

A chronological presentation of the Egypt of three thousand years ago.

Mills, Dorothy. *Book of the Ancient World for Younger Readers.* G. P. Putnam's Sons, 1923. (Grades 7–9)

An account of our common heritage from the dawn of civilization to the coming of the Greeks.

Morison, Samuel Eliot. *Story of the "Old Colony" of New Plymouth, 1620–1692;* illus. by Charles H. Overly. Alfred A. Knopf, 1956. (Grades 6–9)

A history of the Plymouth Colony from its beginnings in England until its incorporation into the Massachusetts Bay Colony in 1692.

Petersham, Maud and Miska. *The Silver Mace; a Story of Williamsburg.* Macmillan, 1956. (Grades 3–5)

A colorful picture story of historic Williamsburg, Virginia.

Quennell, Marjorie and Charles. *Everyday Things in Ancient Greece;* 2nd ed. rev. by Kathleen Freeman. G. P. Putnam's Sons, 1954. (Grades 7–9)

A condensation into one volume of the three books on Greece: Homeric, Archaic, and Classical. Also, *The History of Everyday Things in England.*

Salomon, Julia. *Book of Indian Crafts and Indian Lore.* Harper & Brothers, 1928. (Grades 6–9)

An invaluable book on Indian lore. Illustrated.

Seeger, Elizabeth. *Pageant of Chinese History;* illus. by Bernard Watkins. Longmans, Green, 3rd ed. 1947. (Grades 7–9)

The best history of China available for boys and girls.

Shippen, Katherine. *New Found World;* illus. by C. B. Falls. Viking Press, 1945. (Grades 7–9)

South America is presented to young people in eloquent prose.

Tappan, Eva March. *When Knights Were Bold.* Houghton Mifflin, 1911. (Grades 6–9)

Interesting picture of life in castles, manor houses, monasteries, and towns during the Middle Ages.

Thorne-Thomsen, Gudrun. *In Norway;* illus. by Eyvind Earle. Viking Press, 1948. (Grades 7–9)

The author was brought up in Norway and writes of that country today against its background of history and tradition.

Tunis, Edwin. *Colonial Living.* World, 1957. (Grades 7–12)

The author-artist of *Wheels* and *Weapons* now presents a pictorial history of everyday life in America during the 17th and 18th centuries.

Van Loon, Hendrik Willem. *Story of Mankind.* Liveright, new enl. ed. 1951. (Grades 7–9)

A detailed outline of universal history from the time of the cave man to the beginning of the Second World War. The revised edition contains a supplement written by the author's son.

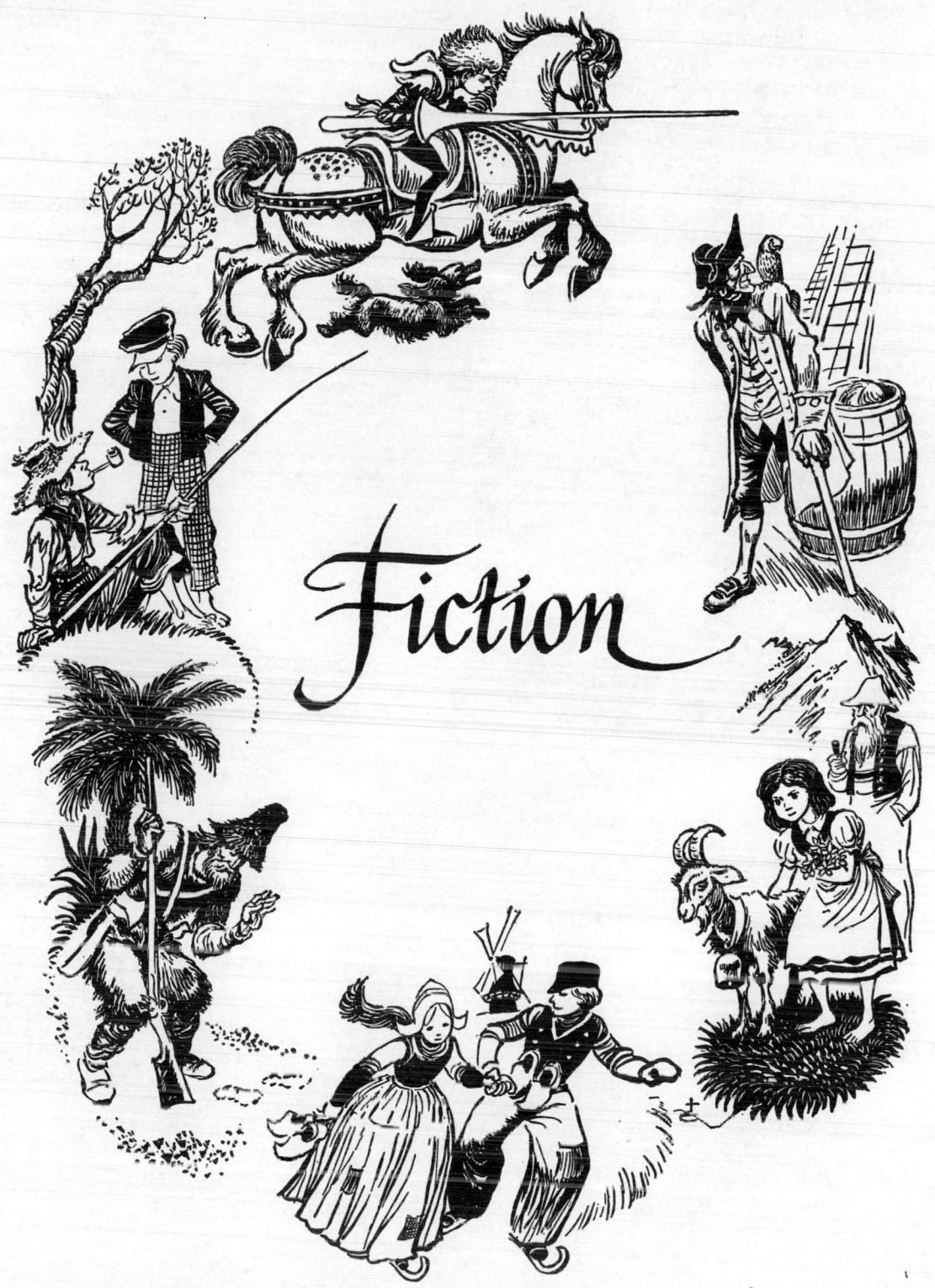

Fiction

Fiction

"The only human activity which has always been of extreme importance to the world is imaginative literature. It is of supreme importance because it is the only means by which humanity can express at once emotion and ideas."[1]

THE FICTION OF CHILDHOOD IS NOT only a preparation for the great stories and novels to come, the glory of English and American literature, but it is also an accomplishment of some dimension in its own right. *The Adventures of Tom Sawyer, Kim, Little Women,* and *Treasure Island* are fair exchange between children and their elders for *Pilgrim's Progress, Gulliver's Travels,* and *Robinson Crusoe.*

Since Fantasy has been discussed elsewhere in this book, Fiction may be defined as stories told in a setting of reality, without the interference of magic and supernatural marvels. The laws of nature, time, and space are accepted as the actuality in which the story moves.

For children, as for the race in its childhood, the first appeal of fiction is in the story, the sequence of events, the plot. But events do not occur, even in the celestial realms beyond us, without involving human beings, or their symbolic equivalent, and the desire to know "what happened?" leaps to include "And to whom?" Then one must know where it happened, and how, and finally, why, and what's to be made of it? What is the point of the story?

The child begins his reading with a primal interest in plot, but even *Little Toot*[2] and *Andy and the Lion*[3] convey an attitude, suggest a line of action, evoke a response that lies outside the function of mere plot. When he becomes involved with Huckleberry Finn, or Big Tiger; with Jancy Larkin, or Laura of the Little House series;[4] when he has read the books in which these characters appear, and hundreds of others that constitute the literature of childhood, he is swept up into the great concepts of Aristotle's *Poetics:* "*Mythos* or plot, *ethos,* which includes both character and setting, and *dianoia* or 'thought'. . . . Every work of literature has both a fictional and a thematic

[1] Ford Madox Ford.
[2] By Hardie Gramatky.
[3] By James Daugherty.
[4] In *The Adventures of Tom Sawyer* and *Adventures of Huckleberry Finn,* by Samuel L. Clemens (Mark Twain); *Big Tiger and Christian,* by Fritz Mühlenweg; *Blue Willow,* by Doris Gates; *Little House in the Big Woods,* by Laura Ingalls Wilder.

aspect, and the question of which is more important is often simply a matter of opinion or emphasis in interpretation."[5]

In books for children, the fictional aspect is emphasized, but children are aware of the wholeness of a book. They seek a good story, to be sure, but they ask that the characters bear some resemblance to life, and not be as wooden as checkers, to be moved into position. They learn to recognize the difference between the books in which the story comes to a logical and inevitable conclusion, and those which spin out the action, incident upon incident, in order to hold the attention of the reader as long as possible. They come to appreciate character and character development in the books they read. They seek action, adventure, the extravagant exploit, but they also appreciate the "tiny flashes of significant moments," the endearing details, the gift for particularization which is a mark of the novelist's genius. Children welcome "thought" when it is inherent in the story, and not propaganda or contrivance. Even the art of good writing commands their attention, and the subtleties of approach, the sustaining of a mood are understood. They do not name these qualities, nor discuss them in the language of the book reviewer or the critic, but if one listens, one can gather evidence of the sureness of their judgments.

The Children's Rooms of Public Libraries offer opportunity for a free exchange of opinions between child and child, between children and librarian. In the give and take of this atmosphere, children give indication of the growth of their appreciation, and of the inner drives which commit them to read for pleasure.

"I never read a book that begins with the weather," a boy remarked, with a tone of bitterness.

"I like books where the girl is one way at the beginning, and then she changes at the end." There is the desire to explore the greatest gift of the storyteller's art, the portrayal of character development.

"I'm tired of girls who are always throwing their long hair over their shoulders, and have heart-shaped faces." Here is a child grown weary at last of the series she had been reading.

"This book made me feel so nice." It was Eleanor Estes' book of atmosphere and warmth and reality — *The Moffats*.

Like perceptive, reading adults, children expect of their best storytellers intensity of feeling; inventiveness in creating plot, situation, and the atmosphere of time and place; skill in building the structure which holds the tale together; the creation of convincing characters; masterful use of language; and the flash of meaning with which the imagination illumines life. Children ask to be united, by the act of reading, with the ebb and flow of the human spirit.

[5] Northrup Frye, *Anatomy of Criticism* (Princeton University Press, 1957), pp. 52-53.

FICTION

Poppy Seed Cakes[1]

Margery Clark

◆§ *This is the first of the gay little tales from the book* Poppy Seed Cakes. *The stories have a true folk-tale quality and are illustrated with bright pictures which remind one of the Czecho-slovakian and Russian picture books.*

Once upon a time there was a little boy and his name was Andrewshek. His mother and his father brought him from the old country when he was a tiny baby.

Andrewshek had an Auntie Katushka and she came from the old country, too, on Andrewshek's fourth birthday.

Andrewshek's Auntie Katushka came on a large boat. She brought with her a huge bag filled with presents for Andrewshek and his father and his mother. In the huge bag were a fine feather bed and a bright shawl and five pounds of poppy seeds.

The fine feather bed was made from the feathers of her old green goose at home. It was to keep Andrewshek warm when he took a nap.

The bright shawl was for Andrewshek's Auntie Katushka to wear when she went to market.

The five pounds of poppy seeds were to sprinkle on little cakes which Andrewshek's Auntie Katushka made every Saturday for Andrewshek.

One lovely Saturday morning Andrewshek's Auntie Katushka took some butter and

[1] From Margery Clark (pseud.), *Poppy Seed Cakes* (Doubleday, 1929).

some sugar and some flour and some milk and seven eggs and she rolled out some nice little cakes. Then she sprinkled each cake with some of the poppy seeds which she had brought from the old country.

While the nice little cakes were baking, she spread out the fine feather bed on top of the big bed, for Andrewshek to take his nap. Andrewshek did not like to take a nap.

Andrewshek loved to bounce up and down and up and down on his fine feather bed.

Andrewshek's Auntie Katushka took the nice little cakes out of the oven and put them on the table to cool; then she put on her bright shawl to go to market. "Andrewshek," she said, "please watch these cakes while you rest on your fine feather bed. Be sure that the kitten and the dog do not go near them."

"Yes, indeed! I will watch the nice little cakes," said Andrewshek. "And I will be sure that the kitten and the dog do not touch them." But all Andrewshek really did was to bounce up and down and up and down on the fine feather bed.

"Andrewshek!" said Andrewshek's Auntie Katushka, "how can you watch the poppy seed cakes when all you do is bounce up and down and up and down on the fine feather bed?" Then Andrewshek's Auntie Katushka, in her bright shawl, hurried off to market.

But Andrewshek kept bouncing up and down and up and down on the fine feather bed and paid no attention to the little cakes sprinkled with poppy seeds.

Just as Andrewshek was bouncing up in the air for the ninth time, he heard a queer noise that sounded like "Hs-s-s-s-sss," at the front door of his house.

"Oh, what a queer noise!" cried Andrewshek. He jumped down off the fine feather bed and opened the front door. There stood a great green goose as big as Andrewshek himself. The goose was very cross and was scolding as fast as he could. He was wagging his head and was opening and closing his long red beak.

"What do you want?" said Andrewshek. "What are you scolding about?"

"I want all the goose feathers from your fine feather bed," quacked the big green goose. "They are mine."

"They are not yours," said Andrewshek. "My Auntie Katushka brought them with her from the old country in a huge bag."

"They are mine," quacked the big green goose. He waddled over to the fine feather bed and tugged at it with his long red beak.

"Stop, Green Goose!" said Andrewshek, "and I will give you one of Auntie Katushka's poppy seed cakes."

"A poppy seed cake!" the green goose quacked in delight. "I love nice little poppy seed cakes! Give me one and you shall have your feather bed."

But one poppy seed cake could not satisfy the greedy green goose.

"Give me another!" Andrewshek gave the green goose another poppy seed cake.

"Give me another!" the big green goose hissed and frightened Andrewshek nearly out of his wits.

Andrewshek gave him another and another and another till all the poppy seed cakes were gone.

Just as the last poppy seed cake disappeared down the long neck of the green goose, Andrewshek's Auntie Katushka appeared at the door, in her bright shawl. "Boo! hoo!" cried Andrewshek. "See! that naughty green goose has eaten all the poppy seed cakes."

"What? All my nice little poppy seed cakes?" cried Andrewshek's Auntie Katushka. "The naughty goose!"

The greedy goose tugged at the fine feather bed again with his long red beak and started to drag it to the door. Andrewshek's Auntie Katushka ran after the green goose and just then there was a dreadful explosion. The greedy goose who had stuffed himself with poppy seed cakes had burst and his feathers flew all over the room.

"Well! well!" said Andrewshek's Auntie Katushka, as she gathered up the pieces of the big green goose. "We soon shall have two fine feather pillows for your fine feather bed."

The Little Wooden Doll [2]

(A Selection)

MARGERY WILLIAMS BIANCO

An old-fashioned wooden doll lay forgotten in a dusty attic until her friends the mice rescued her and found a home for her. Mrs. Bianco told this story to her own little girl, Pamela. At the age of nine Pamela made the delicate drawings which illustrate the book. The first two chapters are given below.

The little wooden doll had lived so long in the attic that no one even knew she was there. Such a number of things get stored away in an attic: broken furniture and disused trunks, tattered books and old preserve jars that have lost their tops, and china that doesn't match — all the things that nobody wants are put up there, and there they stay, among the mice and the cobwebs, and are forgotten.

This attic was just like any other, inasmuch as no one living in the house below really knew what was in it. The little wooden doll lay in a corner, between an old pile of schoolbooks thick with dust and a broken bird cage, and she must have lain there a very long time, indeed, for she was not at all like the dolls that one may see nowadays. All about her the spiders spun their webs, and the little mice scampered to and fro over the attic floor, and there was a pleasant smell of dust and dry rot.

The little wooden doll was seldom lonely, for there was always someone to talk to. The mice in particular were great gossips; they knew all that went on in the house, for they ran everywhere. They knew where the nuts

2 From Margery Williams Bianco, *The Little Wooden Doll* (Macmillan, 1925).

were stored, and how many cakes the cook baked, and why the last lot of preserves went wrong. They knew, too, just where the store-closet key was, that the housewife had been hunting for high and low these past three weeks, for they had seen her put it there. Nothing happened that the mice did not know about; they were natural busybodies, and all their news they brought to the little doll.

The spiders, too, were good company, but they were inclined to be narrow-minded, and dwelt too much on their own affairs. The old, old spider, who had his web just over the doll's head, was a philosopher; he had poked into all the old books that lay on the attic floor, and for that he was considered eccentric. When he chose to talk he could be most interesting, but for the most part he was silent; he disliked chatter, and would shake with rage when the young spiders annoyed him. There was a rumor that he had been disappointed in love, but no one really knew the rights of it.

On summer days, when the sun shone, a beam of light came through the attic window. Golden dust motes danced in the beam, and it was beautiful to see. Sometimes, then, a bumblebee would blunder in, or a great, spotted butterfly, or sometimes a swallow would perch at the open window, and all these had news to bring of the outside world: of the cornfields and the flowers and the blue sky. And sometimes at night, when the moonlight lay on the attic floor, the mice would give parties, and to these the little wooden doll was always invited. Those were gay evenings. All the baby mice were allowed to sit up late, the crickets brought their fiddles to play the dance music, and even the old, fat spider up in the corner would stretch his legs and nod and become quite cheerful.

On the whole the little wooden doll had a pleasant life.

Only sometimes, toward dusk, when the mice were busied on their own affairs, when the spiders dozed in their hammocks, and only the little gray moths fluttered to and fro, a feeling of sadness came over her. For dolls are made for children, and deep in every doll's heart there is a longing to be loved by a child. And at times, when the rain beat on the shingles and the smell of wet earth came up through the attic window, something stirred in the little doll's memory. She recalled dimly a time when someone had really loved her, someone who had carried her about and put her to bed at night, and on rainy days like these played house with her on the nursery floor. It was so long ago that the little wooden doll could not remember very clearly, but she knew that these things had once happened, and she thought that if only some child would come again to the attic, and play with her, she would be quite happy.

But there were no children in the old house, and however eagerly the little doll listened, no one ever came up the attic stairs.

Still, she never quite lost hope. Sitting there in her corner, while the mice played about her, she would think, "Some day, perhaps, a little girl will come up here and find me, and then how pleased she will be!" And she made up a little story to herself of all the things they would do and the games they would play; playing house would be the nicest of all, for every doll loves playing house. She had forgotten what her own name used to be, it was so long ago, but she hoped that the little girl who found her might call her Rose, for that seemed to her the loveliest name in the world, and when she told the mice stories, on winter evenings, that was the name she always gave to the heroine.

Little Girl with Seven Names[3]

MABEL LEIGH HUNT

ᵉᵍ *A kindly and amusing story of a little Quaker girl who had seven names and of how she managed to give two of them away.*

CHAPTER I

There was once a little girl who had a name as long as that of any royal princess.

But she was not a princess.

[3] Complete text from Mabel Leigh Hunt, *Little Girl with Seven Names* (Lippincott, 1936).

She was just a little Quaker girl who lived with her father and mother on an American farm. There were freckles on her nose. A fat little, tight little braid peeped out from behind each ear. Pantalettes, as white as snow, twinkled below the hem of her skirts. And her eyes were the same color as the bluebells that bloomed in the wood just down the road.

As for her name, truly there were so many words in it that only one person ever called her by all of them. That was her Uncle Mark. And he did it just to tease.

When Uncle Mark came to the farmhouse, his little niece always ran to the door to greet him. For she loved him very much, and she thought that surely there could be no other uncle in all the world half so jolly.

And the moment that Uncle Mark clapped eyes on her, he would begin to behave in the strangest manner.

First he would work his arms up and down, limbering up his muscles. He would teeter up and down on his toes, too. Then he would take a very long, deep breath, as if he were getting ready to run a race. He would hold the breath in his mouth until both his big cheeks puffed out like round, red apples.

Then suddenly his cheeks would cave in, with a noise like *P-p-w-u-h!* His mouth would burst open, and out would come tumbling, so fast that all the names seemed to run together into one, the words that had made Uncle Mark's cheeks as fat as round, red apples.

"Good-day-to-thee, Melissa-Louisa-Amanda-Miranda-Cynthia-Jane-Farlow!"

Then he would sigh, fanning himself with his hat, and sink down into the nearest chair. Or he would stagger up against the wall, breathing hard, pretending to be completely worn out with all the work of saying Melissa Louisa's long, long name.

She would run to him with a drink of water, or of sweet cider. He would throw back his head, and swallow the drink in one huge gulp, and clear his throat, and slap his chest.

Then he and Melissa Louisa would burst out laughing. They would laugh and laugh and laugh! The joke was always the same. Yet neither one of them ever grew tired of it.

So that Melissa Louisa Amanda Miranda Cynthia Jane Farlow thought it was great fun to have such a long, long name.

John and Mary Farlow, who were the parents of this little Quaker maid, called her only Melissa Louisa. That was quite enough of a name for everyday use. For how funny it would have been — now wouldn't it? — for them to have said, "Blow thy nose, Melissa Louisa Amanda Miranda Cynthia Jane Farlow." Or, "Melissa Louisa Amanda Miranda Cynthia Jane Farlow, thee may feed the chickens."

But when she was born, they had given her all these names for a very special reason. For they had said, "Since this is the first little girl in the family, we shall name her for her two grandmothers and her four aunts. Then no one's feelings will be hurt, and everyone will be happy."

The two grandmothers and the four aunts were indeed very happy to have the new baby named for them. As she grew up, each one of them, and Uncle Mark, too, secretly thought that there was no child in all the world so dear as Melissa Louisa Amanda Miranda Cynthia Jane Farlow. But they were very careful not to show their love for her out-and-out, for they weren't going to have a child in *their* family with spoiled and unseemly manners.

So that in spite of having a father and a mother and two grandmothers and four aunts and an uncle and no brothers and sisters, nor even any cousins, Melissa Louisa was really quite a good little person.

CHAPTER II

It was from Grandmother Melissa Gray that Melissa Louisa got her first name.

Grandmother Gray was one of the dearest grandmothers a little girl ever had. You had to go around the bend of the road, through the covered bridge, past a crossroads, and over two hills before you reached Grandmother Gray's house. So that Melissa Louisa did not see her as often as she would have liked.

But on First Days, when everyone went to Meeting in the little white meeting-house, Grandmother Gray always managed to sit next to Melissa Louisa. She would hold the little girl's hand in her gentle warm one, and Melissa Louisa would lean her head against Grandmother Gray's soft silken shoulder, and sit as quietly as a mouse, even though her feet sometimes went to sleep.

And every First Day, during Meeting, when it was so still that one could have heard a pin drop, the little girl would begin to wonder what surprise lay hidden this time in the pocket of Grandmother Gray's full skirt. Although she tried with all her might not to think about it, and to send little prayers to the Lord, asking Him to help her to be a better girl, it just seemed that she couldn't ever keep from thinking of Grandmother's pocket.

So that by the time Meeting was over, and everyone was shaking hands, and greeting each other, Melissa Louisa was as hungry as a little bear. But she kept it to herself, and never said a word, for she had been taught to be mannerly.

Then Grandmother Gray would fumble among the folds of her silken skirt, until she found her pocket. And out would come a big brown cooky, or a stick of hoarhound candy, or a peppermint drop. She would hold out the sweet to Melissa Louisa and say, "This will stay thy hunger until thee gets thy dinner, Melissa."

She never bothered about any of the child's other names. The one name of *Melissa* was quite enough for Grandmother Melissa Gray.

Melissa Louisa got her second name from Grandmother Louisa Farlow.

She was a dear grandmother, too, but very different from Grandmother Gray. Her farm adjoined Melissa Louisa's father's farm, so that she lived only a short distance down the road, and Melissa Louisa saw her often. Grandmother Farlow thought that everyone should be good ALL of the time! And no matter how often she saw Melissa Louisa, she would say, "And has thee been a good girl, Louisa-child?"

Grandmother Louisa Farlow never called Melissa Louisa by any other name than *Louisa*.

Aunt Amanda and Aunt Miranda were twins. They lived with Grandmother Gray, for they were her daughters. Melissa Louisa loved them very much. They were slim and pretty, and cared a great deal how they looked when they went to Meeting, or to make calls.

Grandmother Farlow said that "it would be more seemly if Amanda and Miranda Gray spent less time stitching tucks into their petticoats, and more time preparing their souls for the hereafter."

But Melissa Louisa could not help feeling proud of her twin aunts when she saw how very sweet they looked in their dainty sprigged delaines or calicoes, and she thought that their curls peeped out from under their plain little bonnets in the prettiest way imaginable.

It was impossible to tell them apart, for they were as like as two sweet-pea blossoms. So that when Melissa Louisa saw Aunt Amanda, she would say, "Good day to thee, Aunt Amanda-Miranda."

And when she saw Aunt Miranda she would say, "Good day to thee, Aunt Amanda-Miranda."

For that was perfectly safe, as one of them was bound to be either Aunt Amanda or Aunt Miranda.

The dimples would dance in the pink cheeks of the twin aunts, and they would say, "Good day to *thee*, little Amanda Miranda."

It was nice to be named for two such charming aunts. Melissa Louisa wished that she had inherited their curls as well as their names.

Aunt Cynthia and Aunt Jane were Father's sisters, and they lived with Grandmother Farlow in the farmhouse just down the road.

Aunt Cynthia was tall and thin. She was very, very good. She was very, very serious. And she spent a great deal of time teaching Melissa Louisa how to sew, how to be mannerly and, above all, how to be GOOD.

For she said, "First thee must please the Lord. But I want my little namesake to be a credit to me, too."

Aunt Jane was short and stout, and very sensible. She liked to milk, and take care of the chickens and the baby animals on the farm. She could make the best butter and cheese of any woman in the countryside. She was also what people called "a natural-born nurse," so that she was away from home a great deal of the time, taking care of sick people.

Aunt Jane said, "Beween thee and me, child, the name of *Jane* would have been quite enough for thee. It would have suited thee, too. There aren't any fol-de-rols about *Jane*."

Melissa Louisa often wondered if she could ever be as good as Aunt Cynthia. Or as useful as Aunt Jane. She thought it a great honor to be named for them. But sometimes she felt a little worried for fear she would not grow up to be a credit to them.

All of which explains how Melissa Louisa Amanda Miranda Cynthia Jane Farlow happened to have so many names. Seven names she had — and she thought it was very nice until her first day at school.

CHAPTER III

Melissa Louisa had been looking forward to going to school for a long time. She could scarcely wait for the day to come.

But at last one morning her hair was brushed extra smooth, and pulled back into extra tight braids. She put on her starchy pink-and-white checkered pinafore. She took her new slate under her arm, and her lunch basket in her hand. She gave her mother a quick little kiss. Her father took her up behind him on his horse. They rode off to the schoolhouse, and he left her at the door.

She was scarcely a bit afraid. For Aunt Cynthia, in teaching her to be mannerly, had always said, "Thee must ever remember, dear child, that it is almost as rude to be too shy as to be over-bold. Therefore thee must always speak when thee is spoken to."

And then there was Anna Hadley, a nice big girl, who came and took her hand, and began at once to look after her.

Melissa Louisa felt very proud to be sitting there in the school-room, along with all the other new scholars, and with the older children, who had been going to school for a long time. Away in the back of the room there were boys almost as tall as her father. For in the little country schools of long ago, everyone, large and small, sat together in the one room.

Melissa Louisa thought that these big boys

and girls must have learned a great deal at school. But she said to herself that it would not be long until she had learned a great deal, too.

There was a new teacher. He stood up very tall by his desk, and read a chapter from the Bible. Then he said, "We shall now call the roll." And he took up his quill pen, and made ready to write down the names of all the children. "Each scholar," said the teacher, "must stand up, in turn, and give his or her full name."

The teacher began with the biggest boy, away over in the opposite corner from where Melissa Louisa sat. The children stood up by their desks, one by one, and told their names.

There was one girl who was shy of the new teacher. When it came her turn to tell her name, she hung her head and whispered, "Mary Ann." The teacher rapped on his desk quite crossly, and said in a loud tone, "Thy full name, please." The girl blushed, and hung her head a little lower, and said, in a voice that one could scarcely hear, "Scott." The teacher said, "It took thee a long time, Mary Ann Scott, to tell thy full name."

After that, the children knew for certain that the teacher would be cross if he was not promptly told every single name that one owned.

Each of the children had two names, of course. Some had three names. One boy had four names. When it came his turn, he rattled off, "Elbert Elijah Elihu Edwards."

But no one had seven names, as Melissa Louisa had, and underneath her checkered pinafore her heart began to beat like a little trip-hammer, as the time drew nearer and nearer for her to stand up and tell her full name.

At last the teacher looked straight at her.

Aunt Cynthia, and indeed all of the four aunts and the two grandmothers, and Uncle Mark, as well, would have been pleased could they have seen how bravely she stood up, and in what a clear, proud little voice she recited her name.

"Melissa Louisa Amanda Miranda Cynthia Jane Farlow," she said.

The teacher's eyes widened in surprise.

His eyebrows went up. And at that all of the scholars laughed! Some of them giggled, and some of them, especially the big boys, simply shouted!

For a moment Melissa Louisa didn't know what had happened. Had one of her braids turned into a fire-cracker, and exploded just behind her ear, she could not have been more surprised.

Slowly she sank into her seat, her face and neck growing pinker and pinker until she was as pink as her pink pinafore.

The whole school had laughed at her!

And suddenly she wanted to cry, and run home to her mother, and never, never come back to school again. Oh, dear — oh, dear! To think how long she had been wanting to start to school, and now it wasn't nice after all! It was horrid!

The new teacher saw the tears in Melissa Louisa's eyes.

He rapped on his desk. "Silence!" he thundered, and he looked sternly at all of the children. "There is no reason for laughing," he said. "This child was given a name by her parents, and who are you to question the wisdom of your elders?"

He paused, and looked down at the ledger, where he had written Melissa Louisa's full name. "Seven names," said the teacher, "are no more funny than two. And that is not funny at all."

"Now, child," he said, looking kindly down at Melissa Louisa, "by what name is thee called at home?"

There was such a big lump in Melissa Louisa's throat that she could not speak.

Anna Hadley came to the rescue. She raised her hand. "Please, Teacher," she said, "they call her Melissa Louisa."

"Very well," said the teacher. "Next," and he called on the child who sat behind Melissa Louisa.

At recess a hateful boy called over from the boys' side of the playground, "Hello, thee little Melissa Louisa Amanda Miranda Cynthy Jane Mary Patty Polly Susan Rebecca!"

"Never thee mind, honey," said Anna Hadley. "See what I'm doing!"

Melissa Louisa looked up at Anna. She was wrinkling up her nose, making an ugly face at the bad boy. Her tongue stuck away out.

It made Melissa Louisa laugh. She stuck out her tongue, too, but it only came out a tiny bit. Because she happened to remember, just in time, what Grandmother Farlow and Aunt Cynthia would have thought if they could have seen her sticking out her tongue at anybody.

But she felt better, and she skipped into the schoolhouse, holding tight to Anna Hadley's hand.

At home that evening, Mother and Father wanted to know how their little daughter liked school. "I didn't like it much," she said, in a small voice. But she was ashamed to tell what had happened to cause her so much disappointment.

The next time that Uncle Mark came, Melissa Louisa laughed with him again over her name, and *pretended* to think that his "monkey-shines" were just as funny as ever. For Aunt Cynthia had taught her to be kind and polite, and she thought that Uncle Mark would be hurt if she did not laugh as usual. But it was only her face that laughed, and not her heart.

Uncle Mark's joke never again seemed very funny to Melissa Louisa. Never after the day the children laughed at her long, long name.

But of course she had to go to school, whether she liked it or not.

Melissa Louisa thought a great deal about it all. She wished that Father and Mother had not named her for so many people. And she wished that there was someone to whom she might give at least two of her names. Just giving one away would not make enough difference.

But it would never, never do to hurt the feelings of her two grandmothers and her four aunts. Moreover, how could a person give away such a fastened-on thing as a name? It would be almost like giving away one of her braids.

CHAPTER IV

Melissa Louisa had a doll named Ida.

She had a cat named John Doe.

She was very fond of both of them. But sometimes she felt as if she must shake Ida, because she would never answer, although

Melissa Louisa talked to her by the hour, and she was quite sure that the doll heard every word she said.

When she complained about it to Uncle Mark, he said, "It does seem as if Ida will never be a chatterbox. She's a doll of few words, there's no doubt about that. But thee must remember she is a Quaker doll, and Quakers are given to meditation." Melissa Louisa knew all about what *that* meant, and she felt more patient with Ida, for there was no telling what deep thoughts were going on in her child's head.

John Doe, the cat, was a fellow who did just as he pleased. When he wanted to be fed, or petted, he would rub his smooth, furry cheek against Melissa Louisa's ankle, and he would purr as loud as could be, with his tail high over his back, oh, so friendly!

Or when he wanted to be lazy, he would lie soft and limp and cuddly in his mistress' lap.

But let him take a sudden notion, and down he would jump! He would stretch himself, and sharpen his claws on the doorstep. Then off he would go on some secret errand of his own, and no amount of coaxing would bring him back until he was good-and-ready.

Melissa Louisa often said to herself, "If I only had a twin, like Aunt Amanda and Aunt Miranda!" For if she had a twin to play with, she would not have to depend altogether on Ida and John Doe for her fun.

There were no children living near. On one side of her father's farm there was Grandmother Farlow's farm. And on the other side there was Daniel and Susan Wheeler, a young married couple who had no children.

So that Melissa Louisa was sometimes a bit lonely. And since it was now too late to be a twin, she always remembered, when she sat in Meeting, or when she said her prayers at night, to ask the Lord to send her a baby brother or a baby sister.

For there was nothing in the world that Melissa Louisa admired as much as babies. She loved them much better than dolls, or cats. In fact, she like them better than she did children her own age, and when she went to make calls with her mother, if there was a baby in the house, she paid very little atten-

tion to the older brothers and sisters. She would kneel before this tiny one, hiding her face behind her hands to make the baby laugh. Or she would let it pull her braids, or pound her with its chubby fists. Sometimes she would be allowed to hold it carefully on her lap.

Her mother said, "Melissa Louisa seems to have a real *knack* with babies. She's just that much like her Aunt Jane."

One day Melissa Louisa's father came into the house. There was a wide smile on his face. "I was just talking to Dan Wheeler down by the pasture fence," he said, "and thee can't guess, Melissa Louisa, what came to their house last night."

Melissa Louisa ran over and stood at her father's knee. "Was it a little baby calf?" she asked.

"No," said Father.

"Was it a little baby colt?"

"No. Something better than a baby colt. Much, much better."

"Oh, Father!" cried Melissa Louisa, and her eyes began to shine like stars. "Was it a real little baby?"

"Yes," said Father, "it was a real little baby."

"May we go and see it?" asked Melissa Louisa, and she began to hop around on one foot.

"Yes," said Father, "Dan said for thee and thy mother to come over tomorrow and see the new baby."

Melissa Louisa thought that she could never wait for tomorrow to come. She went to bed extra early so that the next day would come more quickly. She lay there thinking what fun it would be to have a baby living just down the road.

"I wonder what they will name it," she said to herself.

And suddenly such a surprising thought came to her that she jumped right out of bed, and stood in the middle of the room in her little nightgown. The new thought caused her heart to beat as hard as if she had been running. "Goodness gracious *ever!*" whispered Melissa Louisa, and she gave a hop and skip and a jump into a little patch of moonlight that fell through the window.

But presently she climbed slowly into her

bed again, for she thought that this was something that she had better keep to herself.

"Yes, I shall ask Susan Wheeler if I may give the new baby two of my names," she whispered to Ida, who shared her pillow. "I shall ask her tomorrow, when I go over there."

"But which ones shall I give away? I can't give away *Melissa* or *Louisa* because they belong to me truly-truly. They belong to me more than any of my other names. And besides, it would never do to hurt the feelings of dear Grandmother Melissa Gray, or of dear Grandmother Louisa Farlow. And that would surely happen if I gave away *Melissa Louisa*."

But Ida was not a bit of help. Perhaps she knew, in her quiet little head, that it is seldom wise to give advice, for she never said a word. So Melissa Louisa had to do all the thinking for herself.

"*Amanda Miranda*. Oh, dear, they are the prettiest names I have! Why, they're almost like poetry!"

Amanda
Miranda.

Yes, they made a tiny, perfect poem.

"Look here, Ida," whispered Melissa Louisa, "if thee had a little poem in thy name, could thee bear to give it away to a perfect stranger? I just know thee couldn't!"

The names she gave away would have to be *Cynthia Jane*, then. She began to think of herself without them, and how she would stand up at school next fall and say that now her name had only five words in it, instead of seven. Surely no one would laugh at her then!

"Melissa Louisa Amanda Miranda — Farlow," she whispered, and for a moment she felt almost as queer as if someone had cut off one of her braids.

But what would Aunt Cynthia think?

What would Aunt Jane think?

Melissa Louisa tossed and turned on her little bed.

"I know! I shall make Aunt Cynthia the very nicest sampler I can make, to let her know that I love her just as much as ever."

Into the sampler she would set her very neatest stitches, those same neat stitches that

Aunt Cynthia had taught her to make. Her A B C's would march along as straight as soldiers. "And I shall make a basket full of apples, red and pink and blue. And all around the sampler there will run a little green vine, for a border." How many, many stitches it would take to make that border! But when it was finished, it would look as if the little green vine had grown around the sampler with magic speed, and caught its own little green tail in its own little green mouth.

"Now what shall I say on the sampler?"

Into Melissa Louisa's head popped the words that she would stitch into the sampler — the beautiful sampler that was to be a peace-offering to Aunt Cynthia.

"The Lord loveth a cheerful giver."

That would be just right! Melissa Louisa sighed with happiness to think it was all settled so nicely.

Now what could she do for Aunt Jane? Melissa Louisa stretched and yawned and rubbed her eyes. Before she could decide anything more, she had fallen fast asleep.

CHAPTER V

The next day was Saturday. There was no school. A light snow lay on the ground. Melissa Louisa stretched and yawned and warmest wraps. They walked down the road, past the wood, and in at the front gate of the Wheeler place, where the new baby had come to live.

The baby was tiny and red and wrinkled. When Melissa Louisa touched its velvety cheek ever so gently with her finger, it squirmed and made a funny face. But she thought it was as dear as could be, and at once she loved it with all her heart.

Now was the time! Her heart beat a little faster. She looked straight at Susan Wheeler, and said, "What was thee going to name her?"

"Her!" echoed Susan, and she laughed. "It's a boy, Melissa Louisa."

A BOY! Melissa Louisa's heart sank. After all her careful plans last night! *Cynthia Jane* would never do for a boy, of course. Oh, dear, she would have to keep her seven names all her life! She would always have to be Melissa Louisa Amanda Miranda Cynthia Jane Farlow! For a moment she was so disappointed that she wanted to cry. Only of course crying did no good.

"We're going to call the baby Tobiah for Dan's father," said Susan. "And thee must come over and see him often, Melissa Louisa. When he gets a little older, thee can play with him, and help me take care of him."

"May I really and truly help?" asked Melissa Louisa, her eyes shining.

"Of course thee may," answered Susan.

After that, Ida grew more quiet than ever, for there was no one to talk to her. What with school, and the new little one at the Wheelers', it seemed as if Melissa Louisa was away from home a great deal of the time. Poor Ida sat in the same position in a corner of the sofa for days and days.

And John Doe, in spite of being such an independent fellow, sometimes went mewing about the house, lonesome for Melissa Louisa.

For nearly every day, especially as spring came on, she stopped after school to see little Tobiah Wheeler. And when summer came, and there was no school, she went more and more often to play with him.

They called him Toby for short, and as he grew fatter and fatter, they sometimes called him Toby Jug.

Toby was always glad to see Melissa Louisa. And she really did help very much in taking care of him, so that Toby's mother was just as glad to see her little neighbor as Toby was. For she was a farmer's wife, and had a great deal to keep her busy.

"I declare, child," said Susan Wheeler, "I don't know what the baby and I would do without thee. Thee is a regular little mother —that's what thee is! Toby thinks as much of thee as he does of me, I do believe. I guess I'll just have to give him to thee."

Melissa Louisa's mouth fell open. "Give him to me! Thee means for keeps, Susan?"

Susan laughed. "Thee will just have to take Toby home with thee some day, and have him for thy baby. I reckon thee'd like that, wouldn't thee?"

Melissa Louisa laughed, too, for sheer joy. "Oh-h, thee knows I would, Susan!"

She squeezed Toby Jug so hard that he squealed and grabbed one of her braids. He pulled and pulled, until she squealed, too, and had to pry her braid out of his tight, fat fist.

When it came time to go home, Melissa Louisa said, "May I take Toby home with me now, Susan?"

"We-ell, perhaps not this time, honey. Perhaps thee'd better ask thy mother first," and Susan laughed again. "Maybe thy mother wouldn't want to bother with such a fat rascal as Toby Jug."

Melissa Louisa's small Quaker feet danced all the way home. To have dear little Toby Jug for her very own!

But she wouldn't tell Mother. It would be such a lovely surprise. She felt very sure that Mother would be delighted to have Toby come and live with them. For now vacation was about over. Soon school would begin again, and Toby would be such company for Mother, for he was almost seven months old now, and he could say "Mum-mum," which meant "Mother."

No, Melissa Louisa would keep this exciting surprise until the time came when she actually carried Toby into the house, to keep for her very own.

CHAPTER VI

The next time that Melissa Louisa went to see Toby his mother said, "Oh, Melissa Louisa, I'm so glad that thee is here! I want to go up into the hill pasture and pick the blackberries. They will go to waste if I don't gather them soon. Will thee take care of Toby while I am gone? I shall be back in a couple of hours, I think."

Melissa Louisa felt very proud at the thought of being left in sole charge of the baby. Just like a grown-up! She listened carefully to all of Susan's directions, and she and Toby waved farewell from the kitchen door.

Susan had been gone only a little while when Melissa Louisa began to feel a bit lonesome. Just the wee-est bit scared in the quiet house, even with Toby there. The very chairs and tables seemed suddenly to be full of strange secrets. The slow *tick-tock* of the grandfather clock was louder than she had ever heard it. Her eyes grew bigger and bigger, and she wished that she were at home with her own mother. And there was Toby, with his mouth crumpling up, as if he were going to cry, if only he had reason enough.

All at once Melissa Louisa said to herself, "Now would be a good time to take Toby home with me, for keeps." And at once she felt as happy as a bird.

Yes, the time had come to give Mother the great surprise. Melissa Louisa's eyes danced as she thought how pleased Mother would be to have a real live baby in the house.

Susan would be surprised, too, when she returned from berry-picking, and found Toby gone. But Susan was so busy with the farm work and the baby to care for. How glad she would be to have him looked after and loved by her good neighbors! Besides, hadn't Susan as good as promised that she, Melissa Louisa, might carry Toby home with her one day?

"Does thee want to go abroad, darling Toby Jug?" she asked.

The baby held up his arms, and crowed.

Melissa Louisa began to gather up a few of his belongings. She could come back tomorrow and get all of his things.

Then she picked him up, and went out of the house, closing the door carefully behind her.

Melissa Louisa walked down the dusty road, carrying the baby. Quite often she had to set him down on the grass and rest herself, for he was as fat as butter, and seemed to grow heavier with every step she took. It was very hot, and it seemed to her as if she would never reach home.

Toby had a wonderful time. He had not been out in the world many times, and this was a great treat for him. He pointed, with his funny, fat finger. He talked, in his funny baby language. He jumped up and down in Melissa Louisa's arms until she was afraid that she would drop him.

When they came to the wood, she decided that she must stop here in the shade until she was really rested.

Toby liked that, too. He crept about in the grass there by the roadside, picking up bits of twigs or tiny pebbles, holding them up proudly for Melissa Louisa to see.

Presently, like John Doe in his friendly moments, Toby climbed into Melissa Louisa's lap. In just a moment he had fallen asleep.

Melissa Louisa was tired enough to sleep, too. But she struggled to her feet, and set forth again. This time Toby was as heavy as lead.

At last she reached home. It was hard to go tiptoeing into the house with such a heavy load in her arms. But tiptoe she did, so that the surprise would be more sudden for Mother.

But Mother was nowhere to be seen. Melissa Louisa guessed that she must be in the hen-house, or out in the barn, gathering the eggs. Very well, she would carry the sleeping baby into her own room. She would put him down on her own soft little bed. She would keep Toby's coming a secret until he woke up. She giggled a little to think how surprised dear Mother would be when she saw Toby, all rosy and fresh after his nap.

Melissa Louisa's room was dark and cool and quiet. She put Toby down in the middle of her bed. My, what a relief! How tired she was! Her arms were quite numb. But how comfortable Toby looked! Melissa Louisa's mouth opened in a wide, pink yawn. Why not lie down beside him and rest herself? Then, when Toby awakened in a strange room he would not be frightened. She climbed up on the bed.

There they lay, she and Toby, fast asleep.

The next thing that she knew was the sound of her mother's voice, calling her to supper. She sat up. There was Mother standing in the doorway.

"My, but that was a long nap!" said Mother. "I guess thee was completely tuckered out carrying the baby all that distance through the heat."

Mother knew about the surprise, then. What a shame she had been asleep when Mother discovered Toby! She looked down at the bed.

Toby was not there.

"Wasn't thee surprised, Mother?" she asked, and the dimples twinkled in her cheeks. "Where's Toby now?"

"His mother came and got him about an hour ago," answered Mother. "You were both asleep here together. Susan didn't know what to think when she came back from berry-picking and found Toby gone. Thee should not have frightened her that way, child."

Melissa Louisa stared. "Susan came and took the baby away? Why, Mother, he's *mine!* Susan said that I could have him, Mother!"

"She was just joking, child, of course. No mother is going to give her baby away to anybody. Come to supper now."

But Melissa Louisa wouldn't come to supper. She flung herself face down on the bed. She sobbed as if her heart would break.

"S-S-Susan said that I c-c-could have him for k-k-keeps," she wailed. "And, oh-h-h, it was to b-be such a g-g-good surprise for thee, Mother. Oh — oh-h-h!"

It took Father and Mother both a long time to quiet their little daughter. They had to explain over and over that Susan was just teasing when she said that Melissa Louisa could have Toby for her very own. They told her that mothers loved their own babies better than anything in the world. They said that it would be very strange, nay, downright wicked of Susan, to give her baby away, even to Melissa Louisa, who loved him so much.

"Just think," they said, "how very, very lonely Daniel and Susan would be without dear little Toby Jug!"

At last Melissa Louisa stopped crying.

Her mother bathed her reddened eyelids, and her swollen nose. She washed the dirty streaks off her cheeks where the tears had run down. She brushed her tumbled hair, and they all sat down to supper.

Uncle Mark came in while they were at the table. For once he did not play his joke about Melissa Louisa's name.

For although he was very polite, and pretended not to notice, he could see by his niece's red eyes and swollen nose, that she had been crying, and that she was in no mood for jokes of any kind whatsoever.

After supper he took her for a fast gallop on his horse. They rode a long way. At last they came to a crossroads store.

Uncle Mark got off his horse, and tied it to a post. He went into the store. And in no time at all he was back again. In two fingers he held a little sugar dove. It was as white and sparkling as hoar frost. It was really almost too pretty to eat.

"This is for a little girl who has a father and a mother and two grandmothers and four aunts and a *nuncle!*" said Uncle Mark.

"That's me," said Melissa Louisa, and she gave the sugar dove a tiny lick with her tongue.

She felt much, much better.

CHAPTER VII

"Well, Melissa Louisa," said Father one morning, "does thee know that school begins in three days?"

"Will there be the same teacher as last year, Father?"

"No, he's going to teach over in town," answered Father. "So there will be a new teacher again this year."

"Oh, dear," thought Melissa Louisa to herself, "the new teacher will have us stand up and say our full names, and all the scholars will laugh at mine, like they did last year.

"Father, I don't believe I want to go to school this year," she said. "Couldn't I just stay at home with thee and Mother all the time?"

"And grow up to be a know-nothing?" cried Father. He looked horrified at the very thought. "Of course thee must go to school. Thee'll like it better this year, I'll just warrant.

"And I'll tell thee what, Daughter — thee's going to have a treat before thee starts to school. Daniel Wheeler's little niece is visiting over there, and they want thee to come over just as soon as thee can get ready, and stay all day, and all night to-night!"

Melissa Louisa had never stayed away from home all night before. She thought it would be fun to go, to play with Toby and Mary Wheeler, and to share Mary's bed at night.

So she put on a clean dress. She tucked her little nightgown and Ida under her arm. She kissed her mother good-bye, and set off for the visit, as happy as could be.

And she did have such a good time that she almost forgot her dread of starting to school. Toby had never been so cunning, and Mary was a very nice little girl, with just the kind of curls that Melissa Louisa most admired. She was scarcely a bit homesick when bedtime came, and she and Mary went to sleep right in the middle of a spell of giggles. She was sorry to say farewell when Father came on horseback the next day to take her home again.

"There is a surprise awaiting thee at home, Daughter," said Father, as they rode along.

"Oh! What it is?" cried Melissa Louisa, and she hugged her father around the waist as tight as she could.

"It won't be a surprise if I tell thee. Now, just bide thy time, and thee shall soon know."

"Do hurry, Father. I can't wait to see the surprise," cried Melissa Louisa. Her braids flew up and thumped the top of her head as she gave an extra bounce or two.

Father made the horse go like the wind. How they flew!

When they reached home, Father lifted Melissa Louisa down. He hitched the horse to the elm tree. He took his daughter's hand, and they went into the house.

There was Grandmother Gray in the kitchen. But Father said, "No, Grandmother Gray is not the surprise," and he kept tight hold of Melissa Louisa's hand. He led her straight into Mother's bedroom.

Mother was lying in the big feather bed.

Father drew Melissa Louisa near, and pulled down the covers.

"Oh-h-h-h-h!" whispered Melissa Louisa. "A *baby*! Is it ours?"

"Yes," said Mother, smiling, "it is ours."

Father led Melissa Louisa around to the other side of the bed, and folded back the covers.

"Oh-h-h-h-h-h-h-h!" whispered Melissa Louisa. Her eyes grew rounder and rounder. She stood on tiptoe and peeped over to the other side of the bed, where she had been a moment ago. On *that* side there was a baby, and on *this* side there was a baby! They were just alike.

"Father! Mother!" she cried, with her eyes almost popping out. "Are there *two* babies?"

"Yes," said Father, "twin girls!"

"Two twins!" gasped Melissa Louisa. It was hard to believe. "May we keep them both, Mother, really and truly? Nobody will come and take them away?"

"No, child," answered Mother, softly, "the Lord has given them to us, to love and to cherish."

Melissa Louisa hung over the bed, trembling with wonder and delight. "Oh, Mother, they are the most beautiful babies that ever were born. I've been asking the Lord to send us a baby for a long time, Father. But I didn't know that He would be so — oh, so *good* about it!"

"The next thing will be finding names for them," said Father.

"Yes," agreed Mother, "we shall all have to be thinking up some nice names for our twin girls."

"Names!" echoed Melissa Louisa. She stared at her father and mother. Her heart began to thump faster than ever.

"Oh, Mother," she cried, "may I name the babies? Please, Father, let me. All by myself!"

Father and Mother smiled at each other. "If thee will choose suitable names, thee may," said Mother. "And remember that twins are generally given names that are somewhat alike."

"Wait a minute, please," said Melissa Louisa.

She dashed from the room, and out of the house. She stood under the big lilac bush, with her fingers over her eyes, thinking very, very hard. Now or never — which should it be?

Why, of course, there was only one answer!

Melissa Louisa prayed a little prayer. "Dear Lord, let Mother and Father like the names I choose. Amen."

She ran back into the bedroom. Yes, the babies were still there, tiny and adorable. Melissa Louisa looked quite pale as she stood by the bed. She took a long breath.

"It didn't take me long to decide," she gasped. "Because, oh, Mother! Oh, Father! I want to give the babies two of *my* names. I want to name them Amanda and Miranda! Don't you see — they're the suitablest names, 'cause they're alike, just like the twins are alike. Oh, Mother! Oh, Father! Please!" Melissa Louisa clasped her hands, and looked from one to the other of her parents.

Father rubbed his chin, thinking. "What does thee say, Mother?" he asked.

"No doubt it would please their Aunt Amanda and Aunt Miranda," murmured Mother. "But, child, doesn't thee mind giving up part of thy own name?"

"Oh, NO, Mother, I'd love to!" cried Melissa Louisa. "I have plenty of names left, all that I shall need forever and ever! And everyone will be happy. Aunt Amanda and Aunt Miranda will be happy. And Aunt Cynthia's and Aunt Jane's feelings won't be hurt. And I won't have to make the sampler!" Melissa Louisa was quite out of breath.

"I don't know what thee is talking about, child, I'm sure," said Mother. "Better calm thyself. We shall name the twins Amanda and Miranda."

"Then that's settled," said Father.

"Yes, that's settled," said Melissa Louisa, and she hopped softly about the room on one foot, full of the greatest joy.

Just then they heard Uncle Mark coming into the house.

Melissa Louisa ran out to meet him. She wanted to be the first to tell him the wonderful and surprising news that now, just since yesterday, she had twin sisters.

When Uncle Mark saw his niece flying toward him, he took a great, deep breath as if he were getting ready to run a race. His cheeks puffed out like fat, red apples. Then the words came tumbling out. "Good-day-to-thee, Melissa-Louisa-Aman —— "

But he got no further, because Melissa Louisa cried out, "Stop! Stop, Uncle Mark!"

And she ran over to him and pulled him down, and clapped her hand over his mouth.

"Thee can't say that any more, Uncle Mark. Never, never any more! I gave away 'Amanda' and 'Miranda' — both of them. Just come and see who has my names now," and she led Uncle Mark proudly into the bedroom.

"See?" she said, pointing. "*There* is Amanda. And *there* is Miranda — two twins!"

No one could have been more surprised than Uncle Mark. "Whew!" he whistled. "Now, whoever heard of the like?" He turned and looked at Melissa Louisa.

"It's too bad I can't tease thee any more. But I think it's pretty nice of thee to give the new babies part of thy name."

"Well," said Melissa Louisa, "I would have minded giving away 'Amanda' and 'Miranda' to strangers. But I was glad to give them to my own dear sisters — thee doesn't know how glad!

"So it wasn't so 'speshly nice of me, 'cause I've been wanting to give *something* away for a long time. But, anyhow, I gave them the prettiest names I had, and — 'The Lord loveth a cheerful giver.' That's what the Bible says. And I do feel very cheerful, Uncle Mark."

"Goodness, child!" said Mother, and a little worry frown puckered her forehead. "She's been saying the strangest things, Mark. This has all been too exciting for her. Come here, child. Let's see if thee is a little feverish."

But Uncle Mark tossed Melissa Louisa up in his arms. He threw back his head and laughed. He laughed so loud that Grandmother Gray came hurrying in from the kitchen.

"Sh-sh-sh! Mark! Thee will frighten the twins out of their wits with thy great laughter."

Uncle Mark stopped laughing until there was nothing left but chuckles and grins. And he said, "Come, thee little cheerful giver, let's go outdoors and celebrate."

He stood Melissa Louisa up on a chair, and he turned his back to her. She put her arms around his neck. He tucked her feet under his elbows, and away he galloped out of the house.

All over the yard, through the barn lot, galloped Uncle Mark, with Melissa Louisa on his back. He pranced. He cavorted. He snorted. He shied and be bucked. He whinnied and he squealed.

Melissa Louisa laughed and laughed. She laughed until her arms grew weak and she could not hold tight to Uncle Mark any longer. She slipped down and down, until at last she slipped off, and tumbled into a pile of leaves.

It was a jolly celebration.

Chapter VIII

The next day Melissa Louisa went to school. It was the first day. She could scarcely bear to leave the little Amanda, and the little Miranda. She flew back twice to kiss their downy heads. Yet she was eager to see the new teacher, too, and for school to take up.

The new teacher read a chapter from the Bible.

Then he said, "We shall now call the roll. Every one will please stand up, each one in turn, and tell me his or her full name."

Melissa Louisa's heart began to beat like a little trip-hammer. She was the very first one the teacher called upon. She stood up by her desk, and spoke in a clear, proud, and happy little voice.

"I don't have as many names as I used to have," she said, "'cause now we have twins at our house. My full name is Melissa Louisa Am — Cynthia Jane Farlow."

And this time not a single scholar laughed! Melissa Louisa felt so happy that it seemed as if she must burst.

"School is going to be nice," she whispered to herself, "very, VERY nice!"

After school Melissa Louisa hurried home as fast as she could. She was quite out of breath when she arrived.

"Oh, Mother," she cried, "I *like* school!"

There were the babies, side by side, in Melissa Louisa's old cradle.

She hung over them, loving them with all her heart.

"Oh, my dear twin sisters Amanda and Miranda," whispered Melissa Louisa, "you came just in the nick of time!"

Little House in the Big Woods

Summertime[4]

LAURA INGALLS WILDER

In Little House in the Big Woods, *the author tells of her early childhood in a log cabin on the edge of the Big Woods in Wisconsin, for she is little Laura in the story. In those pioneer days, each family, living miles from a settlement, was of necessity self-sufficient. Each season brought its special work. In the following chapter, we read of the daily doings that made up life in the summertime.*

[4] From Laura Ingalls Wilder, *Little House in the Big Woods* (Harper, 1932).

Now it was summertime, and people went visiting. Sometimes Uncle Henry, or Uncle George, or Grandpa, came riding out of the Big Woods to see Pa. Ma would come to the door and ask how all the folks were, and she would say:

"Charles is in the clearing."

Then she would cook more dinner than usual, and dinnertime would be longer. Pa and Ma and the visitor would sit talking a little while before they went back to work.

Sometimes Ma let Laura and Mary go across the road and down the hill, to see Mrs. Peterson. The Petersons had just moved in. Their house was new, and always very neat, because Mrs. Peterson had no little girls to muss it up. She was a Swede, and she let Laura and Mary look at the pretty things she had brought from Sweden — laces, and colored embroideries, and china.

Mrs. Peterson talked Swedish to them, and they talked English to her, and they understood each other perfectly. She always gave them each a cooky when they left, and they nibbled the cookies very slowly while they walked home.

Laura nibbled away exactly half of hers, and Mary nibbled exactly half of hers, and the other halves they saved for Baby Carrie. Then when they got home, Carrie had two half-cookies, and that was a whole cooky.

This wasn't right. All they wanted to do was to divide the cookies fairly with Carrie. Still, if Mary saved half her cooky, while Laura ate the whole of hers, or if Laura saved half, and Mary ate her whole cooky, that wouldn't be fair, either.

They didn't know what to do. So each saved half, and gave it to Baby Carrie. But they always felt that somehow that wasn't quite fair.

Sometimes a neighbor sent word that the family was coming to spend the day. Then Ma did extra cleaning and cooking, and opened the package of store sugar. And on the day set, a wagon would come driving up to the gate in the morning and there would be strange children to play with.

When Mr. and Mrs. Huleatt came, they brought Eva and Clarence with them. Eva was a pretty girl, with dark eyes and black curls. She played carefully and kept her dress clean and smooth. Mary liked that, but Laura liked better to play with Clarence.

Clarence was red-headed and freckled, and always laughing. His clothes were pretty, too. He wore a blue suit buttoned all the way up the front with bright gilt buttons, and trimmed with braid, and he had copper-toed shoes.

The strips of copper across the toes were so glittering bright that Laura wished she were a boy. Little girls didn't wear copper-toes.

Laura and Clarence ran and shouted and climbed trees, while Mary and Eva walked nicely together and talked. Ma and Mrs. Huleatt visited and looked at a *Godey's Lady's Book* which Mrs. Huleatt had brought, and Pa and Mr. Huleatt looked at the horses and the crops and smoked their pipes.

Once Aunt Lotty came to spend the day. That morning Laura had to stand still a long time while Ma unwound her hair from the cloth strings and combed it into long curls. Mary was all ready, sitting primly on a chair, with her golden curls shining and her china-blue dress fresh and crisp.

Laura liked her own red dress. But Ma pulled her hair dreadfully, and it was brown instead of golden, so that no one noticed it. Everyone noticed and admired Mary's.

"There!" Ma said at last. "Your hair is curled beautifully, and Lotty is coming. Run meet her, both of you, and ask her which she likes best, brown curls or golden curls."

Laura and Mary ran out of the door and down the path, for Aunt Lotty was already at the gate. Aunt Lotty was a big girl, much taller than Mary. Her dress was a beautiful pink and she was swinging a pink sunbonnet by one string.

"Which do you like best, Aunt Lotty," Mary asked, "brown curls, or golden curls?" Ma had told them to ask that, and Mary was a very good little girl who always did exactly as she was told.

Laura waited to hear what Aunt Lotty would say, and she felt miserable.

"I like both kinds best," Aunt Lotty said, smiling. She took Laura and Mary by the hand, one on either side, and they danced along to the door where Ma stood.

The sunshine came streaming through the windows into the house, and everything was so neat and pretty. The table was covered with a red cloth, and the cookstove was polished shining black. Through the bedroom door Laura could see the trundle bed in its place under the big bed. The pantry door stood wide open, giving the sight and smell of goodies on the shelves, and Black Susan came purring down the stairs from the attic, where she had been taking a nap.

It was all so pleasant, and Laura felt so gay and good that no one would ever have thought she could be as naughty as she was that evening.

Aunt Lotty had gone, and Laura and Mary were tired and cross. They were at the wood-pile, gathering a pan of chips to kindle the fire in the morning. They always hated to pick up chips, but every day they had to do it. Tonight they hated it more than ever.

Laura grabbed the biggest chip, and Mary said:

"I don't care. Aunt Lotty likes my hair best, anyway. Golden hair is lots prettier than brown."

Laura's throat swelled tight, and she could not speak. She knew golden hair was prettier than brown. She couldn't speak, so she reached out quickly and slapped Mary's face.

Then she heard Pa say, "Come here, Laura."

She went slowly, dragging her feet. Pa was sitting just inside the door. He had seen her slap Mary.

"You remember," Pa said, "I told you girls you must never strike each other."

Laura began, "But Mary said —— "

"That makes no difference," said Pa. "It is what I say that you must mind."

Then he took down a strap from the wall, and he whipped Laura with the strap.

Laura sat on a chair in the corner and sobbed. When she stopped sobbing, she sulked. The only thing in the whole world to be glad about was that Mary had to fill the chip pan all by herself.

At last, when it was getting dark, Pa said again, "Come here, Laura." His voice was kind, and when Laura came he took her on his knee and hugged her close. She sat in the crook of his arm, her head against his shoulder and his long brown whiskers partly covering her eyes, and everything was all right again.

She told Pa all about it, and she asked him, "You don't like golden hair better than brown, do you?"

Pa's blue eyes shone down at her, and he said, "Well, Laura, my hair is brown."

She had not thought of that. Pa's hair was brown, and his whiskers were brown, and she thought brown was a lovely color. But she was glad that Mary had had to gather all the chips.

In the summer evenings Pa did not tell stories or play the fiddle. Summer days were long, and he was tired after he had worked hard all day in the fields.

Ma was busy, too. Laura and Mary helped her weed the garden, and they helped her feed the calves and the hens. They gathered the eggs, and they helped make cheese.

When the grass was tall and thick in the woods and the cows were giving plenty of milk, that was the time to make cheese.

Somebody must kill a calf, for cheese could not be made without rennet, and rennet is the lining of a young calf's stomach. The calf must be very young, so that it had never eaten anything but milk.

Laura was afraid that Pa must kill one of the little calves in the barn. They were so sweet. One was fawn-colored and one was red, and their hair was so soft and their large eyes so wondering. Laura's heart beat fast when Ma talked to Pa about making cheese.

Pa would not kill either of his calves, because they were heifers and would grow into cows. He went to Grandpa's and to Uncle Henry's, to talk about the cheese-making, and Uncle Henry said he would kill one of his calves. There would be enough rennet for Aunt Polly and Grandma and Ma.

So Pa went again to Uncle Henry's, and came back with a piece of the little calf's stomach. It was like a piece of soft, grayish-white leather, all ridged and rough on one side.

When the cows were milked at night, Ma set the milk away in pans. In the morning she skimmed off the cream to make into butter later. Then, when the morning's milk

had cooled, she mixed it with the skimmed milk and set it all on the stove to heat.

A bit of the rennet, tied in a cloth, was soaking in warm water.

When the milk was heated enough, Ma squeezed every drop of water from the rennet in the cloth, and she poured the water into the milk. She stirred it well and left it in a warm place by the stove. In a little while it thickened into a smooth, quivery mass.

With a long knife Ma cut this mass into little squares, and let it stand while the curd separated from the whey. Then she poured it all into a cloth and let the thin, yellowish whey drain out.

When no more whey dripped from the cloth, Ma emptied the curd into a big pan and salted it, turning and mixing it well.

Laura and Mary were always there, helping all they could. They loved to eat bits of the curd when Ma was salting it. It squeaked in their teeth.

Under the cherry tree outside the back door, Pa had put up the board to press the cheese on. He had cut two grooves the length of the board, and laid the board on blocks, one end a little higher than the other. Under the lower end stood an empty pail.

Ma put her wooden cheese hoop on the board, spread a clean, wet cloth all over the inside of it, and filled it heaping full of the chunks of salted curd. She covered this with another clean, wet cloth, and laid on top of it a round board, cut small enough to go inside the cheese hoop. Then she lifted a heavy rock on top of the board.

All day long the round board settled slowly under the weight of the rock, and whey pressed out and ran down the grooves of the board into the pail.

Next morning, Ma would take out the round, pale yellow cheese, as large as a milk pan. Then she made more curd, and filled the cheese hoop again.

Every morning she took the new cheese out of the press, and trimmed it smooth. She sewed a cloth tightly around it, and rubbed the cloth all over with fresh butter. Then she put the cheese on a shelf in the pantry.

Every day she wiped every cheese carefully with a wet cloth, then rubbed it all over with fresh butter once more, and laid it down on its other side. After a great many days, the cheese was ripe, and there was a hard rind all over it.

Then Ma wrapped each cheese in paper and laid it away on the high shelf. There was nothing more to do with it but eat it.

Laura and Mary liked cheese-making. They liked to eat the curd that squeaked in their teeth and they liked to eat the edges Ma pared off the big, round, yellow cheeses to make them smooth, before she sewed them up in cloth.

Ma laughed at them for eating green cheese.

"The moon is made of green cheese, some people say," she told them.

The new cheese did look like the round moon when it came up behind the trees. But it was not green; it was yellow, like the moon.

"It's green," Ma said, "because it isn't ripened yet. When it's cured and ripened, it won't be a green cheese."

"Is the moon really made of green cheese?" Laura asked, and Ma laughed.

"I think people say that, because its looks like a green cheese," she said. "But appearances are deceiving." Then, while she wiped all the green cheeses and rubbed them with butter, she told them about the dead, cold moon that is like a little world on which nothing grows.

The first day Ma made cheese, Laura tasted the whey. She tasted it without saying anything to Ma, and when Ma turned around and saw her face, Ma laughed. That night, while she was washing the supper dishes and Mary and Laura were wiping them, Ma told Pa that Laura had tasted the whey and didn't like it.

"You wouldn't starve to death on Ma's whey, like old Grimes did on his wife's," Pa said.

Laura begged him to tell her about Old Grimes. So, though Pa was tired, he took his fiddle out of its box and played and sang for Laura:

"Old Grimes is dead, that good old man,
We ne'er shall see him more,
He used to wear an old gray coat,
All buttoned down before."

"Old Grimes's wife made skim-milk cheese,
Old Grimes, he drank the whey,
There came an east wind from the west,
And blew Old Grimes away."

"There you have it!" said Pa. "She was a mean, tight-fisted woman. If she hadn't skimmed all the milk, a little cream would have run off in the whey, and Old Grimes might have staggered along.

"But she skimmed off every bit of cream, and poor Old Grimes got so thin the wind blew him away. Plumb starved to death."

Then Pa looked at Ma and said, "Nobody'd starve to death when you were around, Caroline."

"Well, no," Ma said. "No, Charles, not if you were there to provide for us."

Pa was pleased. It was all so pleasant, the doors and windows wide open to the summer evening, the dishes making little cheerful sounds together as Ma washed them and Mary and Laura wiped, and Pa putting away the fiddle and smiling and whistling softly to himself.

After a while he said: "I'm going over to Henry's tomorrow morning, Caroline, to borrow his grubbing hoe. Those sprouts are getting waist-high around the stumps in the wheatfield. A man just has to keep everlasting at it, or the woods'll take back the place."

Early next morning he started to walk to Uncle Henry's. But before long he came hurrying back, hitched the horses to the wagon, threw in his axe, the two washtubs, the washboiler and all the pails and wooden buckets there were.

"I don't know if I'll need 'em all, Caroline," he said, "but I'd hate to want 'em and not have 'em."

"Oh, what is it? What is it?" Laura asked, jumping up and down with excitement.

"Pa's found a bee tree," Ma said. "Maybe he'll bring us some honey."

It was noon before Pa came driving home. Laura had been watching for him, and she ran out to the wagon as soon as it stopped by the barnyard. But she could not see into it.

Pa called, "Caroline, if you'll come take this pail of honey, I'll go unhitch."

Ma came out to the wagon, disappointed. She said:

"Well, Charles, even a pail of honey is

something." Then she looked into the wagon and threw up her hands. Pa laughed.

All the pails and buckets were heaping full of dripping, golden honeycomb. Both tubs were piled full, and so was the wash-boiler.

Pa and Ma went back and forth, carrying the two loaded tubs and the wash-boiler and all the buckets and pails into the house. Ma heaped a plate high with the golden pieces, and covered all the rest neatly with cloths.

For dinner they all had as much of the delicious honey as they could eat, and Pa told them how he found the bee tree.

"I didn't take my gun," he said, "because I wasn't hunting, and now it's summer there wasn't much danger of meeting trouble. Panthers and bears are so fat, this time of year, that they're lazy and good-natured.

"Well, I took a short cut through the woods, and I nearly ran into a big bear. I came around a clump of underbrush, and there he was, not as far from me as across this room.

"He looked around at me, and I guess he saw I didn't have a gun. Anyway, he didn't pay any more attention to me.

"He was standing at the foot of a big tree, and bees were buzzing all around him. They couldn't sting through his thick fur, and he kept brushing them away from his head with one paw.

"I stood there watching him, and he put the other paw into a hole in the tree and drew it out all dripping with honey. He licked the honey off his paw and reached in for more. But by that time I had found me a club. I wanted that honey myself.

"So I made a great racket, banging the club against a tree and yelling. The bear was so fat and so full of honey that he just dropped on all fours and waddled off among the trees. I chased him some distance and got him going fast, away from the bee tree, and then I came back for the wagon."

Laura asked him how he got the honey away from the bees.

"That was easy," Pa said. "I left the horses back in the woods, where they wouldn't get stung, and then I chopped the tree down and split it open."

"Didn't the bees sting you?"

"No," said Pa. "Bees never sting me.

"The whole tree was hollow, and filled from top to bottom with honey. The bees must have been storing honey there for years. Some of it was old and dark, but I guess I got enough good, clean honey to last us a long time."

Laura was sorry for the poor bees. She said:

"They worked so hard, and now they won't have any honey."

But Pa said there was lots of honey left for the bees, and there was another large, hollow tree near-by, into which they could move. He said it was time they had a clean, new home.

They would take the old honey he had left in the old tree, make it into fresh, new honey, and store it in their new house. They would save every drop of the spilled honey and put it away, and they would have plenty of honey again, long before winter came.

Heidi

In the Pasture

Johanna Spyri

‚ *Heidi is one of the best-loved characters in children's literature. When she was five years old she was taken up the Alm Mountain in the Swiss Alps to live with her old grandfather, and she quickly won her way into his heart. In the chapter given below, Heidi goes up to the mountain pastures for the first time with Peter, the herdboy. Heidi was first published in 1880 and has been a great favorite ever since.*

Heidi was awakened early the next morning by a loud whistle; the sun was shining through the round window and falling in golden rays on her bed and on the large heap of hay, and as she opened her eyes everything in the loft seemed gleaming with gold. She looked around her in astonishment and could not imagine for a while where she was. But her grandfather's deep voice was now heard outside, and then Heidi began to recall all that had happened; how she had come away from her former home, and was now on the mountain with her grandfather instead of with old Ursula. The latter was nearly stone deaf and always felt cold, so that she sat all day either by the hearth in the kitchen or by the sitting-room stove, and Heidi had been obliged to stay close to her, for the old woman was so deaf that she could not tell where the child was if out of her sight. And Heidi, shut up within the four walls, had often longed to be out of doors. So she felt very happy this morning as she woke up in her new home and remembered all the many new things that she had seen the day before and which she would see again that day, and above all she thought with delight of the two dear goats. Heidi jumped quickly out of bed and a very few minutes sufficed her to put on the clothes which she had taken off the night before, for there were not many of them. Then she climbed down the ladder and ran outside the hut. There stood Peter already with his flock of goats, and the grandfather was just bringing his two out of the shed to join the others. Heidi ran forward to wish good-morning to him and the goats.

"Do you want to go with them onto the mountain?" asked her grandfather. Nothing could have pleased Heidi better, and she jumped for joy in answer.

"But you must first wash and make yourself tidy. The sun that shines so brightly overhead will else laugh at you for being dirty; see, I have put everything ready for you," and her grandfather pointed, as he spoke, to a large tub full of water, which stood in the sun before the door. Heidi ran to it and began splashing and rubbing, till she quite glistened with cleanliness. The grandfather meanwhile went inside the hut, calling to Peter to follow him and bring in his wallet. Peter obeyed with astonishment, and laid down the little bag which held his meager dinner.

"Open it," said the old man, and inside it he put a large piece of bread and an equally large piece of cheese, which made Peter open his eyes, for each was twice the size of the two portions which he had for his own dinner.

"There, now there is only the little bowl to add," continued the grandfather, "for the child cannot drink her milk as you do from the goat; she is not accustomed to that. You must milk two bowlfuls for her when she has

her dinner, for she is going with you and will remain with you till you return this evening: but take care she does not fall over any of the rocks, do you hear?"

Heidi now came running in. "Will the sun laugh at me now, grandfather?" she asked anxiously. Her grandfather had left a coarse towel hanging up for her near the tub, and with this she had so thoroughly scrubbed her face, arms, and neck, for fear of the sun, that as she stood there she was as red all over as a lobster. He gave a little laugh.

"No, there is nothing for him to laugh at now," he assured her. "But I tell you what — when you come home this evening, you will have to get right into the tub, like a fish, for if you run about like the goats you will get your feet dirty. Now you can be off."

She started joyfully for the mountain. During the night the wind had blown away all the clouds; the dark blue sky was spreading overhead, and in its midst was the bright sun shining down on the green slopes of the mountain, where the flowers opened their little blue and yellow cups, and looked up to him smiling. Heidi went running hither and thither and shouting with delight, for here were whole patches of delicate red primroses, and there the blue gleam of the lovely gentian, while above them all laughed and nodded the tender-leaved golden cistus. Enchanted with all this waving field of brightly-colored flowers, Heidi forgot even Peter and the goats. She ran on in front and then off to the side, tempted first one way and then the other, as she caught sight of some bright spot of glowing red or yellow. And all the while she was plucking whole handfuls of the flowers which she put into her little apron, for she wanted to take them all home and stick them in the hay, so that she might make her bedroom look just like the meadows outside. Peter had therefore to be on the alert, and his round eyes, which did not move very quickly, had more work than they could well manage, for the goats were as lively as Heidi; they ran in all directions, and Peter had to follow whistling and calling and swinging his stick to get all the runaways together again.

"Where have you got to now, Heidi?" he called out somewhat crossly.

"Here," called back a voice from somewhere. Peter could see no one, for Heidi was seated on the ground at the foot of a small hill thickly overgrown with sweet-smelling prunella; the whole air seemed filled with its fragrance, and Heidi thought she had never smelt anything so delicious. She sat surrounded by the flowers, drawing in deep breaths of the scented air.

"Come along here!" called Peter again. "You are not to fall over the rocks, your grandfather gave orders that you were not to do so."

"Where are the rocks?" asked Heidi, answering him back. But she did not move from her seat, for the scent of the flowers seemed sweeter to her with every breath of wind that wafted it towards her.

"Up above, right up above. We have a long way to go yet, so come along! And on the topmost peak of all the old bird of prey sits and croaks."

That did it. Heidi immediately sprang to her feet and ran up to Peter with her apron full of flowers.

"You have got enough now," said the boy as they began climbing up again together. "You will stay here for ever if you go on picking, and if you gather all the flowers now there will be none for tomorrow."

This last argument seemed a convincing one to Heidi, and moreover her apron was already so full that there was hardly room for another flower, and it would never do to leave nothing to pick for another day. So she now kept with Peter, and the goats also became more orderly in their behavior, for they were beginning to smell the plants they loved that grew on the higher slopes and clambered up now without pause in their anxiety to reach them. The spot where Peter generally halted for his goats to pasture and where he took up his quarters for the day lay at the foot of the high rocks, which were covered for some distance up by bushes and fir trees, beyond which rose their bare and rugged summits. On one side of the mountain the rock was split into deep clefts, and the grandfather had reason to warn Peter of danger. Having climbed as far as the halting-place, Peter unslung his wallet and put it carefully in a little hollow of the ground, for

he knew what the wind was like up there and did not want to see his precious belongings sent rolling down the mountain by a sudden gust. Then he threw himself at full length on the warm ground, for he was tired after all his exertions.

Heidi meanwhile had unfastened her apron and rolling it carefully round the flowers laid it beside Peter's wallet inside the hollow; she then sat down beside his outstretched figure and looked about her. The valley lay far below bathed in the morning sun. In front of her rose a broad snow-field, high against the dark-blue sky, while to the left was a huge pile of rocks on either side of which a bare lofty peak, that seemed to pierce the blue, looked frowningly down upon her. The child sat without moving, her eyes taking in the whole scene, and all around was a great stillness, only broken by soft, light puffs of wind that swayed the light bells of the blue flowers, and the shining gold heads of the cistus, and set them nodding merrily on their slender stems. Peter had fallen asleep after his fatigue and the goats were climbing about among the bushes overhead. Heidi had never felt so happy in her life before. She drank in the golden sunlight, the fresh air, the sweet smell of the flowers, and wished for nothing better than to remain there for ever. So the time went on, while to Heidi, who had so often looked up from the valley at the mountains above, these seemed now to have faces, and to be looking down at her like old friends. Suddenly she heard a loud harsh cry overhead and lifting her eyes she saw a bird, larger than any she had ever seen before, with great, spreading wings, wheeling round and round in wide circles, and uttering a piercing, croaking kind of sound above her.

"Peter, Peter, wake up!" called out Heidi. "See, the great bird is there — look, look!"

Peter got up on hearing her call, and together they sat and watched the bird, which rose higher and higher in the blue air till it disappeared behind the gray mountain-tops.

"Where has it gone to?" asked Heidi, who had followed the bird's movements with intense interest.

"Home to its nest," said Peter.

"Is his home right up there? Oh, how nice

to be up so high! Why does he make that noise?"

"Because he can't help it," explained Peter.

"Let us climb up there and see where his nest is," proposed Heidi.

"Oh! Oh! Oh!" exclaimed Peter, his disapproval of Heidi's suggestion becoming more marked with each ejaculation, "why, even the goats cannot climb as high as that, besides didn't Uncle say that you were not to fall over the rocks."

Peter now began suddenly whistling and calling in such a loud manner that Heidi could not think what was happening; but the goats evidently understood his voice, for one after the other they came springing down the rocks until they were all assembled on the green plateau, some continuing to nibble at the juicy stems, others skipping about here and there or pushing at each other with their horns for pastime.

Heidi jumped up and ran in and out among them, for it was new to her to see the goats playing together like this and her delight was beyond words as she joined in their frolics; she made personal acquaintance with them all in turn, for they were like separate individuals to her, each single goat having a particular way of behavior of its own. Meanwhile Peter had taken the wallet out of the hollow and placed the pieces of bread and cheese on the ground in the shape of a square, the larger two on Heidi's side and the smaller on his own, for he knew exactly which were hers and which his. Then he took the little bowl and milked some delicious fresh milk into it from the white goat, and afterwards set the bowl in the middle of the square. Now he called Heidi to come, but she wanted more calling than the goats, for the child was so excited and amused at the capers and lively games of her new playfellows that she saw and heard nothing else. But Peter knew how to make himself heard, for he shouted till the very rocks above echoed his voice, and at last Heidi appeared, and when she saw the inviting repast spread out upon the ground she went skipping round it for joy.

"Leave off jumping about, it is time for dinner," said Peter; "sit down now and begin."

Heidi sat down. "Is the milk for me?" she asked, giving another look of delight at the beautifully arranged square with the bowl as a chief ornament in the center.

"Yes," replied Peter, "and the two large pieces of bread and cheese are yours also, and when you have drunk up that milk, you are to have another bowlful from the white goat, and then it will be my turn."

"And which do you get your milk from?" inquired Heidi.

"From my own goat, the piebald one. But go on now with your dinner," said Peter, again reminding her it was time to eat. Heidi now took up the bowl and drank her milk, and as soon as she had put it down empty Peter rose and filled it again for her. Then she broke off a piece of her bread and held out the remainder, which was still larger than Peter's own piece, together with the whole big slice of cheese to her companion, saying, "You can have that, I have plenty."

Peter looked at Heidi, unable to speak for astonishment, for never in all his life could he have said and done like that with anything he had. He hesitated a moment, for he could not believe that Heidi was in earnest; but the latter kept on holding out the bread and cheese, and as Peter still did not take it, she laid it down on his knees. He saw then that she really meant it; he seized the food, nodded his thanks and acceptance of her present, and then made a more splendid meal than he had known ever since he was a goatherd. Heidi the while still continued to watch the goats. "Tell me all their names," she said.

Peter knew these by heart, for having very little else to carry in his head he had no difficulty in remembering them. So he began, telling Heidi the name of each goat in turn as he pointed it out to her. Heidi listened with great attention, and it was not long before she could herself distinguish the goats from one another and could call each by name, for every goat had its own peculiarities which could not easily be mistaken; only one had to watch them closely, and this Heidi did. There was the great Turk with his big horns, who was always wanting to butt the others, so that most of them ran away when they saw him coming and would have nothing to do with their rough companion. Only Greenfinch, the slender nimble little goat, was brave enough to face him, and would make a rush at him, three or four times in succession, with such agility and dexterity, that the great Turk often stood still quite astounded not venturing to attack her again, for Greenfinch was fronting him, prepared for more warlike action, and her horns were sharp. Then there was little White Snowflake, who bleated in such a plaintive and beseeching manner that Heidi already had several times run to it and taken its head in her hands to comfort it. Just at this moment the pleading young cry was heard again, and Heidi jumped up running and, putting her arms round the little creature's neck, asked in a sympathetic voice, "What is it, little Snowflake? Why do you call like that as if in trouble?" The goat pressed closer to Heidi in a confiding way and left off bleating. Peter called out from where he was sitting — for he had not yet got to the end of his bread and cheese, "She cries like that because the old goat is not with her; she was sold at Mayenfeld the day before yesterday, and so will not come up the mountain any more."

"Who is the old goat?" called Heidi.

"Why, her mother, of course," was the answer.

"Where is the grandmother?" called Heidi again.

"She has none."

"And the grandfather?"

"She has none."

"Oh, you poor little Snowflake!" exclaimed Heidi, clasping the animal gently to her, "but do not cry like that any more; see now, I shall come up here with you every day, so that you will not be alone any more, and if you want anything you have only to come to me."

The young animal rubbed its head contentedly against Heidi's shoulder, and no longer gave such plaintive bleats. Peter now having finished his meal joined Heidi and the goats, Heidi having by this time found out a great many things about them. She had decided that by far the handsomest and best-behaved of the goats were undoubtedly the two belonging to her grandfather; they carried themselves with a certain air of distinction and generally went their own way, and

as to the great Turk they treated him with indifference and contempt.

The goats were now beginning to climb the rocks again, each seeking for the plants it liked in its own fashion, some jumping over everything they met till they found what they wanted, others going more carefully and cropping all the nice leaves by the way, the Turk still now and then giving the others a poke with his horns. Little Swan and Little Bear clambered lightly up and never failed to find the best bushes, and then they would stand gracefully poised on their pretty legs, delicately nibbling at the leaves. Heidi stood with her hands behind her back, carefully noting all they did.

"Peter," she said to the boy who had again thrown himself down on the ground, "the prettiest of all the goats are Little Swan and Little Bear."

"Yes, I know they are," was the answer. "Alm-Uncle brushes them down and washes them and gives them salt, and he has the nicest shed for them."

All of a sudden Peter leaped to his feet and ran hastily after the goats. Heidi followed him as fast as she could, for she was too eager to know what had happened to stay behind. Peter dashed through the middle of the flock towards that side of the mountain where the rocks fell perpendicularly to a great depth below, and where any thoughtless goat, if it went too near, might fall over and break all its legs. He had caught sight of the inquisitive Greenfinch taking leaps in that direction, and he was only just in time, for the animal had already sprung to the edge of the abyss. All Peter could do was to throw himself down and seize one of her hind legs. Greenfinch, thus taken by surprise, began bleating furiously, angry at being held so fast and prevented from continuing her voyage of discovery. She struggled to get loose, and endeavored so obstinately to leap forward that Peter shouted to Heidi to come and help him, for he could not get up and was afraid of pulling out the goat's leg altogether.

Heidi had already run up and she saw at once the danger both Peter and the animal were in. She quickly gathered a bunch of sweet-smelling leaves, and then, holding them under Greenfinch's nose, said coaxingly,

"Come, come, Greenfinch, you must not be naughty! Look, you might fall down there and break your leg, and that would give you dreadful pain!"

The young animal turned quickly and began contentedly eating the leaves out of Heidi's hand. Meanwhile Peter got on to his feet again and took hold of Greenfinch by the band round her neck from which her bell was hung, and Heidi taking hold of her in the same way on the other side, they led the wanderer back to the rest of the flock that had remained peacefully feeding. Peter, now he had his goat in safety, lifted his stick in order to give her a good beating as punishment, and Greenfinch seeing what was coming shrank back in fear. But Heidi cried out, "No, no, Peter, you must not strike her; see how frightened she is!"

"She deserves it," growled Peter, and again lifted his stick. Then Heidi flung herself against him and cried indignantly, "You have no right to touch her, it will hurt her, let her alone!"

Peter looked with surprise at the commanding little figure, whose dark eyes were flashing, and reluctantly he let his stick drop. "Well I will let her off if you will give me some more of your cheese tomorrow," he said, for he was determined to have something to make up to him for his fright.

"You shall have it all, tomorrow and every day, I do not want it," replied Heidi, giving ready consent to his demand. "And I will give you bread as well, a large piece like you had today; but then you must promise never to beat Greenfinch, or Snowflake, or any of the other goats."

"All right," said Peter, "I don't care," which meant that he would agree to the bargain. He now let go of Greenfinch, who joyfully sprang to join her companions.

And thus imperceptibly the day had crept on to its close, and now the sun was on the point of sinking out of sight behind the high mountains. Heidi was again sitting on the ground, silently gazing at the blue bell-shaped flowers, as they glistened in the evening sun, for a golden light lay on the grass and flowers, and the rocks above were beginning to shine and glow. All at once she sprang to her feet, "Peter! Peter! everything is on fire! All the rocks are burning and the great snow mountain and the sky! Oh look, look! the high rock up there is red with flame! Oh the beautiful, fiery snow! Stand up, Peter! See, the fire has reached the great bird's nest! look at the rocks! look at the fir trees! Everything, everything is on fire!"

"It is always like that," said Peter composedly, continuing to peel his stick; "but it is not really fire!"

"What is it then?" cried Heidi, as she ran backwards and forwards to look first one side and then the other, for she felt she could not have enough of such a beautiful sight. "What is it, Peter, what is it?" she repeated.

"It gets like that of itself," explained Peter.

"Look, look!" cried Heidi in fresh excitement, "now they have turned all rose color! Look at that one covered with snow, and that with the high, pointed rocks! What do you call them?"

"Mountains have not any names," he answered.

"Oh how beautiful, look at the crimson snow! And up there on the rocks there are ever so many roses! Oh! now they are turning gray! Oh oh now all the color has died away! It's all gone, Peter." And Heidi sat down on the ground looking as full of distress as if everything had really come to an end.

"It will come again tomorrow," said Peter. "Get up, we must go home now." He whistled to his goats and together they all started on their homeward way.

"Is it like that every day, shall we see it every day when we bring the goats up here?" asked Heidi, as she clambered down the mountain at Peter's side; she waited eagerly for his answer, hoping that he would tell her it was so.

"It is like that most days," he replied.

"But will it be like that tomorrow for certain?" Heidi persisted.

"Yes, yes, tomorrow for certain," Peter assured her in answer.

Heidi now felt quite happy again, and her little brain was so full of new impressions and new thoughts that she did not speak any more until they had reached the hut. The grandfather was sitting under the fir-trees, where he had also put up a seat, waiting as usual for his goats which returned down the mountain on this side.

Heidi ran up to him followed by the white and brown goats, for they knew their own master and stall. Peter called out after her, "Come with me again tomorrow! Goodnight!" For he was anxious for more than one reason that Heidi should go with him the next day.

Heidi ran back quickly and gave Peter her hand, promising to go with him, and then making her way through the goats she once more clasped Snowflake round the neck, saying in a gentle soothing voice, "Sleep well, Snowflake, and remember that I shall be with you again tomorrow, so you must not bleat so sadly any more." Snowflake gave her a friendly and grateful look, and then went leaping joyfully after the other goats.

Heidi returned to the fir-trees. "Oh grandfather," she cried, even before she had come up to him, "it was so beautiful. The fire, and the roses on the rocks, and the blue and yellow flowers, and look what I have brought you!" And opening the apron that held her flowers, she shook them all out at her grandfather's feet. But the poor flowers, how changed they were! Heidi hardly knew them again. They looked like dried bits of hay, not a single little flower cup stood open. "O grandfather, what is the matter with them?" exclaimed Heidi in shocked surprise, "they were not like that this morning, why do they look so now?"

"They like to stand out there in the sun and not to be shut up in an apron," said her grandfather.

"Then I will never gather any more. But, grandfather, why did the great bird go on croaking so?" she continued in an eager tone of inquiry.

"Go along now and get into your bath while I go and get some milk; when we are together at supper I will tell you all about it."

Heidi obeyed, and when later she was sitting on her high stool before her milk bowl with her gradfather beside her, she repeated her question, "Why does the great bird go on croaking and screaming down at us, grandfather?"

"He is mocking at the people who live down below in the villages, because they all go huddling and gossiping together, and encourage one another in evil talking and deeds. He calls out, 'If you would separate and each go your own way and come up here and live on a height as I do, it would be better for you!'" There was almost a wildness in the old man's voice as he spoke, so that Heidi seemed to hear the croaking of the bird again even more distinctly.

"Why haven't the mountains any names?" Heidi went on.

"They have names," answered her grandfather, "and if you can describe one of them to me that I know I will tell you what it is called."

Heidi then described to him the rocky mountain with the two high peaks so exactly that the grandfather was delighted. "Just so, I know it," and he told her its name. "Did you see any other?"

Then Heidi told him of the mountain with the great snow-field, and how it had been on fire, and had turned rosy-red and then all of a sudden had grown quite pale again and all the color had disappeared.

"I know that one too," he said, giving her its name. "So you enjoyed being out with the goats?"

Then Heidi went on to give him an account of the whole day, and of how delightful it had all been, and particularly described the fire that had burst out everywhere in the evening. And then nothing would do but her grandfather must tell how it came, for Peter knew nothing about it.

The grandfather explained to her that it was the sun that did it. "When he says goodnight to the mountains he throws his most beautiful colors over them, so that they may not forget him before he comes again the next day."

Heidi was delighted with this explanation, and could hardly bear to wait for another day to come that she might once more climb up with the goats and see how the sun bid goodnight to the mountains. But she had to go to bed first, and all night she slept soundly on her bed of hay, dreaming of nothing but of shining mountains with roses all over them, among which happy little Snowflake went leaping in and out.

The Fair American
The New Cabin Boy [5]

ELIZABETH COATSWORTH

❧ *Sally and Andrew Patterson, whom the reader has already met in two previous books,* Away Goes Sally *and* Five Bushel Farm, *sail for France on the* Fair American, *a ship owned by Captain Patterson, Andrew's father. Meanwhile, the French Revolution has increased in violence. Pierre, who is the sole survivor of an aristocratic French family, manages to escape in disguise with the aid of an old servant and makes his way to the nearest port. In the chapter reprinted below, Captain Patterson takes Pierre on as a cabin boy. After various adventures at sea, they all arrive safely in America. Pierre then goes to Boston to join an uncle. The story is continued in* The White Horse *and* The Wonderful Day.

It was as they stood on the steps above the street that Sally saw the old man and the boy with the cloth about his throat and the little dog. She could not have said why she especially noticed them. Perhaps it was because of something different about them, or perhaps it was because of the fixed way in which they were looking at the captain and Andrew and herself; but she knew immediately that these strangers wanted to speak to them, and were afraid.

She smiled and nodded reassuringly, tugging at Captain Patterson's sleeve.

"Uncle," she said, "those people over there have something to ask you."

"Beggars," replied Captain Patterson, glancing at them carelessly. "The town is full of beggars." But because he had succeeded in procuring his permission to leave the harbor and was in high good humor, he drew a coin from his pocket.

"There, Andrew," he said. "Take it over to those people at the corner. We can help someone, anyhow."

Andrew, walking gravely toward the other boy, held the coin out, saw him draw back almost as from a blow. But the old man

5 From Elizabeth Coatsworth, *The Fair American* (Macmillan, 1940).

spoke to him sharply, and the French boy took the money, his face flushing quickly and then turning pale under the brown. Andrew suddenly thought of a race horse, at once so proud and high-strung. Were beggars like this? he wondered.

But the man, murmuring something, had drawn the boy toward Captain Patterson and was speaking to him earnestly, pointing at his companion. The American stood there, good-natured and handsome.

"Yes, yes, you keep the money!" he smiled, rocking forward onto his toes and back. "Glad for you to have it." But as the old man kept on with his insistent eager words, the captain began to look impatient. He drew another coin from his pocket.

"There, citizen!" he said, handing it to the old man. "Now the children and I must be going." And as the other tried to detain him, he pushed past with a warning, "Enough's enough, my man."

Sally, almost on tiptoe, her mouth a little open, had been listening. It seemed as though she had been listening with all her being, with her eyes, her ears, and her very mouth — as though her heart had been listening.

"Uncle John," she cried, following him. "They're in trouble. I think he was saying, 'Please take him with you. He is the last one left.' He said it so often I began to understand. Uncle John, please don't go so fast. It wasn't money they wanted. They wanted you to take the boy on the *Fair American*."

Captain Patterson had regained his good humor.

"What a little goose you are, Sally," he said, taking her hand again. "I can't take all the boys of France along with us just because they ask. Let them pocket the louis and be satisfied."

Sally pulled her hand free and faced Captain Patterson.

"He's only a little older than Andrew, Uncle John," she remarked gravely. "Suppose it *was* Andrew and he was in trouble." A sudden pain went through Captain Patterson's heart. Andrew *had* been in trouble, a lost child, not knowing if he had a relative in the world; and, out of the indifference of fate, Sally's aunt and Sally had been sent to rescue him. He looked at Andrew, who looked back confidingly, sure that his father would do the thing that was to be done. He felt Sally's impatient, pleading hands pulling at his sleeve, trying to turn him.

"I'll see about this," he muttered, a little threateningly, in his quarter-deck manner, as he turned back toward the group he had just left.

"Now," he said sternly to the old man. "Speak up! What's this all about?"

Again the man tried to tell him, speaking low, repeating his phrases, silent when anyone passed. Again the boy stood, tense and anxious, with the same look of self-control about his lips and dark eyes that asked no favors. Again the little dog retreated against his master's briar-torn legs. This time Captain Patterson, accustomed to judge men, really studied the faces before him, and found out from them more than the two children could make out from the words that were said.

He frowned a little, pinching his lips, while the others waited anxiously. He saw that there might be danger involved, and he had Sally and Andrew with him. He ought to run no risks. But, on the other hand, he could not determine to abandon the French boy, now that he had had a good look at him.

"Well, something must be left to chance," he thought, squaring his shoulders. He nodded to the old man.

"Very well," he said, and put his hand on the boy's shoulder. "I'll sign him on as cabin boy."

Tears rushed to the Frenchman's eyes — tears of relief, that he quickly brushed aside, afraid to show so much emotion in a public place. The boy drew a quivering breath and turned pale again, while Sally hopped up and down silently clapping her hands, her curls bobbing under her bonnet, and Andrew said, "Oh, thank you, sir," in a low voice.

The captain felt he might as well be hanged for a sheep as a lamb. He pointed to the old man and then toward the harbor, and raised his brows questioningly. Did he, too, wish to go? But the other shook his head. His thanks poured out, and his explanations. Sally, quicker than Andrew to understand this new tongue, though slower to speak it,

interpreted, "He says something, Uncle John, about going back to his old village."

"I venture he'll be safe enough, once he gets rid of this boy," the captain said. "He looks like anyone else. But the boy, now, you couldn't hide the breeding back of him from anyone who took the trouble to look."

The good-byes were quickly over. The boy seemed almost stunned by losing his last touch with his old life. As for his companion, relief and sorrow struggled on his face. Bending down, with a sudden gesture, he touched the boy's hand with his lips, slipped a small parcel in the child's unheeding grasp, and, turning, walked rapidly away without a backward glance.

"Jean!" called the boy after him. "Jean!" He started to follow, but Captain Patterson touched his shoulder again and shook his head.

"No," he said. "Come along with us." And the boy, understanding the tone if not the words, fell into step behind his new friends, his heavy shoes stumbling a little sadly over the cobbles.

. . . .

TROUBLE

It was not until they were on the quays that they met any trouble. No one on the streets had given them more than a passing glance, especially after Captain Patterson had taken the precaution of stopping a market woman, and buying a basket of cheeses for the new cabin boy to carry. Except for his wild look of torn clothes and straggling elf locks, he might have been any little servant following his foreign master, in the eyes of the townspeople, each busy about his own affairs.

But on the docks the idlers had no affairs of their own. They sat in the sun, on bales or pierheads, spitting into the water; scratching their matted heads under the liberty caps they wore.

It was an old one-eyed sailor who heaved himself slowly to his feet and swaggered over toward the man and the three children, followed by one or two others.

The captain saw him coming, but neither slowed nor quickened his step, even when the man stopped in his path and, jerking his thumb at the boy, said something which was clearly a question as to who he was and where they might be taking him.

"No parlez-vous," the captain snorted, bearing down at the other. He had dropped the children's hands and now walked a little ahead of them, truculently, his small convoy close at his heels. But the raised voices had gathered a crowd of loafers, always eager for a fight and now made more savage by the scenes they had taken part in during these months of revolution.

The stairs were still somewhat ahead, and the ship's boat lay out of sight at its foot. Captain Patterson saw no sign of the two sailors he had left in charge. They were probably asleep in the thwarts. He considered shouting to them, but knew that to call for help was a sign of weakness, likely to bring on trouble in a rush. His best chance lay in an air of cold indifference, while he got as near to the stairs as he could.

But now there were men behind him as well as in front, and someone had laid his hands on the French boy's shoulders and spun him roughly round. Captain Patterson heard Sally's "Don't you dare touch him — he's ours!" and then the smack of Andrew's small fist, and a roar of teasing laughter. He turned, his own fists doubled; but just then another man appeared on the scene, a tall thin figure with a long nose and a pair of squinting gray eyes, and cocked-up shoulders squeezed into a uniform. This man had boots on and epaulettes, and a sword trailed at his lean side. He appeared to be an officer; but the remarkable thing was that he spoke in English, mixed with a torrent of French — the French addressed to the crowd, which drew back, and the English to Captain Patterson, whom he seized by the hand, shaking it violently.

"Oh, sir!" he exclaimed, "I am proud to meet an American, a citizen of that other Republic for which I also fought. The world has known one great man, a noble human being and a valiant soldier — George Washington!"

Still shaking the captain's hand, he whipped off his hat with its cockade and held it at his breast with his head bowed, as though in prayer.

"George Washington," he repeated, taking Captain Patterson familiarly by the arm. "I saw him often, for I served under Lafayette. A perfect man, citizen. It was an honor to tread the same earth."

The crowd had fallen back; but the leader began snarling some protest in the ear of the officer, who glanced back at the French boy.

"My cabin boy," explained Captain Patterson.

"Of course," said the officer affably. "Nothing more natural."

Then he turned a face suddenly galvanized with fury at the one-eyed man and his companions, and poured forth a torrent of abuse upon them, ending with a savage gesture of a finger across the throat. The crowd melted away — even the leader, surly still.

"Ah," continued the officer, serene again. "They don't like to be reminded that their own necks may come under the guillotine too. General Washington was fortunate in having no such dogs to handle."

Talking of America, he sauntered to the head of the steps and shook hands with the captain for a last time. The sailors below had sprung to their positions and were steadying the boat. As the children passed down the stairs, now shortened by high tide, the officer gave the French boy one appraising glance, shrugged, and said, with a smile, to Captain Patterson, "The great Washington never made war on children. I wish you all a good voyage to America" — and, with a rather sad look on his long face, saluted and walked away.

One of the sailors took the basket of cheeses and helped the new cabin boy into the bow of the boat, for he seemed rather bewildered. The little dog leaped hastily over the gunwale after him and scrambled to his side. The sailor looked questioningly at the captain, who nodded to let the beast be and then stepped into the stern with the other children. The men pushed off with their oars; the boat swayed a little, balanced, and settled down to the short swing of the strokes; and the stone quays, and the stone houses and towers behind them, dropped slowly farther and farther behind.

Suddenly Captain Patterson gave a short, amused laugh.

"What are you thinking of, sir?" asked Sally, leaning against his shoulder.

"I was just thinking, child," said the captain, "that I had promised myself to bring your aunt a present at parting from France, and I think, after all, we have one here much to her liking."

Rufus M. [6]

(A Selection)

ELEANOR ESTES

With the Moffat books, Eleanor Estes has created a family that will be long remembered and loved. The four lively young Moffats and their understanding mother made their first appearance in The Moffats. In Rufus M. the youngest Moffat, now seven years old, proves that he is an individual in his own right. The chapter given below tells how Rufus learns to write his name.

Rufus M. That's the way Rufus wrote his name on his heavy arithmetic paper and on his blue-lined spelling paper. Rufus M. went on one side of the paper. His age, seven, went on the other. Rufus had not learned to write his name in school, though that is one place for learning to write. He had not learned to write his name at home either, though that is another place for learning to write. The place where he had learned to write his name was the library, long ago before he ever went to school at all. This is the way it happened.

One day when Rufus had been riding his scooter up and down the street, being the motorman, the conductor, the passengers, the steam, and the whistle of a locomotive, he came home and found Joey, Jane, and Sylvie, all reading in the front yard. Joey and Jane were sitting on the steps of the porch and Sylvie was sprawled in the hammock, a book in one hand, a chocolate-covered peppermint in the other.

Rufus stood with one bare foot on his scooter and one on the grass and watched

6 From Eleanor Estes, Rufus M. (Harcourt, Brace, 1943).

them. Sylvie read the fastest. This was natural since she was the oldest. But Jocy turned the pages almost as fast and Jane went lickety-cut on the good parts. They were all reading books and he couldn't even read yet. These books they were reading were library books. The library must be open today. It wasn't open every day, just a few days a week.

"I want to go to the library," said Rufus. "And get a book," he added.

"We all just came home from there," said Jane, while Joey and Sylvie merely went on reading as though Rufus had said nothing. "Besides," she added, "why do you want a book anyway? You can't even read yet."

This was true and it made Rufus mad. He liked to do everything that they did. He even liked to sew if they were sewing. He never thought whether sewing was for girls only or not. When he saw Jane sewing, he asked Mama to let him sew too. So Mama tied a thread to the head of a pin and Rufus poked that in and out of a piece of goods. That's the way he sewed. It looked like what Jane was doing and Rufus was convinced that he was sewing too, though he could not see much sense in it.

Now here were the other Moffats, all with books from the library. And there were three more books stacked up on the porch that looked like big people's books without pictures. They were for Mama, no doubt. This meant that he was the only one here who did not have a book.

"I want a book from the library," said Rufus. A flick of the page as Sylvie turned it over was all the answer he got. It seemed to Rufus as though even Catherine-the-cat gave him a scornful glance because he could not read yet and did not have a book.

Rufus turned his scooter around and went out of the yard. Just wait! Read? Why, soon he'd read as fast if not faster than they did. Reading looked easy. It was just flipping pages. Who couldn't do that?

Rufus thought that it was not hard to get a book out of the library. All you did was go in, look for a book that you liked, give it to the lady to punch, and come home with it. He knew where the library was, for he had often gone there with Jane and some of the others. While Jane went off to the shelves to find a book, he and Joey played the game of Find the Duke in the Palmer Cox Brownie books. This was a game that the two boys had made up. They would turn the pages of one of the Brownie books, any of them, and try to be the first to spot the duke, the brownie in the tall hat. The library lady thought that this was a noisy game, and she wished they would not play it there. Rufus hoped to bring a Brownie book home now.

"Toot-toot!" he sang to clear the way. Straight down Elm Street was the way to the library; the same way that led to Sunday School, and Rufus knew it well. He liked sidewalks that were white the best, for he could go the fastest on these.

"Toot-toot!" Rufus hurried down the street. When he arrived at the library, he hid his scooter in the pine trees that grew under windows beside the steps. Christmas trees, Rufus called them. The ground was covered with brown pine needles and they were soft to walk upon. Rufus always went into the library the same way. He climbed the stairs, encircled the light on the granite arm of the steps, and marched into the library.

Rufus stepped carefully on the strips of rubber matting that led to the desk. This matting looked like dirty licorice. But it wasn't licorice. He know because once, when Sylvie had brought him here when he was scarcely more than three, he had tasted a torn corner of it. It was not good to eat.

The library lady was sitting at the desk playing with some cards. Rufus stepped off the matting. The cool, shiny floor felt good to his bare feet. He went over to the shelves and luckily did find one of the big Palmer Cox Brownie books there. It would be fun to play the game of Find the Duke at home. Until now he had played it only in the library. Maybe Jane or Joey would play it with him right now. He laughed out loud at the thought.

"Sh-sh-sh, quiet," said the lady at the desk.

Rufus clapped his chubby fist over his mouth. Goodness! He had forgotten where he was. Do not laugh or talk out loud in the library. He knew these rules. Well, he didn't

want to stay here any longer today anyway. He wanted to read at home with the others. He took the book to the lady to punch.

She didn't punch it, though. She took it and she put it on the table behind her and then she started to play cards again.

"That's my book," said Rufus.

"Do you have a card?" the lady asked.

Rufus felt in his pockets. Sometimes he carried around an old playing card or two. Today he didn't have one.

"No," he said.

"You'll have to have a card to get a book."

"I'll go and get one," said Rufus.

The lady put down her cards. "I mean a library card," she explained kindly. "It looks to me as though you are too little to have a library card. Do you have one?"

"No," said Rufus. "I'd like to, though."

"I'm afraid you're too little," said the lady. "You have to write your name to get one. Can you do that?"

Rufus nodded his head confidently. Writing. Lines up and down. He'd seen that done. And the letters that Mama had tied in bundles in the closet under the stairs were covered with writing. Of course he could write.

"Well, let's see your hands," said the lady.

Rufus obligingly showed this lady his hands, but she did not like the looks of them. She cringed and clasped her head as though the sight hurt her.

"Oh," she gasped. "You'll just have to go home and wash them before we can even think about joining the library and borrowing books."

This was a complication upon which Rufus had not reckoned. However, all it meant was a slight delay. He'd wash his hands and then he'd get the book. He turned and went out of the library, found his scooter safe among the Christmas trees, and pushed it home. He surprised Mama by asking to have his hands washed. When this was done, he mounted his scooter again and returned all the long way to the library. It was not just a little trip to the library. It was a long one. A long one and a hot one on a day like this. But he didn't notice that. All he was bent on was getting his book and taking it home and reading with the others on the front porch. They were all still there, brushing flies away and reading.

Again Rufus hid his scooter in the pine trees, encircled the light, and went in.

"Hello," he said.

"Well," said the lady. "How are they now?"

Rufus had forgotten he had had to wash his hands. He thought she was referring to the other Moffats. "Fine," he said.

"Let me see them," she said, and she held up her hands.

Oh! His hands! Well, they were all right, thought Rufus, for Mama had just washed them. He showed them to the lady. There was a silence while she studied them. Then she shook her head. She still did not like them.

"Ts, ts, ts!" she said. "They'll have to be cleaner than that."

Rufus looked at his hands. Supposing he went all the way home and washed them again, she still might not like them. However, if that is what she wanted, he would have to do that before he could get the Brownie book . . . and he started for the door.

"Well, now, let's see what we can do," said the lady. "I know what," she said. "It's against the rules, but perhaps we can wash them in here." And she led Rufus into a little room that smelled of paste where lots of new books and old books were stacked up. In one corner was a little round sink and Rufus washed his hands again. Then they returned to the desk. The lady got a chair and put a newspaper on it. She made Rufus stand on this because he was not big enough to write at the desk otherwise.

Then the lady put a piece of paper covered with a lot of printing in front of Rufus, dipped a pen in the inkwell and gave it to him.

"All right," she said. "Here's your application. Write your name here."

All the writing Rufus had ever done before had been on big pieces of brown wrapping paper with lots of room on them. Rufus had often covered those great sheets of paper with his own kind of writing at home. Lines up and down.

But on this paper there wasn't much space. It was already covered with writing. How-

ever, there was a tiny little empty space and that was where Rufus must write his name, the lady said. So, little space or not, Rufus confidently grasped the pen with his left hand and dug it into the paper. He was not accustomed to pens, having always worked with pencils until now, and he made a great many holes and blots and scratches.

"Gracious," said the lady. "Don't bear down so hard! And why don't you hold it in your right hand?" she asked, moving the pen back into his right hand.

Rufus started again scraping his lines up and down and all over the page, this time using his right hand. Wherever there was an empty space he wrote. He even wrote over some of the print for good measure. Then he waited for the lady, who had gone off to get a book for some man, to come back and look.

"Oh," she said, as she settled herself in her swivel chair, "is that the way you write? Well . . . it's nice, but what does it say?"

"Says Rufus Moffat. My name."

Apparently these lines up and down did not spell Rufus Moffat to this lady. She shook her head.

"It's nice," she repeated. "Very nice. But nobody but you knows what it says. You have to learn to write your name better than that before you can join the library."

Rufus was silent. He had come to the library all by himself, gone back home to wash his hands, and come back because he wanted to take books home and read them the way the others did. He had worked hard. He did not like to think he might have to go home without a book.

The library lady looked at him a moment and then she said quickly before he could get himself all the way off the big chair, "maybe you can *print* your name."

Rufus looked at her hopefully. He thought he could write better than he could print, for his writing certainly looked to him exactly like all grown people's writing. Still he'd try to print if that was what she wanted.

The lady printed some letters on the top of a piece of paper. "There," she said. "That's your name. Copy it ten times and then we'll try it on another application."

Rufus worked hard. He worked so hard the knuckles showed white on his brown fist.

He worked for a long, long time, now with his right hand and now with his left. Sometimes a boy or girl came in, looked over his shoulder and watched, but he paid no attention. From time to time the lady studied his work and she said, "That's fine. That's fine." At last she said, "Well, maybe now we can try." And she gave him another application.

All Rufus could get, with his large generous letters, in that tiny little space where he was supposed to print his name, was R-U-F. The other letters he scattered here and there on the card. The lady did not like this either. She gave him still another blank. Rufus tried to print smaller and this time he got RUFUS in the space, and also he crowded an M at the end. Since he was doing so well now, the lady herself printed the *offat* part of Moffat on the next line.

"This will have to do," she said. "Now take this home and ask your mother to sign it on the other side. Bring it back on Thursday and you'll get your card."

Rufus's face was shiny and streaked with dirt where he had rubbed it. He never knew there was all this work to getting a book. The other Moffats just came in and got books. Well, maybe they had had to do this once too.

Rufus held his hard-earned application in one hand and steered his scooter with the other. When he reached home, Joey, Jane, and Sylvie were not around any longer. Mama signed his card for him, saying, "My! So you've learned how to write!"

"Print," corrected Rufus.

Mama kissed Rufus and he went back out. The lady had said to come back on Thursday, but he wanted a book today. When the other Moffats came home, he'd be sitting on the top step of the porch, reading. That would surprise them. He smiled to himself as he made his way to the library for the third time.

Once his application blew away. Fortunately it landed in a thistle bush and did not get very torn. The rest of the way Rufus clutched it carefully. He climbed the granite steps to the library again, only to find that the big round dark brown doors were closed. Rufus tried to open them, but he couldn't. He knocked at the door, even kicked it with his foot, but there was no answer. He pounded on the door, but nobody came.

A big boy strode past with his newspapers. "Hey, kid," he said to Rufus, "library's closed!" And off he went, whistling.

Rufus looked after him. The fellow said the library was closed. How could it have closed so fast? He had been there such a little while ago. The lady must still be here. He did want his Brownie book. If only he could see in, he might see the lady and get his book. The windows were high up, but they had very wide sills. Rufus was a wonderful climber. He could shinny up trees and poles faster than anybody on the block. Faster than Joey. Now, helping himself up by means of one of the pine trees that grew close to the building, and by sticking his toes in the ivy and rough places in the bricks, he scrambled up the wall. He hoisted himself up on one of the sills and sat there. He peered in. It was dark inside, for the shades had been drawn almost all the way down.

"Library lady!" he called, and he knocked on the window-pane. There was no answer. He put his hands on each side of his face to shield his eyes, and he looked in for a long, long time. He could not believe that she had left. Rufus was resolved to get a book. He had lost track of the number of times he had been back and forth from home to the library, and the library home. Maybe the lady was in the cellar. He climbed down, stubbing his big toe on the bricks as he did so. He stooped down beside one of the low dirt-spattered cellar windows. He couldn't see in. He lay flat on the ground, wiped one spot clean on the window, picked up a few pieces of coal from the sill and put them in his pocket for Mama.

"Hey, lady," he called.

He gave the cellar window a little push. It wasn't locked, so he opened it a little and looked in. All he could see was a high pile of coal reaching up to this window. Of course he didn't put any of that coal in his pocket, for that would be stealing.

"Hey, lady," he yelled again. His voice echoed in the cellar but the library lady did not answer. He called out, "Hey lady," every few seconds but all that answered him was an echo. He pushed the window open a little wider. All of a sudden it swung wide open and Rufus slid in, right on top of the coal pile and crash, clatter, bang! He slid to the bottom making a great racket.

A little light shone through the dusty windows, but on the whole it was very dark and spooky down here and Rufus really wished that he was back on the outside looking in. However, since he was in the library, why not go upstairs quick, get the Brownie book, and go home? The window had banged shut, but he thought he could climb up the coal pile, pull the window up, and get out. He certainly hoped he could, anyway. Supposing he couldn't and he had to stay in this cellar! Well, that he would not think about. He looked around in the dusky light and saw a staircase across the cellar. Luckily his application was still good. It was torn and dirty, but it still had his name on it, RUFUS M. and that was the important part. He'd leave this on the desk in exchange for the Brownie book.

Rufus cautiously made his way over to the steps, but he stopped halfway across the cellar. Somebody had opened the door at the top of the stairs. He couldn't see who it was, but he did see the light reflected and that's how he knew that somebody had opened the door. It must be the lady. He was just going to say, "Hey, lady," when he thought, "Gee, maybe it isn't the lady. Maybe it's a spooky thing."

Then the light went away, the door was closed, and Rufus was left in the dark again. He didn't like it down here. He started to go back to the coal pile to get out of this place. Then he felt of his application. What a lot of work he had done to get a book and now that he was this near to getting one, should he give up? No. Anyway, if it was the lady up there, he knew her and she knew him and neither one of them was scared of the other. And Mama always said there's no such thing as a spooky thing.

So Rufus bravely made his way again to the stairs. He tiptoed up them. The door at the head was not closed tightly. He pushed it open and found himself right in the library. But goodness! There in the little sink room right opposite him was the library lady!

Rufus stared at her in silence. The library lady was eating. Rufus had never seen her do anything before but play cards, punch books, and carry great piles of them around. Now she was eating. Mama said not to stare at anybody while they were eating. Still Rufus didn't know the library lady ate, so it was hard for him not to look at her.

She had a little gas stove in there. She could cook there. She was reading a book at the same time that she was eating. Sylvie could do that too. This lady did not see him.

"Hey, lady," said Rufus.

The librarian jumped up out of her seat. "Was that you in the cellar? I thought I heard somebody. Goodness, young man! I thought you had gone home long ago."

Rufus didn't say anything. He just stood there. He had gone home and he had come back lots of times. He had the whole thing in his mind; the coming and going, and going and coming, and sliding down the coal pile, but he did not know where to begin, how to tell it.

"Didn't you know the library is closed now?" she demanded, coming across the floor with firm steps.

Rufus remained silent. No, he hadn't known it. The fellow had told him, but he hadn't believed him. Now he could see for himself that the library was closed so the library lady could eat. If the lady would let him take his book, he'd go home and stay there. He'd play the game of Find the Duke with Jane. He hopefully held out his card with his name on it.

"Here this is," he said.

But the lady acted as though she didn't even see it. She led Rufus over to the door.

"All right now," she said. "Out with you!" But just as she opened the door the sound of water boiling over on the stove struck their ears, and back she raced to her little room.

"Gracious!" she exclaimed. "What a day!"

Before the door could close on him, Rufus followed her in and sat down on the edge of a chair. The lady thought he had gone and started to sip her tea. Rufus watched her quietly, waiting for her to finish.

After a while the lady brushed the crumbs off her lap. And then she washed her hands and the dishes in the little sink where Rufus had washed his hands. In a library a lady could eat and could wash. Maybe she slept here, too. Maybe she lived here.

"Do you live here?" Rufus asked her.

"Mercy on us!" exclaimed the lady. "Where'd you come from? Didn't I send you home? No, I don't live here and neither do you. Come now, out with you, young man. I mean it." The lady called all boys "young man" and all girls "Susie." She came out of the little room and she opened the big brown door again. "There," she said. "Come back on Thursday."

Rufus's eyes filled up with tears.

"Here's this," he said again, holding up his application in a last desperate attempt. But the lady shook her head. Rufus went slowly down the steps, felt around in the bushes for his scooter, and with drooping spirits he mounted it. Then for the second time that day, the library lady changed her mind.

"Oh, well," she said, "come back here, young man. I'm not supposed to do business when the library's closed, but I see we'll have to make an exception."

So Rufus rubbed his sooty hands over his face, hid his scooter in the bushes again, climbed the granite steps, and, without circling the light, he went back in and gave the lady his application.

The lady took it gingerly. "My, it's dirty," she said. "You really ought to sign another one."

"And go home with it?" asked Rufus. He really didn't believe this was possible. He wiped his hot face on his sleeve and looked up at the lady in exhaustion. What he was thinking was: All right. If he had to sign another one, all right. But would she just please stay open until he got back?

However, this was not necessary. The lady said, "Well, now, I'll try to clean this old one up. But remember, young man, always have everything clean — your hands, your book, everything, when you come to the library."

Rufus nodded solemnly. "My feet too," he assured her.

Then the lady made Rufus wash his hands again. They really were very bad this time, for he had been in a coal pile, and now at last she gave Rufus the book he wanted — one of the Palmer Cox Brownie books. This one was *The Brownies in the Philippines.*

And Rufus went home.

When he reached home, he showed Mama his book. She smiled at him, and gave his cheek a pat. She thought it was fine that he had gone to the library and joined all by himself and taken out a book. And she thought it was fine when Rufus sat down at the kitchen table, was busy and quiet for a long, long time, and then showed her what he had done.

He had printed RUFUS M. That was what he had done. And that's the way he learned to sign his name. And that's the way he always did sign his name for a long, long time.

Hans Brinker
Hans and Gretel Find a Friend
MARY MAPES DODGE

꿿 Hans Brinker; or, The Silver Skates, *a story of life in Holland, was one of the first stories written for children about a foreign country. It was originally told as a continued story by the author to her young sons after she came home from her office work each night. First published in 1865, the book was an immediate success. Many years later, when the author was in Holland with one of her sons, then grown, she inquired for the best book on Dutch life; and the bookseller handed her a translation of her own* Hans Brinker. *The book still maintains its popularity. The chapter reprinted below tells how Hans and Gretel enter the grand skating match, hoping to win the coveted prize, a beautiful pair of silver skates.*

At noon our young friends poured forth from the schoolhouse intent upon having an hour's practicing upon the canal.

They had skated but a few moments when Carl Schummel said mockingly to Hilda:

"There's a pretty pair just coming upon the ice! The little rag-pickers! Their skates must have been a present from the king direct."

"They are patient creatures," said Hilda,

gently. "It must have been hard to learn to skate upon such queer affairs. They are very poor peasants, you see. The boy has probably made the skates himself."

Carl was somewhat abashed.

"Patient they may be, but, as for skating, they start off pretty well only to finish with a jerk. They could move well to your new staccato piece I think."

Hilda laughed pleasantly and left him. After joining a small detachment of the racers, and sailing past every one of them, she halted beside Gretel who, with eager eyes, had been watching the sport.

"What is your name, little girl?"

"Gretel, my lady," answered the child, somewhat awed by Hilda's rank, though they were nearly of the same age, "and my brother is called Hans."

"Hans is a stout fellow," said Hilda, cheerily, "and seems to have a warm stove somewhere within him, but you look cold. You should wear more clothing, little one."

Gretel, who had nothing else to wear, tried to laugh as she answered:

"I am not so very little. I am past twelve years old."

"Oh, I beg your pardon. You see I am nearly fourteen, and so large for my age that other girls seem small to me, but that is nothing. Perhaps you will shoot up far above me yet; not unless you dress more warmly, though — shivering girls never grow."

Hans flushed as he saw tears rising in Gretel's eyes.

"My sister has not complained of the cold; but this is bitter weather they say —— " and he looked sadly upon Gretel.

"It is nothing," said Gretel, "I am often warm — too warm when I am skating. You are good, jufvrouw, to think of it."

"No, no," answered Hilda, quite angry at herself. "I am careless, cruel; but I meant no harm. I wanted to ask you — I mean — if —— " and here Hilda, coming to the point of her errand, faltered before the poorly clad but noble-looking children she wished to serve.

"What is it, young lady?" exclaimed Hans eagerly. "If there is any service I can do? any —— "

"Oh! no, no," laughed Hilda, shaking off her embarrassment, "I only wished to speak to you about the grand race. Why do you not join it? You both can skate well, and the ranks are free. Anyone may enter for the prize."

Gretel looked wistfully at Hans, who, tugging at his cap, answered respectfully:

"Ah, jufvrouw, even if we could enter, we could skate only a few strokes with the rest. Our skates are hard wood, you see," holding up the sole of his foot, "but they soon become damp, and then they stick and trip us."

Gretel's eyes twinkled with fun as she thought of Hans' mishap in the morning, but she blushed as she faltered out timidly:

"Oh no, we can't join; but may we be there, my lady, on the great day to look on?"

"Certainly," answered Hilda, looking kindly into the two earnest faces, and wishing from her heart that she had not spent so much of her monthly allowance for lace and finery. She had but eight kwartjes left, and they would buy but one pair of skates, at the furthest.

Looking down with a sigh at the two pair of feet so very different in size, she asked:

"Which of you is the better skater?"

"Gretel," replied Hans, promptly.

"Hans," answered Gretel, in the same breath. Hilda smiled.

"I cannot buy you each a pair of skates, or even one good pair; but here are eight kwartjes. Decide between you which stands the best chance of winning the race, and buy the skates accordingly. I wish I had enough to buy better ones — good-bye!" and, with a nod and a smile, Hilda, after handing the money to the electrified Hans, glided swiftly away to rejoin her companions.

"Jufvrouw! jufvrouw von Gleck!" called Hans in a loud tone, stumbling after her as well as he could, for one of his skate strings was untied.

Hilda turned, and with one hand raised to shield her eyes from the sun, seemed to him to be floating through the air, nearer and nearer.

"We cannot take this money," panted Hans, "though we know your goodness in giving it."

"Why not indeed?" asked Hilda flushing.

"Because," replied Hans, bowing like a clown, but looking with the eye of a prince at the queenly girl, "we have not earned it."

Hilda was quick-witted. She had noticed a pretty wooden chain upon Gretel's neck.

"Carve me a chain, Hans, like the one your sister wears."

"That I will, lady, with all my heart, we have white-wood in the house, fine as ivory; you shall have one tomorrow," and Hans hastily tried to return the money.

"No, no," said Hilda, decidedly. "That sum will be but a poor price for the chain," and off she darted, outstripping the fleetest among the skaters.

Hans sent a long, bewildered gaze after her; it was useless, he felt, to make any further resistance.

"It is right," he muttered, half to himself, half to his faithful shadow, Gretel, "I must work hard every minute, and sit up half the night if the mother will let me burn a candle; but the chain shall be finished. We may keep the money, Gretel."

"What a good little lady!" cried Gretel, clapping her hands with delight, "oh! Hans, was it for nothing the stork settled on our roof last summer? Do you remember how the mother said it would bring us luck, and how she cried when Janzoon Kolp shot him? And she said it would bring him trouble. But the luck has come to us at last! Now, Hans, if mother sends us to town tomorrow you can buy the skates in the market-place."

Hans shook his head. "The young lady would have given us the money to buy skates; but if I earn it, Gretel, it shall be spent for wool. You must have a warm jacket."

"Oh!" cried Gretel, in real dismay, "not buy the skates! Why I am not often cold! Mother says the blood runs up and down in poor children's veins humming 'I must keep 'em warm! I must keep 'em warm.'"

"Oh, Hans," she continued with something like a sob, "don't say you won't buy the skates, it makes me feel just like crying — besides, I want to be cold — I mean I'm real, awful warm — so now!"

Hans looked up hurriedly. He had a true Dutch horror of tears, or emotion of any kind, and, most of all, he dreaded to see his sister's blue eyes overflowing.

"Now mind," cried Gretel, seeing her advantage, "I'll feel awful if you give up the skates. I don't want them. I'm not such a stingy as that; but I want you to have them, and then when I get bigger they'll do for me — oh-h — count the pieces, Hans. Did ever you see so many!"

Hans turned the money thoughtfully in his palm. Never in all his life had he longed so intensely for a pair of skates, for he had known of the race and had, boylike, fairly ached for a chance to test his powers with the other children. He felt confident that with a good pair of steel runners, he could readily distance most of the boys on the canal. Then, too, Gretel's argument was so plausible. On the other hand, he knew that she, with her strong but lithe little frame, needed but a week's practice on good runners, to make her a better skater than Rychie Korbes or even Katrinka Flack. As soon as this last thought flashed upon him his resolve was made. If Gretel would not have the jacket, she should have the skates.

"No, Gretel," he answered at last, "I can wait. Some day I may have money enough saved to buy a fine pair. You shall have these."

Gretel's eyes sparkled; but in another instant she insisted, rather faintly:

"The young lady gave the money to you, Hans. I'd be real bad to take it."

Hans shook his head resolutely as he trudged on, causing his sister to half skip and half walk in her effort to keep beside him; by this time they had taken off their wooden "rockers," and were hastening home to tell their mother the good news.

"Oh! I know!" cried Gretel, in a sprightly tone. "You can do this. You can get a pair a little too small for you, and too big for me, and we can take turns and use them. Won't that be fine?" and Gretel clapped her hands again.

Poor Hans! This was a strong temptation, but he pushed it away from him, bravehearted fellow that he was.

"Nonsense, Gretel. You could never get on with a big pair. You stumbled about with these, like a blind chicken, before I curved off the ends. No, you must have a pair to fit exactly, and you must practice every chance you can get, until the 20th comes. My little Gretel shall win the silver skates."

Gretel could not help laughing with delight at the very idea.

"Hans! Gretel!" called out a familiar voice.

"Coming, mother!" and they hastened toward the cottage, Hans still shaking the pieces of silver in his hand.

On the following day, there was not a prouder nor a happier boy in all Holland than Hans Brinker as he watched his sister, with many a dexterous sweep, flying in and out among the skaters who at sundown thronged the canal. A warm jacket had been given her by the kind-hearted Hilda, and the burst-out shoes had been cobbled into decency by Dame Brinker. As the little creature darted backward and forward, flushed with enjoyment, and quite unconscious of the many wondering glances bent upon her, she felt that the shining runners beneath her feet had suddenly turned earth into Fairyland, while "Hans, dear, good Hans!" echoed itself over and over again in her grateful heart.

"By den donder!" exclaimed Peter van Holp to Carl Schummel, "but that little one in the red jacket and patched petticoat skates well. Gunst! she has toes on her heels, and eyes in the back of her head! See her! It will be a joke if she gets in the race and beats Katrinka Flack, after all."

"Hush! not so loud!" returned Carl, rather sneeringly. "That little lady in rags is the special pet of Hilda van Gleck. Those shining skates are her gift, if I make no mistake."

"So! so!" exclaimed Peter, with a radiant smile, for Hilda was his best friend. "She has been at her good work there, too!" And Mynheer van Holp, after cutting a double 8 on the ice, to say nothing of a huge P, then a jump, and an H, glided onward until he found himself beside Hilda.

Hand in hand, they skated together, laughingly at first, then staidly talking in a low tone.

Strange to say, Peter van Holp soon arrived at a sudden conviction that his little sister needed a wooden chain just like Hilda's.

Two days afterwards, on Saint Nicholas' Eve, Hans, having burned three candle-ends, and cut his thumb into the bargain, stood in the market-place at Amsterdam, buying another pair of skates.

Hitty

I Go Up in the World and Am Glad to Come Down Again[7]

RACHEL LYMAN FIELD

Hitty is a little wooden doll carved from stout mountain-ash wood brought from Ireland. She was made for Phoebe Preble by a peddler who spent the winter with Phoebe, her mother, and Andy the chore-boy in the Preble home in Maine. The story is written in the form of Hitty's memoirs, and through the genius of the author, Hitty emerges as a very real character. It is not only a doll story but an adventure story as well, for Hitty gives a thrilling account of her adventures on both land and sea, and the reader catches a vivid picture of the changes in the American scene during the nineteenth century. The strength, beauty, and integrity of the text is extended through the illustrations which are an integral part of the whole. The book was awarded the Newbery medal in 1930. In the chapter given below, Hitty tells of her first summer, when Captain Preble returned home from the sea.

I could fill many pages with accounts of that first summer — of the trips we took with Captain Preble in his gig, to Portland, Bath, and nearer farms; of the expeditions in the old pumpkin-colored dory with the home-made canvas he was teaching Andy to sail; and of the visits from neighbors and relations who often came to spend all day now that the weather was so fine. Such long, blue, sunny days they were, too, and, as happens in northern places where seasons are short, all the flowers seemed to be trying to blossom at once. When buttercups and daisies and

[7] From Rachel Lyman Field, *Hitty: Her First Hundred Years* (Macmillan, 1929).

devil's paint brushes were still bright in all the fields, the wild roses were already opening their petals, and before their last one fell, Queen Anne's lace and early goldenrod were beginning to crowd them out. Then there were the baskets of berries to be picked. Never had there been such a season for them, everyone said, especially for wild raspberries. Indeed, it was thanks to them that I was so nearly lost to the world.

It came about in this way: Mrs. Preble had sent us off to pick another quart or two for her preserving. Andy and Phoebe were to go to a patch not more than a mile or so down the road, where we had picked several days before. Andy carried a big, splint-bottomed basket, while Phoebe had a small one in which I was allowed to ride until it should be time for me to yield my place to the raspberries. She had lined it neatly with plantain leaves that felt pleasantly cool and smooth. It was a hot afternoon in late July, and I was thankful to be out of the dust and glare of the road. It seemed to me that this was one of the many times when it was nice to be a doll. Alas! how soon was I to change my opinion!

But when we reached the berry patch, someone had been before us. The bushes were bent and broken and there was hardly a raspberry left.

"There's a place 'way down by the shore," Andy remembered, just as they were turning away disappointed. "You go over to the Back Cove and walk along the beach until you come to a kind of clearing between the trees. Those raspberries are 'most as big as my two thumbs put together."

"But Mother said we weren't to go off the turnpike," Phoebe reminded him, "not out of sight of it, anyhow."

"Well," Andy wasn't one to give up anything he had his mind set on, "she sent us to get raspberries, didn't she? And there ain't any more here."

There was no denying this, and it took little urging to make Phoebe forget her mother's words. Soon we were headed for the Back Cove through a stretch of very thick spruce woods, with only a thread of a footpath between the close-packed trees.

"I heard Abner Hawks telling your ma last night that there's Injuns round again," Andy told Phoebe. "He said they was Passamaquoddies, a whole lot of 'em. They've got baskets and things to sell, but he said you couldn't trust 'em round the corner. We'd better watch out in case we see any."

Phoebe shivered.

"I'm scared of Injuns," she said.

"Come on," Andy urged, "here's where we turn off to the Cove. We have to walk a ways on the stones."

It was pretty rough going and the stones were well heated after hours in the hot sun. Phoebe complained of them even through her slipper, while Andy, who was barefooted, yelled and jumped from one to another. He kept running down to the water's edge and splashed about to cool his feet off, so that it was some time before they reached the raspberry patch and settled down to picking. Phoebe set me comfortably between the roots of a knotty old spruce tree at the edge of the clearing, where I could see them as they moved among the bushes. Sometimes the brambles grew so high that only their heads showed, like two round apples, one yellow and the other red, bobbing above the greenery.

It was very peaceful and pleasant there by the Back Cove. The spruce woods sloped down to the water, their tips as dark and pointed as hundreds of arrowheads against the sky. The Cove itself was blue and shining, with little white scallops of foam breaking round the edges of distant Cow Island. The air was filled with the sound of bees and birds, of the sea shuffling pebbles alongshore, and the voices of Andy and Phoebe calling to each other as they picked. No other doll in the world felt quite so contented as I.

Then suddenly, without the least warning, I heard Phoebe give a sharp cry.

"Injuns, Andy, Injuns!"

I saw her point toward the woods behind me. Her eyes and Andy's looked as round as doorknobs. But I saw nothing, for I could not turn my head around. Andy seized Phoebe's hand and began running with her in the opposite direction. Pebbles rattled under their feet as they sped along the shingle beach, and raspberries tumbled out of their baskets at every step. Then they disappeared among the trees without a single backward look. At first, I could not believe that they had forgotten me. But there was no doubt about it. It was awful to wait there alone, to hear twigs snapping and voices muttering behind me strange words I could not understand. But feeling things behind one is always so much more terrifying than when they actually appear.

They were only some five or six squaws in moccasins, beads, and blankets, who had come after raspberries, too. No one noticed me between the spruce roots. I watched them filling their woven baskets and thought they looked very fat and kind, though rather brown and somewhat untidy as to hair. One of them had a papoose slung on her back, and its little bright eyes looked out from under her blanket like a woodchuck peering out of its hole. It was almost sunset when they padded off through the trees again with their full baskets.

"Now," thought I to myself, "Andy and Phoebe will come back for me."

But I began to grow a little worried as the sun dropped lower and lower behind the trees. The sky was full of bright clouds now. Companies of sea gulls were flying off toward Cow Island. I could see the sunset on their wings as they moved. It would have seemed very beautiful to me if I had been in the proper company. I felt suddenly bereft and very small indeed. But this was nothing to what I was about to feel.

It happened so quickly that I have no very clear idea of how it actually came about. I had heard distant cawings all that afternoon and I had been vaguely aware that crows were in the nearby trees. But I was used to crows. There were plenty of them round the Preble house, so I thought little of their raucous "caw-caw's" till one sounded alarmingly near my head. At the same time I felt a curious blackness settling down upon me. I knew this could not be night, for the sky was still pink, and, besides, this blackness was heavy and warm. Nor was this all. Before I could do anything to save myself, a sharp, pointed beak was pecking at my face and the wickedest pair of yellow eyes I have ever seen were bent upon me. "Caw, caw, caw!"

Stout ash wood though I was, I quailed at the fierceness of this attack. I felt that my end had come and I was glad to bury my face in the cool moss so that I might be spared the sight of the Crow's cruel expression. Looking back upon it now, I realize that perhaps the Crow was not really cruel. Crows cannot help their blackness or their sharp beaks. But they should be all the more careful about what they seize. Evidently, this one was rather discouraged about eating me, for after several attempts it gave up trying. I could hear it giving vent to a rather unflattering opinion of its latest find in more loud "caw-caw's." But it was a very persistent Crow, determined to put me to some use.

Suddenly I felt myself hoisted into the air by my waistband. I tried to cling to the moss and tree roots, but it was no use. They sank away from me as I rose feet first. The Back Cove, the spruce woods, and the raspberry patch were a queer jumble under me. My skirts crackled in the wind as it rushed past, and now I felt myself go up, now down, according to the Crow's fancy.

"This is certainly the end of me!" I thought, expecting each moment to go spinning through space.

But strange, indeed, are the ways of Providence and of crows!

I came to rest at last and when I had collected my wits enough to look about I found myself in a great untidy nest at the top of a pine tree, staring into the surprised faces of three half-grown crows. If it had been trying to have one crow pecking and peering, it was still more so to have three all fighting over me at once. They may not have been so large and fierce as their mother, but they made up for this by their hoarse cries for food and their gaping red gullets. Their beaks were continually open and I even began to have some sympathy for the Mother Crow when I saw the amount of food she had to keep dropping down those yawning caverns. But hardly was a morsel swallowed before it was "squawk, squawk, squawk" again and off she must fly for more. Never have I seen such appetites, and I had plenty of time to see, for I must have spent the better part of two days and nights in that nest.

A more uncomfortable position I have never found myself in. The nest was large of its kind but not nearly big enough for three restless crows already nearing the fledgling stage. I was jostled and crowded and poked and shoved till it seemed there would be nothing left of me. To add to the crowded quarters the Mother Crow folded herself over the lot of us and I nearly suffocated down at the bottom of the nest with baby crows' claws scratching and sharp spikes of twig sticking into me. How I ever survived that first night I do not know.

But morning came at last and the Mother Crow began her foragings for food. It was strange to see the sun rise behind the topmost branches of a pine, instead of through decent window-panes, and to feel the nest rocking as the branches swayed in the wind. Rather a pleasant sensation when one grows used to it. This motion combined with the crows' jostlings made my position even more precarious, and I knew I must keep my feet braced firmly between the crisscross twigs if I did not wish to be crowded out. Little by little I learned to change my place and to climb higher so that I might peer out over the nest's edge. This terrified me at first, so that I dared not look down from such a vast height. That was why it took me such a long time to discover that I was not far from home, as I had supposed, but within a stone's throw of my own front door. The Crow had carried me to the very ancestral pine that grew beside the Preble house. I could scarcely believe my eyes when I saw the smoke rising from that familiar chimney and saw old knobble-kneed Charlie grazing near the barn.

There was comfort in this at first. Later, it seemed only to make things harder. To see the Preble family moving about below me, to hear the voices of Andy and Phoebe, and yet to be unable to attract their attention was tantalizing. And still the baby crows squawked and shoved and fought over the insides of mussel shells and sea urchins. I grew more uncomfortable and lonely as the day wore on.

Now I saw the sunset between pine needles. The wind moved through them with a deep, rushing noise. This may sound very beautiful when one listens to it in safety on firm ground, but it is a very different matter to hear it from such a perilous perch as mine. I could see curls of blue smoke going up from the Preble chimney and I knew supper must be cooking in the big fireplace. Soon they would be gathering round the table to eat it. But I should not be with them.

"Phoebe would certainly cry if she could see where her doll is now," I thought to myself disconsolately, poking my arm between two twigs as the most active of the crows jostled me.

I was none too quick, either, for the young crows were becoming more and more restless. They begrudged me even the smallest corner until I began to realize that my hours in their nest were numbered.

Night came on. The stars shone very clear and big, like snow crystals sprinkled across the dark. A despair settled down upon me, heavier than the Crow's wing, blacker than the night sky.

"I cannot bear it any longer," I told myself at last. "Better be splintered into kindling wood than endure this for another night."

I knew that any move must be made at once before the Mother Crow returned from a last late foraging expedition, so I began working my way toward the edge of the nest. I must confess that I have never been more frightened in my life than when I peered down into that vast space below and thought of deliberately hurling myself into it. About this time I also remembered a large gray boulder below the tree trunk where Phoebe and I had often sat. Just for a moment my courage failed me.

"Nothing venture, nothing have," I reminded myself. It was a favorite motto of Captain Preble's and I repeated it several times as I made ready. "After all, it isn't as if I were made of ordinary wood."

It would have been easier if I could have let go by degrees, if I could have put first one arm and then a leg over, but the nature of my pegging forbade this. My legs and arms must move together or not at all.

"Caw, caw, caw!"

I heard the Mother Crow coming and knew there was not a moment to lose. Fortunately for me, the young crows heard this, too, and began flinging themselves about the nest so violently that I could not have stayed in if I had wanted. Up went my two feet, out went my arms, and plop! I dropped over the edge!

The darkness seemed like a bottomless pit into which I was falling. Stiff pine needles and cones scratched my face and sharp twigs tore at me as I fell — down, down, down. I do not believe that falling from the moon itself would have seemed any farther to me. By the time I stopped I thought I must certainly have reached the bottom. Still, I felt pine needles and branches about me and when I stretched out my arms there was no comforting solid earth beneath them.

But the new position in which I found myself when morning came was little better than my old one. Instead of falling clear of the old pine, as I had expected, I had become entangled in one of the outer branches. There I dangled ignominiously in midair with my head down and my petticoats over it. My discomfort was great, but it was nothing compared to the humiliation I felt at this unladylike attitude, which I could do nothing to change. Indeed, I could scarcely move at all, so firmly was I caught.

And now an even more trying experience awaited me. I soon discovered that although I could see plainly everything that went on about the Preble house, I might have been a pine cone for all the notice I got. The pine tree was tall and bare of branches halfway up the trunk. It never occurred to one of the family to stand underneath and look for me in such a place. So I hung there for a number of days and nights, headfirst, drenched by rains and buffeted by every wind that blew by. But the greatest hardship of all was when I must see Phoebe Preble moving about below me, sitting on the boulder directly beneath my branch so that its very shadow fell on her curls, and yet be unable to make her look up.

"Suppose," I thought sadly, "I have to hang here till my clothes fall into tatters. Suppose they never find me till Phoebe is grown up and too old for dolls."

I know she missed me. I heard her tell Andy so, and he promised to go once more with her to look for me in the raspberry patch. They were sure the Indians had carried me away and I think this made Phoebe even more distressed about my loss. And all the time I hung just overhead with my skirts turned down till I must have looked like an umbrella inside out.

Curiously enough, it was the crows who were the means of reuniting us in the end. During the days immediately following my departure from their nest they had begun to try their own wings. Such flappings and cawing as they made, too. Never have I heard anything like it since, but then I never knew any other crows so intimately as those. Mrs. Preble said their goings-on were driving her distracted, and Andy spent most of his time aiming at them with pebbles and a sling shot. He never by any chance hit one, but they cawed as if he had. Finally, one morning when he stood right under the old pine with his sling shot all poised and ready, he caught sight of me. I suppose the yellow of my dress attracted his attention, but even then it was some time before he made out what I was.

"Phoebe!" he screamed, when he suddenly realized his find, "come and see what's growin' on the old pine."

He dropped his sling shot and ran to fetch her. Soon the whole family were all gathered in a group under me discussing the best way to bring me back to earth. It was a very serious problem, for the tree trunk was enormous and even if Captain Preble lifted Andy on his shoulders there was not a single branch for him to climb by. No ladder was long enough to reach me, and as I hung far out toward the tip, it looked as if the only way would be to cut down the whole tree. This Mrs. Preble steadily refused to consider. She said it was an ancestral pine and belonged to the family as much as the brass door-knocker or the pine dresser. Andy tried shying green apples, but I was hooked too firmly for these to dislodge me and they dared not use stones. I began to feel desperate.

Then Captain Preble, who had been gone some time, reappeared with a long birch pole he had cut. This was tall enough to reach me, but though both he and Andy worked for over an hour they could not bring me down, for no matter how sharply they whittled the end of the wood, I was too firmly hooked to be dislodged. At last, Phoebe's mother appeared at the kitchen door with a long frying fork in one hand and a plate of fresh doughnuts in the other. That gave the Captain an idea.

"Just you let me try lashin' that fork on here," he said, "and we'll grapple for her."

Quick as a wink he had the doughnut fork tied to the sapling. The steel prongs looked rather terrifying at such close range, but I was in no mood to be critical. I did not wince when I felt them sticking into me even more sharply than the Crow's claws. To my joy I felt myself lifted free of the pine bough.

"More'n one way to harpoon your whale!" he laughed as he put me in Phoebe's hands, "and more'n one use for a doughnut fork!" he added as he gave it back.

"I wouldn't wonder but those pesky crows fetched her 'way over here from the Back Cove," Andy told Phoebe. "It don't seem hardly possible; still, they do say they're awful thieves."

But Phoebe was too happy to have me back to bother about that or even to grieve much over the sad state of my clothes. As for me, I had no other wish than to stay in her lap forever and ever.

Blue Willow
The Shack [8]

DORIS GATES

❧ Blue Willow *is a tender, perceptive story of Janey Larkin, the only child of a migrating family of the San Joaquin Valley in California. Janey longs for a permanent home. The most beautiful thing in her life is a blue willow plate, a symbol of the home she can only dimly remember. Fine family relationships and a vivid sense of place combine to make this an outstanding realistic story.*

Janey Larkin paused on the top step of the shack and looked down at her shadow. Just now it was a very short shadow even for

[8] From Doris Gates, *Blue Willow* (Viking Press, 1940).

a ten-year-old girl who wasn't nearly as tall as she should be. The squatty dark blotch running out from under Janey's feet didn't reach to the edge of the cracked boards. It was noon and the sun hung white and fierce almost directly overhead. It beat down upon Janey, the shack, and all the wide flat country stretching away for miles and miles in every direction. It was hot, so terribly hot that when Janey cupped her hands and blew into her sweaty palms her warm breath seemed cooler than the air she was breathing.

But it was better here on the steps than inside the stifling one-room shack where the heat of a wood-stove added its bit to the best that the sun could do. Besides, here you could look out across the shimmering heat waves to the west, where the mountains were supposed to be. And somewhere on the other side of the mountains was a blue ocean. At this season the heat hid the mountains, which were far off, anyway, and not even a breath from the ocean could find a way through the hidden ranges into this wide and scorching San Joaquin Valley. But earlier in the day, while they were driving here, Janey's father had told her there was an ocean to the west. So, lowering herself onto the top step, she sat humped and listless while she tried to find comfort in thinking about it. She looked very small and very lonely sitting there. Even her shadow, now she had seated herself, had shrunk almost to the vanishing point, abandoning her to the heat.

Across the road was another board shack a little larger and more substantial-looking than the one in which the Larkin family had found shelter. Already Janey had learned that a Mexican family named Romero lived there. Dad had gone over to talk with them soon after the Larkins had arrived here this morning. Janey wondered without much interest what their neighbors were like. Dad hadn't said whether there were any children or not. Of course there would be, though. Every family had children. Every family except the Larkins, that is. Sometimes, as now, Janey regretted her lack of brothers and sisters. Big families always seemed to have a better time of it than she did. Even when they were fighting.

Of course she might scrape acquaintance with the family across the road. Janey considered this possibility for a moment before she discarded it. No, it wouldn't be any use. She wouldn't be here long enough to make it worth her while. Besides, it was just as well not to get too thick with strangers. Saved you a lot of trouble.

"Takes two to make a quarrel," Mom always said. "Mind your own business and the other fellow won't have to mind it for you."

Mom was right, Janey supposed. Mom was nearly always right. Still, there were times when this stand-offishness seemed vaguely wrong. It was at best a lonesome business. Right at this particular moment, for instance, she would have welcomed a quarrel as a pleasant break in the monotony of sitting here on the front step staring listlessly at a house across the road.

Suddenly her sagging shoulders straightened a little and an expectant look widened her blue eyes. A little girl with a baby in her arms had just come out of the Romero house and was now starting across the road toward the Larkin shack. For a moment Janey intently watched her approach and, when she was sure the girl and baby were really coming her way, she called a warning over her shoulder.

"Here comes one of the Romeros with a baby."

There was no answer from inside, only the sound of a garment being rubbed along a washboard. Mrs. Larkin was taking advantage of the present halt to do the washing. It wasn't a very big job, since the Larkins didn't possess a great quantity of clothes. But it takes a little time to rub out even one tubful, and this was the first real chance she had had to do it in many days.

With some surprise, Janey watched the Mexican girl pick her way amongst the greasewood and tumbleweed. It hadn't occurred to her that one of the Romeros might seek her out. When the stranger was within easy hailing distance, Janey called "Hello," with careful indifference. But her eyes were alert.

"Hello," came the answer, rather shyly given. The newcomer stopped in front of the

steps as if she were awaiting judgment and shifted the baby in her arms.

"My name is Lupe Romero," she said. "This is Betty" — giving the baby another bounce. "She's kind of bashful, so I brought her over. It's good for her to see people."

Janey had expected the girl to offer an excuse for her visit. You didn't go out of your way to meet strangers without good reason. Betty seemed a satisfactory one.

"I'm Janey Larkin. Why don't you sit down?"

Lupe lowered herself onto the bottom step and deposited Betty beside her.

For a moment neither of them could think of anything to say, then, "It's sure hot, isn't it?" Lupe ventured.

"Yes," said Janey. "Awful hot."

"I saw you when you got here this morning," said Lupe. "I would have come over right away, but my mother said to wait. How long are you going to stay?"

Janey was used to this question. She had answered it many times in the past five years, and always she gave the same answer as she now gave to Lupe.

"As long as we can," said Janey.

"Did they say you could move in here?"

"No," Janey replied. "Dad said it didn't look as if anyone had been staying here for a long time, so we thought maybe it wouldn't matter if we did."

"My father says this house belongs to the man who owns that herd in the next field where the windmill is," Lupe explained. "No one has lived in this house for a long time."

"How long have you lived over there?" Janey nodded toward the house across the road.

"A little over a year."

Janey's cloak of indifference fell away from her.

"Have you been staying in that place for a whole year?" she asked in astonishment. It was a wonderful thing for a family to remain put for so long a time."

"Sure," said Lupe, making a grab for Betty, who had wiggled off the step. Then, "Where did you come from?" she asked when Betty was safe again.

"Do you mean in the beginning or just lately?" asked Janey. It made a difference in the length of the answer, for the whole story of the wanderings of the Larkin family since they had left northern Texas to come to California would have taken longer than Lupe might have cared to listen.

"I mean where did you stay last before you came here?"

"We camped down by Porterville last night. Dad came up here to work in the cotton."

"Have you any brothers or sisters?" Lupe asked pleasantly.

Janey shook her head and tried to look as if she didn't care.

"I have a brother" — Lupe's voice was smug — "and of course Betty. It is a good thing to have brothers and sisters," she added importantly. "It is too bad you have none." This last was in a tone of exaggerated regret.

Lupe was, of course, merely trying to make a teasing brother and a bothersome baby sound attractive. But Janey didn't know that and decided at once that Lupe was giving herself airs. Since it was a part of Janey's code never to feel inferior to anyone, something began to stir in her. Something that was a mixture of resentment and pride. She began to wonder if perhaps Lupe, though a stranger, already sensed her loneliness. Perhaps she was even feeling sorry for her. Well, she didn't need to! She would make that clear once and for all. Lifting her chin, Janey sent her words as from a great height to Lupe.

"I have a willow plate," she said. "A willow plate is better than brothers or sisters or anything."

Lupe's interest was caught on the instant. She was even impressed. But not in the way Janey had intended.

"You mean a plate made of willows? I have not heard of that before."

Janey gave her a pitying look, and felt much better for it. Lupe might have a brother and a sister. She might even have stayed in one house for a whole year. But she didn't even know what a willow plate looked like!

"Come inside," said Janey, tolerantly but with an eagerness that rather spoiled the effect. "I'll show it to you."

Lupe rose quickly, her dark eyes bright with curiosity. She picked up Betty and followed close on Janey's bare heels.

As they entered the house, a tall, thin woman with a tired face glanced up at them over a tub of steaming suds. The odor of soap and wet clothes in the stifling little room made the air seem too heavy to breathe.

"Mom, this is Lupe Romero, and her sister Betty."

Embarrassed, Lupe pressed her face against the baby in her arms.

"There's quite a family of you Romeros, isn't there?" Mrs. Larkin gave Lupe the ghost of a smile. "How old is the baby?"

"Six months," replied Lupe, answering the last question first, and daring to look at the grown-up. "I have a brother, but I'm the oldest. I'm ten."

"Janey's all the child we've got and she's a runty little thing. Skinny as a June shad." There were worry lines between her eyes as Mrs. Larkin studied Janey's blue-overalled figure. "It's moving about from pillar to post does it," she continued. " 'Tisn't any way to raise a young one, but a family's got to live somehow."

Janey acted as if she hadn't heard. She knew the words weren't really meant for her and Lupe, anyway. She knew Mom was just talking to herself as she did every now and then.

Lupe seemed to understand, too, and covered the awkward moment by looking curiously all about her. No detail of the room escaped her soft eyes.

The shack was not much to look at either for itself or for its furnishings. The sides were rough, unfinished boards. Every crack and seam and knothole was there in plain view. It was exactly like the inside of a chicken coop, and not much larger.

In one corner was an iron bedstead with more rust than paint on it. The mattress, which spent most of its time traveling on the top of the Larkin car, had been dumped onto it along with a mixed heap of household things, including a roll of bedding. Across the room was a small stove as rusty as the bed. Two chairs placed facing each other were doing duty just now as a rest for the washtub. A wobbly table was the only other piece of furniture.

"You can hang these things over the fence pretty soon," Mrs. Larkin said to Janey. "I'll be needing another bucket of water, too." She wrung the last garment. "Help me dump this tub," she said, and Janey sprang to take hold of a handle.

Together they carried the tub to the back door and poured its contents out onto the parched ground.

"Do you want me to hang out the clothes right now, or can I show Lupe the plate first?" Janey asked.

"No, I'll save the last tub of suds for scrubbing up and I'll rinse after that. Then they'll be ready to hang out."

There would be plenty of time to show Lupe the plate, Janey decided thankfully. She needed a lot of time to show anyone the plate. Indeed, she never hurried in showing it to herself, for it was no ordinary plate. It meant to her what a doll might have meant if she had had one. Or brothers and sisters. And it meant much more, besides.

To begin with, it had belonged to Janey's great-great-grandmother, so it was very old. Then it had belonged to Janey's mother. But that was a long, long time ago before that mother had died and Mom had come to take her place. The memory of her mother was so shadowy to Janey that if she tried to hold it even for a second, it faded away altogether. It was like a bit of music you can hear within yourself, but which leaves you when you try to make it heard. Mixed up with this faint memory were Mother Goose rhymes and gay laughter and a home of their own. And because the willow plate had once been a part of all this, it had seemed actually to become these things to Janey. It was the hub of her universe, a solid rock in the midst of shifting sands.

In addition to everything else, the willow plate was the only beautiful thing the Larkins owned. It was a blue willow plate, and in its pattern of birds and willows and human figures it held a story that for Janey never grew old. Its color, deep and unchanging, brought to her the promise of blue skies even on the grayest days and of blue oceans even in an arid wasteland. She never grew tired of looking at it.

But, strangely enough, not once since the drought and dust storm had driven them out of Texas had the blue plate ever been used as a dish or for any other purpose. Never had it been unpacked except for brief moments. And never, Mrs. Larkin had declared long ago, would it be put out as a household ornament until they had a decent home in which to display it. In the meantime it was kept safely tucked away, a reminder of happier days before its owners had become wanderers in search of a livelihood.

Janey rummaged amongst the heap of things on the bed and succeeded finally in hauling forth a scarred and battered suitcase. She worked it to one side of the roll of bedding, leaving a cleared space on the springs.

"You two sit there," she directed Lupe, who still held Betty in her arms. She tried to keep her voice matter-of-fact in spite of her growing excitement. She couldn't remember when she had ever been more eager to exhibit her treasure than on this occasion. Lupe would be dazzled. Never again would she boast of brothers and sisters in Janey's presence. Of course she couldn't be expected to appreciate the plate's whole significance. Nobody could except Janey herself. But no one could be indifferent to its great beauty. Not even Lupe Romero.

While Lupe and Betty made themselves as comfortable as possible on the wobbly bedsprings, Janey opened the suitcase and carefully rolled back a top layer of folded things. Reaching in, she slowly lifted up the blue willow plate.

For an instant she held it at arm's length, her head tilted a little to one side so that the ends of her slightly wavy tow-colored hair bent against her shoulder. Then she drew the plate up level with her pointed chin and blew an imaginary speck of dust off it. Still holding it in her two hands, she placed it on the bed beside Lupe, and slowly let go of it. Not saying a word, she stood back, her eyes still feasting on the treasure, and something in her rapt face cast a silence over Lupe too.

As a matter of fact, so interested was Lupe in watching Janey's strange conduct that she didn't even so much as glance at the thing responsible for it. She was a little bothered by the way Janey was acting. Never outside of church had Lupe seen just such a look on anybody's face. It made her feel uneasy, and, clutching Betty to her, she at last slid her eyes toward the plate, half fearful of what she might see there.

But it was just a plate, after all, Lupe discovered. A pretty enough plate, to be sure, but certainly nothing to make such a fuss about. Its color she found distinctly disappointing. Why couldn't it have been red with a yellow pattern and perhaps a touch of green? But the gentle Lupe did not reveal her thoughts. Something in Janey's face forbade it. At the same time she was too disappointed to be able to say anything fitting. She had expected something marvelous and she had been shown what to her was a very ordinary plate.

Only to Janey did the willow plate seem perfect. Only for her did it have the power to make drab things beautiful and to a life of dreary emptiness bring a feeling of wonder and delight.

Bending over it now, she could feel the cool shade of willows, she could hear the tinkling of the little stream as it passed under the arched bridge, and all the quiet beauty of a Chinese garden was hers to enjoy. It was as if she had stepped inside the plate's blue borders into another world as real as her own and much more desirable.

For the moment she had quite forgotten Lupe, and it was only when a grimy finger descended upon the arched bridge and a small voice said doubtfuly, "It's pretty," that Janey was jerked back to her real world of heat and soapsuds and poverty.

Lupe's questioning dark eyes were lifted to Janey's blue ones, as deeply blue now in their excitement as the plate itself. "But why does it have such funny-looking houses and people on it?" Lupe was trying to be polite.

"They all mean something," Janey explained. "You see, the plate has a story. Dad has told me about it lots of times." Then eagerly: "Would you like to hear it?"

Lupe nodded without much interest, but Janey didn't notice. Had Lupe been so cruel as to shout: "No!" it is more than likely that Janey would have insisted on telling the story anyway. It was nice, of course, that Lupe had

nodded, but not absolutely necessary so far as Janey was concerned.

"Once upon a time over in China there was a rich man who had a beautiful daughter," she began.

"Were they Chinamen?" asked Lupe incredulously.

"Sure. They lived in China, didn't they?" Janey was annoyed at the interruption. She scowled at her listener, who looked apologetic and was silent as Janey went on.

"Well, this rich old man had promised another rich man to let him marry the beautiful daughter. But the daughter was already in love with a poor man who was very handsome. And when the father found it out, he shut his daughter up in a tower. See, here it is in the picture. But the handsome man stole her away, and they ran across the bridge to an island and there they lived for quite a while. But the father found out about it and went to the island to kill them."

At this point, Lupe furtively looked in the direction of Mrs. Larkin. But Mom wasn't listening to Janey's chatter. She was too busy with her own affairs.

Janey, noting that Lupe's interest had wavered for the moment, paused until her visitor's round dark eyes should be once more directed at the plate. Lupe misunderstood the pause and, eager to know the outcome, asked breathlessly: "Did he kill them?"

Janey ignored the question. This was the great moment in the story; she couldn't think of giving it away with a paltry "yes" or "no."

"He went to the island to kill them," she repeated, relishing the suspense, "and he would have done it, too, but just as he got to their house, something changed the lovers into two white birds, and so they escaped and lived happily ever after."

"What changed them?" asked Lupe as soon as Janey had finished.

"I don't know, but something did."

"It was a miracle," Lupe announced awesomely.

"I don't know much about miracles," Janey confessed. "But Mom says things just happen and you have to make the best of it, so I guess that's what the lovers did. Anyway, it would be sort of fun to be a bird," she added dreamily, bending over the plate.

"What kind of trees are those?" Lupe pointed to some waving, frond-like branches that swept almost across one side of the plate.

"Willows. That's why it's called a willow plate."

"I know what willows are; there's lots of them along the river, but they don't look anything like those on that dish," declared Lupe stoutly, defending her ignorance.

Janey chose not to argue the matter. "Whereabouts is the river?" she asked instead.

Lupe slid off the bed and took Betty into her arms again.

"Right over there," she said, balancing the baby on one hip in order to point from out the back door with her free arm.

Janey came and stood beside her in the doorway. Away to the east she could see a billowy line of foliage which distance had shrouded in a misty blue. It seemed to begin nowhere and to end in nothing. That was because one curve of the river swept it within her sight and another drew it away again.

"That's the river," Lupe informed her, adding with a wistful sigh, "I wish it was closer."

"How far away it is?" Janey asked.

"About a mile."

"We must have come by there this morning," said Janey, speaking more to herself than to Lupe. "It's nice to know there are willows here just as there are in the plate."

Lupe turned on Janey dark eyes in which there lay a mild hint of vexation. "But they aren't anything like those in the plate," she said reprovingly.

Janey didn't answer for a moment. A wise smile played at the corners of her mouth as she continued to gaze dreamily toward the river, indifferent to Lupe's troubled glances.

"From here they are exactly the same," she said at last, her voice almost a whisper. "They're even blue like the plate. Maybe there's a little arched bridge near them too."

Lupe's face brightened. "Yes," she said, relieved that Janey was beginning to talk sense, "there's a bridge where the highway crosses the river, only it hasn't got any arch."

Janey looked at her with heavy scorn. "Can't you ever make-believe about things?" she asked. "I don't mean an old highway bridge. I mean a little bridge with a house by it like there is in the plate."

Lupe shook her head slowly. "I don't know about that. Maybe there's a house there. I can ask my father."

"No, don't." Janey spoke quickly. "I'd rather not know if there isn't one. And if I don't know for sure, I can keep on playing there's one."

Lupe surveyed Janey with real interest. It was funny the way this strange girl talked almost as if she saw things other people couldn't see. Lupe wasn't altogether certain that it was safe to be too friendly with that kind of person. Maybe she was just queer and therefore to be avoided. But she didn't look queer, and it was sort of fun to hear her talk. You couldn't tell what she would say next. She sounded like somebody out of a story-book or a movie. Lupe had never been around anyone like this before and she found the experience rather pleasantly exciting. In Janey, thoughtful now over something which Lupe was at a loss to understand, she could sense a difference that set this new-comer apart from all other people. Weighing the matter slowly and carefully, Lupe decided at last that she liked Janey in spite of her difference. On the heels of that decision came the hope that the Larkins wouldn't soon move away.

A tired voice behind them put an end to Lupe's thoughts and recalled Janey from her daydreams.

"You can hang these clothes out along the fence now, Janey."

Lupe hesitated for a moment, undecided what her position as visitor demanded in such a situation, then her natural courtesy came to the rescue. "I'd help you, Janey, only, if I put Betty down, she'll start to cry."

"That's all right," said Janey absently. Her eyes were still on the river.

Lupe edged out the back door. "Come over to my house when you get through," she said adding, "The plate is real pretty, and I hope you stay here a long time."

Janey didn't reply immediately, but continued to stand quietly gazing out the back door. Puzzled, Lupe began to move away, wondering if her polite little speech had been heard at all. At length, with a start, Janey became aware of her guest's departure and turned to Lupe like someone just awakened from sleep. The little Mexican girl with Betty in her arms had already covered half the distance to the corner of the house, the baby looking back owlishly over her sister's shoulder.

"Thanks, Lupe. I hope we stay here, too," Janey called to her just as Lupe rounded the corner and disappeared from sight.

Then Janey went over to the tub of clean clothes, picked it up, and started with it to the back door. But she didn't go directly outside. Instead, she halted in the doorway and stood there musing while the tub pulled her thin arms straight. At that very instant there had come over her the distinct feeling that something fine had happened. Not just the feeling she always had when looking at the willow plate that something fine was about to happen. This time it actually had. Lupe had said she hoped they would stay! It was the first time anyone had ever said that to Janey. A new warmth was encircling her heart, the kind of warmth that comes there only when one has found a friend. She stood perfectly still to let the full joy of the discovery travel all through her. It didn't really matter now that Lupe had thought the river willows different from those in the plate. Lupe had actually said she hoped they would stay! At that moment Janey would have forgiven her anything.

She turned back into the room. "Lupe's nice, isn't she?" She sounded almost fearful. Everything depended on Mom's answer.

"She's a very well-mannered child," said Mrs. Larkin without enthusiasm.

But Janey was more than satisfied. She started away with the tub, a smile on her lips. While the Larkins remained in this place, Janey would have a friend. No longer would she have to feel lonely. There would be Lupe as well as the willow plate. And with that thought, Janey walked out into the blazing sunlight, her step as light as the washtub would permit.

The Wheel on the School [9]

(A Selection)

MEINDERT DE JONG

Lina, the only girl among six school children in Shora, a Dutch fishing village, wrote a composition about storks in which she said, "I do not know much about storks because they never come to Shora." That set the pupils wondering. Why didn't storks come to Shora when they built nests on the roofs of neighboring villages? Storks brought good luck, and a fine thing it would be to have storks on every roof in Shora. Their teacher said, "Sometimes when we wonder we can make things happen." Things did begin to happen. The children worked hard searching the village for a wagon wheel to put on the schoolhouse roof so storks could build a nest on it. At times everything seemed to be against them, even the weather, but the children never gave up. In the selection below, the children scheme to get their fathers to help them.

On Monday morning the storm hadn't stopped. It raged in fury against the dike. The sea was upended; the spume and roiled spindrift still flew high above the dike, landing in gray dirty flecks in the streets and on the roofs. If anything, the storm was more jerky and fitful. Odd sudden lulls seemed to fall momentarily between the high shrieks and moans of the wind, although behind the dike the sea thundered on. Enormous breakers hurled themselves up and washed in a last, thin, hissing line almost to the crest of the dike. Now and then the spent water of an unusually large wave managed to spill over the dike.

In the houses the fishermen sat loafing in the corners of their kitchens, behind the stoves if possible, to be out of the way of their busy wives and of their children getting ready for school. They were given no peace. In all Shora the fisherman fathers were pestered by their children. The wheel had to go up on the school, storm or no storm.

[9] From Meindert DeJong, *The Wheel on the School* (Harper, 1954).

"Just suppose some storks came through tomorrow," Lina argued with her father in the kitchen.

"Yes, just suppose and suppose," her father barked back. "Just suppose you let me be nice and quiet in my little corner. It feels good to be dry and warm and to do nothing for a change."

"Yes, but just suppose the storm ends, then you'll be going out to sea again, and we won't have a wheel up on the roof of the school. There's nobody else but Janus and old Douwa, and they can't get on roofs."

"They're lucky!" her father said impatiently. "It'll be a long storm, I've told you. There's plenty of time. That storm isn't just going to shut off like a faucet. Can't I wait at least for a quieter day?" He disappeared behind his week-old newspaper, which, since he had been at sea for weeks, was news to him — news and a refuge to hide behind.

He was given no chance to read it. Lina's little sister, Linda, at that moment insisted on climbing into his lap, and on the other side of the newspaper Lina still argued with him. "The teacher said Saturday that if the wheel could go up today, there'd be no school. So we can all help you," she said to the newspaper. "With all of us helping, it shouldn't take long."

"What does that teacher know about wind and storms? Let him get on that roof in a storm then! And it's off to school with you right now. There'll come a quieter day before we can take off for sea again, and then we'll see. But off with you, so I can have a quiet day today."

It was final. Lina indignantly shoved her feet into her wooden shoes. She knew better than to argue further. She had gone as far as she dared. She buttoned her jacket tightly up around her throat and stamped out of the house.

"Listen, Jella, how often do I have to tell you? I'm not stirring from this house today, and that's final. A man ought to have a couple days of rest after weeks out at sea without having to sit on top of a school. Now beat it! Get in that school and learn something instead of sitting on top of it."

"But the teacher said there'd be no school today if we put the wheel up."

"Well, you can't get the wheel up in this storm, so there is school, and I say so. Or do I have to take you there by the scruff of your neck and the seat of your pants?"

Jella shoved his feet disgustedly into his wooden shoes and slammed the door hard behind him.

"Listen, Pier and Dirk — that's the trouble with twins, a man gets a double dose of everything — one more yammer or argument out of the two of you, and I'll knock your two heads together so hard you'll be lucky if you have one head left between you. Even so, that ought to be enough — you don't use your two heads. The answer is: No, No, NO! NO wheel on NO school in NO storm!"

"But we'd help all you men. The teacher said no school if . . ."

"And I say there is school, and you two will be in it if only so I don't have to hear another word about storks. On your way!"

Pier and Dirk looked at each other. They glumly shoved their feet into their shoes and moved to the door, muttering dire things to each other. Behind his week-old newspaper their father sat grinning at their fuming threats. "Learn your lesson well today," he teased them. "I hear it's going to be about storks."

"Just so it isn't about lazy, stubborn fishermen," Pier said stormily. Afraid he'd said too much, he scooted to the door with Dirk close behind him. Their father rustled the newspaper. Dirk pushed Pier through the door and almost tumbled over him to get out as fast as he could. The door fell shut.

"Listen, Auka, don't you ever let up on me? If I hear another word about another stork, I'll . . . I'll take your neck and stretch it until you look like a stork. Then you can go and sit up on a wheel on top of a roof. Storks got more sense than to do that in a storm. How do you expect me to lug a wheel up that roof in a storm? I haven't got wings! And if I should slide down a slippery roof in this high wind and land on my head, who's going to earn the money so you can go to school and fool around with storks? You get to that school!"

"But there is no school if we put the wheel up."

"Well, nobody is going to put that wheel up today, so there is school. Bye, Auka."

There was nothing left for Auka to do but to put his shoes on and move off silently. His father watched him. "If you stick that lower lip out much farther in your pout, you can put that wagon wheel on there instead of on the roof," he teased.

Auka said a few wicked things to himself and looked stonily at his father as he closed the door very slowly to let in as much wind and draft as possible.

Eelka's father, sitting dozily beside the stove in the kitchen, peered around his newspaper to watch Eelka slowly putting on his shoes, buttoning his jacket, and pulling up the collar. "Where do you think you're going, son?"

"To school," Eelka said. "It's Monday, you know, but it's much too stormy to put that wheel up on the roof of the school today. So I suppose it'll be school." He sighed. "I never did have much luck. Bye, Pop."

Eelka hunched himself to meet the wind that was driving down the street. Ahead of him were all the other school children, bent over, boring into the wind. Unwilling and angry and defeated, each one walked alone on the hard way to school. No one hurried to catch up with any of the others; each one hated to have to admit that he'd gone down in defeat. And Eelka was too slow and far behind and full of breakfast to make the effort.

It had been a scheme, hatched and planned after church yesterday. That was what Pier and Dirk had said to do about fathers — pester them until they gave in. If all the children worked at it, nagged and pleaded . . . Oh, your father would growl and act angry and make wisecracks, but that's the way men are, different from mothers. You didn't get to know your father very well — always out at sea — but that's the way it had to be done. Joke a little and tease and nag, and nag and tease. Wait and see! In spite of

what your father said or growled, sooner or later he'd do what you wanted.

Some of the others had had their misgivings, Eelka especially. He'd said that *his* father would say, "Oh, sure, Eelka," and then not do it. But Pier and Dirk had knowingly assured them all that it was much easier than with mothers. You'd get a sound box on the ear from your mother if you kept on pestering her like that. But then your mother had you yapping around her all the time so she had less patience.

The others, all but Eelka, had been easily convinced, especially since the success of the scheme meant that not only would the wheel be put up on the school, but they'd also have the rest of the day free from lessons. It was worth a good try. But Eelka had said his father was just too good-natured, he wouldn't be pestered.

The scheme had failed miserably. Now each child on his way to school hated to admit to the others that he had failed, not knowing that the others had failed just as completely.

The storm was never going to stop. They knew it! There wouldn't be a stork left after this storm. Everything was hopeless and useless. Even if there should be one or two storks left over from the storm, what was the good of that? There'd be no wheel on the school anyway — just because of their fathers.

They had to face each other in the portal of the school. It was cold in the portal, but at least here they were sheltered from the vicious wind. They all made great pretense of blowing and stamping and beating their arms; they all breathed heavily. "Whew, what a wind!" somebody said. The others said nothing. They eyed each other while they flailed their arms across their chests in a great pretense of cold and chill.

Finally Jella turned on Dirk and Pier as the authors of the scheme. "Well," he demanded, "is your dad coming?"

Pier and Dirk looked at each other. "No-oo," Pier admitted slowly. "I guess not."

That cleared the air. "Mine isn't either. You should have heard him!"

"Neither is mine. He isn't coming at all. Said he'd just as soon try to sail the sea in a bushel basket in this storm as sit on the sharp roof of this school. Now maybe — he said — if we had a saddle, he might try it. But what good was a fisherman split in two on the ridge of a sharp roof in a high wind? The two halves of him — he didn't think — could go out fishing afterwards and catch double the amount of fish."

In spite of themselves they all laughed at the sally. Now that they'd all admitted failure, they tried to outdo each other in repeating what their fathers had said. Now they could laugh about it. And Eelka didn't say, "What did I tell you?" He was laughing too hard.

Jella summed it up for all them. "Guess it *is* too windy for old men like our dads."

The teacher suddenly stood in the doorway.

Lina burst out with it for the group. "None of our fathers — not a single one — would come," she said. "Not a one would get from behind the stove. There they sit, baking!"

"So," the teacher said. "So is that the grievance? Wise men, I'd say. You'll have to learn, too, sooner or later, that you can't defy a storm — that you can't hurt a wall with just your head. So let's go inside; let's start right in on our lessons to get our minds on other things. Your fathers will come through. You know that. If not today, the first possible day that the storm will let them. They'll put up the wheel before they set out to sea again."

"Did they tell you that?" Lina asked eagerly.

"No, they didn't tell me. I know that. And all of you ought to know it, too. Fathers always come through when it's possible. It's the way of fathers and mothers. You're just impatient, but the wheel can wait now. The storks will be waiting out the storm. Let's be just as patient and wise as the storks."

The lessons didn't go too well in spite of the teacher's reassurances. The wind, howling and shrieking around the corners of the exposed school, kept reminding them of the storm sweeping across the sea and the land. The wagon wheel leaning against the blackboard kept reminding them of storks. The howl of the wind made it difficult to understand the teacher and made it even more difficult to concentrate on answers. Who could think out arithmetic problems when hundreds of storks coming from Africa were maybe going down in the sea? How many storks would drown and never come to Shora? That was the outrageous arithmetic problem the wind seemed to be howling at them.

The teacher asked Auka how much sixteen times sixteen were. Auka had to jerk his attention away from the window where a tuft of hay was held against the glass by the relentless wind. "There won't be a single stork can come through a storm like this," Auka answered.

Nobody smiled at Auka's mistake. All eyes went anxiously to the window and from the window to the huge wagon wheel leaning against the front blackboard. Even the teacher looked somber.

"It's getting still worse," somebody in a back seat muttered.

"It only seems that way," the teacher said slowly, "because we feel so helpless. Because we're just sitting still and doing nothing about the wheel. Inaction is hard, and still, Auka, the only problem before us that we can do anything about is: How much are sixteen times sixteen?"

There was a long pause. Auka had to jerk his mind from his own inside woes, and then figure out the answer. He got it wrong.

"Oh," he said moodily to himself, "I thought he said sixteen times eighteen."

Nobody but Auka cared that his answer was wrong. Not even the teacher! The teacher himself was standing listening to the sounds outside. The wind seemed to be making new noises. Muttering, grumbling noises penetrated the classroom door. Outside the portal there was a sound as of something crashing down. Now there were stumbling noises in the portal. The wind must have blown something in and was rolling it around.

Everybody's head was cocked toward the classroom door. There came a hard knock. There were voices.

"Our dads!" Lina cried.

The teacher hurried to open the door. There stood the men of Shora. "It isn't sane. It's insane," one of the men said to the teacher. It sounded like Eelka's father. "First the kids nag you every waking minute, so you chase the kids off to school. What happens then? Their mothers start in on you! Nobody's got anything on the brain but those blasted storks on that wagon wheel. Well, they nagged us all out of our houses, so we got together and decided it was less grief putting up that wheel than facing a bunch of nagging women and children."

The teacher grinned at the men. "Solomon found that out a few thousand years before you. Didn't he in his Proverbs say that it was better to sit on the roof of a house than with a nagging woman inside the house?"

Auka's father turned to the men behind him. "Did you hear that? If his wives had even wise old Solomon up on a roof, what are a few dumb fishermen going to do?"

"Get on the roof with Solomon," somebody said in the portal. "He knew when he was licked."

The schoolroom tittered. The men were joking, and, in spite of the storm, they were going to try to put the wheel up. And they weren't unhappy about it — you could tell that — not if they were making wisecracks. That was always a good sign.

Jella's hefty father peered over the head of the teacher into the classroom. "It seems I was told," he boomed, "that part of the deal was that if we put that wheel on the roof, there'd be no school today. Was I correctly informed, or was that just Jella and his endless love for school?"

"No-oo," the whole room sang out. "No school. He promised!"

They did not wait for the teacher so much as to nod his head; they could see it in his face — anything went today. They streamed from the room and got into jackets and stocking caps and wooden shoes.

From the portal they saw that their fathers had even brought ladders and lumber and ropes. The stuff lay in a helter-skelter pile in the schoolyard where it had been dropped.

"Out of the way! Out of the way all you mortals," Jella came shouting. Jella alone had remembered. He had jumped to the front of the room to get the wagon wheel instead of just rushing out with the rest.

Now he sent the wheel rolling wildly into the portal. Everybody had to scatter. The wheel wobbled in an uncertain path, somehow found the outside doorway, plunged into the yard, and settled itself on the pile of beams and ropes and ladders.

"Well, it's all here now," a man shouted. "Now roll out your storks."

The men laughed, but not the children. Happy and relieved and eager as they were, now that their fathers were actually going to put up the wheel, it was not a good joke. The low, sweeping sky, scudding and racing with clouds that looked as angry as capped waves on the sea, threatened bad things. There was nothing in the sky but storm; there wasn't a bird anywhere, not even a sparrow. A rain squall slashed down. The wind hurled the rain into the portal.

"Will there be any storks left after a storm like this?" Dirk asked the group of men around the pile in the schoolyard.

The men looked up at the sky and shrugged. "Maybe, if the storm doesn't hang on too long," Lina's father said. "Maybe a couple of them will have sense enough to go bury their heads in sand until this blows over."

"That's ostriches!" Lina, standing right beside him, said scornfully. She was half-ashamed of the ignorance of her father — and right before the teacher! "Ostriches are *supposed* to bury their heads in the sand, only they don't."

"I guess that takes care of you and your ostriches," Eelka's father said.

"Yeah," Lina's father said, nettled. "Maybe I'd better go bury my head in some sand. These modern-day school kids — they know everything, don't they? Me, all I know is fish." He grinned suddenly. "You kids wouldn't be satisfied with a couple of fish on the roof?" he asked plaintively. "Say a couple of sharks in a wash tub?"

The children hooted, and he grinned broadly. He sobered, stepped back, and eyed the sharp school roof. "Well, come on you Solomons," he said impatiently. "Let's get on the roof and get that wheel up."

The men stood studying the steep roof. "Wet and steep and windy, it'll be slipperier than a deckful of jellyfish," one of them said.

"But up with a ladder, and we'll see what the climate is up there."

Two men raised the long ladder high and straight. As they carried it upright around a corner of the school, a blast of wind caught the high ladder. The two men struggled, but they couldn't hold it up. The ladder swayed and twisted and threatened to come crashing down.

Everybody stood anxiously watching the top of the ladder, expecting it to smash to pieces against the ground at any moment. "Watch it. Watch it," somebody yelled. "If you can't even set a ladder up, how do you expect to get a wheel up there? Get into it all of you; don't stand there staring at the top rung. Let it down! Let it down, I say. There. Now carry it flat around that windy corner. That isn't a flag you're carrying in a parade."

It was Janus! There he came in his wheel chair, forcing it ahead against the wind by sheer strength and at the same time loudly scolding everybody.

The men let the ladder down. Then they turned to face Janus, a bit peeved at being bawled out before their own children. But Janus was grinning broadly; he was having a fine time in spite of the wind and the struggle to move against it. He rolled up to the group in his wheel chair. "When it comes to doing anything on land, you guys are about as helpless as the fish are," he told them. He turned his chair so as to face the roof. "Now then, let's use our heads. Better yet, I'll use my head."

"So now we've got an overseer," one of the men said.

"All right, now lay that ladder down," Janus directed. "Place one end against the wall, then raise the other end. Get under it; walk your hands from spoke to spoke until it's up straight against the wall. Then all you have to do is pull out the bottom end. See, that way you don't fight the wind."

"Well, that worked," one of the men said.

When the ladder was up, the men automatically turned to Janus for further instruction. Janus looked at the pile of lumber and the one ladder beside it.

"Now the other ladder and push it up on the roof. But first tie a coil of rope on the top rung, so you can let the rope down the other side of the roof to fasten the ladder down. Then lash the second ladder to the first, otherwise the wind will just sweep it right off the roof. Meanwhile, you kids get me that wagon wheel."

While he waited for the children to roll the big wheel to him, Janus kept looking at the pile of beams and boards still lying in the schoolyard. "What's the big pile for?" he yelled up to the roof.

"To brace up the wheel. Got to have some brackets or braces or something to hold the wheel on the sharp ridge of this roof," Auka's father explained.

"Yeah, but you're just going to have storks up there, not elephants," Janus said scornfully. "The way I've doped it out — that wheel's got to be up there nice and simple. With all your beams and boards and two-by-fours sticking in every direction, storks flying overhead will think it's a trap, not a nest. But just get on with that ladder, Janus will fix it nice and neat and simple."

"Yes, sir, yes, sir," Auka's father said. "Up with the second ladder, men, Janus says."

Jella, Auka, and Lina rolled the wagon wheel before Janus. "Now where's that saw?" Janus said impatiently. "Somewhere I hung a saw on this wheel chair contraption."

"There it is," Pier said behind him. "You brought a hammer, too. You're sitting on it."

"The hammer, too," Janus said. "The hammer first." Then paying no attention to the alarmed looks of the children, he took the hammer and drove the steel rim off the inner wooden rim of the wheel. After studying the pitch of the roof and the ridge, he began sawing a deep V into the side of the wooden rim. The children had to hold the wheel steady for him while he sawed. "See, I'll cut two deep V's; that way the rim will fit snug on the ridge," he explained. "Then we'll fit the iron rim just partly over the wooden one so it won't cover the V notches. The iron doesn't have to cover the whole wooden rim — this wheel isn't going rolling any place — it'll even be better that way. With the iron rim sticking up, it'll make a sort of pan of the wheel — storks are awfully sloppy nest builders. This may help them to hold all the stuff they'll lug up on this wheel."

The teacher came up. "Janus, don't you want to go inside? No sense in your sitting here in the wind when you can do your work just as well inside."

"If those men can sit on that windy roof, I can sit here where it's practically cozy," Janus said shortly, his whole grim attention on his sawing.

The teacher, realizing Janus wanted no favors, said no more. "Anything I can do?" he asked. "I feel sort of useless with everybody else busy."

"Well, I need a brace and bit — a long bit so it will go through the ridge boards on both sides of the roof."

"My dad's got a brace and all kinds of bits, all sizes," Jella said eagerly. "I'll go get them."

"Well, there goes Jella and the job you had for me," the teacher said.

"Hold it," Janus said. "I also need two heavy iron rods — long enough so the two edges of the wheel rim can rest on them. You see, we'll drill the holes through the ridge, shove the rods through them, and then rest the wheel on the rods. The two notches I cut in the wooden rim will fit snugly over the ridge. Then all we'll need to do is to wire the rim to the two supporting rods, and there'll be the wheel, steady and level and solid as a house. But I can't think of anybody in Shora who would have a couple of heavy rods like that."

"Hah!" the teacher said. "You're talking to the right man. It seems to me I've seen a couple of rods like that in the tower when I go there to ring the bell. I'm almost sure."

"Just so they're long enough," Janus said.

"I'll go look, and nobody can take this job away from me. As the official bellringer for the village, I'm the only one to have a key to the tower." The teacher pulled the big ancient key out of his pocket and held it up. He hurried off.

"Glad I found something for him to do," Janus said to Lina. "He makes me nervous watching so closely. He's just as jittery and excited as you kids." He had finished cutting the notches. Now came the job of fitting the iron rim partially over the wooden rim. The

boys and Lina had all they could do to hold the wheel upright and steady as Janus struggled with the close-fitting rim.

Jella returned with the brace and all the bits. A few minutes later the teacher came back with two large, rusty rods. Janus studied the rods. "They should do. Good and thick and solid. Plenty long enough for the wheel. Good thing you remembered them," he said to the teacher. "It must be the only pair of loose rods in Shora. It was the one thing had me worried — me with my fine plans and no rods. I'd have been the laughing-stock around here."

Jella was sent up the ladder to carry the brace and bit to his father. The teacher was sent off to find some heavy wire that could be used to secure the wheel to the rods. "Got to keep him busy," Janus said with a sly wink at Lina.

At last the wheel was ready. The children rolled it to the ladder. The men began hoisting the huge wagon wheel up the ladder, while Jella's father drilled the two holes for the rods in the ridge of the roof.

It was a slow, hard struggle against the tugging of the wind. Two of the fishermen now straddled the ridge, ready to lift the wheel on to the rods when it reached them. A sudden hard hail and rain squall slashed down again. The men straddling the ridge had to press themselves flat; they lay with faces against the roof and clung with one hand to the ladder. The men working the wheel up the roof had to stop and be content just to hold the wheel in place on the ladder. The squall passed as suddenly as it had come, and the struggle went on again.

Janus watched every move with eagle eyes. He was so intent he seemed unaware of the sweep of wind and rain and hail. Yet from time to time Janus glanced down the road to the village. Suddenly he bellowed out, "Look at that, men! Look what's coming! The women! What do you know? Wind or hail — here come the women. Pots of hot coffee for you. This is going to turn into a picnic. Hurray for women!"

All work stopped on the roof. Everybody sat looking down the road; they called the women on. The women came in a close group, trying to protect their steaming coffee from the cold wind. Then a new blast of hail had the men hanging on to the roof and the ladders again.

The moment the squall passed, they looked down the road again. "No use looking," Janus shouted. "No hot coffee, no nothing, until that wheel is up and secure."

"Janus, you're a slave driver," one of the men on the ridge complained. "All you need is a whip."

"Don't need a whip," Janus called back. "Got my tongue."

"Yeah," Pier and Dirk's father yelled down. "Too bad that shark didn't get your tongue instead of your legs."

Down below Janus flushed red and embarrassed. He looked away and then glowered up from under the peak of his cap to see how Pier's father had meant the joke. Pier's father saw the look; he gave Janus a good-natured grin. All of Janus eased in the chair. He let out his breath. "Well, all I can tell you is," he called out slowly, "that shark *was* eyeing my tongue. Got a good look at it, too—all I was telling him! But it looked too tough even for him, I guess. He must have decided my sea boots were tenderer. So he took my boots. How could that poor dumb fish know my legs were inside of them?"

Everybody laughed, and Janus sat back, relieved. He seemed to test the laugh, almost as if he were tasting it. Then he looked at Pier, hovering anxiously beside his chair. "Good kid," he said. "Don't think I don't know everybody's accepting that crazy story because it's good for me. And it is good!" he added fiercely. "Good."

The wheel was being fitted over the ridge. Janus riveted his whole attention on the operation. "It's got to work, my idea with just two rods," he muttered anxiously. "Otherwise my name is mud. They'll razz me out of Shora."

The teacher came hurrying up with a handful of wires. Janus picked out the heaviest and sent Pier up the ladder with them. "Nothing more for you to do," Janus told the teacher. "But the women have hot coffee on the stove in the schoolroom. Go get yourself a cup. You aren't used to being out in this kind of weather."

"Aye, aye, sir," the teacher said. He saluted smartly and trotted off.

Jella's father, lying full-length on the ladder on the roof, was twisting the wire around the rods and the rim of the wheel. It was awkward, slow, overhead work. The cold and the salt, stinging wind were numbing all the men and slowing their movements. The two men straddling the ridge were holding the wheel in place. One of them had to let go his hold to rest his numbed arm. He wearily rubbed a hand over his face to wipe away the icy wetness. He took a new hold, but now the wheel was tilted.

"Jan, hold that wheel straight," Janus said. "Those storks need a nest, not a chute."

"Look," Jan answered irritably, before he gave a thought to what he was saying, "if you think you can do it better, you come up here and hold it."

There was an awkward, stunned pause. Everybody looked at Janus. Lina, beside his chair, laid her hand on Janus' shoulder. But to her astonishment Janus was delighted. "Did you hear that?" he asked Lina. "He forgot I've got no legs. Bless his ornery old hide. That's the way it's got to be."

Now Jan, who had been preoccupied with the wheel and his precarious position, realized what he'd said. He looked down at Janus. A slow grin spread over his face. "Stay there," he said. "I'm not giving you a chance to come up here and show me up. I'll show you I'm as much a man as you are."

He hadn't apologized or even tried to cover it up. They were treating Janus man to man. He was one of them again. Janus bent low to straighten out the pin in his folded-over trousers leg. He fumbled with it. When he straightened up, his eyes were bright. "Bless his ornery old hide," he mumbled.

Lina took her hand off his shoulder. Even she mustn't baby Janus.

"Would you dare?" Janus asked suddenly. "We've got to test that wheel, and you're the only one who is about the weight of two storks. I've got to know whether it'll hold their nest without tilting or wobbling. The men will hold you up on the wheel."

Janus wasn't babying her either. "Sure," Lina said stoutly.

On the ridge Jan held Lina's hand as she climbed on the wheel. Janus directed from down below. Lina walked along the rim of the wheel as far as Jan could reach and still keep his hold on her. Janus watched her closely. "You can come down now," he said. "It'll hold. It didn't so much as stir, even with you walking on the edge. Everybody down now! Take the ropes and ladders down and go get your coffee."

Lina made use of that moment of distraction to pull free from Jan's hand. She climbed up on the hub of the wheel. She flapped her arms. "I'm a stork, I'm a stork," she cried. The next moment a gust of wind caught her, and she had to let herself fall, clutching for the spokes of the wheel and grabbing wildly for Jan's outstretched hand. She hung on for dear life.

"Some stork!" the boys jeered up at her. "Let's see you fly down."

"Jan, come on down and bring that stork with you under your arms," Janus said, "before she tries to fly. I wouldn't put it past her."

It was a picnic — steaming coffee and cakes and fatballs. It was a feast! Hot chocolate milk for the boys and Lina! That was what made it really a picnic and a feast. You had hot chocolate milk only on the Queen's Birthday and fatballs only on Santa Claus Day. But now fatballs and chocolate all the same day! And the rest of the day free — it was a holiday.

The school room buzzed. Janus was in the midst of it in his wheel chair. His voice carried above all the others. But everybody was in high spirits. They'd wrestled the wheel up on the roof in spite of storm and cold and hail and squalls. It made it a holiday.

No school the rest of the day, and their fathers home with games to play. They'd all play dominoes with their dads. The five boys and Lina decided it among themselves as they sat in their seats, sipping hot chocolate while the grownups crowded around the warm stove.

It happened so seldom, having their fathers home. Always they were out at sea or, if home, busy with nets and sails and the readying of the boats. Now they'd have almost a whole day with their dads. The storm had made it a holiday for them, a chance for games and jokes with their fathers.

Everybody was talking, and Janus was in the midst of everything. Now he noticed the boys and Lina in their corner. "How is it?" he asked. "Is this a feast or isn't it?"

"Hot chocolate milk and hot fatballs!" Pier told him smartly. "Hey, Janus, all it lacks is some cherries."

Janus laughed. "To get them you'd have to go where the wind took them — over a couple of provinces or so, I think, or maybe into Germany. Well, there're a few under the tree, if you like salt cherries."

Lina hastily told the boys that she was going to ask Janus to play dominoes, too. He and Jana had no children. Janus ought to be invited, too. They all agreed eagerly; they all wanted Janus in their houses.

"Oh, no, you don't," Lina said. "I thought of it first!"

Caddie Woodlawn
Breeches and Clogs [1]

CAROL RYRIE BRINK

❧ *This fine story of frontier life in Wisconsin in 1860 is based on the childhood of the author's grandmother, who was the original "Caddie." Mrs. Brink says: "Most of the story is as it really happened. Even the breeches and clogs, the portrait of the little red-haired boy, and the father's story of his English ancestry are as Caddie remembers them." The chapter which she mentions is given below. The book was awarded the Newbery medal in 1936.*

The long winter evenings in the farmhouse were very pleasant times. Grouped about the fire and the lamp, the Woodlawns made their own society, nor wanted any better. One evening soon after Caddie's adventure in the attic, they were all gathered together thus. Everyone who belonged was there — except

[1] From Carol Ryrie Brink, *Caddie Woodlawn* (Macmillan, 1935).

Nero. Caddie missed the faithful head resting against her knee. They were recalling old adventures that they had had, and now Clara was speaking in her gentle voice.

"Yes," she said, "it was the first winter we were out here. We lived at Eau Galle then, near the mill, and we had school in the tavern. Caddie and Tom were little then, and Warren was a baby."

"Where was *I*?" demanded Hetty.

"You hadn't come yet."

"Go on and tell," urged the other children. They all sat about the big stove, cracking butternuts between hammer and stones, and dropping the meats into a wooden bowl.

"There isn't much to tell," continued Clara, in her soft voice, "only I came through the woods one day and I saw a bear eating a little pig."

"Where did he get it?" asked Warren.

"From one of the farms, I guess."

"Were you scared?" asked Hetty.

"Oh!" said Clara, putting her slim hand against her heart. "I was so scared! It makes my heart thump yet to think of it!"

"I wouldn't have been so scared," boasted Tom. "Remember, Caddie, when we saw the wolves?"

"*Uh-huh!*" said Caddie, her mouth full of butternuts.

"Tell about that," said Warren. "I wish I'd been there."

"Well, one time the cows got into the swamp, and Caddie and I went after them to bring them home, and right in the swamp we met a wolf."

"Did he bite you?" asked little Minnie breathlessly.

"No, he just stood and looked at us, and we looked at him."

"I'd have shot him or hit him with a rock," said Warren.

"You hold your tongue, Warren," said Tom. "I guess you'd have done the same as us, if you'd been there. I don't know what would have happened next, if two big hounds hadn't come along and chased him away."

"Aw, you're making it up," said Warren, who was always skeptical of any adventures which Tom and Caddie had without him.

"No, honest," said Tom. "Caddie will tell you the same thing. The hounds were after him — that's why he acted so funny. They belonged to a man down the river."

"Robert Ireton can tell a better one than that," said Warren. "He says there was a fiddler coming home through the woods late one night from a dance, and a pack of wolves took after him. He saw he couldn't get away from them, so he stopped and played his fiddle to them, and they all went away and let him go home in peace."

"I know!" said Tom. "It's true, too. Robert had it from a man who married the fiddler's sister."

Mr. Woodlawn smiled at his wife and said: "Ireton knows how to tell a good story as well as sing a good song, I see."

Caddie had been listening to the stories in silence. Now she suddenly jumped up, shaking the nut shells from her apron into the wood basket. Without a word, she caught up one of the candles which burned on a side table and ran upstairs to the attic. She hastily went through the contents of one of the boxes until she found what she was seeking; and downstairs she ran again, almost before the others had ceased gaping over her sudden departure.

"Look!" she said. She held up a small pair of scarlet breeches and two little wooden-soled clogs.

"Well, of all things!" cried Mrs. Woodlawn. "Wherever did you get those?"

"In one of the boxes in the attic."

"What are they? What are they?" cried the children, leaving their nuts to crowd nearer.

"I don't know whose they are," said Caddie. "There must be a story about them, Mother. Do you know it?"

Mrs. Woodlawn looked at her husband. He had taken one of the little shoes in his hand, and it scarcely covered his big palm. He turned it this way and that, smiling an odd, perplexed smile.

"Well, well, well!" he said. "What a funny little shoe!"

The impatient children crowded nearer, and little Minnie clambered onto his knee.

"Father!" cried Caddie, "you know something about them! Tell us!"

"Tell us! Tell us!" echoed the others.

"Yes, Johnny, you had better tell them now," said Mrs. Woodlawn.

Mr. Woodlawn still hesitated, his eyes deep with thoughts of something far away, something beyond the warm room and the ring of bright, expectant faces; something less bright and warm and happy.

Mrs. Woodlawn stirred impatiently. "Those are your father's shoes, children," she said. "He used to dance in them in England, and the little red breeches, too — long, long ago. Do tell them, Johnny. They've a right to know."

"Yes, yes," said Mr. Woodlawn, "they have a right to know and I have always meant to tell them. But it's a long story, children, you had best go back to your hassocks and your nuts."

Eyes round with wonder and anticipation, the young Woodlawns did as they were told. To think of Father ever being small enough to wear those breeches and clogs, and dancing in them, too, in faraway England! How strange it was! They had heard so much of Boston, but nobody spoke of England where the strange little boy, who had grown to be Father, had danced in red breeches and clogs. Caddie thought of what Father had said about England on the night when the Circuit Rider had been with them. How often she had wondered about that since then!

"You have grown up in a free country, children," began Mr. Woodlawn. "Whatever happens I want you to think of yourselves as young Americans, and I want you to be proud of that. It is difficult to tell you about England, because there all men are not free to pursue their own lives in their own ways. Some men live like princes, while other men must beg for the very crusts that keep them alive."

"And your father's father was one of those who live like princes, children," cried Mrs. Woodlawn proudly.

"My father was the second son in a proud, old family," said Mr. Woodlawn. He set the clock he was mending beside him on the table, and his hands, unaccustomed to idleness, rested awkwardly on his knees. "My father's father was a lord of England, and the lands he owned rolled over hills and valleys and through woods."

"Bigger than ours?" wondered Hetty.

"Many times. Yes, many, many times. There was a great stone house with towers and turrets and a moat with swans, and there were peacocks on the lawn."

"Peacocks!" cried Clara, clasping her hands.

"Yes," said the father gravely. "I saw them once when I was a little boy. My mother held me by the hand and I stood on tiptoe to look between the bars of the great gate, and there they were, a dozen of them, stepping daintily, with arched necks, spreading or trailing their great tails upon the grass."

"But, Father," said Caddie, "why were you outside?"

"Well may you ask that question, Caddie!" cried Mrs. Woodlawn. Her earrings trembled with her indignation.

"Old Lord Woodlawn was very proud," said Father, "and he planned a brilliant future for his second son. . . . Thomas, my father's name was — that's where you get your name, Tom. But Thomas Woodlawn wanted to live his own life, and he had fallen in love. His heart had overlooked all the fine young ladies of high degree, and had settled upon the little seamstress who embroidered and mended and stitched away all day in the sewing room of the great house."

"Just like Tom and Kat——" began Hetty, but Caddie suddenly thrust a butternut into her mouth, and the rest of what she had intended to say was lost.

"I cannot blame him for falling in love," said Father. "That little seamstress was very beautiful and sweet. She was my mother. They were married secretly, and then they went to old Lord Woodlawn and told him. They thought that he would forgive them, after it was done and past repair. But they hadn't reckoned on the old man's stubbornness and wounded pride. You see, my mother was the daughter of the village shoemaker. God knows, the old shoemaker earned an honest living and lived an upright life, but to my Grandfather Woodlawn's notion anything connected with such a trade was low and shameful."

"How funny!" said Caddie, "if he was a *good* shoemaker."

"The old lord was beside himself with

anger. He ordered Father to forsake his bride, but that my father would not do, so the old man turned them out together. 'Never come back,' he told my father. 'You are no longer my son.' If my father had been the eldest son, the laws of England would have restored his position to him at the death of the old lord. But a disinherited second son has nothing to look forward to. So now he found himself penniless and with a wife to support."

"But I don't understand!" said Caddie.

"No, my dear," said her father. "It is hard to understand an old man's selfish pride. He had planned his son's life, and he could not endure to have his plans lightly set aside. He might have taken my father back if Father had forsaken Mother, but that was not my father's way. And so the two young things went out into the world to make a living for themselves. My father had been trained to ride a horse to hounds, to read a little Latin, and to grace a drawing room, but he knew no more about any useful trade than baby Joe. There was one thing he could do, however. He had always had some skill at drawing and painting, and, as a boy, his father had humored him by letting him have lessons in the art. Now he found that he could get occasional work by painting panels and murals in taverns and public houses. It was a sorry comedown for the son of a nobleman. Sometimes they paid him only in food and lodging and he and his wife were obliged to stay there eating and sleeping out his earnings. Truly they were glad enough to have a roof over their heads and something in their stomachs, I imagine. I, myself, remember the long walks and the slim dinners and sometimes nights spent under a haycock, when we could not find a tavern which wanted decorating."

"Poor Father!" cried Caddie softly.

"But worse was to come," said Mr. Woodlawn slowly. "The tramping about, the worry and hunger and cold were too much for my father, who did not have the peasant hardiness of my mother and me. I was about ten years old when he died, and I was a little lad who looked scarce half my years."

"And what did you do then?" breathed the little Woodlawns anxiously.

"My mother had no money to take us home again, and what could she have expected for us if she had gone? The old lord was not likely to forgive her after his son was dead, and the shoemaker was as annoyed with his daughter for marrying out of her class as the old lord was himself. And then my mother had her *own* amount of pride. In those days the worst vice in England was pride, I guess — the worst vice of all, because folks thought it was a virtue."

"But, Father, what about the clogs and breeches?" asked Caddie.

"Have patience," said Mrs. Woodlawn. "He'll get to them presently."

"My mother earned what she could as a seamstress. But that was not enough. We had no home of our own and we wandered from lodgings to lodgings always half-hungry and owing money. I did what odd jobs I could, but folks thought me too small and young to be entrusted with much. I was a lively lad, as gay as a cricket, in spite of my troubles. I had learned to dance and I begged my mother for a pair of clogs. The poor, good woman had no money to spare for dancing clogs, as I well know now. But, I dare say, I left her no peace, and suddenly she had an idea for granting my request and at the same time adding something to our income. She bought me the clogs and made me a little green jacket and a pair of red breeches. There was a green cap, too, with a red feather, and so I danced, and people threw me coppers as if I had been a monkey."

"Did you make a lot of money, Father?"

"No, but I made enough to help a bit, and sometimes they even engaged me in cheap music halls to do a week's turn or two. That was a great event."

"Oh, Father, can you still dance?" cried Caddie.

"I've still got two legs," said Mr. Woodlawn, gay once more.

"Oh, do! do!" the children cried, seizing him by the hands and pulling him out of his chair.

"Oh, Father, dance! Do!"

Mr. Woodlawn laughed. Then suddenly he pursed his lips and began to whistle an old-fashioned jig. Tap! tap! tap! went toe and heel, and suddenly he was jigging and clogging and snapping his fingers to the astonishment of the open-mouthed children. They formed a delighted ring about him, clapping and shouting, and keeping time with their feet.

Mrs. Woodlawn got up quickly and went into her bedroom. Nobody missed her, nor heard her opening the drawers in the chest where the linen was kept. When the dance was over, and Father sank, breathless and laughing, into his chair, Mrs. Woodlawn came out with a small oil painting in her hands.

"Your father will never show you this," she said, "so I am going to."

"No, no, Harriet," begged Mr. Woodlawn, still laughing and panting. "It's too foolish."

"The children shall judge of that," said his wife, and she propped the canvas up on the table. It was a dim picture, painted in an old style, of a very funny little boy. The little boy seemed scarcely more than a baby and he was dressed in a quaint little sailor suit with a wide-brimmed hat. Two tufts of bright, red hair were pulled down on either side of the face, beneath the brim of the hat. Everybody began to laugh. And yet there was something sad and wistful, too, in the eyes of the strange little boy who looked at them.

"It's your father," said Mrs. Woodlawn, "and it was *his* poor, dear father who painted it. Your father was only three years old."

The children shouted with laughter, but Caddie felt a little bit as if she wanted to cry, too, and she reached for Father's hand and squeezed it.

"It's a wicked shame!" continued Mrs. Woodlawn tartly. "All that land in England, that great stone house, even the peacocks — they ought to belong in part to your father, perhaps entirely. Who knows? Think, children, all of you might have been lords and ladies!"

"No, no, Harriet," said Mr. Woodlawn, growing grave again. "It was a hard struggle, but what I have in life I have earned with my own hands. I have done well, and I have an honest man's pride. I want no lands and honors which I have not won by my own good sense and industry."

Just then the clocks all over the house began to chime ten.

"Ah! my dears!" cried Mrs. Woodlawn. "When have you ever gone so late to bed! Scamper now, as fast as you can!"

Frightened by the idea of sitting up so late, the little children scurried to obey. Clara and Caddie went more slowly upstairs together. Clara's slender shoulders were lifted with a new pride and her dark eyes shone.

"Peacocks on the lawn, Caddie," she whispered. "Just think!"

"Peacocks!" repeated Caddie softly, and then suddenly she scowled and clenched her fists. For she was seeing the peacocks through a great, barred gate, with a funny little boy in a sailor suit and a wide-brimmed hat, whose wistful eyes looked sadly out between his odd tufts of red hair.

Downright Dencey
The Former Time [2]

CAROLINE DALE SNEDEKER

◄§ *Downright Dencey is a tale of old Nantucket filled with vitality and a tang of the sea. It is the story of Dionis (Dencey) Coffyn, a courageous little Quaker girl, and her staunch loyalty to the village waif whom she befriends. The life of Nantucket over a hundred years ago is seen from Lydia Coffyn's home with the love of husband and wife at its core. The selection given below tells of the courtship of Lydia and Tom Coffyn, Dencey's parents.*

When the white fire of New England life sprang up along the Massachusetts coast, a spark of it blew far out to sea and became — Nantucket.

Here was to be seen, as in a diminishing glass, a tiny New England, delicately outlined — intensified — in a word, islanded. Here were the New England character and hardihood, its God-fearing and mental eagerness, yet all sensitively changed, individualized, so that they became Nantucket and no

2 From Caroline Dale Snedeker, *Downright Dencey* (Doubleday, 1927).

other. Instead of the stony fields of New England, the Nantucketers plowed the wide ocean, and at this period of their history, their harvest was gathered from pole to pole. By its industry, this low, sandy island, eighteen miles long, produced enough whale oil to light half the cities of the world, including London.

Clearly defined smallness on the one hand, world wideness on the other, made the Nantucket life different from all others.

The legend of Nantucket's founding is a twice-told tale, but it is so true to the character of the Island as always to need retelling. How Thomas Macey of Salisbury, Massachusetts, gave shelter overnight to three fleeing Quakers, how for this act of humanity he was fined, questioned, and hectored by the Puritan authorities, until the New England in him rose in wrath against New England; and taking an open boat, he, with two others, put out for the small island off the coast. All Puritanism was a protest, but Nantucket was a protest against protest.

Later on, mainly through the inspiration of one powerful woman, Mary Starbuck, Nantucket became almost entirely Quaker. Imagine it, the tiny gray island clothing itself in gray, unafraid of austerity because of the colorful spirit within.

In this little and complete world, the Coffins had lived since 1660. At one time there were five hundred persons of the name of Coffin living on the Island — "not countin' the Coffin family that wa'n't real Coffins" — that line being founded by a Portuguese cabin boy whom a Coffin captain adopted.

Tom Coffyn was, needless to say, of the genuine variety. He spelled his name with a *y* as did the first Coffyn founder. He it was who afterward was to become Dionis's father. Lydia Severance, afterward her mother, had always lived there, she and her ancestors before her.

Their meeting was at meeting.

To say that they first met there is hardly true, for they had seen each other, as all Island young folk did, at sheep-shearing, at corn-huskings, or passing in the street. But Tom Coffyn was of the First Congregationalist Church and Lydia Severance of the Friends' Meeting on Pleasant Street. So they went to different schools, and the youthful acquaintance was slight. Love at first sight, then, this encounter might be called, a thing not unusual in Nantucket, where happy meetings followed the four-year loneliness of the whaling voyage. From such a voyage Tom Coffyn had just returned when on that First Day morning he chose to go to Quaker meeting with his voyage comrade, Caleb Severance.

Into the gray room filed the gray and silent people, the women on one side, the men on the other, with certain honorable ones facing the meeting from a row of higher benches. The room was perfectly bare save for the candlesticks set at intervals along the walls. The large windows let in all the glare. Only this morning a poplar, golden with autumn, standing outside in the sunlight, threw its glory into the place and filled the gray room with a spell of gold.

Tom did not at all recognize the maiden who seated herself third from the aisle in the fifth row. She must be from Rhode Island or perhaps the "Continent." There she sat among the drab and quiet sisterhood. "Heavens!" thought Tom, "how futile to dress the women all alike when one can shine out from the rest so star-like and distinguished." He must have forgotten in the long four-year glimpses of heathen women how beautiful a woman could be, how wide-set and sweet her gray eyes, how rosy and demure her mouth. In what way Tom managed to see all this across the straight-seated rows is a mystery. But he did so manage.

The Quaker silence began. So many people sitting together not communicating with each other by any word, but waiting — waiting for something outside of themselves. There was awe in the silent room. Obedience made visible. Tom could hear the poplar rustling softly in the sea wind. And once a solitary pedestrian passed in the street, was heard from far, coming, and his footsteps persisted a great distance toward town. Still the Quakers sat. Gracious, that girl was beautiful, with her downcast eyes and folded hands. There seemed an actual light in her face. Tom decided that he approved of this Quaker silence. Was there always such happiness in it? he wondered. The Divine love was played upon by a tender human dawning until both were roseate together. Now he saw the girl sway in her seat — ever so slightly, like a flower in a breath of wind. Her hands moved, she blushed slowly red. By Jove, he had been staring. He must stop it.

But the honored ones who faced the meeting knew well the signs of one whom the Spirit moves. Lydia Severance had never spoken in meeting before. A faint stir of expectation could just be felt in the deeps of meditation.

Lydia rose, swaying flower-like as before, her hands, touching the rail in front of her, passed back and forth softly as willow branches touching the grass. Then, startlingly upon the silence, her voice began — an inner voice, nothing earthly about it. Ah, surely she was "in the Spirit."

"I feel drawings in my mind to thank Thee, O Lord, for the return of the *White Wave*. Lord, only Thou didst bring her out of the stormy seas and cruel hurricane. Only Thou didst know the preciousness of her souls to bring them home."

The *White Wave!* Tom's own ship. But this was a miracle. Why on earth was she doing it? What was she saying?

Her speech was not speech but chanting. All of the sentences on one tone save the last word, which dropped strangely to *almost* a tone below. Then, suddenly, a sentence began a delicate third higher, as though some new impulse of the Spirit had sent it up, and slowly drooped again to the original chanting tone. Singing, no less! Exquisite music denied by the rigid creed of their sect, yet finding its way unmarked to their very holy of holies.

And all her chanting was of the *White Wave* and her return from perilous seas.

Tom was lost in wonder. Like a flickering light, her blessings ran from bow to stern of the ship, from keel to masthead. At her touch, the sordid things grew sacred — the filthy ports they had made and escaped from, the storms they had ridden out swearing at the bitter effort, the very whales they had caught — all these were, somehow, in her prayer.

As the meeting broke up with shaking of hands and solemn greetings, Tom pulled his comrade's arm.

"Who is that wonderful girl over there — fifth row?" Why, his voice was actually trembling!

"That one with the brown eyes?" asked Caleb. "Abigail Folger — yes, she's —"

"Heavens, no! The gray-eyed one — the one who spoke."

"Oh, that one! Lydia, my sister."

Even yet, Tom thought the "speech" was for him. "Then I know her," he exclaimed.

Without more word, he shouldered his way across and caught up with her at the door. He put out his hand. The golden poplar was not brighter than his smile.

"Good-morning, Miss Lydia. Do you know who I am?" he asked.

"Yes. Tom Coffyn. But thee didn't know me at first."

"How did you know I didn't? You must have been looking at me in meeting."

The rogue! He was delighted with the confusion this caused under the Quaker bonnet.

"May I walk home with you?" he pleaded. "I'd like to very much."

"It's quite out of thy way," she began.

"No, it isn't. Your way couldn't be that for me."

Truly a forward youth!

He did not go into her house that day. Sabbaths, or First Days, were not congenial for visiting or pleasures. But the next day he called upon her and stayed to supper, too. The next day and the next he was there. At the husking he sat by Lydia — saw no one else in the barn. He even took her to a quilting party in the middle of the afternoon. He scandalized the Congregationalists by going to Quaker meeting three Sabbaths in succession.

Lydia bloomed like a wild rose under the sudden adoration. Bloomed though she spent many prayerful hours trying to stem the tide that was carrying her along. Marrying out of meeting was the supreme wrong in Quakerism. She would be disowned. The sorrow and disgrace of it would spread through all her kith and kin.

"Lydia," said her mother severely, "how long is thee going to accept the attentions of Lias Coffyn's son? Are there not enough good boys of Friends' Meeting to please thee? Soon I shall have to forbid him the house."

Lydia tried her best. But what could she do? She could not shut the door in Tom's face — that bright and laughing face that seemed to bring the very sunshine in with it. And if she went down town on any errand, he was sure to find her and accompany her home. All too soon came the fateful evening.

All the family and friends were invited to Cousin William's, who had just returned from a whaling voyage. Lydia stayed at home for conscience's sake, knowing that Tom would be there. She had out her spinning wheel and paced before it, holding the outstretched thread in the warm firelight. Oh, she was trying to still her thoughts — trying not to dream so happily — when the big brass knocker knocked on her heart louder than on the door.

Trembling, she opened the door. Of course, it was he.

"You didn't come to the party," he said, as they came into the room. "I'm glad, for I'd rather see you here."

He was scared, too. Mark how his dear hand trembled, holding his hat. Why, she had forgot her manners.

"Will thee give me thy hat?" she ventured, with outstretched hand. But he dropped his hat, caught her hand in both of his, gazing into her eyes until her soul drew out to his.

And what is he saying? Oh, the dreadful, doomful words, for Lydia cannot marry out of Meeting, throw herself into outer darkness, almost damnation. It would break Mother's heart, and, oh Father's wrath when he comes home from sea! Impossible — impossible!

"Oh, no, no!" — Lydia cries it out with horror and shrinking. "I can't marry you — I can't."

"You don't love me," said Tom fatally. "I — I never thought you could — an angel like you giving yourself — to me."

He stooped blindly to pick up his hat — his tall best beaver, worn for her sake — even that touched her. He would go now, that was best. Why couldn't she keep still? But he must not go. He must not go away thinking that lie.

"I do love thee, Tom. Oh, Tom, I do."

Then she cannot help it. He has her in his arms, sweeping her into heavenly places and spaces. Oh, surely it is wrong to kiss like that. For she must not marry him. No — no — no!

After this fateful evening, Lydia did not even go abroad on the street. She would not see Tom when he came to the house, and only the severe Mrs. Severance met him at the door. Her brother Caleb was no help.

"Of course, Lydia's all right," he declared. "I don't wonder thee likes her. But she'll never marry out of Meeting — Lydia won't. She's the most pious of all the family."

Tom was desperate. Ten days passed, and he did not even see her face. He was sure Mrs. Severance took his letters, for he received no answers. Darkness settled on his soul. He was sure he would die.

Mrs. Severance, looking out at the side window, said, with exasperation:

"There's that Coffyn boy going by again. I should think he'd be ashamed. He looks as though he were condemned to the gallows."

And Lydia tangled her thread on the distaff — tried and tried to untangle it. But who can untangle a thread through blinding tears?

She even stayed home from meeting, for her headaches were not feigned. Sorrow and imprisonment are not healthful exercises. But she had to go into the garden for the vegetables, and one day, Tom, passing along the fenced lane, saw her among the pumpkin vines. He leaped over the high fence at a bound. He had not climbed the shrouds on the high seas for naught.

Lydia stopped, rooted to the spot, holding the pumpkin like a full moon in her arms.

"Lydia, how could you!" he cried. "How could you hide from me!"

For a moment she could not speak. To see him again! It somehow made such a commotion, such a glare of happiness.

"I don't dare," she whispered. "Oh, Tom, if I see thee, I — I — "

"Lydia, I couldn't throw you over for anything. What if I am a Congregationalist? I'd love you if you were a Fiji — if you were a — a — oh, heaven, I can't imagine your being anything I wouldn't love. I love you, love you. I'll love you till I die."

She closed her eyes, overcome with the sweetness and pain of his words. Oh, dear, would he throw his arms about her there in the garden, pumpkin and all? But she wanted him to. She longed for him just to touch her hand.

"I've told Mother," she spoke falteringly. "She is in deep grief over me. She says the wrong is mine, not thine, and it is — it is. They would read me out of Meeting. Oh, Tom, why did thee come here?"

"Lydia, they need not despise me, these Quakers. I am a good man, Lydia. At least, I'm not wicked."

"Oh, Tom, haven't I known that from the beginning?"

"Most people don't think so," he acknowledged. For Tom's gayety sat not well in the pious community.

"But I *know*," she answered.

Great heaven, the faith of her. Great heaven, the trust of her in him. He'd be good now, if he never saw her again.

"Do you want to break my heart?" he asked.

She could not answer this.

"Do you love me, Lydia?"

Her head bowed and he saw her shoulders quiver, though there was no sobbing.

"You said so once. Won't you say it again?"

"Yes, Tom. Oh, yes — yes. But I would be wicked to love anyone better than God and the true worship of God. And, oh, oh, I must not, I cannot be read out of Meeting."

"You would be disgraced, of course."

"Yes," she breathed.

"Are you quite sure it is not the disgrace that's holding you back? You know that God can be truly worshipped anywhere and by any true soul. Didn't your George Fox say something like that? Couldn't you love God and me too, Lydia?"

Tom had thought out all these arguments. Had he not lain awake nights thinking them? It was all so clear to him. But well he knew the stone wall of Quakerism against which he beat. That stone wall was here now.

He was astonished at the horror with which she looked up. The pumpkin slid from her arms down to the path. Then she hid her face in her two hands.

What had he done? Had he offended her so deeply as that?

But Tom asked none of these questions. They faded before he could speak them — faded because, somehow, he knew she was suddenly separated from him, by a great gulf — a trance of the spirit. In his far voyages he had not been farther away from her than at this moment. It was all over with him. She would never marry him, now.

Would she never speak to him? Must he go away?

But now quietly Lydia lifted her head.

"Thee has shown me my error," she said in a small clear voice. "And the Lord has shown it me too. It was pride, not faith, that held me from thee. I shall marry thee, Tom Coffyn, whatever comes."

The unexpectedness of it! The dizziness of it! Tom seemed to be hurled upward like an arrow from black depth into bewildering light.

"Lydia — you don't mean — " He stumbled at it like an astonished boy. "Lydia, you darling saint!"

"Tom, oh, thee mustn't," she protested. "They'll see thee from the windows."

"Tell them it's your future husband kissing you," he answered rapturously.

Tom came to his senses and picked up the pumpkin.

"Shall we go in and tell them?" he asked.

"Yes," she answered steadily. But somehow the very joy in her eyes showed him the depth of her renunciation — the stark courage with which she meant to face her kith and kin.

"You sha'n't marry me out of Meeting, Lydia," he told her.

"Yes, I shall. I have decided."

"Bless your dear plucky heart. But you're not going to marry me out of Meeting, I tell you, I'm a Quaker now. From this moment I'm a Friend."

"Tom Coffyn." She drew away from him. "How dares thee jest at sacred things?"

"I'm not joking. I'm serious. I'm going to join the Quakers."

"But thee cannot become a Friend that way, just — just for love."

"Why not?" he demanded.

"Tom, Tom!" she cried in real distress. "Thee cannot do it to gain an end."

"But, Lydia, I'd gained the end beforehand. Look here, are you trying to drive me away from your faith?"

Something in his voice touched her with his real meaning. Tom had seen her religion in action. What did it mean, that deep withdrawal into the Unseen and the return with certain knowledge? A knowledge so wise, so happy for himself? It was real — that thing. It awed him.

And only think, last night he had made up his mind to test Lydia's love. Let her give up her Quakerism, if she loved him. If not — well, Tom had been angry. How crude that all seemed now.

"Yes, I'm a Friend," he said quietly. "We'll be married in Meeting, Lydia."

The Good Master
The Round-up [3]

KATE SEREDY

⮕ The Good Master *is a colorful story of life on a large horse farm on the great plains of Hungary. It tells of the fun and adventures of Jancsi and his lively cousin Kate from Budapest. Under the wise and understanding guidance of "The Good Master," as Jancsi's father is called, tomboy Kate develops into a fine, dependable girl. Perhaps the extraordinary vitality of the story stems from the fact that the book is based on the author's own childhood. The drawings are full of beauty and action. The chapter below tells of a thrilling adventure when the children help round up some wild horses.*

The apple tree was in full bloom. White strawberry blossoms covered the edge of the pastures. The farmyard was teeming with new life. Baby chicks swarmed in the grass, pink piglets squealed in an enclosure. Máli, the cow, had a brown-and-white calf, marked like a chestnut. It was tottering and tumbling after Máli, getting in everybody's way.

[3] From Kate Seredy, *The Good Master* (Viking Press, 1935).

Mother's vegetable garden was coming along splendidly. The fresh green plants were standing in even rows, like so many pert little green soldiers. Swallows darted between the squatty white pillars of the porch, repairing their nest. Early one morning the stork couple came home from the south. Soon mother stork was spending all her time sitting in their nest on top of the chimney.

"The old lady is sitting on her eggs," said Mother. "It's time to start my flower garden."

Kate remembered when Mother had planted the vegetable garden. She remembered the flat wooden boxes full of tiny seedlings. She knew that the seedlings had been transplanted into the soil. Now Mother said she was planting a flower garden, but she didn't have any seedlings.

Kate watched her make furrows with a little stick, and scatter something like sand into them. She looked up at Kate. "These will be rosemaries. Now I'll put snapdragons in the next bed."

"How can you tell, Auntie?"

"Good gracious, child," exclaimed Mother, "I saved the seeds myself from last year."

Kate watched her in silence. Plant life was a mystery to her.

"Auntie! If I put some of that sand into the ground, would flowers grow for me?"

"Seeds, you mean. Of course they would. You can have a garden of your own if you want to."

Kate wanted to. Mother gave her a spade and a rake and showed her how to dig up the soil and rake it smooth. Kate worked hard. After a while she paused.

"I know, Auntie. The seeds are the eggs of the flowers, aren't they?"

Mother laughed. "I never thought of it that way, but they are."

She gave Kate little bags of seeds. Each bag had the name of the flower written on it — hollyhocks, sunflowers, blue-bonnets, marigolds, carnations.

"Don't plant them deep — just so the seeds are covered."

"What next?" asked Kate when all her seeds were planted.

"We'll water them now, very carefully, so the water doesn't wash away the seeds."

"And then what?" was the next question.

"Well, we'll have to water the soil twice a day, and just wait until they grow."

When Father and Jancsi came home, Kate ran to meet them. "Uncle Márton, you know what? I laid some flower eggs today. I am going to have a garden!"

She was a very busy little person from now on. Jancsi let her take care of the whole poultry yard; then there was Milky to feed and clean and exercise. She was very conscientious about watering her garden. Every morning before sunrise, every evening after the sun went down, Mother often found her flat on her stomach, "waiting for the flowers to come up."

Days passed, sunny days, rainy days. Then one morning Kate roused the household, crying at the top of her voice: "Auntie-e-e! Uncle! Jancsi! Come quick!"

They came running from all directions, Mother from the kitchen, Father from the stables, Jancsi from the cow-barn. "Where is she? What happened?"

Kate was kneeling in her garden, waving her hands, yelling for all she was worth: "Look! Look what happened!" They looked.

The black soil she had tended so carefully showed the first promise of a future garden. Tiny seedlings, hardly visible, were pushing up bravely.

"Phoo!" cried Jancsi, when he understood that he had been brought here just to look at seedlings. "A person would think that something wonderful had happened. And here you raise all this fuss for a few seedlings. Seedlings!"

"You know, Jancsi, I think something wonderful has happened," said Father thoughtfully. "It's such an everyday story to us. We know that seeds will grow into plants. But how? Why? What makes them? To Kate it's a miracle — and so it is. Look at those tiny seedlings. See how they struggle up through heavy clumps of earth to reach the light and sun. We are so used to it that we take it for granted, instead of getting on our knees to thank the Lord for another gift!"

He smiled at Kate. "Little monkey, you are teaching me a lesson, too."

"And now," he went on, "I have a surprise for all of you. I met the judge yesterday, and he told me that the big county fair will be held near our village this year — one week from today."

"Oh! And can we all go?" asked Jancsi eagerly.

"Of course we will go, but I have to get some horses for the animal show. I'm riding out to the herds across the river to round up about twenty. I want to sell some at the fair. Jancsi, you're coming with me. And if Kate wants to leave her garden for a day, she may come along."

Kate looked at Mother. "Will the baby flowers be safe if I leave them?" she asked.

"Don't you worry, child, I'll take good care of them," said Mother, smiling.

They rode out of the yard while the morning dew was still sparkling on the grass. The north road they took today wasn't at all like the one leading to the sheep herds. There were large wheat and rye fields on both sides. Narrow paths forked out of the main road, leading to white cottages nestling under shade trees. From the distance they looked like small white mushrooms under their heavy thatched roofs. The scenery was changing gradually. There were more and more trees. They crossed many small wooden bridges, spanning brooks. Soon they could see the river Tisza, like a wild blue ribbon on the green velvet of the fields. Jancsi rode ahead. Suddenly he waved and cried: "The *Komp* is in. Hurry, Father, they're waiting for us." They spurred their horses and clattered onto the floating ferry, the *Komp*. It was attached to stout ropes on both sides. The ropes stretched across the river and were wound on large wooden pulleys. There were several wagons and riders on the wide platform of the *Komp*.

Kate, following the example of Father and Jancsi, got off her horse and tied him to a hitching-post. "How will we get across? Row?" she asked.

"Watch these men, Kate. They'll pull the *Komp* across by the ropes. We can help, too," said Jancsi. A bell sounded. Another answered from across the river. Everybody walked to the ropes. "Here, Kate. Grab this rope! Pull when they say 'Hooo-ruck!'"

"Hooo-ruck!" Kate pulled for all she was

worth. "Hooo-ruck!" they cried with every pull. The *Komp* began to move. "Hooo-ruck! Hooo-ruck!" chanted everybody, pulling and slacking. The far bank seemed to come nearer and nearer. They could see other wagons and riders waiting. There was a scraping sound when the *Komp* touched bottom and came to a stop. A man on the bank fastened it to a high post.

"Coming back tonight, Mister Nagy?" he asked Father when they rode past him.

"Yes, Géza, we'll bring about twenty horses. Wait for us."

The road led through a small forest of acacia trees. Their branches were heavy with clusters of white flowers. The air was drenched with their sweet, heady perfume. White petals drifted in the breeze, covering the ground like snow.

As soon as they left the forest, they saw the first corrals. They were huge grassy squares, surrounded by tall fences. Long, low stables and a few white cottages were scattered among them. Corrals and buildings formed an immense triangle. In the distance hundreds of horses were grazing placidly. Here and there a horse-herder sat his horse, motionless as a statue against the blue sky. One of them saw Father and rode to him. He was an old man, but straight-shouldered and strong, with snow-white hair and a clearly modeled, sunburned face. Under bushy white eyebrows his black eyes were sharp as an eagle's.

"Welcome, Mister Nagy. We got your message. The boys are ready for the round-up." He looked at Kate and Jancsi. "The young ones could stay with my wife, out of harm's way."

Father shook his head. "Jancsi is working with us this year; he is old enough to know what it's all about. But — Kate, I think you'd better stay with Árpád's wife."

"Oh, Uncle Márton, please let me go too. Please!" cried Kate.

Father looked at the old herder. Árpád shook his head. "If those horses stampede, Mister Nagy, you know what it means! A round-up is no place for a girl child."

"She isn't a girl child. She's almost as good as a boy," said Jancsi stoutly. "Father, let Kate ride with me. I can take care of her."

Father hesitated for a second. Then he said: "Kate, you kept your word to me once. Will you promise me now to keep close to Jancsi and not to scream or yell no matter what happens?" He was very serious. "If these wild horses hear one of your famous screams, they'll run right off the face of the earth."

"I promise!" said Kate, looking straight into his eyes.

"Very well, you may go with Jancsi. Árpád! You take two men and start the drive from the north. Send four men to me. Two will go with Jancsi and Kate and drive from the east. I'll take two men to the west."

Even Árpád's straight back expressed his disapproval as he rode away. They saw him stop and speak to the men.

"Jancsi." Father's voice rang sharp — he was giving orders now. "You are one of the men today. Do you know what to do?"

"Yes, Father. I ride slowly to the east fields, about two miles from here. When I pass the last herds, I turn and start the drive back to the corrals. If they stampede, I ride with them and try to take the lead to turn the herd."

"If they stampede, you take Kate out of the way and let the herders turn them. Understand?"

Then Father gave his orders to the waiting herders, and they rode off.

Kate and Jancsi followed the two young herders in silence. They rode slowly, keeping well away from the grazing horses. Kate watched the men. She wondered if they ever got off their horses or were grown to them. Straight, yet supple, their bodies followed the swinging movement of the horses in perfect, smooth rhythm.

Jancsi touched her arm and whispered: "You won't scream, Kate? Promise?" He looked worried.

"I won't make a sound, no matter what happens. Thank you for sticking up for me."

A tall split-rail fence showed in the distance. "Here's where we spread out," said one of the herders.

Kate was terribly excited. They were riding along the fence now, about fifty feet from each other. "Stampede, stampede," kept ringing in her ears. What if they stampede?

But everything went well. They turned back toward the corrals. At their approach there was a ripple of movement in the herd. They stopped grazing, neighed uneasily, but weren't frightened. Slowly they began to move in the direction of the corrals. Jancsi and Kate were directly behind them, the herders slightly to the sides.

Jancsi took off his hat and wiped his forehead. His first round-up was going off well and he felt very proud. The herd was moving peacefully — surely there wouldn't be any trouble. But — what was the sudden stir in front there? He stood up in the stirrups, saw a flock of partridges fly up, heard the sharp, frightened neighing of the leaders, saw the whole herd sway and swerve . . .

"They're turning! Get out of the way, Kate! Follow me!" he yelled. It was too late. The frightened herd was thundering down on them. He couldn't stop to help Kate. His own horse was caught in the panic and raced at breakneck speed. Looking around, he saw Milky go like a white flash in the other direction, with Kate bent close to his neck. He yelled: "To the left, Kate!" It was useless. He could hardly hear his own voice in the deafening tumult. His own words flashed in his memory. "If they stampede, I take the lead to turn the herd!"

With a desperate struggle he pulled at the reins, his horse swerved to the right. The herd followed! "Now back to the corrals, if I can only keep ahead of them! Come on, Bársony!" He dug his heels into the horse's sides. Almost flying over the pasture, he turned his head to look for Milky. Why, the herd must have split in half! There was Kate to his far right, racing ahead of more horses than he had behind him! She was leading them to the corrals!

"What a girl!" shouted Jancsi. "Hurray!"

He was almost at the first corral gate. He checked his horse, pulling him sharply to one side. The wild horses thundered past him and raced around into the enclosure. He closed the gate quickly, just as the rest of the herd rushed into the adjoining corral. Milky, shivering and snorting, pressed close to Bársony. Kate grinned at Jancsi as she closed the gates. "Look at the herders," she said with a wink; "we beat them to it."

The two men looked rather sheepish and bewildered. There was no time for conversation, though. Father's herd came in, closely followed by old Árpád from the north. When all the horses were safely closed behind the gates, a cottage door opened and Árpád's wife came out ringing a bell. "Dinner ready," she cried.

Father turned to the silent herders. "How did my youngsters behave?"

The herders grinned sheepishly. "Behave, Mister Nagy? Behave? Why, the two of them turned the worst stampede we ever saw and brought the herd in, before we knew what happened."

"What?" cried Árpád and Father together.

"I didn't scream, Uncle Márton, did I, Jancsi?" cried Kate.

"She didn't, Father. A flock of partridges started them off. But can she ride! She rides 'most as good as you!"

"That's saying a lot, Sonny," smiled old Árpád. "Your father is the best horseman in seven counties. But tell us all about it while we eat."

They dismounted and walked to the cottage. In the doorway Árpád took off his hat. "Welcome to my house and table," he said.

"Welcome, and thank the Lord you are all here," cried his wife. "When I saw this girl child ahead of the horses, I thought we'd be picking her up in little pieces instead of sitting down to dinner! My, my, what is this world coming to! When I was her age, and a stout husky girl I was, I had to sit by the window and sew all day, and here she is, no bigger than a flea, racing with the best of you. Oh, oh, forgive my chatter, sit down and eat hearty, you must be starved!"

"Womenfolks talk more than magpies — sit down and welcome," said Árpád.

He said a prayer and a huge pot of steaming stew was set on the table.

"Now, let's hear the story," said Father when everybody was served.

Jancsi laughed. "The story of a flea on horseback. She has a new name, Father. We can't call her screaming monkey any more!"

Little by little the story was pieced together. "But how did you know what to do, Kate?" asked Father.

"There was nothing else to do," she said calmly. "I remembered what Jancsi said about taking the lead if they stampeded. I didn't have to take it — they chased me!" She grinned. "Then we came to the horse-yards ——"

"Corrals, Kate," interrupted Jancsi.

"Corrals, then. Anyway, I saw you pull Bársony to one side. So I did the same thing. It was easy!"

Old Árpád shook his head. "A guardian angel watched over you, child. You were in great danger."

"Maybe — maybe it was my mother," whispered Kate with sudden tears in her eyes.

There was a long silence. Father spoke then in a husky voice: "I shouldn't have let you go, Kate, but now that everything is over, I am very proud of both of you."

Lassie Come-Home
A Long Journey's Beginning [4]

ERIC KNIGHT

Lassie Come-Home *is a deeply moving story of a dog's devotion to his young master. When the Carraclough family go on the dole, they are forced to sell their valuable collie to a duke, who takes the dog to northern Scotland. Lassie manages to escape from the kennels, and, in the chapter given below, she starts her long journey home to the master she loves. She endures grueling hardships, but driven on by an unerring instinct, she travels four hundred miles back to her home in Yorkshire, England. The story is told with a fine restraint and shows the author's great love for and understanding of dogs.*

It was growing dusk as Lassie came down the dusty road. Now she trotted more slowly, and there was indecision in her gait. She halted and then turned back toward the direction from which she had come. She lifted her head, for she was badly puzzled.

Now the pull of the time sense was leaving her. A dog knows nothing of maps and of

[4] From Eric Knight, *Lassie Come-Home* (Winston, 1940).

distances as a man does. By this time Lassie should have met the boy, and they should now be on their way home again — home to eat.

It was time to eat. The years of routine told Lassie that. Back in the kennels there would be a platter of fine beef and meal set before her. But back in the kennel also was a chain that made a dog a prisoner.

Lassie stood in indecision, and then another sense began to waken. It was the homing sense — one of the strongest of all instincts in animals. And home was not the kennel she had left. Home was a cottage where she lay on the rug before the fire, where there was warmth and where voices and hands caressed her. Now that she was lost, that was where she would go.

She lifted her head as the desire for her true home woke in her. She scented the breeze as if asking directions. Then without hesitation, she struck down the road to the south. Do not ask any human being to explain how she should know this. Perhaps, thousands upon thousands of years ago, before man "educated" his brain, he too had the same homing sense; but if he had it, it is gone now. Not with all his brain development can man tell how a bird or an animal can be crated, taken miles away in darkness, and when released, strike straight back toward its home. Man only knows that animals can do what he can neither do himself nor explain.

And in Lassie there was no hesitation. Her senses were now aware of a great satisfaction, for there was peace inside her being. She was going home. She was happy.

There was no one to tell her, and no way for her to learn that what she was attempting was almost in the realm of the impossible — that there were hundreds of miles to go over wild land — a journey that would baffle most men going afoot.

A man could buy food on the way, but what coin has a dog to pay for food? No coin except the love of his master. A man can read signs on the road — but a dog must go blindly, on instinct. A man would know how to cross the entire country, barring the way of any animal going south. And how could a dog know that she was valuable, and that in villages and towns lived hundreds of men of keen eye, who would wish to capture her for that reason?

There were so many things that a dog could not know, but by experience a dog might learn.

Happily Lassie set out. The journey had begun.

In the last of the long Northern twilight two men sat outside their cottage. It was like the other cottages of the village which line the old, narrow street. The walls were thick with the whitewash coating of years.

The elder man, clad in rough homespun, lit his pipe carefully and lifted his head as it drew freely. He watched the puffs of smoke eddying away in the still, evening air. Then he felt the sudden clasp of the younger man's hand on his arm.

"Wullie, see yonder!"

The older man looked where the other was pointing. He sat for some time until his eyes saw more plainly in the evening. It was a dog coming toward them.

The younger man, who wore leggings and a corduroy suit, stood up.

"Looks like a good 'un, Wullie," he said.

"Aye, Geordie — a fine collie."

Their eyes followed it as it trotted near. Then the younger man stirred.

"Havers, Wullie. It looks like that fine collie belongin' tae the laird. It is! I'll sweer on it. I saw it twa days back when I were up chinnin' to McWheen aboot the salmon season. It'll be escaped, no doot . . ."

"Och, and then there'll be . . ."

"Aye, a rewarrd for the mon that finds . . ."

"Losh, aye!"

"Hi!"

The younger man flung this last cry over his shoulder, for he was dashing out into the street. He barred the dog's way.

"Here, lass," he called. "Here, lass!"

He patted his hand on his knee in a gesture of friendliness.

Lassie looked up at him. Her ear had caught the sound which was almost her name: lass. Had the man walked toward her, she might have let him place his hand on her. But he moved too quickly. Suddenly Lassie was reminded of Hynes. She veered slightly,

and without altering her trot, ran past him. The man dove at her. Her muscles flexed, and, like a football star, she put on a spurt that upset his timing. She loped a few steps and then went back to the purposeful trot.

But the man raced after her down the village street. Lassie quickened her pace again and broke into a steady gallop. The more he chased her, the more firmly it was becoming fixed in her mind that she must not let any human being put his hands on her. To chase a dog is merely to teach it to run away.

When the Scot saw that he had no chance of catching the dog by speed, he halted and picked up a loose flint. He thought he could hurl it ahead of Lassie, so that the sound of the falling stone might head her off and turn her back toward him. He drew back his arm and threw.

The aim was bad. The stone fell almost at Lassie's shoulder. Even as it was falling, she changed her gallop as a well-trained polo pony does, leading with the other forefoot. She veered away into the ditch. Belly-close, she went at an amazing speed. There was a gap in a hedge. She faded through it and shot away from the road up into the bleak back-country.

Once there, she turned south again and went back to the steady trot.

But now Lassie had learned one thing. She must keep away from men. For some reason that she could not understand, their hands were against her. Their voices now were rough and angry. They shouted and threw things. There was menace in men. Therefore, she must keep away from them. The thought stayed firmly with her. Lassie had learned her first lesson in the first day.

That first night Lassie traveled steadily. Never before in her five years of life had she been out alone at night. So there was no training to help her, only her instinct.

But the instinct within her was keen and alert. Steadily she followed a path over the heather-clad land. The path filled her with a warm satisfaction, for it was going south. She trotted along it confidently and surely.

At last she reached a rise and then, in the hollow below, she saw the dim shapes of farm buildings. She halted, abruptly, with her ears thrown forward and her nose trembling. Her magnificently acute senses read the story of the habitation below as clearly as a human being might read a book.

She read of horses standing in the barns, of sheep, of another dog, of food, of humans. She started down the slope warily. The smell of food was pleasant, and she had gone a long time without eating. But she knew she must be cautious, for men were there, too. And it was becoming fixed in her mind that she must keep away from them. She trotted down the path.

Then there came a sudden challenging bark of the other dog. She could hear him racing toward her. She stood, waiting. Perhaps he was friendly.

But he was not. He came tearing up the path, his mane erect, his ears flat. Lassie crouched to meet him. As he sprang, she stepped aside. He turned, giving loud voice in hysterical rage. His tones were saying: "This is my home — you are an intruder. It is my home and I will defend it."

Then, from the farm below, came the muffled voice of a man.

"What is it, Tammie? Sic 'em up!"

At the sound of the human voice, Lassie wheeled. She trotted away. This was not *her* home. She was an outcast there.

The rough-coated shepherd charged at her as she loped away, worrying at her flanks. She turned quickly, her lip curling. As if that menace were enough, the other dog drew back.

Steadily she trotted on. The farm was soon left behind. She went over the wild country, following the animal paths. Finally in a depression she scented water. She found the small, cold stream and lapped greedily. The sky was graying in the east. She looked about her.

By a rock she scratched gently with her forepaw. She turned around three times and then curled herself up. Behind her was the protecting overhang of the rock. Her head faced outward. Now, even though she slept, her nose and ears would warn her of any approaching danger.

She put her head on her paw and sighed loudly.

Early the next morning, Lassie was on her way again. She went steadily at a swinging trot that drove at the miles. Her muscles paced with inexorable rhythm, uphill, downhill. She did not pause or hesitate. Whenever a path ran to the south, she followed it. If it veered away, she left it, keeping to animal paths through the dense heather and brush.

When a path led toward a town or a farm, she shied away, circling the habitations to keep away from man. So at the places where men lived she went warily, instinctively keeping under cover, gliding like a ghost under the shadow of thicket and brush, taking advantage of any woodland.

For the most part her ground lay uphill, for ahead of her was a range of blue mountains. Unerringly she headed for the lowest dip where there would be a pass. As the day wore on and she gained higher ground and higher, the sky became overcast. The clouds looked leaden.

Then suddenly there was a flash, and thunder pealed. Lassie hesitated and whined in a quick, querulous tone. She was frightened. It is little use to blame a dog for having fear. A dog has so many braveries that its few fears do not cancel them out. And truth to tell, there are few collies that can stand thunder and lightning.

There are many dogs that do not mind such noise. There are breeds of hunting dogs that are never so happy as when a gun is sounded. But not a collie. It seems as if this breed, having worked so long as man's companion, has learned that such sharp, savage sounds may mean hurt. And the crack of a gun will send most collies running for cover. Other foes they will face, but not the unknown danger of noise.

So Lassie hesitated. The rolling peals of thunder echoed through the mountains, and the torrents of rain lashed down in one of the wild storms of North Scotland. For a long time she fought her fear, but at last it was too much. She trotted to a place on the boulder-strewn pass where overhanging ledges made a dry cave. There she crouched, pressing herself back against the rock as the thunder drummed and echoed like a barrage of guns.

But if she had halted her journey, it was not for long. As the storm went muttering away down the mountain range, she got to her feet. For a second she stood, head high, questing the breeze. Then again she started, going in that long, swinging trot.

The rain and the splashed earth now made the beautiful expanse of her coat tarnished and spotted. But she kept on going steadily, going to the south.

Homer Price
The Doughnuts[5]

Robert McCloskey

≼ *Robert McCloskey has created a very real American boy in the character of Homer Price who has a talent for getting himself involved in fantastic and incredible situations. This story of the non-stop doughnut machine is rollicking good fun.*

One Friday night in November Homer overheard his mother talking on the telephone to Aunt Agnes over in Centerburg. "I'll stop by with the car in about half an hour and we can go to the meeting together," she said, because tonight was the night the Ladies' Club was meeting to discuss plans for a box social and to knit and sew for the Red Cross.

"I think I'll come along and keep Uncle Ulysses company while you and Aunt Agnes are at the meeting," said Homer.

So after Homer had combed his hair and his mother had looked to see if she had her knitting instructions and the right size needles, they started for town.

Homer's Uncle Ulysses and Aunt Agnes have a very up and coming lunch room over in Centerburg, just across from the court house on the town square. Uncle Ulysses is a man with advanced ideas and a weakness for labor saving devices. He equipped the lunch room with automatic toasters, automatic coffee maker, automatic dish washer, and an automatic doughnut maker. All just the latest thing in labor saving devices. Aunt

5 From Robert McCloskey, *Homer Price* (Viking Press, 1943).

Agnes would throw up her hands and sigh every time Uncle Ulysses bought a new labor saving device. Sometimes she became unkindly disposed toward him for days and days. She was of the opinion that Uncle Ulysses just frittered away his spare time over at the barber shop with the sheriff and the boys, so, what was the good of a labor saving device that gave you more time to fritter?

When Homer and his mother got to Centerburg they stopped at the lunch room, and after Aunt Agnes had come out and said, "My, how that boy does grow!" which was what she always said, she went off with Homer's mother in the car. Homer went into the lunch room and said, "Howdy, Uncle Ulysses!"

"Oh, hello, Homer. You're just in time," said Uncle Ulysses. "I've been going over this automatic doughnut machine, oiling the machinery and cleaning the works . . . wonderful things, these labor saving devices."

"Yep," agreed Homer, and he picked up a cloth and started polishing the metal trimmings while Uncle Ulysses tinkered with the inside workings.

"Opfwo-oof!!" sighed Uncle Ulysses and, "Look here, Homer, you've got a mechanical mind. See if you can find where these two pieces fit in. I'm going across to the barber shop for a spell, 'cause there's somethin' I've got to talk to the sheriff about. There won't be much business here until the double feature is over and I'll be back before then."

Then as Uncle Ulysses went out the door he said, "Uh, Homer, after you get the pieces in place, would you mind mixing up a batch of doughnut batter and put it in the machine? You could turn the switch and make a few doughnuts to have on hand for the crowd after the movie . . . if you don't mind."

"O.K.," said Homer, "I'll take care of everything."

A few minutes later a customer came in and said, "Good evening, Bud."

Homer looked up from putting the last piece in the doughnut machine and said, "Good evening, Sir, what can I do for you?"

"Well, young feller, I'd like a cup 'o coffee and some doughnuts," said the customer.

"I'm sorry, Mister, but we won't have any doughnuts for about half an hour, until I can mix some dough and start this machine. I could give you some very fine sugar rolls instead."

"Well, Bud, I'm in no real hurry so I'll just have a cup o' coffee and wait around a bit for the doughnuts. Fresh doughnuts are always worth waiting for is what I always say."

"O.K.," said Homer, and he drew a cup of coffee from Uncle Ulysses' super automatic coffee maker.

"Nice place you've got here," said the customer.

"Oh, yes," replied Homer, "this is a very up and coming lunch room with all the latest improvements."

"Yes," said the stranger, "must be a good business. I'm in business too. A traveling man in outdoor advertising. I'm a sandwich man, Mr. Gabby's my name."

"My name is Homer. I'm glad to meet you, Mr. Gabby. It must be a fine profession, traveling and advertising sandwiches."

"Oh no," said Mr. Gabby, "I don't advertise sandwiches, I just wear any kind of an ad, one sign on front and one sign on behind, this way . . . Like a sandwich. Ya know what I mean?"

"Oh, I see. That must be fun, and you travel too?" asked Homer as he got out the flour and the baking powder.

"Yeah, I ride the rods between jobs, on freight trains, ya know what I mean?"

"Yes, but isn't that dangerous?" asked Homer.

"Of course there's a certain amount a risk, but you take any method a travel these days, it's all dangerous. Ya know what I mean? Now take airplanes for instance . . ."

Just then a large shiny black car stopped in front of the lunch room and a chauffeur helped a lady out of the rear door. They both came inside and the lady smiled at Homer and said, "We've stopped for a light snack. Some doughnuts and coffee would be simply marvelous."

Then Homer said, "I'm sorry, Ma'm, but the doughnuts won't be ready until I make this batter and start Uncle Ulysses' doughnut machine."

"Well now aren't you a clever young man to know how to make doughnuts!"

"Well," blushed Homer, "I've really never done it before but I've got a receipt to follow."

"Now, young man, you simply must allow me to help. You know, I haven't made doughnuts for years, but I know the best receipt for doughnuts. It's marvelous, and we really must use it."

"But, Ma'm . . ." said Homer.

"Now just wait till you taste these doughnuts," said the lady. "Do you have an apron?" she asked, as she took off her fur coat and her rings and her jewelry and rolled up her sleeves. "Charles," she said to the chauffeur, "hand me that baking powder, that's right, and, young man, we'll need some nutmeg."

So Homer and the chauffeur stood by and handed things and cracked the eggs while the lady mixed and stirred. Mr. Gabby sat on his stool, sipped his coffee, and looked on with great interest.

"There!" said the lady when all of the ingredients were mixed. "Just wait till you taste these doughnuts!"

"It looks like an awful lot of batter," said Homer as he stood on a chair and poured it into the doughnut machine with the help of the chauffeur. "It's about ten times as much as Uncle Ulysses ever makes."

"But wait till you taste them!" said the lady with an eager look and a smile.

Homer got down from the chair and pushed a button on the machine marked, "Start." Rings of batter started dropping into the hot fat. After a ring of batter was cooked on one side an automatic gadget turned it over and the other side would cook. Then another automatic gadget gave the doughnut a little push and it rolled neatly down a little chute, all ready to eat.

"That's a simply fascinating machine," said the lady as she waited for the first doughnut to roll out.

"Here, young man, you must have the first one. Now isn't that just too delicious!? Isn't it simply marvelous?"

"Yes, Ma'm, it's very good," replied Homer as the lady handed doughnuts to Charles and to Mr. Gabby and asked if they didn't think they were simply divine dough-nuts.

"It's an old family receipt!" said the lady with pride.

Homer poured some coffee for the lady and her chauffeur and for Mr. Gabby, and a glass of milk for himself. Then they all sat down at the lunch counter to enjoy another few doughnuts apiece.

"I'm so glad you enjoy my doughnuts," said the lady. "But now, Charles, we really must be going. If you will just take this apron, Homer, and put two dozen dough-nuts in a bag to take along, we'll be on our way. And, Charles, don't forget to pay the young man." She rolled down her sleeves and put on her jewelry, then Charles man-aged to get her into her big fur coat.

"Good night, young man, I haven't had so much fun in years. I *really* haven't!" said the lady, as she went out the door and into the big shiny car.

"Those are sure good doughnuts," said Mr. Gabby as the car moved off.

"You bet!" said Homer. Then he and Mr. Gabby stood and watched the automatic doughnut machine make doughnuts.

After a few dozen more doughnuts had rolled down the little chute, Homer said, "I guess that's about enough doughnuts to sell to the after theater customers. I'd better turn the machine off for a while."

Homer pushed the button marked *Stop* and there was a little click, but nothing hap-pened. The rings of batter kept right on dropping into the hot fat, and an automatic gadget kept right on turning them over, and another automatic gadget kept right on giv-ing them a little push and the doughnuts kept right on rolling down the little chute, all ready to eat.

"That's funny," said Homer, "I'm sure that's the right button!" He pushed it again but the automatic doughnut maker kept right on making doughnuts.

"Well I guess I must have put one of those pieces in backwards," said Homer.

"Then it might stop if you pushed the but-ton marked *Start,*" said Mr. Gabby.

Homer did, and the doughnuts still kept rolling down the little chute, just as regular as a clock can tick.

"I guess we could sell a few more dough-nuts," said Homer, "but I'd better telephone Uncle Ulysses over at the barber shop." Homer gave the number and while he waited for someone to answer he counted thirty-seven doughnuts roll down the little chute.

Finally someone answered "Hello! This is the sarber bhop, I mean the barber shop."

"Oh, hello, sheriff. This is Homer. Could I speak to Uncle Ulysses?"

"Well, he's playing pinochle right now," said the sheriff. "Anythin' I can tell 'im?"

"Yes," said Homer. "I pushed the button marked *Stop* on the doughnut machine but the rings of batter keep right on dropping into the hot fat, and an automatic gadget keeps right on turning them over, and an-other automatic gadget keeps giving them a little push, and the doughnuts keep right on rolling down the little chute! It won't stop!"

"O.K. Wold the hire, I mean, hold the wire and I'll tell 'im." Then Homer looked over his shoulder and counted another twenty-one doughnuts roll down the little chute, all ready to eat. Then the sheriff said, "He'll be right over. . . . Just gotta finish this hand."

"That's good," said Homer. "G'by, sheriff."

The window was full of doughnuts by now so Homer and Mr. Gabby had to hustle around and start stacking them on plates and trays and lining them up on the counter.

"Sure are a lot of doughnuts!" said Homer.

"You bet!" said Mr. Gabby. "I lost count at twelve hundred and two and that was quite a while back."

People had begun to gather outside the lunch room window, and someone was say-ing, "There are almost as many doughnuts as there are people in Centerburg, and I wonder how in tarnation Ulysses thinks he can sell all of 'em!"

Every once in a while somebody would come inside and buy some, but while some-body bought two to eat and a dozen to take home, the machine made three dozen more.

By the time Uncle Ulysses and the sheriff arrived and pushed through the crowd, the lunch room was a calamity of doughnuts! Doughnuts in the window, doughnuts piled high on the shelves, doughnuts stacked on plates, doughnuts lined up twelve deep all along the counter, and doughnuts still rolling down the little chute, just as regular as a clock can tick.

"Hello, sheriff, hello, Uncle Ulysses, we're having a little trouble here," said Homer.

"Well, I'll be dunked!!" said Uncle Ulysses.

"Dernd ef you won't be when Aggy gits home," said the sheriff. "Mighty fine doughnuts though. What'll you do with 'em all, Ulysses?"

Uncle Ulysses groaned and said, "What will Aggy say? We'll never sell 'em all."

Then Mr. Gabby, who hadn't said anything for a long time, stopped piling doughnuts and said, "What you need is an advertising man. Ya know what I mean? You got the doughnuts, ya gotta create a market . . . Understand? . . . It's balancing the demand with the supply . . . That sort of thing."

"Yep!" said Homer. "Mr. Gabby's right. We have to enlarge our market. He's an advertising sandwich man, so if we hire him, he can walk up and down in front of the theater and get the customers."

"You're hired, Mr. Gabby!" said Uncle Ulysses.

Then everybody pitched in to paint the signs and to get Mr. Gabby sandwiched between. They painted "SALE ON DOUGHNUTS" in big letters on the window too.

Meanwhile the rings of batter kept right on dropping into the hot fat, and an automatic gadget kept right on turning them over, and another automatic gadget kept right on giving them a little push, and the doughnuts kept right on rolling down the little chute, just as regular as a clock can tick.

"I certainly hope this advertising works," said Uncle Ulysses, wagging his head. "Aggy'll certainly throw a fit if it don't."

The sheriff went outside to keep order, because there was quite a crowd by now — all looking at the doughnuts and guessing how many thousand there were, and watching new ones roll down the little chute, just as regular as a clock can tick. Homer and Uncle Ulysses kept stacking doughnuts. Once in a while somebody bought a few, but not very often.

Then Mr. Gabby came back and said,

"Say, you know there's not much use o' me advertisin' at the theater. The show's all over, and besides almost everybody in town is out front watching that machine make doughnuts!"

"Zeus!" said Uncle Ulysses. "We must get rid of these doughnuts before Aggy gets here!"

"Looks like you will have ta hire a truck ta waul 'em ahay, I mean haul 'em away!!" said the sheriff who had just come in. Just then there was a noise and a shoving out front and the lady from the shiny black car and her chauffeur came pushing through the crowd and into the lunch room.

"Oh, gracious!" she gasped, ignoring the doughnuts, "I've lost my diamond bracelet, and I know I left it here on the counter," she said, pointing to a place where the doughnuts were piled in stacks of two dozen.

"Yes, Ma'm, I guess you forgot it when you helped make the batter," said Homer.

Then they moved all the doughnuts around and looked for the diamond bracelet, but they couldn't find it anywhere. Meanwhile the doughnuts kept rolling down the little chute, just as regular as a clock can tick.

After they had looked all around the sheriff cast a suspicious eye on Mr. Gabby, but Homer said, "He's all right, sheriff, he didn't take it. He's a friend of mine."

Then the lady said, "I'll offer a reward of one hundred dollars for that bracelet! It really *must* be found! . . . it *really* must!"

"Now don't you worry, lady," said the sheriff. "I'll get your bracelet back!"

"Zeus! This is terrible!" said Uncle Ulysses. "First all of these doughnuts and then on top of all that, a lost diamond bracelet . . ."

Mr. Gabby tried to comfort him, and he said, "There's always a bright side. That machine'll probably run outta batter in an hour or two."

If Mr. Gabby hadn't been quick on his feet Uncle Ulysses would have knocked him down, sure as fate.

Then while the lady wrung her hands and said, "We must find it, we *must!*" and Uncle Ulysses was moaning about what Aunt Agnes would say, and the sheriff was eyeing Mr. Gabby, Homer sat down and thought hard.

Before twenty more doughnuts could roll down the little chute he shouted, "SAY! I know where the bracelet is! It was lying here on the counter and got mixed up in the batter by mistake! The bracelet is cooked inside one of these doughnuts!"

"Why . . . I really believe you're right," said the lady through her tears. "Isn't that *amazing?* Simply *amazing!*"

"I'll be durn'd!" said the sheriff.

"OhH-h!" moaned Uncle Ulysses. "Now we have to break up all of these doughnuts to find it. Think of the *pieces!* Think of the *crumbs!* Think of what *Aggy* will say!"

"Nope," said Homer. "We won't have to break them up. I've got a plan."

So Homer and the advertising man took some cardboard and some paint and printed another sign. They put this sign in the window, and the sandwich man wore two more signs that said the same thing and walked around in the crowd out front.

FRESH DOUGHNUTS
2 for 5¢
WHILE THEY LAST
$100.00 PRIZE
FOR FINDING
A BRACELET
INSIDE A DOUGHNUT
P.S. YOU HAVE TO GIVE THE BRACELET BACK

THEN . . . The doughnuts began to sell! *Everybody* wanted to buy doughnuts, *dozens* of doughnuts!

And that's not all. Everybody bought coffee to dunk the doughnuts in too. Those that didn't buy coffee bought milk or soda. It kept Homer and the lady and the chauffeur and Uncle Ulysses and the sheriff busy waiting on the people who wanted to buy doughnuts.

When all but the last couple of hundred doughnuts had been sold, Rupert Black shouted, "I GAWT IT!!" and sure enough . . . there was the diamond bracelet inside of his doughnut!

Then Rupert went home with a hundred dollars, the citizens of Centerburg went home full of doughnuts, the lady and her chauffeur drove off with the diamond bracelet, and Homer went home with his mother when she stopped by with Aunt Aggy.

As Homer went out of the door he heard Mr. Gabby say, "Neatest trick of merchandising I ever seen," and Aunt Aggy was looking sceptical while Uncle Ulysses was saying "The rings of batter kept right on dropping into the hot fat, and the automatic gadget kept right on turning them over, and the other automatic gadget kept right on giving them a little push, and the doughnuts kept right on rolling down the little chute just as regular as a clock can tick — they just kept right on a comin', an' a comin', an' a comin', an' a comin'."

Call It Courage

Drums [6]

ARMSTRONG SPERRY

Call It Courage *is based on a Polynesian legend which the author heard as a boy from his great-grandfather who followed the sea. It is the story of Mafatu, who, though he was the son of a great chief, feared the sea from which the Polynesians all drew their living. Determined to conquer his terror, the boy set forth on that sea, alone in a canoe to face the thing he feared. Adrift, with only his dog Uri, he was cast by a furious storm on an uninhabited island where cannibals came to make their sacrifices. Single-handed he managed to wrest food, shelter, clothing, and weapons from the island, and after he had proved his victory over himself, he returned home triumphant. Armstrong Sperry, during his life in the South Seas, stowed away a rich store of atmosphere, legend, and story which form the background for this book. His illustrations have the same simplicity and strength that distinguish the text. The book was awarded the Newbery medal in 1941.*

In the chapter given below, Mafatu starts to make a canoe to replace the one destroyed by the storm, and he wins his first victory over his fear of the sea.

The very next morning Mafatu set about building his canoe. He had banked his fire the night before in the natural shelter of a

---

[6] From Armstrong Sperry, Call It Courage (Macmillan, 1940).

cave and he resolved never to let the sparks die out. For it was altogether too difficult to make fire with the firestick, and it required too much time. In Hikueru, for that reason, the fires were always kept burning, and it was the special charge of the younger members of a family to see that fuel was ever at hand. Woe unto the small boy who let the family fires go out!

While his breakfast roasted in the coals, the boy cleared the brush away from the base of the great *tamanu*. There was no wood better for canoe-building than this. It was tough, durable, yet buoyant in the water. Mafatu could fell his tree by fire, and burn it out, too. Later he would grind an adze out of basalt for the finished work. The adze would take a long time, but he had made them often in Hikueru and he knew just how to go about it. The boy was beginning to realize that the hours he had spent fashioning utensils were to stand him now in good stead. Nets and knives and sharkline, implements and shell fishhooks — he knew how to make them all. How he had hated those tasks in Hikueru! He was quick and clever with his hands, and now he was grateful for the skill which was his.

The fire crackled and snapped about the base of the *tamanu* tree. When at length it had eaten well into the trunk, Mafatu climbed aloft and crept cautiously out upon a large branch that overhung the beach. Then taking firm hold of the branches above his head, he began to jump up and down. As the fire ate deeper into the trunk, the tree began to lean under the boy's weight. With a snap and a crash it fell across the sand. As it fell, Mafatu leaped free of the branches, as nimbly as a cat.

"That's enough for today, Uri," he decided. "Tomorrow we'll build our fires down the trunk and start burning it out. When the eaters-of-men come, we will be ready!"

In the meantime there were many other things to do: a fish trap of bamboo, a net of sennit, a fishhook, too, if only he could find some bone. And while the canoe was building, how could Mafatu get out to the distant reef to set his trap, unless first he made a raft of bamboo?

The boy decided that the raft was of first importance. He chose a score or more of fine bamboos as large around as his arm, felling them by fire; then he lashed them together with strips of *purau* bark, making a sturdy raft of two thicknesses. It would serve him well until his canoe should be finished.

As he worked, his mind returned again and again to the wild pig he was determined to kill. How could he go back to Hikueru without a boar's-tooth necklace? Why, that necklace was almost as important as a canoe! For by that token men would know his strength and courage. When the day came that he should leave this high island, he would sail to the north and east. Somewhere in that quarter lay the Cloud of Islands; the great Tuamotu Archipelago which extends across a thousand miles of ocean and ten degrees of latitude. Within those reef-spiked channels floated Hikueru, his homeland. There was no doubt in his mind that he would find it; for Maui, who had led him safe to this shore, would some day guide him home again. But first, Mafatu knew, he must prove himself worthy. Men should never again call him Mafatu, the Boy Who Was Afraid. And Tavana Nui should say with pride: "Here is my son, come home from the sea."

Kivi, the albatross, came and went on his mysterious errands, emerging out of blue space, vanishing into it again. At sundown, regularly, the white bird came wheeling and circling, to alight clumsily on the beach almost at Mafatu's side, while Uri pranced about and greeted his friend after his own fashion. As for Uri, he was having the time of his life; for there were countless sea-birds nesting along the shore to be chased and put to rout; and wild goats and pigs in the mountains to make life exciting enough for any dog.

Mafatu had discovered a mulberry tree. He stripped off the bark and removed the inner white lining. Then he wet the fiber and laid it upon a flat stone and set about beating it with a stick of wood. The fiber spread and grew thinner under the persistent beating. The boy added another strip, wet it, and beat it into the first one; then another and another. Soon he had a yard of "cloth" to serve as a *pareu*. It was soft and white, and now at last he was clothed.

"Before I go home I will make a dye of *ava* and paint a fine design on my *pareu*," the boy promised himself. "I must not go back ill-clothed and empty-handed. Men must know that I have conquered the sea, and made the land serve me as well."

The days passed in a multitude of tasks that kept Mafatu busy from dawn till dark. His lean-to grew into a three-sided house with bamboo walls and a thatch of palm leaves. The fourth wall was open to the breezes of the lagoon. It was a trim little house and he was proud of it. A roll of woven mats lay on the floor; there was a shelf in the wall with three bowls cut from coconut shells; bone fishhooks dangled from a peg; there was a coil of tough sennit, many feet long; an extra *pareu* of *tapa* water-proofed with gum of the *artu* tree, for wet weather. All day long the wind played through the openings in the bamboo walls and at night lizards scurried through the thatch with soft rustlings.

One morning, wandering far down the beach, Mafatu came upon a sheltered cove. His heart gave a leap of joy; for there, white-gleaming in the sun, was all that remained of the skeleton of a whale. It might not have meant very much to you or to me; but to Mafatu it meant knives and fishhooks galore, splintered bone for darts and spears, a shoulder blade for an axe. It was a veritable treasure-trove. The boy leaped up and down in his excitement. "Uri!" he shouted. "We're rich! Come — help me drag these bones home!"

His hands seemed all thumbs in his eagerness; he tied as many bones as he could manage into two bundles. One bundle he shouldered himself. The other Uri dragged behind him. And thus they returned to the camp site, weary, but filled with elation. Even the dog seemed to have some understanding of what this discovery meant; or if not, he was at least infected with his master's high spirits. He leaped about like a sportive puppy, yapping until he was hoarse.

Now began the long process of grinding the knife and the axe. Hour after long hour, squatting before a slab of basalt, Mafatu worked and worked, until his hands were raw and blistered and the sweat ran down into his eyes. The knife emerged first, since that was the most imperative. Its blade was ten inches long, its handle a knob of joint. It was sharp enough to cut the fronds of coconut trees, to slice off the end of a green nut. *Ai,* but it was a splendid knife! All Mafatu's skill went into it. It would be a fine weapon as well, the boy thought grimly, as he ground it down to a sharp point. Some sea-robber had been breaking into his bamboo trap and he was going to find out who the culprit was! Probably that old hammerhead shark who was always cruising around. . . . Just as if he owned the lagoon!

Fishing with a line took too long when you were working against time. Mafatu could not afford to have his trap robbed. Twice it had been broken into, the stout bamboos crushed and the contents eaten. It was the work either of a shark or of an octopus. That was certain. No other fish was strong enough to snap the tough bamboo.

Mafatu's mouth was set in a grim line as he worked away on his knife. That old hammerhead — undoubtedly *he* was the thief! Mafatu had come to recognize him; for every day, when the boy went out with his trap, that shark, larger than all the others, was circling around, wary and watchful. The other sharks seemed to treat the hammerhead with deference.

Hunger alone drove Mafatu out to the reef to set his trap. He knew that if he was to maintain strength to accomplish all that lay ahead he must have fish to add to his diet of fruit. But often as he set his trap far out by the barrier-reef, the hammerhead would approach, roll over slightly in passing, and the cold gleam of its eye filled Mafatu with dread and anger.

"Wait, you!" the boy threatened darkly, shaking his fist at the *ma'o.* "Wait until I have my knife! You will not be so brave then, *Ma'o.* You will run away when you see it flash."

But the morning that the knife was finished, Mafatu did not feel so brave as he would have liked. He hoped he would never see the hammerhead again. Paddling out to the distant reef, he glanced down from time to time at the long-bladed knife where it hung about his neck by a cord of sennit. It wasn't, after all, such a formidable weapon. It was only a knife made by a boy from a whale's rib.

Uri sat on the edge of the raft, sniffing at the wind. Mafatu always took his dog along, for Uri howled unmercifully if he were left behind. And Mafatu had come to rely upon the companionship of the little yellow dog. The boy talked with the animal as if he were another person, consulting with him, arguing, playing when there was time for play. They were very close, these two.

This morning as they approached the spot where the fish trap was anchored, Mafatu saw the polished dorsal of the hated hammerhead circling slowly in the water. It was like a triangle of black basalt, making a little furrow in the water as it passed.

"Aiá, Ma'o!" the boy shouted roughly, trying to bolster up his courage. "I have my knife today, see! Coward who robs traps — catch your own fish!"

The hammerhead approached the raft in leisurely fashion; it rolled over slightly, and its gaping jaws seemed to curve in a yawning grin. Uri ran to the edge of the raft, barking furiously; the hair on the dog's neck stood up in a bristling ridge. The shark, unconcerned, moved away. Then with a whip of its powerful tail it rushed at the bamboo fish trap and seized it in its jaws. Mafatu was struck dumb. The hammerhead shook the trap as a terrier might shake a rat. The boy watched, fascinated, unable to make a move. He saw the muscles work in the fish's neck as the great tail thrashed the water to fury. The trap splintered into bits, while the fish within escaped only to vanish into the shark's mouth. Mafatu was filled with impotent rage. The hours he had spent making that trap —— But all he could do was shout threats at his enemy.

Uri was running from one side of the raft to the other, furious with excitement. A large wave sheeted across the reef. At that second the dog's shift in weight tipped the raft at a perilous angle. With a helpless yelp, Uri slid off into the water. Mafatu sprang to catch him, but he was too late.

Instantly the hammerhead whipped about. The wave slewed the raft away. Uri, swimming frantically, tried to regain it. There was desperation in the brown eyes — the puzzled eyes so faithful and true. Mafatu strained forward. His dog. His companion. . . . The hammerhead was moving in slowly. A mighty rage stormed through the boy. He gripped his knife. Then he was over the side in a clean-curving dive.

Mafatu came up under his enemy. The shark spun about. Its rough hide scraped the flesh from the boy's shoulder. In that instant Mafatu stabbed. Deep, deep into the white belly. There was a terrific impact. Water lashed to foam. Stunned, gasping, the boy fought for life and air.

It seemed that he would never reach the surface. Aué, his lungs would burst! . . . At last his head broke water. Putting his face to the surface, he saw the great shark turn over, fathoms deep. Blood flowed from the wound in its belly. Instantly gray shapes rushed in — other sharks, tearing the wounded hammerhead to pieces.

Uri — where was he? Mafatu saw his dog then. Uri was trying to pull himself up on the raft. Mafatu seized him by the scruff and dragged him up to safety. Then he caught his dog to him and hugged him close, talking to him foolishly. Uri yelped for joy and licked his master's cheek.

It wasn't until Mafatu reached shore that he realized what he had done. He had killed the ma'o with his own hand, with naught but a bone knife. He could never have done it for himself. Fear would have robbed his arm of all strength. He had done it for Uri, his dog. And he felt suddenly humble, with gratitude.

Adam of the Road
A Blush of Boys [7]

Elizabeth Janet Gray

Adam of the Road *is an absorbing tale of thirteenth-century England. Eleven-year-old Adam accompanies his father, Roger the minstrel, who is attached to Sir Edmund de Lisle's*

[7] From Elizabeth Janet Gray, *Adam of the Road* (Viking Press, 1942).

entourage. Taking the highway to London, Roger and Adam ride the war horse Bayard, a gift from the knight to his minstrel. Sir Edmund and his followers stop at his manor-house near London. The chapter given below tells how Adam makes friends with Sir Edmund's three nephews and the other boys at the de Lisle house. Then Roger and his son take the road to Winchester and the great Fair of St. Giles. On the way, Adam's dog Nick is stolen and Adam in his frantic pursuit to recover his spaniel, becomes separated from his father. Many months pass before the three are happily reunited in Oxford. Into this colorful pageantry of medieval England, the author has interwoven minstrel songs and stories, courage and laughter, faith in human kindness, and the love between father and son. The book was awarded the Newbery medal in 1943.

Adam sat on the brick wall of the stable-yard and pretended that he was not lonely. Here he was, he told himself, sitting in the sunshine with Nick beside him; Roger was in the house talking to Sir Edmund, and Bayard was in the stable. Why was his heart so heavy?

Well, he missed Perkin. That was a courtly sorrow. Roland longing for Oliver, Damon for Pythias, Horn for Athulf: history and romance were full of noble friends grieving because they were separated. Shouts and a burst of laughter from the alley behind him, which was used as a tiltyard, stung him to greater honesty with himself. Even if Perkin had been sitting right there on the wall beside him, still his heart would be heavy because behind and below in the tilt-yard was a band of boys his own age having a good time without him.

He had been here nearly three days now, and they paid no more attention to him than if he had been a fly. The first day he had walked up to them happily and expectantly, and they all, led by Hugh, immediately went somewhere else. The second day they were nowhere to be seen. Adam stayed with Roger most of the day, learning the singing parts of a new romance from France. Simon was with them for a little while, and that had been a great joy to Adam. This morning he had perched himself up on the wall with his back to the boys so that they could see him and

call him if they wanted him. He had played his harp, and he had talked rather loudly to Nick, and then he had just sat. Never before had his friendly advances been turned down; never before had he, Roger the minstrel's son, been ignored. It made him feel very low in his mind.

Suddenly he thought of one of the famous Proverbs of Alfred:

> "If thou hast a sorrow,
> Tell it not to thy foe,
> But whisper it to thy saddle-bow
> And ride forth singing."

He shook himself almost the way Nick did, and, thought being practically action with Adam, jumped down into the stable-yard. A pretty sort of thing he'd been doing, he told himself, sitting up on the wall for all to see his loneliness, when Roger had said he could take Bayard out and give him some exercise!

Bayard was a war horse; he was big and broad and strong enough to carry a great weight of man and armor, but he was no fiery steed. He was well past his mettlesome youth, and Roger was satisfied for Adam to ride him.

Adam whistled as he set about saddling and bridling Bayard, and in his struggle with the harness, which was really too big and heavy for him to manage, he forgot about the other boys. A stableman came to his assistance finally and heaved the big saddle onto Bayard's back; he shortened the stirrups himself, and then mounted by climbing on the edge of the water trough. Just as he was turning around to ride out of the yard, Simon Talbot came through the door in the wall, with his lanneret on his fist.

Adam was pleased to know the word lanneret. Some words were like pets to him, and especially the new words that Simon was teaching him. A lanneret was the kind of falcon that a squire was permitted to own. A king had a gerfalcon, a lady — like Emilie — a merlin, and a yeoman a goshawk. Simon had taught Adam, too, the right words for flocks of different kinds of birds. If you saw, for instance, a number of swallows together, you spoke of a *flight* of swallows, but you said a *walk* of snipe, and a *gaggle* of geese.

Now Adam sat, all eyes and eagerness, on

Bayard and waited for Simon to notice him. Of all the six or seven young squires who served Sir Edmund, Adam most loved and admired Simon.

"Ho, Rob!" called Simon. "Saddle Pommers for me." Pommers within the stable whinnied at the sound of his master's voice.

The squire stooped to pat Nick and then came over to Adam. He held up his right hand with the heavy leather glove that came nearly to his elbow; on it perched a small hawk with his hooded head hunched down into his feathers and his talons clasped around Simon's wrist. Little leather thongs called jesses were fastened to the bird's legs and passed between the fingers of Simon's hand. On each leg was a small bell.

"I'm going to Westminster," said Simon. "There's a fellow there who's going to let me have a pair of Milanese bells cheap."

"You've already got some bells," said Adam.

"I know, but they're not right. One ought to be a semi-tone higher than the other. Where are you going on your war horse?"

"Nowhere special," said Adam breathlessly. Perhaps, he thought, his heart leaping under the stripes of his surcoat, perhaps Simon would ask him to go to Westminster with him.

"There's a blush of boys out there in the tiltyard. A blush of boys, you remember what I told you? — and a what of girls?"

"A bevy of girls," answered Adam promptly.

"Right. Well, they're tilting at the quintain on foot because that sorry nag of Hugh's is lame. Now you've got a real war horse. I believe that if you were disposed to be generous with him, they'd be glad to see you."

Rob brought out Pommers all sleek and shining and prancing delicately, and Simon mounted and rode off. Adam turned Bayard and rode slowly out of the yard.

He knew that Roger would not mind if the boys rode Bayard, for they all rode as well as Adam did, and some rode better, but he did not know whether he himself was willing to lend his horse to that uppish fellow Hugh. He was quite sure that he did not want to offer Bayard to Hugh. Let him ask

politely for it as a favor! Still undecided, he rode into the tiltyard.

Tiltyard was rather a fancy name for what was just part of a wide alley with a quintain halfway down its length. The quintain was a post with a battered old shield hanging on it. The idea was to strike the shield with a lance in such a way as to knock it to the ground. It was much more fun, of course, and much swifter, to ride at it on horseback than to run at it on foot.

Six boys were scattered up and down the alley: Hugh and his younger brothers, Godfrey and Ralph, who were nephews of Sir Edmund; William and Martin, the sons of the falconer, and Matthew, the bailiff's son. Adam tumbled himself down from Bayard and said offhandedly to Godfrey, who was shorter and blunter and much jollier-looking than Hugh, "Why don't you ride at the quintain? You can have Bayard, if you like."

Godfrey looked at him uncertainly for a moment, and then gave a shrill shout. "Hugh! Come here! Minstrel's son says we can ride Bayard!"

Hugh, who was halfway down the alley, turned and came back, carrying the blunt-ended ash wood pole that they used for a lance. For the second time he and Adam looked squarely at each other.

Well, sir, Adam was saying within himself, I don't care so very much for you, but I like your crowd and I want to belong to it; I'll do my share and a bit over.

What Hugh was thinking behind those rather glittery blue eyes of his, Adam could not tell. Hugh's glance wavered first. He turned to Bayard, and Adam knew from the way he looked at the horse and touched him that Hugh loved Bayard almost as Adam himself loved Nick.

"He's getting old," said Hugh, "but he's a great horse still. He was in battle at Acre in the Holy Land. Uncle got him in exchange for a white Spanish jennet and then he was sorry afterward because he liked the jennet better, but I'd rather have Bayard any day."

He mounted nimbly and Ralph handed his lance up to him. Two of the boys ran to raise the shield higher on the post. Nobody questioned Hugh's right to the first turn.

Godfrey said to Adam, while Hugh was

riding Bayard up and down to get the feel of him again, "Hugh thought maybe Uncle would give Bayard to him, but he didn't."

Then Adam understood why Hugh had been so disagreeable. Suppose somebody else had got Nick! "By Saint Simon," he said, copying Simon Talbot, "I'm sorry." Some other horse would have done as well for Roger; time was when they didn't have a horse at all.

Hugh rode twice at the quintain; the first time he missed, but the second time he sent the shield clattering to the ground. Then Godfrey had his turn, and Hugh, glowing, came to talk to Adam. He looked a different boy; all the ill-humor seemed to have been shaken out of him.

"Will Roger let you have Bayard again?" he asked eagerly.

"I'm sure he will when I tell him — I mean you ride better than I do, so if he'd let me he'd let you."

Hugh watched Godfrey critically. "He'll miss. You'll see. He's good, but Bayard doesn't like him as well as he likes me. Bayard and I understand each other. At Ludlow we've got a real tiltyard, and the quintain isn't just a shield. It's a wooden Saracen on a pivot, with a sword in his hand. If you hit him in the middle of the forehead, he falls over, but if you hit him anywhere else he swings around and whacks you in the back with his sword. By Saint Hugh, that's real tilting!"

Godfrey came back, and, declaring that Ralph, who was not yet ten, was too small, Hugh sent Martin off next, and then William.

"Do you want a turn?" he thought at last to say to Adam.

"Hugh!" cried Godfrey reproachfully. "It's his horse!"

Hugh blushed. "Oh, well," he said, trying to cover his confusion. "Minstrels don't joust or ride in tournaments, or go to war."

"Taillefer did," said Adam stoutly. "He was the Conqueror's minstrel, but he was a warrior too. At the battle of Senlac he asked leave of William to begin the onset, and he rode before the whole army juggling with his sword and chanting the Song of Roland. Then he rushed on the English and was killed."

So Adam had his turn. Before he went to Saint Alban's he had had some practice here and there, mostly, it is true, one Easter in London; he had not done badly then. It gave him confidence to remember that. He cradled his lance in his arm and he spoke to Bayard. Nearer and nearer the shield they came. Adam gathered himself together and thrust — and the battered, dingy shield dropped to the ground and wobbled over onto its face. Trying not to grin too broadly, Adam rode back to the others. He could not keep his head from wagging a bit.

"Well done!" said Hugh, with respect in his voice. He had been kneeling on one knee and holding Nick's collar while Adam rode; now he stood up and said, dusting off his knee very briskly. "This is a good dog, Adam. He's got a fine ear-carriage and a straight back. We haven't any dogs at Ludlow any better than he is — at least, not any spaniels."

It was wonderful how much better that made Adam feel. After Matthew had had his first turn and Hugh his second, the shadow of the pear tree reached the wall and it was time to stop. Adam led Bayard back to the stable, and the others went off toward the house with their heads together. In a moment Godfrey left them and came running back to Adam.

"We've a sort of company, we six, when we're in London," he panted. "Hugh and I are knights, and Ralph's a squire, and Will and Matthew and Martin are yeomen, and Margery is our liege lady. We've never had a minstrel, but Hugh says we need one and we all think so. You could be Taillefer!"

After that they were together every minute that they could be. None of the seven went to school — Sir Edmund's three nephews considered learning only for milksops who were not fit to be knights or for poor boys whose sole hope of advancement was through the Church — but they were all subject to instruction of one kind or another from grown-ups. Hugh and Godfrey and Ralph had a tutor who trained them in pursuits necessary for boys who looked forward to being knights: tilting and riding and sword-play and hawking and hunting. They had a great deal of tiresome practicing to do, the same exercises over and over again, with very little praise to sweeten it and even less sympathy when they got tired. The falconer's boys were often busy in the mews, where the moulting hawks were kept, and they had to learn how to make hoods and jesses out of skins and how to school the young hawks and to care for the ailing ones. Matthew, the bailiff's son, must struggle with figures and learn to cast accounts and to know what was expected of everybody in a large and complicated household like Sir Edmund's. As for Adam, he had his work too. The northern minstrels were famous for singing together, one in the bass and the other in the treble. Roger had brought home new songs from France which Adam must learn and they had many old ones to practice as well. Adam had his harping to work on, too, and Roger taught him to do some new tumbling tricks and to juggle knives.

"It's not real minstrelsy, but it catches the crowd," said Roger. "Some people can't appreciate a good story well told, but they like to have a lithe young lad dazzle their slow eyes with tricks. You needn't use them unless you have to, but it's well to have a second string to your bow."

When they were free to be together, the seven boys had endless fun. They were tilting at the quintain, or diving and swimming in the river, or running foot-races, or having wrestling matches. In the long twilights after supper they played games in the garden, and Margery and Emilie and some of the squires would join them. They played prisoners' base and hoop and hide and hoodman's blind, and, when the girls insisted, London Bridge. Adam would play on his harp for that, and his voice soared high above the others in the singing.

> "London Bridge is broken down,
> Dance over my Lady Lea.
> London Bridge is broken down,
> With a gay lady."

The joke of it was, though the song was such an old one and the wooden London Bridge had fallen down more than a hundred years before and been built up in "stone so strong," it was likely to come true again. For years and years the old Queen Eleanor had

collected fees from all who passed over it, and never spent a penny of them on repairs. Now the stones were worn into holes in some of the arches so that you could see the water rushing beneath.

> "Build it up with silver and gold,
> Dance over my Lady Lea,
> Build it up with silver and gold,
> With a fair lady" —

the ones inside the ring would sing, and those outside would answer:

> "Silver and gold will be stolen away,
> Dance over my Lady Lea,
> Silver and gold will be stolen away,
> With a gay lady!"

Adam would twang his harp and look across the beds of roses and gillyflowers and lilies to the river and London Bridge misty in the distance with a faint light or two in the windows in the houses on it. A bridge is a kind of sacred thing, he thought, as Roger said a road was. There was a chapel to Saint Thomas of Canterbury in the middle of London Bridge, and Saint Thomas was a great saint and his chapel was holy. Yet the old queen had not cared enough about the bridge to keep it safe, and boys and girls never gave it a thought when they sang joyfully:

> "London Bridge is broken down,
> With a gay lady!"

Men of Iron [8]

(A Selection)

HOWARD PYLE

This book gives a fine portrayal of life in the great castles and of the training of young nobles for knighthood in fifteenth-century England. The reader should know that before this story takes place, lords who had been elevated under King Richard II were degraded to their former titles under Henry IV. A group plotted to kill the king, but the plot failed, and the conspirators were executed. In some cases, their friends, who had nothing to do with the

[8] From Howard Pyle, *Men of Iron* (Harper, 1891).

plot, were ruined too. Such a one was the father of Myles Falworth, and this is the situation at the opening of the first chapter of Men of Iron, *which is given below. Eventually Myles wins his spurs and succeeds in vanquishing his own and his father's enemy.*

Myles Falworth was but eight years of age at that time, and it was only afterwards, and when he grew old enough to know more of the ins and outs of the matter, that he could remember by bits and pieces the things that afterwards happened; how one evening a knight came clattering into the courtyard upon a horse, red-nostriled and smeared with the sweat and foam of a desperate ride — Sir John Dale, a dear friend of the blind lord.

Even though so young, Myles knew that something very serious had happened to make Sir John so pale and haggard, and he dimly remembered leaning against the knight's iron-covered knees, looking up into his gloomy face, and asking him if he was sick to look so strange. Thereupon those who had been too troubled before to notice him, bethought themselves of him, and sent him to bed, rebellious at having to go so early.

He remembered how the next morning, looking out of a window high up under the eaves, he saw a great troop of horsemen come riding into the courtyard beneath, where a powdering of snow had whitened everything, and of how the leader, a knight clad in black armor, dismounted and entered the great hall doorway below, followed by several of the band.

He remembered how some of the castle women were standing in a frightened group upon the landing of the stairs, talking together in low voices about a matter he did not understand, excepting that the armed men who had ridden into the courtyard had come for Sir John Dale. None of the women paid any attention to him; so, shunning their notice, he ran off down the winding stairs, expecting every moment to be called back again by some one of them.

A crowd of castle people, all very serious and quiet, were gathered in the hall, where a number of strange men-at-arms lounged upon the benches, while two billmen in steel caps and leathern jacks stood guarding the great door, the butts of their weapons resting upon the ground, and the staves crossed, barring the doorway.

In the anteroom was the knight in black armor whom Myles had seen from the window. He was sitting at the table, his great helmet lying upon the bench beside him, and a quart beaker of spiced wine at his elbow. A clerk sat at the other end of the same table, with inkhorn in one hand and pen in the other, and a parchment spread in front of him.

Master Robert, the castle steward, stood before the knight, who every now and then put to him a question, which the other would answer, and the clerk write the answer down upon the parchment.

His father stood with his back to the fireplace, looking down upon the floor with his blind eyes, his brows drawn moodily together, and the scar of the great wound that he had received at the tournament at York — the wound that had made him blind — showing red across his forehead, as it always did when he was angered or troubled.

There was something about it all that frightened Myles, who crept to his father's side, and slid his little hand into the palm that hung limp and inert. In answer to the touch, his father grasped the hand tightly, but did not seem otherwise to notice that he was there. Neither did the black knight pay any attention to him, but continued putting his questions to Master Robert.

Then, suddenly, there was a commotion in the hall without, loud voices, and a hurrying here and there. The black knight half-arose, grasping a heavy iron mace that lay upon the bench beside him, and the next moment Sir John Dale himself, as pale as death, walked into the antechamber. He stopped in the very middle of the room. "I yield me to my lord's grace and mercy," said he to the black knight, and they were the last words he ever uttered in this world.

The black knight shouted out some words of command, and swinging up the iron mace in his hand, strode forward clanking toward Sir John, who raised his arm as though to shield himself from the blow. Two or three of those who stood in the hall without came running into the room with drawn swords and bills, and little Myles, crying out with terror, hid his face in his father's long gown.

The next instant came the sound of a heavy blow and of a groan, then another blow and the sound of one falling upon the ground. Then the clashing of steel, and in the midst Lord Falworth crying, in a dreadful voice, "Thou traitor! thou coward! thou murderer!"

Master Robert snatched Myles away from his father, and bore him out of the room in spite of his screams and struggles, and he remembered just one instant's sight of Sir John lying still and silent upon his face, and of the black knight standing above him, with the terrible mace in his hand stained a dreadful red.

It was the next day that Lord and Lady Falworth and little Myles, together with three of the more faithful of their people, left the castle.

His memory of past things held a picture for Myles of old Diccon Bowman standing over him in the silence of midnight with a lighted lamp in his hand, and with it a recollection of being bidden to hush when he would have spoken, and of being dressed by Diccon and one of the women, bewildered with sleep, shuddering and chattering with cold.

He remembered being wrapped in the sheepskin that lay at the foot of his bed, and of being carried in Diccon Bowman's arms down the silent darkness of the winding stairway, with the great black giant shadows swaying and flickering upon the stone wall as the dull flame of the lamp swayed and flickered in the cold breathing of the night air.

Below were his father and mother and two or three others. A stranger stood warming his hands at a newly made fire, and little Myles, as he peeped from out the warm sheepskin, saw that he was in riding-boots and was covered with mud. He did not know till long years afterwards that the stranger was a messenger sent by a friend at the king's court, bidding his father fly for safety.

They who stood there by the red blaze of the fire were all very still, talking in whispers and walking on tiptoes, and Myles' mother

hugged him in her arms, sheepskin and all, kissing him, with the tears streaming down her cheeks, and whispering to him, as though he could understand their trouble, that they were about to leave their home forever.

Then Diccon Bowman carried him out into the strangeness of the winter midnight.

Outside, beyond the frozen moat, where the osiers stood stark and stiff in their winter nakedness, was a group of dark figures waiting for them with horses. In the pallid moonlight Myles recognized the well-known face of Father Edward, the Prior of Saint Mary's.

After that came a long ride through that silent night upon the saddle-bow in front of Diccon Bowman; then a deep, heavy sleep, that fell upon him in spite of the galloping of the horses.

When next he woke the sun was shining, and his home and his whole life were changed.

The Trumpeter of Krakow

The Man Who Wouldn't Sell His Pumpkin [9]

ERIC PHILBROOK KELLY

&❧ The Trumpeter of Krakow *is a story of fifteenth-century Poland, a colorful and turbulent period with its fierce hatreds, its persecution and cruelty. It is a tense, vibrant story of political intrigue that caught fifteen-year-old Joseph Charnetski in its toils. The following chapter tells how, in spite of disaster, Joseph and his father smuggle the ill-starred Tarnov Crystal into the city of Krakow, by hiding it in a great yellow pumpkin. Later they were able to take it safely to the king. Eric Kelly got his inspiration for the story while he was in Poland after World War I. This book was awarded the Newbery medal in 1929.*

It was in late July of the year 1461 that the sun rose one morning red and fiery as if ushering in midsummer's hottest day. His rays fell upon the old city of Krakow and the roads leading up to it, along which rolled

[9] From Eric Philbrook Kelly, *The Trumpeter of Krakow* (Macmillan, 1928).

and rocked a very caravan of peasants' wagons. They were drawn mostly by single horses hitched into place by the side of a rough pole that served for shaft; for wheels there were stout pieces of board nailed tightly together and cut round about, baked with fire at the rim to harden them; for body they had but rude cross boards as a floor, with sides and ends of plaited willow reeds, so that the wagons had the appearance of large baskets traveling on wheels. As they moved along a road often rough from holes and stones, out through fields sometimes, and even across streams, the wagons pitched about like little boats on a wind-swept sea.

In many cases the drivers were walking alongside the carts, flicking their long whips now and then above the horses' backs to give the animals a little encouragement, while upon the seats sat the patient figures of women and children.

In the wagons was all manner of merchandise — vegetables, flowers, ducks, hens and geese, pigs, butter and milk. Here a driver was conveying a load of skins, here one had nothing but black earth for enriching city gardens. Another, driving a load of poultry, wore around his neck, like beads, garland after garland of dried mushrooms strung upon strings. At the back of the picture rose the foothills of the Carpathians, misty and golden in the early sun, and at a distance the Vistula River curved like a silver bracelet about the Wawel Hill. All about was the early-morning smell of wet grass and fresh earth and growing things.

Market day had begun. All night some of these wagons had been traveling along the highways that spread out from the great highway that was the Krakow, Tarnov, Lvov, Kiev route. Some had been on the march for two days and two nights, so distant were the borders of the province. Here were men and women in town dress from the larger centers, here were barefooted peasants in long coats and round hats, here were peasant women in rough garments but with head scarfs and shawls of dazzling colors, here were the inhabitants of a Jewish village, twelve men in black robes and black hats, with the characteristic orthodox curls hanging down in front of their ears.

Here were boys belonging to the retinue of a local szlachcic or country gentleman, their leather costumes showing up to advantage beside the rather dingy dress of the male portion of the peasantry. Here and there were women with little babies, here and there were old people trudging by the sides of their wagons up to market, as they had done for thirty or forty years past.

But every man in that caravan carried some sort of weapon, either a short knife at the belt, or quarterstaff in the hand, or huge-headed ax at the bottom of the wagon. For thieves were abroad in great number at times of market, and it was even said that there were country gentlemen of ruined fortune who were not above recouping themselves now and then at the expense of some such caravan. Usually, however, it was on the return trip that the thieves were numerous, for then each villager and peasant had gold or silver as the result of the day's bargaining.

Although practically all these wagons carried cargoes of goods, there was one which seemed strangely empty for market day. It had two horses instead of the usual one, its shaft pole was stouter than those of the other wagons, its occupants were better dressed than the peasants and seemed somehow not like actual workers of the soil. In it rode the driver, a man of perhaps forty-five years, a woman — his wife — some ten years younger, and a boy who sat at the open end of the wagon, dangling his legs above the dirt and mud of the highway.

"Now, wife," said the man, snapping a long whip at the off horse — his wife was sitting beside him on a rude seat at the front of the wagon — "that high tower you see is a watch tower on the Wawel Hill of Krakow. Should we go as flies the stork we should reach there by the eighth hour. See, in the distance are the two towers of the Church of Our Lady. It is a welcome sight to my eyes after these three weeks on a rocking cart."

The woman threw back a gray hood from her face and looked ahead with longing eyes. "It is Krakow, then," she said, "the city of my mother. Often has she told me of its glory, and yet I never had hoped to see it. God knows I wish I might see it differently and with less pain in my heart. But God gives, and man receives, and we are here at last."

"Yes," said the man.

For a long time they traveled along in silence. The man was musing on his early experiences in Krakow, the woman on her lost home in the Ukraine, and the boy letting his imagination run riot in speculation as to the sights that he should see in the great city.

Their thoughts were brought suddenly from their own affairs to a commotion among the carts behind them. Drivers were reining in their horses and swinging them to the left of the road, narrow as it was, in order to let someone pass. The man whose thoughts had been thus interrupted turned around, trying to discern who it might be who was pushing forward through the long line of carts, and in a moment he saw that it was a rider on a small horse.

"Way, way," the rider was shouting. "Do you peasants think that the whole road belongs to you? . . . Stay on your farm, where you belong," he shouted angrily at a peasant driver whose horse reared suddenly from the edge of the road to the middle. "Give me room to pass. You have no business on the highroad with an animal that jumps about like that."

"I had gone in the ditch else," replied the peasant without surliness.

The rider glanced sharply at the contents of the man's wagon and being assured that it contained nothing but fresh straw to be sold to the brick makers, dashed ahead until he was even with the cart which held the man and woman and boy.

The last named had been watching his advance curiously. Now this boy, Joseph Charnetski, was in his fifteenth year. He was not by any means handsome, though he could not be called ugly. His hair and his eyes were dark and his face was somewhat round and very pleasant. He wore rather rich, though travel-soiled, nether garments, not leather like those of the retainers, nor of coarse sacking like the peasants' clothes, but of a good quality of homespun, and a thick, buttoned coat of the same material, which fell shirt-like nearly to the knees. On his feet were

brown leather boots, whose tops were soft and loose, and so high that they reached almost to the bottom of the coat. On his head he wore a round hat like a turban.

The instant the rider perceived the boy, "Chlopak, chlopak (boy, boy)," he exclaimed in a rather croaky voice, "tell your old man to hold his horses. You come and hold mine."

The boy obeyed, but as he leaped from the wagon and grasped at the horse's bit thong, he came to the conclusion that the stranger was no friend. In those days when the world was just emerging from a period of darkness and cruelty, it was a necessity that each man should be constantly upon his guard against other men. Robbers abounded — jealous friends often descended to mean tricks; men of noble birth and breeding thought nothing of defrauding poor peasants, and among the poor peasants themselves were those who would commit crimes for the sake of gold.

Therefore when Joseph grasped at the horse's bit rein he had already come to the conclusion, perhaps from something in the stranger's looks or speech or manner, that he was one to be treated with caution. He was attired in a retainer's suit of thick cloth. The jacket was short but concealed a coat of very light chain armor beneath. He wore for breeches not knickerbockers but a single leather garment that combined doublet and hose in one. The cap was round, with a hanging jewel, probably glass, dangling behind against his neck.

It was the face, however, that betrayed the soul beneath. It was a dark, oval, wicked face — the eyes were greenish and narrow and the eyebrow line above them ran straight across the bridge of the nose, giving the effect of a monkey rather than a man. One cheek was marked with a buttonlike scar, the scar of the button plague that is common in the lands east of the Volga, or even the Dnieper, and marks the bearer as a Tartar or a Cossack or a Mongol. The ears were low-set and ugly. The mouth looked like the slit that boys make in the pumpkins they carry on the eve of All-hallows. Above the mouth was a cropped mustache which hung down at the ends and straggled into a scanty beard. The man carried at his waist a short curved sword and from the inside of his jacket could be seen protruding the jeweled handle of an Oriental dagger.

No sooner had the boy caught at his rein than the man was off his horse and with a leap had gained the wagon. Joseph's father reached quickly under the wagon seat for a short cross-hilted sword.

"Not one step nearer," he shouted as the man came toward him with hand outstretched as if to take his hand. "Who you may be I know not, but I stand as a Christian till I find out what your errand is."

The stranger stopped, smiled at the ready sword still in its scabbard, though with a sudden respect in his smile, then pulled off his hat and made a bow. "I take it that you are Andrew Charnetski," he said.

"You take too much," answered the driver. "To strangers I am Pan* Andrew Charnetski."

The stranger bowed again. "I spoke as to an equal," he said. "I am Stefan Ostrovski of Chelm. But now I am come from Kiev where I have been on state business. It is known that one Muscovite has some important business with our Lithuanian provinces and I, though I may not say by whom, was sent to learn ——" He broke off suddenly as if wishing to give the impression that his business was such that he might not speak of it in public fashion. "But on my way some men told me that a band of Tartars had come north from the Krim pillaging much of the country about. Among the houses which they had burned and the fields which they had destroyed were the house and fields of one Andrew Charnetski — nay, I ask pardon — of Pan Andrew Charnetski, who was reported to have escaped with his wife and son in the direction of Krakow, where they were said to have friends. This being true, and since I was traveling in the same direction, I sought a description of Pan Andrew and his family, and this morning when I saw a true Ukranian cart, drawn by two horses and not by one, and bearing a man and woman and boy such as had been described to me, I took the assurance to present myself and make my greetings to you."

Pan Charnetski scrutinized the face, the

* Pan is a formal Polish term signifying Sir or Mr.

clothing, and the figure of the stranger closely. "The half is not yet told," he said.

"Nay," answered the other, "but the rest is perhaps a tale for you and me behind some heavy door when we reach the city of Krakow just ahead. I have heard ——" He spoke significantly, then with his hands he described a circle in the air.

Charnetski watched him with his eyelids drawn half shut so that he could focus his attention upon the man and see naught of the world outside. His heart was not so cold and steady, however, as one might think from looking at his calm, composed features. In truth at the stranger's gesture his heart was beating a tattoo against his ribs. He knew that almost every word the man had uttered was false; he knew that his name was not Ostrovski even though there had been members of that family in Chelm — not one feature of the man's countenance was Polish. And there was that in the tone of the last words that had suggested a threat. Charnetski realized also that here was no chance meeting. It was fourteen days and more since they had left the border. This man, he reasoned, had followed them all that distance, or had perhaps been sent by some person of higher rank to intercept them before they gained entrance to the city.

"You have heard naught that concerns me," he answered shortly. "And now since the carts are leaving me behind, will you kindly return to your horse? I have nothing to say that will be of importance to you, nor do you interest me in any way."

Charnetski spoke truly, for the carts ahead were already some distance away and the drivers behind were shouting at him angrily for blocking the traffic.

"On the contrary," answered the stranger, "you have that which interests me greatly. And I will not leave you until we are safe behind some door in the city. Here, boy," he shouted at Joseph, "lead my horse along behind the wagon, for I intend to ride the rest of the way."

Pan Charnetski's cheeks blazed. "Now, by the lightning, you make yourself too free here," he articulated. "State what business you have quickly and be done."

The man glanced around the cart and he

saw on the wooden floor just in front of the driver's seat a huge yellow pumpkin. "Ha," he said, "a pumpkin, and at this time of the year. I suppose they raise pumpkins in the winter on the steppe. What shall be the price of that pumpkin?"

"It is not for sale," answered Charnetski.

"No?"

"I said no."

"What if I offer its weight in gold?"

"All's one."

"You will not sell?"

"I tell you, no."

"Then" — the stranger drew his sword quickly — "then you will fight for it!" And he stepped forward toward the driver.

Charnetski hesitated no longer. In the flash of an eye he had vaulted across the seat, dodged a blow of the saber, and caught the stranger's right wrist in a grip of steel. The sword dropped with a clang. Charnetski did not let the man go, however. He threw his left hand into the small of the stranger's leg and with clutch upon arm and leg hoisted him high and tossed him out of the cart. He fell in the mud, sputtering with rage and calling curses of every description upon Charnetski's head. And at this minute Joseph, with admirable foresight, swung the man's horse about and struck him smartly upon the right flank. The horse reared and capered, then dashed off down the road in the direction from which the wagons had come; at the same instant the boy leaped upon the cart and shouted to his father who climbed back to the seat and swung the long lash over the horses' heads. They were off in a second, leaving the stranger in the middle of the highway, turning now to the right and now to the left as if uncertain whether to pursue his horse or his enemy. And Charnetski, swinging about, picked up the sword from the bottom of the cart and hurled it into the road.

Some time later they reached the Kazimierz, the Jewish city founded by King Kazimir more than one hundred years earlier. Passing through this, they came to the bridge across the Vistula which would admit them to the city of Krakow itself. Finding, however, that this bridge was undergoing repairs, they were forced to take the next bridge to

the north; hence they proceeded to the fortified gate called Mikolayska, where they were challenged by the gatekeeper.

Master Simon's Garden
The Edge of the World[1]

Cornelia Lynde Meigs

⋸ *The beautiful garden which Master Simon planted about his home in the New World forms the background for a story covering three generations of his descendants. The book gives a splendid picture of a New England colony from Puritan times through Revolutionary days. The selection given below is the first chapter in the book and tells how the garden stands serenely for beauty, and against intolerance and rigid Puritanism.*

Old Goody Parsons, with her cleanest white kerchief, her most sorrowful expression of face and her biggest brown basket, had gone down through the village and across the hill to tell Master Simon what a long, hard winter it had been and how her cupboard was as bare, indeed, as Mother Hubbard's own. Now, as she made her way up the stony path again, her wrinkled old face was wreathed in smiles and her burden sagged heavily from her arm, for once more it had been proved that no one who came hungry to Master Simon's door ever went away unsatisfied. He had piled her basket high with good things from his garden, his wife had added three loaves of freshly baked bread and a jar of honey, and his little daughter Margaret had walked part of the way up the hill to help the old woman on her homeward road.

"Good-bye to you, little Mistress," Goody Parsons called after her when they parted at last, "and may the blessings on your dear father and mother be as many as are the good gifts in my basket."

Margaret, since her father needed her, did not wait to reply, but scampered away down the path again. The old woman stood on the

[1] From Cornelia Lynde Meigs, *Master Simon's Garden* (Macmillan, 1929).

hill-crest looking down at the scattered houses of the little Puritan town, at the spreading, sloping meadows and the wide salt marshes growing yellow-green under the pleasant April sunshine.

"These hills and meadows will never look as fair to me as those of England," she sighed, "but after all it is a goodly land that we have come to. Even if there be hunger and cold and want in it, are there not also freedom and kindness and Master Simon?"

The little town of Hopewell had been established long enough to have passed by those first terrible years when suffering and starvation filled the New England colonies. There were, however, many hard lessons to be learned before those who knew how to live and prosper in the Old World could master the arts necessary to the keeping of body and soul together in the New. Men who had tilled the rich smooth fields of England and had followed the plow down the furrows that their great-grandfathers had trod before them, must now break out new farm lands in those boulder-strewn meadows that sloped steeply down to the sea. Grievous work they surely found it, and small the returns for the first hard years. Yet, whenever food or fire or courage failed, the simplest remedy in the world for every trouble was to go in haste to Master Simon Radpath. His grassy meadow was always green, his fields rich every harvest time with bowing grain, his garden always crowded with herbs and vegetables, and gay the whole summer long with flowers, scarlet and white and yellow.

The old woman who had been his visitor today watched Margaret's yellow head disappear down the lane, and then turned to rest her basket on the rude stone wall, not because the burden was too heavy for her stout old arm, but because she heard footsteps behind her and she did dearly love to stop a neighbor on the road for a bit of talk.

"Good morrow, friend," she cried out, almost before she saw to whom she was speaking.

Her face fell a little when she discovered that it was only Samuel Skerry, the little crooked-backed shoemaker who lived with his apprentice in a tiny cottage, one field away from Master Simon's garden. A scowling, morose fellow the shoemaker was, but Goody Parsons's eager tongue could never be stopped by that.

"Spring is surely coming at last, neighbor," she began, quite undisturbed by Skerry's sullen greeting. "Here is another winter gone where it can trouble old bones no longer."

"Spring indeed," snarled the shoemaker, in his harsh voice, "why, the wind is cold as January and every keyhole in my house was shrieking aloud all last night! Where see you any spring?"

"I have been, but now, to visit Master and Mistress Radpath," she returned, "and their garden is already green, with a whole row of golden daffodils nodding before the door."

"Ah," answered her companion, "trust Master Simon to have some foolish, useless blossoms in his garden the moment the sun peeps out of the winter clouds. Does he never remember that so much time spent on what is only bright and gaudy is not strictly in accord with our Puritan law?"

"It was with herbs from that same garden that he healed you and many of the rest of us during that dreadful season of sickness," retorted Goody Parsons, "and did you not lie ill for two months of that summer and yet have a better harvest than any year before, because he had tended your fields along with his own?"

"Aye, and preached to me afterwards about every nettle and bramble that he found there, as though each had been one of the seven deadly sins. No, no, I like not his ways and I am weary of all this talk of how great and good a man is Master Simon. I fear me that all is not well in that bright-flowering garden of his." The shoemaker nodded craftily, as though he knew much that he would not tell.

Goody Parsons edged nearer. She was grateful to that gentle-voiced, kind-faced Master Simon who had helped her so often in trouble; she loved him much but, alas, she loved gossip more.

"Tell me what they say, good neighbor," she coaxed.

Samuel Skerry was provokingly silent for a space.

"They say," he said at last, "that in that garden — beyond the tulip bed — behind the hedge —— "

"Yes, yes!" she gasped as he paused again.

"There is Something hid," he concluded — "Something that no one of us ever sees but that neighbors hear, sometimes, crying aloud."

"But what is it?" she begged to know, in an agony of curiosity.

"Hush, I will whisper in your ear," he said. "It were not meet to speak such a thing aloud."

Goody Parsons bent her gray head to listen, and started back at the Shoemaker's low-spoken words.

"Ah, surely that cannot be true of so good a Puritan!" she cried in horror.

"You may believe me or not, according to your will," returned the shoemaker testily. "You were there but now; did you hear naught?"

Loyalty to her dear Master Simon and love of giving information struggled for a moment in the Goody's withered face, but at last the words simply burst from her.

"I did hear a strange cry," she said. "Ah, woe is me to think ill of so good a man! Come with me toward my house, Neighbor Skerry, and I will tell you what the sound was like."

So off the two went together, their heads bent close, their lips moving busily, as they gossiped with words that were to travel far.

Only Master Simon, his wife and his daughter, Margaret, knew the real reason why his garden and fields had greater success than any other's, knew of the ceaseless labor and genuine love that he expended upon his plants and flowers. Margaret loved them also, and would often rise early and go out with him to weed the hills of Indian corn, water the long beds of sweet-smelling herbs or coax some drooping shrub back to life and bloom. It was pleasant to be abroad then, when the gray mists lying over the wide, quiet harbor began to lift and turn to silver, when the birds were singing in the great forest near-

by and the dark-leaved bayberry bushes dropped their dew like rain when she brushed against them. Then she would see also mysterious forms slipping out of the dark wood, the graceful, silent figures of the friendly Indians, who also got up before the dawn and came hither for long talks with their good friend, Master Simon. They brought him flowers, roots and herbs that grew in this new country, while he, in turn, gave them plants sprung from English seed, taught them such of the white men's lore as might better their way of living and offered much sage counsel as to the endless quarrels that were always springing up among them between tribe and tribe.

"It is strange and not quite fitting that those heathen savages should follow you about like dogs," the villagers used to tell him, a little jealous, perhaps, that he should be as kind to his red-skinned friends as he was to his Puritan comrades. But Master Simon would only smile and go on his way, undisturbed by what they said.

When the long, warm evenings came and Margaret and her mother brought their spinning wheels to the doorstep that they might use the last ray of daylight for their work, Master Simon would labor beside them, tending now the roses and the yellow evening-primroses before the cottage. And he would tell, as he worked, of those other primroses that grew in English lanes, of blossoming hedgerows and soaring larks and all the other strange beauties of that dear country across the sea. Sometimes Margaret's mother would bend her head low over her spinning to hide the quiet tears, as he told of the great, splendid garden where he had learned his skill with plants and herbs, a garden of long terraces and old gray sundials and banks of blooming flowers. It was there that he and she had walked together in the moonlight, and had planned, with hearts all unafraid, for the day when they would be married and should set sail for that new land that seemed so far away. But there was no sadness or regret in Master Simon's heart.

"Some day," he would say, straightening up from his work and looking about him with a happy smile; "some day we shall have just such another garden planted here in the wilderness, at the very edge of the world that white men know."

This year, however, as he and Margaret planted the garden in unsuspecting peace of mind, there was strange talk about them running through the village. Much as the good Puritans had left behind them in England, there was bound to travel with them beyond the seas, their love of gossip about a neighbor. The whispered words of Samuel Skerry had traveled from Goody Parsons to those who dwelt nearest her, and from them to others, until soon the whole town was buzzing with wonder concerning Master Simon's garden and that secret thing that lay hidden in its midst. There were many people who owed him friendship and gratitude for past kindness, but there was not one who, on hearing the news, could refrain from rushing to the nearest house and bursting in with the words:

"Oh, neighbor, have you heard — ?" the rest always following in eager whispers.

Thus the talk had gone the rounds of the village until it reached the pastor of the church, where it fell like sparks into tow.

"I was ever mistrustful of Simon Radpath," cried the minister, Master Hapgood, when he heard the rumor. "That overbright garden of his has long been a blot upon our Puritan soberness. Others have their dooryards and their garden patches, yes, but these sheets of bloom, these blazes of color, I have always said that they argued something amiss with the man. He had also an easy way of forgiving sinners and rendering aid to those on whom our community frowned, that I liked none too well. Now we know, in truth, what he really is."

And off he set, post-haste, to speak to the Governor of the Colony about this dreadful scandal in Hopewell.

Trouble, therefore, was coming upon Master Simon on that pleasant morning of late May when Margaret went out to swing on the white gate and listen to the robins singing in the linden tree. It was trouble in the form of a stern company of dark-clad men, who came striding down the lane beneath the young white-blooming apple saplings. There were the church deacons, the minister, the assistants, and the great Governor himself, come to inquire into this business of the garden and its mysteries. Beside the Governor walked a stranger, a famous preacher from Scotland, whose strictness of belief and fierce denunciations of all those who broke the law, were known and dreaded throughout New England. Margaret dropped off the gate and ran full of wonder and alarm to tell her father.

It seemed, however, that the thoughts of these sober-faced public officers were not concerned entirely with Master Simon and his wickedness. The Governor bore a letter in his hand and was discussing with his friend from Scotland, Master Jeremiah Macrae, the new and great danger that was threatening the Colony. The friendly Indians, the peaceable Wampanoags, were becoming restless and holding themselves aloof from their former free intercourse with the people of the settlements. Other tribes more fierce and savage than they, were pressing upon them and crowding them more and more into the territory occupied by the whites. The Wampanoags, it was said, were being harassed by the Mohegans, old and often-fought enemies, while they, in turn, were being driven from their homes by the terrible Nascomi tribes, who dwelt far away but were so warlike and cruel that their name had ever been used as a byword to frighten naughty Indian babies into good behavior. Should such an avalanche of furious red-skinned warriors descend upon them, what could the little Colony of Puritans, with its four cannon and only fifty fightingmen, do to defend their lives and the homes that they had built with such courageous toil?

It was small wonder, then, that all the beauty and freshness of the full-flowering spring could not arouse the heavy thoughts of the Governor and his companions. Then, at the turn of the lane, they came in sight of a strange group, so sinister and alarming that the whole company stood still and more than one man laid his hand on his sword. Full in the way stood three tall, silent Indians, mightier of limb and fiercer of aspect than any the white men had ever seen before, their hawk-like faces daubed with gaudy colors and their strange feathered war-bonnets sweeping to their very heels. A trembling Wampanoag, brought as interpreter, advanced at the bidding of his imperious masters and strove vainly to find words with which to repeat his message.

"Come," said the Governor, "speak out. What can these strangers have to say to us?"

The interpreter, after more than one effort, managed to explain as he was ordered. These Indians had come from far away across the mountains and were of those dreaded Nascomis, a branch of the terrible Five Nations. They had heard of the new settlers and had come to look at their lands, intending, if they found them too good for aliens, to return later with all their warriors and drive the white men forth.

"And true it is that they will do so," added the Wampanoag, dropping from halting English into his own tongue when he found that one or two of those present could understand him. "There is no Indian of our tribe who does not hear all his life terrifying stories of these Nascomis, and of how, once in long periods of time, they change their hunting grounds and have no mercy on those who dwell in the land of their desire."

The Governor, in spite of the deep misgiving that all knew must be weighing at his heart, spoke his answer with unmoved calm.

"We will have speech with you later," he said through the interpreter, "for the present we have grave business with Master Simon Radpath. If you wish you may follow and come afterward to my house where we will treat further of this errand of yours."

The Indians, with unchanging faces, turned and walked down the lane beside the Puritan company. They talked together in their strange guttural language, pointing out this or that peculiarity of the white men's dress and seeming to regard them with far less of awe than mere curiosity. It was a short and bitterly uncomfortable journey that brought the gathering of elders, in small humor for any kindness of heart, to Master Simon's gate.

As Margaret stood beside her father, greeting these unexpected and disturbing guests,

she happened to glance across the sunlit field and saw Skerry, the shoemaker, and the boy who was his apprentice, standing before the door of their cottage. The little cobbler was shading his eyes with his hand and watching the dark procession as eagerly as though he had some deep concern in their errand. The ragged boy, however, seemed to have no interest in the matter, or no liking for it, since he stood with head turned away, staring down at the blue harbor and the wide-winged, skimming sea-gulls. The little girl observed them for only one moment, the next, and all her thoughts were drowned in wonder and alarm at the Governor's words.

"It has come to our ears, sir," he was saying sternly, "that you have here a garden too gay for proper Puritan minds, a place too like the show gardens of the Popish monasteries, or of the great lords that dwell amid such sinful luxury in England. In this Colony men and women have sat in the stocks for wasting precious hours over what shows only beauty to the eye and brings no benefit to the mind and heart. But what is that?" he broke off abruptly, sniffing suddenly at a vague sweet perfume that drifted down the May breeze.

"Please, sir, 'tis hawthorn," said Margaret, who was losing her terror of the Governor in curiosity at the sight of the Indians. "There was but a little sprig that Father brought from England grown now to a great, spreading bush."

A sudden change came over the Governor's stern face. Had he a stabbing memory of wide, smooth English meadows, yellow daffodils upon a sunny slope and hedges sweet with hawthorn blossom in the spring? None of the Pilgrims ever spoke of the homesickness that often assailed their steadfast hearts, but, as the Governor and Master Simon looked into each other's eyes, each knew of what the other was thinking. It was of some much-loved and never-forgotten home in England, perhaps, some bit of woods or meadow or narrow lane leading up a windy hill. The offending garden would have been in a fair way toward being forgiven had not the Scotch minister come forward and plucked the Governor by the sleeve.

"See, see!" he said, pointing. "Just look yonder."

Truly that was no sight for sober Puritan eyes! There beside the linden tree was a great bed of tulips, a blaze of crimson and gold, like a court lady's scarf or the cloak of a king's favorite. Against the green of the hedge, the deep red and clear yellow were fairly dazzling in the sunshine. The Governor scowled and drew back.

"Of what use," cried the minister in his loud, harsh voice. "Of what use on earth can be such a display of gaudy finery?"

There were three members of that company who could answer him. The Indian ambassadors, laughing aloud like children, dropped upon their knees before the glowing flower bed, plucked great handfuls of the brilliant blossoms, filled their quivers, their wampum belts, and their blankets with the shining treasure and turned to gaze with visible awe at the owner of all these riches.

"Do you not see," said Master Simon to the minister, an unsubdued twinkle in his eye, "that there is nothing permitted to grow upon this good, green earth that has not its use?"

"Such a flaunting of color," said the Governor severely, yet perhaps with the ghost of a smile held sternly in check, "has not our approval. Now I would see what lies behind that hedge."

Little Margaret looked up at her father and turned pale; even Master Simon hesitated and was about to frame an excuse, but it was too late. A shrill, terrible scream arose from behind the thick bushes.

"There, there, did I not tell you?" cried one of the deacons, and the whole company pressed forward into the inner garden.

They saw, at first, only a smooth square of grass, rolled and cut close like the lawns in England. Four cypress trees, dug up in the forest and trimmed to some semblance of the clipped yew that grace formal gardens, stood in a square about the hewn stone column that bore a sundial. Quiet, peaceful and innocent enough the place seemed — but there again was that terrible scream. Out from behind a shrub came strutting slowly the chief ornament of the place, Margaret's pet,

Master Simon's secret, a full-grown, glittering peacock. Seeing a proper company of spectators assembled, the stately bird spread its tail and walked up and down, turning itself this way and that to show off its glories, the very spirit of shallow and empty vanity. For pure amazement and horror, the Governor and his companions stood motionless and without speech.

But if the Englishmen were frozen to the spot, it was far otherwise with the Indians. They flung themselves upon their faces before the terrifying apparition, they held up their hands in supplication that it would do them no harm. Then, after a moment of stricken fear and upon the peacock's raising its terrible voice again, they sprang to their feet, fled through the gate and up the lane, and paused not once in their headlong flight until they had disappeared into the sheltering forest. The Governor drew a long breath, caught Master Simon's eye, and burst into a great roar of laughter.

"You have done us a good turn, you and your silly, empty-headed bird," he said, "though I was of a mind for a moment to put it to death and to set you in the pillory for harboring such a creature of vanity. Yet for the sake of his help against a dreaded foe, you shall both be spared. Now see that you order your garden more soberly and that no further complaints come to my ears."

He turned to go.

"If you please, may we keep the tulips?" begged Margaret, curtsying low, her voice shaking with anxiety.

"Yes, little maid," was the gracious answer, "you may keep your tulips, since you cannot use them for gold as those poor savages thought they could. And go, pluck me a branch of that hawthorn blossom that smells so sweet. It grew — ah, how it grew in the fair green lanes of my own dear Nottinghamshire!"

With the sprig of hawthorn in his gray coat, and with a bow to Margaret as though she had been some great lady, the Governor passed out into the lane, followed by all his company, deacons, assistants, and Master Hapgood. Only the minister, Jeremiah Macrae, lingered inside the gate. Suddenly he lifted both his arms toward heaven and spoke out loudly in his great, harsh voice. With his dark cloak flying about him and his deep-set eyes lit by a very flame of wrath, he looked to Margaret like one of the prophets of old, such as were pictured in her mother's great Bible. She trembled and crept nearer to her father.

"Think not, Simon Radpath," the minister thundered, "that, although you have won the Governor's forgiveness by a trick, there the matter ends. Woe be unto you, O sinful man, unless you destroy the gaudy vanity of this wicked garden. Change your ways or fire and sword shall waste this place, blood shall be spilled upon its soil, and those who come after you shall walk, mourning, among its desolate paths."

Margaret gasped with terror, but Master Simon, though a little pale, stood his ground undaunted.

"I, too, have made a prophecy concerning my garden," he answered. "It is carved yonder about the edge of the sundial, and the climbing roses are reaching up to cover the words, for it will be long before their truth is proved. It may be that this spot will see flame and sword and the shedding of blood, for new countries and new ideas must be tried in the fire before they can live. But my prophecy is for peace and growth, yours for war and destruction — a hundred years from now men shall know which of us spoke truly."

"A hundred years from now!" repeated the minister scornfully. "Think you that, after the half of that time, there will be any man who remembers you, or your word, or your garden?"

He strode across the lawn, plucked aside roughly the trailing rose-vines at the edge of the sundial and read the words carved deep in the gray stone.* Then, with no comment, nor any word of leave-taking, he went out through the gate and up the lane. Margaret stood long watching him as he climbed the steep path. His figure looked very black in the clear, white sunshine, very ill-omened and forbidding even as it grew small in the distance and finally vanished over the crest of the hill.

* Sundial motto: "I have planted, you have watered, God will give the increase."

Rolling Wheels
Over the Divide [2]

KATHARINE GREY

Based on authentic accounts of the California migration, Rolling Wheels *is an exceptionally realistic story of the adventurous journey made by the Lambert family in a prairie schooner from Indiana to California in the eighteen-forties. Interest centers in twelve-year-old Jerd and his younger sister Betsy and their reactions to the adventures and hardships of the trip.*

For days the caravan climbed gradually up the headwaters of the Sweetwater River. The way was so lovely that they hardly knew the road was leading up. Willows and cotton-woods grew along the water's edge. Sometimes the cañon walls hung with moss where a waterfall leapt over and cast its spray.

And then ——

Jeff could hardly be made to believe the truth of it. He stood by his tired mules and let his eye wander over a vast green meadow that stretched from mountain base to mountain base, while mountains, rising to snow-capped heights, reached into peaks on the north and south.

"Do you believe it?" he kept saying. "Can you believe we're tiptop on the Rocky Mountains?"

"You knew we were comin' to South Pass," Jerd said. Jerd was the only one who would listen to Jeff that day.

They stood there, the weary band, close together to look upon the beauties of the world. Ahead lay a panorama of untold wonders. Vast mountain ranges, with innumerable curves and pinnacles, stretched away to be lost in the haze of distance. Thither was the way to the West. Down among the ravines and cañons of those mountains the wagons would have to go, down out of the Rocky Mountains.

Betsy slipped her hand in Granny's. "I can hardly get my breath, Granny."

"It'll come back to you."

[2] From Katharine Grey, Rolling Wheels (Little, Brown, 1937).

Someone called out, "Look back over the way we came."

There behind them lay grandeur, too. Passing through the long weary way, they had not realized fully its loveliness. Mountains sloped down from splendid heights into a vast plain that looked as level as a floor.

"Aye, but we know the ridges and gullies in it," Jeff said. "We can't be fooled by what we've tromped over."

Joel shouted so all could hear: "Take a long look, everybody. Say good-bye to the East. When we start down from here, we belong to the West. We belong to the West forever."

Jerd jerked off his hat and waved it. Betsy climbed on a wagon wheel and waved her sunbonnet. Everybody in the train waved hands, hats, or sunbonnets. Then they turned again to the West and were silent. They had no word of greeting for the sublime and solemn grandeur of that scene.

Jerd looked at Mother. Her back was toward the East. She stood straight and still, facing the West. Her hands were clasped against her breast. Jerd knew that a prayer was in her heart. Hot tears came into his eyes as he watched her. Oh, he would make her glad she came West to Californy. He would make her glad——

Joel shouted again, "Say your last good-byes. We've got to hurry on home — to California."

Jerd brushed the tears from his eyes with his coat-sleeve and let the long whip curl over the backs of his oxen. All along the line men were chirruping and cracking whips. The train moved over South Pass and started down.

Two miles beyond lay Pacific Springs, a fine big spring of cold water set in the midst of a great green meadow.

"We'll sleep tonight here in our own front yard," Father said.

"If they run us out'n Californy, this may come to be the back-yard fence," George Harlan said. "We may have to skitter over it in a hurry."

"I can't even take thought of what goes on in Californy," Father said. "I can think only of a few days' rest here in the lap of the great Rockies."

On the way down from Pacific Springs the next day, Jerd saw more skeletons of cattle and horses than he had ever seen before in so short a distance. "They just naturally wore out," he thought. "They got to the top, though. Too bad they had to die then." He knew how weak and spent were all the cattle of the train. He stroked his team with a great tenderness. "I'm glad I had the little bit of corn for you. It helped, didn't it?"

Every day or so someone lost an ox or a cow. Jeff's mules were worn to skin and bones. Selim and Milly had not been hitched to the wagon long enough to have suffered so much. Young oxen were taken from the loose herd and broken to the yoke to take the place of the faithful oxen that died.

"We'll have no milk, soon," Mother said. "We can't expect to drain the poor cows when we can count their ribs."

The country became more and more dry and desolate. There was little feed for the cattle. They relished bunch grass even more than green grass, though, and always there was hope of finding green pastures and good water.

Down they came to the waters of Little Sandy River, a fine camping ground already occupied by ravenous mosquitoes. Fires were kindled out in the sagebrush with the hope that the smoke would drive away the mosquitoes from the switching, stamping cattle.

Little Sandy was a shallow stream. Children could wade and plunge about in it. The men and boys found a deep hole in the river a mile below camp and all jumped in and had a fine swim. As they were on the way back to camp, Ring flushed a fine flock of sage hens.

"Shoot!" Someone always carried a gun.

Sage hens for supper were a fine change from salt bacon and deer meat, though deer meat was scarce now and no one had seen a buffalo since they came up from the plains into South Pass.

Such camping grounds were not often come upon. There followed long, dusty, weary miles across the barren earth with never a sight of water.

One day when throats of dust-covered men and beasts were parched past enduring, Johnny Wimmer ran ahead shouting,

"There's a lake over there — a lake of water. It's a sight to this world."

Such a lake! A lake rimmed with green trees — green, waving trees. A jewel of blue water rimmed with green.

"We'll have fish for supper," Jerd said.

Betsy studied the lake, puzzled. "Jerd, don't you think it's funny for a lake like that to be here where there's no river to empty into it?"

"Well, there's the lake. What do you say to that?"

"Why, it's gone. The lake's gone, Jerd."

"It couldn't be gone! A lake couldn't just get up and move away."

Joel passed the wagon just then, Jerd called and Joel reined in his horse. "Joel, did you see a lake! Right over there it was — with trees all around it."

"I was just explaining to Nancy about a mirage," Joel said.

"What is a mirage?"

"That lake was a mirage. It wasn't real at all. You've heard Mr. Ray tell about seeing lakes and towns and rivers when he passed this way before. All mirages they were; all just pictures in the air."

Jeff had listened to what Joel said. He took off his hat and pulled at his long hair. "I'll be dumsquizzled! I had my mouth all set for fried fish."

Betsy was ready to cry. "It ain't fair. It ain't fair to make a picture like that for thirsty folks to look at."

"It won't hurt us if we understand. I think it's nice. We can have the fun of looking at the water anyway."

"Don't forget that Mr. Ray said men have followed after a sight of water till they dropped. Don't let yourself be fooled by it."

Over the divide next, to the Big Sandy River and good grass with acres of lupines making the earth a lovely blue. On from the Big Sandy to the Green River where the water ran wide, shallow, swift. An easy crossing they found there and a great surprise a mile farther on down the river. Houses — with walls and roofs. Houses built by white men.

Mart Horton saw the cabins first and called back for folks to look. "It's just about a town," he said.

"A handful of cabins don't make a town, Mart," George said.

The cabins were empty, abandoned by the trappers who built them in the grove of cottonwood trees. But even an empty cabin was a fair sight, especially on an afternoon when the sky was piled full of clouds that trampled each other in their milling about.

"If it rains," Jerd said, "we can shelter under a roof and sit by a chimney fire. We could stay here a week and let it rain every day."

In answer to that a lance of lightning struck through the dark clouds so that the noise of thunder rolled in echoes among the bluffs. Jerd was for taking the bedding into the cabins, but Mother preferred the shelter under the wagon covers. Others agreed with her; their beds in the wagons were like home.

A terrific storm broke that night. Such a storm that the horses went into the cabins and stood with each other while rain pelted the roof. The cattle came up and huddled against the protected sides of the cabins until the swirling, roaring storm had spent itself.

Morning dawned upon a world with its face new-washed. When the sun shone, men were ready to take the road again.

The Adventures of Tom Sawyer

Tom Meets Becky [3]

MARK TWAIN

The Adventures of Tom Sawyer *is an American classic of boy life. Mark Twain based the story on his own boyhood in Missouri. When he sent the manuscript to his friend William Dean Howells for criticism, Mr. Howells pronounced it* "altogether the best boy's story I have ever read." *The book was first published in 1876 and still maintains its leadership among the most popular books for boys. In the chapter given below, the reader meets Becky Thatcher, and is also introduced for the first time to Huck Finn. The story is continued in* Adventures of Huckleberry Finn.

[3] From Samuel L. Clemens (Mark Twain), *The Adventures of Tom Sawyer* (Harper).

Monday morning found Tom Sawyer miserable. Monday morning always found him so — because it began another week's slow suffering in school. He generally began that day with wishing he had had no intervening holiday, it made the going into captivity and fetters again so much more odious.

Tom lay thinking. Presently it occurred to him that he wished he was sick; then he could stay home from school. Here was a vague possibility. He canvassed his system. No ailment was found, and he investigated again. This time he thought he could detect colicky symptoms, and he began to encourage them with considerable hope. But they soon grew feeble, and presently died wholly away. He reflected further. Suddenly he discovered something. One of his upper front teeth was loose. This was lucky; he was about to begin to groan, as a "starter," as he called it, when it occurred to him that if he came into court with that argument, his aunt would pull it out, and that would hurt. So he thought he would hold the tooth in reserve for the present, and seek further. Nothing offered for some little time, and then he remembered hearing the doctor tell about a certain thing that laid up a patient for two or three weeks and threatened to make him lose a finger. So the boy eagerly drew his sore toe from under the sheet and held it up for inspection. But now he did not know the necessary symptoms. However, it seemed well worth while to chance it, so he fell to groaning with considerable spirit.

But Sid slept on unconscious.

Tom groaned louder, and fancied that he began to feel pain in the toe.

No result from Sid.

Tom was panting with his exertions by this time. He took a rest and then swelled himself up and fetched a succession of admirable groans.

Sid snored on.

Tom was aggravated. He said, "Sid, Sid!" and shook him. This course worked well, and Tom began to groan again. Sid yawned, stretched, then brought himself up on his elbow with a snort, and began to stare at Tom. Tom went on groaning. Sid said:

"Tom! Say, Tom! [No response.] Here, Tom! *Tom!* What is the matter, Tom?" And he shook him and looked in his face anxiously.

Tom moaned out:

"Oh, don't, Sid. Don't joggle me."

"Why, what's the matter, Tom? I must call Auntie."

"No — never mind. It'll be over by and by, maybe. Don't call anybody."

"But I must! *Don't* groan so, Tom, it's awful. How long you been this way?"

"Hours. Ouch! Oh, don't stir so, Sid, you'll kill me."

"Tom, why didn't you wake me sooner? Oh, Tom, *don't!* It makes my flesh crawl to hear you. Tom, what *is* the matter?"

"I forgive you everything, Sid. [Groan.] Everything you've ever done to me. When I'm gone ——"

"Oh, Tom, you ain't dying, are you? Don't, Tom — oh, don't. Maybe ——"

"I forgive everybody, Sid. [Groan.] Tell 'em so, Sid. And Sid, you give my window-sash, and my cat with one eye to that new girl that's come to town, and tell her ——"

But Sid had snatched his clothes and gone. Tom was suffering in reality, now, so handsomely was his imagination working, and so his groans had gathered quite a genuine tone.

Sid flew downstairs and said:

"Oh, Aunt Polly, come! Tom's dying!"

"Dying!"

"Yes'm. Don't wait — come quick!"

"Rubbage! I don't believe it!"

But she fled upstairs, nevertheless, with Sid and Mary at her heels. And her face grew white, too, and her lip trembled. When she reached the bedside she gasped out:

"You, Tom! Tom, what's the matter with you?"

"Oh, Auntie, I'm ——"

"What's the matter with you — what *is* the matter with you, child?"

"Oh, Auntie, my sore toe's mortified!"

The old lady sank down into a chair and laughed a little, then cried a little, then did both together. This restored her and she said:

"Tom, what a turn you did give me! Now you shut up that nonsense and climb out of this."

The groans ceased and the pain vanished

from the toe. The boy felt a little foolish, and he said:

"Aunt Polly, it *seemed* mortified, and it hurt so I never minded my tooth at all."

"Your tooth, indeed! What's the matter with your tooth?"

"One of them's loose, and it aches perfectly awful."

"There, there, now, don't begin that groaning again. Open your mouth. Well — your tooth *is* loose, but you're not going to die about that. Mary, get me a silk thread, and a chunk of fire out of the kitchen."

Tom said:

"Oh, please, Auntie, don't pull it out! It don't hurt any more. I wish I may never stir if it does. Please don't, Auntie. *I* don't want to stay home from school."

"Oh, you don't, don't you? So, all this row was because you thought you'd get to stay home from school and go a-fishing? Tom, Tom, I love you so, and you seem to try every way you can to break my old heart with your outrageousness." By this time the dental instruments were ready. The old lady made one end of the silk thread fast to Tom's tooth with a loop and tied the other to the bedpost. Then she seized the chunk of fire and suddenly thrust it almost into the boy's face. The tooth hung dangling by the bedpost, now.

But all trials bring their compensations. As Tom wended to school after breakfast, he was the envy of every boy he met because the gap in his upper row of teeth enabled him to expectorate in a new and admirable way. He gathered quite a following of lads interested in the exhibition; and one that had cut his finger and had been a center of fascination and homage up to this time now found himself suddenly without an adherent and shorn of his glory. His heart was heavy, and he said with a disdain which he did not feel that it wasn't anything to spit like Tom Sawyer; but another boy said "Sour grapes!" and he wandered away a dismantled hero.

Shortly Tom came upon the juvenile pariah of the village, Huckleberry Finn, son of the town drunkard. Huckleberry was cordially hated and dreaded by all the mothers of the town, because he was idle and lawless and vulgar and bad — and because all their children admired him so, and delighted in his forbidden society, and wished they dared to be like him. Tom was like the rest of the respectable boys, in that he envied Huckleberry his gaudy outcast condition, and was under strict orders not to play with him. So he played with him every time he got a chance. Huckleberry was always dressed in the cast-off clothes of full-grown men, and they were in perennial bloom and fluttering with rags. His hat was a vast ruin with a wide crescent lopped out of its brim; his coat, when he wore one, hung nearly to his heels and had the rearward buttons far down the back; but one suspender supported his trousers; the seat of the trousers bagged low and contained nothing; the fringed legs dragged in the dirt when not rolled up.

Huckleberry came and went, at his own free will. He slept on doorsteps in fine weather and in empty hogsheads in wet; he did not have to go to school or to church, or call any being master or obey anybody; he could go fishing or swimming when and where he chose, and stay as long as it suited him; nobody forbade him to fight; he could sit up as late as he pleased; he was always the first boy that went barefoot in the spring and the last to resume leather in the fall; he never had to wash, nor put on clean clothes; he could swear wonderfully. In a word, everything that goes to make life precious that boy had. So thought every harassed, hampered, respectable boy in St. Petersburg.

Tom hailed the romantic outcast:

"Hello, Huckleberry!"

"Hello yourself, and see how you like it."

"What's that you got?"

"Dead cat."

"Lemme see him, Huck. My, he's pretty stiff. Where'd you get him?"

"Bought him off'n a boy."

"What did you give?"

"I give a blue ticket and a bladder that I got at the slaughter-house."

"Where'd you get the blue ticket?"

"Bought it off'n Ben Rogers two weeks ago for a hoopstick."

"Say — what is dead cats good for, Huck?"

"Good for? Cure warts with."

"No! Is that so? I know something that's better."

"I bet you don't. What is it?"

"Why, spunk-water."

"Spunk-water! I wouldn't give a dern for spunk-water."

"You wouldn't, wouldn't you? D'you ever try it?"

"No, I hain't. But Bob Tanner did."

"Who told you so?"

"Why, he told Jeff Thatcher, and Jeff told Johnny Baker, and Johnny told Jim Hollis, and Jim told Ben Rogers, and Ben told a nigger, and the nigger told me. There now!"

"Well, what of it? They'll all lie. Leastways all but the nigger. I don't know *him*. But I never see a nigger that *wouldn't* lie. Shucks! Now you tell me how Bob Tanner done it, Huck."

"Why, he took and dipped his hand in a rotten stump where the rainwater was."

"In the daytime?"

"Certainly."

"With his face to the stump?"

"Yes. Least I reckon so."

"Did he *say* anything?"

"I don't reckon he did. I don't know."

"Aha! Talk about trying to cure warts with spunk-water such a blame-fool way as that! Why, that ain't a-going to do any good. You got to go all by yourself, to the middle of the woods, where you know there's a spunk-water stump, and just as it's midnight you back up against the stump and jam your hand in and say:

> Barley-corn, barley-corn, injun-meal shorts,
> Spunk-water, spunk-water, swaller these warts,

and then walk away quick, eleven steps, with your eyes shut, and then turn around three times and walk home without speaking to anybody. Because if you speak the charm's busted."

"Well, that sounds like a good way; but that ain't the way Bob Tanner done."

"No, sir, you can bet he didn't, becuz he's the wartiest boy in this town; and he wouldn't have a wart on him if he'd knowed how to work spunk-water. I've took off thousands of warts off of my hands that way, Huck. I play with frogs so much that I've always got considerable many warts. Sometimes I take 'em off with a bean."

"Yes, bean's good. I've done that."

"Have you? What's your way?"

"You take and split the bean, and cut the wart so as to get some blood, and then you put the blood on one piece of the bean and take and dig a hole and bury it 'bout midnight at the crossroads in the dark of the moon, and then you burn up the rest of the bean. You see that piece that's got the blood on it will keep drawing and drawing, trying to fetch the other piece to it, and so that helps the blood to draw the wart, and pretty soon off she comes."

"Yes, that's it, Huck—that's it; though when you're burying it if you say, 'Down bean; off wart; come no more to bother me!' it's better. That's the way Joe Harper does, and he's been nearly to Coonville and most everywheres. But say—how do you cure 'em with dead cats?"

"Why, you take your cat and go and get in the graveyard 'long about midnight when somebody that was wicked has been buried; and when it's midnight a devil will come, or maybe two or three, but you can't see 'em, you can only hear something like the wind, or maybe hear 'em talk; and when they're taking that feller away, you heave your cat after 'em and say, 'Devil follow corpse, cat follow devil, warts follow cat, *I'm* done with ye!' That'll fetch *any* wart."

"Sounds right. D'you ever try it, Huck?"

"No, but old Mother Hopkins told me."

"Well, I reckon it's so, then. Becuz they say she's a witch."

"Say! Why, Tom, I *know* she is. She witched Pap. Pap says so his own self. He come along one day, and he see she was a-witching him, so he took up a rock, and if she hadn't dodged, he'd 'a' got her. Well, that very night he rolled off'n a shed wher' he was a-layin' drunk, and broke his arm."

"Why, that's awful. How did he know she was a-witching him?"

"Lord, Pap can tell easy. Pap says when they keep looking at you right stiddy, they're a-witching you. 'Specially if they mumble. Becuz when they mumble they're saying the Lord's Prayer back'ards."

"Say, Hucky, when you going to try the cat?"

"Tonight. I reckon they'll come after old Hoss Williams tonight."

"But they buried him Saturday. Didn't they get him Saturday night?"

"Why, how you talk! How could their charms work till midnight? — and *then* its Sunday. Devils don't slosh around much of a Sunday, I don't reckon."

"I never thought of that. That's so. Lemme go with you?"

"Of course — if you ain't afeard."

"Afeard! 'Tain't likely. Will you meow?"

"Yes — and you meow back, if you get a chance. Last time, you kep' me a-meowing around till old Hays went to throwing rocks at me and says 'Dern that cat!' and so I hove a brick through his window — but don't you tell."

"I won't. I couldn't meow that night, becuz Auntie was watching me, but I'll meow this time. Say — what's that?"

"Nothing but a tick."

"Where'd you get him?"

"Out in the woods."

"What'll you take for him?"

"I don't know. I don't want to sell him."

"All right. It's a mighty small tick, anyway."

"Oh, anybody can run a tick down that don't belong to them. I'm satisfied with it. It's a good enough tick for me."

"Sho, there's ticks a-plenty. I could have a thousand of 'em if I wanted to."

"Well, why don't you? Becuz you know mighty well you can't. This is a pretty early tick, I reckon. It's the first one I've seen this year."

"Say, Huck — I'll give you my tooth for him."

"Less see it."

Tom got out a bit of paper and carefully unrolled it. Huckleberry viewed it wistfully. The temptation was very strong. At last he said:

"Is it genuwyne?"

Tom lifted his lip and showed the vacancy.

"Well, all right," said Huckleberry, "it's a trade."

Tom enclosed the tick in the percussion-cap box that had lately been the pinch-bug's prison, and the boys separated, each feeling wealthier than before.

When Tom reached the little isolated **frame** schoolhouse, he strode in briskly, with the manner of one who had come with all honest speed. He hung his hat on a peg and flung himself into his seat with businesslike alacrity. The master, throned on high in his great splint-bottom armchair, was dozing, lulled by the drowsy hum of study. The interruption roused him.

"Thomas Sawyer!"

Tom knew that when his name was pronounced in full, it meant trouble.

"Sir!"

"Come up here. Now, sir, why are you late again, as usual?"

Tom was about to take refuge in a lie, when he saw two long tails of yellow hair hanging down a back that he recognized by the electric sympathy of love; and by that form was *the only vacant place* on the girls' side of the schoolhouse. He instantly said:

"I STOPPED TO TALK WITH HUCKLEBERRY FINN!"

The master's pulse stood still, and he stared helplessly. The buzz of study ceased. The pupils wondered if this foolhardy boy had lost his mind. The master said:

"You — you did what?"

"Stopped to talk with Huckleberry Finn."

There was no mistaking the words.

"Thomas Sawyer, this is the most astounding confession I have ever listened to. No mere ferule will answer for this offense. Take off your jacket."

The master's arm performed until it was tired and the stock of switches notably diminished. Then the order followed:

"Now, sir, go and sit with the *girls!* And let this be a warning to you."

The titter that rippled around the room appeared to abash the boy, but in reality that result was caused rather more by his worshipful awe of his unknown idol and the dread pleasure that lay in his high good fortune. He sat down upon the end of the pine bench and the girl hitched herself away from him with a toss of her head. Nudges and winks and whispers traversed the room, but Tom sat still, with his arms upon the long, low desk before him, and seemed to study his book.

By and by attention ceased from him, and the accustomed school murmur rose upon the dull air once more. Presently the boy began to steal furtive glances at the girl. She observed it, "made a mouth" at him and gave him the back of her head for the space of a minute. When she cautiously faced around again, a peach lay before her. She thrust it away. Tom gently put it back. She thrust it away again, but with less animosity. Tom patiently returned it to its place. Then she let it remain. Tom scrawled on his slate, "Please take it — I got more." The girl glanced at the words, but made no sign. Now the boy began to draw something on the slate, hiding his work with his left hand. For a time the girl refused to notice; but her human curiosity presently began to manifest itself by hardly perceptible signs. The boy worked on, apparently unconscious. The girl made a sort of non-committal attempt to see it, but the boy did not betray that he was aware of it. At last she gave in and hesitatingly whispered:

"Let me see it."

Tom partly uncovered a dismal caricature of a house with two gable ends to it and a corkscrew of smoke issuing from the chimney. Then the girl's interest began to fasten itself upon the work and she forgot everything else. When it was finished, she gazed a moment, then whispered:

"It's nice — make a man."

The artist erected a man in the front yard, that resembled a derrick. He could have stepped over the house; but the girl was not hypercritical; she was satisfied with the monster, and whispered:

"It's a beautiful man — now make me coming along."

Tom drew an hour-glass with a full moon and straw limbs to it and armed the spreading fingers with a portentous fan. The girl said:

"It's ever so nice — I wish I could draw."

"It's easy," whispered Tom, "I'll learn you."

"Oh, will you? When?"

"At noon. Do you go home to dinner?"

"I'll stay if you will."

"Good — that's a whack. What's your name?"

"Becky Thatcher. What's yours? Oh, I know. It's Thomas Sawyer."

"That's the name they lick me by. I'm Tom when I'm good. You call me Tom, will you?"

"Yes."

Now Tom began to scrawl something on the slate, hiding the words from the girl. But she was not backward this time. She begged to see. Tom said:

"Oh, it ain't anything."

"Yes, it is."

"No, it ain't. You don't want to see."

"Yes, I do, indeed I do. Please let me."

"You'll tell."

"No, I won't — deed and deed and double deed I won't."

"You won't tell anybody at all? Ever, as long as you live?"

"No, I won't ever tell anybody. Now let me."

"Oh, you don't want to see!"

"Now that you treat me so, I will see." And she put her small hand upon his and a little scuffle ensued, Tom pretending to resist in earnest, but letting his hand slip by degrees till these words were revealed: "I love you."

"Oh, you bad thing!" And she hit his hand a smart rap, but reddened and looked pleased, nevertheless.

Just at this juncture the boy felt a slow, fateful grip closing on his ear, and a steady lifting impulse. In that vise he was borne across the house and deposited in his own seat, under a peppering fire of giggles from the whole school. Then the master stood over him during a few awful moments, and finally moved away to his throne without saying a word. But although Tom's ear tingled, his heart was jubilant.

As the school quieted down, Tom made an honest effort to study, but the turmoil within him was too great. In turn he took his place in the reading class and made a botch of it; then in the geography class and turned lakes into mountains, mountains into rivers, and rivers into continents, till chaos was come again; then in the spelling class, and got "turned down," by a succession of mere baby words, till he brought up at the foot and yielded up the pewter medal which he had worn with ostentation for months.

Treasure Island

(A Selection)

ROBERT LOUIS STEVENSON

Treasure Island, first published in 1883, is one of the best adventure stories ever written and it is still one of the most popular. It was originally written for a schoolboy who wanted "something craggy to break his mind upon." In telling how he first started to write the story, Stevenson says: "I made the map of an island; it was elaborately and (I thought) beautifully colored; the shape of it took my fancy beyond expression; it contained harbors that pleased me like sonnets; and with the unconsciousness of the predestined, I ticketed my performance 'Treasure Island.'...As I paused upon my map ...the future characters of the book began to appear there visibly among imaginary woods; and there brown faces and bright weapons peeped out upon me from unexpected quarters as they passed to and fro, fighting and hunting treasure, on these few square inches of a flat projection. The next thing I knew I had some papers before me and was writing out a list of characters."

The *Hispaniola* lay some way out, and we went under the figureheads and round the sterns of many other ships, and their cables sometimes grated underneath our keel, and sometimes swung above us. At last, however, we got alongside, and were met and saluted as we stepped aboard by the mate, Mr. Arrow, a brown old sailor, with earrings in his ears and a squint. He and the squire were very thick and friendly, but I soon observed that things were not the same between Mr. Trelawney and the captain.

This last was a sharp-looking man, who seemed angry with everything on board, and was soon to tell us why, for we had hardly got down into the cabin when a sailor followed us.

"Captain Smollett, sir, axing to speak with you," said he.

"I am always at the captain's orders. Show him in," said the squire.

The captain, who was close behind the messenger, entered at once, and shut the door behind him.

"Well, Captain Smollett, what have you to say? All well, I hope; all shipshape and seaworthy?"

"Well, sir," said the captain, "better speak plain, I believe, even at the risk of offense. I don't like this cruise; I don't like the men; and I don't like my officer. That's short and sweet."

"Perhaps, sir, you don't like the ship?" inquired the squire, very angry, as I could see.

"I can't speak as to that, sir, not having seen her tried," said the captain. "She seems a clever craft; more I can't say."

"Possibly, sir, you may not like your employer, either?" says the squire.

But here Doctor Livesey cut in.

"Stay a bit," said he, "stay a bit. No use of such questions as that but to produce ill-feeling. The captain has said too much or he has said too little, and I'm bound to say that I require an explanation of his words. You don't, you say, like this cruise. Now, why?"

"I was engaged, sir, on what we called sealed orders, to sail this ship for that gentleman where he should bid me," said the captain. "So far so good. But now I find that every man before the mast knows more than I do. I don't call that fair, now, do you?"

"No," said Doctor Livesey, "I don't."

"Next," said the captain, "I learn we are going after treasure — hear it from my own hands, mind you. Now, treasure is ticklish work; I don't like treasure voyages on any account; and I don't like them, above all, when they are secret, and when (begging your pardon, Mr. Trelawney) the secret has been told to the parrot."

"Silver's parrot?" asked the squire.

"It's a way of speaking," said the captain. "Blabbed, I mean. It's my belief neither of you gentlemen know what you are about; but I'll tell you my way of it — life or death, and a close run."

"That is all clear, and, I dare say, true enough," replied Doctor Livesey. "We take the risk; but we are not so ignorant as you believe us. Next, you say you don't like the crew. Are they not good seamen?"

"I don't like them, sir," returned Captain Smollett. "And I think I should have had the choosing of my own hands, if you go to that."

"Perhaps you should," replied the doctor. "My friend should, perhaps, have taken you along with him; but the slight, if there be one, was unintentional. And you don't like Mr. Arrow?"

"I don't sir. I believe he's a good seaman; but he's too free with the crew to be a good officer. A mate should keep himself to himself — shouldn't drink with the men before the mast!"

"Do you mean he drinks?" cried the squire.

"No, sir," replied the captain; "only that he's too familiar."

"Well, now, and the short and long of it, captain?" asked the doctor. "Tell us what you want."

"Well, gentlemen, are you determined to go on this cruise?"

"Like iron," answered the squire.

"Very good," said the captain. "Then, as you've heard me very patiently, saying things that I could not prove, hear me a few words more. They are putting the powder and the arms in the forehold. Now, you have a good place under the cabin; why not put them there? — first point. Then you are bringing four of your own people with you, and they tell me some of them are to be berthed forward. Why not give them the berths beside the cabin? — second point."

"Any more?" asked Mr. Trelawney.

"One more," said the captain. "There's been too much blabbing already."

"Far too much," agreed the doctor.

"I'll tell you what I've heard myself," continued Captain Smollett; "that you have a map of an island; that there's crosses on the map to show where treasure is; and that the island lies ——" And then he named the latitude and longitude exactly.

"I never told that," cried the squire, "to a soul!"

"The hands know it, sir," returned the captain.

"Livesey, that must have been you or Hawkins," cried the squire.

"It doesn't much matter who it was," replied the doctor. And I could see that neither he nor the captain paid much regard to Mr. Trelawney's protestations. Neither did I, to be sure, he was so loose a talker; yet in this case I believe he was really right, and that nobody had told the situation of the island.

"Well, gentlemen," continued the captain, "I don't know who had the map; but I make it a point, it shall be kept secret even from me and Mr. Arrow. Otherwise I would ask you to let me resign."

"I see," said the doctor. "You wish us to keep the matter dark, and to make a garrison of the stern part of the ship, manned with my friend's own people, and provided with all the arms, and powder on board. In other words, you fear a mutiny."

"Sir," said Captain Smollett, "with no intention to take offense, I deny your right to put words into my mouth. No captain, sir, would be justified in going to sea at all if he had ground enough to say that. As for Mr. Arrow, I believe him thoroughly honest; some of the men are the same; all may be for what I know. But I am responsible for the ship's safety and the life of every man Jack aboard of her. I see things going, as I think, not quite right. And I ask you to take certain precautions, or let me resign my berth. And that's all."

"Captain Smollett," began the doctor, with a smile, "did you ever hear the fable of the mountain and the mouse? You'll excuse me, I dare say, but you remind me of that fable. When you came in here, I'll stake my wig you meant more than this."

"Doctor," said the captain, "you are smart. When I came in here I meant to get discharged. I had no thought that Mr. Trelawney would hear a word."

"No more I would," cried the squire. "Had Livesey not been here, I should have seen you to the deuce. As it is, I have heard you. I will do as you desire; but I think the worse of you."

"That's as you please, sir," said the captain. "You'll find I do my duty."

And with that he took his leave.

"Trelawney," said the doctor, "contrary to all my notions, I believe you have managed to get two honest men on board with you — that man and John Silver."

"Silver, if you like," cried the squire; "but as for that intolerable humbug, I declare I think his conduct unmanly, unsailorly, and downright un-English."

"Well," says the doctor, "we shall see."

When we came on deck, the men had begun already to take out the arms and powder, yo-ho-ing at their work, while the captain and Mr. Arrow stood by superintending.

The new arrangement was quite to my liking. The whole schooner had been overhauled; six berths had been made astern, out of what had been the afterpart of the main hold; and this set of cabins was only joined to the galley and forecastle by a sparred passage on the port side. It had been originally meant that the captain, Mr. Arrow, Hunter, Joyce, the doctor, and the squire, were to occupy these six berths. Now, Redruth and I were to get two of them, and Mr. Arrow and the captain were to sleep on deck in the companion, which had been enlarged on each side till you might almost have called it a round-house. Very low it was still, of course; but there was room to swing two hammocks, and even the mate seemed pleased with the arrangement. Even he, perhaps, had been doubtful as to the crew, but that is only guess; for, as you shall hear, we had not long the benefit of his opinion.

We were all hard at work, changing the powder and the berths, when the last man or two, and Long John along with them, came off in a shore boat.

The cook came up the side like a monkey for cleverness, and, as soon as he saw what was doing, "So, ho, mates!" says he, "what's this?"

"We're a-changing of the powder, Jack," answers one.

"Why, by the powers," cried Long John, "if we do, we'll miss the morning tide!"

"My orders!" said the captain shortly. "You may go below, my man. Hands will want supper."

"Aye, aye, sir," answered the cook; and, touching his forelock, he disappeared at once in the direction of his galley.

"That's a good man, captain," said the doctor.

"Very likely," replied Captain Smollett. "Easy with that, men — easy," he ran on, to the fellows who were shifting the powder; and then suddenly observing me examining the swivel we carried amidships, a long brass nine — "Here, you ship's boy," he cried, "out o' that! Off with you to the cook and get some work."

And then, as I was hurrying off, I heard him say, quite loudly, to the doctor:

"I'll have no favorites on my ship."

I assure you I was quite of the squire's way of thinking, and hated the captain deeply.

THE VOYAGE

All that night we were in a great bustle getting things stowed in their place, and boatfuls of the squire's friends, Mr. Blandly and the like, coming off to wish him a good voyage and a safe return. We never had a night at the Admiral Benbow when I had half the work; and I was dog-tired when, a little before dawn, the boatswain sounded his pipe, and the crew began to man the capstan bars. I might have been twice as weary, yet I would not have left the deck; all was so new and interesting to me — the brief commands, the shrill note of the whistle, the men bustling to their places in the glimmer of the ship's lanterns.

"Now, Barbecue, tip us a stave," cried one voice.

"The old one," cried another.

"Aye, aye, mates," said Long John, who was standing by, with his crutch under his arm, and at once broke out in the air and words I knew so well —

"Fifteen men on the Dead Man's Chest ——"

And then the whole crew bore chorus:

"Yo-ho-ho, and a bottle of rum!"

And at the third "ho!" drove the bars before them with a will.

Even at that exciting moment it carried me back to the old Admiral Benbow in a second; and I seemed to hear the voice of the captain piping in the chorus.

But soon the anchor was short up; soon it was hanging dripping at the bows; soon the sails began to draw, and the land and shipping to flit by on either side; and before I could lie down to snatch an hour of slumber the *Hispaniola* had begun her voyage to the Isle of Treasure.

I am not going to relate that voyage in detail. It was fairly prosperous. The ship proved to be a good ship, the crew were capable seamen, and the captain thoroughly understood his business. But before we came the length of Treasure Island, two or three things had happened which require to be known.

Mr. Arrow, first of all, turned out even worse than the captain had feared. He had no command among the men, and people did what they pleased with him. But that was by no means the worst of it; for after a day or two at sea he began to appear on deck with hazy eye, red cheeks, stuttering tongue, and other marks of drunkenness. Time after time he was ordered below in disgrace. Sometimes he fell and cut himself; sometimes he lay all day long in his little bunk at one side of the companion; sometimes for a day or two he would be almost sober and attend to his work at least passably.

In the meantime, we could never make out where he got the drink. That was the ship's mystery. Watch him as we pleased, we could do nothing to solve it; and when we asked him to his face, he would only laugh, if he were drunk, and if he were sober deny solemnly that he ever tasted anything but water.

He was not only useless as an officer, and a bad influence amongst the men, but it was plain that at this rate he must soon kill himself outright; so nobody was much surprised, nor very sorry, when one dark night, with a head sea, he disappeared entirely and was seen no more.

"Overboard!" said the captain. "Well, gentlemen, that saves the trouble of putting him in irons."

But there we were, without a mate; and it was necessary, of course, to advance one of the men. The boatswain, Job Anderson, was the likeliest man aboard, and, though he kept his old title, he served in a way as mate. Mr. Trelawney had followed the sea, and his knowledge made him very useful, for he often took a watch himself in easy weather. And the coxswain, Israel Hands, was a careful, wily, old, experienced seaman, who could be trusted at a pinch with almost anything.

He was a great confidant of Long John Silver, and so the mention of his name leads me on to speak of our ship's cook, Barbecue, as the men called him.

Aboard ship he carried his crutch by a lanyard round his neck, to have both hands as free as possible. It was something to see him wedge the foot of the crutch against a bulkhead; and, propped against it, yielding to every movement of the ship, to get on with his cooking like someone safe ashore. Still more strange was it to see him in the heaviest of weather cross the deck. He had a line or two rigged up to help him across the widest spaces — Long John's earrings, they were called; and he would hand himself from one place to another, now using the crutch, now trailing it alongside by the lanyard, as quickly as another man could walk. Yet some of the men who had sailed with him before expressed their pity to see him so reduced.

"He's no common man, Barbecue," said the coxswain to me. "He had good schooling in his young days, and can speak like a book when so minded; and brave — a lion's nothing alongside of Long John! I seen him grapple four, and knock their heads together — him unarmed."

All the crew respected and even obeyed him. He had a way of talking to each, and doing everybody some particular service. To me he was unweariedly kind; and always glad to see me in the galley, which he kept as clean as a new pin; the dishes hanging up burnished and his parrot in a cage in one corner.

"Come away, Hawkins," he would say; "come and have a yarn with John. Nobody more welcome than yourself, my son. Sit you down and hear the news. Here's Cap'n Flint — I calls my parrot Cap'n Flint, after the famous buccaneer — here's Cap'n Flint perdicting success to our v'yage. Wasn't you, cap'n?"

And the parrot would say, with great rapidity, "Pieces of eight! pieces of eight! pieces of eight!" till you wondered that it was not out of breath, or till John threw his handkerchief over the cage.

"Now, that bird," he would say, "is, maybe, two hundred years old, Hawkins — they lives forever mostly; and if anybody's seen more wickedness, it must be the devil himself.

She's sailed with England, the great Cap'n England, the pirate. She's been at Madagascar, and at Malabar, and Surinam, and Providence, and Portobello. She was at the fishing-up of the wrecked plate ships. It's there she learned 'Pieces of eight,' and little wonder; three hundred and fifty thousand of 'em, Hawkins! She was at the boarding of the *Viceroy of the Indies* out of Goa, she was; and to look at her you would think she was a babby. But you smelt powder — didn't you, cap'n?"

"Stand by to go about," the parrot would scream.

"Ah, she's a handsome craft, she is," the cook would say, and give her sugar from his pocket, and then the bird would peck at the bars and swear straight on, passing belief for wickedness. "There," John would add, "you can't touch pitch and not be mucked, lad. Here's this poor old innocent bird o' mine swearing blue fire, and none the wiser, you may lay to that. She would swear the same, in a manner of speaking, before chaplain." And John would touch his forelock with a solemn way he had, that made me think he was the best of men.

In the meantime, squire and Captain Smollett were still on pretty distant terms with one another. The squire made no bones about the matter; he despised the captain. The captain, on his part, never spoke but when he was spoken to, and then sharp and short and dry, and not a word wasted. He owned, when driven into a corner, that he seemed to have been wrong about the crew, that some of them were as brisk as he wanted to see, and all had behaved fairly well. As for the ship, he had taken a downright fancy to her. "She'll lie a point nearer the wind than a man has a right to expect of his own married wife, sir. But," he would add, "all I say is we're not home again, and I don't like the cruise."

The squire, at this, would turn away and march up and down the deck, chin in air.

"A trifle more of that man," he would say, "and I should explode."

We had some heavy weather, which only proved the qualities of the *Hispaniola*. Every man on board seemed well content, and they must have been hard to please if they had been otherwise; for it is my belief there was never a ship's company so spoiled since Noah put to sea. Double grog was going on the least excuse; there was duff on odd days, as, for instance, if the squire heard it was any man's birthday; and always a barrel of apples standing broached in the waist, for anyone to help himself that had a fancy.

"Never knew good come of it yet," the captain said to Doctor Livesey. "Spoil foc's'le hands, make devils. That's my belief."

But good did come of the apple barrel, as you shall hear: for if it had not been for that, we should have had no note of warning, and might all have perished by the hand of treachery.

This was how it came about.

We had run up the trades to get the wind of the island we were after — I am not allowed to be more plain — and now we were running down for it with a bright lookout day and night. It was about the last day of our outward voyage, by the largest computation; sometime that night, or, at latest, before noon of the morrow, we should sight the Treasure Island. We were heading S.S.W., and had a steady breeze abeam and a quiet sea. The *Hispaniola* rolled steadily, dipping her bowsprit now and then with a whiff of spray. All was drawing alow and aloft; everyone was in the bravest spirits, because we were now so near an end of the first part of our adventure.

Now, just after sundown, when all my work was over, and I was on my way to my berth, it occurred to me that I should like an apple. I ran on deck. The watch was all forward looking out for the island. The man at the helm was watching the luff of the sail, and whistling away gently to himself; and that was the only sound excepting the swish of the sea against the bows and around the sides of the ship.

In I got bodily into the apple barrel, and found there was scarce an apple left; but, sitting down there in the dark, what with the sound of the waters and the rocking movement of the ship, I had either fallen asleep, or was on the point of doing so, when a heavy man sat down with rather a clash close by. The barrel shook as he leaned his shoulders against it, and I was just about to jump up when the man began to speak. It was Silver's voice, and, before I had heard a dozen words, I would not have shown myself for all the world, but lay there, trembling and listening, in the extreme of fear and curiosity; for from these dozen words I understood that the lives of all the honest men aboard depended upon me alone.

What I Heard in the Apple Barrel

"No, not I," said Silver. "Flint was cap'n; I was quartermaster, along of my timber leg. The same broadside I lost my leg, old Pew lost his headlights. It was a master surgeon, him that ampytated me — out of college and all — Latin by the bucket, and what not; but he was hanged like a dog, and sun-dried like the rest, at Corso Castle. That was Roberts's men, that was, and comed of changing names to their ships — *Royal Fortune* and so on. Now, what a ship was christened, so let her stay, I says. So it was with the *Cassandra,* as brought us all safe home from Malabar, after England took the *Viceroy of the Indies;* so it was with the old *Walrus,* Flint's old ship, as I've seen a-muck with the red blood and fit to sink with gold."

"Ah!" cried another voice, that of the youngest hand on board, and evidently full of admiration, "he was the flower of the flock, was Flint!"

"Davis was a man, too, by all accounts," said Silver. "I never sailed along of him; first with England, then with Flint, that's my story; and now here on my own account, in a manner of speaking. I laid by nine hundred safe, from England, and two thousand after Flint. That ain't bad for a man before the mast — all safe in bank. 'Tain't earning now, it's saving does it, you may lay to that. Where's all England's men now? I dunno. Where's Flint's? Why, most on 'em aboard here, and glad to get the duff — been begging before that, some on 'em. Old Pew, as had lost his sight, and might have thought shame, spends twelve hundred pound in a year, like a lord in Parliament. Where is he now? Well, he's dead now and under hatches; but for two year before that, shiver my timbers! the man was starving. He begged, and he

stole, and he cut throats, and starved at that, by the powers!"

"Well, it ain't much use, after all," said the young seaman.

"'Tain't much use for fools, you may lay to it — that, not nothing," cried Silver. "But now, you look here; you're young, you are, but you're as smart as paint. I see that when I set my eyes on you, and I'll talk to you like a man."

You may imagine how I felt when I heard this abominable old rogue addressing another in the very same words of flattery as he had used to myself. I think, if I had been able, that I would have killed him through the barrel. Meantime, he ran on, little supposing he was overheard.

"Here it is about gentleman of fortune. They lives rough, and they risk swinging, but they eat and drink like fighting-cocks, and when a cruise is done, why, it's hundreds of pounds instead of hundreds of farthings in their pockets. Now, the most goes for rum and a good fling, and to sea again in their shirts. But that's not the course I lay. I puts it all away, some here, some there, and none too much anywheres, by reason of suspicion. I'm fifty, mark you; once back from this cruise, I set up gentleman in earnest. Time enough, too, says you. Ah, but I've lived easy in the meantime; never denied myself o' nothing heart desires, and slep' soft and ate dainty all my days, but when at sea. And how did I begin? Before the mast, like you!"

"Well," said the other, "but all the other money's gone now, ain't it? Your daren't show face in Bristol after this."

"Why, where might you suppose it was? asked Silver, derisively.

"At Bristol, in banks and places," answered his companion.

"It were," said the cook; "it were when we weighed anchor. But my old missis has it all by now. And the 'Spy-glass' is sold, lease and goodwill and rigging; and the old girl's off to meet me. I would tell you where, for I trust you; but it 'ud make jealousy among the mates."

"And can you trust your missis?" asked the other.

"Gentlemen of fortune," returned the cook, "usually trusts little among themselves, and right they are, you may lay to it. But I have a way with me, I have. When a mate brings a slip on his cable — one as knows me, I mean — it won't be in the same world with old John. There was some that was feared of Pew, and some that was feared of Flint; but Flint his own self was feared of me. Feared he was, and proud. They was the roughest crew afloat, was Flint's; the devil himself would have been feared to go to sea with them. Well, now, I tell you, I'm not a boasting man, and you seen yourself how easy I keep company; but when I was quartermaster, *lambs* wasn't the word for Flint's old buccaneers. Ah, you may be sure of yourself in old John's ship."

"Well, I tell you now," replied the lad, "I didn't half a quarter like the job till I had this talk with you, John; but there's my hand on it now."

"And a brave lad you were, and smart, too," answered Silver, shaking hands so heartily that all the barrel shook, "and a finer figurehead for a gentleman of fortune I never clapped my eyes on."

By this time I had begun to understand the meaning of their terms. By a "gentleman of fortune" they plainly meant neither more nor less than a common pirate, and the little scene that I had overheard was the last act in the corruption of one of the honest hands — perhaps of the last one left aboard. But on this point I was soon to be relieved, for Silver giving a little whistle, a third man strolled up and sat down by the party.

"Dick's square," said Silver.

"Oh, I know'd Dick was square," returned the voice of the coxswain, Israel Hands. "He's no fool, is Dick." And he turned his quid and spat. "But, look here," he went on, "here's what I want to know, Barbecue: how long are we a-going to stand off and on like a blessed bumboat? I've had a'most enough o' Cap'n Smollett; he's hazed me long enough, by thunder! I want to go into that cabin, I do. I want their pickles and wines, and that."

"Israel," said Silver, "your head ain't much account, nor ever was. But you're able to hear, I reckon; leastways, your ears is big enough. Now, here's what I say: you'll berth forward, and you'll live hard, and you'll

speak soft, and you'll keep sober, till I give the word; and you may lay to that, my son."

"Well, I don't say no, do I?" growled the coxswain. "What I say is, when? That's what I say."

"When! by the powers!" cried Silver. "Well, now, if you want to know, I'll tell you when. The last moment I can manage; and that's when. Here's a first-rate seaman, Cap'n Smollett, sails the blessed ship for us. Here's this squire and doctor with a map and such — I don't know where it is, do I? No more do you, says you. Well, then, I mean this squire and doctor shall find the stuff, and help us to get it aboard, by the powers. Then we'll see. If I was sure of you all, sons of double Dutchmen, I'd have Cap'n Smollett navigate us halfway back again before I struck."

"Why, we're all seamen aboard here, I should think," said the lad Dick.

"We're all foc's'le hands, you mean," snapped Silver. "We can steer a course, but who's to set one? That's what all you gentlemen split on, first and last. If I had my way, I'd have Cap'n Smollett work us back into the trades at least; then we'd have no blessed miscalculations and a spoonful of water a day. But I know the sort you are. I'll finish with 'em at the island, as soon's the blunt's on board, and a pity it is. But you're never happy till you're drunk. Split my sides, I've a sick heart to sail with the likes of you!"

"Easy all, Long John," cried Israel. "Who's a-crossin' of you?"

"Why, how many tall ships, think ye, now, have I seen laid aboard? and how many brisk lads drying in the sun at Execution Dock?" cried Silver — "and all for this same hurry and hurry and hurry. You hear me? I seen a thing or two at sea, I have. If you would on'y lay your course, and a p'int to windward, you would ride in carriages, you would. But not you! I know you. You'll have your mouthful of rum tomorrow, and go hang."

"Everybody know'd you was a kind of a chaplin, John; but there's others as could hand and steer as well as you," said Israel. "They liked a bit o' fun, they did. They wasn't so high and dry, nohow, but took their fling, like jolly companions every one."

"So?" says Silver. "Well, and where are they now? Pew was that sort, and he died a beggarman. Flint was, and he died of rum at Savannah. Ah, they was a sweet crew, they was! on'y, where are they?"

"But," asked Dick, "when we do lay 'em athwart, what are we to do with 'em, anyhow?"

"There's the man for me!" cried the cook, admiringly. "That's what I call business. Well, what would you think? Put 'em ashore like maroons? That would have been England's way. Or cut 'em down like that much pork? That would have been Flint's or Billy Bones's."

"Billy was the man for that," said Israel. "'Dead men don't bite,' says he. Well, he's dead now hisself; he knows the long and short on it now; and if ever a rough hand come to port, it was Billy."

"Right you are," said Silver, "rough and ready. But mark you here: I'm an easy man — I'm quite the gentleman, says you; but this time it's serious. Dooty is dooty, mates. I give my vote — death. When I'm in Parlyment, and riding in my coach, I don't want none of these sea-lawyers in the cabin a-coming home, unlooked for, like the devil at prayers. Wait is what I say; but when the time comes, why, let her rip!"

"John," cried the coxswain, "you're a man!"

"You'll say so, Israel, when you see," said Silver. "Only one thing I claim — I claim Trelawney. I'll wring his calf's head off his body with these hands. Dick!" he added, breaking off, "you just jump up, like a sweet lad, and get me an apple, to wet my pipe like."

You may fancy the terror I was in! I should have leaped out and run for it if I had found the strength; but my limbs and heart alike misgave me. I heard Dick begin to rise, and then someone seemingly stopped him, and the voice of Hands exclaimed: "Oh, stow that! Don't you get sucking of that bilge, John. Let's have a go of the rum."

"Dick," said Silver, "I trust you. I've a gauge on the keg, mind. There's the key; you fill a pannikin and bring it up."

Terrified as I was, I could not help thinking to myself that this must have been how Mr. Arrow got the strong waters that destroyed him.

Dick was gone but a little while, and during his absence Israel spoke straight on in the cook's ear. It was but a word or two that I could catch, and yet I gathered some important news; for, besides other scraps that tended to the same purpose, this whole clause was audible: "Not another man of them'll jine." Hence there were still faithful men on board.

When Dick returned, one after another of the trio took the pannikin and drank — one "To luck"; another with a "Here's to old Flint"; and Silver himself saying, in a kind of song, "Here's to ourselves, and hold your luff, plenty of prizes and plenty of duff."

Just then a sort of brightness fell upon me in the barrel, and, looking up, I found the moon had risen, and was silvering the mizzentop and shining white on the luff of the foresail; and almost at the same time the voice of the lookout shouted "Land-ho!"

Robinson Crusoe

(A Selection)

DANIEL DEFOE

Few books are more famous than this classic adventure story first published in 1719. It is supposed to be founded on the actual experiences of Alexander Selkirk, who was shipwrecked and lived for years on a lonely island. This island has been identified with Juan Fernandez Island in the Pacific Ocean, off the coast of Chile. Robinson Crusoe was the first book Jean Jacques Rousseau permitted his hero to read in Emile, *the work in which Rousseau set forth his theories of education.*

I was now landed, and safe on shore, and began to look up and thank God that my life was saved, in a case wherein there was some minutes before scarce any room to hope. . . .

I cast my eyes to the stranded vessel, when, the breach and froth of the sea being so big, I could hardly see it, it lay so far off; and considered, Lord! how was it possible I could get on shore?

After I had solaced my mind with the comfortable part of my condition, I began to look round me, to see what kind of place I was in, and what was next to be done: and I soon found my comforts abate, and that, in a word, I had a dreadful deliverance: for I was wet, had no clothes to shift me, nor anything either to eat or drink, to comfort me; neither did I see any prospect before me but that of perishing with hunger, or being devoured by wild beasts: and that which was particularly afflicting to me was that I had no weapon, either to hunt and kill any creature for my sustenance, or to defend myself against any other creature that might desire to kill me for theirs. In a word, I had nothing about me but a knife, a tobacco pipe, and a little tobacco in a box. This was all my provision; and this threw me into terrible agonies of mind, that for a while I ran about like a madman. Night coming upon me, I began, with a heavy heart, to consider what would be my lot if there were any ravenous beasts in that country, seeing at night they always come abroad for their prey.

All the remedy that offered to my thoughts at that time, was to get up into a thick, bushy tree, like a fir, but thorny, which grew near me, and where I resolved to sit all night, and consider the next day what death I should die, for as yet I saw no prospect of life. I walked about a furlong from the shore, to see if I could find any fresh water to drink, which I did, to my great joy; and having drunk, and put a little tobacco in my mouth to prevent hunger, I went to the tree, and getting up into it, endeavored to place myself so that if I should sleep I might not fall. And having cut me a short stick, like a truncheon, for my defense, I took up my lodging; and being excessively fatigued, I fell fast asleep, and slept as comfortably as, I believe, few could have done in my condition, and found myself more refreshed with it than I think I ever was on such an occasion.

When I waked it was broad day, the weather clear, and the storm abated, so that the sea did not rage and swell as before; but that which surprised me most was, that the ship was lifted off in the night from the sand where she lay, by the swelling of the tide, and was driven up almost as far as the rock which I at first mentioned, where I had been

so bruised by the wave dashing me against it. This being within about a mile from the shore where I was, and the ship seeming to stand upright still, I wished myself on board, that at least I might save some necessary things for my use.

When I came down from my apartment in the tree, I looked about me again, and the first I found was the boat, which lay, as the wind and sea had tossed her up, upon the land, about two miles on my right hand. I walked as far as I could upon the shore to have got to her; but found a neck or inlet of water between me and the boat which was about a half a mile broad; so I came back for the present, being more intent upon getting at the ship, where I hoped to find something for my present subsistence.

A little after noon I found the sea very calm, and the tide ebbed so far out that I could come within a quarter of a mile of the ship. And here I found a fresh renewing of my grief; for I saw evidently that, if we had kept on board, we had been all safe; that is to say, we had all got safe on shore, and I had not been so miserable as to be left entirely destitute of all comfort and company, as I now was. This forced tears to my eyes again; but as there was little relief in that, I resolved, if possible, to get to the ship. So I pulled off my clothes, for the weather was hot to extremity, and took to the water. But when I came to the ship my difficulty was still greater to know how to get on board; for, as she lay aground, and high out of the water, there was nothing within my reach to lay hold of. I swam round her twice, and the second time I espied a small piece of rope, which I wondered I did not see at first, hanging down by the fore-chains so low that with great difficulty I got hold of it, and by the help of that rope got up into the forecastle of the ship. Here I found that the ship was bulged, and had a great deal of water in her hold; but that she lay so on the side of a bank of hard sand, or rather earth, that her stern lay lifted up upon the bank, and her head low, almost to the water. By this means all her quarter was free and all that was in that part was dry; for you may be sure my first work was to search, and to see what was spoiled and what was free. And, first, I found that all the ship's provisions were dry and untouched by the water, and being very well disposed to eat, I went to the bread room, and filled my pockets with biscuit, and ate it as I went about other things, for I had no time to lose. I also found some rum in the great cabin, of which I took a large dram, and which I had, indeed, need enough of to spirit me for what was before me. Now I wanted nothing but a boat, to furnish myself with many things which I foresaw would be very necessary to me.

It was in vain to sit still and wish for what was not to be had; and this extremity roused my application. We had several spare yards, and two or three large spars of wood, and a spare topmast or two in the ship: I resolved to fall to work with them, and I flung as many of them overboard as I could manage for their weight, tying every one with a rope, that they might not drive away. When this was done, I went down the ship's side, and pulling them to me, I tied four of them together at both ends, as well as I could, in the form of a raft, and laying two or three short pieces of plank upon them, crossways, I found I could walk upon it very well, but that it was not able to bear any great weight, the pieces being too light. So I went to work, and with the carpenter's saw I cut a spare topmast into three lengths, and added them to my raft, with a great deal of labor and pains. But the hope of furnishing myself with necessaries encouraged me to go beyond what I should have been able to have done upon another occasion.

My raft was now strong enough to bear any reasonable weight. My next care was what to load it with, and how to preserve what I laid upon it from the surf of the sea: but I was not long in considering this. I first laid all the planks or boards upon it that I could get, and having considered well what I most wanted, I first got three of the seamen's chests, which I had broken open and emptied, and lowered them down upon my raft; the first of these I filled with provisions — viz., bread, rice, three Dutch cheeses, five pieces of dried goat's flesh (which we lived much upon), and a little remainder of European corn, which had been

laid by for some fowls which we brought to sea with us, but the fowls were killed. There had been some barley and wheat together; but, to my great disappointment, I found afterwards that the rats had eaten or spoiled it all. As for liquors, I found several cases of bottles belonging to our skipper, in which were some cordial waters; and in all, about five or six gallons of arrack. These I stowed by themselves, there being no need to put them into the chest, nor any room for them. While I was doing this, I found the tide began to flow, though very calm; and I had the mortification to see my coat, shirt, and waistcoat, which I had left on shore upon the sand, swim away. As for my breeches, which were only linen, and open-kneed, I swam on board in them and my stockings. However, this put me upon rummaging for clothes, of which I found enough, but took no more than I wanted for present use, for I had other things which my eye was more upon; as, first, tools to work with on shore; and it was after long searching that I found out the carpenter's chest, which was indeed a very useful prize to me, and much more valuable than a shiploading of gold would have been at that time. I got it down to my raft, whole as it was, without losing time to look into it, for I knew in general what it contained.

My next care was for some ammunition and arms. There were two very good fowling pieces in the great cabin, and two pistols. These I secured first, with some powder horns, a small bag of shot, and two old rusty swords. I knew there were three barrels of powder in the ship, but knew not where our gunner had stowed them; but with much search I found them, two of them dry and good, the third had taken water. Those two I got to my raft, with the arms. And now I thought myself pretty well freighted, and began to think how I should get to shore with them, having neither sail, oar, nor rudder; and the least capful of wind would have overset all my navigation.

I had three encouragements: first, a smooth, calm sea; secondly, the tide rising, and setting in to the shore; thirdly, what little wind there was blew me towards the land. And thus, having found two or three broken oars belonging to the boat, and besides the tools which were in the chest, two saws, an ax, and a hammer, with this cargo I put to sea. For a mile, or thereabouts, my raft went very well, only that I found it driven a little distance from the place where I had landed before; by which I perceived that there was some indraft of the water, and consequently, I hoped to find some creek or river there, which I might make use of as a port to get to land with my cargo.

As I imagined, so it was. There appeared before me a little opening of the land. I found a strong current of the tide set into it; so I guided my raft as well as I could, to keep in the middle of the stream.

But here I had like to have suffered a second shipwreck, which if I had, I think verily would have broken my heart; for knowing nothing of the coast, my raft ran aground at one end of it upon a shoal, and not being aground at the other end, it wanted but a little that all my cargo had slipped off towards the end that was afloat, and so fallen into the water. I did my utmost, by setting my back against the chests, to keep them in their places, but could not thrust off the raft with all my strength; neither durst I stir from the posture I was in; but holding up the chests with all my might, I stood in that manner near half an hour, in which time the rising of the water brought me a little more upon a level; and, a little after, the water still rising, my raft floated again, and I thrust her off with the oar I had into the channel, and then driving up higher, I at length found myself in the mouth of a little river, with land on both sides, and a strong current or tide running up. I looked on both sides for a proper place to get to shore, for I was not willing to be driven too high up the river; hoping in time to see some ship at sea, and therefore resolved to place myself as near the coast as I could.

At length I spied a little cove on the right shore of the creek, to which, with great pain and difficulty, I guided my raft, and at last got so near that, reaching ground with my oar, I could thrust her directly in. But here I had like to have dipped all my cargo into

the sea again; for that shore lying pretty steep — that is to say, sloping — there was no place to land, but where one end of my float, if it ran on shore, would lie so high, and the other sink lower, as before, that it would endanger my cargo again. All that I could do was to wait till the tide was at the highest, keeping the raft with my oar like an anchor, to hold the side of it fast to the shore, near a flat piece of ground, which I expected the water would flow over; and so it did. As soon as I found water enough, for my raft drew about a foot of water, I thrust her upon that flat piece of ground, and there fastened or moored her, by sticking my two broken oars into the ground — one on one side, near one end, and one on the other side, near the other end; and thus I lay till the water ebbed away, and left my raft and all my cargo safe on shore . . . I found also that the island I was in was barren, and, as I saw good reason to believe, uninhabited, except by wild beasts, of which, however, I saw none. . . .

I now began to consider that I might yet get a great many things out of the ship which would be useful to me, and particularly some of the rigging and sails, and such other things as might come to land; and I resolved to make another voyage on board the vessel, if possible. And as I knew that the first storm that blew must necessarily break her all in pieces, I resolved to set all other things apart till I got everything out of the ship that I could get. Then I called a council — that is, to say, in my thoughts — whether I should take back the raft; but this appeared impracticable. So I resolved to go as before, when the tide was down; and I did so, only that I stripped before I went from my hut, having nothing on but a checkered shirt, a pair of linen drawers, and a pair of pumps on my feet.

I got on board the ship as before, and prepared a second raft; and having had experience of the first, I neither made this so unwieldy nor loaded it so hard, but yet I brought away several things very useful to me; as, first, in the carpenter's stores I found two or three bags full of nails and spikes, a great screw-jack, a dozen or two of hatchets, and, above all, that most useful thing called a grindstone. All these I secured, together with several things belonging to the gunner, particularly two or three iron crows, and two barrels of musket bullets, seven muskets, and another fowling piece, with some small quantity of powder more, a large bagful of small shot, and a great roll of sheet lead; but this last was so heavy I could not hoist it up to get it over the ship's side.

Besides these things, I took all the men's clothes that I could find, and a spare fore-topsail, a hammock, and some bedding; and with this I loaded my second raft, and brought them all safe on shore, to my very great comfort. I was under some apprehension during my absence from the land that at least my provisions might be devoured on shore; but when I came back I found no sign of any visitor . . .

Having got my second cargo on shore — though I was obliged to open the barrels of powder, and bring them by parcels, for they were too heavy, being large casks — I went to work to make me a little tent, with the sail and some poles which I cut for that purpose; and into this tent I brought everything that I knew would spoil either with rain or sun; and I piled all the empty chests and casks up in a circle round the tent, to fortify it from any sudden attempt, either from man or beast.

When I had done this, I blocked up the door of the tent with some boards within, and an empty chest set up on end without; and spreading one of the beds upon the ground, laying my two pistols just at my head, and my gun at length by me, I went to bed for the first time, and slept very quietly all night. I was very weary and heavy; for the night before I had slept little, and had labored very hard all day, as well to fetch those things from the ship as to get them on shore.

I had the biggest magazine of all kinds now that ever was laid up, I believe, for one man; but still I was not satisfied, for while the ship sat upright in that posture I thought I ought to get everything out of her that I could; so every day, at low water, I went on board, and brought away something or other; but particularly, the third time I went, I brought away as much of the rigging as I could, as also all the small ropes and rope twine I could get, with a piece of spare canvas, which was to mend the sails upon occasion, and the barrel of wet gunpowder. In a word, I brought away all the sails, first and last; only that I was fain to cut them in pieces, and bring as much at a time as I could, for they were no more useful to me for sails, but as mere canvas only.

But that which comforted me more still was, that at last of all, after I had made five or six such voyages as these, and thought I had nothing more to expect from the ship that was worth my meddling with — I say, after all this, I found a great hogshead of bread, three large runlets of rum, or spirits, a box of fine sugar, and a barrel of fine flour: this was surprising to me, because I had given over expecting any more provisions except what was spoiled by the water. I soon emptied the hogshead of the bread, and wrapped it up, parcel by parcel, in pieces of the sails, which I cut out; and, in a word, I got all this safe on shore also, though at several times.

The next day I made another voyage, and now, having plundered the ship of what was portable and fit to hand out, I began with the cable; cutting the great cable into pieces such as I could move, I got two cables and a hawser on shore, with all the ironwork I could get; and having cut down the sprit-sail-yard and the mizzen-yard, and everything I could to make a large raft, I loaded it with all those heavy goods and came away; but my good luck began to leave me, for this raft was so unwieldy, and so overladen, that after I was entered the little cove, where I had landed the rest of my goods, not being able to guide it so handily as I did the other, it overset, and threw me and all my cargo into the water; as for myself, it was no great harm, for I was near the shore; but as to my cargo, it was a great part of it lost, especially the iron, which I expected would have been of great use to me; however, when the tide was out I got most of the pieces of cable ashore, and some of the iron, though with infinite labor; for I was fain to dip for it into the water, a work which fatigued me very much. After this, I went every day on board, and brought away what I could get.

I had now been thirteen days on shore, and

had been eleven times on board the ship, in which time I had brought away all that one pair of hands could well be supposed capable of bringing; though I verily believe, had the calm weather held, I should have brought away the whole ship, piece by piece; but preparing the twelfth time to go on board, I found the wind began to rise; however, at low water I went on board, and though I thought I had rummaged the cabin so effectually that nothing more could be found, yet I discovered a locker with drawers in it, in one of which I found two or three razors, and one pair of large scissors, with some ten or a dozen of good knives and forks; in another I found about thirty-six pounds value in money — some European coin, some Brazil, some pieces of eight, some gold, and some silver.

I smiled to myself at the sight of this money. "Oh, drug!" said I aloud, "what art thou good for? Thou art not worth to me — no, not the taking off the ground; one of those knives is worth all this heap. I have no manner of use for thee; e'en remain where thou art, and go to the bottom, as a creature whose life is not worth saving." However, upon second thoughts, I took it away; and wrapping all in a piece of canvas, I began to think of making another raft; but while I was preparing this, I found the sky overcast, and the wind began to rise, and in a quarter of an hour it blew a fresh gale from the shore. It presently occurred to me that it was in vain to pretend to make a raft with the wind offshore; and that it was my business to be gone before the tide of flood began, otherwise I might not be able to reach the shore at all. Accordingly, I let myself down into the water, and swam across the channel which lay between the ship and the sands, and even that with difficulty enough, partly with the weight of the things I had about me, and partly from the roughness of the water; for the wind rose very hastily, and before it was quite high water it blew a storm. But I was gotten home to my little tent, where I lay, with all my wealth about me very secure. It blew very hard all that night, and in the morning, when I looked out, behold, no more ship was to be seen.

Johnny Tremain
Salt-Water Tea[4]

ESTHER FORBES

Johnny Tremain, *a distinguished story of pre-Revolutionary days in Boston, was awarded the Newbery medal in 1944. As the story opens, Johnny is apprenticed to a silversmith, and he believes with cocky assurance that he will some day be famous for his beautiful craftsmanship. But an accident cripples his hand and embitters his mind. He is obliged to give up the trade he loves, but he finds work as a courier for the patriotic newspaper* The Boston Observer, *and he becomes a messenger for the Sons of Liberty. He grows to manhood at sixteen and learns the meaning of the liberty for which men fight. The following chapter tells of the part played by Johnny and his friend Rab in the famous Boston Tea Party.*

England had, by the fall of 1773, gone far in adjusting the grievances of her American colonies. But she insisted upon a small tax on tea. Little money would be collected by this tax. It worked no hardship on the people's pocketbooks: only threepence the pound. The stubborn colonists, who were insisting they would not be taxed unless they could vote for the men who taxed them, would hardly realize that the tax had been paid by the East India Company in London before the tea was shipped over here. After all, thought Parliament, the Americans were yokels and farmers — not political thinkers. And the East India tea, even after that tax was paid, would be better and cheaper than any the Americans ever had had. Weren't the Americans, after all, human beings? Wouldn't they care more for their pocketbooks than their principles?

Shivering — for the last week in October was bitterly cold — Johnny built up the fire in the attic. From the back window he could see that the roofs of the Afric Queen were white with frost.

A sharp rat-tat on the shop door below woke Rab.

4 From Esther Forbes, *Johnny Tremain* (Houghton Mifflin, 1943).

"What time's it?" he grumbled, as people do who think they are disturbed too early Sunday morning.

"Seven and past. I'll see what's up."

It was Sam Adams himself. When either cold or excited, his palsy increased. His head and hands were shaking. But his strong, seamed face, which always looked cheerful, today looked radiant. Sam Adams was so pleased that Johnny, a little naïvely, thought he must have word that Parliament had backed down again. The expected tea ships had not sailed.

"Look you, Johnny. I know it's Lord's Day, but there's a placard I must have printed and posted secretly tonight. The Sons of Liberty will take care of the posting, but Mr. Lorne must see to the printing. Could you run across and ask him to step over? And Rab — where's he?"

Rab was coming down the ladder.

"What's up?" said Rab sleepily.

"The first of the tea ships, the *Dartmouth,* is entering the harbor. She'll be at Castle Island by nightfall."

"So they dared send them?"

"Yes."

"And the first has come?"

"Yes. God give us strength to resist. That tea cannot be allowed to land."

When Johnny got back with Mr. Lorne, Rab had Mr. Adams's text in his hands, reading it as a printer reads, thinking first of spacing and capitals, not of the meaning.

"I can set that in no time. Two hundred copies? They'll be fairly dry by nightfall."

"Ah, Mr. Lorne," said Adams, shaking hands, "without you printers the cause of liberty would be lost forever."

"Without you" — Mr. Lorne's voice shook with emotion — "there would not have been any belief in liberty to lose. I will, as always, do anything — everything you wish."

"I got word before dawn. It's the *Dartmouth* and she will be as far as Castle Island by nightfall. If that tea is landed — if that tax is paid — everything is lost. The selectmen will meet all day today and I am calling a mass meeting for tomorrow. This is the placard I will put up."

He took it from Rab's hands and read:

Friends! Brethren! Countrymen! That worst of Plagues, the detested tea shipped for this Port by the East India Company, is now arrived in the Harbour: the hour of destruction, of manly opposition to the machinations of Tyranny, stares you in the Face; Every Friend to his Country, to Himself, and to Posterity, is now called upon to meet at Faneuil Hall, at nine o'clock this day [that, of course, is tomorrow Monday], at which time the bells will ring to make united and successful resistance to this last, worst and most destructive measure of Administration....
Boston, Nov. 29, 1773.

Then he said quietly: "Up to the last moment — up to the eleventh hour, we will beg the Governor's permission for the ships' return to London with their cargo. We have twenty days."

Johnny knew that by law any cargo that was not unloaded within twenty days might be seized by the custom-house and sold at auction.

"Mr. Lorne, needless to say the Observers will meet tonight. There are *private* decisions to be made before the mass meeting tomorrow at nine."

Johnny pricked up his ears. Ever since he had come to Mr. Lorne's (and Rab said he might be trusted with anything — possibly with men's lives) he had now and then summoned the members of the Observers' Club. They were so close to treason they kept no list of members. Rab made Johnny memorize the twenty-two names. They met in Rab and Johnny's attic.

The attic where the boys commonly slept looked strange enough with those chairs pulled out and arranged for the meeting. John Hancock sat in the moderator's chair. His face looked white and drawn. Probably his head still ached. Beside him was Sam Adams leaning toward him, whispering and whispering. Johnny thought how the Tories were saying that Sam Adams seduced John Hancock, even as the Devil had seduced Eve — by a constant whispering in his ear.

Sam Adams was standing at the far end of the room and Mr. Hancock still sat, his head in his hands. Adams clapped slightly and instantly conversation stopped.

"Gentlemen," he said, "tonight we have made our decision — and know the method by which the detested tea can be destroyed, if the ships are not allowed to return. Here we have with us two of exactly — ah — the sort of boys or young men we intend to use for our great purpose. Two boys in whom we have implicit trust. If it is the wish of the assembled club members, I suggest we approach them with our proposition tonight . . . enlist their aid. Twenty days will be up before we know. We'd best get on with our plans."

The members once more took their seats, but the pewter cups of punch were passing from hand to hand. Only Will Molineaux was too restless to sit. He was muttering to himself. Ben Church sat alone. He often did. No one really liked him.

All agreed the boys were to be told.

"First," Adams said to the boys, "raise your right hands. Swear by the great name of God Himself never, for as long as you live, to divulge to anyone the secret matters now trusted to you. Do you so swear?"

The boys swore.

Hancock was not looking at them. He sat with his aching head in his hands.

"There's no chance — not one — those ships will be allowed to return. The mass meetings which will be held almost daily demanding the return of the tea are to arouse public opinion and to persuade the world we did not turn to violence until every other course had been blocked to us. When the twenty days are up, on the night of the sixteenth of December, those ships are going to be boarded. That tea will be dumped in Boston Harbor. For each ship, the *Dartmouth,* the *Eleanor,* and the brig, the *Beaver,* we will need thirty stout, honest, fearless men and boys. Will you be one, Rab?"

He did not say Rab and Johnny, as the younger boy noticed. Was this because he thought Johnny too cripple-handed for chopping open sea chests — or merely because he knew Rab better and he was older?

"Of course, sir."

"How many other boys could you find for

the night's work? Strong and trustworthy boys — for if one ounce of tea is stolen, the whole thing becomes a robbery — not a protest?"

Rab thought.

"Eight or ten tonight, but give me a little time so I can feel about a bit and I can furnish fifteen or twenty."

"Boys who can keep their mouths shut?"

"Yes."

Paul Revere said, "I can furnish twenty or more from about North Square."

"Not one is to be told in advance just what the work will be, nor who the others are, nor the names of the men who instigated this tea party — that is, the gentlemen gathered here tonight. Simply, as they love their country and liberty and hate tyranny, they are to gather in this shop on the night of December sixteenth, carrying with them such disguises as they can think of, and each armed with an axe or hatchet."

.   .   .   .

The next day, the sixteenth, Johnny woke to hear the rain drumming sadly on the roof, and soon enough once more he heard all the bells of Boston cling-clanging, bidding the inhabitants come once more, and for the last time, to Old South to demand the peaceful return of the ships to England.

By nightfall, when the boys Rab had selected began silently to congregate in the office of the *Observer,* behind locked doors, the rain stopped. Many of them Johnny knew. When they started to assume their disguises, smooch their faces with soot, paint them with red paint, pull on nightcaps, old frocks, torn jackets, blankets with holes cut for their arms, they began giggling and laughing at each other. Rab could silence them with one look, however. No one passing outside the shop must guess that toward twenty boys were at that moment dressing themselves as "Indians."

Johnny had taken some pains with his costume. He had sewed for hours on the red blanket Mrs. Lorne had let him cut up and he had a fine mop of feathers standing upright in the old knitted cap he would wear on his head, but when he started to put on his disguise, Rab said no, wait a minute.

Then he divided the boys into three groups. Beside each ship at the wharf they would find a band of men. "You," he said to one group of boys, "will join the boarding party for the *Dartmouth*. You for the *Eleanor*. You for the *Beaver*." Each boy was to speak softly to the leader and say, "Me Know You," for that was the countersign. They would know the three leaders because each of them would wear a white handkerchief about the neck and a red string about the right wrist. Then he turned to Johnny.

"You can run faster than any of us. Somehow get to Old South Church. Mr. Rotch will be back from begging once more the Governor's permission for the ships to sail within a half-hour. Now, Johnny, you are to listen to what Sam Adams says next. Look you. If Mr. Adams then says, 'Now may God help my country,' come back here. Then we will take off our disguises and each go home and say nothing. But if he says, 'This meeting can do nothing more to save the country,' you are to get out of that crowd as fast as you can, and as soon as you get into Cornhill begin to blow upon this silver whistle. Run as fast as you are able back here to me and keep on blowing. I'll have boys posted in dark corners, close enough to the church, but outside the crowd. Maybe we'll hear you the first time you blow."

About Old South, standing in the streets, inside the church, waiting for Rotch to return with the very last appeal that could be made to the Governor, was the greatest crowd Boston had ever seen — thousands upon thousands. There was not a chance, not one, Johnny could ever squirm or wriggle his way inside, but he pushed and shoved until he stood close to one of the doors. Farther than this he could not go — unless he walked on people's heads. It was dark already.

Josiah Quincy's voice rang out from within. "I see the clouds roll and the lightning play, and to that God who rides the whirlwind and directs the storm, I commit my country . . ."

The words thrilled Johnny, but this was not what he was waiting for, and it was not Sam Adams speaking. He was bothered with only one thing. Quincy had a beautiful carrying voice. It was one thing to hear him

and another Sam Adams, who did not speak well at all.

The crowd made way for a chaise. "Rotch is back! Make way for Rotch!" Mr. Rotch passed close to Johnny. He was so young he looked almost ready to cry. This was proof enough that the Governor had still refused. Such a turmoil followed Rotch's entry, Johnny could not hear any one particular voice. What chance had he of hearing Sam Adams's words? He had his whistle in his hand, but he was so jammed into the crowd about the door that he did not believe he would be able to get his hand to his mouth.

"Silence." That was Quincy again. "Silence, silence, Mr. Adams will speak." Johnny twisted and turned and brought the whistle to his lips.

And suddenly there was silence. Johnny guessed there were many in that crowd who, like himself, were hanging on those words. Seemingly Mr. Adams was calmly accepting defeat, dismissing the meeting, for now he was saying,

"This meeting can do nothing more to save the country."

Johnny gave his first shrill blast on his whistle, and he heard whistles and cries seemingly in all directions, Indian war whoops, and "Boston Harbor a teapot tonight!" "Hurrah for Griffin's Wharf!" "Salt-water tea!" "Hi, Mohawks, get your axes and pay no taxes!"

Johnny was only afraid all would be over before Rab and his henchmen could get to the wharf. Still shrilling on the whistle, he fought and floundered against the tide of the crowd. It was sweeping toward Griffin's Wharf, he struggling to get back to Salt Lane. Now he was afraid the others would have gone on without him. After all, Rab might have decided that Johnny's legs and ears were better than his hands — and deliberately let him do the work that best suited him. Johnny pushed open the door.

Rab was alone. He had Johnny's blanket coat, his ridiculous befeathered knitted cap in his hands.

"Quick!" he said, and smoothed his face with soot, drew a red line across his mouth running from ear to ear. Johnny saw Rab's eyes through the mask of soot. They were glowing with that dark excitement he had seen but twice before. His lips were parted. His teeth looked sharp and white as an animal's. In spite of his calm demeanor, calm voice, he was charged and surcharged with a will to action, a readiness to take and enjoy any desperate chance. Rab had come terrifyingly alive.

They flung themselves out of the shop.

"Roundabout!" cried Rab. He meant they would get to the wharf by back alleys.

"Come, follow me. *Now* we're really going to run."

He flew up Salt Lane in the opposite direction from the waterfront. Now they were flinging themselves down back alleys (faster and faster). Once they had a glimpse of a blacksmith shop and other "Indians" clamoring for soot for their faces. Now slipping over a back-yard fence, now at last on the waterfront, Sea Street, Flounder Alley. They were running so fast it seemed more like a dream of flying than reality.

The day had started with rain and then there had been clouds, but as they reached Griffin's Wharf the moon, full and white, broke free of the clouds. The three ships, the silent hundreds gathering upon the wharf, all were dipped in the pure white light. The crowds were becoming thousands, and there was not one there but guessed what was to be done, and all approved.

Rab was grunting out of the side of his mouth to a thick-set, active-looking man, whom Johnny would have known anywhere by his walk and the confident lift of his head, was Mr. Revere. "Me Know You."

"Me Know You," Johnny repeated this countersign and took his place behind Mr. Revere. The other boys, held up by the crowd, began arriving, and more men and boys. But Johnny guessed that many who were now quietly joining one of those three groups were acting on the spur of the moment, seeing what was up. They had blacked their faces, seized axes, and come along. They were behaving as quietly and were as obedient to their leaders as those who had been so carefully picked for this work of destruction.

There was a boatswain's whistle, and in silence one group boarded the *Dartmouth*.

The *Eleanor* and the *Beaver* had to be warped in to the wharf. Johnny was close to Mr. Revere's heels. He heard him calling for the captain, promising him, in the jargon everyone talked that night, that not one thing should be damaged on the ship except only the tea, but the captain and all his crew had best stay in the cabin until the work was over.

Captain Hall shrugged and did as he was told, leaving his cabin boy to hand over the keys to the hold. The boy was grinning with pleasure. The "tea party" was not unexpected.

"I'll show you," the boy volunteered, "how to work them hoists. I'll fetch lanterns, mister."

The winches rattled and the heavy chests began to appear — one hundred and fifty of them. As some men worked in the hold, others broke open the chests and flung the tea into the harbor. But one thing made them unexpected difficulty. The tea inside the chests was wrapped in heavy canvas. The axes went through the wood easily enough — the canvas made endless trouble. Johnny had never worked so hard in his life.

. . . .

The work on the *Dartmouth* and the *Eleanor* finished about the same time. The *Beaver* took longer, for she had not had time to unload the rest of her cargo, and great care was taken not to injure it. Just as Johnny was about to go over to see if he could help on the *Beaver*, Mr. Revere whispered to him. "Go get brooms. Clean um' deck."

Johnny and a parcel of boys brushed the deck until it was clean as a parlor floor. Then Mr. Revere called the captain to come up and inspect. The tea was utterly gone, but Captain Hall agreed that beyond that there had not been the slightest damage.

It was close upon dawn when the work on all three ships was done. And yet the great, silent audience on the wharf, men, women, and children, had not gone home. As the three groups came off the ships, they formed in fours along the wharf, their axes on their shoulders. Then a hurrah went up and a fife began to play. This was almost the first sound Johnny had heard since the tea party started — except only the crash of axes into sea chests, the squeak of hoists, and a few grunted orders.

Standing quietly in the crowd, he saw Sam Adams, pretending to be a most innocent bystander. It looked to Johnny as if the dog fox had eaten a couple of fat pullets, and had a third in his mouth.

As they started marching back to the center of town, they passed the Coffin House at the head of Griffin's Wharf. A window opened.

"Well, boys," said a voice, so cold one hardly knew whether he spoke in anger or not, "you've had a fine, pleasant evening for your Indian caper, haven't you? But mind . . . you've got to pay the fiddler yet."

It was the British Admiral Montague.

"Come on down here," someone yelled, "and we'll settle that score tonight."

The Admiral pulled in his head and slapped down the window.

Johnny and Rab knew, and men like the Observers knew, but best of all Sam Adams knew, that the fiddler would have to be paid. England, unable to find the individuals who had destroyed this valuable property, would punish the whole Town of Boston — make every man, woman, and child, Tories and Whigs alike, suffer until this tea was paid for. Nor was she likely to back down on her claim that she might tax the colonists any way she pleased.

Next day, all over Boston, boys and men, some of them with a little paint still showing behind their ears, were so lame they could scarce move their fingers, but none of them — not one — told what it was that had lamed them so. They would stand about and wonder who "those Mohawks" might have been, or what the British Parliament might do next, but never say what they themselves had been doing, for each was sworn to secrecy.

Only Paul Revere showed no signs of the hard physical strain he had been under all the night before. Not long after dawn he had started on horseback for New York and Philadelphia with an account of the Tea Party. He could chop open tea chests all night, and ride all day.

The Silver Pencil [5]

(A Selection)

ALICE DALGLIESH

Janet Laidlaw, born in Trinidad of English parents, goes to school in England, and later comes to America where she trains for kindergarten teaching. When she was a child, her father gave her a silver pencil "for her stories," and this symbolizes the writing theme which runs through the story. The book is important for its excellent portrayal of Janet's development and of the courage with which she meets her problems; the chapter given below is a good example. While convalescing in Nova Scotia, Janet writes her first book.

A sequel, Along Janet's Road, *tells how she becomes editor of children's books in a publishing house.*

In November, the Armistice was signed. The papers carried the news in staring headlines. Cities and towns and villages went wild with joy. The air was filled with snowstorms of torn paper; strangers hugged each other in the streets. The war was over! There would never be another one.

The children were brimming over with excitement; Janet found herself very much out of patience with them. Lately her patience had been running thin. Renny, a nervous boy who simply could not sit still, annoyed her. And even the Armistice did not make her as happy as the rest of the joy-delirious world. Something must be the matter.

Each day she grew more tired and nervous, and then the pain began. At first it was only in her feet and ankles if she stood too long. Then it was in her knees and in her fingers. Finally she found that she could not walk.

"Is it rheumatism?" she asked the doctor. "I'm not old enough for that."

"Arthritis," the doctor said. "You will have to go into a hospital for rest and treatment."

Rest! The word was a relief. But where was the money to come from? If she gave up her work, her very small salary would stop,

[5] From Alice Dalgliesh, *The Silver Pencil* (Scribner, 1944).

and then there would be nothing to pay the hospital expenses.

Fortunately Miss West came to the rescue. "We will pay your salary until the end of the school year," she said. "And I can get you a free room in a hospital, because my father used to be superintendent of that hospital. They have a certain number of rooms kept for people who really can't afford to pay."

Everyone was amazingly kind. In an emergency, then, Americans didn't only promise things. They *did* them. When one was really in trouble, words meant exactly what they said, even more than they said. One week later, Janet was in the hospital. The free room was a dreary little cell, painted an unattractive drab color, with a single window that looked out on a court. But that first week it seemed like Heaven. She could lie there, could sleep all she wanted to, be relieved of all responsibility. She did not have to think, through continuous, gnawing pain, of the development of Renny and nineteen other children. She did not have to force herself to smile and play "Farmer in the Dell" when all she wanted was to sit down and take the weight off her feet.

After the first week, when she was rested and her nerves were quiet, the drab little room was not so pleasant. By the second week, she was really restless, for she didn't seem to be getting any better. By the third week, she was sure she was never going to get better. The doctors were non-committal when she asked them, desperately, when she would be able to work — or if, for that matter, she would ever again be able to *walk*.

"Arthritis is a very stubborn disease," was all they would say. "You are, of course, unlucky to have it at your age."

The end of the first month found her utterly discouraged. To be so young and to be crippled! She lay in bed with the tears trickling down her cheeks.

This time no one helped her but herself — and possibly William Vaughn Moody. She never knew exactly when the turning-point came. There was a day when snatches of the poem kept going through her head.

Of loss and doubt and dread,
And swift oncoming doom

I made a helmet for my head,
And a floating plume.

Some lines of the poem she couldn't remember, and that was tiresome. "I wish you'd look in my suitcase," she said to a young probationer who came into the room. "There's a small brown book that I want awfully. I think it is where you can see it."

The probationer found the book without difficulty. Janet turned the pages, looking for the poem. It was the book in which she had kept the poems and bits of verses that she had used for roll-call in Professor Kern's class.

"Here it is!" There was so much pleasure in her voice that the probationer was startled. Janet read the poem over. "And there's another one I like, right on the next page," she said. "It might have been written for me."

She read it aloud:

"For when the heavy body has grown weak,
There's nothing that can tether the wild mind,
That being moonstruck and fantastical,
Goes where it pleases."

Then she laughed, a laugh that was rusty from disuse. "I copied that when I was in the infirmary with measles! An Irish poet wrote it; his name was Yeats. My mind isn't exactly 'moonstruck and fantastical,' but it *can* go where it pleases!"

The probationer, a stolid Pennsylvania Dutch girl, saw nothing to laugh at. "She's queer," she said to herself. "Lies here looking grouchy all day, and then finds a silly poem and starts laughing at it." She hurried over to the window and pulled up the shade with a jerk, pulled it up too far, so that the sun shone into Janet's eyes. Then, with a rustle of her blue-and-white dress, the probationer went out of the room.

"Number 29 is talking queer," she said to the head nurse. "She says her mind can go where it pleases. And something about being moonstruck. Maybe you'd better go in and take a look at her."

"I've other things to do," said the head nurse. "Number 29 is all right. Just reads too much."

In her room, Janet lay shading her eyes

from the sun, staring at the opposite wall. How foolish of her to think that she had to look at those drab walls all day! Her mind could go where it pleased. It wasn't pacing up and down, now, like a prisoner in a narrow cell. It was free! It traveled back to Trinidad and the day when she had written her own funny little poem. From there it went to Christmas Day and the silver pencil shining on the tree. The picture was so clear that she felt she could reach out her hand to take the pencil. It was there on the branch between a silver trumpet and a rosy, waxen angel. . . . She made herself come back to reality. Where was the pencil now? On the table by her bed lay the writing-case that she had used as a child. Mother had mailed it to her because, she said, it would be light and easy to handle now that she was in bed.

Janet reached over for the case, opened it, ran her fingers through the pockets. She had used this writing-case when she was in England, perhaps the silver pencil . . . Yes, there it was, in a corner of one of the pockets! She took it out eagerly. The pencil was tarnished, it was almost black, but the sunlight from the window still caught a faint gleam of silver.

Idly, she began scribbling on her writing-pad. Perhaps she could write? But what? Thinking about it took her mind off the pain; for the first time in a month she began to have a real interest.

The nurses noticed the difference. Frances, prettiest and gayest of the student-nurses, put it into words.

"I don't know what has happened to you," she said. "I used to hate to come into this room, you were so sad and gloomy. Now here you are smiling and joking with us — yet I can't see you are any better. What *has* happened?"

"I don't exactly know," Janet said truthfully. "You look tired tonight. What is it?"

Frances shook the thermometer, put it in Janet's mouth, sat down by the bed. "I've had a terrible day," she said. "I don't know what made me forget, but I left a mustard-plaster too long on a patient's chest. Burned the skin off him. Almost got fired."

Janet chuckled as best she could with the thermometer in her mouth. "Don't do anything like that to me! But tell me all the things you do to other people!" It was the first time she had thought of the nurses in terms of anything but bed-making and alcohol rubs. Now they became people, with ups and downs of their own. Before long they were telling her about themselves, telling her small amusing things about the other patients.

Time went a little faster. To make it pass even more quickly, Janet took to making up verses — funny ones — about her nurses, about hospital life in general. She wrote them with the silver pencil — just for the sake of sentiment and because it was easier to use than a pen.

"Why on earth don't you do something with those verses?" asked a student-nurse called Marty.

"What *could* I do with them?" Janet wondered.

"I don't know." Marty was thoughtful. "But it seems as if there would be lots of people here who would enjoy them. Write them down, anyway."

That was how the *Hospital News* started. It was a little hard to produce, as Janet was lying almost flat, but she managed it somehow, rather slowly as the joints of her fingers were still swollen. The *Hospital News* was printed by hand on sheets of writing-paper, illustrated, too, with crude cartoon-like drawings. In prose and verse and picture, the little paper poked friendly fun at doctors and nurses, at operations and hospital diet. It circulated among the internes and nurses and went to all patients on that floor. It came back to its editor literally worn to pieces.

And, for Janet, the hospital began to come to life. Each day brought pleasant surprises. Flowers on her breakfast tray. "From the patient in 22," Frances told her. "She liked your verse about the tonsilectomy, because she's going to have one tomorrow."

"Here are some magazines from 25," Marty said, bringing them in. "And the funny old man in 28 says will you write a poem about hardening of the arteries?"

"Mercy!" said Janet. "What next?" The friendly exchanges kept on, with all kinds of suggestions, practical and impractical, with more patients sharing their books and flowers in return for the little paper.

The days were not so long any more, nor the pain so bad. It actually was letting up a little. Perhaps, Janet thought, when I am better I shall be able to write stories again. I feel almost as if I could.

One morning, Frances came in with a wheel chair. "You're going riding!" Her voice was cheerful.

"In that thing?" Janet looked at the chair with distaste. "I shall feel like an old, old lady."

But the chair brought a certain amount of freedom. One afternoon she wheeled it down the corridor and out onto the porch; no one had told her she could go out there, but she was going. And when she got out on the porch, it was spring. The trees were so green that they startled her. She wheeled the chair to the railing and looked down. Yellow and white crocuses starred the grass. Over in the corner the daffodils had fat green-yellow buds. A robin, his red breast bursting with prosperity, tugged hard at a worm. It really was spring — and in a short time they would let her try to walk.

Before long she *did* walk, with slow, unsteady steps. Now the time was coming when she would have to leave the hospital, and she was actually regretful. It had come to be such a safe, friendly little world.

Frances and Marty were on another floor now, but they came back to visit. "What are you going to do when you leave us?" Frances asked. "You haven't any family in this country, have you? And you won't be able to stand on your feet long enough to teach — at least not for a while."

"I'm planning to go back to college and finish the work for my degree," Janet said. "My brother was married some months ago, but he writes that he can still help me financially. What I *don't* know is where to go this summer. Have you a suggestion?"

"I know just the place for you," Marty said eagerly. "I stayed there last summer. It's a farm, a real farm, in a little village in Nova Scotia. You'd love it, and it isn't expensive. The name of the village is Sandy Cove."

"Sandy Cove." The name had a pleasant sound as Janet said it over. "Canada is so far away," she said doubtfully.

"But worth it when you get there," Marty insisted. "Think about it, anyway. I'll give you the address."

All-American
A Lesson in Citizenship[6]
John R. Tunis

◄§ *John R. Tunis not only writes excellent sports stories, but within that framework he deals courageously with modern problems which young people face today. All-American is a vigorous football story set against the background of two rival schools, a private school and a large city high school. Ronald Perry, the football star on the private school team, becomes incensed at the snobbish attitude of his classmates regarding a Jewish fellow and a colored boy on the rival team. Ronald leaves the Academy and enters the Abraham Lincoln High School. He has a difficult time making the readjustment and winning the respect of his former rivals. In the chapter given below, the principal of the high school, Mr. Curry, has a talk with Ronald and helps him to see what living in a democracy really means.*

A feeling of uneasiness hung over the entire room. Chairs squeaked continually, making a chorus of scratchy noises. Voices hummed and buzzed. It was the end of the marking period; the day that came regularly once every few months. And it was the last hour of the day — when in every homeroom each student's report card was issued for the period.

This scene, so different from anything at the Academy, always interested Ronny. At the Academy you did your work every day or else you got a detention and stayed in afternoons until you did. Here you might fail in a subject and not be sure of having failed until the end of the marking period. He looked around the excited class, at the boys in sweaters without neckties or coats, now all familiar figures who had names and

6 From John R. Tunis, *All-American* (Harcourt, Brace, 1942).

personalities attached. At the girls who gave the room that high-pitched tone so strange to him from the start. At Stacey in a kind of shirt with sleeves cut high above the elbows and the school name in green on his breast; at Ned LeRoy, slumped in his seat and staring ahead, apparently prepared for the worst; at Meyer Goldman in the back of the room, laughing nervouly with Mike Fronzak across the aisle. And at Sandra in front. Especially at Sandra. She had on the white shoes with brown tips, and the pink sweater. . . .

Tap-tap. Tap-tap-tap. Mr. Kates standing by his desk tapped severely with his pencil for order. He glanced over the crowded room. "Quiet, please, quiet. Keep it down." For about a minute he stood silently waiting, glancing around the forty seats, every one occupied by a nervous boy or girl. All save one. Gordon Brewster at the side was undisturbed by the sight of the report cards in Mr. Kates's hand. The noise, the chatter, the squeaking of chairs subsided. Slowly the teacher came forward with that little brown package in his fist.

Eager hands reached out. Subdued murmurs of delight or deep silence even more meaningful greeted the cards. He came down the aisle toward Ronald. As he slipped the card down on the desk, he leaned over, whispering, "Will you please step into Mr. Curry's office a minute before you leave, Ronald?"

He knew at once. He knew without opening the small folded card what had happened. He had failed. But he didn't know the whole of it.

At the top of the folded brown cardboard were the words: REPORT CARD. Underneath that, one line: ACCOMPLISHED IN STUDIES. Every pupil had a serial number. His serial number, 1166, was in the upper left-hand corner.

The card was ruled off into squares, one for each week in the marking period. Grades were listed at the side: 95 was high honors, 85 was honors, 70 was passing. At the top were printed the five subjects he took, and checks had been made in red ink in each square. Thus you — not to mention your teachers and your parents who had to sign

the card — could see the progress or lack of it in every subject you took from week to week.

Yes, he knew. He knew all right. He knew as he studied the card that he was below 70 in Latin. But the history, that's bad. Oh, that's bad; definitely, as Sandra would say. Honors in algebra, English, and French. But the Latin and the history. That's bad. No wonder Mr. Curry wanted to see him. Ronald folded up the card and stuffed it into his pocket, discovering with some relief he wasn't in the least terrified at the coming interview as he had been whenever the Duke called him in. Still and all, you couldn't help being a little worried.

"Come in. Sit down, Ronald." Mr. Curry was telephoning, but he put one hand over the mouthpiece and nodded toward a chair. Then he went on talking. "Yes. Yes, I think so. I imagine he will. Yes, I'd agree to that. At the next meeting of the Board? All right. Yes, I will. Yes, if you wish. All right. Very good. Call me Tuesday then. All right. Good-bye."

While he was talking, Ronald watched him. You'd certainly never think he was the principal of a big high school. Rather a colorless man, on the whole. Naturally you weren't exactly terrified when he called you into his office. Still and all, you couldn't help feeling a little worried.

"Ronald, sit down. Glad to see you. This is almost the first chance I've had to talk to you since you got out of the hospital. Everything working out?"

Surprising man. You got ready for a kind of bawling-out, and then you got a question like that. "Uhuh. Yessir."

"I see. That little incident was unpleasant for you; but it sort of cleared the atmosphere, didn't it?"

"Yessir. It sure did."

He smiled. "Let's see now. You've been here four, no five months nearly, haven't you? Tell me, how do you like us on the whole? Do you like this school?"

"Yessir, I like it. I like it now."

"H'm. I imagine it must have been hard for you at first. Different from the Academy." He looked down at the ruler in his hand. He glanced at the papers on his desk and rearranged them. He looked over at the window with the shade half pulled. But he never looked straight at you the way the Duke did. "H'm. Tell me, Ronald, what do you think of your report card this period?"

The question startled him. "Not so hot."

"No, it wasn't, was it? What seems to be the matter?"

"I really don't know, sir."

"Study habits? You surely don't need to be told how to study. You've been taught that already. We've had several boys from the Academy; they all had first-rate study habits."

"Yessir, I mean, nosir."

"Now it's probably true, you had more individual attention in your work at the Academy." Ronald found himself breaking in to explain how things were.

"See, at the Academy you had to do your homework because you had a two-hour study period in Hall every night."

"Exactly. Here you have no study hall at night. You can go to the movies. Or listen to the Aldrich Family or see your girl. Here you're on your own. We can't watch you, we can't baby you. We don't want to. In this school, Ronald, every pupil has to be responsible for himself. That's one of the principles of a democracy, isn't it?"

Well, yes. Yes, he had something there. Obviously this diffident man, so unlike the Duke, had much more on the ball than you'd think at first glance. He wasn't a personality. Yet . . .

"Now there's one thing you've got to learn, everyone here has to learn. In this school you're on your own. *You* are lucky. You don't need to be taught how to study. You've been taught that. But in a democracy each citizen is on his own. It's up to him. You must get used to being on your own and you better do so here, now."

"Yessir." He understood. The man behind the desk leaned back, his hands behind his head, and looked at the shaded window.

"You know, it's a funny thing, I remember you so well last fall in that football game. You were a fine player, and I hope you'll be just as good on our team next year. You were a great little fighter out there, that's why you licked us."

Well, maybe so. Not exactly. But then, yes, maybe.

The principal paused a minute. "I can remember once in that last quarter watching you go through our line — and our line was plenty tough last fall — with Stacey and Goldman on your neck and . . ."

Suddenly he was back. Back on Academy field, and his cleats were digging into the turf, and his heart was pounding, and clutching hands were grabbing at him, and he could hear Goldman's tense breathing in his ear . . . "huff . . . huff . . . huff . . ."

". . . and that's the way you must be in your work, too. You've got to be aggressive, you've got to lick your studies. Or they'll lick you. Have you been really fighting your studies this way in the last six weeks?"

From a feeling of warmth and satisfaction, from the field behind the Academy he came back to earth and the principal's room at Abraham Lincoln High. With him came an uneasy feeling of what was coming. Ronald's respect for this quiet man grew. Nope, he wasn't a personality like the Duke. His clothes, for instance, weren't at all like the Duke's, and somehow he didn't wear them the same way. But he had something.

"Nosir."

"Have you been neglecting your work at all the last few weeks, do you think?"

"Nosir, yessir, maybe . . ."

"What for?"

Ronald was now bewildered. This man was amazing the way he pinned you down to things, the way he got things out of you.

"Do you think possibly you haven't been working as much nights as you should?"

"Yessir, possibly."

"Well, what have you been spending your time on? Girls?"

"Yessir, I mean nosir, I mean, maybe so."

"Any one girl?"

"Yessir."

"It wouldn't be Sandra Fuller, would it?"

There! It was out now. The principal was tapping the ruler gently on the desk and looking down hard at it. Ronny felt warm all over, and he knew red was coming up into his face. But the man behind the desk still stared at the ruler.

"Sandra's a lovely girl. I don't blame you for liking her. Been seeing a good deal of her, do you think, lately?"

"Yessir."

"How much, since you came out of the hospital?"

"Two, three times a week."

"Or more?"

Hang it, this man had something, he really had something. "Yessir, I guess . . . well, maybe."

"I guess so too." He laughed. Ronald laughed. This made things easier. "Yes, I guess so too. Tell you why; reason is I've seen you twice in the last month at the Empire with her, and several times in at Walgren's drinking cokes. Right?"

"Yessir."

"Now see here, Ronald. Sandra's a fine girl. She's a swell kid. But just think a minute. You know, I can remember when your father was in Yale, and I remember seeing him play in the game in the Bowl in '22, was it? No, '23. The one when he ran way out to the side and grabbed the lateral pass in the last minute of play. Right down the field for a touchdown. What a game that was! A heart-breaker for us to lose. When I watched you on the field last fall, I could see your dad every minute; same way of holding your head, of handling the ball, of waiting until the last minute to chuck a pass. Look! That's what you're risking, all that. Yale, that's your job. Just imagine how your dad would feel if you failed to get into Yale. Imagine!"

He leaned over, and for the first time looked Ronald squarely in the face. "You could, you know, if you keep on this way!" Then quickly he leaned back and began turning the ruler over and over in his hands, and staring down at it silently.

Well, there really wasn't much you could say to this sort of thing. He hadn't thought of it that way, never.

"I'm mighty glad you like Sandra. She's one of the finest girls in this school. I'm glad you like us; we like you. You're part of the school, you're one of us. It's true, I know, you had a hard time at first; the boys were a little tough on you. Because you came from the Academy they suspected you, they had to

get to know you. There's cruelty here. It's a kind of primitive cruelty that's hidden away in us all, I guess. We try to keep it down, yet every once in a while it does crop out, and you happened, as I say, to be the victim. But that's over. We all like you and respect you and want you to like us. And we want you to do well here. Only you must do your part. You've got to think first of all of getting into Yale."

"Yessir."

"Just imagine how you'd feel a year from now, how Sandra would look at you if you failed your College Boards. If you want to see Sandra, that's fine. See her week-ends and see her then as much as you like. But keep your evenings all week for work. You had baseball in the afternoon, and you just weren't doing the work. From Monday to Friday, remember, you have a full-time job on your hands. Getting into Yale."

"Yessir."

"Don't forget, I can't study for you; neither can your parents or your teachers. You're old enough now to be on your own. You're a citizen of a democracy. You have responsibilities. See you live up to them."

He stood up. He held out his hand. He looked you in the face, just the trace of a smile on his lips.

"Yessir, I will. You bet I will, Mr. Curry." They shook hands, a firm, hard fist. Ronny liked him, liked everything about him. 'Course, he wasn't a personality as the Duke was. But just the same, he was some gent.

"Oh! One thing more." Ronald turned at the doorway. "Naturally you're ineligible to play baseball until your marks come up in the next period. You understand, that means no more extra-mural sport this year."

He stumbled from the room. He hardly saw the girls typing away behind the counter in the big room outside. He moved into the corridor, bewildered. He was dizzy. No more extra-mural sport! He couldn't play on the baseball team!

Jeepers! That meant he couldn't play next week against the Academy!

BIBLIOGRAPHY

Alcott, Louisa M. *Little Women;* illus. by Barbara Cooney. Thomas Y. Crowell, 1955. (Grades 5–8)

An old favorite in a new edition with drawings made at the Alcott home in Concord, Massachusetts.

Angelo, Valenti. *Nino;* illus. by the author. Viking Press, 1938. (Grades 5–7)

Based on the author-artist's boyhood in a village in Tuscany.

Armer, Laura. *Waterless Mountain;* illus. by Sidney Armer. Longmans, 1931. (Grades 5–8)

A sensitive story of a present day Navajo Indian boy, told with deep feeling for Indian art and lore.

Bell, Margaret. *Watch for a Tall White Sail;* illus. by Louis Darling. William Morrow, 1948. (Grades 7–9)

An unusual story of a sixteen-year-old girl who meets with courage the hardships of pioneer living in Alaska.

Benary-Isbert, Margot. *The Ark;* trans. by Clara and Richard Winston. Harcourt, Brace, 1953. (Grades 6–9)

A deeply moving story of a refugee family who without bitterness rebuild their lives in postwar Germany. Followed by *Rowan Farm.*

Bennett, John. *Master Skylark;* illus. by Reginald B. Birch. Grosset & Dunlap, 1924. (Grades 6–9)

A vivid tale of a boy who is kidnapped and becomes one of the players in Will Shakespeare's company.

Bianco, Margery. *Little Wooden Doll;* illus. by Pamela Bianco. Macmillan, 1925. (Little Library) (Grades 3–4)

An appealing story of a forgotten doll befriended by the attic mice.

Bishop, Claire. *Pancakes-Paris;* illus. by Georges Schreiber. Viking Press, 1947. (Grades 3–6)

A realistic story of French children and American soldiers just after the Second World War. *Twenty and Ten* is a tale of courage and kindness.

Bontemps, Arna. *Fast Sooner Hound;* illus. by Virginia Lee Burton. Houghton Mifflin, 1942. (Grades 2–5)

A delightful tall tale of a long-legged, lop-eared hound.

Brink, Carol. *Caddie Woodlawn;* illus. by Kate Seredy. Macmillan, 1935. (Grades 6–8)

Caddie and her brothers lived on the Wisconsin frontier in Civil War days. Awarded the Newbery medal in 1936.

Buff, Mary and Conrad. *Apple and the Arrow.* Houghton Mifflin, 1951. (Grades 3–6)

The story of William Tell and the Swiss struggle for freedom.

Carr, Mary. *Children of the Covered Wagon;* illus. by Bob Kuhn. Thomas Y. Crowell, 1943. (Grades 4–6)

A story of the old Oregon Trail. *Young Mac of Fort Vancouver* tells of the early days in the state of Washington.

Caudill, Rebecca. *Tree of Freedom;* illus. by Dorothy Bayley Morse. Viking Press, 1949. (Grades 7–9)

Thirteen-year-old Stephanie takes an apple seed with her when she makes the long trek from North Carolina to Kentucky. As it grows into the "tree of freedom" it is symbolic of the family putting down new roots in their home in the wilderness.

Cervantes Saavedra, Miguel de. *The Adventures of Don Quixote de la Mancha;* adapted by Leighton Barret; illus. by Warren Chappell. Alfred A. Knopf, 1939. (Grades 6–9)

Dramatic illustrations give new life to the Spanish satire of the knight-errant who tilted with windmills.

Clark, Ann Nolan. *Blue Canyon Horse;* illus. by Allan Houser. Viking Press, 1954. (Grades 2–4)

A poetic story written with sensitive understanding of the bond between an Indian boy and his horse. *Little Navajo Bluebird* tells of a Navajo Indian girl; *Secret of the Andes,* of an Inca boy in present-day Peru. This last book received the Newbery medal in 1953.

Clark, Margery, *pseud. Poppy Seed Cakes;* illus. by Maud and Miska Petersham. Doubleday, 1924. (Grades 2–4)

Gay little stories about Andrewshek and his Auntie Katushka.

Clemens, Samuel Langhorne. *The Adventures of Tom Sawyer*. Harper, 1917. (Holiday Edition) (Grades 6–9)

An epic of American boyhood, followed by *Adventures of Huckleberry Finn*. Read also *The Prince and the Pauper*.

Coatsworth, Elizabeth. *Away Goes Sally;* illus. by Helen Sewell. Macmillan, 1934. (Grades 4–6)

Sally travels from Massachusetts to Maine in a little house on sleds drawn by twelve oxen.

Cooper, James Fenimore. *The Deerslayer;* illus. by N. C. Wyeth. Charles Scribner's Sons, 1925. (Scribner Illustrated Classics) (Grades 8–9)

This rousing story of warfare between the Iroquois Indians and the white settlers is the first of the Leatherstocking Tales. Followed by *The Last of the Mohicans*.

Dalgliesh, Alice. *The Courage of Sarah Noble;* illus. by Leonard Weisgard. Charles Scribner's Sons, 1954. (Grades 3–5)

A dramatic story of a real little girl who accompanied her father into the Connecticut wilderness while he built a home. *Bears on Hemlock Mountain* is an amusing tall tale. *The Silver Pencil* tells of a girl's development.

De Angeli, Marguerite. *Door in the Wall;* illus. by the author. Doubleday, 1949. (Grades 3–6)

Robin, crippled son of a great lord, proves his bravery and wins his king's recognition. Awarded the Newbery medal in 1950. In *Thee, Hannah!* Mrs. De Angeli has written about the Quakers in Philadelphia, and in *Henner's Lydia* about the Mennonites.

DeJong, Meindert. *Wheel on the School;* illus. by Maurice Sendak. Harper & Brothers, 1954. (Grades 4–7)

A story of the efforts of six school children to bring back the storks to their little Dutch village. Awarded the Newbery medal in 1955. *The House of Sixty Fathers* is a realistic story of China during the early days of the Japanese invasion, told with dramatic power.

Defoe, Daniel. *Robinson Crusoe;* illus. by N. C. Wyeth. Charles Scribner's Sons, 1958. (Scribner Illustrated Classics) (Grades 5–8)

One of the greatest adventure stories ever written. First published in 1719.

Dickens, Charles. *The Christmas Carol;* illus. by Robert Ball. Macmillan, 1950. (New Children's Classics) (Grades 7–9)

One of the most famous of all Christmas stories.

Dodge, Mary Mapes. *Hans Brinker; or, The Silver Skates;* illus. by George W. Edwards. Charles Scribner's Sons, 1915. (Scribner Illustrated Classics) (Grades 4–6)

Written in 1865, this is still one of the best stories of Holland.

Edmonds, Walter. *The Matchlock Gun;* illus. by Paul Lantz. Dodd, Mead, 1941. (Grades 4–6)

A stirring story of courage during an Indian raid. Awarded the Newbery medal in 1942.

Enright, Elizabeth. *The Saturdays;* illus. by the author. Rinehart, 1941. (Grades 4–7)

A highly diverting story of four motherless children, an understanding father, and Cuffy, the housekeeper. *Thimble Summer* won the Newbery medal in 1939, and *Gone Away Lake* was one of the runners-up in 1958.

Estes, Eleanor. *The Moffats;* illus. by Louis Slobodkin. Harcourt, Brace, 1941. (Grades 4–6)

The Moffat family did not have much in the way of worldly goods, but there was always fun and laughter in the little house on New Dollar Street. Followed by *The Middle Moffat* and *Rufus M.* Mrs. Estes won the Newbery medal in 1952 for *Ginger Pye*. In *The Hundred Dresses* she tells a tender story of a little Polish girl.

Farjeon, Eleanor. *The Little Bookroom;* illus. by Edward Adrizzone. Oxford University Press, 1956. (Grades 4–6)

Eleanor Farjeon has selected the favorites of her own short stories. Here are tales richly imaginative, touched with poetry, wisdom, and humor.

Field, Rachel. *Hitty; Her First Hundred Years;* illus. by Dorothy Lathrop. Macmillan, 1937. (Grades 5–8)

Through the eyes of a famous doll the reader sees America one hundred years ago — whaling days, plantation life, Quaker Philadelphia, and New York in the days of Charles Dickens' visit. *Calico Bush* is a story of the rigorous days of Colonial Maine.

Forbes, Esther. *Johnny Tremain;* illus. by Lynd Ward. Houghton Mifflin, 1943. (Grades 7–9)

A young Boston apprentice learns to accept responsibility under the impact of war. Awarded the Newbery medal in 1944.

Gates, Doris. *Blue Willow;* illus. by Paul Lantz. Viking Press, 1940. (Grades 5–8)

A tender story of a little girl who longs for a permanent home as she moves from place to place with her crop-picking family.

Gray, Elizabeth Janet. *Adam of the Road;* illus. by Robert Lawson. Viking Press, 1942. (Grades 7–9)

A minstrel boy in thirteenth-century England. Awarded the Newbery medal in 1943.

Grey, Katharine. *Rolling Wheels;* illus. by Frank Schoonover. Little, Brown, 1937. (Beacon Hill Bookshelf) (Grades 7–9)

This story of an Indiana family who took the long trek by prairie schooner to California in 1845 is based on authentic accounts.

Hale, Lucretia. *The Peterkin Papers;* illus. by Harold M. Brett. Houghton Mifflin, 1924. (Riverside Bookshelf) (Grades 4–6)

A "masterpiece of nonsense." These stories of the Peterkin family and their absurd dilemmas first appeared in the *St. Nicholas Magazine,* 1874–79.

Haywood, Carolyn. *"B" is for Betsy;* illus. by the author. Harcourt, Brace, 1939. (Grades 2–3)

The first of several engaging realistic stories about Betsy and her friends.

Henry, Marguerite. *King of the Wind;* illus. by Wesley Dennis. Rand McNally, 1948. (Grades 5–8)

The thrilling story of the famous Godolphin Arabian, ancestor of Man-o-War, and a mute stable boy's devotion to the stallion. Awarded the Newbery medal in 1949. Equally fascinating are *Misty of Chincoteague,* the story of a wild island pony, and *Brighty of the Grand Canyon,* about a little burro.

Holling, Holling C. *Paddle-to-the-Sea;* illus. by the author. Houghton Mifflin, 1941. (Grades 4–6)

The author presents geography and history in a fresh, imaginative way in this story and in its companion volumes, *Tree in the Trail, Seabird,* and *Minn of the Mississippi.*

Hunt, Mabel Leigh. *Benjie's Hat;* illus. by Grace Paull. J. B. Lippincott, 1938. (Grades 4–6)

Benjie, a little Quaker boy from North Carolina, has his trials with a hand-me-down hat. In *Little Girl with Seven Names,* a little Quaker girl finds that seven names can be a great burden.

James, Will. *Smoky, the Cowhorse;* illus. by the author. Charles Scribner's Sons, 1926. (Grades 6–9)

One of the best books of its kind. Will James tells the story of the smoke-colored cowpony in cowboy vernacular and illustrates it with fresh, spontaneous sketches.

Jewett, Eleanore. *Hidden Treasure of Glaston;* illus. by Frederick T. Chapman. Viking Press, 1946. (Grades 7–9)

Children interested in the legends of King Arthur will delight in this historical mystery. The adventures of two boys in an ancient abbey in medieval England tie in with the Arthurian tradition.

Keith, Harold. *Rifles for Watie;* illus. by Peter Burchard. Thomas Y. Crowell, 1957. (High School)

A mature, objective story of the Western campaign of the Civil War fought in the Missouri-Oklahoma area. Awarded the Newbery medal in 1958.

Kelly, Eric P. *The Trumpeter of Krakow;* illus. by Angela Pruszynska. Macmillan, 1928. (Grades 7–9)

Fifteenth-century Poland forms the background for this story of mystery, intrigue, and courage. Awarded the Newbery medal in 1929.

Kent, Louise. *He Went with Christopher Columbus;* illus. by Paul Quinn. Houghton Mifflin, 1940. (Grades 7–9)

The famous voyage seen through the eyes of a boy who sailed with Columbus.

Kipling, Rudyard. *Captains Courageous.* Doubleday, 1897. (Grades 7–9)

A voyage with a Grand Banks fishing boat changes a spoiled boy into a man. In *Kim* the color and romance of nineteenth-century India unfold before the reader.

Kjelgaard, Jim. *Big Red;* illus. by Bob Kuhn. Holiday House, 1956. (Grades 7–9)

The adventures of an Irish setter and a trapper's son who grow to maturity together.

Knight, Eric. *Lassie Come-Home;* illus. by Cyrus Leroy Baldridge. Winston, 1940. (Grades 6–9)

The famous classic of the devoted collie who found her way back to her home and master across four hundred miles of mountains and moors.

Krumgold, Joseph. *And Now Miguel;* illus. by Jean Charlot. Thomas Y. Crowell, 1953. (Grades 6–9)

A memorable book distinguished for its sensitive portrayal of a young boy's yearning to grow up and for its illuminating picture of life among the sheep-herders in New Mexico. Awarded the Newbery medal in 1954.

Lattimore, Eleanor. *Little Pear;* illus. by the author. Harcourt, Brace, 1931. (Grades 3–5)

The story of a mischievous five-year-old Chinese boy who craves adventure.

Lawrence, Mildred. *Peachtree Island;* illus. by Mary Stevens. Harcourt, Brace, 1948. (Grades 3–5)

A happy, wholesome orphan story which is thoroughly delightful.

Lawson, Robert. *Ben and Me;* illus. by the author. Little, Brown, 1939. (Grades 5–9)

A new and astonishing life of Benjamin Franklin written by Amos, the mouse that lived in Ben's fur cap. *The Great Wheel* is a fine story of an Irish lad who takes part in building the Ferris Wheel for the World's Fair in Chicago in 1893.

Lenski, Lois. *Strawberry Girl;* illus. by the author. J. B. Lippincott, 1945. (Grades 4–6)

The flavor of life among Florida's fruit-farmers is captured in this story of a warm-hearted little girl who helps her father and mother raise strawberries. Awarded the Newbery medal in 1946. *Judy's Journey* is another of the author's regional stories.

Lewis, Elizabeth. *Young Fu of the Upper Yangtze;* illus. by Kurt Wiese. Winston, 1932. (Grades 7–9)

Through all the vicissitudes and adventures of his apprenticeship to a coppersmith, Young Fu meets life with courage, faithfulness, and good will. Awarded the Newbery medal in 1933.

Lindquist, Jennie. *The Golden Name Day;* illus. by Garth Williams. Harper & Brothers, 1955. (Grades 3–6)

A perceptive story full of kindness and wisdom and enriched with Swedish customs, one of which gives the book its title.

McCloskey, Robert. *Homer Price;* illus. by the author. Viking Press, 1943. (Grades 4–7)

Six rollicking tales of the hilarious adventures of Homer Price, a modern American boy. Further adventures are told in *Centerburg Tales.*

Meader, Stephen. *Red Horse Hill;* illus. by Lee Townsend. Harcourt, Brace, 1930. (Grades 7–9)

This author has written many fine stories with authentic American backgrounds. This book tells of New Hampshire life a generation ago, with an interest in amateur horse-racing.

Means, Florence Crannell. *Shuttered Windows;* illus. by Armstrong Sperry. Houghton Mifflin, 1938. (Grades 7–9)

Sympathetic handling of the problems a Negro girl from the North meets when she goes South to live. *Candle in the Mist* tells of a family who leave their home in Wisconsin to become pioneers in Minnesota.

Meigs, Cornelia. *Master Simon's Garden;* illus. by John Rae. Macmillan, 1929. (Grades 7–9)

The meaning of freedom against tyranny and intolerance is strongly presented in this historical story of Colonial America through three generations. *The Willow Whistle* is a story of frontier days in the Middle West.

Milne, A. A. *Winnie-the-Pooh;* illus. by Ernest H. Shepard. E. P. Dutton, 1950. (Grades 3–5)

The author told these stories to his small son, Christopher Robin, and his Teddy Bear, who were enchanted to find themselves characters in the stories. Followed by *The House at Pooh Corner.*

Montgomery, Rutherford. *Kildee House;* illus. by Barbara Cooney. Doubleday, 1949. (Grades 5–7)

Jerome Kildee, seeking seclusion, built a home against a giant redwood, but a rapidly increasing family of skunks and one of raccoons, who also lived in the tree, complicated the situation. Quiet humor and a fine feeling for nature permeate this unique animal story.

Mukerji, Dhan Gopal. *Gay-Neck; the Story of a Pigeon;* illus. by Boris Artzybasheff. E. P. Dutton, 1927. (Grades 5–8)

The author's gentle Indian philosophy is interwoven in this story of a carrier pigeon and the part it played in the First World War. Awarded the Newbery medal in 1928. *Hari, the Jungle Lad* and *Kari, the Elephant,* tales told with vivid beauty, are imbued with the atmosphere of the jungle.

O'Brien, John. *Silver Chief, Dog of the North;* illus. by Kurt Wiese. Winston, 1933. (Grades 6–8)

A magnificent wolf-dog, tamed and trained by a Canadian Mountie, proves his loyalty by helping his master bring a man to justice.

Pyle, Howard. *Otto of the Silver Hand;* illus. by the author. Charles Scribner's Sons, new ed. 1957. (Grades 6–9)

A medieval tale of Otto and how "by gentleness and love and not by strife and hatred, he came at last to stand above other men and to be looked up to by all." *Men of Iron* tells how Miles wins his spurs and vanquishes his own and his father's enemy.

Rankin, Louise. *Daughter of the Mountains;* illus. by Kurt Wiese. Viking Press, 1948. (Grades 5–8)

A Tibetan girl makes a long journey from her mountain home to the coast of India to find her dog that was stolen.

Ransome, Arthur. *Swallows and Amazons;* illus. by Hélène Carter. J. B. Lippincott, 1931. (Grades 5–8)

The lively adventures of six resourceful English

children who spend a vacation camping on a small island.

Rawlings, Marjorie Kinnan. *The Yearling;* illus. by N. C. Wyeth. Charles Scribner's Sons, 1946. (Grades 7–9)

A classic story of the boy Jody and his pet fawn. In having to sacrifice the thing he loved most, Jody left his yearling days behind and gained the stature of a man.

Rounds, Glenn. *Blind Colt;* illus. by the author. Holiday House, 1941. (Grades 5–7)

An unforgettable story of a colt who was born blind, but learned to see with his nose and ears.

Sawyer, Ruth. *Roller Skates;* illus. by Valenti Angelo. Viking Press, 1936. (Grades 6–8)

High-spirited Lucinda has a wonderful time exploring New York City on roller skates in the 1890's. Awarded the Newbery medal in 1937. Read also *This Way to Christmas* and *The Long Christmas.*

Seredy, Kate. *The Good Master;* illus. by the author. Viking Press, 1935. (Grades 5–7)

Irrepressible Kate comes to stay with her cousin Jancsi and her uncle on a large horse farm on the plains of Hungary. Hard work, happy holidays, and the wisdom of "the good master" help develop her into an amenable, likable girl. Followed by *The Singing Tree.*

Shannon, Monica. *Dobry;* illus. by Atanas Katchamakoff. Viking Press, 1934. (Grades 5–8)

What the land means to the people who live on it is revealed in this story of a Bulgarian peasant boy who wanted to be a sculptor instead of a farmer.

Snedeker, Caroline Dale. *Downright Dencey;* illus. by Maginel Wright Barney. Doubleday, 1927. (Grades 6–9)

Nantucket over a hundred years ago is the setting for this uncommonly fine story for older girls.

Sorensen, Virginia. *Miracles on Maple Hill;* illus. by Beth and Joe Krush. Harcourt, Brace, 1956. (Grades 5–7)

A heart-warming story of a family's first year on a Pennsylvania farm enjoying the miracles of nature and the changing seasons.

Sperry, Armstrong. *Call It Courage;* illus. by the author. Macmillan, 1940. (Grades 5–8)

A Polynesian boy conditioned in infancy to terror of the sea sets out alone in a canoe to conquer his fear. His ultimate victory over himself and his triumphal return make a powerful story. Awarded the Newbery medal in 1941.

Spyri, Johanna. *Heidi;* illus. by Agnes Tait.

J. B. Lippincott, 1948. (Lippincott Classics) (Grades 4–6)

Since its publication in 1880, several generations of children have absorbed, through the story, some of the beauty of the Swiss countryside.

Stevenson, Robert Louis. *Kidnapped;* illus. by N. C. Wyeth. Charles Scribner's Sons, 1924. (Scribner Illustrated Classics) (Grades 7–9)

A stirring historical romance with the action laid in the highlands of Scotland. *Treasure Island* is a classic sea story with pirates, buried treasure, and mutiny.

Stong, Phil. *Honk, the Moose;* illus. by Kurt Wiese. Dodd, Mead, 1935. (Grades 4–5)

A hilarious story of two boys who discover a moose in a livery stable in Minnesota.

Taylor, Sydney. *All-of-a-Kind Family;* illus. by Helen John. Follett, 1951. (Grades 4–6)

Five little Jewish girls with understanding parents grow up in New York's Lower East Side before World War I.

Treffinger, Carolyn. *Li Lun, Lad of Courage;* illus. by Kurt Wiese. Abingdon, 1947. (Grades 4–8)

A story of quiet heroism in which a Chinese boy accomplishes a difficult task with courage and persistence.

Tunis, John. *All-American;* illus. by Hans Walleen. Harcourt, Brace, 1942. (Grades 6–9)

Much more significant than most sport stories is this football story which faces unflinchingly problems of democracy that arise in the daily life of a high school.

Van Stockum, Hilda. *Cottage at Bantry Bay;* illus. by the author. Viking Press, 1938. (Grades 5–7)

A gay story of the lively O'Sullivan children who live with their father and mother in a cottage in Ireland.

Verne, Jules. *Twenty Thousand Leagues Under the Sea;* illus. by W. J. Aylward. Charles Scribner's Sons, 1925. (Scribner Illustrated Classics) (Grades 7–9)

The story of Captain Nemo's ingenious submarine boat, first published in 1870, might be called a forerunner of science fiction.

White, Anne. *Junket;* illus. by Robert McCloskey. Viking Press, 1955. (Grades 4–6)

Junket, an airedale with character, teaches a family from the city how to enjoy country life.

Wilder, Laura Ingalls. *Little House in the Big Woods;* illus. by Garth Williams. Harper & Brothers, new ed. 1953. (Grades 3–7)

The author has written many of her childhood experiences in a group of outstanding books which form a vivid chronicle of life in pioneer days in the Middle West. This first title is followed by six books, each one a little more advanced, ending with *These Happy Golden Years*.

Worth, Kathryn. *They Loved to Laugh;* illus. by Marguerite de Angeli. Doubleday, 1942. (Grades 7–9)

A sense of true values characterizes this story of a lonely orphan who comes to live with a Quaker family where five fun-loving boys teach her how to laugh.

Wyss, Johann David. *Swiss Family Robinson;* illus. by Jeanne Edwards. World Publishing Co., 1947. (Grades 5–8)

The very improbability of this tale of a family shipwrecked on a desert island makes it delightful.

Poetry

"All we who make
Things transitory and good
Cannot but take
When walking in a wood
Pleasure in everything
And the maker's solitude,
Knowing the delicacy
Of bringing shape to birth.
We gave and took the ring
And pledged ourselves to the earth." [1]

OREMOST AMONG THE "BRINGERS
of shape to birth" are the poets. Of all the classes of literature, poetry is
perhaps the natural habitat of children. Three elements of poetry seem as
instinctive to children as the air they breathe. With the first breath and the
first heartbeat, rhythm becomes an urge demanding response. Soon hands and
feet move in an ordered cadence to the tune of "Patty cake, Patty cake,
Baker's Man" or "Dance to your Daddy, My little babby; Dance to your
Daddy, My little man."

If no words are said and no songs sung, there are other ways of responding
to the inner urge of rhythm. One can beat on the table with a spoon or kick
the furniture bare of finish. Space and time can be made sport of by breaking
them into "beats which recur in uniform patterns"; there is the definition of
rhythm. The variety of its occurrence is at the heart of everything: music, art,
poetry, life itself.

Add to the appeal of rhythm the felicity of words which agree in their ter-
minal sounds, within the framework of an established meter, and there are the
beginnings of music, magic, and incantation. Rhyme and rhythm appeal to
almost every child. The jingles of nursery rhymes, popular songs, folk songs,
even the catches of the advertising world which infest the air waves, these will
engage the response of children if nothing better is at hand. They invent their
own nonsense rhymes, and many of their games — jumping rope, bouncing
balls, and devices for counting out — are accompanied by verse, some of it salty
and vigorous, much of it having flashes of pure poetry.

The power of the poet to create pictures with words is the third component
of poetry which has immediate appeal for children. Uninhibited by habit in

[1] From *Collected Poems of Edwin Muir, 1921–1951* (Grove Press, New York, 1957), p. 129.

the use of words, they often employ them themselves with a fresh and unorthodox skill, creating images which might well be the envy of the practicing poet.

> O Little Soldier with the golden helmet,
> What are you guarding on my lawn?

So begins "Dandelion," which Hilda Conkling wrote when she was eight years old. This ability to define one object in terms of another and by so doing to create what Jacques Maritain calls "the immediate illuminating image" — this is the genius of poetry, and children are quick to see and to understand it. "Two things are not compared," Maritain continues, "but rather one thing is made known through the image of another."[2] There is a period in childhood when a flair for image-making is well defined. Properly sustained, the pleasure can become a lifelong habit, one which sharpens the perception of the reader, giving him a third eye with which to see the world. Each of us has looked at the head of a lion and seen there something benign, fierce, and beautiful. "Isn't he beautiful?" we say, or "Isn't he wonderful?" But these words have been over-used. We describe everything with them, from the great mysteries to the quality of our cooking. But if, when looking at a lion, we can recall how Marianne Moore described "The lion's ferocious chrysanthemum head,"[3] our own perception is increased immeasurably, and something of her poetic vision has rubbed off onto us. We become, for a while, a part of her creative will.

"Poetry creates for us a being within ourselves," writes Jacques Maritain. "It creates anew the universe after it has been annihilated in our minds by the recurrence of impressions blunted by reiteration."[4]

For children, poetry serves to confirm the newness and wonder of life which habit has not yet destroyed. Rhythm, rhyme, imagery, and the storytelling virtues of ballads and narrative verse, these are the birthright of children. If it is too soon lost in the welter of days, it may be because the choice of poetry made available to children is limited to a few poets whom we consider as writing for them. There is no reason why a wise choice from the whole range of lyric poetry should not be their field of exploration. A like situation exists in music. Certain melodies of Beethoven, Bach, Brahms, and Mozart can well set standards of appreciation at an early age, rather than the insipid melodies contrived by lesser talents for the introduction of children to music. The time when the powers of the imagination are strongest, and the response to the best is most spontaneous, is in the early years of childhood. This is the period when we so often subject children to poetry and music that is weak, sentimental, effusive, and insincere.

Many of the contemporary poets of childhood are men and women whose gifts derive from genuine poetic inspiration. The writing of poetry for children did not begin and end with Robert Louis Stevenson. He broke new ground, and much of his poetry seems to come from the children themselves, so spontaneous is it and so tuned to incidents and objects which are the com-

[2] Jacques Maritain, *Creative Intuition in Art and Poetry* (Meridian Books, New York, 1955).
[3] In "The Monkey Puzzle," *Collected Poems* (Macmillan, New York, 1953), p. 88.
[4] In *Creative Intuition in Art and Poetry.*

mon concern of children. But sometimes he succeeds only in *pretending* to be a child, and the adult observation and condescension are apparent. A. A. Milne, in *When We Were Very Young*, has caught the very rhythm of a young child at play and in motion, but this is verse rather than poetry. It remained for one of the greatest lyric poets of our time, Walter de la Mare, to mirror the inwardness of childhood, its moods of wonder and mysticism and its haunted sense of the past, as well as its outer world of play, its egotism, its delight in music and imagery. His *Peacock Pie* transcends all other poem sequences of childhood. Not since William Blake's *Songs of Innocence* have children found so true a voice bespeaking the emotion of their kind.

There is at present a heartening number of men and women who are writing poetry for children, with complete respect for the minds of their audience. To the established names of A. A. Milne, Dorothy Aldis, Rachel Field, Eleanor Farjeon, and Elizabeth Coatsworth, can now be added the name of Harry Behn, with his original rhyme schemes and his intuitive awareness of the degree of introspection which interests children. There is also David McCord, with his humor and wit in combination with freshness of imagery; and Myra Livingston, whose first little volume of verse, *Whispers* (Harcourt, Brace, 1958), derives from a sure and uncommon sympathy with the mind of the very young child.

Recent years have seen the publication of several anthologies which broaden the scope of children's interests in poetry: among them, Katherine Love's *Pocketful of Rhymes* (Crowell, 1946); *An Inheritance of Poetry* (Houghton Mifflin, 1951), compiled and arranged by Gladys L. Adshead and Annis Duff; Herbert Read's *This Way, Delight* (Pantheon, 1956). Two anthologies unique in organization and subject matter have been compiled by Helen Plotz: *Imagination's Other Place* (Crowell, 1955), poems of science and mathematics; and *Untune the Sky* (Crowell, 1957), poems of music and the dance. All of these anthologies reflect the personal selection of choice minds.

Those who enjoy poetry are apt to insist that others share its beatitude. "But why beauty should have the effect upon us that it does, the strange serene confidence that it inspires in us, none can say." It is Virginia Woolf speaking, in one of her many explorations of the pleasures of reading. "Most people have tried and perhaps one of the invariable properties of beauty is that it leaves in the mind a desire to impart."[5]

For those concerned with ensnaring children in the golden net, the directive might well be: to key up and keep alive one's own susceptibility to poetry; to read it aloud to children; and to remember that there are many doors into the mansion — Mother Goose, nonsense rhymes, humor, storytelling poems, songs, ballads, even poems whose meaning can hardly be fathomed.

> What is Poetry?
> Poetry is like the stars
> Left undiscovered.[6]

So it has been defined by a child of ten.

[5] Virginia Woolf, *The Captain's Death Bed* (Hogarth Press, London, 1950), pp. 164–165.
[6] Quoted in Flora J. Arnstein, *Adventures into Poetry* (Stanford University Press, 1951), p. 41.

FAIRIES, FAY, AND FAR AWAY

The Fairies[1]

WILLIAM ALLINGHAM

Up the airy mountain,
 Down the rushy glen,
We daren't go a-hunting
 For fear of little men;
Wee folk, good folk,
 Trooping all together;
Green jacket, red cap,
 And white owl's feather!

Down along the rocky shore
 Some make their home;
They live on crispy pancakes
 Of yellow tide-foam;
Some in the reeds
 Of the black mountain-lake,
With frogs for their watch-dogs,
 All night awake.

High on the hilltop
 The old King sits;
He is now so old and gray
 He's nigh lost his wits.
With a bridge of white mist
 Columbkill he crosses,
On his stately journeys
 From Slieveleague to Rosses;
Or going up with music
 On cold starry nights,
To sup with the Queen
 Of the gay Northern Lights.

They stole little Bridget
 For seven years long;

When she came down again
 Her friends were all gone.
They took her lightly back
 Between the night and morrow;
They thought that she was fast asleep,
 But she was dead with sorrow.
They have kept her ever since
 Deep within the lake,
On a bed of flag-leaves,
 Watching till she wake.

By the craggy hillside,
 Through the mosses bare,
They have planted thorn-trees
 For pleasure here and there.
Is any man so daring
 As dig them up in spite,
He shall find their sharpest thorns
 In his bed at night.

Up the airy mountain,
 Down the rushy glen,
We daren't go a-hunting
 For fear of little men;
Wee folk, good folk,
 Trooping all together;
Green jacket, red cap,
 And white owl's feather!

The Fairies[2]

ROSE FYLEMAN

There are fairies at the bottom of our garden!
 It's not so very, very far away;

[1] From William Allingham, *Robin Redbreast and Other Verses* (Macmillan).

[2] From Rose Fyleman, *Fairies and Chimneys* (Doubleday).

You pass the gardener's shed and you just
    keep straight ahead —
I do so hope they've really come to stay.
There's a little wood, with moss in it and
    beetles,
And a little stream that quietly runs
    through;
You wouldn't think they'd dare to come
    merry-making there—
        Well, they do.

There are fairies at the bottom of our garden!
    They often have a dance on summer
    nights;
The butterflies and bees make a lovely little
    breeze,
And the rabbits stand about and hold the
    lights.
Did you know that they could sit upon the
    moonbeams
And pick a little star to make a fan,
And dance away up there in the middle of
    the air?
        Well, they can.

There are fairies at the bottom of our garden!
    You cannot think how beautiful they are;
They all stand up and sing when the Fairy
        Queen and King
    Come gently floating down upon their
    car.
The King is very proud and *very* handsome;
    The Queen — now can you guess who that
    could be
(She's a little girl all day, but at night she
    steals away)?
        Well — it's Me!

A Fairy Went A-Marketing[3]

ROSE FYLEMAN

A fairy went a-marketing —
    She bought a little fish,
She put it in a crystal bowl
    Upon a golden dish.
An hour she sat in wonderment
    And watched its silver gleam,
And then she gently took it up
    And slipped it in a stream.

[3] *Ibid.*

A fairy went a-marketing —
    She bought a colored bird;
It sang the sweetest, shrillest song
    That ever she had heard.
She sat beside its painted cage
    And listened half the day,
And then she opened wide the door
    And let it fly away.

A fairy went a-marketing —
    She bought a winter gown
All stitched about with gossamer
    And lined with thistledown.
She wore it all the afternoon
    With prancing and delight,
Then gave it to a little frog
    To keep him warm at night.

A fairy went a-marketing —
    She bought a gentle mouse
To take her tiny messages,
    To keep her tiny house.
All day she kept its busy feet
    Pit-patting to and fro,
And then she kissed its silken ears,
    Thanked it, and let it go.

The Little Elf[4]

JOHN KENDRICK BANGS

I met a little Elf-man, once,
    Down where the lilies blow.
I asked him why he was so small
    And why he didn't grow.

He slightly frowned, and with his eye
    He looked me through and through.
"I'm quite as big for me," said he,
    "As you are big for you."

The Elves' Dance

AUTHOR UNKNOWN

Round about, round about
    In a fair ring-a,
Thus we dance, thus we dance
    And thus we sing-a,

[4] From *St. Nicholas Book of Verse*, ed. by Mary
Budd Skinner and Joseph Osmun Skinner (Appleton-
Century-Crofts).

Trip and go, to and fro
Over this green-a,
All about, in and out,
For our brave Queen-a.

Here We Come A-Piping

TRADITIONAL

Here we come a-piping,
In Springtime and in May;
Green fruit a-ripening,
And Winter fled away.
The Queen she sits upon the strand,
Fair as a lily, white as a wand;
Seven billows on the sea,
Horses riding fast and free,
And bells beyond the sand.

Some One[5]

WALTER DE LA MARE

Some one came knocking
  At my wee, small door;
Some one came knocking,
  I'm sure — sure — sure;
I listened, I opened,
  I looked to left and right,
But nought there was a-stirring
  In the still dark night;
Only the busy beetle
  Tap-tapping in the wall,
Only from the forest
  The screech-owl's call,
Only the cricket whistling
  While the dewdrops fall,
So I know not who came knocking,
  At all, at all, at all.

Overheard on a Saltmarsh[6]

HAROLD MONRO

Nymph, nymph, what are your beads?

Green glass, goblin. Why do you stare at
  them?

[5] From Walter de la Mare, *Peacock Pie* (Holt).
[6] From Harold Monro, *Collected Poems* (Duckworth, London).

Give them me.

No.

Give them me. Give them me.

No.

Then I will howl all night in the reeds,
Lie in the mud and howl for them.

Goblin, why do you love them so?

They are better than stars or water,
Better than voices of winds that sing,
Better than any man's fair daughter,
Your green glass beads on a silver ring.

Hush, I stole them out of the moon.

Give me your beads, I desire them.

No.

I will howl in a deep lagoon
For your green glass beads, I love them so.
Give them me. Give them.

No.

Escape[7]

ELINOR WYLIE

When foxes eat the last gold grape,
And the last white antelope is killed,
I shall stop fighting and escape
Into a little house I'll build.

But first I'll shrink to fairy size,
With a whisper no one understands,
Making blind moons of all your eyes,
And muddy roads of all your hands.

And you may grope for me in vain
In hollows under the mangrove root,
Or where, in apple-scented rain,
The silver wasp-nests hang like fruit.

[7] From Elinor Wylie, *Collected Poems* (Knopf).

"Over Hill, Over Dale"[8]

WILLIAM SHAKESPEARE

Over hill, over dale,
Through bush, through brier,
Over park, over pale,
Through flood, through fire!
I do wander everywhere,
Swifter than the moon's sphere
And I serve the fairy queen,
To dew her orbs upon the green:
The cowslips tall her pensioners be;
In their gold coats spots you see;
Those be rubies, fairy favours,
In those freckles live their savours:
I must go seek some dew-drops here,
And hang a pearl in every cowslip's ear.

"Where the Bee Sucks"[9]

WILLIAM SHAKESPEARE

Where the bee sucks, there suck I;
  In a cowslip's bell I lie;
There I couch when owls do cry,
  On the bat's back I do fly
  After summer merrily;
    Merrily, merrily shall I live now,
    Under the blossom that hangs on the
    bough.

Queen Mab[1]

WILLIAM SHAKESPEARE

O then, I see, Queen Mab hath been with
    you,
She is the fairies' midwife, and she comes
In shape no bigger than an agate-stone
On the forefinger of an alderman,
Drawn with a team of little atomies
Athwart men's noses as they lie asleep:
Her wagon-spokes made of long spinners'
    legs;

[8] From *A Midsummer Night's Dream.*
[9] From *The Tempest.*
[1] From *Romeo and Juliet.*

The cover, of the wings of grasshoppers;
The traces, of the smallest spider's web;
The collars, of the moonshine's watery
    beams;
Her whip of cricket's bone; the lash, of film;
Her wagoner, a small grey-coated gnat,
Not half so big as a round little worm
Pricked from the lazy finger of a maid:
Her chariot is an empty hazel-nut,
Made by the joiner squirrel, or old grub,
Time out o' mind the fairies' coachmakers.
And in this state she gallops night by night
Through lovers' brains, and then they dream
    of love;
O'er courtiers' knees, that dream on court'sies
    straight;
O'er lawyers' fingers, who straight dream on
    fees;
O'er ladies' lips, who straight on kisses dream.

"You Spotted Snakes"[2]

WILLIAM SHAKESPEARE

You spotted snakes with double tongue,
  Thorny hedgehogs, be not seen;
Newts and blind-worms, do no wrong;
  Come not near our fairy queen.

Philomel, with melody,
Sing in our sweet lullaby;
Lulla, lulla, lullaby; lulla, lulla, lullaby;
  Never harm,
  Nor spell nor charm,
Come our lovely lady nigh;
So, good night, with lullaby.

Weaving spiders, come not here;
Hence, you long-legg'd spinners, hence!
Beetles black, approach not near;
Worm nor snail, do no offence.

Philomel, with melody,
Sing in our sweet lullaby;
Lulla, lulla, lullaby; lulla, lulla, lullaby;
  Never harm,
  Nor spell nor charm,
Come our lovely lady nigh;
So, good night, with lullaby.

[2] From *A Midsummer Night's Dream.*

The Song of Wandering Aengus[3]

WILLIAM BUTLER YEATS

I went out to the hazel wood
Because a fire was in my head,
And cut and peeled a hazel wand,
And hooked a berry to a thread;
And when white moths were on the wing,
And moth-like stars were flickering out,
I dropped the berry in a stream,
And caught a little silver trout.

When I had laid it on the floor,
I went to blow the fire a-flame,
But something rustled on the floor,
And someone called me by my name:
It had become a glimmering girl,
With apple-blossom in her hair,
Who called me by my name and ran
And faded through the brightening air.

Though I am old with wandering
Through hollow lands and hilly lands,
I will find out where she has gone,
And kiss her lips and take her hands;
And walk among long dappled grass,
And pluck till time and times are done
The silver apples of the moon,
And golden apples of the sun.

A Song of Sherwood[4]

ALFRED NOYES

Sherwood in the twilight, is Robin Hood
  awake?
Grey and ghostly shadows are gliding
  through the brake,
Shadows of the dappled deer, dreaming of
  the morn,
Dreaming of a shadowy man that winds a
  shadowy horn.

Robin Hood is here again: all his merry
  thieves
Hear a ghostly bugle-note shivering through
  the leaves,

[3] From William Butler Yeats, *Collected Poems*
(Macmillan).
[4] From Alfred Noyes, *Collected Poems* (Lippincott).

Calling as he used to call, faint and far away,
In Sherwood, in Sherwood, about the break
  of day.

Merry, merry England has kissed the lips of
  June;
All the wings of fairyland were here beneath
  the moon,
Like a flight of rose-leaves fluttering in a mist
Of opal and ruby and pearl and amethyst.

Merry, merry England is waking as of old,
With eyes of blither hazel and hair of
  brighter gold;
For Robin Hood is here again beneath the
  bursting spray
In Sherwood, in Sherwood, about the break
  of day.

Love is in the greenwood building him a
  house
Of wild rose and hawthorn and honeysuckle
  boughs;
Love is in the greenwood, dawn is in the
  skies,
And Marian is waiting with a glory in her
  eyes.

Hark! The dazzled laverock climbs the
  golden steep!
Marian is waiting; is Robin Hood asleep?
Round the fairy grass-rings frolic elf and
  fay,
In Sherwood, in Sherwood, about the break
  of day.

Oberon, Oberon, rake away the gold,
Rake away the red leaves, roll away the
  mould,
Rake away the gold leaves, roll away the red,
And wake Will Scarlett from his leafy forest
  bed.

Friar Tuck and Little John are riding down
  together
With quarter-staff and drinking-can and grey
  goose-feather.
The dead are coming back again, the years
  are rolled away
In Sherwood, in Sherwood, about the break
  of day.

Softly over Sherwood the south wind blows.
All the heart of England hid in every rose
Hears across the greenwood the sunny whis-
    per leap,
Sherwood in the red dawn, is Robin Hood
    asleep?

Hark, the voice of England wakes him as of
    old
And, shattering the silence with a cry of
    brighter gold,
Bugles in the greenwood echo from the steep,
*Sherwood in the red dawn, is Robin Hood
    asleep?*

Where the deer are gliding down the
    shadowy glen
All across the glades of fern he calls his
    merry men —
Doublets of the Lincoln green glancing
    through the May
In Sherwood, in Sherwood, about the break
    of day —

Calls them and they answer: from aisles of
    oak and ash
Rings the *Follow! Follow!* and the boughs
    begin to crash,
The ferns begin to flutter and the flowers
    begin to fly,
And through the crimson dawning the robber
    band goes by.

Robin! Robin! Robin! All her merry thieves
Answer as the bugle-note shivers through
    the leaves,
Calling as he used to call, faint and far away,
In Sherwood, in Sherwood, about the break
    of day.

The King of China's Daughter [5]

(Variations on an old nursery rhyme)

EDITH SITWELL

I

The King of China's daughter,
She never would love me
Though I hung my cap and bells upon
Her nutmeg tree.
For oranges and lemons,
The stars in bright blue air,
(I stole them long ago, my dear)
Were dangling there.
The moon did give me silver pence,
The sun did give me gold,
And both together softly blew
And made my porridge cold;
But the King of China's daughter
Pretended not to see
When I hung my cap and bells upon
Her nutmeg tree.

II

The King of China's daughter
So beautiful to see
With her face like yellow water, left
Her nutmeg tree.
Her little rope for skipping
She kissed and gave it me —
Made of painted notes of singing-birds
Among the fields of tea.
I skipped across the nutmeg grove —
I skipped across the sea;
But neither sun nor moon, my dear,
Has yet caught me.

[5] From Edith Sitwell, *Collected Poems* (Vanguard Press).

WIND, WOODS, AND WEATHER

Laughing Song[1]

WILLIAM BLAKE

When the green woods laugh with the voice
   of joy,
And the dimpling stream runs laughing by;
When the air does laugh with our merry
   wit,
And the green hill laughs with the noise of
   it;

When the meadows laugh with lively green,
And the grasshopper laughs in the merry
   scene,
When Mary and Susan and Emily
With their sweet round mouths sing "Ha,
   Ha, He!"

When the painted birds laugh in the shade,
Where our table with cherries and nuts is
   spread,
Come live, and be merry, and join with me,
To sing the sweet chorus of "Ha, Ha, He!"

Waiting[2]

HARRY BEHN

Dreaming of honeycombs to share
With her small cubs, a mother bear
Sleeps in a snug and snowy lair.

Bees in their drowsy, drifted hive
Sip hoarded honey to survive
Until the flowers come alive.

[1] From William Blake, *Songs of Innocence.*
[2] From Harry Behn, *The Little Hill* (Harcourt, Brace).

Sleeping beneath the deep snow
Seeds of honeyed flowers know
When it is time to wake and grow.

Spring[3]

WILLIAM BLAKE

Sound the flute!
Now it's mute!
Birds delight,
Day and night,
Nightingale,
In the dale,
Lark in sky —
Merrily,
Merrily, merrily to welcome in the year.

Little boy,
Full of joy,
Little girl,
Sweet and small;
Cock does crow,
So do you;
Merry voice,
Infant noise;
Merrily, merrily we welcome in the year.

Little lamb,
Here I am;
Come and lick
My white neck;
Let me pull
Your soft wool;
Let me kiss
Your soft face;
Merrily, merrily we welcome in the year.

[3] From William Blake, *Songs of Innocence.*

The Echoing Green[4]

WILLIAM BLAKE

The sun does arise,
And make happy the skies;
The merry bells ring,
To welcome the spring;
The skylark and thrush,
The birds of the bush,
Sing louder around
To the bells' cheerful sound;
While our sports shall be seen
On the echoing green.

Old John, with white hair,
Does laugh away care,
Sitting under the oak,
Among the old folk.
They laugh at our play,
And soon they all say,
"Such, such were the joys
When we all — girls and boys —
In our youth-time were seen
On the echoing green."

Till the little ones, weary,
No more can be merry:
The sun does descend,
And our sports have an end.
Round the laps of their mothers
Many sisters and brothers,
Like birds in their nest,
Are ready for rest,
And sport no more seen
On the darkening green.

In Just-spring[5]

E. E. CUMMINGS

in Just-
spring   when the world is mud-
luscious the little
lame balloonman

whistles   far   and wee

4 From William Blake, *Songs of Innocence*.
b From E. E. Cummings, *Poems, 1923–1954* (Harcourt, Brace).

and eddieandbill come
running from marbles and
piracies and it's
spring

when the world is puddle-wonderful

the queer
old balloonman whistles
far   and   wee
and bettyandisbel come dancing

from hop-scotch and jump-rope and

it's
spring
and
      the
            goat-footed

balloonMan   whistles
far
and
wee

March

WILLIAM WORDSWORTH

The cock is crowing,
The stream is flowing,
The small birds twitter,
The lake doth glitter,
The green field sleeps in the sun;
The oldest and youngest
Are at work with the strongest;
The cattle are grazing,
Their heads never raising;
There are forty feeding like one!

Like an army defeated
The snow hath retreated,
And now doth fare ill
On the top of the bare hill;
The Plowboy is whooping — anon — anon:
There's joy in the mountains;
There's life in the fountains;
Small clouds are sailing,
Blue sky prevailing;
The rain is over and gone!

Little Wind [6]

KATE GREENAWAY

Little wind, blow on the hill-top;
Little wind, blow down the plain;
Little wind, blow up the sunshine,
Little wind, blow off the rain.

Who Has Seen the Wind? [7]

CHRISTINA ROSSETTI

Who has seen the wind?
  Neither I nor you:
But when the leaves hang trembling
  The wind is passing thro'.

Who has seen the wind?
  Neither you nor I:
But when the trees bow down their heads
  The wind is passing by.

The Wind [8]

ROBERT LOUIS STEVENSON

I saw you toss the kites on high
And blow the birds about the sky;
And all around I heard you pass,
Like ladies' skirts across the grass —
    O wind, a-blowing all day long,
    O wind, that sings so loud a song!

I saw the different things you did,
But always you yourself you hid.
I felt you push, I heard you call,
I could not see yourself at all —
    O wind, a-blowing all day long,
    O wind, that sings so loud a song!

O you that are so strong and cold,
O blower, are you young or old?
Are you a beast of field and tree,
Or just a stronger child than me?
    O wind, a-blowing all day long,
    O wind, that sings so loud a song!

Windy Wash Day [9]

DOROTHY ALDIS

The wash is hanging on the line
And the wind's blowing —
Dresses all so clean and fine,
Beckoning
And bowing.

Stockings twisting in a dance,
Pajamas very tripping,
And every little pair of pants
Upside down
And skipping.

The Kite [1]

HARRY BEHN

How bright on the blue
Is a kite when it's new!

With a dive and a dip
It snaps its tail

Then soars like a ship
With only a sail

As over tides
Of wind it rides,

Climbs to the crest
Of a gust and pulls,

Then seems to rest
As wind falls.

When string goes slack
You wind it back

And run until
A new breeze blows

And its wings fill
And up it goes!

How bright on the blue
Is a kite when it's new!

[6] From Kate Greenaway, *Under the Window.*
[7] From Christina Rossetti, *Sing-Song.*
[8] From Robert Louis Stevenson, *A Child's Garden of Verses.*

[9] From *Child Life Magazine.*
[1] From Harry Behn, *Windy Morning* (Harcourt, Brace).

But a raggeder thing
You never will see

When it flaps on a string
In the top of a tree.

Song (April)[2]

WILLIAM WATSON

April, April,
Laugh thy girlish laughter;
Then, the moment after,
Weep thy girlish tears,
April, that mine ears
Like a lover greetest,

If I tell thee, sweetest,
All my hopes and fears.
April, April,
Laugh thy golden laughter,
But, the moment after,
Weep thy golden tears!

April[3]

SARA TEASDALE

The roofs are shining from the rain,
   The sparrows twitter as they fly,
And with a windy April grace
   The little clouds go by.

Yet the back-yards are bare and brown
   With only one unchanging tree —
I could not be so sure of Spring
   Save that it sings in me.

Home Thoughts from Abroad

ROBERT BROWNING

Oh, to be in England
Now that April's there,
And whoever wakes in England
Sees, some morning, unaware,

That the lowest boughs and the brushwood
   sheaf
Round the elm tree bole are in tiny leaf,
While the chaffinch sings on the orchard
   bough
In England — now!

And after April, when May follows,
And the whitethroat builds and all the swal,
   lows!
Hark, where my blossomed pear tree in the
   hedge
Leans to the field and scatters on the clover
Blossoms and dewdrops — at the bent spray's
   edge —
That's the wise thrush; he sings each song
   twice over,
Lest you should think he never could recap-
   ture
The first fine careless rapture!
And though the fields look rough with hoary
   dew,
All will be gay when noontide wakes anew
The buttercups, the little children's dower —
Far brighter than this gaudy melon-flower!

April and May

RALPH WALDO EMERSON

April cold with dropping rain
Willows and lilacs bring again,
The whistle of returning birds,
And trumpet-lowing of the herds;
The scarlet maple-keys betray
What potent blood hath modest May;
What fiery force the earth renews,
The wealth of forms, the flush of hues;
What Joy in rosy waves outpoured,
Flows from the heart of Love, the Lord.

The Pasture[4]

ROBERT FROST

I'm going out to clean the pasture spring;
I'll only stop to rake the leaves away
(And wait to watch the water clear, I may):
I sha'n't be gone long. — You come too.

2 From William Watson, Poems.
3 From Sara Teasdale, Rivers to the Sea (Mac-millan).
4 From Robert Frost, Collected Poems (Holt).

I'm going out to fetch the little calf
That's standing by the mother. It's so young,
It totters when she licks it with her tongue.
I sha'n't be gone long.—You come too.

Dandelion [5]

(Written at the age of eight)

HILDA CONKLING

O Little Soldier with the golden helmet,
What are you guarding on my lawn?
You with your green gun
And your yellow beard,
Why do you stand so stiff?
There is only the grass to fight!

To the Dandelion

JAMES RUSSELL LOWELL

Dear common flower, that grow'st beside
    the way,
Fringing the dusty road with harmless gold,
    First pledge of blithesome May,
Which children pluck, and, full of pride, up-
    hold,
    High-hearted buccaneers, o'erjoyed that
        they
An Eldorado in the grass have found,
    Which not the rich earth's ample round
May match in wealth, thou art more dear
    to me
Than all the prouder summer-blooms may
    be.

Daffodils

WILLIAM WORDSWORTH

I wandered lonely as a cloud
    That floats on high o'er vales and hills,
When all at once I saw a crowd,
    A host, of golden daffodils;

Beside the lake, beneath the trees,
Fluttering and dancing in the breeze.

Continuous as the stars that shine
    And twinkle on the milky way,
They stretched in never-ending line
    Along the margin of a bay:
Ten thousand saw I at a glance,
    Tossing their heads in sprightly dance.

The waves beside them danced, but they
    Outdid the sparkling waves in glee:
A poet could not but be gay,
    In such a jocund company.
I gazed—and gazed—but little thought
    What wealth the show to me had brought;

For oft, when on my couch I lie
    In vacant or in pensive mood,
They flash upon that inward eye
    Which is the bliss of solitude;
And then my heart with pleasure fills,
    And dances with the daffodils.

To Daffodils [6]

ROBERT HERRICK

Fair Daffodils, we weep to see
    You haste away so soon;
As yet the early-rising sun
    Has not attained his noon.
        Stay, stay,
Until the hastening day
        Has run
    But to the even-song;
And, having prayed together, we
    Will go with you along.

We have short time to stay, as you,
    We have as short a spring;
As quick a growth to meet decay,
    As you, or anything.
        We die
As your hours do, and dry
        Away,
    Like to the summer's rain;
Or as the pearls of morning's dew,
    Ne'er to be found again.

[5] From Hilda Conkling, *Poems by a Little Girl* (Lippincott).

[6] From Robert Herrick, *Hesperides*.

Pussy Willows[7]

ROWENA BASTIN BENNETT

I came on them yesterday (merely by chance)
Those newly born pussies, asleep on a
branch;
Each curled up so tight in a fluff of a ball
That I could not see ear-points nor tail-tips
at all;
But I thought that I heard when the March
wind was stirring,
A soft little sound like the note of purring.
I wonder if they would have leaped from
their bough
And arched their wee backs with a frightened
"Meow!"
If I dared to tell them in one warning cry
That a fierce patch of dogwood was growing
close by.

Sweet Peas

JOHN KEATS

Here are sweet peas, on tiptoe for a flight:
With wings of gentle flush o'er delicate white,
And taper fingers catching at all things,
To bind them all about with tiny rings.
Linger awhile upon some bending planks
That lean against a streamlet's rushy banks,
And watch intently Nature's gentle doings:
They will be found softer than ringdove's
cooings.
How silent comes the water round that bend!
Not the minutest whisper does it send
To the o'erhanging sallows: blades of grass
Slowly across the chequer'd shadows pass.

Rain[8]

ROBERT LOUIS STEVENSON

The rain is raining all around,
   It falls on field and tree,
It rains on the umbrellas here,
   And on the ships at sea.

[7] From Rowena Bastin Bennett, *Around a Toad-stool Table* (Follett).
[8] From Robert Louis Stevenson, *A Child's Garden of Verses*.

The Rain[9]

ROWENA BASTIN BENNETT

The rain, they say, is a mouse-gray horse
   That is shod with a silver shoe;
The sound of his hoofs can be heard on the
      roofs
As he gallops the whole night through.

Rubber Boots[1]

ROWENA BASTIN BENNETT

Little boots and big boots,
   Traveling together
On the shiny sidewalks,
   In the rainy weather,
Little boots and big boots,
   Oh, it must be fun
To splash the silver raindrops
   About you as you run,
Or scatter bits of rainbow
   Beneath the April sun!

Big boots and little boots,
   You know how it feels
To have the white clouds drifting
   Far below your heels;
And it is dizzy pleasure,
   Along the way to school,
To walk the lacy tree tops
   That lie in every pool.

Little boots and big boots,
   How you like to putter
In every slender streamlet
   That scampers down the gutter!

The Umbrella Brigade[2]

LAURA E. RICHARDS

"Pitter patter!" falls the rain
On the school-room window-pane.
Such a plashing! such a dashing!
Will it e'er be dry again?

[9] Rowena Bastin Bennett, *Around a Toadstool Table* (Follett).
[1] *Ibid.*
[2] From Laura E. Richards, *Tirra Lirra* (Little, Brown).

Down the gutter rolls a flood,
And the crossing's deep in mud;
And the puddles! oh, the puddles
Are a sight to stir one's blood!

Chorus

But let it rain
Tree-toads and frogs,
Muskets and pitchforks,
Kittens and dogs!
Dash away! plash away!
Who is afraid?
Here we go,
The Umbrella Brigade!

Pull the boots up to the knee!
Tie the hoods on merrily!
Such a hustling! such a jostling!
Out of breath with fun are we.
Clatter, clatter, down the street,
Greeting every one we meet,
With our laughing and our chaffing,
Which the laughing drops repeat.

Chorus

So let it rain
Tree-toads and frogs,
Muskets and pitchforks,
Kittens and dogs!
Dash away! plash away!
Who is afraid?
Here we go,
The Umbrella Brigade!

Cape Ann[3]

T. S. Eliot

O quick quick quick, quick hear the song-
sparrow,
Swamp-sparrow, fox-sparrow, vesper-sparrow
At dawn and dusk. Follow the dance
Of the goldfinch at noon. Leave to chance
The Blackburnian warbler, the shy one. Hail
With shrill whistle the note of the quail, the
bob-white
Dodging by bay-bush. Follow the feet
Of the walker, the water-thrush. Follow the
flight

[3] From T. S. Eliot, *The Complete Poems and Plays*
(Harcourt, Brace).

Of the dancing arrow, the purple martin.
Greet
In silence the bullbat. All are delectable.
Sweet sweet sweet
But resign this land at the end, resign it
To its true owner, the tough one, the sea-
gull.
The palaver is finished.

In Arden Forest[4]

WILLIAM SHAKESPEARE

Under the greenwood tree,
Who loves to lie with me,
And turn his merry note
Unto the sweet bird's throat,
Come hither, come hither, come hither!
Here shall he see
No enemy
But winter and rough weather.

Who doth ambition shun
And loves to live i' the sun,
Seeking the food he eats
And pleased with what he gets,
Come hither, come hither, come hither!
Here shall he see
No enemy
But winter and rough weather.

A Morning Song[5]

WILLIAM SHAKESPEARE

Hark, hark! the lark at heaven's gate sings,
And Phoebus 'gins arise,
His steeds to water at those springs
On chaliced flowers that lies;
And winking Mary-buds begin
To ope their golden eyes;
With everything that pretty is,
My lady sweet, arise;
Arise, arise.

[4] From *As You Like It*.
[5] From *Cymbeline*.

Loveliest of Trees[6]

ALFRED EDWARD HOUSMAN

Loveliest of trees, the cherry now
Is hung with bloom along the bough
And stands about the woodland ride
Wearing white for Eastertide.

Now, of my threescore years and ten,
Twenty will not come again,
And take from seventy springs a score,
It only leaves me fifty more.

And since to look at things in bloom
Fifty springs are little room,
About the woodlands I will go
To see the cherry hung with snow.

Trees[7]

HARRY BEHN

Trees are the kindest things I know,
They do no harm, they simply grow

And spread a shade for sleepy cows,
And gather birds among their boughs.

They give us fruit in leaves above,
And wood to make our houses of,

And leaves to burn on Hallowe'en,
And in the Spring new buds of green.

They are the first when day's begun
To touch the beams of morning sun,

They are the last to hold the light
When evening changes into night,

And when a moon floats on the sky
They hum a drowsy lullaby

Of sleepy children long ago . . .
Trees are the kindest things I know.

[6] From Alfred Edward Housman, *A Shropshire Lad.*

[7] From Harry Behn, *The Little Hill* (Harcourt, Brace).

The Bridge[8]

CHRISTINA ROSSETTI

Boats sail on the rivers,
    And ships sail on the seas;
But clouds that sail across the sky
    Are prettier far than these.

There are bridges on the rivers,
    As pretty as you please;
But the bow that bridges heaven,
    And overtops the trees,
And builds a road from earth to sky,
    Is prettier far than these.

The Painted Desert[9]

ELIZABETH COATSWORTH

The Navajo

Lean and tall and stringy are the Navajo,
Workers in silver and turquoise, herders of
    flocks,
Their sheep and goats cover the hills like
    scattered rocks.
They wear velvet shirts, they are proud, they
    go
Through the sage, upright on thin bright
    horses.
Their speech is low.
At their necks they gather the black smooth
    cataract of their locks.
Quick are their eyes and bright as the eyes
    of a fox.
You may pass close by their encampments
    and never know.

In Walpi

There is an eagle screaming from a roof
In Walpi, a black eagle with pale eyes.
The kitchen smoke
Morning and evening rises in pale columns
About him. At noon the heat beats down
Upon his head and lies like fire on his shoul-
    ders.

[8] From Christina Rossetti, *Sing-Song.*

[9] Elizabeth Coatsworth, *Compass Rose* (Coward-McCann).

He never sees the Indians below him,
His captors, all day, his look goes out
Across the striped reds of the painted desert,
All day he looks far off to cloud-hung mesas,
All day he screams.

Ceremonial Hunt

As the racing circle closed in like a lasso
Of running dogs and horses, as the sage was
    swept,
Out of the turmoil suddenly upward leapt
A jack-rabbit's fawn and jet, with its great
    soft eye
And fantastic ears outlined against the sky,
Hanging in life a strange moment, then fall-
    ing back
From that remote beautiful leap to the teeth
    of the pack,
And the trampling hoofs and the Indians'
    thin halloo.

Yucca [1]

ANN NOLAN CLARK

Yucca
Growing
So tall,
Like candles;
So white,
Like candles;
With a flower
For light.

We twist your little leaves
Into strings of thread;
We knot your strong stems
Into rope.
We weave your fibers
Into mats and baskets;
We pound your roots
For soap to make us clean.

Yucca,
Tall, white Yucca,
You make my heart sing
With your beauty.

[1] Ann Nolan Clark, *In My Mother's House* (Viking
Press).

Fog [2]

CARL SANDBURG

The fog comes
on little cat feet.
It sits looking
over harbor and city
on silent haunches
and then moves on.

Lost [3]

CARL SANDBURG

Desolate and lone
All night long on the lake
Where fog trails and mist creeps,
The whistle of a boat
Calls and cries unendingly,
Like some lost child
In tears and trouble
Hunting the harbor's breast
And the harbor's eyes.

The Branch [4]

ELIZABETH MADOX ROBERTS

We stopped at the branch on the way to the
    hill.
We stopped at the water awhile and played.
We hid our things by the osage tree
And took off our shoes and stockings to wade.

There is sand at the bottom that bites at your
    feet,
And there is a rock where the waterfall goes.
You can poke your foot in the foamy part
And feel how the water runs over your toes.

The little black spiders that walk on the top
Of the water are hard and stiff and cool.
And I saw some wiggletails going around,
And some slippery minnows that live in the
    pool.

[2] From Carl Sandburg, *Chicago Poems* (Holt).
[3] *Ibid.*
[4] From Elizabeth Madox Roberts, *Under the Tree*
(Viking Press).

And where it is smooth there is moss on a
    stone,
And where it is shallow and almost dry,
The rocks are broken and hot in the sun,
And a rough little water goes hurrying by.

Song of the Brook

ALFRED, LORD TENNYSON

I come from haunts of coot and hern,
    I make a sudden sally,
And sparkle out among the fern,
    To bicker down a valley.

By thirty hills I hurry down,
    Or slip between the ridges,
By twenty thorps, a little town,
    And half a hundred bridges.

I chatter over stony ways,
    In little sharps and trebles,
I bubble into eddying bays,
    I babble on the pebbles.

With many a curve my banks I fret
    By many a field and fallow,
And many a fairy foreland set
    With willow-weed and mallow.

I chatter, chatter, as I flow
    To join the brimming river,
For men may come and men may go,
    But I go on forever.

I wind about, and in and out.
    With here a blossom sailing,
And here and there a lusty trout,
    And here and there a grayling,

And here and there a foamy flake
    Upon me, as I travel
With many a silvery water-break
    Above the golden gravel,

And draw them all along, and flow
    To join the brimming river,
For men may come and men may go,
    But I go on forever.

I steal by lawns and grassy plots,
    I slide by hazel covers;
I move the sweet forget-me-nots
    That grow for happy lovers.

I slip, I slide, I gloom, I glance
    Among my skimming swallows,
I make the netted sunbeam dance
    Against my sandy shallows.

I murmur under moon and stars
    In brambly wildernesses;
I linger by my shingly bars;
    I loiter round my cresses;

And out again I curve and flow
    To join the brimming river,
For men may come and men may go,
    But I go on forever.

Minnows[5]

JOHN KEATS

How silent comes the water round that bend;
Not the minutest whisper does it send
To the o'erhanging sallows; blades of grass
Slowly across the chequer'd shadows pass —
Why, you might read two sonnets, ere they
    reach
To where the hurrying freshnesses aye preach
A natural sermon o'er their pebbly beds;
Where swarms of minnows show their little
    heads,
Staying their wavy bodies 'gainst the streams,
To taste the luxury of sunny beams
Tempered with coolness. How they ever
    wrestle
With their own sweet delight, and ever
    nestle
Their silver bellies on the pebbly sand.
If you but scantily hold out the hand,
That very instant not one will remain;
But turn your eye, and they are there again.

The ripples seem right glad to reach those
    cresses,
And cool themselves among the em'rald
    tresses;

[5] From "I Stood Tip-Toe Upon a Little Hill."

The while they cool themselves, they fresh-
    ness give,
And moisture, that the bowery green may
    live.

The Lake Isle of Innisfree[6]

WILLIAM BUTLER YEATS

I will arise and go now, and go to Innisfree,
And a small cabin build there, of clay and
    wattles made;
Nine bean rows will I have there, a hive for
    the honey bee,
    And live alone in the bee-loud glade.

And I shall have some peace there, for peace
    comes dropping slow,
Dropping from the veils of the morning to
    where the cricket sings;
There midnight's all a glimmer, and noon a
    purple glow,
    And evening full of the linnet's wings.

I will arise and go now, for always night and
    day
I hear lake water lapping with low sounds by
    the shore;
While I stand on the roadway, or on the
    pavements gray,
    I hear it in the deep heart's core.

I Meant to Do My Work Today[7]

RICHARD LE GALLIENNE

I meant to do my work today,
But a brown bird sang in the apple-tree,
And a butterfly flitted across the field,
And all the leaves were calling me.

And the wind went sighing over the land,
Tossing the grasses to and fro,
And a rainbow held out its shining hand —
So what could I do but laugh and go?

    6 From William Butler Yeats, *Collected Poems*
(Macmillan).
    7 From Richard Le Gallienne, *The Lonely Dancer
and Other Poems* (Dodd, Mead).

The Cloud

PERCY BYSSHE SHELLEY

I bring fresh showers for the thirsting flowers,
    From the seas and the streams;
I bear light shade for the leaves when laid
    In their noonday dreams.
From my wings are shaken the dews that
    waken
    The sweet buds every one,
When rocked to rest on their mother's breast
    As she dances about the sun.
I wield the flail of the lashing hail,
    And whiten the green plains under,
And then again I dissolve it in rain,
    And laugh as I pass in thunder.

I sift the snow on the mountains below,
    And their great pines groan aghast;
And all the night 'tis my pillow white,
    While I sleep in the arms of the blast.
Sublime on the towers of my skyey bowers,
    Lightning my pilot sits;
In a cavern under is fettered the thunder,
    It struggles and howls at fits;
Over earth and ocean, with gentle motion,
    This pilot is guiding me,
Lured by the love of the genii that move
    In the depths of the purple sea;
Over the rills, and the crags, and the hills,
    Over the lakes and the plains,
Wherever he dream, under mountain or
    stream,
    The Spirit he loves remains;
And I all the while bask in heaven's blue
    smile,
    Whilst he is dissolving in rains.

The sanguine sunrise, with his meteor eyes,
    And his burning plumes outspread,
Leaps on the back of my sailing rack,
    When the morning star shines dead;
As on the jag of a mountain crag,
    Which an earthquake rocks and swings,
An eagle alit one moment may sit
    In the light of its golden wings,
And when sunset may breathe, from the lit
    sea beneath,
    Its ardors of rest and of love,
And the crimson pall of eve may fall
    From the depth of heaven above.

With wings folded I rest, on mine airy nest,
  As still as a brooding dove.

That orbèd maiden with white fire laden,
  Whom mortals call the moon,
Glides glimmering o'er my fleece like floor,
  By the midnight breezes strewn;
And wherever the beat of her unseen feet,
  Which only the angels hear,
May have broken the woof of my tent's thin
    roof,
  The stars peep behind her and peer;
And I laugh to see them whirl and flee,
  Like a swarm of golden bees,
When I widen the rent in my wind-built tent,
  Till the calm rivers, lakes, and seas,
Like strips of the sky fallen through me on
    high,
  Are each paved with the moon and these.

I bind the sun's throne with a burning zone,
  And the moon's with a girdle of pearl;
The volcanoes are dim, and the stars reel and
    swim,
  When the whirlwinds my banner unfurl.
From cape to cape, with a bridge-like shape,
  Over a torrent sea,
Sunbeam-proof, I hang like a roof —
  The mountains its columns be.
The triumphal arch through which I march
  With hurricane, fire and snow,
When the powers of the air are chained to
    my chair,
  Is the million-colored bow;
The sphere-fire above its soft colors wove,
  While the moist earth was laughing below.

I am the daughter of earth and water,
  And the nursling of the sky;
I pass through the pores of the ocean and
    shores;
  I change, but I cannot die.
For after the rain when with never a stain
  The pavilion of heaven is bare,
And the winds and sunbeams with their
    convex gleams
  Build up the blue dome of air,
I silently laugh at my own cenotaph,
  And out of the caverns of rain,
Like a child from the womb, like a ghost
    from the tomb,
  I arise and unbuild it again.

Glimpse in Autumn[8]

JEAN STARR UNTERMEYER

Ladies at a ball
  Are not so fine as these
  Richly brocaded trees
That decorate the fall.

They stand against a wall
  Of crisp October sky,
  Their plumèd heads held high,
Like ladies at a ball.

The Morns Are Meeker than They Were[9]

EMILY DICKINSON

The morns are meeker than they were,
The nuts are getting brown;
The berry's cheek is plumper,
The rose is out of town.

The maple wears a gayer scarf,
The field a scarlet gown.
Lest I should be old-fashioned,
I'll put a trinket on.

Autumn Fires[1]

ROBERT LOUIS STEVENSON

In the other gardens
  And all up the vale,
From the autumn bonfires
  See the smoke trail!

Pleasant summer over
  And all the summer flowers,
The red fire blazes,
  The grey smoke towers.

Sing a song of seasons!
  Something bright in all!
Flowers in the summer,
  Fires in the fall!

[8] From Jean Starr Untermeyer, *Dreams Out of Darkness* (Viking Press).

[9] From *The Poems of Emily Dickinson*, ed. Martha Dickinson Bianchi and Alfred Leete Hampson (Little, Brown).

[1] From Robert Louis Stevenson, *A Child's Garden of Verses*.

A Vagabond Song[2]

BLISS CARMAN

There is something in the autumn that is
    native to my blood —
Touch of manner, hint of mood;
And my heart is like a rhyme,
    With the yellow and the purple and the
    crimson keeping time.

The scarlet of the maples can shake me like
    a cry
Of bugles going by.
And my lonely spirit thrills
To see the frosty asters like a smoke upon
    the hills.

There is something in October sets the gipsy
    blood astir;
We must rise and follow her,
When from every hill of flame
She calls and calls each vagabond by name.

Color in the Wheat[3]

HAMLIN GARLAND

Like a liquid gold the wheat field lies,
    A marvel of yellow and russet and green,
That ripples and runs, that floats and flies,
    With the subtle shadows, the change, the
        sheen,
        That play in the golden hair of a girl—
        A ripple of amber — a flare
    Of light sweeping after — a curl
    In the hollows like swirling feet
        Of fairy waltzers, the colors run
        To the western sun
    Through the deeps of the ripening
        wheat.

Broad as the fleckless, soaring sky,
    Mysterious, fair as the moon-led sea,
The vast plain flames on the dazzled eye
    Under the fierce sun's alchemy.
        The slow hawk stoops
        To his prey in the deeps;
        The sunflower droops
        To the lazy wave; the wind sleeps —

Then swirling in dazzling links and
    loops,
    A riot of shadow and shine,
    A glory of olive and amber and wine,
To the westering sun the colors run
Through the deeps of the ripening
    wheat.

The Last Word of a Bluebird[4]

(As Told to a Child)

ROBERT FROST

As I went out a Crow
In a low voice said, "Oh,
I was looking for you.
How do you do?
I just came to tell you
To tell Lesley (will you?)
That her little Bluebird
Wanted me to bring word
That the north wind last night
That made the stars bright
And made ice on the trough
Almost made him cough
His tail feathers off.
He just had to fly!
But he sent her Good-by,
And said to be good,
And wear her red hood,
And look for skunk tracks
In the snow with an ax —
And do everything!
And perhaps in the spring
He would come back and sing."

Something Told the Wild Geese[5]

RACHEL FIELD

Something told the wild geese
    It was time to go.
Though the fields lay golden
    Something whispered, — "Snow."
Leaves were green and stirring,
    Berries, luster-glossed,
But beneath warm feathers
    Something cautioned, — "Frost."

---

2 From Bliss Carman, *Vagabondia* (Dodd, Mead).
3 From Hamlin Garland, *Prairie Songs*.
4 From Robert Frost, *Mountain Interval* (Holt).
5 From Rachel Field, *Branches Green* (Macmillan).

All the sagging orchards
  Steamed with amber spice,
But each wild breast stiffened
  At remembered ice.
Something told the wild geese
  It was time to fly,
Summer sun was on their wings,
  Winter in their cry

To the Fringed Gentian

WILLIAM CULLEN BRYANT

Thou blossom bright with Autumn dew,
And colored with heaven's own blue,
That openest when the quiet light
Succeeds the keen and frosty night.

Thou comest not when violets lean,
O'er wandering brooks and springs unseen,
Or columbines, in purple dressed
Nod o'er the ground bird's hidden nest.

Thou waitest late and com'st alone,
When woods are bare and birds are flown,
And frosts and shortening days portend,
The aged year is near its end.

Then doth thy sweet and quiet eye,
Look through its fringes to the sky,
Blue, blue — as if that sky let fall,
A flower from its cerulean wall.

I would that thus, when I shall see
The hour of death draw near to me,
Hope, blossoming within my heart,
May look to heaven as I depart.

Hallowe'en [6]

HARRY BEHN

Tonight is the night
When dead leaves fly
Like witches on switches
Across the sky,
When elf and sprite
Flit through the night
On a moony sheen.

Tonight is the night
When leaves make a sound
Like a gnome in his home
Under the ground,
When spooks and trolls
Creep out of holes
Mossy and green.

Tonight is the night
When pumpkins stare
Through sheaves and leaves
Everywhere,
When ghoul and ghost
And goblin host
Dance round their queen.
It's Hallowe'en!

What Am I? [7]

DOROTHY ALDIS

They chose me from my brothers: "That's
    the
Nicest one," they said,
And they carved me out a face and put a
Candle in my head;

And they set me on the doorstep. Oh, the
Night was dark and wild;
But when they lit the candle, then I
Smiled!

God's World [8]

EDNA ST. VINCENT MILLAY

O World, I cannot hold thee close enough!
  Thy winds, thy wide grey skies!
  Thy mists that roll and rise!
Thy woods, this autumn day, that ache and
  sag
And all but cry with colour! That gaunt
  crag
To crush! To lift the lean of that black
  bluff!
World, World, I cannot get thee close
  enough!

[7] From Dorothy Aldis, *Hop! Skip! and Jump!* (Putnam).

[8] From Edna St. Vincent Millay, *Renascence and Other Poems* (Harper).

[6] From Harry Behn, *The Little Hill* (Harcourt, Brace).

Long have I known a glory in it all,
  But never knew I this;
  Here such a passion is
As stretcheth me apart. Lord, I do fear
Thou'st made the world too beautiful this
    year.
My soul is all but out of me — let fall
No burning leaf; prithee, let no bird call.

To Autumn

JOHN KEATS

Season of mists and mellow fruitfulness!
  Close bosom-friend of the maturing sun;
Conspiring with him how to load and bless
  With fruit the vines that round the thatch-
    eaves run.
To bend with apples the moss'd cottage-trees,
  And fill all fruit with ripeness to the core;
    To swell the gourd, and plump the hazel
      shells
    With a sweet kernel; to set budding
      more,
And still more, later flowers for the bees,
Until they think warm days will never cease,
    For summer has o'er-brimm'd their
      clammy cells.

Who hath not seen thee oft amid thy store?
  Sometimes whoever seeks abroad may find
Thee sitting careless on a granary floor,
  Thy hair soft-lifted by the winnowing
    wind;
Or on a half-reap'd furrow sound asleep,
  Drowsed with the fumes of poppies, while
    thy hook
    Spares the next swath and all its twined
      flowers:
And sometimes like a gleaner thou dost keep
  Steady thy laden head across a brook;
  Or by a cider-press, with patient look,
    Thou watchest the last oozings, hours
    by hours.

Where are the songs of Spring? Ay, where
  are they?
  Think not of them, thou hast thy music
    too,
    While barred clouds bloom the soft-
    dying day.
And touch the stubble-plains with rosy hue;

Then in a wailful choir the small gnats
  mourn
Among the river sallows, borne aloft
  Or sinking as the light wind lives or
    dies;
And full-grown lambs loud bleat from hilly
  bourn;
Hedge-crickets sing; and now with treble
  soft
The redbreast whistles from a garden-croft,
  And gathering swallows twitter in the skies.

Wizard Frost [9]

FRANK DEMPSTER SHERMAN

Wondrous things have come to pass
On my square of window-glass.
Looking in it I have seen
Grass no longer painted green,
Trees whose branches never stir,
Skies without a cloud to blur,
Birds below them sailing high,
Church-spires pointing to the sky,
And a funny little town
Where the people, up and down
Streets of silver, to me seem
Like the people in a dream,
Dressed in finest kinds of lace:
'Tis a picture, on a space
Scarcely larger than the hand,
Of a tiny Switzerland,
Which the wizard Frost had drawn
'Twixt the nightfall and the dawn.
Quick! and see what he has done
Ere 'tis stolen by the Sun.

The Frost Pane [1]

DAVID McCORD

What's the good of breathing
On the window
Pane
In summer?
You can't make a frost
On the window pane
In summer.

[9] From Frank Dempster Sherman, *Little-Folk Lyrics*
(Houghton Mifflin).
[1] From David McCord, *Far and Few* (Little, Brown).

You can't write a
Nalphabet,
You can't draw a
Nelephant;
You can't make a smudge
With your nose
In summer.

Lots of good, breathing
On the window
Pane
In winter.
You can make a frost
On the window pane
In winter.
A white frost, a light frost,
A thick frost, a quick frost,
A write-me-out-a-picture-frost
Across the pane
In winter.

The Snowfluke[2]

WALTER DE LA MARE

Before I melt,
Come, look at me!
This lovely icy filigree!
Of a great forest
In one night
I make a wilderness
Of white:
By skyey cold
Of crystals made,
All softly, on
Your finger laid,
I pause, that you
My beauty see:
Breathe, and I vanish
Instantly.

For Snow[3]

ELEANOR FARJEON

Oh the falling Snow!
Oh the falling Snow!
Where does it all come from?
Whither does it go?

Never never laughing,
Never never weeping,
Falling in its Sleep,
Forever ever sleeping —
From what Sleep of Heaven
Does it flow, and go
Into what Sleep of Earth,
The falling, falling Snow?

Velvet Shoes[4]

ELINOR WYLIE

Let us walk in the white snow
  In a soundless space;
With footsteps quiet and slow,
  At a tranquil pace,
  Under veils of white lace.

I shall go shod in silk,
  And you in wool,
White as a white cow's milk,
  More beautiful
  Than the breast of a gull.

We shall walk through the still town
  In a windless peace;
We shall step upon the white down,
  Upon silver fleece,
  Upon softer than these.

We shall walk in velvet shoes;
  Wherever we go
Silence will fall like dews
  On white silence below.
  We shall walk in the snow.

Stopping by Woods on a Snowy Evening[5]

ROBERT FROST

Whose woods these are I think I know.
His house is in the village though;
He will not see me stopping here
To watch his woods fill up with snow.

[2] From Walter de la Mare, *Bells and Grass* (Viking Press).
[3] From Eleanor Farjeon, *Collected Poems*.

[4] From Elinor Wylie, *Collected Poems* (Knopf).
[5] From Robert Frost, *New Hampshire* (Holt).

My little horse must think it queer
To stop without a farmhouse near
Between the woods and frozen lake
The darkest evening of the year.

He gives his harness bells a shake
To ask if there is some mistake.
The only other sound's the sweep
Of easy wind and downy flake.

The woods are lovely, dark and deep.
But I have promises to keep,
And miles to go before I sleep,
And miles to go before I sleep.

Lines from "Snowbound"

JOHN GREENLEAF WHITTIER

Unwarmed by any sunset light
The grey day darkened into night,
A night made hoary with the swarm
And whirlwind of the blinding storm,
As zigzag, wavering to and fro,
Crossed and recrossed the wingèd snow.
And ere the early bed-time came
The white drift piled the window frame,
And through the dark the clothes-line posts
Looked in like tall and sheeted ghosts.

So all night long the storm roared on;
The morning broke without a sun;
In tiny spherule traced with lines
Of Nature's geometric signs,
In starry flake, and pellicle,
All day the hoary meteor fell;
And, when the second morning shone,
We looked upon a world unknown,
On nothing we could call our own.
Around the glistening wonder bent
The blue walls of the firmament,
No clouds above, no earth below, —
A universe of sky and snow!

The old familiar sights of ours
Took marvellous shapes; strange domes and
towers
Rose up where sty or corn-crib stood,
Or garden wall, or belt of wood;

A smooth white mound the brush pile
showed,
A fenceless drift what once was road;
The bridle-post an old man sat
With loose-flung coat and high cocked hat;
The well-curb had a Chinese roof;
And even the long sweep, high aloof,
In its slant splendor, seemed to tell
Of Pisa's leaning miracle.

"When Icicles Hang by the Wall" [6]

WILLIAM SHAKESPEARE

When icicles hang by the wall,
  And Dick the shepherd blows his nail,
And Tom bears logs into the hall,
  And milk comes frozen home in pail,
When blood is nipped and ways be foul,
Then nightly sings the staring owl,
  "Tu-whit, tu-whoo!" A merry note,
While greasy Joan doth keel the pot.

When all aloud the wind doth blow,
  And coughing drowns the parson's saw,
And birds sit brooding in the snow,
  And Marian's nose looks red and raw;
When roasted crabs hiss in the bowl,
Then nightly sings the staring owl,
  "Tu-whit, tu-whoo!" A merry note,
While greasy Joan doth keel the pot.

An Almanac [7]

WILLIAM SHARP

Our Elder Brother is a Spirit of Joy:
Therefore in this new year, Rejoice!

In January the Spirit Dreams,
And in February weaves a Rainbow,
And in March smiles through Rains,
And in April is clad in White and Green,
And in May is the Youth of the World,
And in June is a Glory,
And in July is in two Worlds,
And in August is a Colour,
And in September dreams of Beauty,
And in October Sighs,

[6] From *Love's Labor's Lost*.
[7] From William Sharp, *Poems* (Dodd, Mead).

And in November Wearieth,
And in December sleeps.

The Wakeupworld [8]

COUNTEE CULLEN

Wake up, O World; O World, awake!
The light is bright on hill and lake;
O World, awake; wake up, O World!
The flags of the wind are all unfurled;
Wake up, O World; O World, awake!
Of earth's delightfulness partake.

Wake up, O World, whatever hour;
Sweet are the fields, sweet is the flower!
Wake up, O World; O World, awake;
Perhaps to see the daylight break,
Perhaps to see the sun descend,
The night begin, the daylight end.

But something surely to behold,
Not bought with silver or with gold,
Not shown in any land of dreams.
For open eyes the whole world teems
With lovely things to do or make,
Wake up, O World; O World, awake!

[8] From Countee Cullen, *The Lost Zoo* (Harper).

SURGE OF THE SEA

At the Sea-side [1]

ROBERT LOUIS STEVENSON

When I was down beside the sea,
A wooden spade they gave to me
  To dig the sandy shore.

My holes were empty like a cup.
In every hole the sea came up,
  Till it could come no more.

The Shell [2]

DAVID McCORD

I took away the ocean once,
Spiraled in a shell,
And happily for months and months
I heard it very well.

How it is then that I should hear
What months and months before
Had blown upon me sad and clear,
Down by the grainy shore?

[1] From Robert Louis Stevenson, *A Child's Garden of Verses.*
[2] From David McCord, *Far and Few* (Little, Brown).

A Sea Song

ALLAN CUNNINGHAM

A wet sheet and a flowing sea;
  A wind that follows fast,
And fills the white and rustling sail
  And bends the gallant mast;
And bends the gallant mast, my boys,
  While like the eagle free,
Away the good ship flies, and leaves
  Old England on the lee.

O for a soft and gentle wind!
  I heard a fair one cry;
But give to me the snoring breeze
  And white waves heaving high;
And white waves heaving high, my lads,
  The good ship light and free —
The world of waters is our home,
  And merry men are we.

There's tempest in yon horned moon,
  And lightning in yon cloud;
But hark the music, mariners!
  The wind is piping loud;
The wind is piping loud, my boys,
  The lightning flashes free —

While the hollow oak our palace is,
Our heritage the sea.

Sea-Fever [3]

JOHN MASEFIELD

I must go down to the seas again, to the
lonely sea and the sky,
And all I ask is a tall ship and a star to steer
her by,
And the wheel's kick and the wind's song and
the white sail's shaking,
And a gray mist on the sea's face and a gray
dawn breaking.

I must go down to the seas again, for the call
of the running tide
Is a wild call and a clear call that may not
be denied;
And all I ask is a windy day with the white
clouds flying,
And the flung spray and the blown spume,
and the sea-gulls crying.

I must go down to the seas again to the
vagrant gypsy life,
To the gull's way and the whale's way where
the wind's like a whetted knife;
And all I ask is a merry yarn from a laughing
fellow-rover,
And quiet sleep and a sweet dream when the
long trick's over.

A Wanderer's Song [4]

JOHN MASEFIELD

A wind's in the heart of me, a fire's in my
heels,
I am tired of brick and stone and rumbling
wagon-wheels;
I hunger for the sea's edge, the limits of the
land,
Where the wild old Atlantic is shouting on
the sand.

[3] From John Masefield, *Salt Water Poems and
Ballads* (Macmillan).
[4] *Ibid.*

Oh I'll be going, leaving the noises of the
street,
To where a lifting foresail-foot is yanking
at the sheet;
To a windy, tossing anchorage where yawls
and ketches ride,
Oh I'll be going, going, until I meet the tide.

And first I'll hear the sea-wind, the mewing
of the gulls,
The clucking, sucking of the sea about the
rusty hulls,
The songs at the capstan in the hooker warp-
ing out,
And then the heart of me'll know I'm there
or thereabout.

Oh I am tired of brick and stone, the heart of
me is sick,
For windy green, unquiet sea, the realm of
Moby Dick;
And I'll be going, going, from the roaring of
the wheels,
For a wind's in the heart of me, a fire's in
my heels.

From "Swimmers" [5]

LOUIS UNTERMEYER

Oh, the swift plunge into the cool, green
dark —
The windy waters rushing past me, through
me;
Filled with a sense of some heroic lark,
Exulting in a vigor clean and roomy.
Swiftly I rose to meet the feline sea
That sprang upon me with a hundred claws,
And grappled, pulled me down and played
with me.
Then, tense and breathless in the tightening
pause
When one wave grows into a toppling acre,
I dived headlong into the foremost breaker;
Pitting against a cold and turbulent strife
The feverish intensity of life. . . .
Out of the foam I lurched and rode the wave,
Swimming, hand over hand, against the wind.

[5] From Louis Untermeyer, *This Singing World*
(Harcourt, Brace).

I felt the sea's vain pounding, and I grinned
Knowing I was its master, not its slave!
Oh, the proud total of those lusty hours —
The give-and-take of rough and vigorous
    tussles

With happy sinews and rejoicing muscles;
The knowledge of my own miraculous
    powers;
Feeling the force in one small body bent
To curb and tame this towering element. . . .

LITTLE CREATURES

Little Things[1]

JAMES STEPHENS

Little things that run and quail,
And die, in silence and despair!

Little things that fight and fail,
And fall, on sea and earth and air!

All trapped and frightened little things,
The mouse, the coney, hear our prayer!

As we forgive those done to us,
— The lamb, the linnet, and the hare —

Forgive us all our trespasses,
Little creatures, everywhere!

A Prayer for Little Things[2]

ELEANOR FARJEON

Please God, take care of little things,
The fledglings that have not their wings,
Till they are big enough to fly
And stretch their wings across the sky.

And please take care of little seeds,
So small among the forest weeds,

Till they have grown as tall as trees
With leafy boughs, take care of these.

And please take care of drops of rain
Like beads upon a broken chain,
Till in some river in the sun
The many silver drops are one.

Take care of small new lambs that bleat,
Small foals that totter on their feet,
And all small creatures ever known
Till they are strong to stand alone.

And please take care of children who
Kneel down at night to pray to you,
Oh, please keep safe the little prayer
That like the big ones ask your care.

The Mouse[3]

ELIZABETH COATESWORTH

I heard a mouse
Bitterly complaining
In a crack of moonlight
Aslant on the floor —

"Little I ask
And that little is not granted.
There are few crumbs
In this world any more.

[1] From James Stephens, *Collected Poems* (Macmillan).

[2] From Eleanor Farjeon, *A Prayer for Little Things* (Houghton Mifflin).

[3] From Elizabeth Coatesworth, *Compass Rose* (Coward-McCann).

"The bread-box is tin
And I cannot get in.

"The jam's in a jar
My teeth cannot mar.

"The cheese sits by itself
On the pantry shelf —

"All night I run
Searching and seeking,
All night I run
About on the floor.

"Moonlight is there
And a bare place for dancing,
But no little feast
Is spread any more."

The Little Turtle[6]

VACHEL LINDSAY

There was a little turtle.
He lived in a box.
He swam in a puddle.
He climbed on the rocks.

He snapped at a mosquito.
He snapped at a flea.
He snapped at a minnow.
And he snapped at me.

He caught the mosquito.
He caught the flea.
He caught the minnow.
But he didn't catch me.

The City Mouse[4]

CHRISTINA ROSSETTI

The city mouse lives in a house; —
    The garden mouse lives in a bower,
He's friendly with the frogs and toads,
    And sees the pretty plants in flower.

The city mouse eats bread and cheese; —
    The garden mouse eats what he can;
We will not grudge him seeds and stalks.
    Poor little timid furry man.

Our Mr. Toad[7]

DAVID McCORD

Our Mr. Toad
Has a nice abode
Under the first front step.
When it rains he's cool
In a secret pool
Where the water goes
        drip
        drop
        drep.

Our Mr. Toad
Will avoid the road:
He's a private-cellar man.
And it's not much fun
In the broiling sun
When you *have* a good
        ten
        tone
        tan.

Our Mr. Toad
Has a kind of code
That tells him the coast is clear.
Then away he'll hop
With a stop, stop, stop

Little Snail[5]

HILDA CONKLING

I saw a little snail
Come down the garden walk.
He wagged his head this way . . . that way . . .
Like a clown in a circus.
He looked from side to side
As though he were from a different country.
I have always said he carries his house on his
        back . . .
Today in the rain
I saw that it was his umbrella!

4 From Christina Rossetti, *Sing-Song*.
5 From Hilda Conkling, *Poems by a Little Girl* (Lippincott).

6 From Vachel Lindsay, *Collected Poems* (Macmillan).
7 From David McCord, *Far and Few* (Little, Brown).

When the dusk draws
>nigh
>no
>near.

The Caterpillar [8]

CHRISTINA ROSSETTI

Brown and furry
Caterpillar in a hurry
Take your walk
To the shady leaf or stalk
Or what not,
Which may be the chosen spot.
No toad spy you,
Hovering bird of prey pass by you;
Spin and die,
To live again a butterfly.

Firefly [9]

(A Song)

ELIZABETH MADOX ROBERTS

A little light is going by,
Is going up to see the sky,
A little light with wings.

I never could have thought of it,
To have a little bug all lit
And made to go on wings.

Fireflies [1]

WINIFRED WELLES

Oh, who is lost tonight?
The field and garden are alight
With tiny lanterns, bobbling, winking,
High in the soundless boughs or sinking,
A-flicker in the forests of the grass.
All through the night they pass,

[8] From Christina Rossetti, *Sing-Song.*
[9] From Elizabeth Madox Roberts, *Under the Tree* (Viking Press).
[1] From Winifred Welles, *Skipping Along Alone* (Macmillan).

Silently peering with their cheerful torches
In snails' round doors, and spiders' ruined
>porches,
Blowing a patient spark
In every corner of the dark.

Who's lost they never say,
But in the silver break of day
Their lamps are dimmed, they have des-
cended
The empty air, their long search ended.
They never see the moist and nibbling nose
Of one who guilty goes
With long, slow hops home through the mea-
dow faring,
His fur all ruffled and his round eyes staring,
A dewdrop, bright and clear,
Twinkling in each tall ear.

On the Grasshopper and Cricket

JOHN KEATS

The poetry of earth is never dead:
When all the birds are faint with the hot sun,
And hide in cooling trees, a voice will run
From hedge to hedge about the new-mown
>mead;
That is the Grasshopper's — he takes the lead
In summer luxury — he has never done
With his delights; for when tired out with
>fun
He rests at ease beneath some pleasant weed.

The poetry of earth is ceasing never;
On a lone winter evening, when the frost
Has wrought a silence, from the stove there
>shrills
The Cricket's song, in warmth increasing
>ever,
And seems to one in drowsiness half lost,
The Grasshopper's among some grassy hills.

The Wasp [2]

WILLIAM SHARP

When the ripe pears droop heavily,
>The yellow wasp hums loud and long
His hot and drowsy autumn song:

[2] From William Sharp, *Collected Poems* (Dodd, Mead).

A yellow flame he seems to be,
When darting suddenly from high
He lights where fallen peaches lie.

Yellow and black — this tiny thing's
A tiger-soul on elfin wings.

The Blackbird [3]

HUMBERT WOLFE

In the far corner,
close by the swings,
every morning
a blackbird sings.

His bill's so yellow
his coat's so black,
that he makes a fellow
whistle back.

Ann, my daughter,
thinks that he
sings for us two
especially.

The Sandpiper [4]

CELIA THAXTER

Across the lonely beach we flit,
  One little sandpiper and I,
And fast I gather, bit by bit,
  The scattered driftwood, bleached and dry.
The wild waves reach their hands for it,
  The wild wind raves, the tide runs high,
As up and down the beach we flit,
  One little sandpiper and I.

Above our heads the sullen clouds
  Scud, black and swift, across the sky;
Like silent ghosts in misty shrouds
  Stand out the white lighthouses high.
Almost as far as eye can reach
  I see the close-reefed vessels fly,
As fast we flit along the beach.
  One little sandpiper and I.

I watch him as he skims along,
  Uttering his sweet and mournful cry;
He starts not at my fitful song,
  Nor flash of fluttering drapery.
He has no thought of any wrong,
  He scans me with a fearless eye;
Stanch friends are we, well-tried and strong,
  The little sandpiper and I.

Comrade, where wilt thou be tonight,
  When the loosed storm breaks furiously?
My driftwood fire will burn so bright!
  To what warm shelter canst thou fly?
I do not fear for thee, though wroth
  The tempest rushes through the sky;
For are we not God's children both,
  Thou, little sandpiper, and I?

Bantam Rooster [5]

HARRY BEHN

He woke me with his tiny trill,
And snow was on the window sill.

He only hatched last Spring, but he
Is big as ever he will be.

I wish I could become a man
As quickly as a bantam can,

Why, right this morning I would go
A hundred miles across the snow!

Red Rooster [6]

(Written at the age of seven)

HILDA CONKLING

Red rooster in your gray coop,
O stately creature with tail-feathers red and
    blue,
Yellow and black,
You have a comb gay as a parade
On your head:
You have pearl trinkets
On your feet:

[3] From Humbert Wolfe, *Kensington Gardens* (Doubleday).

[4] From Celia Thaxter, *Stories and Poems for Children*

[5] From Harry Behn, *The Little Hill* (Harcourt, Brace).

[6] From Hilda Conkling, *Poems by a Little Girl* (Lippincott).

The short feathers smooth along your back
Are the dark color of wet rocks,
Or the rippled green of ships
When I look at their sides through water.
I don't know how you happend to be made
So proud, so foolish,
Wearing your coat of many colors,
Shouting all day long your crooked words,
Loud . . . sharp . . . not beautiful!

Every one for what he likes!
We like to be
Heads down, tails up,
Dabbling free!

High in the blue above
Swifts whirl and call —
We are down a-dabbling
Up tails all!

Mrs. Peck-Pigeon [7]

ELEANOR FARJEON

Mrs. Peck-Pigeon
Is picking for bread,
Bob-bob-bob
Goes her little round head.
Tame as a pussy-cat
In the street,
Step-step-step
Go her little red feet.
With her little red feet
And her little round head,
Mrs. Peck-Pigeon
Goes picking for bread.

Duck's Ditty [8]

KENNETH GRAHAME

All along the backwater,
Through the rushes tall,
Ducks are a-dabbling,
Up tails all!

Ducks' tails, drakes' tails,
Yellow feet a-quiver,
Yellow bills all out of sight
Busy in the river!

Slushy green undergrowth
Where the roach swim —
Here we keep our larder,
Cool and full and dim!

Market Square [9]

A. A. MILNE

I had a penny,
A bright new penny,
I took my penny
    To the market square.
I wanted a rabbit,
A little brown rabbit,
And I looked for a rabbit
    'Most everywhere.

For I went to the stall where they sold sweet
    lavender
("Only a penny for a bunch of lavender!").
"Have you got a rabbit, 'cos I don't want
    lavender?"
    But they hadn't got a rabbit, not anywhere
    there.

I had a penny,
And I had another penny,
I took my pennies
    To the market square.
I did want a rabbit,
A little baby rabbit,
And I looked for rabbits
    'Most everywhere.

And I went to the stall where they sold fresh
    mackerel
("Now then! Tuppence for a fresh-caught
    mackerel!").
"Have you got a rabbit, 'cos I don't like
    mackerel?"
    But they hadn't got a rabbit, not anywhere
    there.

[7] From Eleanor Farjeon, *Over the Garden Wall* (Lippincott).

[8] From Kenneth Grahame, *The Wind in the Willows* (Scribner).

[9] From A. A. Milne, *When We Were Very Young* (Dutton).

I found a sixpence,
A little white sixpence.
I took it in my hand
    To the market square.
I was buying my rabbit
(I do like rabbits),
And I looked for my rabbit
'Most everywhere.

So I went to the stall where they sold fine
    saucepans
("Walk up, walk up, sixpence for a sauce-
    pan!").
"Could I have a rabbit, 'cos we've got two
    saucepans?"
    But they hadn't got a rabbit, not anywhere
    there.

I had nuffin',
No, I hadn't got nuffin',
So I didn't go down
    To the market square;
But I walked on the common,
The old-gold common . . .
And I saw little rabbits
    'Most everywhere!

So I'm sorry for the people who sell fine
    saucepans,
I'm sorry for the people who sell fresh mack-
    erel,
I'm sorry for the people who sell sweet laven-
    der,
    'Cos they haven't got a rabbit, not any-
    where there!

The Squirrel[1]

ANONYMOUS

Whisky, frisky,
Hippity hop,
Up he goes
To the tree top!

Whirly, twirly,
Round and round,
Down he scampers
To the ground.

[1] From *Sung Under the Silver Umbrella,* ed. by the Association for Childhood Education.

Furly, curly
What a tail!
Tall as a feather
Broad as a sail!

Where's his supper?
In the shell,
Snappity, crackity,
Out it fell.

Clover for Breakfast[2]

FRANCES FROST

Upon the sunny summer hill,
As I was lying in the grass,
I caught my breath, I held my breath,
To see a mother woodchuck pass.

Behind her trotted four young 'chucks
On anxious and unsteady feet;
When she halted in a clover patch,
You should have seen them eat!

You should have seen them sitting up
With clover blossoms in their paws;
Their infant eyes were bright. I smiled
To see their small and busy jaws.

Oh, red and white and purple bloom —
That was a fragrant morning feast!
Motionless I lay and watched
And didn't scare them in the least.

Milk for the Cat[3]

HAROLD MONRO

When the tea is brought at five o'clock,
    And all the neat curtains are drawn with
    care,
The little black cat with bright green eyes
    Is suddenly purring there.

At first she pretends, having nothing to do,
    She has come in merely to blink by the
    grate,

[2] From Frances Frost, *The Little Whistler* (McGraw-Hill).

[3] From Harold Monro, *Collected Poems* (Duckworth, London).

But, though tea may be late or the milk be
    sour,
    She is never late.

And presently her agate eyes
    Take a soft large milky haze,
And her independent casual glance
    Becomes a stiff hard gaze.

Then she stamps her claws or lifts her ears
    Or twists her tail or begins to stir,
Till suddenly all her lithe body becomes
    One breathing trembling purr.

The children eat and wriggle and laugh;
    The two old ladies stroke their silk:
But the cat is grown small and thin with
    desire,
    Transformed to a creeping lust for milk.

The white saucer like some full moon de-
    scends
    At last from the clouds of the table above;
She sighs and dreams and thrills and glows,
    Transfigured with love.

She nestles over the shining rim,
    Buries her chin in the creamy sea;
Her tail hangs loose; each drowsy paw
    Is doubled under each bending knee.

A long, dim ecstasy holds her life;
    Her world is an infinite shapeless white,
Till her tongue has curled the last holy drop,
    Then she sinks back into the night,

Draws and dips her body to heap
    Her sleepy nerves in the great arm-chair,
Lies defeated and buried deep
    Three or four hours unconscious there.

The Mysterious Cat [4]

VACHEL LINDSAY

I saw a proud, mysterious cat,
I saw a proud, mysterious cat
Too proud to catch a mouse or rat —
Mew, mew, mew.

[4] From Vachel Lindsay, *The Congo and Other
Poems* (Macmillan).

But catnip she would eat, and purr,
But catnip she would eat, and purr,
And goldfish she did much prefer —
Mew, mew, mew.

I saw a cat — 'twas but a dream,
I saw a cat — 'twas but a dream,
Who scorned the slave that brought her
    cream —
Mew, mew, mew.

Unless the slave were dressed in style,
Unless the slave were dressed in style
And knelt before her all the while —
Mew, mew, mew.

Did you ever hear of a thing like that?
Did you ever hear of a thing like that?
Did you ever hear of a thing like that?
Oh, what a proud mysterious cat.
Oh, what a proud mysterious cat.
Oh, what a proud mysterious cat.
Mew . . . Mew . . . Mew.

I Like Little Pussy

ATTRIBUTED TO JANE TAYLOR

I like little Pussy,
    Her coat is so warm;
And if I don't hurt her
    She'll do me no harm.
So I'll not pull her tail,
    Nor drive her away,
But Pussy and I
    Very gently will play;
She shall sit by my side,
    And I'll give her some food:
And she'll love me because
    I am gentle and good.
I'll pat little Pussy,
    And then she will purr,
And thus show her thanks
    For my kindness to her;
I'll not pinch her ears,
    Nor tread on her paw,
Lest I should provoke her
    To use her sharp claw;
I never will vex her,
    Nor make her displeased,
For Pussy don't like
    To be worried or teased.

Mary's Lamb [5]

SARAH JOSEPHA HALE

Mary had a little lamb,
  Its fleece was white as snow;
And everywhere that Mary went
  The lamb was sure to go.

He followed her to school one day;
  That was against the rule;
It made the children laugh and play
  To see a lamb at school.

And so the teacher turned him out,
  But still he lingered near,
And waited patiently about
  Till Mary did appear.

Then he ran to her, and laid
  His head upon her arm,
As if he said, "I'm not afraid —
  You'll keep me from all harm."

"What makes the lamb love Mary so?"
  The eager children cry.
"Oh, Mary loves the lamb, you know,"
  The teacher did reply.

[5] From Sarah Josepha Hale, *Poems for Our Children.*

And you each gentle animal
In confidence may bind,
And make them follow at your call
If you are always kind.

The Lamb [6]

WILLIAM BLAKE

Little lamb, who made thee?
  Dost thou know who made thee?
Gave thee life, and bid thee feed
By the stream and o'er the mead;
Gave thee clothing of delight,
Softest clothing, woolly, bright;
Gave thee such a tender voice,
Making all the vales rejoice?
  Little lamb, who made thee?
  Dost thou know who made thee?

Little lamb, I'll tell thee,
  Little lamb, I'll tell thee:
He is callèd by thy name,
For He calls Himself a Lamb.
He is meek, and He is mild;
He became a little child.
I a child, and thou a lamb,
We are callèd by His name.
  Little lamb, God bless thee!
  Little lamb, God bless thee!

[6] From William Blake, *Songs of Innocence.*

GOOD DAY AND GOOD NIGHT

Softly, Drowsily [1]

WALTER DE LA MARE

Softly, drowsily,
Out of sleep;
Into the world again
Ann's eyes peep;

[1] From Walter de la Mare, *A Child's Day* (Holt).

Over the pictures
Across the walls
One little quivering
Sunbeam falls.
A thrush in the garden
Seems to say,
Wake, little Ann,
'Tis day, 'tis day!

Faint sweet breezes
The casement stir,
Breathing of pinks
And lavender.
At last from her pillow,
With cheeks bright red,
Up comes her round little
Tousled head;
And out she tumbles
From her warm bed.

The Sounds in the Morning[2]

ELEANOR FARJEON

The sounds in the morning
Go all down the street:
The tapping of sticks
And the patter of feet,
The wind in the plane trees
That whisper and rustle,
The pigeons all sleepy,
The newsboys all hustle,
The *clippety-clop*
And the *clip-clop* again
Of soldiers and horses,
More horses than men,
The clatter of milk-cans,
The chatter of maids,
The slop of their buckets,
The sort without spades,
And sometimes the mooing
Of slow-moving cows
Brings the smell of the lowlands
To me as I drowse,
And sometimes the bleating
And scuffle of sheep
Draws down the high hilltops
To me half-asleep,
Dogs barking, bells chiming,
The twitter of sparrows —
Till the sun through the slats
Of my blind shoots his arrows,
And the world of my ears
Seems to dwindle in size
As I jump out of bed
To the world of my eyes.

[2] From Eleanor Farjeon, *Over the Garden Wall*
(Lippincott).

Song for a Little House[3]

CHRISTOPHER MORLEY

I'm glad our house is a little house,
Not too tall nor too wide:
I'm glad the hovering butterflies
Feel free to come inside.

Our little house is a friendly house,
It is not shy or vain;
It gossips with the talking trees
And makes friends with the rain.

And quick leaves cast a shimmer of green
Against our whited walls,
And in the phlox, the courteous bees
Are paying duty calls.

The Swing[4]

ROBERT LOUIS STEVENSON

How do you like to go up in a swing,
 Up in the air so blue?
Oh, I do think it the pleasantest thing
 Ever a child can do!

Up in the air and over the wall,
 Till I can see so wide,
Rivers and trees and cattle and all
 Over the countryside —

Till I look down on the garden green,
 Down on the roof so brown —
Up in the air I go flying again,
 Up in the air and down!

My Shadow[5]

ROBERT LOUIS STEVENSON

I have a little shadow that goes in and out
 with me,
And what can be the use of him is more than
 I can see.

[3] From Christopher Morley, *The Rocking Horse*
(Lippincott).
[4] From Robert Louis Stevenson, *A Child's Garden
of Verses.*
[5] *Ibid.*

He is very, very like me from the heels up to
the head;
And I see him jump before me, when I jump
into my bed.

The funniest thing about him is the way he
likes to grow —
Not at all like proper children, which is al-
ways very slow;
For he sometimes shoots up taller like an
India-rubber ball,
And he sometimes gets so little that there's
none of him at all.

He hasn't got a notion of how children ought
to play,
And can only make a fool of me in every sort
of way.
He stays so close beside me, he's a coward you
can see;
I'd think shame to stick to nursie as that
shadow sticks to me!

One morning very early, before the sun was
up,
I rose and found the shining dew on every
buttercup;
But my lazy little shadow, like an arrant
sleepy-head,
Had stayed at home behind me and was fast
asleep in bed.

The Land of Counterpane[6]

ROBERT LOUIS STEVENSON

When I was sick and lay a-bed,
I had two pillows at my head,
And all my toys beside me lay
To keep me happy all the day.

And sometimes for an hour or so
I watched my leaden soldiers go
With different uniforms and drills,
Among the bed-clothes, through the hills;

And sometimes sent my ships in fleets
All up and down among the sheets;
Or brought my trees and houses out,
And planted cities all about.

[6] *Ibid.*

I was the giant great and still
That sits upon the pillow-hill
And sees before him, dale and plain,
The pleasant land of counterpane.

Pirate Story[7]

ROBERT LOUIS STEVENSON

Three of us afloat in the meadow by the
swing,
Three of us aboard in the basket on the lea.
Winds are in the air, they are blowing in the
spring,
And waves are on the meadow like the
waves there are at sea.

Where shall we adventure, today that we're
afloat,
Wary of the weather and steering by a
star?
Shall it be to Africa, a-steering of the boat,
To Providence, or Babylon, or off to Malabar?

Hi! but here's a squadron a-rowing on the
sea —
Cattle on the meadow a-charging with a
roar!
Quick, and we'll escape them, they're as mad
as they can be,
The wicket is the harbor, and the garden
is the shore.

The Little Land[8]

ROBERT LOUIS STEVENSON

When at home alone I sit
And am very tired of it,
I have just to shut my eyes
To go sailing through the skies —
To go sailing far away
To the pleasant Land of Play;
To the fairy land afar
Where the Little People are;
Where the clover-tops are trees,
And the rain-pools are the seas,

[7] *Ibid.*
[8] *Ibid.*

And the leaves like little ships
Sail about on tiny trips;
And above the daisy tree
    Through the grasses,
High o'erhead the Bumble Bee
    Hums and passes.

In that forest to and fro
I can wander, I can go;
See the spider and the fly,
And the ants go marching by
Carrying parcels with their feet
Down the green and grassy street.
I can in the sorrel sit
Where the lady-bird alit.
I can climb the jointed grass
    And on high
See the greater swallows pass
    In the sky.
And the round sun rolling by
Heeding no such things as I.

Through that forest I can pass
Till, as in a looking-glass,
Humming fly and daisy tree
And my tiny self I see,
Painted very clear and neat
On the rain pool at my feet.
Should a leaflet come to land
Drifting near to where I stand,
Straight I'll board that tiny boat
Round the rain-pool sea to float.

Little thoughtful creatures sit
On the grassy coasts of it;
Little things with lovely eyes
See me sailing with surprise.
Some are clad in armour green —
(These have sure to battle been!)
Some are pied with ev'ry hue,
Black and crimson, green and blue;
Some have wings and swift are gone; —
But they all look kindly on.

When my eyes I once again
Open, and see all things plain:
High bare walls, great bare floor;
Great big knobs on drawer and door;
Great big people perched on chairs,
Stitching tucks and mending tears,
Each a hill that I could climb,
And talking nonsense all the time —

O dear me,
That I could be
A sailor on the rain-pool sea,
A climber on the clover tree,
And just come back, a sleepy head,
Late at night to go to bed.

Bed in Summer [9]

ROBERT LOUIS STEVENSON

In winter I get up at night
And dress by yellow candle-light.
In summer, quite the other way,
I have to go to bed by day.

I have to go to bed and see
The birds still hopping on the tree,
Or hear the grown-up people's feet
Still going past me in the street.

And does it not seem hard to you,
When all the sky is clear and blue,
And I should like so much to play,
To have to go to bed by day?

Pretending [1]

HARRY BEHN

Of course I'm me but after that
Nobody knows that I am a cat.

My kitten does and says, Purr purr,
And I say, Purr purr purr, to her,

And when she stretches I do too,
Then I say Meow, and she says, Mew.

Nobody knows that I am a hill
Sitting and listening very still

To grass and thistles and rustling seeds
Or crickets chirping under weeds.

Nobody knows when I sway and sway
I'm being a tree on a windy day.

[9] *Ibid.*
[1] From Harry Behn, *Windy Morning* (Harcourt, Brace).

And when there's nothing better to do
I'm a fat old cow that says Moo.

Or else I do what any bee does,
I fly to a flower and say, Buzz.

And sometimes in Summer whenever I wish
I'm a waterbug in our pool, or a fish,

Or an all hunched up and grumpy frog
Sitting and grunting on a log.

But best is when the swallows fly
With a chirp and a twitter across the sky,

I am a swallow as swift as they,
And up I go and swoop away,

And O what fun it is to see,
Down in our garden, myself watching me!

Mummy calls me her precious lamb
But never the other things I am,

And I am glad, 'cause who would hug
A frog or a bee or a waterbug!

Hiding [2]

DOROTHY ALDIS

I'm hiding, I'm hiding,
And no one knows where;
For all they can see is my
Toes and my hair.

And I just heard my father
Say to my mother —
"But, darling, he must be
Somewhere or other;

Have you looked in the inkwell?"
And Mother said, "Where?"
"In the INKWELL?" said Father. But
I was not there.

Then "Wait!" cried my mother —
"I think that I see
Him under the carpet." But
It was not me.

[2] From Dorothy Aldis, *Everything and Anything*
(Putnam).

"Inside the mirror's
A pretty good place,"
Said Father and looked, but saw
Only his face.

"We've hunted," sighed Mother,
"As hard as we could,
And I AM so afraid that we've
Lost him for good."

Then I laughed out aloud
And I wiggled my toes
And Father said — "Look, dear,
I wonder if those

Toes could be Benny's?
There are ten of them, see?"
And they WERE SO surprised to find
Out it was me!

Circus [3]

ELEANOR FARJEON

The brass band blares,
The naphtha flares,
The sawdust smells,
Showmen ring bells,
And oh! right into the circus-ring
Comes such a lovely, lovely thing,
A milk-white pony with flying tress,
And a beautiful lady,
A beautiful lady,
A *beautiful* lady in a pink dress!
The red-and-white clown
For joy tumbles down;
Like a pink rose
Round she goes
On her tip-toes
With the pony under —
And then, oh wonder!
The pony his milk-white tresses droops,
And the beautiful lady,
The *beautiful* lady,
Flies like a bird through the paper hoops!
The red-and-white clown for joy falls dead,
Then he waggles his feet and stands on his
      head,
And the little boys on the twopenny seats
Scream with laughter and suck their sweets.

[3] From Eleanor Farjeon, *Joan's Door* (Lippincott).

Whistles[4]

DOROTHY ALDIS

I want to learn to whistle,
I've always wanted to.
I fix my mouth to do it, but
The whistle won't come through.

I think perhaps it's stuck, and so
I try it once again.
Can people swallow whistles?
Where is my whistle then?

The Little Whistler[5]

FRANCES FROST

My mother whistled softly,
My father whistled bravely,
My brother whistled merrily,
And I tried all day long!
I blew my breath inwards,
I blew my breath outwards,
But all you heard was breath blowing
And not a bit of song!

But today I heard a bluebird,
A happy, young, and new bird,
Whistling in the apple tree —
He'd just discovered how!
Then quick I blew my breath in,
And gay I blew my breath out,
And sudden I blew three wild notes —
And I can whistle now!

Troubles[6]

DOROTHY ALDIS

Stockings are a trouble; so many times my
toes
Try to climb in where a heel generally goes.

And mittens are not easy, for lots of days my
thumbs
Go wandering and crawling into other fingers' homes.

But rubbers are the hardest because, it seems
to me,
I always put one rubber where the other one
should be.

Radiator Lions[7]

DOROTHY ALDIS

George lives in an apartment and
His mother will not let
Him keep a dog or polliwog
Or rabbit for a pet.

So he has Radiator-Lions.
(The parlor is the zoo.)
They love to fight but will not bite
Unless he tells them to.

And days when it is very cold
And he can't go outdoors
They glower and they lower and they
Crouch upon all fours.

And roar most awful roarings and
Gurgle loud and mad.
Up their noses water goeses —
THAT'S what makes them bad.

But he loves Radiator-Lions!
He's glad, although they're wild,
He hasn't dogs and polliwogs
Like any other child!

Mumps[8]

ELIZABETH MADOX ROBERTS

I had a feeling in my neck,
    And on the sides were two big bumps;
I couldn't swallow anything
    At all because I had the mumps.

And Mother tied it with a piece,
    And then she tied up Will and John,
And no one else but Dick was left
    That didn't have a mump rag on.

[4] From Dorothy Aldis, *Here, There, and Everywhere* (Minton, Balch).
[5] From Frances Frost, *The Little Whistler*
(McGraw-Hill).
[6] From Dorothy Aldis, *Here, There, and Everywhere* (Minton, Balch).
[7] *Ibid.*
[8] From Elizabeth Madox Roberts, *Under the Tree*
(Viking Press).

He teased at us and laughed at us,
  And said, whenever he went by,
"It's vinegar and lemon-drops
  And pickles!" just to make us cry.

But Tuesday Dick was very sad
  And cried because his neck was sore,
And not a one said sour things
  To anybody any more.

Washing [9]

JOHN DRINKWATER

What is all this washing about,
Every day, week in, week out?
From getting up till going to bed,
I'm tired of hearing the same thing said.
Whether I'm dirty or whether I'm not,
Whether the water is cold or hot,
Whether I like or whether I don't
Whether I will or whether I won't —
"Have you washed your hands, and washed
      your face?"
I seem to *live* in the washing-place.

Whenever I go for a walk or ride,
As soon as I put my nose inside
The door again, there's some one there
With a sponge and soap, and a lot they care
If I have something better to do,
"Now wash your face and your fingers too."

Before a meal is ever begun,
And after ever a meal is done,
It's time to turn on the waterspout.

Please, what *is* all this washing about?

Twos [1]

JOHN DRINKWATER

Why are lots of things in twos?
Hands on clocks, and gloves, and shoes,
Scissor-blades, and water-taps,
Collar studs, and luggage straps,

Walnut shells, and pigeons' eggs,
Arms and eyes and ears and legs —
Will you kindly tell me who's
So fond of making things in twos?

Miss T. [2]

WALTER DE LA MARE

It's a very odd thing —
  As odd as can be —
That whatever Miss T. eats
  Turns into Miss T.;
Porridge and apples,
  Mince, muffins, and mutton,
Jam, junket, jumbles —
  Not a rap, not a button
It matters; the moment
  They're out of her plate,
Though shared by Miss Butcher
  And sour Mr. Bate;
Tiny and cheerful,
  And neat as can be,
Whatever Miss T. eats
  Turns into Miss T.

Tired Tim [3]

WALTER DE LA MARE

Poor tired Tim! It's sad for him.
He lags the long bright morning through,
Ever so tired of nothing to do,
He moons and mopes the livelong day,
Nothing to think about, nothing to say,
Up to bed with his candle to creep,
Too tired to yawn, too tired to sleep;
Poor tired Tim! It's sad for him.

The Barber's [4]

WALTER DE LA MARE

Gold locks, and black locks,
  Red locks and brown,
Topknot to love-curl
  The hair wisps down;

---

9 From John Drinkwater, *More About Me* (Houghton Mifflin).
1 *Ibid.*

2 From Walter de la Mare, *Peacock Pie* (Holt).
3 *Ibid.*
4 *Ibid.*

Straight above the clear eyes,
  Rounded round the ears,
Snip-snap and snick-a-snick,
  Clash the Barber's shears;
Us, in the looking-glass,
  Footsteps in the street,
Over, under, to and fro,
  The lean blades meet;
Bay Rum or Bear's Grease,
  A silver groat to pay —
Then out a-shin-shan-shining
  In the bright, blue day.

Boys' Names[5]

ELEANOR FARJEON

What splendid names for boys there are!
There's Carol like a rolling car,
And Martin like a flying bird,
And Adam like the Lord's First Word,
And Raymond like the harvest Moon,
And Peter like a piper's tune,
And Alan like the flowing on
Of water. And there's John, like John.

Girls' Names[6]

ELEANOR FARJEON

What lovely names for girls there are!
There's Stella like the Evening Star,
And Sylvia like a rustling tree,
And Lola like a melody,
And Flora like a flowery morn,
And Sheila like a field of corn,
And Melusina like the moan
Of water. And there's Joan, like Joan.

General Store[7]

RACHEL FIELD

Some day I'm going to have a store
With a tinkly bell hung over the door,
With real glass cases and counters wide
And drawers all spilly with things inside.
There'll be a little of everything;
Bolts of calico; balls of string;
Jars of peppermint; tins of tea;
Pots and kettles and crockery;
Seeds in packets; scissors bright;
Kegs of sugar, brown and white;
Sarsaparilla for picnic lunches,
Bananas and rubber boots in bunches.
I'll fix the window and dust each shelf,
And take the money in all myself,
It will be my store and I will say:
"What can I do for you today?"

Taxis[8]

RACHEL FIELD

Ho, for taxis green or blue
  Hi, for taxis red,
They roll along the Avenue
  Like spools of colored thread!

  Jack-o-Lantern yellow,
  Orange as the moon,
  Greener than the greenest grass
  Ever grew in June.
  Gayly striped or checked in squares,
  Wheels that twinkle bright,
  Don't you think that taxis make
  A very pleasant sight?
  Taxis shiny in the rain,
  Scudding through the snow,
  Taxis flashing back the sun
  Waiting in a row.

Ho, for taxis red and green,
  Hi, for taxis blue,
I wouldn't be a private car
  In sober black, would you?

Motor Cars[9]

ROWENA BASTIN BENNETT

From a city window, 'way up high,
I like to watch the cars go by.

---

[5] From Eleanor Farjeon, *Poems for Children* (Lippincott).

[6] From Eleanor Farjeon, *Poems for Children* (Lippincott).

[7] From Rachel Field, *Taxis and Toadstools* (Doubleday).

[8] *Ibid.*

[9] From Rowena Bastin Bennett, *Around a Toadstool Table* (Follett).

They look like burnished beetles, black,
That leave a little muddy track
Behind them as they slowly crawl.
Sometimes they do not move at all
But huddle close with hum and drone
As though they feared to be alone.
They grope their way through fog and night
With the golden feelers of their light.

Trucks[1]

JAMES S. TIPPETT

Big trucks for steel beams,
Big trucks for coal,
Rumbling down the broad streets,
Heavily they roll.

Little trucks for groceries,
Little trucks for bread,
Turning into every street,
Rushing on ahead.

Big trucks, little trucks,
In never-ending lines,
Rumble on and rush ahead
While I read their signs.

Song of the Train[2]

DAVID McCORD

Clickety-clack,
Wheels on the track,
This is the way
They begin the attack:
Click-ety-clack,
Click-ety-clack,
Click-ety, *clack*-ety,
Click-ety
Clack.

Clickety-clack,
Over the crack,
Faster and faster
The song of the track:
Clickety-clack,
Clickety-clack,

Clickety, clackety,
Clackety
Clack.

Riding in front,
Riding in back,
Everyone hears
The song of the track:
Clickety-clack,
Clickety-clack,
Clickety, *clickety*,
Clackety
Clack.

Skyscrapers[3]

RACHEL FIELD

Do skyscrapers ever grow tired
    Of holding themselves up high?
Do they ever shiver on frosty nights
    With their tops against the sky?

Do they feel lonely sometimes,
    Because they have grown so tall?
Do they ever wish they could lie right down
    And never get up at all?

Animal Crackers[4]

CHRISTOPHER MORLEY

Animal crackers, and cocoa to drink,
That is the finest of suppers, I think;
When I'm grown up and can have what I
    please
I think I shall always insist upon these.

What do *you* choose when you're offered a
    treat?
When Mother says, "What would you like
    best to eat?"
Is it waffles and syrup, or cinnamon toast?
It's cocoa and animals that *I* love the most!

The kitchen's the cosiest place that I know:
The kettle is singing, the stove is aglow,

---

[1] From James S. Tippett, *I Go A-Traveling* (Harper).

[2] From David McCord, *Far and Few* (Little, Brown).

[3] From Rachel Field, *Taxis and Toadstools* (Doubleday).

[4] From Christopher Morley, *Songs for a Little House* (Lippincott).

And there in the twilight, how jolly to see
The cocoa and animals waiting for me.

Daddy and Mother dine later in state,
With Mary to cook for them, Susan to wait;
But they don't have nearly as much fun as I
Who eat in the kitchen with Nurse standing
    by;
And Daddy once said he would like to be me
Having cocoa and animals once more for tea!

Evening [5]

HARRY BEHN

Now the drowsy sun shine
Slides far away

Into the happy morning
Of someone else's day.

Nod [6]

WALTER DE LA MARE

Softly along the road of evening,
  In a twilight dim with rose,
Wrinkled with age, and drenched with dew
  Old Nod, the shepherd, goes.

His drowsy flock streams on before him,
  Their fleeces charged with gold,
To where the sun's last beam leans low
  On Nod the shepherd's fold.

The hedge is quick and green with briar,
  From their sand the conies creep;
And all the birds that fly in heaven
  Flock singing home to sleep.

His lambs outnumber a noon's roses,
  Yet, when night's shadows fall,
His blind old sheep-dog, Slumber-soon,
  Misses not one of all.

His are the quiet steeps of dreamland,
  The waters of no-more-pain,
His ram's bell rings 'neath an arch of stars,
  "Rest, rest, and rest again."

[5] From Harry Behn, *Windy Morning* (Harcourt, Brace).
[6] From Walter de la Mare, *The Listeners* (Holt).

What the Rattlesnake Said [7]

VACHEL LINDSAY

The moon's a little prairie-dog.
He shivers through the night.
He sits upon his hill and cries
For fear that I will bite.

The sun's a broncho. He's afraid
Like every other thing,
And trembles, morning, noon and night,
Lest I should spring, and sting!

The Moon's the North Wind's Cooky [8]

(*What the Little Girl Said*)

VACHEL LINDSAY

The Moon's the North Wind's cooky.
He bites it, day by day,
Until there's but a rim of scraps
That crumble all away.

The South Wind is a baker.
He kneads clouds in his den,
And bakes a crisp new moon that ... greedy
North ... Wind ... eats ... again!

Full Moon [9]

WALTER DE LA MARE

One night as Dick lay half asleep,
  Into his drowsy eyes
A great still light began to creep
  From out the silent skies.
It was the lovely moon's, for when
  He raised his dreamy head,
Her surge of silver filled the pane
  And streamed across his bed.
So, for a while, each gazed at each —
  Dick and the solemn moon —
Till, climbing slowly on her way,
  She vanished, and was gone.

[7] From Vachel Lindsay, *Collected Poems* (Macmillan).
[8] *Ibid.*
[9] From Walter de la Mare, *Peacock Pie* (Holt).

Silver[1]

WALTER DE LA MARE

Slowly, silently, now the moon
Walks the night in her silver shoon;
This way, and that, she peers, and sees
Silver fruit upon silver trees;
One by one the casements catch
Her beams beneath the silvery thatch;
Couched in his kennel, like a log,
With paws of silver sleeps the dog;
From their shadowy cote the white breasts
　　peep
Of doves in a silver-feathered sleep;
A harvest mouse goes scampering by,
With silver claws, and silver eye;
And moveless fish in the water gleam,
By silver reeds in a silver stream.

The White Window[2]

JAMES STEPHENS

The Moon comes every night to peep
Through the window where I lie:
But I pretend to be asleep;
And watch the Moon go slowly by,
— And she never makes a sound!

She stands and stares! And then she goes
To the house that's next to me,
Stealing by on tippy-toes;
To peep at folk asleep maybe
— And she never makes a sound!

Stars[3]

SARA TEASDALE

　　Alone in the night
　　On a dark hill
　　With pines around me
　　Spicy and still,

　　And a heaven full of stars
　　Over my head,
　　White and topaz
　　And misty red;

　Myriads with beating
　　Hearts of fire
　That aeons
　　Cannot vex or tire;

　Up the dome of heaven
　　Like a great hill,
　I watch them marching
　　Stately and still,

　And I know that I
　　Am honored to be
　Witness
　　Of so much majesty.

Night[4]

SARA TEASDALE

Stars over snow,
　And in the west a planet
Swinging below a star —
　Look for a lovely thing and you will find it.
It is not far —
　It never will be far.

The Night Will Never Stay[5]

ELEANOR FARJEON

The night will never stay,
The night will still go by,
Though with a million stars
You pin it to the sky,
Though you bind it with the blowing wind
And buckle it with the moon,
The night will slip away
Like sorrow or a tune.

Nurse's Song[6]

WILLIAM BLAKE

When the voices of children are heard on the
　　green
　And laughing is heard on the hill,
My heart is at rest within my breast,
　And everything else is still.

---

[1] *Ibid.*
[2] From James Stephens, *Collected Poems* (Macmillan).
[3] From Sara Teasdale, *Stars To-night* (Macmillan).

[4] From Sara Teasdale, *Stars To-night* (Macmillan).
[5] From Eleanor Farjeon, *Gypsy and Ginger*.
[6] From William Blake, *Songs of Innocence*.

"Then come home, my children, the sun is
    gone down,
  And the dews of the night arise;
Come, come, leave off play, and let us away
  Till the morning appears in the skies."

"No, no, let us play, for it is yet day,
  And we cannot go to sleep;
Besides, in the sky the little birds fly,
  And the hills are all covered with sheep."

"Well, well, go and play till the light fades
    away,
  And then go home to bed."
The little ones leaped, and shouted, and
    laughed,
  And all the hills echoed.

Cradle Song [7]

WILLIAM BLAKE

Sleep, sleep, beauty bright,
Dreaming in the joys of night;
Sleep, sleep; in thy sleep
Little sorrows sit and weep.

Sweet babe, in thy face
Soft desires I can trace,
Secret joys and secret smiles,
Little pretty infant wiles.

As thy softest limbs I feel,
Smiles as of the morning steal
O'er thy cheek, and o'er thy breast
Where thy little heart doth rest.

O the cunning wiles that creep
In thy little heart asleep!
When thy little heart doth wake,
Then the dreadful night shall break.

Sleep, Baby, Sleep

ANONYMOUS

Sleep, baby, sleep!
Thy father watches his sheep;
Thy mother is shaking the dreamland tree,
And down comes a little dream on thee:
  Sleep, baby, sleep!

[7] From William Blake, *Songs of Innocence.*

Sleep, baby, sleep!
The large stars are the sheep,
The little stars are the lambs, I guess,
And the gentle moon is the shepherdess:
  Sleep, baby, sleep!

Sleep, baby, sleep!
Our Saviour loves His sheep;
He is the Lamb of God on high,
Who for our sakes came down to die:
  Sleep, baby, sleep!

An Indian Lullaby

ANONYMOUS

Rock-a-by, rock-a-by, little brown baby,
  Safe in the green branch so high,
Shut your bright black eyes and go to sleep,
    baby,
  While the wood-wind sings, 'Hush-a-by-
    by."

"Hush-a-by-hush," 'tis the voice of the forest,
  "Hush-a-by-hush," the leaves seem to say,
"Hush-a-by-hush," sing the wild birds in
    chorus
  Up in the tree-tops so far, far away.

Rock-a-by, rock-a-by, swinging so gently,
  See, from the dark woods so cool and so
    deep,
The little gray squirrel, the timid brown rab-
    bit,
  Are coming to see if papoose is asleep.

Mother will watch by her little brown baby,
  Swinging aloft on the green branch so high,
No harm can come to the little brown baby.
  Hush-a-by, rock-a-by, hush-a-by-by.

Lullaby of an Infant Chief

SIR WALTER SCOTT

(AIR — "Cadul gu lo")

*The words of the air mean "Sleep on till
day." The lullaby was written for Mr. Terry's
dramatization of Scott's novel,* Guy Mannering.

O, hush thee, my babie, thy sire was a knight,
Thy mother a lady both lovely and bright;

The woods and the glens, from the towers
    which we see,
They all are belonging, dear babie, to thee.
    O ho ro, i ri ri, cadul gu lo,
    O ho ro, i ri ri, cadul gu lo.

O, fear not the bugle, though loudly it blows,
It calls but the warders that guard thy repose;
Their bows would be bended, their blades
    would be red,
Ere the step of a foeman draws near to thy
    bed.
    O ho ro, i ri ri, etc.

O, hush thee, my babie, the time soon will
    come,
When thy sleep shall be broken by trumpet
    and drum;
Then hush thee, my darling, take rest while
    you may,
For strife comes with manhood and waking
    with day.
    O ho ro, i ri ri, etc.

Wynken, Blynken, and Nod [8]

Eugene Field

Wynken, Blynken, and Nod one night
    Sailed off in a wooden shoe —
Sailed on a river of crystal light,
    Into a sea of dew.
"Where are you going, and what do you
    wish?"
    The old moon asked the three.
"We have come to fish for the herring fish
    That live in this beautiful sea,
Nets of silver and gold have we!"
    Said Wynken,
    Blynken,
    And Nod.

The old moon laughed and sang a song,
    As they rocked in the wooden shoe,
And the wind that sped them all night long
    Ruffled the waves of dew.
The little stars were the herring fish
    That lived in that beautiful sea —
"Now cast your nets wherever you wish —
    Never afeared are we";

8 From Eugene Field, *Poems of Childhood.*

So cried the stars to the fishermen three:
    Wynken,
    Blynken,
    And Nod.

All night long their nets they threw
    To the stars in the twinkling foam —
Then down from the skies came the wooden
    shoe,
    Bringing the fishermen home;
'Twas all so pretty a sail it seemed
    As if it could not be,
And some folks thought 'twas a dream they'd
    dreamed
    Of sailing that beautiful sea —
But I shall name you the fishermen three:
    Wynken,
    Blynken,
    And Nod.

Wynken and Blynken are two little eyes,
    And Nod is a little head,
And the wooden shoe that sailed the skies
    Is a wee one's trundle bed;
So shut your eyes while mother sings
    Of wonderful sights that be,
And you shall see the beautiful things
    As you rock in the misty sea
Where the old shoe rocked the fishermen
    three: —
    Wynken,
    Blynken,
    And Nod.

Sweet and Low

Alfred, Lord Tennyson

Sweet and low, sweet and low,
    Wind of the western sea.
Low, low, breathe and blow,
    Wind of the western sea!
Over the rolling waters go,
Come from the dying moon, and blow,
    Blow him again to me;
While my little one, while my pretty one,
    sleeps.

Sleep and rest, sleep and rest,
    Father will come to thee soon;

Rest, rest on mother's breast,
    Father will come to thee soon;
Father will come to his babe in the
    nest,
Silver sails all out of the west
    Under the silver moon;
Sleep, my little one, sleep, my pretty one,
    sleep.

Seal Lullaby [9]

RUDYARD KIPLING

Oh! hush thee, my baby, the night is behind
    us,
    And black are the waters that sparkled so
       green.

[9] From Rudyard Kipling, *The Jungle Book*
(Doubleday).

The moon, o'er the combers, looks downward
    to find us
At rest in the hollows that rustle between.
Where billow meets billow, there soft be thy
    pillow;
    Ah, weary wee flipperling, curl at thy ease!
The storm shall not wake thee, nor shark
    overtake thee,
    Asleep in the arms of the slow-swinging
      seas.

Good Night

THOMAS HOOD

Here's a body — there's a bed!
There's a pillow — here's a head!
There's a curtain — here's a light!
There's a puff — and so good night!

CHRISTMAS, CHRISTMAS!

While Shepherds Watched Their Flocks by Night [1]

NAHUM TATE

While shepherds watched their flocks by
    night,
    All seated on the ground,
The angel of the Lord came down,
    And glory shone around.

"Fear not," said he, for mighty dread
    Had seized their troubled mind;
"Glad tidings of great joy I bring
    To you and all mankind.

"To you, in David's town, this day
    Is born, of David's line,

The Saviour, who is Christ the Lord,
    And this shall be the sign:

"The heavenly babe you there shall find
    To human view displayed,
All meanly wrapped in swaddling bands,
    And in a manger laid."

Thus spake the seraph; and forthwith
    Appeared a shining throng
Of angels, praising God, who thus
    Addressed their joyful song:

"All glory be to God on high,
    And to the earth be peace;
Good-will henceforth from Heaven to men
    Begin and never cease."

[1] From Nahum Tate, *Supplement to the New Version of the Psalms of David.*

O Little Town of Bethlehem [2]

PHILLIPS BROOKS

O little town of Bethlehem,
  How still we see thee lie!
Above thy deep and dreamless sleep
  The silent stars go by;
Yet in thy dark streets shineth
  The everlasting Light;
The hopes and fears of all the years
  Are met in thee tonight.

For Christ is born of Mary,
  And, gathered all above,
While mortals sleep, the angels keep
  Their watch of wondering love.
O morning stars, together
  Proclaim the holy birth!
And praises sing to God the King,
  And peace to men on earth.

How silently, how silently,
  The wondrous gift is given!
So God imparts to human hearts
  The blessings of His heaven.
No ear may hear His coming,
  But in this world of sin,
Where meek souls will receive Him still,
  The dear Christ enters in.

O holy Child of Bethlehem!
  Descend to us, we pray;
Cast out our sin, and enter in,
  Be born in us today.
We hear the Christmas angels
  The great glad tidings tell;
Oh, come to us, abide with us,
  Our Lord Emmanuel!

Cradle Hymn [3]

MARTIN LUTHER

Away in a manger, no crib for a bed,
The little Lord Jesus laid down his sweet
    head.
The stars in the bright sky looked down
    where he lay —
The little Lord Jesus asleep on the hay.

The cattle are lowing, the baby awakes,
But little Lord Jesus no crying he makes.
I love Thee, Lord Jesus! look down from the
    sky,
And stay by my cradle till morning is nigh.

Be near me, Lord Jesus, I ask thee to stay
Close by me forever, and love me, I pray.
Bless all the dear children, in Thy tender
    care,
And take us to heaven, to live with Thee
    there.

Christmas Morning [4]

ELIZABETH MADOX ROBERTS

If Bethlehem were here today,
Or this were very long ago,
There wouldn't be a winter time
Nor any cold or snow.

I'd run out through the garden gate,
And down along the pasture walk;
And off beside the cattle barns
I'd hear a kind of gentle talk.

I'd move the heavy iron chain
Aud pull away the wooden pin;
I'd push the door a little bit
And tiptoe very softly in.

The pigeons and the yellow hens
And all the cows would stand away;
Their eyes would open wide to see
A lady in the manger hay,

If this were very long ago
And Bethlehem were here today.

And Mother held my hand and smiled —
I mean the lady would — and she
Would take the woolly blankets off
Her little boy so I could see.

His shut-up eyes would be asleep,
And he would look like our John,
And he would be all crumpled too,
And have a pinkish color on.

I'd watch his breath go in and out.
His little clothes would all be white.

2 From Phillips Brooks, *Christmas Songs and Easter Carols* (Dutton).

3 From Martin Luther, *Sämtliche Deutsche Geistliche Lieder;* translator unknown.

4 From Elizabeth Madox Roberts, *Under the Tree* (Viking Press).

I'd slip my finger in his hand
To feel how he could hold it tight.

And she would smile and say, "Take care,"
The mother, Mary, would, "Take care";
And I would kiss his little hand
And touch his hair.

While Mary put the blankets back
The gentle talk would soon begin.
And when I'd tiptoe softly out
I'd meet the wise men going in.

A Christmas Folk-Song[5]

LIZETTE WOODWORTH REESE

The little Jesus came to town;
　The wind blew up, the wind blew down;
Out in the street the wind was bold;
　Now who would house Him from the cold?

Then opened wide the stable door,
　Fair were the rushes on the floor;
The Ox put forth a horned head:
　"Come, little Lord, here make Thy bed."

Up rose the Sheep were folded near;
　"Thou Lamb of God, come, enter here."
He entered there to rush and reed,
　Who was the Lamb of God indeed.

The little Jesus came to town;
　With ox and sheep He laid Him down;
Peace to the byre, peace to the fold,
　For that they housed Him from the cold!

God Rest Ye Merry, Gentlemen[6]

DINAH MARIA MULOCK CRAIK

God rest ye merry, gentlemen; let nothing
　you dismay,
For Jesus Christ, our Saviour, was born on
　Christmas-day.
The dawn rose red o'er Bethlehem, the stars
　shone through the gray,
When Jesus Christ, our Saviour, was born on
　Christmas-day.

[5] From Lizette Woodworth Reese, *A Wayside Lute* (Mosher).

[6] From Dinah Maria Mulock Craik, *Thirty Years; Being Poems, New and Old.*

God rest ye, little children; let nothing you
　affright,
For Jesus Christ, your Saviour, was born this
　happy night;
Along the hills of Galilee the white flocks
　sleeping lay,
When Christ, the Child of Nazareth, was
　born on Christmas-day.

God rest ye, all good Christians; upon this
　blessed morn
The Lord of all good Christians was of a
　woman born:
Now all your sorrows He doth heal, your sins
　He takes away;
For Jesus Christ, our Saviour, was born on
　Christmas-day.

"Some Say . . ."[7]

WILLIAM SHAKESPEARE

Some say that ever 'gainst that season comes
Wherein our Savior's birth is celebrated,
The bird of dawning singeth all night
　long:
And then, they say, no spirit dare stir abroad,
The nights are wholesome, then no planets
　strike,
No fairy takes nor witch hath power to
　charm,
So hallow'd and so gracious is the time.

I Wonder as I Wander

TRADITIONAL

I wonder as I wander out under the sky
How Jesus, our Saviour, did come for to
　die
For poor orn'ry people like you and like I
I wonder as I wander out under the sky.

When Mary birthed Jesus 'twas in a cow's
　stall
With Wise Men, and shepherds, and farmers
　and all.
But high from God's Heaven a star's light
　did fall
And the promise of ages it then did recall.

[7] From *Hamlet*, Act I, Scene I.

A Visit from St. Nicholas[8]

Clement C. Moore

'Twas the night before Christmas, when all
    through the house
Not a creature was stirring, not even a
    mouse.
The stockings were hung by the chimney
    with care,
In hopes that St. Nicholas soon would be
    there.
The children were nestled all snug in their
    beds,
While visions of sugar-plums danced in their
    heads;
And mamma in her kerchief, and I in my
    cap,
Had just settled our brains for a long win-
    ter's nap —
When out on the lawn there arose such a
    clatter
I sprang from my bed to see what was the
    matter.
Away to the window I flew like a flash,
Tore open the shutter, and threw up the
    sash.
The moon on the breast of the new-fallen
    snow
Gave a lustre of midday to objects below;
When what to my wondering eyes should ap-
    pear
But a miniature sleigh and eight tiny rein-
    deer,
With a little old driver, so lively and quick,
I knew in a moment it must be St. Nick!
More rapid than eagles his coursers they
    came,
And he whistled and shouted and called them
    by name.
"Now, Dasher! now, Dancer! now, Prancer
    and Vixen!
On, Comet! on, Cupid! on, Donder and Blit-
    zen! —
To the top of the porch, to the top of the
    wall,
Now, dash away, dash away, dash away all!"
As dry leaves that before the wild hurricane
    fly,
When they meet with an obstacle mount to
    the sky,

So, up to the housetop the coursers they flew,
With a sleigh full of toys — and St. Nicholas,
    too.
And then, in a twinkling, I heard on the roof
The prancing and pawing of each little hoof.
As I drew in my head and was turning
    around,
Down the chimney St. Nicholas came with a
    bound:
He was dressed all in fur from his head to
    his foot,
And his clothes were all tarnished with ashes
    and soot:
A bundle of toys he had flung on his back,
And he looked like a peddler just opening
    his pack.
His eyes, how they twinkled! his dimples,
    how merry!
His cheeks were like roses, his nose like a
    cherry;
His droll little mouth was drawn up like a
    bow,
And the beard on his chin was as white as
    the snow.
The stump of a pipe he held tight in his
    teeth,
And the smoke, it encircled his head like a
    wreath.
He had a broad face and a little round belly
That shook, when he laughed, like a bowl
    full of jelly.
He was chubby and plump — a right jolly old
    elf:
And I laughed when I saw him, in spite of
    myself;
A wink of his eye, and a twist of his head,
Soon gave me to know I had nothing to
    dread.
He spoke not a word, but went straight to
    his work,
And filled all the stockings: then turned with
    a jerk,
And laying his finger aside of his nose,
And giving a nod, up the chimney he rose.
He sprang to his sleigh, to his team gave a
    whistle,
And away they all flew like the down of a
    thistle.
But I heard him exclaim, ere they drove out
    of sight,
"Happy Christmas to all, and to all a good-
    night!"

[8] From Troy, New York, *Sentinel.*

THE GRACE OF UNDERSTANDING

Measure Me, Sky![1]

LEONORA SPEYER

Measure me, sky!
  Tell me I reach by a song
Nearer the stars;
  I have been little so long.

Weigh me, high wind!
  What will your wild scales record?
Profit of pain,
  Joy by the weight of a word.

Horizon, reach out!
  Catch at my hands, stretch me taut,
Rim of the world:
  Widen my eyes by a thought.

Sky, be my depth,
  Wind, be my width and my height,
World, my heart's span;
  Loveliness, wings for my flight.

Beauty[2]

E YEH-SHURE

(LOUISE ABEITA)

Beauty is seen
In the sunlight,
The trees, the birds,
Corn growing and people working
Or dancing for their harvest.

Beauty is heard
In the night,
Wind sighing, rain falling,
Or a singer chanting
Anything in earnest.

Beauty is in yourself.
Good deeds, happy thoughts
That repeat themselves
In your dreams,
In your work,
And even in your rest.

Barter[3]

SARA TEASDALE

Life has loveliness to sell,
  All beautiful and splendid things,
Blue waves whitened on a cliff,
  Soaring fire that sways and sings,
And children's faces looking up
Holding wonder like a cup.

Life has loveliness to sell,
  Music like a curve of gold,
Scent of pine trees in the rain,
  Eyes that love you, arms that hold,
And for your spirit's still delight,
Holy thoughts that star the night.

Spend all you have for loveliness,
  Buy it and never count the cost;
For one white singing hour of peace
  Count many a year of strife well lost,
And for a breath of ecstasy
Give all you have been, or could be.

1 From Leonora Speyer, *Slow Wall, Poems*, together with *Nor without Music* (Knopf).
2 From E-Yeh-Shure (Louise Abeita, *I Am a Pueblo Indian Girl* (Morrow).
3 From Sara Teasdale, *Love Songs* (Macmillan).

Wings[4]

VICTOR HUGO

Be like the bird, who
Halting in his flight
On limb too slight
Feels it give way beneath him,
Yet sings
Knowing he hath wings.

My Heart Leaps Up

WILLIAM WORDSWORTH

My heart leaps up when I behold
    A rainbow in the sky:
So was it when my life began;
So is it now I am a man;
So be it when I shall grow old,
    Or let me die!
The Child is father of the Man;
And I could wish my days to be
Bound each to each by natural piety.

I Never Saw a Moor[5]

EMILY DICKINSON

I never saw a moor,
I never saw the sea;
Yet know I how the heather looks,
And what a wave must be.

I never spoke with God,
Nor visited in heaven;
Yet certain am I of the spot
As if the chart were given.

Do You Fear the Wind?[6]

HAMLIN GARLAND

Do you fear the force of the wind,
The slash of the rain?
Go face them and fight them,
Be savage again.

Go hungry and cold like the wolf,
Go wade like the crane:
The palms of your hands will thicken,
The skin of your cheeks will tan,
You'll grow ragged and weary and swarthy,
    But you'll walk like a man!

A Song of Greatness[7]

(A Chippewa Indian Song)

TRANSCRIBED BY MARY AUSTIN

When I hear the old men
Telling of heroes,
Telling of great deeds
Of ancient days,
When I hear them telling,
Then I think within me
I too am one of these.

When I hear the people
Praising great ones,
Then I know that I too
Shall be esteemed,
I too when my time comes
Shall do mightily.

A Chant Out of Doors[8]

MARGUERITE WILKINSON

God of grave nights,
God of brave mornings,
God of silent noon,
Hear my salutation!

For where the rapids rage white and scorn-
    ful,
I have passed safely, filled with wonder;
Where the sweet pools dream under wil-
    lows,
I have been swimming, filled with life.

God of round hills,
God of green valleys,
God of clear springs,
Hear my salutation!

4 From Sung Under the Silver Umbrella, ed. by the Association for Childhood Education.
5 From The Poems of Emily Dickinson, ed. by Martha Dickinson Bianchi and Alfred Leete Hampson.
6 From Hamlin Garland, Prairie Songs.
7 From Mary Austin, Children Sing in the Far West (Houghton Mifflin).
8 From Marguerite Wilkinson, Bluestone (Macmillan).

For where the moose feeds, I have eaten
    berries,
Where the moose drinks, I have drunk
    deep.
When the storms crash through broken
    heavens —
And under clear skies — I have known joy.

God of great trees,
God of wild grasses,
God of little flowers,
Hear my salutation!

For where the deer crops and the beaver
    plunges,
Near the river I have pitched my tent;
Where the pines cast aromatic needles
On a still floor, I have known peace.

God of grave nights,
God of brave mornings,
God of silent noon,
Hear my salutation.

Fern Hill [9]

DYLAN THOMAS

Now as I was young and easy under the apple
    boughs
About the lilting house and happy as the
    grass was green,
  The night above the dingle starry,
    Time let me hail and climb
  Golden in the heydays of his eyes,
And honoured among wagons I was prince of
    the apple towns
And once below a time I lordly had the trees
    and leaves
    Trail with daisies and barley
  Down the rivers of the windfall light.

And as I was green and carefree, famous
    among the barns
About the happy yard and singing as the
    farm was home,
  In the sun that is young once only,
    Time let me play and be
  Golden in the mercy of his means,

[9] From Dylan Thomas, *Collected Poems* (New Directions).

And green and golden I was huntsman and
    herdsman, the calves
Sang to my horn, the foxes on the hills
    barked clear and cold,
    And the sabbath rang slowly
  In the pebbles of the holy streams.

All the sun long it was running, it was lovely,
    the hay
Fields high as the house, the tunes from the
    chimneys, it was air
  And playing, lovely and watery
    And fire green as grass.
  And nightly under the simple stars
As I rode to sleep the owls were bearing the
    farm away,
All the moon long I heard, blessed among
    stables, the night-jars
    Flying with the ricks, and the horses
    Flashing into the dark.

And then to awake, and the farm, like a wan-
    derer white
With the dew, come back, the cock on his
    shoulder: it was all
  Shining, it was Adam and maiden,
    The sky gathered again
  And the sun grew round that very day.
So it must have been after the birth of the
    simple light
In the first, spinning place, the spellbound
    horses walking warm
    Out of the whinnying green stable
    On to the fields of praise.

And honoured among foxes and pheasants by
    the gay house
Under the new made clouds and happy as the
    heart was long,
  In the sun born over and over,
    I ran my heedless ways,
  My wishes raced through the house-high
    hay
And nothing I cared, at my sky blue trades,
    that time allows
In all his tuneful turning so few and such
    morning songs
  Before the children green and golden
    Follow him out of grace,

Nothing I cared, in the lamb white days, that
    time would take me
Up to the swallow thronged loft by the
    shadow of my hand,

In the moon that is always rising,
  Nor that riding to sleep
I should hear him fly with the high fields
And wake to the farm forever fled from the
    childless land.
Oh as I was young and easy in the mercy of
    his means,
  Time held me green and dying
Though I sang in my chains like the sea.

Miracles[1]

WALT WHITMAN

Why, who makes much of a miracle?
As for me I know of nothing else but mir-
    acles,
Whether I walk the streets of Manhattan . . .
Or watch honey-bees busy around the hive
    of a summer forenoon,
Or animals feeding in the fields,
Or birds, or the wonderfulness of insects in
    the air,
Or the wonderfulness of the sun-down, or of
    stars shining so quiet and bright,
Or the exquisite, delicate, thin curve of the
    new moon in spring; . . .
To me every hour of the light and dark is a
    miracle,
Every cubic inch of space is a miracle,
Every square yard of the surface of the earth
    is spread with the same . . .
To me the sea is a continual miracle,
The fishes that swim — the rocks — the mo-
    tion of the waves — the ships with men
    in them,
What stranger miracles are there?

Give Me the Splendid Silent Sun[2]

WALT WHITMAN

Give me the splendid silent sun with all his
    beams full-dazzling,
Give me juicy autumnal fruit ripe and red
    from the orchard,

[1] From "Miracles" in Walt Whitman, *Leaves of Grass* (Doubleday).
[2] From Walt Whitman, *Leaves of Grass* (Double-day).

Give me a field where the unmowed grass
    grows,
Give me an arbor, give me the trellised
    grape,
Give me fresh corn and wheat, give me
    serene-moving animals teaching con-
    tent,
Give me nights perfectly quiet as on high
    plateaus west of the Mississippi, and
    I looking up at the stars,
Give me odorous at sunrise a garden of beau-
    tiful flowers where I can walk undis-
    turbed,
Give me for marriage a sweet-breath'd woman
    of whom I should never tire,
Give me to warble spontaneous songs recluse
    by myself, for my own ears only,
Give me solitude, give me Nature, give me
    again, O Nature, your primal sanities!

I Hear America Singing[3]

WALT WHITMAN

I hear America singing, the varied carols I
    hear,
Those of mechanics, each one singing his as
    it should be blithe and strong,
The carpenter singing his as he measures his
    plank or beam,
The mason singing his as he makes ready for
    work, or leaves off work,
The boatman singing what belongs to him in
    his boat, the deckhand singing on the
    steamboat deck,
The shoemaker singing as he sits on his
    bench, the hatter singing as he stands,
The woodcutter's song, the plowboy's on his
    way in the morning, or at noon inter-
    mission or at sundown,
The delicious singing of the mother, or of
    the young wife at work, or of the girl
    sewing or washing,
Each singing what belongs to him or her and
    to none else,
The day what belongs to the day — at night
    the party of young fellows, robust,
    friendly,
Singing with open mouths their strong melo-
    dious songs.

[3] *Ibid.*

The Commonplace[4]

WALT WHITMAN

The commonplace I sing;
How cheap is health! how cheap nobility!
Abstinence, no falsehood, no gluttony.
The open air I sing, freedom, toleration,
(Take here the mainest lesson — less from
    books — less from the schools,)
The common day and night — the common
    earth and waters,
Your farm — your work, trade, occupation,
The democratic wisdom underneath, like
    solid ground for all.

Atlantic Charter: 1620–1942[5]

FRANCIS BRETT YOUNG

What were you carrying, Pilgrims, Pilgrims?
What did you carry beyond the sea?
    We carried the Book, we carried the
        Sword,
    A steadfast heart in the fear of the
        Lord,
    And a living faith in His plighted word
    That all men should be free.

Lincoln[6]

JOHN GOULD FLETCHER

Like a gaunt, scraggly pine
Which lifts its head above the mournful sand-
    hills;
And patiently, through dull years of bitter
    silence,
Untended and uncared for, starts to grow.

Ungainly, laboring, huge,
The wind of the north has twisted and
    gnarled its branches;
Yet in the heat of mid-summer days, when
    thunder clouds ring the horizon,
A nation of men shall rest beneath its shade.

4 *Ibid.*
5 From Francis Brett Young, *The Island* (Farrar, Straus).
6 From John Gould Fletcher, *Selected Poems* (Rinehart).

And it shall protect them all,
Hold everyone safe there, watching aloof in
    silence;
Until at last, one mad stray bolt from the
    zenith
Shall strike it in an instant down to earth.

Abraham Lincoln Walks at Midnight[7]

(In Springfield, Illinois)

VACHEL LINDSAY

It is portentous, and a thing of state
That here at midnight, in our little town
A mourning figure walks, and will not
    rest,
Near the old court-house pacing up and
    down,

Or by his homestead, or in shadowed yards
He lingers where his children used to play,
Or through the market, on the well-worn
    stones
He stalks until the dawn-stars burn away.

A bronzed, lank man! His suit of ancient
    black,
A famous high top hat and plain worn shawl
Make him the quaint great figure that men
    love,
The prairie-lawyer, master of us all.

He cannot sleep upon his hillside now.
He is among us: — as in times before!
And we who toss and lie awake for long
Breathe deep, and start, to see him pass the
    door.

His head is bowed. He thinks on men and
    kings.
Yea, when the sick world cries, how can he
    sleep?
Too many peasants fight, they know not why,
Too many homesteads in black terror weep.

The sins of all the war-lords burn his heart.
He sees the dreadnaughts scouring every
    main.

7 From Vachel Lindsay, *Collected Poems* (Macmillan).

He carries on his shawl-wrapped shoulders
now
The bitterness, the folly and the pain.

He cannot rest until a spirit-dawn
Shall come; — the shining hope of Europe
free:
The league of sober folk, the Workers' Earth,
Bringing long peace to Cornland, Alp and
Sea.

It breaks his heart that kings must murder
still,
That all his hours of travail here for men
Seem yet in vain. And who will bring white
peace
That he may sleep upon his hill again?

Nancy Hanks [8]

ROSEMARY CARR AND STEPHEN VINCENT BENÉT

If Nancy Hanks
Came back as a ghost,
Seeking news
Of what she loved most,
She'd ask first
"Where's my son?
What's happened to Abe?
What's he done?

"Poor little Abe,
Left all alone
Except for Tom,
Who's a rolling stone;
He was only nine
The year I died,
I remember still
How hard he cried.

"Scraping along
In a little shack,
With hardly a shirt
To cover his back,
And a prairie wind
To blow him down,
Or pinching times
If he went to town.

"You wouldn't know
About my son?

[8] From Rosemary and Stephen Vincent Benét, *A Book of Americans* (Rinehart)

Did he grow tall?
Did he have fun?

Did he learn to read?
Did he get to town?
Do you know his name?
Did he get on?"

"When to the Sessions of Sweet Silent Thought"

WILLIAM SHAKESPEARE

When to the sessions of sweet silent thought
I summon up remembrance of things past,
I sigh the lack of many a thing I sought,
And with old woes new wail my dear time's
waste:
Then can I drown an eye, unused to flow,
For precious friends hid in death's dateless
night,
And weep afresh love's long since canceled
woe,
And moan the expense of many a vanished
sight:
Then can I grieve at grievances foregone,
And heavily from woe to woe tell o'er
The sad account of fore-bemoaned moan,
Which I new pay as if not paid before.
But if the while I think on thee, dear
friend,
All losses are restored and sorrows end.

Incident [9]

COUNTEE CULLEN

Once riding in old Baltimore,
Heart-filled, head-filled with glee,
I saw a Baltimorean
Keep looking straight at me.

Now I was eight and very small,
And he was no whit bigger,
And so I smiled, but he poked out
His tongue, and called me, "Nigger."

I saw the whole of Baltimore
From May until December;

[9] From Countee Cullen, *Color* (Harper).

Of all the things that happened there
That's all that I remember.

Ring Around the World[10]

ANNETTE WYNNE

Ring around the world
Taking hands together

10 From Annette Wynne, *All Through the Year* (Lippincott).

All across the temperate
And the torrid weather.
Past the royal palm-trees
By the ocean sand
Make a ring around the world
Taking each other's hand;
In the valleys, on the hill,
Over the prairie spaces,
There's a ring around the world
Made of children's friendly faces.

BALLADS AND TALES

Get Up and Bar the Door[1]

OLD BALLAD

It fell about the Martinmas time,
And a gay time it was then,
When our goodwife got puddings to make,
And she's boild them in the pan.

The wind sae cauld blew south and north,
And blew into the floor;
Quoth our goodman to our goodwife,
"Gae out and bar the door."

"My hand is in my hussyfskap,
Goodman, as ye may see;
An it should nae be barrd this hundred year,
It's no be barrd for me."

They made a paction tween them twa,
They made it firm and sure,
That the first word whaeer shoud speak,
Shoud rise and bar the door.

Then by there came two gentlemen,
At twelve o'clock at night,

1 From *Oxford Book of Ballads*, comp. by A. T. Quiller-Couch.

And they could neither see house nor hall,
Nor coal nor candle-light.

"Now whether is this a rich man's house,
Or whether is it a poor?"
But neer a word wad ane o them speak,
For barring of the door.

And first they ate the white puddings,
And then they ate the black;
Tho muckle thought the goodwife to hersel,
Yet neer a word she spake.

Then said the one unto the other,
"Here, man, tak ye my knife;
Do ye tak aff the auld man's beard,
And I'll kiss the goodwife."

"But there's nae water in the house,
And what shall we do than?"
"What ails ye at the pudding-broo,
That boils into the pan?"

O up then started our goodman,
An angry man was he:
"Will ye kiss my wife before my een,
And scad me wi pudding-bree?"

Then up and started our goodwife,
  Gied three skips on the floor:
"Goodman, you've spoken the foremost word,
  Get up and bar the door."

Sir Patrick Spens [2]

OLD BALLAD

The king sits in Dunfermline town,
  Drinking the blood-red wine:
"O where will I get a skeely skipper
  To sail this new ship of mine?"

O up and spake an eldern knight,
  Sate at the king's right knee —
"Sir Patrick Spens is the best sailor
  That ever sailed the sea."

Our king has written a broad letter,
  And sealed it with his hand,
And sent it to Sir Patrick Spens
  Was walking on the strand.

The first word that Sir Patrick read,
  So loud, loud laughed he;
The next word that Sir Patrick read,
  The tear blinded his ee.

"O who is this has done this deed,
  And told the king o' me,
To send us out, at this time of the year,
  To sail upon the sea?

"Make ready, make ready, my merry men all!
  Our good ship sails the morn."
"Now ever alack, my master dear,
  I fear a deadly storm!

"I saw the new moon, late yestreen,
  With the auld moon in her arm;
And if we gang to sea, master,
  I fear we'll come to harm."

They had not sailed a league, a league,
  A league but barely three,
When the lift grew dark, and the wind blew
    loud,
  And gurly grew the sea.

"Go, fetch a web o' the silken cloth,
  Another o' the twine,
And wap them into our ship's side,
  And let not the sea come in."

O loth, loth, were our good Scotch lords
  To wet their cork-heeled shoon!
But lang ere a' the play was play'd
  They wet their hats aboon.

O long, long may the ladies sit,
  With their fans into their hand,
Before they see Sir Patrick Spens
  Come sailing to the strand!

And long, long may the maidens sit,
  Wi' the goud combs in their hair,
All waiting for their own dear loves —
  For them they'll see no mair.

Half owre, half owre to Aberdour,
  'Tis fifty fathoms deep,
And there lies good Sir Patrick Spens,
  With the Scotch lords at his feet.

Robin Hood and Little John [3]

OLD BALLAD

When Robin Hood was about twenty years
    old,
  With a hey down down and a down
He happened to meet Little John,
A jolly brisk blade, right fit for the trade,
  For he was a lusty young man.

Tho he was calld Little, his limbs they were
    large,
  And his stature was seven foot high;
Where-ever he came, they quak'd at his
    name,
  For soon he would make them to fly.

How they came acquainted, I'll tell you in
    brief,
  If you will but listen a while;
For this very jest, amongst all the rest,
  I think it may cause you to smile.

[2] Adapted from *English and Scottish Popular Ballads*, Vol. II; comp. by Francis James Child.

[3] From *Story-Telling Ballads*, sel. by Frances Jenkins Olcott.

Bold Robin Hood said to his jolly bowmen,
  "Pray tarry you here in this grove;
And see that you all observe well my call,
  While thorough the forest I rove.

"We have had no sport for these fourteen
    long days,
  Therefore now abroad will I go;
Now should I be beat, and cannot retreat,
  My horn I will presently blow."

Then did he shake hands with his merry men
    all,
  And bid them at present good b'w'ye;
Then, as near a brook his journey he took,
  A stranger he chanced to espy.

They happened to meet on a long narrow
    bridge,
  And neither of them would give way;
Quoth bold Robin Hood, and sturdily stood,
  "I'll show you right Nottingham play."

With that from his quiver an arrow he drew,
  A broad arrow with a goose-wing;
The stranger reply'd, "I'll liquor thy hide,
  If thou offerst to touch the string."

Quoth bold Robin Hood, "Thou dost prate
    like an ass,
  For were I to bend but my bow,
I could send a dart quite thro thy proud
    heart,
  Before thou couldst strike me one blow."

"Thou talkst like a coward," the stranger
    reply'd;
  "Well armed with a long bow you stand,
To shoot at my breast, while I, I protest,
  Have nought but a staff in my hand."

"The name of a coward," quoth Robin, "I
    scorn,
  Wherefore my long bow I'll lay by;
And now, for thy sake, a staff will I take,
  The truth of thy manhood to try."

Then Robin Hood step'd to a thicket of
    trees,
  And chose him a staff of ground-oak;
Now this being done, away he did run
  To the stranger, and merrily spoke:

"Lo! see my staff, it is lusty and tough,
  Now here on the bridge we will play;
Whoever falls in, the other shall win
  The battle, and so we'll away."

"With all my whole heart," the stranger re-
    ply'd;
  "I scorn in the least to give out;"
This said, they fell to 't without more dis-
    pute,
  And their staffs they did flourish about.

And first Robin he gave the stranger a bang,
  So hard that it made his bones ring;
The stranger he said, "This must be repaid,
  I'll give you as good as you bring.

"So long as I'm able to handle my staff,
  To die in your debt, friend, I scorn:"
Then to it each goes, and follow'd their
    blows,
  As if they had been threshing of corn.

The stranger gave Robin a crack on the
    crown,
  Which caused the blood to appear;
Then Robin, enrag'd, more fiercely engag'd,
  And follow'd his blows more severe.

So thick and so fast did he lay it on him,
  With a passionate fury and ire,
At every stroke, he made him to smoke,
  As if he had been all on fire.

O then into fury the stranger he grew,
  And gave him a damnable look,
And with it a blow that laid him full low,
  And tumbld him into the brook.

"I prithee, good fellow, O where art thou
    now?"
  The stranger, in laughter, he cry'd;
Quoth bold Robin Hood, "Good faith, in the
    flood,
  And floating along with the tide.

"I needs must acknowledge thou art a brave
    soul;
  With thee I'll no longer contend;
For needs must I say, thou hast got the day,
  Our battel shall be at an end."

Then unto the bank he did presently wade,
　And pulld himself out by a thorn;
Which done, at the last, he blowd a loud
　　blast
　Straitway on his fine bugle-horn.

The echo of which through the vallies did
　　fly,
　At which his stout bowmen appeared,
All clothed in green, most gay to be seen;
　So up to their master they steerd.

"O what's the matter?" quoth William
　　Stutely;
　"Good master, you are wet to the skin":
"No matter," quoth he; "the lad which you
　　see,
　In fighting, hath tumbld me in."

"He shall not go scot-free," the others re-
　　ply'd;
　So strait they were seizing him there,
To duck him likewise; but Robin Hood cries,
　He is a stout fellow, forbear.

"There's no one shall wrong thee, friend, be
　　not afraid;
　These bowmen upon me do wait;
There's threescore and nine; if thou wilt be
　　mine,
　Thou shalt have my livery strait.

"And other accoutrements fit for a man;
　Speak up, jolly blade, never fear;
I'll teach you also the use of the bow,
　To shoot at the fat fallow-deer."

"O here is my hand," the stranger reply'd,
　"I'll serve you with all my whole heart;
My name is John Little, a man of good
　　mettle;
　Nere doubt me, for I'll play my part."

"His name shall be alterd," quoth William
　　Stutely,
　"And I will his godfather be;
Prepare then a feast, and none of the least,
　For we will be merry," quoth he.

They presently fetched in a brace of fat does,
　With humming strong liquor likewise;
They lovd what was good; so, in the green-
　　wood,
　This pretty sweet babe they baptize.

He was, I must tell you but seven foot high,
　And, may be, an ell in the waste;
A pretty sweet lad; much feasting they had;
　Bold Robin the christening grac'd.

With all his bowmen, which stood in a ring,
　And were of the Nottingham breed;
Brave Stutely comes then, with seven yeomen,
　And did in this manner proceed.

"This infant was called John Little," quoth
　　he,
　Which name shall be changed anon;
The words we'll transpose, so wherever he
　　goes,
　His name shall be calld Little John."

They all with a shout made the elements
　　ring,
　So soon as the office was ore;
To feasting they went, with true merriment,
　And tippld strong liquor gillore.

Then Robin he took the pretty sweet babe,
　And cloth'd him from top to the toe
In garments of green, most gay to be seen,
　And gave him a curious long bow.

"Thou shalt be an archer as well as the
　　best,
　And range in the greenwood with us;
Where we'll not want gold nor silver, behold,
　While bishops have ought in their purse.

"We live here like squires, or lords of re-
　　nown,
　Without ere a foot of free land;
We feast on good cheer, with wine, ale and
　　beer,
　And ev'rything at our command."

Then musick and dancing did finish the
　　day;
　At length, when the sun waxed low,
Then all the whole train the grove did re-
　　frain,
　And unto their caves they did go.

And so ever after, as long as he liv'd,
　Although he was proper and tall,
Yet nevertheless, the truth to express,
　Still Little John they did him call.

The Keys of Canterbury

TRADITIONAL

O Madam, I will give to you
The keys of Canterbury,
And all the bells in London
Shall ring to make us merry,
If you will be my joy, my sweet and only dear,
And walk along with me, anywhere.

I shall not, Sir, accept of you
The keys of Canterbury,
Nor all the bells in London
Shall ring to make us merry,
I will not be your joy, your sweet and only
dear,
Nor walk along with you, anywhere.

O Madam, I will give to you
A pair of boots of cork;
The one was made in London,
The other made in York,
If you will be my joy, my sweet and only dear,
And walk along with me, anywhere.

I shall not, Sir, accept of you
A pair of boots of cork,
Though both were made in London,
Or both were made in York.
I will not be your joy, your sweet and only
dear,
Nor walk along with you, anywhere.

O Madam, I will give to you
A little golden bell,
To ring for all your servants
And make them serve you well,
If you will be my joy, my sweet and only dear,
And walk along with me, anywhere.

I shall not, Sir, accept of you
A little golden bell,
To ring for all my servents
To make them serve me well;
I will not be your joy, your sweet and only
dear,
Nor walk along with you, anywhere.

O Madam, I will give to you
A gallant silver chest,

With a key of gold and silver,
And jewels of the best,
If you will be my joy, my sweet and only dear,
And walk along with me, anywhere.

I shall not, Sir, accept of you
A gallant silver chest,
A key of gold and silver
Nor jewels of the best.
I will not be your joy, your sweet and only
dear,
Nor walk along with you, anywhere.

O Madam, I will give to you
A broidered silken gownd,
With nine yards a-drooping
And training on the ground:
If you will be my joy, my sweet and only dear,
And walk along with me, anywhere.

O Sir, I will accept of you
A broidered silken gownd,
With nine yards a-drooping
And training on the ground:
Then I will be your joy, your sweet and only
dear,
And walk along with you, anywhere.

Hiawatha's Childhood[4]

HENRY WADSWORTH LONGFELLOW

By the shores of Gitche Gumee,
By the shining Big-Sea-Water,
Stood the wigwam of Nokomis,
Daughter of the Moon, Nokomis;
Dark behind it rose the forest,
Rose the black and gloomy pine-trees,
Rose the firs with cones upon them;
Bright before it beat the water,
Beat the clear and sunny water,
Beat the shining Big-Sea-Water.
    There the wrinkled, old Nokomis
Nursed the little Hiawatha,
Rocked him in his linden cradle,
Bedded soft in moss and rushes,
Safely bound with reindeer sinews;
Stilled his fretful wail by saying,
"Ewa-yea! my little owlet!"

[4] From The Song of Hiawatha.

Lulled him into slumber, singing,
"Hush! the Naked Bear will hear thee!
Who is this that lights the wigwam?
With his great eyes lights the wigwam?
Ewa-yea! my little owlet!"
    Many things Nokomis taught him
Of the stars that shine in heaven;
Showed him Ishkoodah, the comet,
Ishkoodah, with fiery tresses;
Showed the Death-Dance of the spirits,
Warriors with their plumes and war-clubs,
Flaring far away to northward
In the frosty nights of Winter;
Showed the broad, white road in heaven,
Pathway of the ghosts, the shadows,
Running straight across the heavens,
Crowded with the ghosts, the shadows.
    At the door on summer evenings
Sat the little Hiawatha;
Heard the whispering of the pine-trees,
Heard the lapping of the water,
Sounds of music, words of wonder;
"Minne-wawa!" said the pine-trees,
"Mudway-aushka!" said the water.
    Saw the firefly, Wah-wah-taysee,
Flitting through the dusk of evening,
With the twinkle of its candle
Lighting up the brakes and bushes;
And he sang the song of children,
Sang the song Nokomis taught him:
"Wah-wah-taysee, little firefly,
Little, flitting, white-fire insect,
Little, dancing, white-fire creature,
Light me with your little candle,
Ere upon my bed I lay me,
Ere in sleep I close my eyelids!"
    Saw the moon rise from the water,
Rippling, rounding from the water,
Saw the flecks and shadows on it,
Whispered, "What is that, Nokomis?"
And the good Nokomis answered:
"Once a warrior, very angry,
Seized his grandmother, and threw her
Up into the sky at midnight;
Right against the moon he threw her;
'Tis her body that you see there."
    Saw the rainbow in the heaven,
In the eastern sky, the rainbow,
Whispered, "What is that, Nokomis?"
And the good Nokomis answered:
"'Tis the heaven of flowers you see there;
All the wild-flowers of the forest,

All the lilies of the prairie,
When on earth they fade and perish,
Blossom in that heaven above us."
    When he heard the owls at midnight,
Hooting, laughing in the forest,
"What is that?" he cried in terror;
"What is that?" he said, "Nokomis?"
And the good Nokomis answered:
"That is but the owl and owlet,
Talking in their native language,
Talking, scolding at each other."
    Then the little Hiawatha
Learned of every bird its language,
Learned their names and all their secrets,
How they built their nests in Summer,
Where they hid themselves in Winter,
Talked with them whene'er he met them,
Called them "Hiawatha's Chickens."
    Of all beasts he learned the language,
Learned their names and all their secrets,
How the beavers built their lodges,
Where the squirrels hid their acorns,
How the reindeer ran so swiftly,
Why the rabbit was so timid,
Talked with them whene'er he met them,
Called them "Hiawatha's Brothers."
    Then Iagoo, the great boaster,
He the marvelous story-teller,
He the traveler and the talker,
He the friend of old Nokomis,
Made a bow for Hiawatha;
From a branch of ash he made it,
From an oak-bough made the arrows,
Tipped with flint, and winged with feathers,
And the cord he made of deer-skin.
    Then he said to Hiawatha:
"Go, my son, into the forest,
Where the red deer herd together,
Kill for us a famous roebuck,
Kill for us a deer with antlers!"
    Forth into the forest straightway
All alone walked Hiawatha
Proudly, with his bow and arrows;
And the birds sang round him, o'er him:
"Do not shoot us, Hiawatha!"
Sang the robin, the Opechee,
Sang the bluebird, the Owaissa,
"Do not shoot us, Hiawatha!"
    Up the oak-tree, close beside him,
Sprang the squirrel, Adjidaumo,
In and out among the branches,

Coughed and chattered from the oak-tree,
Laughed, and said between his laughing,
"Do not shoot me, Hiawatha!"
    And the rabbit from his pathway
Leaped aside, and at a distance
Sat erect upon his haunches,
Half in fear and half in frolic,
Saying to the little hunter,
"Do not shoot me, Hiawatha!"
    But he heeded not, nor heard them,
For his thoughts were with the red deer;
On their tracks his eyes were fastened,
Leading downward to the river,
To the ford across the river,
And as one in slumber walked he.
    Hidden in the alder-bushes,
There he waited till the deer came,
Till he saw two antlers lifted,
Saw two eyes look from the thicket,
Saw two nostrils point to windward,
And a deer came down the pathway,
Flecked with leafy light and shadow.
And his heart within him fluttered,
Trembled like the leaves above him,
Like the birch-leaf palpitated,
As the deer came down the pathway.
    Then, upon one knee uprising,
Hiawatha aimed an arrow;
Scarce a twig moved with his motion,
Scarce a leaf was stirred or rustled,
But the wary roebuck started,
Stamped with all his hoofs together,
Listened with one foot uplifted,
Leaped as if to meet the arrow;
Ah! the singing, fatal arrow,
Like a wasp it buzzed and stung him.
    Dead he lay there in the forest,
By the ford across the river;
Beat his timid heart no longer,
But the heart of Hiawatha
Throbbed and shouted and exulted,
As he bore the red deer homeward,
And Iagoo and Nokomis
Hailed his coming with applauses.
    From the red deer's hide Nokomis
Made a cloak for Hiawatha,
From the red deer's flesh Nokomis
Made a banquet in his honor.
All the village came and feasted,
All the guests praised Hiawatha,
Called him Strong-Heart, Soan-ge-taha!
Called him Loon-Heart, Mahn-go-taysee!

Paul Revere's Ride

HENRY WADSWORTH LONGFELLOW

Listen, my children, and you shall hear
Of the midnight ride of Paul Revere,
On the eighteenth of April, in Seventy-five;
Hardly a man is now alive
Who remembers that famous day and year.

He said to his friend, "If the British march
By land or sea from the town tonight,
Hang a lantern aloft in the belfry arch
Of the North Church tower as a signal light —
One, if by land, and two, if by sea;
And I on the opposite shore will be,
Ready to ride and spread the alarm
Through every Middlesex village and farm,
For the country folk to be up and to arm."

Then he said, "Good night!" and with
        muffled oar
Silently rowed to the Charlestown shore,
Just as the moon rose over the bay,
Where swinging wide at her moorings lay
The Somerset, British man-of-war;
A phantom ship, with each mast and spar
Across the moon like a prison bar,
And a huge black hulk, that was magnified
By its own reflection in the tide.

Meanwhile, his friend, through alley and
        street,
Wanders and watches with eager ears,
Till in the silence around him he hears
The muster of men at the barrack door,
The sound of arms, and the tramp of feet,
And the measured tread of the grenadiers,
Marching down to their boats on the shore.

Then he climbed the tower of the Old North
        Church,
By the wooden stairs, with stealthy tread,
To the belfry-chamber overhead,
And startled the pigeons from their perch
On the somber rafters, that round him made
Masses and moving shapes of shade —
By the trembling ladder, steep and tall,
To the highest window in the wall,
Where he paused to listen and look down
A moment on the roofs of the town,
And the moonlight flowing over all.

Beneath, in the churchyard, lay the dead,
In their night-encampment on the hill,
Wrapped in silence so deep and still
That he could hear, like a sentinel's tread,
The watchful night-wind, as it went
Creeping along from tent to tent,
And seeming to whisper, "All is well!"
A moment only he feels the spell
Of the place and the hour, and the secret
    dread
Of the lonely belfry and the dead;
For suddenly all his thoughts are bent
On a shadowy something far away,
Where the river widens to meet the bay —
A line of black that bends and floats
On the rising tide, like a bridge of boats.

Meanwhile, impatient to mount and ride,
Booted and spurred, with a heavy stride
On the opposite shore walked Paul Revere.
Now he patted his horse's side,
Now gazed at the landscape far and near,
Then, impetuous, stamped the earth,
And turned and tightened his saddle-girth;
But mostly he watched with eager search
The belfry-tower of the Old North Church,
As it rose above the graves on the hill,
Lonely and spectral and somber and still.
And lo! as he looks, on the belfry's height
A glimmer, and then a gleam of light!
He springs to the saddle, the bridle he
    turns,
But lingers and gazes, till full on his sight
A second lamp in the belfry burns!

The hurry of hoofs in a village street,
A shape in the moonlight, a bulk in the dark,
And beneath from the pebbles, in passing, a
    spark
Struck out by a steed flying fearless and
    fleet —
That was all! And yet through the gloom
    and the light,
The fate of a nation was riding that night;
And the spark struck out by that steed, in
    his flight,
Kindled the land into flame with its heat.

He has left the village and mounted the
    steep,
And beneath him, tranquil and broad and
    deep,

Is the Mystic, meeting the ocean tides;
And under the alders, that skirt its edge,
Now soft on the sand, now loud on the ledge,
Is heard the tramp of the steed as he rides.

It was twelve by the village clock
When he crossed the bridge into Medford
    town.
He heard the crowing of the cock,
And the barking of the farmer's dog,
And felt the damp of the river-fog
That rises after the sun goes down.

It was one by the village clock
When he galloped into Lexington.
He saw the gilded weathercock
Swim in the moonlight as he passed,
And the meeting-house windows, blank and
    bare,
Gaze at him with a spectral glare,
As if they already stood aghast
At the bloody work they would look upon.

It was two by the village clock
When he came to the bridge in Concord
    town.
He heard the bleating of the flock,
And the twitter of birds among the trees
And felt the breath of the morning breeze
Blowing over the meadows brown.
And one was safe and asleep in his bed
Who at the bridge would be first to fall,
Who that day would be lying dead,
Pierced by a British musket-ball.

You know the rest. In the books you have
    read
How the British Regulars fired and fled —
How the farmers gave them ball for ball,
From behind each fence and farm-yard wall,
Chasing the red-coats down the lane,
Then crossing the fields to emerge again
Under the trees at the turn of the road,
And only pausing to fire and load.

So through the night rode Paul Revere;
And so through the night went his cry of
    alarm
To every Middlesex village and farm —
A cry of defiance and not of fear,
A voice in the darkness, a knock at the door,
And a word that shall echo forevermore!

For, borne on the night-wind of the Past,
Through all our history, to the last,
In the hour of darkness and peril and need,
The people will waken and listen to hear
The hurrying hoof-beats of that steed,
And the midnight message of Paul Revere.

Barbara Frietchie

JOHN GREENLEAF WHITTIER

Up from the meadows rich with corn,
Clear in the cool September morn,

The clustered spires of Frederick stand
Green-walled by the hills of Maryland.

Round about them orchards sweep,
Apple and peach tree fruited deep,

Fair as the garden of the Lord
To the eyes of the famished rebel horde,

On that pleasant morn of the early fall
When Lee marched over the mountain-
    wall —

Over the mountains winding down,
Horse and foot, into Frederick town.

Forty flags with their silver stars,
Forty flags with their crimson bars,

Flapped in the morning wind: the sun
Of noon looked down, and saw not one.

Up rose old Barbara Frietchie then,
Bowed with her fourscore years and ten;

Bravest of all in Frederick town,
She took up the flag the men hauled down;

In her attic window the staff she set,
To show that one heart was loyal yet.

Up the street came the rebel tread,
Stonewall Jackson riding ahead.

Under his slouched hat left and right
He glanced: the old flag met his sight.

"Halt!" — the dust-brown ranks stood fast.
"Fire!" — out blazed the rifle-blast.

It shivered the window, pane and sash;
It rent the banner with seam and gash.

Quick, as it fell, from the broken staff
Dame Barbara snatched the silken scarf.

She leaned far out on the window-sill,
And shook it forth with a royal will.

"Shoot, if you must, this old gray head,
But spare your country's flag," she said.

A shade of sadness, a blush of shame,
Over the face of the leader came;

The nobler nature within him stirred
To life at that woman's deed and word:

"Who touches a hair of yon gray head
Dies like a dog! March on!" he said.

All day long through Frederick street
Sounded the tread of marching feet:

All day long that free flag tost
Over the heads of the rebel host.

Ever its torn folds rose and fell
On the loyal winds that loved it well;

And through the hill-gaps sunset light
Shone over it with a warm good-night.

Barbara Frietchie's work is o'er,
And the Rebel rides on his raids no more.

Honor to her! and let a tear
Fall, for her sake, on Stonewall's bier.

Over Barbara Frietchie's grave,
Flag of Freedom and Union, wave!

Peace and order and beauty draw
Round thy symbol of light and law;

And ever the stars above look down
On thy stars below in Frederick town!

The Flower-fed Buffaloes[5]

VACHEL LINDSAY

The flower-fed buffaloes of the spring
In the days of long ago,
Ranged where the locomotives sing
And the prairie flowers lie low: —
The tossing, blooming, perfumed grass
Is swept away by the wheat,
Wheels and wheels and wheels spin by
In the spring that still is sweet.
But the flower-fed buffaloes of the spring
Left us, long ago.
They gore no more, they bellow no more,
They trundle around the hills no more: —
With the Blackfeet, lying low.
With the Pawnees, lying low,
Lying low.

The Ballad of William Sycamore[6]

1790–1871

STEPHEN VINCENT BENÉT

My father, he was a mountaineer,
His fist was a knotty hammer;
He was quick on his feet as a running
    deer,
And he spoke with a Yankee stammer.

My mother, she was merry and brave,
And so she came to her labor,
With a tall green fir for her doctor grave
And a stream for her comforting neighbor.

And some are wrapped in the linen fine,
And some like a godling's scion;
But I was cradled on twigs of pine
And the skin of a mountain lion.

And some remember a white, starched lap
And a ewer with silver handles;
But I remember a coonskin cap
And the smell of bayberry candles.

5 From Vachel Lindsay, Going to the Stars (Apple-ton-Century-Crofts).
6 From Stephen Vincent Benét, The Collected Works (Rinehart).

The cabin logs, with the bark still rough,
And my mother who laughed at trifles,
And the tall, lank visitors, brown as snuff,
With their long, straight squirrel-rifles.

I can hear them dance, like a foggy song,
Through the deepest one of my slumbers,
The fiddle squeaking the boots along
And my father calling the numbers.

The quick feet shaking the puncheon-floor,
And the fiddle squealing and squealing,
Till the dried herbs rattled above the door
And the dust went up to the ceiling.

There are children lucky from dawn till
    dusk,
But never a child so lucky!
For I cut my teeth on 'Money Musk'
In the Bloody Ground of Kentucky!

When I grew tall as the Indian corn,
My father had little to lend me,
But he gave me his great, old powder-horn
And his woodsman's skill to befriend me.

With a leather shirt to cover my back,
And a redskin nose to unravel
Each forest sign, I carried my pack
As far as a scout could travel.

Till I lost my boyhood and found my wife,
A girl like a Salem clipper!
A woman straight as a hunting-knife
With eyes as bright as the Dipper!

We cleared our camp where the buffalo feed,
Unheard-of streams were our flagons;
And I sowed my sons like the apple-seed
On the trail of the Western wagons.

They were right, tight boys, never sulky or
    slow,
A fruitful, a goodly muster.
The eldest died at the Alamo,
The youngest fell with Custer.

The letter that told it burned my hand,
Yet we smiled and said, 'So be it!'
But I could not live when they fenced my
    land,
For it broke my heart to see it.

I saddled a red, unbroken colt
And rode him into the day there;
And he threw me down like a thunderbolt
And rolled on me as I lay there.

The hunter's whistle hummed in my ear
As the city-men tried to move me,
And I died in my boots like a pioneer
With the whole wide sky above me.

Now I lie in the heart of the fat, black soil,
Like the seed of a prairie-thistle;
It has ashed my bones with honey and oil
And picked them clean as a whistle.

And my youth returns, like the rains of
    Spring,
And my sons, like the wild-geese flying;
And I lie and hear the meadow-lark sing
And have much content in my dying.

Go play with the towns you have built of
    blocks,
The towns where you would have bound me!
I sleep in my earth like a tired fox,
And my buffalo have found me.

Lochinvar [7]

Sir Walter Scott

O, Young Lochinvar is come out of the
    West —
Through all the wide Border his steed was
    the best;
And, save his good broadsword, he weapons
    had none —
He rode all unarmed and he rode all alone.
So faithful in love, and so dauntless in war,
There never was knight like the young Loch-
    invar.

He stayed not for brake, and he stopped not
    for stone,
He swam the Esk river, where ford there was
    none;
But ere he alighted at Netherby gate,
The bride had consented, the gallant came
    late:
For a laggard in love, and a dastard in war,
Was to wed the fair Ellen of brave Lochinvar.

7 From *Marmion*, Canto Fifth.

So boldly he entered the Netherby hall,
'Mong bridesmen, and kinsmen, and broth-
    ers, and all:
Then spoke the bride's father, his hand on
    his sword
(For the poor, craven bridegroom said never
    a word),
"O, come ye in peace here, or come ye in
    war,
Or to dance at our bridal, young Lord Loch-
    invar?"

"I long wooed your daughter — my suit you
    denied; —
Love swells like the Solway, but ebbs like its
    tide;
And now I am come, with this lost love of
    mine,
To lead but one measure, drink one cup of
    wine.
There are maidens in Scotland more lovely
    by far,
That would gladly be bride to the young
    Lochinvar!"

The bride kissed the goblet; the knight took
    it up,
He quaffed off the wine, and he threw down
    the cup.
She looked down to blush, and she looked up
    to sigh,
With a smile on her lips, and a tear in her
    eye.
He took her soft hand, ere her mother could
    bar —
"Now tread we a measure!" said young Loch-
    invar.

So stately his form, and so lovely her face,
That never a hall such a galliard did grace;
While her mother did fret, and her father
    did fume,
And the bridegroom stood dangling his bon-
    net and plume,
And the bridesmaidens whispered, " 'Twere
    better by far
To have matched our fair cousin with young
    Lochinvar."

One touch to her hand, and one word in her
    ear,
When they reached the hall door, and the
    charger stood near;

So light to the croupe the fair lady he swung,
So light to the saddle before her he sprung!
"She is won! we are gone, over bank, bush,
     and scaur;
They'll have fleet steeds that follow," quoth
     young Lochinvar.

There was mounting 'mong Graemes of the
     Netherby clan;
Forsters, Fenwicks, and Musgraves, they rode
     and they ran:
There was racing and chasing, on Cannobie
     Lee,
But the lost bride of Netherby ne'er did they
     see.
So daring in love, and so dauntless in war,
Have ye e'er heard of gallant like young
     Lochinvar?

The Charge of the Light Brigade

ALFRED, LORD TENNYSON

Half a league, half a league,
Half a league onward,
All in the valley of Death
     Rode the six hundred.

"Forward the Light Brigade!
Charge for the guns!" he said.
Into the valley of Death
     Rode the six hundred.

"Forward, the Light Brigade!"
Was there a man dismayed?
Not though the soldier knew
     Some one had blundered.
Theirs not to make reply,
Theirs not to reason why,
Theirs but to do and die.
Into the valley of Death
     Rode the six hundred.

Cannon to right of them,
Cannon to left of them,
Cannon in front of them
     Volleyed and thundered;
Stormed at with shot and shell,
Boldly they rode and well,

Into the jaws of Death,
Into the mouth of hell
     Rode the six hundred.

Flashed all their sabres bare,
Flashed as they turned in air
Sabring the gunners there,
Charging an army, while
     All the world wondered.
Plunged in the battery-smoke
Right through the line they broke;
Cossack and Russian
Reeled from the sabre-stroke
     Shattered and sundered.
Then they rode back, but not,
     Not the six hundred.

Cannon to right of them,
Cannon to left of them,
Cannon behind them
     Volleyed and thundered;
Stormed at with shot and shell,
While horse and hero fell,
They that had fought so well
Came through the jaws of Death,
Back from the mouth of hell,
All that was left of them,
     Left of six hundred.

When can their glory fade?
Oh, the wild charge they made!
     All the world wondered.
Honor the charge they made!
Honor the Light Brigade,
     Noble six hundred!

The Sands of Dee

CHARLES KINGSLEY

"O Mary, go and call the cattle home,
     And call the cattle home,
     And call the cattle home
Across the sands of Dee";
The western wind was wild and dank with
     foam,
     And all alone went she.

The western tide crept up along the sand,
     And o'er and o'er the sand,

And round and round the sand,
As far as eye could see.
The rolling mist came down and hid the
   land:
And never home came she.

"Oh! is it weed, or fish, or floating hair —
   A tress of golden hair,
   A drownèd maiden's hair
Above the nets at sea?
Was never salmon yet that shone so fair
   Among the stakes on Dee."

They rowed her in across the rolling foam,
   The cruel crawling foam,
   The cruel hungry foam,
To her grave beside the sea:
But still the boatmen hear her call the cattle
   home
   Across the sands of Dee.

Annabel Lee

EDGAR ALLAN POE

It was many and many a year ago,
   In a kingdom by the sea
That a maiden there lived, whom you may
   know
By the name of Annabel Lee;
And this maiden she lived with no other
   thought
Than to love and be loved by me.

I was a child and *she* was a child,
   In this kingdom by the sea,
But we loved with a love that was more than
   love —
   I and my Annabel Lee —
With a love that the wingèd seraphs of
   heaven
Coveted her and me.

And this was the reason that, long ago,
   In this kingdom by the sea,
A wind blew out of a cloud, chilling
   My beautiful Annabel Lee;
So that her highborn kinsmen came
   And bore her away from me,
To shut her up in a sepulcher
   In this kingdom by the sea.

The angels, not half so happy in heaven,
   Went envying her and me —
Yes! — that was the reason (as all men know,
   In this kingdom by the sea)
That the wind came out of the cloud by
   night,
Chilling and killing my Annabel Lee.

But our love it was stronger by far than the
   love
   Of those who were older than we —
   Of many far wiser than we —
And neither the angels in heaven above,
   Nor the demons down under the sea,
Can ever dissever my soul from the soul
   Of the beautiful Annabel Lee:

For the moon never beams, without bringing
   me dreams
   Of the beautiful Annabel Lee;
And the stars never rise, but I feel the bright
   eyes
   Of the beautiful Annabel Lee:
And so, all the night-tide, I lie down by the
   side
Of my darling — my darling — my life and
   my bride,
   In the sepulcher there by the sea —
   In her tomb by the sounding sea

The Pied Piper of Hamelin

ROBERT BROWNING

Hamelin Town's in Brunswick,
   By famous Hanover city;
      The river Weser deep and wide
      Washes its wall on the southern side;
      A pleasanter spot you never spied;
   But, when begins my ditty,
      Almost five hundred years ago,
      To see the townsfolk suffer so
   From vermin, was a pity.

   Rats!
They fought the dogs and killed the cats,
   And bit the babies in the cradles,
And ate the cheeses out of the vats,
   And licked the soup from the cooks' own
      ladles.

Split open the kegs of salted sprats,
Made nests inside men's Sunday hats,
And even spoiled the women's chats,
    By drowning their speaking
    With shrieking and squeaking
In fifty different sharps and flats.

At last the people in a body
    To the Town-hall came flocking:
"'Tis clear," cried they, "our Mayor's a
    noddy:
    And as for our Corporation — shocking
    To think we buy gowns lined with ermine
    For dolts that can't or won't determine
    What's best to rid us of our vermin!
    You hope, because you're old and obese,
    To find in the furry civic robe ease!
Rouse up, sirs! Give your brains a racking
To find the remedy we're lacking,
Or, sure as fate, we'll send you packing!"
At this the Mayor and Corporation
Quaked with a mighty consternation.

An hour they sat in council;
    At length the Mayor broke silence:
"For a guilder I'd my ermine gown sell;
    I wish I were a mile hence!
It's easy to bid one rack one's brain —
I'm sure my poor head aches again,
I've scratched it so, and all in vain.
Oh, for a trap, a trap, a trap!"
Just as he said this, what should hap
At the chamber door but a gentle tap?
"Bless us," cried the Mayor, "what's that?"
(With the Corporation as he sat,
Looking little though wondrous fat;
Nor brighter was his eye, nor moister
Than a too-long-opened oyster,
Save when at noon his paunch grew
    mutinous
For a plate of turtle green and glutinous)
"Only a scraping of shoes on the mat?
Anything like the sound of a rat
Makes my heart go pit-a-pat!"

"Come in!" — the Mayor cried, looking big-
    ger —
And in did come the strangest figure!
His queer long coat from heel to head
Was half of yellow and half of red,
And he himself was tall and thin,
With sharp blue eyes, each like a pin,

And light loose hair, yet swarthy skin,
No tuft on cheek nor beard on chin,
But lips where smiles went out and in;
There was no guessing his kith and kin;
And nobody could enough admire
The tall man and his quaint attire.
Quoth one: "It's as my great-grandsire,
Starting up at the Trump of Doom's tone,
Had walked this way from his painted tomb-
    stone!"

He advanced to the council-table:
And, "Please your honors," said he, "I'm
    able,
By means of a secret charm, to draw
    All creatures living beneath the sun,
    That creep or swim or fly or run,
After me so as you never saw!
And I chiefly use my charm
On creatures that do people harm —
The mole, the toad, the newt, the viper:
And people call me the Pied Piper."
(And here they noticed round his neck
A scarf of red and yellow stripe
To match his coat of the self-same cheque;
And at the scarf's end hung a pipe;
And his fingers, they noticed, were ever stray-
    ing
As if impatient to be playing
Upon this pipe, as low it dangled
Over his vesture so old-fangled.)
"Yet," said he, "poor piper as I am,
In Tartary I freed the Cham
Last June from his huge swarms of gnats;
I eased in Asia the Nizam
Of a monstrous brood of vampire-bats;
And as for what your brain bewilders,
If I can rid your town of rats
Will you give me a thousand guilders?"
"One? fifty thousand!" was the exclamation
Of the astonished Mayor and Corporation.

Into the street the Piper stept,
    Smiling first a little smile,
As if he knew what magic slept
    In his quiet pipe the while;
Then like a musical adept,
To blow the pipe his lip he wrinkled,
And green and blue his sharp eyes twinkled,
Like a candle flame where salt is sprinkled;
And ere three shrill notes the pipe uttered,
You heard as if an army muttered;

And the muttering grew to a grumbling;
And the grumbling grew to a mighty rum-
    bling;
And out of the houses the rats came tum-
    bling —
Great rats, small rats, lean rats, brawny
    rats,
Brown rats, black rats, gray rats, tawny
    rats,
Grave old plodders, gay young friskers,
    Fathers, mothers, uncles, cousins,
Cocking tails, and pricking whiskers,
    Families by tens and dozens,
Brothers, sisters, husbands, wives —
Followed the Piper for their lives.
From street to street he piped advancing,
And step for step they followed dancing,
Until they came to the river Weser,
    Wherein all plunged and perished!
— Save one who, stout as Julius Caesar,
Swam across and lived to carry
    (As he, the manuscript he cherished)
To Rat-land home his commentary:
Which was, "At the first shrill notes of the
    pipe,
I heard a sound as of scraping tripe,
And putting apples, wondrous ripe,
Into a cider-press's gripe:
And a moving away of pickle-tub-boards,
And a leaving ajar of conserve-cupboards,
And a drawing the corks of train-oil-flasks,
And a breaking the hoops of butter-casks:
And it seemed as if a voice
    (Sweeter far than by harp or by psaltery
Is breathed) called out, 'O rats, rejoice!
    The world is grown to one vast drysaltery!
So munch on, crunch on, take your nun-
    cheon,
Breakfast, supper, dinner, luncheon!'
And just as a bulky sugar-puncheon,
All ready staved, like a great sun shone
Glorious scarce an inch before me,
Just as methought it said, 'Come, bore me!'
— I found the Weser rolling o'er me."

You should have heard the Hamelin people
Ringing the bells till they rocked the steeple.
"Go," cried the Mayor, "and get long poles,
Poke out the nests, and block up the holes!
Consult with carpenters and builders,
And leave in our town not even a trace
Of the rats!" When suddenly, up the face

Of the Piper perched in the market-place,
With a "First, if you please, my thousand
    guilders!"

A thousand guilders! The Mayor looked
    blue,
So did the Corporation too,
For council dinners made rare havoc
With Claret, Moselle, Vin-de-Grave, Hock;
And half the money would replenish
Their cellar's biggest butt with Rhenish.
To pay this sum to a wandering fellow
With a gypsy coat of red and yellow!
"Beside," quoth the Mayor, with a knowing
    wink,
"Our business was done at the river's brink;
We saw with our eyes the vermin sink,
And what's dead can't come to life, I think.
So, friend, we're not the folks to shrink
From the duty of giving you something for
    drink,
And a matter of money to put in your poke;
But, as for the guilders, what we spoke
Of them, as you very well know, was in joke.
Beside, our losses have made us thrifty:
A thousand guilders! come, take fifty!"

The Piper's face fell, and he cried,
"No trifling! I can't wait! beside
I've promised to visit by dinner-time
Bagdad and accept the prime
Of the head cook's pottage, all he's rich in,
For having left in the caliph's kitchen,
Of a nest of scorpions no survivor.
With him I proved no bargain-driver,
With you, don't think I'll bate a stiver!
And folks who put me in a passion
May find me pipe after another fashion."

"How?" cried the Mayor, "d'ye think I brook
Being worse treated than a Cook?
Insulted by a lazy ribald
With idle pipe and vesture piebald?
You threaten us, fellow? Do your worst,
Blow your pipe there till you burst!"

Once more he stepped into the street,
    And to his lips again
Laid his long pipe of smooth straight cane;
    And ere he blew three notes (such sweet
Soft notes as yet musician's cunning
    Never gave the enraptured air)

There was a rustling that seemed like a bust-
ling
Of merry crowds jostling at pitching and
hustling;
Small feet were pattering, wooden shoes clat-
tering,
Little hands clapping and little tongues chat-
tering,
And, like fowls in a farm-yard when barley
is scattering,
Out came the children running.
All the little boys and girls,
With rosy cheeks and flaxen curls,
And sparkling eyes and teeth like pearls,
Tripping and skipping, ran merrily after
The wonderful music with shouting and
laughter.

The Mayor was dumb, and the Council stood
As if they were changed into blocks of wood,
Unable to move a step, or cry
To the children merrily skipping by
— Could only follow with the eye
That joyous crowd at the Piper's back.
But how the Mayor was on the rack,
And the wretched Council's bosoms beat,
As the Piper turned from the High Street
To where the Weser rolled its waters
Right in the way of their sons and daughters!
However he turned from South to West,
And to Koppelberg Hill his steps addressed,
And after him the children pressed;
Great was the joy in every breast.
"He never can cross that mighty top!
He's forced to let the piping drop,
And we shall see our children stop!"
When, lo, as they reached the mountain-side,
A wondrous portal opened wide,
As if a cavern was suddenly hollowed;
And the Piper advanced and the children fol-
lowed,
And when all were in to the very last,
The door in the mountain-side shut fast.
Did I say, all? No! One was lame,
And could not dance the whole of the way;
And in after years, if you would blame
His sadness, he was used to say —
"It's dull in our town since my playmates
left!
I can't forget that I'm bereft
Of all the pleasant sights they see,
Which the Piper also promised me.

For he led us, he said, to a joyous land,
Joining the town and just at hand,
Where waters gushed and fruit-trees grew,
And flowers put forth a fairer hue,
And everything was strange and new;
The sparrows were brighter than peacocks
here,
And their dogs outran our fallow-deer,
And honey-bees had lost their stings,
And horses were born with eagles' wings;
And just as I became assured
My lame foot would be speedily cured,
The music stopped and I stood still,
And found myself outside the hill,
Left alone against my will,
To go now limping as before,
And never hear of that country more!"

Alas! alas for Hamelin!
    There came into many a burgher's pate
    A text which says, that Heaven's Gate
Opes to the rich at as easy rate
As the needle's eye takes a camel in!
The Mayor sent east, west, north, and south
To offer the Piper by word of mouth,
    Wherever it was men's lot to find him,
Silver and gold to his heart's content,
If he'd only return the way he went,
    And bring the children behind him.
But when they saw 'twas a lost endeavor,
And Piper and dancers were gone forever,
They made a decree that lawyers never
    Should think their records dated duly,
If, after the day of the month and year
These words did not as well appear,
"And so long after what happened here
    On the Twenty-second of July,
Thirteen hundred and seventy-six";
And the better in memory to fix
The place of the children's last retreat,
They called it the Pied Piper's Street —
Where anyone playing on pipe or tabor
Was sure for the future to lose his labor.
Nor suffered they hostelry or tavern
    To shock with mirth a street so solemn;
But opposite the place of the cavern
    They wrote the story on a column,
And on the great church-window painted
The same, to make the world acquainted
How their children were stolen away,
And there it stands to this very day.
And I must not omit to say

That in Transylvania there's a tribe
Of alien people who ascribe
The outlandish ways and dress
On which their neighbors lay such stress,
To their fathers and mothers having risen
Out of some subterraneous prison
Into which they were trepanned
Long time ago in a mighty band
Out of Hamelin town in Brunswick land,
But how or why, they don't understand.

The Admiral's Ghost [8]

ALFRED NOYES

I tell you a tale tonight
  Which a seaman told to me,
With eyes that gleamed in the lanthorn light
  And a voice as low as the sea.

You could almost hear the stars
  Twinkling up in the sky,
And the old wind woke and moaned in the
    spars,
  And the same old waves went by,

Singing the same old song
  As ages and ages ago,
While he froze my blood in that deep-sea
    night
  With the things that he seemed to know.

A bare foot pattered on the deck;
  Ropes creaked; then — all grew still,
And he pointed his finger straight in my face
  And growled, as a sea-dog will.

"Do'ee know who Nelson was?
  That pore little shriveled form
With the patch on his eye and the pinned-up
    sleeve
  And a soul like a North Sea storm?

"Ask of the Devonshire men!
  They know, and they'll tell you true;
He wasn't the pore little chawed-up chap
  That Hardy thought he knew.

"He wasn't the man you think!
  His patch was a dern disguise!

8 From Alfred Noyes, *Collected Poems*, Vol. II
(Lippincott).

For he knew that they'd find him out, d'you
    see,
  If they looked him in both his eyes.

"He was twice as big as he seemed;
  But his clothes were cunningly made.
He'd both of his hairy arms all right!
  The sleeve was a trick of the trade.

"You've heard of sperrits, no doubt;
  Well, there's more in the matter than
    that!
But he wasn't the patch and he wasn't the
    sleeve,
  And he wasn't the laced cocked-hat.

"*Nelson was just — a Ghost!*
  You may laugh! But the Devonshire men
They knew that he'd come when England
    called,
  And they know that he'll come again.

"I'll tell you the way it was
  (For none of the landsmen know),
And to tell it you right, you must go a-starn
  Two hundred years or so.

.   .   .   .

"The waves were lapping and slapping
  The same as they are today;
And Drake lay dying aboard his ship
  In Nombre Dios Bay.

"The scent of the foreign flowers
  Came floating all around;
'But I'd give my soul for the smell o' the
    pitch,'
  Says he, 'in Plymouth Sound.

" 'What shall I do,' he says,
  'When the guns begin to roar,
An' England wants me, and me not there
  To shatter 'er foes once more?'

" (You've heard what he said, maybe,
  But I'll mark you the p'ints again;
For I want you to box your compass right
  And get my story plain.)

" 'You must take my drum,' he says,
  'To the old sea-wall at home;
And if ever you strike that drum,' he says,
  'Why, strike me blind, I'll come!

" 'If England needs me, dead
  Or living, I'll rise that day!
I'll rise from the darkness under the sea
  Ten thousand miles away.'

"That's what he said; and he died;
  An' his pirates, listenin' roun',
With their crimson doublets and jeweled
    swords
  That flashed as the sun went down.

"They sewed him up in his shroud
  With a round-shot top and toe,
To sink him under the salt sharp sea
  Where all good seamen go.

"They lowered him down in the deep,
  And there in the sunset light
They boomed a broadside over his grave,
  As meanin' to say 'Good-night.'

"They sailed away in the dark
  To the dear little isle they knew;
And they hung his drum by the old sea-wall
  The same as he told them to.

. . . .

"Two hundred years went by,
  And the guns began to roar,
And England was fighting hard for her life,
  As ever she fought of yore.

" 'It's only my dead that count,'
  She said, as she says today;
'It isn't the ships and it isn't the guns
  'Ull sweep Trafalgar's Bay.'

"D'you guess who Nelson was?
  You may laugh, but it's true as true!
There was more in that pore little chawed-
    up chap
  Than ever his best friend knew.

"The foe was creepin' close,
  In the dark, to our white-cliffed isle;
They were ready to leap at England's throat,
  When — O, you may smile, you may smile;

"But — ask of the Devonshire men;
  For they heard in the dead of night
The roll of a drum, and they saw *him* pass
  On a ship all shining white.

"He stretched out his dead cold face
  And he sailed in the grand old way!
The fishes had taken an eye and an arm,
  But he swept Trafalgar's Bay.

"Nelson — was Francis Drake!
  O, what matters the uniform,
Or the patch on your eye or your pinned-up
    sleeve,
  If your soul's like a North Sea storm."

The Creation[9]

JAMES WELDON JOHNSON

And God stepped out on space,
And he looked around and said:
I'm lonely —
I'll make me a world.

And far as the eye of God could see
Darkness covered everything,
Blacker than a hundred midnights
Down in a cypress swamp.

Then God smiled,
And the light broke,
And the darkness rolled up on one side,
And the light stood shining on the other,
And God said: That's good!

Then God reached out and took the light in
  his hands,
And God rolled the light around in his hands
Until he made the sun;
And he set that sun a-blazing in the heavens.
And the light that was left from making the
  sun
God gathered it up in a shining ball
And flung it against the darkness,
Spangling the night with the moon and stars.
Then down between the darkness and the
  light
He hurled the world;
And God said: That's good!

Then God himself stepped down —
And the sun was on his right hand,

[9] From James Weldon Johnson, *God's Trombones*
(Viking Press).

And the moon was on his left;
The stars were clustered about his head,
And the earth was under his feet.
And God walked, and where he trod
His footsteps hollowed the valleys out
And bulged the mountains up.

Then he stopped and looked and saw
That the earth was hot and barren.
So God stepped over to the edge of the world
And he spat out the seven seas —
He batted his eyes, and the lightnings
     flashed —
He clapped his hands, and the thunders
     rolled —
And the waters above the earth came down,
The cooling waters came down.

Then the green grass sprouted,
And the little red flowers blossomed,
The pine tree pointed his finger to the sky,
And the oak spread out his arms,
The lakes cuddled down in the hollows of
     the ground,
And the rivers ran down to the sea;
And God smiled again,
And the rainbow appeared,
And curled itself around his shoulder.

Then God raised his arm and he waved his
     hand
Over the sea and over the land,
And he said: Bring forth! Bring forth!
And quicker than God could drop his hand,
Fishes and fowls
And beasts and birds
Swam the rivers and the seas,
Roamed the forests and the woods,

And split the air with their wings
And God said: That's good!

Then God walked around,
And God looked around
On all that he had made.
He looked at his sun,
And he looked at his moon,
And he looked at his little stars;
He looked on his world
With all its living things,
And God said: I'm lonely still.
Then God sat down —
On the side of a hill where he could think;
By a deep, wide river he sat down;
With his head in his hands,
God thought and thought,
Till he thought: I'll make me a man!

Up from the bed of the river
God scooped the clay;
And by the bank of the river
He kneeled him down;
And there the great God Almighty
Who lit the sun and fixed it in the sky,
Who flung the stars to the most far corner of
     the night,
Who rounded the earth in the middle of his
     hand;
This Great God,
Like a mammy bending over her baby,
Kneeled down in the dust
Toiling over a lump of clay
Till he shaped it in his own image;

Then into it he blew the breath of life,
And man became a living soul.
Amen. Amen.

BIBLIOGRAPHY

Anthologies

Adshead, Gladys L., and Annis Duff, comps. *Inheritance of Poetry;* decorations by Nora S. Unwin. Houghton Mifflin, 1948. (All ages)

An anthology of rare distinction that bears testimony to the compilers' deep delight in poetry. Excellent indexes with a list of musical settings.

Arbuthnot, May Hill, comp. *Time for Poetry;* illus. by Arthur Paul. Scott, Foresman, 1952. (All ages)

Mrs. Arbuthnot's excellent selection covers a wide range and makes a book which will be an invaluable addition to the poetry shelf in home, school, and public library collections.

Association for Childhood Education. *Sung Under the Silver Umbrella; Poems for Young Children;* selected by the Literature committee of the Association of Childhood Education; illus. by Dorothy Lathrop. Macmillan, 1935. (Grades 2–5)

A delightful collection with a foreword by Padraic Colum.

Auslander, Joseph, and Frank Ernest Hill, comps. *Winged Horse Anthology.* Doubleday, 1929. (Grades 7–9)

A companion volume to *The Winged Horse; the Story of the Poets and Their Poetry,* which includes the poems mentioned in that book. The arrangement is chronological. Representative selections illustrate the qualities that made each poet great.

Benét, William Rose, comp. *Poems for Youth.* E. P. Dutton, 1925. (Grades 6–9)

American poetry selected by one of America's most distinguished writers.

Brewton, John, comp. *Gaily We Parade; a Collection of Poems About People, Here, There & Everywhere;* illus. by Robert Lawson. Macmillan, 1940. (Grades 3–7)

A spirited collection about a goodly company, ranging from shopkeepers and sailors to fairy folk and neighbors. Equally delightful is Mr. Brewton's *Under the Tent of the Sky,* poems about animals large and small.

Brewton, Sara and John, comps. *Bridled with Rainbows;* poems about many things of earth and sky; decorations by Vera Bock. Macmillan, 1949. (Grades 4–8)

Poems about the weather, nature, and gay adventure. The compilers' *Christmas Bells Are Ringing* is a varied treasury of Christmas poetry.

Daringer, Helen Fern, and Anne Thaxter Eaton. *Poet's Craft;* illus. by Hélène Carter. World Book Company, 1935. (Grades 7–9)

A collection which will help the reader develop an appreciation and understanding of poetry.

Davis, Mary Gould, comp. *The Girl's Book of Verse.* J. B. Lippincott, new ed. 1952. (Grades 6–9)

This new edition of a popular anthology, first published in 1922, contains 66 new poems and a foreword by Amelia Munson.

De la Mare, Walter, comp. *Come Hither; a Collection of Rhymes and Poems for the Young of All Ages;* illustrated by Warren Chappell. Alfred A. Knopf, new ed. 1958. (Grades 6–9)

The collection represents a poet's choice and through the title extends an invitation to explore the delights of poetry. In a characteristic introduction De la Mare suggests that a love of poetry is a matter of growth and should not be forced. Enlightening notes give his observations about the poems.

Eaton, Anne Thaxter, comp. *Welcome Christmas! A Garland of Poems;* decorated by Valenti Angelo. Viking Press, 1955. (Grades 6–9)

A companion volume to the compiler's *The Animals' Christmas.*

Ferris, Helen, ed. *Favorite Poems Old and New;* illus. by Leonard Weisgard. Doubleday, 1957. (All ages)

A book for the entire family that will form the basis for a shared enjoyment of fine poetry.

Fish, Helen Dean, comp. *Boy's Book of Verse; an Anthology.* J. B. Lippincott, rev. ed. 1951. (Grades 6–9)

A treasury of old and new poems which appeal especially to boys.

Geismer, Barbara Peck, and Antoinette Suter, comps. *Very Young Verses;* illus. by Mildred Bronson. Houghton Mifflin, 1945. (Grades 1–3)

From their experience with small children, two nursery school teachers made this compilation.

Harrington, Mildred, comp. *Ring-a-Round; a Collection of Verse for Boys and Girls;* illus. by Corydon Bell. Macmillan, 1930. (Preschool-Grade 5)

The compiler made this collection for her nieces and nephews, but it serves to introduce all children to the delights of poetry.

Hazeltine, Alice I., and Elva Smith, comps. *The Year Around; Poems for Children;* decorations by Paula Hutchison. Abingdon, 1956. (Grades 4–8)

Poems for every season and every month of the year, as well as for holidays.

Huffard, Grace Thompson, and others, comps. *My Poetry Book;* an anthology of modern verse for boys and girls; illus. by Willy Pogány. John C. Winston, rev. ed. 1956. (Grades 6–8)

First published in 1934. The new edition has an introduction by Marguerite de Angeli and adds more than forty new poems.

Love, Katherine, ed. *Pocketful of Rhymes;* illus. by Henrietta Jones. Thomas Y. Crowell, 1946. (Grades 2–4)

A love of poetry and experience of sharing it with children have gone into the making of this collection by a children's librarian of the New York Public Library. In *A Little Laughter* she has gathered a happy selection of light-hearted verse.

Nash, Ogden, ed. *The Moon Is Shining Bright as Day.* J. B. Lippincott, 1953. (Grades 3–6)

An anthology of good-humored verse.

Plotz, Helen, comp. *Imagination's Other Place;* illus. with wood engravings by Clare Leighton. Thomas Y. Crowell, 1955. (High School)

A unique collection of poems of science and mathematics selected with imagination. *Untune the Sky* includes poems of music and the dance.

Read, Sir Herbert, ed. *This Way, Delight; a Book of Poetry for the Young;* illus. by Juliet Kepes. Pantheon Press, 1956. (Grades 4–7)

The editor of this discriminating anthology is a distinguished poet, writer, and critic.

Smith, Janet Adams, comp. *The Faber Book of Children's Verse.* Transatlantic Arts, 1954. (Grades 5–8)

Janet Smith states in a stimulating introduction that she has included not only poems for immediate pleasure but also poems with "reserves of meaning," for she knows understanding will grow with the reader.

Stevenson, Burton E., comp. *Home Book of Verse for Young Folks;* decorations by Willy Pogány. Henry Holt, rev. and enl. ed. 1929. (All ages)

A delightful collection including old favorites and new. *The Home Book of Modern Verse* contains selections from American and English poets of the twentieth century.

Thompson, Blanche Jennings, ed. *Silver Pennies; a Collection of Modern Poems for Boys and Girls;* illus. by Winifred Bromhall. Macmillan, 1925. (Little Library) (Grades 3–8)

A collection which has been popular ever since it was first published. A brief note introduces each poem.

Untermeyer, Louis, ed. *This Singing World; an Anthology of Modern Poetry for Young People;* illus. by Florence Wyman Ivins. Harcourt, Brace, 1923. (Grades 5–9)

This poet-anthologist has made several excellent collections of poetry including *Rainbow in the Sky* and *Stars to Steer By.*

Individual Poets

Aldis, Dorothy. *All Together; a Child's Treasury of Verse;* illus. by Helen D. Jameson, Marjorie Flack, and Margaret Freeman. G. P. Putnam, 1952. (Grades 2–4)

Includes the best-loved verses from Mrs. Aldis's earlier books: *Everything and Anything; Here, There and Everywhere; Hop, Skip and Jump;* and *Before Things Happen.*

Becker, John. *New Feathers for the Old Goose;* illus. by Virginia Campbell. Pantheon Books, 1956. (Pre-school)

An author and his artist wife have combined their talents to produce a book of gay and original nonsense rhymes.

Behn, Harry. *Windy Morning; Poems and Pictures.* Harcourt, Brace, 1953. (Grades 2–4)

Poems which an outstanding contemporary poet wrote for his own children and illustrated with imaginative drawings. Of equal delight are his poems found in *The Little Hill, The House Beyond the Meadow,* and *The Wizard in the Well.*

Benét, Rosemary and Stephen Vincent. *A Book of Americans;* illus. by Charles Child. Rinehart, rev. ed. 1952. (Grades 5–8)

Stirring poems describe the life and character of famous men and women from Columbus to Woodrow Wilson.

Browning, Robert. *Pied Piper of Hamelin;* illus. by Kate Greenaway. Frederick Warne, n. d. (Grades 5–8)

A favorite poem enriched with Kate Greenaway's charming illustrations.

Coatsworth, Elizabeth. *Poems;* decorations by Vee Guthrie. Macmillan, 1957. (Grades 4–7)

Many of the thoughtful poems that first appeared between chapters of the author's stories are found in this collection, along with new ones.

De la Mare, Walter. *Peacock Pie: A Book of Rhymes;* illus. by Barbara Cooney. Henry Holt, new ed. 1957. (All ages)

Poems of gay fantasy, clear imagery, and sheer beauty distinguish this volume.

De la Mare, Walter. *Rhymes and Verses; Collected Poems for Children;* illus. by Elinore Blaisdell. Henry Holt, 1947. (Grades 5–9)

The poet's own selection from his earlier volume: *Songs of Childhood; Peacock Pie; Bells and Grass; This Year; Next Year;* and *Down-Adown-Derry.*

Dickinson, Emily. *Poems for Youth;* ed. by Alfred Leete Hampson; foreword by May Lamberton Becker; illus. by George and Doris Hauman. Little, Brown, 1934. (Grades 7–9)

A selection of the author's nature poems and others which older children will enjoy.

Dunbar, Paul Laurence. *Little Brown Baby; Poems for Young People;* selections, with biographical sketch by Bertha Rodgers; illus. by Erick Berry. Dodd, Mead, 1940. (Grades 4–8)

A delightful introduction to the well-known Negro poet.

Farjeon, Eleanor. *Eleanor Farjeon's Poems for Children.* J. B. Lippincott, 1951. (Grades 4–6)

Brings together all the poems in the author's *Sing for Your Supper, Over the Garden Wall, Joan's Door,* and *Come Christmas,* with the addition of twenty poems not previously published in America.

Field, Eugene. *Poems of Childhood;* illus. by Maxfield Parrish. Charles Scribner's Sons. (Grades 3–5)

First published in 1896, these poems have long been favorites of children.

Field, Rachel. *Poems;* decorations by the author. Macmillan, 1957. (Grades 3–6)

Gathered here in one volume are the author's verses chosen from *Taxis and Toadstools, Pointed People, Branches Green,* and *Christmas Time,* with a few of her other poems.

Frost, Robert. *Road Not Taken;* illus. by John O'Hara Cosgrave, II. Henry Holt, 1951. (Grades 7–9)

"An introduction to Robert Frost; a selection of Robert Frost's poems; with a biographical preface and running comment by Louis Untermeyer." — Subtitle.

Fyleman, Rose. *Fairies and Chimneys.* Doubleday, 1920. (Grades 4–6)

Many of these charming fairy poems first appeared in *Punch.*

Lindsay, Vachel. *Johnny Appleseed, and Other Poems;* illus. by George Richards. Macmillan, 1928. (Children's Classics) (Grades 5–9)

Selections from "The Congo" and the "Chinese Nightingale" are included with rhymes and songs for younger children.

Milne, A. A. *When We Were Very Young;* illus. by E. H. Shepard. E. P. Dutton, 1924. (K–Grade 3)

Endearing verses which Milne wrote for his small son, Christopher Robin. Followed by *Now We Are Six.*

Moore, Clement Clarke. *Night Before Christmas;* illus. by Arthur Rackham. J. B. Lippincott, 1931. (Grades 1–3)

One of the most beloved of all Christmas poems which first appeared in a newspaper in 1823.

Rossetti, Christina. *Sing-Song; a Nursery Rhyme Book, and Other Poems for Children.* Macmillan, 1924. (Grades 3–4)

This small volume of joyous verse by a famous poet, first published in 1872, has become a nursery classic.

Sandburg, Carl. *Early Moon;* illus. by James Daugherty. Harcourt, Brace, 1930. (Grades 6–9)

Contains an interesting chapter on poetry by Mr. Sandburg, followed by seventy of his poems.

Stevenson, Robert Louis. *A Child's Garden of Verses;* illus. by Jessie Willcox Smith. Charles Scribner's Sons, new ed. 1955. (Scribner Illustrated Classics) (Grades 1–4)

These verses, known and loved generation after generation, were first published in England in 1885 under the title *Penny Whistles.*

Teasdale, Sara. *Stars To-night; Verses New and Old for Boys and Girls;* illus. by Dorothy P. Lathrop. Macmillan, 1930. (Grades 5–9)

The poet's joy in nature finds expression in these poems chosen particularly for older girls.

References for the Adult

Auslander, Joseph, and Frank Hill. *Winged Horse, the Story of the Poets and Their Poetry;* illus. by Paul Honoré. Doubleday, 1927.

Barnes, Walter. *The Children's Poets.* World Book Company, 1924.

Brain, Sir Russell. *Tea with Walter de la Mare.* Faber & Faber (London), 1957.

Brown, Stephen James. *The Realm of Poetry.* Macmillan, 1922.

Dixon, W. Macneile. *English Epic and Heroic Poetry.* E. P. Dutton, 1912.

Drew, Elizabeth. *Discovering Poetry.* W. W. Norton, 1933.

Eastman, Max. *Enjoyment of Poetry.* Charles Scribner's Sons, 1951.

Macintyre, Robert, ed. *Ballads Ancient and Modern.* Thomas Nelson & Sons (London), 1935.

Sackville-West, V. *Walter de la Mare, and The Traveller.* Oxford, 1953.

Untermeyer, Louis, and Carter Davidson. *Poetry: Its Appreciation and Enjoyment.* Harcourt, Brace, 1934.

Chapters, Commentary and Articles

Arbuthnot, May Hill. *Children and Books.* Scott, Foresman, rev. ed. 1957.
"Poetry," Chapters 5 through 10, pp. 76–225.

Benét, Laura. "Walter de la Mare: 1873–1956," *Saturday Review,* Sept. 22, 1956, p. 11.

De la Mare, Walter. *Bells and Grass, Poems.* Viking Press, 1942.
Introduction, pp. 5–10.

Walter de la Mare Issue. *The Horn Book Magazine,* June, 1957.
Editorial, by Bertha Mahony Miller; "Walter de la Mare," by Eleanor Farjeon; "Walter de la Mare," by Herbert Read; "Walter de la Mare," by Pamela Bianco.

Duff, Annis. *"Bequest of Wings"; A Family's Pleasures with Books.* Viking Press, 1944.
"Poetry in the Nursery," pp. 58–70; "Poetry for Children," pp. 71–81.

Eaton, Anne Thaxter. *Reading with Children.* Viking Press, 1940.
"Poetry," pp. 119–135.

Meigs, Cornelia, and others. *A Critical History of Children's Literature.* Macmillan, 1953.

"Poetry for Children in the Nineteenth Century," pp. 286–295; "Poets of Childhood," pp. 407–415.

Moore, Anne Carroll. *The Three Owls; a Book about Children's Books.* Macmillan, 1925.
"Walter de la Mare," pp. 40–53; "Poets and Lepracauns," pp. 259–263; "Modern Poetry for Modern Children," pp. 326–333; "Reading Poetry with Children," pp. 333–337.

Moore, Anne Carroll, and Bertha Mahony Miller, eds. *Writing and Criticism.* The Horn Book, Inc., 1951
"De la Mare: An Essay," by Margery Bianco, pp. 67–77.

Moore, Annie E. *Literature Old and New for Children.* Houghton Mifflin, 1934.
"Natural Response of Children to Poetry," Chapter 9, pp. 257–276; "Makers of Poetry for Children," Chapter 10, pp. 276–352.

Read, Sir Herbert, ed. *This Way, Delight.* Pantheon Books, 1956.
"What Is Poetry?" pp. 137–144.

Smith, Janet Adams, comp. *The Faber Book of Children's Verse.* Transatlantic Arts, 1954.
Introduction, pp. 19–23.

Smith, Lillian H. *The Unreluctant Years.* American Library Association, 1953.
"Poetry," Chapter 7, pp. 96–114.

Stedman, Edmund. *Genius and Other Essays.* Moffat Yard, 1911.
"Eugene Field," pp. 183–192.

Untermeyer, Louis, ed. *Yesterday and Today.* Harcourt, Brace, 1927.
Preface, pp. v–viii.

Suggestions for Further Reading

Duffin, Henry Charles. *Walter de la Mare: A Study of His Poetry.* Sedgwick and Jackson (London), 1949.

Masefield, John. *So Long To Learn.* Macmillan, 1952.

Milne, A.A. *Autobiography.* E. P. Dutton, 1939.

Reid, Forrest. *Walter de la Mare, a Critical Study.* Henry Holt, 1929.

Young, Ella. *Flowering Dusk; an Autobiography.* Longmans, Green, 1945.

APPENDIX A

Storytelling

In ONE OF Hans Christian Andersen's merriest tales,[1] the old Troll King of Norway comes to Denmark to visit an Elfin Mount, bringing with him his two sons, to choose brides for the boys from among the Elf King's seven daughters. After the feast, each daughter stepped forth to parade her special accomplishment. The most ethereal of them knew how to disappear altogether, but this was a trait neither father nor sons approved of in a wife. The sons, bored with the procedure, left the gathering abruptly after the appearance of the fourth daughter, but the old king remained until the seventh daughter's turn. "And what could she do?" runs the story. "Why she could tell fairy tales, as many as any one could wish to hear. 'Here are my five fingers,' said the Troll King: 'tell me a story for each finger.'

"And the Elfin Maid took hold of his wrist, and told her stories, and he laughed till his sides ached; and when she came to the finger that wore the gold ring, as though it knew it might be wanted, the Old Troll suddenly exclaimed, 'Hold fast what you have. The hand is yours. I will marry you myself!' "

Although the storyteller's art may win no kings today, the hard work, imagination, and knowledge which must be spent in pursuit of it are worth a king's ransom. The storyteller will find himself welcomed by everyone. All classes of society will be open to him, and everyone — men, women, and children — will willingly listen and beg for more. The appeal of the story is universal. Fiction, drama, journalism, and all the arts of entertainment have as their major concern the telling of a story. What happened, and to whom, and where? These are the elemental motives that bind us together in the web of humanity.

Before the advent of printing, storytelling was the chief means of recording and preserving history as well as ideas and remembered emotion. In the early history of man, the story was probably a simple narrative recounting the day's events: the hunt, the chase, the capture, and the kill. But as man developed, his storytelling came to include an account of the emotions attending the event: the fear and hope, the courage and cowardice, and the desperate search for aid from the unknown. From these beginnings, man developed the ability to tell all that he felt and observed about life, and the behavior of others around him; his premonitions and theories, his beliefs and tabus. He used the telling of tales as a means of giving form to his religion, his laws, his wit and humor, and the practicality of everyday life. Without the art of storytelling, there would be no mythology, no epic literature, no way for the generations to have reached beyond their allotted time to touch and teach the generations yet to come. This is the heritage of storytelling. When children hear these old tales from the great, anonymous, oral tradition, they are aligned, as it were, with the past, better able, therefore, to understand the present and to sense the future.

Storytelling offers a direct approach to children. The events of the appropriately chosen and well-told story can be counted upon to catch and hold their interest. In addition, there is the flattery of sharing, either as an individual listener or as a part of the group, an experience with an adult, on terms of seemingly absolute equality. The warmth of the voice, the intimacy, the sense of direct, sincere, and eager communication between the teller and his listeners; these are responsible for the unique relationship between the storyteller and his audience. Good storytelling breaks down barriers: differences in age, the fear or awe in which children sometimes hold their elders. Tell

[1] "The Elfin Mount," in *Fairy Tales and Legends* (Oxford University Press, New York 1936), p. 61.

a child a story he enjoys, and he looks upon you as an equal, trusts you with revelations he would never have thought of sharing, and attributes to you interests you may not have. "Did you get many toys for Christmas?" a small boy asked an experienced storyteller. They had liked the same stories. It was logical, then, that their interests should run parallel in the matter of Christmas luck.

How greatly the imagination of children is stimulated by this art of storytelling! They must themselves build the scene and setting with their inner eye. There are no moving pictures, no painted backdrops, no sound accompaniments, no mood music, no film strips: only the modulation of the voice and the words, an occasional involuntary gesture, a change of pace, a pause — only these to tell him how to define the threat, the conflict and the resolution. Yet in this art all the emotions find expression, and the imaginary is given the bone and sinew of reality. Through the storyteller's art children learn to appreciate and enjoy the sound of the language. In this day of pictorial emphasis, when the visual is used increasingly as a method of communication, it would seem that the scope of language is lessened. As far as the written language is concerned, the tendency is to simplify its structure, limit its vocabulary, and narrow its subtleties of feeling and color, reducing it to the basic norm of everyday speech. Perhaps for this reason there is a resurgence of interest in storytelling, for here is a means of using language in all its variability. Those who cannot or will not understand the printed page may listen beyond their years and their comprehension. The ancient art of storytelling now is freshly acclaimed as an able partner in this audio-visual age.

The Choice of Story

The first step in the long discipline of becoming a good storyteller is the choice of a story to tell. It should be a tale worthy of the emphasis which the voice and the spoken word give it. Every weakness of structure, every false feeling becomes apparent when the voice and personality of the storyteller add their dimension to the tale.

Many a story which may seem to have charm when it is read collapses and falls flat when it is told.

The story that tells well is the one in which the conflict is well-defined, the action moves directly to the climax of the conflict, and the ending resolves all difficulties with satisfying finality: in short, the dramatic story, the story in which action is paramount, and everything superfluous to the main purpose of the story is omitted. A good story is built like the clear, curving line of an arch, each part closely related to the others, the incidents of the tale, like the stones of the arch, moving up to the keystone — the climax — and then falling away to the other side. Folk tales are, for the most part, constructed in this fashion. It is for this reason that the storyteller will find the basis of his repertoire in folklore. The folk tales were shaped to the tongue by generations of use. The neophyte storyteller will learn to recognize the tellable if he reads deeply in folklore.

The uses one wishes to make of a story may sometimes lead to the choice of a weak or contrived tale. The hunt is always on for stories for special occasions — those minor feasts and holidays which are troublesome to teachers, librarians, and program-makers; Arbor Day, Flag Day, and even Christmas stories present a hazard. The zeal to teach some specific attitude in children or to point up a good habit often leads to a search for stories that were written for the purpose. The temptation may be strong to relax the storyteller's critical judgment in favor of the message. It is the better part of wisdom to hew to the line of structure, to think in terms of the story's integrity: the drama, action, mood, and total effect, and leave lesser messages to a less effective medium than storytelling.

The excellent story, like all excellence in art, is full of meaning, morality, and nourishment of the spirit, but meaning cannot be wrung from it, like water out of a rag and made to render a drop of moisture on a dry spot.

The choice of a story should also be governed by its appeal for the storyteller, for it stands to reason that one's best efforts are commanded by one's own choice. Choose a story then, for which you have a genuine liking, or better still a strong liking. The story will be as much a part of you as your own thumb, by the time you have mastered it, and therefore it had better be a tale you love. The choice of a simple, short folk tale is a wise one for the beginning storyteller. Save for years of experience the longer and more sophisticated tales of Laurence Housman, Oscar Wilde, Hans Christian Andersen, and Frank Stockton.

PREPARATION OF THE STORY

After a choice of the story is made, consider it. Define first, in your own mind, the prime reasons for its appeal to you. What did you like about it? Was it the plot — a tale of adventure, a giant to be overcome, a magnificent array of perils? Was it the mood — poetic, romantic, humorous or nonsensical? Let us assume that the story you have chosen is "Molly Whuppie" from Joseph Jacobs' *English Fairy Tales*.[2] It is rather long, for a first story, but it is so strong a story, so exciting in its series of events, that you choose it. It is that rare thing, an adventure story in which the main character is a heroine rather than a hero, and it is a story that appeals to all ages. You have read it once, and you like it. Read the notes in the back of the book to discover its origins. Many of its motifs you will recognize: the desertion of children, the recurrence of the number three (three children, three tasks); the changing of the sleeper's garb.

The beginning of this story states briefly and immediately how perilous life is. Don't dwell upon this. Don't question whether or not the desertion is going to make some child feel insecure. Don't contrive some other beginning which shows that this is the best of all possible worlds. Accept the story-opening, as children accept it, in its proportionate relation to the story as a whole. The action moves forward. The three children walk out of the great forest seeking shelter. They find a giant's house where the peril is great. There is the first escape from the house. Then Molly must

2 See also page 203 of this anthology.

return to the giant's house three times. Twice she goes on behalf of her two sisters, and the third time on her own behalf. By dint of great courage, and wit and daring, she succeeds and finds husbands for her sisters and a prince for herself into the bargain. There are the bones of the tale. Mull them over in your mind, and ponder on their vitality, the ingenuousness of the invention, the magnificent symbols of adventure. What is the mood of this story? Name it and define it for yourself, in order that when you come to learn the story you will orchestrate it, as it were, within its key mood. The mood of Molly Whuppie is robust and bold, and courage and dauntlessness are the chief characteristics. Sound the mood in your subconscious mind so that it will color and control your telling of the story.

Now read the story over and over. Do not memorize it either word by word or paragraph by paragraph, but read it over and over until you know *absolutely* what are the successive steps in the course of its action. Test yourself by closing the book, and making a list of the *hinges of action* in proper order.

1. Children deserted in wood.
2. They walk to giant's house.
3. Giant's wife lets them in.
4. Giant comes home and asks who is there.
5. Wife replies, "Three lassies" — note first indication that the children are girls.
6. Giant puts necklaces of straw around their necks, gold necklaces for his own three daughters. Commands they all sleep in the same bed.
7. Molly Whuppie notices this — note first time her name is used.
8. Molly exchanges the necklaces.
9. Molly and her sisters escape.
10. Come to King's house.
11. King tells Molly if she returns to giant and gets sword, he will give his oldest son as husband to her older sister.
12. Molly returns, gets sword. Results.
13. Second trip to giant. Molly gets purse. Results.
14. Third trip to giant. Molly gets ring but is captured.
15. Molly tricks giant for the last time and escapes.
16. Happy ending.

By learning the hinges of action in this way, you are sure of your control of the story. It will belong to you forever. If you do not tell the story for years, one quick reading will bring it back to you.

The next step is to build, in your imagination, the landscape, the setting, the scenes of your story. This is of major importance. *The one immutable law of storytelling is to see with your inner eye everything of which you speak.* When you have accomplished this, your story will have such an air of conviction that you will be able to tell it as though you were telling something that happened to you. *This is an imperative quality for the master storyteller: to see what you relate.* You speak of the forest. Bring to your mind's eye the image of any forest, wood, or grove you have yourself known or seen pictured. Feel the word as you say it, and above all see it! Castles, giants, bridges of one hair, these you must imagine, but never fail to see them as you speak their names. Look at pictures of castles and set one up in your mind. Where does the giant's house stand in your telling of the story? To the right, or the left of the picture. Do the children come from left or right? What kind of bed does the giant sleep on? Is it a four-poster or a crude matter of skins stretched across a wooden frame? Train yourself to see and you unconsciously give your audience time to see also. The pace of your story will come to fit action and scene. You must give your story depth and conviction, setting and atmosphere, before you can make it live for your listeners.

It was told of Ibsen, the great Norwegian dramatist, that before he set pen to paper in writing his plays, he sketched out the whole life experience of his characters as he imagined them, documented their lives up to the moment when he was to present them for a given time in his drama. The storyteller must build his setting and characterization in this same manner.

Look at your story once more, this time with an eye to its climactic parts. Where is the highest point? Build toward it, as you tell, and change pace as you near it, so that the audience may know the pleasure of anticipation. What other bits are pleasur-able and invite lingering? When all this is accomplished, it is time to consider the role of memorization. There will be certain turns of phrase you like, and want to remember, or refrains that are important to the story:

"Woe worth ye, Molly Whuppie,
    Never ye come again."
"Twice yet, Carle, I'll come to Spain."

These can be consciously memorized. As for the rest, you will find the story so familiar to you that you begin to think of it as your own brainchild.

Certain stories must be memorized, because the style in which they were conceived is vital to the story. This is true of Kipling's *Just So Stories,* which would lose at least half of their charm were they told in words other than the author's, and certain stories of Carl Sandburg demand the same memorization. But if these stories are studied in the manner suggested here, the memorization will present little difficulty.

The danger of depending on memorization alone is that if you lose one part of the story, a word or phrase, in a moment of panic, or if some occurrence interrupts the even flow of your memory, you are apt to lose the thread of the whole tale. But if you have learned the hinges of action, you can go on under your own steam, come what may.

THE TELLING

By this time, you are saturated with your story, and ready to tell it. It is good practice to tell aloud to one's self, for by this means your own ears are able to tell you whether or not you have variation in pace, or have by use of a judicious pause indicated the climactic points of the story for the greater enjoyment of the audience. The use of a tape recorder is valuable at this stage. It reveals the best of one's speech habits, as well as the worst, and clearly defines the areas that must be worked upon and improved.

Do not be discouraged if the first efforts are something less than your hopes. The element which will hold the children is your *belief* in the story, your *sincerity* in presenting it, your absolute control of all the story is capable of revealing. If you are sure of these elements, the children will forgive you everything else. You will learn from their reactions much that you need to know: the value of a pause; when to speed up the telling of the tale — in the repetitive sequences, for example.

The fascination of storytelling lies in the fact that it is never completed, never finished, for in each telling the story is re-created anew. The audience, the atmosphere of the place, the inner weather of the storyteller: there are dozens of intangible, mysterious forces that contribute to the growth of a story. "I make the story as I tell it," Ella Young, the noted Irish storyteller once said. She did not mean that she created the events of the story. She meant that the story took on the quality of the audience's collective response to it. Sometimes one face in the group will call forth the teller's deepest feeling. Sometimes, when he is unlucky, he will feel that he speaks to stone walls. Each of these experiences increases his power to convey feeling, to build a mood, to catch and transport people beyond themselves.

Certain obvious circumstances may be avoided: a room that is uncomfortable; too many children crowded together; children of too diverse age range. It is foolish to attempt to tell stories to children ranging in ages from three to thirteen in the same story hour. After a storyteller has presumably perfected his art, he has the right to demand certain basic considerations for the telling.

The Modern Storyteller

The storyteller in modern society is something of an anachronism. He holds no place comparable to his position of might in the primitive societies of untaught men. But the old tradition persists in certain regions of our own country (the mountains of the South, for example, and among many of the American Indians), in the Orient, in Mexico, in parts of Europe (Russia, Wales, Ireland). For the unsophisticated or the unlettered, storytelling is still the chief source of entertainment. The public libraries of the country have found it the most effective and direct means of giving children a background of literature, with its many attendant arts.

Schools, playgrounds, camps, and recreation centers use it also. Its unique influence is substantiated even in the face of television, which has not yet discovered proper use of it.

Certain men and women of our time have made the storyteller's art living and vital to the present day. Charles Laughton, the actor, has reintroduced it in his readings, for though he seems to be reading from a book, his method is that of the storyteller, with its direct approach to the audience, its pace, its emphasis on what is spoken rather than what is read. Seumas MacManus, the Irish storyteller, continues to bring to his fortunate listeners in small concert halls a demonstration of what it means to have been born an Irishman in this matter of telling stories, drawing upon one of the richest folklores of the world, the Celtic, and using the rich, exact, and poetic turns of phrase which characterize the Irish speech. Richard Chase, who ferreted out our native pockets of folklore in the mountains of the South in his two collections of tales,[3] is a master storyteller, his style and speech deriving from the region he has made his own. Philip Sherlock, Vice President of the University of the West Indies at Jamaica, an important leader in the founding of the new West Indian Federation, is another distinguished storyteller who has collected the folk tales[4] of his country.

Early in the century, storytelling gained the recognition of advanced educators in both England and America. The English storyteller, Marie Shedlock (1854–1935), whose book [5] remains the classic treatise on the subject, addressed to teachers the lectures which were the basis of the book. She lectured in France, as well as in her own country, and set the standards of excellence for storytelling in the United States. It was her supreme artistry which inspired the establishment of storytelling in the New York Public Library. To this day the annual storytelling symposium in New York is

[3] Richard Chase, *The Jack Tales* (Houghton Mifflin, Boston, 1943) and *Grandfather Tales* (Houghton Mifflin, Boston, 1948).
[4] Philip Sherlock, *Anansi, the Spider Man* (Thomas Y. Crowell, New York, 1954).
[5] Marie Shedlock, *The Art of the Storyteller* (Dover Publications, New York, 1951).

staged on her birthday. Contemporary with Miss Shedlock was Gudrun Thorne-Thomsen (1873–1956), the Norwegian storyteller who, at the University of Chicago under the aegis of John Dewey, explored the uses of the art. Her influence was to be felt across the country, since she taught in library schools, teachers colleges, and universities, and told stories widely. Fortunately, records of her tellings are available through the American Library Association. The recordings give no inkling of the intensity of her personality, nor the beauty of her face as she told, but the timbre of her voice, one of the most moving voices imaginable, is there, as is her approach to the story.

Ruth Sawyer Durand, who won the Newbery medal in 1937, is another whose tellings are recorded by the American Library Association. This many-faceted author and collector of folk tales has written a book on storytelling [6] which, richly informed by her own experience, gives the reader both inspiration and practical help. Still another noted storyteller in her own right is Augusta Baker, Supervisor of Storytelling in the New York Public Library, a fine successor to Anna Cogswell Tyler and Mary Gould Davis, who under the direction of Anne Carroll Moore laid the basis for the half-century of sustained storytelling in that institution.

Each of these storytellers has his own style

[6] Ruth Sawyer, *The Way of the Storyteller* (Viking Press, New York, 1942).

and individuality as a master of the art. But there is one thing they hold in common: a great simplicity. For each, it is the story which speaks first. They are only instruments. There are no great studied gestures here, no tricks of changing voices to suit each character of the story, no costumes or gimmicks to substantiate the tale. Above all, there is no condescension, either to the story or to the children, no pseudo-ecstatic tone of voice which some adults assume when speaking to children, no asking of questions before and after, no insistence on the explanations of the meaning of words, no rewards for listening — except the story itself.

Storytellers learn from one another. There is nothing so helpful as a meeting of the dedicated in a tournament of tales. Such a fête creates incentive, inspiration, and renewed interest in the development of individual style. Each storyteller is encouraged to try the story someone else has found interesting. By this means, he learns what types of stories best suit his own gifts and aptitudes. Certain tales seem to belong to certain storytellers. No one could match Miss Shedlock, for example, in the telling of Andersen; and Mary Gould Davis was inimitable in the telling of stories by Frank Stockton, who might have written them especially for her. All of this is part of the fascination of storytelling. It is a deathless art, lively and diverse, which, like music, refreshes and revives those whom it touches even in its farthest reaches.

BIBLIOGRAPHY

Arbuthnot, May Hill. *Children and Books.* Scott, Foresman, rev. ed. 1957.

Chapter 12, pp. 270–280.

Colum, Padraic. *The Fountain of Youth; Stories To Be Told.* Macmillan, 1927.

"Storytelling New and Old," pp. 193–206.

Colum, Padraic. *Orpheus: Myths of the World.* Macmillan, 1930.

Introduction, "The Significance of Mythology."

Eaton, Anne Thaxter. *Reading with Children.* Viking Press, 1940.

"The World's Great Stories," Chapter 8, pp. 135–156.

Meigs, Cornelia, and others. *A Critical History of Children's Literature.* Macmillan, 1953.

"Howard Pyle," pp. 299–313; "A Rightful Heritage," pp. 321–327; "Looking to the Past — Hero Stories," pp. 460–464.

Moore, Anne Carroll. *New Roads to Childhood.* Doubleday, 1939.

"Storytelling and the Art of Reading," pp. 142–148.

Sawyer, Ruth. *The Way of the Storyteller.* Viking Press, 1942.

Shedlock, Marie. *The Art of the Storyteller.* Dover, 3d rev. ed. 1951.

Smith, Lillian. *The Unreluctant Years.* American Library Association, 1953.

"Heroes of Epic and Saga," Chapter 6, pp. 81–95.

Articles and Pamphlets

Armstrong, Helen. "Hero Tales for Telling," *The Horn Book Magazine,* Vol. 25, Jan. 1949, pp. 9–15.

Britton, Jasmine. "Gudrun Thorne-Thomsen: Storyteller from Norway," *The Horn Book Magazine,* Vol. 34, Feb. 1958, pp. 17–29.

Davis, Mary Gould. "Storytellers' Harvest," *The Horn Book Magazine,* Vol. 13, Nov.-Dec. 1937, pp. 345–354.

Laughton, Charles. "Storytelling," *Atlantic Monthly,* June, 1950, pp. 71–73.

Mahony, Bertha E. "Guide to Treasure," *The Horn Book Magazine,* Vol. 16, May 1940, pp. 177–185.

Nesbitt, Elizabeth. "The Art of Storytelling," *The Horn Book Magazine,* Vol. 21, Nov. 1945, pp. 439–444.

Nesbitt, Elizabeth. "Hold to That Which Is Good," *The Horn Book Magazine,* Vol. 16, May 1940, pp. 7–15.

Sawyer, Ruth. "How to Tell a Story," written for *Compton's Pictured Encyclopedia.* F. E. Compton, 1953.

Sayers, Frances Clarke. "Enriching Literature Through Storytelling." Association for Childhood Education; Leaflet No. 9 of the portfolio "Adventuring in Literature with Children."

Steinmetz, Eulalie. "Storytelling versus Recordings," *The Horn Book Magazine,* Vol. 24, May 1948, pp. 163–172.

Storytelling Number; a Tribute to Marie L. Shedlock, *The Horn Book Magazine,* Vol. 10, May 1934.

Sutcliff, Rosemary. "Beginning with Beowulf," *The Horn Book Magazine,* Vol. 29, Feb. 1953, pp. 36–38.

Thorne-Thomsen, Gudrun. "Storytelling and Stories I Tell; In Memoriam." Viking Press, 1956.

Viguers, Ruth. "Over the Drawbridge and into the Castle," *The Horn Book Magazine,* Vol. 27, Jan. 1951, pp. 54–62.

Lists

Stories; a List of Stories to Tell and to Read Aloud; compiled by Eulalie Steinmetz. New York Public Library, 4th ed. 1949.

Stories to Tell; prepared by the Children's Department of the Enoch Pratt Free Library, Baltimore. 4th ed. rev. and ed. by Isabella Jinnette, 1956.

Stories to Tell to Children. 6th ed. rev. by Laura E. Cathon and others of the Carnegie Library of Pittsburgh, 1949.

The Story of Children's Literature

THE STORY of children's literature has always been a story of conflict, and so it is even in our own time. The main line of battle lies between those who consider childhood primarily as a period of preparation for the future and those who see it as a state of being in its own right, an experience of life like no other in which emotion, imagination, and the response to the wonder of life reach greatest intensity.

For the first group, books and reading are mainly a means of instilling knowledge and establishing concepts of moral and social law. The second group is more concerned with giving children access to the universal elements in literature which will sustain their intuitive powers, with the hope that some "residue of remembered emotion" will carry over into the adult years. The great books of childhood are those written without regard for specific theories or attitudes, being the invention and inspiration of distinctive personalities, who say what they have to say from inner necessity, compulsion, or delight.

The social, educational, and moral history of cultures can be traced in books for children, within these recurring tides of freedom and the resurgence of manipulated opinions, ideas, and instruction. When one examines the evidence, century by century, it becomes apparent that the freedom of children to read at the peak of their abilities must, like other freedoms, be won anew with each generation.

Lesson books, naturally, were the earliest books for the young, and even these were not for children to handle. During the age of chivalry they were books on behavior, prepared for the young pages, who were later to become knights. The most famous of these "courtesy books" was known as the *Babees Boke* and was produced in manuscript from about 1430. Parts of this were among the earliest of Caxton's printing, under the title *Stans Puer ad Mensam;*[1] judging from its many reprints, it must have been very popular. But the first book the child was allowed to handle was the *Hornbook,* first publication date of which has been placed as far back as 1540. We know that one John Webb was licensed to print the *Hornbook* in 1587, and that by 1609, when Thomas Dekker issued his satirical *Gull's Hornbook,* that type of textbook must have been fairly common.

The *Hornbook* was made up of a sheet of paper or pasteboard, on which was printed, first, a small cross in the upper left-hand corner, followed by all the capital letters, the symbols, and the small letters in rows across the top; below were the vowels, and syllables as *ab, eb, ib,* and *ba, be, bi,* etc., in two parallel lists; still below these were the exorcism and part of the Lord's Prayer — all on a space a little less than three by four inches. This printed page was then pasted on a thin sheet of wood, three by four, with a handle, so that the whole looked much like a small square-cornered tennis racquet. The printed matter was covered by a thin layer of horn and held in place by a narrow copper band, tacked down by brass tacks. Thus the printing and paper were protected from easy soiling. Sometimes a hole was made in the handle, so that a string could be put through and the *Hornbook* hung around the child's neck or from his belt.

This was the child's first schoolbook, and to it we are indebted for the saying

> He does not know
> His criss-cross row —

that is, one is too stupid to be able to copy that first row. We are also indebted to this quaint "book" for the symbol &, which on the *Hornbook* looks more like the abbrevia-

[1] Mrs. E. M. Field, *The Child and His Book* (Wells Gardner, London, 1891), p. 99.

tion of *et cetera* than we make it. This symbol came to be called *ampersand*, from *and per se and* — words which the symbol itself signified. One of the earliest examples of the *Hornbook* is shown below; it may be seen in the British Museum.[2]

Another schoolbook, devised by the Moravian bishop Comenius, and translated into English in 1658, was the *Orbis Sensualium*

the story, its number accompanied the reference. Not only does the illustration on the next page show the influence of the *Orbis Pictus*, but the fact that the edition from which this was taken was the twenty-third, and was published in 1807, shows also how long that influence lasted.

During the time of the Tudor kings, *A B C* books were issued. As these were a royal

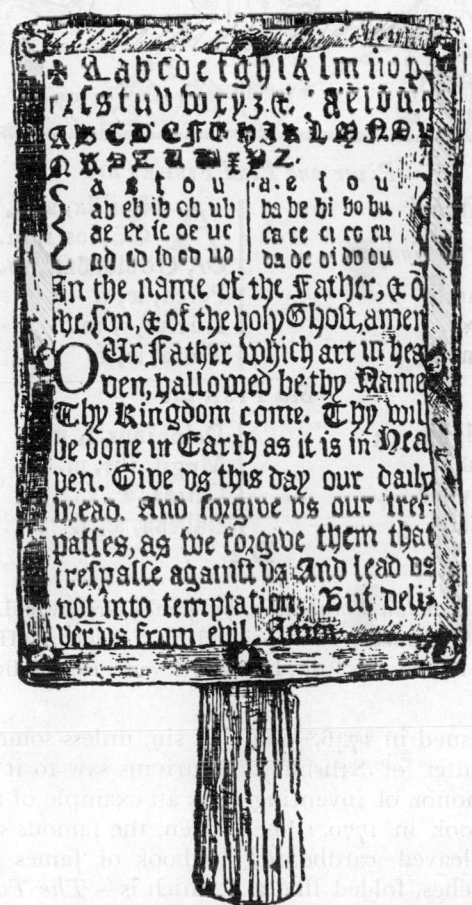

An early hornbook

Pictus, better known as the *Orbis Pictus,* or *The World in Pictures.* With a wood-block picture at the top of each page, it was the child's first picture-book. Each object in the picture was numbered and below it a story was written, originally in High Dutch in one column and in Latin in the other. Whenever any object in the picture was referred to in

[2] *Ibid.,* cover and p. 113.

grant, the religious sentiments changed with that of the royal lessee. When the Stuarts were on the throne, *Primers* — so-called because first used at the hour of "prime" — were popular, and the privilege of printing them was also granted only by royalty.

A different sort of schoolbook was the *Battledore.* Though Clifton Johnson, in his *Old Time Schools and School Books,* says

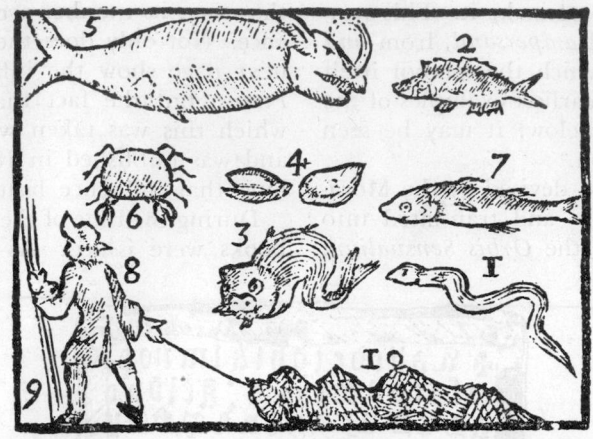

River and Pond FISHES are

A	N Eel 1	A	Nguilla, æ, f.
	A Gudgeon		Gōbius, i, m.
			Or, Gōbio, ōnis, m.
	A Pearch 2		Perca, æ, f.
	A Pike		Lūcïus, i, m.
	A Tench		Tinca, æ, f.

Sea FISH are

A Dolphin 3	Delphĭnus, i, m.
A Mullet	Mugil, ĭlis, m.
An Oyſter 4	Oſtrĕa, æ, f.
A Whale 5	Bālæna, æ, f.

D 2   FISH

From *The London Vocabulary*, by James Greenwood, "late Sur-Master of St. Paul's School, printed for Longmans, Hurst, Rees, and Orme, Paternoster Row, London, Twenty-third Edition, 1807."

that the *Battledore* was issued in 1746,[3] one Benjamin Collins, a printer of Salisbury, claimed for himself the honor of inventing this new type of schoolbook in 1770. The *Battledore* was a three-leaved cardboard, four by six and a half inches, folded like a pocketbook. It had woodcuts, the alphabet, and easy reading matter, but no religious instruction.[4] It was a popular form of textbook as late as 1840.

During the seventeenth century the Puritan influence dominated children's books. The attitude toward the child was that he was conceived in sin, born in sin, filled with sin, would grow to maturity in sin, and die in sin, unless something were done; and the Puritans saw to it that something *was* done. As an example of the sort of stuff given children, the famous stanza below is taken from a book of James Janeway, the title-page of which is — *The Token for Chidren, an exact account of the conversion, holy and exemplary lives, and joyful deaths of several young children.*

When by spectators I am told
What beauty doth adorn me,
Or in a glass when I behold
How sweetly God did form me —
Hath God such comliness bestowed
And on me made to dwell —
What pity such a pretty maid
As I should go to Hell.[5]

[3] Clifton Johnson, *Old Time Schools and School Books* (Macmillan, 1904), p. 63.
[4] Mrs. E. M. Field, p. 121.

[5] *Ibid.*, p. 188.

The Puritan, John Bunyan, wrote one of the masterpieces of English literature; his *Pilgrim's Progress*, written for adults, is an allegory of the spiritual growth of his own immortal soul. Children have claimed this book as their own, reading it as a fairy tale full of marvels and adventure. When Bunyan wrote for children, however, he abandoned inspiration and emotion, and dedicated himself to the religious theories and moral lessons he deemed necessary for children. The result was mournful and deadly; even Puritan children rejected it. The title of the book gave promise of some pleasure, *A Book for Boys and Girls, or Country Rhymes for Children.*[6] But the promise was lost in the author's determination to spell out the moral, as the following extract shows:

MEDITATIONS UPON AN EGG

The Egg's no chick by falling from the Hen
Nor Man no Christian till he's born agen.
The Egg's at first contained in the Shell,
Men, afore Grace, in Sins and Darkness dwell.
The Egg, when laid, by warmth is made a chicken,
And Christ by Grace those dead in Sin doth quicken.
The Egg when first a chick the Shell's its prison,
So's Flesh to the Soul who yet with Christ is risen.
The Shell doth crack; the Chick doth chirp and peep,
The Flesh decays as Men do pray and weep.
The Shell doth break, the Chick's at Liberty,
The Flesh falls off; the Soul mounts up on high;
But both do not enjoy the self-same plight,
The Soul is safe, the Chick now fears the Kite.
But Chicks from rotten Eggs do not proceed,
Nor is a Hypocrit a Saint indeed.
The rotten Egg, though underneath the Hen,

[6] Published in 1686; later issued in 1701 as *Divine Emblems or Temporal Things Spiritualized.*

If cracked Stinks and is loathsome unto Men,
Nor doth her warmth make what is rotten sound,
What's rotten, rotten will at last be found,
The Hypocrit, Sin has him in possession,
He's a rotten Egg under profession.

What a relief Dr. Isaac Watts's *Divine Songs for Children* (1715) must have been. These rhymes are too "moral" from our point of view; yet they were so far superior to the others of the time, that they must have been indeed a blessing. And we must give Dr. Watts credit for a number of our most common sayings:

> How doth the little busy bee
> Improve each shining hour,
>
> For Satan finds some mischief still
> For idle hands to do,
>
> Let dogs delight to bark and bite,

and for his "Cradle Song," which, beginning

> Hush, my child, lie still and slumber,
> Holy angels guard thy bed,

has real poetic feeling in it.

What really happened was that, since children had no literature of their own, they took over what appealed to them in books written for adults. *Pilgrim's Progress* (1678) had been adopted as a fairy tale; likewise Defoe's *Robinson Crusoe* (1719) became their tale of adventure; and in 1726 appeared another adult book, *Gulliver's Travels*, the first two books of which were to them another fantasy. Other adult reading matter of a much lower type became more widely spread — the chapbooks. These were gen-

Illustration for "Meditations upon an Egg," from John Bunyan's book of poems for children (1701 edition).

erally ballads printed cheaply on cheap paper and were peddled about the country by the *chapmen*. Such stories as *The History of Two Children in the Wood* (1700), *Jack and the Gyants* (1708), *Tom Thumb* (1708), and *Tom Hickathrift* must surely have been as eagerly read by the young as by the old.

John Locke (1632–1704), English philosopher and political scientist, touched upon the matter of children's reading in his book *Some Thoughts Concerning Education* (1693). Locke was one of the great minds of the seventeenth century, and many of his political ideas were later to be reflected in the American Declaration of Independence. His ideas on the education of children, too, were to have wide influence. He deplored the use of fairy tales and stories from the old ballads, though he recommended *Aesop's Fables* and the beast epic, *Reynard the Fox,* as having moral value. He was among the first to realize that children could be reasoned with, and might be led to learning rather than being cuffed into submission and made to learn by rote.

The Puritan obsession with sin and infant damnation, the themes of so many books for children in the seventeenth century, was shaken by a blast for freedom which came from France. Charles Perrault, a member of the French Academy, a frequenter of the court of Louis XIV, and superintendent of public works under Colbert, followed the fashion of the Court, which was to retell the stories common among the country people, decking out the tales in all the sophistication of French society. In 1697 he published a book entitled *Histoires du Temps Passé; avec les Moralitez* (Tales of the Past, with Morals). The frontispiece of the book bore the words *Les Contes de ma Mère l'Oye* (Tales of Mother Goose). Perrault was a master storyteller, and the eight tales which first appeared in his book were destined to become immortal. They were: *Cinderella; The Sleeping Beauty; Red Riding-Hood; Blue Beard; Diamonds and Toads; Riquet with the Tuft; Puss in Boots;* and *Hop o' My Thumb.* Scholars cannot agree as to the date when the Perrault tales were first translated into English. But there is evidence that the translation met with authoritative

displeasure. Lord Chesterfield, for one, in his famous letters to his son, advises against reading it.

The chief rescuer of children from the dreariness of the Puritan tradition and of other theorists was John Newbery (1713–1767), the man destined to be called the Father of Children's Literature. Newbery was a self-made man, rising from a printer's apprenticeship to the position of publisher, author, and pharmacist. He was an old friend, and often private banker, to such men as John Gay, Christopher Smart, and Oliver Goldsmith. Even Dr. Samuel Johnson was occasionally in Newbery's debt for a pound or a guinea.[7] But what is of interest here is that he was the first man to realize that children had no *stories* of their own and to attempt to remedy that deficiency. From his publishing office and shop at *The Sign of the Bible and Sun* in St. Paul's churchyard, he issued for children, all told, more than two hundred little books. These were about three by four inches, bound in pasteboard, and covered with pretty Dutch flowered paper; they had crude woodcut illustrations, and were sold very cheaply, none being more than sixpence. They were attractive in appearance and in content, despite their very moral tone. Compared with the twaddle which then was given to children, these books must have been a godsend.

The first book that came from Newbery's shop was called *A Little Pretty Pocket Book;* within its few pages it encompassed old games and riddles, a letter purporting to come from Jack the Giant Killer, and a quotation from Dr. Locke to give the book an appeal for parents. The famous *Mother Goose's Melody* [8] followed soon after. It is interesting for several reasons. It is one of the few early books which have survived to the present; it is the first collection of English

[7] M. Prior, *Life of Oliver Goldsmith,* II, 100.
[8] The complete title of Newbery's Mother Goose is as follows: *Mother Goose's Melody, or Sonnets for the Cradle. In Two Parts; Part I — The Most Celebrated Songs and Lullabies of the Old British Nurses Calculated to amuse Children and excite them to sleep; Part II — Those of that sweet songster and Muse of Art and Humours, Master William Shakespeare.* Adorned with cuts and illustrated with notes and maxims, historical, philosophical, and critical.

"There was an old woman," from a facsimile of
the original *Mother Goose's Melody*, published by
John Newbery (from the earliest extant copy, 1791).

folk-rhymes; it makes use of Shakespeare's songs as suitable for children's reading; it also uses for the first time in English the term *Mother Goose*.

The other famous book from the Newbery press is *The History of Goody Two-Shoes* [9] (1765?). In spite of its romantic impossibilities, its very didactic tone, and its structural weaknesses, the story deserves to have lived so long; for it was still being read far into the nineteenth century. What strikes the modern educator is Mistress Margery's "up-to-date" methods of teaching. But any reader who knows what sort of books for children preceded this will understand its popularity.

[9] The title-page of this little book runs as follows: "*The History of Goody Two-Shoes*, otherwise called, Mistress Margery Two-Shoes, with the means by which she acquired her learning and wisdom, and in consequence thereof her Estate; set forth for the Benefit of those

'Who from a state of Rags and care,
And having Shoes but half a pair;
Their fortune and their Fame, would fix,
And gallop in a Coach and Six.'

See the Original Manuscript in the Vatican at Rome and the cuts by Michael Angelo. Illustrated with the comments of our great Modern Critics." On the next page, the dedication runs: "It is dedicated/To all Young Gentlemen and Ladies who are good, or intend to be good,/This Book is inscribed by their old Friend/In St. Paul's Churchyard." See Appendix C, page 1110.

Because Oliver Goldsmith was doing hack work for John Newbery from 1760 until the publisher's death in 1767, also because these two books out of the two hundred are the only survivors to fame, critics have tried to discover whether Goldsmith had a hand in them, but so far the problem is unsolved.[1] What is more likely is that Goldsmith wrote the maxims that are found after each Mother Goose rhyme, for they show a spirit compatible with his situation at that particular period of his life.

Let us turn again to France, going back a few years. In 1762, Jean Jacques Rousseau (1712–1778) published his *Émile*, in which he sets forth his theory of education. To Rousseau, the child was the hope of the race, provided he was not contaminated by the world.

[1] Prior, in his *Life of Oliver Goldsmith*, said that after making every effort to learn the truth, he did not know. Charles Welsh, in his life of Newbery, thought it possible. Darton, in his chapter on Children's Books in the *Cambridge History of English Literature* [Vol. XI], thought Goldsmith probably had some part in the *Goody Two Shoes* but not in the *Mother Goose*. Florence Barry, in her book *A Century of Children's Books*, thinks the evidence is against Goldsmith's having contributed. Gardner and Ramsay, in their *Handbook of Children's Literature*, suggest the possibility that Goldsmith assisted Newbery. Mrs. Field, in *The Child and His Book*, says "*Goody Two-Shoes* is possibly or probably to be ascribed to Goldsmith, writing about that time for his kind friend Newbery."

With the out-of-doors as his schoolroom, he was to learn from experience through his instincts and feelings. He was to have no books before he was twelve; yet he was to be closely associated with some mature person, such as a parent or tutor, who was qualified to answer all his questions, help him solve his problems, but never direct his actions.

Such, in brief, were the theories that had a great influence not only on English family life of the period, for *Émile* was translated the year after it appeared in France, but upon children's books as well. No longer did writers for children say, "Do this if you wish to go to Heaven," or, "Don't do this, or you will go to Hell." Now the theory was that, if the child could be kept free from the contamination of the world, he would do the natural thing, which would be the right thing; for his instincts were right. In England, however, was added the idea that God would be pleased or displeased accordingly.

The first writer for children, among the followers of Rousseau, was the eccentric Thomas Day (1748–1789) who wrote a three-volume book, *Sandford and Merton* (1783, 1786, 1789), in which the theories worked out perfectly. In his book his boys are about six years old, Harry Sandford being the awful example of goodness to naughty, snobbish Tommy Merton. Their guide is a boresome prig, Mr. Barlow, who helps them acquire facts in physical geography, lets them look through a telescope at the moon, and shows them informational magic-lantern pictures. He tells them historical tales or lets them read fables — all quoted in full — which give rise to long discussions of vices and virtues. The whole is about as uninteresting as a book can be, in spite of occasional spots of naturalness. In the end, however, Tommy is conscious of all his faults and declares to Harry that "all the good I can boast, I owe to you."

But Thomas Day, along with Rousseau, had started a fashion. At the age of nineteen, in 1791, Mary Wollstonecraft also wrote a book for children — her one attempt — called *Original Stories*. Instead of two boys and a tutor, we now see two girls and a governess. The latter, if possible, is more self-righteous than Day's Mr. Barlow, and

certainly more terrifying to her charges. The "bluestocking" Hannah More had also earlier contributed one book — *Sacred Dramas* (1782) — the sole object of which was to teach the poor that it was their duty to be satisfied with their lot in life. Mr. Darton says: "Hannah More had a longer and stronger grip on English minor morals than any other writer since Puritan days." But the most gifted writer of this school was Maria Edgeworth (1767–1849). Her father and Thomas Day became lifelong friends through their common admiration of Rousseau; and after the Days retired to the country, Maria Edgeworth spent much time with them and was thus under Thomas Day's training; and her books written for children show his direct influence.

The story goes that Maria Edgeworth first wrote out her tales on a slate and read them to her seventeen younger brothers and sisters for criticisms. After making the changes they had suggested, she wrote them in the final form. Her first book, *The Parent's Assistant, or, Stories for Children,* was published in 1796. This was the first of half a dozen books from her pen, all of which bring out the same idea: namely, that of letting the child learn through experience.[2]

Maria Edgeworth, however, had talent, and even writing didactic stories for a special purpose could not wholly submerge her natural powers. She has the same character contrasts, the good and the bad, and the same perfect elders, except in the case where there is a *bona fide* adult villain, as the other writers of this school used. Indeed, Rosamond's mother is so annoyingly right and good, you dislike her almost more than her prototype, Mr. Barlow. Even so, many of Maria Edgeworth's characters are more than mere puppets; they are interesting human beings. She also added plot to children's stories and should be remembered for that fact if for nothing else. *The Purple Jar* and

[2] The following are the other titles of Maria Edgeworth's books, *Early Lessons* (Vols. I and II); *Moral Tales,* in 1801. *Early Lessons* (Vols. III and IV), in 1815; *Rosamond, A Sequel to Rosamond in Early Lessons,* in 1821; *Frank, A Sequel to Frank in Early Lessons,* in 1822; and *Harry and Lucy, Concluded; being the last part of Early Lessons* (4 vols.), in 1825.

Waste Not, Want Not are probably the best known of her stories, though others, such as *Simple Susan* and *A Day of Misfortunes* [3] might be more popular with children of today.

In the meantime and simultaneously with the writers of the Rousseau school, another and in a sense counteracting influence was spreading — the Sunday School Movement. In 1780 Robert Raikes, a publisher,[4] started Sunday schools for the slum children in his home town of Gloucester. The idea took like wildfire and within ten years dozens of Sunday schools were started. Originally their purpose was to keep the factory children, who were free on Sundays, from depredations and misbehavior in general. At first they taught only spelling, reading, and writing, but later the Scriptures were added. Because Rousseau in his educational scheme had left out all these studies, it is easy to see that this new religious impulse to teach children would create a demand for stories that would embody the Sunday-school educational theories.

One of the first of such writers was Mrs. Letitia Aikin Barbauld. Her first book, published in 1780, was not yet directly under the influence of the Sunday School Movement, but was rather a protest against some teachings of the Rousseau school. These *Hymns in Prose* [5] attempted to lead the child through Nature to God. "A Child," she says in her introduction to this book, "to feel the full force of the idea of God ought never to remember when he had no such idea. It must come early with no insistence upon dogma, in association with all that he sees and all that he hears, all that affects his mind with wonder and delight." From this statement we can see that Mrs. Barbauld had both schools in mind — that of learning through experience, and that of knowing God. This is really her best book though not

her most famous, which was *Evenings at Home*, written in collaboration with her brother, Dr. Aikin, and published at intervals between 1792 and 1796. Informational, and to us exceedingly boring for the most part, *Evenings at Home* is made up of dialogues, fables, stories, and moralizing doggerels.

Of the Sunday school group, the best known after Mrs. Barbauld was Mrs. Sarah Kirby Trimmer, whose *Fabulous Histories* (1786) is her best work. The experiences of the robin family are really delightfully dealt with in spite of the stilted language the parent robins use. Mrs. Trimmer became so interested in the Sunday School Movement that she not only organized Sunday schools in her home community but wrote textbooks for their use. She had large pictures made, with accompanying explanations, on historical and religious subjects, which could be hung on the wall. These were afterwards greatly reduced and put into book form. She also, for a short time, edited and published two educational magazines.[6]

Among others of this group were Mrs. Mary Belson Elliott, with a list of sixteen titles between 1805 and 1825; Dorothy Kilner and her sister Mary Jane, both of whom wrote from 1783 to 1829. Their titles were at least attractive, however moral their stories: *The Adventures of a Pincushion, The Life and Perambulation of a Mouse, Memoirs of a Peg Top,* and the like. Mrs. Mary Martha Butt Sherwood, whose husband was an officer in East India, wrote the first missionary story, called *Little Henry and His Bearer.* Later she became famous for her *Fairchild Family* (1818), a story that was published as late as 1887, but with most of the religion left out. That same year (1818) Jane Taylor published *Display,* a story which is also a mixture of the two schools.

Most of these writers had not only made it a special point to banish all fairy tales, but had also made it a point to give information, either factual or religious. Charles Lamb was one of the first to protest against "the Barbauld crew, those blights and blasts of all that is human in man and child," as he

---

[3] See Appendix C, page 1123, for this story.

[4] It is interesting to note how these well-known figures are connected. The only sister of Robert Raikes married Francis, the son of John Newbery, whereas Newbery's step-daughter married "Kit" Smart. Thomas Day proposed marriage to two Sneyd sisters, both of whom were the second and third wives successively of Richard Lovell Edgeworth.

[5] See Appendix C, page 1126, for one of these hymns.

[6] F. J. H. Darton, "Children's Books," in *Cambridge History of English Literature,* Vol. XI.

says, in a letter to Coleridge,[7] and asks whether something can't be done toward suppressing them and bringing back *Goody Two-Shoes* and "those wild tales." He does not go on to explain what he means by "wild tales," certainly not *Goody Two-Shoes;* perhaps the ballads and fairy tales.

Meanwhile he and his sister Mary had published the *Tales from Shakespeare* (1807). It would be interesting to know whether the Lambs would have written their stories differently and better if the Godwins had not been their publishers. For despite Lamb's vigorous protest against the "Barbauld crew," he and Mary have some of the same faults. Though they do not give sugar-coated information for the sake of information, they are very moral and certainly condescending. *Mrs. Leicester's School* (1809), by the Lambs, in spite of poetic and truthful touches here and there, does not give girls, in telling their stories, a youthful point of view. The reader is impressed with the heavy moral tone, which overshadows the interesting general plan of the little book. Charles Lamb also wrote a prose version of Ulysses (1809) and that same year he and his sister together issued *Poetry for Young Children.* These poems show little worth.

Lamb, in a letter to Coleridge, says, "You must read them remembering they are task work."[8] Miss Barry suggests they were probably instigated by Mrs. Godwin, their publisher, who wished to issue a rival of the Taylors' *Original Poems.*

William Blake's *Songs of Innocence* (1789) seemed to have little influence on the immediate quality of poetry for children, but their impact, though delayed, was lasting. They were not written for children, but adult and child alike came to recognize in these lyrics the perfect revelation of childhood. It was as though some angelic child were given tongue to speak for the inner world of all children.

An occasional poem such as *The Butterfly's Ball* [9] (1807), written by William Roscoe for his little son's birthday, struck a gay note. This gave one of the earliest peeps into fairyland poetry and brought many imitations. Among these, *The Peacock at Home* by Mrs. Dorset, and *The Wedding among the Flowers* by Ann Taylor, were the best.

Ann (1782–1866) and Jane (1783–1824) Taylor were the true heirs of Dr. Watts, but had their own poetic note. Their first volume, *Original Poems for Infant Minds* (1804), included contributions from the pen of their friend Adelaide O'Keefe. In all, these sisters published three volumes of poetry. Though much of it is too "moral" for modern taste, much rings true. At times they even get the child's point of view, in spite of the fact that their poems are all intended to emphasize "the whole duty of children." Ann's work shows more interest in people and their behavior, as in *Meddlesome Matty.* Jane was more interested in nature; from her pen came *Twinkle, Twinkle, Little Star, The Violet,* and poems about flowers and talking beasts. When one remembers that the Taylors' only rivals in children's poetry were the Lambs, one can easily understand why their verses were very popular.

But a new era is dawning for the English-speaking children. Again the impetus comes from across the channel — this time from Germany. *The Household Tales,* folk tales which Jakob and Wilhelm Grimm had collected and published, were first translated into English by Edgar Taylor with drawings by George Cruikshank in 1823. In 1846 Andersen's *Fairy Tales* were translated by Mary Howitt; that same year, Edward Lear published his first *Nonsense Book.* No didactic literature, whether of the Rousseau cult or of the Sunday school variety, could withstand such a flood of imaginative stories, especially since the world of imagination is the child's natural sphere. Although Sunday school stories lived many years in a sort of *sub rosa* fashion, they never regained their former power and popularity; and didactic literature for children was extinguished, at least for a time.

From now on it is more difficult to discuss

---

[7] Charles Lamb, *Letters,* October 23, 1802. "*Goody Two-Shoes* is almost out of print. Mrs. Barbauld's stuff has banished all the old classics of the nursery. . . . Think what you would have been now, if instead of being fed with tales and old wives' fables in childhood, you had been crammed with geography and natural history."

[8] Charles Lamb, *Letters,* June, 1809.

[9] See Appendix C, page 1127, for this poem.

children's books; their number increases in geometric progression and their variety is almost equally great; consequently only those authors most important historically can be mentioned.

Captain Marryat, a retired naval officer, in disgust over the inaccuracies in *Swiss Family Robinson,* wrote two books of adventure for children. His *Masterman Ready* (1841) was a very religious and moral tale, possibly written to counteract the influence of his *Mr. Midshipman Easy* (1836), which had been written for adults, but which had become equally popular with the children. And why not? Here was a story in which the hero was often disobedient, yet successful! Moreover, there isn't a bit of direct moralizing in the whole book — a daring literary feat! Marryat's *Children of the New Forest* (1847) is even today a readable story with a historical background. In this type of story, however, he was preceded by the "bluestocking" Harriet Martineau, who had published *The Playfellow* (1841) in four volumes. These contained the historical tale, *The Peasant and the Prince;* the first school story, *The Crofton Boys;* and the *Feats on the Fjord,* one of the earliest stories for adolescent boys and girls and one of the first to give a picture of foreign life.

In 1866, a child's magazine for entertainment — *Aunt Judy's Magazine* — was first issued by Mrs. Gatty. The most important contributor was her later-famous daughter, Juliana Horatia (Gatty) Ewing (1841–1885), whose chief right to fame as a writer of children's books is in her character drawing and excellent pictures of the English life of her class. Although *Jackanapes* (1879) is her best story, it is a little too subtle for the young reader. *The Story of a Short Life* (1882) is somewhat melodramatic and sentimental for modern tastes, but *Jan of the Windmill* (1876) and *Daddy Darwin's Dove Cot* (1881) are still interesting. She also wrote a story for adolescent girls, *Six to Sixteen* (1875).

Another woman was writing at the same time as Mrs. Ewing for the adolescent age — Charlotte Mary Yonge (1823–1901). In such books as *The Heir of Redclyffe* (1853) and *Dove in the Eagle's Nest* (1866), dealing with love and chivalry, the author brought ro-

mance into young people's stories, for the first time. Miss Yonge had no particular gift or charm of style, but she is to be remembered for the new turn she gave to children's literature and for the fact that she furnished suitable reading matter for girls of an age which, heretofore, had been little provided for.

What Charlotte M. Yonge did for girls, Thomas Hughes (1822–1896) did for boys. He gave them the first book about real boys in real situations in English public school life. *Tom Brown's School Days* (1856), though preceded by Harriet Martineau's *Crofton Boys* by fifteen years, started a form of boy's story which has come down to the present day.

Meanwhile Charles Kingsley (1819–1875) had turned the new interest in fairy tales to some account by two books: *Glaucus, or the Wonders of the Shore* (1855) and *The Water Babies, a Fairy-tale for a Land-Baby* (1863). Both books were written to interest children in facts of nature, but Kingsley could not let well enough alone and insisted upon occasional preaching.

Then, in 1865, a stunning blow was struck in the cause of spontaneous and unhampered writing for children. Lewis Carroll's *Alice's Adventures in Wonderland* appeared in that year, to be followed six years later by *Through the Looking Glass* (1871). These were books written with no motive of preaching or imparting information; they were the free expression of a whimsical mind, schooled and disciplined in logic and in the reasoned world of mathematics. The author, whose real name was Charles Lutwidge Dodgson (1832–1898), was an Oxford don, a teacher of mathematics and logic. The Alice masterpiece, with its heights of originality, imagination, and wit, remains unsurpassed in English letters. Even Dodgson himself could not repeat the deed, for his third book, *Sylvie and Bruno,* is marred by a tendency to preach. But the Alice books seem to have been written as much for the pleasure and sport of the author as for the child, Alice Liddell, for whom he invented them.

The age of Alice ushered in a trend of refreshing and creative fantasies. George Macdonald (1824–1905), whose children were

since her swim in the pool, and her walk
along the river-bank with its fringe of
rushes and forget-me-nots, and the glass
table and the little door had vanished.

Soon the rabbit
noticed Alice, as
she stood looking
curiously about
her, and at once
said in a quick
angry tone, " why,
Mary Ann! what
are you doing out
here? Go home this
moment, and look
on my dressing-table for my gloves and nosegay,
and fetch them here, as quick as you can

Lewis Carroll's own illustration of Alice and the White Rabbit, together with
his hand-printed text, is shown on this section of a page from *Alice's Adventures
Underground,* the original version of *Alice's Adventures in Wonderland.*
One sees at a glance that Carroll was not much of an artist, and by contrast
one's pleasure in Tenniel's creations is the more enhanced. A comparison
of the Carroll and Tenniel Alices affords an interesting study. Tenniel's
model has been identified, and it has been suggested that Carroll's Alice
resembles Alice Liddell, the little girl for whom he wrote the story. "Carroll's
drawings of her are sweet and gentle, but not otherwise good likenesses of
Alice Liddell. Tenniel's Alice, however, is distinctly someone else, and that
someone else was Miss Mary Hilton Babcock. . . who had bright gold hair
and was quite a different type from the dark, dreamy Alice Liddell." —
Florence Becker Lennon, *Victoria Through the Looking-Glass: The Life of
Lewis Carroll* (Simon and Schuster, 1945), p. 112.

among the first to acclaim Lewis Carroll's *Alice's Adventures Underground,* as the manuscript was titled before it was published, was himself the author of some unusual fantasies for children. His stories, tinged with allegory, touched upon some of the great mysteries of life: good and evil, faith, and even death. *At the Back of the North Wind* (1871), *The Princess and the Goblin* (1872), and *The Princess and Curdie* (1882) are still read by children today.

The genre of fantasy was well served by the Victorian era. The twentieth century in turn was to prove no laggard in this art which is the greatest test of a writer's imagination and creative ability. An early year of the century (1908) saw the emergence of *The Wind in the Willows* by Kenneth Grahame, an ageless book, seemingly about a group of animals — Mr. Toad, Mr. Mole, and Water Rat — but actually a book about the felicity of life, English life, and the world of nature. With its rare quality of observation and wit, it passed into the common heritage of English-speaking people the world over. "It is a Household Book," declared A. A. Milne,[1] "a book which everybody in the household loves, and quotes continually. . . . But I must give you a word of warning. When you sit down to it, don't be so ridiculous as to suppose that you are sitting in judgment . . . on the art of Kenneth Grahame. You are merely sitting in judgment on yourself. . . . It is you who are on trial."

A. A. Milne (1882–1956), playwright and essayist, was himself the author of two well-loved fantasies of toys and childhood, *Winnie-the-Pooh* (1926) and *The House at Pooh Corner* (1928). In addition, his books of verse, *When We Were Very Young* (1924) and *Now We Are Six* (1927), have become a cult among teen-agers as well as the favorite reading of young children.

Rudyard Kipling's *Jungle Books* (1894 and 1895) and *Just So Stories* (1902), as well as *Puck of Pook's Hill* (1906) and *Rewards and Fairies* (1910), established him among the most original of the creators of fantasy. He is, as well, a master of narrative and ad-

venture, as his *Kim* (1901) and *Captains Courageous* (1897) well prove.

Little Boy Lost (1921) by W. H. Hudson, the great naturalist, marked the beginning of a rich period in children's books of high imaginative quality. Hugh Lofting's *Story of Doctor Dolittle* (1920) and its sequels are typical of the vitality of fantasy in the first quarter of the century, culminating in Walter de la Mare's *Three Mulla-Mulgars* (1919), later given the title *Three Royal Monkeys*. The thirties, forties, and fifties have produced fantasies in the grand tradition: P. L. Travers' *Mary Poppins* (1934), J. R. R. Tolkien's *The Hobbit* (1938), and Mary Norton's *The Borrowers* (1953) about a new race of Lilliputians.

One of the giants of the Victorian age was Robert Louis Stevenson, who most certainly could have written a fantasy had it crossed his mind to do so. Not for nothing, however, was he a son of the Scotch border; tales of adventure were his forte. *Treasure Island* (1882), a story of pure adventure with pirates and hidden treasure and a lifelike boy as hero, not only broke down narrow Victorian standards but cast a long shadow across the twentieth century, and centuries to come. Here is a good yarn, written with style, atmosphere, and strong conviction. It sets an incomparable goal for all writers of fiction. Stevenson's *Child's Garden of Verses* (1885) showed an unaccustomed closeness to children's minds and interests, though Christina Rossetti's *Sing-Song* (1872) had given some indication of a comparable understanding of and respect for children.

In America, the story of children's literature paralleled the development in England. In the early years the spirit of Puritanism prevailed more strongly in America than at its source. Consequently, it is not surprising that the earliest books for children were religious books. The first book printed for children in the new country was called *Milk for Babes: Drawn from the Breast of Both Testaments.*

Likewise the earliest textbook, *The New England Primer* (circa 1690), was a revised reprint of an earlier one used in England. The progress of revolt and revolution can be traced in succeeding issues of the *Primer*

[1] In his Introduction to the Limited Editions Club edition, 1940, illustrated by Arthur Rackham.

In Adam's Fall
We finned all.

Thy Life to mend,
This Book attend.

The Cat doth play,
And after flay.

A Dog will bite
A Thief at Night.

An Eagle' flight
Is out of fight.

The idle Fool
Is whipt at SchooL

A page from *The New England Primer*, from a
copy published in the late eighteenth century.

as the spiritual couplets of the alphabet made way for temporal and patriotic substitutes. "Whales in the Sea, God's voice obey," under the letter W, became "Great deeds were done/By Washington."

Isaiah Thomas, printer, first in Boston and later in Worcester, whither he was forced to flee because of his activities traitorous to the Crown, was responsible for the appearance of John Newbery's little books in America. He pirated them, editing them somewhat carelessly to give them an American habitat, by substituting Boston for all references to London, at least in the first few pages of the text, and imprinting his own name on the title page as publisher.

The American landscape and the American character were slow to appear in books for children. Samuel G. Goodrich (1793–1860) published, in 1828, under his pseudonym of Peter Parley, *Peter Parley's Tales About America,* which should have been a good beginning. But Samuel Goodrich had come under the influence of Hannah More, whose *Shepherd of Salisbury Plain* he had read as a boy. As a result, he suppressed a natural talent for writing and observation in the cause of fact, information, and moral instruction. Abandoning America as a subject, he wrote countless volumes of world history, geography, zoology, and astronomy. The Peter Parley books were popular, largely because so little else was available. The name was pirated, and books by imitators flooded the market.

It was Jacob Abbott (1803–1879) who caught the essence of the American scene in his *Franconia Stories* (1850–1853) with their New England setting and their accounts of believable children absorbed in the activities of normal life: winter sports, summer fun, and a community of interests with adults. His twenty-four books comprising the Rollo series were less original, being books of travel in which Rollo eagerly and tirelessly sought information.

There had been a straw in the wind, before the advent of *Franconia,* which gave promise of the emergence of a genuine American literature for children, and that was the publication of a poem that has come to be basic to the American tradition of Christmas; namely, *A Visit from St. Nicholas.* The story, as told by Miss Halsey, runs as follows: "On the 23d of December 1823, there appeared anonymously in the *Troy* (New York) *Sentinel,* a Christmas ballad entitled 'A Visit from St. Nicholas.' This rhymed story of Santa Claus and his reindeer, written one year before its publication by Clement Clarke Moore for his own family, marks the appearance of a truly original story in the literature of the American Nursery." [2] Miss Halsey goes on to say that the American child, under strict Puritan influence, had been given little or no celebration at Christmas time except among the Dutch, who still clung to their traditions; "consequently," she adds, "in 'A Visit from St. Nicholas,' Mr. Moore not only introduced Santa Claus to the young folk of various states, but gave them their first story of any lasting merit whatever. It is worthy of remark that as every impulse to write for juvenile readers has lagged behind the desire to write for adults, so the composition of these familiar verses telling of the arrival in America of the mysterious and welcome visitor on

The night before Christmas, when all through the house
Not a creature was stirring, not even a mouse

fell at the end of that quarter of the nineteenth century to which we are accustomed to refer as the beginning of the national period of American literature." [3]

Among the early women writers of children's books in America were Miss Elizabeth Leslie, Mrs. Sarah J. Hale, and Miss Catherine Sedgwick. Miss Leslie rewrote for the child the adventures of Munchausen, Gulliver, and Sinbad under the title *The Wonderful Traveller;* also *The American Girls' Book* with stories and games for young girls. Mrs. Sarah J. Hale (1788–1879) should be given the credit for the success of *Godey's Lady's Book,* of which she assumed the editorship in 1837, and for the poem *Mary Had a Little Lamb* (1830), the authorship of which she had to defend. The third woman of this period, Miss Catherine Sedgwick (1789–1867), began writing for children in 1827, picturing characteristic New England life in a "sunny, invigorating atmosphere, abounding in local incidents," [4] according to Miss Halsey. But none of these writers are even names today. We know *Mary Had a Little Lamb,* but no one recalls the author; older people remember the Rollo books and no more.

What happened long before in England, when *Robinson Crusoe* and *Gulliver's Travels* became children's books, now took place in America. James Fenimore Cooper's (1789–1851) *Leatherstocking Tales,* Washington Irving's (1783–1859) *The Legend of Sleepy Hollow* and *Rip Van Winkle,* Harriet Beecher Stowe's (1811–1896) *Uncle Tom's Cabin,* and Richard Henry Dana's (1815–1882) *Two Years Before the Mast* are now read almost exclusively by young people, though written for adults.

Nathaniel Hawthorne (1804–1864), on the other hand, wrote also for children: *Grandfather's Chair* (1842), *Tanglewood Tales* (1853), and *A Wonder-Book for Girls and Boys* (1857), the last being the only popular survivor. In this, Hawthorne tells the old Greek myths for children, recasting them so completely, however, that the spirit of the originals is lost.

American scenes and American characters came to full realization in books for children

[2] R. V. Halsey, *Forgotten Books of the American Nursery* (Goodspeed, Boston, 1911), p. 147.

[3] *Ibid.,* p. 148.
[4] *Ibid.,* p. 212.

midway in the nineteenth century. New England continued to be the setting, both for Thomas Bailey Aldrich in his *Story of a Bad Boy* (1860) and for Louisa May Alcott in the books she wrote for boys and girls. Each of these authors showed a new sense of realism, with emphasis on lifelike characterization, natural incidents, and believable drama. What lifts Louisa Alcott's *Little Woman* (1868) into the realm of a classic is the absolute sincerity with which she has written her own life story, together with the intensity of her emotion as she tells it. A fresh sense of mischief and the natural perversity of boys inform the pages of Aldrich's book. But the scene shifts westward for the climactic achievement of the century — to the Mississippi, with Samuel Clemens and his *Adventures of Tom Sawyer* (1876) and *Huckleberry Finn* (1884).

When one recalls Louisa May Alcott, one thinks of her friend and contemporary, Mary Mapes Dodge, who was equally successful in writing a "best juvenile seller," *Hans Brinker, or The Silver Skates,* which is deservedly as popular today as it was when published in 1865. It is interesting to see the modern child devour this story as eagerly as his parents did and as rapidly as his reading powers permit. Mrs. Dodge made another contribution to the American child's literary training, as editor of the *St. Nicholas Magazine* from 1873 to her death. She held her magazine up to a high standard and, to do so, she called in as contributors all the best writers of the period.

The story of children's literature would be incomplete without the mention of magazines for children, yet the history of these periodicals would make a long chapter in itself. The discussion is in place here only because the magazines contributed greatly to children's literature by encouraging writers for young people, in furnishing them a means of getting their work before the public.

In England, *Aunt Judy's Magazine* (1866–1885), which was started by Mrs. Gatty and died at the death of her daughter, Mrs. Ewing, was the first in importance in its effort to appeal to the young reader. Mrs. Ewing published many of her stories first in *Aunt Judy's Magazine.* The periodical *Good Words for the Young* (1869–1877) had such contributors as Charles Kingsley, whose *Madame How and Lady Why* was first published in *Good Words,* and George Macdonald with his *At the Back of the North Wind.* Another magazine, *Our Young Folks Weekly Budget* (1875–1897), existed under various names and first published Stevenson's *Treasure Island* as *The Sea Cook.* Still other magazines, such as *Good Words* (1860–1906) and *Chatterbox* (1866–1942), for different reasons greatly influenced boys and girls; the *Chatterbox,* for example, Barrie confesses, drew him away from his love of the "penny dreadfuls."

In America the story is much the same. Omitting the early periodicals like *Peter Parley's Magazine,* which were not magazines as we think of them, one of the first to offer wholesome entertainment to the child was Mrs. Lydia Maria Child's *Juvenile Miscellany* (1827–1835). *The Youth's Companion* was established that same year (1827) by N. P. Willis and had a phenomenal length of life, for it was the favorite magazine with many children during its whole existence. In 1929, its identity was lost when it was merged with *The American Boy.* It never had, however, as many first-class contributors as some of the others.

The Riverside Magazine (1867–1870), edited by Horace E. Scudder, was very ambitious. It published the fairy tales written by Andersen after 1868, even before they came out in England and Denmark.[5] *Our Young Folks* (1865–1873), edited by J. T. Trowbridge and Lucy Larcom, was one of the best among these early periodicals for children. It had such regular contributors as Thomas Bailey Aldrich, Harriet Beecher Stowe, Edward Everett Hale, and his sister Lucretia P. Hale, whose *Peterkin Papers* first appeared here. In 1868 this same magazine published *Holiday Romance* by Dickens, for which he is said to have received £1000.[6] If so, it was not worth it. If the management paid all contributors at the same rate

[5] Bertha E. Mahony and Elinor Whitney, *Realms of Gold* (Doubleday, New York, 1929), p. 92.

[6] F. J. Harvey Darton, *Children's Books in England* (Macmillan, 1932), p. 299.

as they did Dickens, it is not surprising that the magazine lived only a short time.

The *Harper's Young People* (1880–1894), a weekly, also had a high standard. Among its contributors were Louisa M. Alcott, James Otis Kaler, whose *Toby Tyler* first appeared here as a serial, Howard Pyle, and Sarah Orne Jewett. It existed three years longer as a weekly under the name of *Harper's Round Table;* then it was changed into a monthly.

While it lasted as a weekly, it was a serious rival of the best child's magazine ever published, the *St. Nicholas.* This magazine was founded in 1873 by Mr. Roswell Smith, but its policy was planned by its editor, Mary Mapes Dodge. Mrs. Dodge continued as editor until her death in 1905, and she spared nothing to get the best writers as contributors. Louisa M. Alcott published several of her later books as serials in this magazine; Mark Twain's *Tom Sawyer Abroad* came out in it; Frances Hodgson Burnett's *Sara Crewe, Little Saint Elizabeth,* and the famous *Little Lord Fauntleroy* also first appeared here; Palmer Cox's *Brownies* were watched for eagerly each month during the early eighties; and many of Kipling's *Just So Stories* were first published in this magazine; also those stories that later became *The Jungle Book.* The story goes that Kipling, upon meeting Mrs. Dodge, asked whether he might not write for her magazine. She replied that she didn't know whether he could satisfactorily. He declared he ought to be able to do so, as he and his sister had regularly each month struggled to get first possession of their beloved *St. Nicholas.* His *Just So Stories* are the result. Mrs. Dodge also invited Longfellow, Whittier, and other writers of adult literature to share in this new venture. She spared no pains and she lowered no standards. Later years brought new styles and new interests, but to the end of its days the standard of *St. Nicholas* remained high.

The promise of the nineteenth century was to grow in a hundred directions at once in the succeeding fifty years. The clamor for books was organized with such effect that publishing firms felt and reacted to the pressure. The public library movement, with its development of children's departments, was responsible for a new awareness of what was lacking in books for children. Science, history, biography; what were the seeking children to read? The schools, under the impetus of Progressive Education, with its emphasis on the use of many books, instead of dependence upon textbooks alone, began to draw attention to their needs and to establish school libraries. The youth organizations, such as the Boy Scouts, began to agitate for more books of lasting worth as substitutes for the cheap literature of the newsstand. Publishers responded by organizing separate departments for the publishing of children's books. Macmillan led off with the appointment of Louise Seaman as head of the department in 1919. Doubleday followed with the choice of May Massee, a former children's librarian and editor at the American Library Association. She was later to become the dean of editors as head of the department for the Viking Press. One by one, other publishers followed their example. Children's Book Week (now known as Book Week) was inaugurated by Frederic G. Melcher in cooperation with the American Bookseller's Association, as a focal point for annual meetings and publicity for books and reading. The Newbery medal, named after the proprietor of *The Sign of the Bible and Sun,* was brought into being by Mr. Melcher, and awarded annually to the most distinguished contribution to children's literature. The first award went to Hendrik Van Loon's *Story of Mankind* in 1922. The Caldecott medal was created in 1938, to honor distinguished book illustration. The great renaissance in children's book publishing was under way.

Much of this activity after World War I was due to a new idealism pervading the minds of men, an ideal of peace and new understanding between the nations of the world. It was to reveal itself specifically in children's books by the emergence of stories about life in various parts of the world, written by men and women native to the countries of which they wrote, books rich in life as well as in manners and customs. Kate Seredy's *The Good Master* stems from this period, as do Dhan Gopal Mukerji's fine

F. D. Bedford, with this illustration, introduces a section of poems about children's classics in *Another Book of Verses for Children*, edited by E. V. Lucas (Macmillan, 1907); and those poems give the clue to the characters in the drawing. The reader immediately recognizes Caldecott's Great Panjandrum Himself and two of the Jovial Huntsmen, Tenniel's Alice, Duchess, and Baby, and, on the balcony, some Kate Greenaway children happily engaged in conversation with Puck and a fairy from an Andrew Lang fairy book. Can the "Prillilgirl" (pretty little girl) at the Panjandrum's side and the small boy with the Huntsmen come from Thackeray's *The Rose and the Ring*, or might they be Sylvie and Bruno? The initials stand for Lewis Carroll, Kate Greenaway, Andrew Lang, Harry Furniss (illustrator of Carroll's *Sylvie and Bruno* and of Thackeray's complete works), John Tenniel, William Makepeace Thackeray, and Randolph Caldecott.

books about India, and Elizabeth Cleveland Miller's stories of Albania. Foreign artists found new audiences for picture books of their homelands, and the field of illustration was enriched by innovations in subject matter and techniques.

An interest in the regions of the United States followed the spate of books on other countries. Stories of the South and especially the far West were popular. A vigorous interest in the historical backgrounds of our country resulted in fiction of outstanding value, such as the Little House series of Laura Ingalls Wilder, and in biographies of American heroes.

The whole area of non-fiction received immense stimulus during this period. Higher standards were set for it: absolute accuracy in science and related subjects; qualified authors whose writing was based on first-hand knowledge; simplicity, dignity, and directness in the manner of presentation; and skill in writing in an interesting and provocative fashion.

In these years, too, criticism of books for children was given a place in the weekly and monthly literary journals. Anne Carroll Moore, Anne T. Eaton, and May Lamberton Becker were able to present balanced criticism, rather than brief, inconsequential reviews.

It was a wide and spacious time, the period between the two wars, with an exhilarating development in the format of books, and the resulting publication of books which were works of art in their physical appearance.

After World War II, fear of a resurgence of the Fascist and Nazi ideology fostered some attempts to erase racial bias from the minds of children by means of books which would teach this lesson. Some of the books failed because they were merely crude propaganda, no matter how idealistic the authors or the goal they sought. A few existing books were condemned and banished through misinterpretation of their intent. The net results, however, are on the affirmative side; a dignified literature for the Negro child has come into being, and the concept of mankind's interdependence has received impetus.

Meanwhile the theorists have their day. What are the best methods of teaching reading? What has television done to the mind and taste of the child? What about the comics? Are fairy tales harmful because they are full of violence and terror? Should a child be encouraged to read beyond his experience? Shall the classics be rewritten in words of one syllable, in order to get them read? What about the mass production of books, packaged like merchandise, the emphasis put upon appearance with small regard for editorial responsibility? Should the vocabulary be controlled, the words measured out grade by grade? How shall books be judged for children, by literary and artistic standards or by the graphs and measurements of psychologists? These are subjects for hot debate. Meanwhile, the arts endure. No doubt they will find their audience among the children who stand on the threshold of outer space as surely as they have reached and moved the earth-bound children of the past.

BIBLIOGRAPHY

Ashton, John, ed. *Chap-Books of the Eighteenth Century.* Chatto and Windus (London), 1882.

Barry, Florence. *A Century of Children's Books.* Doran, 1923.

Darton, F. J. Harvey. *Children's Books in England; Five Centuries of Social Life.* Cambridge University Press (London), 1932.

Darton, F. J. Harvey. "Children's Books," in *Cambridge History of English Literature* (15 vols.; G. P. Putnam's Sons, 1914), Vol. XI, Chap. XVI, pp. 407-430.

Eyre, Frank. *20th Century Children's Books;* with twenty-five illustrations in black and white and twelve in color. Published for the British Council by Longmans, Green and Co., 1952.

Field, Mrs. E. M. *The Child and His Book; Some Account of the History and Progress of Children's Literature in England.* Wells Gardner (London), 1891.

Folmsbee, Beulah. *A Little History of the Horn-Book.* Horn Book, Inc., 1942.

Ford, Paul Leicester. *The New England Primer; a History of its Origin;* with a reprint of the unique copy of the earliest known edition. Dodd, 1897.

Gignilliat, George Warren, Jr. *The Author of Sandford and Merton.* Columbia University Press, 1932.

Goodrich, Samuel (Peter Parley). *Recollections of a Lifetime.* 2 vols. Miller and Orton (New York), 1857.

Halsey, R. V. *Forgotten Books of the American Nursery.* Goodspeed (Boston), 1911.

Haviland, Virginia. *The Travelogue Storybook of the Nineteenth Century* (A Caroline Hewins lecture, 1949). The Horn Book, Inc., 1950.

Hazard, Paul. *Books, Children and Men;* trans. from the French by Marguerite Mitchell. The Horn Book, Inc., 1947.

James, Philip. *Children's Books of Yesterday;* ed. by C. Geoffrey Holme. Studio Publications, 1933.

Jordan, Alice. *From Rollo to Tom Sawyer and Other Papers.* The Horn Book, Inc., 1948.

Laski, Marghanita. *Mrs. Ewing, Mrs. Molesworth and Mrs. Hodgson Burnett.* Oxford University Press, 1951.

Lindquist, Jennie D. *Caroline M. Hewins, Her Book;* containing "A Mid-Century Child and Her Books," by Caroline M. Hewins, and "Caroline M. Hewins and Books for Children," by Jennie D. Lindquist. The Horn Book, Inc., 1954.

Meigs, Cornelia; Elizabeth Nesbitt; Anne Eaton; and Ruth Hill Viguers. *A Critical History of Children's Literature;* decorations by Vera Bock. Macmillan, 1953.

Moore, Anne Carroll. *Children's Books of Yesterday.* New York Public Library, 1933.

Moore, Annie E. *Literature Old and New for Children.* Houghton Mifflin, 1934.

Muir, Percy. *English Children's Books, 1600 to 1900.* Frederick A. Praeger, 1954.

Perrault, Charles. *Perrault's Tales of Mother Goose;* the dedication manuscript of 1695 reproduced in collotype facsimile with introduction and critical text by Jacques Barchilon. Vol. I, Text. Vol. II, Facsimile. Pierpont Morgan Library, 1956.

Pierpont Morgan Library. *Children's Literature: Books and Manuscripts.* An Exhibition, November 19, 1954, through February 28, 1955. Pierpont Morgan Library, 1954.

Rosenbach, A. S. W. *Early American Children's Books.* Catalogue of the Rosenbach Collection at the Philadelphia Free Library. Portland, privately printed, 1933.

Scudder, Horace E. *Childhood in Literature and Art.* Houghton Mifflin, 1894.

Shipton, Clifford E. *Isaiah Thomas, Printer, Patriot, and Philanthropist.* Leo Hart, 1948.

Sloane, William. *Children's Books in England & America in the Seventeenth Century; a History and Checklist;* together with *The Young Christian's Library,* the first printed catalogue of books for children. Columbia University Press, 1955.

Smith, Elva Sophronia. *History of Children's Literature: a Syllabus with Selected Bibliographies.* American Library Association, 1937.

Tassin, Algerton. "Books for Children," in *Cambridge History of American History* (3 vols.; Macmillan, 1933), Vol. II, Chap. VII, pp. 396–409.

Tuer, Andrew W. *History of the Horn Book.* 2 vols. Leadenhall Press, 1899–1900.

Welsh, Charles. *A Bookseller of the Last Century, Being some Account of the Life of John Newbery, and of the Books he published with a Notice of the later Newberys.* Griffith, Farran (London), 1885.

Welsh, Charles, ed. *The Renowned History of Little Goody Two-Shoes, Otherwise Called Mrs. Margery Two-Shoes,* attributed to Oliver Goldsmith. D. C. Heath, 1930.

APPENDIX C

Early Writings

COMPARING EARLY WRITING for children with the twentieth-century literature for children will prove an interesting study, and for that purpose the editors have included in this section a few typical examples.

The History of Goody Two-Shoes, often attributed to Oliver Goldsmith, was published by John Newbery in 1765 or 1766. It became very popular and was read for over a hundred years, sometimes in a shortened form. It is given here complete except for two "tales" that Mistress Margery told to point a moral. The reader is surprised that her teaching ideas are so modern and that such absurd and dubious incidents are given with such a straight face.

Maria Edgeworth's Day of Misfortunes is not so well known as her Purple Jar and The Whip Cord, but it is more applicable to a modern child's possible experiences and represents equally well the theory of child training that Maria and her father believed in and wrote about; namely, that a child should learn through experience, for they were devoted followers of Rousseau.

The Hymn in Prose is representative of the work of a group of writers — sometimes called the Sunday School group — of which Mrs. Sarah Kirby Trimmer was the leader. They strongly disapproved of fairy tales and equally strongly of the Rousseau "free thinkers"; instead they emphasized religion.

Mrs. Barbauld thought a child could be led to God through nature, and her Hymns in Prose volume was written for that purpose. If read aloud, these tiny sermons show a rhythm resembling that of the Psalms. Her most popular book was an anthology prepared with her brother and called Evenings at Home. In fact, it was popular even with the Edgeworth children, so Maria writes to an aunt.

The Butterfly's Ball, by William Roscoe, is significant because it was one of the earliest productions written for sheer fun with no moral attached. The author wrote it for his small son's birthday. It appeared in print in The Gentleman's Magazine, November 1906, and was published by John Harris in 1807. Because of its gay rhyme and galloping rhythm the verses became extremely popular. It was the forerunner of similar verses by other authors.

Mrs. Ewing's stories are important in the study of children's literature because she employed a new method: she never wrote down to children. If she wanted to teach something, she did so by example and not by sermonizing. In her literary fairy tale, Murdoch's Rath, each mortal is rewarded according to his just deserts. Mrs. Ewing was unusually successful in imbuing the story with the Irish spirit and the feeling of the folk tale. Many of her stories have real literary merit.

THE RENOWNED HISTORY OF

Little Goody Two-Shoes

COMMONLY CALLED, OLD GOODY TWO–SHOES [1]

ANONYMOUS

All the world must allow, that *Two Shoes* was not her real Name. No; her Father's Name was *Meanwell;* and he was for many Years a considerable Farmer in the Parish where *Margery* was born; but the Misfortunes which he met with in Business, and the wicked Persecutions of Sir *Timothy Gripe,* and an overgrown Farmer called *Graspall,* he was effectually ruined.

The Case was thus. The Parish of *Mould-well* where they lived, had for many Ages been let by the Lord of the Manor into twelve different Farms, in which the Tenants lived Comfortably, brought up large Families, and carefully supported the Poor People who laboured for them; until the Estate by Marriage and by Death came into the Hands of Sir *Timothy.*

This Gentleman, who loved himself better than all his Neighbours, thought it less Trouble to write one Receipt for his Rent than twelve, and Farmer *Graspall* offering to take all the Farms as the Leases expired, Sir *Timothy* agreed with him, and in Process of Time he was possessed of every Farm, but that occupied by little *Margery's* Father; which he also wanted; for as Mr. *Meanwell* was a charitable good Man, he stood up for the Poor at the Parish Meetings, and was unwilling to have them oppressed by Sir *Timothy,* and this avaricious Farmer. — Judge, oh kind, humane and courteous Reader, what a terrible Situation the Poor must be in, when this covetous Man was perpetual Overseer, and every Thing for their Maintenance was drawn from his hard Heart and cruel Hand. But he was not only perpetual Overseer, but perpetual Church-warden, and judge, oh ye Christians, what State the Church must be in, when supported by a Man without Religion or Virtue. He was also perpetual Surveyor of the Highways, and what Sort of Roads he kept up for the Convenience of Travellers, those best know who have had the Misfortune to be obliged to pass thro' that Parish. — Complaints indeed were made, but to what Purpose are Complaints when brought against a Man, who can hunt, drink, and smoak with the Lord of the Manor, who is also Justice of Peace?

[1] To afford an interesting contrast, the first part as given here preserves the eighteenth-century style of capitalization, italics, and the like, whereas Part Two has been modernized in these respects.

The Opposition which little *Margery's* Father made to this Man's Tyranny, gave Offence to Sir *Timothy,* who endeavoured to force him out of his Farm; and to oblige him to throw up the Lease, ordered both a Brick Kiln and a Dog-kennel to be erected in the Farmer's Orchard. This was contrary to Law, and a Suit was commenced, in which *Margery's* Father got the better. The same Offence was again committed three different Times, and as many Actions brought in all of which the Farmer had a Verdict and Costs paid him; but notwithstanding these Advantages, the Law was so expensive, that he was ruined in the Contest, and obliged to give up all he had to his Creditors; which effectually answered the Purpose of Sir *Timothy,* who erected those Nuisances in the Farmer's Orchard with that Intention only. . . .

As soon as Mr. *Meanwell* had called together his Creditors, Sir *Timothy* seized for a Year's Rent, and turned the Farmer, his Wife, little *Margery,* and her Brother out of doors, without any of the Necessaries of Life to support them.

This elated the Heart of Mr. *Graspall,* this crowned his Hopes, and filled the Measure of his Iniquity; for besides gratifying his Revenge, this Man's Overthrow gave him the sole Dominion of the Poor, whom he depressed and abused in a Manner too horrible to mention.

Margery's Father flew into another Parish for Succour, and all those who were able to move left their Dwellings and sought Employment elsewhere, as they found it would be impossible to live under the Tyranny of two such People. The very old, the very lame and the blind, and whether they were starved, or what became of them, History does not say; but the Character of the great Sir *Timothy,* and his avaricious Tenant, were so infamous that nobody would work for them by the Day, and Servants were afraid to engage themselves by the Year, lest any unforseen Accident should leave them Parishioners in a Place, where they knew they must perish miserably; so that great Part of the Land lay untilled for some Years, which was deemed a just Reward for such diabolical Proceedings.

CHAPTER I

How and about Little Margery and her Brother

Care and Discontent shortened the Days of Little *Margery's* Father. — He was forced from his Family, and seized with a violent Fever in a Place where Dr. *James's* Powder was not to be had, and where he died miserably. *Margery's* poor Mother survived the Loss of her Husband but a few days, and died of a broken Heart, leaving *Margery* and her little Brother to the wide World; but, poor Woman, it would have melted your Heart to have seen how frequently she heaved up her Head, while she lay speechless, to survey with languishing Looks her little Orphans, as much as to say, *Do Tommy, do Margery, come with me.* They cried, poor Things, and she sighed away her Soul; and I hope is happy.

It would both have excited your Pity, and have done your Heart good, to have seen how fond these two little ones were of each other, and how, Hand in Hand, they trotted about.

They were both very ragged, and *Tommy* had two Shoes, but *Margery* had but one. They had nothing, poor Things, to support them (not being in their own Parish) but what they picked from the Hedges, or got from the poor People, and they lay every Night in a Barn. Their Relations took no Notice of them; no, they were rich, and ashamed to own such a poor little ragged Girl as *Margery,* and such a dirty little curl-pated Boy as *Tommy.* Our Relations and Friends seldom took Notice of us when we are poor, but as we grow rich they grow fond. And this will always be the Case, while People love Money better than Virtue, or better than they do God Almighty. But such wicked Folks, who love nothing but money, and are proud and despise the Poor, never come to any good in the End, as we shall see by and by.

Chapter II
How and about Mr. Smith

Mr. *Smith* was a very worthy Clergyman, who lived in the Parish where Little *Margery* and *Tommy* were born; and having a Relation come to see him, who was a charitable good Man, he sent for these Children to him. The Gentleman ordered Little *Margery* a new Pair of Shoes, gave Mr. *Smith* some Money to buy her Cloathes; and said, he would take *Tommy* and make him a little Sailor, and accordingly had a Jacket and Trowsers made for him.

After some Days the Gentleman intended to go to *London,* and take little *Tommy* with him, of whom you will know more by and by, for we shall at a proper Time present you with some Part of his History, his Travels and Adventures.

The Parting between these two little Children was very affecting, *Tommy* cried, and *Margery* cried, and they kissed each other an hundred Times. At last *Tommy* thus wiped off her Tears with the end of his Jacket, and bid her cry no more, for that he would come to her again, when he returned from Sea. However, as they were so very fond, the Gentleman would not suffer them to take Leave of each other; but told *Tommy* he should ride out with him, and come back at Night. When night came, Little *Margery* grew very uneasy about her Brother, and after sitting up as late as Mr. *Smith* would let her, she went crying to Bed.

Chapter III
How Little Margery Obtained the Name of Goody Two-Shoes, and What Happened in the Parish

As soon as Little *Margery* got up in the Morning, which was very early, she ran all round the Village, crying for her Brother; and after some Time returned greatly distressed. However, at this Instant, the Shoemaker very opportunely came in with the new Shoes, for which she had been measured by the Gentleman's Order.

Nothing could have supported Little *Margery* under the Affliction she was in for the Loss of her Brother, but the Pleasure she took in her *two* Shoes. She ran out to Mrs. *Smith* as soon as they were put on, and stroking down her ragged Apron thus, cried out, *Two-Shoes, Mame, see two Shoes.* And so she behaved to all the People she met, and by that Means obtained the Name of *Goody Two-Shoes,* though her Playmates called her *Old Goody Two-Shoes.*

Little *Margery* was very happy in being with Mr. and Mrs. *Smith,* who were very charitable and good to her, and had agreed to breed her up with their Family; but as soon as that Tyrant of the Parish, that *Graspall,* heard of her being there, he applied first to Mr. *Smith,* and threatened to reduce his Tythes if he kept her; and after that he spoke to Sir *Timothy,* who sent Mr. *Smith* a peremptory Message by his Servant, that *he should send back* Meanwell's *Girl to be kept by her Relations, and not harbour her in the Parish.* This so distressed Mr. *Smith* that he shed Tears, and cried, *Lord have Mercy on the Poor!*

The Prayers of the Righteous fly upwards, and reach unto the Throne of Heaven, as will be seen in the Sequel.

Mrs. *Smith* was also greatly concerned at being thus obliged to discard poor Little *Margery.* She kissed her and cried; as also did Mr. *Smith,* but they were obliged to send her away; for the People who had ruined her Father could at any Time have ruined them.

CHAPTER IV

How Little Margery Learned to Read, and by Degrees Taught Others

Little *Margery* saw how good, and how wise Mr. *Smith* was, and concluded, that this was owing to his great Learning, therefore she wanted of all Things to learn to read. For this Purpose she used to meet the little Boys and Girls as they came from School, to borrow their Books, and sit down and read till they returned. By this Means she soon got more Learning than any of her Play-mates, and laid the following Scheme for instruct-ing those who were more ignorant than herself. She found, that only the following Letters were required to spell all the Words in the World; but as some of these Letters are large and some small, she with her Knife cut out of several Pieces of Wood ten Setts of each of these:

a b c d e f g h i j k l m n o p q r s t u v w x y z.

And six Setts of these:

A B C D E F G H I J K L M N O P Q R S T
U V W X Y Z.

And having got an old Spelling-Book, she made her Companions set up all the Words they wanted to spell, and after that she taught them to compose Sentences. You know what a Sentence is, my Dear, *I will be good,* is a Sentence, and is made up, as you see, of several Words.

The usual Manner of Spelling, or carrying on the Game, as they called it, was this: Suppose the Word to be spelt was Plum Pudding (and who can suppose a better) the Children were placed in a Circle, and the first brought the Letter *P*, the next *l*, the next *u*, the next *m*, and so on till the Whole was spelt; and if anyone brought a wrong Letter, he was to pay a Fine, or play no more. This was at their Play; and every Morning she used to go round to teach the Children with these Rattle-traps in a Basket. I once went her Rounds with her, and was highly diverted, as you may be, if you please to look into the next Chap-ter.

CHAPTER V

How Little Two-Shoes Became a-Trotting Tutoress, and How She Taught Her Young Pupils

It was about seven o'clock in the Morning when we set out on this important Business, and the first House we came to was Farmer *Wilson's*.

Here *Margery* stopped, and ran up to the Door, *Tap, tap, tap.* Who's there? Only little Goody *Two-Shoes,* answered *Margery,* come to teach *Billy.* Oh Little *Goody,* says Mrs. *Wilson,* with Pleasure in her Face, I am glad to see you, *Billy* wants you sadly, for he has learned all his Lesson. Then out came the little Boy. *How do Doody Two-Shoes,* says he, not able to speak plain. Yet this little Boy had learned all his Letters; for she threw down this Alphabet mixed together thus:

b d f h k m o q s u w y z a c e g i l n p r t v x j

and he picked them up, called them by their right Names, and put them all in order thus:

a b c d e f g h i j k l m n o p q r s t u v w x y z.

She then threw down the Alphabet of Capital Letters in the Manner you here see them.

B D F H K M O Q S U W Y Z A C E G I L N
P R T V X J

and he picked them all up, and having told their Names, placed them thus:

A B C D E F G H I J K L M N O P Q R S T
U V W X Y Z.

Now, pray little Reader, take this Bodkin, and see if you can point out the Letters from these mixed Alphabets, and tell how they should be placed as well as little Boy *Billy.*

The next Place we came to was Farmer *Simpson's. Bow, wow, wow,* says the Dog at the Door. Sirrah, says his Mistress, what do you bark at Little *Two-Shoes.* Come in *Madge;* here, *Sally* wants you sadly, she has learned all her Lesson. Then out came the little one: So *Madge!* says she; so *Sally!* answered the other, have you learned your Lesson? Yes, that's what I have, replied the little one in the Country Manner; and immedi-ately taking the Letters she set up these Syllables:

ba be bi bo bu, ca ce ci co cu, da de di do du,
fa fe fi fo fu

and gave them their exact Sounds as she com-posed them; after which she set up the following:

ac ec ic oc uc, ad ed id od ud, af ef if of uf,
ag eg ig og ug.

And pronounced them likewise. She then sung the Cuzz's Chorus (which may be found in the *Little Pretty Play Thing,* published by Mr. New-bery) and to the same Tune to which it is there set.

After this, Little *Two-Shoes* taught her to spell Words of one Syllable, and she soon set up Pear, Plum, Top, Ball, Pin, Puss, Dog, Hog, Fawn, Buck, Doe, Lamb, Sheep, Ram, Cow, Bull, Cock, Hen, and many more.

The next Place we came to was *Gaffer Cook's* Cottage.

Here a number of poor Children were met to learn, who all came round Little *Margery* at once; and, having pulled out her Letters, she asked the little Boy next her, what he had for Dinner? Who answered, *Bread.* (The poor Children in many Places live very hard.) Well then, says she, set the first Letter. He put up the Letter B, to which the next added r, and the next e, the next a, the next d, and it stood thus, *Bread.*

And what had you *Polly Comb* for your Dinner? *Apple-pye,* answered the little Girl: Upon which the next in Turn set up a great A, the two next a p each, and so on till the two Words Apple and Pye were united and stood thus, *Apple-Pye.*

The next had *Potatoes,* the next *Beef and Turnip* which were spelt with many others, till the Game of Spelling was finished. She then set them another Task, and we proceeded.

The next Place we came to was Farmer *Thompson's,* where there were a great many little ones waiting for her.

So little Mrs. *Goody Two-Shoes,* says one of them, where have you been so long? I have been teaching, says she, longer than I intended, and am afraid I am come too soon for you now. No, but indeed you are not, replied the other; for I have got my Lesson, and so has *Sally Dawson,* and so has *Harry Wilson,* and so we have all; and they capered about as if they were overjoyed to see her. Why then, says she, you are all very good, and God Almighty will love you; so let us begin our Lessons. They all huddled around her, and though at the other Place they were employed about Words and Syllables, here we had People of much greater Understanding who dealt only in Sentences.

The Letters being brought upon the Table, one of the little ones set up the following Sentence.

The Lord have Mercy upon me, and grant that I may be always good, and say my Prayers, and love the Lord my God with all my Heart, with all my Soul, and with all my Strength; and honour the King, and all good Men in Authority under him.

Then the next took the Letters and composed this Sentence.

Lord have Mercy upon me, and grant that I may love my Neighbour as myself, and do unto all Men as I would have them do unto me, and tell no Lies; but be honest and just in all my Dealings.

The third composed the following Sentence.

The Lord have Mercy upon me, and grant that I may honour my Father and Mother, and love my Brothers and Sisters, Relations and Friends, and all my Playmates, and every Body, and endeavour to make them happy.

The fourth composed the following.

I pray God to bless this whole Company, and all our Friends, and all our Enemies.

To this last *Polly Sullen* objected, and said, truly, she did not know why she should pray for her Enemies. Not pray for your Enemies, says little *Margery;* yes, you must, you are no Christian, if you don't forgive your Enemies, and do Good for Evil. *Polly* still pouted; upon which little *Margery* said, though she was poor, and obliged to lie in a Barn, she would not keep Company with such a naughty, proud, perverse Girl as *Polly;* and was going away; however the Difference was made up, and she set them to compose the following.

LESSONS

For the Conduct of LIFE

LESSON I

He that will thrive,
Must rise by Five.
He that hath thriv'n,
May lie till Seven.
Truth may be blam'd,
But cannot be sham'd.
Tell me with whom you go;
And I'll tell what you do.
A Friend in your Need,
Is a Friend indeed.
They ne'er can be wise,
Who good Counsel despise.

LESSON II

A wise Head makes a close Mouth.
Don't burn your Lips with another Man's Broth.
Wit is Folly, unless a wise Man hath the keeping of it.
Use soft Words and hard Arguments.
Honey catches more Flies than Vinegar.
To forget a Wrong is the best Revenge.
Patience is a Plaister for all Sores.
Where Pride goes, Shame will follow.

When Vice enters the Room, Vengeance is near
the Door.

Industry is Fortune's right Hand, and Frugality
her left.

Make much of Three-pence, or you ne'er will be
worth a Groat.

LESSON III

A Lie stands upon one Leg, but Truth upon two.

When a Man talks much, believe but half what
he says.

Fair Words butter no Parsnips.

Bad Company poisons the Mind.

A covetous Man is never satisfied.

Abundance, like Want, ruins many.

Contentment is the best Fortune.

A contented Mind is a continual Feast.

A LESSON IN RELIGION

Love God, for he is good.

Fear God, for he is just.

Pray to God, for all good Things come from him.

Praise God, for great is his Mercy towards us,
and wonderful are all his Works.

Those who strive to be good, have God on their
Side.

Those who have God for their Friend, shall want
nothing.

Confess your Sins to God, and if you repent he
will forgive you.

Remember that all you do, is done in the Presence of God.

The Time will come, my Friends, when we must
give

Account to God, how we on Earth did live.

A MORAL LESSON

A good Boy will make a good Man.

Honour your Parents, and the World will honour
you.

Love your friends, and your Friends will love you.

He that swims in Sin, will sink in Sorrow.

Learn to live, as you would wish to die.

As you expect all Men should deal by you:

So deal by them, and give each Man his Due.

As we were returning Home, we saw a Gentleman, who was very ill, sitting under a shady Tree
at the Corner of his Rookery. Though ill, he
began to joke with Little *Margery*, and said,
laughingly, so, *Goody Two-Shoes*, they tell me
you are a cunning little Baggage; pray, can you
tell me what I shall do to get well? Yes, Sir, says

she, go to Bed when your Rooks do. You see
they are going to Rest already: Do you so likewise, and get up with them in the morning; earn,
as they do, every Day what you eat, and eat and
drink no more than you earn; and you'll get
Health and keep it. What should induce the
Rooks to frequent Gentlemen's Houses only, but
to tell them how to lead a prudent life? They
never build over Cottages or Farm-houses, because they see, that these People know how to
live without their Admonition.

Thus Health and Wit you may improve,
Taught by the Tenants of the Grove.

The Gentleman laughing gave *Margery* Sixpence,
and told her she was a sensible Hussey.

CHAPTER VI
How the Whole Parish Was Frighted

Who does not know Lady *Ducklington,* or
who does not know that she was buried at this
Parish Church? Well, I never saw so grand a
Funeral in all my Life; but the Money they
squandered away, would have been better laid
out in little Books for Children, or in Meat,
Drink, and Cloaths for the Poor.

This is a fine Hearse indeed, and the nodding
Plumes on the Horses look very grand; but what
End does that answer, otherwise than to display
the Pride of the Living, or the Vanity of the
Dead. Fie upon such Folly, say I, and Heaven
grant that those who want more Sense may
have it.

But all the Country round came to see the
Burying, and it was late before the Corpse was
interred. After which, in the Night, or rather
about Four o'Clock in the Morning, the Bells
were heard to jingle in the Steeple, which frightened the People prodigiously, who all thought it
was Lady *Ducklington's* Ghost dancing among
the Bell-ropes. The People flocked to *Will
Dobbins* the Clerk, and wanted him to go and see
what it was; but *William,* said he was sure it was
a Ghost, and that he would not offer to open the
Door. At length Mr. *Long* the Rector, hearing
such an Uproar in the Village, went to the Clerk,
to know why he did not go into the Church, and
see who was there. I go, Sir, says *William,* why
the Ghost would frighten me out of my Wits. —
Mrs. *Dobbins* too cried, and laying hold of her
Husband said, he should not be eat up by the
Ghost. A Ghost, you Blockheads, says Mr. *Long*
in a Pet, did either of you ever see a Ghost, or

know any Body that did? Yes, says the Clerk, my Father did once in the Shape of a Windmill, and it walked all round the Church in a white Sheet, with Jack Boots on, and had a Gun by its Side instead of a Sword. A fine Picture of a Ghost truly, says Mr. *Long*, give me the Key of the Church, you Monkey, for I tell you there is no such Thing now, whatever may have been formerly. Then taking the Key, he went to the Church, all the people following him. As soon as he had opened the Door, what Sort of a Ghost do ye think appeared? Why Little *Two-Shoes*, who being weary, had fallen asleep in one of the Pews during the Funeral Service, and was shut in all Night. She immediately asked Mr. *Long's* Pardon for the Trouble she had given him, told him, she had been locked into the Church, and said, she should not have rung the Bells, but that she was very cold, and hearing Farmer *Boult's* Man go whistling by with his Horses, she was in Hopes he would have went to the Clerk for the Key to let her out.

Chapter VII

Containing an Account of all the Spirits, or Ghosts, She Saw in the Church

The People were ashamed to ask Little *Madge* any Questions before Mr. *Long*, but as soon as he was gone, they all got round her to satisfy their Curiosity, and desired she would give them a particular Account of all that she had heard and seen.

Her Tale

I went to the Church, said she, as most of you did last Night, to see the Burying, and being very weary, I sate me down in Mr. *Jones's* Pew, and fell fast asleep. At Eleven of the Clock I awoke; which I believe was in some measure occasioned by the Clock's striking, for I heard it. I started up, and could not at first tell where I was; but after some Time I recollected the Funeral, and soon found that I was shut in the Church. It was dismal dark, and I could see nothing; but while I was standing in the Pew, something jumped up upon me behind, and laid, as I thought, its Hands over my Shoulders. — I own, I was a little afraid at first; however, I considered that I had always been constant at Prayers and at Church, and that I had done nobody any Harm, but had endeavoured to do what Good I could; and then thought I, what have I to fear? yet I kneeled down to say my Prayers. As soon as I was on my Knees something very cold, as cold as Marble, ay, as cold as Ice, touched my Neck, which made me start; however, I continued my Prayers, and having begged Protection from Almighty God, I found my Spirits come, and I was sensible that I had nothing to fear; for God Almighty protects not only all those who are good, but also all those who endeavour to be good. Nothing can withstand the Power, and exceed the Goodness of God Almighty. Armed with the Confidence of his Protection, I walked down the Church Isle, when I heard something, pit pat, pit pat, pit pat, come after me, and something touched my Hand, which seemed as cold as a Marble Monument. I could not think what this was, yet I knew it could not hurt me, and therefore I made myself easy, but being very cold, and the Church being paved with Stone, which was very damp, I felt my Way as well as I could to the Pulpit, in doing which something brushed by me, and almost threw me down. However I was not frightened, for I knew, that God Almighty would suffer nothing to hurt me.

At last, I found out the Pulpit, and having shut to the Door, I laid me down on the Mat and Cushion to sleep; when something thrust and pulled the Door, as I thought for Admittance, which prevented my going to sleep. At last it cries, *Bow, wow, wow;* and I concluded it must be Mr. *Saunderson's* Dog, which had followed me from their House to Church, so I opened the Door, and called *Snip, Snip,* and the Dog jumped up upon me immediately. After this *Snip* and I lay down together, and had a most comfortable Nap; for when I awoke again it was almost light. I then walked up and down all the Isles of the Church to keep myself warm; and though I went into the Vault, and trod on Lady *Ducklington's* Coffin, I saw no Ghost, and I believe it was owing to the Reason Mr. *Long* has given you, namely, that there is no such thing to be seen. As to my Part, I would as soon lie all Night in the Church as in any other Place; and I am sure that any little Boy or Girl, who is good, and loves God Almighty and keeps his Commandments, may as safely lie in the Church, or the Church-yard, as anywhere else, if they take care not to get Cold, for I am sure there are no Ghosts, either to hurt, or to frighten them; though anyone possessed of Fear might have taken Neighbour *Saunderson's* Dog with his cold Nose for a Ghost; and if they had not been undeceived, as I was, would never have thought otherwise. All the Company acknowledged the Justness of the Observation, and thanked Little *Two-Shoes* for her Advice.

REFLECTION

After this, my dear Children, I hope you will not believe any foolish Stories that ignorant, weak, or designing People may tell you about Ghosts; for the Tales of Ghosts, Witches, and Fairies, are the Frolicks of a distempered Brain. No wise Man ever saw either of them. Little *Margery* you see was not afraid; no, she had *good Sense*, and a *good Conscience*, which is a Cure for all these imaginary Evils.

CHAPTER VIII

Of Something Which Happened to Little Two-Shoes in a Barn, more Dreadful Than the Ghost in the Church; and How She Returned Good for Evil to Her Enemy Sir Timothy

Some Days after this a more dreadful accident befel Little *Madge.* She happened to be coming late from teaching, when it rained, thundered, and lightened, and therefore she took Shelter in a Farmer's Barn at a Distance from the Village. Soon after, the Tempest drove in four Thieves, who, not seeing such a little creep-mouse Girl as *Two-Shoes,* lay down on the Hay next to her, and began to talk over their Exploits, and to settle Plans for future Robberies. Little *Margery* on hearing them, covered herself with Straw. To be sure she was sadly frighted, but her good Sense taught her, that the only Security she had was in keeping herself concealed; therefore, she laid very still, and breathed very softly. About Four o'Clock these wicked People came to a Resolution to break both Sir *William Dove's* House, and Sir *Timothy Gripe's,* and by Force of Arms to carry off all their Money, Plate and Jewels; but as it was thought then too late, they agreed to defer it till the next Night. After laying this Scheme they all set out upon their Pranks, which greatly rejoiced Margery, as it would any other little Girl in her Situation. Early in the Morning she went to Sir *William,* and told him the whole of their Conversation. Upon which, he asked her Name, gave her Something, and bid her call at his House the Day following. She also went to Sir *Timothy,* notwithstanding he had used her so ill; for she knew it was her Duty to *do Good for Evil.* As soon as he was informed who she was, he took no Notice of her; upon which she desired to speak to Lady *Gripe,* and having informed her Ladyship of the Affair, she went her Way. This Lady had more Sense than her Husband, which indeed is not a singular Case; for instead of despising

Little *Margery* and her Information, she privately set People to guard the House. The Robbers divided themselves, and went about the Time mentioned to both Houses, and were surprized by the Guards, and taken. Upon examining these Wretches, one of which turned Evidence, both Sir *William* and Sir *Timothy* found that they owed their Lives to the Discovery made by Little *Margery,* and the first took great Notice of her, and would no longer let her lie in a Barn, but Sir *Timothy* only said, that he was ashamed to owe his Life to the Daughter of one who was his Enemy; so true it is, *that a proud Man seldom forgives those he has injured.*

CHAPTER IX

How Little Margery Was Made Principal of a Country College

Mrs. *Williams,* of whom I have given a particular Account in my *New Year's Gift,* and who kept a College for instructing little Gentlemen and Ladies in the Science of A, B, C, was at this Time very old and infirm, and wanted to decline that important Trust. This being told to Sir *William Dove,* who lived in the Parish, he sent for Mrs. *Williams,* and desired she would examine Little *Two-Shoes,* and see whether she was qualified for the Office. — This was done, and Mrs. *Williams* made the following Report in her Favour, namely, *that Little Margery was the best Scholar, and had the best Head, and the best Heart of anyone she had examined.* All the Country had a great opinion of Mrs. *Williams,* and this Character gave them also a great Opinion of Mrs. *Margery,* for so we must now call her.

This Mrs. *Margery* thought the happiest period of her Life; but more Happiness was in Store for her. God Almighty heaps up Blessings for all those who love him, and though for a Time he may suffer them to be poor and distressed, and hide his good Purposes from human Sight, yet in the End they are generally crowned with Happiness here, and no one can doubt of their being so hereafter.

On this Occasion the following Hymn, or rather a Translation of the twenty-third Psalm, is said to have been written, and was soon after published in the *Spectator.*

I

The Lord my Pasture shall prepare,
    And feed me with a Shepherd's Care:

His Presence shall my Wants supply,
And guard me with a watchful Eye;
My Noon-day Walks he shall attend,
And all my Midnight Hours defend.

II

When in the sultry Glebe I faint,
Or on the thirsty Mountain pant;
To fertile Vales and dewy Meads,
My weary wand'ring Steps he leads;
Where peaceful Rivers, soft and slow,
Amid the verdant Landskip flow.

III

Tho' in the Paths of Death I tread,
With gloomy Horrors overspread,
My steadfast Heart shall fear no Ill.
For thou, O Lord, art with me still;
Thy friendly Crook shall give me Aid,
And guide me thro' the dreadful Shade.

IV

Tho' in a bare and rugged Way,
Thro' devious lonely Wilds I stray,
Thy Bounty shall my Pains beguile:
The barren Wilderness shall smile,
With sudden Green & herbage crown'd,
And streams shall murmur all around.

Here ends the History of Little *Two-Shoes*. Those who would know how she behaved after she came to be Mrs. *Margery Two-Shoes* must read the Second Part of this Work, in which an Account of the Remainder of her Life, her Marriage, and Death are set forth at large, according to Act of Parliament.

PART TWO
Of Her School, Her Ushers or Assistants, and Her Manner of Teaching

We have already informed the reader, that the school where she taught was that which was before kept by Mrs. Williams, whose character you may find in my *New Year's Gift*. The room was large, and as she knew that nature intended children should be always in action, she placed her different letters, or alphabets, all round the school, so that every one was obliged to get up to fetch a letter, or to spell a word, when it came to their turn, which not only kept them in health, but fixed the letters and points firmly in their minds.

She had the following assistants or ushers to help her, and I will tell you how she came by them. Mrs. Margery, you must know, was very humane and compassionate; and her tenderness extended not only to all mankind, but even to all animals that were not noxious, as your's ought to do, if you would be happy here, and go to heaven hereafter. These are God Almighty's creatures as well as we. He made both them and us, and for wise purposes, best known to Himself, placed them in this world to live among us, so that they are our fellow tenants of the globe. How, then, can people dare to torture and wantonly destroy God Almighty's creatures? They as well as you are capable of feeling pain and of receiving pleasure, and how can you, who want to be made happy yourself, delight in making your fellow creatures miserable? Do you think the poor birds, whose nest and young ones that wicked boy Dick Wilson ran away with yesterday, do not feel as much pain as your father and mother would have felt, had any one pulled down their house and ran away with you? To be sure they do. Mrs. Two-Shoes used to speak of those things, and of naughty boys throwing at cocks, torturing flies, and whipping horses and dogs, with tears in her eyes, and would never suffer any one to come to her school who did so.

One day, as she was going through the next village, she met with some wicked boys who had got a young raven, which they were going to throw at. She wanted to get the poor creature out of their cruel hands, and therefore gave them a penny for him, and brought him home. She called his name Ralph, and a fine bird he is. Do look at him, and remember what Solomon says, "The eye that despiseth his father, and regardeth not the distress of his mother, the ravens of the valley shall peck it out, and the young eagles eat it." Now this bird she taught to speak, to spell, and to read, and as he was particularly fond of playing with the large letters, the children used to call this Ralph's alphabet.

ABCDEFGHIJKLMNOPQRST
UVWXYZ.

He always sat at her elbow, as you see in the first picture, and when any of the children were wrong, she used to call out, "Put them right, Ralph."

Some days after she had met with the raven, as she was walking in the fields, she saw some naughty boys, who had taken a pigeon, and tied a string to its leg, in order to let it fly and draw it back again when they pleased; and by this means they tortured the poor animal with the hopes of liberty and repeated disappointment. This pigeon she also bought, and taught him how to spell and read, though not to talk, and he performed all those extraordinary things which are recorded of the famous bird that was some time since advertised in the Haymarket, and visited by most of the great people in the kingdom. This pigeon was a very pretty fellow, and she called him Tom. See, here he is. And as the raven Ralph was fond of the large letters, Tom the pigeon took care of the small ones, of which he composed this alphabet.

a b c d e f g h i j k l m n o p q r s t u v w x y z.

The neighbours, knowing that Mrs. Two-Shoes was very good, as to be sure nobody was better, made her a present of a little skylark, and a fine bird he is.

Now as many people, even at that time, had learned to lie in bed long in the morning, she thought the lark might be of use to her and her pupils, and tell them when to get up.

"For he that is fond of his bed, and lays till noon, lives but half his days, the rest being lost in sleep, which is a kind of death."

Some time after this a poor lamb had lost its dam, and the farmer being about to kill it, she bought it of him, and brought it home with her to play with the children, and teach them when to go to bed, for it was a rule with the wise men of that age (and a very good one, let me tell you) to

"Rise with the lark, and lie down with the lamb."

This lamb she called Will, and a pretty fellow he is; do look at him. No sooner was Tippy the lark and Will the ba-lamb brought into the school, but that sensible rogue, Ralph the raven, composed the following verse, which every little good boy and girl should get by heart.

"Early to bed, and early to rise;
Is the way to be healthy, and wealthy, and wise."

A sly rogue, but it is true enough, for those who do not go to bed early cannot rise early, and those who do not rise early cannot do much business. Pray, let this be told at the Court, and to people who have routs and rackets.

Soon after this, a present was made to Mrs. Margery of little dog Jumper, and a pretty dog he is. Pray, look at him. "Jumper, Jumper, Jumper!" He is always in a good humour, and

playing and jumping about, and therefore he was called "Jumper." The place assigned for Jumper was that of keeping the door, so that he may be called the porter of the College, for he would let nobody go out, or any one come in, without the leave of his mistress. See how he sits, a saucy rogue!

Billy, the ba-lamb, was a cheerful fellow, and all the children were fond of him; wherefore Mrs. Two-Shoes made it a rule, that those who behaved best should have Will home with them at night, to carry their satchel or basket at his back, and bring it in the morning. See what a fine fellow he is, and how he trudges along!

A SCENE OF DISTRESS IN THE SCHOOL

It happened one day, when Mrs. Two-Shoes was diverting the children after dinner, as she usually did with some innocent games, or entertaining and instructive stories, that a man arrived with the melancholy news of Sally Jones's father being thrown from his horse, and thought past all recovery; nay, the messenger said that he was seemingly dying when he came away. Poor Sally was greatly distressed, as indeed were all the school; for she dearly loved her father, and Mrs. Two-Shoes, and all the children dearly loved her. It is generally said that we never know the real value of our parents or friends till we have lost them; but poor Sally felt this by affection, and her mistress knew it by experience. All the school were in tears, and the messenger was obliged to return; but before he went, Mrs. Two-Shoes, unknown to the children, ordered Tom Pigeon to go home with the man, and bring a letter to inform her how Mr. Jones did. They set out together, and the pigeon rode on the man's head (as you see here), for the man was able to carry the pigeon, though the pigeon was not able to carry the man; if he had, they would have been there much sooner, for Tom Pigeon was very good, and never stayed on an errand.

Soon after the man was gone the pigeon was lost, and the concern the children were under for Mr. Jones and little Sally was in some measure diverted, and part of their attention turned after Tom, who was a great favourite, and consequently much bewailed. Mrs. Margery, who knew the great use and necessity of teaching children to submit cheerfully to the will of Providence, bid them wipe away their tears, and then kissing Sally, "You must be a good girl," says she, "and depend upon God Almighty for His blessing and protection; for He is a father to the fatherless, and defendeth all those who put their trust in Him."

. . . .

At this instant something was heard to flap at the window. "Wow, wow, wow," says Jumper, and attempted to leap up and open the door, at which the children were surprised; but Mrs. Margery, knowing what it was, opened the casement, as Noah did the window of the ark, and drew in Tom Pigeon with a letter; and see, here he is.

As soon as he was placed on the table, he walked up to little Sally, and dropping the letter, cried, "Co, co, coo!" as much as to say, "There, read it!" Now this poor pigeon had travelled fifty miles in about an hour, to bring Sally this letter, and who would destroy such pretty creatures? But let us read the letter.

My Dear Sally,

God Almighty has been very merciful, and restored your papa to us again, who is now so well as to be able to sit up. I hear you are a good girl, my dear, and I hope you will never forget to praise the Lord for this His great goodness and mercy to us. What a sad thing it would have been if your father had died, and left both you and me and little Tommy in distress and without a friend! Your father sends his blessing with mine. Be good, my dear child, and God Almighty will also bless you, whose blessing is above all things.

I am, my dear Sally,
Your ever affectionate mother,
MARTHA JONES

Of the Amazing Sagacity and Instinct of a Little Dog

Soon after this a dreadful accident happened in the school. It was on a Thursday morning, I very well remember, when the children having learned their lessons soon, she had given them leave to play, and they were all running about the school, and diverting themselves with the birds and the lamb. At this time the dog, all of a sudden, laid hold of his mistress's apron, and endeavoured to pull her out of the school. She was at first surprised; however, she followed him to see what he intended. No sooner had he led her into the garden, but he ran back, and pulled out one of the children in the same manner; upon which she ordered them all to leave the school immediately, and they had not been out five minutes, before the top of the house fell in. What a miraculous deliverance was here! How

gracious! how good was God Almighty, to save all these children from destruction, and to make use of such an instrument as a little sagacious animal to accomplish His divine will! I should have observed that as soon as they were all in the garden, the dog came leaping round them to express his joy, and when the house was fallen, laid himself down quietly by his mistress.

Some of the neighbours who saw the school fall, and who were in great pain for Margery and the little ones, soon spread the news through the village, and all the parents, terrified for their children, came crowding in abundance; they had, however, the satisfaction to find them all safe, and upon their knees, with their mistress, giving God thanks for their happy deliverance.

. . . .

The downfall of the school was a great misfortune to Mrs. Margery, for she not only lost all her books, but was destitute of a place to teach in; but Sir William Dove, being informed of this, ordered the house to be built at his own expense, and till that could be done, Farmer Grove was so kind as to let her have his large hall to teach in.

The house built by Sir William had a statue erected over the door of a boy sliding on the ice, and under it were these lines, written by Mrs. Two-Shoes, and engraved at her expense.

ON SIN. A SIMILE.

As a poor urchin on the ice,
When he has tumbled once or twice,
With cautious step, and trembling goes,
The drop-stile pendant on his nose,
And trudges on to seek the shore,
Resolv'd to trust the ice no more:
But meeting with a daring mate,
Who often us'd to slide and skate,
Again is into danger led,
And falls again, and breaks his head.

So youth when first they're drawn to sin,
And see the danger they are in,
Would gladly quit the thorny way,
And think it is unsafe to stay;
But meeting with their wicked train,
Return with them to sin again:
With them the paths of vice explore;
With them are ruin'd evermore.

What Happened at Farmer Grove's and How She Gratified Him for the Use of His Room

While at Mr. Grove's, which was in the heart of the village, she not only taught the children in the day-time, but the farmer's servants and all the neighbours to read and write in the evening; and it was a constant practice before they went away to make them all go to prayers, and sing psalms. By this means the people grew extremely regular, his servants were always at home instead of being at the ale-house, and he had more work done than ever. This gave not only Mr. Grove, but all the neighbors an high opinion of her good sense and prudent behaviour. And she was so much esteemed that most of the differences in the parish were left to her decision; and if a man and wife quarrelled which sometimes happened in that part of the kingdom both parties certainly came to her for advice. Every body knows that Martha Wilson was a passionate, scolding jade, and that John, her husband, was a surly, ill-tempered fellow. These were one day brought by the neighbours for Margery to talk to them, when they fairly quarrelled before her, and were going to blows; but she, stepping between them, thus addressed the husband: "John," says she, "you are a man, and ought to have more sense than to fly in a passion at every word that is said amiss by your wife; and Martha," says she, "you ought to know your duty better than to say anything to aggravate your husband's resentment. These frequent quarrels arise from the indulgence of your violent passions, for I know you both love one another notwithstanding what has passed between you. Now, pray tell me John, and tell me Martha, when you have had a quarrel the over-night are you not both sorry for it the next day?" They both declared that they were: "Why, then," says she, "I'll tell you how to prevent this for the future, if you will both promise to take my advice." They both promised her. "You know," says she, "that a small spark will set fire to tinder, and that tinder properly placed will fire a house; an angry word is with you as that spark, for you are both as touchy as tinder, and very often make your own house too hot to hold you. To prevent this, therefore, and to live happily for the future, you must solemnly agree that if one speaks an angry word the other will not answer till he or she has distinctly called over all the letters in the alphabet, and the other not reply till he has told twenty; by this means your passions will be stifled, and reason will have time to take the rule."

This is the best recipe that was ever given for a married couple to live in peace. Though John and his wife frequently attempted to quarrel afterwards they never could get their passions to any considerable height, for there was something so droll in thus carrying on the dispute that before they got to the end of the argument they saw the absurdity of it, laughed, kissed, and were friends.

Just as Mrs. Margery had settled this difference between John and his wife, the children (who had been sent out to play while that business was transacting) returned, some in tears, and others very disconsolate, for the loss of a little dormouse they were very fond of, and which was just dead. Mrs. Margery, who had the art of moralizing and drawing instructions from every accident, took this opportunity of reading them a lecture on the uncertainty of life, and the necessity of being always prepared for death. "You should get up in the morning," says she, "and so conduct yourselves as if that day was to be your last, and lie down at night as if you never expected to see this world any more. This may be done," says she, "without abating of your cheerfulness, for you are not to consider death as an evil, but as a convenience, as a useful pilot, who is to convey you to a place of greater happiness: Therefore, play my dear children, and be merry; but be innocent and good. The good man sets death at defiance, for his darts are only dreadful to the wicked."

After this she permitted the children to bury the little dormouse, and desired one of them to write his epitaph, and here it is.

EPITAPH ON A DORMOUSE, REALLY WRITTEN
BY A LITTLE BOY

I

In a paper case,
Hard by this place,
Dead a poor dormouse lies;
And soon or late,
Summon'd by fate,
Each prince, each monarch dies.

II

Ye sons of verse,
While I rehearse,
Attend instructive rhyme;
No sins had Dor
To answer for,
Repent of yours in time.

. . . .

How Mrs. Margery Was Taken Up for a Witch, and What Happened on That Occasion

And so it is true? And they have taken up Mrs. Margery, then, and accused her of being a witch, only because she was wiser than some of her neighbours! Mercy upon me! people stuff children's heads with stories of ghosts, fairies, witches, and such nonsense when they are young, and so they continue fools all their days. The whole world ought to be made acquainted with her case, and here it is at their service.

The Case of Mrs. Margery

Mrs. Margery, as we have frequently observed, was always doing good, and thought she could never sufficiently gratify those who had done anything to serve her. These generous sentiments naturally led her to consult the interest of Mr. Grove and the rest of her neighbours, and as most of their lands were meadow, and they depended much on their hay, which had been for many years greatly damaged by wet weather, she contrived an instrument to direct them when to mow their grass with safety, and prevent their hay being spoiled. They all came to her for advice, and by that means got in their hay without damage, while most of that in the neighbouring villages was spoiled.

This made a great noise in the country, and so provoked were the people in the other parishes that they accused her of being a witch, and sent Gaffer Goosecap, a busy fellow in other people's concerns, to find out evidence against her. This wiseacre happened to come to her school when she was walking about with the raven on one shoulder, the pigeon on the other, the lark on her hand, and the lamb and the dog by her side, which, indeed, made a droll figure, and so surprised the man that he cried out, "A witch! a witch!" upon this, she laughing, answered, "A conjurer! a conjurer!" and so they parted; but it did not end thus, for a warrant was issued out against Mrs. Margery, and she was carried to a meeting of the justices, whither all the neighbours followed her.

At the meeting one of the justices, who knew little of life and less of the law, behaved very idly, and though nobody was able to prove anything against her, asked who she could bring to her character? "Who can you bring against my character, sir," says she; "there are people enough who would appear in my defence were it necessary, but I never supposed that anyone here could be so weak as to believe there was any such thing as a witch. If I am a witch, this is my charm, and (laying a barometer or weather glass on the table) it is with this," she says, "that I have taught my neighbours to know the state of the weather." All the company laughed, and Sir William Dove, who was on the bench, asked her accusers how they could be such

fools as to think there was any such thing as a witch. "It is true," continued he, "many innocent and worthy people have been abused and even murdered on this absurd and foolish supposition, which is a scandal to our religion, to our laws, to our nation, and to common-sense; but I will tell you a story.

"There was in the West of England a poor industrious woman who laboured under the same evil report which this good woman is accused of. Every hog that died with the murrain, every cow that slipt her calf, she was accountable for: If a horse had the staggers she was supposed to be in his head; and whenever the wind blew a little harder than ordinary, Goody Giles was playing her tricks, and riding on a broomstick in the air. These, and a thousand other phantasies too ridiculous to recite possessed the pates of the common people; horse-shoes were nailed with the heels upwards, and many tricks made use of to mortify the poor creature, and such was their rage against her that they petitioned Mr. Williams, the parson of the parish, not to let her come to church, and at last even insisted upon it: but this he overruled, and allowed the poor woman a nook in one of the isles to herself, where she muttered over her prayers in the best manner she could. The parish, thus disconcerted and enraged, withdrew the small pittance they allowed for her support, and would have reduced her to the necessity of starving had she not been still assisted by the benevolent Mr. Williams.

"But I hasten to the sequel of my story, in which you will find that the true source from whence witchcraft springs is poverty, age, and ignorance, and that it is impossible for a woman to pass for a witch unless she is very poor, very old, and lives in a neighbourhood where the people are void of common-sense.

"Some time after a brother of hers died in London, who, though he would not part with a farthing while he lived, at his death was obliged to leave her five thousand pounds that he could not carry with him. This altered the face of Jane's affairs prodigiously: She was no longer Jane, alias Joan Giles, the ugly old witch, but Madam Giles; her old ragged garb was exchanged for one that was new and genteel; her greatest enemies made their court to her, even the justice himself came to wish her joy; and though several hogs and horses died, and the wind frequently blew afterwards, yet Madam Giles was never supposed to have a hand in it; and from hence it is plain, as I observed before, that a woman must be very poor, very old, and live in a neighbourhood where the people are very stupid, before she can possibly pass for a witch.

" 'Twas a saying of Mr. Williams, who would sometimes be jocose, and had the art of making even satire agreeable, that if ever Jane deserved the character of a witch it was after this money was left her; for that with her five thousand pounds she did more acts of charity and friendly offices than all the people of fortune within fifty miles of the place."

After this Sir William inveighed against the absurd and foolish notions which the country people had imbibed concerning witches and witchcraft, and having proved that there was no such thing, but that all were the effects of folly and ignorance, he gave the court such an account of Mrs. Margery and her virture, good sense, and prudent behaviour, that the gentlemen present were enamoured with her, and returned her public thanks for the great service she had done the country. One gentleman in particular, I mean Sir Charles Jones, had conceived such an high opinion of her that he offered her a considerable sum to take the care of his family and the education of his daughter, which, however, she refused; but this gentleman, sending for her afterwards when he had a dangerous fit of illness, she went, and behaved so prudently in the family, and so tenderly to him and his daughter, that he would not permit her to leave his house, but soon after made her proposals of marriage. She was truly sensible of the honour he intended her, but, though poor, she would not consent to be made a lady till he had effectually provided for his daughter; for she told him that power was a dangerous thing to be trusted with, and that a good man or woman would never throw themselves into the road of temptation.

All things being settled, and the day fixed, the neighbours came in crowds to see the wedding, for they were all glad that one who had been such a good little girl, and was become such a virtuous and good woman, was going to be made a lady; but just as the clergyman had opened his book, a gentleman, richly dressed, ran into the church, and cried, "Stop! stop!" This greatly alarmed the congregation, particularly the intended bride and bridegroom, whom he first accosted, and desired to speak with them apart. After they had been talking some little time the people were greatly surprised to see Sir Charles stand motionless, and his bride cry and faint away in the stranger's arms. This seeming grief, however, was only a prelude to a flood of joy, which immediately succeeded; for you must

know, gentle reader, that this gentleman, so richly dressed and bedizened with lace, was that identical little boy whom you before saw in the sailor's habit; in short, it was little Tom Two-Shoes, Mrs. Margery's brother, who was just come from beyond sea, where he had made a large fortune, and hearing, as soon as he landed, of his sister's intended wedding, had rode post to see that a proper settlement was made on her, which he thought she was now entitled to, as he himself was both able and willing to give her an ample fortune. They soon returned to the communion table, and were married in tears, but they were tears of joy.

. . . .

THE TRUE USE OF RICHES

The harmony and affection that subsisted between this happy couple is inexpressible; but time, which dissolves the closest union, after six years severed Sir Charles from his lady, for being seized with a violent fever he died and left her full of grief, though possessed of a large fortune.

We forgot to remark that after her marriage Lady Jones (for so we must now call her) ordered the chapel to be fitted up, and allowed the chaplain a considerable sum out of her own private purse to visit the sick, and say prayers every day to all the people that could attend. She also gave Mr. Johnson ten guineas a year to preach a sermon annually on the necessity and duties of the marriage state; and on the decease of Sir Charles, she gave him ten more to preach yearly on the subject of death; she had put all the parish into mourning for the loss of her husband; and to those men who attended this yearly service she gave harvest gloves, to their wives shoes and stockings, and to all the children little books and plum cakes. We must also observe that she herself wove a chaplet of flowers, and before the service placed it on his gravestone, and a suitable psalm was always sung by the congregation.

About this time she heard that Mr. Smith was oppressed by Sir Timothy Gripe, the justice, and his friend Graspall, who endeavoured to deprive him of part of his tythes, upon which she, in conjunction with her brother, defended him, and the cause was tried in Westminister Hall, where Mr. Smith gained a verdict; and it appearing that Sir Timothy had behaved most scandalously, as a Justice of the Peace, he was struck off the list, and no longer permitted to act in that capacity. This was a cut to a man of his imperious disposition, and this was followed by one yet more severe; for a relation of his, who had undoubted right to the Mouldwell estate, finding that it was possible to get the better at law of a rich man, laid claim to it, brought his action, and recovered the whole manor of Mouldwell; and being afterwards inclined to sell it, he, in consideration of the aid Lady Margery had lent him during his distress, made her the first offer, and she purchased the whole and threw it into different farms, that the poor might be no longer under the dominion of two overgrown men.

This was a great mortification to Sir Timothy, as well as to his friend Graspall, who from this time experienced nothing but misfortunes, and was in a few years so dispossessed of his ill-gotten wealth, that his family were reduced to seek subsistence from the parish, at which those who had felt the weight of his iron hand rejoiced; but Lady Margery desired that his children might be treated with care and tenderness; "for they," says she, "are no ways accountable for the actions of their father."

At her first coming into power, she took care to gratify her old friends, especially Mr. and Mrs. Smith, whose family she made happy. She paid great regard to the poor, made their interest her own, and to induce them to come regularly to church, she ordered a loaf, or the price of a loaf, to be given to every one who would accept of it. This brought many of them to church, who by degrees learned their duty, and then came on a more noble principle. She also took care to encourage matrimony; and in order to induce her tenants and neighbours to enter into that happy state, she always gave the young couple something towards housekeeping; and stood godmother to all their children, whom she had in parties, every Sunday evening, to teach them their Catechism, and lecture them in religion and morality; after which she treated them with a supper, gave them such books as they wanted, and then despatched them with her blessing. Nor did she forget them at her death, but left each a legacy, as will be seen among other charitable donations when we publish her will, which we may do in some future volume. There is one request, however, so singular, that we cannot help taking notice of it in this place, which is, that of her giving so many acres of land to be planted yearly with potatoes, for all the poor of any parish who would come and fetch them for the use of their families; but if any took them to sell they were deprived of that privilege ever after. And these roots were planted and raised from the rent arising from a farm which she had assigned over for that pur-

pose. In short, she was a mother to the poor, a physician to the sick, and a friend to all who were in distress. Her life was the greatest blessing, and her death the greatest calamity that ever was felt in the neighbourhood. A monument, without inscription, was erected to her memory in the churchyard, over which the poor as they pass weep continually, so that the stone is ever bathed in tears.

On this occasion the following lines were spoken extempore by a young gentleman:

How vain the tears that fall from you,
And here supply the place of dew!
How vain to weep the happy dead,
Who now to heavenly realms are fled!
Repine no more, your plaints forbear,
And all prepare to meet them there.

⟶ ⟵

A Day of Misfortunes [2]

MARIA EDGEWORTH

"Are you getting up so soon?" said Rosamond to her sister. "It seems to be a cold morning: it is very disagreeable to get up from one's warm bed in cold weather. I will not get up yet." So Rosamond, who was covered up warmly, lay quite still looking at Laura, who was dressing herself as quickly as she could.

"It is a cold morning, indeed," said Laura, "therefore I'll make haste, that I may go down and warm myself afterwards at the fire in mamma's dressing-room."

When Laura was about half dressed, she called again to Rosamond, and told her that it was late, and that she was afraid she would not be ready for breakfast.

But Rosamond answered, "I shall be ready, I shall be ready, for you know, when I make a great deal of haste I can dress very quickly indeed. Yesterday morning I did not begin to dress till you were combing the last curl of your hair, and I was ready almost as soon as you were. Nay, Laura, why do you shake your head? I say almost, I don't say quite."

"I don't know what you call almost," said Laura, laughing. "I had been drawing some time before you came downstairs."

"But I looked at your drawing," said Rosamond, "the minute I came into the room, and I saw only three legs and a back of a chair. You

[2] From Maria Edgeworth, *Frank and Rosamond.*

know that was not much — it was hardly worth while to get up early to do so little."

"Doing a little and a little every morning makes something in time," said Laura.

"Very true," replied Rosamond; "you drew the whole of mamma's dressing-room, dressing-table, and glass, and everything, little by little, in — what do you call it? — perspective, before breakfast! I begin to wish that I could get up as you do; but then I can't draw in perspective."

"But, my dear Rosamond, whilst you are talking about perspective, you don't consider how late it is growing," said Laura; "why don't you get up now?"

"Oh, because it is too late to get up early now," argued Rosamond.

Satisfied with this reflection, Rosamond closed her eyes, and turned to go to sleep again. "When you come to the last curl, Laura, call me once more," said she, "and then I'll get up."

But in vain Laura called her again, warning her that she was "come to the last curl."

Rosamond was more sleepy than ever, and more afraid of the cold. At last, however, she was roused by the breakfast-bell. She started up, exclaiming, "Oh, Laura, what shall I do? I shall not be ready, my father will be displeased with me, and I've lost my lace, and I can't find my pocket-handkerchief, and all my things are gone. This will be a day of misfortunes, I'm sure — and the clasp is come out of my shoe," added she, and as she uttered these words in a doleful tone, she sat down upon the side of the bed, and began to cry.

"Nay, don't cry," said Laura, "or else it *will* be a day of misfortunes. Look! here's your pocket-handkerchief."

"But my lace!" said Rosamond, wiping her eyes with her handkerchief; "how can I be ready for breakfast without my lace? and my father will be very, very —— "

"Very what?" said Laura, good-humouredly. "Here's the lace: sit up a minute, and I'll draw it out for you." Rosamond laughed when she found that she was sitting upon her own lace, and she thanked her sister, who was now sewing the clasp into her shoe.

"Well, I don't think it will be a day of misfortunes," said Rosamond. "You see, I'm almost dressed, eh, Laura? and I shall be ready in pretty good time, and I shall be just as well as if I had got up an hour ago, eh, Laura?" But at this moment Rosamond, in her violent haste, pulled the string of her cap into a knot, which she could not untie. Laura was going out of the room, but she called her back in a voice of distress, and begged she would be so very good as to do one thing more for her; and, as Rosamond spoke, she held up her chin and showed the hard knot. Laura, whose patience was not to be conquered even by a hard knot, began very kindly to help her sister; but Rosamond, between her dislike of the cold and her fears that she should not be ready for breakfast, and that her father would be displeased with her, became more and more fretful; she repeated, "This *will* be a day of misfortunes, after all — it tires me, Laura, to hold up my chin so long." Laura knelt down to relieve her chin; but no sooner was this complaint removed, than Rosamond began to shiver extremely, and exclaimed, "It is so cold, I cannot bear it any longer, Laura. This will be a day of misfortunes. I would rather untie the knot myself. Oh, that's my father's voice! He is dressed! he is dressed! and I am not half-dressed!"

Rosamond's eyes were full of tears, and she was a melancholy spectacle, when her mother, at this instant, opened the room door.

"What! not ready yet, Rosamond, and in tears! Look at this cross face," said her mother, leading her to a looking-glass. "Is that an agreeable little girl, do you think?"

"But I'm very cold, mamma; and I can't untie this knot. Laura, I think you have made it worse," said Rosamond, reproachfully.

At these words her mother desired Laura to go downstairs to breakfast. "Rosamond," added she, "you will not gain anything by ill-humour. When you have done crying, and when you have dressed yourself, you may follow us down to breakfast."

As soon as her mother had shut the door and left her, Rosamond began to cry again; but after some time she considered that her tears would neither make her warm nor untie the knot of her cap; she therefore dried her eyes, and once more tried to conquer the grand difficulty. A little patience was all that was necessary: she untied the knot and finished dressing herself, but she felt ashamed to go into the room to her father, and mother, and brothers, and sister. She looked in the glass to see whether her eyes continued red. Yes, they were very red, and her purple cheeks were glazed with tears. She walked backwards and forwards between the door and the looking-glass several times, and the longer she delayed, the more unwilling she felt to do what was disagreeable to her. At length, however, as she stood with the door half-open, she heard the cheerful sound of the voices in the breakfast-room, and she said to herself, "Why should not I be as happy as everybody else is?" She went downstairs, and resolved, very wisely, to tell her father what had happened, and to be good-humoured and happy.

"Well, Rosamond," said her mother, when she came into the room, and when she told her father what had happened, "you look rather more agreeable now than you did when I saw you a little while ago. We are glad to see that you can command yourself. Come, now, and eat some breakfast."

Laura set a chair for her sister at the table near the fire, and Rosamond would have said, "Thank you," but that she was afraid to speak lest she should cry again. She began to eat her breakfast as fast as possible without lifting up her eyes.

"You need not put quite such large pieces in your little mouth," said her mother, "and you need not look quite so dismal: all your misfortunes are over now, are they not?"

But at the word *misfortunes*, Rosamond's face wrinkled up into a most dismal condition, and the large tears, which had gradually collected in her eyes, rolled over her cheeks.

"What is the matter now, Rosamond?" said her mother.

"I don't know, mamma."

"But try to find out, Rosamond," said her mother. "Think, and tell me what it is that makes you look so miserable: if you can find out the cause of this woe, perhaps you will be able to put an end to it. What is the cause, can you tell?"

"The cause is — I believe, mamma — because," said Rosamond, sobbing — "because I think today will be a — will be a day of — a day of — a day of misfortunes."

"And what do you mean by a day of misfortunes, Rosamond? a day on which you are asked not to put large pieces of bread into your mouth?"

"No, mamma," said Rosamond, half laughing; "but — "

"But what? a day when you cannot immediately untie a knot?"

"Not *only* that, mamma," answered Rosamond; "but a day when everything goes wrong."

"When you do not get up in proper time, for instance?"

"Yes, mamma."

"And whose fault was that, Rosamond — yours or the day's?"

"Don't you think it was partly the day's fault,

mamma, because it was so cold? It was the cold that first prevented me from getting up; and then my not getting up was the cause of my being in a great hurry afterwards, and of my losing my lace and my pocket-handkerchief, and of my pulling the strings of my cap into a knot, and of my being cross to Laura, who was so good to me and of your being displeased with me, and of all my misfortunes."

"So the *cold*, you think, was the cause of all these misfortunes, as you call them; but do you think that nobody has felt the cold this morning except yourself? Laura and I have felt the cold, and how comes it that we have had no misfortunes?"

"Oh, mamma!" said Rosamond; "but you and Laura do not mind such little misfortunes. It would be very odd indeed, mamma" — and she burst out laughing at the idea — "it would be very droll indeed, mamma, if I was to find you crying because you could not untie the strings of your cap."

"Or because I was cold," added her mother, laughing with her.

"I was very foolish, to be sure, mamma," resumed Rosamond; "but there are two things I could say for myself, that would be some excuse."

"Say them, then, my dear; I shall be glad to hear them."

"The first is, mamma, that I was a great deal longer in the cold this morning than anybody else; therefore I had more reason to cry, you know. And the second thing I have to say for myself, is — "

"Gently," interrupted her mother: "before you go to your second excuse, let us consider whether your first is a good one. How came you to stay longer in the cold this morning than anybody else did?"

"Because, mamma, you sent Laura downstairs, and told me I must untie the knot myself."

"And why did I send Laura downstairs, and say you must untie the knot for yourself?"

"Because I was cross to Laura, I believe."

"And what made you cross to Laura?"

"I was cross, because I could not untie the knot that the strings of my cap had got into."

"*Had got into*, Rosamond! Did the strings get into a knot of themselves?"

"I mean I pulled them into a knot."

"And how came you to do that?"

"Because I was in a hurry."

"And how came you to be in a hurry?"

"Oh! I see, mamma, that you will say it was

my own fault, that I did not get up in proper time. But now for the second thing I have to say for myself. The strings of my cap are a great, great deal too short, and this, more than the cold, was the cause of all my misfortunes. You and Laura might have felt the cold, as you say, as much as I did; but you neither of you had short strings to your caps, mamma," continued Rosamond, with an emphasis. "But," pausing to reflect, she added, "I do not think that the cold, or the strings, were the *real* cause of my misfortunes. I don't think that I should have cried the first time, and I am almost sure that I should not have cried the second and third time, if it had not been for something else. I am afraid, mamma, to tell you of this *something else,* because I know you will say that was more foolish than all the rest."

"But tell it to me, notwithstanding," said her mother, smiling, "because the way to prevent yourself from being foolish again is to find out what made you so just now. If you tell me what you think and what you feel, perhaps I may help you to manage yourself so as to make you wise, and good, and happy; but unless I know what passes in your little mind, I shall not be able to help you."

"I'll tell you directly, mamma. It was my thinking that today would be a day of misfortunes, that made me cry the second and third time; and do you know, mamma," continued Rosamond, in a faltering, mournful voice, "I don't know why, but I can hardly help feeling almost ready to cry when the same thing comes into my head again now, mamma. Do you think today *will* be a day of misfortunes, mamma?"

"I think, my dear," answered her mother, "that it will depend entirely upon yourself whether it is or no. If you recollect, we have just discovered that all your past *misfortunes,* as you call them ——"

"Were my own fault, you are going to say, mamma," interrupted Rosamond, "that's the worst of it! That makes me more sorry, and not pleased with myself nor with anything else, and ready to cry again, because I can't help it all now."

"Since you cannot help it all now," said her mother, "why should you cry about it? Turn your thoughts to something else. We cannot help what is past, but we can take care of the future."

"The future," repeated Rosamond, "ay, the time to come. Tomorrow, let it be ever so cold, I'll get up in good time, and as for today, I can't get up in good time today; but I may do some-

thing else that is right, and that may make me pleased with myself again, eh, mamma? There's a great deal of this day to come yet, and if I take care, perhaps it will not be a day of misfortunes after all. What do you think I had better do first, mamma?"

"Run about and warm these purple hands of yours, I think," said her mother.

"And after that, mamma, what shall I do next?"

"Do that first," said her mother, "and then we will talk about the next thing."

"But, mamma," said Rosamond, casting a longing, lingering look at the fire, "it is *very* disagreeable to leave this nice warm room, and to go out to run in the cold."

"Don't you remember, Rosamond, how warm you made yourself by running about in the garden yesterday? You said that you felt warm for a great while afterwards, and that you liked that kind of warmth better than the warmth of the fire."

"Yes, it is very true, mamma: one gets cold soon after being at the fire — I mean, soon after one goes away from it; but still, it is disagreeable at first to go out into the cold, don't you think so, mamma?"

"Yes, I do; but I think also that we should be able to do what is a little disagreeable, when we know that it will be for our good afterwards; and by putting off whatever is not quite agreeable to us to do, we sometimes bring ourselves into difficulties. Recollect what happened to a little girl this morning, who did not get up because the cold was disagreeable."

"True, mamma. I will go."

"And I am going to walk," said her mother.

"In the garden, mamma, whilst I run about? I'm very glad of that, because I can talk to you between times, and I don't feel the cold so much when I'm talking. The snow is all swept off the gravel walk, mamma, and there's room for both of us, and I'll run, and set your goloshes at the hall door, ready for your feet to pop into them."

⧫

A Hymn in Prose [3]

LETITIA AIKIN BARBAULD

Come, let us walk abroad; let us talk of the works of God. Take up a handful of sand; number the grains of it; tell them one by one into

[3] "Hymn IX," from Letitia Aikin Barbauld, *Hymns in Prose.*

your lap. Try if you can count the blades of grass in the field, or the leaves on the trees. You cannot count them, they are innumerable; much more the things which God has made.

The fir groweth on the high mountain, and the grey willow bends above the stream.

The thistle is armed with sharp prickles; the mallow is soft and woolly.

The hop layeth hold with her tendrils, and claspeth the tall pole; the oak hath firm root in the ground, and resisteth the winter storm.

The daisy enamelleth the meadows, and groweth beneath the foot of the passenger.

The tulip asketh a rich soil, and the careful hand of the gardener.

The iris and the reed spring up in the marsh; the rich grass covereth the meadows; and the purple heath-flower enliveneth the waste ground.

The water-lilies grow beneath the stream; their broad leaves float on the surface of the water; the wall-flower takes root in the hard stone, and spreads its fragrance amongst broken ruins.

Every leaf is of a different form; every plant hath a separate inhabitant.

Look at the thorns that are white with blossoms, and the flowers that cover the fields, and the plants that are trodden in the green path. The hand of man hath not planted them; the sower hath not scattered the seeds from his hand, nor the gardener digged a place for them with his spade.

Some grow on steep rocks, where no man can climb; in shaking bogs, and deep forests, and desert islands; they spring up everywhere, and cover the bosom of the whole earth.

Who causeth them to grow everywhere, and bloweth the seeds about in winds, and mixeth them with the mould, and watereth them with soft rains, and cherisheth them with dews? Who fanneth them with the pure breath of heaven; and giveth them colours and smells, and spreadeth out their thin transparent leaves?

How doth the rose draw its crimson from the dark brown earth, or the lily its shining white? How can a small seed contain a plant? How doth every plant know its season to put forth? They are marshalled in order: each one knoweth his place, and standeth up in his own rank.

The snow-drop and the primrose make haste to lift their heads above the ground. When the spring cometh, they say, "Here we are." The carnation waiteth for the full strength of the year; and the hardy laurustinus cheereth the winter months.

Every plant produceth its like. An ear of corn will not grow from an acorn; nor will a grape-stone produce cherries; but every one springeth from its proper seed.

Who preserveth them alive through the cold winter, when the snow is on the ground, and the sharp frost bites on the plain? Who soweth a small seed, and a little warmth in the bosom of the earth, and causeth them to spring up afresh, and sap to rise through the hard fibres?

The trees are withered, naked and bare; they are like dry bones.

Who breathed on them with the breath of spring, and they are covered with verdure, and green leaves sprout from the dead wood?

Lo, these are a part of His works; and a little portion of His wonders.

There is little need that I should tell you of God, for everything speaks of Him.

Every field is like an open book; every painted flower hath a lesson written on its leaves.

Every murmuring brook hath a tongue; a voice is in every whispering wind.

They all speak of Him who made them; they all tell us, "He is very good."

We cannot see God, for He is invisible; but we can see His works, and worship His footsteps in the green sod. They that know the most will praise God the best, but which of us can number half His works?

≈§ §≈

The Butterfly's Ball

WILLIAM ROSCOE

"Come, take up your hats, and away let us haste
To the Butterfly's Ball and the Grasshopper's
    Feast,
The Trumpeter, Gadfly, has summon'd the crew,
And the Revels are now only waiting for you."
So said little Robert, and pacing along,
His merry Companions came forth in a throng,
And on the smooth Grass by the side of a Wood,
Beneath a broad oak that for ages had stood,
Saw the Children of Earth and the Tenants of
    Air
For an Evening's Amusement together repair.

And there came the Beetle, so blind and so black,
Who carried the Emmet, his friend, on his back,
And there was the Gnat and the Dragonfly too,
With all their Relations, green, orange and blue.

And there came the Moth, with his plumage of
    down,
And the Hornet in jacket of yellow and brown;
Who with him the Wasp, his companion, did
    bring,
But they promised that evening to lay by their
    sting.
And the sly little Dormouse crept out of his hole,
And brought to the Feast his blind Brother,
    the Mole;
And the Snail, with his horns peeping out of his
    shell,
Came from a great distance, the length of an ell.

A Mushroom, their table, and on it was laid
A water-dock leaf, which a table-cloth made,
The Viands were various, to each of their taste,
And the Bee brought her honey to crown the
    Repast.
Then close on his haunches, so solemn and wise,
The Frog from a corner look'd up to the skies;
And the Squirrel, well pleased such diversion to
    see,
Mounted high overhead and look'd down from a
    tree.

Then out came the Spider, with finger so fine,
To show his dexterity on the tight-line,
From one branch to another his cobwebs he
    slung,
Then quick as an arrow he darted along.
But just in the middle — oh! shocking to tell,
From his rope, in an instant, poor Harlequin
    fell,
Yet he touch'd not the ground, but with talons
    outspread,
Hung suspended in air, at the end of a thread.

Then the Grasshopper came with a jerk and a
    spring,
Very long was his Leg, though but short was his
    Wing;
He took but three leaps, and was soon out of
    sight,
Then chirp'd his own praises the rest of the night.
With step so majestic the Snail did advance,
And promised the Gazers a Minuet to dance;
But they all laughed so loud that he pulled in his
    head,
And went in his own little chamber to bed.

Then as Evening gave way to the shadows of
    Night,
Their Watchman, the Glowworm, came out with
    a light.

"Then Home let us hasten while yet we can see,
For no Watchman is waiting for you and for me."
So said little Robert, and pacing along,
His merry Companions return'd in a throng.

❧ ❧

Murdoch's Rath [4]

Juliana Horatia Ewing

There was not a nicer boy in all Ireland than
Pat, and clever at his trade, too, if only he'd had
one.

But from his cradle he learned nothing (small
blame to him, with no one to teach him) so
when he came to years of discretion he earned his
living by running messages for his neighbors;
and Pat could always be trusted to make the best
of a bad bargain and bring back all the change,
for he was the soul of honesty and good nature.

It's no wonder then that he was beloved by
everyone and got as much work as he could do;
and if the pay had but fitted the work, he'd have
been mighty comfortable; but as it was, what he
got wouldn't have kept him in shoeleather, but
for making both ends meet by wearing his shoes
in his pocket, except when he was in town and
obliged to look genteel for the credit of the
place he came from.

Well, all was going on as peaceable as could
be, till one market-day, when business (or it
might have been pleasure) detained him till the
heel of the evening, and by nightfall, when he
began to make the road short in good earnest, he
was so flustered, rehearsing his messages to make
sure he'd forgotten nothing, that he never bethought him to leave off his brogues, but
tramped on just as if shoe-leather was made to be
knocked to bits on the king's highway.

And this is what he was after saying:

"A dozen hanks of gray yarn for Mistress
Murphy.

"Three gross of bright buttons for the tailor.

"Half an ounce of throat-drops for Father
Andrew, and an ounce of snuff for his housekeeper," and so on.

For these were what he went to the town to
fetch, and he was afraid lest one of the lot might
have slipped his memory.

Now everybody knows there are two ways
home from the town; and that's not meaning the

4 From Juliana Horatia Ewing, *Old Fashioned
Fairy Tales*.

right way and the wrong way, which my grandmother (rest her soul!) said there was to every place but one that it's not genteel to name. (There could only be a wrong way *there,* she said.) The two ways home from the town were the highway and the way by Murdoch's Rath.*

Murdoch's Rath was a pleasant enough spot in the daytime, but not many persons cared to go by it when the sun was down. And in all the years Pat was going backwards and forwards, he never once came home except by the highroad till this unlucky evening, when, just at the place where the two roads part, he got, as one may say, into a sort of confusion.

"Halt!" says he to himself (for his own uncle had been a soldier, and Pat knew the word of command). "The left-hand turn is the right one," says he, and he was going down the highroad as straight as he could go, when suddenly he bethought himself. "And what am I doing?" he says. "This was my left hand going to town, and how in the name of fortune could it be my left going back, considering that I've turned round? It's well that I looked into it in time." And with that he went off as fast down the other road as he had started down this.

But how far he walked he never could tell, before all of a sudden the moon shone out as bright as day, and Pat found himself in Murdoch's Rath.

And this was the smallest part of the wonder; for the Rath was full of fairies.

When Pat got in, they were dancing round and round till his feet tingled to look at them, being a good dancer himself. And as he sat on the side of the Rath, and snapped his fingers to mark the time, the dancing stopped, and a little man comes up, in a black hat and a green coat, with white stockings and red shoes on his feet.

"Won't you take a turn with us, Pat?" says he, bowing till he nearly reached the ground. And, indeed, he had not far to go, for he was barely two feet high.

"Don't say it twice, sir," says Pat. "It's myself will be proud to foot the floor wid ye"; and before you could look round, there was Pat in the circle dancing away for bare life.

At first his feet felt like feathers for lightness, and it seemed as if he could have gone on forever. But at last he grew tired, and would have liked to stop, but the fairies would not, and so they danced on and on. Pat tried to think of

* Rath = a kind of moat-surrounded spot much favored by Irish fairies. The ditch is generally overgrown with furze-bushes.

something *good* to say, that he might free himself from the spell, but all he could think of was:

"A dozen hanks of gray yarn for Mistress Murphy.

"Three gross of bright buttons for the tailor.

"Half an ounce of throat drops for Father Andrew, and an ounce of snuff for his housekeeper," and so on.

And it seemed to Pat that the moon was on the one side of the Rath when they began to dance, and on the other side when they left off; but he could not be sure after all that going round. One thing was plain enough. He danced every bit of leather off the soles of his feet, and they were blistered so that he could hardly stand; but all the little folk did was to stand and hold their sides with laughing at him.

At last the one who spoke before stepped up to him, and — "Don't break your heart about it, Pat," says he, "I'll lend you my own shoes till the morning, for you seem to be a good-natured sort of a boy."

Well, Pat looked at the fairy man's shoes, that were the size of a baby's, and he looked at his own feet; but not wishing to be uncivil, "Thank ye kindly, sir," says he. "And if your honor'll be good enough to put them on for me, maybe you won't spoil the shape." For he thought to himself, "Small blame to me if the little gentleman can't get them to fit."

With that he sat down on the side of the Rath, and the fairy man put on the shoes for him, and no sooner did they touch Pat's feet than they became altogether a convenient size, and fitted him like wax. And, more than that, when he stood up, he didn't feel his blisters at all.

"Bring 'em back to the Rath at sunrise, Pat, my boy," says the little man.

And as Pat was climbing over the ditch, "Look round, Pat," says he. And when Pat looked round, there were jewels and pearls lying at the roots of the furze-bushes on the ditch, as thick as peas.

"Will you help yourself, or take what's given ye, Pat?" says the fairy man.

"Did I ever learn manners?" says Pat. "Would you have me help myself before company? I'll take what your honor pleases to give me, and be thankful."

The fairy man picked a lot of yellow furze-blossoms from the bushes, and filled Pat's pockets.

"Keep 'em for love, Pat, me darlin'," says he.

Pat would have liked some of the jewels, but he put the furze-blossoms by for love.

"Good evening to your honor," says he.

"And where are you going, Pat dear?" says the fairy man.

"I'm going home," says Pat. And if the fairy man didn't know where that was, small blame to him.

"Just let me dust those shoes for ye, Pat," says the fairy man. And as Pat lifted up each foot he breathed on it, and dusted it with the tail of his green coat.

"Home!" says he, and when he let go, Pat was at his own doorstep before he could look round, and his parcels safe and sound with him.

Next morning he was up with the sun, and carried the fairy man's shoes back to the Rath. As he came up, the little man looked over the ditch.

"The top of the morning to your honor," says Pat; "here's your shoes."

"You're an honest boy, Pat," says the little gentleman. "It's inconvenienced I am without them, for I have but the one pair. Have you looked at the yellow flowers this morning?" he says.

"I have not, sir," says Pat; "I'd be loath to deceive you. I came off as soon as I was up."

"Be sure to look when you get back, Pat," says the fairy man, "and good luck to ye!"

With which he disappeared, and Pat went home. He looked for the furze-blossoms, as the fairy man told him, and there's not a word of truth in this tale if they weren't all pure gold pieces.

Well, now Pat was so rich, he went to the shoemaker to order another pair of brogues, and being a kindly, gossiping boy, he soon told the shoemaker the whole story of the fairy man and the Rath. And this so stirred up the shoemaker's greed that he resolved to go the next night himself, to see if he could not dance with the fairies, and have like luck.

He found his way to the Rath all correct, and sure enough the fairies were dancing, and they asked him to join. He danced the soles off his brogues, as Pat did, and the fairy man lent him his shoes, and sent him home in a twinkling.

As he was going over the ditch, he looked round, and saw the roots of the furze-bushes glowing with precious stones as if they had been glow-worms.

"Will you help yourself, or take what's given ye?" said the fairy man.

"I'll help myself, if you please," said the cobbler, for he thought — "If I can't get more than Pat brought home, my fingers must all be thumbs."

So he drove his hand into the bushes, and if he didn't get plenty, it wasn't for want of grasping.

When he got up in the morning, he went straight to the jewels. But not a stone of the lot was more precious than roadside pebbles.

"I ought not to look till I come from the Rath," said he. "It's best to do like Pat all through."

But he made up his mind not to return the fairy man's shoes.

"Who knows the virtue that's in them?" he said. So he made a small pair of red leather shoes, as like them as could be, and he blacked the others upon his feet, that the fairies might not know them, and at sunrise he went to the Rath.

The fairy man was looking over the ditch as before.

"Good morning to you," said he.

"The top of the morning to you, sir," said the cobbler, "here's your shoes." And he handed him the pair that he had made, with a face as grave as a judge.

The fairy man looked at them, but he said nothing, though he did not put them on.

"Have you looked at the things you got last night?" says he.

"I'll not deceive you, sir," says the cobbler. "I came off as soon as I was up. Sorra peep I took at them."

"Be sure to look when you get back," says the fairy man. And just as the cobbler was getting over the ditch to go home, he says: "If my eyes don't deceive me," says he, "there's the least taste in life of dirt on your left shoe. Let me dust it with the tail of my coat."

"That means home in a twinkling," thought the cobbler, and he held up his foot.

The fairy man dusted it, and muttered something the cobbler did not hear. Then, "Sure," says he, "it's the dirty pastures that you've come through, for the other shoe's as bad."

So the cobbler held up his right foot, and the fairy man rubbed that with the tail of his green coat.

When all was done, the cobbler's feet seemed to tingle, and then to itch, and then to smart, and then to burn. And at last he began to dance, and he danced all round the Rath (the fairy man laughing and holding his sides) and then round and round again. And he danced till he cried out with weariness and tried to shake the shoes off. But they stuck fast, and the fairies drove him over the ditch, and through the prickly furze-bushes, and he danced away. Where he danced to, I cannot tell you. Whether he ever got rid of the fairy shoes I do not know. The jewels never were more than wayside pebbles, and they were swept out when his cabin was cleaned, which was not too soon, you may be sure.

All this happened long ago; but there are those who say that the covetous cobbler dances still, between sunset and sunrise, round Murdoch's Rath.

BIBLIOGRAPHY

Aikin, John, and Anna Letitia Aikin Barbauld. *Evenings at Home.* 1792–96. 6 vols.

Barbauld, Anna Letitia Aikin. *Hymns in Prose.* 1781.
Interesting in the study of children's literature.

Berquin, Arnaud. *The Looking-Glass for the Mind.* 1787.
The 1792 edition contains very interesting wood-cuts by John Bewick.

Day, Thomas. *Sandford and Merton.* 1783–89, 3 vols.
Interesting as the first English book illustrating Rousseau's theory of education.

Edgeworth, Maria. *Early Lessons.* 1801–15, 4 vols.
Two books which show Miss Edgeworth at her best are: *Parent's Assistant; or Stories for Children,* illustrated by Chris Hammond (Macmillan); and *Tales,* introduction by Austin Dobson, illustrated by Hugh Thompson (Stokes).

Ewing, Mrs. Juliana Horatia. *Jan of the Windmill.* Bell, London, 1876. (Queen's Treasures Series)
A story of a lad whose talent for painting led to the discovery of his own parentage. Other well-liked books by the same author are: *Brownies and other Stories; Daddy Darwin's Dovecot; Jackanapes; Lob Lie-by-the-fire; Mary's Meadow;* and *Six to Sixteen.* All published in the Queen's Treasures Series)

History of Little Goody Two-Shoes; ed. by Charles Welsh. Heath, 1900.
The first book written especially for children. Sometimes attributed to Oliver Goldsmith. First published by John Newbery in 1765 (?)

Horne, Richard Henry (Mrs. Fairstar, *pseud.*), *Memoirs of a London Doll,* illus. by Emma L. Brock. Macmillan, 1922. (Little Library)
A favorite doll story. First published in 1846.

Lamb, Charles and Mary. *Mrs. Leicester's School;* illus. by Winifred Green. Dent, London, 1899.
The quaint illustrations are in keeping with the text. First published in 1809.

Martineau, Harriet. *Feats on the Fiord;* illus. by Boris Artzybasheff. Macmillan, 1924. (Children's Classics)
An attractive edition of this quaint story of Norwegian smugglers. First published in 1899.

Trimmer, Sarah Kirby. *The History of Robins;* ed. by E. E. Hale. Heath, 1901.
Children still delight in these stories of bird-life. First published in 1786.

Yonge, Charlotte Mary. *The Little Duke, Richard the Fearless;* illus. by Marguerite De Angeli. Macmillan, 1927. (Children Classics)
One of the most popular stories of times of chivalry; first published in 1854. Other books by the same author that are well liked, especially by older boys and girls, are: *Dove in the Eagle's Nest; Chaplet of Pearls;* and *The Prince and the Page.* All of these are published in well-illustrated editions.

APPENDIX D

Illustrators of Children's Books

THE ILLUSTRATED BOOK follows fast on the invention of printing itself. Early in the process of printing came the accompanying attempt to entice and invite the mind of man to the effort of reading by the use of pictures which served to catch the eye and hold the interest. The hand-wrought and hand-copied books of the monasteries were embellished with designs, illuminated initials, minute pictures, and decorative patterns. It was natural that the idea of pictorial decoration should be carried over to the product of the printing press.

The first illustrations made to accompany print consisted of wood blocks: crude, simple pictures drawn on a block of wood, then cut in relief to form an inking and printing surface. The process was closely akin to the method by which letters were cut in relief, and the wood block could be locked in the same form as the letters, or type, and printed at the same time as the text. It was an economical process, one naturally harmonious with print, since there was a balance between the black-and-white line of the picture and the black-on-white line of the type.

William Caxton (1422?–1491), the first English printer, used wood blocks in certain of his books, but these were not addressed to children; and the titles which would seem to be for children, such as *The Book of Courtesy*, designed to give children instruction in manners and behavior, were published without illustration. Caxton's *Aesop's Fables* (1484) was illustrated with 185 "clear and lively woodcuts," which must have delighted children fortunate enough to have access to them, though the fables were intended as adult reading.

It was an inspired teacher, one of the great minds produced by the Reformation, that first understood the necessity of pictorial representation where children were concerned. Comenius (Jan Amos Komensky) was born in 1592 in what is now Czechoslovakia; as a bishop of the Moravian church, the Unity of Brethren, he reformed and invigorated the educational outlook of all Europe, and the text he wrote for children was the chief instrument of that reform. Originally written in High Dutch and Latin, because Latin was the international language of the time, the book bore the title *Orbis Sensualium Pictus, The Visible World: Or, A Picture and Nomenclature of All the Chief Things That Are in the World*. Every object mentioned was illustrated with a picture and numbered in the text for easy identification. The *Orbis Pictus* first appeared in 1658 and was translated into most of the languages of Europe, the Latin text being given on one side of the page and the vernacular on the other. It was first translated into English in 1658 by Charles Hoole.

The battledores — those three-fold cardboard successors to the hornbooks — were often embellished with woodcuts, and these so-called books were entrusted to children. Meanwhile, the ballad sheets and chapbooks, hawked on the streets and at markets and fairs, had their measure of crude woodcut illustration. Often the same cut was made to serve several tales, and an illustration of some maid of ballad fame would make an appearance elsewhere as a portrait of Queen Bess. The astute John Newbery, too, the first to recognize children as buyers and consumers of books, took care to illustrate his little books, and the advertisements of his wares included the promise, "adorned with cuts."

But woodcut illustration was to come to glory as an art under the genius of Thomas Bewick (pronounced Buick). A country lad with his mind full of vivid pictures of the animals and landscapes he had known on his father's farm near Newcastle, Bewick was apprenticed to an engraver and put to work on woodcuts, then considered unimportant, as meeting only a cheap, popular demand. Bewick revived and extended an old art of wood engraving. The common practice was to cut the picture on the flat side of a piece of wood, cutting with the grain. Bewick used the cross section of the wood block, cutting across the grain. He engraved lines *into* the wood. The lines thus engraved represent white spaces between the portions of the block which stand out in relief to hold ink applied to the block for printing. This proc-

THOMAS BEWICK. "The Daw with the Borrowed Feathers," from *Fables* by John Gay (1784). The precise drawing of the birds' claws and delicately jointed legs is typical of Bewick's insistence on a true representation of nature.

ess allowed greater detail and more variety in shading and tone. Bewick was an artist in wood, whose miniature tailpiece landscapes were almost as great in their power to evoke atmosphere and feeling, warmth and coolness, light and shade, as anything a painter could produce with a full palette of color at his command. His portraits of animals and birds are incomparable. His *General History of Quadrupeds* (1790) and *History of British Birds* (1797) were designed for the adult public; but an edition of Aesop illustrated by him, and his pictures for John Gay's *Fables* (1784), must have appealed to

children who had the good fortune to come upon them.

Bewick did not undertake the illustration of books for children until after he was well established as an engraver and had become a partner in the firm. "He is the earliest illustrator in modern times to have earned his living almost exclusively by the illustration of books, and is among the earliest to have his name featured on title pages as an attraction to the purchaser." [1] Among his books for children were *A New Invented Horn Book* (1770); *New Year's Gift for Little Masters and Misses* (1777); *The Mirror, or A Looking Glass for Young People* (1778); and *The Life and Adventures of a Fly* (1789).

When Bewick died in 1828, George Cruikshank, a second master of line and the craft of the wood block, was twenty-four years old. Cruikshank made his first engraving and received pay for it at the age of twelve. An early illustrator of Dickens's books, he achieved success with his nimble gift for caricature and the delineation of action. The outstanding assignment of the day in

[1] Percy Muir, *English Children's Books, 1600 to 1900* (Batsford, London, 1954), p. 173.

the realm of books for children was that of illustrating the first English translation, by Edgar Taylor, of Grimm's *German Popular Tales* (1823 and 1826). These illustrations, by Cruikshank, are well-nigh definitive and are excellent examples, even today, of the extension of the mood of the text in pictorial form. Mrs. Ewing's *The Brownies* (1871) and *Lob-Lie-by-the-Fire* were also enriched by Cruikshank's humor and wit.

Even the most casual perusal of pictures and illustrations cannot but disclose the fact that the medium by which the artist's image is transferred to the page determines the character and form of the resulting illustration. The complicated story of the various methods of reproducing pictures cannot be treated at length in this space. It is a highly technical subject, but even an awareness of its existence contributes to one's enjoyment

of pictures, to one's ability to recognize quality, and to an understanding of the artist's craft as well as of his inspiration. All who would delve more deeply into the subject are indebted to Bertha Mahony Miller, as the Horn Book publisher, for two volumes on *Illustrators of Children's Books* (1947 and 1958). Helen Gentry's article in Volume I, "Graphic Processes in Children's Books," is a notably clear explanation of the basic procedures. A good, simple explanation of modern techniques is given in *Pages, Pictures and Print,* by Joanne Foster (Harcourt, Brace, 1958), a book written for children.

The line drawing, as rendered in woodblock engraving, as we have seen, is by its very nature adapted to the printed page. In the hands of master draughtsmen and engravers, the result is close to perfection. Sir John Tenniel's illustrations for *Alice*

GEORGE CRUIKSHANK. "Rumpelstiltskin," from Grimm's *Popular Stories* (1823). The cartoonist's flair for caricature coupled with control of a sharp and delicate line enabled Cruikshank to depict amusing detail, and emotion as well.

SIR JOHN TENNIEL. From *Alice's Adventures in Wonderland,* by Lewis
Carroll (1865). This picture bears a famous engraver's name in the lower
right-hand corner, Dalziel. Tenniel lived before the invention of photographic
processes and was therefore dependent upon an engraver skilled enough to
transfer accurately the artist's creation to the printing surface.

in Wonderland (1865) and *Through the
Looking-Glass* (1871), for example, represent
the highest art of illustration. Let us study
them in relation to three criteria which Frank
Weitenkampf presents in *The Illustrated
Book* (Harvard University Press, 1938).

First, "How good are the pictures in drawing and composition?" In other words, do
they hold to the tenets of art in their own
right, as well as meet the obligations of illustration? Tenniel's drawing is sheer wiz-
ardry, his line sharp, delicate, and definitive.
How else could he have created the indis-
putable characters of the Mad Hatter, the
Mock Turtle, the Ugly Duchess, and all the
rest? As for composition, notice in *Through
the Looking-Glass* the balanced landscape
in the illustration for " 'Twas brillig, and
the slithy toves/Did gyre and gimble in the
wabe." An unearthly scene it is, and yet
quite like a sensible garden, with the classic
column of the sundial a focal point for all
the animals that never were on sea or land,
its strong perpendicular echoed and reaf-
firmed in the spindly legs of the bird to the
right. Or note, in *Alice,* the recurring angle
V in the agitated kitchen of the Duchess,

with the squalling baby on her angular lap
and the smile of the cat tuned to the same
sharpness.

Second, "Do the pictures *illustrate* or *accompany* or *comment on* or *decorate* the text
sympathetically and with understanding?"
asks Dr. Weitenkampf. Tenniel's drawings
illustrate, and most sympathetically; indeed,
they seem to be part of the author's original
concept, made actual by an act of genius.
Yet Tenniel and Dodgson worked together
in anger and anguish as well as in sympathy,
to judge from all accounts.

Third, and finally, "Do they [the illustra-
tions] go well with the type and the book
generally?" Like glove to hand! The formats of the *Alice* books are timeless.

Twenty years before Tenniel's pictures for
Alice, Edward Lear had set a high example
of good illustration in his own *Nonsense
Book* (1846), with line drawings as sharp,
pungent, and absurdly memorable as the
verse which accompanied them. A study of
Lear's line conditions the beholder to enjoy subsequent mastery of line.

The wood-block line process had its rivals
during the nineteenth century. The engrav-

EDWARD LEAR.   "There was an old man in a tree," from *Nonsense Book,*
written and illustrated by Lear (1846). Lear's mastery of line, combined
with his genius for humor and nonsense, has proved more lasting than
the water colors and oils for which he was famous in his day.

ing of pictures on copper or steel plates persisted over three quarters of the century.
Engravings in this manner permitted an
elaboration of detail which sometimes resulted in overstatement and a florid, sentimental presentation, though these were essentially faults of taste rather than of process. One of the most unusual and beautiful
books of all time had been engraved on cop-

per, William Blake's *Songs of Innocence*
(1789). Blake wrote his poems upon the
plate, drew decorative borders with images
and scenes, printed the pages by hand, and
then hand-colored them. Anne Eaton, in
Illustrators of Children's Books (Horn Book,
1947), tells the story of that creation, with
rare appreciation of the magnitude of the accomplishment.

WALTER CRANE. From Grimm's *Household Stories,* illustrated by
Walter Crane (1882). This decorative tailpiece for "The Bremen Town
Musicians" shows Crane's absorption in design. Complicated, crowded
with action and objects, it holds to the unity of the encircling horn.

RANDOLPH CALDECOTT. "A frog he would a-wooing go," from *Randolph Caldecott's Picture Book No. 3*. The maxim of Caldecott was: "The fewer the lines, the less error committed." The resulting discipline made him a master of action, pace, and mood.

The advent of photography revolutionized the methods of reproducing pictures and all but wiped out the engraver's art, since pictures could be transferred by photographic means onto the metal plates, or printing surfaces, and need not be translated (cut, engraved, or etched) by the highly skilled hand and eye.

The most memorable body of illustrated books for children in the latter half of the nineteenth century came from the printing presses of Edmund Evans, the gifted printer whose development of improved methods in color printing enabled him to produce the books of Randolph Caldecott (1846–1886), Walter Crane (1845–1915), and Kate Greenaway (1846–1901). The remarkable accomplishments of this trio of artists are dis-

KATE GREENAWAY. From *Around the House*, an anthology of poems and stories, illustrated by Kate Greenaway (1888). Here is a typical Greenaway procession, flowers, children, baskets, and bouquets, with its delicacy of line, its rhythmic grouping of the figures, its poetic charm.

cussed in detail elsewhere in this volume.[2] Significantly, these three, working in close cooperation with Evans, gained from him a thorough understanding of the processes by which their work was reproduced, and the felicity of their illustrated books is in no small measure due to their intelligent use of this knowledge.

The twentieth century was ushered in, pictorially, with a rush of picture books. In England, L. Leslie Brooke (1862–1940) followed in the footsteps of Caldecott, with his sure and distinctive line, his delicate color, his humor, and his heightening of such tales as *The Three Bears* and *The Three Little Pigs* and, his own invention, *Johnny Crow.* Arthur Rackham (1867–1939) headed a list of distinguished illustrators: Francis Bedford, Louis Rhead, Charles Hughes. Rackham's work was highly indi-

[2] See pages 68–70.

vidual, however, with its masterly line and its eerie, subdued, and fairy-haunted color. His illustrations of many of the classics of childhood linger in the memory when other illustrations are forgotten.

In the United States, Felix Darley (1822–1888) had given Irving's *Rip Van Winkle* an added dimension by the quality of his exquisitely clear, exact line, and with Thomas Nast, the political cartoonist, had illustrated an early edition of *Hans Brinker.* And fifteen years after the initial appearance of the Uncle Remus stories, A. B. Frost made his unsurpassed illustrations for these tales by Joel Chandler Harris; here again was the perfect matching of text to picture and picture to text.

The prime influence on illustration in America was Howard Pyle. A superb draughtsman, he was a master of line — of color, too, but he was partial to the clean and

L. LESLIE BROOKE. Tailpiece for "The Three Bears," from *The Golden Goose Book,* illustrated by L. Leslie Brooke. This picture is probably engraved in the memories of at least four generations of men and women: the youngest of the Three Bears, wearing Goldilocks' hat. Triumph, mischief, and the mimic's delight in his own arrogance — all are contained in so few lines they can almost be counted.

ARTHUR RACKHAM.   From *English Fairy Tales Retold,* by Flora Annie
Steel, illustrated by Arthur Rackham. This artist was master of color
as well as of line, the tone usually muted, misty with a sense of the
eerie in it. His line is creased, wrinkled, yet minute. It conveys the
supernatural with good effect.

A. B. FROST. "Brer Fox and the Tar-Baby" from one of the *Uncle
Remus* books by Joel Chandler Harris. "The book was mine, but now
you have made it yours, both sap and pith." In these words the author
of Uncle Remus acclaimed the illustrator who gave the book its
definitive illustration fifteen years after its appearance. Frost made every
line count. His art is evocative as well as exact.

HOWARD PYLE. From *The Wonder Clock,* written and illustrated by
Howard Pyle (1888). The clear, direct line of Pyle has an emotional
overtone of light and space. A master of color, he seemed to prefer
the strength and simplicity of black on white.

lyric line of the pen-and-ink drawing, reminiscent of the prints by Albrecht Dürer,
the German wood-block artist of the sixteenth century. Howard Pyle steeped himself in the Middle Ages, writing tales of
chivalry — of King Arthur and Robin Hood
— and illustrating them with such exactitude
that they have made the history of the
period, as well as the literature, a reality for
generations of children. He understood the
function of illustration, and assumed the
obligation to add to the text of the author,
never merely repeating what had already
been stated in words. As a teacher, he put
his mark on future generations of artists.

N. C. Wyeth, Maxfield Parrish, Jessie Willcox
Smith, Frank Schoonover — these were some
of Howard Pyle's students at Chadds Ford,
Delaware. He was responsible for a new
vigor, dignity, and sincerity in illustration.
Integrity was an outstanding attribute of his
character, and it shone forth in every picture
he drew.

When N. C. Wyeth and Maxfield Parrish
came to the years of their greatest produc-
tivity, the fashion in book-making was to
create handsome volumes, with pictures in
color tipped (or glued) into the already
printed book. Wyeth's appeal lay in his brilliant color, his action, his sense of drama,

E. H. Shepard.   An illustration from *When We Were Very Young*, by A. A. Milne (1924). Shepard's illustrations for Milne's books are definitive and perfect accompaniment for the wit, invention, and convincing make-believe of the author's creations.

Wanda Gág.   From *Millions of Cats* (1928). This book, a classic of our time, well-nigh reaches perfection in concept, illustration, and format. The embracing warmth of the circular rhythm, which is characteristic of this artist, is apparent even in this small drawing.

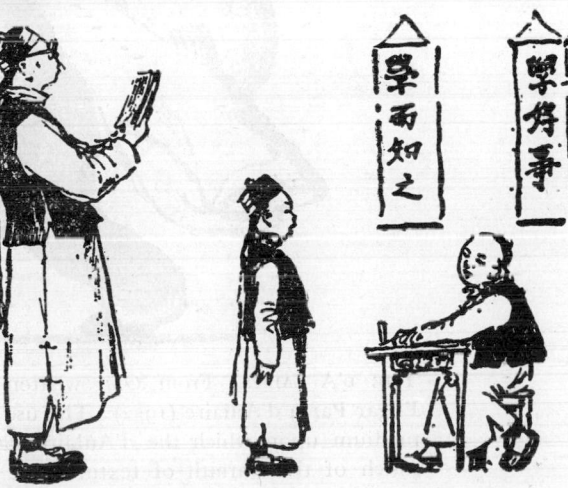

Kurt Wiese.   From *The Chinese Ink Stick* (1929). This artist manages to catch the essence of whatever text he illustrates —here, his own. His line is sensitive, capable of flexibility, and quick to emphasize the humorous and the robust.

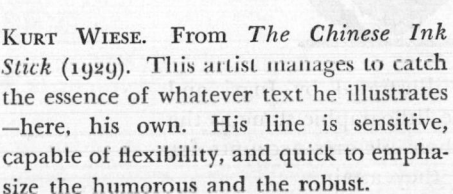

and in the aura of high adventure and romance that suffused his pictures. Parrish, too, was a great colorist and a romanticist. Such illustrations as theirs were really paintings, rather than illustrations, and because they were printed on glossy paper and applied to the book, there was always a breach between text and illustration, accented by the blank, white page on the back of the illustration.

After World War I, a stream of artists from Europe brought new techniques and new ways of illustration to this country. There were Boris Artzybasheff from Russia; Ingri and Edgar d'Aulaire from Switzerland and Norway; Maud and Miska Petersham and Kate Seredy from Hungary; Fritz Eichenberg from Germany, reiterating the strength of the wood block and the print; and Wanda Gág, American-born, but close to her Bohemian heritage. The d'Aulaires, working on lithographic stones, introduced a whole series of brilliantly conceived and executed picture books and picture-story books. The Petershams brought color and folk designs to their illustration, and Artzybasheff was to set new flags on the peaks of book design.

THE PETERSHAMS. From *Poppy Seed Cakes*, by Margery Clark, illustrated by Maud and Miska Petersham (1924). With the publication of this book, a new awareness of European backgrounds became a dominant feature in children's books. Fresh color and the gaiety of peasant art inform the story.

THE D'AULAIRES. From *Ola*, written and illustrated by Ingri and Edgar Parin d'Aulaire (1932). The use of the lithographic stone as the medium upon which the d'Aulaires draw their pictures accounts for much of the warmth of texture and color they attain.

BORIS ARTZYBASHEFF. From *The Fairy Shoe-maker* (1928). A distinctive style, a strong sense of design, and a fresh imagination brought Artzybasheff to the fore among the illustrators of the twenties and thirties.

FRITZ EICHENBERG. From *Padre Porko,* by Robert Davis (1939). A contemporary master of the woodblock, Eichenberg shows in this drawing his delight in and control of line. Note how successfully he portrays character: joviality, authority, and compassion — all conjured up in this portrait of a pig.

KATE SEREDY. From *Caddie Woodlawn,* by Carol Ryrie Brink (1935).
Kate Seredy attains, in her illustrations, a realism that is tinged with
a quality of the idealized and the romantic.

MARJORIE FLACK. From *Angus and the Ducks* (1930). Marjorie Flack is a realist
in illustration, with an expressive line and masterly powers of delineation.

HELEN SEWELL. End-paper drawing for *A First Bible,* selected by
J. W. Maury and illustrated by Helen Sewell (1934). Few illustrators
equal Helen Sewell in ability to absorb the intent of the text and to
restate it, pictorially, in her own style, yet in a medium completely
appropriate to the subject.

The thirties were years of inventive and imaginative illustration and book design. Publishers vied with one another to make books which were individual units of design, with illustration, type, and format combined in living symmetry. Artzybasheff's *Seven Simeons* (Viking, 1937), with its wandering, delicate pictures weaving in and out of the pages and the text, remains as beautiful, as timeless now as it was when it was published. Thomas Handforth's *Mei Li* (Doubleday, 1938) is another book harmonious in every detail of its creation.

The individuality of the illustrator's style was given full scope: for example, Eliza-beth MacKinstry's reed-pen technique (learned through an apprenticeship under Claude Lovat Fraser), and William Nicholson's colored wood blocks. Helen Sewell displayed a remarkable ability to wield her style in changing patterns and modes appropriate to subject matter: her classic illustrations for the *First Bible* (Oxford, 1934), done in the manner of Victorian steel engravings; her stylized, modern decorative illustrations for Bulfinch's *Books of Myths* (Macmillan, 1942); and her illustrations for Eleanor Farjeon's *Ten Saints* (Oxford, 1936) after the mode of the early woodcuts, with their look of having been colored by hand.

ROBERT LAWSON.   From *Adam of the Road,* by Elizabeth Janet Gray (1942).
Gifted writer as well as illustrator, Lawson has been influenced by the same
discipline as was Howard Pyle. The result is a clear-cut line, strength, and a
flair for details that document place, time, and characterization.

VALENTI ANGELO. From *Roller
Skates,* by Ruth Sawyer (1936). For
this artist, the decorative element in
illustration takes precedence over
other attributes. His outline drawings are simple, poetic, and almost
symbolically representative of the
character of the story.

If illustration was dimmed in the decade of the forties, as a result of World War II, the fifties show signs of an exhilarating upsurge. Publishers are embarking upon new schemes of using color, and the use of multicolored papers serves as a fresh source of color. The artists of the period are in a lively mood of experimentation: Antonio Frasconi, with his brilliant use of colored wood blocks, fitted to a modern idiom; Marcia Brown, with her changing and growing variety of styles; William Pène du Bois, with his stunningly effective merging of line and color, as in *Lion* (Viking, 1956); André François, a student of Picasso, with his multiple design, his dissected action, and his sure control of line. New effects are being achieved through the concept of a page as being without boundaries or perspective and horizons; the use of symbolic shapes and geometric structures in place of the slick realism redolent of advertising art; the evocation of joy and action and freedom by the bold use of design and the unaccustomed juxtaposition of objects. The recognition of children's books by the American Institute of Graphic Arts has also had a considerable effect on illustration. The A.I.G.A.'s periodic exhibitions of children's books have been routed around the country, and a new and growing audience has been made aware of excellence in design, of which illustration is a part.

There is much to decry in present-day standards of taste in this country of ours, but among the illustrators and publishers of children's books the yeast of genuine imagination is at work. Surely the public will respond to this creativity and thereby insure for new generations of children the opportunity to relish the work of choice minds in the great tradition of book illustration.

VIRGINIA LEE BURTON. From *The Song of Robin Hood* (1947). Virginia Lee Burton has been a designer of textiles, a water-colorist, and the author-artist of picture books. Here, in illustrations for a book she designed throughout, she shows her mastery of the woodcut effect.

JEAN CHARLOT. From *Two Little Trains*, by Margaret Wise Brown
(1949). The contrast of heavy outline combined with thin and delicate
lines, a gift for universal symbolism (so that, here, no specific train is
drawn, but the essence of all trains), and a closeness to the child's
vision — these elements are richly combined in the drawings of Charlot.

BIBLIOGRAPHY

The Art of Beatrix Potter. With an appreciation
by Anne Carroll Moore. Frederick Warne,
1955.

Bechtel, Louise Seaman. "Helen Sewell," *The
Horn Book Magazine*, Vol. 33, Oct. 1957,
pp. 368–389.

The L. Leslie Brooke Number. *The Horn Book
Magazine*, Vol. 17, May-June 1941.

Crane, Walter. *An Artist's Reminiscences*.
Methuen (London), 1907.

Davis, Mary Gould. *Randolph Caldecott, 1846–
1886; An Appreciation*. Illus. with reproductions of Randolph Caldecott's drawings. J. B.
Lippincott, 1946.

Eaton, Anne Thaxter. *Reading with Children*.
Viking Press, 1940.

"Artists at Work for Children," pp. 281–310.

Ehrlich, Bettina. "Story and Picture in Children's
Books," *The Horn Book Magazine*, Vol. 28,
Oct. 1952, pp. 301–308.

Mahony, Bertha E., and others. *Illustrators of
Children's Books, 1744–1945*. The Horn Book,
Inc., 1947.

Meigs, Cornelia, and others. *A Critical History
of Children's Books*. Macmillan, 1953.

"The Artist as Storyteller," pp. 582–590.

Miller, Bertha Mahony, and Elinor Whitney
Field. *Caldecott Medal Books, 1938–1956*. The
Horn Book, Inc., 1957.

Miller, Bertha Mahony, and others. *Illustrators
of Children's Books, 1946–1956*. The Horn
Book, Inc., 1958.

Moore, Anne Carroll. *A Century of Kate Greenaway; a pamphlet*. Frederick Warne, 1946.

Moore, Anne Carroll. *The Three Owls*. Macmillan, 1925.

"Kate Greenaway and Randolph Caldecott," pp.
173–182.

Oakley, Thornton. "Howard Pyle," *The Horn
Book Magazine*, Vol. 7, May 1931, pp. 91–97.

Pitz, Henry C. *A Treasury of American Book
Illustration*. American Studio Books, 1947.

Smith, Janet Adam. *Children's Illustrated Books*.
Collins (London), 1948.

Smith, Lillian. *The Unreluctant Years*. American
Library Association, 1953.

"Picture Books," pp. 114–130.

Spielmann, M. H., and G. S. Layard. *Kate
Greenaway*. A. & C. Black, 1905.

Ward, Lynd. "The Book Artist and the Twenty-
Five Years," *The Horn Book Magazine*, Vol.
25, Sept.-Oct. 1949, pp. 375–381.

James Daugherty. From *Of Courage Undaunted*
(1951). An accomplished mural painter, Daugherty
often brings over to his book illustrations something of
the grandeur and sweep of the mural style. It well
suits his preoccupation with heroic themes.

Antonio Frasconi. *From See and Say* (1955). A new departure in book design. Here the colored woodcut, in the hands of an original and skilled craftsman-artist, brings multiple objects and four languages together in harmonious pages.

Reiner Zimnik. From *Jonah, the Fisherman* (1956). An exciting adventure in line. Exotic scenes and varied patterns are achieved by the use of a seemingly simple black line on the spacious pages of a highly original picture book.

Garth Williams. From *Little House in the Big Woods*, by Laura Ingalls Wilder (1953 edition). Documentary exactness of period, costume, and utensils is added to the emotional quality which the illustrator successfully evokes.

Thomas Handforth. From *Mei Li* (1938), a milestone in American picture books, with its heightened sense of space, the texture of its drawing, and the inward feeling of the life it portrays.

Georges Schreiber. From *Pancakes-Paris*, by Claire Huchet Bishop (1947). Wash drawings in a muted monotone, sharpened by an accent of line, effectively extend the book's mood and catch the forlorn atmosphere of wartime Paris.

Mario Ets. From *Play with Me* (1955). A distinctive style, strong in its simplicity and charm, is typical of this artist. The child here, with her straight hair and enchanting, plain face, is a fine antidote to the cute, the cuddly, and the coy in illustration.

Hardie Gramatky. From *Little Toot* (1939). The author-artist's gift for animation and drama has made *Little Toot* a classic of childhood.

Françoise. From *Noël for Jeanne-Marie* (1953). The flat surface, the broad outlines, and the clear color characteristic of this artist show her to be close to the naiveté of childhood.

André François. From *Little Boy Brown*, by Isobel Harris (1949). With this book a noted French artist, a student of Picasso, enters the ranks of picture-book makers in America. For all its intricacy of line, the illustration looks as though drawn with one sweep of the pen.

Marcia Brown. From *Dick Whittington* (1950). The rugged, thick line of the linoleum cut is especially suited to a tale which first appeared in chapbook form with crude wood-block illustrations.

The Newbery and Caldecott Awards

JOHN NEWBERY, the famous eighteenth-century bookseller of St. Paul's Churchyard, London, rendered a great service to his age and generation by encouraging the best authors of the day to write for children. It is fitting, therefore, that the name "Newbery," whose owner was the first to recognize that children were a reading public worthy of a publisher, is attached to the medal which since 1922 has been awarded annually to the author of the "most distinguished contribution to American literature for children, published during the preceding year." The donor of this medal is Mr. Frederic Melcher, editor of *Publishers' Weekly*.

During the meeting of the American Library Association held at Swampscott, Massachusetts, in 1921, the idea of presenting the medal took form. In an article published in *The Saturday Review of Literature*, Mr. Melcher says: "I had been asked to give a talk at the Section for Library Work with Children about Children's Book Week, then a new idea but now the oldest of all 'weeks' and still the most useful. I remember looking down from the platform at all those enthusiastic people from every part of the Union and wondering whether they could not, as a group, take one more job, by helping to assure a greater literature for children as well as a wider reading of the then available literature. . . . These people knew the audiences of boys and girls, knew them intimately, knew what boys and girls really wanted. They could help build a greater literature by giving authoritative recognition to those who wrote well. I conceived the plan of an annual award and offered it on the spot with the suggestion that good old John Newbery's name be attached to the medal." Such was the inception of the Newbery award.

The terms of the award are as follows: "The author shall be a citizen or a resident of the United States. Someone living here temporarily is not eligible. His contribution shall be an original and creative piece of work. It shall be the 'most distinguished contribution to American literature for children,' original in conception, fine in workmanship and artistically true. Reprints and compilations are not eligible for consideration. The book need not be written solely for children. The judgment of the voting librarians shall decide whether a book is a 'contribution to the literature for children.' The Committee of Award considers only the books of one calendar year, and does not pass judgment on an author's previous work or other work during that year outside the volume that may be named." The medal is designed by René Paul Chambellan and is cast in bronze.

Again, it was at the suggestion of Mr. Melcher that the Randolph Caldecott award was established in 1937. The Caldecott medal, donated by Mr. Melcher and named in honor of the great English illustrator of children's books, is also designed by René Paul Chambellan and cast in bronze. It is awarded to the illustrator of the most distinguished picture book for children published in the United States during the preceding year. A picture book within the purpose of this award should be the creation of the artist, the product of his initiative and imagination. The text of the volume need not be written by the artist, but must be worthy of the book. It is possible to award the Caldecott medal to artists who work together: e.g., the D'Aulaires, the Haders, the Petershams.

Both awards are now made by a special Newbery-Caldecott awards committee of twenty-three members, consisting of children's and school librarians of the American Library Association. Announcement of the winners of both the Newbery and Caldecott medals is made early in the spring at an informal meeting held in Mr. Melcher's New York office. At that time Mr. Melcher presents the medals to the Children's Services Division (formerly known as the Section of Library Work with Children and later as the Children's Library Section) of the American Library Association. They are accepted in behalf of the division by the chairman of the Newbery-Caldecott awards committee. The formal presentation of the medals to the winners is made at a dinner meeting of the Children's Services Division during the annual conference of the American Library Association, usually held in June.

The Newbery Awards

(to date)

1922   Hendrik Willem Van Loon. *The Story of Mankind;* illus. by the author. Liveright.

1923   Hugh Lofting. *The Voyages of Doctor Dolittle;* illus. by the author. Frederick A. Stokes.

1924   Charles Boardman Hawes. *The Dark Frigate.* Little, Brown.

1925   Charles Joseph Finger. *Tales from Silver Lands;* illus. by Paul Honoré. Doubleday, Doran.

1926   Arthur Bowie Chrisman. *Shen of the Sea;* illus. by Else Hasselriis. E. P. Dutton.

1927   Will James. *Smoky, the Cowhorse;* illus. by the author. Charles Scribner's Sons.

1928   Dhan Gopal Mukerji. *Gay-Neck;* illus. by Boris Artzybasheff. E. P. Dutton.

1929   Eric P. Kelly. *Trumpeter of Krakow;* illus. by Angela Pruszynska. Macmillan.

1930   Rachel Lyman Field. *Hitty, Her First Hundred Years;* illus. by Dorothy P. Lathrop. Macmillan.

1931   Elizabeth Coatsworth. *The Cat Who Went to Heaven;* illus. by Lynd Ward. Macmillan.

1932   Laura Adams Armer. *Waterless Mountain;* illus. by Sidney Armer and the author. Longmans, Green.

1933   Elizabeth Foreman Lewis. *Young Fu of The Upper Yangtze;* illus. by Kurt Wiese. John C. Winston.

1934   Cornelia Lynde Meigs. *Story of the Author of "Little Women": Invincible Louisa.* Little, Brown.

1935   Monica Shannon. *Dobry;* illus. by Atanas Katchamakoff. Viking Press.

1936   Carol Ryrie Brink. *Caddie Woodlawn;* illus. by Kate Seredy. Macmillan.

1937   Ruth Sawyer. *Roller Skates;* illus. by Valenti Angelo. Viking Press.

1938   Kate Seredy. *The White Stag;* illus. by the author. Viking Press.

1939   Elizabeth Enright. *Thimble Summer;* illus. by the author. Farrar and Rinehart.

1940   James Daugherty. *Daniel Boone;* illus. by the author. Viking Press.

1941   Armstrong Sperry. *Call It Courage;* illus. by the author. Macmillan.

1942   Walter Dumaux Edmonds. *The Matchlock Gun;* illus. by Paul Lantz. Dodd, Mead.

1943   Elizabeth Janet Gray. *Adam of the Road;* illus. by Robert Lawson. Viking Press.

1944   Esther Forbes. *Johnny Tremain;* illus. by Lynd Ward. Houghton Mifflin.

1945   Robert Lawson. *Rabbit Hill;* illus. by the author. Viking Press.

1946   Lois Lenski. *Strawberry Girl;* illus. by the author. Lippincott-Stokes.

1947   Carolyn Sherwin Bailey. *Miss Hickory;* illus. by Ruth Gannett. Viking Press.

1948   William Pène du Bois. *The Twenty-One Balloons;* illus. by the author. Viking Press.

1949   Marguerite Henry. *King of the Wind;* illus. by Wesley Dennis. Rand McNally.

1950   Marguerite de Angeli. *The Door in the Wall;* illus. by the author. Doubleday.

1951   Elizabeth Yates. *Amos Fortune, Free Man;* illus. by Nora S. Unwin. Aladdin Books.

1952   Eleanor Estes. *Ginger Pye;* illus. by the author. Harcourt, Brace.

1953   Ann Nolan Clark. *Secret of the Andes;* illus. by Jean Charlot. Viking Press.

1954   Joseph Krumgold. *And Now Miguel;* illus. by Jean Charlot. Thomas Y. Crowell.

1955   Meindert DeJong. *The Wheel on the School;* illus. by Maurice Sendak. Harper.

1956   Jean Lee Latham. *Carry On, Mr. Bowditch;* illus. by John O'Hara Cosgrave II. Houghton Mifflin.

1957   Virginia Sorenson. *Miracles on Maple Hill;* illus. by Beth and Joe Krush. Harcourt, Brace.

1958   Harold Keith. *Rifles for Watie;* illus. by Peter Burchard. Thomas Y. Crowell.

1959 Elizabeth George Speare. *The Witch of Blackbird Pond.* Houghton Mifflin.

1960 Joseph Krumgold. *Onion John;* illus. by Symeon Shimin. Thomas Y. Crowell.

1961 Scott O'Dell. *Island of the Blue Dolphins.* Houghton Mifflin.

1962 Elizabeth George Speare. *The Bronze Bow.* Houghton Mifflin.

1963 Madeleine L'Engle. *A Wrinkle in Time.* Farrar, Straus.

1964 Emily Neville. *It's Like This, Cat;* illus. by Emil Weiss. Harper and Row.

1965 Maia Wojciechowska. *Shadow of a Bull;* illus. by Alvin Smith. Atheneum.

The Caldecott Awards

(to date)

1938 Dorothy Lathrop. *Animals of the Bible;* with text selected by Helen Dean Fish from the King James Bible. Frederick A. Stokes.

1939 Thomas Handforth. *Mei Li;* illus. by the author. Doubleday.

1940 Ingri and Edgar Parin d'Aulaire. *Abraham Lincoln;* illus. by the authors. Doubleday.

1941 Robert Lawson. *They Were Strong and Good;* illus. by the author. Viking Press.

1942 Robert McCloskey. *Make Way for Ducklings;* illus. by the author. Viking Press.

1943 Virginia Lee Burton. *The Little House;* illus. by the author. Houghton Mifflin.

1944 Louis Slobodkin. *Many Moons;* written by James Thurber. Harcourt, Brace.

1945 Elizabeth Orton Jones. *A Prayer for a Child;* written by Rachel Lyman Field. Macmillan.

1946 Maud and Miska Petersham. *The Rooster Crows; a Book of American Rhymes and Jingles;* illus. by the compilers. Macmillan.

1947 Leonard Weisgard. *The Little Island;* written by Golden MacDonald [pseud.]. Doubleday.

1948 Roger Duvoisin. *White Snow, Bright Snow;* written by Alvin Tresselt. Lothrop.

1949 Berta and Elmer Hader. *The Big Snow;* illus. by the authors. Macmillan.

1950 Leo Politi. *Song of the Swallows;* illus. by the author. Charles Scribner's Sons.

1951 Katherine Milhous. *The Egg Tree;* illus. by the author. Charles Scribner's Sons.

1952 Nicolas Mordvinoff. *Finders Keepers;* written by Will and Nicolas [Will Lipkind and Nicolas Mordvinoff]. Harcourt, Brace.

1953 Lynd Ward. *The Biggest Bear;* illus. by the author. Houghton Mifflin.

1954 Ludwig Bemelmans. *Madeline's Rescue;* illus. by the author. Viking Press.

1955 Marcia Brown. *Cinderella;* written by Charles Perrault, trans. and illus. by Marcia Brown. Charles Scribner's Sons.

1956 Feodor Rojankovsky. *Frog Went a-Courtin';* written by John Langstaff. Harcourt, Brace.

1957 Marc Simont. *A Tree Is Nice;* written by Janice Udry. Harper.

1958 Robert McCloskey. *Time of Wonder;* illus. by the author. Viking Press.

1959 Barbara Cooney. *Chanticleer and the Fox;* adapted from the *Canterbury Tales* of Chaucer. Thomas Y. Crowell.

1960 Marie Hall Ets and Aurora Labastida. *Nine Days to Christmas;* illus. by Marie Hall Ets. Viking Press.

1961 Nicolas Sidjakov. *Baboushka and the Three Kings;* written by Ruth Robbins. Parnassus Press.

1962 Marcia Brown. *Once a Mouse . . . ;* a fable cut in wood. Charles Scribner's Sons.

1963 Ezra Jack Keats. *The Snowy Day;* illus. by the author. Viking Press.

1964 Maurice Sendak. *Where the Wild Things Are;* illus. by the author. Harper and Row.

1965 Beni Montresor. *May I Bring a Friend;* written by Beatrice Schenk de Regniers. Atheneum.

APPENDIX F

Graded Reading List

KINDERGARTEN AND GRADES 1 AND 2

(to 8 years of age)

PICTURE BOOKS AND STORIES

Unless otherwise stated, books listed below are both written and illustrated by the author-artist.

Andersen, Hans Christian. *The Steadfast Tin Soldier* trans. by M. R. James; illus. by Marcia Brown. Scribner, 1953. (Grades 1–4)

Anderson, Clarence. *Billy and Blaze.* Macmillan, 1936.

Ardizzone, Edward. *Little Tim and the Brave Sea Captain.* Oxford University Press, new ed. 1955.

Aulaire, Ingri and Edgar Parin d'. *Ola.* Doubleday, 1932. (Grades 1–4)

Bannerman, Helen. *The Story of Little Black Sambo.* Lippincott, 1923.

Bemelmans, Ludwig. *Madeline.* Simon & Schuster, 1939.

———— *Madeline's Rescue.* Viking Press, 1953.

———— *Parsley.* Harper, 1955.

Beskow, Elsa. *Pelle's New Suit.* Harper, n.d.

Bishop, Claire Huchet. *The Five Chinese Brothers;* illus. by Kurt Wiese. Coward-McCann, 1938.

Brooke, L. Leslie. *Golden Goose Book.* Frederick Warne, 1906.

———— *Johnny Crow's Garden.* Frederick Warne, 1904.

———— *Johnny Crow's New Garden.* Frederick Warne, 1935.

———— *Johnny Crow's Party.* Frederick Warne, 1907.

Brown, Marcia. *Dick Whittington and His Cat.* Scribner, 1950.

———— *Little Carousel.* Scribner, 1946.

———— *Stone Soup.* Scribner, 1947. (Grades 1–3)

Brown, Margaret Wise. *The Little Island,* by Golden MacDonald, *pseud.;* illus. by Leonard Weisgard. Doubleday, 1946. (Grades 1–3)

———— *Two Little Trains;* illus. by Jean Charlot. William R. Scott, 1949.

———— *Wheel on the Chimney;* illus. by Tibor Gergely. Lippincott, 1954.

Brunhoff, Jean de. *The Story of Babar, the Little Elephant;* trans. from the French by Merle S. Haas. Random House, 1933.

Burton, Virginia Lee. *Katy and the Big Snow.* Houghton Mifflin, 1943.

———— *The Little House.* Houghton Mifflin, 1942. (Grades 1–4)

———— *Mike Mulligan and His Steam Shovel.* Houghton Mifflin, 1939.

Caldecott, Randolph. *Picture Books.* 4 vols. Frederick Warne, 1878–85.

Charles, Robert. *Roundabout Turn;* illus. by L. Leslie Brooke. Frederick Warne, 1930.

Chönz, Selina. *A Bell for Ursli;* illus. by Alois Carigiet. Oxford University Press, 1950.

De Regniers, Beatrice. *A Little House of Your Own;* illus. by Irene Haas. Harcourt, Brace, 1954.

Eichenberg, Fritz. *Dancing in the Moon.* Harcourt, Brace, 1955.

Elkin, Benjamin. *Gillespie and the Guards;* illus. by James Daugherty. Viking Press, 1956.

Ets, Marie Hall. *In the Forest.* Viking Press, 1944.

———— *Mister Penny's Race Horse.* Viking Press, 1956.

———— *Play with Me.* Viking Press, 1955.

Fatio, Louise. *The Happy Lion;* illus. by Roger Duvoisin. Whittlesey House, 1954.

———— *The Happy Lion Roars;* illus. by Roger Duvoisin. Whittlesey House, 1957.

Fischer, Hans. *The Birthday.* Harcourt, Brace, 1954.

———— *Pitschi.* Harcourt, Brace, 1953.

Flack, Marjorie. *Angus and the Ducks.* Doubleday, 1930.

———— *Ask Mr. Bear.* Macmillan, 1932.

———— *Boats on the River;* illus. by Jay Hyde Barnum. Viking Press, 1946.

———— *The Story of Ping;* illus. by Kurt Wiese. Viking Press, 1933. (Grades 1–3)

Françoise, *pseud.* *Jeanne-Marie Counts Her Sheep.* Scribner, 1951.

———— *Jeanne-Marie in Gay Paris.* Scribner, 1956.

———— *Noël for Jeanne-Marie.* Scribner, 1953.

———— *Springtime for Jeanne-Marie.* Scribner, 1955.

Gág, Wanda. *A B C Bunny;* hand-lettered by Howard Gág. Coward-McCann, 1933.

—— *Millions of Cats.* Coward-McCann, 1928.

—— *Snippy and Snappy.* Coward-McCann, 1931.

Geisel, Theodor Seuss. *And to Think That I Saw It on Mulberry Street.* Vanguard Press, 1937.

—— *Cat in the Hat.* Random House, 1957.

—— *McElligot's Pool.* Random House, 1947.

Graham, Al. *Timothy Turtle;* illus. by Tony Palazzo. Viking Press, 1946.

Gramatky, Hardie. *Little Toot.* Putnam, 1939.

Greenaway, Kate. *A Apple Pie.* Frederick Warne, n.d.

Hader, Berta and Elmer. *The Big Snow.* Macmillan, 1948.

—— *Lost in the Zoo.* Macmillan, 1951.

Handforth, Thomas. *Mei Li.* Doubleday, 1938. (Grades 1–3)

Heyward, Du Bose. *Country Bunny and the Little Gold Shoes.* Houghton Mifflin, 1939.

Kahl, Virginia. *The Duchess Bakes a Cake.* Scribner, 1955.

—— *The Habits of Rabbits.* Scribner, 1957.

—— *Maxie.* Scribner, 1956.

—— *Plum Pudding for Christmas.* Scribner, 1956.

Langstaff, John. *Frog Went A-Courtin';* with pictures by Feodor Rojankovsky. Harcourt, Brace, 1955. (Grades 1–3)

—— *Over in the Meadow;* illus. by Feodor Rojankovsky. Harcourt, Brace, 1957. (Grades 1–3)

Leaf, Munro. *The Story of Ferdinand;* illus. by Robert Lawson. Viking Press, 1936. (Grades 1–4)

Lipkind, William. *Finders Keepers;* illus. by Nicolas Mordvinoff. Harcourt, Brace, 1951.

McCloskey, Robert. *Blueberries for Sal.* Viking Press, 1948.

—— *Make Way for Ducklings.* Viking Press, 1941.

—— *One Morning in Maine.* Viking Press, 1952.

—— *Time of Wonder.* Viking Press, 1957. (Grades 1–4)

McGinley, Phyllis. *All Around the Town;* illus. by Helen Stone. Lippincott, 1948.

Newberry, Clare. *Mittens.* Harper, 1936.

Perrault, Charles. *Cinderella; or the Little Glass Slipper:* A free translation from the French of Charles Perrault; with pictures by Marcia Brown. Scribner, 1954. (Grades 1–3)

Petersham, Maud and Miska. *The Box with the Red Wheels.* Macmillan, 1949.

—— *Circus Baby.* Macmillan, 1950.

Politi, Leo. *A Boat for Peppe.* Scribner, 1950.

—— *Juanita.* Scribner, 1948.

—— *Little Leo.* Scribner, 1951.

—— *The Song of the Swallows.* Scribner, 1949.

Potter, Beatrix. *The Tailor of Gloucester.* Frederick Warne, 1903. (K–Grade 4)

—— *The Tale of Benjamin Bunny.* Frederick Warne, 1904.

—— *The Tale of Peter Rabbit.* Frederick Warne, 1903.

Rey, H. A. *Curious George.* Houghton Mifflin, 1941.

—— *Curious George Rides a Bike.* Houghton Mifflin, 1952.

—— *Curious George Takes a Job.* Houghton Mifflin, 1947.

Ryder, Shirley. *Let's Pretend It's a Birthday;* illus. by Henrietta Bartlett. Lothrop, Lee & Shepard, 1958.

Sawyer, Ruth. *Journey Cake, Ho!;* illus. by Robert McCloskey. Viking Press, 1953.

Sayers, Frances Clarke. *Bluebonnets for Lucinda;* illus. by Helen Sewell. Viking Press, 1934. (Grades 1–3)

Titus, Eve. *Anatole;* illus. by Paul Galdone. Whittlesey House, 1956.

—— *Anatole and the Cat;* illus. by Paul Galdone. Whittlesey House, 1957.

Tresselt, Alvin. *White Snow, Bright Snow;* illus. by Roger Duvoisin. Lothrop, Lee & Shepard, 1947.

Tudor, Tasha. *A Is for Annabelle.* Oxford University Press, 1954.

Udry, Janice. *A Tree Is Nice;* illus. by Marc Simont. Harper, 1956.

Ward, Lynd. *The Biggest Bear.* Houghton Mifflin, 1952.

Yashima, Taro, pseud. *Crow Boy.* Viking Press, 1955.

—— *The Village Tree.* Viking, 1953.

POETRY

Aldis, Dorothy. *All Together; a Child's Treasury of Verse;* illus. by Helen D. Jameson, Marjorie Flack, and Margaret Freeman. G. P. Putnam's Sons, 1952. (Grades 2–4)

Association for Childhood Education. *Sung Under the Silver Umbrella; Poems for Young Children;* illus. by Dorothy Lathrop. Macmillan, 1935. (Grades 2–5)

Behn, Harry. *Little Hill.* Harcourt, Brace, 1949. (Grades 2–4)

—— *Windy Morning.* Harcourt, Brace, 1953. (Grades 2–4)

Brown, Helen, and Harry Heltman. *Let's-Read Together Poems.* Row, Peterson, 1949.

Geismer, Barbara, and Antoinette Suter, comps. *Very Young Verses;* illus. by Mildred Bronson. Houghton Mifflin, 1945.

Livingston, Myra Cohn. *Whispers and Other Poems;* illus. by Jacqueline Chwast. Harcourt, Brace, 1958. (Grades 1–4)

Milne, A. A. *Now We Are Six;* illus. by Ernest H. Shepard. Dutton, 1927.
———— *When We Were Very Young;* illus. by Ernest H. Shepard. Dutton, 1924.

Moore, Clement Clarke. *Night Before Christmas;* illus. by Arthur Rackham. Lippincott, 1931.

Stevenson, Robert Louis. *A Child's Garden of Verses;* illus. by Jessie Willcox Smith. Scribner, 1955. (Grades 1–4)

GRADES 3 AND 4

(8 to 10 years of age)

STORIES

Bemelmans, Ludwig. *Hansi;* illus. by the author. Viking Press, 1934.

Bettina. *Pantaloni;* illus. by the author. Harper, 1957.

Bianco, Margery. *Little Wooden Doll;* illus. by Pamela Bianco. Macmillan, 1925. (Little Library)
———— *The Velveteen Rabbit;* illus. by William Nicholson. Doubleday, 1926.

Bice, Clare. *A Dog for Davie's Hill;* illus. by the author. Macmillan, 1956. (Grades 4–6)

Bishop, Claire. *Pancakes-Paris;* illus. by Georges Schreiber. Viking Press, 1947. (Grades 4–6)

Bontemps, Arna. *Fast Sooner Hound;* illus. by Virginia Lee Burton. Houghton Mifflin, 1942.

Bothwell, Jean. *Little Boat Boy;* illus. by Margaret Ayer. Harcourt, Brace, 1945.
———— *River Boy of Kashmir;* illus. by Margaret Ayer. Morrow, 1946.

Buff, Mary and Conrad. *Apple and the Arrow.* Houghton Mifflin, 1951. (Grades 4–6)
———— *Dancing Cloud.* Viking Press, 1957.
———— *Hah-Nee of the Cliff Dwellers.* Houghton Mifflin, 1956.
———— *Magic Maize.* Houghton Mifflin, 1953. (Grades 4–6)

Cameron, Eleanor. *The Wonderful Flight to the Mushroom Planet;* illus. by Robert Henneberger. Little, Brown, 1954.

Carlson, Natalie S. *Wings Against the Wind;* illus. by Marcea Vasiliu. Harper, 1955.

Clark, Ann Nolan. *Blue Canyon Horse;* illus. by Allan Houser. Viking Press, 1954.
———— *Little Navajo Bluebird;* illus. by Paul Lantz. Viking Press, 1943. (Grades 4–6)
———— *Looking-for-Something;* illus. by Leo Politi. Viking Press, 1952.
———— *Magic Money;* illus. by Leo Politi. Viking Press, 1950. (Grades 4–6)

Clark, Margery, *pseud. Poppy Seed Cakes;* illus. by Maud and Miska Petersham. Doubleday, 1924.

Cleary, Beverly. *Ellen Tebbits;* illus. by Louis Darling. Morrow, 1951.
———— *Henry Huggins;* illus. by Louis Darling. Morrow, 1950.

———— *Henry and Ribsy;* illus. by Louis Darling. Morrow, 1954.

Coatsworth, Elizabeth. *Away Goes Sally;* illus. by Helen Sewell. Macmillan, 1934. (Grades 4–6)

Credle, Ellis. *Down, Down the Mountain;* illus. by the author. Thomas Nelson, 1934.

Dalgliesh, Alice. *Bears on Hemlock Mountain;* illus. by Helen Sewell. Scribner, 1952.
———— *The Courage of Sarah Noble;* illus. by Leonard Weisgard. Scribner, 1954.

Daugherty, James. *Andy and the Lion;* illus. by the author. Viking Press, 1938. (Grades 1–3)

Davis, Lavinia. *Roger and the Fox;* illus. by Hildegard Woodward. Doubleday, 1947.

De Angeli, Marguerite. *Yonie Wondernose;* illus. by the author. Doubleday, 1944.

Du Bois, William Pène. *The Great Geppy;* illus. by the author. Viking Press, 1940.

Emett, Rowland. *New World for Nellie;* illus. by the author. Harcourt, Brace, 1952.

Flora, James. *The Fabulous Firework Family.* Harcourt, Brace, 1955.

Frasconi, Antonio. *See and Say. Guarda e Parla. Regarde et Parle.* Harcourt, Brace, 1955.

Freeman, Don. *Fly High, Fly Low;* illus. by the author. Viking Press, 1957.

Freeman, Lydia. *Pet of the Met;* illus. by Don Freeman. Viking Press, 1953.

Gannett, Ruth Stiles. *My Father's Dragon;* illus. by Ruth Chrisman Gannett. Random House, 1948.

Godden, Rumer. *The Doll's House;* illus. by Dana Saintsbury. Viking Press, 1947.
———— *The Fairy Doll;* illus. by Adrienne Adams. Viking Press, 1956.
———— *Impunity Jane;* illus. by Adrienne Adams. Viking Press, 1954.
———— *Mouse House;* illus. by Adrienne Adams. Viking Press, 1957.
———— *The Mousewife;* illus. by William Pène Du Bois. Viking Press, 1951.

Grahame, Kenneth. *The Reluctant Dragon;* illus. by Ernest H. Shepard. Holiday House, 1953. (Grades 4–6)

Hader, Berta and Elmer. *Spunky;* illus. by the authors. Macmillan, 1933.

Hale, Lucretia. *The Peterkin Papers;* illus. by Harold M. Brett. Houghton Mifflin, 1924. (Riverside Bookshelf) (Grades 4–6)

Haywood, Carolyn. *"B" Is for Betsy;* illus. by the author. Harcourt, Brace, 1939.

—— *Betsy's Busy Summer;* illus. by the author. Morrow, 1956.

—— *Little Eddie;* illus. by the author. Morrow, 1947.

—— *Eddie and the Fire Engine;* illus. by the author. Morrow, 1949.

Hunt, Mabel Leigh. *Benjie's Hat;* illus. by Grace Paull. Lippincott, 1938.

—— *Little Girl with Seven Names;* illus. by Grace Paull. Lippincott, 1936.

—— *Miss Jellytot's Visit;* illus. by Velma Ilsley. Lippincott, 1955.

—— *Stars for Cristy;* illus. by Velma Ilsley. Lippincott, 1956. (Grades 4–6)

Lattimore, Eleanor. *Little Pear;* illus. by the author. Harcourt, Brace, 1931.

Leaf, Munro. *Wee Gillis;* illus. by Robert Lawson. Viking Press, 1938.

Lindquist, Jennie. *The Golden Name Day;* illus. by Garth Williams. Harper, 1955. (Grades 4–6)

Lipkind, William. *Boy of the Islands;* illus. by Nicolas Mordvinoff. Harcourt, Brace, 1954.

Liu, Beatrice. *Little Wu and the Watermelons;* illus. by Graham Peck. Follett, 1954.

McCloskey, Robert. *Lentil;* illus. by the author. Viking Press, 1940.

McGinley, Phyllis. *The Most Wonderful Doll in the World;* illus. by Helen Stone. Lippincott, 1950.

MacKellar, William. *Wee Joseph;* illus. by Ezra Jack Keats. McGraw-Hill, 1957. (Whittlesey House)

Mason, Miriam. *Caroline and Her Kettle Named Maud;* illus. by Kathleen Voute. Macmillan, 1951.

—— *Little Jonathan;* illus. by George and Doris Hauman. Macmillan, 1944.

Meigs, Cornelia. *The Willow Whistle;* illus. by E. Boyd Smith. Macmillan, 1931. (Grades 4–6)

—— *The Wonderful Locomotive;* illus. by Berta and Elmer Hader. Macmillan, 1928.

Milhous, Katherine. *Appolonia's Valentine;* illus. by the author. Scribner, 1954.

—— *The Egg Tree;* illus. by the author. Scribner, 1950.

Milne, A. A. *House at Pooh Corner;* illus. by Ernest H. Shepard. Dutton, 1928.

—— *Winnie-the-Pooh;* illus. by Ernest H. Shepard. Dutton, 1950.

Moore, Anne Carroll. *Nicholas;* illus. by Jay van Everen. Putnam, 1924.

Morrow, Elizabeth. *The Painted Pig; a Mexican Picture Book;* illus. by René d'Harnoncourt. Knopf, 1930.

Parish, Helen. *At the Palace Gates;* illus. by Leo Politi. Viking Press, 1949. (Grades 4–6)

Politi, Leo. *The Butterflies Come;* illus. by the author. Scribner, 1957.

—— *Pedro, the Angel of Olvera Street;* illus. by the author. Scribner, 1946.

Rawlings, Marjorie Kinnan. *The Secret River;* illus. by Leonard Weisgard. Scribner, 1955.

Rhoads, Dorothy. *Corn Grows Ripe;* illus. by Jean Charlot. Viking Press, 1956. (Grades 4–6)

Sayers, Frances Clarke. *Tag-Along Tooloo;* illus. by Helen Sewell. Viking Press, 1941.

Spyri, Johanna. *Heidi;* illus. by Agnes Tait. Lippincott, 1948. (Lippincott Classics) (Grades 4–6)

Stong, Phil. *Honk, the Moose;* illus. by Kurt Wiese. Dodd, Mead, 1935.

Tarry, Ellen. *My Dog Rinty;* illus. by Alexander and Alexandra Alland. Viking Press, 1946.

Tousey, Sanford. *Cowboy Tommy.* Doubleday, 1932.

Wilder, Laura Ingalls. *Farmer Boy;* illus. by Garth Williams. Harper, new ed. 1953. (Grades 4–6)

—— *Little House in the Big Woods;* illus. by Garth Williams. Harper, new ed. 1953. (Grades 3–6)

—— *Little House on the Prairie;* illus. by Garth Williams. Harper, new ed. 1953. (Grades 4–6)

—— *On the Banks of Plum Creek;* illus. by Garth Williams. Harper, new ed. 1953. (Grades 4–6)

FABLES, FOLK AND FAIRY TALES, FANCIFUL STORIES, AND MYTHS

Aesop. *Fables of Aesop;* illus. by Kurt Wiese. Macmillan, 1950. (New Children's Classics)

Andersen, Hans Christian. *The Emperor's New Clothes;* designed and illus. by Virginia Lee Burton. Houghton Mifflin, 1949.

—— *The Ugly Duckling;* trans. by R. P. Keigwin; illus. by Johannes Larsen. Macmillan, 1955.

Artzybasheff, Boris. *Seven Simeons; a Russian Tale;* retold and illus. by Boris Artzybasheff. Viking Press, 1937.

Asbjörnsen, Peter Christen, and Jörgen Moe. *Three Billy Goats Gruff;* illus. by Marcia Brown. Harcourt, Brace, 1957.

Association for Childhood Education. *Told Under the Green Umbrella; Old Stories for New Children;* illus. by Grace Gilkison. Macmillan, 1930.

Atwater, Richard and Florence. *Mr. Popper's Penguins;* illus. by Robert Lawson. Little, Brown, 1938. (Grades 4–6)

Barrie, Sir James Matthew. *Peter Pan;* illus. by Nora S. Unwin. Scribner, new ed. 1950. (Grades 4–6)

Belpré, Pura. *The Tiger and the Rabbit and Other Tales;* illus. by Kay Peterson Parker. Houghton Mifflin, 1946. (Grades 3–6)

Brenner, Anita. *The Boy Who Could Do Anything;* illus. by Jean Charlot. William R. Scott, 1942. (Grades 4–6)

Brown, Abbie Farwell. *In the Days of Giants.* Houghton Mifflin, 1902.

Brown, Marcia. *The Flying Carpet;* told from *The Arabian Nights;* illus. by the author. Scribner, 1956.

Browne, Frances. *Granny's Wonderful Chair;* illus. by Emma L. Brock. Macmillan, 1924. (Children's Classics) (Grades 4–6)

Carlson, Natalie Savage. *Alphonse, That Bearded One;* illus. by Nicolas Mordvinoff. Harcourt, Brace, 1954.

—— *Hortense, the Cow for a Queen;* illus. by Nicolas Mordvinoff. Harcourt, Brace, 1957.

Carroll, Lewis, *pseud. Alice's Adventures in Wonderland, and Through the Looking-Glass;* illus. by Sir John Tenniel. Macmillan, 1950. (New Children's Classics) (All ages)

Chan, Christina. *Magic Monkey;* adapted from an old Chinese legend by Plato and Christina Chan. McGraw-Hill, 1944. (Whittlesey House)

Chase, Richard. *Jack and the Three Sillies;* pictures by Joshua Tolford. Houghton Mifflin, 1950.

Collodi, Carlo, *pseud. Adventures of Pinocchio;* trans. from the Italian by Carol Della Chiesa; illus. by Attilio Mussino. Macmillan, 1951. (New Children's Classics) (Grades 4–6)

Courlander, Harold, and Albert Kof Prempeh. *The Hat-Shaking Dance and Other Tales from the Gold Coast;* illus. by Enrico Arno. Harcourt, Brace, 1956.

Craik, Dinah Marie Mulock. *Adventures of a Brownie;* illus. by Mary Lott Seaman. Macmillan, 1924. (New Little Library)

De la Mare, Walter. *Mr. Bumps and His Monkey;* illus. by Dorothy P. Lathrop. Winston, 1942. (Grades 4–6)

Dickens, Charles. *The Magic Fishbone;* illus. by Louis Slobodkin. Vanguard Press, 1953.

Dobbs, Rose, ed. *Once Upon a Time; Twenty Cheerful Tales to Read and Tell;* illus. by Flavia Gág. Random House, 1950.

Eager, Edward. *Half Magic;* illus. by N. M. Bodecker. Harcourt, Brace, 1954. (Grades 4–6)

—— *Magic by the Lake;* illus. by N. M. Bodecker. Harcourt, Brace, 1954. (Grades 4–6)

—— *The Time Garden;* illus. by N. M. Bodecker. Harcourt, Brace, 1958. (Grades 3–6)

Gibson, Katharine. *Jock's Castle;* illus. by Vera Bock. Longmans, Green, 1957.

—— *To See the Queen;* illus. by Clotilde Embree Funk. Longmans, Green, 1954.

Grimm, Jakob and Wilhelm. *More Tales from Grimm;* freely trans. and illus. by Wanda Gág. Coward-McCann, 1947. (Grades 4–6)

—— *Snow White and the Seven Dwarfs;* freely trans. and illus. by Wanda Gág. Coward-McCann, 1938.

—— *Tales from Grimm;* freely trans. and illus. by Wanda Gág. Coward-McCann, 1936. (Grades 4–6)

—— *Three Gay Tales from Grimm;* freely trans. and illus. by Wanda Gág. Coward-McCann, 1943.

Hutchinson, Veronica, comp. *Chimney Corner Fairy Tales;* illus. by Lois Lenski. Putnam, 1926.

—— *Chimney Corner Stories;* illus. by Lois Lenski. Putnam, 1925.

Jacobs, Joseph, ed. *English Fairy Tales;* illus. by J. D. Batten. Putnam, 3d ed. rev. 1892. (Grades 4–6)

Kipling, Rudyard. *Just So Stories;* illus. by J. M. Gleeson. Doubleday, 1912.

Lang, Andrew, ed. *The Blue Fairy Books;* illus. by Ben Kutcher; foreword by Mary Gould Davis. Longmans, Green, new ed. 1948. (Grades 4–6)

—— *The Red Fairy Book;* illus. by Marc Simont; foreword by Mary Gould Davis. Longmans, Green, new ed. 1948. (Grades 4–6)

Lawson, Robert. *Rabbit Hill;* illus. by the author. Viking Press, 1944. (Grades 3–6)

—— *The Tough Winter;* illus. by the author. Viking Press, 1954. (Grades 3–6)

Lofting, Hugh. *Story of Doctor Dolittle;* illus. by the author. Lippincott, 1920.

McGinley, Phyllis. *The Plain Princess;* illus. by Helen Stone. Lippincott, 1945.

MacGregor, Ellen. *Miss Pickerell Goes to Mars;* illus. by Paul Galdone. McGraw-Hill, 1951. (Whittlesey House) (Grades 4–6)

—— *Miss Pickerell Goes to the Arctic;* illus. by Paul Galdone. McGraw-Hill, 1954. (Whittlesey House) (Grades 4–6)

Norton, Mary. *The Borrowers;* illus. by Beth and Joe Krush. Harcourt, Brace, 1953. (Grades 4–7)

—— *The Borrowers Afield;* illus. by Beth and Joe Krush. Harcourt, Brace, 1955. (Grades 4–7)

Perrault, Charles. *Puss in Boots;* freely trans. and illus. by Marcia Brown. Scribner, 1952.

Reyher, Rebecca. *My Mother Is the Most Beautiful Woman in the World;* pictures by Ruth Gannett. Howell, Soskin, 1945.

Sawyer, Ruth. *Picture Tales from Spain;* illus. by Carlos Sanchez. Lippincott, 1936.

Swayne, Samuel F. *Great-Grandfather in the Honey Tree;* illus. by Zoe Swayne. Viking Press, 1949.

Thorne-Thomsen, Gudrun, ed. *East o' the Sun and West o' the Moon with Other Norwegian Folk Tales.* Row, Peterson, rev. ed. 1946.

Thurber, James. *Many Moons;* illus. by Louis Slobodkin. Harcourt, Brace, 1943.

Travers, Pamela. *Mary Poppins;* illus. by Mary Shepard. Harcourt, Brace, 1934. (Grades 4–7)

—— *Mary Poppins Comes Back;* illus. by Mary Shepard. Harcourt, Brace, 1935. (Grades 4–7)

—— *Mary Poppins in the Park;* illus. by Mary Shepard. Harcourt, Brace, 1952. (Grades 4–7)

—— *Mary Poppins Opens the Door;* illus. by Mary Shepard and Agnes Sims. Reynal, 1943. (Grades 4–7)

Tregarthen, Enys. *The Doll Who Came Alive;* ed. by Elizabeth Yates; illus. by Nora Unwin. John Day, 1942.

Uchida, Yoshiko. *The Magic Listening Cap;* illus. by the author. Harcourt, Brace, 1955.

White, E. B. *Charlotte's Web;* illus. by Garth Williams. Harper, 1952. (Grades 4–6)

SACRED LITERATURE

Bible. Selections. *Animals of the Bible; a Picture Book,* by Dorothy P. Lathrop; with text selected by Helen Dean Fish from the King James Bible. Lippincott, 1937. (A Stokes Book) (Grades 1–4)

—— *Jesus' Story; a Little New Testament;* Bible text selected from the King James Version; illus. by Maud and Miska Petersham. Macmillan, 1942.

—— *Small Rain; Verses from the Bible;* chosen by Jessie Orton Jones; illus. by Elizabeth Orton Jones. Viking Press, 1943. (Grades 1–4)

Bowie, Walter Russell. *Story of Jesus for Young People;* illus. by Robert Lawson. Scribner, 1937.

Farjeon, Eleanor. *A Prayer for Little Things;* pictures by Elizabeth Orton Jones. Houghton Mifflin, 1945. (K–Grade 3)

Field, Rachel Lyman. *Prayer for a Child;* pictures by Elizabeth Orton Jones. Macmillan, 1944. (K–Grade 3)

Fitch, Florence Mary. *A Book About God;* illus. by Leonard Weisgard. Lothrop, Lee & Shepard, 1953. (K–Grade 3)

—— *The Child Jesus;* illus. by Leonard Weisgard. Lothrop, Lee & Shepard, 1955. (K–Grade 3)

Francis of Assisi, Saint. *Song of the Sun; from the Canticle of the Sun;* illus. by Elizabeth Orton Jones. Macmillan, 1952. (K–Grade 4)

Johnson, Emilie Louise. *Little Book of Prayers;* illus. by Maud and Miska Petersham. Viking Press, 1941. (Grades 2–5)

Jones, Jessie Orton, comp. *This is the Way; Prayers and Precepts from World Religions;* illus. by Elizabeth Orton Jones. Viking Press, 1951. (Grades 1–3)

Lines, Kathleen. *Once in Royal David's City; a Picture Book of the Nativity retold from the Gospels,* by Kathleen Lines; drawn by Harold Jones. Franklin Watts, 1956. (K–Grade 3)

Petersham, Maud and Miska. *The Christ Child; as told by Matthew and Luke;* illus. by Maud and Miska Petersham. Doubleday, 1931. (Grades 1–5)

Tudor, Tasha. *First Prayers;* ed. and illus. by Tasha Tudor. Oxford University Press, 1952. (K–Grade 3)

SCIENCE AND NATURE

Bate, Norman. *Who Built the Bridge?;* illus. by the author. Scribner, 1954.

—— *Who Built the Dam?;* illus. by the author. Scribner, 1958.

Bell, Thelma Harrington. *Snow;* illus. by Corydon Bell. Viking Press, 1954. (Grades 3–6)

Bendick, Jeanne. *First Book of Airplanes;* illus. by the author. Franklin Watts, 1952. (Grades 3–6)

Blough, Glenn. *Not only for Ducks: The Story of Rain;* illus. by Jeanne Bendick. McGraw-Hill, 1954. (Whittlesey House)

—— *Wait for the Sunshine: The Story of the Seasons and Growing Things;* illus. by Jeanne Bendick. McGraw-Hill, 1954. (Whittlesey House)

Boulton, Rudyard. *Traveling with the Birds;* illus. by Walter Alois Weber. Donahue, 1933. (Grades 4–6)

Bridges, William. *Zoo Babies;* illus. with photographs. Morrow, 1953. (Grades 3–6)

Bronson, Wilfrid S. *Pollwiggle's Progress;* illus. by the author. Macmillan, 1932.

—— *Turtles;* illus. by the author. Harcourt, Brace, 1945. (Grades 3–6)

Buck, Margaret Waring. *Pets from the Pond;* illus. by the author. Abingdon, 1958. (Grades 3–6)

Buff, Mary and Conrad. *Dash and Dart.* Viking Press, 1942. (Grades 1–4)

—— *Elf Owl.* Viking Press, 1958.

Earle, Olive. *Robins in the Garden;* illus. by the author. Morrow, 1953. (Grades 1–4)

Fenton, Carroll Lane. *Wild Folk in the Mountains;* illus. by Dr. Fenton. John Day, 1958. (Grades 3–6)

Gall, Alice Crew, and Fleming Crew. *Wagtail;* illus. by Kurt Wiese. Oxford University Press, 1932.

George, Jean. *Snow Tracks;* illus. by the author. Dutton, 1958. (Grades 1–3)

Huntington, Harriet E. *Let's Go Outdoors;* illus. by Preston Duncan. Doubleday, 1939. (Grades 1–4)

McClung, Robert M. *Bufo; the Story of a Toad;* illus. by the author. Morrow, 1954. (Grades 1–3)

—— *Luna, the Story of a Moth.* Morrow, 1957.

—— *Ruby Throat; the Story of a Humming Bird;* illus. by the author. Morrow, 1950. (K–Grade 3)

Schneider, Herman and Nina. *You Among the Stars;* illus. by Symeon Shimin. William R. Scott, 1951.

Webb, Addison. *Birds in Their Homes;* pictures by Sabra Kimball. Garden City, 1947.

Webber, Irma. *Thanks to Trees.* William R. Scott, 1952.

—— *Travelers All; the Story of How Plants Go Places;* illus. by the author. William R. Scott, 1944.

Williamson, Margaret. *First Book of Bugs;* illus. by the author. Franklin Watts, 1949.

Zim, Herbert S. *Elephants;* pictures by Joy Buba. Morrow, 1946.

—— *Frogs and Toads;* illus. by Joy Buba. Morrow, 1950. (Grades 4–6)

—— *Lightning and Thunder;* illus. by James Gordon Irving. Morrow, 1952. (Grades 4–7)

—— *Snakes;* illus. by James Gordon Irving. Morrow, 1949. (Grades 4–7)

—— *What's Inside of Me?;* illus. by Herschel Wartik. Morrow, 1952. (Grades 2–5)

—— *What's Inside of Plants?;* illus. by Herschel and William Wartik. Morrow, 1952. (Grades 2–5)

—— *What's Inside the Earth?;* illus. by Raymond Perlman. Morrow, 1953. (Grades 4–6)

BIOGRAPHY, TRAVEL, AND HISTORY

Aulaire, Ingri and Edgar Parin d'. *Abraham Lincoln;* illus. by the authors. Doubleday, 1939.

—— *Benjamin Franklin;* illus. by the authors. Doubleday, 1950.

—— *Buffalo Bill;* illus. by the authors. Doubleday, 1952.

—— *Columbus;* illus. by the authors. Doubleday, 1955.

—— *George Washington;* illus. by the authors. Doubleday, 1936.

—— *Leif the Lucky;* illus. by the authors. Doubleday, 1941.

Averill, Esther. *Daniel Boone;* illus. by Feodor Rojankovsky. Harper, 1945. (Grades 4–6)

Dalgliesh, Alice. *America Begins; the Story of the Finding of the New World;* illus. by Lois Maloy. Scribner, 1938.

—— *America Builds Homes; the Story of the First Colonies;* illus. by Lois Maloy. Scribner, 1938.

—— *The Fourth of July Story;* illus. by Marie Nonnast. Scribner, 1956. (Grades 3–6)

—— *Ride on the Wind;* told from *The Spirit of St. Louis,* by Charles A. Lindbergh; illus. by Georges Schreiber. Scribner, 1956.

—— *The Thanksgiving Story;* illus. by Helen Sewell. Scribner, 1954.

Foster, Genevieve. *Abraham Lincoln;* illus. by the author. Scribner, 1950. (Grades 4–6)

—— *Andrew Jackson;* illus. by the author. Scribner, 1951. (Grades 4–6)

—— *George Washington;* illus. by the author. Scribner, 1949. (Grades 4–6)

Lawson, Robert. *They Were Strong and Good;* illus. by the author. Viking Press, 1940.

Petersham, Maud and Miska. *The Silver Mace; a Story of Williamsburg;* illus. by the authors. Macmillan, 1956.

Politi, Leo. *The Mission Bell;* illus. by the author. Scribner, 1953. (Grades 2–5)

Pyne, Mable. *Little Geography of the United States;* illus. by the author. Houghton Mifflin, 1941.

POETRY

Behn, Harry. *Wizard in the Well;* illus. by the author. Harcourt, Brace, 1956.

De la Mare, Walter. *Peacock Pie: A Book of Rhymes;* illus. by Barbara Cooney. Henry Holt, new ed. 1957. (All ages)

Field, Eugene. *Poems of Childhood;* illus. by Maxfield Parrish. Scribner, 1896.

Field, Rachel Lyman. *Poems;* decorations by the author. Macmillan, 1957. (Grades 3–6)

—— *Taxis and Toadstools.* Doubleday, 1926.

Frost, Frances. *The Little Whistler.* McGraw-Hill, 1949. (Whittlesey House)

Fyleman, Rose. *Fairies and Chimneys.* Doubleday, 1920.

Harrington, Mildred, comp. *Ring-a-Round; a Collection of Verse for Boys and Girls;* illus. by Corydon Bell. Macmillan, 1930. (K–Grade 5)

Love, Katherine, comp. *A Little Laughter;* illus. by Walter H. Lorraine. Crowell, 1957.

—— *Pocketful of Rhymes;* illus. by Henrietta Jones. Crowell, 1946.

MacFarland, Wilma, comp. *For a Child.* Westminster Press, 1947.

Nash, Ogden, ed. *The Moon Is Shining Bright as Day.* Lippincott, 1953. (Grades 3–6)

Peterson, Isabel, comp. *The First Book of Poetry.* Franklin Watts, 1954.

Richards, Laura E. *Tirra Lirra; Rhymes Old and New;* illus. by Marguerite Davis. Little, Brown, new ed. 1955.

Rossetti, Christina. *Sing-Song; a Nursery Rhyme Book, and Other Poems for Children.* Macmillan, 1924.

GRADES 5 AND 6

(*10 to 12 years of age*)

FICTION

Alcott, Louisa May. *Jo's Boys;* illus. by Grace Paull. World Publishing Company, 1957. (Rainbow Classics)

———— *Little Men;* illus. by Reginald Birch. Little, Brown, n.d. (Orchard House Edition)

———— *Little Women;* illus. by Barbara Cooney. Crowell, 1955. (Grades 5–8)

Ames, Evelyn. *My Brother Bird;* illus. by William Pène Du Bois. Dodd, Mead, 1954.

Angelo, Valenti. *Nino;* illus. by the author. Viking Press, 1938.

Armer, Laura. *Waterless Mountain;* illus. by Sidney Armer. Longmans, Green, 1931. (Grades 5–8)

Berry, Erick. *Hay-Foot, Straw-Foot;* illus. by the author. Viking Press, 1954.

———— *Sybil Ludington's Ride;* illus. by the author. Viking Press, 1952.

Bishop, Claire Huchet. *All Alone;* illus. by Feodor Rojankovsky. Viking Press, 1953.

———— *Toto's Triumph.* Viking Press, 1958.

———— *Twenty and Ten;* illus. by William Pène Du Bois. Viking Press, 1952.

Bothwell, Jean. *Little Flute Player;* illus. by Margaret Ayer. Morrow, 1949.

Brink, Carol. *Caddie Woodlawn;* illus. by Kate Seredy. Macmillan, 1935.

———— *Magical Melons;* illus. by Marguerite Davis. Macmillan, 1944.

Buck, Pearl. *The Big Wave;* illus. with prints by Hiroshige and Hokusai. John Day, 1948. (Grades 4–7)

Bunyan, John. *The Pilgrim's Progress;* retold and shortened by Mary Godolphin; illus. by Robert Lawson. Lippincott, 1939.

Carr, Mary. *Children of the Covered Wagon;* illus. by Bob Kuhn. Crowell, 1943.

Clark, Ann Nolan. *Secret of the Andes;* illus. by Jean Charlot. Viking Press, 1952. (Grades 4–7)

Crawford, Phyllis. *"Hello, the Boat!";* pictures by Edward Laning. Holt, 1938.

Daringer, Helen Fern. *Adopted Jane;* illus. by Kate Seredy. Harcourt, Brace, 1947.

De Angeli, Marguerite. *Black Fox of Lorne;* illus. by the author. Doubleday, 1956. (Grades 5–8)

———— *Door in the Wall;* illus. by the author. Doubleday, 1949.

———— *Henner's Lydia;* illus. by the author. Doubleday, 1936.

———— *Thee, Hannah!;* illus. by the author. Doubleday, 1940.

Defoe, Daniel. *Robinson Crusoe;* illus. by N. C. Wyeth. Scribner, 1958. (Scribner Illustrated Classics) (Grades 5 8)

DeJong, Meindert. *Along Came a Dog;* illus. by Maurice Sendak. Harper, 1958. (Grades 5–8)

———— *Hurry Home, Candy;* illus. by Maurice Sendak. Harper, 1953.

———— *Shadrach;* illus. by Maurice Sendak. Harper, 1953.

———— *Wheel on the School;* illus. by Maurice Sendak. Harper, 1954.

Dodge, Mary Mapes. *Hans Brinker; or, The Silver Skates;* illus. by George W. Edwards. Scribner, 1915. (Scribner Illustrated Classics)

Edmonds, Walter. *The Matchlock Gun;* illus. by Paul Lantz. Dodd, Mead, 1941.

———— *Two Logs Crossing;* illus. by Tibor Gergely. Dodd, Mead, 1943. (Grades 5–8)

Enright, Elizabeth. *Gone-Away Lake;* illus. by Beth and Joe Krush. Harcourt, Brace, 1957.

———— *The Saturdays;* illus. by the author. Rinehart, 1941. (Grades 4–7)

———— *Thimble Summer;* illus. by the author. Farrar, 1938.

Estes, Eleanor. *The Hundred Dresses;* illus. by Louis Slobodkin. Harcourt, Brace, 1944.

———— *The Middle Moffat;* illus. by Louis Slobodkin. Harcourt, Brace, 1942.

———— *The Moffats;* illus. by Louis Slobodkin. Harcourt, Brace, 1941.

———— *Pinky Pye;* illus. by Edward Ardizzone. Harcourt, Brace, 1958.

———— *Rufus M.;* illus. by Louis Slobodkin. Harcourt, Brace, 1943.

Evernden, Margery. *The Runaway Apprentice;* illus. by Jeanvee Wong. Random House, 1949.

Farjeon, Eleanor. *The Little Bookroom;* illus. by Edward Ardizzone. Oxford University Press, 1956.

Field, Rachel Lyman. *Hitty: Her First Hundred Years;* illus. by Dorothy Lathrop. Macmillan, 1937. (Grades 5–8)

Fisher, Cyrus. *The Avion My Uncle Flew;* illus. by Richard Floethe. Appleton, 1946.

Freuchen, Pipaluk. *Eskimo Boy;* trans. from the Danish; illus. by Ingrid Vang Nyman. Lothrop, Lee & Shepard, 1951.

Gates, Doris. *Blue Willow;* illus. by Paul Lantz. Viking Press, 1940. (Grades 5–8)

Henry, Marguerite. *Benjamin West and His Cat Grimalkin;* illus. by Wesley Dennis. Bobbs-Merrill, 1947. (Grades 4–6)

———— *Brighty of the Grand Canyon;* illus. by Wesley Dennis. Rand McNally, 1953. (Grades 5–8)

—— *Justin Morgan Had a Horse;* illus. by Wesley Dennis. Rand McNally, 1954. (Grades 4–7)

—— *King of the Wind;* illus. by Wesley Dennis. Rand McNally, 1948. (Grades 5–8)

—— *Misty of Chincoteague;* illus. by Wesley Dennis. Rand McNally, 1947. (Grades 5–8)

Hoff, Carol. *Johnny Texas;* illus. by Bob Meyers. Follett, 1950.

Holling, Holling C. *Minn of the Mississippi;* illus. by the author. Houghton Mifflin, 1951.

—— *Paddle-to-the-Sea;* illus. by the author. Houghton Mifflin, 1941.

—— *Seabird;* illus. by the author. Houghton Mifflin, 1948.

—— *Tree in the Trail;* illus. by the author. Houghton Mifflin, 1942.

Kelly, Eric P. *In Clean Hay;* illus. by Maud and Miska Petersham. Macmillan, 1953.

Knight, Eric. *Lassie Come-Home;* illus. by Cyrus Leroy Baldridge. Winston, 1940. (Grades 6–9)

Lawrence, Isabelle. *Niko, Sculptor's Apprentice;* illus. by Artur Marokvia. Viking Press, 1956.

Lawrence, Mildred. *Peachtree Island;* illus. by Mary Stevens. Harcourt, Brace, 1948.

Lawson, Robert. *Ben and Me;* illus. by the author. Little, Brown, 1939. (Grades 5–9)

—— *Mr. Revere and I;* illus. by the author. Little, Brown, 1953. (Grades 6–8)

Lenski, Lois. *Judy's Journey;* illus. by the author. Lippincott, 1947.

—— *Strawberry Girl;* illus. by the author. Lippincott, 1945.

Lindquist, Willis. *Burma Boy;* illus. by Nicolas Mordvinoff. McGraw-Hill, 1953. (Whittlesey House)

Lippincott, Joseph. *Wilderness Champion;* illus. by Paul Branson. Lippincott, 1944. (Grades 5–8)

McCloskey, Robert. *Centerburg Tales;* illus. by the author. Viking Press, 1951. (Grades 4–7)

—— *Homer Price;* illus. by the author. Viking Press, 1943. (Grades 4–7)

McMeekin, Isabella. *Journey Cake;* illus. by Nicholas Panesis. Messner, 1942. (Grades 5–8)

—— *Kentucky Derby Winner;* illus. by Corinne Dillon. David McKay, 1949.

Menotti, Gian-Carlo. *Amahl and the Night Visitors;* adapted by Frances Frost; illus. by Roger Duvoisin. McGraw-Hill, 1952. (Whittlesey House)

Montgomery, Rutherford. *Kildee House;* illus. by Barbara Cooney. Doubleday, 1949.

Moon, Grace. *Chi-Wee;* illus. by Carl Moon. Doubleday, 1925. (Grades 3–5)

Mukerji, Dhan Gopal. *Gay-Neck; the Story of a Pigeon;* illus. by Boris Artzybasheff. Dutton, 1927. (Grades 5–8)

—— *Hari, the Jungle Lad;* illus. by Morgan Stinemetz. Dutton, 1924.

—— *Kari, the Elephant;* illus. by J. E. Allen. Dutton, 1922.

O'Brien, John. *Silver Chief, Dog of the North;* illus. by Kurt Wiese. Winston, 1933. (Grades 6–8)

Powell, Miriam. *Jareb;* illus. by Marc Simont. Crowell, 1952. (Grades 6–9)

Pyle, Howard. *Men of Iron;* illus. by the author. Harper, 1891. (Grades 6–9)

—— *Otto of the Silver Hand;* illus. by the author. Scribner, new ed. 1957. (Grades 6–9)

Rankin, Louise. *Daughter of the Mountains;* illus. by Kurt Wiese. Viking Press, 1948. (Grades 5–8)

Ransome, Arthur. *Swallows and Amazons;* illus. by Hélène Carter. Lippincott, 1931. (Grades 5–8)

—— *We Didn't Mean to Go to Sea;* illus. by the author. Macmillan, 1938. (Grades 5–8)

Rounds, Glen. *Blind Colt;* illus. by the author. Holiday House, 1941.

Rugh, Belle. *Crystal Mountain;* illus. by Ernest H. Shepard. Houghton Mifflin, 1955. (Grades 4–7)

Salten, Felix. *Bambi;* trans. by Whitaker Chambers. Noble, n.d.

Sauer, Julia. *Light at Tern Rock;* illus. by Georges Schreiber. Viking Press, 1951.

Sawyer, Ruth. *Roller Skates;* illus. by Valenti Angelo. Viking Press, 1936.

—— *This Way to Christmas;* illus. by Maginel Wright Barney. Harper, 1944.

Seredy, Kate. *The Good Master;* illus. by the author. Viking Press, 1935.

—— *Philomena;* illus. by the author. Viking Press, 1955.

Sorensen, Virginia. *Miracles on Maple Hill;* illus. by Beth and Joe Krush. Harcourt, Brace, 1956.

Sperry, Armstrong. *Call It Courage;* illus. by the author. Macmillan, 1940. (Grades 5–8)

Steele, William O. *Lone Hunt;* illus. by Paul Galdone. Harcourt, Brace, 1956.

—— *Winter Danger;* illus. by Paul Galdone. Harcourt, Brace, 1954.

Stuart, Jesse. *Beatinest Boy;* illus. by Robert Henneberger. McGraw-Hill, 1953. (Whittlesey House)

Taylor, Sydney. *All-of-a-Kind Family;* illus. by Helen John. Follett, 1941.

—— *More All-of-a-Kind Family;* illus. by Mary Stevens. Follett, 1954.

Tharp, Louise Hall. *Tory Hole.* Little, Brown, 1940.

Treffinger, Carolyn. *Li Lun, Lad of Courage;* illus. by Kurt Wiese. Abingdon, 1947.

Van Stockum, Hilda. *Cottage at Bantry Bay;* illus. by the author. Viking Press, 1938.

Weil, Ann. *Red Sails to Capri;* illus. by C. B. Falls. Viking Press, 1952. (Grades 5–8)

Weston, Christine. *Bhimsa, the Dancing Bear;* illus. by Roger Duvoisin. Scribner, 1945.

White, Anne. *Junket;* illus. by Robert McCloskey. Viking Press, 1955.

Wiggin, Kate Douglas. *Rebecca of Sunnybrook Farm,* illus. by Helen Mason Grose. Houghton Mifflin, 1925. (Riverside Bookshelf)

Wilson, Leon. *This Boy Cody;* illus. by Ursula Koering. Franklin Watts, 1950.

────── *This Boy Cody and His Friends;* illus. by Ursula Koering. Franklin Watts, 1952.

Wyss, Johann David. *Swiss Family Robinson;* illus. by Harry Roundtree. Macmillan, 1924. (Grades 5–8)

Yates, Elizabeth. *Mountain Born;* illus. by Nora S. Unwin. Coward-McCann, 1943.

FABLES, FOLK AND FAIRY TALES, MYTHS, LEGENDS, AND HERO STORIES

Andersen, Hans Christian. *It's Perfectly True, and Other Stories;* trans. from the Danish by Paul Leyssac; illus. by Richard Bennett. Harcourt, Brace, 1938.

Arabian Nights. *Arabian Nights; Their Best Known Tales;* ed. by Kate Douglas Wiggin and Nora A. Smith; illus. by Maxfield Parrish. Scribner, 1909. (Scribner Illustrated Classics)

Asbjörnsen, Peter Christen, and Jörgen Moe. *East of the Sun and West of the Moon;* illus. by Hedvig Collin. Macmillan, 1953. (New Children's Classics)

Bailey, Carolyn Sherwin. *Miss Hickory;* illus. by Ruth Gannett. Viking Press, 1946.

Baldwin, James. *The Story of Roland;* illus. by Peter Hurd. Scribner, 1930. (Scribner Illustrated Classics)

────── *The Story of Siegfried;* illus. by Peter Hurd. Scribner, 1931. (Scribner Illustrated Classics)

Benary-Isbert, Margot. *The Wicked Enchantment;* trans. by Richard and Clara Winston; illus. by Enrico Arno. Harcourt, Brace, 1955. (Grades 5–8)

Benson, Sally. *Stories of the Gods and Heroes;* illus. by Steele Savage. Dial Press, 1940. (Grades 5–8)

Besterman, Catherine. *The Quaint and Curious Quest of Johnny Longfoot the Shoe King's Son;* illus. by Warren Chappell. Bobbs-Merrill, 1947.

Boston, Lucy Maria. *The Children of Green Knowe;* illus. by Peter Boston. Harcourt, Brace, 1955.

Buff, Mary and Conrad. *The Apple and the Arrow;* illus. by Conrad Buff. Houghton Mifflin, 1951.

Bulfinch, Thomas. *A Book of Myths; Selections from Bulfinch's "Age of Fable";* illus. by Helen Sewell. Macmillan, 1942. (Grades 6–9)

Carlson, Natalie Savage. *The Talking Cat and Other Stories of French Canada;* pictures by Roger Duvoisin. Harper, 1952.

Chase, Richard, ed. *Grandfather Tales; American English Folk Tales;* illus. by Berkeley Williams, Jr. Houghton Mifflin, 1948. (Grades 4–7)

────── *The Jack Tales;* illus. by Berkeley Williams, Jr. Houghton Mifflin, 1943. (Grades 4–7)

Chrisman, Arthur Bowie. *Shen of the Sea;* illus. by Else Hasselriis. Dutton, 1925.

Coatsworth, Elizabeth. *The Cat Who Went to Heaven;* illus. by Lynd Ward. Macmillan, 1930.

Colum, Padraic. *The Adventures of Odysseus and the Tale of Troy;* illus. by Willy Pogány. Macmillan, 1918. (Grades 5–9)

────── *Children of Odin;* illus. by Willy Pogány. Macmillan, 1920.

────── *Forge in the Forest;* illus. by Boris Artzybasheff. Macmillan, 1925.

────── *The Golden Fleece and the Heroes Who Lived Before Achilles;* illus. by Willy Pogány. Macmillan, 1934. (Grades 6–9)

Courlander, Harold. *Terrapin's Pot of Sense;* illus. by Elton Fax. Holt, 1957.

Courlander, Harold, and Wolf Leslau. *Fire on the Mountain, and Other Ethiopian Stories;* illus. by Robert W. Kane. Holt, 1950.

Davis, Mary Gould. *Truce of the Wolf and Other Tales of Old Italy;* illus. by Jay Van Everen. Harcourt, Brace, 1931.

Davis, Robert. *Padre Porko; the Gentlemanly Pig;* illus. by Fritz Eichenberg. Holiday House, 1948.

De la Mare, Walter, ed. *Animal Stories.* Scribner, 1940.

────── *Told Again; Old Tales Told Again;* illus. by A. H. Watson. Knopf, 1927.

Farjeon, Eleanor. *The Glass Slipper;* illus. by Ernest H. Shepard. Viking Press, 1956. (Grades 5–8)

────── *Martin Pippin in the Daisy-Field;* illus. by Isobel and John Morton-Sale. Lippincott, 1937.

────── *The Silver Curlew;* illus. by Ernest Shepard. Viking Press, 1953.

Felton, Harold W. *John Henry and His Hammer;* illus. by Aldren A. Watson. Knopf, 1950. (Grades 5–8)

Finger, Charles. *Tales from Silver Lands;* woodcuts by Paul Honoré. Doubleday, 1924.

French, Allen. *The Story of Grettir the Strong.* Dutton, 1908. (Grades 5–8)

Gaer, Joseph. *The Fables of India.* Little, Brown, 1955.

Galt, Thomas. *The Rise of the Thunderer;* illus. by John Mackey. Crowell, 1954. (Grades 5–8)

Grahame, Kenneth. *Wind in the Willows;* illus. by Ernest H. Shepard. Scribner, new ed. 1953. (All ages)

Grimm, Jakob and Wilhelm. *Household Stories from the Collection of the Brothers Grimm;* trans. from the German by Lucy Crane; illus. by Johannes Troyer. Macmillan, 1954. (New Children's Classics)

Harris, Joel Chandler. *Complete Tales of Uncle Remus;* comp. by Richard Chase; illus. by A. B. Frost and others. Houghton Mifflin, 1955. (Grades 5–9)

Hatch, Mary. *13 Danish Tales;* illus. by Edgun, *pseud.* Harcourt, Brace, 1947.

Hawthorne, Nathaniel. *The Wonder Book and Tanglewood Tales;* illus. by Gustaf Tenggren. Houghton Mifflin, n.d.

Hosford, Dorothy. *By His Own Might; the Battles of Beowulf;* drawings by Lasslo Matulay. Holt, 1947. (Grades 6–8)

—— *Thunder of the Gods;* illus. by Claire and George Louden. Holt, 1952.

Hudson, William Henry. *Little Boy Lost;* illus. by Dorothy Lathrop. Knopf, 1920. (Grades 6–8)

Kelsey, Alice Geer. *Once the Hodja;* illus. by Frank Dobias. Longmans, Green, 1943.

—— *Once the Mullah;* Persian Folk Tales; illus. by Kurt Werth. Longmans, Green, 1954.

Kipling, Rudyard. *The Jungle Book;* illus. by Kurt Wiese. Doubleday, 1932.

Lagerlöf, Selma. *The Wonderful Adventures of Nils;* trans. from the Swedish by Velma Swanston Howard; illus. by H. Baumhauer. Pantheon Books, new ed. 1947.

Lewis, C. S. *The Lion, the Witch, and the Wardrobe;* illus. by Pauline Baynes. Macmillan, 1950.

—— *The Magician's Nephew;* illus. by Pauline Baynes. Macmillan, 1955.

Macdonald, George. *At the Back of the North Wind;* illus. by George and Doris Hauman. Macmillan, new ed. 1953. (New Children's Classics)

MacManus, Seumas. *Well o' the World's End;* illus. by Richard Bennett. Devin-Adair, 1955.

Malcolmson, Anne B. *Yankee Doodle's Cousins;* illus. by Robert McCloskey. Houghton Mifflin, 1941. (Grades 5–8)

Nesbit, E. *The Bastable Children.* Coward-McCann, 1928.

O'Faolain, Eileen. *Miss Pennyfeather and the Pooka;* illus. by Aldren Watson. Random House, 1946.

Parrish, Anne. *Floating Island;* illus. by the author, with sketches by Mr. Doll. Harper, 1930.

Pyle, Howard. *Merry Adventures of Robin Hood of Great Renown in Nottinghamshire;* illus. by the author. Scribner, 1946. (Brandywine Edition) (Grades 5–8)

—— *The Story of King Arthur and His Knights;* illus. by the author. Scribner, 1933. (Brandywine Edition) (Grades 5–8)

—— *The Wonder Clock;* illus. by the author. Harper, 1915.

Ritchie, Alice. *The Treasure of Li-Po;* illus. by T. Ritchie. Harcourt, Brace, 1949.

Rounds, Glen. *Ol' Paul, the Mighty Logger.* Holiday House, 1949.

Ruskin, John. *King of the Golden River;* illus. by Arthur Rackham. Lippincott, 1932.

Sandburg, Carl. *Rootabaga Stories;* illus. by Maud and Miska Petersham. New ed.; 2 vols. in 1. Harcourt, Brace, n.d.

Sauer, Julia. *Fog Magic;* illus. by Lynd Ward. Viking Press, 1943.

Sherlock, Philip M. *Anansi the Spider Man;* illus. by Marcia Brown. Crowell, 1954.

Swift, Jonathan. *Gulliver's Travels into Several Remote Nations of the World;* illus. by Arthur Rackham. E. P. Dutton, new ed. 1952. (Children's Illustrated Classics) (Grades 6–9)

Tarn, W. W. *The Treasure of the Isle of Mist;* illus. by Robert Lawson. Putnam, 1934. (Grades 6–8)

Tolkien, John R. R. *The Hobbit; or There and Back Again;* illus. by the author. Houghton Mifflin, 1938.

Uchida, Yoshiko. *The Dancing Kettle, and Other Japanese Folk Tales, Retold;* illus. by Richard C. Jones. Harcourt, Brace, 1949.

Undset, Sigrid, ed. *True and Untrue and Other Norse Tales;* illus. by Frederick T. Chapman. Knopf, 1945.

Young, Ella. *The Unicorn with the Silver Shoes;* illus. by Robert Lawson. Longmans, Green, 1957 (reissue).

—— *The Wondersmith and His Son;* illus. by Boris Artzybasheff. Longmans, Green, 1957. (reissue).

SACRED LITERATURE

Barnhart, Nancy. *The Lord Is My Shepherd; Stories from the Bible Pictured in Bible Lands;* arranged and illus. by Nancy Barnhart. Scribner, 1949. (Grades 4–7)

A First Bible; illus. by Helen Sewell; selected and arranged by J. W. Maury. Oxford University Press, 1934.

Fitch, Florence Mary. *One God; the Ways We Worship Him.* Lothrop, Lee & Shepard, 1944. (All ages)

SCIENCE AND NATURE

Adler, Irving. *Hurricanes and Twisters,* by Robert Irving, *pseud.* Knopf, 1955. (Grades 4–8)

Andrews, Roy Chapman. *All About Dinosaurs;* illus. by Thomas W. Voter. Random House, 1953. (Grades 5–9)

—— *All About Whales;* illus. by Thomas W. Voter. Random House, 1954. (Grades 5–8)

Beeland, Lee, and Robert Wells. *Space Satellite; the Story of the Man-Made Moon;* illus. by Jack Coggins. Prentice-Hall, 1957. (Grades 5–8)

Beeler, Nelson, and Franklyn Branley. *Experiments with a Microscope;* illus. by Anne Marie Jauss. Crowell, 1957. (Grades 5–9)

—— *Experiments with Electricity;* illus. by A. W. Revell. Crowell, 1949. (Grades 5–8)

Brindze, Ruth. *The Gulf Stream;* illus. by Hélène Carter. Vanguard Press, 1945.

Bronson, Wilfrid S. *Children of the Sea;* illus. by the author. Harcourt, Brace, 1940.

—— *The Wonder World of Ants;* illus. by the author. Harcourt, Brace, 1937.

Buck, Margaret Waring. *In Woods and Fields;* illus. by the author. Abingdon, 1950. (Grades 4–8)

Buff, Mary and Conrad. *Big Tree;* illus. by Conrad Buff. Viking Press, 1946. (Grades 5–9)

Coggins, Jack, and Fletcher Pratt. *By Space Ship to the Moon.* Random House, 1952. (Grades 5–9)

Cooke, David C. *How Atomic Submarines Are Made;* illus. with photographs. Dodd, Mead, 1957.

Cormack, Maribelle. *First Book of Stones;* illus. by M. K. Scott. Franklin Watts, 1950.

—— *First Book of Trees;* illus. by Hélène Carter. Franklin Watts, 1951.

Earle, Olive. *Paws, Hoofs and Flippers;* illus. by the author. Morrow, 1954. (Grades 5–8)

Epstein, Samuel and Beryl. *First Book of Electricity;* illus. by Robin King. Franklin Watts, 1953.

Fenton, Carroll Lane. *Prehistoric World;* with drawings by the author and color plates by James E. Allen. John Day, 1954.

Fenton, Carroll Lane and Mildred. *Worlds in the Sky;* illus. by the authors. John Day, 1950.

Fenton, Carroll Lane, and Dorothy Pallas. *Trees and Their World;* illus. by Carroll Lane Fenton. John Day, 1957.

Fisher, James. *The Wonderful World;* illus. in full color. Garden City, 1954. (Grades 5–8)

—— *The Wonderful World of the Sea;* illus. in color with maps and diagrams. Garden City, 1957. (Grades 5–8)

Freeman, Mae and Ira. *Fun with Astronomy;* illus. with photographs. Random House, 1953. (Grades 4–8)

—— *Fun with Science;* illus. with photographs. Random House, rev. ed. 1956. (Grades 5–8)

Gallant, Roy. *Exploring the Universe;* illus. by Lowell Hess. Garden City, 1956.

George, John and Jean. *Masked Prowler;* illus. by Jean George. Dutton, 1956. (Grades 5–8)

—— *Vulpes the Red Fox;* illus. by Jean George. Dutton, 1948. (Grades 5–8)

Haber, Heinz. *The Walt Disney Story of Our Friend the Atom;* illus. by staff artists of the Walt Disney Studio. Simon & Schuster, 1957 (Grades 5–9)

Henry, Marguerite. *Album of Horses;* illus. by Wesley Dennis. Rand McNally, 1951. (Grades 5–9)

Hoke, Alice Dickinson. *First Book of Plants;* illus. by Paul Wenck. Franklin Watts, 1953.

Lane, Ferdinand. *All About the Sea;* illus. by Fritz Kredel. Random House, 1953. (Grades 5–8)

Lewellen, John. *The Earth Satellite;* illus. by Ida Scheib. Knopf, 1957.

—— *You and Atomic Energy, and Its Wonderful Uses;* illus. by Lois Fisher. Children's Press, 1949. (Grades 5–9)

Liers, Emil E. *An Otter's Story;* illus. by Tony Palazzo. Viking Press, 1953. (Grades 5–8)

McCracken, Harold. *Biggest Bear on Earth;* illus. by Paul Branson. Lippincott, 1943. (Grades 5–8)

Morgan, Alfred. *First Electrical Book for Boys;* illus. by the author. Scribner, rev. ed. 1951. (Grades 5–8)

—— *Pet Book for Boys and Girls;* illus. by the author and Ruth King. Scribner, 1949. (Grades 4–9)

Parker, Bertha Morris. *Golden Treasury of Natural History;* illus. in full color. Simon & Schuster, 1952.

Peattie, Donald Culross. *The Rainbow Book of Nature;* illus. by Rudolf Freund. World Publishing Company, 1957. (Grades 5–9)

Platt, Rutherford. *Walt Disney's Worlds of Nature.* Simon & Schuster, 1957. (Grades 5–8)

Pope, Clifford H. *Reptiles Round the World;* illus. by Helen Damrosch Tee-Van. Knopf, 1957. (Grades 5–8)

Pough, Frederick. *All About Volcanoes and Earthquakes;* illus. by Kurt Wiese. Random House, 1953.

Reed, William Maxwell. *The Earth for Sam; the Story of Mountains, Rivers, Dinosaurs and Men;* drawings by Karl Moseley. Harcourt, Brace, 1930. (Grades 5–8)

—— *Stars for Sam;* ed. by Charles E. St. John; decorations by Karl Moseley. Harcourt, Brace, 1931. (Grades 5–8)

Reed, William Maxwell, and Wilfrid S. Bronson. *The Sea for Sam;* ed. by F. C. Brown and Charles M. Breder, Jr.; illus. by Wilfrid S. Bronson. Harcourt, Brace, 1935. (Grades 5–8)

Rey, H. A. *Find the Constellations.* Houghton Mifflin, 1954. (Grades 4–8)

Schneider, Herman. *Everyday Weather and How It Works;* pictures by Jeanne Bendick. McGraw-Hill, 1951. (Whittlesey House) (Grades 5-8)

Schneider, Herman and Nina. *How Your Body Works;* illus. by Barbara Ivins. William R. Scott, 1949. (Grades 5-8)

―――― *Your Telephone and How It Works;* illus. by Jeanne Bendick. McGraw-Hill, 1952. (Whittlesey House) (Grades 5-9)

Selsam, Millicent. *See Through the Jungle;* illus. by Winifred Lubell. Harper, 1957.

Smith, Frances C. *The First Book of Conservation;* illus. by René Martin. Franklin Watts, 1954.

Sterling, Dorothy. *The Story of Caves;* illus. by Winifred Lubel. Doubleday, 1956. (Grades 5-8)

―――― *The Story of Mosses, Ferns, and Mushrooms.* Doubleday, 1955. (Grades 5-8)

Tannehill, Ivan Ray. *All About the Weather;* illus. by René Martin. Random House, 1953. (Grades 4-8)

Tibbets, Albert B. *The First Book of Bees;* illus. by Hélène Carter. Franklin Watts, 1952.

White, Anne Terry. *Prehistoric America;* illus. by Aldren Watson. Random House, 1951. (Grades 5-8)

Wyler, Rose, and Gerald Ames. *The Golden Book of Astronomy;* illus. by John Polgreen. Simon & Schuster, 1955. (Grades 5-9)

Zim, Herbert S. *Dinosaurs;* illus. by James Gordon Irving. Morrow, 1954.

BIOGRAPHY, TRAVEL, AND HISTORY

Averill, Esther. *Cartier Sails the St. Lawrence;* illus. by Feodor Rojankovsky. Harper, new ed. 1956.

Bailey, Carolyn Sherwin. *Children of the Handcrafts;* illus. by Grace Paull. Viking Press, 1935. (Grades 6-8)

Bishop, Claire Huchet. *Martin de Porres, Hero;* illus. by Jean Charlot. Houghton Mifflin, 1954. (Grades 6-9)

Brindze, Ruth. *Story of the Totem Pole;* illus. by Yeffe Kimball. Vanguard Press, 1951.

De Jong, Dola. *The Level Land;* illus. by Jan Hoowij. Scribner, 1943.

Duvoisin, Roger. *And There Was America;* illus. by the author. Knopf, 1938.

―――― *They Put Out to Sea; the Story of the Map;* illus. by the author. Knopf, 1943. (Grades 5-8)

Eaton, Jeanette. *That Lively Man, Ben Franklin;* illus. by Henry C. Pitz. Morrow, 1948. (Grades 5-8)

Farjeon, Eleanor. *Ten Saints;* illus. by Helen Sewell. Oxford University Press, 1936. (Grades 5-8)

Fisher, Clyde. *The Life of Audubon;* illus. with reproductions of Audubon prints. Harper, 1949.

Forbes, Esther. *America's Paul Revere;* illus. by Lynd Ward. Houghton Mifflin, 1946. (Grades 5-8)

Haviland, Virginia. *William Penn: Founder and Friend;* illus. by Peter Burchard. Abingdon, 1952.

Hillyer, Virgil. *Child's Geography of the World;* rev. by Edward G. Huey; with maps and illus. by Mary Sherwood Wright Jones. Appleton, rev. ed. 1951. (Grades 4-8)

―――― *Child's History of the World.* Appleton, rev. ed. 1951. (Grades 5-8)

Hunt, Mabel Leigh. *"Have You Seen Tom Thumb?";* illus. by Fritz Eichenberg. Lippincott, 1942. (A Stokes Book) (Grades 6-9)

Jewett, Sophie. *God's Troubadour; the Story of Saint Francis of Assisi;* illus. with paintings by Giotto. Crowell, new ed. 1957.

Judson, Clara Ingram. *Benjamin Franklin;* illus. by Robert Frankenburg. Follett, 1957. (Grades 5-8)

―――― *Theodore Roosevelt, Fighting Patriot;* illus. by Lorence F. Bjorklund. Follett, 1953. (Grades 5-8)

La Farge, Oliver. *Cochise of Arizona;* illus. by L. F. Bjorklund. Aladdin, 1953.

McNeer, May. *America's Abraham Lincoln;* illus. by Lynd Ward. Houghton Mifflin, 1957. (Grades 5-8)

―――― *Armed with Courage;* illus. by Lynd Ward. Abingdon, 1957.

―――― *Mexican Story;* illus. by Lynd Ward. Ariel Books, 1953. (Grades 6-9)

―――― *The Story of the Southwest;* illus. by Cornelius H. DeWitt. Harper, 1957. (Regions of American Books)

Masani, Shakuntala. *Nehru's Story;* illus. by the author. Oxford University Press, 1949.

Meadowcroft, Enid. *Gift of the River; a History of Ancient Egypt;* illus. and adapted from Egyptian sources by Katharine Dewey. Crowell, 1937.

Meadowcroft, William. *Boy's Life of Edison;* with autobiographical notes by Mr. Edison. Harper, new ed. 1929. (Grades 6-8)

Petersham, Maud and Miska. *Story of the Presidents of the United States of America;* illus. by the authors. Macmillan, 1953.

Roosevelt, Theodore. *Theodore Roosevelt's Letters to His Children;* ed. by J. B. Bishop. Scribner, 1957 (reissue).

Shippen, Katherine B. *Mr. Bell Invents the Telephone.* Random House, 1952. (Landmark Books)

Wheeler, Opal. *Ludwig Beethoven and the Chiming Tower Bells;* illus. by Mary Greenwalt. Dutton, 1942.

Wheeler, Opal, and Sybil Deucher. *Joseph Haydn, the Merry Little Peasant;* illus. by Mary Greenwalt. Dutton, 1936.

—— *Franz Schubert and His Merry Friends;* illus. by Mary Greenwalt. Dutton, 1939.

POETRY

Arbuthnot, May Hill, comp. *Time for Poetry;* illus. by Arthur Paul. Scott, Foresman, 1952. (All ages)

Brewton, John, comp. *Gaily We Parade; a Collection of Poems About People, Here, There & Everywhere;* illus. by Robert Lawson. Macmillan, 1940. (Grades 4–8)

Brewton, Sara and John, comps. *Bridled with Rainbows; Poems About Many Things of Earth and Sky;* decorations by Vera Bock. Macmillan, 1949. (Grades 4–8)

Browning, Robert. *Pied Piper of Hamelin;* illus. by Kate Greenaway. Frederick Warne, n.d.

Coatsworth, Elizabeth. *Poems;* decorations by Vee Guthrie. Macmillan, 1957.

De la Mare, Walter. *Rhymes and Verses;* illus. by Eleanor Blaisdell. Holt, 1947.

Farjeon, Eleanor. *Eleanor Farjeon's Poems for Children.* Lippincott, 1951.

Hazeltine, Alice I., and Elva Smith, comps. *The Year Around; Poems for Children;* decorations by Paula Hutchison. Abingdon, 1956. (Grades 4–8)

Hullard, Grace. *My Poetry Book; an Anthology of Modern Verse for Boys and Girls;* illus. by Willy Pogány. Winston, rev. ed. 1956. (Grades 6–8)

Lear, Edward. *Complete Nonsense Book;* ed. by Lady Strachey. Dodd, Mead, 1951.

Lindsay, Vachel. *Johnny Appleseed, and Other Poems;* illus. by George Richards. Macmillan, 1928. (Children's Classics) (Grades 5–9)

Longfellow, Henry Wadsworth. *The Children's Longfellow.* Houghton Mifflin, 1908.

Read, Sir Herbert, ed. *This Way, Delight; a Book of Poetry for the Young;* illus. by Juliet Kepes. Pantheon Press, 1956.

Smith, Janet Adams, comp. *The Faber Book of Children's Verse.* Transatlantic Arts, 1954. (Grades 5–8)

Thompson, Blanche Jennings, ed. *Silver Pennies; a Collection of Modern Poems for Boys and Girls;* illus. by Winifred Bromhall. Macmillan, 1925. (Little Library) (Grades 3–8)

JUNIOR HIGH SCHOOL: GRADES 7, 8, AND 9

(*12 to 14 years of age*)

FICTION

Allen, Merritt P. *Johnny Reb;* decorations by Ralph Ray, Jr. Longmans, Green, 1952.

—— *Western Star; a Story of Jim Bridger.* Longmans, Green, 1941.

Austen, Jane. *Pride and Prejudice.* Dodd, Mead. (Great Illustrated Classics) (High School)

Barrie, Sir James Matthew. *The Little Minister.* Grosset, n.d. (High School)

Bell, Margaret. *Watch for a Tall White Sail;* illus. by Louis Darling. Morrow, 1948.

Benary-Isbert, Margot. *The Ark;* trans. by Clara and Richard Winston. Harcourt, Brace, 1953.

—— *Rowan Farm;* trans. by Clara and Richard Winston. Harcourt, Brace, 1954.

Bennett, John. *Master Skylark; a Story of Shakespeare's Time;* illus. by Reginald Birch. Grosset & Dunlap, 1924.

Boyd, James. *Drums,* illus. by N. C. Wyeth. Scribner, 1947.

Breckenfeld, Vivian. *High Trail;* illus. by Leonard Weisgard. Doubleday, 1948.

Bro, Margueritte. *Su-Mei's Golden Year;* illus. by Kurt Wiese. Doubleday, 1950.

Brontë, Charlotte. *Jane Eyre.* Dodd, Mead. (Great Illustrated Classics) (High School)

Cather, Willa. *My Antonia;* illus. by W. T. Benda. Houghton Mifflin, 1918. (High School)

Caudill, Rebecca. *Tree of Freedom;* illus. by Dorothy Bayley Morse. Viking Press, 1949.

Cavanna, Betty. *Going on Sixteen.* Westminster Press, 1946.

Cervantes Saavedra, Miguel de. *The Adventures of Don Quixote de la Mancha;* adapted by Leighton Barret; illus. by Warren Chappell. Knopf, 1939.

Chipperfield, Joseph E. *Storm of Dancerwood;* illus. by Helen Torrey. Longmans, Green, 1949.

Church, Richard. *Five Boys in a Cave.* John Day, 1951.

Chute, Marchette. *Innocent Wayfaring;* illus. by the author. Scribner, 1955.

—— *The Wonderful Winter;* illus. by Grace Golden. Dutton, 1954.

Clark, Ann Nolan. *Santiago;* illus. by Lynd Ward. Viking Press, 1955.

Cleary, Beverly. *Fifteen;* illus. by Joe and Beth Krush. Morrow, 1956.

Clemens, Samuel Langhorne. *Adventures of Huckleberry Finn;* illus. by Worth Brehm. Harper. (Holiday Edition) (Grades 6–9)

—— *Adventures of Tom Sawyer;* illus. by Worth Brehm. Harper. (Holiday Edition) (Grades 6–9)

—— *The Prince and the Pauper;* illus. by Henry Pitz. Harper. (Holiday Edition) (Grades 6–9)

Coatsworth, Elizabeth. *Door to the North;* illus. by Frederick T. Chapman. Winston, 1950.

—— *Here I Stay.* Coward-McCann, 1938. (High School)

—— *Sword of the Wilderness;* illus. by Harvé Stein. Macmillan, 1936.

Coblentz, Catherine. *Beggars' Penny;* illus. by Hilda Van Stockum. Longmans, Green, 1943.

Cooper, James Fenimore. *The Deerslayer;* illus. by N. C. Wyeth. Scribner, 1925. (Scribner Illustrated Classics)

—— *Last of the Mohicans;* illus. by N. C. Wyeth. Scribner, 1924. (Scribner Illustrated Classics)

Dalgliesh, Alice. *The Silver Pencil;* illus. by Katherine Milhous. Scribner, 1944.

Daly, Maureen. *Seventeenth Summer;* illus. by Joy Robinson. Dodd, Mead, 1942.

DeJong, Meindert. *The House of Sixty Fathers;* illus. by Maurice Sendak. Harper, 1956. (Grades 6–8)

Dickens, Charles. *The Christmas Carol;* illus. by Robert Ball. Macmillan, 1950. (New Children's Classics)

—— *David Copperfield;* intro. by May Lamberton Becker; illus. by contemporary artists. Dodd, Mead. (Great Illustrated Classics) (High School)

—— *A Tale of Two Cities;* illus. by "Phiz" and Fred Barnard. Dodd, Mead, 1942. (Great Illustrated Classics) (High School)

Doyle, Sir Arthur Conan. *Boys' Sherlock Holmes;* ed. by Howard Haycraft. Harper, 1936.

Du Bois, William Pène. *Twenty-one Balloons;* illus. by the author. Viking Press, 1947. (Grades 5–9)

Dumas, Alexandre. *The Three Musketeers;* illus. by C. Walter Hodges. World Publishing Company, 1957. (Rainbow Classics) (High School)

Edmonds, Walter. *Cadmus Henry;* illus. by Manning de V. Lee. Dodd, Mead, 1949.

Eifert, Virginia. *The Buffalo Trace;* illus. by Manning de V. Lee. Dodd, Mead, 1955.

Erdman, Loula. *The Wind Blows Free.* Dodd, Mead, 1952.

Field, Rachel. *Calico Bush;* illus. by Allen Davis. Macmillan, 1931.

Forbes, Esther. *Johnny Tremain;* illus. by Lynd Ward. Houghton Mifflin, 1943.

George, John and Jean. *Meph, the Pet Skunk;* illus. by Jean George. Dutton, 1952.

Gipson, Fred. *Old Yeller;* drawings by Carl Burger. Harper, 1956.

Gray, Elizabeth Janet. *Adam of the Road;* illus. by Robert Lawson. Viking Press, 1942.

—— *The Fair Adventure;* illus. by Alice K. Reischer. Viking Press, 1940.

Greener, Leslie. *Moon Ahead;* illus. by William Pène du Bois. Viking Press, 1952. (Grades 6–8)

Grey, Katharine. *Rolling Wheels;* illus. by Frank Schoonover. Little, Brown, 1937. (Beacon Hill Bookshelf)

Harnett, Cynthia. *The Drawbridge Gate;* illus. by the author. Putnam, 1954.

—— *Nicholas and the Wool-Pack;* illus. by the author. Putnam, 1953.

Havighurst, Walter and Marion. *Climb a Lofty Ladder;* illus. by Jill Elgin. Winston, 1952. (Land of the Free Series)

—— *The Song of the Pines;* illus. by Richard Floethe. Winston, 1949. (Land of the Free Series)

Hawes, Charles Boardman. *The Dark Frigate;* illus. by Anton Fischer. Little, Brown, 1934. (Beacon Hill Bookshelf)

—— *The Mutineers;* illus. by Anton Fischer. Little, Brown, 1941. (Beacon Hill Bookshelf)

Heinlein, Robert A. *Between Planets;* illus. by Clifford Geary. Scribner, 1951.

—— *Farmer in the Sky;* illus. by Clifford Geary. Scribner, 1950.

—— *Space Cadet;* illus. by Clifford Geary. Scribner, 1948.

Howard, Elizabeth. *Peddler's Girl.* Morrow, 1951.

Hudson, William Henry. *Green Mansions, a Romance of the Tropical Forest.* Knopf, 1943. (High School)

Hunt, Mabel Leigh. *Singing Among Strangers;* illus. by Irene Gibian. Lippincott, 1954.

Irving, Washington. *Rip Van Winkle and The Legend of Sleepy Hollow;* illus. by Maud and Miska Petersham. Macmillan, 1951. (New Children's Classics) (Grades 6–9)

Jackson, Helen Hunt. *Ramona;* illus. by N. C. Wyeth; intro. by May Lamberton Becker. Little, Brown, 1939. (High School)

James, Will. *Smoky, the Cowhorse;* illus. by the author. Scribner, 1926. (Grades 6–9)

Jewett, Eleanore. *Hidden Treasure of Glaston;* illus. by Frederick T. Chapman. Viking Press, 1946.

Kalashnikoff, Nicholas. *The Defender;* illus. by Claire and George Louden. Scribner, 1951. (Grades 6–9)

Keith, Harold. *Rifles for Watie;* illus. by Peter Burchard. Crowell, 1957.

Kelly, Eric P. *The Trumpeter of Krakow;* illus. by Angela Pruszynska. Macmillan, 1928.

Kent, Louise. *He Went with Christopher Columbus;* illus. by Paul Quinn. Houghton Mifflin, 1940.

Kipling, Rudyard. *Captains Courageous.* Doubleday, 1897.

Kjelgaard, Jim. *Big Red;* illus. by Bob Kuhn. Holiday House, 1956.

—— *Wolf Brother.* Holiday House, 1957.

Krumgold, Joseph. *And Now Miguel;* illus. by Jean Charlot. Crowell, 1953.

Lane, Rose Wilder. *Let the Hurricane Roar.* Longmans, Green, 1953. (High School)

Latham, Jean Lee. *This Dear-Bought Land;* illus. by Jacob Landau. Harper, 1957.

Lathrop, West. *Black River Captive;* illus by Dwight Logan. Random House, 1946.

Lauritzen, Jonreed. *Ordeal of the Young Hunter;* illus. by Hoke Denetsosie. Little, Brown, 1954. (Grades 6-8)

Lawson, Robert. *The Great Wheel;* illus. by the author. Viking Press, 1957.

Leighton, Margaret. *Judith of France;* illus. by Henry Pitz. Houghton Mifflin, 1948.

Lewis, Elizabeth Foreman. *Ho-Ming, Girl of New China;* illus. by Kurt Wiese. Winston, 1934.

—— *To Beat a Tiger, One Needs a Brother's Help.* Winston, 1956.

—— *Young Fu of the Upper Yangtze;* illus. by Kurt Wiese. Winston, 1932.

Lippincott, Joseph. *Wilderness Champion;* illus. by Paul Bransom. Lippincott, 1944. (Grades 5-8)

Lofts, Norah. *Eleanor the Queen: The Story of the Most Famous Woman of the Middle Ages.* Doubleday, 1955. (High School)

London, Jack. *Call of the Wild;* illus. by Paul Bransom. Macmillan, 1912.

Lownsbery, Eloise. *Boy Knight of Reims;* illus. by Elizabeth Wolcott. Houghton Mifflin, 1927.

McGraw, Eloise. *Mara, Daughter of the Nile.* Coward-McCann, 1953.

—— *The Moccasin Trail.* Coward-McCann, 1952.

McLean, Allan Campbell. *Storm Over Skye;* illus. by Shirley Hughes. Harcourt, Brace, 1957.

Masefield, John. *Jim Davis;* illus. by Bob Dean. Macmillan, 1951.

Meader, Stephen. *Boy with a Pack;* illus. by Edward Shenton. Harcourt, Brace, 1939.

—— *The Long Trains Roll;* illus. by Edward Shenton. Harcourt, Brace, 1944.

—— *Red Horse Hill;* illus. by Lee Townsend. Harcourt, Brace, 1930.

Means, Florence Crannell. *Candle in the Mist;* illus. by Marguerite de Angeli. Houghton Mifflin, 1931.

—— *Shuttered Windows;* illus. by Armstrong Sperry. Houghton Mifflin, 1938.

Meigs, Cornelia. *Master Simon's Garden;* illus. by John Rae. Macmillan, 1929.

Melville, Herman. *Moby Dick; or, The White Whale;* illus. by Mead Schaeffer. Dodd, Mead, 1922. (High School)

Mirsky, Reba. *Thirty-One Brothers and Sisters;* illus. by W. T. Mars. Follett, 1952. (Grades 5-8)

Morrison, Lucile. *The Lost Queen of Egypt;* illus. by Franz Geritz. Lippincott, 1937.

Mühlenweg, Fritz. *Big Tiger and Christian;* trans. by Isabel and Florence McHugh; illus. by Rafaello Busoni. Pantheon Books, 1952.

Nolan, Jeannette. *Treason at the Point;* illus. by Henry Pitz. Messner, 1944.

Nordhoff, Charles. *The Pearl Lagoon;* illus. by Anton Fischer. Little, Brown, 1924.

Nordhoff, Charles, and James N. Hall. *Mutiny on the Bounty.* Little, Brown, 1932. (High School)

Norton, Alice. *Scarface,* by Andre Norton, *pseud.;* illus. by Lorence Bjorklund. Harcourt, Brace, 1948.

O'Hara, Mary, *pseud. My Friend Flicka.* Lippincott, 1941. (High School)

Porter, Jane. *Scottish Chiefs;* ed. by Kate Douglas Wiggin and Nora A. Smith; illus. by N. C. Wyeth. Scribner, 1921.

Rawlings, Marjorie Kinnan. *The Yearling;* illus. by N. C. Wyeth. Scribner, 1946. (High School)

Rich, Louise. *Start of the Trail.* Lippincott, 1949.

Richter, Conrad. *Light in the Forest.* Knopf, 1953. (High School)

Robertson, Keith. *The Wreck of the "Saginaw";* illus. by Jack Weaver. Viking Press, 1954.

Robinson, Mabel Louise. *Bright Island;* illus. by Lynd Ward. Random House, 1937.

Robinson, Tom. *Trigger John's Son;* illus. by Robert McCloskey. Viking Press, 1949.

Rush, William M. *Red Fox of the Kinapoo; a Tale of the Nez Percé Indians;* illus. by Charles Banks Wilson. Longmans, Green, 1949.

Sawyer, Ruth. *The Long Christmas;* illus. by Valenti Angelo. Viking Press, 1941.

Scott, Sir Walter. *Ivanhoe;* illus. by E. Boyd Smith. Houghton Mifflin, 1913. (Riverside Bookshelf) (High School)

Seredy, Kate. *The Singing Tree;* illus. by the author. Viking Press, 1939.

Shannon, Monica. *Dobry;* illus. by Atanas Katchamakoff. Viking Press, 1934. (Grades 5-8)

Skinner, Constance Lindsay. *Becky Landers, Frontier Warrior.* Macmillan, 1926.

Snedeker, Caroline Dale. *Downright Dencey;* illus. by Maginel Wright Barney. Doubleday, 1927. (Grades 6-9)

—— *Forgotten Daughter;* illus. by Dorothy Lathrop. Doubleday, 1933.

—— *The White Isle;* illus. by Fritz Kredel. Doubleday, 1940.

Sperry, Armstrong. *Danger to Windward;* illus. by the author. Winston, 1947.

—— *The Rain Forest;* illus. by the author. Macmillan, 1947.

Stapp, Arthur. *Escape on Skis.* Morrow, 1949.

Stevenson, Robert Louis. *Black Arrow;* illus. by

N. C. Wyeth. Scribner. (Scribner Illustrated Classics)

—— *Kidnapped;* illus. by N. C. Wyeth. Scribner, 1924. (Scribner Illustrated Classics)

—— *Treasure Island;* illus. by N. C. Wyeth. Scribner. (Scribner Illustrated Classics)

Stolz, Mary. *Because of Madeline.* Harper, 1957.

Streatfeild, Noel. *Family Shoes.* Random House, 1954.

Sutcliff, Rosemary. *Eagle of the Ninth;* illus. by C. Walter Hodges. Oxford University Press, 1954.

—— *Shield Ring;* illus. by C. Walter Hodges. Oxford University Press, 1957.

Tarkington, Booth. *Penrod, His Complete Story;* illus. by Gordon Grant. Doubleday, 1914.

—— *Seventeen;* illus. by Edward Tunis. Harper. (High School)

Trease, Geoffrey. *Web of Traitors.* Vanguard Press, 1952.

Tunis, John. *All-American;* illus. by Hans Walleen. Harcourt, Brace, 1942.

—— *The Iron Duke;* illus. by Johan Bull. Harcourt, Brace, 1938.

Ullman, James. *Banner in the Sky.* Lippincott, 1954.

Verne, Jules. *Twenty Thousand Leagues Under the Sea;* illus. by W. J. Aylward. Scribner, 1925. (Scribner Illustrated Classics)

Waldeck, Theodore. *Lions on the Hunt;* illus. by Kurt Wiese. Viking Press, 1942.

——*The White Panther;* illus. by Kurt Wiese. Viking Press, 1941.

Weaver, Stella. *The Stranger;* illus. by Genevieve Vaughan-Jackson. Pantheon Books, 1956.

Welch, Ronald. *The Gauntlet;* illus. by T. R. Freeman. Oxford University Press, 1952.

Wilder, Laura Ingalls. *Little Town on the Prairie;* illus. by Garth Williams. Harper, new ed. 1953.

—— *These Happy Golden Years;* illus. by Garth Williams. Harper, new ed. 1953.

Worth, Kathryn. *Middle Button;* illus. by Dorothy Bayley. Doubleday, 1941.

—— *They Loved to Laugh;* illus. by Marguerite de Angeli. Doubleday, 1942.

FAIRY TALES, MYTHS, LEGENDS, AND HERO STORIES

Blair, Walter. *Tall Tale America; a Legendary History of Our Humorous Heroes;* illus. by Glen Rounds. Coward-McCann, 1944. (Grades 5–8)

Bowman, James Cloyd. *Pecos Bill, the Greatest Cowboy of All Time;* pictures by Laura Bannon. Albert Whitman, 1937. (Grades 6–9)

Chanson de Roland. *Song of Roland;* trans. by

Merriam Sherwood; illus. by Edith Emerson. Longmans, Green, 1938.

Church, Alfred. *The Aeneid for Boys and Girls;* retold from Virgil in simple language. Macmillan, 1918. (Grades 5–9)

—— *The Iliad of Homer;* retold by Alfred J. Church; illus. by John Flaxman. Macmillan, 1951. (New Children's Classics) (Grades 5–9)

—— *The Odyssey of Homer;* retold by Alfred J. Church; illus. by John Flaxman. Macmillan, 1951. (New Children's Classics) (Grades 5–9)

Davis, Julia. *Swords of the Vikings; Stories from the Works of Saxo Grammaticus;* retold by Julia Davis Adams; illus. by Suzanne Lasson. Dutton, 1928.

Deutsch, Babette. *Heroes of the Kalevala; Finland's Saga;* illus. by Fritz Eichenberg. Messner, 1940.

Gaer, Joseph. *The Adventures of Rama;* illus. by Randy Monk. Little, Brown, 1954.

Hamilton, Edith. *Mythology;* illus. by Steele Savage. Little, Brown, 1942.

Hosford, Dorothy. *Sons of the Volsungs;* adapted by the author from *Sigurd the Volsung,* by William Morris; illus. by Frank Dobias. Holt, new ed. 1949.

Hull, Eleanor. *The Boys' Cuchulain; Heroic Legends of Ireland;* illus. by Stephen Reid. Crowell, 1910.

Hyde, Mark Powell. *The Singing Sword; the Story of Sir Ogier the Dane;* illus. by Philip Cheney. Little, Brown, 1930. (Grades 6–8)

Irving, Washington. *The Bold Dragoon, and Other Ghostly Tales;* selected and edited by Anne Carroll Moore; with decorative diversions by James Daugherty. Knopf, 1930.

—— *The Alhambra; Palace of Mystery and Splendor;* selected and arranged by Mabel Williams; illus. by Louis Slobodkin. Macmillan, 1953. (New Children's Classics)

Lanier, Sidney, ed. *The Boy's King Arthur;* illus. by N. C. Wyeth. Scribner, 1917. (Scribner Illustrated Classics) (Grades 6–9)

Macleod, Mary. *Book of King Arthur and His Noble Knights;* Stories from Sir Thomas Malory's *Morte d'Arthur;* introduction by Angelo Patri; illus. by Henry C. Pitz. Lippincott, new ed. 1949. (Lippincott Classics)

Malcolmson, Anne, ed. *The Song of Robin Hood;* selected and edited by Anne Malcolmson; music arranged by Grace Castagnetta; designed and illus. by Virginia Lee Burton. Houghton Mifflin, 1947.

Mukerji, Dhan Gopal. *Rama, the Hero of India.* Dutton, 1930.

Norton, Alice. *Huon of the Horn,* by Andre Norton, *pseud.;* illus. by Joe Krush. Harcourt, Brace, 1951.

Saint-Exupéry, Antoine de. *The Little Prince;* illus. by the author; trans. from the French by

Katherine Woods. Reynal & Hitchcock, 1943. (Grades 5-8)

Seredy, Kate. *The White Stag;* illus. by the author. Viking Press, 1937.

Sherwood, Merriam. *The Tale of the Warrior Lord;* illus. by Henry C. Pitz. Longmans, Green, 1957 (reissue).

Young, Ella. *The Tangle-Coated Horse and Other Tales; Episodes from the Fionn Saga;* illus. by Vera Bock. Longmans, Green, 1929.

SACRED LITERATURE

The Book of Books; the King James Version of the English Bible, abridged with editorial comments for young readers, by W. O. Sypherd. Knopf, 1944.

Smith, Ruth, ed. *Tree of Life; Selections from the Literature of the World's Religions;* drawings by Boris Artzybasheff. Viking Press, 1942.

Yates, Elizabeth, ed. *Joseph, the King James Version of a Well-Loved Tale;* illus. by Nora S. Unwin. Knopf, 1947.

Yates, Elizabeth, comp. *Your Prayers and Mine;* decorations by Nora S. Unwin. Houghton Mifflin, 1954.

SCIENCE AND NATURE

Ahnstrom, D. N. *The Complete Book of Jets and Rockets;* illus. with photographs and diagrams. World Publishing Company, 1957.

Asimov, Isaac. *Building Blocks of the Universe.* Abelard-Schuman, 1957.

Baity, Elizabeth Chesley. *America Before Man;* illus. with drawings, maps, charts and diagrams by C. B. Falls and with 31 pages of photographs. Viking Press, 1953.

Baker, Robert. *When the Stars Come Out.* Viking Press, rev. ed. 1954.

Bauman, Hans. *Caves of the Great Hunters;* trans. by Isabel and Florence McHugh. Pantheon Books, 1954.

Bendick, Jeanne. *Electronics for Young People;* illus. by the author. McGraw-Hill, new rev. ed. 1955. (Whittlesey House) (Grades 6-8)

Bendick, Jeanne and Robert. *Television Works Like This.* McGraw-Hill, new rev. ed. 1954. (Whittlesey House) (Grades 6-8)

Billings, Henry. *Bridges;* illus. by the author. Viking Press, 1956.

Blough, Glenn, ed. *Young People's Book of Science;* illus. with photographs. McGraw-Hill, 1958. (Whittlesey House)

Branley, Franklyn M. *Solar Energy.* Crowell, 1957.

Bridges, William. *Wild Animals of the World;* animal portraits by Mary Baker; text by William Bridges; intro. by Roy Chapman Andrews. Garden City, 1948.

Carrighar, Sally. *One Day on Beetle Rock;* illus. by Henry B. Kane. Knopf, 1948.

——— *One Day at Teton Marsh;* illus. by George and Patricia Mattson. Knopf, 1947.

Carson, Rachel L. *The Sea Around Us.* Oxford University Press, 1951. (Grade 8 and up)

Coombs, Charles. *Rockets, Missiles, and Moons;* illus. with photographs. Morrow, 1957.

Crouse, William. *Understanding Science;* illus. by Jeanne Bendick. McGraw-Hill, new rev. ed. 1956. (Whittlesey House)

Darrow, Floyd, and Clarence Hylander. *The Boys' Own Book of Great Inventions.* Macmillan, 1941.

Fenton, Carroll Lane and Mildred. *Rocks and Their Stories;* illus. with photographs. Doubleday, 1951.

Floherty, John J. *The Television Story.* Lippincott, rev. ed. 1957.

Halacy, D. S., Jr. *Fabulous Fireball; the Story of Solar Energy;* illus. with photographs. Macmillan, 1957.

Harpster, Hilda. *Insect World;* illus. by Zhenya Gay. Viking Press, 1947.

Hartman, Gertrude. *Machines and the Men Who Made the World of Industry;* illus. with old prints, photographs and charts. Macmillan, 1939.

Hegner, Robert and Jane. *Parade of the Animal Kingdom.* Macmillan, 1935.

Hogben, Lancelot. *The Wonderful World of Energy;* illus. in full color. Garden City, 1957. (Grades 5-9)

——— *The Wonderful World of Mathematics;* art by André Charles Keeping and Kenneth Symonds; maps by Marjorie Saynor. Garden City, 1955. (Grades 5-9)

Hogner, Dorothy. *Animal Book; American Mammals North of Mexico;* illus. by Nils Hogner. Oxford University Press, 1942.

Hyde, Margaret. *Exploring Earth and Space, the Story of the I.G.Y.* McGraw-Hill, 1957. (Whittlesey House)

Hylander, Clarence J. *Insects on Parade;* illus. with photographs. Macmillan, 1957.

Jessup, Ronald. *The Wonderful World of Archaeology;* illus. in full color. Garden City, 1956. (Grades 5-9)

Kieran, John. *Introduction to Birds;* illus. by Don Eckelberry. Garden City, 1950. (Grades 5-9)

Lehr, Paul, and others. *Weather.* Simon & Schuster, 1957.

Lewellen, John. *Understanding Electronics; From Vacuum Tube to Thinking Machine;* illus. by Ida Scheib. Crowell, 1957.

Ley, Willy. *Engineers' Dreams;* illus. by Isami Kashiwagi. Viking Press, 1954.

Life (Periodical). *The World We Live In;* by the editorial staff of *Life* and Lincoln Barnett; text adapted by Jane Werner Watson. Simon & Schuster, 1956. (Grades 5–9)

Loomis, Frederic. *Field Book of Common Rocks and Minerals.* Putnam, 1923. (Grades 6–8)

Mathews, Ferdinand S. *Book of Birds for Young People.* Putnam, 1921.

——— *Book of Wild Flowers for Young People;* illus. by the author. Putnam, 1923.

Meyer, Jerome S. *The Elements; Builders of the Universe;* illus. with 68 photographs. World Publishing Company, 1957. (High School)

Morgan, Alfred. *Boys' First Book of Radio and Electronics;* illus. by the author. Scribner, 1954.

Neurath, Marie. *New Wonders in Flying.* Lothrop, Lee & Shepard, 1957.

Osmond, Edward. *Animals of the World;* illus. by the author. Oxford University Press, 1956. (Grades 5–9)

Ravielli, Anthony. *Wonders of the Human Body;* illus. by the author. Viking Press, 1954. (Grades 5–8)

Rogers, Frances. *Lens Magic;* illus. by the author. Lippincott, 1957.

Ross, Frank, Jr. *The World of Engineering;* illus. with photographs. Lothrop, Lee & Shepard, 1957. (High School)

Scheele, William E. *First Mammals;* illus. by the author. World Publishing Company, 1955. (Grades 6–9)

Schneider, Herman and Nina. *Rocks, Rivers and the Changing Earth.* William R. Scott, 1952. (Grades 6–9)

Shippen, Katherine B. *Bridle for Pegasus;* illus. by C. B. Falls. Viking Press, 1951.

——— *Bright Design;* illus. by Charles Daugherty. Viking Press, 1949.

——— *The Great Heritage;* illus. by C. B. Falls. Viking Press, 1947.

——— *Men, Microscopes and Living Things;* illus. by Anthony Ravielli. Viking Press, 1955.

Stefferud, Alfred. *The Wonders of Seeds;* illus. by Shirley Briggs. Harcourt, Brace, 1956. (Grades 6–8)

Teale, Edwin Way. *Junior Book of Insects;* illus. by the author. Dutton, 1953. (Grades 6–9)

Yates, Raymond. *Fun with Your Microscope.* Appleton-Century-Crofts, 1943.

Zim, Herbert S. *Rocks and Minerals;* illus. by Raymond Perlman. Simon & Schuster, 1957.

Zim, Herbert S., and Robert H. Baker. *Stars; a Guide to the Constellations, Sun, Moon, Planets and Other Features of the Heavens;* illus. by James Gordon Irving. Simon & Schuster, rev. ed. 1956.

Zim, Herbert S., and Clarence Cottam. *Insects;* illus. by James Gordon Irving. Simon & Schuster, 1951. (Grades 5–9)

Zim, Herbert S., and Iran Gabrielson. *Birds;* illus. by James Gordon Irving. Simon & Schuster, 1949. (Grades 5–9)

Zim, Herbert S., and Donald Hoffmeister. *Mammals; a Guide to Familiar American Species;* illus. by James Gordon Irving. Simon & Schuster. (Grades 5–9)

Zim, Herbert S., and Alexander C. Martin. *Flowers;* illus. by Rudolf Freund. Simon & Schuster, 1950. (Grades 5–9)

——— *Trees;* illus. by Dorothea and Sy Barlow. Simon & Schuster, 1952. (Grades 5–9)

BIOGRAPHY

Averill, Esther. *King Philip: The Indian Chief;* illus. by Vera Belsky. Harper, 1950.

Baker, Nina Brown. *Juarez, Hero of Mexico;* illus. by Marion Greenwood. Vanguard Press, 1942.

——— *Peter the Great;* illus. by Louis Slobodkin. Vanguard Press, 1943.

——— *Sir Walter Raleigh.* Harcourt, Brace, 1950.

Becker, May Lamberton. *Introducing Charles Dickens;* illus. by Oscar Ogg. Dodd, Mead, 1940.

——— *Presenting Miss Jane Austen;* illus. by Edward Price. Dodd, Mead, 1952.

Benét, Laura. *The Boy Shelley;* illus. by James MacDonald. Dodd, Mead, 1937.

——— *Enchanting Jenny Lind;* illus. with decorations by George Gillett Whitney and photographs. Dodd, Mead, 1939.

——— *Stanley, Invincible Explorer;* illus. with photographs. Dodd, Mead, 1955.

Benz, Francis E. *Pasteur, Knight of the Laboratory;* illus. by James MacDonald. Dodd, Mead, 1938.

Commager, Henry Steele. *America's Robert E. Lee;* illus. by Lynd Ward. Houghton Mifflin, 1951. (Grades 6–8)

Cottler, Joseph, and Haym Jaffe. *Heroes of Civilization;* illus. by F. W. Orr. Little, Brown, 1931. (Grades 5–9)

Curie, Eve. *Madame Curie;* trans. by Vincent Sheean. Doubleday, 1937. (Grade 8 and up)

Daugherty, James. *Abraham Lincoln;* illus. by the author. Viking Press, 1943. (Grades 6–9)

——— *Daniel Boone;* illus. by the author. Viking Press, 1939. (Grades 5–9)

——— *Marcus and Narcissa Whitman: Pioneers of Oregon;* illus. by the author, Viking Press, 1953.

——— *Of Courage Undaunted; Across the Continent with Lewis and Clark;* illus. by the author. Viking Press, 1951.

——— *Poor Richard;* illus. by the author. Viking Press, 1941.

Davis, Robert. *Tree Toad: Adventures of the Kid Brother;* illus. by Robert McCloskey with frontispiece by Charles Dana Gibson. Lippincott, 1942.

Deutsch, Babette. *Walt Whitman: Builder for America;* illus. by Rafaello Busoni. Messner, 1941. (High School)

Doorly, Eleanor. *The Radium Woman; a Life of Marie Curie;* illus. by Robert Gibbings. Roy, 1955.

Eaton, Jeanette. *David Livingstone, Foe of Darkness;* illus. by Ralph Ray. Morrow, 1947.

——— *Gandhi; Fighter Without a Sword;* illus. by Ralph Ray. Morrow, 1950.

——— *Leader by Destiny: George Washington, Man and Patriot;* illus. by Jack Manley Rose. Harcourt, Brace, 1938.

——— *Lone Journey; the Life of Roger Williams;* illus. by Woodi Ishmael. Harcourt, Brace, 1944.

——— *Narcissa Whitman, Pioneer of Oregon;* illus. by Woodi Ishmael. Harcourt, Brace, 1941.

Franklin, Benjamin. *Autobiography;* illus. by Kleber Hall. Houghton Mifflin, 1923. (Riverside Bookshelf)

Galt, Thomas. *Peter Zenger, Fighter for Freedom;* illus. by Ralph Ray. Crowell, 1951.

Garst, Doris (Shannon). *Crazy Horse, Great Warrior of the Sioux;* illus. by William Moyers. Houghton Mifflin, 1950.

Godden, Rumer. *Hans Christian Andersen; a Great Life in Brief.* Knopf, 1955. (High School)

Gollomb, Joseph. *Albert Schweitzer, Genius in the Jungle.* Vanguard Press, 1949.

Graham, Shirley, and George Lipscomb. *Dr. George Washington Carver, Scientist;* illus. by Elton C. Fax. Messner, 1944.

Gray, Elizabeth Janet. *Penn;* illus. by George Gillett Whitney. Viking Press, 1938.

——— *Young Walter Scott.* Viking Press, 1935.

Hall, Anna. *Nansen;* illus. by Boris Artzybasheff. Viking Press, 1940.

Hawthorne, Hildegarde. *Romantic Rebel; the Story of Nathaniel Hawthorne;* illus. by W. M. Berger. Appleton, 1932.

Haycraft, Molly Costain. *Queen Victoria.* Messner, 1956.

Hodges, C. Walter. *Columbus Sails;* illus. by the author. Coward-McCann, 1950.

Holbrook, Stewart. *America's Ethan Allen;* illus. by Lynd Ward. Houghton Mifflin, 1949.

Hudson, William Henry. *Far Away and Long Ago.* Dutton, 1924. (High School)

Hunt, Mabel Leigh. *Better Known as Johnny Appleseed;* illus. by James Daugherty; foreword by Louis Bromfield. Lippincott, 1950.

Jackson, Phyllis. *Victorian Cinderella; the Story of Harriet Beecher Stowe;* portraits by Elliott Means. Holiday House, 1947.

Jarden, Mary Louise. *The Young Brontës;* illus. by Helen Sewell. Viking Press, 1938.

Judson, Clara Ingram. *Mr. Justice Holmes;* illus. by Robert Todd. Follett, 1956.

Kamm, Josephine. *Gertrude Bell: Daughter of the Desert.* Vanguard Press, 1956.

Keller, Helen. *The Story of My Life.* Doubleday, new ed. 1954.

Kellogg, Charlotte. *Paderewski.* Viking Press, 1957.

Komroff, Manuel. *Julius Caesar.* Messner, 1956. (High School)

Kugelmass, J. Alvin. *Ralph J. Bunche: Fighter for Peace.* Messner, 1952.

Latham, Jean. *Carry On, Mr. Bowditch;* illus. by John O'Hara Cosgrave, II. Houghton Mifflin, 1955.

Lavine, Sigmund. *Steinmetz: Maker of Lightning;* illus. with photographs. Dodd, Mead, 1955.

Lenski, Lois. *Indian Captive; the Story of Mary Jemison;* illus. by the author. Lippincott, 1941. (Grades 6–9)

Levinger, Elma. *Albert Einstein.* Messner, 1949.

Lindbergh, Charles A. *The Spirit of St. Louis.* Scribner, 1953. (High School)

Lisitzky, Gene. *Thomas Jefferson;* illus. by Harrie Wood. Viking Press, 1933. (Grade 8 and up)

Meigs, Cornelia. *Invincible Louisa.* Little, Brown, 1933.

Moody, Ralph. *Little Britches;* illus. by Edward Shenton. Norton, 1950.

Morgan, James. *Our Presidents; Brief Biographies of Our Chief Magistrates from Washington to Truman: 1789–1949* Macmillan, enl. ed. 1949.

Nolan, Jeannette Covert. *Andrew Jackson;* illus. by Lee Ames. Messner, 1949.

——— *Benedict Arnold; Traitor to His Country.* Messner, 1956.

——— *Florence Nightingale;* illus. by George Avison. Messner, 1946.

——— *George Rogers Clark, Soldier and Hero;* illus. by Lee Ames. Messner, 1954.

——— *The Story of Clara Barton of the Red Cross;* illus. by W. C. Nims. Messner, 1941.

Norman, Charles. *John Muir.* Messner, 1957.

Paine, Albert Bigelow. *Boys' Life of Mark Twain.* Harper, 1916.

——— *Girl in White Armor; the True Story of Joan of Arc.* Macmillan, 1927.

Petry, Ann. *Harriet Tubman, Conductor on the Underground Railroad.* Crowell, 1955.

Purdy, Claire Lee. *He Heard America Sing; the Story of Stephen Foster;* illus. by Dorothea Cooke. Messner, 1940. (Grades 6–9)

Richardson, Ben. *Great American Negroes;* rev. by William A. Fahey; illus. by Robert Hallock. Crowell, 1956.

Robinson, Mabel. *Runner of the Mountain Tops; the Life of Louis Agassiz;* decorations by Lynd Ward. Random House, 1939.

Roos, Ann. *Man of Molokai; the Life of Father Damien;* illus. by Raymond Lufkin. Lippincott, 1943.

Rourke, Constance. *Audubon;* with 12 colored plates from original Audubon prints and illustrations by James MacDonald. Harcourt, Brace, 1936.

—— *Davy Crockett;* illus. by James MacDonald. Harcourt, Brace, 1934.

Sandburg, Carl. *Abe Lincoln Grows Up;* illus. by James Daugherty. Harcourt, Brace, 1928.

—— *Prairie-Town Boy;* taken from *Always the Young Strangers;* illus. by Joe Krush. Harcourt, Brace, 1955.

Shafter, Toby. *Edna St. Vincent Millay: America's Best-Loved Poet.* Messner, 1957. (High School)

Shepard, Ernest H. *Drawn From Memory;* illus. by the author. Lippincott, 1957.

Shippen, Katherine. *Leif Eriksson; First Voyager to America.* Harper, 1951. (Grades 6–9)

—— *Men of Medicine;* illus. by Anthony Ravielli. Viking Press, 1957. (High School)

Sickels, Eleanor. *In Calico and Crinoline;* illus. by Ilse Bischoff. Viking Press, 1935.

Steffens, Lincoln. *Boy on Horseback;* illus. by Sanford Tousey. Harcourt, Brace, 1935.

Stoutenburg, Adrien, and Laura Baker. *Snowshoe Thompson;* illus. by Victor De Pauw. Scribner, 1957.

Swenson, Eric. *The South Sea Shilling; Voyages of Captain Cook, R.N.;* illus. by Charles Michael Daugherty. Viking Press, 1952.

Swift, Hildegarde. *The Edge of April; a Biography of John Burroughs;* illus. by Lynd Ward. Morrow, 1957.

Sze, Mai-Mai. *Echo of a Cry;* illus. by the author. Harcourt, Brace, 1945. (High School)

Teale, Edwin Way. *Dune Boy; the Early Years of a Naturalist;* illus. by Edward Shenton. Dodd, Mead, new ed. 1957.

Trease, Geoffrey. *Sir Walter Raleigh; Captain & Adventurer.* Vanguard Press, 1950.

Vance, Marguerite. *Martha, Daughter of Virginia; the Story of Martha Washington;* illus. by Nedda Walker. Dutton, 1947. (Grades 6–8)

Waite, Helen. *How Do I Love Thee? The Story of Elizabeth Barrett Browning.* Macrae-Smith, 1953.

Waugh, Elizabeth. *Simón Bolívar: A Story of Courage;* illus. by Flora Nash DeMuth. Macmillan, 1941. (Grades 6–8)

Wibberley, Leonard. *John Barry, Father of the Navy.* Farrar, Straus & Cudahy, 1957.

—— *The Life of Winston Churchill.* Farrar, Straus & Cudahy, 1956.

Wood, Laura. *Raymond L. Ditmars; His Exciting Career with Reptiles, Animals and Insects;* illus. with photographs. Messner, 1944.

Yates, Elizabeth. *Amos Fortune, Free Man;* illus. by Nora S. Unwin. Aladdin Books, 1950.

—— *Prudence Crandall, Woman of Courage;* illus. by Nora S. Unwin. Aladdin Books, 1955.

TRAVEL AND HISTORY

Baity, Elizabeth Chesley. *Americans Before Columbus;* illus. with drawings and maps by C. B. Falls and with photographs. Viking Press, 1951.

Busoni, Rafaello. *Stanley's Africa;* illus. by the author. Viking Press, 1944.

Coolidge, Olivia. *The Trojan War;* illus. by Edouard Sandoz. Houghton Mifflin, 1952.

Follett, Helen. *Ocean Outposts;* illus. with maps by Armstrong Sperry and photographs. Scribner, 1942.

Foster, Genevieve. *Abraham Lincoln's World;* illus. by the author. Scribner, 1944.

—— *Augustus Caesar's World; a Story of Ideas and Events from B.C. 44 to 14 A.D.;* illus. by the author. Scribner, 1947.

—— *George Washington's World;* illus. by the author. Scribner, 1941.

Gatti, Ellen and Attilio. *Here Is Africa;* with photographs by Attilio Gatti and others; map by Raymond Lufkin. Scribner, 1943.

Hartman, Gertrude. *The World We Live In, and How It Came To Be;* with illus. from contemporary sources. Macmillan, 1935.

Heyerdahl, Thor. *Kon-Tiki.* Rand McNally, 1950. (High School)

Hoffman, Gail. *Land and People of Israel.* Lippincott, rev. ed. 1955. (Portraits of the Nations Series)

Kelly, Eric P. *Land of the Polish People;* illus. with photographs. Lippincott, rev. ed. 1952. (Portraits of the Nations Series)

Kennedy, Jean. *Here Is India;* photographs by Alice Schalek and others; map by Raymond Lufkin. Scribner, rev. ed. 1954.

Lucas, Mary Seymour. *Vast Horizons;* illus. and maps by C. B. Falls. Viking Press, 1943.

Melbo, Irving Robert. *Our Country's National Parks.* 2 vols. Bobbs-Merrill, 1950. (Grades 6–9)

Mayer, Josephine, and Tom Prideaux. *Never to Die; the Egyptians in Their Own Words.* Viking Press, 1938.

Morison, Samuel Eliot. *Story of the "Old Colony" of New Plymouth, 1620–1692;* illus. by Charles H. Overly. Knopf, 1956. (Grades 6–9)

Paton, Alan. *Land and People of South Africa.* Lippincott, 1955. (Portraits of the Nations Series)

Shippen, Katherine. *New Found World;* illus. by C. B. Falls. Viking Press, 1945.

Stefánsson, Evelyn. *Here Is Alaska;* with a foreword by Vilhjalmur Stefánsson; illus. with photographs by Frederick Machetanz and others. Scribner, 1943.

———— *Here Is the Far North;* illus. with photographs. Scribner, 1957.

Stockton, Frank. *Buccaneers and Pirates of Our Coasts;* illus. by George Varian and B. West Clinedinst. Macmillan, 1898.

Street, Alicia. *Land of the English People;* illus. with photographs. Lippincott, rev. ed. 1953. (Portraits of the Nations Series)

Tappan, Eva March. *When Knights Were Bold.* Houghton Mifflin, 1911. (Grades 6–9)

Thorne-Thomsen, Gudrun. *In Norway;* illus. by Eyvind Earle. Viking Press, 1948.

Van Loon, Hendrik Willem. *Story of Mankind.* Liveright, new and enl. ed. 1951.

Waldeck, Theodore J. *On Safari;* illus. by Kurt Wiese. Viking Press, 1940.

White, Anne Terry. *Lost Worlds; Adventures in Archaeology;* illus. with maps. Random House, 1941.

POETRY

Adshead, Gladys L., and Annis Duff, comps. *Inheritance of Poetry;* decorations by Nora S. Unwin. Houghton Mifflin, 1948. (All ages)

Benét, Rosemary and Stephen Vincent. *A Book of Americans;* illus. by Charles Child. Rinehart, rev. ed. 1952. (Grades 5–8)

Benét, William Rose, comp. *Poems for Youth.* Dutton, 1925. (Grades 6–9)

Daringer, Helen Fern, and Anne Thaxter Eaton. *Poet's Craft;* illus. by Hélène Carter. World Book, 1935.

Davis, Mary Gould, comp. *The Girl's Book of Verse.* Lippincott, new ed. 1952. (Grades 6–9)

De la Mare, Walter, comp. *Come Hither; a Collection of Rhymes and Poems for the Young of All Ages;* embellished by Alec Buckels. Knopf, 1928. (Grades 6–9)

Dickinson, Emily. *Poems for Youth;* ed. by Alfred Leete Hampson; foreword by May Lamberton Becker; illus. by George and Doris Hauman. Little, Brown, 1934.

Ferris, Helen, ed. *Favorite Poems Old and New;* illus. by Leonard Weisgard. Doubleday, 1957. (All ages)

Fish, Helen Dean, comp. *Boy's Book of Verse; an Anthology.* Lippincott, rev. ed. 1951. (Grades 6–9)

Frost, Robert. *Road Not Taken;* illus. by John O'Hara Cosgrave, II. Holt, 1951.

Millay, Edna St. Vincent. *Edna St. Vincent Millay's Poems Selected for Young People.* Harper, 1929.

Plotz, Helen, comp. *Imagination's Other Place;* illus. with wood engravings by Clare Leighton. Crowell, 1955.

———— *Untune the Sky: Poems of Music and the Dance;* illus. with woodcuts by Clare Leighton. Crowell, 1957.

Sandburg, Carl. *Early Moon;* illus. by James Daugherty. Harcourt, Brace, 1930. (Grades 6–9)

Teasdale, Sara. *Stars Tonight; Verses New and Old for Boys and Girls;* illus. by Dorothy P. Lathrop. Macmillan, 1930. (Grades 5–9)

Untermeyer, Louis, comp. *Stars to Steer By;* illus. by Dorothy Bayley. Harcourt, Brace, 1941.

———— *This Singing World; an Anthology of Modern Poetry for Young People;* illus. by Florence Wyman Ivins. Harcourt, Brace, 1923. (Grades 5–9)

Biographical Sketches

ABEITA, LOUISE (1926–   ), whose Indian name is E-Yeh-Shure, meaning "Blue-Corn," is really a Pueblo Indian. As a child, she often accompanied her father on trips to Indian reservations all over the Southwest where his work promoting Indian arts and crafts took him. Because of her travels among other Indians and the fact that her parents are from different Pueblo tribes, Louise speaks three of the most important Indian languages and, as she says, "English for those who can't understand." She led the life of an ordinary Indian girl, going to the public schools in Albuquerque, New Mexico, and owning and riding two Indian ponies so wild no one else could catch them. She was given her English name in school. She was only twelve years old when she wrote *I Am a Pueblo Indian Girl,* from which the poem *Beauty* was taken.

AESOP, whose name is associated with the famous collection of fables, was, according to tradition, a Greek slave who lived in the sixth century B.C. (620?–564? B.C.). He is described as small, misshapen and ugly. Herodotus identifies him in the Greek island of Samos about 570 B.C. Tradition says that he was a slave of two different masters in Samos, and that the second gave him his freedom out of admiration for his nimble wit. Plutarch, in his *Symposium of the Seven Sages,* records that Aesop was a guest at the court of Croesus along with the seven sages of Greece. Some scholars think that Aesop was not one man but several, while others doubt his very existence.

ALDIS, DOROTHY (1897–   ), was born in Chicago. Both of her parents were newspaper reporters. She herself became editor of women's departments of a Chicago newspaper. In 1922 she married Graham Aldis; they have three daughters and a son. Mrs. Aldis has been particularly successful in writing poems which catch the everyday interests of a child's world. Her books of verse for children are *Everything and Anything; Here, There, and Everywhere; Hop, Skip, and Jump; Before Things Happen;* and *All Together* (1952), a collection which includes poems selected from the four previous books. With *Dark Summer,* Mrs. Aldis began writing fiction for young adults.

ALEXANDER, FRANCES, was formerly a professor of English in the Texas College of Arts and Industries. She also taught courses in Children's Literature. Prior to publishing *Mother Goose on the Rio Grande* in 1944, she contributed poems to magazines and published one volume of poetry. She is a member of the Texas Poetry Society, the American Poetry Society, and the Texas Institute of Letters. She is also sponsor of the Border Poets.

ALLINGHAM, WILLIAM (1824–1889), an Irish man of letters, held clerical positions until he became sub-editor of *Fraser's Magazine.* He published several small volumes of poetry which included some charming lyrics with a light touch. His wife, Helen Paterson, was a water color artist. They were friends of the Rossettis and knew many other prominent literary people of the day.

ANDERSEN, HANS CHRISTIAN (1805–1875), was born April 2, in the town of Odense on the island of Fünen, off the coast of Denmark. His father was a poor cobbler who died when Hans was eleven. His mother was a washerwoman full of macabre superstitions. Hans had little schooling; he preferred to stay home and play with his toy theater, make doll clothes, and read. His mother tried to apprentice him to a weaver, a tobacconist, and a tailor, but the boy was interested only in the theater, and in reading and making up stories. He was obsessed with the idea that one day he would become famous, for a gipsy fortune-teller had said that some day his native town would be illuminated in his honor. When he was fourteen, he left home to seek his fortune in Copenhagen. He was a tall, gawky lad, peculiar, dreamy, and sensitive. Years of heart-breaking discouragement followed. He failed as an actor, a dancer, and a singer, but he never completely lost heart. Finally, when he was seventeen, a wealthy patron, Jonas Collin, a Director of the Theater Royal, procured money for his education. In 1833 the King of Denmark gave him a grant, and he traveled through Germany, France, Switzerland, and Italy. He wrote poems, stories, and novels which were far from successful. In 1835 he wrote four little stories for the daughter of the secretary of the Academy of Art.

These tales, *Little Ida's Flowers, The Tinder-box, Little Claus and Big Claus, The Princess and the Pea,* and the fairy tales which he wrote later, were to make him immortal. Perhaps no other author was so honored during his lifetime as was Andersen. On December, 6, 1867, the prophecy of the gipsy fortune-teller came true. The town of Odense was illuminated in his honor: he was made a State Counselor, and on this memorable evening he was the guest of honor at a banquet. Across his chest he wore the Swedish Order of the Knight of the Polar Star; the White Falcon of Weimar; the Red Eagle of Prussia; and the Order of Our Lady of Guadalupe. Today the house where he was born has become a museum. His statue is in the King's Garden in Copenhagen. In 1955, during the celebration of the 150th anniversary of his birth, King Frederick sat at Andersen's desk in the house where he was born and broadcast a tribute to the poet-storyteller over twenty-one broadcasting networks to people all over the world who were honoring the memory of Hans Andersen.

APION (first century A.D.) was born at Oasis in the Libyan Desert. Though he passed himself off as a Greek, he was really an Egyptian. He was twice at Rome, the first time between A.D. 30 and 37, when he made himself useful to the Emperor, and the second in 40. He died in A.D. 48. Apion was a rhetorician and grammarian, very well known. His reputation for not always telling the truth was such that his enemies called him a mountebank. His admirer, Aulus Gellius, who quotes from Apion's *Aegyptiaca,* also acknowledges that the author did not confine himself to the strict limits of veracity.

ARTZYBASHEFF, BORIS (1899–   ), one of the best-known contemporary artists, was born in Kharkov, Russia. His father was a Russian novelist and playwright. When Boris was eight he was sent to Prince Tenisheff's School in St. Petersburg, where he remained nine years, but he says that he spent most of his time drawing pictures. He was planning to go to Paris to study art when the Russian Revolution broke out, and for the next two years he was in the army. In 1919 he shipped as a sailor on a boat bound for Ceylon and India, but the boat's destination was changed and he came to America. He got a job in an engraver's shop, but went to sea again, this time on an oil tanker bound for Mexico and South America. Soon he was back in New York, more determined than ever to become an artist. In 1926 he became an American citizen. He has made distinguished illustrations for *Aesop's Fables; The Arabian Nights;*

Gay-Neck, by Mukerji; *The Forge in the Forest,* by Padraic Colum; and *The Wonder Smith and His Son,* by Ella Young. He himself wrote and illustrated *Seven Simeons.* He is well known for his portraits of people currently in the news drawn for the covers of *Time* magazine.

ASBJÖRNSEN, PETER CHRISTEN (1812–1885), was a collector of Norwegian fairy tales and legends. He tramped through Norway and took down all he could find. His great friend, J. I. Moe, he discovered, was doing the same thing; they decided to work together. As a zoologist, Asbjörnsen had a chance to make investigating voyages, and Moe, who finally became a bishop, hunted for new tales during his vacations. The two wrote their *Norwegian Popular Stories* together. Their collaboration was so successful that it seems like the work of only one person.

AULAIRE, INGRI (1904–   ) AND EDGAR PARIN (1898–   ) D', are a husband-and-wife team who write and illustrate books for young children. Ingri Mortenson was born in Kongsberg, Norway, and received her education in that country. Edgar was born in Campoblenio, Switzerland. His father was a noted portrait painter and his mother was American. He spent his youth among the artists and literary people of Paris, Florence, and Munich. While studying art in Paris, he met Ingri, who was just beginning her art studies, and a year later they were married. They traveled extensively the next four years, painting in France, Italy, Germany, Scandinavia, the Netherlands, Dalmatia, Greece, and North Africa. Edgar divided his time between murals and illustrations. Ingri painted landscapes and portraits of children. In 1929 they came to America and liked it so much they decided to make it their permanent home. Up to this time they had worked separately on their art. It was Anne Carroll Moore who suggested that they combine their talents and make beautiful books for children. Their first book, *The Magic Rug,* grew out of a visit to North Africa. This was followed by colorful picture-story books with a Scandinavian background — *Ola; Ola and Blakken; Children of the Northlights;* and *Leif the Lucky.* One of their most distinguished books is *East of the Sun and West of the Moon,* a collection of twenty-one Norwegian folk tales which they translated and illustrated with glowing lithographs. Later they chose American themes for their books, and made picture-biographies which are a distinct contribution to biographies for younger children. These include *Abraham Lincoln,* for which they received the Caldecott medal in 1940; *Pocahontas; Benjamin Franklin; Buffalo*

Bill; and *Columbus.* These two artists work perfectly together, each complementing the other. Ingri has an intimate knowledge of children and a sense of fun, while Edgar directs their work and gives a dramatic quality to their pictures. They make their own lithographs, using the old technique of the artist-lithographer who did all of his work by hand. The D'Aulaires, with their son Per Ola, live in a hillside farmhouse-studio in Wilton, Connecticut.

AUSTIN, MARY (1868–1934), was an American author who wrote poetry and stories chiefly about Indian life in the Southwest. She was born in Carlinville, Illinois, graduated from Blackburn University in 1888, and moved to California when she was nineteen. For years she lived like an Indian woman on the edge of the Mohave Desert and studied Indian culture. She made her permanent home in Santa Fe, New Mexico.

BAITY, ELIZABETH CHESLEY (1907–   ), was born in Hamilton, Texas. She received her A.B. and B.S. from Texas State College for Women and her M.A. in English from the University of North Carolina. In 1951 she received the New York Herald Tribune Spring Festival award for *Americans Before Columbus,* considered the best book for older children published that spring. She makes her temporary home in Vaud, Switzerland, and her permanent home in Chapel Hill, North Carolina. Her books include *America Before Man* and *Man Is a Weaver.*

BALDWIN, JAMES (1841–1925), was born in Indiana. He was largely self-educated. He started teaching when he was twenty-four and became superintendent of grade schools in Indiana, a position which he held for eighteen years. The last thirty-seven years of his life he was connected with publishing houses, first with Harper and then with the American Book Company, where he was editor of school books for thirty years. It was said at one time that more than half of the school readers then used in the United States were either written or edited by him. He himself wrote many books, including *The Story of Siegfried; The Story of Roland; Fifty Famous Stories; Thirty More Famous Stories; The Story of the Golden Age; Old Greek Stories;* and *The Sampo.* He told the story of his boyhood in his book *In the Days of My Youth,* which was written under the pen name of Robert Dudley.

BANGS, JOHN KENDRICK (1862–1922), was a humorist, lecturer, and editor. After graduating from Columbia, he was associate editor of *Life,* was on *Harper's Magazine,* was editor of *Harper's Weekly* and of *Puck,* and was the first editor of *Munsey's Weekly.* He published over thirty volumes of verse and humor; one of the best known of the latter is *The Houseboat on the Styx.* He was a very popular lecturer. For his activities during World War I he was made a Chevalier of the Legion of Honor.

BARBAULD, LETITIA AIKIN (1743–1825), the daughter of a schoolmaster and Dissenting minister, married a Dissenting minister, and they, too, set up a school. They had no children, but adopted a nephew; many of her children's stories were first tried out on nephews and nieces. Her numerous volumes of *Evenings at Home* were written in collaboration with her brother, Dr. Aikin. They endeavored, by sugar-coating facts and morals, to arouse the child's interest. They must have succeeded, for Maria Edgeworth in a letter tells how happy the stories made her brothers and sisters.

BARRIE, SIR JAMES MATTHEW (1860–1937), a Scottish novelist and dramatist, was born in Kirriemuir, Scotland, the "Thrums" of his stories. He was the son of a weaver. Little is known of his childhood except what he tells in his book *Margaret Ogilvy.* When he was eight he went to school at Glasgow Academy and was there for five years until he was sent to Dumfries Academy. In 1878 Barrie entered Edinburgh University and four years later took his degree. During this time he became greatly interested in the theater — an interest which lasted throughout his life. He began writing and sending articles to the London papers and magazines, and when they were promptly returned, he decided to go to London himself. After a period of discouragement, he began to sell his articles. Then he began writing books — *Auld Licht Idylls; A Window in Thrums; The Little Minister;* and *Sentimental Tommy.* Next he turned to writing plays — *Quality Street; The Admirable Crichton;* and *What Every Woman Knows.* His most famous play, *Peter Pan,* was an unparalleled success. Barrie first introduced the character of Peter Pan in his story *The Little White Bird. Peter Pan in Kensington Gardens* was abridged from *The Little White Bird.* Later he wrote the book *Peter and Wendy* from the play. He continued his career as a dramatist with *A Kiss for Cinderella, Dear Brutus,* and *Mary Rose.* In 1894 Barrie married Mary Ansell, an actress, but later they separated. He became interested in the five sons of Arthur and Sylvia Davies, nephews of Gerald du Maurier, who played the leading part in several of his plays, and on the death of their parents, Barrie adopted the boys. In 1913 King

George V made Barrie a baronet. Barrie arranged for the royalties of the play *Peter Pan* and the books about Peter Pan to go to the Great Ormond Street Hospital for Children. In Kensington Gardens today, there stands a bronze statue of Peter Pan designed by the sculptor Sir George Frampton.

BEEBE, WILLIAM (1877–   ), an American naturalist and author who won fame for his deep-sea explorations, was born in Brooklyn and graduated from Columbia University. Since 1899 he has been curator of ornithology and director of the department of scientific research of the New York Zoological Society. He headed scientific expeditions to Nova Scotia, Mexico, South America, the Himalayas, and Borneo. He has become famous for his scientific investigations of life in the jungle and at the bottom of the sea. He is the author of a number of books including *Beneath the Tropic Seas; Exploring with Beebe; The Arcturus Adventure; Jungle Days;* and *Half Mile Down.*

BEHN, HARRY (1898–   ), was born and grew up near Prescott in the mountainous part of Arizona. Prescott was then a small mining and cattle town with an army post. While at Harvard College he was a member of Professor George P. Baker's "English 47 Workshop," a playwriting course, and after graduating in 1922 he started a Little Theater in Phoenix, Arizona. An American Scandinavian Fellow to Sweden, he traveled in Europe, then went to Hollywood, where he wrote scenarios. He subsequently taught creative writing at the University of Arizona, where he was president of the Faculty Club; organized and directed the University Radio Bureau, where he produced over a thousand programs; founded and edited the *Arizona Quarterly;* and organized the radio station KCNA in Tucson. In 1947 he retired to Connecticut to write. Mr. Behn is best known for his books of poetry — *The Little Hill; Windy Morning;* and *The Wizard in the Well.* Most of these poems he wrote for his own children when they were small. Not until twenty years later were the poems published, with the author's distinctive drawings. Now he enjoys writing for his grandchildren. Besides the books of poetry for children, he has written *All Kinds of Time* and *The Painted Cave.*

BELLOC, HILAIRE, (1870–1953), was born in La Celle, St. Cloud, France, the son of a French barrister and an English mother. He graduated from Oxford University in 1895 and became a British citizen in 1902. As a writer of nonsense and light verse he ranks high. An extremely versatile writer, he has written essays, novels, travel books, history, biography, and criticism. He is known in the field of children's literature for his nonsense rhymes in *A Bad Child's Book of Beasts, More Beasts for Worse Children,* and *Cautionary Verses.*

BENÉT, STEPHEN VINCENT (1898–1943), American poet, novelist, and short-story writer, was born in Bethlehem, Pennsylvania, the son of a U.S. Army officer. He graduated from Yale in 1919. While studying at the Sorbonne, in Paris, he met Rosemary Carr, who was then on the staff of the Paris edition of the Chicago *Tribune,* and later married her. His best-known works are *John Brown's Body,* a narrative poem of the Civil War, which was awarded the Pulitzer Prize in 1929; and *The Devil and Daniel Webster,* which first appeared in the *Saturday Evening Post,* was made into a one-act opera, and later into a motion picture. His poetry includes *A Ballad of William Sycamore; Ballads and Poems;* and *A Book of Americans,* written with Rosemary Benét.

BENNETT, ROWENA BASTIN (1896–   ), born in New Jersey, came to Chicago as a child. She attended the University of Michigan, is married to Kenneth Chisholm Bennett, and has two children — a daughter and a son. She has been publishing poetry for children in magazines for many years and acknowledges that she began writing verse at nine years. She now lives in Highland Park, a North Shore suburb of Chicago.

BESKOW, ELSA (1874–   ), Swedish writer and illustrator of picture books, was born in Stockholm. She was the eldest of six children, and as far back as she can remember she was telling stories to her sisters and brother and illustrating them with her drawings. At the age of seven she decided to "make picture books" when she grew up. Her decision has been abundantly fulfilled, for today her picture books have been published in French, Finnish, Polish, German, Czech, Russian, Danish, Norwegian, Dutch, and English. In 1892, the year that her first picture book, *The Wee Little Old Woman,* was published, she married a minister, Dr. Nathaniel Beskow, who was headmaster of a church school located in a suburb of Stockholm. They have five sons who, when they were small, served as models for their mother's drawings. Her picture books include *Aunt Green, Aunt Brown, and Aunt Lavender; Aunt Brown's Birthday;* and *Pelle's New Suit.*

BIANCO, MARGERY WILLIAMS (1881–1944), author, translator, and critic, was born in London. Her father was a fellow of Merton College, Oxford, and a distinguished classical scholar. When

Margery was nine, she came to America, living first in New York, then on a farm in Pennsylvania. She had little formal schooling, except for two years in the Convent School at Sharon Hill, Pennsylvania. She began to write when she was seventeen; her first novel, *The Late Returning,* was published in England in 1902. In 1904 she married Francesco Bianco, an authority on rare books and fine writing, who was at one time manager of the rare book department at Brentano's in Paris. For three years the Biancos lived in London, where their two children, Cecco and Pamela, were born. In 1914, they settled in Turin, Italy, where they spent the four years of World War I. Francesco Bianco became a captain in the Italian army. Pamela had been drawing since she was five, and in 1919 when the family returned to England, her drawings were shown at the Leicester Galleries in London. In 1921, the Biancos came to America and Pamela's work was exhibited at the Anderson Galleries in New York. Margery Bianco did not begin writing children's books until her own children were born. *The Velveteen Rabbit,* her first book, was followed by *Poor Cecco* and *The Little Wooden Doll,* which was illustrated by Pamela. Mrs. Bianco's interest in pets and gardening is shown in *All About Pets, More About Animals,* and *Green Grows My Garden.* Other favorites include *The Street of Little Shops, The Hurdy-Gurdy Man, The Good Friends, Bright Morning,* and *Winterbound.*

BLAKE, WILLIAM (1757–1827), was an engraver by trade, a poet by inclination, and a mystic by nature. Though London born and bred, he had a keen appreciation of a mystical kind of nature. Trained as a painter, he was an apprentice in the art of engraving, at which he worked all his life along with his water colors and poetry. His *Songs of Innocence* (1789) first attracted small attention, but since the book was privately published and in a small edition, one is not surprised. This and its companion book, *Songs of Experience* (1794), show Blake at his best. Afterwards his poetry with its symbolism and mysticism took second place to his art, until recent years when there was a Blake revival.

BOGGS, RALPH STEELE, (1901–   ), was born in Terre Haute, Indiana. He was educated at the University of Chicago, receiving his Ph.D. in 1930. He has taught at the University of Miami. His works include *Folklore, Index of Spanish Folklore,* and *Outline of Spanish Literature.*

BORSKI, LUCIA MERECKA, was born in Warsaw, Poland, where she received her primary education in private Polish and Russian schools. After World War I, she came to the United States and soon began working in the New York Public Library. Here she learned that children knew very little of Polish folklore. She then began translating this type of story into English and has since published several books of tales. Besides these she has published various articles. She has her A.B. from New York University and her B.S. from the Library School of Columbia. From 1944 to 1946 she was with the Library of Congress. She is married to Stephen Borski Szczepanowicz.

BOWMAN, JAMES CLOYD (1880–1961), was born in Leipsic, Ohio. He received a B.S. from Ohio Northern University. While doing graduate work at Harvard, he became interested in American folklore. Realizing how much he had missed as a boy in not knowing the tall tales, he decided to retell them for boys and girls and wrote *The Adventures of Paul Bunyan.* Next he turned to the legends of cowboys with *Pecos Bill: The Greatest Cowboy of All Time.* A study of the legends of the American Indian resulted in *Winabojo: Master of Life.* When he began spending summers in Florida, he became interested in the popular Negro hero and wrote *John Henry: The Rambling Black Ulysses.* Recalling stories which as a boy he heard his mother tell of her family migrating from "York State" across the Alleghenies to the frontier, he did research on the keel-boat age and wrote *Mike Fink: The Snapping Turtle of the O-bi-oo and the Snag of the Mas-sas-sip.* Besides writing books on American folklore he collaborated with Margery Williams Bianco on a collection of folk tales and fables of Finland, *Tales from a Finnish Tupa.* In addition, Bowman taught English for many years at Iowa State College and Northern State Teachers College in Michigan.

BRENNER, ANITA, was born in Mexico and spent most of her childhood there. She heard the Mexican folk tales and legends that have come down from Indian mythology before the Spanish conquest, and she included twenty-four representative tales in *The Boy Who Could Do Anything.* She has written two other books for children, *A Hero By Mistake* and *Dumb Juan and the Bandits,* and is also the author of *Idols Behind Altars* and *Your Mexican Holiday.*

BRINK, CAROL (1895–   ), was born in the small university town of Moscow, Idaho. Her father was Scotch; her mother's family came from England and New England, moving westward from Boston to Missouri, Wisconsin, and Idaho. Before she was eight, Carol had lost both parents and was reared by an aunt and grandmother in

Wisconsin. There she heard her grandmother tell stories of her pioneer childhood during Civil War days. Many years later Mrs. Brink recalled these stories and they became the basis of *Caddie Woodlawn,* for which she received the Newbery medal in 1936. During high school and college she wrote articles, short stories and poems. Shortly after graduating from the University of California, she married Raymond Brink, a college instructor. They have two children and several grandchildren. It was a year that they spent in France, while her husband was on leave from the University of Minnesota, that suggested Mrs. Brink's first book for children, *Anything Can Happen on the River,* a story of adventure on the Seine. Other books include the fantasy *Baby Island; Magical Melons,* more stories about Caddie Woodlawn; *Family Grandstand* and its sequel, *Family Sabbatical;* and *Lad with a Whistle,* a historical novel of Scotland.

BRONSON, WILFRID SWANCOURT (1894–), was born in Chicago, attended the Art Institute of Chicago, and has been an artist on four scientific marine expeditions: three for the Bingham Oceanographic Collection of the Peabody Museum at Yale and the fourth to the Galapagos Islands. He not only collected specimens, but made paintings of marine life. These trips gave him the material for his own stories, which he illustrated himself.

BROOKE, L. LESLIE (1862–1940), a portrait painter and illustrator of books for children, was born in Birkenhead, England. He received his art training in the Royal Academy Schools. In 1894 he married his cousin, Sybil Diana Brooke. They had two sons, Leonard and Henry, to whom *Johnny Crow's Garden* was dedicated in 1903. Most of Mr. Brooke's picture books were made when his sons were small. Leonard died in action in 1918 while serving in the Royal Air Force in World War I. In later years, Mr. and Mrs. Brooke made their home at Hampstead on the outskirts of London. Aside from the Johnny Crow stories, most of L. Leslie Brooke's books are built on nursery classics — *Ring o' Roses; The Three Bears; The Three Little Pigs; The Golden Goose Book;* and *The History of Tom Thumb.*

BROOKS, PHILLIPS (1835–1893), was born in Boston, educated at Harvard, and became eventually an Episcopal Bishop of Massachusetts. A gifted preacher, he became widely known and loved in his twenty-two-year pastorate at Trinity Church, Boston, as a spiritual leader. As a preacher at Harvard, he had much influence upon the young men. He possessed good judgment and the saving grace of humor, together with a sympathy with other men and other religions that gained him universal confidence and respect.

BROWN, ABBIE FARWELL, was born in Boston about 1875 and died in March, 1927, in the home on Beacon Hill in which she was born. She was educated at a private school and at Radcliffe College. She was a friend of Josephine Preston Peabody, Amy Lowell, and Robert Frost. Besides her two books of rhymes, *Pocketful of Posies* (1902) and *Fresh Posies* (1908), she wrote about twenty-five other books for children.

BROWN, MARCIA, an American illustrator and author, won the Caldecott medal in 1955 for *Cinderella,* which she translated anew from the French of Charles Perrault and illustrated with highly imaginative pastels. She was born in Rochester, New York, and attended the State College for Teachers in Albany. While in college she designed and painted stage sets. With a scholarship she studied two summers under Judson Smith at the Woodstock School of Painting. She taught English and dramatics for a time but was determined to become an artist. She went to New York and took a part-time position in the New York Public Library which gave her an opportunity to work with children and books and to gain experience in storytelling. She studied painting at the New School for Social Research under Kuniyoshi and Stuart Davis and later worked on color wood-block prints under Louis Shanker. Her prints have been exhibited in several galleries, and the Library of Congress purchased one for its permanent collection. *The Little Carousel* was her first picture book. This was followed by *Stone Soup,* which was a runner-up for the Caldecott medal in 1948, as all her books were until she won the medal in 1955. She is a versatile artist with a gift for suiting the style of illustration to her subject. Her picture books include *Henry-Fisherman,* a story of the Virgin Islands; *Dick Whittington and His Cat;* told and cut in linoleum; *Puss in Boots;* and *The Steadfast Tin Soldier.*

BROWNING, ROBERT (1812–1889), the only son of middle-class English people, was born in London. Disliking school, he decided to educate himself by reading and studying music, though he also attended the University of London. His poetic fame came slowly, really after his romantic marriage to another poet, Elizabeth Barrett. Browning took his wife to Italy, where they lived until her death. He then returned to England with their son. His poetry shows him to be a man of enthusiasms, greatly interested in human beings. He is buried in the Poets' Corner of Westminster Abbey.

BRYAN, CATHERINE (Mrs. Mabra Madden) (1907–). As Mr. and Mrs. Madden work together, they will be considered together. Both are native Californians and graduates from the University of California. Mrs. Madden taught art to Mexican children in the fourth, fifth, and sixth grades of the schools in Casa Blanca, a Mexican suburb of Riverside, California. There she met Mabra Madden, and there they wrote two books, *Pito's House* and *The Cactus Fence*. Mr. Madden is principal of one of the schools and, as his wife says, the friend and adviser of the whole community. At present her interests and main efforts are given to her family, but she and her husband look forward to taking up their writing again at some future time.

BRYANT, WILLIAM CULLEN (1794–1878), was born in western Massachusetts. He had little formal education, though he studied hard, hoping his father, a doctor, could send him to Yale. He gave up that hope and he studied law; and though he practiced the profession nine years, he always hated it. Giving up this work, he went into journalism in New York, where he finally became the chief owner of the *Post* with editorial control. But we know him primarily as the author of *Thanatopsis,* written at eighteen, and *To a Waterfowl,* at twenty-one. American poetry is often said to have begun in 1821 with the publication of *Thanatopsis.*

BURROUGHS, JOHN (1837–1921), was a farmer boy who became a businessman but wanted to write. He grew interested in the study of nature and divided his time between literature and experimentation in fruit and vegetable culture. Much of his writing tells in a familiar way the facts he discovered about wild animals and birds. Perhaps his main contribution to the study of nature is his ability to convey the individuality of the bird or animal about which he writes.

BURTON, VIRGINIA LEE (1909–), an American author and illustrator, was born in Newton Center, near Boston, and lived there while her father was dean of the Massachusetts Institute of Technology. When Virginia was seven, the family moved to California, living first in San Diego, then in Carmel, and later in Berkeley. "Jinnee," as she was called, won a scholarship to the California School of Fine Arts, where she studied art and ballet dancing. In 1928 she returned to Massachusetts with her father. She went to art school three nights a week and worked hard at dancing. Circumstances forced her to give up her dream of becoming a ballet dancer, and she concentrated on art. She got a job with the Boston *Transcript* drawing sketches and later worked for *The Bostonian*. She attended Saturday morning art classes at The Boston Museum School, studying under the sculptor, George Demetrios, whom she married in 1931. They lived in Boston for a year and then moved to Folly Cove, Gloucester, where they still live. They have two sons, Aristides and Michael, and it was for them that their mother made her picture books. An engine on the Gloucester branch of the Boston and Maine Railroad became the heroine of *Choo Choo.* "Mary Ann," Mike Mulligan's steam shovel, was the one that dug the cellar of the new Gloucester High School. The idea for *The Little House* came when their own house in Folly Cove was moved from the side of the main road back into an apple orchard on a hill. For this book she was awarded the Caldecott medal in 1943. Besides making picture books, Virginia Lee Burton has done murals and exhibited in Boston. With the help of fellow artists she organized the Folly Cove Designers, whose linoleum block prints on linen, dresses, and curtains have found a popular market in New York and Boston.

CALDECOTT, RANDOLPH (1846–1886), was the English illustrator in whose honor the Caldecott medal has been established. He was born in the old walled town of Chester, England, where he attended the Henry VIII School. When he was fifteen he went to Whitchurch in Shropshire to work in a bank. He lived in the country and sketched hunting scenes, animals, and landscapes. At twenty, he went to Manchester, worked in a bank, and studied at the Manchester School of Art. His sketches appeared in local magazines and papers. In 1872, Caldecott went to London. He began contributing sketches to English periodicals and did art work for *The Graphic* and *Punch.* He took a cottage at Farnham Royal, near Windsor, and worked on illustrations for Washington Irving's *Old Christmas* and *Bracebridge Hall,* two books which established him in the field of illustration. He made two picture-books, *The Diverting History of John Gilpin* (1878) and *The House That Jack Built* (1878), with the engraver Edmund Evans. This partnership proved to be a happy one and produced seventeen picture books which included *The Three Jovial Huntsmen, A Frog He Would a-Wooing Go, Sing a Song of Sixpence, Hey Diddle Diddle* and *The Great Panjandrum Himself.* He drew the illustrations for Mrs. Ewing's *Jackanapes* and *Lob Lie-by-the-*

Fire. In 1880 he married Marion H. Brind and they lived not far from London. In 1886 he and his wife went to Florida hoping the climate would benefit his health, but he died of tuberculosis in St. Augustine in his fortieth year.

CARMAN, WILLIAM BLISS (1861–1929), though born in New Brunswick, Canada, came of Connecticut ancestry; and after finishing his college work at New Brunswick, Edinburgh, and Harvard, he settled in the United States. He studied law and was a teacher, editor, and civil engineer, besides being a poet. He acknowledged his debt to Browning and Matthew Arnold. The keynote of his poetry is a pagan love of nature.

CARRICK, VALERY (1869–1948), was born in St. Petersburg, Russia. His father was a Scotsman and his mother was a Russian writer and journalist. As a boy he heard the old folk tales from his mother, from his nurse, and from the peasants on his father's estate. He began his artistic career as a caricaturist. During a visit to England he made caricatures of well-known British personages for the *Westminster Gazette,* the *Manchester Guardian,* and the *Liverpool Post.* It was not until he was forty that he began writing and illustrating the folk tales he had loved as a boy. These include *Picture Tales from the Russian* and *More Russian Picture Tales.* When the Russian Revolution broke out, Carrick's estate was confiscated and he and his wife migrated to Norway where they made their home in Hvalstad.

CARRIGHAR, SALLY, was born in Cleveland, Ohio. Much of her childhood was spent in the home of her grandparents in northern Ohio. Of those days she says, "My nursery was a meadow with a river along the edge and the smell of Lake Erie over it. From those grandparents I first learned what it was to have an intimate feeling for plants and trees, birds and animals." At Wellesley College she took all the science courses she could. Two summers in the Canadian woods gave her a taste of the real wilderness. With a trapper as guide, she and her brother learned to track wild animals. Then followed trips into northern Michigan, the Rockies, and the Ozarks. For six months she served as guide at an Ozark fishing lodge. Then she turned to writing for motion pictures, radio, advertising, and for a while edited a financial monthly. One night she listened to a singing mouse and began to search for words in which to describe the tiny concert. Suddenly she realized that wild-life writing was the thing she wanted most to do. That was in 1937. For many months at Beetle Rock in Sequoia National Park, in the Sierra Nevada Mountains, she did nothing but watch, "learning every

bush and tree, burrows, dens, and nests, and more important the animals." In 1944 she wrote *One Day on Beetle Rock,* describing the lives of the small animals observed during a single day. In *One Day at Teton Marsh* (1947) she tells about an amazing variety of animals found in a marsh in Jackson Hole, Wyoming. In *Icebound Summer* (1953) she gives an account of the struggle for survival which animals, birds, and human beings share on the northwest coast of Alaska. For three years before the publication of this last book, she gathered material in many parts of Alaska, aided by a Guggenheim fellowship. She lived with the Eskimos in the village of Unalakeet and stayed with the natives of St. Lawrence Island. She worked with and was helped by biologists, arctic explorers, men of the U.S. Fish and Wildlife Service and the Coast Guard, bush pilots, traders, trappers, and miners.

CARROLL, LEWIS. *See* DODGSON, CHARLES LUTWIDGE.

CARRYL, CHARLES EDWARD (1841–1920), was born in New York City and lived there most of his life. He wrote *Davy and the Goblin* for his two small children. The story appeared serially in the *St. Nicholas Magazine* and was later published in book form. Shortly after its publication, he wrote *The Admiral's Caravan* for his daughter Constance. This book also appeared serially in the *St. Nicholas* and a year later was published with illustrations by Reginald Birch. Carryl was a broker by profession, a member of the New York Stock Exchange, and an officer and director of various railroads.

CARSON, RACHEL L. (1907–   ), was born in Springdale, Pennsylvania. She began her literary career at the age of ten with contributions to the St. Nicholas League. Her early ambition to become an author was later overshadowed by her intense interest in natural history. Eventually, however, the two interests merged in bringing to the general reader her vast knowledge of the sea and sea life in beautiful prose. Miss Carson graduated from Pennsylvania College for Women, where she majored in biology. She received her M.A. from Johns Hopkins University and continued her studies at the Marine Biological Laboratory at Woods Hole, Massachusetts. She was a member of the Zoology staff at the University of Maryland, 1931–1936. She has been the recipient of many honorary degrees and literary awards. In 1950 she received the George Westinghouse Science Writing Award and in 1951 the National Book Award in non-fiction for *The Sea Around Us.* She was presented with the Henry Bryant Gold Medal of the Geographic Society of Philadelphia and given the title "Woman of the Year" by the women's editors of Associated Press newspapers. She was granted a Guggenheim fellowship for 1951–52 to make a study of the seashore.

CHAN, CHRISTINA (1930–   ) AND PLATO (1931–   ), a brother-sister team, were born in New York City, where their father was attached to the diplomatic service. They have lived also in Germany, France, England, and China. Christina does the writing and Plato draws the pictures. Christina is especially interested in ballet dancing and has studied that art. Plato could draw before he could talk, and held his first public exhibition in Paris in 1937 for the Chinese Relief Fund. When Paris fell, the father was made a prisoner of war; but the mother got the two children to London and on to the United States.

CHASE, RICHARD (1904–   ), noted folklorist and teller of tales, has made a unique contribution to American folklore by gathering old tales, rhymes, ballads, and dances from the folk themselves who live in remote mountain homes in North Carolina, Virginia, and Kentucky, where storytelling still exists as a folk art. Mr. Chase was born in Huntsville, Alabama. He attended Harvard for two years and graduated from Antioch College in 1929. He has been a recreation consultant in nine states and has been associated with many folk festivals. He first began to collect folk material in 1925. In 1933 he wrote a Negro folk play, *Home to Canaan*, which was produced in Cleveland in 1934. From 1933 to 1936 he was with the Institute of Folk Music at the University of North Carolina and with the White Top Folk Festival from 1934 to 1941. From 1936 to 1949 he was a teacher of American folk songs and dances as Virginia Representative of the Country Dance Society. Since 1940 he has been lecturing on folk music and folk tales in schools and colleges all over the country and has entertained thousands of children and adults by telling folk tales and singing ballads. He recently directed a workshop on folk arts for teachers, church workers, and recreation leaders at Madison College in Harrisonburg, Virginia. His books include *The Jack Tales; Grandfather Tales; Jack and the Three Sillies; Wicked John and the Devil;* and *Hullabaloo,* a book of singing games and dances.

CHRISMAN, ARTHUR BOWIE (1889–1953), was born on a farm "West Brook" near White Post, Virginia. His parents were descended from early colonial settlers. He was one of six children and attended a one-room country school. Later he studied electrical engineering at Virginia Polytechnic Institute. When he was a small boy,

creating and telling stories was a spontaneous part of his being, but he was eighteen before he thought of writing them down and trying to sell them. While he lived in California he loved to explore the state on foot. He became interested in studying the ancient literature and history of India and China. He made the acquaintance of a Chinese shopkeeper and learned from him many folk tales and customs of China. Several years later Chrisman wrote *Shen of the Sea*, a collection of stories so imbued with the atmosphere of China that many thought them translations. With this book he won the Newbery medal in 1926. He wrote two other collections of Chinese stories, *The Wind That Wouldn't Blow* and *Treasures Long Hidden.*

CLARK, ANN NOLAN (1898–   ), an American teacher and writer, was born in New Mexico. She traveled and lived for years in the Indian country learning to know the Indians well. When she was teaching in an Indian school she realized that the textbooks were not adapted to non-English speaking children, so she wrote new ones. The Director of Indian Education persuaded her to spend a year with various tribes and write books from the Indian point of view which could be used in the Indian schools. *In My Mother's House* was the geography she wrote with the help of the Tewa Indian children of the Tesque pueblo near Santa Fe. It was followed by *Little Navajo Bluebird.* The Inter-American Educational Foundation claimed Mrs. Clark's services for five years to travel and live in Mexico, Guatemala, Costa Rica, Ecuador, Peru, and Brazil, to help train native teachers in work with underprivileged children. This experience gave her material for her books *Magic Money, Looking-for-Something,* and *Secret of the Andes.* With this last book Mrs. Clark won the Newbery medal in 1953. Her only son was killed flying over the Pacific in World War II. When she retires she plans to devote her full time to writing on her Red Dog Ranch in Tesque, New Mexico.

CLARK, MARGERY, is the pen name of the collaborators Margaret Quigley (1886–   ) and Mary E. Clark (1887–   ), who wrote *Poppy Seed Cakes.* Miss Quigley was born in Los Angeles and graduated from Vassar. She took a library science course in St. Louis and was on the staff of the St. Louis Public Library. In 1922 she was appointed Chief Librarian of the Public Library in Montclair, New Jersey. Mary E. Clark was born in New York City and attended Columbia University. In 1927 she was made assistant librarian at the Montclair Public Library.

CLEMENS, SAMUEL LANGHORNE (1835–1910), American author and humorist, was born in Florida, Missouri, but spent his boyhood in Hannibal on the Mississippi River. After his father died, Samuel left school at the age of twelve and was apprenticed to a printer. When he was twenty-three he qualified as a river pilot. It was at this time that he took the pen name Mark Twain, a term used in taking soundings to mean that the water was two fathoms deep. He went to California and became a newspaper reporter. His first successful story was *The Jumping Frog of Calaveras County*. His paper sent him to Hawaii to write travel sketches and later sent him to Europe and the Holy Land, after which he wrote *Innocents Abroad*. He married Olivia Langdon of Elmira, New York. For the next twenty years he was at the height of his powers and wrote many books, including *Roughing It; The Prince and the Pauper; Life on the Mississippi;* and *A Connecticut Yankee at King Arthur's Court*. *The Adventures of Tom Sawyer* and its sequel, *Adventures of Huckleberry Finn*, are classics of boyhood and contain many of his childhood experiences in Hannibal.

COATSWORTH, ELIZABETH (1893–), is an American poet, novelist, and author of books for children. She was born in Buffalo, New York, graduated from Vassar, and took her M.A. degree at Columbia. She has traveled extensively in Europe and spent a year in the Orient. She married Henry Beston, a distinguished author in his own right, and they have two daughters. Elizabeth Coatsworth's first story for younger children, *The Cat and the Captain*, was an immediate success and was followed by *The Boy with the Parrot*. In 1931 she received the Newbery medal for *The Cat Who Went to Heaven*, a perceptive reflection of her interest in Buddhism. Her books cover a wide range in both age and subject matter. *Away Goes Sally* was her first period story and is followed by four books about Sally as she grows up — *Five Bushel Farm; The Fair American; The White Horse;* and *The Wonderful Day*. Some of Miss Coatsworth's most exquisite poems link the chapters of these books. *The Golden Horseshoe* has American colonial life as a background. *Sword of the Wilderness* is a story of the French and Indian wars in New England. *The Last Fort*, a story of the French Voyageurs, and *Door to the North*, telling of a Norse expedition to America in the fourteenth century, are both volumes in the Land of the Free Series. Although she wrote *Here I Stay*, a story of Colonial Maine, for adults, older girls enjoy it. Miss Coatsworth has written over

sixty books, more than thirty of which are still in print. Many have also been published in England and twelve have been brought out in European editions. Besides seven volumes of poetry for adults, she has written three for children: *Summer Green; Mouse Chorus;* and *Poems* (1957). The Bestons now live in Chimney Farm at Nobleboro, near Damariscotta, Maine.

COLLODI, CARLO. See LORENZINI, CARLO.

COLUM, PADRAIC (1881–), Irish poet and playwright, was born in Langford, Ireland. As a child he heard folk tales, legends, and bits of poetry until he was steeped in Irish folk literature. As a young man he lived in Dublin when the Celtic Revival was a vital movement. People were urged to learn the Irish language and renew their interest in the old cultural traditions of their country. At this time too, William Butler Yeats was trying to promote an Irish Theater. Colum was drawn into the center of all this activity. With Yeats, George Russell (A.E.), Lady Gregory, and J. M. Synge, he helped found the Irish National Theater. He married Mary Maguire, a literary critic and short-story writer. It was not until Colum came to the United States in 1914 that he began writing books for children. The famous artist, Willy Pogány, suggested that Colum write a children's book which he would illustrate; *The King of Ireland's Son* was the result. Later the Macmillan Company asked Colum to retell the Iliad and the Odyssey in a form that boys and girls would enjoy. Thus began the twenty books he wrote for children. In 1923 he went to Hawaii at the invitation of the government to make a study of Hawaiian folklore and retell the folk tales in an attractive manner. *The Gateways of the Day* and *Bright Islands* were the result of this assignment. Dr. Colum is a lecturer in comparative literature at Columbia University.

CONKLING, HILDA (1910–), was born at Catskill-on-the-Hudson, the daughter of Grace Hazard Conkling, well-known poet and professor emeritus of English at Smith College. At the age of four, Hilda began to "tell" her verses to her mother, who wrote them down without changing them, but arranging them in lines. By the time Hilda was nine, she had created one hundred and fifty verses. These were published in 1920 under the title *Poems by a Little Girl*, with a foreword by Amy Lowell. This was followed two years later by *Shoes of the Wind*. A selection of poems from the two volumes appeared in *Silverhorn*. Hilda was educated at the Mary A. Burnham School and the Northampton School for Girls, and later attended the École de Jeunes Filles at

Versailles, France. For a short time she was a social worker at South End House in Boston. She was manager of the Dartmouth Book Stall in Boston and in 1952 became manager of the Mount Holyoke College Bookstore in South Hadley, Massachusetts.

COURLANDER, HAROLD (1908–   ), a folklorist and musicologist, was born in Indiana. He graduated from the University of Michigan in 1931. He visited Africa, the islands of the Caribbean, and many other places, writing books and magazine articles and recording music. He has been an editor of a series of "Ethnic" music albums issued by the Ethnic Folkways Library. As a folklorist he has been a member of various expeditions under the sponsorship of Columbia University and the American Philosophical Society. Mr. Courlander is an editor in the Publications Division of the United Nations. He is married and has three children. His books include *The Cow-Tail Switch, and Other West African Stories; Fire on the Mountain, and Other Ethiopian Stories; Kantchil's Lime Pit and Other Stories;* and *The Hat-Shaking Dance, and Other Tales from the Gold Coast.*

CRAIK, DINAH MULOCK (1826–1887), an English writer, went to London when about twenty years old, determined to make a living, if not her fortune, by writing fiction for children. The novel *John Halifax, Gentleman* shows the height of her power, though her fairy tales *Adventures of a Brownie* and *Little Lame Prince* are still favorites with children.

CULLEN, COUNTEE (1903–1946), an American Negro poet, was born in New York City, the son of a minister. He received his A.B. from New York University, his M.A. from Harvard, and studied in Paris with a Guggenheim fellowship in 1928. He wrote a number of books of poetry on Negro themes: *Color; Copper Sun; The Ballad of the Brown Girl;* and *The Black Christ.* In 1940 he wrote *The Lost Zoo* for children.

CUMMINGS, EDWARD ESTLIN (1894–   ), was born in Cambridge, Massachusetts. He took his bachelor's degree from Harvard in 1915 and his master's degree in 1916. During World War I, while serving with the Norton Harjes Ambulance Corps, he was detained for three months in a French concentration camp through an error on the part of an official. Out of this experience came his first book, *The Enormous Room,* a classic among war books. Throughout his life Cummings has been interested in a variety of literary and art forms. In his poetry, he is

known for his eccentricity of line arrangement and punctuation, which he employs to indicate the rhythm to the eye of the reader. Mr. Cummings is a painter as well as a poet; he made a collection of drawings and paintings which he called CIOPW because the art work was done in charcoal, ink, oil, pencil, and water color. His plays include *Him,* performed at the Provincetown playhouse in 1928, and *Santa Claus: A Morality.* He also wrote a ballet *Tom,* based on *Uncle Tom's Cabin.* Other books include *Eimi,* a journal of a trip to Soviet Russia; *Anthropos — the Future of Art;* and *Six Nonlectures,* originally delivered as the Charlest Eliot Norton Lectures at Harvard University. *Poems: 1923–1954* brings together all the poems from all the collections of verse Cummings had published to date, presenting in one definitive volume the contents of ten books. He was honored in 1950 by a $5,000 Fellowship of the Academy of American Poets for "great achievement" over a period of years. In 1957 he was the winner of the Boston Arts Festival Poetry Award and was also honored with the 1957 Bollingen Prize in Poetry awarded by Yale University Library.

CUNNINGHAM, ALLAN (1784–1842), was born in Scotland. His father was a neighbor of and had known Burns. Young Cunningham was apprenticed to a stone mason, but later went to London where he supported himself with newspaper work until he obtained a clerkship, which he held until his death. He was not a great poet, but he continued to write, on the side, both poetry and essays all his life. He was the father of five sons, all of whom held responsible positions in national service or in literature or in both.

CURIE, EVE (1904–   ), is an author, musician, and lecturer. She wrote the biography of her famous mother, *Madame Curie,* and it has been translated and published in twenty-four languages. It was also made into a moving picture. In World War II, Eve Curie was a coordinator of women's war activities in France. Several times she came to the United States on a lecture tour for the French cause. In 1942 she was a war correspondent to the battle fronts of Libya, Russia, Burma, and China. She wrote of her experiences in her book *Journey Among Warriors.*

DALGLIESH, ALICE (1893–   ), was born on the island of Trinidad in the West Indies. Her father was Scotch and her mother English. When she was thirteen, they went to live in England and Alice attended the Wimbledon Hill School. By the time she was nineteen, she had decided to be a kindergarten teacher. She came to America and took kindergarten training at Pratt Institute in Brooklyn. She took her A.B. in Education at Teachers College, Columbia University, and taught in the elementary grades for a few years. Then she taught in the Horace Mann Kindergarten in New York, and took her M.A. in English at Columbia. She began teaching a course in Children's Literature in Teachers College. She gave up kindergarten work to become children's book editor at Charles Scribner's Sons. For several years she conducted a column of reviews of children's books in *Parents Magazine*. She is a very versatile writer. Her interest in early America is shown in her books *America Travels; America Builds Homes; America Begins; The Columbus Story; The Fourth of July Story;* and *The Thanksgiving Story.* Summers at Sandy Cove, Nova Scotia, furnished material for her Sandy Cove stories: *The Blue Teapot; Relief's Rocker;* and *Roundabout. A Book for Jennifer* is a story of London children in the eighteenth century and of John Newbery's bookshop. Her many excellent books for younger children include *Bears on Hemlock Mountain; The Courage of Sarah Noble;* and *Ride on the Wind.* For older children she has written two books which are partly autobiographical — *The Silver Pencil* and its sequel, *Along Janet's Road.*

DASENT, SIR GEORGE WEBBE (1817–1896), became interested in Scandinavian studies during a four-year sojourn in Stockholm as secretary to the British envoy Encouraged by Jakob Grimm, he turned to translation of the sagas. Throughout an active career as assistant editor of the London *Times*, advocate at law, and civil service commissioner, he pursued his interest in Norse scholarship. He is best remembered for his translations of the tales collected by Asbjörnsen and Moe.

DAUGHERTY, JAMES (1889–), illustrator, mural painter, and author of books for children, was born in Asheville, North Carolina. His boyhood was spent in Indiana and Ohio. He studied at the Corcoran School of Art in Washington, D.C., at the Pennsylvania Academy of Fine Arts, and in London. He has an amazing gift for recreating in rugged prose and robust pictures the essence of the American spirit. Early in his career he illustrated Washington Irving's *Knickerbocker's History of New York*, edited by Anne Carroll Moore, which contains some of his finest work. Then followed his pictures for Carl Sandburg's *Abe Lincoln Grows Up.* A high peak was reached with books which he both wrote and illustrated — *Andy and the Lion,* his book for younger children, and his *Daniel Boone,* which won the Newbery medal in 1940. Books portraying other early American heroes followed —

Abraham Lincoln; Of Courage Undaunted, the story of the Lewis and Clark expedition; Benjamin Franklin in *Poor Richard;* and *Marcus and Narcissa Whitman.* He has illustrated many books by other authors, including several written by his wife, Sonia Daugherty, a well-known author in her own right. The Daughertys have one son, Charles, who is also an artist.

D'AULAIRE, INGRI AND EDGAR PARIN. *See* AULAIRE, INGRI AND EDGAR PARIN D'.

DAVIS, MARY GOULD (1882–1956), was born in Bangor, Maine, the next to the youngest of eight children. She came from a book-loving family and her mother read aloud to the children in the evenings. She had rather a haphazard education which included a governess and private schools. She began her career in the Brooklyn Public Library and later joined the staff of the New York Public Library, where in 1922 she became Supervisor of Storytelling, a position she held until 1945. Since early childhood she had loved folk tales and in 1923 she decided nothing would be more fascinating than to trace them back to their own country. Her first trip was to England and France to search out the legends of King Arthur and Roland. Another year she spent in Italy, where in Tuscany and Umbria she found the stories which later she put in her book *The Truce of the Wolf.* In 1935 she went to Spain and worked on a collection of folk tales that had been recorded by Dr. Boggs of the University of North Carolina; the following year *Three Golden Oranges* was published. The year 1939 found her on the Island of Skye, seeking Gaelic tales and legends of the early Christian saints. In 1945 she collaborated with Ernest Kalibala in writing *Wakaima and the Clay Man,* folk tales of the Baganda tribe of East Africa. In 1946 she wrote a short biography of the English artist, Randolph Caldecott, which was published in celebration of the one hundredth anniversary of his birth. For several years she was editor of Books for Young People, a department of the *Saturday Review of Literature.*

DAVIS, ROBERT (1881–1949), was born in Beverly, Massachusetts, descended from five generations of Congregational ministers. He attended Union Theological Seminary in New York City and was assistant to Henry Van Dyke. For ten years he was pastor of a suburban church in New York. During World War I he was commissioner for the American Red Cross and editorial writer for the Paris edition of the New York *Herald Tribune.* He was a correspondent and reporter in thirty-one countries. From 1932 to 1936 he was Director of the American Library in Paris. From 1937 to 1939 he was in Spain writing articles for the *Herald Tribune*. While there, he heard old Spanish folk tales which he later used in his book *Padre Porko*. While on an assignment in North Africa, he incidentally collected material which he used in *Pepperfoot of Thursday Market*. He married a Greek wife and they had four sons and three daughters. Along with his career, his chief interest was in his dairy farm and vineyard in France. With the fall of France, he lost all his worldly goods. After months of anxiety, he and his wife and daughters reached the United States. At the age of sixty Mr. Davis started as professor of history at Middlebury College in Vermont. By the time he retired he had become acting president. He went back to France to join his family, who had returned after the war.

DEFOE, DANIEL (1661?–1731), was born and died in London. He had many adventures during that seventy-year span. For a political offense he was sentenced once to the pillory and imprisonment; again he barely escaped imprisonment for debts. After he paid these, he began to fight the law against debtors. He traveled on the Continent; once, also, his ship was saved from pirates only by its capable captain. He was a voluminous writer. His *Robinson Crusoe* still delights the spirit of adventure in boys and serves as a model for all other tales of its kind.

DE JONG, MEINDERT (1906–   ), was born in the village of Wierum, in the province of Friesland, the Netherlands. When he was eight, the family migrated to America and settled in Grand Rapids, Michigan, where they had a struggle to make a living. Meindert attended Christian High School and worked his way through John Calvin College. When he found it difficult to get a job, he went to work on his father's farm. He acquired a whispering duck and its inseparable companion, a honking goose. While peddling eggs to the Public Library, he told the librarians about his pets and they urged him to write a story about them. The result was his first book, *The Big Goose and the Little White Duck*. While persisting at his writing he held a variety of jobs which included bricklayer, janitor, gravedigger, sexton, and college professor. In World War II he served in the Fourteenth Air Force as historian for the Chinese American Wing. He returned with citations and medals but was too depressed to do any writing. Gradually, however, ideas for books began to evolve in his mind and a rich outpouring followed: *The Tower by the Sea*, based on a folk tale of Holland; *Smoke*

Above the Lane; Shadrack; and *Hurry Home, Candy*. The last two were runners-up for the Newbery award in 1954. The following year Mr. De Jong received the Newbery medal for *The Wheel on the School*.

DE LA MARE, WALTER (1873–1956), English poet and writer of imaginative stories for children and adults, was born in the village of Charlton in Kent. He attended St. Paul's Cathedral Choir School in London and while there founded the *Choristers' Journal*, a weekly paper which became a permanent monthly organ of the school. He worked for eighteen years in the London office of the Anglo-American Oil Company. During this period he wrote poems and stories. "Kismet," his first story, was published in a magazine five years after he left school. From that time on, his writings appeared regularly in magazines. It was Andrew Lang who really discovered De la Mare as a poet, for he recommended to Longmans, Green that they publish his *Songs of Childhood*. It was brought out in 1902 under the pen name of Walter Ramal (La Mar spelled backwards). *Peacock Pie: A Book of Rhymes* (1913) brought him real fame. He wrote almost as much prose as poetry. His *Memoirs of a Midget* (1922) won the James Tait Black Memorial Prize, an important literary award in England. *The Three Mulla Mulgars*, first published in 1919, was brought out in a new edition in 1948 under the title *Three Royal Monkeys*. He wrote a fairy play, *Crossings*, for a boys' school in Brighton. As a compiler of anthologies De la Mare stands supreme. He made a unique and distinguished collection of rhymes and poems for "the young of all ages" in *Come Hither*. For *Animal Stories* he selected, edited, and in part re-wrote fifty animal tales showing the development of these stories from Aesop to the present day. In the adult book, *Early One Morning in the Spring*, he brought together chapters of remembered childhood chosen from autobiographies and other writings. In *Told Again* he retells with fresh charm and poetic beauty nineteen favorite fairy tales. De la Mare lived for many years with his wife and four children in Taplow, England. In 1953, Queen Elizabeth II bestowed the Order of Merit upon him. The last years of his life were spent in Twickenham, and he is buried in the crypt of St. Paul's Cathedral in London.

DEUTSCH, BABETTE (1895–   ), poet, writer, and lecturer, was born in New York City. Even before graduation from Barnard College she began contributing poetry and criticism to leading periodicals. She has been a lecturer in English at

Columbia University since 1944 and a guest professor since 1952. She married Dr. Avrahm Yarmolinsky, Chief of the Slavonic Division of the New York Public Library, and they have two sons. Miss Deutsch has published several volumes of poems and novels. She has written two books for young people, *Heroes of the Kalevala, Finland's Saga;* and a biography, *Walt Whitman.* Her *Tales of Faraway Folk* is a collection of tales from Central Asia and the Caucasus, for younger children.

DICKINSON, EMILY (1830–1886), was born and lived most of her quiet, retired life at Amherst, Massachusetts. All her life she was expressing her real self in poetry, the first volume of which was not published until after her death; the second, four years later. Their mystic quality together with their simplicity of form and sincerity of tone have placed these brief lyrics in the front rank of poetry.

DODGE, MARY MAPES (1831–1905), was born in New York City of a well-to-do, book-loving family. Her father, James J. Mapes, was a scholar and scientist, and his home was a center for literary and scientific gatherings. At the age of twenty, Mary Mapes married William Dodge, a prominent attorney, but after seven years she was left a widow with two small boys. To earn a living, she began to write. In 1864 her first book, *Irvington Stories,* was published. While reading Motley's *Rise of the Dutch Republic,* she became interested in Holland and wrote *Hans Brinker, or the Silver Skates.* For this book she received one of the most distinguished literary awards of that day, the Montyon Prize of the French Academy. Within the next thirty years the book was published in more than one hundred editions and was translated into six languages. When the *St. Nicholas Magazine* was organized in 1873, Mrs. Dodge became its editor. She was instrumental in persuading many of the best-known authors to write for it, challenging them to write "something good enough for children."

DODGSON, CHARLES LUTWIDGE (1832–1898), pen name Lewis Carroll, wrote *Alice's Adventures in Wonderland* and *Through the Looking Glass,* two of the best-loved and most often quoted books in the English language. Dodgson was born in the village of Daresbury, in Cheshire, England, the son of a parson. When Charles was eleven, the family moved to Yorkshire, where he lived until he went to Oxford. He was sent to school in Richmond and attended Rugby. At nineteen he entered Christ Church College, Ox-

ford. He graduated in 1854 with high honors and many prizes. He took Holy Orders but did not pursue that career. He became a lecturer on mathematics at Oxford and lived at the college all the rest of his life. He published several scholarly treatises on mathematics, but aside from these he liked to write humorous verse. As he thought it unfitting to publish his nonsense verse under his own name, he invented a pen name. He translated his first two names, Charles Lutwidge, into Latin as Carolus Ludovicus and from that into Carroll Lewis and then transposed the names. Nearly everyone knows that on a hot summer day, July 4, 1862, Dodgson took three little girls for a row on the river and began to tell them the story of Alice's adventures underground. The original manuscript of the story, later penned and illustrated with sketches by Dodgson himself, was sold at auction nearly seventy years later for over £15,000.

DR. SEUSS. *See* GEISEL, THEODOR SEUSS.

DRINKWATER, JOHN (1882–1937), English poet and playright, was born in Leytonstone, Essex, and educated at the Oxford High School. For twelve years he was connected with an insurance business, but his real interest was in the theater. He helped found the Pilgrim Players, now the Birmingham Repertory Theater, for which he wrote the play that brought him fame, *Abraham Lincoln.* His other historical dramas include *Robert E. Lee; Oliver Cromwell;* and *Mary Stuart. Inheritance* and *Discovery* are two autobiographical works. He wrote two books of verse for children, *All About Me* and *More About Me.*

EAGER, EDWARD, playwright, lyricist, and author of books for children, was born in Toledo, Ohio. Since graduating from Harvard, he has been connected with several Broadway productions. He wrote the lyrics for *Dream with Music* and *Sing Out Sweet Land.* He has written adaptations for a number of operas and operettas, including Offenbach's *Orpheus in the Underworld* and Mozart's *The Marriage of Figaro.* The latter was produced by NBC-TV Opera in 1954. He wrote the lyrics for the TV spectacular *Marco Polo,* produced in 1956. Mr. Eager began writing books to please his young son, Fritz. He and his son were devoted admirers of E. Nesbit, the author of *The Bastable Children,* and Mr. Eager's delightful fantasy, *Half Magic,* is written in the E. Nesbit tradition. He says of himself, "When I was eight-to-twelve, I lived across from a family of three girls who are, to a certain extent, the prototypes for Jane and Katharine and Martha of *Half Magic* and *Magic by the Lake. Knight's*

Castle was inspired by my son's model collection of knights and by his games with them after he saw the movie *Ivanhoe*. Fritz is now nearly sixteen, but he still condescends to read my books and pass approval (or not, as the case may be). We live in a house by a small river in Connecticut." Mr. Eager has written *Red Head; Mouse Manor;* and *The Time Garden,* a sequel to *Magic by the Lake.*

EATON, JEANETTE, is best known for the biographies she has written for young people. She was born in Columbus, Ohio, and received her A.B. from Vassar in 1908 and her M.A. from Ohio State University in 1910. After a year of travel in Europe, she began her writing career. She did some editorial work for the New York Board of Education and was editor of *Story Parade* magazine for a time. Her biographies include *Young Lafayette; Leader by Destiny: George Washington, Man and Patriot; Narcissa Whitman, Pioneer of Oregon; David Livingstone; That Lively Man, Ben Franklin;* and *Gandhi, Fighter without a Sword.*

EDGEWORTH, MARIA (1767–1849), was born in Ireland, the second child and oldest daughter of nineteen children. Her father, Richard Lovell Edgeworth, a scientist and civil engineer, was a follower of Rousseau and at one time tried the Frenchman's theory of education in his own family. Maria, besides having the excitement of living with three stepmothers, had a varied life for those times. She tells in her letters how they all had to leave home because of the Irish peasant uprisings; she lived much of her time with the Thomas Days (his influence shows in her writings); she traveled in England, Belgium, and France; she was courted by a Swedish count; and she was her father's right-hand "man." She wrote a successful novel, *Castle Rackrent,* picturing Irish life; a book on education, collaborating with her father; and several volumes of children's stories, in which the Rousseau theories of education were eminently successful.

EICHENBERG, FRITZ (1901–   ), was born in Cologne, Germany. He studied at the School of Applied Arts in Cologne and the State Academy of Graphic Arts in Leipzig. He came to the United States in 1933 and was naturalized in 1941. In Germany he had been staff artist and illustrator for various magazines and newspapers. After coming to the United States he was in the art department of the New School for Social Research and an instructor in the Veterans' Art Center at the Museum of Modern Art. He is professor of art and director of the department of graphic arts and illustration at Pratt Institute, Brooklyn. He has illustrated a great number of books, and his work is represented in major collections. He has won many prizes, among them, the first prize at the Print Exhibit of the National Academy, in 1946, and the Silver Medal of the Limited Editions Club, in 1954. He is the author of *Art and Faith* and the author-illustrator of the picture books *Ape in a Cape* and *Dancing in the Moon.*

ELIOT, THOMAS STEARNS (1888–   ), one of the most influential poets of his day, is also a critic, playwright, and essayist. He was born in St Louis, Missouri, but became a naturalized British subject in 1927 and lives in London. After receiving his A.M. from Harvard, he studied at the Sorbonne in Paris and at Oxford University in England. In 1948 he won the Nobel Prize in literature. He wrote *Murder in the Cathedral,* a dramatization of the murder of Thomas à Becket, for the Canterbury Festival in 1935. The most recent collection of his poems and plays is *The Complete Poems and Plays: 1909–1950.* Both his poetry and his critical essays have had a significant influence on the literary developments of our time. He is a director of Faber & Faber, the London publishers.

EMERSON, RALPH WALDO (1803–1882), was born in New England of famous ancestry. After graduating from Harvard he was a Unitarian minister for three years. Beset by theological doubts, he resigned and gave himself to writing philosophical essays and poetry, to lecturing and to occasional preaching. Of a gentle, earnest, retiring nature, he was fond of children. Louisa M. Alcott tells of what joy they always had when Emerson "played" with them. He became a close friend and an interpreter of Carlyle to America; he admired Landor and Wordsworth but said he found "all of them in different degrees deficient in insight into religious truth." It has been said of him that "among Anglo-Saxons there appears to be no one that stands higher than he as an ethical inspirer or stimulator."

ESTES, ELEANOR (1906–   ), was born in the small New England town of West Haven, Connecticut, very like the town of Cranbury, the scene of her engaging *Moffat* books. When she graduated from the West Haven High School, she worked in the children's department of the New Haven Free Public Library and in 1928 became head of it. In 1931 she was awarded the Caroline M. Hewins scholarship for children's librarians and went to New York to study at the Pratt Institute library school. In 1932 she married Rice Estes, then a student, but later a professor of library science. She worked as a children's librarian in several of the branches of the New York Public Library until 1940, when her first book, *The Moffats*, was accepted. This was followed by *The Middle Moffat* and *Rufus M.* The books have been translated into French, Dutch, Italian, and Norwegian. *The Hundred Dresses*, a compassionate story of a child's suffering caused by thoughtless cruelty in everyday relationships, has also been translated into Turkish. Mrs. Estes and her husband moved to California, where Mr. Estes was made assistant director of the library at the University of Southern California. In 1948 their daughter, Helena, was born. Eleanor Estes won the Newbery medal in 1952 for *Ginger Pye*. In 1958 she wrote more adventures of the Pye family in *Pinkey Pye*. She has also written an adult novel, *The Echoing Green*.

EWING, JULIANA HORATIA (GATTY) (1841–1885), was born in Yorkshire, one of a large family of children. Her father, a clergyman, had been Nelson's chaplain on board the *Victory* at Trafalgar. Her mother, Margaret Gatty, wrote a series of *Parables from Nature* and founded *Aunt Judy's Magazine*, which Juliana edited after her mother's death. Juliana enjoyed telling stories to the younger children and it was not long before she began writing them. She married Major Alexander Ewing, who composed the hymn "Jerusalem the Golden." Mrs. Ewing's best-known stories for children include *Lob Lie-by-the-Fire; Jackanapes*, which was illustrated by Randolph Caldecott; *The Brownies*; and *Jan of the Windmill.*

FABRE, JEAN HENRI (1823–1915), a French natural scientist, was born in a poor peasant family that was almost illiterate. Although he was always a close observer of natural phenomena, he thought at first his main interest was in mathematics. By hard work he managed to get a college education, but while taking his Ph.D. he discovered that the study of the history and habits of insects was really his forte. He married and with his family lived a retired life, giving all his attention to his special study, and writing the results in a charmingly simple and clear style.

FARJEON, ELEANOR (1881–   ), was born in London. Her father, Benjamin Farjeon, was an English novelist and her gifted mother, Maggie Jefferson, was the eldest daughter of Joseph Jefferson, the American actor who became famous in the role of Rip Van Winkle. Although Eleanor and her three brothers had little formal education, they grew up in a literary and artistic

atmosphere. All four children enjoyed writing stories, plays, and poetry. Her eldest brother, Harry, had a decided talent for music and he and Eleanor collaborated in writing and composing several operettas. When their father died in 1903, Joseph Jefferson had the whole family come to him in America. When Harry received an appointment as a professor of harmony and composition at the Royal Academy of Music, the family returned to England and Eleanor continued to write. While living in Sussex, she wrote *Martin Pippin in the Apple Orchard*. This was followed by *Martin Pippin in the Daisy Field*. In 1956, Eleanor Farjeon received the Hans Christian Andersen medal, the first international children's book award, for *The Little Bookroom*. For this same book she also received the Carnegie medal, the British award for "the outstanding book of the year." She has written several books of poetry for children: *Cherrystones; Come Christmas; Sing for Your Supper; Joan's Door;* and *Gypsy and Ginger*. A selection of her verse is contained in *Eleanor Farjeon's Poems for Children*. Two of her plays, which were presented in London, she made into book-length stories — *The Silver Curlew* and *The Glass Slipper*. Also included in her works are *Italian Peepshow; The Tale of Tom Tidler; Ten Saints; Tales of Chaucer; Mighty Men; Kings and Queens;* and an adult biography, *Portrait of a Family*.

FIELD, EUGENE (1850–1895), newspaperman and writer of verse, was born in St. Louis, Missouri. When he was six, his mother died and he grew up in the care of a cousin who lived at Amherst, Massachusetts. After a year each at Williams College, Knox College, and the University of Missouri, he spent a year abroad, then returned to the Middle West and a newspaper career. He married and had several children, who adored their father and were the inspiration for his poems of childhood.

FIELD, RACHEL LYMAN (1894–1942), author, poet, and playwright, was born in New York City. Her childhood was spent in Massachusetts. She studied at Radcliffe College, and while taking Professor George P. Baker's "English 47 Workshop," a playwriting course, she wrote her first successful play, *Three Pills in a Bottle*. After attending Radcliffe, she lived in New York and spent her summers on an island off the coast of Maine. Her first book of poems for children, which she illustrated, was *The Pointed People*. This was followed by *Taxis and Toadstools* and *Branches Green*. Her most famous book, *Hitty: Her First Hundred Years*, won the Newbery medal in 1930. Perhaps her finest story for older children is *Calico Bush,* with colonial Maine as its setting. She wrote several adult novels, one of which, *All This and Heaven Too,* became a best-seller. The last years of her life were spent in California with her husband, Arthur S. Pederson, and their small daughter, Hannah.

FINGER, CHARLES JOSEPH (1871–1941), was born in Willesden, England, on Christmas Day. He attended King's College in London and studied music at Frankfort-on-the-Main, Germany. When he was sixteen he left England in search of adventure. He was shipwrecked in Patagonia, sailed the Straits, and twice rounded Cape Horn. He spent ten years roaming through South America, hunting gold, herding sheep, and listening to old tales and legends which he heard first-hand from the Indians. He went to Africa, traveled to the Klondike Gold Fields in Alaska, explored Canada and Mexico, and saw as much of the United States as he could. His adventures furnished him with rich material for stories and books. At the age of fifty, he bought a farm in the Ozark hills in Arkansas, settled down with his wife and five children, and began to write. His *Tales from Silver Lands* won the Newbery medal in 1924. Among the thirty-five books which he wrote for children and adults are *Tales Worth Telling; Courageous Companions; A Dog at His Heels;* and *Give a Man a Horse.*

FIRDAUSI or FIRDOUSI or FIRDUSI (*circ.* 935–1026) was the pen name of Abu'l Quasim Mansur, the greatest historical poet of ancient Persia. His father was wealthy and of high class, and Firdausi had an education that prepared him for the gigantic task he was given to do, namely, to write the history of Persia from its mythological period through to 1011, in which year he completed his poem of over sixty thousand verses. He spent thirty-five years on the work. Owing to court jealousies and misunderstandings, Firdausi left the court and returned to his childhood home at Tus, a very unhappy and disgruntled man. There he died before he knew that justice had been done him, that the Mohammed had rewarded him and had put to death his enemy.

FLETCHER, JOHN GOULD (1886–1950), was born in Arkansas of an old family and educated at Phillips Exeter and at Harvard. When at his father's death he found himself with little money, he left college to devote himself to literature. He went to Europe, and lived in Italy and England. He married an English girl and had two children. He belongs to the *Imagist* group of poets.

FOOTE, SAMUEL (1720–1777), was an English dramatist, born in Cornwall, of good family. Educated at Oxford, he was sent to study law at the Temple, ran through two fortunes, and finally appeared on the stage, where he made a success as an imitator. Capitalizing on his power for personal satire, he wrote his own skits. These brought him into difficulties, sometimes with the law, but apparently he satirized only what deserved such attention.

FORBES, ESTHER (1894–   ), was born in Westboro, Massachusetts, but has spent most of her life in Worcester, Massachusetts. She grew up in a family surrounded with the atmosphere of books, where the early history of New England was part of the family tradition. She received her education at Bradford Academy and at the University of Wisconsin. While she was a student at college, World War I broke out and she joined a group of volunteer students who answered the call for farm helpers. She worked on a big farm near Harpers Ferry, Virginia, shucking corn, picking apples, and working as a teamster. For six years she was on the editorial staff of Houghton Mifflin Company. Then she married and spent considerable time abroad. Her first successful novel, *Oh Genteel Lady,* was followed by four historical novels of New England. In 1942, she received the Pulitzer Prize for History for *Paul Revere and the World He Lived In.* Only once before had this coveted history prize been awarded to a woman. While working on her Paul Revere book she became interested in the life of the apprentices of this period and later wrote *Johnny Tremain,* an outstanding story of Revolutionary War days in Boston. For this book she was awarded the Newbery medal in 1944.

FOSTER, GENEVIEVE (1893–   ), was born in Oswego, New York, but spent her childhood in Whitewater, Wisconsin. Graduating from the University of Wisconsin, she went to Chicago to attend the Academy of Fine Arts. This was followed by a period of free-lance work as a commercial artist, but when she married she gave up her work for a few years to devote full time to her home and two children. Then she revived her interest in art and began illustrating books for children. Presently she found a way of combining her interest in art with that of history. She wrote and illustrated *George Washington's World,* a book which gives a new approach to history. This was followed by companion volumes, *Abraham Lincoln's World* and *Augustus Caesar's World.* She has written several biographies for younger children in the Initial

Biographies Series. *Birthdays of Freedom: America's Heritage from the Ancient World* and a second volume that brings the history up to 1776 were written to celebrate the seventy-fifth anniversary of the American Library Association.

FRANÇOISE. *See* SEIGNOBOSC, FRANÇOISE.

FRASCONI, ANTONIO, an artist of Italian parentage, was born and brought up in Montevideo, Uruguay. From the time he was a small boy he was interested in drawing, and during his teens he was a political cartoonist on a newspaper, studying and working on his own time in woodcuts and painting. A scholarship to the Art Students League in New York brought him to the United States in 1945. Since coming to America, Mr. Frasconi has made a remarkable record of achievement. Twice he has won the Inter-American Fellowship from the Guggenheim Memorial Foundation to illustrate the poetry of Walt Whitman and Garcia Lorca, as well as six other awards and two scholarships. In 1954, in recognition of his work as an artist, he was given a grant by the National Institute of Arts and Letters. He has had many one-man shows in the United States, Latin America, and Europe, and his work is represented in the permanent collections of many important museums. Mr. Frasconi lives in New York City with his wife, Leona Pierce, also a woodcut artist. They have a small son, Pablo. Mr. Frasconi's first book, *See and Say: A Picture Book in Four Languages,* was published in 1955. His second, *The House That Jack Built,* in French and in English, was published in 1958.

FROST, FRANCES (1905–   ), novelist and poet, was born in St. Albans, Vermont. She was educated at Middlebury College and the University of Vermont. She was an instructor in creative poetry at the university from 1929 to 1931. Her verse has appeared in the *New Yorker, American Mercury,* and the *Saturday Evening Post.* She has written several novels. Her first book for children was published in 1943 when she edited *Legends of the United Nations.* Other books for children include *Windy Foot at the County Fair; Maple Sugar for Windy Foot; Sleigh Bells for Windy Foot; Fireworks for Windy Foot; Then Came Timothy;* and two books of poems, *The Little Whistler* and *This Rowdy Heart.*

FROST, ROBERT (1874–1963), American poet, lecturer, and teacher, has won the Pulitzer Poetry Prize four times—in 1924 for *New Hampshire;* in 1931 for *Collected Poems;* in 1937 for *A Further Range;* and in 1943 for *A Witness Tree.* He was born in San Francisco, but when he was ten his father died and his mother took him to New England. Having to earn his living at an early age, he worked in a shoe shop, a woolen mill, and on a farm. He attended Dartmouth and Harvard but did not graduate from either college. While trying to become established as a poet, he taught and tried farming. In 1912 he went to England to live, and his first book of poetry, *A Boy's Will,* was published there in 1913. His second book, *North of Boston,* published in 1914, established his reputation as a poet. He returned to the United States and found himself famous. Since 1915 he has lived on farms in New England and has been a professor of English at Amherst and professor of poetry at Harvard. In 1957, under the auspices of the International Educational Exchange Service of the Department of State, Robert Frost gave lectures and readings in London, Durham, and Edinburgh, and at Oxford and Cambridge, where he received honorary degrees.

FYLEMAN, ROSE (1877–   ), was born in Nottingham, England. She began to write stories and poems when she was a child. After college she taught for a year or two and then studied singing in Germany, Paris, and London. She sang in concerts and helped with her sister's school. After *Punch* accepted her poem, "Fairies at the Bottom of Our Garden," she was so elated that she decided to devote all her time to writing. She has traveled extensively in Europe and has twice visited the United States and lectured. She founded an English magazine for children, *Merry Go Round.* Her first book of poems, *Fairies and Chimneys,* was published in 1918 and was followed by *The Fairy Flute; The Fairy Green;* and *Gay Go Up.* Her stories include *The Rainbow Cat; Forty Good-Morning Tales;* and *Tea-Time Tales.*

GÁG, WANDA (1893–1946), artist and illustrator of books for children, was born in New Ulm, Minnesota, of a family where drawing and painting were taken for granted. She was the eldest of seven children and they all drew as soon as they could hold pencils. When they were orphaned, well-meaning people suggested that the children be separated and put with different families, but Wanda, then fourteen, determined that somehow she must keep them all together. Long years of hardship and struggle followed. She helped amuse the children by telling them stories and drawing pictures. By means of scholarships she was able to attend art schools in St. Paul and Minneapolis and later studied at the Art Students' League in New York City. She got a job in commercial art which promised a bright future, but she finally broke away from it to develop her own creative talent. Besides drawing and painting she did woodcuts, etchings, and lithographs. It was not long before a New York gallery gave her a one-man show. In 1928 her first picture book, *Millions of Cats*, was published and started her on her author-artist career which has immeasurably enriched the field of children's literature. Her books include *The A B C Bunny; Gone Is Gone; Tales from Grimm; More Tales from Grimm; Three Gay Tales from Grimm;* and *Snow White and the Seven Dwarfs.* She also wrote her autobiography, *Growing Pains.*

GARLAND, HAMLIN (1860–1940), born in Wisconsin of a pioneering family, breathes the spirit of the frontier. Disliking cows, so he says, he made up his mind not to be a farmer, though he once took up a South Dakota claim. He finally went to Boston to devote himself to literary work. His past experience now stood him in good stead, for his best novels are based on the life he had known in boyhood and youth. His pictures of pioneer days on the "Middle Border" are very vivid. His occasional poems also have that vivid touch.

GATES, DORIS (1901–   ), was born at Mountain View in the Santa Clara Valley near San Jose, California. When she was a child she lived on a fruit farm and had a small burro for a pet. Miss Gates' first book, *Sarah's Idea,* is based on this experience. For fifteen years she was head of the Children's Department of Fresno County Free Library, in the heart of California's San Joaquin Valley. From her work with children of "migrants" evolved the idea for her next book, *Blue Willow,* which was runner-up for the Newbery medal in 1940. In 1954 she received the William Allen White children's book award for *Little Vic.* She taught Children's Literature and Library Science at San Jose State College, and has been associated with Ginn and Company, publishers, as editor of the Ginn Enrichment Books. Besides books already mentioned, she has written *Sensible Kate; Trouble for Jerry; North Fork; My Brother Mike;* and *River Ranch.*

GAY, JOHN (1685–1732), was an English poet who aspired to political preferment. Dr. Johnson says all the kindness of Gay's personal friends did not make amends for his political disappointments. Pope's friendship for him as well as that of other important literary and society people may have spoiled him. He is to be remembered for two successes: *The Beggar's Opera* and his rhymed *Fables.* These last were written for a young

member of the Royal Family; but, witty as they are, they failed to get him what his friends considered proper recognition. He is buried in Westminster Abbey.

GEISEL, THEODOR SEUSS (1904–   ), author, illustrator, and cartoonist, was born in Springfield, Massachusetts, where he went to school. When he was a boy he loved to draw fantastic birds and animals. He attended Dartmouth College and went to Oxford University in England to continue his studies in English literature, intending to become a professor. But he kept on drawing. His career began when he sold a drawing of a bear, like no ordinary bear, to the *Saturday Evening Post.* For twelve years he did commercial art work connected with advertising. During World War II he was a captain in the Army, placed in the Education and Information Service. He was sent to Hollywood, where he wrote and designed motion-picture training films which he showed to troops at the Front in France, Belgium, Holland, and Germany. For this work he received the Legion of Merit and rose to the rank of Lieutenant Colonel. After the war he lived in Hollywood where, besides writing and illustrating books for children, he wrote for the motion-picture screen. He has won two Academy Awards, one in 1947 for a documentary film on Japan and another in 1950 for the best motion-picture cartoon. He and his wife live in La Jolla, California. Among his books are *And to Think That I Saw It on Mulberry Street; The Five Hundred Hats of Bartholomew Cubbins; McElligot's Pool; The Cat in the Hat;* and *The Grinch Who Stole Christmas.*

GEORGE, JOHN (1916–   ) AND JEAN (1919–   ), are a husband-and-wife team who write and illustrate books on bird and animal life. John George was born in Milwaukee, Wisconsin, and has devoted himself to natural history since the days when, at high school and later at the University of Wisconsin, he led field parties studying birds for the Milwaukee Museum. In 1939 he received his B.S. degree in wildlife management in the School of Forestry and Conservation of the University of Michigan, and in 1941 an M.S. degree in zoology. He was a graduate assistant in zoology at Michigan. During the summers he was Director of the State 4-H County Camp in West Virginia and Ranger Naturalist in the Great Smokies National Park. During World War II he served for thirty-four months continuous sea duty on the Destroyer *Mervine* in the U.S. Navy. After his discharge in 1946, he returned to his graduate studies at the University of Michigan, where he taught while completing work on his Ph.D. in zoology.

Jean George was born in Washington, D.C. She received her B.A. degree from Pennsylvania State College and then taught modern dancing at the University of Louisiana. During the war, she reported for International News Service in Washington, did feature writing and sketching for the Washington *Post*, was artist for the magazine *Pageant*, and "sketch-text" reporter for Newspaper Enterprise Association. She has also illustrated children's film strips. Dr. and Mrs. George were married in 1944. They have three children and live in Chappaqua, New York. Dr. George is Associate Curator of Mammals of the New York Zoological Society, otherwise known as the Bronx Zoo. The Georges have great fun writing and illustrating their books, which include *Vulpes, the Red Fox; Vison, the Mink; Masked Prowler, the Story of a Raccoon; Bubo, the Great Horned Owl;* and *Dipper of Copper Creek.* This last book won the first Aurianne Award of the American Library Association for the "best juvenile book on animal life which develops humane attitudes." To gather data for it the Georges lived in a one-room cabin at the edge of a waterfall in the ghost town of Gothic in the Colorado Rockies. More recently Mrs. George has both written and illustrated books for younger children, *The Hole in the Tree* and *Snow Tracks.*

GILLHAM, CHARLES EDWARD (1898–   ), lives in Alaska as a biologist for the United States government. The folk tales which he retold in his book, *Beyond the Clapping Mountains,* he heard from the Eskimos.

GODDEN, RUMER (1907–   ), is the pseudonym of the gifted English writer, Margaret Rumer Haynes-Dixon. She was born in Sussex, England, one of four sisters, but was brought up chiefly in India, a country that she regards as a second homeland. She and her sisters had a wonderfully happy childhood in India, sailing, riding, fishing, and writing books. She herself began writing when she was five; by the time she was seven she had completed her life story. She made many trips to England and attended various English schools. When she was grown she returned to India and at one time ran a ballet school in Calcutta. At another time she lived on a farm high up in the Kashmir mountains. She has traveled extensively in Europe and Africa. In 1949, she visited the United States in connection with the motion picture based on her novel, *The River.* Several of her novels have been Book-of-the-Month Club selec-

tions. Her biography, *Hans Christian Andersen,* is a distinguished addition to the series, Great Lives in Brief. She has written several books for children: *The Mousewife,* based on an anecdote in Dorothy Wordsworth's journal; *Impunity Jane; The Doll's House; The Fairy Doll;* and *Mouse House.* In private life she is Mrs. Haynes-Dixon and lives with her husband and two daughters in Buckinghamshire, England.

GOLDSMITH, OLIVER (1728–1774), English poet and man of letters, was born in County Longford, Ireland, the second son of a poor clergyman. He received a degree from Trinity College, Dublin, and studied medicine in Edinburgh. He tried to practice medicine in London, but failed. To make a living he began to do literary hack work. John Newbery, the bookseller who sold books and drugs at The Sign of the Bible and Sun, and who was the first to publish books especially for children, recognized Goldsmith's ability, helped pay his debts, and set him to work writing for his "juvenile library." It is thought that Goldsmith edited *Mother Goose's Melody,* which Newbery published, and *The Renowned History of Little Goody Two-Shoes* has been attributed to him. He became acquainted with Dr. Samuel Johnson and was a member of the famous London Literary Club which gathered around Johnson. It is said that Dr. Johnson sold *The Vicar of Wakefield* for Goldsmith to keep him from being sent to jail for debt. *She Stoops to Conquer* is Goldsmith's best-known play, and *The Deserted Village* his best-known poem.

GOLLOMB, JOSEPH (1881–1950), a Russian-American writer, was born in St. Petersburg. The family left Russia when Joseph was ten years old, and settled in New York City. He was educated at the City College of New York and received his M.A. degree from Columbia University. He taught school, and while he was a teacher at DeWitt Clinton High School he began writing books for boys. After ten years of teaching he became a newspaper reporter and traveled all over Europe. He has written *Albert Schweitzer: Genius of the Jungle; That Year at Lincoln High; Tiger at City High; Up at City High;* and *Window on the World.*

GRAHAME, KENNETH (1859–1932), wrote only four books, and his fame rests principally on one book, *The Wind in the Willows,* which holds a position of eminence shared only by such books as *Alice* and the *Jungle Books.* He was born in Edinburgh, Scotland, of a family directly descended from Robert Bruce. Most of his life was spent at Cookham Dene on the Thames, a river he loved and which was the inspiration and set ting of *Wind in the Willows.* Before he was ten, he was sent to school at St. Edward's, Oxford, where he became head student and captain of the Rugby. He wanted to go on to the University, but his family were not in favor of this, so he took a clerkship in the Bank of England. In his spare time he began writing poems and essays and before long he was a regular contributor to the *National Observer,* whose editor was William E. Henley. Kenneth Grahame's first book, *Pagan Papers,* was published in 1894 and was well received. Two years later *The Golden Age* appeared, and in 1899 *Dream Days.* Shortly after its publication Mr. Grahame was made secretary of the Bank and that same year married Elspeth Thompson. They had one son, Alastair, affectionately known as "Mouse." *The Wind in the Willows* began as bedtime stories which Mr. Grahame told to his small son. When "Mouse" was taken to the seaside the story was continued in the form of letters. Fortunately Alastair's nurse saved the letters, and they became the basis for the book, which was published in 1908. Mrs. Grahame has told how the book came to be written, in *First Whispers of "The Wind in the Willows."* The book was slow in getting a start, but was championed by Theodore Roosevelt, then President of the United States, and by A. A. Milne, who wrote of it, "It is a Household Book . . . which is read aloud to every guest and is regarded as a touchstone of his worth." In spite of its tremendous success, Mr. Grahame wrote no other books. He once told his impatient publishers that he considered himself a spring, not a pump, and could write only when the spring bubbled up. His son, Alastair, was killed while crossing a railroad track when he was a student at Oxford.

GRAMATKY, HARDIE (1907–   ), is a water-color artist well known for his picture books for children. Before launching on this career, he worked in a logging camp and as a deck hand on a freighter. He attended a university for two years, and went to Hollywood as an animator for Walt Disney. Then he married and returned East. He did "pictorial reporting" for *Fortune* magazine. Standing in water up to his hips, he painted on-the-spot pictures of a Mississippi flood; then he was sent to Hudson Bay and painted pictures with the weather thirty degrees below zero. Between assignments he wrote and illustrated *Little Toot,* which was an immediate success. His next book, *Hercules,* was about an old-fashioned fire engine. Then came *Loopy,* the airplane that wanted to fly by itself. Meantime he has taken twenty prizes for water-colors. His

work is represented in the permanent collections of the Chicago Art Institute, the Toledo Museum of Fine Art, and the Brooklyn Museum. He is an associate member of the National Academy. Mr. Gramatky says that his small daughter, Linda, has been the proving ground for his picture books and that she is his severest critic.

GRAY, ELIZABETH JANET (1902–   ), was born in Germantown, Pennsylvania, and attended the Friends School there. She graduated from Bryn Mawr and took a degree in library science at Drexel Institute. A year of teaching and a year of library work followed, but when, at the age of twenty, her first book, *Meredith's Ann,* was published, she knew that she wanted to make writing her career. While working in the University of North Carolina library, she met and married Morgan Vining, a member of the faculty. They had five happy years together, during which time she wrote *Meggy MacIntosh* and *Jane Hope.* As she wanted to write a biography of Sir Walter Scott, she and her husband were planning to go to Scotland. Then suddenly her husband was killed in an automobile accident. It took courage to make the trip alone the following year, but she did and came home to write *Young Walter Scott.* Next she wrote a biography of the beloved Quaker, William Penn. In 1943 she won the Newbery medal for *Adam of the Road,* a story of thirteenth-century England. During World War II she joined the staff of the American Friends Service Committee in Philadelphia and wrote reports and articles about the work of the committee in America, Europe, and Asia. In 1946 she went to Japan as tutor to Crown Prince Akihito. In her adult book, *Windows for the Crown Prince,* she tells of her four remarkable years at the Japanese Court.

GREENAWAY, KATE (1846–1901), was born in London on St. Patrick's Day in the same month and year as her fellow artist, Randolph Caldecott. She was the daughter of a well-known wood engraver and draughtsman who encouraged her interest in art. Memories of her own happy childhood are reflected in her drawings of children in the country, in London streets, or beside the sea. She so disliked the style in which children were dressed in those days that in her drawings she clothed the boys and girls in a manner to harmonize with the English countryside. In so doing she set a fashion. Many lasting friendships grew out of her artistic career. Besides Walter Crane and Randolph Caldecott, she knew the Tennysons and the Brownings, and John Ruskin and Edmund Evans, the color printer, were her devoted friends. Her first book of verse, *Under the Window* (1878), was an immediate success and was also published in France and Germany. *A Apple Pie* is still one of the most beloved alphabet books. Her *Mother Goose* is especially attractive to little girls. Her pictures for Robert Browning's *Pied Piper of Hamelin* are some of the best ever made for that story. She also wrote and illustrated *Marigold Garden; The Language of Flowers;* and *The Kate Greenaway Birthday Book.*

GREY, KATHARINE (1875–1933), was born in Kentucky, where she received her early education. Later she attended both the University of California and New York University. She married a C. F. Smith, a Californian, and was thereafter an out-and-out Westerner. She became a business woman — a cattle rancher, a mine operator, and an orchard grower. But she always found time for civic work; she held a responsible position in the California Federation of Women's Clubs, was a director in the Red Cross, and often a speaker for campaigns and drives.

GRIMM, JAKOB (1785–1863), AND WILHELM (1786–1859), known as the Grimm Brothers, were eminent German philologists who started the science of folklore. Both brothers studied at the University of Marburg. In 1808 Jakob became librarian of the private library of Jerome Bonaparte, the puppet king of Westphalia, and was soon joined by Wilhelm. For several years they were professors at the University of Kassel, and in 1841, at the invitation of Frederick William IV of Prussia, they became professors at Berlin. One day Jakob, in browsing through some books, chanced upon a selection of the German Minnesingers and he caught a vision of what proved to be the life career of the Grimm Brothers. In collecting the old folk tales the brothers complemented each other perfectly. Jakob was more aggressive and supplied the greater initiative. His was the tireless zeal for collecting. Wilhelm, more gentle and gay, labored over the tales with patient devotion, selecting, piecing together, and arranging them. He went over the story-texts and added the characteristic speech and rich phrases he had gathered from the highways and byways. The first volume of the tales came out at Christmas time in 1812, with a dedication to Bettina, the wife of Achim von Arnim, for her little son, Johannes Freimund. Achim von Arnim was a friend interested in collecting folk songs, and he had given the brothers valuable encouragement in their work and had also found a printer in Berlin for their collection of tales. This first volume of tales was eagerly received except in Vienna, where the book was banned

as a work of superstition. But elsewhere the tales were immediately successful. A second volume appeared in 1815, and a third in 1822. The tales were translated into English, Dutch, Italian, Spanish, Czech, Polish, Russian, Bulgarian, Hungarian, Finnish, Esthonian, Hebrew, Armenian, and Esperanto.

HAKLUYT, RICHARD (1552?–1616), was an English geographer and historian, famous for his accounts of the travels and adventures of various explorers and seamen during the reign of Queen Elizabeth. He was born in Herefordshire and educated at Westminster School and Christ Church, Oxford. He took Holy Orders but was more interested in geography than theology. While at Oxford he studied Greek, Latin, Italian, Spanish, Portuguese, and French accounts of travels and voyages. As a result of his research, he published *Divers Voyages Touching the Discovery of America,* a book which attracted the attention of Lord Howard of Effingham, who was the Lord Admiral of the Queen's Navy. Lord Howard's brother, Sir Edward Stafford, who was appointed ambassador to the French Court, took Haykluyt along as his chaplain. During his five years in France, Hakluyt had an excellent opportunity to study records of voyages of French, Portuguese, and Spanish explorers. In making this study, he realized that voyages made by the British had been neglected. When he returned to England, he did research on the various enterprises upon which the English had been engaged and published *The Principal Navigations, Voyages, Traffiques and Discoveries of the English Nation.* The material covered over two hundred voyages and appeared in three volumes. Hakluyt became Archdeacon of Westminster. He helped organize the settling of the Virginia Colony.

HALE, LUCRETIA PEABODY (1820–1900), born in Boston, was a sister of Edward Everett Hale. Her father was an editor, and writing was a common activity in the home. Privately educated, she was accustomed to the social and cultural life of Boston. She claims literary recognition through her Peterkin stories, which she first told to the daughter of her best friend, Mrs. Leslie, who is the original of "The Lady from Philadelphia." She wrote essays, stories, and books on embroidery, knitting, and games. She was one of the first women members of the Boston School Board.

HALE, SARAH J. (1788–1879), an American, is best known as the editor of *Godey's Lady's Book,* though she also edited a magazine for children, called *Juvenile Miscellany.* She was an exceptionally popular writer in her day, but only one poem from her pen is now known and that without her name attached — *Mary Had a Little Lamb.*

HAMILTON, EDITH (1867–   ), one of the world's leading scholars on ancient Greece and Rome, was born in Dresden, Germany, but her parents were United States citizens and she grew up in Fort Wayne, Indiana. Her father was a scholarly man of leisure. At the age of seven Edith began studying Greek and Latin and often held her sisters spellbound by her tales from Sir Walter Scott and her recitations of Keats and Shelley. She attended Miss Porter's Finishing School for Young Ladies in Farmington, Connecticut, and received her A.B. and M.A. degreees from Bryn Mawr. In 1895, following her studies at Bryn Mawr, she and her sister Alice (who later became the first woman professor at Harvard Medical School) set out for Germany, where Edith studied in Leipzig and Munich. At that time Munich University, which was a famous classics center, did not admit women. However, Edith Hamilton was allowed to attend classes, sitting isolated from the men. In 1896 she became headmistress of the Bryn Mawr School in Baltimore, Maryland, where she remained for twenty-six years. But her real career began only after her retirement. At the age of sixty-three she wrote her first book, *The Greek Way.* It was published in 1930 and immediately caught the imagination of both scholars and general readers. In her book she brought the ancient civilization of Greece into brilliant focus. Although she wrote *The Roman Way, Mythology, Spokesman of God,* and *Witness to the Truth,* and translated *Three Greek Plays,* it was not until she was almost ninety that she wrote her seventh book, *The Echo of Greece,* which is a sequel to *The Greek Way.* In August, 1957, she went to Greece to be present at the production of Aeschylus' *Prometheus Bound,* played partly from her translation and partly in modern Greek. On that occasion the Mayor of Athens proclaimed Edith Hamilton an honorary citizen of Athens, and in the name of the King, the Minister of Education decorated her with the Golden Cross of the Order of Benefaction.

HANDFORTH, THOMAS (1897–1948), won the Caldecott medal in 1939 for his book *Mei Li,* which he both wrote and illustrated. He was born in Tacoma, Washington, and spent his childhood on the Pacific Coast. After graduating from high school, he attended the University of Washington for one year, then studied in art schools in New York and Paris. He traveled extensively, sketching wherever he went. In 1931, because of his distinguished etchings of Mt. Popocatepetl in Mexico, he was awarded a Guggenheim fellowship for travel in the Orient. He sailed on a freighter which took a month and a day from New York to Yokohama. For six years he lived in Peking; there he made friends with the little Chinese girl, Mei Li, and other characters that he later put into his book. Besides his work as an illustrator, Mr. Handforth gained wide recognition as an etcher, lithographer, and portrait painter. His works hang in the Metropolitan Museum of Art in New York City, the Library of Congress, the Chicago Art Institute, the Fogg Art Museum in Cambridge, Massachusetts, and the Bibliothèque Nationale in Paris.

HARRIS, JOEL CHANDLER (1848–1908), was born in Georgia. Shortly after his birth his happy-go-lucky father deserted his mother; consequently the boy had little formal education. Instead he had to go to work early, and at fifteen he became an apprenticed typesetter on a Southern plantation newspaper. Here he heard from the old Negroes the stories that later made him famous; here he also educated himself by reading everything in the well-stocked library. After the war he worked on various papers for which he first wrote the Uncle Remus stories, later collected and published in book form. His reputation was made; he published others, and later he and his son Julian published an *Uncle Remus Magazine,* to which Don Marquis and Ludwig Lewisohn were contributors. In spite of an overflowing gaiety, he was really a shy man.

HATCH, MARY COTTAM (1912–   ), was born in Salt Lake City, Utah. She began telling stories at an early age to five younger sisters. She graduated from the University of Utah in 1937, and from Columbia University Library School in 1938. She received her M.A. degree at Columbia University in 1940. For two years she had charge of the collection of children's books at the Columbia University Library School. She is a branch librarian in the New York Public Library and is married to Edgun Valdemr Wulff, a Danish-American artist and illustrator. She has written *Rosamunda,* a picture book, numerous radio scripts, and several short plays. She is the author of two collections of folk tales, *13 Danish Tales* and *More Danish Tales.*

HEARN, LAFCADIO (1850–1904), an exotic and colorful writer, was born of Greek and Irish parentage in the Ionian Islands. At the age of nineteen he came to America and got a job as a newspaper reporter. The editor of the New Orleans *Times Democrat* recognized his talent and sent him to the West Indies as a correspondent. In 1890 he went to Japan and was so charmed by the life and people that he made that country his home. He married a Japanese, became a Buddhist, and was a professor of English literature at the Imperial University of Tokyo from 1894 to 1903. He became known as one of the best interpreters of Japanese culture. In addition to many books for adults, he wrote *Japanese Fairy Tales* for children.

HERRICK, ROBERT (1591–1674), English lyric poet, was born in London and came from a family of goldsmiths, to which trade he was apprenticed. He was educated at St. John's College, Cambridge. After graduating he became vicar of Dean Prior in Devonshire, but in 1647 he was ejected for his Royalist principles and his opposition to the growing Puritan power. After the Restoration in 1662, he regained his position as vicar and held it until he died. His works include *Hesperides* and *Noble Numbers.*

HODGES, C. WALTER (1909–   ), was born in Kent, England. He was educated in Dulwich College, London, and the College School of Art. He first designed scenery and costumes, but his career was interrupted by World War II. Serving in the British Army for five years, he attained the rank of captain. His *Columbus Sails* is the first book he wrote as well as illustrated; but since he has been out of the army, he has written and illustrated *Sky High: The Story of a House that Flew*, and has illustrated books by other authors. He lives in Sussex, England.

HOOD, THOMAS (1799–1845), English poet and humorist, began his writing career by contributing to papers and magazines and eventually became an assistant editor of *The London Magazine.* Though he was noted for his humorous writings during his lifetime, he is now especially remembered for the poems in which he sympathetically portrayed the sufferings of the poor.

HOSFORD, DOROTHY (1900–1952), was born and brought up in Pittsburgh, Pennsylvania. In 1923 she graduated from Margaret Morrison College, Carnegie Institute of Technology. For six years she was secretary of the Carnegie Library School in Pittsburgh. It was through her library work that she became interested in children's literature. She adapted William Morris's *Sigurd the Volsung*, and it was published under the title *Sons of the Volsungs.* She retold the Norse legends in *Thunder of the Gods;* and the battles of Beowulf in *By His Own Might.* In 1924 she married Raymond Hosford, and they had twin sons.

HOUSMAN, A. E. (1859–1936), was one of a talented family. His brother Laurence was an illustrator and man of letters, and his sister Clemence an artist. Alfred, educated at Oxford, became a professor of Latin at the University of London, where he remained until 1911. From then until his death, in 1936, he held a chair of Latin in Trinity College, Cambridge. His work on Latin authors had given him a reputation among classical scholars before his lyric sequence, *The Shropshire Lad*, placed him among the first rank of the poets. In 1922 he published another volume of poetry entitled *Last Poems.*

HUDSON, WILLIAM HENRY (1841–1922), British naturalist and author, was born of American parents on a ranch on the Argentine pampas near Buenos Aires. His father's family was English and Irish but had lived for a generation in Marblehead, Massachusetts. His mother was a New Englander. Hudson spent his boyhood and youth on the South American pampas. When he was thirty he went to England and six years later he became naturalized. He was in ill health, and so poor that his wife, an Englishwoman, kept a boarding house. Memories of his youth spent in the wild beauty of the land he first loved inspired his best writing. In *Far Away and Long Ago*, he tells of his boyhood on the South American pampas and how it was attuned to the wild life about him. *A Little Boy Lost*, an exquisitely imaginative story for children, contains bits of his boyhood fused with the dream of a child. *Green Mansions* is his best-known novel. Other works include *The Purple Land; Adventures Among Birds; A Shepherd's Calendar;* and *A Hind in Richmond Park.*

HUNT, MABEL LEIGH (1892–   ), writer of many books for children, was born in Coatesville, Indiana, and spent her childhood in Greencastle, an Indiana college town. When she was ten the family moved to the Quaker town of Plainfield, and after the death of her father, who was a Quaker country doctor, Mabel and her mother moved to Indianapolis. She attended DePauw University and took library training at Western Reserve. In 1918 she joined the staff of the Indianapolis Public Library as a children's librarian and later as a branch librarian. Her first book, *Lucinda: A Little Girl of 1860*, was published in 1934. It grew out of stories she had heard her mother tell of her Quaker childhood in Indiana of Civil War days. After the publication of three more successful books — *The Boy Who Had No Birthday; Little Girl with Seven Names;* and *Susan Beware!* — Miss Hunt resigned from the library to devote her entire time to writing. Two more Quaker stories followed, *Benjie's Hat* and *Little Grey Gown.* Then in 1940 came a book for older children, *Michel's Island,* an unusual tale of the Great Lakes country in the days of the *voyageurs.* Miss Hunt has received many honors. Two of her books were runners-up for the Newbery medal, *"Have You Seen Tom Thumb?"* in 1942, and *Better Known as Johnny Appleseed* in 1950. This last book was also chosen as one of the books for the White House Library. Twice the New York *Herald Tribune* Spring Festival of Books has included one of Miss Hunt's books in the list of Honor Books — *The Peddler's Clock* in 1943 and *Billy Button's Butter'd Biscuit* in 1941. In 1957 Miss Hunt won the Indiana University Writer's Conference award for the best children's book published that year by an Indiana author. The book so honored was *Stars for Cristy.* A sequel, *Cristy at Skippinghills,* was published in 1958.

HUTCHINSON, W. M. L., was literary secretary for Sir Arthur Quiller-Couch at Cambridge University, England. She was a student at Newnham College, Cambridge, from 1891 to 1895. From 1901 to 1904 she was a research student in the classics. For some years she was an Associate of the College. The Associates are a body of forty-eight elected from past students of Newnham College, calculated to advance Education, Learning, or Research. Miss Hutchinson specialized in Pindar and also in Tacitus. She worked in Greece and at Munich under Furtwängler, and also worked in the British Museum. She was the first woman appointed to a lectureship at Cambridge University, where she was a lecturer in Greek. She wrote two books, *The Golden Porch* and *Orpheus With His Lute,* in which she retold stories from Greek mythology, adapting them to the understanding of children but preserving the original beauty of the tales.

JACOBS, JOSEPH (1854–1916), was an authority on folklore and a collector and writer of fairy tales. He was born in Sydney, Australia, but spent most of his life in England. He graduated from St. John's College, Cambridge. After leaving college, he studied Jewish literature and philosophy in Berlin. In 1900 he came to New York City and became professor of English Literature at the Jewish Theological Seminary of America. From 1906 until his death he was editor of the *American Hebrew.* An interest in folklore grew out of his anthropological studies. In compiling his collections of folk tales, Jacobs made a unique contribution to folklore and to the field of children's literature. He not only retold the stories to interest children, but made the collections of value to scholars by adding a section, "Notes and References," in which he indicates his sources and gives a few parallels and variants. His works include *English Fairy Tales; More English Fairy Tales; Celtic Fairy Tales; More Celtic Fairy Tales;* and *Indian Fairy Tales.* He also edited *Fables of Aesop* and *Arabian Nights' Entertainment.*

JAGENDORF, MORITZ (1888–   ), was born in Austria. At the age of thirteen he came to the United States and attended public schools in New York City. He spent a year at Yale Law School and studied drama and literature at Columbia University, where he took an active part in dramatics. Receiving encouragement from his professors, he embarked upon a theatrical career. Among other plays, he produced some by Lord Dunsany. A long-standing interest in folklore led him into the work for which he is best known: the collecting and retelling of folk tales and legends for young people. He is president of the New York State Folklore Society and vice president of the International Folklore Congress. His books include *The Marvelous Adventures of Johnny Caesar Cicero Darling; New England Bean-Pot; Sand in the Bag: Folk Stories of Ohio, Indiana, and Illinois;* and *Upstate, Downstate: Folk Stories of the Middle Atlantic States.*

JOHNSON, JAMES WELDON (1871–1938), American Negro poet and essayist, was born in Jacksonville, Florida. He received his B.A. and M.A. degrees at Atlanta University and studied for three years at Columbia. In 1897 he was admitted to the Florida bar as the first Negro attorney since the Civil War. He was appointed U. S. Consul in Venezuela and in Nicaragua. He served as secretary of the National Association for the Advancement of Colored People. He was professor of creative literature at Fisk University and a visiting professor of literature at New York University. He edited a book of Negro poetry and two books of spirituals. His books include *God's Trombones; Along the Way;* and *Selected Poems.*

KEATS, JOHN (1795–1821), was born a Cockney Londoner. All his life he struggled with poverty and ill health. At sixteen he left school to become apprentice to a surgeon-apothecary, and four years later he entered Guy's and Thomas's Hospitals in London as a medical student, earning a certificate of proficiency. But poetry soon claimed his full attention. By the time he had published his third volume of poetry at the age of twenty-five, he had reached the first rank of English poets. Swinburne lists his odes *To Autumn* and *On a Grecian Urn* as the most beautiful pieces Keats wrote; *To a Nightingale,* as the most musical. After Keats had nursed his brother Tom, who died of tuberculosis, he himself went to Italy to fight the same disease. He died at Rome and was buried there in the Protestant Cemetery.

KELLY, ERIC PHILBROOK (1884–), author of books for older children, was born in Amesbury, Massachusetts, but spent his boyhood in Denver, Colorado. He attended Dartmouth College and later taught English and journalism there. While doing relief work in Poland after World War I, he became deeply interested in that country. In 1925 he returned to Poland to study and teach at the University of Krakow. His tale of fifteenth-century Poland, *The Trumpeter of Krakow,* won the Newbery medal in 1929. This was followed by two more stories with a Polish background, *The Blacksmith of Vilno* and *From Star to Star.* When World War II broke out, the U. S. State Department sent Mr. Kelly to New Mexico to settle Polish refugees in that state. When the war was over he returned to Dartmouth, retiring in 1954. He spends his summers on the island of Chebeague in Casco Bay, Maine; his winters at Ojo Caliente, New Mexico. His other books include *The Land of the Polish People; At the Sign of the Golden Compass; The Amazing Journey of David Ingram; The Christmas Nightingale;* and *In Clean Hay.*

KELSEY, ALICE GEER, was born in Danvers, Massachusetts, but spent her childhood in Lewiston, Maine. She graduated from Mount Holyoke College in 1918 and the following year married Lincoln David Kelsey. They went to the Near East, where they did relief work with war orphans at Merzifon, Turkey. There Mrs. Kelsey heard the humorous folk tales centering on the character of the Hodja. She collected these tales and retold them in *Once the Hodja.* This was followed by *Once the Mullah,* Persian folk tales about the Persian counterpart of the Hodja. While doing relief work in Greece in 1945, she collected stories about Greek children and published them under the title *Racing the Red Sail.* After a sojourn in the United States, the Kelseys sailed in 1957 for the Philippines, he to be with the Extension and Community Development Department of the College of Agriculture of the University, and she to act as consultant in the Federation of Christian Churches.

KINGSLEY, CHARLES (1819–1875), became a rector in the Church of England after graduating from Oxford. Under the influence of the Christian Socialist movement, he wrote *Alton Locke* (1850). He was an aristocrat by nature but interested in the lower classes and the treatment they received. Two of his greatest books are historical novels, *Hypatia* and *Westward Ho!* His books, *Glaucus* and *Water-Babies,* written to arouse children's interest in nature, fail to be wholly successful because he preaches, but his Greek hero tales and some of his lyrics have better stood the test of time.

KIPLING, RUDYARD (1865–1936), was born in Bombay, India, where his father was for several years professor of sculpture and architecture in art schools at Bombay and Lahore. Kipling was educated in England, attending the United Service College at Westward Ho, Devonshire. At the age of seventeen he returned to India and joined the editorial staff of the Lahore *Civil and Military Gazette.* Later he became assistant editor of the *Pioneer* and during this period published several of his books. In 1892 he married Caroline Starr Balestier of New York and made his home in Brattleboro, Vermont. A few years later, he returned to England with his family and lived there until he died. Kipling's priceless gifts to childhood are the stories contained in the *Jungle Book* (1894), the *Second Jungle Book* (1895), and the *Just So Stories* (1902).

KNIGHT, ERIC (1897–1943), an Englishman by birth, was a wanderer, both literally and figuratively. He was a member of the famous Princess Pat Regiment of Canada in World War I; then, after taking the course in field artillery at Fort Sill, Oklahoma, he became a member of the National Guard. He became a naturalized American citizen in 1942. A major in World War II, he lost his life for his adopted country in a plane crash over the jungles of Dutch Guiana in January, 1943. *Lassie Come-Home* was his first juvenile book and it brought him more fame than anything else he wrote.

LA FONTAINE, JEAN DE (1621–1695), was born at Château-Thierry, a district later made famous in World War I. His father, and later he himself, held the position of deputy ranger of the district. He did not begin his literary work until he was past thirty, when he translated the old Latin comedy *Eunuchus.* For the most part his work is divided into three classes — tales, fables, and miscellaneous, of which his fables are most widely known. As he always seemed to have devoted rich patrons, on the whole his life was easy.

LANG, ANDREW (1844–1912), scholar, poet, and versatile man of letters, was born at Selkirk, Scotland, only a few miles from Abbotsford, the home of Sir Walter Scott. Below his home flowed the river Tweed, where the countryside was haunted by old legends and superstitious beliefs.

The Lang children had an old nurse who regaled them with Scottish tales of fairies, bogies, and hidden gold. Andrew and his brothers and sisters often gathered in an old barn to listen to tales told by an old shepherd. Andrew devoured every book he could lay his hands on. He went to the Selkirk grammar school and later to Edinburgh, then to the universities of St. Andrews and Glasgow. He was a brilliant scholar, winning a First in Classics. He won a scholarship to Balliol College, Oxford, and became a Fellow of Merton College, where he remained seven years. During this period he worked on his famous translation of the *Odyssey*. In 1875 he gave up his Fellowship, married, and settled in Kensington, London, where he lived the rest of his life. His childhood interest in fairy lore intensified and took a scientific turn as he grew older. The study of traditional tales had at this time just begun to be recognized as a science. In 1873 Lang published his famous essay, *Mythology and Fairy Tales,* in which he strongly defended fairy tales and promulgated the theory that folklore was the foundation of literary mythology. Aside from his scholarly interest in traditional lore, he wrote several original fairy stories. Of these *Prince Prigio* is the best known today, although his richly imaginative tale, *The Gold of Fairnilee,* founded on the old Scottish legends and Border ballads, is perhaps his best writing. From his profound knowledge of folklore came his "color" fairy books. *The Blue Fairy Book,* published in 1889, became immensely popular. The *Red, Green,* and *Yellow Fairy Books* followed and were equally enjoyed. From that time on Lang published a yearly volume of fairy tales. In 1907 his *Tales of Troy and Greece* appeared. His scholarly volume, *Custom and Myth,* had already been published in 1884. During the last years of his life he concentrated on Scottish history, folklore, and Homeric scholarship. He died at Banchory, near Aberdeen, and is buried in the cemetery at St. Andrews, the ancient town he loved so well.

LAWSON, ROBERT (1892–1957), was the first person to win both the Caldecott and Newbery awards, the former in 1941 for *They Were Strong and Good,* and the latter in 1945 for *Rabbit Hill.* He was born in New York City, grew up in Montclair, New Jersey, and studied at the New York School of Fine and Applied Art. For three years he drew illustrations for magazines and designed scenery for the Washington Square Players. He served in the Camouflage Section of the Fortieth Engineers in World War I. After the war he drew his first book illustrations for Carl Sandburg's *Rootabaga Stories.* In 1922 he married Marie Abrams, also an illustrator and author. For several years they both worked at commercial art. In 1930 Mr. Lawson took up etching and won the John Taylor Arms Prize awarded by the Society of American Etchers. In that year also he illustrated Arthur Mason's *The Wee Men of Ballywooden* and the next year *From the Horn of the Moon,* by the same author. In 1936 his drawings for Munro Leaf's *Ferdinand* firmly established his reputation as one of the best contemporary illustrators. From then on he devoted his talents entirely to book illustration and writing. In 1938 he wrote his first book, *Ben and Me,* and it was so well received that he began writing most of the books that he illustrated. In all, he illustrated over fifty books, twelve of which were his own. Among the books by other authors which he illustrated are *Mr. Popper's Penguins,* by Richard Atwater; Bunyan's *Pilgrim's Progress; Adam of the Road,* by Elizabeth Janet Gray; and *Wee Gillis,* by Munro Leaf. Shortly after their marriage, Mr. and Mrs. Lawson settled in Westport, Connecticut, where in 1936 they built their home, which they called "Rabbit Hill."

LEAR, EDWARD (1812–1888), was the youngest of twenty-one children and early became an artist. His first work was painting birds and illustrating the works of naturalists. He was only twenty-one when he published a large collection of colored drawings of birds. When doing a similar work for the Earl of Derby, he lived at the Earl's home, where he became very popular with the children of the family because of the absurd poems and drawings he made for them. These afterward became the nucleus of his first *Nonsense Book.* Ruskin thought this one of the most amusing books of his time and Lear's drawings especially original as well as droll. But Lear was a landscape artist, as well, and traveled widely in Greece, Egypt, Palestine, and Albania for new and unusual scenes to paint. He also taught drawing, and Queen Victoria was one of his pupils.

LE GALLIENNE, RICHARD (1866–1947), was born and educated in Liverpool, England. He first went into business, but gave it up to devote himself to writing; he was an essayist as well as a poet and wrote charmingly in both mediums. He lived in the United States for twenty years; but was living in Paris at the time of his death. His daughter, Eva Le Gallienne, became a well-known actress.

LINDBERGH, ANNE MORROW (1906–   ), was born in New Jersey. Her father was a Morgan banker, United States Senator, and Ambassador to Mexico; her mother, a poet, who acted as president of Smith College during an interim. Anne was graduated from Smith with honors. With her famous flying husband, Charles Lindbergh, she has made many trips; but the one she relates in *North to the Orient* was her first long one. Later the Lindberghs made together a forty-thousand-mile flight over five countries to survey transatlantic air routes. Anne Lindbergh received the Cross of Honor of the United States Flag Association and was the first woman given the Hubbard Gold Medal of the National Geographic Society.

LINDSAY, VACHEL (1879–1931), was born in Springfield, Illinois. He attended Hiram College for three years. Then, intending to become an artist, he worked his way through art school in Chicago and New York City. Unable to get a job, he took to the road and became a vagabond poet, reciting and chanting his poems in exchange for food and lodging. His first volume of verse, *General William Booth Enters Heaven*, published in 1913, brought him recognition. The next year *The Congo and Other Poems* appeared, followed by *The Chinese Nightingale* and *Johnny Appleseed and Other Poems for Children*. He traveled all over the country chanting his poems before audiences.

LOFTING, HUGH (1886–1947), the author of the popular *Doctor Dolittle* books for children, was born of Irish-English parents in Maidenhead, England. At the age of sixteen he came to the United States to attend the Massachusetts Institute of Technology, and the following year returned to England to continue his studies at the London Polytechnic. As a civil engineer, Lofting prospected in Canada and worked with the railways in West Africa and Cuba. He then returned to America, married, and had two children. During World War I he served as Captain in the Irish Guards in Flanders and France. It was in letters that Lofting wrote and illustrated to send to his children back home that the character of the kindly country doctor who preferred animals as patients first made his appearance. After the war, at his wife's suggestion, Lofting put the letters into book form, and *The Story of Doctor Dolittle* was published in 1920. With his second book, *Voyages of Doctor Dolittle*, he won the Newbery medal in 1923. He wrote nine books in the series and they have been translated into nine languages. Lofting had just finished *Doctor Dolittle and the Secret Lake* before he died at his home in Santa Monica, California.

LONGFELLOW, HENRY WADSWORTH (1807–1882), was born in Portland, Maine. His mother was descended from John Alden and Priscilla, whose courtship Longfellow described in his poem, "The Courtship of Miles Standish." His was a happy childhood. Before he was fifteen he entered Bowdoin College, where Nathaniel Hawthorne was a classmate. Longfellow was a brilliant student and decided on a literary career. At the age of twenty-two, following a year's study in Europe, he was appointed professor of modern languages and literature at Bowdoin. When in 1834 he was offered a professorship at Harvard, he again went to Europe, this time to Scandinavia to study the Icelandic languages and literature. In the Netherlands his wife, who had accompanied him, fell ill and died. This was his first great sorrow. During the seventeen years he was at Harvard he was greatly beloved. His second wife was Frances Appleton, and their home in Cambridge, Craigie House, had been George Washington's headquarters in 1775. The years that followed were the most productive ones of his life. In 1854 he resigned from Harvard to give his whole time to writing *Hiawatha*. His happy home life was abruptly shattered when his wife was fatally burned. After the Civil War, Longfellow, accompanied by his three daughters, made a final trip to Europe. He was received by Queen Victoria and the Prince of Wales, and dined with William Gladstone.

LORENZINI, CARLO (1831–1890), pen name C. Collodi, lived in Florence, Italy, where he was employed many years as a government official. After he retired from office he gave all his time to writing books for children. The puppet shows originated in Italy; what could be more natural than that a puppet should come to real life in the place of his birth? And so *Pinocchio* was born to delight not only Italian boys and girls but children all over the world.

LOWELL, JAMES RUSSELL (1819–1891), was one of the famous Massachusetts Lowell family. An indifferent student, he graduated from Harvard undecided as to his profession. He chose law, was admitted to the bar, but disliked it. Encouraged by his betrothed, who was later his wife, he began to write poetry, for which he had shown talent. He was always interested in public affairs, and his *Biglow Papers*, begun without design, then carried on, are famous satires on public conditions. He was one of the first editors of the *Atlantic Monthly* and *North American Review*. He succeeded Longfellow in the chair of modern languages at Harvard and was an inspiring lecturer. He became Minister to Spain, and later to England, where he was very popular.

LUCAS, MARY SEYMOUR (1912–   ), born in Old Greenwich, Connecticut, was educated at Rollins College. She also attended the University College of South-West England at Exeter. She has taught in Connecticut and in Oregon.

LUTHER, MARTIN (1483–1546), early showed a brilliant mind. He was educated for the law, but in his preliminary study of philosophy he grew interested in religion and became a monk of the Augustinian Eremites. No one was more surprised than Luther at the furor caused by his ninety-five theses, posted on the cathedral door at Wittenberg — as was the custom — for discussion. He became the real leader of the German Reformation, which involved political as well as religious issues. He left the Church, married an ex-nun and had five children, and devoted the rest of his life to writing commentaries and catechisms, translating the Bible into German, and organizing the Lutheran Protestantism he had instituted.

MABIE, HAMILTON WRIGHT (1846–1916), was born in New York State, graduated from Williams College, and took his law degree at Columbia. At one time he was on the staff of the *Outlook*. He was a lecturer, critic, and essayist, but his one mission was to encourage and spread a love of good reading. His work on the Eddas has been invaluable for children.

McCLOSKEY, ROBERT (1914–   ), was the first artist to receive the Caldecott medal twice, first in 1942 for *Make Way for Ducklings* and again in 1958 for *Time of Wonder*. He was born in Hamilton, Ohio. He won a scholarship to the Vesper George School in Boston and studied at the National Academy of Design in New York City, where he received the President's Award. In 1939 he won the Prix de Rome, but World War II delayed acceptance of it until 1948. He made bas-reliefs for the Municipal building in Hamilton, Ohio, and with Francis Scott Bradford he painted a mural of prominent people of Beacon Hill in Boston. In 1940 he married Margaret Durand, the daughter of Ruth Sawyer, well-known writer and storyteller. During the war, McCloskey joined the Army and spent three years making visual aids for the infantry at Fort McClellan, Alabama. In 1948 the McCloskey family, which now included two small daughters, Sally and Jane, spent a year in Italy. They now live in Maine on an island in Penobscot Bay. The island, the sea, and the coast of Maine have provided the background for *Blueberries for Sal;*

One Morning in Maine; and *Time of Wonder*. Besides writing and illustrating these books, Robert McClockey has put some of his own boyhood interests, such as playing the harmonica, dismantling clocks, and inventing things, into his books *Lentil; Homer Price;* and *Centerburg Tales*. He has illustrated several books by other authors, including Ruth Sawyer's *Journey Cake Ho!*

McCORD, DAVID (1897–   ), was born in New York City. As a boy he lived on a ranch in the Rogue River Valley of Oregon and learned the life of the wilderness. He graduated from Lincoln High School in Portland. He received his A.B. and A.M. degrees from Harvard, and is director of the Harvard Fund. For several years he was on the drama and music staff of the Boston *Transcript*. In 1950, he delivered eight Lowell Lectures on "Edward Lear: A Study of Sense and Nonsense." He has frequently contributed verse to the *Atlantic, Harper's,* the *Saturday Review,* and the *New Yorker*. In 1951 his *Poet Always Next but One* received the William Rose Benét award. His twentieth book, *Far and Few,* is a collection of poems for children.

MacMANUS, SEUMAS (1869–1960), writer and teacher, was born in Ireland and educated in a mountain school. He came to the United States in 1899 but returned each summer to Ireland, where he was well known as a story teller.

MADDEN, MABRA (1900–   ). *See* BRYAN, CATHERINE.

MALORY, SIR THOMAS (d. 1471), if scholars have correctly identified him, was a Warwickshire man, a knight and soldier, and a member of Parliament in 1445. Records show that he spent much of the last twenty years of his life in prison, where he did most of his writing. He took the many different versions and episodes of the Arthurian cycle and rewrote them into a unified whole. William Caxton, the first English printer, published this work in 1485 under the title *Le Morte Darthur*. It is the first English prose epic, one of the early foundations of English prose, and the fountainhead of English Arthurian legend.

MARRIOTT, ALICE LEE (1910–   ), has devoted her life to the study of the American Indians and their ways. She graduated from the University of Oklahoma, where she received training in ethnology. At intervals over a period of ten years she worked with the Kiowa and Cheyenne tribes. As a field research fellow of the Laboratory of Anthropology of Santa Fe, she studied the Northwest tribes, and the Rockefeller and Guggenheim Foundations have further facilitated her research as an ethnographer in the Southwest. Her *Winter-telling Stories* are tales of the Kiowas; *Indians on Horseback* is a factual book on the life of the Plains Indians; and *Indians of the Four Corners* tells of the Anasazi Indians and their modern descendants.

MASEFIELD, JOHN (1871–   ), Poet Laureate of England, lost his parents when young and was brought up by an uncle. Not much of his early life is known. He was on a sailing vessel that rounded the "Horn"; his health broke down, and he landed in New York with five dollars. He did odd jobs in and about the city for nearly three years. He says his proudest moment was the time he shook hands with Bob Fitzsimmons, and his happiest was when he discovered Chaucer's poetry. He then decided to become a poet and went back to London. He is married and has a son, and a daughter who is an illustrator. Besides writing poetry, he writes novels and historical books of adventure for boys.

MEIGS, CORNELIA LYNDE (1884–   ), is professor emeritus of creative writing and American literature at Bryn Mawr College. She was born in Rock Island, Illinois, but grew up in New England, the home of her ancestors. She graduated from Bryn Mawr in 1907. She has written more than twenty-five books for children, most of which are based on incidents in American history. In 1927 she won the $2,000 Beacon Hill Bookshelf Prize for *Trade Wind*, and in 1934 she was awarded the Newbery medal for *Invincible Louisa*, the life of Louisa May Alcott. She was editor-in-chief and an author of *A Critical History of Children's Literature*, published in 1953. Her books include *Master Simon's Garden; The Willow Whistle; Wind in the Chimney;* and *The Wonderful Locomotive*.

MILLAY, EDNA ST. VINCENT (1892–1950), one of the foremost American poets of the early twentieth century, was born in Rockland, Maine. She attended Barnard College and graduated from Vassar in 1917. *Renascence and Other Poems* was published shortly after her graduation; she wrote the title poem when she was only nineteen. Early in her career she lived in Greenwich Village and wrote short stories under the pen name Nancy Boyd. At one time she was associated with the Provincetown Players as playwright and actress. In 1923 she won the Pulitzer Prize for *The Harp Weaver and Other Poems*. She wrote the libretto for the opera *The King's Henchman* (Deems Taylor composed the music) which was produced by the Metropolitan Opera Company in 1927. In 1923 she married Eugen

Jan Boissevain. Her *Collected Sonnets* was published in 1941 and *Collected Lyrics* in 1943. *Edna St. Vincent Millay's Poems Selected for Young People* was published in 1929.

MILNE, ALAN ALEXANDER (1882–1956), essayist, poet, and playwright, was, according to his own statement, a writer of children's books almost by chance. In his *Autobiography*, he tells how he happened to write his first book for children. He and his wife, with their three-year-old son, Christopher Robin, had taken a house with friends in North Wales for the month of August. But with the house full of guests and friends continually dropping in, Milne felt that he must somehow escape. He pleaded urgent inspiration and with pencil and paper fled to a summerhouse. Knowing that he had to write something, he remembered that Rose Fyleman had urged him to write some verses for her new children's magazine. He had refused, but here he was, and he had to write something. Furthermore, it was raining. It rained for eleven days and he wrote eleven sets of verses. Some of these, first printed in *Punch,* were published under the title *When We Were Very Young*. Three years later more poems appeared in *Now We Are Six*. This was followed by two Christopher Robin stories, *Winnie-the-Pooh* and *The House at Pooh Corner*. Milne was born in London and graduated from Cambridge University. He became assistant editor of *Punch* in 1906 and held that position until 1914. While working on *Punch,* he married Dorothy de Sélincourt. During this time also, he began publishing some of his essays. In World War I he served in France, and when he was demobilized, he decided to devote full time to his own writing. He made a play from Kenneth Grahame's *The Wind in the Willows* and called it *Toad of Toad Hall*. His plays for adults include *Mr. Pim Passes By* and *The Dover Road*. Milne's son, Christopher Robin Milne, served in the Royal Air Force in World War II; now he and his wife manage a bookshop in Dartmouth, Devonshire, England.

MONRO, HAROLD EDWARD (1879–1932), an English poet and critic, was born in Brussels, but was of Scottish descent. He was educated at Radley Grammar School and Cambridge University. He established several poetry magazines, *The Poetry Review* in 1912, and *Poetry and Drama* in 1913, refounded after the war as *The Chapbook*. Monro was the first to recognize many poets now famous. His books include *Before Dawn; Trees;* and *Elm Angel*.

MOORE, CLEMENT C. (1779–1863), was born in New York, graduated from Columbia, and held the chair of Biblical learning in the Theological Seminary of New York. Besides studies on his subject, he published a collection of poems. His best-known poem is *A Visit from St. Nicholas,* written one Christmas for his own children and published the next December, 1823, anonymously and without his consent in the Troy (N.Y.) *Sentinel.*

MOORE, MARIANNE (1887–   ), American poet and literary critic, was born in St. Louis, Missouri. She graduated from Bryn Mawr in 1909 and has received many honorary degrees from other colleges. From 1925 to 1929 she was editor of the magazine *The Dial.* Her poetry is distinguished by its wit, intellectual appeal, and precise metrical patterns. She has received many awards; in 1951 alone she was awarded the Bollingen Poetry Prize by Yale University, the National Book Award, and a Pulitzer Prize for her *Collected Poems.* She has written many volumes of poetry, including *The Pangolin and Other Verse; What Are Years?; Predilections;* and *Like a Bulwark.* In 1954 she made a new translation of the *Fables of La Fontaine.*

MORLEY, CHRISTOPHER (1890–1957), poet, novelist, essayist, and playwright, was born in Haverford, Pennsylvania. In 1910 he graduated with honors from Haverford College, where his father was a professor of mathematics. From 1910 to 1913 he was a Rhodes Scholar at Oxford. Early in his career he served on the editorial staffs of Doubleday, Page & Company, the *Ladies' Home Journal,* and the Philadelphia *Evening Public Ledger.* He initiated and conducted a column, "The Bowling Green," in the New York *Evening Post* and in the *Saturday Review of Literature.* In 1934 he helped organize the Baker Street Irregulars, a society devoted to the lore of Sherlock Holmes. For many years he served as a member of the Book-of-the-Month committee. He was a prolific writer, bringing out a book a year for more than thirty years. These include *Parnassus on Wheels; The Haunted Book Shop; Thunder on the Left; The Trojan Horse; Kitty Foyle;* the books of verse *Chimney Smoke* and *The Rocking Horse;* and an autobiography, *John Mistletoe.* He was editor-in-chief of the 1937 and 1948 revised editions of *Bartlett's Familiar Quotations.*

MUKERJI, DHAN GOPAL (1890–1936), was born in a village near Calcutta, India. He was the son of Brahmin parents. From his mother he heard fables and old religious tales of India. These, with his boyhood experiences of life in the jungle, he later used in books which he wrote hoping to make India better understood by boys

and girls. His books include *Hindu Fables; Kari, the Elephant; Hari, the Jungle Lad; Jungle Beasts and Men; Ghond the Hunter; Chief of the Herd;* and *Rama, the Hero of India.* In 1928 he won the Newbery medal for *Gay-Neck,* the story of a carrier pigeon. Mukerji received his education at the University of Calcutta, the University of Tokyo, and Stanford University in California, from which he graduated in 1914. He married an American.

NANKIVELL, JOICE MARY, was born in Queensland, Australia, and is still a citizen of Australia although she now lives in Chalkidhiki, Greece. During World War I she and her husband, Frederick Sydney Loch, were attached to Quaker organizations in various countries. They helped bring Poles out of Hungary and Rumania to Cyprus and Turkey, and afterwards worked with the Poles and the Greeks. For her work she was awarded the Polish Gold Cross of Merit and the Greek Red Cross Medal. When she later returned to Greece, she worked as a doctor to both villagers and monks and followed her interest of extracting vegetable dyes from plants and trees. She heard the villagers tell stories about Christophilos, a goatherd, and these she preserved in her book *Tales of Christophilos.*

NASH, OGDEN (1902–   ), an American writer of humorous verse, was born in Rye, New York. He left Harvard College at the end of his freshman year, taught for a year at St. George's School in Newport, Rhode Island, tried his hand at selling bonds, wrote advertising copy, and worked for publishing firms. His first book of verse, *Hard Times,* was published in 1931. Since then he has written many others, including *Versus; Family Reunion; Parents Keep Out;* and *Good Intentions.* He also edited a collection of humorous verse for children, *The Moon Is Shining Bright as Day.* His light verse frequently is printed in the *New Yorker.*

NOLAN, JEANNETTE COVERT (1896–   ), was born and grew up in Evansville, Indiana. Her grandfather and father were newspapermen and it was her ambition to become a newspaperwoman. During high school, she served as editor of the weekly paper and senior yearbook. After graduation she worked for three years as a reporter and feature writer for the Evansville *Courier.* Then she married Val Nolan, a young lawyer who became United States District Attorney for Indiana. They had three children, two sons and a daughter. When the children were growing up, Mrs. Nolan began writing books for older boys and girls. *The Young Douglas* was published in 1934. This was followed by other stories with a historical setting: *Red Hugh of Ireland; Patriot in the Saddle; Treason at the Point; Hobnailed Boots;* and *The Victory Drum.* Mrs. Nolan has contributed short stories, plays, and serials to children's magazines and has written many successful adult novels, one of which was made into a motion picture. For several years, too, she wrote a column for the Indianapolis *Star.* She has been particularly successful in her biographies for young people; these include lives of Eugene Field, James Whitcomb Riley, Clara Barton, Florence Nightingale, O. Henry, Stephen A. Douglas, Andrew Jackson, John Brown, and Benedict Arnold. In 1954, she won the Indiana University Writers' Conference award for the best children's book by an Indiana author published that year. The book honored was *George Rogers Clark: Soldier and Hero.* For several years Mrs. Nolan taught creative writing at the Indiana University Extension Division in Indianapolis and for five summers directed the Workshop in Juvenile Writing at Writers' Conferences at Indiana University. In 1949 and 1950 she served in a similar capacity at the Writers' Conference at the University of Colorado. She lives in Indianapolis and takes special delight in reading to her five young grandchildren.

NORTON, MARY, was born in England, an only girl with four brothers. She writes of her childhood: "We lived in a house very like the description of Firbank Hall in *The Borrowers,* square and Georgian, staring a little bleakly from the front but, at the back, sunlit and creeper-hung, with lawns which sloped in terraces to the river. At the age of eight, I was sent away to the 'dear Sisters' because our charming nurse could cope with the boys but not so well with 'Miss Mary.' After a year with the Sisters, there were seven years at a more orthodox convent school. Drawing turned out to be my forte, then acting, and lastly, writing." Mrs. Norton was a member of the "Old Vic" Shakespeare Company in the days of the renowned dramatic coach, Lilian Baylis. Upon her marriage to Robert C. Norton, she gave up acting. For some years the Nortons, with their four children, lived in Portugal, where Mr. Norton's business interests were centered. Just before the outbreak of World War II, Mary Norton returned to England for an operation and later signed up with the War Office. As invasion became imminent, she was transferred to New York. Of her stay in America with the four children, she says, "We managed at last to rent a little house in Connecticut and schools were found. But none of this would have been possible without the unforgettable and amazing kindness of American friends. My job did not bring in quite enough to support a house and children, so it was here I began to write in grim earnest — at night, after the children were in bed — short stories, articles, translations from the Portuguese. Later I thought of writing down some of the stories I told my children. We stayed two years instead of one, and in 1943, London again, in the street where we still live. I wrote during the flying-bomb period the book now called *Bed-Knob and Broomstick.*" Mrs. Norton's delightful fantasy, *The Borrowers,* won the Carnegie medal for the most distinguished children's book published in England in 1952. The following year, when it was published in the United States, it was chosen as one of the distinguished books of the year by the American Library Association. In 1955, Mrs. Norton wrote a sequel, *The Borrowers Afield.*

OPIE, PETER AND IONA, are the distinguished editors of the definitive study *The Oxford Dictionary of Nursery Rhymes* and the compilers of *The Oxford Nursery Rhyme Book.* They have three children, James, Bobby, and Letitia, and live at Alton, in Hampshire, England.

PENNEY, GRACE JACKSON, was born in Alabama but grew up in a little coal-mining town in eastern Oklahoma with Indians as friends and neighbors. She received her B.S. and M.A. degrees from the University of Oklahoma, taught social sciences in high school for several years, and then was in charge of the Public Information Department of the University of Oklahoma. She has also been a newspaper correspondent and has written articles for various periodicals. She married Ralph E. Penney, and they have one daughter and two sons. Her great interest in Indian folklore and history is evident in her first published book, *Tales of the Cheyennes.*

PERRAULT, CHARLES (1628–1703), was educated to be a lawyer but practiced little, as he held various government appointive positions. After the death of his patron Colbert, Perrault devoted himself to literature. None of his more pretentious works are now remembered, but his fairy tales, which he attributed to his son, became very popular in his own time and are equally so today. His erudite quarrel with Boileau over ancient and modern literature has contributed less to learning than these stories have to the study of folklore.

PETERSHAM, MAUD (1890–   ) AND MISKA (1889–   ), are a husband-and-wife team who, for almost thirty years, have been writing and illustrating beautiful books for children. Maud was born in Kingston, New York, the daughter of a Baptist minister. She graduated from Vassar and studied at the New York School of Fine and Applied Arts. Her first job was with the International Art Service, where she met Miska Petersham. Miska was born in a little town near Budapest, Hungary. He walked miles each day to art school in Budapest. When he was twenty, he left for England, where he studied art at night while working to earn his living. A few years later he came to New York. The Petershams' first book for younger children was *Miki*, based on Miska's boyhood in Hungary. They spent three months in Palestine before illustrating their distinguished book, *The Christ Child*. Other Bible stories followed. In 1945, they won the Caldecott medal for *The Rooster Crows: A Book of American Rhymes and Jingles*. Other books include *The Box with Red Wheels; Circus Baby; The American ABC;* and *America's Stamps*.

POE, EDGAR ALLAN (1809–1849), was one of America's greatest literary geniuses, but his private life was shadowed by insecurity, poverty, drink, and the long illness and death of his young wife. He was born in Boston, the child of itinerant actors. His mother died when he was not yet three years old, and he was taken into the home of a Mr. and Mrs. Allan, of Richmond, Virginia. His relationship with the Allans was never happy, and eventually there was a total estrangement. After his withdrawal from the University of Virginia and his dismissal from West Point, Poe became a journalist and editor of literary periodicals. As such, he established his reputation as a literary critic. He was a pioneer in developing the short story as a new form of literature; his stories and many of his poems have never been surpassed in their field — that of horror and the haunted mind.

POTTER, BEATRIX (1866–1943), is known all over the world for her "Peter Rabbit" books. Helen Beatrix Potter was born in London and spent a lonely childhood hedged about by Victorian conventions. Her parents considered they had done their duty when they provided her with a clean frock each morning, had a cutlet and rice pudding sent up to the nursery on the third floor for her lunch every day, and had her Scotch nurse take her for a walk each afternoon. So the solitary child made a little world of her own. She amused herself with a paint box, pencils, and a few pets. When Beatrix was seventeen, she had a visiting governess for German, Miss Annie Carter, a charming young woman of about her own age. This delightful interlude of German lessons did not last long, for Miss Carter fell in love, married a Mr. Moore, and proceeded to have a large family. Beatrix used to drive over in her pony carriage behind the coachman to visit her friend. The first baby was a little boy, Noel. At the age of five, he fell ill and one day Beatrix wrote him a letter about a little rabbit named Peter. That was the beginning of *The Tale of Peter Rabbit*. After the publication of the book and its subsequent success, Beatrix Potter bought Hill Top Farm in the little village of Sawrey, between Lake Windermere and Coniston Water. She became a tenant farmer, improving land, buying cows, pigs, and sheep, and then buying more land. In these transactions she was advised by a solicitor, Mr. Heelis. Their friendship grew, and although her family disapproved, she married Mr. Heelis and for the first time found release from her family. As her royalties increased, she bought more and more property and at her death left nearly 4,000 acres of the most lovely countryside in the Lake district to the National Trust. A characteristic clause in her will forbids hunting on the land. The National Trust has made Hill Top Farmhouse into a permanent memorial where a large number of Beatrix Potter's original water colors are exhibited.

PROKOFIEFF, SERGE (1891–1953), escaped from Russia in 1918 after the Revolution, but settled there again in 1938, where he has been honored for his music. He is said to have written *Peter and the Wolf* and to have taken it to Koussevitzky, a fellow countryman and leader of the Boston Symphony Orchestra, saying it was suitably infantile for Boston and its critics, who had severely criticized his Fourth Symphony when played there. He is considered one of the greatest modern composers, but is better known in America for his *Peter and the Wolf* than for his symphonies. Appreciation for his work is growing, however.

PYLE, HOWARD (1853–1911), was born of a Quaker family, near Wilmington, Delaware. He was an imaginative child, who early began to tell stories and draw and whose ambition was to be an artist. Under his mother's encouragement and in spite of the hard times after the Civil War, he had drawing lessons. When, at the age of twenty-three, he actually sold something, he went to New York to study art and sell more. He met many artists and such people as Mary Mapes Dodge. Achieving success, he later moved back home where he established an art school. He always studied the background before writing his historical stories. These and his fairy tales made him the child's own author.

PYLE, KATHARINE (d. 1938). She said of herself that she began making up stories when she was so young that her mother had to write them down for her. She grew up with three brothers in a household of pets. She always illustrated her own work; and though it does not rank so high as that of her famous brother, Howard, it is colorful and generally charming.

REESE, LIZETTE WOODWORTH (1856–1935), was born in Maryland, one of twins. Her father was of Welsh stock; her mother, of German. She lived as a child in the border territory between the North and the South, but her father served in the Confederate Army. She became a school teacher at seventeen, and taught successively in an English-German high school, in a Negro high school, and finally in the Western High School, all of Baltimore. Here she stayed until she gave up teaching twenty years later, and meanwhile she was writing her stories and poems.

RICHARDS, LAURA E. (1850–1943), had a special genius for writing nonsense verses. These have been collected in her book *Tirra Lirra*. She was born in Boston of an illustrious family. Her mother was Julia Ward Howe, who wrote *The Battle Hymn of the Republic*. Her father, Samuel Gridley Howe, founded the Perkins Institution for the Blind. When Laura married and had seven children of her own, she used to make up rhymes and jingles to amuse them. Her husband suggested that she send some of them to the *St. Nicholas Magazine*. They were promptly accepted and she was launched on her writing career. She wrote over seventy books for boys and girls. Perhaps the best known is *Captain January*, which has twice been made into a motion picture. Her books for adults include *Julia Ward Howe*, for which she won the Pulitzer prize in 1917, and *Stepping Westward*, her autobiography.

ROBERTS, ELIZABETH MADOX (1886–1941), was born in Kentucky, lived in the Colorado Rockies, and was educated at Chicago University. She then went to New York to make her living at writing. Those who knew her say her personality was a riddle. While in the university she was one apart, and in New York, though living among the bohemian literary group, she was not of it. She lived alone and is said often to have worked twelve hours at a time.

ROSCOE, WILLIAM P. (1753–1831), was the son of a market gardener at Liverpool. Educating himself while helping his father, he finally became a lawyer and a member of Parliament. He was one of the earliest to write against England's slave trade. He was a historian, botanist, poet. His *Butterfly's Ball* (1807), written for his small son's birthday, was perhaps one of the earliest productions for children with no moral attached.

ROSS, PATRICIA FENT, was born and reared in Eureka, Kansas. She received her early education at the Southern Kansas Academy, attended the University of Kansas, and then went to the Horner Institute of Fine Arts in Kansas City to study drama and fashion art. After completing her work at Horner, she turned to the stage, playing various roles with a stock company. For a period she did fashion drawing, advertising copy, and free-lance writing. Going to Mexico, she decided to take graduate work at Mexico City College, received her Master's degree in anthropology, and became an instructor in the Department of Anthropology at that institution. Mrs. Ross is well equipped to write books on Mexico, for she knows the country intimately and understands the Mexican people, their temperament, their folkways and customs. She makes her permanent home in Mexico City, returning to the United States for frequent visits. Her books include *In Mexico They Say; The Hungry Moon; The Magic Forest;* and *Made in Mexico*.

ROSSETTI, CHRISTINA (1830–1894), was the daughter of Italian exiles in London. She was accustomed from childhood to intellectual but poor surroundings. At one time she helped her mother keep a school; she also sat as a model for her brother, Dante Gabriel, and his friends. She had poor health and had to endure great suffering before her death. Of timid, retiring, and religious disposition, she wrote poems ranging from nursery rhymes to lyrics on death, and from religious poems to a sonnet-sequence on love.

ROURKE, CONSTANCE MAYFIELD (1885–1941), was born in Cleveland, Ohio, went to Vassar, and studied at the Sorbonne and the Bibliothèque Nationale in Paris and at the British Museum. Her home was in Grand Rapids, Michigan. Her article on Paul Bunyan, which appeared in *The New Republic* in 1918, was the first story of this mythical lumberjack in any magazine of general circulation. Her idea of biography was to see the character in relation to his period and background.

RUSKIN, JOHN (1819–1900), an only child, was brought up without toys, was carefully trained in music, drawing, and reading aloud, and was taken traveling when young. Because he was precocious and a bookworm, his parents expected him to go far in the Church. Before leaving Oxford, Ruskin had published articles on nature and art. His first book, *Modern Painters*, produced an immediate sensation and criticism. He believed that the architecture of a people expressed their religion, aspirations, and social habits. No mean drawer himself, he held the chair of Professor of Art at Oxford for ten years. His great contribution to children's literature is *The King of the Golden River*.

SAINT-EXUPÉRY, ANTOINE DE (1900–1944), was born in Lyon, France. As a boy he passed his holidays near a French airport from which he acquired a boyish interest in and information about motors and the like. He took lessons in flying from a civil pilot, entered service at Strasbourg, was sent to Morocco as a cadet, and came back to France an officer. Trying business for a while, he succumbed finally to the life of an aviator. He flew the African mails for three years, but he also had flying experiences in other parts of the world, as *Wind, Sand, and Stars* recounts. He asked for active service in World War II. In August, 1944, he was reported missing in action after a mission over southern France. No trace of him or of his plane was ever found.

SAWYER, RUTH (1880–   ), storyteller and author of books for children, was born in Boston and grew up in New York City. She attended the Garland Kindergarten Training School in Boston and in 1904 graduated from Columbia University, where she majored in folklore and storytelling. As a child she was fortunate in having an Irish nurse, Johanna, who was a wonderful storyteller and instilled in her small charge a deep love of Irish folklore. Later this interest was extended to other countries. Her first opportunity to seek the living source of folk tales came while she was working on the New York *Sun*, when that paper sent her to Ireland in 1905 and again in 1907 to write a series of articles on Irish folklore, Gaelic festivals, and Irish Cottage Industries. In Donegal she heard a tinker tell a story which later she recreated as *The Voyage of the Wee Red Cap*. Later Ruth Sawyer went to Spain and heard tales which she retold in *Picture Tales from Spain*. There too she found material for *Toño Antonio*. In Mexico she found Paco, later to appear in *The Least One*. She has found Christmas stories in many countries and brought them together in *The Long Christmas*. In 1937 she won the Newbery medal for *Roller Skates*, in which she tells of a year in her own childhood. From her rich and varied experience she has written *The Way of*

the Storyteller, a truly inspirational book which deals with storytelling as a creative art. Ruth Sawyer married a physician, Dr. Albert Durand. They have a son and a daughter Margaret, who is the wife of Robert McCloskey, twice winner of the Caldecott medal. Both the Durands and the McCloskeys now live in Maine.

SAXE, JOHN GODFREY (1816–1887), born in Vermont, was a graduate of Middlebury College. He was a lawyer, politician, and editor of different newspapers. He was best known as a writer of satirical, humorous, and society verse, as well as versified fables, of which *The Blind Men and the Elephant* is still remembered. His popularity is now gone, but in his lifetime his verses gave amusement to a large reading public.

SCOTT, ROBERT FALCON (1868–1912), famous English antarctic explorer, commanded the antarctic expedition in the *Discovery* (1901–04). He surveyed South Victoria Land and the interior of the Antarctic Continent. Until 1909 he served in the British Navy. In 1910 he sailed from New Zealand in the ship *Terra Nova* in an attempt to reach the South Pole. He and his four companions reached the Pole shortly after Roald Amundsen's successful expedition, but all perished on the return trip.

SCOTT, SIR WALTER (1771–1832), was born in Edinburgh. Although he became lame in infancy, he was always an active man, even taking long tramps. On these he collected ballads and Scottish legends; he thus became an antiquarian in addition to being a lawyer, public official, publisher, poet, and novelist. The fame he acquired by his literary ballads was surpassed by his novels on legendary and historical subjects. The story of his rapid writing to pay off the debts of the publishing company in which he was a partner is well known. In spite of any weaknesses of plot or character, his novels will always give pleasure for their aliveness and romantic realism.

SEIGNOBOSC, FRANÇOISE (1897–   ), is a French artist who writes and illustrates picture books for very young children under the pen name of Françoise. She was born in Lodève, France. After receiving a Baccalaureate degree in Latin languages, she received a scholarship to study at Monmouth College in Illinois. She attended various art academies and schools, and in 1951 won the New York *Herald Tribune* prize for her picture book *Jeanne-Marie Counts Her Sheep*. Other picture books include *Noël for Jeanne-Marie; Biquette, the White Goat; Small-Trot; Springtime for Jeanne-Marie; The Thank-you*

Book; *Jeanne-Marie in Gay Paris;* and *The Story of Colette.*

SEREDY, KATE (1896   ), was born in Budapest, Hungary. She attended the Academy of Art in that city and studied art in France, Italy and Germany. During the First World War she spent two years as a nurse in a military hospital. In 1922 she came to the United States on a visit but remained to make it her home. While she was trying to earn a living and learn English, she worked in a factory, painted lampshades, and stenciled greeting cards. Willy Pogány, another Hungarian, who was a successful illustrator, helped get her started in art work. Twelve years after coming to America, she wrote and illustrated *The Good Master,* a story based on her own childhood. This was followed a few years later by a sequel, *The Singing Tree.* In 1938 she won the Newbery medal for *The White Stag,* based on the legendary account of the founding of Hungary, when Attila, guided by the white stag and the red eagle, led his people to their promised land. These legends she had heard from her father when she was a child. Her striking drawings in black and white form an integral part of the book. Her other books include *Listening; A Tree for Peter; The Chestry Oak; Gypsy;* and *Philomena.* She has illustrated many books by other authors, among them *Caddie Woodlawn,* by Carol Brink. In 1936 she bought a farm in Montgomery, New York, consisting of one hundred acres surrounding an old house, but the complicated problems of running the farm were too much for her and she moved to the village so as to devote more time to her art.

SHAKESPEARE, WILLIAM (1564–1616), was born at Stratford-on-Avon, England. Little of his boyhood and youth is known; and little of his education. After an early marriage and the birth of three children, he went to London. The records are likewise few about his early life there. He finally became connected with the theater, as actor, reviser of old plays, and manager. He then began writing the original plays which have made him one of the greatest playwrights and poets of all time. Tradition says he was an indifferent actor, an acknowledged poet, and a man well-beloved by his co-workers of the theater. He was successful enough to retire to Stratford and live his last years in comfort.

SHARP, WILLIAM (1855–1905), Scottish man of letters, was not an ordinary boy. Disliking school and the prospect of business, he ran away from school several times, once living with gypsies. He broke down trying to combine law, reading, the theater, and sleep, and sailed to Australia for his health. He went into a bank upon his return to Scotland; but on losing his position, he nearly starved trying to make a living writing. He married, traveled in the United States, Germany, and Italy. While in Italy he met a lady under whose influence he began his metaphysical work under the pen name Fiona Macleod. From this time on he carried on types of writing at the same time under the two names. Heavy work brought illness; he finally died in Italy. His identity with Fiona Macleod was not revealed until after his death.

SHELLEY, PERCY BYSSHE (1792–1822), English poet, was one who, almost from boyhood, repudiated the power of authority and of convention. One must remember this fact to understand what would otherwise seem dastardly behavior; for he was constantly in trouble with his family and society in general because he insisted on living according to his beliefs. As a man, he was extremely sensitive and imaginative. As a poet he ranks high, for his work stands pre-eminent in its musical quality, its passion, and its idealism.

SHERLOCK, PHILIP MANDERSON, was born in Jamaica, British West Indies, the son of a Methodist minister. He grew up in a remote Jamaican village and at an early age became the headmaster of Wolmer's Boys' School. Later he was Secretary of the Institute of Jamaica, a cultural center, and a member of a committee appointed by the British government to report on higher education in the British Caribbean. He has traveled widely in Western Europe and North and Central America. In 1952 Queen Elizabeth II bestowed upon him the honor of Commander of the British Empire. Mr. Sherlock is Vice-Principal and Director of Extra-Mural Studies of the University College of the West Indies, near Kingston. His *Anansi the Spider Man* is a collection of West Indian folk tales which he heard as a child and which he has retold with gaiety and charm.

SHERMAN, FRANK DEMPSTER (1860–1916), was trained as an engineer and architect. He began to write when he was a boy and continued to do so while in college, but it was during enforced idleness from a physical breakdown that he turned to writing poetry seriously. Encouraged by the acceptance of these early poems, he issued several volumes of verse, besides doing other writing.

SHERWOOD, MERRIAM (1892–   ), was born at Ballston Spa, New York. Her father was Professor of Political Economy at Johns Hopkins University. She was graduated from Vassar College and received her Ph.D. from Columbia University. From 1918 to 1920 she was Lectrice d'Anglais at the University of Grenoble, France. Then followed an assistant professorship of Romance languages at Wells College and an instructorship in French at Smith. Since 1924 she has given a course in Old French in the Graduate School of Columbia University, and has done free-lance writing. The spring and summer of 1924 she spent in France and England collecting manuscripts of *Ludgate's Minor Poems, Vol. II* for President H. N. MacCracken of Vassar. She also collected between three and four hundred photographs of medieval manuscript miniatures for a book on medieval town life by President MacCracken. She has written two books for young people, *The Song of Roland* and *The Tale of the Warrior Lord, El Cantar de mio Cid*. She lives in Washington, D.C., and is a translator for the State Department.

SHIPPEN, KATHERINE (1892–   ), was born in Hoboken, New Jersey, graduated from Bryn Mawr, and took her M.A. in history from Columbia University. From 1917 to 1926 she taught history at Miss Beard's School in Orange, New Jersey. She became Curator of the Social Studies Division of the Brooklyn Children's Museum in 1941. Her first book, *New Found World*, about the people of Latin America, was followed by *The Great Heritage*, stories of the origin, discovery, and development of the treasures of the American earth. *Bright Design* tells of the men and women from medieval time to the present who furthered the development and use of electrical energy. Her other books include *Passage to America; Leif Eriksson; A Bridle for Pegasus;* and *Moses.*

SITWELL, DAME EDITH (1887–   ), is an English poet and prose writer known for her irony and wit, and for the originality of rhythm and imagery of her poetry. She was born in Scarborough, England, of a famous literary family of noble ancestry. Her brothers, Osbert and Sacheverell, are both writers. The Sitwells spent most of their childhood at Renishaw Park, a family estate built in (1625). Dame Edith has received honorary degrees from the universities of Leeds, Durham, and Sheffield. Her many books include *A Poet's Notebook; Green Song; Fanfare for Elizabeth; A Notebook on William Shakespeare; Canticle of the Rose;* and *Collected Poems.*

SNEDEKER, CAROLINE DALE (1871–1956), was born in New Harmony, Indiana. She was the great-granddaughter of Robert Owen, the social reformer who purchased the township of New Harmony and brought scientists and educators

from the Old World to start a "Perfect State." Her grandfather, David Dale Owen, was the first United States geologist. Her grandmother told her stories of the early days of New Harmony and its ideals. Three of Mrs. Snedeker's books have New Harmony as a background. Early in life she became interested in the history of Ancient Greece and she recreated this period in several of her books. As a young girl she studied music in Cincinnati, planning to become a musician. However, she married the Rev. Charles H. Snedeker, then dean of the Cathedral in Cincinnati. They moved to Hempstead, Long Island, where she led a busy, happy life. Mrs. Snedeker's books include *The Spartan; Theras and His Town; The Perilous Seat; The Town of the Fearless; Forgotten Daughter; The White Isle; Downright Dencey; Reckoning Road;* and *A Triumph for Flavius,* which she wrote when she was over eighty. A short autobiography, *Trilobite Door, Chapters from My Life,* was printed in *The Horn Book Magazine* in 1947 and 1948.

SPERRY, ARMSTRONG (1897–   ), an American author of children's books which he also illustrates, was born in New Haven, Connecticut. As far back as he can remember he liked to draw, but his greatest joy was listening to his great-grandfather tell hair-raising yarns of his adventures as a sea captain in the South Seas. He made up his mind that someday he would see those islands Captain Armstrong described. Sperry took his first art training at the Yale Art School, but this was interrupted by World War I when he enlisted in the Navy. After the war he studied for three years at the Art Students' League in New York, then went to Paris for a year's study. The next two years he spent in an advertising agency, but always there lurked in the back of his mind the South Sea islands his great-grandfather had made so alluring. In 1925 he sailed for Tahiti and spent the next two years wandering through the South Seas, learning to know the natives and finally deciding that what he wanted most in life was to tell stories in words and pictures. His first book was *One Day with Manu*, followed by *One Day with Jambi* and *One Day with Tuktu*. Then he tried more challenging writing, *All Sails Set,* a story of the clipper ship, "Flying Cloud." In 1941 he received the Newbery medal for *Call It Courage*, based on a Polynesian legend.

SPEYER, LEONORA (1872–1956), was an American poet who won the Pulitzer Prize for poetry in 1927 for her book *Fiddler's Farewell*. She was born in Washington, D.C. Her father was Count

Ferdinand von Stosch, a German nobleman who relinquished his title when he became an American citizen, and who served with the Union forces in the Civil War. Her mother was of American birth. Mrs. Speyer attended Brussels Conservatory where she won first prize with distinction when she was sixteen. She became a concert violinist, toured Europe and America, appeared with the Boston Symphony Orchestra in 1890 and later with the New York Philharmonic. Among her many honors for poetry was a gold medal of the Poetry Society of America awarded in 1955. She was a frequent contributor of poems to the New York *Times*. Her verses have been published in book form in *Canopic Jar* (1921), *The Naked Heel* (1931), and *Slow Wall* (1946). She served many years as president of the Poetry Society of America and, until a few years before her death, taught poetry at Columbia University.

SPYRI, JOHANNA HEUSSER (1827–1901), as a child was living near Zürich, Switzerland when her poor health caused her parents to send her for a summer into the mountains. While there she found the background and inspiration for many of her stories, which she began to write after she was forty. At that time, after the Franco-Prussian War, longing to help war orphans, she decided to try to earn money for this cause by writing. She was so successful that she continued to write for the rest of her life. *Heidi*, however, brought her first real fame and is her best work. It has been translated into many languages.

STEPHENS, JAMES (1882–1950), Irish poet and novelist, was born in Dublin and grew up in poverty. He became an ardent champion of the working people. George William Russell (A.E.) admired his writing and helped him to become better known. *The Crock of Gold*, published in 1912, established him as a writer. His interest in the traditional lore of Ireland, the folk tales, epics, and sagas, is apparent in his *Irish Folk Tales; Deirdre;* and *In the Land of Youth.* His volumes of verse include *The Rocky Road to Dublin; Songs from the Clay;* and *The Hill of Vision.*

STEVENSON, ROBERT LOUIS (1850–1894), born in Edinburgh, spent all his life seeking health, at one time coming to the United States, where he married. He had always wanted to be a writer, but success came slowly. His *Child's Garden of Verses* was one of his first successes, but his *Treasure Island,* written at the request of his stepson for "something interesting," made him so generally popular that his stories were eagerly seized by the public. He was often so ill he had

to write sitting up in bed, but not even tuberculosis of the lungs could subdue his youthful spirit. He died in Samoa.

SWIFT, JONATHAN (1667–1745), was born of English parents in Dublin, where he was educated. Being ambitious, he went into the Church hoping for advancement; but his satire *A Tale of a Tub* so offended the higher powers that, despite the excellent political writing he did for the Tories, he was never offered anything better than the deanship of Dublin Cathedral. This he took and, though he hated the Irish, he hated injustice more, and he so defended them that he became popular with them. His scathing satire on English conditions, *Gulliver's Travels,* is generally read now by children as a fairy story — an irony of fate.

TATE, NAHUM (1652–1715), was born and educated in Ireland. After publishing a volume of poems in London, he began writing for the stage. He is famous for the atrocities he committed on Shakespeare's and other men's plays in his efforts to make them fit the times. He was appointed Poet Laureate in 1692. Two of his hymns, *While Shepherds Watched* and *As Pants the Hart,* are among his best, if not his best poetry.

TEASDALE, SARA (1884–1933), was born in St. Louis, where she went to private school. She was an imaginative, shy child, who was brought up on Mother Goose and found Christina Rossetti's *Christmas Carol* her favorite poem. She was a systematic reader and even as a girl laid out her reading plans. She traveled much in the United States and Europe. Her first book, *Love Songs,* was awarded a prize by Columbia University. Many of her lyrics have been set to music and also translated into Japanese.

TENNYSON, ALFRED, LORD (1809–1892), the son of a rector, was born in the beautiful, rich region of Lincolnshire. The surroundings made an indelible impression upon the youthful poet. At the death of his father, he left Cambridge without taking his degree. His nature was shy and sensitive, and the death of his best friend, Arthur Hallam, made him even more retiring. Tennyson was very fastidious about the quality of his verse, polishing it sometimes to the point of weakening its force. He spent his many years trying to reconcile the new scientific thought with his ideas of religion and God. He became Poet Laureate of England.

THAXTER, CELIA LAIGHTON (1835–1894). Her father, disgusted at politics, withdrew from active life and for ten years was lighthouse keeper on an island off the coast of New Hampshire, where his daughter spent her childhood. She married a devoted student of Robert Browning, and lived the rest of her life on one of the Isles of Shoals. Her lyric poetry deals with sea storms, sails, and the birds and flowers of the shore. Although it is not great poetry, it shows a delicate and sympathetic appreciation, and gives a faithful picture of what she tries to portray.

THOMAS, DYLAN (1914–1953), British poet, was born in Carmarthenshire, Wales. He attended the Swansea Grammar School. His first small volume of poems was published when he was nineteen. In 1938 he won the Oscar Blumenthal Prize offered by *Poetry* magazine of Chicago. His poems appeared frequently in verse magazines of England and the United States. He came to the United States to read his own and other poetry in forty university towns, was stricken with a cerebral ailment, and died in his New York hotel room at the age of thirty-nine. In a tragically short life, he wrote over ten volumes of poetry besides some prose. Philip Toynbee called him "the greatest living poet in the English language." Herbert Read declared his work "the most absolute poetry that has been written in our time." Louis Untermeyer called him "the most powerful and most sensational of the younger British poets." Dylan's works include *New Poems*, 1943; *Deaths and Entrances*, 1946; *Selected Writings*, 1947; *Poems*, 1950; *In Country Sleep and Other Poems*, 1952; and *Collected Poems*, 1953.

THOMPSON, STITH (1885–   ), was born in Kentucky but grew up and was educated in Indiana. He has his doctor's degree from Harvard where he specialized in folklore. His books on the tales of North American Indians are particularly valuable contributions to folklore. His great work, which gives him international recognition as a folklorist, is his *Motif Index of Folk Literature*, published in 1933–35.

THOREAU, HENRY DAVID (1817–1862), of French-Scottish descent, was born in Concord, Massachusetts. A graduate of Harvard and for several years a teacher, he nevertheless decided to live the simple life and for two years he did so. During this time he studied the insects, birds, and animals about Walden Pond, where his cabin stood. He wrote down what he saw, and in *Walden* he produced a work that transcends its account of wood and pond life to become one of the great achievements of American literature.

THURBER, JAMES (1894–1961), one of the best-known American humorists, was born in Columbus, Ohio, and studied at Ohio State University. After being a code clerk in the State Department for two years, he turned to journalism. He began as a reporter on the Columbus *Dispatch* and was with the Chicago *Tribune* in Paris and on the staff of the New York *Evening Post*. He became managing editor of the *New Yorker* magazine in 1926. Seven years later he left the magazine to devote his time to writing and travel, but he continued to contribute articles and drawings. Besides many books for adults, he has written for children *Many Moons*, a fantasy of a little princess who wanted the moon; *The Great Quillow*, in which he used the folk theme of intelligence and courage pitted against brute force; *The White Deer*, a fairy tale with kings and princes, enchanted deer and dark enchantments; and *The Thirteen Clocks*.

TIPPETT, JAMES (1885–   ), was born and educated in Missouri and later at Teachers College, Columbia University, where he also taught. By profession he is a teacher, but has lately been curriculum adviser for the schools of North Carolina. He spends much of his time writing for children, and his verses, simple and childlike, create a new interest for children in the familiar things about them.

TOLKIEN, JOHN RONALD REUEL (1892–   ), is an English scholar, professor and writer. Of Danish extraction, he was born in Bloemfontein, South Africa. He is the Merton Professor of English Language and Literature at Oxford University and is an authority on Anglo-Saxon, Middle English, and Chaucer. He is known for his scholarly works on *Beowulf, Sir Gawain and the Green Knight*, and other early classics of English literature. Tolkien was only four when his father died and his mother took the family back to Birmingham, England, his father's former home. In 1904 his mother died and Tolkien and his brother were put under the care of Father Francis Xavier Morgan, a priest of the Congregation of the Oratory which had been established by Cardinal Newman. Tolkien attended King Edward VI High School in Birmingham and received both his B.A. and M.A. degrees from Exeter College, Oxford. He served with the Lancashire Fusiliers in World War I. For two years he worked as an assistant on the Oxford English Dictionary and in 1920 began his teaching career at the University of Leeds. In 1925 he was appointed professor of Anglo-Saxon at Oxford University and a Fellow of Pembroke College. He married Edith Bratt in 1916 and they have three sons and one daughter. He wrote his unusual fairy story, *The Hobbit*, for his children and read it aloud chapter by chapter as he wrote it. It appeared in book form with his own illustrations in 1938. *Father Giles of Ham* is another tale from the mock-heroic history of Britain before the time of King Arthur. The three books, *The Fellowship of the Ring, The Two Towers,* and *The Return of the King,* which comprise the trilogy *The Lord of the Ring,* are far more complex and have a devoted adult following.

TRAVERS, PAMELA L. (1906–   ), poet and juvenile author, was born in Australia of Irish parents; here she lived during her childhood. She began writing at seventeen. She first told the Mary Poppins stories to two children, and the book *Mary Poppins* has been so popular that it has been translated into German, Swedish, Italian, and Czech, and a Mary Poppins suite for orchestra has been composed by Mortimer Browning. She lived in New York during World War II.

TUNIS, JOHN (1889–   ), was born in Boston and graduated from Harvard, where he played football. He was on the New York *Evening Post* as sports writer for ten years and also broadcast athletics for NBC from London and Paris between 1932 and 1939.

UNTERMEYER, JEAN STARR (1886–   ), was born in Zanesville, Ohio. She was educated in private schools, studied music abroad, and in 1924 made her musical debut in London and Vienna. She specialized in German songs. Besides writing fiction, she has contributed verse to magazines. She translated Bie's *Schubert the Man* which was chosen by the Schubert Centennial Committee as the official biography. She married the poet Louis Untermeyer in 1907.

UNTERMEYER, LOUIS (1885–   ), was born in New York City where he had only fitful schooling. He wanted to be a composer but for twenty years worked in his father's jewelry factory. He even became vice-president. He studied abroad two years, came home, retired from business, and gave his whole attention to literature. He has written poetry, parodies, translations, and critical prose.

VAN LOON, HENDRIK WILLEM (1882–1944), American historian, journalist, and lecturer, was born in Rotterdam, The Netherlands. At the age of twenty he came to the United States. He graduated from Cornell University and studied at the University of Munich. He served as a newspaper correspondent in Russia during the revolution in 1905, and in various European countries during World War I. In 1922 he received the first Newbery medal for *The Story of Mankind,* a book with a fascinating new approach to world history, which helped revolutionize the writing of history. His works include *Ancient Man; Van Loon's Geography; A Short History of Discovery; The Story of the Bible; The Arts; The Songs We Sing;* and *Christmas Carols.*

WADDELL, HELEN (1889–   ), noted scholar of medieval literature, was born in Tokyo, the daughter of the Rev. Hugh Waddell of Manchuria and Japan. She received her education at Victoria College and Queen's University in Belfast, Ireland. She was the Cassell Lecturer for St. Hilda's Hall, Oxford, and also lectured at Bedford College in London. She held the Susette Taylor fellowship of Oxford, in Paris 1923–25. She was made a member of the Irish Academy of Letters and a Corresponding Fellow of the Medieval Academy of America. She did much scholarly writing and her books include *Peter Abelard; The Desert Fathers; The Wandering Scholars; Medieval Latin Lyrics; The Abbé Prévost; Beasts and Saints; Stories from Holy Writ;* and a translation of *Manon Lescaut.*

WATSON, WILLIAM (1858–1935), was brought up in Liverpool. His first book of poetry passed unnoticed, but his later work attracted attention for its poetical qualities. His work shows restraint and careful diction; its form is the classic, rather than the romantic. It has been said that his poetry is contemplative rather than passionate, critical and philosophical rather than lyric.

WATTS, ISAAC (1674–1748), was a precocious child, having learned to read Latin in his fifth year. He obtained his education at a nonconformist academy and shortly after leaving school began to write hymns. He was a tutor, until he became an assistant pastor, then pastor of an Independent church in London. He was only twenty-five years old and held this position until his health broke from overwork. At this time he was taken into the household of Sir Thomas Abney, where he died. As a poet for children, he wrote didactic verse, but it was much more lively and sympathetic than that of any of his predecessors.

WELLES, WINIFRED (1893–1939), was born, educated, and lived in Connecticut. She said that when her son was a child his experiences and reactions made her recall her own; and out of the two combined, she wrote *Skipping Along Alone.* Her work has the simplicity of childhood, and her subject matter is within the child's experience or imagination.

WHEELER, POST (1869–1956), was born in New York, graduated from Princeton, and attended the medical school of the Sorbonne in Paris. He was a very versatile man, being interested in medicine, philology, and geology; but professionally he was a writer and a diplomat. America's first career diplomat, he served in Tokyo, Rome, London, Stockholm, and Rio de Janeiro — also at the former St. Petersburg, where he wrote his *Russian Wonder Tales.* He has written much besides his Russian, Albanian, and Ethiopian folk tales.

WHITMAN, WALT (1819–1892), probably the most original poet in America, is considered by some the greatest. He was born on Long Island, where he lived most of his life. A self-made man, he followed many different occupations before he began publishing his poetry. His first volume, *Leaves of Grass* (1855), created an immediate sensation, and his reputation was made by both the praise and the adverse criticism it received. Whitman was a pacifist, yet he acted as a nurse during the Civil War. He never married.

WHITTIER, JOHN GREENLEAF (1807–1892), was born in Massachusetts, where he lived all his life. As the Quaker Poet, he best represents the American people's feelings and is perhaps best understood by them. With his pen he vigorously fought slavery, but he also portrayed the idyllic life of the New England farmer in such lyrics as *The Barefoot Boy.* His masterpiece depicting that life is *Snow-Bound,* considered by some to be surpassed in its class only by the *Cotter's Saturday Night* of Burns, whose poetry first inspired Whittier to write.

WILDER, LAURA INGALLS (1867–1957), the beloved author of the "Little House" series of children's books, was born in a Wisconsin log cabin described in *Little House in the Big Woods.* This book, published in 1932 when Mrs. Wilder was sixty-five, describes her early childhood. In *Little House on the Prairie* she tells how the family moved to what is now Kansas. Life in Minnesota, how the family set out in a covered wagon for Dakota Territory, and life on the frontier are described in *On the Banks of Plum Creek; By the Shores of Silver Lake; The Long Winter;* and *The Little Town on the Prairie.* At the age of fifteen Laura Ingalls began to teach school, and three years later she married Almanzo Wilder, whose boyhood is the subject of her book *Farmer Boy.* She tells about their marriage in the last book of the series, *These Happy Golden Years,* which was published when the author was seventy-six. The Wilders had one daughter, Rose Wilder Lane, the novelist. In the fall of 1894 the family moved to a farm in Mansfield, Missouri. For twelve years Mrs. Wilder was editor of *The Missouri Ruralist,* and she contributed articles to *Country Gentleman* and *McCall's.* In 1954 the Children's Library Association established the "Laura Ingalls Wilder Award" to be given for "a lasting contribution to literature for children." Mrs. Wilder herself was the first recipient of this award. She died at the age of ninety at her farm home in Missouri.

WILKINSON, MARGUERITE (1883–1928), an American author, was born in Halifax, Nova Scotia. She was educated at the Township High School, Evanston, Illinois, and at Northwestern University. She compiled the poetry anthology *New Voices,* and was author of *The Great Dream* and *Yule Fire.*

WITHERS, CARL, was born on a farm near Sheldon, Missouri. He graduated from Harvard College, where he majored in English. He won a scholarship and studied in Europe, where he became interested in anthropology. He did graduate work at Columbia University. For the past eighteen years he has been writing and doing research in anthropology and folklore. His first major research was in an Ozark foothills community much like his birthplace. He collected over four hundred rhymes, chants, game songs, tongue-twisters, and ear-teasers familiar to children in many parts of the United States today and published them in 1948 under the title *A Rocket in My Pocket.* With Sula Benet he compiled *The American Riddle Book.*

WOLFE, HUMBERT (1885–1940), an English poet, lampoonist, and playwright, was born in Milan, Italy, and was educated at Wadham College, Oxford. He entered the British Civil Service and became Deputy Secretary of the Ministry of Labour. In his writing he took an artist's delight in form, arrangement, line, and cadence; and employed a craftsman's skill in the use of words, rhymes, and meters. His books include *News of the Devil; Requiem; The Upward Anguish;* and *Kensington Gardens.*

WORDSWORTH, WILLIAM (1770–1850), orphaned when young, was brought up by relatives. After his graduation from Cambridge he traveled in France and became sympathetic with the French Revolutionists. His love of the common people and his peculiar attitude toward nature as a "kindly nurse" were the main topics of his poetry with, as he said, "a veil of imagination" thrown over them. His first volume of poems, *Lyrical Ballads,* compiled with his friend Coleridge, was so different from the previous eighteenth-century poetry, that Wordsworth wrote an essay for the second edition, in which he explained his theory of poetry. This *Preface* along with the poems themselves had a lasting influence upon English literature.

WYLIE, ELINOR (Mrs. William Rose Benét) (1885–1928), was born in New Jersey of a distinguished family. She was educated in private schools and during her first marriage lived the life of a society woman. She then went to France and England, alone, to write; and from there she published poetry anonymously. Returning to the United States in 1916, she did war relief work in the New York Red Cross. She wrote four novels, but it is for her poetry she is popular, equally so in England and America. An accident brought sudden death. Her poetry is considered cold, intellectual, and brilliant.

YATES, ELIZABETH (1905–   ), an American writer, was born in Buffalo, New York. Summers were spent on her father's farm south of Buffalo. She was next to the youngest of seven children who shared in tasks of gardening, buttermaking, and caring for many pets. Following graduation from the Franklin School, she attended boarding school and later studied in New York, London, and Paris. Her first job was in New York writing book reviews and articles for newspapers and magazines. When she was twenty-three she married William McGreal, an American, whose business was in London and they lived in England for the next ten years, traveling in France, Germany, Switzerland, Spain, and Iceland. Elizabeth Yates kept up her writing and in 1938 her first book, *High Holiday*, based on a summer in Switzerland, was published. In 1939 she and her husband returned to the United States and they live on a farm outside Peterborough, New Hampshire. In restoring the 125-year-old house, they discovered on the walls the work of an early nineteenth-century journeyman-stenciler, and this inspired the next book, *Patterns on the Wall*. In 1951 she received the Newbery medal for *Amos Fortune*. Other books for children and young people include *Mountain Born; Under the Fir*

Tree; Once in the Year; Children of the Bible; Joseph; The Christmas Story; A Place for Peter; Rainbow Round the World; and *Prudence Crandall*.

YEATS, WILLIAM BUTLER (1865–1939), was born near Dublin. His father was an artist, and he himself studied painting three years at his father's wish. As a boy he spent much of his time on the western coast of Ireland with his maternal grandfather who was a shipowner. He gave up painting at twenty-one, for he preferred reading Gaelic and listening to folk tales. He began to write poetry, and at thirty-five he became interested in the Irish theater and wrote plays in verse. He left the theater when it turned from the mystic to the naturalistic drama. He became the accepted leader of the Irish Movement, living with his wife and two children in an old tower on the western coast of Ireland, and occupying his time with politics, civic duties, and society.

YOUNG, ELLA (1865–1956), an Irish poet and student of mythology, was born in the house of her grandfather in Fenagh, County Antrim, in northern Ireland. Her parents left Antrim when Ella was three and went to Limerick in the southwest part of Ireland. All during her childhood she heard stories of fairies, giants, dragons, and legendary heroes. When years later she went to Dublin, the whole wonderful field of Celtic literature opened up for her. She graduated from the Royal University (later known as the National University). She took part in the Celtic Renaissance and the Rising. Surrounded by poets, artists, writers, and actors, she was in her element. At this time she wrote *Celtic Wonder Tales* and *The Wonder Smith and His Son*. Then she came to America and continued to write both prose and poetry. These books include *The Tangle-Coated Horse; The Unicorn with Silver Shoes;* and two books of verse, *To the Little Princess* and *Smoke of Myrrh*. Her last book was her autobiography, *Flowering Dusk*.

APPENDIX H

Pronouncing Glossary

Aachen ä′ken
Abeita uh-bite-uh
Aeneas ê-nē′ăs
Aesir â′sir; ē′sĭr
Afanasiev ä-fä-nä′syif
Aladdin a-lăd′dĭn
Alberz ăl-bêrz′
Altair ăl-tä′ir
Andaman ăn′dȧ-mȧn
Andromeda ăn-drŏm′ê-dȧ
Andvari än-dwä′rē
Antaeus ăn-tē′ŭs
Aphrodite ăf-rŏ-dī′tê
Apion ā′pĭ-ŏn
Ardizzone är-di-zō′ni
Artzybasheff är-tsĭ-bȧ′shef
Asbjörnsen äs-byûrn′sen
Asclepius ăs-klē′pĭ-ŭs
Asgard äs′gärd
Augean ô-jē′ăn
Aulaire ō-lâr′
Aulnoy ō′nwȧ′
Ayas ä′yäs

Barbauld bär-bôld
Behn bān
Bellerophon bĕ-lĕr′ŏ-fŏn
Belloc, Hilaire bĕl′ŏk, hĭ-lâr′
Benét bĕ-nā′
Beowulf bā′ŏ-woolf
Beskow bes′kō
Bianco bē′an-co
Bidpai bĭd′pī
Bifröst bēf′rŏst
Blancandrin blăn-kăn-drĭn
Boeotia bê-ō′shȧ
Bontemps bŏn-täm′
Borogoves bŏr′row-gōvz
Brahmin brä′min
Brunhilde broōn′hĭlt
Budulinek bu-dū′lin-ĕk

Calypso kȧ-lĭp′sō
Cambulac cam′boo-lac
Cappadocia kăp-ȧ-do′shĭ-ȧ
Cassiopeia kăs-ĭ-ŏ-pē′yȧ
Cepheus sē′fūs; sē′fê-ŭs
Cerberus sûr′bĕr-ŭs
Ceres sē′rēz
Charlot shȧr-lō′

Charnetski chär-nĕt′skĭ
Charon kā′ron; kâ′ron
Chimaera kī-mē′rȧ
Chiron kī′rŏn
Chlopak who (short *o*, almost
    an *a*)-păk′
Chrisman krĭs′măn
Cicons sīk′ŏns
Clymene clī-mē′nē
Coimbra cō-eem′brä
Colum, Padraic kŏl′ŭm,
    pŏd′rĭg
Croisic krwä′zēk
Cruikshank krŏŏk′shăngk
Cullen, Countee kŭl′ĕn,
    koun-tā′
Curie, Eve kü′rē′, âv
Curzola kŭr-zō′lȧ
Cuzco kus′kŏ
Cyclops (sing.),   sī′klŏps,
    Cyclopes (plural) sī-klō′pēz

Daedalus dĕd′ȧ-lus; dē′dȧ-lus
Danaë dăn′ȧ-ē
Daphne dăf′nê
De Jong, Meindert de yung,
    mĭn′dĕrt
De la Mare dē-lȧ-mâr′
Demeter dê-mē′tĕr
Dictys dĭk′tĭs
Diocletian dī-ŏ-klē′shăn
Dionysus dī-o-nī′sŭs
Discobbolos dĭs-cŏb′bŏ-lŏs
Draupner drawp′ner
Du Bois, Pène dū bwäh′, pĕn
Durendal dū′rĕn-däl
Duvoisin dū-vwȧh-zăn′

Echorn ā′cŏrn
Epaphus ĕp′ȧ-fŭs
Epimetheus ĕp-ĭ-mē′thŭs
Eurydice ū-rĭd′ĭ-sē
Eurystheus û-rĭs′thūs;
    û-rĭs′thê-ŭs
Exupéry, St. săn′tāg′zü′pā′rē′
E-Yeh-Shure ee-yeh-shuree

Fabre fä′br′
Fafnir fȧv′nēr

Farjeon fȧr′jȧn
Fatima fä′tê-mä; făt′i-ma
Fian fê′an
Fomalhaut fô-mal-ō′
Françoise frôn-swäz′
Freki frĕk′ĭ
Frey frā
Freya, Freia frā-yä

Gág gäg
Ganelon gȧn′-lôn′
Garenganze gä-rĭng′gän′ze
Garyulies gär-y-ū′lēēz
Geisel, Theodor gī′zl,
    thē′ŏ-dôr
Geppeto jĕ-pĕt′tŏ
Geri gĕr′ĭ
Geryon jēr′rĭ-ŏn; gĕr′i-ŭn
Gimaj gē-mäzh′
Godden, Rumer gŏd′n,
    roō′mēr
Gudbrand goōd′brănt
Gymer gē′mŭr

Hah-yah-no hä-yä′nŏ
Hakluyt hăk′loōt
Halono hăl′ō-nŏ
Hearn, Lafcadio hûrn,
    lăf-kăd′i-ō
Hecate hĕk′ȧ-tē
Heidi hī′dē
Heimdal hām′däl
Hela hĕl′ȧ
Hephaestus hê-fĕs′tŭs
Hesperides hĕs-pĕr′i-dēz
Hiipola hee′pō-lä
Hiordis hyôr′dĭs
Hippodamia hĭp-ŏ-dȧ-mī′a
Hippolyta hĭ-pŏl′ĭ-tȧ
Hippomenes hĭ-pŏm′ĕ-nēz
Hlidskjalf hlidz′kyälf
Hoenir hû′nēr
Holena hol′ay-nȧ
Hrimfaxe hrĕm-fäks′e
Hringhorni hrĭng′hôrn-i
Hrothgar hrōth′gär
Huancanti wan-kän′ti
Hvergelmer hwer-gel′mer
Hyperborean hī′pĕr-bō′rê-ăn
Hyrrockin hy′rrōc-kĭn

1216

Icarus ĭk'ăr-ŭs; ī'kȧ-rŭs
Ichthyosaurus ĭk'thĭ-ō-sô'rŭs
Idun ēē-dōōn'
Ilmarinen ĕl'mä-rē'nĕn
Ishkoodah ĭsh-kŏŏ-dä'

Jancsi yŏn'shi
Jataka jä'tä-kȧ
Jötunheim yô'tŏn-hām
Joyeuse zhwȧ-yûz'

Kantanga kä-täng'gä
Kanya-ti-yo kăn-yȧ-tēē'yô
Karakorum kä'rä-kō'rŭm
Karum kä'rōōm
Kashgar kash'gär
Khorasan kōō-rä-sän'
Khotan kô'tȧn
Kiev kē'yĕf
Krakow krä'kō (English);
      krȧ-koof (Polish)
Kyanian kyän-ē-an

Laertes lȧ-ûr'tēz
La Fontaine lä-fŏn-tän'
Lakshmana läksh'mȧ-nȧ
Lapithai lăp'i-thē
Lethe lē'thē
Leucothoe lū-kŏth'ô-ē
Lie, Haakon lē, hô'kŏn
Loki lō'kē
Lvov lwōōf
Lygni lĭg'nē

MacLeod măk-loud'
Mafatu mä-fä-tū'
Mahabharata mȧ-hä'bä'rȧ-tȧ
Malabar măl'ȧ-bär
Malacca mȧ-lăc'cȧ
Mali mä'lee
Mann-go-tay-see mȧn-gō-tāy'-
      sēē
Marsilius mär-sĭl-ĭ-ŭs
Maruskha mär-ōōsh'kȧ
Medio Pollito mä'dē ō
      pō-lyē'tô
Medusa mē-dū'sȧ
Megalosaurus mĕg'ȧ-lō-sô'rŭs
Meleager mĕl-ē-ā'jĕr
Metanira mĕt-ȧn-nē'rȧ
Micheaux mē'shō'
Mikolayska mĭ-kō-loy'skȧ
Millay mĭ-lā'
Milne mĭln
Mimir mē'mĕr
Min-ne-wa-wa mĭn-nē-wä'wȧ
Minuchihr mĭn-ōō-chär
Mjollnir myôl-nēr
Mordvinoff mord'vin-of
Mubids mōō-bēz

Mudwayaushka mŭd-wāy-
      aush'kȧ
Mukerji,   mōō'kĕr-jē',
      Dhan Gopal   dhän gō'päl

Naioth nā'yoth
Navajo nä'vȧ-hō
Nereus nēr'ūs
Neriman nâr-ē-män
Niflheim nĭv''l-hām
Niord nyôrd
Nukado nōō-kä'dô

Odysseus ô-dĭs'ūs; ô-dĭs'ē-ŭs
Oella o-ĕl'lȧ
Oeneus ē'nŭo
Ogier ō'ji-ĕr; ô-zhyā
Oot-kwa-tah ōōt-kwä'tȧh
Opechee ō-pē'chee
Orion ô-rī'ŏn
Orpheus ôr'fūs; ôr'fē-ŭs
Ostrovski ôs-trôf'skē

Panchatantra pän-chȧ-tän'trȧ
Pecos pā'kŭs
Pegasus pĕg'ȧ-sŭs
Pehliva päh-lä-vē
Pelle pel'lē
Peneus pē-nē'ŭs
Peri pĕ'ree
Perrault pē-rō'
Perseus pûr'sūs; pûr'sē-ŭs
Phaethon fā'ē-thŏn
Phlegon flē'gŏn
Phoebus fē'bŭs
Phrixus frĭk'sŏs
Pinocchio pĭn-ōk'ĭ-ô
Pogány pō-gä'nēē
Politi pō-lē'tē
Polydectes pŏl-y-dĕk'tēz
Polyphemus pŏl-y-fē'mŭs
Poseidon pô-sī'dŏn
Prokofieff,   prŭ-kôf'yĕf,
      Sergei   syēr-gā'ĭ
      Sergeevich syēr-gā'yĕ-vyĭch
Proserpine prô-sûr'pĭ-nȧ;
      prŏs'ĕr-pĭn
Psyche sī'kē
Pyrois pī'rois

Raccas räc'ȧs
Ragnarok räg-nȧ-rŭk'
Rakshasas räk'shȧ-sȧz
Rama rä'mȧ
Ramayana rä-mä'yȧ-nȧ
Ramiro rä-mē'rō
Regin rā'yĭn
Rodrigo rô-drē'gō
Rojankovsky rō-jan-kôf'skē

Roncesvalles rôn-thĕs-väl'yas
Roskva rŏsk'vȧ
Satrap sā'trap; săt'rap
Saum säm
Segovia sȧ-gō'vyä
Scistan sĭs'tän; sēs'tän
Scredy shĕr'ē-dĭ
Seuss, Dr. sois
Shangtu shäng-tū'
Shqyptar shkĕp'tär
Shushan shōō'shăn
Sigurd zē'gōōrt
Simurgh sē-mōōrg'
Sindri sĭn'drē
Skidbladnir skid-bläd'nēr
Skinfaxe shĭn'fäk-si
Skirner skûr'nûr
Skrymir skrim'ēr
Sleipner slĭp'nēr; släp'nēr
Soan-ge-taha sôn-gē-tȧ'hȧ
Spyri, Johanna spee-rēē,
      yō-hän'na
Stymphalian stĭm-fā'lĭ-ăn
Sumuko sū-mōō'kō

Taillefer tä-yĕ-fer
Tenniel tĕn'yĕl
Thiasse tyä'sē; tyā'sē
Thjalfi tyäl'fē
Thor thôr
Thoreau thō'rō; thô-rō'
Thorne-Thomsen Gudrun,
      thôrn tom'-sen, gü'drun
Thrudvang thrōōth'vang
Thrym treem
Towo toy-vō

Utgard-Loke oot'gärd-lō'kē

Vafthrudner väf'thrōō-dner
Vainamoinen vī'nä-mē-ĭ-nen
Valkyrie văl-kĭr'ĭ
Van Loon vän lōn'
Vigrid vĭg'rĭd
Wah-wah-tay-see wä-wä-tā'see
Wampanoag wäm-pȧ-nō'ăg
Wawel vä'vel
Wekotani wä-kō-tä'nē
Wiese, Kurt vē'zĕ, kōōrt

Xanadu zä'na-doo

Yana yä'nä; yä'rä
Yangtse yäng'tzĕ
Yeats yāts; yĕts
Yggdrasill ĭg'drȧ-sĭl

Zaboulstan zȧ-bōōl'ĭs-tän
Zal zôl
Zipango tsēē-păn'gō

CONTENTS BY AGES AND GRADES

Literature cannot be pigeonholed according to children's ages and grades in school. The individual child must always be taken into consideration, for children differ in background, intelligence, and appreciation. Consequently the editors have not graded closely the contents of this book, but have grouped the selections in four broad divisions—Kindergarten and Grades 1 and 2; Grades 3 and 4; Grades 5 and 6; and Junior High School.

Kindergarten and Grades 1 and 2

(to 8 years of age)

Mother Goose Nursery Rhymes	6
Mother Goose Ballads	17
John Newbery's Mother Goose	22
Singing Games, Jingles, Counting-out Rhymes	23
Riddles, Paradoxes, Tongue Trippers	28
Nursery Rhymes of Many Lands	30
American Chants and Jingles	34
Picture Books	
A Apple Pie	72
Johnny Crow's Garden	72
The Story of the Three Bears	73
The Story of the Three Little Pigs	75
The Story of Little Black Sambo	77
Noël for Jeanne-Marie	78
The Tale of Peter Rabbit	79
Millions of Cats	81
Pelle's New Suit	88
Little Toot	83
The Little House	86
Ola	88
Dick Whittington and His Cat	90
The 500 Hats of Bartholomew Cubbins	93
Mei Li	99
Folk Tales	
The Elves	136
The Wolf and the Seven Little Kids	137
The Golden Goose	138
The Bremen Town Musicians	140
The Brother and Sister	142
Hansel and Gretel	145
Snow White and the Seven Dwarfs	156
Little Red Riding-Hood	170
Drakestail	171
Cinderella and the Glass Slipper	174
The Sleeping Beauty	180
The Old Woman and Her Pig	197
Henny-Penny	198
Teeny-Tiny	199
Jack and the Beanstalk	200
The Three Billy-Goats-Gruff	290

The Pancake	291
The Ram and the Pig Who Went into the Woods	292
Poetry	
The Fairies (Fyleman)	1004
A Fairy Went A Marketing	1005
The Little Elf	1005
The Elves' Dance	1005
Here We Come A-Piping	1006
Little Wind	1012
Who Has Seen the Wind?	1012
Windy Wash Day	1012
The Kite	1012
Dandelion	1014
Pussy Willows	1015
Rain (Stevenson)	1015
The Rain (Bennett)	1015
Rubber Boots	1015
The Umbrella Brigade	1015
Fog	1018
The Last Word of a Bluebird	1022
Hallowe'en	1023
What Am I?	1023
The Frost Pane	1024
The Snowflake	1025
At the Sea-side	1027
The Shell	1027
Little Things	1029
A Prayer for Little Things	1029
The City Mouse	1030
Little Snail	1030
The Little Turtle	1030
Our Mr. Toad	1030
Firefly	1031
The Blackbird	1032
Bantam Rooster	1032
Mrs. Peck-Pigeon	1033
The Squirrel	1034
I Like Little Pussy	1035
Mary's Lamb	1036
The Swing	1037

My Shadow   1037
Pirate Story   1038
The Little Land   1038
Bed in Summer   1039
Pretending   1039
Hiding   1040
Whistles   1041
The Little Whistler   1041
Troubles   1041
Radiator Lions   1041
Mumps   1041
Washing   1042
Twos   1042

General Store   1043
Taxis   1043
Motor Cars   1043
Trucks   1044
Song of the Train   1044
Skyscrapers   1044
Evening   1045
The White Window   1046
Sleep, Baby, Sleep   1047
An Indian Lullaby   1047
Good Night   1049
Cradle Hymn   1050

Grades 3 and 4

(8 to 10 years of age)

Nonsense
Little Hermogenes is so small   45
Look at Marcus and take warning   45
I boiled hot water in an urn   45
If a Pig Wore a Wig   45
Mr. Punchinello   45
Three Children Sliding on the Ice   45
Eletelephony   46
The High Barbaree   46
The Monkeys and the Crocodile   46
Mrs. Snipkin and Mrs. Wobblechin   46
The Owl and the Eel and the
   Warming-Pan   47
The Great Panjandrum Himself   47
The Camel's Complaint   47
The Crocodile   49
Nonsense Alphabet   53
The Jumblies   55
The Owl and the Pussy-Cat   56
Mr. and Mrs. Discobbolos   56
The Duck and the Kangaroo   57
The Quangle Wangle's Hat   57
The Table and the Chair   58
The Frog   61
The Yak   61
The Eel   62
The Guppy   62
Fables
The Wind and the Sun   114
A Wolf in Sheep's Clothing   114
A Lion and a Mouse   114
The Shepherd's Boy and the Wolf   114
The Town Mouse and the Country Mouse 115
The Crow and the Pitcher   115
The Dog and His Shadow   115
The Fox and the Crow   115
The Dog in the Manger   115

The Jackdaw and the Borrowed Plumes 116
The Hare and the Tortoise   116
The Goose with the Golden Eggs   116
Folk Tales
The Fisherman and His Wife   149
Rapunzel   154
Rumpelstiltskin   162
Gone Is Gone   164
The Sorcerer's Apprentice   167
Beauty and the Beast   185
Toads and Diamonds   193
The Hare and the Hedgehog   195
Molly Whuppie   203
The Three Sillies   205
Master of All Masters   206
The Well of the World's End   207
The History of Tom Thumb   209
Tamlane   211
The King o' the Cats   212
King O'Toole and His Goose   214
Billy Beg and the Bull   216
The Bee, the Harp, the Mouse, and the
   Bum-Clock   220
The Flea   239
The Tinker and the Ghost   242
The General's Horse   244
The Priceless Cats   247
Seven Simeons   250
The Little Humpbacked Horse   258
Mr. Samson Cat   265
Peter and the Wolf   267
Budulinek   269
The Jolly Tailor Who Became King   276
The Bear Says "North"   280
Mighty Mikko   281
Gudbrand on the Hillside   294
Boots and His Brothers   296

The Princess on the Glass Hill 298
East o' the Sun and West o' the Moon 303
The Lad Who Went to the North Wind 308
The Cat on the Dovrefell 310
The Talking Pot 311
The Magic Monkey 316
The Cat and the Parrot 322
Aladdin and the Wonderful Lamp 324
Three Fridays 331
Mr. Crow Takes a Wife 336
The Wonderful Tar-Baby 339
Brer Rabbit's Astonishing Prank 341
Why the Burro Lives with the Man 355

Myths and Legends
The Magic Apples 422
Thor Gains His Hammer 432
Thor's Unlucky Journey 434
The Quest of the Hammer 438
The Story of the First Woodpecker 446
The Legend of the Palm Tree 456

Heroes of Epic and Romance
Robin Hood and Little John 499

Fantasy
The Real Princess 554
Five Peas in a Pod 554
Thumbelisa 558
The Wild Swans 563
The Steadfast Tin Soldier 571
The Tinder Box 573
The Emperor's New Clothes 582
The Ugly Duckling 584
The Swineherd 589
The Fir Tree 591
Adventures of Pinocchio:
    Pinocchio's First Pranks 596
Peter Pan in Kensington Gardens:
    Lock-Out Time 598
Alice's Adventures in Wonderland:
    Down the Rabbit-Hole and
    The Rabbit Sends in a Little Bill 603
Just So Stories:
    How the Camel Got His Hump 609
The Story of Doctor Dolittle:
    The Rarest Animal of All 610
Rabbit Hill: Little Georgie Sings a Song 612
Many Moons 624
Mary Poppins Opens the Door:
    The Marble Boy 629

Prayers
What God gives, and what we take 710
Lord, purge our eyes to see 710

Earth, Sky, and Sea
Wagtail: Wagtail's World Grows Wider 731

Biography
Abraham Lincoln: His Good Stepmother 793

Fiction
Poppy Seed Cakes 867
The Little Wooden Doll 868
Little Girl with Seven Names 869
Little House in the Big Woods:
    Summertime 881
Heidi: In the Pasture 885
Hans Brinker:
    Hans and Gretel Find a Friend 900

Poetry
The Fairies (Allingham) 1004
Some One 1006
Waiting 1010
Spring 1010
The Wind 1012
Trees 1017
The Bridge 1017
The Branch 1018
Autumn Fires 1021
For Snow 1025
Stopping by Woods on a Snowy Evening 1025
The Mouse 1029
The Caterpillar 1031
Fireflies 1031
Red Rooster 1032
Ducks' Ditty 1033
Market Square 1033
Clover for Breakfast 1034
The Lamb 1036
Softly, Drowsily 1036
The Land of Counterpane 1038
Circus 1040
Miss T. 1042
Tired Tim 1042
The Barber's 1042
Boys' Names 1043
Girls' Names 1043
Animal Crackers 1044
Nod 1045
What the Rattlesnake Said 1045
The Moon's the North Wind's Cooky 1045
Full Moon 1045
Silver 1046
Nurse's Song 1046
Cradle Song 1047
Wynken, Blynken, and Nod 1048
Sweet and Low 1048
Seal Lullaby 1049
Christmas Morning 1050
A Christmas Folk-Song 1051
A Visit from St. Nicholas 1052
Ring Around the World 1059

Grades 5 and 6

(10 to 12 years of age)

Nonsense

The Walrus and the Carpenter	48
'Tis the Voice of the Lobster	49
The White Rabbit's Verses	49
Jabberwocky	50
The Gardener's Song	50
The Beaver's Lesson	51
The Broom, the Shovel, the Poker and the Tongs	59
The Courtship of the Yonghy-Bonghy-Bò	59
Limericks	60

Fables

The Grasshopper and the Ants	116
The Lark and Its Young	116
Belling the Cat	117
The Fox and the Grapes	117
The Miller, His Son, and the Ass	117
The Brâhman's Goat	117
The Poor Man and the Flask of Oil	118
The Crow and the Partridge	118
The Tiger, the Brâhman, and the Jackal	119
The Spirit that Lived in a Tree	120
The Banyan Deer	121
The Hare that Ran Away	122
The Seeds and the Wheat	123
Androcles and the Lion	123
The Dove and the Ant	124
The Fox and the Goat	124
The Camel and the Flotsam	125
The Dairymaid and Her Milk-Pot	125
The Blind Men and the Elephant	126
The Moth and the Star	126

Folk Tales

Jack and the King Who Was a Gentleman	224
Kate Mary Ellen	227
The Children of Lir	230
The Faery Flag of Dunvegan	235
The Twelve Months	271
Hidden Laiva	285
Ah Tcha the Sleeper	313
The Tongue-cut Sparrow	318
Numskull and the Rabbit	319
The Canoe in the Rapids	333
Old Fire Dragaman	343
Paul Bunyan	346
Slue-foot Sue Dodges the Moon	349
The Princess and José	357
The Tale of the Lazy People	358
From Tiger to Anansi	365
The Goat Well	367

Myths and Legends

Demeter	389
Prometheus the Firebringer	391

Pandora	394
The Curse of Echo	396
Cupid and Psyche	399
Orpheus	404
Baucis and Philemon	406
Daphne	407
Phaethon	408
Bellerophon	410
Icarus and Daedalus	412
Atalanta's Race	413
The Judgment of Midas	416
Odin Goes to Mimir's Well	418
How Frey Won Gerda the Giant Maiden	419
Determination of the Seasons	444
How Glooskap Found the Summer	444
The Locust and the Coyote	447
How the Coyote Danced with the Blackbirds	448
Why the Ant Is Almost Cut in Two	450
Origin of the Pleiades	452
How the Seven Brothers Saved Their Sister	452
How Kana Brought Back the Sun and Moon and Stars	457
Why the Monks of Athos Use a Samantron	459
The Seven Sleepers	460

Heroes of Epic and Romance

Odysseus and the Cyclops	474
Perseus	476
Hercules: The Eleventh Task	480
How Jason Lost His Sandal in Anauros	483
Beowulf's Fight with Grendel	487
How St. George Fought the Dragon	492
King Arthur and His Sword	493
The Wonder Smith and His Son	503
Cuchulain's Wooing	507
Sigurd's Youth	512
Fafnir, the Dragon	517

Fantasy

The Candles	556
The Wind in the Willows: The Wild Wood	616
The Borrowers	638
The Hobbit: Riddles in the Dark	645
Half Magic: What Happened to Katharine	652
The King of the Golden River	669

Sacred Writings and Legends of the Saints

The Visit of the Magi	705
The Prodigal Son	705
Charity	706
The Two Paths	706

The Tree and the Chaff 707
The Lord Is My Shepherd 707
The Earth Is the Lord's 707
God Is Our Refuge and Strength 708
Abiding in the Shadow of the Almighty 708
I Will Lift Up Mine Eyes 709
Praise Ye the Lord 709
St. Jerome and the Lion and the Donkey 713
The Truce of the Wolf: A Legend of St.
   Francis of Assisi 715
St. Nicholas 719

Earth, Sky, and Sea
Children of the Sea: The Dolphin's Tale 733
The Cricket 736
Walden: The Battle of the Ants *and*
   The Loon 738
Vulpes the Red Fox 740
Squirrels and Other Fur-Bearers:
   The Mink 745

Biography
Daniel Boone: Boonesborough 787
Invincible Louisa: "Little Women" 802

Fiction
The Fair American:
   The New Cabin Boy 892
Rufus M. 895
Hitty: I Go Up in the World 903
Blue Willow: The Shack 908
The Wheel on the School 914
The Good Master: The Round-up 931
Lassie Come-Home:
   A Long Journey's Beginning 935
Homer Price: The Doughnuts 938
Call it Courage: Drums 942
The Adventures of Tom Sawyer:
   Tom Meets Becky 963
Treasure Island 969
Robinson Crusoe 976

Poetry
"Over Hill, Over Dale" 1007

"Where the Bee Sucks" 1007
A Song of Sherwood 1008
The King of China's Daughter 1009
Laughing Song 1010
The Echoing Green 1011
March 1011
Song: April (Watson) 1013
April (Teasdale) 1013
April and May 1013
The Pasture 1013
To the Dandelion 1014
Daffodils 1014
To Daffodils 1014
Yucca 1018
Lost 1018
I Meant to Do My Work Today 1020
Glimpse in Autumn 1021
Something Told the Wild Geese 1022
Wizard Frost 1024
The Wasp 1031
The Sandpiper 1032
Milk for the Cat 1034
The Mysterious Cat 1035
The Sounds in the Morning 1037
Song for a Little House 1037
Night 1046
The Night Will Never Stay 1046
Lullaby of an Infant Chief 1047
While Shepherds Watched Their Flocks 1049
O Little Town of Bethlehem 1050
Beauty 1053
Barter 1053
Wings 1054
Do You Fear the Wind? 1054
A Song of Greatness 1054
Nancy Hanks 1058
Incident 1058
Robin Hood and Little John 1060
The Keys of Canterbury 1063
Hiawatha's Childhood 1063

Junior High: Grades 7, 8, and 9

(12 to 14 years of age)

Heroes of Epic and Romance
The Song of Roland 522
The Cid 528
The Kalevala: The Two Suitors 533
Rama: The March to Lanka 538
Zal 541

Fantasy
The Little Prince 622
Gulliver's Travels:
   FROM A Voyage to Lilliput 663

Sacred Writings and Legends of the Saints
Joseph and His Brethren 695

The Story of Ruth 703
May the strength of God pilot me 709
Lord, make me an instrument of
   Thy peace 710
God be in my head, and in my
   understanding 710
Give us grace and strength 710
"Golden Words" from Sacred Writings 711

Earth, Sky, and Sea
One Day on Beetle Rock: The Weasel 743
A Hind in Richmond Park: Bird
   Migration on the Pampas 746

Far Away and Long Ago: Flamingoes 749
Beneath the Tropic Seas: Sponges 749
Men, Microscopes, and Living Things:
    Between the Heights and the Depths 751
The Sea Around Us: The Moving Tides 753

Biography

Columbus Sails: The Ambassador 769
Amos Fortune, Free Man: Auctioned
    for Freedom 771
Leader by Destiny: George Washington,
    the Boy 776
Young Lafayette: The Great Adventure
    Begins 782
Audubon: Many Trails and a Snug Cabin 791
Abe Lincoln Grows Up: "Peculiarsome"
    Abe 795
Hans Christian Andersen 798
Clara Barton of the Red Cross 810
Madame Curie: Four Years in a Shed 814
Albert Schweitzer 818

Travel and History

The Story of Mankind: The Setting of
    the Stage 831
Americans Before Columbus:
    The Vikings Find and Lose America 833
Vast Horizons: The Polos 835
Hakluyt's Voyages: The Deliverance 840
Of Courage Undaunted: Lewis and Clark 841
George Washington's World:
    The Declaration of Independence 845
Captain Scott's Last Expedition:
    The Last March 847
North to the Orient: Point Barrow 849
Wind, Sand, and Stars: The Elements 853
The Great Heritage: We Have Tomorrow 858

Fiction

Caddie Woodlawn: Breeches and Clogs 922
Downright Dencey: The Former Time 926
Adam of the Road: A Blush of Boys 945
Men of Iron 949
The Trumpeter of Krakow: The Man
    Who Wouldn't Sell His Pumpkin 951
Master Simon's Garden: The Edge of the
    World 955
Rolling Wheels: Over the Divide 961
Johnny Tremain: Salt-Water Tea 981
The Silver Pencil 986
All-American: A Lesson in Citizenship 989

Poetry

Overheard on a Saltmarsh 1006
Escape 1006
Queen Mab 1007
"You Spotted Snakes" 1007
The Song of Wandering Aengus 1008
In Just-spring 1011
Home Thoughts from Abroad 1013
Sweet Peas 1015

Cape Ann 1016
In Arden Forest 1016
A Morning Song 1016
Loveliest of Trees 1017
The Painted Desert 1017
Song of the Brook 1019
Minnows 1019
The Lake Isle of Innisfree 1020
The Cloud 1020
The Morns Are Meeker than They
    Were 1021
A Vagabond Song 1022
Color in the Wheat 1022
To the Fringed Gentian 1023
God's World 1023
To Autumn 1024
Velvet Shoes 1025
Lines from "Snowbound" 1026
"When Icicles Hang by the Wall" 1026
An Almanac 1026
The Wakeupworld 1027
A Sea Song 1027
Sea-Fever 1028
A Wanderer's Song 1028
From "Swimmers" 1028
On the Grasshopper and Cricket 1031
Stars 1046
God Rest Ye Merry, Gentlemen 1051
"Some Say . . ." 1051
I Wonder as I Wander 1051
Measure Me, Sky! 1053
My Heart Leaps Up 1054
I Never Saw a Moor 1054
A Chant Out of Doors 1054
Fern Hill 1055
Miracles 1056
Give Me the Splendid Silent Sun 1056
I Hear America Singing 1056
The Commonplace 1057
Atlantic Charter: 1620–1942 1057
Lincoln 1057
Abraham Lincoln Walks at Midnight 1057
"When to the Sessions of Sweet Silent
    Thought" 1058
Get Up and Bar the Door 1059
Sir Patrick Spens 1060
Paul Revere's Ride 1065
Barbara Frietchie 1067
The Flower-fed Buffaloes 1068
The Ballad of William Sycamore 1068
Lochinvar 1069
The Charge of the Light Brigade 1070
The Sands of Dee 1070
Annabel Lee 1071
The Pied Piper of Hamelin 1071
The Admiral's Ghost 1075
The Creation 1076

INDEX

Page numbers in italics refer to comments and discussions by the editors; page numbers in ordinary type refer to selections and illustrations.

A Apple Pie, 72
"A bear went over the mountain," 34
"A carrion crow sat on an oak," 14
"A cat came fiddling out of a barn," 10
"A diller, a dollar, a ten o'clock scholar," 8
"A farmer went trotting upon his grey mare," 10
"A Frog he would a-wooing go," 19
"A man in the wilderness asked me," 29
"A wee bird sat upon a tree," 33
Abbott, Jacob, *1103*
Abe Lincoln Grows Up: "Peculiarsome" Abe (Carl Sandburg), 795
Abeita, Louise, *1174;* SEE E-Yeh-Shure
Abiding in the Shadow of the Almighty (Psalm 91), 708
Abraham Lincoln: His Good Stepmother (Genevieve Foster), 793
Abraham Lincoln Walks at Midnight (Vachel Lindsay), 1057
Adam of the Road: A Blush of Boys (E. J. Gray), 945
Admiral's Ghost, The (Alfred Noyes), 1075
Adventures of Pinocchio: Pinocchio's First Pranks (Carlo Collodi), 596
Adventures of Tom Sawyer, The: Tom Meets Becky (Mark Twain), 963
Aesop, *112, 1174;* fables of: *The Wind and the Sun,* 114; *A Wolf in Sheep's Clothing,* 114; *A Lion and a Mouse,* 114; *The Shepherd's Boy and the Wolf,* 114; *The Town Mouse and the Country Mouse,* 114; *The Crow and the Pitcher,* 115; *The Dog and His Shadow,* 115; *The Fox and the Crow,* 115; *The Dog in the Manger,* 115; *The Jackdaw and the Borrowed Plumes,* 116; *The Hare and the Tortoise,* 116; *The Goose with the Golden Eggs,* 116; *The Grasshopper and the Ants,* 116; *The Lark and Its Young,* 116; *Belling the Cat,* 117; *The Fox and the Grapes,* 117; *The Miller, His Son, and the Ass,* 117
Ah Tcha the Sleeper (A. B. Chrisman), 313

Aladdin and the Wonderful Lamp (Andrew Lang), 324
Alaskan (Eskimo) folk tale, 336
Albert Schweitzer (Joseph Gollomb), 818
Alcott, Louisa May, *1104*
Aldis, Dorothy, *1174; Windy Wash Day,* 1012; *What Am I?,* 1023; *Hiding,* 1040; *Whistles,* 1041; *Troubles,* 1041; *Radiator Lions,* 1041
Aldrich, Thomas Bailey, *1104*
Alexander, Frances, *1174;* from *Mother Goose on the Rio Grande,* 32
Alexander's Song, 23
Alice's Adventures in Wonderland (Lewis Carroll): verses from, 49; *Down the Rabbit Hole,* 603; *The Rabbit Sends in a Little Bill,* 606
All-American: A Lesson in Citizenship (J. R. Tunis), 989
Allingham, William, *1174; The Fairies,* 1004
Almanac, An (William Sharp), 1026
American: chants and jingles, 34; regional folk tales, 336–354; Indian myths, 444–455
American Institute of Graphic Arts, *1147*
American Library Association, *1149*
Americans Before Columbus: The Vikings Find and Lose America (E. C. Baity), 833
Amos Fortune, Free Man: Auctioned for Freedom (Elizabeth Yates), 771
"An angel came as I lay in bed," 31
Andersen, Hans Christian, *552, 1174; The Real Princess,* 554; *Five Peas in a Pod,* 554; *The Candles,* 556; *Thumbelisa,* 558; *The Wild Swans,* 563; *The Steadfast Tin Soldier,* 571; *The Tinder Box,* 573; *The Nightingale,* 577; *The Emperor's New Clothes,* 582; *The Ugly Duckling,* 584; *The Swineherd,* 589; *The Fir Tree,* 591
Androcles and the Lion, 123
Angelo, Valenti, illustration by, 1146
Animal Crackers (Christopher Morley), 1044
Annabel Lee (E. A. Poe), 1071
Apion, *1175;* fable from, 123
April (Sara Teasdale), 1013
April and May (R. W. Emerson), 1013

Arabian: nursery rhyme, 30; folk tale, 324

Artzybasheff, Boris, *1142, 1145, 1175; Seven Simeons,* 250; illustration by, 1143

"As I was going to Banbury," 11

"As I was going to St. Ives," 29

"As I was going to sell my eggs," 15

"As round as an apple," 28

"As Tommy Snooks and Bessy Brooks," 8

Asbjörnsen, Peter Christen, *133, 1175; The Three Billy-Goats-Gruff,* 290; *The Pancake,* 291; *The Ram and the Pig Who Went into the Woods,* 292; *Gudbrand on the Hillside,* 295; *Boots and his Brothers,* 296; *The Princess on the Glass Hill,* 298; *East o' the Sun and West o' the Moon,* 303; *The Lad Who Went to the North Wind,* 308; *The Cat on the Dovrefell,* 310

At the Sea-side (R. L. Stevenson), 1027

Atalanta's Race (Padraic Colum), 413

Atlantic Charter (F. B. Young), 1057

Audubon: Many Trails and a Snug Cabin (Constance Rourke), 791

Aulaire, Ingri and Edgar Parin d', 767, *1142, 1175; Ola,* 88; illustration by, 1142

Aulnoy, Mme. d', *134*

Austin, Mary, *1176; A Song of Greatness,* 1054

Autumn Fires (R. L. Stevenson), 1021

"Baa, baa, black sheep," 7

Baity, Elizabeth Chesley, *1176; Americans Before Columbus: The Vikings Find and Lose America,* 833

Baker, Augusta, *1088*

Balder and the Mistletoe (A. F. Brown), 427

Baldwin, James, *1176; Fafnir the Dragon,* 517

Ballad of William Sycamore, The (S. V. Benét), 1068

Bandeira Duarte, Margarida Estrela, *The Legend of the Palm Tree,* 456

Bangs, John Kendrick, *1176; The Little Elf,* 1005

Bannerman, Helen, *The Story of Little Black Sambo,* 77

Bantam Rooster (Harry Behn), 1032

Banyan Deer, The (M. L. Shedlock), 121

Barbara Frietchie (J. G. Whittier), 1067

Barbauld, Letitia Aikin, *1097, 1109, 1176; A Hymn in Prose,* 1126

"Barber, barber, shave a pig," 8

Barber's, The (Walter de la Mare), 1042

Barrie, James M., *1176; Peter Pan in Kensington Gardens: Lock-Out Time,* 598

Barter (Sara Teasdale), 1053

Battledore, 1092, 1132

Baucis and Philemon (Edith Hamilton), 406

Bear Says "North," The (Parker Fillmore), 280

Beaumont, Mme. de, *134*

Beauty (E-Yeh-Shure), 1053

Beauty and the Beast (Andrew Lang), 185

Beaver's Lesson, The (Lewis Carroll), 51

Bed in Summer (R. L. Stevenson), 1039

Bedford, F. D., *1138;* illustration by, 1106

Bee, the Harp, the Mouse, and the Bum-Clock, The (Seumas MacManus), 220

Beebe, William, *1177; Beneath the Tropic Seas: Sponges,* 749

Behn, Harry, *1177; Waiting,* 1010; *The Kite,* 1012; *Trees,* 1017; *Hallowe'en,* 1023; *Bantam Rooster,* 1032; *Pretending,* 1039; *Evening,* 1045

Bellerophon (Padraic Colum), 410

Belling the Cat (Aesop), 117

Belloc, Hilaire, *1177; The Frog,* 61; *The Yak,* 61

Beneath the Tropic Seas: Sponges (William Beebe), 749

Benét, Rosemary Carr and Stephen Vincent, *1177; Nancy Hanks,* 1058

Benét, Stephen Vincent, *1177; The Ballad of William Sycamore,* 1068

Bennett, Rowena Bastin, *1177; Pussy Willows,* 1015; *The Rain,* 1015; *Rubber Boots,* 1015; *Motor Cars,* 1043

Beowulf's Fight with Grendel, 487

Beskow, Elsa, *1177; Pelle's New Suit,* 83

Bett, Henry, from *Nursery Rhymes and Tales,* 27

"Betty Botter bought some butter," 29

Bewick, Thomas, *1132;* illustration by, 1133

Bianco, Margery Williams, *1177; The Little Wooden Doll* (selection), 868

Bible, the, as literature, *691–693; selections,* 695–709

Bidpai fables, *112,* 117

Billy Beg and the Bull (Seumas MacManus), 216

Biography, discussion of, *767–768*

"Black within and red without," 28

Blackbird, The (Humbert Wolfe), 1032

Blake, William, *1098, 1136, 1178; Laughing Song,* 1010; *Spring,* 1010; *The Echoing Green,* 1011; *The Lamb,* 1036; *Nurse's Song,* 1046; *Cradle Song,* 1047

"Bless you, bless you, burnie-bee," 8

Blind Man's Buff (Chinese nursery rhyme), 30

Blind Men and the Elephant, The (J. G. Saxe), 126

Blue Willow: The Shack (Doris Gates), 908

"Bobby Shaftoe's gone to sea," 12

Boggs, Ralph Steele, *1178,* and Mary Gould Davis, *1185; The Tinker and the Ghost,* 242

Boots and His Brothers (Asbjörnsen), 296

Borrowers, The, selection from (Mary Norton), 638

Borski, Lucia, *1178,* and Kate Miller, *The Jolly Tailor Who Became King,* 276

"Bow, wow, wow," 8

Bowman, James Cloyd, *1178; Slue-foot Sue Dodges the Moon,* 349

Bowman, James Cloyd, *1178,* and Margery Bianco, *1177; Hidden Laiva,* 285

"Boys and girls come out to play," 10

Boys' Names (Eleanor Farjeon), 1043

Braekstad, H. L., translation from H. C. Andersen, 591

Bráhman's Goat, The (Arthur Ryder), 117

Branch, The (E. M. Roberts), 1018

Bremen Town Musicians, The (Grimm), 140

Brenner, Anita, *1178; The Princess and José*, 357

Brer Rabbit's Astonishing Prank (J. C. Harris), 341

Bridge, The (Christina Rossetti), 1017

Brink, Carol Ryrie, *1178; Caddie Woodlawn: Breeches and Clogs*, 922

Bronson, Wilfrid S., *1179; Children of the Sea: The Dolphin's Tale*, 733

Brooke, L. Leslie, *1138, 1179; Johnny Crow's Garden*, 72; illustration by, 1138

Brooks, Phillips, *1179; O Little Town of Bethlehem*, 1050

Broom, The Shovel, the Poker, and the Tongs, The (Edward Lear), 59

Brother and Sister, The (Grimm), 142

Brown, Abbie Farwell, *1179; The Magic Apples*, 422; *Balder and the Mistletoe*, 427; *The Quest of the Hammer*, 483

Brown, Marcia, *1147, 1179; Dick Whittington and His Cat*, 90; illustration by, *opposite* 1149

Browning, Robert, *1179; Home Thoughts from Abroad*, 1013; *The Pied Piper of Hamelin*, 1071

Bryan, Catherine, and Mabra Madden, *1180; Why the Burro Lives with the Man*, 355

Bryant, Sara Cone, *The Cat and the Parrot*, 322

Bryant, William Cullen, *1180; To the Fringed Gentian*, 1023

Buckley, Elsie, *The Curse of Echo*, 396

Budulinek (Parker Fillmore), 269

Bunyan, John, *551, 1093*

Burroughs, John, *1180; Squirrels and Other Fur-Bearers: The Mink*, 745

Burton, Virginia Lee, *1180; The Little House*, 86; illustration by, 1147

Butterfly's Ball, The (William Roscoe), 1127

"Bye, baby bunting," 6

Cabullito (Mexican nursery rhyme), 32

Caddie Woodlawn: Breeches and Clogs (C. R. Brink), 922

Caldecott, Randolph, *68, 69, 1137, 1180;* illustration by, 1137

Caldecott award, *1149;* winners listed, *1151*

Call It Courage: Drums (Armstrong Sperry), 942

Camel and the Flotsam, The (La Fontaine), 125

Camel's Complaint, The (C. E. Carryl), 47

"Can you make a cambric shirt," 21

Canadian folk tale, 333

Candles, The (H. C. Andersen), 556

Canoe in the Rapids, The (N. S. Carlson), 333

Cape Ann (T. S. Eliot), 1016

Captain Scott's Last Expedition: The Last March (Robert Scott), 847

Carlson, Natalie Savage, *The Canoe in the Rapids*, 333

Carman, Bliss, *1181; A Vagabond Song*, 1022

Carrick, Valéry, *1181; Mr. Samson Cat*, 265

Carrighar, Sally, *1181; One Day on Beetle Rock: The Weasel*, 743

Carroll, Lewis, *41, 1099; The Walrus and the Carpenter*, 48; *'Tis the Voice of the Lobster*, 49; *The Crocodile*, 49; *The White Rabbit's Verses*, 49; *Jabberwocky*, 50; *The Gardener's Song*, 50; *The Beaver's Lesson*, 51; *Alice's Adventures in Wonderland: Down the Rabbit-Hole*, 603, and *The Rabbit Sends in a Little Bill*, 606; facsimile page from *Alice's Adventures Underground*, 1100. SEE ALSO Dodgson, Charles Lutwidge

Carryl, Charles E., *1181; The Camel's Complaint*, 47

Carson, Rachel L., *1181; The Sea Around Us: The Moving Tides*, 753

Cat and the Parrot, The (S. C. Bryant), 322

Cat on the Dovrefell, The (Asbjörnsen), 310

Caterpillar, The (Christina Rossetti), 1031

Caxton, William, *1132*

Chan, Plato and Christina, *1182; The Magic Monkey*, 316

Chant Out of Doors, A (Marguerite Wilkinson), 1054

Chapbooks, *1093*

Charge of the Light Brigade, The (Tennyson), 1070

Charity (I Corinthians 13), 706

"Charley Wag," 10

Charlot, Jean, illustration by, 1148

Chase, Richard, *1087, 1182; Old Fire Dragaman*, 343

Children of Lir, The (Ella Young), 230

Children of the Sea: The Dolphin's Tale (W. S. Bronson), 733

Chinese: nursery rhymes, 30–31; folk tales, 313–317

Chrisman, Arthur Bowie, *1182; Ah Tcha the Sleeper*, 313

Christmas Folk-Song, A (L. W. Reese), 1051

Christmas Morning (E. M. Roberts), 1050

Cid, The (Merriam Sherwood), 528

Cinderella and the Glass Slipper (Walter de la Mare), 174

Circus (Eleanor Farjeon), 1040

City Mouse, The (Christina Rossetti), 1030

Clara Barton of the Red Cross (J. C. Nolan), 810

Clark, Ann Nolan, *1182; Yucca*, 1018

Clark, Margery, *1182; Poppy Seed Cakes*, 867

Clemens, Samuel L., *1104, 1183;* SEE Twain, Mark

Cloud, The (P. B. Shelley), 1020

Clover for Breakfast (Frances Frost), 1034

Coatsworth, Elizabeth, *1183; The Fair American: The New Cabin Boy*, 892; *The Painted Desert*, 1017; *The Mouse*, 1029

"Cock a doodle doo," 9

Collodi, Carlo, *Adventures of Pinocchio: Pinocchio's First Pranks*, 596. SEE ALSO Lorenzini, Carlo

Color in the Wheat, (Hamlin Garland), 1022

Colum, Padraic *1183; Kate Mary Ellen*, 227; *Orpheus*, 404; *Phaethon*, 408; *Bellerophon*, 410; *Atalanta's*

Race, 413; *Odin Goes to Mimir's Well,* 418; *How Frey Won Gerda the Giant Maiden,* 419; *How Kana Brought Back the Sun and Moon and Stars,* 457; *The Seven Sleepers,* 460; *Odysseus and the Cyclops,* 474; *Sigurd's Youth,* 512

Columbus Sails: The Ambassador (C. W. Hodges), 769

Comenius, *1091, 1132*

Commonplace, The (Walt Whitman), 1057

Conkling, Hilda, *1183; Dandelion,* 1014; *Little Snail,* 1030; *Red Rooster,* 1032

Courlander, Harold, *1184;* and Wolf Leslau, *The Goat Well,* 367

Courtship of the Yonghy-Bonghy-Bò, The (Edward Lear), 59

Cradle Hymn (Martin Luther), 1050

Cradle Song (William Blake), 1047

Craik, Dinah Maria Mulock, *1184; God Rest Ye Merry, Gentlemen,* 1051

Crane, Lucy, translations from Grimm, 136, 140, 142, 162

Crane, Walter, *68, 69, 1137;* illustration by, 1136

Creation, The (J. W. Johnson), 1076

Crew, Fleming H., and Alice Crew Gall, *Wagtail: Wagtail's World Grows Wider,* 731

Cricket, The (J. H. Fabre), 736

Crocodile, The (Lewis Carroll), 49

"Cross patch," 11

Crow and the Partridge, The, 118

Crow and the Pitcher (Aesop), 115

Cruikshank, George, *1133;* illustration by, 1134

Cuchulain's Wooing (Eleanor Hull), 507

Cullen, Countee, *1184; The Wakeupworld,* 1027; *Incident,* 1058

Cummings, E. E., *1184; In Just-spring,* 1011

Cunningham, Allan, *1184; A Sea Song,* 1027

Cupid and Psyche (Edith Hamilton), 399

Curie, Eve, *1184; Madame Curie: Four Years in a Shed,* 814

"Curly locks, Curly locks," 9

Curse of Echo, The (Elsie Buckley), 396

Cushing, Frank Hamilton, *How the Coyote Danced with the Blackbirds,* 448

"Cushy cow, bonny, let down thy milk," 10

Czechoslovakian folk tales, 269–275

Daffodils (William Wordsworth), 1014

Daglish, Alice, and Ernest Rhys, from *The Land of Nursery Rhyme,* 31, 32

Dairymaid and Her Milk-Pot, The (La Fontaine), 125

Dalgliesh, Alice, *767, 1184; The Silver Pencil* (selection), 986

"Dame, get up and bake your pies," 16

"Dance to your daddy," 32

Dandelion (Hilda Conkling), 1014

Daniel Boone: Boonesborough (James Daugherty), 787

Danish nursery rhyme, 31

Daphne (F. J. Olcott), 407

Darley, Felix, *1138*

Dasent, G. W., *133, 1185;* translations from Asbjörnsen, 290, 291, 296, 298, 303, 308, 310

Daugherty, James, *828, 1185; Daniel Boone: Boonesborough,* 787; *Of Courage Undaunted: Lewis and Clark,* 841; illustration by, *opposite* 1148

Davis, Mary Gould, *1185; The Truce of the Wolf,* 715

Davis, Mary Gould, *1185,* and Ralph Steele Boggs, *1178; The Tinker and the Ghost,* 242

Davis, Robert, *1185; The General's Horse,* 244

Day, Thomas, *1096*

Day of Misfortune, A (Maria Edgeworth), 1123

Defoe, Daniel, *1186; Robinson Crusoe* (selection), 976

De Jong, Meindert, *1186; The Wheel on the School* (selection), 914

De la Mare, Walter, *1003, 1101, 1186;* from *Tom Tiddler's Ground,* 45; *Cinderella and the Glass Slipper* (Perrault), 174; *The Sleeping Beauty* (Perrault), 180; *The Hare and the Hedgehog,* 195; *Some One,* 1006; *The Snowflake,* 1025; *Softly, Drowsily,* 1036; *Miss T.,* 1042; *Tired Tim,* 1042; *The Barber's,* 1042; *Nod,* 1045; *Full Moon,* 1045; *Silver,* 1046

Demeter (Edith Hamilton), 389

Determination of the Seasons (Stith Thompson), 444

Deutsch, Babette, *1186; The Kalevala: The Two Suitors,* 533

Dick Whittington and His Cat (Marcia Brown), 90

Dickens, Charles, *41*

Dickinson, Emily, *1187; The Morns Are Meeker than They Were,* 1021; *I Never Saw a Moor,* 1054

"Diddle, diddle, dumpling, my son John," 9

"Ding, dong, bell," 6

Do You Fear the Wind? (Hamlin Garland), 1054

"Doctor Foster went to Gloucester," 13

Dodge, Mary Mapes, *1104, 1105, 1187; Hans Brinker: Hans and Gretel Find a Friend,* 900

Dodgson, Charles Lutwidge, *1187;* SEE Carroll, Lewis

Dog and His Shadow, The (Aesop), 115

Dog in the Manger, The (Aesop), 115

Dove and the Ant, The (La Fontaine), 124

Downright Dencey: The Former Time (C. D. Snedeker), 926

Drakestail (Andrew Lang), 171

Drinkwater, John, *1187; Washing,* 1042; *Twos,* 1042

Du Bois, William Pène, *1147*

Duck and the Kangaroo, The (Edward Lear), 57

Duck's Ditty (Kenneth Grahame), 1033

Dutch nursery rhymes, 31

Eager, Edward, *1187; Half Magic: What Happened to Katharine,* 652

Earth Is the Lord's, The (Psalm 24), 707

East o' the Sun and West o' the Moon (Asbjörnsen), 303

Eaton, Jeanette, *1188; Leader by Destiny: George Washington, the Boy*, 776; *Young Lafayette: The Great Adventure Begins*, 782

Echoing Green, The (William Blake), 1011

Eddas (Icelandic), 387, 469

Edgeworth, Maria, *1096; 1109, 1188; A Day of Misfortunes*, 1123

Edwardes, Marian, translation from Grimm, 138

Eel, The (Ogden Nash), 62

Eichenberg, Fritz, *1112, 1188*; illustration from *Padre Porko*, 1143

"Eins, zwei, Polizei," 27

Eletelephony (L. E. Richards), 46

Eliot, T. S., *1188; Cape Ann*, 1016

"Elizabeth, Elspeth, Betsy, and Bess," 28

Elves, The (Grimm), 136

Elves' Dance, The, 1005

Emerson, Ralph Waldo, *1188; April and May*, 1013

Emett, Rowland, illustration by, *between* 1148–1149

Emperor's New Clothes, The (H. C. Andersen), 582

English: folk tales, 195–213; hero tales, 487–502

Epic, defined, *469*

Escape (Elinor Wylie), 1006

Estes, Eleanor, *1188; Rufus M.* (selection), 895

Ethiopian folk tale, 367

Ets, Marie, illustration by, *between* 1148–1149

Evans, Edmund, *68, 1137*

Evening (Harry Behn), 1045

Ewing, Juliana Horatia, *1099, 1109, 1189; Murdoch's Rath*, 1128

E-Yeh-Shure, *Beauty*, 1053. SEE ALSO Abeita, Louise

Fables, discussion of, *111–113*; Aesop's, 114–117; Jataka, 120–123; La Fontaine's, 124–125; modern, 126–127; Panchatantra and Bidpai, 117–120; Persian, 123

Fabre, Jean Henri, *1189; The Cricket*, 736

Faery Flag of Dunvegan, The (B. K. Wilson), 235

Fafnir, the Dragon (James Baldwin), 517

Fair American, The: The New Cabin Boy (Elizabeth Coatsworth), 892

Fairies, The (William Allingham), 1004

Fairies, The (Rose Fyleman), 1004

Fairy, origin of term, *134*

Fairy tales, *134.* SEE ALSO Fantasy

Fairy Went A-Marketing, A (Rose Fyleman), 1005

Fantasy, discussion of, *551–553*

Far Away and Long Ago: Flamingoes (W. H. Hudson), 749

Farjeon, Eleanor, *1189; St. Nicholas*, 719; *For Snow*, 1025; *A Prayer for Little Things*, 1029; *Mrs. Peck-Pigeon*, 1033; *The Sounds in the Morning*, 1037; *Circus*, 1040; *Boys' Names*, 1043; *Girls' Names*, 1043; *The Night Will Never Stay*, 1046

Fern Hill (Dylan Thomas), 1055

Fiction, discussion of, *865–866*

Field, Eugene, *1189; Wynken, Blynken, and Nod*, 1048

Field, Rachel L., *1189; Hitty: I Go Up in the World and Am Glad to Come Down Again*, 903; *Something Told the Wild Geese*, 1022; *General Store*, 1043; *Taxis*, 1043; *Skyscrapers*, 1044

Fillmore, Parker, *Budulinek*, 269; *The Twelve Months*, 271; *The Bear Says "North,"* 280; *Mighty Mikko*, 281

Finger, Charles J., *1190; The Tale of the Lazy People*, 358

Finnish: folk tales, 280–289; hero tale, 533

Fir Tree, The (H. C. Andersen), 591

Firdusi (Firdausi, Firdousi), *1190; Zal*, 541

Fireflies (Winifred Welles), 1031

Firefly (E. M. Roberts), 1031

Fisherman and His Wife, The (Grimm), 149

Fishing (Danish nursery rhyme), 31

Five Hundred Hats of Bartholomew Cubbins, The (Dr. Seuss), 93

"Five little squirrels sat up in a tree," 34

Five Peas in a Pod (H. C. Andersen), 554

Five Toes, The (Chinese nursery rhyme), 30

Flack, Marjorie, illustration by, 1144

Flea, The (Ruth Sawyer), 239

Fletcher, John Gould, *1190; Lincoln*, 1057

Flower-fed Buffaloes, The (Vachel Lindsay), 1068

Fog (Carl Sandburg), 1018

Folk tales, discussion of, *131–135*; American regional, 336–354; Arabian, 324–331; Canadian, 333–336; Chinese, 313–317; Czechoslovakian, 269–275; English, 195–213; Ethiopian, 367–369; Finnish, 280–289; French, 170–194; German, 136–169; Indian, 319–323; Irish, 214–235; Italian, 247–250; Japanese, 318; Mexican, 355–358; Polish, 276–279; Russian, 250–268; Scandinavian, 290–312; Scottish, 235–239; South American, 358–364; Spanish, 239–247; Turkish, 331–332; West Indian, 365–367

Foote, Samuel, *1190; The Great Panjandrum Himself*, 47

For Snow (Eleanor Farjeon), 1025

Forbes, Esther, *1190; Johnny Tremain: Salt-Water Tea*, 981

Foster, Genevieve, *828, 1190; Abraham Lincoln: His Good Stepmother*, 793; *George Washington's World: The Declaration of Independence*, 845

"Four and twenty tailors," 14

Fox and the Crow, The (Aesop), 115

Fox and the Goat, The (La Fontaine), 124

Fox and the Grapes, The (Aesop), 117

Francis of Assisi, St., a prayer of ("Lord, make me an instrument of Thy peace"), 710

François, André, *1147*; illustration by, *opposite* 1149

Françoise, *Noël for Jeanne-Marie*, 78; illustration by, *between* 1148–1149. SEE ALSO Seignobosc, Françoise

Frasconi, Antonio, *1147, 1191*; illustration by, *between* 1148–1149

French: nursery rhymes, 27, 31; folk tales, 170–194; hero tale, 522

Frog, The (Hilaire Belloc), 61

From Tiger to Anansi (P. M. Sherlock), 365

Frost, A. B., *1138;* illustration by, 1139

Frost, Frances, *1191; Clover for Breakfast,* 1034; *The Little Whistler,* 1041

Frost, Robert, *1191; The Pasture,* 1013; *The Last Word of a Bluebird,* 1022; *Stopping by Woods on a Snowy Evening,* 1025

Frost Pane, The (David McCord), 1024

Full Moon (Walter de la Mare), 1045

Fyleman, Rose, *1191;* from *Picture Rhymes from Foreign Lands,* 30, 31, 32, 33; *The Fairies,* 1004; *A Fairy Went A-Marketing,* 1005

Gág, Wanda, *1142, 1191; Millions of Cats,* 81; *Hansel and Gretel* (Grimm), 145; *The Fisherman and His Wife* (Grimm), 149; *Rapunzel* (Grimm), 154; *Snow White and the Seven Dwarfs* (Grimm), 156; *Gone Is Gone,* 164; illustration by, 1141

Gall, Alice Crew, and Fleming H. Crew, *Wagtail: Wagtail's World Grows Wider,* 731

Gardener's Song, The (Lewis Carroll), 50

Garland, Hamlin, *1192; Color in the Wheat,* 1022; *Do You Fear the Wind?,* 1054

Gates, Doris, *1192; Blue Willow: The Shack,* 908

Gay, John, *1133, 1192*

"Gay go up and gay go down," 24

Geisel, Theodor Seuss, *1192;* SEE Seuss, Dr.

General Store (Rachel Field), 1043

General's Horse, The (Robert Davis), 244

George, John and Jean, *1192; Vulpes, the Red Fox* (selection), 740

George Washington's World: The Declaration of Independence (Genevieve Foster), 845

"Georgie, Porgie, pudding and pie," 7

German: nursery rhymes, 27, 31; folk tales, 136–169; hero tale, 517

Get Up and Bar the Door, 1059

Gillham, Charles E., *1193; Mr. Crow Takes a Wife,* 336

Girls' Names (Eleanor Farjeon), 1043

Give Me the Splendid Silent Sun (Walt Whitman), 1056

"Give us grace and strength" (R. L. Stevenson), 710

Glimpse in Autumn (J. S. Untermeyer), 1021

Goat Well, The (H. Courlander and W. Leslau), 367

Goblin, The (French nursery rhyme), 31

"God be in my head, and in my understanding" (prayer), 710

God Is Our Refuge and Strength (Psalm 46), 708

God Rest Ye Merry, Gentlemen (D. M. M. Craik), 1051

Godden, Rumer, *767, 1193; Han Christian Andersen,* 798

God's World (Edna St. Vincent Millay), 1023

Golden Goose, The (Grimm), 138

"Golden Words" from sacred writings, 711–712

Goldsmith, Oliver, *1095, 1193*

Gollomb, Joseph, *1193; Albert Schweitzer,* 818

Gone Is Gone (Wanda Gág), 164

Good Master, The: The Round-up (Kate Seredy), 931

Good Night (Thomas Hood), 1049

Goodrich, Samuel G., *1102*

Goody Two-Shoes, SEE *Little Goody Two-Shoes*

Goose with the Golden Eggs, The (Aesop), 116

"Goosey, goosey gander," 8

Grahame, Kenneth, *1101, 1193; The Wind in the Willows: The Wild Wood,* 616; *Duck's Ditty,* 1033

Gramatky, Hardie, *1194; Little Toot,* 83; illustration by, *between* 1148–1149

Gray, Elizabeth Janet, *1194; Adam of the Road: A Blush of Boys,* 945

"Gray goose and gander," 12

Grasshopper and the Ants, The (Aesop), 116

"Great A, little a," 8

Great Heritage, The: We Have Tomorrow (K. B. Shippen), 858

Great Panjandrum Himself, The (Samuel Foote), 47

Greek: nonsense rhymes, 45; myths and legends (classical) *388,* 389–417, (modern) 459–463; hero tales, 474–487

Greenaway, Kate, *68, 69, 1137, 1194; Little Wind,* 1012; illustration by, 1137; initials, 3, 41, 67, 111, 131, 385, 469, 551, 691, 729, 767, 827, 865, 1001

Gretchen (Dutch nursery rhyme), 31

Grey, Katharine, *1195; Rolling Wheels: Over the Divide,* 961

Grimm, Jakob and Wilhelm, *132, 1098, 1195; The Elves,* 136; *The Wolf and the Seven Little Kids,* 137; *The Golden Goose,* 138; *The Bremen Town Musicians,* 140; *The Brother and Sister,* 142; *Hansel and Gretel,* 145; *The Fisherman and His Wife,* 149; *Rapunzel,* 154; *Snow White and the Seven Dwarfs,* 156; *Rumpelstiltskin,* 162

Gudbrand on the Hillside (Asbjörnsen), 295

Gulliver's Travels: A Voyage to Lilliput, selection from (Jonathan Swift), 663

Guppy, The (Ogden Nash), 62

"Haily Paily," 33

Hakluyt, Richard, *1195; Hakluyt's Voyages: The Deliverance,* 840

Hakluyt's Voyages: The Deliverance (Richard Hakluyt), 840

Hale, Lucretia, *42, 1195*

Hale, Sarah Josepha, *1103, 1195; Mary's Lamb,* 1036

Half Magic: What Happened to Katharine (Edward Eager), 652

Hallowe'en (Harry Behn), 1023

Hamilton, Edith *1196; Demeter,* 389; *Cupid and Psyche,* 399; *Baucis and Philemon,* 406; *Perseus,* 476

Handforth, Thomas, *1145, 1196; Mei Li,* 99; illustration by, *between* 1148–1149

Hans Brinker: Hans and Gretel Find a Friend (M. M. Dodge), 900

Hans Christian Andersen (Rumer Godden), 798

Hansel and Gretel (Grimm), 145

Hare and the Hedgehog, The (Walter de la Mare), 195

Hare and the Tortoise, The (Aesop), 116

Hare that Ran Away, The (M. L. Shedlock), 122

"Hark, hark, the dogs do bark," 8

Harris, Joel Chandler, *1196; The Wonderful Tar-Baby*, 339; *Brer Rabbit's Astonishing Prank*, 341

Hatch, Mary C., *1196; The Talking Pot*, 311

Hawaiian myth, 457–459

Hawthorne, Nathaniel, *1103*

Headland, I. T., from *Chinese Mother Goose Rhymes*, 30

Hearn, Lafcadio, *1196; The Tongue-cut Sparrow*, 318

Hebrew nursery rhyme, 31

Heidi: In the Pasture (Johanna Spyri), 885

Henny-Penny (Joseph Jacobs), 198

Hercules: The Eleventh Task (Katharine Pyle), 480

Here We Come A-Piping, 1006

"Here's A, B, and C," 22

Hero tales, discussion of, *469–473*; English, 487–502; Finnish, 533–538; French, 522–527; German, 517–521; Greek, 474–487; Indian 538–540; Irish, 503–511; Persian, 541–544; Scandinavian, 512–517; Spanish, 528–532

Herrick, Robert, *1197;* "What God gives and what we take," 710; *To Daffodils*, 1014

"Hey, diddle, diddle," 6

Hiawatha's Childhood (H. W. Longfellow), 1063

"Hick-a-more, Hack-a-more," 28

"Hickety, pickety, my black hen," 7

"Hickory, dickory, dock," 6

Hidden Laiva (J. C. Bowman and Margery Bianco), 285

Hiding (Dorothy Aldis), 1040

High Barbaree, The (L. E. Richards), 46

Hind in Richmond Park, A: Bird Migration on the Pampas (W. H. Hudson), 746

History, discussion of, *827–829*

History of Goody Two-Shoes, The, SEE *Little Goody Two-Shoes*

History of Tom Thumb, The (Joseph Jacobs), 209

Hitty: I Go Up in the World and Am Glad to Come Down Again (Rachel Field), 903

Hobbit, The: Riddles in the Dark (J. R. R. Tolkien), 645

Hodges, C. Walter, *1197; Columbus Sails: The Ambassador*, 769

Holbrook, Florence, *The Story of the First Woodpecker*, 446

Home Thoughts from Abroad (Robert Browning), 1013

Homer, *387*

Homer Price: The Doughnuts (Robert McCloskey), 938

Hood, Thomas, *1197; Good Night*, 1049

Hornbook, *1090;* illustration, 1091

Hosford, Dorothy, *1197; Thor Gains His Hammer*, 432; *Thor's Unlucky Journey*, 434

"Hot-cross buns," 11

Housman, Alfred Edward, *1197; Loveliest of Trees*, 1017

How Frey Won Gerda the Giant Maiden (Padraic Colum), 419

How Glooskap Found the Summer (C. G. Leland), 444

How Jason Lost His Sandal in Anauros (Charles Kingsley), 483

How Kana Brought Back the Sun and Moon and Stars (Padraic Colum), 457

"How many miles to Babylon?" 11

"How much wood would a woodchuck chuck," 29

How St. George Fought the Dragon (Marion Lansing), 492

How the Coyote Danced with the Blackbirds (F. H. Cushing), 448

How the Seven Brothers Saved Their Sister (G. J. Penny), 452

Hudson, W. H., *552, 1101, 1197; A Hind in Richmond Park: Bird Migration on the Pampas*, 746; *Far Away and Long Ago: Flamingoes*, 749

Hughes, Charles, *1138*

Hughes, Thomas, *1099*

Hugo, Victor, *Wings*, 1054

Hull, Eleanor, *Cuchulain's Wooing*, 507

"Humpty Dumpty sat on a wall," 8

Hunt, Mabel Leigh, *1197; Little Girl with Seven Names*, 869

Hunt, Margaret, translation from Grimm, 137

"Hush-a-bye, baby, on the tree top," 6

Husky Hi (Norwegian nursery rhyme), 32

Hutchinson, W. M. L., *1198; Prometheus the Fire-bringer*, 391; *Pandora*, 394

Hymn in Prose, A (L. A. Barbauld), 1126

"I am a gold lock," 26

"I asked my mother for fifty cents," 34

"I boiled hot water in an urn," 45

"I had a little hen," 10

"I had a little husband," 15

"I had a little nut tree," 12

"I had a little pony," 9

"I have a little sister," 28

I Hear America Singing (Walt Whitman), 1056

I Like Little Pussy (Jane Taylor), 1035

"I love sixpence," 12

I Meant to Do My Work Today (Richard Le Gallienne), 1020

I Never Saw a Moor (Emily Dickinson), 1054

"I saw a fishpond all on fire," 29

"I saw a ship a-sailing," 11

"I saw three ships come sailing by," 17

"I went up one pair of stairs," 26

I Will Lift Up Mine Eyes (Psalm 121), 709

I Wonder as I Wander, 1051

"I'll tell you a story," 10

"I'm going to Lady Washington's," 34

"I've got a rocket in my pocket," 34

Icarus and Daedalus (J. P. Peabody), 412

If a Pig Wore a Wig (Christina Rossetti), 45

"If all the seas were one sea," 29

"If all the world was apple pie," 29

"If I had a donkey that wouldn't go," 9

"If I'd as much money as I could spend," 12

Iliad (Homer), *386, 387*

Illustration of children's books, *1132–1148.* SEE ALSO Picture books, discussion of

In Arden Forest (William Shakespeare), 1016

In Just-spring (E. E. Cummings), 1011

"In marble halls as white as milk," 28

Incident (Countee Cullen), 1058

Indian: folk tales, 319–323; hero tale, 538

Indian, North American: myths, 444–455

Indian Lullaby, An, 1047

"Intery, mintery, cutery, corn," 27

Invincible Louisa: "Little Women" (Cornelia Meigs), 802

Irish: folk tales, 214–235; hero tales, 503–511

Italian: nursery rhyme, 32; folk tale, 247

Jabberwocky (Lewis Carroll), 50

"Jack and Jill went up the hill," 9

Jack and the Beanstalk (Joseph Jacobs), 200

Jack and the King Who Was a Gentleman (Seumas MacManus), 224

"Jack be nimble," 8

"Jack Sprat could eat no fat," 9

Jackdaw and the Borrowed Plumes, The (Aesop), 116

Jacobs, Joseph, *112, 133, 1198; The Story of the Three Little Pigs*, 75; *The Old Woman and Her Pig*, 197; *Henny-Penny*, 198; *Teeny-Tiny*, 199; *Jack and the Beanstalk*, 200; *Molly Whuppie*, 203; *The Three Sillies*, 205; *Master of All Masters*, 206; *The Well of the World's End*, 207; *The History of Tom Thumb*, 209; *Tamlane*, 211; *The King o' the Cats*, 212; *King O'Toole and His Goose*, 214

Jagendorf, M. A., *1198; The Priceless Cats*, 247

Japanese: nursery rhyme, 32; folk tale, 318

Jataka tales, *112*, 120–123

"Jenny Wren fell sick," 18

"John Smith's a very guid man," 33

Johnny Crow's Garden (L. L. Brooke), 72

"Johnny shall have a new bonnet," 12

Johnny Tremain: Salt-Water Tea (Esther Forbes), 981

Johnson, James Weldon, *1198; The Creation*, 1076

Jolly Tailor Who Became King, The (L. Borski and K. Miller), 276

Jonathan (Dutch nursery rhyme), 31

Joseph and His Brethren (from Genesis 26–46), 695

Judgment of Midas, The (J. P. Peabody), 416

Jumblies, The (Edward Lear), 55

Just So Stories: How the Camel Got His Hump (Rudyard Kipling), 609

Kalevala, The: The Two Suitors (Babette Deutsch), 533

Kate Mary Ellen (Padraic Colum), 227

Keats, John, *1198; Sweet Peas*, 1015; *Minnows*, 1019; *To Autumn*, 1024; *On the Grasshopper and Cricket*, 1031

Kelly, Eric Philbrook, *1199; The Trumpeter of Krakow: The Man Who Wouldn't Sell His Pumpkin*, 951

Kelsey, Alice Geer, *1199; Three Fridays*, 331

Keys of Canterbury, The, 1063

King Arthur and His Sword (Sidney Lanier), 493

King of China's Daughter, The (Edith Sitwell), 1009

King of the Golden River, The (John Ruskin), 669

King o' the Cats, The (Joseph Jacobs), 212

King O'Toole and His Goose (Joseph Jacobs), 214

Kingsley, Charles, *1099, 1199; How Jason Lost His Sandal in Anauros*, 483; *The Sands of Dee*, 1070

Kipling, Rudyard, *1101, 1199; Just So Stories: How the Camel Got His Hump*, 609; *Seal Lullaby*, 1049

Kite, The (Harry Behn), 1012

Knight, Eric, *1199; Lassie Come-Home: A Long Journey's Beginning*, 935

Krohn, Julius and Kaarle, *133*

Lad Who Went to the North Wind, The (Asbjørnsen), 308

Lady Bug (Chinese nursery rhyme), 30

"Lady, Lady Landers," 33

"Lady Queen Anne she sits in the sun," 25

La Fontaine, *113, 1199; fables of: The Dove and the Ant*, 124; *The Fox and the Goat*, 124; *The Camel and the Flotsam*, 125; *The Dairymaid and Her Milk-Pot*, 125

Lagerlöf, Selma, 552

Lake Isle of Innisfree, The (W. B. Yeats), 1020

Lamb, Charles and Mary, *1097, 1098*

Lamb, The (William Blake), 1036

Land of Counterpane, The (R. L. Stevenson), 1038

Lang, Andrew, *133, 1199; from The Nursery Rhyme Book*, 15, 26; *Drakestail*, 171; *Beauty and the Beast*, 185; *Aladdin and the Wonderful Lamp*, 324

Lanier, Sidney, *King Arthur and His Sword*, 493

Lansing, Marion, *How St. George Fought the Dragon*, 492

Lark and Its Young, The (Aesop), 116

Lassie Come-Home: A Long Journey's Beginning (Eric Knight), 935

Last Word of a Bluebird, The (Robert Frost), 1022

Laughing Song (William Blake), 1010

"Lavender's blue," 12

Lawson, Robert, 552, 1200; *Rabbit Hill: Little Georgie Sings a Song*, 612; illustration by, 1146

Leader by Destiny: George Washington, the Boy (Jeanette Eaton), 776

Lear, Edward, 42, 1135, 1200; *Nonsense Alphabet*, 53; *The Jumblies*, 55; *The Owl and the Pussy-Cat*, 56; *Mr and Mrs. Discobbolos*, 56; *The Duck and the Kangaroo*, 57; *The Quangle Wangle's Hat*, 57; *The Table and the Chair*, 58; *The Broom, the Shovel, the Poker, and the Tongs*, 59; *The Courtship of the Yonghy-Bonghy-Bò*, 59; *Limericks*, 60; illustration by, 1136

Learned Song, A, 22

Le Gallienne, Richard, 1200; *I Meant to Do My Work Today*, 1020

Legend of the Palm Tree, The (M. E. B. Duarte), 456

Legends, SEE Myths and legends

Leland, Charles Godfrey, *How Glooskap Found the Summer*, 444

Leslau, Wolf, and Harold Courlander, *The Goat Well*, 367

Leslie, Elizabeth, 1103

Limericks (Edward Lear), 42, 60

Lincoln (J. G. Fletcher), 1057

Lindbergh, Anne Morrow, 1200; *North to the Orient: Point Barrow*, 849

Lindsay, Vachel, 1201; *The Little Turtle*, 1030; *The Mysterious Cat*, 1035; *What the Rattlesnake Said*, 1045; *The Moon's the North Wind's Cooky*, 1045; *Abraham Lincoln Walks at Midnight*, 1057; *The Flower-fed Buffaloes*, 1068

Lines from "Snowbound" (J. G. Whittier), 1026

Lion and a Mouse, A (Aesop), 114

Little Black Sambo, The Story of (Helen Bannerman), 77

"Little Bo-peep has lost her sheep," 9

"Little Boy Blue," 7

Little Elf, The (J. K. Bangs), 1005

Little Girl (Arabian nursery rhyme), 30

Little Girl with Seven Names (M. L. Hunt), 869

Little Goody Two-Shoes, 1095, 1109, 1110

"Little Hermogenes is so small," 45

Little House, The (V. L. Burton), 86

Little House in the Big Woods: Summertime (L. I. Wilder), 881

Little Humpbacked Horse, The (Post Wheeler), 258

"Little Jack Horner," 7

Little Land, The (R. L. Stevenson), 1038

"Little Miss Muffet," 7

"Little Nancy Etticoat," 28

Little Prince, The, selection from (Antoine de Saint-Exupéry), 622

Little Red Riding-Hood (Perrault), 170

Little Snail (Hilda Conkling), 1030

Little Things (James Stephens), 1029

"Little Tommy Tucker," 7

Little Toot (Hardie Gramatky), 83

Little Turtle, The (Vachel Lindsay), 1030

Little Whistler, The (Frances Frost), 1041

Little Wind (Kate Greenaway), 1012

Little Wooden Doll, The, selection from (M. W. Bianco), 868

Lochinvar (Sir Walter Scott), 1069

Locke, John, 1094

Locust and the Coyote, The (A. B. Nusbaum), 447

Lofting, Hugh, 552, 1101, 1201; *The Story of Doctor Dolittle: The Rarest Animal of All*, 610

"London Bridge is broken down," 24

"Long legs, crooked thighs," 28

Longfellow, Henry Wadsworth, 1201; *Hiawatha's Childhood*, 1063; *Paul Revere's Ride*, 1065

Lönnrot, Elias, 133

"Look at Marcus and take warning," 45

Lord Is My Shepherd, The (Psalm 23), 707

"Lord, make me an instrument of Thy peace" (prayer of St. Francis of Assisi), 710

"Lord, purge our eyes to see" (Christina Rossetti), 710

Lorenzini, Carlo, 1201; SEE Collodi, Carlo

Lost (Carl Sandburg), 1018

Loveliest of Trees (A. E. Housman), 1017

Lowell, James Russell, 1201; *To the Dandelion*, 1014

Lucas, Mrs. Edgar, translations from H. C. Andersen, 554, 558, 563, 571, 573, 577, 582, 584, 589

Lucas, Mary Seymour, 1202; *Vast Horizons: The Polos*, 835

"Lucy Locket lost her pocket," 9

Lullaby of an Infant Chief (Sir Walter Scott), 1047

"Luna, la Luna," 32

Luther, Martin, 1202; *Cradle Hymn*, 1050

Mabie, Hamilton Wright, 1202

McCloskey, Robert, 1202; *Homer Price: The Doughnuts*, 938

McCord, David, 1202; *The Frost Pane*, 1024; *The Shell*, 1027; *Our Mr. Toad*, 1030; *Song of the Train*, 1044

Macdonald, George, 552, 1101

MacKinstry, Elizabeth, 1145

MacManus, Seumas, 1087, 1202; *Billy Beg and the Bull*, 216; *The Bee, the Harp, the Mouse, and the Bum-Clock*, 220; *Jack and the King Who Was a Gentleman*, 224

Madame Curie: Four Years in a Shed (Eve Curie), 814

Madden, Mabra, and Catherine Bryan, 1180; *Why the Burro Lives with the Man*, 355

Magazines for children, 1104–1105

Magic Apples, The (A. F. Brown), 422

Magic Monkey, The (Plato and Christina Chan), 316

Malory, Sir Thomas, 1202. SEE ALSO: *King Arthur and His Sword*

Many Moons (James Thurber), 624

March (William Wordsworth), 1011

Market Square (A. A. Milne), 1033

Marriott, Alice, *1202; Why the Ant Is Almost Cut in Two*, *450*

Marryat, Capt. Frederick, *1099*

Martineau, Harriet, *1099*

"Mary, Mary, quite contrary," 7

Mary Poppins Opens the Door: The Marble Boy (Pamela Travers), 629

Mary's Lamb (S. J. Hale), 1036

Masefield, John, *1203; Sea-Fever*, 1028; *A Wanderer's Song*, 1028

Master of All Masters (Joseph Jacobs), 206

Master Simon's Garden: The Edge of the World (Cornelia Meigs), 955

"May the strength of God pilot me" (prayer of St. Patrick), 709

Measure Me, Sky! (Leonora Speyer), 1053

Mee, Ray, Doh (German nursery rhyme), 31

Mei Li (Thomas Handforth), 99

Meigs, Cornelia, *1203; Invincible Louisa: "Little Women,"* 802; *Master Simon's Garden: The Edge of the World*, 955

Melcher, Frederic, *1149*

Men, Microscopes, and Living Things: Between the Heights and the Depths (K. B. Shippen), 751

Men of Iron, selection from (Howard Pyle), 949

Mexican: nursery rhymes, 32; folk tales, 355–358

Mighty Mikko (Parker Fillmore), 281

Milk for the Cat (Harold Monro), 1034

Millay, Edna St. Vincent, *1203; God's World*, 1023

Miller, Kate, and Lucia Borski, *The Jolly Tailor Who Became King*, 276

Miller, His Son, and the Ass, The (Aesop), 117

Millions of Cats (Wanda Gág), 81

Milne, A. A., *1003, 1101, 1203; Market Square*, 1033

Minnows (John Keats), 1019

Miracles (Walt Whitman), 1056

Miss T. (Walter de la Mare), 1042

Moe, Jörgen, *133*

Molly Whuppie (Joseph Jacobs), 203

"Monday's child is fair of face," 34

Monkeys and the Crocodile, The (L. E. Richards), 46

Monro, Harold, *1203; Overheard on a Saltmarsh*, 1006; *Milk for the Cat*, 1034

Montgomerie, Norah and William, from *Sandy Candy*, 33

Moon's the North Wind's Cooky, The (Vachel Lindsay), 1045

Moore, Clement C., *1103, 1203; A Visit from St. Nicholas*, 1052

Moore, Marianne, *1204; from The Fables of La Fontaine*, 124, 125

More, Hannah, *1096*

Morley, Christopher, *1204; Song for a Little House*, 1037; *Animal Crackers*, 1044

Morning Song, A (William Shakespeare), 1016

Morns Are Meeker than They Were, The (Emily Dickinson), 1021

Moth and the Star, The (James Thurber), 126

Mother Goose, origin of term, 4, 5

Mother Goose's Melody (Newbery), 5, *1094;* selections from, 22–23

Motor Cars (R. B. Bennett), 1043

Mouse, The (Elizabeth Coatsworth), 1029

Mr. and Mrs. Discobbolos (Edward Lear), 56

Mr. Crow Takes a Wife (C. E. Gillham), 336

"Mr. East gave a feast," 14

Mr. Punchinello, 45

Mr. Samson Cat (Valéry Carrick), 265

Mrs. Peck-Pigeon (Eleanor Farjeon), 1033

Mrs. Snipkin and Mrs. Wobblechin (L. E. Richards), 46

Mukerji, Dhan Gopal, *1204; Rama: The March to Lanka*, 538

Mumps (E. M. Roberts), 1041

Murdoch's Rath (J. H. Ewing), 1128

Mushrooms (Russian nursery rhyme), 32

My Heart Leaps Up (William Wordsworth), 1054

"My litle old man and I fell out," 15

My Shadow (R. L. Stevenson), 1037

Mysterious Cat, The (Vachel Lindsay), 1035

Myths and legends, discussion of, *385–387*; Greek, *388*, 389–417; *459–463*; Hawaiian, 457–459; Norse, *417*, 418–443; North American Indian, 444–455; South American, 456–457

Nancy Hanks (R. C. and S. V. Benét), 1058

NanKivell, Joice M., *1204; Why the Monks of Athos Use a Samantron*, 459

Nash, Ogden, 42, *1204; The Eel*, 62; *The Guppy*, 62

Nast, Thomas, *1138*

Nature writing, discussion of, *729–730*

New England Primer, The, *1101;* illustration, 1102

New Year's Day (Japanese nursery rhyme), 32

Newbery, John, 5, *1094, 1132*

Newbery award, *1149;* winners listed, *1150*

Nibelungenlied, *387*

Nicholson, William, *1145*

Night (Sara Teasdale), 1046

Night Will Never Stay, The (Eleanor Farjeon), 1046

Nightingale, The (H. C. Andersen), 577

Nod (Walter de la Mare), 1045

Noël for Jeanne-Marie (Françoise), 78

Nolan, Jeannette Covert, *1204; Clara Barton of the Red Cross*, 810

Nonsense, discussion of, *41–44*

Nonsense Alphabet (Edward Lear), 53

Norse, SEE Scandinavian

North to the Orient: Point Barrow (Anne M. Lindbergh), 849

Norton, Mary, *1101, 1205; The Borrowers* (selection), 638

Norwegian nursery rhymes, 32

Noyes, Alfred, *A Song of Sherwood*, 1008; *The Admiral's Ghost*, 1075

Numskull and the Rabbit (A. W. Ryder), 319
Nursery rhymes, discussion of, *3–5*
Nurse's Song (William Blake), 1046
Nusbaum, Aileen B., *The Locust and the Coyote*, 447

O Little Town of Bethlehem (Phillips Brooks), 1050
Odin Goes to Mimir's Well (Padraic Colum), 418
Odysseus and the Cyclops (Padraic Colum), 474
Odyssey (Homer), 387
Of Courage Undaunted: Lewis and Clark (James Daugherty), 841
"Oh, the brave old Duke of York," 25
Ola (Ingri and Edgar Parin d'Aulaire), 88
Olcott, Frances Jenkins, *Daphne*, 407
Old Chang the Crab (Chinese nursery rhyme), 31
Old Fire Dragaman (Richard Chase), 343
"Old King Cole," 14
"Old Mother Goose when she wanted to wander," 17
"Old Mother Hubbard," 18
Old Woman and Her Pig, The (Joseph Jacobs), 197
On the Grasshopper and Cricket (John Keats), 1031
One Day on Beetle Rock: The Weasel (Sally Carrighar), 743
"One misty, moisty morning," 15
"One, two, buckle my shoe," 23
Opie, Iona and Peter, *5, 1205*; from *The Oxford Nursery Rhyme Book*, 6 ff.; from *The Oxford Dictionary of Nursery Rhymes*, 9, 10, 13, 15, 33, 45
Orbis Pictus, 1091, 1132
Origin of the Pleiades (Stith Thompson), 452
Orpheus (Padraic Colum), 404
Our Mr. Toad (David McCord), 1030
"Over Hill, Over Dale" (William Shakespeare), 1007
Overheard on a Saltmarsh (Harold Monro), 1006
Ovid, 387
Owl and the Eel and the Warming-Pan, The (L. E. Richards), 47
Owl and the Pussy-Cat (Edward Lear), 56

Painted Desert, The (Elizabeth Coatsworth), 1017
Pancake, The (Asbjörnsen), 291
Panchatantra fables, *112*, 117
Pandora (W. M. L. Hutchinson), 394
Parrish, Maxfield, *1140, 1142*
Pasture, The (Robert Frost), 1013
"Pat-a-cake, pat-a-cake," 6
Patrick, St., a prayer of ("May the strength of God pilot me"), 709
Paul Bunyan (Esther Shephard), 346
Paul Revere's Ride (H. W. Longfellow), 1065
Peabody, Josephine Preston, *Icarus and Daedalus*, 412; *The Judgment of Midas*, 416
"Pease porridge hot," 24
Pelle's New Suit (Elsa Beskow), 83
Penney, Grace Jackson, *1205*; *How the Seven Brothers Saved Their Sister*, 452

Perrault, Charles, *4, 134, 1094, 1205*; *Little Red Riding Hood*, 170; *Toads and Diamonds*, 193. SEE ALSO: *Cinderella and the Glass Slipper*, 174; *The Sleeping Beauty*, 180
Perseus (Edith Hamilton), 476
Persian: fable, 123; hero tale, 541
Peter and the Wolf (Serge Prokofieff), 267
Peter Pan in Kensington Gardens: Lock-Out Time (J. M. Barrie), 598
Peter Parley books, 1102
"Peter, Peter, pumpkin eater," 9
"Peter Piper pick'd a peck of pepper," 29
Peter Rabbit, The Tale of (Beatrix Potter), 79
Petersham, Maud and Miska, *1142, 1205*; from *The Rooster Crows*, 29, 34; illustration by, 1142
Phaethon (Padraic Colum), 408
Picture books, discussion of, *67–71*
Pied Piper of Hamelin, The (Robert Browning), 1071
Pirate Story (R. L. Stevenson), 1038
Poe, Edgar Allan, *1206*; *Annabel Lee*, 1071
Poetry, discussion of, *1001–1003*
Polish folk tale, 276
Poor Man and the Flask of Oil, The, 118
Pop Goes the Weasel, 25
Poppy Seed Cakes (Margery Clark), 867
Potter, Beatrix, *69, 70, 1206*; *The Tale of Peter Rabbit*, 79
Praise Ye the Lord (Psalm 150), 709
Prayer for Little Things, A (Eleanor Farjeon), 1029
Prayers, *709–710*
Pretending (Harry Behn), 1039
Priceless Cats, The (M. A. Jagendorf), 247
Primers, *1091*; *New England Primer, 1101*
Princess and José, The (Anita Brenner), 357
Princess on the Glass Hill, The (Asbjörnsen), 298
Prodigal Son, The (from Luke 15), 705
Prokofieff, Serge, *1206*; *Peter and the Wolf*, 267
Prometheus the Firebringer (W. M. L. Hutchinson), 391
"Pussy cat, pussy cat," 7
Pussy Willows (R. B. Bennett), 1015
Pyle, Howard, *1138, 1206*; *Robin Hood and Little John*, 499; *Men of Iron* (selection), 949; illustration by, 1140
Pyle, Katharine, *1207*; *Hercules: The Eleventh Task*, 480

Quangle Wangle's Hat, The (Edward Lear), 57
Queen Mab (William Shakespeare), 1007
Quest of the Hammer, The (A. F. Brown), 438

Rabbit Hill: Little Georgie Sings a Song (Robert Lawson), 612
Rackham, Arthur, *1138*; illustration by, 1139
Radiator Lions (Dorothy Aldis), 1041
Rain (R. L. Stevenson), 1015
Rain, The (R. B. Bennett), 1015

"Rain, rain, go away," 8

Ram and the Pig Who Went into the Woods, The (Asbjörnsen), 292

Rama: The March to Lanka (Dhan Gopal Mukerji), 538

Rapunzel (Grimm), 154

Real Princess, The (H. C. Andersen), 554

Red Rooster (Hilda Conkling), 1032

Reese, Lizette Woodworth, *1207*; *A Christmas Folk-Song*, 1051

Rhead, Louis, *1138*

Richards, Laura E., *42, 1207*; *Eletelephony*, 46; *The High Barbaree*, 46; *The Monkeys and the Crocodile*, 46; *Mrs. Snipkin and Mrs. Wobblechin*, 46; *The Owl and the Eel and the Warming-Pan*, 47; *The Umbrella Brigade*, 1015

"Ride a cock-horse to Banbury Cross," 7

Ring Around the World (Annette Wynne), 1059

Roberts, Elizabeth Madox, *1207*; *The Branch*, 1018; *Firefly*, 1031; *Mumps*, 1041; *Christmas Morning*, 1050

Robin Hood and Little John (old ballad), 1060

Robin Hood and Little John (Howard Pyle), 499

Robinson Crusoe, selection from (Daniel Defoe), 976

"Rock-a-bye, baby, thy cradle is green," 6

Rolling Wheels: Over the Divide (Katharine Grey), 961

Rollo books, *1103*

Romance, the, defined, *469*

Roscoe, William, *1098, 1109, 1207*; *The Butterfly's Ball*, 1127

Ross, Patricia Fent, *1207*; from *The Hungry Moon*, 32

Rossetti, Christina, *1101, 1207*; *If a Pig Wore a Wig*, 45; "Lord, purge our eyes to see," 710; *Who Has Seen the Wind?*, 1012; *The Bridge*, 1017; *The City Mouse*, 1030; *The Caterpillar*, 1031

Rostron, Richard, *The Sorcerer's Apprentice*, 167

Rourke, Constance, *1207*; *Audubon: Many Trails and a Snug Cabin*, 791

Rousseau, Jean-Jacques, *1096*

"Rub-a-dub dub, three men in a tub," 8

Rubber Boots (R. B. Bennett), 1015

Rufus M., selection from (Eleanor Estes), 895

Rumpelstiltskin (Grimm), 162

Ruskin, John, *1207*; *The King of the Golden River*, 669

Russian: nursery rhyme, 32; folk tales, 250–268

Ryder, Arthur, *The Brâhman's Goat*, 117; *Numskull and the Rabbit*, 319

Sacred writings, discussion of, *691–694*

St. Francis of Assisi, a prayer of ("Lord, make me an instrument of Thy peace"), 710

St. Jerome and the Lion and the Donkey (Helen Waddell), 713

St. Nicholas (Eleanor Farjeon), 719

St. Nicholas Magazine, *1105*

St. Patrick, a prayer of ("May the strength of God pilot me"), 709

Saint-Exupéry, Antoine de, *1208*; *The Little Prince* (selection), 622; *Wind, Sand, and Stars: The Elements*, 853

Saints, legends of, 713–722

Sandburg, Carl, *Abe Lincoln Grows Up: "Peculiarsome" Abe*, 795; *Fog*, 1018; *Lost*, 1018

Sandpiper, The (Celia Thaxter), 1032

Sands of Dee, The (Charles Kingsley), 1070

"Sandy Candy," 33

Sawyer, Ruth, *1088, 1208*; *The Flea*, 239

Saxe, John G., *1208*; *The Blind Men and the Elephant*, 126

Scandinavian: folk tales, 290–312; myths, *417, 418*–443; hero tale, 512

Schoonover, Frank, *1140*

Schreiber, Georges, illustration by, *between* 1148–1149

Scott, Robert, *1208*; *Captain Scott's Last Expedition: The Last March*, 847

Scott, Sir Walter, *1208*; *Lullaby of an Infant Chief*, 1047; *Lochinvar*, 1069

Scottish: nursery rhymes, 32–33; folk tale, 235

Scudder, Horace E., *1104*; translation from H. C. Andersen, 556

Sea Around Us: The Moving Tides (R. L. Carson), 753

Sea-Fever (John Masefield), 1028

Sea Song, A (Allan Cunningham), 1027

Seal Lullaby (Rudyard Kipling), 1049

Sedgwick, Catherine, *1103*

"See a pin and pick it up," 14

"See saw, Margery Daw," 22

"See-saw sacradown," 27

Seeds and the Wheat, The, 123

Seignobosc, Françoise, *1208*; SEE Françoise

Seredy, Kate, *1142, 1209*; *The Good Master: The Round-up*, 931; illustration by, 1144

Seuss, Dr., *The Five Hundred Hats of Bartholomew Cubbins*, 93

Seven Simeons (Boris Artzybasheff), 250

Seven Sleepers, The (Padraic Colum), 460

Sewell, Helen, *1145*; illustration by, 1145

Shakespeare, William, *5, 1209*; "Over Hill, Over Dale," 1007; "Where the Bee Sucks," 1007; *Queen Mab*, 1007; "You Spotted Snakes," 1007; *In Arden Forest*, 1016; *A Morning Song*, 1016; "When Icicles Hang by the Wall," 1026; "Some Say . . . ," 1051; "When to the Sessions of Sweet Silent Thought," 1058

Sharp, William, *1209*; *An Almanac*, 1026; *The Wasp*, 1031

Shedlock, Marie L., *113, 1087*; *The Spirit that Lived in a Tree*, 120; *The Banyan Deer*, 121; *The Hare that Ran Away*, 122

Shell, The (David McCord), 1027

Vultes, the Red Fox, selection from (John and Jean George), 740

Waddell, Helen, *1213*; *St. Jerome and the Lion and the Donkey*, 713
Wagtail: Wagtail's World Grows Wider (A. C. Gall and F. H. Crew), 731
Waiting (Harry Behn), 1010
Wakeupworld, The (Countee Cullen), 1027
Walden, selections from (H. D. Thoreau), 738
Walrus and the Carpenter, The (Lewis Carroll), 48
Wanderer's Song, A (John Masefield), 1028
Washing (John Drinkwater), 1042
Wasp, The (William Sharp), 1031
Watson, William, *1213*; *Song: April*, 1013
Watts, Isaac, *1093*, *1213*
"Wee Willie Winkie runs through the town," 12
Well I Never! (Spanish nursery rhyme), 33
Well of the World's End, The (Joseph Jacobs), 207
Welles, Winifred, *1213*; *Fireflies*, 1031
Welsh nursery rhyme, 33
West Indian folk tale, 365
What Am I? (Dorothy Aldis), 1023
"What are little boys made of?" 10
"What God gives, and what we take" (Robert Herrick), 710
What the Rattlesnake Said (Vachel Lindsay), 1045
"What's in the cupboard?" 15
Wheel on the School, The, selection from (Meindert De Jong), 914
Wheeler, Post, *1213*; *The Little Humpbacked Horse*, 258
Wheeler, W. A., from *Mother Goose's Melodies*, 8, 10, 11, 13, 14, 15
"When good King Arthur ruled this land," 4
"When Icicles Hang by the Wall" (William Shakespeare), 1026
"When to the Sessions of Sweet Silent Thought" (William Shakespeare), 1058
"Where are you going, my pretty maid?" 15
"Where the Bee Sucks" (William Shakespeare), 1007
While Shepherds Watched Their Flocks by Night (Nahum Tate), 1049
Whistles (Dorothy Aldis), 1041
White Rabbit's Verses, The (Lewis Carroll), 49
White Window, The (James Stephens), 1046
Whitman, Walt, *1214*; *Miracles*, 1056; *Give Me the Splendid Silent Sun*, 1056; *I Hear America Singing*, 1056; *The Commonplace*, 1057
Whittier, John Greenleaf, *1214*; Lines from *Snowbound*, 1026; *Barbara Frietchie*, 1067
Who Has Seen the Wind? (Christina Rossetti), 1012
"Who killed Cock Robin?" 19
Why the Ant Is Almost Cut in Two (Alice Marriott), 450

Why the Burro Lives with the Man (Catherine Bryan and Mabra Madden), 355
Why the Monks of Athos Use a Samantron (Joice M. NanKivell), 459
Wiese, Kurt, illustration by, 1141
Wild Swans, The (H. C. Andersen), 563
Wilder, Laura Ingalls, *1214*; *Little House in the Big Woods: Summertime*, 881
Wilkinson, Marguerite, *1214*; *A Chant Out of Doors*, 1054
Williams, Garth, illustration by, *between 1148–1149*
Wilson, Barbara Ker, *The Faery Flag of Dunvegan*, 285
Wind, The (R. L. Stevenson), 1012
Wind and the Sun, The (Aesop), 114
Wind in the Willows: The Wild Wood (Kenneth Grahame), 616
Wind, Sand, and Stars: The Elements (Antoine de Saint-Exupéry), 853
Windy Wash Day (Dorothy Aldis), 1012
Wings (Victor Hugo), 1054
Withers, Carl, *1214*; from *A Rocket in My Pocket*, 34
Wizard Frost (F. D. Sherman), 1024
Wolf and the Seven Little Kids, The (Grimm), 137
Wolf in Sheep's Clothing, A (Aesop), 114
Wolfe, Humbert, *1214*; *The Blackbird*, 1032
Wollstonecraft, Mary, *1096*
Wonder Smith and His Son, The (Ella Young), 503
Wonderful Tar-Baby, The (J. C. Harris), 339
Wordsworth, William, *1214*; *March*, 1011; *Daffodils*, 1014; *My Heart Leaps Up*, 1054
Wyeth, N. C., *1140*
Wylie, Elinor, *1215*; *Escape*, 1006; *Velvet Shoes*, 1025
Wynken, Blynken, and Nod (Eugene Field), 1048
Wynne, Annette, *Ring Around the World*, 1059

Yak, The (Hilaire Belloc), 61
"Yankee Doodle went to town," 34
Yates, Elizabeth, *1215*; *Amos Fortune, Free Man: Auctioned for Freedom*, 771
Yeats, William Butler, *1215*; *The Song of Wandering Aengus*, 1008; *The Lake Isle of Innisfree*, 1020
Yonge, Charlotte Mary, *1099*
"You Spotted Snakes" (William Shakespeare), 1007
Young, Ella, *473*, *1215*; *The Children of Lir*, 230; *The Wonder Smith and His Son*, 503
Young, Francis Brett, *Atlantic Charter*, 1057
Young Lafayette: The Great Adventure Begins (Jeanette Eaton), 782
Yucca (A. N. Clark), 1018

Zal (Helen Zimmern), 541
Zimmern, Helen, *Zal*, 541
Zimnik, Reiner, illustration by, *between 1148–1149*